Official Licensed
Publication of FIFA

ALMANACK
OF WORLD
FOOTBALL
2006

Guy Oliver

headline

First published in 2005
by HEADLINE BOOK PUBLISHING

1

A CIP catalogue record for this title is available from the British Library

ISBN 0 7553 1478 6 (hardback)
ISBN 0 7553 1419 0 (trade paperback)

Design: Guy Oliver
Design consultant: Peter Ward
Cover design: Head Design Ltd

Printed and bound in Great Britain by Mackays of Chatham PLC,
Chatham, Kent

Any views expressed in the Almanack of World Football do not necessarily reflect those of FIFA.
The data within the Almanack of World Football has been obtained from a variety of sources, official
and unofficial. Harpastum Publishing cannot vouch for the accuracy of the data in all cases
except for official data provided by FIFA, which is correct as of 20 July 2005.

Headline's policy is to use papers that are natural, renewable and recyclable products and
made from wood grown in sustainable forests. The logging and manufacturing processes
are expected to conform to the environmental regulations of the country of origin.

HEADLINE BOOK PUBLISHING
A division of Hodder Headline
338 Euston Road
London NW1 3BH

www.headline.co.uk
www.hodderheadline.com

CONTENTS

PART ONE – FIFA AND WORLD FOOTBALL

FIFA 1

PART TWO – THE ASSOCIATIONS

PART THREE – THE CONFEDERATIONS

AFC 904

CAF 925

CONCACAF 949

CONMEBOL 965

OFC 989

UEFA 994

FIFA ABBREVIATIONS

The table below shows the order in which the countries are listed within the Almanack. For an alphabetical listing of country names and their page number, please refer to the table on pages vii and viii

	COUNTRY	PAGE		COUNTRY	PAGE
AFG	Afghanistan	200	CTA	Central African Republic	359
AIA	Anguilla	202	CUB	Cuba	361
ALB	Albania	204	CYP	Cyprus	364
ALG	Algeria	207	CZE	Czech Republic	367
AND	Andorra	211	DEN	Denmark	371
ANG	Angola	214	DJI	Djibouti	375
ANT	Netherlands Antilles	217	DMA	Dominica	377
ARG	Argentina	219	DOM	Dominican Republic	379
ARM	Armenia	226	ECU	Ecuador	381
ARU	Aruba	229	EGY	Egypt	385
ASA	American Samoa	231	ENG	England	389
ATG	Antigua and Barbuda	233	EQG	Equatorial Guinea	401
AUS	Australia	235	ERI	Eritrea	403
AUT	Austria	239	ESP	Spain	405
AZE	Azerbaijan	243	EST	Estonia	414
BAH	Bahamas	246	ETH	Ethiopia	417
BAN	Bangladesh	248	FIJ	Fiji	420
BDI	Burundi	251	FIN	Finland	422
BEL	Belgium	253	FRA	France	426
BEN	Benin	258	FRO	Faroe Islands	434
BER	Bermuda	260	GAB	Gabon	437
BFA	Burkina Faso	263	GAM	Gambia	442
BHR	Bahrain	266	GEO	Georgia	444
BHU	Bhutan	270	GER	Germany	447
BIH	Bosnia-Herzegovina	272	GHA	Ghana	456
BLR	Belarus	275	GNB	Guinea-Bissau	459
BLZ	Belize	278	GRE	Greece	461
BOL	Bolivia	280	GRN	Grenada	465
BOT	Botswana	285	GUA	Guatemala	467
BRA	Brazil	290	GUI	Guinea	471
BRB	Barbados	299	GUM	Guam	474
BRU	Brunei Darussalam	302	GUY	Guyana	476
BUL	Bulgaria	304	HAI	Haiti	478
CAM	Cambodia	308	HKG	Hong Kong	481
CAN	Canada	310	HON	Honduras	484
CAY	Cayman Islands	313	HUN	Hungary	488
CGO	Congo	315	IDN	Indonesia	492
CHA	Chad	317	IND	India	495
CHI	Chile	319	IRL	Republic of Ireland	499
CHN	China	325	IRN	Iran	503
CIV	Côte d'Ivoire	331	IRQ	Iraq	507
CMR	Cameroon	334	ISL	Iceland	510
COD	Congo DR	339	ISR	Israel	513
COK	Cook Islands	342	ITA	Italy	517
COL	Colombia	344	JAM	Jamaica	527
CPV	Cape Verde Islands	349	JOR	Jordan	530
CRC	Costa Rica	351	JPN	Japan	533
CRO	Croatia	355	KAZ	Kazakhstan	542

COUNTRY		PAGE		COUNTRY		PAGE
KEN	Kenya	545		ROU	Romania	721
KGZ	Kyrgyzstan	548		RSA	South Africa	725
KOR	Korea Republic	551		RUS	Russia	731
KSA	Saudi Arabia	557		RWA	Rwanda	737
KUW	Kuwait	562		SAM	Samoa	742
LAO	Laos	565		SCA	Serbia and Montenegro	744
LBR	Liberia	567		SCO	Scotland	748
LBY	Libya	569		SEN	Senegal	755
LCA	St Lucia	572		SEY	Seychelles	758
LES	Lesotho	574		SIN	Singapore	760
LIB	Lebanon	576		SKN	St Kitts and Nevis	763
LIE	Liechtenstein	579		SLE	Sierra Leone	766
LTU	Lithuania	581		SLV	El Salvador	768
LUX	Luxembourg	584		SMR	San Marino	771
LVA	Latvia	587		SOL	Solomon Islands	774
MAC	Macao	591		SOM	Somalia	777
MAD	Madagascar	593		SRI	Sri Lanka	779
MAR	Morocco	598		STP	São Tomé e Príncipe	782
MAS	Malaysia	602		SUD	Sudan	784
MDA	Moldova	606		SUI	Switzerland	787
MDV	Maldives	609		SUR	Surinam	791
MEX	Mexico	612		SVK	Slovakia	793
MGL	Mongolia	619		SVN	Slovenia	797
MKD	Macedonia FYR	621		SWE	Sweden	801
MLI	Mali	624		SWZ	Swaziland	805
MLT	Malta	627		SYR	Syria	808
MOZ	Mozambique	630		TAH	Tahiti	812
MRI	Mauritius	633		TAN	Tanzania	814
MSR	Montserrat	636		TCA	Turks and Caicos Islands	817
MTN	Mauritania	638		TGA	Tonga	819
MWI	Malawi	640		THA	Thailand	821
MYA	Myanmar	643		TJK	Tajikistan	824
NAM	Namibia	645		TKM	Turkmenistan	826
NCA	Nicaragua	648		TOG	Togo	829
NCL	New Caledonia	651		TPE	Chinese Taipei	831
NED	Netherlands	653		TRI	Trinidad and Tobago	833
NEP	Nepal	660		TUN	Tunisia	837
NGA	Nigeria	662		TUR	Turkey	841
NIG	Niger	667		UAE	United Arab Emirates	846
NIR	Northern Ireland	669		UGA	Uganda	850
NOR	Norway	673		UKR	Ukraine	853
NZL	New Zealand	678		URU	Uruguay	857
OMA	Oman	681		USA	United States of America	862
PAK	Pakistan	684		UZB	Uzbekistan	869
PAL	Palestine	687		VAN	Vanuatu	873
PAN	Panama	689		VEN	Venezuela	875
PAR	Paraguay	692		VGB	British Virgin Islands	879
PER	Peru	696		VIE	Vietnam	881
PHI	Philippines	700		VIN	St Vincent and the Grenadines	884
PNG	Papua New Guinea	702		VIR	US Virgin Islands	886
POL	Poland	704		WAL	Wales	890
POR	Portugal	708		YEM	Yemen	894
PRK	Korea DPR	714		ZAM	Zambia	897
PUR	Puerto Rico	716		ZIM	Zimbabwe	900
QAT	Qatar	718				

ALPHABETICAL LISTING OF THE ASSOCIATIONS

As the 205 member associations of FIFA are organised in the Almanack according to their trigram and not alphabetically the following table provides a quick alphabetical reference to page numbers.

COUNTRY		PAGE	COUNTRY		PAGE
Afghanistan	AFG	200	Côte d'Ivoire	CIV	331
Albania	ALB	204	Croatia	CRO	355
Algeria	ALG	207	Cuba	CUB	361
American Samoa	ASA	231	Cyprus	CYP	364
Andorra	AND	211	Czech Republic	CZE	367
Angola	ANG	214	Denmark	DEN	371
Anguilla	AIA	202	Djibouti	DJI	375
Antigua and Barbuda	ATG	233	Dominica	DMA	377
Argentina	ARG	219	Dominican Republic	DOM	379
Armenia	ARM	226	Ecuador	ECU	381
Aruba	ARU	229	Egypt	EGY	385
Australia	AUS	235	El Salvador	SLV	768
Austria	AUT	239	England	ENG	389
Azerbaijan	AZE	243	Equatorial Guinea	EQG	401
Bahamas	BAH	246	Eritrea	ERI	403
Bahrain	BHR	266	Estonia	EST	414
Bangladesh	BAN	248	Ethiopia	ETH	417
Barbados	BRB	299	Faroe Islands	FRO	434
Belarus	BLR	275	Fiji	FIJ	420
Belgium	BEL	253	Finland	FIN	422
Belize	BLZ	278	France	FRA	426
Benin	BEN	258	Gabon	GAB	437
Bermuda	BER	260	Gambia	GAM	442
Bhutan	BHU	270	Georgia	GEO	444
Bolivia	BOL	280	Germany	GER	447
Bosnia-Herzegovina	BIH	272	Ghana	GHA	456
Botswana	BOT	285	Greece	GRE	461
Brazil	BRA	290	Grenada	GRN	465
British Virgin Islands	VGB	879	Guam	GUM	474
Brunei Darussalam	BRU	302	Guatemala	GUA	467
Bulgaria	BUL	304	Guinea	GUI	471
Burkina Faso	BFA	263	Guinea-Bissau	GNB	459
Burundi	BDI	251	Guyana	GUY	476
Cambodia	CAM	308	Haiti	HAI	478
Cameroon	CMR	334	Honduras	HON	484
Canada	CAN	310	Hong Kong	HKG	481
Cape Verde Islands	CPV	349	Hungary	HUN	488
Cayman Islands	CAY	313	Iceland	ISL	510
Central African Republic	CTA	359	India	IND	495
Chad	CHA	317	Indonesia	IDN	492
Chile	CHI	319	Iran	IRN	503
China	CHN	325	Iraq	IRQ	507
Chinese Taipei	TPE	831	Israel	ISR	513
Colombia	COL	344	Italy	ITA	517
Congo	CGO	315	Jamaica	JAM	527
Congo DR	COD	339	Japan	JPN	533
Cook Islands	COK	342	Jordan	JOR	530
Costa Rica	CRC	351	Kazakhstan	KAZ	542

HOW TO USE THE ALMANACK

①⇨ **Estadio Centenario, Montevideo**
7-09-2003, 16:00, 39 253, Zamora PER   ⇦②

URU   5   0   BOL ⇦③

④⇨ Forlan ¹⁷, Chevanton 2 ⁴⁰ ⁶¹ ⇦⑤
Abeijon ⁸³, Bueno ⁸⁸

① Stadium and city/town where the match was played.
② *From left to right:* Date, kick-off time, attendance, name and nationality of referee. Assistant referees are included for FIFA tournaments.
③ Teams (using FIFA abbreviations) and scores.

④ Name of goal scorer and the time that the goal was scored.
⑤ Indicates that 2 goals were scored by Chevanton followed by the times of the goals.

	BOLIVIA		
①⇨	FERNANDEZ Leonardo	21	⇦②
	PENA Juan Manuel	2	⇦③
	HOYOS Miguel	4	
	SANCHEZ Oscar	5	
	ROJAS Richard	6	
	CRISTALDO Luis	7	
	MENDEZ Limberg	9	
	CASTILLO Jose	11	
④⇨ 67	RICALDI Alvaro	15	⇦⑤
46	RIBEIRO Luis	17	
⑥⇨ 46	MOREJON Limber	19	
	Tr: ACOSTA Nelson		⇦⑦
46	BALDIVIESO Julio	10	
46	JUSTINIANO Raul	16	⇦⑧

⟷

Estadio Centenario, Montevideo
7-09-2003, 16:00, 39 253, Zamora PER

URU   5   0   BOL

Forlan ¹⁷, Chevanton 2 ⁴⁰ ⁶¹
Abeijon ⁸³, Bueno ⁸⁸

URUGUAY			BOLIVIA		
1	MUNUA Gustavo		FERNANDEZ Leonardo	21	
5	SOSA Marcelo	69	PENA Juan Manuel	2	
6	LOPEZ Diego		HOYOS Miguel	4	
9	BUENO Carlos		SANCHEZ Oscar	5	
10	LIGUERA Martin	77	ROJAS Richard	6	
11	NUNEZ Richard		CRISTALDO Luis	7	
14	GONZALEZ Cristian		MENDEZ Limberg	9	
17	LAGO Eduardo		CASTILLO Jose	11	
19	CHEVANTON Ernesto		67 RICALDI Alvaro	15	
20	RECOBA Alvaro		46 RIBEIRO Luis	17	
21	FORLAN Diego	76	46 MOREJON Limber	19	
	Tr: CARRASCO Juan Ramon		Tr: ACOSTA Nelson		
8	ABEIJON Nelson	69	46 BALDIVIESO Julio	10	
15	SANCHEZ Vicente	76	46 JUSTINIANO Raul	16	
16	OLIVERA Ruben	77			

① Family name in capitals, followed by the player's given name.
② Shirt number.
③ A shaded box indicates that the player was cautioned.
④ A shaded box next to a player who has been sent off (see below), indicates a dismissal for two yellow cards.
A blacked-out box indicates a straight red card.

⑤ A blacked-out box indicates the player was dismissed at the time shown in the centre column.
⑥ Substitution time.
⑦ Team coach/trainer.
⑧ Substitute. The time of the substitution corresponds with the player listed in the starting line-up.

① →   **CLUB DIRECTORY** → ②   ③ ↓   ④↓ ⑤↓ ⑥↓

Club	City	Stadium	Phone	www.	Lge	Cup	CL
Universitatea Craiova	Craiova	Ion Oblemenco 27 915	+40 251 414726	fcuniversitatea.ro	4	6	0
Dinamo Bucuresti	Bucuresti	Dinamo 15 138	+40 21 2106974	fcdinamo.ro	17	12	0
Farul Constanta	Constanta	Gheorghe Hagi 15 520	+40 241 616142	fcfarul.ro	0	0	0

⑦

① Indicates that Universitatea play at the Ion Oblemenco Stadium, which has a capacity of 27, 915.

② Phone number, including international dialing code.

③ Official club website at http://www(given name).

④ National League Championship.

⑤ National Cup

⑥ CL = Champions League of relevant Confederation.

⑦ Indicates that Dinamo Bucuresti have won the National League Championship on 17 occasions.

CHINA PR 2004

① ↓   SUPER LEAGUE   ② ③ ④ ⑤ ⑥ ⑦ ⑧

	Pl	W	D	L	F	A	Pts	Shenzhen	Shandong	Shanghai I	Liaoning	Dalian	Tianjin	Beijing	Shenyang	Sichuan	Shanghai S	Qingdao	Chongqing
Shenzhen Jianlibao †	22	11	9	2	30	13	42		2-1	1-0	3-0	2-2	0-1	2-0	0-0	1-1	3-1	1-0	0-0
Shandong Luneng Tai.	22	10	6	6	44	29	36	1-1		4-2	3-1	2-3	3-1	5-2	4-1	1-2	2-1	1-1	4-1
Shanghai International	22	8	8	6	39	31	32	2-2	2-1		2-1	4-0	3-0	1-1	3-1	3-2	1-1	1-0	1-2
Liaoning Zhongyu	22	10	2	10	39	40	32	1-2	2-3	2-1		1-5	1-5	1-1	1-0	0-0	5-2	3-1	3-0	⇦

⑩ ⇨ 15/05/2004 - 5/12/2004. † Teams qualifying for the AFC Champions League

① Chinese champions of 2004.
All champions are listed in bold. If the club at the top of the table is not listed in bold it means that the table shown represents only part of a season. Relegated clubs are also shown in bold.

② Number of games played.

③ Number of wins.

④ Number of draws.

⑤ Number of losses.

⑥ Number of goals scored.

⑦ Number of goals conceded.

⑧ Number of points gained in the season.

⑨ This result represents the match between Liaoning Zhongyu at home and Chongqing, the away club. The home team score is listed first so Liaoning Zhongyu won 3-0 at home to Chongqing.

⑩ Dates for the kick-off of the season and the final matches.

BRAZIL NATIONAL TEAM RECORDS AND RECORD SEQUENCES

Records			Sequence records						
Victory	10-1	BOL 1949	①	Wins	14	1997	⑤ Clean sheets	8	1989
Defeat	0-6	URU 1920	②	Defeats	4	2001	⑥ Goals scored	47	1994-1997
Player Caps	126	CAFU	③	Undefeated	43	1993-1997	⑦ Without goal	5	1990
Player Goals	77	PELE	④	Without win	7	1983-84, 1990-91	⑧ Goals against	24	1937-1944

① Number of consecutive wins.

② Number of consecutive defeats.

③ Number of consecutive games played without defeat.

④ Number of consecutive games played without a win.

⑤ Number of consecutive games played without conceding a goal.

⑥ Number of consecutive games played in which Brazil scored.

⑦ Number of consecutive games played without scoring.

⑧ Number of consecutive games played with opponent scoring.

EXPLANATION OF OTHER TERMS USED IN THE ALMANACK

In the national team record box for each country the % column is intented as a rough guide to form and is worked out by awarding two points for a win and one for a draw as against the total number of points available.

If there is no referee list within the pages of a country, it can be found in Appendix 1. The column headed Int'l within each box indicates the year in which the referee or assistant referee joined the FIFA list.

INTRODUCTION

One moment in particular brought home to me the unique nature of football. It was in December 1997 and I had just arrived at Cairo airport with a cameraman and £50,000 worth of camera equipment. Unfortunately we didn't have the right paperwork to get the camera into Egypt and you could tell that the overly officious customs officer was rather enjoying our discomfort. To help break the impasse I asked him what team he supported. "Barcelona" was his rather terse reply but when I asked if he was a Zamalek or Al Ahly supporter his demeanour changed. "You know about Zamalek?" he asked. When I replied that we were in Egypt to film at the African Champions League final between Zamalek and Shooting Stars, we got the whole history of Zamalek as well as the current form and players to look out for. More importantly we were whisked through customs and given a personal escort to our hotel in the centre of the city.

Football is a global game but it's a game rooted firmly in local tradition and that is why I believe a book like the *Almanack of World Football* needed to be written. We may all watch the final of the UEFA Champions League but for the majority of fans their football experience and passion for the game lies much closer to home. Every country has a national team and a Championship and both play a role in the culture of that nation. Football has never been and never will be just about the top dozen clubs in Europe and hopefully the *Almanack* will give readers a little insight into the 205 countries that make up the FIFA family.

Another motive for compiling the *Almanack of World Football* has been to provide an historical record for the year. The game of football is a compelling spectacle in its own right but what makes it unique is the historical context. Preserving the historical record for future generations is something that sports like cricket and baseball have done very well but given the global reach of football, just finding a list of champions for some countries has proved difficult enough.

Marius Schneider and his team at FIFA are currently co-ordinating the massive task of providing the first comprehensive official list of international matches that have been played since the first game between England and Scotland in 1872. My hope is that the *Almanack* can contribute to the process that sees football safeguard its heritage. Wherever possible we have relied on official sources for information and of special note is the work done by Charles-Henry Contamine and his team at FIFA.com and FIFAWorldCup.com along with Marius and his team. All of the information relating to FIFA comes from them. For each country the *Almanack* lists a record section detailing record scores and record sequences. At present this information is not official FIFA information and we await the publication of the work Marius is undertaking to verify the information we have listed.

Perhaps the biggest contributors to the *Almanack of World Football* are the thousands of people who make the internet such a lively football community. Without the internet and e-mail it would have been an impossible task to produce the *Almanack*. Most clubs, associations and confederations run websites and the information they provide has proved invaluable as have the many on-line newspapers from around the world. Ten years ago it would have taken weeks for news of the Vietnamese Championship to filter out of the country. On page 883 you will find details of the V-League which finished the weekend the *Almanack* went to the printers.

I would particularly like to praise the extraordinary efforts of those who make the pages of the rsssf.com such a unique contribution to the historical record. I would like to thank each member individually but space prohibits that. Suffice to say that your contribution to the *Almanack* is well appreciated.

Should any reader feel they can correct information, add information where it is missing or simply help keep me up to date with events around the world, please feel free to contact me by e-mail via guy@harpastumpublishing.com.

Guy Oliver, London, August 2005

ACKNOWLEDGMENTS

A number of people have made a significant contribution to the *Almanack of World Football*. David Hobbs helped write many of the country reviews as well as proofing the manuscript, a job that was shared with John English. Thanks to you both. Thank you also to Sharyn for your invaluable help with the input of data; to Oliver and Marion Greenleaves for your efforts in compiling the records section; to Michael Oliver for your valued advice throughout; to Peter Law for the excellent research and to Tom Chittick for your key involvement from the very start. My thanks also to David Wilson, Lorraine Jerram, Wendy McCance and Rachel Geere at Headline; to Paul Marsh who has advised from an early stage and to Peter Ward for helping to make the *Almanack* look as good as it does. At FIFA sincere appreciation to Lars Bretscher, Andrea Meier, Dominique Boyer and Helen de Haan and to Rupert Daniels for listening to the idea for the *Almanack* in the first place. On a personal note deepest gratitude to my family for putting up with the demands on my time that so often took me out of the loop. This is for you but I couldn't have done it without you.

PART ONE

FIFA AND WORLD FOOTBALL

FIFA

Fédération Internationale de Football Association

Celebrating its Centennial in 2004, FIFA's first 100 years in football were often as eventful as the century into which it was born. Now made up of 205 national associations, FIFA today is a far cry from its humble Paris beginnings with seven members in May 1904 and its anniversary was marked with lavish celebrations, the climax being the FIFA Centennial World Player Gala at the Opera House in Zurich in December where Ronaldhino was proclaimed FIFA World Player of the Year. Prior to that, the modern game returned to the French capital for the France v Brazil Centennial Match played on 21 May, exactly 100 years after FIFA was inaugurated and which followed the meeting of the Centennial Congress.

To complement the anniversary there were a number of publications and films released, amongst them *The FIFA 100*, an exhibition of photos of 100 players chosen by Pele (see page 146); the book *100 Years of Football*, written by four respected academics; a DVD called *FIFA Fever*; and the new official film of the 1930 FIFA World Cup™ in which footage of the final between Argentina and Uruguay was restored and coloured. Over the course of the year the celebrations spanned the globe and further events to mark the Centennial included a visit from FIFA to the

THE FIFA BIG COUNT OF 2000

	Male	Female		Male	Female
Registered players	12 487 938	491 296	Referees	678 011	41 833
Non registered players	82 214 931	9 188 610	Officials	3 218 480	428 828
Youth players	15 793 467	2 204 348	Total involved	220 496 336	21 884 254
Children & Occasional	110 000 000	10 000 000	in football	246 747 742	
Professionals	125 304	2 160	Number of clubs	305 060	
Total players	242 380 590		Number of teams	1 548 146	

Football Associations of England, Scotland, Wales and Northern Ireland where President Joseph S. Blatter paid tribute to the United Kingdom as the birthplace of the modern game; the release of commemorative medals and coins; the awarding of a Centennial Order of Merit to a member of each association who had given extraordinary service to the game in that country; and the FIFA Centennial Exhibition at the Olympic Museum in Lausanne.

Not directly connected to the Centennial, but with one eye firmly on the future, the foundation stone for the new FIFA headquarters was laid on 14 May in Zurich with the building due to be inaugurated in May 2006. Once completed all of FIFA's departments and employees will be housed in a single location. The ceremony was followed with the historic announcement that South Africa will be the first African country to host the FIFA World Cup™ when it stages the 2010 event. The celebrations were brought to an end on 20 May, 2005 when a special plaque was presented to the Chinese Football Association in recognition of China's role as the birthplace of football more than 2,000 years ago.

Fédération Internationale de Football Association (FIFA)
FIFA House, PO Box 85, 8030 Zürich, Switzerland
Tel +41 43 222 7777   Fax +41 43 222 7878
info@fifa.org
www.fifa.com
www.fifaworldcup.com
President: Joseph S. Blatter, SUI
General Secretary: Urs Linsi, SUI
Deputy General Secretary, Head of National Associations and Administration: Jérôme Champagne

FIFA EXECUTIVE COMMITTEE

President: BLATTER Joseph S. SUI

Senior Vice-President: GRONDONA Julio ARG   Vice-President: WILL David H. SCO

Vice-President: JOHANSSON Lennart SWE   Vice-President: HAYATOU Issa CMR   Vice-President: CHUNG Mong Joon, Dr KOR

Vice-President: WARNER Jack A. TRI   Vice-President: VILLAR LLONA Angel Maria ESP

ORDINARY MEMBERS OF THE EXECUTIVE COMMITTEE

D'HOOGHE Michel, Dr BEL	SASSO SASSO Isaac David CRC	TEIXEIRA Ricardo Terra BRA
BIN HAMMAM Mohamed QAT	ERZIK Senes TUR	BLAZER Chuck USA
MAKUDI Worawi THA	LEOZ Nicolás, Dr PAR	BHAMJEE Ismaïl BOT
DIAKITE Amadou MLI	KOLOSKOV Viacheslav, Dr RUS	MAYER-VORFELDER Gerhard GER
PLATINI Michel FRA	FUSIMALOHI 'Ahongalu TGA	OGURA Junji JPN
CHIBOUB Slim TUN	Observer: TEMARII Reynald TAH	General Secretary: LINSI Urs, Dr SUI

At the highest level on the field the focus of the men's senior game in this period was on the qualifying rounds for the 2006 FIFA World Cup™. The first countries to qualify were Argentina, Iran, Japan, Korea Republic and Saudi Arabia and the full line up will be known by November 2005 before the draw for the finals is made in Leipzig in December. Before the main event in Germany next year, eight nations competed there for the FIFA Confederations Cup and both Brazil and Argentina posted warnings that a South American nation could win the FIFA World Cup™ in Europe for only the second time, when they reached the final, which the Brazilians won for the second time. The best of the world's younger generation were playing at the FIFA World Youth Championships in the Netherlands at the same time where Argentina continued the South American theme with a record fifth triumph, beating Nigeria in the final. Earlier in the season the second edition of the FIFA U-19 Women's World Championship was played in Thailand and it further demonstrated how far the women's game has developed. It also marked the rise of Germany, who added the U-19 title to their FIFA Women's World Cup victory of 2003. In Chinese Taipei, three-times World Champions Brazil were desperate to regain the FIFA Futsal World Championship, but couldn't prevent Spain retaining the title they won in 2000. The South Americans also had their minds focused on two new World Championships, the FIFA Beach Soccer World Cup and the FIFA Interactive World Cup. With the former being held on the sands of Rio de Janeiro, the host country probably fancied their chances. However, it wasn't to be as France made room in their trophy cabinet for new silverware to sit alongside the European Beach Soccer crown captured in 2004. Better luck for Brazil came in Zurich when Thiago Carrico de Azevedo became the inaugural FIFA Interactive World Cup champion, a competition that attracted thousands of competitors from all over the world.

Off the pitch FIFA's efforts to develop the game globally continued with the expansion of the Goal programme and FIFA's accounts for 2004 illustrate the financial importance of the initiative. Income for its Centennial year reached CHF740 million, the single biggest revenue generator being the CHF404 million from the sale of TV broadcasting rights for the 2006 FIFA World Cup™. Expenditure totalled CHF582 million, of which the Goal programme accounted for CHF25 million, with all development-related expenses worth CHF141 million, nearly a quarter of FIFA's outgoings while event-related expenses cost CHF254 million. Originally Blatter's brainchild, the Goal programme was initiated in 1999 in an effort to provide financial assistance to poorer associations who could then develop football in their countries. By the end of 2004, 170 countries had benefited from the programme through 196 projects, a positive end to FIFA's Centennial year, which while celebrating the organisation's past made clear that the year was also an opportunity to look forward. Some associations unexpectedly needed urgent attention in southern Asia after the devastating Tsunami of December 2004. FIFA and many of its members donated money or equipment to help with reconstruction and with the fundraising highlighted by an all-star match from two teams led by Ronaldhino and Andriy Shevchenko, $7.6 million has so far been given to the affected associations.

A major administrative change came from the decision to postpone the election of FIFA President until after the 2006 FIFA World Cup™. Until now, if the President faced a challenge, as in 2002, the election took place just before the tournament began. To ensure the focus was kept firmly on the football and not the politics, FIFA decided future elections would be held the year after the tournament.

In the 100 years of FIFA, the use of technology in decision-making on the field of play has been resolutely kept on the sidelines – until now. The FIFA U-17 World Championship to be held in Peru in September and October 2005 will witness the first official tests of technical systems that can determine whether the ball has fully crossed the goal line. At its 119th Annual General Meeting in Wales, the game's lawmaking body, the International Football Association Board (IFAB) agreed to try a system with an imbedded electronic chip in the ball and gave FIFA permission to test it in a competitive environment. Approving the decision, Blatter commented that FIFA had a "duty to at least examine whether new technology could be used in football", but with the caveat that any use of technology should not detract from the authority of the match officials.

So often the subject of debates, the offside rule was again at the centre of discussions with the Board deciding that a player's head, body or feet, but not his arms, will be the deciding factors as to whether or not he is nearer to his opponents' goal line than both the ball and the second last opponent. More clarification was given about whether or not a player was regarded as "actively involved in play" and therefore offside. For example, the Board agreed that a player will be deemed culpable when "interfering with an opponent means preventing an opponent from playing or being able to play the ball by clearly obstructing the opponent's line of vision or movements or making a gesture or movement which, in the opinion of the referee, deceives or distracts an opponent." These changes were first introduced in competition at the FIFA Confederations Cup which also featured referees experimenting with the use of yellow cards for unsporting conduct to sanction players who deliberately wasted time. The aim was to prevent players from the penalised side touching the ball after a free-kick had been awarded, but also after conceding a throw-in or a corner or after a goal had been scored. That way, it was hoped altercations between players could be avoided.

The problem of drugs within football has become an issue that has highlighted the differences between FIFA and the World Anti-Doping Agency. In May 2004, delegates at the FIFA Centennial Congress ratified the declaration that underlined FIFA's unconditional support for the fight against doping and its respect for the World Anti-Doping Code. That declaration stopped short of complete acceptance of the Code because FIFA insisted on being able to manage drug cases individually and to impose flexible sanctions on offenders, two issues accepted in his speech to Congress by WADA Chairman Dick Pound.

As to the year ahead, attention at FIFA will now be focused on the successful hosting of the 2006 FIFA World Cup Germany™ which kicks off in Munich on 9 June, 2006 and climaxes in Berlin exactly a month later.

OTHER FIFA COMMITTEES

	Chairman	Organising Committee for...	Chairman
Emergency Committee	BLATTER Joseph S.	The FIFA World Cup™	JOHANSSON Lennart
Finance Committee	GRONDONA Julio H.	The FIFA Confederations Cup	BLAZER Chuck
Internal Audit Committee	CARRARO Franco, Dr	The Olympic Football Tournaments	HAYATOU Issa
Referees' Committee	VILLAR LLONA Angel Maria	The FIFA World Youth Championship	WARNER Jack A.
Technical & Development Committee	PLATINI Michel	The U-17 World Championship	WARNER Jack A.
Sports Medical Committee	D'HOOGHE Michel, Dr	The FIFA Club World Championship	KOLOSKOV Viacheslav, Dr
Players' Status Committee	MAYER-VORFELDER Gerhard	Women's Football and FIFA Women's Competitions	MAKUDI Worawi
Legal Committee	WILL David H.		
Committee for Ethics and Fair Play	ERZIK Senes	Bureau 2006 FIFA World Cup Germany™	JOHANSSON Lennart
Media Committee	MAYER-VORFELDER Gerhard	Futsal Committee	TEIXEIRA Ricardo Terra
Associations Committee	KOLOSKOV Viacheslav, Dr	Marketing and Television Advisory Board	GRONDONA Julio H.
Football Committee	VILLAR LLONA Angel Maria	FIFA Club Task Force	MAYER-VORFELDER Gerhard
Strategic Study Committee	BLATTER Joseph S.	FIFA Medical Assessment and Research Centre	D'HOOGHE Michel, Dr
Goal Bureau	BIN HAMMAM Mohamed	Doping Control Sub-Committee	D'HOOGHE Michel, Dr
Disciplinary Committee	MATHIER Marcel, Me.	Appeal Committee	SALGUERO Rafael

FIFA TOURNAMENTS

FIFA WORLD CUP™

Year	Host Country	Winners	Score	Runners-up	Venue
1930	Uruguay	Uruguay	4-2	Argentina	Centenario, Montevideo
1934	Italy	Italy	2-1	Czechoslovakia	PNF, Rome
1938	France	Italy	4-2	Hungary	Colombes, Paris
1950	Brazil	Uruguay	2-1	Brazil	Maracana, Rio de Janeiro
1954	Switzerland	Germany FR	3-2	Hungary	Wankdorf, Berne
1958	Sweden	Brazil	5-2	Sweden	Råsunda, Stockholm
1962	Chile	Brazil	3-1	Czechoslovakia	Estadio Nacional, Santiago
1966	England	England	4-2	Germany FR	Wembley, London
1970	Mexico	Brazil	4-1	Italy	Azteca, Mexico City
1974	Germany FR	Germany FR	2-1	Netherlands	Olympiastadion, Munich
1978	Argentina	Argentina	3-1	Netherlands	Monumental, Buenos Aires
1982	Spain	Italy	3-1	Germany FR	Bernabeu, Madrid
1986	Mexico	Argentina	3-2	Germany FR	Azteca, Mexico City
1990	Italy	Germany FR	1-0	Argentina	Olimpico, Rome
1994	USA	Brazil	0-0 3-2p	Italy	Rose Bowl, Pasadena
1998	France	France	3-0	Brazil	Stade de France, Paris
2002	Korea Rep/Japan	Brazil	2-0	Germany	International Stadium, Yokohama

The FIFA World Cup™ is the most popular single sports event in the world and ranks alongside the Olympic Games as the focus of sporting attention in the years that the two sporting festivals are held. When FIFA was founded in 1904 it reserved the right to organise a world championship for its members. However, it took more than a quarter of a century for that aim to become reality and it wasn't until the Barcelona Congress of 1929 that a resolution was passed paving the way for the first tournament to be held the following year in Uruguay. The reason the World Cup was such a long time in coming was due to the huge appeal of the Football Tournament of the Olympic Games, the winners of which were regarded as world champions. The Olympic tournament had first been officially organised in 1908 but by the late 1920s there was growing disquiet amongst the members of FIFA that, because of the amateur ethos and the surge of professionalism after 1925, especially within central Europe, the best players were no longer eligible to compete. Although FIFA was responsible for organising the Olympic Football Tournament, the then FIFA President Jules Rimet realised that the best way forward was to organise a separate tournament that was open to anyone. Just 13 teams entered the first tournament, a figure that has risen to over 200 today. It may be the dream of every footballer to take part in the FIFA World Cup™ but only a very select club of players and nations have won the coveted prize – seven nations and 189 players to be precise. Staged every four years, the finals have been hosted by 15 countries with Mexico, Italy, France and Germany each having been granted the honour twice. For many years the hosting would alternate between the Americas and Europe but in 2002 Asia welcomed the tournament for the first time and in 2010 South Africa will entertain as each continent is given a chance on a rotational basis. Much of the excitement of the FIFA World Cup™ can also be found in the qualifying tournaments, which in some parts of the world are now spread over three years. The 32 places in the finals are decided on a continental basis with the hosts, but no longer the holders, qualifying automatically. South America has four guaranteed places, Europe 13, Africa five, Asia four and Central and North America three, with the final two places being decided via a series of play-offs between all the Confederations bar Europe and Africa. For many just making it to the finals is achievement enough although for the elite the aim remains focused on winning the cup itself. Not that the trophy is actually a cup anymore. For the first eight tournaments it was possible to celebrate by drinking champagne from the Jules Rimet trophy, but since 1974 the solid gold trophy is in the form of a globe, held aloft by two players at the moment of victory.

FIFA WOMEN'S WORLD CUP

Year	Host Country	Winners	Score	Runners-up	Venue
1991	China PR	USA	2-1	Norway	Tianhe, Guangzhou
1995	Sweden	Norway	2-0	Germany	Råsunda, Stockholm
1999	USA	USA	0-0 5-4p	China PR	Rose Bowl, Pasadena
2003	USA	Germany	2-1	Sweden	Home Depot Centre, Carson

With the rapid growth of women's football since the 1970s it was a logical step for FIFA to organise a World Cup for women in 1991 to replace the growing number of unofficial tournaments that were being staged around the world. As early as 1970, 40,000 fans in the Stadio Communale in Turin watched Denmark beat Italy to win the Coppa del Mondo while the following year the Danes won the Mundial 1971 in front of 110,000 fans in Mexico City's Azteca Stadium, beating the hosts in the final of a tournament that had been played to packed stadia throughout. The surge in interest in women's football in the Far East and in the Americas in the late 1980s convinced FIFA that the time was right to get involved in the women's game. In 1988 they organised the FIFA Women's Invitation Tournament in China PR. The event, won by Norway, who beat Sweden in the final in Guangzhou, was a huge success although it isn't counted as part of the FIFA Women's World Cup record. The first official tournament was held three years later, in 1991, and again hosted by China PR. The winners were the United States, a major player in the popularisation of the women's game thanks to the seven million women and girls involved with football there. Two of the tournaments since then have been held in the USA although the 2003 tournament should have been held in China but was switched to the States due to the SARS outbreak in the Far East. Many expected the hosts to win the Cup for a third time but the Germans surprised everyone by becoming the third nation to be crowned world champions after the USA and Norway. Played every four years the tournament has firmly established itself as the pinnacle of the women's game. The next edition will be held in China PR in 2007.

FIFA CLUB WORLD CHAMPIONSHIP

Year	Host Country	Winners	Score	Runners-up	Venue
2000	Brazil	Corinthians, BRA	0-0 4-3p	Vasco da Gama, BRA	Maracana, Rio de Janeiro
2005	Japan				

Rarely has there been more controversy engendered by a tournament than the furore surrounding the FIFA Club World Championship; yet the logic behind the tournament is incontrovertible. Every Confederation has a championship for national teams and club sides yet for decades the only world championship has been for national teams. Fans around the world have been denied the chance to watch their teams play against clubs from different Confederations and vie for the title of world champions. European critics railed against FIFA when the FIFA Club World Championship was introduced in 2000 citing an overcrowded fixture list. The argument was put on hold following the bankruptcy of FIFA's marketing partners ISL in 2001 which meant a five year gap before the second edition could be organised. Once again the top European clubs complained, even threatening to boycott the tournament but after taking on their concerns, FIFA announced that the second Club World Championship would take place in Tokyo in December 2005, replacing the annual Toyota Cup played between the European and South American club champions and that it would be held annually every year after. Club fears of a fixture overload were resolved by adopting a straight knock-out format with the Asian, African, Central and North American and Oceania teams playing a preliminary round with the European and South American champions joining in for the semi-finals. To win the first title in 2000, Brazilian club Corinthians had to play four games over nine days, seeing off Real Madrid on goal difference in the group stage and then beating fellow Brazilians Vasco da Gama on penalties in the Maracanã in the final. In December 2004 FC Porto became the final winners of the Toyota Cup, ending a 44 year chapter of European and South American competition and ushering in a new and long overdue era in club football in which the champions of all six Confederations can battle for the mantle of world champions.

FOOTBALL TOURNAMENT OF THE OLYMPIC GAMES

Year	Host City	Winners	Score	Runners-up	Venue
1896	Athens	Demonstration sport			
1900	Paris	Demonstration sport			
1904	St Louis	Demonstration sport			
1906	Athens	Demonstration sport			
1908	London	England	2-0	Denmark	White City, London
1912	Stockholm	England	4-2	Denmark	Stockholms Stadion, Stockholm
1916	Berlin	Games cancelled			
1920	Antwerp	Belgium	2-0	Czechoslovakia	Olympisch Stadion, Antwerp
1924	Paris	Uruguay	3-0	Switzerland	Colombes, Paris
1928	Amsterdam	Uruguay	1-1 2-1	Argentina	Olympisch Stadion, Amsterdam
1932	Los Angeles	No football tournament played			
1936	Berlin	Italy	2-1	Austria	Olympiastadion, Berlin
1940	Tokyo/Helsinki	Games cancelled			
1944	London	Games cancelled			
1948	London	Sweden	3-1	Yugoslavia	Wembley, London
1952	Helsinki	Hungary	2-0	Yugoslavia	Olympiastadion, Helsinki
1956	Melbourne	Soviet Union	1-0	Yugoslavia	Melbourne Cricket Ground
1960	Rome	Yugoslavia	3-1	Denmark	Flamino, Rome
1964	Tokyo	Hungary	2-1	Czechoslovakia	National Stadium, Tokyo
1968	Mexico City	Hungary	4-1	Bulgaria	Azteca, Mexico City
1972	Munich	Poland	2-1	Hungary	Olympiastadion, Munich
1976	Montreal	German DR	3-1	Poland	Olympic Stadium, Montreal
1980	Moscow	Czechoslovakia	1-0	German DR	Centralny, Moscow
1984	Los Angeles	France	2-0	Brazil	Rose Bowl, Pasadena
1988	Seoul	Soviet Union	2-1	Brazil	Olympic Stadium, Seoul
1992	Barcelona	Spain	3-2	Poland	Camp Nou, Barcelona
1996	Atlanta	Nigeria	3-2	Argentina	Sanford Stadium, Athens
2000	Sydney	Cameroon	2-2 5-4p	Spain	Olympic Stadium, Sydney
2004	Athens	Argentina	1-0	Paraguay	Olympic Stadium, Athens

The history of the Football Tournament of the Olympic Games can be divided into three broad phases. Before the introduction of the FIFA World Cup™ in 1930 the winners were lauded as world champions, an honour won twice by Uruguay and England (playing under the banner of Great Britain) and once by Belgium. After 1928 the tournament remained amateur in a world increasingly dominated by professionalism, a situation exploited by countries from the communist bloc who were professionals in all but name. From 1952 until 1980 teams from behind the Iron Curtain walked off with every title, notably the Hungarians, winners in 1952, 1964 and 1968. For the 1984 and 1988 tournaments the amateur restrictions were relaxed with all players who had not taken part in a World Cup eligible to compete, but in 1992 the third major phase began when it became an age-restricted tournament for under-23s although three over-age players were also permitted in the team. Sixteen nations have won Olympic football gold although it is a competition that has been dominated by Europe with only four nations from elsewhere winning the prize. After the legendary triumphs of Uruguay in the 1920s it wasn't until 2004 that another South American team – Argentina – won and the Olympic title remains the only major title not yet won by Brazil. In 1996 Nigeria broke the duck for Africa and that was followed in Sydney four years later by Cameroon. Four previous winners no longer exist as countries – the Soviet Union, East Germany, Czechoslovakia and Yugoslavia while there is also some confusion as to the inaugural winners. The team representing Great Britain was the famous pre-World War One England amateur team that was so instrumental in spreading the game across Europe, hence the listing as England rather than Great Britain. As with the FIFA World Cup™ the finalists for the Olympics are decided by continental qualifying competitions which in 2004 resulted in four finalists from Africa and Europe (including hosts Greece), three from Asia, two from South America, two from the rest of the Americas and one from Oceania.

WOMEN'S OLYMPIC FOOTBALL TOURNAMENT

Year	Host City	Winners	Score	Runners-up	Venue
1996	Atlanta	USA	2-1	China	Sanford Stadium, Athens
2000	Sydney	Norway	3-2	USA	Sydney Football Stadium, Sydney
2004	Athens	USA	2-1	Brazil	Karaiskaki, Piraeus

Women's football is a very recent addition to the list of Olympic sports but in conjunction with the FIFA Women's World Cup it now provides the sport with a second championship of world repute, as, unlike the men's Olympic Football Tournament, the full national teams can enter. The 1996 games in Atlanta were the perfect launch pad for the Women's Olympic Football Tournament with the final between the USA and China witnessed by 76,489 in the Sanford Stadium in Athens, Georgia, while the average for all games was 39,362. The United States have remained the predominant force since winning the first final against China, losing to Norway in Sydney and then winning again in 2004 against Brazil. Whereas the participants for the 1996 tournament qualified by finishing amongst the top eight in the 1995 Women's World Cup, there is now a qualifying tournament run along continental lines.

FIFA CONFEDERATIONS CUP

Year	Host Country	Winners	Score	Runners-up	Venue
1992	Saudi Arabia	Argentina	3-1	Saudi Arabia	King Fahd, Riyadh
1995	Saudi Arabia	Denmark	2-0	Argentina	King Fahd, Riyadh
1997	Saudi Arabia	Brazil	6-0	Australia	King Fahd, Riyadh
1999	Mexico	Mexico	4-3	Brazil	Azteca, Mexico City
2001	Korea/Japan	France	1-0	Japan	International Stadium, Yokohama
2003	France	France	1-0	Cameroon	Stade de France, Paris
2005	Germany	Brazil	4-1	Argentina	Waldstadion, Frankfurt

Conceived in 1992, the Confederations Cup's purpose was to bring together the continental champions from around the world. Initially known as the King Fahd Cup, it was later rebranded the FIFA Confederations Cup in 1997 when it came under FIFA's control. Riyadh in Saudi Arabia staged the first three editions, but from 1999 other countries were give the opportunity to host the tournament in an effort to broaden its appeal and before the 2002 and 2006 FIFA World Cups™ it was used as a timely trial run in Korea Republic and Japan in 2001 and in Germany in 2005. After drawing criticism from within Europe, especially among the big clubs who complained of fixture overcrowding, FIFA responded by not insisting that the European champions take part in future events. However, it is open to conjecture as to whether any national team would not want to take part given the standard of football at the tournament known as the 'Festival of Champions'.

FIFA FUTSAL WORLD CHAMPIONSHIP

Year	Host Country	Winners	Score	Runners-up	Venue
1989	Netherlands	Brazil	2-1	Netherlands	Rotterdam
1992	Hong Kong	Brazil	4-1	United States	Hong Kong
1996	Spain	Brazil	6-4	Spain	Barcelona
2000	Guatemala	Spain	4-3	Brazil	Guatemala City
2004	Chinese Taipei	Spain	2-1	Italy	Taipei City

Futsal, the five-a-side indoor version of football, has become an increasingly important part of FIFA's work and since 1989 there have been five FIFA Futsal World Championships. The first three were won by Brazil, the major power in the game, though that position has been challenged by Spain, who have won the past two titles. Via a series of continental qualifiers, most of which double up as continental championships, 16 teams qualify for the finals. Games consist of two periods of 20 minutes and any of seven substitutes may be brought on or taken off throughout the game as many times as desired.

FIFA WORLD YOUTH CHAMPIONSHIP

Year	Host Country	Winners	Score	Runners-up	Final Venue
1977	Tunisia	Soviet Union	2-2 9-8p	Mexico	El Menzah, Tunis
1979	Japan	Argentina	3-1	Soviet Union	National Stadium, Tokyo
1981	Australia	Germany FR	4-0	Qatar	Sydney Cricket Ground
1983	Mexico	Brazil	1-0	Argentina	Azteca, Mexico City
1985	Soviet Union	Brazil	1-0	Spain	Centralny, Moscow
1987	Chile	Yugoslavia	1-1 5-4p	Germany FR	Estadio Nacional, Santiago
1989	Saudi Arabia	Portugal	2-0	Nigeria	King Fahd, Riyadh
1991	Portugal	Portugal	0-0 4-2p	Brazil	Da Luz, Lisbon
1993	Australia	Brazil	2-1	Ghana	Sydney Football Stadium
1995	Qatar	Argentina	2-0	Brazil	Khalifa, Doha
1997	Malaysia	Argentina	2-1	Uruguay	Shahalam Stadium, Shah Alam
1999	Nigeria	Spain	4-0	Japan	Surulere, Lagos
2001	Argentina	Argentina	3-0	Ghana	Jose Amalfitani, Buenos Aires
2003	UAE	Brazil	1-0	Spain	Zayed Sports City, Abu Dhabi
2005	Netherlands	Argentina	2-1	Nigeria	Galgenwaard, Utrecht

FIFA U-17 WORLD CHAMPIONSHIP

Year	Host Country	Winners	Score	Runners-up	Final Venue
1985	China	Nigeria	2-0	Germany FR	Workers' Stadium, Beijing
1987	Canada	Soviet Union	1-1 3-1p	Nigeria	Varsity Stadium, Toronto
1989	Scotland	Saudi Arabia	2-2 5-4p	Scotland	Hampden Park, Glasgow
1991	Italy	Ghana	1-0	Spain	Comunale, Florence
1993	Japan	Nigeria	2-1	Ghana	National Stadium, Tokyo
1995	Ecuador	Ghana	3-2	Brazil	Monumental, Guayaquil
1997	Egypt	Brazil	2-1	Ghana	National Stadium, Cairo
1999	New Zealand	Brazil	0-0 8-7p	Australia	North Harbour, Auckland
2001	Trinidad	France	3-0	Nigeria	Hasely Crawford, Port of Spain
2003	Finland	Brazil	1-0	Spain	Töölö, Helsinki
2005	Peru				Estadio Nacional, Lima

FIFA U-19 WOMEN'S WORLD CHAMPIONSHIP

Year	Host Country	Winners	Score	Runners-up	Final Venue
2002	Canada	United States	1-0	Canada	Commonwealth, Edmonton
2004	Thailand	Germany	2-0	China PR	Rajamangala National, Bangkok

Aside from the Football Tournament of the Olympic Games FIFA organises three major age-restricted championships. The oldest of these is the FIFA World Youth Championship for players under the age of 20. Since its inception in 1977 in Tunisia, the FIFA World Youth Championship has been held every two years and countries from all six Confederations have hosted the event at least once. That is also the case for the FIFA U-17 World Championship which was introduced in 1985 and which is also held every second year. The winners of the FIFA World Youth Championship have all hailed from Europe or South America with Argentina having won five titles and Brazil four, double the number of closest rivals Portugal. The Brazilians have also been strong in the U-17 event although the Europeans and South Americans have not had it all their way as both Africa and Asia have produced world champion teams. Many were sceptical at first as to the value of these youth tournaments, especially with the problems experienced with over-aged players, although this problem seems largely to have died down and the tournaments are now seen as a vital step in the education of young footballers. They can encounter high pressure tournament conditions and different styles of play early in their careers, experiences that benefit their clubs and full national teams later on. In 2002, due to the growing interest in women's football, the third of FIFA's youth tournaments was launched – the FIFA U-19 Women's World Championship. Two editions have been played so far, in Canada and Thailand, and the rise in standards as a consequence has surprised even those involved in the women's game. In all three tournaments the finalists are determined by a system of continental qualifiers.

FIFA CENTENNIAL WORLD PLAYER GALA 2004

It was a Brazilian samba in Zurich as all but one of the awards went to the South Americans at the FIFA Centennial World Player Gala 2004. Mirroring the dramatic progress of Barcelona, Ronaldhino's efforts for the Spanish club earned him the ultimate accolade when he was named FIFA World Player of the Year, seeing off the challenges of Arsenal's Thierry Henry and Andriy Shevchenko of Milan. Every national team coach can vote, but for its Centennial FIFA also invited the captains of the national teams to cast their verdicts. Ronaldhino beat the French striker by 68 points, but Henry may take some comfort from his consistency – he finished runner up the previous year too. Ronaldhino's achievement reflected Barcelona's new superiority in Spain. Voting was held during December 2004 when the Catalan club were on form in both the Champions League and La Liga. The Brazilian dragged Barcelona back to the top of Spanish football throughout 2004 beginning in January when the club languished 10 points and eight places behind then-leaders Real Madrid. Five months later the side qualified for the Champions League as runners-up to Valencia thanks, in no small part, to Ronaldhino's creativity and skill. The first half of the following season was marked by success in the Champions League Group stages marked by Ronaldhino's spectacular winner against eventual group winners, Milan. Perhaps symbolising the club's resurgence, it was the highlight of his year and led him to comment: "Now we're playing for fun and that's when you know you are doing well." Meanwhile, the FIFA Women's World Player of the Year award bucked the Brazilian trend. One of Germany's finest footballers, 1.FFC Frankfurt striker Birgit Prinz, repeated her success of 2003 comfortably beating former winner Mia Hamm. However, hot on her heels was the rising star of Brazil, 18-year-old Marta, who displayed her talents at the FIFA U-19 Women's World Championship to win the Player of the Tournament accolade. The Brazilian procession continued with Falcao named FIFA Futsal World Player 2004 and Thiago Carico de Azevedo winning FIFA Interactive World Player, while the Brazilian national team was the Top Team of 2004 in the FIFA/Coca-Cola World Ranking.

FIFA FAIR PLAY AWARDS

Year	Recipient	Code
1987	Fans of Dundee United	SCO
1988	Frank Ordenewitz	GER
1988	Fans at the Olympic Football Tournament Seoul '88	
1989	Spectators of Trinidad and Tobago	TRI
1990	Gary Lineker	ENG
1991	Real Federación Española de Fútbol	ESP
1991	Jorginho	BRA
1992	Union Royale Belge des Sociétés de Football Association	BEL
1993	Nandor Hidegkuti	HUN
1994	-	
1995	Jacques Glassmann	FRA
1996	George Weah	LBR
1997	Irish fans at the World Cup qualifier versus Belgium	IRL
1997	Jozef Zovinec	SVK
1997	Julie Foudy	USA
1998	The associations of Iran, the USA and Northern Ireland	
1999	New Zealand's football community	NZL
2000	Lucas Radebe	RSA
2001	Paolo di Canio	ITA
2002	Football communities of Japan and Korea Republic	
2003	Fans of Glasgow Celtic	SCO
2004	Confederação Brasileira de Futebol	BRA

FIFA PRESIDENTIAL AWARD

2004 - HAITI

In acknowledgement of the indispensable role that solidarity plays in the harmony of our world, FIFA conferred the Presidential Award on Haiti. As part of that association's centennial celebrations, and coinciding with the FIFA Centennial, Haiti and Brazil joined forces to stage a match whose impact transcended the boundaries of the football pitch in war-torn Haiti. By recognising the actions of both associations in 2004, FIFA continues the quest that it first embarked on 100 years ago, using football to play a conscious and active role in bringing together peoples and fighting against discrimination in all its guises.

2003 - THE IRAQI FOOTBALL COMMUNITY

The never-say-die spirit of the Iraqi people found in football a vehicle for expression after the Iraq War in 2003. Despite extreme hardship and a dire lack of material provisions, the Iraqi football community, staunchly backed by their prolific coach, German Bernd Stange, stubbornly refused to accept the hand which they had been dealt. Against the odds they have maintained their place in the Top 50 teams of the FIFA/Coca-Cola World Ranking and have their sights firmly set on qualification to the 2006 FIFA World Cup Germany™.

2002 - PARMINDA NAGRA (ENG)

The English actress was given this award by the FIFA President for her starring role in the hugely popular movie Bend It Like Beckham. Her alter ego, Jess, a Punjabi girl growing up in West London, is determined to play football, despite strong objections from her family. The film deals with issues of cultural conformity and serves superbly to bring women's football into the spotlight as a game for all women of all cultures.

2001 - MARVIN LEE (TRI)

The very first FIFA Presidential Award was given to Marvin Lee who was paralysed after an injury sustained in March 2001 in an international game with Trinidad and Tobago's U-20 team, of which he was captain. FIFA President Joseph S. Blatter had the opportunity to meet Marvin Lee at his home during the FIFA U-17 World Championship in September 2001. Tragically, Marvin Lee died on 9 March 2003.

FIFA WORLD PLAYER 2004

Player	Club	Nat	1st	x5	2nd	x3	3rd	x1	Total
RONALDINHO	Barcelona	BRA	89	445	47	141	34	34	620
HENRY Thierry	Arsenal	FRA	79	395	42	126	31	31	552
SHEVCHENKO Andrij	Milan	UKR	34	170	19	57	26	26	253
NEDVED Pavel	Juventus	CZE	12	60	33	99	19	19	178
ZIDANE Zinedine	Real Madrid	FRA	17	85	15	45	20	20	150
ADRIANO	Internazionale	BRA	8	40	15	45	13	13	98
DECO	Barcelona	POR	6	30	18	54	12	12	96
RONALDO	Real Madrid	BRA	6	30	17	51	15	15	96
VAN NISTELROOY Ruud	Manchester United	NED	5	25	10	30	12	12	67
KAKA	Milan	BRA	4	20	11	33	11	11	64
ROONEY Wayne	Manchester United	ENG	2	10	12	36	18	18	64
DROGBA Didier	Chelsea	CIV	5	25	5	15	6	6	46
CRISTIANO RONALDO	Manchester United	POR	5	25	3	9	11	11	45
ETO'O Samuel	Barcelona	CMR	2	10	6	18	14	14	42
FIGO Luis	Real Madrid	POR	0	0	10	30	5	5	35
BECKHAM David	Real Madrid	ENG	4	20	4	12	3	3	35
RAUL	Real Madrid	ESP	2	10	6	18	5	5	33
ZAGORAKIS Theodoros	Bologna	GRE	3	15	2	6	4	4	25
AYALA Roberto	Valencia	ARG	3	15	2	6	3	3	24
OWEN Michael	Real Madrid	ENG	2	10	4	12	0	0	22
ROBERTO CARLOS	Real Madrid	BRA	2	10	2	6	3	3	19
MALDINI Paolo	Milan	ITA	2	10	1	3	6	6	19
BUFFON Gianluigi	Juventus	ITA	1	5	4	12	2	2	19
MAKAAY Roy	Bayern München	NED	1	5	4	12	0	0	17
PIRES Robert	Arsenal	FRA	2	10	1	3	2	2	15
LAMPARD Frank	Chelsea	ENG	2	10	0	0	3	3	13
CAFU	Milan	BRA	2	10	0	0	0	0	10
BALLACK Michael	Bayern München	GER	0	0	2	6	3	3	9
BAROS Milan	Liverpool	CZE	0	0	2	6	3	3	9
IBRAHIMOVIC Zlatan	Juventus	SWE	0	0	1	3	4	4	7
LARSSON Henrik	Barcelona	SWE	1	5	0	0	2	2	7
GIGGS Ryan	Manchester United	WAL	1	5	0	0	1	1	6
NESTA Alessandro	Milan	ITA	0	0	0	0	6	6	6
GERRARD Steven	Liverpool	ENG	0	0	1	3	2	2	5
KAHN Oliver	Bayern München	GER	0	0	1	3	1	1	4

Each first placing earns five points • Each second placing earns three points • Each third placing earns one point

FIFA WOMEN'S WORLD PLAYER 2004

Player	Club	Nat	1st	x5	2nd	x3	3rd	x1	Total
PRINZ Birgit	1.FFC Frankfurt	GER	46	230	39	117	29	29	376
HAMM Mia	US Soccer	USA	40	200	20	60	26	26	286
MARTA	Umeå IK	BRA	39	195	23	69	17	17	281
WAMBACH Abby	US Soccer	USA	16	80	11	33	13	13	126
LILLY Kristine	US Soccer	USA	10	50	14	42	17	17	109
LJUNGBERG Hanna	Umeå IK	SWE	8	40	19	57	12	12	109
BOXX Shannon	US Soccer	USA	14	70	9	27	5	5	102
SVENSSON Victoria	Djurgården/Alvsjö	SWE	6	30	13	39	20	20	89
LINGOR Renate	1.FFC Frankfurt	GER	11	55	8	24	10	10	89
CRISTIANE	1.FFC Turbine Potsdam	BRA	9	45	8	24	11	11	80
PRETINHA		BRA	6	30	11	33	5	5	68
FORMIGA	Santa Isabel	BRA	6	30	6	18	6	6	54
ROTTENBERG Silke	FCR 2001 Duisberg	GER	4	20	6	18	10	10	48
MOSTROEM Malin	Umeå IK	SWE	2	10	9	27	6	6	43
PICHON Marinette	FCF Juvisy	FRA	1	5	7	21	9	9	35
STEGEMANN Kerstin	FFC Heike Rheine	GER	2	10	4	12	4	4	26
DOMINGUEZ Maribel	Barcelona	MEX	1	5	4	12	8	8	25
SCURRY Briana	US Soccer	USA	1	5	3	9	3	3	17
SAWA Homare	Beleza	JPN	0	0	3	9	6	6	15
HOOPER Charmaine	Chicago Cobras	CAN	0	0	3	9	2	2	11
NORDBY Bente	Asker	NOR	1	5	1	3	2	2	10

FIFA WORLD PLAYER 2004 - HOW THEY VOTED

	Coach	1st	2nd	3rd	Captain	1st	2nd	3rd
AIA	Vernon Hodge	Shevchenko	Henry	Ronaldinho	Nigel Connor	Ronaldinho	Henry	Zidane
ALB	no vote	none	none	none	Foto Strakosha	Shevchenko	Kaka	Nesta
ALG	Ali Fergani	Zidane	Ballack	Figo	Dziri Bilal	Zidane	Figo	Ronaldo
AND	David Rodrigo	Ronaldinho	Deco	Zidane	Justo Ruiz	Henry	Ronaldinho	Zidane
ANG	Luis Oliveira Gonçalves	Ronaldinho	Eto'o	Henry	Akwa (Maieco Fabrice)	Ronaldinho	Drogba	V. Nistelrooy
ARG	José Pekerman	Henry	Ronaldo	Maldini	Juan Sorin	Henry	Ronaldinho	Drogba
ARM	Bernard Casoni	Ronaldinho	Drogba	Maldini	Harutyun Vardanyan	Shevchenko	Henry	Adriano
ATG	Mervin Richards	Ronaldinho	Zidane	Shevchenko	no vote	none	none	none
AUS	Frank Farina	Henry	Deco	Nedved	no vote	none	none	none
AUT	Hans Krankl	Shevchenko	Makaay	C. Ronaldo	Andreas Ivanschitz	Adriano	Rooney	Drogba
AZE	Carlos Alberto	Ronaldinho	Adriano	Henry	Gurban Gurbanov	Shevchenko	Ronaldo	Kaka
BAH	Gary White	Ronaldinho	Nedved	Henry	Cameron Hepple	Henry	Rooney	Kaka
BAN	Sarwar S.M. Ghulam	Henry	Buffon	Ronaldinho	Rajani Barman	Zidane	Henry	Ronaldinho
BDI	Ramadhani Maulidi	Ronaldinho	Deco	Nedved	Vladimir Niyonkuru	Ronaldinho	Deco	Rooney
BEL	Aimé Anthuenis	Shevchenko	Kaka	V. Nistelrooy	Bart Goor	Henry	Nedved	Shevchenko
BEN	Gomez Wabi	Henry	V. Nistelrooy	Eto'o	Oumar Tchomogo	Ronaldinho	Owen	Eto'o
BER	Kyle Lightbourne	Henry	Nedved	Rooney	Kentoine Jennings	Nedved	Deco	Adriano
BFA	Ivica Todorov	Shevchenko	Henry	Kaka	Moumouni Dagano	Ronaldinho	Adriano	Nedved
BHR	Srecko Juricic	Ronaldinho	Deco	Lampard	Faisal Mohammed	Ronaldinho	Eto'o	Deco
BHU	K. B. Basnet	Ronaldinho	Rooney	C. Ronaldo	Passang Tshering	Cafu	Beckham	Kahn
BIH	Blaz Sliskovic	Zidane	V. Nistelrooy	Ibrahimovic	Sergei Barbarez	Lampard	Makaay	Nedved
BLR	Anatoly Baidachny	Shevchenko	Kaka	Ronaldinho	Sergei Gurenko	Shevchenko	Deco	Rooney
BLZ	Anthony Adderley	C. Ronaldo	Henry	Ronaldinho	Mervin Flores	Henry	Ronaldinho	Giggs
BOL	Ramiro Blacut	Owen	none	none	Luis Cristaldo	Owen	none	none
BRA	Carlos Alberto Parreira	V. Nistelrooy	Henry	Ballack	Cafu	Maldini	Henry	Shevchenko
BRB	Reinhard Fabisch	Ronaldinho	Buffon	Zidane	John Parris	Shevchenko	Ronaldinho	Zidane
BUL	Hristo Stoitchkov	Shevchenko	Ronaldinho	Deco	no vote	none	none	none
CAN	Frank Yallop	Henry	Nedved	Rooney	Pat Onstad	Henry	Nedved	Ronaldinho
CAY	Marcos Tinoco	Ronaldinho	Zidane	Kaka	Frederick Wilks	Henry	Ronaldinho	C. Ronaldo
CGO	Tschian Gana	Ronaldinho	Nedved	Rooney	Oscar Ewolo	Nedved	Ronaldinho	Rooney
CHI	Juvenal Olmos	Ronaldo	Ronaldinho	Henry	Rafael Olarra	Adriano	Ronaldinho	Henry
CHN	Arie Haan	Kaka	Adriano	Deco	Li Weifeng	Kaka	Adriano	Deco
CIV	Henri Michel	Ronaldinho	Drogba	Adriano	Cyrille Domoraud	Henry	Adriano	Ronaldinho
COK	Alex Napa	Henry	Zagorakis	Zidane	Joseph Chambers	Beckham	Rooney	Luis Figo
COL	Reinaldo Rueda	Kaka	Henry	Nedved	Ivan Cordoba	Raul	Adriano	Zidane
CPV	Alexandre Alhinho	Ronaldinho	Henry	Shevchenko	Pedro Brito	Roberto Carlos	Ronaldinho	Henry
CRC	Jorge Pinto	Henry	Adriano	Nedved	Luis Marin	Ronaldinho	Henry	Adriano
CRO	Zlatko Kranjcar	Shevchenko	Ronaldinho	Deco	Niko Kovac	Shevchenko	Ronaldinho	Buffon
CUB	Armelio Luis Garcia	Henry	Nedved	Ronaldinho	Odelin Molina	Ronaldinho	Kaka	Henry
CYP	Momcilo Vukotic	Ronaldinho	Henry	Zagorakis	Nicos Panayiotou	Zagorakis	Ronaldinho	Adriano
CZE	Karel Brückner	Ronaldinho	Henry	Raul	Tomas Galasek	Ronaldinho	Kaka	Zidane
DEN	Morten Olsen	Ronaldinho	Shevchenko	Henry	Thomas Helveg	Henry	Pires	Shevchenko
DJI	Hasan Kamil	Deco	Ronaldinho	Henry	Mohamed Gmar	Deco	Rooney	Kaka
DOM	Juan Mojica	Ronaldinho	Ronaldo	V. Nistelrooy	Franklin Vasquez	Ronaldinho	Ronaldo	Beckham
ECU	Luis Suarez	Henry	Eto'o	Kaka	Ivan Hurtado	Ronaldo	Ronaldinho	Kaka
ENG	Sven Göran Eriksson	Henry	Deco	Nedved	David Beckham	Henry	Ronaldo	Zidane
EQG	Antonio Dumas	Adriano	Ronaldinho	Ronaldo	Juan Micha Udruz	Ronaldo	Raul	Eto'o
ERI	Negash Teklit Negassi	Ronaldinho	Henry	Shevchenko	Abdu Saleh Suleman	Ronaldinho	Henry	Shevchenko
ESP	Luis Aragones	Adriano	Nedved	Eto'o	Raul	Nedved	Figo	Henry
EST	Jelle Goes	C. Ronaldo	Nedved	V. Nistelrooy	Martin Reim	Ronaldinho	Nedved	Henry
FIJ	invalid votes	none	none	none	invalid votes	none	none	none
FIN	Antti Muurinen	Zagorakis	Ronaldinho	V. Nistelrooy	Jari Litmanen	Ayala	Deco	Henry
FRA	Raymond Domenech	Drogba	Shevchenko	Larsson	Patrick Vieira	Shevchenko	Ronaldinho	Adriano
FRO	Henrik Larsen	Henry	Deco	Nedved	Oli Johannesen	Ronaldinho	Zidane	Henry
GEO	Alain Giresse	Adriano	Shevchenko	Ronaldinho	Kakha Kaladze	Shevchenko	Maldini	Kaka
GER	Jürgen Klinsmann	Nedved	Henry	Shevchenko	Michael Ballack	Nedved	Henry	Ibrahimovic
GHA	Samuel Arday	Nedved	Drogba	Eto'o	no vote	none	none	none
GNB	Baciro Cande	Ronaldinho	Ronaldo	C. Ronaldo	Braima Injai	Henry	Ronaldinho	C. Ronaldo
GRE	Otto Rehhagel	Ronaldinho	Henry	Nedved	Theodoros Zagorakis	Ronaldinho	Nedved	Shevchenko
GUA	Ramon Maradiaga	Henry	Kaka	Ronaldinho	Guillermo Ramirez	Ronaldo	Ronaldinho	Henry
GUI	Patrice Neveu	Zidane	Adriano	Maldini	no vote	none	none	none
GUM	Sugao Kambe	Zagorakis	Ayala	Rooney	no vote	none	none	none
GUY	Neider Dos Santos	Ronaldinho	Zidane	Nedved	Shawn Beveney	V. Nistelrooy	Ronaldinho	Zidane
HKG	Tsang Wai Chung	Nedved	Figo	Ronaldinho	Lee Wai Man	Ronaldinho	Deco	Baros

FIFA WORLD PLAYER 2004 · HOW THEY VOTED

	Coach	1st	2nd	3rd	Captain	1st	2nd	3rd
HON	José de la Paz	Ronaldinho	C. Ronaldo	Ballack	Jorge Samuel Caballero	Adriano	Shevchenko	Zidane
HUN	Lothar Matthäus	Henry	Shevchenko	Ronaldinho	Zoltan Gera	Henry	Kaka	Ronaldinho
IND	Stephen Constantine	Henry	Nedved	Nesta	no vote	-	-	-
IRL	Brian Kerr	Ronaldinho	Henry	Deco	-	-	-	-
IRQ	Adnan Hamad Mageed	Ronaldinho	Ronaldo	V. Nistelrooy	Haidar Majid	Ronaldinho	Nedved	Ayala
ISL	Asgeir Sigurvinsson	Ronaldinho	Henry	Adriano	Eidur Gudjohnsen	Lampard	Henry	Ronaldinho
ISR	Avraham Grant	Henry	Rooney	V. Nistelrooy	Avi Nimni	Beckham	Henry	Rooney
ITA	Marcello Lippi	Shevchenko	Adriano	Henry	Fabio Cannavaro	V. Nistelrooy	Rooney	Adriano
JAM	Sebastiao Lazaroni	Ronaldinho	Nedved	Henry	Theodore Whitmore	Henry	Nedved	Ronaldo
JOR	Mahmoud Al Gohary	Ronaldinho	Rooney	Nedved	Abdullah Abu Zema	Ronaldinho	Beckham	Ronaldo
JPN	Zico	Ronaldinho	Adriano	Kaka	Tsuneyasu Miyamoto	Henry	Nedved	Ayala
KAZ	Sergei Timofeyev	Shevchenko	Henry	Nedved	Samat Smakov	Ronaldinho	Henry	Deco
KGZ	Nematjan Zakirov	Henry	Shevchenko	Zidane	Vladimir Salo	Shevchenko	Zidane	Rooney
KOR	Jo Bonfrere	Raul	Henry	Roberto Carlos	Lee Woon Jae	Giggs	Zidane	Ronaldinho
KSA	Nasser Al Johar	Ronaldinho	Ronaldo	Roberto Carlos	Khamins Al Dossari	Ronaldinho	Ronaldo	Ayala
LAO	Oudompaet Soutsakaone	Ronaldinho	Rooney	Lampard	Sisay Vilaysack	Henry	V. Nistelrooy	Baros
LBY	Mohamed El Seline	Ronaldinho	Kaka	Shevchenko	Abderraouf Bennur	Ronaldinho	Adriano	Baros
LCA	Millar Carson	Ronaldinho	Henry	Maldini	Abraham Mentor	Henry	Ronaldinho	Ronaldo
LIE	Martin Andermatt	Shevchenko	Nedved	Henry	Daniel Hasler	Henry	V. Nistelrooy	Shevchenko
LTU	Algimantas Liubinskas	Nedved	Figo	Zagorakis	Aurelijus Skarbalius	Shevchenko	Raul	Ronaldinho
LUX	Allan Simonsen	Zidane	Nedved	Rooney	Manuel Cardoni	Zidane	Henry	Ronaldinho
LVA	Aleksandrs Starkovs	Ronaldinho	Deco	Shevchenko	Vitalijs Astafjevs	Rooney	C. Ronaldo	Ronaldinho
MAC	João dos Santos Lopes	Zidane	Ronaldinho	Nedved	no vote	-	-	-
MAD	Odon Razafintsalama	Ayala	Ronaldinho	C. Ronaldo	Julian Rakotondrabe	Ronaldinho	Raul	Eto'o
MAR	Zaki Badou	Zidane	Ronaldo	Eto'o	Noureddine Naybet	Zidane	Beckham	Ronaldo
MAS	Bertalan Bicskei	Ronaldinho	Baros	Henry	Rosdi Talib	Henry	Ronaldinho	Ronaldo
MDA	Viktor Pasulko	Shevchenko	Ronaldinho	Henry	Valerii Catinsus	Shevchenko	Ronaldinho	V. Nistelrooy
MDV	Manuel Goncalves	Henry	Ronaldinho	C. Ronaldo	Assad Ghani	Ronaldinho	Henry	Nedved
MEX	Ricardo La Volpe	Kaka	Deco	Henry	Oswaldo Sanchez	Pires	Ayala	Ronaldinho
MGL	Ishdorj Otgonbayar	Henry	Raul	Shevchenko	Lumbengarav Donorov	Henry	Raul	Shevchenko
MKD	Dragan Kanatlarovski	Henry	Nedved	Ronaldinho	Goce Sedloski	Henry	Nedved	V. Nistelrooy
MLI	Mamadou Keita	Henry	Ronaldinho	Rooney	no vote	-	-	-
MLT	Horst Heese	V. Nistelrooy	Shevchenko	Rooney	Gilbert Agius	Henry	Adriano	Shevchenko
MOZ	Ayman El Yamany	Deco	Henry	Rooney	Tico-Tico	Ronaldinho	Rooney	Henry
MRI	Govinden Thorrdop	Ronaldinho	Shevchenko	Kaka	Henry Speville	Ronaldinho	Kaka	Ballack
MSR	Scott Cooper	Henry	Rooney	Shevchenko	Ruel Fox	Henry	Deco	Adriano
MTN	Mohamed Ould Messoud	Ronaldinho	Zidane	Drogba	Samba Gaye	Ronaldinho	Zidane	Drogba
MWI	Kinnah F. Phiri	Drogba	Henry	Beckham	Peter Mponda	Eto'o	Owen	Figo
MYA	Ivan Kolev	Ronaldinho	Shevchenko	Henry	Soe Myat Min	Ronaldinho	Shevchenko	Nedved
NCA	Mauricio Cruz	Ronaldinho	Adriano	Eto'o	Carlos Novoa	Ronaldinho	Ronaldo	Zidane
NCL	Serge Martinengo	Zidane	Nedved	Henry	Gil Elmour	Henry	Shevchenko	V. Nistelrooy
NED	Marco van Basten	Henry	Shevchenko	Ronaldinho	no vote	-	-	-
NEP	Raju Kaji Shakya	Henry	C. Ronaldo	Roberto Carlos	Upendra Singh	Cafu	Kahn	Raul
NIG	Amadou Hamey	Ronaldinho	V. Nistelrooy	Nedved	Abdoulkarim Oumarou	Henry	Kaka	C. Ronaldo
NIR	Lawrie Sanchez	Henry	Ronaldinho	Ronaldo	Aaron Hughes	Ronaldinho	Henry	Deco
NOR	Age Hareide	Henry	Nedved	Nesta	Martin Andersen	Henry	Ronaldinho	Nesta
NZL	Paul Smilley	Henry	Buffon	Deco	Ryan Nelsen	C. Ronaldo	Zagorakis	Rooney
OMA	Milan Macala	Henry	Nedved	Shevchenko	Mohamed Rabia	Zidane	Beckham	Ronaldo
PAK	Tariq Lufti	Henry	Ronaldo	Zidane	Khan Jaffar	Henry	Zidane	Ronaldo
PAL	Ghassan Albalaawi	Ayala	Baros	Drogba	Saeb Jendeya	Ronaldinho	Nedved	Zidane
PAR	Anibal Ruiz	Henry	Ronaldinho	Ronaldo	Carlos Gamarra	Ronaldinho	Henry	Shevchenko
PER	Paulo Autuori	Henry	Nedved	Deco	Nolberto Solano	Ronaldinho	Nedved	Adriano
PHI	José Ariston Caslib	Ronaldinho	Figo	Henry	Roel J. Cener	Ronaldinho	Figo	Henry
PNG	John Davani	Henry	Ronaldo	V. Nistelrooy	no vote	-	-	-
POL	Pawel Janas	Henry	Gerrard	Pires	Tomasz Hajto	Makaay	Rooney	Ibrahimovic
POR	Luiz Felipe Scolari	Ronaldinho	Henry	Nedved	Pauleta	Shevchenko	Henry	Ronaldinho
PUR	Luis Villarejo	Ronaldinho	Figo	Raul	Hector Rivera	Ronaldinho	Owen	Raul
QAT	Dzemaludin Musovic	Henry	V. Nistelrooy	Ronaldinho	Mubarak Fazli	Ronaldinho	Kaka	Henry
ROU	Anghel Iordanescu	Deco	Nedved	Ronaldinho	Cristian Chivu	Deco	Ronaldinho	Shevchenko
RSA	Stuart Baxter	Adriano	Henry	Ronaldinho	Aaron Mokoena	Ronaldinho	Owen	Zidane
SCG	Ilija Petkovic	Shevchenko	Ronaldinho	Adriano	Savo Milosevic	Shevchenko	Adriano	Ronaldinho
SCO	Berti Vogts	Henry	Deco	Zagorakis	Barry Ferguson	Rooney	Henry	Gerrard
SEN	Guy Stephan	Henry	Drogba	Shevchenko	Papa Malick Diop	Henry	Shevchenko	Eto'o
SIN	Radojko Avramovic	Beckham	Raul	Shevchenko	Aide Iskandar	Larsson	V. Nistelrooy	Ronaldinho

FIFA WORLD PLAYER 2004 - HOW THEY VOTED

	Coach	1st	2nd	3rd	Captain	1st	2nd	3rd
SLV	Armando Contreras	Ronaldinho	Ronaldo	Eto'o	Victor Velasquez	Ronaldinho	Ronaldo	Eto'o
SMR	Gianpaolo Mazza	Adriano	Shevchenko	Ibrahimovic	Federico Gasperoni	Maldini	Buffon	Kaka
SRI	invalid votes	-	-	-	invalid votes	-	-	-
STP	Ernesto Vaz de Almeida	C. Ronaldo	Figo	Ronaldinho	Paulino da Costa	C. Ronaldo	Figo	Zidane
SUI	Köbi Kuhn	Shevchenko	Ronaldinho	C. Ronaldo	Johann Vogel	Henry	Deco	Lampard
SVK	Dusan Galis	Henry	Nedved	Shevchenko	Stanislav Varga	Ronaldinho	Zidane	Nedved
SVN	Branko Oblak	Ronaldinho	Zidane	Buffon	Aleksander Knavs	Shevchenko	Ronaldinho	Zidane
SWE	Lars Lagerbäck	Nedved	Henry	Nesta	Olof Mellberg	Ronaldinho	Shevchenko	Ronaldo
SWZ	Dumisa Mahlalela	Nedved	Henry	V. Nistelrooy	Jerry Gamedze	Drogba	Eto'o	Rooney
SYR	Ahmad Refaat	Ronaldinho	Zidane	Ronaldo	Maher Seyed	Zidane	Ronaldo	Ronaldinho
TAH	Gerard Kautai	Shevchenko	Deco	Figo	Samuel Garcia	Shevchenko	Zidane	Ronaldinho
TAN	John Reuben Simkoko	Zidane	Ronaldinho	Eto'o	Joseph Pawasa	Henry	Shevchenko	Ronaldinho
TCA	Paul Crosbie	Ronaldinho	Henry	Deco	Gavin Clinton	Ronaldinho	Nedved	Henry
THA	Siegfried Held	Henry	Makaay	Shevchenko	Therdsak Chaiman	Beckham	Ballack	Nedved
TJK	Zoir Babaev	Shevchenko	Henry	Ronaldo	Aslidin Khabibulloev	Zidane	Figo	Shevchenko
TKM	Rakhim Kurbanmamedov	Shevchenko	Nedved	Henry	Kamil Mingazov	Shevchenko	Nedved	Henry
TOG	Stephane Queshi	Drogba	Roberto Carlos	Shevchenko	Jean Paul Abalo	Drogba	Eto'o	Maldini
TRI	Bertille Saint Clair	Henry	Ronaldinho	Zagorakis	Angus Eve	Deco	Henry	Ronaldinho
TUN	Roger Lemerre	Zidane	Henry	Pires	Khaled Badra	Henry	Ronaldinho	Drogba
TUR	Ersun Yanal	Henry	V. Nistelrooy	Rooney	Bülent Korkmaz	Henry	Ronaldo	Ronaldinho
UAE	Aad de Mos	V. Nistelrooy	Ibrahimovic	C. Ronaldo	no vote	-	-	-
UKR	Oleg Blokhin	Henry	Deco	Adriano	Shevchenko	Zidane	Adriano	Maldini
URU	Jorge Fossati	Ronaldinho	Shevchenko	Eto'o	Pablo Garcia	Ronaldo	V. Nistelrooy	Adriano
USA	Bruce Arena	Henry	Nedved	Shevchenko	Claudio Reyna	Henry	Nedved	Ronaldinho
UZB	Ravshan Khaydarov	Shevchenko	Ronaldinho	Henry	Mirdjalal Kasimov	Shevchenko	Zidane	Beckham
VEN	Richard Paez	Ronaldinho	Shevchenko	Rooney	Luis Vera	Ronaldo	Ronaldinho	Henry
VGB	Ben Davies	Roberto Carlos	Ronaldinho	C. Ronaldo	Avondale Williams	Ronaldinho	Roberto Carlos	Raul
VIE	Edson Tavares	Pires	Zidane	Gerrard	Huynh Duc Le	Henry	Ronaldinho	Nesta
VIN	Zoran Vranes	Buffon	Shevchenko	Deco	Ezra Hendrickson	Eto'o	Ronaldinho	Ronaldo
VIR	Felix St. Rose	Henry	Ronaldinho	Zidane	Dwight Ferguson	Henry	Ronaldinho	Zidane
WAL	L. M. Hughes	Nedved	Makaay	Larsson	Gary Speed	Nedved	Eto'o	Figo
ZAM	Kalusha Bwalya	Henry	V. Nistelrooy	Rooney	Mishek Lungu	Henry	Ronaldinho	Eto'o

FIFA WOMEN'S WORLD PLAYER 2004 - HOW THEY VOTED

	Coach	1st	2nd	3rd	Captain	1st	2nd	3rd
AIA	Colin Johnson	Prinz	Ljungberg	Pretinha	Jaynelle Lake	Wambach	Mostroem	Hamm
ALG	Azzedine Chih	Prinz	Hamm	Pichon	Naïma Laouadi	Prinz	Boxx	Hamm
ANG	André Nzuzi	Lilly	Marta	Prinz	Jacinta Ramos	Hamm	Prinz	Marta
ARG	José Carlos Borrelo	Rottenberg	Hamm	Prinz	Marisa Gerez	Ljungberg	Prinz	Marta
ARM	Mher Mikayelyan	Prinz	Svensson	Lingor	Liana Grigoryan	Prinz	Lingor	Svensson
AUS	Adrian Santrac	Hamm	Marta	Prinz	Cheryl Salisbury	Boxx	Pichon	Lilly
AUT	Ernst Weber	Ljungberg	Lingor	Hamm	Gertrud Stallinger	Rottenberg	Wambach	Dominguez
AZE	Boris Tibilov	Prinz	Lilly	Cristiane	Kifayat Osmanova	Prinz	Lilly	Cristiane
BAH	Gary White	Marta	Prinz	Pichon	Taita Wood	Cristiane	Wambach	Marta
BAN	Abu Yusuf	Lilly	Pretinha	Prinz	Lubna Mahmud	Lilly	Pretinha	Hamm
BDI	Kebe Hakizimana	Hamm	Pretinha	Pichon	F. Makito	Hamm	Lingor	Ljungberg
BEL	Anne Noe-Haesendonck	Svensson	Marta	Rottenberg	Femke Maes	Svensson	Ljungberg	Hamm
BEN	Emmanuel Tcheche	Lilly	Pretinha	Rottenberg	Innocente Nikoue	Pretinha	Rottenberg	Prinz
BER	Vance Brown	Pretinha	Scurry	Prinz	Naquita Dill	Hamm	Pretinha	Scurry
BIH	Dzevad Bekic	Boxx	Ljungberg	Lingor	Sabina Pehic	Hamm	Lilly	Ljungberg
BLR	Oleg Volokh	Marta	Ljungberg	Hamm	Natallia Ryzhevich	Marta	Hamm	Prinz
BLZ	David Griffith	Boxx	Hooper	Lilly	Aretha Flores	Hamm	Hooper	Boxx
BOL	Herman Melgar	Pretinha	none	none	Maitte Zamorano	Pretinha	none	none
BRA	Rene Simoes	Wambach	Nordby	Prinz	Juliana	Prinz	Mostroem	Pichon
BRB	Reinhard Fabisch	Prinz	Pretinha	Hamm	no vote	none	none	none
BUL	Boriana Despodova	Prinz	Cristiane	Hamm	Elena Peeva	Hamm	Cristiane	Lilly
CAN	Even Pellerud	Wambach	Lilly	Prinz	Hooper	Wambach	Prinz	Mostroem
CAY	Thiago Cunha	Marta	Cristiane	Svensson	Shakeina Bush	Hamm	Scurry	Marta
CGO	Jean Paul Mpila	Marta	Prinz	Lilly	Eulode Bikindou	Cristiane	Ljungberg	Lilly
CHN	Haitao Zhang	Cristiane	Marta	Boxx	Fan YunJie	Prinz	Boxx	Lilly
COK	Alex Napa	Prinz	Pretinha	Svensson	Mii Piri	Stegmann	Ljungberg	Mostroem
COL	Myriam Guerrero	-	-	-	-	-	-	-
CRC	Ricardo Rodriguez	Marta	Wambach	Prinz	Monica Salazar	Marta	Prinz	Wambach

FIFA WOMEN'S WORLD PLAYER 2004 - HOW THEY VOTED

	Coach	1st	2nd	3rd	Captain	1st	2nd	3rd
CRO	Kazimir Husic	Hamm	Prinz	Lingor	Branka Kozic	Hamm	Prinz	Lingor
CUB	Rufino Sotolongo	Rottenberg	Prinz	Hamm	M. Gonzales	Hamm	Prinz	Marta
CZE	Dusan Zovinec	Prinz	Mostroem	Marta	Eva Smeralova	Prinz	Mostroem	Ljungberg
DEN	Poul Hojmose	Marta	Stegmann	Wambach	Katrine Pedersen	Marta	Pichon	Cristiane
DJI	Hasan Kamil	Marta	Lilly	Ljungberg	Fozia	Marta	Ljungberg	Lilly
DOM	Santiago Morel	Hamm	Prinz	Cristiane	Ana Odaliz Diaz	Hamm	Prinz	Formiga
ECU	Garis Estupiñan	Prinz	Cristiane	Svensson	Nancy Aguilar	Hamm	Formiga	Prinz
ENG	Hope Powell	Marta	Svensson	Boxx	Faye White	Marta	Wambach	Mostroem
EQG	José David Ekang	Marta	Hamm	Lilly	Fabiola Mathe Nchama	Marta	Hamm	Stegmann
ERI	Negash Teklit	Prinz	Hamm	Wambach	Merhawit Tekeste	Prinz	Hamm	Wambach
ESP	Ignacio Quereda	Prinz	Svensson	Hamm	Arantxa Pel Puerto	Svensson	Hooper	Sawa
EST	Juri Saar	Ljungberg	Prinz	Scurry	Elis Meetua	Hamm	Scurry	Ljungberg
ETH	Shale Melese	Marta	Hamm	Cristiane	Rahel Degefegu	Marta	Hamm	Cristiane
FIN	Michael Käld	Wambach	Marta	Rottenberg	Sanna Valkonen	Marta	Boxx	Lilly
FRA	Elisabeth Loisel	Wambach	Boxx	Marta	Sonia Bompastor	Boxx	Wambach	Marta
FRO	Alvur Hansen	Marta	Mostroem	Wambach	Bara Skaale Klakstein	Marta	Ljungberg	Mostroem
GER	Tina Theune-Meyer	Hamm	Marta	Lilly	Prinz	Marta	Wambach	Formiga
GHA	John Eshun	Boxx	Prinz	Lilly	Memunatu Sulemana	Boxx	Prinz	Lilly
GNB	Artemisa Mendes Cuma	Cristiane	Dominguez	Formiga	Sofia G. Correia de Sa	Cristiane	Formiga	Dominguez
GRE	Xanthi Konstantiniou	Hamm	Marta	Wambach	Eftichia Michailidou	Marta	Wambach	Hamm
GUA	Antonio Garcia	Prinz	Ljungberg	Wambach	Tamara de Leon	Prinz	Rottenberg	Hamm
GUI	Toure Moustapha	Marta	Dominguez	Lilly	Kourouma C. Benjanie	Marta	Lilly	Prinz
GUM	Thomas Cortez	Pretinha	Stegmann	Wambach	Caralyn Blyth Canto	Wambach	Pretinha	Stegmann
GUY	Neider Dos Santos	Cristiane	Hamm	Prinz	Yonette Jeffers	Hamm	Cristiane	Scurry
HKG	Chun Kun Leung	Lingor	Hamm	Prinz	Ho Wing Kam	Hamm	Lingor	Prinz
HON	Miguel Escalante	Hamm	Prinz	Dominguez	Morizan Good	Hamm	Dominguez	Prinz
HUN	Istvan Bacso	Prinz	Pichon	Ljungberg	Aranke Paraoanu	Prinz	Hamm	Svensson
ISL	Helena Olafsdottir	Prinz	Marta	Hamm	Erla Hendrinksdottir	Mostroem	Marta	Svensson
ISR	Alon Schraier	Lingor	Prinz	Svensson	Jeanne Silwie	Prinz	Stegmann	Lingor
ITA	Carolina Morace	Boxx	Hamm	Ljungberg	Manuela Tesse	Boxx	Wambach	Ljungberg
JAM	Christopher Bender	Hamm	Wambach	Prinz	Jodi-Ann McGregor	Wambach	Ljungberg	Prinz
JPN	Ueda Eiji	Boxx	Prinz	Marta	Obe Yumi	Boxx	Hamm	Marta
KAZ	Aitpay Jamantayev	Prinz	Cristiane	Mostroem	Natalya Ivanova	Hamm	Prinz	Svensson
KOR	Back Jong Choul	Prinz	Sawa	Hamm	Lee Myung Hwa	Prinz	Sawa	Hamm
LAO	Kingmano Boutsavath	-	-	-	-	-	-	-
LCA	Trevor Anderson	Prinz	Svensson	Hamm	Shirmain Hyocinth	Prinz	Svensson	Hamm
LTU	Vytautas Tutlys	Lilly	Ljungberg	Marta	Justina Lavrenovaite	Ljungberg	Marta	Svensson
LUX	Jean Romain	Ljungberg	Prinz	Lingor	Paula Das Neves	Prinz	Marta	Lingor
LVA	Agris Bandolis	Prinz	Ljungberg	Marta	Katrine Verreva	Wambach	Rottenberg	Svensson
MAD	Magliore Solofoson	Marta	Wambach	Hooper	Irmine Raharimalala	Marta	Hamm	Svensson
MDA	Evgeni Pusicov	Prinz	Mostroem	Hamm	Ina Budesteanu	Svensson	Hamm	Cristiane
MDV	-	-	-	-	-	-	-	-
MEX	Leonardo Cuellar	Wambach	Marta	Rottenberg	Monica Gonzalez	Wambach	Marta	Sawa
MKD	Dobre Dimovski	Lingor	Stegmann	Pichon	Zorica Stojkovska	Lingor	Prinz	Rottenberg
MLT	Pierre Brincat	Prinz	Formiga	Pretinha	Rebecca Dhagostino	Prinz	Formiga	Pretinha
MOZ	Venâncio Maló	Formiga	Prinz	Boxx	Sandra Kourouma	Formiga	Boxx	Prinz
MRI	Eddy Rose	Marta	Prinz	Wambach	Martine Kelly	Marta	Prinz	Hamm
MSR	Ottley Laborde	-	-	-	-	-	-	-
MWI	Stuart L Mbolembole	Lingor	Lilly	Hamm	Towera Vinkhumbo	Lingor	Lilly	Cristiane
MYA	Maung Aye	Hamm	Lingor	Rottenberg	San San Maw	Hamm	Lingor	Rottenberg
NCA	Edward Urroz	Lingor	Cristiane	Dominguez	Claudia Mojica Méjia	Dominguez	Svensson	Lilly
NED	Vera Pauw	Lilly	Marta	Prinz	Marleen Wissink	Marta	Mostroem	Prinz
NEP	Kishor K. C.	Hamm	Prinz	Sawa	-	-	-	-
NIG	Aminata Cecile Andre	Lilly	Pichon	Prinz	Assanediori Mahaman	Cristiane	Lilly	Marta
NIR	Alfie Wylie	Prinz	Svensson	Wambach	Sara Booth	Prinz	Ljungberg	Boxx
NOR	Age Steen	Wambach	Marta	Cristiane	Nordby	Marta	Boxx	Mostroem
NZL	Paul Smilley	Formiga	Lilly	Hooper	Rebecca Smith	Ljungberg	Prinz	Cristiane
PAR	Esteban Von Lucken	Cristiane	Hamm	Prinz	Lorena Z. Soto	Marta	Prinz	Hamm
PHI	Marlon Maro	Prinz	Pretinha	Sawa	Josephine Loren	Prinz	Pretinha	Sawa
PNG	John Davani	Hamm	Formiga	Prinz	-	-	-	-
POL	Jan Stepczak	Ljungberg	Marta	Prinz	Maria Makowska	Marta	Ljungberg	Pichon
POR	José Augusto	Prinz	Marta	Stegmann	Carla Correia	Lingor	Ljungberg	Hamm
PUR	Oscar Rosa	Hamm	Prinz	Wambach	Tania Guadal. Telleria	Hamm	Prinz	Ljungberg
ROU	Gheorghe Staicu	Lilly	Lingor	Svensson	Daniela Pufulete	Pretinha	Ljungberg	Lilly

FIFA WOMEN'S WORLD PLAYER 2004 - HOW THEY VOTED

	Coach	1st	2nd	3rd	Captain	1st	2nd	3rd
RSA	Fran Hilton-Smith	Marta	Hamm	Dominguez	Portia Modise	Hamm	Marta	Lilly
RUS	Yury Bystritskiy	Prinz	Hamm	Pretinha	Tatiana Egorova	Prinz	Ljungberg	Hamm
SCG	Perica Krstic'	Marta	Svensson	Hamm	Danijela Stojilikovic	Lilly	Marta	Svensson
SCO	Tony Gervaise	Rottenberg	Mostroem	Pichon	Julie Fleeting	Boxx	Pichon	Sawa
SIN	Hassan Ismail	Wambach	Prinz	Ljungberg	Norsuria Damsuri	Wambach	Ljungberg	Prinz
SLV	José Herrera	Hamm	Svensson	Dominguez	Maria Leonor Ramirez	Hamm	Svensson	Dominguez
SRI	Clement de Silva	-	-	-	-	-	-	-
STP	Osvaldo Deus Lima	Marta	Pretinha	Rottenberg	Kaz Zandinai	Formiga	Hamm	Lingor
SUI	Béatrice von Siebenthal	Mostroem	Rottenberg	Marta	Meret Wenger	Lingor	Marta	Svensson
SVK	Frantisek Urvay	Hamm	Svensson	Prinz	Jana Hanzelova	Hamm	Prinz	Svensson
SWE	Marika Domanski Lyfors	Boxx	Marta	Rottenberg	Malin Andersson	Marta	Formiga	Cristiane
SWZ	Naomi Du-Pont	Stegmann	Wambach	Ljungberg	Lunzisile Nxumalo	Hamm	Prinz	Ljungberg
TAH	Gerard Kautai	Boxx	Lilly	Formiga	name missing	Pichon	Boxx	Svensson
TCA	Paul Crosbie	Ljungberg	Prinz	Wambach	Sonia E. Bien-Aime	Svensson	Boxx	Wambach
THA	Prapol Pongpanich	Lingor	Lilly	Nordby	Supaphon Kaeobaen	Lingor	Lilly	Nordby
TJK	Zebo Gasanova	Prinz	Mostroem	Pretinha	Sakhnoza Kholova	Marta	Sawa	Lingor
TRI	Jamaal Shabazz	Wambach	Dominguez	Svensson	Cathy-Ann Nixon	Wambach	Svensson	Marta
TUR	Ersun Yanal	Hamm	Rottenberg	Formiga	-	-	-	-
UKR	Mykola Lytvyn	Prinz	Ljungberg	Pichon	Olena Mazurenko	Prinz	Rottenberg	Marta
URU	Juan Duarte	Formiga	Pichon	Svensson	Carla Quinteros	Formiga	Marta	Rottenberg
USA	April Heinrichs	Marta	Prinz	Pichon	Julie Foudy	Marta	Prinz	Stegmann
VEN	Nelson Sanchez	Hamm	Cristiane	Lilly	Infante Milgaros	Hamm	Lilly	Lingor
VGB	Peterson Azille	Svensson	Prinz	Hamm	Dianne O'Meal	Hamm	Svensson	Prinz
VIE	Chung Duc Mai	Scurry	Lingor	Marta	Doan Thi Kim Chi	Lilly	Prinz	Formiga
VIN	Rodwell Alexander	-	-	-	-	-	-	-
VIR	Yohannes Worede	Prinz	Marta	Dominguez	-	-	-	-
WAL	Andy Beattie	Nordby	Prinz	Svensson	Helen Jones	Prinz	Pichon	Svensson
ZAM	Fredrick Kashimoto	Cristiane	Boxx	Prinz	Enia Matukuta	Boxx	Prinz	Hamm

PAST WINNERS OF THE FIFA WORLD PLAYER AWARD

WOMEN'S WORLD PLAYER 2001

		Votes
HAMM Mia	USA	154
SUN Wen	CHN	79
MILBRETT Tiffeny	USA	47
PRINZ Birgit	GER	40
FITSCHEN Doris	GER	37
SISSI	BRA	35
LJUNBERG Hanna	SWE	29
WIEGMANN Bettina	GER	17
RIISE Hege	NOR	16
MELLGREN Dagny	NOR	13

WOMEN'S WORLD PLAYER 2002

		Votes
HAMM Mia	USA	161
PRINZ Birgit	GER	96
SUN Wen	CHN	58
MILBRETT Tiffeny	USA	45
PICHON Marinette	FRA	42
SINCLAIR Christine	CAN	38
JONES Steffi	GER	19
RIISE Hege	NOR	17
SISSI	BRA	14
BAI Jie	CHN	13

WOMEN'S WORLD PLAYER 2003

		Votes
PRINZ Birgit	GER	268
HAMM Mia	USA	133
LJUNGBERG Hanna	SWE	84
SVENSSON Victoria	SWE	82
MEINERT Maren	GER	69
WIEGMANN Bettina	GER	49
MOSTROEM Malin	SWE	23
KATIA	BRA	14
LINGOR Renate	GER	14
MARTA	BRA	13

WOMEN'S WORLD PLAYER 2004

		Votes
PRINZ Birgit	GER	376
HAMM Mia	USA	286
MARTA	BRA	281
WAMBACH Abby	USA	126
LILLY Kristine	USA	109
LJUNGBERG Hanna	SWE	109
BOXX Shannon	USA	102
SVENSSON Victoria	SWE	89
LINGOR Renate	GER	89
CRISTIANE	BRA	80

FIFA WORLD PLAYER 1991

		Votes
MATTHÄUS Lothar	GER	128
PAPIN Jean-Pierre	FRA	113
LINEKER Gary	ENG	40
PROSINECKI Robert	YUG	38
VAN BASTEN Marco	NED	23
BARESI Franco	ITA	12
ZAMORANO Ivan	CHI	10
BREHME Andreas	GER	9
VIALLI Gianluca	ITA	8
SCIFO Enzo	BEL	7

FIFA WORLD PLAYER 1992

		Votes
VAN BASTEN Marco	NED	151
STOICHKOV Hristo	BUL	88
HÄSSLER Thomas	GER	61
PAPIN Jean-Pierre	FRA	46
LAUDRUP Brian	DEN	44
SCHMEICHEL Peter	DEN	44
BERGKAMP Dennis	NED	29
RIJKAARD Frank	NED	23
PELE Abedi	GHA	10
BARESI Franco	ITA	10

FIFA WORLD PLAYER 1993

		Votes
VAN BASTEN Marco	NED	151
STOICHKOV Hristo	BUL	88
HÄSSLER Thomas	GER	61
PAPIN Jean-Pierre	FRA	46
LAUDRUP Brian	DEN	44
SCHMEICHEL Peter	DEN	44
BERGKAMP Dennis	NED	29
RIJKAARD Frank	NED	23
PELE Abedi	GHA	10
BARESI Franco	ITA	10

FIFA WORLD PLAYER 1994

		Votes
ROMARIO	BRA	346
STOICHKOV Hristo	BUL	100
BAGGIO Roberto	ITA	80
HAGI Georghe	ROU	50
MALDINI Paolo	ITA	40
BEBETO	BRA	16
BERGKAMP Dennis	NED	11
DUNGA Carlos	BRA	9
BARESI Franco	ITA	7
BROLIN Tomas	SWE	7

FIFA WORLD PLAYER 1995

		Votes
WEAH George	LBR	170
MALDINI Paolo	ITA	80
KLINSMANN Jürgen	GER	58
ROMARIO	BRA	50
BAGGIO Roberto	ITA	49
STOICHKOV Hristo	BUL	37
ZAMORANO Ivan	CHI	36
JUNINHO	BRA	28
SAMMER Matthias	GER	23
LAUDRUP Michael	DEN	20

FIFA WORLD PLAYER 1996

		Votes
RONALDO	BRA	329
WEAH George	LBR	140
SHEARER Alan	ENG	123
SAMMER Matthias	GER	109
KLINSMANN Jürgen	GER	54
KANU Nwankwo	NGA	32
MALDINI Paolo	ITA	25
SUKER Davor	CRO	24
BATISTUTA Gabriel	ARG	19
ROMARIO	BRA	13

FIFA WORLD PLAYER 1997

		Votes
RONALDO	BRA	480
ROBERTO CARLOS	BRA	65
BERGKAMP Dennis	NED	62
ZIDANE Zinedine	FRA	62
RAÚL	ESP	51
DEL PIERO Alessandro	ITA	27
SUKER Davor	CRO	20
BATISTUTA Gabriel	ARG	16
SHEARER Alan	ENG	16
LEONARDO	BRA	14

FIFA WORLD PLAYER 1998

		Votes
ZIDANE Zinedine	FRA	518
RONALDO	BRA	164
SUKER Davor	CRO	108
OWEN Michael	ENG	43
BATISTUTA Gabriel	ARG	40
RIVALDO	BRA	37
BERGKAMP Dennis	NED	33
DAVIDS Edgar	NED	26
DESAILLY Marcel	FRA	23
THURAM Lillian	FRA	14

FIFA WORLD PLAYER 1999

		Votes
RIVALDO	BRA	538
BECKHAM David	ENG	194
BATISTUTA Gabriel	ARG	79
ZIDANE Zinedine	FRA	68
VIERI Christian	ITA	39
FIGO Luis	POR	35
SHEVCHENKO Andriy	UKR	34
RAÚL	ESP	31
COLE Andy	ENG	24
YORKE Dwight	TRI	19

FIFA WORLD PLAYER 2000

		Votes
ZIDANE Zinedine	FRA	370
FIGO Luis	POR	329
RIVALDO	BRA	263
BATISTUTA Gabriel	ARG	57
SHEVCHENKO Andriy	UKR	48
BECKHAM David	ENG	41
HENRY Thierry	FRA	35
NESTA Alessandro	ITA	23
KLUIVERT Patrick	NED	22
TOTTI Francesco	ITA	14

FIFA WORLD PLAYER 2001

		Votes
FIGO Luis	POR	250
BECKHAM David	ENG	238
RAÚL	ESP	96
ZIDANE Zinedine	FRA	94
RIVALDO	BRA	92
VERON Juan Sebastian	ARG	71
KAHN Oliver	GER	65
OWEN Michael	ENG	61
SHEVCHENKO Andriy	UKR	46
TOTTI Francesco	ITA	40

FIFA WORLD PLAYER 2002

		Votes
RONALDO	BRA	387
KAHN Oliver	GER	171
ZIDANE Zinedine	FRA	148
ROBERTO CARLOS	BRA	114
RIVALDO	BRA	92
RAÚL	ESP	90
BALLACK Michael	GER	82
BECKHAM David	ENG	51
HENRY Thierry	FRA	38
OWEN Michael	ENG	34

FIFA WORLD PLAYER 2003

		Votes
ZIDANE Zinedine	FRA	264
HENRY Thierry	FRA	186
RONALDO	BRA	176
NEDVED Pavel	CZE	158
ROBERTO CARLOS	BRA	105
VAN NISTELROOY Ruud	NED	86
BECKHAM David	ENG	74
RAÚL	ESP	39
MALDINI Paolo	ITA	37
SHEVCHENKO Andriy	UKR	26

FIFA WORLD PLAYER 2004

		Votes
RONALDINHO	BRA	620
HENRY Thierry	FRA	552
SHEVCHENKO Andriy	UKR	253
NEDVED Pavel	CZE	178
ZIDANE Zinedine	FRA	150
ADRIANO	BRA	98
DECO	POR	96
RONALDO	BRA	96
VAN NISTELROOY Ruud	NED	67
KAKA & ROONEY Wayne		64

WITH APOLOGIES TO SIR BOBBY...

By Guy Oliver

For the past 37 years schoolchildren in England have grown up with the knowledge that Sir Bobby Charlton is the all-time record goalscorer for the England national team. It is a record made all the more memorable by the fact that Charlton scored 49 goals, falling agonisingly short of the half century, a feat very few players ever manage to achieve. It is a record seemingly set in stone, never to be broken and only once has another player come close. A missed penalty against Brazil in one of his last games saw Gary Lineker fail to equal the record and when he retired shortly after he finished his career respectfully one short of Charlton's total. The latest challenge comes from Michael Owen who is fast rising up through the ranks with a good deal of his career still ahead of him, although the biggest threat to Charlton's record may yet come from a most unexpected source, . from a player of the highest quality, respected throughout the land but a player generally forgotten for his remarkable feats on the football pitch. A player who has been dead for 51 years ...

The man in question is Vivian John Woodward. Woodward was born into a world where football was still in its infancy; Old Etonians had just beaten Clapham Rovers in the 1879 FA Cup Final and professionalism was still six years away in England and half a century away in the rest of the world. Amateurs players remained a powerful force during Woodward's childhood and were more than a match for the professionals well into his career with Chelsea and Spurs. It is this relationship between amateurs and professionals that lies at the centre of a mystery that may well see the record books rewritten and Sir Bobby unexpectedly knocked off his pedestal sooner than he might have expected.

This rather bizarre twist of events does not, however, just involve Charlton's record. It also goes to the very heart of England's role as the inventors of the modern game, its spread around the globe and the small matter of two world championship titles won by England for which the team has never received proper recognition. Since winning the FIFA World Cup™ in 1966 Charlton has revelled in the attention that comes with being a world champion and the leading all-time scorer for England. By right Woodward should also be feted not only as a world champion but also as the leading all-time scorer for England. The logic behind the statement runs along the following lines: in 1906 the Football Association created an England amateur team to run alongside what had become the professional national team. The professionals competed in the annual British International championship with Ireland, Wales and Scotland but football on the continent was beginning to take hold and fixtures against English teams were much in demand. Even in those far off days the club v country debate was a hot issue, so rather than risking the wrath of the clubs the FA decided to form an amateur team, where the restriction on players would be less strenuous, to take on the continentals. Although a regular in the professional team, Woodward was an amateur and he was made captain of this new and ambitious England outfit.

On November 1, 1906, Woodward led his team mates onto the pitch at the Parc des Princes in Paris and proceeded to demolish the French national team 15-0 in front of 1,500 inquisitive spectators. Woodward scored four that day, although he was outshone by Stan Harris who scored seven. To this day, the defeat remains the second heaviest defeat suffered by the French national team and therein lies the nub of the problem. The French regard the match as an official international; the Football Association don't. For the next eight years Woodward and his band of amateurs thrilled, entertained and educated footballers and crowds alike on the continent. In April 1907 they travelled to the Hague to play the Dutch, followed by trips to Belgium, Germany, Sweden, Switzerland and Denmark. Opponents also visited England to get a flavour of the game in a country that was still light years ahead of the rest.

Without exception these matches are all regarded as full international matches by England's opponents. The historical significance of these games is immense. Whilst the England professional team largely contented itself with the three matches a year against British opponents, the amateurs were trailblazers, spreading the gospel of the game abroad, sowing the seeds of future success for their opponents. There is a case for saying that Woodward's team was perhaps the most significant team in the history of football until the rise of the extraordinary Austrian Wunderteam in the 1930s. That it has largely been forgotten is understandable given the importance that the Football Association and the public at large bestowed on the professional team at the time. An accusation often levelled at the English is their isolationist standpoint and matches against continental opposition at that time barely registered. The home internationals were all that really mattered. This isolationism was to cost England dearly in future years but it also overshadowed a fact that today England fans would surely like to celebrate. Simply put, Woodward's England team were the first ever world champions!

In the Pathé film archive in Paris there is a remarkable nitrate newsreel that bears witness to an historic event. Time has taken its toll on the film but it shows the Olympic Stadium in Stockholm playing host to England and Denmark in the 1912 Olympic football final. Having beaten Hungary and Finland on the way to the final, England then proceeded to beat the Danes, by far and away the most powerful team on the continent, 4-2, to become world champions for the second time. Sadly no footage remains from four years previously at the London Olympics when they also beat Denmark in the final to win the title for the first time. Woodward is shown being presented to King Gustav of Sweden and well he deserved the honour having also been captain at the 1908 London Olympics.

With the FIFA World Cup™ still 18 years away, the football tournament of the Olympic Games was the world championship for football. The next time you see Uruguay play you will notice four stars above the badge on their shirts representing the four world championships they have won - the Olympic Games of 1924 and 1928 and the FIFA World Cup™ triumphs of 1930 and 1950. England have belatedly introduced a star above their badge but just a single one with no reference, unlike Uruguay, to the two Olympic titles. There has often been confusion with regard to these Olympic triumphs as England played under the banner of Great Britain and temporarily replaced the three lions badge with the Union flag, but this was the England amateur team with Woodward as captain.

All of this may have remained an historical curiosity argued amongst historians but in a major attempt to clear up historical inconsistencies FIFA is compiling a list of every international match that has ever been played. Although there is no confirmation as yet, there is a distinct possibility that FIFA will declare the England Amateur matches as full internationals to be in line with the position of all their opponents. There are many historical precedents for declaring matches recognised by only one association as full international matches so the Football Association faces a potential dilemma. If the matches are classified as full internationals, which should be decided in the Spring of 2006, Bobby Charlton will no longer be the top all-time scorer for England because Woodward, in his 30 games for the amateurs, scored 44 goals. That alone would be enough to put him in joint third place alongside Jimmy Greaves, but he also scored 29 goals in 23 appearances for the professional team between 1903 and 1911, giving him an overall total of 73 goals in just 53 international matches in an England shirt.

If Woodward's feats are acknowledged he may get back from Charlton a title he held for many years. In the 1911 British International Championship match against Wales, Woodward scored twice to overtake Steve Bloomer's record of 28 international goals, and he held on to the record for 47 years until overtaken by a single goal by Tom Finney and Nat Lofthouse in 1958. Jimmy Greaves overtook them in 1964 before relinquishing his record to Charlton in 1968. There will be those who claim that history is being rewritten should Charlton's record be taken away but Woodward's case is strong and there is also the possibility of rectifying a huge historical error. There may even be some consolation for the great Sir Bobby in the fact that the country he represented so valiantly has in fact been world champions not just the once but three times. Perhaps one day two more stars will appear over the three lions crest. If they do, all Englishmen will owe a huge debt of gratitude to the man who made the first two happen - Vivian John Woodward.

FIFA U–19 WOMEN'S WORLD CHAMPIONSHIP 2004

If there is one player who epitomises the inexorable rise of the new generation of women's football today it is Brazil's Marta. When the then-16-year-old first appeared for the Samba Princesses in Canada at the inaugural U-19 Women's World Championship in 2002, all who saw her knew they were witnessing the unveiling of a special talent. Two years on and after guiding Brazil to the Olympic final in Athens she lit up Thailand with her skill and passion, sparking the Championships into life and demonstrating just how far the women's game has developed. Thailand had much to live up to after Canada's success when the home side lost to neighbours USA in the final in front of nearly 48,000 fans. While the host country this time struggled to make any impression on their tournament debut, the Championships witnessed superb displays from established sides such as Germany, USA and Brazil. They all reached the last four again with finalists China proving the best of the rest while Nigeria gave eventual winners Germany a real scare in the quarter-finals. Winning coach Silvia Neid, recognising how fast the game has moved on, paid tribute to the other nations: "There are now very, very good players from all over the world and they have improved in leaps and bounds in recent years. The game is developing so rapidly in many places." Possibly the strongest exponents of women's football, the USA, were especially upset at failing to repeat their success of 2002. Many observers anticipated a glamour final between them and Brazil but the defending champions were outplayed by Germany in the semi-final, suffering their first defeat in the history of the competition. Both coaches had sought to neutralise their opponents' dangers, but after a tight opening few minutes, two goals in quick succession opened the game up. However, the Americans couldn't score again while Germany took full advantage of their chances to win 3-1. Desperate not to leave empty-handed the deposed champions promptly thumped a lacklustre Brazil, still smarting from their defeat to China, 3-0 for third place. Not even Marta and her striking partner Cristiane could summon the energy for a final push and the crushing disappointment was all too evident when the number 10 collected her adidas Golden Ball award as the tournament's top player. Would the Brazilians have given the Germans a sterner test in the final? Quite possibly, but instead the Steel Rosebuds ground out a route to the final through a combination of counter-attacks and a highly organised defence that conceded just four goals. However it was a match too far for the Chinese and they were split asunder as early as the fourth minute by the free-scoring Germans who had already netted 19 times in five games. Although the final score registered 2-0, in truth Germany could have scored a hatful. Germany's performances indicated a definite shift in the balance of power in the women's game at this level, but on closer examination a young Brazilian may have revealed where the true power lies for the future.

FIFA U-19 WOMEN'S WORLD CHAMPIONSHIP 2004

First round groups	Pts	Quarter-finals		Semi-finals		Final	
Germany	7	Germany	3 5p				
Canada	7	Nigeria	3 4p				
Australia	3			Germany	3		
Thailand	0			USA	1		
		Australia	0				
Brazil	6	USA	2				
China PR	6						
Nigeria	4					Germany	2
Italy	1	Brazil	4			China PR	0
		Russia	2				
USA	9			Brazil	0		
Russia	3			China PR	2	Third Place Play-off	
Korea Republic	3	Canada	1			USA	3
Spain	3	China PR	3			Brazil	0

GROUP A	PL	W	D	L	F	A	GD	PTS	GER	CAN	AUS	THA
1 Germany	3	2	1	0	13	3	+10	7		3-3	4-0	6-0
2 Canada	3	2	1	0	12	4	+8	7			2-1	7-0
3 Australia	3	1	0	2	6	6	=	3				5-0
4 Thailand	3	0	0	3	0	18	-18	0				

Rajamangala National, Bangkok, 10-11-2004
17:00, 40 000, Toro COL, Canales ECU, Angulo VEN

THA 0 6 GER

Mittag 10, Goessling 2 11 40
Da Mbabi 2 16 23, Laudehr 43

THAILAND				GERMANY
1 SUDTAVEE Kanyawee			RINKES Tessa	1
3 MAIJAREN Anootsara			KUZNIK Peggy	2
4 WIWASUKHU Thidarat	85		VAN BONN Anne	3
5 KAEOBAEN Supaphon (c)			(c) KRAHN Annike	5
6 JITMANEEROTE Suchada	70		THOMAS Karolin	6
8 SEESRAUM Junpen		62	BEHRINGER Melanie	7
9 NETTHIP Pavinee		62	GOESSLING Lena	8
10 THIANGTHAM Kitiya			MITTAG Anja	9
13 SRIMANEE Orathai			OKOYINO DA MBABI Celia	10
14 TUPSURI Jiraprapa	32	46	LAUDEHR Simone	11
16 KHUEANPET Pikul			HAUER Elena	13
Tr: PONGPANICH Prapol			Tr: NEID Silvia	
7 SRIWASO Niparat	32	62	SCHIEWE Carolin	14
17 MUNGKHALA Siriporn	85	62	FELDBACHER Angelika	17
21 WIPHAKONWIT Suponthip	70	46	BLAESSE Anna	19

Rajamangala National, Bangkok, 10-11-2004
19:45, 40 000, Ihringova SVK, Logarusic CRO, Steinlund NOR

AUS 1 2 CAN

McCallum 49
Timko 2 14 19

AUSTRALIA				CANADA
1 LOGUE Alison	69		VAN BOXMEER Stacey	1
2 COOPER Caitlin			RADCHUCK Katie	2
3 CARROLL Kim			GAYLE Robyn	3
4 DAVISON Emma (c)	46	81	DENNIS Tanya	4
5 BEAUMONT Ellen			CICCHINI Amanda	7
6 SHIPARD Sally		53	IACCHELLI Selenia	10
7 TRISTRAM Jenna	46	62	BELANGER Josee	11
8 COLTHORPE Lauren	46		JAMANI Aysha	14
9 KURALAY Selin			(c) LANG Kara	15
10 McCALLUM Collette			SCHMIDT Sophie	16
14 KHAMIS Leena			TIMKO Brittany	17
Tr: SANTRAC Adrian			Tr: BRIDGE Ian	
12 BAZI Julia	46	53	MARANDA Veronique	8
15 BLAYNEY Leah	46	62	ROBINSON Jodi-Ann	9
17 LEDBROOK Kylie	46	81	LEROUX Sydney	18

Suphachalasai, Bangkok, 13-11-2004
17:00, 5 000, Ortega SLV, Pacheco SLV, Riley JAM

GER 4 0 AUS

Okoyino Da Mbabi 4
Mittag 2 26 73, Blaesse 19 85

GERMANY				AUSTRALIA
1 RINKES Tessa			JACKSON Monique	21
2 KUZNIK Peggy			COOPER Caitlin	2
3 VAN BONN Anne			CARROLL Kim	3
5 KRAHN Annike (c)			BEAUMONT Ellen	5
6 THOMAS Karolin	62		(c) SHIPARD Sally	6
7 BEHRINGER Melanie	78	46	COLTHORPE Lauren	8
8 GOESSLING Lena			KURALAY Selin	9
9 MITTAG Anja	74		McCALLUM Collette	10
10 OKOYINO DA MBABI Celia		78	CANNULI Catherine	11
11 LAUDEHR Simone			BAZI Julia	12
13 HAUER Elena	72		LEDBROOK Kylie	17
Tr: NEID Silvia			Tr: SANTRAC Adrian	
17 FELDBACHER Angelika	78	78	TRISTRAM Jenna	7
19 BLAESSE Anna	74	46	BLAYNEY Leah	15
20 HANEBECK Patricia	62	72	REED Alannah	20

Suphachalasai, Bangkok, 13-11-2004
19:45, 5 500, De Toni ITA, Cini ITA, Parga Rodriguez ESP

CAN 7 0 THA

Dennis 11, Timko 3 25 35 56
Robinson 33, Maranda 46, Jamani 54

CANADA				THAILAND
1 VAN BOXMEER Stacey			SUDTAVEE Kanyawee	1
2 RADCHUCK Katie			MAIJARERN Anootsara	3
3 GAYLE Robyn	46	61	WIWASUKHU Thidarat	4
4 DENNIS Tanya			(c) KAEOBAEN Supaphon	5
7 CICCHINI Amanda			JITMANEEROTE Suchada	6
8 MARANDA Veronique			SRIWASAO Niparat	7
9 ROBINSON Jodi-Ann	74		SEESRAUM Junpen	8
14 JAMANI Aysha	82		NETTHIP Pavinee	9
15 LANG Kara (c)			THIANGTHAM Kitiya	10
16 SCHMIDT Sophie		54	SRIMANEE Orathai	13
17 TIMKO Brittany			KHUEANPET Pikul	16
Tr: BRIDGE Ian			Tr: PONGPANICH Prapol	
11 BELANGER Josee	82	54	SRITALA Duangnapa	12
13 EVERRETT Deana	46	61	MUNGKHALA Siriporn	17
18 LEROUX Sydney	74			

Suphachalasai, Bangkok, 16-11-2004
19:45, 2 500, Girard FRA, De Jong NED, Parga Rodriguez ESP

GER 3 3 CAN

Hanebeck 4, Mittag 2 10 37
Lang 40, Maranda 42, Timko 63

GERMANY				CANADA
1 RINKES Tessa			VAN BOXMEER Stacey	1
2 KUZNIK Peggy			RADCHUCK Katie	2
3 VAN BONN Anne	22		GAYLE Robyn	3
5 KRAHN Annike (c)		46	DENNIS Tanya	4
6 THOMAS Karolin			ZURRER Emily	5
9 MITTAG Anja	46	75	CHICCHINI Amanda	7
11 LAUDEHR Simone	46		MARANDA Veronique	8
16 NIEMEIER Annika		92	JAMANI Aysha	14
17 FELDBACHER Angelika			(c) LANG Kara	15
18 JOKUSCHIES Nina			SCHMIDT Sophie	16
20 HANEBECK Patricia			TIMKO Brittany	17
Tr: NEID Silvia			Tr: BRIDGE Ian	
7 BEHRINGER Melanie	46	75	IACCHELLI Selenia	10
15 MPALASKAS Stephanie	22	46	BELANGER Josee	11
19 BLAESSE Anna	46	92	RABER Sari	21

700th Anniversary Stadium, Chiangmai, 16-11-2004
19:45, 21 600, Oiwa JPN, Fu CHN, Takahashi JPN

AUS 5 0 THA

McCallum 2 10 19, Wiwasukhu OG 26
Ledbrook 45, Kuralay 55

AUSTRALIA				THAILAND
1 LOGUE Alison			SUDTAVEE Kanyawee	1
2 COOPER Caitlin		38	THONGSRI Hathairat	2
3 CARROLL Kim			MAIJARERN Anootsara	3
5 BEAMONT Ellen			WIWASUKHU Thidarat	4
6 SHIPARD Sally (c)			(c) KAEOBAEN Supaphon	5
9 KURALAY Selin			JITMANEEROTE Suchada	6
10 McCALLUM Collette		89	SEESRAUM Junpen	8
11 CANNULI Catherine	52		NETTHIP Pavinee	9
15 BLAYNEY Leah			THIANGTHAM Kitiya	10
17 LEDBROOK Kylie	56		KHUEANPET Pikul	16
19 KHAMIS Leena	63	59	THONGKERN Pattarawan	19
Tr: SANTRAC Adrian			Tr: PONGPANICH Prapol	
7 TRISTRAM Jenna	63	38	SRIWASAO Niparat	7
16 HOLCOMBE Briony	52	59	SRIMANEE Orathai	13
20 REED Alannah	56	89	WIPHAKONWIT Suponthip	21

GROUP B	PL	W	D	L	F	A	GD	PTS	BRA	CHN	NGA	ITA
1 Brazil	3	2	0	1	6	5	+1	6		2-1	2-3	2-1
2 China PR	3	2	0	1	4	3	+1	6	1-0			2-1
3 Nigeria	3	1	1	1	4	4	=	4				1-1
4 Italy	3	0	1	2	3	5	-2	1				

700th Anniversary Stadium, Chiangmai, 10-11-2004
17:00, 6 000, Girard FRA, Kaar AUT, Parga Rodriguez ESP

NGA 0 1 CHN

Zhang Ying 77

NIGERIA		CHINA PR	
18 ONYINANYA Ogechi		ZHANG Yanru	1
2 CHIKWELU Rita		GAO Yan	2
3 SABI Akudo		WANG Kun	4
4 UWAK Cynthia		(c) SUN Yongxia	5
5 NWOSU Chima		SUN Ling	7
6 COLE Lilian		ZHANG Ying	8
12 GODWIN Stella	57	XU Yuan	9
13 SIKE Promise		WANG Dandan	10
16 IKIDI Faith		GUO Yue	12
19 JEROME Ulumma		LOU Xiaoxu	14
20 UDOH Nkese (c)	75	WENG Xinzhi	16
Tr: IBE UKWU Felix		Tr: WANG Haiming	
9 IWUAGWU Akudo	57 88	HOU Lijia	6
15 OKESIE Rosemary	75		

700th Anniversary Stadium, Chiangmai, 13-11-2004
17:00, 6 000, Melksham AUS, Ho AUS, Treloar AUS

CHN 2 1 ITA

Wang Kun 52, Xu Yuan 82   Ricco 24

CHINA PR		ITALY	
1 ZHANG Yanru		(c) MARCHITELLI Chiara	1
2 GAO Yan		RIBOLDI Penelope	2
4 WANG Kun		COSTI Fabiana	3
5 SUN Yongxia (c)		BELLUCCI Diana	4
7 SUN Ling	50	MAGRINI Valeria	5
8 ZHANG Ying		70 BINCOLETTO Anna	6
9 XU Yuan		RICCO Agnese	9
10 WANG Dandan	93	83 COPPOLINO Serena	10
12 GUO Yue		66 CASALI Silvia	11
14 LOU Xiaoxu	75	GUAGNI Alia	15
16 WENG Xinzhi		MANIERI Raffaella	21
Tr: WANG Haiming		Tr: BAVAGNOLI Elisabetta	
6 HOU Lijia	50	70 CARISSIMI Marta	8
11 LIU Sa	75	83 MIANI Cristina	18
17 GAO Ying	93	66 VICCHIARELLO Evelyn	20

Suphachalasai, Bangkok, 16-11-2004
17:00, 2 500, Ihringova SVK, Logarusic CRO, Steinlund NOR

CHN 1 2 BRA

Lou Xiaoxu 53   Marta 38, Cristiane 47

CHINA PR		BRAZIL	
1 ZHANG Yanru		KELLY NUNES	1
2 GAO Yan		TATIANA	2
3 GUO Lin		(c) RENATA DINIZ	4
4 WANG Kun		ALIANE	5
5 SUN Yongxia (c)	46	KAREN	6
6 HOU Lijia	67	KELLY	7
8 ZHANG Ying	64	RENATA COSTA	8
9 XU Yuan	77	ROSANA	9
10 WANG Dandan	50	MARTA	10
14 LOU Xiaoxu		CRISTIANE	11
16 WENG Xinzhi		75 MAURINE	17
Tr: WANG Haiming		Tr: FERREIRA Luiz	
11 LIU Sa	50	46 FRANCINE	14
12 GUO Yue	77	67 ERIKA	18
17 GOA Ying	64	75 SANDRA	19

700th Anniversary Stadium, Chiangmai, 10-11-2004
19:45, 6 000, Hong KOR, Irina UZB, Kim KOR

ITA 1 2 BRA

Ricco 64   Costi OG 11, Kelly 84

ITALY			BRAZIL	
1 MARCHITELLI Chiara (c)			THAIS	12
2 RIBOLDI Penelope			TATIANA	2
3 COSTI Fabiana			ELYSA	3
4 BELLUCCI Diana			ALIANE	5
5 MAGRINI Valeria		46	KAREN	6
6 BINCOLETTO Anna			KELLY	7
8 CARISSIMI Marta			(c) RENATA COSTA	8
9 RICCO Agnese	78	76	ROSANA	9
10 COPPOLINO Serena	59		MARTA	10
15 GUAGNI Alia			CRISTIANE	11
21 MANIERI Raffaella			SANDRA	19
Tr: BAVAGNOLI Elisabetta			Tr: FERREIRA Luiz	
7 BRUTTI Veronica	78	76	ERIKA	18
20 VICCHIARELLO Evelyn	59	46	RAQUEL FARIAS	20

700th Anniversary Stadium, Chiangmai, 13-11-2004
19:45, 7 678, Tovar MEX, Munoz MEX, Douglas CAN

BRA 2 3 NGA

Marta 55, Cristiane 83   Uwak 9, Godwin 14, Sabi 90

BRAZIL			NIGERIA	
12 THAIS			ONYINANYA Ogechi	18
2 TATIANA			CHIKWELU Rita	2
3 ELYSA	35		(c) SABI Akudo	3
4 RENATA DINIZ (c)		80	UWAK Cynthia	4
5 ALIANE	21		COLE Lilian	6
7 KELLY	60		IWUAGWU Akudo	9
8 RENATA COSTA		32	NWABUOKU Evelyn	10
9 ROSANA			GODWIN Stella	12
10 MARTA			IKIDI Faith	16
11 CRISTIANE			AKUSOBI Blessing	17
19 SANDRA	46		JEROME Ulumma	19
Tr: FERREIRA Luiz			Tr: IBE UKWU Felix	
16 DAYANE	60	32 67	YUSUF Ayisat	8
17 MAURINE	46	67	SIKE Promise	13
18 ERIKA	21	80	OKESIE Rosemary	15

700th Anniversary Stadium, Chiangmai, 16-11-2004
17:00, 5 400, Toro COL, Canales ECU, Angulo VEN

ITA 1 1 NGA

Manieri 68   Sabi 88

ITALY			NIGERIA	
1 MARCHITELLI Chiara (c)			ONYINANYA Ogechi	18
2 RIBOLDI Penelope			CHIKWELU Rita	2
3 COSTI Fabiana			(c) SABI Akudo	3
4 BELLUCCI Diana	75		UWAK Cynthia	4
5 MAGRINI Valeria			COLE Lilian	6
6 BINCOLETTO Anna		68	AKINLOSE Semola	7
8 CARISSIMI Marta		76	IWUAGWU Akudo	9
9 RICCO Agnese		83	GODWIN Stella	12
11 CASALI Silvia			IKIDI Faith	16
15 GUAGNI Alia			AKUSOBI Blessing	17
21 MANIERI Raffaella			JEROME Ulumma	19
Tr: BAVAGNOLI Elisabetta			Tr: IBE UKWU Felix	
20 VICCHIARELLO Evelyn	75	83	SIKE Promise	13
		76	OKESIE Rosemary	15
		68	UDOH Nkese	20

GROUP C	PL	W	D	L	F	A	GD	PTS	USA	RUS	KOR	ESP
1 USA	3	3	0	0	8	1	+7	9		4-1	3-0	1-0
2 Russia	3	1	0	2	5	7	-2	3			0-2	4-1
3 Korea Republic	3	1	0	2	3	5	-2	3				1-2
4 Spain	3	1	0	2	3	6	-3	3				

KOR 0 – 3 USA

Sarakul Stadium, Phuket, 11-11-2004
17:00, 9 900, Kokotou GRE, Margariti GRE, De Jong NED

Woznuk 15p, Rodriguez 17, Gray 72

KOREA REPUBLIC

No	Player	
1	JUN Min Kyung	
3	LEE Jin Hwa	
6	PARK Mi Jung (c)	
7	KIM Joo Hee	
8	LEE Jang Mi	
9	PARK Eun Sun	
10	PARK Hee Young	75
13	JUNG Sey Hwa	
16	SONG Yu Na	46
17	HAN Song I	
19	CHA Yun Hee	
	Tr: BAEK Jong Chul	
4	LEE Ye Eun	75
5	YOON Young Geul	46

USA

No	Player	
18	HARRIS Ashlyn (c)	
3	BUEHLER Rachel	
5	GRAY Sheree	91
6	LOPEZ Stephanie	
7	RAPINOE Megan	85
8	LOGTERMAN Stephanie	
10	WOZNUK Angie	
11	SAUERBRUNN Becky	
12	ORAND Alexa	70
16	RODRIGUEZ Amy	
19	HOLMES Meagan	
	Tr: KRIKORIAN Mark	
4	REDMOND Jennifer	70
9	HANKS Kerri	85
13	AVERBUCH Yael	91

RUS 4 – 1 ESP

Sarakul Stadium, Phuket, 11-11-2004
19:45, 5 000, Kamnueng THA, Daw Kaw MYA, Huynh VIE

Terekhova 10, Sochneva 36, Petrova 76, Gil Garcia OG 88

Nuria Zufia 24

RUSSIA

No	Player	
1	TODUA Elvira	
2	SEDOVA Elena	
3	SEMENCHENKO Elena (c)	
6	TITOVA Oxana	
7	SOCHNEVA Ekaterina	82
8	TEREKHOVA Elena	
9	TSIDIKOVA Svetlana	
11	MOROZOVA Elena	
13	TSYBUTOVICH Ksenia	
15	PESHINA Olga	69
16	KHARCHENKO Nadezhda	76
	Tr: GRISHIN Valentin	
4	GOMOZOVA Alexandra	76
10	FOMINA Yana	82
14	PETROVA Olga	69

SPAIN

No	Player	
13	MARIA SANCHEZ	
3	VERONICA BOQUETE	
4	MIRIAM DIEGUEZ	
5	RUTH GARCIA	
7	NATALIA PABLOS	75
8	NURIA ZUFIA	70
9	JADE BOHO	
10	IRAIA ITURREGI (c)	
14	SILVIA DOBLADO	
15	ANE BERGARA	
18	ZURINE GIL GARCIA	
	Tr: QUEREDA Ignacio	
11	ANA ROMERO	75
17	JULIA DE LA PAZ	70

USA 4 – 1 RUS

Sarakul Stadium, Phuket, 14-11-2004
17:00, 8 563, Oiwa JPN, Fu CHN, Takahashi JPN

Woznuk 2p, Rostedt 2 25 60, Rapinoe 63

Sochneva 46

USA

No	Player	
18	HARRIS Ashlyn (c)	
3	BUEHLER Rachel	
5	GRAY Sheree	54
6	LOPEZ Stephanie	
8	LOGTERMAN Stephanie	
10	WOZNUK Angie	
11	SAUERBRUNN Becky	
13	AVERBUCH Yael	
16	RODRIGUEZ Amy	60
17	ROSTEDT Jessica	79
19	HOLMES Meagan	
	Tr: KRIKORIAN Mark	
7	RAPINOE Megan	60
12	ORAND Alexa	54
20	LINDSTROM Stacey	79

RUSSIA

No	Player	
1	TODUA Elvira	
2	SEDOVA Elena	
4	GOMOZOVA Alexandra	54
5	SEMENCHENKO Elena (c)	
6	TITOVA Oxana	
7	SOCHNEVA Ekaterina	
8	TEREKHOVA Elena	80
9	TSIDIKOVA Svetlana	
11	MOROZOVA Elena	
13	TSYBUTOVICH Ksenia	
15	PESHINA Olga	71
	Tr: GRISHIN Valentin	
10	FOMINA Yana	80
16	KHARCHENKO Nadezhda	54
20	GORYACHEVA Anna	71

ESP 2 – 1 KOR

Sarakul Stadium, Phuket, 14-11-2004
19:45, 13 563, Mitchell RSA, Agbavitor GHA, Ejidike NGA

Jade Boho 2 19 57

Park Eun Sun 72

SPAIN

No	Player	
1	LUCIA MUNOZ	
3	VERONICA BOQUETE	90
4	MIRIAM DIEGUEZ	
5	RUTH GARCIA	
7	NATALIA PABLOS	76
8	NURIA ZUFIA	
9	JADE BOHO	82
10	IRAIA ITURREGI (c)	
14	SILVIA DOBLADO	
15	ANE BERGARA	
18	ZURINE GIL GARCIA	
	Tr: QUEREDA Ignacio	
11	ANA ROMERO	76
12	IRUNE MURUA	90
17	JULIA DE LA PAZ	82

KOREA REPUBLIC

No	Player	
1	JUN Min Kyung	
3	LEE Jin Hwa	
4	LEE Ye Eun	
5	YOON Young Geul	
6	PARK Mi Jung (c)	
7	KIM Joo Hee	
8	LEE Jang Mi	
9	PARK Eun Sun	79
16	SONG Yu Na	65
17	HAN Song I	55
19	CHA Yun Hee	
	Tr: BAEK Jong Chul	
11	PARK Eun Jung	65
13	JUNG Sey Hwa	55
20	JEON Jae Min	79

USA 1 – 0 ESP

Sarakul Stadium, Phuket, 18-11-2004
17:00, 9 652, Tovar MEX, Munoz MEX, Douglas CAN

Rostedt 44

USA

No	Player	
18	HARRIS Ashlyn (c)	
3	BUEHLER Rachel	
5	GRAY Sheree	
6	LOPEZ Stephanie	
8	LOGTERMAN Stephanie	
9	HANKS Kerri	
11	SAUERBRUNN Becky	
12	ORAND Alexa	
14	SCHNUR Meghan	58
17	ROSTEDT Jessica	46
19	HOLMES Meagan	
	Tr: KRIKORIAN Mark	
4	REDMOND Jennifer	58
16	RODRIGUEZ Amy	46

SPAIN

No	Player	
1	LUCIA MUNOZ	
3	VERONICA BOQUETE	
4	MIRIAM DIEGUEZ	
5	RUTH GARCIA	
7	NATALIA PABLOS	74
8	NURIA ZUFIA	56
9	JADE BOHO	
10	IRAIA ITURREGI (c)	
14	SILVIA DOBLADO	
15	ANE BERGARA	
18	ZURINE GIL GARCIA	
	Tr: QUEREDA Ignacio	
11	ANA ROMERO	74
12	IRUNE MURUA	56

RUS 0 – 2 KOR

Suphachalasai, Bangkok, 18-11-2004
17:00, 800, Melksham AUS, Ho AUS, Treloar AUS

Lee Jang Mi 21, Park Hee Young 55

RUSSIA

No	Player	
1	TODUA Elvira	
2	SEDOVA Elena	93
5	SEMENCHENKO Elena (c)	
6	TITOVA Oxana	
7	SOCHNEVA Ekaterina	
8	TEREKHOVA Elena	
9	TSIDIKOVA Svetlana	
11	MOROZOVA Elena	
13	TSYBUTOVICH Ksenia	
15	PESHINA Olga	46
16	KHARCHENKO Nadezhda	38
	Tr: GRISHIN Valentin	
3	KOSTYUKOVA Anastasia	93
14	PETROVA Olga	46
17	BUKASHKINA Lyubov	38

KOREA REPUBLIC

No	Player	
1	JUN Min Kyung	
3	LEE Jin Hwa	
4	LEE Ye Eun	
5	YOON Young Geul	
6	PARK Mi Jung (c)	
8	LEE Jang Mi	
9	PARK Eun Sun	46
10	PARK Hee Young	85
16	SONG Yu Na	
17	HAN Song I	
19	CHA Yun Hee	
	Tr: BAEK Jong Chul	
7	KIM Joo Hee	85
20	JEON Jae Min	46

QUARTER-FINALS

700th Anniversary Stadium, Chiang Mai, 21-11-2004
17:00, 8 280, Ortega SLV, Pacheco SLV, Riley JAM

GER (5) 1   1 (4) NGA

Mittag [86]   Udoh [35]

GERMANY			NIGERIA		
1 RINKES Tessa			ONYINANYA Ogechi 18		
2 KUZNIK Peggy			SABI Akudo 3		
3 VAN BONN Anne			UWAK Cynthia 4		
5 KRAHN Annike (c)		79	COLE Lilian 6		
6 THOMAS Karolin			IWUAGWU Akudo 9		
7 BEHRINGER Melanie		53	NWABUOKU Evelyn 10		
8 GOESSLING Lena	46		GODWIN Stella 12		
9 MITTAG Anja			IKIDI Faith 16		
10 OKOYINO DA MBABI Celia	119	107	AKUSOBI Blessing 17		
11 LAUDEHR Simone			JEROME Ulumma 19		
13 HAUER Elena			(c) UDOH Nkese 20		
Tr: NEID Silvia			Tr: IBE UKWU Felix		
16 NIEMEIER Annika	119	79	YUSUF Ayisat 8		
20 HANEBECK Patricia	46	53	SIKE Promise 13		
		107	EGWIM Augusta 14		

700th Anniversary Stadium, Chiang Mai, 21-11-2004
19:45, 8 280, Oiwa JPN, Fu CHN, Takahashi JPN

USA 2   0 AUS

Rodriguez [54], Rapinoe [68]

USA			AUSTRALIA		
18 HARRIS Ashlyn (c)			LOGUE Alison 1		
3 BUEHLER Rachel			COOPER Caitlin 2		
5 GRAY Sheree			CARROLL Kim 3		
6 LOPEZ Stephanie			(c) DAVISON Emma 4		
7 RAPINOE Megan			BEAUMONT Ellen 5		
8 LOGTERMAN Stephanie			SHIPARD Sally 6		
11 SAUERBRUNN Becky			KURALAY Selin 9		
12 ORAND Alexa			McCALLUM Collette 10		
16 RODRIGUEZ Amy		70	SOMI Nicole 14		
17 ROSTEDT Jessica	46	58	BLAYNEY Leah 15		
19 HOLMES Meagan		78	KHAMIS Leena 19		
Tr: KRIKORIAN Mark			Tr: SANTRAC Adrian		
10 WOZNUK Angie	76 46	70	COLTHORPE Lauren 8		
15 KRZYSIK Nikki		76	78	CANNULI Catherine 11		
		58	LEDBROOK Kylie 17		

Suphachalasai, Bangkok, 21-11-2004
17:00, 5 400, Kamnueng THA, Daw Kaw MYA, Huynh VIE

BRA 4   2 RUS

Marta [42], Cristiane [94+],
Sandra 2 [110 113]   Tsybutovich [29], Tsidikova [61]

BRAZIL			RUSSIA		
1 KELLY NUNES			TODUA Elvira 1		
2 TATIANA		74	SEDOVA Elena 2		
4 RENATA DINIZ (c)			(c) SEMENCHENKO Elena 5		
5 ALIANE			TITOVA Oxana 6		
7 KELLY	68		SOCHNEVA Ekaterina 7		
8 RENATA COSTA			TEREKHOVA Elena 8		
9 ROSANA	64		TSIDIKOVA Svetlana 9		
10 MARTA			MOROZOVA Elena 11		
11 CRISTIANE			TSYBUTOVICH Ksenia 13		
17 MAURINE		66	PETROVA Olga 14		
18 ERIKA	46		KHARCHENKO Nadezhda 16		
Tr: FERREIRA Luiz			Tr: GRISHIN Valentin		
14 FRANCINE	46	74	FOMINA Yana 10		
16 DAYANE	68	66 89	PESHINA Olga 15		
19 SANDRA	64	89	GORYACHEVA Anna 20		

Suphachalasai, Bangkok, 21-11-2004
19:45, 5 400, De Toni ITA, Cini ITA, Kaar AUT

CAN 1   3 CHN

Timko [63]   Zhang Ying 2 [3p 21], Liu Sa [65]

CANADA			CHINA PR		
1 VAN BOXMEER Stacey	1		ZHANG Yanru 1		
2 RADCHUCK Katie			GAO Yan 2		
4 DENNIS Tanya	60		GUO Lin 3		
5 ZURRER Emily			WANG Kun 4		
7 CICCHINI Amanda			(c) SUN Yongxia 5		
8 MARANDA Veronique		95	SUN Ling 7		
9 ROBINSON Jodi-Ann	3		ZHANG Ying 8		
14 JAMANI Aysha		64	XU Yuan 9		
15 LANG Kara (c)		81	WANG Dandan 10		
16 SCHMIDT Sophie			LOU Xiaoxu 14		
17 TIMKO Brittany			WENG Xinzhi 16		
Tr: BRIDGE Ian			Tr: WANG Haiming		
13 EVERRETT Deana	60	64	LIU Sa 11		
20 LABBE Stephanie	3	81	GUO Yue 12		
		95	GAO Ying 17		

SEMI-FINALS

Suphachalasai, Bangkok, 24-11-2004
17:00, 10 500, De Toni ITA, Cini ITA, De Jong NED

GER 3   1 USA

Krahn [11], Behringer [69]
Hanebeck [82]   Krahn OG [16]

GERMANY			USA		
1 RINKES Tessa			(c) HARRIS Ashlyn 18		
2 KUZNIK Peggy			BUEHLER Rachel 3		
3 VAN BONN Anne			GRAY Sheree 5		
5 KRAHN Annike (c)			LOPEZ Stephanie 6		
6 THOMAS Karolin			RAPINOE Megan 7		
7 BEHRINGER Melanie	76		LOGTERMAN Stephanie 8		
9 MITTAG Anja			WOZNUK Angie 10		
10 OKOYINO DA MBABI Celia			SAUERBRUNN Becky 11		
11 LAUDEHR Simone		81	ORAND Alexa 12		
13 HAUER Elena			RODRIGUEZ Amy 16		
20 HANEBECK Patricia			HOLMES Meagan 19		
Tr: NEID Silvia			Tr: KRIKORIAN Mark		
17 FELDBACHER Angelika	76	81	ROSTEDT Jessica 17		

Suphachalasai, Bangkok, 24-11-2004
19:45, 10 500, Ihringova SVK, Steinlund NOR, Logarusic CRO

BRA 0   2 CHN

                                    Lou Xiaoxu 2 [11 42]

BRAZIL			CHINA PR		
1 KELLY NUNES			ZHANG Yanru 1		
2 TATIANA			GAO Yan 2		
4 RENATA DINIZ (c)			GUO Lin 3		
5 ALIANE	63		WANG Kun 4		
7 KELLY			(c) SUN Yongxia 5		
8 RENATA COSTA		72	SUN Ling 7		
9 ROSANA	46		ZHANG Ying 8		
10 MARTA			WANG Dandan 10		
11 CRISTIANE		57	LIU Sa 11		
14 FRANCINE	46		LOU Xiaoxu 14		
17 MAURINE			WENG Xinzhi 16		
Tr: FERREIRA Luiz			Tr: WANG Haiming		
18 ERIKA	63	72	HOU Lijia 6		
19 SANDRA	46	57 89	XU Yuan 9		
20 RAQUEL FARIAS	46	89	GUO Yue 12		

Bronze Medal play-off, Rajamangala National, Bangkok
27-11-2004, 16:00, 23 000, Girard FRA, Parga Rodriguez ESP, Kaar AUT

USA   3   0   BRA

Hanks [21], Rapinoe [27], Woznuk [73]

USA				BRAZIL
18	HARRIS Ashlyn (c)			THAIS 12
3	BUEHLER Rachel			TATIANA 2
4	REDMOND Jennifer	46		ELYSA 3
6	LOPEZ Stephanie			(c) RENATA DINIZ 4
7	RAPINOE Megan		32	ALIANE 5
8	LOGTERMAN Stephanie			KELLY 7
9	HANKS Kerri	53		RENATA COSTA 8
10	WOZNUK Angie			ROSANA 9
11	SAUERBRUNN Becky			MARTA 10
15	KRZYSIK Nikki			CRISTIANE 11
16	RODRIGUEZ Amy	46		MAURINE 17
	Tr: KRIKORIAN Mark			Tr: FERREIRA Luiz
2	KRON Stephanie	85	46 66	RAQUEL BUENO 13
5	GRAY Sheree	46	66	DAYANE 16
12	ORAND Alexa	85 53	32	SANDRA 19

PENALTY SHOOT-OUT GER - NGA

Nigeria First		Germany Second	
GODWIN	✔	BEHRINGER	✔
UDOH	✔	THOMAS	✔
IWUAGWU	✘	HAUER	✔
YUSUF	✔	HANEBECK	✔
SIKE	✔	MITTAG	✔

Germany qualified for the semi-finals 5-4 on penalties

ADIDAS GOLDEN BALL

1	MARTA	Brazil
2	WOZNUK Angie	USA
3	MITTAG Anja	Germany

ADIDAS GOLDEN SHOE

			Goals	Assists
1	TIMKO Brittany	Canada	7	2
2	MITTAG Anja	Germany	6	3
3	WOZNUK Angie	USA	3	3

FIFA FAIR PLAY AWARD

1	USA	Ø 776	6 matches
2	Germany	Ø 757	6 matches
3	Australia	Ø 736	4 matches

GOALSCORING AT THAILAND 2004

Total number of goals scored	92
Average per match	3.54
How the Goals were Scored	
Goals scored from inside the penalty area	66
Goals scored from outside of the penalty area	26
Goals scored by headers	8
Goals scored from open play	62
from a passing run	47
from a solo run	11
own goal	4
Goals scored from set pieces	30
after a corner	10
after a free-kick	7
after a throw-in	0
direct from free-kick	10
penalty	3

When the Goals were scored		
1st - 15th minute	18.5%	17
16th - 30th minute	20.7%	19
31st - 45th minute	15.2%	14
46th - 60th minute	15.2%	14
61st - 75th minute	14.1%	13
76th - 90th minute	13.0%	12
91st - 105th minute	1.1%	1
106th - 120th minute	2.2%	2

ATTENDANCES AT THAILAND 2004

Total number of spectators	288 324
Average per match	11 089

Attendances at each venue		
	Total	Average
Bangkok Rajamangala	126 000	31 500
Bangkok Supachalasai	48 100	5 344
Chiang Mai	67 546	8 443
Phuket	46 678	9 335

Largest attendances		
Thailand v Germany	Bangkok Rajamangala	40 000
Australia v Canada	Bangkok Rajamangala	40 000
USA v Brazil	Bangkok Rajamangala	23 000
Germany v China PR	Bangkok Rajamangala	23 000
Australia v Thailand	Chiang Mai	21 600
Spain v Korea Rep	Phuket	13 563
Germany v USA	Bangkok Supachalasai	10 500
Brazil v China PR	Bangkok Supachalasai	10 500
Korea Rep v USA	Phuket	9 900
USA v Spain	Phuket	9 652

Smallest Attendances		
Russia v Korea Rep	Bangkok Supachalasai	800
Germany v Canada	Bangkok Supachalasai	2 500
China PR v Brazil	Bangkok Supachalasai	2 500
Russia v Spain	Bangkok Supachalasai	5 000
Germany v Australia	Phuket	5 000

Women's U-19 2004 Final   **Rajamangala National, Bangkok**   **27-11-2004**

Kick-off: 19:00   Attendance: 23 000

GER   2   0   CHN

Laudehr [4], Behringer [83]

GERMANY				MATCH STATS			CHINA PR		
1	GK	RINKES Tessa					ZHANG Yanru	GK	1
2	DF	KUZNIK Peggy		17	Shots	5	GAO Yan	DF	2
3	DF	VAN BONN Anne		7	Shots on Goal	0	GUO Lin	DF	3
5	DF	KRAHN Annike (c)		12	Fouls Committed	10	WANG Kun	DF	4
6	MF	THOMAS Karolin		3	Corner Kicks	3	(c) SUN Yongxia	MF	5
7	MF	BEHRINGER Melanie		4	Offside	3	36	SUN Ling	MF	7
9	FW	MITTAG Anja		51	Possession %	49	ZHANG Ying	MF	8
10	MF	OKOYINO DA MBABI Celia				74	WANG Dandan	MF	10
11	FW	LAUDEHR Simone	66	MATCH OFFICIALS		57	LIU Sa	FW	11
13	DF	HAUER Elena		REFEREE			LOU Xiaoxu	MF	14
20	FW	HANEBECK Patricia	61	TOVAR Virginia MEX			WENG Xinzhi	DF	16
		Tr: NEID Silvia		ASSISTANTS			Tr: WANG Haiming		
		Substitutes		PACHECO Reina SLV			Substitutes		
8	MF	GOESSLING Lena	61	RILEY Paulette JAM			HOU Lijia	MF	6
12	GK	LAENGERT Kathrin		4TH OFFICIAL		36	XU Yuan	FW	9
14	DF	SCHIEWE Carolin		DAMKOVA Dagmar CZE		57	GUO Yue	DF	12
15	DF	MPALASKAS Stephanie				74	MA Xiaoxu	FW	13
16	MF	NIEMEIER Annika					WANG Cong	MF	15
17	MF	FELDBACHER Angelika	66				GAO Ying	MF	17
18	DF	JOKUSCHIES Nina					WENG Xiaojie	GK	18
19	FW	BLAESSE Anna					GE Yang	DF	19
21	MF	VEEH Carolin					SUN Lisha	MF	20
							SONG Jianqui	GK	21

China played well and made it difficult for us... We knew they would play defensively, but we were able to make and finish some chances like we have done throughout the event. It's a very special achievement to win.

Silva Neid

Going behind that early in the match always makes things more challenging. My players worked hard and showed a lot of spirit... Ultimately, it was not enough against an outstanding German team.

Wang Haiming

MATCH HIGHLIGHTS

4' Zhang saves Mittag's header from a Behringer free-kick but Laudehr strokes home the rebound. **11'** Laudehr shoots just inches wide. **24'** China's first chance but Liu Sa's header goes wide of the post. **43'** Mittag plays a 1-2 with Hannebeck but her shot is deflected just over following confusion in the Chinese defence. **61'** A quick free-kick by Xu Yuan forces a save from Rinkes. **67'** A fierce shot from Behringer from the edge of penalty area hits the side netting. **70'** A great save by Zhang pushes a Goessling shot past the post after a fine run down the left wing and cross by Mittag. **71'** Mittag fires just over from close range after a Behringer cross from the right is only partially cleared by the Chinese defence. **83'** After great persistence by Mittag, Behringer scores with a trademark powerful and accurate shot from just outside the area.

MATCH REPORT

The German women's U-19 team emulated their seniors by becoming world champions and it was done in relatively easy fashion against the Chinese. It was a game that the Germans never seriously looked in danger of losing as the Chinese, resilient as usual in defence, lacked any real firepower up front, failing to get a single shot on target during the entire match. For all their pressure, however, Germany were restricted to just the two goals, scored right at the beginning and at the end of the match.

AUS – AUSTRALIA WOMEN'S U-19 SQUAD

No	Pos	Name	Shirt Name	DoB	Club	Cms	Kg	Games	Mins	Goals	Y	R
1	GK	LOGUE Alison	LOGUE	6-3-1987	Northern NSW Pride	174	1987	3	249			1
2	DF	COOPER Caitlin	COOPER	12-2-1988	NSW Sapphires	170	64	4	360			
3	DF	CARROLL Kim	CARROLL	2-9-1987	Queensland Sting	175	69	4	360			
4	DF	DAVISON Emma (c)	DAVISON	4-5-1985	Queensland Sting	174	69	2	136			
5	DF	BEAUMONT Ellen	BEAUMONT	14-7-1985	Queensland Sting	170	63	4	360			
6	MF	SHIPARD Sally	SHIPARD	20-10-1987	NSW Sapphires	175	64	4	360			
7	FW	TRISTRAM Jenna	TRISTRAM	28-10-1986	Northern NSW Pride	167	58	3	85			
8	MF	COLTHORPE Lauren	COLTHORPE	25-10-1985	Northern NSW Pride	173	59	3	112			
9	FW	KURALAY Selin	KURALAY	25-1-1985	Queensland Sting	161	63	4	360	1		
10	MF	MC CALLUM Collette	MCCALLUM	26-3-1986	Western Waves	165	60	4	360	3		
11	FW	CANNULI Catherine	CANNULI	3-3-1986	NSW Sapphires	163	60	3	142			
12	DF	BAZI Julia	BAZI	20-10-1985	NSW Sapphires	165	63	2	134			
13	DF	BROGAN Danielle	BROGAN	28-6-1988	NSW Sapphires	169	68	0	0			
14	DF	SOMI Nicole	SOMI	19-1-1987	Canberra Eclipse	169	75	1	70			
15	MF	BLAYNEY Leah	BLAYNEY	4-7-1986	NSW Sapphires	156	62	4	236			
16	MF	HOLCOMBE Briony	HOLCOMBE	27-2-1986	NSW Sapphires	167	52	1	38			
17	MF	LEDBROOK Kylie	LEDBROOK	20-3-1986	NSW Sapphires	160	64	4	204	1	1	
18	GK	FAVRETTI Yasmin	FAVRETTI	12-12-1985	NSW Sapphires	170	74	0	0			
19	FW	KHAMIS Leena	KHAMIS	19-6-1986	NSW Sapphires	168	62	3	231			
20	FW	REED Alannah	REED	28-1-1988	Queensland Sting	161	53	2	52			
21	GK	JACKSON Monique	JACKSON	20-12-1985	NSW Sapphires	169	72	1	90			

BRA – BRAZIL WOMEN'S U-19 SQUAD

No	Pos	Name	Shirt Name	DoB	Club	Cms	Kg	Games	Mins	Goals	Y	R
1	GK	KELLY NUNES	KELLY S.	23-2-1986	Marilia	171	66	3	300			
2	DF	TATIANA	TATIANA	18-3-1985	Comercial	166	63	6	570	1		
3	DF	ELYSA	ELYSA	21-6-1987	Uni Santanna	168	65	3	215			1
4	DF	RENATA DINIZ (c)	RENATA D.	1-11-1985	Santos	178	65	5	480	1		
5	DF	ALIANE	ALIANE	30-12-1986	Sao Bernardo	167	61	6	416	2		
6	DF	KAREN	KAREN	17-2-1985	Santos	173	62	2	92	2		
7	FW	KELLY	KELLY C.	8-5-1985	Cepe Caxias	162	63	6	465	1		
8	MF	RENATA COSTA	RENATA C.	8-7-1986	Santos	171	64	6	570	1		
9	MF	ROSANA	ROSANA	27-7-1987	Juventus Atletico	169	66	6	456	1		
10	FW	MARTA	MARTA	19-2-1986	Umea - SWE	169	58	6	570	3		2
11	FW	CRISTIANE	CRISTIANE	15-5-1985	Sao Bernardo	170	62	6	570	3		
12	GK	THAIS	THAIS	19-6-1987	Uni Santanna	173	64	3	270			
13	DF	RAQUEL BUENO	RAQUEL B.	8-1-1985	Sao Caetano	164	50	1	20			
14	DF	FRANCINE	FRANCINE	28-5-1986	Botucatu	157	48	3	164			
15	MF	ADRIANA	ADRIANA	9-4-1985	Uni Santanna	161	55	0	0			
16	FW	DAYANE	DAYANE	13-5-1985	Novo Mundo	165	64	3	106			
17	MF	MAURINE	MAURINE	14-1-1986	Gremio	158	50	5	375			
18	FW	ERIKA	ERIKA	4-2-1988	Juventus Atletico	171	55	5	179			
19	FW	SANDRA	SANDRA	26-6-1985	Sao Bernardo	160	56	6	309	2	1	
20	FW	RAQUEL FARIAS	RAQUEL F.	9-7-1985	Cepe Caxias	169	56	2	88			
21	GK	RITA	RITA	24-6-1987	Gresfi	182	63	0	0			

CAN – CANADA WOMEN'S U-19 SQUAD

No	Pos	Name	Shirt Name	DoB	Club	Cms	Kg	Games	Mins	Goals	Y	R
1	GK	VAN BOXMEER Stacey	VANBOXMEER	10-5-1985	Indiana Univ. - USA	173	63	4	271			1
2	DF	RADCHUCK Katie	RADCHUCK	27-2-1986	Montreal Xtreme	165	61	4	360			
3	DF	GAYLE Robyn	GAYLE	31-10-1985	North Carolina Univ.	170	63	3	226			
4	DF	DENNIS Tanya	DENNIS	26-8-1985	Nebraska Univ. - USA	168	59	4	277	1	1	
5	DF	ZURRER Emily	ZURRER	12-7-1987	Nanaimo Premier	178	68	2	180			
6	DF	LABRECQUE Justine	LABRECQUE	2-7-1987	Montreal Xtreme	168	61	0	0			
7	MF	CICCHINI Amanda	CICCHINI	28-2-1987	Dixie 1986	155	54	4	345			
8	MF	MARANDA Veronique	MARANDA	18-8-1986	Montreal Xtreme	168	61	4	307	2		
9	FW	ROBINSON Jodi-Ann	ROBINSON	17-4-1989	Semiahmoo Spirit	163	63	3	105	1		
10	MF	IACCHELLI Selenia	IACCHELLI	5-6-1986	Edmonton Aviators	173	63	2	68			
11	FW	BELANGER Josee	BELANGER	14-5-1986	Montreal Xtreme	163	63	3	114			
12	MF	BAZOS Kate	BAZOS	15-8-1986	Toronto Inferno	168	54	0	0			
13	FW	EVERRETT Deana	EVERRETT	26-12-1987	Dixie 1986	163	55	2	74			
14	FW	JAMANI Aysha	JAMANI	28-6-1987	Edmonton Aviators	157	53	4	351	1	1	
15	FW	LANG Kara (c)	LANG	22-10-1986	Vancouver Whitecaps	178	68	4	360	1		
16	DF	SCHMIDT Sophie	SCHMIDT	28-6-1988	Abbotsford Rush	170	63	4	360			
17	MF	TIMKO Brittany	TIMKO	5-9-1985	Nebraska Univ. - USA	168	61	4	360	7		
18	FW	LEROUX Sydney	LEROUX	7-5-1990	Coquitlam City Wild	168	55	2	25			
19	GK	MC NULTY Erin	MC NULTY	3-6-1989	Bonivital Flames	178	63	0	0			
20	GK	LABBE Stephanie	LABBE	10-10-1986	Edmonton Aviators	173	63	1	87			1
21	DF	RABER Sari	RABER	1-1-1986	Nebraska Univ. - USA	163	55	1	1			

CHN - CHINA PR WOMEN'S U-19 SQUAD

No	Pos	Name	Shirt Name	DoB	Club	Cms	Kg	Games	Mins	Goals	Y	R
1	GK	ZHANG Yanru	Y.R.ZHANG	10-1-1987	Jiangsu Shuntian	183	83	6	540		1	
2	DF	GAO Yan	Y.GAO	13-10-1985	Shanghai SVA	160	51	6	540			
3	DF	GUO Lin	L.GUO	11-10-1985	Beijing Chengjian	167	55	4	360		3	
4	DF	WANG Kun	K. WANG	20-10-1985	Hebei	175	59	6	540	1	2	
5	DF	SUN Yongxia (c)	Y.X.SUN	19-3-1985	Tianjin Teda	172	63	6	540		1	
6	MF	HOU Lijia	L.J.HOU	3-10-1986	Dalian	167	60	4	150			
7	MF	SUN Ling	L.SUN	12-11-1985	Shanghai SVA	175	63	5	335		2	
8	MF	ZHANG Ying	Y.Zhang	27-6-1985	Shanghai SVA	175	61	6	514	3	1	
9	FW	XU Yuan	Y.XU	17-11-1985	Lanzhou	163	52	6	407	1	1	
10	MF	WANG Dandan	D.D.WANG	1-5-1985	Beijing Chengjian	160	58	6	474			
11	FW	LIU Sa	S.LIU	11-7-1987	Beijing Chengjian	165	62	5	195	1		
12	DF	GUO Yue	Y.GUO	12-12-1985	Changchun	178	66	6	236		1	
13	FW	MA Xiaoxu	X.X.MA	5-6-1988	Dalian	172	62	1	16			
14	MF	LOU Xiaoxu	X.X.LOU	30-5-1986	Changchun	168	57	6	525	2	2	
15	MF	WANG Cong	C.WANG	19-4-1985	Army Club	166	59	0	0			
16	DF	WENG Xinzhi	X.ZH.WENG	15-6-1988	Jiangsu Shuntian	166	57	6	540		2	
17	MF	GAO Ying	Y.GAO	1-7-1985	Beijing Chengjian	164	53	3	28			
18	GK	WENG Xiaojie	X.J.WENG	27-7-1987	Jiangsu Shuntian	174	64	0	0			
19	DF	GE Yang	Y.GE	12-5-1985	Jiangsu Shuntian	172	58	0	0			
20	MF	SUN Lisha	L.SH.SUN	1-9-1985	Lanzhou	165	55	0	0			
21	GK	SONG Jianqiu	J.Q SONG	12-12-1986	Army Club	178	62	0	0			

ESP - SPAIN WOMEN'S U-19 SQUAD

No	Pos	Name	Shirt Name	DoB	Club	Cms	Kg	Games	Mins	Goals	Y	R
1	GK	LUCIA MUNOZ	LUCIA	8-12-1985	Sabadell	168	59	2	180			
2	DF	IRANTZU CASTRILLO	IRANTZU	9-7-1985	Athletic Bilbao	162	60	0	0			
3	FW	VERONICA BOQUETE	VERO	9-4-1987	Xuventu Aguino	163	56	3	269			
4	MF	MIRIAM DIEGUEZ	MIRIAM	4-5-1986	Espanyol Barcelona	169	57	3	270			
5	DF	RUTH GARCIA	RUTH	26-3-1987	Levante	166	60	3	270		1	
6	FW	AINTZANE ENCINAS	AINTZANE	22-4-1988	Real Sociedad	166	58	0	0			
7	MF	NATALIA PABLOS	NATALIA	15-10-1985	Rayo Vallecano	166	55	3	225		1	
8	MF	NURIA ZUFIA	NURIA	4-4-1985	SD Lagunak	169	56	3	216	1		
9	FW	JADE BOHO	JADE	30-8-1986	Torrejon	167	56	3	262	2		
10	MF	IRAIA ITURREGI (c)	IRAIA	24-4-1985	Athletic Bilbao	162	55	3	270		1	
11	MF	ANA ROMERO	ANA	14-6-1987	Hispalis	167	68	3	45			
12	FW	IRUNE MURUA	IRUNE	23-4-1986	Athletic Bilbao	155	57	2	35			
13	GK	MARIA SANCHEZ	MARIA	14-5-1986	Amaya	170	65	1	90			
14	DF	SILVIA DOBLADO	SILVIA	22-3-1987	Rayco	166	60	3	270		1	
15	DF	ANE BERGARA	ANE	3-2-1987	SD Lagunak	169	59	3	270			
16	MF	CARME FERRER	CARME	10-11-1986	Levante	166	55	0	0			
17	MF	JULIA DE LA PAZ	JULIA	9-7-1987	Sporting Plaza Argel	167	67	2	28			
18	DF	ZURINE GIL GARCIA	ZURINE	20-2-1987	Athletic Bilbao	164	56	3	270			
19	FW	JUDITH ACEDO	JUDITH	26-1-1986	FC Barcelona	164	56	0	0			
20	MF	IRENE SAMPIETRO	IRENE	3-11-1986	Transportes Alcaine	166	57	0	0			
21	GK	MARIA RODRIGUEZ	MARI	10-5-1987	Oviedo	163	69	0	0			

GER - GERMANY WOMEN'S U-19 SQUAD

No	Pos	Name	Shirt Name	DoB	Club	Cms	Kg	Games	Mins	Goals	Y	R
1	GK	RINKES Tessa	RINKES	14-9-1986	MTV Mellendorf	182	70	6	570			
2	DF	KUZNIK Peggy	KUZNIK	12-8-1986	FFC Turbine Potsdam	175	73	6	570			
3	DF	VAN BONN Anne	VAN BONN	12-10-1985	FCR Duisburg	168	58	6	502			
4												
5	DF	KRAHN Annike (c)	KRAHN	1-7-1985	FCR Duisburg	174	61	6	570	1		
6	MF	THOMAS Karolin	THOMAS	3-4-1985	FFC Turbine Potsdam	161	58	6	542		1	
7	MF	BEHRINGER Melanie	BEHRINGER	18-11-1985	SC Freiburg	171	67	6	470	2		
8	MF	GOESSLING Lena	GOESSLING	8-3-1986	Guetersloh	171	57	4	227	2		
9	FW	MITTAG Anja	MITTAG	16-5-1985	FFC Turbine Potsdam	169	61	6	510	6		
10	MF	OKOYINO DA MBABI Celia	OKOYINO DA MBABI	27-6-1988	07 Bad Neuenahr	174	65	5	479	3		
11	FW	LAUDEHR Simone	LAUDEHR	12-7-1986	FCR Duisburg	175	59	6	458	2	1	
12	GK	LAENGERT Kathrin	LAENGERT	4-6-1987	FCR Duisburg	176	64	0	0			
13	DF	HAUER Elena	HAUER	13-2-1986	FCR Duisburg	172	60	6	480		1	
14	DF	SCHIEWE Carolin	SCHIEWE	23-10-1988	FFC Turbine Potsdam	179	70	1	28			
15	DF	MPALASKAS Stephanie	MPALASKAS	12-2-1986	FCR Duisburg	162	52	1	68			
16	MF	NIEMEIER Annika	NIEMEIER	15-4-1987	TSV Jahn Calden	165	59	2	91			
17	MF	FELDBACHER Angelika	FELDBACHER	3-6-1986	Wacker Munich	170	62	5	168	1		
18	DF	JOKUSCHIES Nina	JOKUSCHIES	4-8-191986	Holstein Kiel	170	59	1	90		1	
19	FW	BLAESSE Anna	BLAESSE	27-2-1987	USV Jena	167	61	3	104	1		
20	FW	HANEBECK Patricia	HANEBECK	26-2-1986	FCR Duisburg	171	54	5	343	2		
21	MF	VEEH Carolin	VEEH	15-9-191987	TSV Crailsheim	165	51	0	0			

ITA – ITALY WOMEN'S U-19 SQUAD

No	Pos	Name	Shirt Name	DoB	Club	Cms	Kg	Games	Mins	Goals	Y	R
1	GK	MARCHITELLI Chiara (c)	MARCHITELLI	4-5-1985	Atletico Oristano	170	62	3	270			
2	MF	RIBOLDI Penelope	RIBOLDI	2-7-1986	Atalanta Femminile	164	54	3	270			
3	DF	COSTI Fabiana	COSTI	6-10-1986	Reggiana	164	53	3	270	1	1	
4	MF	BELLUCCI Diana	BELLUCCI	11-3-1986	Monti del Matese	164	60	3	255		1	
5	DF	MAGRINI Valeria	MAGRINI	18-2-1985	Vigor Senigallia	157	53	3	270			
6	MF	BINCOLETTO Anna	BINCOLETTO	6-3-1985	Piossasco	175	60	3	250			
7	MF	BRUTTI Veronica	BRUTTI	11-9-1987	Porto Mantovano	162	58	1	12			
8	MF	CARISSIMI Marta	CARISSIMI	3-5-1987	Torino	169	56	3	200		1	
9	FW	RICCO Agnese	RICCO	20-4-1986	Rapid Lugano - SUI	165	65	3	258	2	1	
10	FW	COPPOLINO Serena	COPPOLINO	26-4-1985	Matuziana San Remo	163	50	2	142		2	
11	MF	CASALI Silvia	CASALI	29-1-1985	ACF Milan	160	50	2	156			
12	GK	BIANCHI Paola	BIANCHI	29-8-1986	Bardolino	169	69	0	0			
13	DF	QUITADAMO Sonia	QUITADAMO	10-10-1985	ACF Milan	163	62	0	0			
14	GK	BRAIATO Giorgia	BRAIATO	4-10-1987	Porto Mantovano	170	60	0	0			
15	DF	GUAGNI Alia	GUAGNI	1-10-1987	Firenze	168	63	3	270			
16	FW	SABATINO Daniela	SABATINO	26-6-1985	Monti del Matese	165	57	0	0			
17	DF	MARCHESI Arianna	MARCHESI	1-11-1986	Perugia	158	55	0	0			
18	MF	MIANI Cristina	MIANI	15-9-1985	Rivignano	169	54	1	7			
19	MF	PATU Serena	PATU	24-2-1985	Firenze	169	60	0	0			
20	FW	VICCHIARELLO Evelyn	VICCHIARELLO	24-10-1986	Roseto	169	60	3	70		1	
21	DF	MANIERI Raffaella	MANIERI	21-11-1986	Vigor Senigallia	174	60	3	270	1		

KOR – KOREA REPUBLIC WOMEN'S U-19 SQUAD

No	Pos	Name	Shirt Name	DoB	Club	Cms	Kg	Games	Mins	Goals	Y	R
1	GK	JUN Min Kyung	M K JUN	16-1-1985	Ulsan College	172	74	3	270			
2	GK	WE Sung Hee	S H WE	10-10-1986	Chungwoon HS	169	61	0	0			
3	DF	LEE Jin Hwa	J H LEE	10-10-1986	Yesung HS	162	54	3	270		1	
4	DF	LEE Ye Eun	Y E LEE	2-2-1988	Kangil HS	169	54	3	195			
5	DF	YOON Young Geul	Y G YOON	28-10-1987	Ohsan HS	171	65	3	224		2	
6	DF	PARK Mi Jung (c)	M J PARK	12-1-1985	Youngjin College	167	55	3	270		1	
7	MF	KIM Joo Hee	J H KIM	10-3-1985	Hanyang Univ.	167	53	3	185			
8	MF	LEE Jang Mi	J M LEE	14-11-1985	Youngjin College	157	55	3	270	1	1	
9	DF	PARK Eun Sun	E S PARK	25-12-1986	Wirye HS	177	68	3	270	1	1	
10	FW	PARK Hee Young	H Y PARK	11-6-1985	Youngjin College	168	56	2	160	1		
11	FW	PARK Eun Jung	E J PARK	4-11-1986	Yeasung HS	165	48	1	14			
12	DF	MOON Seul A	S A MOON	15-12-1986	Ohsan HS	164	52	0	0			
13	FW	JUNG Sey Hwa	S H JUNG	19-3-1986	Internet HS	165	55	2	125			
14	MF	RYU Ha Yun	H Y RYU	12-6-1986	Janghowon HS	158	50	0	0			
15	MF	JUNG Mi Jung	M J JUNG	30-8-1986	Hanil HS	170	56	0	0			
16	MF	SONG Yu Na	Y N SONG	1-4-1987	Dongshin HS	156	53	3	201			
17	FW	HAN Song I	S I HAN	28-7-1985	Yeoju	170	62	3	191			
18	MF	PANG A Lang	A L PANG	11-11-1986	Janghowon HS	159	57	0	0			
19	DF	CHA Yun Hee	Y H CHA	26-2-1986	Kwangyang HS	167	57	3	270			
20	DF	JEON Jae Min	J M JEON	7-9-1985	Yeoju	167	62	2	55			
21	GK	KIM Ju Ok	J O KIM	12-1-1987	Aloysius HS	172	70	0	0			

NGA – NIGERIA WOMEN'S U-19 SQUAD

No	Pos	Name	Shirt Name	DoB	Club	Cms	Kg	Games	Mins	Goals	Y	R
1	GK	OKWARA Rose	OKWARA	3-12-1987	Pelican Stars	165	50	0	0			
2	MF	CHIKWELU Rita	CHIKWELU	6-3-1988	FCT Queens	167	58	3	270		2	
3	MF	SABI Akudo	SABI	17-11-1986	Bayelsa Queens	176	68	4	390	2		
4	FW	UWAK Cynthia	UWAK	15-7-1986	FCT Queens	156	55	4	380	1	2	
5	DF	NWOSU Chima	NWOSU	12-3-1986	Inneh Queens	167	58	1	90			
6	DF	COLE Lilian	COLE	1-8-1985	Delta Queens	162	60	4	349		1	
7	FW	AKINLOSE Semola	AKINLOSE	1-9-1985	Delta Queens	170	59	1	68			
8	MF	YUSUF Ayisat	YUSUF	6-3-1985	Delta Queens	162	53	2	76			
9	FW	IWUAGWU Akudo	IWUAGWU	13-10-1986	Delta Queens	160	54	4	319		1	
10	MF	NWABUOKU Evelyn	NWABUOKU	14-11-1985	Bayelsa Queens	165	58	2	85			
11	DF	AMINU Adeola	AMINU	6-8-1986	Delta Queens	160	55	0	0			
12	FW	GODWIN Stella	GODWIN	12-4-1986	Odense - DEN	176	62	4	350	1		
13	FW	SIKE Promise	SIKE	15-1-1987	Delta Queens	160	55	4	187			
14	DF	EGWIM Augusta	EGWIM	30-3-1985	Rivers Angels	170	55	1	13			
15	FW	OKESIE Rosemary	OKESIE	30-11-1986	Bayelsa Queens	170	55	3	39			
16	DF	IKIDI Faith	IKIDI	28-2-1987	Bayelsa Queens	172	63	4	390			
17	DF	AKUSOBI Blessing	AKUSOBI	17-8-1986	Macbeth FC	166	65	3	287			
18	GK	ONYINANYA Ogechi	ONYINANYA	26-5-1985	Pelican Stars	170	65	4	390			
19	DF	JEROME Ulumma	JEROME	11-4-1988	Delta Queens	162	59	4	390		1	
20	FW	UDOH Nkese (c)	UDOH	10-9-1986	Lindsey Wilson - USA	164	50	3	217	1	1	
21	FW	ALAKE Olamide	ALAKE	25-12-1987	Bayelsa Queens	175	60	0	0			

RUS – RUSSIA WOMEN'S U-19 SQUAD

No	Pos	Name	Shirt Name	DoB	Club	Cms	Kg	Games	Mins	Goals	Y	R
1	GK	TODUA Elvira	TODUA	31-1-1986	Rossiyanka Moskva	180	67	4	390			
2	DF	SEDOVA Elena	SEDOVA	11-8-1986	Victoria Belgorod	171	76	4	343	1		
3	DF	KOSTYUKOVA Anastasia	KOSTYUKOVA	15-5-1985	CSK VVS Samara	177	67	1	1			
4	DF	GOMOZOVA Alexandra	GOMOZOVA	8-8-1986	Chertanovo Moskva	163	59	2	68	1		
5	DF	SEMENCHENKO Elena (c)	SEMENTCHENKO	23-1-1985	Chertanovo Moskva	171	56	4	390	1		
6	MF	TITOVA Oxana	TITOVA	17-7-1986	Nadezhda Noginsk	168	58	4	390			
7	MF	SOCHNEVA Ekaterina	SOCHNEVA	12-8-1985	Chertanovo Moskva	168	51	4	382	2	2	
8	MF	TEREKHOVA Elena	TEREKHOVA	5-7-1987	Voronezh	162	54	4	380	1		
9	MF	TSIDIKOVA Svetlana	TSIDIKOVA	4-2-1985	Rossiyanka Moskva	162	53	4	390	1	2	
10	MF	FOMINA Yana	FOMINA	3-11-1986	CSK VVS Samara	165	57	3	64			
11	MF	MOROZOVA Elena	MOROZOVA	15-3-1987	Rossiyanka Moskva	173	62	4	390	1		
12	GK	BAIKINA Svetlana	BAIKINA	25-1-1985	Lada Togliatti	167	75	0	0			
13	DF	TSYBUTOVICH Ksenia	TSYBUTOVICH	26-6-1987	Chertanovo Moskva	175	65	4	390	1		
14	FW	PETROVA Olga	PETROVA	9-7-1986	Rossiyanka Moskva	173	57	3	131	1		
15	MF	PESHINA Olga	PESHINA	15-9-1987	CSK VVS Samara	169	55	4	209		1	
16	MF	KHARCHENKO Nadezhda	KHARCHENKO	27-3-1987	CSK VVS Samara	164	56	4	270	1		
17	DF	BUKASHKINA Lyubov	BUKASHKINA	11-6-1987	Voronezh	162	52	1	52			
18	MF	MAKAROVA Galina	MAKAROVA	10-9-1986	Victoria Belgorod	168	57	0	0			
19	FW	GORBACHEVA Elena	GORBACHEVA	5-6-1987	Voronezh	164	60	0	0			
20	FW	GORYACHEVA Anna	GORYACHEVA	23-2-1986	CSK VVS Samara	171	63	2	50			
21	GK	MEZHAKOVA Nadezhda	MEZHAKOVA	1-12-1987	Victoria Belgorod	169	65	0	0			

THA – THAILAND WOMEN'S U-19 SQUAD

No	Pos	Name	Shirt Name	DoB	Club	Cms	Kg	Games	Mins	Goals	Y	R
1	GK	SUDTAVEE Kanyawee	K.SUDTAVEE	11-5-1986	Khonkean	158	68	3	270			
2	DF	THONGSRI Hathairat	H.THONGSRI	12-6-1987	Samutprakarn	160	50	1	38			
3	DF	MAIJARERN Anootsara	A.MAIJARERN	14-2-1986	Khonkean	163	53	3	270			
4	DF	WIWASUKHU Thidarat	T.WIWASUKHU	18-2-1985	Srisaket	169	55	3	236			
5	DF	KAEOBAEN Supaphon (c)	S.KAEOBAEN	4-3-1985	Bangkok	162	50	3	270			
6	MF	JITMANEEROTE Suchada	S.JITMANEEROTE	31-7-1985	Suphanburi Sports	163	53	3	250			
7	MF	SRIWASAO Niparat	N.SRIWASAO	15-3-1985	Suphanburi Sports	153	45	3	200			
8	MF	SEESRAUM Junpen	J.SEESRAUM	11-5-1987	Khonkean	150	63	3	269	1		
9	MF	NETTHIP Pavinee	P.NETTHIP	1-2-1987	Samchuke	165	47	3	270			
10	FW	THIANGTHAM Kitiya	K.THIANGTHAM	30-6-1986	Banhan	162	58	3	270			
11	DF	KHAYANSAKARN Nantawan	N.KHAYANSAKARN	12-10-1986	Samchuke	162	56	0	0			
12	FW	SRITALA Duangnapa	D.SRITALA	4-2-1986	Sport College	159	58	1	36			
13	FW	SRIMANEE Orathai	O.SRIMANEE	12-6-1988	Khonkean	151	45	3	175			
14	DF	TUPSURI Jiraprapa	J.TUPSURI	30-6-1988	Khonkean	155	65	1	32			
15	MF	KAEWKA Saranya	S.KAEWKA	9-8-1986	Khonkean	171	60	0	0			
16	DF	KHUEANPET Pikul	P.KHUEANPET	20-9-1988	Khonkean	159	45	3	270			
17	DF	MUNGKHALA Siriporn	S.MUNGKHALA	22-1-1986	Khonkean	163	58	2	34			
18	GK	CHANGAUTTHA Benjawan	B.CHANGAUTTHA	21-11-1986	Bangkok	165	58	0	0			
19	FW	THONGKERN Pattarawan	P.THONGKERN	16-4-1986	Khonkean	162	50	1	59			
20	GK	OONSAP Kwannapa	OONSAP	8-5-1987	Samchuke	168	57	0	0			
21	MF	WIPHAKONWIT Suponthip	S.WIPHAKONWIT	20-9-1988	Banhan	161	55	2	21			

USA – UNITED STATES WOMEN'S U-19 SQUAD

No	Pos	Name	Shirt Name	DoB	Club	Cms	Kg	Games	Mins	Goals	Y	R
1	GK	DAVIS Kelsey	DAVIS	14-5-1987	Southern California Utd	179	63	0	0			
2	MF	KRON Stephanie	KRON	20-8-1985	Sereno Eagles	158	57	1	5			
3	DF	BUEHLER Rachel	BUEHLER	26-8-1985	San Diego Surf	164	65	6	540			
4	MF	REDMOND Jennifer	REDMOND	19-4-1986	PDA Galaxy	164	60	3	98			
5	FW	GRAY Sheree	GRAY	12-12-1985	World Class	159	56	6	493	1		
6	DF	LOPEZ Stephanie	LOPEZ	3-4-1986	Elk Grove United	164	59	6	540			
7	FW	RAPINOE Megan	RAPINOE	5-7-1985	Elk Grove United	168	59	5	384	3	1	
8	DF	LOGTERMAN Stephanie	LOGTERMAN	25-2-1986	Warriors Black	166	58	6	540			
9	FW	HANKS Kerri	HANKS	2-9-1985	Dallas Texans	167	55	3	148	1		
10	FW	WOZNUK Angie	WOZNUK	29-3-1985	San Diego Surf	164	55	5	390	3	1	
11	DF	SAUERBRUNN Becky	SAUERBRUNN	6-6-1985	JB Marine	168	62	6	540			
12	FW	ORAND Alexa	ORAND	10-10-1987	Slammers	164	60	6	399			
13	DF	AVERBUCH Yael	AVERBUCH	3-11-1986	World Class	182	65	2	55			
14	FW	SCHNUR Meghan	SCHNUR	16-4-1985	Beadling	164	67	1	58			
15	DF	KRZYSIK Nikki	KRZYSIK	23-5-1987	World Class	168	60	2	104			
16	FW	RODRIGUEZ Amy	RODRIGUEZ	17-2-1987	Calif. Laguna Hills Eclipse	158	61	6	465	2		
17	FW	ROSTEDT Jessica	ROSTEDT	3-3-1986	Internationals	174	65	4	180	3		
18	GK	HARRIS Ashlyn (c)	HARRIS	19-10-1985	Indialantic Force	170	59	6	540			
19	DF	HOLMES Meagan	HOLMES	21-2-1987	Bethesda Excel	160	55	5	450			
20	MF	LINDSTROM Stacy	LINDSTROM	23-2-1985	Southern California Utd	182	68	1	11			
21	GK	COMEAU Laura	COMEAU	13-12-1985	Seacoast	169	60	0	0			

FIFA FUTSAL WORLD CHAMPIONSHIP 2004

Four years after stunning Brazil to claim their first FIFA Futsal World Championship title, Spain retained their crown after a closely contested final with European rivals Italy to confirm their superiority on the world stage. The 2-1 victory in Chinese Taipei followed the holders' penalty shoot-out success against Brazil in a semi-final that effectively ended the South Americans' claims to futsal domination since the World Championships began in 1989. Arguably the key proponents of futsal, the continent suffered double disappointment in the semi-finals with Argentina crashing out 7-4 to Italy. Three-times winners Brazil had arrived in Chinese Taipei intent on exacting revenge for their defeat in Guatemala in 2000 and with maximum points from their first round group games they were odds-on to do just that in spite of Spain, Italy and Argentina also winning their respective groups at a canter. Brazil again dominated their group at the second stage, winning all three matches including a 2-1 defeat of local rivals Argentina while European champions Italy topped the other table thanks to their victory over Spain. Making an impressive debut at the Championships were the Czech Republic, who finished runners-up to Brazil in the first stage after winning two matches. Despite losing all their following games, the Europeans ended eighth in the final rankings. Although the Czechs excelled at the first attempt, other less-established countries still experienced relative levels of success: hosts Chinese Taipei, while failing to win a match, scored two goals on their Futsal World Championship debut; Thailand won their first match (3-2 against Australia); and Japan grabbed their first point in six matches at the Championships. Undisputed star of the fifth FIFA Futsal World Championship was Brazilian striker Falcao, whose 13 goals earned him the adidas Golden Shoe. His scintillating displays made him a firm crowd favourite and he was also awarded the adidas Golden Ball as the outstanding player of the tournament. The 27-year-old stamped his personality on the Championship with a string of spectacular goals and he rounded off his tally with a hat-trick in the third place play-off against Argentina. The adidas Silver and Bronze Shoes went to Falcao's team-mate Indio and Spain's Marcelo respectively, while Vinicius Bacaro of Italy gatecrashed the Spanish-Brazilian domination of awards by taking the adidas Bronze Ball behind Javi Rodriguez of Spain.

FIFA FUTSAL WORLD CHAMPIONSHIP CHINESE TAIPEI 2004

First round groups	Pts	Quarter-final groups	Pts	Semi-finals			Final	
Spain	9							
Ukraine	6							
Egypt	3		Pts					
Chinese Taipei	0	Italy	7					
		Spain	6	Spain	2	5p		
	Pts	Portugal	4	Brazil	2	4p		
Brazil	9	Czech Republic	0					
Czech Republic	6							
Thailand	3							
Australia	0						Spain	2
	Pts						Italy	1
Italy	9							
USA	4							
Paraguay	3		Pts					
Japan	1	Brazil	9					
		Argentina	4	Argentina	4			
	Pts	Ukraine	4	Italy	7			
Argentina	9	USA	0					
Portugal	6						3rd Place Play-off	
Iran	3						Brazil	7
Cuba	0						Argentina	4

GROUP A		PL	W	D	L	F	A	PTS	ESP	UKR	EGY	TPE
1	Spain	3	3	0	0	19	0	9		2-0	7-0	10-0
2	Ukraine	3	2	0	1	12	8	6			5-4	7-2
3	Egypt	3	1	0	2	16	12	3				12-0
4	Chinese Taipei	3	0	0	3	2	29	0				

NTU, Taipei City, 21-11-2004
16:00, 2 125, Paixao BRA, Porritt AUS, Moosavi IRN

TPE   0   12   EGY

Sayed.G 3 [7 20 39], Abdel Mawla 3 [8 13 35], Ibrahim 2 [17 23]
Mohamed M [20], Tseng Tai Lin OG [24], Mahmoud [32], Abdelhamid [34]

CHINESE TAIPEI	EGYPT	
1 CHEN Yung Sheng (GK)	(GK) SAYED Mohamed	2
6 CHANG Chien Ying	SEIF Samir	8
7 WANG Chi Cheng	IBRAHIM Ayman	9
9 TSENG Tai Lin	MOHAMED M. Abdel Hakim	10
13 CHEN Chia Ho	SAYED Gehad	11
2 TSAI Chih Chieh	EL GOHARY Yousef	5
4 CHEN un Shan	ABDEL MAWLA Wael	6
5 CHANG Fu Hsiang	ABDELHAMID Mohamed	7
10 CHANG Chu Yu	MAHMOUD Khaled	14
11 HO Kuo Chen	(GK) NASSEF Ayman	1
14 CHU Chia Wei	EL DARWJ Islam	3
12 YEH Hsien Chung (GK)	EL MALAH Amr	13
Tr: KNABBEN Damien	Tr: ALY Momamed	

LNK, Tao Yuan County, 23-11-2004
18:00, 795, Djiba SEN, Filppu FIN, Cumbo ITA

TPE   0   10   ESP

Alberto Cogorro 2 [6 32], Fran Serrejon [13], Julio [17]
Javi Rodriguez 3 [22p 25 30], Torras [25], Marcelo [37], Limones [39]

CHINESE TAIPEI	SPAIN	
12 YEH Hsien Chung (GK)	(GK) RAFA	12
6 CHANG Chien Ying	JULIO	2
7 WANG Chi Cheng	TORRAS	3
9 TSENG Tai Lin	LIMONES	10
13 CHEN Chia Ho	ALBERTO COGORRO	11
2 TSAI Chih Chieh	FRAN SERREJON	4
4 CHEN un Shan	PIPE	6
5 CHANG Fu Hsiang	JAVI RODRIGUEZ	7
10 CHANG Chu Yu	KIKE	8
11 HO Kuo Chen	ANDREU	9
14 CHU Chia Wei	MARCELO	14
1 CHEN Yung Sheng (GK)	(GK) PACO SEDANO	13
Tr: KNABBEN Damien	Tr: LOZANO Javier	

NTU, Taipei City, 25-11-2004
18:00, 1 850, Konstantinidis USA, Maso Goitisolo CUB, Del Cid GUA

UKR   7   2   TPE

Mansurov 2 [7 20], Koridze 2 [10 38p]   Chen Chia Ho [14]
Shaytanov 2 [14 18], Brunko [38]   Chang Chien Ying [25]

UKRAINE	CHINESE TAIPEI	
2 SYTIN Sergiy (GK)	(GK) CHEN Yung Sheng	1
3 NESTERUK Vitaliy	TSAI Chih Chieh	2
4 KORIDZE Sergiy	CHEN un Shan	4
5 SHAYTANOV Oleg	CHANG Fu Hsiang	5
6 MANSUROV Ramis	CHANG Chien Ying	6
8 KOSENKO Olexandr	WANG Chi Cheng	7
9 BRUNKO Vitaliy	TSENG Tai Lin	9
10 MOSKVYCHOV Igor	CHANG Chu Yu	10
11 PYLYPIV Fedir	HO Kuo Chen	11
12 SUKHOMLINOV Vasyl	(GK) YEH Hsien Chung	12
13 KOVALYOV Artem	CHEN Chia Ho	13
14 VLASENKO Kostyantyn (GK)	CHU Chia Wei	14
Tr: LISENCHUK Gennadiy	Tr: KNABBEN Damien	

NTU, Taipei City, 21-11-2004
16:00, 1 350, Cumbo ITA, Sciancalepore ARG, MASO Goitisolo CUB

ESP   2   0   UKR

Marcelo [5], Andreu [9]

SPAIN	UKRAINE	
1 LUIS AMADO (GK)	(GK) POPOV Olexiy	1
5 OROL	KORIDZE Sergiy	4
7 JAVI RODRIGUEZ	MELNIKOV Georgii	7
8 KIKE	KOSENKO Olexandr	8
14 MARCELO	MOSKVYCHOV Igor	10
2 JULIO	SYTIN Sergiy	2
4 FRAN SERREJON	NESTERUK Vitaliy	3
6 PIPE	MANSUROV Ramis	6
9 ANDREU	BRUNKO Vitaliy	9
10 LIMONES	PYLYPIV Fedir	11
12 RAFA (GK)	KOVALYOV Artem	13
3 TORRAS	(GK) SUKHOMLINOV Vasyl	12
Tr: LOZANO Javier	Tr: LISENCHUK Gennadiy	

LNK, Tao Yuan County, 23-11-2004
20:00, 412, Van Helviort NED, Moosavi IRN, Isokawa JPN

EGY   4   5   UKR

Abdel Mawla 3 [4 18 38], Sayed.G [21]   Koridze 2 [26 38], Sayed OG [29]
                                          Kovalyov [34], Mansurov [35]

EGYPT	UKRAINE	
2 SAYED Mohamed (GK)	(GK) POPOV Olexiy	1
6 ABDEL MAWLA Wael	KORIDZE Sergiy	4
9 IBRAHIM Ayman	MANSUROV Ramis	6
10 MOHAMED M. Abdel Hakim	KOSENKO Olexandr	8
11 SAYED Gehad	PYLYPIV Fedir	11
5 EL GOHARY Yousef	SYTIN Sergiy	2
8 SEIF Samir	NESTERUK Vitaliy	3
12 ABDOU Samir Sabry [36]	SHAYTANOV Oleg	5
1 NASSEF Ayman (GK)	BRUNKO Vitaliy	9
7 ABDELHAMID Mohamed	KOVALYOV Artem	13
14 MAHMOUD Khaled	(GK) VLASENKO Kostyantyn	14
	MELNIKOV Georgii	7
Tr: ALY Momamed	Tr: LISENCHUK Gennadiy	

LNK, Tao Yuan County, 24-11-2004
20:00, 350, Torok HUN, Djiba SEN, Cumbo ITA

EGY   0   7   ESP

                    Marcelo 2 [3 21], Kiki [5], Andreu 2 [10 23]
                    Alberto Cogorro [13], Fran Serrejon [16]

EGYPT	SPAIN	
1 NASSEF Ayman (GK)	(GK) LUIS AMADO	1
2 SAYED Mohamed (GK)	JULIO	2
4 EKRAMY Ibrahim	TORRAS	3
5 EL GOHARY Yousef	FRAN SERREJON	4
6 ABDEL MAWLA Wael	OROL	5
7 ABDELHAMID Mohamed	PIPE	6
8 SEIF Samir	JAVI RODRIGUEZ	7
9 IBRAHIM Ayman	KIKE	8
10 MOHAMED M. Abdel Hakim	ANDREU	9
11 SAYED Gehad	ALBERTO COGORRO	11
14 MAHMOUD Khaled	MARCELO	14
3 EL DARWJ Islam	(GK) RAFA	12
Tr: ALY Momamed	Tr: LOZANO Javier	

	GROUP B	PL	W	D	L	F	A	PTS	BRA	CZE	THA	AUS
1	Brazil	3	3	0	0	23	2	9		4-1	9-1	10-0
2	Czech Republic	3	2	0	1	8	5	6			2-1	5-0
3	Thailand	3	1	0	2	5	13	3				3-2
4	Australia	3	0	0	3	2	18	0				

NTU, Taipei City, 22-11-2004
18:00, 670, Galan ESP, Al Shatti KUW, Djiba SEN

AUS   0 10   BRA

Falcao 2 $^{8\ 25}$, Schumacher ^{12}, Vander ^{13}
Simi ^{18}, Indio 2 $^{21\ 30}$, Fininho ^{28}, Neto 2 $^{35\ 39}$

AUSTRALIA	BRAZIL
1 O'BRIEN Gavin (GK)	(GK) FRANKLIN 2
3 HEWITT Brett	PABLO 6
5 KEITH Simon	EULER 8
10 SINGLETON Ben	SIMI 11
11 WRIGHT Lachlan	FALCAO 12
2 ZWANGOBANI Elliot	SCHUMACHER 3
6 PILAT Damian	NETO 4
8 NOLAN Andrew	MANOEL TOBIAS 5
9 NGALUFE Danny	INDIO 9
14 VIZZARI Adrian	FININHO 10
12 SPATHIS Peter (GK)	VANDER 14
13 HAYDON Luke	(GK) ANGELO 13
Tr: GILLIGAN Scott	Tr: LEITE Fernando

NTU, Taipei City, 22-11-2004
20:00, 740, Valiente PAR, Maso Goitisolo CUB, Sciancalepore ARG

CZE   2 1   THA

Kamenicky ^{34}, Mares ^{35} Innui ^{15}

CZECH REPUBLIC	THAILAND
12 KLIMA Jan (GK)	(GK) CHUENTA Somkid 1
3 RAJNOCH Daniel	JANTA Panuwat 4
4 LEVCIK David	ISSARASUWIPAKORN Ler. 6
7 DLOUHY Martin	NUEANGKORD Joe 10
11 MARES Michal	KHONGKAEW Narongsak 14
2 BLAZEJ Vit	PIEMKUM Pattaya 3
5 SLUKA Tomas	MUNJARERN Anucha 7
9 HAVEL Josef	INNUI Prasert 11
13 SLAMA Zdenek	PUNPOEM Jadet 12
14 KAMENICKY Jaroslav	KHUMTHINKAEW Sermphan 13
1 KRAYZEL Petr (GK)	(GK) PANDEE Parinya 2
10 MUSIAL Roman	POLSAK Ytthana 8
Tr: STRIZ Michal	Tr: DE OLIVEIRA Glaucio

NTU, Taipei City, 24-11-2004
18:00, 639, Konstantinidis USA, Isokawa JPN, Valiente PAR

AUS   0 5   CZE

Havel ^{15}, Mares 3 $^{34\ 36\ 39}$
Dlouhy ^{35}

AUSTRALIA	CZECH REPUBLIC
1 O'BRIEN Gavin (GK)	(GK) KRAYZEL Petr 1
2 ZWANGOBANI Elliot	BLAZEJ Vit 2
3 HEWITT Brett	RAJNOCH Daniel 3
4 MANSON Scott	LEVCIK David 4
5 KEITH Simon	SLUKA Tomas 5
6 PILAT Damian	DLOUHY Martin 7
8 NOLAN Andrew	HAVEL Josef 9
9 NGALUFE Danny	MARES Michal 11
11 WRIGHT Lachlan	SLAMA Zdenek 13
13 HAYDON Luke	KAMENICKY Jaroslav 14
14 VIZZARI Adrian	(GK) KLIMA Jan 12
12 SPATHIS Peter (GK)	MUSIAL Roman 10
Tr: GILLIGAN Scott	Tr: STRIZ Michal

NTU, Taipei City, 24-11-2004
20:00, 810, Torok HUN, Cumbo ITA, Moosavi IRN

BRA   9 1   THA

Schumacher ^{3}, Falcao 2 $^{16\ 36}$
Manoel Tobias ^{24}, Indio 2 $^{26\ 30}$ Issarasuwipakorn ^{37}
Simi 3 $^{35\ 37\ 39}$

BRAZIL	THAILAND
2 FRANKLIN (GK)	(GK) CHUENTA Somkid 1
3 SCHUMACHER	PIEMKUM Pattaya 3
4 NETO	[35] JANTA Panuwat 4
5 MANOEL TOBIAS	POLASAK Anupong 5
6 PABLO	ISSARASUWIPAKORN Ler. 6
7 VINICIUS	MUNJARERN Anucha 7
8 EULER	NUEANGKORD Joe 10
9 INDIO	INNUI Prasert 11
11 SIMI	PUNPOEM Jadet 12
12 FALCAO	KHUMTHINKAEW Sermphan 13
14 VANDER	KHONGKAEW Narongsak 14
1 LAVOISIER (GK)	(GK) PANDEE Parinya 2
Tr: LEITE Fernando	Tr: DE OLIVEIRA Glaucio

NTU, Taipei City, 26-11-2004
20:00, 650, Van Helviort NED, Sciancalepore ARG, Isokawa JPN

THA   3 2   AUS

Munjarern ^{24}, Piemkum ^{37}
Polsak.Y ^{40} Vizzari ^{25}, Singleton ^{40}

THAILAND	AUSTRALIA
1 CHUENTA Somkid (GK)	(GK) O'BRIEN Gavin 1
2 PANDEE Parinya (GK)	ZWANGOBANI Elliot 2
3 PIEMKUM Pattaya	HEWITT Brett 3
6 ISSARASUWIPAKORN Ler.	KEITH Simon 5
7 MUNJARERN Anucha	PILAT Damian 6
8 POLSAK Yytthana	LOMBARDO Paolo 7
10 NUEANGKORD Joe	NOLAN Andrew 8
11 INNUI Prasert	SINGLETON Ben 10
12 PUNPOEM Jadet	WRIGHT Lachlan 11
13 KHUMTHINKAEW Sermphan	(GK) SPATHIS Peter 12
14 KHONGKAEW Narongsak	HAYDON Luke 13
5 POLASAK Anupong	VIZZARI Adrian 14
Tr: DE OLIVEIRA Glaucio	Tr: GILLIGAN Scott

LNK, Tao Yuan County, 26-11-2004
20:00, 1 400, Del Cid GUA, Sheen TPE, Konstantinidis USA

BRA   4 1   CZE

Indio ^{15}, Falcao ^{20}, Neto ^{27}
Vander ^{38} Mares ^{3}

BRAZIL	CZECH REPUBLIC
2 FRANKLIN (GK)	(GK) KLIMA Jan 12
3 SCHUMACHER	BLAZEJ Vit 2
4 NETO	RAJNOCH Daniel 3
5 MANOEL TOBIAS	SLUKA Tomas 5
6 PABLO	DLOUHY Martin 7
7 VINICIUS	HOFFMAN Petr 4
8 EULER	HAVEL Josef 9
9 INDIO	MUSIAL Roman 10
11 SIMI	MARES Michal 11
12 FALCAO	SLAMA Zdenek 13
14 VANDER	KAMENICKY Jaroslav 14
1 LAVOISIER (GK)	(GK) KRAYZEL Petr 1
Tr: LEITE Fernando	Tr: STRIZ Michal

	GROUP C	PL	W	D	L	F	A	PTS	ITA	USA	PAR	JPN
1	Italy	3	3	0	0	15	5	9		6-3	4-2	5-0
2	USA	3	1	1	1	7	8	4			3-1	1-1
3	Paraguay	3	1	0	2	8	11	3				5-4
4	Japan	3	0	1	2	5	11	1				

LNK, Tao Yuan County, 21-11-2004
18:00, 500, Del Cid GUA, Van Helviort, Torok HUN

ITA 6 3 USA

Foglia 2 [13] [28], Bertoni.E 2 [18] [39]
Grana [27], Pellegrini [35]

Torres [11], Dusosky [26], Morris [30]

ITALY		USA	
1	ANGELINI Gianfranco (GK)	(GK) HILEMAN Scott	1
5	ZAFFIRO Salvatore	DUSOSKY Todd	5
6	BERTONI Edgar	BOWERS Sean	6
7	BACARO Vinicius	TORRES Johnny	8
9	FABIANO	BALL John	10
2	GRANA	TSCHANTRET Lee	3
3	PELLEGRINI	BEASLEY Jamar	6
8	VICENTINI Andre	WHITE Pat	7
10	FOGLIA Adriano	HOWES Greg	9
11	MORGADO	SHANKER Joel	13
13	ZANETTI Sandro	MORRIS Pat	14
12	FELLER Alexandre (GK)	(GK) PHILLIPS Brett	12
	Tr: NUCCORINI Alessandro	Tr: TOZER Keith	

LNK, Tao Yuan County, 21-11-2004
20:00, 600, Filppu FIN, Djiba SEN, Galan ESP

JPN 4 5 PAR

Kogure 2 [8] [34], Maeda [17], Higa [17]

Villalba.R [11], Villalba.W 2 [19] [37]
Rotella [31] Velaquez [38]

JAPAN		PARAGUAY	
1	KAWAHARA Hisamitsu (GK)	(GK) ACUNA Cristhian	1
2	SUZUMURA Takuya	ALCARAZ Fabio	3
5	HIGA Rikarudo	CHILAVERT Carlos	5
8	FUJII Kenta	VILLALBA Walter	10
10	KOGURE Kenichiro	BENITEZ Alberto	13
3	MAEDA Yoshifumi	AYALA Emmanuel	2
6	NAMBATA Osamu	VELAZQUEZ Oscar	7
7	KANAYAMA Yuki	ARAUJO Sergio	8
9	ONO Diasuke	VILLALBA Carlos Alberto	9
12	SADANAGA Hisao (GK)	ROTELLA Jose	11
4	KOMIYAMA Yusuke	VILLALBA Rene	14
11	SAGANE Kiyoshi	(GK) MIRANDA Marcos	12
	Tr: FILHO Sergio	Tr: RUIZ Adolfo	

LNK, Tao Yuan County, 23-11-2004
18:00, 800, Porritt AUS, Paixao BRA, Torok HUN

ITA 5 0 JPN

Zanetti [3], Vicentini [7]
Montovaneli 2 [31] [40], Fabiano [33]

ITALY		JAPAN	
12	FELLER Alexandre (GK)	(GK) KAWAHARA Hisamitsu	1
5	ZAFFIRO Salvatore	SUZUMURA Takuya	2
6	BERTONI Edgar	HIGA Rikarudo	5
9	FABIANO	FUJII Kenta	8
13	ZANETTI Sandro	KOGURE Kenichiro	10
2	GRANA	MAEDA Yoshifumi	3
7	MONTOVANELI	KOMIYAMA Yusuke	4
4	BACARO Vinicius	NAMBATA Osamu	6
8	VICENTINI Andre	KANAYAMA Yuki	7
10	FOGLIA Adriano	ONO Diasuke	9
14	BERTONI Rodrigo	SAGANE Kiyoshi	11
1	ANGELINI Gianfranco (GK)	(GK) ISHIWATA Ryota	14
	Tr: NUCCORINI Alessandro	Tr: FILHO Sergio	

LNK, Tao Yuan County, 23-11-2004
20:00, 500, Sciancalepore ARG, Sheen TPE, Farag EGY

USA 3 1 PAR

White [8], Tschantret [33], Torres [38]

Villalba.CA [37]

USA		PARAGUAY	
12	PHILLIPS Brett (GK)	(GK) MIRANDA Marcos	12
5	DUSOSKY Todd	ALCARAZ Fabio	3
6	BOWERS Sean	CHILAVERT Carlos	5
8	TORRES Johnny	VILLALBA Walter	10
10	BALL John	VILLALBA Rene	14
2	GUASTAFERRO Andy	AYALA Gabriel	4
3	TSCHANTRET Lee	GIMENEZ Hebert	6
4	BEASLEY Jamar	ARAUJO Sergio	8
7	WHITE Pat	VILLALBA Carlos Alberto	9
9	HOWES Greg	ROTELLA Jose	11
14	MORRIS Pat	BENITEZ Alberto	13
1	HILEMAN Scott (GK)	(GK) ACUNA Cristhian	1
	Tr: TOZER Keith	Tr: RUIZ Adolfo	

LNK, Tao Yuan County, 25-11-2004
18:00, 550, Farag EGY, Al Shatti KUW, Sheen TPE

PAR 2 4 ITA

Villalba.W [13], Chilavert [28]

Zanetti 2 [17] [36], Bacaro [20]
Morgado [31]

PARAGUAY		ITALY	
1	ACUNA Cristhian (GK)	(GK) ANGELINI Gianfranco	1
3	ALCARAZ Fabio	GRANA	2
4	AYALA Gabriel	PELLEGRINI	3
5	CHILAVERT Carlos	MONTOVANELI	4
7	VELAZQUEZ Oscar	BERTONI Edgar	6
9	VILLALBA Carlos Alberto	BACARO Vinicius	7
10	VILLALBA Walter	VICENTINI Andre	8
11	ROTELLA Jose	FABIANO	9
14	VILLALBA Rene	[40]	MORGADO	11
12	MIRANDA Marcos (GK)	ZANETTI Sandro	13
2	AYALA Emmanuel	BERTONI Rodrigo	14
6	GIMENEZ Hebert	(GK) FELLER Alexandre	12
	Tr: RUIZ Adolfo	Tr: NUCCORINI Alessandro	

LNK, Tao Yuan County, 25-11-2004
20:00, 2 150, Moosavi IRN, Galan ESP, Porritt AUS

USA 1 1 JPN

Guastaferro [14]

Kogure [39]

USA		JAPAN	
12	PHILLIPS Brett (GK)	(GK) KAWAHARA Hisamitsu	1
2	GUASTAFERRO Andy	SUZUMURA Takuya	2
3	TSCHANTRET Lee	MAEDA Yoshifumi	3
5	DUSOSKY Todd	HIGA Rikarudo	5
6	BOWERS Sean	NAMBATA Osamu	6
7	WHITE Pat	KANAYAMA Yuki	7
8	TORRES Johnny	FUJII Kenta	8
9	HOWES Greg	ONO Diasuke	9
10	BALL John	KOGURE Kenichiro	10
11	BUTCHER Steve	SAGANE Kiyoshi	11
14	MORRIS Pat	TAKAHASHI Kensuke	13
1	HILEMAN Scott (GK)	(GK) SADANAGA Hisao	12
	Tr: TOZER Keith	Tr: FILHO Sergio	

	GROUP D	PL	W	D	L	F	A	PTS	ARG	POR	IRN	CUB
1	Argentina	3	3	0	0	10	1	9		1-0	6-1	3-0
2	Portugal	3	2	0	1	9	1	6			4-0	5-0
3	Iran	3	1	0	2	9	13	3				8-3
4	Cuba	3	0	0	3	3	16	0				

LNK, Tao Yuan County, 24-11-2004
18:00, 3 700, Isokawa JPN, T orok HUN, Paixao BRA

IRN   0 4   POR

Luis Silva [10], Leo [14]
Joel Queiros [27], Zezito [38]

IRAN	PORTUGAL
1 NASSERI Reza (GK)	(GK) JOAO BENEDITO 1
6 DADASHI Siamak	IVAN 5
7 MASOUMI Babak	JOEL QUEIROS 6
9 SHAMSAEE Vahid	ANDRE 7
10 HEIDARIAN Mohammad	GONCALO 9
2 LOTFI Mahmoud	LUIS SILVA 2
4 HANIFI Amir	LEO 3
5 HASHEMZADEH Mohammad	MARCELINHO 4
8 MOHAMMADI Kazem	ZEZITO 13
14 FAKHIM Farhad	ISRAEL 11
12 ABRARINIA Hamidreza (GK)	(GK) SANDRO 12
11 RAISE Maged	MAJO 8
Tr: ANSARIFARD Mohammad	Tr: DUARTE Orlando

LNK, Tao Yuan County, 26-11-2004
18:00, 250, Galan ESP, Farag EGY, Van Helviort NED

IRN   8 3   CUB

Shamsaee 3 [2 39 40], Heidarian 2 [8 16]
Mohammadi [17], Lotfi [35], Fakhim [37]

Guerra [23], Saname [33]
Heidarian OG [40]

IRAN	CUBA
1 NASSERI Reza (GK)	(GK) CARBO Wilfredo 1
2 LOTFI Mahmoud	MORALES Amauri 2
4 HANIFI Amir	ROMAN Isven 3
5 HASHEMZADEH Mohammad	OLIVERA Yulier 4
6 DADASHI Siamak	MORALES Eduardo 5
7 MASOUMI Babak	GUERRA Pillin 6
8 MOHAMMADI Kazem	RODRIGUEZ Yampier 7
9 SHAMSAEE Vahid	MESA Yosniel 8
10 HEIDARIAN Mohammad	CHAPMAN Fernando 9
11 RAISE Maged	PORTAL Papi 10
14 FAKHIM Farhad	SANAME Boris 11
12 ABRARINIA Hamidreza (GK)	(GK) POGGI Fernando 12
Tr: ANSARIFARD Mohammad	Tr: REINOSO Clemente

LNK, Tao Yuan County, 28-11-2004
18:00, 700, Filppu FIN, Cumbo ITA, Galan ESP

ARG   6 1   IRN

Sanchez [10p] ,Garcias [33]
Gonzalez [35], Wilhelm 3 [36 36 39]

Shamsaee [16]

ARGENTINA	IRAN
1 GUISANDE Javier (GK)	(GK) NASSERI Reza 1
2 PLANAS Leandro	LOTFI Mahmoud 2
3 ENRIQUEZ Martin	HANIFI Amir 4
4 GIUSTOZZI Diego	DADASHI Siamak 6
5 SANCHEZ Carlos	MASOUMI Babak 7
7 WILHELM Fernando	MOHAMMADI Kazem 8
8 GARCIAS Hernan	SHAMSAEE Vahid 9
9 PETILLO Rodrigo	HEIDARIAN Mohammad 10
10 GIMENEZ Marcelo	(GK) ABRARINIA Hamidreza 12
11 GONZALEZ Esteban	FAKHIM Farhad 14
14 BRESCIANI Cristian	HASHEMZADEH Mohammad 5
12 POGGI Fernando (GK)	RAISE Maged 11
Tr: LARRANAGA Fernando	Tr: ANSARIFARD Mohammad

LNK, Tao Yuan County, 24-11-2004
20:00, 1 200, Farag EGY, Konstantinidis USA, Del Cid GUA

CUB   0 3   ARG

Garcias [30], Planas 2 [32 34]

CUBA	ARGENTINA
1 CARBO Wilfredo (GK)	(GK) GUISANDE Javier 1
6 GUERRA Pillin	PLANAS Leandro 2
9 CHAPMAN Fernando	SANCHEZ Carlos 5
10 PORTAL Papi	WILHELM Fernando 7
11 SANAME Boris	GARCIAS Hernan 8
2 MORALES Amauri	ENRIQUEZ Martin 3
3 ROMAN Isven	BARBONA Gustavo 6
5 MORALES Eduardo	PETILLO Rodrigo 9
7 RODRIGUEZ Yampier	GIMENEZ Marcelo 10
8 MESA Yosniel	RANIERI Pablo 13
12 LOPEZ Francis (GK)	BRESCIANI Cristian 14
4 OLIVERA Yulier	(GK) POGGI Fernando 12
Tr: REINOSO Clemente	Tr: LARRANAGA Fernando

LNK, Tao Yuan County, 26-11-2004
20:00, 400, Al Shatti KUW, Del Cid, Porritt AUS

POR   0 1   ARG

Gonzalez [19]

PORTUGAL	ARGENTINA
1 JOAO BENEDITO (GK)	(GK) GUISANDE Javier 1
2 LUIS SILVA	PLANAS Leandro 2
3 LEO	GIUSTOZZI Diego 4
4 MARCELINHO	SANCHEZ Carlos 5
5 IVAN	BARBONA Gustavo 6
6 JOEL QUEIROS	WILHELM Fernando 7
7 ANDRE	GARCIAS Hernan 8
8 MAJO	PETILLO Rodrigo 9
9 GONCALO	GIMENEZ Marcelo 10
13 ZEZITO	GONZALEZ Esteban 11
12 SANDRO (GK)	BRESCIANI Cristian 14
10 ROGERIO SANTOS	(GK) POGGI Fernando 12
Tr: DUARTE Orlando	Tr: LARRANAGA Fernando

NTU, Taipei City, 28-11-2004
18:00, 532, Paixao BRA, Valiente PAR, Farag EGY

POR   5 0   CUB

Joel Queiros 2 [7 31], Ivan [11]
Majo [26], Andre [39]

PORTUGAL	CUBA
1 JOAO BENEDITO (GK)	(GK) CARBO Wilfredo 1
2 LUIS SILVA	MORALES Amauri 2
3 LEO	ROMAN Isven 3
5 IVAN	MORALES Eduardo 5
6 JOEL QUEIROS	GUERRA Pillin 6
7 ANDRE	RODRIGUEZ Yampier 7
8 MAJO	MESA Yosniel 8
9 GONCALO	CHAPMAN Fernando 9
10 ROGERIO SANTOS	PORTAL Papi 10
11 ISRAEL	SANAME Boris 11
12 SANDRO (GK)	MADRIGAL Carlos 13
13 ZEZITO	(GK) POGGI Fernando 12
Tr: DUARTE Orlando	Tr: REINOSO Clemente

GROUP E	PL	W	D	L	F	A	PTS		ITA	ESP	POR	CZE
1 Italy	3	2	1	0	6	7	7			3-2	0-0	3-0
2 Spain	3	2	0	1	7	6	6				3-1	2-0
3 Portugal	3	1	1	1	9	4	4					8-4
4 Czech Republic	3	0	0	3	4	13	0					

LNK, Tao Yuan County, 28-11-2004
16:00, 350, Moosavi IRN, Filppu FIN, Paixao BRA

ESP   2   0   CZE

Javi Rodriguez 2 [23] [32]

SPAIN	CZECH REPUBLIC	
1 LUIS AMADO (GK)	(GK) KRAYZEL Petr	1
2 JULIO	BLAZEJ Vit	2
3 TORRAS	RAJNOCH Daniel	3
4 FRAN SERREJON	LEVCIK David	4
5 OROL	SLUKA Tomas	5
7 JAVI RODRIGUEZ	DLOUHY Martin	7
8 KIKE	HOFFMAN Petr	8
9 ANDREU	MARES Michal	11
11 ALBERTO COGORRO	(GK) KLIMA Jan	12
14 MARCELO	KAMENICKY Jaroslav	14
12 RAFA (GK)	MUSIAL Roman	10
10 LIMONES	SLAMA Zdenek	13
Tr: LOZANO Javier	Tr: STRIZ Michal	

LNK, Tao Yuan County, 29-11-2004
18:00, 500, Sciancalepore ARG, Paixao BRA, Moosavi IRN

ESP   2   3   ITA

Javi Rodriguez [1], Marcelo [30]   Luis Amado OG [8], Fabiano [19]
Orol OG [20]

SPAIN	ITALY	
1 LUIS AMADO (GK)	(GK) FELLER Alexandre	12
2 JULIO	GRANA	2
3 TORRAS	PELLEGRINI	3
5 OROL	MONTOVANELI	4
7 JAVI RODRIGUEZ	ZAFFIRO Salvatore	5
8 KIKE	BERTONI Edgar	6
9 ANDREU	BACARO Vinicius	7
11 ALBERTO COGORRO	VICENTINI Andre	8
14 MARCELO	FABIANO	9
12 RAFA (GK)	FOGLIA Adriano	10
4 FRAN SERREJON	ZANETTI Sandro	13
6 PIPE	(GK) RIPESI Marco	15
Tr: LOZANO Javier	Tr: NUCCORINI Alessandro	

LNK, Tao Yuan County, 1-12-2004
20:00, 1 100, Torok HUN, Farag EGY, Del Cid GUA

ESP   3   1   POR

Marcelo 2 [6] [30], Fran Serrejon [12]   Joel Queiros [6]

SPAIN	PORTUGAL	
1 LUIS AMADO (GK)	[19] (GK) JOAO BENEDITO	[1]
2 JULIO	LUIS SILVA	2
3 TORRAS	LEO	3
4 FRAN SERREJON	MARCELINHO	4
5 OROL	IVAN	5
7 JAVI RODRIGUEZ	JOEL QUEIROS	6
8 KIKE	ANDRE	7
9 ANDREU	MAJO	8
10 LIMONES	GONCALO	9
11 ALBERTO COGORRO	ISRAEL	11
14 MARCELO	(GK) SANDRO	12
12 RAFA (GK)	ZEZITO	[13]
Tr: LOZANO Javier	Tr: DUARTE Orlando	

LNK, Tao Yuan County, 28-11-2004
18:00, 425, Konstantinidis USA, Torok HUN, Sciancalepore ARG

ITA   0   0   POR

ITALY	PORTUGAL	
1 ANGELINI Gianfranco (GK)	(GK) JOAO BENEDITO	1
2 GRANA	LUIS SILVA	2
3 PELLEGRINI	LEO	3
4 MONTOVANELI	MARCELINHO	4
5 ZAFFIRO Salvatore	IVAN	5
6 BERTONI Edgar	JOEL QUEIROS	6
7 BACARO Vinicius	ANDRE	7
8 VICENTINI Andre	MAJO	8
9 FABIANO	GONCALO	9
10 FOGLIA Adriano	ISRAEL	11
12 FELLER Alexandre (GK)	ZEZITO	13
13 ZANETTI Sandro	(GK) SANDRO	12
Tr: NUCCORINI Alessandro	Tr: DUARTE Orlando	

LNK, Tao Yuan County, 29-11-2004
20:00, 425, Van Helvoirt NED, Farag EGY, Konstantinidis USA

CZE   4   8   POR

Blazej 2 [7] [38], Musial [14], Dlouhy [16]   Joel Queiros 3 [4] [10] [39], Ivan [20]
Andre [22], Goncalo 2 [23] [34], Leo [33]

CZECH REPUBLIC	PORTUGAL	
1 KRAYZEL Petr (GK)	(GK) JOAO BENEDITO	1
2 BLAZEJ Vit	LEO	3
3 RAJNOCH Daniel	MARCELINHO	4
4 LEVCIK David	IVAN	5
5 SLUKA Tomas	JOEL QUEIROS	6
7 DLOUHY Martin	ANDRE	7
9 HAVEL Josef	MAJO	8
10 MUSIAL Roman	GONCALO	9
11 MARES Michal	ROGERIO SANTOS	10
12 KLIMA Jan (GK)	ISRAEL	11
13 SLAMA Zdenek	ZEZITO	13
14 KAMENICKY Jaroslav	(GK) SILVIO	14
Tr: STRIZ Michal	Tr: DUARTE Orlando	

NTU, Taipei City, 1-12-2004
20:00, 1 350, Valiente PAR, Filppu FIN, Paixao BRA

CZE   0   3   ITA

Grana [8], Bertoni [12], Zanetti [30]

CZECH REPUBLIC	ITALY	
1 KRAYZEL Petr (GK)	(GK) FELLER Alexandre	12
2 BLAZEJ Vit	GRANA	2
3 RAJNOCH Daniel	PELLEGRINI	3
4 LEVCIK David	MONTOVANELI	4
5 SLUKA Tomas	BERTONI Edgar	6
7 DLOUHY Martin	BACARO Vinicius	7
8 HOFFMAN Petr	FABIANO	9
9 HAVEL Josef	FOGLIA Adriano	10
10 MUSIAL Roman	MORGADO	11
11 MARES Michal	ZANETTI Sandro	13
12 KLIMA Jan (GK)	BERTONI Rodrigo	14
13 SLAMA Zdenek	(GK) RIPESI Marco	15
Tr: STRIZ Michal	Tr: NUCCORINI Alessandro	

GROUP F	PL	W	D	L	F	A	PTS	BRA	ARG	UKR	USA
1 Brazil	3	3	0	0	16	6	9		2-1	6-0	8-5
2 Argentina	3	1	1	1	3	3	4			0-0	2-1
3 Ukraine	3	1	1	1	3	7	4				3-1
4 USA	3	0	0	3	7	13	0				

NTU, Taipei City, 28-11-2004
16:00, 2 100, Van Helvoirt NED, Valiente PAR, Galan ESP

BRA　　6　0　　UKR

Falcao 3 [7] [21] [24], Indio 2 [14] [25],
Kosenko OG [28]

BRAZIL	UKRAINE	
2 FRANKLIN (GK)	(GK) POPOV Olexiy	1
3 SCHUMACHER	SYTIN Sergiy	2
4 NETO	NESTERUK Vitaliy	3
5 MANOEL TOBIAS	KORIDZE Sergiy	4
7 VINICIUS	SHAYTANOV Oleg	5
8 EULER	MANSUROV Ramis	6
9 INDIO	MELNIKOV Georgii	7
11 SIMI	KOSENKO Olexandr	8
12 FALCAO	BRUNKO Vitaliy	9
14 VANDER	PYLYPIV Fedir	11
1 LAVOISIER (GK)	KOVALYOV Artem	13
10 FININHO	(GK) VLASENKO Kostyantyn	14
Tr: LEITE Fernando	Tr: LISENCHUK Gennadiy	

NTU, Taipei City, 29-11-2004
18:00, 1 650, Galan ESP, Filppu FIN, Cumbo ITA

BRA　　2　1　　ARG

Simi 2 [2] [6]　　　　　　　　　　Garcias [17]

BRAZIL	ARGENTINA	
2 FRANKLIN (GK)	(GK) GUISANDE Javier	1
3 SCHUMACHER	PLANAS Leandro	2
4 NETO	GIUSTOZZI Diego	4
5 MANOEL TOBIAS	SANCHEZ Carlos	5
8 EULER	WILHELM Fernando	7
9 INDIO	GARCIAS Hernan	8
11 SIMI	PETILLO Rodrigo	9
12 FALCAO	GIMENEZ Marcelo	10
1 LAVOISIER (GK)	GONZALEZ Esteban	11
6 PABLO	(GK) POGGI Fernando	12
10 FININHO	ENRIQUEZ Martin	3
14 VANDER	BRESCIANI Cristian	14
Tr: LEITE Fernando	Tr: LARRANAGA Fernando	

NTU, Taipei City, 1-12-2004
18:00, 1 600, Cumbo ITA, Djiba SEN, Maso Goitisolo CUB

BRA　　8　5　　USA

Falcao 2 [5] [25], Fininho [9]
Manoel Tobias [11], Pablo [26]
Schumacher [37], Indio 2 [39] [40]

Butcher [12], Ball [32], White [34]
Torres [38], Beasley [39]

BRAZIL	USA	
1 LAVOISIER (GK)	(GK) HILEMAN Scott	1
2 FRANKLIN (GK)	GUASTAFERRO Andy	2
3 SCHUMACHER	BEASLEY Jamar	4
4 NETO	DUSOSKY Todd	5
5 MANOEL TOBIAS	BOWERS Sean	6
6 PABLO	WHITE Pat	7
8 EULER	TORRES Johnny	8
9 INDIO	BALL John	10
10 FININHO	BUTCHER Steve	11
11 SIMI	MORRIS Pat	14
12 FALCAO	(GK) PHILLIPS Brett	12
14 VANDER		
Tr: LEITE Fernando	Tr: TOZER Keith	

NTU, Taipei City, 28-11-2004
18:00, 1 900, Porritt AUS, Cumbo ITA, Al Shatti KUW

ARG　　2　1　　USA

Giustozzi [5], Wilhelm [20]　　　　　　　Torres [40]

ARGENTINA	USA	
1 GUISANDE Javier (GK)	(GK) PHILLIPS Brett	12
2 PLANAS Leandro	GUASTAFERRO Andy	2
4 GIUSTOZZI Diego	TSCHANTRET Lee	3
5 SANCHEZ Carlos	BEASLEY Jamar	4
6 BARBONA Gustavo	DUSOSKY Todd	5
7 WILHELM Fernando	BOWERS Sean	6
8 GARCIAS Hernan	WHITE Pat	7
9 PETILLO Rodrigo	TORRES Johnny	8
10 GIMENEZ Marcelo	BALL John	10
11 GONZALEZ Esteban	SHANKER Joel	13
14 BRESCIANI Cristian	MORRIS Pat	14
12 POGGI Fernando (GK)	(GK) HILEMAN Scott	1
Tr: LARRANAGA Fernando	Tr: TOZER Keith	

NTU, Taipei City, 29-11-2004
20:00, 1 200, Torok HUN, Del Cid GUA, Valiente PAR

UKR　　3　1　　USA

Sytin 2 [19] [24], Nesteruk [40]　　　　　Torres [20]

UKRAINE	USA	
2 SYTIN Sergiy	(GK) HILEMAN Scott	1
3 NESTERUK Vitaliy	GUASTAFERRO Andy	2
4 KORIDZE Sergiy	BEASLEY Jamar	4
5 SHAYTANOV Oleg	DUSOSKY Todd	5
6 MANSUROV Ramis	BOWERS Sean	6
7 MELNIKOV Georgii　[30]	WHITE Pat	7
8 KOSENKO Olexandr	TORRES Johnny	8
9 BRUNKO Vitaliy	HOWES Greg	9
11 PYLYPIV Fedir	BALL John	10
12 SUKHOMLINOV Vasyl (GK)	BUTCHER Steve	11
1 POPOV Olexiy (GK)	SHANKER Joel	13
13 KOVALYOV Artem	MORRIS Pat	14
Tr: LISENCHUK Gennadiy	Tr: TOZER Keith	

LNK, Tao Yuan County, 1-12-2004
18:00, 750, Moosavi IRN, Al Shatti KUW, Galan ESP

UKR　　0　0　　ARG

UKRAINE	ARGENTINA	
1 POPOV Olexiy (GK)	(GK) GUISANDE Javier	1
2 SYTIN Sergiy	PLANAS Leandro	2
3 NESTERUK Vitaliy	GIUSTOZZI Diego	4
4 KORIDZE Sergiy	SANCHEZ Carlos	5
5 SHAYTANOV Oleg	WILHELM Fernando	7
6 MANSUROV Ramis	GARCIAS Hernan	8
8 KOSENKO Olexandr	PETILLO Rodrigo	9
9 BRUNKO Vitaliy	GIMENEZ Marcelo	10
10 MOSKVYCHOV Igor	GONZALEZ Esteban	11
11 PYLYPIV Fedir	(GK) POGGI Fernando	12
12 SUKHOMLINOV Vasyl (GK)	BARBONA Gustavo	6
13 KOVALYOV Artem	BRESCIANI Cristian	14
Tr: LISENCHUK Gennadiy	Tr: LARRANAGA Fernando	

SEMI-FINALS

NTU, Taipei City, 3-12-2004
18:00, 3 400, Valiente PAR, Torok HUN, Filppu FIN

BRA 4p 2 2 5p ESP

Pablo [26], Simi [35]   Andreu [23], Marcelo [35]

BRAZIL	SPAIN	
2 FRANKLIN (GK)	(GK) LUIS AMADO	1
3 SCHUMACHER	JULIO	2
4 NETO	TORRAS	3
6 PABLO	FRAN SERREJON	4
8 EULER	OROL	5
9 INDIO	JAVI RODRIGUEZ	7
11 SIMI	KIKE	8
12 FALCAO	ANDREU	9
14 VANDER	LIMONES	10
13 ANGELO (GK)	MARCELO	14
5 MANOEL TOBIAS	(GK) RAFA	12
10 FININHO	PIPE	6
Tr: LEITE Fernando	Tr: LOZANO Javier	

NTU, Taipei City, 3-12-2004
20:30, 3 500, Farag EGY, Moosavi IRN, Van Helvoirt NED

ITA 7 4 ARG

Bacaro 3 [2 12 35], Fabiano [9]   Sanchez [28], Gimenez 2 [34 40]
Vicentini [32], Foglia [34]   Wilhelm [35]
Giustozzi OG [38]

ITALY	ARGENTINA	
2 GRANA	(GK) GUISANDE Javier	1
3 PELLEGRINI	PLANAS Leandro	2
4 MONTOVANELI	GIUSTOZZI Diego	4
5 ZAFFIRO Salvatore	SANCHEZ Carlos	5
6 BERTONI Edgar	BARBONA Gustavo	6
7 BACARO Vinicius	WILHELM Fernando	7
8 VICENTINI Andre 33	GARCIAS Hernan	8
9 FABIANO	PETILLO Rodrigo	9
10 FOGLIA Adriano	GIMENEZ Marcelo	10
12 FELLER Alexandre (GK)	GONZALEZ Esteban	11
13 ZANETTI Sandro	(GK) POGGI Fernando	12
15 RIPESI Marco (GK)	BRESCIANI Cristian	14
Tr: NUCCORINI Alessandro	Tr: LARRANAGA Fernando	

THIRD PLACE PLAY-OFF AND FINAL

Bronze medal match, NTU, Taipei City, 5-12-2004
14:00, 3 500, Galan ESP, Cumbo ITA, Del Cid GUA

BRA 7 4 ARG

Falcao 3 [1 6 12], Schumacher 2 [17 36]   Sanchez 2 [9 23], Giustozzi 2 [29 30]
Euler [18], Indio [19]

BRAZIL	ARGENTINA	
2 FRANKLIN (GK)	(GK) GUISANDE Javier	1
3 SCHUMACHER	PLANAS Leandro	2
4 NETO	GIUSTOZZI Diego	4
5 MANOEL TOBIAS	SANCHEZ Carlos	5
6 PABLO	WILHELM Fernando	7
8 EULER	GARCIAS Hernan	8
9 INDIO	PETILLO Rodrigo	9
10 FININHO	GIMENEZ Marcelo	10
11 SIMI	GONZALEZ Esteban	11
12 FALCAO	(GK) POGGI Fernando	12
14 VANDER	ENRIQUEZ Martin	3
13 ANGELO (GK)	BRESCIANI Cristian	14
Tr: LEITE Fernando	Tr: LARRANAGA Fernando	

Final, NTU, Taipei City, 5-12-2004
16:00, 3 500, Sciancalepore ARG, Paixao BRA, Filppu FIN

ESP 2 1 ITA

Kike [24], Marcelo [30]   Zanetti [40]

SPAIN	ITALY	
1 LUIS AMADO (GK)	GRANA	2
2 JULIO	PELLEGRINI	3
3 TORRAS	MONTOVANELI	4
4 FRAN SERREJON	ZAFFIRO Salvatore	5
5 OROL	BERTONI Edgar	6
7 JAVI RODRIGUEZ	BACARO Vinicius	7
8 KIKE	FABIANO	9
9 ANDREU	FOGLIA Adriano	10
10 LIMONES	MORGADO	11
14 MARCELO	(GK) FELLER Alexandre	12
12 RAFA (GK)	ZANETTI Sandro	13
6 PIPE	(GK) RIPESI Marco	15
Tr: LOZANO Javier	Tr: NUCCORINI Alessandro	

ADIDAS GOLDEN BALL		ADIDAS GOLDEN SHOE			FIFA FAIR PLAY AWARD		
1 FALCAO	Brazil			Goals	1 Brazil	Ø 889	8 matches
2 JAVIER RODRIGUEZ	Spain	1 FALCAO	Brazil	13	2 USA	Ø 857	6 matches
3 BACARO Vinicius	Italy	2 INDIO	Brazil	10	3 Czech Republic	Ø 834	6 matches
		3 MARCELO	Spain	9			

GOALSCORING AT CHINESE TAIPEI 2004	
Total number of goals scored	237
Average per match	5.93
How the Goals were Scored	
Goals scored from open play	199
Goals scored from set pieces	38
When the Goals were scored	
1st - 5th minute	6.3%	15
6th - 10th minute	11.4%	27
11th - 15th minute	10.5%	25
16th - 20th minute	13.5%	32
21st - 25th minute	11.0%	26
26th - 30th minute	11.0%	26
31st - 35th minute	16.0%	38
36th - 40th minute	20.3%	48

ATTENDANCES AT CHINESE TAIPEI 2004		
Total number of spectators		50 923
Average per match		1 273
Attendances at each venue		
	Total	Average
NTU, Taipei City	36 423	1 656
Linkou, Tao Yua	14 500	806
Largest attendances		
Spain v Italy	NTU	3 500
Brazil v Argentina	NTU	3 500
Italy v Argentina	NTU	3 500
Smallest Attendances		
Iran v Cuba	Linkou	250
Egypt v Spain	Linkou	350
Spain v Czech Republic	Linkou	350

FIFA INTERACTIVE WORLD CUP 2004

Reflecting that country's footballing heritage, it was perhaps inevitable that a Brazilian would win the inaugural FIFA Interactive World Cup after three months of intense competition across the globe. In a tense final at FIFA House in Zurich, Thiago Carrico de Azevedo triumphed 2-1 over Matija Biljeskovic of USA to win a championship that had attracted more than 2,000 competitors and 6,000 visitors from nine countries and six continents. Qualifying tournaments were staged in eight exotic locations around the world including the Javits Centre in New York, the Equinox Centre in Paris, the Sydney Exhibition Centre and the Rio Centro in Rio, as the hopefuls of all ages aspired to become World Champion of EA Sports' FIFA 2005 on Xbox. The competition was launched in South Africa soon after the announcement that that country had successfully bid to host the 2010 FIFA World Cup™. South African midfielder Benson Mhlongo captured the ethos and spirit of the tournament when he said: "Real footballers and gamers have a lot in common. It's all about patience, interest and fighting spirit and has a lot to do with the love of the game. It's great because kids fall in love with football by playing these games." Atmosphere at the events was boosted with matches played in an interactive football arena to the accompaniment of music provided by top international DJs. Any pre-match nerves needed to be left in the players' tunnel! And for the winner, Thiago, there was the glamour of the trophy presentation at the FIFA World Player Gala in Zurich alongside the likes of Ronaldhino and Thierry Henry.

FIFA INTERACTIVE WORLD CUP 2004

Regional semis	Regional finals	Quarter-final groups	Semi-finals	Final
Thiago Carrico de Azevedo				
Daniel Moreira	Thiago Carrico de Azevedo			
Diego Cesar Rodrigues	Felipe Augusto			
Felipe Augusto				
Simon Pike				
Justin Martin	Simon Pike			
Obaidur Chadri	Paul Gordon	Thiago Carrico de Azevedo		
Paul Gordon		Shimane Morekure		
Shane Magee		Paul Gordon		
Ercan Ersan	Shane Magee	Shane Magee		
George Mikhael	Stephen Coorey			
Stephen Coorey			Thiago Carrico de Azevedo	
Choi Dae Han			Youn See Park	
Jeon Kyung Woon	Choi Dae Han			
Lin Xiaoqang	Youn See Park			
Youn See Park				Thiago Carrico de Azevedo
Shimane Morekure				Matija Biljeskovic
Sandile Motha	Shimane Morekure			
Ndumisco Masango	Luke Hatfield			
Luke Hatfield			Shimane Morekure	
Adrian Martin			Matija Biljeskovic	
Sebastiano Forga	Adrian Martin			
Fabien Legros	Massimiliano Lucchese	Matija Biljeskovic		
Massimiliano Lucchese		Youn See Park		
Kai Kretschman		Massimiliano Lucchese		
Kamil Grzybek	Kai Kretschman	Kai Kretschman		
Andre van Bissenbeck	Rob Day			
Rob Day				
Carlos Briseno				
Jesus Rodriguez	Carlos Briseno			
Paul Canepa	Matija Biljeskovic			
Matija Biljeskovic				

FIFA BEACH SOCCER WORLD CUP 2005

You're nearly 39 years old, you've had an eventful soccer career with one of the world's most famous clubs and you're an occasional film actor, so what's left for a retired football legend? Well, if you're Eric Cantona, you go to the beach. The enigmatic former Manchester United midfielder-turned-coach guided France to victory in the inaugural FIFA Beach Soccer World Cup 2005 on the beaches of Brazil, adding the world title to the European crown they captured the year before. The two victories are the culmination of six years' hard work by Cantona and his brother, Joel. After retiring from mainstream soccer, Cantona has helped France emerge as one of the global giants of the sport. Even in winter, Rio provided the perfect backdrop with its sunshine and 30° temperatures for a week of soccer involving 12 nations ranging from the old masters of Brazil to the relative newcomers from Thailand. The Auriverde of Brazil were at their imperious best for much of the tournament scoring 39 goals in five games including 11 against Japan in the bronze medal playoff. However, the South Americans were overshadowed on their home beaches by the invading Europeans led by France who had won their European crown in a sensational final with Portugal. Their paths met again in the final in Rio after the French had disposed of Japan and Portugal had beaten Brazil, and although an epic battle ran to a penalty shoot out, the French looked like potential champions from the moment they knocked five past Australia in their opening group match. Les Bleus were blessed with a wealth of talent from goalkeeper Jean-Marie Aubry to striker Anthony Mendy. Third in the goalscoring chart and winner of the adidas bronze shoe, Mendy's tournament peaked with a hat-trick in the final. Portugal's defeat was a blow having lost to the French only months earlier, but consolation came from their striker Madjer who claimed both the top player and top goalscorer awards (12) with some exuberant performances. Japan's semi-final spot was one of the surprises of the World Cup and although they suffered against their hosts in the bronze medal play-off, losing 11-2, their fourth place was completely deserved after arriving in Rio as rank outsiders.

FIFA BEACH SOCCER WORLD CUP BRAZIL 2005

First round groups

	ESP	THA	Pts
Brazil	4-1	4-1	6
Spain		4-1	3
Thailand			0

	JPN	USA	Pts
Portugal	4-0	9-3	6
Japan		3-2	3
USA			0

	UKR	RSA	Pts
Uruguay	5-4	7-3	6
Ukraine		8-1	3
South Africa			0

	ARG	AUS	Pts
France	8-2	5-1	6
Argentina		3-1	3
Australia			0

Quarter-finals

France	7
Spain	4

Uruguay	3
Japan	4

Brazil	9
Argentina	3

Ukraine	3
Portugal	5

Semi-finals

France	4
Japan	1

Brazil	6 1p
Portugal	6 2p

Final

France	3 1p
Portugal	3 0p

Third Place Play-off

Brazil	11
Japan	2

FIFA WORLD YOUTH CHAMPIONSHIP 2005

Argentina re-wrote the record books with an historic fifth title in the FIFA World Youth Championship to add to those won in 1995, 1997 and 2001 under Jose Peckerman and the 1979 triumph in which Cesar Luis Menotti coached a team including Diego Maradona. The star of the show was Barcelona's young prodigy Lionel Messi whom the Catalan club signed at the tender age of just 13. Already earning rave reviews with Barcelona he sealed his reputation as one of the most promising talents with a series of fine displays that earned him both the Golden Shoe as top scorer and the Golden Ball as the best player. Despite being played away from the major cities, Dutch fans turned out in good numbers to watch the tournament and in the first round they witnessed a number of surprises, most notably China taking all nine points in Group B and also the Syrian victory over Italy. The Chinese were then beaten in a closely fought match against the Germans in the round of 16 although it proved to be a poor tournament for European nations overall with none making it past the quarter-final stage. Instead the semi-finals saw Argentina against Brazil and Nigeria square up with Morocco. The Argentines were making a habit of scoring late winners in the championship and it was a goal three minutes into injury time by their other star player Pablo Zabaleta which proved to be the difference between them and the Brazilians. The other semi-final was more straightforward with Nigeria easing to a 3-0 win over Morocco and qualifying for their second final. Their attempts to become the first African nation to win the trophy, however, were finally ended by the guile of Messi in the penalty box.

FIFA WORLD YOUTH CHAMPIONSHIP NETHERLANDS 2005

First round groups		Round of 16		Quarter-finals		Semi-finals		Final	
Group A	Pts								
Netherlands	9	Argentina	2						
Japan	2	Colombia	1						
Benin	2			Argentina	3				
Australia	2			Spain	1				
Group B	Pts	Turkey	0						
China PR	9	Spain	3						
Ukraine	4					Argentina	2		
Turkey	4					Brazil	1		
Panama	0	Germany	3						
Group C	Pts	China PR	2						
Spain	9			Germany	1				
Morocco	6			Brazil	2				
Chile	3	Syria	0						
Honduras	0	Brazil	1						
								Argentina	2
								Nigeria	1
Group D	Pts	Morocco	1						
USA	7	Japan	0						
Argentina	6								
Germany	4			Morocco	2 4p				
Egypt	0			Italy	2 2p				
Group E	Pts	USA	1						
Colombia	9	Italy	3						
Syria	4					Morocco	0		
Italy	3					Nigeria	3		
Canada	1	Netherlands	3						
Group F	Pts	Chile	0						
Brazil	7			Netherlands	1 9p				
Nigeria	4			Nigeria	1 10p			3rd place play-off	
Korea Republic	3	Ukraine	0					Brazil	2
Switzerland	3	Nigeria	1					Morocco	1

	GROUP A	PL	W	D	L	F	A	PTS	NED	JPN	BEN	AUS
1	Netherlands	3	3	0	0	6	1	9		2-1	1-0	3-0
2	Japan	3	0	2	1	3	4	2			1-1	1-1
3	Benin	3	0	2	1	2	3	2				1-1
4	Australia	3	0	2	1	2	5	2				

Parkstad Limburg, Kerkrade, 10-06-2005
16:00, 4 500, Medina Cantalejo ESP, Carrasco ESP, Hernandez ESP

BEN 1 1 AUS

Omotoyossi 32 — Ward 59

BENIN				AUSTRALIA
16 DJIDONOU Yoann				FEDERICI Adam 18
2 CHITOU Charaf				MILLIGAN Mark 2
3 OLOU Oscar				(c) MC CLENAHAN Trent 3
5 MOUSSA Traore				TIMPANO Jacob 5
6 RAIMY Florent				MUSIALIK Stuart 6
7 BOCO Romualde (c)				LIA Vince 7
11 MAIGA Abou				CELESKI Billy 8
12 AGBESSI Coffi				SARKIES Kristian 10
5 OMOTOYOSSI Razak	87	77		TADROSSE Chris 11
18 TCHOMOGO Seidath				DOWNES Aaron 13
19 AHOUEYA Jocelin	72			WARD Nick 17
Tr: DEVEZE Serge				Tr: POSTECOGLOU Ange
13 NASSIROU Youssouf	87	77		DILEVSKI Spase 14
14 OSSENI Bachirou	72			

Parkstad Limburg, Kerkrade, 10-06-2005
20:00, 19 500, Ruiz COL, Botero COL, Tamayo ECU

NED 2 1 JPN

Afellay 7, Babel 18 — Hirayama 68

NETHERLANDS				JAPAN
1 VERMEER Kenneth				NISHIKAWA Shusaku 21
2 TIENDALLI Dwight				MIZUMOTO Hiroki 2
3 VLAAR Ron				KOBAYASHI Yuzo 4
4 VAN DER STRUIJK Frank				MASUSHIMA Tatsuya 5
5 DROST Jeroen				NAKAMURA Hokuto 8
6 MADURO Hedwiges (c)				HIRAYAMA Sota 9
7 OWUSU ABEYIE Quincy				(c) HYODO Shingo 10
8 KRUYS Rick	67		41	KOKEGUCHI Takuya 13
10 AFELLAY Ibrahim			64	HONDA Keisuke 14
11 BABEL Ryan	74			NAGIRA Tomokazu 16
18 VINCKEN Tim			78	IENAGA Akihiro 17
Tr: DE HAAN Foppe				Tr: OHKUMA Kiyoshi
9 JOHN Collins	74		41	CULLEN Robert 11
17 AGUSTIEN Kemy	67		64	MIZUNO Koki 12
			78	MORIMOTO Takayuki 20

Parkstad Limburg, Kerkrade, 15-06-2005
17:30, 12 500, Larsen DEN, Hansen DEN, Norrestrand DEN

JPN 1 1 BEN

Mizuno 65 — Maiga 37

JAPAN				BENIN
21 NISHIKAWA Shusaku				DJIDONOU Yoann 16
2 MIZUMOTO Hiroki				CHITOU Charaf 2
4 KOBAYASHI Yuzo		71		OLOU Oscar 3
5 MASUSHIMA Tatsuya				MOUSSA Traore 5
7 KAJIYAMA Yohei	46			BOCO Romualde 7
8 NAKAMURA Hokuto				MAIGA Abou 11
9 HIRAYAMA Sota				AGBESSI Coffi 12
10 HYODO Shingo (c)		73		(c) OSSENI Bachirou 14
11 CULLEN Robert	76			OMOTOYOSSI Razak 15
16 NAGIRA Tomokazu				TCHOMOGO Seidath 18
17 IENAGA Akihiro	84			AHOUEYA Jocelin 19
Tr: OHKUMA Kiyoshi				Tr: DEVEZE Serge
12 MIZUNO Koki	46	73		NASSIROU Youssouf 13
13 KOKEGUCHI Takuya	84			
20 MORIMOTO Takayuki	76			

Parkstad Limburg, Kerkrade, 15-06-2005
20:30, 19 500, Kwon Jong Chul KOR, Liu Tiejun CHN, KIM Dae Young KOR

AUS 0 3 NED

Maduro 20, Emanuelson 46
Kruys 74

AUSTRALIA				NETHERLANDS
18 FEDERICI Adam				VERMEER Kenneth 1
2 MILLIGAN Mark				TIENDALLI Dwight 2
3 MC CLENAHAN Trent				VLAAR Ron 3
5 TIMPANO Jacob				VAN DER STRUIJK Frank 4
6 MUSIALIK Stuart				DROST Jeroen 5
7 LIA Vince (c)				(c) MADURO Hedwiges 6
8 CELESKI Billy	51			OWUSU ABEYIE Quincy 7
10 SARKIES Kristian	61			KRUYS Rick 8
13 DOWNES Aaron		46		JOHN Collins 9
14 DILEVSKI Spase	51	72		BABEL Ryan 11
17 WARD Nick	77			EMANUELSON Urby 15
Tr: POSTECOGLOU Ange				Tr: DE HAAN Foppe
9 LUCAS Jay	61	77		MEDUNJANIN Haris 14
11 TADROSSE Chris	51	46		VINCKEN Tim 18
16 ZADKOVICH Ruben	51	72		RAJCOMAR Prince 19

Parkstad Limburg, Kerkrade, 18-06-2005
16:00, 2 000, Hauge NOR, Holvik NOR, Borgan NOR

JPN 1 1 AUS

Maeda 87 — Townsend 75

JAPAN				AUSTRALIA
21 NISHIKAWA Shusaku				PASFIELD Justin 12
2 MIZUMOTO Hiroki				MILLIGAN Mark 2
4 KOBAYASHI Yuzo				MC CLENAHAN Trent 3
5 MASUSHIMA Tatsuya	80			(c) TIMPANO Jacob 5
7 KAJIYAMA Yohei		72		MUSIALIK Stuart 6
8 NAKAMURA Hokuto				LUCAS Jay 9
9 HIRAYAMA Sota				TADROSSE Chris 11
10 HYODO Shingo (c)	67	64		DILEVSKI Spase 14
11 CULLEN Robert				TOWNSEND Ryan 15
16 NAGIRA Tomokazu		55		ZADKOVICH Ruben 16
17 IENAGA Akihiro	58			WESOLOWSKI James 20
Tr: OHKUMA Kiyoshi				Tr: POSTECOGLOU Ange
12 MIZUNO Koki	67	72		CELESKI Billy 8
19 MAEDA Shunsuke	58	64		SARKIES Kristian 10
20 MORIMOTO Takayuki	80	55		WARD Nick 17

Willem II, Tilburg, 18-06-2005
16:00, 13 700, Al Ghamdi KSA, Arabati JOR, Ghuloum UAE

NED 1 0 BEN

Maduro 47+

NETHERLANDS				BENIN
1 VERMEER Kenneth				DJIDONOU Yoann 16
2 TIENDALLI Dwight		39		CHITOU Charaf 2
3 VLAAR Ron				MOUSSA Traore 5
6 MADURO Hedwiges (c)				BOCO Romualde 7
7 OWUSU ABEYIE Quincy				MAIGA Abou 11
8 KRUYS Rick				AGBESSI Coffi 12
10 AFELLAY Ibrahim	27			NASSIROU Youssouf 13
12 ZUIVERLOON Gianni				(c) OSSENI Bachirou 14
15 EMANUELSON Urby				OMOTOYOSSI Razak 15
18 VINCKEN Tim	46			TCHOMOGO Seidath 18
19 RAJCOMAR Prince				AHOUEYA Jocelin 19
Tr: DE HAAN Foppe				Tr: DEVEZE Serge
17 AGUSTIEN Kemy	27			
20 WISSE Arjan	46			

GROUP B	PL	W	D	L	F	A	PTS		CHN	UKR	TUR	PAN
1 China PR	3	3	0	0	9	4	9			3-2	2-1	4-1
2 Ukraine	3	1	1	1	7	6	4				2-2	3-1
3 Turkey	3	1	1	1	4	4	4					1-0
4 Panama	3	0	0	3	2	8	0					

Galgenwaard, Utrecht, 11-06-2005
17:30, 10 000, Braamharr NED, Garcia ARG, Otero ARG

TUR   1   2   CHN

Gulec [84]   Tan Wangsong [22], Zhao Xuri [95+]

TURKEY			CHINA PR	
1 KIRINTILI Serkan			YANG Cheng	16
3 TEBER Ergun (c)			ZHAO Ming	2
7 YILMAZ Burak			ZHENG Tao	4
8 OZTURK Sezer			(c) FENG Xiaoting	5
10 INAN Selcuk	80		ZHOU Haibin	8
11 ADIN Olcan			CHEN Tao	10
14 OZAVCI Murat		87	ZHU Ting	11
15 TAHTAISLEYEN Ozan		73	LU Lin	13
17 KELES Ergin			TAN Wangsong	17
19 ASLANTAS Hakan	53	66	GAO Lin	18
20 OZTURK Ali	46		CUI Peng	20
Tr: USTAOMER Senol			Tr: KRAUTZEN Eckhard	
2 UCAR Ugur	53	66	ZHAO Xuri	7
6 SAKAR Zafer	46	73	DONG Fangzhuo	9
16 GULEC Gokhan	80	87	HAO Junmin	21

Galgenwaard, Utrecht, 11-06-2005
20:30, 2 500, Al Ghamdi KSA, Arabati JOR, Ghuloum UAE

UKR   3   1   PAN

Aliiev 2 [20p 22], Feshchuk [32]   Arzhanov OG [26]

UKRAINE			PANAMA	
1 MUSIN Leonid			CALDERON Jose	1
3 DOPILKA Oleg			DUNN Tomas	2
4 KITSUTA Anatoliy			(c) GUN Armando	3
5 IATSENKO Oleksandr (c)			TORRES Roman	4
8 ALIIEV Oleksandr			VENEGAS Jose	5
9 SYTNYK Oleksandr	80	82	AROSEMENA Reggie	7
10 MILEVSKYI Artem			VEGA Cristian	8
13 FESHCHUK Maksym	66		AGUILAR Edwin	9
14 ARZHANOV Volodymyr		60	CASTILLO Miguel	10
16 VOROBEI Dmytro	59	46	HILL Hanamell	15
17 SAMBORSKYY Volodymyr			GALLARDO Luis	16
Tr: MIKHAILICHENKO Alexei			Tr: MENDIETA Victor	
6 ROZHOK Sergiy	80	60	POLO Celso	6
7 PROSHYN Andriy	66	82	ARRUE David	11
19 HERASYMYUK Oleh	59	46	SALAZAR Alvaro	17

Galgenwaard, Utrecht, 14-06-2005
17:30, 2 300, Sibrian SLV, Pastrana HON, Salinas HON

CHN   3   2   UKR

Zhu Ting [31], Chen Tao [66p]   Vorobei [19], Aliiev [70p]
Cui Peng [75]

CHINA PR			UKRAINE	
16 YANG Cheng			MUSIN Leonid	1
2 ZHAO Ming			DOPILKA Oleg	3
4 ZHENG Tao	46		KITSUTA Anatoliy	4
5 FENG Xiaoting (c)			IATSENKO Oleksandr	5
7 ZHAO Xuri			ALIIEV Oleksandr	8
10 CHEN Tao		75	SYTNYK Oleksandr	9
11 ZHU Ting	69		MILEVSKYI Artem	10
17 TAN Wangsong		57	ARZHANOV Volodymyr	14
18 GAO Lin		80	YARMASH Grygoriy	15
20 CUI Peng	87		VOROBEI Dmytro	16
21 HAO Junmin	72		SAMBORSKYY Volodymyr	17
Tr: KRAUTZEN Eckhard			Tr: MIKHAILICHENKO Alexei	
3 LIU Yu	46	57	ROZHOK Sergiy	6
6 WANG Hongliang	87	75	FESHCHUK Maksym	13
13 LU Lin	72	80	HERASYMYUK Oleh	19

De Vijverberg, Doetinchem, 17-06-2005
20:30, 9 500, Medina Cantalejo ESP, Carrasco ESP, Hernandez ESP

TUR   2   2   UKR

Ozturk.S 2 [8p 53]   Aliiev 2 [5 19]

TURKEY			UKRAINE	
1 KIRINTILI Serkan			MUSIN Leonid	1
2 UCAR Ugur			GOLOLOBOV Dmytro	2
3 TEBER Ergun (c)			DOPILKA Oleg	3
5 AK Aytac			KITSUTA Anatoliy	4
6 SAKAR Zafer			(c) PROSHYN Andriy	7
7 YILMAZ Burak	80		ALIIEV Oleksandr	8
8 OZTURK Sezer			MILEVSKYI Artem	10
9 ZENGIN Kerim			YARMASH Grygoriy	15
11 ADIN Olcan			SAMBORSKYY Volodymyr	17
14 OZAVCI Murat	54	37	SILYUK Sergiy	18
16 GULEC Gokhan	60	46	HERASYMYUK Oleh	19
Tr: USTAOMER Senol			Tr: MIKHAILICHENKO Alexei	
4 CAKMAK Yasin	54	46	VOROBEI Dmytro	16
18 GURSOY Gurhan	60			
20 OZTURK Ali	80			

Galgenwaard, Utrecht, 14-06-2005
20:30, 6 100, Larrionda URU, Rial URU, Fandino URU

PAN   0   1   TUR

                                    Gulec [24]

PANAMA			TURKEY	
1 CALDERON Jose			KIRINTILI Serkan	1
3 GUN Armando			UCAR Ugur	2
4 TORRES Roman			TEBER Ergun	3
5 VENEGAS Jose			AK Aytac	5
7 AROSEMENA Reggie	72		SAKAR Zafer	6
8 VEGA Cristian			YILMAZ Burak	7
9 AGUILAR Edwin		69	OZTURK Sezer	8
10 LOO Raul			ZENGIN Kerim	9
15 HILL Hanamell			ADIN Olcan	11
16 GALLARDO Luis	58	76	OZAVCI Murat	14
17 SALAZAR Alvaro	81	85	GULEC Gokhan	16
Tr: MENDIETA Victor			Tr: USTAOMER Senol	
11 ARRUE David	72	76	CAKMAK Yasin	4
18 JIMENEZ Eduardo	58	69	GURSOY Gurhan	18
20 DUARTE Mario	81	85	OZTURK Ali	20

Galgenwaard, Utrecht, 17-06-2005
20:30, 4 000, Abd el Fatah EGY, Rashwan EGY, Begashaw ETH

CHN   4   1   PAN

Zhou Haibin [6], Gao Lin [40]   Venegas [37]
Hao Junmin [51], Lu Lin [78]

CHINA PR			PANAMA	
16 YANG Cheng			CALDERON Jose	1
2 ZHAO Ming			(c) GUN Armando	3
5 FENG Xiaoting (c)			TORRES Roman	4
6 WANG Hongliang			VENEGAS Jose	5
8 ZHOU Haibin		46	POLO Celso	6
10 CHEN Tao	83		AROSEMENA Reggie	7
13 LU Lin			AGUILAR Edwin	9
15 YUAN Weiwei			LOO Raul	13
17 TAN Wangsong			HILL Hanamell	15
18 GAO Lin	71	57	SALAZAR Alvaro	17
21 HAO Junmin	75	67	BUITRAGO Ricardo	18
Tr: KRAUTZEN Eckhard			Tr: MENDIETA Victor	
7 ZHAO Xuri	75	67	ARRUE David	11
9 DONG Fangzhuo	71	46	PONCE Eduardo	14
19 ZOU You	83	57	GALLARDO Luis	16

GROUP C

		PL	W	D	L	F	A	PTS	ESP	MAR	CHI	HON
1	Spain	3	3	0	0	13	1	9		3-1	7-0	3-0
2	Morocco	3	2	0	1	7	3	6			1-0	5-0
3	Chile	3	1	0	2	7	8	3				7-0
4	Honduras	3	0	0	3	0	15	0				

De Vijverberg, Doetinchem, 11-06-2005
17:30, 9 863, Larrionda URU, Rial URU, Fandino URU

ESP 3 1 MAR

Llorente 28, Molinero 51, Silva 71 — Doulyazal 84p

SPAIN		MOROCCO	
1 BIEL RIBAS		BOURKADI Mohammed 1	
2 MOLINERO		BENZOUKANE Chakib 3	
3 GARRIDO	52	KANTARI Ahmed 4	
4 ALEXIS		(c) RABEH Youssef 5	
6 RAUL ALBIOL (c)		MSSASSI Abderrahmane 6	
7 JUANFRAN		HERMACH Adil 7	
8 ZAPATER		BENZOUIEN Sofian 8	
9 LLORENTE	61	IAJOUR Mouhssine 9	
10 JONA	46	EL ZHAR Nabil 10	
16 SILVA	74	51 TIBERKANINE Rachid 14	
17 CESC		DOULYAZAL Rida 15	
Tr: SAEZ Inaki		Tr: FATHI Jamal	
11 GAVILAN	74	52 BENDAMOU Tarik 11	
18 VICTOR	61	51 CHIHI Adil 20	
20 ROBERTO	46		

De Vijverberg, Doetinchem, 11-06-2005
20:30 6 800, Busacca DUI, Buragina SUI, Arnet SUI

HON 0 7 CHI

Parada 2 11 71, Fuenzalida 2 30 53
Fernandez 67, Jara 69, Morales 77

HONDURAS			CHILE
1 GUERRA Angel			ARIAS Carlos 12
2 BODDEN Roy			RIQUELME Edzon 2
4 BARDALES Aron			MONTESINOS Sebastian 4
5 NORALES Erick (c)			BASCUNAN Hugo 5
7 RAMOS Luis			VASQUEZ Ivan 8
8 CLAROS Jorge	74	68	CANALES Nicolas 9
10 NUNEZ Ramon			MUNOZ Felipe 13
11 GUITY Jose		82	(c) FERNANDEZ Matias 14
14 CRUZ Jose			JARA Gonzalo 18
17 IZAGUIRRE Emilio	74	80	FUENZALIDA Jose 19
19 SANCHEZ Marvin	46		PARADA Ricardo 20
Tr: GUIFARRO Ruben			Tr: SULANTAY Jose
13 CRUZ Fernando	46	82	MENESES Fernando 7
15 MARTINEZ Maynor	74	68	MORALES Pedro 10
18 NOLASCO Angel	74	80	TUDELA Eduardo 11

De Vijverberg, Doetinchem, 14-06-2005
17:30, 5 985, Al Ghamdi KSA, Arabati JOR, Ghuloum UAE

MAR 5 0 HON

Iajour 2 31 43, Bendamou 55
Benjelloun 81, Chihi 90

MOROCCO		HONDURAS	
1 BOURKADI Mohammed		GUERRA Angel 1	
3 BENZOUKANE Chakib	17	TURCIOS Nery 3	
5 RABEH Youssef		NORALES Erick 5	
6 MSSASSI Abderrahmane		MONCADA Rene 6	
7 HERMACH Adil		46 RAMOS Luis 7	
8 BENZOUIEN Sofian		NUNEZ Ramon 10	
9 IAJOUR Mouhssine		GUITY Jose 11	
10 EL ZHAR Nabil		CRUZ Fernando 13	
11 BENDAMOU Tarik	71	64 CRUZ Jose 14	
16 EL AHMADI Karim	78	MARTINEZ Maynor 15	
17 ZOUCHOU Yassine	50	78 LARA Nataury 16	
Tr: FATHI Jamal		Tr: GUIFARRO Ruben	
15 DOULYAZAL Rida	78	64 CLAROS Jorge 8	
18 BENJELLOUN Abdessalam	71	78 RICE Walter 9	
20 CHIHI Adil	71	46 NOLASCO Angel 18	

De Vijverberg, Doetinchem, 14-06-2005
20:30, 6 600, Archundia MEX, Ramirez MEX, Rebollar MEX

CHI 0 7 ESP

Llorente 4 8 62 78 81, Robuste 51
Silva 2 71 85

CHILE			SPAIN
12 ARIAS Carlos			BIEL RIBAS 1
2 RIQUELME Edzon	41		GARRIDO 3
4 MONTESINOS Sebastian	81		ALEXIS 4
5 BASCUNAN Hugo			ROBUSTE 5
8 VASQUEZ Ivan		46	RAUL ALBIOL 6
9 CANALES Nicolas		66	JUANFRAN 7
13 MUNOZ Felipe			ZAPATER 8
14 FERNANDEZ Matias	85		LLORENTE 9
18 JARA Gonzalo	45		GAVILAN 11
19 FUENZALIDA Jose			CHICA 15
20 PARADA Ricardo	71		CESC 17
Tr: SULANTAY Jose			Tr: SAEZ Inaki
10 MORALES Pedro	85	41	JOSE ENRIQUE 12
11 TUDELA Eduardo	71	66	SILVA 16
16 SANCHEZ Francisco	81	46	MARKEL 20

De Vijverberg, Doetinchem, 17-06-2005
17:30, 3 000, Codjia BEN, Ntagungira RWA, Aderodjou BEN

ESP 3 0 HON

Jona 5, Silva 38, Victor 67

SPAIN			HONDURAS	
13 MANU	76	77	GUERRA Angel 1	
2 MOLINERO		46	BODDEN Roy 2	
5 ROBUSTE (c)			BARDALES Aron 4	
8 ZAPATER	46		NORALES Erick 5	
10 JONA			(c) MONCADA Rene 6	
12 JOSE ENRIQUE			NUNEZ Ramon 10	
14 AGUS			CRUZ Fernando 13	
16 SILVA	60		CRUZ Jose 14	
18 VICTOR			MARTINEZ Maynor 15	
20 BRAULIO			LARA Nataury 16	
20 MARKEL		72	IZAGUIRRE Emilio 17	
Tr: SAEZ Inaki			Tr: GUIFARRO Ruben	
21 ROBERTO	76 79	77	PINEDA Fernando 21	
11 GAVILAN	60	46	GUITY Jose 11	
17 CESC	46	72	RAPALO Julian 20	

Galgenwaard, Utrecht, 17-06-2005
17:30, 11 000, Shield AUS, Gibson, Wilson AUS

MAR 1 0 CHI

Bendamou 47+

MOROCCO			CHILE
1 BOURKADI Mohammed			ROSALES Jose 21
2 EL AMRANI Hicham	92		RIQUELME Edzon 2
3 BENZOUKANE Chakib			BASCUNAN Hugo 5
5 RABEH Youssef (c)			VASQUEZ Ivan 8
7 HERMACH Adil			CANALES Nicolas 9
8 BENZOUIEN Sofian		78	TUDELA Eduardo 11
9 IAJOUR Mouhssine	87		MUNOZ Felipe 13
10 EL ZHAR Nabil			(c) FERNANDEZ Matias 14
11 BENDAMOU Tarik			CARMONA Carlos 15
13 SBAI Salah			FUENZALIDA Jose 19
16 EL AHMADI Karim	53		PARADA Ricardo 20
Tr: FATHI Jamal			Tr: SULANTAY Jose
17 ZOUCHOU Yassine	87	53	MENESES Fernando 7
18 FATAH Said	92	78	MORALES Pedro 10

GROUP D	PL	W	D	L	F	A	PTS	USA	ARG	GER	EGY
1 USA	3	2	1	0	2	0	7		1-0	0-0	1-0
2 Argentina	3	2	1	0	3	1	6			1-0	2-0
3 Germany	3	1	1	1	2	1	4				2-0
4 Egypt	3	0	0	3	0	5	0				

Enschede Stadium, Enschede, 11-06-2005
17:30, 10 500, Hauge NOR, Holvik NOR, Borgan NOR

ARG 0 1 USA

Barrett 39

ARGENTINA			USA	
1 USTARI Oscar			WESTBERG Quentin	1
2 CABRAL Gustavo			WYNNE Marvell	2
3 FORMICA Lautaro		38	SPECTOR Jonathan	3
4 BARROSO Julio			IANNI Patrick	5
6 PALETTA Gabriel			(c) DALBY Greg	6
7 BIGLIA Lucas			FEILHABER Benny	8
8 ZABALETA Pablo (c)	85		BARRETT Chad	9
9 VITTI Pablo			GAVEN Eddie	10
11 ARMENTEROS Emiliano	46		ADU Freddy	11
17 GAGO Fernando	76		FREEMAN Hunter	15
20 OBERMAN Gustavo	60		OCHOA Sammy	18
Tr: FERRARO Francisco			Tr: SCHMID Sigi	
16 CARDOZO Neri	76	38	STURGIS Nathan	4
18 MESSI Lionel	46	60	PETERSON Jacob	13
		85	SZETELA Danny	19

Enschede Stadium, Enschede, 11-06-2005
20:30, 10 500, Sibrian SLV, Pastrana HON, Salinas HON

GER 2 0 EGY

Adler.N 75, Matip 93+

GERMANY			EGYPT		
1 ADLER Rene (c)			SHAABAN Hamada	1	
2 JANKER Christoph		90	MAHMOUD Mohamed	2	
4 MATIP Marvin			TAWFIK Abdelaziz	3	
5 SCHUON Marcel		69	ASHOUR Hossam	4	
7 DELURA Michael			GALAL Abdellah	6	
8 GENTNER Christian		79	FARAG Ahmed	7	
10 SENESIE Sahr	46		ABDELRAZEK Mahmoud	10	
11 JANSEN Marcell			SAID Abdallah	11	
17 FREIS Sebastian	72	83	(c) SHAHAT Abdallah	12	
18 THOMIK Paul	46		MAGDY Ahmed	14	
		87	GHANEM Ahmed	18	
Tr: SKIBBE Michael			Tr: RADWAN Mohamed		
9 ADLER Nicky	72	87	ABDEL ZAHER Ahmed	8	
14 REINHARD Christopher	46	79	OSSAMA Hossam	9	
16 HAMPEL Oliver	46	69	GAMIL Ahmed	20	

Enschede Stadium, Enschede, 14-06-2005
17:30, 8 500, Busacca SUI, Buragina SUI, Arnet SUI

EGY 0 2 ARG

Messi 47, Zabaleta 91+

EGYPT			ARGENTINA	
1 SHAABAN Hamada			USTARI Oscar	1
3 TAWFIK Abdelaziz			CABRAL Gustavo	2
6 GALAL Abdellah			FORMICA Lautaro	3
7 FARAG Ahmed	55		BARROSO Julio	4
9 OSSAMA Hossam	69		TORRES Juan Manuel	5
10 ABDELRAZEK Mahmoud	69		PALETTA Gabriel	6
11 SAID Abdallah (c)			(c) ZABALETA Pablo	8
14 MAGDY Ahmed		77	CARDOZO Neri	16
15 SIAM Islam			GAGO Fernando	17
18 GHANEM Ahmed	84		MESSI Lionel	18
20 GAMIL Ahmed	65		OBERMAN Gustavo	20
Tr: RADWAN Mohamed			Tr: FERRARO Francisco	
8 ABDEL ZAHER Ahmed	69	84	BIGLIA Lucas	7
17 EL HALAWANI Amr	69	77	ARMENTEROS Emiliano	11
19 KHALIFA Ahmed	55	65	AGUERO Sergio	19

Enschede Stadium, Enschede, 14-06-2005
20:30, 10 350, Ruiz COL, Botero COL, Tamayo ECU

USA 0 0 GER

USA			GERMANY	
1 WESTBERG Quentin			ADLER Rene	1
2 WYNNE Marvell			JANKER Christoph	2
4 STURGIS Nathan			MATIP Marvin	4
5 IANNI Patrick			SCHUON Marcel	5
6 DALBY Greg		84	OTTL Andreas	6
8 FEILHABER Benny			DELURA Michael	7
9 BARRETT Chad	91		GENTNER Christian	8
10 GAVEN Eddie		73	ADLER Nicky	9
11 ADU Freddy	81		JANSEN Marcell	11
15 FREEMAN Hunter			REINHARD Christopher	14
18 OCHOA Sammy	63		CIMEN Daniyel	17
Tr: SCHMID Sigi			Tr: SKIBBE Michael	
13 PETERSON Jacob	63	73	SENESIE Sahr	10
14 NGUYEN Lee	81	84	BANECKI Francis	20
20 EVANS Brad	91			

Emmen Stadium, Emmen, 18-06-2005
13:30, 8 600, Archundia MEX, Ramirez MEX, Rebollar MEX

ARG 1 0 GER

Cardozo 43

ARGENTINA			GERMANY	
1 USTARI Oscar			(c) ADLER Rene	1
2 CABRAL Gustavo			JANKER Christoph	2
3 FORMICA Lautaro			MATIP Marvin	4
4 BARROSO Julio			OTTL Andreas	6
5 TORRES Juan Manuel	80	46	SENESIE Sahr	10
6 PALETTA Gabriel		70	JANSEN Marcell	11
8 ZABALETA Pablo (c)			HUBER Alexander	13
16 CARDOZO Neri	92		REINHARD Christopher	14
17 GAGO Fernando		46	FREIS Sebastian	15
18 MESSI Lionel	82		CIMEN Daniyel	17
20 OBERMAN Gustavo	73		THOMIK Paul	18
Tr: FERRARO Francisco			Tr: SKIBBE Michael	
7 BIGLIA Lucas	82	70	COMPPER Marvin	3
11 ARMENTEROS Emiliano	92	46	DELURA Michael	7
19 AGUERO Sergio	73	46	BANECKI Francis	20

Enschede Stadium, Enschede, 18-06-2005
13:30, 7 600, Kwon Jong Chul KOR, LIU Tiejun CHN, Kim Dae Young KOR

USA 1 0 EGY

Peterson 56

USA			EGYPT	
1 WESTBERG Quentin			SHAABAN Hamada	1
4 STURGIS Nathan			TAWFIK Abdelaziz	3
5 IANNI Patrick (c)		77	KANDEL Walid	5
7 KLJESTAN Sacha			GALAL Abdellah	6
8 FEILHABER Benny	83		FARAG Ahmed	7
12 JOHN Will	71		ABDELRAZEK Mahmoud	10
13 PETERSON Jacob	79		SAID Abdallah	11
14 NGUYEN Lee	54		(c) SHAHAT Abdallah	12
15 FREEMAN Hunter			MAGDY Ahmed	14
19 SZETELA Danny			GHANEM Ahmed	18
20 EVANS Brad	35		GAMIL Ahmed	20
Tr: SCHMID Sigi			Tr: RADWAN Mohamed	
9 BARRETT Chad	71	83	ABDEL ZAHER Ahmed	8
11 ADU Freddy	54	77	OSSAMA Hossam	9
18 OCHOA Sammy	79	63	ELHAKAM Ahmed Abd	13

GROUP E	PL	W	D	L	F	A	PTS	COL	SYR	ITA	CAN
1 Colombia	3	3	0	0	6	0	9		2-0	2-0	2-0
2 Syria	3	1	1	1	3	4	4			2-1	1-1
3 Italy	3	1	0	2	5	5	3				4-1
4 Canada	3	0	1	2	2	7	1				

Willem II, Tilburg, 12-06-2005
17:30, 7 000, Shield AUS, Gibson AUS, Wilson AUS

COL 2 0 ITA

Renteria 76, Guarin 93+

COLOMBIA			ITALY	
1 ARENAS Libis			VIVIANO Emiliano	1
3 ZAPATA Cristian			MARZORATTI Lino	2
5 ZUNIGA Juan		61	D AGOSTINO Andrea	3
6 MORALES Harrison			NOCERINO Antonio	4
7 RODALLEGA Hugo	68		CODA Andrea	5
11 OTALVARO Harrison	79		(c) CANINI Michele	6
14 AGUILAR Abel (c)		84	DEFENDI Marino	7
16 VALENCIA Edwin	63		PELLE Graziano	9
17 MARRUGO Cristian			TROIANO Michele	10
18 RENTERIA Wason			GALLOPPA Daniele	11
19 CASIERRA Mauricio		74	BENTIVOGLIO Simone	16
Tr: LARA Eduardo			Tr: BERRETTINI Paolo	
8 TOJA Juan Carlos	63	61	BATTAGLIA Francesco	13
13 GUARIN Fredy	79	74	AGNELLI Cristian	18
15 MORENO Dayro	68	84	COZZOLINO Giuseppe	20

Willem II, Tilburg, 12-06-2005
20:30, 3 500, Larsen DEN, Hansen DEN, Norrestrand DEN

SYR 1 1 CAN

Majed Al Haj 2   Peters 31

SYRIA			CANADA	
1 AL HAFEZ Adnan			WAGENAAR Josh	1
4 KHALAF Abdul	88		RAMALHO Graham	2
5 AL AITONI Hamzeh			(c) LEDGERWOOD Nik	3
6 AL MOSTAFA Hasan			HAINAULT Andrew	4
7 KAILOUNI Meaataz	92	88	PEETOOM Brad	5
8 ALHOUSAIN Abd		55	PETERS Jaime	7
13 JENYAT Aatef			ROSENLUND Tyler	8
14 AL HAJ Majed (c)			GYAKI Ryan	9
15 NAHLOUS Samer	25		JOHNSON Will	10
17 DAKKA Abd		68	DE JONG Marcel	11
20 SHAHROUR Salah			EDGAR David	14
Tr: RADENOVIC Milosav			Tr: MITCHELL Dale	
9 OSSI Mahmoud	92	68	O'NEILL Riley	12
11 AL ABDI Jalal	25	88	LOMBARDO Andrea	17
12 AL KADDOUR Zakariya	88	55	CHAROWSKI Tomek	18

Willem II, Tilburg, 15-06-2005
17:30, 6 500, Abd El Fatah EGY, Rashwan EGY, Begashaw

CAN 0 2 COL

Garcia 81, Guarin 88

CANADA			COLOMBIA	
1 WAGENAAR Josh			ARENAS Libis	1
2 RAMALHO Graham			ZAPATA Cristian	3
3 LEDGERWOOD Nik			ZUNIGA Juan	5
4 HAINAULT Andrew			MORALES Harrison	6
5 PEETOOM Brad			TOJA Juan Carlos	8
8 ROSENLUND Tyler		85	OTALVARO Harrison	11
9 GYAKI Ryan (c)			(c) AGUILAR Abel	14
10 JOHNSON Will	77		MORENO Dayro	15
12 O'NEILL Riley			MARRUGO Cristian	17
14 EDGAR David	84		RENTERIA Wason	18
17 LOMBARDO Andrea	69	69	CASIERRA Mauricio	19
Tr: MITCHELL Dale			Tr: LARA Eduardo	
7 PETERS Jaime	84	69	RODALLEGA Hugo	7
11 DE JONG Marcel	69	77	GARCIA Radamel	9
		85	GUARIN Fredy	13

Willem II, Tilburg, 15-06-2005
20:30, 2 500, Elizondo ARG, Garcia ARG, Otero ARG

ITA 1 2 SYR

Coda 73   Alhousain 37, Al Hamwi 69

ITALY			SYRIA	
1 VIVIANO Emiliano			AL HAFEZ Adnan	1
2 MARZORATTI Lino			KHALAF Abdul	4
3 D AGOSTINO Andrea			AL AITONI Hamzeh	5
4 NOCERINO Antonio			AL MOSTAFA Hasan	6
5 CODA Andrea		94	KAILOUNI Meaataz	7
6 CANINI Michele (c)			ALHOUSAIN Abd	8
7 DEFENDI Marino			OSSI Mahmoud	9
8 CAROTTI Lorenzo			AL HAMWI Mohammad	10
9 PELLE Graziano	72		AL ABDI Jalal	11
10 TROIANO Michele	65	85	(c) AL HAJ Majed	14
11 GALLOPPA Daniele	58		DAKKA Abd	17
Tr: BERRETTINI Paolo			Tr: RADENOVIC Milosav	
16 BENTIVOGLIO Simone	65	85	AL KADDOUR Zakariya	12
19 NIETO Francesco	72	94	NAHLOUS Samer	15
20 COZZOLINO Giuseppe	58			

Parkstad Limburg, Kerkrade, 18-06-2005
13:30, 2 000, Larrionda URU, Rial URU, Fandino URU

ITA 4 1 CAN

Pelle 2 23 68, Galloppa 47   De Jong 49
De Martino 90

ITALY			CANADA	
1 VIVIANO Emiliano (c)			WAGENAAR Josh	1
2 MARZORATTI Lino		81	RAMALHO Graham	2
4 NOCERINO Antonio			(c) LEDGERWOOD Nik	3
5 CODA Andrea			HAINAULT Andrew	4
7 DEFENDI Marino			PEETOOM Brad	5
8 CAROTTI Lorenzo	56		PETERS Jaime	7
9 PELLE Graziano		73	ROSENLUND Tyler	8
11 GALLOPPA Daniele			GYAKI Ryan	9
13 BATTAGLIA Francesco			JOHNSON Will	10
15 AQUILANTI Antonio	84		DE JONG Marcel	11
16 BENTIVOGLIO Simone	71	70	EDGAR David	14
Tr: BERRETTINI Paolo			Tr: MITCHELL Dale	
17 DE MARTINO Raffaele	71	73	SCHIAVONI Carlo	6
18 AGNELLI Cristian	56	81	STEWART Vince	15
19 NIETO Francesco	84	70	LOMBARDO Andrea	17

Willem II, Tilburg, 18-06-2005
13:30, 11 000, Busacca SUI, Buragina SUI, Arnet SUI

COL 2 0 SYR

Rodallega 62, Garcia.R 91+

COLOMBIA			SYRIA	
1 ARENAS Libis			SHAKOSH Moustafa	21
3 ZAPATA Cristian			KHALAF Abdul	4
5 ZUNIGA Juan	73		AL MOSTAFA Hasan	6
6 MORALES Harrison		77	KAILOUNI Meaataz	7
7 RODALLEGA Hugo			OSSI Mahmoud	9
11 OTALVARO Harrison	67		AL ABDI Jalal	11
13 GUARIN Fredy		46	AL KADDOUR Zakariya	12
14 AGUILAR Abel (c)			JENYAT Aatef	13
16 VALENCIA Edwin	85		(c) AL HAJ Majed	14
18 RENTERIA Wason	59		NAHLOUS Samer	15
19 CASIERRA Mauricio			DAKKA Abd	17
Tr: LARA Eduardo			Tr: RADENOVIC Milosav	
9 GARCIA Radamel	59	46	AL HAMWI Mohammad	10
10 HERNANDEZ Sebastian	67	77	SAHIWNI Bwrhan	18
20 MACHACON Daniel	73	85	DILY HASSAN Ahmad	19

GROUP F		PL	W	D	L	F	A	PTS		BRA	NGA	KOR	SUI
1	Brazil	3	2	1	0	3	0	7		0-0	2-0	1-0
2	Nigeria	3	1	1	1	4	2	4				1-2	3-0
3	Korea Republic	3	1	0	2	3	5	3					1-2
4	Switzerland	3	1	0	2	2	5	3					

Emmen Stadium, Emmen, 12-06-2005
17:30, 8 500, Medina Cantalejo ESP, Carrasco ESP, Hernandez ESP

BRA 0 0 **NGA**

BRAZIL				NIGERIA	
1	RENAN (c)			VANZEKIN Ambruse	1
2	RAFAEL			CHINWO Kennedy	2
4	GLADSTONE			TAIWO Taye	3
5	ROBERTO			APAM Onyekachi	4
6	FABIO SANTOS			JAMES Monday	5
7	DIEGO	71	63	ADEDEJI Yinka	6
10	EVANDRO	66		MIKEL John Obi	9
11	RAFAEL SOBIS	74	57	(c) ISAAC Promise	10
14	EDCARLOS		86	OKORONKWO Solomon	11
18	ERNANE			ABWO David	14
20	DIEGO TARDELLI			KAITA Sani	19
Tr: WEBER Rene				Tr: SIASIA Samson	
8	RENATO	66	57	OGBUKE Chinedu	7
16	AROUCA	71	63	SAMBO Soga	15
19	THIAGO QUIRINO	74	86	ATULEWA Gift	16

Emmen Stadium, Emmen, 12-06-2005
20:30, 8 000, Codjia BEN, Ntagungira RWA, Aderodjou BEN

KOR 1 2 **SUI**

Shin Young Rok [25]

Antic [28], Vonlanthen [33]

KOREA REPUBLIC				SWITZERLAND	
1	CHA Ki Seok			LOPAR Daniel	12
2	PARK Hee Chul			BUEHLER Arnaud	3
4	LEE Yoo Han		81	DJOUROU Johan	4
6	KIM Jin Kyu			(c) SENDEROS Philippe	5
7	BAEK Seung Min			SALATIC Veroljub	6
8	BAEK Ji Hoon (c)			BARNETTA Tranquillo	7
9	OH Jang Eun	69	75	ANTIC Goran	8
10	PARK Chu Young			VONLANTHEN Johan	9
18	KIM Seung Yong	56	89	ZAMBRELLA Fabrizio	10
19	SHIN Young Rok	88		ZIEGLER Reto	11
20	LEE Gang Jin			DZEMAILI Blerim	20
Tr: PARK Sung Wha				Tr: SCHUERMANN Pierre-Andre	
14	PARK Jong Jin	69	81	SCHWEGLER Pirmin	16
16	SIM Woo Yeon	56	89	STAHEL Florian	17
17	LEE Sung Hyun	88	75	AFONSO Guilherme	19

Emmen Stadium, Emmen, 15-06-2005
17:30, 8 200, Shield AUS, Gibson AUS, Wilson AUS

SUI 0 1 **BRA**

Gladstone [14]

SWITZERLAND				BRAZIL	
1	KOENIG Swen			(c) RENAN	1
3	BUEHLER Arnaud			RAFAEL	2
4	DJOUROU Johan	71		GLADSTONE	4
5	SENDEROS Philippe (c)			ROBERTO	5
6	SALATIC Veroljub			FABIO SANTOS	6
7	BARNETTA Tranquillo		28	DIEGO	7
8	ANTIC Goran	81	61	EVANDRO	10
9	VONLANTHEN Johan		72	RAFAEL SOBIS	11
10	ZAMBRELLA Fabrizio			EDCARLOS	14
11	ZIEGLER Reto	61		ERNANE	18
20	DZEMAILI Blerim			DIEGO TARDELLI	20
Tr: SCHUERMANN Pierre-Andre				Tr: WEBER Rene	
16	SCHWEGLER Pirmin	71	72	RENATO	8
17	STAHEL Florian	61	28	AROUCA	16
19	AFONSO Guilherme	81	61	FELLYPE GABRIEL	17

Emmen Stadium, Emmen, 15-06-2005
20:30, 8 500, Hauge NOR, Holvik NOR, Borgan NOR

NGA 1 2 **KOR**

Abwo [18]

Park Chu Young [89]
Baek Ji Hoon [92+]

NIGERIA				KOREA REPUBLIC	
1	VANZEKIN Ambruse (c)			CHA Ki Seok	1
2	CHINWO Kennedy		70	AHN Tae Eun	3
3	TAIWO Taye			KIM Jin Kyu	6
4	APAM Onyekachi			BAEK Seung Min	7
5	JAMES Monday			(c) BAEK Ji Hoon	8
7	OGBUKE Chinedu		75	OH Jang Eun	9
9	MIKEL John Obi	87		PARK Chu Young	10
11	OKORONKWO Solomon	73	34	SHIN Hyung Min	13
14	ABWO David	81		KIM Seung Yong	18
15	SAMBO Soga			SHIN Young Rok	19
19	KAITA Sani			LEE Gang Jin	20
Tr: SIASIA Samson				Tr: PARK Sung Wha	
8	BAZUAYE Daddy	87	34	LEE Yoo Han	4
16	ATULEWA Gift	81	70	PARK Jong Jin	14
20	OWOERI John	73	75	LEE Sung Hyun	17

Emmen Stadium, Emmen, 18-06-2005
16:00, 8 600, Larsen DEN, Hansen DEN, Norrestrand DEN

BRA 2 0 **KOR**

Renato [9], Rafael Sobis [57]

BRAZIL				KOREA REPUBLIC	
1	RENAN (c)			CHA Ki Seok	1
2	RAFAEL			AHN Tae Eun	3
3	LEONARDO	73	46	LEE Yoo Han	4
4	GLADSTONE	46		KIM Jin Kyu	6
5	ROBERTO			BAEK Seung Min	7
6	FABIO SANTOS	86		(c) BAEK Ji Hoon	8
8	RENATO		62	OH Jang Eun	9
9	BOBO			PARK Chu Young	10
11	RAFAEL SOBIS			KIM Seung Yong	18
16	AROUCA		82	SHIN Young Rok	19
18	ERNANE			LEE Gang Jin	20
Tr: WEBER Rene				Tr: PARK Sung Wha	
13	JOAO LEONARDO	46	46	PARK Hee Chul	2
14	EDCARLOS	73	82	PARK Jong Jin	14
15	FILIPE	86	62	SIM Woo Yeon	16

Enschede Stadium, Enschede, 18-06-2005
16:00, 8 000, Ruiz COL, Botero COL, Tamayo ECU

NGA 3 0 **SUI**

Ogbuke [49], Mikel [59p], Isaac [85]

NIGERIA				SWITZERLAND	
1	VANZEKIN Ambruse			KOENIG Swen	1
3	TAIWO Taye			BUEHLER Arnaud	3
4	APAM Onyekachi			DJOUROU Johan	4
5	JAMES Monday			(c) SENDEROS Philippe	5
7	OGBUKE Chinedu	64		SALATIC Veroljub	6
9	MIKEL John Obi			BARNETTA Tranquillo	7
10	ISAAC Promise (c)		70	ANTIC Goran	8
13	ADEFEMI Olubayo			VONLANTHEN Johan	9
14	ABWO David	91	46	ZAMBRELLA Fabrizio	10
19	KAITA Sani			ZIEGLER Reto	11
20	OWOERI John	78	68	DZEMAILI Blerim	20
Tr: SIASIA Samson				Tr: SCHUERMANN Pierre-Andre	
6	ADEDEJI Yinka	64	46	SCHWEGLER Pirmin	16
11	OKORONKWO Solomon	78	46	STAHEL Florian	17
18	ANUBI Kola	91	70	AFONSO Guilherme	19

ROUND OF 16

Enschede Stadium, Enschede, 21-06-2005
17:30, 7 000, Abd el Fatah EGY, Rashwan EGY, Begashaw ETH

USA 1   3 ITA

Freeman 44p

Galloppa 54, Pelle 62
Kljestan OG 75

USA			ITALY		
1 WESTBERG Quentin			(c) VIVIANO Emiliano 1		
2 WYNNE Marvell			MARZORATTI Lino 2		
3 SPECTOR Jonathan			NOCERINO Antonio 4		
5 IANNI Patrick			CODA Andrea 5		
6 DALBY Greg (c)	65		CANINI Michele 6		
8 FEILHABER Benny		93	DEFENDI Marino 7		93
9 BARRETT Chad			PELLE Graziano 9		
10 GAVEN Eddie			GALLOPPA Daniele 11		
11 ADU Freddy		46	BATTAGLIA Francesco 13		46
15 FREEMAN Hunter	76		BENTIVOGLIO Simone 16		
18 OCHOA Sammy			DE MARTINO Raffaele 17		
Tr: SCHMID Sigi			Tr: BERRETTINI Paolo		
7 KLJESTAN Sacha	65	93	CAROTTI Lorenzo 8		93
13 PETERSON Jacob	76	46	AQUILANTI Antonio 15		46

Enschede Stadium, Enschede, 21-06-2005
20:30, 11 800, Busacca SUI, Buragina SUI, Arnet SUI

MAR 1   0 JPN

Iajour 92+

MOROCCO			JAPAN		
1 BOURKADI Mohammed			NISHIKAWA Shusaku 21		
3 BENZOUKANE Chakib			MIZUMOTO Hiroki 2		
5 RABEH Youssef (c)			KOBAYASHI Yuzo 4		
7 HERMACH Adil		93	(c) MASUSHIMA Tatsuya 5		93
8 BENZOUIEN Sofian			KAJIYAMA Yohei 7		
9 IAJOUR Mouhssine			NAKAMURA Hokuto 8		
10 EL ZHAR Nabil			HIRAYAMA Sota 9		
11 BENDAMOU Tarik			CULLEN Robert 11		
13 SBAI Salah		72	MIZUNO Koki 12		72
16 EL AHMADI Karim			NAGIRA Tomokazu 16		
20 CHIHI Adil	52	60	IENAGA Akihiro 17		60
Tr: FATHI Jamal			Tr: OHKUMA Kiyoshi		
14 TIBERKANINE Rachid	52	72	HYODO Shingo 10		72
			MAEDA Shunsuke 19		60
			MORIMOTO Takayuki 20		93

Willem II, Tilburg, 21-06-2005
20:30, 11 000, Archundia MEX, Ramirez MEX, Rebollar MEX

BRA 1   0 SYR

Rafael 43p

BRAZIL			SYRIA		
1 RENAN (c)			AL HAFEZ Adnan 1		
2 RAFAEL			AL AITONI Hamzeh 5		
5 ROBERTO			AL MOSTAFA Hasan 6		
6 FABIO SANTOS			KAILOUNI Meaataz 7		
8 RENATO	61		ALHOUSAIN Abd 8		
9 BOBO	69		AL HAMWI Mohammad 10		
11 RAFAEL SOBIS			AL ABDI Jalal 11		
13 JOAO LEONARDO			JENYAT Aatef 13		
14 EDCARLOS			(c) AL HAJ Majed 14		
16 AROUCA			DAKKA Abd 17		
18 ERNANE	82	81	SHAHROUR Salah 20		81
Tr: WEBER Rene			Tr: RADENOVIC Milosav		
10 EVANDRO	61	81	SAHIWNI Bwrhan 18		81
17 FELLYPE GABRIEL	82				
20 DIEGO TARDELLI	69				

Willem II, Tilburg, 21-06-2005
17:30, 9 000, Elizondo ARG, Garcia ARG, Otero ARG

CHN 2   3 GER

Chen Tao 2 4 20p

Gentner 5, Adler 30, Matip 89

CHINA PR			GERMANY		
16 YANG Cheng			(c) ADLER Rene 1		
2 ZHAO Ming			JANKER Christoph 2		
4 ZHENG Tao			MATIP Marvin 4		
5 FENG Xiaoting (c)			SCHUON Marcel 5		
8 ZHOU Haibin	93	91	DELURA Michael 7		91
10 CHEN Tao			GENTNER Christian 8		
13 LU Lin		58	ADLER Nicky 9		58
17 TAN Wangsong			JANSEN Marcell 11		
18 GAO Lin		46	REINHARD Christopher 14		46
20 CUI Peng	93		CIMEN Daniyel 17		
21 HAO Junmin	58		THOMIK Paul 18		
Tr: KRAUTZUN Marcel			Tr: SKIBBE Michael		
7 ZHAO Xuri	58	46	COMPPER Marvin 3		46
9 DONG Fangzhuo	93	58	SENESIE Sahr 10		58
19 ZOU You	93	91	BANECKI Francis 20		91

De Vijverberg, Doetinchem, 22-06-2005
17:30, 9 600, Kwon Jong Chul KOR, Liu Tiejun CHN, Kim Dae Young KOR

NGA 1   0 UKR

Taiwo 80

NIGERIA			UKRAINE		
1 VANZEKIN Ambruse			MUSIN Leonid 1		
2 CHINWO Kennedy	64		DOPILKA Oleg 3		
3 TAIWO Taye			KITSUTA Anatoliy 4		
4 APAM Onyekachi			(c) IATSENKO Oleksandr 5		
5 JAMES Monday		84	PROSHYN Andriy 7		84
7 OGBUKE Chinedu			ALIIEV Oleksandr 8		
9 MIKEL John Obi		84	SYTNYK Oleksandr 9		84
10 ISAAC Promise (c)	85		MILEVSKYI Artem 10		
14 ABWO David			YARMASH Grygoriy 15		
19 KAITA Sani	77		VOROBEI Dmytro 16		77
20 OWOERI John			SAMBORSKYY Volodymyr 17		
Tr: SIASIA Samson			Tr: MIKHAILICHENKO Alexei		
11 OKORONKWO Solomon	85	84	ROZHOK Sergiy 6		84
13 ADEFEMI Olubayo	64	84	GLADKYY Oleksandr 11		84
			FESHCHUK Maksym 13		77

De Vijverberg, Doetinchem, 22-06-2005
20:30, 10 900, Sibrian SLV, Pastrana HON, Salinas HON

NED 3   0 CHI

Babel 3, Owusu Abeyie 73, John 80

NETHERLANDS			CHILE		
1 VERMEER Kenneth			ESPINOZA Carlos 1		
2 TIENDALLI Dwight			RIQUELME Edzon 2		
3 VLAAR Ron			MONTESINOS Sebastian 4		
4 VAN DER STRUIJK Frank			BASCUNAN Hugo 5		
5 DROST Jeroen		46	VASQUEZ Ivan 8		
6 MADURO Hedwiges	87		CANALES Nicolas 9		
7 OWUSU ABEYIE Quincy	77		MUNOZ Felipe 13		
8 KRUYS Rick			FERNANDEZ Matias 14		
11 BABEL Ryan			JARA Gonzalo 18		
15 EMANUELSON Urby	79	79	FUENZALIDA Jose 19		79
18 VINCKEN Tim	74		PARADA Ricardo 20		74
Tr: DE HAAN Foppe			Tr: SULANTAY Jose		
9 JOHN Collins	77	79	MORALES Pedro 10		79
12 ZUIVERLOON Gianni	87	74	TUDELA Eduardo 11		74
14 MEDUNJANIN Haris	79	46	CARMONA Carlos 15		46

Emmen Stadium, Emmen, 22-06-2005
17:30, 8 400, Larsen DEN, Hansen DEN, Norrestrand DEN

COL 1 2 ARG

Otalvaro 52 | Messi 58, Barroso 93

COLOMBIA			ARGENTINA		
1 ARENAS Libis			USTARI Oscar 1		
3 ZAPATA Cristian			CABRAL Gustavo 2		
5 ZUNIGA Juan			FORMICA Lautaro 3		
6 MORALES Harrison			BARROSO Julio 4		
8 TOJA Juan Carlos	72		PALETTA Gabriel 6		
11 OTALVARO Harrison			BIGLIA Lucas 7		
14 AGUILAR Abel (c)			(c) ZABALETA Pablo 8		
15 MORENO Dayro	56	85	ARCHUBI Rodrigo 15		
17 MARRUGO Cristian		89	CARDOZO Neri 16		
18 RENTERIA Wason			MESSI Lionel 18		
19 CASIERRA Mauricio		87	OBERMAN Gustavo 20		
Tr: LARA Eduardo			Tr: FERRARO Francisco		
9 GARCIA Radamel	72	87	VITTI Pablo 9		
13 GUARIN Fredy	56	89	ARMENTEROS Emiliano 11		
		85	GAGO Fernando 17		

Emmen Stadium, Emmen, 22-06-2005
20:30, 8 400, Hauge NOR, Holvik NOR, Borgan NOR

ESP 3 0 TUR

Juanfran 2 28 36, Robuste 69

SPAIN			TURKEY		
1 BIEL RIBAS			(c) OZCAN Sener 12		
2 MOLINERO			UCAR Ugur 2		
4 ALEXIS	38		TEBER Ergun 3		
5 ROBUSTE (c)			CAKMAK Yasin 4		
7 JUANFRAN	77		SAKAR Zafer 6		
8 ZAPATER	75	46	YILMAZ Burak 7		
9 LLORENTE		60	OZTURK Sezer 8		
11 GAVILAN			ZENGIN Kerim 9		
12 JOSE ENRIQUE			ADIN Olcan 11		
17 CESC	63		OZAVCI Murat 14		
20 MARKEL			GULEC Gokhan 16		
Tr: SAEZ Inaki			Tr: USTAOMER Senol		
6 RAUL ALBIOL	74	38	SEZGIN Sezer 13		
10 JONA	77	46	KELES Ergin 17		
16 SILVA	63	60	OZTURK Ali 20		

QUARTER-FINALS

Galgenwaard, Utrecht, 24-06-2005
17:30, 20 000, Kwon Jong Chul KOR, Liu Tiejun CHN, Kim Dae Young KOR

MAR 4p 2 2 2p ITA

El Zhar 26, Battaglia OG 93 | Canini 74, Pelle 112

MOROCCO			ITALY		
1 BOURKADI Mohammed			(c) VIVIANO Emiliano 1		
3 BENZOUKANE Chakib	68		MARZORATTI Lino 2		
5 RABEH Youssef (c)			NOCERINO Antonio 4		
7 HERMACH Adil		85	CODA Andrea 5		
8 BENZOUIEN Sofian		99	CANINI Michele 6		
9 IAJOUR Mouhssine			DEFENDI Marino 7		
10 EL ZHAR Nabil			PELLE Graziano 9		
11 BENDAMOU Tarik	82		GALLOPPA Daniele 11		
13 SBAI Salah			AQUILANTI Antonio 15		
14 TIBERKANINE Rachid	102	66	BENTIVOGLIO Simone 16		
16 EL AHMADI Karim		43	DE MARTINO Raffaele 17		
Tr: FATHI Jamal			Tr: BERRETTINI Paolo		
2 EL AMRANI Hicham	68	43	CAROTTI Lorenzo 8		
15 DOULYAZAL Rida	82	85	BATTAGLIA Francesco 13		
17 ZOUCHOU Yassine	102	66	AGNELLI Cristian 18		

Willem II, Tilburg, 24-06-2005
20:30, 10 000, Shield AUS, Gibson AUS, Wilson AUS

GER 1 2 BRA

Huber 68 | Diego Tardelli 82, Rafael 99

GERMANY			BRAZIL		
1 ADLER Rene (c)			(c) RENAN 1		
2 JANKER Christoph	59		RAFAEL 2		
3 COMPPER Marvin			LEONARDO 3		
4 MATIP Marvin	74		ROBERTO 5		
5 SCHUON Marcel			FABIO SANTOS 6		
6 DELURA Michael			RENATO 8		
8 GENTNER Christian	56		BOBO 9		
9 ADLER Nicky	79	112	EVANDRO 10		
11 JANSEN Marcell			RAFAEL SOBIS 11		
17 CIMEN Daniyel			EDCARLOS 14		
18 THOMIK Paul	93		AROUCA 16		
Tr: SKIBBE Michael			Tr: WEBER Rene		
6 OTTL Andreas	93	112	FELLYPE GABRIEL 17		
13 HUBER Alexander	59	56	THIAGO QUIRINO 19		
19 BROEKER Thomas	79	117 74	DIEGO TARDELLI 20		

Parkstad Limburg, Kerkrade, 25-06-2005
15:30, Elizondo ARG, Garcia ARG, Otero ARG

NGA 10p 1 1 9p NED

Oworei 1 | Vlaar 46

NIGERIA			NETHERLANDS		
1 VANZEKIN Ambruse			VERMEER Kenneth 1		
3 TAIWO Taye			TIENDALLI Dwight 2		
4 APAM Onyekachi			VLAAR Ron 3		
9 MIKEL John Obi		106	VAN DER STRUIJK Frank 4		
10 ISAAC Promise (c)			DROST Jeroen 5		
11 OKORONKWO Solomon	62		(c) MADURO Hedwiges 6		
13 ADEFEMI Olubayo		74	OWUSU ABEYIE Quincy 7		
14 ABWO David	113		KRUYS Rick 8		
17 ADELEYE Dele			BABEL Ryan 11		
19 KAITA Sani		74	EMANUELSON Urby 15		
20 OWOERI John	99		VINCKEN Tim 18		
Tr: SIASIA Samsun			Tr: DE HAAN Foppe		
6 ADEDEJI Yinka	62	74	JOHN Collins 9		
15 SAMBO Soga	113	74	ZUIVERLOON Gianni 12		
16 ATULEWA Gift	99	106	OTTEN Mark 13		

Enschede Stadium, Enschede, 25-06-2005
20:30, 11 200, Archundia MEX, Ramirez MEX, Rebollar MEX

ARG 3 1 ESP

Zabaleta 19, Oberman 71, Messi 73 | Zapater 32

ARGENTINA			SPAIN		
1 USTARI Oscar			BIEL RIBAS 1		
2 CABRAL Gustavo			MOLINERO 2		
3 FORMICA Lautaro			ALEXIS 4		
4 BARROSO Julio			(c) ROBUSTE 5		
5 TORRES Juan Manuel		75	JUANFRAN 7		
6 PALETTA Gabriel	90	83	ZAPATER 8		
8 ZABALETA Pablo (c)		75	LLORENTE 9		
9 VITTI Pablo		46	JOSE ENRIQUE 12		
15 ARCHUBI Rodrigo		63	SILVA 16		
16 CARDOZO Neri			CESC 17		
18 MESSI Lionel			MARKEL 20		
Tr: FERRARO Francisco			Tr: SAEZ Inaki		
13 GARAY Ezequiel	90	75	JONA 10		
17 GAGO Fernando	63	75	GAVILAN 11		
20 OBERMAN Gustavo	46	83	VICTOR 18		

SEMI-FINALS

Galgenwaard, Utrecht, 28-06-2005
17:30, 16 500, Busacca SUI, Buragina SUI, Arnet SUI

BRA	1	2	ARG

Renato [75]

Messi [7], Zabaleta [93+]

BRAZIL		ARGENTINA	
1 RENAN (c)		USTARI Oscar	1
2 RAFAEL		CABRAL Gustavo	2
3 LEONARDO		FORMICA Lautaro	3
5 ROBERTO	56	BARROSO Julio	4
6 FABIO SANTOS		TORRES Juan Manuel	5
8 RENATO		PALETTA Gabriel	6
9 BOBO	67	(c)ZABALETA Pablo	8
10 EVANDRO		CARDOZO Neri	16
11 RAFAEL SOBIS	95	GAGO Fernando	17
14 EDCARLOS		MESSI Lionel	18
16 AROUCA	81	OBERMAN Gustavo	20
Tr: WEBER Rene		Tr: FERRARO Francisco	
17 FELLYPE GABRIEL	67 95	BIGLIA Lucas	7
19 THIAGO QUIRINO	56 81	AGUERO Sergio	19

Parkstad Limburg, Kerkrade, 28-06-2005
20:30, 17 000, Larrionda URU, Rial URU, Fandino URU

MAR	0	3	NGA

Taiwo [34], Adefemi [70], Ogbuke [75]

MOROCCO		NIGERIA	
1 BOURKADI Mohammed		VANZEKIN Ambruse	1
2 EL AMRANI Hicham		TAIWO Taye	3
3 BENZOUKANE Chakib		APAM Onyekachi	4
5 RABEH Youssef		OGBUKE Chinedu	7
8 BENZOUIEN Sofian	91	MIKEL John Obi	9
9 IAJOUR Mouhssine	80	ISAAC Promise	10
10 EL ZHAR Nabil		ADEFEMI Olubayo	13
11 BENDAMOU Tarik	69	ABWO David	14
14 TIBERKANINE Rachid	74	ADELEYE Dele	17
15 DOULYAZAL Rida	91 85	KAITA Sani	19
16 EL AHMADI Karim	60	OWOERI John	20
Tr: FATHI Jamal		Tr: SIASIA Samsun	
17 ZOUCHOU Yassine	60 85	ADEDEJI Yinka	6
19 BENJELLOUN Abdessalam	74 69	BAZUAYE Daddy	8
	91	ANUBI Kola	18

3RD PLACE PLAY-OFF

Galgenwaard, Utrecht, 2-07-2005
17:00, 20 000, Cantalejo ESP, Carrasco ESP, Hernandez ESP

BRA	2	1	MAR

Fabio Santos [88], Edcarlos [91+]

Edcarlos OG [47+]

BRAZIL		MOROCCO	
1 RENAN (c)		(c) BOURKADI Mohammed	1
2 RAFAEL		BENZOUKANE Chakib	3
4 GLADSTONE	54	RABEH Youssef	5
6 FABIO SANTOS		HERMACH Adil	7
8 RENATO		BENZOUIEN Sofian	8
10 EVANDRO	62	EL ZHAR Nabil	10
11 RAFAEL SOBIS	59	BENDAMOU Tarik	11
13 JOAO LEONARDO		SBAI Salah	13
14 EDCARLOS		TIBERKANINE Rachid	14
16 AROUCA		FATAH Said	18
20 DIEGO TARDELLI	53	CHIHI Adil	20
Tr: WEBER Rene		Tr: FATHI Jamal	
15 FILIPE	62	86 53 ZOUCHOU Yassine	17
17 FELLYPE GABRIEL	54		
19 THIAGO QUIRINO	59		

PENALTY SHOOT-OUT

Morocco First		Italy Second	
RABEH Youssef	✔	GALLOPPA Daniele	✔
DOULYAZAL Rida	✘	AGNELLI Cristian	✔
IAJOUR Mouhssine	✔	PELLE Graziano	✘
EL AMRANI Hicham	✔	CAROTTI Lorenzo	✘
EL ZHAR Nabil	✔		

Morocco qualify for the semi-finals 4-2 on penalties

PENALTY SHOOT-OUT

Nigeria First		Netherlands Second	
TAIWO Taye	✔	JOHN Collins	✔
SAMBO Soga	✔	BABEL Ryan	✔
ADEFEMI Olubayo	✔	VLAAR Ron	✔
ATULEWA Gift	✘	KRUYS Rick	✘
ISAAC Promise	✔	MADURO Hedwiges	✔
ADEDEJI Yinka	✘	ZUIVERLOON Gianni	✘
MIKEL John Obi	✔	DROST Jeroen	✔
APAM Onyekachi	✔	VINCKEN Tim	✔
KAITA Sani	✔	OTTEN Mark	✔
ADELEYE Dele	✔	TIENDALLI Dwight	✔
VANZEKIN Ambruse	✔	VERMEER Kenneth	✔
TAIWO Taye	✔	JOHN Collins	✘

Nigeria qualify for the semi-finals 10-9 on penalties

ADIDAS GOLDEN BALL

1 MESSI Lionel	ARG
2 MIKEL John Obi	NGA
3 TAIWO Taye	NGA

ADIDAS GOLDEN SHOE

		Goals	Assists
1 MESSI Lionel	ARG	6	2
2 LLORENTE Fernando	ESP	5	2
3 ALIIEV Oleksandr	UKR	5	2

World Youth Final	Galgenwaard, Utrecht	2-07-2005
Kick-off: 20:00		Attendance: 24 500

ARG   2   1   NGA

Messi 2 [40p 75p]   Ogbuke [53]

ARGENTINA				MATCH STATS			NIGERIA			
1	GK	USTARI Oscar					VANZEKIN Ambruse	GK	1	
3	DF	FORMICA Lautaro		11	Shots	11	TAIWO Taye	DF	3	
4	DF	BARROSO Julio		7	Shots on Goal	3	JAMES Monday	DF	5	
5	MF	TORRES Juan Manuel		22	Fouls Committed	24	OGBUKE Chinedu	MF	7	
6	MF	PALETTA Gabriel		3	Corner Kicks	4	MIKEL John Obi	MF	9	
8	MF	ZABALETA Pablo		2	Offside	8	ISAAC Promise	FW	10	
13	DF	GARAY Ezequiel		49	Possession %	51	ADEFEMI Olubayo	DF	13	
15	MF	ARCHUBI Rodrigo	61			85	ABWO David	FW	14	
17	MF	GAGO Fernando	72	MATCH OFFICIALS			ADELEYE Dele	DF	17	
18	MF	MESSI Lionel		REFEREE			KAITA Sani	MF	19	
20	FW	OBERMAN Gustavo	57	HAUGE Terje NOR			OWOERI John	FW	20	
		Tr: FERRARO Francisco		ASSISTANTS			Tr: SIASIA Samson			
		Substitutes		HOLVIK Steinar NOR			Substitutes			
12	GK	CHAMPAGNE Nereo		BORGAN Ole Hermann NOR			AKPEYI Daniel	GK	12	
21	GK	NAVARRO Nicolas		4TH OFFICIAL			IGE Kola	GK	21	
2	DF	CABRAL Gustavo		ARCHUNDIA Benito MEX			CHINWO Kennedy	DF	4	
7	MF	BIGLIA Lucas	72				APAM Onyekachi	DF	2	
9	FW	VITTI Pablo					ADEDEJI Yinka	MF	6	
10	MF	PEREZ Patricio					BAZUAYE Daddy	MF	8	
11	MF	ARMENTEROS Emiliano	61			85	OKORONKWO Solomon	FW	11	
14	DF	ABRAHAM David					SAMBO Soga	MF	15	
16	FW	CARDOZO Neri					ATULEWA Gift	FW	16	
19	FW	AGUERO Sergio	57				ANUBI Kola	MF	18	

I'm overjoyed to have won this title, It's a personal triumph and will bring great joy to our nation. Messi had a superb championship and deserves all the praise he receives.

Francisco Ferraro

The reason we lost was because of the two penalties. We have got to have better discipline. We lost our concentration. The Argentine players were not in a good position to score, so I don't know why they were brought down.

Samson Siasia

MATCH HIGHLIGHTS

20' Dele Adeleye misses a good chance to open the scoring for Nigeria. **31'** Ambruse Vanzekin fists away a shot from Argentina's Gustavo Oberman. **36'** Oscar Ustari saves from John Owoeri. **40'** Lionel Messi runs from deep with the ball and is fouled by Adeleye in the area. Lionel Messi scores for Argentina from the resulting penalty. **52'** Put through by a neat flick by Promise Isaac, Owoeri squanders the chance to equalise. **53'** Olubayo Adefemi's centre from the rightwing is glanced home from 10 yards by Chinedu Ogbuke to bring the Nigerians level. **57'** Isaac sets up David Abwo but his shot hits the side netting. **60'** Zabaleta fails to get a touch on Messi's dangerous cross goal pass. **62'** Isaac shoots just wide. **74'** Messi scores his second penalty for Argentina after Sergio Aguero is brought down in the box. **84'** Adefemi clears off the line for Nigeria.

MATCH REPORT

A penalty in each half converted by Barcelona's young sensation Lionel Messi earned Argentina a record fifth FIFA World Youth Championship title. In a very tactical match, both teams had good chances throughout but there was only one goal scored from open play. Argentina's first penalty, just before half-time, came when Adeleye brought down Messi after a fine run by the Argentine. Nigeria equalised when Ogbuke converted Adefemi's cross, but when subsitute Sergio Aguera was hauled down in the area with 15 minutes to go, Messi made no mistake to seal the game.

ARG – ARGENTINA YOUTH SQUAD

No	Pos	Name	Shirt Name	DoB	Club	Cms	Kg	Games	Mins	Goals	Y	R
1	GK	USTARI Oscar	USTARI	3-7-1986	Independiente	182	82	7	630			
2	DF	CABRAL Gustavo	CABRAL	14-10-1985	Racing Club	184	78	7	540		3	
3	DF	FORMICA Lautaro	FORMICA	27-1-1986	Newell's Old Boys	172	69	7	630		1	
4	DF	BARROSO Julio	BARROSO	16-1-1985	Boca Juniors	172	72	7	630	1		
5	MF	TORRES Juan Manuel	TORRES	20-6-1985	Racing Club	170	67	5	440		1	1
6	MF	PALETTA Gabriel	PALETTA	15-2-1986	Banfield	183	80	7	629		2	
7	MF	BIGLIA Lucas	BIGLIA	30-1-1986	Independiente	169	67	6	213			
8	MF	ZABALETA Pablo	ZABALETA	16-1-1985	San Lorenzo	173	69	7	630	3	1	
9	FW	VITTI Pablo	VITTI	9-7-1985	Rosario Central	173	64	3	138		1	
10	MF	PEREZ Patricio	PEREZ	27-6-1985	Velez Sarsfield	164	54	0	0			
11	MF	ARMENTEROS Emiliano	ARMENTEROS	18-1-1986	Banfield	179	76	5	89			
12	GK	CHAMPAGNE Nereo	CHAMPAGNE	20-1-1985	San Lorenzo	188	86	0	0			
13	DF	GARAY Ezequiel	GARAY	10-10-1986	Newell's Old Boys	182	87	2	91			
14	DF	ABRAHAM David	ABRAHAM	15-7-1986	Independiente	188	78	0	0			
15	MF	ARCHUBI Rodrigo	ARCHUBI	6-6-1985	Lanus	179	62	3	209		1	
16	FW	CARDOZO Neri	CARDOZO	8-8-1986	Boca Juniors	172	62	6	449	1	2	
17	MF	GAGO Fernando	GAGO	10-4-1986	Boca Juniors	177	65	7	449			
18	MF	MESSI Lionel	MESSI	24-6-1987	Barcelona	170	65	7	571	4	1	
19	FW	AGUERO Sergio	AGUERO	2-6-1988	Independiente	170	69	4	84		1	
20	FW	OBERMAN Gustavo	OBERMAN	25-3-1985	Argentinos Juniors	176	75	7	498	1	1	
21	GK	NAVARRO Nicolas	NAVARRO	25-3-1985	Argentinos Juniors	186	73	0	0			

AUS – AUSTRALIA YOUTH SQUAD

No	Pos	Name	Shirt Name	DoB	Club	Cms	Kg	Games	Mins	Goals	Y	R
1	GK	VUKOVIC Danny	VUKOVIC	27-3-1985	Central Coast	184	78	0	0			
2	DF	MILLIGAN Mark	MILLIGAN	4-8-1985	Sydney FC	177	75	3	270			
3	DF	MC CLENAHAN Trent	MC CLENAHAN	4-2-1985	West Ham United	180	70	3	270			
4	DF	LEIJER Adrian	LEIJER	25-3-1986	Melbourne Victory	184	79	0	0			
5	DF	TIMPANO Jacob	TIMPANO	3-1-1986	Sydney FC	183	80	3	270			
6	MF	MUSIALIK Stuart	MUSIALIK	29-3-1985	Newcastle United AUS	170	72	3	252			
7	MF	LIA Vince	LIA	18-3-1985	Melbourne Victory	176	86	2	180			
8	MF	CELESKI Billy	CELESKI	14-7-1985	Perth Glory	176	73	3	159			
9	FW	LUCAS Jay	LUCAS	14-1-1985	Marconi Stallions	186	87	2	119			
10	MF	SARKIES Kristian	SARKIES	25-10-1986	Melbourne Victory	170	70	2	177			
11	MF	TADROSSE Chris	TADROSSE	10-9-1985	Melbourne Victory	172	75	3	206			
12	GK	PASFIELD Justin	PASFIELD	30-5-1985	Sydney FC	193	97	1	90			
13	DF	DOWNES Aaron	DOWNES	15-5-1985	Chesterfield	190	84	2	180			
14	MF	DILEVSKI Spase	DILEVSKI	13-5-1985	Tottenham Hotspur	180	79	3	128			
15	DF	TOWNSEND Ryan	TOWNSEND	2-9-1985	Burnley	189	82	1	90	1		
16	MF	ZADKOVICH Ruben	ZADKOVICH	23-5-1986	Notts County	182	73	2	94		1	
17	FW	WARD Nick	WARD	24-3-1985	Perth Glory	183	77	3	215		1	
18	GK	FEDERICI Adam	FEDERICI	31-1-1985	Reading	188	90	2	180			
19	FW	WILLIAMS David	WILLIAMS	26-2-1988	Queensland Academy	174	69	0	0			
20	MF	WESOLOWSKI James	WESOLOWSKI	25-8-1987	Leicester City	172	75	1	90		1	
21	DF	TOPOR-STANLEY Nikolai	TOPOR STANLEY	11-3-1985	Belconnen United	190	86	0	0			

BEN – BENIN YOUTH SQUAD

No	Pos	Name	Shirt Name	DoB	Club	Cms	Kg	Games	Mins	Goals	Y	R
1	GK	SALAMI Wassiou	SALAMI	23-12-1989	Mogas 90	173	73	0	0			
2	DF	CHITOU Charaf	CHITOU	21-9-1987	UNB	175	68	3	219			1
3	MF	OLOU Oscar	OLOU	16-11-1987	Mogas 90	176	67	2	161		1	1
4	DF	HOUNTONTO De Gaulle	HONTONTO	20-11-1985	Soleil	172	72	0	0			
5	DF	MOUSSA Traore	TRAORE	31-5-1986	Buffles	168	66	3	270			
6	DF	RAIMY Florent	RAIMY	7-2-1986	Sedan	184	78	1	90		1	
7	MF	BOCO Romualde	BOCO	8-7-1985	Chamois Niortais	178	70	3	270			
8	MF	ADENIYI Mathieu	ADENIYI	26-4-1987	Stade Rennais	176	72	0	0			
9	MF	HONVO Thierry	HONVO	3-1-1987	Clermont	183	75	0	0			
10	MF	AISSI Marvin	AISSI	26-3-1985	Troyes	178	72	0	0			
11	FW	MAIGA Abou	MAIGA	20-9-1985	Creteil	184	75	3	270	1		
12	FW	AGBESSI Coffi	AGBESSI	5-12-1985	Olympic Zawiya	165	65	3	270		1	
13	FW	NASSIROU Youssouf	NASSIROU	14-11-1986	Soleil	162	61	3	110		1	
14	FW	OSSENI Bachirou	OSSENI	15-9-1985	Soleil	175	71	3	181			
15	FW	OMOTOYOSSI Razak	OMOTOYOSSI	8-10-1985	JSA	175	82	3	267	1		
16	GK	DJIDONOU Yoann	DJIDONOU	17-5-1986	Racing Club de Paris	179	70	3	270			
17	MF	ZANOU Medard	ZANOU	6-6-1987	JSC	177	69	0	0			
18	DF	TCHOMOGO Seidath	TCHOMOGO	13-8-1985	Lions	179	70	3	270			
19	MF	AHOUEYA Jocelin	AHOUEYA	19-12-1985	Sion	174	67	3	252	1		
20	GK	TARDIEU Benoit	TARDIEU	21-1-1986	Auxerre	188	84	0	0			
21	DF	AINON Michael	AINON	9-3-1985	Watford	188	82	0	0			

BRA – BRAZIL YOUTH SQUAD

No	Pos	Name	Shirt Name	DoB	Club	Cms	Kg	Games	Mins	Goals	Y	R
1	GK	RENAN	RENAN	24-1-1985	Internacional	187	81	7	660			
2	DF	RAFAEL	RAFAEL	7-9-1985	Coritiba	171	66	7	660		1	1
3	DF	LEONARDO	LEONARDO	19-3-1986	Santos	186	71	3	283			
4	DF	GLADSTONE	GLADSTONE	29-1-1985	Cruzeiro	183	80	4	279		1	1
5	MF	ROBERTO	ROBERTO	18-1-1985	Guarani	177	77	6	490		2	
6	DF	FABIO SANTOS	FABIO SANTOS	16-9-1985	São Paulo	178	73	7	656		1	1
7	MF	DIEGO	DIEGO	17-6-1985	Fluminense	185	86	2	99			
8	MF	RENATO	RENATO	28-4-1985	Atlético Mineiro	186	82	7	493		2	1
9	FW	BOBO	BOBO	9-1-1985	Corinthians	184	83	4	282			
10	MF	EVANDRO	EVANDRO	23-8-1986	Atlético Paranaense	180	66	5	420			
11	FW	RAFAEL SOBIS	RAFAEL SOBIS	17-6-1985	Internacional	173	71	7	595		1	1
12	GK	BRUNO	BRUNO	1-5-1986	São Paulo	190	78	0	0			
13	DF	JOAO LEONARDO	J. LEONARDO	25-6-1985	Guarani	181	79	3	225		2	
14	DF	EDCARLOS	EDCARLOS	10-5-1985	São Paulo	182	77	7	587		1	2
15	DF	FILIPE	FILIPE	9-8-1985	Ajax Amsterdam	181	70	2	32			
16	MF	AROUCA	AROUCA	11-8-1986	Fluminense	170	66	7	561			
17	MF	FELLYPE GABRIEL	FELLYPE G.	6-12-1985	Flamengo	175	61	5	104			
18	MF	ERNANE	ERNANE	2-5-1985	Bahia	178	65	4	352		1	
19	FW	THIAGO QUIRINO	T. QUIRINO	4-1-1985	Atlético Mineiro	180	74	4	145			
20	FW	DIEGO TARDELLI	D. TARDELLI	10-5-1985	São Paulo	175	70	5	337		1	1
21	GK	DIEGO C.	DIEGO C.	24-6-1985	Atlético Mineiro	187	79	0	0			

CAN – CANADA YOUTH SQUAD

No	Pos	Name	Shirt Name	DoB	Club	Cms	Kg	Games	Mins	Goals	Y	R
1	GK	WAGENAAR Josh	WAGENAAR	26-2-1985	Hartwick College	185	90	3	270			
2	DF	RAMALHO Graham	RAMALHO	12-1-1986	Groningen	178	69	3	261			
3	DF	LEDGERWOOD Nik	LEDGERWOOD	16-1-1985	TSV München 1860	179	68	3	270			
4	DF	HAINAULT Andrew	HAINAULT	17-6-1986	Montreal Impact	186	80	3	270			
5	DF	PEETOOM Brad	PEETOOM	2-3-1986	Syracuse University	184	72	3	268			
6	MF	SCHIAVONI Carlo	SCHIAVONI	19-8-1985	University of Alabama	180	79	1	17			
7	MF	PETERS Jaime	PETERS	4-5-1987	Ipswich Town	170	69	3	151	1		
8	MF	ROSENLUND Tyler	ROSENLUND	13-9-1986	Santa Barbara	180	77	3	253			
9	MF	GYAKI Ryan	GYAKI	6-12-1985	Sheffield United	178	71	3	270		1	
10	FW	JOHNSON Will	JOHNSON	21-1-1987	Chicago Fire	180	70	3	270		1	
11	MF	DE JONG Marcel	DE JONG	15-10-1986	Helmond Sport	175	68	3	179	1		
12	FW	O'NEILL Riley	O NEILL	9-9-1985	University of Kentucky	190	84	2	112			
13	DF	BRITNER Matt	BRITNER	17-4-1985	Brown University	185	79	0	0			
14	DF	EDGAR David	EDGAR	19-5-1987	Newcastle United	188	70	3	244	1		
15	DF	STEWART Vince	STEWART	21-1-1986	Simon Fraser University	170	70	1	9			
16	FW	LALLI Franco	LALLI	11-3-1985	US Lucera Calcio	170	65	0	0			
17	FW	LOMBARDO Andrea	LOMBARDO	23-5-1987	Atalanta Bergamo	189	73	3	91			
18	MF	CHAROWSKI Tomek	CHAROWSKI	15-10-1986	Duke University	180	69	1	35			
19	GK	BEGOVIC Asmir	BEGOVIC	20-6-1987	Portsmouth	198	83	0	0			
20	GK	GIACOMI Rob	GIACOMI	1-8-1986	Glasgow Rangers	188	82	0	0			
21	DF	KASSAYE Simon	KASSAYE	19-5-1985	No club affiliation	185	77	0	0			

CHI – CHILE YOUTH SQUAD

No	Pos	Name	Shirt Name	DoB	Club	Cms	Kg	Games	Mins	Goals	Y	R
1	GK	ESPINOZA Carlos	ESPINOZA	23-2-1985	Puerto Montt	188	83	1	90			
2	DF	RIQUELME Edzon	RIQUELME	29-8-1985	Deportes Concepcion	175	73	4	360		1	
3	MF	PAEZ Sebastian	PAEZ	13-8-1986	Deportes la Serena	175	74	0	0			
4	DF	MONTESINOS Sebastian	MONTESINOS	12-3-1986	Colo Colo	182	81	3	261		2	
5	DF	BASCUNAN Hugo	BASCUNAN	11-1-1985	Maracaibo	183	83	4	360		2	
6	MF	DIAZ Marcelo	DIAZ	30-12-1986	Universidad de Chile	168	65	0	0			
7	MF	MENESES Fernando	MENESES	27-9-1985	Colo Colo	170	71	2	45			
8	MF	VASQUEZ Ivan	VASQUEZ	13-8-1985	Universidad Catolica	168	73	4	315			
9	FW	CANALES Nicolas	CANALES	27-6-1985	Universidad de Chile	181	82	4	338			
10	MF	MORALES Pedro	MORALES	25-5-1985	Huachipato	177	72	4	50	1		
11	FW	TUDELA Eduardo	TUDELA	3-3-1986	Cobreloa	178	72	4	123			
12	GK	ARIAS Carlos	ARIAS	4-9-1986	Universidad Catolica	175	76	2	180			
13	DF	MUNOZ Felipe	MUNOZ	4-4-1985	Colo Colo	177	71	4	360		1	
14	MF	FERNANDEZ Matias	FERNANDEZ	15-5-1986	Colo Colo	179	74	4	347	1		
15	MF	CARMONA Carlos	CARMONA	21-2-1987	Coquimbo	177	73	2	135	1		
16	DF	SANCHEZ Francisco	SANCHEZ	6-2-1985	Everton (CHI)	172	71	1	9			
17	MF	VILLANUEVA Carlos	VILLANUEVA	5-2-1986	Audax Italiano	173	71	0	0			
18	DF	JARA Gonzalo	JARA	29-8-1985	Huachipato	178	71	3	225		1	1
19	MF	FUENZALIDA Jose	FUENZALIDA	22-2-1985	Universidad Catolica	169	64	4	339		2	
20	FW	PARADA Ricardo	PARADA	2-1-1985	Deportes Concepcion	175	72	4	288		2	
21	GK	ROSALES Jose	ROSALES	20-9-1985	O'Higgins	181	77	1	90			

CHN - CHINA PR YOUTH SQUAD

No	Pos	Name	Shirt Name	DoB	Club	Cms	Kg	Games	Mins	Goals	Y	R
1	GK	ZHANG Lei	L ZHANG	6-4-1985	Dongguan Nancheng	187	75	0	0			
2	DF	ZHAO Ming	M ZHAO	3-10-1987	Yianbian	189	83	4	360		1	
3	DF	LIU Yu	Y LIU	12-5-1985	Sichuan Guancheng	180	68	1	45			
4	DF	ZHENG Tao	T ZHENG	20-8-1985	Shanghai Guoji	185	74	3	225		1	
5	DF	FENG Xiaoting	X T FENG	22-10-1985	Daian Shide	188	78	4	360		1	
6	MF	WANG Hongliang	H L WANG	14-1-1985	Shanghai Shenhua	174	72	2	93			
7	MF	ZHAO Xuri	X R ZHAO	3-12-1985	Dalian Shide	185	80	4	161	1	1	
8	MF	ZHOU Haibin	H B ZHOU	19-7-1985	Shandong Luneng	185	74	3	269	1		
9	FW	DONG Fangzhuo	F ZH DONG	23-1-1985	Manchester United	188	78	3	37			
10	MF	CHEN Tao	T CHEN	11-3-1985	Shenyang Jinde	178	75	4	353	1	1	
11	FW	ZHU Ting	T ZHU	15-7-1985	Dalian Shide	181	74	2	156	1		1
12	GK	YU Ziqian	Z Q YU	3-6-1985	Dalian Shide	194	86	0	0			
13	MF	LU Lin	L LU	3-2-1985	Guangzhou Rizhiquan	168	68	4	271	1		
14	FW	MAO Biao	B MAO	24-7-1987	Tianjin Teda	184	72	0	0			
15	DF	YUAN Weiwei	W W YUAN	25-11-1985	Shandong Luneng	184	77	1	90			
16	GK	YANG Cheng	CH YANG	11-10-1985	Shandong Luneng	188	78	4	360			
17	DF	TAN Wangsong	W S TAN	19-12-1985	Sichuan Guancheng	180	68	4	360	1	1	
18	FW	GAO Lin	L GAO	14-2-1986	Shanghai Shenhua	185	75	4	317	1		
19	FW	ZOU You	Y ZOU	22-9-1985	Dalian Shide	195	85	2	8			
20	MF	CUI Peng	P CUI	31-5-1987	Shandong Luneng	179	72	3	266	1	3	
21	MF	HAO Junmin	J M HAO	24-3-1987	Tianjin Teda	181	72	4	208	1		

COL - COLOMBIA YOUTH SQUAD

No	Pos	Name	Shirt Name	DoB	Club	Cms	Kg	Games	Mins	Goals	Y	R
1	GK	ARENAS Libis	ARENAS	12-5-1987	Envigado	187	71	4	360			
2	DF	VALDEZ Carlos	C. VALDEZ	22-5-1985	Real Cartagena	184	77	0	0			
3	DF	ZAPATA Cristian	ZAPATA	30-9-1986	Deportivo Cali	188	84	4	360		1	
4	DF	ESTACIO Jimy	ESTACIO	8-1-1986	Deportivo Cali	183	74	0	0			
5	DF	ZUNIGA Juan	ZUNIGA	14-12-1985	Atlético Nacional	170	69	4	343			
6	MF	MORALES Harrison	HARRISON	20-6-1986	Deportes Quindio	186	86	4	360	.		
7	FW	RODALLEGA Hugo	RODALLEGA	25-7-1985	Deportes Quindio	180	69	3	179	1		
8	MF	TOJA Juan Carlos	TOJA	24-5-1985	Independiente Santa Fe	185	78	3	189		1	
9	FW	GARCIA Radamel	F. GARCIA	10-2-1986	River Plate	177	75	3	62	2		
10	MF	HERNANDEZ Sebastian	HERNANDEZ	2-10-1986	Deportes Quindio	178	69	1	23			
11	MF	OTALVARO Harrison	OTALVARO	28-2-1986	América de Cali	177	76	4	321	1		
12	GK	ABELLA Carlos	ABELLA	25-1-1986	Atlético Nacional	186	83	0	0			
13	MF	GUARIN Fredy	GUARIN	30-6-1986	Envigado	183	78	4	140	2		
14	MF	AGUILAR Abel	AGUILAR	6-1-1985	Deportivo Cali	186	82	4	360			
15	FW	MORENO Dayro	D. MORENO	16-9-1985	Once Caldas	178	75	3	155	1		
16	MF	VALENCIA Edwin	VALENCIA	29-3-1985	América de Cali	182	77	2	153			
17	MF	MARRUGO Cristian	MARRUGO	18-7-1985	Atlético Nacional	175	74	3	270	2		
18	FW	RENTERIA Wason	RENTERIA	4-7-1985	Boyaca Chico	186	77	4	329	1		
19	DF	CASIERRA Mauricio	CASIERRA	8-12-1985	Once Caldas	171	61	4	339			
20	MF	MACHACON Daniel	MACHACON	5-1-1985	Junior Barranquilla	172	64	1	17			
21	GK	OSPINA David	OSPINA	31-8-1988	Atlético Nacional	183	76	0	0			

EGY - EGYPT YOUTH SQUAD

No	Pos	Name	Shirt Name	DoB	Club	Cms	Kg	Games	Mins	Goals	Y	R
1	GK	SHAABAN Hamada	HAMADA	1-10-1985	Mansoura	189	78	3	270			
2	DF	MAHMOUD Mohamed	NANO	24-3-1985	Al Ahly	175	73	1	89		1	1
3	MF	TAWFIK Abdelaziz	A. TAWFIK	24-5-1986	Mansoura	172	73	3	270			
4	MF	ASHOUR Hossam	H. ASHOUR	9-3-1986	Al Ahly	172	68	1	69			
5	DF	KANDEL Walid	WALID	24-3-1985	Zamalek	180	78	1	77			
6	DF	GALAL Abdellah	ABDELLAH	20-1-1986	Al Ahly	182	75	3	270			
7	FW	FARAG Ahmed	A. FARAG	20-5-1986	Sochaux	184	80	3	217	1		
8	FW	ABDEL ZAHER Ahmed	A.A. ELZAHER	15-1-1985	Enppi	182	79	3	31			
9	FW	OSSAMA Hossam	H. OSSAMA	30-8-1985	Zamalek	182	81	3	93	1		
10	FW	ABDELRAZEK Mahmoud	SHEKABALA	5-3-1986	PAOK Thessaloniki	183	71	3	249			
11	FW	SAID Abdallah	A. SAID	13-7-1985	Ismaily	176	72	3	270	1		
12	MF	SHAHAT Abdallah	A. SHAHAT	10-5-1985	Ismaily	178	74	2	173	1	1	1
13	DF	ELHAKAM Ahmed Abd	A.A. ELHAKAM	18-3-1985	Mansoura	189	80	1	27			
14	DF	MAGDY Ahmed	A. MAGDY	24-5-1986	Al Ahly	184	79	3	270	1		
15	DF	SIAM Islam	I. SIAM	13-2-1985	Arab Contractors	188	80	1	90			
16	GK	TAWFIK Amir	AMIR	2-10-1985	Al Ahly	179	75	0	0			
17	MF	EL HALAWANI Amr	ELHALAWANI	15-3-1985	Al Ahly	179	72	1	21			
18	MF	GHANEM Ahmed	A. GHANEM	8-4-1986	Zamalek	174	65	3	240			
19	MF	KHALIFA Ahmed	A. KHALIFA	23-3-1985	Ismaily	172	66	1	35			
20	DF	GAMIL Ahmed	A. GAMIL	12-4-1986	Zamalek	179	74	3	146		1	
21	GK	ADEL Ahmed	A. ADEL	10-4-1987	Al Ahly	178	73	0	0			

ESP – SPAIN YOUTH SQUAD

No	Pos	Name	Shirt Name	DoB	Club	Cms	Kg	Games	Mins	Goals	Y	R
1	GK	BIEL RIBAS	BIEL RIBAS	2-12-1985	Espanyol Barcelona	184	80	4	360			
2	DF	MOLINERO	MOLINERO	26-7-1985	Atlético Madrid	179	73	4	360	1		
3	DF	GARRIDO	GARRIDO	15-3-1985	Real Sociedad	180	74	2	131		1	
4	DF	ALEXIS	ALEXIS	4-8-1985	Malaga	185	73	4	360		1	
5	DF	ROBUSTE	ROBUSTE	20-5-1985	Espanyol Barcelona	183	80	4	360	2	1	
6	MF	RAUL ALBIOL	R. ALBIOL	4-9-1985	Getafe	187	77	3	151		1	
7	MF	JUANFRAN	JUANFRAN	9-1-1985	Real Madrid	181	70	4	308	2	1	
8	MF	ZAPATER	ZAPATER	13-6-1985	Real Zaragoza	179	80	5	382	1		
9	FW	LLORENTE	LLORENTE	26-2-1985	Athletic Bilbao	194	88	4	316	5		
10	MF	JONA	JONA	24-9-1985	Espanyol Barcelona	180	72	4	163	1		
11	MF	GAVILAN	J. GAVILAN	12-5-1985	Tenerife	178	72	5	241			
12	DF	JOSE ENRIQUE	JOSE ENRIQUE	23-1-1986	Levante	175	75	4	319			
13	GK	MANU	MANU	9-5-1986	Sporting Gijon	182	76	1	76			
14	DF	AGUS	AGUS	3-5-1985	Albacete	174	70	1	90			
15	DF	CHICA	CHICA	17-5-1985	Espanyol Barcelona	179	76	1	90			
16	MF	SILVA	SILVA	8-1-1986	Eibar	177	76	5	275	4		
17	MF	CESC	CESC	4-5-1987	Arsenal	175	70	5	378		1	
18	FW	VICTOR	VICTOR	28-2-1985	Mallorca	179	78	3	126	1		
19	FW	BRAULIO	BRAULIO	18-9-1985	Atlético Madrid	182	78	1	90			
20	MF	MARKEL	MARKEL	5-5-1986	Real Sociedad	180	74	5	360		1	
21	GK	ROBERTO	ROBERTO	10-2-1986	Atlético Madrid	191	85	1	14			1

GER – GERMANY YOUTH SQUAD

No	Pos	Name	Shirt Name	DoB	Club	Cms	Kg	Games	Mins	Goals	Y	R
1	GK	ADLER Rene	ADLER R.	15-1-1985	Bayer Leverkusen	189	80	5	480			
2	DF	JANKER Christoph	JANKER	14-2-1985	TSV München 1860	185	73	5	419			
3	DF	COMPPER Marvin	COMPPER	14-6-1985	Borussia Mön'gladbach	186	70	3	185		1	
4	DF	MATIP Marvin	MATIP	25-9-1985	1.FC Köln	183	80	5	480	2	2	
5	DF	SCHUON Marcel	SCHUON	28-4-1985	VfB Stuttgart	181	75	4	390		2	
6	MF	OTTL Andreas	OTTL	1-3-1985	Bayern München	185	76	3	201		1	
7	FW	DELURA Michael	DELURA	1-7-1985	Schalke 04	190	83	5	434	1		
8	MF	GENTNER Christian	GENTNER	14-8-1985	VfB Stuttgart	187	73	4	390	1		
9	FW	ADLER Nicky	ADLER N.	23-5-1985	TSV München 1860	182	72	4	228	2	1	
10	MF	SENESIE Sahr	SENESIE	20-6-1985	Grasshopper-Club	173	74	4	140		1	
11	MF	JANSEN Marcell	JANSEN	4-11-1985	Borussia Mön'gladbach	191	72	5	460		2	
12	GK	TSCHAUNER Philipp	TSCHAUNER	3-11-1985	1.FC Nürnberg	196	93	0	0			
13	MF	HUBER Alexander	HUBER	25-2-1985	Eintracht Frankfurt	174	64	2	151	1		
14	DF	REINHARD Christopher	REINHARD	19-5-1985	Eintracht Frankfurt	180	72	4	270		1	
15	FW	FREIS Sebastian	FREIS	23-4-1985	Karlsruher SC	184	76	2	117			
16	MF	HAMPEL Oliver	HAMPEL	2-3-1985	Hamburger SV	170	88	1	45			
17	MF	CIMEN Daniyel	CIMEN	19-1-1985	Eintracht Frankfurt	180	75	5	480			
18	DF	THOMIK Paul	THOMIK	25-1-1985	Bayern München	178	67	4	318			
19	FW	BROEKER Thomas	BROKER	22-1-1985	1.FC Köln	188	81	1	41			
20	DF	BANECKI Francis	BANECKI	17-7-1985	Werder Bremen	192	94	3	51			
21	GK	DOMASCHKE Erik	DOMASCHKE	11-11-1985	FC Sachsen Leipzig	184	79	0	0			

HON – HONDURAS YOUTH SQUAD

No	Pos	Name	Shirt Name	DoB	Club	Cms	Kg	Games	Mins	Goals	Y	R
1	GK	GUERRA Angel	ORELLANA	1-4-1986	Olimpia	185	81	3	257			
2	DF	BODDEN Roy	R. BODDEN	3-2-1986	Estrella	184	73	2	137			
3	DF	TURCIOS Nery	N. TURCIOS	30-4-1985	Groningen	180	76	1	17			1
4	DF	BARDALES Aron	BARDALES	3-12-1985	Olimpia	184	81	2	180			
5	DF	NORALES Erick	E. NORALES	11-2-1985	Vida	180	75	2	270	1		
6	DF	MONCADA Rene	MONCADA	1-6-1985	Olimpia	183	75	2	180			
7	DF	RAMOS Luis	L. RAMOS	11-4-1985	Marathon	178	68	2	135	2		
8	MF	CLAROS Jorge	J. CLAROS	8-1-1986	Vida	176	67	2	100	1		
9	FW	RICE Walter	W. RICE	22-12-1987	Real Espana	182	67	1	12			
10	FW	NUNEZ Ramon	R. NUNEZ	14-11-1985	Dallas	164	68	3	270			
11	FW	GUITY Jose	J. GUITY	19-5-1985	Marathon	184	72	3	225			
12	GK	RIVERA Orlando	O. RIVERA	10-3-1985	Marathon	182	72	0	0			
13	DF	CRUZ Fernando	C. AVILA	8-8-1988	Platense	168	76	3	225			
14	FW	CRUZ Jose	ARMANDO C.	3-1-1985	Real Espana	182	76	3	244	1		
15	DF	MARTINEZ Maynor	MAYNOR M.	8-4-1985	Real Espana	171	62	3	196	2		
16	MF	LARA Nataury	LARA	19-8-1985	La Mesa	165	66	2	168	1		
17	MF	IZAGUIRRE Emilio	E. IZAGUIRRE	10-5-1986	Motagua	178	79	2	146			
18	FW	NOLASCO Angel	NOLASCO	2-11-1986	Platense	180	72	2	61			
19	MF	SANCHEZ Marvin	M. SANCHEZ	2-11-1986	Platense	173	63	1	45			
20	MF	RAPALO Julian	RAPALO	9-8-1986	Villanueva	175	66	1	18			
21	GK	PINEDA Fernando	PINEDA B.	15-2-1985	Villanueva	191	80	1	13			

ITA – ITALY YOUTH SQUAD

No	Pos	Name	Shirt Name	DoB	Club	Cms	Kg	Games	Mins	Goals	Y	R
1	GK	VIVIANO Emiliano	VIVIANO	1-12-1985	Cesena	195	90	5	480		1	
2	DF	MARZORATTI Lino	MARZORATTI	12-10-1986	Milan	181	75	5	480		2	
3	DF	D AGOSTINO Andrea	D AGOSTINO	4-7-1985	Foggia	183	75	2	151		2	
4	MF	NOCERINO Antonio	NOCERINO	9-4-1985	Catanzaro	175	74	5	480		2	
5	DF	CODA Andrea	CODA	25-4-1985	Empoli	188	81	5	445	1	1	
6	DF	CANINI Michele	CANINI	5-6-1985	Sanbenedettese	187	80	4	369	1		1
7	MF	DEFENDI Marino	DEFENDI	19-8-1985	Atalanta Bergamo	174	70	5	473		2	
8	MF	CAROTTI Lorenzo	CAROTTI	31-1-1985	Como	172	75	4	224		1	
9	FW	PELLE Graziano	PELLE	15-7-1985	Catania	193	89	5	462	4		
10	MF	TROIANO Michele	TROIANO	7-1-1985	Modena	188	82	2	155			
11	MF	GALLOPPA Daniele	GALLOPPA	15-5-1985	Triestina	180	71	5	448	2	2	
12	GK	VIRGILI Fabio	VIRGILI	26-4-1986	Parma	186	81	0	0			
13	DF	BATTAGLIA Francesco	BATTAGLIA	26-4-1985	Torino	186	77	4	199			
14	DF	DI DIO Palmiro	DI DIO	6-7-1985	Ternana	185	81	0	0			
15	DF	AQUILANTI Antonio	AQUILANTI	8-11-1985	Fiorentina	177	74	3	249			
16	MF	BENTIVOGLIO Simone	BENTIVOGLIO	29-5-1985	Juventus	183	75	5	326		1	
17	MF	DE MARTINO Raffaele	DE MARTINO	8-4-1986	Bellinzona	181	76	3	152	1	1	
18	MF	AGNELLI Cristian	AGNELLI	23-9-1985	Catanzaro	172	70	2	104		1	
19	FW	NIETO Francesco	NIETO	17-6-1985	Piacenza	182	79	2	24			
20	FW	COZZOLINO Giuseppe	COZZOLINO	12-8-1985	Lecce	181	74	0	38			
21	GK	PADELLI Daniele	PADELLI	25-10-1985	Sampdoria	192	82		0			

JPN – JAPAN YOUTH SQUAD

No	Pos	Name	Shirt Name	DoB	Club	Cms	Kg	Games	Mins	Goals	Y	R
1	GK	MATSUI Kenya	MATSUI	10-9-1985	Jubilo Iwata	186	72	0	0			
2	DF	MIZUMOTO Hiroki	MIZUMOTO	12-9-1985	JEF United Ichihara	183	72	4	360			
3	DF	YOSHIHIRO Mitsuyuki	YOSHIHIRO	4-5-1985	Sanfrecce Hiroshima	181	72	0	0			
4	DF	KOBAYASHI Yuzo	KOBAYASHI	15-11-1985	Kashiwa Reysol	175	72	4	360			
5	DF	MASUSHIMA Tatsuya	MASUSHIMA	22-4-1985	FC Tokyo	180	74	4	349		1	
6	MF	INOHA Masahiko	INOHA	28-8-1985	Hannan University	177	72	0	0			
7	MF	KAJIYAMA Yohei	KAJIYAMA	24-9-1985	FC Tokyo	180	77	3	225			
8	MF	NAKAMURA Hokuto	NAKAMURA	10-7-1985	Avispa Fukuoka	167	64	4	360			
9	FW	HIRAYAMA Sota	HIRAYAMA	6-6-1985	Tsukuba University	190	81	4	360	1	1	
10	MF	HYODO Shingo	HYODO	29-7-1985	Waseda University	170	60	4	265			
11	FW	CULLEN Robert	CULLEN	7-6-1985	Jubilo Iwata	180	72	4	305			
12	DF	MIZUNO Koki	MIZUNO	6-9-1985	JEF United Ichihara	173	58	4	166	1		
13	MF	KOKEGUCHI Takuya	KOKEGUCHI	13-7-1985	Cerezo Osaka	179	71	2	47			
14	FW	HONDA Keisuke	HONDA	13-6-1986	Nagoya Grampus Eight	181	74	1	64			
15	MF	FUNATANI Keisuke	FUNATANI	7-1-1986	Jubilo Iwata	174	63	0	0			
16	DF	NAGIRA Tomokazu	NAGIRA	17-10-1985	Avispa Fukuoka	178	74	4	360			
17	DF	IENAGA Akihiro	IENAGA	13-6-1986	Gamba Osaka	173	70	4	280		1	
18	GK	YAMAMOTO Kaito	YAMAMOTO	10-7-1985	Shimizu S-Pulse	188	78	0	0			
19	FW	MAEDA Shunsuke	MAEDA	9-6-1986	Sanfrecce Hiroshima	173	70	2	62	1	1	
20	FW	MORIMOTO Takayuki	MORIMOTO	7-5-1988	Tokyo Verdy 1969	182	75	4	37			
21	GK	NISHIKAWA Shusaku	NISHIKAWA	18-6-1986	Oita Trinita	183	79	4	360			

KOR – KOREA REPUBLIC YOUTH SQUAD

No	Pos	Name	Shirt Name	DoB	Club	Cms	Kg	Games	Mins	Goals	Y	R
1	GK	CHA Ki Seok	K S CHA	26-12-1986	Chunnam Dragons	195	87	3	270			
2	DF	PARK Hee Chul	H C PARK	7-1-1986	Hongik University	178	70	1	135			
3	DF	AHN Tae Eun	T E AHN	17-9-1985	Mipo Chosun Univ.	177	70	2	160			
4	DF	LEE Yoo Han	Y H LEE	18-12-1985	Incheon United	182	72	3	191			
5	DF	JUNG In Whan	I W JUNG	15-12-1986	Yonsei University	185	76	0	0			
6	DF	KIM Jin Kyu	J K KIM	16-2-1985	Jubilo Iwata	184	80	3	270			
7	MF	BAEK Seung Min	S M BAEK	12-3-1986	Yonsei University	173	65	3	270		1	
8	MF	BAEK Ji Hoon	J H BAEK	28-2-1985	FC Seoul	174	60	3	270	1		
9	MF	OH Jang Eun	J E OH	24-7-1985	Daegu	175	73	3	206			
10	FW	PARK Chu Young	C Y PARK	10-7-1985	FC Seoul	182	70	3	270	1		
11	MF	LEE Gen Ho	G H LEE	11-4-1985	Incheon United	176	72	0	0			
12	GK	JUNG Sung Ryong	S R JUNG	4-1-1985	Pohang Steelers	189	85	0	0			
13	FW	SHIN Hyung Min	H M SHIN	18-7-1986	Hongik University	181	74	1	34			
14	MF	PARK Jong Jin	J J PARK	24-6-1987	Suwon HS	178	65	3	49			
15	MF	HWANG Kyu Hwan	K H HWANG	18-6-1986	Suwon Bluewings	178	73	0	0			
16	FW	SIM Woo Yeon	W Y SIM	3-4-1985	Konkuk University	195	78	2	62	1		
17	FW	LEE Sung Hyun	S H LEE	25-7-1985	Hanyang University	174	67	2	17			
18	FW	KIM Seung Yong	S Y KIM	14-3-1985	FC Seoul	181	73	3	236			
19	FW	SHIN Young Rok	Y R SHIN	27-3-1987	Suwon Bluewings	180	70	3	260	1	1	
20	DF	LEE Gang Jin	G J LEE	25-4-1986	Tokyo Verdy 1969	184	75	3	270			
21	GK	KIM Dae Ho	D H KIM	15-4-1986	Soongsil University	184	75	0	0			

MAR – MOROCCO YOUTH SQUAD

No	Pos	Name	Shirt Name	DoB	Club	Cms	Kg	Games	Mins	Goals	Y	R
1	GK	BOURKADI Mohammed	BOURKADI	22-2-1985	MAS Fes	185	72	7	660		1	
2	DF	EL AMRANI Hicham	EL AMRANI	25-11-1985	Rachad Bernoussi	188	75	3	231		2	
3	MF	BENZOUKANE Chakib	BENZOUKANE	7-8-1986	Kawkab Marakech	183	79	7	608		2	
4	DF	KANTARI Ahmed	KANTARI	28-6-1985	Paris St-Germain	186	78	1	52			
5	DF	RABEH Youssef	RABEH	13-4-1985	FUS Rabat	182	75	7	660		2	
6	DF	MSSASSI Abderrahmane	MSSASSI	24-3-1985	MAS Fes	184	77	2	180			
7	MF	HERMACH Adil	HERMACH	27-6-1986	Lens	178	72	6	570		3	
8	DF	BENZOUIEN Sofian	BENZOUIEN	11-8-1986	Heusden-Zolder	178	68	7	660			
9	FW	IAJOUR Mouhssine	IAJOUR	14-6-1985	Raja Club Athletic	182	80	6	557	3	1	1
10	FW	EL ZHAR Nabil	EL ZHAR	27-8-1986	Saint-Etienne	175	72	7	660	1	1	
11	FW	BENDAMOU Tarik	BENDAMOU	14-1-1985	Raja Club Athletic	171	69	7	551	2	1	
12	GK	IRAQUI Yahia	IRAQUI	29-2-1988	WAC Casablanca	182	71	0	0			
13	DF	SBAI Salah	SBAI	21-8-1985	Ronse	180	72	4	390		3	
14	MF	TIBERKANINE Rachid	TIBERKANINE	28-3-1985	Ajax Amsterdam	173	68	5	355		1	
15	MF	DOULYAZAL Rida	DOULYAZAL	3-9-1985	WAC Casablanca	174	68	4	229		1	1
16	MF	EL AHMADI Karim	EL AHMADI	27-1-1985	Twente Enschede	181	73	5	438			
17	MF	ZOUCHOU Yassine	ZOUCHOU	26-7-1985	WAC Casablanca	180	66	5	138		1	1
18	DF	FATAH Said	FATAH	15-1-1986	Raja Club Athletic	174	60	2	91		1	
19	FW	BENJELLOUN Abdessalam	BENJELLOUN	28-1-1985	MAS Fes	185	81	2	56	1		
20	FW	CHIHI Adil	CHIHI	21-2-1988	1.FC Köln	179	70	4	163	1	1	
21	GK	ATTA Mourad	ATTA	1-1-1985	WAC Casablanca	184	74	0	0			

NED – NETHERLANDS YOUTH SQUAD

No	Pos	Name	Shirt Name	DoB	Club	Cms	Kg	Games	Mins	Goals	Y	R
1	GK	VERMEER Kenneth	VERMEER	10-1-1986	Ajax Amsterdam	182	79	5	480			
2	DF	TIENDALLI Dwight	TIENDALLI	21-10-1985	Utrecht	180	69	5	480		1	
3	DF	VLAAR Ron	VLAAR	16-2-1985	Alkmaar	189	80	5	480	1	1	
4	DF	VAN DER STRUIJK Frank	VAN DER STRUIJK	28-3-1985	Willem II	183	69	4	376			
5	DF	DROST Jeroen	DROST	21-1-1987	Heerenveen	184	74	4	390			
6	DF	MADURO Hedwiges	MADURO	13-2-1985	Ajax Amsterdam	185	72	5	477	2	1	
7	FW	OWUSU ABEYIE Quincy	OWUSU-ABEYIE	15-4-1986	Arsenal	180	74	5	421	1		
8	MF	KRUYS Rick	KRUYS	9-5-1985	Utrecht	177	71	5	457	1		
9	FW	JOHN Collins	JOHN	17-10-1985	Fulham	185	80	4	119	1	1	
10	MF	AFELLAY Ibrahim	AFELLAY	2-4-1986	PSV Eindhoven	180	65	2	117	1	1	
11	FW	BABEL Ryan	BABEL	19-12-1986	Ajax Amsterdam	185	74	4	356	2		
12	DF	ZUIVERLOON Gianni	ZUIVERLOON	30-12-1986	Feyenoord Rotterdam	179	70	3	140			
13	DF	OTTEN Mark	OTTEN	2-9-1985	Excelsior Rotterdam	179	77	1	14			
14	MF	MEDUNJANIN Haris	MEDUNJANIN	8-3-1985	Alkmaar	188	78	2	24			
15	MF	EMANUELSON Urby	EMANUELSON	16-6-1986	Ajax Amsterdam	176	68	4	320	1	1	
16	GK	BRACK Theo	BRACK	10-2-1985	Zwolle	184	74	0	0			
17	MF	AGUSTIEN Kemy	AGUSTIEN	20-8-1986	Willem II	175	70	2	86			
18	FW	VINCKEN Tim	VINCKEN	12-9-1986	Feyenoord Rotterdam	174	65	5	390		2	
19	FW	RAJCOMAR Prince	RAJCOMAR	25-4-1985	Utrecht	185	77	2	108	1		
20	FW	WISSE Arjan	WISSE	10-6-1985	Alkmaar	189	81	1	45			
21	GK	BULTERS Job	BULTERS	22-3-1986	Alkmaar	188	78	0	0			

NGA – NIGERIA YOUTH SQUAD

No	Pos	Name	Shirt Name	DoB	Club	Cms	Kg	Games	Mins	Goals	Y	R
1	GK	VANZEKIN Ambruse	VANZEKIN	14/7/86	Bendel Insurance	178	74	7	660		1	
2	DF	CHINWO Kennedy	CHINWO	29/12/85	Dolphin	158	75	3	244		3	
3	DF	TAIWO Taye	TAIWO	16/4/85	Olympique de Marseille	186	84	7	660	2	1	
4	DF	APAM Onyekachi	APAM	30/12/86	Enugu Rangers	160	75	6	570		2	
5	DF	JAMES Monday	JAMES	19/10/86	Bendel Insurance	177	72	5	450		2	
6	MF	ADEDEJI Yinka	ADEDEJI	24/3/85	Sundsvalls	158	62	4	152			
7	MF	OGBUKE Chinedu	OGBUKE	1/6/86	Lyn	179	65	6	457	3		
8	MF	BAZUAYE Daddy	BAZUAYE	11/12/88	Bendel Insurance	179	80	2	24			
9	MF	MIKEL John Obi	MIKEL	22/4/87	Lyn	160	70	7	656		2	
10	FW	ISAAC Promise	ISAAC	2/12/87	Grays International	177	78	6	532	1	1	
11	FW	OKORONKWO Solomon	OKORONKWO	2/3/87	Hertha Berlin	182	72	6	243	1	1	
12	GK	AKPEYI Daniel	AKPEYI	3/8/86	Gabros International	186	89	0	0			
13	DF	ADEFEMI Olubayo	ADEFEMI	13/8/85	Hapoel Jerusalem	186	80	5	416	1	1	
14	FW	ABWO David	ABWO	10/5/86	Enyimba	150	58	7	617	1		
15	MF	SAMBO Soga	SAMBO	5/10/85	3SC Ibadan	155	75	3	124			
16	FW	ATULEWA Gift	ATULEWA	1/4/86	Bayelsa United	158	60	3	34	1		
17	DF	ADELEYE Dele	ADELEYE	25/12/88	3SC Ibadan	165	72	3	300		1	
18	MF	ANUBI Kola	ANUBI	24/3/87	Bendel Insurance	174	66	2	2		1	
19	MF	KAITA Sani	KAITA	2/5/86	Kano Pillars	169	76	7	655		2	
20	FW	OWOERI John	OWOERI	13/1/87	Bendel Insurance	158	62	6	464	1	1	
21	GK	IGE Kola	KOLA	28/12/85	3SC Ibadan	186	76	0	0			

PAN – PANAMA YOUTH SQUAD

No	Pos	Name	Shirt Name	DoB	Club	Cms	Kg	Games	Mins	Goals	Y	R
1	GK	CALDERON Jose	CALDERON	14-8-1985	San Francisco	183	73	3	270		1	
2	DF	DUNN Tomas	DUNN	14-8-1985	Chepo	181	79	1	90			
3	DF	GUN Armando	GUN	17-1-1986	Chorrillo	175	77	3	270			
4	DF	TORRES Roman	TORRES	20-3-1986	Chepo	181	90	3	270	2		
5	DF	VENEGAS Jose	VENEGAS	20-2-1985	Deportivo Atenas	192	75	3	270	1		
6	MF	POLO Celso	POLO	19-3-1987	Chepo	166	70	2	75			
7	FW	AROSEMENA Reggie	REGGIE	9-9-1986	Tauro	174	59	3	244			
8	FW	VEGA Cristian	VEGA	2-4-1985	Deportes Tolima	181	73	2	180	2		
9	FW	AGUILAR Edwin	AGUILAR	7-8-1985	Tauro	184	75	3	270	1		
10	MF	CASTILLO Miguel	CASTILLO	8-11-1986	Deportivo Atenas	175	76	1	60			
11	FW	ARRUE David	ARRUE	11-4-1985	Deportivo Italia	173	75	3	49			
12	GK	HUGHES Erick	HUGHES	11-9-1986	Tauro	187	75	0	0			
13	MF	LOO Raul	LOO	25-6-1986	Deportivo Arabe Unido	175	80	2	180		13	
14	MF	PONCE Eduardo	PONCE	29-11-1985	Chepo	175	61	1	45			
15	MF	HILL Hanamell	HILL	12-3-1986	San Francisco	169	62	3	225			
16	MF	GALLARDO Luis	GALLARDO	27-6-1986	Columbus Crew	176	78	3	181			
17	FW	SALAZAR Alvaro	SALAZAR	22-11-1985	Deportivo Arabe Unido	171	73	3	183			
18	MF	BUITRAGO Ricardo	BUITRAGO	10-3-1986	Plaza Amador	178	74	1	67			
19	FW	JIMENEZ Eduardo	JIMENEZ	2-4-1986	San Francisco	169	70	1	32			
20	FW	DUARTE Mario	DUARTE	24-8-1985	Atletico Chiriqui	178	65	1	9			
21	GK	RODRIGUEZ Ivan	RODRIGUEZ	18-6-1988	No club affiliation	166	68	0	0			

SUI – SWITZERLAND YOUTH SQUAD

No	Pos	Name	Shirt Name	DoB	Club	Cms	Kg	Games	Mins	Goals	Y	R
1	GK	KOENIG Swen	KÖNIG	3-9-1985	Aarau	185	78	2	180			
2	DF	COKMUS Ferhat	COKMUS	14-2-1985	Young Boys	180	74	0	0			
3	DF	BUEHLER Arnaud	BUEHLER	17-1-1985	Aarau	188	72	3	270		1	
4	MF	DJOUROU Johan	DJOUROU	18-1-1987	Arsenal	192	89	3	242		1	
5	DF	SENDEROS Philippe	SENDEROS	14-2-1985	Arsenal	190	87	3	270		1	
6	DF	SALATIC Veroljub	SALATIC	14-11-1985	Grasshopper-Club	186	88	3	270		1	
7	MF	BARNETTA Tranquillo	BARNETTA	22-5-1985	Hannover 96	176	62	3	270		1	
8	FW	ANTIC Goran	ANTIC	4-7-1985	Wil	180	82	3	226	1	1	
9	FW	VONLANTHEN Johan	VONLANTHEN	1-2-1986	Brescia	175	72	3	270	1	1	
10	MF	ZAMBRELLA Fabrizio	ZAMBRELLA	1-3-1986	Brescia	181	88	3	224			
11	MF	ZIEGLER Reto	ZIEGLER	16-1-1986	Tottenham Hotspur	183	83	3	241			
12	GK	LOPAR Daniel	LOPAR	19-4-1985	Wil	187	84	1	90			
13	DF	SIQUEIRA Henry	SIQUEIRA	15-1-1985	Neuchatel Xamax	180	75	0	0			
14	MF	BURKI Sandro	BURKI	16-9-1985	Wil	188	73	0	0			
15	FW	SCHNEUWLY Marco	SCHNEUWLY	27-3-1985	Young Boys	181	86	0	0			
16	MF	SCHWEGLER Pirmin	SCHWEGLER	9-3-1987	Lucerne	178	74	3	50			
17	DF	STAHEL Florian	STAHEL	10-3-1985	FC Zurich	184	74	3	75			
18	MF	SCHLAURI Christian	SCHLAURI	30-3-1985	Basel	181	75	0	0			
19	FW	AFONSO Guilherme	AFONSO	15-11-1985	Twente Enschede	186	79	3	44			
20	MF	DZEMAILI Blerim	DZEMAILI	12-4-1986	FC Zurich	179	73	3	248		1	
21	GK	GONZALEZ David	GONZALEZ	9-11-1986	Servette	185	75	0	0			

SYR – SYRIA YOUTH SQUAD

No	Pos	Name	Shirt Name	DoB	Club	Cms	Kg	Games	Mins	Goals	Y	R
1	GK	AL HAFEZ Adnan	AL HAFEZ	23-4-1986	Al Karama	184	76	3	270		1	
2	MF	ALDAMEN Mohammad	ALDAMEN	25-1-1986	Al Ittihad	174	64	0	0			
3	MF	ALATASI Safir	ALATASI	11-4-1985	Al Karama	173	70	0	0			
4	DF	KHALAF Abdul	KHALAF	1-1-1986	Al Karama	175	67	3	268			
5	DF	AL AITONI Hamzeh	AL AITONI	16-1-1986	Al Majd	181	70	3	270		1	
6	DF	AL MOSTAFA Hasan	AL MOSTAFA	1-1-1986	Horriya	183	74	4	360		2	
7	MF	KAILOUNI Meaataz	KAILOUNI	10-3-1985	Teshrin	182	71	4	345		2	
8	MF	ALHOUSAIN Abd	ALHOUSAIN	15-9-1986	Horriya	185	79	3	270	1	1	
9	MF	OSSI Mahmoud	OSSI	25-3-1987	Horriya	160	54	3	181			
10	FW	AL HAMWI Mohammad	AL HAMWI	1-1-1986	Al Karama	170	64	3	225	1		
11	FW	AL ABDI Jalal	AL ABDI	1-1-1986	Al Taliya	184	75	4	335		2	
12	DF	AL KADDOUR Zakariya	AL KADDOUR	1-1-1986	Al Ittihad	176	69	3	52		1	
13	MF	JENYAT Aatef	JENYAT	8-5-1986	Al Karama	173	69	3	270		1	
14	FW	AL HAJ Majed	AL HAJ	6-4-1985	Al Jaish	172	69	4	350	1	1	
15	MF	NAHLOUS Samer	NAHLOUS	5-4-1985	Teshrin	186	78	3	116			
16	GK	AL HOLAMI Ali	AL HOLAMI	5-1-1986	Al Fotowa	191	87	0	0			
17	DF	DAKKA Abd	DAKKA	10-1-1985	Teshrin	183	78	4	360		2	
18	MF	SAHIWNI Bwrhan	SAHIWNI	7-4-1986	Umayya	174	69	2	22			
19	FW	DILY HASSAN Ahmad	DILY HASSAN	20-7-1985	Barada	179	73	1	5			
20	DF	SHAHROUR Salah	SHAHROUR	2-1-88	Al Ittihad	198	75	2	171			
21	GK	SHAKOSH Moustafa	SHAKOSH	1-1-1986	Teshrin	189	72	1	90			

TUR – TURKEY YOUTH SQUAD

No	Pos	Name	Shirt Name	DoB	Club	Cms	Kg	Games	Mins	Goals	Y	R
1	GK	KIRINTILI Serkan	SERKAN	15-2-1985	Ankaragucu	185	78	3	270			
2	DF	UCAR Ugur	UGUR	5-4-1987	Galatasaray	178	65	4	307		1	
3	DF	TEBER Ergun	ERGUN	1-9-1985	Kayserispor	181	74	4	308		2	
4	DF	CAKMAK Yasin	YASIN	6-1-1985	Rizespor	186	80	3	140		1	
5	DF	AK Aytac	AYTAC	22-4-1985	Sakaryaspor	187	80	2	180			
6	MF	SAKAR Zafer	ZAFER	25-9-1985	Galatasaray	169	65	3	270		1	
7	MF	YILMAZ Burak	BURAK	15-7-1985	Antalyaspor	188	75	4	305		1	
8	MF	OZTURK Sezer	SEZER OZTURK	3-11-1985	Bayer Leverkusen	176	73	4	309	1		
9	FW	ZENGIN Kerim	KERIM	13-4-1985	Mersin Idman Yurdu	176	71	4	315			
10	MF	INAN Selcuk	SELCUK	10-2-1985	Dardanelspor	180	72	1	80			
11	FW	ADIN Olcan	OLCAN	30-9-1985	Antalyaspor	176	69	4	360		1	
12	GK	OZCAN Sener	SENER	3-3-1985	Genclerbirligi	185	74	1	90			
13	DF	SEZGIN Sezer	SEZER SEZGIN	3-3-1986	Besiktas	170	69	1	52		1	
14	DF	OZAVCI Murat	MURAT	28-6-1985	Dardanelspor	192	78	4	310		1	
15	DF	TAHTAISLEYEN Ozan	OZAN	18-1-1985	Gaziantepspor	188	78	1	90			
16	FW	GULEC Gokhan	GOKHAN	25-9-1985	Gaziantepspor	183	75	4	245	1	2	
17	FW	KELES Ergin	ERGIN	1-1-1987	Trabzonspor	183	75	2	135		1	
18	MF	GURSOY Gurhan	GURHAN	24-9-1987	Fenerbahce	169	67	2	51			
19	DF	ASLANTAS Hakan	HAKAN	26-8-1985	Genclerbirligi	181	77	1	53		1	
20	FW	OZTURK Ali	ALI	28-7-1986	Genclerbirligi	166	68	3	90			
21	GK	KUCUKERTAS Bekir	BEKIR	25-2-1986	Bakirkoyspor	186	81	0	0			

UKR – UKRAINE YOUTH SQUAD

No	Pos	Name	Shirt Name	DoB	Club	Cms	Kg	Games	Mins	Goals	Y	R
1	GK	MUSIN Leonid	MUSIN	19-4-1985	Dynamo Kyiv	200	78	4	360			
2	DF	GOLOLOBOV Dmytro	GOLOLOBOV	1-1-1985	Obolon Kyiv	201	80	1	90		1	
3	DF	DOPILKA Oleg	DOPILKA	12-3-1986	Dynamo Kyiv	182	71	4	360		1	
4	DF	KITSUTA Anatoliy	KITSUTA	22-12-1985	Dynamo Kyiv	183	73	4	360		1	
5	DF	IATSENKO Oleksandr	IATSENKO	24-2-1985	Dynamo Kyiv	183	74	3	270		2	
6	MF	ROZHOK Sergiy	ROZHOK	25-4-1985	Tavria Symferopol	185	77	3	49			
7	DF	PROSHYN Andriy	PROSHYN	19-2-1985	FK Khimki	190	77	3	198			
8	MF	ALIIEV Oleksandr	ALIIEV	3-2-1985	Dynamo Kyiv	172	66	4	360	3	2	
9	MF	SYTNYK Oleksandr	SYTNYK	2-1-1985	Dynamo Kyiv	179	67	3	239		1	
10	FW	MILEVSKYI Artem	MILEVSKYI	12-1-1985	Dynamo Kyiv	190	78	4	360		1	
11	FW	GLADKYY Oleksandr	GLADKYY	24-8-1987	Arsenal Kharkiv	186	75	1	6			
12	GK	SHUST Bohdan	SHUST	4-3-1986	Karpaty Lviv	188	78	0	0			
13	FW	FESHCHUK Maksym	FESHCHUK	25-11-1985	Karpaty Lviv	177	72	3	94	1	1	
14	MF	ARZHANOV Volodymyr	ARZHANOV	29-11-1985	Metalurh Zaporizhzhya	183	79	2	147		2	
15	DF	YARMASH Grygoriy	YARMASH	4-1-1985	Dynamo Kyiv	171	67	3	260		2	
16	FW	VOROBEI Dmytro	VOROBEI	10-5-1985	Dynamo Kyiv	170	66	4	271	1		
17	MF	SAMBORSKYY Volodymyr	SAMBORSKYY	29-8-1985	Arsenal Kharkiv	171	87	4	360			
18	FW	SILYUK Sergiy	SILYUK	5-6-1985	Metalurh Zaporizhzhya	178	71	1	37			1
19	MF	HERASYMYUK Oleh	HERASYMYUK	25-9-1986	Dynamo Kyiv	178	85	3	86			
20	MF	DERKACH Andriy	DERKACH	28-5-1985	Borysfen Boryspol	184	75	0	0			
21	GK	MARTYSHCHUK Yuriy	MARTYSHCHUK	22-4-1986	Spartak Ivano-Frankivsk	187	80	0	0			

USA – USA YOUTH SQUAD

No	Pos	Name	Shirt Name	DoB	Club	Cms	Kg	Games	Mins	Goals	Y	R
1	GK	WESTBERG Quentin	WESTBERG	25-4-1986	Troyes	185	81	4	360			
2	DF	WYNNE Marvell	WYNNE	8-5-1986	UCLA	175	78	3	270		1	
3	DF	SPECTOR Jonathan	SPECTOR	1-3-1986	Manchester United	183	79	2	128			
4	DF	STURGIS Nathan	STURGIS	6-7-1987	Clemson University	180	70	3	232			
5	DF	IANNI Patrick	IANNI	15-6-1985	UCLA	182	81	4	360			
6	DF	DALBY Greg	DALBY	3-11-1985	Univ. Notre Dame	185	79	3	245			
7	MF	KLJESTAN Sacha	KLJESTAN	9-9-1985	Seton Hall University	185	72	2	115			
8	MF	FEILHABER Benny	FEILHABER	19-1-1985	UCLA	175	68	4	360			
9	FW	BARRETT Chad	BARRETT	30-4-1985	Chicago Fire	180	79	4	283	1		
10	MF	GAVEN Eddie	GAVEN	25-10-1986	MetroStars	182	80	3	270		1	
11	FW	ADU Freddy	ADU	2-6-89	DC United	172	68	4	297		1	
12	MF	JOHN Will	JOHN	13-6-1985	Chicago Fire	175	68	1	71			
13	FW	PETERSON Jacob	PETERSON	27-1-1986	Indiana University	177	74	4	150	1		
14	MF	NGUYEN Lee	NGUYEN	7-10-1986	Dallas Texans	172	68	2	63			
15	DF	FREEMAN Hunter	FREEMAN	8-1-1985	Colorado Rapids	180	77	4	346			
16	MF	HARRINGTON Michael	HARRINGTON	24-1-1986	North Carolina Univ.	182	77	0	0			
17	GK	KARTUNEN Andrew	KARTUNEN	7-2-1985	Stanford University	185	79	0	0			
18	FW	OCHOA Sammy	OCHOA	4-9-1986	Tecos UAG	180	81	4	224			
19	MF	SZETELA Danny	SZETELA	17-6-1987	Columbus Crew	180	77	2	95			
20	MF	EVANS Brad	EVANS	20-4-1985	UC Irvine	185	77	2	91		1	
21	GK	HUGHES Justin	HUGHES	23-4-1985	North Carolina Univ.	185	79	0	0			

FIFA CONFEDERATIONS CUP GERMANY 2005

The FIFA Confederations Cup Germany 2005 turned out to be a great success with capacity crowds, thrilling games and a final that will live long in the memory. With a record 56 goals in the 16 games fans were richly entertained, especialy in the final four matches, which produced an average of nearly five goals a game. The tournament also produced a number of pointers to the FIFA World Cup™ finals in Germany next year with Brazil, Argentina, Germany and also surprise package Mexico all showing that they are developing well. German captain Michael Ballack was particulary encouraged. "We needn't worry about lagging miles behind. We are already on a par," he said. Their continuing failure to beat a top 10 nation is still a source of concern but coach Jürgen Klinsmann was optimistic after the tournament, saying "We still have a great deal to learn, but even if we take a step backwards we are always taking two steps forward." Brazil's form in the tournament was patchy with many expecting them to be beaten by Argentina in the final, but they turned on the style against the Argentines with one of the most complete performances seen for a number of years. Ronaldo's decision to sit out the tournament may backfire on him given the stunning performance of Adriano who capped a display of skill, speed and guile with two goals to finish the tournament as the top scorer with five goals. Ronaldinho was the man of the match in the final but all around him there were players at the top of their game, including the defence which looked impenetrable during the final. "Brazil, for the first time will arrive at a FIFA World Cup™ as absolute favourites," Brazil coach Carlos Alberto Parreira stated after the final. "We have to be sure that this does not adversely affect our performance." Despite their humbling by Brazil in the final, Argentina proved that they have built well since the last FIFA World Cup™ with Juan Riquelme an important element in coach Jose Pekerman's plans. The biggest disappointment were European champions Greece who failed to score a goal and finished bottom of their group. Twelve months on from their extraordinary exploits in Portugal the Greeks have come back down to earth with a bump and have even been made to struggle in their FIFA World Cup™ qualifying group. Off the pitch at the FIFA Confederations Cup the organisers were able to carry out a dummy run for next years FIFA World Cup™ finals and if the atmosphere then is anything like it was at this tournament, fans will be in for a real treat in the summer of 2006.

FIFA CONFEDERATIONS CUP GERMANY 2005

First round groups

	Pts
Germany	7
Argentina	7
Tunisia	3
Australia	0

	Pts
Mexico	7
Brazil	4
Japan	4
Greece	1

Semi-finals

Brazil	3	
Germany	2	

Mexico	1	5p
Argentina	1	6p

Final

Brazil	4
Argentina	1

Third Place play-off

Germany	4
Mexico	3

GROUP A	PL	W	D	L	F	A	PTS		GER	ARG	TUN	AUS
1 Germany	3	2	1	0	9	5	7	GER		2-2	3-0	4-3
2 Argentina	3	2	1	0	8	5	7	ARG			2-1	4-2
3 Tunisia	3	1	0	2	3	5	3	TUN				2-0
4 Australia	3	0	0	3	5	10	0	AUS				

FIFA World Cup Stadium, Köln, 15-06-2005
18:00, 28 033, Rosetti ITA, Griselli ITA, Copelli ITA

ARG   2   1   TUN

Riquelme [33]p, Saviola [57]   Guemamdia [72]p

ARGENTINA				TUNISIA	
12	LUX German			FADHEL Khaled	16
3	SORIN Juan (c)	79		YAHIA Alaeddine	2
6	HEINZE Gabriel			ESSEDIRI Karim	3
8	RIQUELME Juan	46		(c) TRABELSI Hatem	6
9	SAVIOLA Javier	66	46	MHADHEBI Imed	7
13	RODRIGUEZ Gonzalo		78	GUEMAMDIA Haykel	9
16	COLOCCINI Fabricio			MNARI Jawhar	12
17	BERNARDI Lucas			CHADLI Adel	14
18	SANTANA Mario			JAIDI Radhi	15
19	RODRIGUEZ Maximiliano			BENACHOUR Slim	18
22	GALLETTI Luciano			AYARI Anis	19
	Tr: PEKERMAN Jose			Tr: LEMERRE Roger	
4	ZANETTI Javier	79	78	JAZIRI Ziad	5
7	TEVEZ Carlos	66	46	SANTOS	11
			46	HAJ MASSAOUD Amir	23

FIFA World Cup Stadium, Köln, 18-06-2005
18:00, 44 377, Prendergast JAM, Garwood JAM, Taylor TRI

TUN   0   3   GER

Ballack [74]p, Schweinsteiger [80]
Hanke [88]

TUNISIA				GERMANY	
1	BOUMNIJEL Ali			LEHMANN Jens	12
4	ABDI Wissem			FRIEDRICH Arne	3
5	JAZIRI Ziad	83		HUTH Robert	4
6	TRABELSI Hatem (c)			SCHWEINSTEIGER Bastian	7
8	NAFTI Mehdi			FRINGS Torsten	8
10	GHODHBANE Kaies	59		DEISLER Sebastian	10
11	SANTOS		62	(c) BALLACK Michael	13
12	MNARI Jawhar		68	ASAMOAH Gerald	14
14	CHADLI Adel			HITZLSPERGER Thomas	16
15	JAIDI Radhi			MERTESACKER Per	17
20	CLAYTON		87	PODOLSKI Lukas	20
	Tr: LEMERRE Roger			Tr: KLINSMANN Jürgen	
13	NAMOUCHI Hamed	59	87	HANKE Mike	9
17	BEN SAADA Chouki	83	68	SCHNEIDER Bernd	19
			62	KURANYI Kevin	22

Zentralstadion, Leipzig, 21-06-2005
20:45, 23 952, Chandia CHI, Julio CHI, Vargas CHI

AUS   0   2   TUN

Santos 2 [26 70]

AUSTRALIA				TUNISIA	
12	PETKOVIC Michael			KASRAOUI Hamdi	22
3	MOORE Craig (c)			SAIDI Karim	2
4	NEILL Lucas			(c) TRABELSI Hatem	6
5	VIDMAR Tony			NAFTI Mehdi	8
8	SKOKO Josip	61		GUEMAMDIA Haykel	9
9	VIDUKA Mark	46	89	SANTOS	11
11	CHIPPERFIELD Scott	38		MNARI Jawhar	12
14	COLOSIMO Simon			NAMOUCHI Hamed	13
15	ALOISI John		55	CHADLI Adel	14
17	MC KAIN Jon		69	BEN SAADA Chouki	17
19	CULINA Jason			AYARI Anis	19
	Tr: FARINA Frank			Tr: LEMERRE Roger	
10	CAHILL Tim	61	89	JAZIRI Ziad	5
20	MILICEVIC Ljubo	38	69	GHODHBANE Kaies	10
22	THOMPSON Archie	46	55	JOMAA Issam	21

Waldstadion, Frankfurt, 15-06-2005
21:00, 46 466, Amarilla PAR, Andino PAR, Bernal PAR

GER   4   3   AUS

Kuranyi [17], Mertesacker [23]
Ballack [60]p, Podolski [88]   Skoko [21], Aloisi 2 [31 92+]

GERMANY				AUSTRALIA	
1	KAHN Oliver			SCHWARZER Mark	1
3	FRIEDRICH Arne			MUSCAT Kevin	2
4	HUTH Robert			(c) MOORE Craig	3
7	SCHWEINSTEIGER Bastian	83		NEILL Lucas	4
8	FRINGS Torsten		57	POPOVIC Tony	6
13	BALLACK Michael (c)			EMERTON Brett	7
16	HITZLSPERGER Thomas			SKOKO Josip	8
17	MERTESACKER Per		74	CAHILL Tim	10
19	SCHNEIDER Bernd	76	83	CHIPPERFIELD Scott	11
20	PODOLSKI Lukas			ALOISI John	15
22	KURANYI Kevin	68		MILICEVIC Ljubo	20
	Tr: KLINSMANN Jürgen			Tr: FARINA Frank	
10	DEISLER Sebastian	76	57	MC KAIN Jon	17
14	ASAMOAH Gerald	68	74	CULINA Jason	19
15	ERNST Fabian	83	83	THOMPSON Archie	22

Franken-Stadion, Nürnberg, 18-06-2005
20:45, 25 618, Maidin SIN, Permpanich THA, Allaberdyev TKM

AUS   2   4   ARG

Aloisi 2 [61p, 70]   Figueroa 3 [12 53 89], Riquelme [31]p

AUSTRALIA				ARGENTINA	
1	SCHWARZER Mark			LUX German	12
2	MUSCAT Kevin	46		SAMUEL Walter	2
3	MOORE Craig (c)			(c) SORIN Juan	3
4	NEILL Lucas			ZANETTI Javier	4
7	EMERTON Brett			HEINZE Gabriel	6
8	SKOKO Josip	74	73	RIQUELME Juan	8
10	CAHILL Tim		86	SAVIOLA Javier	9
11	CHIPPERFIELD Scott			COLOCCINI Fabricio	16
15	ALOISI John			BERNARDI Lucas	17
20	MILICEVIC Ljubo	56	66	SANTANA Mario	18
	Tr: FARINA Frank			FIGUEROA Luciano	21
9	VIDUKA Mark	46	66	Tr: PEKERMAN Jose	
17	MC KAIN Jon	56	73	CAMBIASSO Esteban	5
19	CULINA Jason	74	86	AIMAR Pablo	10
				RODRIGUEZ Gonzalo	13

Franken-Stadion, Nürnberg, 21-06-2005
20:45, 42 088, Michel SUI, Slysko SVK, Balko SVK

ARG   2   2   GER

Riquelme [33], Cambiasso [74]   Kuranyi [29], Asamoah [51]

ARGENTINA				GERMANY	
12	LUX German			HILDEBRAND Timo	23
2	SAMUEL Walter	62		HINKEL Andreas	2
3	SORIN Juan (c)			HUTH Robert	4
4	ZANETTI Javier		70	SCHWEINSTEIGER Bastian	7
5	CAMBIASSO Esteban			DEISLER Sebastian	10
6	HEINZE Gabriel		58	ASAMOAH Gerald	14
7	TEVEZ Carlos	80		ERNST Fabian	15
8	RIQUELME Juan			HITZLSPERGER Thomas	16
16	COLOCCINI Fabricio			MERTESACKER Per	17
17	BERNARDI Lucas	53	46	(c) SCHNEIDER Bernd	19
21	FIGUEROA Luciano			KURANYI Kevin	22
	Tr: PEKERMAN Jose			Tr: KLINSMANN Jürgen	
10	AIMAR Pablo	53	70	ENGELHARDT Marco	6
11	DELGADO Cesar	80	46	FRINGS Torsten	8
18	SANTANA Mario	62	58	HANKE Mike	9

GROUP B		PL	W	D	L	F	A	PTS	MEX	BRA	JPN	GRE
1	Mexico	3	2	1	0	3	1	7		1-0	2-1	0-0
2	Brazil	3	1	1	1	5	3	4	2-2		3-0	
3	Japan	3	1	1	1	4	4	4				1-0
4	Greece	3	0	1	2	0	4	1				

FIFA World Cup Stadium, Hannover, 16-06-2005
18:00, 24 036, Breeze AUS, Cream AUS, Ouliaris AUS

JPN 1 2 MEX

Yanagisawa [12]   Zinha [39], Fonseca [64]

JAPAN			MEXICO	
23	KAWAGUCHI Yoshikatsu		SANCHEZ Oswaldo	1
2	TANAKA Makoto		GALINDO Aaron	2
3	CHANO Takayuki	82	SALCIDO Carlos	3
5	MIYAMOTO Tsuneyasu (c)		OSORIO Ricardo	5
7	NAKATA Hidetoshi		46	TORRADO Gerardo	6
8	OGASAWARA Mitsuo	68		ZINHA	7
10	NAKAMURA Shunsuke	59		(c) PARDO Pavel	8
13	YANAGISAWA Atsushi		BORGETTI Jared	9
14	SANTOS Alessandro		86	FONSECA Jose	17
15	FUKUNISHI Takashi		CARMONA Salvador	18
21	KAJI Akira		46	LOZANO Jaime	21
	Tr: Zico			Tr: LA VOLPE Ricardo	
9	TAMADA Keiji	82	46	PINEDA Gonzalo	14
16	OGURO Masashi	68	86	RODRIGUEZ Juan Pablo	20
18	INAMOTO Junichi	59	46	PEREZ Luis	22

Zentralstadion, Leipzig, 16-06-2005
20:45, 42 507, Michel SVK, Slysko SVK, Balko SVK

BRA 3 0 GRE

Adriano [41], Robinho [46]
Juninho Pernambuco [81]

BRAZIL			GREECE	
1	DIDA		NIKOPOLIDIS Antonios	1
3	LUCIO		46	SEITARIDIS Giourkas	2
4	ROQUE JUNIOR (c)		KYRGIAKOS Sotirios	5
5	EMERSON		BASINAS Angelos	6
6	GILBERTO		73	(c) ZAGORAKIS Theo	7
7	ROBINHO		GIANNAKOPOULOS Stylianos	8
8	KAKA	77	CHARISTEAS Angelos	9
9	ADRIANO	71	46	VRYZAS Zisis	15
10	RONALDINHO	71	GOUMAS Ioannis	18
11	ZE ROBERTO		KARAGOUNIS Georgios	20
13	CICINHO		KATSOURANIS Konstantinos	21
	Tr: PARREIRA Carlos Alberto			Tr: REHHAGEL Otto	
18	JUNINHO PERNAMBUCANO	77	46	VYNTRA Loukas	3
19	RENATO	71	46	PAPADOPOULOS Dimitrios	11
21	RICARDO OLIVEIRA	71	73	AMANATIDIS Ioannis	17

Waldstadion, Frankfurt, 19-06-2005
18:00, 34 314, Fandel GER, Kadach GER, Wezel GER

GRE 0 1 JPN

Oguro [76]

GREECE			JAPAN	
1	NIKOPOLIDIS Antonios		KAWAGUCHI Yoshikatsu	23
4	TAVLARIDIS Efstathios	31	TANAKA Makoto	2
5	KYRGIAKOS Sotirios		(c) MIYAMOTO Tsuneyasu	5
6	BASINAS Angelos		NAKATA Hidetoshi	7
8	GIANNAKOPOULOS Stylianos		74	OGASAWARA Mitsuo	8
9	CHARISTEAS Angelos		66	TAMADA Keiji	9
14	FYSSAS Panagiotis		89	NAKAMURA Shunsuke	10
15	VRYZAS Zisis (c)	46	YANAGISAWA Atsushi	13
20	KARAGOUNIS Georgios		SANTOS Alessandro	14
21	KATSOURANIS Konstantinos		FUKUNISHI Takashi	15
23	LAKIS Vassilios	59	KAJI Akira	21
	Tr: REHHAGEL Otto			Tr: Zico	
10	TSIARTAS Vassilios	31	74	ENDO Yasuhito	4
11	PAPADOPOULOS Dimitrios	59	89	NAKATA Koji	6
22	GEKAS Theofanis	46	66	OGURO Masashi	16

FIFA World Cup Stadium, Hannover, 19-06-2005
20:45, 43 677, Rosetti ITA, Griselli ITA, Copelli ITA

MEX 1 0 BRA

Borgetti [59]

MEXICO			BRAZIL	
1	SANCHEZ Oswaldo		DIDA	1
2	GALINDO Aaron		LUCIO	3
3	SALCIDO Carlos		(c) ROQUE JUNIOR	4
5	OSORIO Ricardo		66	EMERSON	5
7	ZINHA		GILBERTO	6
8	PARDO Pavel (c)		66	ROBINHO	7
9	BORGETTI Jared		76	KAKA	8
11	MORALES Ramon	73	ADRIANO	9
14	PINEDA Gonzalo	69	RONALDINHO	10
17	FONSECA Jose		46	ZE ROBERTO	11
18	CARMONA Salvador		CICINHO	13
	Tr: LA VOLPE Ricardo			Tr: PARREIRA Carlos Alberto	
16	MENDEZ Mario	69	76	JUNINHO PERNAMBUCANO	18
19	MEDINA Alberto	73	66	RENATO	19
22	PEREZ Luis	46	66	RICARDO OLIVEIRA	21

Waldstadion, Frankfurt, 22-06-2005
20:45, 31 285, Amarilla PAR, Andino PAR, Bernal PAR

GRE 0 0 MEX

GREECE			MEXICO	
1	NIKOPOLIDIS Antonios		SANCHEZ Oswaldo	1
3	VYNTRA Loukas		SALCIDO Carlos	3
6	BASINAS Angelos		OSORIO Ricardo	5
7	ZAGORAKIS Theo (c)		46	(c) PARDO Pavel	8
8	GIANNAKOPOULOS Stylianos		MORALES Ramon	11
9	CHARISTEAS Angelos		PINEDA Gonzalo	14
14	FYSSAS Panagiotis		MENDEZ Mario	16
15	VRYZAS Zisis	61	61	FONSECA Jose	17
17	AMANATIDIS Ioannis	46	RODRIGUEZ Juan Pablo	20
18	GOUMAS Ioannis		73	LOZANO Jaime	21
19	KAPSIS Mihalis	74	PEREZ Luis	22
	Tr: REHHAGEL Otto			Tr: LA VOLPE Ricardo	
4	TAVLARIDIS Efstathios	74	73	MARQUEZ Rafael	4
11	PAPADOPOULOS Dimitrios	61	61	TORRADO Gerardo	6
22	GEKAS Theofanis	46	46	MEDINA Alberto	19

FIFA World Cup Stadium, Köln, 22-06-2005
20:45, 44 922, Daami TUN, Adjengui TUN, Tomusange UGA

JPN 2 2 BRA

Nakamura [27], Oguro [88]   Robinho [10], Ronaldinho [32]

JAPAN			BRAZIL	
23	KAWAGUCHI Yoshikatsu		MARCOS	12
2	TANAKA Makoto		LUCIO	3
5	MIYAMOTO Tsuneyasu (c)		ROBINHO	7
7	NAKATA Hidetoshi		62	KAKA	8
8	OGASAWARA Mitsuo	46	62	ADRIANO	9
9	TAMADA Keiji	46	(c) RONALDINHO	10
10	NAKAMURA Shunsuke		78	ZE ROBERTO	11
13	YANAGISAWA Atsushi	73	CICINHO	13
14	SANTOS Alessandro		JUAN	14
15	FUKUNISHI Takashi		LEO	16
21	KAJI Akira		GILBERTO SILVA	17
	Tr: Zico			Tr: PARREIRA Carlos Alberto	
6	NAKATA Koji	46	62	RENATO	19
11	SUZUKI Takayuki	73	62	JULIO BAPTISTA	20
16	OGURO Masashi	46	78	EDU	22

SEMI-FINALS

Franken-Stadion, Nürnberg, 25-06-2005
18:00, 42 187, Chandia CHI, Julio CHI, Vargas CHI

GER　　2　3　　BRA

Podolski [23], Ballack [48+p]　　Adriano 2 [21 76], Ronaldinho [43p]

GERMANY			BRAZIL	
12	LEHMANN Jens		DIDA	1
3	FRIEDRICH Arne	46	MAICON	2
4	HUTH Robert		LUCIO	3
8	FRINGS Torsten		ROQUE JUNIOR	4
10	DEISLER Sebastian	83	EMERSON	5
13	BALLACK Michael (c)		GILBERTO	6
15	ERNST Fabian	87	87 ROBINHO	7
17	MERTESACKER Per		78 KAKA	8
19	SCHNEIDER Bernd		ADRIANO	9
20	PODOLSKI Lukas		(c) RONALDINHO	10
22	KURANYI Kevin	63	ZE ROBERTO	11
	Tr: KLINSMANN Jürgen		Tr: PARREIRA Carlos Alberto	
9	HANKE Mike	83	46 CICINHO	13
14	ASAMOAH Gerald	63	78 RENATO	19
18	BOROWSKI Tim	87	87 JULIO BAPTISTA	20

FIFA World Cup Stadium, Hannover, 26-06-2005
18:00, 40 718, Rosetti ITA, Griselli ITA, Copelli ITA

MEX　5p　1　1　6p　　ARG

Salcido [104]　　Figueroa [110]

MEXICO			ARGENTINA	
1	SANCHEZ Oswaldo		LUX German	12
3	SALCIDO Carlos		(c) SORIN Juan	3
4	MARQUEZ Rafael	93	ZANETTI Javier	4
5	OSORIO Ricardo		CAMBIASSO Esteban	5
7	ZINHA	94	HEINZE Gabriel	6
8	PARDO Pavel (c)		RIQUELME Juan	8
9	BORGETTI Jared		90 SAVIOLA Javier	9
11	MORALES Ramon	72	66 MILITO Gabriel	14
14	PINEDA Gonzalo		COLOCCINI Fabricio	16
16	MENDEZ Mario		76 SANTANA Mario	18
21	LOZANO Jaime	56	116 FIGUEROA Luciano	21
	Tr: LA VOLPE Ricardo		Tr: PEKERMAN Jose	
6	TORRADO Gerardo	94	76 AIMAR Pablo	10
19	MEDINA Alberto	72	66 RODRIGUEZ Maximiliano	19
22	PEREZ Luis	56	116 GALLETTI Luciano	22

PENALTY SHOOT-OUT

Mexico First		Argentina Second	
PEREZ Luis	✔	RIQUELME Juan	✔
PARDO Pavel	✔	RODRIGUEZ Max	✔
BORGETTI Jared	✔	AIMAR Pablo	✔
SALCIDO Carlos	✔	GALLETTI Luciano	✔
PINEDA Gonzalo	✔	SORIN Juan	✔
OSORIO Ricardo	✘	CAMBIASSO Esteban	✔

Argentina qualify for the final 6-5 on penalties

BRONZE MEDAL PLAY-OFF

Zentralstadion, Leipzig, 29-06-2005
17:45, 43 335, Breeze AUS, Cream AUS, Ouliaris AUS

GER　　4　3　　MEX

Podolski [37], Schweinsteiger [41]　　Fonseca [40], Borgetti 2 [58 85]
Huth [79], Ballack [97]

GERMANY			MEXICO	
1	KAHN Oliver		SANCHEZ Oswaldo	1
2	HINKEL Andreas		SALCIDO Carlos	3
4	HUTH Robert		OSORIO Ricardo	5
7	SCHWEINSTEIGER Bastian	83	ZINHA	7
8	FRINGS Torsten		PARDO Pavel	8
9	HANKE Mike	54	BORGETTI Jared	9
10	DEISLER Sebastian	67	81 MORALES Ramon	11
13	BALLACK Michael		PINEDA Gonzalo	14
17	MERTESACKER Per		58 MENDEZ Mario	16
19	SCHNEIDER Bernd		46 FONSECA Jose	17
20	PODOLSKI Lukas	74	PEREZ Luis	22
	Tr: KLINSMANN Jürgen		Tr: LA VOLPE Ricardo	
14	ASAMOAH Gerald	67	81 MARQUEZ LUGO Rafael	13
15	ERNST Fabian	83	58 MEDINA Alberto	19
22	KURANYI Kevin	74	46 RODRIGUEZ Juan Pablo	20

ADIDAS GOLDEN BALL

1	ADRIANO	BRA
2	RIQUELME Juan	ARG
3	BALLACK Michael	GER

ADIDAS GOLDEN SHOE

			Goals	Assists
1	ADRIANO	BRA	5	0
2	BALLACK Michael	GER	4	1
3	ALOISI John	AUS	4	0

Confederations Cup Final   **Waldstadion, Frankfurt**   **29-06-2005**

Kick-off: 20:45   Attendance: 45 591

BRA   4   1   ARG

Adriano 2 ¹¹ ⁶³, Kaka ¹⁶, Ronaldinho ⁴⁷   Aimar ⁶⁵

	BRAZIL			MATCH STATS				ARGENTINA		
1	GK	DIDA						LUX German	GK	12
3	DF	LUCIO		17	Shots	12		SORIN Juan	DF	3
4	DF	ROQUE JUNIOR		10	Shots on Goal	6		ZANETTI Javier	DF	4
5	MF	EMERSON		24	Fouls Committed	25	56	CAMBIASSO Esteban	MF	5
6	DF	GILBERTO		5	Corner Kicks	8		HEINZE Gabriel	DF	6
7	FW	ROBINHO	90	3	Offside	2		RIQUELME Juan	MF	8
8	MF	KAKA	86	47	Possession %	53	81	DELGADO Cesar	FW	11
9	FW	ADRIANO						PLACENTE Diego	DF	15
10	MF	RONALDINHO			MATCH OFFICIALS			COLOCCINI Fabricio	DF	16
11	MF	ZE ROBERTO			REFEREE			BERNARDI Lucas	MF	17
13	DF	CICINHO	86		MICHEL Lubos SVK		72	FIGUEROA Luciano	FW	21
	Tr: PARREIRA Carlos Alberto				ASSISTANTS			Tr: PEKERMAN Jose		
	Substitutes				SLYSKO Roman SVK			Substitutes		
12	GK	MARCOS			BALKO Martin SVK			FRANCO Leonardo	GK	1
23	GK	GOMES			4TH OFFICIAL			CABALLERO Wilfredo	GK	23
2	DF	MAICON	86		PRENDERGAST Peter JAM			SAMUEL Walter	DF	2
14	DF	JUAN					72	TEVEZ Carlos	FW	7
15	DF	LUISAO						SAVIOLA Javier	FW	9
16	DF	LEO					56	AIMAR Pablo	MF	10
17	MF	GILBERTO SILVA						RODRIGUEZ Gonzalo	DF	13
18	MF	JUNINHO PERNAMBUCANO	90					MILITO Gabriel	DF	14
19	MF	RENATO	86					SANTANA Mario	MF	18
20	MF	JULIO BAPTISTA						RODRIGUEZ Maximiliano	FW	19
21	FW	RICARDO OLIVEIRA						DEMICHELIS Martin	DF	20
22	MF	EDU					81	GALLETTI Luciano	FW	22

This was a really important competition for Brazil. The team showed great spirit tonight, we stuck together, defended well, got into space and we broke quickly. I think we deserved to win the competition.

Carlos Alberto Parreira

We just couldn't get back into the game after what happened at the start. Fair play to Brazil though - they were on fire tonight. We lost against the best, or possibly one of the best sides in the world.

Jose Pekerman

MATCH HIGHLIGHTS

11' Adriano scores with a powerful shot from the edge of the penalty area. 16' Riquelme's shot goes just wide. 16' Robinho passes to Kaka who scores from 18 yards into the top right hand corner. 46+' Lucio's overhead kick goes just high and wide following a free-kick. 47' Ronaldinho flicks home a Cicinho cross from six yards. 51' Coloccini shoots over from six yards following Cambiasso's pass. 52' Lux blocks a Kaka shot having been set up by Ronaldinho. 59' A Robinho shot is deflected off Heinze and hits the bar. 63' Cicinho finds Adriano with a cross who heads home. 65' Aimar heads home to reduce the defecit for Argentina. 82' Dida saves well from Sorin.

MATCH REPORT

A compelling match and a fitting end to a superbly entertaining tournament saw Brazil outclass a very good Argentine team to win the FIFA Confederations Cup. Played against the backdrop of a summer thunderstorm, Brazil were 2-0 up with just over a quarter of an hour gone and never relinquished their grip. Their defence stood firm against everything Argentina threw against it and the attack created a number of good chances. The first two goals came from individual skill on the part of Adriano and Kaka whilst Cicinho provided the crosses for the third and fourth goals.

ARG - ARGENTINA SQUAD

No	Pos	Name	Shirt Name	DoB	Club	Cms	Kg	Games	Mins	Goals	Y	R
1	GK	FRANCO Leonardo	FRANCO	20-05-1977	Atlético Madrid	188	79	0	0			
2	DF	SAMUEL Walter	SAMUEL	23-03-1978	Real Madrid	182	73	2	151		2	
3	DF	SORIN Juan	SORIN	5-05-1976	Villarreal	173	65	5	468		1	
4	DF	ZANETTI Javier	ZANETTI	10-08-1973	Internazionale	178	75	5	402			
5	MF	CAMBIASSO Esteban	CAMBIASSO	18-08-1980	Internazionale	178	73	4	290	1	1	
6	DF	HEINZE Gabriel	HEINZE	19-04-1978	Manchester United	179	78	5	480			
7	FW	TEVEZ Carlos	TEVEZ	5-02-1984	Corinthians	168	67	3	123			
8	MF	RIQUELME Juan	RIQUELME	24-06-1978	Villarreal	182	75	5	480	3		
9	FW	SAVIOLA Javier	SAVIOLA	11-12-1981	Monaco	169	62	3	226	1	1	1
10	MF	AIMAR Pablo	AIMAR	3-11-1979	Valencia	170	62	4	136	1		
11	FW	DELGADO Cesar	DELGADO	18-08-1981	Cruz Azul	174	69	2	91		1	
12	GK	LUX German	LUX	7-06-1982	River Plate	186	78	5	480			
13	DF	RODRIGUEZ Gonzalo	RODRIGUEZ G.	10-04-1984	Villarreal	178	70	2	95		1	
14	DF	MILITO Gabriel	MILITO	7-09-1980	Real Zaragoza	176	70	1	65		1	
15	DF	PLACENTE Diego	PLACENTE	24-04-1977	Bayer Leverkusen	176	72	1	90			
16	DF	COLOCCINI Fabricio	COLOCCINI	22-01-1982	Deportivo La Coruña	183	78	5	475		2	
17	MF	BERNARDI Lucas	BERNARDI	27-09-1977	Monaco	172	69	4	322		1	
18	MF	SANTANA Mario	SANTANA	23-12-1981	Palermo	177	71	4	259			
19	FW	RODRIGUEZ Maximiliano	RODRIGUEZ	2-01-1981	Espanyol	173	73	2	145			
20	DF	DEMICHELIS Martin	DEMICHELIS	20-12-1980	Bayern München	184	80	0	0			
21	FW	FIGUEROA Luciano	FIGUEROA	19-05-1981	Villarreal	181	73	4	366	4		
22	FW	GALLETTI Luciano	GALLETTI	9-04-1980	Real Zaragoza	175	75	3	105			
23	GK	CABALLERO Wilfredo	CABALLERO	28-09-1981	Elche	186	80	0	0			

AUS - AUSTRALIA SQUAD

No	Pos	Name	Shirt Name	DoB	Club	Cms	Kg	Games	Mins	Goals	Y	R
1	GK	SCHWARZER Mark	SCHWARZER	6-10-1972	Middlesbrough	194	92	2	180			
2	DF	MUSCAT Kevin	MUSCAT	7-08-1973	Millwall	178	73	2	135			
3	DF	MOORE Craig	MOORE	12-12-1975	Borussia Mön'gladbach	186	76	3	270		1	
4	DF	NEILL Lucas	NEILL	9-03-1978	Blackburn Rovers	185	78	3	270		1	
5	DF	VIDMAR Tony	VIDMAR	4-07-1970	Cardiff City	186	80	2	180			
6	DF	POPOVIC Tony	POPOVIC	4-07-1973	Crystal Palace	194	83	1	56			
7	MF	EMERTON Brett	EMERTON	22-02-1979	Blackburn Rovers	185	85	2	180		1	
8	MF	SKOKO Josip	SKOKO	10-12-1975	Genclerbirligi	177	77	3	223	1		
9	FW	VIDUKA Mark	VIDUKA	9-10-1975	Middlesbrough	188	91	2	90			
10	MF	CAHILL Tim	CAHILL	6-12-1979	Everton	178	65	3	193		2	
11	MF	CHIPPERFIELD Scott	CHIPPERFIELD	30-12-1975	Basel	180	70	3	209			
12	GK	PETKOVIC Michael	PETKOVIC	16-07-1976	Trabzonspor	190	85	1	90			
13	MF	WILKSHIRE Luke	WILKSHIRE	2-10-1981	Bristol City	176	72	0	0			
14	MF	COLOSIMO Simon	COLOSIMO	8-01-1979	Perth Glory	183	74	1	90		1	
15	FW	ALOISI John	ALOISI	5-02-1976	Atletico Osasuna	184	83	3	270	4		
16	FW	ZDRILIC David	ZDRILIC	13-04-1974	Sydney FC	183	80	0	0			
17	DF	MC KAIN Jon	MC KAIN	21-09-1982	National Bucharest	186	78	3	159		1	
18	GK	KALAC Zeljko	KALAC	16-12-1972	Perugia	202	95	0	0			
19	MF	CULINA Jason	CULINA	5-08-1980	Twente Enschede	175	72	3	124			
20	DF	MILICEVIC Ljubo	MILICEVIC	13-02-1981	Thun	193	88	3	198		1	
21	MF	ELRICH Ahmad	ELRICH	30-05-1981	No club affiliation	183	72	0	0			
22	FW	THOMPSON Archie	THOMPSON	23-10-1978	Lierse	179	70	2	53			
23	MF	STERJOVSKI Mile	STERJOVSKI	27-05-1979	Basle	181	80	0	0			

BRA - BRAZIL SQUAD

No	Pos	Name	Shirt Name	DoB	Club	Cms	Kg	Games	Mins	Goals	Y	R
1	GK	DIDA	DIDA	7-10-1973	Milan	195	85	4	360			
2	DF	MAICON	MAICON	26-07-1981	Monaco	184	85	2	50			
3	DF	LUCIO	LUCIO	8-05-1978	Bayern München	188	81	5	450			
4	DF	ROQUE JUNIOR	ROQUE JR	31-08-1976	Bayer Leverkusen	187	76	4	360		2	
5	MF	EMERSON	EMERSON	4-04-1976	Juventus	184	82	4	335		1	
6	DF	GILBERTO	GILBERTO	25-04-1976	Hertha Berlin	180	78	4	360		1	
7	FW	ROBINHO	ROBINHO	25-01-1984	Santos	172	60	5	420	2		
8	MF	KAKA	KAKA	22-04-1982	Milan	183	73	5	374	1		
9	FW	ADRIANO	ADRIANO	17-02-1982	Internazionale	189	86	5	401	5	1	
10	MF	RONALDINHO	RONALDINHO	21-03-1980	Barcelona	181	80	5	430	3	1	
11	MF	ZE ROBERTO	ZE ROBERTO	6-07-1974	Bayern München	172	71	5	437			
12	GK	MARCOS	MARCOS	4-08-1973	Palmeiras	193	86	1	90			
13	DF	CICINHO	CICINHO	24-06-1980	São Paulo	172	68	5	400		2	
14	DF	JUAN	JUAN	1-02-1979	Bayer Leverkusen	180	72	1	90			
15	DF	LUISAO	LUISAO	13-02-1981	Benfica	192	81	0	0			
16	DF	LEO	LEO	6-07-1975	Santos	169	62	1	90			
17	MF	GILBERTO SILVA	G SILVA	7-10-1976	Arsenal	191	78	1	90			
18	MF	JUNINHO PERNAMBUCANO	JUNINHO PE	30-01-1975	Olympique Lyonnais	179	74	3	30	1		
19	MF	RENATO	RENATO	15-05-1979	Sevilla	178	72	5	92			
20	MF	JULIO BAPTISTA	J BAPTISTA	1-10-1981	Sevilla	183	72	2	33			
21	FW	RICARDO OLIVEIRA	R OLIVEIRA	6-05-1980	Betis	183	82	2	45			
22	MF	EDU	EDU	16-05-1978	Arsenal	186	72	1	13			
23	GK	GOMES	GOMES	15-02-1981	PSV Eindhoven	192	79	0	0			

GER - GERMANY SQUAD

No	Pos	Name	Shirt Name	DoB	Club	Cms	Kg	Games	Mins	Goals	Y	R
1	GK	KAHN Oliver	KAHN	15-06-1969	Bayern München	188	88	2	210			
2	DF	HINKEL Andreas	HINKEL	26-03-1982	VfB Stuttgart	183	74	2	210			
3	DF	FRIEDRICH Arne	FRIEDRICH	29-05-1979	Hertha BSC Berlin	185	78	3	270		2	
4	DF	HUTH Robert	HUTH	18-08-1984	Chelsea	188	82	5	480	1	1	
5	DF	OWOMOYELA Patrick	OWOMOYELA	5-11-1979	Arminia Bielefeld	187	80	0	0			
6	MF	ENGELHARDT Marco	ENGELHARDT	2-12-1980	1.FC Kaiserslautern	186	74	1	21		1	
7	MF	SCHWEINSTEIGER Bastian	SCHWEINSTEIGER	1-08-1984	Bayern München	180	76	4	323	2	2	
8	MF	FRINGS Torsten	FRINGS	22-11-1976	Bayern München	182	80	5	435		1	
9	FW	HANKE Mike	HANKE	5-11-1983	Schalke 04	184	75	4	98	1		1
10	MF	DEISLER Sebastian	DEISLER	5-01-1980	Bayern München	182	78	5	343	2		
11	FW	BRDARIC Thomas	BRDARIC	23-01-1975	VfL Wolfsburg	185	78	0	0			
12	GK	LEHMANN Jens	LEHMANN	10-11-1969	Arsenal	190	87	2	180			
13	MF	BALLACK Michael	BALLACK	26-09-1976	Bayern München	189	80	4	390	4	1	
14	FW	ASAMOAH Gerald	ASAMOAH	3-10-1978	Schalke 04	180	85	5	223	1	1	
15	MF	ERNST Fabian	ERNST	30-05-1979	Werder Bremen	183	80	4	222		1	
16	MF	HITZLSPERGER Thomas	HITZLSPERGER	5-04-1982	Aston Villa	183	77	3	247			
17	DF	MERTESACKER Per	MERTESACKER	29-09-1984	Hannover 96	196	85	5	480	1		
18	MF	BOROWSKI Tim	BOROWSKI	2-05-1980	Werder Bremen	194	84	1	4			
19	MF	SCHNEIDER Bernd	SCHNEIDER	17-11-1973	Bayer Leverkusen	176	74	5	353			
20	FW	PODOLSKI Lukas	PODOLSKI	4-06-1985	1.FC Köln	180	81	4	339	3		
21	DF	SCHULZ Christian	SCHULZ	1-04-1983	Werder Bremen	185	79	0	0			
22	FW	KURANYI Kevin	KURANYI	2-03-1982	VfB Stuttgart	189	80	5	295	2	1	
23	GK	HILDEBRAND Timo	HILDEBRAND	5-04-1979	VfB Stuttgart	185	77	1	90			

GRE - GREECE SQUAD

No	Pos	Name	Shirt Name	DoB	Club	Cms	Kg	Games	Mins	Goals	Y	R
1	GK	NIKOPOLIDIS Antonios	NIKOPOLIDIS	14-01-1971	Olympiakos	187	88	3	270			
2	DF	SEITARIDIS Giourkas	GIOURKAS	4-06-1981	FC Porto	185	79	1	45			
3	DF	VYNTRA Loukas	VYNTRA	5-02-1981	Panathinaikos	184	76	2	135			
4	DF	TAVLARIDIS Efstathios	TAVLARIDIS	25-01-1980	Lille	188	83	2	47		1	
5	DF	KYRGIAKOS Sotirios	KYRGIAKOS	23-07-1979	Glasgow Rangers	192	88	2	180		1	
6	MF	BASINAS Angelos	BASINAS	3-01-1976	Panathinaikos	180	76	3	270			
7	MF	ZAGORAKIS Theo	ZAGORAKIS	27-10-1971	Bologna	178	75	2	162			
8	MF	GIANNAKOPOULOS Stylianos	GIANNAKOPOULOS	12-07-1974	Bolton Wanderers	172	70	3	270			
9	FW	CHARISTEAS Angelos	CHARISTEAS	9-02-1980	Ajax	191	82	3	270			
10	MF	TSIARTAS Vassilios	TSIARTAS	12-11-1972	1.FC Köln	186	75	1	60			
11	FW	PAPADOPOULOS Dimitrios	PAPADOPOULOS	20-10-1981	Panathinaikos	177	71	3	107			
12	GK	CHALKIAS Konstantinos	CHALKIAS	30-05-1974	Portsmouth	199	88	0	0			
13	GK	SIFAKIS Michail	SIFAKIS	9-09-1984	OFI Kreta	189	79	0	0			
14	DF	FYSSAS Panagiotis	FYSSAS	12-06-1973	Benfica	188	80	2	180			
15	FW	VRYZAS Zisis	VRYZAS	9-11-1973	Celta Vigo	182	79	3	150			
16	MF	KAFES Pantelis	KAFES	24-06-1978	Olympiacos	180	76	0	0			
17	FW	AMANATIDIS Ioannis	AMANATIDIS	3-12-1981	Kaiserslautern	181	80	2	63		1	
18	DF	GOUMAS Ioannis	GOUMAS	24-05-1975	Panathinaikos	184	76	2	180			
19	DF	KAPSIS Mihalis	KAPSIS	18-10-1973	Girondins de Bordeaux	182	79	1	73			
20	MF	KARAGOUNIS Georgios	KARAGOUNIS	6-03-1977	Internazionale	176	74	2	180		2	
21	MF	KATSOURANIS Konstantinos	KATSOURANIS	21-06-1979	AEK Athens	183	81	2	180			
22	FW	GEKAS Theofanis	GEKAS	23-05-1980	Panathinaikos	179	76	2	90			
23	MF	LAKIS Vassilios	LAKIS	10-09-1976	Crystal Palace	177	71	1	58			

JPN - JAPAN SQUAD

No	Pos	Name	Shirt Name	DoB	Club	Cms	Kg	Games	Mins	Goals	Y	R
1	GK	NARAZAKI Seigo	NARAZAKI	15-04-1976	Nagoya Grampus Eight	185	76	0	0			
2	DF	TANAKA Makoto	TANAKA	8-08-1975	Jubilo Iwata	178	74	3	270			
3	DF	CHANO Takayuki	CHANO	23-11-1976	Jubilo Iwata	177	74	1	81			
4	MF	ENDO Yasuhito	ENDO	28-01-1980	Gamba Osaka	178	75	1	17			
5	DF	MIYAMOTO Tsuneyasu	MIYAMOTO	7-02-1977	Gamba Osaka	176	72	3	270			
6	MF	NAKATA Koji	K. NAKATA	9-07-1979	Olympique Marseille	182	74	2	47			
7	MF	NAKATA Hidetoshi	NAKATA	22-01-1977	Fiorentina	175	72	3	270		1	
8	MF	OGASAWARA Mitsuo	OGASAWARA	5-04-1979	Kashima Antlers	173	72	3	185			
9	FW	TAMADA Keiji	TAMADA	11-04-1980	Kashiwa Reysol	173	67	3	119			
10	MF	NAKAMURA Shunsuke	NAKAMURA	24-06-1978	Reggina	178	69	3	236	1	1	
11	FW	SUZUKI Takayuki	SUZUKI	5-06-1976	Kashima Antlers	182	75	1	18			
12	GK	DOI Yoichi	DOI	25-07-1973	FC Tokyo	184	83	0	0			
13	FW	YANAGISAWA Atsushi	YANAGISAWA	27-05-1977	Messina	177	75	3	252	1	1	
14	DF	SANTOS Alessandro	ALEX	20-07-1977	Urawa Reds	178	69	3	270			
15	MF	FUKUNISHI Takashi	FUKUNISHI	1-09-1976	Jubilo Iwata	181	77	3	270			
16	FW	OGURO Masashi	OGURO	4-05-1980	Gamba Osaka	177	71	3	93	2		
17	DF	MIURA Atsuhiro	MIURA	24-07-1974	Vissel Kobe	175	73	0	0			
18	MF	INAMOTO Junichi	INAMOTO	18-09-1979	West Bromwich Albion	181	75	1	32			
19	MF	MOTOYAMA Masashi	MOTOYAMA	20-06-1979	Kashima Antlers	175	66	0	0			
20	DF	TSUBOI Keisuke	TSUBOI	16-09-1979	Urawa Reds	179	67	0	0			
21	DF	KAJI Akira	KAJI	13-01-1980	FC Tokyo	177	73	3	270		2	
22	DF	NAKAZAWA Yuji	NAKAZAWA	25-02-1978	Yokohama F Marinos	187	78	0	0			
23	GK	KAWAGUCHI Yoshikatsu	KAWAGUCHI	15-08-1975	Jubilo Iwata	179	78	3	270			

MEX – MEXICO SQUAD

No	Pos	Name	Shirt Name	DoB	Club	Cms	Kg	Games	Mins	Goals	Y	R
1	GK	SANCHEZ Oswaldo	O SANCHEZ	21-09-1973	Guadalajara	184	84	5	510		1	
2	DF	GALINDO Aaron *	A GALINDO	8-05-1982	Cruz Azul	182	80	2	180			
3	DF	SALCIDO Carlos	C SALCIDO	2-04-1980	Guadalajara	177	70	5	510	1	1	
4	DF	MARQUEZ Rafael	R MARQUEZ	13-02-1979	Barcelona	182	74	2	108		2	1
5	DF	OSORIO Ricardo	R OSORIO	30-03-1980	Cruz Azul	173	68	5	510		1	
6	MF	TORRADO Gerardo	G TORRADO	30-04-1979	Racing Santander	173	73	3	102			
7	MF	ZINHA	A NAELSON	23-05-1976	Toluca	163	66	4	393	1		
8	MF	PARDO Pavel	P PARDO	26-07-1976	América	175	67	5	465		1	
9	FW	BORGETTI Jared	J BORGETTI	14-08-1973	Pachuca	182	78	4	420	3		
10	FW	BRAVO Omar	O BRAVO	4-03-1980	Guadalajara	174	72	0	0			
11	MF	MORALES Ramon	R MORALES	10-10-1975	Guadalajara	169	62	4	313			
12	GK	MUNOZ Moises	M MUÑOZ	1-02-1980	Monarcas Morelia	185	82	0	0			
13	FW	MARQUEZ LUGO Rafael	R MARQUEZ	2-11-1981	Atlético Morelia	172	68	1	40			
14	MF	PINEDA Gonzalo	G PINEDA	19-10-1982	Pumas UNAM	175	70	5	443		2	
15	DF	SANCHEZ Hugo	H SANCHEZ	8-05-1981	Tigres	175	68	0	0			
16	DF	MENDEZ Mario	M MENDEZ	1-06-1979	Toluca	175	66	4	289		2	
17	FW	FONSECA Jose	F FONSECA	2-10-1979	Cruz Azul	184	79	4	235	2		
18	DF	CARMONA Salvador *	S CARMONA	22-08-1975	Cruz Azul	176	72	2	180			
19	FW	MEDINA Alberto	A MEDINA	29-05-1983	Guadalajara	172	63	4	175			
20	MF	RODRIGUEZ Juan Pablo	JP RODRIGUEZ	7-08-1979	Tecos UAG	166	68	3	170		1	
21	MF	LOZANO Jaime	J LOZANO	29-09-1979	Pumas UNAM	171	65	3	172			
22	MF	PEREZ Luis	L PEREZ	12-01-1981	Monterrey	170	67	5	365		1	
23	GK	CORONA Jose	JJ CORONA	26-01-1981	Tecos UAG	176	70	0	0			

* Player expelled during the competition after testing positive in doping tests carried out by the Mexican Football Federation before the tournament. The results were received on June 20, 2005 after which the player was sent home

TUN – TUNISIA SQUAD

No	Pos	Name	Shirt Name	DoB	Club	Cms	Kg	Games	Mins	Goals	Y	R
1	GK	BOUMNIJEL Ali	BOUMNIJEL	13-04-1966	Club Africain	188	83	1	90			
2	DF	SAIDI Karim	SAIDI	24-03-1983	Feyenoord	186	76	2	180			
3	FW	ESSEDIRI Karim	ESSEDIRI	29-07-1979	Tromso	185	81	1	90			
4	DF	ABDI Wissem	ABDI	2-04-1979	CS Sfaxien	186	81	1	90		1	
5	FW	JAZIRI Ziad	JAZIRI	12-07-1978	Gaziantepspor	171	71	3	97			
6	DF	TRABELSI Hatem	TRABELSI	25-01-1977	Ajax Amsterdam	179	81	3	225			
7	FW	MHADHEBI Imed	MHADHBI	22-03-1976	Etoile du Sahel	175	70	1	45			
8	MF	NAFTI Mehdi	NAFTI	28-11-1978	Birmingham City	179	77	2	180		1	
9	FW	GUEMAMDIA Haykel	GMAMDIA	22-12-1981	CS Sfaxien	177	71	2	167	1		
10	MF	GHODHBANE Kaies	GHODHBANE	7-01-1976	Samsunspor	184	80	2	80			
11	FW	SANTOS	DOS SANTOS	20-03-1979	Toulouse	172	68	3	223	2		
12	MF	MNARI Jawhar	MNARI	8-11-1976	Espérance	183	83	3	270			
13	FW	NAMOUCHI Hamed	NAMOUCHI	14-02-1984	Glasgow Rangers	183	74	2	122			
14	MF	CHADLI Adel	CHEDLI	16-09-1976	Istres	176	72	3	234			
15	DF	JAIDI Radhi	JAIDI	30-08-1975	Bolton Wanderers	189	89	2	180		2	
16	GK	FADHEL Khaled	FADHEL	29-09-1976	Diyarbakirspor	182	78	1	90			
17	FW	BEN SAADA Chouki	BEN SAADA	1-07-1984	Bastia	171	70	2	76	1		
18	MF	BENACHOUR Slim	BEN ACHOUR	8-09-1981	Paris St-Germain	172	69	1	90			
19	DF	AYARI Anis	AYARI	16-02-1982	Samsunspor	179	75	2	180		1	
20	DF	CLAYTON	CLAYTON	21-03-1974	Espérance	180	77	1	90			
21	FW	JOMAA Issam	JOMAA	28-01-1984	Espérance	185	80	1	36			
22	GK	KASRAOUI Hamdi	KASRAOUI	18-01-1983	Espérance	192	87	1	90			
23	DF	HAJ MASSAOUD Amir	HAJ MASSAOUD	8-02-1981	CS Sfaxien	179	68	1	45			

REVIEW OF WOMEN'S FOOTBALL

FIFA WOMEN'S WORLD RANKING 2003 TO 2005

Country	Code	07-2003	08-2003	10-2003	12-2003	03-2004	06-2004	08-2004	12-2004	03-2005	06-2005
Algeria	ALG			97	96	96	74	78	78	79	
Angola	ANG	87	91	91	82	87	86	87	92	92	93
Argentina	ARG	35	35	38	38	38	37	37	37	37	37
Armenia	ARM	95	100	83	103	103	103	104	109	109	109
Australia	AUS	15	15	16	16	16	16	15	15	15	15
Austria	AUT	48	48	48	47	47	47	46	47	47	47
Bahamas	BAH	96	101	100	101	101	101	102	106	106	106
Belgium	BEL	27	27	27	27	28	28	27	27	27	28
Bermuda	BER	106	111	111	111	111	111				
Bosnia-Herzegovina	BIH	78	81	80	79	79	81	82	85	85	86
Belarus	BLR	42	42	42	43	43	42	41	40	40	41
Belize	BLZ	107	112	112	115	115	115	116	120	120	121
Bolivia	BOL	79	82	81	81	81	80	81	86	86	87
Botswana	BOT	102	107	107	107	107	107	109	114	114	115
Brazil	BRA	6	6	6	6	6	4	4	4	4	4
Bulgaria	BUL	47	47	47	48	48	48	48	48	48	48
Canada	CAN	12	12	11	11	11	11	12	11	11	12
Cayman Islands	CAY	108	113	113	114	114	114	115	119	119	120
Congo	CGO							105	110	110	110
Chile	CHI	50	50	51	51	51	51	51	51	51	51
China PR	CHN	4	4	5	5	5	5	6	6	9	8
Cameroon	CMR	80	83	82	80	80	79	80	82	83	84
Congo DR	COD	36			90	89	89	91	96	96	97
Cook Islands	COK	91	96	96	95	94	94	96	101	101	101
Colombia	COL			36	35	35	35	36	36	35	35
Costa Rica	CRC	45	45	45	46	45	45	45	45	45	46
Croatia	CRO	44	44	44	44	44	44	44	44	44	44
Cyprus	CYP	104	109	109	109	109	109	111	116	116	117
Czech Republic	CZE	24	24	23	22	22	20	20	22	22	22
Denmark	DEN	8	8	8	8	8	9	9	7	7	9
Dominica	DMA	82	86	86	85	83	83	84	88	88	89
Dominican Republic	DOM	92	97	97	100	99	99	100	104	104	104
Ecuador	ECU	51	51	52	52	52	52	52	52	52	52
Egypt	EGY										59
England	ENG	13	13	13	13	13	14	14	14	14	14
Spain	ESP	19	19	20	20	21	21	20	20	20	20
Estonia	EST	76	80	78	78	78	78	79	84	84	85
Ethiopia	ETH	77	79	78	112	112	112	113	107	107	107
Fiji	FIJ		70	70	69	69	70	70	72	72	73
Finland	FIN	20	20	19	19	19	18	18	16	16	16
France	FRA	9	9	9	9	9	7	7	9	5	5
Faroe Islands	FRO								70	70	70
Gabon	GAB	104	109	109	109	109	109	111	116	116	117
Germany	GER	3	3	1	1	1	1	1	1	1	1
Ghana	GHA	53	52	50	50	49	49	49	50	50	50
Greece	GRE	57	58	58	57	57	53	53	53	53	53
Guatemala	GUA	72	75	74	75	75	75	76	80	80	81
Guinea	GUI							103	107	107	107
Guam	GUM	66	67	67	66	66	68	68	69	69	72
Haiti	HAI	53	55	55	55	56	57	57	57	57	58
Hong Kong	HKG	64	65	65	64	64	64	64	65	65	66
Honduras	HON	83	88	88	84	85	85	86	90	90	91
Hungary	HUN	26	26	26	26	26	28	27	27	28	32
Indonesia	IDN	58	60	60	60	60	60	60	62	62	65
India	IND	56	57	57	57	58	58	58	58	58	57
Republic of Ireland	IRL	38	38	37	36	36	35	35	35	34	34
Iceland	ISL	17	17	17	17	17	17	17	18	18	18
Israel	ISR	71	72	72	70	69	69	69	71	71	71
Italy	ITA	10	10	10	10	10	10	10	10	10	10
Jamaica	JAM	70	73	73	72	73	73	73	73	76	76
Japan	JPN	14	14	14	14	14	13	13	13	12	11
Kazakhstan	KAZ	60	61	61	61	61	61	61	64	64	63
Korea Republic	KOR	25	25	25	25	24	24	26	26	26	26
St Lucia	LCA	90	94	94	93	92	92	94	98	98	99
Lithuania	LTU								60	60	61
Latvia	LVA								61	61	62
Morocco	MAR	52	52	53	53	53	53	54	54	54	54
Malaysia	MAS	69	71	71	71	71	71	71	74	74	76
Moldova	MDA	85	89	89	88	88	87	88	93	93	94
Maldives	MDV								100	100	111
Mexico	MEX	31	31	31	30	25	26	25	25	25	25
Mali	MLI	62	63	63	73	72	72	72	79	79	80
Malta	MLT		74	102	98	97	97	98	103	103	103
Mozambique	MOZ	102	107	107	107	107	107	109	114	114	115
Myanmar	MYA	46	46	46	45	46	46	46	46	46	45
Namibia	NAM				113	113	113	114	118	118	119
Nicaragua	NCA	86	90	90	89	100	100	101	105	105	105
Netherlands	NED	16	16	15	15	15	15	16	17	17	17
Nigeria	NGA	23	23	24	24	27	25	23	24	23	24
Northern Ireland	NIR	74	77	76	77	77	77	78	83	82	83
Norway	NOR	2	2	3	3	3	3	3	3	3	3
New Zealand	NZL	21	21	21	21	21	22	22	21	20	21
Panama	PAN	63	64	64	63	62	62	62	63	63	64
Paraguay	PAR	65	66	66	65	65	65	65	66	66	67
Peru	PER	39	39	39	39	39	38	38	38	38	38
Philippines	PHI	75	78	77	76	76	76	77	81	81	81
Papua New Guinea	PNG	59	59	59	59	59	59	59	59	59	60
Poland	POL	31	32	33	32	32	32	32	32	32	31
Portugal	POR	33	33	32	34	34	34	34	34	36	36
Korea DPR	PRK	7	7	7	7	8	8	8	8	8	7
Puerto Rico	PUR	100	105	105	105	105	105	107	112	112	113
Romania	ROU	34	34	34	33	33	33	33	33	33	33
South Africa	RSA	61	62	62	62	63	63	63	73	73	74
Russia	RUS	11	11	12	12	12	12	11	12	13	13
Samoa	SAM	94	99	99	99	98	98	99	102	102	102
Serbia & Montenegro	SCG	28	28	29	29	30	30	31	31	31	30
Scotland	SCO	30	30	30	30	31	31	30	29	29	29
Senegal	SEN	97	102	101	102	102	102	90	94	94	95
Singapore	SIN	83	87	86	87	86	88	89	90	90	92
El Salvador	SLV	89	93	93	92	91	91	93	97	97	98
Switzerland	SUI	29	29	28	28	29	27	29	30	30	27
Surinam	SUR	81	85	85	85	83	83	84	88	88	89
Slovakia	SVK	36	36	35	37	37	40	42	42	42	43
Slovenia	SVN								75	75	75
Sweden	SWE	5	5	4	4	4	4	5	5	6	6
Swaziland	SWZ	99	104	104	104	104	104	106	111	111	111
Tahiti	TAH		95	95	94	93	93	95	99	99	100
Tanzania	TAN							117	121	121	122
Tonga	TGA		54	54	54	54	55	55	55	55	55
Thailand	THA	41	41	41	41	41	41	40	41	41	40
Chinese Taipei	TPE	22	22	22	23	23	23	24	23	23	23
Trinidad and Tobago	TRI	40	40	40	40	39	39	39	39	39	
Turkey	TUR	68	69	69	68	68	67	67	68	68	69
Ukraine	UKR	18	18	18	18	18	19	19	19	19	19
Uruguay	URU	67	68	68	67	67	66	66	67	67	68
USA	USA	1	1	2	2	2	2	2	2	1	2
Uzbekistan	UZB	49	49	49	49	50	50	50	49	49	49
Vanuatu	VAN			84	82	82	82	83	87	87	88
Venezuela	VEN	73	76	75	74	74	74	74	77	77	78
Vietnam	VIE	43	43	43	42	42	42	43	43	43	42
St Vincent/Grenadines	VIN	92	97	97	96	95	95	97			
Wales	WAL	56	56	56	55	56	56	56	56	56	56
Zambia	ZAM	101	106	106	106	106	106	108	113	113	114
Zimbabwe	ZIM	88	92	92	91	90	90	92	95	95	96

INTERNATIONALS PLAYED SINCE THE FIFA WOMEN'S WORLD CUP 2003

2003	Venue		Score		Comp	2003	Venue		Score		Comp
12-10	LAGOS	Nigeria B	3-1	Mali	AAG	02-12	HAI PHONG	Vietnam	6-0	Indonesia	SEA
12-10	CAMPINA	Romania	2-0	Bosnia-Herzeg.	ECq	04-12	HAI PHONG	Indonesia	1-1	Philippines	SEA
12-10	KADUNA	South Africa	3-1	Cameroon	AAG	04-12	HAI PHONG	Malaysia	1-3	Vietnam	SEA
15-10	KADUNA	Cameroon	1-0	Mali	AAG	04-12	NAM DINH	Myanmar	3-0	Singapore	SEA
15-10	SINGAPORE	Singapore	1-1	Hong Kong	Fr	05-12	GEORGETOWN	Jamaica	3-0	Cayman Islands	OGq
16-10	ABUJA	Nigeria B	1-0	South Africa	AAG	06-12	NAM DINH	Indonesia	2-2	Malaysia	SEA
17-10	KILKIS	Greece	4-3	Serbia & Mont.	Fr	06-12	POMBAL	Portugal	0-1	Czech Republic	ECq
18-10	MOGILEV	Belarus	1-1	Israel	ECq	06-12	NAM DINH	Singapore	0-2	Thailand	SEA
18-10	BELISCE	Croatia	2-3	Romania	ECq	06-12	HAI PHONG	Vietnam	3-0	Philippines	SEA
18-10	ODENSE	Denmark	3-0	Netherlands	ECq	07-12	GEORGETOWN	Cayman Islands	0-1	Jamaica	OGq
19-10	KRAVARE	Czech Republic	2-0	Scotland	ECq	08-12	HAI PHONG	Myanmar	8-0	Malaysia	SEA
19-10	AXIOUPOLI	Greece	2-2	Serbia & Mont.	Fr	08-12	HAI PHONG	Vietnam	3-1	Thailand	SEA
20-10	SINGAPORE	Hong Kong	4-1	Singapore	Fr	10-12	TEGUCIGALPA	Nicaragua	0-1	Honduras	OGq
21-10	MOSCOW	Russia	2-2	England	Fr	11-12	HAI PHONG	Thailand	6-1	Malaysia	SEA
21-10	SINGAPORE	Singapore	0-5	Thailand	Fr	11-12	HAI PHONG	Vietnam	2-1	Myanmar	SEA
22-10	TA'QALI	Malta	0-9	Ireland Republic	ECq	12-12	TEGUCIGALPA	Mexico	8-0	Nicaragua	OGq
22-10	KANSAS CITY	USA	2-2	Italy	Fr	14-12	TEGUCIGALPA	Honduras	0-6	Mexico	OGq
24-10	TEGUCIGALPA	Honduras	2-2	Guatemala	Fr	**2004**					
25-10	LIVADIA	Greece	7-0	Armenia	ECq	15-01	ATHENS	Greece	1-1	Scotland	Fr
25-10	PRETORIA	South Africa	13-0	Namibia	OGq	17-01	ATHENS	Greece	0-3	Scotland	Fr
26-10	KUMASI	Ghana	2-0	Congo DR	OGq	21-01	ATHENS	Greece	0-3	Italy	Fr
26-10	TEGUCIGALPA	Honduras	1-1	Guatemala	Fr	30-01	SHENZHEN	China PR	2-1	Canada	Fr
26-10	HARARE	Zimbabwe	0-0	Angola	OGq	30-01	SHENZHEN	USA	3-0	Sweden	Fr
28-10	THIVA	Armenia	0-9	Greece	ECq	31-01	IBADAN	Nigeria	1-1	Ghana	OGq
28-10	SWANSEA	Wales	1-1	Portugal	Fr	01-02	SHENZHEN	China PR	0-0	USA	Fr
30-10	LLANELLI	Wales	1-0	Portugal	Fr	01-02	JOHANNESBURG	South Africa	6-2	Angola	OGq
31-10	SAN CRISTOBAL	Dominican Rep.	0-7	Haiti	OGq	01-02	SHENZHEN	Sweden	3-1	Canada	Fr
31-10	GUATEMALA CITY	Guatemala	0-2	Honduras	Fr	03-02	SHENZHEN	China PR	2-2	Sweden	Fr
31-10	KUALA LUMPUR	Malaysia	0-4	Philippines	Fr	03-02	SHENZHEN	USA	2-0	Canada	Fr
31-10	KUALA LUMPUR	Thailand	6-0	Indonesia	Fr	07-02	ALBUFEIRA	Portugal	0-11	Germany	ECq
02-11	ANITGUA	Guatemala	1-1	Honduras	Fr	14-02	LUANDA	Angola	3-2	South Africa	OGq
02-11	SAN CRISTOBAL	Haiti	3-2	Dominican Rep.	OGq	14-02	ACCRA	Ghana	1-1	Nigeria	OGq
02-11	KUALA LUMPUR	Malaysia	3-1	Indonesia	Fr	17-02	VIAREGGIO	Italy	2-1	Netherlands	Fr
02-11	KUALA LUMPUR	Thailand	4-1	Philippines	Fr	18-02	BRISBANE	Australia	2-0	New Zealand	Fr
02-11	DALLAS	USA	3-1	Mexico	Fr	18-02	BRISBANE	China PR	0-3	Korea DPR	Fr
04-11	GUATEMALA CITY	Guatemala	0-2	Mexico	Fr	18-02	SETE	France	1-1	Scotland	Fr
04-11	KUALA LUMPUR	Malaysia	0-4	Thailand	Fr	19-02	PORTSMOUTH	England	2-0	Denmark	Fr
04-11	KUALA LUMPUR	Philippines	5-0	Indonesia	Fr	20-02	ATHENS	Greece	0-2	Russia	Fr
06-11	ANTIGUA	Guatemala	0-5	Mexico	Fr	21-02	BRISBANE	Australia	-	Korea DPR	Fr
06-11	SINGAPORE	Singapore	2-1	Philippines	Fr	21-02	MONTPELLIER	France	6-3	Scotland	Fr
08-11	LUANDA	Angola	1-0	Zimbabwe	OGq	21-02	BRISBANE	New Zealand	0-3	China PR	Fr
08-11	WINDHOEK	Namibia	1-13	South Africa	OGq	22-02	ATHENS	Greece	1-1	Russia	Fr
08-11	PANAMA CITY	Panama	1-3	Mexico	Fr	24-02	BRISBANE	Australia	0-0	China PR	Fr
09-11	KINSHASA	Congo DR	1-2	Ghana	OGq	24-02	BRISBANE	Korea DPR	11-0	New Zealand	Fr
09-11	PARAMARIBO	Surinam	0-2	Trinidad-Tobago	OGq	25-02	SAN JOSE	Mexico	5-0	Haiti	OGq
12-11	PARAMARIBO	Trinidad & Tobago	4-2	Surinam	OGq	25-02	SAN JOSE	Trinidad & Tobago	0-7	USA	OGq
13-11	PRESTON	England	5-0	Scotland	Fr	26-02	HEREDIA	Canada	6-0	Jamaica	OGq
14-11	PANAMA CITY	Panama	4-1	Honduras	Fr	26-02	HEREDIA	Costa Rica	6-1	Panama	OGq
15-11	QUIMPER	France	7-1	Poland	ECq	27-02	HEREDIA	Haiti	0-8	USA	OGq
15-11	REUTLINGEN	Germany	13-0	Portugal	ECq	27-02	HEREDIA	Trinidad & Tobago	1-8	Mexico	OGq
15-11	DRAMA	Greece	3-1	Slovakia	ECq	28-02	SAN JOSE	Canada	6-0	Panama	OGq
15-11	BELGRADE	Serbia & Mont.	0-4	Sweden	ECq	28-02	SAN JOSE	Costa Rica	1-0	Jamaica	OGq
16-11	LAS ROZAS	Spain	0-2	Norway	ECq	29-02	ALGINET	Spain	9-1	Belgium	ECq
16-11	TA'QALI	Malta	1-4	Croatia	ECq	29-02	SAN JOSE	Haiti	2-6	Trinidad & Tobago	OGq
16-11	PANAMA CITY	Panama	4-2	Honduras	Fr	29-02	SAN JOSE	USA	2-0	Mexico	OGq
19-11	GUATEMALA CITY	Belize	0-18	Guatemala	OGq	01-03	HEREDIA	Costa Rica	1-2	Canada	OGq
21-11	GUATEMALA CITY	Panama	15-2	Belize	OGq	01-03	HEREDIA	Jamaica	0-3	Panama	OGq
22-11	EINDHOVEN	Netherlands	3-0	Belgium	ECq	02-03	BA	Fiji	0-2	Papua N. Guinea	OGq
23-11	GUATEMALA CITY	Guatemala	1-1	Panama	OGq	03-03	SAN JOSE	Canada	1-2	Mexico	OGq
29-11	NAOUSSA	Greece	0-2	Austria	ECq	03-03	SAN JOSE	USA	4-0	Costa Rica	OGq
02-12	HAI PHONG	Philippines	0-0	Malaysia	SEA	04-03	BA	Australia	10-0	Papua N. Guinea	OGq
02-12	NAM DINH	Thailand	2-4	Myanmar	SEA	04-03	FURTH	Germany	0-1	China PR	Fr

INTERNATIONALS PLAYED SINCE THE FIFA WOMEN'S WORLD CUP 2003

2004	Venue		Score		Comp
05-03	HEREDIA	Canada	4-0	Costa Rica	OGq
05-03	HEREDIA	Mexico	2-3	USA	OGq
06-03	BA	Fiji	0-7	Australia	OGq
07-03	BRUSSELS	Belgium	1-6	Norway	ECq
07-03	SCHWANDORF	China PR	1-0	Czech Republic	Fr
10-03	LEIDEN	Netherlands	6-0	Republic of Ireland	Fr
12-03	PRETORIA	South Africa	2-2	Nigeria	OGq
13-03	REYKJAVIK	Iceland	5-1	Scotland	Fr
14-03	FERREIRAS	Denmark	0-1	Sweden	ALG
14-03	FARO	Greece	1-0	Wales	ALG
14-03	GUIA	Italy	1-0	China PR	ALG
14-03	GUIA	Norway	4-1	Finland	ALG
14-03	FARO	Portugal	2-0	Northern Ireland	ALG
14-03	FERREIRAS	USA	5-1	France	ALG
16-03	QUARTEIRA	Denmark	0-1	USA	ALG
16-03	OLHAO	Finland	0-4	China PR	ALG
16-03	ALBUFEIRA	Northern Ireland	0-2	Greece	ALG
16-03	OLHAO	Norway	3-0	Italy	ALG
16-03	ALBUFEIRA	Portugal	2-3	Wales	ALG
16-03	QUARTEIRA	Sweden	0-3	France	ALG
18-03	SILVES	Denmark	0-1	France	ALG
18-03	LAGOS	Finland	1-2	Italy	ALG
18-03	SILVES	Norway	0-0	China PR	ALG
18-03	GUIA	Portugal	3-0	Greece	ALG
18-03	LAGOS	Sweden	3-1	USA	ALG
18-03	GUIA	Wales	3-1	Northern Ireland	ALG
20-03	OLHAO	China PR	1-1	Sweden	ALG
20-03	FERREIRAS	Finland	4-0	Wales	ALG
20-03	FARO	Italy	3-3	France	ALG
20-03	MONTECHORO	Northern Ireland	0-2	Greece	ALG
20-03	LOULE	Portugal	0-1	Denmark	ALG
20-03	FARO	USA	4-1	Norway	ALG
21-03	LA RODA	Spain	0-0	Netherlands	ECq
30-03	ABUJA	Nigeria	1-0	South Africa	OGq
31-03	ALBENA	Bulgaria	0-3	Kazakhstan	Fr
31-03	BOZEN	Italy	2-0	Germany	Fr
31-03	ALBENA	Romania	0-5	Russia	Fr
03-04	SETUBAL	Portugal	1-2	Ukraine	ECq
04-04	ALBENA	Russia	5-0	Kazakhstan	Fr
06-04	ALBENA	Bulgaria	1-1	Romania	Fr
09-04	BASEL	Switzerland	0-0	Belgium	Fr
10-04	DUBLIN	Republic of Ireland	8-1	Croatia	ECq
10-04	SIMFEROPOL	Ukraine	1-0	Scotland	ECq
11-04	MAPUTO	Mozambique	3-1	Swaziland	Fr
11-04	BASEL	Switzerland	0-1	Belgium	Fr
18-04	HIROSHIMA	China PR	11-0	Myanmar	OGq
18-04	LUCENA	Spain	0-1	Denmark	ECq
18-04	TOKYO	Japan	7-0	Vietnam	OGq
18-04	HIROSHIMA	Korea Republic	7-0	Guam	OGq
18-04	HIROSHIMA	Korea DPR	5-0	Chinese Taipei	OGq
18-04	HIROSHIMA	Singapore	0-2	Hong Kong	OGq
20-04	HIROSHIMA	Guam	0-9	China PR	OGq
20-04	HIROSHIMA	Hong Kong	0-9	Korea DPR	OGq
20-04	HIROSHIMA	Myanmar	0-7	Korea Republic	OGq
20-04	HIROSHIMA	Chinese Taipei	5-0	Singapore	OGq
20-04	TOKYO	Vietnam	0-0	Thailand	OGq
22-04	HIROSHIMA	China PR	3-0	Korea Republic	OGq
22-04	READING	England	8-0	Nigeria	Fr
22-04	HIROSHIMA	Guam	0-2	Myanmar	OGq
22-04	HIROSHIMA	Hong Kong	1-3	Chinese Taipei	OGq
22-04	HIROSHIMA	Korea DPR	8-0	Singapore	OGq
22-04	TOKYO	Thailand	0-6	Japan	OGq
24-04	OTTENSHEIM	Austria	1-2	Greece	ECq
24-04	HIROSHIMA	China PR	1-0	Korea Republic	OGq
24-04	REIMS	France	6-0	Hungary	ECq
24-04	ANDRIA	Italy	1-1	Finland	ECq
24-04	TOKYO	Korea DPR	0-3	Japan	OGq
24-04	SOLOTHURN	Switzerland	0-2	Sweden	ECq
24-04	BIRMINGHAM, AL	USA	5-1	Brazil	Fr
25-04	LEUVEN	Belgium	0-3	Netherlands	ECq
26-04	HIROSHIMA	Japan	0-1	China PR	OGq
26-04	HIROSHIMA	Korea DPR	5-1	Korea Republic	OGq
28-04	OLDENBURG	Germany	6-0	Ukraine	ECq
29-04	SENEC	Slovakia	2-2	Greece	ECq
01-05	DUNAUJVAROS	Hungary	2-2	Poland	ECq
01-05	BUCHAREST	Romania	1-1	Republic of Ireland	ECq
02-05	MONS	Belgium	2-0	Spain	ECq
02-05	LIVINGSTON	Scotland	1-3	Germany	ECq
08-05	LEOPOLDSDORF	Austria	3-0	Slovakia	ECq
08-05	HAMRUN	Malta	0-8	Romania	ECq
08-05	KWIDZYN	Poland	1-1	Russia	ECq
09-05	SARAJEVO	Bosnia-Herzeg.	1-4	Republic of Ireland	ECq
09-05	UH'SKE HRADISTE	Czech Republic	5-1	Portugal	ECq
09-05	TEL AVIV	Israel	12-1	Estonia	ECq
09-05	ALBUQUERQUE	USA	3-0	Mexico	Fr
12-05	VAXJO	Sweden	5-1	Serbia & Mont.	ECq
14-05	PETERBOROUGH	England	1-0	Iceland	Fr
15-05	LAHTI	Finland	4-0	Serbia & Mont.	ECq
16-05	SLAVONSKI BROD	Croatia	6-0	Bosnia-Herzeg.	ECq
16-05	SELYATINO	Russia	0-3	France	ECq
22-05	FARUM	Denmark	2-0	Spain	ECq
22-05	TRAPANI	Italy	0-0	Switzerland	ECq
22-05	MR WEZEP	Netherlands	0-2	Norway	ECq
23-05	LIVINGSTON	Scotland	2-1	Portugal	ECq
25-05	ASTANA	Kazakhstan	0-2	Belarus	ECq
27-05	ODENSE	Denmark	2-1	Norway	ECq
29-05	SZEKESFEHERVAR	Hungary	0-5	Iceland	ECq
29-05	DAR ES SAALAM	Tanzania	4-0	Eritrea	CN
30-05	MALABO	Equatorial Guinea	2-2	Congo	CN
30-05	HERZLIYYA	Israel	3-1	Kazakhstan	ECq
02-06	REYKJAVIK	Iceland	0-3	France	ECq
05-06	ROUDNICE	Czech Republic	4-1	Ukraine	ECq
05-06	PETROYSA DRAMA	Greece	1-0	Serbia & Mont.	Fr
06-06	LOUISVILLE	USA	1-1	Japan	Fr
07-06	KALABAKI DRAMA	Greece	3-3	Serbia & Mont.	Fr
12-06	BRAZZAVILLE	Congo	2-0	Equatorial Guinea	CN
12-06	ASMARA	Eritrea	1-1	Tanzania	CN
25-06	DUBLIN	Republic of Ireland	5-0	Malta	ECq
26-06	BENEVENTO	Italy	2-1	Sweden	ECq
30-06	BEIJING	China PR	0-2	Australia	Fr
01-07	BEIJING	China PR	1-1	Australia	Fr
03-07	NASHVILLE	USA	1-0	Canada	Fr
06-07	ATHENS	Greece	0-1	Russia	Fr
08-07	MEXICO CITY	Mexico	1-2	Australia	Fr
10-07	DAKAR	Senegal	2-8	Nigeria	CN
11-07	BRAZZAVILLE	Congo	0-2	Cameroon	CN
11-07	CONAKRY	Guinea	0-13	Ghana	CN
11-07	GUADALAJARA	Mexico	2-0	Australia	Fr
11-07	BAMAKO	Mali	2-2	Algeria	CN
11-07	BLANTYRE	Malawi	0-4	Ethiopia	CN
11-07	DAR ES SAALAM	Tanzania	0-3	Zimbabwe	CN
21-07	HOFFENHEIM	Germany	0-1	Norway	Fr
21-07	BLAINE	USA	3-1	Australia	Fr
23-07	BLIDA	Algeria	1-0	Mali	CN

INTERNATIONALS PLAYED SINCE THE FIFA WOMEN'S WORLD CUP 2003

2004	Venue		Score		Comp	2004	Venue		Score		Comp
24-07	OFFENBACH	Germany	3-1	Nigeria	Fr	24-09	PRETORIA	South Africa	1-2	Ethiopia	CN
24-07	ACCRA	Ghana	9-0	Guinea	CN	25-09	JOHANNESBURG	Algeria	1-3	Cameroon	CN
24-07	WARRI	Nigeria	4-1	Senegal	CN	25-09	PRIBRAM	Czech Republic	0-5	Germany	ECq
24-07	UDEVALLA	Sweden	0-4	Norway	Fr	25-09	PRETORIA	Nigeria	3-0	Mali	CN
25-07	YAOUNDE	Cameroon	0-0	Congo	CN	25-09	NIS	Serbia & Mont.	1-2	Italy	ECq
25-07	ADDIS ABEBA	Ethiopia	5-0	Malawi	CN	25-09	ROCHESTER, NY	USA	4-3	Iceland	Fr
25-07	HARARE	Zimbabwe	4-0	Tanzania	CN	26-09	AALBORG	Denmark	6-0	Belgium	ECq
30-07	TOKYO	Japan	3-0	Canada	Fr	26-09	DIJON	France	2-5	Russia	ECq
31-07	ODRANCI	Slovenia	0-2	Czech Republic	Fr	28-09	JOHANNESBURG	Ghana	0-1	Cameroon	CN
01-08	HARTFORD	USA	3-1	China PR	Fr	28-09	JOHANNESBURG	Nigeria	4-0	Ethiopia	CN
06-08	ATHENS	Australia	1-0	Mexico	Fr	29-09	KATWIJK	Netherlands	1-5	Denmark	Fr
06-08	ZEIST	Netherlands	0-2	Japan	Fr	29-09	KRUSEVAC	Serbia & Mont.	1-0	Switzerland	ECq
11-08	THESSALONIKI	Brazil	1-0	Australia	OGr1	29-09	PITTSBURGH	USA	3-0	Iceland	Fr
11-08	PATRAS	Germany	8-0	China PR	OGr1	30-09	HO CHI MINH CITY	Indonesia	1-0	Philippines	Fr
11-08	HERAKLIO	Greece	0-3	USA	OGr1	01-10	JOHANNESBURG	Ghana	0-0	Ethiopia	CN
11-08	VOLOS	Sweden	0-1	Japan	OGr1	01-10	HO CHI MINH CITY	Myanmar	17-0	Maldives	Fr
14-08	PATRAS	China PR	1-1	Mexico	OGr1	02-10	VAASA	Finland	1-1	Sweden	ECq
14-08	HERAKLIO	Greece	0-1	Australia	OGr1	02-10	PORSGRUNN	Norway	2-0	Spain	ECq
14-08	ATHENS	Japan	0-1	Nigeria	OGr1	02-10	HO CHI MINH CITY	Philippines	2-1	Singapore	Fr
14-08	THESSALONIKI	USA	2-0	Brazil	OGr1	02-10	BUCHAREST	Romania	10-0	Croatia	ECq
15-08	SZAMOTULY	Poland	0-2	Finland	Fr	03-10	JOHANNESBURG	Cameroon	0-5	Nigeria	CN
17-08	ATHENS	Germany	2-0	Mexico	OGr1	03-10	RISHON LEZION	Israel	0-2	Belarus	ECq
17-08	PATRAS	Greece	0-7	Brazil	OGr1	03-10	OPOLE	Poland	1-5	France	ECq
17-08	VOLOS	Sweden	2-1	Nigeria	OGr1	03-10	SELYATINO	Russia	4-0	Hungary	ECq
17-08	THESSALONIKI	USA	1-1	Australia	OGr1	03-10	PORTLAND	USA	5-0	New Zealand	Fr
19-08	BRISTOL	England	1-2	Russia	Fr	04-10	HO CHI MINH CITY	Singapore	1-0	Indonesia	Fr
19-08	DINGWALL	Scotland	6-0	Switzerland	Fr	04-10	HO CHI MINH CITY	Vietnam	14-0	Maldives	Fr
20-08	PATRAS	Germany	2-1	Nigeria	OGqf	05-10	HO CHI MINH CITY	Vietnam	1-1	Myanmar	Fr
20-08	UKMERGE	Lithuania	4-1	Latvia	Fr	07-10	HO CHI MINH CITY	Myanmar	7-0	Indonesia	Fr
20-08	HERAKLIO	Mexico	0-5	Brazil	OGqf	09-10	HO CHI MINH CITY	Vietnam	4-1	Indonesia	Fr
20-08	VOLOS	Sweden	2-1	Australia	OGqf	10-10	CINCINNATI	USA	6-0	New Zealand	Fr
20-08	THESSALONIKI	USA	2-1	Japan	OGqf	12-10	KLAKSVIK	Faroe Islands	1-2	Republic of Ireland	Fr
21-08	UKMERGE	Latvia	0-5	Estonia	Fr	14-10	BERLIN	Germany	0-0	Netherlands	Fr
21-08	SENEC	Slovakia	2-3	Austria	ECq	16-10	PIETARSAARI	Finland	1-0	Russia	ECq
22-08	REYKJAVIK	Iceland	0-2	Russia	ECq	16-10	KANSAS CITY	USA	1-0	Mexico	Fr
22-08	UKMERGE	Lithuania	2-2	Estonia	Fr	20-10	MOSCOW	Russia	1-3	Finland	ECq
23-08	PATRAS	Sweden	0-1	Brazil	OGsf	20-10	CHICAGO	USA	5-1	Republic of Ireland	Fr
23-08	HERAKLIO	USA	2-1	Germany	OGsf	23-10	HOUSTON	USA	5-0	Republic of Ireland	Fr
25-08	MINSK	Belarus	8-1	Kazakhstan	ECq	03-11	EAST RUTHERFORD	USA	1-1	Denmark	Fr
26-08	ATHENS	Germany	1-0	Sweden	OG3p	06-11	Philadelphia	USA	1-3	Denmark	Fr
26-08	ATHENS	USA	2-1	Brazil	OGf	10-11	REYKJAVIK	Iceland	2-7	Norway	ECq
28-08	ST. JOHN'S	Antigua-Barbuda	1-0	Anguilla	Fr	13-11	BATTICE	Belgium	5-1	Hungary	Fr
29-08	ST. JOHN'S	Antigua-Barbuda	0-1	Anguilla	Fr	13-11	CROTONE	Italy	2-1	Czech Republic	ECq
29-08	PARNU	Estonia	1-3	Belarus	ECq	13-11	OSLO	Norway	2-1	Iceland	ECq
04-09	BERGEN	Norway	3-1	Italy	Fr	13-11	HO CHI MINH CITY	Vietnam	3-0	Hong Kong	Fr
04-09	VISP	Switzerland	0-2	Finland	ECq	27-11	CASLAV	Czech Republic	0-3	Italy	ECq
05-09	TA'QALI	Malta	0-2	Bosnia-Herzeg.	ECq	01-12	SINGAPORE	Singapore	2-0	Guam	Fr
05-09	DINGWALL	Scotland	3-2	Czech Republic	ECq	08-12	CARSON	USA	5-0	Mexico	Fr
08-09	SLAGELSE	Denmark	2-3	France	Fr	18-12	TOKYO	Japan	11-0	Chinese Taipei	Fr
18-09	HEERHUGOWAARD	Netherlands	1-2	England	Fr	**2005**					
18-09	PRETORIA	South Africa	0-3	Ghana	CN	28-01	QUANZHOU	China PR	3-1	Russia	Fr
18-09	PRETORIA	Zimbabwe	1-1	Ethiopia	CN	28-01	QUANZHOU	Germany	0-1	Australia	Fr
19-09	VOGOSCA	Bosnia-Herzeg.	0-0	Romania	ECq	30-01	QUANZHOU	China PR	3-0	Australia	Fr
19-09	JOHANNESBURG	Cameroon	2-2	Mali	CN	30-01	QUANZHOU	Germany	1-0	Russia	Fr
19-09	ASTANA	Kazakhstan	0-0	Estonia	ECq	01-02	QUANZHOU	China PR	0-2	Germany	Fr
19-09	JOHANNESBURG	Nigeria	4-0	Algeria	CN	01-02	QUANZHOU	Russia	0-5	Australia	Fr
21-09	JOHANNESBURG	Ghana	2-1	Ethiopia	CN	04-02	YIWU	China PR	0-0	Denmark	Fr
21-09	JOHANNESBURG	Zimbabwe	2-1	South Africa	CN	04-02	DUBAI	Czech Republic	4-0	Romania	Fr
22-09	JOHANNESBURG	Algeria	3-0	Mali	CN	07-02	YIWU	China PR	1-1	Denmark	Fr
22-09	JOHANNESBURG	Cameroon	2-2	Nigeria	CN	15-02	LAS PALMAS G.C.	Spain	2-2	Finland	Fr
22-09	TUITJENHOORN	Netherlands	0-1	England	Fr	17-02	MILTON KEYNES	England	4-1	Italy	Fr
24-09	JOHANNESBURG	Ghana	2-0	Zimbabwe	CN	17-02	LAS PALMAS G.C.	Spain	0-0	Netherlands	Fr

INTERNATIONALS PLAYED SINCE THE FIFA WOMEN'S WORLD CUP 2003

2005	Venue		Score		Comp
18-02	LAS PALMAS G.C.	Netherlands	0-1	Finland	Fr
19-02	LA MANGA	Norway	0-2	France	Fr
22-02	LA MANGA	Norway	0-1	France	Fr
23-02	SANTA MARIA	Portugal	0-2	Italy	Fr
07-03	SIMFEROPOL	Ukraine	1-2	Russia	Fr
09-03	FERREIRAS	Denmark	4-1	Finland	ALG
09-03	PADERNE	England	4-0	Northern Ireland	ALG
09-03	FERREIRAS	France	0-1	USA	ALG
09-03	LAGOS	Norway	2-1	China PR	ALG
09-03	QUARTEIRA	Portugal	1-2	Mexico	ALG
09-03	LAGOS	Sweden	1-2	Germany	ALG
11-03	SILVES	China PR	0-2	Sweden	ALG
11-03	GUIA	Denmark	1-2	France	ALG
11-03	FARO	England	4-0	Portugal	ALG
11-03	SILVES	Germany	4-0	Norway	ALG
11-03	FARO	Mexico	2-0	Northern Ireland	ALG
11-03	GUIA	USA	3-0	Finland	ALG
12-03	CORK	Republic of Ireland	2-0	Belgium	Fr
13-03	ALVOR	China PR	0-2	Germany	ALG
13-03	LAGOS	England	5-0	Mexico	ALG
13-03	LOULE	Finland	1-2	France	ALG
13-03	LAGOS	Northern Ireland	2-1	Portugal	ALG
13-03	LOULE	Sweden	1-1	Norway	ALG
13-03	VILA REAL	USA	4-0	Denmark	ALG
15-03	GUIA	England	0-0	China PR	ALG
15-03	FARO-LOULE	Germany	0-1	USA	ALG
15-03	QUARTEIRA	Mexico	1-1	Finland	ALG
15-03	MONTECHORO	Northern Ireland	1-3	Portugal	ALG
15-03	FARO	Norway	2-1	Denmark	ALG
15-03	FARO-LOULE	Sweden	2-3	France	ALG
17-03	TAPOLCA	Hungary	0-3	Poland	Fr
19-03	TAPOLCA	Hungary	0-4	Poland	Fr
25-03	ARLON	Belgium	2-1	Switzerland	Fr
26-03	SYDNEY	Australia	0-2	Japan	Fr
27-03	ETHE	Belgium	0-4	Switzerland	Fr
29-03	MIRANDA	Australia	2-1	Japan	Fr
03-04	ALBENA	Bulgaria	2-0	Kazakhstan	Fr
05-04	VARNA	Korea DPR	6-1	Romania	Fr
09-04	VARNA	Bulgaria	0-5	Korea DPR	Fr
09-04	VARNA	Kazakhstan	2-2	Romania	Fr
12-04	MALE DVORNIKY	Slovakia	2-1	Hungary	Fr
13-04	MONTBELIARD	France	0-0	Netherlands	Fr
13-04	GYOR	Hungary	2-0	Slovakia	Fr
13-04	GENOA	Italy	1-0	Denmark	Fr
19-04	APELDOORN	Netherlands	1-1	Canada	Fr
21-04	TRANMERE	England	2-1	Scotland	Fr
21-04	OSNABRUECK	Germany	3-1	Canada	Fr
24-04	HILDESHEIM	Germany	3-2	Canada	Fr
25-04	CAIRO	Egypt	1-0	Algeria	Fr
27-04	VILDBJERG	Denmark	7-2	Switzerland	Fr
27-04	STRASBOURG	France	0-2	Canada	Fr
27-04	FLUGGI	Italy	0-0	Finland	Fr
30-04	VAXJO	Sweden	0-0	Denmark	Fr
03-05	TRELLEBORG	Sweden	2-0	Netherlands	Fr
06-05	BARNSLEY	England	1-0	Norway	Fr
18-05	VENICE	Italy	2-0	Republic of Ireland	Fr
20-05	TURKU	Finland	2-0	Scotland	Fr
21-05	TOKYO	Japan	6-0	New Zealand	Fr
21-05	KUALA LUMPUR	Malaysia	1-6	Philippines	Fr
21-05	GARIC	Slovenia	7-1	Macedonia FYR	Fr
23-05	KUALA LUMPUR	Philippines	0-5	Myanmar	Fr
24-05	ZALAEGERSZEG	Hungary	2-0	Slovenia	Fr

2005	Venue		Score		Comp
25-05	COPENHAGEN	Denmark	3-4	Canada	Fr
25-05	KUALA LUMPUR	Malaysia	0-16	Myanmar	Fr
25-05	PERTH	Scotland	0-2	Iceland	Fr
26-05	WALSALL	England	4-1	Czech Republic	Fr
26-05	SHELKOVO	Russia	2-4	Japan	Fr
28-05	MOSCOW	Russia	0-2	Japan	Fr
28-05	STOCKHOLM	Sweden	3-1	Canada	Fr
30-05	SINGAPORE	Singapore	0-1	Philippines	Fr
31-05	SARPSBORG	Norway	3-0	Canada	Fr
05-06	MANCHESTER	England	3-2	Finland	ECr1
05-06	BLACKPOOL	Sweden	1-1	Denmark	ECr1
06-06	PRESTON	France	3-1	Italy	ECr1
06-06	WARRINGTON	Germany	1-0	Norway	ECr1
06-06	DUBLIN	Republic of Ireland	2-1	Faroe Islands	Fr
08-06	BLACKBURN	Denmark	2-1	England	ECr1
08-06	BLACKPOOL	Sweden	0-0	Finland	ECr1
09-06	WARRINGTON	France	1-1	Norway	ECr1
09-06	PRESTON	Italy	0-4	Germany	ECr1
11-06	BLACKBURN	England	0-1	Sweden	ECr1
11-06	BLACKPOOL	Finland	2-1	Denmark	ECr1
12-06	WARRINGTON	Germany	3-0	France	ECr1
12-06	HANOI	Guam	0-10	India	ACq
12-06	PRESTON	Norway	5-3	Italy	ECr1
12-06	HANOI	Vietnam	6-1	Philippines	ACq
13-06	HANOI	Indonesia	0-0	Singapore	ACq
13-06	HANOI	Maldives	0-6	Uzbekistan	ACq
14-06	HANOI	India	1-2	Chinese Taipei	ACq
14-06	HANOI	Philippines	1-4	Myanmar	ACq
15-06	PRESTON	Germany	4-1	Finland	ECsf
15-06	HANOI	Singapore	1-5	Thailand	ACq
15-06	HANOI	Uzbekistan	3-0	Hong Kong	ACq
16-06	HANOI	Myanmar	0-1	Vietnam	ACq
16-06	WARRINGTON	Norway	3-2	Sweden	ECsf
16-06	HANOI	Chinese Taipei	11-0	Guam	ACq
17-06	HANOI	Hong Kong	4-0	Maldives	ACq
17-06	HANOI	Thailand	4-0	Indonesia	ACq
19-06	BLACKBURN	Germany	3-1	Norway	ECf
19-06	HANOI	Chinese Taipei	3-0	Singapore	ACq
19-06	HANOI	Vietnam	4-1	Hong Kong	ACq
20-06	HANOI	India	2-3	Thailand	ACq
20-06	HANOI	Myanmar	2-1	Uzbekistan	ACq
26-06	VIRGINIA BEACH	USA	2-0	Canada	Fr
09-07	MOSCOW	Russia	5-1	Republic of Ireland	WCq
10-07	PORTLAND	USA	7-0	Ukraine	Fr
12-07	CUNNINGSBURGH	Bermuda	0-3	Faroe Islands	Fr
16-07	TIANJIN	China PR	1-2	Australia	Fr
19-07	TIANJIN	China PR	2-0	Australia	Fr
22-07	LECZNA	Poland	1-2	Ukraine	Fr
23-07	TOKYO	Japan	4-2	Australia	Fr
24-07	STEZYCA	Poland	0-4	Ukraine	Fr
24-07	CARSONES	USA	3-0	Iceland	Fr
26-07	JEONJU	Korea Republic	0-0	Australia	Fr
28-07	JEONJU	Korea Republic	3-0	Australia	Fr
31-07	PERTH	Scotland	2-1	Northern Ireland	Fr

Fr = Friendly • AAG = All Africa Games • EC = UEFA European Women's Championship • OG = Olympic Games • SEA = Southeast Asian Games ALG = Algarve Cup • CN = CAF African Women's Championship

q = qualifier • r1 = final tournament first round group • qf = quarter-final • sf = semi-final • f = final

CHINA PR 2004-05
SUPER LEAGUE

Northern Group

	Pl	W	D	L	F	A	Pts
Beijing Chengjian	10	7	1	0	2	25	7
Dalian Shide	10	5	1	2	2	17	10
Tianjin Huisun	10	3	3	0	4	18	18
Hebei Huabei Medicine	10	4	0	3	3	12	14
Shandong	10	2	2	2	4	13	20
Henan Jianye	10	1	1	1	7	7	23

Southern Group

	Pl	W	D	L	F	A	Pts
Shanghai SVA	10	8	1	0	1	39	7
Army Yixintai	10	5	1	1	3	23	13
Guangdong Haiyin	10	4	2	0	4	16	17
Jiangsu Huatai	10	4	0	3	3	22	11
Sichuan Jiannanchun	10	4	1	1	4	14	15
Olympic Little Swans	10	0	0	0	10	5	56

Championship Finals
Semi-finals: Shanghai SVA 2-1 2-2 Dalian Shide;
Army Yixintai 0-1 0-2 Beijing Chengjian;
Third place play-off: Dalian Shide 4-0 2-2 Army Yixintai
Final: **Shanghai SVA** 1-0 1-1 Beijing Chengjian

CZECH REPUBLIC 2004-05
FIRST DIVISION

	Pl	W	D	L	F	A	Pts
Sparta Praha	18	18	0	0	103	6	54
Slavia Praha	18	13	2	3	72	23	41
Hradec Králové	18	12	2	4	39	12	38
Otrokovice	18	11	4	3	52	22	37
Brno	18	8	3	7	39	28	27
Kladno	18	6	2	10	29	53	20
Krásná Studánka	18	4	5	9	20	52	17
Rapid Sport	18	3	2	13	12	48	11
Vrchovina N. Mesto	18	3	0	15	12	65	9
Hlucín	18	1	2	15	21	90	5

DENMARK 2004-05
FIRST DIVISION

	Pl	W	D	L	F	A	Pts
Brøndby IF	21	20	0	1	83	9	60
Fortuna Hjørring	21	18	1	2	95	16	55
Skovbakken	21	10	4	7	62	39	34
Skovlunde	21	9	4	8	34	34	31
Vejle	21	8	4	9	40	42	28
OB	21	4	3	14	23	58	15
Team Viborg	21	3	2	16	15	75	11
Horsens SIK	21	2	2	17	11	90	8

Cup Final: Brøndy IF 3-0 Fortuna Hjørring

ENGLAND 2004-05
PREMIER LEAGUE

	Pl	W	D	L	F	A	Pts
Arsenal LFC	18	15	3	0	57	13	48
Charlton Athletic LFC	18	13	2	3	43	17	41
Everton LFC	18	11	4	3	45	24	37
Birmingham City LFC	18	9	3	6	37	28	30
Bristol Rovers WFC	18	9	1	8	35	28	28
Leeds United LFC	18	8	2	8	31	34	26
Fulham FC Ladies	18	3	5	10	18	39	14
Doncaster Belles	18	3	3	12	10	38	12
Liverpool FC Ladies	18	3	2	13	21	49	11
Bristol City WFC	18	2	3	13	12	39	9

Cup Final: Charlton Athletic 1-0 Everton

SPAIN 2004-05
FIRST DIVISION

	Pl	W	D	L	F	A	Pts
Athletic Bilboko	26	20	6	0	77	15	66
Levante	26	20	3	3	74	18	63
RCD Espanyol	26	18	3	5	92	46	57
Torrejón	26	17	4	5	52	28	55
Sevilla	26	16	3	7	75	33	51
Puebla	26	13	4	9	55	37	43
Rayo Vallecano	26	11	1	14	53	54	34
Sabadell	26	8	5	13	59	63	29
Barcelona	26	8	5	13	42	59	29
Oviedo Moderno	26	6	5	15	27	57	23
Lagnuak	26	5	7	14	23	50	22
Estudiantes	26	5	5	16	42	64	20
Pozuelo	26	4	4	18	24	75	16
Nuestra Señora Belén	26	3	1	22	23	119	10

FINLAND 2004
FIRST DIVISION

	Pl	W	D	L	F	A	Pts
FC United Pietarsaari	18	15	2	1	63	10	47
HJK Helsinki	18	13	1	4	59	18	40
FC Espoo	18	12	1	5	41	21	37
SCR Raisio	18	9	2	7	35	26	29
Honka	18	8	5	5	33	29	29
Ilves Tampere	18	8	0	10	26	29	24
MPS Helsinki	18	7	2	9	20	33	23
KMF	18	5	2	11	21	33	17
TiPS Vantaa	18	5	0	13	24	40	15
Kontu	18	0	1	17	7	90	1

Cup Final: United Pietasaari 1-0 HJK Helsinki

FRANCE 2004-05
DIVISION 1

	Pl	W	D	L	F	A	Pts
Montpellier HSC	22	19	3	0	68	9	82
FCF Juvisy	22	18	3	1	78	12	79
FC Lyon Féminin	22	15	2	5	50	20	69
ASJ Soyaux	22	12	2	8	40	33	60
Toulouse FC	22	11	4	7	43	32	59
CNFE Football Fém.	22	10	4	8	40	27	56
FCF Hénin-Beaumont	22	9	2	11	42	46	51
FC Vendenheim	22	6	5	11	21	46	49
St Memmie Olympique	22	4	4	14	23	61	38
Paris-St.-Germain FC	22	3	5	14	24	50	36
Saint-Brieuc	22	3	3	16	25	75	34
FCF Condé/Noireau	22	1	5	16	13	56	30

HUNGARY 2004-05
FIRST DIVISION

	Pl	W	D	L	F	A	Pts
MTK Budapest	20	15	2	3	56	10	47
WHC Viktória	20	12	4	4	39	20	40
1.FC Femina	20	11	4	5	71	24	37
Saturnus	20	10	2	8	44	33	32
Debreceni VSC	20	3	2	15	19	64	11
Miskolci VSC	20	2	0	18	14	92	6

GERMANY 2004-05
FIRST DIVISION

	Pl	W	D	L	F	A	Pts
1.FFC Frankfurt/Main	22	21	0	1	78	16	63
FCR 2001 Duisburg	22	18	2	2	91	20	56
1.FFC Turbine Potsdam	22	16	1	5	79	29	49
FC Bayern München	22	10	3	9	39	37	33
SC 1907 Bad Neuenahr	22	10	3	9	40	42	33
FSV Frankfurt/Main	22	7	5	10	37	51	26
FFC Heike Rheine	22	7	4	11	36	54	25
SC Freiburg	22	7	2	13	30	56	23
Hamburger SV	22	6	2	14	20	48	20
SG Essen-Schönebeck	22	6	2	14	28	63	20
TSV Crailsheim	22	6	0	16	19	49	18
VfL Wolfsburg	22	5	2	15	26	58	17

Cup Final: 1.FFC Turbine Potsdam 3-0 1.FFC Frankfurt

ICELAND 2004
FIRST DIVISION

	Pl	W	D	L	F	A	Pts
Valur	14	13	1	0	56	7	40
IBV	14	10	2	2	69	12	32
KR	14	9	3	2	49	20	30
Breidablik	14	5	0	9	25	35	15
Stjarnan	14	3	5	6	18	40	14
FH	14	4	2	8	14	53	14
Thor/KA/KS	14	1	5	8	14	48	8
Fjölnir	14	1	2	11	7	37	5

Cup Final: IBV 2-0 Valur

ITALY 2004-05
FIRST DIVISION

	Pl	W	D	L	F	A	Pts
Poliplast Bardolino	22	17	2	3	85	18	53
Torres Terra Sarda	22	16	2	4	65	15	50
Torino	22	14	4	4	72	23	46
Reggiana	22	10	5	7	31	32	35
Fiammamonza	22	10	3	9	35	30	33
Agliana Aircargo	22	9	3	10	35	38	30
Milan	22	8	6	8	19	28	30
Atletico Oristano	22	9	2	11	52	46	29
Vigor Senigallia	22	7	4	11	28	35	25
Tavagnacco	22	7	4	11	30	52	25
Vallassinese	22	5	2	15	18	46	17
Lazio Ad Decimum	22	0	3	19	11	118	3

Cup Final: Torres Terra Sada 2-0 Vigor Senigallia

JAPAN 2004
L.LEAGUE

	Pl	W	D	L	F	A	Pts
Saitama Reinas	14	11	3	0	35	8	36
NTV Beleza	14	11	2	1	41	2	35
Tasaki Perule	14	9	1	4	33	9	28
Iga Kunoichi	14	8	1	5	26	16	25
YKK AP Flappers	14	3	3	8	13	21	12
Takarazuka Bunny's	14	4	0	10	9	45	12
Speranza Takatsuki	14	3	2	9	12	26	11
O-hara Gakuen JaSRA	14	0	2	12	4	46	2

NORWAY 2004
FIRST DIVISION

	Pl	W	D	L	F	A	Pts
Røa	18	14	2	2	39	9	44
Trondheims-Ørn	18	13	4	1	46	18	43
Fløya	18	10	3	5	47	22	33
Asker	18	9	4	5	37	23	31
Kolbotn	18	9	1	8	51	34	28
Team Strømmen	18	7	2	9	36	39	23
Sandviken	18	4	6	8	23	44	18
Klepp	18	5	2	11	26	40	17
Arna-Bjørnar	18	4	1	13	31	54	13
Medkila	18	2	1	15	12	65	7

Cup Final: Røa 2-1 Asker

POLAND 2004-05
FIRST DIVISION

	Pl	W	D	L	F	A	Pts
AZS Wroclaw	18	17	0	1	82	9	51
Czarni Sosnowiec	18	15	1	2	102	11	46
Medyk Konin	18	13	1	4	84	10	40
Cisy Naleczów	18	11	2	5	39	22	35
Atena Pozna	18	8	3	7	18	25	27
ZTKKF Stilon Gorzów	18	6	4	8	38	37	22
Gol Czestochowa	18	6	1	11	27	56	19
Praga Warszawa	18	4	2	12	19	75	14
Podgórze Kraków	18	2	2	14	11	59	8
TKKF Checz Gdynia	18	0	0	18	4	120	0

Cup Final: Medyk Konin 2-0 Czarni Sosnowiec

RUSSIA 2004
FIRST DIVISION

	Pl	W	D	L	F	A	Pts
Lada Togliatti	18	10	5	3	46	17	35
Rossiyanka	18	9	5	4	33	20	32
Energiya Voronezh	18	8	7	3	34	12	31
Nadezhda Noginsk	18	5	7	6	18	14	22
CSK VVS Samara	16	6	7	3	26	12	25
Chertanovo Moskva	16	3	6	7	22	24	15
Nika Nizhniy Novgorod	16	0	1	15	5	85	1

Cup Final: Lada Togliatti 1-1 5-2 Rossiyanka

SCOTLAND 2004-05
FIRST DIVISION

	Pl	W	D	L	F	A	Pts
Glasgow City	22	21	0	1	85	16	63
Kilmarnock	22	15	2	5	72	30	47
Hibernian Ladies	17	15	1	1	99	22	46
Raith Rovers Ladies	22	11	3	8	57	46	36
Aberdeen	21	8	5	8	56	56	29
Newburgh	20	8	4	8	58	52	28
Hamilton Academical	18	8	4	6	32	32	28
Whitehill Welfare Ladies	23	8	3	12	56	54	27
Queens Park	21	5	6	10	47	66	21
Cove Rangers	22	4	4	14	51	94	16
Clyde Ladies	21	2	4	15	33	95	10
East Kilbride	19	0	2	17	25	108	2

SWITZERLAND 2004-05
LIGUE NATIONALE A

	Pl	W	D	L	F	A	Pts
SC LUwin.ch	21	14	7	0	58	12	49
FC Rapid Lugano	21	13	3	5	42	32	42
SV Seebach Zürich	21	9	4	8	40	38	31
FC Bern	21	7	8	6	41	34	29
FC Zuchwil	21	7	7	7	40	28	28
Ruggell-Liechtenstein	21	6	7	8	21	25	25
FC Schwerzenbach	21	5	6	10	30	36	21
FC Malters	21	1	2	18	22	89	5

Cup Final: SC LUwin.ch 3-1 SV Seebach Züirich

USA 2005
W-LEAGUE

	Pl	W	D	L	F	A	Pts
Central Conference Atlantic Division							
Charlotte Lady Eagles†	14	11	1	2	37	11	34
Central Florida Krush †	14	11	0	3	32	13	33
Atlanta Silverbacks	14	8	1	5	30	20	25
Richmond K. Destiny	14	6	0	8	20	23	18
Hampton R. Piranhas	14	5	3	6	28	29	18
N. Virginia Majestics	14	5	0	9	22	33	15
Bradenton Athletics	14	4	3	7	12	25	15
Carolina Dynamo	14	1	2	11	10	37	5
Central Conference Midwest Division							
Detroit Jaguars †	14	11	0	3	38	13	33
Cleveland Internationals †	14	9	0	5	36	20	27
London Gryphons	14	8	2	4	31	18	26
Cincinnati Ladyhawks	14	6	1	7	33	40	19
Fort Wayne Fever	14	5	0	9	24	36	15
Chicago Gaels	14	4	2	8	27	38	14
West Michigan Firewomen	14	3	1	10	21	45	10

Conference play-off semi-finals: Central Florida 3-2 Detroit;
Charlotte 6-2 Cleveland; Final: Central Florida 1-0 Charlotte

	Pl	W	D	L	F	A	Pts
Eastern Conference Northeast Division							
New Jersey Wildcats ‡	14	13	0	1	57	2	39
Boston Renegades †	14	9	0	5	43	23	27
Long Isl. Lady Riders †	14	8	0	6	24	14	24
WM Lady Pioneers †	14	7	1	6	17	16	22
New York Magic †	14	5	1	8	19	26	16
New H. Lady Phantoms	14	3	0	11	14	56	6
South Jersey Banshees	14	1	0	13	6	57	3
Eastern Conference Northern Division							
Ottawa Fury †	14	13	0	1	64	7	39
Toronto Lady Lynx †	14	11	0	3	44	16	33
Vermont Lady Voltage†	14	7	0	7	21	21	21
Sudbury Canadians	14	3	0	11	15	50	9
Rochester Ravens	14	3	0	11	14	50	9

Conference play-off first round: Boston 4-0 New York;
Long Island 3-1 WM Lady Pioneers; Toronto 6-0 Vermont;
Semi-finals: Toronto 2-1 Boston, Ottawa 5-1 Long Island
Final: Ottawa 2-0 Toronto

	Pl	W	D	L	F	A	Pts
Western Conference							
Vancouver Whitecaps †	14	13	0	1	47	4	39
Arizona Heatwave †	14	10	1	3	40	17	31
Mile High Mustangs	14	10	0	4	40	20	30
Denver Lady Cougars	14	7	1	6	26	24	22
Seattle Sounders	14	5	1	8	25	27	16
Fort Collins Force	14	2	1	11	13	44	7
San Diego Gauchos	14	0	0	14	4	59	0

Championship Finals

Semi-finals: Ottawa Fury 2-1 Central Florida Krush;
New Jersey Wildcats 2-1 Vancouver Whitecaps
Final: **New Jersey Wildcats** 3-0 Ottawa Fury
† Qualified for the play-offs • ‡ Qualified for the finals

SWEDEN 2004
DAMALLSVENSKAN

	Pl	W	D	L	F	A	Pts
Djurgården/Alvsjö	22	19	2	1	74	23	59
Umeå IK	22	19	1	2	106	17	58
Malmö FF	22	15	4	3	67	23	49
Kopparbergs/Göteborg	22	10	4	8	29	33	34
Hammarby IF DFF	22	10	3	9	44	42	33
Linköpings FC	22	8	4	10	28	37	28
Karlslunds IF DFF	22	7	3	12	32	54	24
Mallbackens IF	22	6	4	12	17	41	22
Sunnanå SK	22	5	5	12	30	47	20
Själevads IK	22	5	5	12	19	49	20
Bälinge IF	22	4	7	11	23	55	17
Stattena IF	22	1	4	17	13	61	7

Cup Final: Djurgården/Alvsjö 2-1 Umeå IK

SLOVAKIA 2004-05
FIRST DIVISION

	Pl	W	D	L	F	A	Pts
Sala	20	20	0	0	116	7	60
PVFA	20	16	1	3	77	10	49
Humenné	20	12	3	5	51	56	39
Ziar nad Hronom	20	11	2	7	39	47	35
Nové Zámky	20	10	3	7	42	38	33
Zilina	20	9	4	7	39	32	31
Malé Dvorníky	20	7	3	10	25	30	24
Rimavská Sobota	20	5	2	13	22	47	17
Trnava	20	2	6	12	17	52	12
Priechod	20	2	2	16	15	75	8
Cadca	20	1	4	15	9	59	7

USA 2005
WPSL

	Pl	W	D	L	F	A	Pts
West Division							
California Storm †	14	13	1	0	45	7	42
Ajax of America	14	12	0	2	42	14	36
Utah Spiders	14	7	2	5	26	22	23
San Diego SeaLions	14	5	0	9	26	24	15
Elk Grove Pride	14	4	3	7	22	20	15
Las Vegas Tabagators	14	4	3	7	21	34	15
San Fran. Nighthawks	14	3	1	10	11	45	10
Lamorinda East Bay	14	1	4	9	15	42	8
East Division							
New England Mutiny †	13	13	0	0	38	7	39
Steel City Sparks †	13	7	3	3	28	22	26
Bay State Select	13	7	1	5	29	17	22
Philadelphia Pirates	13	5	3	5	18	25	18
Massachusetts Stingers	14	3	6	5	20	19	15
Rhode Island Rays	11	2	4	5	13	19	10
Boston-North Aztecs	13	3	1	9	9	28	10
Maryland Pride	12	2	0	10	16	34	6
Central Division							
FC Indiana †	4	4	0	0	20	3	12
Houston Stars	6	2	2	2	10	17	8
Everton FC America	4	0	2	2	6	8	2
St. Louis Archers	2	0	0	2	1	9	0

Championship Finals

Semi-finals: California Storm 3-0 Steel City Sparks
FC Indiana 4-0 New England Mutiny
Final: **FC Indiana** 4-3 California Storm
† Qualified for the finals

2006 FIFA WORLD CUP™ QUALIFIERS

QUALIFYING MATCHES PLAYED IN ASIA

Preliminary Round		

First Group Stage		

Final Group Stage		

Group 1		Pts
Iran	IRN	15
Jordan	JOR	12
Qatar	QAT	9
Laos	LAO	0

Group 2		Pts
Uzbekistan	UZB	16
Iraq	IRQ	11
Palestine	PAL	7
Chinese Taipei	TPE	0

Group 3		Pts
Japan	JPN	18
Oman	OMA	10
India	IND	4
Singapore	SIN	3

Bangladesh	BAN	0	0
Tajikistan	TJK	2	2
Turkmenistan	TKM	11	2
Afghanistan	AFG	0	0
Chinese Taipei	TPE	3	3
Macao	MAC	0	1
Pakistan	PAK	0	0
Kyrgyzstan	KGZ	2	4
Laos	LAO	0	0
Sri Lanka	SRI	0	3
Mongolia	MGL	0	0
Maldives	MDV	1	12
Guam - withdrew	GUM		
Nepal - withdrew	NEP		

Laos qualified as best loser after the
withdrawl of Guam and Nepal.

Group 4		Pts
Kuwait	KUW	15
China PR	CHN	15
Hong Kong	HKG	6
Malaysia	MYS	0

Group 5		Pts
Korea DPR	PRK	11
United Arab Emirates	UAE	10
Thailand	THA	7
Yemen	YEM	5

Group 6		Pts
Bahrain	BHR	14
Syria	SYR	8
Tajikistan	TJK	7
Kyrgyzstan	KGZ	4

Group 7		Pts
Korea Republic	KOR	14
Lebanon	LIB	11
Vietnam SR	VIE	4
Maldives	MDV	4

Group 8		Pts
Saudi Arabia	KSA	18
Turkmenistan	TKM	7
Indonesia	IDN	7
Sri Lanka	SRI	2

Group A		Pts
Saudi Arabia	KSA	11
Korea Republic	KOR	10
Kuwait	KUW	4
Uzbekistan	UZB	2

Remaining fixtures: 17/08/2005
Korea Republic v Saudi Arabia;
Uzbekistan v Kuwait

Group B		Pts
Iran	IRN	13
Japan	JPN	12
Bahrain	BHR	4
Korea DPR	PRK	0

Remaining fixtures : 17/08/2005
Japan v Iran; Bahrain v Korea DPR

Saudi Arabia, Korea Republic,
Iran and Japan qualified for the
finals in Germany. The two third-
placed teams play off with the
winner meeting the fourth-placed
team from CONCACAF

PRELIMINARY ROUND

Mirpur Sher-e-Bangla, Dhaka
26-11-2003, 15:00, 6 000, Khanthachai THA

BAN 0 2 TJK

Khamidov 11, Hakimov 51

#	BANGLADESH	min	min	TAJIKISTAN	#
1	HAQUE Aminul			KHABIBULLOEV Aslidin	1
2	HOSSAIN Firoj		59	KNITEL Denis	3
4	BARMAN Rajani			TOURDEV Akhliddin	4
5	ISLAM Kazi			OEV Dzhamolidin	6
6	MUNWAR Hossian	46	71	LRGASHEV Odil	7
8	ARMAN Mohammed	70		KHOLOMATOV Akmal	8
10	ALFAZ Mohammed	57		NAZAROV Oraz	9
11	KANCHAN Rokonuzzaman			MOUMINOV Takhirdjon	10
15	MUNNA Motiur			HAMIDOV Sukhrob	11
16	BIDDUTH Azul Hossain	67	77	HAKIMOV Numordzhon	15
19	SUJAN Mohammed			MUHIDINOV Dzhamikhon	24
	Tr: GHULAM Sarwar			Tr: NAZAROV Sharif	
7	AL MAMUN Hassan	70	59	ZUVAYDOV Safardion	5
12	SAIF Saiful Islam	46	71	KHUJAMOV Subkhon	12
20	KABIR Ariful	57	77	RABIEV Yusuf	17

Central Stadium, Dushanbe
30-11-2003, 14:00, 12 000, Pereira IND

TJK 2 0 BAN

Kholomatov 15, Rabiev 83

#	TAJIKISTAN	min	min	BANGLADESH	#
1	KHABIBULLOEV Aslidin			HAQUE Aminul	1
3	KNITEL Denis			HOSSAIN Firoj	2
4	TOURDEV Akhliddin			BARMAN Rajani	4
6	OEV Dzhamolidin			ISLAM Kazi	5
7	LRGASHEV Odil			AL MAMUN Hassan	7
8	KHOLOMATOV Akmal	88	88	ARMAN Mohammed	8
9	NAZAROV Oraz	46	46	ALFAZ Mohammed	10
10	MOUMINOV Takhirdjon			KANCHAN Rokonuzzaman	11
11	KHAMIDOV Sukhrob	86		Khan Arif	13
15	HAKIMOV Numordzhon	46	46	MUNNA Motiur	15
24	MUHIDINOV Dzhamikhon	67		SUJAN Mohammed	19
	Tr: NAZAROV Sharif			Tr: GHULAM Sarwar	
17	RABIEV Yusuf	67	88	MUNWAR Hossian	6
25	NEMATOV Shujoat	86	46	SAIF Saiful Islam	12
			46	KABIR Ariful	20

Olympic Stadium, Ashgabat
19-11-2003, 19:00, 12 000, Busurmankulov KGZ

TKM 11 0 AFG

Ovekov 2 6 35, Kuliev 3 8 22 81, Bayramov.N 27
Berdyev 42, Agabaev 3 49 65 67, Urazov 90

#	TURKMENISTAN	min	min	AFGHANISTAN	#
1	NABOYCHENKO Evgeni			JAMSHED Jamshed	1
2	OVEKOV Guvanch	53	58	AHMAD Basher	2
6	DOURDUEV Kourbangeldy		46	AZIZ Rohllah	3
7	MINGAZOV Kamil			AHMAD Rahil	5
15	BERDYEV Omar			ZIA Ahmad	6
19	HAYDAROV Alik		46	ZARIMI Nadjibilah	7
20	KULIEV Begench			MAHMOUDI Raza	8
21	BAYRAMOV Vladimir	46		ZAKI Mohammad	9
22	BAYRAMOV Nazar	75		REZAEE Raza	10
42	AGAYEV Muslim			MARMOOF Abdul	12
48	BORODOLIMOV Yuri		76	KHESRAW Ahmad	19
	Tr: KURBANMAMEDOV Rakhim			Tr: KARGAR Mohamed	
10	URAZOV Didar	53	76	KHEDRI Qais	4
11	AGABAEV Redjep	46	46	TAHIR Sayed	16
14	SAPAROV Rustam	75	46	MUHANDES Eris	16

National Stadium, Kabul
23-11-2003, 13:30, 6 000, Khan PAK

AFG 0 2 TKM

Kuliev 2 85 91

#	AFGHANISTAN	min	min	TURKMENISTAN	#
22	NADER Mohammad			BERDYEV Baramaniyaz	16
3	AZIZ Rohllah		89	OVEKOV Guvanch	6
4	KHEDRI Qais			DOURDUEV Kourbangeldy	6
6	ZIA Ahmad			MINGAZOV Kamil	7
8	MAHMOUDI Raza		57	NAZAROV Artem	8
9	ZAKI Mohammad		31	MIRZOEV Arif	9
10	REZAEE Raza			SAPAROV Rustam	14
12	MARMOOF Abdul			BERDYEV Omar	15
14	AHMAD Ali	84		HAYDAROV Alik	19
16	MUHANDES Eris	46		KULIEV Begench	20
16	FAIZI Ali	46		BAYRAMOV Nazar	22
	Tr: KARGAR Mohamed			Tr: KURBANMAMEDOV Rakhim	
13	OMARI Ali	84	31	NASYROV Mekan	3
15	BRATYAN Mohammad	46	89	HAJIEV Didar	4
			57	MEREDOV Bayramduray	5

Chun Shan, Taipei
23-11-2003, 14:00 2 000, Napitupulu IDN

TPE 3 0 MAC

Chuang 23, Chen.JT 52
Chang 57

#	CHINESE TAIPEI	min	min	MACAO	#
1	YANG Cheng Hsing			CHAN Domingos	1
2	JU Wen Bin			AU Kee Yuen	2
3	CHEN Jeng I			HEITOR Alexandre	4
4	WANG Chien Hsiang			LAM Ka Koi	5
5	TSAI Hui Kai	33	33	SOUSA Chzung	6
6	LIN Kuei Pin			IAN Chi Pang	8
9	CHEN Jiunn Ming	76	58	LEI Fu Weng	9
10	CHUANG Yao Tsung			ARMANDO Manuel	10
12	WU Chun I	63	69	WONG Hon Fai	12
17	Chang Wu Yeh			CHONG Kun Kan	14
20	CHEN Jui Te			HO VENG Fai	16
	Tr: LEE Po Houng			Tr: IMAI Masataka	
13	PAN Kuao Kai	76	33	HOI Man Io	7
30	TSENG Tai Lin	63	58	CHEANG Chon Man	11
			69	CHAN Man HEI	13

Campo Desportivo do Canidromo, Macao
29-11-2003, 15:00, 250, Zhou Weixin CHN

MAC 1 3 TPE

Lei 87
Chen JT 2 14 69, Chiang 66

#	MACAO	min	min	CHINESE TAIPEI	#
1	CHAN Domingos			YANG Cheng Hsing	1
2	AU Kee Yuen		73	JU Wen Bin	2
3	IEONG Lap Tap			CHEN Jeng I	3
4	HEITOR Alexandre			WANG Chien Hsiang	4
7	HOI Man Io	89		TSAI Hui Kai	5
8	IAN Chi Pang			LIN Kuei Pin	6
9	LEI Fu Weng		78	CHEN Jiunn Ming	9
10	ARMANDO Manuel			CHUANG Yao Tsung	10
11	CHEANG Chon Man	72	63	WU Chun I	11
14	CHONG Kun Kan	46		Chang Wu Yeh	17
16	HO VENG Fai			CHEN Jui Te	20
	Tr: IMAI Masataka			Tr: LEE Po Houng	
12	WONG Hon Fai	46	73	TU Ming Feng	8
13	CHAN Man HEI	72	63	CHIANG Shih Lu	11
15	HO Wai Tong	89	78	LIN Chia Sheng	23

People Sports Complex, Karachi
29-11-2003, 15:00, 10 000, Nesar BAN

PAK   0   2   KGZ

Boldygin 36, Chikishev 59

PAKISTAN			KYRGYZSTAN	
1	KHAN Jaffar		DJALILOV Zakair	1
2	MOHAMMED Tariq		VYACHESLAV Amin	2
3	ARIF Masih		KONONOV Vassili	3
4	TANVEER Ahmad		SYDYKOV Ruslan	4
6	SAJJAD Hussain		SHARAPOV Alimordon	5
7	SHAHID	60	KNIAZEV Sergey	6
8	ARIF Mehmood		CHERTKOV Vladimir	7
9	QADEER Ahmad		HARCHENKO Vadim	8
10	ADEEL Ahmad	63	BOLDYGIN Evgeny	11
11	SAJJAD Haider	30 55	ISHMAKOV Rinat	17
12	NASSER Ahmed	70	CHIKISHEV Sergey	19
	Tr: LUFTI Tariq		Tr: ZAKIROV Nematjan	
13	SHAHID Naim	30 63	KORNILOV Roman	9
14	ZAHID Hameed	60 70	SAMSALIEV Talant	13
		55	KASYMOV Marlen	14

Spartak, Bishkek
3-12-2003, 13:00, 12 000, Mamedov TKM

KGZ   4   0   PAK

Chikishev 18, Chertkov 28
Boldygin 67, Krasnov 92

KYRGYZSTAN			PAKISTAN	
1	DJALILOV Zakair		KHAN Jaffar	1
2	VYACHESLAV Amin		ARIF Masih	3
3	KONONOV Vassili		TANVEER Ahmad	4
4	SYDYKOV Ruslan		SAJJAD Hussain	6
5	SHARAPOV Alimordon		SHAHID	7
6	KNIAZEV Sergey		ARIF Mehmood	8
7	CHERTKOV Vladimir	69	QADEER Ahmad	9
8	HARCHENKO Vadim	76	ADEEL Ahmad	10
11	BOLDYGIN Evgeny	88	NASSER Ahmed	12
17	ISHMAKOV Rinat		SHAHID Naim	13
19	CHIKISHEV Sergey	67 41	JAMSHED Anwar	18
	Tr: ZAKIROV Nematjan		Tr: LUFTI Tariq	
9	KORNILOV Roman	67 41	MOHAMMED Tariq	2
12	BELDINOV Aleksandr	76 69	ZAHID Hameed	14

Stade National, Vientiane
29-11-2003, 17:00, 4 500, Luong The Tai VIE

LAO   0   0   SRI

LAOS			SRI LANKA	
20	SENGPHET Vongsayarat		THILAKARATANE Sugath	1
3	SAYYAVONG Khaisone	78	STEINWALL Dudley	6
4	VILAYPHONG Xayavong		CHATURA Siyaguna	7
5	CHALANA Louane Amat		HASSAN Hamza	8
6	TAPSOUVANH Anan	70	RAHEEM Imthyas	9
7	SOUVANHNO Louang Amath	87	EDRIBANDANAGE Channa	10
9	KHANYYAVONG Latthaphone	69	WEERARATHNA Kassun	11
12	PHAYVANH Loung Lath		MOHAMED Azmeer	14
13	CHANTHALOME Phutthadavong		PERERA Isuru	16
16	VIENGAZOUN Bounthaiyavong		PERERA Indika	19
17	SISOMEPHONE Sathongyot		FUARD Kamaldeen	20
	Tr: SAVTHONG Syprasay		Tr: SAMPATH PERERA Kolomage	
8	SOUMPHONPHADY Cholaka	78	87 MUDIYANSELAGE Rathna	15
10	PHONEPHACHAN Kholadeth	69	70 ABEYSEKARA Niroshan	17

Sugathadasa, Colombo
3-12-2003, 18:30, 6 000, Saleem MDV

SRI   3   0   LAO

Edribandanage 35
Weerarathna 59, Hameed 93+

SRI LANKA			LAOS	
1	THILAKARATANE Sugath		SENGPHET Vongsayarat	20
4	FERNANDO Cristeen	46	SAYYAVONG Khaisone	3
6	STEINWALL Dudley		VILAYPHONG Xayavong	4
7	CHATURA Siyaguna		CHALANA Louane Amat	5
8	HASSAN Hamza		TAPSOUVANH Anan	6
10	EDRIBANDANAGE Channa	88	55 SOUVANHNO Louang Amath	7
11	WEERARATHNA Kassun		PHONEPHACHAN Kholadeth	10
14	MOHAMED Azmeer		PHAYVANH Loung Lath	12
16	PERERA Isuru		CHANTHALOME Phutthadavong	13
19	PERERA Indika		VIENGAZOUN Bounthaiyavong	16
20	FUARD Kamaldeen	84	SISOMEPHONE Sathongyot	17
	Tr: FERREIRA George		Tr: SAVTHONG Syprasay	
12	HAMEED Mohamed	88	84 KHANSAY Phakasy	2
			46 SOUMPHONPHADY Cholaka	8
			55 KHOUPHACHANSY Nitsavong	15

Ulaan Baatar Stadium, Ulaan-Baatar
29-11-2003, 13:00, 2 000, Yang Zhiqiang CHN

MGL   0   1   MDV

Nizam 24

MONGOLIA			MALDIVES	
1	JARGALSAIKHAN Enkhbayer		MOHAMED Imran	18
2	BAYASGALAN Garidmagnai	75	FAZEEL Ibrahim	5
3	DONOROV Lumbengarav		NIZAM Mohamed	7
7	DAVAA Bayazorig		LUTHFY Ashraf	8
8	SEMBAATAR Baatarsuren	51	35 THARIQ Ahmed	9
9	SUKHBAATAR Gerelt-Od	68	90 ASHFAG Ali	10
11	CHOUIL Altantogos		AZEEM Yoosuf	12
12	GANBAATAR Tugsbayar		GHANI Assad Abdul	13
14	MUNKHTOGOO Idersaikhan		JAMEEL Mohamed	15
15	GANBAT Bat-Yalalt		GHANEE Anwar Abdul	19
20	CHIMIDDORJ Munkhbat		IBRAHIM Sabah	21
	Tr: OTGONBAYER Ishdorj		Tr: GONCALVES Manuel	
5	KHISHIGDALAI Battulga	51	90 HABEEB Hussain	4
10	ENKHBAYER Chinzorig	68	35 SHIYAM Ibrahim	14
			75 AMIL Ibrahim	16

Galolhu National Stadium, Male
3-12-2003, 15:35, 9 000, Arambekade SRI

MDV   12   0   MGL

Ashfag 4 4 61 63 68, Nizam 42, Fazeel 2 46+ 49+, Ghani 65
Thariq 2 74 78, Khishigdalai OG 75, Nazeeh 80

MALDIVES			MONGOLIA	
18	MOHAMED Imran		16 JARGALSAIKHAN Enkhbayer	1
5	FAZEEL Ibrahim	65	BAYASGALAN Garidmagnai	2
6	GHANEE Anwar Abdul		34 DONOROV Lumbengarav	3
7	NIZAM Mohamed	75	KHISHIGDALAI Battulga	5
10	UMAR Ali		46 GOMBOLKHAM Ariumbayer	6
11	AZEEM Yoosuf	70	DAVAA Bayazorig	7
12	ASHFAG Ali		SUKHBAATAR Gerelt-Od	9
13	GHANI Assad Abdul		CHOUIL Altantogos	11
14	JAMEEL Mohamed		GANBAATAR Tugsbayar	12
17	LUTHFY Ashraf		69 OYUNCHIMEG Chingis	19
21	IBRAHIM Sabah		CHIMIDDORJ Munkhbat	20
	Tr: GONCALVES Manuel		Tr: OTGONBAYAR Ishdorj	
9	ASHFAN Ahmed	70 69	MUNKHTOGOO Idersaikhan	14
16	NAZEEH Mohamed	75 46	GANBAT Bat-Yalalt	15
19	THARIQ Ahmed	65 16	KHIIMOIRISAN Khangal	18

SECOND PHASE GROUP 1	PL	W	D	L	F	A	PTS	IRN	JOR	QAT	LAO
1 Iran	6	5	0	1	22	4	15		0-1	3-1	7-0
2 Jordan	6	4	0	2	10	6	12	0-2		1-0	5-0
3 Qatar	6	3	0	3	16	8	9	2-3	2-0		5-0
4 Laos	6	0	0	6	3	33	0	0-7	2-3	1-6	

Al-Qwaismeh, Amman
18-02-2004, 16:00, 5 000, Al Mozahmi OMA

JOR 5   0 LAO

Aqel [40], Shelbaieh [45]
Al Shagran [63], Ragheb [90], Shehdeh [90]

JORDAN				LAOS
22	MAHAD Issa			KHANYYAVONG Sithalay 1
4	Al AWADAT Rateb	71		VIENGAZOUN Bounthaiyavong 3
6	BANI YASEEN Bashar			VILAYPHONG Xayavong 4
8	QASEM Hassouneh			CHALANA Louane Amat 5
9	SHELBAIEH Mahmoud			TAPSOUVANH Anan 6
10	MANSOUR Moayad			DALAPHONE Valasine 7
11	AL ZBOUN Anas	46		PHAPHOUVANIN Visay 9
13	ABU ALIEH Qosai		70	PHOTHILATH Vilasack 11
16	IBRAHIM Faisal			PHAYVANH Loung Lath 12
17	AQEL Hatem		12	NAMTHAVISAY Kovanh 19
20	AL SHAGRAN Badran	70		CHANTHALOME Phutthadavong 20
	Tr: Al Gohary Mahmoud			Tr: SAVTHONG Syprasay
2	SHEHDEH Mustafa	71	70	THONGPHACHAN Sengphet 14
14	AL SHBOUL Haitham	46	12	PHACHOUMPHON Sunthasine 16
24	RAGHEB Awad	70		

Azadi, Tehran
18-02-2004, 19:00, BCD, Haj Khader SYR

IRN 3   1 QAT

Vahedi [8], Mahdavikia [44]
Daei [62]
Rasoul [70]

IRAN				QATAR
1	MIRZAPOUR Ebrahim			AL MEAMARI Abdulrahman 3
2	MAHDAVIKIA Mehdi			AL SHAMMARI Saud 5
5	REZAEI Rahman			AL SHAMMARI Saad 8
6	NEKOUNAM Javad	50	86	RASOUL Waleed 11
8	KARIMI Ali	88	46	Ahmed Walled 12
10	DAEI Ali			MAHMOUD Yousef 15
11	VAHEDI Alireza	75		AL MEAMARI Selman 19
13	KABEI Hossein			FAZLI Mubarak 20
14	NAVIDKIA Moharram			KONI Abdulla Obaid 21
18	BADAVI Ali			AHMED Mohamed 24
20	NOSRATI Mohammad	83		AL BALOUSHI Mubarak 28
	Tr: IVANKOVIC Branko			Tr: TROUSSIER Philippe
15	TAGHIPOUR Ebrahim	88	83	AL MARRI Ali 7
19	ABBASI Seyed	50	46	BECHIR Sayd Ali 9
21	RAJABZADEH Mehdi	75	86	SIDDIQ Majid 13

Stade National, Vientiane
31-03-2004, 17:00, 7 000, Yang Mu-Sheng TPE

LAO 0   7 IRN

Daei 2 [9] [17p], Enayati 2 [32] [36]
Khouphachansy OG [54], Taghipour 2 [68] [83]

LAOS				IRAN
1	KHANYYAVONG Sithalay			MIRZAPOUR Ebrahim 1
2	KHOTSOMBATH Anousone			TAGHIPOUR Ebrahim 3
4	VILAYPHONG Xayavong			GOLMOHAMMADI Yahya 4
5	CHALANA Louane Amat			NEKOUNAM Javad 6
6	TAPSOUVANH Anan			KARIMI Ali 8
7	DALAPHONE Valasine	81		ENAYATI Reza 9
9	PHAPHOUVANIN Visay			DAEI Ali 10
10	KHOUPHACHANSY Nitsavong	59		VAHEDI Alireza 11
12	PHAYVANH Loung Lath		73	KABEI Hossein 13
19	SOUTHSAKHONE Vongsamany	89	79	BADAVI Ali 18
19	NAMTHAVISAY Kovanh		46	RAJABZADEH Mehdi 24
	Tr: SAVTHONG Syprasay			Tr: IVANKOVIC Branko
3	VIENGAZOUN Bounthaiyavong	81	73	AMIR Mehdi 2
14	THONGPHACHAN Sengphet	89	46	NAVIDKIA Moharram 14
20	CHANTHALOME Phutthadavong	59	79	BORHANI Arash 23

Al-Qwaismeh, Amman
31-03-2004, 18:30, 15 000, Shaban KUW

JOR 1   0 QAT

Mansour [70]

JORDAN				QATAR
1	SHAFI SABBAH Amer			ANYASS Mohammed 22
4	Al AWADAT Rateb			AL KHATER Nayef 2
6	BANI YASEEN Bashar		66	AL SHAMMARI Saad 5
8	QASEM Hassouneh			AL NAEMI Dahi 6
9	SHELBAIEH Mahmoud	80	77	AL KATHIRI Saoud 14
10	MANSOUR Moayad		77	AL BLOOSHI Mohamed 16
14	AL SHBOUL Haitham			FAZLI Mubarak 20
16	IBRAHIM Faisal			KONI Abdulla Obaid 21
17	AQEL Hatem			HASHIM Ahmad Khalifa 23
18	ABU ZEMA Abdullah	18		MUBARK Nasser Kamil 25
20	AL SHAGRAN Badran	56		RAJAB Bilal 30
	Tr: Al Gohary Mahmoud			Tr: TROUSSIER Philippe
11	AL ZBOUN Anas	56	77	BECHIR Sayd Ali 9
13	ABU ALIEH Qosai	18	66	AHMED Waleed 11
19	ABDEL FATTAH Hasan	80	77	ABDULMAJID Wesam 17

Azadi, Tehran
9-06-2004, 18:30, 35 000, Kamikawa JPN

IRN 0   1 JOR

Al Shboul [83]

IRAN				JORDAN
1	MIRZAPOUR Ebrahim			SHAFI SABBAH Amer 1
2	MAHDAVIKIA Mehdi			ALMALTAHA Khaled 3
4	GOLMOHAMMADI Yahya			Al AWADAT Rateb 4
5	REZAEI Rahman	63		BANI YASEEN Bashar 6
6	NEKOUNAM Javad		75	QASEM Hassouneh 8
8	KARIMI Ali		66	SHELBAIEH Mahmoud 9
10	DAEI Ali			MANSOUR Moayad 10
11	VAHEDI Alireza	58		ABU ALIEH Qosai 13
13	KABEI Hossein			IBRAHIM Faisal 16
18	BADAVI Ali			AQEL Hatem 17
20	NOSRATI Mohammad	72		AL SHAGRAN Badran 20
	Tr: FARAKI Hossein			Tr: Al Gohary Mahmoud
14	BORHANI Arash	63	72	AL ZBOUN Anas 11
17	MOBALI Eman	58	66	AL SHBOUL Haitem 14
			75	MAHMOUD Hasan Abdel 19

Al Etehad, Doha
9-06-2004, 19:30, 500, Abu Armana PAL

QAT 5   0 LAO

Fazli 2 [17] [37], Abdulla 2 [69] [86]
Bechir [89]

QATAR				LAOS
22	ABDULLA Abdulaziz			KHANYYAVONG Sithalay 1
2	FAZLI Mubarak			KHOTSOMBATH Anousone 2
5	JADOUA Abumousa			XAYAVONG Vilayphone 4
6	AL Khater Nayef Mubark			CHALANA Louane Amat 5
9	Bechir Sayd Ali		74	DALAPHONE Valasine 7
11	HASSAN Magid	38	90	PHAPHOUVANIN Visay 9
14	AL KATHIRI		43	PHOTHILATH Vilasack 11
15	AHMED Waleed			PHAYVANH Loung Lath 12
16	AL BLOOSHI Mohamed	46		VONGSAMANY Davone 15
23	MUSA Alown	58		NAMTHAVISAY Kovanh 19
27	ABDUL MAJID Wesam			SANASITH Anolack 24
	Tr: TROUSSIER Philippe			Tr: SAVTHONG Syprasay
7	MOOSA Ahmed	46	74	BOUNTHAIYAVONG Davone 3
8	DAD Abdulaziz	58	90	PHACHOUMPHON Sunthasine 16
10	ABDULLA Waleed Jassim	38	43	CHANTHALOME Phutthadavong 20

Stade National, Vientiane
8-09-2004, 17:00, 2 900, Napitupulu IDN

LAO 1 6 QAT

Chanthalome 88 | Abdulmajid 36, Mubarak 42, Bechir 50, Rasoul 70, Abdulla.M 86, Al Shammari 89

	LAOS			QATAR	
1	KHANYYAVONG Sithalay			HASHIM Ahmad Khalifa	28
4	XAYAVONG Vilayphone	71	53	ABDURAHMAN Alkuwari	3
5	CHALANA Louane Amat			BUDAWOOD Meshal	6
6	TAPSOUVANH Anan			AL SHAMMARI Saad	8
7	DALAPHONE Valasine		63	BECHIR Sayd Ali	9
9	PHAPHOUVANIN Visay			ABDULLA Meshal	11
12	PHAYVANH Loung Lath	78		MAHMOUD Yousuf	15
14	THONGPHACHAN Sengphet			MESBEH Selman	19
17	SISOMEPHONE Sathongyot	75	69	MUBARAK Nasser Kamil	20
20	CHANTHALOME Phutthadavong			AL ROMAIHI Hussain	21
24	SANASITH Anolack	15		ABDULMAJID Wesam	27
	Tr: SAVTHONG Syprasay			Tr: MUSOVIC Dzemaludin	
13	SOUTHSAKHONE Vongsamany	75	53	ABDULLA Abdulaziz	5
19	NAMTHAVISAY Kovanh	71	69	RASOUL Waleed	10
78	SIRIVONG Silasay	78	63	AL BUAINAIN Jassim	25

King Hussein Sport Complex, Amman
8-09-2004, 20:00, 20 000, Lu Jun CHN

JOR 0 2 IRN

Vahedi 80, Daei 91+

	JORDAN			IRAN	
1	SHAFI SABBAH Amer			MIRZAPOUR Ebrahim	1
3	ALMALTAAH Khaled	46		GOLMOHAMMADI Yahya	4
4	AL AWADAT Rateb			REZAEI Rahman	5
6	BANI YASEEN Bashar			NEKOUNAM Javad	6
8	QASEM Hassouneh			KARIMI Ali	8
9	SHELBAIEH Mahmoud			HASHEMIAN Vahid	9
10	MANSOUR Moayad	60	91	DAEI Ali	10
13	ABU ALIEH Qosai		69	AZIZI Khodadad	11
16	IBRAHIM Faisal		76	KABEI Hossein	13
17	AQEL Hatem Mohammad			KAMELI Jalal	19
18	ABU ZEMA Abdullah	85		NOSRATI Mohammad	20
	Tr: AL GOHARY Mahmoud			Tr: IVANKOVIC Branko	
11	AL ZBOUN Anas	60	76	KAZEMEYAN Javad	14
14	AL SHOBOUL Haitham	46	69	VAHEDI Alireza	22
20	AL SHAGRAN Badran	85	91	ALAVI Seyed	26

Stade National, Vientiane
13-10-2004, 17:00, 3 000, Gosh BAN

LAO 2 3 JOR

Phaphouvanin 13, Thongphachan 53 | Al Maharmeh 28, Al Shagran 2 73 76

	LAOS			JORDAN	
1	KHANYYAVONG Sithalay	22		TALEB Feras	12
2	KHOTSOMBATH Anousone		63	ALMALTAAH Khaled	3
5	CHALANA Louane Amat			BANI YASEEN Bashar	6
6	TAPSOUVANH Anan			QASEM Hassouneh	8
7	DALAPHONE Valasine		80	SHELBAIEH Mahmoud	9
9	PHAPHOUVANIN Visay	84		ABU ALIEH Qosai	13
12	PHAYVANH Loung Lath			AL SHBOUL Haitham	14
14	THONGPHACHAN Sengphet	81		AL MAHARMEH Abdelhadi	15
17	SISOMEPHONE Sathongyot	71	61	IBRAHIM Faisal	16
19	NAMTHAVISAY Kovanh			AQEL Hatem Mohammad	17
20	CHANTHALOME Phutthadavong			MAHMOUD Hasan Abdel	19
	Tr: SAVTHONG Syprasay			Tr: AL GOHARY Mahmoud	
15	VONGSAMANY Davone	81	61	SHEHDEH Mustafa	2
16	PHACHOUMPHON Sunthasine	71	80	MANSOUR Moayad	10
22	THILAVONGSA Vanhnasith	22	63	AL SHAGRAN Badran	20

Al Etehad, Doha
13-10-2004, 19:30, 8 000, Kwon KOR

QAT 2 3 IRN

Rajab 18, Golmohammadi OG 75 | Hashemian 2 9 89, Borhani 78

	QATAR			IRAN	
24	AHMED Mohamed			RAHMATI Seyed	21
2	KONI Abdulla Obaid			MAHDAVIKIA Mehdi	2
6	BUDAWOOD Meshal			GOLMOHAMMADI Yahya	4
8	AL SHAMMARI Saad			REZAEI Rahman	5
9	BECHIR Sayd Ali			NEKOUNAM Javad	6
10	RASOUL Waleed	40		KARIMI Ali	8
12	MUBARAK Nasser Kamil	76		HASHEMIAN Vahid	9
15	MAHMOUD Yousuf		86	KABEI Hossein	13
17	ABDULMAJID Wesam			NOSRATI Mohammad	20
19	AL MEAMARI Selman		74	VAHEDI Alireza	22
30	RAJAB Bilal		64	ZARE Sattar	27
	Tr: MUSOVIC Dzemaludin			Tr: IVANKOVIC Branko	
5	ABDULLA Waleed	58	86	AZIZI Khodadad	11
20	FAZLI Mubarak	58 40	74	BORHANI Arash	14
23	HASHIM Ahmad Khalifa	76	64	MOBALI Eman	17

Al Etehad, Doha
17-11-2004, 19:00, 800, Yoshida JPN

QAT 2 0 JOR

Al Hamad 60, Al Khater 75

	QATAR			JORDAN	
24	SAQR Mohamed			SHAFI SABBAH Amer	1
2	KONI Abdulla Obaid		81	AL AWADAT Rateb	4
3	AL GHANIM Ibrahim			BASHAR Mustafa	6
8	AL SHAMMARI Saad			QASEM Hassouneh	8
9	BECHIR Sayd Ali	46		SHELBAIEH Mahmoud	9
10	RASOUL Waleed	84		ABU ALIEH Qosai	13
11	AL HAMAD Mohamed		61	AL-MAHARMEH Abdelhadi	15
14	AL KATHIRI Saoud			IBRAHIM Faisal	16
19	SALEH Ali Nasser			AQEL Hatem Mohammad	17
23	ABDULLA Waleed Jassim	74		MAHMOUD Hasan Abdel	19
30	RAJAB Bilal		73	DEEB Amer	23
	Tr: MUSOVIC Dzemaludin			Tr: AL GOHARY Mahmoud	
16	AL KHATER Nayef	46		MANSOUR Moayad	10
17	ABUHAMDA Bilal	74	61	AL ZBOUN Anas	11
20	AL BUAINAIN Jassim	84	81	AL SHBOUL Haitham	14

Azadi, Tehran
17-11-2004, 19:30, 30 000, Mamedov TKM

IRN 7 0 LAO

Daei 4 8 20 28 58, Nekounam 2 63 72, Borhani 69

	IRAN			LAOS	
1	MIRZAPOUR Ebrahim		84	KHANYYAVONG Sithalay	1
4	GOLMOHAMMADI Yahya			KHOTSOMBATH Anousone	2
6	NEKOUNAM Javad			XAYAVONG Vilayphone	4
8	KARIMI Ali			CHALANA Louane Amat	5
10	DAEI Ali			DALAPHONE Valasine	7
13	KABEI Hossein			PHENGSENGSAY Souksavanh	8
14	BORHANI Arash	72	66	SINGTO Lamnoum	10
15	MOBALI Eman	65		THONGPHACHAN Sengphet	14
18	BADAVI Ali			VONGSAMANY Davone	15
20	NOSRATI Mohammad			THONGKHEN Kitsada	25
27	ZARE Sattar	46	73	NAKADY Vannaseng	27
	Tr: IVANKOVIC Branko			Tr: KHENKITISACK Bounlab	
7	KAZEMEYAN Javad	46	66	SOUTHSAKHONE Vongsamany	13
16	KHATIBI Rasoul Paki	65	84	THILAVONGSA Vanhnasith	22
23	SOLEIMANI Masoud	72	73	RATHSACHACK Soulivan	23

SECOND PHASE GROUP 2	PL	W	D	L	F	A	PTS	UZB	IRQ	PAL	TPE
1 Uzbekistan	6	5	1	0	16	3	16		1-1	3-0	6-1
2 Iraq	6	3	2	1	17	7	11	1-2		4-1	6-1
3 Palestine	6	2	1	3	11	11	7	0-3	1-1		8-0
4 Chinese Taipei	6	0	0	6	3	26	0	0-1	1-4	0-1	

Pakhtakor, Tashkent
18-02-2004, 17:00, 24 000, Srinivasan IND

UZB   1   1   IRQ

Soliev [78]

Adwan [57]

	UZBEKISTAN					IRAQ	
1	POLYAKOV Aleksey			22	ABBAS Noor Sabri	
2	ASHURMATOV Bahtiyor			3	KATI Basim	
3	AKOPYANTS Andrey	46	74	4	KADHIM Hayder	
8	DJEPAROV Server		76	9	MOSSA Razak	
10	KARPENKO Victor			11	FAYADH Jassim	
11	SHISHELOV Vladimir	74		12	Taher Haythem	
16	SHATSKIKH Maksim			13	Mohammed Hawar	
17	KHVOSTUNOV Alexandr	65		16	JASSIM Haydar	
18	KADADZE Timur			25	LABID Abdul	
22	SHIRSHOV Nikolai			26	AJEEL Mahdi	
24	ALIKULOV Asror		84	27	ADWAN Ahmad	
	Tr: KHAYDAROV Ravshan				Tr: STANGE Bernd	
4	KASIMOV Mirdjalal	65	84	10	RIDHA Emad	
6	KOSHEKEV Leonid	46	76	18	ASSAD Ahmed	
9	SOLIEV Anvarjon	74				

Al Wakra, Doha
18-02-2004, 18:30, 1 000, Al Yarimi YEM

PAL   8   0   TPE

Alkord [10], Habaib 2 [20 32], Atura [43]
Beshe 2 [52 86], Amar [76], Keshkesh [82]

	PALESTINE					CHINESE TAIPEI	
22	SALEH Ramzi			18	YEH Hsein Chung	
5	JENDEYA Saeb			3	CHEN Jeng I	
6	ABDALLAH Pablo		46	4	WANG Chien Hsiang	
9	BESHE Roberto		83	5	TSAI Hui Kai	
12	ALKORD Ziyad	63		7	CHIANG Shih Lu	
13	MONTERO Edgardo			9	CHUANG Yao Tsung	10
16	AMAR Taysir			12	WU Chun I	
17	ADAUY Roberto		36	16	LI Po Yuan	
20	ATURA Francisco	61		17	LIN Kuei Pin	
21	ABUALIA Osama			27	CHANG Wu Yeh	
24	HABAIB Safwan	69		30	TU Ming Feng	
	Tr: RIEDL Alfred				Tr: LEE Po Houng	
7	ABUJAZAR Ihab	63	46	19	TU Chia Po	
14	FARRAN Adel	69	83	20	KUO Chun Yi	
15	KESHKESH Ahmed	61	36	29	WANG Chia Cheng	

Chung Shan, Taipei
31-03-2004, 15:00, 2 500, Midi Nitrorejo IDN

TPE   0   1   UZB

Koshekev [59]

	CHINESE TAIPEI					UZBEKISTAN	
1	YANG Cheng Hsing			12	NESTEROV Ignatiy	
3	CHEN Jeng I			2	ASHURMATOV Bahtiyor	
5	TSAI Hui Kai			3	FEDOROV Andrei	
6	CHENG Yung Jen		84	6	KOSHEKEV Leonid	
8	CHEN Jui Te			8	DJEPAROV Server	
12	WU Chun I			9	SOLIEV Anvarjon	
17	LIN Kuei Pin	85	46	10	TADJIYEV Zayntdin	
25	CHANG Fu Hsiang	75	73	11	SHISHELOV Vladimir	
26	CHEN Bing Shin	64		18	KADADZE Timur	
27	CHANG Wu Yeh			24	ALIKULOV Asror	
30	TU Ming Feng			28	NIKOLAEV Alexey	
	Tr: LEE Po Houng				Tr: KHAYDAROV Ravshan	
7	CHIANG Shih Lu	85	46	15	GEYNRIKH Alexander	
16	LI Po Yuan	75	84	20	MAGDEEV Ildar	
19	TU Chia Po	64	73	22	BIKMOEV Marat	

Al Wakra, Doha
31-03-2004, 17:05, 500, Al Shoufi SYR

PAL   1   1   IRQ

Beshe [72]

Mossa [20]

	PALESTINE					IRAQ	
22	SALEH Ramzi			22	ABBAS Noor Sabri	
5	JENDEYA Saeb			3	KATI Basim	
9	BESHE Roberto			9	MOSSA Razak	
11	AL HASSAN Rami	70	74	10	RIDHA Emad	
12	ALKORD Ziyad	77		13	TAHER Hawar	
13	MONTERO Edgardo			16	JASSIM Haydar	
17	AMAR Taysir			23	ABOUDY Ousay	
17	ADAUY Roberto		86	25	LABID Abdul	
19	MANSOUR Mohammad			26	AJEEL Mahdi	
20	ATURA Francisco		66	27	ALWAN Ahmed	
21	ABUALIA Osama			30	MAJID Haidar	
	Tr: RIEDL Alfred				Tr: STANGE Bernd	
15	KESHKESH Ahmed	77	66	12	TAHER Haythem	
24	HABAIB Safwan	70	74	20	KHALEF Younes	
			86	22	ABBAS Ahmad	

Al Qwaismeh, Amman
9-06-2004, 18:00, 2 000, Al Hail QAT

IRQ   6   1   TPE

Mossa 2 [2 14], Naji Fawazi [18]
Abbas 2 [50 85], Fayadh [68]

Huang Wei Yi 57

	IRAQ					CHINESE TAIPEI	
22	ABBAS Noor Sabri			1	YANG Cheng Hsing	
2	MAHODER Emad			3	CHEN Jeng I	
9	MOSSA Razak			5	TEAI Hui Kai	
11	FAYADH Jassim			6	CHENG Yung Jen	
15	NAJI FAWAZI Husam	74		12	WU Chun I	
16	JASSIM Haydar		46	16	LI Po Yuan	
18	ASSAD Ahmed			17	LIN Kuei Pin	
19	SALEH Qussi	53	75	27	CHANG Wu Yeh	
23	ABOUDY Qusay Munir			30	TU Ming Feng	
24	ABBAS Ahmed Manajid		65	32	CHENG Sheng Jen	
26	AJEEL Mahdi Karim	46		33	HUANG Wei Yi	
	Tr: KHADUM Sultan				Tr: LEE Po Houng	
7	ALI Said	53	75	20	KUO Chun Yi	
14	AHMED Rafed	46	46	31	CHEN Hstao Wei	
25	LABID Abdul	74	65	38	CHANG Wei Lun	

Pakhtakor, Tashkent
9-06-2004, 19:00, 35 000, Moradi IRN

UZB   3   0   PAL

Ashurmatov [6], Shishelov [42]
Djeparov [89]

	UZBEKISTAN					PALESTINE	
1	POLYAKOV Aleksey			22	SALEH Ramzi	
2	ASHURMATOV Bahtiyor			5	JENDEYA Saeb	
4	KASIMOV Mirdjalal	68	50	9	BESHE Roberto	
7	AKOPYANTS Andrey			12	ALKORD Ziyad	
9	SOLIEV Anvarjon	85		13	MONTERO Edgardo	
11	SHISHelov Vladimir		78	16	AMAR Taysir	
14	PASHININ Oleg			17	ADAUY Roberto	
18	KADADZE Timur			19	MANSOUR Mohammad	
19	KARPENKO Victor	66		20	ATURA Francisco	
24	ALIKULOV Asror			26	BAKROON Fadi	29
28	NIKOLAEV Alexey		41	30	ABUSIDU Majed	
	Tr: KHAYDAROV Ravshan				Tr: RIEDL Alfred	
6	KOSHEKEV Leonid	85	50	26	ASAD Shaker	
8	DJEPAROV Server	68	78	27	ABULATIFA Fady	
10	TADJIYEV Zayntdin	66	41	28	SALAMA Ashraf	

Chung Shan, Taipei
8-09-2004, 15:00, 5 000, Baskar IND

TPE 1 4 IRQ

Huang Wei Yi 82

Salih Sadir 2 4 43
Saad Attiya 75, Khalef 86

CHINESE TAIPEI			IRAQ	
1 YANG Cheng Hsing			UDAY TALIB	18
3 CHEN Jeng I			SAAD ATTIYA	2
5 TSAI Hui Kai		46	BASSIM ABBAS	3
6 CHENG Yung Jen			KADHIM Hayder	4
9 CHEN Jui Te	62		NASHAT AKRAM	5
12 WU Chun I		68	SALIH SADIR	6
17 LIN Kuei Pin			EMAD MOHAMMED	7
30 TU Ming Feng			MOSSA Razak	9
31 CHEN Hsiao Wei			HAWAR MULLA	11
33 HUANG Wei Yi		73	QUSAI MUNIR	13
41 HUANG Che Ming			HAIDAR ABDUL AMIR	14
Tr: LEE Po Houng			Tr: MAGEED Adnan Hamad	
38 CHUANG Wei Lun	62	73	ABDUL WAHAB ABU	8
		46	KHALEF Younes	10
		68	AJEEL Mahdik	15

Al Rayyan, Rayyan
8-09-2004, 18:30, 400, Maidin SIN

PAL 0 3 UZB

Kasimov 9, Djeparov 32
Bikmoev 78

PALESTINE			UZBEKISTAN	
22 SALEH Ramzi			POLYAKOV Aleksey	1
2 CATALDO Hernan			ASHURMATOV Bahtiyor	2
5 JENDEYA Saeb			FEDOROV Andrei	3
6 ABDALLAH Pablo	46	82	KASIMOV Mirdjalal	4
7 ABU JAZAR Ihab			AKOPYANTS Andrey	7
9 BESHE Roberto	79		DJEPAROV Server	8
13 MONTERO Edgardo			SHISHELOV Vladimir	11
15 KESHKESH Ahmed		54	GEYNRIKH Alexander	15
17 ADAUY Roberto		73	MAGDEEV Ildar	20
27 ABULATIFA Fady	46		ALIKULOV Asror	24
31 ROJAS Brono			NIKOLAEV Alexey	28
Tr: RIEDL Alfred			Tr: KHAYDAROV Ravshan	
4 MHENA Patricio	46	54	SOLIEV Anvarjon	9
12 ALKORD Ziyad	46	82	KADADAZE Timur	18
34 ABDALHADI Wasim	79	73	BIKMOEV Marat	73

Al-Qwaismeh, Amman
13-10-2004, 18:00, 10 000, Maidin SIN

IRQ 1 2 UZB

Qusai Munir 29

Shatskikh 10, Geynrikh 22

IRAQ			UZBEKISTAN	
21 AHMED ALI			POLYAKOV Aleksey	1
3 BASSIM ABBAS	46		ASHURMATOV Bahtiyor	2
4 KADHIM Hayder	76		FEDOROV Andrei	3
5 NASHAT AKRAM			KASIMOV Mirdjalal	4
7 EMAD MOHAMMED			AKOPYANTS Andrey	7
8 ABDUL WAHAB ABU	66		DJEPAROV Server	8
10 KHALEF Younes		36	SOLIEV Anvarjon	9
11 TAHER Haythem		75	GEYNRIKH Alexander	15
13 QUSAI MUNIR		93	SHATSKIKH Maksim	16
15 AJEEL Mahdik	28		ALIKULOV Asror	24
20 MAJID Haidar			NIKOLAEV Alexey	28
Tr: MAGEED Adnan Hamad			Tr: KHAYDAROV Ravshan	
2 JAMEEL Saad	46	93	KOSHEKEV Leonid	6
9 MOSSA Razak	66	36	KADADAZE Timur	18
14 HAIDAR ABDUL AMIR	28	75	INNOMOV Islom	25

Chung Shan, Taipei
14-10-2004, 16:00, 500, Rasheed MDV

TPE 0 1 PAL

Amar 90

CHINESE TAIPEI			PALESTINE	
22 LU Kun Chi			SALAMA Ashraf	22
3 CHEN Jeng I			DWAIMA Iyad	3
5 TSAI Hui Kai			JENDEYA Saeb	5
6 CHENG Yung Jen			ABU JAZAR Ihab	7
12 WU Chun I			KESHKESH Ahmed	15
17 LIN Kuei Pin			NAIF Raul	25
26 CHEN Bing Shin	70		ROJAS Brono	28
27 CHANG Wu Yeh		70	ATURA Francisco	29
30 TU Ming Feng			ABUSELEISEL Ammar	35
33 HUANG Wei Yi			ALASHQAR Nahedd	40
41 HUANG Che Ming	77		ALAYADI Akram	41
Tr: LEE Po Houng			Tr: BALAWI Ghassan	
38 CHUANG Wei Lun	70	70	BAKROON Fadi	38
		77	AMAR Taysir	39

Doha Stadium, Doha
16-11-2004, 19:30, 500, Al Mutlaq KSA

IRQ 4 1 PAL

Qusai Munir 2 54 58, Emad Mohammed 65
Nashat Akram 70

Zaatara 71

IRAQ			PALESTINE	
1 NOUR SABRI			ALSIDAWI Abdallah	45
2 SAADATTIYA			MHENA Patricio	4
3 BASSIM ABBAS			AMAR Taysir	16
5 NASHAT AKRAM			ADAUY Roberto	17
6 SALIH SADIR	68	86	KHALIL Omar	18
7 EMAD MOHAMMED			ATURA Francisco	20
9 MOSSA Razak	76	76	HABAYEB Safwan	24
11 HAWAR MULLA MOHAMMED			ALSEIDU Majed	30
13 QUSAI MUNIR			ROJAS Brono	31
14 HAIDAR ABDUL AMIR			ZAATARA Imad	42
20 MAJID Haidar	64	76	RABI Rami	47
Tr: MAGEED Adnan Hamad			Tr: FESKO Tomas	
15 AJEEL Mahdik	64	76	ABUALIA Osama	21
17 ATEA Hassan	68	76	FARID Murad	33
23 LOUAI Hassan	76	86	SALEM Fady	44

Pakhtakor, Tashkent
17-11-2004, 16:00, 20 000, Basma SYR

UZB 6 1 TPE

Geynrikh 5, Kasimov 12, Shatskikh 18
Koshekev 34, Kasimov 2 45 85

Huang Wei Yi 64

UZBEKISTAN			CHINESE TAIPEI	
1 SAFONOV Evgeni		46	LU Kun Chi	22
2 ASHURMATOV Bahtiyor	46		CHEN Jeng I	3
3 FEDOROV Andrei			TSAI Hui Kai	5
4 KASIMOV Mirdjalal			WU Chun I	12
6 KOSHEKEV Leonid	70		LI Po Yuan	16
7 AKOPYANTS Andrey			LIN Kuei Pin	17
14 KIRYAN Vladislav			KUO Chun Yi	20
15 GEYNRIKH Alexander	68		CHANG Wu Yeh	27
16 SHATSKIKH Maksim			CHEN Hsiao Wei	31
23 NIKOLAEV Alexey			HUANG Wei Yi	33
24 ALIKULOV Asror		46	KAO Hao Chieh	37
Tr: KHAYDAROV Ravshan			Tr: LEE Po Houng	
11 SHISHELOV Vladimir	68	46	PAN Wei Chih	1
18 KADADZE Timur	46	46	KUNG Kun Liang	35
22 BIKMOEV Marat	70			

SECOND PHASE GROUP 3	PL	W	D	L	F	A	PTS	JPN	OMA	IND	SIN
1 Japan	6	6	0	0	16	1	18		1-0	7-0	1-0
2 Oman	6	3	1	2	14	3	10	0-1		0-0	7-0
3 India	6	1	1	4	2	18	4	0-4	1-5		1-0
4 Singapore	6	1	0	5	3	13	3	1-2	0-2	2-0	

JPN 1 0 OMA

Saitama Stadium 2002, Saitama
18-02-2004, 19:20, 60 270, Abdul Hamid MAS

Kubo 90

#	JAPAN			OMAN	#
1	NARAZAKI Seigo			ALI ABDULLAH	26
2	YAMADA Nobuhisa			MOHAMED RABIA	2
3	TSUBOI Keisuke			SAEED ASHOON	4
5	MIYAMOTO Tsuneyasu			HAMDI HUBAIS	6
6	INAMOTO Junichi		81	BADER AL MAIMANI	8
7	NAKATA Hidetoshi			FOUZI BASHIR	10
10	NAKAMURA Shunsuke			YOUSEF SHAABAN	11
13	YANAGISAWA Atsushi	46		HASSAN YOUSUF	17
14	SANTOS Alessandro			IMAD ALI	20
19	ENDO Yasuhito	64	71	AHMED HADID	21
20	TAKAHARA Naohiro	82		KHALIFA AYIL	25
	Tr: ZICO			Tr: MACALA Milan	
8	OGASAWARA Mitsuo	64	71	AHMED MUBARAK	13
9	KUBO Tatsuhiko	46	81	NASSER ZAYID	15
11	SUZUKI Takayuki	82			

IND 1 0 SIN

Nehru, Margao
18-02-2004, 16:00, 28 000, Yasrebi IRN

Singh.R 50

#	INDIA			SINGAPORE	#
1	MUKHERJEE Sangram			SUNNY Hassan	30
4	GHOSH Debjit			MUHAMAD Ridhuan	2
5	LAWRENCE Climax		88	ISKANDAR Aide	5
8	SINGH Renedy	75		KHAIZAN Baihakki	6
10	D'CUNHA Alvito Roland	58		LATIFF Ahmad	7
11	ANCHERI Jo Paul	24		SHAH Noh Alam	8
12	BISWAS Ashim		55	BIN DAUD Indra Sahdan	10
14	GAWLI Mahesh			SUBRAMANI Shunmugham	14
15	BHUTIA Baichung			BENNETT Daniel	16
16	NAIK Samir Subash			LENG Tan Kim	22
17	MANDAL Deepak		89	SALLEH Sazali Mohamed	23
	Tr: CONSTANTINE Stephen			Tr: AVRAMOVIC Radojko	
6	SHANMUGAM Venkatesh	24	55	CASMIR Agu	15
7	SINGH Wangkheirakpam	58	89	MANZUR Mustaqim	19
18	CHAKRABORTY Subhas	75	88	FADHIL Syed	24

IND 1 5 OMA

Jawaharla Nehru, Kochin
31-03-2004, 17:45, 48 000, Kim Heng MAS

Singh.R 18
Amad Ali 12, Ahmed Mubarak 2 26 49
Al Hinai 2 60 88

#	INDIA			OMAN	#
1	MUKHERJEE Sangran			AHMED RASHID	1
2	MUTTATH Suresh			MOHAMED RABIA	2
4	GHOSH Debjit		78	SAEED ASHOON	4
5	LAWRENCE Climax			AYIMAN SUROOR	5
7	SINGH Lukram	54	54	MOHAMED Hashim Saleh	9
8	SINGH Renedy			FOUZI BASHIR	10
9	YADAV Abhishek			AHMED MUBARAK	12
10	D'CUNHA Alvito Roland	35		HASSAN YOUSUF	17
14	GAWLI Mahesh			NABIL ASHOOR	19
15	BHUTIA Baichung		41	AMAD ALI	20
17	MANDAL Deepak	75		AHMED HADID	21
	Tr: CONSTANTINE Stephen			Tr: MACALA Milan	
3	BHARTI Satish Kumar	75	41	AL HINAI Mohamed	16
6	SHANMUGHAM Venkatesh	35	54	SULTAN MOHAMED	18
18	SINGH Jatin Bisht	54	78	KHALIFA AYIL	25

SIN 1 2 JPN

Jalan Besar, Singapore
31-03-2004, 20:00, 6 000, Bae Jae Yong KOR

Bin Daud 62
Takahara 33, Fujita 81

#	SINGAPORE			JAPAN	#
30	SUNNY Hassan			NARAZAKI Seigo	1
2	MUHAMAD Ridhuan			TSUBOI Keisuke	5
5	ISKANDAR Aide			MIYAMOTO Tsuneyasu	3
6	KHAIZAN Baihakki			INAMOTO Junichi	6
9	BIN DAUD Indra Sahdan	86		NAKATA Hidetoshi	7
14	SUBRAMANI Shunmugham		75	TAKAHARA Naohiro	9
16	BENNETT Daniel		66	NAKAMURA Shunsuke	10
17	ISHAK Shahril		68	YANAGISAWA Atsushi	13
21	GRABOVAC Mirko	46		SANTOS Alessandro	14
22	LENG Tan Kim			ONO Shinji	18
25	NASIR Nazri	46		KAJI Akira	21
	Tr: AVRAMOVIC Radojko			Tr: Zico	
7	LATIFF Ahmad	46	68	SUZUKI Takayuki	11
11	ALI Noor	86	66	FUJITA Toshiya	16
15	CASMIR Agu	46	75	TAMADA Keiji	20

JPN 7 0 IND

Saitama Stadium 2002, Saitama
9-06-2003, 19:20, 63 000, Huang Junjie CHN

Kubo 12, Fukunishi 25, Nakamura 29
Suzuki 54, Nakazawa 2 65 76, Ogasawara 68

#	JAPAN			INDIA	#
23	KAWAGUCHI Yoshikatsu			MUKHERJEE Sangram	1
3	TSUBOI Keisuke			RAHAMAN Habibur	2
5	MIYAMOTO Tsuneyasu	62	62	LAWRENCE Climax	5
9	KUBO Tatsuhiko	46		SHANMUGHAM Venkatesh	6
10	NAKAMURA Shunsuke			SINGH Renedy	8
14	SANTOS Alessandro			ANCHERI Jo Paul	11
17	FUKUNISHI Takashi		75	BISWAS Ashim	12
18	ONO Shinji	70		BHUTIA Baichung	15
20	TAMADA Keiji			NAIK Samir Subash	16
21	KAJI Akira			MANDAL Deepak	17
22	NAKAZAWA Yuji		46	SINGH Jatin Bisht	19
	Tr: ZICO			Tr: CONSTANTINE Stephen	
8	OGASAWARA Mitsuo	62	75	PRAKASH R.R.	9
11	SUZUKI Takayuki	46	62	SINGH Bijen	10
16	FUJITA Toshiya	70	46	DEBABRATA Roy	20

OMA 7 0 SIN

Sultan Qaboos Sports Complex, Muscat
9-06-2004, 19:45, 2 000, Ebrahim BHR

Bader Al Maimani 4 9 44 64 86
Khalifa Ayil 2 25 53, Ahmed Hadid 39

#	OMAN			SINGAPORE	#
22	SUBAIT Badar Juma			SUNNY Hassan	30
2	MOHAMED Rabia		86	MUHAMAD Ridhuan	2
7	HASSAN YOUSUF			ISKANDAR Aide	5
8	BADER AL MAIMANI			KHAIZAN Baihakki	6
9	MOHAMED Hashim Saleh	46		DAUD Indra Sahdan	10
10	FOUZI BASHIR		55	ALI Noor	11
15	AL MAHROUQI Badar			RAHMAN Noh	13
19	NABIL ASHOOR			CASMIR Agu	15
20	AMAD ALI	77		BENNETT Daniel	16
21	AHMED HADID	70		ISHAK Shahril	17
25	KHALIFA AYIL			NASIR Nazri	25
	Tr: MACALA Milan			Tr: AVRAMOVIC Radojko	
6	HAMDI HUBAIS	70	67	ZAINOL Ishak	4
16	AL HINAI Mohamed	77	86	MOHD Khairul Amri	19
17	AYIMAN SUROOR	46	86	FADHIL Syed	24

Jalan Besar, Singapore
8-09-2004, 19:30, 4 000, Arambekade SRI

SIN 0 2 OMA

Yousef Shaaban [3], Amad Ali [82]

SINGAPORE				OMAN
30	SUNNY Hassan			ALI ABDULLAH 26
3	ZAINOL Ishak	64		MOHAMED RABIA 2
6	KHAIZAN Baihakki			SAEED ASHOON 4
8	SHAH Noh Alam	79	66	BADER AL MAIMANI 8
10	DAUD Indra Sahdan			FOUZI BASHIR 10
13	RAHMAN Noh		88	YOUSEF SHAABAN 11
14	SUBRAMANI Shunmugham			AHMED MUBARAK 12
16	BENNETT Daniel			HASSAN YOUSEF 17
17	ISHAK Shahril			AMAD ALI 20
22	DICKSON Itimi	55	74	AHMED HADID 21
24	CHUAN Goh			KHALIFA AYIL 25
	Tr: AVRAMOVIC Radojko			Tr: MACALA Milan
11	SAHIB Imran	64	74	HAMDI HUBAIS 6
12	BIN MASTURI Masrewan	55	66	MOHAMED Hashim Saleh 9
20	FADHIL Syed	79	88	AL HINAI Mohamed 16

Yuba Bharati Krirangan, Calcutta
8-09-2004, 17:30, 90 000, Hajjar SYR

IND 0 4 JPN

Suzuki [45], Ono [60]
Fukunishi [71], Miyamoto [87]

INDIA				JAPAN
22	NANDY Sandip			KAWAGUCHI Yoshikatsu 23
4	GHOSH Debjit		73	TANAKA Makoto 2
5	LAWRENCE Climax			MIYAMOTO Tsuneyasu 5
6	SHANMUGHAM Venkatesh			SUZUKI Takayuki 11
8	POTSANGBAM Renedy	61		SANTOS Alessandro 14
9	YADAV Abhishek			FUKUNISHI Takashi 15
11	SINGH Jatin Bisht	77		ONO Shinji 18
14	GAWLI Mahesh		83	MOTOYAMA Masashi 19
16	NAIK Samir Subash		67	TAKAHARA Naohiro 20
17	MANDAL Deepak			KAJI Akira 21
19	CHIKKANNA Ravi	82		NAKAZAWA Yuji 22
	Tr: CONSTANTINE Stephen			Tr: ZICO
7	SINGH Wangkheirakpam	77	83	OGASAWARA Mitsuo 8
10	SINGH Bijen	82	67	KUBO Tatsuhiko 9
18	DEBABRATA Roy	61	73	FUJITA Toshiya 16

Jalan Besar, Singapore
13-10-2004, 19:30, 3 609, Husain BHR

SIN 2 0 IND

Daud [73], Mohd [76]

SINGAPORE				INDIA
30	SUNNY Hassan			NANDY Sandip 1
2	MUHAMAD Ridhuan	46	71	RAHAMAN Habibur 2
5	ISKANDAR Aide		38	JOSE Vinu 3
6	KHAIZAN Baihakki			DEBABRATA Roy 5
7	CHUAN Goh			SHANMUGHAM Venkatesh 6
10	DAUD Indra Sahdan	89		SINGH Renedy 8
12	BIN MASTURI Masrewan	90	63	D'CUNHA Alvito Roland 10
13	RAHMAN Noh			GAWLI Mahesh 14
16	BENNETT Daniel			MANDAL Deepak 17
17	ISHAK Shahril			PRAKASH R.R. 19
22	DICKSON Itimi			ZIRSANGA Jerry 23
	Tr: AVRAMOVIC Radojko			Tr: CONSTANTINE Stephen
3	ZAINOL Ishak	89	63	SINGH Gurjinder 4
9	BIN SHARIFF Ashrin	90	38	LAMARE Rocus 16
23	MOHD Khairul Amri	46	71	NABI Syed 18

Sultan Qaboos Sports Complex, Muscat
13-10-2004, 18:30, 35 000, Lu Jun CHN

OMA 0 1 JPN

Suzuki [52]

OMAN				JAPAN
26	ALI ABDULLAH			KAWAGUCHI Yoshikatsu 23
2	MOHAMED RABIA			TANAKA Makoto 2
4	SAEED ASHOON			MIYAMOTO Tsuneyasu 5
8	BADER AL MAIMANI	69		NAKAMURA Shunsuke 10
10	FOUZI BASHIR		92	SUZUKI Takayuki 11
11	YOUSEF SHAABAN			SANTOS Alessandro 14
12	AHMED MUBARAK			FUKUNISHI Takashi 15
17	HASSAN YOUSEF			ONO Shinji 18
19	NABIL ASHOOR	69		TAKAHARA Naohiro 20
20	AMAD ALI			KAJI Akira 21
21	AHMED HADID	80		NAKAZAWA Yuji 22
	Tr: MACALA Milan			Tr: Zico
5	HUSSEIN MUSTAHIL	69	92	TAMADA Keiji 28
6	HAMDI HUBAIS	80		
9	MOHAMED Hashim Saleh	69		

Saitama Stadium 2002, Saitama
17-11-2004, 19:20, 58 881, Torky IRN

JPN 1 0 SIN

Tamada [13]

JAPAN				SINGAPORE
12	DOI Yoichi			LIONEL Lewis 18
3	MATSUDA Naoki			MUHAMAD Ridhuan 2
4	ENDO Yasuhito			KHAIZAN Baihakki 6
5	MIYAMOTO Tsuneyasu			CHUAN Goh 7
6	NAKATA Koji		66	DAUD Indra Sahdan 10
8	OGASAWARA Mitsuo	80	74	RAHMAN Noh 13
16	FUJITA Toshiya	59		SUBRAMANI Shunmugham 14
17	MIURA Atsuhiro		52	MUSHADAD Tengku 15
19	MOTOYAMA Masashi			BENNETT Daniel 16
21	KAJI Akira			ISHAK Shahril 17
28	TAMADA Keiji	72		DICKSON Itimi 22
	Tr: ZICO			Tr: AVRAMOVIC Radojko
11	SUZUKI Takayuki	72	66	SHAH Noh Alam 8
14	SANTOS Alessandro	80	52	MOHD Khairul Amri 23
27	OKUBO Yoshito	59	74	HATTA Jaslee 24

Sultan Qaboos Sports Complex, Muscat
17-11-2004, 18:00, 2 000, Nurilddin Salman IRQ

OMA 0 0 IND

OMAN				INDIA
26	ALI ABDULLAH			MUKHERJEE Sangram 1
3	AL WAHAIBI Juma			RAHAMAN Habibur 2
5	HUSSEIN MUSTAHIL	46		JOSE Vinu 3
6	HAMDI HUBAIS	64		LAWRENCE Climax 5
7	KAMOUNA Abdullah Said		75	SINGH Wangkheirakpam 7
8	BADER AL MAIMANI			YADAV Abhishek 9
11	YOUSEF SHAABAN		84	SINGH Jatin Bisht 11
16	AL MUKHAINI Mohamed	81	61	BISWAS Ashim 12
17	HASSAN YOUSEF			DEBABRATA Roy 13
20	AMAD AI			NAIK Samir Subash 16
21	AHMED HADID			NABI Syed 17
	Tr: MACALA Milan			Tr: CONSTANTINE Stephen
10	FOUZI BASHIR	64	61	D'CUNHA Alvito Roland 10
13	AHMED SALIM	81	75	ZIRSANGA Jerry 14
25	KHALIFA AYIL	46	84	LAMARE Rocus 19

SECOND PHASE GROUP 4	PL	W	D	L	F	A	PTS	KUW	CHN	HKG	MAS
1 Kuwait	6	5	0	1	15	2	15		1-0	4-0	6-1
2 China PR	6	5	0	1	14	1	15	1-0		7-0	4-0
3 Hong Kong	6	2	0	4	5	15	6	0-2	0-1		2-0
4 Malaysia	6	0	0	6	2	18	0	0-2	0-1	1-3	

Tianhe Stadium, Guangzhou
18-02-2004, 19:30, 50 000, Roman UZB

CHN 1 0 KUW

Hao Haidong 15

#	CHINA PR	min		min	KUWAIT	#
1	LIU Yunfei				KANKUNE Shehab	1
3	YANG Pu				ASEL Ali	4
5	ZHENG Zhi			79	AL SHAMMARI Nohayer	5
7	SUN Jihai	84			ZADAH Khaled	7
9	HAO Haidong	92			AL ENEZI Mesaed	13
10	ZHANG Yuning			86	AL SHUWAYE Nawaf	14
12	WEI Xin				AL SHAMMARI Ahmad	15
14	LI Weifeng				AL SHAMMARI Khaled	16
15	ZHAO Junzhe				HUMAIDAN Nawaf	18
17	XIAO Zhanbo			[89]	AL HAMAD Fahad	20
19	ZHENG Bin				AL ATAIQI Jarah	24
	Tr: HAAN Arie				Tr: CARPEGGIANI Paulo Cesar	
16	ZHAO Xuri	84		79	ABDULAZIZ Bashar	9
25	ZHAO Haibin	92		86	AL HARBI Hamad	17

Darul Makmur, Kuantan
18-02-2004, 20:45, 12 000, Nagalingam SIN

MAS 1 3 HKG

Talib 39p

Ng Wai Chiu 17, Chu Siu Kei 84
Kwok Yue Hung 93+

#	MALAYSIA	min		min	HONG KONG	#
21	AHMAD Mohd Hamsani				FAN Chun Yip	19
2	ZAHARI Yuzaiman				MAN Pei Tak	3
3	ZAINAL Faizal				NG Wai Chiu	4
5	MOHD SAAD Syamsul				LAU Chi Keung	6
9	OMAR Hairuddin			90	LAW Chun Bong	7
10	KIT KONG Liew	46		58	AKANDU Lawrance	10
13	ABDUL MANAN Eddy				CHU Siu Kei	12
17	KALIAPPAN Nanthan Kumar			63	SHAM Kwok Keung	14
18	HUSSAIN Muhamad	69			CHAN Wai Ho	15
19	YUSOP Mohd Nizaruddin				LUK Koon Pong	16
20	TALIB Rosdi	93			LEE Wai Man	18
	Tr: KRISHNASAMY Rajagobal				Tr: LAI Sun Cheung	
8	WING HONG Chan	93		90	CHEUNG Sai Ho	8
	VELLU Saravanan	46		63	KWOK Yue Hung	21
15	RAJA Tengku	69		58	CHAN Ho Man	22

Siu Sai Wan Sports Ground, Hong Kong
31-03-2004, 20:00, 9 000, Rungklay THA

HKG 0 1 CHN

Hao Haidong 71

#	HONG KONG	min		min	CHINA PR	#
19	FAN Chun Yip				LIU Yunfei	1
2	LEUNG Chi Wing				YANG Pu	3
4	NG Wai Chiu				ZHENG Zhi	5
5	LAU Chi Keung			70	SUN Jihai	7
8	CHEUNG Sai Ho	84			HAO Haidong	9
12	WONG Chun Yue			66	ZHANG Yuning	10
13	SZETO Man Chun	78		75	WEI Xin	12
18	LEE Wai Man				LI Weifeng	14
21	KWOK Yue Hung				ZHAO Junzhe	15
23	CHU Siu Kei				XIAO Zhanbo	17
25	FENG Ji Zhi	31			ZHENG Bin	19
	Tr: LAI Sun Cheung				Tr: HAAN Arie	
3	MAN Pei Tak	31		66	LI Yi	11
7	LAW Chun Bong	84		70	ZHAO Xuri	16
16	LUK Koon Pong	78		75	XU Yunlong	21

Darul Makmur, Kuantan
31-03-2004, 20:45, 9 327, Matsumura JPN

MAS 0 2 KUW

Al Mutwa 75, Al Harbi 87

#	MALAYSIA	min		min	KUWAIT	#
1	AZRAM Azmin				AL FADHLI Khaled	1
4	SULONG Subri				ASEL Ali	4
5	MISBAH Norhafiz				AL SHAMMARI Nohayer	5
9	OMAR Hairuddin	39			HUMAIDAN Nawaf	7
13	ABDUL MANAN Eddy				ABDULAZIZ Bashar	9
15	MAHAYUDDIN Indra Putra				AL FADLI Abdullah	11
16	AHAMD RAKIL Akmal Rizal				AL ENEZI Mesaed	13
17	KALIAPPAN Nanthan Kumar				AL SHAMMARI Ahmad	15
18	HUSSAIN Muhamad				AL SHAMMARI Khaled	16
19	YUSOP Mohd Nizaruddin	75			AL MUTWA Bader	17
20	TALIB Rosdi	51			AL DAWOOD Abdul	20
	Tr: KRISHNASAMY Rajagobal				Tr: IBRAHIM Mohammed	
10	BIN JAMLUS Mohd Khalid	75			AL HARBI Hamad	19
11	IDRUS Irwan	51			AL NAMASH Ali	14
12	ADAN Muhammad	39			AL MUTAIRI Mohammad	24

Teda, Tianjin
9-06-2004, 19:30, 35 000, Park Sang Gu KOR

CHN 4 0 MAS

Hao Haidong 43, Sun Jihai 62
Li Xiaopeng 2 66 76

#	CHINA PR	min		min	MALAYSIA	#
1	LIU Yunfei				MUSTAFA Mohamad	22
5	ZHENG Zhi				ISMAIL Abd	3
7	SUN Jihai	64		78	SAARI Mohd Fadzli	7
8	ZHENG Bin	81			WAN ISMAIL Wan Rohaimi	9
9	HAO Haidong	68		88	BIN JAMLUS Mohd Khalid	10
12	WEI Xin				IDRUS Irwan	11
14	LI Weifeng				MAHAYUDDIN Indra Putra	13
15	ZHAO Junzhe			69	KALIAPPAN Nanthan Kumar	17
18	LI Xiaopeng				HUSSAIN Muhamad	18
27	ZHOU Ting				YUSOP Mohd Nizaruddin	19
29	LI Jinyu				TALIB Rosdi	20
	Tr: HAAN Arie				Tr: HARRIS Allan	
11	LI Yi	68		88	ABDUL MANAN Eddy	8
13	XU Yunlong	64		69	ADAN Muhammad	12
22	YAN Song	81		78	VELLU Saravanan	14

Kazma, Kuwait City
9-06-2004, 20:30, 9 000, Najm LIB

KUW 4 0 HKG

Seraj 12, Al Mutwa 38
Al Enezi 45, Al Dawood 75

#	KUWAIT	min		min	HONG KONG	#
1	KANKUNE Shehab				FAN Chun Yip	19
2	ABDULLAH Yaqoub				MAN Pei Tak	3
5	AL SHAMMARI Nohayer				NG Wai Chiu	4
7	HUMAIDAN Nawaf	65			LAU Chi Keung	6
8	AL BURAIKI	78			CHEUNG Sai Ho	8
13	AL ENEZI Mesaed				WONG Chun Yue	12
16	AL SHAMMARI Khaled	71			SZETO Man Chun	13
17	AL MUTWA Bader	86			LUK Koon Pong	16
19	SERAJ Husain				POON Yin Cheuk	20
20	AL DAWOOD Abdul	84			KWOK Yue Hung	21
23	AL MUTAIRI Nawaf	67			CHU Siu Kei	23
	Tr: IBRAHIM Mohammed				Tr: LAI Sun Cheung	
6	JARRAGH Mohamad	78		67	AKANDU Lawrence	10
10	AL MUTAIRI Khalaf	65		71	POON Man Tik	24
11	AL HARBI Hamad	86		84	LAI Kai Cheuk	26

Siu Sai Wan Sports Ground, Hong Kong
8-09-2004, 20:00, 1 500, Busurmankulov KGZ

HKG 0 2 KUW

Al Enezi [38], Humaidan [70]

HONG KONG				KUWAIT	
19	FAN Chun Yip			KANKUNE Shehab	1
3	MAN Pei Tak			ABDULLAH Yaqoub	2
6	LAU Chi Keung			ASEL Ali	4
8	CHEUNG Sai Ho			AL BERAIKI Mohammad	6
10	AKANDU Lawrance			HUMAIDAN Nawaf	7
13	SZETO Man Chun	64		AL BURAIKI Saleh	8
16	LUK Koon Pong		84	ABDULAZIZ Bashar	9
20	POON Yin Cheuk			AL ENEZI Mesaed	13
21	KWOK Yue Hung	74		AL ATAIQI Jarah	18
23	CHU Siu Kei	68	75	SERAJ Husain	19
25	FENG Ji Zhi	67	60	AL SHAMMARI Ahmad	25
	Tr: LAI Sun Cheung			Tr: IBRAHIM Mohammed	
7	AU Wai Lun	68	75	AL HARBI Hamad	10
22	CHAN Ho Man	74	84	AL DAWOOD Abdul	20
24	POON Man Tik	64	60	AL MUTAIRI Nawaf	23

Mongkok, Hong Kong
13-10-2004, 20:00, 2 425, Ghandour LIB

HKG 2 0 MAS

Chu Siu Kei [5], Wong Chun Yue [51]

HONG KONG				MALAYSIA	
19	FAN Chun Yip			BIN ABDUL KADIR Azizon	1
3	MAN Pei Tak			BIN JAMIL Mohd	3
4	NG Wai Chiu	65	71	PANDATHAN Gunalan	4
6	LAU Chi Keung			AHMAD Tharmini	5
7	AU Wai Lun			WAN ISMAIL Wan Rohaimi	6
11	LAU Chun Bong	84		CHAN YEW Lim	11
12	WONG Chun Yue		55	MAHAYUDDIN Indra Putra	13
16	LUK Koon Pong			YAHYAH Mohd Amri	17
18	LEE Wai Man			SAARI Modh Fadzli	18
20	POON Yin Cheuk			TALIB Rosdi	19
23	CHU Siu Kei	78	30	OMAR Hairuddin	20
	Tr: LAI Sun Cheung			Tr: BICSKEI Bertalan	
21	KWOK Yue Hung	78	71	DAVA GHAN Suren Dran	7
22	CHAN Ho Man	84	30	BIN MOHD YUSOFF Mohd	10
24	POON Man Tik	65	79 55	AHAMD RAKHIL Akmal	14

Tianhe, Guangzhou
17-11-2004, 21:00, 20 300, Lee Jong Kuk KOR

CHN 7 0 HKG

Li Junyu 2 [8 47], Shao Jiayi 2 [42 44], Xu Yunlong [49]
Yu Genwei [88], Li Weifeng [92+]

CHINA PR				HONG KONG	
1	LIU Yunfei			FAN Chun Yip	19
5	ZHENG Zhi			MAN Pei Tak	3
6	SHAO Jiayi		72	NG Wai Chiu	4
9	HAO Haidong	61		LAU Chi Keung	6
12	WEI Xin	79		CHEUNG Sai Ho	8
13	XU Yunlong		55	AKANDU Lawrance	10
14	LI Weifeng			WONG Chun Yue	12
15	ZHAO Junzhe			LUK Koon Pong	16
22	YAN Song	88		LEE Wai Man	18
27	ZHOU Ting		46	POON Yin Cheuk	20
29	LI Jinyu			CHU Siu Kei	23
	Tr: HAAN Arie			Tr: LAI Sun Cheung	
10	YU Genwei	61	55	AU Wai Lun	7
11	LI Yi	88	46	SZETO Man Chun	13
30	DU Wei	79	72	POON Man Tik	24

City Stadium, Penang
8-09-2004, 20:45, 14 000, Karim BHR

MAS 0 1 CHN

Li Jinyu [67]

MALAYSIA				CHINA PR	
1	MUSTAFA Mohamad			LIU Yunfei	1
4	NORFAZLY Alias			SUN Xiang	3
8	WAN ISMAIL Wan Rohaimi			ZHANG Yaokun	4
9	ABDUL MANAN Eddy		50	ZHENG Zhi	5
11	IDRUS Irwan	57	46	Zheng Bin	8
12	ADAN Muhammad		79	LI Yi	11
14	AHAMD RAKHIL Akmal	84		WEI Xin	12
15	RAJA Tengku	64		ZHAO Junzhe	15
18	HUSSAIN Muhamad			LI Ming	21
19	TALIB Rosdi			LI Jinyu	29
20	SAARI Mohd Fadzli		57	YANG Pu	30
	Tr: BICSKEI Bertalan			Tr: HAAN Arie	
5	SUNDER Selver	57	57	HAO Wei	7
10	VELLU Saravanan	64	79	XU Yunlong	13
17	MOHD Amri	84	46	YAN Song	22

Kazma, Kuwait City
13-10-2004, 19:00, 10 000, Kunsuta THA

KUW 1 0 CHN

Jumah [47]

KUWAIT				CHINA PR	
1	KANKUNE Shehab			LIU Yunfei	1
2	ABDULLAH Yaqoub		76	SUN Xiang	3
3	JARRAGH Mohamad			ZHANG Yaokun	4
4	ASEL Ali			SHAO Jiayi	6
7	HUMAIDAN Nawaf	46		YANG Pu	8
8	AL BURAIKI Saleh		46	HAO Haidong	9
9	ABDULAZIZ Bashar			WEI Xin	12
13	AL ENEZI Mesaed		65	XU Yunlong	13
16	AL SHAMMARI Khaled	78		LI Weifeng	14
19	SERAJ Husain	65		ZHAO Junzhe	15
24	AL MUTAIRI Mohammad			LI Jinyu	29
	Tr: IBRAHIM Mohammed			Tr: HAAN Arie	
14	AL MUTAIRI Nawaf	65	76	SUN Jihai	7
15	JUMAH Waleed	46	46	LI Yi	11
25	AL SHAMMARI Ahmad	78	65	YAN Song	22

Kazma, Kuwait City
17-11-2004, 16:00, 15 000, Lutfullin UZB

KUW 6 1 MAS

Al Mutwa [17], Abdulaziz 2 [60 70]
Saeed 2 [75 85], Al Hamad [82]

Mohd [19]

KUWAIT				MALAYSIA	
1	KANKUNE Shehab			MUSTAFA Mohamad	1
2	ABDULLAH Yaqoub			NORFAZLY Alias	4
3	JARRAGH Mohamad	90	81	BIN CHE OMAR Shariman	6
4	ASEL Ali			WING HONG Chan	8
8	AL BURAIKI Saleh	40	48	MOHD Amri	9
9	ABDULAZIZ Bashar		68	KIT KONG Liew	10
13	AL ENEZI Mesaed	72	86	CHAN YEW Lim	11
14	AL HAMAD Fahad			AHMAD Tharmini	15
16	AL SHAMMARI Khaled			BIN ISMAIL Moud	16
17	AL MUTWA Bader			KALIAPPAN Nanthan Kumar	17
24	AL MUTAIRI Mohammad			BIN MOHD YUSOFF Mohd	19
	Tr: IBRAHIM Mohammed			Tr: BICSKEI Bertalan	
15	JUMAH Waleed	72	86	HONG SENG Leong	12
19	SAEED Faraj	40	81	CHEE WENG Chow	20
22	AL MUTAIRI Nawaf	90	68	PANDATHAN Gunalan	23

SECOND PHASE GROUP 5	PL	W	D	L	F	A	PTS	PRK	UAE	THA	YEM
1 Korea DPR	6	3	2	1	11	5	11		0-0	4-1	2-1
2 United Arab Emirates	6	3	1	2	6	6	10	1-0		1-0	3-0
3 Thailand	6	2	1	3	9	10	7	1-4	3-0		1-1
4 Yemen	6	1	2	3	6	11	5	1-1	3-1	0-3	

Ali Moshen, Sana'a
18-02-2004, 16:00, 15 000, Husain BHR

YEM 1 – 1 PRK

Al Selwi 73   Hong 85

#	YEMEN	Min		Min	#	KOREA DPR
1	ABDULKHALEQ Muaadh				1	SIM Sung Chol
2	AL NAGGAR Zaid				2	RI Myong Sam
3	AL SAFI Abdullah				4	SO Hyok Chol
4	AL BAADANI Yaser	81		81	5	KIM Yong Jun
5	AL BAITI Ali				9	KIM Yong Su
10	AL SELWI Akram	84		46	10	RI Kum Dong
12	BASUKI Yaser	88		82	12	SIN Yong Nam
14	AL SHEKRI Saleh	66			14	HAN Song Chol
16	SHARYAN Abdulelah				15	JANG Sok Chol
20	AL EDRESI Abdo				16	NAM Song Chol
21	ALWAH Mohammed				19	HONG Yong Jo
	Tr: Hussein Amen					Tr: YON Jong Su
8	BALEID Khaled	88 82		82	3	RI Kwang Chon
13	AL QOR Wasim	66 46		46	6	PAK Nam Chol
24	HUSSEIN Ebrahim	84 81		81	8	JI Yun Nam

Al Ain Club, Al Ain City
18-02-2004, 19:15, 4 000, Sun CHN

UAE 1 – 0 THA

Mohamed Rashid 22

#	ARAB EMIRATES	Min		Min	#	THAILAND
1	MUTAZ ABDULLA				18	HATHAIRATTANAKOOL Kosin
2	ABDULRAHEEM JUMAA				3	SIRIWONG Niweat
5	ABDULSALAM JUMA				4	PAJAKKATA Thanongsak
6	RASHID ABDULRAHMAN				6	PROMRUT Choketawee
7	MOHAMED OMAR	70			9	CHAIKAMDEE Sarayoot
10	MOHAMED RASHID	64		71	11	DAMRONG-O Thawatchai
16	SULTAN RASHED				12	SURASIANG Nirut
19	KHALID ALI	84			13	SENAMUANG Kiatisuk
20	ALI MSARRI			58	17	THONGLAO Datsakorn
21	HUMAID FAKHER				21	SINGTHONG Issawa
26	SALEM KHAMIS				23	SUKSOMKIT Sutee
	Tr: JODAR Jean-Francois					Tr: DE CARVALHO Carlos Roberto
3	ABDULLA SUHAIL	84 58		58	16	JOEMDEE Sakda
8	SALAH ABBAS	70 71		71	26	CHOECHIU Pichitpong
9	SALEM SAAD	64				

Kim Il Sung, Pyongyang
31-03-2004, 16:00, 20 000, Zhou Weixin CHN

PRK 0 – 0 UAE

#	KOREA DPR	Min		Min	#	ARAB EMIRATES
1	SIM Sung Chol				17	AL BADRANI Waleed
2	RI Myong Sam				2	ABDULRAHEEM JUMAA
5	JANG Sok Chol				5	ABDULSALAM JUMA
6	PAK Nam Chol				6	RASHID ABDULRAHMAN
9	KIM Yong Su			69	10	MOHAMED RASHID
10	HONG Yong Jo				14	SAEED Basher
12	SIN Yong Nam				16	SULTAN RASHED
13	KIM Chol Ho	54			20	ALI MSARRI
14	HAN Song Chol				21	HUMAID FAKHER
15	KIM Yong Jun				23	MUSABEH Nawaf Mubarak
16	NAM Song Chol				24	KHATIR Subait
	Tr: YON Jong Su					Tr: JODAR Jean-Francois
3	RI Kwang Chon	87 54		54	4	MOHAMED OMAR
7	MUN In Guk	87 54		69	11	AL JABERI Rami

Ali Mohsen, Sana'a
31-03-2004, 16:00, 25 000, Mansour LIB

YEM 0 – 3 THA

Chaikamdee 69, Surasiang 71
Senamuang 88

#	YEMEN	Min		Min	#	THAILAND
1	ABDUL KHALEK Muaadh	57			18	HATHAIRATTANAKOOL Kosin
2	AL NAGGAR Zaid				2	PHORUANDEE Preratat
4	AL BADANI Yaser				3	SIRIWONG Niweat
7	AL AMMARI Fuad	46			6	PROMRUT Choketawee
10	AL SELWI Akram			46	8	CHAIMAN Therdsak
12	BASUKI Yaser				9	CHAIKAMDEE Sarayoot
14	AL SHEKRI Saleh	74		85	11	DAMRONG-O Thawatchai
15	AL WORAFI Akram				12	SURASIANG Nirut
16	SHARYAN Abdulelah				13	SENAMUANG Kiatisuk
18	MOHAMMED Fadhi				17	CHALERMSAN Dusit
23	ATAIFA Nabil				21	SINGTHONG Issawa
	Tr: AL SUNAINI Amen					Tr: DE CARVALHO Carlos Roberto
20	AL EDRESI Abdo	74 46		46	10	SRIPAN Tawan
21	ALWAH Mohammed	46 85		85	35	VACHIRABAN Narongchai
22	AL AUG Anwar	57				

Rajamangala National, Bangkok
9-06-2004, 19:00, 30 000, Tseytlin UZB

THA 1 – 4 PRK

Senamuang 51   Kim Yong Su 42, Sin Yong Nam 52
Hong Yong Jo 67, Kim Yong Su 71

#	THAILAND	Min		Min	#	KOREA DPR
18	HATHAIRATTANAKOOL Kosin				1	SIM Sung Chol
5	SAWANGSRI Rungroj				2	RI Myong Sam
6	PROMRUT Choketawee				3	RI Kwang Chon
9	CHAIKAMDEE Sarayoot	78			5	JANG Sok Chol
11	DAMRONG-O Thawatchai				7	MUN In Guk
12	SURASIANG Nirut	69		77	9	KIM Yong Su
13	SENAMUANG Kiatisuk				10	HONG Yong Jo
17	CHALERMSAN Dusit				12	SIN Yong Nam
21	THONGLAO Datsakorn			41	13	KIM Chol Ho
26	SINGTHONG Issawa				14	HAN Song Chol
26	CHOECHIU Pichitpong	46			16	NAM Song Chol
	Tr: DE CARVALHO Carlos Roberto					Tr: YUN Jong Su
2	PHOURANDEE Preratat	69		41	8	JI Yun Nam
10	SRIPAN Tawan	46				
24	NOYVACH Manit	78				

Al Ain Club, Al Ain City
9-06-2004, 20:00, 5 000, Sapaev TKM

UAE 3 – 0 YEM

Rashid Abdulrahman 24
Mohamed Omar 2 28 73

#	ARAB EMIRATES	Min		Min	#	YEMEN
17	WALEED SALEM				1	ABDUL KHALEK Muaadh
5	ABDULSALAM JUMA			25	2	SALEM Mohammed
6	RASHID ABDULRAHMAN				3	AL FAKIH Ebrahim
7	MOHAMED OMAR			88	4	ABDULLAH Wafi
10	MOHAMED RASHID	70			5	HUSSEIN Asaad
14	BASHEER SAEED				6	EISSA Nashwan
16	SULTAN RASHED				7	AHMED Fathi
18	ISMAIL MATAR			57	8	YAHYA Redwan
21	HUMAID FAKHER	83			11	AL NONO Ali
25	MOHAMMAD QASSIM				18	AL ARAMI Fadhi
26	SALEM KHAMIS	66			20	AL ZURAQI Aziz
	Tr: JODAR Jean-Francois					Tr: Al Sunaini Amen
4	MOHAMED Omran	83 57		57	11	GHAZI Nasser
23	NAWAF MUBARAK	66 25		25	13	AL WADI Ahmed
24	SUBAIT KHATIR	70 88		88	17	SAEED Ahmed

Yanggakdo Stadium, Pyongyang
8-09-2004, 16:00, 20 000, Moradi IRN

PRK	4	1	THA

An Yong Hak 2 49 73, Hong Yong Jo 55
Ri Hyok Chol 60

Suksomkit 72

KOREA DPR			THAILAND	
1 SIM Sung Chol			HATHAIRATTANAKOOL Kosin	18
2 RI Myong Sam			SIRIWONG Niweat	3
3 RI Kwang Chon	75		PROMRUT Choketawee	6
5 JANG Sok Chol			CHAIMAN Therdsak	8
7 MUN In Guk			TIEBMA Paitoon	15
10 HONG Yong Jo			THONGLAO Datsakorn	19
12 SIN Yong Nam	67		SUKSOMKIT Sutee	23
14 HAN Song Chol		46	NOYYACH Manit	24
15 KIM Yong Jun		9	CHOECHIU Pichitpong	26
18 AN Yong Hak			SUWANNASIRI Worachai	27
19 CHOE Ung Chon	46		YUNTRASRI Sakchai	38
Tr: YUN Jong Su			Tr: PAHOLPAT Chatchai	
11 KIM Kwang Hyok	67	46	CHAIKAMDEE Sarayoot	9
16 NAM Song Chol	75	9 32	KEELALAY Tada	30
17 RI Hyok Chol	46	32	JITSAWAD Jetsada	31

Ali Moshen, Sana'a
8-09-2004, 16:00, 17 000, Al Ghamdi KSA

YEM	3	1	UAE

Al Nono 2 22 77, Abduljabar 49

Mohamed Omar 26

YEMEN			ARAB EMIRATES	
1 ABDUL KHALEK Muaadh			MUTAZ ABDULLA	22
3 ALWAH Mohammed			SALEH OBEID	2
4 ABDO MOHAMED Khaled		46	ABDULSALAM JUMA	5
5 HUSSEIN Asaad			RASHID ABDULRAHMAN	6
10 AL NONO Ali			MOHAMED OMAR	7
11 GHAZI Nasser	87	88	MOHAMED RASHID	10
13 AL WADI Ahmed			SULTAN RASHED	16
14 AL SHEHRI Saleh	46	46	ISMAIL MATAR	18
17 AMWAS Ahmed			ALI MSARRI	20
19 ESSAM MOHAMMED	84	75	HUMAID FAKHER	21
20 AL KUHALI Ebrahim			SUBAIT KHATIR	24
Tr: SAADANE Rabah			Tr: DE MOS Aad	
6 AL ZURAQI Ahmed	84	46	ALI Haidar Alo	8
7 FATEHI Hasan	87	75	SAEED HASSAN	19
9 ABDULJABAR Radwan	46	46	NAWAF MUBARAK	23

Yanggakdo Stadium, Pyongyang
13-10-2004, 15:30, 15 000, Vo Minh Tri VIE

PRK	2	1	YEM

Ri Han Ja 1, Hong Yong Jo 64

Jaber 76

KOREA DPR			YEMEN	
1 SIM Sung Chol			ABDUL KHALEK Muaadh	1
2 RI Myong Sam			AL FAQEH Ibrahim	3
3 RI Kwang Chon	62		AFARAH Khalid	4
5 JANG Sok Chol			HUSSEIN Asaad	5
9 KIM Yong Su			YAHYA Redwan	9
10 HONG Yong Jo		83	AL NONO Ali	10
12 SIN Yong Nam	38	72	GHAZI Nasser	11
13 RI Han Ja			AL QERSHI Esmail	13
14 HAN Song Chol			AMWAS Ahmed	17
15 KIM Yong Jun		70	AWN Essam	19
18 AN Yong Hak	74		AL KUHALI Ebrahim	20
Tr: PAEK Kil Son			Tr: AL RAEA Ahmad	
7 MUN In Guk	38	72	JABER Fathi	7
11 KIM Kwang Hyok	74	70	AL ZURAQI Ahmed	12
16 NAM Song Chol	62	83	AL SHEHRI Saleh	14

Rajamangala National, Bangkok
13-10-2004, 19:00, 15 000, Nishimura JPN

THA	3	0	UAE

Jakapong 10, Nanok 30
Chaiman 67

THAILAND			ARAB EMIRATES	
18 HATHAIRATTANAKOOL Kosin			MOHAMED ABDULLA	22
2 NANOK Anon			ABDULLA Abdulla Essa	3
3 SIRIWONG Niweat			ABDULLA ALI	4
4 JAKAPONG Jiensathawong	65		ALI Haider Alo	8
6 FUPLOOK Nakarin		71	SEBAIT Faisal Khalil	11
7 SAISANG Narasak		38	SHEHAB AHMED	13
8 CHAIMAN Therdsak			BASHEER SAEED	14
14 THONGMAN Piyawat			FAHED MASOUD	15
17 CHUWONG Prathum	73		SULTAN RASHED	16
22 PUANAKUNMEE Jetsada	82		SUBAIT KHATIR	24
23 SUKSOMKIT Sutee		59	SALEM KHAMIS	26
Tr: HELD Siegfried			Tr: DE MOS Aad	
9 INTHASEN Ekaphan	82	71	SALEM SAAD	9
11 KRAIKIAT Beadtaku	73	38	ISMAIL MATAR	18
12 BUNKHAM Jakkrit	65	59	MOHAMED SALEM	19

Rajamangala National, Bangkok
17-11-2004, 19:00, 15 000, Baskar IND

THA	1	1	YEM

Siriwong 95+

Al Shehri 69

THAILAND			YEMEN	
18 HATHAIRATTANAKOOL Kosin			ABDUL KHALEK Muaadh	1
2 NANOK Anon			AL WADI Ahmed	2
3 SIRIWONG Niweat			AL FAQEH Ibrahim	3
4 JAKAPONG Jiensathawong			HUSSEIN Assad	5
5 NONSRICHAI Thritthi		61	GHAZI Nasser	11
6 FUPLOOK Nakarin		90	JABER Fathi	7
7 SAISANG Narasak	42	76	AL SHEHRI Saleh	14
8 CHAIMAN Therdsak			AMWAS Ahmed	17
14 THONGMAN Piyawat			AL AROMI Fadhl	18
19 THONGLAO Datsakorn	84		AWN Essam	19
20 CHAOKLA Preecha	62		AL KUHALI Ebrahim	21
Tr: HELD Sigi			Tr: AL-RAEA Ahmad	
9 INTHASEN Ekaphan	62	76	AL GHURBANI Abdulsalam	8
11 KRAIKIAT Beadtaku	42	61	ABDULJABAR Radwan	13
15 YODYINGYONG Banluesak	84	90	AL QOR Wasim	16

Al Ahli Club, Dubai
17-11-2004, 18:30, 2 000, Abdul Hamid MAS

UAE	1	0	PRK

Saleh Obeid 58

ARAB EMIRATES			KOREA DPR	
17 ISMAIL RABEE			SIM Sung Chol	1
2 SALEH OBEID			RI Myong Sam	2
4 ABDULLA ALI		63	RI Kwang Chon	3
9 SALEM SAAD			JANG Sok Chol	5
12 SALAH ABBAS	85		MUN In Guk	7
13 ABDULSALAM Jumaa			KIM YONG Su	9
15 FAHED MASOUD		69	SIN Yong Nam	12
18 ISMAIL MATAR	76		HAN Song Chol	14
23 YOUSEF ABDULAZIZ			KIM Yong Jun	15
24 SUBAIT KHATIR			NAM Song Chol	16
25 MOHAMMAD QASSIM		34	CHOE Ung Chon	19
Tr: DE MOS Aad			Tr: YUN Jong Su	
5 ABDULRAHEEM JUMAA	85	69	PAK Nam Chol	6
19 REDHA ABDULHADI	76	34	JI Yun Nam	8
		63	KIM Kwang Hyok	11

SECOND PHASE GROUP 6	PL	W	D	L	F	A	PTS	BHR	SYR	TJK	KGZ
1 Bahrain	6	4	2	0	15	4	14		2-1	4-0	5-0
2 Syria	6	2	2	2	7	7	8	2-2		2-1	0-1
3 Tajikistan	6	2	1	3	5	9	7	0-0	0-1		2-1
4 Kyrgyzstan	6	1	1	4	5	12	4	1-2	1-1	1-2	

Spartak, Bishkek
18-02-2004, 15:00, 14 000, Lutfullin UZB

KGZ 1 2 TJK

Berezovsky [12]

Burkhanov 2 [31 53]

KYRGYZSTAN			TAJIKISTAN	
1 DJALILOV Zakair			KHABIBULLOEV Aslidin	1
2 VYACHESLAV Amin			FOUZAILOV Rakhmatoullo	2
3 SALO Vladimir			TOURDEV Akhliddin	3
4 SYDYKOV Ruslan			ZUVAYDOV Safardion	4
5 SHARAPOV Alimordon	84		TOUKHTAEV Alicher	6
7 CHERTKOV Vladimir			KHOLOMATOV Akmal	8
8 HARCHENKO Vadim	31		NORKULOV Anvar	9
10 BEREZOVSKY Valeri	70		BURKHANOV Pirmurod	10
11 BOLDYGIN Evgeny	82		LRGASHEV Odil	19
12 PHILIPAS Evgeny	46	69	SHAMSIEV Shubrat	20
17 ISHMAKOV Rinat			UMARBAEV Abdullo	21
Tr: ZAKIROV Nematjan			Tr: BABAEV Zoir	
6 KNIAZEV Sergey	70	69	SHARIPOV Fakhritdin	7
16 ISHENBAEV Azamat	82	84	KHAKBERDIEV Alisher	11
18 PRIANISHNIKOV Viacheslav	46	31	RAHIMOV Nizom	22

Muharraq, Muharraq
18-02-2004, 18:30, 5 000, Khanthama THA

BHR 2 1 SYR

Hubail.A 2 [64 73]

Shekh Eleshra [80]

BAHRAIN			SYRIA	
5 ALMOSWEI Hasan Ali			SAEED Samer	1
6 ALKHWARI Ghazi		85	MOHAMMAD Rafat	2
7 JALAL Sayed			DYAB Ali	3
8 ALDOSARI Rashed		87	REDAWI Dirar	5
10 SALMEEN Mohamed	55	60	AL-AMNAH Mahmoud	8
12 BASHEER Mohamed			AL AFASH Mohamad	10
13 YUSUF MOHAMED Talal			AL KHATIB Feras	11
17 HASAN Hussein Ali			ZAHER Khaled	14
19 ALI AHMED Husain			AQRAA Yaseen	15
22 SAEED Ali		68	SARI Anas	18
30 HUBAIL Alaa Ahmed	79		SHEKH ELESHRA Yousef	21
Tr: JURICIC Srecko			Tr: WOJCIK Janusz	
15 FARHAN Saleh Ahmed	79	60	SAYED Maher	9
31 Hubail Mohamed Ahmed	55	87	ALI Akram	17
		68	RAFE Raja	20

Spartak, Bishkek
31-03-2004, 16:00, 17 000, Bose IND

KGZ 1 1 SYR

Ishenbaev [55]

Kailouni [86]

KYRGYZSTAN			SYRIA	
1 DJALILOV Zakair			SAEED Samer	1
2 SAMSALIEV Talant			ESMAEEL Feras	4
3 SALO Vladimir			KASSAB Jihab	5
4 SYDYKOV Ruslan		85	REDAWI Dirar	6
5 AMIN Viacheslav	47	72	ALHOUSSAIN Jehad	8
6 PILIPAS Evgeny		76	SAYED Maher	9
7 CHERTKOV Vladimir			AL KHATIB Feras	10
8 PRIANISHNIKOV Viacheslav	74		ISTANBALI Mohammad	12
9 BEREZOVSKY Valeri			JENYAT Aatef	13
10 ISHENBAEV Azamat	79		AQRAA Yaseen	15
11 KUDRENKO Igor			REFAEE Ali	18
Tr: ZAKIROV Nematjan			Tr: REFAAT Ahmad	
12 SHARAPOV Alimordon	47	72	KAILOUNI Meaataz	7
15 BOLDYGIN Evgeny	74	85	ALKADDOR Mouhammad	17
17 CHIKISHEV Sergey	79	76	RAFE Raja	24

National Stadium, Dushanbe
31-03-2004, 16:00, 17 000, Maidin SIN

TJK 0 0 BHR

TAJIKISTAN			BAHRAIN	
1 KHABIBULLOEV Aslidin			SAEED Ali	22
2 FOUZAILOV Rakhmatoullo			ALKHWARI Ghazi	6
3 TOURDEV Akhliddin			ALDOSARI Rashed	8
4 ZUVAYDOV Safardion	39		SALMEEN Mohamed	10
6 TOUKHTAEV Alicher	77		MOHAMMED Feisal	11
8 KHOLOMATOV Akmal			BASHEER Mohamed	12
10 BURKHANOV Pirmurod			YUSUF MOHAMED Talal	13
18 MUHIDINOV Dzhamikhon			GHULOOM Salman	14
20 SHAMSIEV Shubrat	48		MAHFOODH Sayed	16
21 UMARBAEV Abdullo		69	ALI AHMED Husain	19
22 RAHIMOV Nizom		58	HUBAIL Alaa Ahmed	30
Tr: BABAEV Zoir			Tr: JURICIC Srecko	
9 BOBOEV Osimdjon	77	58	AL HANFI Mahmood	3
17 TABAROV Rustam	39	69	JALAL Sayed	7
19 IRGASHEV Odil	48			

Muharraq, Muharraq
9-06-2004, 19:15, 2 800, Al Saeedi UAE

BHR 5 0 KGZ

Hubail.A 3 [12 45 60], Ahmed [66]
Duaij [82]

BAHRAIN			KYRGYZSTAN	
22 SAEED Ali			DJALILOV Zakair	1
6 ALKHWARI Ghazi	55		AMIN Viacheslav	2
8 ALDOSARI Rashed			SALO Vladimir	3
9 AHMED Husain	80		SYDYKOV Ruslan	4
10 SALMEEN Mohamed		66	CHERTKOV Vladimir	7
11 MOHAMMED Feisal		46	PRIANISHNIKOV Viacheslav	8
12 BASHEER Mohamed			ISHENBAEV Azamat	10
13 YUSUF MOHAMED Talal	75	70	BEREZOVSKY Valeri	11
14 GHULOOM Salman			HARCHENKO Vadim	12
16 ADNAN Sayed			KUDRENKO Igor	13
30 HUBAIL Alaa Ahmed			PILIPAS Evgeniy	18
Tr: JURICIC Srecko			Tr: ZAKIROV Nematjan	
7 JALAL Sayed	75	66	KORNILOV Roman	9
23 DUAIJ Naser	80	70	HOLKOVSKY Oleg	14
31 HUBAIL Mohamed Ahmed	55	46	SAMSALIEV Talant	17

Al-Basel, Homs
10-06-2004, 17:15, 18 000, Al Fadhli KUW

SYR 2 1 TJK

Al Mohamed [76], Rafe [80]

Kholomatov [35]

SYRIA			TAJIKISTAN	
16 KARKAR Mahmowd			KHABIBULLOEV Aslidin	1
2 DYAB Ali			TABAROV Rustam	2
6 ALHOUSSAIN Jehad	63	77	UMARBAEV Abdullo	4
8 AL-AMNAH Mahmoud			KHABIBULLOEV Umed	5
9 SAYED Maher			KHOLOMATOV Akmal	8
13 JENYAT Aatef			NORKULOV Anvar	9
14 AL RASHED Maen	46	83	HAMIDOV Sukhrob	10
17 ALKADDOR Mouhammad	85		NASIKHOV Eradzh	12
21 SHEKH ELESHRA Yousef			OEV Dzhamolidin	17
23 ESMAEEL Feras			MUHIDINOV Dzhamikhon	18
24 RAFE Raja			IRGASHEV Odil	19
Tr: REFAAT Ahmad			Tr: BABAEV Zoir	
7 KAILOUNI Meaataz	63	77	KHADJAEV Roustam	7
18 ALREFAIZ Ali	85	83	SHARIPOV Fakhritdin	11
19 Al Mohamed Yahia	46	70	KHAKBERDIEV Alisher	14

Central Stadium, Dushanbe
8-09-2004, 16:00, 18 000, Mohd Salleh MAS

TJK 0 1 SYR

Rafe [35]

TAJIKISTAN				SYRIA		
1 KHABIBULLOEV Aslidin					KARKAR Mahmowd	16
2 FOUZAILOV Rakhmatoullo					DYAB Ali	2
3 TABAROV Rustam			50		GHSSAN Mohamed	3
4 KNITEL Denis	46		46		REDAWI Dirar	5
8 KHOLOMATOV Akmal					AL-AMNAH Mahmoud	8
9 NORKULOV Anvar					SAYED Maher	9
12 NASIKHOV Eradzh					AQRAA Yaseen	15
19 IRGASHEV Odil	65	88	88		ALKADDOR Mouhammad	17
20 RABIEV Yusuf					SHEKH ELESHRA Yousef	21
21 HAKIMOV Numordzhon					ESMAEEL Feras	23
22 RAHIMOV Nizom	44	59	59		RAFE Raja	24
Tr: BABAEV Zoir				Tr: REFAAT Ahmad		
5 NEGMATOV Alexsei	46	88	88		BODAKA Mohammed	7
15 BAROTOV Rahmonaly	65	59	59		AL KHATIB Feras	10
17 OEV Dzhamolidin	44	50	50		JENYAT Aatef	13

Spartak, Bishkek
8-09-2004, 17:00, 10 000, Rungklay THA

KGZ 1 2 BHR

Kenjisariev [86]   Ahmed [23], Hubail.M [58]

KYRGYZSTAN				BAHRAIN		
1 DJALILOV Zakair					ABDULLA Rhaman	16
2 SARDAROV Kanat	70				BAHZAD Mohammed	2
3 SALO Vladimir					JALAL Sayed	7
4 SYDYKOV Ruslan	87				ALDOSARI Rashed	8
5 AMIN Viacheslav		84			AHMED Husain	9
8 PRIANISHNIKOV Viacheslav					MOHAMMED Faisal	11
10 ISHENBAEV Azamat	63	79	79		BABA Hussain	17
13 KUDRENKO Igor					ABDULLA Ali	22
14 HOLKOVSKLY Igor	46				HUBAIL Mohamed Ahmed	29
18 PILIPAS Evgeniy					HUBAIL Alaa Ahmed	30
19 HARCHENKO Vadim		89	89		AMER Yaser	31
Tr: ZAKIROV Nematjan				Tr: JURCIC Srecko		
7 CHERTKOV Vladimir	46	79	79		BASHEER Mohamed	12
12 KRASNOV Andrey	63	84	84		ALZAIN Mohammed	19
20 KENJISARIEV Emil	70	89	89		HAMAD Humood	24

National Stadium, Dushanbe
13-10-2004, 15:00, 11 000, Al Enezi KUW

TJK 2 1 KGZ

Rabiev [19], Hakimov [37]   Chikishev [84]

TAJIKISTAN				KYRGYZSTAN		
1 KHABIBULLOEV Aslidin					DJALILOV Zakair	1
3 MAMADJONOV Shuhrat					AMIN Viacheslav	2
4 RUSTAMOW Maruf			68		SALO Vladimir	3
5 NEGMATOV Alexsei					CHERTKOV Vladimir	6
7 UMARBAEV Abdullo	46		46		PRIANISHNIKOV Viacheslav	8
8 KHOLOMATOV Akmal					KORNILOV Roman	9
9 NORKULOV Anvar					VODOPIANOV Radik	13
10 HAKIMOV Mansurdzhon					HOLKOVSKY Oleg	14
15 BAROTOV Rahmonaly	59				SAMSALIEV Talant	17
17 OEV Dzhamolidin			46		BELDINOV Aleksandr	18
20 RABIEV Yusuf	61				HARCHENKO Vadim	19
Tr: BABAEV Zoir				Tr: ZAKIROV Nematjan		
11 MUHIDINOV Dzhamikhon	61	68	68		VALIEV Timur	4
19 IRGASHEV Odil	59	46	46		KENJISARIEV Emil	10
21 RABIMOV Ibragim	46	46	46		CHIKISHEV Sergey	11

Al-Abbasiyin, Damascus
13-10-2004, 18:00, 35 000, Moradi IRN

SYR 2 2 BHR

Shekh Eleshra [12], Alhoussain [18]   Mahfoodh [27], Mohamed [92+]

SYRIA				BAHRAIN		
1 SAEED Samer					ABDULLA Ali	22
2 MOHAMMAD Rafat					BAHZAD Mohammed	2
3 GHASSAN Mohamed					JALAL Sayed	7
4 DYAB Ali					ALDOSARI Rashed	8
6 ALHOUSSAIN Jehad			60		AHMED Husain	9
8 AL-AMNAH Mahmoud					SALMEEN Mohamed	10
9 SAYED Maher	79				MOHAMED Talal	13
15 AQRAA Yaseen					MAHFOODH Sayed	16
21 SHEKH ELESHRA Yousef					BABA Hussain	17
23 ESMAEEL Feras			80		HUBAIL Mohamed Ahmed	29
24 RAFE Raja	77		80		HUBAIL Alaa Ahmed	30
Tr: REFAAT Ahmad				Tr: JURICIC Srecko		
7 AL OMAIR Ahmad	79		80		MARZOOKI Abdulla	3
11 AL ZENO Mohamed	77		60		FARHAN Saleh	15
			80		DUAIJ Naser	23

Al-Abbasiyin, Damascus
17-11-2004, 17:00, 1 000, Tongkhan THA

SYR 0 1 KGZ

Amin [47]

SYRIA				KYRGYZSTAN		
16 KARKAR Mahmowd					DJALILOV Zakair	1
4 DYAB Ali					SALO Vladimir	3
6 ALHOUSSAIN Jehad	85				SYDYKOV Ruslan	4
8 AL-AMNAH Mahmoud	68				AMIN Viacheslav	5
9 SAYED Maher					CHERTKOV Vladimir	6
11 AL ZENO Mohamed	56		85		CHIKISHEV Sergey	11
13 JENYAT Aatef					PILIPAS Evgeniy	12
15 AQRAA Yaseen					BEREZOVSKY Valeri	15
17 ALKADDOR Mouhammad					SAMSALIEV Talant	17
21 SHEKH ELESHRA Yousef			91		BELDINOV Aleksandr	18
23 ESMAEEL Feras					HARCHENKO Vadim	19
Tr: REFAAT Ahmad				Tr: ZAKIROV Nematjan		
5 REDAWI Dirar	68		85		PRIANISHNIKOV Viacheslav	8
18 AL ATASI Safir	85		91		HOLKOVSKY Oleg	14
24 RAFE Raja	56					

National Stadium, Manama
17-11-2004, 18:00, 15 000, Sun Baojie CHN

BHR 4 0 TJK

Mohamed.T [9], Mohamed.H [40],
Hubail.M 2 [42 77]

BAHRAIN				TAJIKISTAN		
21 JAFFER Sayed					KHABIBULLOEV Aslidin	1
2 MOHAMED Husain					RUSTAMOW Maruf	3
3 MARZOOKI Abdulla	70	46	46		MAMADJONOV Shuhrat	4
7 JALAL Sayed					NEGMATOV Alexsei	5
8 ALDOSARI Rashed					KHOLOMATOV Akmal	8
9 AHMED Husain					NORKULOV Anvar	9
10 SALMEEN Mohamed	75	76	76		HAKIMOV Mansurdzhon	10
13 MOHAMED Talal					OEV Dzhamolidin	17
17 ALI Hassan			65		IRGASHEV Odil	19
29 HUBAIL Mohamed Ahmed					RABIEV Yusuf	20
30 HUBAIL Alaa Ahmed	80				MAKHMUDOV Khurshed	21
Tr: JURICIC Srecko				Tr: BABAEV Zoir		
6 MOHAMED Abdulla	75	46	46		TOUKHTASOUNOV Daler	2
16 ADNAN Sayed	70	65	65		ORTIKOV Ilhomdzhon	7
23 DUAIJ Naser	80	76	76		BAROTOV Rahmonaly	15

SECOND PHASE GROUP 7	PL	W	D	L	F	A	PTS	KOR	LIB	VIE	MDV
1 Korea Republic	6	4	2	0	9	2	14		2-0	2-0	2-0
2 Lebanon	6	3	2	1	11	5	11	1-1		0-0	3-0
3 Vietnam	6	1	1	4	5	9	4	1-2	0-2		4-0
4 Maldives	6	1	1	4	5	14	4	0-0	2-5	3-0	

My Dinh, Hanoi
18-02-2004, 17:00, 25 000, Fong HKG

VIE 4 0 MDV

Phan.VTE 2 [9] 60, Nguyen.MH [13]
Pham.VQ 80p

VIETNAM				MALDIVES			
1	NGUYEN The Anh			MOHAMED Imran	18		
2	LE Van Troung	82		FAZEEL Ibrahim	5	82	
3	NGUYEN Huy Hoang	35		NAAZ Ahmed	6	35	
7	TRAN Truong Giang	70		NIZAM Mohamed	7		
8	NGUYEN Minh Hai			JAMEEL Mohamed	8		
10	PHAM Van Quyen			AZEEM Yoosuf	11		
11	LE Hong Minh	71		GHANI Assad Abdul	13		
12	NGUYEN Minh Phuong	80		GHANEE Anwar Abdul	15		
14	NGUYEN Huu Thang			LUTHFY Ashraf	17		
15	NGUYEN Manh Dung	67		THARIQ Ahmed	19		
22	PHAN Van Tai Em			IBRAHIM Sabah Mohamed	21		
	Tr: Nguyen Thanh Vinh			Tr: GONCALVES Manuel			
4	PHUNG Van Nhien	80	82	SHIYAM Ibrahim	9	82	
6	NGUYEN Trung Kien	70	67	IBRAHIM Ilyas	14	67	
20	LE Quoc Vuong	71	35	NAZEEH Mohamed	20	35	

Suwon World Cup Stadium, Suwon
18-02-2004, 19:00, 22 000, Al Dosari KSA

KOR 2 0 LIB

Cha Di Ri 32, Cho Byung Kuk 51

KOREA REPUBLIC				LEBANON			
1	LEE Woon Jae			EL SAMAD Mohamad	1		
4	CHOI Jin Cheul			YOUSSEF Mohamad	3		
5	KIM Nam Il			KENAAN Abbas	5		
7	KIM Tae Young	77		ALI AIWI Abbas	10	77	
8	PARK Ji Sung			EL ATTAR Ali	14		
9	SEOL Ki Hyeon	53		FERNANDEZ Luis	15		
12	LEE Young Pyo	56		KASSAS Mohammad	16		
16	CHA Du Ri			HALAWEH Mohamad	18		
19	AHN Jung Hwan			EL ATTAR Oday	19		
22	SONG Chong Gug			HAMIEH Khaled	21		
24	CHO Byung Kuk	82		CHAHOUD Mahmoud	23		
	Tr: COELHO Humberto			Tr: HAMOUD Mahmoud			
14	LEE Chun Soo	53		HASSOUN Malek	8	82	
				NASSEREDINE Ali	17	56	
				AL JAMAL Nasrat	20	77	

Galolhu National Stadium, Male
31-03-2004, 16:00, 12 000, Vidanagamage SRI

MDV 0 0 KOR

MALDIVES				KOREA REPUBLIC			
18	MOHAMED Imran			LEE Woon Jae	1		
3	LUTHFEE Hussain	68		CHOI Jin Cheul	4		
5	FAZEEL Ibrahim	.93		KIM Nam Il	5		
7	NIZAM Mohamed	61		KIM Tae Young	7	61	
8	JAMEEL Mohamed			SEOL Ki Hyeon	9		
10	UMAR Ali			CHUNG Kyung Ho	11		
13	GHANI Assad Abdul			LEE Young Pyo	12		
14	IBRAHIM Ilyas	91		LEE Eul Yong	13	82	
15	GHANEE Anwar Abdul	74		AHN Jung Hwan	19	74	
17	LUTHFY Ashraf			SONG Chong Gug	22		
21	IBRAHIM Sabah Mohamed			CHO Byung Kuk	24		
	Tr: GONCALVES Manuel			Tr: COELHO Humberto			
4	NASIR Mohamed	68	74	PARK Yo Seb	2	74	
16	MOHAMED Ismail	93	82	LEE Kwan Woo	10	82	
23	MOHAMED Fareed	91	61	KIM Dae Eui	18	61	

Thien Truong, Nam Dinh
31-03-2004, 17:00, 25 000, Irmatov UZB

VIE 0 2 LIB

Antar 83, Hamieh 88

VIETNAM				LEBANON			
1	NGUYEN The Anh			EL SAMAD Ziad	1		
2	LE Van Truong	57		YOUSSEF Mohamad	3		
3	NGUYEN Huy Hoang			KENAAN Abbas	5		
6	NGUYEN Trung Kien	46	78	ALI ATWI Abbas	10	78	
9	PHAM Van Quyen			ATTAR Ali	14		
11	LE Hong Minh			FERNANDEZ Luis	15		
12	NGUYEN Minh Phuong			NAJARIN Bilal	18		
14	NGUYEN Huu Thang	57	90	EL ATTAR Oday	19		
15	NGUYEN Manh Dung			ANTAR Roda	20		
18	PHAN Thanh Binh			HAMIEH Khaled	21		
22	PHAN Van Tai Em	61		CHAHOUD Mahmoud	23	61	
	Tr: TAVARES Edson			Tr: HAMOUD Mahmoud			
16	TRAN Hai Lam	57	78	SALAME Khodor	2	78	
17	TRINH Xuan Thanh	46	90	CHAHROUR Mohamad	4	90	
20	LE Quoc Vuong	57	61	NASSEREDINE Ali	17	61	

Daejeon World Cup Stadium, Daejeon
9-06-2004, 19:00, 40 019, Al Mehannah KSA

KOR 2 0 VIE

Ahn Jung Hwan 29, Kim Do Heon 61

KOREA REPUBLIC				VIETNAM			
1	LEE Woon Jae			TRAN Minh Quang	25		
2	PARK Jin Sub	52		PHUNG Van Nhien	4	52	
4	CHOI Jin Cheul			PHAM Hung Dung	5		
5	KIM Nam Il	46		LE Hong Minh	11		
6	Yoo Sang Chul			NGUYEN Minh Phuong	12		
12	KIM Eun Jung	76	65	NGUYEN Huu Thang	14	65	
13	LEE Eul Yong			LE Huynh Duc	21		
15	KIM Dong Jin	86		PHAN Van Tai Em	22		
19	AHN Jung Hwan			LE Anh Dung	23		
21	PARK Ji Sung	67		LE Quang Trai	26	67	
24	CHO Byung Kuk			THACH Bao Khanh	28		
	Tr: PARK Sung Wha			Tr: TAVARES Edson			
8	KIM Do Heon	46	65	LE Cong Vinh	9	65	
9	SEOL Ki Hyeon	76	52	VU Duy Hoang	17	52	
14	KIM Jung Woo	86	67	NGUYEN Van Dan	27	67	

Municipal Stadium, Beirut
9-06-2004, 20:30, 18 000, Nurilddin Salman IRQ

LIB 3 0 MDV

Zein 21, Antar 87, Nasseredine 93+

LEBANON				MALDIVES			
1	EL SAMAD Ziad			MOHAMED Imran	18		
3	MOHAMAD Youssef			LUTHFEE Hussain	3		
5	KENAAN Abbas			FAZEEL Ibrahim	5	25	
9	ZEIN Haitham	66		JAMEEL Mohamed	8		
10	ALI ATWI Abbas	89		UMAR Ali	10	75	
14	ATTAR Ali			ASHFAG Ali	12	70	
18	NAJARIN Bilal			GHANI Assad	13		
19	EL ATTAR Oday			IBRAHIM Ilyas	14	51	
20	ANTAR Roda			GHANEE Anwar	15		
21	HAMIEH Khaled			LUTHFY Ashraf	17		
23	CHAHOUD Mahmoud	81		FIRAZ Ahmed	20		
	Tr: HAMOUD Mahmoud			Tr: GONCALVES Manuel			
17	NASSEREDINE Ali	81	75	NASIR Mohamed	4	75	
24	AL JAMAL Nasrat	66	25	NIZAM Mohamed	7	25	
26	AZAR Rony	89	51	MOHAMED Ismail	16	51	

Galolhu National Stadium, Male
8-09-2004, 16:00, 12 000, Al Ajmi OMA

MDV	**2**	**5**	**LIB**

Fazeel 79, Umar 88 | Nasseredine 2 4 58, Antar.F 44 / Chahoud 63, Antar.R 75

MALDIVES				LEBANON
18 MOHAMED Imran				EL SAMAD Ziad 1
3 LUTHFEE Hussain				MOHAMAD Youssef 3
5 FAZEEL Ibrahim	82		65	ANTAR Faysal 6
7 NIZAM Mohamed	46			BAALBAKI Nabil 7
8 JAMEEL Mohamed	46			NAJARIN Bilal 8
10 UMAR Ali			77	CHAHOUD Mahmoud 9
13 GHANI Assad				NASSEREDINE Ali 10
15 GHANEE Anwar		58		ISSA Issa 15
16 SHAREEF Adam				EL ATTAR Ali 16
17 LUTHFY Ashraf				HALAWEH Mohamad 18
21 IBRAHIM Sabah				ANTAR Roda 20
Tr: GONCALVES Manuel				Tr: HAMOUD Mahmoud
4 NASIR Mohamed	46	58		ALOZIAN Krikor 17
9 SUNAIN Ahmed	82	65		HAMIEH Khaled 21
14 HABEEB Hussain	46	77		AZAR Rony 23

Thong Nhat, Ho Chi Minh City
8-09-2004, 17:00, 25 000, Yoshida JPN

VIE	**1**	**2**	**KOR**

Phan.VTE 49 | Lee Dong Gook 63, Lee Chun Soo 76

VIETNAM				KOREA REPUBLIC
25 TRAN Minh Quang				LEE Woon Jae 1
5 PHAM Hung Dung			66	LEE Min Sung 2
7 TRAN Truong Giang	72			PARK Jae Hong 3
9 LE Cong Vinh				CHOI Jin Cheul 4
10 PHAM Van Quyen	80			SEOL Ki Hyeon 9
12 NGUYEN Minh Phuong			43	CHA Du Ri 11
15 NGUYEN Manh Dung				LEE Young Pyo 12
21 LE Huynh Duc	80			LEE Chun Soo 14
22 PHAN Van Tai Em			87	AHN Jung Hwan 19
26 LE Quang Trai			73	LEE Dong Gook 20
27 NGUYEN Van Dron				SONG Chong Gug 22
Tr: TAVARES Edson				Tr: BONFRERE Jo
11 LE Hong Minh	72	66		KIM Do Heon 8
19 TRINH Xuan Thanh	80	73		CHOI Sung Kuk 10
28 THACH Bao Khanh	80	87		KIM Jung Woo 15

Galolhu National Stadium, Male
13-10-2004, 15:45, 10 000, Haq IND

MDV	**3**	**0**	**VIE**

Thariq 29, Ashfaq 2 68 85

MALDIVES				VIETNAM
18 MOHAMED Imran				TRAN Minh Quang 25
4 NASIR Mohamed			71	NGUYEN Huy Hoang 3
5 FAZEEL Ibrahim	82			PHAM Hung Dung 5
8 JAMEEL Mohamed				TRAN Truong Giang 7
10 UMAR Ali		46		PHAM Van Quyen 10
12 ASHFAQ Ali	88			NGUYEN Minh Phuong 12
13 GHANI Assad				NGUYEN Manh Dung 15
14 HABEEB Hussain				LE Huynh Duc 21
15 GHANEE Anwar	83			PHAN Van Tai Em 22
19 THARIQ Ahmed				THACH Bao Khanh 28
21 IBRAHIM Sabah				NGUYEN Duc Thang 33
Tr: GONCALVES Manuel				Tr: TAVARES Edson
3 LUTHFEE Hussain	83	46		LE Cong Vinh 9
9 SUNAIN Ahmed	82	71		NGUYEN Van Dan 27
20 MOHAMED Ismail	88			

Municipal Stadium, Beirut
13-10-2004, 18:00, 38 000, Irmatov UZB

LIB	**1**	**1**	**KOR**

Nasseredine 27 | Choi Jin Cheul 8

LEBANON				KOREA REPUBLIC
1 EL SAMAD Ziad				LEE Woon Jae 1
3 MOHAMAD Youssef				LEE Min Sung 2
6 ANTAR Faysal				PARK Jae Hong 3
9 CHAHOUD Mahmoud	75			CHOI Jin Cheul 4
13 ISSA Issa	80			YOO Sang Chul 6
15 KENAAN Abbas			46	SEOL Ki Hyeon 9
17 ALOZIAN Krikor				LEE Young Pyo 12
18 HALAWEH Mohamad				LEE Chun Soo 14
20 ANTAR Roda			30	KIM Jung Woo 15
21 HAMIEH Khaled	72			Ahn Jung Hwan 19
30 NASSEREDINE Ali				SONG Chong Gug 22
Tr: HAMOUD Mahmoud				Tr: BONFRERE Jo
14 HAIDAR Ossama	72	30		KIM Do Heon 8
10 ALI ATWI Abbas	75	46		LEE Dong Gook 20
7 BAALBAKI Nabil	80			

Seoul World Cup Stadium, Seoul
17-11-2004, 20:00, 64 000, Lazar SIN

KOR	**2**	**0**	**MDV**

Kim Do Heon 66, Lee Dong Gook 80

KOREA REPUBLIC				MALDIVES
1 LEE Woon Jae				MOHAMED Imran 18
3 PARK Jae Hong				NASIR Mohamed 4
4 CHOI Jin Cheul			95	FAZEEL Ibrahim 5
7 YOO Sang Chul				JAMEEL Mohamed 8
8 KIM Do Heon				UMAR Ali 10
12 LEE Young Pyo			83	ASHFAG Ali 12
14 LEE Chun Soo				GHANI Assad 13
19 AHN Jung Hwan	27	56		HABEEB Hussain 14
20 LEE Dong Gook				GHANEE Anwar 15
21 PARK Ji Sung				SHAREEF Adam 16
22 SONG Chong Gug	72			IBRAHIM Sabah 21
Tr: BONFRERE Jo				Tr: GONCALVES Manuel
9 SEOL Ki Hyeon	72	56		LUTHFY Ashraf 17
18 CHO Jae Jin	27	83		THARIQ Ahmed 19
		95		MOHAMED Ismail 20

Municipal Stadium, Beirut
17-11-2004, 18:00, 1 000, Ebrahim BHR

LIB	**0**	**0**	**VIE**

LEBANON				VIETNAM
1 EL SAMAD Ziad				TRAN Minh Quang 25
2 NAJARIN Bilal				NGUYEN Huy Hoang 3
6 ANTAR Faysal				TRAN Truong Giang 7
7 BAALBAKI Nabil			76	LE Cong Vinh 9
9 CHAHOUD Mahmoud	46		76	LE Hong Minh 11
10 ALI ATWI Abbas	81			NGUYEN Minh Phuong 12
13 ISSA Issa				NGUYEN Manh Dung 15
15 KENAAN Abbas				LE Huynh Duc 21
18 HALAWEH Mohamad				PHAN Van Tai Em 22
19 ATTAR Ali	53			LE Quang Trai 26
30 NASSEREDINE Ali				THACH Bao Khanh 28
Tr: HAMOUD Mahmoud				Tr: TAVARES Edson
11 EL CHOUM Ahmad	81	76		NGUYEN Van Dan 27
17 ALOZIAN Krikor	46	76		DANG Van Thanh 30
26 AZAR Rony	53			

SECOND PHASE GROUP 8	PL	W	D	L	F	A	PTS	KSA	TKM	IDN	SRI
1 Saudi Arabia	6	6	0	0	14	1	18		3-0	3-0	3-0
2 Turkmenistan	6	2	1	3	8	10	7	0-1		3-1	2-0
3 Indonesia	6	2	1	3	8	12	7	1-3	3-1		1-0
4 Sri Lanka	6	0	2	4	4	11	2	0-1	2-2	2-2	

Kopetdag, Ashgabat
18-02-2004, 19:00, 11 000, Al Bannai UAE

TKM   2   0   SRI

Ovekov [40], Bayramov [56]

TURKMENISTAN			SRI LANKA	
1	BERDIYEV Baramaniyaz		THILAKARATNE Sugath	1
3	GOCHKULIEV Gochkuli		MUDIYANSELAGE Samantha	3
6	DOURDUEV Kourbangeldy	46	FERNANDO Cristeen	4
10	URAZOV Didar	61	GEEGANGE Nalin	5
13	OVEKOV Guvanch		STEINWALL Dudley	6
14	SAPAROV Rustam		RAHEEM Imthyas	9
15	BERDYEV Omar	73	EDRIBANDANAGE Channa	10
18	AGAYEV Muslim		WEERARATHNA Kassun	11
19	HAYDAROV Alik		MOHAMED Azmeer Lathif	14
21	BAYRAMOV Vladimir		MUDIYANSELAGE Rathnayake	15
22	BAYRAMOV Nazar		MOHAMED Imran	21
Tr: KURBANMAMEDOV Rakhim			Tr: SAMPATH PERERA Kolomage	
4	BORODOLIMOV Yuri	46	8 ACHARIGE R.	2
11	AGABAEV Redjep	61		
20	KULIEV Begench	73		

Sugathadasa, Colombo
31-03-2004, 18:30, 6 000, Chynybekov KGZ

SRI   0   1   KSA

Al Shahrani [51]

SRI LANKA			SAUDI ARABIA	
1	THILAKARATNE Sugath		ZAID Mabrouk	21
2	JAYAVILAL B.A.R		AL DOSARI Ahmed Dukhi	2
3	MUDIYANSELAGE Samantha		AL MONTASHARI Hamad	4
5	GEEGANGE Nalin		AL QADI Naif	5
6	STEINWALL Dudley		AL SHAHRANI Ibrahim	7
9	RAHEEM Imthyas	55	AL GIZANI Waleed	9
10	EDRIBANDANAGE Channa	82	AL SHLHOUB Mohammad	10
11	WEERARATHNA Kassun		KHARIRI Saud	14
12	HAMEED Mohamed		AL DOSSARI Khamis	16
16	PERERA Isuru		AL JANOUBI Abdul Aziz	20
20	FUARD Kamaldeen		AL MESHAL Talal	29
Tr: SAMPATH PERERA Kolomage			Tr: VAN DER LEM Gerard	
		55	ALBASHA Yusri	11
		82	ALKHAIBARI Saod	13

Gelora Bung Karno, Jakarta
9-06-2004, 19:00, 30 000, Nesar BAN

IDN   1   0   SRI

Aiboi [30]

INDONESIA			SRI LANKA	
1	KARTIKO Hendro		THILAKARATNE Sugath	1
2	SETYABUDI Agung	87	MUDIYANSELAGE Samantha	3
6	ARDI Warsidi		GEEGANGE Nalin	5
8	AIBOI Elie	84	CHATURA Siyaguna	7
11	ASTAMAN Ponario		RAHEEM Imthyas	9
13	SUDARSONO Budi	69	EDRIBANDANAGE Channa	10
16	BACHRI Syamsul		WEERARATHNA Kassun	11
17	SAPUTRA Hary		MOHAMED Azmeer Lathif	14
18	AGUS Firmansyah		PERERA Isuru	16
20	PAMUNGKAS Bambang		FUARD Kamaldeen	20
26	SOFYAN Ismed		WEWAGE Dilshan	29
Tr: KOLEV Ivan			Tr: SAMPATH PERERA Kolomage	
25	PULALO Alexandr	87		
28	IVAK Eduard	84		
29	ALIYUDIN	69		

King Fahd International, Riyadh
18-02-2004, 20:15, 1 000, Al-Ghafary JOR

KSA   3   0   IDN

Al Shahrani 2 [4 39], Al Kahtani [45]

SAUDI ARABIA			INDONESIA	
22	SHARIFI Mohammad		KARTIKO Hendro	1
2	AL DOSARI Ahmed Dukhi		SETYABUDI Agung	2
3	TUKAR Redha		ALI Isnan	3
4	AL MONTASHARI Hamad		SUGIANTORO Bejo	5
7	AL SHAHRANI Ibrahim	79	NAWAWI Uston	9
8	NOOR Mohammed	70	ASTAMAN Ponario	11
9	AL KAHTANI Yaser	79	73	SUDARSONO Budi	13
14	KHARIRI Saud		GEDE Putu	14
15	ABUSHGEER Manaf		LAALA Jet Donald	15
16	AL DOSSARI Khamis		SAPUTRA Hary	17
19	AL SAQRI Saleh	81	89	PAMUNGKAS Bambang	20
Tr: VAN DER LEM Gerard			Tr: KOLEV Ivan	
11	AL DOSARI Bander	70	89	TECUARI Aples	4
20	AL JANOUBI Abdul Aziz	81	73	AIBOI Elie	8
29	AL MESHAL Talal	79	79	KURNIAWAN Dwi	10

Olympic Stadium, Ashgabat
31-03-2004, 19:00, 5 000, Sahib Shakir IRQ

TKM   3   1   IDN

Bayramov 2 [10 74], Kuliev [35]   Sudarsono [30]

TURKMENISTAN			INDONESIA	
30	HARCHIK Pavel		CHRISTIAN Yandri	12
3	GOCHKULIEV Gochkuli		88 SETYABUDI Agung	2
6	DOURDUEV Kourbangeldy		SUGIANTORO Bejo	5
7	MINGAZOV Kamil		ARDI Warsidi	6
11	AGABAEV Redjep	79	70 ICHWAN Muhammad	7
12	REJEPOV Guvanch		ASTAMAN Ponario	11
15	BERDYEV Omar		SUDARSONO Budi	13
19	HAYDAROV Alik	59	89 BACHRI Syamsul	16
20	KULIEV Begench		SAPUTRA Hary	17
21	BAYRAMOV Vladimir		PAMUNGKAS Bambang	20
22	BAYRAMOV Nazar		PULALO Alexandr	25
Tr: KURBANMAMEDOV Rakhim			Tr: KOLEV Ivan	
8	NAZAROV Artem	79	88 TECUARI Aples	4
9	MIRZOEV Arif	59	70 AIBOI Elie	8
			89 KURNIAWAN Agus	22

King Fahd International, Riyadh
9-06-2004, 21:00, 1 000, Khanthama THA

KSA   3   0   TKM

Al Meshal 2 [27 45], Noor [32]

SAUDI ARABIA			TURKMENISTAN	
21	ZAID Mabrouk		NABOYCHENKO Evgeni	16
2	AL DOSARI Ahmed Dukhi		MEREDOV Bayramduray	5
3	TUKAR Redha	34	DURDIYEV Gurbangeldi	6
4	AL MONTASHARI Hamad		MINGAZOV Kamil	7
7	AL SHAHRANI Ibrahim	84	74 REJEPOV Guvanch	12
8	NOOR Mohammed		52 OVEKOV Guvanch	13
9	AL KAHTANI Yaser		BERDYEV Omar	15
12	AL ABDALI Ali		HAYDAROV Alik	19
14	AL ABDULLHA Saheb		82 KULIEV Begench	20
16	AL DOSSARI Khamis		BAYRAMOV Vladimir	21
29	AL MESHAL Talal	69	BAYRAMOV Nazar	22
Tr: VAN DER LEM Gerard			Tr: KURBANMAMEDOV Rakhim	
5	AL QADI Naif	34	82 NAZAROV Artem	8
15	AL OTAIBI Marzouq	84	52 MIRZOEV Arif	9
18	AL DOSSARI Saeed	69	74 ALIKPEROV Vitaliy	45

Sugathadasa, Colombo
8-09-2004, 18:30, 4 000, Marshoud JOR

SRI	2	2	IDN

Steinwall [81], Karunaratne [82] — Jaya 8, Sofyan [51]

SRI LANKA			INDONESIA	
1 THILAKARATNE Sugath			KARTIKO Hendro	1
2 JAYAVIIAL BA Rajitha	56		ALI Isnan	3
3 WICKREMATHILAKE SP	74	85	AIBOI Elie	8
5 GEEGANGE Nalin			ASTAMAN Ponario	11
6 STEINWALL Dudley			LAALA Jet Donald	15
7 WEERASINGHE Chatura			BACHRI Syamsul	16
10 EDRIBANDANAGE Kassun			SAPUTRA Hary	17
14 MOHAMED Azmeer Lathif	76		INDARTO Aris	19
16 PERERA Isuru			SOFYAN Ismed	26
20 FUARD Kamaldeen			SALOSSA Ortizan	29
29 DILSHAN Maduranga		75	JAYA Ilham	32
Tr: SAMPATH PERERA Kolomage			Tr: WITHE Peter	
28 KARUNARATNE Galboda	76	85	SUDARSONO Budi	13
30 NAUFER Isadeen	74	56	GEDE Putu	14
		75	PAMUNGKAS Bambang	20

Olympic Stadium, Ashgabat
8-09-2004, 19:00, 5 000, Kwon Jong Chul KOR

TKM	0	1	KSA

Al Kahtani [47]

TURKMENISTAN			SAUDI ARABIA	
30 HARCHIK Pavel			BABKR Mohammed	22
3 GOCHKULIEV Gochkuli			AL DOSARI Ahmed	2
6 DURDIYEV Gurbangeldi			FALLATHA Redha	3
7 MINGAZOV Kamil	79		AL QADI Naif	5
10 URAZOV Didar	83	89	NOOR Mohammed	8
14 SAPAROV Rustam			AL KAHTANI Yaser	9
15 BERDYEV Omar			AUTEF Abdoh	11
20 KULIEV Begench		69	KHARIRI Saud	14
21 BAYRAMOV Vladimir			AL DOSSARI Khamis	16
22 BAYRAMOV Nazar	81	73	AL SUWAILH Ahmed	20
27 ZEMSKOV Yevgeniy	63		SULIMANI Hussein	24
Tr: KURBANMAMEDOV Rakhim			Tr: AL-ABODULAZIZ Nasser	
9 MIRZOEV Arif	63	89	HAGAWI Jaber	4
19 HAYDAROV Alik	79	73	AL DOSARI Abdullah	7
32 URAZOV Dayanch	83	69	AL GHANNAM Abdullatif	17

Sugathadasa, Colombo
9-10-2004, 18:30, 4 000, Al Bannai UAE

SRI	2	2	TKM

Perera [47], Mudiyanselage.R [57] — Bayramov.D [20], Nazarov [70]

SRI LANKA			TURKMENISTAN	
1 THILAKARATNE Sugath			BERDIYEV Baramaniyaz	16
3 PRABATH Samantha	85		BOROVIK Boris	2
5 GEEGANGE Nalin			CHONKAEV Gahrymanberdy	3
6 STEINWALL Dudley		59	REJEPOV Guvanch	4
7 MADURANGA Chathura	72		DURDIYEV Gurbangeldi	6
11 WEERARATHNA Kassun			NAZAROV Artem	7
15 MUDIYANSELAGE Rathnayake			ALIKPEROV Vitaliy	8
16 PERERA Isuru		56	MIRZOEV Arif	9
20 FUARD Kamaldeen		73	BAYRAMOV Dovlet	14
29 DILSHAN Maduranga			ATAYEV Dovletmurad	20
30 NAUFER Isadeen			MEREDOV Bayramduray	28
Tr: SAMPATH PERERA Kolomage			Tr: KURBANMAMEDOV Rakhim	
34 PRASANNA	85	73	URAZOV Dayanch	11
		56	KARADANOV Mamedaly	13
		59	ZEMSKOV Yevgeniy	26

Gelora Bung Karno, Jakarta
12-10-2004, 19:30, 30 000, Mohd Salleh MAS

IDN	1	3	KSA

Jaya [50] — Al Meshal 9, Sulaimani [13], Al Qahtani [80]

INDONESIA			SAUDI ARABIA	
1 KARTIKO Hendro			AL MUGREN Rashed	1
8 AIBOI Elie			AL DOSARI Ahmed	2
11 ASTAMAN Ponario			AL QADI Naif	5
15 LAALA Jet Donald		65	AL SAEED Mishal	6
16 BACHRI Syamsul		55	AL SHARANI Sowed	7
19 INDARTO Aris	84		AL QAHTANI Saeed	9
26 SOFYAN Ismed	45		AL HARBI Osamah	13
29 SALOSSA Ortizan			FALLATAH Hassan	14
32 JAYA Ilham	63	77	AL DOSSARI Khamis	16
34 SALOSSA Boas			SULAIMANI Omar	24
37 YULIANTO Charis			AL MESHAL Saeed	29
Tr: WITHE Peter			Tr: AL-ABODULAZIZ Nasser	
10 KURNIAWAN Dwi	63	55	AL SAHRANI Hussain	17
38 SALIMIN Supriyono	84	77	AL GHANNAM Abdullatif	18
		65	AL HARTHI Meshal	19

Gelora Bung Karno, Jakarta
17-11-2004, 19:30, 15 000, Shaban KUW

IDN	3	1	TKM

Jaya 3 [20 47 59] — Durdiyev [25]

INDONESIA			TURKMENISTAN	
12 CHRISTIAN Yandri			BERDIYEV Baramaniyaz	16
8 AIBOI Elie		50	REJEPOV Guvanch	4
11 ASTAMAN Ponario			DURDIYEV Gurbangeldi	6
16 BACHRI Syamsul			NAZAROV Artem	8
29 SALOSSA Ortizan		46	MIRZOEV Arif	9
32 JAYA Ilham	71		URAZOV Dayanch	11
34 SALOSSA Boas	69		BAYRAMOV Dovlet	14
36 MAULY Mohammad		78	MEREDOV Bayramduray	15
37 YULIANTO Charis			KULIEV Begench	20
38 SALIMIN Supriyono			ALIKPEROV Vitaliy	22
39 JACOB KOMBOY Kamasan	88		CHONKAEV Gahrymanberdy	26
Tr: WITHE Peter			Tr: KURBANMAMEDOV Rakhim	
19 INDARTO Aris	88	50	MINGAZOV Kamil	7
42 SINAGA Saktiawan	69	78	HAMRAYEV Murad	24
43 PANGGABEAN Mahyadi	71	46	HAJIEV Didar	25

Prince Mohammed Bin Fahd Bin Abdul Aziz, Dammam
17-11-2004, 20:00, 2 000, Muflah OMA

KSA	3	0	SRI

Al Harthi [6], Al Shlhoub [45p]
Fallata [65]

SAUDI ARABIA			SRI LANKA	
12 AL EISA Hamad			THILAKARATNE Sugath	1
3 JAHDALI Walid			JAYAVIIAL BA Rajitha	2
4 AL MONTASHARI Hamad	86		KUMARA Nandana	5
6 AL SAEED Mishal			STEINWALL Dudley	6
7 FALLATA Fahad			WEERARATHNA Kassun	11
10 AL SHLHOUB Mohammad	69		Mohamed Azmeer Lathif	14
14 FALLATAH Hassan			MUDIYANSELAGE Rathnayake	15
15 ALHARTHI Saad	58		PERERA Isuru	16
18 AL JASSAM Taiseer		53	FUARD Kamaldeen	20
19 AL ABDULLHA Saheb			DILSHAN Maduranga	29
22 KHOJAH Mohammad			NAUFER Isadeen	30
Tr: AL-ABODULAZIZ Nasser			Tr: SAMPATH PERERA Kolomage	
16 AL BISHI Abdulrahman	58			
17 ALTHAGAFI Mansour	86			
20 ALMOHAMMEDI Saleh	69			

THIRD PHASE GROUP A

Pakhtakor, Tashkent
9-02-2005, 15:45, 45 000, Kamikawa JPN

UZB	1 1	KSA

Soliev 93+   Al Jaber 76

UZBEKISTAN		SAUDI ARABIA	
1 POLYAKOV Aleksey		ZAID Mabrouk 21	
2 ASHURMATOV Bahtiyor		AL MONTASHARI Hamad 4	
3 FEDOROV Andrei	82	AL BAHRI Ahmed 5	
5 ALIKULOV Asror	78	ABUSHGEER Manaf 6	
7 AKOPYANTS Andrey	88	AL SHLHOUB Mohammad 10	
8 DJEPAROV Server		KHARIRI Saud 14	
10 MAMINOV Vladimir		AL THAKER Khaled 16	
11 SHISHELOV Vladimir	89	AL JASSAM Taiseer 17	
14 PASHININ Oleg		SHARIFY Hadi 18	
16 SHATSKIKH Maksim	73	AL QAHTANI Yasser 20	
17 NIKOLAEV Alexey		SULIMANI Hussein 24	
Tr: GEODE Heinz-Juergen		Tr: CALDERON Gabriel	
9 SOLIEV Anvarjon	89 73	AL JABER Sami 9	
13 BIKMOEV Marat	82	AL SAGRI Safeh 19	88
		AL SHAMRANI Nassir 26	78

World Cup Stadium, Seoul
9-02-2005, 20:05, 53 287, Maidin SIN

KOR	2 0	KUW

Lee Dong Gook 24, Lee Young Pyo 81

KOREA REPUBLIC		KUWAIT	
1 LEE Woon Jae		AL FADLI Khaled 23	
2 YOU Kyoung Youl		ASEL Ali 4	
3 PARK Jae Hong		AL SHAMMARI Nohayer 5	
5 KIM Nam Il	54	AL MUTAIRI Nawaf 11	
7 PARK Ji Sung		AL ENEZI Mesaed 13	
9 SEOL Ki Hyeon		JUMAH Waleed 15	
12 LEE Young Pyo		AL SHAMMARI Khaled 16	
13 KIM Dong Jin		AL MUTWA Bader 17	
14 LEE Chun Soo	70	61 AL DAWOOD Abdul 20	
20 LEE Dong Gook		AL MUTAIRI Mohammad 24	
23 PARK Dong Hyuk		AL SHAMMARI Ahmad 25	
Tr: BONFRERE Jo		Tr: PAVKOVIC Sloboadan	
16 CHUNG Kyung Ho	70	61 ABDULAZIZ Bashar 9	
		54 AL HAMAD Fahad 10	

Kazma, Kuwait City
25-03-2005, 19:45, 12 000, Sun Baojie CHN

KUW	2 1	UZB

Abdulaziz 2 7 62   Geynrikh 77

KUWAIT		UZBEKISTAN	
1 KANKUNE Shehab		POLYAKOV Aleksey 1	
3 JARRAGH Mohamad		ASHURMATOV Bahtiyor 2	
4 ASEL Ali		KASIMOV Mirdjalal 4	
5 AL SHAMMARI Nohayer	67	ALIKULOV Asror 5	
6 ZAYED Yousef	37	AKOPYANTS Andrey 7	
9 ABDULAZIZ Bashar	77 67	MAMINOV Vladimir 10	
10 AL HAMAD Fahad		PASHININ Oleg 14	
12 AL TAYYAR Hamad		GEYNRIKH Alexander 15	
13 JUMAH Waleed		SHATSKIKH Maksim 16	
17 AL MUTWA Bader	60	NIKOLAEV Alexey 17	
25 AL SHAMMARI Ahmad	30	MAGDEEV Ildar 20	
Tr: PAVKOVIC Sloboadan		Tr: GEODE Heinz-Juergen	
8 AL SHAMMARI Husain	77 37	KOSHEKEV Leonid 6	
11 SAIHAN Abdullah	60 67	DJEPAROV Server 8	
30 AL MUTAIRI Nawaf	30 67	SOLIEV Anvarjon 9	

Prince Mohammed Bin Fahad Bin Abdul Aziz, Dammam
25-03-2005, 19:45, 25 000, Mohd Salleh MAS

KSA	2 0	KOR

Khariri 29, Al Qahtani 74

SAUDI ARABIA		KOREA REPUBLIC	
21 ZAID Mabrouk		LEE Woon Jae 1	
3 FALLATHA Redha		PARK Jae Hong 3	
4 AL MONTASHARI Hamad		KIM Nam Il 6	
6 ABUSHGEER Manaf	75	69 YOO Sang Chul 7	
9 AL JABER Sami		88 LEE Chun Soo 8	
12 KHATHRAN Abdulaziz		LEE Young Pyo 10	
14 KHARIRI Saud		75 SEOL Ki Hyeon 12	
15 AL BAHRI Ahmed		KIM Dong Jin 14	
16 AL THAKER Khaled		PARK Dong Hyuk 18	
17 AL JASSAM Taiseer	83	LEE Dong Gook 19	
20 AL QAHTANI Yasser	86	PARK Ji Sung 21	
Tr: CALDERON Gabriel		Tr: BONFERE Jo	
10 AL SHLHOUB Mohammad	75	75 NAMKUNG Do 11	
11 AL SHAMRANI Nassir	86	88 KIM Do Heon 13	
25 AL ABDULLHA Saheb	83	69 CHUNG Kyung Ho 17	

Kazma, Kuwait City
30-03-2005, 19:45, 25 000, Moradi IRN

KUW	0 0	KSA

KUWAIT		SAUDI ARABIA	
1 KANKUNE Shehab		ZAID Mabrouk 21	
3 JARRAGH Mohamad		FALLATHA Redha 3	
4 ASEL Ali		AL MONTASHARI Hamad 4	
5 AL SHAMMARI Nohayer	91	ABUSHGEER Manaf 6	
9 ABDULAZIZ Bashar	73	AL JABER Sami 9	
10 AL HAMAD Fahad	75	KHATHRAN Abdulaziz 12	
12 AL TAYYAR Hamad		AL BAHRI Ahmed 15	
13 AL ENEZI Mesaed		AL THAKER Khaled 16	
15 JUMAH Waleed		AL JASSAM Taiseer 17	
19 SAEED Faraj	64	AL QAHTANI Yasser 20	
26 AL NAMASH Ali		AL ABDULLHA Saheb 25	
Tr: PAVKOVIC Sloboadan		Tr: CALDERON Gabriel	
11 SAIHAN Abdullah	75	73 AL SHLHOUB Mohammad 10	
18 MATAR Khaled	64	91 AL SHAMRANI Nassir 11	

World Cup Stadium, Seoul
30-03-2005, 20:45, 62 857, Najm LIB

KOR	2 1	UZB

Lee Young Pyo 54, Lee Dong Gook 61   Geynrikh 78

KOREA REPUBLIC		UZBEKISTAN	
1 LEE Woon Jae		NESTEROV Ignatiy 12	
2 YOU Kyoung Youl		FEDOROV Andrei 3	
6 YOO Sang Chul		ALIKULOV Asror 5	
7 PARK Ji Sung		81 KOSHEKEV Leonid 6	
9 SEOL Ki Hyeon	85	DJEPAROV Server 8	
11 CHA Du Ri		SOLIEV Anvarjon 9	
12 LEE Young Pyo		MAMINOV Vladimir 10	
13 KIM Dong Jin		PASHININ Oleg 14	
20 LEE Dong Gook	75	GEYNRIKH Alexander 15	
23 PARK Dong Hyuk		NIKOLAEV Alexey 17	
36 KIM Jin Kyu		50 MAGDEEV Ildar 20	
Tr: BONFRERE Jo		Tr: GEODE Heinz-Juergen	
17 CHUNG Kyung Ho	75	81 AKOPYANTS Andrey 7	
19 NAMKUNG Do	85	50 BIKMOEV Marat 13	

Pakhtakor, Tashkent
3-06-2005, 18:00, 40 000, Moradi IRN

UZB	1	1	KOR

Shatskikh [63]   Park Chu Young [90]

UZBEKISTAN			KOREA REPUBLIC	
1 SAFONOV Evgeni			LEE Woon Jae	1
2 ASHURMATOV Bahtiyor			YOU Kyoung Youl	2
4 KASIMOV Mirdjalal	86		KIM Han Yoon	3
5 ALIKULOV Asror		89	YOO Sang Chul	6
6 KOSHEKEV Leonid			PARK Ji Sung	7
10 KARPENKO Victor			PARK Chu Young	10
15 GEYNRIKH Alexander	60	70	CHA Du Ri	11
16 SHATSKIKH Maksim			LEE Young Pyo	12
17 NIKOLAEV Alexey			KIM Dong Jin	13
18 KADADAZE Timur		58	AHN Jung Hwan	19
22 SHIRSHOV Nikolai			PARK Dong Hyuk	21
Tr: KHAYDAROV Ravshan			Tr: BONFRERE Jo	
9 SOLIEV Anvarjon	60	89	KIM Do Heon	8
14 KIRYAN Vladislav	86	70	CHUNG KYyung Ho	16
		58	LEE Dong Gook	20

Kazma, Kuwait City
8-06-2005, 20:45, 15 000, Khanthama THA

KUW	0	4	KOR

Park Chu Young [19], Lee Dong Gook [29]
Chung Kyung Ho [55], Park Ji Sung [61]

KUWAIT			KOREA REPUBLIC	
1 KANKUNE Shehab			LEE Woon Jae	1
2 ABDULLAH Yaqoub	70		YOU Kyoung Youl	2
4 ASEL Ali	58		KIM Han Yoon	3
5 AL SHAMMARI Nohayer			PARK Ji Sung	7
7 ZADAH Khaled			PARK Chu Young	10
8 AL SHAMMARI Husain		54	CHA Du Ri	11
9 ABDULAZIZ Bashar			LEE Young Pyo	12
11 SHAHEEN Fahad	45	68	KIM Dong Jin	13
13 AL ENEZI Mesaed			KIM Jung Woo	15
18 AL HAMAD Fahad		80	LEE Dong Gook	20
19 AL MUTAIRI Nawaf			KIM Jin Kyu	36
Tr: PAVKOVIC Sloboadan			Tr: BONFRERE Jo	
16 AL SHAMMARI Khaled	58	54	CHUNG Kyung Ho	16
17 AL MUTWA Bader	45	80	AHN Jung Hwan	19
27 AL OTHMAN Nasser	70	68	KWAK Hee Ju	24

King Fahd International, Riyadh
3-06-2005, 21:05, 72 000, Kamikawa JPN

KSA	3	0	KUW

Al Shlhoub 2 [19] [50], Al Harthi [82]

SAUDI ARABIA			KUWAIT	
1 ZAID Mabrouk			KANKUNE Shehab	1
3 FALLATHA Redha			JARRAGH Mohamad	3
4 AL MONTASHARI Hamad	68		ASEL Ali	4
8 HAIDAR Mohammied	75		AL SHAMMARI Nohayer	5
9 AL JABER Sami		46	ABDULAZIZ Bashar	9
10 AL SHLHOUB Mohammad			AL ENEZI Mesaed	13
12 KHATHRAN Abdulaziz		71	JUMAH Waleed	15
14 KHARIRI Saud	80		AL MUTWA Bader	17
15 AL BAHRI Ahmed			AL MUTAIRI Nawaf	19
16 AL THAKER Khaled		75	AL HAMAD Fahad	20
20 AL QAHTANI Yasser	86	65	AL NAMASH Ali	26
Tr: CALDERON Gabriel			Tr: PAVKOVIC Sloboadan	
7 AL SHARANI Sowed	86	68	ABDULLAH Yaqoub	2
11 AL HARTHI Saad	75	46	ZADAH Khaled	7
25 AL DOSARI Bander Tamim	80	75	AL SHAMMARI Husain	8

King Fahd International, Riyadh
8-06-2005, 21:05, 72 000, Huang Junjie CHN

KSA	3	0	UZB

Al Jaber 2 [8] [61], Al Harthi [88]

SAUDI ARABIA			UZBEKISTAN	
1 ZAID Mabrouk			SAFONOV Evgeni	1
4 AL MONTASHARI Hamad			FEDOROV Andrei	3
5 AL QADI Naif		73	KASIMOV Mirdjalal	4
6 ABUSHGEER Manaf	60		ALIKULOV Asror	5
9 AL JABER Sami	67		KOSHEKEV Leonid	6
10 AL SHLHOUB Mohammad		46	KARPENKO Victor	10
12 KHATHRAN Abdulaziz		53	KHOLMURADOV Zafar	11
14 KHARIRI Saud			SHATSKIKH Maksim	16
15 AL BAHRI Ahmed			NIKOLAEV Alexey	17
16 AL THAKER Khaled	85		KADADAZE Timur	18
20 AL QAHTANI Yasser			SHIRSHOV Nikolai	22
Tr: CALDERON Gabriel			Tr: KHAYDAROV Ravshan	
7 AL SHARANI Sowed	85	73	BAYRAMOV Renat	8
11 AL HARTHI Saad	67	53	SOLIEV Anvarjon	9
19 AL ABDULLHA Saheb	60	46	KIRYAN Vladislav	14

THIRD PHASE GROUP A	PL	W	D	L	F	A	PTS	KSA	KOR	KUW	UZB
1 Saudi Arabia	5	3	2	0	9	1	11		2-0	3-0	3-0
2 Korea Republic	5	3	1	1	9	4	10			2-0	2-1
3 Kuwait	5	1	1	3	2	10	4	0-0	0-4		2-1
4 Uzbekistan	5	0	2	3	4	9	2	1-1	1-1		

Table as of 16 August 2005. Remaining fixtures: 17-08-2005 Korea Republic v Saudi Arabia; Uzbekistan v Kuwait

THIRD PHASE GROUP B

National Stadium, Manama
9-02-2005, 18:35, 25 000, Mohd Salleh MAS

BHR 0 0 IRN

#	BAHRAIN			IRAN	#
1	ALI Hassan			MIRZAPOUR Ebrahim	1
3	MARZOOKI Abdulla			MAHDAVIKIA Mehdi	2
7	JALAL Sayed			GOLMOHAMMADI Yahya	4
8	ALDOSARI Rashed			REZAEI Rahman	5
10	SALMEEN Mohamed			NEKOUNAM Javad	6
13	MOHAMED Talal			KARIMI Ali	8
14	GHULOOM Salman		86	HASHEMIAN Vahid	9
16	MAHFOODH Sayed			DAEI Ali	10
17	BABA Hussain		62	ZANDI Ferydoon	12
23	DUAIJ Naser	86		KABEI Hossein	13
19	HUBAIL Alaa			NOSRATI Mohammad	20
	Tr: JURICIC Srecko			Tr: IVANKOVIC Branko	
9	AHMED Husain	86	62	NAVIDKIA Moharram	14
			86	MOBALI Eman	23

Saitama Stadium 2002, Saitama
9-02-2005, 19:30, 60 000, Al Ghamdi KSA

JPN 2 1 PRK

Ogasawara 4, Oguro 92+ — Nam Song Chol 61

#	JAPAN			KOREA DPR	#
23	KAWAGUCHI Yoshikatsu			SIM Sung Chol	1
2	TANAKA Makoto	66		RI Myong Sam	2
4	ENDO Yasuhito			JANG Sok Chol	5
5	MIYAMOTO Tsuneyasu			MUN In Guk	7
8	OGASAWARA Mitsuo		84	RI Han Ja	8
11	SUZUKI Takayuki	64		HONG Yong Jo	10
14	SANTOS Alessandro			HAN Song Chol	14
15	FUKUNISHI Takashi			KIM Yong Jun	15
21	KAJI Akira			AN Yong Hak	17
22	NAKAZAWA Yuji		43	PAK In Chol	20
28	TAMADA Keiji	79	29	CHOE Chol Man	21
	Tr: Zico			Tr: YUN Jong Su	
10	NAKAMURA Shunsuke	66	84	PAK Nam Chol	6
20	TAKAHARA Naohiro	64	29	KIM Yong Su	9
31	OGURO Masashi	79	43	NAM Song Chol	16

Kim Il Sung, Pyongyang
25-03-2005, 15:35, 50 000, Rungklay THA

PRK 1 2 BHR

Pak Song Gwan 63 — Ahmed 2 [7 58]

#	KOREA DPR			BAHRAIN	#
23	KIM Myong Gil			ALI Hassan	1
3	RI Kwang Chon			MOHAMMED Husain	2
5	JANG Sok Chol			MARZOOKI Abdulla	3
7	MUN In Guk	76		JALAL Sayed	7
9	KIM Yong Su			ABDUL RAHMAN Rashed	8
14	HAN Song Chol		72	AHMED Husain	9
15	KIM Yong Jun			SALMEEN Mohamed	10
16	NAM Song Chol			MOHAMED Talal	13
17	AN Yong Hak			GHULOOM Salman	14
18	KIM Chol Ho		84	ADNAN Sayed	16
25	PAK Song Gwan	84		HUBAIL Mohammed	29
	Tr: YUN Jong Su			Tr: SIDKA Wolfgang	
21	CHOE Chol Man	76	72	DUAIJ Naser	23
			84	HAMAD Humood	24

Azadi, Tehran
25-03-2005, 18:05, 110 000, Maidin SIN

IRN 2 1 JPN

Hashemian 2 [13 66] — Fukunishi 33

#	IRAN			JAPAN	#
1	MIRZAPOUR Ebrahim			NARAZAKI Seigo	1
2	MAHDAVIKIA Mehdi			MIYAMOTO Tsuneyasu	5
4	GOLMOHAMMADI Yahya			NAKATA Hidetoshi	7
5	REZAEI Rahman			NAKAMURA Shunsuke	10
6	NEKOUNAM Javad			FUKUNISHI Takashi	15
8	KARIMI Ali	78		MIURA Atsuhiro	17
9	HASHEMIAN Vahid		79	ONO Shinji	18
10	DAEI Ali	43	82	TAKAHARA Naohiro	20
12	ZANDI Ferydoon	65		KAJI Akira	21
13	KABEI Hossein		62	NAKAZAWA Yuji	22
20	NOSRATI Mohammad			TAMADA Keiji	28
	Tr: IVANKOVIC Branko			Tr: ZICO	
14	NAVIDKIA Moharram	43	79	OGASAWARA Mitsuo	8
22	VAHEDI Alireza	78	62	YANAGISAWA Atsushi	13
26	ALAVI Seyed	65	82	OGURO Masashi	31

Kim Il Sung, Pyongyang
30-03-2005, 15:35, 55 000, Kousa SYR

PRK 0 2 IRN

Mahdavikia 32, Nekounam 79

#	KOREA DPR			IRAN	#
23	KIM Myong Gil			MIRZAPOUR Ebrahim	1
2	RI Myong Sam			MAHDAVIKIA Mehdi	2
5	JANG Sok Chol			GOLMOHAMMADI Yahya	4
9	KIM Yong Su			REZAEI Rahman	5
14	HAN Song Chol			NEKOUNAM Javad	6
15	KIM Yong Jun			KARIMI Ali	8
16	NAM Song Chol	87	93	HASHEMIAN Vahid	9
17	AN Yong Hak		60	ZANDI Ferydoon	12
18	KIM Chol Ho	36		KABEI Hossein	13
20	PAK Chol Jin	56		NOSRATI Mohammad	20
21	CHOE Chol Man	56		ALAVI Seyed	26
	Tr: YUN Jong Su			Tr: IVANKOVIC Branko	
3	RI Kwang Chon	56	93	NAVIDKIA Moharram	14
7	MUN In Guk	36	60	VAHEDI Alireza	22
25	PAK Song Gwan	56			

Saitama Stadium 2002, Saitama
30-03-2005, 19:30, 67 549, Irmatov UZB

JPN 1 0 BHR

Salmeen OG 71

#	JAPAN			BAHRAIN	#
1	NARAZAKI Seigo			ALI Hassan	1
2	TANAKA Makoto			MOHAMMED Husain	2
5	MIYAMOTO Tsuneyasu			MARZOOKI Abdulla	3
7	NAKATA Hidetoshi			ABDUL RAHMAN Rashed	8
10	NAKAMURA Shunsuke	90		AHMED Husain	9
11	SUZUKI Takayuki	69		SALMEEN Mohamed	10
14	SANTOS Alessandro			GHULOOM Salman	14
15	FUKUNISHI Takashi			MAHFOODH Sayed	16
20	TAKAHARA Naohiro			BABA Hussain	17
21	KAJI Akira		59	MAKKI Hussain	18
22	NAKAZAWA Yuji		64	HUBAIL Mohammed	29
	Tr: ZICO			Tr: SIDKA Wolfgang	
28	TAMADA Keiji	69	59	TALEB Ahmed	20
29	INAMOTO Junichi	90	64	DUAIJ Naser	23

Azadi, Tehran
3-06-2005, 19:05, 35 000, Al Ghamdi KSA

IRN 1 0 PRK

Rezaei [45]

IRAN			KOREA DPR	
1	MIRZAPOUR Ebrahim		KIM Myong Gil	23
2	MAHDAVIKIA Mehdi		RI Myong Sam	2
4	GOLMOHAMMADI Yahya		RI Kwang Chon	3
5	REZAEI Rahman		JANG Sok Chol	5
6	NEKOUNAM Javad		RI Han Ja	8
8	KARIMI Ali	82	35	JON Chol	11
9	HASHEMIAN Vahid	90		SIN Yong Nam	12
10	DAEI Ali			KIM Yong Jun	15
12	ZANDI Ferydoon	69	45	KIM Song Chol	18
13	KABEI Hossein			PAK Chol Jin	20
27	ZARE Sattar			CHA Jong Hyok	22
	Tr: IVANKOVIC Branko			Tr: YUN Jong Su	
11	VAHEDI Alireza	82	45	HONG Yong Jo	10
20	NOSRATI Mohammad	90	35	CHOE Chol Man	21
26	ALAVI Seyed	69			

National Stadium, Manama
3-06-2005, 19:30, 32 000, Mohd Salleh MAS

BHR 0 1 JPN

Ogasawara [34]

BAHRAIN			JAPAN	
1	ALI Hassan		KAWAGUCHI Yoshikatsu	23
3	MARZOOKI Abdulla	74		TANAKA Makoto	2
7	JALAL Sayed			MIYAMOTO Tsuneyasu	5
8	ABDUL RAHMAN Rashed			NAKATA Hidetoshi	7
9	AHMED Husain		87	OGASAWARA Mitsuo	8
10	SALMEEN Mohamed	46	76	NAKAMURA Shunsuke	10
12	BASHEER Mohamed		90	YANAGISAWA Atsushi	13
13	MOHAMED Talal			SANTOS Alessandro	14
14	ISA Salman			FUKUNISHI Takashi	15
16	ADNAN Sayed			KAJI Akira	21
29	HUBAIL Mohammed	46		NAKAZAWA Yuji	22
	Tr: SIDKA Wolfgang			Tr: Zico	
20	TALEB Ahmed	46	76	NAKATA Koji	6
23	DUAIJ Naser	74	90	TAMADA Keiji	28
25	SALEM Rashad	46	87	INAMOTO Junichi	29

Suphachalasai, Bangkok
8-06-2005, 17:35, 0 (BCD), De Bleeckere BEL

PRK 0 2 JPN

Yanagisawa [67], Oguro [89]

KOREA DPR			JAPAN	
23	KIM Myong Gil		KAWAGUCHI Yoshikatsu	23
2	RI Myong Sam		TANAKA Makoto	2
3	RI Kwang Chon		MIYAMOTO Tsuneyasu	5
4	JANG Sok Chol		NAKATA Koji	6
8	RI Han Ja		OGASAWARA Mitsuo	8
10	HONG Yong Jo	46	SUZUKI Takayuki	11
11	JON Chol	27	85	YANAGISAWA Atsushi	13
14	HAN Song Chol		FUKUNISHI Takashi	15
15	KIM Yong Jun		KAJI Akira	21
20	PAK Chol Jin	46	NAKAZAWA Yuji	22
21	CHOE Chol Man	61	INAMOTO Junichi	29
	Tr: PAK Jong Hun		Tr: Zico	
6	PAK Nam Chol	61	85	ENDO Yasuhito	4
9	KIM Yong Su	27	91	46	OGURO Masashi	31
18	KIM Song Chol	46			

Azadi, Tehran
8-06-2005, 19:05, 80 000, Kwon Jong Chul

IRN 1 0 BHR

Nosrati [47]

IRAN			BAHRAIN	
1	MIRZAPOUR Ebrahim		ALI Hassan	1
2	MAHDAVIKIA Mehdi		MOHAMMED Husain	2
4	GOLMOHAMMADI Yahya		MARZOOKI Abdulla	3
6	NEKOUNAM Javad		78	JALAL Sayed	7
8	KARIMI Ali	87	68	ABDUL RAHMAN Rashed	8
9	HASHEMIAN Vahid			AHMED Husain	9
10	DAEI Ali			MOHAMED Talal	13
12	ZANDI Ferydoon	64		ISA Salman	14
13	KABEI Hossein			ADNAN Sayed	16
20	NOSRATI Mohammad			BABA Hussain	17
27	ZARE Sattar		60	DUAIJ Naser	23
	Tr: IVANKOVIC Branko			Tr: SIDKA Wolfgang	
19	KAMELI Jalal	87	78	MAKKI Husain	18
26	ALAVI Seyed	64	60	SALEM Rashad	25
			68	HUBAIL Mohammed	29

THIRD PHASE GROUP B		PL	W	D	L	F	A	PTS	IRN	JPN	BHR	PRK
1	Iran	5	4	1	0	6	1	13		2-1	1-0	1-0
2	Japan	5	4	0	1	7	3	12			1-0	2-1
3	Bahrain	5	1	1	3	2	4	4	0-0	0-1		
4	Korea DPR	5	0	0	5	2	9	0	0-2	0-2	1-2	

Table as of 16 August 2005. Remaining fixtures: 17-08-2005 Bahrain v Korea DPR; Japan v Iran

QUALIFYING MATCHES PLAYED IN AFRICA

Preliminary Round

Congo	CGO	1	1
Sierra Leone	SLE	0	1
Seychelles	SEY	0	1
Zambia	ZAM	4	1
Equatorial Guinea	EQG	1	0
Togo	TOG	0	2
Gambia	GAM	2	0
Liberia	LBR	0	3
Guinea-Bissau	GNB	1	0
Mali	MLI	2	2
Burkina Faso	BFA	w-o	
Central African Republic	CTA		
Ghana	GHA	5	2
Somalia	SOM	0	0
Swaziland	SWZ	1	0
Cape Verde Islands	CPV	1	3
Uganda	UGA	3	1
Mauritius	MRI	0	3
Madagascar	MAD	1	2
Benin	BEN	1	3
Sudan	SUD	3	0
Eritrea	ERI	0	0
São Tomé e Príncipe	STP	0	0
Libya	LBY	1	8
Niger	NIG	0	0
Algeria	ALG	1	6
Chad	CHA	3	0
Angola	ANG	1	2
Burundi	BDI	0	1
Gabon	GAB	0	4
Zimbabwe	ZIM	3	1
Mauritania	MTN	0	2
Rwanda	RWA	3	1
Namibia	NAM	0	1
Tanzania	TAN	0	0
Kenya	KEN	0	3
Guinea	GUI	1	4
Mozambique	MOZ	0	3
Ethiopia	ETH	1	0
Malawi	MWI	3	0
Botswana	BOT	4	0
Lesotho	LES	1	0

Group Stage

Group 1		Pts
Togo	TOG	17
Zambia	ZAM	16
Senegal	SEN	15
Congo	CGO	10
Mali	MLI	5
Liberia	LBR	4

Still to play: 2/09/2005: Zambia v Senegal, Mali v Congo, Togo v Liberia; 7/10/2005: Liberia v Zambia, Congo v Togo, Senegal v Mali

Group 2		Pts
Ghana	GHA	15
South Africa	RSA	15
Congo DR	COD	12
Cape Verde Islands	CPV	10
Burkina Faso	BFA	9
Uganda	UGA	7

Still to play: 2/09/2005: Congo DR v Cape Verde, Ghana v Uganda, Burkina Faso v South Africa; 7/10/2005: Uganda v Burkina Faso, South Africa v Congo DR, Cape Verde v Ghana

Group 3		Pts
Côte d'Ivoire	CIV	19
Cameroon	CMR	17
Egypt	EGY	13
Libya	LBY	11
Benin	BEN	2
Sudan	SUD	2

Still to play: 17/08/2004: Sudan v Benin; 2/09/2005: Egypt v Benin, Libya v Sudan, Côte d'Ivoire v Cameroon; 7/10/2005: Benin v Libya, Cameroon v Egypt, Sudan v Côte d'Ivoire

Group 4		Pts
Angola	ANG	15
Nigeria	NGA	15
Zimbabwe	ZIM	12
Gabon	GAB	9
Algeria	ALG	7
Rwanda	RWA	5

Still to play: 2/09/2005: Zimbabwe v Rwanda, Angola v Gabon, Algeria v Nigeria; 7/10/2005: Nigeria v Zimbabwe, Rwanda v Angola, Gabon v Algeria

Group 5		Pts
Morocco	MAR	16
Tunisia	TUN	14
Guinea	GUI	11
Kenya	KEN	10
Botswana	BOT	9
Malawi	MWI	3

Still to play: 17/08/2005: Tunisia v Kenya; 2/09/2005: Morocco v Botswana, Guinea v Malawi, Kenya v Tunisia; 7/10/2005: Tunisia v Morocco, Botswana v Guinea, Malawi v Kenya

No team has yet qualified in the five places allocated to Africa for the finals. The qualifying system involved a preliminary knock-out round for 42 teams. The 21 winners joined the nine seeded teams - Cameroon, Nigeria, South Africa, Senegal, Tunisia, Morocco, Egypt, Côte d'Ivoire and Congo DR - in the group stage with the five group winners qualifying for the finals.

PRELIMINARY ROUND

Stade Alphonse Massamba, Brazzaville
12-10-2003, 15:30, 4 800, Mana NGA

CGO   1   0   SLE

Mvoubi 89p

CONGO			SIERRA LEONE	
1	MOUYABI Kiyari		TAYLOR Jonathan	1
2	YOKA Arsene		MANSARAY Sidique	2
3	BEAULIA Hermann	49	LANSANA Alpha	4
4	MVOUBI Mbiamcie	53	SESAY Hassan	6
5	NDZI Fortune	63	SESAY Alimamy	7
6	NZEBELE Narcisse		KAMARA Mohamed	8
7	EWOLO Oscar		KALLON Mohamed	10
9	MAKITA-PASY Fabry	71	SESAY Mowahid	11
11	MAVOUNGOU Loemba	64	KAMARA Ernest	14
12	LOLO Patrick		SESAY Koeman	15
13	BHEBEY Rudy	59	YUNIS Osman	16
	Tr: MINGA Noel		Tr: SHERRINGTON John	
10	LIKIBI Cesack	64 71	MANSARAY Alusine	9
14	AYESSA Romeo	59 53	JALLOH Yayah	13
17	MASSOUANGA Bhaudry	49 63	FODAY Albert	17

Freetown Stadium, Freetown
16-11-2003, 16:30, 20 000, Monteiro Lopes CPV

SLE   1   1   CGO

Koroma 58   Nguie 67

SIERRA LEONE				CONGO	
1	TAYLOR Jonathan			ITOUA Old	1
2	MANSARAY Sidique	88		YOKA Arsene	2
4	LANSANA Alpha			MVOUBI Mbiamcie	3
6	KARGBO Ibrahim			OPONGA Camille	4
7	SILLAH Alpha	53 85		MINGA Edson Dico	5
8	BAH Mahmadu			EWOLO Oscar	7
10	KOROMA Ibrahim	86		MAKITA-PASSY Fabry	9
11	KANU Abu	94		NGUIE Mien Rolf	10
14	KAMARA Mohamed	64		BAKOUMA Walter	11
15	CONTEH Kewullay			NDZI Fortune	13
18	WOBAY Julius			ENDZANGA Wilfrid	14
	Tr: SHERRINGTON John			Tr: MINGA Noel	
9	BARLAY Samuel	88 94		NZEBELE Narcisse	8
13	CONTEH Julius	53 64		LOLO Patrick	12
16	SESAY Hassan	86 85		BATOTA Gervais	18

Stade Linite, Victoria
11-10-2003, 15:00, 2 700, Lim Kee Chong MRI

SEY   0   4   ZAM

Kampamba 8, Fichite 44
Milanzi 52, Numba 75

SEYCHELLES			ZAMBIA	
1	SOPHA Eric Nelson		PHIRI Davies	1
2	LARUE Allen		SINKALA Andrew	3
3	BIBI Jonathan	66	MWILIMA Justine	4
6	BELLE Denis		MUMBA Lloyd	6
7	NIBOURETTE Alex		FICHITE Dadley	9
8	LABICHE Marcel		MILANZI Harry	12
10	BALDE Alpha	66	BAKALA Ian	14
12	BARBE Denis	64	MUSONDA Joseph	15
13	ZIALOR Philip	25	KAMPAMBA Gift	17
18	ROSE Verna		CHALWE Sashi	18
19	ROSE Yelvahny	71	SICHONE Moses	19
	Tr: NEES Michael		Tr: BWALYA Kalusha	
5	CEASAR Danny	64 66	NUMBA Mumamba	5
9	BONNE James	25 66	CHASWE Nsofwa	10
11	DORASMY Che	71		

Independence Stadium, Lusaka
15-11-2003, 15:00, 30 000, Abdulkadir TAN

ZAM   1   1   SEY

Milanzi 7   Suzette 69

ZAMBIA				SEYCHELLES	
1	PHIRI Davies			SOPHA Eric Nelson	1
4	CHALWE Sashi			LARUE Allen	2
5	MUMBA Lloyd			LIBANOTIS Harry	3
7	MUSONDA Joseph			BRUTUS Wilnes	7
8	MWILIMA Justine			LABICHE Marcel	8
11	KATONGO Christopher	55		ANNACOURA Don	9
12	MILANZI Harry			BARBE Denis	12
13	LUNGU Mishek			ZIALOR Philip	13
14	NUMBA Mumamba			BIBI Jonathan	14
15	BAKALA Ian		66	ESTHER Ted	15
19	FICHITE Dadley	68	79	SUZETTE Robert	17
	Tr: BWALYA Kalusha			Tr: NEES Michael	
3	CHALWE Songwe	68 79		ROSE Yelvahny	10
6	Mbesuma Collins	55 66		NIBOURETTE Alex	11

La Libertad, Bata
11-10-2003, 15:30, Evehe CMR

EQG   1   0   TOG

Barila 25p

EQUATORIAL GUINEA			TOGO	
1	ECOLO Silvestre		AGASSA Kossi	16
2	RONDO Jose Luis		ATTE-OUDEYI Zanzan	3
3	ELA Ruslan	81	ADEBAYOR Sheyi	4
4	ONDO Santiago		MAMAH Abdul Gafar	5
5	BARILA Sergio Javier		AZIAWONOU KAKA Yao	6
6	EDJOGO Juvenal		FERREIRA Henio	7
7	ELA Francisco Salvador		AMEWOU Komlan	8
8	MAKUBA Lino		AKOTO Eric	13
9	BODIPO Rodolfo		ABALO Yaovi	14
10	ZARANDONA Ivan	75	DE SOUZA Jeferson	15
11	CUYAMI Juan Remigio	57 53	ATTE-OUDEYI Ismaila	18
	Tr: ENGONGA Oscar		Tr: DUMAS Antonio	
14	NCOGO Jose	81 75	BATSA Albert	11
15	DYOWE Juan Epitie	57 53	LANGUEH Senam	17

Kegue, Lomé
16-11-2003, 15:30, 12 000, Mandzioukouta CGO

TOG   2   0   EQG

Adebayor 43, Salifou 53

TOGO				EQUATORIAL GUINEA	
16	AGASSA Kossi			ECOLO Silvestre	1
3	ATTE-OUDEYI Zanzan			RONDO Jose Luis	2
4	ADEBAYOR Sheyi	46		ELA Ruslan	3
5	MAMAH Abdul Gafar			ONDO Santiago	4
6	AZIAWONOU KAKA Yao			BARILA Sergio Javier	5
8	AMEWOU Komlan			EDJOGO Juvenal	6
10	MAMAM Cherif-Toure			ELA Francisco Salvador	7
11	DOGBE Kouadji	56 87		MAKUBA Lino	8
12	AKOTO Eric			BODIPO Rodolfo	9
14	ABALO Yaovi	84		ZARANDONA Ivan	10
15	SALIFOU Moustapha	67		DYOWE Juan Epitie	11
	Tr: DUMAS Antonio			Tr: ENGONGA Oscar	
9	OURO AKPO Abdou	56 84		OLO Benjamin	12
18	ENIFOUL Komlan	67 87		ENZEMA Damian	13
			46	GREGORLO Manuel	14

Independence Stadium, Bakau
12-10-2003, 17:00, 20 000, Codjia BEN

GAM	2	0		LBR

Njie [64], Sonko [79]

	GAMBIA				LIBERIA	
1	TOURAY Pa Dembo				SEAH Sunday	1
2	COLLEY Lamin	74	62		BOAKAI Varney	2
4	LOUM Momodou				SONKALEY Tarkpor	3
5	CORR Abdoulie		63		KPOTO Varmah	4
6	SOLEY Seyfo				VAH Frederick	6
7	SONKO Idrissa				BARLEE Shelton	7
10	CEESAY Jatto				BENSON Esaiah	8
11	SILLAH Ebrima		86		MENNOH Steven	13
14	BADJIE Simon				SETON Josiah	14
15	GOMEZ Arthur	81			BARYOUR Morris	17
17	NYANG Aziz Corr	55			LAFFOR Anthony	18
	Tr: NDONG Sang				Tr: KROMAH Kadalah	
8	NJIE Abdou-Rahman	55	62		TONDO Issac	10
9	JANNEH Latiff	81	63		GOBAH Henry	11
18	GAI Amadou	74	86		GRIMES Solomon	12

Antoinette Tubman, Monrovia
16-11-2003, 16:00, 10 000, Coulibaly MLI

LBR	3	0		GAM

Roberts [10], Tondo 2 [76 83]

	LIBERIA				GAMBIA	
1	SEAH Sunday				TOURAY Pa Dembo	1
2	BOAKAI Varney	57			COLEY Lamin	2
3	SONKALEY Tarkpor				CONATEH Abdurahman	3
4	KPOTO Varmah				LOUM Momodou	4
5	BARYOUR Morris	82			CORR Abdoulie	5
7	SETON Josiah	66			SOLEY Seyfo	6
8	BENSON Esaiah		36		SONKO Idrissa	7
9	Roberts Zizi		81		NJIE Abdou-Rahman	8
11	BARLEE Shelton				GOMEZ Arthur	9
17	GEBRO George				CEESAY Jatto	10
18	LAFFOR Anthony				SILLAH Ebrima	11
	Tr: KROMAH Kadalah				Tr: NDONG Sang	
10	TONDO Issac	66	81		BAH Dawda	13
13	MENNOH Steven	57	36		NYANG Aziz Corr	17
15	WESSEH Solomon	82				

Stade du 24 Septembre, Bissau
10-10-2003, 16:00, 22 000, Sowe GAM

GNB	1	2		MLI

Fernandes [50]   Keita [8], Coulibaly.S [69]

	GUINEA-BISSAU				MALI	
1	SILVA Crodonilson				SIDIBE Mahamadou	1
2	NANCASSA Rui				TRAORE Sammy	3
3	BALDE Mamadi				KANTEH Cedric	4
4	ENCADA Ankyofna				THIAM Brahim	5
5	DOS SANTOS Antonio		79		DIARRA Mahamadou	6
6	MENDES Euclides		60		TRAORE Dramane	7
7	INJAI Braima	88			TOURE Bassala	8
9	CAMARA Sanussi				BAGAYOKO Mamadou	9
10	FERNANDES Dionisio	82			COULIBALY Soumaila	10
11	GOMEZ Cuvilito	34			KEITA Seydou	12
14	TALHADO Juvenico				DOUKANTIE Vincent	14
	Tr: CANDE Baciro				Tr: DIALLO Sekou	
15	CASSAMA Diondino	34	79		SIDIBE Djibril	11
17	BALDE Amadu	82	60		COULIBALY Dramane	17
18	CO Anibal	88				

Stade du 26 Mars, Bamako
14-11-2003, 20:00, 13 251, Seydou MTN

MLI	2	0		GNB

Coulibaly.S [15], Sidibe [84p]

	MALI				GUINEA-BISSAU	
1	SIDIBE Mahmadou				SILVA Crodonilson	1
2	DIAMOUTENE Souleymane				LOPES Evaldo	2
4	COULIBALY Adama				BALDE Mamadi	3
5	KANTEH Cedric				ENCADA Ankyofna	4
6	DIARRA Mahamadou				DOS SANTOS Antonio	5
8	TRAORE Mamary	48	80		CAMARA Sanussi	7
9	BAGAYOKO Mamadou		86		FERNANDES Dionisio	10
10	COULIBALY Soumaila	78	46		GOMEZ Cuvilito	11
11	SIDIBE Djibril				TALHADO Juvenico	14
12	KEITA Seydou	61			INJAI Braima	16
13	COULIBALY David				MENDES Euclides	17
	Tr: DIALLO Sekou				Tr: CANDE Baciro	
3	DIAWARA Fousseini	78	46		FADEIRA Adilson	8
14	DOUKANTIE Vincent	48	80		BA Dauda	9
17	ABOUTA Janvier	61	86		JASSI Demba	18

Accra Stadium, Accra
16-11-2003, 15:00, 19 447, Bebou TOG

SOM	0	5		GHA

Arhin Duah 2 [2 25 56]
Boakye 2 [69 89], Gyan [82]

	SOMALIA				GHANA	
1	ABDULKADIR Sheik				ADJEI Sammy	1
2	YASIN Ali		62		ANSAH Aziz	2
3	MOHAMUD ABDULAHI				PAPPOE Emmanuel	3
4	HUSSEIN Meigag	52			KUFFOUR Samuel	4
5	ABDIASIS Salad				MENSAH John	5
6	MUSTAF Hassan				MOHAMMED Hamza	6
7	OSMAN Omar		77		ARHIN DUAH Nana	7
9	ISSE Aden				ESSIEN Michael	8
11	YUSUF Ali				BOAYE Isaac	9
16	MOHAMED Abdullahi	34	80		APPIAH Stephen	10
18	ABDULKADIR Omar				DONG-BORTEY Benard	11
	Tr: ABDI FARAH Ali				Tr: ZUMDICK Ralf	
10	ABDULAHI Abdi	34	80		YAKUBU Abukari	15
17	ABDIFITAH Mohamed	52	77		GYAN Asamoah	16
			62		ADJEI Lawrence	18

Kumasi Stadium, Kumasi
19-11-2003, 16:00, 12 000, Chaibou NIG

GHA	2	0		SOM

Appiah [27], Adjei.L [90]

	GHANA				SOMALIA	
1	OWU George	46			ABDULKADIR Sheik	1
2	ANSAH Aziz				YASIN Ali	2
3	Pappoe Emmanuel				MOHAMUD ABDULAHI	3
5	MENSAH John				HUSSEIN Meigag	4
6	MOHAMMED Hamza		60		ABDIASIS Salad	5
7	ARHIN DUAH Nana	74			MUSTAF Hassan	6
9	BOAKYE Isaac	62			OSMAN Omar	7
10	APPIAH Stephen				ISSE Aden	9
11	DONG-BORTEY Benard	59			ABDULAHI Abdi	10
15	YAKUBU Abukari				YUSUF Ali	11
18	ADJEI Lawrence				ABDULKADIR Omar	18
	Tr: ZUMDICK Ralf				Tr: ABDI FARAH Ali	
8	POKU Kwadwo	74	60		ABDULKADIR Ahmed	8
12	ADJEI Sammy	46				
16	GYAN Asamoah	62				

SWZ 1 1 CPV

Somhlolo National Stadium, Mbabane
12-10-2003, 15:00, 5 000, Teshome ERI

Dlamini.Sz [64]   Morais [55]

SWAZILAND			CAPE VERDE ISLANDS	
1 DLADLA Bongani			CRUZ Anilton	1
2 KUNENE Manqoba			MONTEIRO Rui	2
3 MXOLISI Mtsetfwa			BARROS Jose	3
5 NGUBANE Mlungisi			DUARTE Adriano	5
6 GAMEDZE Jerry			BRITO Pedro	6
7 DLAMINI Siza			VEIGA Nelson	7
8 MASEKO Jabulani	46		SEMEDO Arlindo	9
10 MDLULI Bongani	63	89	AGUIAR Claudio	11
12 NHLEKO Wonder			MODESTE Jimmy	14
15 DLAMINI Sibusiso			DA LUZ Emerson	17
17 MASANGANE Bongani		82	MORAIS Carlos	18
Tr: BANDA Francis			Tr: ALHINHO Alexander	
4 ZIKALALA Maxwell	63	89	BRITO Carlos	10
9 TSABEDZE Thulani	46	82	VICENTE Artur	16

CPV 3 0 SWZ

Estadio da Varzea, Praia
16-11-2003, 16:00, 6 000, Aboubacar CIV

Semedo 2 [51] [65], Morais [90]

CAPE VERDE ISLANDS			SWAZILAND	
1 CRUZ Anilton			DUBE Sipho	1
2 MONTEIRO Rui			DLAMINI Sibusiso	4
3 BARROS Jose			KUNENE Manqoba	5
5 DUARTE Adriano			GAMEDZE Jerry	6
6 BRITO Pedro			DLAMINI Siza	7
7 VEIGA Nelson			MKHWANAZI Patrick	8
9 SEMEDO Arlindo			TSABEDZE Thulani	9
11 AGUIAR Claudio			NHLEKO Wonder	10
14 MODESTE Jimmy			MSIBI Zweli	11
17 DA LUZ Emerson			DUBE Calvin	14
18 MORAIS Carlos			NXUMALO Wandile	18
Tr: ALHINHO Alexander			Tr: BANDA Francis	
4 TAVARES Jose				

UGA 3 0 MRI

Nakivubo, Kampala
11-10-2003, 16:30, 6 800, Tangawarima ZIM

Bajope [52], Mubiru [68], Obua [92]

UGANDA			MAURITIUS	
1 MUGISHA Ibrahim			DORO Nicolas	1
2 OBWIN Philip			EDOUARD Guiliano	2
3 TABULA Abubakari			L'ENFLE Stephan	3
4 SEKAJJA Ibrahim		49	MARMITTE Johan	4
5 KABETA Henry			SPEVILLE Henry	7
6 TENYWA Sulaiman			BAYARAM Jean Gilbert	8
7 WATSON Edgar	55	88	APPOU Kersley	9
10 MUBIRU Hassan			MOURGINE Cyril	11
11 KASULE Noah			LOUIS Jerry	12
12 BAJOPE Assani		72	PERLE Christopher	17
13 OBUA David			PUNCHOO Ashik	18
Tr: ADRAA Leo			Tr: PATEL Ackbar	
15 SSALI Godrey	55	49	NABOTH Giovanni	5
		88	GODON Kervin	10
		72	NABOTH Ricardo	13

MRI 3 1 UGA

King George V, Curepipe
16-11-2003, 16:30, 2 465, Maillet SEY

Naboth.R [37], Mourgine [70]
Louis [82]   Obua [113]

MAURITIUS			UGANDA	
16 DORO Nicolas			MUGISHA Ibrahim	18
2 EDOUARD Guillano			OBWIN Philip	2
3 L'ENFLE Stephan			TABULA Abubakari	3
5 BAX Jean Sebastien			SEKAJJA Ibrahim	5
6 PERIATAMBEE Desire	46		TENYWA Sulaiman	6
7 SPEVILLE Henry			WATSON Edgar	7
8 BAYARAM Jean Gilbert			BAJOPE Assani	8
11 MOURGINE Cyril		50	SSALI Godrey	9
14 CUNDASAMI Jimmy		102	KABETA Henry	10
15 NABOTH Ricardo	73		OBUA David	13
17 PERLE Christopher	86	71	KAWEESA Kiseny Huudu	15
Tr: PATEL Ackbar			Tr: ADRAA Leo	
9 APPOU Kersley	73	50	KABANDA Robert	11
12 LOUIS Jerry	46	102	LUBEGA Zakaria	12
13 FRANCOIS Tony	86	71	MAWEJJE Tony	17

MAD 1 1 BEN

Mahamasina, Antananarivo
11-10-2003, 14:30, 5 131, Maillet SEY

Edmond [28]   Adjamossi [74]

MADAGASCAR			BENIN	
1 RAHARISON Jean			CHITOU Rachad	1
3 RABARIVONY Franck			LATOUNDJI Moussa	2
5 RAKOTONDRABE Julian			CHRYSOSTOME Damien	5
6 AHAMADA Jambay			OKETOLA Jonas	6
7 RADONAMAHAFALISON JJ		81	MOUSSORO Kabirou	7
8 JOHAN Paul	67		TOCLOMITI Stanislas	8
9 MENAKELY Ruphin	87		SINGBO Felicien	12
10 RAKOTONDRAMANANA AI	61	69	MOUSTAPHA Agnede	13
13 RAJAONARIVELO Augustin		64	GASPOZ Alain	14
14 EDMOND Robert			ADJAMONSI Anicet	15
19 RAKOTONARIVO Emilson			AHOUEYA Jocelin	17
Tr: RAUX Auguste			Tr: ATTQUAYEFIO Cecil	
11 RAKOTOMANDIMBY Rija	61	81	ADOME JOCELYN	3
17 RALAIKOA Bob	87	69	COREA Jaures	10
18 RAKOTONIAINA Harinjaka	67	64	OGUNBIYI Muri	11

BEN 3 2 MAD

Stade de l'Amitié, Cotonou
16-11-2003, 16:00, 20 000, Imiere NGA

Tchomogo.O 3 [33p] [62] [90]   Radonamahafalison [15]
Rakotondramanana [23]

BENIN			MADAGASCAR	
1 CHITOU Rachad			RAHARISON Jean	1
2 LATOUNDJI Moussa			RAKOTONDRABE Julian	5
5 CHRYSOSTOME Damien		57	JAMBAY Ahamada	6
9 AHOUEYA Jocelin			RADONAMAHAFALISON JJ	7
10 TCHOMOGO Oumar			JOHAN Paul	8
11 OGUNBIYI Muri		72	MENAKELY Ruphin	9
12 SINGBO Felicien	46	85	RAKOTONDRAMANANA AI	10
13 MOUSTAPHA Agnede			RAZAFINDRAKOTO Maru	14
14 AKPAKOUN Rodrigue	46		EDMOND Robert	18
15 ADJAMONSI Anicet		89	RADAFISON Jimmy	20
18 TCHOMOGO			RAZAFIMAHATRATRA J	21
Tr: ATTQUAYEFIO Cecil			Tr: RAUX Auguste	
6 OKETOLA Jonas	46	85	RAJAONARIVELO Agustin	3
7 MOUSSORO Kabirou	46	57	VALENTIN MAZINOT	13
		72	RALAIKOA Bob	17

National Stadium, Khartoum
12-10-2003, 20:00, 18 000, Tamuni LBY

SUD 3 0 ERI

Tambal 68, El Rasheed 72, Ahmed.M 89p

#	SUDAN					ERITREA	#
18	ABDALLA Elmuez					SULEMAN Abdu Saleh	1
3	SAEED Anwaar					SHIMANGUS Yidnekachew	3
5	AHMED Salih					GOITOM Haile	4
7	KARBOS Jundi					WELDEGHEBRIEL Dawit	5
8	KARAR Haitham	61				AGHADE Medhanie	6
9	KABIR Motaz	46				BERHE Frezghi	8
10	TAMBAL Haytham					FESEHAYE Yonas	9
12	ABDALLA Bader					MESFUN Natnael	14
14	AHMED Mugahid			87		DEBESA Elias	15
15	KOKU Amir	35				DAWIT Efrem	25
16	LADO Richard	65				MEBRAHTU Mana	28
	Tr: LAZAREK Wojciech					Tr: ABRAHA Tekie	
11	EL RASHEED Haitham	61	75		75	AREGAI Berhane	2
13	EL FATIH Ahmed	46	65		69	ZEROM Daniel	22
17	EL BASHIR Hamouda	35					

Asmara Stadium, Asmara
16-11-2003, 16:00, 12 000, Abdulle Ahmed SOM

ERI 0 0 SUD

#	ERITREA					SUDAN	#
1	SULEMAN Abdu Saleh					ABDALLA Elmuez	18
4	GOITOM Haile					ABDEL FARAG Elnazir	2
5	WELDEGHEBRIEL Dawit		60	60		SAEED Anwaar	3
6	AGHADE Medhanie	80				AHMED Salih	5
8	BERHE Frezghi			47		TAMBAL Haytham	10
9	FESEHAYE Binyam					EL RASHEED Haitham	11
12	SHINESHI Ghirmai	44				KATOUL Alaadin	12
14	MESFUN Natnael					ABDALLA Bader Eldin	13
15	TZEREZGHI Yosief					EL FAKI Mughaid	14
17	GEBREMICHAEL Yohanas	67				LADO Richard	16
21	MOHAMED Suleman		77	77		El BASHIR Hamouda	20
	Tr: ABRAHA Tekie					Tr: LAZAREK Wojciech	
2	AREGAI Berhane	80	60	60		BOSHRA Abdel Elah	6
9	NEGASH Tedros	44	47	47		AHMED Haitham	8
22	ZEROM Daniel	67	77	77		KABIR Motaz	9

Estadio 12 de Julho, São Tomé
11-10-2003, 16:00, 4 000, Yameogo BFA

STP 0 1 LBY

Masli 85

#	SAO TOME					LIBYA	#
1	DUMBY Abidulay					EL AMNI Abdalla	12
2	NEVES Derilson					ELGAAID Sami	2
3	SANTIAGO Celestino					Al Mohamed Mohamed	4
4	VELOSO Staydner					SULIMAN Marei	6
5	DA COSTA Paulino					ABOMOOD Akrm	7
6	APRESENTACAO Neridson	69				KAZIRI Mustafa	8
7	ALFREDO Bonfin					MASLI Ahmed Frag	9
8	NEVES Gervasio					OSMAN Ahmed	10
9	SEMEDO Jairson	71				EL TAIB Tareq	14
10	MONTEIRO Orlando					AL AJNEF Abubaker	16
11	BRITO Osvaldo					AL SHIBANI Younus	18
	Tr: FERRAZ Jose					Tr: LONCAREVIC Ilija	
				71		KARA Nader	15
				69		SAFTAR Mahmud	17

28 March Stadium, Benghazi
16-11-2003, 22:00, 20 000, Guirat TUN

LBY 8 0 STP

Masli 3 14 17 20, El Taib 2 45 63,
Suliman 54, Osman.A 74, El Rabty 88

#	LIBYA					SAO TOME	#
12	El AMNI Abdalla					TONGA Joao	1
4	AL MOHAMED Mohamed					NEVES Derilson	2
5	MARIEMI Omar					GOMES Ronaldinho	3
7	ABOMOOD Akrm	46	6	6		DA COSTA Paulino	4
9	MASLI Ahmed Frag	59				VELOSO Staydner	5
10	OSMAN Ahmed			46		NANA Agilson	6
13	MILAD Rida					ALFREDO Bonfin	7
14	EL TAIB Tareq					APRESENTACAO Neridson	8
16	OSMAN Walid					NEVES Gervasio	9
17	BOUBAKR Abdul Salam					LIMA Antonio	10
19	KAZIRI Mustafa	46				BRITO Osvaldo	11
	Tr: LONCAREVIC Ilija					Tr: FERRAZ Jose	
3	ABDUSADEQ Suleman	59	46	46		JOAQUIM Jorge	13
6	SULIMAN Marei	46	69	69		COSTA Lasset	15
8	EL RABTY Mohamed	46	46	46		RAMOS Julio	17

Stade General Seyni Kountche, Niamey
11-10-2003, 16:00, 20 126, Coulibaly MLI

NIG 0 1 ALG

Boutabout 62

#	NIGER					ALGERIA	#
16	ABDOURAHIME Aboudou					MEZAIR Hicham	1
2	ADELEKE Gafaru	78				BOUTABOUT Mansour	2
3	ABDOULAYE Ide					HADDOU Moulay	3
5	TIECOURA Ousmane		65	65		MAMOUNI Maamar	4
6	LAUALI IDRISSA					ARIBI Salim	5
8	MUYEI Mohammed					MANSOUR Yazid	6
9	MUSSA Mohamed					ACHIOU Hocine	10
11	IDRISSA Issoufou	66				ZAFOUR Brahim	13
12	ALHASSAN Haruna	52	75			HADJADJ Fodil	14
15	ALASSANE Ismael		82			AKROUR Nassim	15
18	ALHASSANE Issoufou					RAHO Slimane	18
	Tr: YEO Martial					Tr: SAADANE Rabah	
4	SADIKOU Abdellatif	52	82	82		GHAZI Karim	7
7	IDRISSA Sadou	78	65	65		KRAOUCHE Nasreddine	8
10	TANKARY Ibrahim	66	75	75		ZIANI Karim	9

Complexe du 5 Juillet, Alger
14-11-2003, 21:30, 50 000, El Arjoun MAR

ALG 6 0 NIG

Cherrad 2 16 21, Boutabout 2 41 71,
Mamouni 47+, Akrour 82

#	ALGERIA					NIGER	#
1	MEZAIR Hicham					ABDOURAHIME Aboudou	1
3	HADDOU Moulay					DAOUDA Ibrahim	2
4	MAMOUNI Maamar	69				ISSA Dodo	5
5	ARIBI Salim					MUYEI Mohammed	8
6	MANSOURI Yazid	57		57		ANISET Pascal	11
7	CHERRAD Abdelmalek	64	65	65		MAHAMADOU Issaka	13
8	KRAOUCHE Nasreddine	76				MOUSSA Issoufou	14
10	ACHIOU Hocine					ALASSANE Ismael	15
12	BOUTABOUT Mansour					ALHASSAN Haruna	16
13	ZAFOUR Brahim					BULUS Jimmy	17
18	RAHO Slimane			69		MUSSA Mohamed	18
	Tr: SAADANE Rabah					Tr: YEO Martial	
11	HADJADJ Fodil	69	57	57		GALEY Komla	4
14	GHAZI Karim	76	65	65		LAUALI Idrissa	6
15	AKROUR Nassim	64	69	69		IDRISSA Issoufou	10

Stade Omnisports, N'Djamena
12-10-2003, 15:30, 30 000, Nahi CIV

CHA 3 1 ANG

Oumar 3 [53] [74] [83]   Bruno Mauro [49]

CHAD			ANGOLA	
18	NGUEADI Religues		MARITO	17
2	LAMA Pierre	73	ELISIO	2
3	MBAI Didier Timothee		DIAS CAIRES	4
4	DJERABE Armand		KALI	5
6	KRABE Mbanguingar	85	YAMBA ASHA	6
9	OUMAR Francis		FIGUEREDO	7
10	SEID Mahamat Idriss	55	ANDRE	8
11	HISSEIN Mahamat		FLAVIO	9
13	NDONINGA Kalwaye	55	67	BRUNO MAURO	10
16	ABAKAR Oumar		GILBERTO	11
17	YAMBE Rufin	68	FILIPE	17
	Tr: DJIM Yann		Tr: KURTZ Ismael	
7	MEDEGO Ahmed Evariste	68	85	DELGADO	3
8	MBAIAM Nekiambe	55	67	LOVE	13
14	HABIB Mahamat Saleh	55	73	MENDONCA	14

Cidadela, Luanda
16-11-2003, 16:00, 30 000, Buenkadila COD

ANG 2 0 CHA

Akwa [42], Bruno Mauro [57]

CHAD				ANGOLA	
1	MARITO		55	NGUEADI Religues	18
4	DIAS CAIRES		36	GASTOM Mobati	2
5	KALI			MBAI Didier Timothee	3
6	YAMBA ASHA			DJERABE Armand	4
7	FIGUEREDO	31		OTTOBAYE Djangtoloum	5
8	ANDRE			KRABE Mbanguingar	6
10	AKWA			OUMAR Francis	9
11	GILBERTO			HISSEIN Mahamat	10
14	MENDONCA	37		MEDEGO Ahmed Evariste	11
15	MANUEL		60	HABIB Mahamat Saleh	14
17	BRUNO MAURO	88		ABAKAR Oumar	16
	Tr: KURTZ Ismael			Tr: DJIM Yann	
3	LOVE	31	55	NDEIDOUM Ndakom	1
13	RATS	37	60	MBAIAM Nekiambe	8
18	AVELINO LOPES	88	36	NDONINGA Kalwaye	13

Stade Prince Louis Rwagasore, Bujumbura
12-10-2003, 15:15, 10 000, Itur, KEN

BDI 0 0 GAB

BURUNDI			GABON	
1	KITENGE Aime		OVONO EBANG Didier	16
2	SALEH Amissi	46	78	NZIGOU Shiva	3
3	NZEYIMANA Gabriel		60	NSI AKOUE Rene	5
4	NDIKUMANA Saidi		MOUYOUMA Dieudonne	6
6	HAKIZIMANA Jean		ZUE NGUEMA Theodore	7
8	NDIZEYE Alain		EKOUMA Jeannot	8
10	MASUDI Juma	85	MOUNDOUNGA Rodrigue	9
12	NDAYISHIMIYE Sutch		DJISSIKADIE Alain	10
13	BIZIMANA Didier	60	KESSANY Paul	11
15	MWINYI Rajabu		58	ANTCHOUET Henri	15
16	MBAZUMUTIMA Henri		MOUBAMBA Cedric	18
	Tr: RIBAKARE Baudouin		Tr: MBOUROUNOT Claude	
5	MANIRAMBONA Jaffar	60	78	LARY Yannick	4
7	NDAYISHIMIYE Christophe	85	60	MBANANGOYE ZITA Bruno	13
9	BAHATI Olivier	46	58	MUE MINTSA Claude	14

Stade Omnisports, Libreville
15-11-2003, 16:00, 15 000, Ndoye SEN

GAB 4 1 BDI

Nzigou [2], Mwinyi OG [16]   Nzeyimana.G [90p]
Nguema 2 [38] [80]

GABON			BURUNDI	
16	OVONO Didier		KITENGE Aime	1
2	AMBOUROUET Georges	18	TWITE Valery	3
5	NSI-AKOUE Rene		RAMADHANI Waso	5
6	MOUYOUMA Thierry		24	HAKIZIMANA Jean	6
7	ZUE Theodore		70	NDIZEYE Alain	8
8	NZIGOU Shiva	80	48	MBANZA Felicien	9
9	MOUNDOUNGA Rodrigue		MUSSA Omar	11
13	MBANANGOYE Zita	18	JUMA Mossi	13
15	NGUEMA Stephane		MWINYI Rajabu	15
17	ISSIEMOU Thierry		20	BIZIMANA Didier	17
18	MOUBAMBA Cedric		NDAYIZEYE Jimmy	18
	Tr: MBOUROUNOT Claude		Tr: RIBAKARE Baudouin	
3	OKOGO Saturnin	18	20	NZEYIMANA Hussein	4
4	LARY Yannick	80	24	NZEYIMANA Gabriel	7
11	KESSANY Paul	18	48	MASUDI Juma	10

National Stadium, Harare
12-10-2003, 15:00, 55 000, Damon RSA

ZIM 3 0 MTN

Ndlovu.A [23], Tembo [47], Ndlovu.P [57]

ZIMBABWE			MAURITANIA	
1	MURAMBADORO Energy	46	GAYE Samba	1
2	MPOFU Dumisani		87	TIMBO Omar	2
3	NYANDORO Esrom		DESCOMBES Eric	3
5	KAPENYA Dezidewo		KANDE Moise	4
6	TEMBO Kaitano		GOURVILLE Pascal	5
7	MASHIRI Edmore	73	SIDIBE Bilal	6
11	YOHANE Charles		70	DIAME Gaston	7
12	NDLOVU Peter		26	BENYACHOU Mohamed	8
13	NDLOVU Adam		SIDIBE Ahmed	9
14	MBWANDO George		TAVARES Antonio	10
15	SIBANDA Ronald		LANGLET Yohan	11
	Tr: MARIMO Sunday		Tr: TOSI Noel	
10	MBANO Albert	73	70	KETCHANKE Bertrand	12
16	KAPINI Tapuwa	46	26	SOW Sidi	13
			87	SIDI Ould Achour	14

Stade Olympique, Nouakchott
14-11-2003, 16:30, 3 000, Keita GUI

MTN 2 1 ZIM

Langlet [3], Sidibe.A [10]   Mbwando [81]

MAURITANIA			ZIMBABWE	
1	GAYE Samba		MURAMBADORO Energy	1
2	TIMBO Oscar		NYANDORO Esrom	3
3	DESCOMBES Eric	67	NDLOVU Bhekithemba	4
4	KANDE Moise	76	KAPENYA Dezidewo	5
5	GOURVILLE Pascal		TEMBO Kaitano	6
6	SIDIBE Bilal		MUHONE Lazarus	8
7	BENYACHOU Mohamed	67	YOHANE Charles	11
8	SIDIBE Ahmed		NDLOVU Adam	13
9	DABO Ahmed		MBWANDO George	14
10	TAVARES Antonio		73	CHORUMA Richard	17
11	LANGLET Yohan		61	SAWU Agent	18
	Tr: TOSI Noel		Tr: MARIMO Sunday	
14	SOW Sidi	67	73	KURAUZIONE Leo	9
17	DIAME Gaston	67	61	MBANO Albert	10

Stade Amahoro, Kigali
12-10-2003, 16:00, 22 000, Abdulkadir TAN

RWA   3   0   NAM

Elias [43], Karekezi [52], Lomani [58]

RWANDA			NAMIBIA	
1 MOHAMMUD Mossi			TJIUORO Esau	16
3 NDIKUMANA Hamad			NAUSEB Robert	2
5 NTAGANDA Elias			TOROMA Hartman	3
6 KALISA Claude	26	71	GARISEB Richard	4
7 BIZAGWIRA Leandre			DIERGAARDT Floris	9
11 KAREKEZI Olivier			RISSER Oliver	10
14 SAID Abed			OUSEB Mohamed	12
15 MBONABUCYA Desire	61		NAUSEB Nicro	13
16 NSHIMIYMANA Eric		73	HINDJOU Johannes	15
17 LOMANI John	79		SHJYUKA Amos	17
18 ELIAS Joao Rafael			HUMMEL George	18
Tr: LATOMIR			Tr: UEBERJAHN Peter	
4 LITA Mana	26	71	NDJAVERA Erastus	6
10 GATETE Jean Michel	79	73	ROMAN Geoffrey	7
12 MUNYANEZA Henri	61			

Windhoek Stadium, Windhoek
15-11-2003, 16:00; 9 000, Mbera GAB

NAM   1   1   RWA

Shipanga [39]   Lomani [37]

NAMIBIA			RWANDA	
16 TJIUORO Esau			MOHAMMUD Mossi	1
2 OUSEB Mohamed		56	MUKUKO Benoit	2
4 GARISEB Richard			NDIKUMANA Hamad	3
7 BENJAMIN Collin			LITA Mana	4
8 RISSER Oliver	31	71	ELIAS Joao Rafael	6
9 DIERGAARDT Floris		82	KAREKEZI Olivier	11
10 MANNETTI Ricardo	70		NTAGANDA Elias	13
11 TJIKUZU Razundara			LOMANI John	14
12 BIWA Richard	54		MBONABUCYA Desire	15
15 HINDJOU Johannes			NSHIMIYIMANA Eric	16
18 HUMMEL George			BIZAGWIRA Leandre	19
Tr: UEBERJAHN Peter			Tr: LATOMIR	
3 GEINGOB Nelson	54	56	HABYARIMANA Paul	5
5 NDJAVERA Erastus	70	82	GATETE Jean Michel	10
6 SHIPANGA Paulus	31	71	MULISA Jimmy	20

National Stadium, Dar es Salaam
11-10-2003, 16:00, 8 864, Tessema ETH

TAN   0   0   KEN

TANZANIA			KENYA	
1 KASEJA Juma			ONYISO Francis	13
2 KISIGA Shaban			WAWERU Japheth	2
5 ALEX Christopher			ISSA Kassim	3
6 COSTA Victor			OTIENO Musa	4
7 MACHO Yusuph			MULAMA Titus	7
9 LISEKI Monja	53	46	SHABAN Adan	8
11 KANIKI Joseph	85	60	OYUGA Paul Mbuya	9
12 MAXIME Mecky			MACHETHA John	10
13 KASSIM Issa			MATHENGE Antony	14
14 MWAKINGWE Ulimboka			OPIYO Philip	15
17 MAYAY Ally		46	OMULAKO Francis	16
Tr: HAFIDH Badru			Tr: MULEE Jacob	
4 JUMA Abdallah	85	46	OWINO Lawrence	5
10 GABRIEL Emanuel	53	60	BARASA John	11
		46	OLIECH Dennis	18

Moi International Sports, Nairobi
15-11-2003, 16:00, 14 000, El Beltagy EGY

KEN   3   0   TAN

Oliech 2 [9 32], Okoth Origi [30]

KENYA			TANZANIA	
13 ONYISO Francis			KASEJA Juma	1
2 WAWERU Japheth			PAWASA Joseph	4
3 ISSA Kassim	39		MWAKINGWE Ulimboka	7
4 OTIENO Musa			NGOYE Herry Morris	8
5 OUNDO Thomas Juma		73	GABRIEL Emanuel	10
7 MULAMA Titus	73	80	KANIKI Joseph	11
8 SHABAN Adan			MAXIME Mecky	12
9 OKOTH ORIGI Michael			KASSIM Issa	13
10 MACHETHE John	82	63	KASSIM Abdi	14
17 MAMBO Robert			MATOLA Seleman	16
18 OLIECH Dennis			MAYAY Ally	17
Tr: MULEE Jacob			Tr: HAFIDH Badru	
12 NGOKA Maurice	82	73	JUMA Abdallah	3
14 OWINO Lawrence	73	63	COSTA Victor	6
16 NYABARO Evans	39	80	LISEKI Monja	9

Stade du 28 Septembre, Conakry
12-10-2003, 16:30, 13 400, Ndoye SEN

GUI   1   0   MOZ

Bangoura [70]

GUINEA			MOZAMBIQUE	
16 CAMARA Kemoko			ANTONINHO	12
2 FEINDOUNO Pascal			BAUTE	3
3 SOW Abdoul			DARIO	4
5 BALDE Dianbobo			TO	6
6 SYLLA Mohamed			MANO-MANO	8
7 MANSARE Fode	46		TICO-TICO	9
9 BANGOURA Sambegou		73	ARMANDO	10
10 BAH Schuman		73	PAITO	11
11 YOULA Souleymane		77	MACAMITO	13
13 CONTE Ibrahima Sory II		51	KITO	15
17 SOUMAH Morlaye			CAMPIRA	18
Tr: DUSSUYER Michel			Tr: BONDARENKO Victor	
14 CAMARA Ousmane	46	73	FAIFE	2
		77	TOMAS	5
		73	JOSSIAS	7

Estadio Machava, Maputo
16-11-2003, 15:30, 50 000, Mochubela RSA

MOZ   3   4   GUI

Monteiro Dario 3 [75 80 89]   Youla [14], Bangoura 3 [21 35 54]

MOZAMBIQUE			GUINEA	
12 ANTONINHO	46		CAMARA Kemoko	16
4 DARIO			FEINDOUNO Pascal	2
5 PAITO			SOW Abdoul	3
7 ARMANDO			BALDE Dianbobo	5
8 MANO-MANO	34	60	BAH Schuman	7
9 TICO-TICO			SYLLA Kanfory	8
10 MONTEIRO DARIO			BANGOURA Sambegou	9
14 NANDO			YOULA Souleymane	11
16 GENITO			CAMARA Ousmane	14
17 MANO			SOUMAH Morlaye	17
18 CAMPIRA	25	68	SYLLA Abdoulkarim	19
Tr: BONDARENKO Victor			Tr: DUSSUYER Michel	
1 KAPANGO	46	60	CAMARA Abdoulkader	6
2 FAIFE	25	68	SOUMAH Issiagua	15
15 TO	34			

Addis Abeba Stadium, Addis Abeba
12-10-2003, 16:00, 20 000, Abd El Fatah EGY

ETH 1 3 MWI

Getu [81p]   Kanyenda 2 [39 55], Mgangira [88]

ETHIOPIA		MALAWI	
1 ASGEDOM Tsegazeab		NYASULU Philip	1
2 SIRAJ Anwar		MABEDI Patrick	5
3 ZEWDU Bekele		CHIPATALA Emmanuel	6
4 ABEBE Tamrat	69	MPONDA Peter	7
5 MULUGETA Samson		MWAFULIRWA Russel	9
6 HUSSEIN Ibrahim		MADUKA John	10
7 GETU Teshome		KANYENDA Essau	11
8 MENSUR Hyder	46	NUNDWE Itay	15
9 ASHENAFI Girma	46	MGANGIRA Peter	17
11 NIGUSSIE Andualem	83	MUNTHALI Heston	18
17 YORDANOS Abay		KONDOWE Fisher	20
Tr: KEBEDE Seyoum		Tr: GILLET Allan	
10 ASSEFA Mesfin	46 83	NGAMBI Robert	19
	69		
14 REGASSA Mulualem	46		

Lilongwe Stadium, Lilongwe
15-11-2003, 15:00, 20 000, Abdel Rahman SUD

MWI 0 0 ETH

MALAWI			ETHIOPIA	
1 NYASULU Philip			GETACHEW Tadios	1
4 CHIPATALA Emmanuel			SIRAJ Anwar	2
5 MABEDI Patrick		62	ZEWDU Bekele	3
6 KAMANGA Allan		82	ASSEFA Mesfin	6
7 MPONDA Peter			TESFAYE Tafese	8
9 MWAFULIRWA Russel	80		NIGUSSIE Andualem	9
10 MADUKA John	41		MULUKEN Yohanes	10
13 PHIRI Victor	68		GETU Teshome	12
14 KAMWENDO Joseph			DEBEBE Degu	13
17 MGANGIRA Peter			MENSUR Hyder	15
20 KONDOWE Fisher			HABTAMU Daniel	17
Tr: NGONAMO Eddington			Tr: KEBEDE Seyoum	
12 GONDWE Ziwange	68	62	ABEBE Tamrat	4
18 CHIRWA Maxwell	80	82	ISMAEL Abubakar	5
19 NGAMBI Robert	41			

National Stadium, Gaborone
11-10-2003, 15:00, 10 000, Manuel Joao ANG

BOT 4 1 LES

Molwantwa [7], Gabolwelwe [44]   Ramafole [64]
Selolwane 2 [50 53]

BOTSWANA		LESOTHO	
16 MARUMO Modiri	54	NTSOANE Tumelo	1
3 MOTLHABANE Khumo		NTOBO Mohapi	2
6 GABOLWELWE Nelson		MARAI Mpitsa	4
7 KGOPOLELO Duncan	82	HLOJENG Tsepo	6
9 KGOSIANG Kabelo		LEHOHLA Shalane	9
10 BUTALE Phazha		RAMAFOLE Moses	10
11 SELOLWANE Diphetogo		PHEKO Malefetsane	11
12 MOLWANTWA Tshepiso	82	SESINYI Khoto	12
14 AMOS Ernest		MAJARA Masupha	46
17 KOLAGANO Pius		SEEMA Lehlohonolo	17
18 GABONAMONG Mogogi	80	POTSE Refiloe	18
Tr: JELUSIC Veselin		Tr: RAMAKAU Mafa	
13 MABOGO Mpho	82 80	MOSOTHOANE Kabelo	3
15 BANGWE Richard	82 46	MPAKANYANE Paballo	14
	54	MOTSOAI Shokhoe	16

Maseru Stadium, Maseru
16-11-2003, 15:00, 9 000, Shikapande ZAM

LES 0 0 BOT

LESOTHO			BOTSWANA	
13 MATHETHA Tsepo			MARUMO Modiri	16
2 LESOETSA Maliele			LETSHOLATHEBE Ndiapo	2
5 MPHONGOA Lebajoa			MOTLHABANE Khumo	3
6 MASEELA Motlatsi			GABOLWELWE Nelson	6
9 LEHOHLA Shalane		61	KGOPOLELO Duncan	7
10 RAMAFOLE Moses			MOTLHABANKWE Tshepo	8
11 PHEKO Malefetsane			KGOSIANG Kabelo	9
14 MARAI Mpitsa		77	BUTALE Phazha	10
15 MOLETSANE Bushi	62		SELOLWANE Diphetogo	11
17 KOLISANG Makhetha	71		AMOS Ernest	14
18 SHALE Motlatsi	46		KOLAGANO Pius	17
Tr: RAMAKAU Mafa			Tr: JELUSIC Veselin	
3 MPAKANYANE Paballo	71	77	MOTHUSI Tebogo	5
7 NTHONYANA Kutloisiso	62	61	MOLWANTWA Tshepiso	12
16 MAJARA Masupha	46			

GROUP STAGE

GROUP 1

Independence Stadium, Lusaka
5-06-2004, 15:00, 40 000, Damon RSA

ZAM 1 0 TOG

Mulenga [11]

ZAMBIA			TOGO	
1 KAKONJE Kalililo			TCHAGNIROU Ouro	1
2 MULENGA Jacob			ADEBAYOR Sheyi	4
3 MUSONDA Joseph			ATTE-OUDEYI Zanzan	5
6 MUMBA Lloyd			AZIAWONOU KAKA Yao	6
7 MWILIMA Justine	36	53	SALOU Tadjou	7
10 BAKALA Ian	53		AMEWOU Komlan	8
11 MBESUMA Collins	76		TOURE Sherif	10
12 MILANZI Harry		63	MAMAM Souleymane	13
13 LUNGU Mishek			OLUFADE Adekanmi	14
17 SINKALA Andrew			AKOTO Eric	16
18 MWANZA Billy			MAMAH Abdul	17
Tr: BWALYA Kalusha			Tr: KESHI Stephan	
3 MWILA Boyd	76	63	SENAYA Junior	3
14 NUMBA Mumamba	53	53	NIBOMBE Dare	18
15 KATONGO Christopher	36			

Stade Léopold Sédar Senghor, Dakar
5-06-2004, 16:30, 18 000, Benouza ALG

SEN 2 0 CGO

Diatta [59], Ndiaya [77]

SENEGAL			CONGO	
1 SYLVA Tony			MOUKO Barel	1
2 BEYE Habib			YOKA Arsene	2
3 FAYE Ibrahima		62	DIAMESSO Luc	3
4 DIOP Papa Malick			MVOUBI Mbiamcie	4
6 SARR Papa			KIMBEMBE Christel	5
7 CAMARA Henri			BOUANGA Michel	8
8 NDIAYE Sylvain			MIYAMOU Rodalec	9
10 GUEYE Babacar	70		GUIE-MIEN Rolf	10
12 FAYE Amdy	79	86	ENDZANGA Wilfrid	14
13 DIATTA Lamine		70	EMBINGOU Roch	15
18 NIANG Mamadou	46		ONGOLY Teddy	18
Tr: GUY Stephan			Tr: LETARD Christian	
9 KAMARA Diomansy	46	62	TSOUMOU Denis	6
14 NDIAYA Moussa	70	70	BAKOUMA Walter	11
17 DIOP Papa Bouba	79	86	NTSIKA Compeige	13

Samuel Doe Sports Complex, Monrovia
6-06-2004, 16:00, 30 000, Codjia BEN

LBR 1 0 MLI

Kieh 85

LIBERIA			MALI	
1 SEAH Sunday			SIDIBE Mahamadou	1
4 KPOTO Varmah			DIAMOUTENE Souleymane	2
5 DIXON Jimmy			COULIBALY Adama	4
6 TEEKLON Ben			TAMBOURRA Adamaa	6
7 SEATOR Frank	53	65	SISSOKO Mohamed	8
8 BENSON Esaiah			KANOUTE Frederic	9
9 WILLIAMS Dio			COULIBALY Soumaila	10
10 DEBBAH James	84		CHELLE Eric	13
11 DAYE Prince	77		TRAORE Dramane	14
17 GEBRO George	71		DIARRA Boubacar	15
18 LAFFOR Anthony			TRAORE Sammy	17
Tr: KROMAH Kadalah			Tr: MOIZAN Alain	
2 JOHNSON Fallah	71	84	SIDIBE Djibril	11
13 KIEH Alvin	53	65	DIALLO Mamadou	12
14 TONDO Isaac	77			

Stade du 26 mars, Bamako
19-06-2004, 19:00, 19 000, Sowe GAM

MLI 1 1 ZAM

Kanoute 80

Milanzi 25

MALI			ZAMBIA	
16 TANGARA Fousseni			KAKONJE Kalililo	1
3 DIAWARA Fousseiny	56		MULENGA Jacob	2
4 COULIBALY Adama			MUSONDA Joseph	4
6 DIARRA Mahamadou			CHANSA Isaac	8
10 COULIBALY Soumaila	68		FICHITE Dadley	9
12 DIALLO Mamadou	43	80	MILANZI Harry	12
13 TAMBOURA Adama			LUNGU Mishek	13
15 DIARRA Boubacar	67		NUMBA Mumamba	14
18 SISSOKO Momo			MUMBA Lloyd	15
19 KANOUTE Frederic		59	PHIRI Edwin	17
20 TRAORE Dramane	77		MWANZA Billy	18
Tr: MOIZAN Alain			Tr: BWALYA Kalusha	
9 ABOUTA Sedonoude	77	68	CHHALWE SASHI	6
11 SIDIBE Djibril	43	80	CHALWE Songwe	10
17 TRAORE Sammy	67	56	KATONGO Christopher	11

Stade Alphonse Massamba, Brazzaville
20-06-2004, 15:30, 25 000, Ould Lemghambodj MTN

CGO 3 0 LBR

Bouanga 52, Mamouna-Ossila 55
Batota 66

CONGO			LIBERIA	
1 MOUKO Barel			SEAH Sunday	1
2 YOKA Arsene			SONKALEY Tarkpor	3
3 DIAMESSO Luc			KPOTO Varmah	4
4 ONGOLY Teddy			WRIGHT Eric	5
5 KIMBEMBE Christel			TEEKLON Ben	6
8 EWOLO Oscar			FORKEY Francis	10
8 BOUANGA Michel	84	62	KIEH Alvin	13
9 MIYAMOU Rodalec	62	72	TONDO Isaac	14
10 NGUIE Mien Rolf			BARLEE Shelton	15
12 MAMOUNA-OSSILA Armel			GEBRO George	17
15 EMBINGOU Roch	46	84	LAFFOR Anthony	18
Tr: LETARD Christian			Tr: KROMAH Kadalah	
13 MAKIITA-PASSY Fabry	84	72	BARYOUR Morrisss	2
17 MOUKASSA Sylvain	62	84	GOBAH Henry	8
18 BATOTA Gervais	46	62	VAH Frederick	9

Kegue, Lorné
20-06-2004, 16:00, 25 000, El Arjoun MAR

TOG 3 1 SEN

Adebayor 30, Senaya 2 76 85

Pape Diop 81

TOGO			SENEGAL	
16 AGASSA Kossi			SYLVA Tony	1
2 NIBOMBE Dare			BEYE Habib	2
3 ABALO Yaovi			FAYE Ibrahima	3
4 ADEBAYOR Sheyi			DIOP Pape Malick	4
5 ATTE-OUDEYI Zanzan			SARR Papa	6
8 AZIAWONOU KAKA Yao		46	CAMARA Henri	7
8 MAMAH Abdul Gafar		46	NDIAYE Sylvain	8
10 TOURE Sherif			KAMARA Diomansy	9
13 AMEWOU Komlan	70		GUEYE Babacar	10
14 OLUFADE Adekamni	69	63	FAYE Amdy	12
15 SALIFOU Moustapha			DIATTA Lamine	13
Tr: KESHI Stephen			Tr: GUY Stephan	
9 AKOTO Eric	70	46	NDIAYE Moussa	14
18 SENAYA Junior	69	46	FAYE Abdoulaye	15
		63	DIOP Pape	17

Stade Léopold Sédar Senghor, Dakar
3-07-2004, 16:30, 50 000, Monteiro Duarte CPV

SEN 1 0 ZAM

Gueye 21

SENEGAL			ZAMBIA	
1 SYLVA Tony			KAKONJE Kalililo	1
4 DIOP Pape Malick	52		MULENGA Jacob	2
5 DIAWARA Souleymane			MUSONDA Joseph	4
8 NDIAYE Sylvain			TANA Elijah	5
9 KAMARA Diomansy	79		CHANSA Isaac	8
10 GUEYE Babacar			FICHITE Dadley	9
13 DIATTA Lamine	76	83	MILANZI Harry	12
14 NDIAYE Moussa	57		LUNGU Mishek	13
18 FAYE Abdoulaye			NUMBA Mumamba	14
19 DIOP Papa Bouba		75	MUMBA Lloyd	15
21 BEYE Habib			MWANZA Billy	18
Tr: STEPHAN Guy			Tr: BWALYA Kalusha	
3 FAYE Ibrahima	76	83	MWILA Boyd	3
7 CAMARA Henri	57	52	CHALWE Songwe	10
18 NIANG Mamadou	79	75	MBESUMA Collins	17

Stade Alphonse Massamba, Brazzaville
4-07-2004, 15:30, 20 000, Evehe CMR

CGO 1 0 MLI

Mamouna-Ossila 30

CONGO			MALI	
1 MOUKO Barel			TANGARA Fousseiny	16
2 YOKA Arsene		82	DIAMOUTENE Souleymane	2
4 ONGOLY Teddy			DIAWARA Fousseiny	3
5 KIMBEMBE Christel			THIAM Brahim	5
7 EWOLO Oscar		53	DIARRA Mahamadou	6
8 BOUANGA Michel			COULIBALY Soumaila	10
9 MIYAMOU Rodalec	36		SIDIBE Djibril	11
10 MOUKILA Jaures	86		DIALLO Mamadou	12
12 MAMOUNA-OSSILA Armel			TAMBOURA Adama	13
13 MAKITA-PASSY Fabry			TRAORE Sammy	17
18 BATOTA Gervais			KANOUTE Frederic	19
Tr: LETARD Christian			Tr: MOIZAN Alain	
11 BAKOUMA Walter	80 36	82	ABOUTA Janvier	9
15 POSSOKABA Simplice	80	53	TRAORE Dramane	20
17 MOUKASSA Sylvain	86			

Samuel Doe Sports Complex, Monrovia
4-07-2004, 16:00, 30 000, Soumah GUI

LBR	0	0	TOG

LIBERIA			TOGO	
1 SEAH Sunday			AGASSA Kossi	16
2 JOHNSON Fallah			ABALO Yaovi	3
4 KPOTO Varmah		65	ADEBAYOR Sheyi	4
5 MENYONGAI John			ATTE-OUDEYI Zanzan	5
6 TEEKLON Ben			AZIAWONOU Yao	6
8 BENSON Esaiah			MAMAH Abdul	8
10 DEBBAH James	71		TOURE Sherif	10
11 SARWIEH Jonah	56	88	AKOTO Eric	12
15 FORKEY Francis	80		AMEWOU Komlan	13
17 GEBRO George		75	OLUFADE Adekamni	14
18 LAFFOR Anthony		88	SALIFOU Moustapha	15
Tr: KROMAH Kadalah			Tr: KESHI Stephen	
3 SONKALEY Tarkpor	56	65	OURO-AKPO Abdou	9
12 KIEH Alvin	80	88	ENINFUL Komlan	17
14 TONDO Isaac	71	75	SENAYA Junior	18

Independence Stadium, Lusaka
4-09-2004, 15:00, 30 000, Nchengwa BOT

ZAM	1	0	LBR

Bwalya 91+

ZAMBIA			LIBERIA	
1 KAKONJE Kalililo			CRAYTON Louis	1
2 MULENGA Jacob	80		JOHNSON Fallah	2
4 MUSONDA Joseph		81	JOHNSON Dulee	3
5 TANA Elijah			KPOTO Varmah	4
7 MWANDILA Noel	46		DIXON Jimmy	5
8 CHANSA Isaac		21	TEEKLON Ben	6
9 FICHITE Dadley	68		MENYONGAI John	8
13 LUNGU Mishek			WILLIAMS Dio	9
14 PHIRI Edwin		61	TARLEY Duncan	10
15 MBESUMA Collins			BALLAH Anthony	13
17 KAMPAMBA Gift			FORKEY Francis	15
Tr: BWALYA Kalusha			Tr: KROMAH Kadalah	
6 KATONGO Christopher	46	21	BARLEE Shelton	11
11 BWALYA Kalusha	68	81	TONDO Isaac	14
12 MILANZI Harry	80	61	MC COLM Cephas	17

Kegué, Lome
5-09-2004, 16:00, 20 000, Mbera GAB

TOG	2	0	CGO

Adebayor 2 37 80

TOGO			CONGO	
16 AGASSA Kossi			ITOUA Old	1
2 NIBOMBE Dare			YOKA Arsene	2
3 ABALO Yaovi		72	DIAMESSO Luc	3
4 ADEBAYOR Sheyi	76	29	KIMBEMBE Christel	5
5 ATTE-OUDEYI Zanzan			EWOLO Oscar	7
6 AZIAWONOU Yao		60	BOUANGA Michel	8
8 MAMAH Abdul			MIYAMOU Rodalec	9
10 TOURE Sherif			MOUKILA Jaures	10
12 KASSIM Guyazou			MAMOUNA-OSSILA Armel	12
17 COUBADJA Abdel	76		MAKITA-PASSY Fabry	13
18 SENAYA Junior	82		BATOTA Gervais	18
Tr: KESHI Stephen			Tr: LETARD Christian	
7 KADDAFI Ali	82	29	SAMBA VEIJEANY Christopher	4
9 FARIAS Alessandro	76	72	VIEIRA Batchi	11
14 OLUFADE Adekamni	76	60	TSOUMOU Denis	15

Stade du 26 mars, Bamako
5-09-2004, 17:00, 45 000, Guezzaz MAR

MLI	2	2	SEN

Diallo 4, Kanoute 54   Camara.H 45, Dia 84

MALI			SENEGAL	
1 SIDIBE Mahamadou			SYLVA Tony	1
4 COULIBALY Adama			FAYE Ibrahima	3
5 KANTE Cedric			DIOP Papa Malick	4
7 DIALLO Mamadou			DIAWARA Souleymane	5
8 SISSOKO Momo	88		CAMARA Henri	7
9 KANOUTE Frederic		81	GUEYE Babacar	10
10 COULIBALY Soumaila		66	NDIAYE Moussa	14
11 SIDIBE Djibril			DIAO Salif	15
12 KEITA Seydou			DIOP Papa Bouba	19
17 COULIBALY Dramane	57	66	FAYE Abdoulaye	20
21 TRAORE Abdou			BEYE Habib	21
Tr: KEITA Mamadou			Tr: GUY Stephan	
3 TAMBOURA Adama	57	66	CAMARA Souleymane	9
14 DOUKANTIE Vincent	88	66	BA Issa	11
		81	DIA Papa	18

Stade Alphonse Massamba, Brazzaville
10-10-2004, 15:30, 20 000, Yacoubi TUN

CGO	2	3	ZAM

Bouanga 75, Mamouna-Ossila 81   Mbesuma 3 2 37 65

CONGO			ZAMBIA	
1 MOUKO Barel			MWEENE Kennedy	1
2 YOKA Arsene			HACHILESA Clive	3
3 DIAMESSO Luc			MUSHOTA Kunda	4
4 ONGOLY Teddy	60		KATONGO Christopher	5
5 N'GUEMBETHE Jean Marie			MBESUMA Collins	6
7 EWOLO Oscar			CHANSA Isaac	8
8 BOUANGA Michel	75		BAKALA Ian	10
9 MIYAMOU Rodalec	75	55	MILANZI Harry	12
10 MOUKILA Jaures	46		LUNGU Mishek	13
12 MAMOUNA-OSSILA Armel		50	NUMBA Mumamba	14
14 MAKITA-PASSY Fabry			MWANZA Billy	18
Tr: LETARD Christian			Tr: BWALYA Kalusha	
6 LEBALLY Ngassilat	60	50	MULENGA Jacob	2
13 LEONCE Andzouana	75	75	PHIRI Ackson	7
17 SAMBA VEIJEANY Christopher	46	55	KILAMBE Rotson	15

Samuel Doe Sports Complex, Monrovia
10-10-2004, 16:00, 26 000, Aboubacar CIV

LBR	0	3	SEN

Diop.PB 41, Camara.H 2 50 73

LIBERIA			SENEGAL	
1 CRAYTON Louis			SYLVA Tony	1
2 JOHNSON Fallah		80	DAF Omar	2
3 JOHNSON Dulee	74		DIOP Papa Malick	4
4 GBANDI Christopher			DIAWARA Souleymane	5
5 DIXON Jimmy	58		CAMARA Henri	7
6 TEEKLON Ben		58	GUEYE Babacar	10
8 MENYONGAI John			DIATTA Lamine	13
9 WILLIAMS Dio		85	NDIAYE Moussa	14
13 BALLAH Anthony			DIAO Salif	15
17 MC COLM Cephas			DIOP Papa Bouba	19
18 LAFFOR Anthony			FAYE Abdoulaye	20
Tr: KROMAH Kadalah			Tr: GUY Stephan	
11 AMOAH Joseph	58	80	FAYE Ibrahima	3
15 FORKEY Francis	74	58	NDIAYE Sylvain	8
		85	CAMARA Souleymane	9

Kegue, Lomé
10-10-2004, 16:00, 45 000, Njike CMR

TOG 1   0 MLI

Adebayor 23

TOGO				MALI
16	AGASSA Kossi			BATHILY Cheick 16
2	NIBOMBE Dare			TRAORE Djimi 2
3	ABALO Yaovi			TAMBOURA Adama 3
4	ADEBAYOR Sheyi			KANTE Cedric 5
6	AZIAWONOU Yao			DIALLO Mamadou 6
8	MAMAH Abdul			NDIAYE Tenema 7
10	TOURE Sherif		85	COULIBALY Soumaila 10
12	KASSIM Guyazou			SIDIBE Djibril 11
14	OLUFADE Adekamni	66	63	KEITA Seydou 12
15	TCHANGAI Massamasso			SISSOKO Momo 14
17	COUBADJA Abdel	83	55	COULIBALY Moussa 18
Tr: KESHI Stephen				Tr: KEITA Mamadou
7	SALIFOU Moustapha	66	55	KONE Boubacar 4
11	DOSSEVI Thomas	83	85	NDIAYE Mallal 9
			63	COULIBALY Dramane 17

Chililabombwe Stadium, Chililabombwe
26-03-2005, 15:00, 20 000, Maillet SEY

ZAM 2   0 CGO

Tana 1, Mbesuma 44

ZAMBIA				CONGO
16	MWEENE Kennedy			MOUKO Barel 1
2	KASONDE Francis			YOKA Arsene 2
4	MUSONDA Joseph			NGO Patrick 3
5	TANA Elijah		46	ITOUA Endzongo 4
6	SINYANGWE Mark		60	KIMBEMBE Christel 5
7	KATONGO Christopher			TSOUMOU Denis 6
9	MBESUMA Collins			EWOLO Oscar 7
10	BAKALA Ian	62		MATIKA-PASSY Fabry 9
13	LUNGU Mishek		82	BHEBEY Rudy 11
19	MWAPE Davies	62		MAMOUNA-OSSILA Armel 12
20	KATONGO Felix			LAKOU Belisaire 14
Tr: BWALYA Kalusha				Tr: TCHIANGANA Gaston
14	MUTAPA Perry	62	82	LOLO Patrick 8
15	MWILA Boyd	62	60	BOUNKOULOU 15
			46	LEONCE Andzouana 18

Stade Léopold Sédar Senghor, Dakar
26-03-2005, 16:30, 50 000, Shelmani LBY

SEN 6   1 LBR

Fadiga 19, Diouf 2 45p 84
Faye.Ab 56, Camara.H 72, Ndiaye 75

Tondo 86

SENEGAL				LIBERIA
1	SYLVA Tony			JACKSON Lartee 1
2	DAF Omar			DOE Sackie 2
5	DIAWARA Souleymane			KPOTO Varmah 4
7	CAMARA Henri	74		BARLEE Shelton 5
10	FADIGA Khalilou	78		MENYONGAI John 8
11	DIOUF El Hadji		81	ZEO Gardiehbey 9
12	FAYE Amdy			MAKOR Oliver 12
13	DIATTA Lamine			GRANUE Patrick 13
18	NIANG Mamadou	61		SEBWE Kelvin 14
20	FAYE Abdoulaye			GEBRO George 17
21	BEYE Habib	59		LAFFOR Anthony 18
Tr: STEPHAN Guy				Tr: SAYON Joseph
9	GUEYE Babacar	74	81	KEITA Sekou 7
14	NDIAYE Moussa	61	59	TONDO Isaac 10
17	BA Issa	78		

Stade du 26 mars, Bamako
27-03-2005, 18:00, 45 000, Agbenyega GHA

MLI 1   2 TOG

Coulibaly 12

Salifou 78, Mamam 91+

MALI				TOGO
16	TANGARA Fousseni			AGASSA Kossi 16
4	COULIBALY Adama			NIBOMBE Dare 2
5	THIAM Brahim			ABALO Yaovi 3
6	DIARRA Mahamadou			ADEBAYOR Sheyi 4
7	KANOUTE Frederic			ATTE-OUDEYI Ismaila 5
9	BAGAYOKO Mamadou	85	78	SALIFOU Moustapha 7
10	COULIBALY Soumaila			MAMAM Cherif-Toure 10
12	KEITA Seydou	46		AKOTO Eric 12
14	KANTE Cedric			MATHIAS Emmanuel 14
17	TRAORE Sammy			COUBADJA Abdel 15
18	SISSOKO Momo	78	88	SENAYA Junior 18
Tr: LECHANTRE Pierre				Tr: KESHI Stephen
8	TOURE Bassala	78	78	OYAWOLE Djima 6
11	SIDIBE Djibril	46	88	OUADJA Lantame 8
13	DIALLO Mamadou	85		

Stade Alphonse Massamba, Brazzaville
5-06-2005, 15:30, 40 000, Damon RSA

CGO 0   0 SEN

CONGO				SENEGAL
1	MOUKO Barel			SYLVA Tony 1
2	YOKA Arsene			FAYE Ibrahima 3
5	KIMBEMBE Christel			DIAKHATE Pape 4
6	TSOUMOU Denis			SECK Mamadou 5
7	EWOLO Oscar		63	CAMARA Henri 7
8	DJIMBI Landry	50	71	FADIGA Khalilou 10
9	MAKITA-PASSY Fabry			DIOUF El Hadji 11
11	BHEBEY Rudy		76	NDIAYE Moussa 14
12	MAMOUNA-OSSILA Armel			COLY Ferdinand 17
17	ONTSONDO Bienvenu			DIOP Papa Bouba 19
18	LEONCE Andzouana			FAYE Abdoulaye 20
Tr: TCHIANGANA Gaston				Tr: STEPHAN Guy
10	BATSIMBA Jean	50	71	CISSE Aliou 6
			76	BA Issa 15
			63	NIANG Mamadou 18

Kegue, Lomé
5-06-2005, 15:30, 15 000, Guezzaz MAR

TOG 4   1 ZAM

Adebayor 2 14 94
Mamam 47, Coubadja 61

Kampamba 15

TOGO				ZAMBIA
16	AGASSA Kossi			KAKONJE Kalililo 1
2	NIBOMBE Dare			KASONDE Francis 2
3	ABALO Yaovi			MUSONDA Joseph 4
4	ADEBAYOR Sheyi			NKETANI Kennedy 5
5	ATTE-OUDEYI Zanzan			KATONGO Christopher 7
7	SALIFOU Moustapha	34		CHANSA Isaac 8
10	MAMAM Cherif-Toure			MBESUMA Collins 9
12	AKOTO Eric	72	66	BAKALA Ian 10
14	MATHIAS Emmanuel	77		LUNGU Mishek 13
17	COUBADJA Abdel			KAMPAMBA Gift 15
18	SENAYA Junior	46		KATONGO Felix 20
Tr: KESHI Stephen				Tr: BWALYA Kalusha
6	AZIAWONOU Yao	34	46	MWAPE Davies 12
8	OUADJA Lantame	72	66	MULENGA Clifford 14
15	KASSIM Guyazou	77		

Stade Amary-Daou, Segou
5-06-2005, 17:00, 11 000, Pare BFA

MLI 4 1 LBR

Coulibaly 2 [7p 34]
Diamoutene [48p], Diarra [75]

Toe [54]

	MALI				LIBERIA	
16	TANGARA Fousseni				SWEN Saylee	16
2	DIAKITE Daouda	67	56		LOMELL James	2
3	DIAWARA Fousseiny				KPOTO Varmah	4
4	KANTE Cedric				GRANUE Patrick	5
5	KONE Boubacar				SANDO Abu	6
6	DIARRA Mahamadou	80			DOE Sackie	8
8	TOURE Bassala		54		KEITA Sekou	9
11	SIDIBE Djibril		74		TOE Arcardia	10
13	DIALLO Mamadou				GARWO Prince	14
14	DIAMOUTENE Souleymane				BARLEE Shelton	15
17	COULIBALY Dramane	85			DORBOR Gizzie	18
	Tr: LECHANTRE Pierre				Tr: SAYON Joseph	
7	TRAORE Mahrahane	80	56		PENIE Aloysius	11
9	DIABATE Cheick	85	74		MILLER George	12
12	TAMBOURA Adama	67	54		SALUE Rufus	17

Chililabombwe Stadium, Chililabombwe
18-06-2005, 15:00, 29 000, Colembi ANG

ZAM 2 1 MLI

Chalwe [26], Mbesuma [85]

Coulibaly [73]

	ZAMBIA				MALI	
16	MWEENE Kennedy				TANGARA Fousseni	16
3	HACHILESA Clive		87		DIAWARA Fousseiny	3
4	MUSONDA Joseph				KANTE Cedric	4
5	TANA Elijah				DIARRA Mahamadou	6
7	KATONGO Christopher		74		TOURE Bassala	8
8	CHANSA Isaac	81			COULIBALY Soumaila	10
9	MBESUMA Collins				SIDIBE Djibril	11
14	MUTAPA Perry	55			DIALLO Mamadou	13
15	CHALWE Linos				DIAMOUTENE Souleymane	14
18	NKETANI Kennedy				BERTHE Sekou	15
20	KATONGO Felix	59	66		COULIBALY Dramane	17
	Tr: BAMPUCHILE Ben				Tr: LECHANTRE Pierre	
10	BAKALA Ian	55	74		DIAKITE Daouda	2
12	MULENGA Clifford	59	87		DIABATE Cheick	9
17	KALABA Rainford	81	66		DISSA Mahamadou	18

Stade Léopold Sédar Senghor, Dakar
18-06-2005, 17:00, 50 000, Guirat TUN

SEN 2 2 TOG

Niang [15], Camara.H [30]

Olufade [11], Adebayor [71]

	SENEGAL				TOGO	
1	SYLVA Tony				AGASSA Kossi	16
3	FAYE Ibrahima				NIBOMBE Dare	2
4	DIAKHATE Pape				ABALO Yaovi	3
6	CISSE Aliou	76			ADEBAYOR Sheyi	4
7	CAMARA Henri				ATTE-OUDEYI Zanzan	5
11	DIOUF El Hadji		50		SALIFOU Moustapha	7
13	DIATTA Lamine				MAMAM Cherif-Toure	10
15	BA Issa	75	67		AKOTO Eric	12
17	COLY Ferdinand				MATHIAS Emmanuel	13
18	NIANG Mamadou	83			OLUFADE Adekanmi	14
19	DIOP Papa Bouba				SENAYA Junior	18
	Tr: STEPHAN Guy				Tr: KESHI Stephan	
9	MENDY Frederic	75	50		AZIAWONOU Yao	6
12	NDOYE Ousmane	76	67		OUADJA Lantame	8
14	NDIAYE Moussa	83				

Samuel K. Doe Sports Stadium, Paynesville
19-06-2005, 16:00, 5 000, Sillah GAM

LBR 0 2 CGO

Bhebey 2 [3 73]

	LIBERIA				CONGO	
16	SWEN Saylee				MOUKO Barel	1
2	LOMELL James				NGO Patrick	3
4	KPOTO Varmah				KIMBEMBE Christel	5
6	SANDO Abu	70			TSOUMOU Denis	6
8	DOE Sackie				FILANCKEMBO	7
10	SALUE Rufus	55	56		MAKITA-PASSY Fabry	9
13	TEAH Robert				BHEBEY Rudy	11
14	GARWO Prince		66		MAMOUNA-OSSILA Armel	12
15	BARLEE Shelton				ONTSONDO Bienvenu	17
17	SALUE Rufus	75			LEONCE Andzouana	18
18	DORBOR Gizzie				Tr: TCHIANGANA Gaston	
	Tr: SAYON Joseph					
5	GRANUE Patrick	70	56		LAKOU Belisaire	14
7	POPO Isaac	75	66		SEMBOLO Francky	15
12	MILLER George	55				

SECOND PHASE GROUP 1		PL	W	D	L	F	A	PTS	TOG	ZAM	SEN	CGO	MLI	LBR
1	Togo	8	5	2	1	14	6	17		4-1	3-1	2-0	1-0	
2	Zambia	8	5	1	2	11	9	16	1-0		2-0	2-1		1-0
3	Senegal	8	4	3	1	17	8	15	2-2	1-0		2-0		6-1
4	Congo	8	3	1	4	8	9	10	2-3	0-0			1-0	3-0
5	Mali	8	1	2	5	9	11	5	1-2	1-1	2-2			4-1
6	Liberia	8	1	1	6	3	19	4	0-0		0-3	0-2	1-0	

Table as of 1 September 2005. Remaining fixtures: 2-09-2005 Zambia v Senegal, Mali v Congo, Togo v Liberia; 7-10-2005 Liberia v Zambia, Congo v Togo, Senegal v Mali

GROUP 2

Vodacom Park, Bloemfontein
5-06-2004, 15:00, 30 000, Tessema ETH

RSA   2   1   CPV

Mabizela 2 40 68   Martins 73

SOUTH AFRICA			CAPE VERDE		
1 VONK Hans			VEIGA Jose	1	
3 WINSTANLEY Neil	82		BARROS Jose	3	
4 MOKOENA Aaron			VEIGA Nelson	5	
5 MABIZELA Mbulelo			BRITO Pedro	6	
7 MORRIS Nasief	66	60	MIRANDA Adriano	7	
8 FISH Mark			AGUIAR Claudio	11	
9 BARTLETT Shaun			MARTINS Janicio	14	
14 NOMVETHE Siyabonga		76	MENDES Sandrom	16	
15 VILAKAZI Benedict			DA LUZ Emerson	17	
17 VAN HEERDEN Elrio	86		MORAIS Carlos	18	
18 BUCKLEY Delron			MODESTE Jimmy	21	
Tr: BAXTER Stuart			Tr: ALHINHO Alexander		
2 MOLEFE Thabang	66	76	FURTADO Dario	2	
11 ZWANE Japhet	82	60	GOMES Domingos	8	
12 MHLONGO Benson	86				

Stade du 4 aout, Ouagadougou
5-06-2004, 18:00, 25 000, Chukwujekwu NGA

BFA   1   0   GHA

Zongo 79

BURKINA FASO			GHANA		
1 KABORE Mohamed			KINGSTON Richard	1	
2 OUATTARA Moussa		60	MUNTARI Sulley	2	
5 TRAORE Lamine			AMANKWA MIREKU Yaw	3	
6 TOURE Amadou	54		KUFFOUR Samuel	4	
7 COULIBALY Amadou			MENSAH John	5	
9 DAGANO Moumouni			PAPPOE Emmanuel	6	
11 OUEDRAOGO Alassane	72	78	ADJEI Lawrence	7	
12 BARRO Tanguy	83		ESSIEN Michael	8	
13 KAMBOU Bebe			APPIAH Stephen	10	
17 ROUAMBA Florent		11	BOATENG Derek	11	
18 OUATTARA Abdramane			OBODAI Anthony	13	
Tr: TODOROV Ivica			Tr: BARRETO Mariano		
8 KERE Mahamoudou	83	78	ARHIN DUAH Nana	9	
10 ZONGO Mamadou	54	60	DUAH Emmanuel	12	
14 OUEDRAOGO Hyacinthe	72	62	MORGAN Ablade	18	

National Stadium, Kampala
6-06-2004, 16:00, 45 000, Maillet SEY

UGA   1   0   COD

Sekajja 75

UGANDA			CONGO DR		
1 MUGISHA Ibrahim			NKELA Nkatu	12	
2 KIZITO Nestroy		22	NDIWA Kangana	2	
3 TABULA Abubakari	67		TSHIOLOLA Tshinyama	4	
4 BATABAIRE Timothy			MILAMBO Mutamba	6	
6 TENYWA Sulaiman			KABAMBA Musasa	7	
8 BAJOPE Assani	53	74	KALUYITU Kadioko	9	
10 MUBIRU Hassan			MUBIALA Kitambala	11	
13 OBUA David			BAGETA Dikilu	13	
14 SEKAJJA Ibrahim			ILONGO Ngasanya	14	
16 ODOCH James	75		NKULUKUTA Miala	16	
17 KASULE Noah		86	NSUMBU Dituabanza	18	
Tr: MUTEBI Mike			Tr: LE ROY Claude		
9 MUBIRU Dan	75	86	KAMATA Makiadi	5	
11 SSOZI Phillip	53	22	MULEKELAY Kanku	10	
12 KADOGO Alimansi	67	74	MBALA Mbuta	17	

Estadio da Varzea, Praia
19-06-2004, 16:00, 5 000, Coulibaly MLI

CPV   1   0   UGA

Semedo 42

CAPE VERDE			UGANDA		
1 VEIGA Jose			MUGISHA Ibrahim	1	
3 BARROS Jose			BATABAIRE Timothy	4	
5 VEIGA Nelson		67	KABAGAMBE Joseph	7	
6 BRITO Pedro			BAJOPE Assani	8	
7 MIRANDA Adriano			MUBIRU Hassan	10	
9 SEMEDO Arlindo			KADOGO Alimansi	11	
11 AGUIAR Claudio	88		OBUA David	13	
14 MARTINS Janicio	81		SEKAJJA Ibrahim	14	
17 DA LUZ Emerson		83	BAGOLE Johnson	15	
18 MORAIS Carlos	65		MUBIRU Dan	16	
21 MODESTE Jimmy			KASULE Noah	17	
Tr: ALHINHO Alexander			Tr: MUTEBI Mike		
4 TAVARES Jose	81	83	TABULA Abubakari	3	
8 GOMES Domingos	65	67	MAWEJJE Tony	6	
10 BRITO Carlos	88				

Kumasi Stadium, Kumasi
20-06-2004, 15:00, 32 000, Diatta SEN

GHA   3   0   RSA

Muntari 13, Appiah 2 55 78

GHANA			SOUTH AFRICA		
1 ADJEI Sammy			JOSEPH Moneeb	1	
2 QUAYE Daniel			LEKGETHO Jacob	2	
3 GYAN Baffour			MOKOENA Aaron	4	
4 KUFFOUR Samuel			MABIZELA Mbulelo	5	
5 MENSAH John			MORRIS Nasief	7	
6 PAPPOE Emmanuel			FISH Mark	8	
8 ESSIEN Michael		70	KOUMANTARAKIS George	9	
10 APPIAH Stephen	86		PIENAAR Stephen	10	
11 MUNTARI Sulley	63		MHLONGO Benson	13	
13 TIERO William			NOMVETHE Siyabonga	14	
18 TANKO Ibrahim	80	60	BUCKLEY Delron	18	
Tr: BARRETO Mariano			Tr: BAXTER Stuart		
7 ASAMPONG Charles	86	70	RASELEMANE Abram	12	
9 POKU Kwadwo	80	60	VAN HEERDEN Elrio	17	
17 YAHUZA Abubakar	63				

Stade de Martyrs, Kinshasa
20-06-2004, 15:30, 75 000, Djaoupe TOG

COD   3   2   BFA

Mbajo 12, Mbala 75, Bageta 88p   Toure.A 26, Dagano 85

CONGO DR			BURKINA FASO		
16 NKELA Nkatu			KABORE Mohamed	1	
2 NKULUKUTA Miala			OUATTARA Moussa	2	
3 MUBIALA Kitambala			TRAORE Lamine	5	
6 TSHIOLOLA Tshinyama			COULIBALY Amadou	7	
6 MILAMBO Mutamba			KERE Mahamoudou	8	
11 MBAJO Kibemba			DAGANO Moumouni	9	
12 KIMOTO Okitankoy			OUEDRAOGO Alassane	11	
13 BAGETA Dikilu		80	BARRO Tanguy	12	
14 ILONGO Ngasanya			KAMBOU Bebe	13	
17 TUTUANA Gemi	48		TASSEMBEDO Soumaila	14	
18 KALUYITU Kadioko	72	63	TOURE Amadou	18	
Tr: LE ROY Claude			Tr: TODOROV Ivica		
7 KABAMBA Musasa	72	80	KONE Yssouf	4	
9 MBALA Mbuta	48	63	TRAORE Ousmane	15	

FNB, Johannesburg
3-07-2004, 15:00, 25 000, Ramaampamonjy MAD

RSA   **2**   **0**   **BFA**

Pienaar [14], Bartlett [42]

	SOUTH AFRICA				BURKINA FASO	
1	VONK Hans				KABORE Mohamed	1
3	CARNELL Bradley		78		OUATTARA Moussa	2
4	MOKOENA Aaron		46		OUATTARA Abdramane	4
5	MABIZELA Mbulelo				TRAORE Lamine	5
6	SIBAYA MacBeth				COULIBALY Amadou	7
7	MORRIS Nasief				SANOU Issouf	8
9	BARTLETT Shaun	83			DAGANO Moumouni	9
10	PIENAAR Steven		83		ZONGO Mamadou	10
11	ZWANE Japhet	77			OUEDRAOGO Alassane	11
15	VILAKAZI Benedict	83			BARRO Tanguy	12
17	MC CARTHY Benedict				TASSEMBEDO Soumaila	14
	Tr: BAXTER Stuart				Tr: TODOROV Ivica	
8	VAN HEERDEN Elrio	77	78		NOGO Salif	3
13	MHLONGO Benson	83	83		OUEDRAOGO Hyacinthe	15
14	NOMVETHE Siyabonga	83	46		TOURE Amadou	18

Estadio da Varzea, Praia
3-07-2004, 16:00, 3 800, Nahi CIV

CPV   **1**   **1**   **COD**

Modeste [26]   Kaluyitu [1]

	CAPE VERDE				CONGO DR	
1	VEIGA Jose				NKELA Nkatu	16
5	VEIGA Nelson				NKULUKUTA Miala	2
6	BRITO Pedro				MUBIALA Kitambala	3
7	MIRANDA Adriano	81			TSHIOLOLA Tshinyama	4
9	SEMEDO Arlindo	87	82		LUALUA Lomana	9
11	AGUIAR Claudio		46		MULEKELAY Kanku	10
14	MARTINS Janicio		85		KABAMBA Musasa	11
16	MENDES Sandrom				KIMOTO Okitankoy	12
17	DA LUZ Emerson				BAGETA Dikilu	13
18	MORAIS Carlos				ILONGO Ngasanya	14
21	MODESTE Jimmy				KALUYITU Kadioko	18
	Tr: ALHINHO Alexander				Tr: LE ROY Claude	
4	TAVARES Jose	81	82		MILAMBO Mutamba	6
10	BRITO Carlos	87	85		MAZAWA Nsumbu	8
			46		MBALA Mbuta	15

National Stadium, Kampala
3-07-2004, 16:30, 20 000, El Beltagy EGY

UGA   **1**   **1**   **GHA**

Obua [46+]   Gyan [88]

	UGANDA				GHANA	
1	MUGISHA Ibrahim				ADJEI Sammy	1
2	KIZITO Nestroy		75		QUAYE Daniel	2
4	BATABAIRE Timothy				GYAN Bafffour	3
6	BAJOPE Assani				KUFFOUR Samuel	4
8	KYAMBADDE Jamil	46			AMPONSAH Kofi	5
10	MUBIRU Hassan				PAPPOE Emmanuel	6
11	SSOZI Phillip		57		ESSIEN Michael	8
13	OBUA David		55		POKU Kwadwo	9
14	MWESIGWA Andrew				APPIAH Stephen	10
8	BAGOLE Johnson				MUNTARI Sulley	11
17	KASULE Noah				TIERO William	15
	Tr: MUTEBI Mike				Tr: BARRETO Mariano	
12	KADOGO Alimansi	72	75		ASAMPONG Charles	7
16	OJARA Tonny	72 46	55		GYAN Asamoah	17
			57		MOHAMMED Hamza	19

Stade du 4 aout, Ouagadougou
4-09-2004, 18:00, 30 000, Ould Lemghambodj MTN

BFA   **2**   **0**   **UGA**

Dagano [34], Nikiema [79]

	BURKINA FASO				UGANDA	
1	KABORE Mohamed				MUGISHA Ibrahim	1
2	OUATTARA Moussa				MASABA Simon	2
5	TRAORE Lamine				TABULA Abubakari	3
6	OUEDRAOGO Rahim				BATABAIRE Timothy	4
8	KERE Mahamoudou		81		KABAGAMBE Joseph	7
9	DAGANO Moumouni		86		MUBIRU Hassan	10
10	ZONGO Mamadou	60			SSOZI Phillip	11
11	OUEDRAOGO Alassane	75			ODOCH James	12
12	BARRO Tanguy				NSUBUGA Muhamad	13
14	TASSEMBEDO Soumaila				MWESIGWA Andrew	14
18	TOURE Amadou	80			BAGOLE Johnson	15
	Tr: TODOROV Ivica				Tr: MUTEBI Mike	
7	SANOU Wilfred	75	86		SERUNKUMA Geofrey	8
13	KAMBOU Bebe	80	81		OJARA Tonny	16
17	NIKIEMA Abdoul Aziz	60				

National Sports Council, Kumasi
5-09-2004, 15:00, 35 000, Tamuni LBY

GHA   **2**   **0**   **CPV**

Essien [24p], Veiga OG [62]

	GHANA				CAPE VERDE	
1	ADJEI Sammy				VEIGA Jose	1
2	AMPONSAH Kofi	65			BARROS Jose	3
3	GYAN Bafffour	69			VEIGA Nelson	5
4	KUFFOUR Samuel				BRITO Pedro	6
5	MENSAH John				MIRANDA Adriano	7
6	PAPPOE Emmanuel				SEMEDO Arlindo	9
8	ESSIEN Michael				AGUIAR Claudio	11
9	GYAN Asamoah				MARTINS Janicio	14
13	TIERO William				DA LUZ Emerson	17
15	EDUSEI Mark				MORAIS Carlos	18
16	TANKO Ibrahim	54	73		MODESTE Jimmy	21
	Tr: BARRETO Mariano				Tr: ALHINHO Alexander	
17	AMANKWA MIREKU Yaw	65	73		LORES Margeus	10
19	POKU Kwadwo	69				
20	MOHAMMED Hamza	54				

Stade de Martyrs, Kinshasa
5-09-2004, 15:30, 85 000, Hicuburundi BDI

COD   **1**   **0**   **RSA**

Kabamba [86]

	CONGO DR				SOUTH AFRICA	
1	KALEMBA Lukoki				VONK Hans	1
2	MUBIALA Kitambala				WINSTANLEY Neil	2
4	TSHIOLOLA Tshinyama				CARNELL Bradley	3
6	MILAMBO Mutamba				MOKOENA Aaron	4
10	KALUYITU Kadioko	46			MABIZELA Mbulelo	5
11	MBAJO Kibemba	82			SIBAYA MacBeth	6
12	KIMOTO Okitankoy	46	89		PIENAAR Steven	10
13	BAGETA Dikilu		75		NOMVETHE Siyabonga	14
14	ILONGO Ngasanya				VILAKAZI Benedict	15
15	ILUNGA Herita				MC CARTHY Benedict	17
17	GLADYS Bokede		73		BUCKLEY Delron	18
	Tr: LE ROY Claude				Tr: BAXTER Stuart	
5	MBALA Musasa	46	73		VAN HEERDEN Elrio	8
8	MPUTU Mabi	82	75		MNGOMENI Thando	9
9	KABAMBA Musasa	46	89		ARENDSO Tyron	11

Estadio da Varzea, Praia
9-10-2004, 16:00, 6 000, Aziaka TOG

CPV 1 0 BFA

Semedo 2

CAPE VERDE				BURKINA FASO		
1	VEIGA Jose			KABORE Mohamed	1	
3	BARROS Jose			NOGO Salif	3	
5	VEIGA Nelson			TRAORE Lamine	5	
7	MIRANDA Adriano	86		OUEDRAOGO Rahim	6	
9	SEMEDO Arlindo	85		SANOU Wilfred	7	
11	AGUIAR Claudio			KERE Mahamoudou	8	
14	MARTINS Janicio		88	DAGANO Moumouni	9	
15	DUARTE Adriano		46	OUEDRAOGO Alassane	11	
16	MENDES Sandrom			BARRO Tanguy	12	
17	DA LUZ Emerson			TASSEMBEDO Soumaila	14	
18	MORAIS Carlos	79	36	TOURE Amadou	18	
	Tr: ALHINHO Alexander			Tr: TODOROV Ivica		
4	TAVARES Jose	85	36	PANANDETIGUIRI Saidou	2	
10	LOPES Mateus	86	88	OUATTARA Abdramane	4	
13	SANCHES Manuel	79	46	OUEDRAOGO Hyacinthe	17	

National Sports Council, Kumasi
10-10-2004, 15:00, 30 000, Coulibaly MLI

GHA 0 0 COD

GHANA				CONGO DR		
1	ADJEI Sammy			KALEMBA Lukoki	1	
2	QUAYE Daniel			MUBIALA Kitambala	3	
3	GYAN Baffour	80		TSHIOLOLA Tshinyama	4	
4	KUFFOUR Samuel			MILAMBO Mutamba	6	
5	MENSAH John			KABAMBA Musasa	9	
6	YEBOAH Godfred			MBAJO Kibemba	11	
8	ESSIEN Michael		60	KIMOTO Okitankoy	12	
10	APPIAH Stephen			BAGETA Dikilu	13	
11	MUNTARI Sulley	70	64	ILONGO Ngasanya	14	
17	CHIBSAH Yussif			NSUMBU Dituabanza	15	
18	TANKO Ibrahim	46		NKULUKUTA Miala	19	
	Tr: ARDAY Samuel			Tr: LE ROY Claude		
7	GAWU Eric	80	60	MBALA Mbuta	5	
9	POKU Kwadwo	70	64	KALUYITUKA Djoko	10	
13	DONG-BORTEY Bernard	46				

National Stadium, Kampala
10-10-2004, 16:30, 50 000, Gasingwa RWA

UGA 0 1 RSA

McCarthy 68p

UGANDA				SOUTH AFRICA		
18	OMWONY Posnet			VONK Hans	1	
2	KIZITO Nestroy			NZAMA Cyril	2	
4	BATABAIRE Timothy			RAMMILE Thabiso	3	
5	SHAKA Okello	82		MOKOENA Aaron	4	
8	BAJOPE Assani			MORRIS Nasief	5	
9	SENTONGO Robert	65		FORTUNE Quinton	7	
11	SSOZI Phillip	53		VILAKAZI Benedict	8	
12	ODOCH James		78	PIENAAR Steven	10	
13	OBUA David		76	ARENDSO Tyron	11	
14	SEKAJJA Ibrahim		85	ZUMA Sibusiso	15	
15	NSUBUGA Muhamad			MC CARTHY Benedict	17	
	Tr: ABBAS Mohammed			Tr: BAXTER Stuart		
3	LWEBUGA Peter	82	78	SIBAYA MacBeth	6	
10	MUBIRU Hassan	65	85	VAN HEERDEN Elrio	12	
16	MAGUMBA Hakimu	53	76	BUCKLEY Delron	18	

FNB, Johannesburg
26-03-2005, 15:45, 20 000, Chukwujekwu NGA

RSA 2 1 UGA

Fortune 21p, Pienaar 71

SOUTH AFRICA				UGANDA		
1	VONK Hans			OMWONY Posnet	1	
2	NZAMA Cyril			KIZITO Nestroy	2	
3	RAMMILE Thabiso			MASABA Simon	3	
4	MOKOENA Aaron			BATABAIRE Timothy	4	
5	MORRIS Nasief			SEKAJJA Ibrahim	5	
7	FORTUNE Quinton		76	TENYWA Sulaiman	7	
8	VILAKAZI Benedict		91	OBOTE Dan	8	
9	BARTLETT Shaun	88		MUBIRU Hassan	10	
10	PIENAAR Steven	79		OBUA David	14	
15	ZUMA Sibusiso	75		BALYEJJUSA Emmanuel	16	
18	BUCKLEY Delron		87	SERUNKUMA Geofrey	17	
	Tr: BAXTER Stuart			Tr: ABBAS Mohammed		
12	VAN HEERDEN Elrio	79	91	BAGOLE Johnson	11	
13	SIPHIKA Siyabonga	88	76	KALUNGI David	12	
17	MC CARTHY Benedict	75	87	LAWRENCE Segawa	13	

Stade du 4 aout, Ouagadougou
26-03-2005, 18:00, 27 500, Evehe CMR

BFA 1 2 CPV

Dagano 71

Morais 2 48 87

BURKINA FASO				CAPE VERDE		
16	SOULAMA Abdulaye			VEIGA Jose	1	
3	OUATTARA Amara	60		MONTEIRO Rui	2	
5	TRAORE Lamine			TAVARES Jose	4	
8	KERE Mahamoudou			NEVES Fernando	5	
9	DAGANO Moumouni			BRITO Pedro	6	
10	ZONGO Mamadou	61	78	MIRANDA Adriano	7	
11	OUEDRAOGO Alassane	74		SEMEDO Arlindo	9	
12	PANANDETIGUIRI Saidou	80		AGUIAR Claudio	11	
13	BANCE Aristide	66		DUARTE Adriano	15	
15	TRAORE Ousmane			DA LUZ Emerson	17	
18	CISSE Abdoulaye			MORAIS Carlos	18	
	Tr: BERNARD Simondi			Tr: ALHINHO ALexander		
2	OUATTARA Moussa	60	74	GOMES Domingos	8	
4	CONOMBO Henock	66	80	LOPES Mateus	10	
7	ZOUNDI Patrick	61	78	SANCHES Manuel	13	

Stade de Martyrs, Kinshasa
27-03-2005, 15:30, 80 000, Sowe GAM

COD 1 1 GHA

Nonda 50

Gyan 30

CONGO DR				GHANA		
1	KALEMBA Lukoki			ADJEI Sammy	1	
2	LEMBI Nzelo			SARPEI Hans	2	
3	MUBIALA Kitambala			GYAN Asamoah	3	
4	TSHIOLOLA Tshinyama			MENSAH John	5	
6	MILAMBO Mutamba			PAPPOE Emmanuel	6	
9	KABAMBA Musasa	60		KINGSTON Richard	7	
10	NONDA Shabani			APPIAH Stephen	10	
11	MBAJO Kibemba	73	85	MUNTARI Sulley	11	
15	ILUNGA Herita			AMOAH Matthew	14	
17	FUAMBA Kinkela	45		COLEMAN Daniel	15	
18	MAKONDELE Muzola	82	76	ABUBAKARI Gariba	18	
	Tr: LE ROY Claude			Tr: DUJKOVIC Ratomir		
5	MBALA Mbuta	45	76	HAMZA Mohammed	8	
12	KIMOTO Okitankoy	73	60	AGYEMAN Louis	9	
14	ILONGO Ngasanya	82	85	ATTRAM Godwin	13	

Estadio da Vareza, Praia
4-06-2005, 16:00, 6 000, Benouza ALG

CPV   1   2   RSA

Gomes 77 | McCarthy 10, Buckley 12

CAPE VERDE			SOUTH AFRICA	
1 MONTEIRO Jose			VONK Hans	1
2 ALMEIDA Rui	63		MOKOENA Aaron	4
5 TAVARES Nelson			MABIZELA Mbulelo	5
6 BRITO Pedro	67		MORRIS Nasief	6
7 MIRANDA Adriano	46	84	ZWANE Arthur	7
9 GOMES Arlindo			VILAKAZI Benedict	8
11 AGUIAR Claudio		84	PIENAAR Steven	10
15 DA LUZ Adriano			KATZA Ricardo	13
16 MENDES Sandrom			PAGAXA Siboniso	15
18 MORIAS Carlos			MC CARTHY Benedict	17
21 NEVES Fernando		84	BUCKLEY Delron	18
Tr: ALHINHO			Tr: BAXTER Stuart	
10 LOPEZ Mateus	63	84	RAMMILE Thabiso	3
14 GOMES Janicio	46	84	MHLONGO Benson	9
19 RAMOS DA GRACA Rumerito	67	84	CULABANGH Lerato	12

National Sports Council, Kumasi
5-06-2005, 15:00, 11 920, Abd El Fatah EGY

GHA   2   1   BFA

Appiah 66, Amoah 83 | Dagano 30

GHANA			BURKINA FASO	
1 ADJEI Sammy			SOULAMA Abdulaye	16
4 PANTSIL John		79	OUATTARA Moussa	2
5 MENSAH John			KAMBOU Bebe	4
6 PAPPOE Emmanuel			TASSEMBEDO Soumaila	5
9 GYAN Asamoah	54		KERE Mahamoudou	8
10 APPIAH Stephen			DAGANO Moumouni	9
12 ATTRAM Godwin	63	86	CISSE Abdoulaye	10
14 AMOAH Matthew		53	OUEDRAOGO Alassane	11
18 YAKUBU Abukari			PANANDETIGUIRI Saidou	12
19 AMPONSAH Kofi	36		OUATTARA Boureima	13
24 EDUSEI Daniel			ROUAMBA Florent	17
Tr: DUJKOVIC Ratomir			Tr: BERNARD Simondi	
13 MOHAMMED Hamza	63	79	GNAMOU Ibrahim	3
21 ISSAH Gabriel	36	86	MINOUNGOU Dieubonne	14
25 ASAMOAH Frimpong	54	53	TOURE Amadou	18

Stade de Martyrs, Kinshasa
5-06-2005, 15:30, 80 000, Daami TUN

COD   4   0   UGA

Nonda 2 2 69p, Ilongo 58
Matumdna 78

CONGO DR			UGANDA	
1 KALEMBA Lukoki			OMWONY Posnet	1
2 MUBIALA Kitambala			KIZITO Nestroy	2
3 NSUMBU Dituabanza			BATABAIRE Timothy	4
4 TSHIOLOLA Tshinyama			SEKAJJA Ibrahim	6
5 MBALA Mbuta	71		KALUNGI David	7
6 MILAMBO Mutamba	46		OBOTE Dan	8
9 LUALUA Lomana			OBUA David	13
10 NONDA Shabani	87	22	SHAKA Okello	15
11 MBAJO Kibemba	76		BALYEJJUSA Emmanuel	16
14 ILONGO Ngasanya	85		MASABA Simon	19
15 ILUNGA Herita			MUBIRU Hassan	20
Tr: LE ROY Claude			Tr: ABBAS Mohammed	
12 MATUMDNA Zola	76	71	TABULA Abubakari	3
13 KABAMBA Musasa	87	46	OCHAMA Morley	10
17 MUKANDILA Tshitenge	85	22	SSEJJEMBA Robert	14

FNB, Johannesburg
18-06-2005, 15:30, 50 000, Guezzaz MAR

RSA   0   2   GHA

Amoah 59, Essien 91+

SOUTH AFRICA			GHANA	
1 MARLIN Calvin			OWU George	1
2 LEKGWATHI Lucky			PANTSIL John	4
4 MOKOENA Aaron			MENSAH John	5
5 MABIZELA Mbulelo			EDUSEI Daniel	6
6 MORRIS Nasief		70	LARYEA Kingston	7
8 VILAKAZI Benedict			ESSIEN Michael	8
9 BARTLETT Shaun			ASAMOAH Frimpong	9
10 PIENAAR Steven	89		APPIAH Stephen	10
15 KATZA Ricardo		78	MUNTARI Sulley	11
17 CULABANGH Lerato	69	94	AMOAH Matthew	14
18 BUCKLEY Delron	85		ISSAH Gabriel	17
Tr: BAXTER Stuart			Tr: DUJKOVIC Ratomir	
11 ZWANE Arthur	85	94	OSEI Emmanuel	3
12 MPHELA Katlego	89	70	HAMZA Mohammed	13
14 NOMVETHE Siyabonga	69	78	YAKUBU Abukari	18

National Stadium, Kampala
18-06-2005, 16:30, 5 000, Kidane ERI

UGA   1   0   CPV

Serunkuma 36

UGANDA			CAPE VERDE	
1 ONYANGO Denis			MONTEIRO Jose	1
2 KIZITO Nestroy			ALMEIDA Rui	2
5 SSOZI Phillip	60		BARROS Jose	3
6 OCHAMA Morley	78		NEVES Fernando	5
11 BAGOLE Johnson		58	BRITO Pedro	6
13 OBUA David		73	GOMES Domingos	8
14 MWESIGWA Andrew		63	AGUIAR Claudio	11
15 SHAKA Okello			GOMES Janicio	14
16 BALYEJJUSA Emmanuel	89		DA LUZ Adriano	15
17 SERUNKUMA Geofrey			DA LUZ Emerson	17
20 MUBIRU Hassan			MORIAS Carlos	18
Tr: ABBAS Mohammed			Tr: ALHINHO Alexandre	
4 NSEREKO Stephen	60	73	GOMES Arlindo	9
8 OBOTE Dan	89	63	LOPES Mateus	10
9 KASULE Noah	78	58	DA VEIGA Jose	19

Stade du 4 aout, Ouagadougou
18-06-2005, 18:00, 25 000, Shelmani LBY

BFA   2   0   COD

Panandetiguiri 3, Dagano 68

BURKINA FASO			CONGO DR	
16 SOULAMA Abdulaye	86		KALEMBA Lukoki	1
2 HABOUNA Bamogo			MUBIALA Kitambala	2
4 KAMBOU Bebe			NSUMBU Dituabanza	3
5 TASSEMBEDO Soumaila		50	MBALA Mbuta	5
6 BARRO Tanguy		71	MILAMBO Mutamba	6
9 DAGANO Moumouni			BUKASA Kasonga	7
10 CISSE Abdoulaye	77		LUALUA Lomana	9
11 OUEDRAOGO Alassane	61		NONDA Shabani	10
12 PANANDETIGUIRI Saidou		55	MBAJO Kibemba	11
13 OUATTARA Boureima			ILONGO Ngasanya	14
14 ROUAMBA Florent			ILUNGA Herita	15
Tr: BERNARD Simondi			Tr: LE ROY Claude	
1 KABORE Mohamed	86	71	MATUMDNA Zola	12
15 KEBE Yahia	77	50	KABAMBA Musasa	13
17 NIKIEMA Abdoul Aziz	61	55	MAKONDELE Muzola	18

SECOND PHASE GROUP 2	PL	W	D	L	F	A	PTS	GHA	RSA	COD	CPV	BFA	UGA
1 Ghana	8	4	3	1	11	4	15		3-0	0-0	2-0	2-1	
2 South Africa	8	5	0	3	9	9	15	0-2			2-1	2-0	2-1
3 Congo DR	8	3	3	2	10	7	12	1-1	1-0			3-2	4-0
4 Cape Verde Islands	8	3	1	4	7	9	10		1-2	1-1		1-0	1-0
5 Burkina Faso	8	3	0	5	9	10	9	1-0		2-0	1-2		2-0
6 Uganda	8	2	1	5	4	11	7	1-1	0-1	1-0	1-0		

Table as of 1 September 2005. Remaining fixtures: 2-09-2005 Congo DR v Cape Verde Islands, Ghana v Uganda, Burkina Faso v South Africa;
7-10-2005 Uganda v Burkina Faso, South Africa v Congo DR, Cape Verde Islands v Ghana

GROUP 3

Stade Omnisport, Yaoundé
6-06-2004, 15:30, 40 000, Mbera GAB

CMR 2 1 BEN

Eto'o [42], Song [45]   Tchomogo [11]

CAMEROON			BENIN	
1 KAMENI Idris			AGUEH Maxime	1
2 PERRIER DOUMBE Jean Joel			BOCO Romuald	3
3 WOME Pierre		63	OKETOLA Jonas	6
4 SONG Rigobert		81	TOCLOMITI Stanislas	8
5 ATOUBA Thimothee			OGUNBIYI Muri	11
7 FEUTCHINE Guy	65		ADJAMONSI Anicet	15
8 GEREMI			SESSEGNON Stephane	17
9 ETO'O Samuel			TCHOMOGO Seidah	18
10 MBAMI Modeste			AHOUEYA Jocelin	19
12 TUM Herve	83		CHRYSOSTOME Damien	23
23 TCHATO Bill		74	SEKA Noel	24
Tr: SCHAEFER Winnie			Tr: ATTUQUAYEFIO Cecil	
15 WEBO Achille	83	74	AMOUSSOU Sevi	10
19 DJEMBA DJEMBA Eric	65	63	OSSENI Bachirou	21
		81	YOUSSOUF Nassirou	22

Stade Félix Houphouët-Boigny, Abidjan
6-06-2004, 16:00, 40 827, Colembi ANG

CIV 2 0 LBY

Dindane [35], Drogba [63p]

COTE D'IVOIRE			LIBYA	
1 TIZIE Jean-Jacques			EL AMMI Abdalla	12
3 BOKA Etienne Arthur			SHUSHAN Naji Said	3
4 TOURE Abib			OSMAN Ahmed	10
5 ZOKORA Didier			EL TAIB Tareq	14
6 KOUASSI Blaise		73	KARA Nader	15
7 GUEL Tchiressoa	75		ABDUSSALAH Nadder	16
8 KALOU Bonaventure			SAFTER Mahmud	17
10 DIE Serge	46		HAMADI Osama	18
11 DROGBA Didier	86		BOUBAKR Abdul Salam	19
15 DINDANE Aruna		73	AL SHIBANI Younus	23
17 DOMORAUD Cyrille		73	ELBESKINI Emad	26
Tr: MICHEL Henri			Tr: LONCAREVIC Ilija	
7 AKALE Kanga	46	73	MOHAMED Khaled	8
9 KONE Arouna	86	73	KHAMIS Fathi	22
13 DEMEL Guy	75			

National Stadium, Khartoum
6-06-2004, 20:00, 10 000, Kidane Tesfu ERI

SUD 0 3 EGY

Ali [6], Aboutraika [53],
Abdel Wahab [88]

SUDAN			EGYPT	
18 ABDALLA Emuez Mahgoub			EL HADRY Essam	1
3 ABD IAZIZ Ranadan	59		ABDEL WAHAB Mohamed	3
5 AHMED Salih		70	ABD RABO Hosni	4
6 LADO Richard Gastin			EL SAQUA Abdel	5
10 TAMBAL Haytham	46		ELSHATER Islam	6
12 ABDALLA Bader Eldin			MOUSTAFA Hassan	7
15 DAMAR Amir			SHAWKY Mohamed	11
17 BUSTAWI Mohamed		63	SOLIMAN Mohamed	12
19 EL FAITH Ahmed	46		EL-TABEI Besheer	15
20 EL BASHIR Hamouda		84	ALI Abel	19
22 SAEED Anwaar			ABOUTRAIKA Mohamed	20
Tr: LAZAREK Wojciech			Tr: TARDELLI Marco	
11 EL RASHEED Haitham	46	84	AYED Ahmed	2
13 ELDIN BABIKER Alaa	59	70	TAREK EL SAYED Mohamed	13
16 MAOROUF Noureldin	46	63	EMAM Hazem	14

Misurata Stadium, Misurata
18-06-2004, 19:30, 7 000, Lim Kee Chong MRI

LBY 0 0 CMR

LIBYA			CAMEROON	
12 EL AMMI Abdalla			KAMENI Idris	1
2 OSMAN Walid			PERRIER DOUMBE Jean Joel	2
3 SHUSHAN Naji Said			WOME Pierre	3
6 SULIMAN Marei	65		SONG Rigobert	4
10 OSMAN Ahmed			ATOUBA Thimothee	5
14 EL TAIB Tareq		60	FEUTCHINE Guy	7
16 ABDUSSALAH Nadder	86		GEREMI	8
17 SAFTER Mahmud	60		ETO'O Samuel	9
18 HAMADI Osama		86	MBAMI Modeste	10
19 BOUBAKR Abdul Salam			METTOMO Lucien	13
23 AL SHIBANI Younus		65	WEBO Achille	15
Tr: LONCAREVIC Ilija			Tr: SCHAEFER Winnie	
4 SENUSSI Senussi	60	65	NDIEFI Pius	11
20 REWANI Salem	86	86	MAKOUN Jean	14
26 ELBESKINI Emad	65	60	EMANA Achille	18

Stade de l'Amitié, Cotonou
20-06-2004, 16:00, 20 000, Guezzaz

BEN 1 1 SUD

Ogunbiyi [30]   Abd Iaziz [47+]

BENIN			SUDAN		
1	AGUEH Maxime		ABDELLAH Mohamed	1	
3	BOCO Romuald		ABDEL FARAG Elnazir	2	
5	CHRYSOSTOME Damien		ABD IAZIZ Ranadan	3	
6	OKETOLA Jonas	60	ISMAIL Anwar	4	
8	TOCLOMITI Stanislas	58	AHMED Salih	5	
10	TCHOMOGO Oumar	35	LADO Richard Gastin	6	
11	OGUNBIYI Muri		KHALIB Ibrahim	8	
15	ADJAMONSI Anicet		KABIR Motaz	9	
17	SESSEGNON Stephane	73	ELDIN BABIKER Alaa	12	
18	TCHOMOGO Seidah		KOKU Amir Damar	15	
19	AHOUEYA Jocelin	83	EL BASHIR Hamouda	20	
	Tr: ATTUQUAYEFIO Cecil		Tr: LAZAREK Wojciech		
2	YOUSSOUF Nassirou	60	SAEED James Joseph	10	73
			EL FAITH Ahmed	19	35
			MAAROUF Noureldin	21	58

Alexandria Stadium, Alexandria
20-06-2004, 20:00, 13 000, Guirat TUN

EGY 1 2 CIV

Aboutraika [55]   Dindane [22], Drogba [75]

EGYPT			COTE D'IVOIRE		
1	EL HADRY Essam		TIZIE Jean-Jacques	16	
3	ABDEL WAHAB Mohamed		BOKA Etienne Arthur	3	
4	ABD RABO Hosni		TOURE Abib	4	
5	EL SAQUA Abdel		ZOKORA Didier	5	
6	AYED Ahmed	81	GUEL Tchiressoa	7	
7	MOUSTAFA Hassan		72	KALOU Bonaventure	8	
11	SHAWKY Mohamed		90	DIE Serge	10	
15	EL-TABEI Besheer		DROGBA Didier	11	
18	GHALI Hossam	78	72	TEBILY Olivier	14	
19	ALI Abel	80	DINDANE Aruna	15	
20	ABOUTRAIKA Mohamed		DOMORAUD Cyrille	17	
	Tr: TARDELLI Marco		Tr: MICHEL Henri		
9	ZAKI Amr	80	90	TOURE Yaya	2	
13	TAREK EL SAYED Mohamed	78	72	KOUASSI Blaise	6	
17	HASSAN Ahmed	81	72	YAPI Gilles	12	

National Stadium, Khartoum
3-07-2004, 20:00, 10 000, Bennett RSA

SUD 0 1 LBY

                                              Kara [93+]

SUDAN			LIBYA		
18	ABDALLA Elmuez		46	EL AMMI Abdalla	12	
2	ABDEL Elnazeir		SHUSHAN Naji	3	
3	ABDEL Amar		OSMAN Ahmed	10	
4	KABASHIISMAIL Anour		EL TAIB Tareq	14	
5	AHMED Salih		ABDUSSALAH Nader	16	
6	LADO Richard Gastin	46	SAFTAR Mahmud	17	
9	KABIR Motaz		HAMADI Osama	18	
12	ABDALLA Bader		BOUBAKR Abdul Salam	19	
14	KARBOS Jundi	27	59	REWANI Salem	20	
15	KOKU Amir		AL SHIBANI Younus	23	
19	EL FAITH Ahmed	73	65	ELBESKINI Emad	26	
	Tr: LAZAREK Wojciech		Tr: LONCAREVIC Ilija		
8	KHALIB Ibrahim	46	46	GHZALLA Muftah	1	
10	SAEED James Joseph	73	65	MOHAMED Khaled	8	
13	ELDIN BABIKER Alaa	27	59	KARA Nader	15	

Stade Omnisport, Yaoundé
4-07-2004, 15:30, 80 000, Guezzaz MAR

CMR 2 0 CIV

Eto'o [80], Feutchine [82]

CAMEROON			COTE D'IVOIRE		
16	SOULEYMANOU Hamidou		TIZIE Jean-Jacques	16	
2	PERRIER DOUMBE Jean Joel		BOKA Etienne Arthur	3	
4	SONG Rigobert		TOURE Abib	4	
5	ATOUBA Thimothee		92	ZOKORA Didier	5	
8	GEREMI		77	GUEL Tchiressoa	7	
10	MBAMI Modeste		KALOU Bonaventure	8	
13	METTOMO Lucien	56	83	DIE Serge	10	
17	ETO'O Samuel		DROGBA Didier	11	
18	IDRISSOU Mohamadou	64	MEITE Abdoulaye	12	
19	DJEMBA DJEMBA Eric	42	TIZIE Jean-Jacques	15	
23	TCHATO Bill		BOKA Etienne Arthur	17	
	Tr: SCHAEFER Winnie		Tr: MICHEL Henri		
6	ABANDA Patrice	56	83	KONE Arouna	9	
7	FEUTCHINE Guy	42	77	YAPI Gilles	14	
11	NDIEFI Pius	64				

Stade de l'Amitié, Cotonou
4-07-2004, 16:00, 15 000, Chukwujekwu NGA

BEN 3 3 EGY

Tchomogo [8p], Ahoueya [46],   Hassan.A [66], Aboutraika [75],
Ogunbiyi [68]   Moustafa [80]

BENIN			EGYPT		
1	AGUEH Maxime		EL HADRY Essam	1	
3	ADOME Jocelyn		28	ABDALLA Mohamed	2	
6	OKETOLA Jonas	78	46	ABDEL WAHAB Mohamed	3	
7	BOCO Romuald		MOUSTAFA Hassan	4	
8	TOCLOMITI Stanislas		EL SAQUA Abdel	5	
10	TCHOMOGO Oumar	81	ELSHATER Islam	6	
14	OSSENI Bachirou		SHAWKY Mohamed	11	
17	SESSEGNON Stephane	57	GHALI Hossam	14	
18	TCHOMOGO Seidah		EL-TABEI Besheer	15	
19	AHOUEYA Jocelin		ALI Abel	19	
20	AMOUSSOU Sevi	46	ABOUTRAIKA Mohamed	20	
	Tr: GOMEZ Wabi		Tr: TARDELLI Marco		
5	SEKA Noel	78	46	TAREK EL SAYED Mohamed	13	
9	MAIGA Abou	81	28	HASSAN Ahmed	17	
11	OGUNBIYI Muri	46	57	HOSNI Osama	18	

11th June Stadium, Tripoli
3-09-2004, 19:00, 30 000, Kidane Tesfu ERI

LBY 4 1 BEN

Al Shibani [9], Kara [47],
Osman.A [51], Suliman [70]   Osseni [12]

LIBYA			BENIN		
12	EL AMMI Abdalla		AGUEH Maxime	1	
2	OSMAN Walid		BOCO Romuald	3	
3	SHUSHAN Naji		82	CHRYSOSTOME Damien	5	
7	MONTASSER Jehad	75	54	OKETOLA Jonas	8	
8	MOHAMED Khaled	65	TCHOMOGO Oumar	10	
10	OSMAN Ahmed		OSSENI Bachirou	14	
15	KARA Nader	86	OMOTOYOSSI Razak	15	
16	ABDUSSALAH Nader		62	TCHOMOGO Seidah	18	
18	HAMADI Osama		AHOUEYA Jocelin	19	
19	BOUBAKR Abdul Salam		ADOME Jocelyn	20	
23	AL SHIBANI Younus		Tr: REVELLI Herve		
	Tr: EL SELINE Mohamed		AMOUSSOU Sevi	7	
6	SULIMAN Marei	65	82	OLAOFE	9	
13	KASMBA Rida	75	62	OGUNBIYI Muri	11	
17	BUZBEDA Walid	86	54			

Stade Félix Houphouët-Boigny, Abidjan
5-09-2004, 16:00, 20 000, Mana NGA

CIV 5   0   SUD

Drogba 12p, Dindane 2 15 64
Yapi 25, Kone 56

#	COTE D'IVOIRE	m	m	SUDAN	#
1	TIZIE Jean-Jacques			ABDALLA Elmuez	18
3	BOKA Etienne Arthur		33	MUSA Salahel	2
4	TOURE Abib	46		HAGANA Merghani	3
6	KOUASSI Blaise	76		KABASHIISMAIL Anour	4
7	GUEL Tchiressoa		46	ABDEL Amar	5
8	KALOU Bonaventure		65	KARBOS Jundi	7
11	DROGBA Didier	40		EL BASHIR Hamouda	8
12	MEITE Abdoulaye			SAEED James Joseph	10
14	DEMEL Guy			ABDALLA Bader	12
15	DINDANE Aruna			ALI Khalid	14
18	YAPI Gilles			DAMAR Amir	15
	Tr: MICHEL Henri			Tr: AHMED Mohamed	
2	EBOUE Emmanuel	76	46	ELDIN Alaa	6
9	KONE Bakary	40	65	EL RASHEED Haitham	11
17	DOMORAUD Cyrille	46	33	EL FAITH Ahmed	19

Arab Contractors Stadium, Cairo
5-09-2004, 20:00, 25 000, Lim Kee Chong MRI

EGY 3   2   CMR

Shawky 45, Hassan.A 74p, Tarek El Sayed 86
Tchato 88, Eto'o 89

#	EGYPT	m	m	CAMEROON	#
1	EL SAYED Nader			KAMENI Idris	1
3	ABDEL WAHAB Mohamed			PERRIER DOUMBE Jean Joel	2
4	ABD RABO Hosni			TCHATO Bill	3
7	FATHI Ahmed	86		SONG Rigobert	4
9	ZAKI Amr	87		ATOUBA Thimothee	5
11	SHAWKY Mohamed			GEREMI	8
12	RAMY Adel			ETO'O Samuel	9
15	EL TABEI Besheer		80	MBAMI Modeste	10
17	HASSAN Ahmed	76		METTOMO Lucien	13
20	GOMAA Wael		65	TUM Herve	18
22	ABOUTRAIKA Mohamed		76	JOB Joseph-Desire	21
	Tr: TARDELLI Marco			Tr: SCHAEFER Winnie	
13	TAREK EL SAYED Mohamed	76	65	FEUTCHINE Guy	7
14	MOUSTAFA Hassan	86	76	NDIEFI Pius	11
19	ABOUTRAIKA Mohamed	87	80	MAKOUN Jean	14

11th June Stadium, Tripoli
8-10-2004, 19:00, 40 000, Haimoudi ALG

LBY 2   1   EGY

Kara 31, Osman.A 85
Zaki 57

#	LIBYA	m	m	EGYPT	#
1	ABOUD Samir			EL SAYED Nader	1
3	SHUSHAN Naji		85	ABDEL WAHAB Mohamed	3
8	MOHAMED Khaled	55		ABD RABO Hosni	4
10	OSMAN Ahmed	89	46	FATHI Ahmed	7
14	EL TAIB Tareq			ZAKI Amr	9
15	KARA Nader	77		SHAWKY Mohamed	11
16	ABDUSSALAH Nader	87		RAMY Adel	12
18	HAMADI Osama			EL TABEI Besheer	15
19	BOUBAKR Abdul Salam			HASSAN Ahmed	17
23	AL SHIBANI Younus			GOMAA Wael	20
26	OSMAN Walid			ABOUTRAIKA Mohamed	22
	Tr: EL SELINE Mohamed			Tr: TARDELLI Marco	
7	ALHAMALI Akram	55	85	ABOUTRAIKA Mohamed	10
17	SAFTAR Mahmud	89	46	EL SAYED Tarek	13
20	REWANI Salem	77			

El Meriekh, Omdurman
9-10-2004, 20:30, 30 000, Buenkadila COD

SUD 1   1   CMR

Agab Sido 17
Job 92+

#	SUDAN	m	m	CAMEROON	#
18	ABDALLA Elmuez			SOULEYMANOU Hamidou	16
2	ABDEL Elnazeir			PERRIER DOUMBE Jean Joel	2
3	ABDEL Amar		61	TCHATO Bill	3
5	HADO Alaa Eldin			SONG Rigobert	4
6	LADO Ritshard			ATOUBA Thimothee	5
8	ALA ELDIN Ahmed	78		FEUTCHINE Guy	7
9	KARAR Haitham	60		GEREMI	8
10	TAMBAL Haytham	72		MAKOUN Jean	14
12	ABDALLA Bader		46	TUM Herve	18
16	KOKU Amir			DJEMBA DJEMBA Eric	19
17	AGAB SIDO Faisal			JOB Joseph-Desire	21
	Tr: AHMED Mohamed			Tr: SCHAEFER Winnie	
11	EL RASHEED Haitham	72	61	ROUDOLPHE Mbela	10
19	EL BASHIR Hamouda	78	46	TOMOU Bertin	12
20	IBRAHIM Ahmed Ali	60	46	MBAMI Modeste	23

Stade de l'Amitié, Cotonou
10-10-2004, 16:00, 25 000, Sowe GAM

BEN 0   1   CIV

Dindane 48

#	BENIN	m	m	COTE D'IVOIRE	#
1	CHITOU Rachad			TIZIE Jean-Jacques	1
2	OMOTOYOSSI Razak			TOURE Abib	4
3	BOCO Romuald	63		ZOKORA Didier	5
8	TOCLOMITI Stanislas			KOUASSI Blaise	6
10	TCHOMOGO Oumar			GUEL Tchiressoa	7
13	SEKA Noel			KALOU Bonaventure	8
14	GASPOZ Alain	85	61	YAPI Gilles	10
15	ADJAMONSI Anicet			MEITE Abdoulaye	12
17	SESSEGNON Stephane		79	DINDANE Aruna	15
18	OSSENI Bachirou			DOMORAUD Cyrille	17
24	CHRYSOSTOME Damien			TOURE Yaya	18
	Tr: REVELLI Herve			Tr: MICHEL Henri	
9	MAIGA Abou	85	79	KONE Arouna	9
19	AHOUEYA Jocelin	63	61	KONE Bakary	14

Stade Ahmadou Ahidjo, Yaoundé
27-03-2005, 15:30, 30 000, Diatta SEN

CMR 2   1   SUD

Geremi 34, Webo 90

#	CAMEROON	m	m	SUDAN	#
1	KAMENI Idris			MOHAMED Abu Baker	1
4	SONG Rigobert		72	ELNAZIR Mahmoud	2
5	ATOUBA Thimothee	72		ABDEL Amar	3
6	ANGBWA Benoit			HADO Alaa Eldin	4
8	GEREMI			ALADIN Ahmed	7
9	ETO'O Samuel		78	AHMED Haitham	8
13	METTOMO Lucien	46		TAMBAL Haytham	10
18	DOUALA Rudolphe	58	55	AHMED Mugahid	14
19	SAIDOU Aboun		66	DAMAR Amir	15
20	OLEMBE Salomon			AGAB SIDO Faisal	17
21	JOB Joseph-Desire			ALI Khalid	19
	Tr: JORGE Artur			Tr: AHMED Mohamed	
3	DEUMI Armand	46	55	LADO Richard	6
7	KOMW Daniel	58	72	ALI Ahmed	12
15	WEBO Achille	72	78	MOHAMED Ali Al Khidir	20

Stade Félix Houphouët-Boigny, Abidjan
27-03-2005, 16:00, 35 000, Guirat TUN

CIV 3 0 BEN

Kalou 7, Drogba 2 19 59

#	COTE D'IVOIRE			BENIN	#
1	TIZIE Jean-Jacques			CHITOU Rachad	1
3	BOKA Etienne Arthur		64	CHITOU Charaf	2
4	TOURE Abib			OLOU Oscar	3
5	ZOKORA Didier			BOCO Romuald	7
7	GUEL Tchiressoa	68		MAIGA Abou	9
8	KALOU Bonaventure		75	OGUNBIYI Muri	11
11	DROGBA Didier	83		AGBESSI Coffi	12
13	ZORO Marc			SEKA Noel	13
15	DINDANE Aruna			ADJAMONSI Anicet	15
17	DOMORAUD Cyrille			SESSEGNON Stephane	17
18	TIENE Siaka	60		TCHOMOGO Seidah	18
	Tr: MICHEL Henri			Tr: DEVEZ Serge	
2	AKALE Kanga	60	75	OMOTOYOSSI Razak	8
9	FAE Emerse	68	64	OSSENI Bachirou	14
14	KONE Bakary	83			

Arab Contractors Stadium, Cairo
27-03-2005, 20:00, 30 000, Poulat FRA

EGY 4 1 LBY

Hossam Mido 55, Motab 2 56 80
Hassan.A 76
Ferjani 50

#	EGYPT			LIBYA	#
16	EL SAYED Abdel			GHZALLA Muftah	12
7	FATHI Ahmed			SHUSHAN Naji	3
8	ABD RABO Hosni		53	FERJANI Othman	4
9	HOSSAM MIDO Ahmed	73		MONTASSER Jehad	7
10	MOTAB Emad			OSMAN Ahmed	10
11	SHAWKY Mohamed		85	EL TAIB Tareq	14
12	BARKAT Mohamed		65	KARA Nader	15
15	EL TABEI Besheer			HAMADI Osama	18
20	GOMAA Wael			BOUBAKR Abdul Salam	19
22	ABOUTRAIKA Mohamed	86		AL SHIBANI Younus	23
29	ABOU MOSLEM Ahmed	57		OSMAN Walid	26
	Tr: SHEHATA Hassan			Tr: El Seline Mohamed	
5	EL SAQUA Abdel	86	85	ABDUSADEQ Suleman	8
17	HASSAN Ahmed	73	65	REWANI Salem	20
28	ABDELMALK Ahmed	57	53	SUIUENEI Abubaker	22

11 June Stadium, Tripoli
3-06-2005, 19:00, 45 000, Lim Kee Chong MRI

LBY 0 0 CIV

#	LIBYA			COTE D'IVOIRE	#
12	ALEJANDRO Ruben			TIZIE Jean-Jacques	1
6	SULIMAN Marei			TOURE Abib	4
9	MASLI Ahmed Frag	88		ZOKORA Didier	5
14	OSMAN Ahmed	64	86	GUEL Tchiressoa	7
16	EL TAIB Tareq		72	KALOU Bonaventure	8
16	ABDUSSALAH Nader		78	DROGBA Didier	11
17	SAFTAR Mahmud			MEITE Abdoulaye	12
18	HAMADI Osama			ZORO Marc	13
19	BOUBAKR Abdul Salam			DINDANE Aruna	15
22	OSMAN Walid			DOMORAUD Cyrille	17
23	AL SHIBANI Younus			TIENE Siaka	18
	Tr: LONCAREVIC Ilija			Tr: MICHEL Henri	
15	KARA Nader	88	78	KONE Bakary	2
20	REWANI Salem	64	72	YAPI Gilles	10
			86	FAE Emerse	14

Stade de l'Amitié, Cotonou
4-06-2005, 16:00, 20 000, El Arjoun MAR

BEN 1 4 CMR

Agbessi 81
Song 19, Webo 51, Geremi 64
Etoo 69

#	BENIN			CAMEROON	#
1	TARDIEU Benoit			SOULEYMANOU Hamidou	16
2	CHITOU Charaf			WOME Pierre	3
3	OLOU Oscar			SONG Rigobert	4
5	MOUSSA Traore	61		SAIDOU Alioum	5
7	BOCO Romuald			ANGBWA Benoit	6
11	MAIGA Abou	87	80	GEREMI	8
12	AGBESSI Coffi		76	ETO'O Samuel	9
14	OSSENI Bachirou	73		DEUMI Armand	12
17	SESSEGNON Stephane		67	WEBO Achille	15
18	TCHOMOGO Seidah			DOUALA Rudolphe	18
19	AHOUEYA Jocelin			OLEMBE Salomon	20
	Tr: DEVEZE Serge			Tr: JORGE Artur	
6	RAIMY Florent	61	67	KOME Daniel	7
13	NASSIROU Youssouf	73	80	MAKOUN Jean	14
15	OMOTOYOSSI Razak	87	76	DJEMBA DJEMBA Eric	19

Arab Contractors Stadium, Cairo
5-06-2005, 21:00, 20 000, Mususa ZIM

EGY 6 1 SUD

Ali 2 8 31, Zaki 2 28 50
El Sayed 62, Abdelmalk 71
Tambal 83

#	EGYPT			SUDAN	#
1	EL SAYED Nader			MOHAMED Abu	1
8	ABD RABO Hosni			ELNAZIR Mahmoud	2
9	ZAKI Amr	55		ABDEL Amar	3
11	SHAWKY Mohamed		46	MOHAMED Ali	4
12	BARKAT Mohamed			HADO Alaa Eldin	5
13	EL SAYED Tarek			ALADIN Ahmed	7
15	EL TABEI Besheer		46	KARAR Haitham	8
17	HASSAN Ahmed	60		TAMBAL Haytham	10
20	GOMAA Wael		73	ABDALLA Bader	12
22	ABOUTRAIKA Mohamed			ALI Khalid	15
24	ALI Abel	75		AGAB SIDO Faisal	17
	Tr: SHEHATA Hassan			Tr: AHMED Mohamed	
10	ZIDAN Mohamed	60	46	LADO Richard	6
14	EMAM Hazem	75	73	IBRAHIM Ahmed	11
30	ABDELMALK Ahmed	55	46	SAEED James	16

Stade Omnisport, Yaoundé
19-06-2005, 15:30, 36 000, Coulibaly MLI

CMR 1 0 LBY

Webo 37

#	CAMEROON			LIBYA	#
16	SOULEYMANOU Hamidou			ALEJANDRO Ruben	12
3	WOME Pierre			SHASHAN Naji	3
4	SONG Rigobert		80	MASLI Ahmed Frag	9
6	ANGBWA Benoit		78	OSMAN Ahmed	10
8	GEREMI			EL TAIB Tareq	14
9	ETO'O Samuel			ABDUSSALAH Nader	16
12	SAIDOU Alioum			HAMADI Osama	18
14	SAIDOU Alioum			BOUBAKR Abdul Salam	19
15	WEBO Achille	90	80	REWANI Salem	20
18	DOUALA Rudolphe	83		OSMAN Walid	22
20	OLEMBE Salomon	88		AL SHIBANI Younus	23
	Tr: JORGE Artur			Tr: LONCAREVIC Ilija	
5	MAKOUN Jean	88	78	SULIMAN Marei	6
7	KOME Daniel	83	80	MOHAMED Khaled	8
19	DJEMBA DJEMBA Eric	90	80	KARA Nader	15

Stade Félix Houphouët-Boigny, Abidjan
19-06-2005, 16:00, 30 000, Damon RSA

CIV   2 0   EGY

Drogba 2 [41] [49]

COTE D'IVOIRE				EGYPT	
1	TIZIE Jean-Jacques			EL SAYED Nader	1
3	BOKA Etienne		71	EL-NAHHAS Emad	4
4	TOURE Abib		49	FATHI Ahmed	7
5	ZOKORA Didier			ABD RABO Hosni	8
7	GUEL Tchiressoa			SHAWKY Mohamed	11
8	KALOU Bonaventure	65		BARKAT Mohamed	12
11	DROGBA Didier	82		EL SAYED Tarek	13
13	ZORO Marc	60		EL TABEI Besheer	15
15	DINDANE Aruna			GOMAA Wael	20
17	DOMORAUD Cyrille			ABOUTRAIKA Mohamed	22
18	TIENE Siaka		55	ALI Abel	24
	Tr: MICHEL Henri			Tr: SHEHATA Hassan	
2	AKALE Kanga	65	49	HOSSAM MIDO Ahmed	9
12	MEITE Abdoulaye	60	55	ZAKI Amr	10
14	KONE Bakary	82	71	HASSAN Ahmed	17

SECOND PHASE GROUP 3	PL	W	D	L	F	A	PTS	CIV	CMR	EGY	LBY	BEN	SUD
1 Côte d'Ivoire	8	6	1	1	15	3	19			2-0	2-0	3-0	5-0
2 Cameroon	8	5	2	1	14	7	17	2-0		1-0	2-1	2-1
3 Egypt	8	4	1	3	21	13	13	1-2	3-2		4-1		6-1
4 Libya	8	3	2	3	8	9	11	0-0	0-0	2-1		4-1	
5 Benin	7	0	2	5	7	18	2	0-1	1-4	3-3			1-1
6 Sudan	7	0	2	5	4	19	2		1-1	0-3	0-1		

Table as of 16 August 2005. Remaining fixtures: 17-08-2005 Sudan v Benin; 2-09-2005 Egypt v Benin, Libya v Sudan, Côte d'Ivoire v Cameroon; 7-10-2005 Benin v Libya, Cameroon v Egypt, Sudan v Côte d'Ivoire

GROUP 4

Stade Omnisports, Libreville
5-06-2004, 16:00, 25 000, Quartey GHA

GAB   1 1   ZIM

Nzue [52]

Kaondera [82]

GABON				ZIMBABWE	
1	NGUEMA Bekale			MURAMBADORO Energy	1
2	AMBOUROUET Georges			MPOFU Dumisani	2
5	NZENG Guy		68	NYANDORO Esrom	3
7	NZUE Theodore			NDLOVU Bhekithemba	4
8	NZIGOU Shiva	65		KAPENYA Dezidewo	5
11	NGUEMA Stephane	65		MAKONESE Zvenyika	6
13	MBANANGOYE Zita			NENGOMASHA Tinashe	8
15	NSI AKOUE Rene			YOHANE Charles	11
18	MOUBAMBA Cedric	73	75	NDLOVU Peter	12
19	ISSIEMOU Thierry		60	NDLOVU Adam	13
21	MOUNDOUNGA Rodrigue			LUPAHLA Joel	17
	Tr: JAIRZINHO			Tr: GUMBO Allen	
10	LONDO Dieudonne	73	75	KAONDERA Shingayi	10
20	DO MARCOLINO Fabrice	65	60	SIBANDA Ronald	15
23	AKIEREMY Georges	65	68	CHORUMA Richard	18

National Stadium, Abuja
5-06-2004, 16:00, 35 000, Pare BFA

NGA   2 0   RWA

Martins 2 [55] [88]

NIGERIA				RWANDA	
1	ENYEAMA Vincent			NKUNZINGOMA Ramazan	18
2	YOBO Joseph			NDIKUMANA Hamadi	3
6	ENAKAHIRE Joseph			GASANA Philipe	4
7	UTAKA John			BIZAGWIRA Leandre	5
8	OBODO Chris		58	KAMANZI Michel	8
9	MARTINS Obafemi		54	GATETE Jean Michel	10
10	EKWUEME Ifeanyi			KAREKEZI Olivier	11
11	LAWAL Garba		77	NTAGANDA Elias	13
14	OLOFINJANA Seyi			SAID Abed	14
15	ABBEY George		79	KIZITO Manfred	15
18	OGBECHE Bartholomew		75	GASERUKA Alua	16
	Tr: CHUKWU Christian			Tr: DUJKOVIC Ratomir	
5	OLAJENGBESI Seyi	79	79	SIBOMANA Abdul	6
17	DOSUNMU Tosin	75	58	MULISA Jimmy	7
			54	LOMAMI John	17

Stade 19 Mai 1956, Annaba
5-06-2004, 19:00, 55 000, Daami TUN

ALG 0 0 ANG

ALGERIA				ANGOLA
1 BEN HAMOU Mohamed				JOAO Pereira 1
2 YAHIA Antar	23			JAMBA 3
3 BELHADJ Nadir				KALI 5
6 MANSOURI Yazid				YAMBA ASHA 6
7 CHERRAD Abdelmalek			89	FIGUEREDO 7
10 BELMADI Djamel	63			ANDRE 8
12 ARRACHE Salim				FREDDY 9
13 ZAFOUR Brahim				MAURITO 10
14 KERKAR Karim	46			PEREIRA Jacinto 15
15 ZIANI Karim			90	BRUNO MAURO 17
18 RAHO Slimane			58	LOVE 18
Tr: WASEIGE Robert				Tr: DE OLIVEIRA GONCALVES Luis
5 ARIBI Salim	23	58		FLAVIO 11
9 BADACHE Mohamed	46	89		RATS 13
17 ACHIOU Hocine	63	90		CHINHO 16

Stade Amahoro, Kigali
19-06-2004, 16:00, 16 325, Abdulkadir TAN

RWA 3 1 GAB

Said 2 4 64, Mulisa 27 — Zue 20

RWANDA				GABON
18 NKUNZINGOMA Ramazan				OVONO Didier 16
3 NDIKUMANA Hamadi				OKOGO Saturnin 3
6 SIBOMANA Abdul			78	NZENG Guy 5
7 MULISA Jimmy	86		46	BOUTAMBA-IBINGA Ulrich 6
9 MULENDA Abedi	46			ZUE Theodore 7
11 KAREKEZI Olivier			46	LONDO Dieudonne 10
13 NTAGANDA Elias				MBANANGOYE Zita 13
14 SAID Abed				NSI-AKOUE Rene 15
15 KIZITO Manfred				ISSIEMOU Thierry 17
16 GASERUKA Alua	46			MOUBAMBA Cedric 18
17 LOMAMI John				MOUNDOUNGA Rodrigue 23
Tr: DUJKOVIC Ratomir				Tr: JAIRZINHO
4 KAKULE Abdallah	86	46		MVE-MINTSA Claude-Cedric 4
5 BIZAGWIRA Leandre	46	78		TCHICAYA Thibaut 14
8 KAMANZI Michel	46	46		DO MARCOLINO Fabrice 20

National Stadium, Harare
20-06-2004, 15:00, 65 000, Ntambidila COD

ZIM 1 1 ALG

Raho OG 60 — Cherrad 3

ZIMBABWE				ALGERIA
16 KAPINI Tapuwa				BEN HAMOU Mohamed 1
2 MPOFU Dumisani				BELHADJ Nadir 3
4 NDLOVU Bhekithemba	70			YAHIA Antar 5
6 TEMBO Kaitano				MANSOURI Yazid 6
8 NENGOMASHA Tinashe				CHERRAD Abdelmalek 7
10 KAONDERA Shingayi	87			GHAZI Karim 8
11 YOHANE Charles		61		BEZZAZ Yacine 9
12 NDLOVU Peter				BOUGHERRA Majid 12
14 DICKSON Ghoto	35	43		ZIANI Karim 15
5 SIBANDA Ronald		75		ACHIOU Hocine 17
18 LUPAHLA Joel				RAHO Slimane 18
Tr: GUMBO Allen				Tr: WASEIGE Robert
3 NYANDORO Esrom	35	43		BRAHMI Mohamed Fadhil 4
9 KATHANA Newton	70	61		BELMADI Djamel 10
13 NDLOVU Adam	87	75		DAOUD Boabdellah 19

Cidadela, Luanda
20-06-2004, 15:30, 40 000, Nkole ZAM

ANG 1 0 NGA

Akwa 84

ANGOLA				NIGERIA
1 JOAO Pereira				ENYEAMA Vincent 1
2 PEREIRA Jacinto				YOBO Joseph 2
3 JAMBA				OBIEFULE Paul 4
5 KALI				ENAKAHIRE Joseph 6
6 YAMBA ASHA				UTAKA John 7
7 FIGUEREDO	54	88		ALIYU Mohammed 8
8 ANDRE		81		EKWUEME Ifeanyi 10
9 FREDDY				LAWAL Garba 11
10 AKWA				OLOFINJANA Seyi 14
15 MAURITO	61			ABBEY George 15
17 BRUNO MAURO	74		16	BAITA Rabiu 16
Tr: DE OLIVEIRA GONCALVES Luis				Tr: CHUKWU Christian
11 GILBERTO	54	88		OLAJENGBESI Seyi 5
14 ZE KALANGA	74	81		AKARUYE Robert 9
18 LOVE	61	63		WAHAB Adewale 18

Stade Amahoro, Kigali
3-07-2004, 16:00, Chilinda MWI

RWA 0 2 ZIM

Ndlovu.P 41, Nengomasha 79

RWANDA				ZIMBABWE
18 NKUNZINGOMA Ramazan				KAPINI Tapuwa 19
2 SIBOMANA Abdul				MPOFU Dumisani 2
3 NDIKUMANA Hamadi				NYANDORO Esrom 3
4 GASANA Philipe				NDLOVU Bhekithemba 4
7 MULISA Jimmy	75			MAKONESE Zvenyika 5
8 KAMANZI Michel	46			NENGOMASHA Tinashe 8
9 ELIAS Joao Rafael		58		KATHANA Newton 9
11 KAREKEZI Olivier				NDLOVU Peter 12
13 NTAGANDA Elias				KASINAUYO Edzai 14
15 KIZITO Manfred				SHERENI Harlington 17
17 LOMAMI John				LUPAHLA Joel 18
Tr: HIGIRO Thomas				Tr: GUMBO Allen
12 MUNYANEZA Henri	46	58		MGUNI Musa 10
14 MULENDA Abedi	75			

Stade Omnisports, Libreville
3-07-2004, 16:00, 20 000, Louzaya CGO

GAB 2 2 ANG

Issiemou 44, Zue 49 — Akwa 19, Marco Paulo 81

GABON				ANGOLA
16 OVONO Didier				JOAO Pereira 1
2 AMBOUROUET Georges				PEREIRA Jacinto 2
5 NZENG Guy	72			JAMBA 3
7 ZUE Theodore				KALI 5
8 AKIEREMY Georges				YAMBA ASHA 6
13 MBANANGOYE Zita	82	55		FIGUEREDO 7
15 NSI-AKOUE Rene				ANDRE 8
17 ISSIEMOU Thierry	55			FREDDY 9
18 MOUBAMBA Cedric				AKWA 10
21 MOUSSAVOU-MAPAGHA	57			GILBERTO 11
24 MOUNDOUNGA Rodrigue	79			MAURITO 15
Tr: JAIRZINHO				Tr: DE OLIVEIRA GONCALVES Luis
3 AKOUASSAGA Ernest	72	55		ZE KALANGA 14
6 BOUTAMBA-IBINGA Ulrich	82	79		MARCO PAULO 16
14 TCHICAYA Thibaut	57	55		LOVE 18

National Stadium, Abuja
3-07-2004, 16:00, 35 000, Hisseine CHA

NGA	1	0	ALG

Yobo [84]

NIGERIA			ALGERIA
1 ENYEAMA Vincent			BEN HAMOU Mohamed 1
2 YOBO Joseph		81	BOUGHERRA Majid 2
3 UDEZE Ifeanyi	71		BELHADJ Nadir 3
6 ENAKAHIRE Joseph			BRAHAMI Mohamed Fadhil 4
7 UTAKA John	90		GHAZI Karim 8
8 AIYEGBENI Yakubu			BOUTABOUT Mansour 11
9 MARTINS Obafemi	79		ARRACHE Salim 12
10 OKOCHA Jay Jay		79	ZIANI Karim 15
11 LAWAL Garba			ACHIOU Hocine 17
14 OLAJENGBESI Seyi		62	MAMOUNI Maamar 19
15 ABBEY George			YAHIA Antar 21
Tr: CHUKWU Christian			Tr: WASEIGE Robert
17 AGHAHOWA Julius	79	81	ZEGHDOUD Mounir 5
19 EKWUEME Ifeanyi	71	62	BELKAID Farouk 6
20 ODEMWINGIE Peter	90	79	KERKER Karim 14

National Stadium, Harare
5-09-2004, 15:00, 60 000, Mandzioukouta CGO

ZIM	0	3	NGA

Aghahowa [3], Enakahire [28], Aiyegbeni [48p]

ZIMBABWE			NIGERIA
16 KAPINI Tapuwa			ENYEAMA Vincent 1
2 MPOFU Dumisani			ODIAH Chidi 2
3 NYANDORO Esrom			NWANERI Obinna 4
4 NDLOVU Bhekithemba			ENAKAHIRE Joseph 6
5 MAKONESE Zvenyika		69	UTAKA John 7
7 KASINAUYO Edzai	58	77	AIYEGBENI Yakubu 8
8 NENGOMASHA Tinashe			OKOCHA Jay Jay 10
9 MWARUWARI Benjamin			LAWAL Garba 11
12 NDLOVU Peter	75		OLAJENGBESI Seyi 14
17 SHERENI Harlington	71		AGHAHOWA Julius 17
18 LUPAHLA Joel		60	EKWUEME Ifeanyi 19
Tr: GUMBO Allen			Tr: CHUKWU Christian
10 KAONDERA Shingayi	75	60	OBODO Chris 16
11 YOHANE Charles	71	77	OGBECHE Bartholomew 18
15 SIBANDA Ronald	58	69	ODENWIGIE Osaze 20

Cidadela, Luanda
5-09-2004, 15:30, 30 000, Damon RSA

ANG	1	0	RWA

Freddy [52]

ANGOLA			RWANDA
1 JOAO Pereira			NKUNZINGOMA Ramazan 18
3 JAMBA		69	NDIKUMANA Hamadi 3
5 KALI			BIZAGWIRA Leandre 4
6 YAMBA ASHA			GASANA Philipe 5
7 FIGUEREDO	53	88	SIBOMANA Abdul 8
8 ANDRE			UJENEZA Robert 9
9 FREDDY	93		KAREKEZI Olivier 11
10 MAURITO	66	56	UWIMANA Abdoul 12
11 GILBERTO			NTAGANDA Elias 13
15 MANUEL			SAID Abedi 14
16 FLAVIO			GASERUKA Alua 16
Tr: DE OLIVEIRA GONCALVES Luis			Tr: PALMGREN Roger
13 SIMAO	93	69	MULISA Jimmy 7
14 ZE KALANGA	53	88	GATETE Jean Michel 10
18 LOVE	66	56	KIZITO Manfred 15

Stade 19 Mai 1956, Annaba
5-09-2004, 20:15, 51 000, Ndoye SEN

ALG	0	3	GAB

Aubame [56], Akieremy [73], Bito'o [84]

ALGERIA			GABON
1 BEN HAMOU Mohamed			OVONO Didier 16
3 BELHADJ Nadir		85	AMBOUROUET Georges 2
4 BELOUFA Samir			NZENG Guy 5
6 MANSOURI Yazid	46		MOUYOUMA Dieudonne 6
7 CHERRAD Abdelmalek		79	AKIEREMY Georges 8
10 SAIFI Rafik			BITO'O Etienne 11
12 ARRACHE Salim	57	59	AUBAME Catilina 13
17 ACHIOU Hocine			KESSANY Paul 14
19 RAHO Slimane	79		NSI-AKOUE Rene 15
19 MAMOUNI Maamar			ISSIEMOU Thierry 17
21 YAHIA Antar			MOUBAMBA Cedric 18
Tr: WASEIGE Robert			Tr: JAIRZINHO
8 GHAZI Karim	46	85	MBOUSSY Waldi 3
9 DAOUD Boabdellah	57	79	OTTOMO Juste 4
13 BOUGUECHE Hadj	79	59	MVE-MINTSA Claude-Cedric 12

Stade Amahoro, Kigali
9-10-2004, 16:00, 20 000, Abdel Rahman SUD

RWA	1	1	ALG

Said [9]

Bourahli [14]

RWANDA			ALGERIA
18 NKUNZINGOMA Ramazani	45		BEN HAMOU Mohamed 1
2 UJENEZA Robert			BELHADJ Nadir 3
3 GASERUKA Alua			BELOUFA Samir 4
5 GASANA Philipe		70	MANSOURI Yazid 6
7 MULISA Jimmy			BRAHAMI Mohamed Fadhil 7
10 GATETE Jean Michel	65		BILAL Dziri 8
11 KAREKEZI Olivier			BOURAHLI Issaad 9
14 SAID Abedi		75	SAIFI Rafik 10
16 BITANA Remy		88	ARRACHE Salim 12
17 KALISA Claude			MAMOUNI Maamar 19
MANAMA Raphael			YAHIA Antar 21
Tr: PALMGREN Roger			Tr: FERGANI Ali
1 BIGIRIMANA Jean	45	88	BOUTABOUT Mansour 11
6 LOMAMI John	65	75	ZAFOUR Brahim 13
		70	ACHIOU Hocine 17

Stade Omnisports, Libreville
9-10-2004, 16:30, 26 000, Yameogo BFA

GAB	1	1	NGA

Issiemou [29]

Aiyegbeni [50]

GABON			NIGERIA
16 OVONO Didier			ENYEAMA Vincent 1
2 AMBOUROUET Georges	84		YOBO Joseph 2
5 NZENG Guy			UDEZE Ifeanyi 3
6 MOUYOUMA Thierry		73	KANU Nwankwo 4
11 BITO'O Etienne			ENAKAHIRE Joseph 6
12 AUBAME Catilina	64	85	UCHE Kalu 7
14 KESSANY Paul			AIYEGBENI Yakubu 8
15 NSI-AKOUE Rene		59	EKWUEME Ifeanyi 11
17 ANTCHOUET Henri	67		OLOFINJANA Seyi 14
18 MOUBAMBA Cedric			ODIAH Chidi 15
21 ISSIEMOU Thierry			OBODO Chris 16
Tr: JAIRZINHO			Tr: CHUKWU Christian
7 ZUE Theodore	64	73	OGBECHE Bartholomew 9
9 MOUNDOUNGA Rodrigue	84	85	KAKU Blessing 13
20 DO MARCOLINO Fabrice	67	59	ODEMWINGIE Peter 18

Cidadela, Luanda
10-10-2004, 15:30, 17 000, Lwanja MWI

ANG 1 0 ZIM

Flavio 53

ANGOLA				ZIMBABWE		
1	JOAO PEREIRA			MURAMBADORO Energy		1
2	PEREIRA Jacinto			MPOFU Dumisani		2
3	JAMBA			NYANDORO Esrom		3
5	LELO LELO			MAKONESE Zvenyika		5
6	YAMBA ASHA		78	NENGOMASHA Tinashe		8
7	MAURITO	65		SENGU David		10
8	ANDRE			YOHANE Charles		11
9	FREDDY	82		NDLOVU Peter		12
10	AKWA		88	CHIMEDZA Cephas		13
11	GILBERTO			TSIPA Leonard		17
16	FLAVIO	70		LUPAHLA Joel		18
Tr: DE OLIVEIRA GONCALVES Luis				Tr: MHLAURI Charles		
13	MATEUS	82	78	GOMBAMI Honour		7
14	ZE KALANGA	65	63	BADZA Brian		9
17	MARCO PAULO	70	88	KASINAUYO Edzai		19

Liberation Stadium, Port Harcourt
26-03-2005, 19:00, 16 489, Hicuburundi BDI

NGA 2 0 GAB

Aghahowa 79, Kanu 81

NIGERIA				GABON		
1	ENYEAMA Vincent			OVONO Didier		1
2	YOBO Joseph			AMBOUROUET Georges		2
3	UDEZE Ifeanyi		68	NZIGOU Shiva		4
5	ODIAH Chidi			NZENG Guy		5
7	UTAKA John	70		MOUYOUMA Thierry		6
9	MARTINS Obafemi	77		MOUNDOUNGA Rodrigue		9
10	OKOCHA Jay Jay		84	NGUEMA-BEKALE Claude		10
11	LAWAL Garba	89	55	LONDO Dieudonne		11
14	OLOFINJANA Seyi			MBANANGOYE Zita		13
17	AGHAHOWA Julius			NSI-AKOUE Rene		15
21	NWANERI Obinna			MOUBAMBA Cedric		18
Tr: CHUKWU Christian				Tr: JAIRZINHO		
4	KANU Nwankwo	77	55	ZUE Theodore		7
8	AIYEGBENI Yakubu	70	68	AUBAME Catilina		12
13	ATANDA Yusuf	89	84	MOULOUNGUI Eric		17

National Stadium, Harare
27-03-2005, 15:00, Codjia BEN

ZIM 2 0 ANG

Kaondera 60, Mwaruwari 69

ZIMBABWE				ANGOLA		
1	MURAMBADORO Energy			JOAO PEREIRA		1
2	MPOFU Dumisani			JACINTO		2
3	NYANDORO Esrom			JAMBA		3
5	DINHA Edelbert	54		KALI		5
6	MAKONESE Zvenyika			YAMBA ASHA		6
9	MWARUWARI Benjamin			MACANGA Andre		8
11	YOHANE Charles		57	FREDDY		9
12	NDLOVU Peter		64	MAURITO		10
15	SIBANDA Ronald	62		GILBERTO		11
17	KASINAUYO Edzai	46		FLAVIO		16
18	LUPAHLA Joel		64	MARCO PAULO		17
Tr: MHLAURI Charles				Tr: DE OLIVEIRA GONCALVES Luis		
8	NENGOMASHA Tinashe	54	64	CHINHO		7
10	KAONDERA Shingayi	46	57	ZE KALANGA		14
13	CHIMEDZA Cephas	62	64	LOVE		18

Stade Ahmed Zabana, Oran
27-03-2005, 19:00, 20 000, Abd El Fatah EGY

ALG 1 0 RWA

Boutabout 48

ALGERIA				RWANDA		
1	MEZAIR Hicham			NKUNZINGOMA Ramazani		18
2	BOUGHERRA Madjid			NDIKUMANA Hamadi		3
3	BELHADJ Nadir			GASANA Philipe		5
4	BELOUFA Samir			KIZITO Manfred		6
6	MANSOURI Yazid			HABIMANA Dany		7
8	DZIRI Billal		79	ELIAS Joao Rafael		9
10	SAIFI Rafik	76		KABONGO Honore		10
11	BOUTABOUT Mansour	82		KAREKEZI Olivier		11
12	ARRACHE Salim	46	88	SAID Abedi		14
15	ZIANI Karim			MBONABUCYA Desire		15
18	RAHO Slimane			GASERUKA Alua		16
Tr: FERGANI Ali				Tr: PALMGREN Roger		
13	ZAFOUR Brahim	82	88	MUNYANEZA Henri		12
17	ACHIOU Hocine	76	79	LOMAMI John		17
19	DAOUD Sofiane	46				

National Stadium, Harare
5-06-2005, 15:00, 55 000, Ssegonga UGA

ZIM 1 0 GAB

Ndlovu 52

ZIMBABWE				GABON		
1	MURAMBADORO Energy			OVONO Didier		1
2	MPOFU Dumisani			AMBOUROUET Georges		2
3	NYANDORO Esrom			MOUNDOUNGA Rodrigue		3
5	DINHA Edelbert		89	NZIGOU Shiva		4
6	MATOLA James			NZENG Guy		5
7	MOYO Zenzo	59		MOUYOUMA Dieudonne		6
8	NENGOMASHA Tinashe			NGUEMA Stephane		10
10	KAONDERA Shingayi	80	82	LONDO Dieudonne		12
11	YOHANE Charles	61	82	MBANANGOYE Zita		13
12	NDLOVU Peter			NSI-AKOUE Rene		15
18	LUPAHLA Joel			MOUBAMBA Cedric		18
Tr: MHLAURI Charles:				Tr: JAIRZINHO		
9	BADZA Brian	80	82	AKIEREMY George		9
13	CHIMEDZA Cephas	61	89	MOUSSAVOU-MAPAGHA		14
17	MASHIRI Edmore	59	82	MASHIRI Edmore		17

Cidadela, Luanda
5-06-2005, 15:30, 27 000, Hicuburundi BDI

ANG 2 1 ALG

Flavio 50, Akwa 58

Boutabout 63

ANGOLA				ALGERIA		
1	JOAO PEREIRA			MEZAIR Hicham		1
3	JAMBA			ZAZOU Samir		2
5	KALI			BOUGHERRA Madjid		4
6	YAMBA ASHA		79	DISS Smaine		5
7	FIGUEIREDO	77		MANSOURI Yazid		6
8	MACANGA Andre		70	DZIRI Billal		8
10	AKWA			BOUTABOUT Mansour		11
11	GILBERTO	60		BRAHAMI Mohamed Fadhil		14
13	LOCO		58	ZIANI Karim		15
14	MENDONCA			YACEF Hanza		19
16	FLAVIO	71		YAHIA Antar		21
Tr: DE OLIVEIRA GONCALVES Luis				Tr: FERGANI Ali		
9	MANTORRAS	71	79	DAOUD Sofiane		10
17	ZE KALANGA	60	58	ACHIOU Hocine		17
18	PAULO	77	70	KRAOUCHE Nasreddine		18

Stade Amahoro, Kigali
5-06-2005, 16:00, 30 000, Kidane ERI

RWA	1	1	NGA

Gatete [53]

Martins [78]

RWANDA			NIGERIA	
18 NKUNZINGOMA Ramazani			ENYEAMA Vincent	1
2 UJENEZA Robert			YOBO Joseph	2
3 NDIKUMANA Hamadi			UDEZE Ifeanyi	3
6 FRITZ Emeran		61	KANU Nwankwo	4
8 SIBOMANA Abdul			ODIAH Chidi	5
9 ELIAS Joao Rafael	65	79	OBIEFULE Paul	6
10 GATETE Jean Michel			MARTINS Obafemi	9
11 KAREKEZI Olivier			LAWAL Garba	11
13 NTAGANDA Elias			EJIDE Austin	12
14 SAID Abedi	88		SHITTU Dlusola	13
16 KABONGO Honore	82		ABBEY George	15
Tr: PALMGREN Roger			Tr: CHUKWU Christian	
5 BULANGA Alafu	82	79	AMUNEKE Onyekachi	16
7 MULISA Jimmy	65	61	AYODELE Makinwa	19
17 LOMAMI John	88			

Omnisports President Omar Bongo, Libreville
18-06-2005, 15:30, 10 000, El Arjoun MAR

GAB	3	0	RWA

Djissikadie [10], Londo [55]
Zue [60]

GABON			RWANDA	
1 OVONO Didier			NKUNZINGOMA Ramadhani	18
2 AMBOUROUET Georges			NDIKUMANA Hamadi	3
3 MOUNDOUNGA Rodrigue	77	40	BULANGA Alafu	4
5 NZENG Guy			GASANA Philipe	5
7 ZUE Theodore			FRITZ Emeran	6
10 DJISSIKADIE Alain	60		SIBOMANA Abdul	8
12 LONDO Dieudonne			GATETE Jean Michel	10
13 MBANANGOYE Zita			KAREKEZI Olivier	11
15 NSI-AKOUE Rene			NTAGANDA Elias	13
18 MOUBAMBA Cedric		63	SAID Abedi	14
20 DO MARCOLINO Fabrice	51	70	KABONGO Honore	16
Tr: JAIRZINHO			Tr: PALMGREN Roger	
8 MBOUSSY Waldi	60	40	BIGIRIMANA Jean	1
11 EDOU Djimiri	51	70	MULISA Jimmy	7
26 MOUYOUMA Thierry	77	63	LOMAMI John	17

Sani Abacha, Kano
18-06-2005, 16:00, 17 000, Abd El Fatah EGY

NGA	1	1	ANG

Okocha [5]

Figueiredo [60]

NIGERIA			ANGOLA	
1 ENYEAMA Vincent			JOAO PEREIRA	1
2 YOBO Joseph			JACINTO	2
3 UDEZE Ifeanyi	59		JAMBA	3
5 ODIAH Chidi			KALI	5
8 AIYEGBENI Yakubu	75		YAMBA ASHA	6
10 OKOCHA Jay Jay		71	FIGUEIREDO	7
11 LAWAL Garba		85	JOAQUIN	8
14 OLOFINJANA Seyi			AKWA	10
19 AYODELE Makinwa	54		GILBERTO	11
20 ODEMWINGIE Peter			MENDONCA	14
21 NWANERI Obinna		54	FLAVIO	16
Tr: CHUKWU Christian			Tr: DE OLIVEIRA GONCALVES Luis	
4 KANU Nwankwo	54	71	FREDDY	9
17 AMUNEKE Onyekachi	59	85	LOCO	13
18 OBODO Chris	75	54	MAURITO	15

Stade Ahmed Zabana, Oran
19-06-2005, 20:30, 15 000, Pare Lassina BFA

ALG	2	2	ZIM

Yahia [17], Daoud [48]
Kaondera [33], Ndlovu [87]

ALGERIA			ZIMBABWE	
1 MEZAIR Hicham			KAPINI Tapuwa	20
3 BELHADJ Nadir			MPOFU Dumisani	2
5 DISS Smaine			NYANDORO Esrom	3
6 MANSOURI Yazid			MAKONESE Zvenyika	6
7 YACEF Hanza	69		MWARUWARI Beniamin	9
11 BOUTABOUT Mansour	46	46	KAONDERA Shingayi	10
15 ZIANI Karim		62	YOHANE Charles	11
17 ACHIOU Hocine	85		NDLOVU Peter	12
21 YAHIA Antar			MBWANDO George	14
23 KRAOUCHE Nasreddine			SIBANDA Ronald	15
24 HAMDOUD Mohamed		86	LUPAHLA Joel	18
Tr: FERGANI Ali			Tr: MHLAURI Charles	
8 DZIRI Billal	85	86	MASHIRI Edmore	7
10 DAOUD Sofiane	46	46	CHIMEDZA Cephas	13
18 RAHO Slimane	69	62	BADZA Brian	17

SECOND PHASE GROUP 4

		PL	W	D	L	F	A	PTS	ANG	NGA	ZIM	GAB	ALG	RWA
1	Angola	8	4	3	1	8	6	15		1-0	1-0		2-1	1-0
2	Nigeria	8	4	3	1	11	4	15	1-1			2-0	1-0	2-0
3	Zimbabwe	8	3	3	2	9	8	12	2-0	0-3		1-0	1-1	
4	Gabon	8	2	3	3	11	10	9	2-2	1-1	1-1			3-0
5	Algeria	8	1	4	3	6	10	7	0-0		2-2	0-3		1-0
6	Rwanda	8	1	2	5	5	12	5		1-1	0-2	3-1	1-1	

Table as of 1 September 2005. Remaining fixtures: 2-09-2005 Zimbabwe v Rwanda, Angola v Gabon, Algeria v Nigeria; 7-10-2005 Nigeria v Zimbabwe, Rwanda v Angola, Gabon v Algeria

SECOND PHASE GROUP 5

		PL	W	D	L	F	A	PTS	MAR	TUN	GUI	KEN	BOT	MWI
1	Morocco	8	4	4	0	14	5	16		1-1	1-0	5-1		4-1
2	Tunisia	7	4	2	1	20	7	14			2-0		4-1	7-0
3	Guinea	8	3	2	3	10	8	11	1-1	2-1		1-0	4-0	
4	Kenya	7	3	1	3	8	11	10	0-0		2-1		1-0	3-2
5	Botswana	8	3	0	5	9	15	9	0-1	1-3		2-1		2-0
6	Malawi	8	0	3	5	8	23	3	1-1	2-2	1-1		1-3	

Table as of 16 August 2005. Remaining fixtures: 17-08-2005 Tunisia v Kenya; 2-09-2005 Morocco v Botswana, Guinea v Malawi, Kenya v Tunisia; 7-10-2005 Tunisia v Morocco, Botswana v Guinea, Malawi v Kenya

GROUP 5

Chichiri, Blantyre
5-06-2004, 15:00, 30 040, Mususa ZIM

MWI	1	1	MAR

Munthali [35]   Safri [25]

MALAWI			MOROCCO	
16	NYASULU Phillip			FOUHAMI Khalid	1
2	KONDOWE Fisher			REGRAGUI Hoalid	2
4	CHILAPONOWA James			KACEMI Noureddine	3
5	MABEDI Patrick			OUADDOU Abdeslem	4
6	KAMANGA Allan			EL KARKOURI Talal	5
7	MPONDA Peter			KISSI Abdelkrim	8
8	KAMWENDO Joseph	46	EL YAAGOUBI Mohammed	11
11	KANYENDA Essau	75		SAFRI Youssef	15
13	MWAKASUNGULA Hellings	80		CHAMARH Marouane	17
14	MWAFULIRWA Russel	23	63	FAHMI Abdelilah	18
15	MSOWOYA Maupo			HADJI Youssef	20
	Tr: KAPUTA John			Tr: BADOU Zaki	
12	ZAKAZAKA Jimmy	80	75	KHARJA Houssine	13
18	MUNTHALI Heston	23	46	MOKHTARI Youssef	16
			63	CHIHAB Tariq	21

National Stadium, Gaborone
19-06-2004, 15:00, 15 000, Awuye UGA

BOT	2	0	MWI

Selolwane [7], Gabolwelwe [25]

BOTSWANA			MALAWI	
16	MARUMO Modiri		76	SANUDI Swadic	1
2	LETSHOLATHEBE Ndiapo			KONDOWE Fisher	2
4	MOGALADI Michael			CHILAPONOWA James	4
5	NTSHINGANE Masego	67		MABEDI Patrick	5
6	GABOLWELWE Nelson			KAMANGA Allan	6
8	MOTLHABANKWE Tshepo			MPONDA Peter	7
11	SELOLWANE Diphetogo			KAMWENDO Joseph	9
12	MOLWANTWA Tshepiso	76	54	MWAKASUNGULA Hellings	13
14	AMOS Ernest		35	MWAFULIRWA Russel	14
17	KOLAGANO Pius			MSOWOYA Maupo	17
18	GABONAMONG Mogogi			MUNTHALI Heston	18
	Tr: JELUSIC Veselin			Tr: KAPUTA John	
13	BOLELENG Malepa	67	35	ZAKAZAKA Jimmy	12
15	MOLOI Pontsho	76	54	NUNDWE Itay	15
			76	NYASULU Phillip	16

National Stadium, Gaborone
3-07-2004, 15:00, 22 000, Dlamini SWZ

BOT	0	1	MAR

Mokhtari [30]

BOTSWANA			MOROCCO	
1	TSHELAMETSI Kagiso			LAMYAGHRI Nadir	12
2	LETSHOLATHEBE Ndiapo			REGRAGUI Hoalid	2
4	MOGALADI Michael			KACEMI Noureddine	3
5	NTSHINGANE Masego	59		OUADDOU Abdeslem	4
6	GABOLWELWE Nelson	77		EL KARKOURI Talal	5
7	KGOPOLELO Duncan	59		KISSI Abdelkrim	8
8	MOTLHABANKWE Tshepo		66	BHAH Nabil	9
11	SELOLWANE Diphetogo			KHARJA Houssine	13
14	AMOS Ernest		88	MOKHTARI Youssef	16
17	KOLAGANO Pius		77	HADJI Youssef	20
18	GABONAMONG Mogogi			CHIHAB Tariq	21
	Tr: JELUSIC Veselin			Tr: BADOU Zaki	
12	MOLWANTWA Tshepiso	59	88	AHNAFOUF Abdelaziz	7
13	BOLELENG Malepa	59	77	EL YAAGOUBI Mohammed	11
15	MOLOI Pontsho	77	66	CHAMARH Marouane	17

Stade 7 Novembre, Tunis
5-06-2004, 19:15, 2 844, Abdel Rahman SUD

TUN	4	1	BOT

Ribabro [9], Hagui 2 [35 79],   Selolwane [65]
Zitouni [74]

TUNISIA			BOTSWANA	
16	FADHEL Khaled			MARUMO Modiri	16
2	BADRA Khaled			LETSHOLATHEBE Ndiapo	2
3	HAGUI Karim		63	MOTLHABANE Khumo	3
8	NAFTI Mehdi	64		MOTHUSI Tebogo	5
9	BRAHAM Najeh	61	83	GABOLWELWE Nelson	6
12	MNARI Jaohar		87	MOTLHABANKWE Tshepo	8
14	CHEDLI Adel			KGOSIANG Kabelo	9
15	JAIDI Radhi			SELOLWANE Diphetogo	11
17	JEDIDI Mohamed			AMOS Ernest	14
18	BENACHOUR Slim	85		KOLAGANO Pius	17
20	RIBABRO Jose			GABONAMONG Mogogi	18
	Tr: LEMERRE Roger			Tr: JELUSIC Veselin	
6	ESSEDIRI Karim	85	83	MOLOI Pontsho	7
11	ZITOUNI Ali	61	87	MOATIHARING Moemedi	10
21	SGHAIER Wajih	64	63	MOLWANTWA Tshepiso	12

Stade du 28 septembre, Conakry
20-06-2004, 16:30, 15 300, Codjia BEN

GUI	2	1	TUN

Kaba 2 [12 46]   Braham [67]

GUINEA			TUNISIA	
16	CAMARA Kemoko			BOUMNIJEL Ali	1
2	FEINDOUNO Pascal			BADRA Khaled	2
3	SOW Abdoul			HAGUI Karim	3
5	BALDE Dianbobo			YAHIA Alaeddine	4
7	MANSARE Fode		75	BRAHAM Najeh	9
8	SYLLA Kanfory			ZITOUNI Ali	11
10	SYLLA Abdoulkarim	72		MNARI Jawhar	12
12	CISSE Morlaye	64	58	BOUAZIZI Riadh	13
14	CAMARA Ousmane			CHEDLI Adel	14
17	DIALLO Mamadou			JAIDI Radhi	15
19	KABA Diawara	64	80	BENACHOUR Slim	18
	Tr: NEVEU Patrice			Tr: LEMERRE Roger	
6	KEITA Alseny	64	58	ESSEDIRI Karim	6
11	YOULA Souleymane	64	75	JEDIDI Mohamed	17
13	CISSE Mohamed	72	80	SGHAIER Wajih	23

Civo, Lilongwe
3-07-2004, 15:00, 11 383, Abdulkadir TAN

MWI	1	1	GUI

Mpinganjira [71]   Kaba [80]

MALAWI			GUINEA	
16	NYASULU Phillip			CAMARA Kemoko	16
2	KONDOWE Fisher	88		SOW Abdoul	3
5	MABEDI Patrick			BALDE Dianbobo	5
6	KAMANGA Allan		86	MANSARE Fode	7
7	MPONDA Peter			SYLLA Kanfory	8
11	KANYENDA Essau		72	SYLLA Abdoulkarim	10
12	MKANDAWIRE Noel	63		YOULA Souleymane	11
13	MWAKASUNGULA Hellings			CISSE Morlaye	12
14	CHIPATALA Emmanuel	23		CAMARA Ousmane	14
17	MSOWOYA Maupo			DIALLO Mamadou	17
18	MUNTHALI Heston			KABA Diawara	19
	Tr: KAPUTA John			Tr: NEVEU Patrice	
4	CHILAPONOWA James	88	72	BANGOURA Ousmane	18
9	KAMWENDO Joseph	23	86	CISSE Mohamed	20
10	MPINGANJIRA Albert	63			

Moi International, Nairobi
4-09-2004, 16:00, 13 000, Mwanza ZAM

KEN   3   2   MWI

Barasa 2 [21] [29], Oliech [25]   Munthali [41], Mabedi [90p]

	KENYA				MALAWI	
1	OCHIENG Duncan		30	NYASULU Phillip	16
4	OTIENO Musa			MSOWOYA Maupo	3
5	JUMA Tom			MABEDI Patrick	5
6	SHABAN Adan			KAMANGA Allan	6
7	MULAMA Titus			MPONDA Peter	7
11	BARASA John	85	43	MWAKASUNGULA Hellings	9
14	OYOMBE Andrew			MADUKA John	10
15	OPIYO Philip			KANYENDA Essau	11
17	MAMBO Robert	62		CHIPATALA Emmanuel	13
18	OLIECH Dennis		61	MKANDAWIRE Malumbo	17
19	AKE Emmanuel	78		MUNTHALI Heston	18
	Tr: MULEE Jacob			Tr: KAPUTA John	
10	SIRENGO Mark	62	30	SANUDI Swadic	1
13	MARIAGA Macdonald	78	43	CHILAPONOWA James	4
16	OMONDI James	85	61	MPINGANJIRA Albert	12

Prince Moulay Abdellah, Rabat
4-09-2004, 19:30, 45 000, Auda EGY

MAR   1   1   TUN

El Karkouri [74]   Santos [11]

	MOROCCO				TUNISIA	
22	LAMYAGHRI Nadir			BOUMNIJEL Ali	1
3	EL KADDOURI Badr	53		BADRA Khaled	2
4	OUADDOU Abdeslem			HAGUI Karim	3
5	EL KARKOURI Talal		77	JAZIRI Ziad	5
6	NAYBET Noureddine			NAFTI Mehdi	8
7	ZAIRI Jaouad		94	SANTOS	11
8	KISSI Abdelkrim	69		MNARI Jawhar	12
10	HDIOUAD Mourad			BOUAZIZI Riadh	13
13	KHARJA Houssine		86	CHEDLI Adel	14
16	MOKHTARI Youssef	85		JAIDI Radhi	15
17	CHAMARH Marouane		75	CLAYTON	20
	Tr: BADOU Zaki			Tr: LEMERRE Roger	
11	EL YAAGOUBI Mohammed	53	86	TRAOUI Majdi	7
14	AHNAFOUF Abdelaziz	85	94	GHODHBANE Kaies	10
20	HADJI Youssef	69	77	AYARI Anis	19

Stade du 28 septembre, Conakry
5-09-2004, 16:30, 25 000, Agbenyega Agbeko GHA

GUI   4   0   BOT

Feindouno [44], Youla [54], Kaba [60], Mansare [82]

	GUINEA				BOTSWANA	
16	CAMARA Kemoko			MARUMO Modiri	16
2	FEINDOUNO Pascal			LETSHOLATHEBE Ndiapo	2
3	SOW Abdoul			MOTLHABANE Khumo	3
4	JABI Daouda			MOGALADI Michael	4
5	BALDE Dianbobo		64	GABOLWELWE Nelson	6
6	MANSARE Fode	82		KGOPOLELO Duncan	7
8	SYLLA Kanfory			SELOLWANE Diphetogo	11
11	YOULA Souleymane	61	51	NYATHI Talinda	13
17	DIALLO Mamadou			AMOS Ernest	14
18	BAH Schuman	39	76	MOATLHAPING Moemedi	17
19	KABA Diawara			GABONAMONG Mogogi	18
	Tr: NEVEU Patrice			Tr: JELUSIC Veselin	
6	SYLLA Mohamed	61	64	MOTLHABANKWE Tshepo	8
14	CAMARA Ousmane	39	51	BUTALE Phazha	10
15	BANGOURA Pathe	82	76	MOLOI Pontsho	15

Chichiri, Blantyre
9-10-2004, 15:00, 20 000, Awuye UGA

MWI   2   2   TUN

Mwafulirwa [19], Chipatala [37]   Jaziri [82], Ghodhbane [89]

	MALAWI				TUNISIA	
1	SANUDI Swadic			FADHEL Khaled	16
2	KONDOWE Fisher		46	BADRA Khaled	2
3	MSOWOYA Maupo			YAHIA Alaeddine	4
6	KAMANGA Allan	76		JAZIRI Ziad	5
7	MPONDA Peter		53	NAFTI Mehdi	8
10	KAMWENDO Joseph	82		GHODHBANE Kaies	10
11	MWAFULIRWA Russel	63		SANTOS	11
12	MALIDADI Dick	77		MNARI Jawhar	12
13	CHIPATALA Emmanuel		66	CHEDLI Adel	14
14	KAFWAFWA Clement			JAIDI Radhi	15
15	NGAMBI Robert			BOUSSAIDI Anis	19
	Tr: OSMAN Yasin			Tr: LEMERRE Roger	
8	MSUKU Sherry	77	66	ZITOUNI Ali	9
18	MUNTHALI Heston	63	53	BOUAZIZI Riadh	13
19	CHAVULA Moses	82	46	SAIDI Karim	21

National Stadium, Gaborone
9-10-2004, 16:00, 16 500, Colembi ANG

BOT   2   1   KEN

Molwantwa [51], Selolwane [58]   Oliech [5]

	BOTSWANA				KENYA	
16	MARUMO Modiri			OCHIENG Duncan	1
2	LETSHOLATHEBE Ndiapo			OTIENO Musa	4
3	MOTLHABANE Khumo			JUMA Tom	5
4	MOGALADI Michael			MULAMA Titus	7
5	NTSHINGANE Masego	86		SHABAN Adan	8
6	GABOLWELWE Nelson	82	66	BARASA John	11
8	MOTLHABANKWE Tshepo			OYOMBE Andrew	14
11	SELOLWANE Diphetogo			OPIYO Philip	15
12	MOLWANTWA Tshepiso		79	MAMBO Robert	17
14	AMOS Ernest			OLIECH Dennis	18
18	GABONAMONG Mogogi		59	AKE RICHARD Muttendango	19
	Tr: JELUSIC Veselin			Tr: MULEE Jacob	
17	MOATLHAPING Moemedi	86	79	BARASA Nyongesa Michael	9
			59	MARIAGA Macdonald	13
			66	OMONDI James	16

Stade du 28 septembre, Conakry
10-10-2004, 16:30, 25 000, Monteiro Duarte CPV

GUI   1   1   MAR

Mansare [50]   Chamarh [5]

	GUINEA				MOROCCO	
16	CAMARA Kemoko			LAMYAGHRI Nadir	22
2	FEINDOUNO Pascal		46	OUADDOU Abdeslem	4
4	JABI Daouda			EL KARKOURI Talal	5
5	BALDE Dianbobo			NAYBET Noureddine	6
6	SYLLA Mohamed	46	70	ZAIRI Jaouad	7
7	MANSARE Fode			HDIOUAD Mourad	10
8	SYLLA Kanfory		63	EL YAAGOUBI Mohammed	11
10	SYLLA Abdoulkarim	62		KHARJA Houssine	13
17	DIALLO Mamadou			SAFRI Youssef	15
18	BAH Schuman			MOKHTARI Youssef	16
19	KABA Diawara	84		CHAMARH Marouane	17
	Tr: NEVEU Patrice			Tr: BADOU Zaki	
11	YOULA Souleymane	62	63	DIANE Mounir	2
13	CAMARA Ousmane	84	46	CHIHAB Tariq	19
14	CONTE Ibrahima Sory II	46	70	HADJI Youssef	20

Nyayo National Stadium, Nairobi
17-11-2004, 16:00, 16 000, Abd El Fatah EGY

KEN 2 1 GUI

Oliech 10, Mukenya 61

No.	KENYA	min		min	GUINEA	No.
1	OCHIENG Duncan				CAMARA Youssouf	1
2	MUKENYA Edwin				FEINDOUNO Pascal	2
5	OUNDO Thomas Juma				SOW Abdoul	3
7	MULAMA Titus	83			KEITA Alseny	4
10	ABDALLA Mohamed	87			BALDE Dianbobo	5
11	BARASA John	66	64		THIAM Pablo	6
13	MARIAGA Macdonald				MANSARE Fode	7
14	OYOMBE Andrew				SYLLA Kanfory	8
15	OPIYO Philip		77		KABA Diawara	10
17	AMANAKA Zablon Davies				CISSE Morlaye	12
18	OLIECH Dennis		89		BAH Schuman	18
	Tr: MUHIDDIN Twahir				Tr: NEVEU Patrice	
6	MATHENGE Antony	87	77		YOULA Souleymane	11
8	AKE RICHARD Muttendango	66	64		YATTARA Ibrahima	13
9	BARASA Nyongesa Michael	83	89		SYLLA Mohamed	14

Prince Moulay Abdellah, Rabat
9-02-2005, 19:30, 40 000, Tamuni LBY

MAR 5 1 KEN

Zairi 3 12 39 90, Diane 46, Hadji 81　　　Otieno 93+

No.	MOROCCO	min		min	KENYA	No.
1	SINOUH Khaled				OCHIENG Duncan	1
4	OUADDOU Abdeslem				MUKENYA Edwin	2
5	EL KADDOURI Badr				HUSSEIN Mohamed	3
6	NAYBET Noureddine				OTIENO Musa	4
7	ZAIRI Jaouad				OUNDO Thomas Juma	5
8	REGRAGUI Hoalid				MULAMA Titus	7
13	KHARJA Houssine			82	ABDALLA Mohamed	8
16	ABDESSADKI Yassine	63			MARIAGA Macdonald	10
17	CHAMARH Marouane	68	86		BARASA John	11
18	DIANE Mounir	72			AMANAKA Zablon Davies	17
20	HADJI Youssef				OLIECH Dennis	18
	Tr: BADOU Zaki				Tr: MUHIDDIN Twahir	
10	SEKTIOUI Tarik	72		82	YUSUF Mohamoud Ali	13
14	AHNAFOUF Abdelaziz	68		86	NGAYWA Asman	15
15	ABOUCHAROUANE Hicham	63				

Kasarani, Nairobi
26-03-2005, 16:00, 15 000, Buenkadila COD

KEN 1 0 BOT

Oliech 44

No.	KENYA	min		min	BOTSWANA	No.
1	ORIGI Arnold				MARUMO Modiri	16
2	AKE Emmanuel	42			LETSHOLATHEBE Ndiapo	2
3	HUSSEIN Mohamed	79			MOTLHABANE Khumo	3
4	OTIENO Musa		72		MOGALADI Michael	4
7	MULAMA Titus				THUMA Mompati	6
8	BREIKH Ali				MOTLHABANKWE Tshepo	8
10	MARIAGA Macdonald				SELOLWANE Diphetogo	11
11	BARASA John	86	61		PHARO Kgakgamstso	13
13	MULINGE Ndeto				AMOS Ernest	14
14	AMANAKA Zablon Davies		17		MOGOROSI Joel	17
18	OLIECH Dennis				GABONAMONG Mogogi	18
	Tr: KHERI Mohammed				Tr: JELUSIC Veselin	
9	JUMA Tom	79	72		RABITHOME Koegathe	5
9	SIRENGO Mark	86	61		MOATLHAPING Moemedi	10
12	SIMIYU Sammy Wanyonyi	42	46		MOLWANTWA Tshepiso	12

Stade 7 Novembre, Tunis
26-03-2005, 19:15, 30 000, Awuye UGA

TUN 7 0 MWI

Guemamdia 3, Santos 4 12 52 75 77
Clayton 60p, Ghodhbane 80

No.	TUNISIA	min		min	MALAWI	No.
1	BOUMNIJEL Ali				SANUDI Swadic	1
3	HAGUI Karim			72	KONDOWE Fisher	2
6	TRABELSI Hatem				KAMWENDO Joseph	5
9	GUEMAMDIA Haykel	62			MSOWOYA Maupo	6
10	GHODHBANE Kaies				MPONDA Peter	7
11	SANTOS				MADUKA John	10
12	MNARI Jawhar	55			KANYENDA Essau	11
14	NAMOUCHI Hamed				NDHOLVU Wisdom	12
15	JAIDI Radhi			72	CHIPATALA Emmanuel	13
18	BENACHOUR Slim				KAFWAFWA Clement	14
20	CLAYTON	78	39		NGAMBI Robert	15
	Tr: LEMERRE Roger				Tr: OSMAN Yasin	
4	YAHIA Alaeddine	78	72		CHILAPONOWA James	4
7	BEN SAADA Chaouki	62	72		MWAFULIRWA Russel	9
13	BOUAZIZI Riadh	55	39		MUNTHALI Heston	18

Prince Moulay Abdellah, Rabat
26-03-2005, 19:30, 70 000, Coulibaly MLI

MAR 1 0 GUI

Hadji 62

No.	MOROCCO	min		min	GUINEA	No.
1	SINOUH Khaled				CAMARA Kemoko	22
2	REGRAGUI Hoalid				FEINDOUNO Pascal	2
4	OUADDOU Abdeslem		42		BALDE Dianbobo	5
5	EL KARKOURI Talal				THIAM Pablo	6
6	NAYBET Noureddine		77		MANSARE Fode	7
7	ZAIRI Jaouad	68			SYLLA Kanfory	8
13	KHARJA Houssine	89	43		KABA Diawara	11
15	SAFRI Youssef		70		KEITA Alhassane	12
17	CHAMARH Marouane				JABI Daouda	13
20	HADJI Youssef				KALABANE Oumar	15
21	DIANE Mounir	65			SYLLA Mohamed	18
	Tr: BABOU Zaki				Tr: NEVEU Patrice	
10	SEKTIOUI Tarik	68	70		BANGOURA Sambegou	9
11	EL YAAGOUBI Mohammed	89	77		SYLLA Abdoulkarim	10
19	BOU SABOUN Abdelali	65	43		CAMARA Ousmane	14

National Stadium, Gaborone
4-06-2005, 15:00, 20 000, Mana NGA

BOT 1 3 TUN

Gabonamong 12　　　Nafti 27, Santos 43, Abdi 78

No.	BOTSWANA	min		min	TUNISIA	No.
1	TSHELAMETSI Kagiso				BOUMNIJEL Ali	1
2	LETSHOLATHEBE Ndiapo				ABDI Wissem	4
3	MOTLHABANE Khumo				JAZIRI Ziad	5
4	MOGALADI Michael				TRABELSI Hatem	6
5	MOTHUSI Tebogo	66			BEN SAADA Chaouki	7
6	THUMA Mompati				NAFTI Mehdi	8
10	MOATLHAPING Moemedi	88			SANTOS	11
11	SELOLWANE Diphetogo	77	66		CHADLI Adel	14
12	MOLWANTWA Tshepiso				JAIDI Radhi	15
14	AMOS Ernest				CLAYTON	20
18	GABONAMONG Mogogi				JOMAA Issam	21
	Tr: JELUSIC Veselin				Tr: LEMERRE Roger	
13	MOLOI Pontsho	77	66		GHODHBANE Kaies	10
			66		MNARI Jawhar	12
			88		ZITOUNI Ali	23

Prince Moulay Abdellah, Rabat
4-06-2005, 20:00, 48 000, Buenkadila COD

MAR 4 1 MWI

Chamarh 16, Hadji 2 21 75, Kharja 72
Chipatala 10

MOROCCO		MALAWI	
1 SINOUH Khaled		SANUDI Swadic 1	
3 KACEMI Noureddine		MSOWOYA Maupo 3	
4 OUADDOU Abdeslem		CHILAPONOWA James 4	
5 EL KARKOURI Talal		KAMANGA Allan 6	
6 NAYBET Noureddine		ZAKAZAKA Jimmy 9	82
9 ABDESSADKI Yassine	82	MADUKA John 10	81
11 EL YAAGOUBI Mohammed	59	KANYENDA Essau 11	
13 KHARJA Houssine		CHIPATALA Emmanuel 13	
15 SAFRI Youssef		KAFWAFWA Clement 14	
17 CHAMARH Marouane	81	NDHOLVU Wisdom 15	
20 HADJI Youssef	87	MUNTHALI Heston 18	
Tr: BADOU Zaki		Tr: OSMAN Yasin	
7 ZAIRI Jaouad	87 82	KONDOWE Fisher 2	82
14 BOU SABOUN Abdelali	59 81	CHAVULA Moses 17	81
16 MOKHTARI Youssef	81		

Stade du 28 septembre, Conakry
5-06-2005, 16:30, 21 000, Mbera GAB

GUI 1 0 KEN

Bangoura 68

GUINEA		KENYA	
16 CAMARA Kemoko		OTIENO Arnold 1	
2 FEINDOUNO Pascal		HUSSEIN Mohamed 3	
3 CAMARA Ibrahima		OTIENO Musa 4	
4 JABI Daouda	89	ABDALLA Ali Mohamed 8	84
6 THIAM Pablo	84	SIRENGO Mark 9	
8 SYLLA Kanfory		MARIAGA Macdonald 10	
9 BANGOURA Sambegou	75	MULINGE Ndeto 13	
15 KALABANE Oumar		SIMIYU Sammy Wanyonyi 14	
17 DIALLO Mamadou		AMANAKA Zablon Davies 17	
18 SYLLA Mohamed	63	MWALALA Bernard 18	
21 KEITA Alhassane	57		
Tr: NEVEU Patrice		Tr: KHERI Mohammed	
5 SYLLA Aboubacar	75 84	OWINO George 5	84
10 SYLLA Abdoulkarim	63 89	ABDURAZAK Hussein 11	89
19 KABA Diawara	57		

Stade 7 Novembre, Tunis
11-06-2005, 19:15, 30 000, Lim Kee Chong MRI

TUN 2 0 GUI

Clayton 36, Chadli 78

TUNISIA		GUINEA	
1 BOUMNIJEL Ali		CAMARA Kemoko 16	
4 ABDI Wissem		FEINDOUNO Pascal 2	
5 JAZIRI Ziad	72	CAMARA Ibrahima 3	
6 TRABELSI Hatem		THIAM Pablo 6	
8 NAFTI Mehdi		MANSARE Fode 7	
10 GHODHBANE Kaies		SYLLA Kanfory 8	79
11 SANTOS		BANGOURA Sambegou 9	
12 MNARI Jawhar		CAMARA Ousmane 14	
13 JAIDI Radhi		KALABANE Oumar 15	
17 BEN SAADA Chouki	49	DIALLO Mamadou 17	
20 CLAYTON	86	SYLLA Mohamed 18	40
Tr: LEMERRE Roger		Tr: NEVEU Patrice	
14 CHADLI Adel	72 65	KABA Diawara 10	65
19 AYARI Anis	86 40 65	CAMARA Sekouba 13	40 65
21 JOMAA Issam	49		

Kamuzu, Blantyre
18-06-2005, 15:00, 20 000, Evehe CMR

MWI 1 3 BOT

Mwafulirwa 48
Molwantwa 8, Selolwane 40, Motlhabankwe 88

MALAWI		BOTSWANA	
1 SANUDI Swadic		TSHELAMETSI Kagiso 1	
2 KONDOWE Fisher		MOGALADI Michael 4	
3 MSOWOYA Maupo		MOTHUSI Tebogo 5	
4 CHILAPONOWA James		THUMA Mompati 6	
6 KAMANGA Allan		MOTLHABANKWE Tshepo 8	
7 MPONDA Peter		MOATLHAPING Moemedi 10	
9 CHITSULO Daniel	46	SELOLWANE Diphetogo 11	
10 MADUKA John		MOLWANTWA Tshepiso 12	
11 ZAKAZAKA Jimmy		AMOS Ernest 14	
13 CHIPATALA Emmanuel	71	GABANAKGOSI Seabo 15	
15 NDHOLVU Wisdom	46	GABONAMONG Mogogi 18	90
Tr: OSMAN Yasin		Tr: JELUSIC Veselin	
14 KAMWENDO Joseph	71		
17 MWAFULIRWA Russel	46		
18 NGAMBI Robert	46		

Nyayo National Stadium, Nairobi
18-06-2005, 16:00, 50 000, Diatta SEN

KEN 0 0 MAR

KENYA		MOROCCO	
1 OTIENO Arnold		LAMYAGHRI Nadir 1	
3 SHABAN Adan		REGRAGUI Hoalid 2	
4 OTIENO Musa		KACEMI Noureddine 3	
5 AMANAKA Zablon Davies		OUADDOU Abdeslem 4	
8 ABDALLA Ali Mohamed		EL KARKOURI Talal 5	
9 SIRENGO Mark		ZAIRI Jaouad 7	76
13 MULINGE Ndeto		ABDESSADKI Yassine 9	83
14 SIMIYU Sammy Wanyonyi	71	KHARJA Houssine 13	
15 MWALALA Bernard		MOKHTARI Youssef 16	
17 MAMBO Robert	70	DIANE Mounir 18	15
18 OLIECH Dennis		HADJI Youssef 20	
Tr: KHERI Mohammed		Tr: BADOU Zaki	
10 MACHETHE John	71	EL YAAGOUBI Mohammed 11	15
11 BARASA John	70	BOU SABOUN Abdelali 14	76
		ERBATE Elamine 21	83

QUALIFYING MATCHES PLAYED IN CENTRAL AMERICA, NORTH AMERICA AND THE CARIBBEAN

First Preliminary Round

Grenada	GRN	5 3
Guyana	GUY	0 1

Bermuda	BER	13 7
Montserrat	MSR	0 0

Haiti	HAI	5 2
Turks and Caicos Isl.	TCA	0 0

British Virgin Islands	VGB	0 0
St Lucia	LCA	1 9

Cayman Islands	CAY	1 0
Cuba	CUB	2 3

Aruba	ARU	1 1
Surinam	SUR	2 8

Antigua and Barbuda	ATG	2 0
Netherlands Antilles	ANT	0 3

Dominica	DMA	1 3
Bahamas	BAH	1 1

US Virgin Islands	VIR	0 0
St Kitts and Nevis	SKN	4 7

Dominican Republic	DOM	0 6
Anguilla	AIA	0 0

Second Preliminary Round

Grenada	GRN	3 3
USA	USA	0 2

Bermuda	BER	1 2
El Salvador	SLV	2 2

Haiti	HAI	1 0
Jamaica	JAM	1 3

St Lucia	LCA	0 0
Panama	PAN	4 3

Cuba	CUB	2 1
Costa Rica	CRC	2 1

Surinam	SUR	1 1
Guatemala	GUA	1 3

Netherlands Antilles	ANT	1 0
Honduras	HON	2 4

Canada	CAN	4 4
Belize	BLZ	0 0

Dominica	DMA	0 0
Mexico	MEX	10 8

St Kitts and Nevis	SKN	2 3
Barbados	BRB	0 2

Dominican Republic	DOM	0 0
Trinidad & Tobago	TRI	2 4

Nicaragua	NCA	2 1
St Vincent/Grenadines	VIN	2 4

First Group Stage

Group 1	Pts
USA	12
Panama	8
Jamaica	7
El Salvador	4

Group 2	Pts
Costa Rica	10
Guatemala	10
Honduras	7
Canada	5

Group 3	Pts
Mexico	18
Trinidad & Tobago	12
St Vincent/Grenadines	6
St Kitts and Nevis	0

Final Group Stage

Final Group	Pts
Mexico	13
USA	12
Costa Rica	7
Guatemala	4
Trinidad & Tobago	4
Panama	2

As of 16 August 2005 only half of the group matches had been played. Remaining fixtures to be played on 17/08/2005, 3/09/2005, 7/09/2005, 8/10/2005 and 12/10/2005

No team has yet qualified. The top three from the final group stage qualify for the finals in Germany. The fourth-placed team enters a play-off against an Asian side. The prleiminary rounds consisted of 12 groups, 10 of which had three teams. The seeded team received a bye into the Second preliminary round

PRELIMINARY ROUNDS

GROUP 1

Grenada National Stadium, St. George's
28-02-2004, 19:00, 7 000, Archundia MEX

GRN   5   0   GUY

Bishop [34], Phillip [39], Augustine [72]
Modeste.A [81], Rennie [91]

	GRENADA			GUYANA	
1	BAPTISTE Kellon			HENDRICKS Marlon	1
4	JAMES Jason			LOWE Howard	3
5	BAPTISTE Franklyn			JILGEOUS Orlando	4
8	BISHOP Nigel	75		MOORE Walter	5
9	JOSEPH Shalrie			CARROLL Orville	6
11	MODESTE Anthony			MC KINNON Kayode	9
12	MODESTE Patrick	60	70	HERNANDEZ Neil	10
14	BENJAMIN Brian		87	RICHARDSON Gregory	11
15	PHILLIP Kennedy	64		BEVENEY Shawn	13
16	BUBB Byron			ARCHER Dirk	14
19	CHARLES Ricky		62	JEROME Randolph	17
	Tr: DEBELLOTTE Alister			Tr: DOS SANTOS Neider	
7	RENNIE Denis	75	87	ABRAMS Anthony	15
13	AUGUSTINE Anthony	64	62	DURANT Andrew	18
19	MORRIS Ricky	60	70	HARRIS Carey	19

Blairmont Community Centre, Blairmont
14-03-2004, 15:00, 1 200, Quesada Cordero CRC

GUY   1   3   GRN

Harris [29]   Charles [15], Roberts [69], Bubb [87]

	GUYANA			GRENADA	
1	DURANT Andrew			BAPTISTE Kellon	1
3	CADOGAN Slawin			JAMES Jason	4
4	JILGEOUS Orlando			BAPTISTE Franklyn	5
5	MOORE Walter			JOSEPH Shalrie	9
6	CARROLL Orville	46	80	CHARLES Ricky	10
9	MC KINNON Kayode	73		MODESTE Anthony	11
10	CODRINGTON Nigel	86		MODESTE Patrick	12
11	RICHARDSON Gregory			BENJAMIN Brian	14
12	HARRIS Carey		81	BEDEAU Antony	20
13	BEVENEY Shawn		51	LEE Dlane	27
14	ARCHER Dirk			ROBERTS Jason	30
	Tr: DOS SANTOS Neider			Tr: DEBELLOTTE Alister	
2	WATERTON Travis	46	80	BISHOP Nigel	8
15	ABRAMS Anthony	86	51	PHILLIP Kennedy	15
18	BROWN Elton	73	81	BUBB Byron	16

Columbus Crew Stadium, Columbus
13-06-2004, 13:00, 10 000, Navarro CAN

USA   3   0   GRN

Beasley 2 [45 71], Vanney [90]

	USA			GRENADA	
18	KELLER Kasey			BAPTISTE Kellon	1
3	VANNEY Greg			BAPTISTE Franklyn	5
4	BOCANEGRA Carlos			JOSEPH Shalrie	9
6	CHERUNDOLO Steve			CHARLES Ricky	10
9	CASEY Conor	20		MODESTE Anthony	11
10	REYNA Claudio			MODESTE Patrick	12
14	ARMAS Chris	72	51	WATTS Everette	13
17	BEASLEY DaMarcus		65	BENJAMIN Brian	14
20	MC BRIDE Brian	90	73	PHILLIP Kennedy	15
21	DONOVAN Landon			BEDEAU Antony	20
23	POPE Eddie			ROBERTS Jason	30
	Tr: ARENA Bruce			Tr: DEBELLOTTE Alister	
7	LEWIS Eddie	72	65	GEORGE Eric	2
8	STEWART Earnie	90	51	BISHOP Nigel	8
11	KIROVSKI Jovan	20	73	BUBB Byron	16

Grenada National Stadium, St. George's
20-06-2004, 16:00, 10 000, Brizan TRI

GRN   2   3   USA

Roberts [12], Charles [77]   Donovan [6], Wolff [19], Beasley [76]

	GRENADA			USA	
1	BAPTISTE Kellon			KELLER Kasey	18
5	BAPTISTE Franklyn			HEJDUK Frankie	2
9	JOSEPH Shalrie	63	77	REYNA Claudio	10
10	CHARLES Ricky			GIBBS Cory	12
11	MODESTE Anthony			ARMAS Chris	14
12	MODESTE Patrick		87	CONVEY Bobby	15
14	BENJAMIN Brian	54	61	WOLFF Josh	16
15	PHILLIP Kennedy	58		BEASLEY Da Marcus	17
16	BUBB Byron	88		MC BRIDE Brian	20
20	BEDEAU Antony			DONOVAN Landon	21
30	ROBERTS Jason			MASTRNENI Pablo	25
	Tr: DEBELLOTTE Alister			Tr: ARENA Bruce	
19	MORRIS Ricky	88	87	VANNEY Greg	3
21	BAIN Kitson	58	77	ZAVAGNIN Kerry	5
23	NECKLES Arkenson	63	61	STEWART Earnie	8

GROUP 2

National Stadium, Hamilton
29-02-2004, 15:00, 3 000, Kennedy USA

BER   13   0   MSR

Ming 3 [5 20 50], Nusum 3 [15 54 60], Smith [36]
Bean 2 [41 52], Steede [43], Wade [77], Simons [83], Burgess [87]

	BERMUDA			MONTSERRAT	
1	HALL Troy			JOYCE Kurt	1
2	THOMAS David		66	THOMPSON Charles	2
3	JENNINGS Kentoine		45	MC LEAN Samuel	3
4	BURGESS Shannon			RODNEY Courtney	4
5	LEWIS Stanton			WILLIAMS Elton	5
6	STEEDE Otis	68		ANTOINE Willix	7
8	WADE Meshach			FARRELL Vladimir	8
9	NUSUM John		76	PONDE Kelvin	9
10	BEAN Ralph	70		DYER Wayne	10
11	SMITH Khano	62		HOWSON Sean	11
17	MING Damon			CLIFFORD Joseph	12
	Tr: THOMPSON Kenny			Tr: LEWIS William	
7	CODDINGTON Domico	62	66	BUFFONGE Crenston	6
14	HILL Clevon	68	76	HENRY Michael	15
16	SIMONS Rohann	70	45	LABORDE Ottley	20

Blakes Estate Football Ground, Plymouth
21-03-2004, 15:00, 250, Charles DMA

MSR   0   7   BER

Hill [15], Nusum 2 [21 44], Bean [39]
Smith 2 [45 46], Ming [76]

	MONTSERRAT			BERMUDA	
1	JOYCE Kurt	65		HALL Troy	1
4	RODNEY Courtney			THOMAS David	2
5	WILLIAMS Elton			BURGESS Shannon	3
7	ANTOINE Willix			JENNINGS Kentoine	4
8	FARRELL Vladimir		68	STEEDE Otis	6
9	PONDE Kelvin			HILL Clevon	8
10	DYER Wayne		68	NUSUM John	9
12	JOSEPH Clifford			BEAN Ralph	10
16	HARPER Dorian		72	SMITH Khano	11
17	FARRELL Charleston	81		DILL Kofi	15
20	LABORDE Ottley	75		MING Damon	17
	Tr: LEWIS William			Tr: THOMPSON Kenny	
2	THOMPSON Charles	81	68	HUNT Musceo	5
21	WRIGHT Derrick	65	72	SMITH Carlos	18
			68	ASTWOOD Stephen	19

Estadio Cuscatlan, San Salvador
13-06-2004, 15:00, 12 000, Campos NCA

SLV 2 1 BER

Martinez [14], Velasquez [54] — Nusum [30]

EL SALVADOR				BERMUDA	
1	RIVERA Santos Noel			FIGURIEDO Timothy	1
3	GONZALEZ Marvin			RICHARDS Kevin	2
5	VELASQUEZ Victor			BURGESS Shannon	3
6	PRADO Erick			JENNINGS Kentoine	4
7	SANCHEZ Ramon	46		LEWIS Stanton	5
10	GOCHEZ Ernesto	81		STEEDE Otis	6
14	CORRALES Rudis	66		MING Damon	7
18	MURGAS Gilberto			LIGHTBOURNE Kyle	8
19	PACHECO Alfredo			SMITH Khano	11
20	TORRES William		41	NUSUM John	18
23	MARTINEZ Jose		59	GOATER Shaun	19
	Tr: PAREDES Juan			Tr: THOMPSON Kenny	
11	GALDAMEZ Naun	81	77	BEAN Ralph	10
21	ERAZO Alex	46	41 77	ASTWOOD Stephen	16
24	MARTINEZ Jose Manuel	66	59	SMITH Carlos	17

National Stadium, Hamilton
20-06-2004, 19:00, 4 000, Whittaker CAY

BER 2 2 SLV

Burgess [4], Nusum [22] — Pacheco 2 [20 41]

BERMUDA				EL SALVADOR	
1	FIGURIEDO Timothy			GOMEZ Juan	22
2	RICHARDS Kevin			CARRANZA Edwin	2
3	BURGESS Shannon			VELASQUEZ Victor	5
4	JENNINGS Kentoine 42			PRADO Erick	6
5	LEWIS Stanton	82		GOCHEZ Ernesto	10
6	STEEDE Otis	70		CORRALES Rudis	14
7	MING Damon	31		OCHOA Roberto	15
8	WADE Meshach			MURGAS Gilberto	18
9	NUSUM John			PACHECO Alfredo	19
10	BEAN Ralph	70		TORRES William	20
11	SMITH Khano	63		MARTINEZ Jose	23
	Tr: THOMPSON Kenny			Tr: PAREDES Juan	
16	ASTWOOD Stephen	63	70	CAMPOS Juan	8
17	SMITH Carlos	70	31	MEJIA Diego	9
			82	GALDAMEZ Naun	11

GROUP 3

Orange Bowl, Miami
18-02-2004, 20:30, 3 000, Stott USA

HAI 5 0 TCA

Peguero [6], Descouines 3 [43 45 50]
Wadson [71]

HAITI				TURKS AND CAICOS	
1	FENELON Gabard			GREGG Gerard	1
2	DESIR Roosevelt			CLINTON Duan	2
3	FRANTZ Gilles			SLATTERY Paul	3
5	DAVID Sancius			GANNON Christopher	4
7	WADSON Corriolan	77		REID Christian	5
9	PEGUERO Jean-Philippe	66	27	CROSBIE Paul	6
10	DESCOUINES Johnny			THOMPSON Steve	7
11	JEAN Boucicaut	80		COOK Charles	8
13	BRUNY Pierre Richard			CLINTON Gavin	9
14	MONES Chery		66	CHARLES Errion	10
16	TEMPS Dorcelus	46		HARVEY Lawrence	11
	Tr: CLAVIJO Fernando			Tr:	
6	LOUIS Max	80	66	BRUNO Chris	12
15	TURLIEN Romulus	46	77	SAVAGE Steve	14
19	ROODY Loimera	66	27	SHEARER Phillip	15

Ted Hendricks, Hialeah
21-02-2004, 20:00, 3 000, Valenzuela USA

TCA 0 2 HAI

Roody [10], Harvey OG [41]

TURKS AND CAICOS				HAITI	
1	GREGG Gerard			DESIR Roosevelt	2
2	THOMPSON Steve			FRANTZ Gilles	3
3	SLATTERY Paul			GERMAIN Peter	4
4	GANNON Christopher			DAVID Sancius	5
5	CROSBIE Paul		67	WADSON Corriolan	7
6	HARVEY Lawrence		53	THELAMOUR Dieuphene	12
7	CLINTON Duan			BRUNY Pierre Richard	13
8	COOK Charles		63	TURLIEN Romulus	15
9	BRUNO Chris	86		GRACIEN Marc Herold	16
10	CHARLES Errion	77		LUIOGI Beauzile	17
11	SHEARER Phillip	80		ROODY Loimera	19
	Tr:			Tr: CLAVIJO Fernando	
13	DUFFY Ryan	86	63	LOUIS Max	6
16	SLATTERY James	80	67	MONES Chery	14
17	STOKES Jerry	77	53	ULCENAT Richardson	21

Orange Bowl, Miami
12-06-2004, 19:30, Stott USA

HAI 1 1 JAM

Peguero [50] — King [39]

HAITI				JAMAICA	
1	FENELON Gabard			RICKETTS Donovan	30
3	FRANTZ Gilles			STEWARD Damian	3
5	PIERRE Jean Jacques			GOODISON Ian	5
7	WADSON Corriolan		76	KING Marlon	6
9	PEGUERO Jean-Philippe			HYDE Micah	8
10	DESCOUINES Johnny	58	88	FULLER Ricardo	10
11	BOURCICAUT Jean-Michel	79		GARDNER Ricardo	15
13	BRUNY Pierre Richard			REID Garfield	21
16	TEMPS Dorcelus	87	68	DAVIS Fabian	22
17	DAVID Sancius			ZIADIE Craig	23
20	DESIR Roosevelt			DAVIS Claude	25
	Tr: CLAVIJO Fernando			Tr: BROWN Carl	
8	TURLIEN Romulus	87	68	WHITMORE Theodore	11
12	GRACIEN Marc	79	88	BURTON Deon	18
18	THELAMOUR Dieuphene	58	76	RALPH Damani	20

National Stadium, Kingston
20-06-2004, 18:00, Sibrian SLV

JAM 3 0 HAI

King 3 [4 14 31]

JAMAICA				HAITI	
30	RICKETTS Donovan			FENELON Gabard	1
3	STEWARD Damian		46	FRANTZ Gilles	3
5	GOODISON Ian			PIERRE Jean Jacques	5
6	KING Marlon			WADSON Corriolan	7
8	LAWRENCE James			PEGUERO Jean-Philippe	9
9	WILLIAMS Andrew	85		DESCOUINES Johnny	10
11	WHITMORE Theodore		65	BOURCICAUT Jean-Michel	11
15	GARDNER Ricardo			BRUNY Pierre Richard	13
20	RALPH Damani	80	46	TEMPS Dorcelus	16
21	REID Garfield	70		DAVID Sancius	17
23	ZIADIE Craig		83	DESIR Roosevelt	20
	Tr: BROWN Carl			Tr: CLAVIJO Fernando	
10	FULLER Ricardo	80	65	TURLIEN Romulus	8
12	JOHNSON Jermaine	85	46	GRACIEN Marc	12
			46	ROODY Loimera	21

GROUP 4

A.O. Shirley Recreational Field, Tortola
22-02-2004, 16:00, 800, Stewart JAM

VGB 0 1 LCA

Elva [55]

BRITISH VIRGIN ISL.			ST. LUCIA	
1	BUTLER Desire		DETERVILLE Giovanni	1
2	WILLIAMS Troy	90	EMMANUEL Sheldon	2
5	PARRIS Ron	59	TOBIE Faustas	3
6	NOBEL Tyrone	59	JOSEPH Elijah	5
10	SIMMONS Kenmore		KIRTON Sean	6
11	THOMAS Fitzroy	65	MARK Sheldon	7
12	HALL Gary		JEAN Earl	9
16	MORRIS Jairo		ELVA Titus	11
16	WILLIAMS Prince		VALCIN Germal	13
17	ISAAC Nole	68	JOSEPH Valencius	15
18	CAIN Ranelie	79	SKEETE Jarvin	16
	Tr: TULLACH Michael		Tr: ARMSTRONG Kingsley	
4	GREENE Alex	59 90	ALCIDE Curtis	8
8	ROACH Quaver	59 68	CADET Marciano	14
9	LENNON Rohan	65 79	SAMUEL Junior	17

National Stadium, Vieux Fort
28-03-2004, 17:00, 665, Corrivault CAN

LCA 9 0 VGB

Emmanuel 2 [13 66], Joseph [26], Jean 2 [28 52]
Skeete 2 [49 55], Elva [69], Baptiste [90]

ST. LUCIA			BRITISH VIRGIN ISL.	
1	DETERVILLE Giovanni		BUTLER Desire	1
3	TOBIE Faustas	46	WILLIAMS Troy	2
4	LASTIC Francis		HALL Gary	6
5	JOSEPH Elijah		SAVAGE Merrick	7
6	EMMANUEL Sheldon	49	SIMMONS Kenmore	10
7	MARK Sheldon		ALEXANDER Roger	12
9	JEAN Earl	80	MORRIS Jairo	14
10	SKEETE Jarvin		WILLIAMS Prince	15
11	ELVA Titus	79 58	WEARMOUTH James	16
13	VALCIN Germal		CAIN Ranelie	18
15	JOSEPH Valencius	60	HAYNES Michael	19
	Tr: CASSIM Louis		Tr: TULLOCH Michael	
14	LAURENCIN Junior	79 49	LENNON Rohan	9
16	BLANCHARD Shane	80 58	ROACH Quaver	17
17	BAPTISTE Andy	60 46	AZILLE Peterson	27

Estadio Rommel Fernandez, Panama City
13-06-2004, 16:00, Phillip GRN

PAN 4 0 LCA

Dely Valdez [5], Tejada [18]
Phillips [39], Brown [75]

PANAMA			ST. LUCIA	
1	JAMES Ricardo		DETERVILLE Giovanni	1
2	MIRANDA Victor		POLIUS Mogabi	2
3	BALOY Felipe		LASTIC Francis	4
4	HENRIQUEZ Luis	42	JOSEPH Elijah	5
5	RIVERA Carlos		MARK Sheldon	7
6	GOMEZ Gabriel		JEAN Earl	9
7	MITRE Engin		SKEETE Jarvin	10
8	TEJADA Luis	61 87	ELVA Titus	11
9	DELY VALDEZ Julio		VALCIN Germal	13
10	MEDINA Julio	53	BAPTISTE Andy	17
11	PHILLIPS Ricardo	46 55	EMMANUEL Sheldon	20
	Tr: HERNANDEZ Jose Eugenio		Tr: ARMSTRONG Kingsley	
15	BLANCO Alberto	42 55	TOBIE Faustas	6
16	ZAPATA Alberto	61 87	ALCIDE Curtis	8
19	BROWN Roberto	46 53	SAMUEL Junior	16

National Stadium, Vieux Fort
20-06-2004, 17:00, 400, Gurley VIN

LCA 0 3 PAN

Tejada [14], Dely [88], Blanco [89]

ST. LUCIA			PANAMA	
1	DETERVILLE Giovanni		JAMES Ricardo	1
2	POLIUS Mogabi	85	MIRANDA Victor	2
4	LASTIC Francis		BALOY Felipe	3
5	JOSEPH Elijah		HENRIQUEZ Luis	4
6	TOBIE Faustas		RIVERA Carlos	5
7	MARK Sheldon		GOMEZ Gabriel	6
9	JEAN Earl	59	BLANCO Alberto	7
11	ELVA Titus	65 75	TEJADA Luis	8
13	FLAVIUS David		DELY VALDEZ Julio	9
16	SAMUEL Junior	71	MEDINA Julio	10
20	EMMANUEL Sheldon	59 58	PHILLIPS Ricardo	11
	Tr: CASSIM Louis		Tr: HERNANDEZ Jose Eugenio	
3	VALCIN Germal	85 75	RAMOS Gary	13
10	SKEETE Jarvin	65 71	LOMBARDO Angel	15
18	WALTER Benner	59 58	BROWN Roberto	19

GROUP 5

Truman Bodden, Grand Cayman
22-02-2004, 19:00, 1 789, Sibrian SLV

CAY 1 2 CUB

Elliot [72]

More [53], Marten [89]

CAYMAN ISLANDS			CUBA	
1	COLEMAN Franklin		MOLINA Odelin	1
2	WILKS Frederick		MINOSO Silvio	2
4	BERRY Phillip		MARQUEZ Jeniel	3
5	ELLIOT Thomas		CRUZATA Alexander	5
7	FISHER Junior	7	PEREZ Livan	6
9	WHITTAKER Leon		CERVANTES Alain	9
10	BROWN Eric		MORE Lester	10
11	HILL Nikolai	67 80	HERRERA Raul	13
17	THOMAS Romeo	65	PEREIRA Pedro	16
20	ANDERSON Garth	82 46	VERGARA Javier	17
21	WALTER Mario		MARTEN Luis	18
	Tr: TINOCO Marcos		Tr: COMPANY Miguel	
12	ROWE Colin	82 46	PEDRAZA Mario	4
16	KELLY John	7 72 80	RAMIREZ Jorge	7
23	CHALLENGER Alfredo	67 65	AQUINO Disney	8

Pedro Marrero, Havana
27-03-2004, 15:00, 3 500, Rodriguez MEX

CUB 3 0 CAY

More 3 [7 50 66]

CUBA			CAYMAN ISLANDS	
1	MOLINA Odelin		COLEMAN Franklin	1
2	MINOSO Silvio		WILKS Frederick	2
3	MARQUEZ Jeniel	37	FISHER Junior	4
5	CRUZATA Alexander		ELLIOT Thomas	5
6	PEREZ Livan	46	PIERRE Justin	7
9	CERVANTES Alain	89	BROWN Eric	10
10	MORE Lester	69	FORBES Aldene	13
11	HERRERA Raul		WALTER Mario	15
13	GALINDO Maikel	64	LINDO Ian	16
14	COLONE Jaime	46	THOMAS Romeo	17
16	PEREIRA Pedro	60	ANDERSON Garth	20
	Tr: COMPANY Miguel		Tr: TINOCO Marcos	
4	PEDRAZA Mario	46 89	CHALLENGER Alfredo	6
17	MORALES Gisbel	60 64	ROWE Colin	12
18	MARTEN Luis	69 46	FORBES Marshall	19

Pedro Marrero, Havana
12-06-2004, 16:30, 18 500, Archundia MEX

CUB	2	2	CRC

More 2 [24] [75]   Sequeira [12], Saborio [42]

CUBA		COSTA RICA	
1 MOLINA Odelin		GONZALEZ Ricardo 23	
3 MARQUEZ Jeniel		MARIN Luis 3	
4 PEDRAZA Mario		MARTINEZ Gilberto 5	
5 CRUZATA Alexander		SEQUEIRA Douglas 6	
6 PEREIRA Pedro	58	SOLIS Mauricio 8	
8 AQUINO Disney	60	CENTENO Walter 10	
9 CERVANTES Alain	70	65	BRYCE Stevens 17
10 MORE Lester		32	GOMEZ Ronald 19
13 GALINDO Maikel		CHINCHILLA Pablo 20	
14 COLONE Jaime		79	LEDEZMA Froylan 21
17 FAIFE Pedro		CASTRO Carlos 22	
Tr: COMPANY Miguel		Tr: SAMPSON Steve	
2 MORALES Gisbel	70	65	SOLIS Alonso 7
15 HERNANDEZ Osmin	58	32	SABORIO Alvaro 9
18 MARTEN Luis	60	79	SCOTT Eric 14

Alejandro Mojera Soto, Alajuela
20-06-2004, 1:00, 12 000, Prendergast JAM

CRC	1	1	CUB

Gomez [31]   Cervantes [46]

COSTA RICA		CUBA	
23 GONZALEZ Ricardo		MOLINA Odelin 1	
3 MARIN Luis		MARQUEZ Jeniel 3	
5 MARTINEZ Gilberto		PEDRAZA Mario 4	
8 SOLIS Mauricio		CRUZATA Alexander 5	
10 CENTENO Walter		AQUINO Disney 8	
11 GONZALEZ Ronald		65	CERVANTES Alain 9
12 GONZALEZ Leonardo	46	MORE Lester 10	
14 SCOTT Eric	77	GALINDO Maikel 13	
16 BENNETTE Tray		COLONE Jaime 14	
21 LEDEZMA Froylan	62	50	HERNANDEZ Osmin 15
22 CASTRO Carlos		65	FAIFE Pedro 17
Tr: SAMPSON Steve		Tr: COMPANY Miguel	
9 SABORIO Alvaro	77	65	MORALES Gisbel 2
17 BRYCE Stevens	62	50	PEREIRA Pedro 6
20 CHINCHILLA Pablo	46	65	RAMIREZ Jorge 18

GROUP 6

Guillermo Prospero Trinidad, Oranjestad
28-02-2004, 19:00, 2 108, Moreno PAN

ARU	1	2	SUR

Escalona [89]   Felter [54], Zinhagel [63]

ARUBA		SURINAM	
1 PANTOPHLET Geoland		BLOKLAND Harold 1	
2 CELAIRE Eldrick		DOELBAKIR Riff 2	
3 VALDEZ Juan		AMELO Mick 3	
4 FIGAROA Andy		FELTER Marlon 4	
5 ESCALONA Daniel		LINGER Ulrich 5	
6 LAKE Rodney		79	URALIME Siegfried 8
7 RUIZ Theric	46	SANDVLIET Clifton 10	
8 GOMEZ Frederick		PANKA Dwight 12	
10 ESCALONA Maurice		LUPSON Rinaldo 13	
11 LAMPE Roderick	75	85	VAN ENGEL Gregory 15
19 ZSCHUBSCHEN Enrique	69	61	LOSWIJK Carlos 17
Tr: MUNOZ Marcelo		Tr: BONE BALDI Edgardo	
14 CABRERA Germain	69	79	KINSAINI Gordon 7
15 MACKAY Mark	46	61	ZINHAGEL Patrick 11
17 BRISON Derek	75	85	CEDER Ronny 16

National Stadium, Paramaribo
27-03-2004, 17:00, 4 000, Prendergast JAM

SUR	8	1	ARU

Kinsaini 2 [6] [49], Loswijk [14], Felter 3 [18] [65] [66]   Escalona [24]
Sandvliet [42], Zinhagel [90]

SURINAM		ARUBA	
1 BLOKLAND Harold		PANTOPHLET Geoland 1	
2 DOELBAKIR Riff		VALDEZ Juan 3	
3 AMELO Mick		ZIMMERMANN Gerald 4	
4 FELTER Marlon		ESCALONA Daniel 5	
5 LINGER Ulrich	72	LAKE Rodney 6	
7 KINSAINI Gordon		GOMEZ Frederick 8	
8 URALIME Siegfried		ESCALONA Maurice 10	
10 SANDVLIET Clifton	76	NOUWEN Ronnie 11	
12 PANKA Dwight	75	PIMIENTA Raymondt 15	
13 LUPSON Rinaldo		28	LOPEZ Ikel 17
17 LOSWIJK Carlos	59	65	CELAIRE Eldrick 19
Tr: BONE BALDI Edgardo		Tr: MUNOZ Marcelo	
6 GROOTFAAM Orlando	76	28	CONNOR RUBIO 13
11 ZINHAGEL Patrick	59	72	CABRERA Germain 14
14 EMANUELSON Rouche	75		

Andre Kamperveen Stadium, Paramaribo
12-06-2004, 16:30, 5 500, Jimenez CRL

SUR	1	1	GUA

Purperhart [14]   Ramirez [36]

SURINAM		GUATEMALA	
1 BLOKLAND Harold		TRIGUENO Ricardo 22	
2 BAINO Dennis		MELGAR Pablo 3	
3 AMELO Mick		CHEN Denis 4	
4 FELTER Marlon		FLORES Manuel 5	
5 LINGER Ulrich		THOMPSON Fredy 7	
7 KINSAINI Gordon		75	ROMERO Gonzalo 8
8 URALIME Siegfried	46	ACEVEDO Mario 9	
10 SANDVLIET Clifton		68	RAMIREZ Guillermo 11
12 PURPERHART Dennis	58	MARTINEZ Nestor 13	
12 PANKA Dwight		PEZZAROSSI Dwight 17	
13 LUPSON Rinaldo	44	RODRIGUEZ Mario 19	
Tr: BONE BALDI Edgardo		Tr: MARADIAGA Ramon	
14 EMANUELSON Rouche	44	68	FIGUEROA Carlos 12
15 IVES VLIJTER Arno	46	75	GUEVARA Sergio 24
17 BRANDON Gino	58		

Mateo Flores, Guatemala City
20-06-2004, 11:00, 19 610, Rodriguez MEX

GUA	3	1	SUR

Ruiz 2 [21] [85], Pezzarossi [80]   Brandon [82]

GUATEMALA		SURINAM	
22 TRIGUENO Ricardo		TEMPO Roel 22	
3 MELGAR Pablo		BAINO Dennis 2	
4 CHEN Denis		AMELO Mick 3	
6 CABRERA Gustavo		FELTER Marlon 4	
7 THOMPSON Fredy		GROOTFAAM Orlando 6	
11 RAMIREZ Guillermo	87	KINSAINI Gordon 7	
13 MARTINEZ Nestor		PURPERHART Dennis 11	
16 ANTONIO Jose		42	PANKA Dwight 12
17 PEZZAROSSI Dwight		LUPSON Rinaldo 13	
19 RODRIGUEZ Mario	67	77	IVES VLIJTER Arno 15
20 RUIZ Carlos		54	CEDER Romeo 16
Tr: MARADIAGA Ramon		Tr: BONE BALDI Edgardo	
12 FIGUEROA Carlos	67	42	CHRISTOPH Wensley 9
21 HURTARTE Sergio	87	54	SANDVLIET Clifton 10
		77	BRANDON Gino 17

GROUP 7

Recreation Ground, St. Johns
18-02-2004, 16:00, 1 500, Navarro CAN

ATG 2 0 ANT

Roberts 39, Clarke 89

ANTIGUA/BARBUDA			NETH. ANTILLES		
1 SIMON Janiel			HOMOET Raymond 1		
2 CYRILLIEN Ashton		63	CIJNTJE Ryangelo 2		
6 ANTHONY Steveroy			MARTHA Eugene 3		
11 SKEPPLE Kerry			MAURIS Lennox 4		
13 THOMAS Tamorley	78		WINKLAAR Djuric 5		
15 JEFFERS Neil			ROOS Raymond 6		
16 CHRISTIAN Ranja			WAU Nuelson 7		
17 DUBLIN George		76	VICTORIA Raymond 8		
18 CLARKE Quentin			HOSE Brutil 9		
19 JULIAN Lennox	69	32	KANTELBERG Leon 10		
22 ROBERTS Winston	56		HERNANDEZ Ferdino 11		
Tr: WILLIAMS Rolston			Tr: VERBEEK Peter		
4 BYERS Peter	56	63	FRANKEN Giovanni 12		
8 GREGORY Gayson	78	32	SIBERIE Richman 14		
14 SIMON Tyio	69	76	BRUNKARD Criston 18		

Ergilio Hato, Willemstad
31-03-2004, 20:30, 9 000, Piper TRI

ANT 3 0 ATG

Siberie 27, Martha 46, Hose 48

NETH. ANTILLES			ANTIGUA/BARBUDA		
1 PISAS Marcello			ANTHONY Elvis 1		
2 RIJAARD Daniel			CYRILLIEN Ashton 2		
3 MONGEN Tayron	79		ANTHONY Steveroy 6		
4 MARTHA Eugene			JAMES Arnold 7		
5 WINKLAAR Djuric			SKEPPLE Kerry 11		
6 JONES Shalimar		46	THOMAS Tamorley 13		
7 FRANKEN Giovanni			JEFFERS Schyan 15		
8 ROOS Raymond		75	CHRISTIAN Ranja 16		
9 SIBERIE Richmar			DUBLIN George 17		
10 HOSE Brutil	68	68	CLARKE Quentin 18		
11 HERNANDEZ Ferdino	46	81	FREDERICK Kelly 22		
Tr: VERBEEK Peter			Tr: WILLIAMS Rolston		
14 FORBUIS Shargene	68	81	BYERS Peter 4		
15 MAURIS Lennox	46 52	46	GONSALVES Garfield 5		
18 CIJNTJE Angelo	79	68	WATTS Kevin 9		

Ergilio Hato, Willemstad
12-06-2004, 20:00, 12 000, McArthur GUY

ANT 1 2 HON

Hose 75 ; Suazo 2 9 68

NETH. ANTILLES			HONDURAS		
1 PISAS Marcello			MEDINA Hector 1		
2 MARTHA Eugene			FIGUEROA Maynor 3		
3 JONES Shalimar			SUAZO David 7		
4 MONGEN Tayron	69	81	LEON Julio 10		
5 WINKLAAR Djuric			SUAZO Maynor 12		
6 VICTORIA Raymond		89	MARTINEZ Saul 14		
7 RIJAARD Daniel			GUERRERO Ivan 19		
8 ROOS Raymond	69		GUEVARA Amado 20		
9 HOSE Brutil			ALVAREZ Edgar 21		
10 FRANKEN Giovanni			SABILLON Mauricio 23		
11 SIBERIE Richmar	78		BERNARDEZ Victor 24		
Tr: VERBEEK Peter			Tr: MILUTINOVIC Bora		
12 HERNANDEZ Ferdino	78	81	MARIN Elmer 5		
14 CICILIA Kenneth	69	89	PAVON Carlos 9		
15 CIJNTJE Angelo	69				

Estadio Olimpico, San Pedro Sula
19-06-2004, 19:30, 30 000, Alcala MEX

HON 4 0 ANT

Guevara 7, Suazo 22, Alvarez 50, Pavon 70

HONDURAS			NETH. ANTILLES		
1 MEDINA Hector			PISAS Marcello 1		
3 FIGUEROA Maynor			MARTHA Eugene 2	34	
7 SUAZO David	63	48	JONES Shalimar 3		
10 LEON Julio	72	69	HERNANDEZ Ferdino 4		
12 SUAZO Maynor			WAU Nuelson 5		
14 MARTINEZ Saul	63		VICTORIA Raymond 6		
19 GUERRERO Ivan			RIJAARD Daniel 7		
20 GUEVARA Amado			ROOS Raymond 8		
21 ALVAREZ Edgar		40	SIBERIE Richman 9		
23 SABILLON Mauricio			HOSE Brutil 10		
24 BERNARDEZ Victor			WINKLAAR Djuric 11		
Tr: MILUTINOVIC Bora			Tr: VERBEEK Peter		
9 PAVON Carlos	63	69	BERNARDUS Shayron 15		
11 NUNEZ Milton	63	48	KANTELBERG Leon 16		
13 MARTINEZ Emil	72	40	CIJNTJE Angelo 17		

GROUP 8

Richardson Stadium, Kingston (Ontario)
13-06-2004, 16:30, 8 245, Batres GUA

CAN 4 0 BLZ

Peschisolido 38, Radzinski 54, McKenna 75, Brennan 83

CANADA			BELIZE		
1 ONSTAD Pat			MOODY Shane 1		
3 JAZIC Ante			SMITH Elroy 2		
4 WATSON Mark			SYMMS Vallan 3		
5 DE VOS Jason			MARIANO Peter 4		
6 DE GUZMAN Julian			ROWLEY Edon 5		
7 STALTERI Paul			LESLIE Mark 7		
8 IMHOF Daniel			MUSCHAMP Robert 8		
9 RADZINSKI Tomasz		60	SERANO Dennis 12		
10 PESCHISOLIDO Paul	70	60	FLOWERS Dion 14		
16 HUME Iain	65	74	FRAZER Dion 16		
17 DE ROSARIO Dwayne			ALVAREZ Jarbi 20		
Tr: YALLOP Frank			Tr: ADDERLY Anthony		
2 MC KENNA Kevin	70	60	HENDRICKS Oliver 11		
11 BRENNAN Jim	65	74	MORALES Victor 18		
		60	LYONS Orland 24		

Richardson Stadium, Kingston (Ontario)
16-06-2004, 19:00, 5 124, Gordon TRI

BLZ 0 4 CAN

Radzinski 45, De Rosario 2 63 73, Brennan 85

BELIZE			CANADA		
1 MOODY Shane			ONSTAD Pat 1		
2 SMITH Elroy			MC KENNA Kevin 3		
3 SYMMS Vallan			DE VOS Jason 5		
5 MARIANO Peter	60	46	IMHOF Daniel 8		
7 LESLIE Mark		46	RADZINSKI Tomasz 9		
8 MUSCHAMP Robert			BRENNAN Jim 11		
10 ROACHES Harrison			BERNIER Patrice 12		
11 HENDRICKS Oliver	80		BIRCHAM Marc 13		
15 LYONS Orland	55		HUTCHINSON Atiba 14		
18 MORALES Victor	72		KLUKOWSKI Mike 15		
21 ALVAREZ Jarbi			DE ROSARIO Dwayne 17		
Tr: ADDERLY Anthony			Tr: YALLOP Frank		
9 DORADO Jorge	72	46	PESCHISOLIDO Paul 10		
16 FRAZER Dion	80	84 46	HUME Iain 16		
17 LESLIE Rodwell	55				

GROUP 9

BFA National Development Center, Nassau
26-03-2004, 19:00, 800, Forde BRB

DMA 1 1 BAH

Casimir [88]   Horton [66]

DOMINICA			BAHAMAS	
22	ANGOL Nathaniel		44	MULLINGS Harvey 1
2	ETTIENNE Bishara		65	SWABY Deron 2
6	DYER Terry	78		NEVILLE Damien 3
7	CUFFY Elry			DEGREGORY Kamal 4
8	MARSHALL Shane			CHRISTIE Gavin 5
9	JOSEPH Yanik			ALTIDOR Mackinson 6
11	PETERS Kelly	84	89	BETHEL Vaughn 7
13	FRANCIS Derwin			MOUSSIS George 8
14	VICTOR Paul			DAVIS Theron 9
15	DANGLER George			JEAN Nesley 10
18	CASIMIR Vincent			HORTON Damani 11
	Tr: LEOGAL Don			Tr: WHITE Gary
17	SMITH Ergel	84	89	MCKENZIE Trevor 12
	GEORGE Sherwin	78	65	ROLLE Shivargo 13
			44	WHYLLY Dwayne 22

BFA National Development Center, Nassau
28-03-2004, 15:00, 900, Pineda HON

BAH 1 3 DMA

Jean [67]   Casimir 2 [39 86], Peters [85]

BAHAMAS			DOMINICA	
22	WHYLLY Dwayne			ANGOL Nathaniel 22
2	SWABY Deron		39	ETTIENNE Bishara 2
3	NEVILLE Damien	67		PIERRE-LOUIS Rosie 3
4	DEGREGORY Kamal		62	CUFFY Elry 7
5	CHRISTIE Gavin			MARSHALL Shane 8
6	ALTIDOR Mackinson	75		JOSEPH Yanik 9
7	BETHEL Vaughn	57		GEORGE Sherwin 17
8	MOUSSIS George		89	CASIMIR Vincent 18
10	JEAN Nesley			DANGLER George 19
11	HORTON Damani	35	65	SMITH Ergel 21
16	HEPPLE Cameron			FRANCIS Derwin 23
	Tr: WHITE Gary			Tr: LEOGAL Don
9	DAVIS Theron	67	65	PETERS Kelly 11
12	MCKENZIE Trevor	35	62	WILLIAMS Russel 12
15	SMITH Julian	57	89	TOUSSAINT Don 16

Alamodome, San Antonio (Texas)
19-06-2004, 19:00, 36 451, Callender BAB

DMA 0 10 MEX

Bautista 2 [9 38], Borgetti 2 [11 36], Marquez [16], Osorno [49]
Lozano 2 [74 87], Davino [77], Palencia [92]

DOMINICA			MEXICO	
22	ANGOL Nathaniel			SANCHEZ Oswaldo 1
3	PIERRE-LOUIS Rosie	63		MARQUEZ Rafael 4
6	DYER Terry	46		DAVINO Duilio 5
7	CUFFY Elry		62	TORRADO Gerardo 6
8	MARSHALL Shane			VALDEZ Octavio 7
9	JOSEPH Yanik			PARDO Pavel 8
10	CASIMIR Vincent		46	BORGETTI Jared 9
11	PETERS Kelly			BAUTISTA Adolfo 10
13	FRANCIS Derwin			PALENCIA Francisco 17
14	VICTOR Paul	31		OSORIO Ricardo 20
15	DANGLER George		62	ALTAMIRANO Hector 22
	Tr: LEOGAL Don			Tr: LA VOLPE Ricardo
4	FREDERICK Fitz	63	46	OSORNO Daniel 11
5	SMITH Ergel	46	62	LOZANO Jaime 19
17	GEORGE Sherwin	31	62	ARELLANO Jesus 21

Victoria, Aguascalientes
27-06-2004, 12:00, 17 000, Stott USA

MEX 8 0 DMA

Bautista 2 [2 36], Lozano 2 [17 61]
Borgetti 2 [33 38], Oteo [59], Altamirano [76]

MEXICO			DOMINICA	
12	PEREZ Oscar			ANGOL Nathaniel 22
4	MARQUEZ Rafael	46		ETTIENNE Bishara 2
5	DAVINO Duilio			PIERRE-LOUIS Rosie 3
6	TORRADO Gerardo	60		CUFFY Elry 7
8	PARDO Pavel			MARSHALL Shane 8
9	BORGETTI Jared			JOSEPH Yanik 9
10	BAUTISTA Adolfo		60	TOUSSAINT Don 16
11	OSORNO Daniel			GEORGE Sherwin 17
19	LOZANO Jaime	71	76	CASIMIR Vincent 18
20	OSORIO Ricardo			DANGLER George 19
22	ALTAMIRANO Hector			FRANCIS Derwin 23
	Tr: LA VOLPE Ricardo			Tr: LEOGAL Don
14	MORALES Ramon	60	76	PETERS Kelly 11
15	OTEO David	46	60	WILLIAMS Russel 12
17	PALENCIA Francisco	71		

GROUP 10

Lionel Roberts, St Thomas/St John
18-02-2004, 19:00, 225, Brizan TRI

VIR 0 4 SKN

Huggins [26], Lake 2 [50 64], Isaac [62]

US VIRGIN ISLANDS			ST KITTS AND NEVIS	
1	JONES Terrence		88	BENJAMIN Kayian 1
2	THOMAS Dwayne			LAWRANCE Shelda 3
3	TAYLOR MacDonald	68		LEWIS Lance 4
4	ARNOLD Jarrel			JEFFERS Iroy 6
7	BAILEY Lishati			ISAAC George 7
8	PEREZ Francisco		72	SARGEANT Vernon 10
9	BABB Wallace			LAKE Ian 11
10	WRENSFORD Kareem		72	SADDLER Keithroy 12
11	BANNIS David	74		RILEY Toussaint 15
15	APPLETON Leonard	58		HODGE Floyd 16
17	FERGUSON Dwight			HUGGINS Austin 19
	Tr: RAMIREZ Francisco William			Tr: BROWNE Elvis
12	FRANSECA Francisco	58	72	FRANCIS Jevon 9
13	DOMINIQUE Gene	68	88	TAYLOR Dion 13
16	ALPHONSE Brian	74	72	WARNER Alister 17

Warner Park, Basseterre
31-03-2004, 19:00, 800, Recinos SLV

SKN 7 0 VIR

Lake 5 [8 38 46 56 77], Isaac 2 [80 90]

ST KITTS AND NEVIS			US VIRGIN ISLANDS	
1	BENJAMIN Kayian			JONES Terrence 1
2	EDDY Keithroy			THOMAS Dwayne 2
3	RILEY Toussaint			TAYLOR MacDonald 3
4	LEWIS Lance			ARNOLD Jarrel 4
5	LEADER Thrizen			FERGUSON Dwight 6
7	ISAAC George		46	BAILEY Lishati 7
9	FRANCIS Jevon	53		CORNELIUS Keithroy 8
11	LAKE Ian		54	LABADIE Benny 9
12	SADDLER Keithroy	69		WRENSFORD Kareem 10
14	WILLIAMS Shawn			APPLETON Leonard 15
19	HODGE Floyd	58	63	STEPHENS Elvis 16
	Tr: BROWNE Elvis			Tr: RAMIREZ Francisco William
8	JARVIS Dachan	69	46	ADJOHA Denver 5
10	GREAUX Larrier	53	54	BANNIS David 11
15	HUGGINS Austin	58	63	WALTERS Ian 13

Waterford National Stadium, Bridgetown
13-06-2004, 20:00, 3 700, Alfaro SLV

BRB	0	2	SKN

Gumbs [78], Newton [88]

	BARBADOS			ST KITTS AND NEVIS	
1	CHASE Adrian			BYRON Akil	1
2	BURROWES Randy			EDDY Keithroy	2
4	JAMES Dyson			LEWIS Lance	4
7	IFILL Paul			LEADER Thrizen	5
9	LUCAS Ryan	65		NEWTON Adam	6
10	GOODRIDGE Gregory	65		ISAAC George	7
14	HALL Kent		73	WILLOCK Calum	10
16	SOBERS Wayne			GUMBS Keith	11
17	PARRIS John		75	HUGGINS Austin	15
20	GROSVENOR Sheridan			BURTON Sagi	17
21	FORDE Norman		87	GOMEZ Daryl	18
	Tr: LAYNE Kenville			Tr: LAKE Lennie	
11	RILEY Llewellyn	83 65	87	RILEY Toussaint	3
19	LOVELL Paul	65	73	LAKE Ian	8
24	SKINNER Kenroy	83	75	HODGE Floyd	19

Warner Park, Basseterre
19-06-2004, 20:00, 3 500, Pineda HON

SKN	3	2	BRB

Gomez [16], Willock 2 [22 29]   Skinner [33], Goodridge [45]

	ST KITTS AND NEVIS			BARBADOS	
1	BYRON Akil			CHASE Adrian	1
2	EDDY Keithroy			JAMES Dyson	4
4	LEWIS Lance			COX Kirk	5
5	LEADER Thrizen			IFILL Paul	7
6	NEWTON Adam		60	LUCAS Ryan	9
7	ISAAC George	83		GOODRIDGE Gregory	10
10	WILLOCK Calum	67		HALL Kent	14
11	GUMBS Keith			PARRIS John	17
15	HUGGINS Austin		54	LOVELL Paul	19
17	BURTON Sagi			BRATHWAITE Romell	23
18	GOMEZ Daryl	61	73	SKINNER Kenroy	24
	Tr: LAKE Lennie			Tr: LAYNE Kenville	
3	RILEY Toussaint	83	60	FORDE Michael	11
8	LAKE Ian	67	54	HAWKESWORTH John	18
19	HODGE Floyd	61	73	GROSVENOR Rudolph	20

GROUP 11

Juan Pablo Duarte, Santo Domingo
19-03-2004, 15:30, 400, Mattus CRC

DOM	0	0	AIA

	DOMINICAN REPUBLIC			ANGUILLA	
1	LLOYD Miguel			CONNOR Marvin	1
4	MEDINA Freddy			CONNOR Nigel	2
5	TAVERAS Flavio			HAWLEY Kevin	4
6	SEVERINO Kervin			ABBOTT Jaiden	5
8	REYES Feliciano	46		CONNOR Girdon	7
9	ZAPATA Omar			JEFFERS Leon	8
10	SANCHEZ Omar	62	70	ROGERS Terrence	9
11	CONTRERA Juan			BENJAMIN Walwyn	10
14	ARIAS Samuel	75		EDWARDS Ian	11
15	TEJADA Wilkys		84	CONNER Lester	12
16	ALVAREZ Samuel			KENTISH Shomari	15
	Tr: BENNETT William			Tr: HODGE Vernon	
7	MORILLO Pablo	62	70	BENJAMIN Iston	16
17	CASQUEZ Luis	75	84	FLEMMING Lucian	17
18	REYES Carlos	46			

Juan Pablo Duarte, Santo Domingo
21-03-2004, 15:30, 850, Porras CRC

AIA	0	6	DOM

Zapata [15], Severino 2 [38 61]
Contrera 2 [57 90], Casquez [77]

	ANGUILLA			DOMINICAN REPUBLIC	
1	CONNOR Marvin			TAVERAS Flavio	5
2	CONNOR Nigel			LLOYD Miguel	1
3	KENTISH Kieran			VASQUEZ Franklin	2
4	HAWLEY Kevin			MEDINA Freddy	4
5	ABBOTT Jaiden		64	SEVERINO Kervin	6
7	CONNOR Girdon		75	ZAPATA Omar	9
8	JEFFERS Leon			SANCHEZ Omar	10
10	BENJAMIN Walwyn	45		CONTRERA Juan	11
12	CONNER Lester		53	ARIAS Samuel	14
15	KENTISH Shomari	70		TEJADA Wilkys	15
16	BENJAMIN Iston	73		ALVAREZ Samuel	16
	Tr: HODGE Vernon			Tr: BENNETT William	
6	HODGE Jermain	70	75	KOURY Mario	13
17	FLEMMING Lucian	45	64	CASQUEZ Luis	17
18	SMITH Rocarlo	73	53	REYES Carlos	18

Estadio Olimpico, Santo Domingo
13-06-2004, 15:30, 2 500, Moreno

DOM	0	2	TRI

Andrews [62], Stern [90]

	DOMINICAN REPUBLIC			TRINIDAD/TOBAGO	
1	MEJIA Oscar			INCE Clayton	21
2	VASQUEZ Franklin			FITZWILLIAMS Hayden	3
4	MEDINA Freddy			ANDREWS Marvin	4
5	TAVERAS Flavio		72	SANCHO Brent	5
6	SEVERINO Kervin		54	EDWARDS Carlos	7
7	ESPINAL Edwards			EVE Angus	8
10	SANCHEZ Luis	68		JEMMOT Kerwyn	10
11	CONTRERA Juan			ROUGIER Anthony	12
14	ARIAS Samuel	60		JOHN Stern	14
15	TEJADA Wilkys		85	THOMAS Keyeno	15
16	ALVAREZ Samuel			LAWRENCE Dennis	16
	Tr: BENNETT William			Tr: SAINT CLAIR Bertille	
13	PEREZ Manuel	60	72	ROJAS Marlon	2
18	REYES Carlos	68	54	THEOBALD Densil	13
			85	BAPTISTE Kerry	18

Manny Ramjohn Stadium, Marabella
20-06-2004, 16:00, 5 500, Pinas SUR

TRI	4	0	DOM

Scotland [49], Stern [71]
Theobald [73], Sealt [85]

	TRINIDAD/TOBAGO			DOMINICAN REPUBLIC	
21	INCE Clayton			MEJIA Oscar	1
2	ROJAS Marlon			VASQUEZ Franklin	2
4	ANDREWS Marvin			MEDINA Freddy	4
7	RAHIM Brent	78		TAVERAS Flavio	5
8	EVE Angus			SEVERINO Kervin	6
9	SCOTLAND Jason	66		ESPINAL Edwards	7
11	THEOBALD Densil		23	ZAPATA Omar	9
12	ROUGIER Anthony			CONTRERA Juan	11
14	JOHN Stern	88		PEREZ Manuel	13
16	LAWRENCE Dennis		62	TEJADA Wilkys	15
20	JONES Kenwyne		88	ALVAREZ Samuel	16
	Tr: SAINT CLAIR Bertille			Tr: BENNETT William	
10	SEALT Scott	78	88	REYES Feliciano	8
13	GLENN Cornell	66	23	SANCHEZ Luis	10
18	BAPTISTE Kerry	88	62	ARIAS Samuel	14

GROUP 12

Cacique Diriangen, Diriamba
13-06-2004, 15:00, 7 500, Delgado CUB

NCA   2   2   VIN

Palacio 37, Calero 79   Haynes 9, Samuel 43

NICARAGUA			ST VINCENT	
1	CHAMORRO Sergio		ANDREWS Melvin	1
2	QUINTANILLA Hevel	66	SAMUELS Brent	2
5	RUIZ Jamie		FORDE Matthew	3
6	ALONSO Carlos		JOHN Wesley	4
7	ACEVEDO Tyron	58	HENDRICKSON Ezra	5
8	LOPEZ Franklin	73	CHARLES Matthew	6
9	CALERO Rudel	68	GONSALVES Kenlyn	7
10	PALACIO Emilio		PRINCE Tyrone	8
12	ROCHA Jose	56	SAMUEL Shandel	9
18	RODRIGUEZ Sergio	54	HAYNES Renson	10
20	SOLORZANO David		JOSEPH Benford	11
	Tr: BATISTINI Mauricio		Tr: SHAW Adrian	
11	NOVOA Carlos	56 68	BALLANTYNE Jamal	68 12
16	ACEVEDO Mario	58 54	GUY Alwyn	54 14
19	MARTINEZ David	73 66	JOHN Vincent	66 18

Arnos Vale Playing Ground, Kingstown
20-06-2004, 15:00, 5 000, Brohim DMA

VIN   4   1   NCA

Samuel 2 14, 79, James 15,
Alonso OG 86   Palacio 60

ST VINCENT			NICARAGUA	
1	ANDREWS Melvin		CHAMORRO Sergio	1
2	HUGGINS Cornelius	46	QUINTANILLA Hevel	2
3	FORDE Matthew		RUIZ Jamie	5
4	JOHN Wesley		ALONSO Carlos	6
5	HENDRICKSON Ezra		CALERO Rudel	9
6	CHARLES Matthew		PALACIO Emilio	10
7	BALLANTYNE Jamal	90 46	ROCHA Jose	46 12
8	PRINCE Tyrone		ACEVEDO Mario	16
9	SAMUEL Shandel	83 83	RODRIGUEZ Sergio	83 18
10	JAMES Marlon	75	SOLORZANO David	20
11	VELOX Kendal		LOPEZ Francisco	23
	Tr: SHAW Adrian		Tr: BATISTINI Mauricio	
12	HAYNES Renson	83 46	NOVOA Carlos	11
15	GONSALVES Kenlyn	90 83	SANCHEZ Miguel	13
16	GUY Alwyn	75 46	MARTINEZ David	19

FIRST GROUP STAGE

SECOND STAGE GROUP 1	PL	W	D	L	F	A	PTS	USA	PAN	JAM	SLV
1 USA	6	3	3	0	13	3	12		6-0	1-1	2-0
2 Panama	6	2	2	2	8	11	8	1-1		1-1	3-0
3 Jamaica	6	1	4	1	7	5	7	1-1	1-2		0-0
4 El Salvador	6	1	1	4	2	11	4	0-2	2-1	0-3	

National Stadium, Kingston
18-08-2004, 18:00, 30 000, Mattus CRC

JAM   1   1   USA

Goodisson 49   Ching 88

JAMAICA			USA	
30	RICKETTS Donovan		KELLER Kasey	18
5	GOODISON Ian		HEJDUK Frankie	2
6	KING Marlon	66	VANNEY Greg	3
8	HYDE Micah		BOCANEGRA Carlos	4
9	WILLIAMS Andrew	67	STEWART Earnie	8
11	WHITMORE Theodore		REYNA Claudio	10
14	MARSHALL Tyrone	76	ARMAS Chris	14
15	GARDNER Ricardo		BEASLEY DaMarcus	17
17	RALPH Damani	60	MC BRIDE Brian	20
22	DAVIS Fabian		DONOVAN Landon	21
25	DAVIS Claude		POPE Eddie	23
	Tr: LAZARONI Sebastiao		Tr: ARENA Bruce	
10	FULLER Ricardo	66 76	LEWIS Eddie	76 7
			JONES Cobi	67 13
			CHING Brian	60 25

Estadio Cuscatlan, San Salvador
18-08-2004, 19:30, 11 400, Navarro CAN

SLV   2   1   PAN

Velasquez 7, Rodriguez 45   Dely 36

EL SALVADOR			PANAMA	
1	RIVERA Noel		JAMES Ricardo	1
4	GUEVERA Mario		MIRANDA Victor	2
5	VELASQUEZ Victor		MORENO Luis	3
6	PRADO Erick		HENRIQUEZ Luis	4
10	GOCHEZ Ernesto	51	RIVERA Carlos	5
11	CERRITOS Ronald		MITRE Engin	6
17	RODRIGUEZ Jorge	39	LOMBARDO Angel	39 7
18	MURGAS Gilberto		BLANCO Alberto	60 8
19	PACHECO Alfredo		DELY Julio	9
21	GALDAMEZ Naun	89	MEDINA Julio	10
23	MARTINEZ Jose	43	PHILLIPS Ricardo	73 11
	Tr: PAREDES Juan		Tr: HERNANDEZ Jose	
3	GONZALEZ Marvin	87 39	AGUILAR William	39 16
9	MEJIA Diego	89 60	GARCES Jose	60 17
15	SILVA Nildeson	51 87	DELY Jorge	73 18

7 August 2004. Workers Stadium, Beijing, China. Japan celebrate winning the AFC Asian Cup after beating hosts China 3–1 in the final.

18 August 2004. Stade Sylvio Cator, Port-au-Prince, Haiti. Brazil's superstars beat Haiti 6–0 in the 'Football for Peace' match.

26 August 2004. Karaiskaki, Piraeus, Greece. Golden girl Mia Hamm crowns a glorious career with a second Olympic gold medal after the USA beat Brazil 2–1 in the women's final.

27 August 2004. Kaftanzoglio, Thessaloniki, Greece. Despite missing out on a bronze medal after losing to Italy in the third place play-off, Iraqi fans enjoy their moment in the limelight.

28 September 2004. Old Trafford, Manchester, England. Wayne Rooney scores his first goal for Manchester United in a 5–2 win against Fenerbahçe in the UEFA Champions League.

Gillette Stadium, Foxboro/Boston
4-09-2004, 16:00, 25 266, Brizan TRI

USA 2 0 SLV

Ching 5, Donovan 68

USA				EL SALVADOR	
1 HOWARD Tim				RIVERA Noel	1
4 BOCANEGRA Carlos				GUEVERA Mario	4
5 ZAVAGNIN Kerry	82			VELASQUEZ Victor	5
6 CHERUNDOLO Steve	69			PRADO Erick	6
9 CASEY Conor	77		46	GONZALEZ Edwin	8
10 REYNA Claudio				CERRITOS Ronald	11
12 GIBBS Cory			27	ALAS MORALES Dennis	12
15 CONVEY Bobby				RODRIGUEZ Jorge	17
17 BEASLEY Da Marcus				MURGAS Gilberto	18
21 DONOVAN Landon				PACHECO Alfredo	19
25 CHING Brian			46	GALDAMEZ Naun	21
Tr: ARENA Bruce				Tr: PAREDES Juan	
11 MATHIS Clint	82		46	MERINO Victor Hugo	7
13 JONES Cobi	69		46	MEJIA Diego	9
20 MC BRIDE Brian	77				

National Stadium, Kingston
4-09-2004, 19:00, 24 000, Batres GUA

JAM 1 2 PAN

Ralph 77 / Brown 2, Dely 90

JAMAICA				PANAMA	
30 RICKETTS Donovan				PENEDO Jaime	12
5 GOODISON Ian	32			MIRANDA Victor	2
6 KING Marlon	64			MORENO Luis	3
8 HYDE Micah				HENDRIQUEZ Luis	4
10 FULLER Ricardo				TORRES Josa	5
11 WHITMORE Theodore		54		MITRE Engin	6
14 MARSHALL Tyrone		59		RAMOS Gary	7
15 GARDNER Ricardo				BLANCO Alberto	8
19 REID Garfield	46			DELY Julio	9
22 DAVIS Fabian	75	73		MEDINA Julio	10
25 DAVIS Claude				BROWN Roberto	11
Tr: LAZARONI Sebastiao				Tr: HERNANDEZ Jose	
9 WILLIAMS Andrew	75	54		TORRES Manuel	14
12 JOHNSON Jermaine	64	73		TEJADA Luis	16
20 RALPH Damani	46	59		ZAPATA Alberto	17

Estadio Cuscatlan, San Salvador
8-09-2004, 19:30, 25 000, Alcala MEX

SLV 0 3 JAM

King 2 3 38, Hyde 40

EL SALVADOR				JAMAICA	
1 RIVERA Noel				RICKETTS Donovan	30
4 GUEVERA Mario	66			STEWARD Damian	3
5 VELASQUEZ Victor	83			KING Marlon	6
6 PRADO Erick				LAWRENCE James	8
7 MERINO Victor Hugo	88	76		FULLER Ricardo	10
11 CERRITOS Ronald				WHITMORE Theodore	11
15 SILVA Nildeson	61			MARSHALL Tyrone	14
17 RODRIGUEZ Jorge				GARDNER Ricardo	15
18 MURGAS Gilberto				HYDE Micah	17
19 PACHECO Alfredo				RALPH Damani	20
23 MARTINEZ Jose		13		DAVIS Claude	25
Tr: AGUILAR Miguel Angel				Tr: LAZARONI Sebastiao	
2 ESCOBAR Alexander	88	76		WILLIAMS Andrew	9
20 TORRES William	66	83		JOHNSON Jermaine	12
21 GALDAMEZ Naun	61	13		ZIADIE Craig	23

Estadio Rommel Fernandez, Panama City
8-09-2004, 20:00, 15 000, Rodriguez Moreno MEX

PAN 1 1 USA

Brown 69 / Jones 91

PANAMA				USA	
1 GONZALEZ Donaldo				KELLER Kasey	18
2 RIVERA Carlos				HEJDUK Frankie	2
3 MORENO Luis				VANNEY Greg	3
4 HENDRIQUEZ Luis				BOCANEGRA Carlos	4
5 TORRES Josa		61		CASEY Conor	9
6 MITRE Engin				REYNA Claudio	10
7 ZAPATA Alberto	38	56		MATHIS Clint	11
8 TORRES Manuel	78			BEASLEY Da Marcus	17
9 DELY Julio	71			DONOVAN Landon	21
10 MEDINA Julio				POPE Eddie	23
11 BROWN Roberto		77		CHING Brian	25
Tr: HERNANDEZ Jose				Tr: ARENA Bruce	
14 CUBILLAS Juan Carlos	78	77		LEWIS Eddie	7
15 PHILLIPS Ricardo	38	56		JONES Cobi	13
18 DELY Jorge	71	61		MC BRIDE Brian	20

Estadio Cuscatlan, San Salvador
9-09-2004, 19:30, 20 000, Batres GUA

SLV 0 2 USA

McBride 29, Johnson 75

EL SALVADOR				USA	
1 ALFARO Misael				KELLER Kasey	18
2 TOBAR Rafael				HEJDUK Frankie	2
3 GONZALEZ Marvin				BERHALTER Gregg	3
4 BENITEZ Marvin				ZAVAGNIN Kerry	5
5 VELASQUEZ Victor		67		MATHIS Clint	11
7 MERINO Victor Hugo				GIBBS Cory	12
8 CABRERA Santos	79	87		WOLFF Josh	16
9 GONZALEZ Fredy	69			BEASLEY Da Marcus	17
11 CERRITOS Ronald		70		MC BRIDE Brian	20
13 UMANZOR Deris				DONOVAN Landon	21
17 RODRIGUEZ Jorge	79			POPE Eddie	23
Tr: CONTRERAS Armando				Tr: ARENA Bruce	
16 SARAVIA Isaac	79	67		LEWIS Eddie	7
21 GALDAMEZ Naun	79	87		JONES Cobi	13
23 MARTINEZ Jose	69	70		JOHNSON Ed	19

Estadio Rommel Fernandez, Panama City
9-10-2004, 20:00, 16 000, Pineda HON

PAN 1 1 JAM

Brown 24 / Whitmore 75

PANAMA				JAMAICA	
1 GONZALEZ Donaldo		60		RICKETTS Donovan	30
2 RIVERA Carlos		62		KING Marlon	6
3 MORENO Luis		46		LAWRENCE James	8
4 HENDRIQUEZ Luis				FULLER Ricardo	10
5 TORRES Josa				WHITMORE Theodore	11
6 MITRE Engin	63			MARSHALL Tyrone	14
7 PHILLIPS Ricardo				GARDNER Ricardo	15
8 BLANCO Alberto				HYDE Micah	17
9 DELY Julio				RALPH Damani	20
10 MEDINA Julio	79			ZIADIE Craig	23
11 BROWN Roberto	86			DAVIS Claude	25
Tr: HERNANDEZ Jose				Tr: LAZARONI Sebastiao	
13 MIRANDA Victor	79	46		GOODISON Ian	5
14 TORRES Manuel	63	62		WILLIAMS Andrew	9
18 DELY Jorge	86	60		LAWRENCE Aaron	13

National Stadium, Kingston
13-10-2004, 19:00, 12 000, Quesada Cordero CRC

JAM 0 0 SLV

JAMAICA		EL SALVADOR	
13 LAWRENCE Aaron		46 ALFARO Misael	1
5 GOODISON Ian		TOBAR Rafael	2
6 KING Marlon	70	BENITEZ Marvin	4
8 LAWRENCE James		VELASQUEZ Victor	5
10 FULLER Ricardo	82	PRADO Erick	6
11 WHITMORE Theodore		MERINO Victor Hugo	7
14 MARSHALL Tyrone	64	GONZALEZ Fredy	9
15 GARDNER Ricardo	83	CERRITOS Ronald	11
20 RALPH Damani		ALAS MORALES Dennis	12
23 ZIADIE Craig		UMANZOR Deris	13
25 DAVIS Claude	73	RODRIGUEZ Jorge	17
Tr: LAZARONI Sebastiao		Tr: CONTRERAS Armando	
9 WILLIAMS Andrew	64 83	CABRERA Santos	8
12 JOHNSON Jermaine	82 73	SARAVIA Isaac	16
18 RICKETTS Donovan	70 46	RIVERA Noel	25

RFK Memorial Stadium, Washington DC
13-10-2004, 19:30, 22 000, Ramdhan TRI

USA 6 0 PAN

Donovan 2 [21][56]
Johnson 3 [69][84][86], Torres OG [89]

USA		PANAMA	
18 KELLER Kasey		GONZALEZ Donaldo	1
2 HEJDUK Frankie		RIVERA Carlos	2
3 BERHALTER Gregg	61	MORENO Luis	3
4 BOCANEGRA Carlos	40	HENRIQUEZ Luis	4
5 ZAVAGNIN Kerry	73	TORRES Antony	5
7 LEWIS Eddie	74	TORRES Manuel	6
16 WOLFF Josh	65	PHILLIPS Ricardo	7
17 BEASLEY Da Marcus		BLANCO Alberto	8
20 MC BRIDE Brian		DELY Julio	9
21 DONOVAN Landon		MEDINA Julio	10
23 POPE Eddie	86	BROWN Roberto	11
Tr: ARENA Bruce		Tr: HERNANDEZ Jose	
6 ONYEWU Oguchi	86 40	MIRANDA Victor	13
19 JOHNSON Ed	65 74	MITRE Engin	14
25 MASTROENI Pablo	73 61	ZAPATA Alberto	17

Columbus Crew Stadium, Columbus
17-11-2004, 19:30, 9 088, Navarro CAN

USA 1 1 JAM

Johnson [15]

Williams [26]

USA		JAMAICA	
18 KELLER Kasey		RICKETTS Donovan	30
3 CORRALES Ramiro	67 23	STEWARD Damian	3
5 ALBRIGHT Chris		GOODISON Ian	5
6 ONYEWU Oguchi	74	LAWRENCE James	8
7 JOHNSON Ed	88	WILLIAMS Andrew	9
10 DONOVAN Landon		FULLER Ricardo	10
12 GIBBS Cory	72	WHITMORE Theodore	11
14 RALSTON Steve	77	MARSHALL Tyrone	14
20 MC BRIDE Brian		GARDNER Ricardo	15
22 SANNAH Tony	68	RALPH Damani	20
25 MASTROENI Pablo		ZIADIE Craig	23
Tr: ARENA Bruce		Tr: LAZARONI Sebastiao	
2 DEMPSEY Clint	67 68	KING Marlon	6
4 SPECTOR Jonathan	77 72	EUELL Jason	7
16 TWELLMAN Taylor	88 23	HUE Jermaine	17

Estadio Rommel Fernandez, Panama City
17-11-2004, 19:30, 9 502, Archundia MEX

PAN 3 0 SLV

Brown 4, Baloy 7, Garces 21

PANAMA		EL SALVADOR	
1 GONZALEZ Donaldo		ALFARO Misael	1
2 RIVERA Carlos		BENITEZ Marvin	4
3 MORENO Luis		VELASQUEZ Victor	5
4 TORRES Antony		PRADO Erick	6
5 BALOY Felipe	74	CABRERA Santos	8
6 MITRE Engin		CERRITOS Ronald	11
8 BLANCO Alberto		UMANZOR Deris	13
10 MEDINA Julio	33	CORRALES Rudis	14
11 BROWN Roberto	29	CASTRO Julio	15
15 PHILLIPS Ricardo	81	RODRIGUEZ Jorge	17
19 GARCES Jose	74 46	PEDROZO Emiliano	18
Tr: HERNANDEZ Jose		Tr: CONTRERAS Armando	
7 DELY Jorge	29 46	GONZALEZ Fredy	9
9 DELY Julio	81 33	ALAS MORALES Dennis	12
17 PEREZ Blas	74	ALVAREZ Cristian	19

SECOND STAGE GROUP 2	PL	W	D	L	F	A	PTS	CRC	GUA	HON	CAN
1 Costa Rica	6	3	1	2	12	8	10		5-0	2-5	1-0
2 Guatemala	6	3	1	2	7	9	10	2-1		1-0	0-1
3 Honduras	6	1	4	1	9	7	7	0-0	2-2		1-1
4 Canada	6	1	1	3	4	8	5	1-3	0-2	1-1	

Swangard, Vancouver
18-08-2004, 19:00, 6 500, Sibrian SLV

CAN 0 2 GUA

Ruiz 2 [7][59]

CANADA		GUATEMALA	
1 ONSTAD Pat		TRIGUENO Ricardo	22
2 PIZZOLITTO Nevio		MELGAR Pablo	3
3 JAZIC Ante		CHEN Denis	4
4 WATSON Mark		CABRERA Gustavo	6
6 DE GUZMAN Julian	44	THOMPSON Fredy	7
7 STALTERI Paul		ROMERO Gonzalo	8
8 IMHOF Daniel		RAMIREZ Guillermo	11
10 PESCHISOLIDO Paul		MARTINEZ Nestor	13
11 SIMPSON Josh	59	PEZZAROSSI Dwight	17
14 DE ROSARIO Dwayne		RODRIGUEZ Mario	19
17 OCCEAN Olivier		RUIZ Carlos	20
Tr: YALLOP Frank		Tr: MARADIAGA Ramon	
12 SERIOUX Adrian	44		
13 PETERS Jamie	59		

Alejandro Mojera Soto, Alajuela
18-08-2004, 20:00, 14 000, Rodriguez Moreno MEX

CRC 2 5 HON

Herron 2 [20][36]

Suazo [22], Leon [35], Guevara [77],
Guerrero [87], Martinez 89

COSTA RICA		HONDURAS	
23 GONZALEZ Ricardo		VALLADARES Noel	22
2 ARNAEZ Luis		FIGUEROA Maynor	3
3 MARIN Luis		IZAGUIRRE Junior	4
4 CASTRO Alexander	83	SUAZO David	7
5 MARTINEZ Gilberto		PALACIOS Wilson	8
8 SOLIS Mauricio	80	LEON Julio	10
9 WANCHOPE Paulo		SUAZO Maynor	12
10 CENTENO Walter	74	GUEVARA Amado	20
17 BRYCE Stevens	77	ALVAREZ Edgar	21
20 HERRON Andy	63	GUERRERO Ivan	23
22 CATRO Carlos		BERNARDEZ Victor	24
Tr: PINTO Jorge		Tr: MARTINEZ Raul	
7 SOLIS Alonso	80 77	MARIN Elmer	5
11 GOMEZ Ronald	63 83	MARTINEZ Saul	18
15 SOTO Jafet	74		

Commonwealth Stadium, Edmonton
4-09-2004, 19:00, 8 000, Archundia MEX

CAN 1 1 HON

De Vos 82   Guevara 88p

No	CANADA				HONDURAS	No
1	ONSTAD Pat				VALLADARES Noel	22
3	JAZIC Ante				FIGUEROA Maynor	3
4	WATSON Mark				PALACIOS Milton	6
5	DE VOS Jason		89	89	SUAZO David	7
6	DE GUZMAN Julian				PALACIOS Wilson	8
7	STALTERI Paul	90	85	85	LEON Julio	10
8	IMHOF Daniel				SUAZO Maynor	12
9	RADZINSKI Tomasz				GUEVARA Amado	20
10	PESCHISOLIDO Paul	46			ALVAREZ Edgar	21
14	DE ROSARIO Dwayne	78			GUERRERO Ivan	23
15	HUTCHINSON Atiba				BERNARDEZ Victor	24
	Tr: YALLOP Frank				Tr: MARTINEZ Raul	
11	SIMPSON Josh	73	89	89	PAVON Carlos	9
13	PETERS Jaime	46 73	85	85	MARTINEZ Saul	18
17	OCCEAN Olivier	78				

Mateo Flores, Guatemala City
5-09-2004, 12:00, 27 460, Stott USA

GUA 2 1 CRC

Plata 2 58 73   Solis 24

No	GUATEMALA				COSTA RICA	No
22	TRIGUENO Ricardo				PORRAS Jose	18
3	MELGAR Pablo	66			MARIN Luis	3
6	CABRERA Gustavo				CASTRO Alexander	4
7	THOMPSON Fredy				MARTINEZ Gilberto	5
8	ROMERO Gonzalo	71	59	59	SOLIS Alonso	7
11	RAMIREZ Guillermo				LOPEZ Jose Luis	8
13	MARTINEZ Nestor				WANCHOPE Paulo	9
17	PEZZAROSSI Dwight				GONZALEZ Leonardo	12
19	RODRIGUEZ Mario		75	75	BADILLA Cristian	14
20	RUIZ Carlos		59	59	BRYCE Stevens	17
26	SANABRIA Angel	46		18	HERRON Andy	20
	Tr: MARADIAGA Ramon				Tr: PINTO Jorge	
15	PLATA Juan Carlos	46	59	59	CENTENO Walter	10
29	MORALES Nelson	66	59	59	BENNETTE Tray	16
31	DAVILA Maynor	71	75	75	SABORIO Alvaro	22

Estadio Olimpico, San Pedro Sula
8-09-2004, 20:00, 40 000, Prendergast JAM

HON 2 2 GUA

Guevara 51, Suazo 65   Ruiz 20, Pezzarossi 49

No	HONDURAS				GUATEMALA	No
22	VALLADARES Noel				TRIGUENO Ricardo	22
3	FIGUEROA Maynor				CABRERA Gustavo	6
6	PALACIOS Milton				ROMERO Gonzalo	8
7	SUAZO David			82	RAMIREZ Guillermo	11
8	PALACIOS Wilson				MARTINEZ Nestor	13
9	PAVON Carlos	84			PEZZAROSSI Dwight	17
10	LEON Julio	86		91	RODRIGUEZ Mario	19
12	SUAZO Maynor				RUIZ Carlos	20
20	GUEVARA Amado				SANABRIA Angel	29
23	GUERRERO Ivan				MORALES Nelson	29
24	BERNARDEZ Victor				DAVILA Maynor	31
	Tr: MARTINEZ Raul				Tr: MARADIAGA Ramon	
18	MARTINEZ Saul	84		91	PLATA Juan Carlos	15
21	ALVAREZ Edgar	86		82	GUAVARA Sergio	24

Ricardo Saprissa, San Jose
8-09-2004, 20:00, 13 000, Ramdhan TRI

CRC 1 0 CAN

Wanchope 46

No	COSTA RICA				CANADA	No
18	PORRAS Jose				ONSTAD Pat	1
3	MARIN Luis				JAZIC Ante	3
5	MARTINEZ Gilberto				WATSON Mark	4
7	SOLIS Alonso	78			GERVAIS Gabriel	5
8	LOPEZ Jose Luis				DE GUZMAN Julian	6
12	GONZALEZ Leonardo			62	HUME Iain	7
14	BADILLA Cristian	54			IMHOF Daniel	8
16	BENNETTE Tray				RADZINSKI Tomasz	9
20	BRYCE Stevens		83		HUTCHINSON Atiba	13
22	SCOTT Eric			78	DE ROSARIO Dwayne	14
	Tr: PINTO Jorge				GRANDE Sandro	16
					Tr: YALLOP Frank	
6	FONSECA Danny	78	83	83	PETERS Jaime	11
9	WANCHOPE Paulo	46	78	78	SIMPSON Josh	15
10	CENTENO Walter	54	62	62	OCCEAN Olivier	17

Estadio Olimpico, San Pedro Sula
9-10-2004, 15:00, 42 000, Stott USA

HON 1 1 CAN

Turcios 92   Hutchinson 73

No	HONDURAS				CANADA	No
22	VALLADARES Noel				ONSTAD Pat	1
6	MEDINA Ninrod				JAZIC Ante	3
8	PALACIOS Wilson	46			WATSON Mark	4
9	PAVON Carlos				DE VOS Jason	5
10	LEON Julio		74	74	DE GUZMAN Julian	6
12	SUAZO Maynor	80	65	65	HUME Iain	7
16	MENDOZA Sergio				IMHOF Daniel	8
20	GUEVARA Amado				RADZINSKI Tomasz	9
21	ALVAREZ Edgar	74			HUTCHINSON Atiba	13
23	GUERRERO Ivan				DE ROSARIO Dwayne	14
24	BERNARDEZ Victor		78		GRANDE Sandro	16
	Tr: MARTINEZ Raul				Tr: YALLOP Frank	
13	MARTINEZ Emil	80	78	78	BERNIER Patrice	12
18	MARTINEZ Saul	46	74	74	SIMPSON Josh	15
19	TURCIOS Elvis	74	65	65	OCCEAN Olivier	17

Ricardo Saprissa, San Jose
9-10-2004, 19:30, 18 000, Archundia MEX

CRC 5 0 GUA

Hernandez 19
Wanchope 3 36 62 69, Fonseca 83

No	COSTA RICA				GUATEMALA	No
18	PORRAS Jose				TRIGUENO Ricardo	22
3	MARIN Luis				MELGAR Pablo	3
5	MARTINEZ Gilberto	75			CABRERA Gustavo	6
8	LOPEZ Jose Luis				THOMPSON Fredy	7
9	WANCHOPE Paulo				RAMIREZ Guillermo	11
12	GONZALEZ Leonardo				MARTINEZ Nestor	13
15	WALLACE Harold		79		PLATA Juan Carlos	15
16	HERNANDEZ Carlos		63	79	PEZZAROSSI Dwight	17
17	BRYCE Stevens			63	RODRIGUEZ Mario	19
21	HERRON Andy	71	71		SANABRIA Angel	26
	Tr: PINTO Jorge			71	DAVILA Maynor	31
					Tr: MARADIAGA Ramon	
7	FONSECA Rolando	71	79	79	ESTRADA Walter	17
10	CENTENO Walter	67	71	71	CABRERA Eddy	32
20	CHINCHILLA Pablo	75	63	63	CASTILLO Carlos	34

| 11 | SOLIS Alonso | 67 | | | | |

Swangard, Vancouver
13-10-2004, 19:00, 4 000, Prendergast JAM

CAN	1	3	CRC

De Rosario [12]

Wanchope [49], Sunsing [81]
Hernandez [87]

	CANADA		COSTA RICA	
1	ONSTAD Pat		MESEN Alvaro	1
3	JAZIC Ante	76	MARIN Luis	3
4	WATSON Mark		MARTINEZ Gilberto	5
5	DE VOS Jason		LOPEZ Jose Luis	8
6	DE GUZMAN Julian		SOLIS Alonso	11
7	HUME Iain	58	GONZALEZ Leonardo	12
8	IMHOF Daniel		BADILLA Cristian	14
9	RADZINSKI Tomasz	70	BRYCE Stevens	17
13	HUTCHINSON Atiba		CHINCHILLA Pablo	20
14	DE ROSARIO Dwayne	29	HERRON Andy	21
16	GRANDE Sandro	70 76	SCOTT Eric	22
	Tr: YALLOP Frank		Tr: PINTO Jorge	
10	CORAZZIN Carlo	58 29	WANCHOPE Paulo	9
11	PETERS Jaime	76 70	HERNANDEZ Carlos	16
17	OCCEAN Olivier	70 76	SUNSING William	19

Francisco Morazan, San Pedro Sula
17-11-2004, 17:00, 18 000, Sibrian SLV

HON	0	0	CRC

	HONDURAS		COSTA RICA	
1	COELLO Victor		MESEN Alvaro	1
2	BEATA Mario		MARIN Luis	3
3	FIGUEROA Maynor		LOPEZ Jose Luis	8
6	MENDOZA Sergio	90	WANCHOPE Paulo	9
9	CARCAMO Juan	65 59	SOLIS Alonso	11
10	TURCIOS Elvis		GONZALEZ Leonardo	12
15	SABILLON Mauricio	86	BADILLA Cristian	14
17	VALLECILLO Erick		WALLACE Harold	15
18	MARTINEZ Saul	83	BRYCE Stevens	17
20	GUEVARA Amado		CHINCHILLA Pablo	20
23	GUERRERO Ivan	75	HERRON Andy	21
	Tr: DE LA PAZ Jose		Tr: PINTO Jorge	
12	HERNANDEZ Walter	90 83	MARTINEZ Gilberto	5
13	MARTINEZ Emil	86 59	CENTENO Walter	10
19	PALACIOS Jerry	65 75	HERNANDEZ Carlos	16

Mateo Flores, Guatemala City
13-10-2004, 20:00, 26 000, Brizan TRI

GUA	1	0	HON

Ruiz [44]

	GUATEMALA		HONDURAS	
30	KLEE Miguel		VALLADARES Noel	22
3	MELGAR Pablo		MEDINA Ninrod	6
6	CABRERA Gustavo	76	LEON Julio	10
7	THOMPSON Fredy		SUAZO Maynor	12
8	ROMERO Gonzalo		MORALES Rony	14
11	RAMIREZ Guillermo	46	LOPEZ Walter	15
13	MARTINEZ Nestor		MENDOZA Sergio	16
17	PEZZAROSSI Dwight	70	MARTINEZ Saul	18
19	RODRIGUEZ Mario	90	GUEVARA Amado	20
20	RUIZ Carlos	82	GUERRERO Ivan	23
26	SANABRIA Angel		BERNARDEZ Victor	24
	Tr: MARADIAGA Ramon		Tr: MARTINEZ Raul	
31	DAVILA Maynor	82 70	PAVON Carlos	9
34	CASTILLO Carlos	90 46	NUNEZ Milton	11
		76	TURCIOS Elvis	19

Mateo Flores, Guatemala-City
17-11-2004, 20:15, 18 000, Rodriguez MEX

GUA	0	1	CAN

De Rosario [57]

	GUATEMALA		CANADA	
30	KLEE Miguel		HIRSCHFELD Lars	1
3	MELGAR Pablo		GERVAIS Gabriel	2
6	CABRERA Gustavo	66	MC KENNA Kevin	4
7	THOMPSON Fredy	65 75	SERIOUX Adrian	6
8	ROMERO Gonzalo		GRANDE Sandro	7
11	RAMIREZ Guillermo		BERNIER Patrice	8
15	PLATA Juan Carlos	45 71	OCCEAN Olivier	9
19	RODRIGUEZ Mario		PETERS Jaime	11
20	RUIZ Carlos		HUTCHINSON Atiba	13
32	CABRERA Eddy		DE ROSARIO Dwayne	14
			SIMPSON Josh	15
	Tr: MARADIAGA Ramon		Tr: YALLOP Frank	
17	PEZZAROSSI Dwight	45 75	POZNIAK Chris	16
34	CASTILLO Carlos	65		

SECOND STAGE GROUP 3	PL	W	D	L	F	A	PTS	MEX	TRI	VIN	SKN
1 Mexico	6	6	0	0	27	1	18		3-0	7-0	8-0
2 Trinidad and Tobago	6	4	0	2	12	9	12	1-3		2-1	5-1
3 St Vincent and the Grenad.	6	2	0	4	5	12	6	0-1	0-2		1-0
4 St Kitts and Nevis	6	0	0	6	2	24	0	0-5	1-2	0-3	

Arnos Vale Playing Ground, Kingstown
18-08-2004, 16:00, 5 000, Vaughn USA

VIN	0	2	TRI

McFarlane 2 [80 85]

	ST VINCENT		TRINIDAD/TOBAGO	
1	DWIGHT Bramble		WILLIAMS Daurance	1
2	FORDE Matthew		ROJAS Marlon	2
3	HUGGINS Cornelius		ANDREWS Marvin	4
4	PRINCE Tyrone	55	SANCHO Brent	5
5	HENDRICKSON Ezra		EVE Angus	8
6	CHARLES Matthew	84	DWARIKA Arnold	9
7	GONSALVES Kenlyn	86	ROUGIER Anthony	12
8	JOHN Vincent	88	MC FARLANE Errol	13
9	SAMUEL Shandel	60	JOHN Stern	14
10	JACK Rodney		LAWRENCE Dennis	18
11	VELOX Kendal	61	JONES Kenwyne	19
	Tr: SHAW Adrian		Tr: SAINT CLAIR Bertille	
14	GUY Alwyn	60 88	SEALT Scott	10
15	WILLIAMS Howie	55 61	RAHIM Brent	11
18	BALLANTYNE Jamal	86 84	SPANN Silvio	18

Warner Park, Basseterre
4-09-2004, 20:00, 2 800, Castillo GUA

SKN	1	2	TRI

Isaac [40]

McFarlane [45], John [89]

	ST KITTS AND NEVIS		TRINIDAD/TOBAGO	
1	BYRON Akil		JACK Kelvin	1
2	RICHARDS Keithroy		ROJAS Marlon	2
3	RILEY Toussaint		ANDREWS Marvin	4
4	RILEY Alexander		SANCHO Brent	5
5	LEADER Thrizen	71	BOUCAUD Andre	7
7	ISAAC George		DWARIKA Arnold	9
10	LAKE Ian	79 89	RAHIM Brent	11
11	GUMBS Keith		JOHN Stern	14
13	GOMEZ Daryl	88 82	MC FARLANE Errol	15
15	HUGGINS Austin		LAWRENCE Dennis	16
17	HODGE Floyd		JONES Kenwyne	19
	Tr: LAKE Lennie		Tr: SAINT CLAIR Bertille	
12	SADDLER Keithroy	88 89	MASON Stokely	3
14	CONNONIER Seritse	79 82	THEOBALD Densil	12
		71	GLENN Cornell	13

Hasely Crawford Stadium, Port of Spain
8-09-2004, 18:00, 20 000, Navarro CAN

TRI 1 – 3 MEX

Stern 39

Areilano 2 1, 80, Borgetti 19

#	TRINIDAD/TOBAGO	min
1	JACK Kelvin	
2	ROJAS Marlon	
4	ANDRWES Marvin	
5	SANCHO Brent	
8	EVE Angus	
9	DWARIKA Arnold	
11	RAHIM Brent	72
14	JOHN Stern	
15	MC FARLANE Errol	80
16	LAWRENCE Dennis	
19	JONES Kenwyne	60
	Tr: SAINT CLAIR Bertille	
7	BOUCAUD Andre	60
10	SCOTLAND Jason	80
13	GLENN Cornell	72

min	MEXICO	#
	SANCHEZ Oswaldo	1
	RODRIGUEZ Francisco	2
	PEREZ Mario	3
74	SALCIDO Carlos	6
	PARDO Pavel	8
	BORGETTI Jared	9
84	NAELSON Antonio	10
	SANCHEZ Hugo	15
	CARMONA Salvador	18
	ARELLANO Jesus	21
	PEREZ Luis	23
	Tr: LA VOLPE Ricardo	
74	PINEDA Gonzalo	14
84	ALTAMIRANO Hector	22

Arnos Vale Playing Ground, Kingstown
10-09-2004, 15:00, 4 000, Delgado CUB

VIN 1 – 0 SKN

Jack 23

#	ST VINCENT	min
1	ANDREWS Melvin	
2	SAMUELS Brent	66
3	HUGGINS Cornelius	
4	JOHN Wesley	
5	HENDRICKSON Ezra	
6	CHARLES Matthew	
8	PIERRE Randy	77
9	JACK Rodney	
10	HAYNES Renson	63
11	VELOX Kendal	76
18	BALLANTYNE Jamal	
	Tr: SHAW Adrian	
12	FORDE Matthew	66
14	SAMUEL Shandei	63
16	WILLIAMS Howie	76

min	ST KITTS AND NEVIS	#
	BYRON Akil	1
	RICHARDS Keithroy	2
	RILEY Toussaint	3
	LEADER Thrizen	5
	ISAAC George	7
	HARRIS Atiba	8
77	LAKE Ian	11
	GUMBS Keith	12
88	GOMEZ Daryl	13
	HUGGINS Austin	15
59	HODGE Floyd	19
	Tr: LAKE Lennie	
59	SARGEANT Vernon	9
88	CONNONIER Seritse	14
77	WARNER Alister	17

Miguel Hidalgo, Pachuca
6-10-2004, 17:00, 21 000, Liu CAN

MEX 7 – 0 VIN

Borgetti 4 31, 68, 77, 89
Lozano 2 54, 63, Santana 81

#	MEXICO	min
1	SANCHEZ Oswaldo	
2	RODRIGUEZ Francisco	
4	MARQUEZ Rafael	
5	LOPEZ Israel	
6	SALCIDO Carlos	
7	NAELSON Antonio	66
9	BORGETTI Jared	
10	BLANCO Cuauhtemoc	
16	MENDEZ Mario	66
19	LOZANO Jaime	
21	ARELLANO Jesus	72
	Tr: LA VOLPE Ricardo	
8	GARCIA Rafael	66
17	SANTANA Sergio	72
23	PEREZ Luis	66

min	ST VINCENT	#
	ANDREWS Melvin	1
46	SAMUELS Brent	3
	HENDRICKSON Ezra	5
	JACK Rodney	9
	VELOX Kendal	11
	WILLIAMS Howie	12
35	GONSALVES Kenlyn	14
65	GUY Alwyn	15
69	JOSEPH Benford	17
	BALLANTYNE Jamal	18
	FORDE Matthew	20
	Tr: VRANES Zoran	
46	FRANCOIS Rodney	2
35	FRANCIS Darren	6
65	SAMUEL Shandel	10

Manny Ramjohn Stadium, Marabella
10-10-2004, 15:30, 7 000, Valenzuela USA

TRI 5 – 1 SKN

Stern 2 24, 80, Glenn 71, Nixon 88
Riley OG 8

Gumbs 43p

#	TRINIDAD/TOBAGO	min
1	HISLOP Skaka	
2	ROJAS Marlon	36
3	COX Ian	
4	ANDREWS Marvin	
5	SANCHO Brent	80
8	EVE Angus	
12	ROUGIER Anthony	
13	GLENN Cornell	79
14	JOHN Stern	
16	THEOBALD Densil	58
19	JONES Kenwyne	
	Tr: SAINT CLAIR Bertille	
10	RAHIM Brent	36
11	NIXON Jerren	79
18	SPANN Silvio	58

min	ST KITTS AND NEVIS	#
	BYRON Akil	1
	RICHARDS Keithroy	2
	RILEY Toussaint	3
	RILEY Alexander	4
80	LEADER Thrizen	5
	NEWTON Adam	6
	ISAAC George	7
	LAKE Ian	11
	GUMBS Keith	12
	GOMEZ Daryl	13
	HUGGINS Austin	15
	Tr: LAKE Lennie	
85	HARRIS Atiba	8
80	FRANCIS Jevon	9
51	SARGEANT Vernon	10

Arnos Vale Playing Ground, Kingstown
10-10-2004, 16:00, 2 500, Alfaro SLV

VIN 0 – 1 MEX

Borgetti 25

#	ST VINCENT	min
1	ANDREWS Melvin	
3	HUGGINS Cornelius	
4	JOHN Wesley	61
5	HENDRICKSON Ezra	
6	CHARLES Matthew	
8	WILLIAMS Howie	
9	JACK Rodney	46
11	VELOX Kendal	
12	BALLANTYNE Jamal	74
14	JAMES Marlon	41
19	FORDE Matthew	
	Tr: VRANES Zoran	
7	JOHN Vincent	74
10	SAMUEL Shandel	46
17	PRINCE Tyrone	61

min	MEXICO	#
	SANCHEZ Oswaldo	1
	RODRIGUEZ Francisco	2
	MARQUEZ Rafael	4
18	LOPEZ Israel	5
	SALCIDO Carlos	6
64	NAELSON Antonio	7
	BORGETTI Jared	9
78	BLANCO Cuauhtemoc	10
	MENDEZ Mario	16
	LOZANO Jaime	19
	ARELLANO Jesus	21
	Tr: LA VOLPE Ricardo	
64	OSORNO Daniel	11
18	SANCHEZ Hugo	15
78	PEREZ Luis	23

Warner Park, Basseterre
13-10-2004, 20:00, 500, Whittaker

SKN 0 – 3 VIN

Velox 2 19, 85, Samuel 65

#	ST KITTS AND NEVIS	min
1	BENJAMIN Kayian	
2	RICHARDS Keithroy	
3	RILEY Toussaint	67
4	RILEY Alexander	
5	LEADER Thrizen	78
6	NEWTON Adam	
8	HARRIS Atiba	79
11	LAKE Ian	60
12	GUMBS Keith	
13	GOMEZ Daryl	
15	HUGGINS Austin	
	Tr: LAKE Lennie	
9	FRANCIS Jevon	67
10	SARGEANT Vernon	60
17	CHALLENGER Avalon	78

min	ST VINCENT	#
	ANDREWS Melvin	22
	HUGGINS Cornelius	3
	JOHN Wesley	4
	HENDRICKSON Ezra	5
	CHARLES Matthew	6
	SAMUEL Shandel	9
	HAYNES Renson	11
	VELOX Kendal	11
	BALLANTYNE Jamal	12
	GUY Alwyn	14
	FORDE Matthew	19
	Tr: VRANES Zoran	
86	JOHN Vincent	7
79	BURGIN Bevan	13
90	PRINCE Tyrone	14

Cuauhtemoc, Puebla
13-10-2004, 20:30, 37 000, Sibrian SLV

MEX   3   0   TRI

Naelson [19], Lozano 2 [55] [84]

MEXICO					TRINIDAD/TOBAGO
1	SANCHEZ Oswaldo				HISLOP Skaka 1
2	RODRIGUEZ Francisco				COX Ian 3
6	SALCIDO Carlos				ANDREWS Marvin 4
7	NAELSON Antonio	84			SANCHO Brent 5
8	GARCIA Rafael	83	67		BOUCAUD Andre 7
9	BORGETTI Jared				EVE Angus 8
15	SANCHEZ Hugo				RAHIM Brent 10
16	MENDEZ Mario		76		GLENN Cornell 13
19	LOZANO Jaime				JOHN Stern 14
21	ARELLANO Jesus	81	80		LAWRENCE Dennis 16
23	PEREZ Luis				JONES Kenwyne 19
	Tr: LA VOLPE Ricardo				Tr: SAINT CLAIR Bertille
14	PINEDA Gonzalo	83	76		MC FARLANE Errol 9
17	SANTANA Sergio	84	67		THEOBALD Densil 15
18	ARCE Fernando	81	80		SPANN Silvio 18

Orange Bowl, Miami
13-11-2004, 20:30, 18 312, Moreno PAN

SKN   0   5   MEX

Altamirano [31], Fonseca 2 [40] [57]
Santana 2 [49] [91]

ST KITTS AND NEVIS				MEXICO
1	JONES Adolphus			MUNOZ Moises 1
2	RICHARDS Keithroy			RODRIGUEZ Francisco 2
4	RILEY Alexander	66		PEREZ Mario 3
5	LEADER Thrizen			GALINDO Aaron 4
7	ISAAC George			RODRIGUEZ Juan Pablo 5
8	HARRIS Atiba	78		GARCIA Rafael 8
9	FRANCIS Jevon	64		OLALDE Jesus 9
10	SARGEANT Vernon	66		FONSECA Josa 10
13	GOMEZ Daryl	65		PINEDA Gonzalo 14
14	CONNONIER Seritse	77		SANTANA Sergio 17
17	MEADE Nathan			ALTAMIRANO Hector 22
	Tr: LAKE Lennie			Tr: LA VOLPE Ricardo
3	RILEY Toussaint	77	78	VALDEZ Octavio 7
6	ISAAC Shashi	65	66	OSORNO Daniel 11
19	JARVIS Dachan	66	64	MEDINA Alberto 20

Hasely Crawford Stadium, Port of Spain
17-11-2004, 19:00, 10 000, Batres GUA

TRI   2   1   VIN

Sam [84], Eve [91]
Haynes [49]

TRINIDAD/TOBAGO					ST VINCENT
21	INCE Clayton				ANDREWS Melvin 22
2	JOHN Avery	93			HUGGINS Cornelius 3
3	COX Ian				JOHN Wesley 4
4	ANDREWS Marvin		62		HENDRICKSON Ezra 5
5	SANCHO Brent		89		CHARLES Matthew 6
7	RAHIM Brent	69	75		SAMUEL Shandel 10
9	MC FARLANE Errol	69			VELOX Kendal 11
11	NIXON Jerren	78			BALLANTYNE Jamal 12
16	ROUGIER Anthony		46		JAMES Marlon 14
16	LAWRENCE Dennis				GUY Alwyn 15
19	JONES Kenwyne				FORDE Matthew 19
	Tr: SAINT CLAIR Bertille				Tr: VRANES Zoran
8	EVE Angus	69	46		HAYNES Renson 13
10	SAM Hector	69	75		GONSALVES Kenlyn 16
15	SEALT Scott	78	62		JOSEPH Benford 17

Tecnologico, Monterrey
17-11-2004, 21:00, 12 000, Stott USA

MEX   8   0   SKN

Altamirano [10]p, Perez 3 [21] [49] [78]
Fonseca 2 [44] [56], Osorno [52], Santana [67]

MEXICO				ST KITTS AND NEVIS
1	MUNOZ Moises			JONES Adolphus 1
2	RODRIGUEZ Francisco	52		RICHARDS Keithroy 2
3	PEREZ Mario	31	71	LEADER Thrizen 5
5	RODRIGUEZ Juan Pablo			ISAAC George 7
8	GARCIA Rafael	58		HARRIS Atiba 8
9	OLALDE Jesus	46		FRANCIS Jevon 9
10	FONSECA Francisco	55		SARGEANT Vernon 10
14	PINEDA Gonzalo			GOMEZ Daryl 13
15	SANCHEZ Hugo			SADDLER Keithroy 15
22	ALTAMIRANO Hector			JARVIS Dachan 19
23	PEREZ Luis			FRANCIS Brian 22
	Tr: LA VOLPE Ricardo			Tr: LAKE Lennie
11	OSORNO Daniel	31	55	RILEY Toussaint 3
17	SANTANA Sergio	58	52	ISAAC Shashi 6
20	MEDINA Alberto	46	71	ROGERS Glen 11

FINAL GROUP STAGE

Queen's Park Oval, Port of Spain
9-02-2005, 15:38, 11 000, Archundia

TRI   1   2   USA

Eve [87]
Johnson [23], Lewis [53]

TRINIDAD/TOBAGO				USA
1	HISLOP Shaka			KELLER Kasey 18
2	ROJAS Marlon			BOCANEGRA Carlos 4
4	ANDREWS Marvin			CHERUNDOLO Steve 6
5	SANCHO Brent		81	LEWIS Eddie 7
7	FITZPATRICK Leslie	71	86	JOHNSON Ed 9
10	ROUGIER Anthony	46		DONOVAN Landon 10
11	EDWARDS Carlos	74		GIBBS Cory 12
14	JOHN Stern			BEASLEY DaMarcus 17
15	JONES Kenwyne			MC BRIDE Brian 20
16	PIERRE Anton			POPE Eddie 23
19	YORKE Dwight		66	MASTROENI Pablo 25
	Tr: SAINT CLAIR Bertille			Tr: ARENA Bruce
8	EVE Angus	46	86	BERHALTER Gregg 3
12	THEOBALD Densil	74	81	ALBRIGHT Chris 5
13	GLENN Cornell	71	66	DEMPSEY Clint 8

Estadio Rommel Fernandez
9-02-2005, 19:00, 20 000, Prendergast JAM

PAN   0   0   GUA

PANAMA				GUATEMALA
1	GONZALEZ Donaldo			TRIGUENO Ricardo 22
2	RIVERA Carlos			MORALES Nelson 2
3	MORENO Luis			MELGAR Pablo 3
4	TORRES Antony			CHEN Denis 4
5	BALOY Felipe			THOMPSON Fredy 7
6	MITRE Engin	67	78	ROMERO Gonzalo 8
7	RODRIGUEZ Orlando	59		RAMIREZ Guillermo 11
8	BLANCO Alberto			MARTINEZ Nestor 13
9	GARCES Jose			PEZZAROSSI Dwight 17
10	MEDINA Julio			RODRIGUEZ Mario 19
11	BROWN Roberto	72		RUIZ Carlos 20
	Tr: HERNANDEZ Jose			Tr: MARADIAGA Ramon
14	GOMEZ Gabriel	67	78	CASTILLO Carlos 9
16	AGUILAR William	59		
19	PEREZ Blas	72		

Ricardo Saprissa, San Jose
9-02-2005, 20:00, 22 000, Batres GUA

CRC 1 2 MEX

Wanchope 38 — Lozano 2 8 10

COSTA RICA				MEXICO	
1 MESEN Alvaro				PEREZ Oscar	1
2 MONTERO Christian	60			MARQUEZ Rafael	4
3 MARIN Luis				SALCIDO Carlos	6
8 LOPEZ Jose Luis				NAELSON Antonio	7
9 WANCHOPE Paulo				PARDO Pavel	8
10 CENTENO Walter		62		BORGETTI Jared	9
11 GOMEZ Ronald	69	78		BLANCO Cuauhtemoc	10
12 GONZALEZ Leonardo				SANCHEZ Hugo	15
15 WALLACE Harold				FONSECA Francisco	17
17 SOTO Jafet	46			CARMONA Salvador	18
20 CHINCHILLA Pablo		85		LOZANO Jaime	19
Tr: LONIS Erick				Tr: LA VOLPE Ricardo	
7 FONSECA Rolando	69	85		PINEDA Gonzalo	14
16 HERNANDEZ Carlos	46	78		MEDINA Alberto	16
21 SOLIS Alonso	60	62		ALTAMIRANO Hector	22

Ricardo Saprissa, San Jose
26-03-2005, 18:00, 8 000, Rodriguez MEX

CRC 2 1 PAN

Wilson 40, Myre 91 — Brown 58

COSTA RICA				PANAMA	
1 MESEN Alvaro				PENEDO Jaime	12
3 MARIN Luis				RIVERA Carlos	2
5 MARTINEZ Gilberto				MORENO Luis	3
7 WILSON Whayne	63			TORRES Antony	4
8 LOPEZ Jose Luis	47			BALOY Felipe	5
9 WANCHOPE Paulo	73	81		GOMEZ Gabriel	6
10 CENTENO Walter				BLANCO Alberto	8
12 GONZALEZ Leonardo				GARCES Jose Luis	9
15 WALLACE Harold				MEDINA Julio	10
16 HERNANDEZ Carlos	61	86		BROWN Roberto	11
20 SEQUEIRA Douglas		82		PHILLIPS Ricardo	15
Tr: LONIS Erick				Tr: HERNANDEZ Jose	
6 MYRE Roy	61	82		AGUILAR William	16
19 SUNSING William	63	81		SOLIS Juan Ramon	17
21 LEDEZMA Froylan	73	86		RODRIGUEZ Orlando	19

Mateo Flores, Guatemala City
26-03-2005, 20:00, 22 506, Stott USA

GUA 5 1 TRI

Ramirez 17, Ruiz 2 30 38
Pezzarossi 2 78 87 — Edwards 32

GUATEMALA				TRINIDAD/TOBAGO	
22 TRIGUENO Ricardo				HISLOP Shaka	1
3 MELGAR Pablo				HENRY Nigel	3
4 CHEN Denis	32			SANCHO Brent	5
6 CABRERA Gustavo			48	FITZPATRICK Leslie	7
7 THOMPSON Fredy				EVE Angus	8
8 ROMERO Gonzalo	80			EDWARDS Carlos	11
11 RAMIREZ Guillermo				LAWRENCE Dennis	13
12 FIGUEROA Carlos				JOHN Stern	14
13 MARTINEZ Nestor			68	JONES Kenwyne	15
17 PEZZAROSSI Dwight				PIERRE Anton	16
20 RUIZ Carlos	86			YORKE Dwight	19
Tr: MARADIAGA Ramon				Tr: SAINT CLAIR Bertille	
15 PLATA Juan Carlos	86	48		SAM Hector	10
18 QUINONEZ Carlos	32	68		NAKHID David	12
24 DAVILA Maynor	80				

Azteca, Mexico City
27-03-2005, 12:07, 84 000, Sibrian SLV

MEX 2 1 USA

Borgetti 30, Naelson 32 — Lewis 58

MEXICO				USA	
1 SANCHEZ Oswaldo				KELLER Kasey	18
4 MARQUEZ Rafael				BERHALTER Gregg	3
5 OSORIO Ricardo		75		BOCANEGRA Carlos	4
6 SALCIDO Carlos		82		CHERUNDOLO Steve	6
7 NAELSON Antonio				LEWIS Eddie	7
8 PARDO Pavel				JOHNSON Ed	9
9 BORGETTI Jared	65			REYNA Claudio	10
10 BLANCO Cuauhtemoc	69			BEASLEY DaMarcus	17
17 FONSECA Francisco				DONOVAN Landon	21
18 CARMONA Salvador				ONYEWU Oguchi	22
19 LOZANO Jaime	69	71		MASTROENI Pablo	25
Tr: LA VOLPE Ricardo				Tr: ARENA Bruce	
11 MORALES Ramon	69	75		NOONAN Pat	13
16 MEDINA Alberto	65	71		RALSTON Steve	14
23 PEREZ Luis	69	82		MC BRIDE Brian	20

Hasely Crawford Stadium, Port of Spain
30-03-2005, 16:30, 8 000, Navarro CAN

TRI 0 0 CRC

TRINIDAD/TOBAGO				COSTA RICA	
21 INCE Clayton				MESEN Alvaro	1
2 ROJAS Marlon				MARIN Luis	3
4 CHARLES Atiba				MARTINEZ Gilberto	5
8 EVE Angus	63		63	WILSON Whayne	7
9 SPANN Silvio	63			CENTENO Walter	10
11 EDWARDS Carlos	71		50	SOLIS Alonso	11
12 LAWRENCE Dennis				GONZALEZ Leonardo	12
13 GLENN Cornell	74			BADILLA Cristian	14
14 JOHN Stern				WALLACE Harold	15
16 PIERRE Anton			67	ROJAS Oscar	17
19 YORKE Dwight				SEQUEIRA Douglas	20
Tr: SAINT CLAIR Bertille				Tr: PINTO Jorge	
7 FITZPATRICK Leslie	63	67		WANCHOPE Paulo	9
10 SAM Hector	71	50		HERNANDEZ Carlos	16
18 PIERRE Nigel	74	63		HERRON Andy	21

Legion Field, Birmingham, AL
30-03-2005, 19:00, Ramdhan TRI

USA 2 0 GUA

Johnson 11, Ralston 69

USA				GUATEMALA	
18 KELLER Kasey				TRIGUENO Ricardo	22
4 BOCANEGRA Carlos				MELGAR Pablo	3
6 CHERUNDOLO Steve		46		CHEN Denis	4
7 LEWIS Eddie	85			CABRERA Gustavo	6
9 JOHNSON Ed		46		THOMPSON Fredy	7
12 GIBBS Cory				ROMERO Gonzalo	8
14 RALSTON Steve				RAMIREZ Guillermo	11
19 CHING Brian	79			MARTINEZ Nestor	13
21 DONOVAN Landon	90			PEZZAROSSI Dwight	17
22 ONYEWU Oguchi			69	RODRIGUEZ Mario	19
25 MASTROENI Pablo				RUIZ Carlos	20
Tr: ARENA Bruce				Tr: MARADIAGA Ramon	
2 DEMPSEY Clint	90	46		QUINONEZ Carlos	18
13 NOONAN Pat	85	69		SANDOVAI Hernan	23
16 WOLFF Josh	79	46		DAVILA Maynor	24

Estadio Rommel Fernandez, Panama City
30-03-2005, 20:30, 13 000, Pineda HON

PAN 1 1 MEX

Tejada [75]   Morales [26]

PANAMA			MEXICO		
12 PENEDO Jaime			SANCHEZ Oswaldo 1		
3 MORENO Luis			MARQUEZ Rafael 4		
4 TORRES Antony			OSORIO Ricardo 5		
5 BALOY Felipe			SALCIDO Carlos 6		
6 SOLIS Juan Ramon	79		NAELSON Antonio 7		
8 BLANCO Alberto		57	PARDO Pavel 8		
9 GARCES Jose Luis		70	BORGETTI Jared 9		
10 MEDINA Julio		58	BLANCO Cuauhtemoc 10		
11 BROWN Roberto	53	56	MORALES Ramon 11		
14 GUN Armando			CARMONA Salvador 18		
15 PHILLIPS Ricardo	88		ALTAMIRANO Hector 22		
Tr: HERNANDEZ Jose			Tr: LA VOLPE Ricardo		
13 SOLANILLA Joel	88	56	PINEDA Gonzalo 14		
18 TEJADA Luis	53	70	MEDINA Alberto 16		
20 MITRE Engin	79	58	GARCIA Rafael 20		

Rice Eccles, Salt Lake City
4-06-2005, 17:30, 40 586, Batres GUA

USA 3 0 CRC

Donovan 2 [10] [62], McBride [87]

USA			COSTA RICA		
18 KELLER Kasey			MESEN Alvaro 1		
4 BOCANEGRA Carlos			DRUMMOND Jervis 2		
6 CHERUNDOLO Steve			MARTINEZ Gilberto 5		
7 BEASLEY DaMarcus	86	66	ROJAS Oscar 7		
10 DONOVAN Landon			SOTO Jafet 10		
14 RALSTON Steve		39	GONZALEZ Leonardo 12		
15 CONVEY Bobby	74		CORDERO Victor 13		
16 WOLFF Josh	64		HERNANDEZ Carlos 16		
20 MC BRIDE Brian			WRIGHT Mauricio 19		
23 POPE Eddie		90	SEQUEIRA Douglas 20		
25 ZAVAGNIN Kerry		61	SOLIS Alonso 21		
Tr: ARENA Bruce			Tr: GUIMARAES Alexandre		
2 HEJDUK Frankie	74	66	WANCHOPE Paulo 9		
8 DEMPSEY Clint	86	61	GOMEZ Ronald 11		
17 NOONAN Pat	64	39	BRYCE Stevens 17		

Hasely Crawford Stadium, Port of Spain
4-06-2005, 18:30, 18 000, Prendergast JAM

TRI 2 0 PAN

John [34], Lawrence [71]

TRINIDAD/TOBAGO			PANAMA		
1 JACK Kelvin			GONZALEZ Donaldo 1		
3 JOHN Avery		60	RIVERA Carlos 2		
4 ANDREWS Marvin			MORENO Luis 3		
5 CHARLES Atiba			TORRES Jose Anthony 4		
6 LAWRENCE Dennis			GOMEZ Gabriel 6		
8 BIRCHALL Christopher			BLANCO Alberto 8		
9 WHITLEY Aurtis			MEDINA Julio 10		
11 EDWARDS Carlos		46	BROWN Roberto 11		
14 JOHN Stern	72	72	SOLANILLA Joel 13		
18 THEOBALD Densil			PHILLIPS Ricardo 15		
19 YORKE Dwight			TEJADA Luis 18		
Tr: BEENHAKKER Leo			Tr: HERNANDEZ Jose		
15 JONES Kenwyne	72	72	HENRIQUEZ Amilcar 7		
		46	GARCES Jose Luis 9		
		60	JIMENEZ Joel 16		

Mareo Flores, Guatemala City
4-06-2005, 19:00, 26 723, Hall USA

GUA 0 2 MEX

Naelson [41], Cabrera OG [45]

GUATEMALA			MEXICO		
22 TRIGUENO Ricardo			SANCHEZ Oswaldo 1		
3 MELGAR Pablo			SALCIDO Carlos 3		
6 CABRERA Gustavo		72	MARQUEZ Rafael 4		
8 ROMERO Gonzalo			OSORIO Ricardo 5		
10 VILLATORO Roberto			NAELSON Antonio 7		
11 RAMIREZ Guillermo			BORGETTI Jared 9		
12 FIGUEROA Carlos	65	68	FONSECA Francisco 17		
13 MARTINEZ Nestor	85		CARMONA Salvador 18		
15 PLATA Juan Carlos	79		RODRIGUEZ Juan Pablo 20		
16 GIRON Julio	55	74	LOZANO Jaime 21		
26 SANABRIA Angel			PEREZ Luis 22		
Tr: MARADIAGA Ramon			Tr: LA VOLPE Ricardo		
7 THOMPSON Fredy	55	72	GALINDO Aaron 2		
19 RODRIGUEZ Mario	65	74	BRAVO Omar 10		
23 SANDOVAL Hernan	79	68	PINEDA Gonzalo 14		

Universitario, Monterrey
8-06-2005, 19:00, 32 833, Stott USA

MEX 2 0 TRI

Borgetti [63], Perez [88]

MEXICO			TRINIDAD/TOBAGO		
1 SANCHEZ Oswaldo			JACK Kelvin 1		
2 GALINDO Aaron			JOHN Avery 3		
3 SALCIDO Carlos			ANDREWS Marvin 4		
5 OSORIO Ricardo			CHARLES Atiba 5		
7 ZINHA	62		LAWRENCE Dennis 6		
9 BORGETTI Jared		84	BIRCHALL Christopher 8		
16 MENDEZ Mario	36	54	WHITLEY Aurtis 9		
17 FONSECA Jose	84		EDWARDS Carlos 11		
20 RODRIGUEZ Juan Pablo			JOHN Stern 14		
21 LOZANO Jaime		80	THEOBALD Densil 18		
22 PEREZ Luis			YORKE Dwight 19		
Tr: LA VOLPE Ricardo			Tr: BEENHAKKER Leo		
10 BRAVO Omar	84	80	SAM Hector 10		
11 MORALES Ramon	62	54	RAHIM Brent 12		
19 MEDINA Alberto	36	84	GLASGOW Gary 15		

Estadio Rommel Fernandez, Panama City
8-06-2005, 20:30, 15 000, Navarro CAN

PAN 0 3 USA

Bocanegra 6, Donovan [19]
McBride [39]

PANAMA			USA		
1 GONZALEZ Donaldo			KELLER Kasey 18		
2 HENRIQUEZ Amilcar	75		HEJDUK Frankie 2		
4 TORRES Jose Anthony			BOCANEGRA Carlos 4		
5 BALOY Felipe			CHERUNDOLO Steve 6		
6 GOMEZ Gabriel		63	BEASLEY DaMarcus 7		
8 BLANCO Alberto			DONOVAN Landon 10		
9 GARCES Jose Luis			RALSTON Steve 14		
10 MEDINA Julio		80	NOONAN Pat 17		
11 BROWN Roberto			MC BRIDE Brian 20		
15 PHILLIPS Ricardo	38	86	POPE Eddie 23		
16 JIMENEZ Joel	38		ZAVAGNIN Kerry 25		
Tr: HERNANDEZ Jose			Tr: ARENA Bruce		
7 MITRE Engin	75	86	BERHALTER Gregg 3		
13 SOLANILLA Joel	38	63	DEMPSEY Clint 8		
18 TEJADA Luis	38	80	CONVEY Bobby 15		

Ricardo Saprissa, San Jose
8-06-2005, 20:00, 0 (BCD), Archundia MEX

CRC 3 2 GUA

Hernandez [34], Gomez [65]
Wanchope [92+]

Villatoro Roberto [74], Rodriguez [77]

COSTA RICA		
1	MESEN Alvaro	
2	DRUMMOND Jervis	
3	MARIN Luis	
5	MARTINEZ Gilberto	
8	SOLIS Mauricio	
9	WANCHOPE Paulo	
11	GOMEZ Ronald	
13	CORDERO Victor	82
16	HERNANDEZ Carlos	
17	BOLANOS Christian	
22	SOTO Jafet	54
Tr: GUIMARAES Alexandre		
10	CENTENO Walter	54
21	SOLIS Alonso	82

	GUATEMALA	
	MOLINA Luis Pedro	1
	MORALES Nelson	2
	MELGAR Pablo	3
	CABRERA Gustavo	6
	THOMPSON Fredy	7
62	ROMERO Gonzalo	8
72	RAMIREZ Guillermo	11
46	PLATA Juan Carlos	15
	RODRIGUEZ Mario	19
	RUIZ Carlos	20
	SANABRIA Angel	26
Tr: MARADIAGA Ramon		
62	CASTILLO Carlos	9
46	VILLATORO Roberto	10
72	GOMEZ Rigoberto	21

THE FIFA 100

The top 100 living players as selected by Pele for the FIFA Centennial

ARG - ARGENTINA
BATISTUTA Gabriel Omar
CRESPO Hernan
KEMPES Mario
MARADONA Diego Armando
PASSARELLA Daniel
SAVIOLA Javier
SIVORI Omar
DI STEFANO Alfredo
VERON Juan Sebastien
ZANETTI Javier

BEL - BELGIUM
CEULEMANS Jan
PFAFF Jean-Marie
VAN DER ELST Franky

BRA - BRAZIL
CARLOS ALBERTO
CAFU
ROBERTO CARLOS
FALCAO
JUNIOR
PELE
RIVALDO
RIVELINO Roberto
ROMARIO
RONALDINHO
RONALDO
DJALMA SANTOS
NILTON SANTOS
SOCRATES
ZICO

BUL - BULGARIA
STOICHKOV Hristo

CHI - CHILE
FIGUEROA Elias
ZAMORANO Ivan

CMR - CAMEROON
MILLA Roger

COL - COLOMBIA
VALDERRAMA Carlos

CRO - CROATIA
SUKER Davor

CZE - CZECH REPUBLIC
MASOPUST Josef
NEDVED Pavel

DEN - DENMARK
LAUDRUP Brian
LAUDRUP Michael
SCHMEICHEL Peter

ENG - ENGLAND
BANKS Gordon
BECKHAM David
CHARLTON Bobby
KEEGAN Kevin
LINEKER Gary
OWEN Michael
SHEARER Alan

ESP - SPAIN
BUTRAGUENO Emilio
LUIS ENRIQUE
RAUL

FRA - FRANCE
CANTONA Eric
DESAILLY Marcel
DESCHAMPS Didier
FONTAINE Just
HENRY Thierry
KOPA Raymond
PAPIN Jean-Pierre
PIRES Robert
PLATINI Michel
THURAM Lilian
TRESOR Marius
TREZEGUET David
VIEIRA Patrick
ZIDANE Zinedine

GER - GERMANY
BALLACK Michael
BECKENBAUER Franz
BREITNER Paul
KAHN Oliver

KLINSMANN Jürgen
MAIER Sepp
MATTHAUS Lothar
MULLER Gerd
RUMMENIGGE Karl-Heinz
SEELER Uwe

GHA - GHANA
ABEDI PELE

HUN - HUNGARY
PUSKAS Ferenc

IRL - REPUBLIC OF IRELAND
KEANE Roy

ITA - ITALY
BAGGIO Roberto
BARESI Franco
BERGOMI Giuseppe
BONIPERTI Giampiero
BUFFON Gianluigi
FACCHETTI Giacinto
MALDINI Paolo
NESTA Alessandro
DEL PIERO Alessandro
RIVERA Gianni
ROSSI Paolo
TOTTI Francesco
VIERI Christian
ZOFF Dino

JPN - JAPAN
NAKATA Hidetoshi

KOR - KOREA REPUBLIC
HONG Myung Bo

LBR - LIBERIA
WEAH George

MEX - MEXICO
SANCHEZ Hugo

NED - NETHERLANDS
BERGKAMP Dennis
CRUIJFF Johann
DAVIDS Edgar
GULLIT Ruud
VAN DER KERKHOF Willy

VAN DER KERKHOF Rene
KLUIVERT Patrick
NEESKENS Johann
VAN NISTELROOIJ Ruud
RENSENBRINK Rob
RIJKAARD Frank
SEEDORF Clarence
VAN BASTEN Marco

NGA - NIGERIA
OKOCHA Jay-Jay

NIR - NORTHERN IRELAND
BEST George

PAR - PARAGUAY
ROMERITO

PER - PERU
CUBILLAS Teofilo

POL - POLAND
BONIEK Zbigniew

POR - PORTUGAL
RUI COSTA Manuel
EUSEBIO
FIGO Luis

ROM - ROMANIA
HAGI Gheorghe

RUS - RUSSIA
DASSAYEV Rinat

SCO - SCOTLAND
DALGLISH Kenny

SEN - SENEGAL
DIOUF El Hadji

TUR - TURKEY
EMRE
RUSTU Recber

UKR - UKRAINE
SHEVCHENKO Andriy

URU - URUGUAY
FRANCESCOLI Enzo

USA - USA
AKERS Michelle
HAMM Mia

QUALIFYING MATCHES PLAYED IN SOUTH AMERICA

Qualification for the 2006 FIFA World Cup™ from South America involves all 10 members of CONMEBOL playing each other home and away. The top four teams in the group qualify automatically whilst the fifth team has to play off against the winners from Oceania.

Estadio Monumental, Buenos Aires
6-09-2003, 16:00, 35 372, Aquino PAR

ARG 2 2 CHI

Gonzalez [32], Aimar [36]   Mirosevic [60], Navoa [77]

ARGENTINA			CHILE	
12 CAVALLERO Pablo			TAPIA Nelson	1
2 AYALA Roberto		87	ALVAREZ Cristian	2
4 VIVAS Nelson			PEREZ Rodrigo	4
6 SAMUEL Walter	87		CONTRERAS Pablo	5
8 ZANETTI Javier			MARTEL Fernando	8
9 CRESPO Hernan	72	92	NAVIA Reinaldo	9
11 VERON Juan	69	55	GONZALEZ Mark	11
15 D'ALESSANDRO Andres			GONZALEZ Marcos	14
16 AIMAR Pablo		38	MELENDEZ Rodrigo	18
18 GONZALEZ Cristian			OLARRA Rafael	19
21 DELGADO Cesar	55		TAPIA Hector	22
Tr: BIELSA Marcelo			Tr: OLMOS Juvenal	
5 ALMEYDA Matias	69	55	ACUNA Jorge	6
19 SAVIALOA Javier	72	55	PINILLA Mauricio	15
		38	MIROSEVIC Milovan	17

Estadio Nacional, Lima
6-09-2003, 20:20, 42 557, Baldassi ARG

PER 4 1 PAR

Solano [34], Mendoza [42], Soto [83]   Gamarra [24]
Farfan [90]

PERU			PARAGUAY	
1 DELGADO Erick			TAVARELLI Ricardo	22
3 REBOSIO Miguel			ARCE Francisco	2
4 SOTO Jorge			CACERES Julio Cesar	3
5 HIDALGO Martin			GAMARRA Carlos	4
7 SOLANO Nolberto	88	59	TOLEDO Delio	5
8 JAYO Juan		80	BONET Carlos	6
10 PALACIOS Roberto	76		SANTA CRUZ Roque	9
14 PIZARRO Claudio			PAREDES Carlos	13
16 MENDOZA Andres	70		DA SILVA Paulo	14
20 ZEGARRA Pablo			ENCISO Julio Cesar	16
22 GALLIQUIO John			CARDOZO Jose	20
Tr: ATUORI Paulo			Tr: RUIZ Anibal	
6 SOTO Jose	88	59	ALVARENGA Guido	10
17 FARFAN Jefferson	70	80	CUEVAS Nelson	23
19 CIURLIZZA Marco	76			

Metropolitano, Barranquilla
7-09-2003, 16:15, 47 600, Elizondo ARG

COL 1 2 BRA

Angel [38]   Ronaldo [22], Kaka [61]

COLOMBIA			BRAZIL	
1 CORDOBA Oscar			DIDA	1
2 CORDOBA Ivan			CAFU	2
3 YEPES Mario			LUCIO	3
9 ANGEL Juan Pablo			ROQUE JUNIOR	4
10 HERNANDEZ Giovanni			GILBERTO SILVA	5
16 LOPEZ Jorge			ROBERTO CARLOS	6
17 PATINO Jairo	76	60	EMERSON	7
19 GRISALES Freddy		60	ALEX	8
20 BEDOYA Gerardo	35		RONALDO	9
21 RESTREPO John	63	87	RIVALDO	10
23 MARTINEZ Gonzalo			ZE ROBERTO	11
Tr: MATURANA Francisco			Tr: PARREIRA Carlos Alberto	
6 PEREA Luis Amaranto	35	60	RENATO	15
7 BECERRA Elson	63	60	KAKA	16
8 MOLINA Mauricio	76	87	DIEGO	17

Estadio Olimpico Atahualpo, Quito
6-09-2003, 16:00, 14 997, Albornoz CHI

ECU 2 0 VEN

Espinoza [5], Tenorio.C [72]

ECUADOR			VENEZUELA	
1 CEVALLOS Jose			ANGELUCCI Gilberto	1
3 HURTADO Ivan			VALLENILLA Pacheco	2
4 DE LA CRUZ Ulises			REY Jose Manuel	3
5 OBREGON Alfonso			ALVARADO Wilfredo	4
9 TENORIO Carlos			MEA VITALI Rafael	5
10 AGUINAGA Alex	43	63	URDANETA Gabriel	10
15 AYOVI Marlon		52	PAEZ Ricardo	11
16 CHALA Clever			JIMENEZ Leopoldo	14
17 ESPINOZA Giovanny		66	MORAN Ruberth	16
18 REASCO Neicer			ROJAS Jorge	17
19 MENDEZ Edison			ARANGO Juan	18
Tr: GOMEZ Hernan Dario			Tr: PAEZ Richard	
14 TENORIO Otilino	43	52	NORIEGA Daniel	7
		63	GONZALEZ Hector	20
		66	CASSERES Cristian	23

Estadio Centenario, Montevideo
7-09-2003, 16:00, 39 253, Zamora PER

URU 5 0 BOL

Forlan [17], Chevanton 2 [40] [61]
Abeijon [83], Bueno [88]

URUGUAY			BOLIVIA	
1 MUNUA Gustavo			FERNANDEZ Leonardo	21
5 SOSA Marcelo	69		PENA Juan Manuel	2
6 LOPEZ Diego			HOYOS Miguel	4
9 BUENO Carlos			SANCHEZ Oscar	5
10 LIGUERA Martin	77		ROJAS Richard	6
11 NUNEZ Richard			CRISTALDO Luis	7
14 GONZALEZ Cristian			MENDEZ Limberg	9
17 LAGO Eduardo			CASTILLO Jose	11
19 CHEVANTON Ernesto		67	RICALDI Alvaro	15
20 RECOBA Alvaro		46	RIBEIRO Luis	17
21 FORLAN Diego	76	46	MOREJON Limber	19
Tr: CARRASCO Juan Ramon			Tr: ACOSTA Nelson	
8 ABEIJON Nelson	69	46	BALDIVIESO Julio	10
15 SANCHEZ Vicente	76	46	JUSTINIANO Raul	16
16 OLIVERA Ruben	77			

Olimpico, Caracas
9-09-2003, 19:00, 24 783, Vazques Broquetas URU

VEN 0 3 ARG

Aimar [7], Crespo [25], Delgado [32]

VENEZUELA			ARGENTINA	
1 ANGELUCCI Gilberto			CAVALLERO Pablo	12
3 REY Jose Manuel			AYALA Roberto	2
4 ALVARADO Wilfredo			PLACENTE Diego	3
7 NORIEGA Daniel			VIVAS Nelson	4
8 VERA Luis			ZANETTI Javier	8
11 PAEZ Ricardo			CRESPO Hernan	9
14 JIMENEZ Leopoldo			VERON Juan	11
16 MORAN Ruberth	46	85	D'ALESSANDRO Andres	15
17 ROJAS Jorge		63	AIMAR Pablo	16
18 ARANGO Juan	61		GONZALEZ Cristian	18
20 GONZALEZ Hector	46	81	DELGADO Cesar	21
Tr: PAEZ Richard			Tr: BIELSA Marcelo	
2 VALLENILLA Pacheco	46	81	ALMEYDA Matias	5
10 URDANETA Gabriel	46	63	HEINZE Gabriel	6
26 MORENO Wilfredo	61	85	GONZALEZ Luis	20

Estadio Nacional, Santiago
9-09-2003, 21:10, 54 303, Gimenez ARG

CHI 2 1 PER

Pinilla [35], Norambuena [70]   Mendoza [57]

#	CHILE			#	PERU	
1	TAPIA Nelson				DELGADO Erick	1
4	PEREZ Rodrigo				REBOSIO Miguel	3
5	CONTRERAS Pablo				SOTO Jorge	4
6	ACUNA Jorge				HIDALGO Martin	5
14	GONZALEZ Marcos	46	81		SOLANO Nolberto	7
15	PINILLA Mauricio				JAYO Juan	8
16	ROJAS Ricardo		75		PALACIOS Roberto	10
17	MIROSEVIC Milovan				PIZARRO Claudio	14
19	OLARRA Rafael				MENDOZA Andres	16
21	MARTEL Fernando	46			ZEGARRA Pablo	20
23	TAPIA Hector	67			GALLIQUIO John	22
	Tr: OLMOS Juvenal				Tr: AUTUORI Paulo	
8	PIZARRO David	46	81		SOTO Jose	6
22	NORAMBUENA Arturo	67	75		FRAFAN Jefferson	17
24	GONZALEZ Boris	46				

Hernando Siles, La Paz
10-09-2003, 16:00, 23 200, Oliveira BRA

BOL 4 0 COL

Baldivieso [11p], Botero 3 [27 49 59]

#	BOLIVIA				COLOMBIA	
21	FERNANDEZ Leonardo	46			CORDOBA Oscar	1
2	PENA Juan Manuel		64		CORDOBA Ivan	2
3	GARCIA Juan				YEPES Mario	3
5	SANCHEZ Oscar				CORTES Roberto	4
6	ROJAS Richard	75	46		VARGAS Fabian	5
7	CRISTALDO Luis				ANGEL Juan Pablo	9
9	MENDEZ Limburg		46		HERNANDEZ Giovanni	10
10	BALDIVIESO Julio				ARISTIZABAL Victor	11
11	SUAREZ Roger	63			VIAFARA John Eduis	15
17	RIBEIRO Luis		46		PATINO Jairo	17
20	BOTERO Joaquin				MARTINEZ Gonzalo	23
	Tr: ACOSTA Nelson				Tr: MATURANA Francisco	
8	JUSTINIANO Raul	63	46		MOLINA Mauricio	8
14	GARCIA Ronald	75	46		CASTILLO Rafael	13
23	FERNANDEZ Jose	46	46		RESTREPO John	21

Defensores del Chaco, Asuncion
10-09-2003, 19:00, 15 000, Ruiz COL

PAR 4 1 URU

Cardozo 3 [26 58 72], Paredes [53]   Chevanton [24]

#	PARAGUAY				URUGUAY	
12	VILLAR JUSTO				MUNUA Gustavo	1
2	ARCE Francisco				AGUIAR Jesus Cono	2
3	CACERES Julio Cesar				SORONDO Gonzalo	3
4	GAMARRA Carlos		77		REGUEIRO Mario	7
6	BONET Carlos				ABEIJON Nelson	8
11	CAMPOS Jorge	79	57		BUENO Carlos	9
13	PAREDES Carlos				GONZALEZ Cristian	14
14	DA SILVA Paulo				OLIVERA Ruben	17
16	ENCISO Julio Cesar	90	46		GIACOMAZZI Guillermo	18
20	CARDOZO Jose				CHEVANTON Ernesto	19
24	SANTA CRUZ Roque				FORLAN Diego	21
	Tr: RUIZ Anibal				Tr: CARRASCO Juan Ramon	
8	GAVILAN Diego	79	46		LIGUERA Martin	10
17	ORTIZ Angel	90	77		NUNEZ Richard	11
			57		RECOBA Alvaro	20

Vivaldo Lima, Manaus
10-09-2003, 20:45, 36 601, Soloranzo Torres VEN

BRA 1 0 ECU

Ronaldinho [13]

#	BRAZIL				ECUADOR	
1	DIDA				CEVALLOS Jose	1
2	CAFU				HURTADO Ivan	3
3	LUCIO				DE LA CRUZ Ulises	4
4	ROQUE JUNIOR				OBREGON Alfonso	5
5	GILBERTO SILVA		83		TENORIO Carlos	9
6	ROBERTO CARLOS				AYOVI Marlon	15
7	RONALDINHO	68			CHALA Clever	16
8	EMERSON	62			ESPINOZA Giovanny	17
9	RONALDO				REASCO Neicer	18
10	RIVALDO	90			MENDEZ Edison	19
11	ZE ROBERTO				TENORIO Edwin	20
	Tr: PARREIRA Carlos Alberto				Tr: GOMEZ Hernan Dario	
15	RENATO	62	83		TENORIO Otilino	14
16	KAKA	68				
17	ALEX	90				

Centenario, Montevideo
15-11-2003, 15:00, 60 000, Martin ARG

URU 2 1 CHI

Chevanton [31], Romero [49]   Melendez [21]

#	URUGUAY				CHILE	
1	MUNUA Gustavo				TAPIA Nelson	1
5	SOSA Marcelo				RAMIREZ Miguel	3
6	LOPEZ Diego				PEREZ Rodrigo	4
8	MUNHOZ Pablo	45	74		NAVIA Reinaldo	9
9	BUENO Carlos				PINILLA Mauricio	15
10	LIGUERA Martin	70			ROJAS Ricardo	16
11	NUNEZ Richard				MELENDEZ Rodrigo	18
14	GONZALEZ Cristian				OLARRA Rafael	19
17	LAGO Eduardo		54		GONZALEZ Mark	20
19	CHEVANTON Ernesto		54		MARTEL Fernando	21
21	FORLAN Diego	45			MUNOZ Raul	24
	Tr: CARRASCO Juan Ramon				Tr: OLMOS Juvenal	
15	ROMERO Adrian	45	54		ORMAZABAL Patricio	6
20	RECOBA Alvaro	70	54		MIROSEVIC Milovan	17
22	HORNOS German	45	74		NORAMBUENA Arturo	22

Metropolitano, Barranquilla
15-11-2003, 16:00, 20 000, Chandia CHI

COL 0 1 VEN

Arango [8]

#	COLOMBIA				VENEZUELA	
22	MONDRAGON Farid				ANGELUCCI Gilberto	1
3	YEPES Mario				VALLENILLA Luis	2
4	VIVEROS Alexander				REY Jose Manuel	3
5	VALLEJO Gerardo		6		MEA VITALI Miguel	5
6	BOLANO Jorge	54			CICHERO Alejandro	6
7	BECERRA Elson				NORIEGA Daniel	7
8	LOZANO John		56		URDANETA Gabriel	10
9	ANGEL Juan Pablo		56		PAEZ Ricardo	11
10	HERNANDEZ Giovanni	46			JIMENEZ Leopoldo	14
14	PEREA Luis Amaranto				ARANGO Juan	18
19	GRISALES Freddy				HERNANDEZ Jonay	27
	Tr: MATURANA Francisco				Tr: PAEZ Richard	
11	ARRIAGA Eudalio	54	6		VIELMA Leonel	13
17	PATINO Jairo	46	56		Rojas Jorge	17
			56		GONZALEZ Hector	20

Defensores del Chaco, Asuncion
15-11-2003, 19:20, 12 000, Paniagua Arandia BOL

PAR 2 – 1 ECU

Santa Cruz 29, Cardozo 75 — Mendez 58

#	PARAGUAY			ECUADOR	#
12	VILLAR Justo			CEVALLOS Jose	1
2	ARCE Francisco			HURTADO Ivan	3
3	CACERES Julio Cesar			DE LA CRUZ Ulises	4
4	GAMARRA Carlos			COROZO Klever	6
6	BONET Carlos	73		GOMEZ Luis	7
11	CAMPOS Jorge	62		ORDONEZ Ebelio	8
13	PAREDES Carlos			CHALA Clever	16
17	ORTIZ Angel			ESPINOZA Giovanny	17
20	CARDOZO Jose	87		MENDEZ Edison	19
21	CANIZA Denis		83	TENORIO Edwin	20
24	SANTA CRUZ Roque		73	AMBROSI Vicente	22
	Tr: RUIZ Anibal			Tr: GOMEZ Hernan Dario	
8	GAVILAN Diego	73	73	SALAS Franklin	11
10	ALVARENGA Guido	87	83	FERNANDEZ Angel	13
23	CUEVAS Nelson	62			

Estadio Monumental, Buenos Aires
15-11-2003, 21:30, 30 042, Hidalgo Zamora PER

ARG 3 – 0 BOL

D'Alessandro 56, Crespo 61, Aimar 63

#	ARGENTINA			BOLIVIA	#
12	CAVALLERO Pablo			FERNANDEZ Leonardo	21
2	AYALA Roberto			PAZ Juan	2
4	ALMEYDA Matias			RICALDI Alvaro	4
5	SAMUEL Walter	89		SANCHEZ Oscar	5
6	ZANETTI Javier			JUSTINIANO Raul	6
8	CRESPO Hernan	69	69	SUAREZ Roger	11
9	CAVALLERO Pablo	80		REYES Leonel	14
15	D'ALESSANDRO Andres	84		RALDES Ronald	16
16	AIMAR Pablo			RIBEIRO Luis	17
18	GONZALEZ Cristian		64	MERCADO Miguel Angel	19
19	DELGADO Cesar		64	BOTERO Joaquin	20
	Tr: BIELSA Marcelo			Tr: ACOSTA Nelson	
3	SORIN Juan	84	64	MENDEZ Limberg	9
7	SAVIOLA Javier	80	69	ETCHEVERRY Marco	10
14	CAMBIASSO Esteban	89	64	CASTILLO Jose	18

Monumental, Lima
16-11-2003, 16:00, 70 000, Ruiz COL

PER 1 – 1 BRA

Solano 50 — Rivaldo 20

#	PERU			BRAZIL	#
1	IBANEZ Oscar			DIDA	1
3	REBIOSO Miguel			CAFU	2
4	SOTO Jorge			LUCIO	3
5	HIDALGO Martin	51		ROQUE JUNIOR	4
7	SOLANO Nolberto			GILBERTO SILVA	5
8	JAYO Juan			JUNIOR	6
10	PALACIOS Roberto	75	74	KAKA	7
14	PIZARRO Claudio		61	EMERSON	8
16	MENDOZA Andres			RONALDO	9
19	CIURLIZZA Marco		81	RIVALDO	10
22	GALLIQUIO John			ZE ROBERTO	11
	Tr: AUTOURI Paulo			Tr: PARREIRA Carlos Alberto	
15	SALAS Guillermo	51	61	RENATO	15
25	GARCIA Julio	75	74	ALEX	17
			81	LUIS FABIANO	18

Pachenricho Romero, Maracaibo
18-11-2003, 19:00, 30 000, Reinoso ECU

VEN 2 – 1 BOL

Rey 90, Arango 92+ — Botero 60

#	VENEZUELA			BOLIVIA	#
1	ANGELUCCI Gilberto			FERNANDEZ Leonardo	21
2	VALLENILLA Luis			PAZ Juan	2
3	REY Jose Manuel			SANCHEZ Oscar	5
6	CICHERO Alejandro			JUSTINIANO Raul	6
7	NORIEGA Daniel	51	70	SUAREZ Roger	11
10	ILDANETA Gabriel			REYES Leonel	14
11	PAEZ Ricardo			ALVAREZ Lorgio	15
14	JIMENEZ Leopoldo		80	RALDES Ronald	16
16	MORAN Ruberth	59		RIBEIRO Luis	17
18	ARANGO Juan		65	MERCADO Miguel	19
27	HERNANDEZ Jonay	61		BOTERO Joaquin	20
	Tr: PAEZ Richard			Tr: ACOSTA Nelson	
17	ROJAS Jorge	61	80	SANDY Marco	3
24	RONDON Alexander	59	65	VACA Joselito	8
26	MORENO Wilfredo	51	70	MENDEZ Limberg	9

Estadio Nacional, Santiago
18-11-2003, 22:05, 61 923, Mendez Gonzalez URU

CHI 0 – 1 PAR

Paredes 30

#	CHILE			PARAGUAY	#
1	TAPIA Nelson			VILLAR Justo	12
2	ALVAREZ Cristian	45		ARCE Francisco	2
3	RAMIREZ Miguel			CACERES Julio Cesar	3
4	PEREZ Rodrigo			GAMARRA Carlos	4
5	CONTRERAS Pablo		81	BONET Carlos	6
8	PIZARRO David		89	PAREDES Carlos	13
9	NAVIA Reinaldo	63		ENCISO Julio Cesar	16
14	GONZALEZ Marcos	45		ORTIZ Angel	17
15	PINILLA Mauricio		88	CARDOZO Jose	20
17	MIROSEVIC Milovan			CANIZA Denis	21
19	OLARRA Rafael			SANTA CRUZ Roque	24
	Tr: OLMOS Juvenal			Tr: RUIZ Anibal	
6	ORMAZABAL Patricio	45	81	GAVILAN Diego	8
18	MELENDEZ Rodrigo	45	88	ALVARENGA Guido	10
22	NORAMBUENA Arturo	63	89	DA SILVA Paulo	14

Olimpico Atahualpa, Quito
19-11-2003, 17:00, 34 361, Gonzalez Chaves PAR

ECU 0 – 0 PER

#	ECUADOR			PERU	#
1	CEVALLOS Jose			IBANEZ Oscar	1
3	HURTADO Ivan			REBOSIO Miguel	3
4	DE LA CRUZ Ulises			SOTO Jorge	4
5	OBREGON Alfonso	66		JAYO Juan	8
8	ORDONEZ Ebelio	45	54	PALACIOS Roberto	10
9	TENORIO Carlos			PIZARRO Claudio	14
15	AYOVI Marlon			SALAS Guillermo	15
16	CHALA Clever	79	45	MENDOZA Andres	16
17	ESPINOZA Giovanny			CIURLIZZA Marco	19
18	REASCO Neicer			GALLIQUIO John	22
19	MENDEZ Edison			GARCIA Julio	25
	Tr: GOMEZ Hernan Dario			Tr: AUTOURI Paulo	
10	AGUINAGA Alex	79	45	FARFAN Jefferson	17
11	SALAS Franklin	45	54	MOZON Alessandro	24
13	FERNANDEZ Angel	66			

Metropolitano, Barranquilla
19-11-2003, 21:00, 19 034, Simon BRA

COL	1	1	ARG

Angel [47]   Crespo [27]

	COLOMBIA				ARGENTINA	
1	CORDOBA Oscar				CAVALLERO Pablo	12
2	CORDOBA Ivan				AYALA Roberto	2
3	YEPES Mario				QUIROGA FACUNDO	4
4	VIVEROS Alexander				ALMEYDA Matias	5
8	LOZANO John	26			SAMUEL Walter	6
9	ANGEL Juan Pablo				ZANETTI Javier	8
10	MONTOYA David	71	71		CRESPO Hernan	9
15	VIAFARA John Eduis				PLACENTE Diego	13
17	PATINO Jairo	45	71		AIMAR Pablo	16
19	GRISALES Freddy				GONZALEZ Cristian	18
23	MARTINEZ Gonzalo		45		DELGADO Cesar	19
	Tr: MATURANA Francisco				Tr: BIELSA Marcelo	
6	BOLANO Jorge	26	71		SAVIOLA Javier	7
7	BECERRA Elson	71	45		VERON Juan	11
11	ARRIAGA Eudalio	45	71		D'ALESSANDRO Andres	15

Pinheiro, Curitiba
19-11-2003, 21:50, 28 000, Elizondo ARG

BRA	3	3	URU

Kaka [20], Ronaldo 2 [28 87]   Forlan 2 [57 76]
                                          Gilberto Silva OG [78]

	BRAZIL				URUGUAY	
1	DIDA				MUNUA Gustavo	1
2	CAFU				BIZERA Joe	3
3	LUCIO				SOSA Marcelo	5
4	ROQUE JUNIOR				LOPEZ Diego	6
5	RENATO	79	36		ABEIJON Nelson	7
6	JUNIOR				LIGUERA Martin	10
7	KAKA	72	45		ROMERO Adrian	15
8	GILBERTO SILVA				ZALAYETA Marcelo	16
9	RONALDO				LAGO Eduardo	17
10	RIVALDO	79			FORLAN Diego	21
11	ZE ROBERTO		54		HORNOS German	22
	Tr: PARREIRA Carlos Alberto				Tr: CARRASCO Juan Ramon	
16	JUNINHO PERNAMBUCO	79	36		NUNEZ Richard	11
17	ALEX	72	54		CHEVANTON Ernesto	19
18	LUIS FABIANO	79	45		RECOBA Alvaro	20

Hernando Siles, La Paz
30-03-2004, 16:00, 40 000, Martin ARG

BOL	0	2	CHI

Villarroel [37], Gonzalez.M [59]

	BOLIVIA				CHILE	
23	FERNANDEZ Jose				TAPIA Nelson	1
2	PENA Juan Manuel				PEREZ Rodrigo	4
3	PIZARRO Limbert		55		GALAZ Patricio	10
5	SANCHEZ Oscar				SALAS Marcelo	11
7	REYES Leonel	62			VARGAS Jorge	13
11	SUAREZ Roger	46	55		VILLARROEL Moises	14
14	DA ROSA Alex				ROJAS Ricardo	16
17	PACHI Danner				MELENDEZ Rodrigo	18
18	CASTILLO Jose Alfredo				OLARRA Rafael	19
20	BOTERO Joaquin	46			GONZALEZ Mark	20
21	ANGULO Carmelo		74		MARTEL Fernando	21
	Tr: ACOSTA Nelson				Tr: OLMOS Juvenal	
9	MENDEZ Limberg	46	55		MALDONADO Claudio	3
10	VACA Joselito	62	74		VALENZUELA Rodrigo	7
13	RIBEIRO Luis	46	55		PINILLA Mauricio	15

Estadio Monumental, Buenos Aires
30-03-2004, 20:30, 55 000, Vazquez URU

ARG	1	0	ECU

Crespo [60]

	ARGENTINA				ECUADOR	
12	CAVALLERO Pablo				CEVALLOS Jose	1
2	AYALA Roberto				HURTADO Ivan	3
3	SORIN Juan				DE LA CRUZ Ulises	4
4	RODRIGUEZ Clemente				OBREGON Alfonso	5
5	GONZALEZ Luis		73		TENORIO Carlos	14
6	HEINZE Gabriel				AYOVI Marlon	15
9	CRESPO Hernan		63		CHALA Clever	16
15	D'ALESSANDRO Andres				ESPINOZA Giovanny	17
16	AIMAR Pablo	55			REASCO Neicer	18
18	GONZALEZ Mariano	46			MENDEZ Edison	19
19	DELGADO Cesar	66	67		TENORIO Edwin	20
	Tr: BIELSA Marcelo				Tr: GOMEZ Hernan Dario	
8	RIQUELME Juan	55	73		SALAS Franklin	8
11	TEVEZ Carlos	46	67		KAVIEDES Ivan	9
14	BURDISSO Nicolas	66	63		DELGADO Agustin	11

Estadio Centenario, Montevideo
31-03-2004, 19:40, 40 094, Ortube BOL

URU	0	3	VEN

Urdaneta [19], Gonzalez.H [67]
Arango [77]

	URUGUAY				VENEZUELA	
1	MUNUA Gustavo				ANGELUCCI Gilberto	1
3	SORONDO Gonzalo				VALLENILLA Luis	2
4	RODRIGUEZ Dario				REY Jose Manuel	3
5	SOSA Marcelo				CICHERO Alejandro	6
6	LOPEZ Diego	74			VERA Luis	8
8	HORNOS German	46	61		URDANETA Gabriel	10
10	LIGUERA Martin		61		PAEZ Ricardo	11
11	NUNEZ Richard				JIMENEZ Leopoldo	14
19	CHEVANTON Ernesto	59	83		ARANGO Juan	18
20	RECOBA Alvaro				RONDON Alexander	24
21	FORLAN Diego	72			HERNANDEZ Jonay	27
	Tr: CARRASCO Juan Ramon				Tr: PAEZ Richard	
7	PANDIANI Walter	46	61		ROJAS Jorge	17
9	BUENO Carlos	72	83		GONZALEZ Andree	19
22	CORREA Fernando	59	61		GONZALEZ Hector	20

Defensores de Chaco, Asuncion
31-03-2004, 21:45, 40 000, Ruiz COL

PAR	0	0	BRA

	PARAGUAY				BRAZIL	
22	TAVAELLI Ricardo				DIDA	1
2	ARCE Francisco				CAFU	2
3	CACERES Julio Cesar	73			LUCIO	3
4	GAMARRA Carlos				ROQUE JUNIOR	4
6	BONET Carlos	30	67		RENATO	5
13	PAREDES Carlos				ROBERTO CARLOS	6
15	TOLEDO Delio	56			RONALDINHO	7
16	ENCISO Julio Cesar				GILBERTO SILVA	8
20	CARDOZO Jose				RONALDO	9
21	CANIZA Denis				KAKA	10
24	SANTA CRUZ Roque				ZE ROBERTO	11
	Tr: RUIZ Anibal				Tr: PARREIRA Carlos Alberto	
11	CAMPOS Jorge	56	67		JUNINHO PERNAMBUCO	17
14	DA SILVA Paulo	73				
17	ORTIZ Angel	30				

Estadio Nacional, Lima
31-03-2004, 21:45, 29 325, Rezende BRA

PER	0	2	COL

Grisales 30, Oviedo 42

	PERU			COLOMBIA	
1	IBANEZ Oscar			CALERO Miguel	1
3	REBIOSO Miguel			CORDOBA Ivan	2
4	SOTO Jorge			YEPES Mario	3
5	HIDALGO Martin	46		VARGAS Fabian	6
8	JAYO Juan			OVIEDO Frankie	8
10	PALACIOS Roberto	58		ANGEL Juan Pablo	9
11	QUINTEROS Henry	46	72	MURILLO Elkin	11
14	PIZARRO Claudio			PEREA Luis Amaranto	14
16	MENDOZA Andres		90	RAMIREZ Juan	18
19	CIURLIZZA Marco		78	GRISALES Freddy	19
22	GALLIQUIO John			BEDOYA Gerardo	20
	Tr: AUTUORI Paulo			Tr: RUEDA Reinaldo	
9	Silva Roberto	58	72	VIVEROS Alexander	4
15	SALAS Guillermo	46	90	VIAFARA John Eduis	15
17	FARFAN Jefferson	46	78	PATINO Jairo	17

Hernando Siles, La Paz
1-06-2004, 16:00, 23 013, Rezende BRA

BOL	2	1	PAR

Cristaldo 8, Suarez 72   Cardozo 33

	BOLIVIA				PARAGUAY	
21	FERNANDEZ Leonardo				VILLAR Justo	1
2	PENA Juan Manuel	69			ESPINOLA Carlos	2
3	JAUREGUI Sergio				GAMARA Carlos	4
4	ALVAREZ Lorgio	60	82		LUGO Carlos	5
5	SANCHEZ Oscar		70		DUARTE Troadio	6
7	CRISTALDO Luis				GONZALEZ Edgar	8
10	BALDIVIESO Julio				DA SILVA Paulo	14
16	RALDES Ronald				ENCISO Julio Cesar	16
17	RIBEIRO Luis	85			ORTIZ Angel	17
20	BOTERO Joaquin				CARDOZO Jose	20
22	GUTIERREZ Limberg	87	63		SANTACRUZ Roque	24
	Tr: BLACUT Ramiro				Tr: RUIZ Anibal	
6	ANGULO Carmelo	87	82		CABANAS Salvador	7
11	SUAREZ Roger	60	70		DOS SANTOS Julio	10
15	SOLIZ Herman	85	63		RAMIREZ Cesar	11

Pueblo Nuevo, San Cristobal
1-06-2004, 19:00, 23 040, Torres PAR

VEN	0	1	CHI

Pinilla 83

	VENEZUELA			CHILE	
1	ANGELUCCI Gilberto			TAPIA Nelson	1
2	VALLENILLA Luis	64		MALDONADO Claudio	3
3	REY Jose Manuel			PEREZ Rodrigo	4
6	CICHERO Alejandro		79	PIZARRO David	8
10	URDANETA Gabriel	46		NAVIA Reinaldo	9
11	PAEZ Ricardo			VARGAS Jorge	13
13	VIELMA Leonel	75		ROJAS Ricardo	16
14	JIMENEZ Leopoldo			MELENDEZ Rodrigo	18
18	ARANGO Juan			OLARRA Rafael	19
24	RONDON Alexander		57	GONZALEZ Mark	20
27	HERNANDEZ Jonay		46	GALAZ Patricio	25
	Tr: HERNANDEZ Ramon			Tr: OLMOS Juvenal	
19	GONZALEZ Andree	75	79	VALENZUELA Rodrigo	7
20	GONZALEZ Hector	64	46	PINILLA Mauricio	15
29	MARGIOTTA Massimo	46	57	MIROSEVIC Milovan	17

Estadio Centenario, Montevideo
1-06-2004, 21:40, 30 000, Selman CHI

URU	1	3	PER

Forlan 72   Solano 13, Pizarro 18, Farfan 61

	URUGUAY			PERU	
1	MUNUA Gustavo			IBANEZ Oscar	1
2	LEMBO Alejandro			ACASIETE Santiago	2
3	SORONDO Gonzalo	32	80	REBOSIO Miguel	3
4	DE SOUZA Marcelo			VILCHEZ Walter	6
5	SOSA Marcelo			SOLANO Nolberto	7
6	GUIGOU Gianni	46		JAYO Juan	8
7	PANDIANI Walter	62	58	PALACIOS Roberto	10
10	PACHECO Antonio	46	46	PIZARRO Claudio	14
11	NUNEZ Richard			FARFAN Jefferson	17
16	GARCIA Pablo			ZEGARRA Carlos	20
19	CHEVANTON Ernesto			GALLIQUIO John	22
	Tr: FOSSATI Jorge			Tr: AUTUORI Paulo	
9	SILVA Dario	62	58	SOTO Jorge	4
15	ROMERO Adrian	46	46	MENDOZA Andres	16
21	FORLAN Diego	46	80	GARCIA Julio	25

Estadio Olimpico Atahualpa, Quito
2-06-2004, 16:00, 31 484, Baldassi ARG

ECU	2	1	COL

Delgado 3, Salas 66   Oviedo 57

	ECUADOR			COLOMBIA	
1	ESPINOZA Jacinto			CALERO Miguel	1
3	HURTADO Ivan			CORDOBA Ivan	2
4	DE LA CRUZ Ulises			YEPES Mario	3
6	AMBROSI Vicente			VARGAS Fabian	6
11	DELGADO Agustin			OVIEDO Frankie	8
15	AYOVI Marlon	86	46	VIAFARA John	13
16	CHALA Clever			PEREA Luis Amaranto	14
17	ESPINOZA Giovanny			RAMIREZ Juan	17
19	MENDEZ Edison	64		REY Luis	18
20	TENORIO Edwin		69	VALENTIERRA Arnulfo	19
24	FIGUEROA Gustavo	50	77	BEDOYA Gerardo	20
	Tr: GOMEZ Hernan Dario			Tr: RUEDA Reinaldo	
7	SALAS Franklin	50	46	VIVEROS Alexander	4
10	AGUINAGA Alex	64	77	FERREIRA David	7
23	LASTRA Mario	86	69 87	MURILLO Elkin	11

Estadio Magalhaes Pinto, Belo Horizonte
2-06-2004, 21:45, 60 000, Ruiz COL

BRA	3	1	ARG

Ronaldo 3 16p 67p 96+p   Sorin 79

	BRAZIL			ARGENTINA	
1	DIDA			CAVALLERO Pablo	12
2	CAFU			HEINZE Gabriel	2
3	JUAN			SORIN Juan	3
4	ROQUE JUNIOR			QUIROGA Facundo	4
5	EDMILSON			MASCHERANO Javier	5
6	ROBERTO CARLOS			SAMUEL Walter	6
7	JUNINHO PERNAMBUCO	74		ZANETTI Javier	8
8	KAKA	74		CRESPO Hernan	9
9	RONALDO		61	GONZALEZ Luis	14
10	LUIS FABIANO	92		GONZALEZ Cristian	18
11	ZE ROBERTO		36	DELGADO Cesar	19
	Tr: PARREIRA Carlos Alberto			Tr: BIELSA Marcelo	
15	JULIO BAPTISTA	74	61	SAVIOLA Javier	7
16	ALEX	74	61	AIMAR Pablo	16
17	EDU	92	36	ROSALES Mauro	21

Estadio Olimpico Atahualpa, Quito
5-06-2004, 16:00, 30 020, Brand VEN

ECU 3 – 2 BOL

Soliz OG 27, Delgado 32, De la Cruz 38
Gutierrez 57, Castillo 74

No	ECUADOR	Min	Min	BOLIVIA	No
1	ESPINOZA Jacinto			FERNANDEZ Leonardo	21
3	HURTADO Ivan		46	SOLIZ Herman	3
4	DE LA CRUZ Ulises			ALVAREZ Lorgio	4
5	OBREGON Alfonso	70		SANCHEZ Oscar	5
6	AMBROSI Vicente	80	46	ANGULO Carmelo	8
7	SALAS Franklin			BALDIVIESO Julio	10
11	DELGADO Agustin	66		SUAREZ Roger	14
16	CHALA Clever	65		JAUREGUI Sergio	15
17	ESPINOZA Giovanny			RALDES Ronald	16
18	REASCO Neicer			GUTIERREZ Limberg	20
20	TENORIO Carlos			BOTERO Joaquin	24
	Tr: GOMEZ Hernan Dario			Tr: BLACUT Ramiro	
10	AGUINAGA Alex	70	46	RIBEIRO Luis	17
15	AYOVI Marlon	80	66	CASTILLO Jose	18
19	MENDEZ Edison	65	46	GALINDO Gonzalo	19

Estadio Monumental, Buenos Aires
6-06-2004, 15:00, 37 000, Simon BRA

ARG 0 – 0 PAR

No	ARGENTINA	Min	Min	PARAGUAY	No
1	ABBONDANZIERI Robert			VILLAR Justo	1
2	AYALA Roberto			CACERES Julio Cesar	3
3	SORIN Juan			GAMARRA Carlos	4
5	MASCHERANO Javier	63		TOLEDO Delio	5
6	SAMUEL Walter	89		GAVILAN Diego	10
9	SAVIOLA Javier			DA SILVA Paulo	14
9	CRESPO HERNAN			ENCISO Julio Cesar	16
11	TEVEZ Carlos	61		ORTIZ Angel	17
14	GONZALEZ Luis	66	84	CARDOZO Jose	20
15	HEINZE Gabriel			CANIZA Denis	21
18	GONZALEZ Cristian			SANTACRUZ Roque	24
	Tr: BIELSA Marcelo			Tr: RUIZ Anibal	
21	ROSALES Mauro	66	63	GONZALEZ Edgar	8
			84	RAMIREZ Cesar	11
			89	SARABIA Pedro	15

Estadio Nacional, Lima
6-06-2004, 15:00, 40 000, Larrionda URU

PER 0 – 0 VEN

No	PERU	Min	Min	VENEZUELA	No
1	IBANEZ Oscar			ANGELUCCI Gilberto	1
2	ACASIETE Santiago			VALLENILLA Luis	2
3	REBOSIO Miguel			REY Jose Manuel	3
4	SOTO Jorge			MEA VITALI Miguel	5
5	HIDALGO Martin	67		CICHERO Alejandro	6
7	SOLANO Nolberto		79	URDANETA Gabriel	10
8	JAYO Juan		66	PAEZ Ricardo	11
10	PALACIOS Roberto	67		JIMENEZ Leopoldo	14
16	MENDOZA Andres	79		ARANGO Juan	18
17	FARFAN Jefferson		60	RONDON Alexander	24
20	ZEGARRA Carlos			HERNANDEZ Jonay	27
	Tr: AUTUORI Paulo			Tr: PAEZ Richard	
6	VILCHEZ Walter	67	60	MORAN Ruberth	16
9	SILVA Roberto	79	66	GONZALEZ Hector	20
23	OREJUELA Carlos	67	79	MARGIOTTA Massimo	29

Estadio Metropolitano, Barranquilla
6-06-2004, 17:10, 7 000, Amarilla PAR

COL 5 – 0 URU

Pacheco 2 17 31, Moreno 20, Restrepo 81, Herrera 86

No	COLOMBIA	Min	Min	URUGUAY	No
1	CALERO Miguel			MUNUA Gustavo	1
3	YEPES Mario			LEMBO Alejandro	2
8	OVIEDO Frankie	73		GONZALEZ Cristian	3
9	HERRERA Sergio		62	DE SOUZA Marcelo	4
10	PACHECO Victor	84		DELGADO Javier	8
14	PEREA Luis Amaranto		46	CANOBBIO Fabian	10
17	RAMIREZ Juan			ROMERO Marcelo	14
19	MORENO Malher	73	46	ROMERO Adrian	15
20	BEDOYA Gerardo			GARCIA Pablo	16
21	RESTREPO John			CHEVANTON	19
24	PALACIO Haider			RECOBA Alvaro	20
	Tr: RUEDA Reinaldo			Tr: FOSSATI Jorge	
6	VARGAS Fabian	73	46	DE LOS SANTOS Gonzalo	4
7	FERREIRA David	84	62	LAGO Eduardo	17
11	ARRIAGA Eudalio	73	46	FORLAN Diego	21

Estadio Nacional, Santiago
6-06-2004, 21:30, 62 503, Elizondo ARG

CHI 1 – 1 BRA

Navia 89p
Luis Fabiano 16

No	CHILE	Min	Min	BRAZIL	No
1	TAPIA Nelson			DIDA	1
3	MALDONADO Claudio			CAFU	2
4	PEREZ Rodrigo			JUAN	3
8	PIZARRO David			ROQUE JUNIOR	4
9	NAVIA Reinaldo		80	EDMILSON	5
16	ROJAS Ricardo	46		ROBERTO CARLOS	6
18	MELENDEZ Rodrigo		85	JUNINHO PERNAMBUCO	7
19	OLARRA Rafael		72	KAKA	8
20	GONZALEZ Mark	56		RONALDO	9
21	MARTEL Fernando	46		LUIS FABIANO	10
22	FUENTES Luis			EDU	11
	Tr: OLMOS Juvenal			Tr: PARREIRA Carlos Alberto	
2	ALVAREZ Cristian	46	72	JULIO BAPTISTA	15
17	MIROSEVIC Milovan	56	85	ALEX	16
25	GALAZ Patricio	46	80	GILBERTO SILVA	17

Estadio Monumental, Lima
4-09-2004, 19:00, 28 000, Simon BRA

PER 1 – 3 ARG

Soto 62
Rosales 14, Coloccini 66, Sorin 92+

No	PERU	Min	Min	ARGENTINA	No
1	IBANEZ Oscar			ABBONDANZIERI Roberto	1
2	ACASIETE Santiago			MILITO Gabriel	2
4	SOTO Jorge	76		COLOCCINI Fabricio	4
6	VILCHEZ Walter			MASCHERANO Javier	5
7	SOLANO Nolberto			HEINZE Gabriel	6
8	JAYO Juan			ROSALES Mauro	7
10	PALACIOS Roberto	75		ZANETTI Javier	8
15	SALAS Guillermo		83	TEVEZ Carlos	11
16	MENDOZA Andres	16		D'ALESSANDRO Andres	15
17	FARFAN Jefferson		45	GONZALES Cristian	18
22	GALLIQUIO John		69	DELGADO Cesar	19
	Tr: AUTUORI Paulo			Tr: BIELSA Marcelo	
9	MAESTRI Flavio	16 45	69	SORIN Juan	3
11	OLCESE Aldo	75	63	MILITO Diego	9
25	GARCIA Julio	76	83	MEDINA Nicolas	20

Estadio Centenario, Montevideo
5-09-2004, 15:15, 28 000, Hidalgo PER

URU   1   0   ECU

Bueno [57]

URUGUAY			ECUADOR		
1 VIERA Sebastian			VILLAFUERTE Edwin	1	
2 BIZERA Joe			HURTADO Ivan	3	
3 RODRIGUEZ Dario			DE LA CRUZ Ulises	4	
4 MONTERO Paolo		70	SOLEDISPA Leonardo	5	
5 SOSA Marcelo			MENDEZ Edison	8	
9 SILVA Dario	24		TENORIO Carlos	9	
10 RECOBA Alvaro	78	82	AYOVI Walter	10	
11 RODRIGUEZ Cristian	61	59	BALDEON Johnny	14	
16 DELGADO Javier			AYOVI Marlon	15	
17 DIOGO Carlos			ESPINOZA Giovanny	17	
20 BUENO Carlos			REASCO Neicer	18	
Tr: FOSSATI Jorge			Tr: SUAREZ Luis		
13 ESTOYANOFF Fabian	61	70	QUINONEZ Carlos	7	
15 PEREZ Diego	78	59	DELGADO Agustin	11	
22 SANCHEZ Vicente	24	82	VALENCIA Luis	16	

Morumbi, São Paulo
5-09-2004, 17:10, 60 000, Baldassi ARG

BRA   3   1   BOL

Ronaldo [1], Ronaldinho [12p]   Cristaldo 48
Adriano [44]

BRAZIL			BOLIVIA		
1 JULIO CESAR			FERNANDEZ Leonardo	21	
2 BELLETTI			PENA Juan Manuel	2	
3 EDMILSON			ALVAREZ Lorgio	4	
4 ROQUE JUNIOR			SANCHEZ Oscar	5	
5 JUNINHO PERNAMBUCO	60		CRISTALDO Luis	7	
6 ROBERTO CARLOS		76	GUTIERREZ Limberg	10	
7 ADRIANO		46	COLQUE Percy	14	
8 GILBERTO SILVA			PIZARRO Limbert	15	
9 RONALDO			RALDES Ronald	16	
10 RONALDINHO	60	46	RIBEIRO Luis	17	
11 EDU	73		BOTERO Joaquin	20	
Tr: PARREIRA Carlos Alberto			Tr: BLACUT Ramiro		
15 RENATO	60	46	TUFINO Ruben	8	
17 ALEX	60	76	COIMBRA Milton	9	
18 ROBINHO	73	46	ARANA Ronald	22	

Defensores del Chaco, Asuncion
5-09-2004, 18:20, 30 000, Mendez URU

PAR   1   0   VEN

Gamarra [52]

PARAGUAY			VENEZUELA		
1 VILLAR Justo			ANGELUCCI Gilberto	1	
2 SARABIA Pedro			VALLENILLA Luis	2	
3 CACERES Julio Cesar			REY Jose Manuel	3	
4 GAMARRA Carlos	82		CICHERO Alejandro	6	
10 GAVILAN Diego	77	76	CASTELLIN Rafael	7	
13 PAREDES Carlos			VERA Luis	8	
14 DA SILVA Paulo		70	URDANETA Gabriel	10	
16 ENCISO Julio Cesar		67	PAEZ Ricardo	11	
20 CARDOZO Jose	57		JIMENEZ Leopoldo	14	
23 CUEVAS Nelson			ROJAS Jorge	17	
24 SANTACRUZ Roque			ARANGO Juan	18	
Tr: RUIZ Anibal			Tr: PAEZ Richard		
7 RAMIREZ Cesar	57	67	RONDON Alexander	9	
8 BARRETO Edgar	77	70	GONZALEZ Hector	20	
15 MANZUR Julio	82	76	MORENO Wilfredo	26	

Estadio Nacional, Santiago
5-09-2004, 21:00, 62 523, Souza BRA

CHI   0   0   COL

CHILE			COLOMBIA		
1 TAPIA Nelson			CALERO Miguel	1	
3 MALDONADO Claudio	17		CORDOBA Ivan	2	
4 PEREZ Rodrigo	70		YEPES Mario	3	
6 ACUNA Jorge			VARGAS Fabian	6	
8 PIZARRO David	59	55	HERNANDES Giovanni	7	
9 NAVIA Reinaldo	46	87	OVIEDO Frankie	8	
14 VILLARROEL Moises			PEREA Luis Amaranto	14	
15 PINILLA Mauricio		17	VIAFARA John	15	
17 MIROSEVIC Milovan	59		CASTILLO Jairo	18	
19 OLARRA Rafael			BEDOYA Gerardo	20	
22 FUENTES Luis		65	PRECIADO Leider	23	
Tr: OLMOS Juvenal			Tr: RUEDA Reinaldo		
7 VALENZUELA Rodrigo	59	65	MURILLO Elkin	11	
11 SALAS Marcelo	46	70	55 PATINO Jairo	17	
25 TELLO Rodrigo	59	87	DIAZ Oscar	21	

Estadio Monumental, Buenos Aires
9-10-2004, 15:00, 50 000, Souza BRA

ARG   4   2   URU

Gonzalez.L [6], Figueroa 2 [32 54]   Rodriguez.C [63], Chevanton [86p]
Zanetti [44]

ARGENTINA			URUGUAY		
1 ABBONDANZIERI Roberto			VIERA Sebastian	1	
2 SAMUEL Walter		57	BIZERA Joe	2	
3 SORIN Juan			RODRIGUEZ Dario	3	
4 ZANETTI Javier			LEMBO Alejandro	4	
5 CAMBIASSO Esteban			SOSA Marcelo	5	
6 HEINZE Gabriel		55	SILVA Dario	9	
7 SAVIOLA Javier			RODRIGUEZ Cristian	11	
8 RIQUELME Juan		55	PEREZ Diego	15	
15 COLOCCINI Fabricio			DELGADO Javier	16	
16 GONZALEZ Luis	68		DIOGO Carlos	17	
19 FIGUEROA Luciano	80		CHEVANTON Ernesto	19	
Tr: PEKERMAN Jose			Tr: FOSSATI Jorge		
9 INSUA Federico	80	57	LAGO Eduardo	6	
11 RODRIGUEZ Maximiliano	68	55	GARCIA Pablo	8	
		55	FORLAN Diego	21	

Hernando Siles, La Paz
9-10-2004, 16:00, 23 729, Reinoso ECU

BOL   1   0   PER

Botero [56]

BOLIVIA			PERU		
21 FERNANDEZ Leonardo			IBANEZ Oscar	1	
5 SANCHEZ Oscar			ACASIETE Santiago	2	
6 GARCIA Ronald			SOTO Jorge	4	
7 CRISTALDO Luis			JAYO Juan	8	
10 GUTIERREZ Limberg	91		GUERRERO Jose	9	
11 COLQUE Percy			SALAS Guillermo	15	
16 RALDES Ronald			FARFAN Jefferson	17	
17 RIBEIRO Luis	82	62	CIURLIZZA Marco	19	
20 BOTERO Joaquin		71	GALLIQUIO John	22	
22 ARANA Ronald			RODRIGUEZ Alberto	24	
37 SANCHEZ Erwin	85	56	GARCIA Julio	25	
Tr: BLACUT Ramiro			Tr: AUTUORI Paulo		
8 TUFINO Ruben	85	56	PALACIOS Roberto	10	
24 GALINDO Gonzalo	91	71	LA ROSA Juan Carlos	20	
		62	MONSERRATE German	23	

Metropolitano, Barranquilla
9-10-2004, 17:10, 25 000, Elizondo ARG

COL	1	1	PAR

Grisales [17]   Gavilan [77]

COLOMBIA				PARAGUAY			
1	CALERO Miguel			VILLAR Justo	1		
2	CORDOBA Ivan			CACERES Julio Cesar	3		
3	YEPES Mario			MANZUR Julio	4		
6	DIAZ Oscar	81	59	BAREIRO Fredy	9		
8	OVIEDO Frankie		78	TORRES Aureliano	11		
9	ANGEL Juan Pablo			PAREDES Carlos	13		
10	PACHECO Victor			DA SILVA Paulo	14		
14	PEREA Luis Amaranto			ENCISO Julio Cesar	16		
19	GRISALES Freddy	67	46	ORTIZ Angel	17		
20	BEDOYA Gerardo			CARDOZO Jose	20		
21	RESTREPO John			CANIZA Denis	21		
	Tr: RUEDA Reinaldo			Tr: AMARILLA Raul			
7	MORENO Malher	67	46	GAVILAN Diego	10		
11	RODRIGUEZ Milton	81	59	CUEVAS Nelson	23		
			78	MONGES Mauro	24		

Pachenricho Romero, Maracaibo
9-10-2004, 21:00, 26 133, Chandia CHI

VEN	2	5	BRA

Moran 2 [79 90]   Kaka 2 [5 34], Ronaldo 2 [48 50]
                                                        Adriano [75]

VENEZUELA				BRAZIL			
1	ANGELUCCI Gilberto			DIDA	1		
2	VALLENILLA Luis			CAFU	2		
3	REY Jose Manuel			JUAN	3		
6	CICHERO Alejandro			ROQUE JUNIOR	4		
8	VERA Luis	68		RENATO	5		
14	JIMENEZ Leopoldo			ROBERTO CARLOS	6		
16	MORAN Ruberth		68	KAKA	7		
17	ROJAS Jorge		61	JUNINHO PERNAMBUCO	8		
18	ARANGO Juan		71	RONALDO	9		
27	HERNANDEZ Jonay	54		RONALDINHO	10		
29	MARGIOTTA Massimo	46		ZE ROBERTO	11		
	Tr: PAEZ Richard			Tr: PARREIRA Carlos Alberto			
13	VIELMA Leonel	54	61	EDU	15		
15	GONZALEZ Cesar	68	71	ALEX	16		
20	GONZALEZ Hector	46	68	ADRIANO	17		

Estadio Olimpico Atahualpa, Quito
10-10-2004, 17:00, 27 956, Ortube BOL

ECU	2	0	CHI

Kaviedes [49], Mendez [64]

ECUADOR				CHILE			
1	VILLAFUERTE Edwin			TAPIA Nelson	1		
3	HURTADO Ivan			CONTRERAS Pablo	5		
4	DE LA CRUZ Ulises		58	VALENZUELA Rodrigo	7		
5	AYOVI Walter	46		SALAS Marcelo	11		
6	GUERRON Raul			ROJAS Ricardo	16		
8	MENDEZ Edison			MELENDEZ Rodrigo	18		
9	ORDONEZ Ebelio	61		OLARRA Rafael	19		
10	KAVIEDES Ivan	89	46	MARTEL Fernando	21		
15	AYOVI Marlon			FUENTES Luis	22		
17	ESPINOZA Giovanny			GONZALEZ Luis	24		
20	TENORIO Edwin		78	GALAZ Patricio	25		
	Tr: SUAREZ Luis			Tr: OLMOS Juvenal			
7	SALAS Franklin	46	58	MIROSEVIC Milovan	17		
13	FERNANDEZ Angel	89	78	QUINTEROS Luis	20		
14	AMBROSI Vicente	61	46	BEAUSEJOUR Coliqueo	23		

Hernando Siles, La Paz
12-10-2004, 16:00, 24 349, Rezende BRA

BOL	0	0	URU

BOLIVIA				URUGUAY			
21	FERNANDEZ Leonardo			VIERA Sebastian	1		
3	CARBALLO Marcelo	65		LAGO Eduardo	3		
4	ALVAREZ Lorgio	76		RODRIGUEZ Dario	6		
5	SANCHEZ Oscar			VARELA Gustavo	7		
6	GARCIA Ronald	46		GARCIA Pablo	8		
7	CRISTALDO Luis		72	REGUEIRO Mario	10		
10	GUTIERREZ Limberg			RODRIGUEZ Guillermo	11		
16	RALDES Ronald		73	POUSO Omar	16		
20	BOTERO Joaquin			DIOGO Carlos	17		
22	ARANA Ronald		76	MORALES Richard	18		
37	SANCHEZ Erwin		75	SANCHEZ Vicente	22		
	Tr: BLACUT Ramiro			Tr: FOSSATI Jorge			
11	COLQUE Percy	65	75	SOSA Marcelo	5		
24	GALINDO Gonzalo	76	76	CHEVANTON Ernesto	19		
27	CABRERA Diego	46	72	PARODI Juan	20		

Defensores del Chaco, Asuncion
13-10-2004, 17:00, 30 000, Ruiz COL

PAR	1	1	PER

Paredes [13]   Solano [74]

PARAGUAY				PERU			
1	VILLAR Justo			IBANEZ Oscar	1		
3	CACERES Julio Cesar			ACASIETE Santiago	2		
4	MANZUR Julio			REBOSIO Miguel	3		
10	GAVILAN Diego	82		SOTO Jorge	4		
11	TORRES Aureliano	53		VARGAS Juan	5		
13	PAREDES Carlos		86	SOLANO Nolberto	7		
14	DA SILVA Paulo			JAYO Juan	8		
16	ENCISO Julio Cesar			PALACIOS Roberto	10		
18	HAEDO VALDEZ Nelson		66	MENDOZA Andres	16		
20	CARDOZO Jose	72		FARFAN Jefferson	17		
21	CANIZA Denis		46	GALLIQUIO John	22		
	Tr: RUIZ Anibal			Tr: AUTUORI Paulo			
9	BAREIRO Fredy	82	66	GUERRERO Jose	9		
23	CUEVAS Nelson	53	86	COMINGES Juan	18		
24	MONGES Mauro	72	46	CIURLIZZA Marco	19		

Estadio Nacional, Santiago
13-10-2004, 20:00, 57 671, Amarilla PAR

CHI	0	0	ARG

CHILE				ARGENTINA			
1	TAPIA Nelson			ABBONDANZIERI Roberto	1		
2	ALVAREZ Cristian			SAMUEL Walter	2		
5	CONTRERAS Pablo			SORIN Juan	3		
7	VALENZUELA Rodrigo			ZANETTI Javier	4		
9	NAVIA Reinaldo			CAMBIASSO Esteban	5		
11	SALAS Marcelo			HEINZE Gabriel	6		
13	VARGAS Jorge		76	SAVIOLA Javier	7		
14	VALDIVIA Jorge	72		RIQUELME Juan	8		
16	ROJAS Ricardo	46	46	GONZALEZ Luis	14		
18	MELENDEZ Rodrigo	58	62	FIGUEROA Luciano	19		
22	FUENTES Luis			COLOCCINI Fabricio	22		
	Tr: OLMOS Juvenal			Tr: PEKERMAN Jose			
17	MIROSEVIC Milovan	58	62	TEVEZ Carlos	9		
19	OLARRA Rafael	46	76	D'ALESSANDRO Andres	15		
20	QUINTEROS Luis	72	46	MASCHERANO Javier	18		

Estadio Reo Pele, Maceio
13-10-2004, 21:50, 20 000, Larrionda URU

BRA 0 0 COL

BRAZIL			COLOMBIA	
1 DIDA			CALERO Miguel	1
2 CAFU			CORDOBA Ivan	2
3 JUAN			YEPES Mario	3
4 ROQUE JUNIOR			DIAZ Oscar	6
5 RENATO		86	OVIEDO Frankie	8
6 ROBERTO CARLOS			ANGEL Juan Pablo	9
7 ALEX	58	77	PACHECO Victor	10
8 MAGRAO	58		PEREA Luis Amaranto	14
9 RONALDO		86	GRISALES Freddy	19
10 RONALDINHO			BEDOYA Gerardo	20
11 ZE ROBERTO	84		RESTREPO John	21
Tr: PARREIRA Carlos Alberto			Tr: RUEDA Reinaldo	
15 EDU	84	77	VIVEROS Alexander	4
16 ELANO	58	86	MORENO Malher	7
17 ADRIANO	58	86	LEAL Juan	23

Pueblo Nuevo, San Cristobal
14-10-2004, 19:00, 13 800, Lecca PER

VEN 3 1 ECU

Urdaneta [20p], Moran 2 [72 80]   Ayovi.M [41p]

VENEZUELA			ECUADOR	
22 DUDAMEL Rafael			VILLAFUERTE Edwin	1
2 VALLENILLA Luis	68		HURTADO Ivan	3
3 REY Jose Manuel		75	AMBROSI Vicente	4
6 CICHERO Alejandro			GUERRON Raul	6
8 VERA Luis		70	SALAS Franklin	7
9 RONDON Alexander	60		MENDEZ Edison	8
10 URDANETA Gabriel			KAVIEDES Ivan	10
14 JIMENEZ Leopoldo	64		AYOVI Marlon	15
16 MORAN Ruberth			ESPINOZA Giovanny	17
17 ROJAS Jorge			REASCO Neicer	18
18 ARANGO Juan			TENORIO Edwin	20
Tr: PAEZ Richard			Tr: SUAREZ Luis	
7 GARCIA Juan	60	75	ORDONEZ Ebelio	9
11 PAEZ Ricardo	64	70	BALDEON Johnny	14
20 GONZALEZ Hector	68			

Estadio Olimpico Atahualpa, Quito
17-11-2004, 16:00, 38 308, Ruiz COL

ECU 1 0 BRA

Mendez [77]

ECUADOR			BRAZIL	
1 VILLAFUERTE Edwin			DIDA	1
3 HURTADO Ivan			CAFU	2
4 DE LA CRUZ Ulises			JUAN	3
8 MENDEZ Edison			ROQUE JUNIOR	4
10 KAVIEDES Ivan	75		RENATO	5
11 DELGADO Agustin	90		ROBERTO CARLOS	6
13 AMBROSI Vicente		74	JUNINHO PERNAMBUCO	7
14 URRUTIA Patricio	46	81	KAKA	8
15 AYOVI Marlon			RONALDO	9
17 ESPINOZA Giovanny			RONALDINHO	10
20 TENORIO Edwin		64	KLEBERSON	11
Tr: SUAREZ Luis			Tr: PARREIRA Carlos Alberto	
5 AYOVI Walter	75	74	DUDU	15
7 SALAS Franklin	46	64	RICARDINHO	17
18 REASCO Neicer	90	81	ADRIANO	18

Metropolitano, Barranquilla
17-11-2004, 18:00, 25 000, Torres PAR

COL 1 0 BOL

Yepes [18]

COLOMBIA			BOLIVIA	
1 CALERO Miguel			FERNANDEZ Leonardo	21
2 CORDOBA Ivan		80	PENA Juan Manuel	2
3 YEPES Mario			JAUREGUI Sergio	3
4 VIVEROS Alexander			ALVAREZ Lorgio	4
8 OVIEDO Frankie	62		CRISTALDO Luis	7
9 ANGEL Juan Pablo		76	TUFINO Ruben	8
10 PACHECO Victor	76	45	COIMBRA Milton	9
11 MURILLO Elkin	70		GUTIERREZ Limberg	10
14 PEREA Luis Amaranto			RALDES Ronald	16
19 GRISALES Freddy			BOTERO Joaquin	20
21 RESTREPO John			ARANA Ronald	22
Tr: RUEDA Ronald			Tr: BLACUT Ramiro	
6 PEREZ Andres	62	80	ARCE Juan Carlos	17
15 HERNANDEZ Giovanni	76	76	VACA DIEZ Getulio	18
18 FERREIRA David	70	45	GALINDO Gonzalo	19

Estadio Nacional, Lima
17-11-2004, 20:00, 39 752, Baldassi ARG

PER 2 1 CHI

Farfan [56], Guerrero [85]   Gonzalez [91+]

PERU			CHILE	
1 IBANEZ Oscar			TAPIA Nelson	1
2 ACASIETE Santiago	41		ALVAREZ Cristian	2
3 SOTO Jorge		75	MALDONADO Claudio	3
5 VARGAS Juan			CONTRERAS Pablo	5
7 SOLANO Nolberto		46	VALENZUELA Rodrigo	7
8 JAYO Juan			PIZARRO David	8
10 PALACIOS Roberto			PINILLA Mauricio	15
14 PIZARRO Claudio	71	41	MELENDEZ Rodrigo	18
17 FARFAN Jefferson		62	OLARRA Rafael	19
19 CIURLIZZA Marco	37		GONZALEZ Mark	20
24 RODRIGUEZ Alberto			FUENTES Luis	22
Tr: AUTUORO Paulo			Tr: OLMOS Juvenal	
9 GUERRERO Jose	71	62	GONZALEZ Sebastian	9
20 ZEGARRA Carlos	62 37	75	VALDIVIA Jorge	14
23 VILLALTA Miguel	62	46	GONZALEZ Luis	24

Estadio Centenario, Montevideo
17-11-2004, 20:45, 35 000, Simon BRA

URU 1 0 PAR

Montero [78]

URUGUAY			PARAGUAY	
1 VIERA Sebastian			VILLAR Justo	1
2 LUGANO Diego			CACERES Julio Cesar	3
3 RODRIGUEZ Guillermo			GAMARRA Carlos	4
4 MONTERO Paolo		80	MONGES Mauro	6
5 GARCIA Pablo		80	BARRETO Edgar	8
6 LOPEZ Diego			PAREDES Carlos	13
7 VARELA Gustavo	67		DA SILVA Paulo	14
9 SILVA Dario	46		ORTIZ Angel	17
10 RECOBA Alvaro	70		CARDOZO Jose	20
16 DELGADO Javier			CANIZA Denis	21
19 CHEVANTON Ernesto		68	CUEVAS Nelson	23
Tr: FOSSATI Jorge			Tr: RUIZ Anibal	
13 ESTOYANOFF Fabian	67	68	RAMIREZ Cesar	7
18 MORALES Richard	46	80	BAREIRO Fredy	9
22 SANCHEZ Vicente	70	80	GAVILAN Diego	10

Monumental, Buenos Aires
17-11-2004, 21:45, 30 000, Hidalgo PER

ARG 3 2 VEN

Rey OG [3], Riquelme [46+]
Saviola [65]

Moran [31], Vielma [72]

ARGENTINA				VENEZUELA	
1	ABBONDANZIERI Roberto			DUDAMEL Rafael	22
2	RODRIGUEZ Gonzalo			VALLENILLA Luis	2
3	SORIN Juan			REY Jose Manuel	3
4	ZANETTI Javier			CICHERO Alejandro	6
5	MASCHERANO Javier			VERA Luis	8
6	MILITO Gabriel		70	PAEZ Ricardo	11
8	RIQUELME Juan		77	JIMENEZ Leopoldo	14
9	FIGUEROA Luciano			MORAN Ruberth	16
11	SOLARI Santiago	65		ROJAS Jorge	17
19	CAMBIASSO Esteban	79		ARANGO Juan	18
21	DELGADO Cesar	58	52	HERNANDEZ Jonay	27
Tr: PEKERMAN Jose			Tr: PAEZ Richard		
7	SAVIOLA Javier	58	52	URDANETA Gabriel	10
13	PLACENTE Diego	79	70	VIELMA Leonel	13
16	GONZALEZ Luis	65	77	CASSERES Cristian	23

Hernando Siles, La Paz
26-03-2005, 16:00, 25 000, Larrionda URU

BOL 1 2 ARG

Castillo [49]

Figueroa [57], Galletti [63]

BOLIVIA				ARGENTINA	
21	FERNANDEZ Leonardo			ABBONDANZIERI Roberto	1
4	ALVAREZ Lorgio			BURDISSO Nicolas	2
5	SANCHEZ Oscar			RODRIGUEZ Clemente	3
6	ANGULO Carmelo	69	75	MILITO Gabriel	6
10	SANCHEZ Erwin			FIGUEROA Luciano	9
11	COLQUE Percy	46	63	RODRIGUEZ Maximiliano	11
15	PIZARRO Limbert			CUFRE Leandro	14
16	RALDES Ronald			DUSCHER Aldo	15
18	CASTILLO Jose		84	GALLETTI Luciano	18
20	BOTERO Joaquin			CAMBIASSO Esteban	19
24	GALINDO Gonzalo	85		SCALONI Lionel	20
Tr: MESA Ovidio			Tr: PEKERMAN Jose		
8	GARCIA Ronald	85	63	PONZIO Leonardo	4
26	PACHI Danner	46	84	PALACIO Rodrigo	7
27	CABRERA Diego	69	75	ZARATE Rolando	16

Pachenricho Romero, Maracaibo
26-03-2005, 19:00, 18 000, Simon BRA

VEN 0 0 COL

VENEZUELA				COLOMBIA	
22	DUDAMEL Rafael			CALERO Miguel	1
3	REY Jose Manuel			CORDOBA Ivan	2
6	CICHERO Alejandro			YEPES Mario	3
7	CASTELLIN Rafael	56		OROZCO Andres	5
10	URDANETA Gabriel	65		PEREA Edixon	7
13	VIELMA Leonel		73	HERNANDEZ Giovanni	15
14	JIMENEZ Leopoldo		71	RAMIREZ Juan	17
18	MALDONADO Giancarlos		87	CASTILLO Jairo	18
20	GONZALEZ Hector			FERREIRA David	19
27	HERNANDEZ Jonay			BEDOYA Gerardo	20
29	MARGIOTTA Massimo	74		RESTREPO John	21
Tr: PAEZ Richard			Tr: RUEDA Reinaldo		
15	NORIEGA Daniel	74	71	VARGAS Fabian	6
19	GONZALEZ Andree	65	87	HERRERA Sergio	9
21	GONZALEZ Cesar	56	73	PACHECO Victor	10

Estadio Nacional, Santiago
26-03-2005, 22:00, 55 000, Ruiz COL

CHI 1 1 URU

Mirosevic [47]

Regueiro [4]

CHILE				URUGUAY	
1	TAPIA Nelson			VIERA Sebastian	1
2	ALVAREZ Cristian			LUGANO Diego	2
3	MALDONADO Claudio			RODRIGUEZ Dario	3
5	CONTRERAS Pablo	46		MONTERO Paolo	4
8	PIZARRO David			GARCIA Pablo	5
11	SALAS Marcelo			LOPEZ Diego	6
15	PINILLA Mauricio		69	ZALAYRTA Marcelo	9
16	ROJAS Ricardo		58	OLIVERA Ruben	10
17	MIROSEVIC Milovan	82	82	REGUEIRO Mario	11
20	GONZALEZ Mark	82		DIOGO Carlos	17
22	FUENTES Luis			FORLAN Diego	21
Tr: OLMOS Juvenal			Tr: FOSSATI Jorge		
7	VALENZUELA Rodrigo	82	58	SOSA Marcelo	8
14	VALDIVIA Jorge	46	69	MORALES Richard	18
32	GONZALEZ Sebastian	82	82	SANCHEZ Vicente	22

Serra Dourada, Goiania
27-03-2005, 16:00, 49 163, Amarilla PAR

BRA 1 0 PER

Kaka [74]

BRAZIL				PERU	
1	DIDA			IBANEZ Oscar	1
2	CAFU			REBOSIO Miguel	3
3	LUCIO			SOTO Jorge	4
4	JUAN			VILCHEZ Walter	6
5	EMERSON		68	SOLANO Nolberto	7
6	ROBERTO CARLOS			JAYO Juan	8
7	KAKA	83	46	PALACIOS Roberto	10
8	JUNINHO PERNAMBUCO	46		PIZARRO Claudio	14
9	RONALDO			FARFAN Jefferson	17
10	RONALDINHO			ZEGARRA Carlos	20
12	ZE ROBERTO		72	RODRIGUEZ Alberto	24
Tr: PARREIRA Carlos Alberto			Tr: AUTUORI Paulo		
15	RENATO	83	46	OLCESE Aldo	11
17	ROBINHO	46	68	COMINGUES Juan	18
			72	GUADALUPE RIVAD. Luis	22

Olimpico Atahualpa, Quito
27-03-2005, 16:10, 32 449, Mendez URU

ECU 5 2 PAR

Valencia 2 [32] [49], Mendez 2 [47+] [47]
Ayovi.M [77p]

Cardozo [10p], Cabanas [14]

ECUADOR				PARAGUAY	
1	VILLAFUERTE Edwin			VILLAR Justo	1
3	HURTADO Ivan			SARABIA Pedro	2
4	DE LA CRUZ Ulises			GAMARRA Carlos	4
8	MENDEZ Edison			BONET Carlos	6
11	DELGADO Agustin	78		CABANAS Salvador	9
13	AMBROSSI Paul		52	GAVILAN Diego	10
14	TENORIO Otilino	57		DA SILVA Paulo	14
15	AYOVI Marlon		52	MONGES Mauro	16
16	VALENCIA Luis			ORTIZ Angel	17
17	ESPINOZA Giovanny			CARDOZO Jose	20
20	TENORIO Edwin	78		CANIZA Denis	21
Tr: SUAREZ Luis			Tr: RUIZ Anibal		
7	SALAS Franklin	57	52	BARRETO Edgar	8
10	KAVIEDES Ivan	78	52	CUEVAS Nelson	23
19	CAICEDO Luis	78			

Hernando Siles, La Paz
29-03-2005, 16:00, 7 908, Lecca PER

BOL 3 1 VEN

Cichero OG [2], Castillo [25], Vaca [84] Maldonado [71]

BOLIVIA			VENEZUELA	
21 FERNANDEZ Leonardo			DUDAMEL Rafael	1
3 JAUREGUI Sergio			REYT Jose Manuel	3
4 ALVAREZ Lorgio			FUENMAYOR Juan	4
5 SANCHEZ Oscar		46	CICHERO Alejandro	6
8 GARCIA Ronald	20		VERA Luis	8
10 SANCHEZ Erwin	80	57	URDANETA Gabriel	10
15 PIZARRO Limbert		71	DE ORNELAS Fernando	17
16 RALDES Ronald			MALDONADO Giancarlos	18
18 CASTILLO Jose	58		GONZALEZ Andree	19
20 BOTERO Joaquin			GONZALEZ Hector	20
24 GALINDO Gonzalo			HERNANDEZ Jonay	27
Tr: MESA Ovidio			Tr: PAEZ Richard	
22 VACA Joselito	20	71	RONDON Alexander	9
26 PACHI Danner	80	46	NORIEGA Daniel	15
27 CABRERA Diego	58	57	GONZALEZ Cesar	16

Defensores del Chaco, Asuncion
30-03-2005, 19:00, 10 000, Elizondo ARG

PAR 2 1 CHI

Morinigo [37], Cardoza [59] Pinilla [72]

PARAGUAY			CHILE	
1 VILLAR Justo			TAPIA Nelson	1
3 CACERES Julio Cesar			MALDONADO Claudio	3
4 GAMARRA Carlos		46	PEREZ Rodrigo	4
6 BONET Carlos			SALAS Marcelo	11
9 CABANAS Salvador			PINILLA Mauricio	15
11 NUNEZ Jorge			ROJAS Ricardo	16
13 PAREDES Carlos	82	65	MIROSEVIC Milovan	17
14 DA SILVA Paulo		53	MELENDEZ Rodrigo	18
17 ORTIZ Angel			OLARRA Rafael	19
20 CARDOZO Jose	71		GONZALEZ Mark	20
25 MORINGO Gustavo	60		FUENTES Luis	22
Tr: RUIZ Anibal			Tr: OLMOS Juvenal	
8 BARRETO Edgar	60	46	ALVAREZ Cristian	2
10 GAVILAN Diego	82	53	PIZARRO David	8
18 HAEDO Valdez Nelson	71	65	GONZALEZ Sebastian	32

Monumental, Buenos Aires
30-03-2005, 20:00, 40 000, Amarilla PAR

ARG 1 0 COL

Crespo [65]

ARGENTINA			COLOMBIA	
1 ABBONDANZIERI Roberto			CALERO Miguel	1
2 AYALA Roberto			CORDOBA Ivan	2
3 SORIN Juan			YEPES Mario	3
4 ZANETTI Javier			OROZCO Andres	5
5 MASCHERANO Javier	54	42	VARGAS Fabian	6
6 HEINZE Gabriel		68	PEREA Edixon	7
7 SAVIOLA Javier	79		OVIEDO Frankie	8
8 RIQUELME Juan			VIAFARA John	14
9 CRESPO Hernan		46	HERNANDEZ Giovanni	15
16 GONZALEZ Luis			BEDOYA Gerardo	20
19 CAMBIASSO Esteban		79	RESTREPO John	21
Tr: PEKERMAN Jose			Tr: RUEDA Reinaldo	
13 PLACENTE Diego	79	46	VIVEROS Alexander	4
18 GALLETTI Luciano	54	79	PACHECO Victor	10
		68	CASTILLO Jairo	18

Estadio Nacional, Lima
30-03-2005, 20:00, 40 000, Chandia CHI

PER 2 2 ECU

Guerrero [1], Farfan [58] De la Cruz [4], Valencia [45]

PERU			ECUADOR	
1 IBANEZ Oscar			VILLAFUERTE Edwin	1
2 ACASIETE Santiago			HURTADO Ivan	3
3 REBOSIO Miguel			DE LA CRUZ Ulises	4
4 SOTO Jorge	60	86	MENDEZ Edison	8
7 SOLANO Nolberto	85	46	BALDEON Johnny	9
8 JAYO Juan			DELGADO Agustin	11
9 GUERRERO Jose			AMBROSSI Paul	13
14 PIZARRO Claudio		71	AYOVI Marlon	15
17 FARFAN Jefferson			VALENCIA Luis	16
20 ZEGARRA Carlos	61		ESPINOZA Giovanny	17
23 VARGAS Juan			TENORIO Carlos	20
Tr: AUTUORI Paulo			Tr: SUAREZ Luis	
10 PALACIOS Roberto	61	86	AYOVI Walter	5
15 SALAS Guillermo	60	46	SALAS Franklin	7
16 MENDOZA Andres	85	71	CAICEDO Luis	19

Centenario, Montevideo
30-03-2005, 21:30, 60 000, Baldassi ARG

URU 1 1 BRA

Forlan [48] Emerson [67]

URUGUAY			BRAZIL	
1 VIERA Sebastian			DIDA	1
2 LUGANO Diego			CAFU	2
3 RODRIGUEZ Dario			LUCIO	3
4 MONTERO Paolo			LUISAO	4
5 GARCIA Pablo			EMERSON	5
6 LOPEZ Diego			ROBERTO CARLOS	6
7 ZALAYETA Marcelo	63		RICARDO OLIVEIRA	7
10 OLIVERA Ruben	72		KAKA	8
11 REGUEIRO Mario	58		RONALDO	9
17 DIOGO Carlos	87		RONALDINHO	10
21 FORLAN Diego		68	ZE ROBERTO	11
Tr: FOSSATI Jorge			Tr: PARREIRA Carlos Alberto	
15 DELGADO Javier	58	68	RENATO	15
16 DE LOS SANTOS Gonzalo	87	63	ROBINHO	17
19 CHEVANTON Ernesto	72			

Metropolitano, Barranquilla
4-06-2005, 15:00, 15 000, Torres PAR

COL 5 0 PER

Rey [29], Soto [55], Angel [58], Restrepo [75], Perea.E [78]

COLOMBIA			PERU	
22 MONDRAGON Farid			FLORES Juan	1
3 YEPES MArio	80		ACASIETE Santiago	2
8 ANGEL Juan Pablo	65		REBOSIO Miguel	3
10 MORENO Malher			VARGAS Juan	5
11 SOTO Elkin		45	VILCHEZ Walter	6
14 PEREA Luis			SOLANO Nolberto	7
15 VIAFARA John		59	JAYO Juan	8
18 REY Luis	72	63	PALACIOS Roberto	10
20 BEDOYA Gerardo			PIZARRO Claudio	14
21 RESTREPO John		63	FARFAN Jefferson	17
23 PALACIO Haider			LA ROSA Juan Carlos	20
Tr: RUEDA Reinaldo			Tr: TERNERO Freddy	
4 MENDOZA Humberto	80	63	MENDOZA Jose	4
7 PEREA Edixon	65	45	GUERRERO Jose	9
24 ARZUAGA Martin	72	63	COMINGES Juan	18

Olimpico Atahualpa, Quito
4-06-2005, 16:00, 37 583, Selman CHI

ECU 2 0 ARG

Lara [53], Delgado [89]

ECUADOR				ARGENTINA	
1	VILLAFuerte Edwin			FRANCO Leonardo	1
3	HURTADO Ivan			COLOCCINI Fabricio	2
4	DE LA CRUZ Ulises		68	MILITO Gabriel	3
5	VALENCIA Luis	84		ZANETTI Javier	4
6	ESPINOZA Giovanny		31	DUSCHER Aldo	5
7	GOMEZ Christian	46		SAMUEL Walter	6
11	DELGADO Agustin			GALLETTI Luciano	7
13	AMBROSSI Paul			RODRIGUEZ Maximiliano	11
15	AYOVI Marlon		74	AIMAR Pablo	16
18	REASCO Neicer	75		GONZALEZ Cristian	18
20	TENORIO Edwin		88	CAMBIASSO Esteban	19
	Tr: SUAREZ Luis			Tr: PEKERMAN Jose	
10	LARA Christian	46	31	TEVEZ Carlos	9
14	TENORIO Carlos	84	74	D'ALESSANDRO Andres	15
16	QUIROZ Mario	75	68	FIGUEROA Luciano	20

Pachenricho Romero, Maracaibo
4-06-2005, 19:00, 12 504, Brazenas ARG

VEN 1 1 URU

Maldonado [74]   Forlan [2]

VENEZUELA				URUGUAY	
22	DUDAMEL Rafael			VIERA Sebastian	1
3	REY Jose Manuel			LUGANO Diego	2
6	CICHERO Alejandro		63	RODRIGUEZ Dario	3
8	VERA Luis			MONTERO Paolo	4
9	MALDONADO Giancarlos			SOSA Marcelo	5
11	PAEZ Ricardo	63		LOPEZ Diego	6
13	VIELMA Leonel	38		ZALAYETA Marcelo	9
16	MORAN Ruberth			OLIVERA Ruben	10
17	ROJAS Jorge	68	42	REGUEIRO Mario	11
18	ARANGO Juan		28	DIOGO Carlos	17
20	GONZALEZ Hector		84	FORLAN Diego	21
	Tr: PAEZ Richard			Tr: FOSSATI Jorge	
4	HERNANDEZ Jonay	68	42	PEREZ Diego	15
10	URDANETA Gabriel	38	84	CHEVANTON Ernesto	19
23	CASSERES Cristian	63	63	DE LOS SANTOS Gonzalo	22

Estadio Nacional, Santiago
4-06-2005, 21:00, 46 729, Rezende BRA

CHI 3 1 BOL

Fuentes 2 [8 34], Salas [66]   Castillo [83p]

CHILE				BOLIVIA	
1	TAPIA Nelson			FERNANDEZ Leonardo	21
3	MALDONADO Claudio		80	JAUREGUI Sergio	3
4	ROJAS Francisco			ALVAREZ Lorgio	4
8	PIZARRO David			ARANA Ronald	5
11	SALAS Marcelo	70	34	GARCIA Ronald	6
15	VILLARROEL Moises			COIMBRA Milton	9
16	ROJAS Ricardo			GUTIERREZ Limburg	10
21	MELENDEZ Rodrigo	14		JUSTINIANO Raul	15
21	JIMENEZ Luis	72		RALDES Ronald	16
22	FUENTES Luis			CASTILLO Jose	18
32	GONZALEZ Sebastian	31	46	PACHI Danner	26
	Tr: ACOSTA Nelson			Tr: MESA Ovidio	
6	ACUNA Jorge	14	80	PARADA Enrique	14
7	GALAZ Patricio	70	46	ARCE Juan Carlos	17
10	TELLO Rodrigo	72	34	VACA Joselito	22

Beira Rio, Porto Alegre
5-06-2005, 16:00, 45 000, Vazquez URU

BRA 4 1 PAR

Ronaldinho 2 [32p 41p]
Ze Roberto [70], Robinho [82]   Santacruz [72]

BRAZIL				PARAGUAY	
1	DIDA			VILLAR Justo	1
2	BELLETTI			GAMARRA Carlos	4
3	LUCIO	79	46	MANZUR Julio	5
4	ROQUE JUNIOR		63	BONET Carlos	6
5	EMERSON	75		CABANAS Salvador	9
6	ROBERTO CARLOS			TORRES Aureliano	11
7	ROBINHO	82		PAREDES Carlos	13
8	KAKA			DA SILVA Paulo	14
9	ADRIANO	75		ORTIZ Angel	17
10	RONALDINHO			CANIZA Denis	21
11	ZE ROBERTO			SANTACRUZ Roque	24
	Tr: PARREIRA Carlos Alberto			Tr: RUIZ Anibal	
13	JUAN	82	46	BARRETO Edgar	8
15	GILBERTO SILVA	75	63	CUEVAS Nelson	23
18	RICARDO OLIVEIRA	75			

Estadio Nacional, Lima
7-06-2005, 20:00, 31 515, Baldassi ARG

PER 0 0 URU

PERU				URUGUAY	
1	FLORES Juan			VIERA Sebastian	1
3	REBOSIO Miguel			LUGANO Diego	2
4	MENDOZA Jose			RODRIGUEZ Dario	3
6	VILCHEZ Walter			GARCIA Pablo	5
9	GUERRERO Jose		31	LOPEZ Diego	6
14	PIZARRO Claudio		83	RODRIGUEZ Guillermo	8
16	GUADALUPE Luis			ZALAYETA Marcelo	9
17	FARFAN Jefferson			OLIVERA Ruben	10
18	COMINGES Juan	63		DELGADO Javier	16
20	LA ROSA Juan Carlos	86	71	CHEVANTON Ernesto	19
22	VILLALTA Miguel			FORLAN Diego	21
	Tr: TERNERO Freddy			Tr: FOSSATI Jorge	
7	SOLANO Nolberto	86	71	ESTOYANOFF Fabian	13
10	PALACIOS Roberto	63	31	PEREZ Diego	15
			83	MORALES Richard	18

Metropolitano, Barranquilla
8-06-2005, 15:00, 20 402, Simon BRA

COL 3 0 ECU

Yepes [7], Reasco [80], Caicedo [86]

COLOMBIA				ECUADOR	
22	MONDRAGON Farid			VILLAFUERTE Edwin	1
3	YEPES Mario			HURTADO Ivan	3
5	BENITEZ Jair			DE LA CRUZ Ulises	4
9	ANGEL Juan Pablo		53	VALENCIA Luis	5
10	MORENO Malher	68		ESPINOZA Giovanny	6
11	SOTO Elkin	39		DELGADO Agustin	11
14	PEREA Luis		59	AMBROSSI Paul	13
15	VIAFARA John			TENORIO Carlos	14
18	REY Luis	66	45	AYOVI Marlon	15
21	RESTREPO John			QUIROZ Mario	16
25	PALACIO Haider			REASCO Neicer	18
	Tr: RUEDA Reinaldo			Tr: SUAREZ Luis	
6	VARGAS Fabian	39	53	AYOVI Walter	8
16	HURTADO Hector	66	59	LARA Christian	10
24	ARZUAGA Martin	68	45	CAICEDO Luis	19

Defensores del Chaco, Asuncion
8-06-2005, 19:15, 5 534, Brand VEN

PAR 4 1 BOL

Gamarra [17], Santacruz [46+]
Caceres [54], Nunez [68]

Galindo [30]

PARAGUAY			BOLIVIA		
1 VILLAR Justo			GALARZA Sergio 25		
2 NUNEZ Jorge			JAUREGUI Sergio 3		
3 CACERES Juan Daniel			ALVAREZ Lorgio 4		
4 GAMARA Carlos		78	MOJICA Gualberto 8		
5 CACERES Julio Cesar			GUTIERREZ Limberg 10		
8 BARRETO Edgar	74		FLORES Walter 12		
9 CABANAS Salvador	77	46	PARADA Enrique 14		
13 PAREDES Carlos			RALDES Ronald 16		
17 ORTIZ Angel		65	CASTILLO Jose 18		
20 CARDOZO Jose	64		ZENTENO Edward 19		
24 SANTACRUZ Roque			GALINDO Gonzalo 24		
Tr: RUIZ Anibal			Tr: MESA Ovidio		
10 GAVILAN Diego	74	46	COIMBRA Milton 9		46
18 SALCEDO Santiago	64	65	ARCE Juan Carlos 17		65
23 CUEVAS Nelson	77	78	VACA Joselito 22		78

Estadio Nacional, Santiago
8-06-2005, 19:00, 35 506, Torres PAR

CHI 2 1 VEN

Jimenez 2 [31 60]

Moran [82]

CHILE			VENEZUELA		
1 TAPIA Nelson			DUDAMEL Rafael 22		
3 MALDONADO Claudio			REY Jose Manuel 3		
4 ROJAS Francisco			HERNANDEZ Jonay 4		
5 CONTRERAS Pablo			CICHERO Alejandro 6		
6 ACUNA Jorge			URDANETA Gabriel 10		
7 GALAZ Patricio	62		JIMENEZ Leopoldo 14		
8 PIZARRO David	88		MORAN Ruberth 16		
15 VILLARROEL Moises			ARANGO Juan 18		
16 ROJAS Ricardo	71		GONZALEZ Andree 19		71
21 JIMENEZ Luis	81		CASSERES Cristian 23		57
22 FUENTES Luis			DE ORNELAS Fernando 24		46
Tr: ACOSTA Nelson			Tr: PAEZ Richard		
14 VALDIVIA Jorge	81	46	VALLENILLA Luis 2		46
17 VILLANUEVA Jose Luis	62	57	GONZALEZ Cesar 7		57
24 GONZALEZ Luis	88	71	PEREZ Giovanny 15		71

Monumental, Buenos Aires
8-06-2005, 21:45, 49 497, Mendez URU

ARG 3 1 BRA

Crespo 2 [3 40], Riquelme [18]

Roberto Carlos [71]

ARGENTINA			BRAZIL		
1 ABBONDANZIERI Roberto			DIDA 1		
2 AYALA Roberto			CAFU 2		
3 SORIN Juan			JUAN 3		
5 MASCHERANO Javier			ROQUE JUNIOR 4		
6 HEINZE Gabriel			EMERSON 5		
7 SAVIOLA Javier	82		ROBERTO CARLOS 6		
8 RIQUELME Juan	61		ROBINHO 7		61
9 CRESPO Hernan			KAKA 8		
18 GONZALEZ Cristian			ADRIANO 9		
21 GONZALEZ Luis	71		RONALDINHO 10		
22 COLOCCINI Fabricio			ZE ROBERTO 11		
Tr: PEKERMAN Jose			Tr: PARREIRA Carlos Alberto		
4 ZANETTI Javier	71	61	RENATO 16		61
11 TEVEZ Carlos	82				

		PL	W	D	L	F	A	PTS	ARG	BRA	ECU	PAR	COL	CHI	URU	PER	VEN	BOL
1	Argentina	15	9	4	2	27	15	31		3-1	1-0	0-0	1-0	2-2	4-2		3-2	3-0
2	Brazil	15	7	6	2	26	16	27	3-1		1-0	4-1	0-0		3-3	1-0		3-1
3	Ecuador	15	7	2	6	21	18	23	2-0	1-0		5-2	2-1	2-0		0-0	2-0	3-2
4	Paraguay	15	6	4	5	21	22	22		0-0	2-1			2-1	4-1	1-1	1-0	4-1
5	Colombia	15	5	5	5	20	12	20	1-1	1-2	3-0	1-1		5-0	5-0	0-1	1-0	
6	Chile	15	5	5	5	17	16	20	0-0	1-1	0-1	0-0			1-1	2-1	2-1	3-1
7	Uruguay	15	4	6	5	19	26	18	1-1	1-0	1-0		2-1			1-3	0-3	5-0
8	Peru	15	3	6	6	15	21	15	1-3	1-1	2-2	4-1	0-2	2-1	0-0		0-0	
9	Venezuela	15	4	3	8	16	23	15	0-3	2-5	3-1							2-1
10	Bolivia	15	1	4	10	17	30	13	1-2			2-1	4-0	0-2	0-0	1-0	3-1	

Table as of 2 September 2005. Remaining fixtures: 3-09-2005 Paraguay v Argentina, Brazil v Chile, Bolivia v Ecuador, Venezuela v Peru, Uruguay v Colombia; 8-10-2005 Bolivia v Brazil, Argentina v Peru, Ecuador v Uruguay, Venezuela v Paraguay, Colombia v Chile; 11-10-2005 Uruguay v Argentina, Paraguay v Colombia, Brazil v Venezuela, Peru v Bolivia, Chile v Ecuador

QUALIFYING MATCHES PLAYED IN OCEANIA

Preliminary Round

Group 1		Pts
Solomon Islands	SOL	10
Tahiti	TAH	8
New Caledonia	NCL	7
Tonga	TGA	3
Cook Islands	COK	0

Group 2		Pts
Vanuatu	VAN	10
Fiji	FIJ	9
Papua New Guinea	PNG	7
Samoa	SAM	3
American Samoa	ASA	0

Group Stage

		Pts
Australia	AUS	13
Solomon Islands	SOL	10
New Zealand	NZL	9
Fiji	FIJ	4
Tahiti	TAH	4
Vanuatu	VAN	4

Play-off

Australia	AUS
Solomon Islands	SOL

Winner of the matches played on 3
and 6 September qualifies to meet
the CONMEBOL fifth placed team

PRELIMINARY ROUND

	GROUP 1	PL	W	D	L	F	A	PTS	SOL	TAH	NCL	TGA	COK
1	Solomon Islands	4	3	1	0	14	1	10		1-1	2-0	6-0	5-0
2	Tahiti	4	2	2	0	5	1	8			0-0	2-0	2-0
3	New Caledonia	4	2	1	1	16	2	7				8-0	8-0
4	Tonga	4	1	0	3	2	17	3					2-1
5	Cook Islands	4	0	0	4	1	17	0					

Lawson Tama, Honiara
10-05-2004, 14:00, 12 385, Attison VAN

SOL   6   0   TGA

Faarodo 3 [12 30 77]
Maemae 2 [62 76], Samani [79]

SOLOMON ISLANDS			TONGA	
1 RAY Felix			SAAFI Heneli	1
2 LEO Leslie		82	HUIHAHAU Kaya	2
3 HOUKARAWA Mahlon	69		MOEAKI Makatuu	3
7 MAEMAE Alick			MAFI Sitenilesili	4
9 MENAPI Commins			MAAMALOA Siua	5
13 LUI George	55	75	UHATAHI Mark	7
16 WAITA Stanley	56		UELE Kilifi	8
17 OMOKIRIO Gideon			PAPANI Kamaliele	10
18 FAARODO Henry			TEVI Maamalua	11
19 KAKAI Paul			MOALA Lafaele	13
21 SURI George		67	MOA Solomone	17
Tr: GILLET Allan			Tr: JANKOVIC Milan	
4 RUHASIA Martin	69	75	FONUA Ipeni	6
8 KONOFILIA Joel	55	67	FOTU Mekilani	12
14 SAMANI Moses	56	82	MOEAKI Folio	14

Lawson Tama, Honiara
10-05-2004, 16:00, 12 000, Singh FIJ

TAH   2   0   COK

Temataua [2], Moretta [80]

TAHITI			COOK ISLANDS	
20 SAMIN Xavier			JAMIESON Tony	1
2 TCHEN Angelo			JAMIESON Mark	3
3 KUGOGNE Pierre			PAREANGA John	4
4 KAUTAI Iotua	79		TATUAVAEugenie	5
5 LI WAUT Jean-Yves		31	SAMUEL Victor	6
7 GARCIA Samuel		79	TAUIRA Christian	7
8 MATAITAI Billy			CHAMBERS Joseph	9
10 TEMATAUA Axel	63	46	SHEPHERD Daniel	11
11 NEUFFEr Taufa	79		TISAM Tuka	12
12 TEUIRA Farahia			OTI Albert	15
15 MARMOUYET Larry			SHEPHERD Adrian	16
Tr: KAUTAI Gerard			Tr: JERKS Tim	
9 WAJOKA Gabriel	63	46	MATEARIKI Teariki	10
13 SIMON Vincent	79	79	PUTERE Teatu-Rangi	13
14 MORETTA Rino	79	31	STRICKLAND Geoffrey	17

Lawson Tama, Honiara
12-05-2004, 14:00, 14 000, Fred VAN

SOL   5   0   COK

Waita [21], Omokirio [27]
Samani [45], Maemae [70], Leo [81]

SOLOMON ISLANDS			COOK ISLANDS	
1 RAY Felix			JAMIESON Tony	1
3 HOUKARAWA Mahlon	74		JAMIESON Mark	3
6 SALE Nelson			PAREANGA John	4
7 MAEAMAE Alick			TATUAVA Eugenie	5
9 MENAPI Commins	46	70	SAMUAL Victor	6
10 SURI Batram	30		TAUIRA Christian	7
16 WAITA Stanley			CHAMBERS Joseph	9
17 OMOKIRIO Gideon			MATEARIKI Teariki	10
18 FAARODO Henry	70		TISAM Tuka	12
19 KAKAI Paul	46		PUTERE Teatu-Rangi	13
21 SURI George			OTI Albert	15
Tr: GILLET Allan			Tr: JERKS Tim	
2 LEO Leslie	74	70	UNE Rourururoa	8
14 SAMANI Jack	30	46	SHEPHERD Daniel	11
15 TOATA Moses	46	70	ANGENE David	14

Lawson Tama, Honiara
12-05-2004, 16:00, 14 000, Rakaroi FIJ

TAH   0   0   NCL

TAHITI			NEW CALEDONIA	
20 SAMIN Xavier			HNE Michel	1
2 TCHEN Angelo			SINEDO Andre	4
3 KUGOGNE Pierre			WIAKO Jacky	6
5 LI WAUT Jean-Yves			ELMOUR Gil	8
7 GARCIA Samuel			OIREJOIN Frank	9
8 MATAITAI Billy			WEA Jules	11
9 WAJOKA Gabriel	46		HMAE Jose	13
10 TEMATAUA Axel			HMAE Michel	13
11 NEUFFER Taufa		46	WAJOKA Pierre	14
12 TEUIRA Farahia		60	DJAMALI Ramon	16
13 SIMON Vincent		69	KABEU Iamel	18
Tr: KAUTAI Gerard			Tr: MARTINENGO Serge	
14 MORETTA Rino	46	69	DAHOTE Jacques	7
		60	POATINDA Paul	17
		46	LONGUE Steve	22

Lawson Tama, Honiara
15-05-2004, 14:00, 15 000, Sosongan PNG

TGA 2 1 COK

Uhatahi 46, Vaitaki 61 | Pareanga 59

TONGA				COOK ISLANDS
1	SAAFI Heneli			JAMIESON Tony 1
2	HUIHAHAU Kaya			JAMIESON Mark 3
3	MOEAKI Makatuu			PAREANGA John 4
4	MAFI Sitenilesili			TATUAVA Eugenie 5
5	MAAMALOA Siua			SAMUEL Victor 6
6	FONUA Ipeni	57		TAUIRA Christian 7
7	UHATAHI Mark	53	68	CHAMBERS Joseph 9
8	UELE Kilifi		53	MATEARIKI Tteariki 10
10	PAPANI Kamaliele			PUTERE Teatu-Rangi 13
13	MOALA Lafaele		46	OTI Albert 15
19	VAITAKI Viliami	68		STRICKLAND Geoffrey 17
	Tr: JANKOVIC Milan			Tr: JERKS Tim
12	FOTU Mekilani	57	46	UNE Rourvroaroa 8
14	MOEAKI Folio	53	53	TISAM Tuka 12
17	MOA Solomone	68	68	SHEPHERD Adrian 16

Lawson Tama, Honiara
15-05-2004, 16:00, 20 000, Attison VAN

SOL 2 0 NCL

Omokirio 10, Suri 42

SOLOMON ISLANDS				NEW CALEDONIA
1	RAY Felix			HNE Michel 1
3	HOUKARAWA Mahlon	26		SINEDO Andre 4
6	SALE Nelson	48		KECINE Alain 5
7	MAEMAE Alick	72		WIAKO Jacky 6
9	MENAPI Commins			WEA Jules 11
10	SURI Batram			OUKA Nicolas 12
16	WAITA Stanley	73		HMAE Michel 13
17	OMOKIRIO Gideon			WAJOKA Pierre 14
18	FAARODO Henry		42	POATINDA Paul 17
19	KAKAI Paul			HMAE Jose 18
21	SURI George			LONGUE Steve 22
	Tr: GILLET Allan			Tr: MARTINENGO Serge
2	LEO Leslie	26	72	DAHOTE Jacques 7
14	SAMANI Jack	73	48	OIREJOIN Frank 9
			42	DJAMALI Ramon 16

Lawson Tama, Honiara
17-05-2004, 14:00, 400, Singh FIJ

NCL 8 0 COK

Wajoka 3, Hmae.M 5 20 40 42 52 85
Djamali 25, Hmae 35

NEW CALEDONIA				COOK ISLANDS
20	DREMON Francis			JAMIESON Tony 1
2	HAPELAMA Jacques			JAMIESON Mark 3
3	PIAN Theodore			PAREANGA John 4
9	OIREJOIN Frank			TATUAVA Eugenie 5
10	WADRIAKO Robert	70	45	SAMUEL Victor 6
11	WEA Jules			TAUIRA Christian 7
13	HMAE Michel			UNE Rourvroaroa 8
14	WAJOKA Pierre	45	60	MATEARIKI Tteariki 10
16	DJAMALI Ramon	45		PUTERE Teatu-Rangi 13
18	HMAE Jose			ANGENE David 14
19	KABEU Iamel		60	SHEPHERD Adrian 16
	Tr: MARTINENGO Serge			Tr: JERKS Tim
7	DAHOTE Jacques	70	45	VAN EIJK Paul 2
15	KAUME Robert	45	60	TISAM Tuka 12
17	POATINDA Paul	45	60	STRICKLAND Geoffrey 17

Lawson Tama, Honiara
17-05-2004, 16:00, 400, Sosongan PNG

TAH 2 0 TGA

Wajoka 1, Temataua 78

TAHITI				TONGA
1	TIEN WAH Stanley			SAAFI Heneli 1
2	TCHEN Angelo			HUIHAHAU Kaya 2
4	KAUTAI Iotua			MOEAKI Makatuu 3
5	LI WAUT Jean-Yves	18	70	MAFI Sitenilesili 4
6	TONG SANG Harry			MAAMALOA Siua 5
8	GARCIA Samuel		61	UHATAHI Mark 7
9	WAJOKA Gabriel	69		UELE Kilifi 8
12	TEUIRA Farahia			PAPANI Kamaliele 10
13	SIMON Vincent		83	TEVI Maamalua 11
14	MORETTA Rino	46		MOEAKI Folio 14
15	MARMOUYET Larry			MOA Solomone 17
	Tr: KAUTAI Gerard			Tr: JANKOVIC Milan
3	KUGOGNE Pierre	18	61	MOALA Lafaele 13
10	TEMATAUA Axel	69	70	FINAU Feao 16
16	TAGAWA Felix	46	83	VAITAKI Viliami 19

Lawson Tama, Honiara
19-05-2004, 14:00, 14 000, Fred VAN

NCL 8 0 TGA

Hmae.J 4, Poatinda 3 26 42 79, Hmae.M 45
Wajoka 2 54 58, Kaume 72

NEW CALEDONIA				TONGA
23	SAMEK Louis		66	SAAFI Heneli 1
4	SINEDO Andre			HUIHAHAU Kaya 2
5	KECINE Alain			MOEAKI Makatuu 3
11	WEA Jules	46		MAAMALOA Siua 5
12	OUKA Nicolas			UELE Kilifi 8
13	HMAE Michel	46		PAPANI Kamaliele 10
14	WAJOKA Pierre			TEVI Maamalua 11
15	KAUME Robert		46	FOTU Mekilani 13
17	POATINDA Paul			MOALA Lafaele 13
18	HMAE Jose	46		MOA Solomone 17
22	LONGUE Steve		39	TUAKALAU Alalaite 18
	Tr: MARTINENGO Serge			Tr: JANKOVIC Milan
3	PIAN Theodore	46	46	MAFI Sitenilesili 4
7	DAHOTE Jacques	46	39	FOTU Suliasi 15
9	OIREJOIN Frank	46	66	TAFOLO Sitiveni 20

Lawson Tama, Honiara
19-05-2004, 16:00, 18 000, Rakaroi FIJ

SOL 1 1 TAH

Suri 80 | Simon 30

SOLOMON ISLANDS				TAHITI
22	ARUWAFU Francis			TIEN WAH Stanley 1
2	LEO Leslie			TCHEN Angelo 2
6	SALE Nelson			KUGOGNE Pierre 3
7	MAEMAE Alick			LI WAUT Jean-Yves 5
8	KONOFILIA Joel	60		GARCIA Samuel 7
9	MENAPI Commins			MATAITAI Billy 8
10	SURI Batram			TEMATAUA Axel 10
14	SAMANI Jack	60	81	NEUFFER Taufa 11
17	OMOKIRIO Gideon			TEUIRA Farahia 12
18	FAARODO Henry			SIMON Vincent 13
21	SURI George			TAGAWA Felix 16
	Tr: GILLET Allan			Tr: KAUTAI Gerard
16	WAITA Stanley	60	81	MORETTA Rino 14
19	KAKAI Paul	60		

GROUP 2

		PL	W	D	L	F	A	PTS	VAN	FIJ	PNG	SAM	ASA
1	Vanuatu	4	3	1	0	16	2	10		3-0	1-1	3-0	9-1
2	Fiji	4	3	0	1	19	5	9			4-2	4-0	11-0
3	Papua New Guinea	4	2	1	1	17	6	7				4-1	10-0
4	Samoa	4	1	0	3	5	11	3					4-0
5	American Samoa	4	0	0	4	1	34	0					

Toleafoa J.S. Blatter Complex, Apia
10-05-2004, 14:00, 500, Breeze AUS

PNG 1 1 VAN

Wasi [73] | Lauru [92]

PAPUA NEW GUINEA				VANUATU		
1	POSMAN Tapas				CHILIA David	1
3	IMANG Geoffrey	20	64		TABE Manley	3
5	ELIZAH Selan				BIBI Lexa	4
6	FRED Hans				LAURU Simon	5
7	WASI Mauri				DEMAS Graham	6
9	DANIEL Richard				IAUTU Turei	8
10	DAVANi Reginald				CHILIA Seimata	9
13	LEPANI Andrew	64			MERMER Etienne	10
14	MOYAP Francis		54		IWAI Richard	13
16	TOMDA Yanding				MAKI Pita	14
19	KOMU Adrian	88	60		MAKI Gerard	18
Tr: PEKA Ludwig				Tr: BUZZETTI Juan Carlos		
8	ENOCh Abraham	88	64	64	GETE Geoffrey	2
11	LEPANI Nathaniel	64	60	60	THOMPSEN Lorry	12
17	KOMBOI Paul	20	54	54	MALEB Jean	17

Toleafoa J.S. Blatter Complex, Apia
10-05-2004, 16:00, 500, Afu SOL

SAM 4 0 ASA

Bryce [12], Fasavalu 2 [30 53]
Michael [66]

SAMOA				AMERICAN SAMOA		
20	NUMIA Fatuvalu				SALAPU Nicky	22
4	BRYCE Dennis	60			SEGAIGA Ben	2
6	FASAVALU Tama	57			MOLESI Maika	3
7	MICHAEL Junior				SINAPATI Travis	4
8	MAPOSUA Iosefa				HELETA Uasi	5
12	TAYLOR Lionel		46		LEPOU Ovite	6
14	LEMANA Pualele		65		NATIA Natia	7
15	FUIMAONO Sakaria				VAOFANUA Viliamu	8
17	TUMUA Penitito	77			OTT Ramin	9
18	VICTOR Peko	82			AFU Savaliga	17
19	PESA Setefano				ATUELEVAO Duane	18
Tr: BRAND David				Tr: CROOK Ian		
2	TUSITALA Afasene	60	82	82	FATU Filimaua	12
5	TYRELL Edwin	57	46	46	MULIPOLA Sam	15
11	EPA Lene	77	65	65	TANU Tanu	16

Toleafoa J.S. Blatter Complex, Apia
12-05-2004, 14:00, 400, Fox NZL

ASA 1 9 VAN

Natia [39] | Qorig 2 [30 47], Mermer 3 [37 56 91+]
Poida [55], Chilia [65], Maleb 2 [80 92+]

AMERICAN SAMOA				VANUATU		
22	SALAPU Nicky				CHILIA David	1
3	MOLESI Maika		71		BIBI Lexa	4
4	SINAPATI Travis	65			LAURU Simon	5
5	HELETA Uasi		47		IAUTU Turei	8
6	LEPOU Ovite				CHILIA Seimata	9
7	NATIA Natia	57			MERMER Etienne	10
8	VAOFANUA Viliamu		55		THOMPSON Lorry	12
9	OTT Ramin				IWAI Richard	13
15	MULIPOLA Sam	20			ALICK Daniel	15
17	AFU Savaliga				QORIG Alphose	16
18	ATUELEVAO Duane				MALEB Jean	17
Tr: CROOK Ian				Tr: BUZZETTI Juan Carlos		
2	SEGAIGA Ben	20	47	47	GETE Geoffrey	2
12	FATU Filimaua	65	71	71	VAVA Fedy	7
16	TANU Tanu	57	55	55	POIDA Moise	11

Toleafoa J.S. Blatter Complex, Apia
12-05-2004, 16:00, 400, Diomis AUS

FIJ 4 2 PNG

Rabo [24], Toma [48], Gataurua [78]
Rokotakala [90] | Davani [12], Komboi [44]

FIJI				PAPUA NEW GUINEA		
1	TAMANISAU Simione				POSMAN Tapas	1
4	AVINESH Alvin				ELIZAH Selan	5
5	BALEINUKU Emosi				FRED Hans	6
8	KAINIHEWE Malakai	26			WASI Mauri	7
10	TOMA Veresa				DANIEL Richard	9
11	RABO Pita	43			DAVANI Reginald	10
12	MASINISAU Esala		39		LEPANI Nathaniel	11
13	WAQA Taniela		60		LEPANI Andrew	13
17	TOMA Viliame				MOYAP Francis	14
18	ROKOTAKALA Seveci				TOMDA Yanding	16
19	GATAURUA Laisiasa				KOMBOI Paul	17
Tr: BUESNEL Tony				Tr: PEKA Ludwig		
3	RAOMA Nikola	26	39	39	LOHAI Michael	12
9	VULIVULI Thomas	43	19	19	KOMU Adrian	19

Toleafoa J.S. Blatter Complex, Apia
15-05-2004, 14:00, 300, Fox NZL

FIJ 11 0 ASA

Toma 3 [7 11 16], Vulivuli [24], Rokotakala 2 [32 38]
Sabutu 2 [46 81], Masinisau [60], Gatauroa 2 [75 77]

FIJI						AMERICAN SAMOA
23	KUMAR Shamal					SALAPU Nicky 1
2	DAU Lorima					MOLESI Maika 3
3	RAOMA Nikola			30		SINAPATI Travis 4
7	MORREL Stephen					HELETA Uasi 5
9	VULIVULI Thomas					LEPOU Ovite 6
10	TOMA Veresa	65				VAOFANUA Viliamu 8
12	MASINISAU Esala	81				OTT Ramin 9
16	TOMA Viliame	63	42			NUUSILA Vaueli 11
17	ROKOTAKALA Seveci		82			TANU Tanu 16
21	ERENIO Pene					AFU Savaliga 17
22	SABUTU Waisake					ATUELEVAO Duane 18
	Tr: BUESNEL Tony					Tr: CROOK Ian
14	DYER Lagi	63	42			SEGAIGA Ben 2
18	GATAURUA Laisiasa	65	82			SUA Geoffrey 13
15	WAKQA Maika	81	30			SAELUA Johnny 14

Toleafoa J.S. Blatter Complex, Apia
15-05-2004, 16:00, 650, Breeze AUS

SAM 0 3 VAN

Mermer [13], Chillia [55], Maleb [57]

SAMOA						VANUATU
1	TOKUMA Moresi					CHILIA David 1
4	BRYCE Dennis					GETE Geoffrey 2
5	TYRELL Edwin					BIBI Lexa 4
6	FASAVALU Tama	48				LAURU Wilkins 5
7	MICHAEL Junior			16		LAUTU Turei 8
12	TAYLOR Lionel	65				CHILLIA Seimata 9
14	LEMANA Pualele					MERMER Etienne 10
15	FUIMAONO Sakaria					POIDA Moise 11
17	TUMUA Penitito					ALICK Daniel 15
18	VICTOR Peko	77	75			MALEB Jean 17
19	PESA Setefano					JOE Roger 19
	Tr: BRAND David					Tr: BUZZETTI Juan Carlos
3	ASAFO Amby	48		16	41	TABE Manley 3
8	MAPOSUA Iosefo	77		41		DEMAS Graham 6
16	TOGAMOA Sio	65		75		MAKI Peter 14

Toleafoa J.S. Blatter Complex, Apia
17-05-2004, 14:00, 150, Afu SOL

ASA 0 10 PNG

Davani 4 [23 24 40 79], Lepani 3 [26 28 64]
Wasi [34], Komboi [37], Lohai [71]

AMERICAN SAMOA					PAPUA NEW GUINEA
1	SALAPU Nicky				POSMAN Tapas 1
2	SEGAIGA Ben	70			ELIZAH Selan 5
3	MOLESI Maika				FRED Hans 6
4	SINAPATI Travis	11	60		WASI Mauri 7
5	HELETA Uasi				DANIEL Richard 9
6	LEPOU Ovite	75			DAVANI Reginald 10
8	VAOFANUA Viliamu		75		LEPANI Nathaniel 11
9	OTT Ramin				LEPANI Andrew 13
16	TANU Tanu				MOYAP Francis 14
17	AFU Savaliga				TOMDA Yanding 16
18	ATUELEVAO Duane				KOMBOI Paul 17
	Tr: CROOK Ian				Tr: PEKA Ludwig
10	FAATAUALOFA Willie	75	60		LOHAI Michael 12
11	NUUSILA Vaueli	11	75		KOMU Adrian 19
19	AMEPEROSA Roy	70			

Toleafoa J.S. Blatter Complex, Apia
17-05-2004, 16:00, 450, Diomis AUS

SAM 0 4 FIJ

Toma [17], Sabutu [52]
Masinisau [82], Rokotakala [84]

SAMOA					FIJI
1	TOKUMA Moresi				TAMANISAU Simione 1
3	ASAFO Amby				DAU Lorima 2
4	BRYCE Dennis	74	79		AVINESH Alvin 4
5	TYRELL Edwin				BALEINUKU Emosi 5
7	MICHAEL Junior				KAINIHEWE Malakai 8
8	MAPOSUA Iosefa	85	70		VULIVULI Thomas 10
10	TAUA Jerome				TOMA Veresa 10
14	LEMANA Pualele				MASINISAU Esala 12
16	TOGAMOA Sio	60			WAQA Taniela 13
18	VICTOR Peko				TOMA Viliame 16
19	PESA Setefano	65			SABUTU Waisake 22
	Tr: BRAND David				Tr: BUESNEL Tony
2	TUSITALA Afasene	85	70		DYER Lagi 14
9	IOANE Iosefo	74	79		ROKOTAKALA Seveci 17
13	HUNT Otto	60	65		ERENIO Pene 21

Toleafoa J.S. Blatter Complex, Apia
19-05-2004, 14:00, 200, Breeze AUS

FIJ 0 3 VAN

Thompson [46], Lauru 2 [63 65]

FIJI					VANUATU
1	TAMANISAU Simione				CHILIA David 1
2	DAU Lorima				GETE Geoffrey 2
3	RAOMA Nikola	25			BIBI Lexa 4
8	KAINIHEWE Malakai	75	82		LAURU Wilkins 5
9	VULIVULI Thomas				DEMAS Graham 6
12	MASINISAU Esala				CHILLIA Seimata 9
13	WAQA Taniela				MERMER Etienne 10
16	TOMA Viliame		60		POIDA Moise 11
17	ROKOTAKALA Seveci	71			THOMPSEN Lorry 12
18	GATAURUA Laisiasa				IWAI Richard 13
22	SABUTU Waisake		64		ALICK Daniel 15
	Tr: BUESNEL Tony				Tr: BUZZETTI Juan Carlos
4	AVINESH Alvin	75	82		VAVA Fedy 7
5	BALEINUKU Emosi	25	60		MALEB Jean 17
21	ERENIO Pene	71	64		JOE Roger 19

Toleafoa J.S. Blatter Complex, Apia
19-05-2004, 16:00, 300, Diomis AUS

SAM 1 4 PNG

Michael [69]

Davani [16], Lepani. A [37]
Lepani.N [55], Komeng [68]

SAMOA				PAPUA NEW GUINEA
20	NUMIA Fatuvalu	24		BANIAU Geoffrey 20
3	ASAFO Amby			TUHIANA Brian 7
4	BRYCE Dennis			ELIZAH Selan 5
5	TYRELL Edwin			DANIEL Richard 9
6	FASAVALU Tama			DAVANI Reginald 10
7	MICHAEL Junior			LEPANI Nathaniel 11
13	HUNT Oto			LOHAI Michael 12
14	LEMANA Pualele	67		LEPANI Andrew 13
17	TUMUA Penitito			MOYAP Francis 14
18	VICTOR Peko			TOMDA Yanding 16
19	PESA Setefano			KOMBOI Paul 17
	Tr: BRAND David			Tr: PEKA Ludwig
8	MAPOSUA IOSEFA	24		POSMAN Tapas 1
9	IOANE Iosefo	70		MARNHI Spencer 15
11	EPA Lene	67		KOMENG Eric 18

GROUP STAGE

GROUP 1	PL	W	D	L	F	A	PTS	AUS	SOL	NZL	FIJ	TAH	VAN
1 Australia	5	4	1	0	21	3	13		2-2	1-0	6-1	9-0	3-0
2 Solomon Islands	5	3	1	1	9	6	10			0-3	2-1	4-0	1-0
3 New Zealand	5	3	0	2	17	5	9				2-0	10-0	2-4
4 Fiji	5	1	1	3	3	10	4					0-0	1-0
5 Tahiti	5	1	1	3	2	24	4						2-1
6 Vanuatu	5	1	0	4	5	9	3						

Marden Sports Complex, Adelaide
29-05-2004, 14:00, 200, Shield AUS

VAN 0 1 SOL

Suri [51]

VANUATU			SOLOMON ISLANDS	
1 CHILIA David			AEFI Severino	20
2 GETE Geoffrey		89	HOUKARAWA Mahlon	3
4 BIBI Lexa			KILIFA Nelson	6
5 LAURU Wilkins	70	83	MAEMAE Alick	7
8 IAUTU Turei			SURI Batram	10
9 CHILLIA Seimata			MENAPI Commins	11
10 MERMER Etienne		69	WAITA Stanley	16
11 POIDA Moise	75		OMOKIRIO Gideon	17
13 IWAI Richard			FAARODO Henry	18
14 MAKI Pita	46		KAKAI Paul	19
15 ALICK Daniel			SURI George	21
Tr: BUZZETTI Juan Carlos			Tr: GILLET Allan	
7 VAVA Fedy	70	89	LEO Leslie	2
16 QORIG Alphose	46	69	SAMANI Jack	14
17 MALEB Jean	75	83	TOATA Moses	15

Hindmarsh, Adelaide
29-05-2004, 17:30, 3000, Farina ITA

TAH 0 0 FIJ

TAHITI			FIJI	
19 TAPETA Daniel			TAMANISAU Simione	1
2 TCHEN Angelo	75		DAU Lorima	2
3 KUGOGNE Pierre			BALEINUKU Emosi	5
5 LI WAUT Jean-Yves			KAINIHEWE Malakai	7
7 GARCIA Samuel		86	VULIVULI Thomas	9
8 MATAITAI Billy			TOMA Veresa	10
10 TEMATAUA Axel			MASINISAU Esala	12
11 NUFFER Taufa	65		WAQA Taniela	13
12 TEUIRA Farahia		76	KUMAR Sailesh	15
13 SIMON Vincent			TOMA Viliame	16
16 TAGAWA Felix	84		ROKOTAKALA Seveci	17
Tr: KAUTAI Gerard			Tr:	
4 KAUTAI Iotua	75	76	GATAURUA Laisiasa	18
9 WAJOKA Gabriel	84	86	SABUTU Waisake	22
17 LABASTE Hiro	65			

Hindmarsh, Adelaide
29-05-2004, 20:00, 12 100, Larsen DEN

AUS 1 0 NZL

Bresciano [40]

AUSTRALIA			NEW ZEALAND	
18 KALAC Zeljko			PASTON Mark	1
3 LAYBUTT Steve	72		MULLIGAN David	3
4 COLOSIMO Simon	53		OLD Steven	4
5 VIDMAR Tony			BUNCE Che	5
7 EMERTON Brett			LOCHHEAD Tony	6
8 SKOKO Josip			VICELICH Ivan	7
9 ALOISI John		50	HICKEY Noah	9
11 LAZARIDIS Stan		69	BERTOS Leo	11
13 GRELLA Vince			ELLIOTT Simon	12
19 VIERI Max	67		COVENY Vaughan	16
23 BRESCIANO Marco		77	DE GREGORIO Raf	17
Tr: FARINA Frank			Tr: WAITT Mick	
2 NORTH Jade	53	77	OUGHTON Duncan	2
15 STERJOVSKI Mile	67	50	FISHER Brent	13
20 MADASCHI Adrian	72	69	SMELTZ Shane	18

Marden Sports Complex, Adelaide
31-05-2004, 14:00, 217, Iturralde Gonzalez ESP

NZL 3 0 SOL

Fisher [36], Oughton [81], Lines [90]

NEW ZEALAND			SOLOMON ISLANDS	
1 PASTON Mark			AEFI Severino	20
3 MULLIGAN David			HOUKARAWA Mahlon	3
4 OLD Steven			KILIFA Nelson	6
5 BUNCE Che			MAEMAE Alick	7
6 LOCHHEAD Tony			SURI Batram	10
7 VICELICH Ivan			MENAPI Commins	11
8 LINES Aaran		66	WAITA Stanley	16
10 BROWN Tim	80		OMOKIRIO Gideon	17
12 ELLIOTT Simon	85		FAARODO Henry	18
13 FISHER Brent			KAKAI Paul	19
16 COVENY Vaughan	73		SURI George	21
Tr: WAITT Mick			Tr: GILLET Allan	
2 OUGHTON Duncan	80	66	SAMANI Jack	14
11 BERTOS Leo	73			
15 WILSON Mike	85			

Match 1

Hindmarsh, Adelaide
31-05-2004, 17:30, 1 200, Attison VAN

AUS 9 0 TAH

Cahill 2 [14 47], Skoko [43], Simon OG [44]
Sterjovski 3 [51 61 74], Zdrilic [85], Chipperfield [89]

	AUSTRALIA			TAHITI	
18	KALAC Zeljko			TAPETA Daniel	19
2	NORTH Jade			TCHEN Angelo	2
5	VIDMAR Tony			KUGOGNE Pierre	3
6	CHIPPERFIELD Scott		80	LI WAUT Jean-Yves	5
8	SKOKO Josip	46		GARCIA Samuel	7
9	ALOISI John	46		MATAITAI Billy	8
10	CAHILL Tim			TEMATAUA Axel	10
11	LAZARIDIS Stan	46		TEUIRA Farahia	12
13	GRELLA Vince		61	SIMON Vincent	13
17	ZDRILIC David			TAGAWA Felix	16
20	MADASCHI Adrian		58	LABASTE Hiro	17
	Tr: FARINA Frank			Tr: KAUTAI Gerard	
14	KISNORBO Patrick	46	58	NEUFFER Taufa	11
15	STERJOVSKI Mile	46	61	MARMOUYET Larry	15
21	ELRICH Ahmad	46	80	PITOEFF Georges	18

Match 2

Hindmarsh, Adelaide
31-05-2004, 20:00, 500, Ariiotima TAH

FIJ 1 0 VAN

Toma [73]

	FIJI			VANUATU	
23	TUBA Laisenia			CHILIA David	1
2	DAU Lorima		82	GETE Geoffrey	2
7	KAINIHEWE Malakai			BIBI Lexa	4
9	VULIVULI Thomas			DEMAS Graham	6
10	TOMA Veresa			VAVA Fedy	7
12	MASINISAU Esala	81		CHILLIA Seimata	9
13	WAQA Taniela			MERMER Etienne	10
15	KUMAR Sailesh		86	POIDA Moise	11
16	TOMA Viliame	46		THOMSEN Lorry	12
17	ROKOTAKALA Seveci		46	IWAI Richard	13
18	GATAURUA Laisiasa			ALICK Daniel	15
	Tr: BUESNEL Tony			Tr: BUZZETTI Juan Carlos	
5	BALEINUKU Emosi	81	82	QORIG Alphose	16
11	VIDOVI Luke	46	46	MALEB Jean	17
			86	JOE Roger	19

Match 3

Marden Sports Complex, Adelaide
2-06-2004, 14:00, 2 200, Iturralde Gonzalez ESP

AUS 6 1 FIJ

Madaschi 2 [6 50], Cahill 3 [39 66 75]
Elrich [89]   Gataurua [19]

	AUSTRALIA			FIJI	
18	KALAC Zeljko		43	TUBA Laisenia	23
2	NORTH Jade			DAU Lorima	2
5	VIDMAR Tony			BALEINUKU Emosi	5
6	CHIPPERFIELD Scott	46		VESIKULA Jone	6
7	EMERTON Brett	46	82	KAINIHEWE Malakai	7
10	CAHILL Tim			VULIVULI Thomas	9
13	GRELLA Vince		56	VIDOVI Luke	11
14	KISNORBO Patrick			WAQA Taniela	13
15	STERJOVSKI Mile			KUMAR Sailesh	15
19	VIERI Max	59	58	GATAURUA Laisiasa	18
20	MADASCHI Adrian			SABUTU Waisake	22
	Tr: FARINA Frank			Tr: BUESNEL Tony	
12	BROSQUE Alex	46	43	TAMANISAU Simione	1
17	ZDRILIC David	59	82	AVINESH Alvin	4
21	ELRICH Ahmad	46	56	ERENIO Pene	21

Match 4

Hindmarsh, Adelaide
2-06-2004, 17:30, 50, Rakaroi FIJ

TAH 0 4 SOL

Faarodo [9], Menapi 2 [14 80], Suri [42]

	TAHITI			SOLOMON ISLANDS	
1	TIEN WAH Stanley			RAY Felix	1
2	TCHEN Angelo			LEO Leslie	2
4	KAUTAI Iotua			HOUKARAWA Mahlon	3
5	LI WAUT Jean-Yves			KILIFA Nelson	6
7	GARCIA Samuel			MAEMAE Alick	7
9	WAJOKA Gabriel	46	89	SURI Batram	10
11	NEUFFER Taufa	46		MENAPI Commins	11
12	TEUIRA Farahia			WAITA Stanley	16
13	SIMON Vincent			OMOKIRIO Gideon	17
17	LABASTE Hiro	63		FAARODO Henry	18
18	PITOEFF Georges			KAKAI Paul	19
	Tr: KAUTAI Gerard			Tr: GILLET Allan	
8	MATAITAI Billy	46	89	SAMANI Jack	14
10	TEMATAUA Axel	63			
16	TAGAWA Felix	46			

Match 5

Hindmarsh, Adelaide
2-06-2004, 20:00, 356, Farina ITA

NZL 2 4 VAN

                                    Chillia [37], Bibi [64], Maleb [72]
Coveny 2 [61 75]   Qorig [88]

	NEW ZEALAND			VANUATU	
1	PASTON Mark			CHILIA David	1
2	OUGHTON Duncan		81	GETE Geoffrey	2
5	BUNCE Che			BIBI Lexa	4
6	LOCHHEAD Tony			DEMAD Graham	6
7	VICELICH Ivan			VAVA Fedy	7
8	LINES Aaran	56		CHILLIA Seimata	9
11	BERTOS Leo	72	84	POIDA Moise	11
13	FISHER Brent			THOMSEN Lorry	12
14	NELSEN Ryan			QORIG Alphose	16
15	WILSON Mike	52		MALEB Jean	17
21	PUNA Rupesh			MANSES Tom	21
	Tr: WAITT Mick			Tr: BUZZETTI Juan Carlos	
16	COVENY Vaughan	52	84	TABE Manley	3
17	DE GREGORIO Raf	72	81	JOE Roger	19
18	SMELTZ Shane	56			

Match 6

Marden Sports Complex
4-06-2004, 14:00, 200, Shield AUS

NZL 10 0 TAH

Coveny 3 [6 38 46], Fisher 3 [16 22 63]
Jones [72], Oughton [74], Nelsen 2 [82 87]

	NEW ZEALAND			TAHITI	
1	PASTON Mark			SAMIN Xavier	20
2	OUGHTON Duncan			TCHEN Angelo	2
4	OLD Steven			KUGOGNE Pierre	3
5	BUNCE Che	46	46	GARCIA Samuel	7
6	LOCHHEAD Tony			TEMATAUA Axel	10
8	LINES Aaran	35		TEUIRA Farahia	12
13	FISHER Brent			SIMON Vincent	13
14	NELSEN Ryan		79	MORETTA Rino	14
15	WILSON Mike			MARMOUYET Larry	15
16	COVENY Vaughan	65		TAGAWA Felix	16
17	DE GREGORIO Raf		69	PITOEFF Georges	18
	Tr: WAITT Mick			Tr: KAUTAI Gerard	
11	BERTOS Leo	35	79	KAUTAI Iotua	4
12	ELLIOTT Simon	46	69	LI WAUT Jean-Yves	5
19	JONES Neil	65	46	NEUFFER Taufa	11

Hindmarsh, Adelaide
4-06-2004, 17:30, 1 500, Attison VAN

FIJ 1 2 SOL

Toma 21

Kakai 16, Houkarawa 82

FIJI			SOLOMON ISLANDS		
23 TUBA Laisenia			RAY Felix 1		
2 DAU Lorima			LEO Leslie 2		
5 BALEINUKU Emosi			HOUKARAWA Mahlon 3		
7 KAINIHEWE Malakai	83		KILIFA Nelson 6		
9 VULIVULI Thomas			MAEMAE Alick 7		
10 TOMA Veresa	87		SURI Batram 10		
12 MASINISAU Esala			MENAPI Commins 11		
13 WAQA Taniela		51	WAITA Stanley 16		
15 KUMAR Sailesh			FAARODO Henry 18		
16 TOMA Viliame			KAKAI Paul 19		
17 ROKOTAKALA Seveci	85		SURI George 21		
Tr: BUESNEL Tony			Tr: GILLET Allan		
6 VESIKULA Jone	83	51	SAMANI Jack 14		
21 ERENIO Pene	85				
22 SABUTU Waisake	87				

Hindmarsh, Adelaide
4-06-2004, 20:00, 4 000, Ariiotima TAH

VAN 0 3 AUS

Aloisi 2 25 85, Emerton 81

VANUATU			AUSTRAILIA		
1 CHILIA David			KALAC Zeljko 18		
4 BIBI Lexa			NORTH Jade 2		
6 DEMAS Graham			VIDMAR Tony 5		
7 VAVA Fedy			EMERTON Brett 7		
9 CHILLIA Seimata			SKOKO Josip 8		
11 POIDA Moise	43		ALOISI John 9		
12 THOMPSEN Lorry			LAZARIDIS Stan 11		
16 QORIG ALPHOSE	74	64	BROSQUE Alex 12		
17 MALEB Jean	61		GRELLA Vince 13		
19 JOE Roger			TARKA David 16		
21 MANSES Tom		64	ZDRILIC David 17		
Tr: BUZZETTI Juan Carlos			Tr: FARINA Frank		
10 MERMER Etienne	74	64	STERJOVSKI Mile 15		
13 IWAI Richard	61	64	ELRICH Ahmad 21		
14 MAKI Pita	43				

Marden Sports Complex, Adelaide
6-06-2004, 14:00, 300, Rakaroi FIJ

TAH 2 1 VAN

Temataua 40, Wajoka 89

Iwai 23

TAHITI			VANUATU		
19 TAPETA Daniel			KALSANEI Charly 20		
2 TCHEN Angelo		67	TABE Manley 3		
3 KUGOGNE Pierre			BIBI Lexa 4		
7 GARCIA Samuel	54		DEMAS Graham 6		
8 MATAITAI Billy			VAVA Fedy 7		
9 WAJOKA Gabriel		63	CHILLIA Seimata 9		
10 TEMATAUA Axel			MERMER Etienne 10		
12 TEUIRA Farahia		77	THOMPSEN Lorry 12		
13 SIMON Vincent			IWAI Richard 13		
15 MARMOUYET Larry			MAKI Pita 14		
16 TAGAWA Felix			JOE Roger 19		
Tr: KAUTAI Gerard			Tr: BUZZETTI Juan Carlos		
		67	GETE Geoffrey 2		
		77	IAUTU Turei 8		
		63	MALEB Jean 17		

Hindmarsh, Adelaide
6-06-2004, 17:30, 300, Larsen DEN

FIJ 0 2 NZL

Bunce 8, Coveny 56

FIJI			NEW ZEALAND		
1 TAMANISAU Simione			PASTON Mark 1		
2 DAU Lorima			OUGHTON Duncan 2		
6 VESIKULA Jone			OLD Steven 4		
7 KAINIHEWE Malakai	33		BUNCE Che 5		
9 VULIVULI Thomas	81		LOCHHEAD Tony 6		
12 MASINISAU Esala	51		VICELICH Ivan 7		
13 WAQA Taniela			LINES Aaran 8		
15 KUMAR Sailesh		81	FISHER Brent 13		
16 TOMA Viliame			NELSEN Ryan 14		
18 GATAURUA Laisiasa			COVENY Vaughan 16		
21 ERENIO Pene		60	DE GREGORIO Raf 17		
Tr: BUEANEL Tony			Tr: WAITT Mick		
11 VIDOVI Luke	33	60	BERTOS Leo 11		
17 ROKOTAKALA Seveci	81	81	JONES Neil 19		
22 SABUTU Waisake	51				

Hindmarsh, Adelaide
6-06-2004, 20:00, 1 500, Iturralde Gonzalez ESP

SOL 2 2 AUS

Menapi 2 43 75

Cahill 50, Emerton 52

SOLOMON ISLANDS			AUSTRALIA		
1 RAY Felix			KALAC Zeljko 18		
2 LEO Leslie			NORTH Jade 2		
3 HOUKARAWA Mahlon			EMERTON Brett 7		
6 KILIFA Nelson			SKOKO Josip 8		
7 MAEMAE Alick			ALOISI John 9		
10 SURI Batram			CAHILL Tim 10		
11 MENAPI Commins		46	BROSQUE Alex 12		
14 SAMANI Jack	63	52	KISNORBO Patrick 14		
18 FAARODO Henry		46	TARKA David 16		
19 KAKAI Paul	63	46	VIERI Max 19		
21 SURI George			MADASCHI Adrian 20		
Tr: GILLET Allan			Tr: FARINA Frank		
13 LUI George	63	46	COLOSIMO Simon 4		
16 WAITA Stanley	63	46	STERJOVSKI Mile 15		
		46	ELRICH Ahmad 21		

QUALIFYING MATCHES PLAYED IN EUROPE

Group 1		Pts
Netherlands	NED	22
Czech Republic	CZE	21
Romania	ROU	16
Finland	FIN	9
Macedonia FYR	MKD	8
Armenia	ARM	4
Andorra	AND	4

Group 2		Pts
Ukraine	UKR	23
Turkey	TUR	16
Greece	GRE	15
Denmark	DEN	12
Albania	ALB	9
Georgia	GEO	5
Kazakhstan	KAZ	0

Group 3		Pts
Portugal	POR	20
Slovakia	SVK	17
Russia	RUS	14
Latvia	LVA	13
Estonia	EST	11
Liechtenstein	LIE	4
Luxembourg	LUX	0

Group 4		Pts
Ireland Republic	IRL	13
Switzerland	SUI	12
Israel	ISR	11
France	FRA	10
Cyprus	CYP	1
Faroe Islands	FRO	1

Group 5		Pts
Italy	ITA	13
Norway	NOR	9
Slovenia	SVN	9
Belarus	BLR	7
Scotland	SCO	6
Moldova	MDA	2

Group 6		Pts
Poland	POL	18
England	ENG	16
Austria	AUT	11
Northern Ireland	NIR	3
Wales	WAL	2
Azerbaijan	AZE	2

Group 7		Pts
Spain	ESP	13
Serbia/Montenegro	SCG	12
Lithuania	LTU	9
Belgium	BEL	8
Bosnia-Herzegovina	BIH	7
San Marino	SMR	0

Group 8		Pts
Croatia	CRO	16
Sweden	SWE	15
Hungary	HUN	10
Bulgaria	BUL	8
Iceland	ISL	4
Malta	MLT	1

Play-offs

No teams have qualified so far for the finals. Europe has 13 places in Germany with the group winners and the two best second-placed teams guaranteed to play at the finals. The remaining six second-placed teams play a single knock-out round to determine the final three places. Second-placed teams will be ranked according to their record against the first, third, fourth, fifth and sixth-placed teams in their groups

Remaining fixtures to be played on 17/08/2005, 3/09/2005, 7/09/2005, 8/10/2005 and 12/10/2005 with the play-offs held in November

GROUP 1

City Stadium, Skopje
18-08-2004, 20:00, 4 375, Guenov BUL

MKD	3	0		ARM

Pandev [5], Sakiri [37], Sumolikoski [90]

MACEDONIA FYR				ARMENIA	
1	MILOSEVSKI Petar			AMBARTSUMYAN Armen	1
2	STAVREVSKI Goran			MELIKYAN Eghishe	2
3	KRSTEV Mile		81	DOKHOYAN Karen	3
4	SEDLOSKI Goce			HOVSEPYAN Sargis	4
5	MITRESKI Igor			VARDANYAN Harutyun	5
6	MITRESKI Aleksandar		46	KHACHATRYAN Romik	6
7	TRAJANOV Vanco	65	65	PETROSYAN Artur	7
8	SUMOLIKOSKI Velice			NAZARYAN Rafayel	8
9	PANDEV Goran			SARGSYAN Albert	9
10	SAKIRI Artim	85		KARAMYAN Arman	10
11	DIMITROVSKI Gragan	46		MOVSISYAN Andrey	11
	Tr: KANATLAROVSKI Dragan			Tr: CASONI Bernard	
15	VASOSKI Aleksander	65	46	ALEKSANYAN Karen	15
17	JANSEVSKI Igor	46	65	HAKOBYAN Ara	17
18	TOLESKI Goce	85	81	TATEOSIAN Alexander	18

Giulesti, Bucharest
18-08-2004, 20:30, 17 500, Gilewski POL

ROU	2	1		FIN

Mutu [50], Petre [90]　　　　Eremenko [93+]

ROMANIA				FINLAND	
1	LOBONT Bogdan			NIEMI Antti	1
2	STOICAN Flavius	85	61	PASANEN Petri	2
3	RAT Razvan			SAARINEN Janne	3
4	BARCAUAN Cosmin	78		HYYPIA Sami	4
5	GHIONEA Sotin		83	VAYRYNEN Mika	6
6	RADOI Mirel		83	NURMELA Mika	7
7	DICA Nicolae	76	58	LITMANEN Jari	10
8	PETRE Florentin			KOLKKA Joonas	11
9	CARAMARIN Gabriel	46		KUIVASTO Toni	14
10	MUTU Adrian			RIIHILAHTI Aki	16
11	DANCIULESCU Ionel			JOHANSSON Jonathan	21
	Tr: IORDANESCU Anghel			Tr: MUURINEN Antti	
15	IENCSI Adrian	85	61	KOPPINEN Mika	13
17	SOAVA Florin	76	83	KOPTEFF Peter	17
18	CERNAT Florin	46	58	EREMENKO Alexei Jun	20

Ratina Stadium, Tampere
4-09-2004, 17:00, 7 437, Siric CRO

FIN	**3**	**0**	**AND**

Eremenko 2 [42][64], Riihilahti [58]

FINLAND			ANDORRA	
1 MIEMI Antti			ALVAREZ Jesus	1
2 PASANEN Perti			AYALA Josep	2
4 HYYPIA Sami			GARCIA Josep	3
7 NURMELA Mika			FERNANDEZ Juli	4
9 FORSSELL Mikael			LIMA Antoni	5
10 LITMANEN Jari	73		SONEJEE Oscar	6
11 KOLKKA Joonas	82	89	PUJOL Marc	7
14 KUIVASTO Toni		74	SANCHEZ Juli	8
15 POHJA Antti	59		SIVERA Antoni	9
16 RIIHILAHTI Aki			MORENO Sergi	10
20 EREMENKO Alexei Jun		70	RUIZ Justo	11
Tr: MUURINEN Antti			Tr: RODRIGO David	
17 KOPTEFF Peter	59	89	REIRA Gabriel	15
21 JOHANSSON Johnathan	73	70	JIMENEZ Manel	16
23 HEIKKINEN Markus	82	74	SILVA Fernando	18

Ion Oblemenco, Craiova
4-09-2004, 20:30, 14 500, Plautz AUT

ROU	**2**	**1**	**MKD**

Pancu [15], Mutu [88]   Vasoski [70]

ROMANIA			MACEDONIA FYR	
1 LOBONT Bogdan			MILOSEVSKI Petar	1
2 STOICAN Flavius		46	KRSTEV Mile	3
3 RAT Razvan			STIJANOVSKI Milan	4
4 IENCSI Adrian			MITRESKI Igor	5
5 MOLDOVAN Flavius			MITRESKI Aleksander	6
6 SOAVA Florin		89	SUMOLIKOSKI Velice	8
7 DICA Nicolae	79		PANDEV Goran	9
8 PETRE Florentin		85	SAKIRI Artim	10
9 PANCU Daniel	64		VASOSKI Aleksandar	15
10 MUTU Adrian			POPOV Goran	16
11 DANCIULESCU Ionel	46	90	JANCEVSKI Igor	17
Tr: IORDANECU Anghel			Tr: KANATLAROVSKI Dragan	
14 NEGA Adrian	79	90	TRAJANOV Vanco	7
15 CERNAT Florin	46	46	BOZINOVSKI Vasko	14
17 MARICA Ciprian	64	85	TOLESKI Goce	18

Comunal, Andorra-la-Vella
8-09-2004, 16:00, 1 100, Kircher GER

AND	**1**	**5**	**ROU**

Pujol [28p]   Cernat 2 [1][17], Pancu 2 [5][83]
                              Niculae [70]

ANDORRA			ROMANIA	
1 ALVAREZ Jesus			LOBONT Bogdan	1
2 GARCIA Josep			STOICAN Flavius	2
3 BERNAUS Marc			RAT Razvan	3
4 FERNANDEZ Juli	74		IENCSI Adrian	4
5 LIMA Antoni			BARCAUAN Cosmin	5
6 LIMA Ildefons	80		SOAVA Florin	6
7 SANCHEZ Juli		62	NEGA Adrian	7
8 AYALA Josep	14	83	CARAMARIN Gabriel	8
9 SIVERA Antoni			PANCU Daniel	9
10 PUJOL Marc			CERNAT Florin	10
11 RUIZ Justo	80	76	NICULAE Marius	11
Tr: RODRIGO David			Tr: IORDANECU Anghel	
15 JIMENEZ Manel	14	83	PARASCHIV Sorin	13
16 SONEJEE Oscar	74	62	MARICA Ciprian	17
17 MORENO Sergi	80	76	DICA Nicolae	18

Republican, Yerevan
8-09-2004, 21:00, 2 864, Malzinskas LTU

ARM	**0**	**2**	**FIN**

                              Forssell [24], Eremenko [67]

ARMENIA			FINLAND	
1 AMBARTSUMYAN Armen			MIEMI Antti	1
2 MELIKYAN Eghishe			PASANEN Perti	2
3 DOKHOYAN Karen			HYYPIA Sami	4
4 HOVSEPYAN Sargis			VAYRYNEN Mika	6
5 MKRTCHYAN Artur			NURMELA Mika	7
6 KHACHATRYAN Romik			FORSSELL Mikael	9
7 PETROSYAN Artur		46	LITMANEN Jari	10
8 NAZARYAN Rafayel	75	86	KOLKKA Joonas	11
9 SARGSYAN Albert	54		KUIVASTO Toni	14
10 KARAMYAN Arman	77		RIIHILAHTI Aki	16
11 MOVSISYAN Andrey		75	EREMENKO Alexei Jun	20
Tr: CASONI Bernard			Tr: MUURINEN Antti	
13 MANUCHARYAN Edgar	54	86	POHJA Antti	15
15 ALEKSANYAN Karen	75	75	KOPTEFF Peter	17
16 GRIGORYAN David	77	46	LAGERBLOM Pekka	18

Amsterdam ArenA, Amsterdam
8-09-2004, 20:30, 48 488, Merk GER

NED	**2**	**0**	**CZE**

Van Hooijdonk 2 [34][84]

NETHERLANDS			CZECH REPUBLIC	
1 VAN DER SAR Edwin			CECH Petr	1
2 HEITINGA John			BOLF Rene	5
3 OOIJER Andre			JANKULOVSKI Marek	6
4 SNEIJDER Wesley			KOLLER Jan	9
5 DE JONG Nigel			ROSICKY Tomas	10
6 VAN BOMMEL Marc		58	JIRANEK Martin	13
7 CASTELEN Romeo	74		BAROS Milan	15
8 DAVIDS Edgar		62	HUBSCHMAN Tomas	17
9 VAN HOOIJDONK Pierre	86		HEINZ Marek	18
10 VAN DER VAART Rafael	64	75	TYCE Roman	19
11 KUYT Dirk			UJFALUSI Tomas	21
Tr: VAN BASTEN Marco			Tr: BRUECKNER Karel	
12 BOULAHROUZ Khalid	64	58	GRYGERA Zdenek	2
15 VAN BRONCKHORST Gio.	86	75	LOKVENC Vratislav	12
18 MAKAAY Roy	74	62	VACHOUSEK Stepan	14

Toyota Arena, Prague
9-10-2004, 17:00, 16 028, Rosetti ITA

CZE	**1**	**0**	**ROU**

Koller [36]

CZECH REPUBLIC			ROMANIA	
1 CECH Petr			LOBONT Bogdan	1
4 GALASEK Tomas			STOICAN Flavius	2
5 BOLF Rene			RAT Razvan	3
6 JANKULOVSKI Marek			IENCSI Adrian	4
9 KOLLER Jan		46	BARCAUAN Cosmin	5
10 ROSICKY Tomas	92		SOAVA Florin	6
13 JIRANEK Martin			CODREA Paul	7
14 VACHOUSEK Stepan		58	PETRE Florentin	8
18 BAROS Milan	84	75	PANCU Daniel	9
18 HEINZ Marek	69		MUTU Adrian	10
21 UJFALUSI Tomas			MARICA Ciprian	11
Tr: BRUECKNER Karel			Tr: IORDANECU Anghel	
3 KOVAC Radoslav	92	46	MOLDOVAN Flavius	14
19 SIONKO Libor	69	75	DICA Nicolae	15
20 JAROSIK Jiri	84	58	CERNAT Florin	16

Ratina Stadium, Tampere
9-10-2004, 17:00, 7 894, Fandel GER

FIN 3 1 **ARM**

Kuqi 2 [9] [87], Eremenko [28]   Shahgeldyan [32]

FINLAND			ARMENIA	
1 MIEMI Antti			AMBARTSUMYAN Armen	12
2 PASANEN Perti			DOKHOYAN Karen	3
3 SAARINEN Janne	68		HOVSEPYAN Sargis	4
4 HYYPIA Sami			VARDANYAN Harutyun	5
6 VAYRYNEN Mika		36	KHACHATRYAN Romik	6
7 NURMELA Mika			NAZARYAN Rafayel	8
11 KOLKKA Joonas	83		MKHITARYAN Hamlet	9
14 KUIVASTO Toni	46		SHAHGELDYAN Armen	10
16 RIIHILAHTI Aki		84	MOVSISYAN Andrey	11
18 KUQI Shefki		59	GRIGORYAN David	16
20 EREMENKO Alexei Jun			TATEOSIAN Alexander	18
Tr: MUURINEN Antti			Tr: CASONI Bernard	
8 TAINIO Teemu	46	59	MANUCHARYAN Edgar	13
19 KALLIO Toni	68	36	ALEKSANYAN Karen	15
21 JOHANSSON Jonathan	83	84	HAKOBYAN Ara	17

City Stadium, Skopje
9-10-2004, 20:30, 15 000, Frojdfeldt SWE

MKD 2 2 **NED**

Pandev [45], Stojkov [71]   Bouma [42], Kuyt [65]

MACEDONIA FYR			NETHERLANDS	
1 NIKOLOSKI Jane			VAN DER SAR Edwin	1
3 KRSTEV Mile			BOULAHROUZ Khalid	2
4 SEDLOSKI Goce			DE JONG Nigel	3
5 MITRESKI Igor		61	COCU Phillip	4
6 MITRESKI Aleksander			BOUMA Wilfred	5
9 PANDEV Goran	88	81	VAN BOMMEL Marc	6
10 SAKIRI Artim			CASTELEN Romeo	7
11 STOJKOV Aco	76		DAVIDS Edgar	8
14 BOZINOVSKI Vasko		61	VAN HOOIJDONK Pierre	9
15 VASOSKI Aleksandar			SNEIJDER Wesley	10
17 JANCEVSKI Igor	73		KUYT Dirk	11
Tr: KANATLAROVSKI Dragan			Tr: VAN BASTEN Marco	
7 TRAJANOV Vanco	73	81	LANDZAAT Denny	14
8 BAJEVSKI Aleksandar	76	61	VAN DER VAART Rafael	15
16 GROZDANOVSKI Vlatko	88	61	MAKAAY Roy	17

Comunal, Andorra-la-Vella
13-10-2004, 15:00, 350, Podeschi SMR

AND 1 0 **MKD**

Bernaus [60]

ANDORRA			MACEDONIA FYR	
1 ALVAREZ Jesus			NIKOLOSKI Jane	1
2 ESCURA Jordi			STAVREVSKI Goran	2
3 GARCIA Josep			STOJANOVSKI Milan	4
4 FERNANDEZ Juli			MITRESKI Igor	5
5 LIMA Antoni		78	MITRESKI Aleksander	6
6 SONEJEE Oscar		46	TRAJANOV Vanco	7
7 PUJOL Marc	78		PANDEV Goran	9
8 SILVA Fernando	85		SAKIRI Artim	10
9 SIVERA Antoni			STOJKOV Aco	11
10 BERNAUS Marc			GROZDANOVSKI Vlatko	16
11 RUIZ Justo	90		JANCEVSKI Igor	17
Tr: RODRIGO David			Tr: KANATLAROVSKI Dragan	
12 ALONSO Robert	90	46	BAJEVSKI Aleksandar	8
14 SANCHEZ Juli	85	78	BOZINOVSKI Vasko	14
16 GARCIA Genis	78			

Republican, Yerevan
13-10-2004, 20:20, 3 205, Granat POL

ARM 0 3 **CZE**

Koller 2 [3] [75], Rosicky [30]

ARMENIA			CZECH REPUBLIC	
1 BETE Edel			CECH Petr	1
2 MELIKYAN Eghishe			GRYGERA Zdenek	2
3 DOKHOYAN Karen	46	55	GALASEK Tomas	4
4 HOVSEPYAN Sargis			BOLF Rene	5
5 VARDANYAN Hatutyun			JANKULOVSKI Marek	6
7 PETROSYAN Artur		83	KOLLER Jan	9
8 NAZARYAN Rafayel			ROSICKY Tomas	10
9 MKHITARYAN Hamlet		73	VACHOUSEK Stepan	14
10 SHAHGELDYAN Armen	81		HEINZ Marek	18
13 MANUCHARYAN Edgar			SIONKO Libor	19
15 ALEKSANYAN Karen	64		UJFALUSI Tomas	21
Tr: CASONI Bernard			Tr: BRUECKNER Karel	
6 SARGSYAN Albert	64	55	KOVAC Radoslav	3
11 MOVSISYAN Andrey	81	83	LOKVENC Vratislav	12
14 MKRTCHYAN Artur	46	73	JAROSIK Jiri	20

Amsterdam ArenA, Amsterdam
13-10-2004, 20:30; 50 000, Bennett ENG

NED 3 1 **FIN**

Sneijder [39], Van Nistelrooij 2 [41] [63]   Tainio [13]

NETHERLANDS			FINLAND	
1 VAN DER SAR Edwin			NIEMI Antti	1
2 DE JONG Nigel			PASANEN Petri	2
3 HEITINGA John		85	HYYPIA Sami	4
4 COCU Phillip			VAYRYNEN Mika	6
5 LANDZAAT Denny			NURMELA Mika	7
6 SNEIJDER Wesley	83		TAINIO Teemu	8
7 CASTELEN Romeo	77		KOLKKA Joonas	11
8 DAVIDS Edgar			KUIVASTO Toni	14
9 VAN NISTELROOIJ Ruud		60	RIIHILAHTI Aki	16
10 VAN DER VAART Rafael	72		KUQI Shefki	18
11 KUYT Dirk		72	EREMENKO Alexei Jun.	20
Tr: VAN BASTEN Marco			Tr: MUURINEN Antti	
14 VAN BRONCKHORST Gio.	72	72	SAARINEN Janne	3
15 VAN BOMMEL Marc	83	85	POHJA Antti	15
18 MAKAAY Roy	77	60	JOHANSSON Jonathan	21

Mini-Estadi, Barcelona
17-11-2004, 20:30, 2 000, Yefet ISR

AND 0 3 **NED**

Cocu [21], Robben [31], Sneijder [78]

ANDORRA			NETHERLANDS	
1 ALVAREZ Jesus			VAN DER SAR Edwin	1
2 GARCIA Josep			MELCHIOT Mario	2
3 ESCURA Jordi			OOIJER Andre	3
4 FERNANDEZ Juli		83	COCU Phillip	4
5 LIMA Antoni			VAN BRONCKHORST Gio.	5
6 LIMA Ildefons			LANDZAAT Denny	6
7 SILVERA Antoni	86		KUYT Dirk	7
8 SONEJEE Oscar			SNEIJDER Wesley	8
9 SILVA Fernando	72	36	VAN NISTELROOIJ Ruud	9
10 JIMENEZ Manel	79	68	VAN GALEN Benny	10
11 RUIZ Justo			ROBBEN Arjen	11
Tr: RODRIGO David			Tr: VAN BASTEN Marco	
12 SANCHEZ Juli	72	83	MATHYSEN Yoris	12
16 AYALA Josep	79	68	VAN HOOIJDONK Pierre	17
17 GARCIA Genis	86	36	MAKAAY Roy	18

Republican, Yerevan
17-11-2004, 19:00, 1 403, De Bleeckere BEL

ARM 1 1 **ROU**

Dokhoyan [60]   Marica [29]

ARMENIA				ROMANIA	
1	BETE Edel			STELEA Bogdan	1
3	DOKHOYAN Karen			STOICAN Flavius	2
4	HOVSEPYAN Sargis			DANCIA Cristian	3
5	VARDANYAN Harutyun			MOLDOVAN Flavius	4
8	NAZARYAN Rafayel			TARARACHE Mihai	5
9	MKHITARYAN Hamlet			BARCAUAN Cosmin	6
10	SHAHGELDYAN Armen	87	46	CARAMARIN Gabriel	7
13	MANUCHARYAN Edgar	75		PARASCHIV Sorin	8
14	VOSKANYAN Aram	76		MARICA Ciprian	9
16	GRIGORYAN David	74	62	CERNAT Florin	10
18	TATEOSIAN Alexander			NEGA Adrian	11
	Tr: CASONI Bernard			Tr: IORDANESCU Anghel	
6	MKRTCHYAN Aghvan	74	46	DICA Nicolae	14
11	KARAMYAN Arman	76	75	BRATU Florin	15
15	ALEKSANYAN Karen	87	62	MALDARASANU Marius	17

City Stadium, Skopje
17-11-2004, 17:30, 7 000, Meier SUI

MKD 0 2 **CZE**

                                    Lokvenc [88], Koller [90]

MACEDONIA FYR				CZECH REPUBLIC	
1	MILOSEVSKI Petar			CECH Petr	1
3	NOVESKI Nikolce		77	GRYGERA Zdenek	2
4	SEDLOSKI Goce			GALASEK Tomas	4
5	MITRESKI Igor			BOLF Rene	5
6	MITRESKI Aleksandar			JANKULOVSKI Marek	6
8	KRSTEV Mile	46		POBORSKY Karel	8
9	PANDEV Goran			KOLLER Jan	9
10	SAKIRI Artim	77		ROSICKY Tomas	10
11	CADIKOVSKI Dragan	64	59	VACHOUSEK Stepan	14
14	BOZINOVSKI Vasko		16	BAROS Milan	15
15	VASOSKI Aleksandar			UJFALUSI Tomas	21
	Tr: KANATLAROVSKI Dragan			Tr: BRUECKNER Karel	
16	IGNATOV Stojan	77	77	LOKVENC Vratislav	12
17	JANCEVSKI Igor	46	16	HEINZ Marek	18
18	STOJKOV Aco	64	59	JUN Tomas	19

City Stadium, Skopje
9-02-2005, 16:00, 5 000, Verbist BEL

MKD 0 0 **AND**

MACEDONIA FYR				ANDORRA	
1	MILOSEVSKI Petar			ALVAREZ Jesus	1
3	NOVESKI Nikolce			GARCIA Josep	2
4	SEDLOSKI Goce			ESCURA Jordi	3
6	MITRESKI Aleksandar			SONEJEE Oscar	4
8	KRSTEV Mile			LIMA Antoni	5
9	PANDEV Goran			LIMA Ildefons	6
10	SAKIRI Artim	90		PUJOL Marc	7
11	CADIKOVSKI Dragan			SIVERA Antoni	8
14	BOZINOVSKI Vasko	74	60	SILVA Fernando	9
15	VASOSKI Aleksandar	42		BERNAUS Marc	10
18	STOJKOV Aco	67	85	RUIZ Justo	11
	Tr: KANATLAROVSKI Dragan			Tr: RODRIGO David	
2	STAVREVSKI Goran	42	90	JONAS Roberto	14
5	POPOV Goran	74	60	SANCHEZ Juli	16
7	BAJEVSKI Aleksandar	67	85	GARCIA Genis	18

Republican, Yerevan
26-03-2005, 18:00, 2 100, Attard MLT

ARM 2 1 **AND**

Hakobyan [30], Khachatryan [73]   Silva 56

ARMENIA				ANDORRA	
1	BEREZOVSKI Roman			ALVAREZ Jesus	1
2	MELIKYAN Eghishe			AYALA Josep	2
3	DOKHOYAN Karen			ESCURA Jordi	3
5	ARZUMANYAN Robert			GARCIA Josep	4
6	KHACHATRYAN Romik			FERNANDEZ Juli	5
7	HAKOBYAN Ara	93		SONEJEE Oscar	6
8	NAZARYAN Rafayel	73		PUJOL Marc	7
9	MKHITARYAN Hamlet		88	SIVERA Antoni	8
10	SHAHGELDYAN Armen		93	SILVA Fernando	9
11	KARAMYAN Arman	71	79	JIMENEZ Manel	10
15	ALEKSANYAN Karen			RUIZ Justo	11
	Tr: CASONI Bernard			Tr: RODRIGO David	
4	JENEBYAN Romeo	73	88	SANCHEZ Juli	12
13	MKRTCHYAN Aghvan	71	93	MARTIN SANCHEZ Xavi	14
14	VOSKANYAN Valeri	93	79	GARCIA Genis	16

Na Stinadlech, Teplice
26-03-2005, 17:00, 16 200, Larsen DEN

CZE 4 3 **FIN**

Baros [7], Rosicky [34], Polak [58]   Litmanen [46], Riihilahti [73]
Lokvenc [87]   Johansson [79]

CZECH REPUBLIC				FINLAND	
1	CECH Petr			JAASKELAINEN Jussi	12
3	POLAK Jan	82		PASANEN Petri	2
5	BOLF Rene			HYYPIA Sami	4
6	JANKULOVSKI Marek			TIHINEN Hannu	5
7	SIONKO Libor	73		NURMELA Mika	7
8	POBORSKY Karel		10	LITMANEN Jari	10
10	ROSICKY Tomas		11	KOLKKA Joonas	11
12	LOKVENC Vratislav			ILOLA Jari	15
13	JIRANEK Martin			RIIHILAHTI Aki	16
15	BAROS Milan	53		KOPTEFF Peter	17
21	UJFALUSI Tomas			KUQI Shefki	18
	Tr: BRUCKNER Karel			Tr: MUURINEN Antti	
2	JUN Tomas	82	60	EREMENKO Alexei Jun	20
18	JAROSIK Jiri	73	78	JOHANSSON Jonathan	21
20	PLASIL Jaroslav	53			

Giulesti, Bucharest
26-03-2005, 20:00, 19 000, Medina Cantalejo ESP

ROU 0 2 **NED**

                                    Cocu [1], Babel [84]

ROMANIA				NETHERLANDS	
1	LOBONT Bogdan			VAN DER SAR Edwin	1
2	OGARARU George			KROMKAMP Jan	2
3	MARIN Petre			BOULAHROUZ Khalid	3
4	GHIOANE Tiberiu	46		MATHYSEN Yoris	4
5	CHIVU Cristian			VAN BRONCKHORST Gio.	5
6	RADOI Mirel			LANDZAAT Denny	6
7	PETRE Florentin		90	KUYT Dirk	7
8	MUNTEANU Dorinel		73	VAN BOMMEL Marc	8
9	MOLDOVAN Viorel	69		VAN NISTELROOIJ Ruud	9
10	PANCU Daniel			COCU Phillip	10
11	ILIE Adrian	85	23	ROBBEN Arjen	11
	Tr: PITURCA Victor			Tr: VAN BASTEN Marco	
14	PLESAN Mihaita	46	73	MADURO Hedwiges	14
15	CRISTEA Andrei	69	90	CASTELEN Romeo	17
18	BUCUR Gheorghe	85	23	BABEL Ryan	18

Comunal, Andorra-la-Vella
30-03-2005, 16:50, 900, Messner AUT

AND 0 4 CZE

Jankulovski 31p, Baros 40
Lokvenc 53, Rosicky 92+p

ANDORRA				CZECH REPUBLIC	
1	ALVAREZ Jesus			CECH Petr	1
2	ESCURA Jordi			JANKULOVSKI Marek	6
3	GARCIA Josep	60		POBORSKY Karel	8
4	SONEJEE Oscar			ROSICKY Tomas	10
5	LIMA Antoni			LOKVENC Vratislav	12
6	LIMA Ildefons	75		JIRANEK Martin	13
7	PUJOL Marc			VACHOUSEK Stepan	14
8	SIVERA Antoni	60		BAROS Milan	15
9	SILVA Fernando	66	46	TYCE Roman	19
10	BERNAUS Marc			UJFALUSI Tomas	21
11	RUIZ Justo	67		ROZEHNAL David	22
	Tr: RODRIGO David			Tr: BRUECKNER Karel	
12	FERNANDEZ Juli	67	60	JUN Tomas	2
14	SANCHEZ Juli	66	46	POLAK Jan	3
18	AYALA Josep	60	75	PLASIL Jaroslav	20

Philips Stadion, Eindhoven
30-03-2005, 20:30, 35 000, Trefoloni ITA

NED 2 0 ARM

Castelen 3, Van Nistelrooij 33

NETHERLANDS				ARMENIA	
1	VAN DER SAR Edwin			BEREZOVSKI Roman	1
2	KROMKAMP Jan			MELIKYAN Eghishe	2
3	BOULAHROUZ Khalid			DOKHOYAN Karen	3
4	MATHYSEN Yoris			HOVSEPYAN Sargis	4
5	VAN BRONCKHORST Gio.	85		ARZUMANYAN Robert	5
6	LANDZAAT Denny	50		KHACHATRYAN Romik	6
7	CASTELEN Romeo	50	46	HAKOBYAN Ara	7
8	VAN BOMMEL Marc			MKHITARYAN Hamlet	9
9	VAN NISTELROOIJ Ruud			SHAHGELDYAN Armen	10
10	COCU Phillip		59	GRIGORYAN David	16
11	KUYT Dirk	80		VOSKANYAN Aram	17
	Tr: VAN BASTEN Marco			Tr: CASONI Bernard	
15	VAN DER VAART Rafael	50	46	NAZARYAN Rafayel	8
17	HESSELINK Jan	80	59	KARAMYAN Arman	13
18	BABEL Ryan	50	85	TATEOSIAN Alexander	18

City Stadium, Skopje
30-03-2005, 20:00, 15 000, Ovrebo NOR

MKD 1 2 ROU

Maznov 31
Mitea 2 18 58

MACEDONIA FYR				ROMANIA	
1	MILOSEVSKI Petar			LOBONT Bogdan	1
2	POPOV Robert			CONTRA Cosmin	2
3	PETROV Robert	46		RAT Razvan	3
4	SEDLOSKI Goce			GALCA Constantin	4
5	VASOSKI Aleksandar		46	CHIVU Cristian	5
6	MITRESKI Aleksandar			RADOI Mirel	6
7	KRSTEV Mile			PETRE Florentin	7
8	SUMOLIKOSKI Velice	73		MUNTEANU Dorinel	8
9	MAZNOV Goran		78	MOLDOVAN Viorel	9
16	GROZDANOVSKI Vlatko	82		PANCU Daniel	10
17	JANCEVSKI Igor		70	MITEA Nicolae	11
	Tr: SANTRAC Slobodan			Tr: PITURCA Victor	
11	IGNATOV Stojan	73	70	BUCUR Gheorghe	13
14	BOZINOVSKI Vasko	46	46	GHIONEA Sorin	14
18	BAJEVSKI Aleksandar	82	78	CRISTEA Andrei	15

U Nisy, Liberec
4-06-2005, 17:00, 9 520, Dereli TUR

CZE 8 1 AND

Lokvenc 2 12 92, Koller 30, Smicer 37
Galasek 52, Baros 79, Rosicky 84, Polak 86
Riera 36

CZECH REPUBLIC				ANDORRA	
1	CECH Petr			ALVAREZ Jesus	1
2	GRYGERA Zdenek			GARCIA Josep	2
4	GALASEK Tomas			ESCURA Jordi	3
7	SMICER Vladimir	46		SONEJEE Oscar	4
8	POBORSKY Karel			LIMA Antoni	5
9	KOLLER Jan	61		FERNANDEZ Juli	6
10	ROSICKY Tomas		78	SIVERA Antoni	7
12	LOKVENC Vratislav			AYALA Josep	8
15	BAROS Milan		68	RIERA Gabriel	9
21	UJFALUSI Tomas		85	JIMENEZ Manel	10
22	ROZEHNAL David	46	63	RUIZ Justo	11
	Tr: BRUECKNER Karel			Tr: RODRIGO David	
3	POLAK Jan	46	85	MORENO Sergi	14
18	JUN Tomas	61	78	GARCIA Genis	16
20	PLASIL Jaroslav	46	68	ANDORRA Xavier	17

Republican, Yerevan
4-06-2005, 20:00, 2 870, Mikulski POL

ARM 1 2 MKD

Manucharyan 55
Pandev 2 29p 47

ARMENIA				MACEDONIA FYR	
1	BEREZOVSKI Roman			MADZOVSKI GK	1
3	DOKHOYAN Karen			LAZAREVSKI Sasko	2
4	HOVSEPYAN Sargis		59	POPOV Goran	3
6	KHACHATRYAN Romik			SEDLOSKI Goce	4
8	MKRTCHYAN Aghvan			VASOSKI Aleksandar	5
9	MKHITARYAN Hamlet			MITRESKI Aleksandar	6
10	SHAHGELDYAN Armen			PETROV Robert	7
14	VOSKANYAN Aram	71	85	SUMOLIKOSKI Velice	8
15	ALEKSANYAN Karen	79		PANDEV Goran	9
17	SARGSYAN Albert	52		GROZDANOVSKI Vlatko	10
18	TATEOSIAN Alexander		68	MAZNOV Goran	11
	Tr: WISMAN Hendrik			Tr: SANTRAC Slobodan	
7	HAKOBYAN Ara	71	85	KRALEVSKI Igor	13
13	MANUCHARYAN Edgar	52	59	KRSTEV Mile	16
16	JENEBYAN Romeo	79	68	ISMAILI Ismail	17

Feyenoord Stadium, Rotterdam
4-06-2005, 20:30, 47 000, De Santis ITA

NED 2 0 ROU

Robben 26, Kuyt 47

NETHERLANDS				ROMANIA	
1	VAN DER SAR Edwin			LOBONT Bogdan	1
2	LUCIUS Theo			CONTRA Cosmin	2
3	HEITINGA John			STOICA Pompiliu	3
4	OPNAM Barry			TAMAS Gabriel	4
5	VAN BRONCKHORST Gio.			CHIVU Cristian	5
6	LANDZAAT Denny		65	MITEA Nicolae	6
7	KUYT Dirk			PETRE Florentin	7
8	VAN BOMMEL Marc	49		MUNTEANU Dorinel	8
9	VAN NISTELROOIJ Ruud	63		NICULAE Marius	9
10	VAN DER VAART Rafael	85	85	MUTU Adrian	10
11	ROBBEN Arjen			PANCU Daniel	11
	Tr: VAN BASTEN Marco			Tr: PITURCA Victor	
14	DE JONG Nigel	49	65	NICULAE Marius	14
15	MADURO Hedwiges	85	85	COMAN Gigel	15
18	VAN PERSIE Robin	63			

Farul, Constanta
8-06-2005, 20:30, 5 146, Briakos GRE

ROU 3 0 ARM

Petre [29], Bucur 2 [40] [78]

#	ROMANIA			#	ARMENIA	
1	LOBONT Bogdan				BEREZOVSKI Roman	1
2	CONTRA Cosmin	66			MELIKYAN Eghishe	2
3	RAT Razvan				DOKHOYAN Karen	3
4	TAMAS Gabriel				HOVSEPYAN Sargis	4
5	CHIVU Cristian				KHACHATRYAN Romik	6
6	PETRE Ovidiu				HAKOBYAN Ara	7
7	PLESAN Mihaita		80		MKHITARYAN Hamlet	9
8	MUNTEANU Dorinel	83			SHAHGELDYAN Armen	10
9	NICULAE Marius		54		MANUCHARYAN Edgar	13
10	COMAN Gigel	77	46		VOSKANYAN Aram	14
11	BUCUR Gheorghe				TATEOSIAN Alexander	18
	Tr: PITURCA Victor				Tr: WISMAN Hendrik	
14	MAZILU Ionut	83	46		ARZUMYAN Robert	5
16	MITEA Nicolae	77	80		GRIGORYAN David	8
17	STOICAN Flavius	66	54		KARAMYAn Arman	11

Na Stinadlech, Teplice
8-06-2005, 17:00, 14 150, Dauden Ibanez ESP

CZE 6 1 MKD

Koller 4 [41] [45] [48] [52]
Rosicky [73p], Baros [87]   Pandev [13]

#	CZECH REPUBLIC			#	MACEDONIA FYR	
1	CECH Petr				MADZOVSKI GK	1
2	GRYGERA Zdenek				LAZAREVSKI Vlade	2
4	GALASEK Tomas				POPOV Goran	3
7	SMICER Vladimir	60			SEDLOSKI Goce	4
8	POBORSKY Karel	77			VASOSKI Aleksandar	5
9	KOLLER Jan				MITRESKI Aleksandar	6
10	ROSICKY Tomas				PETROV Robert	7
12	LOKVENC Vratislav	45	69		SUMOLIKOSKI Velice	8
15	BAROS Milan		65		PANDEV Goran	9
17	HIBSCHMAN Tomas				MAZNOV Goran	11
21	UJFALUSI Tomas		73		KRSTEV Mile	16
	Tr: BRUCKNER Karel				Tr: SANTRAC Slobodan	
3	POLAK Jan	45	65		GROZDANOVSKI Vlatko	10
19	ZELENKA Lukas	77	69		KRALEVSKI Igor	13
20	PLASIL Jaroslav	60	73		BAHDUZIEV Toni	18

Olympic Stadium, Helsinki
8-06-2005, 21:00, 37 786, Hamer LUX

FIN 0 4 NED

Van Nistelrooij [36], Kuyt [76]
Cocu [85], Van Persie [87]

#	FINLAND			#	NETHERLANDS	
1	JAASKELAINEN Jussi				VAN DER SAR Edwin	1
3	SAARINEN Janne		26		LUCIUS Theo	2
4	HYYPIA Sami				HEITINGA John	3
5	TIHINEN Hannu				OPNAM Barry	4
6	VAYRYNEN Mika				VAN BRONCKHORST Gio.	5
7	NURMELA Mika				LANDZAAT Denny	6
8	TAINIO Teemu	74			KUYT Dirk	7
10	LITMANEN Jari	28	86		DE JONG Nigel	8
16	RIIHILAHTI Aki		87		VAN NISTELROOIJ Ruud	9
18	KUQI Shefki				COCU Phillip	10
20	EREMENKO Alexei Jun	81			ROBBEN Arjen	11
	Tr: MUURINEN Antti				Tr: VAN BASTEN Marco	
9	FORSSELL Mikael	74	26		MELCHIOT Mario	12
17	KOPTEFF Peter	81	86		MADURO Hedwiges	15
21	JOHANSSON Jonathan	28	87		VAN PERSIE Robin	18

GROUP 2

Qemal Stafa, Tirana
4-09-2004, 20:45, 15 800, Iturralde Gonzalez ESP

ALB 2 1 GRE

Murati [2], Aliaj [11]   Giannakopoulos [38]

#	ALBANIA			#	GREECE	
1	STRAKOSHA Fotis				NIKOPOLIDIS Antonios	1
2	BEQIRI Elvin				SEITARIDIS Giourkas	2
5	CANA Lorik		32		FYSSAS Panagiotis	3
6	HASI Besnik		16		NTAMPIZAS Nikolaos	4
7	MURATI Edwin				KAPSIS Michail	5
9	MYRTAJ Florian	76			BASINAS Angelos	6
11	ALIAJ Adrian				ZAGORAKIS Theodoros	7
13	SKELA Ervin				KATSOURANIS Konstantinos	8
14	LALA Altin				CHARISTEAS Angelos	9
17	TARE Igli				KARAGOUNIS Georgios	10
18	DURO Klodian	86	65		VRYZAS Zizis	11
	Tr: BRIEGEL Hans-Peter				Tr: REHHAGEL Otto	
16	DRAGUSHA Mehmet	76	16		GIANNAKOPOULOS Stylianos	13
21	BEQIRI Ardit	86	32		TSARTAS Vassilios	14
			65		PAPADOPOULOS Dimitrios	16

Parken, Copenhagen
4-09-2004, 20:00, 36 335, Meier SUI

DEN 1 1 UKR

Jorgensen [9]   Husin [56]

#	DENMARK			#	UKRAINE	
1	SORENSEN Thomas				SHOVKOVSKI Alexandr	1
2	BOGELUND Kasper	43			NESMACHNY Andriy	2
3	POULSEN Christian	65			RUSOL Andrey	3
4	KROLDRUP Per				TYMOSHYUK Anatoliy	4
5	JENSEN Niclas				YEZERSKI Vladimir	5
6	HELVEG Thomas				SHELAEV Oleg	6
7	GRAVESEN Thomas				SHEVCHENKO Andriy	7
8	GRONKJAER Jesper		67		HUSIN Andrii	8
9	TOMASSON Jon Dahl		75		HUSYEV Oleh	9
10	JORGENSEN Martin				STAROSTYAK Mikhail	10
11	MADSEN Peter	79	84		VOROBEY Andriy	11
	Tr: OLSEN Morten				Tr: BLOKHIN Oleg	
12	PRISKE Brian	43	84		RADCHENKO Aleksandr	14
14	JENSEN Claus	65	67		MATIUKHIN Sergey	15
18	PEDERSEN Henrik	79	75		ZADOROZHNY Sergiy	19

Avni Aker, Trabzon
4-09-2004, 20:00, 10 169, Medina Cantalejpo ESP

TUR 1 1 GEO

Tekke [49]   Asatiani [85]

#	TURKEY			#	GEORGIA
1	RECBER Rustu				DEVADZE Akaki	1
2	BALCI Serkan				MJAVANADZE Kakhaber	2
3	BARIS Deniz	89			KHIZANISHVILI Zurab	3
4	TORAMAN Ibrahim				KALADZE Kakha	4
5	BELOZOGLU Emre				KHIZANEISHVILI Otar	5
6	OZAT Umit				KVIRKVELIA Dato	6
7	BURUK Okan				TSIKITISHVILI Levan	7
8	SANLI Tuncay	72	79	REKHVIASHVILI Alexander	8
9	SUKUR Hakan	79	74	DEMETRADZE George	9
10	TEKKE Fatih	72		JAMARAULI Gocha	10
11	SAS Hasan	58		ARVELADZE Shota	11
	Tr: YANAL Ersun			Tr: GIRESSE Alain	
13	KARADENIZ Gokdeniz	72	89	KVARASTSKHELIA Givi	15
14	CIMSIR Huseyin	72	79	ASATIANI Malkhaz	16
15	KAHVECI Nihat	79	74	JAKOBIA Lasha	17

Lokomotivi, Tbilisi
8-09-2004, 20 000, 20 000, Courtney NIR

GEO 2 0 ALB

Iashvili [15], Demetradze [91+]

#	GEORGIA			ALBANIA	#
1	DEVADZE Akaki			STRAKOSHA Foto	1
2	MJAVANADZE Kakhaber	81		BEQIRI Elvin	2
3	KHIZANEISHVILI Otar			CANA Lorik	5
4	KALADZE Kakha			HASI Besnik	6
6	SALUKVADZE Lasha	79		MURATI Edvin	7
7	TSIKITISHVILI Levan	66		MYRTAJ Florian	9
9	IASHVILI Alexander			ALIAJ Ardian	11
10	JAMARAULI Gocha	77		SKELA Ervin	13
11	ARVELADZE Shota	88		LALA Altin	14
16	ASATIANI Malkhaz	58		TARE Igli	17
17	KOBIASHVILI Levan		56	DURO Klodian	18
	Tr: GIRESSE Alain			Tr: BRIEGEL Hans-Peter	
5	KVIRKVELIA Dato	77	66	BUSHI Alban	8
13	KANKAVA Jaba	58	56	DRAGUSHA Mehmet	16
18	DEMETRADZE George	88	79	SHKEMBI Blendi	20

Karaiskaki, Piraeus
8-09-2004, 21:45, 32 182, Frisk SWE

GRE 0 0 TUR

#	GREECE			TURKEY	#
1	NIKOPOLIDIS Antonios			RECBER Rustu	1
2	SEITARIDIS Giourkas			TORAMAN Ibrahim	2
6	BASINAS Angelos			BARIS Deniz	3
7	ZAGORAKIS Theodoros			CETIN Servet	4
8	GIANNAKOPOULOS Stylianos	81		BELOZOGLU Emre	5
9	CHARISTEAS Angelos			OZAT Umit	6
14	FYSSAS Panagiotis	81	73	BURUK Okan	7
15	VRYZAS Zizis			KARADENIZ Gokdeniz	8
19	KAPSIS Michail	93		KAHVECI Nihat	9
20	KARAGOUNIS Georgios	90		TEKKE Fatih	10
21	KATSOURANIS Konstantinos			BALCI Serkan	11
	Tr: REHHAGEL Otto			Tr: YANAL Ersun	
10	TSARTAS Vassilios	81	73	CIMSIR Huseyin	15
17	PAPADOPOULOS Dimitrios	81	90	ALTINTOP Hamit	16
			93	AKIN Serhat	18

Central Stadium, Almaty
8-09-2004, 21:00, 23 000, Oliveira Alves Garcia POR

KAZ 1 2 UKR

Karpovich [34]   Byelik [14], Rotan [90]

#	KAZAKHSTAN			UKRAINE	#
1	NOVIKOV Yuriy			SHOVKOVSKI Alexandr	1
4	BALTIYEV Ruslan			NESMACHNY Andriy	2
6	DUBINSKIY Renat			RUSOL Andrey	3
7	AVDEYEV Igor			TYMOSHYUK Anatoliy	4
8	SMAKOV Samat	70		YEZERSKI Vladimir	5
9	KARPOVICH Andrey			ZAKARLYUKA Sergiy	6
11	NIZOVTSEV Maxim		92	BYELIK Olekcii	7
15	FAMILTSEV Alexander		66	HUSIN Andrii	8
16	CHICHULIN Anton	50		HUSYEV Oleh	9
17	IRISMETOV Farkhadbek		49	STAROSTYAK Mikhail	10
20	TLESHEV Murat	65		VOROBEY Andriy	11
	Tr: TIMOFEYEV Sergei			Tr: BLOKHIN Oleg	
2	MUSSIN Oleg	70	49	VORONIN Andrey	15
12	RADIONOV Denis	65	92	SHELAEV Oleg	16
21	URAZBAKHTIN Rafael	50	66	ROTAN Ruslan	17

Olympic, Kyiv
9-10-2004, 19:15, 56 000, Mejuto Gonzalez ESP

UKR 1 1 GRE

Shevchenko [48]   Tsartas [83]

#	UKRAINE			GREECE	#
1	SHOVKOVSKI Alexandr			NIKOPOLIDIS Antonios	1
2	NESMACHNY Andriy			SEITARIDIS Giourkas	2
3	FEDOROV Sergiy			DELLAS Traianos	5
4	TYMOSHYUK Anatoliy		80	BASINAS Angelos	6
5	YEZERSKI Vladimir			ZAGORAKIS Theodoros	7
6	RUSOL Andrey		61	GIANNAKOPOULOS Stylianos	8
7	SHEVCHENKO Andriy		70	FYSSAS Panagiotis	14
8	SHELAEV Oleg	86		VRYZAS Zizis	15
9	HUSYEV Oleh			KAPSIS Michail	19
10	VORONIN Andrey	92		KARAGOUNIS Georgios	20
11	VOROBEY Andriy	65		KATSOURANIS Konstantinos	21
	Tr: BLOKHIN Oleg			Tr: REHHAGEL Otto	
14	HUSIN Andrii	65	61	CHARISTEAS Angelos	9
17	BYELIK Olekcii	92	70	TSARTAS Vassilios	10
18	ZAKARLYUKA Sergiy	86	80	GEORGIADIS Georgios	11

Sükrü Saracoglu, Istanbul
9-10-2004, 20:00, 39 900, Hrinak SVK

TUR 4 0 KAZ

Karadeniz [17], Kahveci [50]
Tekke 2 [90] [93+]

#	TURKEY			KAZAKHSTAN	#
1	RECBER Rustu		52	NOVIKOV Yuriy	1
2	SEYHAN Tolga			LYAPKIN Dmitri	2
4	CETIN Servet			DUBINSKIY Renat	6
6	OZAT Umit			AVDEYEV Igor	7
8	KAHVECI Nihat	84	59	SMAKOV Samat	8
9	TEKKE Fatih			KARPOVICH Andrey	9
10	KARADENIZ Gokdeniz	69		BULESHEV Alibek	10
13	BARIS Deniz			NIZOVTSEV Maxim	11
14	BALCI Serkan	64		FAMILTSEV Alexander	15
16	CIMSIR Huseyin	33		CHICHULIN Anton	16
18	ATES Necati			IRISMETOV Farkhadbek	17
	Tr: YANAL Ersun			Tr: TIMOFEYEV Sergei	
11	SAS Hasan	64	59	KOZULIN Sergey	3
17	SANLI Tuncay	69	33	BALTIYEV Ruslan	14
20	ALTINTOP Hamit	84	52	MOREV Andrey	18

Qemql Stafa, Tirana
9-10-2004, 20:45, 14 500, Baskakov RUS

ALB 0 2 DEN

Jorgensen [52], Tomasson [72]

ALBANIA			DENMARK	
1 STRAKOSHA Foto			SKOV-JENSEN Peter	1
5 CANA Lorik			POULSEN Christian	2
6 HASI Besnik			PRISKE Brian	3
7 MURATI Edvin			KROLDRUP Per	4
13 SKELA Ervin			JENSEN Niclas	5
14 LALA Altin			HELVEG Thomas	6
15 MUKAJ Oevi	79		GRAVESEN Thomas	7
17 TARE Igli		78	GRONKJAER Jesper	8
18 OURO Klodian			TOMASSON Jon Dahl	9
21 BEQIRI Ardit		83	JORGENSEN Martin	10
23 HAXHI Altin	67	46	PEDERSEN Henrik	11
Tr: BRIEGEL Hans-Peter			Tr: OLSEN Morten	
8 BUSHAJ Alban	79	83	KRISTIANSEN Jan	12
16 DRAGUSHA Mehmet	67	78	KAHLENBERG Thomas	15
		46	ROMMEDAHL Dennis	17

Karpaty, Lviv
13-10-2004, 19:15, 28 000, Stark GER

UKR 2 0 GEO

Byelik [12], Shevchenko [79]

UKRAINE			GEORGIA	
1 SHOVKOVSKI Alexandr			DEVADZE Akaki	1
2 NESMACHNY Andriy		46	MJAVANADZE Kakhaber	2
3 FEDOROV Sergyi			KHIZANEISHVILI Otar	3
4 TYMOSHYUK Anatoliy			SALUKVADZE Lasha	6
5 YEZERSKI Vladimir	46		TSIKITISHVILI Levan	7
6 RUSOL Andrey			IASHVILI Alexander	9
7 SHEVCHENKO Andriy		85	JAMARAULI Gocha	10
9 HUSYEV Oleh			ARVELADZE Shota	11
10 VORONIN Andrey	39		KHIZANISHVILI Zurab	13
11 BYELIK Olekcii			ASATIANI Malkhaz	16
14 HUSIN Andrii			KOBIASHVILI Levan	17
Tr: BLOKHIN Oleg			Tr: GIRESSE Alain	
8 SHELAEV Oleg	64 39	46	BURDULI Vladimir	8
13 CHECHER Vyacheslav	46	85	DEMETRADZE George	18
18 ZAKARLYUKA Sergiy	64			

Central Stadium, Almaty
13-10-2004, 20:00, 12 300, Stuchlik AUT

KAZ 0 1 ALB

Bushaj [61]

KAZAKHSTAN			ALBANIA	
18 MOREV Andrey			STRAKOSHA Foto	1
2 LYAPKIN Dmitri			CANA Lorik	5
6 DUBINSKIY Renat			HASI Besnik	6
7 AVDEYEV Igor		87	BUSHAJ Alban	8
8 SMAKOV Samat	55		SKELA Ervin	13
9 KARPOVICH Andrey	64		LALA Altin	14
11 NIZOVTSEV Maxim		54	MUKAJ Oevi	15
14 BALTIYEV Ruslan		94	DRAGUSHA Mehmet	16
15 FAMILTSEV Alexander			TARE Igli	17
17 IRISMETOV Farkhadbek			BEQIRI Ardit	21
19 URAZBAKHTIN Rafael	58		HAXHI Altin	23
Tr: TIMOFEYEV Sergei			Tr: BRIEGEL Hans-Peter	
4 SHEVCHENKO Maxim	64	87	RAKLLI Altin	10
5 KAMELOV Dias	55	94	SHKEMBI Blendi	20
10 BULESHEV Alibek	58	54	LICI Suad	24

Parken, Copenhagen
13-10-2004, 20:00, 41 331, De Santis ITA

DEN 1 1 TUR

Tomasson [27p]   Kahveci [70]

DENMARK			TURKEY	
1 SKOV-JENSEN Peter			RECBER Rustu	1
2 POULSEN Christian			SEYHAN Tolga	2
3 PRISKE Brian		68	CETIN Servet	4
4 KROLDRUP Per			BELOZOGLU Emre	5
5 JENSEN Niclas			OZAT Umit	6
6 HELVEG Thomas			BURUK Okan	7
7 GRAVESEN Thomas			KAHVECI Nihat	8
8 GRONKJAER Jesper	31		TEKKE Fatih	9
9 TOMASSON Jon Dahl		83	KARADENIZ Gokdeniz	10
10 JORGENSEN Martin	80	46	UZULMEZ Ibrahim	15
11 PEREZ Kenneth	62		CIMSIR Huseyin	16
Tr: OLSEN Morten			Tr: YANAL Ersun	
12 KRISTIANSEN Jan	80	83	BALCI Serkan	14
17 ROMMEDAHL Dennis	62	46	SANLI Tuncay	17
		68	ATES Necati	18

Sükrü Saracoglu, Istanbul
17-11-2044, 20:30, 40 468, Cardoso Batista POR

TUR 0 3 UKR

Husyev [8], Shevchenko 2 [17 88]

TURKEY			UKRAINE	
1 RECBER Rustu			SHOVKOVSKI Alexandr	1
2 SEYHAN Tolga			NESMACHNY Andriy	2
4 CETIN Servet	28		FEDOROV Sergyi	3
5 BELOZOGLU Emre			YEZERSKI Vladimir	5
6 OZAT Umit			RUSOL Andrey	6
7 BURUK Okan		92	SHEVCHENKO Andriy	7
8 KAHVECI Nihat			SHELAEV Oleg	8
9 TEKKE Fatih			HUSYEV Oleh	9
11 KARADENIZ Gokdeniz	54	61	VORONIN Andrey	10
14 BARIS Deniz			HUSIN Andrii	14
16 CIMSIR Huseyin	67	75	VOROBEY Andriy	16
Tr: YANAL Ersun			Tr: BLOKHIN Oleg	
10 BASTURK Yildiray	54	61	RIKUN Aleksandr	15
17 SANLI Tuncay	28	92	NAZARENKO Sergey	17
18 ATES Necati	67	75	DMITRULIN Yuri	18

Lokomotivi, Tbilisi
17-11-2004, 21:00, 20 000, Ceferin SVN

GEO 2 2 DEN

Demetradze [33], Asatiani [76]   Tomasson 2 [7 64]

GEORGIA			DENMARK	
1 DEVADZE Akaki			SORENSEN Thomas	1
2 MJAVANADZE Kakhaber			POULSEN Christian	2
3 KHIZANISHVILI Otar			PRISKE Brian	3
4 KALADZE Kakha			KROLDRUP Per	4
7 TSIKITISHVILI Levan			JENSEN Niclas	5
9 IASHVILI Alexander	72		LUSTU Steven	6
10 DEMETRADZE George			GRAVESEN Thomas	7
13 KHIZANISHVILI Zurab		89	JENSEN Daniel	8
16 ASATIANI Malkhaz			TOMASSON Jon Dahl	9
17 KOBIASHVILI Levan		89	JORGENSEN Martin	10
18 JIKIA Mamuka	72	46	PEREZ Kenneth	11
Tr: GIRESSE Alain			Tr: OLSEN Morten	
5 KVIRKVELIA Dato	72	89	LOVENKRANDS Peter	15
11 ARVELADZE Shota	72	46	ROMMEDAHL Dennis	17
		89	SKOUBO Morten	18

Karaiskaki, Piraeus
17-11-2004, 21:30, 31 838, Kostadinov BUL

GRE	3	1	KAZ

Charisteas 2 [24][46+]
Katsouranis [85]

GREECE		KAZAKHSTAN	
1 NIKOPOLIDIS Antonios		NOVIKOV Yuriy	1
2 SEITARIDIS Giourkas		LYAPKIN Dmitri	2
5 DELLAS Traianos		DUBINSKIY Renat	6
6 BASINAS Angelos		SMAKOV Samat	8
7 ZAGORAKIS Theodoros	70	KARPOVICH Andrey	9
9 CHARISTEAS Angelos	66	BULESHEV Alibek	10
10 TSARTAS Vassilios	72	BALTIYEV Ruslan	14
14 FYSSAS Panagiotis	68	ZHALMAGAMBETOV Maxim	15
15 VRYZAS Zizis		CHICHULIN Anton	16
19 KAPSIS Michail	59	IRISMETOV Farkhadbek	17
20 KARAGOUNIS Georgios	51	URAZBAKHTIN Rafael	19
Tr: REHHAGEL Otto		Tr: TIMOFEYEV Sergei	
11 GEORGIADIS Georgios	72 68	KAMELOV Dias	5
16 KAFES Pantelis	70 66	SHEVCHENKO Maxim	11
21 KATSOURANIS Konstantinos	59 51	RADIONOV Denis	12

Qemal Stafa, Tirana
9-02-2005, 19:45, 12 000, Bennett ENG

ALB	0	2	UKR

Rusol [40], Gusin [59]

ALBANIA		UKRAINE	
1 STRAKOSHA Foto		SHOVKOVSKI Alexandr	1
2 DALLKU Armend		NESMACHNY Andriy	2
3 CIPI Geri	56	TYMOSHYUK Anatoliy	4
5 CANA Lorik		YEZERSKI Vladimir	5
8 BUSHAJ Alban	76	RUSOL Andrey	6
11 ALIAJ Ardian		SHEVCHENKO Andriy	7
13 SKELA Ervin		SHELAEV Oleg	8
14 LALA Altin		HUSYEV Oleh	9
17 TARE Igli	65 82	VORONIN Andrey	10
18 DURO Klodian	67	ROTAN Ruslan	11
23 HAXHI Altin		GUSIN Andrei	14
Tr: BRIEGEL Hans-Peter		Tr: BLOKHIN Oleg	
4 OSMANI Tefik	56 67	VOROBEY Andriy	16
9 MYRTAJ Florian	76 82	RIKUN Aleksandr	18
25 BOGDANI Erion	65		

Karaiskaki, Piraeus
9-02-2005, 21:30, 32 430, Collina ITA

GRE	2	1	DEN

Zagorakis [25], Basinas [32p]   Rommedahl [46+]

GREECE		DENMARK	
1 NIKOPOLIDIS Antonios		SORENSEN Thomas	1
2 SEITARIDIS Giourkas		POULSEN Christian	2
5 DELLAS Traianos		KROLDRUP Per	3
6 BASINAS Angelos	65	LUSTU Steven	4
7 ZAGORAKIS Theodoros	46 70	JENSEN Niclas	5
8 GIANNAKOPOULOS Stylianos		PRISKE Brian	6
9 CHARISTEAS Angelos		GRAVESEN Thomas	7
14 FYSSAS Panagiotis		ROMMEDAHL Dennis	8
15 VRYZAS Zizis	83	TOMASSON Jon Dahl	9
20 KARAGOUNIS Georgios	61	JENSEN Daniel	10
21 KATSOURANIS Konstantinos	46	PEREZ Kenneth	11
Tr: REHHAGEL Otto		Tr: OLSEN Morten	
16 KAFES Pantelis	61 65	NIELSEN Per	13
25 KYRGIAKOS Sotiros	46 46	JORGENSEN Martin	14
33 AMANATIDIS Ioannis	83 70	MADSEN Morten	17

Parken, Copenhagen
26-03-2005, 20:00, 20 980, Gilewski POL

DEN	3	0	KAZ

Moller 2 [10][48], Poulsen [33]

DENMARK		KAZAKHSTAN	
1 SORENSEN Thomas		NOVIKOV Yuriy	1
2 POULSEN Christian		LYAPKIN Dmitri	2
3 PRISKE Brian	78	UTABAYEV Kairat	4
4 LAURSEN Martin		AVDEYEV Kairat	7
5 JENSEN Niclas		SMAKOV Samat	8
6 HELVEG Thomas		KARPOVICH Andrey	9
7 JENSEN Daniel	46	RADIONOV Denis	12
8 GRONKJAER Jesper	74	BALTIYEV Ruslan	14
9 TOMASSON Jon Dahl	46	FAMILTSEV Alexander	15
10 JORGENSEN Martin	46	CHICHULIN Anton	16
11 MOLLER Peter	57	TRAVIN Andrey	17
Tr: BORDINGGAARD Keld		Tr: TIMOFEYEV Sergei	
13 SILBERBAUER Michael	74 78	DUBINSKIY Renat	20
14 JENSEN Claus	46 46	LARIN Sergey	23
17 PEREZ Kenneth	46 57	BAIZHANOV Maxat	25

Besiktas Inönü, Istanbul
26-03-2005, 20:00, 32 000, Plautz AUT

TUR	2	0	ALB

Ates [3p], Basturk [5]

TURKEY		ALBANIA	
1 RECBER Rustu		LIKA Ilion	1
2 SEYHAN Tolga		BEQIRI Elvin	2
4 TORAMAN Ibrahim		DALLKU Armend	3
5 BELOZOGLU Emre	84	CANA Lorik	5
6 OZAT Umit		ALIAJ Ardian	11
9 TEKKE Fatih	62	SKELA Ervin	13
10 BASTURK Yildiray		LALA Altin	14
11 ALTINTOP Hamit	76	TARE Igli	17
14 BALCI Serkan	78	DURO Klodian	18
15 AVCI Koray		BOGDANI Erion	22
18 ATES Necati		HAXHI Altin	23
Tr: YANAL Ersun		Tr: BRIEGEL Hans-Peter	
3 KORKMAZ Bulent	84 78	BUSHAJ Alban	8
16 KARADENIZ Gokdeniz	76		
20 AKMAN Ayhan	62		

Lokomotivi, Tbilisi
26-03-2005, 20:30, 23 000, Rosetti ITA

GEO	1	3	GRE

Asatiani [22]   Kapsis [43], Vryzas [44]
Giannakopoulos [53]

GEORGIA		GREECE	
1 LOMAIA George		NIKOPOLIDIS Antonios	1
2 MJAVANADZE Kakhaber		SEITARIDIS Giourkas	2
3 KHIZANEISHVILI Otar		BASINAS Angelos	6
4 KALADZE Kakha		ZAGORAKIS Theodoros	7
5 KVIRKVELIA Dato		GIANNAKOPOULOS Stylianos	8
10 DEMETRADZE George		CHARISTEAS Angelos	9
11 ARVELADZE Shota	59	VRYZAS Zizis	15
13 KHIZANISHVILI Zurab		GOUMAS Ioannis	18
14 GOGUA Gogita	46	KAPSIS Milalis	19
16 ASATIANI Malkhaz		KARAGOUNIS Georgios	20
17 KOBIASHVILI Levan		KATSOURANIS Konstantinos	21
Tr: GIRESSE Alain		Tr: REHHAGEL Otto	
7 TSIKITISHVILI Levan	46		
9 IASHVILI Alexander	59		

Olympic Stadium, Kyiv
30-03-2005, 19:15, 60 000, Michel SVK

UKR 1 0 DEN

Voronin 68

UKRAINE				DENMARK			
1	SHOVKOVSKI Alexandr					SORENSEN Thomas	1
2	NESMACHNY Andriy					POULSEN Christian	2
3	SVIDERSKKY Vyacheslav					PRISKE Brian	3
4	TYMOSHYUK Anatoliy					KROLDRUP Per	4
5	YEZERSKI Vladimir		70		70		JENSEN Niclas	5
6	RUSOL Andrey					HELVEG Thomas	6
8	KOSYRIN Aleksandr	60				GRAVESEN Thomas	7
9	HUSYEV Oleh					GRONKJAER Jesper	8
10	VORONIN Andrey	90				TOMASSON Jon Dahl	9
11	VOROBEY Andriy			84		JORGENSEN Martin	10
14	GUSIN Andrei			75		ROMMEDAHL Dennis	11
	Tr: BLOKHIN Oleg					Tr: OLSEN Morten	
13	MATIUKHIN Sergey	90		75		SILBERBAUER Michael	13
15	RADCHENKO Aleksandr	84		84	84	CHRISTIANSEN Jesper	14
17	BYELIK Olekcii	84	60		70	MOLLER Peter	18

Lokomotivi, Tbilisi
30-03-2005, 20:30, 10 000, Hauge NOR

GEO 2 5 TUR

Amisulashvili 13, Iashvili 40

Seyhan 12, Tekke 2 20 35
Avci 72, Sanli 89

GEORGIA				TURKEY			
12	DEVADZE Akaki	22				RECBER Rustu	1
2	MJAVANADZE Kakhaber					SEYHAN Tolga	2
3	KHIZANEISHVILI Otar	17				TORAMAN Ibrahim	4
4	KALADZE Kakha					BELOZOGLU Emre	5
7	TSIKITISHVILI Levan	76				OZAT Umit	6
9	IASHVILI Alexander		88			TEKKE Fatih	9
11	ASHVETIA Mikhail		46			BASTURK Yildiray	10
14	GOGUA Gogita		83			ALTINTOP Hamit	11
15	AMISULASHVILI Aleksander					AVCI Koray	15
16	ASATIANI Malkhaz					KARADENIZ Gokdeniz	16
17	KOBIASHVILI Levan		63			ATES Necati	18
	Tr: GIRESSE Alain					Tr: YANAL Ersun	
1	LOMAIA George	22	46			CIMSIR Huseyin	8
6	SALUKVADZE Lasha	17	63			SANLI Tuncay	17
8	BURDULI Vladimir	76	88			ALTINTOP Halil	21

Karaiskaki, Piraeus
30-03-2005, 21:30, 31 700, Layec FRA

GRE 2 0 ALB

Charisteas 33, Karagounis 84

GREECE				ALBANIA			
1	NIKOPOLIDIS Antonios					LIKA Ilion	1
2	SEITARIDIS Giourkas					BEQIRI Elvin	2
5	BASINAS Angelos					OSMANI Tefik	4
7	ZAGORAKIS Theodoros					CANA Lorik	5
8	GIANNAKOPOULOS Stylianos	87				SKELA Ervin	13
9	CHARISTEAS Angelos					LALA Altin	14
15	VRYZAS Zizis	89	46			MUKA Oevi	15
18	GOUMAS Ioannis		85			DURO Klodian	18
20	KARAGOUNIS Georgios		65			BOGDANI Erion	22
21	KATSOURANIS Konstantinos					HAXHI Altin	23
25	KYRGIAKOS Sotiris					LICI Suat	24
	Tr: REHHAGEL Otto					Tr: BRIEGEL Hans-Peter	
33	AMANATIDIS Ioannis	87	85	85		DALLKU Armend	3
44	GEKAS Theofanis	89	46	46		RAKLLI Altin	10
			65	65		TARE Igli	17

Qemal Stafa, Tirana
4-06-2005, 20:30, BCD, Tudor ROU

ALB 3 2 GEO

Tare 2 6 56, Skela 33

Burduli 85, Kobiashvili 94

ALBANIA				GEORGIA			
1	LIKA Ilion					STURUA Zviadi	1
2	BEQIRI Elvin					SALUKVADZE Lasha	3
6	HASI Besnik					KALADZE Kakha	4
8	JUPI Redi					KVIRKVELIA Dato	5
11	ALIAJ Ardian					REKHVIASHVILI Alexander	7
13	SKELA Ervin	85	76			DEMETRADZE George	9
17	TARE Igli					KOBIASHVILI Levan	10
18	DURO Klodian					KHIZANISHVILI Zurab	13
19	OSMANI Tefik					JAKOBIA Lasha	14
22	BOGDANI Erion	66	58			ASATIANI Malkhaz	16
23	HAXHI Altin	28	66			MAGHRADZE Levan	18
	Tr: BRIEGEL Hans-Peter					Tr: GIRESSE Alain	
3	CIPI Geri	28	66	66		BURDULI Vladimir	8
9	MYRTAJ Florian	66	76	76		BOBOKHIDZE Michael	11
20	SHKEMBI Blendi	85	58	58		DARASELIA Vitali	15

Besiktas Inönü, Istanbul
4-06-2005, 21:00, 26 700, Merk GER

TUR 0 0 GRE

TURKEY			GREECE		
1	RECBER Rustu		NIKOPOLIDIS Antonios	1	
2	SEYHAn Tolga		SEITARIDIS Giourkas	2	
5	BELOZOGLU Emre	79	BASINAS Angelos	6	
6	OZAT Umit		GIANNAKOPOULOS Stylianos	8	
8	AVCI Koray	46	CHARISTEAS Angelos	9	
9	TEKKE Fatih		FYSSAS Panagiotis	14	
10	BASTURK Yildiray	90	VRYZAS Zizis	15	
11	ALTINTOP Hamit		GOUMAS Ioannis	18	
17	CIMSIR Huseyin		KAPSIS Mihalis	19	
16	KARADENIZ Gokdeniz	61	KARAGOUNIS Georgios	20	
19	TORAMAN Ibrahim		KATSOURANIS Konstantinos	21	
	Tr: YANAL Ersun		Tr: REHHAGEL Otto		
4	YAVUZ Erdinc	79			
17	SANLI Tuncay	46			
18	ATES Necati	61			

Olympic Stadium, Kyiv
4-06-2005, 19:15, 45 000, Lehner AUT

UKR 2 0 KAZ

Shevchenko 18, Avdeyev OG 83

UKRAINE				KAZAKHSTAN			
1	SHOVKOVSKI Alexandr					NOVIKOV Yuriy	1
2	NESMACHNY Andriy					LYAPKIN Dmitri	2
4	TYMOSHYUK Anatoliy					BAIZHANOV Maxat	6
5	YEZERSKi Vladimir	83				AVDEYEV Igor	7
6	RUSOL Andrey			56		SMAKOV Samat	8
7	SHEVCHENKO Andriy					KARPOVICH Andrey	9
8	ROTAN Ruslan			31		RADIONOV Denis	12
9	HUSYEV Oleh					BALTIYEV Ruslan	14
10	VORONIN Andrey	70	79			FAMILTSEV Alexander	15
11	VOROBEY Andriy					DUBINSKIY Renat	17
18	RADCHENKO Aleksandr	46				KROKHMAL Alexandr	21
	Tr: BLOKHIN Oleg					Tr: TIMOFEYEV Sergei	
3	FEDOROV Sergyi	83	56	56		NIZOVTSEV Maxim	11
14	GUSIN Andrei	46	31	31		CHICHULIN Anton	16
17	BYELIK Olekcii	70	79	79		TRAVIN Andrey	19

Central Stadium, Almaty
8-06-2005, 21:00, 20 000, Kassai HUN

KAZ   **0**   **6**   **TUR**

Tekke 2 [13] [85], Toraman [15]
Sanli 2 [41] [90], Altintop [88]

KAZAKHSTAN				TURKEY
1 NOVIKOV Yuriy				CATKIC Omer 12
2 LYAPKIN Dmitri				SEYHAN Tolga 2
6 BAIZHANOV Maxat	46		66	BELOZOGLU Emre 5
7 AVDEYEV Igor				OZAT Umit 6
9 KARPOVICH Andrey				TEKKE Fatih 9
11 NIZOVTSEV Maxim				ALTINTOP Hamit 11
12 RADIONOV Denis	66			CIMSIR Huseyin 15
14 BALTIYEV Ruslan			86	KARADENIZ Gokdeniz 16
15 FAMILTSEV Alexander	59			SANLI Tuncay 17
20 DUBINSKIY Renat			46	ATES Necati 18
21 KROKHMAL Alexandr				TORAMAN Ibrahim 19
Tr: TIMOFEYEV Sergei				Tr: YANAL Ersun
8 SMAKOV Samat	59		66	BALCI Serkan 14
10 LITVINENKO Oleg	66		46	ALTINTOP Halil 21
16 CHICHULIN Anton	46		86	AKIN Serhat 22

Parken, Copenhagen
8-06-2005, 20:00, 26 366, Frojdfeldt SWE

DEN   **3**   **1**   **ALB**

Larsen 2 [5] [47], Jorgensen [55]   Bogdani [73]

DENMARK				ALBANIA
1 SORENSEN Thomas				LIKA Ilion 1
2 POULSEN Christian				BEQIRI Elvin 2
3 KROLDRUP Per				CANA Lorik 5
4 NIELSEN Per				HASI Besnik 6
5 JENSEN Niclas			92	JUPI Redi 8
6 HELVEG Thomas				ALIAJ Ardian 11
7 GRAVESEN Thomas	60		66	SKELA Ervin 13
8 LARSEN Soren				LALA Altin 14
9 TOMASSON Jon Dahl	87		82	TARE Igli 17
10 JORGENSEN Martin				OSMANI Tefik 19
11 ROMMEDAHL Dennis	71			BOGDANI Erion 22
Tr: OLSEN Morten				Tr: BRIEGEL Hans-Peter
14 JENSEN Daniel	60		82	MYRTAJ Florian 9
15 PEREZ Kenneth	87		66	DURO Klodian 18
17 SILBERBAUER Michael	71		92	SINA Elvis 25

Karaiskaki, Piraeus
8-06-2005, 21:30, 33 500, Temmink NED

GRE   **0**   **1**   **UKR**

Gusin [82]

GREECE				UKRAINE
1 NIKOPOLIDIS Antonios				SHOVKOVSKI Alexandr 1
2 SEITARIDIS Giourkas				NESMACHNY Andriy 2
6 BASINAS Angelos				FEDOROV Sergyi 3
7 ZAGORAKIS Theo				TYMOSHYUK Anatoliy 4
8 GIANNAKOPOULOS Stylianos				YEZERSKi Vladimir 5
9 CHARISTEAS Angelos				RUSOL Andrey 6
14 FYSSAS Panagiotis		92		SHEVCHENKO Andriy 7
15 VRYZAS Zisis				HUSYEV Oleh 9
18 GOUMAS Ioannis	86	90		VORONIN Andrey 10
19 KAPSIS Mihalis	56	57		VOROBEY Andriy 11
20 KARAGOUNIS Georgios	35			GUSIN Andrei 14
Tr: REHHAGEL Otto				Tr: Blokhin Oleg
10 TSIARTAS Vassilios	35	57		ROTAN Ruslan 8
17 PAPADOPOULOS Dimitrios	86	92		BYELIK Olekcii 17
24 VYNTRA Loukas	56	90		SHELAEV Oleg 19

GROUP 3

Rheinpark, Vaduz
18-08-2004, 20:15, 912, Bozinovski MKD

LIE   **1**   **2**   **EST**

D'Elia [49]   Viikmae [34], Lindpere [80]

LIECHTENSTEIN				ESTONIA
1 HEEB Martin				KOTENKO Artur 1
2 TELSER Martin				ALLAS Teet 2
3 STOCKLASA Michael				JAAGER Enar 3
4 HASLER Daniel				PIIROJA Raio 4
5 RITTER Christof	24			ROOBA Urmes 5
6 STOCKLASA Martin				RAHN Taavi 6
7 BECK Roger	64		66	SMIRNOV Maksim 7
8 GERSTER Andreas	90			REIM Martin 8
9 BECK Thomas	80			VIIKMAE Kristen 9
10 FRICK Mario			92	ZAHOVAIKO Vjatseslav 10
11 D'ELIA Fabio			60	TEREKHOV Sergei 11
Tr: ANDERMATT Martin				Tr: PIJPERS Arno
14 ROHRER Raphael	64		60	LINDPERE Joel 14
17 VOGT Franz-Josef	80		66	HAAVISTU Kert 15
			92	TEEVER Ingemar 16

Tehelné Pole, Bratislava
18-08-2004, 20:15, 5 016, Kassai HUN

SVK   **3**   **1**   **LUX**

Vittek [26], Gresko [48], Demo [89]   Strasser [2]

SLOVAKIA				LUXEMBOURG
1 KONIG Miroslav				BESIC Alija 1
2 GRESKO Vratislav				PETERS Rene 2
3 ZABAVNIK Radioslav				REITER Claude 3
4 KRATOCHVIL Roman				HOFFMANN Eric 4
5 VARGA Stanislav				STRASSER Jeff 5
6 KARHAN Miroslav				REMY Sebastien 6
7 MINTAL Marek				SCHAULS Manuel 7
8 NEMETH Szilard	84		61	LEWECK Alphonse 8
9 MICHALIK Rastislav	46		61	BRAUN Gordon 9
10 JANOCKO Vladimir	68			CARDONI Manuel 10
11 VITTEK Robert			74	HUSS Daniel 11
Tr: GALIS Dusan				Tr: SIMONSEN Allan
15 SESTAK Stanislav	84		74	LEWECK Charles 13
16 CHECH Marek	46		61	MANNON Paul 15
18 DEMO Igor	68		61	MOLITOR Greg 16

Le Coq Arena, Tallinn
4-09-2005, 18:00, 3 000, Kelly IRL

EST 4 - 0 LUX

Teever 7, Schauls OG 41, Oper 61
Viikmae 67

ESTONIA			LUXEMBOURG
1 POOM Mart			BESIC Alija 1
2 ALLAS Teet			PETERS Rene 2
3 JAAGER Enar		90	REITER Claude 3
4 PIIROJA Raio			HOFFMANN Eric 4
5 ROOBA Urmes			STRASSER Jeff 5
6 RAHN Taavi			REMY Sebastien 6
7 TEEVER Ingemar			SCHAULS Manuel 7
8 REIM Martin	75		LEWECK Alphonse 8
9 VIIKMAE Kristen		67	BRAUN Gordon 9
10 ZAHOVAIKO Vjatseslav	46	81	CARDONI Manuel 10
11 LINDPERE Joel	62	34	HUSS Daniel 11
Tr: PIJPERS Arno			Tr: SIMONSEN Allan
13 LEETMA Liivo	75	67	LEWECK Charles 13
14 OPER Andres	46	81	DI DOMENICO Sven 14
15 KLAVAN Ragnar	62	90	HELLENBRAND Xavier 17

Dinamo, Moscow
4-09-2004, 19:00, 11 500, Mejuto Gonzalez ESP

RUS 1 - 1 SVK

Bulykin 14
Vittek 87

RUSSIA			SLOVAKIA
1 MALAFEEV Vyacheslav			CONTOFALSKY Kamil 1
2 ANYUKOV Aleksandr			GRESKO Vratislav 2
3 SHARONOV Roman		83	HANEK Michal 3
4 SMERTIN Alexei			KRATOCHVIL Roman 4
5 EVSEEV Vadim	46		VARGA Stanislav 5
6 KOLODINE Denis			KARHAN Miroslav 6
7 ALENICHEV Dmitry			MINTAL Marek 7
8 KHOKHLOV Dmitry	66	76	NEMETH Szilard 8
9 BULYKIN Dmtri		76	MICHALIK Rastislav 9
10 KARYAKA Andrei			ZABAVNIK Radioslav 10
11 KERZHAKOV Alexander			VITTEK Robert 11
Tr: YARTSEV Georgy			Tr: GALIS Dusan
15 SENNIKOV Dmitri	46	76	BRESKA Mario 14
18 BOYARINTSEV Denis	66	76	CECH Marek 16
		83	REITER Lubomir 17

Skonto, Riga
4-09-2004, 20:15, 9 500, Poll ENG

LVA 0 - 2 POR

Cristiano Ronaldo 57, Pauleta 58

LATVIA			PORTUGAL
1 KOLINKO Alexandrs			RICARDO 1
2 STEPANOVS Igors			PAULO FERREIRA 2
3 ASTAFJEVS Vitalijs			JORGE ANDRADE 4
4 ZEMLINSKIS Mihails			COSTINHA 6
5 LAIZANS Juris			PAULETA 9
6 LOBANOVS Valentins		68	SIMAO SABROSA 11
7 ISAKOVS Aleksandrs		73	VALENTE Nuno 14
8 BLEIDELIS Imants			RICARDO CARVALHO 16
9 VERPAKOVSKIS Maris		82	CRISTIANO RONALDO 17
10 RUBINS Andrejs			MANICHE 18
11 PROHORENKOVS Andrejs	76		DECO 20
Tr: STARKOVS Aleksandrs			Tr: SCOLARI Luiz Felipe
14 RIMKUS Vits	76	82	PETIT 8
		73	CANEIRA 15
		68	BOA MORTE 25

Josy-Barthel, Luxembourg
8-09-2004, 20:00, 2 125, Kasnaferis GRE

LUX 3 - 4 LVA

Braun 11, Leweck 55, Cardoni 62
Verpakovskis 4, Zemlinskis 40p, Hoffman OG 65, Prohorenkovs 67

LUXEMBOURG			LATVIA
1 BESIC Alija			KOLINKO Alexandrs 1
2 PETERS Rene	93		STEPANOVS Igors 2
3 HELLENBRAND Xavier			ASTAFJEVS Vitalijs 3
4 HOFFMANN Eric			ZEMLINSKIS Mihails 4
5 STRASSER Jeff			LAIZANS Juris 5
6 REMY Sebastien			LOBANOVS Valentins 6
7 SCHAULS Manuel			ISAKOVS Aleksandrs 7
8 LEWECK Alphonse	88	32	BLEIDELIS Imants 8
9 BRAUN Gordon	77		VERPAKOVSKIS Maris 9
10 CARDONI Manuel			RUBINS Andrejs 10
11 MOLITOR Greg		63	RIMKUS Vits 11
Tr: SIMONSEN Allan			Tr: ANDREJEVS Jurijs
13 LEWECK Charles	77	32	PROHORENKOVS Andrejs 14
14 DI DOMENICO Sven	93	63	SEMJONOVS Igors 15
16 COLLETTE Dan	88		

Tehelné Pole, Bratislava
8-09-2004, 20:15, 5 620, Delevic SCG

SVK 7 - 0 LIE

Vittek 3 15 59 81, Karhan 42
Nemeth 84, Mintal 85, Zabavnik 92

SLOVAKIA			LIECHTENSTEIN
1 CONTOFALSKY Kamil			HEEB Martin 1
2 GRESKO Vratislav	62		TELSER Martin 2
3 HANEK Michal			VOGT Franz-Josef 3
4 KRATOCHVIL Roman	46		D'ELIA Fabio 4
5 DEMO Igor	46		BURGMEIER Patrick 5
6 KARHAN Miroslav			STOCKLASA Martin 6
7 MINTAL Marek			BECK Roger 7
8 NEMETH Szilard		76	BUCHEL Martin 8
9 CECH Marek			BECK Thomas 9
10 ZABAVNIK Radioslav			FRICK Mario 10
11 VITTEK Robert		70	ROHRER Raphael 11
Tr: GALIS Dusan			Tr: ANDERMATT Martin
13 PETRAS Martin	46	76	ALABOR Claudio 14
14 BRESKA Mario	62	70	FRICK Christoph 16
15 JANOCKO Vladimir	46		

Dr. Magalhaes Pessoa, Leiria
8-09-2004, 21:15, 27 214, Demirlek TUR

POR 4 - 0 EST

Cristiano Ronaldo 75
Helder Postiga 2 83 91+, Pauleta 86

PORTUGAL			ESTONIA
1 RICARDO			POOM Mart 1
2 PAULO FERREIRA			ALLAS Teet 2
4 RUI JORGE	55		JAAGER Enar 3
5 JORGE ANDRADE			PIIROJA Raio 4
6 COSTINHA		46	ROOBA Urmes 5
9 PAULETA			LEETMA Liivo 6
11 SIMAO SABROSA	71	64	TEEVER Ingemar 7
16 RICARDO CARVALHO			REIM Martin 8
17 CRISTIANO RONALDO			OPER Andres 9
18 MANICHE	46		LINDPERE Joel 10
20 DECO		71	TEREKHOV Sergei 11
Tr: SCOLARI Luiz Felipe			Tr: PIJPERS Arno
13 MIGUEL	55	71	ZAHOVAIKO Vjatseslav 14
23 HELDER POSTIGA	46	46	KLAVAN Ragnar 15
25 BOA MORTE	71	64	VIIKMAE Kristen 16

Josy-Barthel, Luxembourg
9-10-2004, 17:00, 3 670, Braamhaar NED

LUX 0 4 RUS

Sychev 3 [56] [69] [86], Arshavin [62]

LUXEMBOURG				RUSSIA	
1 BESIC Alija				MALAFEEV Vyacheslav	1
2 PETERS Rene				ANYUKOV Aleksandr	2
3 FEDERSPIEL Ben				BUGAEV Aleksej	3
4 HOFFMANN Eric				SMERTIN Alexei	4
5 STRASSER Jeff				EVSEEV Vadim	5
6 REMY Sebastien				IGNASHEVICH Sergei	6
7 SCHAULS Manuel	59	46		KANTONISTOV Lubomir	7
8 LEWECK Alphonse		75		GUSEV Rolan	8
9 BRAUN Gordon		67		BULYKIN Dmtri	9
10 CARDONI Manuel	77			ARSHAVIN Andrei	10
11 MOLITOR Greg	77			SYCHEV Dmitri	11
Tr: SIMONSEN Allan				Tr: YARTSEV Georgy	
13 LEWECK Charles	77	46		BOYARINTSEV Denis	14
16 MANNON Paul	77	75		ALDONIN Evgeni	16
18 SCHNELL Tom	59	67		KIRICHENKO Dmitri	18

Tehelné Pole, Bratislava
9-10-2004, 17:30, 13 025, Farina ITA

SVK 4 1 LVA

Nemeth [46], Reiter [50]
Karhan 2 [55] [87]

Verpakovskis [3]

SLOVAKIA				LATVIA	
1 CONTOFALSKY Kamil				KOLINKO Alexandrs	1
2 GRESKO Vratislav		90		ASTAFJEVS Vitalijs	3
3 HANEK Michal				KORABLOVS Igors	4
4 KRATOCHVIL Roman	46			LAIZANS Juris	5
5 VARGA STanislav				ZIRNIS Dzintaris	6
6 KARHAN Miroslav				ISAKOVS Aleksandrs	7
7 MINTAL Marek	46	86		BLEIDELIS Imants	8
8 NEMETH Szilard				VERPAKOVSKIS Maris	9
9 MICHALIK Rastislav	75	76		RIMKUS Vits	11
10 ZABAVNIK Radoslav				LOBANOVS Valentins	14
11 VITTEK Robert				SMIRNOVS Maris	18
Tr: GALIS Dusan				Tr: ANDREJEVS Jurijs	
15 JANOCKO Vladimir	46	90		KOLESNICENKO Vladimirs	10
16 CECH Marek	75	86		SEMJONOVS Igors	15
17 REITER Lubomir	46	76		MIHOLAPS Mihails	16

Rheinpark, Vaduz
9-10-2004, 19:15, 3 548, Panic BIH

LIE 2 2 POR

Burgmeier [48], Beck.T [76]

Pauleta [23], Hasler OG [39]

LIECHTENSTEIN				PORTUGAL	
1 JEHLE Peter				RICARDO	1
2 TELSER Martin				PAULO FERREIRA	2
3 STOCKLASA Michael				JORGE ANDRADE	4
4 HASLER Daniel		46		COSTINHA	6
5 RITTER Christof				PAULETA	9
6 STOCKLASA Martin		57		SIMAO SABROSA	11
7 ROHRER Raphael	46			RICARDO CARVALHO	16
8 GERSTER Andreas		62		CRISTIANO RONALDO	17
9 BECK Thomas	88			MANICHE	18
10 FRICK Mario	91			DECO	20
11 BURGMEIER Franz				JORGE RIBEIRO	25
Tr: ANDERMATT Martin				Tr: SCOLARI Luiz Felipe	
14 BECK Roger	46	57		PETIT	8
16 FRICK Daniel	91	46		TIAGO	19
17 BUCHEL Ronny	88	62		HELDER POSTIGA	23

Skonto, Riga
13-10-2004, 18:00, 8 500, Meyer GER

LVA 2 2 EST

Astafjevs [65], Laizans [82]

Oper [72], Teever [79]

LATVIA				ESTONIA	
1 KOLINKO Alexandrs				POOM Mart	1
2 STEPANOVS Igors	46			ALLAS Teet	2
3 ASTAFJEVS Vitalijs				JAAGER Enar	3
4 ZEMLINSKIS Mihails				PIIROJA Raio	4
5 LAIZANS Juris				ROOBA Urmes	5
6 ZIRNIS Dzintaris				RAHN Taavi	6
7 ISAKOVS Aleksandrs		85		TEEVER Ingemar	7
8 BLEIDELIS Imants	81			LINDPERE Joel	8
9 VERPAKOVSKIS Maris				VIIKMAE Kristen	9
11 PROHORENKOVS Andrejs				OPER Andres	10
14 LOBANOVS Valentins		85		TEREKHOV Sergei	11
Tr: ANDREJEVS Jurijs				Tr: GOES Jelle	
10 RUBINS Andrejs	46	85		KRUGLOV Dmitri	15
18 RIMKUS Vits	81	85		LEETMA Liivo	16

Josy-Barthel, Luxembourg
13-10-2004, 20:00, 3 478, Jara CZE

LUX 0 4 LIE

Martin Stocklasa [41]
Burgmeier 2 [44] [85], Frick [57p]

LUXEMBOURG				LIECHTENSTEIN	
1 BESIC Alija				JEHLE Peter	1
2 FEDERSPIEL Ben				TELSER Martin	2
3 HELLENBRAND Xavier				STOCKLASA Michael	3
4 HOFFMANN Eric				HASLER Daniel	4
5 STRASSER Jeff				RITTER Christof	5
6 REMY Sebastien				STOCKLASA Martin	6
7 LEWECK Charles		57		BECK Roger	7
8 LEWECK Alphonse	73			GERSTER Andreas	8
9 BRAUN Gordon		88		BECK Thomas	9
10 CARDONI Manuel		82		FRICK Mario	10
11 MOLITOR Greg	46			BURGMEIER Franz	11
Tr: SIMONSEN Allan				Tr: ANDERMATT Martin	
14 DI DOMENICO Sven	73	82		ROHRER Raphael	14
17 COLLETTE Dan	46	88		BUCHEL Martin	17
		57		D'ELIA Fabio	18

Jose Alvalade, Lisbon
13-10-2004, 21:15, 27 258, Vassaras GRE

POR 7 1 RUS

Pauleta [26], Cristiano Ronaldo 2 [39] [69]
Deco [45] Simao Sabrosa [82], Petit 2 [89] [92+]

Arshavin [79]

PORTUGAL				RUSSIA	
1 RICARDO				MALAFEEV Vyacheslav	1
2 PAULO FERREIRA				ANYUKOV Aleksandr	2
4 JORGE ANDRADE				BUGAEV Aleksej	3
6 COSTINHA				SMERTIN Alexei	4
9 PAULETA	67			EVSEEV Vadim	5
11 SIMAO SABROSA				IGNASHEVICH Sergei	6
13 MIGUEL		46		SENNIKOV Dmtri	7
16 RICARDO CARVALHO		71		ALDONIN Evgeni	8
17 CRISTIANO RONALDO	85			BULYKIN Dmtri	9
18 MANICHE	72			ARSHAVIN Andrei	10
20 DECO		46		SYCHEV Dmitri	11
Tr: SCOLARI Luiz Felipe				Tr: YARTSEV Georgy	
8 PETIT	72	71		BOYARINTSEV Denis	14
21 NUNO GOMES	67	46		GUSEV Rolan	17
28 BOA MORTE	85	46		KIRICHENKO Dmitri	18

Rheinpark, Vaduz
17-11-2004, 19:00, 1 460, Szabo HUN

LIE 1   3 LVA

Frick.M 32

Verpakovskis 7, Zemlinskis 57
Prohorenkovs 89

#	LIECHTENSTEIN				LATVIA	#
1	JEHLE Peter				KOLINKO Alexandrs	1
2	VOGT Franz-Josef	88			STEPANOVS Igors	2
3	STOCKLASA Michael				ASTAFJEVS Vitalijs	3
4	HASLER Daniel				ZEMLINSKIS Mihails	4
5	RITTER Christof			90	LAIZANS Juris	5
6	STOCKLASA Martin				ZIRNIS Dzintaris	6
7	BECK Roger	64			ISAKOVS Aleksandrs	7
8	GERSTER Andreas	80			BLEIDELIS Imants	8
9	BECK Thomas				VERPAKOVSKIS Maris	9
10	FRICK Mario			92	RUBINS Andrejs	10
11	BURGMEIER Franz			59	RIMKUS Vits	11
	Tr: ANDERMATT Martin				Tr: ANDREJEVS Jurijs	
14	ROHRER Raphael	64		90	LOBANOVS Valentins	14
15	FRICK Daniel	80		92	ZAKRESEVSKIS Arturs	16
16	BUCHEL Ronny	88		59	PROHORENKOVS Andrejs	18

Kuban Stadium, Krasnodar
17-11-2004, 19:00, 29 000, Busacca SUI

RUS 4   0 EST

Karyaka 23, Izmailov 25
Sychev 32 Loskov 67p

#	RUSSIA				ESTONIA	#
1	MALAFEEV Vyacheslav				KAALMA Martin	1
2	EVSEEV Vadim				ALLAS Teet	2
3	BUGAEV Aleksej				JAAGER Enar	3
4	SMERTIN Alexei				PIIROJA Raio	4
5	BEREZUTSKY Vassili				ROOBA Urmes	5
6	IZMAILOV Marat				RAHN Taavi	6
7	KHOKHLOV Dmitri	88	90		TEEVER Ingemar	7
8	LOSKOV Dmitri	81			LINDPERE Joel	8
9	KARYAKA Andrei				VIIKMAE Kristen	9
10	KERZHAKOV Alexander				OPER Andres	10
11	SYCHEV Dmitri		81		TEREKHOV Sergei	11
	Tr: YARTSEV Georgy				Tr: GOES Jelle	
14	GUSEV Rolan	88	81		KLAVAN Ragnar	14
15	SEMSHOV Igor	81	90		KRUGLOV Dmitri	15

Josy-Barthel, Luxembourg
17-11-2004, 20:00, 8 045, Godulyan UKR

LUX 0   5 POR

Federspiel OG 11, Cristiano Ronaldo 28
Maniche 52, Pauleta 2 67 82

#	LUXEMBOURG				PORTUGAL	#
1	BESIC Alija				RICARDO	1
2	FEDERSPIEL Ben				PAULO FERREIRA	2
3	REITER Claude				JORGE ANDRADE	4
4	HOFFMANN Eric		58		COSTINHA	6
5	SCHAULS Manuel				PAULETA	9
6	REMY Sebastien				RICARDO CARVALHO	16
7	PETERS Rene				CRISTIANO RONALDO	17
8	LEWECK Alphonse		71		MANICHE	18
9	MANNON Paul	78			DECO	20
10	LEWECK Charles				JORGE RIBEIRO	25
11	HUSS Daniel	78	46		BOA MORTE	28
	Tr: SIMONSEN Allan				Tr: SCOLARI Luiz Felipe	
14	DI DOMENICO Sven	78	58		PETIT	8
17	COLLETTE Dan	78	71		TIAGO	19
			46		RICARDO QUARESMO	27

Rheinpark, Vaduz
26-03-2005, 17:00, 2 400, Berntsen NOR

LIE 1   2 RUS

Beck.T 40

Kerzhakov 23, Karyaka 37

#	LIECHTENSTEIN				RUSSIA	#
1	JEHLE Peter				MALAFEEV Vyacheslav	1
2	TELSER Martin				EVSEEV Vadim	2
3	STOCKLASA Michael				BEREZUTSKY Vassili	3
4	HASLER Daniel				BEREZUTSKY Alexei	4
5	RITTER Christof				KARYAKA Andrei	5
6	D'ELIA Fabio	53			IGNASHEVICH Sergei	6
7	BECK Roger	60	67		BYSTROV Vladimir	7
8	GERSTER Andreas		78		KHOKHLOV Dmitri	8
9	BECK Thomas	55			ARSHAVIN Andrei	9
10	FRICK Mario				LOSKOV Dmitri	10
11	BURGMEIER Franz				KERZHAKOV Alexander	11
	Tr: ANDERMATT Martin				Tr: YARTSEV Georgy	
14	VOGT Franz-Josef	60	78		ALDONIN Evgeni	15
17	BUCHEL Ronny	53	67		IZMAILOV Marat	16
			55		SYCHEV Dmitri	17

Le Coq Arena, Tallinn
26-03-2005, 18:00, 3 051, Frojdfeldt SWE

EST 1   2 SVK

Oper 57

Mintal 58, Reiter 65

#	ESTONIA				SLOVAKIA	#
1	KOTENKO Artur				CONTOFALSKY Kamil	1
2	ALLAS Teet				PETRAS Martin	2
3	STEPANOV Andrei				VALACHOVIC Jozef	3
4	JAAGER Enar				HLINKA Peter	4
5	ROOBA Urmes	80			VARGA Stanislav	5
6	REIM Martin				KARHAN Miroslav	6
7	TEREKHOV Sergei	80	55		KISEL Karol	7
8	LINDPERE Joel	87	90		NEMETH Szilard	8
9	VIIKMAE Kristen		46		MICHALIK Rastislav	9
10	OPER Andres				ZABAVNIK Radoslav	10
11	KRUGLOV Dmitri				MINTAL Marek	11
	Tr: GOES Jelle				Tr: GALIS Dusan	
14	KLAVAN Ragnar	80	90		CECH Marek	13
17	ZAHOVAIKO Vjatseslav	87	55		JAKUBKO Martin	16
18	TEEVER Ingemar	80	46		REITER Lubomir	17

Le Coq Arena, Tallinn
30-03-2005, 18:00, 8 850, Paparesta ITA

EST 1   1 RUS

Terekhov 63

Arshavin 18

#	ESTONIA				RUSSIA	#
1	KOTENKO Artur				AKINFEEV Igor	1
2	ALLAS Teet				BEREZUTSKY Alexei	2
3	STEPANOV Andrei				BEREZUTSKY Vassili	3
4	JAAGER Enar				SMERTIN Alexei	4
5	KRUGLOV Dmitri		72		ZHIRKOV Yury	5
6	RAHN Taavi				IGNASHEVICH Sergei	6
7	TEREKHOV Sergei	84			BYSTROV Vladimir	7
8	REIM Martin		63		KHOKHLOV Dmitri	8
9	VIIKMAE Kristen	90	66		ARSHAVIN Andrei	9
10	OPER Andres				LOSKOV Dmitri	10
11	LINDPERE Joel	24			KERZHAKOV Alexander	11
	Tr: GOES Jelle				Tr: YARTSEV Georgy	
15	KLAVAN Ragnar	24	63		KOLODINE Denis	14
17	SMIRNOV Maksim	84	72		KARYAKA Andrei	15
18	TEEVER Ingemar	90	66		SYCHEV Dmitri	17

Tehelné Pole, Bratislava
30-03-2005, 19:00, 21 000, Sars FRA

SVK 1 1 POR

Karhan [8p] — Helder Postiga [62]

#	SLOVAKIA			PORTUGAL	#
1	CONTOFALSKY Kamil			RICARDO	1
2	PETRAS Martin		63	PAULO FERREIRA	2
3	HANEK Michal	80		JORGE ANDRADE	4
4	HLINKA Peter			COSTINHA	6
5	VARGA Stanislav		57	PAULETA	9
6	KARHAN Miroslav		89	SIMAO SABROSA	11
7	JAKUBKO Martin	65		NUNO VALENTE	14
8	NEMETH Szilard			RICARDO CARVALHO	16
9	MICHALIK Rastislav	36		CHRISTIANO RONALDO	17
10	ZABAVNIK Radoslav			MANICHE	18
11	MINTAL Marek			DECO	20
	Tr: GALIS Dusan			Tr: SCOLARI Luiz Felipe	
14	HAD Marian	36	63	MIGUEL	13
16	KISEL Karol	80	57	HELDER POSTIGA	23
17	REITER Lubomir	65	89	HUGO VIANA	30

Skonto, Riga
30-03-2005, 19:00, 8 203, Kovacic CRO

LVA 4 0 LUX

Bleidelis [32], Laizans [38p], Verpakovskis 2 [73] [90]

#	LATVIA			LUXEMBOURG	#
1	KOLINKO Alexandrs			OBERWEIS Marc	1
2	STEPANOVS Igors		82	SCHAULS Manuel	2
3	ASTAFJEVS Vitalijs			HEINZ Tim	3
4	ZIRNIS Dzintars			HOFFMANN Eric	4
5	LAIZANS Juris			STRASSER Jeff	5
6	SMIRNOVS Maris			FERREIRA Joao	6
7	MOROZS Viktors		50	PETERS Rene	7
8	BLEIDELIS Imants	66		REMY Sebastien	8
9	VERPAKOVSKIS Maris			DURRER Phillippe	9
10	RUBINS Andrejs	39	89	PACE Carlo	10
11	PROHORENKOVS Andrejs	82		COLLETTE Dan	11
	Tr: ANDREJEVS Jurijs			Tr: HELLERS Guy	
13	ZAVORONKOVS Vladimirs	39	50	LEWECK Charles	15
15	MIHOLAPS Mihails	66	89	MANNON Paul	16
18	RIMKUS Vits	82	82	LANG Benoit	18

Petrovski, St. Petersburg
4-06-2005, 18:00, 21 575, Poulat FRA

RUS 2 0 LVA

Arshavin [56], Loskov [78p]

#	RUSSIA			LATVIA	#
1	AKINFEEV Igor			PIEDELS Andrejs	1
2	BEREZUTSKY Alexei			STEPANOVS Igors	2
3	BEREZUTSKY Vassili			ASTAFJEVS Vitalijs	3
4	SMERTIN Alexei			LAIZANS Juris	5
5	ZHIRKOV Yury			ZIRNIS Dzintaris	6
6	ANYUKOV Aleksandr		85	ISAKOVS Aleksandrs	7
7	SEMSHOV Igor	66		BLEIDELIS Imants	8
8	ALDONIN Evgeni	54		RUBINS Andrejs	9
9	ARSHAVIN Andrei	80	77	PROHORENKOVS Andrejs	10
10	LOSKOV Dmitri			VERPAKOVSKIS Maris	11
11	KERZHAKOV Alexander			SMIRNOVS Maris	14
	Tr: SYOMIN Yuri			Tr: ANDREJEVS Jurijs	
15	SENNIKOV Dmitri	66	85	ZAVORONKOVS Vladimirs	15
16	IZMAILOV Marat	80	77	RIMKUS Vits	18
18	BYSTROV Vladimir	54			

A. Le Coq Arena, Tallinn
4-06-2005, 18:00, 3 000, Whitby WAL

EST 2 0 LIE

Stepanov [27], Oper [57]

#	ESTONIA			LIECHTENSTEIN	#
1	KOTENKO Artur			JEHLE Peter	1
2	ALLAS Teet			TELSER Martin	2
3	STEPANOV Andrei		82	D'ELIA Fabio	3
4	JAAGER Enar			HASLER Daniel	4
5	KRUGLOV Dmitri			RITTER Christof	5
6	REIM Mart			STOCKLASA Martin	6
7	TEREKHOV Sergei	88		BECK Roger	7
8	LINDPERE Joel		56	GERSTER Andreas	8
9	VIIKMAE Kristen	70		BECK Thomas	9
10	OPER Andres			FRICK Mario	10
11	KLAVAN Ragnar	87		BURGMEIER Franz	11
	Tr: GOES Jelle			Tr: ANDERMATT Martin	
16	SMIRNOV Maksim	88	82	ALABOR Claudio	15
17	SAHAROV Aleksandr	87	56	BUCHEL Ronny	16
18	TEEVER Ingemar	70			

Estadio da Luz, Lisbon
4-06-2005, 19:45, 64 000, Collina ITA

POR 2 0 SVK

Fernando Meira [21], Cristiano Ronaldo [42]

#	PORTUGAL			SLOVAKIA	#
1	RICARDO			CONTOFALSKY Kamil	1
4	JORGE ANDRADE			PETRAS Martin	2
7	LUIS FIGO		64	HANEK Michal	3
8	PETIT			HLINKA Peter	4
9	PAULETA	79		VARGA Stanislav	5
15	CANEIRA			KARHAN Miroslav	6
17	CRISTIANO RONALDO	76		HAD Marian	7
18	MANICHE		59	NEMETH Szilard	8
20	DECO	88	59	JAKUBKO Martin	9
29	FERNANDO MEIRA			ZABAVNIK Radoslav	10
34	ALEX			MINTAL Marek	11
	Tr: SCOLARI Luiz Felipe			Tr: GALIS Dusan	
19	TIAGO	88	59	SLOVAK Samuel	14
23	HELDER POSTIGA	79	64	KISEL Karol	16
27	RICARDO QUARESMA	76	59	VITTEK Robert	18

Skonto, Riga
8-06-2005, 18:30, 8 000, Eriksson SWE

LVA 1 0 LIE

Bleidelis [17]

#	LATVIA			LIECHTENSTEIN	#
1	PIEDELS Andrejs			JEHLE Peter	1
2	STEPANOVS Igors			TELSER Martin	2
3	ASTAFJEVS Vitalijs		56	D'ELIA Fabio	3
5	LAIZANS Juris			HASLER Daniel	4
6	ZAVORONKOVS Vladimirs			RITTER Christof	5
7	KORABLOVS Igors			STOCKLASA Martin	6
8	BLEIDELIS Imants		77	BECK Roger	7
9	VERPAKOVSKIS Maris		92	BUCHEL Ronny	8
10	RUBINS Andrejs			BECK Thomas	9
11	PROHORENKOVS Andrejs	60		FRICK Mario	10
16	SMIRNOVS Maris			BURGMEIER Franz	11
	Tr: ANDREJEVS Jurijs			Tr: ANDERMATT Martin	
18	RIMKUS Vits	60	56	VOGT Franz-Josef	14
			92	BUCHEL Martin	15
			77	ROHRER Raphael	16

Josy-Barthel, Luxembourg
8-06-2005, 20:00, 2 108, Styles ENG

LUX 0 4 SVK

Nemeth [5], Mintal [15]
Kisel [54], Reiter [60]

#	LUXEMBOURG				#	SLOVAKIA
1	OBERWEIS Marc				1	CONTOFALSKY Kamil
2	FEDERSPIEL Ben	62	58		2	PETRAS Martin
3	REITER Claude				3	HANEK Michal
4	HOFFMANN Eric		46		4	HLINKA Peter
5	HEINZ Tim	22			5	VARGA Stanislav
6	LEWECK Charles				6	KARHAN Miroslav
7	STRASSER Jeff				7	KISEL Karol
8	REMY Sebastien				8	NEMETH Szilard
9	LEWECK Alphonse		46		9	HAD Marian
11	COLLETTE Dan				10	MINTAL Marek
18	LANG Benoit				11	VITTEK Robert
	Tr: HELLERS Guy					Tr: GALIS Dusan
10	PACE Carlo	90 22	46		14	SLOVAK Samuel
13	DURRER Phillippe	90	46		15	SNINSKY Dusan
15	SABOTIC Ernad	62	58		17	REITER Lubomir

A. Le Coq Arena, Tallinn
8-06-2005, 20:15, 10 280, Riley ENG

EST 0 1 POR

Cristiano Ronaldo [32]

#	ESTONIA					PORTUGAL	#
1	KOTENKO Artur					RICARDO	1
2	ALLAS Teet					JORGE ANDRADE	4
3	STEPANOV Andrei					COSTINHA	6
4	JAAGER Enar					LUIS FIGO	7
5	ROOBA Urmes		66			PAULETA	9
6	RAHN Taavi					CANEIRA	15
7	TEREKHOV Sergei	78	88			CRISTIANO RONALDO	17
8	REIM Martin		71			NUNO GOMES	18
9	VILKMAE Kristen	55				DECO	20
10	OPER Andres					FERNANDO MEIRA	29
11	KRUGLOV Dmitri	87				ALEX	34
	Tr: GOES Jelle					Tr: SCOLARI Luiz Felipe	
14	KLAVAN Ragnar	87	71			PETIT	8
17	SAHAROV Aleksandr	78	88			TIAGO	19
18	ZAHOVAIKO Vjatseslav	55	66			HELDER POSTIGA	23

GROUP 4

Lansdowne Road, Dublin
4-09-2004, 15:00, 36 000, Paniashvili GEO

IRL 3 0 CYP

Morrison [33], Reid [38], Keane [54]

#	REP OF IRELAND					CYPRUS	#
1	GIVEN Shay					PANAYIOTOY Nikos	1
2	CARR Stephen	71	65			CHARALAMBOUS Elias	3
3	O SHEA John	83				KAKOYIANNIS Loizos	4
4	CUNNINGHAM Kenny					MAKRIDIS Konstantinos	6
5	O BRIEN Andy					THEODOTOU Georgios	7
6	KAVANAGH Graham					SATSIAS Marinos	8
7	REID Andy		78			OKKAS Ioannis	9
8	KILBANE Kevin		71			CHARALAMPIDIS Konstinos	10
9	MORRISON Clinton	81				KONSTANTINOU Michael	11
10	KEANE Robbie					OKKARIDES Stelios	15
11	DUFF Damien					LAMBROU Lambros	18
	Tr: KERR Brian					Tr: VUKOTIC Momcilo	
13	MAYBURY Alan	83	71			MICHAIL Chrysostomos	13
14	FINNAN Steve	71	78			KRASSAS Asimakis S.	16
18	LEE Alan	81	65			ILIA Marios	17

St. Jakob-Park, Basel
4-09-2004, 17:30, 11 880, Tudor ROU

SUI 6 0 FRO

Vonlanthen 3 [10 14 57]
Rey 3 [29 44 55]

#	SWITZERLAND					FAROE ISLANDS	#
1	ZUBERBUHLER Pascal					KNUDSEN Jens	1
2	HAAS Bernt					OLSEN Suni	2
3	SPYCHER Christoph	46				JOHANNESEN Oli	3
4	MULLER Patrick					THORSTEINSSON Pol	4
5	YAKIN Murat					JACOBSEN Jon Roi	5
7	VOGEL Johann		69			JORGENSEN Claus Bech	6
7	CABANAS Ricardo	62				BENJAMINSEN Frodi	7
8	WICKY Raphael					JOHNSSON Julian	8
9	REY Alexandre	74	63			BORG Jakup	9
10	YAKIN Hakan		55			PETERSEN John	10
11	VONLANTHEN Johan					FREDERIKSBERG Jonhard	11
	Tr: KUHN Koebi					Tr: LARSEN Henrik	
16	HUGGEL Benjamin	62	55			JACOBSEN Rogvi	12
18	HAEBERLI Thomas	74	69			HANSEN Johan	13
19	MAGNIN Ludovic	46	63			DANIELSEN Atli	18

Stade de France, Saint-Denis/Paris
4-09-2004, 21:00, 43 527, Temmink NED

FRA 0 0 ISR

#	FRANCE					ISRAEL	#
23	COUPET Gregory					DAVIDOVITCH Nir	1
3	EVRA Patrice					BENADO Arik	4
4	VIEIRA Patrick					BEN HAIM Tal	5
5	GALLAS William		71			AFEK Omri	9
6	MAKELELE Claude					BADEER Valeed	10
12	HENRY Thierry					TAL Idan	11
14	ROTHEN Jerome	66				GOLAN Omer	12
16	MENDY Bernard	58	13			ANTEBI Igal	14
17	SQUILACI Sebastien		80			BENAYOUN Yossi	15
19	GIVET Gael					KATAN Yaniv	20
20	SAHA Louis					SABAN Klemi	21
	Tr: DOMENECH Raymond					Tr: GRANT Avraham	
7	PIRES Robert	66	13			KEISI Adoram	6
21	GIULY Ludovic	58	80			NIMNI Avi	8
			71			GAZAL Ravid	19

Tórsvøllur, Tórshavn
8-09-2004, 17:00, 5 917, Thomson SCO

FRO 0 2 FRA

Giuly [32], Cisse [73]

#	FAROE ISLANDS					FRANCE	#
1	MIKKELSEN Jakup					COUPET Gregory	23
2	OLSEN Suni					EVRA Patrice	3
4	THORSTEINSSON Pol		65			VIEIRA Patrick	4
5	JACOBSEN Jon Roi					GALLAS William	5
6	JACOBSEN Rogvi	75				PIRES Robert	7
7	BENJAMINSEN Frodi		63			HENRY Thierry	12
8	JOHNSSON Julian					SQUILACI Sebastien	17
9	BORG Jakup					PEDRETTI Benoit	18
11	FREDERIKSBERG Jonhard	68				GIVET Gael	19
12	JORGENSEN Claus Bech	83	8			SAHA Louis	20
13	JOHANNESEN Oli					GIULY Ludovic	21
	Tr: LARSEN Henrik					Tr: DOMENECH Raymond	
10	PETERSEN John	68	8			CISSE Djibril	9
14	FLOTUM Andrew	75	63			DHORASOO Vikash	13
18	DANIELSEN Atli	83					

St. Jakob-Park, Basel
8-09-2004, 20:30, 28 000, Vassarasa Kyros GRE

SUI	1 1	IRL

Yakin.H [17]

Morrison [8]

	SWITZERLAND			REP OF IRELAND	
1	ZUBERBUHLER Pascal			GIVEN Shay	1
2	HAAS Bernt			CARR Stephen	2
3	MAGNIN Ludovic			FINNAN Steve	3
4	MULLER Patrick			CUNNINGHAM Kenny	4
5	YAKIN Murat			O BRIEN Andy	5
6	VOGEL Jonann			KEANE Roy	6
7	CABANAS Ricardo	72		REID Andy	7
8	BARNETTA Tranquillo			KILBANE Kevin	8
9	REY Alexandre	84		MORRISON Clinton	9
10	YAKIN Hakan			KEANE Robbie	10
11	VONLANTHEN Johan	72		DUFF Damien	11
	Tr: KUHN Koebi			Tr: KERR Brian	
16	LONFAT Johann	72	72	KAVANAGH Graham	14
			84	DOHERTY Gary	17

Ramat Gan, Tel Aviv
8-09-2004, 20:50, 21 872, Shmolik BLR

ISR	2 1	CYP

Benayoun [64], Badeer [75]

Konstantinou [59]

	ISRAEL				CYPRUS	
1	DAVIDOVITCH Nir				PANAYIOTOY Nikos	1
4	BENADO Arik				KAKOYIANNIS Loizos	3
5	BEN HAIM Tal				NIKOLAOU Nikos	4
6	KEISI Adoram				MAKRIDIS Konstantinos	6
8	NIMNI Avi	57	31		THEODOTOU Georgios	7
10	BADEER Valeed				SATSIAS Marinos	8
11	TAL Idan	72	80		OKKAS Ioannis	9
12	GOLAN Omer		73	CHARALAMPIDIS Konst'inos		10
15	BENAYOUN Yossi				KONSTANTINOU Michael	11
20	KATAN Yaniv	83			OKKARIDES Stelios	15
21	SABAN Klemi				ILIA Marios	16
	Tr: GRANT Avraham				Tr: VUKOTIC Momcilo	
7	BALILI Pini	57	31		GEORGIOU Stavros	2
9	AFEK Omri	72	73	MICHAIL Chrysostomos		13
19	GAZAL Ravid	83	80	YIASOUMI Yiasoumis		14

G.S.P., Nicosia
9-10-2004, 20:00, 1 400, Gadiyev AZE

CYP	2 2	FRO

Konstantinou [15], Okkas [81]

Jorgensen [21], Jacobsen.R [43]

	CYPRUS				FAROE ISLANDS	
1	PANAYIOTOY Nikos				MIKKELSEN Jakup	1
3	NIKOLAOU Nikos				OLSEN Suni	2
6	OKKARIDES Stelios	61			THORSTEINSSON Pol	4
7	MAKRIDIS Konstantinos	68			JACOBSEN Jon Roi	5
9	OKKAS Ioannis		76		JACOBSEN Rogvi	6
10	CHARALAMPIDIS Konst'inos				BENJAMINSEN Frodi	7
11	KONSTANTINOU Michael				JOHNSSON Julian	8
13	CHARALAMBOUS Elias				BORG Jakup	9
14	GEORGIOU Stavros		70	FREDIKSBERG Jonhard		11
15	ILIA Marios		46	JORGENSEN Claus Bech		12
16	KRASSAS Asimakis	46			JOHANNESEN Oli	13
	Tr: VUKOTIC Momcilo				Tr: LARSEN Henrik	
2	KAIAFAS Costas	61	76		PETERSEN John	10
8	NEOFYTOU Marios	68	70		FLOTUM Andrew	14
17	SATSIAS Marinos	46	46		DANIELSEN Atli	15

Ramat Gan, Tel Aviv
9-10-2004, 20:05, 37 976, Sheild AUS

ISR	2 2	SUI

Benayoun 2 [9 48]

Frei [26], Vonlanthen [34]

	ISRAEL				SWITZERLAND	
1	DAVIDOVITCH Nir				ZUBERBUHLER Pascal	1
3	BEN HAIM Tal				HAAS Bernt	2
4	BENADO Arik				MAGNIN Ludovic	3
5	GERSHON Shimon	76			MULLER Patrick	4
6	KEISI Adoram		61		YAKIN Murat	5
7	BALILI Pini	59			VOGEL Jonann	6
10	BADEER Valeed				CABANAS Ricardo	7
11	TAL Idan		33		BARNETTA Tranquillo	8
15	BENAYOUN Yossi				FREI Alexander	9
18	AFEK Omri		79		YAKIN Hakan	10
19	GAZAL Ravid	46			VONLANTHEN Johan	11
	Tr: GRANT Avraham				Tr: KUHN Koebi	
8	NIMNI Avi	46	61	HENCHOZ Stephane		14
12	GOLAN Omer	59	79		LONFAT Johann	15
21	SABAN Klemi	76	33		GYGAX Daniel	17

Stade de France, Saint-Denis/Paris
9-10-2004, 21:00, 78 863, Dauden Ibanez ESP

FRA	0 0	IRL

	FRANCE			REP OF IRELAND	
16	BARTHEZ Fabien			GIVEN Shay	1
5	GALLAS William			CARR Stephen	2
7	PIRES Robert			O SHEA John	3
6	CISSE Djibril	81		CUNNINGHAM Kenny	4
11	WILTORD Sylvain			O BRIEN Andy	5
12	HENRY Thierry			KEANE Roy	6
13	SILVESTRE Mikael			FINNAN Steve	7
14	SQUILACI Sebastien			KILBANE Kevin	8
15	MAVUBA Rio	40		MORRISON Clinton	9
17	DACOURT Olivier	62		KEANE Robbie	10
19	GIVET Gael			DUFF Damien	11
	Tr: DOMENECH Raymond			Tr: KERR Brian	
6	DIARRA Alou	62	40	REID Andy	17
22	GOVOU Sidney	81			

Lansdowne Road, Dublin
13-10-2004, 19:30, 36 000, Lajuks LVA

IRL	2 0	FRO

Keane.Rb 2 [14 32]

	REP OF IRELAND				FAROE ISLANDS	
1	GIVEN Shay				MIKKELSEN Jakup	1
2	CARR Stephen				OLSEN Suni	2
3	O SHEA John	57			THORSTEINSSON Pol	4
4	CUNNINGHAM Kenny				JACOBSEN Jon Roi	5
5	O BRIEN Andy		58		JACOBSEN Rogvi	6
6	KEANE Roy				BENJAMINSEN Frodi	7
7	FINNAN Steve				JOHNSSON Julian	8
8	KILBANE Kevin		85		BORG Jakup	9
9	REID Andy	76			PETERSEN John	10
10	KEANE Robbie		82	FREDIKSBERG Jonhard		11
11	DUFF Damien				JOHANNESEN Oli	13
	Tr: KERR Brian				Tr: LARSEN Henrik	
15	MILLER Liam	57	58		LAKJUNI Hedin	3
18	DOHERTY Gary	76	82		FLOTUM Andrew	14
			85		DANIELSEN Atli	15

G.S.P., Nicosia
13-10-2004, 21:45, 3 319, Larsen DEN

CYP 0 2 FRA

Wiltord [38], Henry [72]

#	CYPRUS			#	FRANCE
1	PANAYIOTOU Nikos			16	BARTHEZ Fabien
3	NIKOLAOU Nikos	76		4	VIEIRA Patrick
5	KAKOYIANNIS Loizos			5	GALLAS William
6	OKKARIDES Stelios		46	7	PIRES Robert
9	OKKAS Ioannis			11	WILTORD Sylvain
10	CHARALAMPIDIS Konst'inos	56		12	HENRY Thierry
11	KONSTANTINOU Michael			13	SILVESTRE Mikael
13	CHARALAMBOUS Elias			14	SQUILACI Sebastien
14	GEORGIOU Stavros	82	90	17	DACOURT Olivier
15	ILIA Marios			19	GIVET Gael
17	SATSIAS Marinos		66	20	LUYINDULA Peguy
	Tr: VUKOTIC Momcilo				Tr: DOMENECH Raymond
4	LAMBROU Lambros	76	66	3	EVRA Patrice
7	MAKRIDIS Konstantinos	56	90	6	DIARRA Alou
18	YIASOUMI Yiasoumis	82	46	8	MOREIRA Daniel

G.S.P., Nicosia
17-11-2004, 19:00, 1 624, Kaldma EST

CYP 1 2 ISR

Okkas [45]

Keisi [17], Nimni [86]

#	CYPRUS			#	ISRAEL
1	PANAYIOTOU Nikos			1	DAVIDOVITCH Nir
2	KAIAFAS Costas			3	BEN HAIM Tal
5	KAKOYIANNIS Loizos			4	BENADO Arik
6	OKKARIDES Stelios			6	KEISI Adoram
7	MAKRIDIS Konstantinos		53	7	BALILI Pini
9	OKKAS Ioannis	56		8	NIMNI Avi
10	CHARALAMPIDIS Konst'inos	85		10	BADEER Valeed
11	KONSTANTINOU Michael			15	BENAYOUN Yossi
13	CHARALAMBOUS Elias		79	18	AFEK Omri
14	GEORGIOU Stavros	71	65	20	KATAN Yaniv
15	ILIA Marios			21	SABAN Klemi
	Tr: VUKOTIC Momcilo				Tr: GRANT Avraham
8	NEOFYTOU Marios	85	65	11	SOUAN Abbas
17	GOUMENOS Demosthenis	71	53	12	GOLAN Omer
18	YIASOUMI Yiasoumis	56	79	19	REVIVO David

Ramat Gan, Tel Aviv
26-03-2005, 19:50, 32 150, Ivanov RUS

ISR 1 1 IRL

Souan [90]

Morrison [43]

#	ISRAEL			#	REP OF IRELAND
1	AOUATE Dudu			1	GIVEN Shay
3	BEN HAIM Tal			2	CARR Stephen
4	BENADO Arik			3	O SHEA John
5	GERSHON Shimon			4	CUNNINGHAM Kenny
6	KEISI Adoram			5	O BRIEN Andy
10	BADEER Valeed			6	KEANE Roy
11	TAL Idan	65		7	FINNAN Steve
12	GOLAN Omer	74		8	KILBANE Kevin
15	BENAYOUN Yossi		85	9	MORRISON Clinton
18	AFEK Omri	65		10	KEANE Robbie
20	KATAN Yaniv			11	DUFF Damien
	Tr: GRANT Avraham				Tr: KERR Brian
7	BALILI Pini	65	85	14	HOLLAND Matt
8	NIMNI Avi	65			
19	SOUAN Abbas	74			

Stade de France, Saint-Denis/Paris
26-03-2005, 21:00, 79 373, De Santis ITA

FRA 0 0 SUI

#	FRANCE			#	SWITZERLAND
16	BARTHEZ Fabien			1	ZUBERBUHLER Pascal
2	BOUMSONG Jean-Alain			6	VOGEL Johann
4	VIEIRA Patrick			7	CABANAS Ricardo
5	GALLAS William			9	FREI Alexander
8	GIULY Ludovic			17	SPYCHER Christoph
11	WILTORD Sylvain	81	28	18	LONFAT Johann
13	DHORASOO Vikash	58		20	MUELLER Patrick
17	GIVET Gael		92	21	GYGAX Daniel
19	PEDRETTI Benoit			24	SENDEROS Philippe
19	SAGNOL Willy		69	25	ZIEGLER Reto
20	TREZEGUET David			26	DEGEN Philipp
	Tr: DOMENECH Raymond				Tr: KUHN Koebi
10	MERIEM Camel	58	69	3	MAGNIN Ludovic
22	GOVOU Sidney	81	92	4	HENCHOZ Stephane
			28	14	HUGGEL Benjamin

Hardturm, Zurich
30-03-2005, 20:30, 16 066, Dougal SCO

SUI 1 0 CYP

Frei [87]

#	SWITZERLAND			#	CYPRUS
1	ZUBERBUHLER Pascal		92	1	PANAYIOTOU Nikos
6	VOGEL Johann			2	LOUKA Loukas
7	CABANAS Ricardo			4	LAMBROU Lambros
9	FREI Alexander		64	7	MAKRIDIS Konstantinos
17	SPYCHER Christoph	82	80	8	KRASSAS Asimakis
18	LONFAT Johann	62		9	OKKAS Ioannis
20	MUELLER Patrick			10	CHARALAMPIDIS Konst'inos
21	GYGAX Daniel			11	KONSTANTINOU Michael
24	SENDEROS Philippe			13	MICHAIL Chrysostomos
25	ZIEGLER Reto	42		19	ILIA Marios
26	DEGEN Philipp		92	20	GARPOZIS Alexandros
	Tr: KUHN Koebi				Tr: ANASTASIADIS Angelos
3	MAGNIN Ludovic	82	64	17	SATSIAS Marinos
10	YAKIN Hakan	62	80	18	YIASOUMI Yiasoumis
22	VONLANTHEN Johan	42	92	21	ALONEFTIS Efstathios

Ramat Gan, Tel Aviv
30-03-2005, 20:50, 32 150, Merk GER

ISR 1 1 FRA

Badeer [83]

Trezeguet [50]

#	ISRAEL			#	FRANCE
1	AOUATE Dudu			16	BARTHEZ Fabien
3	BEN HAIM Tal			2	BOUMSONG Jean-Alain
5	GERSHON Shimon			4	VIEIRA Patrick
6	KEISI Adoram			5	GALLAS William
7	BALILI Pini			7	MALOUDA Florent
8	NIMNI Avi		92	11	WILTORD Sylvain
10	BADEER Valeed			15	DIARRA Alou
11	TAL Idan	67		17	GIVET Gael
15	BENAYOUN Yossi			19	PEDRETTI Benoit
20	KATAN Yaniv			19	SAGNOL Willy
21	SABAN Klemi		55	20	TREZEGUET David
	Tr: GRANT Avraham				Tr: DOMENECH Raymond
18	AFEK Omri	67	92	13	DHORASOO Vikash

Svangaskard, Toftir
4-06-2005, 16:30, 2 047, Gumienny BEL

FRO	1	3		SUI

Jacobsen.R [70]   Wicky [25], Frei 2 [72 84]

FAROE ISLANDS			SWITZERLAND	
1 MIKKELSEN Jakup			ZUBERBUHLER Pascal	1
2 OLSEN Suni			MAGNIN Ludovic	3
3 DANIELSEN Atli			VOGEL Johann	6
4 HANSEN Johan		89	WICKY Raphael	8
5 JACOBSEN Jon Roi			FREI Alexander	9
6 JACOBSEN Rogvi		68	BARNETTA Tranquillo	16
7 BENJAMINSEN Frodi			MUELLER Patrick	20
9 BORG Jakup	66		GYGAX Daniel	21
10 JORGENSEN Claus Bech	75	77	VONLANTHEN Johan	22
11 FLOTUM Andrew	63		DEGEN Philipp	26
13 JOHANNESEN Oli			ROCHAT Alain	28
Tr: LARSEN Henrik			Tr: KUHN Koebi	
12 JACOBSEN Christian	63	89	LONFAT Johann	18
14 LAKJUNI Hedin	75	77	ZIEGLER Reto	25
15 FREDERIKSBERG Jonhard	66	68	MARGAIRAZ Xavier	31

Lansdowne Road, Dublin
4-06-2005, 19:30, 36 000, Vassaras GRE

IRL	2	2		ISR

Harte [5], Keane.Rb [11]   Yemiel [39], Nimni [46]

REP OF IRELAND			ISRAEL	
1 GIVEN Shay			AOUATE Dudu	1
2 O SHEA John			YEMIEL Avi	3
3 HARTE Ian			BENADO Arik	4
4 CUNNINGHAM Kenny			GERSHON Shimon	5
5 O BRIEN Andy		84	KEISI Adoram	6
6 HOLLAND Matt		78	NIMNI Avi	8
7 REID Andy	65		TAL Idan	11
8 KILBANE Kevin			BENAYOUN Yossi	15
9 MORRISON Clinton			SOUAN Abbas	19
10 KEANE Robbie	26	67	KATAN Yaniv	20
11 DUFF Damien			SABAN Klemi	21
Tr: KERR Brian			Tr: GRANT Avraham	
15 KAVANAGH Graham	26	67	BALILI Pini	7
18 DOHERTY Gary	65	78	GOLAN Omer	12

Tórsvøllur, Tórshavn
8-06-2005, 19:30, 5 180, Guenov BUL

FRO	0	2		IRL

Harte [51p], Kilbane [59]

FAROE ISLANDS			REP OF IRELAND	
1 MIKKELSEN Jakup			GIVEN Shay	1
2 OLSEN Suni			CARR Stephen	2
3 DANIELSEN Atli			HARTE Ian	3
4 HANSEN Johan			CUNNINGHAM Kenny	4
6 JACOBSEN Rogvi			O SHEA John	5
7 BENJAMINSEN Frodi	76		KEANE Roy	6
8 JOHNSSON Julian			REID Andy	7
10 JORGENSEN Claus Bech	76		KILBANE Kevin	8
11 FLOTUM Andrew	59		ELLIOT Stephen	9
13 JOHANNESEN Oli		78	MORRISON Clinton	10
14 LAKJUNI Hedin			DUFF Damien	11
Tr: LARSEN Henrik			Tr: KERR Brian	
9 BORG Jakup	76	78	DOHERTY Gary	17
12 JACOBSEN Christian	59			
17 AKSELSEN Tor Ingar	76			

GROUP 5

Sportni Park, Celje
4-09-2004, 20:15, 3 620, Hyytia FIN

SVN	3	0		MDA

Acimovic 3 [5 27 48]

SLOVENIA			MOLDOVA	
1 MAVRIC Borut			HMARUC Evgheni	1
3 KARIC Amir		71	COVALENCO Alexandr	2
4 MAVRIC Matej			LASCENCOV Serghei	3
6 KNAVS Aleksander			OLEXICI Ghenadie	4
9 SILJAK Ermin			CATINSUS Valerii	5
10 CEH Nastja	89		PRIGANIUC Iurie	6
11 KOMAC Andrej	74		COVALCIUC Serghei	7
15 POKORN Jalen	86	46	SAVINOV Alexei	8
16 ACIMOVIC Milenko		82	ROGACIOV Serghei	9
19 SESLAR Simon			CEBOTARI Boris	10
20 DEDIC Zlatko			MITEREV Iurie	11
Tr: OBLAK Branko			Tr: PASULKO Viktor	
2 TANJIC Almir	74	71	IVANOV Stanislav	15
7 SUKALO Goran	86	46	LUNGU Vladislav	16
8 KOREN Robert	89	82	DADU Serghei	18

Renzo Barbera, Palermo
4-09-2004, 20:45, 21 463, Sars FRA

ITA	2	1		NOR

De Rossi [4], Toni [80]   Carew [1]

ITALY			NORWAY	
1 BUFFON Gianluigi			JOHNSEN Espen	1
2 BONERA Daniele			BASMA Ole Christer	2
3 FAVALLI Giuseppe	70		RISETH Vidar	3
4 GATTUSO Gennaro			LUNDEKVAM Claus	4
5 MATERAZZI Marco			RIISE John Arne	5
6 NESTA Alessandro		87	SORENSEN Jan Derek	6
7 FIORE Stefano			ANDRESEN Martin	7
8 DE ROSSI Daniele		89	HOSET Magne	8
9 GILARDINO Alberto	59		JOHNSEN Frode	9
10 MICCOLI Fabrizio	74	74	CAREW John	10
11 ZAMBROTTA Gianluca			RUDI Petter	11
Tr: LIPPI Marcello			Tr: HAREIDE Age	
13 DIANA Aimo	70	89	SOLLI Jan	16
18 TONI Luca	74	87	PEDERSEN Morten	17
19 CORRADI Bernardo	59	74	RUSHFELDT Sigurd	18

Hampden Park, Glasgow
8-09-2004, 20:00, 38 279, Larsen DEN

SCO 0 0 SVN

No	SCOTLAND				SLOVENIA	No
1	GORDON Craig				MAVRIC Borut	1
2	CALDWELL Gary				KARIC Amir	3
3	NAYSMITH Gary	59			MAVRIC Matej	4
4	WEBSTER Andy				KNAVS Aleksander	6
5	MACKAY Malky		64		SILJAK Ermin	9
6	FERGUSON Barry				CEH Nastja	10
7	FLETCHER Darren				KOMAC Andrej	11
8	MC NAMARA Jackie				POKORN Jalen	15
9	DICKOV Paul	80			ACIMOVIC Milenko	18
10	QUASHIE Nigel				SESLAR Simon	19
11	MC FADDEN James		79		DEDIC Zlatko	20
	Tr: VOGTS Berti				Tr: OBLAK Branko	
15	HOLT Gary	59	79		SUKALO Goran	7
16	CRAWFORD Stephen	80	64		LAVRIC Klemen	17

Ullevaal, Oslo
8-09-2004, 20:00, 25 272, Costa POR

NOR 1 1 BLR

Riseth 39 — Kutuzov 78

No	NORWAY					BELARUS	No
1	MYHRE Thomas					KHOMUTOVSKY Vasily	1
2	HOILAND Jon					KULCHY Aleksandr	2
3	RISETH Vidar					YASKOVICH Sergei	3
4	LUNDEKVAM Claus					OMELYANCHUK Sergei	4
5	RIISE John Arne					SHTANYUK Sergei	5
6	PEDERSEN Morten					GURENKO Sergei	6
7	ANDRESEN Martin					LAVRIK Andrei	7
8	HOSET Magne	78	62			BULYGA Vitaly	8
9	JOHNSEN Frode					ROMASHCHENKO Maksim	9
10	RUSHFELDT Sigurd	81	44			HLEB Vyacheslav	10
11	RUDI Petter	46				KUTUZOV Vitaly	11
	Tr: HAREIDE Age					Tr: BAIDACHNY Anatoly	
15	SOLLI Jan	78		94	BLIZNIUK Henadzi 44		14
17	CAREW John	81	62		SASHCHEKA Dzianis		15
18	SORENSEN Jan Derek	46	94		SUCHKOV Aleksei		17

Republican Stadium, Chisinau
8-09-2004, 21:45, 5 200, Benes CZE

MDA 0 1 ITA

Del Piero 32

No	MOLDOVA				ITALY	No
1	HMARUC Evgheni				BUFFON Gianluigi	1
2	LUNGU Vladislav		84		BONERA Daniele	2
3	LASCENCOV Serghei				ZAMBROTTA Gianluca	3
4	OLEXICI Ghenadie				GATTUSO Gennaro	4
5	CATINSUS Valerii				MATERAZZI Marco	5
6	PRIGANIUC Iurie				NESTA Alessandro	6
7	COVALCIUC Serghei				DEL PIERO Alessandro	7
8	IVANOV Stanislav		73		AMBROSINI Massimo	8
9	ROGACIOV Serghei	81	80		GILARDINO Alberto	9
10	BURSUC Iulian				PIRLO Andrea	10
11	MITEREV Iurie	62			DIANA Aimo	11
	Tr: PASULKO Viktor				Tr: LIPPI Marcello	
16	CEBOTARI Boris	81	73		ODDO Massimo	13
17	DADU Serghei	62 78	84		BLASI Manuele	15
			80		TONI Luca	18

Hampden Park, Glasgow
9-10-2004, 15:00, 51 000, Allaerts BEL

SCO 0 1 NOR

Iversen 54p

No	SCOTLAND				NORWAY	No
1	GORDON Craig				MYHRE Thomas	1
2	CALDWELL Gary				BERGDOLMO Andre	2
3	NAYSMITH Gary				HAGEN Erik	3
4	ANDERSON Russell				LUNDEKVAM Claus	4
5	WEBSTER Andy				RIISE John Arne	5
6	FERGUSON Barry		73		SORENSEN Jan Derek	6
7	FLETCHER Darren				SOLLI Jan	7
8	HOLT Gary	80	58		HOSET Magne	8
9	DICKOV Paul	75			LARSEN Tommy	9
10	MC FADDEN James	53			CAREW John	10
11	HUGHES Richard	63	88		IVERSEN Steffen	11
	Tr: VOGTS Berti				Tr: HAREIDE Age	
13	THOMPSON Steven	80	73		ANDRESEN Martin	14
15	PEARSON Stephen	63	88		JOHNSEN Frode	16
17	MILLER Kenny	75	58		PEDERSEN Morten	17

Dynamo, Minsk
9-10-2004, 19:00, 21 000, Dereli TUR

BLR 4 0 MDA

Omelyanchuk 45, Kutuzov 65
Bulyga 75, Romashchenko 91

No	BELARUS				MOLDOVA	No
1	KHOMUTOVSKY Vasily				HMARUC Evgheni	1
2	KULCHY Aleksandr	79			SAVINOV Alexei	2
3	YASKOVICH Sergei				LASCENCOV Serghei	3
4	OMELYANCHUK Sergei				OLEXICI Ghenadie	4
5	SHTANYUK Sergei				CATINSUS Valerii	5
6	GURENKO Sergei		79		BARISEV Victor	6
7	LAVRIK Andrei		84		COVALCIUC Serghei	7
8	BELKEVICH Valentin	82			IVANOV Stanislav	8
9	ROMASHCHENKO Maksim				ROGACIOV Serghei	9
10	KORYTKO Vladimir				BURSUC Iulian	10
11	KUTUZOV Vitaly	65	75		MITEREV Iurie	11
	Tr: BAIDACHNY Anatoly				Tr: PASULKO Viktor	
13	KOVBA Denis	79	75		GOLBAN Alexandru	14
17	BULYGA Vitaly	65	79		POGREBAN Serghei	15
18	KOVEL Leanid	82	84		EPUREANU Sergiu	17

Sportni Park, Celje
9-10-2004, 21:00, 9 262, De Bleeckere BEL

SVN 1 0 ITA

Cesar 82

No	SLOVENIA				ITALY	No
1	MAVRIC Borut				BUFFON Gianluigi	1
3	KARIC Amir	69			BONERA Daniele	2
4	MAVRIC Matej				ZAMBROTTA Gianluca	3
6	MITRAKOVIC Zeljko	76			GATTUSO Gennaro	4
7	SUKALO Goran				CANNAVARO Fabio	5
9	SILJAK Ermin				NESTA Alessandro	6
10	CEH Nastja	88	83		CAMORANESI Mauro	7
11	KOMAC Andrej				DE ROSSI Daniele	8
15	POKORN Jalen		68		GILARDINO Alberto	9
18	ACIMOVIC Milenko				TOTTI Francesco	10
19	SESLAR Simon		68		ESPOSITO Mauro	11
	Tr: OBLAK Branko				Tr: LIPPI Marcello	
5	CESAR Bostjan	76	68		FIORE Stefano	16
8	LAZIC Igor	88	68		TONI Luca	18
20	DEDIC Zlatko	69	83		DI VAIO Marco	19

Ullevaal, Oslo
13-10-2004, 19:00, 24 907, Ivanov RUS

NOR **3 0** **SVN**

Carew [7], Pedersen [60]
Odegaard [89]

NORWAY			SLOVENIA	
1 MYHRE Thomas			MAVRIC Borut	1
2 BERGDOLMO Andre			MAVRIC Matej	4
3 HAGEN Erik			CESAR Bostjan	5
4 LUNDEKVAM Claus			MITRAKOVIC Zeljko	6
5 RIISE John Arne			SUKALO Goran	7
6 ANDRESEN Martin			SILJAK Ermin	9
7 SOLLI Jan			CEH Nastja	10
8 PEDERSEN Morten	80		POKORN Jalen	15
9 LARSEN Tommy		78	LAVRIC Klemen	17
10 CAREW John	76		ACIMOVIC Milenko	18
11 IVERSEN Steffen	88	66	SESLAR Simon	19
Tr: HAREIDE Age			Tr: OBLAK Branko	
16 JOHNSEN Frode	88	66	KOMAC Andrej	11
17 RUSHFELDT Sigurd	76	78	DEDIC Zlatko	20
18 ODEGAARD Alexander	80			

Ennio Tardini, Parma
13-10-2004, 21:00, 19 833, Megia Davila ESP

ITA **4 3** **BLR**

Totti 2 [26p 74], De Rossi [32]
Gilardino [86]

Romashchenko 2 [52 88]
Bulyga [76]

ITALY			BELARUS	
1 BUFFON Gianluigi			KHOMUTOVSKY Vasily	1
2 ODDO Massimo	68	83	KULCHY Aleksandr	2
3 PANCARO Giuseppe		89	YASKOVICH Sergei	3
4 GATTUSO Gennaro			TARLOVSKY Igor	4
5 MATERAZZI Marco			SHTANYUK Sergei	5
6 NESTA Alessandro			GURENKO Sergei	6
7 DIANA Aimo	64	75	LAVRIK Andrei	7
8 DE ROSSI Daniele	74		BELKEVICH Valentin	8
9 GILARDINO Alberto			ROMASHCHENKO Maksim	9
10 TOTTI Francesco		35	KORYTKO Vladimir	10
11 ZAMBROTTA Gianluca			KUTUZOV Vitaly	11
Tr: LIPPI Marcello			Tr: BAIDACHNY Anatoly	
13 CANNAVARO Fabio	68	75	KOVBA Denis	13
14 BLASI Manuele	74	35	BULYGA Vitaly	17
15 PERROTTA Simone	64	83	KOVEL Leanid	18

Republican Stadium, Chisinau
13-10-2004, 21:00, 7 000, Jakobsson ISL

MDA **1 1** **SCO**

Dadu [28]

Thompson [31]

MOLDOVA			SCOTLAND	
1 HMARUC Evgheni			GORDON Craig	1
2 SAVINOV Alexei			CALDWELL Gary	2
3 LASCENCOV Serghei		46	NAYSMITH Gary	3
4 OLEXICI Ghenadie	39		CALDWELL Gary	4
5 CATINSUS Valerii			WEBSTER Andy	5
6 PRIGANIUC Iurie			FERGUSON Barry	6
7 COVALCIUC Serghei		66	FLETCHER Darren	7
8 IVANOV Stanislav			HOLT Gary	8
9 ROGACIOV Serghei	86	86	THOMPSON Steven	9
10 BURSUC Iulian			CRAWFORD Stephen	10
11 DADU Serghei			CAMERON Colin	11
Tr: PASULKO Viktor			Tr: VOGTS Berti	
15 MITEREV Iurie	86	66	MILLER Kenny	16
16 CEBOTARI Boris	39	46	MURRAY Ian	17
		86	MC CULLOCH Lee	18

Giuseppe Meazza, Milan
26-03-2005, 20:45, 45 000, Vassaras GRE

ITA **2 0** **SCO**

Pirlo 2 [35 85]

ITALY			SCOTLAND	
1 BUFFON Gianluigi		39	DOUGLAS Robert	1
2 BONERA Daniele			MC NAMARA Jackie	2
3 CHIELLINI Giorgio			NAYSMITH Gary	3
4 GATTUSO Gennaro			PRESSLEY Steven	4
5 CANNAVARO Fabio			WEIR David	5
6 MATERAZZI Marco			FERGUSON Barry	6
7 CAMORANESI Mauro		76	HARTLEY Paul	7
8 PIRLO Andrea			CALDWELL Gary	8
9 GILARDINO Alberto		87	MILLER Kenny	9
10 TOTTI Francesco	70		QUASHIE Nigel	10
11 CASSANO Antonio	82		MC CULLOCH Lee	11
Tr: LIPPI Marcello			Tr: SMITH Walter	
16 DE ROSSI Daniele	70	39	GORDON Craig	12
19 TONI Luca	82	76	CRAWFORD Stephen	16
		87	O CONNER Garry	17

Petrol Arena, Celje
30-03-2005, 20:15, 6 450, Al Ghamdi KSA

SVN **1 1** **BLR**

Rodic [44]

Kulchy [49]

SLOVENIA			BELARUS	
12 HANDANOVIC Samir			ZHAUNOU Yury	1
2 CIPOT Fabijan			KULCHY Aleksandr	2
3 FILEKOVIC Suad	54		KOVBA Denis	3
4 MAVRIC Matej			OMELYANCHUK Sergei	4
6 KNAVS Aleksander			LAVRIK Andrei	5
10 CEH Nastja			GURENKO Sergei	6
11 KOMAC Andrej		85	KHATSKEVICH Aleksandr	7
14 CIMIROTIC Sebastijan	27		BELKEVICH Valentin	8
18 ACIMOVIC Milenko		75	ROMASHCHENKO Maksim	9
19 SESLAR Simon	70		HLEB Aleksandr	10
20 ILIC Branko		63	KUTUZOV Vitaly	11
Tr: OBLAK Branko			Tr: BAIDACHNY Anatoly	
9 SILJAK Ermin	54	85	OSTROVSKY Andrei	13
15 POKORN Jalen	70	75	KALACHEV Timofei	16
16 RODIC Aleksandar	27	63	BULYGA Vitaly	17

Republican Stadium, Chisinau
30-03-2005, 20:45, 5 000, Meyer GER

MDA **0 0** **NOR**

MOLDOVA			NORWAY	
1 HMARUC Evgheni			MYHRE Thomas	1
2 SAVINOV Alexei			BERGDOLMO Andre	2
3 LASCENCOV Serghei	85		HAGEN Erik	3
4 OLEXICI Ghenadie			LUNDEKVAM Claus	4
5 CATINSUS Valerii			RIISE John Arne	5
6 PRIGANIUC Iurie			SOLLI Jan	6
8 IVANOV Stanislav			LARSEN Tommy	7
9 ROGACIOV Serghei	89	59	HOSET Magne	8
10 BORET Vadim			IVERSEN Steffen	9
11 DADU Serghei		81	RUSHFELDT Sigurd	10
15 IEPUREANU Serghei	81		PEDERSEN Morten	11
Tr: PASULKO Viktor			Tr: HAREIDE Age	
13 FRUNZA Viorel	89	81	KARADAS Azar	17
14 COVALENCO Alexandr	85	59	CAREW John	19
16 BARISEV Victor	81			

Hampden Park, Glasgow
4-06-2005, 15:00, 45 317, Braamhaar NED

SCO	2	0	MDA

Dailly [52], McFadden [88]

SCOTLAND			MOLDOVA	
1 GORDON Craig			HMARUC Evgheni	1
2 GRAHAM Alexander			SAVINOV Alexei	2
3 MC NAMARA Jackie	26	46	LASCENCOV Serghei	3
4 PRESSLEY Steven			OLEXICI Ghenadie	4
5 WEIR David		60	CATINSUS Valerii	5
6 FERGUSON Barry			PRIGANIUC Iurie	6
7 FLETCHER Darren			IEPUREANU Serghei	7
8 WEBSTER Andy			IVANOV Stanislav	8
9 MILLER Kenny		82	ROGACIOV Serghei	9
10 HARTLEY Paul			BORET Vadim	10
11 MC CULLOCH Lee	74		DADU Serghei	11
Tr: SMITH Walter			Tr: PASULKO Viktor	
14 DAILLY Christian	26	46	COVALENCO Alexandr	14
17 MC FADDEN James	74	60	COVALCIUC Serghei	16
		82	FRUNZA Viorel	17

Dynamo, Minsk
4-06-2005, 20:00, 29 042, Hansson SWE

BLR	1	1	SVN

Belkevich [18] Ceh [17]

BELARUS			SLOVENIA	
1 ZHAUNOU Yury			HANDANOVIC Samir	12
2 KHATSKEVICH Aleksandr			CIPOT Fabijan	2
3 YASKOVICH Sergei	75		FILEKOVIC Suad	3
4 OMELYANCHUK Sergei	84		MAVRIC Matej	4
5 SHTANYUK Sergei			CESAR Bostjan	5
6 GURENKO Sergei			CEH Nastja	10
7 KOVBA Denis		93	KOMAC Andrej	11
8 BELKEVICH Valentin			POKORN Jalen	15
9 BULYGA Vitaly		58	RODIC Aleksandar	16
10 HLEB Aleksandr			LAVRIC Klemen	17
11 KUTUZOV Vitaly	71	68	ILIC Branko	20
Tr: BAIDACHNY Anatoly			Tr: OBLAK Branko	
14 TARLOVSKY Igor	84	93	ZLOGAR Anton	6
15 LAVRIK Andrei	75	68	SUKALO Goran	7
18 KORNILENKO Sergei	71	58	CIMIROTIC Sebastijan	14

Ullevaal, Oslo
4-06-2005, 20:30, 24 829, Mejuto Gonzalez ESP

NOR	0	0	ITA

NORWAY			ITALY	
1 MYHRE Thomas			BUFFON Gianluigi	1
2 BERGDOLMO Andre			BONERA Daniele	2
3 HAGEN Erik			GROSSO Fabio	3
4 LUNDEKVAM Claus			DE ROSSI Daniele	4
5 RIISE John Arne			CANNAVARO Fabio	5
6 SOLLI Jan	71	79	MATERAZZI Marco	6
7 ANDERSEN Martin			CAMORANESI Mauro	7
8 HAESTAD Kristoffer			PIRLO Andrea	8
9 PEDERSEN Morten		56	VIERI Christian	9
10 CAREW John		68	CASSANO Antonio	10
11 IVERSEN Steffen	83		ZAMBROTTA Gianluca	11
Tr: HAREIDE Age			Tr: LIPPI Marcello	
16 JOHNSEN Frode	83	79	DIANA Aimo	14
17 KARADAS Azar	71	56	TONI Luca	18
		68	IAQUINTA Vincenzo	19

Dynamo, Minsk
8-06-2005, 21:00, 28 287, Benquerenca POR

BLR	0	0	SCO

BELARUS			SCOTLAND	
1 ZHAUNOU Yury			GORDON Craig	1
2 KALACHEV Timofei	59		DAILLY Christian	2
3 YASKOVICH Sergei			GRAHAM Alexander	3
4 OMELYANCHUK Sergei			PRESSLEY Steven	4
5 SHTANYUK Sergei			WEIR David	5
6 GURENKO Sergei			FERGUSON Barry	6
7 KOVBA Denis			FLETCHER DARREN	7
8 BELKEVICH Valentin			WEBSTER Andy	8
9 BULYGA Vitaly	85		MILLER Kenny	9
10 HLEB Aleksandr			CALDWELL Gary	10
11 KORNILENKO Sergei		76	MC CULLOCH Lee	11
Tr: BAIDACHNY Anatoly			Tr: SMITH Walter	
13 KULCHY Aleksandr	85	76	MC FADDEN James	14
17 HLEB Vyacheslav	59			

GROUP 6

Windsor Park, Belfast
4-09-2004, 15:00, 12 487, Wegereef NED

NIR	0	3	POL

Zurawski [4], Wlodarczyk [36], Krzynowek [56]

NORTHERN IRELAND			POLAND	
1 TAYLOR Maik			DUDEK Jerzy	1
3 CAPALDI Tony		75	MILA Sebastian	2
4 CRAIGAN Stephen			RZASA Tomasz	3
5 WILLIAMS Mark			ZEWLAKOW Michal	4
6 WHITLEY Jeff			GLOWACKI Arkadiusz	5
7 JOHNSON Damien			BAK Jacek	6
8 HUGHES Michael	53		ZIENCZUK Marek	7
9 HEALY David		69	KRZYNOWEK Jacek	8
10 QUINN James	72	84	ZURAWSKI Maciej	9
11 ELLIOTT Stuart	62		LEWANDOWSKI Mariusz	10
18 HUGHES Aaron			WLODARCZYK Piotr	11
Tr: SANCHEZ Lawrie			Tr: JANAS Pawel	
14 SMITH Andy	72	75	RADOMSKI Arkadiusz	16
15 MC VEIGH Paul	62	69	GORAWSKI Damian	17
16 JONES Steve	53	84	KRYSZALOWICZ Pawel	18

Ernst Happel Stadion, Vienna
4-09-2004, 20:30, 48 000, Michel SVK

AUT	2	2	ENG

Kollmann [71], Ivanschitz [72] Lampard [24], Gerrard [65]

AUSTRIA			ENGLAND	
1 MANNINGER Alexander			JAMES David	1
2 STANDFEST Joachim			NEVILLE Gary	2
3 HIDEN Martin			COLE Ashley	3
4 STRANZL Martin		82	GERRARD Steven	4
5 POGATETZ Emanuel			TERRY John	5
6 AUFHAUSER Rene	74		KING Ledley	6
7 SICK Gernot			BECKHAM David	7
8 KUHBAUER Dietmar			LAMPARD Frank	8
9 HAAS Mario	90	76	SMITH Alan	9
10 IVANSCHITZ Andreas			OWEN Michael	10
11 GLIEDER Eduard	68	84	BRIDGE Wayne	11
Tr: KRANKL Hans			Tr: ERIKSSON Sven Goran	
14 HIEBLINGER Mario	90	82	CARRAGHER Jamie	12
16 KIESENEBNER Markus	74	84	COLE Joe	15
18 KOLLMANN Roland	68	76	DEFOE Jermain	17

Tofik Bakhramov, Baku
4-09-2004, 21:00, 8 000, Trivkovic CRO

AZE 1 1 WAL

Sadigov 55   Speed 47

#	AZERBAIJAN	min	min	WALES	#
1	KRAMARENKO Dmitriy			JONES Paul	1
2	AGHAYER Emin			DELANEY Mark	2
3	HAJIYEV Altandil			GABBIDON Danny	3
4	SHUKUROV Mohir			MELVILLE Andy	4
6	HUSEYNOV Vusal	73		PAGE Robert	5
7	GURBANOV Makhmud		46	PEMBRIDGE Mark	6
8	KERIMOV Aslan			SAVAGE Robbie	7
9	GURBANOV Gurban			BELLAMY Craig	8
10	PANAMARYOV Anotoliy	83		HARTSON John	9
11	ALIYEV Samir	71		SPEED Gary	10
14	SADIGOV Rashad		88	KOUMAS Jason	11
	Tr: CARLOS ALBERTO			Tr: HUGHES Mark	
15	MAMMADOV Ismayil	73	46	OSTER John	15
17	NABIYER Nadir	71	88	EARNSHAW Rob	18
18	GURBANOV Ilgar	83			

Millennium, Cardiff
8-09-2004, 20:00, 63 500, Messina ITA

WAL 2 2 NIR

Hartson 32, Earnshaw 74   Whitley 10, Healy 21

#	WALES	min	n-min	NORTHERN IRELAND	#
1	JONES Paul			TAYLOR Maik	1
2	DELANEY Mark	27	93	CAPALDI Tony	3
3	THATCHER Ben	62		MURDOCK Colin	4
4	COLLINS James			WILLIAMS Mark	5
5	GABBIDON Danny			JOHNSON Damien	6
6	OSTER John			CLYDE Mark	7
7	SAVAGE Robbie	(9)		WHITLEY Jeff	8
8	BELLAMY Craig		22	HEALY David (9)	9
9	HARTSON John	57		QUINN James	10
10	SPEED Gary	(9)		HUGHES Michael	11
11	KOUMAS Jason			HUGHES Aaron	18
	Tr: HUGHES Mark			Tr: SANCHEZ Lawrie	
15	PARRY Paul	62	57 88	SMITH Andy	14
18	EARNSHAW Rob	27	88	MC VEIGH Paul	15
			93	MC CARTNEY George	17

Slaski, Chorzow
8-09-2004, 20:30, 30 000, Farina ITA

POL 1 2 ENG

Zurawski 47   Defoe 36, Glowacki OG 57

#	POLAND	min	e-min	ENGLAND	#
1	DUDEK Jerzy			ROBINSON Paul	1
2	MILA Sebastian	62	30	NEVILLE Gary	2
3	RZASA Tomasz			COLE Ashley	3
4	ZEWLAKOW Michael			GERRARD Steven	4
5	GLOWACKI Arkadiusz			TERRY John	5
6	BAK Jacek			KING Ledley	6
7	RASIAK Grzegorz	68	89	BECKHAM David	7
8	KRZYNOWEK Jacek			LAMPARD Frank	8
9	ZURAWSKI Maciej		87	DEFOE Jermain	9
10	LEWANDOWSKI Mariusz			OWEN Michael	10
11	KOSOWSKI Kamil	79		BRIDGE Wayne	11
	Tr: JANAS Pawel			Tr: ERIKSSON Sven Goran	
14	KUKIELKA Mariusz	62	30	CARRAGHER Jamie	12
16	NIEDZIELAN Andrzej	68	89	HARGREAVES Owen	14
17	GORAWSKI Damian	79	87	DYER Kieron	15

Ernest Happel Stadion, Vienna
8-09-2004, 20:30, 26 400, Sammut MLT

AUT 2 0 AZE

Stranzl 23, Kollmann 44

#	AUSTRIA	min	a-min	AZERBAIJAN	#
1	MANNINGER Alexander			KRAMARENKO Dmitriy	1
2	STANDFEST Joachim			AGHAYER Emin	2
3	STRANZL Martin			HAJIYEV Altandil	3
4	HIDEN Martin			SHUKUROV Mohir	4
5	POGATETZ Emanuel			HUSEYNOV Vusal	5
6	AUFHAUSER Rene		46	GURBANOV Makhmud	7
7	SCHOPP Markus	57		KERIMOV Aslan	8
8	KUHBAUER Dietmar			GURBANOV Gurban	9
9	HAAS Mario	72	46	PANAMARYOV Anotoliy	10
10	IVANSCHITZ Andreas		46	ALIYEV Samir	11
11	KOLLMANN Roland	79		SADIGOV Rashad	14
	Tr: KRANKL Hans			Tr: CARLOS ALBERTO	
14	GLIEDER Eduard	72	46	MAMMADOV Ismayil	16
16	DOLLINGER Matthias	57	46	NABIYER Nadir	17
17	LINZ Roland	79	46	GURBANOV Ilgar	18

Old Trafford, Manchester
9-10-2004, 15:00, 65 224, Hauge NOR

ENG 2 0 WAL

Lampard 4, Beckham 76

#	ENGLAND	min	w-min	WALES	#
1	ROBINSON Paul			JONES Paul	1
2	NEVILLE Gary			DELANEY Mark	2
3	COLE Ashley			THATCHER Ben	3
4	BUTT Nicky			GABBIDON Danny	5
5	FERDINAND Rio		59	PEMBRIDGE Mark	6
6	CAMPBELL Sol			DAVIES Simon	7
7	BECKHAM David	85		BELLAMY Craig	8
8	LAMPARD Frank			HARTSON John	9
9	ROONEY Wayne	87		SPEED Gary	10
10	OWEN Michael			GIGGS Ryan	11
11	DEFOE Jermain	70	74	KOUMAS Jason	17
	Tr: ERIKSSON Sven Goran			Tr: HUGHES Mark	
12	KING Ledley	87	59	ROBINSON Carl	15
15	HARGREAVES Owen	85	74	EARNSHAW Rob	18
18	SMITH Alan	70			

Ernest Happel Stadion, Vienna
9-10-2004, 20:30, 46 100, Cardoso Batista POR

AUT 1 3 POL

Schopp 30   Kaluzny 10, Krzynowek 78, Frankowski 90

#	AUSTRIA	min	p1	p2	POLAND	#
1	MANNINGER Alexander				DUDEK Jerzy	1
2	STANDFEST Joachim	46			ZAJAC Marcin	2
3	STRANZL Martin				RZASA Tomasz	3
4	HIDEN Martin				BASZCZYNSKI Marcin	4
5	POGATETZ Emanuel			71	KALUZNY Radoslaw	5
6	AUFHAUSER Rene	46			BAK Jacek	6
7	SCHOPP Markus				HAJTO Tomasz	7
8	KUHBAUER Dietmar				KRZYNOWEK Jacek	8
9	HAAS Mario	38			ZURAWSKI Maciej	9
10	IVANSCHITZ Andreas				MILA Sebastian	10
11	VASTIC Ivica	80		67	RASIAK Grzegorz	11
	Tr: KRANKL Hans				Tr: JANAS Pawel	
15	KIESENEBNER Markus	46	87	71	RADOMSKI Arkadiusz	16
17	MAYRLEB Christian	80		67	FRANKOWSKI Tomas	17
18	KOLLMANN Roland	38		38	KOSOWSKI Kamil	18

Tofik Bakhramov, Baku
9-10-2004, 21:30, 6 460, Hanacsek HUN

AZE 0 0 NIR

#	AZERBAIJAN				NORTHERN IRELAND	#
1	HASANZADA Cahangir				TAYLOR Maik	1
2	AMIRBAYOV Rafael				CLYDE Mark	3
3	HAJIYEV Altandil				MURDOCK Colin	4
4	SHUKUROV Mohir				WILLIAMS Mark	5
5	GULIYEV Emin				JOHNSON Damien	6
6	GULIYEV Kamal				BAIRD Chris	7
7	GURBANOV Makhmud	58			DOHERTY Tommy	8
11	NABIYER Nadir		9		WHITLEY Jeff	9
14	SADIGOV Rashad		76		QUINN James	11
16	MAMMADOV Ismayil	53			ELLIOTT Stuart	11
17	ALIYEV Samir	76			HUGHES Aaron	18
	Tr: CARLOS ALBERTO				Tr: SANCHEZ Lawrie	
9	GURBANOV Gurban	76	76		SMITH Andy	14
10	PANAMARYOV Anotoliy	58	9		GILLESPIE Keith	17
18	GURBANOV Ilgar	53				

Windsor Park, Belfast
13-10-2004, 19:45, 11 810, Shield AUS

NIR 3 3 AUT

Healy 36, Murdock 58, Elliott 93   Schopp 2 14 72, Mayrleb 59

#	NORTHERN IRELAND				AUSTRIA	#
1	CARROLL Roy				MANNINGER Alexander	1
3	MC CARTNEY George				IBERTSBERGER Andreas	2
4	MURDOCK Colin	79			HIDEN Martin	4
5	WILLIAMS Mark				POGATETZ Emanuel	5
6	JOHNSON Damien				KIESENEBNER Markus	6
7	GILLESPIE Keith		82		SCHOPP Markus	7
8	DOHERTY Tommy	85			KUHBAUER Dietmar	8
9	HEALY David		81		MAYRLEB Christian	9
10	QUINN James		64		KIRCHLER Roland	10
11	WHITLEY Jeff	89			VASTIC Ivica	11
18	HUGHES Aaron				FELDHOFER Ferdinand	17
	Tr: SANCHEZ Lawrie				Tr: KRANKL Hans	
15	ELLIOTT Stuart	79	82		SICK Gernot	14
16	JONES Steve	85	64		IVANSCHITZ Andreas	16
17	MC VEIGH Paul	89	81		KOLLMANN Roland	18

Millennium, Cardiff
13-10-2004, 20:00, 56 685, Sars FRA

WAL 2 3 POL

Earnshaw 56, Hartson 90   Frankowski 72, Zurawski 81, Krzynowek 85

#	WALES				POLAND	#
1	JONES Paul				DUDEK Jerzy	1
2	DELANEY Mark				RZASA Tomasz	2
3	THATCHER Ben				KOSOWSKI Kamil	3
4	COLLINS James				BASZCZYNSKI Marcin	4
5	GABBIDON Danny		70		KALUZNY Radoslaw	5
6	DAVIES Simon		46		BAK Jacek	6
7	SAVAGE Robbie				HAJTO Tomasz	7
8	BELLAMY Craig				KRZYNOWEK Jacek	8
9	EARNSHAW Rob				ZURAWSKI Maciej	9
10	SPEED Gary	88			SZYMKOWIAK Miroslav	10
11	KOUMAS Jason	85	59		WLODARCZYK Piotr	11
	Tr: HUGHES Mark				Tr: JANAS Pawel	
17	PARRY Paul	58	70		MILA Sebastian	15
18	HARTSON John	88	59		FRANKOWSKI Tomas	17
			46		KLOS Tomasz	18

Tofik Bakhramov, Baku18
13-10-2004, 21:30, 17 000, Hamer LUX

AZE 0 1 ENG

Owen 22

#	AZERBAIJAN				ENGLAND	#
1	HASANZADA Cahangir				ROBINSON Paul	1
2	AMIRBAYOV Rafael				NEVILLE Gary	2
3	HAJIYEV Altandil				COLE Ashley	3
4	SHUKUROV Mohir				BUTT Nicky	4
5	GULIYEV Emin	75			FERDINAND Rio	5
6	GULIYEV Kamal				CAMPBELL Sol	6
8	KERIMOV Aslan		72		JENAS Jermaine	7
10	PANAMARYOV Anotoliy				LAMPARD Frank	8
11	NABIYER Nadir	80	85		ROONEY Wayne	9
14	SADIGOV Rashad				OWEN Michael	10
17	ALIYEV Samir	59	55		DEFOE Jermain	11
	Tr: CARLOS ALBERTO				Tr: ERIKSSON Sven Goran	
9	GURBANOV Gurban	59	85		COLE Joe	16
15	ABDULLAYER Rashad	80	72		WRIGHT-PHILLIPS Shaun	17
18	GURBANOV Ilgar	75	55		SMITH Alan	18

Old Trafford, Manchester
26-03-2005, 15:00, 62 239, Stark GER

ENG 4 0 NIR

Cole J 47, Owen 2 52, Baird OG 54, Lampard 62

#	ENGLAND				NORTHERN IRELAND	#
1	ROBINSON Paul				TAYLOR Maik	1
2	NEVILLE Gary				BAIRD Chris	2
3	COLE Ashley				CAPALDI Tony	3
4	GERRARD Steven	72			MURDOCK Colin	5
5	FERDINAND Rio				JOHNSON Damien	6
6	TERRY John				GILLESPIE Keith	7
7	BECKHAM David	72	60		DOHERTY Tommy	8
8	LAMPARD Frank		88		HEALY David	9
9	ROONEY Wayne	81	88		WHITLEY Jeff	10
10	OWEN Michael				ELLIOTT Stuart	11
11	COLE Joe				HUGHES Aaron	18
	Tr: ERIKSSON Sven Horan				Tr: SANCHEZ Lawrie	
15	DYER Kieron	72	88		KIRK Andrew	13
16	HARGREAVES Owen	72	60		DAVIS Steve	14
18	DEFOE Jermain	81	88		JONES Steve	15

Millennium, Cardiff
26-03-2005, 15:00, 47 760, Allaerts BEL

WAL 0 2 AUT

Vastic 81, Stranzl 85

#	WALES				AUSTRIA	#
1	COYNE Danny				PAYER Helge	1
2	DELANEY Mark				KATZER Markus	2
3	RICKETTS Samuel				STRANZL Martin	3
4	GABBIDON Danny				POGATETZ Emanuel	4
5	PAGE Robert				EHMANN Anton	5
6	ROBINSON Carl				AUFHAUSER Rene	6
7	FLETCHER Carl				DOSPEL Ernst	7
8	BELLAMY Craig				KIRCHLER Roland	8
9	HARTSON John		87		MAYRLEB Christian	9
10	DAVIES Simon	75	90		IVANSCHITZ Andreas	10
11	GIGGS Ryan	78			HAAS Mario	11
	Tr: TOSHACK John				Tr: KRANKL Hans	
18	EARNSHAW Rob	75	90		HEIBLINGER Mario	14
			87		MAIR Wolfgang	17
			78		VASTIC Ivica	18

Legia, Warsaw
26-03-2005, 18:00, 9 000, Vollquartz DEN

POL 8 0 AZE

Frankowski 3 [12 63 66], Hajiyev OG [16]
Kosowski [40], Krzynowek [72], Saganowski 2 [84 90]

POLAND			AZERBAIJAN	
1 DUDEK Jerzy			KRAMARENKO Dmitriy	1
2 KLOS Tomasz			AMIRBAYOV Rafael	2
3 RZASA Tomasz			HAJIYEV Altandil	3
4 BASZCZYNSKI Marcin			SHUKUROV Mohir	4
5 KOSOWSKI Kamil	46	20	GULIYEV Emin	5
6 BAK Jacek			GULIYEV Kamal	6
7 SOBOLEWSKI Radoslaw		46	NADIROV Iugar	7
8 KRZYNOWEK Jacek			KERIMOV Aslan	8
9 ZURAWSKI Maciej	75		GURBANOV Gurban	9
10 SZYMKOWSKI Miroslav		46	NABIYEV Nadir	11
11 FRANKOWSKI Tomas	68		SADIGOV Rashad	14
Tr: JANAS Pawel			Tr: CARLOS ALBERTO	
16 SMOLAREK Ebi	46	20	MALIKOV Rail	15
17 SAGANOWSKI Marek	75	46	AXHTYAMOV Daniel	17
18 NIEDZIELAN Andrzej	68	46	GURBANOV Ilgar	18

St James' Park, Newcastle
30-03-2005, 19:45, 49 046, Costa POR

ENG 2 0 AZE

Gerrard [51], Beckham [62]

ENGLAND			AZERBAIJAN	
1 ROBINSON Paul			KRAMARENKO Dmitriy	1
2 NEVILLE Gary		46	AMIRBAYOV Rafael	2
3 COLE Ashley			HAJIYEV Altandil	3
4 GERRARD Steven			HASHIMOV Zaur	4
5 FERDINAND Rio	78		BAKHSHIYEV Elmar	5
6 TERRY John			ABDURAKHMONOV Ilgar	6
7 BECKHAM David	84		MALIKOV Rail	7
8 LAMPARD Frank			KERIMOV Aslan	8
9 ROONEY Wayne	78	78	GURBANOV Gurban	9
10 OWEN Michael		78	NABIYEV Nadir	11
11 COLE Joe			SADIGOV Rashad	14
Tr: ERIKSSON Sven Goran			Tr: CARLOS ALBERTO	
14 KING Ledley	78	78	PANAMARYOV Anotoliy	10
15 DYER Kieron	78	46	GULIYEV Vugar	15
18 DEFOE Jermain	84	78	AXHTYAMOV Daniel	17

Legia, Warsaw
30-03-2005, 20:00, 13 515, Frojdfeldt SWE

POL 1 0 NIR

Zurawski [87]

POLAND			NORTHERN IRELAND	
1 DUDEK Jerzy			TAYLOR Maik	1
2 KLOS Tomasz			BAIRD Chris	2
3 RZASA Tomasz	47		CAPALDI Tony	3
4 BASZCZYNSKI Marcin			MURDOCK Colin	4
5 KALUZNY Radoslaw	68	89	WILLIAMS Mark	5
6 BAK Jacek			DAVIS Steve	6
7 KARWAN Bartosz	75		GILLESPIE Keith	7
8 KRZYNOWEK Jacek			WHITLEY Jeff	8
9 ZURAWSKI Maciej		81	HEALY David	9
10 SZYMKOWSKI Miroslav		36	QUINN James	10
11 FRANKOWSKI Tomas			HUGHES Aaron	18
Tr: JANAS Pawel			Tr: SANCHEZ Lawrie	
13 MILA Sebastian	68	11	ELLIOTT Stuart	89
14 KIELBOWICZ Tomasz	47	13	SMITH Andy	81
18 RASAIK Grzegorz	75	36	FEENEY Warren	17

Ernst Happel Stadion, Vienna
30-03-2005, 20:30, 29 500, Mejuto Gonzalez ESP

AUT 1 0 WAL

Aufhauser [87]

AUSTRIA			WALES	
1 PAYER Helge			COYNE Danny	1
2 KATZER Markus			DELANEY Mark	2
3 STRANZL Martin			RICKETTS Samuel Derek	3
4 DOSPEL Ernst	83		GABBIDON Danny	4
5 EHMANN Anton		57	COLLINS James	5
6 AUFHAUSER Rene			ROBINSON Carl	6
7 KIRCHLER Roland	77		FLETCHER Carl	7
8 KUEHBAUER Dietmar			BELLAMY Craig	8
9 MAYRLEB Christian			PARTRIDGE David	9
10 IVANSCHITZ Andreas			DAVIES Simon	10
11 HAAS Mario	54		GIGGS Ryan	11
Tr: KRANKL Hans			Tr: TOSHACK John	
15 KIESENEBNER Markus	83	57	PAGE Robert	16
17 MAIR Wolfgang	77			
18 VASTIC Ivica	54			

Tofik Bakhramov, Baku
4-06-2005, 20:00, 10 458, Undiano Mallenco ESP

AZE 0 3 POL

Frankowski [28], Klos [57]
Zurawski [81]

AZERBAIJAN			POLAND	
1 HASANZADA Cahangir			DUDEK Jerzy	1
2 ABDURAKHMONOV Ilgar	77		KLOS Tomasz	2
3 HAJIYEV Altandil			RZASA Tomasz	3
4 SHUKUROV Mohir			BASZCZYNSKI Marcin	4
5 GULIYEV Emin			KOSOWSKI Kamil	5
6 GULIYEV Kamal			BAK Jacek	6
7 ABDULLAYER Rashad			SOBOLEWSKI Radoslaw	7
8 KERIMOV Aslan	77	84	MILA Sebastian	8
9 GURBANOV Gurban			ZURAWSKI Maciej	9
14 SADIGOV Rashad		90	SZYMKOWSKI Miroslav	10
15 MALIKOV Rail	60	57	FRANKOWSKI Tomas	11
Tr: CARLOS ALBERTO			Tr: JANAS Pawel	
10 RAMAZANOV Zaur	60	84	ZIENCZUK Marek	13
11 GURBANOV Alim	77	57	NIEDZIELAN Andrzej	16
16 ISMAYLOV Farrukh	77	90	RADOMSKI Arkadiusz	17

GROUP 7

Stade du Pays de Charleroi, Charleroi
4-09-2004, 20:15, 19 218, Loizou CYP

BEL 1 1 LTU

Sonck [61]

Jankauskas [73]

	BELGIUM			LITHUANIA	
1	PEERSMAN Tristan			KARCHEMARSKAS Zhidrunas	1
2	DEFLANDRE Eric	46		STANKEVICIUS Marius	2
3	SIMONS Timmy			DZIAUKSTAS Rolandas	3
4	VAN BUYTEN Daniel			BARASA Nerijus	4
5	DHEEDENE Didier			SKERLA Andrius	5
6	CLEMENT Philippe	59		VENCEVICIUS Donatas	6
8	GOOR Bart	10		SKARBALIUS Aurelijus	7
9	SONCK Wesley			CESNAUSKIS Edgaras	8
10	BUFFEL Thomas	67		DANILEVICIUS Tomas	9
11	MPENZA Mbo	23		POSKUS Robertas	10
14	VERMANT Sven	74		JANKAUSKAS Edgaras	11
	Tr: ANTHUENIS Aime			Tr: LIUBINSKAS Algimantas	
13	DUFER Gregory	23	67	MIKOLIUNAS Saulius	13
16	PIERONI Luigi	74	59	RAZANAUSKAS Tomas	14
27	KOMPANY Vincent	46	10	MORINAS Igoris	15

Stadio Olimpico, Serravalle
4-09-2004, 20:30, 1 137, Kholmatov KAZ

SMR 0 3 SCG

Vukic [4], Jestrovic 2 [15 83]

	SAN MARINO			SERBIA/MONTENEGRO	
1	GASPERONI Federico			JEVRIC Dragoslav	1
2	VALENTINI Carlo			DRAGUTINOVIC Ivica	3
3	MARANI Michele		82	MLADENOVIC Dragan	4
4	BACCIOCCHI Simone			VIDIC Nemanja	5
5	DELLA VALLE Alessandro			GAVRANCIC Goran	6
6	CRESCENTINI Federico	46		KOROMAN Ognjen	7
7	DOMENICONI Marco		68	MILOSEVIC Savo	9
8	GASPERONI Alex	87		STANKOVIC Dejan	10
9	CIACCI Nicola			JESTROVIC Nenad	11
10	VANNUCCI Damiano		85	VUKIC Zvonimir	18
11	UGOLINI Andrea	26		KRSTAJIC Mladen	20
	Tr: MAZZA Gianpaolo			Tr: PETKOVIC Ilija	
14	MAIANI Giacomo	87	68	KEZMAN Mateja	8
15	MONTAGNA Paolo	26	82	DULJAJ Igor	15
17	MORETTI Michele	46	85	BRNOVIC Nenad	19

S Darius & S Girenas, Kaunas
8-09-2004, 19:15, 4 000, Jareci ALB

LTU 4 0 SMR

Jankauskas 2 [18 50]
Danilevicius [65], Gedgaudas [92]

	LITHUANIA			SAN MARINO	
1	KARCHEMARSKAS Zhidrunas			GASPERONI Federico	1
2	STANKEVICIUS Marius			VALENTINI Carlo	2
3	DZIAUKSTAS Rolandas			MARANI Michele	3
4	BARASA Nerijus			BACCIOCCHI Simone	4
5	SKERLA Andrius			DELLA VALLE Alessandro	5
6	VENCEVICIUS Donatas		87	ALBANI Nicola	6
7	MIKOLIUNAS Saulius	72		DOMENICONI Marco	7
8	CESNAUSKIS Edgaras	46		GASPERONI Alex	8
9	DANILEVICIUS Tomas			CIACCI Nicola	9
10	POSKUS Robertas		81	VANNUCCI Damiano	10
11	JANKAUSKAS Edgaras	68	65	MONTAGNA Paolo	11
	Tr: LIUBINSKAS Algimantas			Tr: MAZZA Gianpaolo	
15	RADZINEVICIUS Tomas	68	87	MAIANI Giacomo	13
16	MORINAS Igoris	46	65	MORETTI Michele	15
17	GEDGAUDAS Andrius	72	81	NANNI Luca	16

Bilino Polje, Zenica
8-09-2004, 20:15, 14 380, De Santis ITA

BIH 1 1 ESP

Bolic [79]

Vicente [65]

	BOSNIA-HERZEGOVINA			SPAIN	
1	HASAGIC Kenan			IKER CASILLAS	1
2	GRUJIC Vladan	65		SALGADO Michel	2
3	MUSIC Vedin			ROMERO	3
4	SPAHIC Emir		70	ALBELDA	4
5	BAJIC Branimir			PUYOL	5
6	MISIMOVIC Zvjezdan			HELGUERA Ivan	6
7	BOLIC Elvir	83		RAUL	7
8	BESLIJA Mirsad		58	BARAJA	8
9	BARBAREZ Sergej			REYES	9
10	SALIHAMIDZIC Hasan		50	VICTOR	10
11	BALJIC Elvir	62		VICENTE	11
	Tr: SLISKOVIC Blaz			Tr: ARAGONES Luis	
15	KERKEZ Dusan	65	58	VALERON	12
17	BLATNJAK Dragan	62	50	MORIENTES Fernando	14
18	HALILOVIC Nedim	83	70	XABI ALONSO	18

Kosevo, Sarajevo
9-10-2004, 20:15, 22 440, Veissiere FRA

BIH 0 0 SCG

	BOSNIA-HERZEGOVINA			SERBIA/MONTENEGRO	
1	TOLJA Almir			JEVRIC Dragoslav	1
2	SPAHIC Emir			DRAGUTINOVIC Ivica	3
3	PAPAC Sasa	61		DULJAJ Igor	4
4	GRLIC Ivica			GAVRANCIC Goran	6
5	MISIMOVIC Zvjezdan		90	KOROMAN Ognjen	7
6	BAJIC Branimir	78		VUKIC Zvonimir	8
7	BOLIC Elvir		77	MILOSEVIC Savo	9
8	BLATNJAK Dragan			STANKOVIC Dejan	10
9	BARBAREZ Sergej		57	DJORDJEVIC Nenad	14
11	BALJIC Elvir	80		LJUBOJA Danijel	18
14	BESLIJA Mirsad			KRSTAJIC Mladen	20
	Tr: SLISKOVIC Blaz			Tr: PETKOVIC Ilija	
13	CRNOGORAC Gradimir	61	57	MARKOVIC Marjan	2
15	LAGO SANTOS Ricardo	80	77	PANTELIC Marko	11
16	HRGOVIC Mirko	78	90	BRNOVIC Nenad	13

El Sardinero, Santander
9-10-2004, 21:45, 17 000, Nielsen DEN

ESP 2 0 BEL

Luque [60], Raul [65]

	SPAIN			BELGIUM	
1	IKER CASILLAS			PEERSMAN Tristan	1
2	SALGADO Michel		29	DEFLANDRE Eric	2
3	DEL HORNO Asier			VAN BUYTEN Daniel	4
4	MARCHENA Carlos			DESCHACHT Olivier	5
5	PUYOL			CLEMENT Philippe	6
6	ALBELDA	58	68	GOOR Bart	8
7	RAUL			SONCK Wesley	9
8	XAVI	75	79	BUFFEL Thomas	10
9	FERNANDO TORRES	53	75	MPENZA Mbo	11
10	JOAQUIN		60	BISCONTI Roberto	17
11	REYES			KOMPANY Vincent	27
	Tr: ARAGONES Luis			Tr: ANTHUENIS Aime	
14	XABI ALONSO	58	60	DOLL Olivier	14
16	LUQUE	53	75	HUYSEGEMS Stein	15
17	BARAJA	75	79	DUFER Gregory	16

FK Crvena Zvezda, Belgrade
13-10-2004, 20:00, 4 000, Isaksen FRO

SCG	5 0	SMR

Milosevic [35], Stankovic 2 [46+ 50]
Koroman [53], Vukic [69]

SERBIA/MONTENEGRO			SAN MARINO	
1 JEVRIC Dragoslav			GASPERONI Federico	1
2 MARKOVIC Marjan			VALENTINI Carlo	2
3 DRAGUTINOVIC Ivica	61		MARANI Michele	3
4 DULJAJ Igor	46		BACCIOCCHI Simone	4
6 GAVRANCIC Goran			DELLA VALLE Alessandro	5
7 KOROMAN Ognjen			ALBANI Nicola	6
8 VUKIC Zvonimir		90	DOMENICONI Marco	7
9 MILOSEVIC Savo			VANNUCCI Damiano	8
10 STANKOVIC Dejan		78	CIACCI Nicola	9
18 LJUBOJA Danijel	72		GASPERONI Alex	10
20 KRSTAJIC Mladen		64	MORETTI Michele	11
Tr: PETKOVIC Ilija			Tr: MAZZA Gianpaolo	
11 PANTELIC Marko	72	78	DE LUIGI Marco	15
13 BRNOVIC Nenad	46	64	GASPERONI Bryan	16
15 VITAKIC Milivoje	61	90	MORETTI Lorenzo	17

Zalgiris, Vilnius
13-10-2004, 12:15, 9 114, Poulat FRA

LTU	0 0	ESP

LITHUANIA			SPAIN	
1 KARCHEMARSKAS Zhidrunas			IKER CASILLAS	1
2 STANKEVICIUS Marius			SALGADO Michel	2
3 DZIAUKSTAS Rolandas	79		CAPDEVILA	3
4 BARASA Nerijus			MARCHENA Carlos	4
5 SKERLA Andrius			PUYOL	5
6 VENCEVICIUS Donatas			ALBELDA	6
7 SKARBALIUS Aurelijus			RAUL	7
8 CESNAUSKIS Edgaras	65		BARAJA	8
9 GEDGAUDAS Andrius	75	53	VICTOR	9
10 DANILEVICUS Tomas	81		LUQUE	10
11 JANKAUSKAS Edgaras			XAVI	11
Tr: LIUBINSKAS Algimantas			Tr: ARAGONES Luis	
16 MIKOLIUNAS Saulius	75	65	REYES	15
18 RADZINEVICIUS Tomas	81	79	FERNANDO TORRES	17
		53	TAMUDO Raul	18

King Baudouin Stadium, Brussels
17-11-2004, 20:15, 28 350, Frojdfeldt SWE

BEL	0 2	SCG

Vukic [7], Kezman [60]

BELGIUM			SERBIA/MONTENEGRO	
1 PROTO Silvio			JEVRIC Dragoslav	1
3 SIMONS Timmy			DRAGUTINOVIC Ivica	3
5 VAN DER HEYDEN Peter		78	MLADENOVIC Dragan	4
6 CLEMENT Philippe			VIDIC Nemanja	5
7 BASEGGIO Walter			GAVRANCIC Goran	6
9 SONCK Wesley	66	56	KOROMAN Ognjen	7
10 BUFFEL Thomas		28	MILOSEVIC Savo	9
15 DESCHACHT Olivier	28		STANKOVIC Dejan	10
17 BISCONTI Roberto	58		DJORDJEVIC Predrag	11
19 DE COCK Olivier			VUKIC Zvonimir	18
27 KOMPANY Vincent			MARKOVIC Marjan	20
Tr: ANTHUENIS Aime			Tr: PETKOVIC Ilija	
11 DAERDEN Koen	28	28	KEZMAN Mateja	8
16 PIERONI Luigi	58	78	DJORDJEVIC Nenad	14
18 HUYSEGEMS Stein	66	56	DULJAJ Igor	15

Stadio Olimpico, Serravalle
17-11-2004, 20:30, 1 457, Nalbandyan ARM

SMR	0 1	LTU

Cesnauskis.D [41]

SAN MARINO			LITHUANIA	
1 GASPERONI Federico			KARCHEMARSKAS Zhidrunas	1
2 VALENTINI Carlo			SEMBERAS Deividas	2
3 MARANI Michele			DZIAUKSTAS Rolandas	3
4 BACCIOCCHI Simone			STANKEVICIUS Marius	4
5 DELLA VALLE Alessandro		85	GEDGAUDAS Andrius	5
6 ALBANI Nicola			ZVIRGZDAUSKAS Tomas	6
7 MUCCIOLI Riccardo	67		SKARBALIUS Aurelijus	7
8 GASPERONI Alex		75	CESNAUSKIS Edgaras	8
9 DE LUIGI Marco	83		DANILEVICUS Tomas	9
10 SELVA Andy	56		CESNAUSKIS Deividas	10
11 VANNUCCI Damiano		46	RADZINEVICIUS Tomas	11
Tr: MAZZA Gianpaolo			Tr: LIUBINSKAS Algimantas	
13 BONIFAZI Luca	83	75	MIKOLIUNAS Saulius	13
14 CIACCI Nicola	56	85	VENCEVICIUS Donatas	14
16 DOMENICONI Marco	67	46	MORINAS Igoris	15

Estadio Mediterraneo, Almeria
9-02-2005, 21:45, 12 580, Clark SCO

ESP	5 0	SMR

Joaquin [15], Fernando Torres [32]
Raul [42], Guti [61], Del Horno [75]

SPAIN			SAN MARINO	
1 IKER CASILLAS			GASPERONI Federico	1
2 SALGADO Michel			VALENTINI Carlo	2
3 DEL HORNO Asier		56	ANDREINI Matteo	3
4 MARCHENA Carlos			ALBANI Nicola	4
5 PUYOL			DELLA VALLE Alessandro	5
6 XAVI			BACCIOCCHI Simone	6
7 RAUL	46	71	DOMENICONI Marco	7
8 DE LA PENA Ivan	73		VANNUCCI Damiano	8
9 FERNANDO TORRES		88	GASPERONI Alex	9
10 JOAQUIN			SELVA Andy	10
11 LUQUE	46		MARANI Michele	11
Tr: ARAGONES Luis			Tr: MAZZA Gianpaolo	
14 GUTI	46	88	CIACCI Nicola	13
17 GUAYRE	73	56	GASPERONI Bryan	15
18 VILLA David	46	71	MORETTI Michele	17

King Baudouin Stadium, Brussels
26-03-2005, 20:15, 36 700, Hrinak SVK

BEL	4 1	BIH

Mpenza.E 2 [15 54], Daerden [44]
Buffel [77]

Bolic [1]

BELGIUM			BOSNIA-HERZEGOVINA	
1 PROTO Silvio			HASAGIC Kenan	1
2 DOLL Olivier			BAJIC Branimir	2
3 SIMONS Timmy		58	PAPAC Sasa	3
4 VAN BUYTEN Daniel			SPAHIC Emir	4
5 VAN DER HEYDEN Peter			BAJRAMOVIC Zlatan	5
7 DAERDEN Koen			MILENKOVIC Ninoslav	6
8 VANDERHAEGHE Yves			BOLIC Elvir	7
9 MPENZA Emile	90	72	GRLIC Ivica	8
10 BUFFEL Thomas	90		BARBAREZ Sergej	9
16 PIERONI Luigi	87	58	BALJIC Elvir	11
27 KOMPANY Vincent			BESLIJA Mirsad	14
Tr: ANTHUENIS Aime			Tr: SLISKOVIC Blaz	
6 CLEMENT Philippe	90	58	MISIMOVIC Zvjezdan	10
11 VANDENBERGH Kevin	87	72	GRUJIC Vladan	16
17 BISCONTI Roberto	90	58	HALILOVIC Nedim	17

Kosevo, Sarajevo
30-03-2005, 20:00, 6 000, Baskakov RUS

BIH	1	1	LTU

Misimovic [21]

Stankevicius [60]

BOSNIA-HERZEGOVINA			LITHUANIA	
1 HASAGIC Kenan			KARCHEMARSKAS Zhidrunas	1
2 BAJIC Branimir	73		SEMBERAS Deividas	2
3 VIDIC Velimir			DZIAUKSTAS Rolandas	3
4 SPAHIC Emir		65	STANKEVICIUS Marius	4
5 BAJRAMOVIC Zlatan			SKERLA Andrius	5
6 MILENKOVIC Ninoslav		91	CESNAUSKIS Deividas	6
7 BOLIC Elvir			SKARBALIUS Aurelijus	7
8 GRLIC Ivica		56	CESNAUSKIS Edgaras	8
9 BARBAREZ Sergej			POSKUS Robertas	9
10 MISIMOVIC Zvjezdan	65	93	DANILEVICUS Tomas	10
11 BALJIC Elvir	46		JANKAUSKAS Edgaras	11
Tr: SLISKOVIC Blaz			Tr: LIUBINSKAS Algimantas	
14 BESLIJA Mirsad	46	91	MIKOLIUNAS Saulius	13
16 GRUJIC Vladan	65	56	BARASA Nerijus	14
17 HALILOVIC Nedim	73	93	VENCEVICIUS Donatas	18

Stadio Olimpico, Serravalle
30-03-2005, 20:30, 871, Kasnaferis GRE

SMR	1	2	BEL

Selva [41]

Simons [18p], Van Buyten [65]

SAN MARINO			BELGIUM	
1 GASPERONI Federico			PROTO Silvio	1
2 VALENTINI Carlo		58	DOLL Olivier	2
3 MARANI Michele			SIMONS Timmy	3
4 ALBANI Nicola			VAN BUYTEN Daniel	4
5 DELLA VALLE Alessandro			VAN DER HEYDEN Peter	5
6 BACCIOCCHI Simone			DAERDEN Koen	7
7 GASPERONI Alex			VANDERHAEGHE Yves	8
8 DOMENICONI Marco	88		MPENZA Emile	9
9 CIACCI Nicola	62	38	BUFFEL Thomas	10
10 SELVA Andy		84	PIERONI Luigi	16
11 VANNUCCI Damiano			KOMPANY Vincent	27
Tr: MAZZA Gianpaolo			Tr: ANTHUENIS Aime	
15 GASPERONI Bryan	62	58	VANDENBERGH Kevin	11
16 MONTAGNA Paolo	88	84	BISCONTI Roberto	17
		38	CHATELLE Thomas	20

FK Crvena Zvezda, Belgrade
30-03-2005, 21:00, 48 910, Busacca SUI

SCG	0	0	ESP

SERBIA/MONTENEGRO			SPAIN	
1 JEVRIC Dragoslav			IKER CASILLAS	1
3 DRAGUTINOVIC Ivica			PABLO	2
5 VIDIC Nemanja			DEL HORNO Asier	3
6 GAVRANCIC Goran		46	PUYOL	5
7 KOROMAN Ognjen	77		ALBELDA	6
8 KEZMAN Mateja	80	62	XAVI	8
9 MILOSEVIC Savo	65		REYES	9
10 STANKOVIC Dejan		46	DE LA PENA Ivan	11
11 DJORDJEVIC Predrag			FERNANDO TORRES	14
15 DULJAJ Igor			JOAQUIN	17
20 KRSTAJIC Mladen			SERGIO RAMOS	19
Tr: PETKOVIC Ilija			Tr: ARAGONES Luis	
17 BASTA Dusan	77	62	ANTONIO LOPEZ	4
18 JESTROVIC Nenad	80	46	RAUL	7
22 ILIC Sasa	65	46	JUANITO	20

FK Crvena Zvezda, Belgrade
4-06-2005, 20:15, 16 662, Ivanov RUS

SCG	0	0	BEL

SERBIA/MONTENEGRO			BELGIUM	
1 JEVRIC Dragoslav			PROTO Silvio	1
3 DRAGUTINOVIC Ivica			VAN BUYTEN Daniel	4
5 VIDIC Nemanja			DESCHACHT Olivier	5
6 GAVRANCIC Goran			CLEMENT Philippe	6
7 KOROMAN Ognjen	82	79	DAERDEN Koen	7
8 VUKIC Zvonimir			VANDERHAEGHE Yves	8
9 LJUBOJA Danijel			MPENZA Emile	9
10 STANKOVIC Dejan	84	88	BUFFEL Thomas	10
11 JESTROVIC Nenad	53	84	MPENZA Mbo	11
15 DULJAJ Igor			BISCONTI Roberto	17
20 KRSTAJIC Mladen			VANDENBORRE Anthony	20
Tr: PETKOVIC Ilija			Tr: ANTHUENIS Aime	
4 MLADENOVIC Dragan	84	79	LEONARD Philippe	3
17 VUKCEVIC Simon	82	88	PIERONI Luigi	16
18 VUCINIC Mirko	53	84	VANDENBERGH Kevin	18

Stadio Olimpico, Serravalle
4-06-2005, 20:30, 750, Demirlek

SMR	1	3	BIH

Selva [39]

Salihamidzic 2 [17 38]
Barbarez [75]

SAN MARINO			BOSNIA-HERZEGOVINA	
1 CECCOLI Michele			TOLJA Almir	1
2 VALENTINI Carlo	63		BERBEROVIC Dzemal	2
3 MARANI Michele			MILENKOVIC Ninoslav	3
4 CRESCENTINI Federico			VIDIC Velimir	4
5 DELLA VALLE Alessandro		80	BAJRAMOVIC Zlatan	5
6 BACCIOCCHI Simone			PAPAC Sasa	6
7 DOMENICONI Marco			GRLIC Ivica	8
8 GASPERONI Alex			BARBAREZ Sergej	9
9 DE LUIGI Marco	71		SALIHAMIDZIC Hasan	10
10 SELVA Andy	85	59	MISIMOVIC Zvjezdan	11
11 VANNUCCI Damiano		57	BESLIJA Mirsad	14
Tr: MAZZA Gianpaolo			Tr: SLISKOVIC Blaz	
13 ANDREINI Matteo	71	80	KERKEZ Dusan	15
15 GASPERONI Bryan	63	57	BARTOLOVIC Mladen	16
16 MONTAGNA Paolo	85	59	HALILOVIC Nedim	17

Mestalla, Valencia
4-06-2005, 21:30, 25 000, Farina ITA

ESP	1	0	LTU

Luque [68]

SPAIN			LITHUANIA	
1 IKER CASILLAS			KARCHEMARSKAS Zhidrunas	1
2 SALGADO Michel			PAULAUSKAS Gediminas	2
3 DEL HORNO Asier	60		DZIAUKSTAS Rolandas	3
4 MARCHENA Carlos			BARASA Nerijus	4
5 PUYOL			SKERLA Andrius	5
6 ALBELDA			ZVIRGZDAUSKAS Tomas	6
7 RAUL	74	46	KUCYS Aurimas	7
8 XAVI		72	CESNAUSKIS Deividas	8
9 FERNANDO TORRES	57		DANILEVICIUS Tomas	9
11 VICENTE		72	MORINAS Igoris	10
17 JOAQUIN			POSKUS Robertas	11
Tr: ARAGONES Luis			Tr: LIUBINSKAS Algimantas	
15 SERGIO RAMOS	74	72	MIKOLIUNAS Saulius	13
18 JAVIER GARCIA	60	72	CESNAUSKIS Edgaras	15
19 LUQUE	57	46	PREIKSAITIS Aidas	16

Mestalla, Valencia
8-06-2005, 22:00, 38 041, Bennett ENG

ESP	1	1	BIH
Marchena 96+			Misimovic 39

	SPAIN			BOSNIA-HERZEGOVINA	
1	IKER CASILLAS			TOLJA Almir	1
2	SALGADO Michel		76	VIDIC Velimir	2
4	MARCHENA Carlos			MUSIC Vedin	3
5	PUYOL		8	SPAHIC Emir	4
6	ALBELDA			BAJRAMOVIC Zlatan	5
7	RAUL			BAJIC Branimir	6
8	XAVI			GRLIC Ivica	8
9	FERNANDO TORRES	35		BARBAREZ Sergej	9
10	ANTONIO LOPEZ	62	64	MISIMOVIC Zvjazdan	10
11	VICENTE		74	GRUJIC Vladan	11
17	JOAQUIN		95	BESLIJA Mirsad	14
	Tr: ARAGONES Luis			Tr: SLISKOVIC Blaz	
14	XABI ALONSO	62	76	MILENKOVIC Ninoslav	13
19	LUQUE	35	74	DAMJANOVIC Dario	16
20	JUANITO	8	87 64	HALILOVIC Nedim	18

GROUP 8

Laugardalsvollur, Reykjavik
4-09-2004, 16:00, 5 014, Hamer LUX

ISL	1	3	BUL
Gudjohnsen 51p			Berbatov 2 35 49, Yanev 62

	ICELAND			BULGARIA	
1	ARASON Arni			IVANKOV Dimitar	27
2	BJARNASON Olafur			KISHISHEV Radostin	2
3	SIGURDSSON Kristjan			KIRILOV Rosen	3
4	GUNNARSSON Brynjar	84		PETKOV Ivaylo	4
5	SIGURDSSON Indridi	64	80	YANKOV Caaandar	8
6	GRETARSSON Arnar	56		BERBATOV Dimitar	9
7	HREIDARSSON Hermann		42	LAZAROV Zdravko	11
8	EINARSSON Gylfi			HRISTOV Marian	15
9	GUDJOHNSSON Eidur			PETROV Stilian	19
10	GUDJONSSON Thordur		72	BOJINOV Valeri	20
11	HELGUSON Heidar	70		STOYANOV Ilian	22
	Tr: SIGURVINSSON Asgeir			Tr: STOITCHKOV Hristo	
14	VIDARSSON Arnar	64	42	YENEV Hristo	7
16	GUDJONSSON Johannes	56	72	BUKAREV Asen	13
17	SIGURDSSON Helgi	70	80	KAMBUROY Martin	14

Maksimir, Zagreb
4-09-2004, 20:30, 20 853, Riley ENG

CRO	3	0	HUN
Prso 2 31 54, Gyepes OG 80			

	CROATIA			HUNGARY	
1	BUTINA Tomislav			KIRALY Gabor	1
2	SRNA Darijo	84		BODNAR Laszlo	2
3	SIMUNIC Josip	11		HUSZTI Szabolcs	3
4	KOVAC Robert			JUHASZ Roland	4
5	TUDOR Igor		59	STARK Peter	5
6	VRANJES Jurica		81	TOTH Andras	6
8	BABIC Marko			MOLNAR Balasz	7
9	PRSO Dado	74		ROSA Denes	8
10	KOVAC Niko			SZABICS Imre	9
17	KLASNIC Ivan			GERA Zoltan	10
19	KRANJCAR Niko	72	11	SIMEK Peter	11
	Tr: KRANJCAR Zlatko			Tr: MATTHAEUS Lothar	
7	MORNAR Ivica	84	59	GYEPES Gabor	13
13	LEKO Jerko	72	18	LOW Zsolt	15
18	OLIC Ivica	74	81	KOVACS Peter	18

National Stadium, Ta'Qali
4-09-2004, 20:45, 4 200, Jakov ISR

MLT	0	7	SWE
*			Ibrahimovic 4 4 11 14 71
			Ljungberg 2 46, Larsson 76

	MALTA			SWEDEN	
1	MUSCAT Mario			ISAKSSON Andreas	1
2	BRIFFA Roderick		62	LUCIC Teddy	2
3	AZZOPARDI Ian			MELLBERG Olof	3
4	PULLICINO Peter		49	HANSSON Petter	4
5	SAID Brian			EDMAN Erik	5
6	DIMECH Luke			LINDEROTH Tobias	6
7	WOODS Ivan	79	77	WILHELMSSON Christian	7
8	GIGLIO Stefan			SVENSSON Anders	8
9	MIFSUD Michael			LJUNGBERG Fredrik	9
10	GALEA Michael			IBRAHIMOVIC Zlatan	10
11	ZAHRA Antoine	57		LARSSON Henrik	11
	Tr: HEESE Horst			Tr: LAGERBACK Lars	
13	AGIUS Gilbert	57	49	OSTLUND Alexander	13
15	MALLIA George	79	62	NILSSON Mikael	15
			77	JONSON Mattias	18

Nya Ullevi, Gothenburg
8-09-2004, 20:15, 40 023, Dauden Ibanez ESP

SWE	0	1	CRO
			Srna 64

	SWEDEN			CROATIA	
1	ISAKSSON Andreas			BUTINA Tomislav	1
2	OSTLUND Alexander			SRNA Darijo	2
3	MELLBERG Olof			SIMUNIC Josip	3
4	LUCIC Teddy	79		KOVAC Robert	4
5	EDMAN Erik			TUDOR Igor	5
6	LINDEROTH Tobias			VRANJES Jurica	6
7	WILHELMSSON Christian			BABIC Marko	8
8	SVENSSON Anders	73	92	PRSO Dado	9
9	LJUNGBERG Fredrik			KOVAC Niko	10
10	IBRAHIMOVIC Zlatan		46	KLASNIC Ivan	17
11	LARSSON Henrik		62	KRANJCAR Niko	19
	Tr: LAGERBACK Lars			Tr: KRANJCAR Zlatko	
17	ALLBACK Marcus	79	92	TOKIC Mario	11
18	JONSON Mattias	73	62	LEKO Jerko	16
			46	OLIC Ivica	18

Ujpesti, Budapest
8-09-2004, 21:15, 5 461, Ovrebo NOR

HUN 3 2 ISL

Gera 62, Torghelle 75, Szabics 79   Gudjohnsen 39, Sigurdsson.I 78

	HUNGARY				ICELAND	
1	KIRALY Gabor				ARASON Arni	1
2	SZELESI Zoltan	46			BJARNASON Olafur	2
3	BODNAR Laszlo				SIGURDSSON Kristjan	3
4	JUHASZ Roland				VIDARSSON Arnar	4
5	GYEPES Gabor				SIGURDSSON Indridi	5
6	TOTH Andras		86		GRETARSSON Arnar	6
7	MOLNAR Balasz				HREIDARSSON Hermann	7
8	ROSA Denes				GUDJONSSON Johannes	8
9	KOVACS Peter	67	86		GUDJOHNSEN Eidur	9
10	GERA Zoltan		76		GUDJONSSON Thordur	10
11	SIMEK Peter	90			HELGUSON Heidar	11
	Tr: MATTHAEUS Lothar				Tr: SIGURVINSSON Asgeir	
13	LOW Zsolt	90	76		EINARSSON Gylfi	16
17	SZABICS Imre	46	86		SIGURDSSON Helgi	17
18	TORGHELLE Sandor	67	86		GUNNARSSON Veigar	18

Rasunda, Stockholm
9-10-2004, 17:00, 32 288, Dougal SCO

SWE 3 0 HUN

Ljungberg 26, Larsson 50
Svensson 67

	SWEDEN				HUNGARY	
1	ISAKSSON Andreas				KIRALY Gabor	1
2	OSTLUND Alexander		80		BODNAR Laszlo	2
3	MELLBERG Olof				BODOR Boldiszar	3
4	MJJALLBY Johan	46			GYEPES Gabor	4
5	LUCIC Teddy				STARK Peter	5
6	LINDEROTH Tobias				TOTH Andras	6
7	WILHELMSSON Christian	74	55		MOLNAR Balasz	7
8	SVENSSON Anders	80			DARDAI Pal	8
9	LJUNGBERG Frederik		67		TORGHELLE Sandor	9
10	ALLBACK Marcus				GERA Zoltan	10
11	LARSSON Henrik				SZABICS Imre	11
	Tr: LAGERBACK Lars				Tr: MATTHAEUS Lothar	
13	NILSSON Mikael	46	80		FEHER Csaba	14
15	ALEXANDERSSON Niclas	74	55		HAJNAL Tamas	16
16	KAELLSTROM Kim	80	67		KOVACS Peter	18

National Stadium, Ta'Qali
9-10-2004, 18:15, 1 130, Corpodean ROM

MLT 0 0 ISL

	MALTA				ICELAND	
1	HABER Justin				ARASON Arni	1
2	CIANTAR Ian				BJARNASON Olafur	2
3	AZZOPARDI Ian				SIGURDSSON Kristjan	3
4	BRIFFA Roderick		78		GUNNARSSON Brynjar	4
5	SAID Brian		60		SIGURDSSON Indridi	5
6	DIMECH Luke				VIDARSSON Arnar	6
7	AGIUS Gilbert	65			HREIDARSSON Hermann	7
8	GIGLIO Stefan				EINARSSON Gylfi	8
9	MIFSUD Michael				GUDJOHNSEN Eidur	9
10	WOODS Ivan	78	70		GUDJONSSON Thordur	10
11	MATTOCKS Claude				HELGUSON Heidar	11
	Tr: HEESE Horst				Tr: SIGURVINSSON Asgeir	
16	GALEA Michael	78	78		GRETARSSON Arnar	16
17	MALLIA George	65	60		SIGURDSSON Helgi	17
			70		GUNNARSSON Veigar	18

Maksimir, Zagreb
9-10-2004, 20:15, 31 565, Collina ITA

CRO 2 2 BUL

Srna 2 15 31p   Petrov.M 77, Berbatov 86

	CROATIA				BULGARIA	
1	BUTINA Tomislav				IVANKOV Dimitar	27
2	SRNA Darijo		55		KISHISHEV Radostin	2
3	SIMUNIC Josip				PETKOV Ivaylo	4
4	KOVAC Robert	76			MARKOV Georgi	5
5	TOKIC Mario				YANKOV Caaandar	8
6	VRANJES Jurica				BERBATOV Dimitar	9
8	BABIC Marko		90		GEORGIEV Blagoy	15
9	PRSO Dado				PETROV Martin	17
10	KOVAC Niko				PETROV Stilian	19
17	KLASNIC Ivan	55	55		BOJINOV Valeri	20
19	KRANJCAR Niko	68			STOYANOV Ilian	22
	Tr: KRANJCAR Zlatko				Tr: STOITCHKOV Hristo	
14	BANOVIC Ivica	76	90		PASKOV Ivan	6
16	LEKO Jerko	55	55		YANEV Hristo	7
18	BALABAN Bosko	68	55		MANCHEV Vladimir	10

Vasilij Levski, Sofia
13-10-2004, 18:00, 16 800, Richards WAL

BUL 4 1 MLT

Berbatov 2 43 55, Yanev 47
Yankov 88   Mifsud 11

	BULGARIA				MALTA	
27	IVANKOV Dimitar				HABER Justin	1
4	PETKOV Ivaylo				CIANTAR Ian	2
7	YANEV Hristo	72			AZZOPARDI Ian	3
8	YANKOV Caaandar		46		BRIFFA Roderick	4
9	BERBATOV Dimitar				SAID Brian	5
10	MANCHEV Vladimir	65			DIMECH Luke	6
15	GEORGIEV Blagoy				AGIUS Gilbert	7
17	PETROV Martin				GIGLIO Stefan	8
19	PETROV Stilian				MIFSUD Michael	9
20	BOJINOV Valeri	67	10		WOODS Ivan	10
22	STOYANOV Ilian		11		MATTOCKS Claude	11
	Tr: STOITCHKOV Hristo				Tr: HEESE Horst	
3	KIRILOV Rosen	72	75		PULLICINO Peter	13
13	SAKALIEV Stdyko	67	80		COHEN Andrew	17
18	GARGOROV Emil	65	46		ZAHRA Antoine	18

Laugardalsvollur, Reykjavik
13-10-2004, 18:10, 7 037, Busacca SUI

ISL 1 4 SWE

Gudjohnsen 66   Larsson 2 24 39, Allback 27
Wilhelmsson 45

	ICELAND				SWEDEN	
1	ARASON Arni		30		ISAKSSON Andreas	1
2	BJARNASON Olafur	56			OSTLUND Alexander	2
3	SIGURDSSON Kristjan				MELLBERG Olof	3
4	GUNNARSSON Brynjar				LUCIC Teddy	4
5	SIGURDSSON Indridi	25			NILSSON Mikael	5
6	MARTEINSSON Petur				LINDEROTH Tobias	6
7	HREIDARSSON Hermann				WILHELMSSON Christian	7
8	EINARSSON Gylfi				SVENSSON Anders	8
9	GUDJOHNSEN Eidur		56		LJUNGBERG Fredrik	9
10	GUDJONSSON Johannes				ALLBACK Marcus	10
11	HELGUSON Heidar	80	53		LARSSON Henrik	11
	Tr: SIGURVINSSON Asgeir				Tr: LAGERBACK Lars	
14	GUDJONSSON Thordur	56	30		HEDMAN Magnus	12
15	JONSSON Hjalmar	25	56		ALEXANDERSSON Niclas	15
17	GUNNARSSON Veigar	80	53		IBRAHIMOVIC Zlatan	17

National Stadium, Ta'Qali
17-11-2004, 19:30, 14 500, Asumaa FIN

MLT 0 2 **HUN**

Gera [39], Kovacs [93]

MALTA			HUNGARY	
1 HABER Justin			KIRALY Gabor	1
2 CIANTAR Ian		92	ROSA Denes	2
3 AZZOPARDI Ian			HUSZTI Szabolcs	3
4 BRIFFA Roderick			JUHASZ Roland	4
5 SAID Brian			STARK Peter	5
6 DIMECH Luke			HAJNAL Tamas	6
7 AGIUS Gilbert	86		FEHER Csaba	7
8 GIGLIO Stefan			DARDAI Pal	8
9 MIFSUD Michael		67	TORGHELLE Sandor	9
10 WOODS Ivan	74		GERA Zoltan	10
11 MATTOCKS Claude	60	79	WALTNER Robert	11
Tr: HEESE Horst			Tr: MATTHAEUS Lothar	
16 GALEA Michael	60	79	LIPCSEI Peter	16
17 COHEN Andrew	74	92	GYEPES Gabor	17
18 BARBARA Etienne	86	67	KOVACS Peter	18

Vasilij Levski, Sofia
26-03-2005, 17:30, 42 530, Fandel GER

BUL 0 3 **SWE**

Ljungberg 2 [17 92+p]
Edman [74]

BULGARIA			SWEDEN	
27 IVANKOV Dimitar			ISAKSSON Andreas	1
2 KISHISHEV Radostin	74		OSTLUND Alexander	2
4 PETKOV Ivaylo			MELLBERG Olof	3
5 MARKOV Georgi	59		LUCIC Teddy	4
8 YANKOV Caaandar			EDMAN Erik	5
9 BERBATOV Dimitar			LINDEROTH Tobias	6
11 LAZAROV Zdravko	62	60	ALEXANDERSSON Niclas	7
15 GEORGIEV Blagoy			SVENSSON Anders	8
18 BORIMIROV Daniel	76		LJUNGBERG Fredrik	9
20 IVANOV Georgi			IBRAHIMOVIC Zlatan	10
22 STOYANOV Ilian		11	JONSON Mattias	11
Tr: STOITCHKOV Hristo			Tr: FANDEL Herbert	
3 KIRILOV Rosen	74	60	WILHELMSSON Christian	15
7 YANEV Hristo	76	80	ALLBACK Marcus	17
21 TOPUZAKOV Elin	62			

Maksimir, Zagreb
26-03-2005, 18:00, 17 912, Damon RSA

CRO 4 0 **ISL**

Kovac 2 [38 75], Simunic [70]
Prso [91+]

CROATIA			ICELAND	
1 BUTINA Tomislav			ARASON Arni	1
2 SRNA Darijo			SIGURDSSON Kristjan	2
3 SIMUNIC Josip			SIGURDSSON Indridi	3
4 TOMAS Stjepan			BJARNASON Olafur	4
5 TUDOR Igor		73	MARTEINSSON Petur	5
7 LEKO Ivan	79	47	VIDARSSON Arnar	6
9 PRSO Dado			HREIDARSSON Hermann	7
10 KOVAC Niko			GUNNARSSON Brynjar	8
17 KLASNIC Ivan	67		HELGUSON Heidar	9
21 KRANJCAR Niko		60	GUDJONSSON Johannes	10
20 SERIC Anthony	85		EINARSSON Gylfi	11
Tr: KRANJCAR Zlatko			Tr: SIGURVINSSON Asgeir	
14 BOSNJAK Ivan	85	73	GISLASON Stefan	13
16 LEKO Jerko	79	47	STEINSSON Gretar	16
18 OLIC Ivica	67	60	GUDJONSSON Bjarni	17

Maksimir, Zagreb
30-03-2005, 18:00, 15 510, Kapitanis CYP

CRO 3 0 **MLT**

Prso 2 [22 35], Tudor [79]

CROATIA			MALTA	
1 BUTINA Tomislav			HABER Justin	1
2 TOMAS Stjepan			PULLICINO Peter	2
4 KOVAC Robert	45		AZZOPARDI Ian	3
5 TUDOR Igor			SAMMUT Kevin	4
7 LEKO Ivan		58	SAID Brian	5
8 BABIC Marko			DIMECH Luke	6
9 PRSO Dado			AGIUS Gilbert	7
10 KOVAC Niko	76		GIGLIO Stefan	8
14 BOSNJAK Ivan	67	67	MIFSUD Michael	9
17 KLASNIC Ivan		45	GRIMA Massimo	10
19 KRANJCAR Niko			MATTOCKS Claude	11
Tr: KRANJCAR Zlatko			Tr: HEESE Horst	
6 VRANJES Jurica	76	67	BARBARA Etienne	13
11 TOKIC Mario	67	45	WOODS Ivan	14
18 OLIC Ivica	45	58	MALLIA George	15

Ferenc Puskas Stadium, Budapest
30-03-2005, 20:45, 11 586, Wegereef NED

HUN 1 1 **BUL**

Rajczi [90]
Petrov.S [51]

HUNGARY			BULGARIA	
1 KIRALY Gabor			IVANKOV Dimitar	27
3 BODNAR Laszlo			KIRILOV Rosen	3
4 JUHASZ Roland			PETKOV Ivaylo	4
5 STARK Peter		62	YANKOV Caaandar	8
7 SZABICS Imre			BERBATOV Dimitar	9
8 BOOR Zoltan		75	LAZAROV Zdravko	11
9 TORGHELLE Sandor			GEORGIEV Blagoy	15
10 VINCZE Otto	84	83	PETROV Martin	17
11 KORSOS Gyorgy	74		PETROV Stilian	19
14 HUSZTI Szabolcs			TOPUZAKOV Elin	21
17 KOMLOSI Adam			STOYANOV Ilian	11
Tr: MATTHAEUS Lothar			Tr: STOITCHKOV Hristo	
15 RAJCZI Peter	84	62	MANCHEV Vladimir	10
18 KEREKES Zsombor	74	75	BORIMIROV Daniel	18
		83	IVANOV Georgi	20

Nya Ullevi, Gothenburg
4-06-2005, 17:15, 35 593, Ivanov RUS

SWE 6 0 **MLT**

Jonson [6], Svensson [18], Wilhelmsson [29]
Ibrahimovic [40], Ljungberg [57], Elmander [81]

SWEDEN			MALTA	
1 ISAKSSON Andreas			HABER Justin	1
2 ALEXANDERSSON Niclas			PULLICINO Peter	2
3 MELLBERG Olof			PULIS Adrian	3
4 LUCIC Teddy			SAID Brian	5
5 EDMAN Erik			DIMECH Luke	6
6 LINDEROTH Tobias		75	AGIUS Gilbert	7
7 WILHELMSSON Christian	78		GIGLIO Stefan	8
8 SVENSON Anders	63		MIFSUD Michael	9
9 LJUNGBERG Fredrik		46	COHEN Andrew	10
10 IBRAHIMOVIC Zlatan			WOODS Andrew	14
11 JONSON Mattias	63		SAMMUT Kevin	17
Tr: LAGERBACK Lars			Tr: HEESE Horst	
16 KALLSTROM Kim	63	46	BRIFFA Roderick	4
17 ALLBACK Marcus	63	75	MALLIA George	11
18 ELMANDER Johan	78			

Vasilij Levski, Sofia
4-06-2005, 18:00, 35 000, Nielsen DEN

BUL	1	3	CRO

Petrov.M [72]   Babic [19], Tudor [57], Kranjcar [80]

	BULGARIA				CROATIA	
27	IVANKOV Dimitar				BUTINA Tomislav	1
2	KISHISHEV Radostin	55			SRNA Darijo	2
3	KIRILOV Rosen				SIMUNIC Josip	3
5	ILIEV Valentin				KOVAC Robert	4
8	YANKOV Chavdar				TUDOR Igor	5
9	BERBATOV Dimitar				BABIC Marko	8
15	GEORGIEV Blagoy				PRSO Dado	9
17	PETROV Martin				KOVAC Niko	10
19	PETROV Stilian				TOMAS Stjepan	13
20	IVANOV Georgi	46	90		OLIC Ivica	18
22	STOYANOV Ilian		82		KRANJCAR Niko	19
	Tr: STOITCHKOV Hristo				Tr: KRANJCAR Zlatko	
10	BOJINOV Valeri	46	82		LEKO Jerko	16
11	LAZAROV Zdravko	55	90		BALABAN Bosko	21

Laugardalsvollur, Reykjavik
4-06-2005, 18:05, 4 613, Cortez Batista POR

ISL	2	3	HUN

Gudjohnsen [17], Sigurdsson.K [68]   Gera 2 [45p 56p], Huszti [73]

	ICELAND				HUNGARY	
1	ARASON Arni				KIRALY Gabor	1
2	SIGURDSSON Kristjan				BODNAR Laszlo	2
3	SIGURDSSON Indridi				HUSZTI Szabolcs	3
4	BJARNASON Olafur	55	13		VANCZAK Vilmos	4
5	MARTEINSSON Petur	25			STARK Peter	5
6	GUNNARSSON Brynjar				TAKACS Akos	6
7	GISLASON Stefan		75		BARANYOS Zsolt	7
8	EINARSSON Gylfi	51			HAJNAL Tamas	8
9	GUDJOHNSEN Eidur				KEREKES Zsombor	9
10	VIDARSSON Arnar				GERA Zoltan	10
11	STEINSSON Gretar	46	91		TOTH Norbert	11
	Tr: OLAFSSON/SIGURVINSSON				Tr: MATTHAEUS Lothar	
13	ARNASON Haraldur	25	13		BALOG Zoltan	14
14	ARNASON Kari	46	75		SZABICS Imre	17
17	THORVALDSSON Gunnar	51	91		RAJCZI Peter	18

Laugardalsvollur, Reykjavik
8-06-2005, 18:05, 4 887, Skomina SVN

ISL	4	1	MLT

Thorvaldsson [27], Gudjohnsen [33]
Gudmundsson [74], Gunnarsson.V [84]   Said [58]

	ICELAND				MALTA	
1	ARASON Arni				GAUCI Reuben	1
2	STEINSSON Gretar				PULLICINO Peter	2
3	VIDARSSON Arnar				PULIS Adrian	3
4	GISLASON Stefan				BRIFFA Roderick	4
5	HELGASON Audun				SAID Brian	5
6	GUNNARSSON Brynjar				DIMECH Luke	6
7	GUNNARSSON Veigar				AGIUS Gilbert	7
8	ARNASON Kari	63			MATTOCKS Claude	8
9	GUDJOHNSEN Eidur	81			MIFSUD Michael	9
10	THORVALDSSON Gunnar	83	59		SAMMUT Kevin	10
11	GUDMUNDSSON Tryggvi				MALLIA George	11
	Tr: OLAFSSON/SIGURVINSSON				Tr: HEESE Horst	
14	DABNIELSSON Helgi	81	59		COHEN Andrew	15
15	HARDARSON Johannes	63				
17	SIGURDSSON Hannes	83				

PART TWO

THE
ASSOCIATIONS

AFG – AFGHANISTAN

NATIONAL TEAM RECORD
JULY 1ST 2002 TO JUNE 30TH 2005

PL	W	D	L	F	A	%
7	1	0	6	2	24	14.3

FIFA/COCA-COLA WORLD RANKING

1993	1994	1995	1996	1997	1998	1999	2000	2001	2002	2003	2004	High		Low	
-	-	-	-	-	-	-	-	-	-	196	200	196	12/03	204	01/03

2004-2005											
08/04	09/04	10/04	11/04	12/04	01/05	02/05	03/05	04/05	05/05	06/05	07/05
198	198	198	198	200	200	200	200	200	200	200	200

At the FIFA Congress the roll call always starts with Afghanistan but for many years it was met with silence as the seats reserved for the Afghanistan Football Federation remained empty. During the years of the Taliban what football there had been in Afghanistan all but ceased to exist. Since the fall of the regime, however, huge efforts have been made to re-establish the game. The Goal programme is financing a new centre for Afghan football in Kabul, whilst the associations in England, Germany and Iran have helped to start leagues as well as put together national teams at youth level and the full senior team. Seven matches were played in 2003 including a first home

INTERNATIONAL HONOURS
None

match in Kabul for 44 years when Turkmenistan visted for a FIFA World Cup™ qualifier. There have been no matches played since then as efforts have concentrated on unifying the structure of the game throughout the provinces along with developing the essentials such as coaching and refereeing. There is huge interest in football, with local competitions drawing crowds of up to 20,000 for the big games, whilst girls have also started playing, helping the struggle of women to regain acceptance in Afghan society. The twin long-term aims are to establish a national league and to field representative teams in both Asian and world tournaments.

THE FIFA BIG COUNT OF 2000

	Male	Female		Male	Female
Registered players	3 000	0	Referees	75	0
Non registered players	3 000	0	Officials	50	0
Youth players	5 600	0	Total involved	11 725	
Total players	11 600		Number of clubs	440	
Professional players	0	0	Number of teams	450	

Afghanistan Football Federation (AFF)
PO Box 5099, Kabul, Afghanistan
Tel +93 20 210 2417   Fax +93 20 210 2417
e-mail none   www. none
President: KOHISTANI Alim, Gen   General Secretary: MUZAFARI Sayed Zia
Vice-President: MAWLAHI Farid Ahmed   Treasurer: TBD   Media Officer: WADEED Mohammad Nadir
Men's Coach: KARGAR Mohamed   Women's Coach: None
AFF formed: 1933   AFC: 1954   FIFA: 1948
Colours: White with red lines, White with red lines, White with red lines or Green, Green, Green

GAMES PLAYED BY AFGHANISTAN IN THE 2006 FIFA WORLD CUP™ CYCLE

2002	Opponents	Score		Venue	Comp	Scorers	Att	Referee
No international matches played in 2002								
2003								
10-01	Sri Lanka	L	0-1	Dhaka	SAFr1			
12-01	India	L	0-4	Dhaka	SAFr1			
14-01	Pakistan	L	0-1	Dhaka	SAFr1			
16-03	Kyrgyzstan	W	2-1	Kathmandu	ACq	Sayeed Tahir 26, Farid Azimi 76		
18-03	Nepal	L	0-4	Kathmandu	ACq			
19-11	Turkmenistan	L	0-11	Ashgabat	WCq		12 000	Busurmankulov KGZ
23-11	Turkmenistan	L	0-2	Kabul	WCq		6 000	Khan PAK
2004								
No international matches played in 2004								
2005								
No international matches played in 2005 before August								

SAF = South Asian Football Federation Cup • AC = Asian Cup • WC = FIFA World Cup™ • q = qualifier • r1 = first round group

RECENT LEAGUE AND CUP RECORD

Championship		Cup	
Year	Champions		Winners
No championship has been organised in Afghanistan since the 1970s			

FIFA REFEREE LIST 2005

	Int'l	DoB
Afghanistan does not have any referees or assistant referees on the FIFA lists		

AFGHANISTAN NATIONAL TEAM RECORDS AND RECORD SEQUENCES

Records			Sequence records				
Victory	2-1	KYR 2003	Wins	1		Clean sheets	1	
Defeat	0-11	TKM 2003	Defeats	12	1948-1975	Goals scored	3	1954-59, 1979
Player Caps	n/a		Undefeated	1		Without goal	6	1941-1951
Player Goals	n/a		Without win	26	1941-2003	Goals against	21	1948-1984

AFGHANISTAN COUNTRY INFORMATION

Capital	Kabul	Independence	1919 from the UK	GDP per Capita	$700
Population	28 513 677	Status	Islamic Republic of Afghanistan	GNP Ranking	109
Area km²	647 500	Language	Pushtu, Dari	Dialling code	+93
Population density	44 per km²	Literacy rate	36%	Internet code	.af
% in urban areas	20 %	Main religion	Sunni Muslim 80%	GMT +/−	+4.5
Towns/Cities ('000)	Kabul 3 043; Kandahar 391; Mazar-e-Sharif 303; Herat 272; Jalabad 200; Kunduz 161; Ghazni 143; Bamiyan 125; Balkh 114; Baglan 108; Ghardez 103; Khost 96; Maymaneh 79				
Neighbours (km)	Iran 936; Turkmenistan 744; Uzbekistan 137; Tajikistan 1 206; China 76; Pakistan 2 430				
Main stadia	Kabul National Stadium – Kabul 25 000				

AIA – ANGUILLA

NATIONAL TEAM RECORD
JULY 1ST 2002 TO JUNE 30TH 2005

PL	W	D	L	F	A	%
3	0	1	2	1	8	16.7

FIFA/COCA-COLA WORLD RANKING

1993	1994	1995	1996	1997	1998	1999	2000	2001	2002	2003	2004	High		Low	
-	-	-	-	190	197	202	197	194	196	198	197	189	06/97	202	02/00

					2004-2005						
08/04	09/04	10/04	11/04	12/04	01/05	02/05	03/05	04/05	05/05	06/05	07/05
197	197	197	197	197	197	197	197	197	197	197	197

Anguilla is one of the true minnows of world football. With a population of just 13 000 – only neighbours Montserrat have less – the country does surprisingly well in international competition though games are few and far between given that all of the players have many other commitments. A first round exit in the FIFA World Cup™ qualifiers in March 2004 against the Dominican Republic saw the national team go into hibernation again but not before they had forced a draw in Santo Domingo. Both games were played away from home but in future Anguilla will be able to entertain teams at a new national stadium which is being built with Goal Programme finance to the

INTERNATIONAL HONOURS
None

tune of US$ 600,000 and which will be finished in early 2006. The stadium will also provide a top class venue for the two senior leagues run by the AFA, for men and women. In December 2004 Spartans International won the Championship for a second time, and it is this tournament that provides the focus for football on the island, along with the women's league now in its second year. The hope is that clubs will also be able to use the new stadium to compete in the CONCACAF Champions Cup while the national team will play Digicel Caribbean Cup matches there. Anguilla did not take part in the latest editions of either.

THE FIFA BIG COUNT OF 2000 FOR ANGUILLA

	Male	Female		Male	Female
Registered players	140	0	Referees	15	0
Non registered players	100	0	Officials	20	0
Youth players	320	200	Total involved	805	
Total players	760		Number of clubs	4	
Professional players	0	0	Number of teams	9	

Anguilla Football Association (AFA)
PO Box 1318, The Valley, Anguilla
Tel +1 264 497 7323   Fax +1 264 497 7324
axafa@yahoo.com   www. none
President: GUISHARD Raymond   General Secretary: HUGHES Damian
Vice-President: RICHARDSON Ambrel   Treasurer: HODGE Max   Media Officer: HUGHES Damian
Men's Coach: HODGE Vernon   Women's Coach: JOHNSON Colin
AFA formed: 1990   CONCACAF: 1996   FIFA: 1996
Colours: Turquoise & white, Turquoise & white, Turquoise or Orange & blue, Orange & blue, Orange

GAMES PLAYED BY ANGUILLA IN THE 2006 FIFA WORLD CUP™ CYCLE

2002	Opponents	Score		Venue	Comp	Scorers	Att	Referee
6-07	British Virgin Islands	L	1-2	Tortola	Fr			
2003								
No international matches played in 2003								
2004								
19-03	Dominican Republic	D	0-0	Santo Domingo	WCq		400	Mattus CRC
21-03	Dominican Republic	L	0-6	Santo Domingo	WCq		850	Porras CRC
2005								
No international matches played in 2005 prior to August								

Fr = Friendly match • WC = FIFA World Cup™ • q = qualifier

ANGUILLA NATIONAL TEAM RECORDS AND RECORD SEQUENCES

Records			Sequence records					
Victory	4-1	MSR 2001	Wins	1		Clean sheets	1	
Defeat	0-14	GUY 1998	Defeats	17	1991-1998	Goals scored	5	2000-2002
Player Caps	n/a		Undefeated	1		Without goal	7	1991-1994
Player Goals	n/a		Without win	18	1991-1998	Goals against	27	1991-2002

FIFA REFEREE LIST 2005

	Int'l	DoB
BRYAN Leroy	1999	11-10-1960
ROUSE Trevor	1998	1-04-1962

RECENT LEAGUE RECORD

Year	Champions
1996	No tournament played
1997	No tournament played
1998	Spartans International
1999	Attackers
2000	No tournament played due to Hurricane Lenny
2001	Roaring Lions
2002	Roaring Lions
2003	Roaring Lions
2004	Spartans International

ANGUILLA COUNTRY INFORMATION

Capital	The Valley	Independence	Overseas territory of the UK	GDP per Capita	$8 600
Population	13 008	Status		GDP Ranking	n/a
Area km²	102	Language	English	Dialling code	+1 264
Population density	128 per km²	Literacy rate	95%	Internet code	.ai
% in urban areas	n/a	Main religion	Christian 88%	GMT +/−	-4
Towns/Cities ('000)	North Side 1; The Valley 1; Stoney Ground 1; The Quarter 1				
Neighbours (km)	Caribbean Sea 61				
Main stadia	Webster Park – The Valley 4 000				

ALB – ALBANIA

ALBANIA NATIONAL TEAM RECORD
JULY 1ST 2002 TO JUNE 30TH 2005

PL	W	D	L	F	A	%
27	9	3	15	35	47	38.9

FIFA/COCA-COLA WORLD RANKING FOR ALBANIA

1993	1994	1995	1996	1997	1998	1999	2000	2001	2002	2003	2004	High	Low
92	100	91	116	116	106	83	72	96	93	89	86	**72** 12/00	**124** 08/97

2004-2005											
08/04	09/04	10/04	11/04	12/04	01/05	02/05	03/05	04/05	05/05	06/05	07/05
94	94	89	87	86	86	93	89	88	87	86	86

The 2004–05 season in Albania got off to a sensational start when the national team beat neighbours Greece, fresh from their European Championship triumph in Portugal, in the opening FIFA World Cup™ qualifier in Tirana. Any thoughts of emulating the Greek heroics were, however, quickly quashed in perhaps the strongest of all the European qualifying groups with home defeats at the hands of Ukraine and Denmark, although the Albanians have become a much more consistent outfit under former German international Hans-Peter Briegel. Gone are the days when they would go for six years without a win as happened in the 1980s. Briegel also oversees the youth development

INTERNATIONAL HONOURS
Balkan Cup 1946

in Albania and the aim is to build strength in depth, which is lacking at present. The return of a number of players like Alban Bushi and Altin Rrakli to clubs in Albania after long careers abroad has given a boost to the domestic league but good young players still make their way into the bigger leagues in Europe. SK Tirana were chased all the way by Elbasani in the Championship but although they ended comfortable winners they were denied the double by Teuta who beat them in the final on penalties. It was a third Cup triumph for Teuta with all three won on penalties after a 0-0 draw. Indeed, in eight appearances in the final Teuta have yet to score a goal.

THE FIFA BIG COUNT OF 2000 FOR ALBANIA

	Male	Female		Male	Female
Registered players	9 000	0	Referees	1 000	0
Non registered players	30 000	0	Officials	1 000	0
Youth players	9 000	0	Total involved	50 000	
Total players	48		Number of clubs	400	
Professional players	0	0	Number of teams	900	

The Football Association of Albania (FSHF)
Federata Shqiptare e Futbolit, Rruga Labinoti, Pallati perballe Shkolles, "Gjuhet e Huaja", Tirana, Albania
Tel +355 43 46601   Fax +355 43 46 609
fshf@albaniaonline.net   www.fshf.org
President: DUKA Armand   General Secretary: BICI Arben
Vice-President: NURI Luti   Treasurer: KASMI Bujar   Media Officer: NURISHMI Lysien
Men's Coach: BRIEGEL Hans-Peter   Women's Coach: None
FSHF formed: 1930   UEFA: 1954   FIFA: 1932
Colours: Red, Black, Red or White, White, White

GAMES PLAYED BY ALBANIA IN THE 2006 FIFA WORLD CUP™ CYCLE

2002	Opponents	Score		Venue	Comp	Scorers	Att	Referee
12-10	Switzerland	D	1-1	Tirana	ECq	Murati [79]	15 000	Erdemir TUR
16-10	Russia	L	1-4	Volgograd	ECq	Duro.K [13]	18 000	Sundell SWE
2003								
12-02	Vietnam	W	5-0	Bastia Umbra - ITA	Fr	Bushi [16], Myrtaj 2 [21 38], Dragusha [53], Pinari [85]		Nikoluci ITA
29-03	Russia	W	3-1	Shkoder	ECq	Rraklli [20], Lala [79], Tare [82]	16 000	Allaerts BEL
2-04	Republic of Ireland	D	0-0	Tirana	ECq		20 000	Farina ITA
30-04	Bulgaria	L	0-2	Sofia	Fr		9 325	Vidlak CZE
7-06	Republic of Ireland	L	1-2	Dublin	ECq	Skela [8]	33 000	Mikulski POL
11-06	Switzerland	L	2-3	Geneva	ECq	Lala [23], Skela [86p]	26 000	Bennett ENG
20-08	Macedonia	L	1-3	Prilep	Fr	Skela [74]	3 000	Mihajlevic SCM
6-09	Georgia	L	0-3	Tbilisi	ECq		18 000	Vollquartz DEN
10-09	Georgia	W	3-1	Tirana	ECq	Hasi [52], Tare [54], Bushi [80]	10 500	Salomir ROM
11-10	Portugal	L	3-5	Lisbon	Fr	Aliaj 2 [13 59], Tare [43]	5 000	Garibian FRA
15-11	Estonia	W	2-0	Tirana	Fr	Aliaj [26], Bushi [81]	5 000	Douros GRE
2004								
18-02	Sweden	W	2-1	Tirana	Fr	Skela [69], Aliaj [75]	15 000	Paparesta ITA
31-03	Iceland	W	2-1	Tirana	Fr	Aliaj [42], Bushi [78]	12 000	Bertini ITA
28-04	Estonia	D	1-1	Tallinn	Fr	Aliaj [51]	1 500	Sipailo LVA
18-08	Cyprus	L	1-2	Nicosia	Fr	Rraklli [64]	200	Kapitanis CYP
4-09	Greece	W	2-1	Tirana	WCq	Murati [2], Aliaj [11]	15 800	Gonzalez ESP
8-09	Georgia	L	0-2	Tbilisi	WCq		20 000	Courtney NIR
9-10	Denmark	L	0-2	Tirana	WCq		14 500	Baskarov RUS
13-10	Kazakhstan	W	1-0	Almaty	WCq	Bushi [61]	12 300	Stuchlik AUT
2005								
9-02	Ukraine	L	0-2	Tirana	WCq		12 000	Bennett ENG
26-03	Turkey	L	0-2	Istanbul	WCq		32 000	Plautz AUT
30-03	Greece	L	0-2	Piraeus	WCq		31 700	Layec FRA
29-05	Poland	L	0-1	Szczecin	Fr		14 000	Weiner GER
4-06	Georgia	W	3-2	Tirana	WCq	Tare 2 [6 56], Skela [33]	BCD	Tudor ROM
8-06	Denmark	L	1-3	Copenhagen	WCq	Bogdani [73]	26 366	Frojdfeldt SWE

Fr = Friendly match • EC = UEFA EURO 2004 • WC = FIFA World Cup™ • q = qualifier • BCD = behind closed doors

NATIONAL CAPS		NATIONAL GOALS		NATIONAL COACH	
	Caps		Goals		Years
STRAKOSHA Foto	73	BUSHI Alban	13	SHULA Argon	-1987
RRAKLLI Altin	63	RRAKLLI Altin	11	RRELI Shyqri	1988-'90
TARE Igli	60	KUSHTA Sokol	10	SHULA Argon	1990
VATA Rudi	59	TARE Igli	9	BIRCE Bejkush	1990-'94
BUSHI Alban	56	ALIAJ Ardian	7	BAJKO Neptun	1994-'96
XHUMBA Arben	48	KOLA Bledar	6	HAFIZI Astrit	1996-'99
DEMOLLARI Sulejman	45	BORICI Loro	6	ZHEGA Medin	2000-'01
HAXHI Altin	45	SKELA Ervin	6	DEMOLLARI Sulejman	2001-'02
LALA Altin	43	PERNASKA Ilir	5	DOSSENA Giuseppe	2002
SHULKU Ilir	41	VATA Rudi	5	BRIEGEL Hans-Peter	2002-

ALBANIA COUNTRY INFORMATION

Capital	Tirana (Tiranë)	Independence	1912	GDP per Capita	$4 500
Population	3 544 808	Status	Republic	GNP Ranking	118
Area km[2]	28 748	Language	Albanian	Dialling code	+355
Population density	123 per km[2]	Literacy rate	86%	Internet code	.al
% in urban areas	37%	Main religion	Muslim 70%	GMT + / -	+1
Towns/Cities ('000)	Tirana 374; Durrës 122; Elbasan 100; Shkodër 89; Vlorë 89; Fier 59; Korçë 58; Berat 47				
Neighbours (km)	Greece 282; Macedonia 151; Serbia and Montenegro 287				
Main stadia	Qemal Stafa – Tirana 18 000; Loro Boriçi – Shkodër 16 000; Tomori – Berat 14 500; Ruzhdi Bizhuta – Elbasan 13 000; Selman Stermasi – Tirana 12 500				

ALBANIA NATIONAL TEAM RECORDS AND RECORD SEQUENCES

Records			Sequence records					
Victory	5-0	VIE 2003	Wins	4	1999-2000	Clean sheets	3	Three times
Defeat	0-12	HUN 1950	Defeats	10	1989-1991	Goals scored	7	1973-1980
Player Caps	59	STRAKOSHA Foto	Undefeated	4	Four times	Without goal	6	1987-88, 1990-91
Player Goals	10	RRAKLII Altin	Without win	25	1985-1991	Goals against	14	1988-1991

ALBANIA 2004-05

KATEGORIA SUPERIORE

	Pl	W	D	L	F	A	Pts	Tirana	Elbasani	Dinamo	Vllaznia	Teuta	Shkumbini	Lushnja	Partizani	Egnatia	Laçi
SK Tirana †	36	26	6	4	82	32	84		2-2 0-1	3-1 0-2	2-1 2-2	2-0 2-2	1-0 2-0	3-0 1-1	3-3 4-0	3-1 3-1	1-0 6-0
SK Elbasani ‡	36	24	7	5	59	27	79	3-1 2-2		0-0 1-1	1-0 1-0	2-0 2-0	2-1 4-2	2-0 3-1	2-1 2-1	1-0 2-1	2-0 7-0
Dinamo Tiranë	36	18	8	10	51	30	62	2-1 0-1	0-0 0-0		0-1 1-0	0-1 0-2	3-2 2-1	1-1 1-0	3-2 2-0	1-0 3-1	6-1 4-0
Vllaznia Shkodër	36	19	4	13	80	47	61	1-2 0-2	4-1 2-1	2-1 0-2		6-1 2-0	2-0 3-3	2-0 4-2	3-1 4-2	3-2 2-0	7-0 8-0
Teuta Durrës ‡	36	14	6	16	47	49	52	0-2 3-5	1-0 0-1	1-0 2-2	3-2 3-2		1-2 1-0	1-1 2-1	0-1 1-2	1-0 1-0	6-1 5-0
Shkumbini Peqin	36	14	6	16	49	47	48	0-1 1-2	1-2 1-0	2-1 1-0	3-5 0-1	1-0 3-1		2-0 0-0	2-0 4-3	1-1 1-1	5-1 1-0
KS Lushnja	36	13	9	14	43	47	48	0-3 1-3	0-1 3-2	0-2 2-2	2-0 2-0	1-0 1-1	3-1 1-0		1-0 1-3	2-1 3-1	1-1 5-0
Partizani Tiranë	36	13	7	16	59	58	46	2-5 0-1	2-2 0-2	0-1 0-2	**2-0** 1-1	2-1 1-0	1-1 1-0	3-0 1-1		2-1 4-1	4-1 5-5
Egnatia Rrogozhinë	36	7	7	22	26	48	28	0-2 0-1	0-1 0-1	2-1 0-0	1-0 1-1	1-2 0-2	0-2 0-0	0-2 0-0	1-0 0-0		1-0 2-0
Laçi	36	0	2	34	13	124	2	0-3 0-5	0-1 0-1	0-3 0-1	1-7 1-2	0-1 0-1	1-3 0-2	0-1 0-3	0-4 0-5	0-2 0-3	

21/08/2004 - 21/05/2005 • † Qualified for the UEFA Champions League • ‡ Qualified for the UEFA Cup • Matches in bold awarded 2-0

ALBANIA 2004-05 KATEGORIA E PARE (2)

	Pl	W	D	L	F	A	Pts
Besa Kavajë	22	14	5	3	39	18	47
Skënderbeu Korçë	22	15	2	5	36	15	47
Apolonia Fier	22	12	5	5	38	15	41
Tomori Berat	22	9	8	5	27	19	35
Erzeni Shijak	22	9	7	6	22	18	34
Kastrioti Krujë	22	8	7	7	25	18	31
Besëlidhja Lezhë	22	8	6	8	24	23	30
Luftëtari Gjirokastër	22	8	6	8	23	25	30
Flamurtari Vlorë	22	8	3	11	24	29	27
Pogradeci	22	6	6	10	21	21	24
Naftëtari Kuçovë	22	4	2	16	12	33	14
Bylis Ballshi	22	2	1	19	13	70	7

12/09/2004 - 14/05/2005. Title play-off: Skënderbeu 1-0 Besa

TOP SCORERS

BYLYKBASHI Dorian	Partizani	24
XHAFA Daniel	Teuta	21

KUPA E SHQIPERISE 2004-05

Quarter-finals		Semi-finals		Final	
Teuta Durrës	3 1				
Elbasani *	3 0	Teuta Durrës *	1 1		
Flamurtari *	1 0	Partizani Tiranë	0 2		
Partizani Tiranë	2 1			Teuta Durrës ‡	0 6p
Vllaznia Shkodër	1 2			SK Tirana	0 5p
Shkumbini *	0 2	Vllaznia Shkodër	0 1	11-05-2005, Ref: Janku
Lushnja *	1 0	SK Tirana *	1 3	Ruzhdi Bizhuda, Elbasan
SK Tirana	0 3			* Home team 1st leg • ‡ Qualified for the UEFA Cup

CLUB DIRECTORY

Club	Town/City	Stadium	Phone	www.	Lge	Cup	E1
Dinamo	Tiranë	Selman Stërmasi 12 500	+355 4 230336		16	13	0
Egnatia	Rrogozhinë		+355 5 772031		0	0	0
Elbasani	Elbasan	Ruzhdi Bizhuda 13 000	+355 54 53253		1	2	0
Laçi	Laç	Prane Bashkise 5 000			0	0	0
Lushnja	Lushnjë	Roza Haxhiu 12 000	+355 3 522512		0	0	0
Partizani	Tiranë	Selman Stërmasi 12 500	+355 4 250910		15	15	0
Shkumbini	Peqin	Fusha Sportive 5 000	+355 5 123200		0	0	0
Teuta	Durrës	Niko Dovana 12 000	+355 5 224748		1	3	0
SK Tirana	Tiranë	Selman Stërmasi 12 500	+355 4 256899	sktirana.com	22	12	0
Vllaznia	Shkodër	Loro Borici 16 000	+355 2 247470		9	5	0

RECENT LEAGUE AND CUP RECORD

	Championship						Cup		
Year	Champions	Pts	Runners-up	Pts	Third	Pts	Winners	Score	Runners-up
2000	SK Tirana	52	Tomori Berat	52	Teuta Durrës	49	Teuta Durrës	0-0 5-4p	Lushnjë
2001	Vllaznia Shkodër	56	SK Tirana	54	Teuta Durrës	52	SK Tirana	5-0	Teuta Durrës
2002	Dinamo Tiranë	63	SK Tirana	62	Partizani Tiranë	46	SK Tirana	1-0	Dinamo Tiranë
2003	SK Tirana	60	Vllaznia Shkodër	49	Partizani Tiranë	46	Dinamo Tiranë	1-0	Teuta Durrës
2004	SK Tirana	80	Dinamo Tiranë	71	Vllaznia Shkodër	68	Partizani Tiranë	1-0	Dinamo Tiranë
2005	SK Tirana	84	SK Elbasani	79	Dinamo Tiranë	62	Teuta Durrës	0-0 6-5p	SK Tirana

ALG – ALGERIA

NATIONAL TEAM RECORD
JULY 1ST 2002 TO JUNE 30TH 2005

PL	W	D	L	F	A	%
35	11	13	11	41	39	50

FIFA/COCA-COLA WORLD RANKING

1993	1994	1995	1996	1997	1998	1999	2000	2001	2002	2003	2004	High		Low	
35	57	48	49	59	71	86	82	75	68	62	73	30	09/93	88	11/99

2004-2005											
08/04	09/04	10/04	11/04	12/04	01/05	02/05	03/05	04/05	05/05	06/05	07/05
58	61	66	70	73	74	75	75	76	77	80	81

From being one of the major powers on the African continent the Algerian national team now finds itself in something of a crisis. The past year has even seen the team struggle to make it into the top three of the FIFA World Cup™ qualifying group who would offer the consolation of a place in next year's CAF African Cup of Nations in Egypt. As for qualifying for the FIFA World Cup™ that was never a realistic task after the opening month of the campaign. In June 2005 Ali Fergani became the latest in a long line of managers to be shown the door, following Robert Waseige, the coach at the start of the qualifiers who quit after the embarrassing home defeat to Gabon in September 2004.

INTERNATIONAL HONOURS
Qualified for the FIFA World Cup™ finals 1982 1986 CAF African Cup of Nations 1990

CAF Youth Cup 1979 All Africa Games 1978 African Champions League Mouloudia Alger 1976, JS Kabylie 1981 1990

There was little more encouragement at club level where USM Alger failed to qualify from the 2004 Champions League group stage whilst no Algerian club made it to the group stage of either the Champions League or Confederation Cup in 2005. There were a number of surprises on the domestic front, however, especially when Third Division USM Sétif made it to the Cup Final before falling to ASO Chlef in front of a capacity crowd in Algiers. The Championship proved to be a stroll for USM Alger who were rarely threatened finishing a comfortable 13 points clear of 2004 champions JS Kabylie.

THE FIFA BIG COUNT OF 2000

	Male	Female		Male	Female
Registered players	125 260	976	Referees	530	38
Non registered players	225 600	104	Officials	20 505	310
Youth players	58 900	0	Total involved	432 223	
Total players	410 840		Number of clubs	252	
Professional players	260	0	Number of teams	2 329	

Fédération Algérienne de Football (FAF)
Chemin Ahmed Ouaked, Case Postale 39, Dely-Ibrahim, Alger, Algeria

Tel +213 21 372929   Fax +213 21 367266

admfaf@mail.wissal.dz   www.faf.org.dz

President: RAOURAOUA Mohamed   General Secretary: BOUCHEMLA Mourad

Vice-President: CHAABANE Abdelkader   Treasurer: MECHRARA Mohamed   Media Officer: DERRADJI Hafid

Men's Coach: TBD   Women's Coach: CHIH Azzedine

FAF formed: 1962   CAF: 1964   FIFA: 1963

Colours: Green, White, Green or White, Green, White

GAMES PLAYED BY ALGERIA IN THE 2006 FIFA WORLD CUP™ CYCLE

2002	Opponents	Score		Venue	Comp	Scorers	Att	Referee
20-08	Congo DR	D	1-1	Blida	Fr	Haddou 61p		Benaissa ALG
7-09	Namibia	W	1-0	Windhoek	CNq	OG 4	13 000	Tangawarima ZIM
24-09	Uganda	D	1-1	Annaba	Fr	Amaouche 46		Benaissa ALG
11-10	Chad	W	4-1	Annaba	CNq	Akrour 2 26 72p, Belmadi 2 54 69	20 000	El Beltagy EGY
2003								
25-01	Uganda	W	1-0	Kampala	Fr	Ammour 64	5 000	Aouuby UGA
12-02	Belgium	L	1-3	Annaba	Fr	Belmadi 89	40 000	Baraket TUN
29-03	Angola	D	1-1	Luanda	Fr	Akrour 85	8 000	Mavunza ANG
24-04	Madagascar	W	3-1	Amiens	Fr	Fellahi 26, Belkaid 60, Cherrad 76	1 000	Garibian FRA
29-05	Burkina Faso	L	0-1	Avion	Fr		1 050	Gannard FRA
20-06	Namibia	W	1-0	Blida	CNq	Kraouche 5	30 000	Auda EGY
6-07	Chad	D	0-0	N'Djamena	CNq			
4-09	Qatar	W	1-0	Dinard	Fr	Cherrad 26	400	
24-09	Gabon	D	2-2	Algiers	Fr	Fellahi 51, Achiou 59, W 4-3p	2 000	Zekrini ALG
26-09	Burkina Faso	D	0-0	Algiers	Fr	W 4-3p	1 500	Benouza ALG
11-10	Niger	W	1-0	Niamey	WCq	Boutabout 63	20 126	Coulibaly MLI
14-11	Niger	W	6-0	Algiers	WCq	Cherrad 2 16 22, Boutabout 2 42 70, Mamouni 45, Akrour 82	50 000	El-Arjoun MOR
2004								
15-01	Mali	L	0-2	Algiers	Fr		7 000	Zehmoun TUN
25-01	Cameroon	D	1-1	Sousse	CNr1	Zafour 51	20 000	Codjia BEN
29-01	Egypt	W	2-1	Sousse	CNr1	Mamouni 13, Achiou 85	15 000	Hamer LUX
3-02	Zimbabwe	L	1-2	Sousse	CNr1	Achiou 72	10 000	Maillet SEY
8-02	Morocco	L	1-3	Sfax	CNqf	Cherrad 83	20 000	Shelmani LBY
28-04	China PR	L	0-1	Clermont-Ferrand	Fr		1 600	Poulat FRA
30-05	Jordan	D	1-1	Annaba	Fr	Cherrad 60	20 000	Zahmoul TUN
5-06	Angola	D	0-0	Annaba	WCq		55 000	Daami TUN
20-06	Zimbabwe	D	1-1	Harare	WCq	Cherrad 3	65 000	Ntambidila COD
3-07	Nigeria	L	0-1	Abuja	WCq		35 000	Hisseine CHA
17-08	Burkina Faso	D	2-2	Blida	Fr	Tahraoui 33, Arrache 54	15 000	Tahri MAR
5-09	Gabon	L	0-3	Annaba	WCq		51 000	Ndoye SEN
9-10	Rwanda	D	1-1	Kigali	WCq	Bourahli 14	20 000	Abdel Rahmen SUD
17-11	Senegal	L	1-2	Toulon	Fr	Daoud 77	4 000	Bata FRA
2005								
9-02	Burkina Faso	W	3-0	Algiers	Fr	Saifi 2 29 42, Sofiane 72	5 000	Benaissa ALG
27-03	Rwanda	W	1-0	Oran	WCq	Boutabout 48	20 000	Abd El Fatah EGY
5-06	Angola	L	1-2	Luanda	WCq	Boutabout 63	27 000	Hicuburundi BDI
12-06	Mali	L	0-3	Arles	Fr			
19-06	Zimbabwe	D	2-2	Oran	WCq	Yahia 17, Daoud 48	15 000	Pare BFA

Fr = Friendly match • CN = CAF African Cup of Nations • WC = FIFA World Cup™ • q = qualifier • r1 = first round group • qf = quarter-final

ALGERIA COUNTRY INFORMATION

Capital	Algiers (Alger)	Independence	1962	GDP per Capita	$6 000
Population	32 129 324	Status	Republic	GNP Ranking	47
Area km²	2 381 740	Language	Arabic	Dialling code	+213
Population density	13 per km²	Literacy rate	60%	Internet code	.dz
% in urban areas	56%	Main religion	Muslim 99%	GMT + / –	+1
Towns/Cities ('000)	Algiers 1 980; Oran 646; Constantine 450; Batna 280; Bab Azwar 277; Setif 226; Al Jilfah 213; Annaba 206; Biskra 196; Sidi Bel Abbès 191; Tibissah 182; Tiyarat 176; Al Buni 171				
Neighbours (km)	Tunisia 965; Libya 982; Niger 956; Mali 1 376; Mauritania 463; Western Sahara 42; Morocco 1 559; Mediterranean Sea 998				
Main stadia	Stade 5 Juillet – Algiers 66 000; Stade 19 Mai – Annaba 50 000; Ahmed Zabana - Oran 50 000; Stade 24 Février – Sidi Bel Abbes 50 000; Frères Brakni – Blida 35 000				

ALGERIA NATIONAL TEAM RECORDS AND RECORD SEQUENCES

Records			Sequence records					
Victory	15-1	YEM 1973	Wins	5	1981-1982, 1990	Clean sheets	4	Five times
Defeat	0-5	BFA 1975, GDR 1976	Defeats	5	1974	Goals scored	16	2000-2001
Player Caps	n/a		Undefeated	15	1989-1991	Without goal	5	1989
Player Goals	n/a		Without win	11	2004	Goals against	9	2000-2001

NATIONAL COACH

	Years
DJADAOUI Abdelghani	2000-'01
ZOUBA Hamid & KERMALI Abdelhamid	2001
MADJER Rabah	2001-'02
ZOUBA Hamid	2002-'03
BOURATTA Rachid	2003
LEEKENS George	2003
SAADANE Rabah	2003
WASEIGE Robert	2003-'04
FERGANI Ali	2004

FIFA REFEREE LIST 2005

	Int'l	DOB
BENAISSA Mohamed Lamine	2001	25-09-1970
BENOUZA Mohamed	2001	26-09-1972
BERBER Kamel	1998	22-06-1962
BOUBAKOUR Samir		16-06-1970
DJABALLAH Touati	2001	11-11-1970
HAIMOUDI Djamel		10-12-1970
ZEKRINI Mohamed	2001	19-07-1962

FIFA ASSISTANT REFEREE LIST 2005

	Int'l	DoB
BELBECIR Mohamed Lamine	2000	16-07-1961
BERRAHMOUNE Karim	2001	12-07-1968
DJEZZAR Brahim	1995	23-01-1963
KAID Ahmed	2000	28-07-1963
KERRAI Mazari	2005	10-10-1969
SEDRATI Ahmed	2001	23-04-1963
TALBI Amar		3-05-1968

CLUB DIRECTORY

Club	Town/City	Stadium	Phone	www.	Lge	Cup	A1
CR Belouizdad	Algiers	20 Août 1955 20 000	+213 21 677644	chabab-belcourt.com	6	5	0
CS Constantine	Constantine	Chahid Hamlaoui 40 000	+213 31 929436		1	0	0
ES Setif	Setif	8 Mai 1945 25 000	+213 36 903333		2	6	0
GC Mascara	Mascara	Unité Africaine 5 000	+213 45 812908		1	0	0
JS Kabylie	Tizi Ouzou	1 Novembre 1954 25 000	+213 26 215272	js-kabylie.com	12	4	2
MC Alger	Algiers	5 Juillet 1962 80 000	+213 21 634743	mcalger.com	6	4	1
MC Oran	Oran	Ahmed Zabana 50 000	+213 41 331846	mouloudia.com	4	4	0
NA Hussein Dey	Algiers	Frères Zioui 7 000	+213 21 777930	nasria.com	1	1	0
USM Alger	Algiers	Omar Hammadi 15 000	+213 21 966684	usma-alger.com	5	7	0
WA Tlemcen	Tlemcen	Frères Zerga 6 000	+213 43 276149	watlemcen.com	0	2	0

CR = Chabab Riadhi • CS = Club Sportif • ES = Entente Sportive • GC = Ghali Club • JS = Jeunesse Sportive • MC = Mouloudia Chaabia (Alger) • MC = Mouloudia Club (Oran) • NA = Nasr Athletic • USM = Union Sportive Madinet • WA = Widad Athletic

RECENT LEAGUE AND CUP RECORD

	Championship						Cup		
Year	Champions	Pts	Runners-up	Pts	Third	Pts	Winners	Score	Runners-up
1990	JS Kabylie	40	MC Oran	36	MC Alger	34	Tournament not held		
1991	MO Constantine	38	AS Ain Mlila	36	ASM Oran	36	USM Bel Abbés	2-0	JS Kabylie
1992	MC Oran	39	USM El Harrach	35	WA Tlemcen	35	JS Kabylie	1-0	ASO Chlef
1993	MC Oran	38	NA Hussein Dey	37	US Chaouia	36	Tournament not held		
1994	US Chaouia	35	JS Kabylie	35	JS Bordj Menaiel	35	JS Kabylie	1-0	AS Ain Mlila
1995	JS Kabylie	40	MC Oran	35	USM Blida	33	CR Belouizdad	2-1	OM Médéa
1996	USM Algiers	60	MC Oran	58	WA Tlemcen	51	MC Oran	1-0	Ittihad Blida
1997	CS Constantine	56	MC Oran	55	USM Algiers	49	USM Algiers	1-0	CA Batna
1998	USM El Harrach	3-2	USM Algiers				WA Tlemcen	1-0	MC Oran
1999	MC Alger	1-0	JS Kabylie				USM Alger	2-0	JS Kabylie
2000	CR Belouizdad	47	MC Oran	38	MC Constantine	38	MC Ouargla	2-1	WA Tlemcen
2001	CR Belouizdad	62	USM Algiers	55	JS Kabylie	52	USM Alger	1-0	CR Méchria
2002	USM Alger	57	JS Kabylie	52	WA Tlemcen	51	WA Tlemcen	1-0	MC Oran
2003	USM Alger	58	USM Blida	51	NA Hussein Dey	51	USM Alger	2-1	CR Belouizdad
2004	JS Kabylie	61	USM Alger	58	NA Hussein Dey	49	USM Alger	0-0 5-4p	JS Kabylie
2005	USM Alger	67	JS Kabylie	54	MC Alger	49	ASO Chlef	1-0	USM Sétif

ALGERIA 2004-05

PREMIERE DIVISION

	Pl	W	D	L	F	A	Pts	USM Alger	JS Kabylie	MC Alger	CA Bordj BA	NA HD	USM Blida	ASO Chlef	CO Constine	MC Oran	WA Tlemcen	ES Sétif	USM Annaba	CR Bel'dad	OMR El An.	GC Mascara	US Chaouia
USM Alger †	30	21	4	5	55	27	67		2-1	1-2	2-0	1-0	4-1	1-0	3-0	2-1	2-1	3-2	2-2	0-1	4-1	1-0	3-0
JS Kabylie †	30	16	6	8	44	22	54	2-1		6-1	2-0	0-0	1-0	3-0	4-1	1-0	2-0	1-0	0-0	3-0	1-0	3-1	3-0
MC Alger	30	14	7	9	39	44	49	1-2	2-1		0-1	0-0	1-0	2-1	1-4	2-1	1-1	3-0	0-0	1-0	2-3	1-0	2-0
CA Bordj Bou Arreridj	30	10	13	7	32	25	43	3-0	0-0	3-1		0-0	2-0	0-0	1-1	2-0	2-1	1-0	3-0	0-1	0-0	1-0	1-0
NA Hussein Dey	30	11	10	9	29	19	43	1-2	1-0	0-1	1-1		1-1	2-0	0-1	1-0	2-0	0-1	1-0	2-1	1-0	1-2	5-0
USM Blida	30	11	9	10	36	28	42	0-2	2-1	3-1	1-1	0-1		2-2	4-1	1-1	2-0	3-0	1-1	1-0	0-0	2-0	3-0
ASO Chlef	30	10	11	9	30	32	41	1-2	1-1	0-0	1-1	1-1	1-0		1-0	2-1	0-0	1-0	1-0	1-0	1-1	1-0	2-1
CS Constantine	30	11	7	12	33	42	40	1-3	1-1	2-4	1-0	0-0	0-1	2-2		0-1	1-0	2-0	1-0	3-0	3-2	2-1	1-1
MC Oran	30	10	9	11	36	37	39	2-1	2-1	2-2	2-2	0-0	0-0	3-2	3-0		0-0	1-0	3-0	1-1	0-3	2-1	4-0
WA Tlemcen	30	9	11	10	36	27	38	0-1	3-1	8-1	2-1	0-0	0-0	1-2	0-1	2-0		1-1	1-1	1-0	1-1	5-1	1-0
ES Sétif	30	11	5	14	37	36	38	1-2	2-0	0-2	2-2	1-2	2-1	2-0	0-1	3-1	1-1		1-2	2-0	3-0	5-3	3-1
USM Annaba	30	9	10	11	30	37	37	1-1	0-2	3-1	2-0	2-2	2-2	1-1	2-1	0-1	1-0	1-0		1-0	2-2	0-1	2-1
CR Belouizdad	30	10	6	14	25	34	36	0-3	0-1	0-0	2-0	0-2	0-3	2-1	2-1	2-0	3-2	1-1	1-1		4-0	1-1	2-1
OMR El Anasser	30	8	11	11	32	35	35	1-3	1-1	1-2	0-0	1-0	0-1	2-1	3-0	1-1	0-1	0-1	2-1	0-0		4-2	0-0
GC Mascara	30	8	6	16	34	48	30	1-1	1-0	1-2	3-3	1-0	1-0	1-3	1-1	1-1	1-1	0-0	1-3	1-0	1-0		4-1
US Chaouia §	30	5	7	18	15	49	19	0-0	0-1	0-0	0-0	2-1	1-3	0-0	1-1	0-3	0-3	1-0	1-0	0-1	0-1	2-1	

20/08/2004 - 23/05/2005 • † Qualified for the CAF Champions League • § Chaouia deducted 3 points

ALGERIA 2004-05 — SECONDE DIVISION (2)

	Pl	W	D	L	F	A	Pts
US Biskra	34	19	10	5	39	19	67
Paradou AC Hidra	34	18	9	7	57	36	63
CA Batna	34	18	8	8	45	24	62
USM El Harrach	34	18	5	11	39	25	59
ASM Oran	34	16	9	9	51	38	57
AS Khroub	34	15	9	10	47	37	54
MC El Eulma	34	13	11	10	43	34	50
Bou Saada	34	14	7	13	44	40	49
JSM Béjaia	34	13	8	13	40	42	47
MO Béjaia	34	10	13	11	28	32	43
SA Mohammadia	34	11	9	14	28	38	42
WA Boufarik	34	10	10	14	33	37	40
MO Constantine	34	10	10	14	38	45	40
MC Saida	34	9	11	14	34	39	38
RC Kouba	34	8	13	13	28	33	37
ES Mostaganem	34	10	7	17	42	55	37
USM Bel Abbès	34	7	12	15	28	46	33
HB Chelghoum Laid §	34	5	3	26	20	64	15

27/08/2004 - 3/06/2005 • § Deducted 3 points

TOP SCORERS

BERGUIGUA Hamid	JSK	18
DZIRI Billel	USMAl	11
DEHAM Noureddine	MCA	11
HEMANI Nabil	OMR	11
EL HADI Adel	USMAn	10
DAOUD Sofiane	MCO	10
FENIER Hocine	CSC	10

COUPE D'ALGERIE 2004-05

Round of 16

ASO Chlef *	1 6p
US Chaouia	1 5p
CS Constantine	1
MC Alger *	2
MC Oran	2
ASM Oran *	1
JSC Sig	0
USM Annaba *	1
WA Tlemcen *	3
MC El Eulma	1
ES Berrouaghia	1
OMR El Anasser *	2
USM Blida *	1 3p
Bou Saada	1 2p
Hamra Annaba	1
USM Sétif *	2

Quarter-finals

ASO Chlef	2
MC Alger *	1
MC Oran	0
USM Annaba *	1
WA Tlemcen *	1
OMR El Anasser	0
USM Blida	0
USM Sétif *	1

* Home team

Semi-finals

ASO Chlef	3
USM Annaba	0
WA Tlemcen	0 6p
USM Sétif	0 7p

Final

ASO Chlef	1
USM Sétif	0

CUP FINAL

21-06-2005, Att: 70 000
Stade 5 Juillet, Algiers

Scorer - Messaoudi 95 for ASO Chlef

AND – ANDORRA

NATIONAL TEAM RECORD
JULY 1ST 2002 TO JUNE 30TH 2005

PL	W	D	L	F	A	%
21	1	2	18	5	56	9.5

FIFA/COCA-COLA WORLD RANKING

1993	1994	1995	1996	1997	1998	1999	2000	2001	2002	2003	2004	High		Low	
-	-	-	187	185	171	145	145	140	137	147	138	**137**	12/02	**188**	06/97

2004-2005											
08/04	09/04	10/04	11/04	12/04	01/05	02/05	03/05	04/05	05/05	06/05	07/05
149	148	147	143	138	141	139	139	139	138	135	135

October 13, 2004 will go down in Andorran football folklore as the day the national team – after eight years of trying – finally won a competitive international match. The 1-0 victory at home against the relative might of FYR Macedonia in the 2006 FIFA World Cup™ qualifiers was then followed by a 0-0 draw in Skopje. It may be a while before an Andorran team posts a positive record against another nation in a qualifying campaign given Andorra's record of just three wins in total since international matches were first played in 1996. Aside fom the FYR Macedonia games it was business as usual in the rest of the FIFA World Cup™ qualifiers although apart from

INTERNATIONAL HONOURS
None

a heavy reverse in the Czech Republic, the defeats were not as bad as expected in a very strong group. In domestic football there was a thrilling Championship race between Sant Julia and Rangers, breaking the stranglehold of Santa Coloma. Both clubs had hired locally based Argentine players giving the Championship an unusual flavour and the title race went to the wire with Sant Julia winning a crucial game between the two with two weeks to go. Between them the pair lost just five games, all but one of them inflicted on each other. There was some consolation for Santa Coloma when they beat Sant Julia in the Cup Final for the third year running.

THE FIFA BIG COUNT OF 2000

	Male	Female		Male	Female
Registered players	623	0	Referees	24	3
Non registered players	700	0	Officials	86	4
Youth players	386	23	Total involved	1 849	
Total players	1 732		Number of clubs	19	
Professional players	0	0	Number of teams	35	

Federació Andorrana de Fútbol (FAF)
Avinguda Carlemany 67, 3er pis, Apartado postal 65, Escaldes-Engordany, Principat d'Andorra
Tel +376 805830   Fax +376 862006
administracio@fedanfut.com   www.fedanfut.com
President: AMAT ESCOBAR Francesc   General Secretary: GEA Tomas
Vice-President: QUINONES Miquel Angel   Treasurer: GARCIA Josep   Media Officer: TURNER Lucy
Men's Coach: RODRIGO David   Women's Coach: RODRIGO David
FAF formed: 1994   UEFA: 1996   FIFA: 1996
Colours: Yellow, Red, Blue or Blue, Blue, Blue

GAMES PLAYED BY ANDORRA IN THE 2006 FIFA WORLD CUP™ CYCLE

2002	Opponents	Score		Venue	Comp	Scorers	Att	Referee
21-08	Iceland	L	0-3	Rejkjavik	Fr		2 900	Isaksen FRO
12-10	Belgium	L	0-1	Andorra la Vella	ECq		700	Nalbandyan ARM
16-10	Bulgaria	L	1-2	Sofia	ECq	Lima.A [80]	42 000	Richards WAL
2003								
2-04	Croatia	L	0-2	Varazdin	ECq		8 500	Salomir ROM
30-04	Estonia	L	0-2	Andorra la Vella	ECq		500	Aydin TUR
7-06	Estonia	L	0-2	Tallinn	ECq		3 500	Juhos HUN
11-06	Belgium	L	0-3	Gent	ECq		12 000	Shmolik BLR
13-06	Gabon	L	0-2	Andorra la Vella	Fr			
6-09	Croatia	L	0-3	Andorra la Vella	ECq		800	Liba CZE
10-09	Bulgaria	L	0-3	Andorra la Vella	ECq		1 000	Mikulski POL
2004								
14-04	China PR	D	0-0	Peralada	Fr			
28-05	France	L	0-4	Montpellier	Fr		27 750	Daami TUN
5-06	Spain	L	0-4	Getafe	Fr		14 000	Trefolini ITA
4-09	Finland	L	0-3	Tampere	WCq		7 437	Siric CRO
8-09	Romania	L	1-5	Andorra la Vella	WCq	Pujol [28p]	1 100	Kircher GER
13-10	FYR Macedonia	W	1-0	Andorra la Vella	WCq	Bernaus [60]	350	Podeschi SMR
17-11	Netherlands	L	0-3	Andorra la Vella	WCq		2 000	Yefet ISR
2005								
9-02	FYR Macedonia	D	0-0	Skopje	WCq		5 000	Verbist BEL
26-03	Armenia	L	1-2	Yerevan	WCq	Silva [56]	2 100	Attard MLT
30-03	Czech Republic	L	0-4	Andorra la Vella	WCq		900	Messner AUT
4-06	Czech Republic	L	1-8	Liberec	WCq	Riera [36]	9 520	Dereli TUR

Fr = Friendly match • EC = UEFA EURO 2004™ • WC = FIFA World Cup™ • q = qualifier

NATIONAL CAPS

	Caps
TXEMA Josep	54
SONEJEE Oscar	54
SANCHEZ Juli	51
ALVAREZ Jesus Luis 'Koldo'	50
RUIZ Justo	50
LIMA Antonio	42
JIMENEZ Manolo	41
LIMA Ildefons	39
ESCURA Jordi	37
GONZALEZ Emiliano	37

NATIONAL GOALS

	Goals
LIMA Ildefons	3
LUCENDO Jesus Julian	3
LIMA Antonio	2
GONZALEZ Emiliano	2
RUIZ Justo	2
SANCHEZ Juli	2

NATIONAL COACH

	Years
CODINA Isidrea	1996
MILOIE Manuel	1997-'99
RODRIGO David	1999-

FIFA REFEREE LIST 2005

	Int'l	DoB
MENGUAL PRADES Jose Luis		16-03-1962

FIFA ASSISTANT REFEREE LIST 2005

	Int'l	DoB
GONCALVES BARBOSA Jose		9-04-1961

ANDORRA COUNTRY INFORMATION

Capital	Andorra la Vella	Independence	1278	GDP per Capita	$19 000
Population	69 865	Status	Principality	GNP Ranking	150
Area km²	468	Language	Catalan (official), French	Dialling code	+376
Population density	149 per km²	Literacy rate	99%	Internet code	.ad
% in urban areas	63%	Main religion	Christian 94%	GMT +/−	+1
Towns/Cities ('000)	Andorra la Vella 22; Les Escaldes 13; Encamp 9				
Neighbours (km)	France 56; Spain 63				
Main stadia	Comunal – Andorra la Vella 1 140				

ANDORRA NATIONAL TEAM RECORDS AND RECORD SEQUENCES

Records			Sequence records				
Victory	2-0	BLR 2000, ALB 2002	Wins	1		Clean sheets	2	2000
Defeat	1-7	POR 2001	Defeats	11	2002-2003	Goals scored	2	Three times
Player Caps	41	TXEMA Josep	Undefeated	3	2000	Without goal	10	2003-2004
Player Goals	3	LIMA I, LUCENDO	Without win	23	1996-2000	Goals against	11	2000-02, 2002-03

ANDORRA 2004-05
LLIGA ANDORRANA PRIMERA DIVISIO

	Pl	W	D	L	F	A	Pts	Sant Julia	Rangers	S'ta Coloma	Principat	Inter	Lusitans	Atlètic	Encamp
Sant Julia ‡	20	18	0	2	61	14	54		3-2 1-2	2-0 3-2	1-0 8-0	3-2	5-1	4-0	3-1
Rangers	20	17	0	3	59	15	51	0-3 0-1		3-2 2-0	2-0 3-0	5-0	5-1	8-0	3-0
Santa Coloma	20	12	1	7	50	26	37	1-0 1-2	0-1 0-1		3-2 2-2	4-1	3-1	5-0	3-1
Principat	20	6	2	12	23	45	20	0-2 1-4	0-1 0-5	0-5 1-2		4-3	2-0	5-2	1-1
Inter d'Escaldes	20	7	4	9	36	44	25	0-5	3-8	2-3	1-0		1-1 2-2	5-3 0-1	0-0 2-1
Lusitans	20	5	2	13	24	48	17	1-7	0-2	0-3	0-1	1-2 0-3		0-1 3-0	2-3 2-1
Atlètic Escaldes	20	5	0	15	19	58	15	0-2	1-4	0-5	0-2	0-4 3-2	1-3 1-2		3-0 3-0
Encamp	20	4	3	13	19	41	15	0-2	0-2	2-6	0-2	0-3 0-0	1-2 4-2	2-0 2-0	

19/09/2004 - 1/05/2005 • ‡ Qualified for the UEFA Cup

ANDORRA 2004-05
SEGONA DIVISIO

	Pl	W	D	L	F	A	Pts
Santa Coloma B	18	13	3	2	49	16	42
Engordany	18	11	4	3	35	22	37
Extremenya	18	10	3	5	40	28	33
Massana	14	6	1	7	19	21	19
Sporting Escaldes	14	5	2	7	22	25	17
Benfica	14	4	1	9	13	24	13
Lusitans B	14	4	0	10	21	35	12
Principat B	14	2	0	12	16	44	6

18/09/2004 - 24/04/2005 • Santa Coloma ineligible for promotion

COPA CONSTITUCIO 2004-05

Quarter-finals		Semi-finals		Final	
Santa Coloma	7				
Lusitans	1	Santa Coloma	1		
Santa Coloma B	0	Principat	0		
Principat	1			Santa Coloma	2
Rangers	4			Sant Julia	1
Inter d'Escaldes	0	Rangers	3 2p	22-05-2005, Aixovall	
Encamp	0	Sant Julia	3 3p	Scorers - Ayala [14], Imbernón [71] for Santa Coloma; Roig [90] for Sant Julia	
Sant Julia	4				

RECENT LEAGUE AND CUP RECORD

Championship						Cup		
Year	Champions	Pts	Runners-up	Pts	Third	Pts	Winners	Score	Runners-up
1996	Encamp	47	Principat	45	Santa Coloma	42	Principat	2-0	Santa Coloma
1997	Principat	61	Veterans d'Andorra	59	Encamp	41	Principat	7-0	Sant Julia
1998	Principat	56	Santa Coloma	55	Encamp	38	Principat	4-3	Santa Coloma
1999	Principat	62	Santa Coloma	54	Encamp	43	Principat	3-1	Santa Coloma
2000	Constelació	64	Santa Coloma	28	Inter d'Escaldes	20	Constelació	6-0	Encamp
2001	Santa Coloma	24	Sant Julia	22	Inter d'Escaldes	12	Santa Coloma	2-0	Sant Julia
2002	Encamp	44	Sant Julia	43	Santa Coloma	42	Lusitans	2-0	Inter d'Escaldes
2003	Santa Coloma	49	Encamp	48	Sant Julia	38	Santa Coloma	5-3	Sant Julia
2004	Santa Coloma	45	Sant Julia	43	Rangers	34	Santa Coloma	1-0	Sant Julia
2005	Sant Julia	54	Rangers	51	Santa Coloma	37	Santa Coloma	2-1	Sant Julia

ANG – ANGOLA

NATIONAL TEAM RECORD
JULY 1ST 2002 TO JUNE 30TH 2005

PL	W	D	L	F	A	%
29	13	9	7	37	29	60.3

FIFA/COCA-COLA WORLD RANKING

1993	1994	1995	1996	1997	1998	1999	2000	2001	2002	2003	2004	High		Low	
102	106	80	70	58	50	52	55	55	76	83	72	45	07/00	124	06/94

2004-2005											
08/04	09/04	10/04	11/04	12/04	01/05	02/05	03/05	04/05	05/05	06/05	07/05
78	82	75	73	72	73	73	72	74	73	72	68

Angola have confirmed their position as a rising force in African football with the national team putting in a major bid to reach the 2006 FIFA World Cup™. With only two defeats in their last 15 games, the Palancas Negras have also set their sights on a third appearance at the African Cup of Nations where they would now expect to register their first win. Coached by Luis De Oliveira Goncalves, the team, which has some excellent players including Mantorras of Benfica, have proved strong opponents on their travels as well as at home. Angola are the current holders of the COSAFA Cup, beating Zambia on penalties in the 2004 final. In the 2004 Girabola League,

INTERNATIONAL HONOURS
CAF Youth Championship 2001 COSAFA Cup 1999 2001 2004

Atletico Sport Aviação won their third straight title, three points ahead of Sagrada Esperança and also setting a new League victory record when they beat Primeiro de Agosto 8-1. In the Cup competition, the Taca Nacional, Desportivo Sonangol lifted the trophy for the second time when they beat 1° de Agosto 2-0 in the final. Angola had reached the FIFA World Youth Championship in 2002, but campaigns this year proved disappointing. The U-19s featured at the finals in Benin, but left without a win against Morocco, Lesotho and Egypt and bottom of the group, while the U-17s were eliminated in the preliminary stage thanks to home and away defeats to Nigeria.

THE FIFA BIG COUNT OF 2000

	Male	Female		Male	Female
Registered players	5000	0	Referees	250	0
Non registered players	35 000	0	Officials	1 900	0
Youth players	3 000	0	Total involved	45 150	
Total players	43 000		Number of clubs	100	
Professional players	0	0	Number of teams	500	

Federaçao Angolana de Futebol (FAF)
Compl. da Cidadela Desportiva, Luanda - 3449, Angola
Tel +244 2 264948   Fax +244 2 260566
fafutebol@ebonet.net   www.fafutebol.com
President: FERNANDES Justino Dr   General Secretary: PEREIRA DA SILVA Augusto
Vice-President: MANGUEIRA Antonio   Treasurer: GOMES FURTADO Antonio   Media Officer: MACEDO Arlindo
Men's Coach: DE OLIVEIRA GONCALVES Luis   Women's Coach: NZUZI Andre
FAF formed: 1979   CAF: 1996   FIFA: 1980
Colours: Red, Black, Red

GAMES PLAYED BY ANGOLA IN THE 2006 FIFA WORLD CUP™ CYCLE

2002	Opponents	Score		Venue	Comp	Scorers	Att	Referee
25-08	Gabon	W	1-0	Luanda	Fr	Malamba [64]	10 000	
8-09	Nigeria	D	0-0	Luanda	CNq		10 000	Mathabela RSA
12-10	Malawi	L	0-1	Lilongwe	CNq		40 000	Tangawarima ZIM
2003								
29-03	Algeria	D	1-1	Luanda	Fr	Gilberto [5p]	8 000	Mavunza ANG
20-04	Zimbabwe	L	0-1	Harare	CCr1		20 000	Nkuna ZAM
21-06	Nigeria	D	2-2	Benin City	CNq	Figueiredo [9], Akwa [55]		
6-07	Malawi	W	5-1	Luanda	CNq	Msowoya [2], Akwa [3], Flavio [33], Stopirra [76], Chinho [89]	10 000	
20-08	Congo DR	L	0-2	Luanda	Fr			
7-09	Namibia	W	2-0	Luanda	Fr	Delgado [44], Flavio [63]	5 000	De Sousa ANG
20-09	Namibia	W	3-1	Windhoek	Fr	Jaburu, Avelino Lopes, Akwa [80]		
12-10	Chad	L	1-3	N'Djamena	WCq	Bruno Mauro [49]	30 000	Nahi CIV
16-11	Chad	W	2-0	Luanda	WCq	Akwa [42], Bruno Mauro [57]	30 000	Buenkadila COD
2004								
31-03	Morocco	L	1-3	Casablanca	Fr	Norberto [84]	7 000	Helal EGY
28-04	Ghana	D	1-1	Accra	Fr	Fofana [55]		Kotey GHA
9-05	Namibia	W	2-1	Luanda	CCr1	Love 2 [26 67]	4 000	Ngcamphalala SWZ
23-05	Congo DR	W	3-1	Kinshasa	Fr	Gilberto [8], Bruno Mauro [40], Maurito [89]	60 000	
5-06	Algeria	D	0-0	Annaba	WCq		55 000	Daami TUN
20-06	Nigeria	W	1-0	Luanda	WCq	Akwa [84]	40 000	Nkole ZAM
3-07	Gabon	D	2-2	Libreville	WCq	Akwa [19], Marco Paulo [81]	20 000	Louzaya CGO
18-07	Botswana	D	1-1	Luanda	CCqf	Flavio [3]. W 5-3p	6 000	Phomane LES
5-09	Rwanda	W	1-0	Luanda	WCq	Freddy [52]	30 000	Damon RSA
19-09	Mozambique	W	1-0	Maputo	CCsf	Flavio [68]	50 000	Jovinala MWI
10-10	Zimbabwe	W	1-0	Luanda	WCq	Flavio [53]	17 000	Lwanja MWI
20-11	Zambia	D	0-0	Lusaka	CCf	W 5-4p		Lwanja MWI
2005								
22-02	Congo	W	2-0	Brazzaville	Fr			
27-03	Zimbabwe	L	0-2	Harare	WCq			Codjia BEN
27-05	Tunisia	L	1-4	Tunis	Fr	Flavio [77p]	4 000	
3-06	Algeria	W	2-1	Luanda	WCq	Flavio [50], Akwa [58]	27 000	Hicuburundi BDI
17-06	Nigeria	D	1-1	Kano	WCq	Figueiredo [60]	17 000	Abd El Fatah EGY

Fr = Friendly match • CN = CAF African Cup of Nations • CC = COSAFA Castle Cup • WC = FIFA World Cup™
q = qualifier • r1 = first round group • qf = quarter-final • sf = semi-final • f = final

FIFA REFEREE LIST 2005

	Int'l	DoB
ANTONIO DE SOUSA Jose	1999	5-08-1966
BRAGA MAVUNZA Jose		23-06-1964
CACHIQUENGUE Frederico	2001	2-03-1963
CARMELINO Belmiro		9-08-1965
COLEMBI Eugenio	1998	5-06-1963
MATOS Venancio	2005	21-10-1969
MULUTA PRATA Agostinho	2001	26-06-1963

FIFA ASSISTANT REFEREE LIST 2005

	Int'l	DoB
ANTONIO Inacio	1996	17-03-1962
CANOMBO Pedro	2004	24-04-1970
DA SILVA MARIA Manuel	1996	2-05-1962
MANUEL ANTONIO Luciano	1993	8-08-1963
MANUEL CANDIDO Inacio	2005	27-01-1971
MUSSUNGO Pedro		16-06-1961
ZEFERINO MUANDA Jose	1996	22-07-1963

ANGOLA COUNTRY INFORMATION

Capital	Luanda	Independence	1975	GDP per Capita	$1 900
Population	10 978 552	Status	Republic	GNP Ranking	102
Area km²	1 246 700	Language	Portuguese	Dialling code	+244
Population density	9 per km²	Literacy rate	45%	Internet code	.ao
% in urban areas	32%	Main religion	Christian 90%	GMT +/–	+1
Towns/Cities ('000)	Luanda 2 776; Huambo 226; Lobito 207; Benguela 151; Kuito 113; Lubango 102; Malanje 87				
Neighbours (km)	Congo 201; Congo DR 2 511; Zambia 1 110; Namibia 1 376; Atlantic Ocean 1 600				
Main stadia	Cidadela – Luanda 60 000; Do Santos – Viana 17 000; Nossa Senhora do Monte – Lubango 14 000				

ANGOLA NATIONAL TEAM RECORDS AND RECORD SEQUENCES

Records			Sequence records					
Victory	7-1	SWZ 2000	Wins	3	1993-1994, 1999	Clean sheets	3	1999
Defeat	0-6	POR 1989	Defeats	6	1989-1990	Goals scored	11	2001
Player Caps	n/a		Undefeated	11	1999-2000	Without goal	3	1980-1981
Player Goals	n/a		Without win	13	1980-1982	Goals against	8	1989-90, 1998-91

ANGOLA 2004

CAMPEONATO NACIONAL GIRABOLA 1º DIVISAO

	Pl	W	D	L	F	A	Pts	Aviação	Sagrada	Inter	Petro At.	Sonangol	1º Agosto	Petro H'bo	1º Maio	Cabinda	Lobito	Progrsso	Soyo	Benfica	Bravos
Atlético Aviação	26	16	8	2	53	13	56		2-1	0-0	1-1	2-0	8-1	4-1	6-0	3-0	4-1	2-0	2-0	3-0	4-1
Sagrada Esperança †	26	15	8	3	32	10	53	1-1		0-0	1-2	2-1	0-0	2-0	3-0	2-0	2-1	2-0	2-0	2-0	1-0
Inter Clube	26	15	6	5	36	21	51	2-0	0-0		1-4	2-1	0-1	2-1	1-0	3-2	0-0	1-0	1-0	2-0	4-0
Petro Atlético	26	13	9	4	41	18	48	0-1	0-0	2-0		2-0	2-0	2-0	3-0	2-2	2-2	0-1	3-0	1-0	2-0
Sonangol	26	7	12	7	32	28	33	0-0	0-0	2-2	0-2		1-1	2-1	1-1	3-2	4-0	2-3	2-1	1-1	3-0
Primeiro de Agosto	26	9	6	11	21	29	33	0-1	0-1	1-0	2-2	1-3		0-2	1-0	1-0	1-0	0-0	0-1	0-0	1-0
Petro Huambo	26	8	7	11	27	36	31	1-1	0-3	3-2	1-0	1-1	1-0		0-1	1-1	1-1	0-2	3-0	3-3	1-0
Primeiro de Maio	26	8	7	11	20	33	31	0-2	0-2	1-3	2-2	0-0	2-1	0-1		1-2	1-0	0-0	3-0	1-2	
Sporting Cabinda	26	6	12	8	30	31	30	0-0	1-0	0-1	3-1	0-0	1-3	3-0	1-1		1-1	1-0	1-1	1-1	**3-0**
Académica Lobito	26	7	9	10	28	31	30	0-1	0-0	0-1	0-2	0-0	2-0	0-2	1-2	1-1		0-0	4-3	2-1	6-0
Progresso Sambizanga	26	6	12	8	22	26	30	0-0	1-2	1-1	0-0	1-1	0-0	1-1	0-0	3-3	1-1		2-2	1-0	2-1
Académica Soyo	26	6	10	10	22	32	28	2-0	1-1	0-1	1-1	2-1	0-3	0-0	1-1	0-0	1-2	1-0		1-0	1-1
Benfica Lubango	26	6	8	12	22	33	26	1-1	0-1	1-4	0-0	1-1	2-1	3-1	0-1	1-0	0-2	3-0	1-1		2-0
Bravos Maquis	26	2	2	22	10	55	8	0-4	0-1	1-2	**0-3**	0-2	0-2	2-1	0-1	1-1	0-1	1-3	0-2	0-1	

14/02/2004 - 7/11/2004 • † Qualified for CAF Champions League • ‡ Qualified for CAF Confederation Cup • Matches in bold awarded 3-0

ANGOLA 2004 2º DIVISAO

Zona A	Pl	W	D	L	F	A	Pts
Benfica Luanda	10	9	1	0	18	3	28
Santos	10	6	2	2	13	6	20
Kabuscorp Palanca	10	4	3	3	19	12	15
Atlético Kissama	10	2	4	4	11	12	10
21 de Janeiro	10	1	2	7	7	15	5
Benfica Milunga	10	1	2	7	4	24	5

Zona B	Pl	W	D	L	F	A	Pts
Desportivo Huíla	10	6	4	0	16	4	22
17 de Setembro	10	3	5	2	9	11	14
Militar Keves	10	4	1	5	12	17	13
Ferroviário Huíla	10	1	8	1	7	6	11
Recreativo Caála	10	2	3	5	7	7	9
Sporting Sumbe	10	2	3	5	10	16	9

17/07/2004 - 20/11/2004 • Championship play-offs:
Benfica 1-0 Petróleos; Huíla 1-0 Benfica; Huíla 0-0 Petróleos; Huíla win the Second Division Championship

TACA NACIONAL 2004

Quarter-finals		Semi-finals		Final	
Sonangol	w/o				
Sporting Cabinda		Sonangol	1		
Petro Huambo	1	Inter Clube	0		
Inter Clube	2			Sonangol	2
Desportivo Huíla	5			1º de Agosto	0
Atlético Kissama	1	Desportivo Huíla	0		
Petro Atlético	2 3p	1º de Agosto	1	Cidadela, Luanda	
1º de Agosto	2 4p			11-11-2004	
				Scorers - Capique 34, Nuno 83	

Zona C	Pl	W	D	L	F	A	Pts
At. Petróleos Bié	12	10	1	1	28	2	31
Sport Ritondo	12	7	4	1	17	7	25
Lacrau Army Sport	11	5	4	2	16	10	19
Africa Sport	11	4	1	6	9	20	13
Heróis da Baixa	10	2	3	5	7	12	9
Pecandec Sport	11	1	3	7	4	16	6
15 de Setembro	11	1	2	8	2	16	5

RECENT LEAGUE AND CUP RECORD

	Championship							Cup		
Year	Champions	Pts	Runners-up	Pts	Third	Pts		Winners	Score	Runners-up
1998	Primeiro de Agosto	62	Petro Atlético	58	Atlético Aviação	50		Petro Atlético	4-1	Primeiro de Agosto
1999	Primeiro de Agosto	59	Académica Lobito	51	Inter Clube	49		Sagrada Esperança	1-0	Atlético Aviação
2000	Petro Atlético	63	Atlético Aviação	44	Petro Huambo	42		Petro Atlético	1-0	Inter Clube
2001	Petro Atlético	57	Atlético Aviação	50	Petro Huambo	42		Sonangol	3-2	Sporting Cabinda
2002	Atlético Aviação	57	Primeiro de Agosto	53	Petro Atlético	51		Petro Atlético	3-0	Desportivo Hulla
2003	Atlético Aviação	53	Petro Atlético	52	Petro Huambo	46		Inter Clube	1-0	Sagrada Esperança
2004	Atlético Aviação	56	Sagrada Esperança	53	Inter Clube	51		Sonangol	2-0	Primeiro de Agosto

ANT – NETHERLANDS ANTILLES

NATIONAL TEAM RECORD
JULY 1ST 2002 TO JUNE 30TH 2005

PL	W	D	L	F	A	%
12	5	2	5	19	17	50

FIFA/COCA-COLA WORLD RANKING

1993	1994	1995	1996	1997	1998	1999	2000	2001	2002	2003	2004	High		Low	
128	152	125	142	156	156	167	175	183	177	188	163	**118**	07/95	**188**	12/03

2004-2005											
08/04	09/04	10/04	11/04	12/04	01/05	02/05	03/05	04/05	05/05	06/05	07/05
168	166	165	165	163	163	166	165	166	166	166	166

Since losing to Honduras in the second qualifying round of the 2006 FIFA World Cup™ qualifiers there has been little activity on the international front with Netherlands Antilles withdrawing from the newly created Digicel Caribbean Cup, which doubled up as a qualifying tournament for the 2005 CONCACAF Gold Cup. The only international activity involved the qualifiers for the FIFA World Youth Championship in the Netherlands and the FIFA U-17 Championship in Peru. Both the youth team and the juniors played their groups in Haiti with the youth team finishing second behind the hosts. The development of youth football has been given a high priority in the country

INTERNATIONAL HONOURS
None

helped by the opening of the US$400,000 Mordy L. Maduro Centre in January 2003 which was funded by the Goal programme. Hosting both the NAVU offices and the Curaçao Football Federation, the facilities also boast accommodation for players and coaches. The Curaçao Championship was once again the main feature of the domestic season with Centro Barber winning a fourth title in succession when they beat Victory Boys in the final for the second year running. Real Rincon were the 2004 champions of Bonaire, however, the Kopa Antiano for teams from both Bonaire and Curacao has not been organised recently.

THE FIFA BIG COUNT OF 2000

	Male	Female		Male	Female
Registered players	600	0	Referees	38	0
Non registered players	2 200	0	Officials	306	0
Youth players	740	0	Total involved	3 884	
Total players	3 540		Number of clubs	36	
Professional players	0	0	Number of teams	71	

Nederlands Antilliaanse Voetbal Unie (NAVU)
Bonamweg 49, Curaçao
Tel +599 97365040   Fax +599 97365047
navusoccer@interneeds.net   www.navusoccer.com
President: RIGNAAL Francisca   General Secretary: AUBREY Sealy
Vice-President: TBD   Treasurer: NELSON Maria   Media Officer: None
Men's Coach: VERBEEK Peter   Women's Coach: None
NAVU formed: 1921   CONCACAF: 1961   FIFA: 1932
Colours: White, Red, Red or Blue, Blue, Red

GAMES PLAYED BY NETHERLANDS ANTILLES IN THE 2006 FIFA WORLD CUP™ CYCLE

2002	Opponents		Score	Venue	Comp	Scorers	Att	Referee
28-07	Guyana	L	1-2	Georgetown	GCq	Muzo [14]		
11-08	Guyana	W	1-0	Willemstad	GCq	Martis [43], W 3-2p		Villar Polo ARU
20-11	Antigua and Barbuda	D	1-1	Port-au-Prince	GCq	Forbuis [88]		Bowen CAY
22-11	Haiti	L	0-3	Port-au-Prince	GCq			Bowen CAY
2003								

No international matches played in 2003

2004								
10-01	Surinam	D	1-1	Paramaribo	Fr	Forbuis [38]		Jol NED
17-01	Surinam	W	2-0	Willemstad	Fr	Silberie, Christina		
28-01	Aruba	W	6-1	Willemstad	Fr			
18-02	Antigua and Barbuda	L	0-2	St John's	WCq		1 500	Navarro CAN
31-03	Antigua and Barbuda	W	3-0	Willemstad	WCq	Siberie [27], Martha [46], Hose [48]	9 000	Piper TRI
27-04	Dominican Republic	W	3-1	Willemstad	Fr	Bernardus 2 [6 32], Cicilia [7]		Faneite ANT
12-06	Honduras	L	1-2	Willemstad	WCq	Hose [75]	12 000	McArthur GUY
19-06	Honduras	L	0-4	San Pedro Sula	WCq		30 000	Alcala MEX
2005								

No international matches played in 2005 before August

Fr = Friendly match • GC = CONCACAF Gold Cup™ • WC = FIFA World Cup™ • q = qualifier

NETHERLANDS ANTILLES NATIONAL TEAM RECORDS AND RECORD SEQUENCES

Records			Sequence records					
Victory	15-0	PUR 1959	Wins	5	Three times	Clean sheets	3	1961-1962, 1966
Defeat	0-8	NED 1962, MEX 1973	Defeats	6	1973-1980	Goals scored	30	1926-1948
Player Caps	n/a		Undefeated	9	1959-1961	Without goal	3	Four time
Player Goals	n/a		Without win	17	1969-1980	Goals against	19	1968-1980

FIFA REFEREE LIST 2005

	Int'l	DoB
CHANCE Valentino		4-10-1961
FANEIJTE Urvin	1991	26-05-1965
MARTIS Jgranoth	2005	14-02-1973
THOMAS Charlton	2000	1-12-1968

FIFA ASSISTANT REFEREE LIST 2005

	Int'l	DoB
ELLIS Antonio	2001	9-12-1961
MERCERA Marcial	2001	16-04-1964
ROJER Roderick	2001	30-04-1972

RECENT LEAGUE AND CUP RECORD

	Kopa Antiano				Curacao Champions				Bonaire Champions		
Year	Winners	Score	Runners-up		Winners	Score	Runners-up		Winners	Score	Runners-up
1997	Jong Colombia	2-1	Undeba		Undeba	2-1 2-1	Jong Colombia		Real Rincon	1-0	Estrellas
1998	No competition				-				-		
1999	Sithoc	0-0 3-2p	Jong Holland		Jong Holland	0-0 4-2p	Sithoc				
2000	No competition				Jong Colombia	2-1	Centro Barber		Estrellas	4-1	Uruguay
2001	Jong Colombia	3-0	Juventus		-				Estrellas	2-0	Real Rincon
2002	Centro Barber	1-0	SUBT		Centro Barber	2-1	SUBT		Estrellas	1-0	Real Rincon
2003	Centro Barber	2-1	Jong Colombia		Centro Barber	1-0	Jong Colombia		Real Rincon	3-0	Juventus
2004					Centro Barber	1-0	Victory Boys		Real Rincon	0-0 1-0	Estrellas
2005					Centro Barber	4-1	Victory Boys				

NETHERLANDS ANTILLES COUNTRY INFORMATION

Capital	Willemstad	Independence		Part of the Netherlands with autonomy in internal affairs		GDP per Capita	$11 400
Population	218 126	Status				GNP Ranking	n/a
Area km²	960	Language	Dutch			Dialling code	+599
Population density	227 per km²	Literacy rate	96%			Internet code	.an
% in urban areas	n/a	Main religion	Christian			GMT +/−	-4
Towns/Cities ('000)	Willemstad (Curaçao) 97; Princess Quarter (Sint Maarten) 13; Kraleendijk (Bonaire) 3;						
Neighbours (km)	Netherlands Antilles is a group of Caribbean islands consisting of Bonaire, Curaçao, Saba, Sint Eustatius & Sint Maarten						
Main stadia	Ergilio Hato – Willemstad 15 000; Municipal – Kraleendijk 3 000						

ARG – ARGENTINA

NATIONAL TEAM RECORD
JULY 1ST 2002 TO JUNE 30TH 2005

PL	W	D	L	F	A	%
42	26	10	6	81	46	73.8

After the disappointment of the 2002 FIFA World Cup™ finals, the Argentina national team has rebuilt under new coach Jose Pekerman and there is now genuine optimism for the finals in 2006, based on some excellent performances in the 2004-05 season. In the space of 12 months Argentina entered four competitions and reached each final. Not bad for a team that also led the marathon South American qualifying campaign for the 2006 FIFA World Cup™ qualifiers from the start. In early August 2004 Argentina came within seconds of winning the Copa América in Peru in what would have been their first South American title since 1993, but they conceded a goal deep into injury time against Brazil and then lost on penalties. Later in the month the under 23 team made up for that disappointment by winning gold at the Athens Olympics when they beat Paraguay in an all South American final - the first since Argentina and Uruguay played each other in the now legendary 1928 final in Amsterdam. By winning gold the Argentines finally won the only title that had eluded them. Then after becoming the first nation to qualify for the finals in Germany, having soundly beaten Brazil in a qualifier in Buenos Aires, they made it to the final of the FIFA

INTERNATIONAL HONOURS
FIFA World Cup™ 1978 1986
Olympic Gold 2004   FIFA World Youth Championship 1979 1995 1997 2001 2005
Copa América 1910 1921 1925 1927 1929 1937 1941 1945 1946 1947 1955 1957 1959 1991 1993
Sudamericana Sub-20 1967 1997 1999 2003   Sudamericana Sub-17 1985 2003
Copa Toyota Libertadores Independiente 1964 1965 1972 1973 1974 1975 1984, Racing Club 1967, Estudiantes 1968 1969 1970,
Boca Juniors 1977 1978 2000 2001 2003, Argentinos Juniors 1985, River Plate 1986 1996, Vélez Sarsfield 1994

Confederations Cup. Once again, however, the Brazilians sent Argentina home empty-handed but that disappointment was short-lived as a very good Argentina Under-20 team won a record fifth title at the FIFA World Youth Championship in the Netherlands. Domestically the picture has not been so rosy with violence still a major problem amongst fans in the stadiums resulting in one case of a Newell's Old Boys' fan being shot dead by a rival Newell's hooligan group. It is estimated that there have now been 177 football-related fatalities in the past 66 years. It was also a depressing season for traditional giants River Plate and Boca Juniors, neither of whom could make it past the semi-finals of the Copa Libertadores nor make an impact in the Championship. Instead it was Newell's, bolstered by the return to Argentina of Ariel Ortega, who won the Apertura, whilst Velez won the Clausura and had the best seasonal record overall. There was one international honour to celebrate at club level when Boca got their centenary celebrations off to a good start by winning the 2004 Copa Sudamericana in December after beating Bolivar in the final.

Asociación del Fútbol Argentino (AFA)
Viamonte 1366/76, Buenos Aires - 1053
Tel +54 11 43727900   Fax +54 11 43754410
info@afa.org.ar   www.afa.org.ar
President: GRONDONA Julio H.   General Secretary: MEISZNER Jose Luis
Vice-President: AGUILAR Jose Maria   Treasurer: DOMINGUEZ Hector   Media Officer: TBD
Men's Coach: PEKERMAN Jose   Women's Coach: BORRELO Jose Carlos
AFA formed: 1893   CONMEBOL: 1916   FIFA: 1912
Colours: Light blue and white stripes, Dark blue, White or Dark blue, Black, White

GAMES PLAYED BY ARGENTINA IN THE 2006 FIFA WORLD CUP™ CYCLE

2002	Opponents	Score	Venue	Comp	Scorers	Att	Referee
20-11	Japan	W 2-0	Tokyo	Fr	Sorin 46, Crespo 48	61 816	Mane KUW
2003							
31-01	Honduras	W 3-1	San Pedro Sula	Fr	Milito 15, Gonzalez.L 2 53 56		Recinos SLV
4-02	Mexico	W 1-0	Los Angeles	Fr	Rodriguez.G		Stott USA
8-02	USA	W 1-0	Miami	Fr	Gonzalez.L	27 196	Batres GUA
12-02	Netherlands	L 0-1	Amsterdam	Fr		40 090	Milton Nielsen DEN
30-04	Libya	W 3-1	Tripoli	Fr	Saviola 21, Riquelme 66, Aimar 88	25 000	Zahmoul TUN
8-06	Japan	W 4-1	Osaka	KC	Saviola 30, Zanetti 45, Romeo 79, Rodriguez.M 82	42 508	Fandel GER
11-06	Korea Republic	W 1-0	Seoul	Fr	Saviola 44	30 000	Rungklay THA
16-07	Uruguay	D 2-2	La Plata	Fr	Milito 2 4 10	35 000	Gonzalez PAR
20-08	Uruguay	W 3-2	Florence	Fr	Veron 45, Samuel 86, D'Alessandro 89	3 000	De Santis ITA
6-09	Chile	D 2-2	Buenos Aires	WCq	Kily Gonzalez 31, Aimar 35	38 000	Aquino PAR
9-09	Venezuela	W 3-0	Caracas	WCq	Aimar 7, Crespo 25, Delgado 31	36 000	Vazquez URU
15-11	Bolivia	W 3-0	Buenos Aires	WCq	D'Alessandro 56, Crespo 61, Aimar 63	30 042	Hidalgo PER
19-11	Colombia	D 1-1	Barranquilla	WCq	Crespo 26	30 000	Simon BRA
2004							
30-03	Ecuador	W 1-0	Buenos Aires	WCq	Crespo 60	55 000	Vazquez URU
28-04	Morocco	W 1-0	Casablanca	Fr	Kily Gonzalez 52	60 000	Ndoye SEN
2-06	Brazil	L 1-3	Belo Horizonte	WCq	Sorin 81	50 000	Ruiz COL
6-06	Paraguay	D 0-0	Buenos Aires	WCq		43 000	Simon BRA
27-06	Colombia	L 0-2	New York	Fr			Terry USA
30-06	Peru	W 2-1	New York	Fr	Kily Gonzalez 25p, Saviola 72	41 013	Stott USA
7-07	Ecuador	W 6-1	Chiclayo	CAr1	Kily Gonzalez 5p, Saviola 3 64 74 79, D'Alessandro 84, Gonzalez.L 90	24 000	Amarilla PAR
10-07	Mexico	L 0-1	Chiclayo	CAr1		25 000	Rezende BRA
13-07	Uruguay	W 4-2	Piura	CAr1	Kily Gonzalez 19p, Figueroa 2 20 89, Ayala 80	24 000	Selman CHI
17-07	Peru	W 1-0	Chiclayo	CAqf	Tevez 60	25 000	Amarilla PAR
20-07	Colombia	W 3-0	Lima	CAsf	Tevez 32, Gonzalez.L 51, Sorin 80	22 000	Hidalgo PER
25-07	Brazil	D 2-2	Lima	CAf	Kily Gonzalez 21p, Delgado 87	43 000	Amarilla PAR
18-08	Japan	W 2-1	Shizuoka	Fr	Galletti 4, Santana 40	45 000	Lu CHN
4-09	Peru	W 3-1	Lima	WCq	Rosales 14, Coloccini 66, Sorin 92	28 000	Simon BRA
9-10	Uruguay	W 4-2	Buenos Aires	WCq	Gonzalez.L 6, Figueroa 2 32 54, Zanetti 44	50 000	Souza BRA
13-10	Chile	D 0-0	Santiago	WCq		57 671	Amarilla PAR
16-11	Venezuela	W 3-2	Buenos Aires	WCq	Rey OG 3, Riquelme 46+, Saviola 65	30 000	Hidalgo PER
2005							
9-02	Germany	D 2-2	Dusseldorf	Fr	Crespo 2 40p 81	52 000	Farina ITA
9-03	Mexico	D 1-1	Los Angeles	Fr	Zarate 67	51 345	Hall USA
26-03	Bolivia	W 2-1	La Paz	WCq	Figueroa 57, Galletti 63	25 000	Larrionda URU
30-03	Colombia	W 1-0	Buenos Aires	WCq	Crespo 65	40 000	Amarilla PAR
4-06	Ecuador	L 0-2	Quito	WCq		37 583	Selman CHI
8-06	Brazil	W 3-1	Buenos Aires	WCq	Crespo 2 3 40, Riquelme 18	49 497	Mendez URU
15-06	Tunisia	W 2-1	Köln	CCr1	Riquelme 33p, Saviola 57	28 033	Rosetti ITA
18-06	Australia	W 4-2	Nürnberg	CCr1	Figueroa 3 12 53 89, Riquelme 31p	25 618	Maidin SIN
21-06	Germany	D 2-2	Nürnberg	CCr1	Riquelme 33, Cambiasso 74	42 088	Michel SVK
26-06	Mexico	D 1-1	Hanover	CCsf	Figueroa 110	40 718	Rosetti ITA
29-06	Brazil	L 1-4	Frankfurt	CCf	Aimar 65	45 591	Michel SVK

Fr = Friendly match • KC = Kirin Cup • CA = Copa América • CC = FIFA Confederations Cup • WC = FIFA World Cup™
q = qualifier • r1 = 1st round • qf = quarter-final • sf = semi-final • f = final

FIFA/COCA-COLA WORLD RANKING

1993	1994	1995	1996	1997	1998	1999	2000	2001	2002	2003	2004	High	Low
8	10	7	22	17	5	6	3	2	5	5	3	2	24 08/96

2004-2005											
08/04	09/04	10/04	11/04	12/04	01/05	02/05	03/05	04/05	05/05	06/05	07/05
4	4	3	3	3	3	3	3	3	3	3	2

ARGENTINA NATIONAL TEAM RECORDS AND RECORD SEQUENCES

Records			Sequence records					
Victory	12-0	ECU 1942	Wins	9	1941-1942	Clean sheets	8	1998
Defeat	1-6	CZE 1958	Defeats	4	1911-1912	Goals scored	42	1942-1954
Player Caps	106	SIMEONE Diego	Undefeated	31	1991-1993	Without goal	8	1989-1990
Player Goals	56	BATISTUTA Gabriel	Without win	10	1989-1990	Goals against	13	1906-1910

NATIONAL CAPS

	Caps
SIMEONE Diego	106
ZANETTI Javier	101
RUGGERI Oscar	97
AYALA Roberto	93
MARADONA Diego	91
ORTEGA Ariel	86
BATISTUTA Gabriel	78
GALLEGO America	73
PASSARELLA Daniel	70
SORIN Juan	64

NATIONAL GOALS

	Goals
BATISTUTA Gabriel	56
MARADONA Diego	34
CRESPO Hernan	28
ARTIME Luis	24
PASSARELLA Daniel	22
LUQUE Leopold	22
MASANTONIO Herminio	21
SANFILLIPO Jose	21
KEMPES Mario	20

NATIONAL COACH

	Years
PEDERNERA Adolfo	1969
PIZZUTI Juan Jose	1970-'72
SIVORI Omar	1972-'73
CAP Vladislao	1974
MENOTTI Cesar Luis	1974-'82
BILARDO Carlos	1983-'90
BASILE Alfi	1990-'94
PASSARELLA Daniel	1994-'98
BIELSA Marcelo	1999-'04
PEKERMAN Jose	2004-

THE FIFA BIG COUNT OF 2000

	Male	Female		Male	Female
Registered players	140 000	3 000	Referees	3 255	5
Non registered players	1 100 000	15 000	Officials	34 283	400
Youth players	245 467	2 000	Total involved	1 543 410	
Total players	1 505 467		Number of clubs	2 994	
Professional players	2 500	0	Number of teams	17 826	

FIFA REFEREE LIST 2005

	Int'l	DoB
BALDASSI Hector	2000	5-01-1966
BRAZENAS Gabriel	1997	29-11-1967
ELIZONDO Horacio	1994	4-11-1963
FAVALE Gabriel	2004	19-07-1967
FURCHI Rafael	2004	28-01-1966
GIMENEZ Daniel	1996	15-07-1961
MARTIN Claudio	1998	31-01-1962
PEZZOTTA Sergio	2000	28-11-1967
POMPEI Juan	2004	18-09-1968
SEQUEIRA Oscar	1997	4-07-1960

FIFA ASSISTANT REFEREE LIST 2005

	Int'l	DoB
CAGNI Sergio	2002	22-08-1965
CASAS Ricardo	2004	17-04-1967
GARCIA Dario	1996	29-10-1961
HERRERO Horacio	2004	06-06-1964
OTERO Rodolfo	1998	14-12-1962
REBOLLO Juan Carlos	2002	20-04-1962
ROCCHIO Francisco	2003	22-07-1964
ROSSI Claudio	1995	19-05-1961
TADDEO Gilberto	2000	27-12-1961
VELAZ Walter	2004	21-04-1965

ARGENTINA COUNTRY INFORMATION

Capital	Buenos Aires	Independence	1816	GDP per Capita	$11 200
Population	39 144 753	Status	Republic	GNP Ranking	18
Area km²	2 766 890	Language	Spanish	Dialling code	+54
Population density	14 per km²	Literacy rate	96%	Internet code	.ar
% in urban areas	88%	Main religion	Christian 92%	GMT + / –	-3
Towns/Cities ('000)	Buenos Aires 11 548; Cordoba 1 441; Rosario 1 218; Mendoza 973; Tucuman 828; La Plata 684; Mar del Plata 645; Salta 548; San Juan 469; Santa Fe 456; Resistencia 406				
Neighbours (km)	Bolivia 832; Paraguay 1 880; Brazil 1 224; Uruguay 579; Chile 5 150; Atlantic Ocean 4 989				
Main stadia	Monumental – Buenos Aires 66 449; Cilindro – Buenos Aires 64 161; La Bombonera – Buenos Aires 60 245; Independiente – Buenos Aires 57 901; Jose Amalfitani – Buenos Aires 49 747				

ARGENTINA 2004-05

PRIMERA DIVISION TORNEO APERTURA

Team	Pl	W	D	L	F	A	Pts	New	Vél	Riv	Est	SLo	Ros	Col	Boc	Ban	Rac	Lan	Gim	Ars	Qui	Ind	Arg	Alm	Oli	Ins	Hur
Newell's Old Boys †	19	10	6	3	22	11	36		0-1	1-0						1-1	1-0	0-0	2-0		2-0				1-1	3-0	1-0
Vélez Sarsfield	19	10	4	5	21	16	34	1-0					0-1	2-3			2-1	2-0	1-1	4-0		1-1		1-0			
River Plate	19	9	6	4	28	19	33	2-2				1-1	1-2	2-0	3-3	2-0									3-0	1-0	0-2
Estudiantes LP	19	7	9	3	22	14	30		0-2					1-0	5-0	0-0	0-0	1-1							3-2	3-1	1-1
San Lorenzo	19	8	6	5	29	22	30	1-2	1-0				0-0				3-1	4-1	3-0					1-1	1-1	2-0	4-1
Rosario Central	19	8	6	5	19	15	30	0-1				2-1		1-0		1-0	3-1			0-0			0-1			0-0	2-2
Colón Santa Fe	19	7	6	6	24	22	27	0-0				1-1	3-0		1-2		1-0	1-1		0-0			0-0				2-1
Boca Juniors	19	7	5	7	22	16	26	1-3	6-0			0-0	3-0			1-1	2-1		2-1			1-1				0-0	2-1
Banfield	19	6	8	5	24	22	26	0-0	2-2						1-1		4-0	0-0	1-0		0-2		2-0				3-1
Racing Club	19	8	2	9	23	22	26	1-2	1-2	0-1		0-2	2-1		4-0					1-0					2-1	1-0
Lanús	19	6	8	5	25	26	26	1-0		2-3	1-1	1-0	0-0		3-3				3-1	1-0	4-2	0-0
Gimnasia La Plata	19	6	7	6	16	23	25	0-0		1-1	2-0		2-1	1-1			0-3	0-0		2-1	2-1				1-0
Arsenal Sarandi	19	5	9	5	17	16	24	0-0		1-2		1-1	3-1	0-0	1-0		0-0		2-1	0-1	2-2
Quilmes	19	6	6	7	14	18	24		2-2		1-1	0-0	0-1	0-1		0-0		2-0		1-0	1-0	1-0
Independiente	19	6	5	8	23	26	23	2-0	0-2		2-2	2-2		2-1	1-3	1-0		3-0		1-1	4-0
Argentinos Juniors	19	6	4	9	17	18	22	1-2		0-1	1-0	0-2	3-1	1-0		3-0		0-0		1-2
Almagro	19	4	10	5	15	18	22	1-0	0-0		0-1		0-2	0-2	2-2	0-0		1-1	3-1	1-1
Olimpo	19	4	5	10	21	29	17		2-3		1-0	2-4	0-2		1-3	2-0		1-0	4-2	0-1	1-1
Instituto	19	2	8	9	16	30	14	2-0	0-2		1-1		2-2	2-2	0-1	0-2		1-1		2-2
Huracán Tres Arroyos	19	2	6	11	19	34	12	0-1	0-0		2-3		1-3	1-2	1-1	0-1		3-1		2-1

13/08/2004 - 12/12/2004 • † Qualified for Copa Libertadores 2006

APERTURA TOP SCORERS

LOPEZ Lisandro	Racing Club	12
MIRANDA Osvaldo	Almagro	8
CAGGIANO Jeremias	Huracán TA	8
GRAF Claudio	Lanús	8
ZARATE Rolando	Vélez Sarsfield	8

CLAUSURA TOP SCORERS

PAVONE Mariano	Estudiantes LP	16
FUERTES Esteban	Colón Santa Fé	11
FRUTOS Nicolás	Independiente	10
CALDERON José Luis	Arsenal	9
LUJAMBIO Josemir	Instituto	9

ARGENTINA 2004-05 NACIONAL B (2) APERTURA

Team	Pl	W	D	L	F	A	Pts
Tiro Federal Rosario	19	10	6	3	30	15	36
Huracán BA	19	10	4	5	27	21	34
Nueva Chicago	19	9	5	5	24	16	32
Atlético Rafaela	19	9	5	5	28	24	32
Gimnasia Jujuy	19	9	2	8	32	30	29
Ferro Carril Oeste	19	8	5	6	22	22	29
San Martin San Juan	19	7	7	5	23	22	28
El Porvenir	19	7	6	6	22	18	27
San Martin Mendoza	19	7	6	6	31	28	27
Racing Club Córdoba	19	7	6	6	21	22	27
Belgrano Córdoba	19	8	3	8	18	20	27
CA Infantiles	19	7	5	7	30	27	26
Unión Santa Fe	19	6	7	6	19	21	25
Godoy Cruz	19	6	4	9	27	27	22
Defensa y Justicia	19	6	4	9	20	25	22
Talleres Córdoba	19	5	6	8	18	19	21
Juventud Antoniana	19	6	3	10	23	27	21
Chacarita Juniors	19	4	7	8	23	31	19
Defensores Belgrano	19	4	6	9	23	29	18
Sarmiento Junin	19	4	5	10	20	37	17

12/08/2004 - 18/12/2004

ARGENTINA 2004-05 PRIMERA B (3) APERTURA

Team	Pl	W	D	L	F	A	Pts
Tigre	20	12	7	1	33	11	43
Platense	20	11	5	4	24	13	38
Deportivo Italiano	20	10	7	3	27	16	37
Tristán Suárez	20	10	4	6	32	23	34
All Boys	20	8	8	4	22	20	32
Atlanta	20	10	2	8	30	29	32
Temperley	20	9	4	7	31	23	31
Los Andes	20	8	7	5	33	33	31
Deportivo Morón	20	7	9	4	20	13	30
Central Córdoba	20	6	10	4	26	21	28
Deportivo Armenia	20	7	6	7	21	17	27
Talleres Escalada	20	6	8	6	20	22	26
Almirante Brown	20	4	12	4	21	21	24
Estudiantes BA	20	5	9	6	22	25	24
Defensores Cambaceres	20	4	11	5	16	18	23
Brown Adrogué	20	5	6	9	19	25	21
Deportivo Laferrere	20	5	5	10	24	36	20
Argentino Rosario	20	5	4	11	22	37	19
Deportivo Español	20	5	2	11	20	32	17
San Telmo	20	3	5	12	24	36	14
Flandria	20	2	4	14	16	32	10

31/07/2004 - 5/12/2004

ARGENTINA 2004-05

PRIMERA DIVISION — TORNEO CLAUSURA

Team	Pl	W	D	L	F	A	Pts	Vél	Ban	Rac	Est	Ros	Ars	Gim	Lan	Ins	Riv	Col	Ind	Oli	New	Boc	SLo	AJu	Qui	Alm	Hur
Vélez Sarsfield †	19	11	6	2	32	14	39			2-0	2-1	3-0		2-3			3-1	0-0	2-0	2-0						0-0	2-0
Banfield ‡	19	10	3	6	25	16	33				1-0	0-0	3-0				1-0	0-0	1-1		0-1	3-2	1-0			4-1	
Racing Club	19	9	5	5	25	17	32						1-0	2-1	2-0			3-1	2-0	3-3	1-0	0-1				2-1	1-1
Estudiantes LP ‡	19	8	7	4	28	23	31					2-2	1-1	2-2				2-1	3-1			3-2	0-0	0-1	1-3		3-2
Rosario Central ‡	19	8	7	4	27	24	31	1-1	0-2					2-1	2-1	3-3	3-0	0-0	1-0					1-1	1-0		
Arsenal	19	8	6	5	27	22	30	1-1		2-1		0-0		1-2	2-2	2-1				3-0				2-1			1-1
Gimnasia y Esgrima	19	9	2	8	25	25	29	2-4	0-2	4-1								0-0		1-0	0-1	3-1				2-1	2-0
Lanús	19	7	7	5	36	27	28	1-2	2-4	0-0						3-0	4-3			5-0	0-0					6-0	3-1
Instituto	19	8	4	7	32	30	28					0-1	0-3	1-2			2-0	0-0			4-3	3-1	1-1	3-2			3-2
River Plate	19	8	3	8	31	29	27	0-1	1-0	1-0				2-0	1-2	1-1		3-1		0-2				4-0			1-0
Colón Santa Fe	19	6	8	5	30	23	26	1-1		2-2					2-0	4-2	2-0		0-1	2-3	1-0	3-3	2-1				3-0
Independiente	19	6	8	5	29	26	26						2-0	4-2	2-0	0-1	1-1			2-3	1-1	3-2		0-0			
Olimpo	19	7	5	7	18	22	26		1-1		2-0	0-2				1-0					1-1	3-0			1-0		3-1
Newell's Old Boys ‡	19	5	9	5	22	21	24	0-0			0-0	1-1	1-1				1-0					1-1					2-1
Boca Juniors	19	6	4	9	26	30	22	4-1				1-3	2-2		2-1		1-1						3-1				0-0
San Lorenzo	19	6	4	9	23	29	22			1-3				1-2			3-1		3-1	0-0	2-4			3-0		0-2	2-0
Argentinos Juniors	19	5	6	8	28	30	21	0-3	1-2	1-0				1-1	1-2	0-2		3-3			0-0					0-1	5-1
Quilmes	19	5	5	9	16	23	20	2-0	1-0				1-4				1-1	0-0	1-2		1-1	2-0					3-0
Almagro	19	3	4	12	22	44	13				1-4	1-2	2-5			0-5	2-2	**3-2**	3-1						2-0		2-0
Huracán Tres Arroyos	19	0	5	14	12	42	5		0-2			0-0							2-2								

11/02/2005 - 3/07/2005 • † Qualified for Copa Libertadores 2006 • ‡ Qualified for Copa Sudamericana 2005 • Match in bold abandoned and awarded as a defeat to both teams • Relegation decided on average points over three years • Argentinos Juniors and Instituto entered a play-off

PRIMERA/NACIONAL B PROMOTION AND RELEGATION

Tiro Federal	1 1				
Gimnasia Jujuy	0 1	Gimnasia Jujuy	1 0		
		Huracán BA	0 0	Huracán BA	1 0
				Instituto	2 1

San Martin Mendoza	3 1				
CA Infantiles	1 2	San Martin Mendoza	0 1		
Nueva Chicago	0 1	Atlético Rafaela	0 4	Atlético Rafaela	2 0
Atlético Rafaela	0 2			Argentinos Juniors	1 3

Clubs in bold promoted

ARGENTINA 2004-05 — NACIONAL B (2) CLAUSURA

Team	Pl	W	D	L	F	A	Pts
Gimnasia Jujuy †	19	10	5	4	30	17	35
CA Infantiles ‡	19	8	10	1	26	18	34
Atlético Rafaela ‡	19	7	8	4	26	23	29
Talleres Córdoba	19	6	10	3	27	18	28
Belgrano Córdoba	19	8	4	7	22	23	28
Chacarita Juniors	19	7	6	6	30	28	27
Huracán BA ‡	19	8	3	8	25	23	27
Tiro Federal Rosario †	19	6	9	4	14	17	27
San Martin Mendoza ‡	19	6	8	5	29	24	26
Juventud Antoniana	19	6	8	5	23	20	26
San Martin San Juan	19	6	7	6	18	16	25
Godoy Cruz	19	6	7	6	23	27	25
Unión Santa Fe	19	5	10	4	23	28	25
Ferro Carril Oeste	19	5	9	5	24	20	24
Nueva Chicago	19	5	8	6	21	20	23
Racing Club Córdoba	19	4	7	8	22	27	19
El Porvenir	19	4	7	8	14	22	19
Defensores Belgrano	19	4	7	8	18	27	19
Defensa y Justicia	19	3	9	7	15	20	18
Sarmiento Junin	19	3	5	11	25	37	14

4/02/2005 - 18/06/2005 • † Qualified for the play-offs as Apertura/Clausura winners • ‡ Qualified on season record

ARGENTINA 2004-05 — PRIMERA B (3) CLAUSURA

Team	Pl	W	D	L	F	A	Pts
Tigre	20	15	5	0	39	13	50
Platense	20	10	5	5	33	21	35
Atlanta	20	9	8	3	29	18	35
Los Andes	20	9	6	5	43	34	33
Deportivo Armenia	20	9	6	5	31	24	33
Deportivo Morón	20	9	5	6	24	25	32
Brown Adrogué	20	9	5	6	23	26	32
Talleres Escalada	20	9	4	7	32	28	31
Tristán Suárez	20	8	4	8	24	22	28
All Boys	20	7	7	6	20	18	28
Deportivo Italiano	20	7	7	6	27	26	28
Flandria	20	7	6	7	22	16	27
Deportivo Español	20	7	6	7	20	20	27
Estudiantes BA	20	7	5	8	30	34	26
San Telmo	20	6	5	9	25	31	23
Central Córdoba	20	5	7	8	22	26	22
Temperley	20	4	8	8	15	19	20
Defensores Cambaceres	20	3	8	9	19	32	17
Argentino Rosario	20	5	2	13	20	36	17
Almirante Brown	20	2	8	10	15	28	14
Deportivo Laferrere	20	2	5	13	14	30	11

11/12/2004 - 28/05/2005

NEWELL'S OLD BOYS 2004-2005

Date	Opponents	Score		Comp	Scorers
15-08-2004	Vélez Sarsfield	L 0-1	H	TAP	
22-08-2004	Rosario Central	W 1-0	A	TAP	Maidana 77
25-08-2004	Huracán Tres Arroyos	W 1-0	H	TAP	Marino 90
28-08-2004	Colón Santa Fe	D 0-0	A	TAP	
12-09-2004	Banfield	D 1-1	H	TAP	Scocco 23
19-09-2004	Argentinos Juniors	W 2-1	A	TAP	Belluschi 17, Ré 27
23-09-2004	Instituto Córdoba	W 3-0	H	TAP	Borghello 12, Steinert 75, Belluschi 79
26-09-2004	River Plate	D 2-2	H	TAP	Capria 5, Penta 58
1-10-2004	Estudiantes La Plata	W 1-0	H	TAP	Ortega 55p
15-10-2004	Arsenal	D 0-0	A	TAP	
20-10-2004	Racing Club	W 1-0	H	TAP	Belluschi 42
24-10-2004	Quilmes	W 2-0	H	TAP	Marino 30, Ortega 34p
31-10-2004	Almagro	L 0-1	A	TAP	
7-11-2004	Lanús	D 0-0	H	TAP	
12-11-2004	San Lorenzo	W 2-1	A	TAP	Scocco 14, Borghello 79
21-11-2004	Olimpo Bahia Blanca	D 1-1	H	TAP	Ortega 45
28-11-2004	Boca Juniors	W 3-1	A	TAP	Borghello 2 30 35, Maidana 52
5-12-2004	Gimnasia y Esgrima La Plata	W 2-0	H	TAP	Belluschi 31, Marino 33
12-12-2004	Independiente	L 0-2	A	TAP	
12-02-2005	Vélez Sarsfield	D 0-0	A	TCL	
20-02-2005	Rosario Central	D 0-0	H	TCL	
27-02-2005	Huracán Tres Arroyos	W 2-0	A	TCL	Zapata 5, Esnaider 78
4-03-2005	Colón Santa Fe	D 1-1	H	TCL	Belluschi 16
12-03-2005	Banfield	W 1-0	A	TCL	Belluschi 17
19-03-2005	Argentinos Juniors	D 1-1	H	TCL	Spolli 74
3-04-2005	Instituto Córdoba	L 3-4	A	TCL	Vella 21, Spolli 37, Capria 64
10-04-2005	River Plate	W 4-2	H	TCL	Belluschi 3 5 52 90, Ortega 66
17-10-2005	Estudiantes La Plata	L 2-3	A	TCL	Scocco 12, Maidana 19
24-04-2005	Arsenal	D 0-0	H	TCL	
29-04-2005	Racing Club	D 3-3	A	TCL	Capria 63, Zapata 71, Ortega 84
7-05-2005	Quilmes	L 0-2	A	TCL	
15-05-2005	Almagro	W 2-1	H	TCL	Borghello 28, Ceresetto 84
20-05-2005	Lanús	D 0-0	A	TCL	
28-05-2005	San Lorenzo	D 1-1	H	TCL	Vella 62
11-06-2005	Olimpo Bahia Blanca	L 0-1	A	TCL	
19-06-2005	Boca Juniors	W 1-0	H	TCL	Borghello 47
25-06-2005	Gimnasia y Esgrima La Plata	L 0-1	A	TCL	
2-07-2005	Independiente	D 1-1	H	TCL	Ceresetto 36

TAP = Torneo Apertura • TCL = Torneo Clausura

RECENT LEAGUE RECORD

Torneo Clausura					Torneo Apertura			
Year	Champions	Pts	Runners-up	Pts	Champions	Pts	Runners-up	Pts
1990					Newell's Old Boys	28	River Plate	26
1991	Boca Juniors	32	San Lorenzo	27	River Plate	31	Boca Juniors	24
1992	Newell's Old Boys	29	Vélez Sarsfield	27	Boca Juniors	27	River Plate	25
1993	Vélez Sarsfield	27	Independiente	24	River Plate	24	Vélez Sarsfield	23
1994	Independiente	26	Huracán	25	River Plate	31	San Lorenzo	26
1995	San Lorenzo	30	Gimnasia LP	29	Vélez Sarsfield	41	Racing Club	35
1996	Vélez Sarsfield	40	Gimnasia LP	39	River Plate	46	Independiente	37
1997	River Plate	41	Colón Santa Fe	35	River Plate	45	Boca Juniors	44
1998	Vélez Sarsfield	46	Lanús	40	Boca Juniors	45	Gimnasia LP	36
1999	Boca Juniors	44	River Plate	37	River Plate	44	Rosario Central	43
2000	River Plate	42	Independiente	36	Boca Juniors	41	River Plate	37
2001	San Lorenzo	47	River Plate	41	Racing Club	42	River Plate	41
2002	River Plate	43	Gimnasia LP	37	Independiente	43	Boca Juniors	40
2003	River Plate	43	Boca Juniors	39	Boca Juniors	39	San Lorenzo	36
2004	River Plate	40	Boca Juniors	36	Newell's Old Boys	36	Vélez Sarsfield	34
2005	Vélez Sarsfield	39	Banfield	33				

The system of two leagues in a year - the Apertura and Clausura - was adopted in mid 1990 • Newell's beat Boca in a play-off in 1991 but there have been no play-offs since • The season runs from August to July with the Apertura played at the end of the calendar year and the Clausura at the beginning of the calendar year

VELEZ SARSFIELD 2004-2005

Date	Opponents	Score		Comp	Scorers
15-08-2004	Newell's Old Boys	W 1-0	A	TAP	Zárate.R [45]
21-08-2004	Quilmes	W 4-0	H	TAP	Valdemarín [35], Zárate.R 3 [69 76 90]
24-08-2004	Almagro	D 0-0	A	TAP	
27-08-2004	Lanús	W 2-1	H	TAP	Batalla [25], Zárate.R [87]
11-09-2004	San Lorenzo	L 0-1	A	TAP	
19-09-2004	Olimpo	W 1-0	H	TAP	Valdemarín [90]
22-09-2004	Boca Juniors	L 0-6	A	TAP	
26-09-2004	Gimnasia y Esgrima La Plata	W 1-0	H	TAP	Castroman [69]
2-10-2004	Independiente	W 2-0	A	TAP	Abraham OG [38], Zárate.R [84]
16-10-2004	Racing Club	W 2-1	A	TAP	Valdemarín [15p], Zárate.M [62]
19-10-2004	Rosario Central	L 0-1	H	TAP	
22-10-2004	Huracán Tres Arroyos	W 1-0	A	TAP	Castroman [42]
30-10-2004	Colón Santa Fe	L 2-3	H	TAP	Valdemarín [15p], Cubero [82]
6-11-2004	Banfield	D 0-0	A	TAP	
13-11-2004	Argentinos Juniors	D 1-1	H	TAP	Zárate.R [63]
19-11-2004	Instituto Córdoba	L 0-1	A	TAP	
28-11-2004	River Plate	W 1-0	H	TAP	Zárate.R [31]
5-12-2004	Estudiantes La Plata	W 2-0	A	TAP	Cubero [12], Bravo [38]
12-12-2004	Arsenal	D 1-1	H	TAP	Fuentes [18]
12-02-2005	Newell's Old Boys	D 0-0	H	TCL	
18-02-2005	Quilmes	L 0-2	A	TCL	
25-02-2005	Almagro	D 0-0	H	TCL	
4-03-2005	Lanús	W 2-1	H	TCL	Zárate.R [60], Martínez.J [63]
12-03-2005	San Lorenzo	W 2-0	A	TCL	Gracián [2], Zárate.R [36]
20-03-2005	Olimpo	D 1-1	H	TCL	Zárate.R [37]
3-04-2005	Boca Juniors	W 2-0	H	TCL	Cubero [59], Castromán [90]
9-04-2005	Gimnasia y Esgrima La Plata	W 4-1	A	TCL	Zárate.R 2 [24 89], Cubero [63], Gracián [71]
17-10-2005	Independiente	W 3-1	H	TCL	Gracián [20], Zárate.R [42], Bravo [45]
23-04-2005	Racing Club	W 2-1	H	TCL	Castromán [28p], Gracián [88]
30-04-2005	Rosario Central	D 1-1	A	TCL	Castromán [90]
7-05-2005	Huracán Tres Arroyos	W 2-0	H	TCL	Pellegrino [11], Bravo [84]
15-05-2005	Colón Santa Fe	D 1-1	A	TCL	Bravo [8]
21-05-2005	Banfield	W 2-0	H	TCL	Castromán [68], Zárate.M [90]
29-05-2005	Argentinos Juniors	W 3-0	A	TCL	Castromán [1p], Pellerano [65], Gracián [84]
12-06-2005	Instituto Córdoba	L 2-3	H	TCL	Castromán [2p], Gracian [60]
19-06-2005	River Plate	W 1-0	A	TCL	Castromán [13p]
26-06-2005	Estudiantes La Plata	W 3-0	H	TCL	Cubero [18], Zárate.R [22], Castromán [26]
3-07-2005	Arsenal	D 1-1	A	TCL	Zárate.R [39]

TAP = Torneo Apertura • TCL = Torneo Clausura

CLUB DIRECTORY

Club	Town/City	Stadium	Members	Phone	www.	Lge	CL
Almagro	Buenos Aires	Almagro 19 000	4 500	+54 11 48634901	None	0	0
Argentinos Juniors	Buenos Aires	Diego Maradona 24 800	5 000	+54 11 45516887	argentinosjuniors.com.ar	2	1
Arsenal	Buenos Aires	Viaducto 16 300	1 800	+54 11 42040755	None	0	0
Banfield	Buenos Aires	Florencio Sola 33 351	6 000	+54 11 42421209	clubabanfield.com.ar	0	0
Boca Juniors	Buenos Aires	La Bombonera 57 395	43 320	+54 11 43094700	bocajuniors.com.ar	26	5
Colón	Santa Fe	Cementerio Elefantes 32 500	9 500	+54 342 4598025	None	0	0
Estudiantes	La Plata	Jorge Luis Hirsch 20 000	13 500	+54 221 4255716	estudiantesdelp.com.ar	4	3
Gimnasia y Esgrima	La Plata	Bosque 33 000	13 000	+54 221 4222510	gelp.com.ar	1	0
Huracán	Tres Arroyos	Roberto Bottino 7 000	1 400	+54 2983 427020	huracansas.com.ar	0	0
Independiente	Buenos Aires	Doble Visera 57 901	42 583	+54 11 42011875	independiente.co.ar	16	7
Instituto	Cordoba	Monumental 26 535	7 500	+54 351 4740447	None	0	0
Lanús	Buenos Aires	La Fortaleza 44 000	24 635	+54 11 42414239	lanusclubatletico.com.ar	0	0
Newell's Old Boys	Rosario	Coloso 42 000	9 000	+54 341 4117725	pasionrojinegra.com	5	0
Olimpo	Bahía Blanca	Roberto Carminatti 15 000	-	+54 291 4525290	aurinegro.com.ar	0	0
Quilmes	Buenos Aires	Centenario 33 000	4 925	+54 11 42531014	quilmesac.com	2	0
Racing Club	Buenos Aires	Cilindro 64 161	25 000	+54 11 42226388	racingclub.com	16	1
River Plate	Buenos Aires	Monumental 76 687	51 000	+54 11 47881200	cariverplate.com.ar	33	2
Rosario Central	Rosario	Gigante 41 654	16 500	+54 341 4389595	rosariocentral.com	4	0
San Lorenzo	Buenos Aires	Nuevo Gasometro 43 480	17 265	+54 11 49192470	sanlorenzo.com.ar	12	0
Vélez Sarsfield	Buenos Aires	El Fortin 49 540	27 545	+54 11 46415663	velezsarsfield.com.ar	6	1

ARM – ARMENIA

NATIONAL TEAM RECORD
JULY 1ST 2002 TO JUNE 30TH 2005

PL	W	D	L	F	A	%
23	5	3	15	19	46	28.3

FIFA/COCA-COLA WORLD RANKING

1993	1994	1995	1996	1997	1998	1999	2000	2001	2002	2003	2004	High		Low	
-	141	113	106	105	100	85	90	95	107	113	119	**79**	09/00	**159**	07/94

2004-2005											
08/04	09/04	10/04	11/04	12/04	01/05	02/05	03/05	04/05	05/05	06/05	07/05
116	119	123	123	119	120	120	120	120	121	121	119

The qualification of the Armenian U-20 team for the UEFA U-20 European Championship in Northern Ireland in 2005 was a major breakthrough for football in the country and was helped by the decision to bring the Malatia youth academy under the control of the football federation with the aid of Goal Programme. The scene was not so rosy with the senior team. Frenchman Bernard Casoni lasted just eight months before he was replaced by Dutchman Hendrik Wisman as national team coach. Nine defeats in Casoni's first 11 matches with just one victory – over Andorra – meant he had little support amongst the local fans, especially with the team battling Andorra to avoid the

INTERNATIONAL HONOURS
None

wooden spoon in the FIFA World Cup™ qualifying group. Wiseman's appointment also saw him take the reins at reigning champions Pyunik Yerevan who had an outstanding 2004 and had they not lost their penultimate match against Kilikia, they would have gone consecutive seasons unbeaten. Their run of 59 league games spanning 25 months was an impressive achievement, the fourth longest unbeaten streak in top flight European football. There was no Cup joy for Pyunik, however, after Kilikia knocked them out in the quarter-finals of the 2005 competition which was won by League runners-up Mika Ashtarak, their fourth Cup triumph in six years.

THE FIFA BIG COUNT OF 2000

	Male	Female		Male	Female
Registered players	1 600	100	Referees	64	10
Non registered players	35 000	100	Officials	140	20
Youth players	2 550	160	Total involved	39 744	
Total players	39 510		Number of clubs	56	
Professional players	550	0	Number of teams	78	

Football Federation of Armenia (FFA)
Khanjyan str. 27, Yerevan 375 010, Armenia
Tel +374 1 568 883   Fax +374 1 539 517
ffarm@arminco.com   www.ffa.am
President: HAYRAPETYAN Ruben   General Secretary: MINASYAN Armen
Vice-President: TBD   Treasurer: PAPIKYAN Gevorg   Media Officer: MANUKYAN Arayik
Men's Coach: WISMAN Hendrik   Women's Coach: MIKAYELYAN Mher
FFA formed: 1992   UEFA: 1993   FIFA: 1992
Colours: Red, Blue, Orange or White, White, White

GAMES PLAYED BY ARMENIA IN THE 2006 FIFA WORLD CUP™ CYCLE

2002	Opponents	Score	Venue	Comp	Scorers	Att	Referee
7-09	Ukraine	D 2-2	Yerevan	ECq	Petrosyan.Art [73], Sarkisyan [90p]	9 000	Vuorela FIN
16-10	Greece	L 0-2	Athens	ECq		6 000	Ceferin SVN
2003							
12-02	Israel	L 0-2	Tel Aviv	Fr		8 000	Trentlange ITA
29-03	Northern Ireland	W 1-0	Yerevan	ECq	Petrosyan.Art [86]	10 321	Beck LIE
2-04	Spain	L 0-3	Leon	ECq		13 500	Yefet ISR
7-06	Ukraine	L 3-4	Lviv	ECq	Sarkisyan 2 [14p 52], Petrosyan.Art [74]	35 000	Albrecht GER
6-09	Greece	L 0-1	Yerevan	ECq		6 500	Temmink NED
10-09	Northern Ireland	W 1-0	Belfast	ECq	Karamyan.Arm [29]	8 616	Stredak SVK
11-10	Spain	L 0-4	Yerevan	ECq		15 000	Meier SUI
2004							
18-02	Hungary	L 0-2	Paphos	Fr		400	Gerasimou CYP
19-02	Kazakhstan	D 3-3	Paphos	Fr	Petrosyan.G [52], Karamyan.Art 2 [73 80] L 2-3p	100	
21-02	Georgia	W 2-0	Nicosia	Fr	Karamyan.Arm [42], Karamyan.Art [52]		
28-04	Turkmenistan	W 1-0	Yerevan	Fr	Hakopyan [68]	7 500	
18-08	FYR Macedonia	L 0-3	Skopje	WCq		4 375	Guenov BUL
8-09	Finland	L 0-2	Yerevan	WCq		2 864	Malzinskas LTU
9-10	Finland	L 1-3	Tampere	WCq	Shahgeldyan [32]	7 894	Fandel GER
13-10	Czech Republic	L 0-3	Yerevan	WCq		3 205	Granat POL
17-11	Romania	D 1-1	Yerevan	WCq	Dokhoyan [62]	1 403	De bleeckere BEL
2005							
18-03	Kuwait	L 1-3	Al Ain	Fr	Mkhitaryan [87p]		
26-03	Andorra	W 2-1	Yerevan	WCq	Hakobyan [30], Khachatryan.R [73]	2 100	Attard MLT
30-03	Netherlands	L 0-2	Eindhoven	WCq		35 000	Trefoloni ITA
4-06	FYR Macedonia	L 1-2	Yerevan	WCq	Manucharyan [55]	2 870	Mikulski POL
8-06	Romania	L 0-3	Constanta	WCq		5 146	Briakos GRE

Fr = Friendly match • EC = UEFA EURO 2004™ • WC = FIFA World Cup™ • q = qualifier

NATIONAL CAPS

	Caps
HOVSEPYAN Sargis	73
PETROSYAN Artur	69
VARDANYAN Harutyun	62
SHAHGELDYAN Armen	43
BEREZOVSKI Roman	41
KHACHATRYAN Romik	39
MKHITARYAN Hamlet	38
SUKIASYAN Yervand	36
SARKISYAN Albert	33

NATIONAL GOALS

	Goals
PETROSYAN Artur	11
SHAHGELDYAN Armen	6
KARAMYAN Arman	4
YESAYAN Tigran	4
SARKISYAN Albert	3
ASSADOURYAN Eric	3
KARAMYAN Artavzad	3

NATIONAL COACH

	Years
DARBINYAN Samvel	1995-'96
HOVANNISYAN Khoren	1996-'98
BARSEGYAN Suren	1998-'99
SUKIASYAN Varuzhan	1999-'01
ADAMYAN Andravik	2002
LOPEZ Oscar	2002
STOICHITA Mihai	2003-'04
CASONI Bernard	2004-'05
WISMAN Hendrik	2005-

FIFA REFEREE LIST 2005

	Int'l	DoB
HOVSEPYAN Tigran	2003	14-03-1978
NALBANDYAN Karen	1993	27-08-1964
TSHAGHARYAN Ararat	2003	5-10-1967

FIFA ASSISTANT REFEREE LIST 2005

	Int'l	DoB
ARTOYAN Hakob	2003	5-08-1970
GHUSHCHYAN Arman	2005	6-03-1979
IGITYAN Artur	2003	4-09-1972
KNYAZYAN Arshak	2003	29-03-1967
MAHTESYAN Kamo	2005	4-01-1972
VARDANYAN Gegham	2005	5-12-1970

ARMENIA COUNTRY INFORMATION

Capital	Yerevan	Independence	1991	GDP per Capita	$3 500
Population	2 991 360	Status	Republic	GNP Ranking	136
Area km²	29 800	Language	Armenian	Dialling code	+374
Population density	100 per km²	Literacy rate	99%	Internet code	.am
% in urban areas	69%	Main religion	Christian 98%	GMT + / –	+4
Towns/Cities ('000)	Yerevan 1 093; Gyumri 148; Vanadzor 101; Vagharshapat 49; Hrazdan 40; Abovyan 35				
Neighbours (km)	Georgia 164; Azerbaijan 787; Iran 35; Turkey 268				
Main stadia	Hrazdan – Yerevan 48 250; Hanrapetakan – Yerevan 14 968; Kotayk – Abovyan 5 500				

ARMENIA NATIONAL TEAM RECORDS AND RECORD SEQUENCES

Records			Sequence records					
Victory	3-0	ALB 1997, AND 1999	Wins	2	2004	Clean sheets	2	2004
Defeat	0-7	CHI 1997, GEO 1997	Defeats	5	1995-1996	Goals scored	6	1999-2000
Player Caps	73	HOVSEPYAN Sargis	Undefeated	3	Four times	Without goal	7	1999
Player Goals	11	PETROSYAN Artur	Without win	10	1996-1997	Goals against	13	1994-1996

ARMENIA 2004

PREMIER LEAGUE

	Pl	W	D	L	F	A	Pts	Pyunik	Mika	Banants	Ararat	Dinamo	Kilikia	Kotayk	Shirak
Pyunik Yerevan †	28	22	5	1	89	25	71		3-1 3-0	3-0 3-2	3-1 3-1	3-0 7-0	7-2 0-1	3-1 1-0	4-0 6-1
Mika Ashtarak ‡	28	16	7	5	41	23	55	2-2 0-1		2-1 4-0	3-1 2-0	1-0 1-0	1-0 5-1	2-1 1-1	2-1 0-1
Banants Yerevan ‡	28	12	7	9	40	39	43	1-3 1-1	0-1 1-1		3-2 1-1	2-0 4-0	1-0 2-1	2-1 1-1	1-1 1-1
Ararat Yerevan	28	12	7	9	40	33	43	1-4 1-2	1-1 0-2	1-0 1-2		1-1 2-0	3-2 1-0	5-1 1-0	2-0 3-0
Dinamo-Zenit Yerevan	28	7	6	15	23	51	27	2-2 1-5	2-1 1-2	1-1 0-3	0-0 1-4		1-0 0-1	2-1 2-3	0-1 1-0
Kilikia Yerevan	28	7	5	16	32	49	26	1-1 2-2	0-1 1-1	4-0 3-2	0-2 0-0	2-3 0-1		1-0 2-3	1-1 2-1
Kotayk Abovyan	28	6	6	16	31	54	24	1-6 1-6	1-3 0-0	1-2 0-2	0-2 0-1	1-1 2-1	2-0 2-0		3-3 3-1
Shirak Gyumri	28	4	9	15	27	49	21	0-1 1-4	0-1 0-0	1-2 1-2	2-2 0-0	0-1 1-1	3-4 3-1	1-1 2-0	

8/04/2004 - 11/11/2004 • † Qualified for the UEFA Champions League • ‡ Qualified for the UEFA Cup • Shirak not relegated due to expansion of league

ARMENIA 2004 SECOND DIVISION

	Pl	W	D	L	F	A	Pts
Pyunik-2 Yerevan *	30	27	2	1	98	21	83
Lernayin Yerevan	30	22	6	2	82	20	72
Gandzasar Yerevan	30	17	6	7	52	32	57
Vagharshapat	30	17	3	10	61	42	54
Mika-2 Ashtarak	30	15	9	6	48	25	54
Araks Ararat	30	16	3	11	57	31	51
Ararat-2 Yerevan	30	16	1	13	83	50	49
Banants-2 Yerevan	30	13	9	8	40	30	48
Pyunik-3 Yerevan	30	13	4	13	56	47	43
Banants-3 Yerevan	30	11	6	13	46	48	39
Lokomotiv Yerevan	30	8	6	16	29	51	30
Dinamo Yerevan	30	9	1	20	52	72	28
Dinamo VZ Yerevan	30	7	3	20	46	83	24
Lori Vanadzor	30	7	6	17	35	68	24
Zenit Charentsavyan	30	6	3	21	34	89	21
Norq-Marash Yerevan	30	2	0	28	7	117	3

23/04/2004 - 6/11/2004

TOP SCORERS

Edgar Manucharian	Pyunik	21
Galust Petrosian	Pyunik	21
Nshan Erzrumian	Kilikia	18
Levon Pachajian	Pyunik	13
Armen Shahgeldian	Mika	12

FFA CUP 2005

Quarter-finals			Semi-finals			Final		
Mika Ashtarak	1	1						
Dinamo-Zenit	0	0	Mika Ashtarak	1	2			
Ararat Yerevan	1	0	Kotayk Abovyan	2	0			
Kotayk Abovyan	1	1				Mika Ashtarak ‡		2
Banants Yerevan	5	1				Kilikia Yerevan		0
Shirak Gyumri	2	0	Banants Yerevan	2	2	Hanrapetakan, Yerevan		
Pyunik Yerevan	0	0	Kilikia Yerevan	3	1	9-05-2005, Att: 6 000		
Kilikia Yerevan	1	0	‡ Qualified for UEFA Cup			Scorers - OG 52, Magdiev 77		

RECENT LEAGUE AND CUP RECORD

	Championship						Cup		
Year	Champions	Pts	Runners-up	Pts	Third	Pts	Winners	Score	Runners-up
1992	Shirak Kumajri*	37	Homenetmen*	37	Banants Kotiak	36	Banants Aboyan	2-0	Homenetmen
1993	Ararat Yerevan	51	Shirak Gyumri	49	Banants Kotiak	48	Ararat Yerevan	3-1	Shirak Gyumri
1994	Shirak Gyumri	52	AOSS Yerevan	47	Ararat Yerevan	47	Ararat Yerevan	1-0	Shirak Gyumri
1995							Ararat Yerevan	4-2	Kotayk Abovyan
1996	Pyunik Yerevan	60	Shirak Gyumri	51	FK Yerevan	44	Pyunik Yerevan	3-2	Kotayk Abovyan
1997	Pyunik Yerevan	59	Ararat Yerevan	52	FK Yerevan	50	Ararat Yerevan	1-0	Pyunik Yerevan
1998	Tsement Ararat	64	Shirak Gyumri	61	FK Yerevan	48	Tsement Ararat	3-1	FK Yerevan
1999	Shirak Gyumri	73	Ararat Yerevan	72	Tsement Ararat	71	Tsement Ararat	3-2	Shirak Yerevan
2000	Araks Ararat	61	Ararat Yerevan	59	Shirak Gyumri	58	Mika Ashtarak	2-1	Zvarnots Yerevan
2001	Pyunik Yerevan	53	Zvarnots Yerevan	48	Spartak Yerevan	48	Mika Ashtarak	1-1 4-3p	Ararat Yerevan
2002	Pyunik Yerevan	59	Shirak Gyumri	51	Banants Yerevan	50	Pyunik Yerevan	2-0	Zvarnots Yerevan
2003	Pyunik Yerevan	74	Banants Yerevan	66	Shirak Gyumri	53	Mika Ashtarak	1-0	Banants Yerevan
2004	Pyunik Yerevan	71	Mika Ashtarak	55	Banants Yerevan	43	Pyunik Yerevan	0-0 6-5p	Banants Yerevan
2005							Mika Ashtarak	2-0	Kilikia Yerevan

*Championship shared • Due to a change in the calendar season there was a spring championship in 1995 won by Shirak & Ararat • In 1997 there was an autumn championship won by FK Yerevan • Tsement Ararat changed their name to Araks Ararat and then Spartak Yerevan. They merged with Banants to become Banants Yerevan in 2002 • Pyunik previously known as Homenetmen and AOSS.

ARU – ARUBA

NATIONAL TEAM RECORD

JULY 1ST 2002 TO JUNE 30TH 2005

PL	W	D	L	F	A	%
5	0	0	5	3	24	0

FIFA/COCA-COLA WORLD RANKING

1993	1994	1995	1996	1997	1998	1999	2000	2001	2002	2003	2004	High		Low	
165	173	171	181	177	180	191	184	185	189	195	198	**164**	02/94	**198**	12/04

2004-2005											
08/04	09/04	10/04	11/04	12/04	01/05	02/05	03/05	04/05	05/05	06/05	07/05
196	196	196	196	198	198	198	198	198	198	198	198

Lying 198th in the FIFA Coca-Cola World rankings, Aruba's decline has been long and steady since reaching a high of 164 more than ten years ago. The position reflects the national team's results in recent years with only five matches played since 2002, all of them defeats. The 4-2 home win against Puerto Rico in March 2000 in the qualifiers for the 2002 FIFA World Cup™ was their last victory, so it was no surprise when Aruba lost to Surinam in the preliminaries of the 2006 edition, although having lost by the odd goal in three at home, the 1-8 collapse in Paramaribo was perhaps worse than expected. Hopes rest with the country's links with the Dutch association, the KNVB,

INTERNATIONAL HONOURS

None

which has provided technical and material assistance, but coach Marcelo Munoz faces a strong challenge if the country's fortunes are to improve. Both youth teams entered the regional international tournaments with the U-20s performing best. They beat Surinam 4-3 on aggregate in the preliminary round, but struggled in the group stages only managing a draw with Netherlands Antilles. Meanwhile, the U-17s lost all three of their group games. In the domestic Championship there was a first Division di Honor title for SV Britannia in 2005 who beat Racing Club Aruba 3-1 on aggregate in the final.

THE FIFA BIG COUNT OF 2000

	Male	Female		Male	Female
Registered players	2 200	0	Referees	24	3
Non registered players	900	0	Officials	130	10
Youth players	3 200	0	Total involved	6 467	
Total players		6 300	Number of clubs	54	
Professional players	0	0	Number of teams	127	

Arubaanse Voetbal Bond (AVB)

Ferguson Street Z/N, PO Box 376, Oranjestad, Aruba

Tel +297 829550   Fax +297 829550

avaruba@setarnet.aw   www.avaruba.aw

President: KELLY Rufo   General Secretary: LACLE Egbert

Vice-President: FARO Bernardo A   Treasurer: CROES Adrian   Media Officer: CROES Adrian

Men's Coach: MUNOZ Marcelo   Women's Coach: None

AVB formed: 1932   CONCACAF: 1961   FIFA: 1988

Colours: Yellow, Blue, Yellow/Blue

GAMES PLAYED BY ARUBA IN THE 2006 FIFA WORLD CUP™ CYCLE

2002	Opponents		Score	Venue	Comp	Scorers	Att	Referee
28-07	Surinam	L	0-2	Oranjestad	GCq			Faneijte ANT
11-08	Surinam	L	0-6	Paramaribo	GCq		2 500	Mercera ANT
2003								
No international matches played in 2003								
2004								
28-01	Netherlands Antilles	L	1-6	Willemstad	Fr			
28-02	Surinam	L	1-2	Oranjestad	WCq	Escalona 89	2 108	Moreno PAN
27-03	Surinam	L	1-8	Paramaribo	WCq	Escalona 24	4 000	Prendergast JAM
2005								
No international matches played in 2005 before August								

Fr = Friendly match • GC = CONCACAF Gold Cup™ • WCq = FIFA World Cup™ • q = qualifier

ARUBA NATIONAL TEAM RECORDS AND RECORD SEQUENCES

Records				Sequence records				
Victory	4-1	CUB 1953	Wins	1		Clean sheets	1	
Defeat	1-8	SUR 2004	Defeats	11	1953-1996	Goals scored	9	1944-1953
Player Caps	n/a		Undefeated	3	1944-1953	Without goal	5	1991-1992
Player Goals	n/a		Without win	12	1953-1996	Goals against	24	1934-1997

FIFA REFEREE LIST 2005

	Int'l	DoB
BANT Willem	1996	29-07-1963
VILLAR-POLO Harlem	1995	23-02-1962

FIFA ASSISTANT REFEREE LIST 2005

	Int'l	DoB
ANGELA Rudolph	2005	23-07-1970
DE WINDT Humphrey	2002	17-12-1965
PAESCH Egbert	2005	28-06-1974

RECENT LEAGUE RECORD

Year	Winners	Score	Runners-up
1996	Estrella		Racing Club
1997	Riverplate		Racing Club
1998	Estrella	2-1	Dakota
1999	Estrella	2-1	Nacional
2000	Nacional	1-1 1-1 1-0	Dakota
2001	Nacional	3-1 1-0	Racing Club
2002	Racing Club	†	Nacional
2003	Nacional	1-0 2-1	Estrella
2004	No tournament due to season readjustment		
2005	Britannia	2-1 1-0	Racing Club

† Played on a league basis

ARUBA COUNTRY INFORMATION

Capital	Oranjestad	Independence		Part of the Netherlands with	GDP per Capita	$28 000
Population	71 218	Status		autonomy in internal affairs	GNP Ranking	n/a
Area km²	193	Language	Dutch		Dialling code	+297
Population density	369 per km²	Literacy rate	97%		Internet code	.aw
% in urban areas	n/a	Main religion	Christian 90%		GMT + / –	-5
Towns/Cities ('000)	Oranjestad 29; Sint Nicolaas 17; Druif; Santa Cruz; Barcadera;					
Neighbours (km)	Caribbean Sea 68					
Main stadia	Guillermo Trinidad – Oranjestad 5 500					

ASA – AMERICAN SAMOA

NATIONAL TEAM RECORD
JULY 1ST 2002 TO JUNE 30TH 2005

PL	W	D	L	F	A	%
4	0	0	4	1	34	0

FIFA/COCA-COLA WORLD RANKING

1993	1994	1995	1996	1997	1998	1999	2000	2001	2002	2003	2004	High		Low	
-	-	-	-	-	193	199	203	201	201	202	204	192	10/98	205	03/05

2004-2005											
08/04	09/04	10/04	11/04	12/04	01/05	02/05	03/05	04/05	05/05	06/05	07/05
203	203	203	204	204	204	204	205	205	205	205	205

For the people of the small pacific island of American Samoa there is no escaping the fact that since March 2005 their national team has officially been the worst in the world. That was when they sunk below Guam in the FIFA Coca-Cola World Ranking. It's not easy being a football fan in the country – it's 22 years since American Samoa last won a game while in 2001 they were on the wrong end of a 31-0 defeat at the hands of Australia, the biggest defeat ever suffered by a national team. As the motto says it is the taking part that counts, though efforts are being made to improve the standard of football in a country where rugby is also very popular. US$500,000 has been spent on building

INTERNATIONAL HONOURS
None

a headquarters for the national association along with integrated playing fields in the capital Pago Pago, giving League clubs a venue at which they can play and giving the national team a location to prepare for matches. Since May 2004 and the World Cup qualifiers in Apia, however, American Samoa have not played any games and nor did the youth teams enter the OFC U-20 or OFC U-17 championships. Instead the only fooball has been in the domestic League, which in 2005 was won by PanSa for the fourth time in six seasons. The 2003 champions Manumea did enter the OFC Champions Cup but they pulled out before their match against Auckland City.

THE FIFA BIG COUNT OF 2000

	Male	Female		Male	Female
Registered players	1 000	0	Referees	50	0
Non registered players	400	0	Officials	100	0
Youth players	1 000	0	Total involved	2 550	
Total players	2 400		Number of clubs	30	
Professional players	0	0	Number of teams	100	

American Samoa Football Association (ASFA)
PO Box 1300, Faga'alu Main Road, Pago Pago AS 96799, American Samoa
Tel +684 6337975   Fax +684 6337976
richardott@samoatelco.com   www.none
President: OTT Richard   General Secretary: SOLOFA Paul K.
Vice-President: CHRICHTON Clarence   Treasurer: MAYERS Oscar   Media Officer: None
Men's Coach: CROOK Ian   Women's Coach: None
ASFA formed: 1984   OFC: 1994   FIFA: 1998
Colours: Navy blue, White, Red

GAMES PLAYED BY AMERICAN SAMOA IN THE 2006 FIFA WORLD CUP™ CYCLE

2002	Opponents	Score	Venue	Comp	Scorers	Att	Referee
No international matches played in 2002							
2003							
No international matches played in 2003							
2004							
10-05	Samoa	L 0-4	Apia	WCq		500	Afu SOL
12-05	Vanuatu	L 1-9	Apia	WCq	Natia 39	400	Fox NZL
15-05	Fiji	L 0-11	Apia	WCq		300	Fox NZL
17-05	Papua New Guinea	L 0-10	Apia	WCq		150	Afu SOL
2005							
No international matches played in 2005 before August							

WC = FIFA World Cup™ • q = qualifier

AMERICAN SAMOA NATIONAL TEAM RECORDS AND RECORD SEQUENCES

Records			Sequence records					
Victory	3-0	Wallis/Futuna 1983	Wins	1		Clean sheets	1	
Defeat	0-31	AUS 2001	Defeats	28	1983-	Goals scored	3	1983, 1994
Player Caps	n/a		Undefeated	1		Without goal	5	2001-2002
Player Goals	n/a		Without win	28	1983-	Goals against	28	1983-

FIFA ASSISTANT REFEREE LIST 2005

	Int'l	DoB
AFU Savaliga	2004	2-10-1970
ALATASI Lemusa	2004	28-05-1974
ALIVA Uinifareti	2004	17-10-1980
CHRICHTON David		20-05-1967
FUIMANO Laulo		19-03-1962
TALAIA Atufili	2001	19-05-1976

RECENT LEAGUE RECORD

Year	Winners
1996	No tournament
1997	Pago Eagles
1998	No tournament
1999	Konica Machine
2000	PanSa & Wild Wild West
2001	PanSa
2002	PanSa
2003	Manumea
2004	No tournament
2005	PanSa

AMERICAN SAMOA COUNTRY INFORMATION

Capital	Pago Pago	Independence	Unincorporated territory of the USA	GDP per Capita	$8 000
Population	57 902	Status		GNP Ranking	n/a
Area km²	199	Language	Samoan	Dialling code	+684
Population density	291 per km²	Literacy rate	97%	Internet code	.as
% in urban areas	n/a	Main religion	Christian	GMT +/-	-10
Towns/Cities ('000)	Tafuna 11; Nu'uuli 5; Pago Pago 4; Leone 4; Faleniu 3; Ili'ili 3				
Neighbours (km)	South Pacific Ocean 116				
Main stadia	Veterans Memorial – Pago Pago 10 000				

ATG – ANTIGUA AND BARBUDA

NATIONAL TEAM RECORD
JULY 1ST 2002 TO JUNE 30TH 2005

PL	W	D	L	F	A	%
16	5	2	9	19	28	37.5

FIFA/COCA-COLA WORLD RANKING

1993	1994	1995	1996	1997	1998	1999	2000	2001	2002	2003	2004	High		Low	
117	136	137	145	159	137	147	144	157	155	170	153	**116**	02/94	**170**	01/04

					2004-2005						
08/04	09/04	10/04	11/04	12/04	01/05	02/05	03/05	04/05	05/05	06/05	07/05
163	162	161	155	153	153	153	154	155	154	154	154

Germany 2006 was the eighth FIFA World Cup™ campaign Antigua and Barbuda had embarked on, but the team weren't able to repeat the relative success of four years previously when they knocked out Bermuda and St Vincent before losing to Guatemala. This time the team exited at the first attempt against Netherlands Antilles. After winning the first leg 2-0, Antigua squandered the lead in the away tie to lose 3-2 on aggregate. Since then games have included a morale-boosting first win over Trinidad and Tobago, a side ranked more than 100 places above them, and three games in the Digicel Caribbean Cup although they failed to make it out of their qualifying group.

INTERNATIONAL HONOURS
None

With a small population the country has always struggled in international football, but domestically there are plans for a semi-professional league structure for 2006 as well as for women's and youth leagues. The 2004 Premier League was won by Bassa who pipped Hoppers to the title on goal difference. Bassa's progress in the Champions League was short-lived, losing 4-2 on aggregate to Tivoli Gardens of Jamaica after winning the first leg 2-1. The U-20s finished bottom of their Youth Tournament group whilst the U-17s thumped British Virgin Islands 14-1 on aggregate in the preliminary round of the Junior Tournament before failing at the group stage.

THE FIFA BIG COUNT OF 2000

	Male	Female		Male	Female
Registered players	1 000	0	Referees	30	0
Non registered players	700	0	Officials	100	0
Youth players	1 000	0	Total involved	2 830	
Total players	2 700		Number of clubs	15	
Professional players	0	0	Number of teams	50	

Antigua and Barbuda Football Association (ABFA)
Suite 19, Vendors Mall, PO Box 773, St John's, Antigua
Tel +1 268 5626012   Fax +1 268 5626016
abfa@candw.ag   www.abfa.org.ag
President: RICHARDS Mervyn   General Secretary: DERRICK Gordon
Vice-President: GATESWORTH James   Treasurer: GARDNER Dwight   Media Officer: DERRICK Gordon
Men's Coach: EDWARDS SNR. Veron   Women's Coach: None
ABFA formed: 1928   CONCACAF: 1980   FIFA: 1970
Colours: Red/Black/Yellow/Blue, Red/Black/Yellow/Blue, Red/Black/Yellow/Blue

GAMES PLAYED BY ANTIGUA AND BARBUDA IN THE 2006 FIFA WORLD CUP™ CYCLE

2002	Opponents	Score		Venue	Comp	Scorers	Att	Referee
29-10	St Kitts and Nevis	D	1-1	St John's	Fr			
8-11	St Lucia	L	1-2		Fr			
18-11	Haiti	L	0-1	Port-au-Prince	GCq			Bowen CAY
20-11	Netherlands Antilles	D	1-1	Port-au-Prince	GCq	Jeffers 77		Bowen CAY
2003								
26-03	Trinidad and Tobago	L	0-2	Port of Spain	GCq			James GUY
28-03	Cuba	L	0-2	Macoya	GCq			James GUY
30-03	Guadeloupe	L	0-2	Marabella	GCq			Callender BRB
2004								
31-01	St Kitts and Nevis	W	1-0		Fr			
18-02	Netherlands Antilles	W	2-0	St John's	WCq	Roberts 42, Clarke 89	1 500	Navarro CAN
21-03	St Kitts and Nevis	W	3-2	Basseterre	Fr			
31-03	Netherlands Antilles	L	0-3	Willemstad	WCq		9 000	Piper TRI
2-11	Montserrat	W	5-4	Basseterre	GCq	OG 30, Frederick 53, Gonsalves 67 82, Thomas 72		Phillip GRN
4-11	St Kitts and Nevis	L	0-2	Basseterre	GCq			Phillip GRN
6-11	St Lucia	L	1-2	Basseterre	GCq	Dublin 65		Bedeau GRN
2005								
12-01	Trinidad and Tobago	W	2-1	St John's	Fr	Byers 48, Isaac 57	2 000	
6-02	Barbados	L	2-3	Bridgetown	Fr	Thomas 2, Byers 74	4 000	

Fr = Friendly match • GC = CONCACAF Gold Cup™ • WCq = FIFA World Cup™ • q = qualifier

ANTIGUA AND BARBUDA NATIONAL TEAM RECORDS AND RECORD SEQUENCES

Records			Sequence records					
Victory	8-0	MSR 1994	Wins	3	1992, 1997, 2004	Clean sheets	3	1992, 1999
Defeat	1-11	TRI 1972	Defeats	7	1972-1984	Goals scored	8	1995-97, 1998
Player Caps	n/a		Undefeated	6	2000	Without goal	3	1990, 2003
Player Goals	n/a		Without win	8	2002-2003	Goals against	12	2000-2001

FIFA REFEREE LIST 2005

	Int'l	DoB
WILLETT Bryan	1999	13-08-1971

FIFA ASSISTANT REFEREE LIST 2005

	Int'l	DoB
GOVIA Anthony	2003	12-03-1979
WALSH Audwin	2002	15-12-1970

ANTIGUA AND BARBUDA 2004-05 PREMIER LEAGUE

	Pl	W	D	L	F	A	Pts
Bassa	21	12	7	2	47	24	43
Hoppers	21	13	4	4	45	22	43
Empire	21	11	6	4	53	32	39
Villa Lions	21	8	4	9	42	45	28
Sap	21	8	2	11	42	49	26
Parham §	21	6	10	5	33	28	25
Wadadli	21	3	4	14	16	47	13
English Harbour §	21	3	3	15	28	59	9

29/08/2004 - 14/01/2005 • § 3 points deducted

RECENT LEAGUE RECORD

	Championship					
Year	Champions	Pts	Runners-up	Pts	Third	Pts
1998	Empire	32	English Harbour	29	Sap	29
1999	Empire					
2000	Empire	2-0	English Harbour			
2001	Empire	58	Bassa	37	Sap	33
2002	Parham	57	Empire	53	Sap	37
2003	Parham	38	Sap	37	Hoppers	35
2004	Bassa	34	Sap	28	Parham	23
2005	Bassa	43	Hoppers	43	Empire	39

ANTIGUA AND BARBUDA COUNTRY INFORMATION

Capital	St John's	Independence	1981	GDP per Capita	$11 000
Population	68 320	Status	Commonwealth	GNP Ranking	164
Area km²	443	Language	English	Dialling code	+1 268
Population density	154 per km²	Literacy rate	95%	Internet code	.ag
% in urban areas	36%	Main religion	Christian 96%	GMT +/–	-4.5
Towns/Cities ('000)	St John's 25; All Saints 2; Liberta 1; Potters Village 1				
Neighbours (km)	Caribbean Sea & North Atlantic Ocean 153				
Main stadia	Recreation Ground – St John's 18 000; Police Ground – St George's 3 000				

AUS – AUSTRALIA

AUSTRALIA NATIONAL TEAM RECORD
JULY 1ST 2002 TO JUNE 30TH 2005

PL	W	D	L	F	A	%
27	16	4	7	78	29	66.7

Despite the almost complete absence of competitive football in Australia for almost a year following Perth's triumph in the last ever NFL in April 2004, the sport has hardly been out of the headlines. Headed by millionaire Frank Lowy and former Australian rugby union chief John O'Neill, a new broom has swept through the game in an attempt to revitalise its fortunes. The word soccer has gone to be replaced by football, in line with much of the rest of the world, but of more significance was the launch of the Hyundai A-League in August 2005 and the move from the Oceania Football Confederation to the Asian Football Confederation in January 2006. Both are seen as vital in order to raise the standard of football in Australia by firstly providing more incentives for young players to stay in Australia instead of moving to the European leagues and to provide the national team with a better standard of opposition on a more regular basis. Eight franchises were offered for the new League and were taken up by existing clubs such as Perth Glory and Auckland Kingz along with new clubs such as Sydney FC and Melbourne Victory. The absence of any league football for 17 months did not help the situation but the new League has attracted significant interest and has

INTERNATIONAL HONOURS
Qualified for the FIFA World Cup™ 1974
Oceania Nations Cup 1980 1996 2000 2004   Oceania Women's Championship 1995 1998 2003
Oceania Youth Cup 1978 1982 1985 1987 1988 1990 1994 1996 1998 2001 2003
Oceania U-17 1983 1986 1989 1991 1993 1995 1999 2001 2003
Oceania Champions Cup Adelaide City 1987, South Melbourne 1999, Wollongong Wolves 2001

drawn players from Europe like Dwight Yorke who signed for Sydney. Sydney started the season well by winning a qualification tournament to take part in the OFC Champions Cup and then by becoming Oceania champions and qualifying for the FIFA Club World Championship in Tokyo. To qualify again they will have to win the AFC Champions League and by joining the AFC Australia has also passed up the opportunity to qualify with ease for FIFA age-restricted competitions although this is a price that the Federation believes is worth paying. Time will tell if it is harder or easier to qualify for the FIFA World Cup™ or not but once again the national team made it through the initial Oceania qualifiers with ease, qualifying for a play-off with the Soloman Islands with the prospect of a play-off against the fifth ranked South American nation. Australia also played the Solomon Islands in the 2004 OFC Nations Cup emerging as easy victors, 11-1 on aggregate, to qualify for the FIFA Confederations Cup in Germany. Whilst there they played some entertaining football but finished bottom of their group, prompting Frank Farina to resign after six years as national team coach.

Football Federation Australia Limited (FFA)
Suite 701 Level 7, 26 College Street, Locked Bag A4071, Sydney South, NSW 2000 1235, Australia
Tel +61 2 83545555   Fax +61 2 83545590
info@footballaustralia.com.au   www.footballaustralia.com.au
President: LOWY Frank   General Secretary: O'NEILL John
Vice-President: SCHWARTZ Brian   Treasurer: WALKER Mark   Media Officers: HODGE Stuart & SMITH Peter
Men's Coach: HIDDINK Guus   Women's Coach: SERMANNI Tom
FFA formed: 1961   OFC: 1966-72 & 1978-2005   AFC: 2006   FIFA: 1963
Colours: Green, Green, Green

GAMES PLAYED BY AUSTRALIA IN THE 2006 FIFA WORLD CUP™ CYCLE

2002	Opponents		Score	Venue	Comp	Scorers	Att	Referee
6-07	Vanuatu	W	2-0	Auckland	OCr1	Mori [69], Despotovski [85]	1 000	Ariiotima TAH
8-07	New Caledonia	W	11-0	Auckland	OCr1	Despotovski 4 [2 56p 76 77], Horvat [15], Chipperfield 2 [22 35], Mori [34], Costanzo [83], Porter [86], Trimboli [90]	200	Rugg NZL
10-07	Fiji	W	8-0	Auckland	OCr1	Milicic [5], Porter 4 [8 13 44 53], Juric [36], Trimboli [47], De Amicis [89]	1 000	Sosongan PNG
12-07	Tahiti	W	2-1	Auckland	OCsf	Durakovic [88], Mori [96]	400	Rugg NZL
14-07	New Zealand	L	0-1	Auckland	OCf		3 000	Ariiotima TAH
2003								
12-02	England	W	3-1	London	Fr	Popovic [17], Kewell [42], Emerton [84]	34 590	Gonzalez ESP
19-08	Republic of Ireland	L	1-2	Dublin	Fr	Viduka [49]	37 200	Vidlak CZE
7-09	Jamaica	W	2-1	Reading	Fr	Bresciano [19], Kewell [58]	8 050	D'Urso ENG
2004								
18-02	Venezuela	D	1-1	Caracas	Fr	Agostino [18]	12 000	Ruiz COL
30-03	South Africa	W	1-0	London	Fr	Bresciano [19]	16 108	Halsey ENG
21-05	Turkey	L	1-3	Sydney	Fr	Bresciano [49p]	28 326	Kamikawa JPN
24-05	Turkey	L	0-1	Melbourne	Fr		28 953	Rugg NZL
9-05	New Zealand	W	1-0	Adelaide	WCq	Bresciano [40]	12 100	Larsen DEN
31-05	Tahiti	W	9-0	Adelaide	WCq	Cahill 2 [14 47], Skoko [43], OG [44], Sterjovski 3 [51 61 74], Zdrilic [85], Chipperfield [89]	1 200	Attison VAN
2-06	Fiji	W	6-1	Adelaide	WCq	Madaschi 2 [6 50], Cahill 3 [39 66 75], Elrich [89]	2 200	Gonzalez ESP
4-06	Vanuatu	W	3-0	Adelaide	WCq	Aloisi 2 [25 85], Emerton [81]	4 000	Ariiotima TAH
6-06	Solomon Islands	D	2-2	Adelaide	WCq	Cahill [50], Emerton [52]	1 500	Gonzalez ESP
9-10	Solomon Islands	W	5-1	Honaria	OCf	Skoko 2 [5 28], Milicic [19], Emerton [44], Elrich [79]	21 000	O'Leary NZL
12-10	Solomon Islands	W	6-0	Sydney	OCf	Milicic [5], Kewell [9], Vidmar.T [60], Thompson [79], Elrich [80], Emerton [89]	19 208	Rakaroi FIJ
16-11	Norway	D	2-2	London	Fr	Cahill [45], Skoko [58]	7 364	Styles ENG
2005								
9-02	South Africa	D	1-1	Durban	Fr	Chipperfield [70]	25 000	Lim Kee Chong MRI
26-03	Iraq	W	2-1	Sydney	Fr	Bresciano [22], Elrich [72]	30 258	O'Leary NZL
29-03	Indonesia	W	3-0	Perth	Fr	Milicic 2 [25 57], Zdrilic [85]	13 719	Yamanishi JPN
9-06	New Zealand	W	1-0	London	Fr	Colosimo [86]	9 023	Dean ENG
15-06	Germany	L	3-4	Frankfurt	CCr1	Skoko [21], Aloisi 2 [31 92+]	46 466	Amarilla PAR
18-06	Argentina	L	2-4	Nürnberg	CCr1	Aloisi 2 [61p 70]	25 618	Maidin SIN
21-06	Tunisia	L	0-2	Leipzig	CCr1		23 952	Chandia CHI

Fr = Friendly match • OC = OFC Oceania Nations Cup • CC = FIFA Confederations Cup • WC = FIFA World Cup™
q = qualifier • r1 = first round group • sf = semi-final • f = final

FIFA/COCA-COLA WORLD RANKING

1993	1994	1995	1996	1997	1998	1999	2000	2001	2002	2003	2004	High		Low	
49	58	51	50	35	39	89	73	48	50	82	58	31	07/97	92	06/00

2004-2005											
08/04	09/04	10/04	11/04	12/04	01/05	02/05	03/05	04/05	05/05	06/05	07/05
57	58	64	49	58	58	58	59	56	56	57	60

THE FIFA BIG COUNT OF 2000

	Male	Female		Male	Female
Registered players	60 000	6 000	Referees	3 000	50
Non registered players	250 000	8 000	Officials	4 000	400
Youth players	60 000	5 000	Total involved	396 450	
Total players	389 000		Number of clubs	1 200	
Professional players	200	0	Number of teams	12 000	

NATIONAL CAPS

	Caps
TOBIN Alex	87
WADE Paul	84
VIDMAR Tony	71
WILSON Peter	64
ABONYI Attila	61
KOSMINA John	60
IVANOVIC Milan	59
ROONEY Jimmy	57
ARNOLD Graham	56
LAZARIDIS Stan	56

NATIONAL GOALS

	Goals
MORI Damian	29
ABONYI Attila	25
KOSMINA John	25
ZDRILIC David	21
ALOISI John	21
ARNOLD Graham	19
BAARTZ Ray	18
VIDMAR Aurelio	17
THOMPSON Archie	17

NATIONAL COACH

	Years
SHOULDER Jim	1976-'78
GUTENDORF Rudi	1979-'81
SCHEINFLUG Les	1981-'83
AROK Frank	1983-'98
THOMSON Eddie	1990-'96
BLANCO Raul	1996
VENABLES Terry	1997-'98
BLANCO Raul	1998
FARINA Frank	1999-'05
SMITH Ron	2005-

AUSTRALIA NATIONAL TEAM RECORDS AND RECORD SEQUENCES

Records			Sequence records					
Victory	31-0	ASA 2001	Wins	14	1996-1997	Clean sheets	6	2000, 2001
Defeat	0-8	RSA 1955	Defeats	5	1955	Goals scored	31	1924-1954
Player Caps	87	TOBIN Alex	Undefeated	20	1996-1997	Without goal	4	Three times
Player Goals	29	MORI Damian	Without win	6	Five times	Goals against	11	1936-1947

FIFA ASSISTANT REFEREE LIST 2005

	Int'l	DoB
ANAZ Hakan	2005	4-08-1969
CREAM Matthew	2000	19-06-1975
ELDRIDGE Paul	2002	14-07-1972
GIBSON Nathan	2001	17-08-1972
OULIARIS Jim	2002	22-07-1966
PEACOCK John	2002	6-12-1962
POWER Jason	2005	31-03-1977
STREATER Jonathan	2004	23-09-1973
VRTKOVSKI Peter	2003	10-08-1975
WILSON Ben	2000	26-06-1975

FIFA REFEREE LIST 2005

	Int'l	DoB
BREEZE Matthew	2001	10-06-1972
DIOMIS Con	2003	13-10-1960
MICALLEF Simon	1998	21-07-1970
SHIELD Mark	1999	2-09-1973
WILLIAMS Benjamin	2005	14-04-1977

AUSTRALIA COUNTRY INFORMATION

Capital	Canberra	Independence	1901 from the UK	GDP per Capita	$29 000
Population	19 913 144	Status	Commonwealth	GNP Ranking	15
Area km²	7 686 850	Language	English	Dialling code	+61
Population density	2 per km²	Literacy rate	99%	Internet code	.au
% in urban areas	85%	Main religion	Christian 76%	GMT + / –	+10
Towns/Cities ('000)	Sydney 4 394; Melbourne 3 730; Brisbane 1 843; Perth 1 446; Adelaide 1 074; Gold Coast 501; Newcastle 497; Canberra 324; Wollongong 260; Hobart 204; Cairns 154; Geelong 150				
Neighbours (km)	Indian Ocean and the South Pacific Ocean 25 760				
Main stadia	Telstra Stadium – Sydney 83 500; Energy Australia – Newcastle 28 000; Members Equity – Perth 18 450; Hindmarsh – Adelaide 15 000				

HYUNDAI A-LEAGUE CLUB DIRECTORY

Club	City	Stadium	Phone	www.
Adelaide United FC	Adelaide	Hindmarsh Stadium 15 000	+61 8 83403000	adelaideunited.com.au
Central Coast Mariners	Gosford	Central Coast Stadium 20 000	+61 1300 767442	ccmariners.com.au
New Zealand Knights FC	Albany	North Harbour Stadium 25 000	+64 9 4143671	knightsfc.com
Melbourne Victory	Melbourne	Olympic Park 20 000	+61 3 99413145	melbournevictory.com.au
Newcastle United Jets	Newcastle	Energy Australia Stadium 27 000	+61 2 49622755	nufc.com.au
Perth Glory FC	Perth	Members Equity Stadium 18 450	+61 8 94926000	perthglory.com.au
Queensland Roar FC	Brisbane	Suncorp Stadium 52 579	+61 7 37123333	qldroar.com.au
Sydney FC	Sydney	Aussie Stadium 40 792	+61 2 93874233	sydneyfc.com

The 2003-2004 National Soccer League season, which culminated in a second championship for Perth Glory, was the last in the 28-year history of the League. Set up in 1977 as the first national tournament to cover this huge country, it had often been plagued by indifference and poor standards. The immigrant ethnic identity of many of the clubs (and accompanying violence at some matches) was often regarded as a major reason why the majority of Australians tended to stick with Aussie rules and rugby league as the favoured spectator sports. Efforts were made to broaden the appeal of the clubs - hence Melbourne Croatia became Melbourne Knights – but the previous associations were hard to lose. In a bid to take this one stage further, the NSL was scrapped after the 2003-04 season and replaced with the A-League which consists of eight new franchised clubs representing the eight major football centres in the country.

AUSTRALIAN NATIONAL SOCCER LEAGUE HISTORY

Year	Champions/First	Pts	Second	Pts	Third	Pts	Champions	Score	Runners-up
1977	Eastern Suburbs	37	Marconi Fairfield	37	Fitzroy	32			
1978	West Adelaide	36	Eastern Suburbs	35	South Melbourne	32			
1979	Marconi Fairfield	40	Fitzroy	36	Sydney City	34			
1980	Sydney City	37	Heidelberg United	36	South Melbourne	35			
1981	Sydney City	43	South Melbourne	39	Brisbane City	35			
1982	Sydney City	45	St George	36	Wollongong Wolves	35			
1983	St George	55	Sydney City	54	Preston	52			
1984							South Melbourne	2-1 2-1	Sydney Olympic
1985							Brunswick	1-0 1-0	Sydney City
1986							Adelaide City	0-1 3-1	Sydney Olympic
1987	APIA Leichhardt	35	Preston	29	St George	29			
1988	Wollongong Wolves	34	Sydney CSC	34	South Melbourne	34	Marconi Fairfield	2-2 5-4p	Sydney CSC
1989	Marconi Fairfield	38	St George	32	Sydney Olympic	31	Marconi Fairfield	1-0	Sydney Olympic
1990	Marconi Fairfield	38	South Melbourne	36	Melbourne CSC	35	Sydney Olympic	2-0	Marconi Fairfield
1991	Melbourne CSC	37	South Melbourne	34	Adelaide City	33	South Melbourne	1-1 5-4p	Melbourne CSC
1992	Melbourne CSC	35	Sydney Olympic	34	South Melbourne	31	Adelaide City	0-0 4-2p	Melbourne CSC
1993	South Melbourne	58	Marconi Fairfield	53	Adelaide City	41	Marconi Fairfield	1-0	Adelaide City
1994	Melbourne Knights	53	South Melbourne	47	Sydney United	46	Adelaide City	1-0	Melbourne Knights
1995	Melbourne Knights	70	Adelaide City	69	Sydney United	68	Melbourne Knights	2-0	Adelaide City
1996	Marconi Fairfield	60	Melbourne Knights	59	Sydney Olympic	59	Melbourne Knights	2-1	Marconi Fairfield
1997	Sydney United	56	Brisbane Strikers	47	South Melbourne	46	Brisbane Strikers	2-0	Sydney United
1998	South Melbourne	48	Carlton	45	Adelaide City	43	South Melbourne	2-1	Carlton
1999	Sydney United	58	South Melbourne	57	Perth Glory	53	South Melbourne	3-2	Sydney United
2000	Perth Glory	64	Wollongong Wolves	60	Carlton Blues	58	Wollongong Wolves	3-3 7-6p	Perth Glory
2001	South Melbourne	57	Wollongong Wolves	61	Perth Glory	61	Wollongong Wolves	2-1	South Melbourne
2002	Perth Glory	55	Newcastle United	42	Sydney Olympic	40	Sydney Olympic	1-0	Perth Glory
2003	Sydney Olympic	51	Perth Glory	50	Parramatta Power	40	Perth Glory	2-0	Olympic Sharks
2004	Perth Glory	57	Parramatta Power	51	Adelaide United	40	Perth Glory	1-0	Parramatta Power

A single round robin championship was played from 1977-1983 and in 1987 • From 1984-1986 the league was split into two conferences with a Grand Final to determine the champions • From 1987 the season was split into a regular season from which the top clubs qualified for the play-offs, culminating in a Grand Final to determine the champions • Eastern Suburbs became Sydney City • Fitzroy became Heidelberg United • Melbourne CSC became Melbourne Knights

AUT – AUSTRIA

NATIONAL TEAM RECORD
JULY 1ST 2002 TO JUNE 30TH 2005

PL	W	D	L	F	A	%
25	9	7	9	39	35	50

FIFA/COCA-COLA WORLD RANKING

1993	1994	1995	1996	1997	1998	1999	2000	2001	2002	2003	2004	High		Low	
36	49	39	34	25	22	28	44	56	65	67	83	17	05/99	90	09/04

2004-2005											
08/04	09/04	10/04	11/04	12/04	01/05	02/05	03/05	04/05	05/05	06/05	07/05
89	90	85	82	83	82	82	80	72	72	74	71

The success of regional clubs has been one of the most startling features of Austrian football over the past two decades with Salzburg, Graz and Innsbruck all producing Championship-winning teams at the expense of Vienna, a city that for years dominated to the exclusion of all others. The 2005 season, however, was just like the old days again with Rapid winning their first Bundesliga for nine years and FK Austria winning the Cup. Not since 1985 had these two grand old clubs from the capital shared the major honours between them and they completed their domination of the season by meeting in the Cup Final, the first time they had done so since 1990. FK Austria proved

INTERNATIONAL HONOURS
Qualified for the FIFA World Cup™ 1934 1954 1958 1978 1982 1990 1998 International Cup 1932
FIFA Junior Tournament 1950 UEFA Junior Tournament 1957 Mitropa Cup SK Rapid 1930, First Vienna 1931, FK Austria 1933 1936

their revival wasn't a fluke by also progressing through five rounds of the UEFA Cup before losing to Parma in the quarter-finals. There was also a mini revival of sorts for the national team in the FIFA World Cup™ qualifiers although a home defeat against Poland proved costly in the attempt to keep up with the English and the Poles in a tough group. Since the 1980s the national team has established a pattern of qualifying for the finals every other tournament but having missed out in 2002 Austrian fans also look set to miss out on the chance of a short trip across the border to neighbours Germany in 2006.

THE FIFA BIG COUNT OF 2000

	Male	Female		Male	Female
Registered players	290 360	4 200	Referees	2 400	18
Non registered players	250 000	10 000	Officials	390 000	200
Youth players	90 100	2 800	Total involved	1 040 078	
Total players	647 460		Number of clubs	4 497	
Professional players	360	0	Number of teams	10 535	

Osterreichischer Fussball-Bund (OFB)
Ernst Happel Stadion, Sektor A/F, Postfach 340, Meiereistrasse 7, Wien 1021, Austria
Tel +43 1 727180   Fax +43 1 7281632
office@oefb.at   www.oefb.at
President: STICKLER Friedrich   General Secretary: LUDWIG Alfred
Vice-President: EHRENBERGER Kurt   Treasurer: TALOS Rudolf, HR Mag   Media Officer: GOLLATZ Ronald
Men's Coach: KRANKL Hans   Women's Coach: WEBER Ernst
OFB formed: 1904   UEFA: 1954   FIFA: 1907
Colours: Red, White, Red or White, Black, White

GAMES PLAYED BY AUSTRIA IN THE 2006 FIFA WORLD CUP™ CYCLE

2002	Opponents	Score		Venue	Comp	Scorers	Att	Referee
21-08	Switzerland	L	2-3	Basle	Fr	Wallner 2 [11] [81]	23 500	Rosetti ITA
7-09	Moldova	W	2-0	Vienna	ECq	Herzog 2 [4p] [30p]	18 300	Dougal SCO
12-10	Belarus	W	2-0	Minsk	ECq	Schopp [57], Akagunduz [90]	15 000	Poulat FRA
16-10	Netherlands	L	0-3	Vienna	ECq		46 300	Collina ITA
20-11	Norway	L	0-1	Vienna	Fr		15 800	Abraham HUN
2003								
26-03	Greece	D	2-2	Graz	Fr	Schopp [52], Haas [81]	8 500	Ovrebo NOR
2-04	Czech Republic	L	0-4	Prague	ECq		20 000	Nieto ESP
30-04	Scotland	W	2-0	Glasgow	Fr	Kirchler [28], Haas [34]	12 189	Vollquartz DEN
7-06	Moldova	L	0-1	Tiraspol	ECq		10 000	Silva POR
11-06	Belarus	W	5-0	Innsbruck	ECq	Aufhauser [33], Haas [47], Kirchler [52], Wallner [62], Cerny [70]	8 100	Frojdfeldt SWE
20-08	Costa Rica	W	2-0	Vienna	Fr	Glieder [34p], Wallner [70]	16 000	Hamer LUX
6-09	Netherlands	L	1-3	Rotterdam	ECq	Pogatetz [34]	47 000	Poulat FRA
11-10	Czech Republic	L	2-3	Vienna	ECq	Haas [51], Ivanschitz [77]	32 350	Kasnaferis GRE
2004								
31-03	Slovakia	D	1-1	Bratislava	Fr	Kollmann [90]	4 500	Vidlak CZE
28-04	Luxembourg	W	4-1	Innsbruck	Fr	Kirchler [5], Kiesenebner [9], Haas [85], Kollmann [88]	9 400	Skomina SVN
25-05	Russia	D	0-0	Graz	Fr		9 600	Vuorela FIN
18-08	Germany	L	1-3	Vienna	Fr	Amerhauser [10]	37 900	Collina ITA
4-09	England	D	2-2	Vienna	WCq	Kollmann [71], Ivanschitz [72]	48 000	Lubos SVK
8-09	Azerbaijan	W	2-0	Vienna	WCq	Stranzl [23], Kollmann [44]	26 400	Sammut MLT
9-10	Poland	L	1-3	Vienna	WCq	Schopp [30]	46 100	Batista POR
13-10	Northern Ireland	D	3-3	Belfast	WCq	Schopp 2 [14] [72], Mayrleb [59]	11 810	Shield AUS
2005								
8-02	Cyprus	D	1-1	Limassol	Fr	Kirchler [43], L 4-5p	300	Hyytia FIN
9-02	Latvia	D	1-1	Limassol	Fr	Sariyar [41]	50	Theodotou CYP
26-03	Wales	W	2-0	Cardiff	WCq	Vastic [81], Stranzl [85]	47 760	Allaerts BEL
30-03	Wales	W	1-0	Vienna	WCq	Aufhauser [87]	29 500	Mejuto Gonzalez ESP

Fr = Friendly match • EC = UEFA EURO 2004™ • WC = FIFA World Cup™ • q = qualifier

AUSTRIA NATIONAL TEAM RECORDS AND RECORD SEQUENCES

Records			Sequence records					
Victory	9-0	MLT 1977	Wins	7	1933-1934	Clean sheets	5	1931, 1996
Defeat	1-11	ENG 1908	Defeats	6	1946-1947	Goals scored	28	1931-1934
Player Caps	103	HERZOG Andreas	Undefeated	14	1931-1932	Without goal	3	
Player Goals	44	POLSTER Anton	Without win	9	1973-1974	Goals against	17	1919-22, 1954-56

AUSTRIA COUNTRY INFORMATION

Capital	Vienna (Wien)	Independence	1918	GDP per Capita	$30 000
Population	8 174 762	Status	Republic	GNP Ranking	22
Area km²	83 870	Language	German	Dialling code	+
Population density	97 per km²	Literacy rate	99%	Internet code	.at
% in urban areas	56%	Main religion	Christian 83%	GMT + / −	+1
Towns/Cities ('000)	Vienna 1 569; Graz 222; Linz 181; Salzburg 145; Innsbruck 112; Klagenfurt 90; Villach 58; Wels 57; Sankt Pölten 49; Dornbirn 43; Steyr 39; Wiener Neustadt 38; Bregenz 26				
Neighbours (km)	Czech Republic 362; Slovakia 91; Hungary 366; Slovenia 330; Italy 430; Switzerland 164; Liechtenstein 35; Germany 784				
Main stadia	Ernst Happel – Vienna 44 844; Linzer – Linz 21 328; Salzburg – Salzburg 18 686; Gerhard Hanappi – Vienna 18 456; Tivoli Neu – Innsbruck 17 400; Arnold Schwarzenegger – Graz 15 400				

NATIONAL CAPS

	Caps
HERZOG Andreas	103
POLSTER Anton	95
HANAPPI Gerhard	93
KOLLER Karl	86
KONCILLA Friedl	84
PEZZEY Bruno	84
PROHASKA Herbert	83
KRANKL Hans	69
WEBER Heribert	68
STOGER Peter	65

NATIONAL GOALS

	Goals
POLSTER Anton	44
KRANKL Hans	34
HOF Erich	28
HORVATH Hans	28
SCHALL Anton	28
SINDELAR Matthias	27
HERZOG Andreas	26
ZISCHEK Karl	24
SCHACHNER Walter	23
WAGNER Theodor	22

NATIONAL COACH

	Years
HOF Erich	1982-'84
ELSNER Branko	1984-'87
HICKERSBERGER Josef	1988-'90
RIEDL Alfred	1990-'91
CONSTANTINI Dietmar	1991
HAPPEL Ernst	1992
CONSTANTINI Dietmar	1992
PROHASKA Herbert	1993-'99
BARIC Otto	1999-'01
KRANKL Hans	2002-

FIFA REFEREE LIST 2005

	Int'l	DoB
BRUGGER Bernhard	1999	25-12-1966
DRABEK Dietmar	1997	30-06-1965
EINWALLER Thomas	2005	25-04-1977
LEHNER Gerald		12-03-1968
MESSNER Stefan	2001	13-12-1964
PLAUTZ Konrad	1996	16-10-1964
STUCHLIK Fritz	1994	11-02-1966

FIFA ASSISTANT REFEREE LIST 2005

	Int'l	DoB
BEREUTER Egon	1993	11-05-1963
BUCH Raimund		3-05-1964
FELLINGER Andreas		3-08-1971
GORGON Wojciech	1999	7-08-1963
KRENN Herbert	1999	20-06-1962
LAMBERT Andreas	2004	8-03-1969
MAYR Markus	1997	8-09-1964
SCHWAB Norbert		30-12-1967
STAUDINGER Walter	1996	23-11-1960
ZAUNER Bernhard		9-01-1965

CLUB DIRECTORY

Club	Town/City	Stadium	Phone	www.	Lge	Cup	CL
Admira	Mödling	Südstadt 12 000	+43 2236 48710	admirazone.com	8	5	0
FK Austria	Wien	Franz-Horr-Stadion 11 800	+43 1 6880150	fk-austria.at	22	24	0
Schwarz-Weiss	Bregenz	Casino-Stadion 15 000	+43 5574 42795	swbregenz.at	0	0	0
Grazer AK	Graz	Schwarzenegger-Stadion 15 428	+43 316 483030	gak.at	1	4	0
SV Mattersburg	Mattersburg	Pappelstadion 19 700	+43 2626 62510	svm.at	0	0	0
SV Pasching	Pasching	Waldstadion 5 650	+43 7229 62390	fcsuperfund.at	0	0	0
SK Rapid	Wien	Gerhard-Hanappi-Stadion 19 600	+43 1 910220	skrapid.at	31	14	0
SV Austria Salzburg	Salzburg	Wals-Siezenheim 18 686	+43 662 433332	austria-salzburg.at	3	0	0
SK Sturm	Graz	Schwarzenegger-Stadion 15 428	+43 316 7717710	sksturm.at	2	3	0
FC Wacker Tirol	Innsbruck	Tivoli Neu 17 400	+43 512 5888770	fc-wacker-tirol.at	10	7	0

RECENT LEAGUE AND CUP RECORD

	Championship						Cup		
Year	Champions	Pts	Runners-up	Pts	Third	Pts	Winners	Score	Runners-up
1990	FC Tirol Innsbruck	38	FK Austria Wien	31	Admira-Wacker	29	FK Austria Wien	3-1	SK Rapid Wien
1991	FK Austria Wien	36	FC Tirol Innsbruck	35	SK Sturm Graz	32	SV Stockerau	2-1	SK Rapid Wien
1992	FK Austria Wien	33	SV Austria Salzburg	33	FC Tirol Innsbruck	33	FK Austria Wien	1-0	Admira-Wacker
1993	FK Austria Wien	36	SV Austria Salzburg	36	Admira-Wacker	28	Wacker Innsbruck	3-1	SK Rapid Wien
1994	SV Austria Salzburg	51	FK Austria Wien	49	Admira-Wacker	44	FK Austria Wien	4-0	FC Linz
1995	SV Austria Salzburg	47	SK Sturm Graz	47	SK Rapid Wien	46	SK Rapid Wien	1-0	DSV Leoben
1996	SK Rapid Wien	73	SV Austria Salzburg	67	FC Tirol Innsbruck	62	SK Sturm Graz	3-1	Admira-Wacker
1997	SV Austria Salzburg	69	SK Rapid Wien	66	SK Sturm Graz	55	SK Sturm Graz	2-1	First Vienna FC
1998	SK Sturm Graz	81	SK Rapid Wien	62	Grazer AK	61	SV Ried	3-1	SK Sturm Graz
1999	SK Sturm Graz	73	SK Rapid Wien	70	Grazer AK	65	SK Sturm Graz	1-1 4-2	LASK Linz
2000	FC Tirol Innsbruck	74	SK Sturm Graz	74	SK Rapid Wien	66	Grazer AK	2-2 4-3p	SV Austria Salzburg
2001	FC Tirol Innsbruck	68	SK Rapid Wien	60	Grazer AK	57	FC Kärnten	2-1	FC Tirol Innsbruck
2002	FC Tirol Innsbruck	75	SK Sturm Graz	65	Grazer AK	63	Grazer AK	3-2	SK Sturm Graz
2003	FK Austria Wien	70	Grazer AK	57	SV Austria Salzburg	56	FK Austria Wien	3-0	FC Kärnten
2004	Grazer AK	72	FK Austria Wien	71	SV Pasching	63	Grazer AK	3-3 5-4p	FK Austria Wien
2005	SK Rapid Wien	71	Grazer AK	70	FK Austria Wien	69	FK Austria Wien	3-1	SK Rapid Wien

AUSTRIA 2004-05

BUNDESLIGA

	Pl	W	D	L	F	A	Pts	Rapid	GAK	FK Austria	Pasching	Matt'burg	Wacker	Sturm	Admira	Salzburg	Bregenz
SK Rapid Wien †	36	21	8	7	67	31	71		2-1 1-0	1-1 0-1	3-0 2-1	3-0 2-1	4-1 2-2	2-0 4-1	2-1 6-0	0-0 5-0	2-1 4-1
Grazer AK ‡	36	21	7	8	58	28	70	2-2 3-1		0-1 0-0	2-1 1-2	1-1 5-1	2-1 2-1	1-0 4-0	0-0 5-2	1-0 1-0	3-0 2-2
FK Austria Wien ‡	36	19	12	5	64	24	69	1-1 1-0	0-0 0-3		1-2 4-0	2-0 0-0	2-2 1-0	3-0 2-2	2-1 5-1	2-0 3-1	2-0 1-1
SV Pasching ‡	36	17	9	10	53	48	60	2-1 1-1	1-2 0-3	2-1 1-1		4-0 1-0	3-2 1-1	3-0 2-1	0-3 1-1	2-1 1-1	4-0 2-0
SV Mattersburg	36	12	9	15	48	58	45	0-0 1-0	0-1 3-1	0-0 2-1	3-0 1-1		2-1 1-1	1-1 1-3	3-0 2-3	5-3 2-0	5-2 2-2
FC Wacker Tirol	36	11	11	14	48	48	44	0-2 1-2	1-0 1-1	0-2 0-3	2-1 0-0	5-1 2-1		1-0 0-0	3-1 3-1	0-0 2-0	
SK Sturm Graz	36	10	10	16	37	47	40	0-1 1-1	1-0 1-1	0-2 1-0	1-2 3-0	3-1 2-3	3-1 0-0		1-0 0-0	3-1 3-1	0-0 2-0
VfB Admira/Wacker	36	10	8	18	36	63	38	1-0 0-1	2-0 1-4	0-5 2-2	2-4 0-2	3-1 0-1	0-2 1-0	0-0 1-1		0-2 1-1	3-0 0-1
SV Austria Salzburg	36	9	9	18	37	51	36	0-1 4-1	0-1 0-1	1-1 0-1	1-0 1-2	0-1 1-2	0-0 1-1	1-0 1-0	4-2 0-1		4-2 2-1
Schwarz-Weiß Bregenz	36	4	9	23	30	80	21	1-5 0-2	1-3 0-1	0-9 0-1	2-3 1-2	1-0 0-3	2-0 3-0	2-1 1-1	1-1 0-1	1-1 1-2	

13/07/2004 - 26/05/2005 • † Qualified for the UEFA Champions League • ‡ Qualified for the UEFA Cup

AUSTRIA 2004-05
ERSTE LIGA (2)

	Pl	W	D	L	F	A	Pts
SV Reid im Innkreis	36	24	5	7	79	38	77
Kapfenberger SV	36	21	8	7	64	37	71
FC Kärnten	36	17	7	12	68	41	58
SC Austria Lustenau	36	14	14	8	55	43	56
DSV Leoben	36	12	11	13	43	49	47
SC Rheindorf Altach	36	9	14	13	37	45	41
LASK Linz	36	8	15	13	38	64	39
SC Untersiebenbrunn	36	9	7	20	45	66	34
FC Gratkorn	36	6	14	16	43	58	32
SV Wörgl	36	7	11	18	32	63	32

23/07/2004 - 24/05/2005

TOP SCORERS

MAYRLEB	SV Pasching	21
RUSHFELDT	FK Austria	19
BAZINA	Grazer AK	15
KOLLMAN	Grazer AK	15
LAWAREE	SK Rapid Wien	13
KOEJOE	Wacker Tirol	12
MAIR	Wacker Tirol	12

OFB POKAL 2004-05

Round of sixteen

FK Austria Wien	0 5p
SK Sturm Graz	0 3p
SV Austria Salzburg	1
SKN Sankt Pölten	5
LASK Linz	3
SV Hall	0
Kapfenburg SV	0
FC Kärnten	3
Grazer AK	4
Kremser SC	1
SV Pasching	2 7p
SC Austria Lustenau	2 8p
SV Mattersburg	3
Blau-Weiß Linz	0
SV Austria Salzburg Am	0
SK Rapid Wien	2

Quarter-finals

FK Austria Wien	6
SKN Sankt Pölten	0
LASK Linz	2
FC Kärnten	3
Grazer AK	3
SC Austria Lustenau	1
SV Mattersburg	1
SK Rapid Wien	3

Semi-finals

FK Austria Wien	3
FC Kärnten	0
Grazer AK	1
SK Rapid Wien	4

Final

FK Austria Wien ‡	3
SK Rapid Wien	1

‡ Qualified for the UEFA Cup

CUP FINAL

1-06-2005, Att: 28 000
Ernst Happel Stadion, Vienna

Scorers - Mila 20, Vastic 55, Sionko 65 for FK Austria; Burgstaller 5 for Rapid

AZE – AZERBAIJAN

NATIONAL TEAM RECORD
JULY 1ST 2002 TO JUNE 30TH 2005

PL	W	D	L	F	A	%
33	4	11	18	23	64	28.8

FIFA/COCA-COLA WORLD RANKING

1993	1994	1995	1996	1997	1998	1999	2000	2001	2002	2003	2004	High		Low	
-	147	141	125	123	99	97	115	113	113	119	113	97	06/99	170	07/94

2004-2005											
08/04	09/04	10/04	11/04	12/04	01/05	02/05	03/05	04/05	05/05	06/05	07/05
118	116	114	116	113	115	117	116	116	116	116	116

With just five points separating the top five teams at the end of the season, the championship in Azerbaijan proved to be the most exciting to date, climaxing with a Golden Match between Neftchi and Khazar to decide the title after the two had finished level on points. A near capacity crowd packed the stadium to witness Neftchi consolidate their recent revival with a 2-1 victory and claim the championship for the second year running. The Cup Final was contested by two clubs with new names - FK Baku, previously Dinamo Baku and Inter Baku, previously Khazar Baku - and it was the former who won their first ever honour. In contrast to the domestic scene, the national team had

INTERNATIONAL HONOURS
None

a nightmare season that cost Carlos Alberto Torres his job. Admittedly in a very difficult FIFA World Cup™ group, the Azeris struggled to find any form at all and in 13 games over the course of the season they failed to win a single match. An 8-0 defeat in Warsaw against Poland was a severe embarrassment although it wasn't until after the home defeat against the Poles in June that the Brazilian was given his marching orders. His replacement Vagif Sadykov was promoted from the U-21s for his second spell in charge but with little chance of hauling the team off the bottom of the qualifying group.

THE FIFA BIG COUNT OF 2000

	Male	Female		Male	Female
Registered players	1 146	85	Referees	90	15
Non registered players	75 000	155	Officials	320	16
Youth players	158	60	Total involved	77 045	
Total players	76 604		Number of clubs	76	
Professional players	650	0	Number of teams	512	

Association of Football Federations of Azerbaijan (AFFA)
37 Khojali Avenue, Baku AZ 1025, Azerbaijan
Tel +994 12 908308   Fax +994 12 989393
affa@azeronline.com   www.none
President: MIRZAYEV Ramiz   General Secretary: ASADOV Fuad
Vice-President: ZEYNALOV Oktay   Treasurer: ABBASOVA Sadafxanim   Media Officer: NOVRUZOV Latif
Men's Coach: SADYKOV Vagif   Women's Coach: TIBILOV Boris
AFFA formed: 1992   UEFA: 1994   FIFA: 1994
Colours: White, Blue, White or Blue, Blue, Blue

GAMES PLAYED BY AZERBAIJAN IN THE 2006 FIFA WORLD CUP™ CYCLE

2002	Opponents	Score		Venue	Comp	Scorers	Att	Referee
3-07	Estonia	D	0-0	Kuressaare	Fr		2 200	Vollquartz DEN
6-07	Latvia	D	0-0	Riga	Fr		2 000	Miezelis LTU
8-08	Iran	D	1-1	Tabriz	Fr	Ismailov [16]	25 000	Rahimi Moghadam IRN
21-08	Uzbekistan	W	2-0	Baku	Fr	Aliyev.S [39], Ismaelov [79]	7 000	Abdullayev AZE
7-09	Italy	L	0-2	Baku	ECq		37 000	Vassaras GRE
12-10	Finland	L	0-3	Helsinki	ECq		11 853	Hamer LUX
20-11	Wales	L	0-2	Baku	ECq		8 000	Huyghe BEL
2003								
12-02	Serbia & Montenegro	D	2-2	Podgorica	ECq	Gurbanov.G 2 [59] [78]	8 000	Granat POL
29-03	Wales	L	0-4	Cardiff	ECq		72 500	Leuba SUI
11-06	Serbia & Montenegro	W	2-1	Baku	ECq	Gurbanov.G [86]p, Ismailov [90]	5 000	Fisker DEN
6-09	Finland	L	1-2	Baku	ECq	Ismailov [89]	7 500	Hrinak SVK
11-10	Italy	L	0-4	Reggio Calabria	ECq		30 000	Dougal SCO
14-12	United Arab Emirates	D	3-3	Dubai	Fr	Nabiyev 2 [35] [90], Kerimov [85]		Mohamed UAE
18-12	Oman	L	0-1	Muscat	Fr			
20-12	Saudi Arabia	L	0-1	Riyadh	Fr			
2004								
18-02	Israel	L	0-6	Tel Aviv	Fr		13 250	Paraty POR
31-03	Moldova	L	1-2	Chisinau	Fr	Gurbanov.G [20]	5 500	Godulyan UKR
28-04	Kazakhstan	W	3-2	Almaty	Fr	Nabiyev [31], Guliev [57], Sadigov [80]	20 000	Chynybekov KGZ
28-05	Uzbekistan	W	3-1	Baku	Fr	Gurbanov.G [31], Gurbanov.I [64], Guliev [75]	12 000	
6-06	Latvia	D	2-2	Riga	Fr	Guliev [55], Gurbanov.G [74]p	8 000	Maisonlahti FIN
18-08	Jordan	D	1-1	Amman	Fr	Ponomarev [23]	4 000	
4-09	Wales	D	1-1	Baku	WCq	Sadigov [55]	8 000	Trivkovic CRO
8-09	Austria	L	0-2	Vienna	WCq		26 400	Sammut MLT
9-10	Northern Ireland	D	0-0	Baku	WCq		6 460	Hanacsek HUN
13-10	England	L	0-1	Baku	WCq		17 000	Hamer LUX
17-11	Bulgaria	D	0-0	Baku	Fr		10 000	Sipailo LVA
2005								
21-01	Trinidad and Tobago	L	0-1	Port of Spain	Fr		500	
23-01	Trinidad and Tobago	L	0-2	Marabella	Fr		1 000	Gordon TRI
9-02	Moldova	D	0-0	Baku	Fr		3 000	
26-03	Poland	L	0-8	Warsaw	WCq		9 000	Vollquartz DEN
30-03	England	L	0-2	Newcastle	WCq		49 046	Costa POR
29-05	Iran	L	1-2	Tehran	Fr	Gurbanov.G [67]		
4-06	Poland	L	0-3	Baku	WCq		10 458	Undiano Mallenco ESP

Fr = Friendly match • EC = UEFA EURO 2004™ • WCq = FIFA World Cup™ • q = qualifier

NATIONAL CAPS

	Caps
AKHMEDOV Tarlan	72
AGAEV Emin	64
GURBANOV Gurban	63
GURBANOV Makhmud	61
KERIMOV Aslan	53

NATIONAL GOALS

	Goals
GURBANOV Gurban	12
ISMAILOV Farrukh	5
RZAEV Vidadi	5
SULEYMANOV Nazim	5
TAGIZADE Zaur	5
LICHKIN Vyacheslav	4

NATIONAL COACH

	Years
PONOMAREV Igor	2000-'02
TUAEV Kazbek	2002
SADYGOV Vagif	2002-'03
ABDULLAYEV Asgar	2003
CARLOS ALBERTO	2003-'05
SADYGOV Vagif	2005-

AZERBAIJAN COUNTRY INFORMATION

Capital	Baku	Independence	1991	GDP per Capita	$3 400
Population	7 868 385	Status	Republic	GNP Ranking	111
Area km²	86 600	Language	Azerbaijani	Dialling code	+994
Population density	90 per km²	Literacy rate	96%	Internet code	.az
% in urban areas	56%	Main religion	Muslim 93%	GMT +/−	+5
Towns/Cities ('000)	Baku 1 116; Gäncä 303; Sumqayit 265; Mingäçevir 95; Qaraçuxur 72; Ali Bayramli 70				
Neighbours (km)	Iran 179; Turkey 9; Armenia 787; Georgia 322; Russia 284				
Main stadia	Tofik Bakhramov – Baku 29 858; Mehdi Huseyn-zade – Sumqayit 16 000				

AZERBAIJAN NATIONAL TEAM RECORDS AND RECORD SEQUENCES

Records			Sequence records				
Victory	4-0	LIE 1999	Wins	2	1998, 2004	Clean sheets	2
Defeat	0-10	FRA 1995	Defeats	11	1994-1995	Goals scored	6	2004
Player Caps	72	AKHMEDOV Tarlan	Undefeated	4	2002	Without goal	9	1999-2000
Player Goals	12	GURBANOV Gurban	Without win	15	1994-1996	Goals against	19	2002-2004

AZERBAIJAN 2004-05

YUKSAK LIGA (1)

	Pl	W	D	L	F	A	Pts	Nef	Kha	Kar	Tur	Bak	Krb	Int	MKT	Kap	Krt	Gey	Gen	Sha	Shd	MOI	Adl	Bkl	Shf
Neftchi Baku †	34	24	6	4	52	18	78		2-1	2-1	2-1	0-0	1-0	1-1	2-2	2-0	2-0	1-0	3-0	1-0	1-0	0-0	2-0	2-0	2-0
Khazar Lenkoran ‡	34	24	6	4	68	15	78	1-1		1-0	1-0	2-0	3-0	0-0	1-1	2-0	3-0	3-0	6-0	2-0	5-0	1-0	6-1	1-0	2-1
Karvan Yevlakh	34	23	7	4	66	18	76	1-1	0-1		3-0	0-0	0-1	2-0	2-0	1-1	2-0	4-1	3-0	4-1	3-0	3-0	1-0	3-0	3-0
Turan Tovuz	34	22	7	5	64	21	73	1-0	1-1	1-1		3-0	4-0	1-0	2-0	2-0	2-1	3-0	1-0	2-0	1-1	3-0	4-0	1-0	4-0
FK Baku ‡	34	21	10	3	60	14	73	2-0	2-0	0-0	0-0		1-1	2-0	1-0	1-0	4-2	6-0	1-0	1-0	4-1	2-0	4-0	2-0	3-0
Karabakh Baku	34	22	5	7	61	31	71	2-1	3-1	1-2	1-0	2-0		3-1	1-2	1-1	3-1	4-2	1-0	3-2	2-1	1-0	3-0	1-1	3-0
Inter Baku	34	19	9	6	44	24	66	2-1	1-0	0-0	4-3	0-0	1-0		0-0	2-0	2-0	1-0	1-1	2-1	2-0	1-0	2-1	2-0	3-0
MKT-Araz Imishli	34	16	9	9	35	23	57	0-1	0-0	0-2	1-0	0-2	1-1	0-0		0-0	1-1	2-1	2-1	2-0	3-0	1-0	2-1	0-1	3-0
Kapaz Ganja	34	11	9	14	37	37	42	0-1	0-1	0-3	0-3	0-2	0-1	0-1	0-1		4-1	3-1	6-1	1-1	2-0	1-0	1-1	1-0	3-0
Karat Baku	34	12	4	18	40	62	40	0-4	0-2	0-2	1-3	0-1	0-3	3-2	1-0	2-3		2-2	0-5	0-2	2-0	1-0	1-0	3-1	4-1
Geyazan Gazakh	34	9	6	19	30	52	33	0-1	0-0	1-0	0-0	1-3	0-2	0-1	0-2	0-0	2-1		0-2	0-0	0-1	1-0		3-1	3-0
Genclerbirliyi Sumgayit	34	9	6	19	32	58	33	1-2	0-5	0-2	0-2	1-1	0-2	1-1	1-0	1-1	0-1	1-0		1-1	1-0	0-3	3-1	3-1	2-1
FK Shamkir	34	9	5	20	34	48	32	1-2	0-4	1-2	1-1	0-2	1-2	1-2	0-2	0-1	1-2	0-2	1-0		2-3	0-1	3-1	3-0	3-1
Shahdag Gusar	34	8	8	18	29	51	32	1-2	1-3	0-2	0-3	0-0	0-0	1-0	0-2	0-0	3-1	3-1	0-1	0-0		0-0	0-2	3-1	1-1
MOIK Baku	34	7	9	18	24	34	30	0-1	0-1	0-2	1-2	1-1	0-3	0-0	1-0	0-1	0-0	1-3	1-2	2-0	0-0		0-0	0-2	3-1
Adliyye Baku	34	7	4	23	24	66	25	0-2	0-2	1-3	0-1	0-6	2-1	0-1	0-1	2-1	2-3	1-0	0-0	1-1	1-1	0-6		1-1	3-0
Bakili Baku	34	3	5	26	22	71	14	0-3	0-3	0-1	0-5	1-2	2-7	0-3	1-5	1-4	0-2	1-3	0-3	0-1	1-0	0-2	0-3		0-3
Shafa Baku	34	2	1	31	16	95	7	0-3	0-3	1-2	0-3	0-3	1-5	1-4	0-2	1-3	0-3	1-2	0-3	0-3	1-4	0-3	3-1	0-3	

7/08/2004 - 24/05/2005 • † Qualified for the UEFA Champions League • ‡ Qualified for the UEFA Cup • Shafa Baku withdrew after the winter break •
Matches in bold awarded 3-0
Championship play-off: Neftchi 2-1 Khazar (10-06-2005, Ganja, Att: 25 000, Scorers: Abbasov 68 Tagizada 73 for Neftchi, Gurbanov.A 42 for Khazar

AZERBAIJAN 2004-05 BIRINCI DASTA (2)

	Pl	W	D	L	F	A	Pts
AMMK Baku	14	10	3	1	25	9	33
Energetik Mingacevir	14	10	1	3	34	13	31
Khazar-2 Lenkoran	14	7	3	4	25	18	24
Goyca Baku	14	5	5	4	25	22	20
Ansad Petrol	14	5	5	4	22	19	20
Vilas Masalli	14	5	0	9	18	27	15
Ganclik-95 Sumgayit	14	2	1	11	17	36	7
Boyuk Vadi Baku	14	1	4	9	10	32	7

9/10/2004 - 15/05/2005

FFA CUP 2004

Quarter-finals			Semi-finals			Final	
FK Baku	2	1					
Karat Baku	1	0	FK Baku	1	1		
Genclerbirliyi	0	1	MKT-Araz	0	1		
MKT-Araz	0	3				FK Baku	2
Khazar Lenkoran	1	1				Inter Baku	1
MOIK Baku	0	0	Khazar Lenkoran	1	1		
Neftchi Baku	0	3p	Inter Baku	2	1		
Inter Baku	0	4p					

Tofik Bakhramov, Baku
28-05-2005, Att: 10 000
Scorers - Gomes 5, Ladega 114 for FK; Makouski 52 for Inter

RECENT LEAGUE AND CUP RECORD

	Championship						Cup		
Year	Champions	Pts	Runners-up	Pts	Third	Pts	Winners	Score	Runners-up
1992	Neftchi Baku	62	Khazar Sumgayit	57	Turan Tauz	56	Inshaatchi Baku	2-1	Kur Mingəçevir
1993	Karabakh Agdam	1-0	Khazar Sumgayit				Karabakh Agdam	1-0	Insh. Sabirabad
1994	Turan Tauz	50	Karabakh Agdam	49	Kapaz Ganja	47	Kapaz Ganja	2-0	Khazar Lenkoran
1995	Kapaz Ganja	42	Turan Tauz	40	Neftchi Baku	38	Neftchi Baku	1-0	Kur-Nur
1996	Neftchi Baku	36	Khazri Buzovna	33	Kapaz Ganja	32	Neftchi Baku	3-0	Karabakh Agdam
1997	Neftchi Baku	74	Karabakh Agdam	71	Khazri Buzovna	66	Kapaz Ganja	1-0	Khazri Buzovna
1998	Kapaz Ganja	70	Dinamo Baku	54	Shamkir	54	Kapaz Ganja	2-0	Karabakh Agdam
1999	Kapaz Ganja	58	Karabakh Agdam	54	Dinamo Baku	52	Neftchi Baku	0-0 5-4p	Shamkir
2000	Shamkir	55	Kapaz Ganja	44	Neftchi Baku	43	Kapaz Ganja	2-1	Karabakh Agdam
2001	Shamkir	51	Neftchi Baku	51	Vilash Masalli	38	Shafa Baku	2-1	Neftchi Baku
2002	Championship abandoned with eight rounds to play						Neftchi Baku	W-O	Shamkir
2003	No championship played						No tournament played		
2004	Neftchi Baku	69	Shamkir	64	Karabakh Agdam	60	Neftchi Baku	1-0	Shamkir
2005	Neftchi Baku	78	Khazar Lenkoran	78	Karvan Yevlakh	76	FK Baku	2-1	Inter Baku

BAH – BAHAMAS

NATIONAL TEAM RECORD
JULY 1ST 2002 TO JUNE 30TH 2005

PL	W	D	L	F	A	%
3	0	1	2	2	10	16.7

FIFA/COCA-COLA WORLD RANKING

1993	1994	1995	1996	1997	1998	1999	2000	2001	2002	2003	2004	High		Low	
167	-	-	-	-	-	189	178	184	187	193	192	166	08/93	197	03/99

2004-2005											
08/04	09/04	10/04	11/04	12/04	01/05	02/05	03/05	04/05	05/05	06/05	07/05
191	191	191	190	192	193	193	193	192	193	192	192

Organising football in a country made up of hundreds of tiny islands is no easy task, but the Bahamas Football Association have proved sound administrators complemented by an impressive new National Centre for Football Development, built with FIFA Goal finance. From such sound foundations hopes were high going into the qualifiers for the 2006 FIFA World Cup™ especially with both games against first round opponents Dominica – ranked only 25 places above them in the FIFA rankings – to be played in the Bahamas. Disappointment followed, however, with a draw in the first tie and then a 1-3 defeat in the second and since then, the Bahamanians have not played

INTERNATIONAL HONOURS
None

a match, withdrawing from their group in the 2005 Digicel Caribbean Cup. National coach Gary White has developed a link with his old club, Southampton, and has reorganised the internal structure for the players including a new U-15 side although the U-17s were on the wrong end of a 14-1 scoreline against Trinidad and Tobago in the CONCACAF Junior Tournament. The national championship final between the winners of the six-team Grand Bahama League, Haitian Superstars, and the eight-team New Providence competition, Bears FC, wasn't contested in 2004, the second time in three years there has been no season finale.

THE FIFA BIG COUNT OF 2000

	Male	Female		Male	Female
Registered players	396	242	Referees	21	9
Non registered players	2 000	250	Officials	45	20
Youth players	850	160	Total involved	3 993	
Total players		3 898	Number of clubs	30	
Professional players	0	0	Number of teams	104	

Bahamas Football Association (BFA)
Plaza on the Way, West Bay Street, PO Box N-8434, Nassau, NP, Bahamas
Tel +1 242 3225897　　　Fax +1 242 3225898
lehaven@bahamas.net.bs　　　www.bahamasfootballassoc.com
President: SEALEY Anton　　General Secretary: HAVEN Lionel E.
Vice-President: LUNN Fred　　Treasurer: LAFLEUR Pierre　　Media Officer: LENIHAN Craig
Men's Coach: WHITE Gary　　Women's Coach: GREEN Matthew
BFA formed: 1967　　CONCACAF: 1981　　FIFA: 1968
Colours: Yellow, Black, Yellow

GAMES PLAYED BY BAHAMAS IN THE 2006 FIFA WORLD CUP™ CYCLE

2002 Opponents	Score	Venue	Comp	Scorers	Att	Referee
No international matches played in 2002						
2003						
27-12 Haiti	L 0-6	Miami	Fr			
2004						
26-03 Dominica	D 1-1	Nassau	WCq	Casimir 88	800	Forde BRB
28-03 Dominica	L 1-3	Nassau	WCq	Jean 67	900	Pineda HON
2005						
No international matches played in 2005 before August						

Fr = Friendly match • WC = FIFA World Cup™ • q = qualifier

BAHAMAS NATIONAL TEAM RECORDS AND RECORD SEQUENCES

Records			Sequence records					
Victory	3-0	TCA 1999	Wins	2	2000	Clean sheets	2	1999
Defeat	0-9	HAI 2000	Defeats	4	1999, 2000-2003	Goals scored	2	2000, 2004
Player Caps	n/a		Undefeated	2	1999, 2000	Without goal	4	2000-2003
Player Goals	n/a		Without win	6	2000-present	Goals against	12	1999-present

FIFA REFEREE LIST 2005

	Int'l	DoB
MCNAB Caudel	1994	7-07-1960

FIFA ASSISTANT REFEREE LIST 2005

	Int'l	DoB
DOUGLAS Lynden	2000	17-07-1969
MESSAM Paul	2001	3-09-1971

RECENT LEAGUE RECORD

Year	Winners	Score	Runners-up
1996	Freeport FC	3-0	JS Johnson United
1997	Cavalier FC		
1998	Cavalier FC		
1999	Cavalier FC		
2000	Abacom United	2-1	Cavalier FC
2001	Cavalier FC	2-1	Abacom United
2002	Final between Bears & Abacom United not played		
2003	Bears FC	2-1	Abacom United
2004	Final not contested		

The National Championship is played between the champions
of New Providence and the champions of Grand Bahama

BAHAMAS COUNTRY INFORMATION

Capital	Nassau	Independence	1973	GDP per Capita	$16 700
Population	299 697	Status	Commonwealth	GNP Ranking	117
Area km²	13 940	Language	English	Dialling code	+1 242
Population density	21 per km²	Literacy rate	96%	Internet code	.bs
% in urban areas	87%	Main religion	Christian 94%	GMT +/-	-5
Towns/Cities ('000)	Nassau 227; Freeport 46; Coppers Town 8; Marsh Harbour 5; Freetown 4; High Rock 3				
Neighbours (km)	North Atlantic Ocean 3 542				
Main stadia	Thomas Robinson – Nassau 9 100; Grand Bahama – Freeport 3 100				

BAN – BANGLADESH

NATIONAL TEAM RECORD
JULY 1ST 2002 TO JUNE 30TH 2005

PL	W	D	L	F	A	%
9	4	2	3	11	10	55.6

FIFA/COCA-COLA WORLD RANKING

1993	1994	1995	1996	1997	1998	1999	2000	2001	2002	2003	2004	High	Low
116	130	138	136	141	157	130	151	146	159	151	167	**110** 04/96	**168** 02/05

2004-2005											
08/04	09/04	10/04	11/04	12/04	01/05	02/05	03/05	04/05	05/05	06/05	07/05
158	158	160	161	167	167	168	168	168	168	168	

Unlike much of the rest of the Indian sub-continent Bangladesh is passionate about football so with a population of over 140 million it is surprising that success for the national team has been so thin on the ground. The South Asian Football Federation Cup triumph in January 2003 could have seen the start of better times but it was followed by a quick exit in both the AFC Asian Cup and the 2006 FIFA World Cup™ qualifiers against opposition Bangladesh should be looking to beat. A new headquarters for the national association, paid for largely via the FIFA Goal programme, ought to help the football authorities control better the often chaotic nature of the game in Bangladesh. 2004

INTERNATIONAL HONOURS
Qualified for AFC Asian Cup Finals 1980   Represented in the Football Tournament of the Asian Games 1978 1982 1986 1990
South Asian Federation Games 1999   South Asian Football Federation Cup 2003

saw the fourth staging of the National Football League which brings together the best clubs from the many regional leagues that dominate the game in the country. Having won the powerful Dhaka League in March, Brothers Union added the national title in September and then the Federation Cup in March 2005 to complete a treble of major tournaments. The building of a new national stadium has encouraged the football federation to put in a bid to host the 2006 AFC Asian Youth Championship.

THE FIFA BIG COUNT OF 2000

	Male	Female		Male	Female
Registered players	95 350	0	Referees	2 950	0
Non registered players	5 000 000	0	Officials	64 000	32 000
Youth players	135 000	0	Total involved	5 329 800	
Total players	5 230 850		Number of clubs	3 800	
Professional players	0	0	Number of teams	7 000	

Bangladesh Football Federation (BFF)
BFF House, Dhaka 1000, Bangladesh
Tel +880 2 7161582   Fax +880 2 7160270
bffbd@citechco.net   www.bffonline.com
President: SULTAN S.A.   General Secretary: HUQ Anwarul
Vice-President: AHMED Monir   Treasurer: ALAM CHOWDHURY Shah   Media Officer: none
Men's Coach: S.M. GHULAM Sarwar   Women's Coach: S.M. GHULAM Sarwar
BFF formed: 1972   AFC: 1974   FIFA: 1974
Colours: Green, Green, Green

GAMES PLAYED BY BANGLADESH IN THE 2006 FIFA WORLD CUP™ CYCLE

2002	Opponents	Score	Venue	Comp	Scorers	Att	Referee
No international matches played in 2002							
2003							
11-01	Nepal	W 1-0	Dhaka	SAr1	Ahmed Alfaz [30]		Kunsuta THA
13-01	Maldives	W 1-0	Dhaka	SAr1	Arif Khan [89]		Vidanagamage SRI
15-01	Bhutan	W 3-0	Dhaka	SAr1	Ariful Kabir Farhad 2 [4 54], Rukunuzzaman Kanchan [79]		Balu IND
18-01	India	W 2-1	Dhaka	SAsf	Rukunuzzaman Kanchan [78], Matiur Munna [98 GG]		Kunsuta THA
20-01	Maldives	D 1-1	Dhaka	SAf	Rukunuzzaman Kanchan [14] W 5-3p		Vidanagamage SRI
27-03	Laos	L 1-2	Hong Kong	ACq	Ariful Kabir Farhad [90]		Liu Sung Ho TPE
30-03	Hong Kong	D 2-2	Hong Kong	ACq	Mahmud Hossein Titu [66], Hossein Monwar [78]		
26-11	Tajikistan	L 0-2	Dhaka	WCq		6 000	Khanthachai THA
30-11	Tajikistan	L 0-2	Dushanbe	WCq		12 000	Pereira IND
2004							
No international matches played in 2004							
2005							
No international matches played in 2005 before August							

SA = South Asian Football Federation Cup • AC = AFC Asian Cup • WCq = FIFA World Cup™
q = qualifier • r1 = first round group • sf = semi-final • f = final • GG = Golden Goal

RECENT LEAGUE RECORD

	Dhaka League						National Championship		
Year	Champions	Pts	Runners-up	Pts	Third	Pts	Winners	Score	Runners-up
1992	Abahani	37	Mohammedan	33	Brothers Union	27			
1993	Mohammedan	30	Abahani	29	Brothers Union	23			
1994	Abahani	28	Muktijoddha	25	Mohammedan	25			
1995	Abahani	43	Mohammedan	42	Muktijoddha	33			
1996	Mohammedan	48	Abahani	43	Muktijoddah	33			
1997	No championship due to a readjustment in the timings of the season								
1998	Muktijoddha	52	Mohammedan	50	Abahani	42			
1999	Mohammedan	40	Abahani	37	Muktijoddha	34			
2000	Muktijoddha	40	Abahani	37	Mohammedan	33			
2001	Abahani	41	Mohammedan	27	Rahmatganj	18			
2002	Mohammedan	33	Abahani	31	Muktijoddha	29			
2003	No championship due to a readjustment in the timings of the season								
2004	Brothers Union	40	Sheikh Russell	38	Abahani	33			

† played on a league system

Abahani	†	Mohammedan	
Not played			
Mohammedan	0-0 6-5p	Abahani	
Muktijoddha	1-1 3-2p	Mohammedan	
Brothers Union	0-0 4-2p	Muktijoddha	

FIFA REFEREE LIST 2005

	Int'l	DoB
GOSH Ram	1996	30-06-1962
MIRON Abdul	2004	8-08-1974
SHAMSUZZAMAN Tayeb	1999	9-01-1970
SIKDER Mohammad	2000	3-06-1960

FIFA ASSISTANT REFEREE LIST 2005

	Int'l	DoB
BACHCHU Shahidul		1-05-1963
ISLAM Shahidul	2004	12-01-1965
NRIPEN Nripen	2002	24-09-1964
RAHMAN Mahbubur	2001	10-10-1968
SARKER Abdul	2005	1-06-1968

BANGLADESH COUNTRY INFORMATION

Capital	Dhaka	Independence	1971	GDP per Capita	$1 900
Population	141 340 476	Status	Republic	GNP Ranking	51
Area km²	144 000	Language	Bengali	Dialling code	+880
Population density	98 per km²	Literacy rate	40%	Internet code	.bd
% in urban areas	18%	Main religion	Muslim 87%	GMT +/−	+6
Towns/Cities ('000)	Dhaka 6 493; Chittagong 3 672; Khulna 1 342; Rajshahi 700; Comilla 389; Tungi 337; Mymensingh 330; Sylhet 326; Rangpur 285; Narsinghdi 281; Barisal 280;				
Neighbours (km)	India 4 053; Burma 193; Bay of Bengal 580				
Main stadia	Bangabandhu – Dkaka 36 000; Sher-e-Bangla Mirpur – Dhaka 30 000; MA Aziz – Chittagong 20 000; Kamlapur – Dhaka 20 000				

BANGLADESH NATIONAL TEAM RECORDS AND RECORD SEQUENCES

Records			Sequence records					
Victory	8-0	MDV 1985	Wins	4	2003	Clean sheets	3	1984, 1999, 2003
Defeat	0-9	KOR 1979	Defeats	7	1979-1981	Goals scored	8	1984, 2001-2003
Player Caps	n/a		Undefeated	6	2001-2003	Without goal	5	1980-82, 2000-01
Player Goals	n/a		Without win	19	1973-1979	Goals against	34	1973-1983

BANGLADESH 2004

4TH NATIONAL FOOTBALL LEAGUE

First Stage Group A

	Pl	W	D	L	F	A	Pts	Abahani	Muktijoddha	Moham. Ch.	Najirpara	BU Panch	Kararchar
Abahani Ltd Dhaka †	5	4	1	0	11	1	13		0-0	2-0	1-0	4-1	4-0
Muktijoddha Sangsad Dhaka †	5	3	2	0	10	2	11			1-0	0-0	7-1	2-1
Mohammedan SC Chittagong †	5	2	1	2	5	4	7				3-0	2-1	0-0
Najirpara KC Chandpur	5	1	2	2	4	5	5					0-0	4-1
Brothers Union Panchagarh	5	1	1	3	8	14	4						5-1
Kararchar KC Narshingdi	5	0	1	4	3	15	1						

First Stage Group B

	Pl	W	D	L	F	A	Pts	BU Dhaka	Moham. Dh.	Sh. Russell	Moham. Jh.	Air Force	Unmochon
Brothers Union Dhaka †	5	4	1	0	12	3	13		0-0	2-1	2-1	3-0	5-1
Mohammedan SC Dhaka †	5	3	2	0	12	2	11			1-1	3-0	5-1	3-0
Sheikh Russell Dhaka †	5	3	1	1	9	4	10				2-1	4-0	1-0
Mohammedan SC Jhenaidah	5	2	0	3	6	7	6					2-0	2-0
Bangladesh Air Force	5	1	0	4	5	17	3						4-3
Unmochon Club Bagerhat	5	0	0	5	4	15	0						

Second Stage (in Dhaka)

	Pl	W	D	L	F	A	Pts	Muktijoddha	Brothers Union	Abahani	Mohammedan D.	Sheikh Russell	Mohammedan C.
Muktijoddha Sangsad Dhaka †	5	3	1	1	7	5	10		2-4	*0-0*	2-1	2-0	*1-0*
Brothers Union Dhaka †	5	2	3	0	6	3	9			0-0	*0-0*	*2-1*	0-0
Abahani Ltd Dhaka †	5	2	3	0	3	0	9				0-0	1-0	*2-0*
Mohammedan SC Dhaka †	5	1	3	1	6	6	6					*1-1*	4-3
Sheikh Russell Dhaka	5	1	1	2	5	7	4						3-1
Mohammedan SC Chittagong	5	0	1	4	4	10	1						

25/06/2004 - 9/09/2004 • † Teams qualifying for the next stage • 6 regional qualifiers were played to determine the final 12 • * Teams took head to head records against first stage qualifiers into the second stage

CHAMPIONSHIP PLAY-OFFS

Semi-finals		Final	
Brothers Union	2	Dhaka, 9-9-2004, 20,000	
Abahani Ltd	1	**Brothers Union**	0 4p
Mohammedan	0	Muktijoddha	0 2p
Muktijoddha	2		

FEDERATION CUP 2005

Semi-finals		Final	
Brothers Union	1	Dhaka, 3-05-2005, 10 000	
Abahani Ltd	0	**Brothers Union**	1
Mohammedan SC	0	Muktijoddha	0
Muktijoddha	1		

BANGLADESH 2004

DHAKA PREMIER LEAGUE

	Pl	W	D	L	F	A	Pts	Brothers U	Sh. Russell	Abahani	Muktijo'dan	Moham'dan	Arambagh	Wanderers	Victoria	Badda	Dhanmondi
Brothers Union	18	12	4	2	44	11	40		2-0	1-2	1-0	0-0	4-2	3-0	4-0	5-0	1-0
Sheikh Russell	18	11	5	2	22	9	38	1-0		2-1	1-2	0-0	0-0	2-1	1-0	2-0	2-1
Abahani Ltd	18	9	6	3	35	16	33	3-3	1-1		0-0	2-1	1-0	6-1	2-0	0-0	7-3
Muktijoddha Sangsad	18	9	5	4	25	12	32	0-0	1-2	1-0		0-2	2-1	4-1	0-1	3-0	2-2
Mohammedan SC	18	8	8	2	32	8	31	1-1	0-0	1-0	0-2		3-0	1-1	5-0	4-0	6-0
Arambagh	18	7	5	6	17	20	26	0-5	0-0	0-0	1-1	0-0		1-0	1-0	1-0	2-0
Dhaka Wanderers	18	6	4	8	15	27	22	0-2	0-2	1-1	0-1	0-0	2-1		1-0	1-0	1-0
Victoria SC	18	5	2	11	12	28	17	1-4	0-1	0-1	0-0	1-2	1-2	1-1		2-1	2-1
Badda Jagarani	18	5	2	15	5	41	5	0-1	0-3	0-3	0-4	0-5	0-2	1-2	1-2		2-1
Dhanmondi Club	18	0	3	15	13	48	3	1-7	0-2	1-5	0-2	1-1	1-3	1-2	0-1	0-0	

17/12/2003 - 12/03/2004 • The following season didn't kick-off until May 2005

BDI – BURUNDI

NATIONAL TEAM RECORD
JULY 1ST 2002 TO JUNE 30TH 2005

PL	W	D	L	F	A	%
18	4	4	10	17	33	33.3

FIFA/COCA-COLA WORLD RANKING

1993	1994	1995	1996	1997	1998	1999	2000	2001	2002	2003	2004	High		Low	
101	126	146	137	152	141	133	126	139	135	145	152	96	08/93	160	07/98

2004-2005											
08/04	09/04	10/04	11/04	12/04	01/05	02/05	03/05	04/05	05/05	06/05	07/05
152	153	156	158	152	145	145	146	146	145	144	144

Football in Burundi has just emerged from a troubled period culminating in new leadership of the country's Federation headed by possibly the only princess to have been in charge of a FIFA national association, Lydia Nsekora. The transfer of power from the old regime has been acrimonious and Nsekora has had to pull together disparate elements in the country, but can do so confident that she has the full backing of Joseph S. Blatter. The FIFA President visited Burundi within months of Nsekora taking over to lay the foundation stone for the Federation's new headquarters, funded by the FIFA Goal programme from where it is hoped the country's footballing fortunes will improve

INTERNATIONAL HONOURS
None

when the domestic scene is reorganised. At the moment there are a number of low-key and truncated competitions, including a league programme that was won by Atletico Olympique in 2004. Three Cup competitions were held to keep fixtures alive with Inter Star winning two editions of the Coupe de President Ndayizeye and Bafalo capturing the Coupe PSI. The same year brought great success for the national team, the Sparrows, who finished runners-up to hosts Ethiopia in the CECAFA Cup. It was the only action the team saw all year following their early exit from the FIFA World Cup™ qualifiers which also doubled as CAF Cup of Nations qualifiers.

THE FIFA BIG COUNT OF 2000

	Male	Female		Male	Female
Registered players	4 582	384	Referees	399	13
Non registered players	17 000	400	Officials	9 134	86
Youth players	6 151	102	Total involved	38 251	
Total players	28 619		Number of clubs	165	
Professional players	0	0	Number of teams	189	

Fédération de Football du Burundi (FFB)
Building Nyogozi, Boulevard de l'Uprona, Case postale 3426, Bujumbura, Burundi
Tel +257 928762   Fax +257 242892
lydiansekera@yahoo.fr   www.none
President: NSEKERA Lydia   General Secretary: TBD
Vice-President: SAMUGABO Mustapha   Treasurer: NDEBERI Robert   Media Officer: None
Men's Coach: MAULIDI Ramadhani   Women's Coach: HAKIZIMANA Kebe
FFB formed: 1948   CAF: 1972   FIFA: 1972
Colours: Red/white, White/red, Green

GAMES PLAYED BY BURUNDI IN THE 2006 FIFA WORLD CUP™ CYCLE

2002	Opponents	Score		Venue	Comp	Scorers	Att	Referee
12-10	South Africa	L	0-2	Bloemfontein	CNq		30 000	Madarbocus MRI
1-12	Eritrea	D	1-1	Arusha	CCrl	Juma 83		Juma Ali TAN
3-12	Kenya	D	1-1	Arusha	CCrl	Nduimana 75p		Hassan Mohamed SOM
5-12	Tanzania	L	0-2	Arusha	CCrl			
7-12	Sudan	L	1-2	Arusha	CCrl	Msabah 22		
2003								
15-03	Rwanda	L	2-4	Kigali	Fr			
26-03	Burkina Faso	D	0-0	Bujumbura ·	Fr			
30-03	Côte d'Ivoire	L	0-1	Bujumbura	CNq			
8-06	Côte d'Ivoire	L	1-6	Abidjan	CNq	Shabani 88	50 000	Monteiro Duarte CPV
6-07	South Africa	L	0-2	Bujumbura	CNq		8 000	Teshome ETH
12-10	Gabon	D	0-0	Bujumbura	WCq		10 000	Itur KEN
15-11	Gabon	L	1-4	Libreville	WCq	Nzeyimana 90	15 000	Ndoye SEN
2004								
11-12	Ethiopia	L	1-2	Addis Abeba	CCrl	Hakizimana 75p		
13-12	Rwanda	W	3-1	Addis Abeba	CCrl	Hakizimana 51p, Ntibazonkizia 54, Nzohabonayo 83		
15-12	Tanzania	W	2-0	Addis Abeba	CCrl	Kubis 2 46 90		
17-12	Zanzibar †	W	2-1	Addis Abeba	CCrl	Nahimana 43, Hakizimana 78p		
22-12	Sudan	W	2-1	Addis Abeba	CCsf	Ntibazonkizia 22, Kubis 75		
25-12	Ethiopia	L	0-3	Addis Abeba	CCf			
2005								

No international matches played in 2005 before August

Fr = Friendly match • CN = CAF African Cup of Nations qualifier • CC = CECAFA Cup • WCq = FIFA World Cup™
q = qualifier • rl = 1st round • † Not a full international

BURUNDI NATIONAL TEAM RECORDS AND RECORD SEQUENCES

Records			Sequence records					
Victory	6-2	RWA 1976	Wins	5	1996-1998	Clean sheets	6	1993-1998
Defeat	1-6	CIV 2003	Defeats	4	1999	Goals scored	9	1982-1992
Player Caps	n/a		Undefeated	8	1993-1998	Without goal	3	1982, 1993
Player Goals	n/a		Without win	14	2001-2004	Goals against	10	1975-1981

RECENT LEAGUE AND CUP RECORD

Year	Champions	Cup Winners
1996	Fantastique	Vital'O
1997	Maniema	Vital'O
1998	Vital'O	Elite
1999	Vital'O	Vital'O
2000	Vital'O	Atletico Olympique
2001	Prince Louis	
2002	Muzinga	
2003	Championship abandoned	
2004	Atletico Olympique	Bafalo Muramvya

BURUNDI COUNTRY INFORMATION

Capital	Bujumbura	Independence	1962	GDP per Capita	$600
Population	6 231 221	Status	Republic	GNP Ranking	161
Area km²	27 830	Language	Kirundi/French	Dialling code	+257
Population density	224 per km²	Literacy rate	45%	Internet code	.bi
% in urban areas	8%	Main religion	Muslim 43%	GMT + / –	+2
Towns/Cities ('000)	Bujumbura 330; Muyinga 71; Ruyigi 38; Gitega 23; Ngozi 21; Rutana 20; Bururi 19;				
Neighbours (km)	Rwanda 290, Tanzania 451, Congo DR 233. Burundi also borders Lake Tanganyika				
Main stadia	Prince Louis Rwagasore – Bujumbura 22 000				

BEL – BELGIUM

NATIONAL TEAM RECORD
JULY 1ST 2002 TO JUNE 30TH 2005

PL	W	D	L	F	A	%
24	10	6	8	31	34	54.2

FIFA/COCA-COLA WORLD RANKING

1993	1994	1995	1996	1997	1998	1999	2000	2001	2002	2003	2004	High		Low	
25	24	24	42	41	35	33	27	20	17	16	45	16	01/03	50	07/05

2004-2005											
08/04	09/04	10/04	11/04	12/04	01/05	02/05	03/05	04/05	05/05	06/05	07/05
31	29	35	38	45	44	44	51	41	42	47	50

Club Brugge won their 13th league title in 2005 and they had the huge satisfaction of clinching it on their own ground against fierce rivals Anderlecht. Brugge have now finished in the top two of the league in each of the past 10 seasons and are by far the most consistent performers in Belgian football. However, their dip in form at the end of the season did cost them the double when they lost the Cup Final to Germinal Beerschot. It was the Antwerp club's first trophy since its creation in 1999 through the merger of Beerschot and Germinal Ekeren although both clubs had won honours, including the Cup, before then. It proved to be a disappointing year for Belgian clubs in

INTERNATIONAL HONOURS
Qualified for the FIFA World Cup™ finals 1930 1934 1938 1954 1970 1982 1986 1990 1994 1998 2002 Olympic Gold 1920

Europe with Anderlecht failing to pick up a single point in their UEFA Champions League group, the only club to come away empty-handed whilst Brugge were eliminated in the preliminary round by Shakhter Donetsk. It was also a disappointing season for the national team which got off to a terrible start in the FIFA World Cup™ qualifiers. A draw at home to Lithuania was followed by an away defeat to Spain and then, most damaging of all, a defeat in Brussels to Serbia and Montenegro. That left Belgium playing catch up for the rest of the qualifiers in the quest to keep up their record of having qualified for every finals since 1982.

THE FIFA BIG COUNT OF 2000

	Male	Female		Male	Female
Registered players	84 816	3 772	Referees	6 378	158
Non registered players	125 000	800	Officials	77 478	3 618
Youth players	240 119	8 096	Total involved	550 235	
Total players	462 603		Number of clubs	2 002	
Professional players	386	0	Number of teams	16 780	

Union Royale Belge des Sociétés de Football Association / Koninklijke Belgische Voetbalbond (URBSFA/KBVB)
145 Avenue Houba de Strooper, Bruxelles 1020, Belgium
Tel +32 2 4771211   Fax +32 2 4782391
urbsfa.kbvb@footbel.com   www.footbel.com
President: PEETERS Jan   General Secretary: HOUBEN Jean-Paul
Vice-President: VANDEN STOCK Roger   Treasurer: LANDSHEERE Germain   Media Officer: CORNU Nicolas
Men's Coach: ANTHUENIS Aime   Women's Coach: NOE-HAESENDONCK Anne
URBSFA/KBVB formed: 1895   UEFA: 1954   FIFA: 1904
Colours: Red, Red, Red or Blue, Blue, Blue

GAMES PLAYED BY BELGIUM IN THE 2006 FIFA WORLD CUP™ CYCLE

2002	Opponents	Score		Venue	Comp	Scorers	Att	Referee
21-08	Poland	D	1-1	Szczecin	Fr	Sonck [42]	19 000	Ingvarsson SWE
7-09	Bulgaria	L	0-2	Brussels	ECq		20 000	Hauge NOR
12-10	Andorra	W	1-0	Andorra La Vella	ECq	Sonck [61]	700	Nalbandyan ARM
16-10	Estonia	W	1-0	Tallinn	ECq	Sonck [2]	2 500	Riley ENG
2003								
12-02	Algeria	W	3-1	Annaba	Fr	Mpenza.E 2 [2 57], Sonck [7]	40 000	Baraket TUN
29-03	Croatia	L	0-4	Zagreb	ECq		25 000	Fandel GER
30-04	Poland	W	3-1	Brussels	Fr	Sonck [28], Buffel [56], Soetaers [86]	27 000	McDonald SCO
7-06	Bulgaria	D	2-2	Sofia	ECq	OG [31], Clement [56]	42 000	Collina ITA
11-06	Andorra	W	3-0	Gent	ECq	Goor 2 [20 68], Sonck [44]	12 000	Shmolik BLR
20-08	Netherlands	D	1-1	Brussels	Fr	Sonck [39]	38 000	Fandel GER
10-09	Croatia	W	2-1	Brussels	ECq	Sonck 2 [34 42]	35 000	Poll ENG
11-10	Estonia	W	2-0	Liège	ECq	OG [45], Buffel [61]	26 000	Busacca SUI
2004								
18-02	France	L	0-2	Brussels	Fr		43 160	Halsey ENG
31-03	Germany	L	0-3	Cologne	Fr		46 500	Wegereef NED
28-04	Turkey	L	2-3	Brussels	Fr	Sonck [33], Dufer [85]	25 000	Van Egmond NED
29-05	Netherlands	W	1-0	Eindhoven	Fr	Goor [77p]	32 500	Colombo FRA
18-08	Norway	D	2-2	Oslo	Fr	Buffel 2 [25 34]	16 669	Stupik POL
4-09	Lithuania	D	1-1	Charleroi	WCq	Sonck [61]	19 218	Loizou CYP
9-10	Spain	L	0-2	Santander	WCq		17 000	Nielsen DEN
17-11	Serbia & Montenegro	L	0-2	Brussels	WCq		28 350	Frojdfeldt SWE
2005								
9-02	Egypt	L	0-4	Cairo	Fr		5 000	Beltagi EGY
26-03	Bosnia-Herzegovina	W	4-1	Brussels	WCq	Mpenza.E 2 [15 54], Daerden [44], Buffel [77]	36 700	Hrinak SVK
30-03	San Marino	W	2-1	Serravalle	WCq	Simons [18p], Van Buyten [65]	871	Kasnaferis GRE
4-06	Serbia & Montenegro	D	0-0	Belgrade	WCq		16 662	Ivanov.V RUS

Fr = Friendly match • EC = UEFA EURO 2004™ • WCq = FIFA World Cup™ • q = qualifier

BELGIUM NATIONAL TEAM RECORDS AND RECORD SEQUENCES

Records			Sequence records					
Victory	10-1	SMR 2001	Wins	7	1979-1980	Clean sheets	5	1972-1973, 1989
Defeat	2-11	ENG 1909	Defeats	7	1927-1928	Goals scored	21	1937-1945
Player Caps	96	CEULEMANS Jan	Undefeated	11	1988-1989	Without goal	5	1999
Player Goals	30	VAN HIMST & VOORHOOF	Without win	13	1933-1935	Goals against	38	1928-1933

BELGIUM COUNTRY INFORMATION

Capital	Brussels	Independence	1830	GDP per Capita	$29 100
Population	10 348 276	Status	Kingdom	GNP Ranking	20
Area km²	30 528	Language	Flemish/French	Dialling code	+32
Population density	339 per km²	Literacy rate	99%	Internet code	.be
% in urban areas	97%	Main religion	Christian 90%	GMT + / –	+1

Towns/Cities ('000)	Brussels 1 019; Antwerp 459; Ghent 231; Charleroi 200; Liège 182; Brugge 116; Namur 106; Leuven 92; Mons 91; Aalst 77; Mechelen 77; La Louvière 76; Kortrijk 73; Hasselt 69; Ostend 69; Sint-Niklaas 69; Tournai 67; Genk 63; Seraing 60; Roeselare 56; Mouscron 52
Neighbours (km)	Netherlands 450; Germany 167; Luxembourg 148; France 620; North Sea 66
Main stadia	Roi Baudouin (Heysel) – Brussels 50 000; Jan Breydel – Brugge 29 975; Sclessin – Liège 29 173; Constant Vanden Stock – Brussels 26 361; Pays de Charleroi – Charleroi 25 149

NATIONAL CAPS

	Caps
CEULEMANS Jan	96
GERETS Eric	86
VAN DER ELST Franky	86
SCIFO Enzo	84
VAN HIMST Paul	81
GRUN Georges	77
STAELENS Lorenzo	70
WILMOTS Marc	70
MEES Vic	68

NATIONAL GOALS

	Goals
VAN HIMST Paul	30
VOORHOOF Bernard	30
WILMOTS Marc	28
MERMANS Joseph	27
BRAINE Raymond	26
DE VEEN Robert	26
CEULEMANS Jan	23
DEGRYSE Marc	23
COPPENS Henrik	21

NATIONAL COACH

	Years
GOETHALS Raymond	1968-'76
THYS Guy	1976-'89
MEEUWS Walter	1989-90
THYS Guy	1990-'91
VAN HIMST Paul	1991-'96
VAN MOER Wilfred	1996-'97
LEEKENS Georges	1997-'99
WASIEGE Robert	1999-'02
ANTHUENIS Aime	2002-

FIFA REFEREE LIST 2005

	Int'l	DoB
ALLAERTS Paul	2000	9-07-1964
DE BLEECKERE Frank	1998	1-07-1966
GUMIENNY Serge	2003	14-04-1972
VAN DE VELDE Joeri	2004	14-02-1971
VER EECKE Johny	2001	22-06-1962
VERBIST Johan	2001	13-04-1966
VERVECKEN Peter	2003	9-12-1967

FIFA ASSISTANT REFEREE LIST 2005

	Int'l	DoB
DE SPIEGELEER Vincent	2004	29-06-1972
GREGOIRE Claude	2002	16-09-1960
HENNISSEN Rombout	1997	12-09-1961
HERMANS Peter	2002	27-06-1966
HUENS Danny	2005	1-09-1970
LANNOY Jean-Philippe	2003	26-07-1965
SIMONS Mark	2002	29-12-1966
VANDERHOVEN Danny	2001	10-09-1961
VERSTRAETEN Alex	2005	10-08-1965
VROMANS Walter	2005	21-04-1968

CLUB DIRECTORY

Club	Town/City	Stadium	Phone	www.	Lge	Cup	CL
RSC Anderlecht	Brussels	Vanden Stock 28 063	+32 2 5229400	rsca.be	27	8	0
KSK Beveren	Antwerp	Freethiel 13 290	+32 3 7759000	kskbeveren.be	2	2	0
FC Brussels	Brussels	Machtens 15 266	+32 2 4116886	fcmbs.be	1	0	0
KSV Cercle Brugge	Brugge	Jan Breydel 29 268	+32 50 389193	cerclebrugge.be	3	2	0
Club Brugge KV	Brugge	Jan Breydel 29 268	+32 50 402121	clubbrugge.be	13	9	0
RSC Charleroi	Charleroi	Pays de Charleroi 20 000	+32 71 319126	rcsc.be	0	0	0
Excelsior Mouscron	Mouscron	Le Canonnier 10 692	+32 56 860600	excelsior.be	0	0	0
KRC Genk	Genk	Feniksstadion 22 989	+32 89 841608	krcgenk.be	2	2	0
KAA Gent	Gent	Ottenstadion 18 215	+32 9 2306610	kaagent.be	0	2	0
Germinal Beerschot	Antwerp	Olympic Stadion 12 500	+32 3 2484845	germinal-beerschot.be	0	1	0
Lierse SK	Lier	Vanderpoorten 14 538	+32 3 4801370	lierse.com	4	2	0
KSC Lokeren	Lokeren	Daknam 12 000	+32 9 3483905	sporting.be	0	0	0
RAA La Louvière	La Louvière	Tivoli 13 300	+32 64 211975	raal.be	0	1	0
RAEC Mons	Mons	Tondreau 9 000	+32 65 221111	raec-mons.be	0	0	0
KV Oostende	Oostende	Albertparkstadion 10 709	+32 59 703610	kvo.be	0	0	0
K Sint-Truidense VV	Sint-Truiden	Staaien 12 861	+32 11 683829	stvv.com	0	0	0
R Standard Liège	Liège	Sclessin 30 000	+32 4 2522122	standardliege.com	8	5	0
KVC Westerlo	Westerlo	't Kuipipe 10 278	+32 14 545288	kvcwesterlo.be	0	1	0

RECENT LEAGUE AND CUP RECORD

Year	Champions	Pts	Runners-up	Pts	Third	Pts	Winners	Score	Runners-up
1990	Club Brugge	57	RSC Anderlecht	53	KV Mechelen	50	RFC Liège	2-1	Germinal Ekeren
1991	RSC Anderlecht	53	KV Mechelen	50	Club Brugge	47	Club Brugge	3-1	KV Mechelen
1992	Club Brugge	53	RSC Anderlecht	49	Standard CL	46	Royal Antwerp FC	2-2 9-8p	KV Mechelen
1993	RSC Anderlecht	58	Standard CL	45	KV Mechelen	42	Standard CL	2-0	RSC Charleroi
1994	RSC Anderlecht	55	Club Brugge	53	RFC Seraing	43	RSC Anderlecht	2-0	Club Brugge
1995	RSC Anderlecht	52	Standard CL	51	Club Brugge	49	Club Brugge	3-1	Germinal Ekeren
1996	Club Brugge	81	RSC Anderlecht	71	Germinal Ekeren	53	Club Brugge	2-1	Cercle Brugge
1997	Lierse SK	73	Club Brugge	71	Excelsior Mouscron	61	Germinal Ekeren	4-2	RSC Anderlecht
1998	Club Brugge	84	KRC Genk	66	Germinal Ekeren	58	KRC Genk	4-0	Club Brugge
1999	KRC Genk	73	Club Brugge	71	RSC Anderlecht	70	Lierse SK	3-1	Standard Liège
2000	RSC Anderlecht	75	Club Brugge	67	KAA Gent	63	KRC Genk	4-1	Standard Liège
2001	RSC Anderlecht	83	Club Brugge	78	Standard Liège	60	KVC Westerlo	1-0	KFC Lommelse
2002	KRC Genk	72	Club Brugge	72	RSC Anderlecht	66	Club Brugge	3-1	Excelsior Mouscron
2003	Club Brugge	79	RSC Anderlecht	71	KSC Lokeren	60	La Louvière	3-1	Sint-Truidense
2004	RSC Anderlecht	81	Club Brugge	72	Standard Liège	65	Club Brugge	4-2	KSK Beveren
2005	Club Brugge	79	RSC Anderlecht	76	Standard Liège	80	Germinal Beerschot	2-1	Club Brugge

BELGIUM 2004-05

LIGUE JUPILER

Team	Pl	W	D	L	F	A	Pts	Brugge	Anderlecht	Standard	Genk	Charleroi	Gent	Louvière	Lokeren	GBA	Lierse	Cercle	Westerlo	Mouscron	St Truiden	Brussels	Beveren	Oostende	Mons
Club Brugge †	34	24	7	3	83	25	79		2-2	1-1	1-1	1-1	5-0	2-0	0-0	6-0	1-0	5-0	2-0	3-0	5-1	4-1	3-1	7-3	3-1
RSC Anderlecht †	34	23	7	4	75	34	76	2-1		3-2	4-2	3-0	2-0	2-1	2-0	3-0	5-1	5-2	4-0	2-0	2-1	3-0	5-2	0-1	2-1
Standard Liège	34	21	7	6	64	30	70	1-4	1-0		1-0	1-2	3-0	1-0	3-0	4-1	4-0	2-0	4-1	1-3	3-0	5-0	2-0		
KRC Genk ‡	34	21	7	6	59	37	70	2-1	2-4	1-1		2-0	1-1	1-0	2-1	2-1	3-0	2-1	3-2	0-0	1-0	4-1	2-1	2-2	2-2
RSC Charleroi	34	19	7	8	47	34	64	0-1	2-1	0-0	2-0		3-2	2-5	2-1	1-0	1-0	5-1	0-1	2-0	0-0	1-2	2-1	1-0	1-0
KAA Gent	34	18	5	11	46	36	59	0-1	0-0	1-1	0-1	3-1		2-1	3-1	5-0	1-0	1-2	1-0	1-0	2-1	3-0	1-0	2-1	2-1
RAA La Louvière	34	12	8	14	43	43	44	0-2	1-1	0-1	2-0	0-0	0-1		0-0	1-1	3-2	1-1	3-1	1-0	1-3	0-3	2-0	4-0	
KSC Lokeren	34	11	11	12	36	38	44	0-2	2-2	0-0	1-3	1-1	0-1	1-0		0-1	0-2	4-0	3-1	1-1	4-3	1-0	1-1	1-0	0-0
Germinal Beerschot ‡	34	12	6	16	36	45	42	0-1	0-1	1-0	3-1	0-1	0-0	1-1	1-2		2-2	2-3	1-0	3-1	3-1	2-0	3-1	4-0	2-0
Lierse SK	34	12	5	17	57	60	41	0-2	1-1	1-1	1-5	1-1	3-2	7-0	2-0	2-0		2-0	3-0	0-1	0-1	5-1	1-2	1-1	4-1
KSV Cercle Brugge	34	12	5	17	45	74	41	1-2	1-3	1-3	1-3	0-4	2-1	2-2	2-2	2-2			0-0	1-0	5-1	1-2	1-1	2-0	2-0
KVC Westerlo	34	11	6	17	34	54	39	1-3	2-1	1-3	0-0	2-1	2-1	0-2	1-1	1-0	2-1	1-2		0-1	2-1	1-0	0-2	0-1	
Excelsior Mouscron	34	10	6	18	40	43	36	0-1	2-0	0-3	1-2	0-1	0-2	1-1	1-1	0-1	1-3	6-0	3-0		4-0	2-0	1-0	1-1	5-1
Sint-Truidense VV	34	10	6	18	40	58	36	3-2	2-2	4-1	0-2	2-2	0-2	2-1	2-0	1-1	4-0	0-1	1-0	3-2		2-0	0-1	0-0	0-0
FC Brussels	34	10	3	21	32	60	33	1-6	0-1	0-1	0-1	1-2	1-1	1-2	0-2	2-1	3-2	2-1	0-1	2-1	0-1		1-3	2-2	2-1
KSK Beveren	34	8	8	18	43	59	32	1-1	0-1	2-3	0-1	1-2	1-0	2-0	2-0	1-0	2-0	5-1	4-1	2-2	3-1	0-1		2-2	0-4
KV Oostende	34	6	9	19	31	62	27	1-2	1-3	1-1	1-3	1-2	1-2	2-1	0-2	0-0	2-3	0-1	3-3	1-0	1-0	1-0	1-1		1-0
RAEC Mons	34	7	5	22	39	58	26	0-0	1-2	2-3	1-2	0-1	0-4	1-0	4-1	1-3	3-2	0-2	4-1	1-2	2-2	2-0			

6/08/2004 - 21/05/2005 • † Qualified for the UEFA Champions League • ‡ Qualified for the UEFA Cup (Genk beat Standard 1-3 3-0 in a play-off)

BELGIUM 2004-05 — TWEEDE CLASSE (2)

Team	Pl	W	D	L	F	A	Pts
SV Zulte-Waregem	34	22	7	5	71	35	73
KSV Roeselare ‡	34	16	12	6	51	31	60
Verbroedering Geel	34	16	8	10	49	36	56
Royal Antwerp ‡	34	15	5	14	48	40	50
Red Star Waasland ‡	34	14	8	12	51	55	50
AFC Tubize	34	14	6	14	54	49	48
KV Kortrijk	34	13	9	12	56	48	48
KSK Ronse	34	13	9	12	42	51	48
Beringen-Heusden-Zolder	34	12	11	11	41	41	47
KMSK Deinze	34	11	10	13	47	59	43
KFC VW Hamme	34	10	11	13	50	47	41
Excelsior Virton	34	10	11	13	43	54	41
AS Eupen	34	9	14	11	52	46	41
Union Saint-Gilloise	34	10	9	15	41	53	39
KFC Dessel Sport	34	9	12	13	31	46	39
CS Visé	34	10	7	17	52	54	37
Patro Maasmechelen	34	10	10	15	35	53	37
Eendracht Aalst	34	7	13	14	41	57	34

11/08/2004 - 15/05/2004 • ‡ Qualified for play-offs

TOP SCORERS

JESTROVIC Nenad	Anderlecht	18
VANDENBERGH Kevin	Genk	17
LANGE Rune	Club Brugge	15
BANGOURA Sembegou	Standard Liège	15
THOMPSON Archie	Lierse	14
DINDANE Aruna	Anderlecht	14
ZEWLAKOW Marcin	Mouscron	14
DATI Mohammed	Mons	14

BELGIUM 2004-05 — TWEEDE CLASSE PLAY-OFFS

Team	Pl	W	D	L	F	A	Pts	Roeselare	Geel	Antwerp	Red Star
KSV Roeselare	6	5	1	0	10	1	16		1-0	1-0	3-0
Verbroedering Geel	6	3	2	1	12	5	11	1-1		3-1	1-1
Royal Antwerp	6	1	1	4	6	14	4	0-2	1-5		2-1
Red Star Waasland	6	0	2	4	4	12	2	0-2	0-2	2-2	

COUPE DE BELGIQUE 2004-05

Eighth-finals

Germinal Beerschot	1
RAEC Mons *	0
RSC Anderlecht	1
KRC Genk *	2
KAA Gent	1
Excelsior Mouscron *	0
Sint-Truidense	1
KSC Lokeren *	2
Lierse SK	7
AS Eupen *	0
Standard Liège *	1 3p
RSC Charleroi	1 4p
RAA Louviéroise *	3
KSK Beveren	2
Charleroi-Marchienne	0
Club Brugge *	4

Quarter-finals

Germinal Beerschot	1	3
KRC Genk *	1	1
KAA Gent	1	0
KSC Lokeren *	2	1
Lierse SK	1	2
RSC Charleroi *	3	0
RAA Louviéroise	2	2
Club Brugge *	2	3

Semi-finals

Germinal Beerschot	1	0
KSC Lokeren *	1	0
Lierse SK	0	0
Club Brugge *	1	1

Final

Germinal Beerschot ‡	2
Club Brugge	1

CUP FINAL

28-05-2005, Att: 40 000, Ref: De Bleeckere
Roi Baudoiun, Brussels
Scorers - Snoeckx [23], De Wree [55] for Germinal Beerschot; Verheyen [53] for Brugge

* Home team/home team in 1st leg • ‡ Qualified for the UEFA Cup

CLUB BRUGGE 2004-2005

Date	Opponents	Score		Comp	Scorers	Att
28-07-2004	Lokomotiv Plovdiv	W 2-0	H	CLpr2	Balaban $^{71\ 87}$	
4-08-2004	Lokomotiv Plovdiv	W 4-0	A	CLpr2	Balaban $^{13\ 43}$, Saeternes ^{73}, Ceh ^{83}	
7-08-2004	KSK Beveren	D 1-1	A	JL	Balaban ^{7}	7 000
11-08-2004	Shakhtar Donetsk	L 1-4	A	CLpr3	Balaban ^{49}	25 000
15-08-2004	KAA Gent	W 5-0	H	JL	Balaban ^{20}, Verheyen ^{40}, Simons ^{66}, Victor ^{70}, Cornelius ^{90}	24 173
21-08-2004	KV Oostende	W 2-1	A	JL	Stoica ^{54}, Victor ^{81}	9 000
25-08-2004	Shakhtar Donetsk	D 2-2	H	CLpr3	Ceh $^{14\ 33}$	16 000
28-08-2004	Lierse SK	W 1-0	H	JL	Lange ^{79}	24 316
11-09-2004	RSC Charleroi	W 1-0	A	JL	Balaban ^{48}	9 575
16-09-2004	Châteauroux	W 4-0	H	UCr1	Clement ^{17}, Simons ^{43}, Verheyen ^{80}, Stoica ^{88}	10 000
19-09-2004	KSV Cercle Brugge	W 5-0	H	JL	Lange ^{44}, Ceh $^{47\ 54}$, Cornelis ^{82}, Van Tornhout ^{87}	25 265
25-09-2004	FC Brussels	W 6-1	A	JL	Balaban $^{35\ 53\ 56\ 78}$, Verheyen ^{39}	7 500
30-09-2004	Châteauroux	W 2-1	A	UCr1	Lange ^{14}, Gvozdenovic ^{31}	8 100
3-10-2004	KRC Genk	D 1-1	H	JL	Gvozdenovic ^{37}	25 040
17-10-2004	KSC Lokeren	W 2-0	A	JL	Victor ^{1}, Van Tornhout ^{90}	8 000
21-10-2004	Dnipropetrovsk	L 2-3	A	UCgC	Ceh ^{37}, Balaban ^{43}	22 000
24-10-2004	RAA La Louvière	W 2-0	H	JL	Ceh ^{44}, Englebert ^{80}	23,558
29-10-2004	Standard Liège	W 4-1	A	JL	Balaban ^{24}, Englebert $^{63\ 78}$, Simons ^{88}	21 000
5-11-2004	KVC Westerlo	W 2-0	H	JL	Balaban ^{18}, Verheyen ^{35}	23,501
10-11-2004	Germinal Beerschot	W 1-0	A	JL	Van der Heyden ^{17}	8 500
21-11-2004	Eendracht Aalst	W 3-0	A	CDBr1	Lange $^{17\ 67}$, Van Tornhout ^{75}	5 712
25-11-2004	FC Utrecht	W 1-0	H	UCgC	Lange ^{63}	21 961
28-11-2004	Excelsior Mouscron	W 3-0	H	JL	Simons $^{2\ 56}$, Lange ^{35}	23 041
1-12-2004	FK Austria Wien	D 1-1	A	UCgC	Lange ^{90}	19 000
4-12-2004	RAEC Mons	W 3-1	H	JL	Simons ^{19}, Englebert ^{60}, Verheyen ^{65}, Gousse ^{78}	23 018
11-12-2004	RSC Anderlecht	L 1-2	A	JL	Ceh ^{20}	25 693
16-12-2004	Real Zaragoza	D 1-1	H	UCgC		23 000
19-12-2004	Sint-Truidense VV	W 5-1	H	JL	Verheyen $^{2\ 10\ 57}$, Simons ^{13p}, Blondel ^{30}, Lange ^{62}	22 557
15-01-2005	KSK Beveren	W 3-1	H	JL	Blondel ^{7}, Lange ^{32}, Van der Heyden ^{75}	24 166
18-01-2005	Olympique Charleroi	W 4-0	H	CDBr2	Ishiaku $^{2\ 5\ 40}$, Vlaeminck ^{75}, Van Tornhout ^{78}	
23-01-2005	KAA Gent	W 1-0	A	JL	Lange ^{65}	10 840
29-01-2005	KV Oostende	W 7-3	H	JL	Ishiaku ^{6}, Clement $^{3\ 8\ 28\ 75}$, Verheyen $^{2\ 15\ 25}$, Lange ^{31}	23 931
2-02-2005	RAA La Louvière	D 2-2	H	CDBqf	Simons ^{71p}, Lange ^{73}	2 000
5-02-2005	Lierse SK	W 2-0	A	JL	Ceh ^{27}, Victor ^{83}	10 800
13-02-2005	RSC Charleroi	D 1-1	H	JL	Lange ^{46}	22 988
20-02-2005	KSV Cercle Brugge	W 2-1	A	JL	Lange ^{75}, Yulu-Matondo ^{77}	12 450
9-03-2005	FC Brussels	W 4-1	H	JL	Ceh ^{14}, Van der Heyden ^{37}, Lange $^{2\ 44\ 90}$	
12-03-2005	KRC Genk	L 1-2	A	JL	Balaban ^{58}	23 532
19-03-2005	KSC Lokeren	D 0-0	H	JL		25 926
2-04-2005	RAA La Louvière	W 2-0	A	JL	Verheyen $^{2\ 58\ 87}$	5 576
6-04-2005	RAA La Louvière	W 3-2	A	CDBqf	Verheyen ^{40}, Lange ^{70}, Rozehnal ^{82}	6 000
10-04-2005	Standard Liège	D 1-1	H	JL	Verheyen ^{39}	27 341
15-04-2005	KVC Westerlo	W 3-1	A	JL	Clement ^{14}, Lange $^{2\ 59\ 81}$	8 500
20-04-2005	Lierse SK	W 1-0	H	CDBsf	Clement ^{9}	
23-04-2005	Germinal Beerschot	W 6-0	H	JL	Lange ^{23}, Ceh $^{2\ 28\ 48}$, Verheyen $^{2\ 34\ 41}$, Simons ^{60}	26 864
30-04-2005	Excelsior Mouscron	W 1-0	A	JL	Balaban ^{78}	10 000
6-05-2005	RAEC Mons	D 0-0	H	JL		9 000
10-05-2005	Lierse SK	W 1-0	A	CDBsf	Ceh ^{30}	7 000
15-05-2005	RSC Anderlecht	D 2-2	H	JL	Ceh $^{2\ 1\ 38}$	27 734
21-05-2005	Sint-Truidense VV	L 2-3	A	JL	Rozehnal ^{19}, Van Tournhout ^{86}	11 000
28-05-2005	Germinal Beerschot	L 1-2	N	CDBf	Verheyen ^{53}	40 000

JL = Jupiler League • CDB = Coupe de Belgique • CL = UEFA Champions League • UC = UEFA Cup
pr2 = second preliminary round • pr3 = third preliminary round • gG = group G • r1 = first round • r2 = second round • qf = quarter-final •
sf = semi-final • f = final

BEN – BENIN

NATIONAL TEAM RECORD
JULY 1ST 2002 TO JUNE 30TH 2005

PL	W	D	L	F	A	%
32	8	6	18	34	57	34.4

FIFA/COCA-COLA WORLD RANKING

1993	1994	1995	1996	1997	1998	1999	2000	2001	2002	2003	2004	High		Low	
130	143	161	143	137	127	140	148	152	146	121	122	120	07/04	165	07/96

2004-2005												
08/04	09/04	10/04	11/04	12/04	01/05	02/05	03/05	04/05	05/05	06/05	07/05	
121	120	120	121	122	122	122	122	123	123	125	125	

Benin has witnessed something of a transformation on the international scene, most notably the first appearance by the national team at the CAF African Cup of Nations in 2004. They then edged past Madagascar in the preliminary round of the 2006 FIFA World Cup™ qualifiers thanks to a last minute goal from striker Oumar Tchomogo, but the Squirrels found themselves in a difficult group that included Cameroon, Egypt and Cote d'Ivoire, a situation reflected in their subsequent poor results. In January 2005 Benin hosted their first major international tournament – the CAF African Youth Championship - resulting in an historic first qualification for a world tournament although

INTERNATIONAL HONOURS
None

the U-20s couldn't make it past the first round of the FIFA World Youth Championship in the Netherlands. While there has been some progress internationally, football inside Benin has floundered. In 2000 and 2001 there was no League programme, a Championship only reappearing in 2002. Forced to contend with a heavy schedule the game's administrators decided to abandon the 2004 Superleague playoffs after the 18 clubs had completed the regular season in which JS Pobe and Donjo FC topped their respective groups. The only trophy left to play for was the Coupe de l'Independence, which was won by Mogas 90 for the second year.

THE FIFA BIG COUNT OF 2000

	Male	Female		Male	Female
Registered players	4 500	0	Referees	200	0
Non registered players	15 000	0	Officials	1 400	0
Youth players	2 500	0	Total involved	23 600	
Total players	22 000		Number of clubs	100	
Professional players	0	0	Number of teams	400	

Fédération Béninoise de Football (FBF)
Stade René Pleven d'Akpakpa, Case Postale 965, Cotonou 01, Benin
Tel +229 330537   Fax +229 330537
www.none
President: ADJAGODO Martin   General Secretary: DIDAVI Bruno Arthur
Vice-President: ANJORIN Moucharafou   Treasurer: AHOUANVOEBLA Augustin   Media Officer: None
Men's Coach: TBD   Women's Coach: None
FBF formed: 1962   CAF: 1969   FIFA: 1962
Colours: Green, Yellow, Red

GAMES PLAYED BY BENIN IN THE 2006 FIFA WORLD CUP™ CYCLE

2002	Opponents	Score		Venue	Comp	Scorers	Att	Referee
8-09	Tanzania	W	4-0	Cotonou	CNq	Adjamonsi 2 [9] [40], Tchomogo.O [74p], Latoundji [80]	10 000	Chukwujekwu NGA
12-10	Zambia	D	1-1	Lusaka	CNq	Oladikpikpo [44]	30 000	Mochubela ZIM
2003								
26-01	Ghana	L	0-3	Kumasi	Fr			Amedior GHA
15-02	Ghana	W	1-0	Cotonou	Fr	Gaspoz [17]		Lamidi BEN
7-03	Niger	D	1-1	Cotonou	Fr	W 3-1p		
9-03	Burkina Faso	W	3-0	Cotonou	Fr	Akpakoun 2 [31p] [74], Adjamonsi [42p]		Aguidissou BEN
25-03	Ethiopia	L	0-3	Addis Abeba	Fr			
29-03	Sudan	L	0-3	Khartoum	CANq		15 000	Buenkadila COD
8-06	Sudan	W	3-0	Cotonou	CANq	Tchomogo.O 2 [55p] [72], Ogunbiyi [90]		Coulibaly MLI
22-06	Tanzania	W	1-0	Dar es Salaam	CANq	Kabirou [66]	20 000	
6-07	Zambia	W	3-0	Cotonou	CANq	Tchomogo.O 2 [20] [33p], Latoundji [75]	40 000	Monteiro Duarte CPV
24-09	Burkina Faso	L	0-1	Algiers	Fr			
26-09	Gabon	L	0-4	Algiers	Fr			
11-10	Madagascar	D	1-1	Antananarivo	WCq	Adjamonsi [74]	5 131	Maillet SEY
16-11	Madagascar	W	3-2	Cotonou	WCq	Tchomogo.O 3 [33p] [62] [90+2]	20 000	Imiere NGA
2004								
14-01	Tunisia	L	0-2	Djerba	Fr		6 000	
17-01	Tunisia	L	1-2	Tunis	Fr	Ahoueya [60]	25 000	
27-01	South Africa	L	0-2	Sfax	CNr1		12 000	Coulibaly MLI
31-01	Morocco	L	0-4	Sfax	CNr1		20 000	Maillet SEY
4-02	Nigeria	L	1-2	Sfax	CNr1	Latoundji [90]	15 000	Abd El Fatah EGY
20-05	Togo	L	0-1	Cotonou	Fr			
23-05	Togo	D	1-1	Lome	Fr	Amoussou [9]		
26-05	Burkina Faso	W	1-0	Cotonou	Fr	Maiga [75]		
6-06	Cameroon	L	1-2	Yaoundé	WCq	Tchomogo.S [11]	40 000	Mbera GAB
13-06	Burkina Faso	L	2-4	Ouagadougou	Fr	Amoussou [33], Adjamonsi [44p]		
20-06	Sudan	D	1-1	Cotonou	WCq	Ogunbiyi [30]	20 000	Guezzaz MAR
4-07	Egypt	D	3-3	Cotonou	WCq	Tchomogo.O [8p], Ahoueya [46], Ogunbiyi [68]	15 000	Chukwujekwu NGA
3-09	Libya	L	1-4	Tripoli	WCq	Osseni [12]	30 000	Kidane Tesfu ERI
3-10	Gabon	L	0-2	Libreville	Fr			
10-10	Côte d'Ivoire	L	0-1	Cotonou	WCq		25 000	Sowe GAM
2005								
27-03	Côte d'Ivoire	L	0-3	Abidjan	WCq		35 000	Guirat TUN
4-06	Cameroon	L	1-4	Cotonou	WCq	Agbessi [81]	20 000	El Arjoun MAR

Fr = Friendly match • CN = CAF African Cup of Nations • WCq = FIFA World Cup™ • q = qualifier • r1 = first round group

RECENT LEAGUE AND CUP RECORD

	Championship						Coupe de l'Independence		
Year	Champions	Pts	Runners-up	Pts	Third	Pts	Winners	Score	Runners-up
2000	No championship held						Mogas 90	1-0	Buffles Borgou
2001	No championship held						Buffles Borgou	1-0	Dragons
2002	Dragons	15	Requins	15	Postel	13	Jeunesse Pobe	0-0 1-1 4-3p	Mogas 90
2003	Dragons	21	Buffles Borgou	19	Postel	14	Mogas 90	1-0	Soleil
2004	Championship unfinished						Mogas 90	1-0	Requins

BENIN COUNTRY INFORMATION

Capital	Porto-Novo	Independence	1960	GDP per Capita	$1 100
Population	7 250 033	Status	Republic	GNP Ranking	135
Area km²	112 620	Language	French, Fon, Yoruba	Dialling code	+229
Population density	64 per km²	Literacy rate	40%	Internet code	.bj
% in urban areas	31%	Main religion	Indigenous 50%	GMT +/−	+1
Towns/Cities ('000)	Cotonou 690; Abomey 385; Porto Novo 234; Djougou 202; Parakou 163; Bohicon 125				
Neighbours (km)	Niger 226; Nigeria 773; Togo 644; Burkina Faso 306; Atlantic Ocean (Bight of Benin) 121				
Main stadia	Stade de l'Amitié – Cotonou 35 000; Stade Municipale – Porto Novo 20 000				

BER – BERMUDA

NATIONAL TEAM RECORD
JULY 1ST 2002 TO JUNE 30TH 2005

PL	W	D	L	F	A	%
18	5	3	10	37	33	36.1

FIFA/COCA-COLA WORLD RANKING

1993	1994	1995	1996	1997	1998	1999	2000	2001	2002	2003	2004	High		Low	
84	102	140	167	176	185	163	153	166	172	183	157	**76**	08/93	**185**	12/98

2004-2005											
08/04	09/04	10/04	11/04	12/04	01/05	02/05	03/05	04/05	05/05	06/05	07/05
161	160	159	159	157	157	156	158	158	159	156	157

Bermuda's 2006 FIFA World Cup™ qualifying campaign started with a bang as they demolished Montserrat 20-0 over two legs. The crushing victories set the side up for a second round clash with the more powerful El Salvador and Kenny Thompson's side rose to the challenge, leaving San Salvador with a creditable 2-1 defeat and hope for the return leg. However, in Hamilton they were leading 2-1 until the visitors won a penalty and duly equalised to force the draw and progress at their hosts' expense. The result was a boost for Bermuda though, whose national side had not played for nearly two years. Former Coventry City player Kyle Lightbourne was appointed coach

INTERNATIONAL HONOURS
None

and his first task was to take part in the Digicel Caribbean Cup. Bermuda won, drew and lost in their group to finish third and out of the competition. Refusing to leave without a fight, Bermuda questioned the nationality of three British Virgin Islands players although one of them, Avondale Williams, had played against Bermuda in 2000 without drawing any protest. The eight-team domestic League ended with Devonshire Cougars as champions after losing just twice, while North Village won the FA Cup for the fourth year in a row. Meanwhile, one of Bermuda's U-17 leagues was abandoned mid-season because of the increasing violence at matches.

THE FIFA BIG COUNT OF 2000

	Male	Female		Male	Female
Registered players	1 804	180	Referees	30	2
Non registered players	700	0	Officials	200	10
Youth players	1 500	30	Total involved	4 456	
Total players	4 214		Number of clubs	47	
Professional players	4	0	Number of teams	95	

Bermuda Football Association (BFA)
48 Cedar Avenue, Hamilton, HM 12, Bermuda
Tel +1 441 2952199   Fax +1 441 2950773
bfa@northrock.bm   www.bfa.bm
President: MUSSENDEN Larry   General Secretary: SABIR David
Vice-President: FURBERT Chris   Treasurer: O'BRIEN Delroy   Media Officer: None
Men's Coach: LIGHTBOURNE Kyle   Women's Coach: BROWN Vance
BFA formed: 1928   CONCACAF: 1966   FIFA: 1966
Colours: Blue, Blue, Blue

GAMES PLAYED BY BERMUDA IN THE 2006 FIFA WORLD CUP™ CYCLE

2002	Opponents	Score	Venue	Comp	Scorers	Att	Referee
No international matches played in 2002							
2003							
26-12	Barbados	L 1-2	Hamilton	Fr	Nusum [79]		Mouchette BER
2004							
1-01	Barbados	L 0-4	Hamilton	Fr			Raynor BER
10-02	Trinidad and Tobago	L 0-1	Hamilton	Fr		3 000	Raynor BER
12-02	Trinidad and Tobago	D 2-2	Hamilton	Fr	Smith.C [36], Simons [76]		Crockwell BER
29-02	Montserrat	W 13-0	Hamilton	WCq	Ming 3 [5 20 50], Nusum 3 [15 54 60], Smith.K [36], Bean.R 2 [41 52], Steede [43], Wade [77], Simons [83], Burgess [87]	3 000	Kennedy USA
21-03	Montserrat	W 7-0	Plymouth	WCq	Hill [15], Nusum 2 [21 44], Bean.R [39], Smith.K 2 [45 46], Ming [76]	250	Charles DOM
31-03	Nicaragua	W 3-0	Hamilton	Fr	Goater 2 [33 65p], Simons [90]		Crockwell BER
2-04	Nicaragua	W 2-1	Hamilton	Fr	Nusum 2 [47 67]		Raynor BER
28-04	Panama	L 1-4	Panama City	Fr	Ashwood [14]		
30-04	Nicaragua	L 0-2	Diriamba	Fr		800	
2-05	Nicaragua	L 0-2	Esteli	Fr			
13-06	El Salvador	L 1-2	San Salvador	WCq	Nusum [30]	12 000	Campos NCA
20-06	El Salvador	D 2-2	Hamilton	WCq	Burgess [5p], Nusum [21]	4 000	Whittaker CAY
24-11	Cayman Islands	W 2-1	Kingstown	GCq	Smith.K [4], Hill [34]	200	Mathews SKN
26-11	St Vincent/Grenadines	D 3-3	Kingstown	GCq	Smith.K [42], Lowe [82], Ming [90p]		
28-11	British Virgin Islands	L 0-2	Kingstown	GCq		400	Mathews SKN
2005							
25-05	Trinidad and Tobago	L 0-4	Port of Spain	Fr		400	
27-05	Trinidad and Tobago	L 0-1	Marabella	Fr			

Fr = Friendly match • GC = 2005 CONCACAF Gold Cup™ • WC = FIFA World Cup™ • q = qualifier

BERMUDA NATIONAL TEAM RECORDS AND RECORD SEQUENCES

Records			Sequence records					
Victory	13-0	MSR 2004	Wins	4	2004	Clean sheets	3	2004
Defeat	0-6	DEN 1969, CAN 1983	Defeats	6	1968-1969	Goals scored	17	1990-1992
Player Caps	n/a		Undefeated	7	1990-1991	Without goal	2	
Player Goals	n/a		Without win	10	1964-1969	Goals against	12	1968-1971

FIFA REFEREE LIST 2005

	Int'l	DoB
CROCKWELL Stuart	1995	9-03-1962

FIFA ASSISTANT REFEREE LIST 2005

	Int'l	DoB
MOUCHETTE Anthony	1998	21-07-1962

BERMUDA COUNTRY INFORMATION

Capital	Hamilton	Independence	British Crown Colony	GDP per Capita	$36 000
Population	64 935	Status		GNP Ranking	n/a
Area km²	53.3	Language	English	Dialling code	+1 441
Population density	1 218 per km²	Literacy rate	99%	Internet code	.bm
% in urban areas	100%	Main religion	Christian	GMT + / −	-4
Towns/Cities ('000)	Hamilton 1; St George 1				
Neighbours (km)	North Atlantic Ocean				
Main stadia	National Stadium – Hamilton 8 500; White Hill – Sandys				

BERMUDA 2004-05

PREMIER DIVISION

	Pl	W	D	L	F	A	Pts	Cougars	Dandy Town	Zebras	Blazers	Nth Village	Trojans	Eagles	Rangers
Devonshire Cougars	14	10	2	2	35	23	32		1-2	2-1	3-2	3-1	2-0	5-3	2-0
Dandy Town	14	9	3	2	33	16	30	2-2		2-2	1-1	2-0	3-0	3-2	3-0
PHC Zebras	14	8	2	4	32	18	26	1-2	1-2		1-0	2-0	1-2	3-2	2-2
Boulevard Blazers	14	6	3	5	23	21	21	3-3	1-0	1-4		2-1	1-1	2-0	4-1
North Village	14	7	0	7	24	23	21	0-3	2-1	0-3	1-0		4-1	5-1	5-1
Somerset Trojans	14	5	2	7	21	25	17	4-1	2-3	2-4	3-4	1-0		0-0	2-0
Somerset Eagles	14	2	3	9	17	32	9	2-3	1-3	0-3	1-0	2-3	1-0		1-1
Southampton Rangers	14	0	3	11	13	40	3	2-3	1-6	1-4	1-2	1-2	1-3	1-1	

3/10/2004 - 27/03/2005

FRIENDSHIP TROPHY 2004-05

Quarter-finals		Semi-finals		Final	
Devonshire Cougars	4				
Southampton Rangers	2	Devonshire Cougars	2		
Somerset Trojans	2 4p	Boulevard Blazers	1	3-04-2005	
Boulevard Blazers	2 5p			Devonshire Cougars	3
North Village †	2			PHC Zebras	1
Dandy Town	2	North Village	0		
Somerset Eagles	1	PHC Zebras	1		
PHC Zebras	4	† North Village qualified. Dandy Town withdrew			

FA CUP 2004-05

Round of sixteen		Quarter-finals		Semi-finals		Final	
North Village	3						
Boulevard Blazers	2	North Village	3 3				
Lobster Pot	0	Devonshire Cougars	3 2				
Devonshire Cougars	9			North Village	1		
MR Onions	1 2			PHC Zebras	0		
Southampton Rangers	1 1	MR Onions	0				
Dandy Town	1	PHC Zebras	3			North Village	2
PHC Zebras	3					Hamilton Parish	0
Somerset Trojans	4						
Wolves	1	Somerset Trojans	5				
Robin Hood	0	Ireland Rangers	0				
Ireland Rangers	3			Somerset Trojans	1		
Prospect	1			Hamilton Parish	2		
Valley	0	Prospect	1				
Key West Rangers	3 0	Hamilton Parish	3				
Hamilton Parish	3 1						

CUP FINAL

10-04-2005, Ref: Raynor
Scorers - Bean [69], Tankard [86] for North Village

RECENT LEAGUE AND CUP RECORD

	Championship							Cup		
Year	Champions	Pts	Runners-up	Pts	Third	Pts		Winners	Score	Runners-up
1997	Devonshire Colts	41	Vasco da Gama	34	Dandy Town	31		Boulevard Blazers	3-2	Wolves
1998	Vasco da Gama		Dandy Town		Boulevard Blazers			Vasco da Gama	2-1	Devonshire Colts
1999	Vasco da Gama	41	Dandy Town	33	North Village	32		Devonshire Colts	1-0	Dandy Town
2000	PHC Zebras	39	North Village	37	Dandy Town	32		North Village	2-1	Devonshire Colts
2001	Dandy Town	29	North Village	28	Devonshire Colts	26		Devonshire Colts	3-1	North Village
2002	North Village	27	Dandy Town	23	Devonshire Cougars	22		North Village	3-0	Dandy Town
2003	North Village	29	Devonshire Cougars	23	Boulevard Blazers	20		North Village	5-1	Prospect
2004	Dandy Town	31	Devonshire Cougars	30	Boulevard Blazers	25		North Village	3-3 2-1	Devonshire Cougars
2005	Devonshire Cougars	32	Dandy Town	30	PHC Zebras			North Village	2-0	Hamilton Parish

BFA – BURKINA FASO

NATIONAL TEAM RECORD
JULY 1ST 2002 TO JUNE 30TH 2005

PL	W	D	L	F	A	%
37	12	7	18	37	46	41.9

FIFA/COCA-COLA WORLD RANKING

1993	1994	1995	1996	1997	1998	1999	2000	2001	2002	2003	2004	High		Low	
127	97	101	107	106	75	71	69	78	75	78	84	62	08/98	127	12/93

2004-2005											
08/04	09/04	10/04	11/04	12/04	01/05	02/05	03/05	04/05	05/05	06/05	07/05
79	83	82	83	84	84	84	84	88	90	91	90

The rise of Burkina Faso over the past 10 years has been dramatic with the national side transformed from West African minnows to a side that has reached the CAF African Cup of Nations finals every time between 1996 and 2004. However, the Stallions' chances of continuing that impressive record looks under threat after a run of poor results in a tough qualifying group for the FIFA World Cup™ that also acts as a Nations Cup qualifying group. Even a change in coach with Frenchman Bernard Simondi replacing Ivica Todorov of Serbia didn't bring a positive outcome. As a result, Burkina Faso have slipped down the FIFA/Coca-Cola World Rankings from their high of

INTERNATIONAL HONOURS
None

62 seven years ago to 91. However, with the calibre of the two strikers Mamadou 'Bebeto' Zongo and Moumouni Dagano in the squad, the Stallions can look forward to more success. Rail Club du Kadiogo won the 2005 Championship, ending ASFA's hopes of a fourth consecutive title, whilst the end of season Coupe Nationale du Faso was won for the first time by USO. The successes of the Burkinabe junior sides have been impressive recently, but both the U-20 and U-17 sides failed to make an impact in the 2005 CAF competitions. The U-20s missed out on reaching the finals after defeat to Nigeria while the U-17s finished bottom of their group in the finals in Gambia.

THE FIFA BIG COUNT OF 2000

	Male	Female		Male	Female
Registered players	1 065	400	Referees	92	5
Non registered players	40 500	1 700	Officials	2 100	200
Youth players	555	350	Total involved	46 967	
Total players	44 570		Number of clubs	87	
Professional players	10	0	Number of teams	775	

Fédération Burkinabé de Foot-Ball (FBF)
01 Case postale 57, Ouagadougou 01, Burkina Faso
Tel +226 50 318815   Fax +226 50 318843
febefoo@fasonet.bf   www.fasofoot.com
President: DIAKITE Seydou   General Secretary: ZANGREYANOGHO Joseph
Vice-President: SAWADOGO Benoit   Treasurer: TRAORE SOME Clemence   Media Officer: BARRY Alpha
Men's Coach: BERNARD Simondi   Women's Coach: None
FBF formed: 1960   CAF: 1964   FIFA: 1964
Colours: Green/red/white, Green/red/white, Green/red/white

GAMES PLAYED BY BURKINA FASO IN THE 2006 FIFA WORLD CUP™ CYCLE

2002	Opponents	Score		Venue	Comp	Scorers	Att	Referee
8-09	Congo	D	0-0	Brazzaville	CNq		60 000	Itur KEN
12-10	Central African Rep	W	2-1	Ouagadougou	CNq	Toure.A [60], Minoungou [75]	25 000	Camara GUI
2003								
9-03	Benin	L	0-3	Cotonou	Fr			
26-03	Burundi	D	0-0	Bujumbura	Fr			
30-03	Mozambique	L	0-1	Maputo	CNq			Nunko MRI
29-05	Algeria	W	1-0	Amiens	Fr	Dagano [90]	1 050	Gannard FRA
7-06	Mozambique	W	4-0	Ouagadougou	CNq	Dagano 2 [6 8], Toure.A [34], Minoungou [88]	25 000	Ould Mohamed MTN
21-06	Congo	W	3-0	Ouagadougou	CNq	Toure.A [54p], Ouedraogo.R [61], Minoungou [75]	36 000	Mana NGA
6-07	Central African Rep	W	3-0	Bangui	CNq	Dagano 2 [30 71], Minoungou [90]		
24-09	Benin	W	1-0	Algiers	Fr	Balbone [57]		
26-09	Algeria	D	0-0	Algiers	Fr	L 3-4p	1 500	Benouza ALG
23-10	Zimbabwe	L	1-4	Hyderabad	AAG	Samba [16]		
25-10	Uzbekistan	L	0-1	Hyderabad	AAG			
27-10	Iran	W	2-1	Hyderabad	AAG			
8-11	Gabon	D	0-0	Moanda	Fr			
15-11	Morocco	L	0-1	Meknes	Fr		25 000	Boukhtir TUN
2004								
17-01	Egypt	D	1-1	Port Said	Fr	Dagano [35]	8 000	
20-01	Guinea	L	0-1	Sainte-Maxime	Fr			
26-01	Senegal	D	0-0	Tunis	CNr1		2 000	Guezzaz MAR
30-01	Mali	L	1-3	Tunis	CNr1	Minoungou [50]	1 500	Shelmani LBY
2-02	Kenya	L	0-3	Bizerte	CNr1		4 550	Sowe GAM
26-05	Benin	L	0-1	Cotonou	Fr			
30-05	Libya	W	3-2	Ouagadougou	Fr	Kone.Y [11], Kabore.I [34], Diabate [70]		
5-06	Ghana	W	1-0	Ouagadougou	WCq	Zongo [79]	25 000	Chukwujekwu NGA
13-06	Benin	W	4-2	Ouagadougou	Fr	Toure.A [41], Coulibaly.A [55], Dagano [89], Ouedraogo.A [90]		
20-06	Congo DR	L	2-3	Kinshasa	WCq	Toure.A [26], Dagano [85]	75 000	Djaoupe TOG
3-07	South Africa	L	0-2	Johannesburg	WCq		25 000	Ramanampamonjy MAD
17-08	Algeria	D	2-2	Blida	Fr	Zongo [50p], Ouedraogo.H [67]	15 000	Tahri MAR
4-09	Uganda	W	2-0	Ouagadougou	WCq	Dagano [34], Nikiema [79]	30 000	Lemghambodj MTN
9-10	Cape Verde Islands	L	0-1	Praia	WCq		6 000	Aziaka TOG
17-11	Morocco	L	0-4	Rabat	Fr		5 000	Keita.M MLI
2005								
9-02	Algeria	L	0-3	Algiers	Fr		3 000	Benaissa ALG
20-03	Korea Republic	L	0-1	Dubai	Fr			
26-03	Cape Verde Islands	L	1-2	Ouagadougou	WCq	Dagano [71]	27 500	Evehe CMR
29-05	Togo	L	0-1	Lome	Fr			
5-06	Ghana	L	1-2	Kumasi	WCq	Dagano [30]	11 920	Abd El Fatah EGY
18-06	Congo DR	W	2-0	Ouagadougou	WCq	Panandetiguiri [3], Dagano [68]	25 000	Shelmani LBY

Fr = Friendly match • CN = CAF African Cup of Nations • AAG = Afro-Asian Games • WC = FIFA World Cup™ • q = qualifier, r1 = first round group

BURKINA FASO NATIONAL TEAM RECORDS AND RECORD SEQUENCES

Records			Sequence records					
Victory	4-0	MOZ 2003	Wins	6	1988	Clean sheets	6	2003
Defeat	0-7	ALG 1981	Defeats	10	1976-1981	Goals scored	24	1998-2000
Player Caps	n/a		Undefeated	7	1999	Without goal	4	1978-81, 1986
Player Goals	n/a		Without win	13	1976-82, 1994-96	Goals against	13	1960-1967

BURKINA FASO COUNTRY INFORMATION

Capital	Ouagadougou	Independence	1960	GDP per Capita	$1 100
Population	13 574 820	Status	Republic	GNP Ranking	133
Area km²	274 200	Language	French	Dialling code	+226
Population density	49 per km²	Literacy rate	26%	Internet code	.bf
% in urban areas	27%	Main religion	Muslim 50%	GMT +/–	0
Towns/Cities ('000)	Ouagadougou 1 031; Bobo-Dioulasso 370; Koudougou 86; Banfora 63; Ouahigouya 61				
Neighbours (km)	Mali 1,000; Niger 628; Benin 306; Togo 126; Ghana 549; Côte d'Ivoire 584				
Main stadia	Stade du 4 Août – Ouagadougou 40 000; Stade Municipal – Bobo-Dioulasso 30 000				

FIFA REFEREE LIST 2005

	Int'l	DoB
BANAO Seydou	1997	11-06-1966
DIPAMA Pascal	2004	2-03-1965
ILBOUDO Serge	2004	22-06-1968
KANGBEGA Lambert	2003	3-01-1975
PARE Lassina	1997	27-08-1964
YAMEOGO Koudougou	2000	29-10-1961

FIFA ASSISTANT REFEREE LIST 2005

	Int'l	DoB
DIABY Lalama	2001	1-01-1967
KABRE Philemon	2002	14-05-1966
MILLOGO Brama	1993	21-03-1960
OUATTARA Aly	2002	23-08-1963
PARE Adolphe	2003	18-12-1970
PARE Lossene	1997	27-08-1964
TIEMTORE Amadou	2004	31-12-1963

BURKINA FASO 2004-05

PREMIERE DIVISION

	Pl	W	D	L	F	A	Pts	RCK	USO	USFA	EFO	ASFAY	Santos	USCO	ASFB	RCB	SONABEL	USFRAN	ASEC-K	JCB	Sanmatenga
Rail Club Kadiogo	26	16	9	1	38	8	57	–	0-1	1-1	1-0	1-0	2-2	3-0	1-0	0-0	3-0	**3-0**	1-0	3-0	2-1
US Ouagadougou	26	14	8	4	38	13	50	0-0	–	0-1	1-0	1-2	3-0	1-1	1-1	0-0	3-1	1-0	5-0	1-1	4-0
US Forces Armées	26	15	5	6	48	25	50	1-2	1-2	–	1-0	1-2	3-0	3-0	2-1	3-2	1-1	2-0	4-0	2-1	5-0
Etoile Filante	26	14	5	7	36	15	47	0-1	0-2	2-3	–	4-0	4-2	1-0	0-0	3-0	2-1	2-1	4-1	0-0	1-0
ASFA/Yennenga	26	13	7	6	40	20	46	0-1	0-0	1-1	0-1	–	0-0	2-0	1-0	2-1	5-1	1-1	4-1	2-1	4-1
Santos	26	11	9	6	42	37	42	0-2	2-3	1-4	1-0	1-1	–	3-3	3-2	3-2	1-1	2-1	1-0	5-1	3-2
US Comoé	26	9	10	7	23	23	37	0-0	1-0	2-1	0-1	1-0	0-0	–	1-0	1-0	2-0	0-0	0-1	0-0	1-0
ASF Bobo-Dioulasso	26	9	7	10	26	25	34	0-0	0-1	1-0	0-2	0-3	0-0	2-2	–	0-1	2-0	1-0	2-0	3-0	2-1
Racing Club B-D	26	9	6	11	28	28	33	0-0	2-0	1-1	0-2	1-0	0-1	2-2	0-3	–	0-1	0-0	2-1	3-0	2-0
AS SONABEL	26	10	2	14	22	45	32	1-5	0-2	1-0	0-4	0-4	1-4	2-1	0-1	1-0	–	0-3	2-0	3-1	1-0
USFRAN	26	4	10	12	20	29	22	0-2	0-2	2-2	0-0	0-1	0-0	0-0	1-2	1-2	0-2	–	2-1	3-1	3-0
ASEC Koudougou	26	3	10	13	12	41	19	0-0	0-0	1-2	0-0	0-0	0-3	1-1	1-1	**0-3**	1-0	1-1	–	0-0	1-0
Jeunesse Club B-D	26	2	8	16	19	55	14	1-4	0-4	0-1	0-3	0-4	2-2	0-3	0-1	1-3	0-1	1-1	1-1	–	5-2
Sanmatenga Kaya	26	2	6	18	14	44	12	0-0	0-0	1-2	0-0	1-1	0-2	0-1	3-1	2-1	0-1	0-0	0-0	0-1	–

11/12/2004 - 10/07/2005 • Matches in bold awarded 3-0

COUPE NATIONALE DU FASO 2004-05

Round of 16

US Ouagadougou	5
AS SONABEL *	1
Jeuness Club B-D *	0
Etoile Filante	3
US Comoé	1
Racing Club B-D *	0
BPFC Koudougou	0
ASFA/Yennenga *	1
Santos	2
AS Douanes *	0
US Forces Armeés	2
Rail Club Kadiogo *	0
USFRAN *	0 4p
ASF Bobo-Dioulasso	0 5p

Quarter-finals

US Ouagadougou *	1 5p
Etoile Filante	1 4p
US Comoé *	0
ASFA/Yennenga	1
Santos	†
US Forces Armeés *	0
ASF Bobo-Dioulasso	2

Semi-finals

US Ouagadougou *	1
ASFA/Yennenga	0
Santos *	1
ASF Bobo-Dioulasso	2

Final

US Ouagadougou	2
ASF Bobo-Dioulasso	0

CUP FINAL
5-08-2005
Stade du 4 Août, Ouagadougou

* Home team • † Bye

RECENT LEAGUE AND CUP RECORD

Championship

Year	Champions	Pts	Runners-up	Pts	Third	Pts
1997	Racing Club B-D					
1998	US Forces Armées		Etoile Filante			
1999	ASFA Yennenga	53	Etoile Filante	47	US Forces Armées	43
2000	US Forces Armées	44	Etoile Filante	41	ASFA Yennenga	39
2001	Etoile Filante	51	ASFA Yennenga	49	US Forces Armées	41
2002	ASFA Yennenga	49	US Forces Armées	44	Etoile Filante	39
2003	ASFA Yennenga	51	US Ouagadougou	47	Etoile Filante	45
2004	ASFA Yennenga	43	US Ouagadougou	40	Etoile Filante	39
2005	Rail Club Kadiogo	57	US Ouagadougou	50	US Forces Armées	50

Cup

	Winners	Score	Runners-up
1997	ASF Bobo-Dioulasso		
1998	ASF Bobo-Dioulasso	0-0 7-6p	USFRAN
1999	Etoile Filante	3-2	US Forces Armées
2000	Etoile Filante	3-1	US Ouagadougou
2001	Etoile Filante	3-1	ASF Bobo-Dioulasso
2002	US Forces Armées	2-0	ASF Bobo-Dioulasso
2003	Etoile Filante	0-0 5-4p	ASFA Yennenga
2004	ASF Bobo-Dioulasso	0-0 3-2p	US Forces Armées
2005	US Ouagadougou	2-0	ASF Bobo-Dioulasso

BHR – BAHRAIN

BAHRAIN NATIONAL TEAM RECORD
JULY 1ST 2002 TO JUNE 30TH 2005

PL	W	D	L	F	A	%
65	26	19	20	108	83	54.6

FIFA/COCA-COLA WORLD RANKING FOR BAHRAIN

1993	1994	1995	1996	1997	1998	1999	2000	2001	2002	2003	2004	High		Low	
78	73	99	118	121	119	136	138	110	105	64	49	**44**	09/04	138	12/00

2004-2005											
08/04	09/04	10/04	11/04	12/04	01/05	02/05	03/05	04/05	05/05	06/05	07/05
45	44	47	48	49	50	52	52	50	49	51	50

Fans in Bahrain have never known a spell quite like the one enjoyed by their national team since mid-2003. Such a volume of games played can often have a negative effect but coach Srecko Juricic used it to build a great team spirit that saw Bahrain qualify for the AFC Asian Cup for only the second time in their history. But that was just the start of the story because in China the Bahrainis exceeded all expectations by reaching the semi-finals where, in a thrilling match, they lost 3-4 to eventual winners Japan. The good form carried over into the 2006 FIFA World Cup™ qualifiers with Bahrain topping their first round group to qualify for the final stage of the Asian

INTERNATIONAL HONOURS
Qualified for the AFC Asian Cup finals 1988 2004 Represented at the Asian Games 1974 1978 1986 1994 2002

qualifiers. It was with some surprise that Juricic quit in March 2005 to be replaced by former coach Wolfgang Sidka. His failure to secure an automatic place in the finals brought to an end his brief spell in charge and it was left to the Belgian Luka Peruzovic to guide the team through the play-offs. Some of the Bahraini players, notably key striker Alaa Ahmed Hubail, play in the strong Q-League in Qatar and this has helped raise standards in the country but the League in Bahrain has also grown in strength in recent years. In 2005 Riffa reclaimed the title they lost in 2004 from Muharraq, whose disappointment was tempered by triumphs in both cup competitions.

THE FIFA BIG COUNT OF 2000

	Male	Female		Male	Female
Registered players	770	0	Referees	98	0
Non registered players	1 650	0	Officials	616	0
Youth players	2 970	0	Total involved	6 104	
Total players	5 390		Number of clubs	44	
Professional players	0	0	Number of teams	110	

Bahrain Football Association (BFA)
Bahrain National Stadium, PO Box 5464, Manama, Bahrain
Tel +973 17 689569   Fax +973 17 781188
bhrfa@batelco.com.bh   www.bahrainfootball.org
President: AL-KHALIFA Sheik Salman Bin Ibrahim   General Secretary: JASSEM Ahmed Mohammed
Vice-President: AL-KHALIFA Sheik Ali Bin Khalifa   Treasurer: ABBAS Abdul Razzaq Mohd.   Media Officer: MADKOOR Majid
Men's Coach: PERUZOVIC Luka   Women's Coach: SANNSARU Taqawi
BFA formed: 1957   AFC: 1970   FIFA: 1966
Colours: Red, Red, Red or White, White, White

GAMES PLAYED BY BAHRAIN IN THE 2006 FIFA WORLD CUP™ CYCLE

2002	Opponents	Score		Venue	Comp	Scorers	Att	Referee
23-11	Iraq	D	2-2	Doha	Fr	Ghuloom [7], Al Dosari.R [56p]		Al Hail QAT
7-12	Jordan	L	0-3	Manama	Fr			Al Dosari KSA
9-12	Syria	L	2-3	Manama	Fr	Talib [30], Al Dosari.R [32p]		Al Hail QAT
12-12	China PR	D	2-2	Manama	Fr	Salmeen [22], Mohammed Hussain [36]		Shaban KUW
17-12	Saudi Arabia	L	1-2	Kuwait City	ARr1	Yousuf [44]	7 000	Guezzaz MAR
19-12	Syria	W	2-0	Kuwait City	ARr1	Talib [82], Al Dosari.R [90p]		Shaban KUW
21-12	Yemen	W	3-1	Kuwait City	ARr1	Talib 3 [45 83 90]	1 000	El Beltagi EGY
26-12	Lebanon	D	0-0	Kuwait City	ARr1		1 000	Guirat TUN
28-12	Jordan	W	2-1	Kuwait City	ARsf	Ali Ahmed.H 2 [85 90]	2 000	Shaban KUW
30-12	Saudi Arabia	L	0-1	Kuwait City	ARf		7 500	Zekrini ALG
2003								
10-09	Oman	L	0-1	Muscat	Fr			
19-09	Lebanon	W	4-3	Manama	Fr	Hubail.A [17], Yousuf [19], Al Marzouqi [37], Ali Ahmed.H [63]		
27-09	United Arab Emirates	W	4-1	Sharjah	Fr	Bilal [18], Ghuloom [49], Yousuf [57], Jamal [88]		
8-10	Iraq	L	1-5	Kuala Lumpur	ACq	Farhan [71]		Matsumura JPN
10-10	Myanmar	W	3-1	Kuala Lumpur	ACq	Yousuf [14], Hubail.A [49], Ali Ahmed.H [76]		Nagalingham SIN
12-10	Malaysia	D	2-2	Kuala Lumpur	ACq	Ebrahim [5], Husain Bahzad [45]		Matsumura JPN
20-10	Myanmar	W	4-0	Manama	ACq	Al Marzouqi [22], Ali Ahmed.H [27], Jalal [44], Farhan [45p]		Al Harrassi OMA
22-10	Malaysia	W	3-1	Manama	ACq	Ali Ahmed.H 2 [30 45], Yousuf [39p]		Najm LIB
24-10	Iraq	W	1-0	Manama	ACq	Hubail.A [12]		Al Saeedi UAE
12-12	Iraq	D	2-2	Manama	Fr	Ghuloom [12], Hubail.A [33]	15 000	
15-12	Egypt	L	0-1	Manama	Fr		20 000	
18-12	Kenya	W	2-1	Manama	Fr	Jamal [82], Baba [90]		
27-12	Qatar	D	0-0	Kuwait City	GC			Kassai HUN
30-12	Yemen	W	5-1	Kuwait City	GC	Salmeen [2], Hubail.A 2 [19 47], Yousuf [40], Al Dosari.R [75]		Al Hamdan KSA
2004								
1-01	Saudi Arabia	L	0-1	Kuwait City	GC			
3-01	Oman	W	1-0	Kuwait City	GC	Salmeen [13]		
7-01	UAE	W	3-1	Kuwait City	GC	Farhan [27], Yousuf 2 [28 60]		
10-01	Kuwait	W	4-0	Kuwait City	GC	Yousuf 2 [6 65], Hubail [17], Salmeen [51]		
8-02	Lebanon	L	1-2	Beirut	Fr	Yousuf [5]		
13-02	Qatar	L	0-2	Doha	Fr			
18-02	Syria	W	2-1	Muharraq	WCq	Hubail.A 2 [64 73]	5 000	Khanthama THA
21-03	Jordan	D	0-0	Muharraq	Fr			
23-03	Jordan	L	0-2	Muharraq	Fr			
31-03	Tajikistan	D	0-0	Dushanbe	WCq		17 000	Maidin SIN
26-05	Lebanon	D	2-2	Beirut	Fr	Yousuf [33], Ali Ahmed.H [41]		
31-05	United Arab Emirates	W	3-2	Dubai	Fr			
9-06	Kyrgyzstan	W	5-0	Muharraq	WCq	Hubail.A 3 [12 45 60], Ali Ahmed.H [66], Duaij [82]	2 800	Al Saeedi UAE
5-07	Thailand	W	2-0	Bangkok	Fr	Hubail.A, Ali Ahmed.H		
10-07	Korea Republic	L	0-2	Gwangju	Fr		35 241	Fong HKG
17-07	China PR	D	2-2	Beijing	ACr1	Hubail.M [41], Ali Ahmed.H [89]	40 000	Mohd Salleh MAS
21-07	Qatar	D	1-1	Beijing	ACr1	Hubail.M [90]		Kamizawa JPN
25-07	Indonesia	W	3-1	Jinan	ACr1	Ali Ahmed.H [43], Hubail.A [57], Yousuf [82]	20 000	Codjia BEN
30-07	Uzbekistan	D	2-2	Chengdu	ACqf	Hubail.A 2 [71 76]	18 000	Kwon KOR
3-08	Japan	L	3-4	Jinan	ACsf	Hubail.A 2 [6 71], Duaij [85]		Maidin SIN
6-08	Iran	L	2-4	Beijing	AC3p	Yousuf [48], Farhan [57]		Al Marzouqi UAE
26-08	Kuwait	D	0-0	Muharraq	Fr			
2-09	Palestine	W	1-0	Muharraq	Fr			
8-09	Kyrgyzstan	W	2-1	Bishkek	WCq	Ali Ahmed.H [23], Hubail.M [58]	10 000	Rungklay THA
13-10	Syria	D	2-2	Damascus	WCq	Mahfoodh [27], Mohamed.T [90+2]	35 000	Moradi IRN
17-11	Tajikistan	W	4-0	Manama	WCq	Mohamed.T [9], Mohamed.H [40], Hubail.M 2 [42 77]	15 000	Sun CHN
1-12	Finland	L	1-2	Manama	Fr	Ali Ahmed.H [6]	10 000	
3-12	Latvia	D	2-2	Manama	Fr	Mohammed.S 2 [?], Ali Ahmed.H [72], W 4-2p	2 000	Al Hilali OMA
11-12	Yemen	D	1-1	Doha	GCr1	Yousuf [25]		
14-12	Kuwait	D	1-1	Doha	GCr1	Ali Ahmed.H [45]		

GAMES PLAYED BY BAHRAIN IN THE 2006 FIFA WORLD CUP™ CYCLE (CONT'D)

2004	Opponents		Score	Venue	Comp	Scorers	Att	Referee
17-12	Saudi Arabia	W	3-0	Doha	GCr1	Al Marzouki [64], Ghuloom [78], Yousef [90]		
20-12	Oman	L	2-3	Doha	GCsf	Jalal [51], Duaij [77]		
23-12	Kuwait	W	3-1	Doha	GC3p	Nada OG [31], Hubail.A [56], Duaij [90]		
2005	Opponents							
25-01	Norway	L	0-1	Manama	Fr			
2-02	Lebanon	W	2-1	Doha	Fr	Jamil, Ali Ahmed.H		
9-02	Iran	D	0-0	Manama	WCq		25 000	Mohd Salleh MAS
25-03	Korea DPR	W	2-1	Pyongyang	WCq	Ali Ahmed.H 2 [7 58]	50 000	Rungklay THA
30-03	Japan	L	0-1	Saitama	WCq		67 549	Irmatov UZB
27-05	Saudi Arabia	D	1-1	Riyadh	Fr	Adnan [18p]		
3-06	Japan	L	0-1	Manama	WCq		32 000	Mohd Salleh MAS
8-06	Iran	L	0-1	Tehran	WCq		80 000	Kwon Jong Chul KOR

Fr = Friendly match • AR = Arab Cup • AC = AFC Asian Cup • GC = Gulf Cup • WC = FIFA World Cup™
q = qualifier • r1 = first round group • qf = quarter-final • sf = semi-final • f = final • 3p = third place play-off

BAHRAIN NATIONAL TEAM RECORDS AND RECORD SEQUENCES

Records			Sequence records				
Victory	6-0	SRI 1991	Wins	5	2001	Clean sheets	5	1988
Defeat	1-10	IRQ 1966	Defeats	9	1974-1975	Goals scored	9	1996-1998
Player Caps	n/a		Undefeated	6	1993, 2001	Without goal	7	1988-1990
Player Goals	n/a		Without win	12	1988-1990	Goals against	12	1974-1976

FIFA REFEREE LIST 2005

	Int'l	DoB
AL DELAWAR Rahman	2001	26-04-1964
AL DOSERI Khalifa		5-04-1963
AL KHABBAZ Jaafar Mahdi	1999	30-10-1967
ALI Hasan	2005	1-01-1970
EBRAHIM Abdulhameed	1998	30-12-1962
HUSAIN Yousuf		21-12-1969
KARIM Jasim		28-05-1967
MAHFOODH Jaafar	2005	16-12-1975
MOHAMED Khalid	2005	1-01-1968
ZUHAIR Ali Salman		29-11-1967

FIFA ASSISTANT REFEREE LIST 2005

	Int'l	DoB
AL ALLAN Khaled		4-11-1973
AL-ALI Saad Sultan		15-11-1960
ALWAZEER Yusuf	2005	1-01-1965
EBRAHIM Sameer		1-01-1968
HASAN Abdul	1998	30-11-1962
HUSAIN Akber		1-01-1967
MALALLA Ali	1998	29-11-1960
MOHAISH Khalifa	2005	1-01-1967
MOHAMED Jaafar		18-11-1965

BAHRAIN COUNTRY INFORMATION

Capital	Manama	Independence	1971	GDP per Capita	$16 900
Population	677 886	Status	Kingdom	GNP Ranking	101
Area km²	665	Language	Arabic	Dialling code	+973
Population density	1 019 per km²	Literacy rate	89%	Internet code	.bh
% in urban areas	90%	Main religion	Muslim 100%	GMT + / −	+3
Towns/Cities ('000)	Manama 147; Al-Muharraq 97; Al-Riffa 94; Madinat 65; Al-Wusta 51; Ali 55; Issa 38				
Neighbours (km)	Persian Gulf 161				
Main stadia	National Stadium – Manama 30 000; Issa Town – Issa 20 000; Al Muharraq – Muharraq 10 000				

BAHRAIN 2005

FIRST DIVISION

	Pl	W	D	L	F	A	Pts	Riffa	Muharraq	Al Ahli	Al Shabab	Al Namja	Busaiteen	Bahrain	East Riffa	Manama	Al Hala
Riffa	18	13	1	4	40	18	40		2-2	3-2	4-1	1-0	2-1	2-0	3-1	4-2	1-2
Muharraq	18	10	6	2	36	18	36	1-2		2-1	0-0	1-1	3-1	2-1	4-1	3-1	2-0
Al Ahli	18	10	3	5	30	26	33	1-0	0-0		2-2	0-3	1-0	2-1	3-2	3-4	2-1
Al Shabab	18	9	5	4	33	28	32	1-5	0-2	2-3		3-1	0-0	5-2	2-1	1-1	2-1
Al Najma	18	9	4	5	33	18	31	1-0	2-2	0-2	0-1		3-1	3-0	1-1	2-1	3-0
Busaiteen	18	6	5	7	25	28	23	3-0	2-2	1-1	2-2	1-5		3-0	1-0	3-2	2-1
Bahrain	18	5	3	10	21	30	18	0-2	1-2	**3-0**	1-2	1-0	3-1		1-1	3-1	2-2
East Riffa	18	5	2	11	26	33	17	0-2	3-1	1-3	1-3	1-4	0-1	0-1		1-0	5-1
Manama	18	4	3	11	22	41	15	0-4	0-5	1-2	1-2	1-1	0-0	2-1	1-4		2-1
Al Hala	18	2	2	14	16	42	8	0-3	0-2	0-2	1-4	1-3	3-2	0-0	1-3	1-2	

5/01/2005 - 6/05/2005 • Match in bold awarded 3-0

BAHRAIN 2004 SECOND DIVISION

	Pl	W	D	L	F	A	Pts
Setra	14	11	1	2	28	6	34
Malikiya	14	10	2	2	29	5	32
Al Tadamun	14	8	3	3	20	10	27
Al Sahel	14	6	3	5	28	18	21
Al Ittihad	14	5	3	6	19	22	18
Issa Town	14	6	0	8	16	27	18
Budaia	14	2	2	10	5	35	8
Al Ittifaq	14	1	0	13	11	33	3

8/01/2005 - 8/05/2005

FA CUP 2004

Semi-finals		Final	
Muharraq	4	18-12-2004	
Al Ahli	2	**Muharraq**	2
Bahrain	1	Busaiteen	1
Busaiteen	3		

1st round consisted of three groups of six teams

CROWN PRINCE CUP 2005

Semi-finals		Final	
Riffa	2	16-05-2005	
Al Shabab	1	**Riffa**	3
Muharraq	0	Al Ahli	1
Al Ahli	2		

Played between the top four in the League

KINGS CUP 2005

Quarter-finals		Semi-finals		Final
Muharraq	2			
Setra	0	**Muharraq**	1	
Al Najma	1	Al Ahli	0	20-06-2005
Al Ahli	2			**Muharraq**
Riffa	3			Al Shabab
Al Sahel	2	Riffa	1	
East Riffa	1	**Al Shabab**	3	
Al Shabab	3			

RECENT LEAGUE AND CUP RECORD

	Championship						King's Cup		
Year	Champions	Pts	Runners-up	Pts	Third	Pts	Winners	Score	Runners-up
1996	Al Ahli	9	Muharraq	6	Bahrain	3	Muharraq	0-0 4-3p	Bahrain
1997	West Riffa						Muharraq	2-1	East Riffa
1998	West Riffa	45	Muharraq	38	East Riffa	36	West Riffa	2-1	Budaia
1999	Muharraq	39	Al-Ahli	30	West Riffa	28	East Riffa	1-0	Al-Hala
2000	West Riffa	4-0	East Riffa				East Riffa	3-1	Qadisiya
2001	Muharraq	52	Besaiteen	45	West Riffa	40	Al-Ahli	1-0	Essa Town
2002	Muharraq	46	Al-Ahli	46	Riffa	36	Muharraq	0-0 4-2p	Al-Ahli
2003	Riffa	40	Muharraq	34	Al-Ahli	32	Al-Ahli	2-1	Muharraq
2004	Muharraq	48	Riffa	36	Al-Ahli	30	Al Shabab	2-1	Busaiteen
2005	Riffa	40	Muharraq	36	Al Ahli	33	Muharraq	1-0	Al Shabab

BHU – BHUTAN

NATIONAL TEAM RECORD
JULY 1ST 2002 TO JUNE 30TH 2005

PL	W	D	L	F	A	%
11	1	1	9	6	37	13.6

FIFA/COCA-COLA WORLD RANKING

1993	1994	1995	1996	1997	1998	1999	2000	2001	2002	2003	2004	High		Low	
-	-	-	-	-	-	-	201	202	199	187	187	**187**	12/03	**202**	05/01

2004-2005											
08/04	09/04	10/04	11/04	12/04	01/05	02/05	03/05	04/05	05/05	06/05	07/05
189	189	188	187	187	188	188	188	188	188	188	188

With archery the national sport in Bhutan, a visit by FIFA officials in June 2005 revealed that football suffered from "no marketing, virtually no sponsors and negligible government aid" leaving the football authorities to survive on the FIFA grant alone. As with many smaller nations FIFA is helping to build a new headquarters for the national association along with a youth academy and a new pitch, all in one location, with most of the US$500,000 coming from the FIFA Goal programme. A long-term development plan is, however, being drafted which should see national team coach Khare Basnet able to arrange more fixtures for the national team, which has been

INTERNATIONAL HONOURS
None

inactive since the AFC Asian Cup qualifiers in October 2003. Both the U-17 and U-20 teams did enter the 2004 Asian qualifiers and although both finished bottom of their groups the U-20s did manage a draw against Sri Lanka. The Bhutan Football Federation organises a number of competitions across age ranges for both men and women, including a senior Championship which in 2004 was won by Transport United. They deposed Druk Pol, the team of the Royal Bhutan Police, who are traditionally the strongest outfit in the country. For the 2005 season the championship has been extended from four to seven teams playing on a traditional round robin format.

THE FIFA BIG COUNT OF 2000

	Male	Female		Male	Female
Registered players	500	0	Referees	50	0
Non registered players	1 000	0	Officials	100	0
Youth players	500	0	Total involved	2 150	
Total players	2 000		Number of clubs	30	
Professional players	0	0	Number of teams	60	

Bhutan Football Federation (BFF)
PO Box 365, Thimphu, Bhutan
Tel +975 2 322350   Fax +975 2 321131
bff@druknet.net.bt   www.none
President: WANGCHUK Lyonpo Khandu HE   General Secretary: WANGCHUK Ugyen
Vice-President: TSHERING Dasho Gyom   Treasurer: DORJI B.T.   Media Officer: None
Men's Coach: BASNET Khare   Women's Coach: None
BFF formed: 1983   AFC: 1993   FIFA: 2000
Colours: Yellow, Yellow, Yellow or Red, Red, Red

GAMES PLAYED BY BHUTAN IN THE 2006 FIFA WORLD CUP™ CYCLE

2002	Opponents	Score		Venue	Comp	Scorers	Att	Referee
No international matches played in 2002 after June								
2003								
11-01	Maldives	L	0-6	Dhaka	SAFr1			Vidanagamage SRI
13-01	Nepal	L	0-2	Dhaka	SAFr1		25 000	Magheshwaran IND
15-01	Bangladesh	L	0-3	Dhaka	SAFr1		15 000	Magheshwaran IND
23-04	Guam	W	6-0	Thimphu	ACq	Dorji 2 [31 33], Chetri [59], Tshering [76p], Chophel [88] Nedup [89]		
27-04	Mongolia	D	0-0	Thimphu	ACq			
6-10	Indonesia	L	0-2	Jeddah	ACq			
8-10	Saudi Arabia	L	0-6	Jeddah	ACq			
10-10	Yemen	L	0-8	Jeddah	ACq			
13-10	Indonesia	L	0-2	Jeddah	ACq			
15-10	Saudi Arabia	L	0-4	Jeddah	ACq			
17-10	Yemen	L	0-4	Jeddah	ACq			
2004								
No international matches played in 2004								
2005								
No international matches played in 2005 before August								

SAF = South Asian Football Federation Cup • AC = AFC Asian Cup • q = qualifier • r1 = first round group

BHUTAN NATIONAL TEAM RECORDS AND RECORD SEQUENCES

Records			Sequence records					
Victory	6-0	GUM 2003	Wins	1		Clean sheets	2	2003
Defeat	0-20	KUW 2000	Defeats	15	1984-2001	Goals scored	3	2000-2003
Player Caps	n/a		Undefeated	2	2003	Without goal	7	2003-
Player Goals	n/a		Without win	15	1984-2001	Goals against	15	1984-2001

FIFA ASSISTANT REFEREE LIST 2005

	Int'l	DoB
CHOPHEL Tshering	2005	1-09-1969
DORJI Kinley	2005	2-12-1981
YESHI Karma	2005	12-09-1974

RECENT LEAGUE RECORD

Year	Champions
1996	Druk Pol
1997	Druk Pol
1998	Druk Pol
1999	Druk Pol
2000	Druk Pol
2001	Druk Pol
2002	Druk Star
2003	Druk Pol
2004	Transport United

BHUTAN COUNTRY INFORMATION

Capital	Thimphu	Independence	1949	GDP per Capita	$1 300
Population	2 185 569	Status	Kingdom	GNP Ranking	170
Area km²	47 000	Language	Dzongkha	Dialling code	+975
Population density	46 per km²	Literacy rate	44%	Internet code	.bt
% in urban areas	6%	Main religion	Buddhist 70%	GMT +/−	+6
Towns/Cities ('000)	Thimphu 66; Phuntsholing 65; Punakha 18; Samdrup Jongkhar 14; Geylegphug 7; Jakar 4				
Neighbours (km)	China 470; India 605				
Main stadia	Changlimithang – Thimphu 15 000; PSA Phuntsholing – Phuntsholing 6 000				

BIH – BOSNIA-HERZEGOVINA

NATIONAL TEAM RECORD
JULY 1ST 2002 TO JUNE 30TH 2005

PL	W	D	L	F	A	%
22	7	8	7	22	26	50

FIFA/COCA-COLA WORLD RANKING

1993	1994	1995	1996	1997	1998	1999	2000	2001	2002	2003	2004	High	Low
-	-	-	152	99	96	75	78	69	87	59	79	**53** 10/03	**173** 09/96

2004-2005											
08/04	09/04	10/04	11/04	12/04	01/05	02/05	03/05	04/05	05/05	06/05	07/05
76	69	81	79	79	79	78	77	81	81	78	77

Having come so desperately close to qualifying for UEFA EURO 2004™, Bosnia-Herzegovina were hopeful of an equally good 2006 FIFA World Cup™ qualifying campaign and had it not been for a Spanish equaliser six minutes into injury time in Valencia their prospects of reaching the finals in Germany would have been very much better in what has turned out to be a very close group. With many of the top players based in Germany, notably Hasan Salihamidzic at Bayern, Sergej Barbarez at Hamburger SV and Zvjezdan Misimovic at Bochum, the squad is capable of causing an upset against anyone and the fact that the different ethnic factions in the association

INTERNATIONAL HONOURS
None

have now been unified can only make the team stronger. The area where this has had the biggest impact has been in the League which in 2005 produced the fourth different winner in the five seasons it has been running. Zrinjski Mostar led from the start, in a two-way race with Zeljeznicar from Sarajevo, to win their first title but the remarkable thing about the League was that only five points separated relegated Borac Banja Luka and deposed champions Siroki in third place. With only 28 away wins recorded all season – 11 of them by the top two – home advantage is a big factor in the League.

THE FIFA BIG COUNT OF 2000

	Male	Female		Male	Female
Registered players	12 290	162	Referees	776	0
Non registered players	37 000	800	Officials	11 990	510
Youth players	30 430	109	Total involved	94 067	
Total players	80 791		Number of clubs	775	
Professional players	420	0	Number of teams	1 980	

Football Federation of Bosnia-Herzegovina (FFBH)

Nogometni/Fudbalski Savez Bosne i Hercegovine, Ferhadija 30, Sarajevo - 71000, Bosnia-Herzegovina
Tel +387 33 276660   Fax +387 33 444332
nsbih@bih.net.ba   www.nsbih.ba
President: DOMINKOVIC Iljo   General Secretary: USANOVIC Munib
Vice-President: JAHIC Fadil   Treasurer: KURES Miodrag   Media Officer: PECIKOZA Slavica
Men's Coach: SLISKOVIC Blaz   Women's Coach: BEKIC Dzevad
FFBH formed: 1992   UEFA: 1996   FIFA: 1996
Colours: White, Blue, White or Blue, White, Blue

GAMES PLAYED BY BOSNIA-HERZEGOVINA IN THE 2006 FIFA WORLD CUP™ CYCLE

2002	Opponents	Score		Venue	Comp	Scorers	Att	Referee
21-08	Yugoslavia	L	0-2	Sarajevo	Fr		9 000	Siric CRO
7-09	Romania	L	0-3	Sarajevo	ECq		4 000	Batista POR
11-10	Germany	D	1-1	Sarajevo	Fr	Baljic 21	5 000	De Santis ITA
16-10	Norway	L	0-2	Oslo	ECq		24 169	Benes CZE
2003								
12-02	Wales	D	2-2	Cardiff	Fr	Baljic 5, Barbarez 64	25 000	Malcolm NIR
29-03	Luxembourg	W	2-0	Zenica	ECq	Bolic 53, Barbarez 79	10 000	Hyytia FIN
2-04	Denmark	W	2-0	Copenhagen	ECq	Barbarez 23, Baljic 29	30 845	Stredak SVK
7-06	Romania	L	0-2	Craiova	ECq		36 000	Bossen NED
6-09	Norway	W	1-0	Zenica	ECq	Bajramovic 86	18 000	Bre FRA
10-09	Luxembourg	W	1-0	Luxembourg	ECq	Barbarez 36	3 500	Kapitanis CYP
11-10	Denmark	D	1-1	Sarajevo	ECq	Bolic 39	35 500	Barber ENG
2004								
18-02	Macedonia FYR	L	0-1	Skopje	Fr		8 000	Vrajkov BUL
31-03	Luxembourg	W	2-1	Luxembourg	Fr	Misimovic 63, Bolic 71	2 000	Rogalla SUI
28-04	Finland	W	1-0	Zenica	Fr	Misimovic 88	20 000	Bozinovski MKD
18-08	France	D	1-1	Rennes	Fr	Grlic 37	26 527	McDonald SCO
8-09	Spain	D	1-1	Zenica	WCq	Bolic 79	14 380	De Santis ITA
9-10	Serbia & Montenegro	D	0-0	Sarajevo	WCq		22 440	Veissiere FRA
2005								
2-02	Iran	L	1-2	Tehran	Fr	Bolic 17	15 000	
26-03	Belgium	L	1-4	Brussels	WCq	Bolic 1	36 700	Hrinak SVK
30-03	Lithuania	D	1-1	Sarajevo	WCq	Misimovic 21	6 000	Baskakov RUS
4-06	San Marino	W	3-1	Serravalle	WCq	Salihamidzic 2 17 38, Barbarez 75	750	Demirlek TUR
8-06	Spain	D	1-1	Valencia	WCq	Misimovic 39	38 041	Bennett ENG

Fr = Friendly match • EC = UEFA EURO 2004™ • WC = FIFA World Cup™ • q = qualifier

NATIONAL CAPS

	Caps
BOLIC Elvir	46
SALIHAMIDZIC Hasan	40
BALJIC Elvir	39
KONJIC Muhamed	38
BARBAREZ Sergej	36
HIBIC Mirsad	36

NATIONAL GOALS

	Goals
BOLIC Elvir	16
BALJIC Elvir	14
BARBAREZ Sergej	12
SALIHAMIDZIC Hasan	6
MISIMOVIC Zvjezdan	4
KODRO Meho	3
KONJIC Muhamed	3

NATIONAL COACH

	Years
MUZUROVIC Fuad	1995-'98
MUSOVIC Dzemaludin	1998-'99
HADZIBEGIC Faruk	1999
SMAJLOVIC Drago	1999-'01
SLISKOVIC Blaz	2002-

FIFA REFEREE LIST 2005

	Int'l	DoB
MRKOVIC Rusmir	2003	2-07-1968
PANIC Novo	2003	4-01-1970
ZRNIC Sinisa	2001	15-06-1970

FIFA ASSISTANT REFEREE LIST 2005

	Int'l	DoB
CULE Drago	2003	4-07-1966
LEPIR Goran	2003	22-03-1966
MIRIC Miroslav	2003	6-11-1966
SELIMOVIC Edin	1999	7-07-1964
STANIC Mato	2003	9-12-1967
TUTUN Mujo	2002	1-10-1965

BOSNIA-HERZEGOVINA COUNTRY INFORMATION

Capital	Sarajevo	Independence	1992	GDP per Capita	$6 100
Population	4 007 608	Status	Republic	GNP Ranking	114
Area km²	51 129	Language	Bosnian, Croatian, Serbian	Dialling code	+387
Population density	78 per km²	Literacy rate	93%	Internet code	.ba
% in urban areas	49%	Main religion	Christian 46%, Muslim 40%	GMT + / −	+1
Towns/Cities ('000)		Sarajevo 696; Banja Luka 221; Zenica 164; Tuzla 142; Mostar 104; Bihac 75; Bugojno 41; Brcko 38; Bijeljina 37; Prijedor 36, Trebinje 33; Travnik 31; Doboj 27; Cazin 21;			
Neighbours (km)	Croatia 932; Serbia and Montenegro 527; Adriatic Sea 20				
Main stadia	Olimpijski Kosevo – Sarajevo 37 500; Bijeli Brijeg – Mostar 20 000				

BOSNIA-HERZEGOVINA NATIONAL TEAM RECORDS AND RECORD SEQUENCES

Records			Sequence records					
Victory	5-0	LIE 2001	Wins	3	1999-2000	Clean sheets	2	Five times
Defeat	0-5	ARG 1998	Defeats	3	Four times	Goals scored	10	1998-1999
Player Caps	46	BOLIC Elvir	Undefeated	4	1997, 2004	Without goal	3	Three times
Player Goals	16	BOLIC Elvir	Without win	7	2002-2003	Goals against	7	2002-2003

BOSNIA-HERZEGOVINA 2004-05

PREMIER LIGE

	Pl	W	D	L	F	A	Pts	Zrinjski	Zeljeznicar	Siroki	Sarajevo	Travnik	Modrica	Orasje	Buducnost	Posusje	Sloboda	Slavija	Zepce	Celik	Leotar	Borac	Rudar
Zrinjski Mostar †	30	19	4	7	56	30	61		1-0	0-0	2-0	5-0	0-0	2-1	2-0	5-0	1-0	3-2	3-0	3-1	2-0	4-3	2-1
Zeljeznicar Sarajevo ‡	30	15	6	9	31	22	51	2-1		3-0	1-1	2-0	2-1	3-0	2-0	1-0	1-0	0-0	1-2	1-0	1-0	1-2	0-0
Siroki Brijeg	30	12	9	9	42	33	45	2-3	1-0		2-0	2-2	1-3	1-1	4-0	1-0	0-0	3-2	3-0	3-1	1-0	2-0	2-1
Sarajevo ‡	30	13	6	11	39	37	45	2-3	0-1	3-2		2-4	0-0	3-0	2-1	2-0	2-0	2-1	4-1	1-0	2-1	2-1	
Travnik	30	14	2	14	42	47	44	1-2	2-0	2-3	0-0		4-1	3-1	4-1	4-1	1-0	2-0	3-1	1-0	1-0	2-1	3-1
Modrica Maksima	30	11	9	10	38	32	42	1-0	1-2	1-1	0-0	2-1		1-1	2-0	4-0	2-2	1-0	4-0	0-0	2-0	1-0	2-0
Orasje	30	13	3	14	45	43	42	1-3	1-2	2-1	5-3	3-0	1-1		2-0	4-0	2-1	2-1	1-0	3-1	3-1	3-0	4-1
Buducnost	30	13	3	14	37	40	42	2-0	1-1	**0-3**	3-0	3-0	3-1	1-0		3-1	1-1	1-0	1-0	3-0	5-1	1-0	3-1
Posusje	30	13	3	14	34	43	42	0-1	1-1	2-0	1-0	2-0	2-1	1-0	2-1		1-0	3-2	3-0	2-0	0-0	3-0	1-0
Sloboda Tuzla	30	11	8	11	30	28	41	2-2	2-0	0-0	1-1	2-1	2-1	2-0	0-0	2-0		2-0	1-0	2-0	1-0	3-1	1-0
Slavija Istocno Sarajevo	30	12	5	13	36	34	41	2-2	0-0	3-2	0-0	1-0	2-1	3-1	2-0	2-1	1-0		0-0	3-1	2-0	**3-0**	4-1
Zepce Limorad	30	13	2	15	33	35	41	2-1	2-0	0-0	0-1	5-0	2-1	3-1	2-0	3-0	1-0			0-1	0-1	2-0	2-1
Celik Zenica	30	13	2	15	29	37	41	1-0	1-0	1-1	2-1	0-1	2-1	2-0	2-1	3-1	1-0	1-0	1-2		3-0	1-0	2-0
Leotar Trebinje	30	13	2	15	34	45	41	3-2	2-1	2-1	0-0	2-0	3-1	1-0	2-1	0-2	3-2	1-2	3-1	2-0		0-0	4-2
Borac Banja Luka §	30	13	2	15	36	39	40	1-0	0-1	1-0	**3-0**	3-0	1-2	1-2	1-0	4-3	0-0	3-1	1-0	1-0	5-1		1-0
Rudar Ugljevik	30	7	4	19	26	43	25	0-1	0-1	0-0	0-2	1-0	0-0	3-0	1-2	0-0	2-0	2-0	1-0	1-0	3-1	1-2	

7/08/2004 - 28/05/2005 • † Qualified for the UEFA Champions League • ‡ Qualified for the UEFA Cup • § Borac deducted one point • Matches in bold awarded 3-0

KUP BIH 2004-05

Round of sixteen			Quarter-finals			Semi-finals			Final		
Sarajevo	1	4									
Borac Banja Luka *	2	1	Sarajevo *	1	1						
Leotar Trebinje *	3	0	Orasje	1	0						
Orasje	0	7				Sarajevo	2	3			
Radnik Bijeljina *	2	5				Slavija Istocno Sarajevo *	0	1			
Branitelj Rodoc	0	2	Radnik Bijeljina	0	1						
Sloga Doboj *	1	0	Slavija Istocno Sarajevo *	1	2						
Slavija Istocno Sarajevo	2	1							Sarajevo ‡	1	1
Zrinjski Mostar	0 3	7p							Siroki Brijeg *	0	1
Celik Zenica *	3 0	6p	Zrinjski Mostar	1	3						
Posusje	0	3	SASK Napredak *	1	0						
SASK Napredak *	2	1				Zrinjski Mostar	0	2			
Zeljeznicar Sarajevo *	3	2				Siroki Brijeg *	1	1			
Velez Mostar	0	2	Zeljeznicar Sarajevo	0	0						
Ljubic Prnjavor	2	1	Siroki Brijeg *	2	1						
Siroki Brijeg *	4	3									

* Home team in the 1st leg • ‡ Qualified for the UEFA Cup

CUP FINALS

1st leg. 11-05-2005
Scorers - Obuca [10] for Sarajevo

2nd leg. 17-05-2005
Scorers - Obuca [42] for Sarajevo; Juricic [66] for Siroki

RECENT LEAGUE AND CUP RECORD

	Championship						Cup		
Year	Champions	Pts	Runners-up	Pts	Third	Pts	Winners	Score	Runners-up
1999	No overall winner. Sarajevo won NSBiH league						Sarajevo	0-0 1-0	Orasje
2000	Brotnjo Citluk beat Buducnost in a play-off between the various leagues						Zeljeznicar	3-1	Sloboda Tuzla
2001	Zeljeznicar	91	Brotnjo Citluk	84	Sarajevo	81	Zeljeznicar	3-2	Sarajevo
2002	Zeljeznicar	62	Siroki Brijeg	51	Brotnjo Citluk	47	Sarajevo	2-1	Zeljeznicar
2003	Leotar Trebinje	85	Zeljeznicar	82	Sarajevo	69	Zeljeznicar	0-0 2-0	Leotar Trebinje
2004	Siroki Brijeg	61	Zeljeznicar	59	Sarajevo	56	Modrica Maksima	1-1 4-2p	Borac Banja Luka
2005	Zrinjski Mostar	61	Zeljeznicar	51	Siroki Brijeg	45	Sarajevo	1-0 1-1	Siroki Brijeg

BLR – BELARUS

NATIONAL TEAM RECORD

JULY 1ST 2002 TO JUNE 30TH 2005

PL	W	D	L	F	A	%
27	13	5	9	45	40	57.4

FIFA/COCA-COLA WORLD RANKING

1993	1994	1995	1996	1997	1998	1999	2000	2001	2002	2003	2004	High		Low	
137	121	88	90	110	104	95	96	85	74	90	69	62	06/05	142	07/94

2004-2005											
08/04	09/04	10/04	11/04	12/04	01/05	02/05	03/05	04/05	05/05	06/05	07/05
83	77	73	69	69	68	64	66	63	63	62	62

Belarus's progress up the FIFA/Coca-Cola World Ranking to their current highest ever position disguises the more sobering fact that in 14 competitive matches between September 2002 and June 2005 the national team won just twice - both times against Moldova - so whilst the overall record remains encouragingly positive this has largely been because of excellent results in friendly matches. Coach Anatoly Baidachny has made a big impact since taking over in 2003 and he can call on a growing band of players based abroad, notably in Russia, but also in Italy where Vitaly Kutuzov plays for Sampdoria and in England where star striker Alexander Hleb has just signed for Arsenal.

INTERNATIONAL HONOURS

None

It remains a close run thing for the play-off spot in their 2006 FIFA World Cup™ qualifying group but if Baidachny can instil more consistency into the team in competitive matches Belarus could be a potential threat in the future. Domestically, former Soviet champions Dinamo Minsk won the League after a gap of six years whilst MTZ-RIPO Minsk won the Cup, their first trophy, beating eternal runners-up BATE Borisov in the final. With so many players moving abroad clubs have struggled to progress in European competitions and none made it past the first stage in either the UEFA Champions League or the UEFA Cup.

THE FIFA BIG COUNT OF 2000

	Male	Female		Male	Female
Registered players	7 880	286	Referees	1 032	10
Non registered players	110 000	94	Officials	1 090	48
Youth players	11 550	100	Total involved	132 090	
Total players	129 910		Number of clubs	80	
Professional players	1 380	106	Number of teams	418	

Belarus Football Federation (BFF)

Kirova Street 8/2, Minsk 223 030, Belarus

Tel +375 17 2270802   Fax +375 17 2272920

info@bff.by   www.bff.by

President: NEVYGLAS Gennady   General Secretary: DMITRANITSA Leonid

Vice-President: VERGEENKO Mikhail   Treasurer: KOLTOVICH Valentina   Media Officer: TOMIN Alexandr

Men's Coach: BAIDACHNY Anatoly   Women's Coach: VOLOKH Oleg

BFF formed: 1989   UEFA: 1993   FIFA: 1992

Colours: Red, Green, Red or White, White, White

GAMES PLAYED BY BELARUS IN THE 2006 FIFA WORLD CUP™ CYCLE

2002	Opponents	Score		Venue	Comp	Scorers	Att	Referee
21-08	Latvia	W	4-2	Riga	Fr	Kutuzov [16], Kulchy [30], Romaschenko.Ma 2 [64 86]	4 200	Kaasik EST
7-09	Holland	L	0-3	Eindhoven	ECq		34 000	Barber ENG
12-10	Austria	L	0-2	Minsk	ECq		15 000	Poulat FRA
16-10	Czech Republic	L	0-2	Teplice	ECq		12 850	Fleischer GER
2003								
29-03	Moldova	W	2-1	Minsk	ECq	Kutuzov [43], Gurenko [58]	7 500	Verbist BEL
2-04	Uzbekistan	D	2-2	Minsk	Fr	Tsygalko [26], Rozhkov [52]	4 000	Lauks LVA
30-04	Uzbekistan	W	2-1	Tashkent	Fr	Shuneiko [15], Kutuzov [55]	4 000	Kolpakov KGZ
7-06	Holland	L	0-2	Minsk	ECq		28 000	Ovrebo NOR
11-06	Austria	L	0-5	Innsbruck	ECq		8 100	Frojdfeldt SWE
20-08	Iran	W	2-1	Minsk	Fr	Romaschenko.Ma [10p], Shtanyuk [41]	10 000	Ivanov.N RUS
6-09	Czech Republic	L	1-3	Minsk	ECq	Bulyga [14]	11 000	McCurry SCO
10-09	Moldova	L	1-2	Tiraspol	ECq	Vasilyuk [89p]	7 000	Selevic SCM
2004								
14-02	Estonia	L	1-2	Valletta	Fr	Tarasenko [89]	200	Casha MLT
16-02	Moldova	W	1-0	Valletta	Fr	Hleb.V [39]	40	Attard MLT
18-02	Malta	W	4-0	Valletta	Fr	Kornilenko [12], Tsygalko [30], Biahanski [71], Lashankou [85]		Kaldma EST
18-02	Cyprus	W	2-0	Achnas	Fr	Romaschenko.Ma 2 [56 70]	500	Kalis CYP
21-02	Latvia	W	4-1	Limassol	Fr	Bulyga [20], Romaschenko.Ma 3 [73p 87p 90]	100	
28-04	Lithuania	W	1-0	Minsk	Fr	Blizniuk [75]	8 000	Ivanov RUS
18-08	Turkey	W	2-1	Denizli	Fr	Hleb.V [67], Kouba [90]	18 000	Mrkovic BIH
8-09	Norway	D	1-1	Oslo	WCq	Kutuzov [77]	25 272	Gomes Costa POR
9-10	Moldova	W	4-0	Minsk	WCq	Omelyanchuk [45], Kutuzov [65], Bulyga [75], Romashchenko.Ma [90]	21 000	Dereli TUR
13-10	Italy	L	3-4	Parma	WCq	Romashchenko 2 [52 88], Bulyga [76]	19 833	Megia Davila ESP
22-11	United Arab Emirates	W	3-2	Dubai	Fr	Shkabara [44], Kovel [60], Kulchy [90]	600	Al Delawar BHR
2005								
9-02	Poland	W	3-1	Warsaw	Fr	Hleb.A [8], Hleb.V [84], Lavrik [92+]	6 000	Zuta LTU
30-03	Slovenia	D	1-1	Celje	WCq	Kulchy [49]	6 450	Al Ghamdi KSA
4-06	Slovenia	D	1-1	Minsk	WCq	Belkevich [18]	29 042	Hansson SWE
8-06	Scotland	D	0-0	Minsk	WCq		28 287	Benquerenca POR

Fr = Friendly match • EC = UEFA EURO 2004™ • WC = FIFA World Cup™ • q = qualifier

NATIONAL CAPS

	Caps
GURENKO Sergei	76
SHTANYUK Sergei	55
BELKEVICH Valentin	53
OSTROVSKIY Andrei	50
KULCHIY Alexandr	50
ROMASHCHENKO Maxym	47

NATIONAL GOALS

	Goals
ROMASHCHENKO Maxym	13
BELKEVICH Valentin	10
GERASIMETS Sergei	7
VASILYUK Roman	7
KUTUZOV Vitaly	7

NATIONAL COACH

	Years
VERGEYENKO Mikhail	1992-'94
BOROVSKIY Sergei	1994-'96
VERGEYENKO Mikhail	1996-'99
BOROVSKIY Sergei	1999-'00
MALOFEYEV Eduard	2000-'03
BAIDACHNY Anatoli	2003-

FIFA REFEREE LIST 2005

	Int'l	DoB
CHYKUN Aleh	1999	5-08-1960
SHMOLIK Siarhei	1993	12-01-1965
VIALICHKA Valery	2002	12-09-1966

FIFA ASSISTANT REFEREE LIST 2005

	Int'l	DoB
BYKOV Viachaslau	1998	25-12-1972
DUPANOV Yuri	1993	7-06-1962
KALINOVSKI Vasili	1999	16-09-1964
SAVITSKI Stanislau	2003	12-11-1976
SIAMIONAU Dzmitry	2003	29-08-1971
ZHUK Siarhei	1997	7-10-1963

BELARUS COUNTRY INFORMATION

Capital	Minsk	Independence	1991	GDP per Capita	$6 100
Population	10 310 520	Status	Republic	GNP Ranking	81
Area km²	207 600	Language	Belorussian	Dialling code	+375
Population density	49 per km²	Literacy rate	99%	Internet code	.by
% in urban areas	71%	Main religion	Christian 80%	GMT +/-	+2
Towns/Cities ('000)	Minsk 1 742; Gomel 480; Mogilev 365; Vitebsk 342; Grodno 317; Brest 300				
Neighbours (km)	Russia 959; Ukraine 891; Poland 407; Lithuania 502; Latvia 141				
Main stadia	Dinamo – Minsk 42 375; Neman – Grodno 15 000; Dinamo – Brest 15 000				

BELARUS NATIONAL TEAM RECORDS AND RECORD SEQUENCES

Records			Sequence records					
Victory	5-0	LTU 1998	Wins	3	2004, 2004	Clean sheets	3	1998, 2004
Defeat	0-5	AUT 2003	Defeats	8	1997	Goals scored	7	2003-2004
Player Caps	76	GURENKO Sergei	Undefeated	5	2000-2001	Without goal	3	1995, 1997, 2002
Player Goals	13	ROMASHCHENKO Maxym	Without win	14	1998-2000	Goals against	13	2002-2004

BELARUS 2004

PREMIER LEAGUE

	Pl	W	D	L	F	A	Pts	Dinamo	BATE	Shakhtyor	Zhodino	Gomel	Torpedo	Neman	Brest	Dnepr	Naftan	Darida	Slavia	Zvezda	Lokomotiv	MTZ-RIPO	Belshina
Dinamo Minsk †	30	24	3	3	64	18	75		2-0	1-0	2-1	1-0	0-1	1-0	3-0	2-1	6-1	2-2	4-2	4-0	2-1	1-0	5-0
BATE Borisov ‡	30	22	4	4	59	25	70	1-1		0-1	2-1	3-1	3-1	1-0	2-1	1-0	1-1	4-1	4-0	2-3	3-2	3-0	2-1
Shakhtyor Soligorsk	30	19	8	3	55	21	65	0-1	5-1		2-1	2-1	0-0	0-0	5-2	1-0	1-0	4-1	2-1	1-0	4-1	3-3	2-0
Torpedo Zhodino	30	19	2	9	57	28	59	0-1	0-2	1-2		4-0	1-0	1-0	2-1	3-0	3-1	2-0	3-1	5-2	4-1	3-0	3-0
FC Gomel	30	13	7	10	42	41	46	2-0	0-1	1-0	3-0		0-0	1-0	1-1	0-4	2-2	1-1	2-1	0-0	2-0	2-1	4-1
Torpedo-SKA Minsk	30	13	7	10	37	31	46	2-0	0-3	0-0	1-0	2-4		1-2	2-5	2-1	5-1	1-1	1-0	1-0	1-0	2-1	3-0
Neman Grodno	30	11	7	12	37	33	40	0-2	1-1	1-2	2-1	4-1	2-2		0-1	2-1	0-2	2-2	1-0	2-0	1-1	0-1	1-1
Dinamo Brest	30	10	9	11	39	41	39	0-3	1-1	0-0	2-2	0-1	3-1	2-0		3-1	3-0	0-3	0-1	2-2	0-1	4-0	2-2
Dnepr Trans. Mogilev	30	11	4	15	29	37	37	0-1	0-1	1-1	0-1	1-2	1-0	3-2	0-0		0-3	0-1	1-3	2-1	1-0	1-1	2-0
Naftan Novopolotsk	30	10	5	15	45	50	35	1-3	0-2	0-1	1-3	1-0	2-2	3-1	3-1	0-2		1-2	3-1	5-1	0-3	2-2	3-0
Darida	30	9	8	13	38	48	35	0-4	2-3	2-2	1-2	1-1	0-1	1-0	0-1	1-1	1-3		3-0	3-1	0-3	2-0	1-0
Slavia Mozyr	30	9	4	17	32	51	31	1-3	0-1	0-5	0-2	1-0	2-2	1-3	4-1	2-0	2-0	3-1		0-0	3-1	1-1	2-1
Zvezda Minsk	30	7	8	15	31	56	29	0-3	0-2	0-0	0-2	3-0	1-0	0-1	1-2	0-3	0-1	2-0	2-4		1-1	2-0	2-1
Lokomotiv Vitebsk	30	8	3	19	34	54	27	1-3	0-1	0-3	0-0	0-1	0-1	1-2	2-3	0-1	1-3	2-1	2-1	2-1		2-2	2-1
MTZ-RIPO Minsk ‡	30	6	9	15	32	56	27	0-0	0-3	1-4	0-5	5-2	0-3	0-2	1-2	0-1	2-1	2-0	1-4	0-0	6-0		2-1
Belshina Bobruisk	30	2	6	22	21	62	12	1-3	0-5	1-2	0-1	1-4	0-1	0-3	0-0	0-1	0-0	2-2	0-0	4-1	2-1	1-2	

15/04/2004 - 7/11/2004 • † Qualified for the UEFA Champions League • ‡ Qualified for the UEFA Cup

BELARUS 2004 SECOND DIVISION

	Pl	W	D	L	F	A	Pts
Lokomotiv Minsk	30	24	3	3	75	25	75
Vedrych-97 Rechitsa	30	18	8	4	46	21	62
Smorgon	30	14	11	5	49	21	53
Granit Mikashevichi	30	12	10	8	31	22	46
Zlin Gomel	30	12	10	8	31	18	46
Veras Nyasvizh	30	14	2	14	35	34	44
Baranavichy	30	13	5	12	41	39	44
Lida	30	11	7	12	37	30	40
Khimik Svetlogorsk	30	9	13	8	19	18	40
Bereza	30	10	7	13	39	45	37
Kommunalnik Slonim	30	9	7	14	33	47	34
Torpedo Mogilev	30	7	11	12	31	45	32
Molodechno 2000	30	9	4	17	27	54	31
Dnepr Rogachev	30	9	3	18	27	54	30
Vertykal Kalinkavichy	30	7	8	15	29	49	29
Dinamo Juni Minsk	30	6	3	21	27	55	21

17/04/2004 - 6/11/2004

PLAY-OFFS
Relegation

MTZ-RIPO Minsk	4
Lokomotiv Vitsyebsk	1

TOP SCORERS

STRIPEIKIS Valery	Naftan	18
VASILUK Roman	Dinamo Minsk	17
SOKOLOV Aleksandr	Darida	16
ZUYEU Yauhen	Zhodino	15

BFF CUP 2005

Quarter-finals			Semi-finals			Final	
MTZ-RIPO Minsk*	0	2					
Baranavichy	0	1	MTZ-RIPO Minsk*	2	3		
Belshina Bob'sk	1	1	Neman Grodno	0	1		
Neman Grodno*	0	2				MTZ-RIPO Minsk	2
Darida	1	0				BATE Borisov	1
FC Gomel*	1	0	Darida*	0	0		
Dnepr Mogilev	0	2	BATE Borisov	1	1		
BATE Borisov*	1	1					

22-05-2005, Att: 10 000
Dinamo, Minsk, Ref: Kulbakou

Scorers - Fyodorov 42, Kantsevy 73 for MTZ-RIPA; Lebyadzeu 28 for BATE

* Home team in the first leg

RECENT LEAGUE AND CUP RECORD

Championship

Year	Champions	Pts	Runners-up	Pts	Third	Pts
1999	BATE Borisov	77	Slavia Mozyr	65	FC Gomel	63
2000	Slavia Mozyr	74	BATE Borisov	64	Dinamo Minsk	62
2001	Belshina Bobruisk	56	Dinamo Minsk	53	BATE Borisov	51
2002	BATE Borisov	56	Neman Grodno	56	Shakhtyor Soligorsk	51
2003	FC Gomel	74	BATE Borisov	66	Dinamo Minsk	64
2004	Dinamo Minsk	75	BATE Borisov	70	Shakhtyor Soligorsk	65
2005						

Cup

Winners	Score	Runners-up
Belshina Bobruisk	1-1 4-2p	Slavia Mozyr
Slavia Mozyr	2-1	Torpedo-SKA Minsk
Belshina Bobruisk	1-0	Slavia Mozyr
FC Gomel	2-0	BATE Borisov
Dinamo Minsk	2-0	Lokomotiv Minsk
Shakhtyor Soligorsk	1-0	FC Gomel
MTZ-RIPO Minsk	2-1	BATE Borisov

BLZ – BELIZE

NATIONAL TEAM RECORD
JULY 1ST 2002 TO JUNE 30TH 2005

PL	W	D	L	F	A	%
5	0	0	5	0	15	0

FIFA/COCA-COLA WORLD RANKING

1993	1994	1995	1996	1997	1998	1999	2000	2001	2002	2003	2004	High		Low	
-	-	173	182	179	186	190	186	167	158	174	181	**157**	05/02	**190**	02/00

2004-2005											
08/04	09/04	10/04	11/04	12/04	01/05	02/05	03/05	04/05	05/05	06/05	07/05
180	180	180	180	181	181	181	180	180	180	180	

The lowest ranked nation in Central America, Belize does not have the resources to take on the more established teams in the region as the recent FIFA World Cup™ qualifiers demonstrated. Paired with Canada, Belize found themselves in a David and Goliath situation and any hopes of progression soon disappeared when the Belize Football Federation agreed to play both games in Ontario, both of which were lost 0-4. Matters didn't improve during the qualifying rounds for the Gold Cup. Held in Guatemala, Belize lost all three games in the UNCAF Cup and made an early exit. For coach Tony Adderley, progress in the country is difficult when he has to rely on mostly

INTERNATIONAL HONOURS
None

part-time players. League football in Belize has been plagued in recent years by a break-away of the leading clubs from the Federation although the differences were put aside for the 2005 season which saw all of the clubs compete in the national League, a tournament won by Juventus who beat holders Sagitún in the final. The League is comprised of eight clubs with the top four qualifying for the play-offs followed by the final. Kulture Yabra and Boca Juniors competed in the Central American Zone of the 2005 CONCACAF Champions Cup, both losing their first round matches to Alianza of El Salvador and Olimpia of Honduras respectively.

THE FIFA BIG COUNT OF 2000

	Male	Female		Male	Female
Registered players	1 436	0	Referees	60	1
Non registered players	2 000	500	Officials	400	50
Youth players	471	0	Total involved	4 918	
Total players		4 407	Number of clubs	22	
Professional players	236	0	Number of teams	116	

Football Federation of Belize (FFB)
26 Hummingbird Highway, Belmopan, PO Box 1742, Belize City
Tel +501 822 3410   Fax +501 822 3377
bchimilio@yahoo.com   www.none
President: CHIMILIO Bertie Dr   General Secretary: HULSE Marguerite
Vice-President: DAVIS Ray   Treasurer: BAXTER Matthews   Media Officer: None
Men's Coach: ADDERLEY Anthony   Women's Coach: MORK Ian
FFB formed: 1980   CONCACAF: 1986   FIFA: 1986
Colours: Red/White/Blue, Red/White/Blue, Red/White/Blue

GAMES PLAYED BY BELIZE IN THE 2006 FIFA WORLD CUP™ CYCLE

2002	Opponents	Score		Venue	Comp	Scorers	Att	Referee
No international matches played after June 2002								
2003								
No international matches played in 2003								
2004								
13-06	Canada	L	0-4	Kingston, Ontario	WCq		8 245	Batres GUA
16-06	Canada	L	0-4	Kingston, Ontario	WCq		5 124	Gordon TRI
2005								
19-02	Guatemala	L	0-2	Guatemala City	GCq		10 000	Quesada CRC
21-02	Honduras	L	0-4	Guatemala City	GCq		3 000	Campos NCA
23-02	Nicaragua	L	0-1	Guatemala City	GCq		3 000	Campos NCA

GC = CONCACAF Gold Cup™ • WC = FIFA World Cup™ • q = qualifier

BELIZE NATIONAL TEAM RECORDS AND RECORD SEQUENCES

Records			Sequence records					
Victory	7-1	NCA 2002	Wins	3	2001-2002	Clean sheets	2	2000-2001
Defeat	0-7	CRC 1999	Defeats	6	1997-2000	Goals scored	5	2001-2002
Player Caps	n/a		Undefeated	3	2000-01, 2001-02	Without goal	5	2004-2005
Player Goals	n/a		Without win	12	1995-2000	Goals against	11	1995-2000

FIFA REFEREE LIST 2005

	Int'l	DoB
HENRY Gerald	2001	14-11-1972
JONES David	1990	10-01-1961
WILLIAMS Victor	2001	19-11-1964

FIFA ASSISTANT REFEREE LIST 2005

	Int'l	DoB
AKE Ricardo	2003	27-12-1978
CHIRINOS Armando	1994	1-02-1962
CONTRERAS Eugene	1998	15-01-1968
TRAPP Earl	2005	1-12-1967

RECENT LEAGUE RECORD

Year	Winners	Score	Runners-up
1996	Juventus	4-1 1-1	Real Verdes
1997	Juventus		
1998	Juventus	2-0 6-1	Acros
1999	Juventus	2-1 1-1	La Victoria Dolphins
2000	Sagitún	0-2 2-0 3-0	Grigamandala
2001	Kulture Yabra	1-0 2-0	Belmopan Bandits
2002	Kulture Yabra	1-1 4-2p 2-1	Juventus
2003		Not played	
2004		Not played	
2005	Juventus	1-0 1-0	Sagitún

In 2002 the leading clubs of the BPFL withdrew from the Football Federation of Belize and set up a rival league

2002	Sagitún	1-1 1-1 3-2p	Belmopan Bandits
2003	Kulture Yabra	2-0 2-1	Belmopan Bandits
2004	Sagitún	0-2 3-2 1-0	Juventus

BELIZE COUNTRY INFORMATION

Capital	Belmopan	Independence	1981	GDP per Capita	$4 900
Population	272 945	Status	Commonwealth	GNP Ranking	159
Area km²	22 966	Language	English	Dialling code	+501
Population density	11 per km²	Literacy rate	75%	Internet code	.bz
% in urban areas	47%	Main religion	Christian 77%	GMT +/−	-6
Towns/Cities ('000)	Belize City 61; San Ignacio 16; Orange Walk 15; Belmopan 13; Dangriga 10; Corozal 8				
Neighbours (km)	Mexico 250; Guatemala 266; Caribbean Sea 386				
Main stadia	People's Stadium – Orange Walk 3 000; MCC Grounds – Belize City 2 500				

BOL – BOLIVIA

NATIONAL TEAM RECORD
JULY 1ST 2002 TO JUNE 30TH 2005

PL	W	D	L	F	A	%
24	6	3	15	24	43	31.2

FIFA/COCA-COLA WORLD RANKING

1993	1994	1995	1996	1997	1998	1999	2000	2001	2002	2003	2004	High		Low	
58	44	53	39	24	61	61	65	70	92	99	94	18	07/97	114	08/03

2004-2005											
08/04	09/04	10/04	11/04	12/04	01/05	02/05	03/05	04/05	05/05	06/05	07/05
93	93	99	94	94	95	97	96	94	94	97	99

The past five years have seen a dramatic slump in the fortunes of the Bolivian national team. From a top 20 ranking in 1997, Bolivia is now struggling to maintain a place in the top 100. Qualification for the 1994 FIFA World Cup™ looked to have ushered in a new era, helped along by the exceptional talents emerging from the Tahuichi academy in Santa Cruz, but 11 years on Bolivia finds itself propping up the South American qualifying group for the 2006 FIFA World Cup™ in Germany. Fortress La Paz, once the most feared destination in world football for visiting teams because of the high altitude, no longer seems to pose the threat it did in the past. Current coach

INTERNATIONAL HONOURS
Qualified for the FIFA World Cup™ finals 1930 1950 1994　**Copa América** 1963

Ovidio Mesa is the third to guide the team through the qualifiers with the previous incumbents complaining of a poor relationship with the Federation. Domestically there was some cheer with leading club Bolivar reaching the final of the 2004 Copa Sudamericana, the first Bolivian club to make it to a major club final, but despite winning the first leg 1-0 against Boca Juniors they went down 2-0 in the return in Buenos Aires. In the championship Bolivar won the Apertura with The Strongest winning the Clausura. A transitional tournament was held in early 2005 so that in the future the Bolivian season will follow the European calendar from September to June.

THE FIFA BIG COUNT OF 2000

	Male	Female		Male	Female
Registered players	14 698	1 080	Referees	480	30
Non registered players	210 000	0	Officials	95	20
Youth players	30 240	0	Total involved	256 643	
Total players	256 018		Number of clubs	809	
Professional players	360	0	Number of teams	999	

Federación Boliviana de Fútbol (FBF)
Av. Libertador Bolivar 1168, Cochabamba, Bolivia
Tel +591 4 4244982　　　Fax +591 4 4282132
fbfcba@entelnet.bo　　　www.fbf.com.bo
President: CASTEDO Walter　　General Secretary: REINOSO Mario
Vice-President: MENDEZ Mauricio　　Treasurer: JIMENEZ Pedro　　Media Officer: SILVER Javier
Men's Coach: MESA Ovidio　　Women's Coach: MELGAR Herman
FBF formed: 1925　　CONMEBOL: 1926　　FIFA: 1926
Colours: Green, White, Green

GAMES PLAYED BY BOLIVIA IN THE 2006 FIFA WORLD CUP™ CYCLE

2002	Opponents	Score	Venue	Comp	Scorers	Att	Referee
21-08	Venezuela	L 0-2	Caracas	Fr		25 000	Ibarra VEN
2003							
19-03	Mexico	L 0-2	Dallas	Fr		40 000	Terry USA
10-06	Portugal	L 0-4	Lisbon	Fr		10 000	Kenan ISR
31-08	Panama	W 3-0	La Paz	Fr	Mendez [21], Ricaldi [51], Gutierrez.L [84]	8 000	Ortube BOL
7-09	Uruguay	L 0-5	Montevideo	WCq		45 000	Hidalgo PER
10-09	Colombia	W 4-0	La Paz	WCq	Baldivieso [12p], Botero 3 [27 48 58]	30 000	Oliveira BRA
11-10	Honduras	W 1-0	Washington	Fr	Pena.JM [89]	20 000	Kennedy USA
15-11	Argentina	L 0-3	Buenos Aires	WCq		30 042	Hidalgo PER
18-11	Venezuela	L 1-2	Maracaibo	WCq	Botero [60]	25 000	Reinoso ECU
2004							
30-03	Chile	L 0-2	La Paz	WCq		42 000	Martin ARG
1-06	Paraguay	W 2-1	La Paz	WCq	Cristaldo [8], Suarez.R [72]	23 013	Rezende BRA
5-06	Ecuador	L 2-3	Quito	WCq	Gutierrez.L [58], Castillo [75]	30 020	Brand VEN
6-07	Peru	D 2-2	Lima	CAr1	Botero [36], Alvarez [57]	45 000	Baldassi ARG
9-07	Colombia	L 0-1	Lima	CAr1		35 000	Ramos ECU
12-07	Venezuela	D 1-1	Trujillo	CAr1	Galindo [32]	25 000	Mattus CRC
5-09	Brazil	L 1-3	Sao Paulo	WCq	Cristaldo [48]	60 000	Baldassi ARG
9-10	Peru	W 1-0	La Paz	WCq	Botero [56]	23 729	Reinoso ECU
12-10	Uruguay	D 0-0	La Paz	WCq		24 349	Rezende BRA
13-11	Guatemala	L 0-1	Washington DC	Fr		22 000	Prus USA
17-11	Colombia	L 0-1	Barranquilla	WCq		25 000	Torres PAR
2005							
26-03	Argentina	L 1-2	La Paz	WCq	Castillo [49]	25 000	Larrionda URU
29-03	Venezuela	W 3-1	La Paz	WCq	Cichero OG [2], Castillo [25], Vaca [84]	7 908	Lecca PER
4-06	Chile	L 1-3	Santiago	WCq	Castillo [83p]	46 729	Rezende BRA
8-06	Paraguay	L 1-4	Asuncion	WCq	Galindo [30]	5 534	Brand VEN

Fr = Friendly match • CA = Copa América • WC = FIFA World Cup™ • q = qualifier • r1 = first round group

BOLIVIA NATIONAL TEAM RECORDS AND RECORD SEQUENCES

Records			Sequence records					
Victory	9-2	HAI 2000	Wins	5	1963, 1993, 1998	Clean sheets	3	1998, 1999
Defeat	1-10	BRA 1949	Defeats	9	1926-1930	Goals scored	15	1995-1996
Player Caps	93	SANDY Marco Antonio	Undefeated	9	1997	Without goal	7	1994
Player Goals	16	UGARTE Victor Agustín	Without win	19	1945-1948	Goals against	18	1977-1980

BOLIVIA COUNTRY INFORMATION

Capital	Sucre; La Paz	Independence	1825	GDP per Capita	$2 400
Population	8 724 156	Status	Republic	GNP Ranking	95
Area km²	1 098 580	Language	Spanish	Dialling code	+591
Population density	8 per km²	Literacy rate	87%	Internet code	.bo
% in urban areas	61%	Main religion	Christian	GMT +/-	-4
Towns/Cities ('000)	Santa Cruz 1 342; Cochabamba 900; El Alto 834; La Paz 812; Sucre 224; Oruro 208; Tarija 159; Potosi 141; Montero 88; Trinidad 84; Yacuiba 82; Riberalta 74; Guayaramerin 36				
Neighbours (km)	Brazil 3 400; Paraguay 750; Argentina 832; Chile 861; Peru 900				
Main stadia	Hernando Siles - La Paz 42 000; Ramón Tahuichi Aguilera - Santa Cruz 38 000; Felix Capriles - Cochabamba 32 000; Olimpico Patria - Sucre 30 000				

NATIONAL CAPS

	Caps
SANDY Marco Antonio	93
CRISTALDO Luis Héctor	91
MELGAR José Milton	89
BORJA Carlos Fernando	88
BALDIVIESO Julio César	83
RIMBA Miguel Angel	80
SANCHEZ Oscar	77
PENA Juan Manuel	76
ETCHEVERRY Marco Antonio	71
MORENO Jaime	63

NATIONAL GOALS

	Goals
UGARTE Víctor Agustín	16
ARAGONES Carlos	15
BALDIVIESO Julio César	15
SANCHEZ Erwin	15
ALCOCER Máximo	13
ETCHEVERRY Marco Antonio	13
BOTERO Joaquín	12
AGUILAR Miguel	10
RAMALLO Luis William	9
MEZZA Ovidio	8

NATIONAL COACH

	Years
VIERA Hector	1998
LOPEZ Antonio	1999
ARAGONES Carlos	2000-'01
HABEGGER Jorge	2001
TRUCCO Carlos Leonel	2001-'02
ROCHA	2003
GIOVAGNOLI Dalcio	2003
ACOSTA Nelson	2003-'04
BLACUT Ramiro	2004-'05
MESA Ovidio	2005-

FIFA REFEREE LIST 2005

	Int'l	DoB
ANTEQUERA Joaquin	2005	20-09-1973
CLOQUE Jhonny	2005	12-02-1966
GAMBOA Ivan		16-07-1965
GARCIA Gil		4-01-1966
MALDONADO Oscar	2005	13-04-1972
ORTUBE Rene	1992	26-12-1964
PANIAGUA Juan	1996	20-10-1964

FIFA ASSISTANT REFEREE LIST 2005

	Int'l	DoB
ARROYO Juan	1997	24-06-1965
CALDERON Jorge	2001	25-10-1966
CHIRINOS Gregorio	2005	16-11-1961
LEDEZMA Alian	2005	22-04-1977
LIMPIAS Carlos	2005	4-06-1970
SORIA Oscar	1995	29-09-1960
VALDA Arol	1998	10-12-1970

CLUB DIRECTORY

Club	Town/City	Stadium	Phone	www.	Lge	CL
Aurora	Cochabamba	Tahuichi 40 000	+591 4 4589399	clunaurora.com.bo	1	0
Blooming	Santa Cruz	Tahuichi 40 000	+591 3 369435		3	0
Bolivar	La Paz	Hernando Siles 55 000	+591 22 2786665	clubbolivar.com	16	0
Jorge Wilsterman	Cochabamba	Felix Capriles 35 000	+591 4 4221631		9	0
La Paz FC	La Paz	Hernando Siles 55 000	+591 2782824		0	0
Oriente Petrolero	Santa Cruz	Tahuichi 40 000	+591 3 355581		4	0
Real Potosi	Potosi	Guzman 15 000	+591 2 6225835	clubrealpotosi.com	0	0
Real Santa Cruz	Santa Cruz	Camba 12 000			0	0
San Jose	Oruro	Monumental 33 000	+591 2 5247300		1	0
The Strongest	La Paz	Achumani 40 000	+591 22 2001891		8	0
Universidad Iberoamericana	La Paz	Libertador Bolivar	+591 22 2372077		0	0
Union Central	Tarija	Centenario 20 000	+591 4 6647494		0	0

RECENT LEAGUE RECORD

Year	Championship Champions	Pts	Runners-up	Pts	Third	Pts
1993	The Strongest	14	Bolivar	13	Blooming	12
1994	Bolivar	15	Jorge Wilsterman	11	The Strongest	10
1995	San Jose					
1996	Bolivar	17	Oriente Petrolero	17	The Strongest	15
1997	Bolivar	25	Oriente Petrolero	18	Blooming	16
1998	Blooming		Jorge Wilsterman			
1999	Blooming		The Strongest			
2000	Jorge Wilsterman		Oriente Ptrolero			
2001	Oriente Petrolero		Bolivar			
2002	Bolivar					
2003ap	The Strongest	46	Bolivar	45	Jorge Wilsterman	40
2003cl	The Strongest	13	Jorge Wilsterman	10	Bolivar	9
2004ap	Bolivar	53	Aurora	38	Jorge Wilsterman	53
2004cl	The Strongest	27	Oriente Petrolero	27	Real Potosí	24
2005ap						

Championship Play-off Champions	Score	Runners-up
Bolivar	3-1	Oriente Petrolero
Blooming	3-0 1-0	Jorge Wilsterman
Blooming	3-2 3-2	The Strongest
Jorge Wilsterman	4-1 0-4 2-2	Oriente Petrolero
Oriente Petrolero	1-4 4-3 2-0	Bolivar
The Strongest	1-3 2-1 1-1	Oriente Petrolero

Since 1994 the league has consisted of Apertura and Clausura tournaments • In 1995 San Jose won both, as did Bolivar in 2002 so no play-off was necessary • In 1996 and 1997 the play-off consisted of a hexagonal final whilst between 1998 and 2001 the winners of the Apertura and Clausura played off against each other • From 2003 the winners of the Apertura and the Clausura are champions in their own right • In 2000 Jorge Wilsterman won the championship 4-3 on penalties

BOLIVIA 2004

TORNEO APERTURA

	Pl	W	D	L	F	A	Pts	Bolívar	Aurora	Wilsterman	Potosí	San José	Oriente	La Paz	Unión	Santa Cruz	Strongest	Blooming	Ibero.
Bolívar †	22	17	2	3	51	21	53		2-0	0-2	2-1	4-1	6-1	5-1	2-1	4-0	2-1	4-0	4-2
Aurora	22	11	5	6	42	32	38	1-0		1-0	4-2	1-1	2-2	3-1	1-3	2-0	3-0	5-1	5-1
Jorge Wilsterman	22	11	3	8	40	28	36	1-2	2-3		1-2	0-0	1-0	5-1	2-0	4-2	3-2	6-2	1-0
Real Potosí	22	10	3	9	43	38	33	0-1	2-3	2-1		2-1	4-3	3-1	1-1	3-0	3-2	7-1	1-0
San José	22	9	5	8	35	36	32	1-1	2-1	2-3	4-3		3-1	3-2	2-1	5-1	1-1	2-1	2-0
Oriente Petrolero	22	8	7	7	43	38	31	1-1	4-1	2-2	1-1	4-0		3-1	3-0	2-2	3-1	4-2	4-0
La Paz FC	22	9	4	9	33	38	31	0-2	0-0	0-1	2-1	3-2	2-0		1-1	2-2	1-0	2-0	2-2
Unión Central	22	8	6	8	27	29	30	1-2	3-1	2-1	3-1	0-0	2-1	0-2		1-1	1-1	1-0	2-0
Real Santa Cruz	22	7	5	10	28	40	26	0-2	3-1	1-0	1-1	0-1	1-1	1-3	0-1		1-0	3-1	3-1
The Strongest	22	7	3	12	31	31	24	3-0	1-2	2-1	3-0	4-1	1-2	0-2	1-1	2-0		1-0	0-1
Blooming	22	5	4	13	28	52	19	1-2	1-1	2-2	2-1	2-1	1-1	2-1	5-2	2-3	2-1		0-0
Univ. Iberoamericana	22	5	3	14	23	41	18	2-3	1-1	0-1	1-2	1-0	4-0	2-3	1-0	1-3	1-4	2-0	

14/02/2004 - 24/06/2004 • † Qualified for the Copa Libertadores

BOLIVIA 2004

TORNEO CLAUSURA 1ST STAGE

Group A

	Pl	W	D	L	F	A	Pts	Bolívar	San José	Strongest	Potosí	Ibero	La Paz
Bolívar ‡	10	4	6	0	11	6	18		2-0	1-1	1-1	1-1	2-2
San José ‡	10	5	2	3	19	10	17	0-0		4-0	3-0	1-2	2-2
The Strongest ‡	10	4	2	4	10	14	14	0-1	2-0		2-6	0-0	2-0
Real Potosí ‡	10	3	3	4	19	17	12	0-1	1-3	2-0		4-1	1-1
Univ. Iberoamericana	10	3	3	4	11	16	12	0-1	0-4	0-1	2-2		3-1
La Paz FC	10	1	4	5	12	19	7	1-1	1-2	0-2	3-2	1-2	

Group B

	Pl	W	D	L	F	A	Pts	Blooming	Unión	Wilsterman	Oriente	Aurora	Santa Cruz
Blooming ‡	10	5	3	2	19	14	18		1-2	0-2	1-1	4-2	3-2
Unión Central ‡	10	5	1	4	15	14	16	0-2		1-1	1-0	2-3	3-1
Jorge Wilsterman ‡	10	4	3	3	13	10	15	2-3	2-0		1-0	1-0	1-2
Oriente Petrolero ‡	10	3	4	3	13	11	13	1-3	3-2	1-1		4-0	1-1
Aurora	10	3	3	4	10	16	12	0-0	0-2	1-1	0-0		2-1
Real Santa Cruz	10	2	2	6	14	19	8	2-2	1-2	2-1	1-2	1-2	

24/07/2004 - 26/09/2004 • ‡ Qualified for the 2nd stage

BOLIVIA 2004

TORNEO CLAUSURA 2ND STAGE

	Pl	W	D	L	F	A	Pts	Oriente	Strongest	Potosí	San José	Wilsterman	Bolívar	Blooming	Unión
Oriente Petrolero † §	14	9	0	5	31	18	27		0-1	3-0	3-2	1-3	9-0	2-0	2-0
The Strongest † §	14	9	0	5	27	14	27	1-0		2-1	3-0	0-1	7-0	1-0	4-1
Real Potosí	14	7	3	4	32	27	24	3-2	3-2		5-2	3-1	2-2	4-3	3-1
San José	14	7	3	4	28	27	24	4-1	3-4	2-2		2-1	2-2	2-1	2-2
Jorge Wilsterman	14	5	5	4	15	14	20	0-1	1-0	1-1	1-2		1-0	1-1	2-2
Bolívar	14	5	3	6	22	32	18	1-2	2-0	2-0	0-1	1-1		6-2	3-1
Blooming	14	4	1	9	22	28	13	1-2	1-0	4-2	1-2	0-1	2-0		3-4
Unión Central	14	1	3	10	18	35	6	2-3	1-2	0-3	1-2	0-0	2-3	1-3	

16/10/2004 - 19/12/2004 • † Qualified for the Copa Libertadores • § Championship play-off

CLAUSURA PLAY-OFF

The Strongest	1	2	1	4p
Oriente Petrolero	3	1	1	3p

The Strongest win the Clausura Championship 4-3 on penalties

LIBERTADORES PLAY-OFF

Between Apertura & Clausura runners-up

Oriente Petrolero	3	2
Aurora	1	2

Oriente qualify for the Copa Libertadores

TOP SCORERS 2004

MENACHO José	Real Potosí	24
ESCOBAR Pablo	San José	19
SOSA Hugo	San José	19
GUTIERREZ Limberg	Bolívar	18
BENTOS Gustavo	Real Potosí	17

BOLIVAR 2004

Date	Opponents	Score		Comp	Scorers	Att
15-02-2004	Oriente Petrolero	D 1-1	A	TAP	Chiorazzo [80]	7 177
18-02-2004	Boca Juniors	W 3-1	H	CLg7	Castillo 3 [17 34 57]	
25-02-2004	San José	W 4-1	H	TAP	Sandy [13], Castillo 2 [28 58], Suarez [82]	3 183
28-02-2004	La Paz FC	W 2-0	A	TAP	Castillo [27], Mercado [71]	3 053
2-03-2004	Deportivo Cali	L 1-3	A	CLg7	Gutierrez.L [73]	
7-03-2004	Jorge Wilsterman	L 0-2	H	TAP		7 174
10-03-2004	Unión Central	W 2-1	A	TAP	Castillo 2 [13 28]	10 704
14-03-2004	Blooming	W 2-1	A	TAP	Castillo 2 [42 71]	7 893
18-03-2004	Colo Colo	W 2-0	H	CLg7	Suarez [4], Castillo [46]	
25-03-2004	Colo Colo	L 0-2	A	CLg7		
3-04-2004	Real Potosí	W 2-1	H	TAP	Sandy [38], Mercado [76]	1 929
7-04-2004	Deportivo Cali	W 1-0	H	CLg7	Castillo [21]	
11-04-2004	Real Santa Cruz	W 2-0	A	TAP	Suarez [5], Ribeiro	2 443
18-04-2004	Universidad Iberoamericana	W 4-2	H	TAP	Gutierrez.L 3 [7p 42 90], Chiorazzo [23]	2 318
21-04-2004	Boca Juniors	L 0-3	A	CLg7		
25-04-2004	Aurora	L 0-1	A	TAP		
29-04-2004	The Strongest	W 2-1	H	TAP	Gutierrez.L [21], Mercado [40]	29 246
2-05-2004	Oriente Petrolero	W 6-1	H	TAP	Suarez [7], Gutierrez.L 2 [12 66], Galindo [23], Sanchez [34], Mercado [46]	6 791
5-05-2004	San José	D 1-1	A	TAP	Suarez [79]	16 463
9-05-2004	La Paz FC	W 5-1	H	TAP	Tufiño [31], Suarez [33], Sanchez [56], Ribeiro 2 [86 90]	5 851
13-05-2004	Jorge Wilsterman	W 2-1	A	TAP	Gutierrez [1], Suarez [30]	19 373
16-05-2004	Unión Central	W 2-1	H	TAP	Guiberguis [21], Ferreira [84]	5 930
19-05-2004	Blooming	W 4-0	H	TAP	Castillo [5], Tufiño [43], Ferreira [54], Gutierrez [69]	4 589
10-06-2004	Real Potosí	W 1-0	H	TAP	Gutierrez [37p]	7 200
13-06-2004	Real Santa Cruz	W 4-0	H	TAP	Guiberguis [46], Mercado [59], Pachi [64], Chiorazzo [74]	5 394
17-06-2004	Universidad Iberoamericana	W 3-2	A	TAP	Gutierrez [55], Guiberguis [63], Mercado [86]	1 223
20-06-2004	Aurora	W 2-0	H	TAP	Chiorazzo [61], Mercado [74]	13 472
24-06-2004	The Strongest	L 0-3	A	TAP		3 410
1-08-2004	La Paz FC	D 2-2	H	TCL1	Suarez [14], Gutierrez [88]	2 071
8-08-2004	San José	D 0-0	A	TCL1		23 357
12-08-2004	Aurora - BOL	W 2-1	H	CSr1	Sandy [53], Tufiño [82]	
15-08-2004	The Strongest	D 1-1	H	TCL1	Sandy [30]	18 748
19-08-2004	Aurora - BOL	W 3-1	H	CSr1	Suarez 2 [60 95], Gutierrez [91]	
22-08-2004	Real Potosí	W 1-0	H	TCL1	Suarez [90]	5 032
26-08-2004	Universidad Iberoamericana	W 1-0	A	TCL1	Gutierrez [51]	1 617
28-08-2004	La Paz FC	D 1-1	A	TCL1	Guiberguis [85]	2 261
5-09-2004	Universidad Iberoamericana	D 1-1	H	TCL1	Mercado [41]	1 349
12-09-2004	San José	W 2-0	H	TCL1	Chiorazzo 2 [39 78]	6 102
19-09-2004	The Strongest	W 1-0	A	TCL1	Colque [87]	
26-09-2004	Real Potosí	D 1-1	H	TCL1	Gutierrez.L [39]	2 219
28-09-2004	Universidad de Concepción - CHI	D 0-0	A	CSr2		
16-10-2004	San José	D 2-2	H	TCL2	Guiberguis [55], Gutierrez.L [87]	13 019
19-10-2004	Universidad de Concepción - CHI	W 4-2	H	CSr2	Garcia [16], Chiorazzo [26], Gutierrez.L [30], Suarez [39]	
24-10-2004	Real Potosí	D 2-2	A	TCL2	Chiorazzo 2 [34 44]	4 173
28-10-2004	Arsenal - ARG	L 0-1	A	CSqf		
31-10-2004	Unión Central	W 3-2	A	TCL2	Guiberguis 2 [39 54], Suarez [48]	5 351
4-11-2004	Arsenal - ARG	W 3-0	H	CSqf	Ferreira [36], Chiorazzo [49], Tufiño [54]	
7-11-2004	The Strongest	W 2-0	H	TCL2	Gutierrez.L 2 [61 81]	22 631
10-11-2004	Blooming	W 6-2	H	TCL2	Gutierrez.L 2 [3p 34], Suarez [32], Tufiño [36], Chiorazzo 2 [48 62]	4 101
21-11-2004	Jorge Wilsterman	L 0-1	A	TCL2		15 204
25-11-2004	LDU Quito - ECU	D 1-1	A	CSsf	Chiorazzo [69]	
28-11-2004	San José	L 0-1	H	TCL2		3 592
1-12-2004	Blooming	L 0-2	A	TCL2		2 297
2-12-2004	LDU Quito - ECU	W 2-1	H	CSsf	Chiorazzo [11], Garcia [48]	
4-12-2004	Real Potosí	W 2-0	H	TCL2	Reyes [44], Nuñez [90]	917
7-12-2004	Oriente Petrolero	L 1-2	H	TCL2	Apaza [70]	1 007
8-12-2004	Boca Juniors - ARG	W 1-0	H	CSf		
8-12-2004	The Strongest	L 0-7	A	TCL2		5 537
11-12-2004	Unión Central	W 3-1	H	TCL2	Colque 2 [7 54], Suarez [34]	415
15-12-2004	Oriente Petrolero	L 0-9	H	TCL2		2 660
17-12-2004	Boca Juniors - ARG	L 0-2	A	CSf		
19-12-2004	Jorge Wilsterman	D 1-1	H	TCL2	Ricaldo OG [85]	615

TAP = Torneo Apertura • TCL1 = Torneo Clausura stage one • TCL2 = Torneo Clausura stage two • CS = Copa Sudamericana
r1 = first round • r2 = 2nd round • qf = quarter-final • sf = semi-final • f = final

BOT – BOTSWANA

NATIONAL TEAM RECORD
JULY 1ST 2002 TO JUNE 30TH 2005

PL	W	D	L	F	A	%
36	8	15	13	27	36	43.1

FIFA/COCA-COLA WORLD RANKING

1993	1994	1995	1996	1997	1998	1999	2000	2001	2002	2003	2004	High		Low	
140	145	155	161	162	155	165	150	153	136	112	102	**100**	11/04	**165**	02/00

2004-2005											
08/04	09/04	10/04	11/04	12/04	01/05	02/05	03/05	04/05	05/05	06/05	07/05
105	107	107	100	102	103	105	103	105	105	104	101

With the arrival of Serbian coach Veselin Jelusic three years ago, Botswana's national team have discovered some stability and ambition fuelled by their first victory in a COSAFA Cup match in 2003 against Namibia. Currently lying just outside the top 100 in the FIFA/Coca-Cola World Ranking after a steady climb, the Zebras of Botswana look like a team on the up, and reaching the final round of the 2006 FIFA World Cup™ qualifiers was another milestone. Although unable to qualify for Germany, Jelusic is developing a solid young team with MLS based striker Diphetogo Selolwane emerging as a useful striker. As one of the richer and more politically stable countries

INTERNATIONAL HONOURS
None

in Africa, Botswana does have potential although a small population provides a major stumbling block. After winning the double in 2004, Botswana Defence Force had moved to within within one of Township Rollers' record haul of eight titles. That seemed to spur Rollers on for the 2004-05 Championship and after nearly a decade without winning a major trophy they just beat Police to the finishing line to win the League for only the second time since 1985. After winning their preliminary round match, Defence Force's foray into the Confederation Cup ended at the next stage when they lost 2-1 on aggregate to St Eloi Lupopo of Congo DR.

THE FIFA BIG COUNT OF 2000

	Male	Female		Male	Female
Registered players	6 000	0	Referees	200	0
Non registered players	8 000	0	Officials	800	0
Youth players	3 000	0	Total involved	18 000	
Total players	17 000		Number of clubs	50	
Professional players	0	0	Number of teams	400	

Botswana Football Association (BFA)
PO Box 1396, Gaborone, Botswana
Tel +267 3900279   Fax +267 3900280
bfa@info.bw   www.none
President: MAKGALEMELE Dikgang Philip   General Secretary: NTSHINOGANG Thabo
Vice-President: RAMOTLHWA Segolame   Treasurer: KANDJII David   Media Officer: NTSHINOGANG Thabo
Men's Coach: JELUSIC Veselin   Women's Coach: None
BFA formed: 1970   CAF: 1976   FIFA: 1978
Colours: Blue with white & black stripes, Blue, Blue

GAMES PLAYED BY BOTSWANA IN THE 2006 FIFA WORLD CUP™ CYCLE

2002	Opponents	Score		Venue	Comp	Scorers	Att	Referee
26-08	Lesotho	L	0-1	Gaborone	Fr			
7-09	Swaziland	D	0-0	Gaborone	CNq			Moeketsi RSA
13-10	Congo DR	L	0-2	Kinshasa	CNq			Mandzioukouta CGO
14-12	Zambia	W	1-0	Gaborone	Fr	Selolwane 20		
2003								
9-03	Lesotho	L	0-1	Gaborone	Fr			
16-03	Namibia	W	1-0	Windhoek	CCr1	Molwantwa 4		Fakudze SWZ
30-03	Libya	D	0-0	Tripoli	CNq			Lassina Pare BFA
16-05	Lesotho	W	2-1	Maseru	Fr	Ntshingane 2		
25-05	Malawi	D	1-1	Gaborone	CCqf	Ntshingane 21. L 1-3p	25 000	Infante MOZ
7-06	Libya	L	0-1	Gaborone	CNq			Nunkoo MRI
10-06	Trinidad and Tobago	D	0-0	Gaborone	Fr		5 000	
22-06	Swaziland	L	2-3	Mbabane	CNq	Mogaladi 41, Kolagano 56	10 000	
5-07	Congo DR	D	0-0	Gaborone	CNq			
6-09	Swaziland	W	3-0	Mbabane	Fr			
11-10	Lesotho	W	4-1	Gaborone	WCq	Molwantwa 7, Gabolwelwe 44, Selolwane 2 50 53	10 000	Manuel Joao ANG
16-11	Lesotho	D	0-0	Maseru	WCq		9 000	Shikapande ZAM
13-12	Zimbabwe	L	0-2	Selibe-Phikwe	Fr		7 000	
2004								
29-02	Lesotho	D	0-0	Maseru	CCr1	W 11-10p	10 000	Mufeti NAM
28-04	Namibia	D	0-0	Windhoek	Fr		1 500	
26-05	Mozambique	D	0-0	Maputo	Fr		2 000	
5-06	Tunisia	L	1-4	Tunis	WCq	Selolwane 65	2 844	Abdel Rahman SUD
19-06	Malawi	W	2-0	Gaborone	WCq	Selolwane 7, Gabolwelwe 25	15 000	Awuye UGA
3-07	Morocco	L	0-1	Gaborone	WCq		22 000	Dlamini SWZ
18-07	Angola	D	1-1	Luanda	CCqf	Motlhabankwe 25. L 3-5p	6 000	Phomane LES
18-08	Zimbabwe	L	0-2	Bulawayo	Fr		5 000	
5-09	Guinea	L	0-4	Conakry	WCq		25 000	Agbenyega GHA
9-10	Kenya	W	2-1	Gaborone	WCq	Molwantwa 51, Selolwane 58	16 500	Colembi ANG
15-12	Lesotho	D	1-1	Maseru	Fr			
2005								
26-02	Zambia	D	0-0	Gaborone	Fr			
16-03	Zimbabwe	D	1-1	Harare	Fr	Moathiaping 72	3 000	
26-03	Kenya	L	0-1	Nairobi	WCq		15 000	Buenkadila COD
16-04	Namibia	D	1-1	Windhoek	CCr1	Moathiaping 90. L		Sentso LES
17-04	Zimbabwe	L	0-2	Windhoek	CCr1			Mavunza ANG
4-06	Tunisia	L	1-3	Gaborone	WCq	Gabonamong 12	20 000	Mana NGA
18-06	Malawi	W	3-1	Blantyre	WCq	Molwantwa 8, Selolwane 40, Motlhabankwe 88	20 000	Evehe CMR
1-07	Congo DR	D	0-0	Gaborone	Fr			

Fr = Friendly match • CN = CAF African Cup of Nations • CC = COSAFA Cup • WC = FIFA World Cup™ • q = qualifier • r1 = first round group • qf = quarter-final

FIFA REFEREE LIST 2005

	Int'l	DoB
CHIDODA Biggie	2003	4-08-1967
DISANG Thapelo	2003	5-04-1972
MALEPA Israel	2005	18-01-1972
MPOFU Boniface	2001	17-12-1965
NCHENGWA Kuedza	1999	27-11-1964

FIFA ASSISTANT REFEREE LIST 2005

	Int'l	DoB
JOHANNES Lekgotla	2001	11-06-1971
KEOAGILE Moletlanyi	1996	5-11-1968
LEBOTSE Harris	1999	23-06-1960
MALAPELA Oratile	2001	15-10-1965
PHATSHWANE Johnson	2002	28-05-1962
RASETSOGA Phodiso	2002	25-03-1972
SILAS Moora	2003	4-01-1970

BOTSWANA COUNTRY INFORMATION

Capital	Gaborone	Independence	1966	GDP per Capita	$9000
Population	1 561 973	Status	Republic	GDP Ranking	
Area km²	600 370	Language	English, Setswana	Dialling code	+267
Population density	2 per km²	Literacy rate	74%	Internet code	.bw
% in urban areas	28%	Main religion	Indigenous 85%	GMT +/–	+2
Towns/Cities ('000)	Gaborone 208; Francistown 89; Molepolole 63; Selibe Phikwe 53; Maun 49; Serowe 47				
Neighbours (km)	Zimbabwe 813; South Africa 1,840; Namibia 1,360				
Main stadia	National Stadium – Gaborone 22,500				

BOTSWANA NATIONAL TEAM RECORDS AND RECORD SEQUENCES

Records			Sequence records					
Victory	6-2	SWZ 2002	Wins	4	2001-2002	Clean sheets	3	Three times
Defeat	1-8	MWI 1968	Defeats	8	1968-1986	Goals scored	4	Three times
Player Caps	n/a		Undefeated	5	2001-2002	Without goal	6	1990-91, 2002
Player Goals	n/a		Without win	24	1994-1999	Goals against	14	1983-1995

BOTSWANA 2004-05 PREMIER LEAGUE

	Pl	W	D	L	F	A	Pts
Township Rollers	30	14	10	6	42	25	52
Police XI	30	16	3	11	61	39	51
Centre Chiefs	30	11	12	7	37	31	45
Mogoditshane Fighters	30	10	15	5	32	28	45
TASC	30	13	5	12	34	39	44
Notwane	30	11	10	9	45	32	43
Defence Force	30	11	10	9	32	27	43
Prisons XI	30	12	7	11	36	33	43
ECCO City Green	30	10	10	10	46	46	40
Nico United	30	10	9	11	32	40	39
Satmos	30	11	6	13	35	46	39
Botswana Meat Comm.	30	9	11	10	41	32	38
Lobtrans Gunners	30	11	5	14	30	43	38
Santos	30	9	9	12	26	32	36
TAFIC	30	6	9	15	27	47	27
Orapa Wanderers	30	5	11	14	35	51	26

5/11/2004 - 1/08/2005

COCA-COLA CUP 2004

Round of 16		Quarter-finals		Semi-finals		Final	
Defence Force	1						
Space Moonlanders *	0	Defence Force *	0 4p				
Jwaneng Comets	0	BMC	0 3p				
BMC *	1			Defence Force	3 5p		
Police	3			Notwane	3 4p		
Extension Gunners *	1	Police *	0				
TASC	0	Notwane	2				
Notwane *	1					Defence Force	2
Satmos	4					Mogoditshane	1
Boteti Young Fighters*	1	Satmos	1				
Wonder Sporting *	2	TAFIC *	0			CUP FINAL	
TAFIC	4			Satmos	0		
Township Rollers *	3			Mogoditshane	3		
Red Sparks	0	Township Rollers *	1			28-08-2004	
Prisons	0	Mogoditshane	2			National Stadium, Gaborone	
Mogoditshane *	2	* Home Team					

RECENT LEAGUE AND CUP RECORD

	Championship						Cup		
Year	Champions	Pts	Runners-up	Pts	Third	Pts	Winners	Score	Runners-up
1997	Defence Force	40	Gaborone United	35	PG Notwane	35	PG Notwane	2-0	Mokgosi Fighters
1998	PG Notwane	39	Defence Force	39	Police XI	35	Defence Force	1-0	Jwaneng Cosmos
1999	Mogodishane	25	Defence Force	21	Centre Chiefs	21	Mogodishane	3-0	Satmos
2000	Mogoditshane	42	Centre Chiefs	40	Defence Force	37	Mogodishane	1-1 5-4p	Gaborone United
2001	Mogoditshane	45	Defence Force	44	Police XI	43	TASC	2-0	Extension Gunners
2002	Defence Force	47	Mogoditshane	38	Centre Chiefs	36	Tafic	0-0 6-5p	TASC
2003	Mogoditshane	2-1	Police XI				Mogodishane	1-0	Township Rollers
2004	Defence Force		Police XI		TASC	39	Defence Force	2-1	Mogoditshane
2005	Township Rollers	52	Police XI	51	Centre Chiefs	45			

12 October 2004. Sydney Football Stadium, Sydney, Australia. Harry Kewell helps Australia to an 11–1 aggregate victory over the Solomon Islands in the final of the OFC Nations Cup.

13 October 2004. Comunal, Andorra la Vella, Andorra. Goalscorer Marc Bernaus is mobbed by celebrating team-mates. His goal gave Andorra their first win in a competitive international.

24 October 2004. Old Trafford, Manchester, England. Arsene Wenger is unhappy as Arsenal's extraordinary record unbeaten run comes to an end at 49 matches with defeat against Manchester United.

Above **14 November 2004. Home Depot Centre, Carson, USA.** DC United's Jaime Moreno congratulates goalscorer Alecko Eskandarian in their team's 2–1 victory over Kansas City Wizards in the 2004 MLS Cup final.

Top **17 November 2004. Tianhe Stadium, Guangzhou, China PR.** Despair for China PR. Despite winning their final FIFA World Cup™ qualifier 7–0 against Hong Kong they are eliminated by Kuwait on goal difference.

Above **20 November 2004. Camp Nou, Barcelona, Spain.** Barcelona President Juan Laporta enjoys the final word as his team beat Florentino Perez's Real Madrid 3–0 to set the tone for the Spanish League season.

Left **27 November 2004. Rajamangala National, Bangkok, Thailand.** Germany celebrate winning the FIFA U-19 Women's World Championship with a 2–0 victory over China PR in the final.

BRA – BRAZIL

NATIONAL TEAM RECORD
JULY 1ST 2002 TO JUNE 30TH 2005

PL	W	D	L	F	A	%
48	24	15	9	89	43	65.6

Prior to the 1994 World Cup, sceptics wondered if Brazil would ever re-emerge as a world power. Eleven years on the notion seems ridiculous and in August 2005 the only international title not held by Brazil was the Olympic title. 2004 saw the addition of the Copa América to the trophy cabinet along with the FIFA Futsal World Cup and then the FIFA Confederations Cup in 2005. Unsurprisingly the men maintained their lead in the FIFA/Coca-Cola World Ranking at the end of 2004 whilst Ronaldinho was elected FIFA World Player, one of three Brazilians to pick up an annual award, along with Falcao for futsal and Thiago for winning the inaugural FIFA Interactive World Cup. The Seleção maintained their progress in the FIFA World Cup™ South American qualifiers though there were some tricky moments along the way with defeats in Ecuador and Argentina, but that can be expected in such a long campaign. Ronaldo and Ronaldinho dominated the frontline for the national team but it was the emergence of Inter's Adriano that caused most excitement. His last-minute equaliser saved Brazil from defeat in the final of the Copa América against Argentina, a tournament in which he finished as top scorer, and he was the player of the tournament as Brazil

BRAZIL INTERNATIONAL HONOURS
FIFA World Cup™ 1958 1962 1970 1994 2002   **FIFA Confederations Cup** 1997 2005
FIFA World Youth Championship 1983 1985 1993 2003   **FIFA U-17 World Championship** 1997 1999 2003
Copa América 1919 1922 1949 1989 1997 1999 2004   **South American Women's Championship** 1991 1995 1998 2003
Sudamericana Sub-20 1974 1983 1985 1988 1991 1992 1995 2001   **Sudamericana Sub-17** 1988 1991 1995 1997 1999 2001
FIFA Club World Championship Corínthians 2000   **Copa Toyota Libertadores** Santos 1962 1963 Cruzeiro 1976 1997
Flamengo 1981 Grêmio 1983 1995 São Paulo 1992 1993 2005 Vasco da Gama 1998 Palmeiras 1999

won the FIFA Confederations Cup in Germany, where he again finished as top scorer. Domestically Santos were the dominant force, winning their second Championship in three years, with both Diego and Robinho influential in a team led by Wanderlei Luxemburgo who won his fifth title as a coach. It may be a while before Serie A can match the pulling power of Europe – over 900 players left in 2004 – but the CBF is determined to bring some order into an often chaotic domestic scene. A European-style championship was maintained although a minimum ticket price of $5 meant crowds fell to an average of 8,085 from 10,342 in 2003. Surprises in the Championship included the relegation of Grêmio whilst in the Copa do Brasil Second Division Paulista stunned Fluminense in the final in what turned out to be another wretched year for clubs from Rio de Janeiro. The 2005 Copa Libertadores proved to be a major fillip for Brazilian clubs when both São Paulo and Atlético Paranaense qualified for the final, the first time a final had been contested by two clubs from the same country, with São Paulo winning the title for a third time.

Confederação Brasileira de Futebol (CBF)
Rua Victor Civita 66, Bloco 1 - Edifício 5 - 5 Andar, Barra da Tijuca, Rio de Janeiro 22.775-040, Brazil
Tel +55 21 35359610   Fax +55 21 35359611
CBF@cbffutebol.com.br   www.cbfnews.com.br
President: TEIXEIRA Ricardo Terra   General Secretary: TEIXEIRA Marco Antonio
Vice-President: BASTOS Jose Sebastiao   Treasurer: OSORIO LOPES DA COSTA Antonio   Media Officer: PAIVA Rodrigo
Men's Coach: PARREIRA Carlos Alberto   Women's Coach: FERREIRA Luiz
CBF formed: 1914   CONMEBOL: 1916   FIFA: 1923
Colours: Yellow, Blue, White or Blue, White, White

GAMES PLAYED BY BRAZIL IN THE 2006 FIFA WORLD CUP™ CYCLE

2002 Opponents	Score	Venue	Comp	Scorers	Att	Referee
21-08 Paraguay	L 0-1	Fortaleza	Fr		30 000	Ruiz COL
20-11 Korea Republic	W 3-2	Seoul	Fr	Ronaldo 2 $^{16\ 68}$, Ronaldinho ^{90p}	63 000	Lu Jun CHN
2003						
12-02 China PR	D 0-0	Guangzhou	Fr		80 000	Kim Tae Young KOR
29-03 Portugal	L 1-2	Oporto	Fr	Ronaldinho ^{64p}		Yefet ISR
30-04 Mexico	D 0-0	Guadalajara	Fr		60 000	Ruiz COL
11-06 Nigeria	W 3-0	Abuja	Fr	Gil ^{34}, Luis Fabiano ^{38}, Adriano ^{81}	30 000	Quartey GHA
19-06 Cameroon	L 0-1	Paris	CCr1		46 719	Ivanov RUS
21-06 USA	W 1-0	Lyon	CCr1	Adriano ^{22}	20 306	Batista POR
23-06 Turkey	D 2-2	Saint-Etienne	CCr1	Adriano ^{23}, Alex ^{90}	29 170	Merk GER
13-07 Mexico	L 0-1	Mexico City	GCr1		60 000	Sibrian SLV
15-07 Honduras	W 2-1	Mexico City	GCr1	Maicon ^{16}, Diego ^{84}		Navarro CAN
19-07 Colombia	W 2-0	Miami	GCqf	Kaka 2 $^{42\ 67}$	23 425	Stott USA
23-07 USA	W 2-1	Miami	GCsf	Kaka ^{89}, Diego ^{100p}	35 211	Batres GUA
27-07 Mexico	L 0-1	Mexico City	GCf		80 000	Navarro CAN
7-09 Colombia	W 2-1	Barranquilla	WCq	Ronaldo ^{23}, Kaka ^{62}	50 000	Elizondo ARG
10-09 Ecuador	W 1-0	Manaus	WCq	Ronaldinho ^{13}	35 000	Solorzano VEN
12-10 Jamaica	W 1-0	Leicester	Fr	Roberto Carlos ^{14}	32 000	Styles ENG
16-11 Peru	D 1-1	Lima	WCq	Rivaldo ^{20p}	70 000	Ruiz COL
19-11 Uruguay	D 3-3	Curitiba	WCq	Kaka ^{19}, Ronaldo 2 $^{29\ 87}$	30 000	Elizondo ARG
2004						
18-02 Republic of Ireland	D 0-0	Dublin	Fr		44 000	Frisk SWE
31-03 Paraguay	D 0-0	Asuncion	WCq		40 000	Ruiz COL
28-04 Hungary	W 4-1	Budapest	Fr	Kaka ^{33}, Luis Fabiano 2 $^{36\ 45}$, Ronaldinho ^{76}	45 000	De Santis ITA
20-05 France	D 0-0	Paris	FIFA		79 344	Gonzalez ESP
2-06 Argentina	W 3-1	Belo Horizonte	WCq	Ronaldo 3 $^{16p\ 67p\ 90p}$	50 000	Ruiz COL
6-06 Chile	D 1-1	Santiago	WCq	Luis Fabiano ^{15}	62 503	Elizondo ARG
8-07 Chile	W 1-0	Arequipa	CAr1	Luis Fabiano ^{89}	35 000	Rodriguez MEX
11-07 Costa Rica	W 4-1	Arequipa	CAr1	Adriano 3 $^{45\ 54\ 68}$, Juan ^{49}	12 000	Baldassi ARG
14-07 Paraguay	L 1-2	Arequipa	CAr1	Luis Fabiano ^{35}	8 000	Hidalgo PER
18-07 Mexico	W 4-0	Piura	CAqf	Alex ^{26p}, Adriano 2 $^{65\ 78}$, Ricardo Oliveira ^{87}	22 000	Ruiz COL
21-07 Uruguay	D 1-1	Lima	CAsf	Adriano ^{46} W 5-3p	10 000	Rodriguez MEX
25-07 Argentina	D 2-2	Lima	CAf	Luisao ^{45}, Adriano ^{90}	43 000	Amarilla PAR
18-08 Haiti	W 6-0	Port-au-Prince	Fr	Roger 2 $^{17\ 40}$, Ronaldinho 3 $^{33\ 70\ 80}$, Nilmar ^{89}	15 000	Oliveira BRA
5-09 Bolivia	W 3-1	Sao Paulo	WCq	Ronaldo ^{1}, Ronaldinho ^{12p}, Adriano ^{44}	60 000	Baldassi ARG
8-09 Germany	D 1-1	Berlin	Fr	Ronaldinho ^{9}	74 315	Meier SUI
9-10 Venezuela	W 5-2	Maracaibo	WCq	Kaka 2 $^{5\ 34}$, Ronaldo 2 $^{48\ 50}$, Adriano ^{75}	26 133	Chandia CHI
13-10 Colombia	D 0-0	Maceio	WCq		20 000	Larrionda URU
16-11 Ecuador	L 0-1	Quito	WCq		38 308	Ruiz COL
2005						
9-02 Hong Kong	W 7-1	Hong Kong	Fr	Lucio ^{19}, Roberto Carlos ^{30}, Ricardo Oliveira 2 $^{45\ 57}$ Ronaldinho ^{49}, Robinho ^{77}, Alex ^{79p}		
27-03 Peru	W 1-0	Goiania	WCq	Kaka ^{74}	49 163	Amarilla PAR
30-03 Uruguay	D 1-1	Montevideo	WCq	Emerson ^{67}	60 000	Baldassi ARG
27-04 Guatemala	W 3-0	Sao Paulo	Fr	Anderson ^{4}, Romario ^{16}, Grafite ^{65}	36 235	Vazquez URU
5-06 Paraguay	W 4-1	Porto Alegre	WCq	Ronaldinho 2 $^{32p\ 41p}$, Ze Roberto ^{70}, Robinho ^{82}	45 000	Vazquez URU
8-06 Argentina	L 1-3	Buenos Aires	WCq	Roberto Carlos ^{71}	49 497	Mendez URU
16-06 Greece	W 3-0	Leipzig	CCr1	Adriano ^{41}, Robinho ^{46}, Juninho Pernambuco ^{81}	42 507	Michel SVK
19-06 Mexico	L 0-1	Hanover	CCr1		43 677	Rosetti ITA
22-06 Japan	D 2-2	Köln	CCr1	Robinho ^{10}, Ronaldinho ^{32}	44 922	Daami TUN
26-06 Germany	W 3-2	Nürnberg	CCsf	Adriano 2 $^{21\ 76}$, Ronaldinho ^{43p}	42 187	Breeze AUS
29-06 Argentina	W 4-1	Frankfurt	CCf	Adriano 2 $^{11\ 63}$, Kaka ^{16}, Ronaldinho ^{47}	45 591	Michel SVK

Fr = Friendly match • CC = FIFA Confederations Cup • GC = CONCACAF Gold Cup • CA = Copa America • WC = FIFA World Cup™
FIFA = FIFA Centennial celebration match • q = qualifier • r1 = 1st round • qf = quarter-final • sf = semi-final • f = final

FIFA/COCA-COLA WORLD RANKING

1993	1994	1995	1996	1997	1998	1999	2000	2001	2002	2003	2004	High	Low
3	1	1	1	1	1	1	1	3	1	1	1	1	8 08/93

2004-2005											
08/04	09/04	10/04	11/04	12/04	01/05	02/05	03/05	04/05	05/05	06/05	07/05
1	1	1	1	1	1	1	1	1	1	1	1

THE FIFA BIG COUNT OF 2000

	Male	Female		Male	Female
Registered players	275 000	4 000	Referees	3 000	46
Non registered players	5 500 000	30 000	Officials	40 000	1 000
Youth players	1 222 828	2 000	Total involved	7 077 874	
Total players	7 033 828		Number of clubs	6 000 *	
Professional players	14 709	152	Number of teams	20 000	

NATIONAL CAPS

	Caps
CAFU	126
ROBERTO CARLOS	107
CLAUDIO TAFFAREL	101
DJALMA SANTOS	98
GILMAR	94
PELE	92
ROBERTO RIVELINO	92
CARLOS DUNGA	91
RONALDO	82
ALDAIR & JAIRZINHO	81

NATIONAL GOALS

	Goals
PELE	77
RONALDO	54
ROMARIO	54
ZICO	48
BEBETO	39
RIVALDO	34
JAIRZINHO	33
ADEMIR DE MENEZES	32
TOSTÃO	32
ZIZINHO	30

NATIONAL COACH

	Years
SILVA Carlos Alberto	1987-'88
LAZARONI Sebastião	1989-'90
FALCAO Roberto	1990-'01
PAULO Ernesto	1991
PARREIRA Carlos Alberto	1991-'94
ZAGALLO Mario	1994-'98
LUXEMBURGO Wanderlay	1998-'00
LEAO Emerson	2000-'01
SCOLARI Luis Felipe	2001-'02
PARREIRA Carlos Alberto	2002-

BRAZIL NATIONAL TEAM RECORDS AND RECORD SEQUENCES

Records			Sequence records					
Victory	10-1	BOL 1949	Wins	14	1997	Clean sheets	8	1989
Defeat	0-6	URU 1920	Defeats	4	2001	Goals scored	47	1994-1997
Player Caps	126	CAFU	Undefeated	43	1993-1997	Without goal	5	1990
Player Goals	77	PELE	Without win	7	1983-84, 1990-91	Goals against	24	1937-1944

BRAZIL COUNTRY INFORMATION

Capital	Brasilia	Independence	1822 from Portugal	GDP per Capita	$7 600
Population	184 101 109	Status	Republic	GNP Ranking	1
Area km²	8 511 965	Language	Portuguese	Dialling code	+55
Population density	21 per km²	Literacy rate	84%	Internet code	.br
% in urban areas	78%	Main religion	Christian 95%	GMT +/–	-3
Towns/Cities ('000)	São Paulo 19 091; Rio de Janeiro 11 719; Belo Horizonte 4 919; Porto Alegre 3 762; Recife 3 540; Salvador 3 415; Fortaleza 3 131; Curitiba 3 042; Brasilia 2 207; Belém 2 252; Brasilia 2 207; Goiânia 1 855; Santos 1 664; Manaus 1 598; Vitória 1 512; Campinas 1 443; São Luis 1 224; Natal 1 172, Maceió 1 064; Teresina 1 014; João Pessoa 975; Ribeirão Preto 840; Florianópolis 790				
Neighbours (km)	Venezuela 2 200; Guyana 1 119; Surinam 597; French Guiana 673; Uruguay 985; Argentina 1 224; Paraguay 1 290; Bolivia 3 400; Peru 1 560; Colombia 1 643; Atlantic Ocean 7 491				
Main stadia	Maracanã – Rio 103 045; Mineirão – Belo Horizonte 81 987; Morumbi – São Paulo 80 000; Castelão – São Luis 75 000; Castelão – Fortaleza 69 000; Fonte Nova – Salvador 66 000				

BRAZIL 2004

SERIE A

	Pl	W	D	L	F	A	Pts	Santos	Atlético	São Paulo	Palmeiras	Corínth'ns	Goiás	Juventude	Inter	Flu	Ponte P.	Fig'ense	Coritiba	Cruzeiro	Paysandu	Paraná	Vasco	Flamengo	Caetano	Atlético	Botafogo	Criciúma	Guarani	Vitória	Grêmio
Santos † ‡	46	27	8	11	103	58	**89**		1-1	2-1	0-4	1-1	2-1	2-1	3-0	5-0	4-0	4-1	4-2	1-3	6-0	5-1	2-1	2-0	0-1	2-0	2-0	5-2	2-1	4-1	5-1
Atlético Paranaense †	46	25	11	10	93	56	**86**	1-0		1-0	0-0	3-1	6-0	4-1	2-1	4-1	4-0	0-3	1-1	3-1	2-0	1-1	2-0	2-1	5-2	5-0	1-1	6-1	2-0	1-3	0-0
São Paulo † ‡	46	24	10	12	78	43	**82**	1-0	1-0		2-1	1-1	4-0	4-0	2-1	1-0	2-0	2-1	2-3	0-0	7-0	2-2	1-0	1-1	4-2	1-0	5-2	2-0	3-3	2-1	3-2
Palmeiras †	46	22	13	11	72	47	**79**	1-2	3-1	2-1		0-1	0-3	4-1	3-1	3-2	3-0	0-0	2-0	1-3	1-0	1-1	2-2	1-2	3-1	0-0	2-1	3-2	0-2	2-2	2-0
Corinthians ‡	46	20	14	12	54	54	**74**	2-3	0-5	0-0	0-4		1-0	1-2	0-0	1-1	2-0	5-2	0-0	1-0	2-1	1-0	3-1	1-1	2-0	1-0	2-2	1-0	1-0	1-0	1-1
Goiás ‡	46	21	9	16	81	68	**72**	3-3	2-0	2-0	0-0	1-1		1-2	1-0	4-0	5-0	1-0	1-2	2-2	3-2	3-0	3-2	2-2	3-2	1-0	3-1	2-1	2-0	4-0	4-0
Juventude ‡	46	20	10	16	60	66	**70**	1-2	3-3	1-2	0-2	1-0	1-1		2-3	2-1	1-2	0-0	1-0	1-0	1-2	4-0	1-1	1-0	2-2	1-1	1-0	1-0	2-0	3-2	1-1
Internacional ‡	46	20	7	19	66	59	**67**	2-1	6-0	1-1	1-0	3-0	1-0	1-2		0-0	1-2	4-0	1-1	2-0	1-0	2-1	1-3	0-0	1-0	4-1	3-1	3-0	1-3	2-1	2-0
Fluminense ‡	46	18	13	15	65	68	**67**	1-0	1-2	1-0	1-1	2-0	1-4	7-1	3-1		1-0	0-2	1-1	0-0	1-1	3-1	1-0	2-1	1-0	1-1	1-4	1-1	1-1	1-0	2-0
Ponte Preta	46	19	7	20	43	73	**64**	0-4	2-3	0-1	0-0	3-2	2-0	0-1	1-2	3-2		0-2	0-0	1-0	3-0	0-2	3-2	1-0	0-3	1-1	1-1	1-0	3-1	1-0	1-0
Figueirense	46	17	12	17	57	59	**63**	2-1	1-1	1-0	0-1	0-1	3-2	1-0	1-0	2-1	0-1		1-1	0-0	1-1	0-0	2-2	3-2	1-0	2-1	3-1	2-0	1-1	2-1	2-0
Coritiba	46	15	17	14	53	48	**62**	0-1	1-2	1-2	0-0	1-2	1-0	2-3	1-1	2-0	2-0	2-0		1-1	1-1	1-1	0-1	1-0	1-0	0-1	1-0	1-0	1-0	5-1	2-1
Cruzeiro ‡	46	16	8	22	69	81	**56**	4-4	2-4	2-1	2-1	0-1	1-3	2-1	2-0	2-3	5-0	3-3	0-3		1-0	1-4	3-2	2-0	0-1	0-3	3-2	2-2	2-0	4-0	2-0
Paysandu	46	14	14	18	56	76	**56**	1-1	0-3	1-0	1-0	2-1	4-2	0-1	2-1	3-3	3-0	3-1	0-0	3-1		1-1	1-2	2-2	0-0	2-1	2-0	2-2	4-2	4-2	1-3
Paraná	46	15	9	22	52	73	**54**	3-2	1-0	0-2	1-2	1-2	2-1	1-2	1-2	0-1	0-1	2-1	1-0	2-0	2-0		2-1	2-1	0-1	1-0	1-1	0-3	0-0	4-1	1-0
Vasco da Gama	46	14	12	20	64	68	**54**	2-3	1-0	0-0	2-5	1-3	3-1	1-1	2-0	1-1	2-2	1-0	2-3	3-2	0-1	0-0		1-0	1-2	3-0	4-0	0-1	0-1	3-1	1-1
Flamengo	46	13	15	18	51	53	**54**	1-1	3-0	1-0	0-1	0-0	4-0	0-1	1-2	1-2	0-0	0-3	0-0	6-2	4-1	2-1	0-1		1-1	0-0	0-0	3-1	1-0	2-0	3-0
São Caetano §	46	23	8	15	65	49	**53**	0-3	0-3	0-0	1-1	2-1	2-0	1-0	2-0	2-0	0-1	1-0	1-0	4-1	3-0	2-1	3-2	0-1		1-1	1-2	5-0	3-0	1-0	2-0
Atlético Mineiro	46	12	17	17	60	66	**53**	3-3	0-1	0-5	1-2	2-2	0-2	1-1	1-1	2-1	1-2	3-1	2-1	2-0	0-0	4-1	1-1	6-1	3-0		1-1	2-2	3-2	1-1	3-0
Botafogo	46	11	18	17	62	71	**51**	2-0	1-1	1-0	1-1	1-2	1-4	0-1	5-1	3-3	0-1	1-1	4-1	2-1	2-2	4-3	2-2	0-0	1-1	2-2		1-1	1-0	1-1	2-1
Criciúma	46	13	11	22	61	78	**50**	1-1	4-1	1-1	1-2	1-1	7-2	2-0	2-1	0-2	3-1	2-1	3-3	1-2	1-0	1-2	1-0	1-1	0-4	4-2	1-0		1-1	2-0	1-2
Guarani	46	11	16	19	43	55	**49**	0-1	0-0	2-3	1-0	0-1	1-1	3-1	2-1	1-1	0-0	2-1	0-0	2-0	0-0	1-0	1-1	0-1	1-1	1-1	0-2	2-1		0-0	2-0
Vitória	46	13	9	24	68	87	**48**	1-2	2-3	1-4	2-2	1-1	0-0	1-1	2-1	2-3	1-2	3-1	2-2	3-2	4-1	6-1	4-1	5-1	1-2	2-1	1-0	1-0	3-2		2-0
Grêmio	46	9	12	25	60	80	**39**	3-1	3-3	2-1	2-3	4-0	1-1	2-4	1-3	2-3	6-1	2-2	1-1	2-3	1-1	4-0	1-2	0-0	1-2	0-1	2-2	2-0	1-1	4-0	

21/04/2004 - 19/12/2004 • † Teams qualifying for the Copa Libertadores 2005 • ‡ Teams qualifying for the Copa Sudamericana 2005 • § São Caetano deducted 24 points for fielding Serginho on 27 October, who died during the match. São Caetano had knowledge of his heart condition.

TOP SCORERS

Washington	Atlético PR	34
Alex Dias	Goiás	22
Deivid	Santos	21
Robinho	Santos	21
Cláudio Pitbull	Grêmio	19

BRAZIL 2004 SERIE B PRIMEIRA FASE

	Pl	W	D	L	F	A	Pts
Brasiliense †	23	13	7	3	43	22	**46**
Náutico †	23	14	3	6	46	27	**45**
Bahia †	23	13	4	6	38	24	**43**
Ituano †	23	12	6	5	41	20	**42**
Fortaleza †	23	11	6	6	43	29	**39**
Marília †	23	10	6	7	38	29	**36**
Avaí †	23	10	6	7	28	30	**36**
Santa Cruz †	23	10	5	8	35	25	**35**
Paulista	23	10	5	8	32	32	**35**
Caxias RS	23	10	4	9	30	32	**34**
Portuguesa	23	8	7	8	31	31	**31**
Ceará	23	9	3	11	30	33	**30**
Anapolina	23	9	3	11	25	29	**30**
Santo André §(-12)	23	12	5	6	38	28	**29**
CRB	23	7	8	8	32	33	**29**
São Raimundo	23	8	4	11	31	36	**28**
Sport Recife	23	7	7	9	24	31	**28**
Vila Nova	23	7	6	10	34	38	**27**
América RN	23	7	5	11	22	36	**26**
Remo	23	5	10	8	30	40	**25**
América MG	23	6	5	12	25	40	**23**
Joinville	23	6	0	17	24	42	**18**
Mogi Mirim	23	2	12	9	26	38	**18**
Londrina	23	4	5	14	19	40	**17**

7/08/2004 - 7/05/2005 • † Qualified for semi-final stage

SERIE B FASE SEMI-FINAL

Group A	Pl	W	D	L	F	A	Pts	Fortal.	Brasil.	Ituano	SC
Fortaleza †	6	2	2	2	8	7	**8**		3-0	1-1	1-1
Brasiliense †	6	2	2	2	6	6	**8**	2-0		2-0	1-1
Ituano	6	2	2	2	7	9	**8**	0-2	2-1		2-1
Santa Cruz	6	1	4	1	8	7	**7**	3-1	0-0	2-2	

1/10/2004 - 30/10/2004 • † Qualified for final stage

SERIE B FASE SEMI-FINAL

Group B	Pl	W	D	L	F	A	Pts	Bahia	Avaí	Náut.	Maríl.
Bahia †	6	4	1	1	8	5	**13**		1-0	1-0	4-1
Avaí †	6	3	1	2	6	4	**10**	0-0		1-0	1-0
Náutico	6	2	1	3	7	6	**7**	4-1	2-1		0-0
Marília	6	1	1	4	4	10	**4**	0-1	1-3	2-1	

1/10/2004 - 30/10/2004 • † Qualified for final stage

SERIE B FASE FINAL

Group A	Pl	W	D	L	F	A	Pts	Brasil.	Fortal.	Avaí	Bahia
Brasiliense	6	4	0	2	8	5	**12**		1-0	2-0	2-1
Fortaleza	6	2	2	2	4	4	**8**	1-0		2-0	1-1
Avaí	6	2	2	2	4	5	**8**	1-0	0-0		2-0
Bahia	6	1	2	3	7	9	**5**	2-3	2-0	1-1	

6/11/2004 - 11/12/2004

COPA DO BRASIL 2005

First Round			Second Round			Third Round		
Paulista *	1	1						
Juventude	0	1	Paulista *	1	2			
São Raimundo *		1	Botafogo - RJ	1	2			
Botafogo - RJ		4				Paulista	0 1	4p
Friburgense *	4	1				Internacional *	1 0	2p
Caldense	1	2	Friburgense *	1	0			
SER Chapadão *	1	0	Internacional	1	4			
Internacional	2	2						
Corinthians	1	3						
Sampaio Corrêa *	1	0	Corinthians	0	5			
CENE	1	1	Cianorte *	3	1			
Cianorte *	2	1				Corinthians *	2 0	2p
Remo	1	4				Figueirense	0 2	3p
Grêmio Coariense *	1	2	Remo	1	2			
América - RJ	0	2	Figueirense *	0	4			
Figueirense *	1	1						
Baraúnas *	2 1	4p						
América - MG	1 2	2p	Baraúnas *	1	2			
Confiança	1	0	Vitória	0	1			
Vitória	0	3				Baraúnas *	2	3
Moto Clube		3				Vasco da Gama	2	0
Rio Branco *		1	Moto Clube *	1	0			
União Rondonópolis *	2	0	Vasco da Gama	2	6			
Vasco da Gama	2	2						
Santa Cruz		4						
Potiguar *		0	Santa Cruz *	2	0			
CRAC *	0	1	Guarani	0	0			
Guarani	0	2				Santa Cruz	0	1
Ipatinga *	2	2				Cruzeiro *	4	0
Americano	0	2	Ipatinga *		0			
Sergipe *	0	0	Cruzeiro		3			
Cruzeiro	1	7						
Ceará	0	3						
4 de Julho *	0	2	Ceará	0	4			
União Cacoalense *	0	1	Paysandu *	2	0			
Paysandu	1	3				Ceará	2	1
Ypiranga *	2	1				Flamengo *	0	1
São Raimundo - AM *	0	3	Ypiranga *		0			
River	1	1	Flamengo		2			
Flamengo	1	3						
Ituano		0						
Atlético Hermann Aichinger *§		0	Ituano *	2	1			
Coruripe *	1	1	Fortaleza	0	2			
Fortaleza	1	3				Ituano *	0	1
Brasiliense	2	4				Atlético Mineiro	0	3
Serra *	2	2	Brasiliense *		1			
Estrela do Norte *	3	0	Atlético Mineiro		3			
Atlético Mineiro	4	6						
Treze	0	5						
Ulbra *	3	0	Treze *	2	1			
Corinthians Maceió *		0	São Caetano	1	1			
São Caetano		2				Treze	1	1
Náutico	1	3				Coritiba *	2	0
Palmas *	0	1	Náutico *	1	0			
CFZ de Brasília *		0	Coritiba	0	3			
Coritiba		2						
Grêmio	1	1						
Bahia *	2	0	Grêmio	1	3			
Cuiabá *	1	0	Vila Nova *	1	1			
Vila Nova	1	2				Grêmio	0	0
Esportivo *	4	0				Fluminense *	3	1
Londrina	1	2	Esportivo *	1	0			
Campinense *	1	1	Fluminense	2	1			
Fluminense	0	3						

If the away team wins the first leg by two goals no second leg is played • § Atlético disqualified

COPA DO BRASIL 2005

Quarter-finals **Semi-finals** **Final**

Paulista	0 1 3p
Figueirense *	1 0 1p

Paulista *	3 2
Cruzeiro	1 3

Baraúnas *	3 0
Cruzeiro	7 5

Paulista *	2 0
Fluminense	0 0

Ceará	1 2
Atlético Mineiro *	1 0

Ceará	2 1
Fluminense *	2 4

Treze	0 1 8p
Fluminense *	1 0 9p

* Home team in the first leg

CLUB DIRECTORY

Club	Town/City	Stadium	Phone	www.	Lge	Cup	SC	CL
Atlético Mineiro	Belo Horizonte	Mineirão 81 987	+55 31 32916060	atletico.com.br	1	0	38	0
Atlético Paranaense	Curitiba	Arena da Baixada 32 000	+55 41 21055600	atleticopr.com.br	1	0	21	0
Botafogo	Rio de Janeiro	Caio Martins 12 000	+55 21 27145582	botafogonocoracao.com.br	1	0	18	0
Corinthians	São Paulo	São Jorge 12 000	+55 11 61953000	sccorinthians.com.br	3	2	25	0
Coritiba	Curitiba	Pinheirão 56 793	+55 41 3623234	coritiba.com.br	1	0	32	0
Criciúma	Criciúma	Heribelto Hulse 28 749	+55 48 4373844	criciumaec.com.br	0	1	7	0
Cruzeiro	Belo Horizonte	Mineirão 81 987	+55 31 32955200	cruzeiro.com.br	1	4	33	2
Figueirense	Florianópolis	Orlando Scarpelli 21 069	+55 48 2443956	figueirense.com.br	0	0	13	0
Flamengo	Rio de Janeiro	Raulino de Oliveira 20 000	+55 21 25290100	flamengo.com.br	4	1	28	1
Fluminense	Rio de Janeiro	Laranjeiras 8 000	+55 21 25532898	fluminense.com.br	1	0	29	0
Goiás	Goiânia	Serra Dourada 54 048	+55 62 5464848	goiasesporteclube.com.br	0	0	20	0
Grêmio	Porto Alegre	Olímpico 51 081	+55 51 32182837	gremio.com.br	2	4	33	2
Guarani	Campinas	Brinco de Ouro 30 988	+55 19 37947900	guaranifc.com.br	1	0	2	0
Internacional	Porto Alegre	Beira Rio 58 306	+55 51 32304600	internacional.com.br	3	1	36	0
Juventude	Caxias do Sul	Alfredo Jaconi 30 519	+55 54 30278700	juventude.com.br	0	1	1	0
Palmeiras	São Paulo	Parque Antartica 32 000	+55 11	palmeiras.com.br	4	1	21	1
Paraná	Curitiba	Vila Capanema 22 500	+55 41 30294747	paranaclube.com.br	0	0	0	0
Paysandu	Belém	Mangueirão 12 000	+55 91 2124474	paysandu.com.br	0	0	6	0
Ponte Preta	Campinas	Moisés Lucarelli 20 080	+55 19 21017201	pontepretaesportes.com.br	0	0	0	0
Santos	Santos	Vila Belmiro 2- 120	+55 13 32574000	Santosfc.com.br	2	0	15	2
São Caetano	São Caetano do Sul	Municipal 22 738	+55 11 42324688	adsaocaetano.com.br	0	0	1	0
São Paulo	São Paulo	Morumbi 80 000	+55 11	spfc.com.br	3	0	21	2
Vasco da Gama	Rio de Janeiro	São Januário 35 000	+55 21 25807373	crvascodagama.com	3	0	22	1
Vitória	Salvador	Barradão 35 000	+55 71 3735200	ecvitoria.com.br	0	0	23	0

Lge = National Championship since the first tournament in 1971 • Cup = Copa do Brasil since the first tournament in 1989 • SC = State Championship • Clubs in Rio also use the Maracanã (103 045) for the bigger games • Clubs in São Paulo also use the Pacaembu (45 000)

2005 STATE CHAMPIONSHIPS

State	Winners	Score	Runners-up
Acre	Rio Branco	3-0 1-1 0-0	Adesg
Alagoas	ASA	‡	
Amapá			
Amazonas	Grêmio Coariense	‡	
Bahia	Vitória	2-2 0-0	Bahia
Ceará	Fortaleza	1-3 2-0	Icasa
Distrito Federal	Brasiliense	†	
Espírito Santo	Serra	2-3 4-2	Estrela do Norte
Goiás	Vila Nova	1-1 0-0 3-1p	Goiás
Maranhão			
Mato Grosso	Vila Aurora	2-2 3-1	Operário
Mato Grosso Sul	CENE	‡	
Minas Gerais	Ipatinga	1-1 2-1	Cruzeiro
Pará	Paysandu	‡	

2005 STATE CHAMPIONSHIPS

State	Winners	Score	Runners-up
Paraíba	Treze	‡	
Paraná	Atlético Paranaense	0-1 1-0 4-2p	Coritiba
Pernambuco	Santa Cruz	‡	
Piauí			
Rio de Janeiro	Fluminense	3-4 3-1	Volta Redonda
Rio Grande Nor.	São Goncalo	0-0 3-2p	Santa Cruz
Rio Grande Sul	Internacional	2-0 2-3	15 de Novembro
Rondônia	Vilhena	1-2 4-2	Ji-Paraná
Roraima	São Raimundo	1-1 4-3p	Baré
Santa Catarina	Criciúma	1-1 1-0	Hermann Aichinger
São Paulo	São Paulo FC	†	
Sergipe	Itabaiana	†	
Tocantins	Colinas	2-2 2-1	Araguaína

‡ Won both stages so no final needed. † Played on a league basis

RECENT LEAGUE AND CUP RECORD

National Championship

Year	Champions	Score/Runners-up	Runners-up/Third	
1989	Vasco da Gama	1-0	São Paulo FC	
1990	Corinthians	1-0 1-0	São Paulo FC	
1991	São Paulo FC	1-0 0-0	Bragantino	
1992	Flamengo	3-0 2-2	Botafogo	
1993	Palmeiras	1-0 2-0	Vitória	
1994	Palmeiras	3-1 1-1	Corinthians	
1995	Botafogo	2-1 1-1	Santos	
1996	Grêmio	0-2 2-0	Portuguesa	
1997	Vasco da Gama	0-0 0-0	Palmeiras	
1998	Corinthians	2-2 1-1 2-0	Cruzeiro	
1999	Corinthians	2-3 2-0 0-0	Atlético Mineiro	
2000	Vasco da Gama	1-1 3-1	São Caetano	
2001	Atlético Paranaense	4-2 1-0	São Caetano	
2002	Santos	2-0 3-2	Corinthians	
2003	Cruzeiro	100	Santos	87	São Paulo FC	78
2004	Santos	89	Atlético Paranaense	86	São Paulo FC	82
2005				

Cup

Winners	Score	Runners-up
Grêmio	0-0 2-1	Sport Recife
Flamengo	1-0 0-0	Goiás
Criciúma	1-1 0-0	Grêmio
Internacional	1-2 1-0	Fluminense
Cruzeiro	0-0 2-1	Grêmio
Grêmio	0-0 1-0	Ceará
Corinthians	2-1 1-0	Grêmio
Cruzeiro	1-1 2-1	Palmeiras
Grêmio	0-0 2-2	Flamengo
Palmeiras	0-1 2-0	Cruzeiro
Juventude	2-1 0-0	Botafogo
Cruzeiro	0-0 2-1	São Paulo FC
Grêmio	2-2 3-1	Corinthians
Corinthians	2-1 1-1	Brasiliense
Cruzeiro	1-1 3-1	Flamengo
Santo André	2-2 2-0	Flamengo
Paulista	2-0 0-0	Fluminense

SANTOS 2004

Date	Opponents	Score		Comp	Scorers	Att
5-02-2004	Jorge Wilstermann - BOL	W 3-2	A	CLg7	Basilio 2 [14][24], Alex [86]	
18-02-2004	Guarani - PAR	D 2-2	H	CLg7	Robgol [1], Lopes [89]	
3-03-2004	Barcelona - ECU	W 3-1	A	CLg7	Renato [44], Basilio [48], Robinho [85]	
11-03-2004	Barcelona - ECU	W 1-0	H	CLg7	Robinho [69]	
25-03-2004	Guarani - PAR	W 2-1	A	CLg7	Basilio [63], Robgol [65]	
14-04-2004	Jorge Wilstermann - BOL	W 5-0	H	CLg7	Diego 2 [20p][73], Elano [40], Casagrande [55], Robinho [87p]	
21-04-2004	Paraná	L 2-3	A	SA	Léo [25], Robinho [82]	6 744
25-04-2004	Botafogo	W 2-0	H	SA	Diego 2 [55][72]	3 115
28-04-2004	Figueirense	L 1-2	A	SA	Robinho [28]	16 579
2-05-2004	Cruzeiro	L 1-3	H	SA	Diego [62p]	10 788
5-05-2004	LDU Quito - ECU	L 2-4	A	CLr2	Robinho [2], Elano [4]	
8-05-2004	Juventude	W 2-1	H	SA	Basilio [34], Deivid [87]	4 154
11-05-2004	LDU Quito - ECU	W 2-0	H	CLr2	Diego 2 [2][49], Won 5-3p	18 821
15-05-2004	Atlético Paranaense	L 0-1	A	SA		15 958
19-05-2004	Once Caldas - COL	D 1-1	H	CLqf	Basilio [83]	12 855
23-05-2004	Palmeiras	L 0-4	H	SA		10 271
27-05-2004	Once Caldas - COL	L 0-1	A	CLqf		
30-05-2004	Atlético Mineiro	D 3-3	A	SA	Diego [17], Léo [60], Deivid [67]	11 171
13-06-2004	Vitória	W 2-1	A	SA	Claiton [16], Basilio [81]	2 714
20-06-2004	Internacional	W 3-0	H	SA	Robinho [12], Basilio [81], Garcia [89]	6 669
26-06-2004	Guarani	W 2-1	H	SA	Deivid [25], Paulo César [90]	20 713
4-07-2004	Corinthians	W 3-2	A	SA	Elano [7], Basilio [68], Deivid [86]	14 215
7-07-2004	Ponte Preta	W 4-0	A	SA	Elano [2], Casagrande [66], Basilio [71], Robinho [73]	6 148
10-07-2004	São Paulo FC	W 2-1	H	SA	Deivid [33], Ricardinho [90]	14 663
13-07-2004	Flamengo	W 2-0	H	SA	Robinho [80], Basilio [88]	12 611
17-07-2004	Fluminense	L 0-1	A	SA		6 128
20-07-2004	Criciúma	W 5-2	H	SA	Robinho 2 [26][68], Deivid [34], Elano [36], Ricardinho [90]	2 630
24-07-2004	Goiás	D 3-3	A	SA	Robinho [13], OG [27], Deivid [35]	23 824
29-07-2004	Coritiba	W 4-2	H	SA	Deivid [13], Elano 2 [31][52], Basilio [43]	7 618
1-08-2004	Paysandu	W 6-0	H	SA	Robinho 2 [10][44], Elano [15], Ricardinho [42], Basilio [60], Fabinho [83]	12 960
4-08-2004	Grêmio	L 1-3	A	SA	Basilio [61]	12 628
7-08-2004	São Caetano	L 0-1	H	SA		12 770
11-08-2004	Vasco da Gama	W 3-2	A	SA	Deivid 2 [4][66], Robinho [82]	1 866
15-08-2004	Paraná	W 5-1	H	SA	Robinho 2 [2][62], Léo [31], Basilio 2 [41][90]	9 156
18-08-2004	Botafogo	L 0-2	A	SA		2 557
22-08-2004	Figueirense	W 4-1	*H*	SA	Elano [7], Robinho 2 [20][76], Deivid [48]	13 824
25-08-2004	Paraná	L 1-2	A	CSpr1	Marcinho [37]	
29-08-2004	Cruzeiro	D 4-4	A	SA	Robinho 2 [13][20], Deivid [58], Elano [63]	12 907
1-09-2004	Juventude	W 2-1	A	SA	Elano [11], Ricardinho [88]	9 182
4-09-2004	Paraná	W 3-0	H	CSpr1	Elano [43], Basilio [59], William [68]	
8-09-2004	Atlético Paranaense	D 1-1	H	SA	Basilio [49]	8 075
12-09-2004	Palmeiras	W 2-1	A	SA	Deivid [41], Elano [45]	19 109
16-09-2004	Flamengo	D 0-0	H	CSpr2		3 611
18-09-2004	Atlético Mineiro	W 2-0	H	SA	Domingos [7], Elano [57]	13 384
22-09-2004	Flamengo	D 2-2	A	CSpr2	Basilio [36], Deivid [89], Won 5-4p	10 439
26-09-2004	Vitória	W 4-1	H	SA	Elano [4], Robinho 2 [17][47], Ricardinho [84]	11 535
29-09-2004	Internacional	L 1-2	A	SA	Elano [33]	13 924
2-10-2004	Guarani	W 1-0	A	SA	Deivid [62]	6 134
6-10-2004	Corinthians	D 1-1	H	SA	Casagrande [22]	18 987
10-10-2004	São Paulo FC	W 1-0	H	CSpr3	Elano [76]	12 260
16-10-2004	Ponte Preta	W 4-0	H	SA	Deivid [11], Casagrande [22], Ricardinho 2 [58][63]	9 929
20-10-2004	São Paulo FC	D 1-1	A	CSpr3	Casagrande [82]	8 196
24-10-2004	São Paulo FC	L 0-1	A	SA		20 913
27-10-2004	Flamengo	D 1-1	A	SA	Deivid [30]	5 666
30-10-2004	Fluminense	W 5-0	*H*	SA	Robinho 2 [7][55], Laerte OG [19], Deivid 2 [47][81]	21 763
3-11-2004	LDU Quito - ECU	L 2-3	A	CSqf	William [20], Basilio [51]	
7-11-2004	Criciúma	D 1-1	A	SA	Deivid [5]	15 279
10-11-2004	LDU Quito - ECU	L 1-2	H	CSqf	Elano [83]	
14-11-2004	Goiás	W 2-1	H	SA	Basilio [83], William [85]	21 344
21-11-2004	Coritiba	W 1-0	A	SA	Deivid [64]	9 972
28-11-2004	Paysandu	D 1-1	A	SA	William [81]	24 385
5-12-2004	Grêmio	W 5-1	*H*	SA	Ricardinho 2 [7p][26], Cristiano Avalos [12], Deivid [28], Basilio [71]	12 620
12-12-2004	São Caetano	W 3-0	A	SA	Elano [31], Ricardinho [51p], Basilio [60]	11 616
19-12-2004	Vasco da Gama	W 2-1	H	SA	Ricardinho [4], Elano [29]	36 426

SA = Serie A • CL = Copa Libertadores • CS = Copa Sudamericana
H = Vila Belmiro • **H** = Pacaembu • *H* = Mogi Mirim • H̲ = Presidente Prudente • *H* = Rio Preto • A = Pacaembu

ATLETICO PARANAENSE 2004

Date	Opponents	Score		Comp	Scorers	Att
22-04-2004	São Paulo FC	L 0-1	A	SA		5 038
25-04-2004	Figueirense	L 0-3	H	SA		2 421
28-04-2004	Paysandu	W 3-0	A	SA	Jadson 51, Ilan 64p, Ramalho 81	6 629
2-05-2004	Coritiba	D 1-1	H	SA	Dagoberto 2	16 510
8-05-2004	Guarani	D 0-0	A	SA		1 762
15-05-2004	Santos	W 1-0	H	SA	Washington 72	15 958
23-05-2004	Corinthians	W 5-0	A	SA	Jadson 3 25 26 59, Dagoberto 2 35 86	5 760
30-05-2004	Cruzeiro	W 3-1	H	SA	Dagoberto 42, Washington 51 60	12 222
13-06-2004	Flamengo	L 0-3	A	SA		5 718
19-06-2004	Vitória	L 1-3	H	SA	Dagoberto 77	6 914
27-06-2004	Atlético Mineiro	W 1-0	A	SA	Washington 36	5 973
3-07-2004	Juventude	W 4-1	H	SA	Washington 3 12 25 66, Ilan 77	7 428
7-07-2004	Paraná	L 0-1	A	SA		5 835
10-07-2004	Palmeiras	D 0-0	H	SA		15 668
13-07-2004	Goiás	W 6-0	H	SA	Fagoberto 29, Washington 3 40 55 68, Ilan 57, Dennys 81	7 178
17-07-2004	Internacional	L 0-6	A	SA		8 667
20-07-2004	Fluminense	W 4-1	H	SA	Jadson 2, Dagoberto 3 25 45 81p	6 059
24-07-2004	Criciúma	L 1-4	A	SA	Marcão 38	4 524
28-07-2004	Ponte Preta	W 4-0	H	SA	Fernandinho 70, Jadson 83, Washington 90, Ivan 90	7 260
31-07-2004	Grêmio	D 0-0	H	SA		16 369
4-08-2004	São Caetano	W 3-0	A	SA	Dagoberto 34, Marinho 62, Washington 64	951
8-08-2004	Vasco da Gama	W 2-0	H	SA	Jadson 12, Dagoberto 87	16 394
12-08-2004	Botafogo	D 1-1	A	SA	Washington 34	7 316
15-08-2004	São Paulo FC	W 1-0	H	SA	Dagoberto 37	18 865
18-08-2004	Figueirense	D 1-1	A	SA	Raulen 63	7 605
22-08-2004	Paysandu	W 2-0	H	SA	Igor 42, Washington 56	9 063
29-08-2004	Coritiba	W 2-1	A	SA	Fernandinho 82, Washington.S 85	20 960
2-09-2004	Guarani	W 2-0	H	SA	Fernandinho 14, Washington.S 80	10 349
8-09-2004	Santos	D 1-1	A	SA	Marinho 46	8 075
12-09-2004	Corinthians	W 3-1	H	SA	Valdson OG 55, Jadson 72, Washington 90	18 990
19-09-2004	Cruzeiro	W 4-2	A	SA	Washington 2 45p 76p, Ivan 51, Jadson 52	10 777
26-09-2004	Flamengo	W 2-1	H	SA	Washington 2 88 90p	19 544
29-09-2004	Vitória	W 3-2	A	SA	Washington 2 45p 82p, Fernandinho 54	5 784
2-10-2004	Atlético Mineiro	W 5-0	H	SA	Jadson 3 32 45 65, Washington 61, Dennys 80	14 606
7-10-2004	Juventude	D 3-3	A	SA	Ivan 28, Washington 40, Fernandinho 45	8 718
17-10-2004	Paraná	D 1-1	H	SA	Jadson 57	17 369
23-10-2004	Palmeiras	L 1-3	A	SA	Dênis 23	18 755
26-10-2004	Goiás	L 0-2	A	SA		10 432
30-10-2004	Internacional	W 2-1	H	SA	Washington 2 12p 73p	1 350
7-11-2004	Fluminense	W 2-1	A	SA	Fernandinho 2 63 90	3 890
14-11-2004	Criciúma	W 6-1	H	SA	Fernandinho 31 Alan Bahia 43, Washington 2 50 65, Morais 83, Dênis 90	16 768
21-11-2004	Ponte Preta	W 3-2	A	SA	Washington 2 9 77, Marinho 30	4 372
28-11-2004	Grêmio	D 3-3	A	SA	Dênis 23, Fernandinho 2 27 59	8 222
5-12-2004	São Caetano	W 5-2	H	SA	Dênis 2 63 90, Jadson 2 64 79, Washington 89p	21 165
12-12-2004	Vasco da Gama	L 0-1	A	SA		14 540
19-12-2004	Botafogo	D 1-1	H	SA	Washington 78	20 061

SA = Serie A • H = Goiânia

FIFA REFEREE LIST 2005

	Int'l	DoB
ALMEIDA Luciano	1998	6-02-1959
AZEVEDO Wagner		23-06-1964
CARVALHO Edilson		4-08-1962
LOPES Heber		13-07-1972
OLIVEIRA Paulo	1999	16-12-1973
PENA Alicio		1-02-1968
QUELHAS Alvaro		1-04-1963
REZENDE Marcio	1991	22-12-1960
SIMON Carlos	1998	3-09-1965
SOUZA Wilson	1994	16-08-1964

FIFA ASSISTANT REFEREE LIST 2005

	Int'l	DoB
CORONA Ednilson	1997	4-02-1965
DOS SANTOS Milton	1995	16-12-1963
HAUSMANN Altemir	2004	5-12-1968
MELONIO Jose de Ribamar	1997	1-08-1959
OLIVEIRA Jorge	1994	23-04-1959
REIS Valter	1995	16-03-1962
ROCHA Alessandro	2001	10-02-1976
RODRIGUES Hilton	1998	30-12-1968
TAVARES Aristeu	1998	17-10-1962
TRINDADE Marcos		20-03-1962

BRB – BARBADOS

NATIONAL TEAM RECORD
JULY 1ST 2002 TO JUNE 30TH 2005

PL	W	D	L	F	A	%
27	11	6	10	39	36	51.9

FIFA/COCA-COLA WORLD RANKING

1993	1994	1995	1996	1997	1998	1999	2000	2001	2002	2003	2004	High		Low	
114	107	103	110	113	121	113	104	107	99	124	121	93	06/00	126	06/95

2004-2005											
08/04	09/04	10/04	11/04	12/04	01/05	02/05	03/05	04/05	05/05	06/05	07/05
115	117	118	119	121	121	121	121	122	122	122	120

The positive record of the national team since the 2002 FIFA World Cup™ cannot mask the fact that the past three years have been desperately disappointing for Barbados. With a first round exit at the hands of St Kitts and Nevis in the 2006 FIFA World Cup™ qualifiers the frustration was exacerbated by the spurning of a golden chance to make it to the 2005 CONCACAF Gold Cup finals by finishing last in the final tournament of the Digicel Caribbean Cup – a competition they hosted. Given that there were only four teams in the finals and three of them qualified for the Gold Cup, the outcome was especially crushing for a nation that believes it should be able to compete

INTERNATIONAL HONOURS
None

with the likes of Trinidad, Jamaica and Cuba, the other three finalists. In an attempt to help raise standards, a new training centre, which also houses the national association offices, was opened in 2004 which will give the various national teams up to date facilities as they prepare for tournaments. In domestic football Notre Dame won the Premier Division in 2004 to take their sixth title in eight seasons and rounded off a good year by capturing the FA Cup, defeating Silver Sands 3-2 in one of the best finals for some years. However, the double winners were not able to take matters further as they declined to enter the CONCACAF Champions Cup.

THE FIFA BIG COUNT OF 2000

	Male	Female		Male	Female
Registered players	2 500	0	Referees	70	0
Non registered players	2 600	0	Officials	400	0
Youth players	2 500	0	Total involved	8 070	
Total players	7 600		Number of clubs	80	
Professional players	0	0	Number of teams	200	

Barbados Football Association (BFA)
Hildor, No. 4, 10th Avenue, PO Box 1362, Belleville, St Michael, Barbados
Tel +1 246 2281707   Fax +1 246 2286484
barbadosfootball@caribsurf.com   www.barbadossoccer.com
President: JONES Ronald   General Secretary: TBD
Vice-President: BARROW Keith   Treasurer: HUNTE Curtis   Media Officer: Beckles Patrick
Men's Coach: TBD   Women's Coach: TBD
BFA formed: 1910   CONCACAF: 1968   FIFA: 1968
Colours: Royal blue/gold, Gold, White/gold/blue

GAMES PLAYED BY BARBADOS IN THE 2006 FIFA WORLD CUP™ CYCLE

2002	Opponents		Score	Venue	Comp	Scorers	Att	Referee
25-07	Trinidad & Barbados	D	0-0	Basseterre	Fr		700	
27-07	St Kitts & Nevis	L	0-3	Basseterre	Fr			
6-10	St Lucia	W	3-2	Bridgetown	Fr	Valencius, Xavier, Forde.M		
9-11	Jamaica	D	1-1	St George's	GCq	Goodridge 88	3 000	
11-11	Grenada	W	2-0	St George's	GCq	Lucas 66, Goodridge 90	2 500	Murray TRI
13-11	Guadeloupe	L	0-1	St George's	GCq		3 250	Brizan TRI
2003								
12-01	Jamaica	W	1-0	Bridgetown	Fr	Williams 61	7 500	
26-01	Finland	D	0-0	Bridgetown	Fr			Bynoe TRI
12-02	Martinique	D	3-3	Bridgetown	Fr	Lucas 5, Williams 9, Straker 48		
23-03	Jamaica	L	1-2	Kingston	Fr	Cox 59		Bowen CAY
26-12	Bermuda	W	2-1	Hamilton	Fr	Lovell 2 39 43		Mouchette BER
2004								
1-01	Bermuda	W	4-0	Hamilton	Fr	Parris 6, Riley 51, Goodridge 2 74 76		Raynor BER
11-01	Grenada	W	2-0	Bridgetown	Fr	Forde.N 35, Riley 58	2 000	Small BRB
18-01	Canada	L	0-1	Bridgetown	Fr			Forde BRB
31-01	Grenada	W	1-0	St George's	Fr	Riley 70		
15-02	Guyana	L	0-2	Bridgetown	Fr		1 200	Small BRB
12-03	Dominica	W	2-1	Bridgetown	Fr	OG 28, Burrowes 85	46	
30-05	Northern Ireland	D	1-1	Bridgetown	Fr	Skinner 40	8 000	Brizan TRI
13-06	St Kitts & Nevis	L	0-2	Bridgetown	WCq		3 700	Alfaro SLV
19-06	St Kitts & Nevis	L	2-3	Basseterre	WCq	Skinner 33, Goodridge 45	3 500	Pineda HON
2005								
23-01	Guyana	W	3-0	Bridgetown	Fr	Forde.M 41, OG 53, Goodridge 58,		
30-01	St Vincent/Grenadines	W	3-1	Bridgetown	Fr	Riley 2 47 82, Goodridge 80	3 000	
6-02	Antigua & Barbuda	W	3-2	Bridgetown	Fr	Forde.M 10, Stanford 40, Goodridge 57	4 000	
13-02	Guyana	D	3-3	Bridgetown	Fr	Forde.N 5, Lucas 29, James 56	6 000	Callender BRB
20-02	Cuba	L	0-3	Bridgetown	GCq		5 000	Prendergast JAM
22-02	Jamaica	L	0-1	Bridgetown	GCq			Brizan TRI
24-02	Trinidad & Tobago	L	2-3	Bridgetown	GCq	Forde.N 32, Lucas 86	3 000	Prendergast JAM

Fr = Friendly match • GC = CONCACAF Gold Cup • WC = FIFA World Cup™ • q = qualifier

FIFA REFEREE LIST 2005

	Int'l	DoB
CALLENDER Barney	2000	26-06-1963
FORDE Mark	1991	3-10-1964
SMALL Royon	2002	16-11-1968

FIFA ASSISTANT REFEREE LIST 2005

	Int'l	DoB
GOODRIDGE Winston	1998	27-02-1971
HOLDER Kenville	2002	9-09-1970
MOSES Mark	2002	6-09-1968
TAYLOR Jeremy	2005	18-08-1973

BARBADOS COUNTRY INFORMATION

Capital	Bridgetown	Independence	1966 from the UK	GDP per Capita	$15 700
Population	278 289	Status	Commonwealth	GNP Ranking	132
Area km²	431	Language	English	Dialling code	+1 246
Population density	645 per km²	Literacy rate	98%	Internet code	.bb
% in urban areas	47%	Main religion	Christian 71%	GMT + / -	-4
Towns/Cities ('000)	Bridgetown 98; Speightstown 3; Oistins 2, Bathsheba 1; Holetown 1; Bulkeley 1; Crane 1				
Neighbours (km)	Barbados is an island bordered by the Caribbean Sea and the Atlantic Ocean				
Main stadia	Waterford National Stadium – Bridgetown 15 000				

BARBADOS NATIONAL TEAM RECORDS AND RECORD SEQUENCES

Records			Sequence records					
Victory	6-1	CAY 1993	Wins	3	Five times	Clean sheets	3	1990, 1996
Defeat	0-7	USA 2000	Defeats	5	2000	Goals scored	8	1998-99, 2000
Player Caps	n/a		Undefeated	8	2000	Without goal	3	Three times
Player Goals	n/a		Without win	10	1976-88	Goals against	15	2000-01

BARBADOS 2004
PREMIER DIVISION

	Pl	W	D	L	F	A	Pts
Notre Dame	22	16	4	2	56	15	52
Beverly Hills	22	13	3	6	44	30	42
Youth Milan	22	13	1	8	50	29	40
Silver Sands	22	12	4	6	37	24	40
Paradise	22	11	6	5	31	28	39
Gall Hill	22	10	8	4	42	27	38
BDF	22	11	4	7	32	21	37
Eden Stars	22	6	4	12	32	43	22
Ivy Rovers	22	6	3	13	29	52	21
Ellerton	22	4	5	13	22	40	17
St John's Sonnets	22	2	7	13	18	48	13
Haynesville	22	2	3	17	21	57	9

29/01/2004 - 16/08/2004

FA CUP 2004

Round of sixteen		Quarter-finals		Semi-finals		Final	
Notre Dame	6						
Weymouth Wales	0	Notre Dame					
BDF		Haynesville					
Haynesville				Notre Dame	2		
				Gall Hill	1		
		Empire					
		Gall Hill				5-09-2004	
						Notre Dame	3
Ellerton	3					Silver Sands	2
Parish Land	2	Ellerton					
		Cave Hill					
				Ellerton	1		
Pinelands	3 2p			Silver Sands	2		
Benfica	3 4p	Pinelands	2				
Youth Milan	0	Silver Sands	6				
Silver Sands	2						

RECENT LEAGUE AND CUP RECORD

	Championship							Cup		
Year	Champions	Pts	Runners-up	Pts	Third	Pts		Winners	Score	Runners-up
1997	Notre Dame							Notre Dame	1-0	Paradise
1998	Notre Dame	39	Budg-Buy	38	Bayer Pride			Bayer Pride	1-0	Notre Dame
1999	Notre Dame							Gall Hill	2-1	Paradise
2000	Notre Dame	35	Paradise	31	Youth Milan			Paradise	2-1	Notre Dame
2001	Paradise	43	Youth Milan	41	Notre Dame	35		Notre Dame	1-0	Youth Milan
2002	Notre Dame	44	Paradise	32	Youth Milan	30		Youth Milan	2-1	Notre Dame
2003	Paradise	*	BDF					Paradise	1-0	Weymouth Wales
2004	Notre Dame	52	Beverly Hills	42	Youth Milan	40		Notre Dame	3-2	Silver Sands

*Paradise beat Barbados Defence Force 4-1 on penalties in the Championship final

BRU – BRUNEI DARUSSALAM

NATIONAL TEAM RECORD
JULY 1ST 2002 TO JUNE 30TH 2005

PL	W	D	L	F	A	%
2	0	1	1	1	6	25

FIFA/COCA-COLA WORLD RANKING

1993	1994	1995	1996	1997	1998	1999	2000	2001	2002	2003	2004	High	Low
151	165	167	170	178	183	185	193	189	194	194	199	145 08/93	199 12/04

						2004-2005					
08/04	09/04	10/04	11/04	12/04	01/05	02/05	03/05	04/05	05/05	06/05	07/05
195	195	195	195	199	199	199	199	199	199	199	198

It is an enigma that a country as rich as Brunei is only ranked 198 in the world. What makes it even more extraordinary is that football is very popular in the country and there is a well funded, thriving League. The problem lies in the fact that historically Brunei has taken part in the prestigious Malaysia Cup, a tournament until recently reserved for state selections and in 1999, amid much celebration, the team even won the tournament. As a result the Brunei selection, with a liberal helping of foreign players, has become the de facto national team. Not even the allure of the 2006 FIFA World Cup™ qualifiers could tempt the proper national team out of hibernation and just two

INTERNATIONAL HONOURS
None

matches have been played since 2002. Remarkably, the national association has applied for help from the Goal Bureau to build a technical centre, which will also house the association headquarters, a project that was approved in February 2005. The aim is to help develop local talent that can then progress through the national teams as well as to further strengthen the B-League, which began in 2002. There is certainly the will to develop the national team and in March 2005 Brunei hosted the ASEAN U-21 Championship. Teams in the B-League, won comfortably in 2004 by DPMM, are allowed three imports but must also fill a quota of U-21 players.

THE FIFA BIG COUNT OF 2000

	Male	Female		Male	Female
Registered players	300	0	Referees	30	0
Non registered players	1 000	0	Officials	100	0
Youth players	500	0	Total involved	1 930	
Total players		1 800	Number of clubs	20	
Professional players	0	0	Number of teams	40	

The Football Association of Brunei Darussalam (BAFA)
PO Box 2010, Bandar Seri Begawan, BS 8674, Brunei Darussalam
Tel +673 2 382761   Fax +673 2 382760
bruneifasg@yahoo.com   www.bafa.org.bn
President: HUSSAIN YUSSOFF Pehin Dato Haji   General Secretary: MATUSIN MATASAN Pengiran Haji
Vice-President: HASSAN ABAS Pengiran Haji   Treasurer: PANG Jeffery   Media Officer: None
Men's Coach: YUNOS Haji   Women's Coach: None
BAFA formed: 1959   AFC: 1970   FIFA: 1969
Colours: Yellow, Black, Black/white

GAMES PLAYED BY BRUNEI DARUSSALAM IN THE 2006 FIFA WORLD CUP™ CYCLE

2002	Opponents		Score	Venue	Comp	Scorers	Att	Referee
No international matches played in 2002								
2003								
21-03	Maldives	D	1-1	Male	ACq	Faldin 89		
23-03	Myanmar	L	0-5	Male	ACq			
2004								
No international matches played in 2004								
2005								
No international matches played in 2005 before August								

AC = AFC Asian Cup • q = qualifier

BRUNEI DARUSSALAM NATIONAL TEAM RECORDS AND RECORD SEQUENCES

Records			Sequence records					
Victory	2-0	PHI 1980, PHI 1989	Wins	2	1980	Clean sheets	1	
Defeat	0-12	UAE 2001	Defeats	12	1972-80, 1999-01	Goals scored	4	1998-99
Player Caps	n/a		Undefeated	2		Without goal	11	1999-01
Player Goals	n/a		Without win	22	1999-05	Goals against	26	1982-87

BRUNEI 2004

B-LEAGUE

	Pl	W	D	L	F	A	Pts	DPMM	AH United	Armed Forces	Wijaya	QAF	Kasuka	Jerudong	Indera	Sengkurong	Kota Ranger
DPMM	18	17	1	0	81	7	**52**		0-0	5-2	3-0	2-1	7-0	8-0	6-1	3-0	2-0
AH United	18	13	3	2	56	19	**42**	1-4		1-1	2-1	3-1	3-1	10-0	4-2	5-0	7-1
Armed Forces Tutong	18	11	4	3	43	22	**37**	0-1	1-2		3-1	3-1	3-0	3-2	5-1	3-0	2-1
Wijaya	18	7	4	7	42	31	**25**	1-3	1-3	1-1		5-1	1-3	2-3	6-1	6-0	1-1
QAF	18	7	3	8	37	37	**24**	0-5	1-1	1-1	2-2		1-3	1-3	1-2	7-3	4-1
Kasuka	18	7	2	9	36	47	**23**	0-5	2-3	1-2	1-3	1-2		4-3	5-1	1-1	4-1
Jerudong	18	7	1	10	30	51	**22**	0-5	1-0	1-5	1-1	1-3	3-0		2-1	0-1	3-1
Indera	18	5	2	11	32	57	**17**	0-6	1-3	3-3	1-3	1-2	2-2	3-1		5-2	2-1
Sengkurong	18	4	1	13	18	51	**13**	1-5	0-4	0-2	0-1	0-1	3-4	2-1	3-1		1-0
Kota Ranger	18	1	1	16	18	71	**4**	0-11	1-4	0-3	2-6	0-7	3-4	1-6	2-4	2-1	

9/05/2004 - 13/10/2004 • NBT Berakas and Bandaran Kuala Belait promoted from B-League Two

RECENT LEAGUE AND CUP RECORD

Championship						
Year	**Champions**	**Pts**	**Runners-up**	**Pts**	**Third**	**Pts**
2000	Kasuka					
2001	Kasuka	3-1	DPMM			
2002	DPMM	19	Armed Forces	16	Kasuka	9
2003	Wijaya	25	DPMM	22	Armed Forces	21
2004	DPMM	52	AH United	42	Armed Forces	37

Cup		
Winners	**Score**	**Runners-up**
Wijaya	1-0	Armed Forces
Armed Forces	3-0	Kota Ranger
DPMM	0-0 3-1p	Armed Forces

BRUNEI DARUSSALAM COUNTRY INFORMATION

Capital	Bandar Seri Begawan	Independence	1984 from the UK	GDP per Capita	$18 600
Population	365 251	Status	Sultanate	GNP Ranking	97
Area km²	5 770	Language	Malay	Dialling code	+673
Population density	63 per km²	Literacy rate	90%	Internet code	.bn
% in urban areas	70%	Main religion	Muslim 67%	GMT + / –	+8
Towns/Cities ('000)	Bandar Seri Begawan 64; Kuala Belait 31; Pekan Seria 30; Tutong 19; Bangar 3				
Neighbours (km)	Malaysia 381; South China Sea 161				
Main stadia	Sultan Hassal Bolkiah – Bandar Ser Begawan 30 000				

BUL – BULGARIA

NATIONAL TEAM RECORD
JULY 1ST 2002 TO JUNE 30TH 2005

PL	W	D	L	F	A	%
32	13	10	9	44	37	56.2

FIFA/COCA-COLA WORLD RANKING

1993	1994	1995	1996	1997	1998	1999	2000	2001	2002	2003	2004	High	Low
31	16	17	15	36	49	37	53	51	42	34	37	8 06/95	58 08/02

2004-2005											
08/04	09/04	10/04	11/04	12/04	01/05	02/05	03/05	04/05	05/05	06/05	07/05
42	41	41	37	37	37	39	39	40	43	45	46

Not since 1958 has a team gone through a season unbeaten in Bulgaria but having remained undefeated for the first 29 games – itself a record – and having been ahead three times against outgoing champions Lokomotiv Plovdiv in the final match of the season, CSKA Sofia looked to be on target to do just that. Then with just four minutes of the season left they conceded a goal, scored by Velko Hristev, to lose the match 4-3. It had been an enthralling campaign for the two big Sofia teams with Levski finishing just three points behind having lost a decisive encounter between the two at the end of April. There was some consolation for Levski when they beat CSKA 2-1 in

INTERNATIONAL HONOURS
European Youth Tournament 1959 1969 1974, **Balkan Cup** 1932 1935 1976

the Cup Final just before the end of the League campaign. The national team looked to have got off to a solid start in the 2006 FIFA World Cup™ qualifiers but then lost twice at home to Sweden and Croatia to leave themselves with an almost impossible task of qualifying for the finals. Given their fine record at home in recent years the results were not only disappointing but also very surprising. Having been part of the team that finished fourth at the 1994 FIFA World Cup™ in the USA and which qualified for the finals four years later, coach Hristo Stoitchkov looks like missing out on a tournament he once graced as a player.

THE FIFA BIG COUNT OF 2000

	Male	Female		Male	Female
Registered players	32 024	143	Referees	2 989	25
Non registered players	80 000	150	Officials	1 835	45
Youth players	10 632	25	Total involved	127 868	
Total players	122 974		Number of clubs	541	
Professional players	960	0	Number of teams	1 418	

Bulgarian Football Union (BFU)
Bulgarski Futbolen Soius, 26 Tzar Ivan Assen II Str., Sofia - 1124, Bulgaria
Tel +359 2 9426202   Fax +359 2 9426200
bfu@bfunion.bg   www.bfunion.bg
President: SLAVKOV Ivan   General Secretary: KAPRALOV Stefan
Vice-President: MIHAILOV Borislav   Treasurer: PEEV Todor   Media Officer: KARAIVANOV Atanas
Men's Coach: STOITCHKOV Hristo   Women's Coach: DIMITROV Lachezar
BFU formed: 1923   UEFA: 1954   FIFA: 1924
Colours: White, Green, White or Red, Green, White

GAMES PLAYED BY BULGARIA IN THE 2006 FIFA WORLD CUP™ CYCLE

2002	Opponents	Score		Venue	Comp	Scorers	Att	Referee
21-08	Germany	D	2-2	Sofia	Fr	Berbatov [21], Balakov [50p]	10 000	Bre FRA
7-09	Belgium	W	2-0	Brussels	ECq	Jankovic [17], Petrov.S	20 000	Hauge NOR
12-10	Croatia	W	2-0	Sofia	ECq	Petrov.S [22], Berbatov [37]	43 000	Frisk SWE
16-10	Andorra	W	2-1	Sofia	ECq	Chilikov [37], Balakov [58]	42 000	Richards WAL
20-11	Spain	L	0-1	Granada	Fr		20 000	Coue FRA
2003								
12-02	Hungary †	W	1-0	Laranaca	Fr	Jancovic [36], Abandoned after 45' due to weather	200	Theodotou CYP
27-03	Serbia & Montenegro	W	2-1	Krusevac	Fr	Petrov.S [14], Todorov [56]	10 000	Lazarevski MKD
2-04	Estonia	D	0-0	Tallinn	ECq		4 000	Plautz AUT
30-04	Albania	W	2-0	Sofia	Fr	Berbatov 2 [3 34]	9 325	Vidlak CZE
7-06	Belgium	D	2-2	Sofia	ECq	Berbatov [52], Todorov [72p]	42 000	Collina ITA
20-08	Lithuania	W	3-0	Sofia	Fr	Dimitrov 2 [25p 45], Berbatov [33]	2 000	Bolognino ITA
6-09	Estonia	W	2-0	Sofia	ECq	Petrov.M [16], Berbatov [67]	25 128	Wack GER
10-09	Andorra	W	3-0	Andorra la Vella	ECq	Berbatov 2 [10 23], Hristov [58]	1 000	Mikulski POL
11-10	Croatia	L	0-1	Zagreb	ECq		37 000	Veissiere FRA
18-11	Korea Republic	W	1-0	Seoul	Fr	Manchev [19]	38 257	Saleh MAS
2004								
18-02	Greece	L	0-2	Athens	Fr		6 000	Poll ENG
31-03	Russia	D	2-2	Sofia	Fr	Berbatov 2 [15 66]	14 938	Garcia POR
28-04	Cameroon	W	3-0	Sofia	Fr	Berbatov 2 [7 54p], Lazarov [56]	13 987	Verbist BEL
2-06	Czech Republic	L	1-3	Prague	Fr	Petkov.M [90]	6 627	Stredak SVK
14-06	Sweden	L	0-5	Lisbon	ECr1		31 652	Riley ENG
18-06	Denmark	L	0-2	Braga	ECr1		22 000	Cortez Batista POR
22-06	Italy	L	1-2	Guimaraes	ECr1	Petrov.M [45p]	16 002	Ivanov RUS
18-08	Republic of Ireland	D	1-1	Dublin	Fr	Bojinov [70]	31 887	Brines SCO
4-09	Iceland	W	3-1	Reykjavik	WCq	Berbatov [35 49], Yanev [62]	5 014	Hamer LUX
9-10	Croatia	D	2-2	Zagreb	WCq	Petrov.M [77], Berbatov [86]	31 565	Collina ITA
13-10	Malta	W	4-1	Sofia	WCq	Berbatov 2 [43 55], Yanev [47], Yankov [88]	16 800	Richards WAL
17-11	Azerbaijan	D	0-0	Baku	Fr		3 000	Sipailo LVA
29-11	Egypt	D	1-1	Cairo	Fr	Gargorov [90]		
2005								
9-02	Serbia & Montenegro	D	0-0	Sofia	Fr		2 957	Genov BUL
26-03	Sweden	L	0-3	Sofia	WCq		42 530	Fandel GER
30-03	Hungary	D	1-1	Budapest	WCq	Petrov.S [51]	11 586	Wegereef NED
4-06	Croatia	L	1-3	Sofia	WCq	Petrov.M [72]	35 000	Nielsen DEN

Fr = Friendly match • EC = UEFA EURO 2004™ • WC = FIFA World Cup™ • q = qualifier • r1 = first round group • † Not a full international

BULGARIA COUNTRY INFORMATION

Capital	Sofia	Independence	1908 from Ottoman Empire	GDP per Capita	$7 600
Population	7 517 973	Status	Republic	GNP Ranking	79
Area km²	110 910	Language	Bulgarian	Dialling code	+359
Population density	67 per km²	Literacy rate	98%	Internet code	.bg
% in urban areas	71%	Main religion	Christian 85%	GMT +/–	+2
Towns/Cities ('000)	Sofia 1 044; Plovdiv 324; Varna 304; Burgas 186; Ruse 156; Pleven 128				
Neighbours (km)	Romania 608; Turkey 240; Greece 494; Macedonia FYR 148; Serbia & Montenegro 318; Black Sea 354				
Main stadia	Plovdiv Stadion – Plovdiv 48 000; Vassil Levski – Sofia 43 384; Hristo Botev – Vratza 32 000				

BULGARIA NATIONAL TEAM RECORDS AND RECORD SEQUENCES

Records			Sequence records					
Victory	7-0	NOR 1957, MLT 1982	Wins	5	1983 & 1987	Clean sheets	4	1963
Defeat	0-13	ESP 1933	Defeats	7	1924-1927	Goals scored	18	1934-1938
Player Caps	102	MIKHAILOV Borislav	Undefeated	11	1972-1973	Without goal	4	1984 & 1998
Player Goals	47	BONEV Hristo	Without win	16	1977-1978	Goals against	24	1924-1932

NATIONAL CAPS

	Caps
MIKHAILOV Borislav	102
BONEV Christo	96
BALAKOV Krasimir	92
PENEV Dimitar	90
STOITCHKOV Hristo	83
SIRAKOV Nasko	81
SADKOV Anyo	80
YANKOV Zlatko	79
DIMITROV Georgi	77
IVANOV Trifon	76

NATIONAL GOALS

	Goals
BONEV Christo	47
STOITCHKOV Hristo	37
KOSTADINOV Emil	26
JEKOV Petar	25
KOLEV Ivan	25
SIRAKOV Nasko	23
BERBATOV Dimitar	21
MILANOV Dimitar	20
ASPAROUKHOV Georgi	19
DERMENDJIEV Dinko	19

NATIONAL COACH

	Years
VOUTSOV Ivan	1982-'86
MLADENOV Hristo	1986-'88
ANGUELOV Boris	1988-'89
VOUTSOV Ivan	1989-'91
PENEV Dimitar	1991-'96
BONEV Christo	1996-'99
DIMITROV Dimitar	1999
MLADENOV Stoicho	1999-'01
MARKOV Plamen	2002-'04
STOITCHKOV Hristo	2004

CLUB DIRECTORY

Club	Town/City	Stadium	Phone	www.	Lge	Cup	CL
Belasitza Petrich	Petrich	Tsar Samuil 12 000	+359 74 523554	rondia-bg.com	0	0	0
Beroe Stara Zagora	Stara Zagora	Beroe 17 800	+359 42 603492		1	0	0
Cherno More Varna	Varna	Ticha 12 000	+359 52 302243		0	0	0
CSKA Sofia	Sofia	Bulgarska Armia 24 000	+359 2 9633477	cska.bg	30	8	0
Levski Sofia	Sofia	Georgi Asparukhov 29 698	+359 2 9892156	levski.bg	23	11	0
Litex Lovech	Lovech	Lovech 7 000	+359 68 601704	fclitex-lovech.bg	2	2	0
Lokomotiv Plovdiv	Plovdiv	Lokomotiv 20 000	+359 32 627373	lokopd.com	1	0	0
Lokomotiv Sofia	Sofia	Lokomotiv 25 000	+359 2 378479		3	1	0
Marek Dupnitza	Dupnitza	Bonchuk 12 500	+359 701 32007	marek.matrix-bg.net	0	0	0
Naftex Burgas	Burgas	Neftochimik 18 000	+359 56 800320	pfcnaftex.bg/bg	0	0	0
PFC Nesebar	Nesebar		+359 554 45878		0	0	0
Pirin Blagoevgrad	Blagoevgrad	Hristo Botev 15 000	+359 73 884072		0	0	0
Rodopa Smolian	Smolian	Septemvri 6 000	+359 301 65848		0	0	0
Spartak Varna	Varna	Spartak 7 500	+359 2 9831774		0	0	0
Slavia Sofia	Sofia	Slavia 28 000	+359 2 8569197	pfcslavia.com	7	1	0
Vidima Rakovski	Sevlievo	Rakovski 5 000	+359 675 30815		0	0	0

RECENT LEAGUE AND CUP RECORD

Year	Champions	Pts	Runners-up	Pts	Third	Pts	Winners	Score	Runners-up
1990	CSKA Sofia	47	Levski Sofia	36	Slavia Sofia	36	Sliven	2-0	CSKA Sofia
1991	Etar Veliko Tarnovo	44	CSKA Sofia	37	Slavia Sofia	37	Levski Sofia	2-1	Botev Plovdiv
1992	CSKA Sofia	47	Levski Sofia	45	Botev Plovdiv	37	Levski Sofia	5-0	Pirin Blagoevgrad
1993	Levski Sofia	50	CSKA Sofia	42	Botev Plovdiv	38	CSKA Sofia	1-0	Botev Plovdiv
1994	Levski Sofia	71	CSKA Sofia	54	Botev Plovdiv	50	Levski Sofia	1-0	Pirin Blagoevgrad
1995	Levski Sofia	79	Lokomotiv Sofia	68	Botev Plovdiv	60	Lokomotiv Sofia	4-2	Botev Plovdiv
1996	Slavia Sofia	67	Levski Sofia	62	Lokomotiv Sofia	58	Slavia Sofia	1-0	Levski Sofia
1997	CSKA Sofia	71	Neftohimik Burgas	67	Slavia Sofia	57	CSKA Sofia	3-1	Levski Sofia
1998	Liteks Lovech	69	Levski Sofia	64	CSKA Sofia	61	Levski Sofia	5-0	CSKA Sofia
1999	Liteks Lovech	73	Levski Sofia	71	Levski Kjustendil	57	CSKA Sofia	1-0	Litex Lovech
2000	Levski Sofia	74	CSKA Sofia	64	Velbazhd	55	Levski Sofia	2-0	Neftohimik Burgas
2001	Levski Sofia	69	CSKA Sofia	62	Velbazhd	57	Litex Lovech	1-0	Velbazhd
2002	Levski Sofia	65	Litex Lovech	55	Lokomotiv Plovdiv	53	Levski Sofia	3-1	CSKA Sofia
2003	CSKA Sofia	66	Levski Sofia	60	Litex Lovech	55	Levski Sofia	2-1	Litex Lovech
2004	Lokomotiv Plovdiv	75	Levski Sofia	72	CSKA Sofia	65	Litex Lovech	2-2 4-3p	CSKA Sofia
2005	CSKA Sofia	79	Levski Sofia	76	Lokomotiv Plovdiv	58	Levski Sofia	2-1	CSKA Sofia

BULGARIA 2004-05

'A' PFG

	Pl	W	D	L	F	A	Pts	CSKA	Levski	Lok Plovdiv	Litex	Slavia	Lok Sofia	Naftex	Cherno M.	Marek	Beroe	Belasitsa	Rodopa	Pirin	Vidima	Nesebar	Spartak
CSKA Sofia †	30	25	4	1	81	16	79		2-2	0-0	3-1	4-0	5-1	3-0	1-0	5-0	4-1	2-0	1-0	2-1	3-0	5-0	6-0
Levski Sofia ‡	30	24	4	2	76	19	76	0-1		2-1	0-1	3-0	5-0	4-1	2-1	3-2	3-1	8-1	5-1	4-0	2-0	2-0	4-1
Lokomotiv Plovdiv ‡	30	18	4	8	65	34	58	4-3	2-2		4-3	1-0	4-0	1-0	2-0	3-0	3-0	3-0	4-0	4-4	4-0	4-1	5-0
Litex Lovech ‡	30	16	4	10	45	27	52	0-1	0-1	0-1		1-1	2-0	0-1	2-0	3-0	1-1	2-0	2-0	4-2	1-0	2-1	4-1
Slavia Sofia	30	13	9	8	43	33	48	1-4	0-2	2-0	2-2		1-0	3-0	3-1	0-0	3-2	4-0	1-3	0-0	4-1	4-1	2-1
Lokomotiv Sofia §	30	14	7	9	43	35	46	0-1	0-0	2-0	2-1	1-0		1-0	2-1	4-2	2-1	5-1	2-1	0-0	5-2	0-0	3-1
Naftex Burgas	30	10	5	15	24	38	35	0-4	0-2	1-1	1-0	0-2	0-0		2-1	2-1	1-0	3-0	0-0	0-1	2-0	1-2	5-1
Cherno More Varna	30	10	5	15	30	38	35	1-2	0-0	2-0	1-3	1-1	0-1	2-0		3-2	1-0	3-0	1-0	1-1	1-0	2-1	1-0
Marek Dupnitza	30	9	8	13	34	44	35	2-2	0-1	1-0	0-1	0-2	1-1	2-1	2-1		1-0	1-0	2-1	2-1	2-2	4-1	4-1
Beroe Stara Zagora	30	9	8	13	32	36	35	1-3	0-1	2-1	1-1	2-0	2-1	1-1	2-0	1-0		1-1	2-0	4-0	0-0	2-1	1-0
Belasitsa Petrich	30	9	7	14	25	48	34	1-4	0-1	2-1	1-0	0-0	1-0	2-0	0-0	0-0	0-0		1-0	0-0	1-0	3-0	4-0
Rodopa Smolian	30	6	15	9	33	43	33	0-1	1-2	4-2	0-1	0-0	1-1	1-0	2-3	0-0	2-1	3-1		2-0	1-1	3-1	2-0
Pirin Blagoevgrad	30	7	12	11	31	40	33	0-3	0-1	1-4	1-0	2-2	0-0	0-1	3-0	1-1	0-0	1-1	4-2		1-1	3-1	2-0
Vidima Rakovski	30	9	5	16	32	51	32	0-4	1-4	1-2	1-2	0-1	2-0	3-0	2-1	2-1	1-0	1-1	0-0	2-0		2-1	2-1
Nesebar	30	5	5	20	26	63	20	0-2	2-3	1-2	0-3	1-4	0-4	0-0	1-1	1-1	2-1	2-3	2-0	1-0	1-2		1-0
Spartak Varna	30	5	3	22	18	73	18	0-0	0-7	0-2	0-2	0-0	0-5	0-1	1-0	1-0	2-2	1-0	0-1	1-2	3-2	2-1	

6/08/2004 - 28/05/2005 • † Qualified for the UEFA Champions League • ‡ Qualified for the UEFA Cup • § Lokomotiv Sofia deducted 3 points

BULGARIA 2004-05 'B' PFG

	Pl	W	D	L	F	A	Pts
Vihren Sandanski	30	21	6	3	57	20	69
Botev Plovdiv	30	21	5	4	64	21	68
Pirin 1922	30	20	7	3	63	18	67
Spartak Pleven	30	19	4	7	61	27	61
Rilski Sportist Samokov	30	15	6	9	47	35	51
Svetkavitsa	30	14	6	10	48	45	48
Minyor Bobov dol	30	12	5	13	46	42	41
Pomorie	30	11	7	12	38	39	40
Shumen 2001	30	12	4	14	43	45	40
Koneliano	30	11	6	13	31	40	39
Etar 1924	30	10	6	14	38	46	36
Dobrudzha Dobrich	30	10	5	15	34	53	35
Dorostol 2003	30	5	10	15	24	43	25
Akademik Svishtov	30	6	6	18	21	53	24
Chernomorets Burgas	30	5	4	21	29	64	19
Lokomotiv Gorna O.	30	4	1	25	16	69	13

7/08/2004 - 28/05/2005

TOP SCORERS

KAMBUROV Martin	Lok Plovdiv	27
YANEV Hristo	CSKA	22
ZLATINOV Vladislav	Pirin	14
GENKOV Tsvetan	Lok Sofia	12

BFU CUP 2004-05

Round of 16		Quarter-finals		Semi-finals		Final	
Levski Sofia	3						
Etar 1924 *	0	Levski Sofia *	3				
Litex Lovech	0	Naftex Burgas	0				
Naftex Burgas *	2			Levski Sofia	2 2		
Botev Plovdiv	1			Lokomotiv Plovdiv *	0 1		
Spartak '94 Plovdiv *	0	Botev Plovdiv *	1				
Lokomotiv Sofia	0	Lokomotiv Plovdiv	2				
Lokomotiv Plovdiv *	2					Levski Sofia ‡	2
Pirin 1922 *	3					CSKA Sofia	1
Belasitza Petrich	0	Pirin 1922 *	0 4p				
Minyor *	0	Marek Dupnitza	0 2p				
Marek Dupnitza	1			Pirin 1922 *	0 3		
Hebar Pazardzhik *	1			CSKA Sofia	2 3		
Svetkavitsa	0	Hebar Pazardzhik *	0				
Rilski Sportist Samokov*	2	CSKA Sofia	1				
CSKA Sofia	3						

CUP FINAL

25-05-2005, Vasil Levski, Sofia

Scorers - Borimirov 52, Domovchiyski 75 for Levski; Yanev 82p for CSKA

* Home team/home team in the first leg • ‡ Qualified for the UEFA Cup

CAM – CAMBODIA

NATIONAL TEAM RECORD
JULY 1ST 2002 TO JUNE 30TH 2005

PL	W	D	L	F	A	%
9	1	0	8	7	45	11.1

FIFA/COCA-COLA WORLD RANKING

1993	1994	1995	1996	1997	1998	1999	2000	2001	2002	2003	2004	High		Low	
-	-	180	186	170	162	168	169	169	176	178	184	156	07/98	186	04/97

2004-2005											
08/04	09/04	10/04	11/04	12/04	01/05	02/05	03/05	04/05	05/05	06/05	07/05
184	184	185	185	184	184	184	185	185	185	185	185

Making only their second international appearance since the 2002 FIFA World Cup™ qualifiers, Cambodia's experience at the 2004 ASEAN Tiger Cup couldn't match their previous outing in 2002 where they actually won a match. In 2004 the Cambodians were on the end of two sound thrashings - against Vietnam and Indonesia - and they shipped 22 goals in just four games. Given the lack of experience in the squad the football federation decided not to enter the 2006 FIFA World Cup™ or the 2004 AFC Asian Cup preferring instead to devote scarce resources on building up a youth programme. There was a creditable 4-2 win by the U-17s over the Philippines in the AFC

INTERNATIONAL HONOURS
None

qualifiers, but a 5-0 defeat at home to Laos in the U-20 AFC qualifiers shows the mountain that football in Cambodia still has to climb before there is the prospect of respectable results at senior level. A new training centre and association headquarters opened in 2003 is a step in the right direction but Cambodia is a country still coming to terms with genocide and civil war in which football almost ceased to exist for 20 years. It is hoped that club football will benefit from the scheduled introduction of the AFC President's Cup, which will be contested by the weaker nations on the continent and after a gap of two years the Championship got underway again in April 2005.

THE FIFA BIG COUNT OF 2000

	Male	Female		Male	Female
Registered players	1 000	0	Referees	64	0
Non registered players	5 000	0	Officials	150	0
Youth players	500	0	Total involved	6 714	
Total players	6 500		Number of clubs	60	
Professional players	0	0	Number of teams	400	

Cambodian Football Federation (CFF)
Chaeng Maeng Village Rd, Kab Srov, Sangkat Samrong Krom, Khan Dangkor, Phnom Penh, Cambodia
Tel +855 23 364889   Fax +855 23 220780
the-cff@everyday.com.kh   www.none
President: KHEK Ravy   General Secretary: CHHEANG Yean
Vice-President: KEO Sarin   Treasurer: CHAN Soth   Media Officer: None
Men's Coach: FICKERT Joachim   Women's Coach: None
CFF formed: 1933   AFC: 1957   FIFA: 1953
Colours: Blue, Blue, Blue

GAMES PLAYED BY CAMBODIA IN THE 2006 FIFA WORLD CUP™ CYCLE

2002	Opponents	Score	Venue	Comp	Scorers	Att	Referee
11-12	Malaysia	L 0-5	Kuala Lumpur	Fr			
15-12	Vietnam SR	L 2-9	Jakarta	TCr1	Hok Sochetra 27, Ung Kanyanith 53	5 000	Nagalingham SIN
17-12	Indonesia	L 2-4	Jakarta	TCr1	Hok Sochetra 2 10 44	20 000	Khantachai THA
19-12	Myanmar	L 0-5	Jakarta	TCr1		2 000	Ebrahim BHR
21-12	Philippines	W 1-0	Jakarta	TCr1	Ung Kanyanith 90	2 500	Napitupulu IDN
2003							
No international matches played in 2003							
2004							
9-12	Vietnam SR	L 1-9	Ho Chi Minh City	TCr1	Hang Sokunthea 44	8 000	Supian MAS
11-12	Laos	L 1-2	Ho Chi Minh City	TCr1	Hing Darith 27	20 000	Kwon Jong Chul KOR
13-12	Indonesia	L 0-8	Ho Chi Minh City	TCr1		17 000	Sun Baojie CHN
15-12	Singapore	L 0-3	Ho Chi Minh City	TCr1		2 000	Ebrahim BHR
2005							
No international matches played to the end of June 2005							

Fr = Friendly match • TC = ASEAN Tiger Cup • r1 = first round group

CAMBODIA NATIONAL TEAM RECORDS AND RECORD SEQUENCES

Records			Sequence records				
Victory	11-0	YEM 1966	Wins	1		Clean sheets	1	
Defeat	0-10	IDN 1995	Defeats	10	1995-1997	Goals scored	3	1997
Player Caps	n/a		Undefeated	1		Without goal	5	1996-1997
Player Goals	n/a		Without win	17	1998-2002	Goals against	20	1997-2000

FIFA REFEREE LIST 2005

	Int'l	DoB
CHHUN Try	1999	1-02-1965
METH Sambath	1999	11-04-1966
NUON YIN Monarath	1999	5-02-1972

FIFA ASSISTANT REFEREE LIST 2005

	Int'l	DoB
DOUNG Sochet		14-02-1969
KOUNG Ly		30-04-1976
LY Ratana	1999	20-07-1972
SRENG Haody		19-09-1969
TUY Vichhika		15-11-1979

RECENT LEAGUE RECORD

Year	Champions
1990	Ministry of Transport
1991	Department of Municipal Contstruction
1992	Department of Municipal Contstruction
1993	Ministry of Defense
1994	Civil Aviation
1995	Civil Aviation
1996	Body Guards Club
1997	Body Guards Club
1998	Royal Dolphins
1999	Royal Dolphins
2000	National Police
2001	No tournament played
2002	Samart United
2003	No tournament played
2004	No tournament played

CAMBODIA COUNTRY INFORMATION

Capital	Phnom Penh	Independence	1953	GDP per Capita	$1 900
Population	13 363 421	Status	Kingdom	GNP Ranking	127
Area km²	181 040	Language	Khmer	Dialling code	+855
Population density	73 per km²	Literacy rate	66%	Internet code	.kh
% in urban areas	21%	Main religion	Buddhist 95%	GMT +/−	+7
Towns/Cities ('000)	Phnom Penh 1 573; Preah Sihanouk 157; Bat Dambang 150; Siem Reab 148				
Neighbours (km)	Laos 541; Vietnam 1,228; Thailand 803; Gulf of Thailand 443				
Main stadia	National Olympic – Phnom Penh 50 000				

CAN – CANADA

NATIONAL TEAM RECORD
JULY 1ST 2002 TO JUNE 30TH 2005

PL	W	D	L	F	A	%
26	8	2	16	29	47	34.6

FIFA/COCA-COLA WORLD RANKING

1993	1994	1995	1996	1997	1998	1999	2000	2001	2002	2003	2004	High		Low	
44	63	65	40	66	101	81	63	92	70	87	90	40	12/96	101	12/98

2004-2005											
08/04	09/04	10/04	11/04	12/04	01/05	02/05	03/05	04/05	05/05	06/05	07/05
96	99	95	95	90	90	85	84	84	83	85	84

The past two years have been hugely disappointing for the Canadian national team with a lacklustre showing in the 2006 FIFA World Cup™ qualifiers and a lame first round exit in the 2005 CONCACAF Gold Cup. Much more was hoped for from a team with a number of high profile players based in Europe and MLS and from Frank Yallop, one of the most respected young coaches in the game. Paired with three Central American nations in the first group stage of the FIFA World Cup™ qualifiers the Canadians didn't win until the last match and scored just three goals. A problem for the national team is that football comes way down the list of favourite sports in the country,

INTERNATIONAL HONOURS
Qualified for the FIFA World Cup™ 1986 Qualified for the FIFA Women's World Cup 1995 1999 2003 Olympic Gold 1904 (Unofficial)
CONCACAF Gold Cup 2000 CONCACAF Women's Gold Cup 1998 CONCACAF U-20 Championship 1986 1996

behind ice hockey, baseball, basketball and Canadian and American football. It is hoped that the awarding of the 2007 FIFA World Youth Championship to Canada will help the profile of the game in a country where there is not even a national league. The top clubs compete in the American A-League, the tier just below MLS, and 2004 proved to be a good year, showing that football in Canada does have potential with Vancouver Whitecaps reaching the play-off semi-finals and Montreal Impact beating Seattle Sounders in the final to win the Championship.

THE FIFA BIG COUNT OF 2000

	Male	Female		Male	Female
Registered players	62 100	35 000	Referees	7 000	6 000
Non registered players	400 000	200 000	Officials	100 000	50 000
Youth players	418 000	235 000	Total involved	1 513 100	
Total players	1 350 100		Number of clubs	5 900	
Professional players	100	0	Number of teams	51 000	

The Canadian Soccer Association (CSA)

Place Soccer Canada, 237 Metcalfe Street, Ottawa, Ontario, K2P 1R2, Canada
Tel +1 613 2377678   Fax +1 613 2371516
info@soccercan.ca   www.canadasoccer.com
President: SHARPE Andy   General Secretary: PIPE Kevan
Vice-President: MONTAGLIANI Victor   Treasurer: NEWMANN Adrian   Media Officer: QUARRY Morgan
Men's Coach: YALLOP Frank   Women's Coach: PELLERUD Even
CSA formed: 1912   CONCACAF: 1978   FIFA: 1912-28, 1946
Colours: Red, Red, Red

GAMES PLAYED BY CANADA IN THE 2006 WORLD CUP™ CYCLE

2002	Opponents	Score		Venue	Comp	Scorers	Att	Referee
15-10	Scotland	L	1-3	Edinburgh	Fr	De Rosario [9p]	16 207	Huyghe BEL
2003								
18-01	USA	L	0-4	Fort Lauderdale	Fr		6 549	Sibrian SLV
12-02	Libya	W	4-2	Tripoli	Fr	McKenna [18], Brennan [34], Stalteri [47], Canizalez [81]	45 000	
29-03	Estonia	L	1-2	Tallinn	Fr	Stalteri [47]	2 500	Hansson SWE
1-06	Germany	L	1-4	Wolfsburg	Fr	McKenna [20]	24 000	Poulat FRA
12-07	Costa Rica	W	1-0	Foxboro	GCr1	Stalteri [59]	33 652	Piper TRI
14-07	Cuba	L	0-2	Foxboro	GCr1		8 780	Prendergast JAM
11-10	Finland	L	2-3	Tampere	Fr	Radzinski [75], De Rosario [85]	5 350	
15-11	Czech Republic	L	1-5	Teplice	Fr	Radzinski [89]	8 343	Sundell SWE
18-11	Republic of Ireland	L	0-3	Dublin	Fr		23 000	Whitby WAL
2004								
18-01	Barbados	W	1-0	Bridgetown	Fr	Corazzin [10]		Ford BRB
30-05	Wales	L	0-1	Wrexham	Fr		10 805	McKeon IRE
13-06	Belize	W	4-0	Kingston	WCq	Peschisolido [39], Radzinski [55], McKenna [75], Brennan [83]	8 245	Batres GUA
16-06	Belize	W	4-0	Kingston	WCq	Radzinski [45], De Rosario 2 [63 73], Brennan [85]	5 124	Gordon TRI
18-08	Guatemala	L	0-2	Vancouver	WCq		6 725	Sibrian SLV
4-09	Honduras	D	1-1	Edmonton	WCq	De Vos [82]	9 654	Archundia MEX
8-09	Costa Rica	L	0-1	San Jose	WCq		13 000	Ramdhan TRI
9-10	Honduras	D	1-1	San Pedro Sula	WCq	Hutchinson [73]	42 000	Stott USA
13-10	Costa Rica	L	1-3	Vancouver	WCq	De Rosario [12]	4 728	Prendergast JAM
17-11	Guatemala	W	1-0	Guatemala City	WCq	De Rosario [57]	18 000	Rodriguez MEX
2005								
9-02	Northern Ireland	W	1-0	Belfast	Fr	Occean [31]	11 156	Attard MLT
26-03	Portugal	L	1-4	Barcelos	Fr	McKenna [85]	13 000	Ishchenko UKR
2-07	Honduras	L	1-2	Vancouver	Fr	McKenna [70]	4 105	Valenzuela USA
7-07	Costa Rica	L	0-1	Seattle	GCr1		15 831	Prendergast JAM
9-07	USA	L	0-2	Seattle	GCr1		15 109	Brizan TRI
12-07	Cuba	W	2-1	Foxboro	GCr1	Gerba [69], Hutchinson [87]	15 211	Moreno PAN

Fr = Friendly match • GC = CONCACAF Gold Cup • WC = FIFA World Cup™ • q = qualifier • r1 = first round group

NATIONAL CAPS

	Caps
SAMUEL Randy	82
WATSON Mark	72
HOOPER Lyndon	66
BUNBURY Alex	65
DASOVIC Nick	62
MILLER Colin	61
SWEENEY Mike	61
CORAZZIN Carlo	58
WILSON Bruce	57
FORREST Craig	56

NATIONAL GOALS

	Goals
CATLIFF John	19
MITCHELL Dale	19
BUNBURY Alex	16
CORAZZIN Carlo	11
VRABLIC Igor	11
PESCHISOLIDO Paul	10
McKENNA Kevin	8
DE ROSARIO Dwayne	7
PARSONS Les	7
RADZINSKI Tomasz	7

NATIONAL COACH

	Years
WAITERS Tony	1983-'87
BEARPARK Bob	1986-'87
TAYLOR Tony	1988
LENARDUZZI Bob	1989
WAITERS Tony	1990-'91
LENARDUZZI Bob	1992-'97
TWAMLEY Bruce	1998
OSIECK Holger	1999-'03
MILLER Colin	2003
YALLOP Frank	2003-

CANADA COUNTRY INFORMATION

Capital	Ottawa	Independence	1867	GDP per Capita	$29 800
Population	32 507 874	Status	Commonwealth	GNP Ranking	8
Area km²	9 984 670	Language	English/French	Dialling code	+1
Population density	3 per km²	Literacy rate	99%	Internet code	.ca
% in urban areas	77%	Main religion	Christian 82%	GMT +/–	-3.5 / -8
Towns/Cities ('000)	Toronto 4 612; Montreal 3 268; Vancouver 1 837; Calgary 968; Ottawa 874; Edmonton 822; Hamilton 653; Quebec 645; Winnipeg 632; Kitchener 409; London 346; Victoria 289				
Neighbours (km)	USA 8 893; Arctic Ocean, Atlantic Ocean & Pacific Ocean 202 020				
Main stadia	Commonwealth Stadium – Edmonton 60 217; York University – Toronto 25 000 (from 2007)				

PART TWO – THE ASSOCIATIONS

CANADA NATIONAL TEAM RECORDS AND RECORD SEQUENCES

Records			Sequence records					
Victory	7-0	USA 1904	Wins	6	2000	Clean sheets	5	1996
Defeat	0-8	MEX 1993	Defeats	9	1974-1976	Goals scored	10	1980-1983 & 1985
Player Caps	82	SAMUEL Randy	Undefeated	15	1999-2000	Without goal	5	1986 & 2000
Player Goals	19	CATLIFF & MITCHELL	Without win	12	1974-1976	Goals against	17	1988-1992

FIFA REFEREE LIST 2005

	Int'l	DoB
DEPIERO Steven	2002	24-01-1970
FARIAS Jose	1996	15-01-1962
LIU Hu	2001	6-07-1961
NAVARRO Mauricio	2000	7-04-1966
PETRESCU Silviu	2001	6-10-1968

FIFA ASSISTANT REFEREE LIST 2005

	Int'l	DoB
DE LUCA Amato	2002	24-04-1962
FEARN Simon	1999	24-01-1968
KRISTO Zoran	1999	20-07-1962
ROY Eric	1993	9-06-1966
SCHOFIELD Neil	1999	28-01-1962
VERGARA Hector	1993	15-12-1966

CLUB DIRECTORY

Club	Town/City	Stadium	Phone	www.	League
Calgary Mustangs	Calgary	McMahon Stadium 36 000	+1 403 2626664	calgarymustangs.com	USL A-League
Edmonton Aviators	Edmonton				USL A-League
Montreal Impact	Montreal	Claude Robillard 14 000	+1 514 3283668	impactmontreal.com	USL A-League
Toronto Lynx	Toronto	Centennial Stadium 3 500	+1 416 2514625	lynxsoccer.com	USL A-League
Vancouver Whitecaps	Vancouver	Swangard, Burnaby 6 100	+1 604 6699283	whitecapsfc.com	USL A-League

2004 saw five Canadian clubs play in the United Soccer Leagues (USL) First Division, also known as the A-League, in what is the second tier of football in the USA behind the MLS. Montreal won the title in 2005 for the second time. At the start of the 2005 season, however, both Calgary and Edmonton lost their franchises, leaving just three Canadian clubs in the league. See USA for results.

CAY – CAYMAN ISLANDS

NATIONAL TEAM RECORD
JULY 1ST 2002 TO JUNE 30TH 2005

PL	W	D	L	F	A	%
9	2	0	7	4	20	22.2

FIFA/COCA-COLA WORLD RANKING

1993	1994	1995	1996	1997	1998	1999	2000	2001	2002	2003	2004	High		Low	
154	150	131	148	164	153	148	159	165	164	181	176	127	11/95	184	03/04

2004-2005											
08/04	09/04	10/04	11/04	12/04	01/05	02/05	03/05	04/05	05/05	06/05	07/05
183	183	183	183	176	176	176	176	176	176	177	177

The 2006 FIFA World Cup™ qualifiers saw the Cayman Islands face up to Cuba for the third tournament in a row. Having lost 6-0 on aggregate in 1996 and 4-0 in 2000, it was the same story in 2004. A 1-2 defeat in Grand Cayman against a side ranked more than 100 places above them was no disgrace, but back in Havana the Cubans took control and won 3-0. Attention then turned to the Digicel Caribbean Cup which doubled up as CONCACAF Gold Cup qualifiers. In a group with Bermuda, St Vincent and the Grenadines and the British Virgin Islands, the Cayman Islands beat the latter, but two defeats sent them packing and since then the side has lain dormant.

INTERNATIONAL HONOURS
None

Meanwhile, the support system for the country's football programme received a boost from FIFA with funds from the Goal Project provided to aid construction of a national training centre. Combine that with a growing junior programme and a player exchange system with Vasco da Gama in Brazil and the foundations for growth are well laid. After a battering from Hurricane Ivan last year, getting the 13 teams in the Fosters National League to compete was achievement in itself. Played in two zones, the top two in each group met in the semi-finals with Scholars International and Western Union reaching the final which Union won on penalties after a goalless draw.

THE FIFA BIG COUNT OF 2000

	Male	Female		Male	Female
Registered players	592	224	Referees	48	3
Non registered players	1 000	0	Officials	180	16
Youth players	540	140	Total involved	2 743	
Total players	2 496		Number of clubs	39	
Professional players	0	0	Number of teams	48	

Cayman Islands Football Association (CIFA)
Truman Bodden Sports Complex, Olympic Way, Off Walkers Road, PO Box 178, GT, Grand Cayman, Cayman Islands
Tel +1 345 9495775   Fax +1 345 9457673
cifa@candw.ky   www.caymanfootball.ky
President: WEBB Jeffrey   General Secretary: BLAKE Bruce
Vice-President: FREDERICK David   Treasurer: WATSON Canover   Media Officer: MORGAN Kenisha
Men's Coach: TINOCO Marcos   Women's Coach: CUNHA Thiago
CIFA formed: 1966   CONCACAF: 1993   FIFA: 1992
Colours: Red/white, Blue/white, White/red

GAMES PLAYED BY CAYMAN ISLANDS IN THE 2006 FIFA WORLD CUP™ CYCLE

2002	Opponents		Score	Venue		Scorers	Att.	Referee
17-11	Nicaragua	L	0-1	Grand Cayman	Fr			
27-11	Cuba	L	0-5	Grand Cayman	GCq			Prendergast JAM
29-11	Dominican Republic	W	1-0	Grand Cayman	GCq	Forbes 27		Grant HAI
1-12	Martinique	L	0-3	Grand Cayman	GCq			Prendergast JAM
2003								

No international matches played in 2003

2004								
22-02	Cuba	L	1-2	Grand Cayman	WCq	Elliot 72	1 789	Sibrian SLV
27-03	Cuba	L	0-3	Havana	WCq		3 500	Rodriguez MEX
24-11	Bermuda	L	1-2	Kingstown	GCq	Berry 48	200	Matthew SKN
26-11	British Virgin Islands	W	1-0	Kingstown	GCq	Whittaker 49		
28-11	St Vincent/Grenadines	L	0-4	Kingstown	GCq		850	Prendergast JAM
2005								

No international matches played in 2005 before August

Fr = Friendly match • GC = CONCACAF Gold Cup • WC = FIFA World Cup™ • q = qualifier

CAYMAN ISLANDS NATIONAL TEAM RECORDS AND RECORD SEQUENCES

Records			Sequence records					
Victory	5-0	VGB 1994	Wins	3	1994	Clean sheets	2	1994, 1995
Defeat	2-9	TRI 1995	Defeats	8	1991-1993	Goals scored	5	1993-94, 2000
Player Caps	n/a		Undefeated	4	1994-1995	Without goal	5	2000
Player Goals	n/a		Without win	9	1991-93, 1995-98	Goals against	10	1991-1993

FIFA REFEREE LIST 2005

	Int'l	DoB
BOWEN Godfrey	1982	25-10-1961
WHITTAKER Alfredo	2003	1-02-1966

FIFA ASSISTANT REFEREE LIST 2005

	Int'l	DoB
BAILEY Livingston	2004	18-05-1968
BERRY Ernest	1999	29-09-1970
WILLIAMS Noel	1997	19-08-1970

RECENT LEAGUE AND CUP RECORD

	Championship				Cup		
Year	Champions	Score	Runners-up		Winners	Score	Runners-up
1998	Scholars International				George Town		
1999	George Town						
2000	Western Union						
2001	Scholars International	†	George Town		Bodden Town		
2002	George Town	2-1	Future		George Town	4-0	Scholars International
2003	Scholars International	3-1	Sunset		Scholars International	2-1	Bodden Town
2004	Latinos	3-2	Scholars International		Latinos	2-1	George Town
2005	Western Union	0-0 3-2p	Scholars International				

† Played on a league system

CAYMAN ISLANDS COUNTRY INFORMATION

Capital	George Town	Independence		British Crown Colony	GDP per Capita	$35 000
Population	43 103	Status			GNP Ranking	n/a
Area km²	262	Language	English		Dialling code	+1 345
Population density	164 per km²	Literacy rate	98%		Internet code	.ky
% in urban areas	%	Main religion	Christian		GMT +/–	-5
Towns/Cities ('000)	George Town 27; West Bay 10; Bodden Town 6; East End 1; North Side 1					
Neighbours (km)	The Cayman Islands consist of three islands in the Caribbean Sea					
Main stadia	Truman Boden – George Town 7 000; ED Bush – West Bay 2 500					

CGO – CONGO

NATIONAL TEAM RECORD
JULY 1ST 2002 TO JUNE 30TH 2005

PL	W	D	L	F	A	%
28	9	8	11	23	30	46.4

FIFA/COCA-COLA WORLD RANKING

1993	1994	1995	1996	1997	1998	1999	2000	2001	2002	2003	2004	High		Low	
103	114	119	100	101	112	94	86	94	97	108	117	85	11/00	139	04/96

2004-2005											
08/04	09/04	10/04	11/04	12/04	01/05	02/05	03/05	04/05	05/05	06/05	07/05
98	100	100	105	117	118	115	118	117	117	111	112

Apart from coming agonisingly close to qualifying for the 1998 FIFA World Cup™, when they lost out to South Africa, Congo's recent international career has had few highlights. The Red Devils have missed out again for Germany 2006 and are also in danger of not qualifying for the CAF Cup of Nations. Coach Christian Letard, after presiding over disappointing performances and results, publicly aired the grievances he had with his employers and soon found himself out of a job. Although not at their lowest ebb, Congo's national side is not progressing at any great rate and the chances of a repeat of the Nations Cup triumph of more than 30 years ago look a distant dream.

INTERNATIONAL HONOURS
CAF African Cup of Nations 1972 African Games 1965 CAF Champions League CARA Brazzaville 1974

The country may need to pin its hopes on a new generation that is being assisted with the opening of two youth academies. Unfortunately, there has been too little to show for it so far with the U-20s withdrawn from the African Youth Championship first round qualifier match with Cameroon while the U-17s lost in the preliminary round of the U-17 Championship, beaten 3-1 on aggregate by Central African Republic. Diables Noirs won the domestic title for the fifth time, beating AS Police 2-1 in the final of the national play-offs to register their first League success since 1993. Muni Sport won the Cup, inflicting a second successive final defeat on Vita Club Mokanda.

THE FIFA BIG COUNT OF 2000

	Male	Female		Male	Female
Registered players	5 625	250	Referees	125	10
Non registered players	25 000	150	Officials	625	30
Youth players	2 400	115	Total involved	34 300	
Total players	33 540		Number of clubs	266	
Professional players	0	0	Number of teams	278	

Fédération Congolaise de Football (FECOFOOT)
BP 11, Brazzaville, Congo
Tel +242 811563   Fax +242 812524
fecofoot@congonet.cg   www.none
President: MBONGO Sylvestre   General Secretary: OTENDA Charles
Vice-President: MABOUNDA Magloire   Treasurer: NGUIE Gregoire   Media Officer: MALONGA Roger
Men's Coach: LETARD Christian   Women's Coach: MPILA Jean Paul
FECOFOOT formed: 1962   CAF: 1966   FIFA: 1962
Colours: Green, Yellow, Red

GAMES PLAYED BY CONGO IN THE 2006 FIFA WORLD CUP™ CYCLE

2002	Opponents		Score	Venue	Comp	Scorers	Att	Referee
25-08	Congo DR	L	1-3	Brazzaville	Fr			
1-09	Gabon	D	0-0	Brazzaville	Fr			
8-09	Burkina Faso	D	0-0	Brazzaville	CNq		60 000	Itur KEN
13-10	Mozambique	W	3-0	Maputo	CNq	Tsoumou [49], Nguie [70], Bakouma [73]		Lwanja MWI
2003								
9-03	Congo DR	L	0-3	Kinshasa	Fr			
4-05	Central African Rep.	W	2-1	Brazzaville	CNq	Embingou [6], Owolo [52]		
8-06	Central African Rep.	D	0-0	Bangui	CNq			Hissene CHA
21-06	Burkina Faso	L	0-3	Ouagadougou	CNq		36 000	Mana NGA
6-07	Mozambique	D	0-0	Brazzaville	CNq			
12-10	Sierra Leone	W	1-0	Brazzaville	WCq	Mvoubi [89p]	4 800	Mana NGA
16-11	Sierra Leone	D	1-1	Freetown	WCq	Nguie [67]	20 000	Monteiro Lopez CPV
5-12	Gabon	W	3-2	Brazzaville	CMr1	Ayessa [25], Ndey [56], Beaulia [67]		Tchoumba CMR
9-12	Gabon	D	1-1	Brazzaville	CMr1	Ayessa [56]		
10-12	Cameroon	L	0-2	Brazzaville	CMsf			Mbera GAB
13-12	Gabon	W	1-0	Brazzaville	CM3p			
2004								
5-06	Senegal	L	0-2	Dakar	WCq		18 000	Benouza ALG
20-06	Liberia	W	3-0	Brazzaville	WCq	Bouanga [52], Mamouna-Ossila [55], Batota [66]	25 000	Lemghambodj MTN
4-07	Mali	W	1-0	Brazzaville	WCq	Mamouna-Ossila [30]	20 000	Evehe CMR
5-09	Togo	L	0-2	Lome	WCq		20 000	Mbera GAB
10-10	Zambia	L	2-3	Brazzaville	WCq	Bouanga [75], Mamouna-Ossila [81]	20 000	Yacoubi TUN
2005								
5-02	Central African Rep.	W	1-0	Libreville	CMr1	Bhebey [10]		
8-02	Gabon	L	0-1	Libreville	CMr1			
12-02	Gabon	L	1-2	Libreville	CM3p	Lakou [35]		
22-02	Angola	L	0-2	Brazzaville	Fr			
19-03	Gabon	D	0-0	Libreville	Fr			
26-03	Zambia	L	0-2	Chililabombwe	WCq		20 000	Maillet SEY
5-06	Senegal	D	0-0	Brazzaville	WCq		40 000	Damon RSA
19-06	Liberia	W	2-0	Paynesville	WCq	Bhebey 2 [3 73]	5 000	Sillah GAM

Fr = Friendly match • CN = African Cup of Nations • CM = CEMAC Cup • WC = FIFA World Cup™
q = qualifier • r1 = first round game • sf = semi-final • 3p = third place play-off

CONGO NATIONAL TEAM RECORDS AND RECORD SEQUENCES

Records			Sequence records				
Victory	11-0	STP 1976	Wins	5	1983	Clean sheets	4	1983, 1998-1999
Defeat	1-8	MAD 1960	Defeats	5	1968, 1973, 1993	Goals scored	11	1975-1977
Player Caps	n/a		Undefeated	8	1963-1965	Without goal	7	1992-1993
Player Goals	n/a		Without win	9	2001-2002	Goals against	14	1965-1968

RECENT LEAGUE AND CUP RECORD

	Championship				Cup		
Year	Champions	Score	Runners-up		Winners	Score	Runners-up
2000	Etoile du Congo	†			Etoile du Congo	5-1	Vita Club Mokanda
2001	Etoile du Congo	1-0	La Mancha		AS Police	1-0	Etoile du Congo
2002	AS Police	2-1	Etoile du Congo		Etoile du Congo	2-1	FC Abeilles
2003	St Michel Ouenzé	0-0	La Mancha		Diables Noirs	0-0 3-2p	Vita Club Mokanda
2004	Diables Noirs	2-1	AS Police		Muni Sport	0-0 3-0p	Vita Club Mokanda

† Played on a league system

CONGO COUNTRY INFORMATION

Capital	Brazzaville	Independence	1960 from France	GDP per Capita	$700
Population	2 998 040	Status	Republic	GNP Ranking	137
Area km²	342 000	Language	French	Dialling code	+242
Population density	8 per km²	Literacy rate	77%	Internet code	.cg
% in urban areas	59%	Main religion	Christian 50%	GMT +/–	+1
Towns/Cities ('000)	Brazzaville 1 115; Pointe-Noire 628; Loubomo 70; Nkayi 70; Loandjili 26; Madingou 22				
Neighbours (km)	Central African Republic 467; Congo DR 2 410; Angola 201; Gabon 1 903; Cameroon 523; Atlantic Ocean 169				
Main stadia	Stade de la Révolution – Brazzaville 50 000				

CHA – CHAD

NATIONAL TEAM RECORD
JULY 1ST 2002 TO JUNE 30TH 2005

PL	W	D	L	F	A	%
13	4	3	6	15	22	42.3

FIFA/COCA-COLA WORLD RANKING

1993	1994	1995	1996	1997	1998	1999	2000	2001	2002	2003	2004	High		Low	
166	175	180	188	184	178	166	163	176	173	152	168	152	11/03	190	09/97

2004-2005											
08/04	09/04	10/04	11/04	12/04	01/05	02/05	03/05	04/05	05/05	06/05	07/05
159	160	162	163	168	168	160	160	161	160	159	159

Since joining FIFA nearly 20 years ago, Chad have languished in the lower echelons of the world rankings, but there have been definite shoots of growth from one of the continent's lesser footballing outposts. Competing in only their second FIFA World Cup™ they upset Angola, ranked nearly 100 places above them, in the preliminary qualifiers for 2006 beating them 3-1 in N'Djamena thanks to a hat-trick from Francis Oumar. They were cruelly denied a place in the next round though when they lost on away goals as Angola took the return leg 2-0. There were no further internationals until the 2005 CEMAC Cup where Chad took part with notable success. Two

INTERNATIONAL HONOURS
None

draws in the group games and a 3-2 semi-final victory over Gabon set Chad up for a final against defending champions Cameroon Amateurs. A hard fought contest was settled by a single penalty for the Amateurs, but coach Yann Djim and his side are clearly making progress. Money problems are a feature in Chad affecting the league programme. In its absence, a regional competition was played in 2004 won by Renaissance FC while the Coupe de la Ligue du Chari-Baguirmi was won by Gazelle. Both teams exited the continental cups at the first hurdle, but Renaissance pushed Libya's Al Olympique close losing 3-4 on aggregate, while Gazelle lost to FC 105 on away goals.

THE FIFA BIG COUNT OF 2000

	Male	Female		Male	Female
Registered players	5 000	0	Referees	200	0
Non registered players	20 000	0	Officials	1 500	0
Youth players	2 500	0	Total involved	29 200	
Total players	27 500		Number of clubs	100	
Professional players	0	0	Number of teams	500	

Fédération Tchadienne de Football (FTF)
Case postale 886, N'Djamena, Chad
Tel +235 518740   Fax +235 523806
www.none
President: MAHAMAT Saleh Issa   General Secretary: RAMADANE Daouda
Vice-President: TBD   Treasurer: DJIMEZO Abdelkader   Media Officer: ZOUTANE DABA Martin
Men's Coach: DJIM Yann   Women's Coach: None
FTF formed: 1962   CAF: 1962   FIFA: 1988
Colours: Blue, Yellow, Red

GAMES PLAYED BY CHAD IN THE 2006 FIFA WORLD CUP™ CYCLE

2002	Opponents	Score		Venue	Comp	Scorers	Att	Referee
26-07	Sudan	L	0-2	Khartoum	Fr			Abdel Rahman SUD
28-07	Ethiopia	W	3-2	Khartoum	Fr			Rassas Lebrato SUD
30-07	Uganda	L	0-2	Khartoum	Fr			Salih SUD
11-10	Algeria	L	1-4	Annaba	CNq	Naay 70	20 000	El Beltagy EGY
2003								
30-03	Namibia	W	2-0	N'Djamena	CNq	Hissein 2 57 89p		Dimanche CTA
7-06	Namibia	L	1-2	Windhoek	CNq	Hissein 35	5 000	Colembi ANG
6-07	Algeria	D	0-0	N'Djamena	CNq			
12-10	Angola	W	3-1	N'Djamena	WCq	Oumar 3 53 74 83	30 000	Nahi CIV
16-11	Angola	L	0-2	Luanda	WCq		30 000	Buenkadila COD
2004								
No international matches played in 2004								
2005								
8-02	Equatorial Guinea	D	0-0	Libreville	CMr1			
10-02	Gabon	W	3-2	Libreville	CMsf	Djenet 3, Doumbe 8, Nguembaye 56		
22-05	Sudan	L	1-4	Khartoum	Fr			
27-05	Sudan	D	1-1	Khartoum	Fr			

Fr = Friendly match • CN = African Cup of Nations • CM = CEMAC Cup • WC = FIFA World Cup™ • q = qualifier • r1 = first round group • sf = semi-final

CHAD NATIONAL TEAM RECORDS AND RECORD SEQUENCES

Records			Sequence records				
Victory	5-0	STP 1976	Wins	3	1999	Clean sheets	2	1986, 1999
Defeat	2-6	BEN 1963	Defeats	7	1991-1997	Goals scored	4	Three times
Player Caps	n/a		Undefeated	4	1984-1985	Without goal	5	1992-1997
Player Goals	n/a		Without win	12	1976-86, 1991-99	Goals against	9	1978-86, 1991-98

FIFA REFEREE LIST 2005

	Int'l	DOB
ADELIL Abakar	1996	15-08-1963
CORDIER Adam	2005	8-07-1972
MAHAMAT Saeh	2001	29-11-1971
NDOUBAHIDI Napoleon	2005	10-12-1978
NDOUBANGAR Saradoum	2001	24-05-1968

FIFA ASSISTANT REFEREE LIST 2005

	Int'l	DoB
ADOUM Kette	1998	14-11-1963
BIMBAYE Edmond	2001	14-10-1967
BRAHIM Vovo	2005	12-03-1970
LARGUE Jonas	1994	28-04-1968
MAOGOMBAYE Mbaissagem	1998	15-04-1968
WALDABET Koissoual		10-03-1976
ZAKARIA Lawadji		21-05-1971

RECENT LEAGUE RECORD

Year	Champions
1996	AS Coton Chad
1997	Tourbillon
1998	AS Coton Chad
1999	Renaissance
2000	Tourbillon
2001	Tourbillon
2002	No tournament
2003	No tournament
2004	No tournament

CHAD COUNTRY INFORMATION

Capital	N'Djamena	Independence	1960 from France	GDP per Capita	$1 200
Population	9 538 544	Status	Republic	GNP Ranking	145
Area km²	1 284 000	Language	French, Arabic	Dialling code	+235
Population density	7 per km²	Literacy rate	47%	Internet code	.td
% in urban areas	21%	Main religion	Muslim 51%, Christian 35%	GMT +/–	+1
Towns/Cities ('000)	N'Djamena 721; Moundou 135; Sarh 102; Abeche 74; Kelo 42; Koumra 36; Pala 35				
Neighbours (km)	Libya 1 055; Sudan 1 360; Central African Republic 1 197; Cameroon 1 094; Nigeria 87; Niger 1 175				
Main stadia	Stade National – N'Djamena 30 000				

CHI – CHILE

NATIONAL TEAM RECORD
JULY 1ST 2002 TO JUNE 30TH 2005

PL	W	D	L	F	A	%
28	10	9	9	32	28	51.8

FIFA/COCA-COLA WORLD RANKING

1993	1994	1995	1996	1997	1998	1999	2000	2001	2002	2003	2004	High		Low	
55	47	36	26	16	16	23	19	39	84	80	74	**8**	04/98	**84**	12/02

2004-2005											
08/04	09/04	10/04	11/04	12/04	01/05	02/05	03/05	04/05	05/05	06/05	07/05
67	66	79	80	74	75	74	74	76	76	77	72

After the huge embarrassment of finishing bottom of the South American qualifying group for the 2002 FIFA World Cup™ Chile's national team restored a certain sense of pride with a solid mid-table performance in the 2006 qualifying group, which in South America holds out the possibility of qualification for the finals. Three coaches were used during the campaign which included the return of the hugely successful Nelson Acosta who guided the team to the 1998 finals in France, the only time Chile have qualified since 1982. The victory over Bolivia in June 2005 was notable not just because it was Acosta's first match back in charge but because it also saw veteran Marcelo

INTERNATIONAL HONOURS
Qualified for the FIFA World Cup™ 1930 1950 1962 1966 1974 1982 1998 Copa Libertadores Colo Colo 1991

Salas score a goal that took him past Ivan Zamorano as the all-time leading goalscorer for Chile. Nowhere in the world in 2004 was there a more prolific striker in League football than Patricio Galaz. His 42 goals helped Cobreloa to the final of both the Apertura and Clausura and although they lost the Apertura to Universidad de Chile on penalties they won the Clausura by beating Union Española over the two legs. Both Universidad and Cobreloa represented Chile in the 2005 Copa Libertadores and although Universidad made it out of the group stage they lost in the second round to Santos. For the second year running Cobreloa failed to make it to the knock-out stage.

THE FIFA BIG COUNT OF 2000

	Male	Female		Male	Female
Registered players	519 983	950	Referees	5 002	0
Non registered players	400 000	0	Officials	14 500	200
Youth players	264 293	1 000	Total involved	1 205 928	
Total players	1 186 226		Number of clubs	4 931	
Professional players	1 125	0	Number of teams	29 498	

Federación de Fútbol de Chile (FFCH)
Avenida Quilin No. 5635, Comuna Peñalolén, Casilla No. 3733, Central de Casillas, Santiago de Chile, Chile
Tel +56 2 3975000   Fax +56 2 2843510
ffch@anfpchile.cl   www.anfp.cl
President: SANCHEZ Reinaldo   General Secretary: LAFRENTZ Jorge
Vice-President: JELVEZ Sergio   Treasurer: TBD   Media Officer: None
Men's Coach: ACOSTA Nelson   Women's Coach: QUINTILIANI Claudio
FFCH formed: 1895   CONMEBOL: 1916   FIFA: 1913
Colours: Red, Blue, White

GAMES PLAYED BY CHILE IN THE 2006 FIFA WORLD CUP™ CYCLE

2002	Opponents		Score	Venue	Comp	Scorers	Att	Referee
10-12	Palestine	W	3-1	Santiago	Fr			
2003								
30-03	Peru	W	2-0	Santiago	Fr	Mirosevic [44], Pinilla [64]	39 662	Amarilla PAR
2-04	Peru	L	0-3	Lima	Fr		25 000	Ruiz COL
30-04	Costa Rica	W	1-0	Santiago	Fr	Contreras [61]	8 618	Aquino PAR
8-06	Costa Rica	L	0-1	San Jose	Fr		14 000	Pineda HON
11-06	Honduras	W	2-1	San Pedro Sula	Fr	Tapia [44p], Gonzalez.M [60]	25 000	Burgos GUA
20-08	China	D	0-0	Tianjin	Fr		20 000	Huang CHN
6-09	Argentina	D	2-2	Buenos Aires	WCq	Mirosevic [60], Navia [77]	38 000	Aquino PAR
9-09	Peru	W	2-1	Santiago	WCq	Pinilla [35], Norambuena [70]	60 000	Elizondo ARG
15-11	Uruguay	L	1-2	Montevideo	WCq	Melendez [20]	60 000	Martin ARG
18-11	Paraguay	L	0-1	Santiago	WCq		63 000	Mendez URU
2004								
18-02	Mexico	D	1-1	Carson	Fr	Navia [46]	20 173	Cruz USA
30-03	Bolivia	W	2-0	La Paz	WCq	Villarroel [38], Gonzalez.M [60]	42 000	Martin ARG
28-04	Peru	D	1-1	Antofagasta	Fr	Fuentes [56]	23 000	Amarilla PAR
1-06	Venezuela	W	1-0	San Cristobal	WCq	Pinilla [84]	30 000	Torres PAR
6-06	Brazil	D	1-1	Santiago	WCq	Navia [89p]	65 000	Elizondo ARG
8-07	Brazil	L	0-1	Arequipa	CAr1		35 000	Rodriguez MEX
11-07	Paraguay	D	1-1	Arequipa	CAr1	Gonzalez.S [71]	35 000	Mendez URU
14-07	Costa Rica	L	1-2	Tacna	CAr1	Olarra [40]	20 000	Ortube BOL
5-09	Colombia	D	0-0	Santiago	WCq		62 523	Souza BRA
10-10	Ecuador	L	0-2	Quito	WCq		27 956	Ortube BOL
13-10	Argentina	D	0-0	Santiago	WCq		57 671	Amarilla PAR
17-11	Peru	L	1-2	Lima	WCq	Gonzalez.S [91+]	39 752	Baldassi ARG
2005								
9-02	Ecuador	W	3-0	Vina del Mar	Fr	Maldonado [25], Gonzalez.M [35], Pinilla [83]	15 000	Favale ARG
26-03	Uruguay	D	1-1	Santiago	WCq	Mirosevic [47]	55 000	Ruiz COL
30-03	Paraguay	L	1-2	Asuncion	WCq	Pinilla [72]	10 000	Elizondo ARG
4-06	Bolivia	W	3-1	Santiago	WCq	Fuentes 2 [8 34], Salas [66]	46 729	Rezende BRA
8-06	Venezuela	W	2-1	Santiago	WCq	Jimenez 2 [31 60]	35 506	Torres PAR

Fr = Friendly match • CA = Copa América • WC = FIFA World Cup™ • q = qualifier • r1 = first round group

CHILE COUNTRY INFORMATION

Capital	Santiago	Independence	1818 from Spain	GDP per Capita	$9 900
Population	15 823 957	Status	Republic	GNP Ranking	43
Area km²	756 950	Language	Spanish	Dialling code	+56
Population density	20 per km²	Literacy rate	95%	Internet code	.cl
% in urban areas	84%	Main religion	Christian 99%	GMT +/–	-4
Towns/Cities ('000)	Santiago 4 837; Puente Alto 510; Antofagasta 309; Vina del Mar 294; Valparaiso 282; Talcahuano 282; San Bernardo 249; Temuco 238; Iquique 227; Concepción 215; Rancagua 212				
Neighbours (km)	Peru 160; Bolivia 861; Argentina 5 150; South Pacific Ocean 6 435				
Main stadia	Estadio Nacional – Santiago 77 000; Monumental – Santiago 62 500; Municipal – Concepción 35 000; Estadio Regional – Antofagasta 26 339; Santa Laura – Santiago 25 000				

CHILE NATIONAL TEAM RECORDS AND RECORD SEQUENCES

Records			Sequence records					
Victory	7-0	VEN 1979	Wins	5	1950-1952	Clean sheets	8	1983-1985
Defeat	0-7	BRA 1959	Defeats	10	1922-1924	Goals scored	18	1995-1997
Player Caps	84	SANCHEZ Leonel	Undefeated	10	1995-1996	Without goal	4	Three times
Player Goals	35	SALAS Marcelo	Without win	33	1910-1924	Goals against	41	1910-1928

NATIONAL CAPS

	Caps
SANCHEZ Leonel	84
FOUILLOUX Alberto	70
ESTAY Fabian	69
ZAMORANO Ivan	69
TAPIA Nelson	64
MARGAS Javier	63
RAMIREZ Miguel	62
ACUNA Clarence	61
SALAS Marcelo	60
LETELIER Juan Carlos	57

NATIONAL GOALS

	Goals
SALAS Marcelo	35
ZAMORANO Ivan	34
CASZELY Carlos	29
SANCHEZ Leonel	23
ARAVENA Jorge	22
LETELIER Juan Carlos	18
HORMAZABAL Enrique	17
BANDA Jaime Ramirez	12
RUBIO Hugo	12
TORO Raul	12

NATIONAL COACH

	Years
ARAVENA Orlendo	1987-'89
SALAH Arturo	1990-'93
JOZIC Mirko	1994
AZKARGORTA Xavier	1995-'96
ACOSTA Nelson	1996-'00
GARCIA Pedro	2001
GARCES Jorge	2001
VACCIA Cesar	2002
OLMOS Juvenal	2003-'05
ACOSTA Nelson	2005-

CLUB DIRECTORY

Club	Town/City	Stadium	Phone	www.	Lge	CL
Audax Italiano	Santiago	Municipal 8 500	+56 2 2872547	audax.cl	4	0
Cobreloa	Calama	Municipal 20 180	+56 55 341775	cdcobreloa.cl	7	0
Cobresal	El Salvador	El Cobre 20 752	+56 52 472392		0	0
Colo Colo	Santiago	Monumental 62 500	+56 2 2947300	colocolo.cl	23	1
Coquimbo Unido	Coquimbo	Sanchez Rumoroso 15 000	+56 51 321311		0	0
Everton	Viña del Mar	Sausalito 18 037	+56 32 689504		3	0
Huachipato	Talcahuano	Las Higueras 10 000	+56 41 582100	cdhuachipato.cl	1	0
La Serena	La Serena	La Portada 18 000	+56 51 218143		0	0
Palestino	Santiago	La Cisterna 12 000	+56 2 5590211	palestino.cl	2	0
Puerto Montt	Puerto Montt	Chinquihue 10 000	+56 65 254110		0	0
Rangers	Talca	Fiscal 17 020	+56 71 227030	rangers.cl	0	0
Unión San Felipe	San Felipe	Municipal 13 162	+56 34 915345		1	0
Temuco	Temuco	German Becker 20 930	+56 45 210242		0	0
Universidad Católica	Santiago	San Carlos 20 000	+56 2 4124400	lacatolica.cl	8	0
Universidad Concepción	Concepción	Municipal 35 000	+56 41232836	udeconcefutbol.cl	0	0
Universidad de Chile	Santiago	Nacional 77 000	+56 2 2393338		12	0
Unión Española	Santiago	Santa Laura 25 000	+56 2 7354110		5	0
Santiago Wanderers	Valparaíso	Playa Ancha 19 000	+56 32 217210	santiagowanderers.cl	3	0

PRIMERA DIVISION RESULTS 2004

Apertura results shaded darker than Clausura results

	Audax	Cobreloa	Cobresal	Colo Colo	Coquimbo	Everton	Huachip.	La Serena	Palestino	P. Montt	Rangers	S. Felipe	Temuco	Católica	Concep.	U de Ch.	Española	Wanderers
Audax Italiano		2-2	4-0	1-2	5-2	1-1	3-0	3-3	0-0	2-2	3-1	3-1	4-0	2-3	0-2	1-1	1-1	1-1
Cobreloa	1-1		1-1	3-0	3-1	6-0	2-0	1-1	6-1	2-1	5-2	3-1	3-0	2-1	2-3	3-0	2-2	5-1
Cobresal	1-1	2-3		0-1	2-1	0-1	1-3	6-1	3-3	4-2	2-1	2-2	0-3	0-1	3-2	0-1	3-4	5-1
Colo Colo	2-1	2-2	4-0		2-1	1-1	2-4	3-1	2-1	1-0	0-0	1-1	2-1	1-1	0-2	0-4	4-1	4-1
Coquimbo Unido	1-3	3-3	2-1	1-0		2-0	3-2	4-3	2-2	4-0	4-2	0-0	4-3	3-2	2-0	1-3	2-2	3-2
Everton	4-2	1-3	1-0	0-2	2-0		2-0	2-0	0-1	1-1	4-0	0-1	5-0	2-0	2-1	0-0	0-0	0-1
Huachipato	2-0	1-2	3-1	2-2	1-0	2-4		4-2	3-2	3-1	4-0	0-0	2-2	1-2	2-2	2-1	0-1	1-2
La Serena	3-1	1-2	4-3	1-1	2-1	3-0	1-3		3-2	0-1	1-1	3-0	2-2	1-4	0-1	1-3	2-4	3-2
Palestino	3-5	1-1	1-0	2-3	2-3	4-0	2-3	5-1		2-0	0-0	2-1	1-0	3-0	0-1	2-3	2-1	2-4
Puerto Montt	0-2	1-1	4-0	3-3	0-2	3-2	2-1	1-2	1-0		3-0	1-1	0-1	1-1	0-0	2-0	4-1	1-0
Rangers	1-2	0-2	2-4	1-2	0-0	1-0	2-2	1-4	2-3	3-2		1-1	2-3	2-1	2-1	0-1	3-2	4-2
Unión San Felipe	1-1	1-3	1-1	1-5	2-1	1-1	1-0	2-0	2-3	1-2	0-2		1-1	1-0	1-0	1-0	0-2	0-2
Temuco	2-1	4-4	3-3	0-1	1-1	2-1	1-3	3-3	2-1	4-2	2-2	1-0		1-0	0-5	3-3	2-2	3-3
Univ. Católica	3-2	2-1	0-1	1-2	3-3	5-0	4-1	2-1	0-0	0-0	4-0	3-2			3-4	1-2	0-4	0-1
Univ. Concepción	1-3	3-0	0-0	2-0	5-0	2-4	2-0	5-0	2-0	1-1	0-0	1-1	0-0	4-1		0-0	1-0	2-1
Univ. de Chile	0-1	2-1	2-0	0-1	1-0	0-0	2-1	3-1	4-1	6-1	2-1	3-0	2-2	0-0	3-1		2-2	2-2
Unión Española	2-0	2-0	1-2	3-0	2-1	2-1	2-1	1-1	3-5	0-0	1-2	2-2	2-3	1-2	2-2	3-1		0-1
Santiago Wanderers	3-2	1-0	2-0	1-2	2-2	4-0	0-2	5-0	2-0	5-0	3-0	2-4	2-0	1-3	0-1	1-2	0-1	

CHILE 2004
PRIMERA DIVISION APERTURA

Grupo 1	Pl	W	D	L	F	A	Pts
Colo Colo †	17	10	3	4	29	25	33
Audax Italiano †	17	5	6	6	31	28	21
Unión San Felipe †	17	4	5	8	15	27	17
Cobresal	17	1	3	13	19	40	6

Grupo 2	Pl	W	D	L	F	A	Pts
Univ. Concepción †	17	9	5	3	37	17	32
Temuco †	17	7	3	7	24	34	24
Rangers	17	5	3	9	21	33	18
La Serena	17	5	3	9	32	46	18
Palestino	17	4	2	11	34	42	14

Grupo 3	Pl	W	D	L	F	A	Pts
Cobreloa †	17	11	4	2	39	19	37
Coquimbo Unido †	17	9	2	6	39	37	29
Unión Española †	17	7	5	5	35	32	26
Everton †	17	6	3	8	22	25	21
Universidad Católica	17	6	1	10	29	29	19

Grupo 4	Pl	W	D	L	F	A	Pts
Santiago Wanderers †	17	11	3	3	37	15	36
Universidad de Chile†	17	9	3	5	32	21	30
Huachipato †	17	8	3	6	35	31	27
Puerto Montt †	17	5	5	7	27	36	20

† Qualified for the play-offs

CHILE 2004
PRIMERA DIVISION CLAUSURA

Grupo 1	Pl	W	D	L	F	A	Pts
Audax Italiano †	17	7	5	5	33	24	26
Cobreloa †	17	6	7	4	37	26	25
Unión Española †	17	6	5	6	24	20	23
Deportes La Serena	17	4	4	9	23	38	16

Grupo 2	Pl	W	D	L	F	A	Pts
Coquimbo Unido †	17	4	6	7	21	26	18
Unión San Felipe † ‡	17	5	6	6	18	25	18
Puerto Montt † ‡	17	5	5	7	16	20	17
Santiago Wanderers	17	4	2	11	24	36	14

Grupo 3	Pl	W	D	L	F	A	Pts
Colo Colo †	17	9	5	3	28	18	32
Universidad de Chile † §	17	9	6	2	27	14	30
Temuco †	17	4	9	4	34	36	21
Palestino	17	6	3	8	23	28	21
Rangers	17	3	6	8	19	33	15

Grupo 4	Pl	W	D	L	F	A	Pts
Universidad Católica †	17	9	5	3	32	19	32
Cobresal †	17	8	4	5	32	26	28
Univ. Concepción †	17	8	4	5	22	16	28
Everton †	17	6	4	7	20	26	22
Huachipato	17	6	2	9	24	26	20

† Qualified for the play-offs • § 3 points deducted

APERTURA PLAY-OFFS 2004

Preliminary Play-off
Rangers 3-1 Puerto Montt
Unión San Felipe 2-1 Everton
First Round
Unión San Felipe 0-2 1-2 **Cobreloa**
Rangers 1-1 0-3 **Santiago Wanderers**
Unión Española 3-1 1-1 **Universidad de Chile**
Huachipato 3-2 3-0 Coquimbo Unido
Temuco 0-1 1-1 **Universidad de Concepción**
Audax Italiano 0-1 0-1 **Colo Colo**

Quarter-finals		Semi-finals		Final	
Univ. de Chile*	1 1				
Univ. Concepción	0 2	Univ. de Chile *	1 2		
Unión Española *	2 0 1p	Santiago Wand.	1 0		
Santiago Wand.	1 2 3p			Univ. de Chile *†	0 1 4p
Huachipato *	1 1			Cobreloa	0 1 2p
Colo Colo	1 0	Huachipato *	2 2		
Temuco *	1 1	Cobreloa	2 3		
Cobreloa	1 3				

* At home in the first leg • The two best losers from the first round also qualify for the quarter-finals • † Universidad de Chile are Apertura champions and qualify for the Copa Libertadores 2005

APERTURA SCORERS

GALAZ Patricio	Cobreloa	23
RIVEROS Jaime	Wanderers	22
FLORES Felipe	La Serena	17
MANCILLA Hector	Huachipato	16

CLAUSURA SCORERS

GALAZ Patricio	Cobreloa	19
SUAZO Humberto	Audax	17
DIAZ Cesar	Temuco	13
COMAS Alex	La Serena	12
GIOINO Sergio	Univ. de Chile	12

CLAUSURA PLAY-OFFS 2004

Preliminary Play-off
Puerto Montt 1-2 **Everton**
First Round
Cobreloa 5-2 2-1 Audax Italiano
Everton 3-2 0-1 1-3p **Cobresal**
Coquimbo Unido 3-7 1-1 **Colo Colo**
Unión San Felipe 2-2 0-3 **Universidad Católica**
Temuco 2-0 0-2 3-5p **Universidad de Chile**
Unión Española 0-0 1-1 3-1p Universidad de Concepción

Quarter-finals		Semi-finals		Final	
Cobreloa*	2 2				
Cobresal	1 2	Cobreloa*	4 1		
Everton*	1 4	Colo Colo	1 1		
Colo Colo	3 3			Cobreloa †	3 0
Univ. Católica	1 6			Unión Española*	1 0
Temuco*	3 2	Univ. Católica	1 3 3p		
Univ. de Chile	3 3 2p	Unión Española*	3 1 4p		
Unión Española*	4 2 4p				

* At home in the first leg • The two best losers from the first round also qualify for the quarter-finals • † Cobreloa are Clausura champions and qualify for the Copa Libertadores 2005 • No relegation due to expansion of league to 20 teams.

UNIVERSIDAD DE CHILE 2004

Date	Opponents	Score		Comp	Scorers
8-02-2004	Colo Colo	W 4-0	A	TAP	Rivarola [26], Iturra [50], Gioino 2 [71 81]
14-02-2004	Rangers	W 2-0	H	TAP	Gioino [25], Rivarola [48]
21-02-2004	Unión Española	L 1-3	A	TAP	Rojas [41]. Abandoned 87' Result stood
28-02-2004	Puerto Montt	W 6-1	H	TAP	Rivarola 2 [11 88], Tampe [25], Espinola [56], Olea [77], Gioino [90p]
6-03-2004	Unión San Felipe	L 0-1	A	TAP	
9-03-2004	Everton	D 0-0	H	TAP	
14-03-2004	Palestino	W 3-2	A	TAP	Rivarola [48], Olea [69], Gioino [85]
20-03-2004	La Serena	W 3-1	H	TAP	Amaya [13], Rivarola [33], Olea [69]
3-04-2004	Huachipato	L 1-2	A	TAP	Rivarola [26]
10-04-2004	Cobresal	W 1-0	A	TAP	Rivarola [83]
13-04-2004	Audax Italiano	L 0-1	H	TAP	
18-04-2004	Cobreloa	L 0-3	A	TAP	
21-04-2004	Universidad de Concepción	W 3-1	H	TAP	Rivarola 2 [10 36], Amaya [89p]
24-04-2004	Temuco	D 3-3	A	TAP	Henriquez [23], Olea [59], Gioino [76]
30-04-2004	Santiago Wanderers	D 2-2	H	TAP	Olea [53], Gioino [89p]
4-05-2004	Universidad Católica	W 2-1	A	TAP	Rivarola [52], Gioino [55]
9-05-2004	Coquimbo Unido	W 1-0	H	TAP	Rivarola [78]
16-05-2004	Unión Española	L 1-3	H	TAPr1	Olea [67]
23-05-2004	Unión Española	D 1-1	H	TAPr1	Gioino [44]. Univ. de Chile qualify as best loser
7-06-2004	Universidad de Concepción	W 1-0	H	TAPqf	Gioino [5]
12-06-2004	Universidad de Concepción	L 1-2	A	TAPqf	Gioino [116]. Univ. de Chile qualify via golden goal
17-06-2004	Santiago Wanderers	D 1-1	H	TAPsf	Rivarola [25]
20-06-2004	Santiago Wanderers	W 2-0	A	TAPsf	Olea [70], Muñoz [90]
23-06-2004	Cobreloa	D 0-0	H	TAPf	
27-06-2004	Cobreloa	D 1-1	A	TAPf	OG [52]. Univ. de Chile won 4-2 on penalties
7-07-2004	Unión Española	L 0-1	A	LGr1	
18-07-2004	Unión Española	D 0-0	H	LGr1	
1-08-2004	Colo Colo	L 0-1	H	TCL	
7-08-2004	Rangers	W 1-0	A	TCL	Gioino [5]
11-08-2004	Unión Española	D 2-2	H	TCL	Rivarola [6], Gioino [90]
14-08-2004	Puerto Montt	L 0-2	A	TCL	
21-08-2004	Unión San Felipe	W 3-0	H	TCL	Gioino [45p]
29-08-2004	Everton	D 0-0	A	TCL	
8-09-2004	Palestino	W 4-1	H	TCL	Gioino 2 [32 64], Pinto [67], Olea [87]
12-09-2004	La Serena	W 3-1	A	TCL	Rivarola [6], Garcia [47], Gioino [59]
17-09-2004	Huachipato	W 2-1	H	TCL	Rivarola [32], Gioino [76]
26-09-2004	Cobresal	W 2-0	H	TCL	Garcia [38], Ponce [89]
3-10-2004	Audax Italiano	D 1-1	A	TCL	Olea [72]
17-10-2004	Cobreloa	W 2-1	H	TCL	Garcia.G [54], Barrera [84]
20-10-2004	Universidad de Concepción	D 0-0	H	TCL	
24-10-2004	Temuco	D 2-2	H	TCL	Cancino [21], Olea [39]
27-10-2004	Santiago Wanderers	W 2-1	A	TCL	Pinto [71p], Olea [90]
3-11-2004	Universidad Católica	D 0-0	H	TCL	
7-11-2004	Coquimbo Unido	W 3-1	A	TCL	Gioino [5], Rivarola [38], Olea [90]
24-11-2004	Temuco	L 0-2	A	TCLr1	
28-11-2004	Temuco	W 2-0	H	TCLr1	Olea [51], Barrera [61]. W 5-3p
2-12-2004	Unión Española	L 3-4	A	TCLqf	Olea [33], Gioino 2 [51 84p]
5-12-2004	Unión Española	W 3-2	H	TCLqf	Gioino 2 [43p 79], Muñoz [86]. L 2-4p

TAP = Torneo Apertura • LG = Liguilla pre Copa Sudamericana • TCL = Torneo Clausura
r1 = first round • qf = quarter-final • sf = semi-final • f = final

RECENT LEAGUE RECORD

	Championship						Play-offs		
Year	Champions	Pts	Runners-up	Pts	Third	Pts	Champions	Score	Runners-up
1998	Colo Colo	64	Univ. de Chile	63	Univ. Católica	53			
1999	Univ. de Chile	47	Univ. Católica	44	Cobreloa				
2000	Univ. de Chile	61	Cobreloa	52	Colo Colo	49			
2001	Santiago Wanderers	66	Univ. Católica	60	Univ. de Chile	57			
2002ap							Univ. Católica	1-1 4-0	Rangers
2002cl							Colo Colo	2-0 3-2	Univ. Católica
2003ap							Cobreloa	0-0 4-0	Colo Colo
2003cl							Cobreloa	2-2 2-1	Colo Colo
2004ap							Univ. de Chile	0-0 1-1 4-2p	Cobreloa
2004cl							Cobreloa	3-1 0-0	Unión Española

ap = Apertura • cl = Clausura

COBRELOA 2004

Date	Opponents	Score		Comp	Scorers
6-02-2004	Santiago Wanderers	L 0-1	A	TAP	
10-02-2004	LDU Quito - ECU	L 0-2	H	CLg4	
15-02-2004	Universidad Católica	W 2-1	H	TAP	Cisternas [5], Galaz [76]
21-02-2004	Coquimbo Unido	D 3-3	A	TAP	Fernandez.D 2 [13 65], Cornejo [61]
26-02-2004	São Paulo - BRA	L 1-3	A	CLg4	Cicinho OG [48]
29-02-2004	Colo Colo	W 3-0	H	TAP	Galaz 3 [23 65 86]
4-03-2004	Alianza Lima - PER	L 0-2	A	CLg4	
7-03-2004	Rangers	W 2-0	A	TAP	Galaz 2 [45 80]
10-03-2004	Alianza Lima - PER	L 0-1	H	CLg4	
14-03-2004	Puerto Montt	D 1-1	A	TAP	Estigarribia [40]
17-03-2004	Unión Española	D 2-2	H	TAP	Galaz [73], Fernandez.D [77p]
21-03-2004	Unión San Felipe	W 3-1	H	TAP	Galaz 2 [22 55], Dinamarca [86]
24-03-2004	São Paulo - BRA	L 0-1	H	CLg4	Dinamarca [27p]
4-04-2004	Everton	W 3-1	A	TAP	Galaz [11], Cisternas [26], Villanueva [88]
7-04-2004	LDU Quito - ECU	L 1-5	A	CLg4	Galaz [85]
11-04-2004	Palestino	W 6-1	H	TAP	Dinamarca [3p], Galaz 3 [14 27 64], Cisternas [66], Gonzalez.E [79]
15-04-2004	La Serena	W 2-1	A	TAP	Dinamarca [67], Vigna [90]
18-04-2004	Universidad de Chile	W 3-0	H	TAP	Rojas OG [15], Dinamarca [18], Galaz [88]
21-04-2004	Cobresal	W 3-2	A	TAP	Galaz 3 [9 27 42]
25-04-2004	Audax Italiano	D 1-1	H	TAP	Cisternas [89]
2-05-2004	Huachipato	W 2-1	A	TAP	Perez.D [81], Dinamarca [83p]
4-05-2004	Universidad de Concepción	L 0-3	A	TAP	
9-05-2004	Temuco	W 3-0	H	TAP	Galaz 2 [36 40], Cisternas [53]
15-05-2004	Unión San Felipe	W 2-0	A	TAPr1	Estigarribia [71], Galaz [90]
23-05-2004	Unión San Felipe	W 2-1	H	TAPr1	Estigarribia [5], Galaz [37p]
8-06-2004	Temuco	D 1-1	A	TAPqf	Cisternas [37]
13-06-2004	Temuco	W 3-1	H	TAPqf	Estigarribia [27], Galaz [38], Perez.R [79]
17-06-2004	Huachipato	D 2-2	A	TAPsf	Cisternas [17], Galaz [32]
20-06-2004	Huachipato	W 3-2	H	TAPsf	Cisternas [62], Cornejo [82], Perez.R [119]
23-06-2004	Universidad de Chile	D 0-0	A	TAPf	
27-06-2004	Universidad de Chile	D 1-1	H	TAPf	Fuentes [35]
7-07-2004	Cobresal	D 2-2	A	LGr1	Cornejo 2 [50 73]
18-07-2004	Cobresal	L 1-2	H	LGr1	Dinamarca [50]
31-07-2004	Santiago Wanderers	D 1-1	H	TCL	Cornejo [69]
7-08-2004	Universidad Católica	L 1-2	A	TCL	Galaz [57]
11-08-2004	Coquimbo Unido	W 3-1	H	TCL	Galaz 3 [24 77 86]
15-08-2004	Colo Colo	D 2-2	A	TCL	Cisternas [20], Dinamarca [52]
22-08-2004	Rangers	W 5-2	H	TCL	Norambuena 3 [31 68 72], Galaz [59], Perez.R [64p]
28-08-2004	Unión Española	L 0-2	A	TCL	
8-09-2004	Puerto Montt	W 2-1	H	TCL	Dinamarca [45], Galaz [55]
11-09-2004	Unión San Felipe	W 3-1	A	TCL	Dinamarca [37], Diaz.J [46], Robledo OG [59]
17-09-2004	Everton	W 6-0	H	TCL	Galaz 2 [34 45], Dinamarca [37], Diaz.J [58], Gonzalez.J [86], Perez.D [87]
24-09-2004	Palestino	D 1-1	A	TCL	Galaz [37]
3-10-2004	La Serena	D 1-1	H	TCL	Galaz [66p]
17-10-2004	Universidad de Chile	L 1-2	A	TCL	Galaz [28]
20-10-2004	Cobresal	D 1-1	H	TCL	Diaz.J [72]
23-10-2004	Audax Italiano	D 2-2	A	TCL	Perez.D 2 [43 61]
28-10-2004	Huachipato	W 2-0	H	TCL	Diaz.J [48], Estigarribia [84]
3-11-2004	Universidad de Concepción	L 2-3	H	TCL	Perez.D [17], Cisternas [86]
7-11-2004	Temuco	D 4-4	A	TCL	Galaz 3 [11 26 90], Perez.D [76]
24-11-2004	Audax Italiano	W 5-2	H	TCLr1	Perez.D 3 [5 15 43], Diaz.J [33], Galaz [48]
27-11-2004	Audax Italiano	L 1-2	A	TCLr1	Estigarribia [70]
1-12-2004	Cobresal	W 2-1	H	TCLqf	Galaz 2 [33p 56]
4-12-2004	Cobresal	D 2-2	A	TCLqf	Diaz.J [52], Perez.D [55]
8-12-2004	Colo Colo	W 4-1	H	TCLsf	Diaz.J 2 [36 63], Galaz 2 [41 70]
11-12-2004	Colo Colo	D 1-1	A	TCLsf	Diaz.J [36]
16-12-2004	Unión Española	W 3-1	A	TCLf	Perez.D [28], Perez.R [52], Miranda OG [80]
19-12-2004	Unión Española	D 0-0	H	TCLf	

TAP = Torneo Apertura • CL = Copa Libertadores • LG = Liguilla pre Copa Sudamericana • TCL = Torneo Clausura
g4 = group 4 • r1 = first round • qf = quarter-final • sf = semi-final • f = final

CHN – CHINA PR

NATIONAL TEAM RECORD
JULY 1ST 2002 TO JUNE 30TH 2005

PL	W	D	L	F	A	%
37	19	10	8	61	31	64.9

FIFA/COCA-COLA WORLD RANKING

1993	1994	1995	1996	1997	1998	1999	2000	2001	2002	2003	2004	High		Low	
53	40	66	76	55	37	88	75	54	63	86	54	37	12/98	88	12/99

2004-2005											
08/04	09/04	10/04	11/04	12/04	01/05	02/05	03/05	04/05	05/05	06/05	07/05
51	48	49	49	54	54	55	57	58	58	61	56

China's qualification for the 2002 FIFA World Cup™ represented a major breakthrough for the underachieving national team but it was followed by two major disappointments – defeat against Japan in the final of the AFC Asian Cup in 2004, a tournament the Chinese hosted and were hoping to win for the first time, and the failure to reach the final qualifying group stage for Germany 2006. Their first round group turned into a two-horse race with the Kuwaitis which was decided on goal difference. In a frantic final match against Hong Kong at home, a 7-0 victory left the pair level on points, but the Kuwaitis were group winners by a single goal. Coach Arie Haan was then replaced

INTERNATIONAL HONOURS
Qualified for the FIFA World Cup™ 2002   AFC Asian Women's Championship 1986 1989 1991 1993 1995 1997 1999
Asian U-19 Championship 1985   Asian U-17 Championship 1992 2004   AFC Asian Champions League Liaoning 1990

by Zhu Guanghu who had led Shenzhen Jianlibao to their first China Super League title losing just two of their 22 matches along the way. However, the league was marred with allegations of corruption and player protests and title sponsors Siemens did not renew for the enlarged 2005 League. On the bright side the U-20 national team won all its group matches at the 2005 FIFA World Youth Championship, before losing to a last minute goal against Germany in the next round, whilst the U-17 team won the Asian Championship held in Japan to qualify for the finals in Peru.

THE FIFA BIG COUNT OF 2000

	Male	Female		Male	Female
Registered players	75 000	490	Referees	4 713	56
Non registered players	7 000 000	40 000	Officials	2 548	420
Youth players	125 000	3 851	Total involved	7 252 078	
Total players	7 244 341		Number of clubs	2 347	
Professional players	1 492	256	Number of teams	16 536	

Football Association of the People's Republic of China (CFA)
2 Tiyuguan Road, Beijing 100763, China PR
Tel +86 10 67117019   Fax +86 10 67142533
li_chen@fa.org.cn   www.fa.org.cn
President: YUAN Weimin   General Secretary: YALONG Xie
Vice-President: TBD   Treasurer: NAN Yong   Media Officer: LU Ting & DONG Hua
Men's Coach: ZHU Guanghu   Women's Coach: ZHANG Haitao
CFA formed: 1924   AFC: 1974   FIFA: 1931-58 & 1974
Colours: White, White, White

GAMES PLAYED BY CHINA PR IN THE 2006 FIFA WORLD CUP™ CYCLE

2002 Opponents	Score	Venue	Comp	Scorers	Att	Referee
7-12 Syria	W 3-1	Manama	Fr	Zhao Junzhe 32, Wang Xinxin 38, Xu Yunlong 41		Al Khabbaz BHR
9-12 Jordan	D 0-0	Manama	Fr			Husain BHR
12-12 Bahrain	D 2-2	Manama	Fr	Wang Xinxin 16, Qu Bo 61		Shaban KUW
2003						
12-02 Brazil	D 0-0	Guangzhou	Fr		80 000	Kim Tae Young KOR
16-02 Estonia	W 1-0	Wuhan	Fr	Li Weifeng 67	20 000	
20-08 Chile	D 0-0	Tianjin	Fr		15 000	Sun Baojie CHN
31-08 Haiti	L 3-4	Fort Lauderdale	Fr	Qi Hong 15, Xiao Zhanbo 39p, Li Jinyu 43		Ruty USA
7-09 Costa Rica	L 0-2	Fort Lauderdale	Fr			Stott USA
4-12 Japan	L 0-2	Tokyo	EAC		41 742	Nagalingam SIN
7-12 Korea Republic	L 0-1	Saitama	EAC		27 715	Abdul Hamid MAS
10-12 Hong Kong	W 3-1	Yokohama	EAC	Zhao Xuri 20, Liu Jindong 21, Yang Chen 44	17 400	Piromya THA
2004						
27-01 FYR Macedonia	D 0-0	Shanghai	Fr		24 000	Lu Jun CHN
29-01 FYR Macedonia	W 1-0	Shanghai	Fr	Zheng Zhi 88	17 500	Yang Zhiqiang CHN
3-02 Finland	W 2-1	Guangzhou	Fr	Zhang Yuning 42, Hao Haidong 53		
7-02 Finland	W 2-1	Shenzhen	Fr	Zhang Yuning 8, Zheng Zhi 41		
18-02 Kuwait	W 1-0	Guangzhou	WCq	Hao Haidong 75	50 000	Roman UZB
17-03 Myanmar	W 2-0	Guangzhou	Fr	Zheng Zhi 16, Xu Yunlong 29		
31-03 Hong Kong	W 1-0	Hong Kong	WCq	Hao Haidong 71	9 000	Rungklay THA
14-04 Andorra	D 0-0	Peralada	Fr			
28-04 Algeria	W 1-0	Clermont-Ferrand	Fr	Xiao Zhanbo 26	1 600	Poulat FRA
1-06 Hungary	W 2-1	Beijing	Fr	Zhou Haibin 44, Zheng Zhi 88p	18 000	Chiu HKG
9-06 Malaysia	W 4-0	Tianjin	WCq	Hao Haidong 43, Sun Jihai 62, Li Xiaopeng 2 66 76	35 000	Park Sang Gu KOR
3-07 Lebanon	W 6-0	Chongqing	Fr	Li Jinyu 2 15 50, Yan Song 61, Li Ming 69, Zhang Shuo 79, Li Yi 86		
10-07 United Arab Emirates	D 2-2	Hohhot	Fr	Zheng Zhi 2 63 90p		
17-07 Bahrain	D 2-2	Beijing	ACr1	Zheng Zhi 58, Li Jinyu 66p	40 000	Subkhiddin MAS
21-07 Indonesia	W 5-0	Beijing	ACr1	Shao Jiayi 2 24 65, Hao Haidong 39, Li Ming 51, Li Yi 80		Talaat LIB
25-07 Qatar	W 1-0	Beijing	ACr1	Xu Yunlong 78	60 000	Moradi IRN
30-07 Iraq	W 3-0	Beijing	ACqf	Hao Haidong 8, Zheng Zhi 2 79p 90p	60 000	Maidin SIN
3-08 Iran	D 1-1	Beijing	ACsf	Shao Jiayi 19 W 4-3p	51 000	Talaat LIB
7-08 Japan	L 1-3	Beijing	ACf	Li Ming 31	62 000	Al Fadhi KUW
8-09 Malaysia	W 1-0	Penang	WCq	Li Jinyu 67	14 000	Karim BHR
13-10 Kuwait	L 0-1	Kuwait City	WCq		10 000	Kunsuta THA
17-11 Hong Kong	W 7-0	Guangzhou	WCq	Li Jinyu 2 8 47, Shao Jiayi 2 42 44, Xu Yunlong 49, Yu Genwei 88, Li Weifeng 90+2	20 300	Lee Jong Kuk KOR
2005						
26-03 Spain	L 0-3	Salamanca	Fr		17 000	Batista POR
29-03 Republic of Ireland	L 0-1	Dublin	Fr		35 222	Casha MLT
19-06 Costa Rica	D 2-2	Changsa	Fr	Zhang Yaokun 27, Sun Xiang 79	20 000	Lee Gi Young KOR
22-06 Costa Rica	W 2-0	Guangzhou	Fr	Zheng Zhi 44p, Xie Hui 54	15 000	Yu Byung Seob KOR

Fr = Friendly match • EAC = East Asian Championship • AC = AFC Asian Cup • WC = FIFA World Cup™
q = qualifier • r1 = first round group • qf = quarter-final • sf = semi-final • f = final

CHINA PR NATIONAL TEAM RECORDS AND RECORD SEQUENCES

Records			Sequence records					
Victory	19-0	GUM 2000	Wins	10	1919-1930	Clean sheets	8	1998-2000
Defeat	0-5	USA 1992	Defeats	5	1982, 2002	Goals scored	20	1915-1934
Player Caps	115	HAO Haidong	Undefeated	19	2003-2004	Without goal	5	2002
Player Goals	41	HAO Haidong	Without win	7	1996, 2000-2001	Goals against	9	1934-1957

Includes records dating back to the Far-Eastern Games of 1913-1934

CLUB DIRECTORY

Club	Town/City	Stadium	Lge	Cup	CL
Beijing Hyundai	Beijing	Worker's 72 000	5	5	0
Chongqing Qiche	Chongqing	Olympic 58 680	0	1	0
Dalian Shide	Dalian	People's 55 000	7	2	0
Liaoning Zhongyu	Fushun	Lei Feng 30 000	8	2	1
Qingdao Beilaite	Qingdao	Yizhong 60 000	0	1	0
Shandong Luneng	Jinan	Shandong 43 700	1	3	0
Shanghai International	Shanghai	Shanghai 80 000	0	0	0
Shanghai Shenhua	Shanghai	Hongkou 35 000	4	3	0
Shenyang Ginde	Shenyang	Wulihe 65 000	0	0	0
Shenzhen Jianlibao	Shenzhen	Shenzhen 33 000	0	0	0
Sichuan Guancheng	Chengdu	Sichuan 40 000	0	0	0
Tianjin Kangshifu	Tianjin	Teda 36 000	3	1	0

FIFA REFEREE LIST 2005

	Int'l	DoB
HE Zhibiao	1996	12-11-1968
HUANG Junjie	1998	20-08-1966
LI Yuhong	2004	
SUN Baojie	1997	2-01-1965
TAN Hai	2004	27-11-1970
WAN Daxue	2004	10-03-1969
YANG Zhiqiang		16-01-1966
ZHANG Lei	2004	4-02-1967
ZHOU Weixin	2003	22-03-1967

FIFA ASSISTANT REFEREE LIST 2005

	Int'l	DoB
HAN Wei	2004	10-02-1968
LI Dongnan	2000	8-02-1970
LI Zhizhong	1998	17-03-1963
LIU Qingwei	2004	5-09-1969
LIU Tiejun	1997	31-03-1963
SU Jige	2004	30-06-1967
YU Duo	1998	5-06-1964
ZHENG Weixiang	2000	16-09-1968
ZHOU Dequan	2000	28-04-1963

CHINA PR COUNTRY INFORMATION

Capital	Beijing	Independence	221 BC	GDP per Capita	$5 000
Population	1 298 847 624	Status	Republic	GNP Ranking	6
Area km²	9 596 960	Language	Mandarin	Dialling code	+86
Population density	135 per km²	Literacy rate	90%	Internet code	.cn
% in urban areas	30%	Main religion	Atheist	GMT +/–	+8
Towns/Cities ('000)	Shanghai 12 762; Beijing 7 490; Wuhan 4 191; Chengdu 3 999; Chongqing 3 975; Xian 3 959; Tianjin 3 791; Shenyang 3 519; Harbin 3 234; Guangzhou 3 146; Nanjing 3 095; Taiyuan 2 727; Changchun 2 541; Changsha 2 074; Jinan 2 073; Tangshan 2 057; Dalian 2 039				
Neighbours (km)	Mongolia 4 677; Russia 3 645; Korea DPR 1 416; Vietnam 1 281; Laos 423; Burma 2 185; Bhutan 470; Nepal 1 236; India 3 380; Pakistan 523; Tajikistan 414; Kyrgyzstan 858; Kazakhstan 1 533; Afghanistan 76; Yellow Sea & South and East China Seas 14 500				
Main stadia	Guangdong Olympic – Guangzhou 80 012; Shanghai Stadium – Shanghai 80 000; Worker's Stadium – Beijing 72 000; Wulihe Stadium – Shenyang 65 000; Wuhan Stadium – Wuhan 60 000; Qingdao Yizhong Center – Qingdao 60 000				

CHINA PR 2004

SUPER LEAGUE

	Pl	W	D	L	F	A	Pts	Shenzhen	Shandong	Shanghai I	Liaoning	Dalian	Tianjin	Beijing	Shenyang	Sichuan	Shanghai S	Qingdao	Chongqing
Shenzhen Jianlibao †	22	11	9	2	30	13	42		2-1	1-0	3-0	2-2	0-1	2-0	0-0	1-1	3-1	1-0	0-0
Shandong Luneng †	22	10	6	6	44	29	36	1-1		4-2	3-1	2-3	3-1	5-2	4-1	1-2	2-1	1-1	4-1
Shanghai International	22	8	8	6	39	31	32	2-2	2-1		2-1	4-0	3-0	1-1	3-1	3-2	1-1	1-0	1-2
Liaoning Zhongyu	22	10	2	10	39	40	32	1-2	2-3	2-1		1-5	1-5	1-1	1-0	0-0	5-2	3-1	3-0
Dalian Shide §§	22	10	6	6	33	26	30	0-0	1-0	1-1	0-4		0-1	2-1	0-3*	5-1	2-2	0-0	2-0
Tianjin Kangshifu	22	7	8	7	28	29	29	0-2	1-1	2-2	2-0	0-4		3-0	3-0	1-1	0-2	1-1	0-0
Beijing Hyundai §	22	8	7	7	35	33	28	1-4	1-1	2-0	2-0	1-0	2-0		4-1	1-1	3-0	2-0	4-1
Shenyang Ginde	22	7	5	10	23	29	26	0-0	1-1	0-3	1-3	1-0		3-0*		4-0	1-1	1-0	2-0
Sichuan Guancheng	22	4	11	7	29	37	23	0-1	0-2	2-2	6-3	1-2	1-1	3-2	4-2		1-1	1-1	0-0
Shanghai Shenhua	22	4	10	8	28	37	22	0-2	2-1	3-2	0-1	0-1	4-4	2-2	0-0	1-1		0-1	1-1
Qingdao Beilaite	22	4	9	9	21	28	21	1-0	0-2	2-2	1-2	1-1	0-1	3-3	1-0	1-1	3-3		1-2
Chongqing Qiche	22	4	9	9	14	31	21	1-1	1-1	1-1	0-4	0-2	1-1	0-0	1-0	0-0	0-1	0-2	

15/05/2004 - 5/12/2004 • † Teams qualifying for the AFC Champions League • No relegation due to expansion of the league to 14 clubs in 2005 • § Beijing 3 points deducted • §§ Dalian 6 points deducted • *Shenyang awarded match 3-0 after Beijing left the field after 80' with the score at 1-1 • * Shenyang awarded match 3-0 after Dalian left the field after 85' with the score at 2-2.

CHINA PR 2004
JIAJIDUI (SECOND DIVISION)

	Pl	W	D	L	F	A	Pts
Wuhan Huanghelou	32	19	9	4	54	28	66
Zhuhai Zhongbang	32	19	5	8	56	36	62
Xiamen Lanshi	32	13	14	5	38	26	53
Guangzhou Rizhiqan	32	12	16	4	47	29	52
Changchun Yatai	32	13	12	7	53	34	51
Jiangsu Shuntian	32	13	11	8	35	24	50
Henan Jianye	32	11	12	9	29	27	45
Zhejiang Lucheng	32	12	9	11	38	39	45
Nanjing Yoyo	32	10	11	11	44	47	41
Shenzhen Kejian	32	9	12	11	44	40	39
Qingdao Hailifeng	32	10	9	13	36	39	39
Ningbo Guoli	32	11	6	15	44	61	39
Chengdu Wuniu	32	6	13	13	46	57	31
Hunan Xiangjun	32	7	10	15	34	51	31
Dalian Changbo	32	6	12	14	22	35	30
Dongguan Dongcheng	32	7	9	16	38	56	30
Xi'an Anxinyuan	32	4	10	18	30	59	22

TOP SCORERS

AYEW Kwame GHA	Shanghai Int'l	17
LI Jinyu	Shandong LT	13
JELIC Branko BIH	Beijing Hyundai	11
LI Xiaopeng	Shandong LT	10
OYAWOLE Djima TGO	Shenzhen J	9
NANNSKOG Daniel SWE	Sichuan G	9
SILJAK Ermin SVN	Dalian Shide	9
Tao Wei	Beijing Hyundai	9

RECENT LEAGUE AND CUP RECORD

Year	Champions	Pts	Runners-up	Pts	Third	Pts
1994	Dalian	33	Guangzhou	27	Shanghai Shenhua	26
1995	Shanghai Shenhua	46	Beijing	42	Dalian	42
1996	Dalian	46	Shanghai Shenhua	39	August 1st	35
1997	Dalian	51	Shanghai Shenhua	40	Beijing	34
1998	Dalian	62	Shanghai Shenhua	45	Beijing	43
1999	Shandong	48	Liaoning	47	Sichuan	45
2000	Dalian	56	Shanghai Shenhua	50	Sichuan	44
2001	Dalian	53	Shanghai Shenhua	48	Liaoning	48
2002	Dalian	57	Shenzhen	52	Beijing	52
2003	Shanghai Shenhua	55	Shanghai Int'l	54	Dalian	53
2004	Shenzhen	42	Shandong	36	Shanghai Int'l	32

FA Cup

Winners	Score	Runners-up
No Tournament		
Jinan	2-0	Shanghai Shenhua
Beijing	4-1	Jinan
Beijing	2-1	Shanghai Shenhua
Shanghai Shenhua	2-1 2-1	Liaoning
Shandong	2-1 2-1	Dalian
Chongqing	0-1 4-1	Beijing
Dalian	1-0 2-1	Beijing
Qingdao	1-3 2-0	Liaoning
Beijing	3-0	Dalian
Shandong	2-1	Sichuan

LANDI FA CUP 2004

First Round

Team	Score
Shandong Luneng Taishan	1
Zhejiang Lucheng *	0
Chongqing Lifan *	1
Shenzhen Kejian	2
Beijing Hyundai	bye
Jiangsu Shuntian *	0
Wuhan Huanghelou	1
Qingdao Bellaite *	1 5p
Chengdu Wunlu	1 3p
Dalian Pearl	1
Shanghai International *	2
Zhuhai Zhongbang *	2
Hunan Xiangjun	0
Xi'an Anximyuan *	0
Shenzhen Jianlibao	1
Shanghai Shenhua	0 5p
Dongguan Dongcheng *	0 4p
Nanjing Yoyo *	0 5p
Tianjin Kangshifu	0 6p
Shaanxi Guoli *	2
Guangzhou Rizhiquan	0
Shenyang Ginde	bye
Dalian Shide	bye
Changchun Yatai	1
Henan Jianye *	2
Qingdao Hailifeng *	1
Liaoning Zhongyu	0
Xiamen Shishi	1
Sichuan Guancheng *	4

Second Round

Team	Score
Shandong Luneng Taishan	5 4
Shenzhen Kejian *	1 1
Beijing Hyundai	1 0
Wuhan Huanghelou *	2 2
Qingdao Bellaite *	3 0 3p
Shanghai International	0 3 1p
Zhuhai Zhongbang *	1 1
Shenzhen Jianlibao	4 4
Shanghai Shenhua	1 3
Tianjin Kangshifu *	1 1
Shaanxi Guoli *	1 0
Shenyang Ginde	2 1
Dalian Shide	1 4
Henan Jianye *	1 0
Qingdao Hailifeng *	1 0
Sichuan Guancheng	1 3

Quarter-finals

Team	Score
Shandong Luneng Taishan	4 0
Wuhan Huanghelou *	0 1
Qingdao Bellaite *	1 2
Shenzhen Jianlibao	1 4
Shanghai Shenhua *	6 2
Shenyang Ginde	1 1
Dalian Shide	1 1
Sichuan Guancheng *	2 3

Semi-finals

Team	Score
Shandong Luneng Taishan *	1 3
Shenzhen Jianlibao	1 3
Shanghai Shenhua	1 2
Sichuan Guancheng *	2 3

Final

Team	Score
Shandong Luneng Taishan	2
Sichuan Guancheng	1

CUP FINAL

18-12-2004, He Long Stadium, Changsha

Scorers
Li Jinyu 24, Shu Chang 84 for Shandong;
Yan Feng 18 for Sichuan

* Home team/home team in the first leg

SHENZHEN JIANLIBAO 2004

Date	Opponents		Score		Comp	Scorers
10-04-2004	Xi'an Anxinyuan	W	1-0	A	FACr1	Yang Chen 50
29-04-2004	Zhuhai Zhongbang	W	4-1	A	FACr2	Yang Chen 45, Zheng Zhi 3 47 53 60
5-05-2004	Zhuhai Zhongbang	W	4-1	H	FACr2	Li Yi 2 5 65, Yang Chen 2 7 48
16-05-2004	Shenyang Ginde	D	0-0	A	SL	
23-05-2004	Liaoning Zhongyu	W	3-0	H	SL	Kovacs 20, Yang Chen 27, Lu Bofei 48
26-05-2004	Qingdao Beilaite	L	0-1	A	SL	
29-05-2004	Shandong Luneng Taishan	W	2-1	H	SL	Li Ming 24, Oyawole 76
13-06-2004	Beijing Hyundai	W	4-1	A	SL	Kovacs 2 27 72, Oyawole 32, Xin Feng 35
16-06-2005	Chongqing Qiche	D	0-0	H	SL	
20-06-2004	Tianjin Kangshifu	W	2-0	A	SL	Zheng Zhi 64, Oyawole 90
26-06-2004	Sichuan Guancheng	D	1-1	H	SL	Oyawole 5
1-07-2004	Sichuan Guancheng	W	2-0	H	SLCqf	Oyawole 22p, Kovacs 64
4-07-2004	Sichuan Guancheng	L	2-3	A	SLCqf	Zhang Xinxin 23, Oyawole 63
7-07-2004	Qingdao Beilaite	D	1-1	A	FACqf	Zhang Xinxin 61
11-07-2004	Qingdao Beilaite	W	4-2	H	FACqf	Oyawole 3 49 55 68, Huang Fengtao 82
8-08-2004	Shandong Luneng Taishan	D	1-1	A	FACsf	Li Yi 90
14-08-2004	Shandong Luneng Taishan	D	3-3	H	FACsf	Li Yi 2 2 54, Zheng Zhi 11. Lost on away goals
18-08-2004	Tianjin Kangshifu	D	3-3	A	SLCsf	Li Yi 11, Wen Guanghui 29, Zheng Zhi 37p
21-08-2004	Tianjin Kangshifu	W	4-2	H	SLCsf	Kovacs 2 16 76, Li Yi 22, Oyawole 23
26-08-2004	Dalian Shide	D	0-0	A	SL	
11-09-2004	Shanghai Shenhua SVA	W	2-0	A	SL	Oyawole 74, Lu Bofei 78p
15-09-2004	Shanghai International	W	1-0	H	SL	Zheng Bin 27
26-09-2004	Shenyang Ginde	D	0-0	H	SL	
29-09-2004	Liaoning Zhongyu	W	2-1	A	SL	Oyawole 2 81 88
2-10-2004	Qingdao Beilaite	W	1-0	H	SL	Oyawole 13
16-10-2004	Shandong Luneng Taishan	D	1-1	A	SL	Zheng Zhi 38
20-10-2004	Beijing Hyundai	W	2-0	H	SL	Xin Feng 63, Vitakic 79
24-10-2004	Chongqing Qiche	D	1-1	A	SL	Yin Xiaolong 81
31-10-2004	Tianjin Kangshifu	L	0-1	H	SL	
4-11-2004	Sichuan Guancheng	W	1-0	A	SL	Li Yi 38
24-11-2004	Shanghai Shenhua SVA	W	3-1	H	SL	Li Weifeng 56, Li Yi 2 76 88
28-11-2004	Shanghai International	D	2-2	A	SL	Xin Feng 57, Oyawole 65p
5-12-2004	Dalian Shide	D	2-2	H	SL	Li Jianhua 42, Li Ming 59
11-12-2004	Shandong Luneng Taishan	L	0-2	N	SLCf	

FAC = FA Cup • SL = Super League • SLC = Super League Cup
r1 = first round • r2 = second round • qf = quarter-final • sf = semi-final • f = final

SUPER LEAGUE CUP 2004

Round of sixteen		Quarter-finals		Semi-finals		Final	
Shandong LT *	5 1						
Beijing Hyundai	0 2	**Shandong LT ***	0 1				
		Dalian Shide	0 1				
Dalian Shide	bye			**Shandong LT ***	1 2		
Liaoning Zhongyu	1 2			Shanghai Shenhua	0 3		
Qingdao Beilaite *	2 0	Liaoning Zhongyu *	0 1				
		Shanghai Shenhua	0 4				
Shanghai Shenhua	bye					**Shandong LT**	2
Tianjin Kangshifu *	4 7					Shenzhen Jianlibao	0
Shenyang Ginde	0 0	**Tianjin Kangshifu ***	5 0				
		Shanghai Internat'al	2 1				
Shanghai Internat'al	bye			Tianjin Kangshifu *	3 2	**CUP FINAL**	
Sichuan Guancheng *	4 1			**Shenzhen Jianlibao**	3 4	11-12-2004, Jinan	
Chongqing Qiche	0 3	Sichuan Guancheng	0 3				
		Shenzhen Jianlibao *	2 2			Scorers - Shu Chang 33, Wang Chao 50 for Shandong	
Shenzhen Jianlibao	bye	Open to Super League clubs only • * Home team in the first leg					

CIV – COTE D'IVOIRE

NATIONAL TEAM RECORD
JULY 1ST 2002 TO JUNE 30TH 2005

PL	W	D	L	F	A	%
20	13	3	4	39	15	72.5

FIFA/COCA-COLA WORLD RANKING

1993	1994	1995	1996	1997	1998	1999	2000	2001	2002	2003	2004	High		Low	
33	25	20	51	52	44	53	51	44	64	70	40	20	12/95	75	05/04

2004-2005											
08/04	09/04	10/04	11/04	12/04	01/05	02/05	03/05	04/05	05/05	06/05	07/05
64	58	45	42	40	41	41	42	44	44	46	44

After raising a few eyebrows by not qualifying for the 2004 African Cup of Nations, the Elephants of Côte d'Ivoire have been revitalised and dominated their qualifying group for the 2006 FIFA World Cup™. Experienced French coach Henri Michel inherited some quality players when he took charge including Kolo Toure, Aruna Dindane and Didier Drogba, who have all contributed to a series of positive results and the tantalising prospect of a possible first appearance in the FIFA World Cup™ finals. Already assured of a place at next year's African Cup of Nations, the team are an interesting bet to win the title 14 years after their first triumph. At youth level the U-17 team

INTERNATIONAL HONOURS
African Cup of Nations 1992 CAF African Champions League ASEC Mimosas 1998

finished third in the African Championship to book a place in the FIFA U-17 Championship in Peru. The dominance of ASEC Mimosas in the national Championship was underlined again when the club won their fifth successive title after going through the season unbeaten. It was ASEC's 13th title in the past 15 years thanks in no small part to their youth academy in Abidjan. However, they were knocked out of the Coupe Nationale by local rivals Stade Abidjan who then lost to CO Bouafle in the final. ASEC had a poor campaign in the 2004 CAF Champions League when they were knocked out in the first round but they did qualify for the league stage in 2005.

THE FIFA BIG COUNT OF 2000

	Male	Female		Male	Female
Registered players	11 000	0	Referees	500	0
Non registered players	75 000	0	Officials	3 500	0
Youth players	10 000	0	Total involved	100 000	
Total players	96 000		Number of clubs	200	
Professional players	50	0	Number of teams	1 200	

Fédération Ivoirienne de Football (FIF)
01 Case postale 1202, Abidjan 01, Côte d'Ivoire
Tel +225 21240027   Fax +225 21259552
fifci@aviso.ci   www.fif.ci
President: ANOUMA Jacques   General Secretary: DIABATE Sory
Vice-President: FEH Kesse Lambert   Treasurer: ABINAN Pascal   Media Officer: None
Men's Coach: MICHEL Henri   Women's Coach: None
FIF formed: 1960   CAF: 1960   FIFA: 1960
Colours: Orange, White, Green

GAMES PLAYED BY COTE D'IVOIRE IN THE 2006 FIFA WORLD CUP™ CYCLE

2002	Opponents	Score		Venue	Comp	Scorers	Att	Referee
8-09	South Africa	D	0-0	Abidjan	CNq		30 000	Coulibaly MLI
2003								
11-02	Cameroon	W	3-0	Chateauroux	Fr	Guel [37], Drogba [45], Kalou [83p]	3 000	Ennjini FRA
30-03	Burundi	W	1-0	Bujumbura	CNq	Bakari [57]		Gasingwa RWA
30-04	Morocco	W	1-0	Rabat	Fr	Kalou [83p]	20 000	El Arjoun MAR
8-06	Burundi	W	6-1	Abidjan	CNq	Drogba 3 [7 27 32], Bakari 2 [56 78], Dindane [70]	50 000	Monteiro Duarte CPV
22-06	South Africa	L	1-2	Johannesburg	CNq	Kalou [41]	35 000	Maillet SEY
10-09	Tunisia	L	2-3	Tunis	Fr	Dindane [88], Kalou [90p]	17 000	Djaballah ALG
15-11	Senegal	L	0-1	Dakar	Fr		50 000	Daami TUN
2004								
31-03	Tunisia	W	2-0	Tunis	Fr	Drogba 2 [34 65]	10 000	Haimoudi ALG
28-04	Guinea	W	4-2	Aix-les-Bains	Fr	Drogba [8], Toure [32], Kalou [45], Bakari [68]	2 000	
6-06	Libya	W	2-0	Abidjan	WCq	Dindane [35], Drogba [63p]	40 827	Colembi ANG
20-06	Egypt	W	2-1	Alexandria	WCq	Dindane [22], Drogba [75]	13 000	Guirat TUN
4-07	Cameroon	L	0-2	Yaounde	WCq		80 000	Guezzaz MAR
18-08	Senegal	W	2-1	Avignon	Fr	Boka [32], Dindane [68]	5 000	
5-09	Sudan	W	5-0	Abidjan	WCq	Drogba [12p], Dindane 2 [15 64], Yapi [25], Kone [56]	20 000	Mana NGA
10-10	Benin	W	1-0	Cotonou	WCq	Dindane [48]	25 000	Sowe GAM
2005								
8-02	Congo DR	D	2-2	Rouen	Fr	Dindane [39], Kalou [88p]	4 000	Duhamel FRA
27-03	Benin	W	3-0	Abidjan	WCq	Kalou [7], Drogba 2 [19 59]	35 000	Guirat TUN
3-06	Libya	D	0-0	Tripoli	WCq		45 000	Lim Kee Chong MRI
19-06	Egypt	W	2-0	Abidjan	WCq	Drogba 2 [41 49]	30 000	Damon RSA

Fr = Friendly match • CN = African Cup of Nations • WC = FIFA World Cup™ • q = qualifier

COTE D'IVOIRE NATIONAL TEAM RECORDS AND RECORD SEQUENCES

Records			Sequence records					
Victory	6-0	Four times	Wins	7	1984	Clean sheets	9	1991
Defeat	2-6	GHA 1971	Defeats	6	1977-1979	Goals scored	15	1983-1984
Player Caps	n/a		Undefeated	16	1987-1989	Without goal	3	1985, 1989
Player Goals	n/a		Without win	7	1985	Goals against	11	1980-1983

FIFA REFEREE LIST 2005

	Int'l	DoB
ABOUBACAR Sharaf	2000	4-01-1963
BOHUI Zako	2004	30-05-1964
CHICOTO Koffi	2002	1-01-1966
DOUE Noumandiez	2004	29-09-1970
KONAN Kouakou	1999	16-05-1963
NAHI Monetchet	1999	6-11-1965

FIFA ASSISTANT REFEREE LIST 2005

	Int'l	DoB
ETTIEGNE Mian	1999	11-07-1963
GNAGNE Sem	2001	2-09-1962
KOFFI Kablan	2000	13-06-1963
KOUADIO N'Guessan	2000	15-05-1966
TEHE Guei	1996	12-08-1964
YAO Kossonou	1996	8-10-1961
YEO Songuifolo	2004	1-01-1970

COTE D'IVOIRE COUNTRY INFORMATION

Capital	Yamoussoukro	Independence	1960	GDP per Capita	$1 400
Population	17 327 724	Status	Republic	GNP Ranking	85
Area km²	322 460	Language	French	Dialling code	+225
Population density	53 per km²	Literacy rate	43%	Internet code	.ci
% in urban areas	44%	Main religion	Traditional 40%	GMT + / –	0
Towns/Cities ('000)	Abidjan 3 692; Bouaké 572; Daloa 217; Yamoussoukro 200; San Pedro 195; Korhogo 172				
Neighbours (km)	Mali 532; Burkina Faso 584; Ghana 668; Liberia 716; Guinea 610; Atlantic Ocean 515				
Main stadia	Houphouët-Boigny – Abidjan 45 000; Robert Champroux – Abidjan 20 000				

COTE D'IVOIRE 2004

PREMIERE DIVISION

	Pl	W	D	L	F	A	Pts	ASEC	Africa Sport	Stella	JCA	Sabé	Stade	Réveil	Bouaflé	Satellite	Denguélé	Séwé	Bingerville	Korhogo	Man
ASEC Mimosas †	26	21	5	0	60	7	68		0-0	1-0	1-1	3-0	2-0	6-0	3-1	3-1	2-0	3-0	3-0	2-0	5-1
Africa Sport †	26	15	9	2	38	16	48	1-2		2-0	0-0	2-1	1-2	0-0	4-1	3-1	2-1	1-0	3-0	2-1	3-1
Stella Adjamé ‡	26	11	10	5	32	21	43	0-3	1-1		2-2	1-0	3-1	0-1	2-0	2-0	1-1	2-0	2-0	4-1	2-0
Jeunesse Abidjan	26	8	11	7	34	25	35	0-0	0-1	1-2		3-0	0-0	0-1	1-1	4-1	2-0	2-1	4-1	1-1	1-1
Sabé Sports Bouna	26	8	11	7	21	18	35	0-0	1-1	1-1	0-0		1-0	2-0	1-1	1-0	1-0	0-0	0-0	1-2	1-1
Stade Abidjan	26	8	10	8	25	28	34	1-2	1-1	0-0	0-0	0-0		2-2	1-1	2-0	1-1	2-0	0-2*	4-1	1-0
Réveil Daloa	26	9	7	10	24	31	34	0-2	0-1	1-1	0-2	1-0	2-0		2-0	0-1	2-2	1-2	2-1	0-0	1-0
CO Bouaflé ‡	26	7	10	9	24	26	31	0-0	0-0	0-0	1-0	0-0	0-0	2-1		5-0	0-1	0-4	2-0	0-2	2-1
Satellite FC	26	9	4	13	22	42	31	0-5	0-2	0-1	4-1	0-5	0-0	2-1	1-0		1-0	1-1	1-1	2-1	1-1
Denguélé Odienné	26	6	12	8	24	27	30	0-2	0-1	1-1	2-2	1-0	4-1	2-1	1-1	1-0		0-0	1-1	1-1	1-1
Séwé San Pedro	26	7	8	11	20	30	29	1-2	2-2	2-1	3-2	0-0	1-0	0-1	1-0	1-2	2-1		1-1	0-1	1-0
Entente Bingerville	26	6	9	11	21	37	27	0-4	1-1	1-1	0-2	0-1	0-2	2-2	0-1	1-0	0-0	1-1		2-0	2-1
CO Korhogo	26	5	6	15	22	42	21	0-2	0-2	0-1	0-1	1-3	1-3	0-0	2-1	0-2	1-1	2-0	0-1		2-3
Man FC	26	2	8	16	17	37	14	0-2	0-1	1-1	2-1	0-1	0-1	1-2	0-0	0-1	0-1	0-0	0-1	2-2	

21/02/2004 - 20/10/2004 • † Qualified for the CAF Champions League • ‡ Qualified for the CAF Confederation Cup • * Stade walked off with the score at 2-0. The result stood for Bingerville but Stade were penalised with a 0-5 defeat • Issia Wazi and Sporting Club Gagnoa promoted

COUPE NATIONALE 2004

Round of sixteen

CO Bouaflé	2
Satellite FC	0
CO Korhogo	
Rio Sport	
Séwé San Pedro	4
Moossou FC	2
Jeunesse Abidjan	0 4p
SO Armée	0 5p
ASEC Mimosas	2
Man FC	1
RFC Daoukro	Bye
Stella Adjamé	0
Stade Abidjan	1

Quarter-finals

CO Bouaflé	1
Rio Sport	0
Séwé San Pedro	0 3p
SO Armée	0 4p
ASEC Mimosas	1
RFC Daoukro	0
Stade Abidjan	Bye

‡ Qualified for the CAF Confederation Cup

Semi-finals

CO Bouaflé	1
SO Armée	0
ASEC Mimosas	1 2p
Stade Abidjan	1 3p

Final

| CO Bouaflé ‡ | 2 |
| Stade Abidjan | 1 |

CUP FINAL
Houphouët-Boigny, Abidjan, 7-08-2004

Scorers - Digba Zah 2 [56] [76] for Bouaflé; Kambou [60p] for Stade

RECENT LEAGUE AND CUP RECORD

	Championship						Cup		
Year	Champions	Pts	Runners-up	Pts	Third	Pts	Winners	Score	Runners-up
1990	ASEC Mimosas						ASEC Mimosas	2-0	SC Gagnoa
1991	ASEC Mimosas	57	Africa Sports	54	SC Gagnoa	34	No final played		
1992	ASEC Mimosas						No final played		
1993	ASEC Mimosas						Africa Sports	2-1	ASC Bouaké
1994	ASEC Mimosas	18	Africa Sports	18	SO Armée	9	Stade Abidjan	4-2	Africa Sports
1995	ASEC Mimosas	23	SO Armée	18	Africa Sports	15	ASEC Mimosas	2-0	Stade Abidjan
1996	Africa Sports						SO Armée	0-0 10-9p	Africa Sports
1997	ASEC Mimosas	26	SO Armée	15	Africa Sports	12	ASEC Mimosas	4-0	Africa Sports
1998	ASEC Mimosas	24	FC Man	16	Africa Sports	13	Africa Sports	3-0	Stade Abidjan
1999	Africa Sports	28	ASEC Mimosas	23	Stade Abidjan	16	ASEC Mimosas	5-0	Séwé San Pedro
2000	ASEC Mimosas	21	Sabé Bouna	16	Africa Sports	16	Stade Abidjan	2-1	ASEC Mimosas
2001	ASEC Mimosas	55	Satellite FC	45	Africa Sports	41	Alliance Bouaké	2-0	ASC Bouaké
2002	ASEC Mimosas	22	Jeunesse Abidjan	18	Satellite FC	16	Africa Sports	2-0	Renaissance
2003	ASEC Mimosas	21	Africa Sports	19	Stella Adjamé	15	ASEC Mimosas	1-1 4-2p	Africa Sports
2004	ASEC Mimosas	68	Africa Sport	48	Stella Adjamé	43	CO Bouaflé	2-1	Stade Abidjan

CMR – CAMEROON

NATIONAL TEAM RECORD
JULY 1ST 2002 TO JUNE 30TH 2005

PL	W	D	L	F	A	%
28	13	7	8	34	29	58.9

FIFA/COCA-COLA WORLD RANKING

1993	1994	1995	1996	1997	1998	1999	2000	2001	2002	2003	2004	High		Low	
23	31	37	56	53	41	58	39	38	16	14	23	12	07/03	62	04/97

2004-2005											
08/04	09/04	10/04	11/04	12/04	01/05	02/05	03/05	04/05	05/05	06/05	07/05
16	16	21	22	23	23	23	25	26	26	26	27

The four-times African Cup of Nations winners are facing a tough battle with Côte d'Ivoire to reach the 2006 FIFA World Cup™finals, a task that would have been far more daunting if FIFA had not overturned its decision to dock Cameroon six points before the qualifiers had even begun because of the illegal kit worn at the 2004 Nations Cup. Even with current African footballer of the year, Barcelona's Samuel Eto'o, the Lions dropped points early on leading to coach Winfried Schafer being replaced by Artur Jorge. Currently the highest ranked African nation, if Cameroon do fail to qualify for Germany it would be only the second time since 1982 that they would have

INTERNATIONAL HONOURS
Qualified for the FIFA World Cup™ finals 1982 1990 1994 1998 2002   African Cup of Nations 1984 1988 2000 2002   African Games 1991 1999 2003
African Youth 1995   African U-17 2003   CAF African Champions League Oryx Doula 1965, Canon Yaounde 1971 1978 1980, Union Douala 1979

missed out on the finals. Domestically Cotonsport of Garoua made it a second double in a row when the club won the Super Ligue Nationale ahead of Racing Bafoussam for their fifth title and then beat Union Douala 1-0 in the Coupe de Cameroun in front of a 60,000-strong crowd. Neither Cotonsport nor Racing Bafoussam made an impression in the 2004 CAF Champions League, both falling in the first round, while Bamboutos reached the third stage of the Confederation Cup, a round further than Union Douala.

THE FIFA BIG COUNT OF 2000

	Male	Female		Male	Female
Registered players	12 450	500	Referees	2 000	30
Non registered players	75 000	1 000	Officials	5 000	0
Youth players	10 000	0	Total involved	105 980	
Total players	98 950		Number of clubs	720	
Professional players	450	0	Number of teams	3 000	

Fédération Camerounaise de Football (FECAFOOT)
Avenue du 27 aout 1940, Tsinga-Yaoundé, Case Postale 1116, Yaoundé, Cameroon
Tel +237 2210012   Fax +237 7991393
fecafoot@fecafootonline.com   www.cameroon.fifa.com
President: IYA Mohammed   General Secretary: ATANGANA Jean Rene
Vice-President: PENNE Robert   Treasurer: ALIOUM Alhadji Hamadou   Media Officer: None
Men's Coach: JORGE Artur   Women's Coach: KAMDEM Charles
FECAFOOT formed: 1959   CAF: 1963   FIFA: 1962
Colours: Green, Red, Yellow or Red, Green, Yellow

GAMES PLAYED BY CAMEROON IN THE 2006 FIFA WORLD CUP™ CYCLE

2002	Opponents	Score		Venue	Comp	Scorers	Att	Referee
	No international matches played after June 2002							
2003								
11-02	Côte d'Ivoire	L	0-3	Chateauroux	Fr		3 000	Ennjini FRA
27-03	Madagascar	W	2-0	Tunis	Fr	Eto'o [15], Job [43]		Zahmoul TUN
30-03	Tunisia	L	0-1	Tunis	Fr			Guezzaz MAR
19-06	Brazil	W	1-0	Paris	CCr1	Eto'o [83]	46 719	Ivanov RUS
21-06	Turkey	W	1-0	Paris	CCr1	Geremi [90p]	43 743	Amarilla PAR
23-06	United States	D	0-0	Lyon	CCr1		19 206	Shield AUS
26-06	Colombia	W	1-0	Lyon	CCsf	N'Diefi [9]	12 352	Merk GER
29-06	France	L	0-1	Paris	CCf		51 985	Ivanov RUS
19-11	Japan	D	0-0	Oita	Fr		38 627	Lu CHN
7-12	Central African Rep.	D	2-2	Brazzaville	CM r1	Mokake [60]		
9-12	Central African Rep.	L	0-1	Brazzaville	CMr1			
10-12	Congo	W	2-0	Brazzaville	CMsf	Ambassa [45], Abada [90]		Youssouf GAB
13-12	Central African Rep.	W	3-2	Brazzaville	CMf	Mevengue [16p], Mokake.M [69], Mokake.E [78]		Bantsimba CGO
2004								
25-01	Algeria	D	1-1	Sousse	CNr1	Mboma [44]	20 000	Codjia BEN
29-01	Zimbabwe	W	5-3	Sfax	CNr1	Mboma 3 [31 44 64], Mbami 2 [39 66]	15 000	Aboubacar CIV
3-02	Egypt	D	0-0	Monastir	CNr1		20 000	Bujsaim UAE
8-02	Nigeria	L	1-2	Monastir	CNqf	Eto'o [42]	18 000	Guezzaz MAR
28-04	Bulgaria	L	0-3	Sofia	Fr		13 987	Verbist BEL
6-06	Benin	W	2-1	Yaoundé	WCq	Eto'o [42], Song [45]	40 000	Mbera GAB
18-06	Libya	D	0-0	Misurata	WCq		7 000	Lim Kee Chong MRI
4-07	Côte d'Ivoire	W	2-0	Yaoundé	WCq	Eto'o [80], Feutchine [82]	80 000	Guezzaz MAR
5-09	Egypt	L	2-3	Cairo	WCq	Tchato [88], Eto'o [90]	25 000	Lim Kee Chong MRI
9-10	Sudan	D	1-1	Omdurman	WCq	Job [90+2]	30 000	Buenkadila COD
17-11	Germany	L	0-3	Leipzig	Fr		4 200	De Santis ITA
2005								
9-02	Senegal	W	1-0	Creteil	Fr	Geremi [87]	8 000	Lhermite FRA
27-03	Sudan	W	2-1	Yaoundé	WCq	Geremi [34], Webo [90]	30 000	Diatta SEN
4-06	Benin	W	4-1	Cotonou	WCq	Song [19], Webo [51], Geremi [64], Eto'o [69]	20 000	El Arjoun MAR
19-06	Libya	W	1-0	Yaoundé	WCq	Webo [37]	36 000	Coulibaly MLI

Fr = Friendly match • CC = FIFA Confederations Cup • CN = African Cup of Nations • CM = CEMAC Championship • WC = FIFA World Cup™
q = qualifier • r1 = 1st round • sf = semi-final • f = final

CAMEROON NATIONAL TEAM RECORDS AND RECORD SEQUENCES

Records			Sequence records					
Victory	9-2	SOM 1960	Wins	7	2002	Clean sheets	7	2002
Defeat	1-6	NOR 1990, RUS 1994	Defeats	3	Five times	Goals scored	24	1967-1972
Player Caps	n/a		Undefeated	16	1981-1983	Without goal	4	1981, 2001
Player Goals	33	MBOMA Patrick	Without win	9	1994-1995	Goals against	11	1969-1972

CAMEROON COUNTRY INFORMATION

Capital	Yaoundé	Independence	1960 from UN Trusteeship	GDP per Capita	$1 800
Population	16 063 678	Status	Republic	GNP Ranking	91
Area km²	475 440	Language	French, English	Dialling code	+237
Population density	33 per km²	Literacy rate	72%	Internet code	.cm
% in urban areas	45%	Main religion	Indigenous 40% Christian 40%	GMT +/−	+1
Towns/Cities ('000)	Douala 1 338; Yaoundé 1 299; Garoua 436; Kousseri 435; Bamenda 393; Bafoussam 290				
Neighbours (km)	Central African Republic 797; Chad 1 094; Congo 523; Equatorial Guinea 189; Gabon 298; Nigeria 1,690				
Main stadia	Amadou Ahidjo – Yaoundé 80 000; Stade de la Réunification – Douala 30 000				

CAMEROON 2004

PREMIERE DIVISION (FIRST STAGE)

Poule A

	Pl	W	D	L	F	A	Pts	Cotonsport	Sable	Fovu	Tonnerre	Mt Cam	Unisport	Kadji	Univ. Ng.	Cintra
Cotonsport Garoua †	16	11	5	0	25	1	38		2-0	1-0	0-0	2-0	1-0	4-0	3-0	5-0
Sable Batié †	16	6	6	4	14	9	24	0-0		0-0	1-0	0-0	3-0	1-2	1-0	1-1
Fovu Baham †	16	6	5	5	14	10	23	0-0	0-0		0-1	0-0	3-2	2-0	1-1	1-0
Tonnerre Yaoundé †	16	6	5	5	17	18	23	1-1	1-0	1-3		2-2	2-2	1-1	1-0	1-2
Mt Cameroun Buéa ‡	16	6	4	6	16	14	22	0-1	0-1	0-1	0-1		4-1	2-1	1-0	2-1
Unisport Bafang ‡	16	4	6	6	17	21	18	0-1	0-3	1-0	2-0	2-0		0-0	4-0	1-1
Kadji Sport Douala ‡	16	4	6	6	16	20	18	0-0	1-0	1-3	1-2	0-2	0-0		4-1	1-1
Univ. Ngaoundéré ‡	16	4	4	8	16	24	16	0-1	1-1	1-0	2-0	1-0	2-2	1-1		5-1
Cintra Yaoundé	16	3	3	10	16	34	12	0-3	1-2	1-0	1-3	2-3	1-2	0-3	3-1	

Poule B

	Pl	W	D	L	F	A	Pts	Racing	Bamboutos	Canon	Union	Botafogo	Victoria	Espérance	PWD	Renaissance
Racing Bafoussam †	16	9	3	4	16	8	30		0-0	0-1	1-0	1-0	3-0	2-0	1-0	2-0
Bamboutos Mbouda †	16	7	5	4	18	10	26	0-0		0-2	0-0	1-1	2-0	4-0	1-0	1-0
Canon Yaoundé †	16	8	2	6	15	12	26	0-1	0-1		1-1	0-1	2-1	2-0	1-0	0-0
Union Douala †	16	6	5	5	19	18	23	0-2	0-4	0-1		1-0	2-0	2-1	4-2	1-1
Botafogo Buéa ‡	16	6	5	5	14	14	23	1-0	1-1	1-0	1-1		1-2	1-1	3-2	1-0
Victoria Utd Limbe ‡	16	6	2	8	15	20	20	4-0	1-2	0-2	2-1	0-0		1-0	2-0	2-1
Espérance Guider ‡	16	6	2	8	14	19	20	1-0	1-0	3-0	0-2	0-1	1-0		2-1	3-1
PWD Bamenda ‡	16	5	2	9	18	22	17	0-0	2-0	2-1	1-3	2-1	3-0	1-0		1-2
Renaissance	16	3	6	7	14	20	15	1-3	2-1	1-2	1-1	2-0	0-0	1-1	1-1	

16/08/2003 - 15/05/2004 • † Qualified for the Super Ligue Nationale • ‡ Qualified for the Ligue Nationale

CAMEROON 2004

SUPER LIGUE NATIONALE

	Pl	W	D	L	F	A	Pts	Cotonsport	Racing	Union	Bamboutos	Fovu	Sable	Canon	Tonnerre
Cotonsport Garua †	14	9	3	2	30	9	**30**		2-1	1-2	1-0	5-0	4-2	**3-0**	3-1
Racing Bafoussam †	14	8	4	2	18	6	28	0-0		4-0	2-1	2-1	0-0	2-0	2-0
Union Douala ‡	14	7	5	2	18	13	26	2-1	0-0		0-0	1-0	2-2	2-0	2-1
Bamboutos Mbouda ‡	14	3	8	3	8	7	17	0-0	2-1	1-0		0-0	0-0	0-0	2-0
Fovu Baham	14	3	4	7	9	18	13	0-0	0-0	1-2	1-1		1-3	0-1	1-0
Sable Batié ‡ §	14	3	6	5	14	19	12	0-2	0-1	**0-3**	1-1	2-0		0-0	2-1
Canon Yaoundé	14	2	5	7	4	17	11	0-4	0-2	0-0	0-0	0-2	3-1		0-0
Tonnerre Yaoundé	14	2	3	9	10	22	9	1-4	0-1	2-2	1-0	1-2	1-1	1-0	

18/07/2004 - 5/12/2004 • † Qualified for the CAF Champions League • ‡ Qualified for the CAF Confederation Cup • Matches in bold awarded 3-0
§ Three points deducted

CAMEROON 2004

LIGUE NATIONALE

	Pl	W	D	L	F	A	Pts	Mt Cam	Unisport	PWD	Kadji	Univ. Ng.	Espérance	Victoria Utd	Botafogo
Mt Cameroun Buéa	14	5	6	3	18	11	21		0-0	7-1	2-0	2-0	1-0	1-1	0-0
Unisport Bafang	14	6	3	5	15	12	21	0-1		1-1	4-1	2-0	2-0	1-0	1-3
PWD Bamenda	14	6	3	5	17	20	21	0-0	2-1		3-1	0-2	3-1	2-0	1-0
Kadji Sport Douala	14	6	2	6	23	17	20	2-1	0-1	2-0		4-0	5-0	3-1	1-1
Univ. Ngaoundéré	14	6	2	6	13	15	20	3-1	0-0	2-1	1-1		2-0	1-0	1-0
Espérance Guider	14	6	2	6	15	18	20	2-0	1-0	1-1	1-0	1-0		2-2	4-0
Victoria Utd Limbe	14	5	3	6	20	20	18	2-2	3-1	0-1	2-1	2-1	1-0		5-2
Botafogo Buéa	14	4	3	7	12	20	15	0-0	0-1	2-1	0-2	1-0	1-2	2-1	

18/07/2004 - 5/12/2004

FIFA REFEREE LIST 2005

	Int'l	DoB
ABIMNI Andrew	2003	4-01-1967
BODO NDZOMO Desire	1999	15-10-1963
EVEHE Divine	1998	24-10-1964
EYENE Lambert	2004	9-04-1968
NJIKE Gilbert	1994	29-12-1961
OMGBA ZING Martin	2000	30-06-1969
TCHOUMBA Alain	2001	5-12-1973

FIFA ASSISTANT REFEREE LIST 2005

	Int'l	DoB
BOUNGANI DODA Patrice	2000	25-05-1970
EFFA Englebert	2005	11-04-1970
ENDENG Zogo	1997	11-10-1962
GAMBO Abdoulaye	2004	25-05-1968
KABA Charles	2004	8-05-1969
MENKOUANDE Evarist	2004	14-11-1974
MOUSSA Yanoussa	2005	13-03-1973

CAMEROON 2004
TOURNOI INTER POULES (2)

Pool A - in Yaoundé	Pl	W	D	L	F	A	Pts
Astres FC Douala	4	3	1	0	7	3	10
Sahel FC Maroua	4	2	1	1	10	6	7
Young Stars Bamenda	4	1	3	0	5	4	6
Etoile Filante Garoua	4	1	1	2	4	5	4
AS Kadey Batouri	4	0	0	4	1	9	0

Pool B - in Douala	Pl	W	D	L	F	A	Pts
Foudre d'Akonolinga	4	3	0	1	13	4	9
Aigle Royale Menoua	4	3	0	1	10	9	9
Asmy FC d'Ebolowa	4	2	0	2	7	9	6
Girondins Ngaoundéré	4	1	0	3	6	8	3
Electsport de Limbe	4	1	0	3	3	9	3

Astres, Sahel, Foudre & Aigle Royale promoted

COUPE DE CAMEROUN 2004

Round of 16

| Cotonsport Garua * | 2 |
| PWD Bamenda | 0 |

| Espérance Guider | 0 1 |
| University Ngaoundéré* | 1 1 |

| Canon Yaoundé * | 1 1 |
| Victoria Utd Limbe | 0 2 |

| Bamboutos Mbouda * | 1 0 2p |
| Impôt Yaoundé | 0 1 3p |

| Fovu Baham | 1 2 |
| Foudre d'Akonolinga * | 0 1 |

| Racing Bafoussam | 0 |
| Tonnerre Yaoundé * | 2 |

| Mount Cameroun | 1 1 |
| Panthère Bangangté * | 0 1 |

| Botafogo Buéa * | 1 1 |
| Union Douala | 4 2 |

Quarter-finals

| Cotonsport Garua * | 3 2 |
| University Ngaoundéré | 0 0 |

| Canon Yaoundé | 0 0 |
| Impôt Yaoundé * | 0 4 |

| Fovu Baham * | 5 1 |
| Tonnerre Yaoundé | 1 0 |

| Mount Cameroun | 1 0 |
| Union Douala * | 1 1 |

* Home team in the first leg

Semi-finals

| Cotonsport Garua * | 2 2 |
| Impôt Yaoundé | 0 1 |

| Fovu Baham * | 3 2 2p |
| Union Douala | 3 2 3p |

Final

| Cotonsport Garua | 1 |
| Union Douala | 0 |

CUP FINAL
28-12-2004, Att: 60 000
Stade Ahmadou Ahidjo, Yaoundé

Scorer - Aloma [68p] for Cotonsport

CLUB DIRECTORY

Club	Town/City	Stadium	Phone	Lge	Cup	CL
Bamboutos	Mbouda	Stade Municipal 11 000		0	0	0
Botafogo	Buéa	Moliko Stadium 8 000		0	0	0
Canon Sportif	Yaoundé	Stade Ahmadou Ahidjo 80 000	+237 303167	10	12	3
Cintra	Yaoundé	Stade Ahmadou Ahidjo 80 000	+237 2210139	0	0	0
Cotonsport	Garoua	Stade Omnisport Poumpoum Rey 22 000	+237 2272303	5	2	0
Espérance	Guider	Stade Municipal 10 000		0	0	0
Fovu Club	Baham	Stade Municipal 7 000	+237 444402	1	1	0
Kadji Sport Academy	Douala	Stade de la Reunification 30 000		0	0	0
Mount Cameroun FC	Buéa	Moliko Stadium 8 000	+237 3429228	0	1	0
Ngaoundéré University FC	Ngaoundéré	Stade Municipal 10 000		0	0	0
PWD (Public Works Dept)	Bamenda	Stade Municipal 10 000		0	0	0
Racing Club	Bafoussam	Stade Municipal de Bamendzi 5 000	+237 9925903	4	1	0
Renaissance	Ngoumou	Stade Ahmadou Ahidjo 80 000		0	0	0
Sable	Batié	Stade de la Reunification 30 000	+237 443681	1	0	0
Tonnerre Kalara Club	Yaoundé	Stade Ahmadou Ahidjo 80 000	+237 2221475	5	0	0
Union Sportive	Douala	Stade de la Reunification 30 000	+237 374470	4	5	1
Unisport	Bafang	Stade Municipal 5 000	+237 9903541	1	0	0
Victoria United	Limbe	Stade Municipal 12 000		0	0	0

COTONSPORT GARUA 2004

Date	Opponents	Score		Comp	Scorers
28-02-2004	Kadji Sport Academy Douala	D	0-0	A	LGs1	
7-03-2004	Ngaoundéré University FC	W	1-0	A	LGs1	Vital 79p
14-03-2004	Sable de Batié	W	2-0	H	LGs1	Tchango 5, Minusu 70
21-03-2004	Unisport de Bafang	W	1-0	A	LGs1	Buba 32
24-03-2004	Fovu de Baham	W	1-0	H	LGs1	Buba 60
28-03-2004	Tonnerre Kalara Yaoundé	D	1-1	A	LGs1	Tchango 44
1-04-2004	Mount Cameroun FC de Buéa	W	2-0	H	LGs1	Tchango 34p, Amungwa 80
11-04-2004	Saint Michel d'Ouenzé - CGO	W	4-1	H	CLr1	Amungwa 2 43 83, Minusu 65, Dikoume 73
18-04-2004	Cintra de Yaoundé	W	5-0	H	LGs1	Mbangue 4 25 48 66 70, Amungwa 55
25-04-2004	Saint Michel d'Ouenzé - CGO	L	0-1	A	CLr1	
2-05-2004	Kadji Sport Academy Douala	W	4-0	H	LGs1	Ntsogo 12, Aloma 2 23 77, Gambo 35
5-05-2004	Ngaoundéré University FC	W	3-0	H	LGs1	Sadjo 2 8 53, Aloma 88
9-05-2004	Sable de Batié	D	0-0	A	LGs1	
15-05-2004	Espérance Sportive Tunis - TUN	L	0-3	A	CLr2	
23-05-2003	Unisport de Bafang	W	1-0	H	LGs1	Mbangue 61
30-05-2004	Espérance Sportive Tunis - TUN	W	1-0	H	CLr2	Kameni 41p
5-06-2004	Fovu de Baham	D	0-0	A	LGs1	
13-06-2004	Tonnerre Kalara Yaoundé	D	0-0	H	LGs1	
17-06-2004	Mount Cameroun FC de Buéa	W	1-0	A	LGs1	Mbangue 62
24-06-2004	Cintra de Yaoundé	W	3-0	A	LGs1	Nassourou 67, Gambo 74, Amungwa 90
11-07-2004	Green Buffaloes - ZAM	W	3-0	H	CCir	Soussia 23, Nassourou 2 56 79
14-07-2004	Gro-Ngolona de Yagoua	W	3-0	H	CUPr1	Kemeni 36p, Nassourou 88, Aloma 89
18-07-2004	Sable de Batié	W	4-2	H	LGE	Aloma 2, Amungwa 19, Oumarou 26, Mbangue 62
24-07-2004	Green Buffaloes - ZAM	D	1-1	A	CCir	Mbangue 32
1-08-2004	Fovu de Baham	D	0-0	A	SLN	
4-08-2004	Union de Douala	L	1-2	A	SLN	Minusu 1
8-08-2004	Bamboutos de Mbouda	W	1-0	H	SLN	Oumarou 30
15-08-2004	Canon de Yaoundé	W	4-0	A	SLN	Aloma 3 17 55 69, Nassourou 88
18-08-2004	Racing de Bafoussam	D	0-0	H	SLN	
22-08-2004	PWD de Bamenda	W	2-0	H	CUPr2	Abandoned 42 minutes. Match awarded 2-0 to Cotonsport
29-08-2004	Sable de Batié - CMR	D	0-0	A	CCgB	
5-09-2004	Tonnerre Kalara Yaoundé	W	3-1	H	SLN	Kameni 16p, Soussia 29, Sadjo 48
12-09-2004	Hearts of Oak - GHA	D	0-0	H	CCgB	
15-09-2004	Ngaoundéré University FC	W	3-0	H	CUPqf	Mbangue 54, Sadjo 65, Dikoume 80
19-09-2004	Sable de Batié	W	2-0	A	SLN	Aloma 8, Soussia 86
25-09-2004	Cape Town Santos - RSA	W	4-0	H	CCgB	Ngomna 18, Minufu 39, D'Koume 60, Soussia 69
26-09-2004	Ngaoundéré University FC	W	2-0	A	CUPqf	Mbangue 55, Oumarou 88
3-10-2004	Fovu de Baham	W	5-0	H	SLN	Ngomna 14, Bitrus 2 34 37, Nassourou 51, Mbangue 90
6-10-2004	Union de Douala	L	1-2	H	SLN	Gaha 82
16-10-2004	Cape Town Santos - RSA	W	2-0	A	CCgB	Aloma 3, Sanda 85
21-10-2004	Bamboutos de Mbouda	D	0-0	A	SLN	
31-10-2004	Sable de Batié - CMR	W	1-0	H	CCgB	Hamadou 16
4-11-2004	Canon de Yaoundé	W	3-0	H	SLN	Abandoned after 79' with score at 0-0. Awarded to Cotonsport
8-11-2004	Impôt FC de Yaoundé	W	2-0	H	CUPsf	Hamadou 10, Boya 49
13-11-2004	Hearts of Oak - GHA	L	2-3	A	CCgB	Makadji 89, Nzame 90+3
18-11-2004	Impôt FC de Yaoundé	D	0-0	A	CUPsf	Abandoned after 87' due to rain with the score at 0-0
28-11-2004	Racing de Bafoussam	W	2-1	H	SLN	Aloma 2 54 75
2-12-2004	Impôt FC de Yaoundé	W	2-1	A	CUPsf	
5-12-2004	Tonnerre Kalara Yaoundé	W	4-1	A	SLN	Ateba 83, Aloma 3 13 87 90p, Hamadou 27
28-12-2004	Union de Douala	W	1-0	N	CUPf	Aloma 68p

LGs1 = League Championship 1st stage • SLN = Super Ligue Nationale (League 2nd stage) • CL = CAF Champions League
CC = CAF Confederation Cup • CUP = Coupe de Cameroun
r1 = first round • r2 = second round • ir = intermediate round • gB = group B • qf = quarter-final • sf = semi-final • f = final

RECENT LEAGUE AND CUP RECORD

	Championship						Cup		
Year	Champions	Pts	Runners-up	Pts	Third	Pts	Winners	Score	Runners-up
1994	Aigle Nkongsamba	42	Cotonsport Garoua	38	Union Douala	36	Olympique Mvolyé	1-0	Tonnerre Yaoundé
1995	Racing Bafoussam	52	Léopard Douala	48	Unisport Bafang	48	Canon Yaoundé	1-0	Océan Kribi
1996	Unisport Bafang	56	Cotonsport Garoua	47	Canon Yaoundé	47	Racing Bafoussam	1-0	Stade Banjoun
1997	Cotonsport Garoua	62	Stade Bandjoun	60	Union Douala	55	Union Douala	2-1	Ports FC Douala
1998	Cotonsport Garoua	54	Canon Yaoundé	53	Tonnerre Yaoundé	51	Dynamo Douala	1-0	Canon Yaoundé
1999	Sable Batié	58	Cotonsport Garoua	56	Racing Bafoussam	49	Canon Yaoundé	2-1	Cotonsport Garoua
2000	Fovu Baham	59	Cotonsport Garoua	53	Union Douala	51	Kumbo Strikers	1-0	Unisport Bafang
2001	Cotonsport Garoua	58	Tonnerre Yaoundé	53	Fovu Baham	50	Fovu Baham	3-2	Cintra Yaoundé
2002	Canon Yaoundé	55	Cotonsport Garoua	53	Bamboutos Mbouda	50	Mt Cameroun	2-1	Sable Batié
2003	Cotonsport Garoua	62	Canon Yaoundé	51	PWD Bamenda	51	Cotonsport Garoua	2-1	Sable Batié
2004	Cotonsport Garoua	30	Racing Bafoussam	28	Union Douala	26	Cotonsport Garoua	1-0	Union Douala

COD – CONGO DR

NATIONAL TEAM RECORD
JULY 1ST 2002 TO JULY 1ST 2005

PL	W	D	L	F	A	%
30	11	11	8	43	36	55

FIFA/COCA-COLA WORLD RANKING

1993	1994	1995	1996	1997	1998	1999	2000	2001	2002	2003	2004	High		Low	
71	68	68	66	76	62	59	70	77	65	56	78	51	09/03	81	07/01

2004-2005											
08/04	09/04	10/04	11/04	12/04	01/05	02/05	03/05	04/05	05/05	06/05	07/05
71	79	76	77	78	78	76	76	75	77	68	78

A disastrous performance at the 2004 CAF African Cup of Nations in Tunisia led to accusations of mismanagement and poor administration with players like Shabani Nonda and Tresor Lualua caught in the middle of a bitter dispute between various official bodies. However, since the appointment of the experienced French coach Claude Le Roy in June 2004 there has been progress, including training camps and matches in France to make preparations easier for the European-based players. In the FIFA World Cup™ qualifiers, Congo DR found themselves in a tough group containing South Africa and Ghana but which turned out to be incredibly close with no single team

INTERNATIONAL HONOURS
Qualified for the FIFA World Cup™ finals 1974
African Cup of Nations 1968 1974   CAF Champions League TP Mazembe 1967 1968 AS Vita Club 1973

dominating. With Cape Verde upsetting many of the odds, not even a top three finish and a place in the 2006 Cup of Nations in Egypt can be counted on. DC Motema Pembe, based in the capital Kinshasa, won their 10th Ligue Nationale du Football title in 2004 although it was their first in five years while in the Coupe du Congo, CS Cilu from Luakala beat AS Saint-Luc 1-0 for the title. There was little progress in continental competitions with no team from Congo DR making it to the group stage in either the Champions League or the Confederation Cup in either 2004 or 2005.

THE FIFA BIG COUNT OF 2000

	Male	Female		Male	Female
Registered players	25 000	0	Referees	1 000	0
Non registered players	150 000	0	Officials	7 000	0
Youth players	20 000	0	Total involved	203 000	
Total players	195 000		Number of clubs	700	
Professional players	0	0	Number of teams	3 000	

Fédération Congolaise de Football-Association (FECOFA)
31 Avenue de la Justice, c/Gombe, Case postale 1284, Kinshasa 1, Congo DR
Tel +243 9939635   Fax +243 813013527
nzilafanan@hotmail.com   www.none
President: SELEMANI Omari   General Secretary: MASAMBA Malunga
Vice-President: TSHIMANGA MWAMBA Donatien   Treasurer: MASAMBA Malunga   Media Officer: NZILA Fanan
Men's Coach: LE ROY Claude   ·   Women's Coach: MOSI Mosi
FECOFA formed: 1919   ,   CAF: 1973   FIFA: 1962
Colours: Blue, Blue, Blue or Yellow, Yellow, Yellow

GAMES PLAYED BY CONGO DR IN THE 2006 WORLD CUP CYCLE

2002	Opponents	Score		Venue	Comp	Scorers	Att	Referee
20-08	Algeria	D	1-1	Blida	Fr	Yemo 36		Benaissa ALG
25-08	Congo	W	3-1	Brazzaville	Fr			
8-09	Libya	L	2-3	Tripoli	CNq	Nonda 22, Kikeba 52		El Arjoun MAR
13-10	Botswana	W	2-0	Kinshasa	CNq	Lua Lua 5, Mpiana 22		Mandzioukouta CGO
2003								
22-02	Malawi	D	1-1	Blantyre	Fr			
23-02	Malawi	W	3-2	Lilongwe	Fr			
5-03	Sudan	W	3-1	Khartoum	Fr			
9-03	Congo	W	3-0	Kinshasa	Fr			
16-03	Lesotho	D	2-2	Maseru	Fr			
30-03	Swaziland	D	1-1	Mbabane	CNq	Musasa 65		Katjimune NAM
8-06	Swaziland	W	2-0	Kinshasa	CNq	Mpiana 18, Musasa 71	60 000	Ravelotslam MRI
22-06	Libya	W	2-1	Kinshasa	CNq	Masudi 29, Mpiana 83		
5-07	Botswana	D	0-0	Gaborone	CNq			
20-08	Angola	W	2-0	Luanda	Fr	Massaro 46, Mbotale 52		
2004								
14-01	Egypt	D	2-2	Port Said	Fr	Dinzey 52, Mbala 70	10 000	Kamal EGY
25-01	Guinea	L	1-2	Tunis	CNr1	Masudi 30	3 000	Aboubacar CIV
28-01	Tunisia	L	0-3	Tunis	CNr1		20 000	Damon RSA
1-02	Rwanda	L	0-1	Bizerte	CNr1		700	Ndoye SEN
23-05	Angola	L	1-3	Kinshasa	Fr	Kalulika 30p	60 000	Ntambidila COD
6-06	Uganda	L	0-1	Kampala	WCq		45 000	Maillet SEY
20-06	Burkina Faso	W	3-2	Kinshasa	WCq	Mbajo 12, Mbala 75, Bageta 88p	75 000	Djaoupe TOG
3-07	Cape Verde Islands	D	1-1	Praia	WCq	Kaluyitu 1	3 800	Nahi CIV
18-08	Mali	L	0-3	Paris	Fr			Derrien FRA
5-09	South Africa	W	1-0	Kinshasa	WCq	Kabamba 86	85 000	Hicuburundi BDI
10-10	Ghana	D	0-0	Kumasi	WCq		30 000	Coulibaly MLI
2005								
8-02	Côte d'Ivoire	D	2-2	Rouen	Fr	Makendele 44, Nonda 92+	4 000	Duhamel FRA
27-03	Ghana	D	1-1	Kinshasa	WCq	Nonda 50	80 000	Sowe GAM
5-06	Uganda	W	4-0	Kinshasa	WCq	Nonda 2 2 69p, Ilongo 58, Matumdna 78	80 000	Daami TUN
18-06	Burkina Faso	L	0-2	Ouagadougou	WCq		25 000	Shelmani LBY
1-07	Botswana	D	0-0	Gaborone	Fr			

Fr = Friendly match • CN = CAF African Cup of Nations • WC = FIFA World Cup™ • q = qualifier • r1 = first round group

FIFA REFEREE LIST 2005

	Int'l	DoB
ANGOYAE Bongo	2004	16-02-1970
BUENKADILA Bisingu	1992	4-01-1962
MBILA Ieya	2004	11-05-1966
MUSUNGAYI Mpunga	2004	8-06-1969
NTAMBIDILA Wa	1989	18-08-1960
TSHIAMALA Kalala	1996	15-10-1960
UMBA Day	2001	30-10-1962

FIFA ASSISTANT REFEREE LIST 2005

	Int'l	DoB
KANYONGA Kazadi	1998	27-08-1960
LONGA Longa	1997	25-12-1964
LUKOJI Banza	2000	15-12-1963
MATALA Tala	2004	22-09-1965
MIBOTI Moise	2004	15-08-1974
NGALAMULUME Tshioka	2001	10-10-1967
NTUNKU Mukangala	2004	7-01-1969

CONGO DR COUNTRY INFORMATION

Capital	Kinshasa	Independence	1960 from Belgium	GDP per Capita	$700
Population	58 317 930	Status	Republic	GNP Ranking	120
Area km²	2 345 410	Language	French	Dialling code	+243
Population density	24 per km²	Literacy rate	65%	Internet code	.zr
% in urban areas	29%	Main religion	Christian 70%	GMT +/−	+1
Towns/Cities ('000)	Kinshasa 7 787; Lubumbashi 1 374; Kolwezi 910; Mbuji-Mayi 874; Kisangani 539; Kananga 463; Likasi 422; Boma 344; Tshikapa 267; Bukavu 225; Mwene-Ditu 189; Kikwit 186				
Neighbours (km)	Congo 2 410; Central African Republic 1 577; Sudan 628; Uganda 765; Rwanda 217; Burundi 233; Tanzania 459; Zambia 1 930; Angola 2 511; Atlantic Ocean 37				
Main stadia	Stade des Martyrs – Kinshasa 80 000; Stade Municipal – Lubumbashi 35 000; Stade Municipal – Kinshasa 20 000; Stade de Virunga – Goma 8 000				

CONGO DR NATIONAL TEAM RECORDS AND RECORD SEQUENCES

Records			Sequence records				
Victory	10-1	ZAM 1969	Wins	5	1973-1974	Clean sheets	4	Four times
Defeat	0-9	YUG 1974	Defeats	5	2004	Goals scored	38	1976-1985
Player Caps	n/a		Undefeated	12	2002-2004	Without goal	4	1990
Player Goals	n/a		Without win	7	1989, 1997	Goals against	13	1964-1966

CONGO DR 2004

LIGUE NATIONAL DE FOOTBALL
PRELIMINARY ROUND

Poule A - Kinshasa

	Pl	W	D	L	F	A	Pts			
TP Mazembe †	6	5	0	1	23	4	15	3-1	5-1	7-0
DC Motema Pembe †	6	4	1	1	13	8	13	2-1		2-0 2-2
OC Bukavu Dawa	6	1	1	4	5	14	4	0-3 1-3		3-1
TS Malekesa	6	0	2	4	4	19	2	0-4 1-3 0-0		

Poule B - Lubumbashi

	Pl	W	D	L	F	A	Pts			
FC St-Eloi Lupopo †	6	3	3	0	7	2	12	0-0 1-0		*
AS Vita Club †	6	2	4	0	6	2	10	0-0		1-1 2-0
SC Cilu Lukala	6	2	2	2	11	7	8	0-2 1-1		4-0
AC Capaco Sport	6	0	1	5	4	7	1	2-2 0-2 2-5		

25/07/2004 - 8/08/2004 • † Qualified for final stage • * Awarded 2-0 to Lupopo after Capaco walked off

CONGO DR 2004

LIGUE NATIONAL DE FOOTBALL
FINAL ROUND

	Pl	W	D	L	F	A	Pts			
DC Motema Pembe †	6	4	2	0	11	7	14	1-1	2-1 1-1
TP Mazembe †	6	3	2	1	12	8	11	2-3	4-2 3-1
FC St-Eloi Lupopo ‡	6	2	0	4	5	8	6	0-1 0-1	1-0
AS Vita Club	6	0	2	4	5	10	2	2-3 1-1 0-1

12/09/2004 - 21/11/2004 • † Qualified for the CAF Champions League • ‡ Qualified for the CAF Confederation Cup

CONGO DR 2004
KINSHASA LEAGUE (EPFKIN)

	Pl	W	D	L	F	A	Pts
AS Vita Club	30	19	7	4	52	20	58
DC Motema Pembe	30	17	6	7	50	28	54
AS Canon Bureaumeca	30	14	7	9	39	28	49
Olympic Club	30	13	9	8	42	25	48
SC Inter	30	12	12	6	34	19	48
AS Dragons	30	14	6	10	33	28	48
Bel 'Or FC	30	15	3	12	39	40	48
CS Style du Congo	30	12	11	7	30	24	47
FC Les Stars	30	12	9	9	35	26	45
FC Tornado	30	12	8	10	28	28	44
AC Sodigraf	30	13	4	13	38	38	43
FC Standard de Lemba	30	9	7	14	25	29	34
DC St François	30	10	4	16	34	40	34
AC Kintainers	30	9	6	15	23	37	33
AS Paulino	30	4	2	24	17	63	14
National SCC	30	3	3	24	18	64	12

17/03/2004 - 25/10/2004 • Vita Club deducted six points • Daring Club Motema Pembe deducted three points

CONGO DR 2004

COUPE DU CONGO
FINAL ROUND

Poule A

	Pl	W	D	L	F	A	Pts		
SC Cilu Lukala †	2	2	0	0	4	0	6	1-0	3-0
CS Makiso	2	1	0	1	1	1	3		1-0
TS Malekesa	2	0	0	2	0	4	0		

Poule B

	Pl	W	D	L	F	A	Pts		
AS St Luc Kananga †	2	1	1	0	1	0	4	1-0	0-0
OC Mbongo Sport	2	1	0	1	2	2	3		2-1
AS Dragons	2	0	1	1	1	2	1		

14/11/2004 - 21/11/2004 • † Qualified for the final • Tournament played in Boma

Final: **SC Cilu** 1-0 AS St Luc (scorer Mbungu [49p])

RECENT LEAGUE AND CUP RECORD

	Championship							Cup		
Year	Champions	Pts	Runners-up	Pts	Third	Pts		Winners	Score	Runners-up
1997	AS Vita Club	†	DC Motema Pembe					AS Dragons	2-1	AS Vita Club
1998	DC Motema Pembe	13	AS Vita Club	8	SM Sanga Balende	6		AS Dragons	1-0	AS Sucrière
1999	DC Motema Pembe		TP Mazembe		AS Vita Club			AS Dragons	3-2	AS Paulino
2000	TP Mazembe	16	SM Sanga Balende	8	AS Vita Club	5		TP Mazembe	2-0	AS St-Luc Kananga
2001	TP Mazembe	†	FC St-Eloi Lupopo					AS Vita Club	3-0	AS Veti Matadi
2002	FC St-Eloi Lupopo	25	TP Mazembe	23	AS Vita Club	18		US Kenya	2-1	SM Sanga Balende
2003	AS Vita Club	27	SC Cilu	18	FC St-Eloi Lupopo	17		DC Motema Pembe	2-0	TP Mazembe
2004	DC Motema Pembe	14	TP Mazembe	11	FC St-Eloi Lupopo	6		CS Cilu Lukala	1-0	AS St Luc Kananga

† Knock-out format • Toute Puissant Mazembe beat FC Saint-Eloi Lupopo 1-1 3-1 in the 2001 final

COK – COOK ISLANDS

NATIONAL TEAM RECORD
JULY 1ST 2002 TO JUNE 30TH 2005

PL	W	D	L	F	A	%
5	0	1	4	1	17	10

FIFA/COCA-COLA WORLD RANKING

1993	1994	1995	1996	1997	1998	1999	2000	2001	2002	2003	2004	High		Low	
-	-	-	188	192	173	182	170	179	182	190	190	169	07/00	192	05/04

2004-2005											
08/04	09/04	10/04	11/04	12/04	01/05	02/05	03/05	04/05	05/05	06/05	07/05
190	190	190	190	190	191	191	191	192	192	192	193

With a population of just 21,000 spread out over 15 islands, the Cook Islands are one of the true minnows of world football. The majority live on the main island of Rarotonga with rugby union and rugby league the most popular sports. Football has, however, managed to establish a foothold and in 2005 a new centre for football was completed with an academy, training pitches and offices for the national association with the US$643,000 cost met by the Goal Programme and the Financial Assistance Programme. High on the list of priorities will be women's football which is increasingly popular in the country and now that Australia is no longer a member of Oceania,

INTERNATIONAL HONOURS
None

qualification for the FIFA Women's World Cup has opened up considerably. It may be a while before the Cook Islands can be considered serious contenders in that tournament or in any other tournament in Oceania but the various national teams are no longer the pushover they once were. The local Championship is fiercely contested with winners Nikao Sokattack entering the Oceania Champions Cup. In a preliminary round they were drawn against eventual finalists AS Magenta and lost 1-9 on aggregate but with the tournament to be played every year, as a preliminary for the FIFA Club World Championship, the hope is that the standard of club football will improve.

THE FIFA BIG COUNT OF 2000

	Male	Female		Male	Female
Registered players	700	250	Referees	60	20
Non registered players	150	50	Officials	70	0
Youth players	900	300	Total involved	2 500	
Total players	2 350		Number of clubs	35	
Professional players	0	0	Number of teams	113	

Cook Islands Football Association (CIFA)
Matavora Main Road, PO Box 29, Tupapa, Rarotonga, Cook Islands
Tel +682 28980   Fax +682 28981
cifa@cisoccer.org.ck   www.none
President: HARMON Lee   General Secretary: ELIKANA Tingika
Vice-President: PARKER Allen   Treasurer: NUMANGA Jake   Media Officer: TONGA Vainga
Men's Coach: JERKS Tim   Women's Coach: TILLOTSON Maurice
CIFA formed: 1971   OFC: 1994   FIFA: 1994
Colours: Green with white sleeves, Green, White

GAMES PLAYED BY COOK ISLANDS IN THE 2006 FIFA WORLD CUP™ CYCLE

2002	Opponents		Score	Venue	Comp	Scorers	Att	Referee
No international matches played in 2002								
2003								
No international matches played in 2003								
2004								
5-05	Samoa	D	0-0	Auckland	Fr			
10-05	Tahiti	L	0-2	Honiara	WCq		12 000	Singh FIJ
12-05	Solomon Islands	L	0-5	Honiara	WCq		14 000	Fred VAN
15-05	Tonga	L	1-2	Honiara	WCq	Pareanga 59	15 000	Sosongan PNG
17-05	New Caledonia	L	0-8	Honiara	WCq		400	Singh FIJ
2005								
No international matches played in 2005 before August								

Fr = Friendly match • WC = FIFA World Cup™ • q = qualifier

COOK ISLANDS NATIONAL TEAM RECORDS AND RECORD SEQUENCES

Records			Sequence records			
Victory	3-0	ASA 2000	Wins	2	1998, 2000	Clean sheets	1	
Defeat	0-30	TAH 1971	Defeats	6	2000-2001	Goals scored	4	1996-1998
Player Caps	n/a		Undefeated	3	1998	Without goal	5	2001-2004
Player Goals	n/a		Without win	11	2000-	Goals against	16	1971-2000

FIFA REFEREE LIST 2005

	Int'l	DoB
LYNCH Paul	2002	24-07-1964

FIFA ASSISTANT REFEREE LIST 2005

	Int'l	DoB
GOODWIN Teariki	1998	6-12-1964
MOUAURI Michael	1999	5-08-1967
PAREANGA John		2-10-1980

RECENT LEAGUE AND CUP RECORD

	Championship	Cup		
Year	Champions	Winners	Score	Runners-up
1996	Avatiu FC	Avatiu FC		
1997	Avatiu FC	Avatiu FC		
1998	No Tournament	Teau-o-Tonga		
1999	Tupapa FC	Tupapa FC		
2000	Avatiu FC	Avatiu FC	3-1	Tupapa FC
2001	Nikao Sokattacck	Avatiu FC	3-1	Nikao Sokattack
2002	Tupapa FC	Tupapa FC	5-1	Avatiu FC
2003	Tupapa FC	Nikao Sokattack	3-2	Tupapa FC
2004	Tupapa FC	Nikao Sokattack	3-1	Tupapa FC
2005	Nikao Sokattack	Tupapa FC	3-3 3-1p	Nikao Sokattack

COOK ISLANDS COUNTRY INFORMATION

Capital	Avarua	Independence	Self-governing in free association with New Zealand	GDP per Capita	$5 000
Population	21 200	Status		GNP Ranking	n/a
Area km²	240	Language	English, Maori	Dialling code	+682
Population density	88 per km²	Literacy rate	95%	Internet code	.ck
% in urban areas	n/a	Main religion	Christian	GMT +/−	-10
Towns/Cities ('000)	Avarua 13; Mangaia; Amuri; Omoka; Atiu; Mauke				
Neighbours (km)	South Pacific Ocean 120				
Main stadia	National Stadium – Avarua 3 000				

COL – COLOMBIA

NATIONAL TEAM RECORD
JULY 1ST 2002 TO JUNE 30TH 2005

PL	W	D	L	F	A	%
43	14	15	14	45	38	50

FIFA/COCA-COLA WORLD RANKING

1993	1994	1995	1996	1997	1998	1999	2000	2001	2002	2003	2004	High		Low	
21	17	15	4	10	34	25	15	5	37	39	26	4	12/96	41	03/04

2004-2005											
08/04	09/04	10/04	11/04	12/04	01/05	02/05	03/05	04/05	05/05	06/05	07/05
28	28	28	28	26	26	26	26	27	28	25	25

With a terrible start to the 2006 FIFA World Cup™ qualifiers the Colombian national team have made a late bid to qualify for the finals, something that did not look even remotely on the cards in June 2004 when after six games they had just four points. Having missed out on the 2002 finals, failure to qualify for Germany would be a major disaster. Ever since the early 1990s Colombia have been touted as the team of the future in South America, something backed up by their recent record in youth tournaments, but that promise has yet to be realised on a consistent basis. With the possibility of five South American nations qualifying for the FIFA World Cup™ finals, Colombian

INTERNATIONAL HONOURS
Qualified for the FIFA World Cup™ finals 1962 1990 1994 1998 **Copa América** 2001 **Juventud de América** 1987 2005 **South America U-17** 1993
Copa Toyota Libertadores Atlético Nacional Medellin 1989 Once Caldas 2004

fans now expect their team to be amongst that number. Expectations at club level were also raised by the unexpected success of Once Caldas in winning the Copa Libertadores in 2004, though the spectre of the drug cartels still hangs over the domestic game. Atlético Nacional reached the final of both the Apertura and Clausura, but lost both on penalties – to city rivals Independiente and Atlético Junior from Barranquilla, neither of whom made it beyond the first knock-out stage of the 2005 Copa Libertadores.

THE FIFA BIG COUNT OF 2000

	Male	Female		Male	Female
Registered players	80 000	1 000	Referees	2 000	0
Non registered players	1 300 000	10 000	Officials	12 000	400
Youth players	150 000	1 000	Total involved	1 556 400	
Total players	1 542 000		Number of clubs	2 500	
Professional players	2 500	0	Number of teams	7 000	

Federación Colombiana de Fútbol (COLFUTBOL)
Avenida 32, No. 16-22 Piso 4°, Apdo Aéreo 17602, Bogotá, Colombia
Tel +57 1 2889838   Fax +57 1 2889559
info@colfutbol.org   www.colfutbol.org
President: ASTUDILLO Oscar Dr   General Secretary: SIERRA Celina
Vice-President: CAMARGO Gabriel   Treasurer: MORENO Gustavo   Media Officer: ROSAS Victor
Men's Coach: RUEDA Reinaldo   Women's Coach: GUERRERO Myriam
COLFUTBOL formed: 1924   CONMEBOL: 1940   FIFA: 1936
Colours: Yellow, Blue, Red

GAMES PLAYED BY COLOMBIA IN THE 2006 FIFA WORLD CUP™ CYCLE

2002 Opponents	Score	Venue	Comp	Scorers	Att	Referee
20-11 Honduras	L 0-1	San Pedro Sula	Fr		25 000	Sabillon HON
2003						
12-02 Mexico	D 0-0	Phoenix	Fr		28 764	Valenzuela USA
27-03 Korea Republic	D 0-0	Busan	Fr		56 000	Katayama JPN
30-04 Honduras	D 0-0	Miami	Fr		10 441	Kennedy USA
8-06 Ecuador	D 0-0	Madrid	Fr		12 000	Perez ESP
18-06 France	L 0-1	Lyon	CCr1		38 541	Batista POR
20-06 New Zealand	W 3-1	Lyon	CCr1	Lopez [58], Yepes [75], Hernandez [85]	22 811	Batres GUA
22-06 Japan	W 1-0	Saint-Etienne	CCr1	Hernandez [68]	24 541	Larrionda URU
26-06 Cameroon	L 0-1	Lyon	CCsf		12 352	Merk GER
28-06 Turkey	L 1-2	Saint-Etienne	CC3p	Hernandez [63]	18 237	Shield AUS
13-07 Jamaica	W 1-0	Miami	GCr1	Patino [42]	15 423	Stott USA
17-07 Guatemala	D 1-1	Miami	GCr1	Molina [79]	13 000	Porras CRC
19-07 Brazil	L 0-2	Miami	GCqf		23 425	Stott USA
20-08 Slovakia	D 0-0	New Jersey	Fr		16 000	Stott USA
7-09 Brazil	L 1-2	Barranquilla	WCq	Angel [38]	47 600	Elizondo ARG
10-09 Bolivia	L 0-4	La Paz	WCq		23 200	Oliveira BRA
15-11 Venezuela	L 0-1	Barranquilla	WCq		20 000	Chandia CHI
19-11 Argentina	D 1-1	Barranquilla	WCq	Angel [47]	19 034	Simon BRA
2004						
18-02 Honduras	D 1-1	Tegucigalpa	Fr	Herrera [58]	8 000	Alfaro SLV
31-03 Peru	W 2-0	Lima	WCq	Grisales [30], Oviedo [42]	29 325	Rezende BRA
28-04 El Salvador	W 2-0	Washington	Fr	Rey [52], Oviedo [61]	21 000	Vaughan USA
2-06 Ecuador	L 1-2	Quito	WCq	Oviedo [57]	31 484	Baldassi ARG
6-06 Uruguay	W 5-0	Barranquilla	WCq	Pacheco 2 [17 31], Moreno [20], Restrepo [81], Herrera [86]	7 000	Carlos PAR
27-06 Argentina	W 2-0	Miami	Fr	Moreno [21], Herrera [75]	32 415	Terry USA
6-07 Venezuela	W 1-0	Lima	CAr1	Moreno [22p]	45 000	Rezende BRA
9-07 Bolivia	W 1-0	Lima	CAr1	Perea [90]	35 000	Ramos ECU
12-07 Peru	D 2-2	Trujillo	CAr1	Congo [34], Aguilar [52]	25 000	Rodriguez MEX
17-07 Costa Rica	W 2-0	Trujillo	CAqf	Aguilar [41], Moreno [45p]	18 000	Mendez URU
20-07 Argentina	L 0-3	Lima	CAsf		22 000	Hidalgo PER
24-07 Uruguay	L 1-2	Cusco	CA3p	Herrera [70]	35 000	Ortube BOL
5-09 Chile	D 0-0	Santiago	WCq		62 523	Souza BRA
9-10 Paraguay	D 1-1	Barranquilla	WCq	Grisales [17]	25 000	Elizondo ARG
13-10 Brazil	D 0-0	Maceio	WCq		20 000	Larrionda ARG
17-11 Bolivia	W 1-0	Barranquilla	WCq	Yepes [18]	25 000	Torres PAR
2005						
15-01 Korea Republic	W 2-1	Los Angeles	Fr	Castillo [41p], Perea [75]	20 000	
17-01 Guatemala	D 1-1	Los Angeles	Fr	Hurtado [80]	15 000	Vaughn USA
23-02 Mexico	D 1-1	Culiacan	Fr	Perea [58]	10 000	Gasso MEX
9-03 USA	L 0-3	Fullerton	Fr		7 086	Moreno MEX
26-03 Venezuela	D 0-0	Maracaibo	WCq		18 000	Simon BRA
30-03 Argentina	L 0-1	Buenos Aires	WCq		40 000	Amarilla PAR
31-05 England	L 2-3	New Jersey	Fr	Yepes [45], Ramirez.A [78]	58 000	Hall USA
4-06 Peru	W 5-0	Barranquilla	WCq	Rey [29], Soto [55], Angel [58], Restrepo [75], Perea [78]	15 000	Torres PAR
8-06 Ecuador	W 3-0	Barranquilla	WCq	Moreno 2 [5 9], Arzuaga [70]	20 402	Simon BRA
6-07 Panama	L 0-1	Miami	GCr1		10 311	Batres GUA
10-07 Honduras	L 1-2	Miami	GCr1	Moreno [30p]	17 292	Hall USA
12-07 Trinidad and Tobago	W 2-0	Miami	GCr1	Aguilar [77], Hurtado [79]	11 000	Rodriguez MEX
17-07 Mexico	W 2-1	Houston	GCqf	Castrillón [58], Aguilar [74]	60 050	Sibrian SLV
21-07 Panama	L 2-3	New Jersey	GCsf	Patiño 2 [62 88]	41 721	Sibrian SLV

Fr = Friendly match • CC = FIFA Confederations Cup • GC = CONCACAF Gold Cup • CA = Copa América • WC = FIFA World Cup™
q = qualifier • r1 = first round group • qf = quarter-final • sf = semi-final • 3p = third place play-off

NATIONAL CAPS

	Caps
VALDERRAMA Carlos	111
ALVAREZ Leonel	101
RINCÓN Freddy	84
PEREA Luis	78
CÓRDOBA Oscar	71
HIGUITA René	69
IGUARÁN Arnoldo	68
MENDOZA Alexis	68
ARISTIZÁBAL Victor	66
HERRERA Luis	62

NATIONAL GOALS

	Goals
IGUARÁN Arnoldo	25
ASPRILLA Faustino	20
RINCÓN Freddy	17
ARISTIZÁBAL Victor	15
VALENCIA José	14
VALENCIANO Iván	13
ORTIZ Willington	13
DE AVILA Anthony	13
VALDERRAMA Carlos	11
HERRERA Hernán	9

NATIONAL COACH

	Years
GARCIA Luis	1991
ORTIZ Humberto	1992
MATURANA Francisco	1993-'94
DARÍO GÓMEZ Hernán	1995-'98
ALVAREZ Javier	1999
GARCIA Luis	2000-'01
MATURANA Francisco	2001
RUEDA Reynaldo	2002
MATURANA Francisco	2002-'03
RUEDA Reynaldo	2004-

FIFA REFEREE LIST 2005

	Int'l	DoB
BETANCUR Carlos Alberto	2005	20-03-1964
DUARTE Albert	2004	13-07-1969
DUQUE Alberto	1996	15-11-1969
HOYOS Jorge	2000	13-02-1971
LOPEZ Carlos	2000	16-02-1963
PANESO Fernando	1994	8-08-1962
RUIZ Oscar	1995	1-11-1969

FIFA ASSISTANT REFEREE LIST 2005

	Int'l	DoB
BEDOYA Juan Carlos	2004	4-04-1964
BOTERO Eduardo	1994	3-05-1961
NAVIA Jose	2004	5-12-1963
PERDOMO Dember	1993	10-04-1960
ROMAN Jose	2004	2-08-1963
SIERRA Carlos	2000	11-04-1960
ZAPATA Jovani de Jesus	2004	13-10-1968

CLUB DIRECTORY

Club	Town/City	Stadium	Phone	www.	Champs	CL
América	Cali	Pascual Guerrero 45 000	+57 2 5130417	america.com.co	12	0
Atlético Bucaramanga	Bucaramanga	Alfonso Lopez 33 000	+57 7 6331415		0	0
Deportivo Cali	Cali	Pascual Guerrero 45 000	+57 92 6670976	deporcali.com	7	0
Chicó	Bogotá	Alfonso Lopez 12 000	+57 1 4835435	chicofc.com	0	0
Envigado	Envigado	Polideportivo Sur 12 000	+57 94 3319742	envigadofutbolclub.com	0	0
Atlético Huila	Neiva	Guillermo Alcid 15 000	+57 8 8756439	elatleticohuila.com	0	0
Atlético Junior	Barranquilla	Metropolitano 58 000	+57 5 3562752		5	0
Independiente Medellin	Medellin	Atanasio Girardot 52 700	+57 94 2603355	dim.com.co	4	0
Millonarios	Bogota	El Campin 48 600	+57 1 3477080	millonarios.com.co	13	0
Atlético Nacional	Medellin	Atanasio Girardot 52 700	+57 94 3702700	atlnacional.com.co	7	1
Once Caldas	Manizales	Palogrande 33 000	+57 96 8813482	oncecaldas.com.co	2	1
Deportivo Pasto	Pasto	Libertad 14 000	+57 92 7204122	deporpasto.com	0	0
Deportivo Pereira	Pereira	Olimpico 34 000	+57 6 3294441	clubdeportivopereira.com	0	0
Deportes Quindio	Armenia	Centenario 29,000	+57 6 7476268		1	0
Independiente Santa Fé	Bogotá	El Campin 48,600	+57 1 5446670	independientesantafe.com	6	0
Deportes Tolima	Ibagué	Manuel Toro 19,000	+57 8 2644954	deportestolima.com	1	0
Corporación Tuluá	Tuluá	12 de Octubre 12,000	+57 92 2252902	cortulua.com.co	0	0
Unión Magdalena	Santa Marta	Eduardo Santos 23,000	+57 5 4214591		1	0

COLOMBIA COUNTRY INFORMATION

Capital	Bogotá	Independence	1810 from Spain	GDP per Capita	$6 300
Population	42 310 775	Status	Republic	GNP Ranking	40
Area km²	1 138 910	Language	Spanish	Dialling code	+57
Population density	37 per km²	Literacy rate	91%	Internet code	.co
% in urban areas	73%	Main religion	Christian	GMT + / –	-5

Towns/Cities ('000)	Bogotá 7 102; Cali 2 392; Medellin 2 000; Barranquilla 1 380; Cartagena 952; Cúcuta 721; Bucaramanga 571; Pereira 440; Santa Marta 431; Ibagué 421; Pasto 382; Manizales 357
Neighbours (km)	Venezuela 2 050; Brazil 1 643; Peru 1 496; Ecuador 590; Panama 225; North Pacific Ocean 1 448; Caribbean Sea 1 760
Main stadia	Metropolitano – Barranquilla 58 000; Atanasio Giradot – Medellin 52 700; El Campin – Bogotá 48 600; Pascual Guerrero – Cali 45 000; Centenario – Armenia 29 000

COLOMBIA NATIONAL TEAM RECORDS AND RECORD SEQUENCES

Records			Sequence records					
Victory	5-0	ARG 1993, URU 2004	Wins	7	1988-1989	Clean sheets	6	2001
Defeat	0-9	BRA 1957	Defeats	7	1947-1949	Goals scored	15	1995-1997
Player Caps	111	VALDERRAMA Carlos	Undefeated	27	1992-1994	Without goal	6	2002-2003
Player Goals	25	IGUARAN Arnoldo	Without win	15	1947-1957	Goals against	14	1938-46, 1961-63

COLOMBIA 2004 TORNEO APERTURA

	Pl	W	D	L	F	A	Pts
América Cali †	18	12	1	5	30	17	37
Deportivo Cali †	18	10	4	4	23	15	34
Atlético Nacional †	18	10	3	5	30	23	33
Once Caldas †	18	9	4	5	23	14	31
Atlético Junior †	18	8	6	4	26	16	30
Indep. Medellín †	18	8	5	5	20	19	29
Deportivo Pasto †	18	8	3	7	18	19	27
Chicó FC †	18	7	6	5	25	24	27
Deportes Pereira	18	7	5	6	21	18	26
Millonarios	18	7	5	6	23	22	26
Deportes Tolima	18	6	8	4	20	17	26
Atlético Bucaramanga	18	5	6	7	22	25	21
Indep. Santa Fé	18	4	8	6	18	22	20
Corporación Tuluá	18	5	4	9	27	32	19
Atlético Huila	18	4	4	10	19	29	16
Deportes Quindío	18	3	6	9	11	23	15
Envigado	18	2	8	8	19	26	14
Unión Magdalena	18	2	4	12	15	29	10

7/02/2004 - 16/05/2004 • † Qualified for the second stage

COLOMBIA 2004 TORNEO APERTURA SECOND STAGE

Group A	Pl	W	D	L	F	A	Pts			
Atlético Nacional †	6	3	1	2	12	8	10		1-2 4-3 1-1
Deportivo Pasto	6	3	1	2	9	6	10	2-1	4-0 0-1
América Cali	6	2	1	3	7	10	7	0-1 2-0	1-1
Atlético Junior	6	1	3	2	4	8	6	0-4 1-1 0-1	

Group B	Pl	W	D	L	F	A	Pts			
Indep. Medellín †	6	3	1	2	15	8	10		4-0 3-3 1-2
Once Caldas	6	3	0	3	7	11	9	0-2	2-0 1-0
Deportivo Cali	6	2	2	2	9	11	8	0-3 3-1	2-2
Chicó FC	6	2	1	3	9	10	7	3-2 2-3 0-1	

19/05/2004 - 20/06/2004 • † Qualified for the final

COLOMBIA 2004 TORNEO APERTURA FINAL

Home team first leg	Score	Home team second leg
Independiente Medellin	2-1 0-0	Atlético Nacional

COLOMBIA 2004 TORNEO CLAUSURA

	Pl	W	D	L	F	A	Pts
América Cali †	18	13	3	2	32	14	42
Atlético Bucaramanga†	18	10	4	4	23	16	34
Deportes Tolima †	18	10	3	5	27	20	33
Deportivo Cali †	18	9	3	6	24	17	30
Atlético Nacional †	18	9	3	6	24	18	30
Indep. Medellín †	18	8	5	5	24	13	29
Once Caldas †	18	8	4	6	30	19	28
Atlético Junior †	18	7	7	4	26	21	28
Envigado	18	7	5	6	26	20	26
Indep. Santa Fé	18	7	4	7	25	24	25
Deportes Quindío	18	7	4	7	21	29	25
Corporación Tuluá	18	6	4	8	14	19	22
Atlético Huila	18	5	3	10	21	25	18
Chicó FC	18	4	6	8	15	24	18
Unión Magdalena	18	5	2	11	11	27	17
Deportivo Pasto	18	3	8	7	10	16	17
Millonarios	18	3	4	11	14	29	13
Deportes Pereira	18	3	4	11	9	25	13

1/08/2004 - 7/11/2004 • † Qualified for the second stage

COLOMBIA 2004 TORNEO CLAUSURA SECOND STAGE

Group A	Pl	W	D	L	F	A	Pts			
Atlético Nacional †	6	3	2	1	6	3	11		0-0 2-0 0-0
América Cali	6	2	2	2	10	8	8	2-1	2-3 1-2
Deportes Tolima	6	2	1	3	9	9	7	1-2 1-1	4-1
Once Caldas	6	2	1	3	5	10	7	0-1 1-4 1-0	

Group B	Pl	W	D	L	F	A	Pts			
Atlético Junior †	6	4	1	1	11	5	13		3-0 2-0 2-1
Deportivo Cali	6	2	2	2	6	6	8	1-1	1-1 2-0
Indep. Medellín	6	2	2	2	9	10	8	3-2 0-2	5-3
Atlético Bucaramanga	6	1	1	4	5	10	4	0-1 1-0 0-0	

21/11/2004 - 12/11/2004 • † Qualified for the final

COLOMBIA 2004 TORNEO CLAUSURA FINAL

Home team first leg	Score	Home team second leg
Atlético Junior	3-0 2-5 5-4p	Atlético Nacional

COLOMBIA 2004
PRIMERA B (2) FIRST ROUND

	Pl	W	D	L	F	A	Pts
Expreso Rojo †	34	18	8	8	49	24	62
Real Cartagena †	34	18	8	8	59	39	62
Centauros Villavicencio†	34	16	10	8	51	32	58
Cúcuta Deportivo †	34	16	9	9	47	32	57
Deportivo Antioquía †	34	15	11	8	48	36	56
Alianza Petrolera †	34	16	6	12	57	40	54
Patriotas †	34	14	12	8	49	25	54
Valledupar †	34	13	12	9	39	34	51
Bajo Cauca	34	14	6	14	42	41	48
Los Pumas Casanare	34	13	8	13	40	32	47
CD La Equidad	34	12	6	16	46	49	42
Real Sincelejo	34	11	8	15	37	60	41
Girardot	34	10	10	14	39	52	40
Johann	34	9	10	15	36	49	37
Bogotá	34	9	8	17	28	47	35
Bello	34	9	8	17	30	60	35
Deportivo Rionegro	34	8	7	19	35	56	31
Chía	34	5	13	16	22	46	28

† Qualified for the second stage

COLOMBIA 2004
PRIMERA B SECOND STAGE

Group A	Pl	W	D	L	F	A	Pts			
Deportivo Antioquía †	6	2	3	1	9	9	9		2-1	2-1 2-2
Centauros Villavicencio	6	2	2	2	6	5	8	0-0		2-0 2-1
Patriotas	6	2	1	1	7	9	7	3-1 1-0		1-1
Expreso Rojo	6	1	4	1	10	9	7	2-2 1-1 3-1		

Group B	Pl	W	D	L	F	A	Pts			
Real Cartagena †	6	3	1	2	9	4	10		3-0	1-0 0-0
Cúcuta Deportivo	6	3	1	2	9	7	10	3-0		3-1 1-0
Alianza Petrolera	6	2	1	3	6	9	7	1-0 1-1		3-2
Valledupar	6	2	1	3	6	10	7	0-5 2-1 2-0		

† Qualified for the final

COLOMBIA 2004
PRIMERA B FINAL

Home team first leg	Score	Home team second leg
Deportivo Antioquía	1-0 0-3	**Real Cartagena**

Real Cartagena promoted to replace Corporación Tuluá

COLOMBIA 2004 RELEGATION TABLE AND RESULTS

PRIMERA A

	2002		2003		2004			Cali	América	Nacional	Caldas	Medellín	Bucaramanga	Pasto	Tolima	Junior	Santa Fé	Pereira	Magdalena	Millonarios	Quindío	Huila	Envigado	Chicó	Tuluá
	Pl	Pts	Pl	Pts	Pl	Av																				
Deportivo Cali	44	86	36	62	36	64	1.828	3-1 0-1	2-0	2-0	3-1	2-1	2-0	1-0	0-0	1-0	2-0	1-0	2-0	3-0	2-1	1-0	4-2	0-0
América Cali	44	67	36	53	36	79	1.716	3-1 3-0		4-1	1-0	0-0	2-1	0-0	3-3	4-1	1-0	2-1	3-0	1-0	4-0	2-1	2-1	3-1	3-2
Atlético Nacional	44	70	36	52	36	63	1.595	3-1	0-1		2-0	0-2 2-1	2-1	1-0	2-0	2-1	0-1	2-0	1-1	2-2	4-0	1-1	2-4	0-2	2-1
Once Caldas	44	64	36	53	36	59	1.517	2-0	3-0	2-3		0-0	3-1	1-0	2-2	1-2	1-1	0-1 1-2	2-0	4-0	6-1	4-0	2-2	0-0	2-1
Indep. Medellín	44	56	36	53	36	58	1.440	2-0	1-0	0-2 0-1	2-0		1-1	3-1	0-1	2-2	1-2	1-0	5-1	1-0	3-0	1-0	2-2	1-0	3-0
Atlético Bucaramanga	44	66	36	42	36	55	1.405	2-1	0-1	1-0	0-2	0-0		1-0	3-1	0-1	4-0	1-0	1-2	1-0	3-1	2-2	2-1 0-0	3-3
Deportivo Pasto	44	70	36	47	36	44	1.388	0-1	1-0	2-0	2-1	1-2	1-1		1-0	1-1	1-0	2-0	0-0	2-1	3-1	1-1	0-0	0-1
Deportes Tolima	44	51	36	49	36	59	1.371	2-1	2-1	2-2	1-0	0-0	1-1	0-0		1-1	2-1	0-1	1-0	2-0	0-2 3-2	2-1	0-0	0-1
Atlético Junior	44	47	36	52	36	58	1.353	0-3	2-2	2-0	1-4	5-0	1-1	2-0	1-2		2-0	0-0	2-1 3-0	2-1	2-3	1-2	4-0	0-2
Indep. Santa Fé	44	70	36	42	36	45	1.353	0-0	0-2	1-1	2-2	1-1	3-1	1-1	1-0	2-0		2-1 1-1	4-1	2-3	2-1	1-2	1-2	1-1
Deportes Pereira	44	58	36	51	36	39	1.276	0-1	1-0	1-4	1-1 0-2	1-1	1-2	2-0	2-2	0-0	2-1		4-1	1-0	0-2	1-0	0-0	1-0	0-1	3-1
Unión Magdalena	44	66	36	54	36	27	1.267	1-1	3-2	2-3	1-2	0-1	0-0	0-0 0-2	0-1	1-0		0-1	0-2	2-3	1-0
Millonarios	44	46	36	57	36	39	1.224	2-0	0-2	1-1	0-1	0-3	1-2	5-3	2-1	0-1	1-1 1-1	2-1	1-0		0-0	3-0	3-0	2-2	2-0
Deportes Quindío	44	58	36	38	36	40	1.172	1-1	0-2	1-2	0-0	1-2	1-0	1-0	1-1	1-0	3-0	1-1	2-1		2-0	1-1 1-1	1-2	1-0
Atlético Huila	44	47	36	50	36	34	1.129	2-2	0-1	0-3	0-1	3-1	0-1	2-1 1-4	1-1	1-3	0-2	3-0	1-1	2-0		1-1	0-1	1-0
Envigado	44	51	36	40	36	40	1.129	1-1	0-1	2-1	0-1	3-1	0-1	0-0	1-2	2-2	1-1	3-1	4-0	1-1	1-2 3-0	2-1		1-0	4-3
Chicó FC	44	49	36	32	36	45	1.086	1-2	1-2	1-2	1-0	0-0	3-1 0-2	1-1	1-1	2-2	1-1	1-0	2-4	2-2	2-1	1-0		1-2
Corporación Tuluá	44	49	36	32	36	41	1.051	1-0	1-2	3-2	1-1	3-1	1-2	1-0 0-0	1-3	1-2	3-1	1-1	3-1	1-0	1-1	3-1	1-0	1-0	0-3	

Relegation is based on average points over three seasons • Corporación Tuluá relegated • Match in bold awarded 3-0 after a 1-1 draw • Results in shaded boxes were played in the Apertura • Local rivals play each other four times in the regular season • The Apertura result is listed above the Clausura result in this instance

RECENT LEAGUE AND CUP RECORD

	Championship Play-off/Apertura from 2002				Clausura		
Year	Champions	Score	Runners-up		Winners	Score	Runners-up
1997	América Cali	1-0 2-0	Atlético Bucaramanga				
1998	Deportivo Cali	4-0 0-0	Once Caldas				
1999	Atlético Nacional	1-1 0-0 4-2p	América Cali				
2000	América Cali	‡	Atlético Junior				
2001	América Cali	1-0 2-0	Independiente Medellín				
2002	América Cali	2-1 1-0	Independiente Medellín		Independiente Medellín	2-0 1-1	Deportivo Pasto
2003	Once Caldas	0-0 1-0	Atlético Junior		Deportes Tolima	2-0 1-3 4-2p	Deportivo Cali
2004	Independiente Medellín	2-1 0-0	Atlético Nacional		Atlético Junior	3-0 2-5 5-4p	Atlético Nacional

Colombia adopted the format of two Championships per year in 2002 • ‡ Final tournament played as a league

CPV – CAPE VERDE ISLANDS

NATIONAL TEAM RECORD
JULY 1ST 2002 TO JUNE 30TH 2005

PL	W	D	L	F	A	%
19	7	3	9	22	23	44.7

FIFA/COCA-COLA WORLD RANKING

1993	1994	1995	1996	1997	1998	1999	2000	2001	2002	2003	2004	High	Low
147	161	144	155	171	167	177	156	159	154	143	129	**119** 05/05	**182** 04/00

2004-2005											
08/04	09/04	10/04	11/04	12/04	01/05	02/05	03/05	04/05	05/05	06/05	07/05
133	133	131	125	129	129	129	129	121	119	119	123

The Cape Verde Islands national team is currently enjoying its most successful period. With a highest position of 119 in the FIFA/Coca-Cola World Ranking, the national team surpassed all expectations in their 2006 FIFA World Cup™ qualifying group when at one point they threatened to lead the table ahead of established nations including Ghana and South Africa. A former Portuguese colony, Cape Verde are coached by former Portuguese international, Carlos Alhinho, who has worked wonders with a relatively inexperienced group of players putting the country on the football map after a number of barren years. The regional Amilcar Cabral tournament used to provide most of

INTERNATIONAL HONOURS
Copa Amilcar Cabral 2000

the side's international football before the country entered mainstream competitions. Former coach Oscar Duarte tried to encourage eligible players living abroad to commit to the country's cause, but it is under Alhinho that this process has moved on with the carrot of a Nations Cup place dangling in front of the team even if qualifying for Germany 2006 has been a step too far. Nine of the ten islands that make up the country run leagues, the winners of which take part in the Campeonato Nacional. The 2005 championship was won by Derby from Mindelo on São Vicente island who beat Sporting da Praia from the capital 5-4 on aggreagte.

THE FIFA BIG COUNT OF 2000

	Male	Female		Male	Female
Registered players	6 350	0	Referees	191	2
Non registered players	5 200	0	Officials	550	0
Youth players	2 810	0	Total involved	15 103	
Total players	14 360		Number of clubs	89	
Professional players	600	0	Number of teams	154	

Federação Caboverdiana de Futebol (FCF)
Praia Cabo Verde, FCF CX, Case postale 234, Praia, Cape Verde Islands
Tel +238 2 611362   Fax +238 2 611362
fcf@cvtelecom.cv   www.none
President: SEMEDO Mario   General Secretary: REZENDE Jose João
Vice-President: ALMEIDA Fernando   Treasurer: REZENDE Jose João   Media Officer: None
Men's Coach: ALHINHO Alexandre   Women's Coach: none
FCF formed: 1982   CAF: 1986   FIFA: 1986
Colours: Blue, Blue, Blue or White, White, Red

GAMES PLAYED BY CAPE VERDE ISLANDS IN THE 2006 FIFA WORLD CUP™ CYCLE

2002	Opponents	Score		Venue	Comp	Scorers	Att	Referee
6-09	Mauritania	W	2-0	Nouakchott	CNq	Zelilo [45], Duarte [60]		Sillah GAM
13-10	Kenya	L	0-1	Praia	CNq			Aboubacar CIV
20-11	Luxembourg	D	0-0	Hesperange	Fr		2 750	Leduntu FRA
2003								
29-03	Togo	W	2-1	Praia	CNq	Duarte [68], Morais [80]		Nandigna GNB
31-05	Senegal	L	1-2	Dakar	Fr	Morais [40]	20 000	Carlos Santos GNB
8-06	Togo	L	2-5	Lome	CNq	Aguiar [6], Morais [26]		Pare BFA
21-06	Mauritania *	W	3-0	Praia	CNq	Zelito [65], Morais 2 [76p 82]		
5-07	Kenya	L	0-1	Nairobi	CNq		35 000	
12-10	Swaziland	D	1-1	Mbabane	WCq	Morais [55]	5 000	Teshome ERI
16-11	Swaziland	W	3-0	Praia	WCq	Semedo 2 [51 65], Morais [90]	6 000	Aboubacar CIV
2004								
5-06	South Africa	L	1-2	Bloemfontein	WCq	Martins [73]	30 000	Tessema ETH
13-06	Senegal	L	1-3	Praia	Fr	Emerson [68]	10 000	
19-06	Uganda	W	1-0	Praia	WCq	Semedo [42]	5 000	Coulibaly MLI
3-07	Congo DR	D	1-1	Praia	WCq	Modeste [26]	3 800	NAHI CIV
5-09	Ghana	L	0-2	Kumasi	WCq		35 000	Tamuni LBY
9-10	Burkina Faso	W	1-0	Praia	WCq	Semedo [2]	6 000	Aziaka TOG
2005								
26-03	Burkina Faso	W	2-1	Ouagadougou	WCq	Morais 2 [48 87]	27 500	Evehe CMR
4-06	South Africa	L	1-2	Praia	WCq	Gomes [77]	6 000	Benouza ALG
18-06	Uganda	L	0-1	Kampala	WCq		5 000	Kidane ERI

Fr = Friendly match • CN = CAF African Cup of Nations • WC = FIFA World Cup™
q = qualifier • * Abandoned after 85 minutes when Mauritania were reduced to six players - the result stood

CAPE VERDE ISLANDS NATIONAL TEAM RECORDS AND RECORD SEQUENCES

Records			Sequence records					
Victory	3-0	GNB 81, MTN 03, SWZ 03	Wins	3	2000	Clean sheets	3	2000
Defeat	2-5	SEN 1981	Defeats	4	1982-83, 1985-87	Goals scored	7	2000
Player Caps	n/a		Undefeated	7	2000	Without goal	5	1985-87, 1998-2000
Player Goals	n/a		Without win	9	1997-2000	Goals against	9	1988-1989

RECENT LEAGUE RECORD

Year	Champions	Pts	Runners-up	Pts	Third	Pts		Champions	Score	Runners-up
1999	Amarante São Vicente							Amarante São Vicente	2-0 1-1	Vulcânicos São Filipe
2000	Derby São Vicente							Derby São Vicente	1-1 1-0	Académica B'vista
2001	Onze Unidos	14	Académica do Sal	13	Botafogo	11				
2002	Sporting da Praia	19	Batuque	19	Académica Fogo	16				
2003	Académico do Sal							Académico do Sal	3-1 3-2	FC Ultramarina
2004	Sal-Rei SC							Sal-Rei SC	2-0 1-2	Académica Praia
2005	Derby São Vicente							Derby São Vicente	1-1 4-3	Sporting da Praia

Championship / Championship Play-off

CAPE VERDE ISLANDS COUNTRY INFORMATION

Capital	Praia	Independence	1975 from Portugal	GDP per Capita	$1 400	
Population	415 294	Status	Republic	GNP Ranking	166	
Area km²	4 033	Language	Portuguese	Dialling code	+238	
Population density	102 per km²	Literacy rate	76%	Internet code	.cv	
% in urban areas	54%	Main religion	Christian	GMT +/-	-1	
Towns/Cities ('000)	Praia 111; Mindelo 69; Santa Maria 16; Pedra Badejo 9; São Filipe 8; Assomada 7					
Neighbours (km)	Cape Verde consists of a group of 13 islands in the North Atlantic Ocean					
Main stadia	Estadio da Varzea – Praia 8 000; Estadio Municipal Adérito Sena – Midelo 5 000					

CRC – COSTA RICA

NATIONAL TEAM RECORD
JULY 1ST 2002 TO JUNE 30TH 2005

PL	W	D	L	F	A	%
47	20	10	17	69	61	53.2

FIFA/COCA-COLA WORLD RANKING

1993	1994	1995	1996	1997	1998	1999	2000	2001	2002	2003	2004	High		Low	
42	65	78	72	51	67	64	60	30	21	17	27	17	05/03	93	07/96

2004-2005											
08/04	09/04	10/04	11/04	12/04	01/05	02/05	03/05	04/05	05/05	06/05	07/05
28	33	32	27	27	27	27	21	22	21	24	23

Costa Rica has firmly established itself as the leading nation behind Mexico and the USA in the CONCACAF region. The national team is in a position to qualify for successive finals of the FIFA World Cup™, something that has not happened before, whilst Costa Rican clubs have matched the record of Mexican clubs over the past 12 years in the CONCACAF Champions Cup. In February 2005 the national team won the UNCAF Championship in Guatemala City to become Central American champions for the 12th time since 1941 and qualify for the CONCACAF Gold Cup in

INTERNATIONAL HONOURS

Qualified for the FIFA World Cup™ finals 1990 2002 Central American Championship 1941 1946 1948 1953 1955 1960 1961 1963
UNCAF Championship 1991 1997 1999 2003 2005 CONCACAF U-20 Championship 1954 1960 1988 CONCACAF U-17 Championship 1994
CONCACAF Club Championship LD Alajuelense 1986 2004 Deportivo Saprissa 1993 1995 2005 CS Cartiginés 1995

the process. In the final tournament in America, however, there was the disappointment of a 2-3 defeat at the hands of Honduras which cost them a place in the semi-finals. The 2004-05 Championship was won by Liga Deportiva Alajuelense who beat surprise Apertura winners Pérez Zeledón in the Championship final at the end of May. At the same time the 2004 champions Deportivo Saprissa were beating Mexico's UNAM Tigres in the final of the CONCACAF Champions Cup to win that title for a third time.

THE FIFA BIG COUNT OF 2000

	Male	Female		Male	Female
Registered players	2 740	1 200	Referees	120	5
Non registered players	35 000	1 500	Officials	1 500	20
Youth players	28 248	0	Total involved	70 333	
Total players	68 688		Number of clubs	128	
Professional players	1 040	0	Number of teams	5 760	

Federación Costarricense de Fútbol (FEDEFUTBOL)
Costado Norte Estatua, León Cortés, Sabana Este, San José 670-1000, Costa Rica
Tel +506 2221544   Fax +506 2552674
ejecutivo@fedefutbol.com   www.fedefutbol.com
President: HERMES Navarro Vargas   General Secretary: CASTRO SERRANO Milton
Vice-President: MOREIRA ARAYA Orlando   Treasurer: GONZALEZ EDUARTE Rodrigo   Media Officer: HIDALGO Marvin
Men's Coach: GUIMARAES Alexandre   Women's Coach: RODRIGUEZ Ricardo
FEDEFUTBOL formed: 1921   CONMEBOL: 1962   FIFA: 1927
Colours: Red, Blue, White

GAMES PLAYED BY COSTA RICA IN THE 2006 FIFA WORLD CUP™ CYCLE

2002	Opponents		Score	Venue	Comp	Scorers	Att	Referee
16-10	Ecuador	D	1-1	San Jose	Fr	Bryce [53]	8 000	Badilla CRC
20-11	Ecuador	D	2-2	Quito	Fr	Chinchilla [29], Herron [45]	35 000	Ramos ECU
2003								
11-02	El Salvador	W	1-0	Panama City	GCq	Scott [62]	500	Batres GUA
13-02	Guatemala	D	1-1	Panama City	GCq	Centeno [24p]		Rizo MEX
15-02	Nicaragua	W	1-0	Colón	GCq	Scott [16]	600	Aguilar SLV
20-02	Honduras	W	1-0	Panama City	GCq	Bryce [45]	200	Batres GUA
23-02	Panama	W	1-0	Panama City	GCq	Solis [73]	550	Batres GUA
29-03	Paraguay	W	2-1	Alajuela	Fr	Parks [36], Bennett [89]	17 000	Quesada CRC
30-04	Chile	L	0-1	Santiago	Fr		8 618	Aquino PAR
8-06	Chile	W	1-0	San Jose	Fr	Fonseca.R [88]	14 000	Pineda HON
12-07	Canada	L	0-1	Foxboro	GCr1		33 652	Piper TRI
16-07	Cuba	W	3-0	Foxboro	GCr1	Centeno [45], Bryce [72], Scott [77]	10 361	Archundia MEX
19-07	El Salvador	W	5-2	Foxboro	GCqf	Scott [11], Centeno 3 [45 68p 90p], Bryce [71]	15 627	Ramos MEX
24-07	Mexico	L	0-2	Mexico City	GCsf		35 000	Alfaro SLV
26-07	USA	L	2-3	Miami	GC3p	Fonseca 2 [24 39]	5 093	Piper TRI
20-08	Austria	L	0-2	Vienna	Fr		16 000	Hamer LUX
7-09	China PR	W	2-0	Fort Lauderdale	Fr	Saborio [13], Bryce [25]		Stott USA
11-10	South Africa	L	1-2	Johannesburg	Fr	OG [79]	17 000	Bwanya ZIM
19-11	Finland	W	2-1	San Jose	Fr	Marin [16], Saborio [74]		Batres GUA
2004								
31-03	Mexico	L	0-2	Carson	Fr		27 000	Stott USA
4-06	Nicaragua	W	5-1	San Carlos	Fr	Scott [19], Ledezma [30], Parks.W 2 [46 57], Solis.A [90]	BCD	
12-06	Cuba	D	2-2	Havana	WCq	Sequeira [12], Saborio [42]	18 500	Archundia MEX
20-06	Cuba	D	1-1	Alajuela	WCq	Gomez [31]	12 000	Prendergast JAM
8-07	Paraguay	L	0-1	Arequipa	CAr1		30 000	Ruiz COL
11-07	Brazil	L	1-4	Arequipa	CAr1	Marin [81]	12 000	Baldassi ARG
14-07	Chile	W	2-1	Tacna	CAr1	Wright [59], Herron [90]	20 000	Ortube BOL
17-07	Colombia	L	0-2	Trujillo	CAqf		18 000	Mendez URU
18-08	Honduras	L	2-5	Alajuela	WCq	Herron 2 [20 36]	14 000	Rodriguez MEX
5-09	Guatemala	L	1-2	Guatemala City	WCq	Solis [24]	27 460	Stott USA
8-09	Canada	W	1-0	San Jose	WCq	Wanchope [46]	13 000	Ramdhan TRI
9-10	Guatemala	W	5-0	San Jose	WCq	Hernandez.C [19], Wanchope 3 [36 62 69], Fonseca [83]	18 000	Archundia MEX
13-10	Canada	W	3-1	Vancouver	WCq	Wanchope [49], Sunsing [81] Hernandez.C [87]	4 000	Prendergast JAM
17-11	Honduras	D	0-0	San Pedro Sula	WCq		18 000	Sibrian SLV
2005								
12-01	Haiti	D	3-3	San Jose	Fr	Centeno [2], Scott [10], Herron [13p]		Porras CRC
9-02	Mexico	L	1-2	San Jose	WCq	Wanchope [38]	22 000	Batres GUA
16-02	Ecuador	L	1-2	Heredia	Fr	Alfaro [46]	1 000	Duran CRC
21-02	El Salvador	W	2-1	Guatemala City	GCq	Wilson [75], Myrie [90]	3 000	Batres GUA
23-02	Panama	W	1-0	Guatemala City	GCq	Myrie [83]	3 000	Archundia MEX
25-02	Guatemala	W	4-0	Guatemala City	GCq	Segura [9], Sequeira [22], Wilson [41], Scott [61]	11 159	Archundia MEX
27-02	Honduras	D	1-1	Guatemala City	GCq	Wilson [68]. W 7-6p	1 491	Batres GUA
26-03	Panama	W	2-1	San Jose	WCq	Wilson [40p], Myre [91+]	8 000	Rodriguez MEX
30-03	Trinidad and Tobago	D	0-0	Port of Spain	WCq		8 000	Navarro CAN
24-05	Norway	L	0-1	Oslo	Fr		21 251	Van Egmond NED
4-06	USA	L	0-3	Salt Lake City	WCq		40 586	Batres GUA
8-06	Guatemala	W	3-2	San Jose	WCq	Hernandez.C [34], Gomez [65], Wanchope [92+]	BCD	Archundia MEX
19-06	China PR	D	2-2	Changsha	Fr	Solis [57], Gomez [75]	20 000	Lee Gi Young KOR
22-06	China PR	L	0-2	Guangzhou	Fr		15 000	Yu Byung Seob KOR
7-07	Canada	W	1-0	Seattle	GCr1	Soto.J [30p]	15 831	Prendergast JAM
9-07	Cuba	W	3-1	Seattle	GCr1	Brenes 2 [61 85p], Soto.J [81p]	15 109	Archundia MEX
12-07	USA	D	0-0	Foxboro	GCr1		15 211	Archundia MEX
16-07	Honduras	L	2-3	Foxboro	GCqf	Bolaños [39], Ruiz [81]	22 108	Archundia MEX

Fr = Friendly match • GC = CONCACAF Gold Cup • CA = Copa América • WC = FIFA World Cup™
q = qualifier • r1 = first round group • qf = quarter-finals • BCD = behind closed doors

COSTA RICA NATIONAL TEAM RECORDS AND RECORD SEQUENCES

Records			Sequence records					
Victory	12-0	PUR 1946	Wins	11	1960-1961	Clean sheets	5	1961, 2001-2002
Defeat	0-7	MEX 1975	Defeats	4	1990, 1991, 1995	Goals scored	28	1935-1946
Player Caps	112	MARIN Luis	Undefeated	12	1965	Without goal	4	1980-1983
Player Goals	42	FONSECA/WANCHOPE	Without win	8	1997	Goals against	12	Three times

NATIONAL CAPS

	Caps
MARÍN Luis	112
SOLIS Mauricio	102
FONSECA Rolando	96
MEDFORD Hernán	89
CENTENO Walter	84
LONNIS Erick	76
LÓPEZ Wilmer	76
RAMÍREZ Oscar	75
GÓMEZ Ronald	72
WALLACE Harold	71

NATIONAL GOALS

	Goals
FONSECA Rolando	42
WANCHOPE Paulo	42
ULLOA Juan	27
MONGE Jorge	23
GÓMEZ Ronald	22
MEDFORD Hernán	18
MADRIGAL Rafael	15
HERRERA Rodolfo	14
CENTENO Walter	13
SAÉNZ Roy	12

CLUB DIRECTORY

Club	Town/City	Stadium	Phone	www.	Lge	CL
Liga Deportiva Alajuelense	Alajuela	Alejandro Morera Soto 22 500	+506 4431617	ldacr.org	23	2
AD Belén	Heredia	Polideportivo Belén 10 500			0	0
Brujas Escazú FC	San José	Nicolas Macis 4 500			0	0
AD Carmelita	Alajuela	Carlos Alvarado 4 000	+506 4416688		0	0
Club Sport Cartaginés	Cartago	Fello Meza 18 000	+506 5920102	cartagines.co.cr	3	1
Club Sport Herediano	Heredia	Eladio Rosabal Cordero 8 144	+506 2603322	herediano.com	21	0
Municipal Liberia	Liberia	Edgardo Baltodano 5 000	+506 6667171		0	0
AD Pérez Zeledón	San Isidro	Municipal 5 500	+506 7714548		0	0
Puntarenas FC	Puntarenas	Lito Pérez 8 700			0	0
AD Ramonense	Alajuela	Guillermo Vargas 5 000			0	0
Santos de Guápiles	Guápiles	Ebal Rodrigues 3 000	+506 7104534		1	0
Deportivo Saprissa	San José	Ricardo Saprissa 21 260	+506 2354733	saprissa.co.cr	23	2

RECENT LEAGUE RECORD

Year	Winners	Score	Runners-up
1995	Deportivo Saprissa	3-1 0-1	Liga Deportiva Alajuelense
1996	Liga Deportiva Alajuelense	3-1 1-1	CS Cartaginés
1997	Liga Deportiva Alajuelense	3-2 1-1	Deportivo Saprissa
1998	Deportivo Saprissa	0-1 2-0	Liga Deportiva Alajuelense
1999	Deportivo Saprissa	†	
2000	Liga Deportiva Alajuelense	†	
2001	Liga Deportiva Alajuelense	0-1 3-0	CS Herediano
2002	Liga Deportiva Alajuelense	2-2 4-0	Santos de Guápiles
2003	Liga Deportiva Alajuelense	†	
2004	Deportivo Saprissa	1-1 2-1	CS Herediano
2005	Liga Deportiva Alajuelense	3-1 1-0	AD Pérez Zeledón

† Won both Apertura and Clausura so automatic champions

COSTA RICA COUNTRY INFORMATION

Capital	San José	Independence	1821 from Spain	GDP per Capita	$9 100
Population	3 956 507	Status	Republic	GNP Ranking	74
Area km²	51 100	Language	Spanish	Dialling code	+506
Population density	77 per km²	Literacy rate	96%	Internet code	.cr
% in urban areas	50%	Main religion	Christian 92%	GMT +/–	-6
Towns/Cities ('000)	San José 335; Limón 63; San Francisco 55; Alajuela 47; Liberia 45; Paraiso 39				
Neighbours (km)	Nicaragua 309; Panama 330; Caribbean Sea & Pacific Ocean 1 290				
Main stadia	Alejandro Soto – Alajuela 22 500; Ricardo Saprissa – San José 21 260				

COSTA RICA 2004-05
TORNEO APERTURA

Group A	Pl	W	D	L	F	A	Pts
CS Herediano †	16	11	4	1	33	12	37
LD Alajuelense †	16	11	3	2	40	16	36
AD Carmelita	16	5	5	6	18	30	20
AD Ramonense	16	4	3	9	16	27	15
Puntarenas FC	16	3	3	10	20	35	12
Municipal Liberia	16	2	6	8	18	33	12

Group B	Pl	W	D	L	F	A	Pts
Deportivo Saprissa †	16	9	3	4	24	16	30
AD Pérez Zeledón †	16	8	5	3	28	20	29
CS Cartaginés	16	7	2	7	27	17	23
Brujas Escazú FC	16	6	3	7	20	19	21
Santos de Guápiles	16	5	6	5	18	24	21
AD Belén	16	2	3	11	16	29	9

21/08/2004 - 12/12/2004 • † Qualified for the play-offs

COSTA RICA 2004-05
TORNEO CLAUSURA

Group A	Pl	W	D	L	F	A	Pts
Deportivo Saprissa †	16	7	7	2	21	10	28
CS Herediano †	16	8	4	4	21	12	28
AD Carmelita	16	8	2	6	27	21	26
Puntarenas FC	16	6	5	5	31	24	23
Municipal Liberia	16	4	3	9	17	26	15
AD Ramonense	16	4	3	9	17	27	15

Group B	Pl	W	D	L	F	A	Pts
LD Alajuelense †	16	7	6	3	30	21	27
CS Cartaginés †	16	5	9	2	22	19	24
Brujas Escazú FC	16	6	4	6	25	28	22
AD Pérez Zeledón	16	4	6	6	17	25	18
AD Belén	16	3	7	6	19	26	16
Santos de Guápiles	16	3	6	7	16	24	15

15/01/2005 - 24/04/2005 • † Qualified for the play-offs

APERTURA PLAY-OFFS

Semi-finals

AD Pérez Zeledón	0	3
CS Herediano	1	0

LD Alajuelense	1	1	3p
Deportivo Saprissa	1	1	4p

Final

23-12-2004 & 29-12-2004

AD Pérez Zeledón	0	1
Deportivo Saprissa	0	0

APERTURA PLAY-OFFS

Semi-finals

LD Alajuelense	1	1
CS Herediano	1	0

CS Cartaginés	0	1
Deportivo Saprissa	0	2

Final

8-05-2005 & 16-05-2005

LD Alajuelense	1	2
Deportivo Saprissa	0	2

COSTA RICA 2004-05
PRIMERA DIVISION CHAMPIONSHIP FINAL

Home team first leg	Score	Home team second leg
AD Pérez Zeledón	1-3 0-1	**Liga Deportiva Alajuelense**

First leg: 22-05-2005, Ricardo Saprissa, San Jose. Scorers - Segura [21] for Pérez Zeledón; Hernandez.C [1], Lopez.W [52], Fonseca.R [85] for LD Alajuelense

Second leg: 28-05-2005. Alejandro Morera Soto, Alajuela. Scorer - Ledezma [91+] for LD Alajuelense

COSTA RICA RESULTS 2004-05

	LDA	Belén	Brujas	Carmelita	Cartaginés	Herediano	Liberia	Pérez Zeledón	Puntarenas	Ramonense	Santos	Saprissa
LD Alajuelense		1-0	1-1 2-0	3-1 3-4	4-1	3-1 0-0	4-0 3-2	2-0	4-2	4-1 3-2	3-1 3-3	1-0
AD Belén	1-2 3-3		1-3 1-1	1-3	1-0 1-1	3-1	1-0	1-2 1-1	1-1	1-0	1-1 1-0	2-3
Brujas Escazú FC	1-1	2-1 3-0‡		0-3	0-3 3-2	3-2	1-1	1-2 3-0	2-0	1-2	0-0 2-0	0-1 1-1
AD Carmelita	1-5	2-0	1-0		1-4	1-1 0-1	1-0 2-1	3-1	3-2 1-1	1-1 2-1	0-0	1-3 2-0
CS Cartaginés	0-0 0-0	2-1 2-1	0-2 1-1	1-0		1-1	3-0	3-0 1-1	4-1	1-0	4-0 1-0	1-3
CS Herediano	2-1	3-1	3-1	3-0 1-0	1-0		2-2 4-1	3-0	3-0 1-0	3-2 2-0	2-0	1-0 0-1
Municipal Liberia	0-4	2-2	2-0	1-2 1-0	1-1	0-2 3-2		5-2	0-0 1-2	1-1 2-2	1-0	0-2
AD Pérez Zeledón	2-2 1-1	3-1 4-2	1-0 4-3	5-1	3-1 1-1	0-0	1-0		2-1	1-1 1-0	1-1	0-0
Puntarenas FC	1-2	2-1	6-2	1-1 5-2	2-1	0-5 0-1	2-0 4-2	2-2		4-1 4-1	2-1	0-0
AD Ramonense	2-1 2-0	3-1	0-1	0-0 1-5	1-0	1-3 0-0	2-3 2-0	0-2	2-0 1-0		0-1	3-1
Santos de Guápiles	1-4	2-1 1-1	1-3 3-1	1-1	2-1 2-5	0-0	2-2	1-3 0-0	2-1	2-0		2-1 1-1
Deportivo Saprissa	1-0	0-0 1-1	1-3	3-0	1-1 1-1	0-0	3-1 0-0	1-0 2-0	3-2 5-1	2-0 2-0	2-1	

Clausura matches listed in bold • ‡ Match awarded 3-0

CRO – CROATIA

NATIONAL TEAM RECORD
JULY 1ST 2002 TO JUNE 30TH 2005

PL	W	D	L	F	A	%
33	17	10	6	52	30	66.7

FIFA/COCA-COLA WORLD RANKING

1993	1994	1995	1996	1997	1998	1999	2000	2001	2002	2003	2004	High	Low
122	62	41	24	19	4	9	18	19	32	20	23	3 01/99	125 03/94

2004-2005											
08/04	09/04	10/04	11/04	12/04	01/05	02/05	03/05	04/05	05/05	06/05	07/05
25	25	23	23	23	23	23	24	21	21	22	22

Aiming for a third successive appearance in the FIFA World Cup™ finals, Croatia were handed a tough group in the 2006 qualifiers with European Championship finalists Bulgaria and Sweden. However, with just one point dropped in their first six games the Croats look odds-on for a top two finish and either automatic qualification or the lottery of the play-offs. Much of the Croats' consistent form stems from the fact that they have never lost a competitive international at home, covering a total of 28 games between September 1994 and June 2005. With more consistency away the current generation may even begin to match the exploits of the team that finished third at the FIFA

INTERNATIONAL HONOURS
Qualified for the FIFA World Cup™ finals 1998 2002

World Cup™ finals in France. The Croatian Championship produced a major surprise in 2005 when seven-times champions Dinamo Zagreb found themselves in the relegation group when the Championship split after 22 rounds. It was left for Hajduk Split, one of only two other clubs to have won a title, to win a sixth, although it was a close run thing with Inter Zapresic finishing just two points behind with the clubs level on points going into the final fixtures. Three days earlier Hajduk had lost the Cup Final to Rijeka who won their first trophy since winning back-to-back Yugoslav Cups in 1978 and 1979.

THE FIFA BIG COUNT OF 2000

	Male	Female		Male	Female
Registered players	28 322	430	Referees	2 802	15
Non registered players	210 000	0	Officials	14 975	85
Youth players	458 204	0	Total involved	714 833	
Total players	696 956		Number of clubs	1 186	
Professional players	605	0	Number of teams	3 205	

Croatian Football Federation (HNS)
Hrvatski nogometni savez, Rusanova 13, Zagreb 10 000, Croatia
Tel +385 1 2361555   Fax +385 1 2441501
info@hns-cff.hr   www.hns-cff.hr
President: MARKOVIC Vlatko   General Secretary: SREBRIC Zorislav
Vice-President: ZEC Vlado   Treasurer: TBD   Media Officer: ROTIM Ivan
Men's Coach: KRANJCAR Zlatko   Women's Coach: HUSIC Kazimir
HNS formed: 1912   UEFA: 1993   FIFA: 1992
Colours: Red and white chequered shirts, White, Blue or Blue, Blue, Blue

GAMES PLAYED BY CROATIA IN THE 2006 FIFA WORLD CUP™ CYCLE

2002	Opponents	Score		Venue	Comp	Scorers	Att	Referee
21-08	Wales	D	1-1	Varazdin	Fr	Petric [79]	6 000	Frolich GER
7-09	Estonia	D	0-0	Osijek	ECq		12 000	Marin ESP
12-10	Bulgaria	L	0-2	Sofia	ECq		43 000	Frisk SWE
20-11	Romania	W	1-0	Timisoara	Fr	Maric.T [48]	40 000	Megyebiro HUN
2003								
9-02	FYR Macedonia	D	2-2	Sibenik	Fr	Maric.M [35p], Andric [72]	4 000	Zrnic BIH
12-02	Poland	D	0-0	Split	Fr		1 000	Wack GER
29-03	Belgium	W	4-0	Zagreb	ECq	Srna [9], Prso [55], Maric.T [70], Leko.J [76]	25 000	Fandel GER
2-04	Andorra	W	2-0	Varazdin	ECq	Rapajic 2 [10p 43]	8 500	Salomir ROM
30-04	Sweden	W	2-1	Stockholm	Fr	Olic [6], Zivkovic [58]	15 109	Van Egmond NED
11-06	Estonia	W	1-0	Tallinn	ECq	Kovac.N [77]	7 000	Hamer LUX
20-08	England	L	1-3	Ipswich	Fr	Mornar [77]	28 700	Larsen DEN
6-09	Andorra	W	3-0	Andorra-la-Vella	ECq	Kovac [4], Simunic [16], Rosso [71]	800	Liba CZE
10-09	Belgium	L	1-2	Brussels	ECq	Simic [35]	35 000	Poll ENG
11-10	Bulgaria	W	1-0	Zagreb	ECq	Olic [48]	37 000	Veissiere FRA
15-11	Slovenia	D	1-1	Zagreb	ECpo	Prso [5]	35 000	Merk GER
19-11	Slovenia	W	1-0	Ljubljana	ECpo	Prso [61]	9 000	Meier SUI
2004								
18-02	Germany	L	1-2	Split	Fr	Neretljak [86]	15 000	Frojdfeldt SWE
31-03	Turkey	D	2-2	Zagreb	Fr	Sokota [2], Srna [76]	12 000	Ferreira POR
28-04	FYR Macedonia	W	1-0	Skopje	Fr	Klasnic [33]	15 000	Arzuman TUR
29-05	Slovakia	W	1-0	Rijeka	Fr	Olic [29]	5 000	Kassai HUN
5-06	Denmark	W	2-1	Copenhagen	Fr	Sokota [27], Olic [39]	30 843	Stuchlik AUT
13-06	Switzerland	D	0-0	Leiria	ECr1		24 000	Cortez Batista POR
17-06	France	D	2-2	Leiria	ECr1	Rapajic [48p], Prso [52]	28 000	Milton Nielsen DEN
21-06	England	L	2-4	Lisbon	ECr1	Kovac.N [5], Tudor [73]	62 000	Collina ITA
18-08	Israel	W	1-0	Zagreb	Fr	Simunic [29]	10 000	Granat POL
4-09	Hungary	W	3-0	Zagreb	WCq	Prso 2 [31 54], Gyepes OG [80]	20 853	Riley ENG
8-09	Sweden	W	1-0	Gothenburg	WCq	Srna [64]	40 023	Dauden Ibanez ESP
9-10	Bulgaria	D	2-2	Zagreb	WCq	Srna 2 [15 31]	31 565	Collina ITA
16-11	Republic of Ireland	L	0-1	Dublin	Fr		33 200	Orrason ISL
2005								
9-02	Israel	D	3-3	Jerusalem	Fr	Klasnic 2 [15 78], Srna [55p]	4 000	Kailis CYP
26-03	Iceland	W	4-0	Zagreb	WCq	Kovac.N 2 [38 75], Simunic [70], Prso [91+]	17 912	Damon RSA
30-03	Malta	W	3-0	Zagreb	WCq	Prso 2 [22 35], Tudor [79]	15 510	Kapitanis CYP
4-06	Bulgaria	W	3-1	Sofia	WCq	Babic [19], Tudor [57], Kranjcar [80]	35 000	Nielsen DEN

Fr = Friendly match • EC = UEFA EURO 2004™ • WC = FIFA World Cup™
q = qualifier • po = play-off • r1 = first round group

CROATIA COUNTRY INFORMATION

Capital	Zagreb	Independence	1991 from Yugoslavia	GDP per Capita	$10 600
Population	4 496 869	Status	Republic	GNP Ranking	63
Area km²	56 542	Language	Croatian	Dialling code	+385
Population density	79 per km²	Literacy rate	98%	Internet code	.hr
% in urban areas	64%	Main religion	Christian 92%	GMT +/−	+1
Towns/Cities ('000)	Zagreb 698; Split 176; Rijeka 141; Osijek 88; Zadar 71; Slavonski Brod 60; Pula 59				
Neighbours (km)	Slovenia 670; Hungary 329; Serbia & Montenegro 266; Bosnia & Herzegovina 932; Adriatic Sea 1 777				
Main stadia	Poljud – Split 39 941; Maksimir – Zagreb 38 923; Gradski – Osijek 19 500				

CROATIA NATIONAL TEAM RECORDS AND RECORD SEQUENCES

Records			Sequence records					
Victory	7-0	AUS 1998	Wins	5	1994-95, 1995-96	Clean sheets	4	1994, 2002
Defeat	1-5	GER 1941, GER 1942	Defeats	2	Four times	Goals scored	21	1996-1998
Player Caps	81	JARNI Robert	Undefeated	12	2000-2001	Without goal	2	
Player Goals	45	SUKER Davor	Without win	6	1999	Goals against	8	1996-1997

NATIONAL CAPS

	Caps
JARNI Robert	81
SIMIC Dario	70
SUKER Davor	69
ASANOVIC Aljosa	62
SOLDO Zvonimir	61
LADIC Drazen	59
STIMAC Igor	53
BOBAN Zvonimir	51
VLAOVIC Goran	51

NATIONAL GOALS

	Goals
SUKER Davor	45
VLAOVIC Goran	15
BOBAN Zvonimir	12
WÖLFL Franjo	12
BOKSIC Alen	10
PROSINECKI Robert	10
CIMERMANCIC Zvonimir	8
KOVAC Niko	8
PRSO Dado	8

NATIONAL COACH

	Years
JERKOVIC Drazen	1990-'91
POKLEPOVIC Stanko	1992
MARKOVIC Vlatko	1992-'93
BLAZEVIC Miroslav	1994-'00
JOZIC Mirko	2000-'02
BARIC Otto	2002-'04
KRANJCAR Zlatko	2004-

CROATIA 2004-05

PRVA HNL OZUJSKO (1)

	Pl	W	D	L	F	A	Pts	Hajduk	Inter	Zagreb	Rijeka	Varteks	Slaven	Dinamo	Kamen	Osijek	Pula	Medimurje	Zadar
Hajduk Split †	32	16	8	8	58	33	56		2-0 5-1	2-4 0-1	2-0 1-1	3-1 6-0	2-1 0-0	1-0	2-0	1-1	1-1	2-0	4-0
Inter Zapresic ‡	32	15	9	8	44	39	54	1-3 1-1		1-0 1-1	2-2 3-2	3-2 2-0	2-0 2-1	1-0	0-0	1-3	0-0	3-0	4-0
Zagreb	32	15	5	12	50	42	50	2-0 3-2	0-1 3-3		2-1 2-1	0-1 3-1	0-2 7-1	2-1	1-0	1-0	2-0	0-1	4-1
Rijeka ‡	32	11	14	7	52	40	47	2-0 1-1	2-0 3-3	2-1 4-2		3-0 1-1	1-1 0-0	4-2	2-1	4-0	1-1	3-1	2-0
Varteks Varazdin	32	14	3	15	53	50	45	0-4 1-2	0-1 1-2	1-0 3-1	2-0 3-1		6-0 2-0	2-2	3-0	4-0	1-0	5-0	3-0
Slaven Belupo	32	12	9	11	37	41	45	1-0 1-1	2-1 0-1	1-1 2-0	0-0 1-1	0-1 2-2		3-1	4-1	1-2	1-0	2-0	1-0
Dinamo Zagreb	32	12	11	9	55	37	47	3-0	2-0	1-2	1-1	2-1	1-2		2-1 0-0	0-3 3-3	3-0 0-0	4-1 5-1	2-1 7-0
Kamen Ingrad Velika	32	12	5	15	36	39	41	2-1	0-1	4-1	3-2	3-2	2-0	0-0 0-1		3-1 2-0	1-0 1-1	2-0 0-1	2-0 1-0
Osijek	32	9	14	9	41	45	41	2-2	2-0	1-1	1-1	1-3	1-1	1-1 0-0	2-0 3-0		2-1 1-0	0-0 1-2	3-1 1-1
Pula 1856	32	7	14	11	28	31	35	0-1	1-1	1-1	0-0	3-0	2-0	3-3 0-0	1-0 1-1	2-0 1-1		2-1 0-0	2-0 3-1
Medimurje Cakovec	32	9	6	17	29	52	33	1-3	0-0	0-1	1-2	2-0	0-1	1-3 2-1	1-4 1-0	2-2 2-2	1-1 1-0		4-0 1-0
Zadar	32	10	2	20	36	70	32	1-3	0-2	2-1	2-2	3-1	1-5	3-4 1-0	2-1 3-1	2-4 2-0	3-0 2-1	2-1 1-0	

21/07/2004 - 28/05/2005 • † Qualified for the UEFA Champions League • ‡ Qualified for the UEFA Cup • Each team plays each other twice before the top six play each other twice again in the Championship group and the bottom six play each other twice in the relegation group • This system is also used in the Second Division • Relegation play-off between the second bottom team and the losers of the Second Division play-off: Medimurje 2-0 1-1 Novalja - Medimurje remain in the First Division

HRVATSKOG NOGOMETNOG KUPA 2004-05

Round of sixteen		Quarter-finals			Semi-finals			Final		
Rijeka *	2									
Crikvenica	1	Rijeka *	1	2						
Budainka *	1	Slaven Belupo	1	2						
Slaven Belupo	4				Rijeka *	3	3			
Dinamo Zagreb *	3				Varteks Varazdin	2	2			
Belisce	2	Dinamo Zagreb	0	0						
Koprivnica	0	Varteks Varazdin *	1	0						
Varteks Varazdin	4							Rijeka ‡	2	1
Osijek *	2							Hajduk Split	1	0
Slobada Varazdin	0	Osijek *	0	1						
Pomorac Kostrena	1	Pula 1856	0	0						
Pula 1856 *	3				Osijek	1	1			
Zagreb *	3				Hajduk Split *	2	1			
Medimurje Cakovec	2	Zagreb *	1	0						
Nehaj *	2	Hajduk Split *	0	2						
Hajduk Split	3									

* Home team/home team in the first leg • ‡ Qualified for the UEFA Cup

CUP FINAL

First leg. 11-05-2005, Att: 7 000
Kantrida, Rijeka
Scorers - Mitu 58, Erceg 61 for Rijeka; Dolonga 22 for Hajduk
Second leg. 25-05-2005, Att: 15 000
Poljud, Split
Scorer - Mitu 80 for Rijeka

CROATIA 2004-05
GRUPA SJEVER (2)

	Pl	W	D	L	F	A	Pts
Cibalia Vinkovci † §	32	21	8	3	65	23	65
Marsonia Slavonski Brod	32	16	8	8	50	36	56
Cakovec	32	13	9	10	45	41	48
Belisce	32	12	7	13	48	41	43
Metalac Osijek	32	11	9	12	45	38	42
Dilj Vinkovci	32	11	8	13	31	41	41
Koprivnica	32	12	8	12	50	48	44
Bjelovar	32	11	8	13	54	53	41
Slavonija S'ska Pozega	32	12	4	16	37	57	40
Vukovar '91	32	10	9	13	37	46	39
Graficar V'vod Osijek	32	9	7	16	46	53	34
Valpovka Valpovo	32	10	3	19	29	60	33

21/08/2004 - 22/05/2005 • † play-off versus Jug (Southern
Group) winner • § Six points deducted
Play-off: **Cibalia Vinkovci** 4-0 1-1 Novalja

CROATIA 2004-05
GRUPA JUG (2)

	Pl	W	D	L	F	A	Pts
Novalja †	32	17	8	7	51	29	59
Hrvatski Zagreb	32	17	8	7	62	39	59
Solin Grada	32	14	8	10	54	53	50
Sibenik §	32	13	12	7	42	26	48
Segesta Sisak	32	12	12	8	51	38	48
Mosor Zrnovnica	32	11	11	10	48	49	44
Pomorac Kostrena	32	13	7	12	37	36	46
Naftas Ivanic Grad	32	12	4	16	44	52	40
Croatia Sesvete	32	10	8	14	41	47	38
Imotski	32	10	7	15	36	46	37
GOSK 1919 Dubrovnik	32	9	7	16	30	50	34
Uskok Klis	32	5	6	21	27	58	21

21/08/2004 - 21/05/2005 • † play-off versus Sjever (Northern
Group) winner • § Three points deducted

FIFA REFEREE LIST 2005

	Int'l	DoB
BEBEK Ivan	2003	30-05-1977
KOVACIC Drazenko	1999	8-10-1966
SIRIC Zeljko	1996	1-12-1960
STRAHONJA Marijo	2004	21-08-1975
SUPRAHA Alojzije	2000	29-11-1963
TRIVKOVIC Edo	1996	11-07-1964

FIFA ASSISTANT REFEREE LIST 2005

	Int'l	DoB
BOROVEC Predrag	2002	21-03-1963
BUIC Sinisa	2004	26-06-1970
GRGEC Zeljko	2002	28-06-1966
KRMAR Igor	2005	2-04-1973
LUSETIC Armando	2005	2-05-1965
NOVOSEL Zeljko	2001	25-01-1968
PETROVIC Tomislav	2001	4-09-1973
PREMUZAJ Sinisa	2005	1-04-1973
SETKA Tomislav	2005	25-08-1967
SLIVAR Darko	2000	19-01-1961

CLUB DIRECTORY

Club	Town/City	Stadium	Phone	www.	Lge	Cup	CL
NK Dinamo Zagreb	Zagreb	Maksimir 38 923	+385 1 2386120	nk-dinamo.hr	7 - 4	7 - 7	0
HNK Hajduk Split	Split	Poljud 39 941	+385 21 381244	hnkhajduk.hr	6 - 9	4 - 9	0
NK Inter Zapresic	Zapresic	Inter 8 000	+385 1 3310464	nk-inter.com	0	1	0
NK Kamen Ingrad	Velika	Kamen Ingrad 4 000	+385 34 230122		0	0	0
NK Medimurje	Cakovec	Mladost 4 000	+385 40 329209		0	0	0
NK Osijek	Osijek	Gradski Vrt 19 500	+385 31 570300		0	1	0
NK Pula 1856	Pula	Gradski 7 000	+385 52 210496		0	0	0
HNK Rijeka	Rijeka	Kantrida 10 275	+385 51 261622	nk-rijeka.hr	0	1 - 2	0
NK Slaven Belupo	Koprivnica	Gradski 3 054	+385 48 623960	nk-slaven-belupo	0	0	0
NK Varteks	Varazdin	Varteksa 9 300	+385 42 240250	nk-varteks.hr	0	0	0
NK Zadar	Zadar	Stanovi 8 000	+385 23 312792		0	0	0
NK Zagreb	Zagreb	Kranjceviceva 12 000	+385 1 3668111		1	0	0

Where two figures are shown in the League and Cup column, the second indicates trophies won in the Yugoslav League and Cup

RECENT LEAGUE AND CUP RECORD

	Championship						Cup		
Year	Champions	Pts	Runners-up	Pts	Third	Pts	Winners	Score	Runners-up
1992	Hajduk Split	36	NK Zagreb	33	NK Osijek	27	Inker Zapresic	1-1 1-0	HASK Gradjanski
1993	Croatia Zagreb	49	Hajduk Split	42	NK Zagreb	40	Hjaduk Split	4-1 1-2	Croatia Zagreb
1994	Hajduk Split	50	NK Zagreb	49	Croatia Zagreb	48	Croatia Zagreb	2-0 0-1	NK Rijeka
1995	Hajduk Split	65	Croatia Zagreb	64	NK Osijek	59	Hajduk Split	3-2 1-0	Croatia Zagreb
1996	Croatia Zagreb	26	Hajduk Split	26	Varteks Varazdin	24	Croatia Zagreb	2-0 1-0	Varteks Varazdin
1997	Croatia Zagreb	81	Hajduk Split	60	Dragovoljac Zagreb	49	Croatia Zagreb	2-1	NK Zagreb
1998	Croatia Zagreb	49	Hajduk Split	36	NK Osijek	32	Croatia Zagreb	1-0 2-1	Varteks Varazdin
1999	Croatia Zagreb	45	NK Rijeka	44	Hajduk Split	39	NK Osijek	2-1	Cibalia Vinkovci
2000	Dinamo Zagreb	75	Hajduk Split	61	NK Osijek	53	Hajduk Split	2-0 0-1	Dinamo Zagreb
2001	Hajduk Split	66	Dinamo Zagreb	65	NK Osijek	57	Dinamo Zagreb	2-0 1-0	Hajduk Split
2002	NK Zagreb	67	Hajduk Split	65	Dinamo Zagreb	59	Dinamo Zagreb	1-1 1-0	Varteks Varazdin
2003	Dinamo Zagreb	78	Hajduk Split	70	Varteks Varazdin	57	Hajduk Spit	1-0 4-0	Uljanik Pula
2004	Hajduk Split	78	Dinamo Zagreb	76	NK Rijeka	42	Dinamo Zagreb	1-1 0-0†	Varteks Varazdin
2005	Hajduk Split	56	Inter Zapresic	54	NK Zagreb	50	Rijeka	2-1 1-0	Hajduk Split

Dinamo Zagreb previously known as HASK Gradjanski and then as Croatia Zagreb • † Dinamo won on away goals

CTA – CENTRAL AFRICAN REPUBLIC

NATIONAL TEAM RECORD
JULY 1ST 2002 TO JUNE 30TH 2005

PL	W	D	L	F	A	%
12	2	3	7	10	19	29.2

FIFA/COCA-COLA WORLD RANKING

1993	1994	1995	1996	1997	1998	1999	2000	2001	2002	2003	2004	High		Low	
157	174	180	183	188	192	175	176	182	179	177	180	**153**	08/93	**197**	10/99

2004-2005											
08/04	09/04	10/04	11/04	12/04	01/05	02/05	03/05	04/05	05/05	06/05	07/05
178	178	179	179	180	180	180	181	181	181	181	180

After many years of isolation the Central African Republic has started to take steps to re-integrate into the international football community with participation in the CEMAC Cup, the tournament for central African nations, the main focus of activity. In 2003 the Low-Ubangui Fawns, as the national team is known, even reached the final where they lost 2-3 in Brazzaville to a Cameroon team without any of its European-based professionals. Lack of funds, however, forced the team to withdraw from the 2006 FIFA World Cup™ qualifiers and in the 44 years since the national association was formed the national team has played in just two FIFA World Cup™ matches. With the

INTERNATIONAL HONOURS
None

Republic experiencing internal troubles it is not surprising that the League has been disrupted with the 1998 and 2002 seasons abandoned. The 2004 title was won for the eighth time by Olympique Réal, one of two clubs that dominate the Championship, the other being Tempête Mocaf who successfully defended the Coupe de la Ligue de Bangui, beating SCAF 2-0 in the final. There has been little involvement with continental competitions at club and junior level with the exception of the U-17s, who beat Congo 3-0 in the preliminary rounds of the Africa U-17 Championship. However, with the finals in sight, the dream was ended by a 4-1 aggregate defeat to Mali.

THE FIFA BIG COUNT OF 2000

	Male	Female		Male	Female
Registered players	4 500	350	Referees	150	10
Non registered players	10 000	800	Officials	1 500	300
Youth players	500	110	Total involved	18 220	
Total players	16 260		Number of clubs	263	
Professional players	0	0	Number of teams	263	

Fédération Centrafricaine de Football (RCA)
Avenue de Martyrs, Case Postale 344, Bangui, Central African Republic
Tel +236 619545   Fax +236 615660
dameca@intnet.cf   www.none
President: KAMACH Thierry   General Secretary: GBATE Jeremie
Vice-President: SAKILA Jean-Marie   Treasurer: MABOGNA Patrick   Media Officer: NDOTAH Christian
Men's Coach: YANGUERE Francois Cesar   Women's Coach: NGBANGANDIMBO Camille
RCA formed: 1961   CAF: 1965   FIFA: 1963
Colours: Blue, White, Blue

GAMES PLAYED BY CENTRAL AFRICAN REPUBLIC IN THE 2006 FIFA WORLD CUP™ CYCLE

2002	Opponents		Score	Venue	Comp	Scorers	Att	Referee
9-09	Mozambique	D	1-1	Bangui	CNq	Tamboula 72		Ndong EQG
12-10	Burkina Faso	L	1-2	Ouagadougou	CNq	Ouefio 38	25 000	Camara GUI
2003								
4-05	Congo	L	1-2	Brazzaville	CNq	Makita 84		
8-06	Congo	D	0-0	Bangui	CNq			Hissene CHA
22-06	Mozambique	L	0-1	Maputo	CNq		15 000	
6-07	Burkina Faso	L	0-3	Bangui	CNq			
7-12	Cameroon	D	2-2	Brazzaville	CMr1	Oroko 10, Sandjo 30		Mbera GAB
9-12	Cameroon	W	1-0	Brazzaville	CMr1	Sandjo 85		Mandioukouta CGO
11-12	Gabon	W	2-0	Brazzaville	CMsf			
13-12	Cameroon	L	2-3	Brazzaville	CMf	Oroko 63, Destin 74		Bansimba CGO
2004								
No international matches played in 2004								
2005								
3-02	Gabon	L	0-4	Libreville	CMr1			
5-02	Congo	L	0-1	Libreville	CMr1			

CN = CAF African Cup of Nations • CM = CEMAC Cup • q = qualifier • r1 = first round group • sf = semi-final • f = final

CENTRAL AFRICAN REPUBLIC NATIONAL TEAM RECORDS AND RECORD SEQUENCES

Records			Sequence records					
Victory	4-0	CHA 1999	Wins	2	1976, 1999, 2003	Clean sheets	2	2003
Defeat	1-7	CMR 1984	Defeats	9	1985-1987	Goals scored	7	1990-1999
Player Caps	n/a		Undefeated	3	2003	Without goal	4	1988-1989
Player Goals	n/a		Without win	16	1976-1987	Goals against	19	1976-1988

FIFA REFEREE LIST 2005

	Int'l	DoB
DIMANCHE Maurice		11-11-1963
KOLISSOKO Jean François	2004	4-08-1968
NGANA Barthelemy		24-08-1971
TANGA Patrick		9-09-1973

FIFA ASSISTANT REFEREE LIST 2005

	Int'l	DoB
DJEGUELET Placide	1998	5-10-1960
GONDA-BATTI Sylvain-Nestor		6-12-1970
SENDEOLI Jean Claude		10-09-1960
SORRO Robert-Blandin	2005	1-01-1968
ZIALI-BANICOLO Dieudonne		23-12-1963

RECENT LEAGUE AND CUP RECORD

League		Cup		
Year	Champions	Winners	Score	Runners-up
1996	Tempête Mocaf			
1997	Tempête Mocaf	USCA	2-0	Anges de Fatima
1998	Championship not finished	Anges de Fatima	3-0	AS Petroca
1999	Tempête Mocaf	Olympique Réal		
2000	Olympique Réal	Anges de Fatima	2-1	Olympique Réal
2001	Olympique Réal	Stade Centrafricain	2-1	Tempête Mocaf
2002	Championship annulled			
2003	Tempête Mocaf	Tempête Mocaf	8-0	Ouham Pendé
2004	Olympique Réal	Tempête Mocaf	2-0	SCAF

CENTRAL AFRICAN REPUBLIC COUNTRY INFORMATION

Capital	Bangui	Independence	1960 from France	GDP per Capita	$1100
Population	3 742 482	Status	Republic	GNP Ranking	154
Area km2	622 984	Language	French	Dialling code	+236
Population density	6 per km2	Literacy rate	42%	Internet code	.cf
% in urban areas	39%	Main religion	Christian 50%	GMT +/–	+1
Towns/Cities ('000)	Bangui 684; Carnot 83; Kaga-Bandoro 82; Mbaiki 76; Berbérati 59; Bouar 55; Bouar 55				
Neighbours (km)	Sudan 1 165; Congo DR 1 577; Congo 467; Cameroon 797; Chad 1 197				
Main stadia	Barthelemy Boganda – Bangui 35 000				

CUB – CUBA

NATIONAL TEAM RECORD
JULY 1ST 2002 TO JUNE 30TH 2005

PL	W	D	L	F	A	%
27	15	6	6	44	29	66.7

FIFA/COCA-COLA WORLD RANKING

1993	1994	1995	1996	1997	1998	1999	2000	2001	2002	2003	2004	High		Low	
159	175	96	68	88	107	77	77	76	71	75	76	51	08/96	175	12/94

2004-2005										
08/04	09/04	10/04	11/04	12/04	01/05	02/05	03/05	04/05	05/05	06/05	07/05
74	74	77	81	76	72	71	60	64	64	70	

Cuba has maintained its position as one of the leading Caribbean footballing nations but once the national team ventures beyond the region it struggles to make any impact at all. Despite the traditional antagonism towards the United States, Cubans very much follow the American sports culture with football way down the list. FIFA has helped put the game on a sound footing with the establishment of an academy and new national association headquarters at the Pedro Marrero stadium in Havana while agreement has also been reached for the creation of an academy for women's football. Should that bear fruit in future years the USA women's team could face a new

INTERNATIONAL HONOURS
Qualified for the FIFA World Cup™ finals 1938
CONCACAF U-17 Championship 1988   Central American and Caribbean Games 1930 1974 1978 1986

threat given the success Cuba has managed to achieve across the sporting spectrum in the past. The men's national team were runners-up in the Digicel Caribbean Cup but made a quick first round exit in the CONCACAF Gold Cup finals. In the well-established Campeonato Nacional League Villa Clara and Pinar del Rio reached the play-off final after seeing off Las Tunas and Holguin respectively in the semis. Pinar won the first leg 1-0, but Villa Clara asserted themselves in the return, winning 3-0 to claim a record 10th League title.

THE FIFA BIG COUNT OF 2000

	Male	Female		Male	Female
Registered players	26 220	200	Referees	199	0
Non registered players	1 000 000	0	Officials	5 000	0
Youth players	12 000	100	Total involved	1 043 719	
Total players	1 038 520		Number of clubs	338	
Professional players	0	0	Number of teams	1 470	

Asociación de Fútbol de Cuba (AFC)
Calle 41 No. 4109 e/ 44 y 46, La Habana, Cuba
Tel +53 7 2076440   Fax +53 7 2043563
futbol@inder.co.cu   www.none
President: HERNANDEZ Luis   General Secretary: GARCES Antonio
Vice-President: ARAGON Victor   Treasurer: LOPEZ LOPEZ Pedro   Media Officer: None
Men's Coach: COMPANY Miguel   Women's Coach: SOTOLONGO Rufino
AFC formed: 1924   CONCACAF: 1961   FIFA: 1932
Colours: Red, Red, Red or White, White, White

GAMES PLAYED BY CUBA IN THE 2006 FIFA WORLD CUP™ CYCLE

2002	Opponents	Score		Venue	Comp	Scorers	Att	Referee
27-11	Cayman Islands	W	5-0	Grand Cayman	GCq	Driggs [21], Moré 2 [23 77], Dalcourt [80], Galindo [86]		Prendergast JAM
29-11	Martinique	W	2-1	Grand Cayman	GCq	Moré [38], Dalcourt [60]		Prendergast JAM
1-12	Dominican Republic	W	2-1	Grand Cayman	GCq	OG [63], Prado [57]		Grant HAI
2003								
11-03	Jamaica	D	0-0	Havana	Fr		10 000	
13-03	Jamaica	W	1-0	Havana	Fr	Galindo [43]	15 000	Hernandez CUB
26-03	Guadeloupe	W	3-2	Port of Spain	GCq	Galindo 2 [17 83], Dalcourt [30]	6 000	Callendar BRB
28-03	Antigua and Barbuda	W	2-0	Macoya	GCq	Moré 2 [65 78]	4 000	James GUY
30-03	Trinidad and Tobago	W	3-1	Marabella	GCq	Ramirez [26], Moré [72], Galindo [77]	5 000	James GUY
27-06	Panama	L	0-2	Panama City	Fr			Moreno PAN
29-06	Panama	L	0-1	Panama City	Fr			Vidal PAN
6-07	Jamaica	W	2-1	Kingston	Fr	Fernandez [20], Marquez [38]	8 500	Bowen CAY
14-07	Canada	W	2-0	Foxboro	GCr1	Moré 2 [15 46]	8 780	Prendergast JAM
16-07	Costa Rica	L	0-3	Foxboro	GCr1		10 361	Archundia MEX
19-07	USA	L	0-5	Foxboro	GCqf		15 627	Prendergast JAM
19-11	Trinidad and Tobago	L	1-2	Port of Spain	Fr	Galindo [47]	8 000	
2004								
22-02	Cayman Islands	W	2-1	Grand Cayman	WCq	Moré [53], Marten [89]	1 789	Sibrian SLV
16-03	Panama	D	1-1	Havana	Fr	Moré [33]		Rojas Corbeas CUB
18-03	Panama	W	3-0	Havana	Fr	Colome [36], Galindo [49], Moré [55]		Yero Rodriguez CUB
27-03	Cayman Islands	W	3-0	Havana	WCq	Moré 3 [7 50 66]	3 500	Rodriguez MEX
20-05	Grenada	D	2-2	Havana	Fr	Galindo [15], Faife [23]		
12-06	Costa Rica	D	2-2	Havana	WCq	Moré 2 [24 75]	18 500	Archundia MEX
20-06	Costa Rica	D	1-1	Alajuela	WCq	Cervantes [46+]	12 000	Prendergast JAM
2005								
9-01	Haiti	W	1-0	Port-au-Prince	GCq	Galindo [51]	15 000	Minyetti DOM
16-01	Haiti	D	1-1	Havana	GCq	Marquez [112]		Brizan TRI
20-02	Barbados	W	3-0	Bridgetown	GCq	Moré 2 [24 71], Galindo [90]	7 000	Prendergast JAM
22-02	Trinidad and Tobago	W	2-1	Bridgetown	GCq	Moré 2 [23 48]	2 100	Lancaster GUY
24-02	Jamaica	L	0-1	Bridgetown	GCq		3 000	Brizan TRI
7-07	USA	L	1-4	Seattle	GCr1	Moré [18]	15 831	Pineda HON
9-07	Costa Rica	L	1-3	Seattle	GCr1	Galindo [72]	15 109	Archundia MEX
12-07	Canada	L	1-2	Foxboro	GCr1	Cervantes [90]	15 211	Moreno PAN

Fr = Friendly match • GC = CONCACAF Gold Cup • WC = FIFA World Cup™ • q = qualifier • r1 = first round group

FIFA REFEREE LIST 2005

	Int'l	DoB
DELGADO Roberto	1999	29-11-1964
DUQUE Francisco	1998	22-08-1961
ROJAS Lazaro	2000	25-12-1963
TAMAYO Atilio	2004	13-09-1968
YERO Luis	1996	11-03-1960

FIFA ASSISTANT REFEREE LIST 2005

	Int'l	DoB
ABREU Roger	2004	18-01-1967
BETANCOURT Carlos	2000	6-11-1960
CASTILLO Ricardo	2000	14-11-1967
HIERREZUELO Modesto	2000	4-11-1966
MICHEL Orestes	2001	24-11-1968
RICARDO Aristides	2002	13-04-1964
SCULL Julio	2000	19-04-1965

CUBA COUNTRY INFORMATION

Capital	Havana	Independence	1902 from Spain	GDP per Capita	$2 900
Population	11 308 764	Status	Republic	GNP Ranking	69
Area km²	110 860	Language	Spanish	Dialling code	+53
Population density	102 per km²	Literacy rate	97%	Internet code	.cu
% in urban areas	76%	Main religion	None	GMT +/–	-5
Towns/Cities ('000)	Havana 2 163; Santiago 555; Camagüey 347; Holguín 319; Guantánamo 272; Santa Clara 250				
Neighbours (km)	North Atlantic Ocean, Caribbean Sea and the Gulf of Mexico 3 735				
Main stadia	Estadio Panamericano – Havana 34 000; Pedro Marrero – Havana 28 000				

CUBA NATIONAL TEAM RECORDS AND RECORD SEQUENCES

Records			Sequence records				
Victory	9-0	PUR 1995	Wins	7	1998-1999	Clean sheets	7	1996
Defeat	0-8	SWE 1938	Defeats	18	1949-1960	Goals scored	10	1995-96, 1998-99
Player Caps	n/a		Undefeated	11	1981-1983	Without goal	4	1957, 1983, 2002
Player Goals	n/a		Without win	20	1949-1960	Goals against	26	1949-1961

CUBA 2004
CAMPEONATO NACIONAL

Group A West	Pl	W	D	L	F	A	Pts
Pinar del Río †	12	8	2	2	17	6	26
Ciudad La Habana †	14	5	5	4	21	14	20
Provincia La Habana	14	3	2	9	9	29	11
Isla La Juventud	14	0	2	12	7	29	2

Group B Central-West	Pl	W	D	L	F	A	Pts
Villa Clara †	12	9	3	0	28	7	27
Cienfuegos †	14	7	5	2	20	8	26
Matanzas †	14	6	2	6	16	15	20
Industriales	14	4	3	7	11	21	15

Group C Central-East	Pl	W	D	L	F	A	Pts
Camagüey †	14	7	3	4	10	9	24
Ciego de Avila †	14	6	5	3	14	8	23
Sancti Spiritus	14	5	4	5	15	12	19
Azucareros	14	2	1	11	7	23	7

Group D East	Pl	W	D	L	F	A	Pts
Holguín †	14	6	5	3	15	10	23
Las Tunas †	14	6	4	4	16	13	22
Granma Bayamo †	14	5	5	4	11	9	20
Santiago de Cuba	14	4	3	7	14	18	13

1/08/2004 - 22/09/2004 • † Clubs qualifying for the Second Round

CUBA 2004
SECOND ROUND

	Pl	W	D	L	F	A	Pts
Villa Clara †	17	11	2	4	32	14	35
Pinar del Río †	17	8	6	3	26	13	30
Holguín †	18	8	5	5	17	12	29
Las Tunas †	18	8	5	5	21	21	29
Cienfuegos	18	6	9	3	20	13	27
Granma Bayamo	18	7	6	5	20	15	27
Ciego de Avila †	18	6	5	7	22	20	23
Ciudad La Habana	16	3	7	6	20	23	16
Matanzas	16	3	3	10	18	36	12
Camagüey	16	1	2	13	11	40	5

29/09/2004 - 29/12/2004 • † Clubs qualifying for the play-offs

PLAY-OFFS 2004

Semi-finals			Final	
Villa Clara	3	1		
Las Tunas *	1	2	26-01-2005 & 30-01-2005	
			Villa Clara	0 3
			Pinar del Río *	1 0
Holguín *	0	1		
Pinar del Río	0	2	* Home team in first leg	

CLUB DIRECTORY

Club	Town/City	Stadium	Phone	Lge	CL
Camagüey	Camagüey	Terreno de Futbol de Florida	+53 32 98894	0	0
Ciego de Avila	Ciego de Avila	CVD Deportivo	+53 32 22512	6	0
Cienfuegos	Cienfuegos		+53 432 8646	2	0
Ciudad de La Habana	Havana	Pedro Marrero	+53 7 292991	6	0
Granma	Bayamo	Conrado Benitez	+53 3 481932	0	0
Holguín	Holguín	Turcio Lima	+53 5 24424	0	0
Industriales	Havana	Campo Armada	+53 29 2991	4	0
Las Tunas	Victoria de Las Tunas	Ovidio Torres	+53 14 5203	0	0
Matanzas	Matanzas	Terreno de Futbol de Colon	+53 5 25087	0	0
Pinar del Río	Pinar del Río	La Bombonera	+53 82 4290	6	0
Santiago de Cuba	Santiago de Cuba	Antonio Maceo	+53 226 42651	0	0
Villa Clara	Santa Clara	Camilo Cienfuegos	+53 42 24700	10	0

RECENT LEAGUE RECORD

Year	Winners	Score	Runners-up
1996	Villa Clara	2-3 4-0	Cienfuegos
1997	Villa Clara	1-2 2-0	Pinar del Río
1998	Ciudad de La Habana	2-1 1-0	Villa Clara
1999	No championship due to season readjustment		
2000	Pinar del Río	0-1 2-1†	Ciudad de La Habana
2001	Ciudad de La Habana	2-1 0-0	Villa Clara
2002	Ciego de Avila	1-0 0-0	Granma Bayamo
2003	Villa Clara	1-0 2-0	Ciudad de La Habana
2003	Ciego de Avila	1-1 2-0	Villa Clara
2004	Villa Clara	0-1 3-0	Pinar del Río

† Won on away goals

CYP – CYPRUS

NATIONAL TEAM RECORD
JULY 1ST 2002 TO JUNE 30TH 2005

PL	W	D	L	F	A	%
26	6	6	14	26	45	34.6

FIFA/COCA-COLA WORLD RANKING

1993	1994	1995	1996	1997	1998	1999	2000	2001	2002	2003	2004	High		Low	
72	67	73	78	82	78	63	62	79	80	97	108	**58**	02/99	**113**	03/05

2004-2005											
08/04	09/04	10/04	11/04	12/04	01/05	02/05	03/05	04/05	05/05	06/05	07/05
104	101	101	105	108	109	108	113	109	109	109	109

From 1966 to 1991 the Cyprus national team won just four matches, a figure that was equalled in 1992 alone thanks to the swelling of UEFA's ranks with countries smaller and less experienced. There have even been some notable victories including a 3-2 home win against Spain in the EURO 2000™ qualifiers, but no such heroics in the 2006 FIFA World Cup™ qualifiers against France, Switzerland, the Republic of Ireland and Israel. Instead the duel with the Faroe Islands to avoid the wooden spoon has provided the main focus of attention. The annual Cyprus International Tournament has become an important feature in the fixture list with a number of nations taking

INTERNATIONAL HONOURS
None

advantage of their winter breaks to visit the island. After beating Austria in the semi-final on penalties the Cypriots then lost to Finland in the 2005 final. Anorthosis Famagusta, who found themselves forced out of their home town following the partition of the island in 1974, continue to flourish in exile and after securing a first Championship post-partition in 1997, they have now won five of the past nine after beating defending champions APOEL in a closely fought race to clinch the 2005 title. The most successful club in the history of the league, Omonia Nicosia, made up for a disappointing campaign by beating Digenis Morfu in the Cup Final.

THE FIFA BIG COUNT OF 2000

	Male	Female		Male	Female
Registered players	33 250	104	Referees	162	1
Non registered players	10 487	0	Officials	1 869	75
Youth players	7 000	74	Total involved	53 022	
Total players	50 915		Number of clubs	321	
Professional players	450	1	Number of teams	506	

Cyprus Football Association (CFA)
1 Stasinos Street, Engomi, PO Box 25071, Nicosia 2404, Cyprus
Tel +357 22 590960   Fax +357 22 590544
cyprusfa@cytanet.com.cy   www.none
President: KOUTSOKOUMNIS Costakis   General Secretary: GEORGIADES Chris
Vice-President: KATSIKIDES Tassos   Treasurer: KIZIS Theodoros   Media Officer: GIORGALIS Kyriakos
Men's Coach: ANASTASIADIS Angelos   Women's Coach: None
CFA formed: 1934   UEFA: 1962   FIFA: 1948
Colours: Blue, White, Blue or White, White, White

GAMES PLAYED BY CYPRUS IN THE 2006 FIFA WORLD CUP™ CYCLE

2002	Opponents	Score		Venue	Comp	Scorers	Att	Referee
21-08	Northern Ireland	D	0-0	Belfast	Fr		6 922	Jones WAL
7-09	France	L	1-2	Nicosia	ECq	Okkas [15]	10 000	Fandel GER
20-11	Malta	W	2-1	Nicosia	ECq	Rauffmann [50], Okkas [74]	5 000	Guenov BUL
2003								
29-01	Greece	L	1-2	Larnaca	Fr	Konstantinou.M [28p]	2 000	Loizou CYP
12-02	Russia	L	0-1	Limassol	Fr		300	Efthimiadis GRE
13-02	Slovakia	L	1-3	Larnaca	Fr	Rauffmann [40]	250	Kapitanis CYP
29-03	Israel	D	1-1	Limassol	ECq	Rauffmann [61]	8 500	McCurry SCO
2-04	Slovenia	L	1-4	Ljubljana	ECq	Konstantinou.M [10]	5 000	Costa POR
30-04	Israel	L	0-2	Palermo	ECq		1 000	Benes CZE
7-06	Malta	W	2-1	Ta'Qali	ECq	Konstantinou.M 2 [22p 53]	3 000	Brugger AUT
6-09	France	L	0-5	Paris	ECq		55 000	Irvine NIR
11-10	Slovenia	D	2-2	Limassol	ECq	Georgiou.S [74], Yiasoumi [84]	2 346	Ovrebo NOR
2004								
18-02	Belarus	L	0-2	Achnas	Fr		500	Kailis CYP
19-02	Georgia	W	3-1	Nicosia	Fr	Charalampidis 2 [44 55], Ilia [73]	200	Kapitanis CYP
21-02	Kazakhstan	W	2-1	Larnaca	Fr	Charalampidis [3], Michail.C [8]	300	Lajuks LVA
19-05	Jordan	D	0-0	Nicosia	Fr		2 500	Loizou CYP
18-08	Albania	W	2-1	Nicosia	Fr	Konstantinou.M 2 [13p 48]	200	Kapitanis CYP
4-09	Republic of Ireland	L	0-3	Dublin	WCq		36 000	Paniashvili GEO
8-09	Israel	L	1-2	Tel Aviv	WCq	Konstantinou.M [59]	21 872	Shmolik BLR
9-10	Faroe Islands	D	2-2	Nicosia	WCq	Konstantinou.M [15], Okkas [81]	1 400	Gadiyev AZE
13-10	France	L	0-2	Nicosia	WCq		3 319	Larsen DEN
17-11	Israel	L	1-2	Nicosia	WCq	Okkas [45]	1 624	Kaldma EST
2005								
8-02	Austria	D	1-1	Limassol	Fr	Charalampidis [90]. W 5-4p	300	Hyytia FIN
9-02	Finland	L	1-2	Nicosia	Fr	Michail.C [24]	300	Lajuks LVA
26-03	Jordan	W	2-1	Larnaca	Fr	Charalampidis [9], Okkas [28]	200	Kapitanis CYP
30-03	Switzerland	L	0-1	Zurich	WCq		16 066	Dougal SCO

Fr = Friendly match • EC = UEFA EURO 2004™ • WC = FIFA World Cup™ • q = qualifier

NATIONAL CAPS

	Caps
PITTAS Pambos	82
PANAYIOTOU Nikos	73
YIANGOUDAKIS Yiannakis	68
OKKAS Ioannis	61
CHARALAMBOUS Marios	60
THEODOTOU Gheorghios	56
IOANNOU Dimitris	50
SAVVIDES George	47
KONSTANTINOU Michael	46
PANTZIARAS Nikos	46

NATIONAL GOALS

	Goals
KONSTANTINOU Michael	19
OKKAS Ioannis	12
AGATHOKLEOUS Mariojos	10
GOGIC Sinisa	8
SOTIRIOU Andros	8
VRAHIMIS Phivos	8
ENGOMITIS Panayiotis	7
PITTAS Pambos	7
KAIAFAS Sotiris	6
IOANNOU Yiannakis	6

NATIONAL COACH

	Years
IOAKOVOU Panikos	1984-'87
CHARALAMBOUS Takis	1987
IOAKOVOU Panikos	1988-'91
MICHAILIDIS Andreas	1991-'96
PAPADOPOULOS Stavros	1997
GEORGIOU Panikos	1997-'99
PAPADOPOULOS Stavros	1999-'01
CHARALAMBOUS Takis	2001
VUKOTIC Momcilo	2001-'04
ANASTASIADIS Angelos	2004-

CYPRUS COUNTRY INFORMATION

Capital	Nicosia	Independence	1960 from the UK	GDP per Capita	$19 200
Population	775 927	Status	Republic	GNP Ranking	89
Area km²	9 250	Language	Greek, Turkish	Dialling code	+357
Population density	83 per km²	Literacy rate	97%	Internet code	.cy
% in urban areas	54%	Main religion	Christian 82%	GMT +/-	+2
Towns/Cities ('000)	Nicosia 242; Limassol 154; Larnaka 48; Gazimagusa 42; Paphos 35; Girne 26; Güzelyurt 14				
Neighbours (km)	Mediterranean Sea 648				
Main stadia	Neo GSP – Nicosia 23 400; Tsirion – Limassol 13 152; Zenon – Larnaca 13 032				

CYPRUS NATIONAL TEAM RECORDS AND RECORD SEQUENCES

Records			Sequence records				
Victory	5-0	AND 2000	Wins	3	1992, 1998, 2000	Clean sheets	2	1992-93, 1994,1996
Defeat	0-12	GER 1969	Defeats	19	1973-1978	Goals scored	7	1997-1998
Player Caps	82	PITTAS Pambos	Undefeated	6	1997-1998	Without goal	6	1975, 1987-1988
Player Goals	19	KONSTANTINOU Michael	Without win	39	1984-1992	Goals against	36	1973-1981

CYPRUS 2004-05

DIVISION A

	Pl	W	D	L	F	A	Pts	Anorthosis	APOEL	Omonia	Olympiakos	Digenis	Nea S'mina	Apollon	ENP	AEK	AEL	Ethnikos	AEP	Alki	Aris
Anorthosis Famagusta †	26	19	5	1	64	23	62		1-1	2-0	5-0	0-0	4-2	§	3-2	3-1	2-0	3-0	2-1	7-2	2-0
APOEL Nicosia ‡	26	17	7	2	56	21	58	2-3		3-1	4-0	2-1	2-0	4-2	2-1	2-0	5-0	1-1	3-0	5-1	1-0
Omonia Nicosia ‡	26	13	8	5	47	29	47	2-4	1-1		3-0	1-0	1-0	1-0	1-0	0-0	2-1	1-1	7-0	3-0	4-1
Olympiakos Nicosia	26	11	6	9	36	38	39	1-1	1-2	2-0		2-0	1-3	2-1	0-0	2-1	2-1	2-2	2-2	0-1	2-0
Digenis Morfu	26	10	6	10	36	31	36	1-3	1-1	0-1	0-1		1-1	0-1	1-0	3-3	0-2	1-1	2-1	6-2	2-0
Nea Salamina	26	11	3	12	36	40	36	0-2	1-2	0-1	2-1	0-4		1-1	3-2	2-0	1-0	4-1	2-1	0-0	4-1
Apollon Limassol	26	10	5	10	43	35	35	0-1	0-0	1-1	1-0	1-2	2-3		4-1	1-2	0-3	6-0	0-2	5-0	4-1
ENP Paralimni	26	7	11	8	38	39	32	1-1	3-3	3-0	2-2	1-0	2-1	2-3		1-1	2-0	3-2	2-2	1-1	2-1
AEK Larnaca	26	7	11	8	26	34	32	0-0	2-1	1-1	0-0	1-1	1-0	0-0	1-1		0-5	2-0	2-1	0-2	2-0
AEL Limassol	26	8	7	11	36	38	31	3-1	1-1	2-2	2-3	0-1	2-1	1-4	2-2	1-1		0-2	0-0	2-2	2-1
Ethnikos	26	8	6	12	31	40	30	1-3	0-1	0-0	1-0	1-2	3-0	0-0	0-1	3-2	0-1		1-2	2-0	5-2
AEP Paphos	26	8	5	13	38	52	29	2-3	0-3	3-4	1-2	3-1	0-2	1-3	2-2	1-1	3-2	1-0		3-2	2-1
Alki Larnaca	26	8	5	13	39	55	29	0-4	0-1	3-3	2-3	1-2	3-0	6-1	2-0	3-1	0-0	0-1	3-1		3-2
Aris Limassol	26	1	1	24	22	73	4	1-4	0-3	1-6	1-5	1-4	2-3	1-2	1-1	0-1	0-3	2-3	0-3	2-0	

18/09/2004 - 15/05/2004 • † Qualified for the UEFA Champions League • ‡ Qualified for the UEFA Cup • § Anorthosis v Apollon declared void

CYPRUS 2004-05 DIVISION B

	Pl	W	D	L	F	A	Pts
APOP	26	17	6	3	70	22	57
APEP	26	14	7	5	37	22	49
THOI Lakatamia	26	14	5	7	47	27	47
Anagennisis Yermasoyia	26	12	7	7	34	25	43
Ayia Napa	26	11	5	10	37	34	38
Halkanoras Dhaliou	26	10	6	10	43	44	36
Doxa Katokopia	26	10	5	11	32	28	35
Omonia Aradippou	26	9	8	9	39	45	35
Onisillos Sotiras	26	9	7	10	38	32	34
MEAP Nisou	26	8	10	8	35	33	34
Ethnikos Ashia	26	8	9	9	35	38	33
ASIL Lysi	26	8	5	13	35	49	29
Ermis Aradippou	26	5	10	11	31	35	25
Akritas Chloraka	26	2	0	24	19	98	6

18/09/2004 - 3/04/2005

TOP SCORERS

SOSIN Lukasz	Apollon	21
FROUSSOS Nikolaos	Anorthosis	17
JOVANOVIC Sasa	AEP	17
KETSBAIA Temuri	Anorthosis	16
NEOPHITOU Marios	APOEL	14

CUP 2004

Quarter-finals			Semi-finals			Final	
Omonia	2	1					
AEK *	1	0	Omonia	2	3		
ENP *	2	0	Apollon *	2	0		
Apollon	1	3				Omonia	2
APOEL	2	3				Digenis	0
Aris *	2	0	APOEL *	0	1		
AEL	1	1	Digenis	0	3	22-05-2005, GSP, Nicosia	
Digenis *	4	0	* Home team in the first leg			Scorers - Mguni [45], Papaioannoau [74] for Omonia	

RECENT LEAGUE AND CUP RECORD

	Championship						Cup		
Year	Champions	Pts	Runners-up	Pts	Third	Pts	Winners	Score	Runners-up
1996	APOEL Nicosia	64	Anorthosis F'gusta	55	Omonia Nicosia	53	APOEL Nicosia	2-0	AEK Larnaca
1997	Anorthosis F'gusta	65	Apollon Limassol	52	Omonia Nicosia	46	APOEL Nicosia	2-0	Omonia Nicosia
1998	Anorthosis F'gusta	66	Omonia Nicosia	62	Apollon Limassol	55	Anothosis F'gusta	3-1	Apollon Limassol
1999	Anorthosis F'gusta	67	Omonia Nicosia	67	APOEL Nicosia	59	APOEL Nicosia	2-0	Anorthosis F'gusta
2000	Anorthosis F'gusta	65	Omonia Nicosia	59	APOEL Nicosia	46	Omonia Nicosia	4-2	APOEL Nicosia
2001	Omonia Nicosia	57	Olympiakos	54	AEL Limassol	52	Apollon Limassol	1-0	NEA Salamina
2002	APOEL Nicosia	59	Anorthosis F'gusta	58	AEL Limassol	54	Anorthosis F'gusta	1-0	Ethnikos Achnas
2003	Omonia Nicosia	60	Anorthosis F'gusta	59	APOEL Nicosia	55	Anorthosis F'gusta	0-0 5-3p	AEL Limassol
2004	APOEL Nicosia	65	Omonia Nicosia	62	Apollon Limassol	49	AEK Larnaca	2-1	AEL Limassol
2005	Anorthosis F'gusta	62	APOEL Nicosia	58	Omonia Nicosia	47	Omonia Nicosia	2-0	Digenis Morfu

CZE – CZECH REPUBLIC

NATIONAL TEAM RECORD
JULY 1ST 2002 TO JUNE 30TH 2005

PL	W	D	L	F	A	%
34	26	4	4	95	28	82.4

FIFA/COCA-COLA WORLD RANKING

1993	1994	1995	1996	1997	1998	1999	2000	2001	2002	2003	2004	High	Low	
-	34	14	5	3	8	2	5	14	15	6	4	2	67	03/94

2004-2005											
08/04	09/04	10/04	11/04	12/04	01/05	02/05	03/05	04/05	05/05	06/05	07/05
5	5	6	5	4	4	4	4	2	2	2	4

The Czech Republic's rise to second place in the FIFA/Coca-Cola World Ranking has come on the back of a series of outstanding results. In the three years after the 2002 FIFA World Cup™ the national team won 26 of the 34 matches played with just four defeats, a record that Brazil do not come close to matching. Key defeats against Greece in the semi-final of Euro 2004 and against the Netherlands in the 2006 FIFA World Cup™ qualifiers have cost the Czechs dearly, although even if they do finish second behind the Dutch they would expect to automatically qualify for a first finals given their record of seven wins in their first eight matches. The strength of the team lies in

INTERNATIONAL HONOURS
UEFA U-21 Championship 2002

the phenomenal goalscoring record with the tall Jan Koller overtaking the Czechoslovakian record of 34 international goals set by Antonin Puc in 1938. In domestic football Sparta reclaimed the League title from Banik Ostrava with considerable ease earning direct qualification to the UEFA Champions League group stage. Despite losing their League crown Banik did win a trophy, beating Slovacko in the Cup Final. The challenge for the Czechs, not made any easier after recent match-fixing scandals, is to maintain the increase in standards and to eventually rival the likes of the Dutch and Portuguese leagues, enabling some of the more talented players to stay at home.

THE FIFA BIG COUNT OF 2000

	Male	Female		Male	Female
Registered players	241 235	2 984	Referees	3 600	5
Non registered players	100 000	3 000	Officials	8 000	200
Youth players	236 988	3 038	Total involved	599 050	
Total players	587 245		Number of clubs	2 000	
Professional players	1 208	0	Number of teams	3 940	

Football Association of Czech Republic (CMFS)
Diskarska 100, Praha 6 - 16017, Czech Republic
Tel +420 2 33029111   Fax +420 2 33353107
cmfs@fotbal.cz   www.fotbal.cz
President: OBST Jan   General Secretary: FOUSEK Petr
Vice-President: MOKRY Pavel   Treasurer: TBD   Media Officer: MACHO Daniel
Men's Coach: BRUECKNER Karel   Women's Coach: ZOVINEC Dusan
CMFS formed: 1901   UEFA: 1954   FIFA: 1907 & 1994
Colours: Red, White, Blue or White, White, White

GAMES PLAYED BY CZECH REPUBLIC IN THE 2006 FIFA WORLD CUP™ CYCLE

2002	Opponents	Score		Venue	Comp	Scorers	Att	Referee
21-08	Slovakia	W	4-1	Olomouc	Fr	Koller 2 [32 65], Rosicky 2 [71 79]	11 986	Douros GRE
6-09	Yugoslavia	W	5-0	Prague	Fr	Smicer [2], Ujfalusi 2 [21 55], Baros 2 [51 80]	5 435	Baskakov RUS
12-10	Moldova	W	2-0	Chisinau	ECq	Jankulovski [69p], Rosicky [79]	4 000	Irvine NIR
16-10	Belarus	W	2-0	Teplice	ECq	Poborsky [6], Baros [23]	12 850	Fleischer GER
20-11	Sweden	D	3-3	Teplice	Fr	Fukal [8], Vachousek [45], Baros [63]	10 238	Bosat TUR
2003								
12-02	France	W	2-0	Paris	Fr	Grygera [7], Baros [62]	57 366	Stark GER
29-03	Netherlands	D	1-1	Rotterdam	ECq	Koller [68]	51 180	Nielsen DEN
2-04	Austria	W	4-0	Prague	ECq	Nedved [19], Koller 2 [32 62], Jankulovski [56p]	20 000	Nieto ESP
30-04	Turkey	W	4-0	Teplice	Fr	Rosicky [2], Koller [21], Smicer [27], Baros [38]	14 156	Szabo HUN
11-06	Moldova	W	5-0	Olomouc	ECq	Smicer [41], Koller [73p], Stajner [82], Lokvenc 2 [88 90]	12 097	Jakobsson ISL
6-09	Belarus	W	3-1	Minsk	ECq	Nedved [37], Baros [54], Smicer [85]	11 000	McCurry SCO
10-09	Netherlands	W	3-1	Prague	ECq	Koller [15p], Poborsky [38], Baros [90]	18 356	Batista POR
11-10	Austria	W	3-2	Vienna	ECq	Jankulovski [27], Vachousek [79], Koller [90]	32 350	Kasnaferis GRE
15-11	Canada	W	5-1	Teplice	Fr	Jankulovski [26p], Heinz [49], Poborsky [55], Sionko [63], Skacel [82]	8 343	Sundell SWE
2004								
18-02	Italy	D	2-2	Palermo	Fr	Stajner [42], Rosicky [89]	20 935	Braamhaar NED
31-03	Republic of Ireland	L	1-2	Dublin	Fr	Baros [81]	42 000	Fisker DEN
28-04	Japan	L	0-1	Prague	Fr		11 802	McKeon IRE
2-06	Bulgaria	W	3-1	Prague	Fr	Baros [54], Plasil [74], Rosicky [81]	6 627	Stredak SVK
6-06	Estonia	W	2-0	Teplice	Fr	Baros 2 [6 22]	11 873	Bruggwer AUT
15-06	Latvia	W	2-1	Aveiro	ECr1	Baros [73], Heinz [85]	21 744	Veissiere FRA
19-06	Netherlands	W	3-2	Aveiro	ECr1	Koller [23], Baros [71], Smicer [88]	29 935	Gonzalez ESP
23-06	Germany	W	2-1	Lisbon	ECr1	Heinz [30], Baros [77]	46 849	Hauge NOR
27-06	Denmark	W	3-0	Porto	ECqf	Koller [49], Baros 2 [63 65]	41 092	Ivanov RUS
1-07	Greece	L	0-1	Porto	ECsf		42 449	Collina ITA
18-08	Greece	D	0-0	Prague	Fr		15 050	Dougal SCO
8-09	Netherlands	L	0-2	Amsterdam	WCq		48 488	Merk GER
9-10	Romania	W	1-0	Prague	WCq	Koller [36]	16 028	Rosetti ITA
13-10	Armenia	W	3-0	Yerevan	WCq	Koller 2 [3 75]	3 205	Granat POL
17-11	FYR Macedonia	W	2-0	Skopje	WCq	Lokvenc [88], Koller [90]	7 000	Meier SUI
2005								
9-02	Slovenia	W	3-0	Celje	Fr	Koller [10], Jun [47], Polak [79]	4 000	Strahonja CRO
26-03	Finland	W	4-3	Teplice	WCq	Baros [7], Rosicky [34], Polak [58], Lokvenc [87]	16 200	Larsen DEN
30-03	Andorra	W	4-0	Andorra la Vella	WCq	Jankulovski [31p], Baros [40], Lokvenc [53], Rosicky [92+p]	900	Messner AUT
4-06	Andorra	W	8-1	Liberec	WCq	Lokvenc 2 [12 92], Koller [30], Smicer [37], Galasek [52], Baros [79], Rosicky [84], Polak [86]	9 520	Dereli TUR
8-06	FYR Macedonia	W	6-1	Teplice	WCq	Koller 4 [41 45 48 52], Rosicky [73p], Baros [87]	14 150	Dauden Ibanez ESP

Fr = Friendly match • EC = UEFA EURO 2004™ • WC = FIFA World Cup™ • q = qualifier • r1 = first round group • qf = quarter-final • sf = semi-final

CZECH REPUBLIC NATIONAL TEAM RECORDS AND RECORD SEQUENCES

Records			Sequence records				
Victory	6-0	MLT 1996, BUL 2001	Wins	7	2003	Clean sheets	4	1999
Defeat	0-3	SUI 1994	Defeats	3	2000	Goals scored	17	2002-2004
Player Caps	105	POBORSKY Karel	Undefeated	20	2002-2004	Without goal	3	2004
Player Goals	39	KOLLER Jan	Without win	3	Four times	Goals against	8	1999-2000, 2003-04

CZECH REPUBLIC COUNTRY INFORMATION

Capital	Prague (Praha)	Independence	1993 split from Slovakia	GDP per Capita	$15 700
Population	10 246 178	Status	Republic	GNP Ranking	45
Area km²	78 866	Language	Czech	Dialling code	+420
Population density	129 per km²	Literacy rate	99%	Internet code	.cz
% in urban areas	65%	Main religion	Christian 43%, Atheist 40%	GMT +/–	+1
Towns/Cities ('000)	Praha 1 154; Brno 377; Ostrava 317; Plzen 165; Olomouc 102; Liberec 99; Ceske Budejovice 97				
Neighbours (km)	Poland 658; Slovakia 215 Austria 362; Germany 646				
Main stadia	Strahov – Praha 20 565; Na Stinadlech – Teplice 18 428; Andruv – Olomouc 12 119				

CZECH REPUBLIC 2004-05

I. GAMBRINUS LIGA

	Pl	W	D	L	F	A	Pts	Sparta	Slavia	Teplice	Olomouc	Liberec	Jablonec	Ostrava	1.FKD	Pribram	Brno	Zlin	Blsany	Slovacko	Boleslav	Budejovice	Opava
Sparta Praha †	30	20	4	6	53	28	64		2-0	1-2	2-0	2-1	3-1	2-1	2-0	4-2	2-0	2-0	4-2	1-1	0-1	2-0	5-1
Slavia Praha †	30	15	8	7	39	25	53	1-1		2-0	3-2	1-0	1-1	1-0	2-1	5-1	3-0	1-0	0-0	0-0	2-2	0-2	1-0
FK Teplice ‡	30	14	11	5	36	27	53	0-0	1-0		1-0	0-1	0-0	2-0	2-1	1-0	3-1	2-1	0-0	1-1	1-1	5-2	1-0
Sigma Olomouc	30	15	6	9	39	34	51	0-2	2-1	3-3		2-2	0-1	2-2	4-1	3-0	2-1	1-0	1-0	1-0	2-0	2-1	0-1
Slovan Liberec	30	14	10	6	45	26	46	0-1	1-1	4-0	3-0		1-1	1-0	0-2	2-0	1-0	1-1	3-0	1-1	1-3	3-2	3-0
FK Jablonec 97	30	12	9	9	33	27	45	3-0	1-1	1-1	0-1	1-2		1-1	1-0	3-1	2-0	1-0	3-0	1-1	2-0	1-2	0-1
Baník Ostrava ‡	30	9	10	11	33	36	37	0-2	0-2	1-2	4-0	0-4	0-0		2-2	2-1	1-1	3-1	1-0	2-2	2-0	2-0	0-0
1.FK Drnovice §	30	9	8	13	30	34	35	2-3	2-1	2-0	0-0	1-1	0-1	1-0		0-1	1-3	2-0	0-0	1-0	2-0	2-0	1-1
Marila Pribram	30	9	8	13	30	41	35	3-1	0-1	0-2	0-0	1-1	3-1	1-2	1-2		1-3	0-0	2-1	0-0	2-1	1-0	2-1
1.FC Brno	30	9	6	15	30	42	33	0-1	0-1	1-3	0-1	1-2	1-2	2-0	1-0	1-2		1-1	1-1	1-0	2-0	0-0	2-1
Tescoma Zlin	30	7	12	11	29	35	33	1-1	1-0	2-0	0-2	1-0	1-2	1-1	3-1	0-0	3-3		0-0	1-0	2-2	2-2	3-0
Chmel Blsany	30	7	11	12	25	38	32	1-3	0-3	2-2	2-2	1-1	0-0	0-2	1-1	3-2	0-1	2-0		2-0	2-0	1-0	1-0
1.FC Slovácko	30	10	14	6	30	22	32	2-0	2-0	0-0	1-0	1-0	1-0	3-1	2-1	1-1	1-2	3-1	1-0		1-1	0-0	1-0
Mladá Boleslav	30	6	13	11	26	35	31	2-1	1-1	0-0	1-2	0-1	1-1	0-1	0-0	0-0	4-0	1-1	1-1	0-0		1-0	1-1
Ceske Budejovice	30	6	7	17	28	39	25	1-2	1-2	0-1	1-2	1-2	0-1	0-1	2-1	0-0	1-1	0-0	3-0	0-2	3-0		2-0
SFC Opava	30	5	9	16	25	42	18	0-1	1-2	0-0	1-2	1-1	4-1	1-1	0-0	0-2	2-0	1-2	1-2	2-2	2-1	2-2	

7/08/2004 - 28/05/2005 • † Qualified for the UEFA Champions League • ‡ Qualified for the UEFA Cup • § 1.FK Drnovice withdrew at the end of the season • Liberec and Opava deducted six points • Slovacko deducted 12 points

CZECH REPUBLIC 2004-05 II. LIGA

	Pl	W	D	L	F	A	Pts
Siad Most	28	17	10	1	58	30	61
Vysocina Jihlava	28	13	9	6	46	30	48
Viktoria Plzen	28	12	10	6	32	23	46
SK Kladno	28	11	10	7	37	22	43
1.FC Brno B	28	10	6	12	33	31	36
Viktoria Zizkov §1	28	14	4	10	42	36	34
Hradec Kralove	28	9	7	12	37	38	34
FC Vitkovice §2	28	10	12	6	35	30	33
FK Kunovice	28	8	9	11	29	42	33
Sparta Praha B	28	7	11	10	24	30	32
Sigma Olomouc B	28	7	10	11	32	39	31
Usti nad Labem	28	7	9	12	27	40	30
Hanacka Kromeriz	28	6	10	12	29	45	28
AS Pardubice	28	6	9	13	20	34	27
Tatran Prachatice	28	6	8	14	28	39	26

8/08/2004 - 12/06/2005 • Bohemians Praha withdrew after 15 matches • §1 Deducted 12 points • §2 Deducted nine points

TOP SCORERS

JUN Tomas	Sparta	14
ZELENKA Ludek	Brno	12
MASEK Jiri	Teplice	10
VLCEK Stanislav	Slavia	10
POSPISIL Michal	Slovan Liberec	9

POHAR CMFS 2004-05

Round of 16		Quarter-finals		Semi-finals		Final	
Baník Ostrava	1						
Unicov *	0	Baník Ostrava *	5				
Slavcin *	0	Slavia Praha	1				
Slavia Praha	6			Baník Ostrava	0 3p		
Siad Most *	1			Viktoria Plzen	0 0p		
Mladá Boleslav	0	Siad Most	1 3p				
HFK Olomouc *	0	Viktoria Plzen *	1 4p				
Viktoria Plzen	1					Baník Ostrava ‡	2
Slovan Liberec	1					1.FC Slovácko	1
SK Kladno *	0	Slovan Liberec *	4				
Ceské Budejovice *	1	FK Jablonec 97	1				
FK Jablonec 97	2			Slovan Liberec	2 2p		
FK Teplice	2			1.FC Slovácko	2 3p		
Tescoma Zlin *	1	FK Teplice	0 8p				
Hlucin *	1 1p	1.FC Slovácko *	0 9p				
1.FC Slovácko	1 4p	* Home team • ‡ Qualified for the UEFA Cup					

CUP FINAL

31-05-2005, Att: 11 251, Ref: Sedivy Andruv, Olomouc
Scorers - Metelka [54], Papadopoulos [88] for Baník, Dostalek [90] for Slovácko

NATIONAL CAPS

	Caps
POBORSKY Karel	105
KUKA Pavel	87
NEMEC Jiri	84
NEDVED Pavel	83
SMICER Vladimir	74
LOKVENC Vratislav	69
KADLEC Miroslav	64
KOLLER JAN	63

Appearances for Czechoslovakia:
Kuka 24/87, Nemec 40/84, Kadlec 38/64

NATIONAL GOALS

	Goals
KOLLER Jan	39
KUKA Pavel	29
SMICER Vladimir	26
BAROS Milan	25
BERGER Patrick	18
NEDVED Pavel	17
SKUHRAVY Tomas	17
ROSICKY Tomas	13

Goals for Czechoslovakia:
Kuka 7/29, Skuhravy 14/17

NATIONAL COACH

	Years
JEZEK Vaclav	1993
UHRIN Dusan	1994-'97
CHOVANEC Jozef	1998-'01
BRUECKNER Karel	2001-

FIFA REFEREE LIST 2005

	Int'l	DoB
BENES Michal	1998	26-11-1967
CURIN Tomas	2005	5-05-1970
JARA Jaroslav	1998	21-02-1964
KRALOVEC Pavel	2005	16-08-1977
MATEJEK Radek	2004	5-02-1973
SEDIVY Milan	2003	17-06-1967

FIFA ASSISTANT REFEREE LIST 2005

	Int'l	DoB
CHYTIL Ivo	2005	16-09-1967
FILGAS Jan	2005	17-06-1974
FILIPEK Patrik	2000	18-12-1968
HOLUB Vitezslav	2003	20-07-1967
KORDULA Antonin	2005	25-01-1969
POKORNY Ivan	2001	14-01-1967
TULINGER Miroslav	1999	8-05-1960
VODICKA Jiri	1997	27-04-1962
WILCZEK Martin	2005	23-05-1970
ZLAMAL Miroslav	2001	14-05-1973

CLUB DIRECTORY

Club	Town/City	Stadium	Phone	www.	Lge	Cup	CL
FC Banik Ostrava	Ostrava	Bazaly 18 020	+420 596 241804	fcb.cz	1 - 3	0 - 3	0
FK Chmel Blsany	Blsany	Chmel 2 300	+420 415 214523	fkblsany.cz	0	0	0
1.FC Brno	Brno	Na Srbské 12 500	+420 541 233582	1fcbrno.cz	0 - 1	0	0
SK Dynamo	Ceské Budéjovice	Na Steleckem Ostrove 6 129	+420 387 312502	dynamocb.cz	0	0	0
1.FK Drnovice	Drnovice	Drnovice 6 400	+420 517 353265	fkdrnovice.cz	0	0	0
FK Jablonec 97	Jablonec nad Nisou	Strelnice 15 577	+420 483 318943	fkjablonec97.cz	0	1 - 0	0
FK Marila Pribram	Pribram	Marila 8 000	+420 318 626173	fkmarila.cz	0	0	0
FK Mladá Boleslav	Mladá Boleslav	Mestsky 4 280	+420 326 719041	fk-mladaboleslav.cz	0	0	0
SFC Opava	Opava	Mestsky 17 687	+420 553 616390	sfc.cz	0	0	0
SK Sigma Olomouc	Olomouc	Andruv 12 119	+420 585 222956	sigmafotbal.cz	0	0	0
SK Slavia Praha	Prague	Evzena Rosickeho 19 336	+420 2 33081764	slavia.cz	5 - 9	3 - 15	0
1.FC Slovácko	Uherské Hradiste	Mestsky Futbalovy 8 121	+420 572 551801	fc.synot.cz	0	0	0
FC Slovan Liberec	Liberec	U Nisy 9 090	+420 485 103714	fcslovanliberec.cz	1 - 0	1 - 0	0
AC Sparta Praha	Prague	Strahov (Toyota Arena) 20 565	+420 2 96111111	sparta.cz	10 - 19	2 - 22	0
FK Teplice	Teplice	Na Stinadlech 18 428	+420 417 507401	fkteplice.cz	0	1 - 0	0
FC Tescoma Zlín	Zlín	Letná 4 541	+420 577 210506	fctescomazlin.cz	0	0	0

Where there are two figures in the League or Cup column, the first shows titles won in Czech tournaments, the second in Czechoslovakian tournaments

RECENT LEAGUE AND CUP RECORD

	Championship						Cup		
Year	Champions	Pts	Runners-up	Pts	Third	Pts	Winners	Score	Runners-up
1990							Dukla Praha	5-3	Uherske Hradiste
1991							Banik Ostrava	4-2	Dy. Ceske Budejovice
1992							Sparta Praha	2-1	Banik Ostrava
1993							Sparta Praha	2-0	FC Boby Brno
1994	Sparta Praha	45	Slavia Praha	39	Banik Ostrava	36	Viktoria Zizkov	2-2 6-5p	Sparta Praha
1995	Sparta Praha	70	Slavia Praha	64	Boby Brno	54	SK Hradec Kralové	0-0 3-1p	Viktoria Zizkov
1996	Slavia Praha	70	Sigma Olomouc	61	Jablonec nad Nisou	53	Sparta Praha	4-0	Petra Drnovice
1997	Sparta Praha	65	Slavia Praha	61	Jablonec nad Nisou	56	Slavia Praha	1-0	Dukla Praha
1998	Sparta Praha	71	Slavia Praha	59	Sigma Olomouc	55	FK Jablonec	2-1	Petra Drnovice
1999	Sparta Praha	60	FK Teplice	55	Slavia Praha	55	Slavia Praha	1-0	Slovan Liberec
2000	Sparta Praha	76	Slavia Praha	68	FK Drnovice	48	Slovan Liberec	2-1	Banik Ratiskovice
2001	Sparta Praha	68	Slavia Praha	52	Sigma Olomouc	52	Viktoria Zizkov	2-1	Sparta Praha
2002	Slovan Liberec	64	Sparta Praha	63	Viktoria Zizkov	63	Slavia Praha	2-1	Sparta Praha
2003	Sparta Praha	65	Slavia Praha	64	Viktoria Zizkov	50	FK Teplice	1-0	FK Jablonec
2004	Banik Ostrava	63	Sparta Praha	58	Sigma Olomouc	55	Sparta Praha	2-1	Banik Ostrava
2005	Sparta Praha	64	Slavia Praha	53	FK Teplice	53	Banik Ostrava	2-1	1.FC Slovácko

Prior to 1994 clubs played in the Czechoslovakian League, whilst the winners of the Czech Cup played the winners of the Slovak Cup

DEN – DENMARK

NATIONAL TEAM RECORD

JULY 1ST 2002 TO JUNE 30TH 2005

PL	W	D	L	F	A	%
35	17	11	7	56	35	64.3

FIFA/COCA-COLA WORLD RANKING

1993	1994	1995	1996	1997	1998	1999	2000	2001	2002	2003	2004	High		Low	
6	14	9	6	8	19	11	22	18	12	13	14	3	05/97	27	05/98

2004-2005											
08/04	09/04	10/04	11/04	12/04	01/05	02/05	03/05	04/05	05/05	06/05	07/05
15	15	15	13	14	14	15	17	18	19	16	19

In their attempt to qualify for the FIFA World Cup™ finals for an unprecedented third time in succession the Danes found themselves in a hugely difficult group containing the European champions Greece, Turkey, who finished third in the 2002 finals, and one of the current form teams on the continent - Ukraine. With the Ukrainians running away at the top the group has resembled a dogfight between the rest for a play-off spot. Should they fail to qualify it will be only the third major tournament that they will have missed out on since qualifying for the finals of Euro 1984. There have been significant changes to the domestic calendar in Scandinavia with the inauguration

INTERNATIONAL HONOURS

Qualified for the FIFA World Cup™ finals 1986 1998 2002   Qualified for the FIFA Women's World Cup finals 1991 1995 1999
UEFA European Championship 1992

of the Royal League tournament and it was FC København, the only Danish team to qualify for the final stage, who won it, beating IFK Göteborg on penalties in the final on 26 May. That was some consolation for the double winners of 2004 who had seen their fierce Copenhagen rivals Brøndby win the 2005 Cup Final earlier in the month. Coached by Michael Laudrup, Brøndby beat Midtjylland 3-2 after extra-time in an exciting match and then 10 days later they thrashed FC København 5-0 to effectively seal the title and the double.

THE FIFA BIG COUNT OF 2000

	Male	Female		Male	Female
Registered players	175 000	25 285	Referees	4 450	20
Non registered players	80 000	20 000	Officials	8 000	200
Youth players	70 000	25 000	Total involved	407 955	
Total players	395 285		Number of clubs	1 000	
Professional players	940	15	Number of teams	1 599	

Dansk Boldspil-Union (DBU)

DBU Allé 1, Brøndby 2605, Denmark
Tel +45 43 262222   Fax +45 43 262245
dbu@dbu.dk   www.dbu.dk
President: HANSEN Allan   General Secretary: HANSEN Jim
Vice-President: MOLLER Jesper   Treasurer: MOGENSEN Torben   Media Officer: BERENDT Lars
Men's Coach: OLSEN Morten   Women's Coach: HOJMOSE Poul
DBU formed: 1889   UEFA: 1954   FIFA: 1904
Colours: Red, White, Red or White, Red, White

GAMES PLAYED BY DENMARK IN THE 2006 FIFA WORLD CUP™ CYCLE

2002	Opponents	Score			Venue	Comp	Scorers	Att	Referee
21-08	Scotland	W	1-0		Glasgow	Fr	Sand [8]	28 766	Irvine NIR
7-09	Norway	D	2-2		Oslo	ECq	Tomasson 2 [23 72]	25 141	Dallas SCO
12-10	Luxembourg	W	2-0		Copenhagen	ECq	Tomasson [52p], Sand [72]	40 259	Bede HUN
20-11	Poland	W	2-0		Copenhagen	Fr	Tomasson [23], Larsen [72]	15 364	Bossen HOL
2003									
1-02	Iran	L	0-1		Hong Kong	Fr		15 100	Chiu Sin Chuen HKG
12-02	Egypt	W	4-1		Cairo	Fr	Jensen.C 3 [31 68 70], Tomasson [59]	30 000	El Fatah EGY
29-03	Romania	W	5-2		Bucharest	ECq	Rommedahl 2 [9 90], Gravesen [53], Tomasson [72], OG [74]	55 000	Gonzalez ESP
2-04	Bosnia-Herzegovina	L	0-2		Copenhagen	ECq		30 845	Stredak SVK
30-04	Ukraine	W	1-0		Copenhagen	Fr	Gravesen [37]	14 599	Mikulski POL
7-06	Norway	W	1-0		Copenhagen	ECq	Gronkjaer [5]	41 824	Poll ENG
11-06	Luxembourg	W	2-0		Luxembourg	ECq	Jensen.C [22], Gravesen [50]	6 869	Baskakov RUS
20-08	Finland	D	1-1		Copenhagen	Fr	Gonkjaer [42]	14 882	McCurry SCO
10-09	Romania	D	2-2		Copenhagen	ECq	Tomasson [35p], Lauresen [90]	42 049	Meier GER
11-10	Bosnia-Herzegovina	D	1-1		Sarajevo	ECq	Jorgensen.M [12]	35 500	Barber ENG
16-11	England	W	3-2		Manchester	Fr	Jorgensen.M 2 [8 30p], Tomasson [82]	64 159	Hrinak SVK
2004									
18-01	USA	D	1-1		Carson	Fr	Larsen [28p]	10 461	Moreno MEX
18-02	Turkey	W	1-0		Adana	Fr	Jorgensen.M [32]	15 000	Wack GER
31-03	Spain	L	0-2		Gijon	Fr		18 600	Costa POR
28-04	Scotland	W	1-0		Copenhagen	Fr	Sand [61]	22 485	Ingvarsson SWE
30-05	Estonia	D	2-2		Tallinn	Fr	Tomasson [28], Perez [80]	3 000	Bossen HOL
5-06	Croatia	L	1-2		Copenhagen	Fr	Sand [56]	30 843	Stuchlik AUT
14-06	Italy	D	0-0		Guimaraes	ECr1		19 595	Gonzalez ESP
18-06	Bulgaria	W	2-0		Braga	ECr1	Tomasson [44], Gronkjaer [90]	24 131	Baptista POR
22-06	Sweden	D	2-2		Porto	ECr1	Tomasson 2 [28 66]	26 115	Merk GER
27-06	Czech Republic	L	0-3		Porto	ECqf		41 092	Ivanov RUS
18-08	Poland	W	5-1		Poznan	Fr	Madsen 3 [23 30 90], Gaardsoe [51], Jensen.C [86]	4 500	Bebek CRO
4-09	Ukraine	D	1-1		Copenhagen	WCq	Jorgensen.M [9]	36 335	Meier SUI
9-10	Albania	W	2-0		Tirana	WCq	Jorgensen.M [52], Tomasson [72]	14 500	Baskakov RUS
13-10	Turkey	D	1-1		Copenhagen	WCq	Tomasson [27p]	41 331	De Santis ITA
17-11	Georgia	D	2-2		Tbilisi	WCq	Tomasson 2 [7 64]	20 000	Ceferin SVN
2005									
9-02	Greece	L	1-2		Athens	WCq	Rommedahl [46+]	32 430	Collina ITA
26-03	Kazakhstan	W	3-0		Copenhagen	WCq	Moller.P 2 [10 48], Poulsen [33]	20 980	Gilewski POL
30-03	Ukraine	L	0-1		Kyiv	WCq		60 000	Michel SVK
2-06	Finland	W	1-0		Tampere	Fr	Silberhauser [90]	9 238	Wegereef NED
8-06	Albania	W	3-1		Copenhagen	WCq	Larsen.S 2 [5 47], Jorgensen.M [55]	26 366	Frojdfeldt SWE

Fr = Friendly match • EC = UEFA EURO 2004™ • WC = FIFA World Cup™ • q = qualifier • r1 = first round group • qf = quarter-final

DENMARK COUNTRY INFORMATION

Capital	Copenhagen	Independence	950 as a unified state	GDP per Capita	$31 100
Population	5 413 392	Status	Kingdom	GNP Ranking	25
Area km²	43 094	Language	Danish	Dialling code	+45
Population density	125 per km²	Literacy rate	99%	Internet code	.dk
% in urban areas	85%	Main religion	Christian 98%	GMT + / −	+1
Towns/Cities ('000)	København 1 089; Aarhus 226; Odense 145; Aalborg 122; Esbjerg 72; Randers 55				
Neighbours (km)	Germany 68; North Sea & Baltic Sea 7 314				
Main stadia	Parken – Copenhagen 41 781; Brøndby – Copenhagen 29 000; Idrætspark – Aarhus 21 000				

DENMARK 2004-05

SAS LIGAEN

	Pl	W	D	L	F	A	Pts	Brøndby	København	Midtjylland	AaB	Esbjerg	OB	Viborg	Silkeborg	AGF	Nordsjælland	Herfølge	Randers
Brøndby IF †	33	20	9	4	61	23	69		5-0	2-1 0-1	1-1	4-0	1-2 2-1	2-0 1-0	1-0 0-0	4-0	0-0 2-0	7-0	2-0 2-0
FC København ‡	33	16	9	8	53	39	57	1-3 3-0		4-0	3-2 4-0	2-2 1-0	1-1 1-1	0-0	0-1	2-1 2-3	2-0	2-0 1-1	4-0
FC Midtjylland ‡	33	17	6	10	49	40	57	3-1	2-0 1-0		4-1	4-3	2-1 0-0	1-1 1-2	2-1 0-0	1-1 2-0	1-0	1-1 2-0	3-1 2-1
AaB Aalborg	33	15	8	10	59	45	53	1-1 3-3	1-1	1-2 2-1		0-0	1-1	1-2 5-3	1-0 3-1	3-1	2-0 2-0	3-0	3-0 1-1
Esbjerg FB	33	13	10	10	61	47	49	2-2 0-0	1-1	3-0 0-0	1-0 2-3		2-4 3-2	4-1	4-0	1-2 3-1	3-1	7-2 5-1	1-0
OB Odense	33	13	9	11	61	41	48	1-1	1-2	3-1	1-3 1-2	0-1		0-2 0-0	3-0	0-2 3-0	4-0 7-1	5-0 2-0	5-1 1-0
Viborg FF	33	13	9	11	43	45	48	0-2	3-2 0-2	2-1	2-1	2-0 2-2	1-0		1-1 1-1	2-1	0-1 1-2	2-1	0-1 2-1
Silkeborg IF	33	13	8	12	50	52	47	0-1	2-2 4-1	0-1	1-0	2-1 2-1	1-2 4-2	3-2		3-1 1-1	2-1	2-4 3-0	2-2
AGF Aarhus	33	11	6	16	47	53	39	0-0 1-2	1-2	3-1 2-2	2-2 2-1	0-1	3-3	1-2 1-2	1-3		2-1	2-0 2-1	4-0
FC Nordsjælland	33	8	6	19	36	59	30	0-1	1-2 2-3	3-2	0-1	2-1 2-3	0-0	3-2	2-3 0-0	1-1		0-0	2-2 2-0
Herfølge BK	33	6	7	20	29	71	25	1-4 1-2	0-1	0-1 1-3	2-1 2-4	1-1	2-3	0-0 1-1	1-1	1-0 0-2 1-0			3-2
Randers FC	33	5	9	19	30	64	24	0-2	0-0 0-1	0-3	0-4	1-1 2-2	1-1	2-2	4-3 4-0	0-3 1-0	2-1	0-1 1-1	

24/07/2004 - 19/06/2005 • † Qualified for the UEFA Champions League • ‡ Qualified for the UEFA Cup

DENMARK 2004-05 — 1. DIVISION (2)

	Pl	W	D	L	F	A	Pts
Sønderjyske	30	19	7	4	75	31	64
AC Horsens	30	19	6	5	51	23	63
Frem	30	17	8	5	61	30	59
Køge	30	16	8	6	67	34	56
Vejle BK	30	14	7	9	59	51	49
Skjold	30	15	4	11	47	45	49
Hellerup IK	30	12	11	7	58	41	47
Fremad Amager	30	12	10	8	50	39	46
FC Frederica	30	10	8	12	48	50	38
Nykøbing	30	10	6	14	50	59	36
Akademisk Boldklub	30	10	5	15	49	52	35
Brønshøj	30	8	7	15	48	65	31
Olstykke	30	7	6	17	39	68	30
Dalum	30	7	3	20	47	81	27
Næstved	30	6	2	22	30	71	20
B 93	30	3	8	19	41	80	17

31/07/2004 - 18/06/2005

TOP SCORERS

HOJER Steffen	OB	20
BERGLUND Fredrik	Esbjerg	18
MITI Mwape	OB	16
MOTA Jose Roberto	Viborg	14
JUNKER Mads	Nordsjælland	13
KAHLENBERG Thomas	Brøndby	13
OLSEN Tommy	Nordsjælland	13

DONG CUP 2004-05

Round of 16

Brøndby IF	1
Esbjerg FB *	0
Frem *	0
Skjold	2
Fremad Amager *	3
FC Nordsjælland	2
OB Odense	1
FC København *	2
AC Horsens *	2
AaB Aalborg	1
Køge *	1
AGF Aarhus	2
Olstykke	3
Sønderjyske	1
Herfølge *	1
FC Midtjylland	4

Quarter-finals

Brøndby IF	2
Skjold *	0
Fremad Amager *	1
FC København	3
AC Horsens *	3
AGF Aarhus	1
Olstykke *	0
FC Midtjylland	3

Semi-finals

Brøndby IF *	1 2
FC København	0 2
AC Horsens *	0 0
FC Midtjylland	4 1

Final

Brøndby IF	3
FC Midtjylland ‡	2

CUP FINAL

5-05-2005, Att: 34 026, Ref: Fisker Parken, Copenhagen
Scorers - Skoubo 40, Daugaard 74, Bagger 110 for Brøndby; Hansen.M 47, Pimpong 59 for Midtjylland

* Home team/home team in the first leg • ‡ Qualified for the UEFA Cup

DENMARK NATIONAL TEAM RECORDS AND RECORD SEQUENCES

Records			Sequence records					
Victory	17-1	FRA 1908	Wins	11	1912-1916	Clean sheets	4	1993, 1995
Defeat	0-8	GER 1937	Defeats	7	1970-1971	Goals scored	26	1942-1948
Player Caps	129	SCHMEICHEL Peter	Undefeated	12	1992-1993	Without goal	7	1970-1971
Player Goals	52	NIELSEN Poul	Without win	14	1969-1971	Goals against	21	1939-1946

NATIONAL CAPS

	Caps
SCHMEICHEL Peter	129
LAUDRUP Michael	104
OLSEN Morten	102
HELVEG Thomas	95
SIVEBAEK John	87
HEINTZE Jan	86

NATIONAL GOALS

	Goals
NIELSEN Poul	52
JØRGENSEN Pauli	44
MADSEN Ole	42
ELKJAER-LARSEN Preben	38
LAUDRUP Michael	37
TOMASSON Jon Dahl	35

NATIONAL COACH

	Years
STRITTICH Rudi	1970-'75
NIELSEN Kurt	1976-'79
PIONTEK Sepp	1979-'90
MØLLER-NIELSEN Richard	1990-'96
JOHANSSON Bo	1996-'00
OLSEN Morten	2000-

FIFA REFEREE LIST 2005

	Int'l	DoB
FISKER Knud	1994	17-09-1960
LARSEN Claus Bo	1996	28-10-1965
LAURSEN Emil	2002	23-09-1970
NIELSEN Kim Milton	1988	3-08-1960
POULSEN Tonny	2001	2-07-1965
SVENDSEN Michael	2004	31-05-1967
VOLLQUARTZ Nicolai	1999	7-02-1965

FIFA ASSISTANT REFEREE LIST 2005

	Int'l	DoB
ABILDGAARD Bo	2001	20-05-1963
HANSEN Bill	1998	15-03-1963
HANSEN Ole	1994	27-06-1963
JENSEN Torben	2003	31-07-1965
JEPSEN Jorgen	1998	30-09-1961
NORRESTRAND Anders	2004	18-09-1975
PEDERSEN Bo Blankholm	2000	4-06-1960
PETERSEN Jesper	2004	13-04-1970
SONDERBY Henrik	2005	12-12-1972
UDSEN Palle	2002	6-10-1965

CLUB DIRECTORY

Club	Town/City	Stadium	Phone	www.	Lge	Cup	CL
AaB	Aalborg	Aalborg 16 000	+45 96 355900	ab-fodbold.dk	2	2	0
AGF	Aarhus	Aarhus Idrætspark 21 000	+45 86 112733	agf.co.dk	5	9	0
Brøndby IF	København	Brøndby 29 000	+45 43 630810	brondby.com	9	4	0
Esbjerg FB	Esbjerg	Esbjerg Idrætspark 14 500	+45 75 453355	efb.dk	5	2	0
Herfølge BK	Herfølge	Herfølge 7 5000	+45 56 276021	hb.dk	1	0	0
FC København	København	Parken 41 781	+45 35 437422	fck.dk	4	3	0
FC Midtjylland	Herning	SAS Arena 12 500	+45 96 271040	fc-mj.dk	0	0	0
FC Nordsjælland	Farum	Farum Park 10,000	+45 44 342500	fcnfodbold.dk	0	0	0
OB	Odense	Odense 15 633	+45 63 119090	ob.dk	3	4	0
Randers FC	Randers	Randers 18 000	+45 86 611122	randersfc.dk	3	0	0
Silkeborg IF	Silkeborg	Silkeborg 9 800	+45 86 804477	sif-support.dk	1	1	0
Viborg FF	Viborg	Viborg 9 796	+45 86 601066	vff.dk	0	1	0

KB won 15 championships and one Cup whilst B1903 won seven Championships and two Cups before the clubs merged in 1992 to form FC København

RECENT LEAGUE AND CUP RECORD

Championship							Cup		
Year	Champions	Pts	Runners-up	Pts	Third	Pts	Winners	Score	Runners-up
1990	Brøndby IF	42	B 1903 København	31	Ikast FS	30	Lyngby BK	0-0 6-1	AGF Aarhus
1991	Brøndby IF	26	Lyngby BK	24	AGF Aarhus	20	OB Odense	0-0 4-3p	AaB Aalborg
1992	Lyngby BK	32	B 1903 København	29	Frem København	26	AGF Aarhus	3-0	B 1903 København
1993	FC København	32	OB Odense	31	Brøndby IF	30	OB Odense	2-0	AaB Aalborg
1994	Silkeborg IF	31	FC København	29	Brøndby IF	27	Brøndby IF	0-0 3-1p	Naestved IF
1995	AaB Aalborg	31	Brøndby IF	29	Silkeborg IF	24	FC København	5-0	Akademisk
1996	Brøndby IF	67	AGF Aarhus	66	OB Odense	60	AGF Aarhus	2-0	Brøndby IF
1997	Brøndby IF	68	Vejle BK	54	AGF Aarhus	52	FC København	2-0	Ikast FS
1998	Brøndby IF	76	Silkeborg IF	63	FC København	61	Brøndby IF	4-1	FC København
1999	AaB Aalborg	64	Brøndby IF	61	Akademisk	56	Akademisk	2-1	AaB Aalborg
2000	Herfølge BK	56	Brøndby IF	54	Akademisk	52	Viborg FF	1-0	AaB Aalborg
2001	FC København	63	Brøndby IF	58	Silkeborg IF	56	Silkeborg IF	4-1	Akademisk
2002	Brøndby IF	69	FC København	69	FC Midtjylland	57	OB Odense	2-1	FC København
2003	FC København	61	Brøndby IF	56	Farum BK	51	Brøndby IF	3-0	FC Midtjylland
2004	FC København	68	Brøndby IF	67	Esbjerg FB	62	FC København	1-0	AaB Aalborg
2005	Brøndby IF	69	FC København	57	FC Midtjylland	57	Brøndby IF	3-2	FC Midtjylland

DJI – DJIBOUTI

NATIONAL TEAM RECORD

JULY 1ST 2002 TO JUNE 30TH 2005

PL	W	D	L	F	A	%
0	0	0	0	0	0	-

FIFA/COCA-COLA WORLD RANKING

1993	1994	1995	1996	1997	1998	1999	2000	2001	2002	2003	2004	High		Low	
-	169	177	185	189	191	195	189	193	195	197	201	169	12/94	201	12/04

2004-2005											
08/04	09/04	10/04	11/04	12/04	01/05	02/05	03/05	04/05	05/05	06/05	07/05
199	199	200	200	201	201	201	201	201	201	201	201

Remarkably for a team that has not played an international game since December 2001, Djibouti are not propping up the FIFA Coca-Cola World Ranking. Instead they lie fourth from bottom in 201st, but with good reason; four years ago the country decided to pull out of the international arena to concentrate on developing its youth structure. Affiliated to FIFA for only 11 years, Djibouti's results when they were playing international matches were notably underwhelming, and with results such as 1-10 and 0-7 against Uganda in 2001 and 1998 and 1-9 v Kenya in 1998, morale dropped. There had been a glimmer of hope during the preliminary round of qualifiers for

INTERNATIONAL HONOURS
None

the 2002 FIFA World Cup™ when the Young Red Sea, as the national team is known, held Congo DR to a 1-1 draw but the embarrassment forced the Congolese to call up their European-based players and the return leg finished 9-1. The Federation has declined to take part in recent CECAFA Cups claiming the team is unprepared and have seen no reason to change that stance, hence the decision not to enter the 2006 FIFA World Cup™. However, domestic football continues and Gendarmerie Nationale won the 10-team local League for the second year running, while Chemin de Fer convincingly won the Coupe National beating AS Boreh 6-2 in the final.

THE FIFA BIG COUNT OF 2000

	Male	Female		Male	Female
Registered players	900	132	Referees	70	0
Non registered players	2 000	0	Officials	400	0
Youth players	996	0	Total involved	4 498	
Total players	4 028		Number of clubs	40	
Professional players	0	0	Number of teams	90	

Fédération Djiboutienne de Football (FDF)

Stade el Haoj Hassan Gouled, Case postale 2694, Djibouti

Tel +253 341964   Fax +253 341963

fdf@intnet.dj   www.none

President: FADOUL Houssein   General Secretary: TBD

Vice-President: YACIN Mohamed   Treasurer: AHMED Youssouf   Media Officer: None

Men's Coach: KAMIL Hasan   Women's Coach: KAMIL Hasan

FDF formed: 1979   CAF: 1986   FIFA: 1994

Colours: Green, White, Blue

GAMES PLAYED BY DJIBOUTI IN THE 2006 FIFA WORLD CUP™ CYCLE

2002 Opponents	Score	Venue	Comp	Scorers	Att	Referee
No international matches played in 2002						
2003						
No international matches played in 2003						
2004						
No international matches played in 2004						
2005						
No international matches played in 2005 before August						

DJIBOUTI NATIONAL TEAM RECORDS AND RECORD SEQUENCES

Records			Sequence records				
Victory	4-1	YEM 1988	Wins	1		Clean sheets	1	
Defeat	1-10	UGA 2001	Defeats	7	1994-1999	Goals scored	6	1998-2000
Player Caps	n/a		Undefeated	1		Without goal	2	1994-1998, 2000
Player Goals	n/a		Without win	18	1994-	Goals against	20	1983-2000

FIFA REFEREE LIST 2005

	Int'l	DoB
ALI Hassan	2001	7-09-1973
RIRACHE Hassan	1998	2-07-1971

FIFA ASSISTANT REFEREE LIST 2005

	Int'l	DoB
ABDALLAH Mahamoda	1998	11-08-1966
ALI Abdo	1996	1-09-1969
MOUSSA Hassan	2000	4-05-1971
SAID Aboubaker	2005	5-05-1968

RECENT LEAGUE AND CUP RECORD

	League	Cup		
Year	Champions	Winners	Score	Runners-up
1996	Force Nationale de Police	Balbala		
1997	Force Nationale de Police	Force Nationale de Police		
1998	Force Nationale de Police	Force Nationale de Police		
1999	Force Nationale de Police	Balbala		
2000	CDA Djibouti			
2001	Force Nationale de Police	Chemin de Fer		
2002	AS Borreh	Jeunesse Espoir		Chemin de Fer
2003	Gendarmerie Nationale	AS Borreh	1-1 5-4p	AS Ali-Sabieh
2004	Gendarmerie Nationale	Chemin de Fer	6-2	AS Borreh

DJIBOUTI COUNTRY INFORMATION

Capital	Djibouti	Independence	1977 from France	GDP per Capita	$1 300
Population	768 200	Status	Republic	GNP Ranking	167
Area km²	23 000	Language	Arabic, French	Dialling code	+253
Population density	20 per km²	Literacy rate	49%	Internet code	.dj
% in urban areas	83%	Main religion	Muslim 94%	GMT + / –	+3
Towns/Cities ('000)	Djibouti 623; Ali Sabieh 40; Tadjoura 22; Obock 17; Dikhil 12				
Neighbours (km)	Somalia 58; Ethiopia 349; Eritrea 109; Red Sea & Gulf of Aden 314				
Main stadia	Stade du Ville – Djibouti 10 000				

DMA – DOMINICA

JULY 1ST 2002 TO JUNE 30TH 2005

PL	W	D	L	F	A	%
8	4	1	3	13	23	56.2

FIFA/COCA-COLA WORLD RANKING

1993	1994	1995	1996	1997	1998	1999	2000	2001	2002	2003	2004	High		Low	
-	-	158	138	139	133	149	152	161	174	185	165	**129**	7/98	**185**	12/03

					2004-2005						
08/04	09/04	10/04	11/04	12/04	01/05	02/05	03/05	04/05	05/05	06/05	07/05
165	165	165	166	165	166	167	167	167	167	167	167

Football may be the number one sport on the tiny island of Dominica, but there is a long way to go if there is to be progress internationally. However, the situation has been helped with the opening of the Dominica Football Association's new headquarters in Roseau. Built with assistance from the Goal Programme and the FIFA Financial Assistance Programme it provides a much improved base on an island with few facilities. The road to Germany 2006 began with a tie against the Bahamas with both games switched to Nassau and thanks to a late equaliser, Don Leogal's side escaped with a 1-1 draw in the first match. The return leg proved equally competitive until the last 10 minutes

INTERNATIONAL HONOURS
None

when two late goals gave Dominica a 3-1 victory and a date with Mexico. The first game was played in San Antonio, USA, in front of 36,000 fans who watched the Tricolores trounce the islanders 10-0. In the second leg, Mexico, ranked sixth in the world, ran in another eight goals without reply. The Gold Cup provided little comfort subsequently as Dominica lost to Martinique, Guadeloupe and French Guyana in the qualifying group, conceding 16 goals while scoring just one. Only eight clubs contested the 2004-05 League season with Dublanc Strikers finishing as champions, while Harlem won the Patrick John Knockout Cup defeating Zebians 3-0.

THE FIFA BIG COUNT OF 2000

	Male	Female		Male	Female
Registered players	463	30	Referees	35	0
Non registered players	500	0	Officials	21	0
Youth players	652	0	Total involved	1 701	
Total players	1 645		Number of clubs	15	
Professional players	0	0	Number of teams	19	

Dominica Football Association (DFA)
Bath Estate, PO Box 372, Roseau, Dominica
Tel +1 767 4487577   Fax +1 767 4487587
domfootball@cwdom.dm   www.none
President: JOHN Patrick   General Secretary: CELAIRE Clifford
Vice-President: NIBBS Justin   Treasurer: WHITE Philip   Media Officer: FRAMPTON Ferdinand
Men's Coach: LEOGAL Don   Women's Coach: ROBERTSON Hypolite
DFA formed: 1970   CONMEBOL: 1994   FIFA: 1994
Colours: Emerald, Black, Green

GAMES PLAYED BY DOMINICA IN THE 2006 FIFA WORLD CUP™ CYCLE

2002	Opponents		Score	Venue	Comp	Scorers	Att	Referee
No international matches played in 2002								
2003								
No international matches played in 2003								
2004								
28-01	British Virgin Islands	W	1-0	Tortola	Fr	Cuffy 34		Matthew SKN
31-01	US Virgin Islands	W	5-0	St Thomas	Fr	OG 12, Marshall 42, Dangler 68, Casimir 87, George 90		Matthew SKN
1-02	British Virgin Islands	W	2-1	Tortola	Fr	Marshall 44, Peters 70		Charles DMA
12-03	Barbados	L	1-2	Bridgetown	Fr	Peters 88	46	
26-03	Bahamas	D	1-1	Nassau	WCq	Casimir 88	800	Forde BRB
28-03	Bahamas	W	3-1	Nassau	WCq	Casimir 2 39 86, Peters 85	900	Pineda HON
19-06	Mexico	L	0-10	San Antonio, USA	WCq		36 451	Callender BRB
27-06	Mexico	L	0-8	Aguascalientes	WCq		17 000	Stott USA
10-11	Martinique †	L	1-5	Fort de France	GCq	Peltier 42		Arthur LCA
12-11	Guadeloupe †	L	0-7	Rivière-Pilote	GCq			Arthur LCA
14-11	French Guyana †	L	0-4	Fort de France	GCq		5 800	Fenus LCA
2005								
No international matches played in 2005 before August								

Fr = Friendly match • WC = FIFA World Cup™ • q = qualifier • † Not a full international

DOMINICA NATIONAL TEAM RECORDS AND RECORD SEQUENCES

Records			Sequence records				
Victory	6-1	VGB 1997	Wins	3	1997, 1999, 2004	Clean sheets	2	1997 2004
Defeat	0-10	MEX 2004	Defeats	5	1998-99, 2001-02	Goals scored	8	1999-2000
Player Caps	n/a		Undefeated	4	1998	Without goal	3	1994-1995, 2001
Player Goals	n/a		Without win	8	2001-2002	Goals against	17	1997-1999

FIFA REFEREE LIST 2005

	Int'l	DoB
BROHIM Ibrahim	1998	27-06-1960
CHARLES Martin	1998	4-12-1966

FIFA ASSISTANT REFEREE LIST 2005

	Int'l	DoB
LESLIE Daniel	1998	16-09-1970
PROSPER Leford	2001	26-11-1964
SAMUEL Steve	1996	12-07-1963
WILLIAMS Nehron	2001	8-08-1974

RECENT LEAGUE AND CUP RECORD

Year	Championship Champions	Pts	Runners-up	Pts	Third	Pts	Cup Winners	Score	Runners-up
1997	Harlem Bombers	22	Black Rocks	19	Pointe Michel	12	Harlem Bombers	1-0	Black Rocks
1998	Pointe Michel						Pointe Michel	1-0	ACS Zebians
1999	Harlem Bombers	46	Superwoods United						
2000	Harlem Bombers	13	Dublanc Strikers	13					
2001	Harlem Bombers	22	Dublanc Strikers	22	South East	19			
2002	St Joseph	12	ACS Zebians	12	Harlem Bombers	10	South East	1-0	Antilles Kensbro
2003	Harlem Bombers	†	ACS Zebians				Harlem Bombers		
2004	Harlem Bombers						Harlem Bombers	3-0	ACS Zebians
2005	Dublanc Strikers	31	Pointe Michel	29	South East	29			

† Bombers beat Zebians in the final

DOMINICA COUNTRY INFORMATION

Capital	Roseau	Independence	1978 from the UK	GDP per Capita	$5 400
Population	69 278	Status	Republic/Commonwealth	GNP Ranking	181
Area km²	754	Language	English	Dialling code	+1767
Population density	91 per km²	Literacy rate	94%	Internet code	.dm
% in urban areas	69%	Main religion	Christian 92%	GMT + / −	-4
Towns/Cities ('000)	Roseau 16; Berekua 3; Portsmouth 3; Marigot 2; Atkinson 2; La Plaine 2; Mahaut 2				
Neighbours (km)	Caribbean Sea and the North Atlantic 148				
Main stadia	Windsor Park – Roseau 6 000				

DOM – DOMINICAN REPUBLIC

NATIONAL TEAM RECORD
JULY 1ST 2002 TO JUNE 30TH 2005

PL	W	D	L	F	A	%
10	3	1	6	19	18	35

FIFA/COCA-COLA WORLD RANKING

1993	1994	1995	1996	1997	1998	1999	2000	2001	2002	2003	2004	High		Low	
153	164	159	130	144	152	155	157	160	149	171	170	116	05/96	173	03/04

2004-2005											
08/04	09/04	10/04	11/04	12/04	01/05	02/05	03/05	04/05	05/05	06/05	07/05
170	170	170	170	170	170	171	171	171	171	171	172

One of the Caribbean islands that must contend with the overwhelming popularity of baseball, the Dominican Republic's national association believes the country has the potential to build a national team capable of reaching the FIFA World Cup™ finals. Coach William Bennett cites Jamaica as the example to follow and with a population of nearly nine million, there is a market waiting to be tapped. With the opening of the new centre for football development in 2003, the infrastructure to realise that dream has been laid but it remains a long-term goal. The 2006 World Cup™ qualifiers provided little satisfaction with a 0-6 aggregate defeat at the hands of Trinidad and Tobago's Soca

INTERNATIONAL HONOURS
None

Warriors seeing elimination in the preliminary qualifying rounds. The national team then withdrew from their Digicel Caribbean Cup group in Cuba, along with Guyana and Netherlands Antilles, leaving the Cubans to qualify for the next stage by default. That left the national team's fixture list very thin, hardly the programme for a team aspiring to play in the FIFA World Cup™ finals. In the 2004-05 Liga Mayor there was an unlikely combination of champions being relegated and a promoted team winning the title when Deportivo Pantoja captured the title in their first season and Jarabacoa ignominiously left the League.

THE FIFA BIG COUNT OF 2000

	Male	Female		Male	Female
Registered players	607	200	Referees	30	10
Non registered players	80 000	1 000	Officials	200	20
Youth players	15 002	600	Total involved	97 669	
Total players	97 409		Number of clubs	495	
Professional players	7	0	Number of teams	710	

Federación Dominicana de Fútbol (FEDOFUTBOL)
Centro Olimpico Juan Pablo Duarte, Ensanche Miraflores, Apartado postale 1953, Santo Domingo, Dominican Republic
Tel +1 809 5426923   Fax +1 809 5475363
fedofutbol.f@codetel.net.do   www.none
President: GUZMAN Osiris   General Secretary: MIRANDA Angel Rolando
Vice-President: OGANDO Isaac   Treasurer: LEDESMA Felix   Media Officer: SANCHEZ CABRERA Angel
Men's Coach: BENNETT William   Women's Coach: MOREL Santiago
FEDOFUTBOL formed: 1953   CONCACAF: 1964   FIFA: 1958
Colours: Navy blue, White, Red

GAMES PLAYED BY DOMINICAN REPUBLIC IN THE 2006 FIFA WORLD CUP™ CYCLE

2002	Opponents		Score	Venue	Comp	Scorers	Att	Referee
16-08	US Virgin Islands	W	6-1	Santo Domingo	GCq	Zapata 16, Contreras 28, Almanza 33, Mejia 2 38 67, Odalis.R 62		Forde BRB
18-08	US Virgin Islands	W	5-1	Santo Domingo	GCq	Lopez 12, Zapata 14, Sanchez 43, Valenzuela 67, Mejia 88		Jean-Lesley HAI
27-11	Martinique	L	0-4	Grand Cayman	GCq			Grant HAI
29-11	Cayman Islands	L	0-1	Grand Cayman	GCq			Grant HAI
1-12	Cuba	L	1-2	Grand Cayman	GCq	Marino 20		Grant HAI
2003								
No international matches played in 2003								
2004								
19-03	Anguilla	D	0-0	Santo Domingo	WCq		400	Mattus CRC
21-03	Anguilla	W	6-0	Santo Domingo	WCq	Zapata 15, Severino 2 38 61, Contrera 2 57 90, Casquez 77	850	Porras CRC
27-04	Netherlands Antilles	L	1-3	Willemstad	Fr	Zapata 9		Faneijte ANT
13-06	Trinidad and Tobago	L	0-2	Santo Domingo	WCq		2 500	Moreno PAN
20-06	Trinidad and Tobago	L	0-4	Marabella	WCq		5 500	Pinas SUR
2005								
No international matches played in 2005 before August								

Fr = Friendly match • GC = CONCACAF Gold Cup • WC = FIFA World Cup™ • q = qualifier

DOMINICAN REPUBLIC NATIONAL TEAM RECORDS AND RECORD SEQUENCES

Records			Sequence records					
Victory	6-0	AIA 2004	Wins	4	1999-2000	Clean sheets	3	1999-2000
Defeat	0-8	HAI 1967, TRI 1996	Defeats	5	1974-1976	Goals scored	5	1987-91, 1991-93
Player Caps	n/a		Undefeated	4	1999-2000	Without goal	3	Three times
Player Goals	n/a		Without win	16	1987-1992	Goals against	15	1991-1996

FIFA ASSISTANT REFEREE LIST 2005

	Int'l	DoB
ALCANTARA Robert	1996	23-09-1969
CASTILLO Alberto	2001	13-10-1973
GARCIA Jose Maria	1996	22-12-1960
LUIS Watson	1997	3-09-1965
MENDOZA Jorge	2000	1-11-1966
RODRIGUEZ Jose	2000	26-12-1967
SANDY Vasquez		22-02-1977

FIFA REFEREE LIST 2005

	Int'l	DoB
MARTINEZ Jose	2005	18-07-1973
RONY Labour	2000	15-01-1974

RECENT LEAGUE AND CUP RECORD

	Championship						Cup		
Year	Champions	Pts	Runners-up	Pts	Third	Pts	Winners	Score	Runners-up
1997	San Cristóbal	21	Moca	17	Bancredicard	15			
1998	No tournament played								
1999	FC Don Bosco								
2000	No tournament played								
2001	CD Pantoja	21	Baninter Jarabacoa	19	Bancredicard	13	Domingo Savio	2-2 5-4p	CD Pantoja
2002	Baninter Jarabacoa	25	Moca	19	Bancredicard	14	Bancredicard	1-0	Cañabrava
2003	Baninter Jarabacoa	31	Bancredicard	26	Moca	23			
2004	No tournament played								
2005	Deportivo Pantoja	40	Barcelona	39	Don Bosco	39			

Bancredicard renamed Barcelona

DOMINICAN REPUBLIC COUNTRY INFORMATION

Capital	Santo Domingo	Independence	1865	GDP per Capita	$6 000
Population	8 833 634	Status	Republic	GNP Ranking	67
Area km²	48 730	Language	Spanish	Dialling code	+1 809
Population density	181 per km²	Literacy rate	84%	Internet code	.do
% in urban areas	65%	Main religion	Christian 95%	GMT +/−	-4
Towns/Cities ('000)	Santo Domingo 2 240; Santiago 505; La Romana 171; San Pedro de Macorís 152; Puerto Plata 135				
Neighbours (km)	Haiti 360; Atlantic Ocean & Caribbean Sea 1 288				
Main stadia	Olimpico – Santo Domingo 35 000; Quisqueya – Santo Domingo 30 000				

ECU – ECUADOR

NATIONAL TEAM RECORD
JULY 1ST 2002 TO JUNE 30TH 2005

PL	W	D	L	F	A	%
38	14	9	15	47	55	48.7

FIFA/COCA-COLA WORLD RANKING

1993	1994	1995	1996	1997	1998	1999	2000	2001	2002	2003	2004	High		Low	
48	55	55	33	28	63	65	54	37	31	37	39	26	05/98	76	06/95

2004-2005											
08/04	09/04	10/04	11/04	12/04	01/05	02/05	03/05	04/05	05/05	06/05	07/05
39	42	48	44	39	39	37	36	34	34	34	33

The early 21st century may go down in history as one of the best ever periods for football in Ecuador. In 2002 there was a first qualification for the finals of the FIFA World Cup™ and that was followed up by a good campaign in the 2006 qualifiers in which they at times led the 'best of the rest' chase behind leaders Argentina and Brazil. Once again their hopes of qualification were enhanced by a solid home record at altitude in Quito where both Brazil and Argentina were beaten. The performances away from home, however, remain a worry, especially if the team makes it to the finals in Germany. On a sad note international striker Otilino Tenorio was killed in a car crash

INTERNATIONAL HONOURS
Qualified for the FIFA World Cup™ finals 2002

just three days after playing in Ecuador's 1-0 win over Paraguay in May 2005. In domestic football there was a first championship for Deportivo Cuenca in December 2004 who became only the second provincial team to win the title. They were coached by the Argentine Julio Asad who also led Olmedo to the title in 2000 when they became the first team to break the stranglehold of the clubs from Quito and Guayaquil. Having held out longer than most South American countries, Ecuador has finally succumbed to the lure of having two Championships a year, a system that kicked off in February 2005.

THE FIFA BIG COUNT OF 2000

	Male	Female		Male	Female
Registered players	11 639	300	Referees	276	14
Non registered players	1 000 000	1 300	Officials	657	200
Youth players	8 934	200	Total involved	1 023 520	
Total players	1 022 373		Number of clubs	1 000	
Professional players	9 656	26	Number of teams	3 361	

Federación Ecuatoriana de Fútbol (FEF)
Km 4 1/2 Via a la Costa, Avenida las Aguas y Calle, Alianza, PO Box 09-01-7447, Guayaquil, Ecuador
Tel +593 42 880610   Fax +593 42 880615
fef@gye.satnet.net   www.ecuafutbol.org
President: CHIRIBOGA Luis   General Secretary: ACOSTA ESPINOSA Francisco
Vice-President: VILLACIS Carlos   Treasurer: MORA Hugo   Media Officer: MUNOZ PEDRO Mauricio
Men's Coach: SUAREZ Luis   Women's Coach: ESTUPINAN Garis
FEF formed: 1925   CONMEBOL: 1930   FIFA: 1926
Colours: Yellow, Blue, Red

GAMES PLAYED BY ECUADOR IN THE 2006 FIFA WORLD CUP™ CYCLE

2002	Opponents	Score		Venue	Comp	Scorers	Att	Referee
16-10	Costa Rica	D	1-1	San Jose	Fr	Tenorio.C [83]	8 000	Badilla CRC
20-10	Venezuela	L	0-2	Caracas	Fr		28 000	Brand VEN
20-11	Costa Rica	D	2-2	Quito	Fr	Aguinaga [75p], Kaviedes [85]	35 000	Ramos ECU
2003								
9-02	Estonia	W	1-0	Guayaquil	Fr	Hurtado.I [89p]	12 000	Ramos ECU
12-02	Estonia	W	2-1	Quito	Fr	Baldeon 2 [25 48]		Vasco ECU
30-04	Spain	L	0-4	Madrid	Fr		35 000	Kvaratskhelia GEO
8-06	Colombia	D	0-0	Madrid	Fr		12 000	Perez ESP
11-06	Peru	D	2-2	New Jersey	Fr	Kaviedes [26], Tenorio.O [64]		Terry USA
20-08	Guatemala	W	2-0	Ambato	Fr	Baldeon [6], Aguinaga [50]	25 000	Diaz ECU
6-09	Venezuela	W	2-0	Quito	WCq	Espinoza.G [5], Tenorio.C [72]	14 997	Selman CHI
10-09	Brazil	L	0-1	Manaus	WCq		36 601	Solorzano VEN
15-11	Paraguay	L	1-2	Asuncion	WCq	Mendez [58]	12 000	Paniagua BOL
19-11	Peru	D	0-0	Quito	WCq		34 361	Gonzalez PAR
2004								
10-03	Mexico	L	1-2	Tuxtla Gutierrez	Fr	Mendez [33p]	20 000	Batres GUA
30-03	Argentina	L	0-1	Buenos Aires	WCq		55 000	Vazquez URU
28-04	Honduras	D	1-1	Fort Lauderdale	Fr	Ordonez [81]	15 000	Saheli USA
2-06	Colombia	W	2-1	Quito	WCq	Delgado [3], Salas [66]	31 484	Baldassi ARG
5-06	Bolivia	W	3-2	Quito	WCq	Soliz OG [27], Delgado [32], De la Cruz [38]	32 020	Brand VEN
7-07	Argentina	L	1-6	Chiclayo	SCr1	Delgado [62]	24 000	Amarilla PAR
10-07	Uruguay	L	1-2	Chiclayo	SCr1	Salas [73]	25 000	Brand VEN
13-07	Mexico	L	1-2	Piura	SCr1	Delgado [71]	21 000	Lecca PER
5-09	Uruguay	L	0-1	Montevideo	WCq		28 000	Hidalgo PER
10-10	Chile	W	2-0	Quito	WCq	Kaviedes [49], Mendez.E [64]	27 956	Ortube BOL
14-10	Venezuela	L	1-3	San Cristobal	WCq	Ayovi.M [41p]	13 800	Lecca PER
20-10	Jordan	L	0-3	Tripoli	Fr			
22-10	Nigeria	D	2-2	Tripoli	Fr	Poroso [65], W 5-4p		
27-10	Mexico	L	1-2	New Jersey	Fr	Calle [80]		Prus USA
17-11	Brazil	W	1-0	Quito	WCq	Mendez.E [77]	38 308	Ruiz COL
2005								
26-01	Panama	W	2-0	Ambato	Fr	Tenorio.O [88 91+]	5 000	Vasco ECU
29-01	Panama	W	2-0	Babahoyo	Fr	Kaviedes [45], Tenorio.O [56]		
9-02	Chile	L	0-3	Vina del Mar	Fr		15 000	Favale ARG
16-02	Costa Rica	W	2-1	Heredia	Fr	Ayovi [60p], Guagua [86]	1 000	Duran CRC
27-03	Paraguay	W	5-2	Quito	WCq	Valencia 2 [32 49], Mendez 2 [47+ 47], Ayovi [77p]	32 449	Mendez URU
30-03	Peru	D	2-2	Lima	WCq	De la Cruz [4], Valencia [45]	40 000	Chandia CHI
4-05	Paraguay	W	1-0	East Rutherford	Fr	Mendez [51]	26 491	
4-06	Argentina	W	2-0	Quito	WCq	Lara [53], Delgado [89]	37 583	Selman CHI
8-06	Colombia	L	0-3	Barranquilla	WCq		20 402	Simon BRA
11-06	Italy	D	1-1	East Rutherford	Fr	Ayovi [18p]	27 583	Vaughn USA

Fr = Friendly match • SC = Copa América • WC = FIFA World Cup™ • q = qualifier • r1 = first round group

ECUADOR COUNTRY INFORMATION

Capital	Quito	Independence	1822 from Spain	GDP per Capita	$3 300
Population	13 212 742	Status	Republic	GNP Ranking	77
Area km²	283 560	Language	Spanish	Dialling code	+593
Population density	46 per km²	Literacy rate	92%	Internet code	.ec
% in urban areas	58%	Main religion	Christian	GMT +/−	-5
Towns/Cities ('000)	Guayaquil 1 952; Quito 1 399; Cuenca 276; Santo Domingo 200; Machala 198; Manta 183				
Neighbours (km)	Colombia 590; Peru 1 420; Pacific Ocean 2 237				
Main stadia	Monumental – Guayaquil 59 283; La Casa Blanca – Quito 41 596				

ECUADOR NATIONAL TEAM RECORDS AND RECORD SEQUENCES

Records			Sequence records					
Victory	6-0	PER 1975	Wins	6	1996	Clean sheets	3	Five times
Defeat	0-12	ARG 1942	Defeats	18	1938-1945	Goals scored	16	1991-1993
Player Caps	114	HURTADO Iván	Undefeated	8	1996, 2000-2001	Without goal	5	1985-1987
Player Goals	26	DELGADO Augustín	Without win	34	1938-1949	Goals against	28	1953-1963

NATIONAL CAPS

	Caps
HURTADO Iván	125
AGUINAGA Alex	109
CAPURRO Luis	100
CHALA Cléber	86
DE LA CRUZ Ulises	78
CEVALLOS José	77
FERNANDEZ Angel	77
HURTADO Eduardo	74

NATIONAL GOALS

	Goals
DELGADO Agustín	27
HURTADO Eduardo	26
AGUINAGA Alex	23
AVILES Raúl	16
GRAZIANI Ariel	15
FERNANDEZ Angel	12
KAVIEDES Iván	12
MENDEZ Edison	10

ECUADOR 2004 SERIE A TORNEO APERTURA

	Pl	W	D	L	F	A	Pts
Aucas †	18	10	6	2	31	15	36
LDU Quito †	18	9	3	6	33	26	30
Deportivo Cuenca †	18	8	5	5	21	15	29
Emelec	18	9	1	8	26	21	28
El Nacional	18	7	5	6	26	25	26
Deportivo Quito	18	7	4	7	28	32	25
Olmedo	18	6	6	6	23	23	24
Barcelona	18	4	6	8	20	25	18
Espoli	18	3	8	7	14	23	17
Macará	18	2	6	10	16	33	12

6/02/2004 - 23/05/2004 • † Qualified for the Liguilla Final •
Bonus points to take forward - Aucas 2, LDU 1, Cuenca 0.5

ECUADOR 2004 SERIE A TORNEO FINALIZACION

	Pl	W	D	L	F	A	Pts
Barcelona †	18	10	4	4	36	22	34
Olmedo †	18	8	7	3	34	25	31
El Nacional †	18	9	4	5	21	17	31
Deportivo Quito	18	8	6	4	37	26	30
Deportivo Cuenca	18	8	4	6	24	21	28
Aucas	18	7	5	6	22	20	26
Emelec	18	5	7	6	27	33	22
LDU Quito	18	6	2	10	23	27	20
Macará	18	3	6	9	17	32	15
Espoli	18	2	3	13	15	33	9

11/06/2004 - 3/10/2004 • † Qualified for the Liguilla Final •
Bonus points to take forward - Barcelona 2, Olmedo 1, Nacional 0.5

SERIE A RESULTS 2004

Apertura results listed first	Aucas	Barcelona	D Cuenca	D Quito	Emelec	Espoli	LDU	Macará	Nacional	Olmedo
Aucas		1-1 2-1	1-0 1-0	2-2 1-1	2-0 2-0	1-0 1-0	5-1 1-1	3-1 0-0	4-2 1-1	2-0 3-4
Barcelona	2-3 2-1		1-0 1-0	0-2 4-1	2-1 2-0	0-0 0-0	5-2 2-1	0-0 3-1	2-0 2-0	0-1 3-2
Deportivo Cuenca	0-0 3-1	2-0 2-2		3-1 1-0	2-0 2-2	2-2 3-2	0-1 0-1	2-2 1-0	0-0 0-1	1-0 0-0
Deportivo Quito	2-1 1-2	1-1 3-3	3-2 3-2		2-0 7-1	2-1 3-2	2-3 2-1	1-1 3-2	3-2 1-1	1-2 3-1
Emelec	1-0 1-0	2-2 2-3	0-1 3-1	4-1 1-1		2-0 1-1	2-0 1-0	4-2 6-1	1-0 1-0	3-0 2-2
Espoli	0-0 0-2	1-1 0-4	1-2 1-3	2-1 2-1	2-4 3-1		0-0 0-2	1-0 0-0	2-1 0-2	0-2 1-3
LDU Quito	2-3 0-1	3-1 2-1	0-1 2-3	1-2 0-2	2-0 5-2	3-0 2-1		3-1 2-2	2-0 3-2	2-2 1-3
Macará	0-2 2-1	2-1 1-1	0-1 1-2	0-0 1-1	1-0 2-2	0-0 1-0	1-6 1-0		2-3 0-1	0-1 1-5
El Nacional	0-0 1-0	2-1 2-1	2-1 0-1	3-1 0-3	2-1 1-1	1-1 1-0	1-1 1-0	2-0 2-1		2-2 5-2
Olmedo	1-1 2-2	2-0 2-1	1-1 0-0	4-1 1-1	0-1 0-0	1-1 3-2	0-1 2-0	3-3 2-0	1-3 0-0	

ECUADOR 2004 LIGUILLA FINAL

	Pl	W	D	L	F	A	Pts	Cu	Ol	Qu	Na	Ba	Au
Deportivo Cuenca †	10	6	1	3	16	13	19.5		1-3	1-1	3-0	1-0	2-1
Olmedo †	10	6	0	4	16	14	19	0-1		4-2	2-1	1-0	2-1
LDU Quito †	10	5	2	3	13	9	18	1-2	2-0		1-1	1-0	1-0
El Nacional	10	4	3	3	17	16	15.5	3-1	1-2	1-0		3-3	2-2
Barcelona	10	3	2	5	14	16	13	2-1	3-1	0-2	2-3		2-1
Aucas	10	1	2	7	11	19	7	2-3	2-1	0-2	0-2	2-2	

23/10/2004 - 19/12/2004 • † Qualified for the Copa Libertadores

TOP SCORERS

ORDONEZ Evelio	El Nacional	28
RODRIGUEZ Fernando	Olmedo	23
CARNERO Christian	Deportivo Quito	21
FIGUEROA Gustavo	Aucas	19
RICARD Hamilton	Emelec	17

ECUADOR 2004
SERIE B TORNEO APERTURA

	Pl	W	D	L	F	A	Pts
Deportivo Quevedo †	18	9	7	2	30	22	34
LDU de Loja †	18	8	7	3	29	23	31
Técnico Universitario §	18	10	3	5	21	12	27
Manta FC	18	8	3	7	23	19	27
LDU Portoviejo	18	7	6	5	23	23	27
Deportivo Saquisili	18	5	5	8	29	32	20
Santa Rita	18	4	8	6	26	30	20
Audaz Octubrino	18	5	4	9	21	25	19
Delfin	18	5	4	9	28	34	19
Universidad Católica	18	4	3	11	18	28	15

20/02/2004 - 6/06/2004 • † Qualified for the Liguilla Final •
§ Six points deducted • Bonus points to take forward -
Quevedo 2, LDU Loja 1

ECUADOR 2004
SERIE B TORNEO FINALIZACION

	Pl	W	D	L	F	A	Pts
LDU de Loja †	18	11	3	4	35	26	36
Técnico Universitario †	18	10	5	3	31	14	35
LDU Portoviejo †	18	10	3	5	28	20	33
Deportivo Quevedo	18	9	3	6	30	22	30
Universidad Católica	18	8	4	6	28	20	28
Manta FC	18	6	4	8	20	19	22
Santa Rita	18	5	5	8	15	22	20
Delfin	18	4	5	9	27	37	17
Audaz Octubrino	18	4	4	10	28	35	16
Deportivo Saquisili	18	3	4	11	15	42	13

11/06/2004 -26/09/2004 • † Qualified for the Liguilla Final
• Bonus points to take forward - LDU Loja 2, Universitario 1

ECUADOR 2004
SERIE B LIGUILLA FINAL

	Pl	W	D	L	F	A	Pts	Qu	Lo	Un	Po
Deportivo Quevedo	6	3	1	2	11	8	12		4-1	0-0	3-1
LDU de Loja	6	2	3	1	13	11	12	4-2		1-1	4-1
Técnico Universitario	6	2	3	1	6	3	10	2-0	1-1		2-0
LDU Portoviejo	6	1	1	4	5	13	4	0-2	2-2	1-0	

2/10/2004 - 7/11/2004 • Quevedo and Loja promoted in place of
Espoli and Macará who finished Serie A with the worst overall record

ECUADOR 2004
SERIE B LIGUILLA RELEGATION

	Pl	W	D	L	F	A	Pts	De	Ca	Sa	Au
Delfin	6	4	1	1	11	5	12		3-2	3-0	3-1
Universidad Católica	6	3	1	2	9	8	8	1-0		3-0	2-1
Deportivo Saquisili	6	2	0	4	6	9	4	0-1	4-1		*2-0*
Audaz Octubrino	6	1	2	3	4	8	4	1-1	0-0	1-0	

2/10/2004 - 6/11/2004 • Saquisili and Audaz relegated • Match in
italics awarded 2-0 to Saquisili after Audaz did not turn up

CLUB DIRECTORY

Club	Town/City	Stadium	Phone	www.	Lge	CL
Aucas	Quito	Chillogallo 21 489	+593 2 2461605	aucas.com	0	0
Barcelona	Guayaquil	Monumental 59 283	+593 4 2203252	barcelonaac.com	13	0
Deportivo Cuenca	Cuenca	Alejandro Aguilar 18 830	+593 7 833800		1	0
Deportivo Olmedo	Riobamba	Olimpico Riobamba 18 936	+593 3 969902		1	0
Deportivo Quevedo	Quevedo	7 de Octubre 16 000	+593 757201		0	0
Deportivo Quito	Quito	Olimpico Atahualpa 40 948	+593 2 2476560	sdquito.com	2	0
Emelec	Guayaquil	George Capwell 18 222	+593 4 2404318	csemelec.com	10	0
LDU de Loja	Loja		+593 7 2574200		7	0
LDU de Quito	Quito	Casablanca 41 596	+593 2 2527206	clubldu.com	0	0
Nacional	Quito	Olimpico Atahualpa 40 948	+593 2 2456586	elnacional.com	11	0

RECENT LEAGUE RECORD

	Championship						Championship Play-off		
Year	Champions	Pts	Runners-up	Pts	Third	Pts	Champions	Score	Runners-up
1990	LDU Quito	7	Barcelona	6	Emelec	6			
1991	Barcelona	10	Valdez	5	El Nacional	5			
1992	El Nacional	15	Barcelona	15	Emelec	13	El Nacional	2-1 1-1	Barcelona
1993	Emelec	19	El Nacional	18	Barcelona	18			
1994	Emelec	14	El Nacional	13.5	Barcelona	11			
1995	Barcelona						Barcelona	2-0 1-0	Espoli
1996	El Nacional						El Nacional	2-1 2-0	Emelec
1997	Barcelona	19	Deportivo Quito	19	Emelec	15			
1998	LDU Quito						LDU Quito	0-1 7-0	Emelec
1999	El Nacional	20	LDU Quito	19	Emelec	18			
2000	Olmedo	23	El Nacional	20	Emelec	20			
2001	Emelec	22	El Nacional	21	Olmedo	20			
2002	Emelec	20	Barcelona	19	El Nacional	18			
2003	LDU Quito	26	Barcelona	23	El Nacional	20			
2004	Deportivo Cuenca	19.5	Olmedo	19	LDU Quito	18			

Although Ecuador has long used the Apertura and Clausura system popular across the Americas, until 2005 there has always been an end of season tournament to decide the overall champions. In 1995, 1996 and 1998 this involved a grand final and not the traditional league format. A play-off happened in 1992 after El Nacional and Barcelona finished equal on points.

EGY – EGYPT

NATIONAL TEAM RECORD
JULY 1ST 2002 TO JUNE 30TH 2005

PL	W	D	L	F	A	%
44	28	8	8	90	37	72.7

FIFA/COCA-COLA WORLD RANKING

1993	1994	1995	1996	1997	1998	1999	2000	2001	2002	2003	2004	High		Low	
26	22	23	28	32	28	38	33	41	39	32	34	17	05/98	44	05/03

2004-2005											
08/04	09/04	10/04	11/04	12/04	01/05	02/05	03/05	04/05	05/05	06/05	07/05
34	35	30	32	34	33	32	31	28	27	28	26

The 2004-05 season in Egypt was a tale of two unbeaten runs. Zamalek hadn't lost in 52 league matches, dating back to December 2002 when they met fierce rivals Al Ahly in November 2004. Meanwhile Al Ahly were embarking on an equally spectacular run and their 4-2 victory over Zamalek that day turned out to be just one of 17 consecutive victories from the start of the season. Remarkably they had tied up the Championship by January, with Zamalek falling apart and ending up in sixth place, the lowest ranking in their history and only the third time they have finished

INTERNATIONAL HONOURS
Qualified for the FIFA World Cup™ finals 1934 1990 **CAF African Cup of Nations** 1957 1959 1986 1998 **African Games** 1987 1991
CAF African Youth Championship 1981 1991 2003 **CAF African U-17 Championship** 1997
CAF African Champions League Ismaili 1969, Al Ahly 1982 1987 2001, Zamalek 1984 1986 1993 1996 2002

outside of the top four. There was not good news on the national team front in the FIFA World Cup™ qualifiers with the Egyptians missing out on a place in the finals. However, in their defence their group proved to be the toughest with both Cameroon and Côte d'Ivoire having outstanding campaigns. There is genuine hope that the Pharaohs can win a record fifth African Cup of Nations when they host the finals in 2006 as their record since 2002 has been very good – apart from those slip ups in the key FIFA World Cup™ qualifers.

THE FIFA BIG COUNT OF 2000

	Male	Female		Male	Female
Registered players	13 768	223	Referees	1 731	0
Non registered players	250 000	0	Officials	102	0
Youth players	6 648	0	Total involved	272 472	
Total players	270 639		Number of clubs	545	
Professional players	350	0	Number of teams	6 000	

Egyptian Football Association (EFA)
5 Gabalaya Street, Gezira, El Borg Post Office, Cairo, Egypt
Tel +20 2 7351793   Fax +20 2 7367817
www.efa.com.eg
President: ZAHER   General Secretary: EL KIYEI Adly
Vice-President: SHOUBEIR Ahmed   Treasurer: ABBAS Mamdouh   Media Officer: None
Men's Coach: SHEHATA Hassan   Women's Coach: None
EFA formed: 1921   CAF: 1957   FIFA: 1923
Colours: Red, White, Black

GAMES PLAYED BY EGYPT IN THE 2006 FIFA WORLD CUP™ CYCLE

2002	Opponents	Score		Venue	Comp	Scorers	Att	Referee
8-08	Ethiopia	W	4-1	Alexandria	Fr	Barkat [4], Belal [6], Halim Ali [80], Hamdi [88]		
20-08	Uganda	W	2-0	Alexandria	Fr	Belal 2 [2 36]		
23-08	Sudan	W	3-0	Cairo	Fr	Youssef [32], Barkat 2 [43p 75]		
27-08	Libya	L	0-1	Alexandria	Fr			
8-09	Madagascar	L	0-1	Antananarivo	CNq			Nkole ZAM
20-11	Tunisia	D	0-0	Tunis	Fr			Ambaya LBY
25-11	Nigeria	D	1-1	Lagos	Fr	El Yamani [26]		
16-12	United Arab Emirates	W	2-1	Abu Dhabi	Fr	Abdel Hafiz [6], Belal [90]		
22-12	Ghana	D	0-0	Cairo	Fr			
2003								
12-02	Denmark	L	1-4	Cairo	Fr	Hassan.A [20]	30 000	Abd El Fatah EGY
19-03	Qatar	W	6-0	Port Said	Fr	Hamza 3 [14 35 37], El Sayed [42], OG [48], Halim Ali [77p]		El Beltagy EGY
29-03	Mauritius	W	1-0	Port Louis	CNq	Hossam Mido [45]	800	Masole BOT
30-04	France	L	0-5	Paris	Fr		54 554	Busacca SUI
8-06	Mauritius	W	7-0	Cairo	CNq	Hossam Mido 2 [7p 22], El Sayed [18], Hamza [53], Emam [61], Hassan.A 2 [72 89]	40 000	Abdalla LBY
20-06	Madagascar	W	6-0	Port Said	CNq	El Tabei [1], Belal 4 [9 24 56 83], Hossam Mido [41]		
10-10	Senegal	W	1-0	Cairo	Fr	Hossam Mido [58]	20 000	
15-11	South Africa	W	2-1	Cairo	Fr	Abdel Hady [73], Hossam Mido [90]	10 000	Salim LBY
18-11	Sweden	W	1-0	Cairo	Fr	Belal [10]	15 000	Abdalla LBY
12-12	Kenya	W	1-0	Manama	Fr	El Sayed [8]		
15-12	Bahrain	W	1-0	Manama	Fr	Youssef [90]	20 000	
18-12	Iraq	W	2-0	Manama	Fr	Belal 2 [21 50]		
2004								
8-01	Rwanda	W	5-1	Port Said	Fr	Belal [16], Abdel Hamid [26], El Tabei [39], Hassan.A 2 [59 68]	10 000	
14-01	Congo DR	D	2-2	Port Said	Fr	Belal 2 [40 53]	10 000	Helal EGY
17-01	Burkina Faso	D	1-1	Port Said	Fr	Belal [53]	8 000	
25-01	Zimbabwe	W	2-1	Sfax	CNr1	Abdel Hamid [58], Barkat [62]	22 000	Lassina Pare BFA
29-01	Algeria	L	1-2	Sousse	CNr1	Belal [26]	15 000	Hamer LUX
3-02	Cameroon	D	0-0	Monastir	CNr1		20 000	Bujsaim UAE
31-03	Trinidad and Tobago	W	2-1	Cairo	Fr	Aboutraika [60], Halim Ali [65]	5 000	El Beltagy EGY
24-05	Zimbabwe	W	2-0	Cairo	Fr	Aboutraika [73], Hosny [83]	10 000	
29-05	Gabon	W	2-0	Cairo	Fr	Hassan.H 2 [90 95]	15 000	Auda EGY
6-06	Sudan	W	3-0	Khartoum	WCq	Abel H [6], Aboutraika [53], Abdel Wahab [88]	10 000	Kidane Tesfu ERI
20-06	Côte d'Ivoire	L	1-2	Alexandria	WCq	Aboutraika [55]	13 000	Guirat TUN
4-07	Benin	D	3-3	Cotonou	WCq	Hassan.A [66], Aboutraika [75], Moustafa.H [80]	15 000	Chukwujekwu NGA
5-09	Cameroon	W	3-2	Cairo	WCq	Shawky [45], Hassan.A [74p], El Sayed [86]	25 000	Lim Kee Chong MRI
8-10	Libya	L	1-2	Tripoli	WCq	Zaki [57]	40 000	Haimoudi ALG
29-11	Bulgaria	D	1-1	Cairo	Fr	Motab [85]		
2005								
8-01	Uganda	W	3-0	Cairo	Fr	Zaki 2 [38 67p], Shawky [63]		
4-02	Korea Republic	W	1-0	Seoul	Fr	Emad [14]	16 054	
9-02	Belgium	W	4-0	Cairo	Fr	Motab 2 [39 50], Abdelmalk [52], Hosny [80]	5 000	El Beltagy EGY
14-03	Saudi Arabia	W	1-0	Dammam	Fr	Motab [64]		
27-03	Libya	W	4-1	Cairo	WCq	Hossam Mido [55] Motab 2 [56 80], Hassan.A [76]	30 000	Poulat FRA
27-05	Kuwait	W	1-0	Kuwait City	Fr	Hassan.A [52]		
5-06	Sudan	W	6-1	Cairo	WCq	Abel Ali 2 [8 31], Zaki 2 [28 50], El Sayed [62], Abdelmalk [71]	20 000	Mususa ZIM
17-06	Côte d'Ivoire	L	0-2	Abidjan	WCq		30 000	Damon RSA

Fr = Friendly match • CN = CAF African Cup of Nations • WC = FIFA World Cup™ • q = qualifier • r1 = first round group

EGYPT COUNTRY INFORMATION

Capital	Cairo	Independence	1936	GDP per Capita	$4 000
Population	76 117 421	Status	Republic	GNP Ranking	37
Area km²	1 001 450	Language	Arabic	Dialling code	+20
Population density	76 per km²	Literacy rate	57%	Internet code	.eg
% in urban areas	45%	Main religion	Muslim 94%	GMT + / –	+2
Towns/Cities ('000)	Cairo 7 734; Alexandria 3 811; Giza 2 443; Shubra 991; Port Said 538; Suez 488; Mehalla al Kubra 431; Assiout 420; Luxor 422; Mansoura 420; Tanta 404; El Faiyum 306; Ismailya 284				
Neighbours (km)	Gaza Strip 11; Israel 266; Sudan 1 273; Libya 1 115; Mediterranean Sea & Red Sea 2 450				
Main stadia	International – Cairo 75 750; Port Said – Port Said 45 00; Alexandria – Alexandria 25 000				

EGYPT 2004-05

PREMIER LEAGUE

	Pl	W	D	L	F	A	Pts	Ahly	ENPPI	Sawahel	Ismaily	Suez C.	Zamalek	Masry	Ghazl	Ittihad	Jaish	Assiout	Baladeyet	Tersana	Mansoura
Al Ahly †	26	24	2	0	59	13	74		1-1	2-1	1-0	2-0	3-0	0-0	2-1	3-2	1-0	3-0	1-0	2-0	1-0
ENPPI †	26	11	10	5	43	26	43	1-2		1-1	1-0	5-2	1-1	3-1	2-1	2-1	3-0	3-0	2-2	3-0	2-0
Sawahel ‡	26	10	9	7	42	33	39	1-2	2-2		1-1	0-2	1-0	1-0	1-0	4-0	3-1	2-1	3-3	4-1	1-1
Ismaily	26	10	9	7	30	25	39	0-6	2-1	2-2		3-1	1-2	2-1	1-0	2-0	0-0	2-0	1-0	1-0	1-2
Suez Cement	26	10	7	9	29	31	37	0-3	0-2	1-0	0-0		2-1	1-1	2-1	0-1	0-0	2-0	2-0	1-1	3-0
Zamalek	26	9	9	8	37	30	36	2-4	1-1	2-1	1-0	0-1		1-1	4-1	3-0	1-1	0-1	4-1	3-0	0-1
Al Masry	26	7	11	8	29	22	32	0-2	1-1	3-1	0-0	3-1	1-1		1-1	1-1	4-0	0-1	1-2	0-0	1-0
Ghazl Al Mehalla	26	8	7	11	25	28	31	1-2	1-0	1-1	1-1	1-1	0-0	1-0		2-1	3-1	1-0	3-0	1-0	2-1
Ittihad	26	9	4	13	25	37	31	0-4	1-0	0-0	1-3	1-2	1-0	1-0	1-0		1-2	3-1	2-0	2-3	1-0
Al Jaish	26	7	9	10	23	33	30	1-3	2-3	1-2	2-1	0-0	1-3	0-0	2-1	2-1		2-0	0-1	0-0	2-1
Assiout Cement	26	7	8	11	24	36	29	1-3	2-2	2-2	0-4	0-0	1-1	1-1	2-0	1-1	0-0		1-0	1-0	3-0
Baladeyet Al Mehalla	26	6	8	12	27	42	26	1-2	1-1	1-4	1-1	1-3	2-2	0-2	1-1	1-0	0-0	2-1		4-3	2-0
Al Tersana	26	6	7	13	25	42	25	0-3	1-0	1-2	0-0	3-1	3-3	0-2	1-0	0-1	1-1	1-3	1-0		2-2
Mansoura	26	4	8	14	18	38	20	0-1	0-0	2-1	1-1	2-1	0-1	0-4	0-0	1-1	0-2	1-1	1-1	2-3	

16/09/2004 - 29/04/2005 • † Qualified for the CAF Champions League • ‡ Qualified for the Confederation Cup

CUP 2004-05

Round of 16		Quarter-finals		Semi-finals		Final	
ENPPI	1 3p						
Sawahel *	1 0p	ENPPI	1 1				
Petrojet	0	Bani-Suef *	1 0				
Bani-Suef *	1			ENPPI *	1 2		
Ghazl Al Mehalla *	1 4p			Mansoura	1 1		
Al Ahly	1 3p	Ghazl Al Mehalla	0 1				
Suez Cement *	1	Mansoura *	2 0				
Mansoura	2					ENPPI	1
Al Masry	4					Ittihad	0
Baladeyet Al Mehalla *	3	Al Masry *	2 2				
Tanta	1	Zamalek	1 2				
Zamalek *	3			Al Masry *	0 0 7p		
Al Jaish *	1			Ittihad	0 0 8p		
Qanat	0	Al Jaish *	0 1				
Gounah	0	Ittihad	1 1				
Ittihad *	1	* Home team/home team in the first leg					

CUP FINAL

20-05-2005, Ref: Kabil
Mokawloon, Cairo

Scorer - Amagdy Abdel Aaty [108] for ENPPI

RECENT LEAGUE AND CUP RECORD

	Championship							Cup		
Year	Champions	Pts	Runners-up	Pts	Third	Pts		Winners	Score	Runners-up
1990	Unfinished due to Egypt's participation in the 1990 FIFA World Cup™							Mokawloon	2-1	Suez Canal
1991	Ismaily	51	Al Ahly	51	Zamalek	50		Al Ahly	1-0	Aswan
1992	Zamalek	40	Ismaily	37	Ghazl Al Mehalla	33		Al Ahly	2-1	Zamalek
1993	Zamalek	45	Al Ahly	39	Ghazl Al Mehalla	31		Al Ahly	3-2	Ghazl Al Mehalla
1994	Al Ahly	39	Ismaily	39	Zamalek	35			Not held	
1995	Al Ahly	58	Zamalek	50	Ismaili	43		Mokawloon	2-0	Ghazl Al Mehalla
1996	Al Ahly	70	Zamalek	66	Ismaili	52		Al Ahly	3-1	Mansoura
1997	Al Ahly	69	Zamalek	60	Mansoura	49		Ismaily	1-0	Al Ahly
1998	Al Ahly	68	Zamalek	62	Mokawloon	54		Al Masry	4-3	Mokawloon
1999	Al Ahly	68	Zamalek	41	Ismaily	40		Zamalek	3-1	Ismaily
2000	Al Ahly	60	Ismaily	54	Zamalek	52		Ismaily	4-0	Mokawloon
2001	Zamalek	65	Al Ahly	57	Al Masry	46		Al Ahly	2-0	Ghazl Al Mehalla
2002	Ismaily	66	Al Ahly	64	Zamalek	53		Zamalek	1-0	Baladeyet Mehalla
2003	Zamalek	67	Al Ahly	66	Ismaily	46		Al Ahly	1-1 4-3p	Ismaily
2004	Zamalek	68	Al Ahly	59	Ismaily	51		Mokawloon	2-1	Al Ahly
2005	Al Ahly	74	ENPPI	43	Sawahel	39		ENPPI	1-0	Ittihad

AL AHLY 2004-05

Date	Opponents	Score		Comp	Scorers
17-09-2004	Suez Cement	W 3-0	A	Lge	Motab 2 [9] [13], Hosny [35]
25-09-2004	Al Tersana	W 2-0	H	Lge	Aboutraika [42], Bebo [77]
13-10-2004	Mansoura	W 1-0	A	Lge	Motab [45]
17-10-2004	Ittihad	W 3-2	H	Lge	Maky [61], Motab [62], Castello [84]
22-10-2004	Al Masry	W 2-0	A	Lge	Belal [54], El Nahhas [83]
31-10-2004	Baladeyet Al Mehalla	W 1-0	H	Lge	El Nahhas [85]
4-11-2004	Zamalek	W 4-2	A	Lge	Aboutraika 2 [32] [51], Gilberto [57], Motab [63]
11-11-2004	Assiout Cement	W 3-0	H	Lge	El Nahhas [57], Hassan.A [69], Gomaa [84]
17-11-2004	ENPPI	W 2-1	A	Lge	El Nahhas [10], Hosny [83p]
21-11-2005	Al Jaish	W 1-0	H	Lge	Barkat [83]
5-12-2004	Talaran	W 4-0	H	Cupr1	Makino, Motab, Moustafa, Belal
10-12-2004	Ghazl Al Mehalla	D 1-1	A	Cupr2	Said. L 3-4p
15-12-2004	Sawahel	W 2-1	A	Lge	Shawky [6], Moteab [90+4p]
19-12-2005	Ismaily	W 1-0	H	Lge	Shawky [47]
23-12-2004	Ghazl Al Mehalla	W 2-1	A	Lge	Shiko [30], Hosny [61p]
27-12-2004	Suez Cement	W 2-0	H	Lge	Barkat [20], Hassan.A [33]
31-12-2004	Al Tersana	W 3-0	A	Lge	Barkat [20], Moustafa [22], Motab [80]
4-01-2005	Mansoura	W 1-0	H	Lge	Aboutraika [68]
14-01-2005	Ittihad	W 4-0	A	Lge	Barkat [20], Aboutraika [31], Shawky [49], Hosny [66]
21-01-2005	Al Masry	D 0-0	H	Lge	
28-01-2005	Baladeyet Al Mehalla	W 2-1	A	Lge	Motab [45+3] [90+3]
12-02-2005	Zamalek	W 3-0	H	Lge	Motab [61], Aboutraika 2 [68] [72]
18-02-2005	Assiout Cement	W 3-1	A	Lge	Motab [24], Bebo [63], Castello [87]
25-02-2005	ENPPI	D 1-1	H	Lge	Motab [27]
4-03-2005	SC Villa - UGA	D 0-0	A	CLr1	
10-03-2005	Al Jaish	W 3-1	A	Lge	Castello [31], Belal [65], Aboutraika [82]
19-03-2005	SC Villa - UGA	W 6-0	H	CLr1	Imed [23], Barket 2 [56] [90], Aboutraika 2 [65] [87], El Nahhas [85]
31-03-2005	Sawahel	W 2-1	H	Lge	Barkat [84], Motab [88]
8-04-2005	USM Alger - ALG	W 1-0	A	CLr2	Barkat [6]
14-04-2005	Ismaily	W 6-0	A	Lge	Barkat 3 [17] [36] [50], Motab [63], Aboutraika [78], Hosny [85]
22-04-2005	USM Alger - ALG	D 2-2	H	CLr2	El Nahhas [45], Motab [55]
29-04-2005	Ghazl Al Mehalla	W 2-1	H	Lge	El Nahhas [45], Hosny [46]

Lge = Egyptian League • Cup = Egyptian Cup • CL = CAF Champions League • r1 = first round • r2 = second round

CLUB DIRECTORY

Club	Town/City	Stadium	Lge	Cup	CL
Al Ahly	Cairo	Ahly Sports Club 25 000	30	33	3
Assiout Cement	Assiout		0	0	0
Baladeyet	Al Mehalla		0	0	0
ENPPI (Petroleum)	Cairo		0	1	0
Ghazl	Al Mehalla		0	0	0
Ismaily	Ismailya	Ismailiya Stadium 30 000	3	2	1
Ittihad	Alexandria	Alexandria Stadium 22 500	0	6	0
Al Jaish (Army Club)	Cairo		0	0	0
Al Masry	Port Said	Port Said Stadium 45 000	0	1	0
Sawahel (Border Guards)	Alexandria	Alexandria Stadium 22 500	0	0	0
Al Tersana (Arsenal)	Cairo	Mit Okba 25 000	1	6	0
Zamalek	Cairo	Zamalek 25 000	11	20	5

EGYPT NATIONAL TEAM RECORDS AND RECORD SEQUENCES

Records			Sequence records				
Victory	15-0	LAO 1963	Wins	9	2003-2004	Clean sheets	10	1989
Defeat	3-11	ITA 1928	Defeats	4	1990	Goals scored	22	1963-1964
Player Caps	163	HASSAN Hossam	Undefeated	15	1963-64, 2000-01	Without goal	4	1985, 1990
Player Goals	64	HASSAN Hossam	Without win	9	1981-1983	Goals against	13	1972-1973

FIFA REFEREE LIST 2005

	Int'l	DoB
ABD EL FATAH Esam	2001	30-12-1965
ABDALLA Fahim	2005	20-09-1969
AUDA Ahmed	1997	25-09-1963
HELAL Mohamed		2-02-1961
IBRAHIM Mohamed		10-09-1965
KABIL Naser		25-08-1962
OSMAN Samir	2005	8-08-1972

FIFA ASSISTANT REFEREE LIST 2005

	Int'l	DoB
ABDEL NABY Nasser Sadek	2004	23-01-1971
ABDEL-KADER Sobhy		11-12-1964
ABO Ahmed	2005	19-08-1971
DEGEASH Ayman	2005	26-07-1970
ELGARHY Ahmed	2005	8-12-1965
IBRAHIM Walid	2004	3-09-1967
RASHWAN Beshr		15-08-1963

ENG – ENGLAND

NATIONAL TEAM RECORD
JULY 1ST 2002 TO JUNE 30TH 2005

PL	W	D	L	F	A	%
33	20	8	5	64	32	72.7

2005 may prove to be a seminal year for English football with the national team establishing itself as a genuine force on the international scene once again and the Abramovic millions transforming the League which for the past decade had become the private reserve of Arsenal and Manchester United. There was also that extraordinary night in Istanbul which saw Liverpool crowned European champions for the fifth time, thanks in no small part to the fanatical support they took with them to the game. One man, however, dominated the headlines - Chelsea manager Jose Mourinho, the 'Special One'. He more than lived up to the accolade winning two trophies in his first season including the Championship, Chelsea's first for 50 years. Had it not been for Liverpool's controversial goal in the UEFA Champions League semi-final defeat at Anfield, they might have also won the European Cup too. The season had begun with Arsenal continuing their remarkable unbeaten run and looking unstoppable in the defence of their title but a defeat at Old Trafford in November not only brought an end to their run - at 49 games - but it also sent their season off the rails although there was the consolation of a third FA Cup triumph in the past four sea-

INTERNATIONAL HONOURS
FIFA World Cup™ 1966
Qualified for the FIFA World Cup™ 1950 1954 1958 1962 1966 (hosts) 1970 1982 1986 1990 1998 2002 Qualified for the FIFA Women's World Cup 1995
European U-21 Championship 1982 1984   European Junior Championship 1948 1963 1964 1971 1972 1973 1975 1980 1993
UEFA Champions League Manchester United 1968 1999 Liverpool 1977 1978 1981 1984 2005 Nottingham Forest 1979 1980 Aston Villa 1982

sons for Arséne Wenger's team. Speculation of a takeover did not help Manchester United, a drama that culminated in the club being purchased by Malcolm Glazer for £790m, much of which was borrowed and is now a debt against the club. The takeover of England's most popular club did not go down well with most of the fans and a warning of how the mighty can fall came with the relegation of Nottingham Forest to the third level of English football, an ignominy no other former European Champion has ever had to face. The revolution at Chelsea has had a hugely positive side effect for the England national team with John Terry, Frank Lampard and Joe Cole emerging as players of genuine international class. England lost just one match all season, a nasty, intimidating affair in Madrid during which England's black players were subjected to a barrage of racist abuse. In the FIFA World Cup™ qualifiers, an away win in Poland handed England the advantage in their group but the Poles kept up the pressure with the pair breaking away from the rest. In June 2005 the North West of England hosted the UEFA Women's Championship but despite record crowds England were knocked out by Sweden and Finland in what turned out to be an incredibly tight first round group.

The Football Association (The FA)
25 Soho Square, London W1D 4FA, United Kingdom
Tel +44 20 77454545   Fax +44 20 77454546
info@TheFA.com   www.TheFA.com
President: THOMPSON Geoffrey   General Secretary: BARWICK Brian
Vice-President: DEIN David   Treasurer: None   Media Officer: BEVINGTON Adrian
Men's Coach: ERIKSSON Sven Goran   Women's Coach: POWELL Hope
The FA formed: 1863   UEFA: 1954   FIFA: 1905-20 & 1945
Colours: White, Navy blue, White or Red, White, Red

GAMES PLAYED BY ENGLAND IN THE 2006 FIFA WORLD CUP™ CYCLE

2002	Opponents	Score		Venue	Comp	Scorers	Att	Referee
7-09	Portugal	D	1-1	Birmingham	Fr	Smith.A [40]	40 058	Ovrebo NOR
12-10	Slovakia	W	2-1	Bratislava	ECq	Beckham [64], Owen [82]	30 000	Messina ITA
16-10	Macedonia	D	2-2	Southampton	ECq	Beckham [13], Gerrard [35]	32 095	Ibanez ESP
2003								
12-02	Australia	L	1-3	London	Fr	Jeffers [70]	34 590	Gonzalez ESP
29-03	Liechtenstein	W	2-0	Vaduz	ECq	Owen [28], Beckham [53]	3 548	Kasnaferis GRE
2-04	Turkey	W	2-0	Sunderland	ECq	Vassell [76], Beckham [90p]	47 667	Meier SUI
22-05	South Africa	W	2-1	Durban	Fr	Southgate [1], Heskey [64]	48 000	Chong MRI
3-06	Serbia & Montenegro	W	2-1	Leicester	Fr	Gerrard [35], Cole.J [82]	30 900	Allaerts BEL
11-06	Slovakia	W	2-1	Middlesbrough	ECq	Owen 2 [62p 73]	35 000	Stark GER
20-08	Croatia	W	3-1	Ipswich	Fr	Beckham [9p], Owen [51], Lampard [80]	28 700	Larsen DEN
6-09	Macedonia	W	2-1	Skopje	ECq	Rooney [53], Beckham [63p]	20 500	De Bleeckere BEL
10-09	Liechtenstein	W	2-0	Manchester	ECq	Owen [46], Rooney [52]	64 931	Fisker DEN
11-10	Turkey	D	0-0	Istanbul	ECq		45 000	Collina ITA
16-11	Denmark	L	2-3	Manchester	Fr	Rooney [5], Cole.J [9]	64 159	Hrinak SVK
2004								
18-02	Portugal	D	1-1	Faro	Fr	King [48]	27 000	Kassai HUN
31-03	Sweden	L	0-1	Gothenburg	Fr		40 464	Ovrebo NOR
1-06	Japan	D	1-1	Manchester	Fr	Owen [22]	38 581	Rosetti ITA
5-06	Iceland	W	6-1	Manchester	Fr	Lampard [25], Rooney 2 [27 38], Vassell 2 [57 77], Bridge [68]	43 500	Wegereef NED
13-06	France	L	1-2	Lisbon	ECr1	Lampard [38]	62 487	Merk GER
17-06	Switzerland	W	3-0	Coimbra	ECr1	Rooney 2 [23 75], Gerrard [82]	28 214	Ivanov RUS
21-06	Croatia	W	4-2	Lisbon	ECr1	Scholes [40], Rooney 2 [45 68], Lampard [79]	57 047	Collina ITA
24-06	Portugal	D	2-2	Lisbon	ECqf	Owen [3], Lampard [115], L 5-6p	62 564	Meier SUI
18-08	Ukraine	W	3-0	Newcastle	Fr	Beckham [28], Owen [50], Wright-Phillips [70]	35 387	McCurry SCO
4-09	Austria	D	2-2	Vienna	WCq	Lampard [24], Gerrard [63]	48 500	Lubos SVK
8-09	Poland	W	2-1	Chorzow	WCq	Defoe [37], Glowacki OG [58]	38 000	Farina ITA
9-10	Wales	W	2-0	Manchester	WCq	Lampard [4], Beckham [76]	65 224	Hauge NOR
13-10	Azerbaijan	W	1-0	Baku	WCq	Owen [22]	15 000	Hamer LUX
17-11	Spain	L	0-1	Madrid	Fr		48 000	Kasnaferis GRE
2005								
9-02	Netherlands	D	0-0	Birmingham	Fr		40 705	Frojdfeldt SWE
26-03	Northern Ireland	W	4-0	Manchester	WCq	Cole.J [47], Owen 2 [52], Baird OG [54], Lampard [62]	62 239	Stark GER
30-03	Azerbaijan	W	2-0	Newcastle	WCq	Gerrard [51], Beckham [62]	49 046	Costa POR
28-05	USA	W	2-1	Chicago	Fr	Richardson 2 [4 44]	47 637	Archundia MEX
31-05	Colombia	W	3-2	New Jersey	Fr	Owen 3 [35 44 58]	58 000	Hall USA

Fr = Friendly match • EC = UEFA EURO 2004™ • WC = FIFA World Cup™ • q = qualifier • r1 = first round group • qf = quarter-final

FIFA/COCA-COLA WORLD RANKING

1993	1994	1995	1996	1997	1998	1999	2000	2001	2002	2003	2004	High	Low
11	18	21	12	4	9	12	17	10	7	8	8	4 12/97	27 02/96

2004-2005											
08/04	09/04	10/04	11/04	12/04	01/05	02/05	03/05	04/05	05/05	06/05	07/05
7	7	7	7	8	8	8	8	6	6	7	8

THE FIFA BIG COUNT OF 2000

	Male	Female		Male	Female
Registered players	1 502 500	18 200	Referees	33 000	450
Non registered players	1 000 000	17 000	Officials	34 800	500
Youth players	750 000	23 000	Total involved	3 379 450	
Total players	3 310 700		Number of clubs	42 000	
Professional players	2 500	0	Number of teams	64 850	

NATIONAL CAPS

	Caps
SHILTON Peter	125
MOORE Bobby	108
CHARLTON Bobby	106
WRIGHT Billy	105
ROBSON Bryan	90
SANSOM Kenny	86
WILKINS Ray	84
BECKHAM David	81
LINEKER Gary	80
BARNES John	79

NATIONAL GOALS

	Goals
CHARLTON Bobby	49
LINEKER Gary	48
GREAVES Jimmy	43
OWEN Michael	32
FINNEY Tom	30
LOFTHOUSE Nat	30
SHEARER Alan	30
WOODWARD Vivian †	29
BLOOMER Steve	28
† also scored 44 goals for England amateurs	

NATIONAL COACH

	Years
REVIE Don	1974-'77
GREENWOOD Ron	1977-'82
ROBSON Bobby	1982-'90
TAYLOR Graham	1990-'93
VENABLES Terry	1994-'96
HODDLE Glenn	1996-'99
WILKINSON Howard	1999
KEEGAN Kevin	1999-'00
TAYLOR Peter	2000
ERIKSSON Sven Goran	2000-

ENGLAND NATIONAL TEAM RECORDS AND RECORD SEQUENCES

Records			Sequence records					
Victory	15-0	FRA 1906	Wins	23	1908-1909	Clean sheets	7	1908-1909
Defeat	1-7	HUN 1954	Defeats	3	Six times	Goals scored	53	1884-1901
Player Caps	125	SHILTON Peter	Undefeated	36	1906-1910	Without goal	4	1981
Player Goals	49	CHARLTON Bobby	Without win	7	1958	Goals against	13	1873-81, 1959-60

These statistics include data from the England Amateur team that played between 1906 and 1923 which the FA do not regard as full internationals. The associations of their opponents, however, do regard the games as full internationals

FIFA REFEREE LIST 2005

	Int'l	DoB
BENNETT Stephen	2001	17-01-1961
D'URSO Andy	2001	30-11-1963
DEAN Michael	2003	2-07-1968
HALSEY Mark	2001	8-07-1961
MESSIAS Matthew	2002	7-05-1964
POLL Graham	1996	29-07-1963
RILEY Michael	1999	17-12-1964
STYLES Robert	2002	21-04-1964
WEBB Howard	2005	14-07-1971

FIFA ASSISTANT REFEREE LIST 2005

	Int'l	DoB
BABSKI David	1997	5-09-1961
BRYAN David	1999	1-07-1962
DEVINE James	1999	17-04-1962
EAST Roger	2005	12-05-1965
GREEN Antony	2000	20-08-1962
LEWIS Robert	2005	22-04-1969
PIKE Kevin	2001	2-05-1961
SHARP Phillip	1997	5-04-1964
TINGEY Mike	2004	10-08-1967
TURNER Glen	2002	6-11-1964

ENGLAND COUNTRY INFORMATION

Capital	London	Independence	Part of the United Kingdom	GDP per Capita	$29 600
Population	49 561 800	Status	Kingdom	GNP Ranking	4
Area km²	130 439	Language	English	Dialling code	+44
Population density	380 per km²	Literacy rate	99%	Internet code	.uk
% in urban areas	89%	Main religion	Christian	GMT +/-	0
Towns/Cities ('000)	London 7 172; West Midlands (Birmingham) 2 555; Greater Manchester 2 482; West Yorkshire (Leeds, Bradford) 2 079; Merseyside (Liverpool) 1 362; South Yorkshire (Sheffield) 1 266; Tyne & Wear (Newcastle, Sunderland) 1 075				
Neighbours (km)	Scotland 164; Wales 468				
Main stadia	Wembley – London 90 000 (from 2006); Old Trafford – Manchester 68 174; Emirates Stadium – London 60 000 (from 2006); St James' Park – Newcastle 52 142; Villa Park – Birmingham 43 275				

ENGLAND 2004-05

PREMIER LEAGUE

Team	Pl	W	D	L	F	A	Pts	Ars	Che	MUn	Eve	Liv	Bol	Mid	MCi	Spu	Vil	Cha	Bir	Ful	New	Bla	Por	WBA	Pal	Nor	Sou
Chelsea †	38	29	8	1	72	15	95	0-0		1-0	1-0	1-0	2-2	2-0	0-0	0-0	1-0	1-0	1-1	3-1	4-0	4-0	3-0	1-0	4-1	4-0	2-1
Arsenal †	38	25	8	5	87	36	83		2-2	2-4	7-0	3-1	2-2	5-3	1-1	1-0	3-1	4-0	3-0	2-0	1-0	3-0	3-0	1-1	5-1	4-1	2-2
Manchester United †	38	22	11	5	58	26	77	1-3	2-0		0-0	2-1	2-0	1-1	0-0	0-0	3-1	2-0	2-0	1-0	2-1	0-0	2-1	1-1	5-2	2-1	3-0
Everton †	38	18	7	13	45	46	61	0-1	1-4	1-0		1-0	3-2	1-0	2-1	0-1	1-1	1-0	1-1	1-1	1-0	2-0	0-1	2-1	2-1	4-0	1-0
Liverpool †	38	17	7	14	52	41	58	0-1	2-1	0-1	2-1		1-0	1-1	2-1	2-2	2-1	0-0	0-1	3-1	3-1	0-0	1-1	3-0	3-2	3-0	1-0
Bolton Wanderers ‡	38	16	10	12	49	44	58	0-2	1-0	2-2	3-2	1-0		0-0	0-1	3-1	1-2	4-1	1-1	3-1	2-1	0-1	0-1	1-1	1-0	1-1	1-1
Middlesbrough ‡	38	14	13	11	53	46	55	0-1	0-1	0-2	1-1	2-0	1-1		3-2	1-0	3-0	2-2	2-1	1-1	2-2	1-0	1-1	4-0	2-1	2-0	1-3
Manchester City	38	13	13	12	47	39	52	1-0	0-1	0-1	2-0	1-1	0-0	1-1		0-1	2-0	4-0	3-0	1-1	1-1	1-2	0-1	1-1	3-1	1-1	2-1
Tottenham Hotspur	38	14	10	14	47	41	52	0-2	4-5	0-1	5-2	1-1	1-2	2-2	0-1		5-1	2-1	3-1	0-2	1-0	0-0	3-1	1-1	1-1	0-0	5-1
Aston Villa	38	12	11	15	45	52	47	0-0	1-3	0-1	1-3	1-1	1-1	2-0	1-2	1-0		0-0	1-2	2-0	4-2	1-0	3-0	1-1	1-1	3-0	2-0
Charlton Athletic	38	12	10	16	42	58	46	0-4	1-3	0-4	2-0	1-2	1-2	1-2	2-2	2-0	3-0		3-1	2-1	1-1	0-2	1-1	1-4	2-2	4-0	0-0
Birmingham City	38	11	12	15	40	46	45	0-1	2-1	0-0	0-1	2-0	1-2	0-1	1-0	1-2	0-1	1-2		2-2	1-0	0-4	0-0	1-1	1-2	1-1	2-1
Fulham	38	12	8	18	52	60	44	1-4	0-3	1-1	0-2	2-4	2-0	2-1	2-0	1-0	1-2	0-1	1-3		3-1	1-1	3-1	1-1	6-0	1-0	5-2
Newcastle United	38	10	14	14	47	57	44	1-1	0-1	1-3	1-1	1-0	2-1	0-0	4-3	0-1	0-3	1-0	3-1	1-4		3-0	1-1	3-1	0-0	2-2	2-1
Blackburn Rovers	38	9	15	14	32	43	42	0-1	0-1	1-0	0-0	2-2	0-1	0-4	0-0	0-1	2-2	1-0	3-3	1-3	2-2		1-0	1-1	0-3	3-0	1-0
Portsmouth	38	10	9	19	43	59	39	0-2	0-1	2-0	1-1	1-2	1-2	1-1	1-3	1-0	1-2	4-2	1-4	4-3	1-1	0-1		3-2	3-1	1-1	4-1
West Bromwich Albion	38	6	16	16	36	61	34	1-4	0-2	0-3	1-0	0-5	2-1	1-2	2-0	1-1	1-1	0-1	2-0	1-0	2-1	0-1	1-2		2-2	0-0	0-0
Crystal Palace	38	7	12	19	41	62	33	0-2	1-1	0-0	1-3	1-0	0-1	1-2	3-0	2-0	0-1	2-0	2-0	0-2	0-0	0-1	3-0	1-2		3-3	2-2
Norwich City	38	7	12	19	42	77	33	1-3	1-4	2-0	2-3	1-2	3-2	4-4	2-3	0-0	2-0	1-0	0-1	2-1	1-1	2-2	3-2	1-1	2-3		2-1
Southampton	38	6	14	18	45	66	32	1-3	1-1	1-2	2-2	2-0	1-2	2-2	0-0	1-0	2-3	0-0	3-3	1-2	3-2	2-1	2-2	2-4	4-3		

14/08/2004 - 15/05/2005 • † Qualified for the UEFA Champions League • ‡ Qualified for the UEFA Cup

TOP SCORERS

Player	Club	
HENRY Thierry	Arsenal	25
JOHNSON Andrew	Crystal Palace	21
PIRES Robert	Arsenal	14
DEFOE Jermain	Tottenham Hotspur	13
HASSELBAINK Jimmy Floyd	Middlesbrough	13
LAMPARD Frank	Chelsea	13
YAKUBU Ayegbeni	Portsmouth	13

ENGLAND 2004-05

THE CHAMPIONSHIP (2)

Team	Pl	W	D	L	F	A	Pts	Sun	Wig	Ips	Der	PNE	WHa	Rea	ShU	Wol	Mil	QPR	Sto	Bur	Lee	Lei	Car	Ply	Wat	Cov	Bri	Cre	Gil	For	Rot
Sunderland	46	29	7	10	76	41	94		1-1	2-0	0-0	3-1	0-2	1-2	1-0	3-1	1-0	2-2	1-0	2-1	2-3	2-1	2-1	5-1	4-2	1-0	2-0	3-1	1-1	2-0	4-1
Wigan Athletic	46	25	12	9	79	35	87	0-1		1-0	1-2	5-0	1-2	3-1	4-0	2-0	0-0	0-0	0-0	3-0	0-0	2-1	0-2	2-2	4-1	3-0	4-1	2-0	1-1	2-0	1-1
Ipswich Town ‡	46	24	13	9	85	56	85	2-2	2-1		3-2	3-0	0-2	1-5	2-1	2-0	0-0	3-0	0-0	1-3	2-1	3-2	1-0	5-2	1-0	1-0	5-2	1-0	6-1	4-3	
Derby County ‡	46	22	10	14	71	60	76	0-2	1-1	3-2		3-1	1-1	2-1	0-1	3-3	0-3	0-0	3-1	1-1	2-0	1-0	1-0	1-0	2-2	2-2	3-0	2-4	2-0	3-0	3-2
Preston North End ‡	46	21	13	12	67	58	75	3-2	1-1	1-3	0-1		2-1	1-0	0-1	3-3	0-0	3-0	3-1	1-2	0-1	1-2	0-1	2-3	2-4	0-3	1-0	1-0	3-2	2-0	
West Ham United ‡	46	21	10	15	66	56	73	1-2	1-3	1-1	1-2	1-2		1-0	0-2	1-1	2-1	1-2	1-0	2-2	3-0	0-1	2-2	1-0	5-0	3-2	3-0	0-1	1-1	3-2	1-0
Reading	46	19	13	14	51	44	70	1-0	1-1	1-0	1-0	3-1	3-1		0-0	1-2	2-1	1-0	1-0	0-1	1-0	0-0	3-0	1-2	3-2	3-2	4-0	3-1	1-0	1-0	1-0
Sheffield United	46	18	13	15	57	56	67	1-0	0-2	0-2	0-1	1-1	1-2	0-1		3-3	0-1	3-2	0-0	2-2	0-2	2-0	2-1	1-1	1-1	1-2	4-0	0-0	1-1	1-0	
Wolverhampton W	46	15	21	10	72	59	66	1-1	3-3	2-0	2-0	2-2	4-2	4-1	4-2		1-2	2-1	1-1	2-0	0-0	1-2	3-1	1-1	4-0	2-0	2-0	1-2	3-2	4-0	2-1
Millwall	46	18	12	16	51	45	66	2-0	0-2	3-1	3-1	1-0	1-0	1-0	1-2	0-2		1-1	0-0	0-1	1-1	1-0	0-0	2-2	3-0	0-2	1-1	4-3	2-1	1-0	2-0
Queens Park Rangers	46	17	11	18	54	58	62	1-3	1-0	2-4	0-2	1-2	1-0	0-0	0-0	1-1	1-1		1-0	3-0	1-1	3-2	1-3	2-2	3-0	0-2	4-3	2-1	1-0	1-2	
Stoke City	46	17	10	19	36	38	61	0-1	0-1	3-2	1-0	0-0	0-1	0-1	2-0	2-1	1-0	0-1		0-1	0-1	3-2	1-3	2-0	0-1	1-0	2-0	0-0	0-1	2-1	
Burnley	46	15	15	16	38	39	60	1-2	1-0	0-0	2-2	2-0	1-1	0-0	1-0	0-1	1-1	1-1	6-2		0-1	0-0	0-3	1-1	2-2	1-3	1-1	0-1	2-1	3-0	
Leeds United	46	14	18	14	49	52	60	0-1	0-2	1-1	1-0	1-0	0-1	3-0	1-0	1-6	1-0	0-1	1-1	0-2		1-1	2-1	2-0	1-1	0-2	1-0	2-0	0-0	1-0	
Leicester City	46	12	21	13	49	46	57	0-0	2-2	1-0	1-0	0-0	3-2	1-1	3-1	1-0	1-0	2-0		1-2	1-0		3-0	1-1	2-0	1-1		2-0	0-1		
Cardiff City	46	13	15	18	48	51	54	0-1	0-2	0-1	4-1	2-0	1-0	1-0	1-0	0-1	0-0	0-0		0-1	0-3	2-1	1-0	1-3	1-3	1-0	2-0				
Plymouth Argyle	46	14	11	21	52	64	53	2-1	1-2	1-2	0-2	0-2	1-2	2-3	1-2	0-0	2-0	0-0	0-0	1-0		1-0	1-1	5-1	3-0	2-1	3-2	1-1			
Watford	46	12	16	18	52	59	52	1-1	0-0	2-2	2-2	0-2	1-2	0-1	0-0	1-1	3-0	0-1	0-1	1-2	2-2	0-0	3-1		2-3	1-1	3-0	2-1	2-0		
Coventry City	46	13	13	20	61	73	52	1-1	0-0	2-2	2-2	0-2	1-2	1-2	1-2	2-2	0-0	1-2	1-1	1-1	1-0		2-1	2-1		1-2	2-0	2-0	0-0		
Brighton & Hove Alb	46	13	12	21	40	65	51	2-1	2-4	1-2	3-1	0-2	0-1	1-0	1-0	2-3	0-1	0-1	1-1	0-1	0-1	2-1	1-1		2-1		1-3	2-1	0-0		
Crewe Alexandra	46	12	14	20	66	86	50	0-1	1-3	2-2	1-2	1-2	2-3	1-1	1-4	2-1	0-2	0-1	1-2	2-2	2-2	3-0	3-0	2-1	3-1		4-1		1-1	1-1	
Gillingham	46	12	14	20	45	66	50	0-4	2-1	0-0	0-2	0-0	1-3	1-0	0-0	0-1	2-1	0-1	0-0	1-1	1-0	1-0	0-1	1-1	1-0	2-1			2-1	3-1	
Nottingham Forest	46	9	17	20	42	66	44	1-2	1-1	1-1	2-2	2-0	2-1	1-0	1-1	1-0	1-2	2-1	1-0	2-1	0-1	1-1	1-0	0-3	1-1	3-4	0-1	2-2	2-2		2-2
Rotherham United	46	5	14	27	35	69	29	0-1	0-2	0-2	1-3	1-2	2-2	1-0	2-2	1-2	1-1	0-1	1-1	0-0	1-0	0-2	2-2	0-1	0-1	1-2	0-1	2-3	1-3	0-0	

7/08/2004 - 8/05/2005 • ‡ Qualified for the play-offs

ENGLAND 2004-05
LEAGUE ONE (3)

	Pl	W	D	L	F	A	Pts
Luton Town	46	29	11	6	87	48	98
Hull City	46	26	8	12	80	53	86
Tranmere Rovers ‡	46	22	13	11	73	55	79
Brentford ‡	46	22	9	15	57	60	75
Sheffield Wed'day ‡	46	19	15	12	77	59	72
Hartlepool United ‡	46	21	8	17	76	66	71
Bristol City	46	18	16	12	74	57	70
Bournemouth	46	20	10	16	77	64	70
Huddersfield Town	46	20	10	16	74	65	70
Doncaster Rovers	46	16	18	12	65	60	66
Bradford City	46	17	14	15	64	62	65
Swindon Town	46	17	12	17	66	68	63
Barnsley	46	14	19	13	69	64	61
Walsall	46	16	12	18	65	69	60
Colchester United	46	14	17	15	60	50	59
Blackpool	46	15	12	19	54	59	57
Chesterfield	46	14	15	17	55	62	57
Port Vale	46	17	5	24	49	59	56
Oldham Athletic	46	14	10	22	60	73	52
Milton Keynes Dons	46	12	15	19	54	68	51
Torquay United	46	12	15	19	55	79	51
Wrexham	46	13	14	19	62	80	43
Peterborough Utd	46	9	12	25	49	73	39
Stockport County	46	6	8	32	49	98	26

7/08/2004 - 7/05/2005 • ‡ Qualified for the play-offs

PLAY-OFFS
THE CHAMPIONSHIP
Semi-finals

West Ham United	2 2
Ipswich Town	2 0
Preston NE	2 0
Derby County	0 0

Final

West Ham United	1
Preston NE	0

LEAGUE ONE
Semi-finals

Sheffield Wed	1 2
Brentford	0 1
Hartlepool	2 0 6p
Tranmere Rovers	0 2 5p

Final

Sheffield Wed	4
Hartlepool	2

LEAGUE TWO
Semi-finals

Northampton Town	0 0
Southend United	0 1
Lincoln City	1 1
Macclesfield Town	0 1

Final

Southend United	2
Lincoln City	0

ENGLAND 2004-05
LEAGUE TWO (4)

	Pl	W	D	L	F	A	Pts
Yeovil Town	46	25	8	13	90	65	83
Scunthorpe United	46	22	14	10	69	42	80
Swansea City	46	24	8	14	62	43	80
Southend United ‡	46	22	12	12	65	46	78
Macclesfield Town ‡	46	22	9	15	60	49	75
Lincoln City ‡	46	20	12	14	64	47	72
Northampton Town ‡	46	20	12	14	62	51	72
Darlington	46	20	12	14	57	49	72
Rochdale	46	16	18	12	54	48	66
Wycombe Wand'ers	46	17	14	15	58	52	65
Leyton Orient	46	15	15	15	65	67	63
Bristol Rovers	46	13	21	12	60	57	60
Mansfield Town	46	15	15	16	56	56	60
Cheltenham Town	46	16	12	18	51	54	60
Oxford United	46	16	11	19	50	63	59
Boston United	46	14	16	16	62	58	58
Bury	46	14	16	16	54	54	58
Grimsby Town	46	14	16	16	51	52	58
Notts County	46	13	13	20	46	62	52
Chester City	46	12	16	18	43	69	52
Shrewsbury Town	46	11	16	19	48	53	49
Rushden & Diamonds	46	10	14	22	42	63	44
Kidderminster Har's	46	10	8	28	39	85	38
Cambridge United	46	8	16	22	39	62	30

7/08/2004 - 7/05/2005 • ‡ Qualified for the play-offs

CLUB DIRECTORY

Club	Town/City	Stadium	Phone	www.	Lge	Cup	CL
Arsenal	London	Highbury 38 500	+44 20 77044000	arsenal.com	13	10	0
Aston Villa	Birmingham	Villa Park 42 573	+44 121 3272299	avfc.co.uk	7	7	1
Birmingham City	Birmingham	St Andrews 29 949	+44 121 7720101	bcfc.com	0	0	0
Blackburn Rovers	Blackburn	Ewood Park 31 367	+44 8701 113232	rovers.co.uk	3	6	0
Bolton Wanderers	Bolton	The Reebok 27 879	+44 1204 673673	bwfc.co.uk	0	4	0
Charlton Athletic	London	The Valley 26 875	+44 20 83334000	cafc.co.uk	0	1	0
Chelsea	London	Stamford Bridge 42 449	+44 870 3001212	chelseafc.com	2	3	0
Crystal Palace	London	Selhurst Park 26 500	+44 20 87686000	cpfc.co.uk	0	0	0
Everton	Liverpool	Goodison Park 40 565	+44 151 3302200	evertonfc.com	9	5	0
Fulham	London	Craven Cottage 22 400	+44 870 4421222	fulhamfc.com	0	0	0
Liverpool	Liverpool	Anfield 45 362	+44 151 2632361	liverpoolfc.tv	18	6	5
Manchester City	Manchester	City of Manchester 48 000	+44 870 0621894	mcfc.co.uk	2	4	0
Manchester United	Manchester	Old Trafford 68 190	+44 161 8688000	manutd.com	15	11	2
Middlesbrough	Middlesbrough	The Riverside 35 120	+44 1642 877700	mfc.co.uk	0	0	0
Newcastle United	Newcastle	St James' Park 52 193	+44 191 2018400	nufc.co.uk	4	6	0
Norwich City	Norwich	Carrow Road 24 349	+44 1603 760760	canaries.co.uk	0	0	0
Portsmouth	Portsmouth	Fratton Park 20 228	+44 2392 731204	pompeyfc.co.uk	2	1	0
Southampton	Southampton	St Mary's 32 689	+44 870 2200000	saintsfc.co.uk	0	1	0
Tottenham Hotspur	London	White Hart Lane 36 252	+44 20 83655000	spurs.co.uk	2	8	0
West Bromwich Albion	West Bromwich	The Hawthorns 28 000	+44 121 5258888	wbafc.co.uk	1	5	0

RECENT LEAGUE AND CUP RECORD

	Championship						Cup		
Year	Champions	Pts	Runners-up	Pts	Third	Pts	Winners	Score	Runners-up
1990	Liverpool	79	Aston Villa	70	Tottenham Hotspur	63	Manchester United	3-3 1-0	Crystal Palace
1991	Arsenal	83	Liverpool	76	Crystal Palace	69	Tottenham Hotspur	2-1	Nottingham Forest
1992	Leeds United	82	Manchester United	78	Sheffield Wed'day	75	Liverpool	2-0	Sunderland
1993	Manchester United	84	Aston Villa	74	Norwich City	72	Arsenal	1-1 2-1	Sheffield Wed'day
1994	Manchester United	92	Blackburn Rovers	84	Newcastle United	77	Manchester United	4-0	Chelsea
1995	Blackburn Rovers	89	Manchester United	88	Nottingham Forest	77	Everton	1-0	Manchester United
1996	Manchester United	82	Newcastle United	78	Liverpool	71	Manchester United	1-0	Liverpool
1997	Manchester United	75	Newcastle United	68	Arsenal	68	Chelsea	2-0	Middlesbrough
1998	Arsenal	78	Manchester United	77	Liverpool	65	Arsenal	2-0	Newcastle United
1999	Manchester United	79	Arsenal	78	Chelsea	75	Manchester United	2-0	Newcastle United
2000	Manchester United	91	Arsenal	73	Leeds United	69	Chelsea	1-0	Aston Villa
2001	Manchester United	80	Arsenal	70	Liverpool	69	Liverpool	2-1	Arsenal
2002	Arsenal	87	Liverpool	80	Manchester United	77	Arsenal	2-0	Chelsea
2003	Manchester United	83	Arsenal	78	Newcastle United	69	Arsenal	1-0	Southampton
2004	Arsenal	90	Chelsea	79	Manchester United	75	Manchester United	3-0	Millwall
2005	Chelsea	95	Arsenal	83	Manchester United	77	Arsenal	0-0 5-4p	Manchester United

FA CUP 2004-05

Third Round

Arsenal *	2
Stoke City	1
Millwall	0
Wolverhampton Wanderers *	2
West Ham United *	1
Norwich City	0
Aston Villa	1
Sheffield United *	3
Fulham	1 2
Watford *	1 0
Wigan Athletic	1
Derby County *	2
Oldham Athletic *	1
Manchester City	0
Ipswich Town *	1
Bolton Wanderers	3
Leicester City *	2 1
Blackpool	2 0
Swansea City	1 0
Reading *	1 1
Yeovil Town	3
Rotherham United *	0
Rochdale	1
Charlton Athletic *	4
Burnley *	1
Liverpool	0
Chester City	1
AFC Bournemouth *	2
Colchester United	2
Hull City *	0
Cardiff City *	1 2
Blackburn Rovers	1 3
Newcastle United	2
Yeading * †	0
Crewe Alexandra	0
Coventry City *	3
Birmingham City *	3
Leeds United	0
Scunthorpe United	1
Chelsea *	3
Nottingham Forest	3
Queens Park Rangers *	0
Milton Keynes Dons *	0
Peterborough United	2
West Bromwich Albion	2
Preston North End *	0
Brighton & Hove Albion	1
Tottenham Hotspur *	2
Southampton	3
Northampton Town *	1
Gillingham	0
Portsmouth *	1
Hartlepool United	0 1
Boston United	0 0
Luton Town *	0
Brentford	2
Everton	3
Plymouth Argyle *	1
Crystal Palace	1
Sunderland *	2
Middlesbrough	2
Notts County *	1
Exeter City	0 0
Manchester United *	0 2

Fourth Round

Arsenal *	2
Wolverhampton Wanderers	0
West Ham United *	1 1 1p
Sheffield United	1 1 3p
Fulham	1 4
Derby County *	1 2
Oldham Athletic	0
Bolton Wanderers *	1
Leicester City	2
Reading *	1
Yeovil Town	2
Charlton Athletic *	3
Burnley *	2
AFC Bournemouth	0
Colchester United	0
Blackburn Rovers *	3
Newcastle United *	3
Coventry City	1
Birmingham City	0
Chelsea *	2
Nottingham Forest *	1
Peterborough United	0
West Bromwich Albion *	1 1
Tottenham Hotspur	1 3
Southampton *	2
Portsmouth	1
Hartlepool United	0 0
Brentford *	0 1
Everton *	3
Sunderland	0
Middlesbrough	0
Manchester United *	3

Fifth Round

Arsenal *	1 0 4p
Sheffield United	1 0 2p
Fulham	0
Bolton Wanderers *	1
Leicester City	2
Charlton Athletic *	1
Burnley *	0 1
Blackburn Rovers	0 2
Newcastle United *	1
Chelsea	0
Nottingham Forest	1 0
Tottenham Hotspur *	1 3
Southampton *	2 3
Brentford	2 1
Everton *	0
Manchester United	2

* Home team • † Played at QPR

FA CUP 2004-05

Quarter-finals   **Semi-finals**   **Final**

| Arsenal | 1 |
| Bolton Wanderers * | 0 |

| Arsenal | 3 |
| Blackburn Rovers | 0 |

| Leicester City | 0 |
| Blackburn Rovers * | 1 |

| Arsenal | 0 5p |
| Manchester United | 0 4p |

| Newcastle United * | 1 |
| Tottenham Hotspur | 0 |

| Newcastle United | 1 |
| Manchester United | 4 |

FA CUP FINAL 2005

Millennium Stadium, Cardiff, 21-05-2005, Att: 71 876, Referee: Styles

| Southampton * | 0 |
| Manchester United | 4 |

Arsenal   0 5p

Manchester United   0 4p

Arsenal - Lehmann - Lauren, Toure, Senderos, Cole - Fabregas (Van Persie 86), Vieira, Silva, Pires (Edu 105) - Bergkamp (Ljungberg 65), Reyes. Tr: Wenger
Man Utd - Carroll - Brown, Ferdinand, Silvestre, O'Shea (Fortune 77) - Fletcher (Giggs 91), Keane, Scholes, Ronaldo - Van Nistelrooy, Rooney. Tr: Ferguson
Penalties: Van Nistelrooy scored, Lauren scored, Scholes saved by Lehmann, Ljungberg scored, Ronaldo scored, Van Persie scored, Rooney scored, Cole scored, Keane scored, Vieira scored. Sent-off: Reyes 120

Semi-finals played at the Millennium Stadium, Cardiff

CARLING LEAGUE CUP 2004-05

Third Round		Fourth Round		Quarter-finals		Semi-finals			Final	
Chelsea *	1	Chelsea	2	Chelsea	2	Chelsea *	0	2	Chelsea	3
West Ham United	0	Newcastle United *	0	Fulham *	1	Manchester United	0	1	Liverpool	2
Norwich City	1									
Newcastle United *	2									
Nottingham Forest	2	Nottingham Forest *	2							
Doncaster Rovers *	0	Fulham	4							
Birmingham City *	0									
Fulham	1									
Arsenal	2	Arsenal *	3	Arsenal	0					
Manchester City *	1	Everton	1	Manchester United *	1					
Preston North End	0									
Everton *	2									
Crystal Palace	2	Crystal Palace	0							
Charlton Athletic *	1	Manchester United *	2							
Crewe Alexandra *	0									
Manchester United	3									
Watford	0 4p	Watford *	5	Watford *	3	Watford	0	0		
Sheffield United *	0 2p	Southampton	2	Portsmouth	0	Liverpool *	1	1		
Colchester United	2									
Southampton *	3									
Cardiff City	3 5p	Cardiff City *	0							
Bournemouth *	3 4p	Portsmouth	2							
Leeds United	1									
Portsmouth *	2									
Tottenham Hotspur	4	Tottenham Hotspur	3	Tottenham Hotspur *	1 3p					
Bolton Wanderers	3	Burnley *	0	Liverpool	1 4p					
Aston Villa	1									
Burnley *	3									
Middlesbrough *	3	Middlesbrough	0							
Coventry City	0	Liverpool *	2							
Millwall *	0									
Liverpool	3									

CARLING CUP FINAL

27-02-2005, Att. 78,000
Millennium Stadium, Cardiff
Scorers - Gerrard OG 79, Drogba 107, Kezman 112 for Chelsea; Riise 1, Nunez 113 for Liverpool

Chelsea - Cech, Ferreira, Carvalho, Terry, Gallas (Kezman 74), Jarosik (Gudjohnsen 45), Lampard, Makelele, Cole (Johnsen 81), Drogba, Duff. Tr. Mourinho

Liverpool - Dudek, Finnan, Carragher, Hyypia, Traore (Biscan 67), Luis Garcia, Gerrard, Hamann, Riise, Kewell (Nunez 56), Morientes (Baros 74). Tr. Benitez

* Home team/home team in the first leg of the semi-finals

CHELSEA 2004-05

Date	Opponents	Score		Comp	Scorers	Att
15-08-2004	Manchester United	W 1-0	H	PL	Gudjohnsen [15]	41 813
21-08-2004	Birmingham City	W 1-0	A	PL	Cole [68]	28 559
24-08-2004	Crystal Palace	W 2-0	A	PL	Drogba [28], Mendes [72]	24 953
28-08-2004	Southampton	W 2-1	H	PL	Beatttie OG [34], Lampard [41p]	40 864
11-09-2004	Aston Villa	D 0-0	A	PL		36 691
14-09-2004	Paris Saint Germain - FRA	W 3-0	A	CLgH	Terry [29], Drogba 2 [45 75]	40 000
19-09-2004	Tottenham Hotspur	D 0-0	H	PL		42 246
25-09-2004	Middlesbrough	W 1-0	A	PL	Drogba [81]	32 341
29-09-2004	FC Porto - POR	W 3-1	H	CLgH	Smertin [7], Drogba [50], Terry [70]	39 237
3-10-2004	Liverpool	W 1-0	H	PL	Cole [64]	42 028
16-10-2004	Manchester City	L 0-1	H	PL		45 047
20-10-2004	CSKA Moskva - RUS	W 2-0	H	CLgH	Terry [9], Gudjohnsen [45]	33 945
23-10-2004	Blackburn Rovers	W 4-0	H	PL	Gudjohnsen 3 [37 38 51p], Duff [74]	41 546
27-10-2004	West Ham United	W 1-0	H	LCr3	Kezman [57]	41 774
30-10-2004	West Bromwich Albion	W 4-1	A	PL	Gallas [45], Gudjohnsen [51], Duff [59], Lampard [81]	27 399
2-11-2004	CSKA Moskva - RUS	W 1-0	A	CLgH	Robben [24]	20 000
6-11-2004	Everton	W 1-0	H	PL	Robben [72]	41 965
10-11-2004	Newcastle United	W 2-0	A	LCr4	Gudjohnsen [100], Robben [112]	38 055
13-11-2004	Fulham	W 4-1	A	PL	Lampard [33], Robben [59], Gallas [73], Tiago [81]	21 877
20-11-2004	Bolton Wanderers	D 2-2	H	PL	Duff [1], Tiago [48]	42 203
24-11-2004	Paris Saint Germain - FRA	D 0-0	H	CLgH		39 626
27-11-2004	Charlton Athletic	W 4-0	A	PL	Duff [4], Terry 2 [47 50], Gudjohnsen [59]	26 355
30-11-2004	Fulham	W 2-1	A	LCqf	Duff [55], Lampard [88]	14 531
4-12-2004	Newcastle United	W 4-0	H	PL	Lampard [63], Drogba [69], Robben [89], Kezman [90p]	42 328
7-12-2004	FC Porto - POR	L 1-2	A	CLgH	Duff [33]	42 409
12-12-2004	Arsenal	D 2-2	A	PL	Terry [17], Gudjohnsen [46]	38 153
18-12-2004	Norwich City	W 4-0	H	PL	Duff [10], Lampard [34], Robben [44], Drogba [83]	42 071
26-12-2004	Aston Villa	W 1-0	H	PL	Duff [30]	41 950
28-12-2004	Portsmouth	W 2-0	A	PL	Robben [79], Cole [90]	20 210
1-01-2005	Liverpool	W 1-0	A	PL	Cole [80]	43 886
4-01-2005	Middlesbrough	W 2-0	H	PL	Drogba 2 [15 17]	40 982
8-01-2005	Scunthorpe United	W 3-1	H	FACr3	Kezman [26], Crosby OG [58], Gudjohnsen [86]	40 019
12-01-2005	Manchester United	D 0-0	HH	LCsf		41 492
15-01-2005	Tottenham Hotspur	W 2-0	A	PL	Lampard 2 [39p 90]	36 105
22-01-2005	Portsmouth	W 3-0	H	PL	Drogba 2 [15 39], Robben [21]	42 267
26-01-2005	Manchester United	W 2-1	A	LCsf	Lampard [29], Duff [85]	67 000
30-01-2005	Birmingham City	W 2-0	H	FACr4	Huth [6], Terry [80]	40 379
2-02-2005	Blackburn Rovers	W 1-0	A	PL	Robben [5]	23 414
6-02-2005	Manchester City	D 0-0	H	PL		42 093
12-02-2005	Everton	W 1-0	A	PL	Gudjohnsen [69]	40 270
20-02-2005	Newcastle United	L 0-1	A	FACr5		45 740
23-02-2005	Barcelona - ESP	L 1-2	A	CLr2	Belletti OG [33]	89 000
27-02-2005	Liverpool	W 3-2	N	LCf	Gerrard OG [79], Drogba [107], Kezman [112]	78 000
5-03-2005	Norwich City	W 3-1	A	PL	Cole [22], Kezman [71], Carvalho [79]	24 506
8-03-2005	Barcelona - ESP	W 4-2	H	CLr2	Gudjohnsen [8], Lampard [17], Duff [19], Terry [76]	41 515
15-03-2005	West Bromwich Albion	W 1-0	H	PL	Drogba [26]	41 713
19-03-2005	Crystal Palace	W 4-1	H	PL	Lampard [29], Cole [54], Kezman 2 [78 90]	41 667
2-04-2005	Southampton	W 3-1	A	PL	Lampard [22], Gudjohnsen 2 [39 83]	31 919
6-04-2005	Bayern München - GER	W 4-2	H	CLqf	Cole [4], Lampard 2 [60 70], Drogba [81]	40 253
9-04-2005	Birmingham City	D 1-1	H	PL	Drogba [82]	42 043
12-04-2005	Bayern München - GER	L 2-3	A	CLqf	Lampard [30], Drogba [80]	59 000
20-04-2005	Arsenal	D 0-0	H	PL		41 621
23-04-2005	Fulham	W 3-1	H	PL	Cole [17], Lampard [64], Gudjohnsen [87]	42 081
27-04-2005	Liverpool - ENG	D 0-0	H	CLsf		40 497
30-04-2005	Bolton Wanderers	W 2-0	A	PL	Lampard 2 [60 76]	27 653
3-05-2005	Liverpool - ENG	L 0-1	A	CLsf		42 529
7-05-2005	Charlton Athletic	W 1-0	H	PL	Makelele [90]	42 065
10-05-2005	Manchester United	W 3-1	A	PL	Tiago [17], Gudjohnsen [61], Cole [82]	67 832
15-05-2005	Newcastle United	W 1-0	A	PL	Lampard [35p]	52 326

PL = FA Premier League (Barclays Premiership) • CL = UEFA Champions League • FAC = FA Cup • LC = Carling League Cup
gH = Group H • r3 = 3rd round • r4 = 4th round • r5 = 5th round • qf = quarter-final • sf = semi-final • f = final • N = Millennium Stadium

ARSENAL 2004-05

Date	Opponents	Score			Scorers	Att
8-08-2004	Manchester United	W 3-1	N	CS	Gilberto 49, Reyes 59, Silvestre OG 79	63 317
15-08-2004	Everton	W 4-1	A	PL	Bergkamp 23, Reyes 39, Ljungberg 54, Pires 83	35 521
22-08-2004	Middlesbrough	W 5-3	H	PL	Henry 2 25 90, Bergkamp 54, Pires 65, Reyes 65	37415
25-08-2004	Blackburn Rovers	W 3-0	H	PL	Henry 50, Fabregas 58, Reyes 79	37 946
28-08-2004	Norwich City	W 4-1	A	PL	Reyes 22, Henry 36, Pires 40, Bergkamp 90	23 944
11-09-2004	Fulham	W 3-0	A	PL	Ljungberg 62, Knight OG 65, Reyes 71	21 681
14-09-2004	PSV Eindhoven - NED	W 1-0	H	CLgE	Alex OG 42	34 068
18-09-2004	Bolton Wanderers	D 2-2	H	PL	Henry 31, Pires 66	37 010
25-09-2004	Manchester City	W 1-0	A	PL	Cole 14	47 015
29-09-2004	Rosenborg BK - NOR	D 1-1	A	CLgE	Ljungberg 6	21 195
2-10-2004	Charlton Athletic	W 4-0	H	PL	Ljungberg 33, Henry 2 48 69, Reyes 70	38 103
16-10-2004	Aston Villa	W 3-1	H	PL	Pires 2 19 72, Henry 45	38 137
20-10-2004	Panathinaikos - GRE	D 2-2	A	CLgE	Ljungberg 17, Henry 74	12 346
24-10-2004	Manchester United	L 0-2	A	PL		67 862
27-10-2004	Manchester City	W 2-1	H	LCr3	Van Persie 78, Karbassiyon 90	21 708
30-10-2004	Southampton	D 2-2	H	PL	Henry 67, Van Persie 90	38 141
2-11-2004	Panathinaikos - GRE	D 1-1	H	CLgE	Henry 16p	35 137
6-11-2004	Crystal Palace	D 1-1	A	PL	Henry 63	26 193
9-11-2004	Everton	W 3-1	H	LCr4	Owusu-Abeyie 25, Lupoli 2 52 85	27 791
13-11-2004	Tottenham Hotspur	W 5-4	A	PL	Henry 45, Lauren 55p, Vieira 60, Ljungberg 69, Pires 81	36 095
20-11-2004	West Bromwich Albion	D 1-1	H	PL	Pires 54	38 109
24-11-2004	PSV Eindhoven - NED	D 1-1	A	CLgE	Henry 31	26 100
28-11-2004	Liverpool	L 1-2	A	PL	Vieira 57	47 730
1-12-2004	Manchester United	L 0-1	A	LCqf		67 103
4-12-2004	Birmingham City	W 3-0	H	PL	Pires 33, Henry 2 80 86	38 064
7-12-2004	Rosenborg BK - NOR	W 5-1	H	CLgE	Reyes 3, Henry 24, Fabregas 29, Pires 41p, Van Persie 84	35 421
12-12-2004	Chelsea	D 2-2	H	PL	Henry 2 2 29	38 153
19-12-2004	Portsmouth	W 1-0	A	PL	Campbell 75	20 170
26-12-2004	Fulham	W 2-0	H	PL	Henry 12, Pires 71	38 047
29-12-2004	Newcastle United	W 1-0	A	PL	Vieira 45	52 320
1-01-2005	Charlton Athletic	W 3-1	H	PL	Ljungberg 2 35 48, Van Persie 67	26 711
4-01-2005	Manchester City	D 1-1	H	PL	Ljungberg 75	38 086
9-01-2005	Stoke City	W 2-1	H	FACr3	Reyes 50, Van Persie 70	36 579
15-01-2005	Bolton Wanderers	L 0-1	A	PL		27 514
23-01-2005	Newcastle United	W 1-0	H	PL	Bergkamp 19	38 137
29-01-2005	Wolverhampton Wanderers	W 2-0	H	FACr4	Vieira 53, Ljungberg 82	37 153
1-02-2005	Manchester United	L 2-4	H	PL	Vieira 8, Bergkamp 36	38 164
5-02-2005	Aston Villa	W 3-1	A	PL	Ljungberg 10, Henry 14, Cole 28	42 593
14-02-2005	Crystal Palace	W 5-1	H	PL	Bergkamp 32, Reyes 35, Henry 2 39 77, Vieira 54	38 065
19-02-2005	Sheffield United	D 1-1	H	FACr5	Pires 78	36 891
22-02-2005	Bayern München - GER	L 1-3	A	CLr2	Toure 88	59 000
26-02-2005	Southampton	D 1-1	A	PL	Ljungberg 45	31 815
1-03-2005	Sheffield United	D 0-0	A	FACr5	W 4-2p	27 595
5-03-2005	Portsmouth	W 3-0	H	PL	Henry 3 39 53 85	38 079
9-03-2005	Bayern München - GER	W 1-0	H	CLr2	Henry 66	35 463
12-03-2005	Bolton Wanderers	W 1-0	A	FACqf	Ljungberg 3	23 523
19-03-2005	Blackburn Rovers	W 1-0	H	PL	Van Persie 43	22 992
2-04-2005	Norwich City	W 4-1	H	PL	Henry 3 19 22 66, Ljungberg 50	38 066
9-04-2005	Middlesbrough	W 1-0	A	PL	Pires 73	33 874
16-04-2005	Blackburn Rovers	W 3-0	N	FACsf	Pires 42, Van Persie 2 86 90	52 077
20-04-2005	Chelsea	D 0-0	A	PL		41 621
25-04-2005	Tottenham Hotspur	W 1-0	H	PL	Reyes 22	38 147
2-05-2005	West Bromwich Albion	W 2-0	A	PL	Van Persie 66, Edu 90	27 351
8-05-2005	Liverpool	W 3-1	H	PL	Pires 25, Reyes 29, Fabregas 90	38 119
11-05-2005	Everton	W 7-0	H	PL	Van Persie 8, Pires 2 12 50, Vieira 37, Edu 70p, Bergkamp 77, Flamini 85	38 073
15-05-2005	Birmingham City	L 1-2	A	PL	Bergkamp 88	29 302
21-05-2005	Manchester United	D 0-0	N	FACf	W 5-4p	71 876

CS = Community Shield • PL = FA Premier League (Barclays Premiership) • CL = UEFA Champions League • FAC = FA Cup • LC = Carling League Cup
gE = Group E • r3 = 3rd round • r4 = 4th round • r5 = 5th round • qf = quarter-final • sf = semi-final • f = final • N = Millennium Stadium

MANCHESTER UNITED 2004-05

Date	Opponents		Score			Scorers	Att
8-08-2004	Arsenal	L	1-3	N	CS	Smith 55	63 317
11-08-2004	Dinamo Bucuresti - ROM	W	2-1	A	CLpr3	Giggs 37 Alistar OG 70	58 000
15-08-2004	Chelsea	L	0-1	A	PL		41 813
21-08-2004	Norwich City	W	2-1	H	PL	Bellion 32, Smith 50	67 812
25-08-2004	Dinamo Bucuresti - ROM	W	3-0	H	CLpr3	Smith 2 47 49, Bellion 70	61 041
28-08-2004	Blackburn Rovers	D	1-1	A	PL	Smith 90	26 155
30-08-2004	Everton	D	0-0	H	PL		67 803
11-09-2004	Bolton Wanderers	D	2-2	A	PL	Heinze 44, Bellion 90	27 766
15-09-2004	Olympique Lyonnais - FRA	D	2-2	A	CLgD	Van Nistelrooy 2 56 61	36 000
20-09-2004	Liverpool	W	2-1	H	PL	Silvestre 2 20 66	67 857
25-09-2004	Tottenham Hotspur	W	1-0	A	PL	Van Nistelrooy 42p	36 103
28-09-2004	Fenerbahçe - TUR	W	6-2	H	CLgD	Giggs 7, Rooney 3 17 28 54, Van Nistelrooy 74, Bellion 81	67 128
3-10-2004	Middlesbrough	D	1-1	H	PL	Smith 81	67 988
16-10-2004	Birmingham City	D	0-0	A	PL		29 221
19-10-2004	Sparta Praha - CZE	D	0-0	A	CLgD		20 654
24-10-2004	Arsenal	W	2-0	H	PL	Van Nistelrooy 73p	67 862
26-10-2004	Crewe Alexandra	W	3-0	A	LCr3	Smith 10, Miller 57, Foster OG 59	10 103
30-10-2004	Portsmouth	L	0-2	A	PL		20 190
3-11-2004	Sparta Praha - CZE	W	4-1	H	CLgD	Van Nistelrooy 4 14 25p 60 90	66 706
7-11-2004	Manchester City	D	0-0	H	PL		67 863
10-11-2004	Crystal Palace	W	2-0	H	LCr4	Saha 22, Richardson 39	48 891
14-11-2004	Newcastle United	W	3-1	A	PL	Rooney 2 7 90, Van Nistelrooy 74p	52 320
20-11-2004	Charlton Athletic	W	2-0	H	PL	Giggs 41, Scholes 50	67 704
23-11-2004	Olympique Lyonnais - FRA	W	2-1	A	CLgD	Neville.G 19, Van Nistelrooy 53	66 398
27-11-2004	West Bromwich Albion	W	3-0	A	PL	Scholes 2 53 82, Van Nistelrooy 72	27 709
1-12-2004	Arsenal	W	1-0	H	LCqf	Bellion 1	67 103
4-12-2004	Southampton	W	3-0	H	PL	Scholes 53, Rooney 58, Ronaldo 87	67 921
8-12-2004	Fenerbahçe - TUR	L	0-3	A	CLgD		35 000
13-12-2004	Fulham	D	1-1	A	PL	Smith 33	21 940
18-12-2004	Crystal Palace	W	5-2	H	PL	Scholes 2 22 49, Smith 35, Boyce OG 48, O'Shea 90	67 814
26-12-2004	Bolton Wanderers	W	2-0	H	PL	Giggs 10, Scholes 89	67 867
28-12-2004	Aston Villa	W	1-0	A	PL	Giggs 41	42 593
1-01-2005	Middlesbrough	W	2-0	A	PL	Fletcher 9, Giggs 79	34 199
4-01-2005	Tottenham Hotspur	D	0-0	H	PL		67 962
8-01-2005	Exeter City	D	0-0	H	FACr3		67 551
12-01-2005	Chelsea	D	0-0	A	LCsf		41 492
15-01-2005	Liverpool	W	1-0	H	PL	Rooney 21	44 183
19-01-2005	Exeter City	W	2-0	A	FACr3	Ronaldo 9, Rooney 87	9 033
22-01-2005	Aston Villa	W	3-1	H	PL	Ronaldo 8, Saha 69, Scholes 70	67 859
26-01-2005	Chelsea	L	1-2	H	LCsf	Giggs 67	67 000
29-01-2005	Middlesbrough	W	3-0	H	FACr4	O'Shea 10, Rooney 2 67 82	67 251
1-02-2005	Arsenal	W	4-2	H	PL	Giggs 18, Ronaldo 2 54 58, O'Shea 89	38 164
5-02-2005	Birmingham City	W	2-0	H	PL	Keane 55, Rooney 78	67 838
13-02-2005	Manchester City	W	2-0	A	PL	Rooney 68, Dunne OG 75	47 111
19-02-2005	Everton	W	2-0	H	FACr5	Fortune 23, Ronaldo 58	38 664
23-02-2005	Milan - ITA	L	0-1	H	CLr2		67 162
26-02-2005	Portsmouth	W	2-1	H	PL	Rooney 2 8 81	67 989
5-03-2005	Crystal Palace	D	0-0	A	PL		26 021
8-03-2005	Milan - ITA	L	0-1	H	CLr2		78 957
12-03-2005	Southampton	W	4-0	A	FACqf	Keane 2, Ronaldo 45, Scholes 2 48 87	30 971
19-03-2005	Fulham	W	1-0	H	PL	Ronaldo 21	67 959
2-04-2005	Blackburn Rovers	D	0-0	H	PL		67 939
9-04-2005	Norwich City	L	0-2	A	PL		25 522
17-04-2005	Newcastle United	W	4-1	N	FACsf	Van Nistelrooy 2 19 58, Scholes 45, Ronaldo 76	69 280
20-04-2005	Everton	L	0-1	A	PL		37 160
24-04-2005	Newcastle United	W	2-1	H	PL	Rooney 57, Brown 75	67 845
1-05-2005	Charlton Athletic	W	4-0	A	PL	Scholes 34, Fletcher 44, Smith 62, Rooney 67	26 789
7-05-2005	West Bromwich Albion	D	1-1	H	PL	Giggs 21	67 827
10-05-2005	Chelsea	L	1-3	H	PL	Van Nistelrooy 7	67 832
15-05-2005	Southampton	W	2-1	A	PL	Fletcher 19, Van Nistelrooy 63	32 066
21-05-2005	Arsenal	D	0-0	N	FACf	L 4-5p	71 876

CS = Community Shield • PL = FA Premier League (Barclays Premiership) • CL = UEFA Champions League • FAC = FA Cup • LC = Carling League Cup
gD = Group D • r3 = 3rd round • r4 = 4th round • r5 = 5th round • qf = quarter-final • sf = semi-final • f = final • N = Millennium Stadium

LIVERPOOL 2004-05

Date	Opponents	Score			Scorers	Att
10-08-2004	Grazer AK - AUT	W 2-0	A	CLpr3	Gerrard 2 [23] [79]	15 400
14-08-2004	Tottenham Hotspur	D 1-1	A	PL	Cisse [38]	35 105
21-08-2004	Manchester City	W 2-1	H	PL	Baros [48], Gerrard [75]	42 831
24-08-2004	Grazer AK - AUT	L 0-1	H	CLpr3		42 950
29-08-2004	Bolton Wanderers	L 0-1	A	PL		27 880
11-09-2004	West Bromwich Albion	W 3-0	H	PL	Gerrard [16], Finnan [42], Luis Garcia [60]	42 947
15-09-2004	AS Monaco - FRA	W 2-0	H	CLgA	Cisse [22], Baros [84]	33 517
20-09-2004	Manchester United	L 1-2	A	PL	O'Shea OG [54]	67 857
25-09-2004	Norwich City	W 3-0	H	PL	Baros [23], Luis Garcia [26], Cisse [64]	43 152
28-09-2004	Olympiacos - GRE	L 0-1	A	CLgA		33 000
3-10-2004	Chelsea	L 0-1	A	PL		42 028
16-10-2004	Fulham	W 4-2	A	PL	Knight OG [50], Baros [71], Alonso [79], Biscan [90]	21 884
19-10-2004	Deportivo La Coruña - ESP	D 0-0	H	CLgA		40 236
23-10-2004	Charlton Athletic	W 2-0	H	PL	Riise [52], Luis Garcia [74]	41 625
26-10-2004	Millwall	W 3-0	A	LCr3	Diao [18], Baros 2 [70] [90]	17 655
30-10-2004	Blackburn Rovers	D 2-2	A	PL	Riise [7], Baros [54]	26 314
3-11-2004	Deportivo La Coruña - ESP	W 1-0	A	CLgA	Andrade OG [14]	32 000
6-11-2004	Birmingham City	L 0-1	H	PL		42 669
10-11-2004	Middlesbrough	W 2-0	H	LCr4	Mellor 2 [83] [89]	28 176
13-11-2004	Crystal Palace	W 3-2	H	PL	Baros 3 [23p] [45] [90p]	42 862
20-11-2004	Middlesbrough	L 0-2	A	PL		34 751
23-11-2004	AS Monaco - FRA	L 0-1	A	CLgA		15 000
28-11-2004	Arsenal	W 2-1	H	PL	Alonso [41], Mellor [90]	43 730
1-12-2004	Tottenham Hotspur	D 1-1	A	LCqf	Pongolle [117]. W 4-3p	36 100
4-12-2004	Aston Villa	D 1-1	A	PL	Kewell [16]	42 593
8-12-2004	Olympiacos - GRE	W 3-1	H	CLgA	Pongolle [47], Mellor [80], Gerrard [86]	42 045
11-12-2004	Everton	L 0-1	H	PL		40 552
14-12-2004	Portsmouth	D 1-1	H	PL	Gerrard [70]	35 064
19-12-2004	Newcastle United	W 3-1	H	PL	Bramble OG [35], Mellor [38], Baros [61]	43 856
26-12-2004	West Bromwich Albion	W 5-0	A	PL	Riise 2 [17] [82], Pongolle [51], Gerrard [55], Luis Garcia [89]	27 533
28-12-2004	Southampton	W 1-0	H	PL	Pongolle [44]	42 382
1-01-2005	Chelsea	L 0-1	H	PL		43 886
3-01-2005	Norwich City	W 2-1	A	PL	Luis Garcia [58], Riise [64]	24 503
11-01-2005	Watford	W 1-0	H	LCsf	Gerrard [56]	35 739
15-01-2005	Manchester United	L 0-1	H	PL		44 183
18-01-2005	Burnley	L 0-1	A	FACr3		19 033
22-01-2005	Southampton	L 0-2	A	PL		32 017
25-01-2005	Watford	W 1-0	A	LCsf	Gerrard [77]	19 797
1-02-2005	Charlton Athletic	W 2-1	A	PL	Morientes [61], Riise [79]	27 102
5-02-2005	Fulham	W 3-1	H	PL	Morientes [9], Hyypia [63], Baros [77]	43 534
12-02-2005	Birmingham City	L 0-2	A	PL		29 318
22-02-2005	Bayer Leverkusen - GER	W 3-1	H	CLr2	Garcia [15], Riise [35], Hamann [90]	40 952
27-02-2005	Chelsea	L 2-3	N	LCf	Riise [1], Nunez [113]	71 622
5-03-2005	Newcastle United	L 0-1	H	PL		52 323
9-03-2005	Bayer Leverkusen - GER	W 3-1	A	CLr2	Garcia 2 [26] [32], Baros [66]	22 500
16-03-2005	Blackburn Rovers	D 0-0	H	PL		37 765
20-03-2005	Everton	W 2-1	H	PL	Gerrard [27], Garcia [32]	44 224
2-04-2005	Bolton Wanderers	W 1-0	H	PL	Biscan [85]	43 755
5-04-2005	Juventus - ITA	W 2-1	H	CLqf	Hyypia [10], Garcia [25]	41 216
9-04-2005	Manchester City	L 0-1	A	PL		47 203
13-04-2005	Juventus - ITA	D 0-0	A	CLqf		55 464
16-04-2005	Tottenham Hotspur	D 2-2	H	PL	Garcia [44], Hyypia [63]	44 029
20-04-2005	Portsmouth	W 2-1	A	PL	Morientes [4], Garcia [44]	20 205
23-04-2005	Crystal Palace	L 0-1	A	PL		26 043
27-04-2005	Chelsea	D 0-0	A	CLsf		40 497
30-04-2005	Middlesbrough	D 1-1	H	PL	Gerrard [52]	43 250
3-05-2005	Chelsea	W 1-0	H	CLsf	Garcia [4]	42 529
8-05-2005	Arsenal	L 1-3	A	PL	Gerrard [51]	38 119
15-05-2005	Aston Villa	W 2-1	H	PL	Cisse 2 [20] [27]	43 406
25-05-2005	Milan - ITA	D 3-3	N	CLf	Gerrard [54], Smicer [56], Alonso [59]. W 3-2p	75 000

PL = FA Premier League (Barclays Premiership) • CL = UEFA Champions League • FAC = FA Cup • LC = Carling League Cup
pr3 = third preliminary round • gA = Group A • r3 = 3rd round • r4 = 4th round • r5 = 5th round • qf = quarter-final • sf = semi-final • f = final
N = Millennium Stadium • *N* = Atatürk Olympiyat Stadi - Istanbul

EQG – EQUATORIAL GUINEA

NATIONAL TEAM RECORD
JULY 1ST 2002 TO JUNE 30TH 2005

PL	W	D	L	F	A	%
10	3	1	6	7	19	35

FIFA/COCA-COLA WORLD RANKING

1993	1994	1995	1996	1997	1998	1999	2000	2001	2002	2003	2004	High		Low	
-	-	-	-	-	195	188	187	190	192	160	171	**160**	12/03	**195**	12/98

2004-2005											
08/04	09/04	10/04	11/04	12/04	01/05	02/05	03/05	04/05	05/05	06/05	07/05
166	167	168	169	171	171	170	170	170	170	170	171

The emergence of an oil industry has brought wealth to Equatorial Guinea, but this has not spilled over to the sports budget in a country lying 170 in the FIFA/Coca-Cola World Ranking and 43rd in Africa. A FIFA member since 1986, progress has been slow and although the national side registered a creditable 1-0 home victory against Togo in the 2006 FIFA World Cup™ preliminary qualifying round, they fell 2-0 in the return leg thereby ending their 2006 Nations Cup hopes as well because the result counted for both. Since that defeat, Equatorial Guinea have played just two matches, both in the CEMAC Cup in Gabon where, having been drawn in the same group as

INTERNATIONAL HONOURS
None

eventual winners and runners-up Cameroon Amateurs and Chad respectively, it was no great surprise they progressed no further. In a country split between Atlantic Ocean islands and territory on the African mainland, a coherent league structure is difficult to maintain, but in 2004 Renacimiento FC clinched their first league title by four points from CD Ela Nguema. The latter were rewarded with the National Cup title though, albeit in unusual circumstances, when the flood-lights at the final with Akonangui failed after Nguema had scored. With less than 20 minutes left to play the match was abandoned and Nguema were awarded the Cup for the seventh time.

THE FIFA BIG COUNT OF 2000

	Male	Female		Male	Female
Registered players	1 000	200	Referees	70	4
Non registered players	3 000	150	Officials	40	0
Youth players	1 000	0	Total involved	5 464	
Total players	5 350		Number of clubs	30	
Professional players	0	0	Number of teams	68	

Federación Ecuatoguineana de Fútbol (FEGUIFUT)
Carretera LUBA, Malabo 1071, Equatorial Guinea
Tel +240 9 1874   Fax +240 9 1874
feguifut@wanadoo.gq   www.none
President: MANGA OBIANG Bonifacio   General Secretary: MARTIN PEDRO Ndong
Vice-President: ESONO MELCHOR Edjo   Treasurer: MANUEL Nsi Nguema   Media Officer: BORABOFA Clemente
Men's Coach: DUMAS Antonio   Women's Coach: EKANG Jose Davio
FEGUIFUT formed: 1960   CAF: 1986   FIFA: 1986
Colours: Red, Red, Red

GAMES PLAYED BY EQUATORIAL GUINEA IN THE 2006 FIFA WORLD CUP™ CYCLE

2002	Opponents		Score	Venue	Comp	Scorers	Att	Referee
8-09	Sierra Leone	L	1-3	Malabo	CNq	Mavidi 82		Tavares Neto STP
13-10	Morocco	L	0-5	Rabat	CNq			Boukthir TUN
2003								
29-03	Gabon	L	0-4	Libreville	CNq			Tavares Neto STP
8-06	Gabon	W	2-1	Malabo	CNq	Mba 22, Mangongo 50		Buenkadila COD
22-06	Sierra Leone	L	0-2	Freetown	CNq			
6-07	Morocco	L	0-1	Malabo	CNq			
11-10	Togo	W	1-0	Bata	WCq	Barila 25p	25 000	Evehe CMR
12-11	São Tomé e Príncipe	W	3-1	Malabo	Fr			
16-11	Togo	L	0-2	Lome	WCq		12 000	Mandzioukouta CGO
2004								
No international matches played in 2004								
2005								
8-02	Chad	D	0-0	Libreville	CMr1			

Fr = Friendly match • CN = CAF African Cup of Nations • CM = CEMAC Cup • WC = FIFA World Cup™ • q = qualifier • r1 = first round group

EQUATORIAL GUINEA NATIONAL TEAM RECORDS AND RECORD SEQUENCES

Records			Sequence records					
Victory	4-2	CAR 1999	Wins	2	2003	Clean sheets	1	
Defeat	0-6	CGO 1990	Defeats	9	1999-2003	Goals scored	2	
Player Caps	n/a		Undefeated	2	1984, 2003	Without goal	2	Five times
Player Goals	n/a		Without win	22	1984-1999	Goals against	22	1988-2003

FIFA REFEREE LIST 2005

	Int'l	DoB
ESONO Jose	1996	3-03-1964
MORO Expedito	2005	21-06-1978
NGUEMA Acacio	2005	18-01-1974
ONDO Antonio	1994	18-02-1969

FIFA ASSISTANT REFEREE LIST 2005

	Int'l	DoB
EDJANG Bienvenido	2004	16-02-1975
ESONO Antonio	2004	17-04-1975
MBA Ricardo		14-11-1975
MBA Valero	2004	1-07-1976
MICHA Victoriano		26-02-1969
NGUEMA Roberto	1998	1-12-1961
OBAMA Pablo-Moises	1998	7-08-1969

RECENT LEAGUE AND CUP RECORD

Year	Champions	Cup Winners
1996	Cafe Bank Sportif Malabo	FC Akonangui
1997	Deportivo Mongomo	Union Vesper
1998	CD Ela Nguema	Union Vesper
1999	FC Akonangui	CD Unidad
2000	CD Ela Nguema	CD Unidad
2001	FC Akonangui	Atlético Malabo
2002	CD Ela Nguema	FC Akonangui
2003	Atlético Malabo	Deportivo Mongomo
2004	Renacimiento FC	CD Ela Nguema

EQUATORIAL GUINEA COUNTRY INFORMATION

Capital	Malabo	Independence	1968 from Spain	GDP per Capita	$2 700
Population	523 051	Status	Republic	GNP Ranking	175
Area km²	28 051	Language	Spanish	Dialling code	+240
Population density	18 per km²	Literacy rate	80%	Internet code	.gq
% in urban areas	42%	Main religion	Christian	GMT +/-	+1
Towns/Cities ('000)	Malabo 101; Bata 82; Ebebiyin 13; Mbini 12; Luba 7				
Neighbours (km)	Cameroon 189; Gabon 350; Bight of Biafra 296. Malabo is on the island of Bioko in the Atlantic				
Main stadia	Internacional – Malabo 6 000				

ERI - ERITREA

NATIONAL TEAM RECORD
JULY 1ST 2002 TO JUNE 30TH 2005

PL	W	D	L	F	A	%
13	2	2	9	8	21	23.1

FIFA/COCA-COLA WORLD RANKING

1993	1994	1995	1996	1997	1998	1999	2000	2001	2002	2003	2004	High		Low	
-	-	-	-	-	189	169	158	171	157	155	169	153	11/03	189	12/98

2004-2005											
08/04	09/04	10/04	11/04	12/04	01/05	02/05	03/05	04/05	05/05	06/05	07/05
162	163	164	164	169	169	169	169	169	169	169	169

When it was part of Ethiopia, Eritrea enjoyed a fair amout of success in football with clubs from the area proving competitive and providing a number of international players. However, since independence, one of FIFA's newest African members has made slow progress since affiliation in 1998 slipping to 169th in the FIFA/Coca-Cola World Ranking because of a dearth of international matches since late 2003. Their FIFA World Cup™ debut wasn't the embarrassment many had predicted though; paired with Nigeria for the 2002 preliminary round, Eritrea held the Super Eagles to a creditable goalless draw in Asmara, only to lose 4-0 in the away leg. Hoping to get further in

INTERNATIONAL HONOURS
None

qualifying for the 2006 FIFA World Cup™, the Red Sea Boys were drawn with Sudan, when after a 3-0 defeat in Khartoum they again ground out a 0-0 draw at home. In the CECAFA Cup, Eritrea have frequently narrowly failed to win or draw giving the impression that the country's national team is making headway, but with finance also a major problem it may still be a long journey for coach Rene Feller as he targets a place at the African Cup of Nations. Red Sea FC Asmara, part of the state owned Red Sea Corporation, got back into winning ways again by beating off the challenge of the Ministry of Defence team, Denden, to win the 2005 Championship.

THE FIFA BIG COUNT OF 2000

	Male	Female		Male	Female
Registered players	2 700	150	Referees	214	0
Non registered players	180 000	70 000	Officials	850	10
Youth players	1 267	300	Total involved	255 491	
Total players	254 417		Number of clubs	15	
Professional players	0	0	Number of teams	204	

Eritrean National Football Federation (ENFF)
Sematat Avenue 29-31, PO Box 3665, Asmara, Eritrea
Tel +291 1 120335   Fax +291 1 126821
www.none
President: SIUM Solomon   General Secretary: GHEBREMARIAM Yemane
Vice-President: GEBREYESUS Tesfaye   Treasurer: GEUSH Tikue   Media Officer: LIJAM Amamel
Men's Coach: FELLER Rene   Women's Coach: TEKLIT Negash
ENFF formed: 1996   CAF: 1998   FIFA: 1998
Colours: Blue, Red, Green

GAMES PLAYED BY ERITREA IN THE 2006 FIFA WORLD CUP™ CYCLE

2002 Opponents		Score	Venue	Comp	Scorers	Att	Referee
8-09	Seychelles	L 0-1	Victoria	CNq			
12-10	Zimbabwe	L 0-1	Asmara	CNq			
1-12	Burundi	D 1-1	Arusha	CCr1	Yonnas Tesfaye [87]		
4-12	Sudan	W 2-1	Arusha	CCr1	Elias Dedesaye [14], Aram Negash [45]		
6-12	Kenya	L 1-4	Arusha	CCr1	Berhane Aergaye [78]		
2003							
30-03	Mali	L 0-2	Asmara	CNq			
7-06	Mali	L 0-1	Bamoko	CNq			
21-06	Seychelles	W 1-0	Asmara	CNq	Yonnas Fessehaye [62]		
5-07	Zimbabwe	L 0-2	Harare	CNq			
12-10	Sudan	L 0-3	Khartoum	WCq		18 000	Tamuni LBY
16-11	Sudan	D 0-0	Asmara	WCq		12 000	Abdulle Ahmed SOM
30-11	Uganda	L 1-2	Kassala	CCr1	Ghirmay Shinash [70]		
2-12	Kenya	L 2-3	Kassala	CCr1	Tesfaldet Goitom 2 [30] [48]		
2004							

No international matches played in 2004

2005

No international matches played in 2005 before August

CN = CAF African Cup of Nations • CC = CECAFA Cup • WC = FIFA World Cup™ • q = qualifier • r1 = first round group

ERITREA NATIONAL TEAM RECORDS AND RECORD SEQUENCES

Records			Sequence records					
Victory	2-0	KEN 1994	Wins	2	1994	Clean sheets	3	1994
Defeat	0-5	GHA 1999	Defeats	3	1994-98, 2001-02	Goals scored	4	2002
Player Caps	n/a		Undefeated	3	1994	Without goal	6	1999-2000
Player Goals	n/a		Without win	10	2000-2002	Goals against	9	2001-2003

FIFA REFEREE LIST 2005

	Int'l	DoB
DAGNEW Berhane	2004	1-01-1967
EYOB Amanuel	2004	1-01-1974
GHEBREMICHAEL Luelseghed	2004	1-01-1972
KIDANE Kubrom	1999	10-12-1964
KIFLE Tedros	2005	13-05-1970
TEKESTE Neguse	1999	2-06-1965
TESFU Mussie	2005	21-05-1969

FIFA ASSISTANT REFEREE LIST 2005

	Int'l	DoB
ABRHA Fanus		23-09-1967
KIFLAY Amanuel		1-01-1968
KIROS Redae		24-10-1966
OGBAMARIAM Angesom	1999	13-09-1971
TESFAGIORGHIS Berhe		12-12-1975
YOHANES Dawit	1999	13-09-1963
YOHANNES Ghirmai		1-01-1967

RECENT LEAGUE AND CUP RECORD

Year	Champions	Cup Winners
1998	Red Sea FC Asmara	Hintsa Asmara
1999	Red Sea FC Asmara	
2000	Red Sea FC Asmara	
2001	Hintsa Asmara	
2002	Red Sea FC Asmara	
2003	Anseba Sports Club Keren	
2004	Adulis Club Asmara	
2005	Red Sea FC Asmara	

ERITREA COUNTRY INFORMATION

Capital	Asmara	Independence	1993	GDP per Capita	$700
Population	4 447 307	Status	Transitional	GNP Ranking	162
Area km²	121 320	Language	Tigrinya, Arabic	Dialling code	+291
Population density	36 per km²	Literacy rate	80%	Internet code	.er
% in urban areas	17%	Main religion	Christian, Muslim	GMT +/-	+3
Towns/Cities ('000)	Asmara 563; Assab 78; Keren 58; Mitsiwa 39; Addi Ugri 17; Barentu 15; Addi Keyih 13				
Neighbours (km)	Djibouti 109; Ethiopia 912; Sudan 605; Red Sea 2 234				
Main stadia	ChicChero – Asmara 12 000				

ESP – SPAIN

NATIONAL TEAM RECORD
JULY 1ST 2002 TO JUNE 30TH 2005

PL	W	D	L	F	A	%
34	21	11	2	62	16	77.9

The 2004-05 Spanish season was dominated by a resurgent Barcelona who led the Championship race from start to finish to win their first honour of any description this century. It had been a long wait for the Barca fans who had witnessed the club spiralling into debt and into mid-table obscurity since last winning the title in 1999. Key to the revival was star attraction Ronaldinho but the signing of striker Samuel Eto'o in the summer of 2004 proved to be just as important. Not only were his goals vital in the Championship race but his comments that he had no interest in joining Real Madrid, a club that part owned him, gave a strong indication that the balance of power was shifting away from the capital. Indeed, Real's Galactico policy backfired once again as the club went a second season without a trophy. Real Betis, on the other hand, had an excellent season and after qualifying for the UEFA Champions League won the Copa del Rey for only the second time in their history in a hard fought encounter against Osasuna. For the first time since the creation of the UEFA Champions League in 1992 there were no Spanish clubs in the quarter-finals with Real losing tamely to Juventus in the second round while Barcelona lost to Chelsea at the same stage in

INTERNATIONAL HONOURS
Qualified for the FIFA World Cup™ finals 1934 1950 1962 1966 1978 1982 (hosts) 1986 1990 1994 1998 2002
Olympic Gold 1992   **FIFA Futsal World Championship** 2000 2004
FIFA World Youth Championship 1999   **FIFA Junior Tournament** 1952 1954
UEFA U-21 Championship 1986 1998   **UEFA U-19 Championship** 1995 2002 2004   **UEFA U-17 Championship** 1986 1988 1991 1997 1999 2001
UEFA Champions League Real Madrid 1956 1957 1958 1959 1960 1966 1998 2000 2002 Barcelona 1992

a game that paired perhaps the best two teams in Europe at the time. Had they won there was a genuine feeling that Barcelona could have gone all the way. On the national team front Spain went the season undefeated although the incidents during the Spain v England match in November cast a long shadow over the progress made by the team. During that match England's black players were subjected to a torrent of racist abuse by the fans in Madrid while the build-up had been soured by the derogatory remarks made by coach Luis Aragones to Jose Antonio Reyes about his Arsenal team mate Thierry Henry. It took a goal six minutes into injury-time at home against Bosnia-Herzegovina to maintain that unbeaten record since UEFA EURO 2004 and the Spanish have had to fight hard in a close FIFA World Cup™ qualifying group from which five of the six teams were still in with a chance of qualifying going into the final stages. With talented youngsters like Reyes, Fernando Torres and Joaquin breaking into the team there is a growing belief that should the Spanish qualify for the finals they might, for once, live up to their billing amongst the pre-tournament favourites, although that is a story heard countless times before.

Real Federación Española de Fútbol (RFEF)
Ramon y Cajal s/n, Apartado postale 385, Las Rozas 28230, Madrid, Spain
Tel +34 91 4959800   Fax +34 91 4959801
rfef@rfef.es   www.rfef.es
President: VILLAR LLONA Angel Maria   General Secretary: PEREZ ARIAS Jorge
Vice-President: PADRON MORALES Juan   Treasurer: LARREA Juan   Media Officer: NUNEZ Rogelio
Men's Coach: ARAGONES Luis   Women's Coach: QUEREDA Ignacio
RFEF formed: 1913   UEFA: 1954   FIFA: 1904
Colours: Red, Blue, Blue or Blue, Blue, Blue

GAMES PLAYED BY SPAIN IN THE 2006 FIFA WORLD CUP™ CYCLE

2002	Opponents	Score		Venue	Comp	Scorers	Att	Referee
21-08	Hungary	D	1-1	Budapest	Fr	Tamudo 55	20 000	Fleischer GER
7-09	Greece	W	2-0	Athens	ECq	Raúl 8, Valeron 77	16 500	Merk GER
12-10	Northern Ireland	W	3-0	Albacete	ECq	Baraja 2 19 89, Guti 59	16 000	Michel SVK
16-10	Paraguay	D	0-0	Logrono	Fr		15 000	Benquerenca POR
20-11	Bulgaria	W	1-0	Granada	Fr	Jose Mari 10	20 000	Coue FRA
2003								
12-02	Germany	W	3-1	Palma	Fr	Raúl 2 31 76p, Guti 82	20 000	Riley ENG
29-03	Ukraine	D	2-2	Kyiv	ECq	Raúl 83, Etxeberria 87	82 000	Riley ENG
2-04	Armenia	W	3-0	Leon	ECq	Diego Tristan 52, Helguera 68, Joaquin 90	13 500	Yefet ISR
30-04	Ecuador	W	4-0	Madrid	Fr	De Pedro 15, Morientes 3 21 23 64	35 000	Kvaratskhelia GEO
7-06	Greece	L	0-1	Zaragoza	ECq		32 000	Sars FRA
11-06	Northern Ireland	D	0-0	Belfast	ECq		11 365	Larsen DEN
6-09	Portugal	W	3-0	Lisbon	Fr	Etxeberria 11, Joaquin 64, Diego Tristan 76	21 176	Salomir ROU
10-09	Ukraine	W	2-1	Elche	ECq	Raúl 2 59 71	38 000	Hauge NOR
11-10	Armenia	W	4-0	Yerevan	ECq	Valeron 7, Raúl 76, Reyes 2 87 90	15 000	Meier SUI
15-11	Norway	W	2-1	Valencia	ECpo	Raúl 20, Berg OG 85	53 000	Poll ENG
19-11	Norway	W	3-0	Oslo	ECpo	Raúl 34, Vicente 49, Etxeberria 55	25 106	Collina ITA
2004								
18-02	Peru	W	2-1	Barcelona	Fr	Etxeberria 30, Baraja 32	23 580	Layec FRA
31-03	Denmark	W	2-0	Gijon	Fr	Morientes 22, Raúl 60	18 600	Almeida Costa POR
28-04	Italy	D	1-1	Genoa	Fr	Torres 53	30 300	Poll ENG
5-06	Andorra	W	4-0	Getafe	Fr	Morientes 25, Baraja 45, Cesar 65, Valeron 89	14 000	Trefolini ITA
12-06	Russia	W	1-0	Faro-Loule	ECr1	Valeron 60	28 100	Meier SUI
16-06	Greece	D	1-1	Porto	ECr1	Morientes 28	25 444	Michel SVK
20-06	Portugal	L	0-1	Lisbon	ECr1		52 000	Frisk SWE
18-08	Venezuela	W	3-2	Las Palmas	Fr	Morientes 40, Tamudo 2 56 67	32 500	Rodomonti ITA
3-09	Scotland	D	1-1	Valencia	Fr	Raúl 56p, Abandoned 59' after floodlight failure	11 000	Bre FRA
8-09	Bosnia-Herzegovina	D	1-1	Zenica	WCq	Vicente 65	14 380	De Santis ITA
9-10	Belgium	W	2-0	Santander	WCq	Luque 60, Raúl 65	17 000	Nielsen DEN
13-10	Lithuania	D	0-0	Vilnius	WCq		9 114	Pouat FRA
17-11	England	W	1-0	Madrid	Fr	Del Horno 9	70 000	Kasnaferis GRE
2005								
9-02	San Marino	W	5-0	Almeria	WCq	Joaquin 15, Torres 32, Raúl 42, Guti 61, Del Horno 75	12 580	Clark SCO
26-03	China	W	3-0	Salamanca	Fr	Torres 3p, Xavi 32, Joaquin 53	17 000	Cortes POR
30-03	Serbia & Montenegro	D	0-0	Belgrade	WCq		48 910	Busacca SUI
4-06	Lithuania	W	1-0	Valencia	WCq	Luque 68	25 000	Farina ITA
8-08	Bosnia-Herzegovina	D	1-1	Valencia	WCq	Marchena 96+	38 041	Bennett ENG

Fr = Friendly match • EC = UEFA EURO 2004™ • WC = FIFA World Cup™ • q = qualifier • po = play-off • r1 = first round group

FIFA/COCA-COLA WORLD RANKING

1993	1994	1995	1996	1997	1998	1999	2000	2001	2002	2003	2004	High		Low	
5	2	4	8	11	15	4	7	7	3	3	5	**2**	12/94	**25**	03/98

2004-2005											
08/04	09/04	10/04	11/04	12/04	01/05	02/05	03/05	04/05	05/05	06/05	07/05
3	3	4	4	5	5	5	5	7	8	9	8

THE FIFA BIG COUNT OF 2000

	Male	Female		Male	Female
Registered players	117 438	10 307	Referees	553	7
Non registered players	1 700 000	150 000	Officials	60 000	2 000
Youth players	478 884	1 025	Total involved	2 520 214	
Total players	2 457 654		Number of clubs	33 555	
Professional players	1 362	0	Number of teams	101 906	

NATIONAL CAPS

	Caps
ZUBIZARRETA Andoni	126
HIERRO Fernando	89
RAUL	85
CAMACHO José Antonio	81
GORDILLO Rafael	75
BUTRAGUEÑO Emilio	69
ARCONADA Luis	68
MICHEL	66
LUIS ENRIQUE	62
NADAL Miguel Angel	62

NATIONAL GOALS

	Goals
RAÚL	41
HIERRO Fernando	29
BUTRAGUEÑO Emilio	26
MORIENTES Fernando	24
DI STÉFANO Alfredo	23
SALINAS Julio	22
MICHEL	21
ZARRA	20
LÁNGARA Isidrio	17
PIRRI & REGUEIRO Luis	16

NATIONAL COACH

	Years
Committee	1969
KUBALA Ladislao	1969-'80
SANTAMARIA José	1980-'82
MUÑOZ Miguel	1982-'88
SUAREZ Luis	1988-'91
MIERA Vicente	1991-'92
CLEMENTE Javier	1992-'98
CAMACHO José Antonio	1998-'02
SÁEZ Iñaki	2002-'04
ARAGONES Luis	2004-

SPAIN NATIONAL TEAM RECORDS AND RECORD SEQUENCES

Records			Sequence records				
Victory	13-0	BUL 1933	Wins	9	1924-1927	Clean sheets	7	1992
Defeat	1-7	ITA 1928, ENG 1931	Defeats	3	Five times	Goals scored	20	1947-1951
Player Caps	126	ZUBIZARRETA Andoni	Undefeated	30	1994-1997	Without goal	3	1985, 1992
Player Goals	41	Raúl	Without win	10	1980	Goals against	11	1952 1955

FIFA REFEREE LIST 2005

	Int'l	DoB
CARMONA MENDEZ Fernando	2000	23-01-1961
DAUDEN IBANEZ Arturo	1997	9-07-1964
GONZALEZ VAZQUEZ Bernardino	2005	29-03-1966
ITURRALDE GONZALEZ Eduardo	1998	20-02-1967
MEDINA CANTALEJPO Luis		1-03-1964
MEGIA DAVILA Carlos		7-07-1966
MEJUTO GONZALEZ Manuel	1999	16-04-1965
PEREZ BURRULL Alfonso		15-09-1965
RODRIGUEZ SANTIAGO Julian	2001	8-02-1965
UNDIANO MALLENCO Alberto		8-10-1973

FIFA ASSISTANT REFEREE LIST 2005

	Int'l	DoB
ARTERO GALLARDO Antonio	2005	21-09-1966
AYETE PLOU Clemente	2001	31-10-1965
CALVO GUADAMURO Jesus		6-09-1968
GIRALDEZ CARRASCO Victoriano	1995	18-09-1964
GUERRERO Rafael	1998	20-04-1963
LOPEZ VILLATE Carlos	2005	17-11-1965
MARTINEZ Fermin		4-07-1966
MARTINEZ SAMANIEGO Oscar	1999	27-12-1965
MEDINA HERNANDEZ Pedro		17-12-1962
YUSTE JIMENEZ Juan Carlos		25-11-1975

SPAIN COUNTRY INFORMATION

Capital	Madrid	Independence	1492	GDP per Capita	$22 000
Population	40 280 780	Status	Kingdom	GNP Ranking	9
Area km²	504 782	Language	Spanish	Dialling code	+34
Population density	79 per km²	Literacy rate	97%	Internet code	.es
% in urban areas	76%	Main religion	Christian	GMT +/–	+1
Towns/Cities ('000)	Madrid 3 102; Barcelona 1 570; Valencia 769; Sevilla 686; Zaragoza 635; Málaga 557; Murcia 410; Palma 378; Las Palmas 365; Bilbao 349; Alicante 327, Valladolid 315; Córdoba 311; Vigo 286, Gijón 262; Granada 248; La Coruña 236; Elche 227; Vitoria 224; Oviedo 198				
Neighbours (km)	France 623; Andorra 63; Gibraltar 1; Portugal 1 214; Morocco 15; Mediterranean Sea & North Atlantic Ocean 4 964				
Main stadia	Camp Nou – Barcelona 98 934; Bernabeu – Madrid 80 354; La Cartuja – Sevilla 72 000; Mestalla – Valencia 53 000; San Mamés – Bilbao 39 750; Romareda – Zaragoza 34 700				

SPAIN 2004-05

PRIMERA DIVISION

Team	Pl	W	D	L	F	A	Pts	Barcelona	Real Madrid	Villarreal	Betis	Espanyol	Sevilla	Valencia	Deportivo	Athletic	Malaga	Atlético M	Zaragoza	Getafe	Sociedad	Osasuna	Racing	Mallorca	Levante	Numancia	Albacete
Barcelona †	38	25	9	4	73	29	84		3-0	3-3	3-3	0-0	2-0	1-1	2-1	2-0	4-0	0-2	4-1	2-0	1-0	3-0	3-0	2-0	2-1	1-0	2-0
Real Madrid †	38	25	5	8	71	32	80	4-2		2-1	3-1	4-0	0-1	1-0	0-1	0-2	1-0	0-0	3-1	2-0	2-1	1-0	5-0	3-1	5-0	1-0	6-1
Villarreal †	38	18	11	9	69	37	65	3-0	0-0		0-0	4-1	0-0	3-1	0-2	3-1	3-0	3-2	2-0	4-0	0-0	3-0	2-1	2-1	4-1	4-0	1-0
Real Betis †	38	16	14	8	62	50	62	2-1	1-1	2-1		1-4	1-0	1-1	2-0	2-1	1-1	1-0	3-2	2-2	2-3	3-1	2-1	2-0	2-2	4-0	2-1
RCD Espanyol ‡	38	17	10	11	54	46	61	0-1	1-0	0-0	2-2		1-3	2-1	2-1	1-2	0-1	0-2	3-1	2-0	2-2	4-1	2-1	2-1	2-1	3-0	2-1
Sevilla ‡	38	17	9	12	44	41	60	0-4	2-2	2-1	2-1	1-0		2-2	2-0	2-0	0-2	2-1	0-1	0-0	2-1	0-1	2-2	1-1	3-0	1-0	1-0
Valencia	38	14	16	8	54	39	58	0-2	1-1	2-1	2-1	3-0	1-2		1-2	2-2	2-2	2-1	0-0	3-1	3-1	1-0	2-0	2-0	2-1	1-0	0-0
RC Deportivo	38	12	15	11	46	50	51	0-1	2-0	1-1	1-1	4-1	2-1	1-5		1-1	1-0	2-0	2-3	2-1	2-2	1-3	1-4	0-3	1-0	1-1	0-0
Athletic Bilbao	38	14	9	15	59	54	51	1-1	2-1	2-1	4-4	1-1	3-2	2-1	1-2		1-0	1-0	2-0	1-2	3-0	4-3	3-0	4-0	3-1	0-2	3-1
Malaga	38	15	6	17	40	48	51	0-4	0-2	0-2	1-2	3-2	1-0	0-2	1-1	1-0		1-0	0-0	1-1	1-5	2-0	2-0	0-0	1-0	4-1	0-2
Atlético Madrid	38	13	11	14	40	34	50	1-1	0-3	1-0	1-2	0-0	3-0	1-0	1-0	1-2	0-0		1-1	2-2	1-0	3-2	1-0	4-0	0-0	0-2	3-1
Real Zaragoza	38	14	8	16	52	57	50	1-4	1-3	1-0	1-0	0-1	3-2	2-2	2-0	1-0	0-0			3-1	2-1	5-1	1-0	0-1	4-3	4-1	4-3
Getafe	38	12	11	15	38	46	47	1-2	2-1	1-2	0-2	1-0	0-0	1-0	1-1	3-1	1-0	1-1	3-0		2-0	0-0	2-0	1-2	1-0	1-0	1-0
Real Sociedad	38	13	8	17	47	56	47	0-0	0-2	0-4	1-0	0-2	1-0	0-3	3-1	0-3	2-1	3-1	2-1	1-1		2-0	0-1	2-1	1-1	2-1	0-2
Osasuna ‡	38	12	10	16	46	65	46	0-1	1-2	3-2	3-2	1-1	4-1	0-0	1-1	1-6	1-0	2-2	2-1	1-0			1-0	1-1	0-1	2-0	3-2
Racing Santander	38	12	8	18	41	58	44	0-2	2-3	1-1	1-1	1-3	0-0	1-0	2-2	0-2	2-1	2-1	1-0	2-1	1-3	1-1		3-0	2-2	2-0	1-0
RCD Mallorca	38	10	9	19	42	63	39	1-3	0-1	1-1	1-1	3-2	0-1	0-0	2-2	4-3	1-2	1-0	0-2	3-1	3-2	1-2	1-2		1-2	3-2	2-1
Levante	38	9	10	19	39	58	37	1-1	0-2	2-4	1-2	0-2	0-3	0-0	0-1	1-0	0-1	1-0	0-0	0-0	2-1	4-0	3-1	2-0		1-1	1-1
Numancia	38	6	11	21	30	61	29	1-1	1-2	1-1	1-0	0-2	1-1	1-1	1-1	1-0	1-0	0-2	2-2	2-1	1-1	2-2	2-3	1-2	1-3		0-0
Albacete	38	6	10	22	33	56	28	1-2	1-2	2-2	0-0	1-0	0-2	0-1	0-1	1-0	1-2	0-2	2-1	1-1	2-2	1-1	0-0	0-0	3-1	1-2	

28/08/2004 – 29/05/2005 • † Qualified for the UEFA Champions League • ‡ Qualified for the UEFA Cup

TOP SCORERS

FORLAN Diego	Villarreal	25
ETO'O Samuel	Barcelona	24
OLIVEIRA Ricardo	Betis	22
RONALDO	Real Madrid	21
BAPTISTA Cesar Julio	Sevilla	18

SPAIN 2004-05

SEGUNDA DIVISION A (2)

Team	Pl	W	D	L	F	A	Pts	Cádiz	Celta	Alavés	Eibar	Recreativo	Valladolid	Gimnastic	Xerez	Tenerife	Elche	Sporting	Murcia	Ejido	Almería	Lleida	Ferrol	Malaga	C. Murcia	Córdoba	Terrassa	Salamanca	Pontevedra
Cádiz	42	21	13	8	68	30	76		2-0	0-1	1-2	0-6	1-2	0-1	0-1	4-1	3-1	0-0	0-1	3-0	2-1	0-2	2-0	4-0	0-0	4-1	3-1	0-0	4-0
Celta Vigo	42	22	10	10	55	38	76	0-2		2-2	1-2	1-2	0-0	2-1	1-1	2-2	1-0	1-0	1-0	1-0	0-1	0-1	0-1	0-1	2-1	2-1	2-0	2-0	
Deportivo Alavés	42	23	7	12	62	47	76	1-3	0-3		0-2	0-2	2-4	1-1	2-0	1-0	1-0	1-0	2-3	2-0	2-1	2-0	2-1	3-1	1-1	1-1	4-1	2-1	3-2
Eibar	42	20	13	9	53	39	73	2-1	2-1	1-2		1-2	2-0	2-0	0-0	0-5	2-1	0-1	0-1	1-1	1-0	3-0	0-1	0-2	1-0	2-1	0-1	1-2	
Recreativo Huelva	42	19	14	9	48	32	71	1-1	1-2	0-0	0-0		2-0	1-0	1-0	0-0	2-1	1-1	1-0	1-1	3-0	0-1	0-3	1-2	3-2	1-2	1-0	0-2	
Real Valladolid	42	18	9	15	56	56	63	0-1	3-3	1-0	1-2	1-0		1-0	1-1	2-1	1-2	2-0	0-2	2-1	0-1	1-1	3-0	2-1	0-1	3-2	2-3	2-0	
Gimnastic Tarragona	42	16	12	14	49	45	60	1-1	0-2	1-0	3-2	4-0	1-0		1-0	1-0	2-0	1-0	2-0	1-4	1-2	2-1	1-1	0-2	0-0	1-1	3-2	2-0	0-0
Xerez	42	14	17	11	39	36	59	0-2	**3-0**	0-1	0-3	0-0	0-1	1-1		1-1	1-1	1-0	0-1	1-0	1-0	2-2	1-0	3-5	1-0	0-1	1-1		
Tenerife	42	13	18	11	42	45	57	2-0	3-1	1-1	2-0	1-1	2-0	0-0	1-1		1-0	1-0	1-1	3-1	1-1	1-1	0-0	2-1	1-1	0-2	2-1	1-4	0-0
Elche	42	16	9	17	51	52	57	1-1	0-1	1-2	1-0	0-1	3-2	3-3	1-2	0-0		4-0	1-0	3-1	0-0	2-1	2-1	2-1	3-1	1-2	1-0	0-2	2-0
Sporting Gijón	42	15	12	15	41	39	57	1-0	1-0	1-2	0-0	0-1	1-1	0-3	0-0	1-1	3-1		2-0	1-0	1-0	1-3	2-2	0-2	3-1	2-0	1-3	2-3	
Real Murcia	42	15	9	18	40	52	54	0-2	1-1	5-1	0-1	3-0	1-1	0-1	1-0	1-3	3-3	0-1		3-3	0-1	0-0	1-1	0-0	1-0	0-1	0-2		
Polideportivo Ejido	42	12	16	14	41	45	52	0-0	0-3	0-1	4-1	1-4	0-0	3-1	0-0	0-2	2-1	0-1	1-1		2-0	2-0	0-0	1-2	2-2	2-0	0-0	1-1	1-0
Almería	42	13	12	17	36	44	51	0-1	0-1	0-1	2-1	1-1	0-0	0-1	1-1	2-0	1-2	2-1	0-1	0-1		1-1	1-6	0-1	0-0	2-2	0-1	1-0	
Lleida	42	13	11	18	46	54	50	1-3	0-2	0-1	1-1	2-3	2-0	2-0	1-1	1-1	1-1	2-0	2-5	1-0	1-1		1-2	2-1	0-0	1-2	4-2	2-1	3-0
Racing Club Ferrol	42	12	13	17	55	54	49	1-1	1-2	2-1	1-0	2-1	3-1	4-1	2-2	2-0	0-0	3-1	2-0	1-3				1-0	4-0	0-0	3-2	0-3	
Malaga B	42	12	12	18	33	51	48	1-0	1-1	1-0	0-0	0-1	0-2	0-1	0-3	2-1	1-0	0-0	2-1	0-1	1-1				3-1	3-2	0-0	1-3	1-1
Ciudad Murcia	42	10	17	15	49	57	47	0-0	2-2	0-1	1-2	2-2	2-1	1-0	2-0	0-0	0-0	2-1	3-1	3-0	1-2	3-0				1-0	2-0	2-1	2-3
Córdoba	42	12	10	20	43	52	46	0-2	0-1	1-2	0-0	3-4	2-0	1-2	2-0	0-0	2-0	1-2	1-3	3-0	1-1	5-2					2-1	0-0	
Terrassa	42	12	8	22	45	63	44	3-2	1-4	0-2	2-3	1-2	2-1	0-1	0-0	0-1	0-0	1-1	0-0	2-2	1-3	0-3						3-0	1-0
Salamanca	42	12	8	22	50	63	44	1-3	0-1	3-3	1-2	1-0	1-2	0-1	1-1	4-5	2-0	2-1	3-1	1-1	3-2	2-0	3-3						2-0
Pontevedra	42	10	14	18	52	60	44	1-1	3-1	1-3	2-3	0-0	3-0	3-1	2-1	1-1	2-2	1-2	0-1	0-1	0-2	5-0	1-1	1-1	2-2	1-1	3-3	4-1	

28/08/2004 – 18/06/2005 • Match in bold awarded 3-0

SPAIN 2004-05
SEGUNDA DIVISION B (3) PLAY-OFFS

First Round		Second Round		Promoted Clubs
Alcalá *	1 1			
Ponferradina	1 0	Alcalá *	1 1	Hércules promoted to
Ceuta *	0 0	Hércules	3 1	Segunda Division A
Hércules	1 2			
Zamora *	0 1			
Sevilla B	0 1	Zamora *	2 0	Castellón promoted to
Castellón *	0 2	Castellón	1 1	Segunda Division A
Universid. Las Palmas	0 1			
Lorca Deportiva *	1 2			
Alicante	0 1	Lorca Deportiva *	1 3	Lorca Deportiva promoted to
Rayo Vallecano *	1 0	Real Unión Irún	2 1	Segunda Division A
Real Unión Irún	1 1			
Real Madrid B	0 2			
Real Zaragoza B *	0 0	Real Madrid B	2 1	Real Madrid B promoted to
Burgos *	0 0	Conquense *	0 0	Segunda Division A
Conquense	0 1	* Home team in the first leg		

CLUB DIRECTORY

Club	Town/City	Stadium	Socios	Phone	www.	Lge	Cup	CL
Albacete	Albacete	Carlos Belmonte 17 000	12 800	+34 967 521100	albacetebalompiesad.com	0	0	0
Athletic Club	Bilbao	San Mamés 39 750	34 373	+34 94 4240877	athletic-club.net	8	23	0
Atlético Madrid	Madrid	Vicente Calderón 54 851	42 000	+34 91 3664707	clubatleticodemadrid.com	9	9	0
Barcelona	Barcelona	Camp Nou 98 260	118 699	+34 902 189900	fcbarcelona.com	17	24	1
Real Betis	Sevilla	Ruiz de Lopera 52 500	35 000	+34 954 610340	realbetisbalompie.es	1	2	0
RC Deportivo	La Coruña	Riazor 34 178	30 160	+34 981 259500	canaldeportivo.com	1	2	0
Espanyol	Barcelona	Olímpic de Montjuïc 55 000	28 500	+34 93 2927700	rcdespanyo.com	0	3	0
Getafe	Madrid	Coliseum 14 400	6 000	+34 91 6959771	getafecf.com	0	0	0
Levante	Valencia	Ciutat de Valencia 17 000	14 123	+34 96 3379530	levanteud.es	0	0	0
Málaga	Málaga	La Rosaleda 22 800	19 043	+34 952 613750	malagacf.es	0	0	0
RCD Mallorca	Palma	Son Moix 24 142	15 000	+34 971 221221	rcdmallorca.es	0	1	0
Numancia	Soria	Los Pajaritos 9 500	5 000	+34 975 227303	cdnumancia.com	0	0	0
Osasuna	Pamplona	El Sadar 19 980	13 867	+34 948 152636	osasuna.es	0	0	0
Racing	Santander	El Sardinero 22 500	14 800	+34 942 282828	realracingclub.es	0	0	0
Real Madrid	Madrid	Santiago Bernabeu 80 000	69 000	+34 91 3984300	realmadrid.com	29	17	9
Real Sociedad	San Sebastián	Anoeta 32 082	28 530	+34 943451109	realsociedad.com	2	2	0
Sevilla	Sevilla	Sánchez Pizjuán 43 000	35 000	+34 954 535353	sevillafc.es	1	3	0
Valencia	Valencia	Mestalla 55 000	39 000	+34 96 3372626	valenciacf.es	6	6	0
Villarreal	Villarreal	El Madrigal 23 500	17 500	+34 964 500250	villarrealcf.es	0	0	0
Real Zaragoza	Zaragoza	La Romareda 34 596	30 000	+34 976 567777	realzaragoza.com	0	6	0

RECENT LEAGUE AND CUP RECORD

	Championship						Cup		
Year	Champions	Pts	Runners-up	Pts	Third	Pts	Winners	Score	Runners-up
1990	Real Madrid	62	Valencia	53	Barcelona	51	Barcelona	2-0	Real Madrid
1991	Barcelona	57	Atlético Madrid	47	Real Madrid	46	Atlético Madrid	1-0	Mallorca
1992	Barcelona	55	Real Madrid	54	Atlético Madrid	53	Atlético Madrid	2-0	Real Madrid
1993	Barcelona	58	Real Madrid	57	Deportivo	54	Real Madrid	2-0	Real Zaragoza
1994	Barcelona	56	Deportivo	56	Real Zaragoza	46	Real Zaragoza	0-0 5-4p	Celta Vigo
1995	Real Madrid	55	Deportivo	51	Real Betis	46	Deportivo	2-1	Valencia
1996	Atlético Madrid	87	Valencia	83	Barcelona	80	Atlético Madrid	1-0	Barcelona
1997	Real Madrid	92	Barcelona	90	Deportivo	77	Barcelona	3-2	Real Betis
1998	Barcelona	74	Athletic Bilbao	65	Real Sociedad	63	Barcelona	1-1 4-3p	Mallorca
1999	Barcelona	79	Real Madrid	68	Mallorca	66	Valencia	3-0	Atlético Madrid
2000	Deportivo	69	Barcelona	64	Valencia	64	Espanyol	2-1	Atlético Madrid
2001	Real Madrid	80	Deportivo	73	Mallorca	71	Real Zaragoza	3-1	Celta Vigo
2002	Valencia	75	Deportivo	68	Real Madrid	66	Deportivo	2-1	Real Madrid
2003	Real Madrid	78	Real Sociedad	76	Deportivo	72	Mallorca	3-0	Recreativo Huelva
2004	Valencia	77	Barcelona	72	Deportivo	71	Real Zaragoza	3-2	Real Madrid
2005	Barcelona	84	Real Madrid	80	Villarreal	65	Real Betis	2-1	Osasuna

COPA DEL REY 2004-05

Second Round

Real Betis	0	4p
Alcalá	0	2p
Polideportivo Ejido	0	
Cádiz *	4	
Real Sociedad	3	
Burgos *	1	
Salamanca	2	
Mirandés *	3	
Lleida *	1	
Valencia	0	
Espanyol	1	2p
Terrassa *	1	4p
Levante	1	
Badalona *	0	
Barcelona	0	
Gramenet *	1	
Real Valladolid	0	4p
Eibar *	0	2p
Amurrio *	2	
Racing Santander	3	
Tenerife *	3	
Celta Vigo	1	
Leganés *	1	
Real Madrid	2	
Lanzarote *	3	
Racing Club Ferrol	2	
Rayp *	0	
RCD Mallorca	1	
Cultural *	1	3p
Deportivo Alavés	1	2p
Segoviana *	0	
Athletic Bilbao	1	
Atlético Madrid	3	
Ourense *	0	
Real Zaragoza	1	
Nastic *	2	
Malaga	2	
Don Benito *	0	
Real Murcia	1	
Lorca Deportiva *	4	
Elche	2	
Sporting Gijón *	1	
Cerceda *	0	
RC Deportivo	2	
Córdoba *	0	4p
Almería	0	3p
Recreación *	0	
Numancia	3	
Sevilla	1	
Algeciras *	0	
Xerez *	0	
Ciudad Murcia	1	
Albacete	1	
Ceuta *	0	
Conquense *	0	
Recreativo Huelva	2	
Getafe	1	
Las Palmas *	0	
Vecindario *	2	
Pontevedra	3	
Girona *	2	
Villarreal	1	
Castellón *	0	2p
Osasuna	0	4p

Third Round

Real Betis	2	
Cadiz *	0	
Real Sociedad	0	3p
Mirandés *	0	4p
Lleida	2	4p
Terrassa *	2	2p
Levante	1	
Gramenet *	2	
Real Valladolid *	2	
Racing Santander	1	
Tenerife *	1	
Real Madrid	2	
Lanzarote *	2	
RCD Mallorca	1	
Cultural *	1	
Athletic Bilbao	2	
Atlético Madrid	1	
Nastic *	0	
Malaga	2	
Lorca Deportiva *	5	
Elche *	1	
RC Deportivo	0	
Córdoba *	1	3p
Numancia	1	4p
Sevilla	2	
Ciudad Murcia *	1	
Albacete	0	
Recreativo Huelva *	1	
Getafe	2	
Pontevedra *	1	
Girona *	0	
Osasuna	1	

Fourth Round

Real Betis	3	0
Mirandés *	1	0
Lleida	0	1
Gramenet *	2	0
Real Valladolid *	0	1
Real Madrid	0	1
Lanzarote *	2	0
Athletic Bilbao	1	6
Atlético Madrid	3	2
Lorca Deportiva *	1	0
Elche *	1 0	3p
Numancia	0 1	5p
Sevilla	2	2
Recreativo Huelva *	0	1
Getafe	0	3
Osasuna *	2	2

* Home team/home team in the first leg

COPA DEL REY 2004-05

Quarter-finals	Semi-finals	Final

Real Betis | 2 4
Gramenet * | 2 3

Real Betis * | 0 0 5p
Athletic Bilbao | 0 0 4p

Real Valladolid | 2 0
Athletic Bilbao * | 3 1

Real Betis | 2
Osasuna ‡ | 1

Atlético Madrid | 0 1
Numancia * | 0 0

Atlético Madrid | 0 0
Osasuna * | 1 0

COPA DEL REY FINAL 2005

Vicente Calderon, Madrid, 11-06-2005, Att: 50 000, Referee: Perez Burrull

Real Betis   2   Ricardo Oliveira [75], Dani [115]
Osasuna   1   Aloisi [84]

Real Betis - Antonio Doblas; Melli, Juanito, David Rivas (Daniel Lembo 79), Luis Fernández; Arzu (Fernando Varela 68), Marcos Assuncao; Joaquín Sanchez, Fernando Miguel, Edu (Dani 90); Ricardo Oliveira. Tr: Lorenzo Serrer Ferrer
Osasuna - Juan Elía; Unai Expósito, Cesar Cruchaga, Josetxo Romero, Rafael Clavero; Pablo García, Patxi Puñal (David López 77); Valdo, Pierre Webó (John Aloisi 79), Ludovic Delporte; Richard Morales (Savo Milosevic 72). Tr: Javier Aguirre

Sevilla * | 2 1
Osasuna | 1 3

‡ Qualified for the UEFA Cup

BARCELONA 2004-05

Date	Opponents	Score		Comp	Scorers	Att
29-08-2004	Racing Santander	W 2-0	A	PD	Giuly [68], Eto'o [73p]	17 589
11-09-2004	Sevilla	W 2-0	H	PD	Giuly [35], Larsson [77]	61 204
14-09-2004	Celtic - SCO	W 3-1	A	CLgF	Deco [20], Giuly [77], Larsson [82]	60 500
19-09-2004	Atlético Madrid	D 1-1	A	PD	Van Bronkhorst [21]	55 000
23-09-2004	Real Zaragoza	W 4-1	H	PD	Eto'o 2 [26 46], Xavi [67], Van Bronkhorst [79]	74 600
26-09-2004	Mallorca	W 3-1	A	PD	Larsson [10], Eto'o 2 [38 40]	23 620
29-09-2004	Shakhtar Donetsk - UKR	W 3-0	H	CLgF	Deco [15], Ronaldinho [64p], Eto'o [89]	64 000
3-10-2004	Numancia	W 1-0	H	PD	Larsson [70]	79 447
16-10-2004	Espanyol	W 1-0	A	PD	Deco [9]	34 400
20-10-2004	Milan - ITA	L 0-1	A	CLgF		76 502
24-10-2004	Osasuna	W 3-0	H	PD	Eto'o 2 [39 89], Ronaldinho [43]	67 461
27-10-2004	Gramanet	L 0-1	A	CDRr1		6 000
31-10-2004	Athletic Bilbao	D 1-1	A	PD	Eto'o [11]	39 000
2-11-2004	Milan - ITA	W 2-1	H	CLgF	Eto'o [37], Ronaldinho [88]	94 682
6-11-2004	Deportivo La Coruña	W 2-1	H	PD	Xavi [23], Eto'o [35]	81 284
14-11-2004	Real Betis	L 1-2	A	PD	Gerard [72]	45 000
20-11-2004	Real Madrid	W 3-0	H	PD	Eto'o [29], Van Bronckhorst [43], Ronaldinho [76p]	97 000
24-11-2004	Celtic - SCO	D 1-1	H	CLgF	Eto'o [24]	74 119
27-11-2004	Getafe	W 2-1	A	PD	Marquez [20], Deco [23]	14 000
4-12-2004	Málaga	W 4-0	H	PD	Eto'o 2 [25 90], Deco [29], Iniesta [72]	67 226
7-12-2004	Shakhtar Donetsk - UKR	L 0-2	A	CLgF		25 000
11-12-2004	Albacete	W 2-1	A	PD	Iniesta [2], Xavi [84]	17 000
18-12-2004	Valencia	D 1-1	H	PD	Ronaldinho [79]	82 000
21-12-2004	Levante	W 2-1	H	PD	Deco [29], Eto'o [87]	51 368
9-01-2005	Villarreal	L 0-3	A	PD		22 000
16-01-2005	Real Sociedad	W 1-0	H	PD	Eto'o [80]	68 700
22-01-2005	Racing Santander	W 3-0	H	PD	Eto'o [8], Ronaldinho [74], Deco [76]	67 043
29-01-2005	Sevilla	W 4-0	A	PD	Eto'o [48], Julio Baptista OG [53], Ronaldinho [58], Giuly [76]	45 000
6-02-2005	Atlético Madrid	L 0-2	H	PD		67 112
12-02-2005	Real Zaragoza	W 4-1	A	PD	Toledo OG [1], Giuly [29], Eto'o [39], Márquez [71]	34 000
19-02-2005	Mallorca	W 2-0	H	PD	Deco 2 [16 56]	71 038
23-02-2005	Chelsea - ENG	W 2-1	H	CLr2	López [67], Eto'o [73]	89 000
26-02-2005	Numancia	D 1-1	A	PD	Márquez [48]	10 000
1-03-2005	Espanyol	D 0-0	H	PD		49 285
5-03-2005	Osasuna	W 1-0	A	PD	Eto'o [40]	17 521
8-03-2005	Chelsea - ENG	L 2-4	A	CLr2	Ronaldinho 2 [27p 38]	41 515
12-03-2005	Athletic Bilbao	W 2-0	H	PD	Deco [20], Giuly [38]	81 701
19-03-2005	Deportivo La Coruña	W 1-0	A	PD	Giuly [10]	35 000
3-04-2005	Real Betis	D 3-3	H	PD	Eto'o 2 [15p 82p], Van Bronkhorst [94+]	86 352
10-04-2005	Real Madrid	L 2-4	A	PD	Eto'o [28], Ronaldinho [73]	75 000
17-04-2005	Getafe	W 2-0	H	PD	Ronaldinho [30], Giuly [55]	68 946
24-04-2005	Málaga	W 4-0	A	PD	Oleguer [21], Giuly 2 [34 67], Gerard [90]	23 000
1-05-2005	Albacete	W 2-0	H	PD	Eto'o [66], Messi [90]	91 174
8-05-2005	Valencia	W 2-0	A	PD	Ronaldinho [27], Eto'o [30]	55 000
14-05-2005	Levante	D 1-1	A	PD	Eto'o [60]	25 000
22-05-2005	Villarreal	D 3-3	H	PD	Ronaldinho [33], Giuly 2 [37 47]	84 537
28-05-2005	Real Sociedad	D 0-0	A	PD		25 861

PD = Primera División • CL = UEFA Champions League • CDR = Copa del Rey • gF = Group F • r1 = first round • r2 = second round

REAL MADRID 2004-05

Date	Opponents	Score			Comp	Scorers	Att
11-08-2004	Wisla Krakow - POL	W	2-0	A	CLpr3	Morientes 2 72 90	10 000
25-08-2004	Wisla Krakow - POL	W	3-1	H	CLpr3	Ronaldo 2 3 30, Pavon 84	60 000
29-08-2004	Mallorca	W	1-0	A	PD	Ronaldo 51	23 000
11-09-2004	Numancia	W	1-0	H	PD	Beckham 16	70 000
15-09-2004	Bayer Leverkusen - GER	L	0-3	A	CLgB		22 500
18-09-2004	Espanyol	L	0-1	A	PD		39 500
21-09-2004	Osasuna	W	1-0	H	PD	Beckham 60	65 000
25-09-2004	Athletic Bilbao	L	1-2	A	PD	Raúl 51	38 000
28-09-2004	Roma - ITA	W	4-2	H	CLgB	Raúl 2 38 71, Figo 53p, Roberto Carlos 79	60 000
3-10-2004	Deportivo La Coruña	L	0-1	H	PD		67 415
16-10-2004	Real Betis	D	1-1	A	PD	Ronaldo 65	45 000
19-10-2004	Dynamo Kyiv - UKR	W	1-0	H	CLgB	Owen 35	45 000
23-10-2004	Valencia	W	1-0	H	PD	Owen 7	78 326
26-10-2004	Leganés	W	2-1	A	CDRr1	Morientes 19, Owen 49	4 000
31-10-2004	Getafe	W	2-0	H	PD	Owen 28, Ronaldo 78	75 000
3-11-2004	Dynamo Kyiv - UKR	D	2-2	A	CLgB	Raúl 37, Figo 44p	78 000
7-11-2004	Málaga	W	2-0	A	PD	Figo 24p, Owen 79	30 000
10-11-2004	Tenerife	W	2-1	A	CDRr2	Solari 2 44 118	18 300
14-11-2004	Albacete	W	6-1	H	PD	Ronaldo 2 2 90, Zidane 29, Raúl 31, Samuel 48, Owen 88	79 000
20-11-2004	Barcelona	L	0-3	A	PD		97 000
23-11-2004	Bayer Leverkusen - GER	D	1-1	A	CLgB	Raúl 70	40 000
28-11-2004	Levante	W	5-0	H	PD	Ronaldo 2 43 52, Figo 50, Beckham 55, Owen 87	76 000
5-12-2004	Villarreal	D	0-0	A	PD		20 000
8-12-2004	Roma - ITA	W	3-0	H	CLgB	Ronaldo 9, Figo 2 60p 82	BCD
12-12-2004	Real Sociedad	W	2-1	H	PD	Ronaldo 41, Zidane 90p. Abandoned 87'. Finished on 5-01-2005	70 000
18-12-2004	Racing Santander	W	3-2	A	PD	Owen 34, Raúl 61, Zidane 90	17 383
22-12-2004	Sevilla	L	0-1	H	PD		65 000
9-01-2005	Atlético Madrid	W	3-0	A	PD	Ronaldo 2 14 84, Solari 81	54 000
12-01-2005	Valladolid	D	0-0	A	CDRr3		13 000
16-01-2005	Real Zaragoza	W	3-1	H	PD	Raúl 41, Ronaldo 53, Owen 84	65 000
19-01-2005	Valladolid	D	1-1	H	CDRr3	Owen 67	45 000
23-01-2005	Mallorca	W	3-1	H	PD	Figo 35p, Samuel 80, Solari 90	60 000
30-01-2005	Numancia	W	2-1	A	PD	Beckham 62, Salgado 82	9 500
5-02-2005	Espanyol	W	4-0	H	PD	Zidane 13, Figo 29, Raúl 74, Graveson 83	73 000
13-02-2005	Osasuna	W	2-1	A	PD	Owen 77, Helguera 80	16 899
19-02-2005	Athletic Bilbao	L	0-2	H	PD		75 000
22-02-2005	Juventus - ITA	W	1-0	H	CLr2	Helguera 31	78 000
26-02-2005	Deportivo La Coruña	L	0-2	A	PD		35 000
2-03-2005	Real Betis	W	3-1	H	PD	Owen 9, Roberto Carlos 40, Helguera 61	70 000
5-03-2005	Valencia	D	1-1	A	PD	Ronaldo 28	50 000
9-03-2005	Juventus - ITA	L	0-2	A	CLr2		59 000
13-03-2005	Getafe	L	1-2	A	PD	Solari 90	14 400
20-03-2005	Málaga	W	1-0	H	PD	Roberto Carlos 61	75 000
3-04-2005	Albacete	W	2-1	A	PD	Helguera 15, Owen 45	13 000
10-04-2005	Barcelona	W	4-2	H	PD	Zidane 6, Ronaldo 20, Raúl 45, Owen 65	75 000
17-04-2005	Levante	W	2-0	A	PD	Ronaldo 2 36 83	19 129
23-04-2005	Villarreal	W	2-1	H	PD	Ronaldo 69, Michel Salgado 73	80 000
30-04-2005	Real Sociedad	W	2-0	A	PD	Ronaldo 2 83 92+	26 588
7-05-2005	Racing Santander	W	5-0	H	PD	Owen 28, Ronaldo 2 36p 90, Raúl 2 53 71	78 000
14-05-2005	Sevilla	D	2-2	A	PD	Javi Navarro OG 41, Zidane 73	45 000
21-05-2005	Atlético Madrid	D	0-0	H	PD		75 000
28-05-2005	Real Zaragoza	W	3-1	A	PD	Owen 25, Roberto Carlos 53, Ronaldo 92+	27 000

PD = Primera División • CL = UEFA Champions League • CDR = Copa del Rey • gB = Group B • r1 = first round • r2 = second round • r3 = third round

EST – ESTONIA

NATIONAL TEAM RECORD
JULY 1ST 2002 TO JUNE 30TH 2005

PL	W	D	L	F	A	%
46	12	11	23	42	69	38

FIFA/COCA-COLA WORLD RANKING

1993	1994	1995	1996	1997	1998	1999	2000	2001	2002	2003	2004	High		Low	
109	119	129	102	100	90	70	67	83	60	68	81	60	12/02	135	02/96

2004-2005											
08/04	09/04	10/04	11/04	12/04	01/05	02/05	03/05	04/05	05/05	06/05	07/05
83	81	77	76	81	80	80	82	82	81	82	82

2004 saw a shift in the balance of power in Estonian club football away from Flora Tallinn to Levadia Tallinn, who emphatically ended Flora's run of three successive Championships. Starting with their Cup Final victory over TVMK in May 2004 Levadia had an outstanding 12 months, winning a hat-trick of trophies. The Cup triumph was followed by a close race in the Championship in which they again beat TVMK into second place, losing just one game all season and they rounded off a great year by winning the 2005 Cup Final in May with TVMK again the victims. It was not a good year for Flora, who, for only the second time since independence, finished outside of the

INTERNATIONAL HONOURS
Baltic Cup 1929 1931 1938

top two in the championship, although spare a thought for Lootus who won just one game all season, lost their last 16 games and then relegated themselves two divisions instead of just the one. In contrast the national team enjoyed some success; although never threatening a top two place in their FIFA World Cup™ qualifying group they did a least pull away from Luxembourg and Liechtenstein at the bottom and even held Russia to a 1-1 draw in Tallinn. Such is the experience now in the team that both Marko Kristal and Martin Reim are joint eighth in the all-time list of international caps, 30 short of the record held by Al-Deayea of Saudi Arabia.

THE FIFA BIG COUNT OF 2000

	Male	Female		Male	Female
Registered players	2 764	103	Referees	152	3
Non registered players	14 000	500	Officials	400	20
Youth players	2 770	64	Total involved	20 776	
Total players	20 201		Number of clubs	163	
Professional players	110	0	Number of teams	264	

Estonian Football Association (EFA)
Eesti Jalgpalli Liit, Rapla 8/10, Tallinn 11312, Estonia
Tel +372 6 512720   Fax +372 6 512729
efa@jalgpall.ee   www.estonia.fifa.com
President: KANNIK Indrek   General Secretary: SIREL Tonu
Vice-President: TARMAK Mart   Treasurer: TBD   Media Officer: None
Men's Coach: GOES Jelle   Women's Coach: SAAR Juri
EFA formed: 1921   UEFA: 1992   FIFA: 1923-43 & 1992
Colours: Blue, Black, White or White, Black, Blue

GAMES PLAYED BY ESTONIA IN THE 2006 FIFA WORLD CUP™ CYCLE

2002	Opponents	Score		Venue	Comp	Scorers	Att	Referee
3-07	Azerbaijan	D	0-0	Kuressare	Fr		2 200	Vollquartz DEN
7-07	Kazakhstan	D	1-1	Almaty	Fr	Rooba.M [40]	15 000	Kapanin KAZ
21-08	Moldova	W	1-0	Tallinn	Fr	Allas [53]	1 500	Kaldma EST
7-09	Croatia	D	0-0	Osijek	ECq		12 000	Marin ESP
12-10	New Zealand	W	3-2	Tallinn	Fr	Anniste [9], Viikmäe [52], Zelinski [81]	800	Pedersen NOR
16-10	Belgium	L	0-1	Tallinn	ECq		2 500	Riley ENG
20-11	Iceland	W	2-0	Tallinn	ECq	Viikmäe [75], Oper [84]	478	Haverkort NED
2003								
9-02	Ecuador	L	0-1	Guayaquil	Fr		12 000	Ramos ECU
12-02	Ecuador	L	1-2	Quito	Fr	Zahhovaiko [68]		Vasco Villacis ECU
16-02	China	L	0-1	Wuhan	Fr		20 000	
29-03	Canada	W	2-1	Tallinn	Fr	Oper 2 [72 90]	2 500	Hansson SWE
2-04	Bulgaria	D	0-0	Tallinn	ECq		4 000	Plautz AUT
30-04	Andorra	W	2-0	Andorra la Vella	ECq	Zelinski 2 [27 75]	500	Aydin TUR
7-06	Andorra	W	2-0	Tallinn	ECq	Allas [22], Viikmäe [30]	3 500	Juhos HUN
11-06	Croatia	L	0-1	Tallinn	ECq		7 000	Hamer LUX
3-07	Lithuania	L	1-5	Valga	BC	Sirel [57]	800	Ingvarsson SWE
5-07	Latvia	D	0-0	Tallinn	BC			Ingvarsson SWE
20-08	Poland	L	1-2	Tallinn	Fr	Lemsalu [90]	4 500	Johannesson SWE
6-09	Bulgaria	L	0-2	Sofia	ECq		25 128	Wack GER
11-10	Belgium	L	0-2	Liege	ECq		26 000	Busacca SUI
15-11	Albania	L	0-2	Tirana	Fr		5 000	Douros GRE
19-11	Hungary	W	1-0	Budapest	Fr	Rooba.M [86]	1 200	Sedivy CZE
17-12	Saudi Arabia	D	1-1	Dammam	Fr	Zahhovaiko [40]	1 500	Al-Mehannah KSA
20-12	Oman	L	1-3	Muscat	Fr	Zelinski [45]	1 000	Al-Harrassi OMA
2004								
14-02	Belarus	W	2-1	Ta'Qali	Fr	Rooba.M [13], Lemsalu [45]	200	Casha MLT
16-02	Malta	L	2-5	Ta'Qali	Fr	Zahhovaiko [16], Piiroja [44]		Orlic MDA
18-02	Moldova	W	1-0	Ta'Qali	Fr	Lindpere [58]	100	Sammut MLT
31-03	Northern Ireland	L	0-1	Tallinn	Fr		2 900	Petteri FIN
28-04	Albania	D	1-1	Tallinn	Fr	Viikmäe [80]	1 500	Sipailo LVA
27-05	Scotland	L	0-1	Tallinn	Fr		4 000	Poulsen DEN
30-05	Denmark	D	2-2	Tallinn	Fr	Viikmäe [77], Lindpere [90]	3 000	Bossen NED
6-06	Czech Republic	L	0-2	Teplice	Fr		11 873	Brugger AUT
11-06	Macedonia FYR	L	2-4	Tallinn	Fr	Zahhovaiko [54], Teever [65]	2 200	Frojdfeldt SWE
18-08	Liechtenstein	W	2-1	Vaduz	WCq	Viikmäe [34], Lindpere [80]	912	Bozinovski MKD
4-09	Luxembourg	W	4-0	Tallinn	WCq	Teever [7], Schauls OG [41], Oper [61], Viikmäe [67]	3 000	Kelly IRL
8-09	Portugal	L	0-4	Leiria	WCq		27 214	Demirlek TUR
13-10	Latvia	D	2-2	Riga	WCq	Oper [72], Teever [79]	8 500	Meyer GER
17-11	Russia	L	0-4	Krasnodar	WCq		29 000	Busacca SUI
30-11	Thailand	D	0-0	Bangkok	Fr	L 3-4p	35 000	Mat Amin MAS
2-12	Hungary	L	0-5	Bangkok	Fr		800	Tongkhan THA
2005								
9-02	Venezuela	L	0-3	Maracaibo	Fr		8 000	Vasco Villacis ECU
26-03	Slovakia	L	1-2	Tallinn	WCq	Oper [57]	3 051	Frojdfeldt SWE
30-03	Russia	D	1-1	Tallinn	WCq	Terekhov [63]	8 850	Paparesta ITA
20-04	Norway	L	1-2	Tallinn	Fr	Saharov [81]	2 500	Vink NED
4-06	Liechtenstein	W	2-0	Tallinn	WCq	Stepanov [27], Oper [57]	3 000	Whitby WAL
8-06	Portugal	L	0-1	Tallinn	WCq		10 280	Riley ENG

Fr = Friendly match • EC = UEFA EURO 2004™ • BC = Baltic Cup • WC = FIFA World Cup™ • q = qualifier

ESTONIA COUNTRY INFORMATION

Capital	Tallinn	Independence	1991 from the Soviet Union	GDP per Capita	$12 300
Population	1 341 664	Status	Republic	GNP Ranking	110
Area km²	425 226	Language	Estonian	Dialling code	+372
Population density	3 per km²	Literacy rate	99%	Internet code	.ee
% in urban areas	73%	Main religion	Christian	GMT +/−	+2
Towns/Cities ('000)	Tallinn 394; Tartu 101; Narva 66; Kothla-Järve 46; Pärnu 44; Viljandi 20; Rakvere 16				
Neighbours (km)	Russia 294; Latvia 339; Baltic Sea & Gulf of Finland 3 794				
Main stadia	A. Le Coq Arena – Tallinn 10 300				

ESTONIA NATIONAL TEAM RECORDS AND RECORD SEQUENCES

Records			Sequence records				
Victory	6-0	LTU 1928	Wins	3	2000	Clean sheets	3	1999, 2000, 2003
Defeat	2-10	FIN 1922	Defeats	13	1994-1995	Goals scored	13	1928-30, 1999-00
Player Caps	143	KRISTAL/REIM	Undefeated	6	Three times	Without goal	11	1994-1995
Player Goals	26	ZELINSKI Indrek	Without win	34	1993-1996	Goals against	19	1934-1937

NATIONAL CAPS

	Caps
KRISTAL Marko	143
REIM Martin	143
POOM Mart	101
ZELINSKI Indrek	101
VIIKMÄE Kristen	95
OPER Andreas	94
LEMSALU Marek	84
KIRS Urmas	80

NATIONAL GOALS

	Goals
OPER Andreas	27
ZELINSKI Indrek	26
ELLMAN-EELMA Eduard	21
PIHLAK Arnold	17
KUREMAA Richard	16
REIM Martin	14
SIIMENSON Georg	14

NATIONAL COACH

	Years
PIIR Uno	1992-'93
UBAKIVI Roman	1994-'95
SARAP Aavo	1995
THÓRDARSON Teitur	1996-'99
RÜÜTLI Tarmo	1999-'00
LILLEVERE Aivar	2000
PIJPERS Arno	2000-'04
GOES Jelle	2004-

ESTONIA 2004

MEISTRILIIGA

	Pl	W	D	L	F	A	Pts	Levadia	TVMK	Flora	Trans Narva	Merkuur	Viljandi	Valga	Lootus
Levadia Tallinn †	28	21	6	1	82	14	69		3-0 0-0	2-2 2-0	2-0 0-1	6-0 0-0	6-1 1-0	3-0 3-0	4-0 7-0
TVMK Tallinn ‡	28	19	6	3	89	29	63	0-0 2-2		1-4 1-1	2-0 2-0	5-1 1-3	3-1 2-1	3-1 4-0	5-0 13-0
Flora Tallinn ‡	28	18	4	6	83	25	58	0-2 0-2	2-2 2-3		2-0 1-3	3-0 3-0	4-0 0-1	1-0 2-0	6-0 9-0
Trans Narva	28	15	2	11	43	39	47	1-1 0-6	1-4 2-3	0-2 0-2		1-2 2-2	1-0 2-0	2-1 3-1	1-0 1-0
Merkuur Tartu	28	10	5	13	47	58	35	1-3 2-5	0-2 1-5	0-1 3-5	0-2 2-1		2-1 0-0	4-0 1-2	1-1 4-1
Viljandi Tulevik	28	6	7	15	30	47	25	0-1 1-4	0-3 1-1	1-5 0-0	0-3 1-2	1-4 2-2		2-0 2-1	0-0 5-0
Valga	28	5	2	21	30	35	17	1-5 2-4	2-5 0-5	0-6 1-6	0-2 1-3	2-0 1-7	3-3 2-2		0-1 5-1
Lootus Alutaguse	28	1	2	25	11	25	5	0-5 0-3	0-2 1-10	1-8 0-6	2-6 0-3	1-2 1-3	0-1 1-3	0-2 0-2	

13/03/2004 - 31/10/2004 • † Qualified for the UEFA Champions League • ‡ Qualified for the UEFA Cup

ESTONIA 2004 ESILIIGA (2)

	Pl	W	D	L	F	A	Pts
Tammeka Tartu	28	17	7	4	73	34	58
Levadia Tallinn II	28	17	6	5	75	37	57
Tervis Pärnu	28	18	2	8	70	50	56
Dünamo Tallinn	28	12	2	14	49	66	38
Kuressaare	28	11	2	15	56	70	35
Estel Tallinn	28	10	2	16	66	66	32
TVMK Tallinn II	28	8	3	17	46	54	27
Tallinna JK	28	5	4	19	29	87	19

2/04/2004 - 30/10/2004 • Levadia ineligible for promotion

FFA CUP 2004-05

Quarter-finals

Levadia Tallinn *	5	0
Viljandi Tulevik	1	0
Lootus Alutaguse	1	0
Flora Tallinn *	1	10
Trans Narva *	3	1
Merkuur Tartu	0	1
Valga *	0	0
TVKM Tallinn	4	5

Semi-finals

Levadia Tallinn *	4	2
Flora Tallinn	0	0
Trans Narva *	0	1
TVMK Tallinn	2	3

* Home team in first leg

Final

Levadia Tallinn	1
TVMK Tallinn	0

18-05-2005, Att: 1 500
Kadrioru
Scorer - Leitan [86]

RECENT LEAGUE AND CUP RECORD

	Championship						Cup		
Year	Champions	Pts	Runners-up	Pts	Third	Pts	Winners	Score	Runners-up
1995	Flora Tallinn	41	Lantana-Marlekor	40	Trans Narva	26	Flora Tallinn	2-0	Lantana-Marlekor
1996	Lantana Tallinn	37	Flora Tallinn	31	Tevalte-Marlekor	31	Tallinna Sadam	2-0	EP Jõhvi
1997	Lantana Tallinn	41	Flora Tallinn	38	Tallinna Sadam	24	Tallinna Sadam	3-2	Lantana Tallinn
1998	Flora Tallinn	42	Tallinna Sadam	32	Lantana-Tallinn	25	Flora Tallinn	3-2	Lantana Tallinn
1998	Flora Tallinn	35	Tallinna Sadam	34	Lantana Tallinn	25			
1999	Levadia Maardu	73	Tulevik Viljandi	53	Flora Tallinn	47	Levadia Maardu	4-1	Flora Tallinn
2000	Levadia Maardu	74	Flora Tallinn	55	TVMK Tallinn	48	Levadia Maardu	2-0	Tulevik Viljandi
2001	Flora Tallinn	68	TVMK Tallinn	56	Levadia Maardu	55	Trans Narva	1-0	Flora Tallinn
2002	Flora Tallinn	64	Levadia Maardu	62	TVMK Tallinn	53	Levadia Tallinn	2-0	Levadia Maardu
2003	Flora Tallinn	76	TVMK Tallinn	65	Levadia Maardu	49	TVMK Tallinn	2-2 4-1p	Flora Tallinn
2004	Levadia Tallinn	69	TVMK Tallinn	63	Flora Tallinn	58	Levadia Tallinn	3-0	TVMK Tallinn
2005							Levadia Tallinn	1-0	TVMK Tallinn

Levadia Tallinn known as Levadia Maardu until 2003 • The orginal Levadia Tallinn are now Merkuur Tartu

ETH – ETHIOPIA

NATIONAL TEAM RECORD
JULY 1ST 2002 TO JUNE 30TH 2005

PL	W	D	L	F	A	%
23	7	5	11	22	31	41.3

FIFA/COCA-COLA WORLD RANKING

1993	1994	1995	1996	1997	1998	1999	2000	2001	2002	2003	2004	High		Low	
96	115	105	108	126	145	142	133	155	138	130	151	**90**	10/93	**155**	12/01

2004-2005											
08/04	09/04	10/04	11/04	12/04	01/05	02/05	03/05	04/05	05/05	06/05	07/05
139	141	143	148	151	131	131	132	132	129	129	126

With one of the biggest populations in Africa, Ethiopia has the potential to become one of the giants of the continental game again, although in recent years it has been a continual struggle just to maintain a leading role in East Africa. Most of the football played by the national team has been in the CECAFA Cup, a tournament they have won three times, most recently as tournament hosts in 2004 where they progressed undefeated to the final with Burundi to be cheered on to a comfortable 3-0 victory by a 35,000-strong crowd. The success made up for the disappointment of exiting the 2006 FIFA World Cup™ qualifiers in the preliminary round to Malawi with particular dismay at a

INTERNATIONAL HONOURS
CAF African Cup of Nations 1962   **CECAFA Cup** 1987 2001 2004

3-1 reversal at home. Forty years have passed since their only Nations Cup title, but the Walyas, led by coach Seyoum Kebede, have a place at the 2008 CAF African Cup of Nations as a medium-term target. In domestic football St George claimed their third League title in four years, running away with the Championship by finishing 18 points clear of second-placed Trans Ethiopia and winning 20 of their 26 matches. Last year's champions Awassa City were knocked out of the Champions League in the preliminary round, but won the Ethiopia Cup on penalties after a 2-2 draw with Muger Cement.

THE FIFA BIG COUNT OF 2000

	Male	Female		Male	Female
Registered players	19 000	0	Referees	1 000	0
Non registered players	180 000	0	Officials	7 000	0
Youth players	10 000	0	Total involved	217 000	
Total players	209 000		Number of clubs	500	
Professional players	0	0	Number of teams	3 000	

Ethiopian Football Federation (EFF)
Addis Abeba Stadium, PO Box 1080, Addis Abeba, Ethiopia
Tel +251 1 514453   Fax +251 1 515899
eff@telecom.net.et   www.none
President: WOLDEGIORGIS Ashebir Dr   General Secretary: BEGASHAW Luleseged
Vice-President: TBD   Treasurer: TBD   Media Officer: None
Men's Coach: KEBEDE Seyoum   Women's Coach: MELESE Shale
EFF formed: 1943   CAF: 1957   FIFA: 1953
Colours: Green, Yellow, Red

GAMES PLAYED BY ETHIOPIA IN THE 2006 FIFA WORLD CUP™ CYCLE

2002	Opponents	Score		Venue	Comp	Scorers	Att	Referee
26-07	Uganda	D	0-0	Khartoum	Fr			Salih SUD
28-07	Chad	L	2-3	Khartoum	Fr			Rassas Lebrato SUD
30-07	Sudan	L	0-3	Khartoum	Fr			Abdel Rahmab SUD
8-08	Egypt	L	1-4	Alexandria	Fr	Saber OG 86		
7-09	Niger	L	1-3	Niamey	CNq	Girma 16	35 000	Pare BFA
12-10	Guinea	W	1-0	Addis Abeba	CNq	Abege 63		Itur KEN
2-12	Zanzibar †	D	0-0	Arusha	CCr1			
4-12	Uganda	L	0-3	Arusha	CCr1			Abdulkadir TAN
7-12	Somalia	L	0-1	Arusha	CCr1			
9-12	Rwanda	L	0-1	Arusha	CCr1			
2003								
25-03	Benin	W	3-0	Addis Abeba	Fr	Regassa 18, Mulu 39, Mulugeta 67	15 000	
30-03	Liberia	W	1-0	Addis Abeba	CNq	Felekah 80	40 000	Ali Mohamed DJI
8-06	Liberia	L	0-1	Monrovia	CNq		14 000	Aguidissou BEN
22-06	Niger	W	2-0	Addis Abeba	CNq	Azad OG 15, Kidanu 51	25 000	
6-07	Guinea	L	0-3	Conakry	CNq			
12-10	Malawi	L	1-3	Addis Abeba	WCq	Getu 81p	20 000	Abd El Fatah EGY
15-11	Malawi	D	0-0	Lilongwe	WCq		20 000	Abdel Rahman SUD
2004								
11-12	Burundi	W	2-1	Addis Abeba	CCr1	Shegere 20, Tefera 22		
15-12	Rwanda	D	0-0	Addis Abeba	CCr1		20 000	
17-12	Tanzania	W	2-0	Addis Abeba	CCr1	Alamerew 55, Tesfaye 90		
19-12	Zanzibar †	W	3-0	Addis Abeba	CCr1	Tefera 50, Girma 54, Mensur 64		
22-12	Kenya	D	2-2	Addis Abeba	CCsf	Alamerew 24, Tesfaye 58, W 5-4p	50 000	Ssegonga UGA
25-12	Burundi	W	3-0	Addis Abeba	CCf	Niguse 25, Tesfaye 32, Alamerew 49	30 000	
2005								
12-03	Sudan	L	1-3	Khartoum	Fr			

Fr = Friendly match • CN = CAF African Cup of Nations • CC = CECAFA Cup • WC = FIFA World Cup™
q = qualifier • r1 = first round group • sf = semi-final • f = final • † Not an official A International as Zanzibar are not full members of FIFA

ETHIOPIA NATIONAL TEAM RECORDS AND RECORD SEQUENCES

Records			Sequence records					
Victory	8-1	DJI 1983	Wins	5	1967-1968	Clean sheets	3	1984
Defeat	0-13	IRQ 1992	Defeats	4	Five times	Goals scored	1	1995-97, 2000-02
Player Caps	n/a		Undefeated	11	1984-1988	Goals against	5	1995
Player Goals	n/a		Without win	9	1996-1999	Goals against	18	1956-1962

ETHIOPIA COUNTRY INFORMATION

Capital	Addis Abeba	Independence	Occupied by Italy 1936-41	GDP per Capita	$700
Population	67 851 281	Status	Republic	GNP Ranking	103
Area km²	1 127 127	Language	Amharic	Dialling code	+251
Population density	60 per km²	Literacy rate	42%	Internet code	.et
% in urban areas	13%	Main religion	Muslim 45%, Christian 40%	GMT + / -	+3
Towns/Cities ('000)	Addis Abeba 2 757; Dire Dawa 252; Nazret 214; Bahir Dar 168; Gondar 153; Mek'ele 151; Dese 136; Awassa 133; Jimma 128; Debre Zeyit 104; Kembolcha 93; Harer 90				
Neighbours (km)	Eritrea 912; Djibouti 349; Somalia 1 600; Kenya 861; Sudan 1 606				
Main stadia	Addis Abeba Stadium – Addis Abeba 35 000; Awassa Kenema – Awassa 25 000				

ETHIOPIA 2004-05

PREMIER LEAGUE

	Pl	W	D	L	F	A	Pts	St George	Trans Eth	Awassa City	Banks	Defence	Coffee	Muger	Harar Beer	Metehara	Wonji	Guna	EEPCO	Adama City	Arba Minch
St George	26	20	4	2	56	16	**64**		4-3	6-1	2-0	1-0	4-3	1-0	2-1	2-1	2-2	1-1	3-0	2-0	3-0
Trans Ethiopia	26	13	7	6	36	25	46	2-1		1-0	1-0	0-0	3-1	2-1	1-0	2-0	1-1	3-3	1-1	1-0	3-0
Awassa City	26	13	5	8	32	24	44	0-2	2-0		1-1	2-1	1-0	0-2	3-0	1-0	0-0	1-0	2-1	2-0	6-0
Banks SC	26	11	8	7	38	19	41	1-1	0-1	4-0			1-0	1-0	0-0	1-1	1-0	2-0	4-1	1-0	3-0
Defence	26	11	7	8	28	21	40	0-1	2-1	0-2	3-2		0-3	0-1	3-0	2-0	3-1	1-1	3-3	3-0	1-0
Ethiopian Coffee	26	11	4	11	36	28	37	0-2	1-0	1-1	1-1	0-0		2-0	0-1	1-2	3-0	3-4	2-0	4-1	3-0
Muger Cement	26	9	9	8	27	23	36	0-0	1-1	3-1	2-1	0-1	1-2		0-1	1-1	2-0	3-3	1-1	0-0	2-1
Harar Beer	26	9	9	8	22	27	36	0-5	1-0	1-0	1-1	1-0	1-1	0-0		0-1	2-1	1-0	0-0	1-1	4-0
Metehara Sugar	26	9	7	10	27	28	34	0-2	0-0	1-0	1-0	0-0	0-2	2-0	0-2		4-4	0-1	2-2	4-0	2-0
Wonji Sugar	26	9	7	10	32	39	34	1-0	2-1	0-2	0-5	0-0	3-0	0-0	1-0	2-3		5-0	1-0	2-6	2-1
Guna Trading	26	8	8	10	29	42	32	0-3	1-3	0-1	1-0	0-1	1-0	2-1	0-0	1-1	2-1		0-0	2-1	2-1
EEPCO Mebrat Hail	26	7	10	9	34	27	31	0-2	1-1	0-0	1-1	1-1	1-0	0-1	3-1	2-0	0-1	4-1		4-0	1-0
Adama City	26	4	5	17	18	48	17	0-3	1-2	0-2	0-2	0-1	0-1	1-3	1-1	0-0	0-0	2-1	2-1		1-0
Arba Minch Textile	26	1	4	21	9	57	7	0-1	1-2	0-0	1-1	0-2	0-2	0-2	1-1	0-2	**0-2**	1-1	0-7	2-1	

31/10/2004 - 4/06/2005 • Match in bold awarded 2-0

RECENT LEAGUE AND CUP RECORD

Year	Champions	Pts	Runners-up	Pts	Third	Pts
1998	EELPA Mebrat Hail	32	Medhin	32	Ethiopian Coffee	29
1999	St George	47	Awassa City	39	Ethiopian Coffee	33
2000	St George	46	EEPCO Mebrat Hail	39	Ethiopian Coffee	38
2001	EEPCO Mebrat Hail	59	St George	49	Ethiopian Coffee	48
2002	St George	61	Ethiopian Coffee	50	EEPCO Mebrat Hail	45
2003	St George	56	Arba Minch Textile	55	Ethiopian Coffee	44
2004	Awassa City	48	Ethiopian Coffee	46	Trans Ethiopia	45
2005	St George	64	Trans Ethiopia	46	Awassa City	44

Cup Winners	Score	Runners-up
Ethiopian Coffee	4-2	St George
St George		
Ethiopian Coffee	2-1	Awassa City
EEPCO Mebrat Hail	2-1	Guna Trading
Medhin	6-3p	EEPCO Mebrat Hail
Ethiopian Coffee	2-0	EEPCO Mebrat Hail
Banks	1-0	Ethiopian Coffee
Awassa City	2-2 wop	Muger Cement

In 1999 EELPA were renamed EEPCO - Ethiopian Electric Light & Power Authority (also known as Mebrat Hail) • wop = won on penalties

FIJ – FIJI

NATIONAL TEAM RECORD
JULY 1ST 2002 TO JUNE 30TH 2005

PL	W	D	L	F	A	%
16	8	2	6	30	27	56.3

FIFA/COCA-COLA WORLD RANKING

1993	1994	1995	1996	1997	1998	1999	2000	2001	2002	2003	2004	High		Low	
107	120	139	157	146	124	135	141	123	140	149	135	**94**	07/94	**161**	09/98

2004-2005											
08/04	09/04	10/04	11/04	12/04	01/05	02/05	03/05	04/05	05/05	06/05	07/05
134	134	132	135	135	137	138	136	136	138	139	141

Fiji has traditionally been the third football power in Oceania so the decision of the Australians to leave the OFC has given them a chance to move up the pecking order, although this has been countered by a rise in standards of other nations, notably the Solomon Islands. Football also faces huge competition from rugby union, a sport in which Fiji has achieved notable international success. The Goal Programme has aimed to give youth football a firm footing with help in funding the construction of the Dr M. S. Sahu Khan Football School which was opened in February 2003 while a second Goal Programme project will see the construction of a new facility to include a

INTERNATIONAL HONOURS
Melanesian Cup 1988 1989 1992 1998 2000 **South Pacific Games** 1991 2003

headquarters for the national association along with a training complex. Since their FIFA World Cup™ exit in the OFC final tournament in Adelaide the national team has not played a game with the focus on the OFC U-17 and OFC Youth qualifiers instead. The U-20 team reached the semi-finals of the youth championship where they lost to Australia but the U-17s failed to get out of their group. In domestic football the Football Association formed a new franchised League which was won by 4R Electric Ltd of Ba who entered the OFC Club Championship. They failed to make it to the finals in Tahiti after losing to Makuru of the Solomon Islands in a preliminary round.

THE FIFA BIG COUNT OF 2000

	Male	Female		Male	Female
Registered players	9 838	303	Referees	90	0
Non registered players	5 000	0	Officials	2 500	50
Youth players	15 000	710	Total involved	33 491	
Total players	30 851		Number of clubs	300	
Professional players	0	0	Number of teams	1 775	

Fiji Football Association (FFA)
73 Knolly Street, PO Box 2514, Suva, Fiji
Tel +679 3300453   Fax +679 3304642
bobkumar@fijifootball.com.fj   www.fijifootball.com
President: SAHU KHAN Muhammad Dr   General Secretary: KUMAR Bob Sant
Vice-President: KEWAL Hari Dr   Treasurer: TBD   Media Officer: None
Men's Coach: BUESNEL Tony   Women's Coach: None
FFA formed: 1938   OFC: 1966   FIFA: 1963
Colours: White, Blue, Blue

GAMES PLAYED BY FIJI IN THE 2006 FIFA WORLD CUP™ CYCLE

2002	Opponents	Score		Venue	Comp	Scorers	Att	Referee
6-07	New Caledonia	W	2-1	Auckland	OCr1	Toma.Ve [23], Bukaudi [49]	1 000	Rugg NZL
8-07	Vanuatu	L	0-1	Auckland	OCr1		800	Sosognan PNG
10-07	Australia	L	0-8	Auckland	OCr1		1 000	Sosognan PNG
2003								
30-06	Vanuatu	D	0-0	Suva	SPr1			Taga VAN
7-07	Solomon Islands	W	2-1	Lautoka	SPr1	Toma.Ve [4], Masi.E [13]	6 000	Ariiotima TAH
9-07	Tahiti	W	2-1	Lautoka	SPsf	Waqa [9], Toma.Ve [106]	8 000	Attison VAN
11-07	New Caledonia	W	2-0	Suva	SPf	Masi.M [30], Masi.E [63]	10 000	Attison VAN
2004								
12-05	Papua New Guinea	W	4-2	Apia	WCq	Rabo [24], Toma.Ve [48+], Gataurua [78], Rokotakala [90]	400	Diomis AUS
15-05	American Samoa	W	11-0	Apia	WCq	Toma.Ve 3 [7 11 16], Vulivulu [24], Rokotakala 2 [32 38], Sabutu 2 [46+ 81], Masinisau [60], Gataurua 2 [75 77]	300	Fox NZL
17-05	Samoa	W	4-0	Apia	WCq	Toma.Ve [17], Sabutu [52], Masinisau [82], Rokotakala [84]	450	Diomis AUS
19-05	Vanuatu	L	0-3	Apia	WCq		200	Breeze AUS
29-05	Tahiti	D	0-0	Adelaide	WCq		3 000	Farina ITA
31-05	Vanuatu	W	1-0	Adelaide	WCq	Toma.Ve [73]	500	Ariiotima TAH
2-06	Australia	L	1-6	Adelaide	WCq	Gataurua [19]	2 200	Iturralde Gonzalez ESP
4-06	Solomon Islands	L	1-2	Adelaide	WCq	Toma.Ve [21]	1 500	Attison VAN
6-06	New Zealand	L	0-2	Adelaide	WCq		300	Larsen DEN
2005								

No international matches played in 2005 before July

OC = Oceania Nations Cup • SP = South Pacific Games • WC = FIFA World Cup™ • q = qualifier • r1 = first round group • sf = semi-final • f = final

FIJI NATIONAL TEAM RECORDS AND RECORD SEQUENCES

Records			Sequence records				
Victory	15-1	GUM 1991, COK 1971	Wins	6	2003-2004	Clean sheets	4	1992, 1989-90
Defeat	0-13	NZL 1981	Defeats	8	1985-1986	Goals scored	15	1985-1989
Player Caps	n/a		Undefeated	13	1989-1991	Without goal	5	1985
Player Goals	n/a		Without win	12	1983-1988	Goals against	13	1983-1988

FIFA REFEREE LIST 2005

	Int'l	DoB
RAKAROI Leone	2002	3-07-1965
SHAH Intaz	1992	19-03-1960
SINGH Rajendra	2002	9-02-1964
VARMAN Rakesh	2000	2-01-1968

FIFA ASSISTANT REFEREE LIST 2005

	Int'l	DoB
ACHARI Andrew	2005	28-02-1973
DAYAL Rohitesh	2005	7-01-1975
KEWAL Dhirendra	2002	16-04-1964

RECENT LEAGUE AND CUP RECORD

	League	Inter-District Competition			Battle of the Giants			FA Cup		
Year	Winners	Winners	Score	Finalist	Winners	Score	Finalist	Winners	Score	Finalist
1997	Suva	Ba	2-0	Nadi	Labasa	1-0	Nadi	Labasa	0-0	Ba
1998	Nadi	Nadi	3-1	Lautoka	Ba	3-0	Nadi	Ba	3-0	Nadi
1999	Ba	Nadi	1-0	Ba	Ba	1-0	Tavua	Labasa	2-1	Lautoka
2000	Nadi	Ba	1-0	Nadi	Ba	2-0	Labasa	Lautoka	2-0	Nadroga
2001	Ba	Rewa	1-0	Ba	Ba	2-0	Lautoka	Nadroga	1-1 7-6p	Labasa
2002	Ba	Nadi	1-1 4-2p	Rewa	Nadroga	2-1	Labasa	Lautoka	1-1 3-2p	Nasinu
2003	Olympians	Ba	1-0	Nadi	Rewa	1-0	Ba	Navua	1-0	Rewa
2004	Ba	Ba	3-0	Rewa	Rewa	2-0	Nadi	Ba	2-0	Suva
2005	4R Electric							Ba	1-0	Nadi

FIJI COUNTRY INFORMATION

Capital	Suva	Independence	1970 from the UK	GDP per Capita	$5 800
Population	880 874	Status	Republic	GNP Ranking	141
Area km²	18 270	Language	English, Fijian	Dialling code	+679
Population density	48 per km²	Literacy rate	93%	Internet code	.fj
% in urban areas	41%	Main religion	Christian 52%, Hindu 38%	GMT +/–	+12
Towns/Cities ('000)	Suva 199; Nadi 53; Lautoka 49; Labasa 33; Nausori 32; Lami 21; Ba 20; Sigatoka 12				
Neighbours (km)	Fiji consists of two large islands, Viti Levu and Vanua Levu, along with 880 islets in the South Pacific				
Main stadia	National Stadium – Suva 5 000; Govind Park – Ba 4 000; Churchill Park – Lautoka 2 000				

FIN – FINLAND

NATIONAL TEAM RECORD
JULY 1ST 2002 TO JUNE 30TH 2005

PL	W	D	L	F	A	%
38	17	4	17	51	51	50

FIFA/COCA-COLA WORLD RANKING

1993	1994	1995	1996	1997	1998	1999	2000	2001	2002	2003	2004	High		Low	
45	38	44	79	60	55	56	59	46	43	40	43	**36**	03/05	**79**	12/96

2004-2005											
08/04	09/04	10/04	11/04	12/04	01/05	02/05	03/05	04/05	05/05	06/05	07/05
49	53	45	43	43	43	38	36	37	37	40	43

A highest ever FIFA/Coca-Cola World Ranking of 36 in March 2005 for the Finland national team would seem to be a cause for celebration but within three months long serving coach Antti Muurinen had been fired after a third consecutive defeat in the 2006 FIFA World Cup™ qualifying campaign. It is a measure of how far the Finns have progressed in recent years that mid-table is no longer seen as acceptable. For many years the Finns were by far the weakest of the Scandinavian nations but now with almost the whole team playing in strong leagues abroad - Sami Hyypia won a European Cup winners medal with Liverpool in May 2005 - there is a growing expectation that

INTERNATIONAL HONOURS
None

qualification for a major finals is a possibility. However, with both the Czech Republic and the Netherlands in such irresistible form it was always going to be a tough group to negotiate. The women's team made up for some of the disappointment when they surprised everyone by qualifying for the UEFA Women's European Championship finals and then proceded to knock out the hosts England and neighbours Denmark to unexpectedly reach the semi-finals where they lost to eventual winners Germany. In the Veikkausliiga, Haka won a ninth Championship with the Cup honours going to MyPa-47.

THE FIFA BIG COUNT OF 2000

	Male	Female		Male	Female
Registered players	17 112	964	Referees	2 303	230
Non registered players	83 000	7 000	Officials	10 500	3 000
Youth players	64 265	12 540	Total involved	200 914	
Total players	184 881		Number of clubs	1 865	
Professional players	325	0	Number of teams	4 365	

Suomen Palloliitto (SPL/FBF)
Urheilukatu 5, PO Box 191, Helsinki 00251, Finland
Tel +358 9 742151   Fax +358 9 74215200
firstname.lastname@palloliitto.fi   www.palloliitto.fi
President: HAMALAINEN Pekka   General Secretary: HOLOPAINEN Teuvo
Vice-President: GUSTAFSSON Jukka   Treasurer: HOLOPAINEN Teuvo   Media Officer: TERAVA Sami
Men's Coach: TBD   Women's Coach: KALD Michael
SPL/FBF formed: 1907   UEFA: 1954   FIFA: 1908
Colours: White, Blue, White or Blue, White, Blue

GAMES PLAYED BY FINLAND IN THE 2006 FIFA WORLD CUP™ CYCLE

2002	Opponents	Score		Venue	Comp	Scorers	Att	Referee
21-08	Republic of Ireland	L	0-3	Helsinki	Fr		12 225	Pedersen NOR
7-09	Wales	L	0-2	Helsinki	ECq		35 833	Plautz AUT
12-10	Azerbaijan	W	3-0	Helsinki	ECq	Agaev OG [13], Tihinen [50], Hyypia [72]	11 853	Hamer LUX
16-10	Yugoslavia	L	0-2	Belgrade	ECq		30 000	Wegereef NED
2003								
26-01	Barbados	D	0-0	Bridgetown	Fr		5 000	Bynoe TRI
29-01	Trinidad and Tobago	W	2-1	Port of Spain	Fr	Kottila [79], Niemi.J [82]	4 000	Forde BRB
12-02	Northern Ireland	W	1-0	Belfast	Fr	Hyypia [49]	6 137	McDonald SCO
29-03	Italy	L	0-2	Palermo	ECq		34 074	Ivanov RUS
30-04	Iceland	W	3-0	Helsinki	Fr	Litmanen [55p], Forssell [57], Johansson.J [79]	4 005	Frojdfeldt SWE
22-05	Norway	L	0-2	Oslo	Fr		13 436	Clark SCO
7-06	Serbia & Montenegro	W	3-0	Helsinki	ECq	Hyypia [19], Kolkka [45], Forssell [56]	17 343	Colombo FRA
11-06	Italy	L	0-2	Helsinki	ECq		36 850	Siric CRO
20-08	Denmark	D	1-1	Copenhagen	Fr	Riihilahti [88]	14 882	McCurry SCO
6-09	Azerbaijan	W	2-1	Baku	ECq	Tainio [52], Nurmela [76]	8 000	Hrinak SVK
10-09	Wales	D	1-1	Cardiff	ECq	Forssell [79]	72 500	Dauden Ibanez ESP
11-10	Canada	W	3-2	Tampere	Fr	Forssell [14], Kolkka [16], Tainio [32]	5 350	Richmond SCO
16-11	Honduras	W	2-1	Houston	Fr	Tainio [60], Hakanpaa [68]	26 000	Hall USA
19-11	Costa Rica	L	1-2	San Jose	Fr	Nurmela [61p]	11 000	Batres CRC
2004								
3-02	China	L	1-2	Guangzhou	Fr	Eremenko [51]	15 000	Lee Gi Young KOR
7-02	China	L	1-2	Shenzhen	Fr	Kopteff [37]	18 000	Bae Jae Young KOR
31-03	Malta	W	2-1	Ta'Qali	Fr	Eremenko [51], Litmanen [86]	1 100	Trefoloni ITA
28-04	Bosnia-Herzegovina	L	0-1	Zenica	Fr		20 000	Bozinovski MKD
28-05	Sweden	L	1-3	Tammerfors	Fr	Litmanen [8p]	16 500	Undiano Mallenco ESP
18-08	Romania	L	1-2	Bucharest	WCq	Eremenko [90+3]	17 500	Gilewski POL
4-09	Andorra	W	3-0	Tampere	WCq	Eremenko 2 [42 64], Riihilahti [58]	7 437	Siric CRO
8-09	Armenia	W	2-0	Yerevan	WCq	Forssell [24], Eremenko [67]	2 864	Malzinskas LTU
9-10	Armenia	W	3-1	Tampere	WCq	Kuqi 2 [9 87], Eremenko [28]	7 894	Fandel GER
13-10	Netherlands	L	1-3	Amsterdam	WCq	Tainio [13]	50 000	Bennett ENG
17-11	Italy	L	0-1	Messina	Fr		7 043	Tudor ROU
1-12	Bahrain	W	2-1	Manama	Fr	Pohja [9], Huusko [67]	10 000	Najm LIB
3-12	Oman	D	0-0	Manama	Fr	L 3-4p	3 000	Masoudi IRN
2005								
8-02	Latvia	W	2-1	Nicosia	Fr	Johansson.J [31], Huusko [72]	102	Kailis CYP
9-02	Cyprus	W	2-1	Nicosia	Fr	Roiha 2 [66 70]	1 502	Romans LVA
12-03	Kuwait	W	1-0	Kuwait City	Fr	Kuqi.N [16]	1 500	Al Shatti KUW
18-03	Saudi Arabia	W	4-1	Dammam	Fr	Kuivasto [4], Kuqi.N 2 [71 78], Nurmela [76]	8 000	Al Amri KSA
26-03	Czech Republic	L	3-4	Teplice	WCq	Litmanen [46], Riihilahti [73], Johansson.J [79]	16 200	Larsen DEN
2-06	Denmark	L	0-1	Tampere	Fr		9 238	Wegereef NED
8-06	Netherlands	L	0-4	Helsinki	WCq		37 786	Hamer LUX

Fr = Friendly match • EC = UEFA EURO 2004™ • WC = FIFA World Cup™ • q = qualifier

FINLAND COUNTRY INFORMATION

Capital	Helsinki	Independence	1917 from Russia	GDP per Capita	$27 400
Population	5 214 512	Status	Republic	GNP Ranking	29
Area km²	338 145	Language	Finnish	Dialling code	+358
Population density	15 per km²	Literacy rate	99%	Internet code	.fi
% in urban areas	63%	Main religion	Christian 90%	GMT +/-	+2
Towns/Cities ('000)	Helsinki 558; Espoo 229; Tampere 202; Vantaa 188; Turku 175; Oulu 128; Lahti 98				
Neighbours (km)	Norway 736; Russia 1 340; Sweden 614; Baltic Sea, Gulf of Bothnia & Gulf of Finland 1 250				
Main stadia	Olympiastadion – Helsinki 42 062; Lahden – Lahti 14 500; Finnair – Helsinki 10 770				

FINLAND NATIONAL TEAM RECORDS AND RECORD SEQUENCES

Records			Sequence records					
Victory	10-2	EST 1922	Wins	3	Six times	Clean sheets	3	1924, 1993
Defeat	0-13	GER 1940	Defeats	14	1967-1969	Goals scored	14	1925-1927
Player Caps	100	HJELM Arie	Undefeated	10	2001-2002	Without goal	5	1937, 1971-1972
Player Goals	24	LITMANEN Jari	Without win	27	1939-1949	Goals against	44	1936-1949

NATIONAL CAPS

	Caps
HJELM Ari	100
LITMANEN Jari	95
PETAJA Erkka	83
TOLSA Arto	76
PAATELAINEN Mika-Matti	70
RANTA Esko	69
PELTONEN Juhani	68
HYYPIA Sami	68

NATIONAL GOALS

	Goals
LITMANEN Jari	25
HJELM Ari	20
PAATELAINEN Mika-Matti	18
EKLOF Verner	17
KOPONEN Aulis	16
ASTROM Gunnar	16
KANERVA William	13
VAIHELA Jorma	13

NATIONAL COACH

	Years
RYTKONEN Aulis	1975-'78
MALM Esko	1979-'81
KUUSELA Martti	1982-'87
VAKKILA Jukka	1988-'92
LINDHOLM Tommy	1993-'94
IKALAINEN Jukka	1994-'96
MØLLER NIELSEN Richard	1996-'99
MUURINEN Antti	2000-'05

FIFA REFEREE LIST 2005

	Int'l	DoB
ASUMAA Tony	2003	15-09-1968
HIETALA Jouni	2005	4-02-1971
HYYTIA Jouni	1997	24-06-1964
KARI Petteri	1999	5-04-1971
VUORELA Mikko	1995	8-11-1967

FIFA ASSISTANT REFEREE LIST 2005

	Int'l	DoB
IIVAVAINEN Janne	2002	25-01-1973
IKONEN Jouko	2003	25-10-1967
KOSKELA Jukka-Pekka	2003	28-04-1978
KOTINURMI Teijo	2004	5-03-1969
LAHTI Lassi	1999	15-05-1963
TIENSUU Markku	1995	5-07-1966
TURKKI Ari	2000	22-03-1964
VEHVILAINEN Esa	2001	6-07-1970

CLUB DIRECTORY

Club	City/Town	Stadium	Phone	www.	Lge	Cup	CL
Allianssi	Vantaa	Pohjola Stadion 4 700	+358 9 4366510	acallianssi.com	0	0	0
Haka	Valkeakoski	Tehtaan kenttä 6 400	+358 3 5845364	fchaka.fi	9	11	0
HJK	Helsinki	Finnair Stadion 10 770	+358 94 774550	hjk.fi	21	8	0
IFK	Mariehamn	Idrottsparken 1 500	+358 18 531436	ifkmariehamn.com	0	0	0
Inter	Turku	Veritas Stadion 9 000	+358 22 792700	fcinter.com	0	0	0
Jaro	Pietarsaari	Keskuskenttä 5 000	+358 67 247936	ffjaro.fi	0	0	0
KooTeePee	Kotka	Arto Tolsa Areena 4 780	+358 5 217044	fckooteepee.fi	0	0	0
KuPS	Kuopio	Väinölänniemi 9 800	+358 17 2668560	kups.fi	5	2	0
Lahti	Lahti	Lahden Stadion 14 500	+358 3 880810	fclahti.fi	0	0	0
MyPa-47	Anjalankoski	Jalkapallokenttä 4 067	+358 53 656686	mypa.fi	0	3	0
RoPS	Rovaniemi	Keskuskenttä 4 000	+358 400 690815	rops.fi	0	1	0
Tampere United	Tampere	Ratina Stadion 16 850	+358 32 554454	tampereunited.com	3	2	0
TP-47	Tornio	Pohjan Stadion 3 000	+358 16 445247	tp47.com	0	0	0
TPS	Turku	Veritas Stadion 9 000	+358 22 731116	tps.fi	8	2	0

RECENT LEAGUE AND CUP RECORD

	Championship						Cup		
Year	Champions	Pts	Runners-up	Pts	Third	Pts	Winners	Score	Runners-up
1991	Kuusysi Lahti	59	MP Mikkeli	58	Haka Valkeakoski	54	TPS Turku	0-0 5-3p	Kuusysi Lahti
1992	HJK Helsinki	66	Kuusysi Lahti	63	Jazz Pori	63	MyPa-47	2-0	Jaro Pietarsaari
1993	Jazz Pori	41	MyPa-47	54	HJK Helsinki	49	HJK Helsinki	2-0	RoPS Rovaniemi
1994	TVP Tampere	52	MyPa-47	50	HJK Helsinki	43	TPS Turku	2-1	HJK Helsinki
1995	Haka Valkeakoski	59	MyPa-47	53	HJK Helsinki	52	MyPa-47	1-0	FC Jazz Pori
1996	FC Jazz Pori	47	MyPa-47	45	TPS Turku	44	HJK Helsinki	0-0 4-3p	TPS Turku
1997	HJK Helsinki	58	VPS Vaasa	48	FinnPa Helsinki	39	Haka Valkeakoski	2-1	TPS Turku
1998	Haka Valkeakoski	48	VPS Vaasa	45	PK-35 Helsinki	44	HJK Helsinki	3-2	PK-35 Helsinki
1999	Haka Valkeakoski	67	HJK Helsinki	65	MyPa-47	47	Jokerit Helsinki	2-1	FF Jaro Pietarsaari
2000	Haka Valkeakoski	66	Jokerit Helsinki	62	MyPa-47	61	HJK Helsinki	1-0	KTP Kotka
2001	Tampere United	68	HJK Helsinki	67	MyPa-47	62	Atlantis Helsinki	1-0	Tampere United
2002	HJK Helsinki	65	MyPa-47	60	Haka Valkeakoski	52	Haka Valkeakoski	4-1	FC Lahti
2003	HJK Helsinki	57	Haka Valkeakoski	53	Tampere United	47	HJK Helsinki	2-1	Allianssi Vantaa
2004	Haka Valkeakoski	59	Allianssi Vantaa	48	Tampere United	47	MyPa-47	2-1	Hämeenlinna

Jokerit Helsinki known as PK-35 until 1999

FINLAND 2004

VEIKKAUSLIIGA (1)

	Pl	W	D	L	F	A	Pts	Haka	Allianssi	Tampere	Inter	TPS	HJK	Lahti	MyPa	KooTeePee	TP-47	Jaro	RoPS	Jazz	Hämeenlinna
Haka Valkeakoski †	26	18	5	3	54	20	59		2-3	0-1	4-0	1-2	3-2	2-0	4-3	4-1	4-2	2-0	1-0	1-0	1-1
Allianssi Vantaa ‡	26	14	6	6	36	28	48	0-0		0-0	1-0	0-0	1-0	1-2	0-3	0-0	3-2	4-0	1-0	3-1	3-1
Tampere United	26	14	5	7	39	24	47	1-3	1-0		2-2	3-1	1-4	0-0	1-1	2-0	3-2	2-0	5-1	6-0	1-0
Inter Turku	26	13	5	8	42	34	44	0-0	4-0	1-0		0-1	1-4	4-2	0-1	1-1	2-1	5-1	4-0	3-0	1-0
TPS Turku	26	12	6	8	36	31	42	0-0	3-1	0-1	2-0		2-2	2-2	1-0	1-0	3-2	3-1	1-0	1-2	2-3
HJK Helsinki	26	9	12	5	42	31	39	0-0	0-1	0-0	0-1	3-2		2-2	0-0	3-2	1-1	2-1	2-1	4-1	3-0
Lahti	26	9	11	6	37	33	38	1-2	3-3	2-1	2-1	1-2	1-1		1-1	1-1	1-1	1-0	2-1	4-0	1-0
MyPa-47 ‡	26	9	8	9	33	31	35	0-4	0-1	1-2	1-1	1-2	1-1	0-0		1-1	2-0	2-1	1-2	2-1	3-1
KooTeePee	26	8	8	10	28	28	32	0-1	0-2	0-1	0-1	3-0	2-2	1-1	2-0		2-1	2-0	3-0	1-1	1-0
TP-47 Tornio	26	8	4	14	34	44	28	1-4	1-2	1-0	0-1	1-0	1-2	3-1	2-0	1-0		0-4	3-0	3-2	2-0
Jaro Pietarsaari	26	8	4	14	31	43	28	0-3	1-2	0-3	1-1	1-0	2-2	2-1	1-1	3-1	3-0		1-2	3-1	1-1
RoPS Rovaniemi	26	7	4	15	28	45	25	1-3	1-0	2-0	4-0	0-2	2-0	2-2	1-2	1-3	1-1	0-2		1-2	2-2
Jazz Pori	26	4	7	15	28	53	19	0-2	1-1	3-1	3-4	1-1	0-0	0-1	0-4	0-0	2-2	0-1	0-1		5-1
Hämeenlinna	26	3	7	16	28	51	16	1-3	2-3	0-1	3-4	2-2	2-2	0-2	1-2	0-1	1-0	2-1	2-2	2-2	

6/05/2004 - 2/10/2004 • † Qualified for the UEFA Champions League • ‡ Qualified for the UEFA Cup
Play-off: IFK Mariehamn 1-0 2-2 Jazz Pori • Jazz relegated

FINLAND 2004 — YKKÖNEN (2)

	Pl	W	D	L	F	A	Pts
KuPS Kuopio	26	16	6	4	51	22	54
IFK Mariehamn	26	16	2	8	52	32	50
FC Honka	26	13	4	9	55	38	43
FC Viikingit	26	11	9	6	40	33	42
AC Oulu	26	10	9	7	39	33	39
VPS Vaasa	26	11	6	9	32	26	39
MP Mikkeli	26	9	11	6	46	40	38
Rakuunat	26	10	8	8	37	34	38
PP-70 Tampere	26	9	8	9	36	30	35
P-Iirot Rauma	26	10	5	11	32	41	35
VG-62 Naantali	26	9	6	11	34	40	33
Närpes Kraft	26	6	6	14	37	47	24
FC Kuusankoski	26	4	6	16	28	54	18
GBK Kokkola	26	3	4	19	26	75	13

6/05/2004 - 2/10/2004

TOP SCORERS

POHJA Antti	Tampere Utd	16
ADRIANO	Allianssi	11
LEHTINEN Toni	Haka	11

SUOMEN CUP 2004

Round of 16		Quarter-finals		Semi-finals		Final	
MyPa-47 *	3						
HJK Helsinki	2	MyPa-47	2				
TP Seinäjoki *	0	Allianssi Vantaa *	1				
Allianssi Vantaa	7			MyPa-47	6		
Lahti *	3 4p			Haka Valkeakoski	3		
MP Mikkeli	3 3p	Lahti	1				
KäPä *	0	Haka Valkeakoski *	2				
Haka Valkeakoski	2					MyPa-47 ‡	2
Klubi-04 *	1					Hämeenlinna	1
FC Kuusankoski	0	Klubi-04	3				
VPS Vaasa *	2	PP-70 Tampere *	1				
PP-70 Tampere	3			Klubi-04	1		
RoPS Rovaniemi *	2			Hämeenlinna	2		
KooTeePee	0	RoPS Rovaniemi	1 6p				
Huima *	0	Hämeenlinna *	1 5p				
Hämeenlinna	3						

* Home team • ‡ Qualified for the UEFA Cup

CUP FINAL

30-10-2004
Finnair Stadion, Helsinki
Scorers - Puhakainen [23], Aho [50] for MyPa;
Byrnes [51] for Hämeenlinna

FRA – FRANCE

NATIONAL TEAM RECORD
JULY 1ST 2002 TO JUNE 30TH 2005

PL	W	D	L	F	A	%
38	25	11	2	78	17	80.3

Under new coach Raymond Domenech the French national team went through the 2004-05 season unbeaten and in the three years following the debacle at the 2002 FIFA World Cup™ France have lost just two matches. That run has included record sequences of 14 consecutive wins and 11 clean sheets but Domenech has faced a crisis from a most unexpected source since taking over from Jacques Santini in the aftermath of UEFA EURO 2004™ - the goals have dried up. With just nine scored in his first 10 matches in charge Domenech watched his side draw seven times, four of them 0-0, and as a result the team has slipped out of the top three of the FIFA/Coca-Cola World Ranking for only the second time since winning the FIFA World Cup™ in 1998. It has also made what was a tough group in the 2006 qualifiers much harder with Switzerland, the Republic of Ireland, Israel and the French all neck and neck for the one automatic qualification spot. Having guided the U-21 team to unprecedented success over the previous decade, Domenech seemed the obvious man for the job, but after a year in charge the jury is still out. The domestic scene in France was once again dominated by Olympique Lyonnais who won a fourth consecutive Championship to match the

INTERNATIONAL HONOURS
FIFA World Cup™ 1998   Qualified for the FIFA Women's World Cup finals 2003
Qualified for the FIFA World Cup™ finals 1930 1934 1938 1954 1958 1966 1978 1982 1986 1998 2002
FIFA Junior Tournament 1949   FIFA U-17 World Championship 2001   UEFA European Championship 1984 2000
UEFA U-21 Championship 1988 UEFA U-19 Championship 1983 1996 1997 2000 UEFA U-17 Championship 2004
UEFA Champions League Olympique Marseille 1993

feats of the great Saint-Etienne team of the late 1960s and the Marseille team of the early 1990s; not bad going for a club that had not even won the title before 2002. Even with a number of high profile players based abroad the French League has developed great strength in depth and will only get stronger following the €1.8bn paid by Canal Plus for the rights to televise the League for three years from 2005, a huge increase on the €375m paid for the previous three years. Auxerre won the Coupe de France for the fourth time in 12 years thanks to an injury-time winner from Côte d'Ivoire international Bonaventure Kalou against Second Division Sedan, while Strasbourg won the Coupe de La Ligue for the second time, beating Caen 2-1 in the final. The challenge now for French clubs is to keep the best players and make a sustained push for honours in European football, an area where they have often lagged behind their major rivals. Lyon are proving to be good role models and they had an excellent UEFA Champions League campaign, including an astonishing 10-2 aggregate victory over German champions Werder Bremen, and it was only due to a penalty shoot-out defeat at the hands of PSV that they missed out on a place in the semis.

Fédération Française de Football (FFF)
60 Bis Avenue d'Iéna, Paris 75116, France
Tel +33 1 44317300   Fax +33 1 47208296
www.fff.fr
President: ESCALETTES Jean-Pierre   General Secretary: LAMBERT Jacques Mosnieur
Vice-President: THIRIEZ Frederic   Treasurer: DESUMER Bernard   Media Officer: TOURNON Philippe
Men's Coach: DOMENECH Raymond   Women's Coach: LOISEL Elisabeth
FFF formed: 1919   UEFA: 1954   FIFA: 1904
Colours: Blue, White, Red or White, Blue, Red

GAMES PLAYED BY FRANCE IN THE 2006 FIFA WORLD CUP™ CYCLE

2002	Opponents	Score		Venue	Comp	Scorers	Att	Referee
21-08	Tunisia	D	1-1	Rades	Fr	Silvestre [18]	59 223	Bolognino ITA
7-09	Cyprus	W	2-1	Nicosia	ECq	Cisse [39], Wiltord [53]	14 000	Fandel GER
12-10	Slovenia	W	5-0	Paris	ECq	Vieira [10], Marlet 2 [34 64], Wiltord [79], Govou [85]	77 561	Nielsen DEN
16-10	Malta	W	4-0	Ta'Qali	ECq	Henry 2 [25 35], Wiltord [59], Carriere [84]	10 000	Tudor ROU
20-11	Yugoslavia	W	3-0	Paris	Fr	Carriere 2 [11 49], Kapo [69]	59 958	Iturralde Gonzales ESP
2003								
12-02	Czech Republic	L	0-2	Paris	Fr		57 354	Stark GER
29-03	Malta	W	6-0	Lens	ECq	Wiltord [37], Henry 2 [39 54], Zidane 2 [57p 80], Trezeguet [71]	40 775	Bozinovski MKD
2-04	Israel	W	2-1	Palermo	ECq	Trezeguet [23], Zidane [45]	4 000	Barber ENG
30-04	Egypt	W	5-0	Paris	Fr	Henry 2 [25 34], Pires [46], Cisse [62], Kapo [78]	54 554	Busacca SUI
18-06	Colombia	W	1-0	Lyon	CCr1	Henry [39p]	38 541	Cardoso Batista POR
20-06	Japan	W	2-1	St-Etienne	CCr1	Pires [43p], Govou [65]	33 070	Shield AUS
22-06	New Zealand	W	5-0	Paris	CCr1	Kapo [17], Henry [20], Cisse [71], Giuly [90+1], Pires [90+3]	36 842	Moradi IRN
26-06	Turkey	W	3-2	Paris	CCsf	Henry [11], Pires [26], Wiltord [43]	41 195	Larrionda URU
29-06	Cameroon	W	1-0	Paris	CCf	Henry [97]	51 985	Ivanov RUS
20-08	Switzerland	W	2-0	Geneva	Fr	Wiltord [13], Marlet [55]	30 000	Allaerts BEL
6-09	Cyprus	W	5-0	Paris	ECq	Trezeguet 2 [7 80], Wiltord 2 [19 40], Henry [59]	50 132	Irvine NIR
10-09	Slovenia	W	2-0	Ljubljana	ECq	Trezeguet [9], Dacourt [71]	8 000	Messina ITA
11-10	Israel	W	3-0	Paris	ECq	Henry [9], Trezeguet [25], Boumsong [43]	57 009	Bolognino ITA
15-11	Germany	W	3-0	Gelsenkirchen	Fr	Henry [21], Trezeguet 2 [54 81]	53 574	Farina ITA
2004								
18-02	Belgium	W	2-0	Brussels	Fr	Govou [46], Saha [76]	43 160	Halsey ENG
31-03	Netherlands	D	0-0	Rotterdam	Fr		52 000	Stark GER
20-05	Brazil	D	0-0	Paris	FIFA		79 334	Mejuto Gonzalez ESP
28-05	Andorra	W	4-0	Montpellier	Fr	Wiltord 2 [44 56], Saha [68], Marlet [73]	27 753	Daami TUN
6-06	Ukraine	W	1-0	Paris	Fr	Zidane [87]	66 646	Ceferin SVN
13-06	England	W	2-1	Lisbon	ECr1	Zidane 2 [90 90+3]	65 272	Merk GER
17-06	Croatia	D	2-2	Leiria	ECr1	Tudor OG [22], Trezeguet [64]	29 160	Nielsen DEN
21-06	Switzerland	W	3-1	Coimbra	ECr1	Zidane [20], Henry 2 [76 84]	28 111	Michel SVK
25-06	Greece	L	0-1	Lisbon	ECqf		45 390	Frisk SWE
18-08	Bosnia-Herzegovina	D	1-1	Rennes	Fr	Luyindula [7]	26 527	McDonald SCO
4-09	Israel	D	0-0	Paris	WCq		43 527	Temmink NED
8-09	Faroe Islands	W	2-0	Tórshavn	WCq	Giuly [32], Cisse [73]	5 917	Thomson SCO
9-10	Ireland Republic	D	0-0	Paris	WCq		78 863	Dauden Ibañez ESP
13-10	Cyprus	W	2-0	Nicosia	WCq	Wiltord [38], Henry [72]	3 319	Larsen DEN
17-11	Poland	D	0-0	Paris	Fr		50 480	Benquerença POR
2005								
9-02	Sweden	D	1-1	Paris	Fr	Trezeguet [35]	56 923	Rodriguez Santiago ESP
26-03	Switzerland	D	0-0	Paris	WCq		79 373	De Santis ITA
30-03	Israel	D	1-1	Tel Aviv	WCq	Trezeguet [50]	32 150	Merk GER
31-05	Hungary	W	2-1	Metz	Fr	Cisse [10], Malouda [35]	26 000	Allaerts BEL

Fr = Friendly match • EC = UEFA EURO 2004™ • CC = FIFA Confederations Cup • FIFA = FIFA Centennial match • WC = FIFA World Cup™
q = qualifier • r1 = first round group • qf = quarter-final • sf = semi-final • f = final

FIFA/COCA-COLA WORLD RANKING

1993	1994	1995	1996	1997	1998	1999	2000	2001	2002	2003	2004	High		Low	
15	19	8	3	6	2	3	2	1	2	2	2	**1**	05/01	**25**	04/98

2004-2005											
08/04	09/04	10/04	11/04	12/04	01/05	02/05	03/05	04/05	05/05	06/05	07/05
2	2	2	2	2	2	2	2	4	4	5	7

THE FIFA BIG COUNT OF 2000

	Male	Female		Male	Female
Registered players	795 596	13 338	Referees	25 606	100
Non registered players	1 100 000	21 000	Officials	60 000	500
Youth players	1 042 830	21 659	Total involved	3 080 629	
Total players	2 994 423		Number of clubs	19 835	
Professional players	1 331	0	Number of teams	142 600	

NATIONAL CAPS

	Caps
DESAILLY Marcel	116
DESCHAMPS Didier	103
THURAM Lilian	103
BLANC Laurent	97
LIZARAZU Bixente	97
ZIDANE Zinedine	93
AMOROS Manuel	82
DJORKAEFF Youri	82
PIRES Robert	79
BOSSIS Maxime	76

NATIONAL GOALS

	Goals
PLATINI Michel	41
FONTAINE Just	30
PAPIN Jean-Pierre	30
TREZEGUET David	29
HENRY Thierry	28
DJORKAEFF Youri	28
ZIDANE Zinedine	26
WILTORD Sylvian	23
VINCENT Jean	22
NICOLAS Jean	21

NATIONAL COACH

	Years
BOULOGNE Georges	1969-'73
KOVACS Stefan	1973-'75
HIDALGO Michel	1976-'84
MICHEL Henri	1984-'88
PLATINI Michel	1988-'92
HOULLIER Gérard	1992-'93
JACQUET Aimé	1994-'98
LEMERRE Roger	1998-'02
SANTINI Jacques	2002-'04
DOMENECH Raymond	2004-

FRANCE NATIONAL TEAM RECORDS AND RECORD SEQUENCES

Records			Sequence records					
Victory	10-0	AZE 1995	Wins	14	2003-2004	Clean sheets	11	2003-2004
Defeat	1-17	DEN 1908	Defeats	12	1908-1911	Goals scored	17	1999-2000
Player Caps	116	DESAILLY Marcel	Undefeated	30	1994-1996	Without goal	4	1924-1925, 1986
Player Goals	41	PLATINI Michel	Without win	15	1908-1911	Goals against	24	1905-1912

FIFA REFEREE LIST 2005

	Int'l	DoB
BRE Stephane	1998	29-03-1966
COLOMBO Claude	1995	1-10-1960
COUE Bruno	1999	12-04-1966
DERRIEN Bruno	1999	9-04-1964
DUHAMEL Laurent	1999	10-10-1968
GARIBIAN Pascal	1996	22-03-1961
LAYEC Bertrand	2002	3-07-1965
PICCIRILLO Hervé	2005	6-03-1967
POULAT Eric	1999	8-12-1963
SARS Alain	1993	30-04-1961

FIFA ASSISTANT REFEREE LIST 2005

	Int'l	DoB
ARNAULT Frederic	1997	30-04-1961
BEHAGUE Philippe	2005	19-03-1965
CHAUDRE Jean-Paul	2004	14-02-1965
DAGORNE Lionel	1997	9-07-1961
FAYE Bruno	1998	21-09-1962
IZZO Jean-Philippe	2001	27-04-1963
MARTINEZ Claude	2001	8-09-1964
REINBOLD Patrick	2002	22-04-1962
TEXIER Vincent	1999	25-11-1962
THOISON Christian	2000	11-03-1964

FRANCE COUNTRY INFORMATION

Capital	Paris	Independence	France unified in 486	GDP per Capita	$27 600
Population	60 424 213	Status	Republic	GNP Ranking	5
Area km²	547 030	Language	French	Dialling code	+33
Population density	110 per km²	Literacy rate	99%	Internet code	.r
% in urban areas	73%	Main religion	Christian	GMT + / –	+1
Towns/Cities ('000)	Paris 2 110; Marseille 792; Lyon 463; Toulouse 411; Nice 341; Nantes 284; Strasbourg 273; Montpellier 238, Bordeaux 219; Rennes 213; Reims 192; Lille 189; Le Havre 188; Saint-Etienne 170; Angers 158; Grenoble 154, Toulon 154; Dijon 153; Brest 150, Le Mans 147				
Neighbours (km)	Belgium 620; Luxembourg 73; Germany 451; Switzerland 573; Italy 488; Monaco 4; Spain 623; Andorra 56; North Atlantic & Mediterranean Sea 3 427				
Main stadia	Stade de France – Saint-Denis, Paris 79 959; Vélodrome – Marseille 60 031; Parc des Princes – Paris 48 712; Gerland – Lyon 41 184; De la Beaujoire – Nantes 38 486;				

FRANCE 2004-05

LIGUE 1

	Pl	W	D	L	F	A	Pts	Lyon	Lille	Monaco	Rennes	Marseille	St-Etienne	Lens	Auxerre	PSG	Sochaux	Strasbourg	Nice	Toulouse	Ajaccio	Bordeaux	Metz	Nantes	Caen	Bastia	Istres
Olympique Lyonnais †	38	22	13	3	56	22	79		1-0	0-0	2-1	1-1	3-2	1-0	2-1	0-1	1-1	1-1	1-0	0-0	4-0	2-1	5-1	2-0	2-0	4-0	0-0 2-1
Lille OSC †	38	18	13	7	52	29	67	2-1		1-1	0-0	1-2	1-0	2-1	2-1	2-0	1-0	0-0	1-1	1-0	1-1	0-2	0-0	4-0	2-1	2-0	2-1 8-0
AS Monaco †	38	15	18	5	52	35	63	1-1	2-0		2-0	2-1	1-1	2-0	0-0	2-0	1-3	3-4	0-4	4-1	1-1	2-2	1-1	0-0	2-1	5-2	5-2 2-1
Stade Rennais ‡	38	15	10	13	49	42	55	1-2	0-1	0-0		1-0	2-2	3-1	1-0	2-1	3-4	4-0	4-1	1-1	2-0	2-0	3-1	1-0	1-1	1-0	3-1
Olympique Marseille	38	15	10	13	47	42	55	0-1	3-0	1-3	1-3-1		1-1	2-1	0-1	1-1	0-2	2-0	2-0	1-0	1-1	0-1	1-3	3-1	2-3	1-0	1-1
AS Saint-Etienne	38	12	17	9	47	34	53	2-3	0-0	0-1	1-0	2-0		0-0	3-1	0-0	1-0	1-1	2-1	0-0	3-0	0-0	0-0	0-0	5-0	3-0	2-0
RC Lens	38	13	13	12	45	39	52	0-1	1-1	1-1	5-2	0-0	3-0		3-1	2-2	3-2	2-1	0-0	1-0	1-1	2-0	2-0	2-0	0-1	2-1	0-0
AJ Auxerre ‡	38	14	10	14	48	47	52	0-3	1-3	2-2	3-1	0-0	2-2	3-0		1-1	2-0	0-0	4-3	3-2	1-0	0-0	4-0	2-1	1-0	4-1	0-0
Paris Saint-Germain	38	12	15	11	40	41	51	0-0	1-1	0-1	1-0	2-2	0-2	0-1	1-0		2-2	1-0	3-1	0-0	1-0	1-1	3-0	1-0	2-2	1-0	2-2
Sochaux-Montbéliard	38	13	11	14	42	41	50	0-2	0-2	1-1	3-0	2-0	2-1	1-2	1-2	1-2		1-2	0-0	2-0	1-0	4-0	2-1	1-0	1-0	1-0	1-1
RC Strasbourg ‡	38	12	12	14	42	43	48	0-1	1-2	0-0	1-0	1-0	1-1	2-2	3-1	3-1	0-0		3-1	1-4	1-0	1-0	3-1	0-2	5-0	2-0	1-1
OGC Nice	38	10	16	12	38	45	46	0-1	1-1	2-1	2-0	1-1	2-0	1-1	1-0	1-1	2-1	0-0		1-0	3-0	3-3	1-1	0-0	0-1	1-1	0-0
Toulouse FC	38	12	10	16	36	43	46	0-2	1-0	0-0	0-2	1-3	0-2	0-0	1-2	2-1	0-0	2-0	1-0		3-1	1-0	1-1	2-1	2-3	1-0	2-1
AC Ajaccio	38	10	15	13	36	40	45	1-1	0-0	3-0	1-1	2-0	1-1	0-0	4-3	1-0	3-1	2-2	0-1	1-0		0-0	1-2	1-1	2-2	1-0	0-0
Girondins Bordeaux	38	8	20	10	37	41	44	0-0	1-3	1-1	0-0	3-3	2-0	1-1	0-0	0-0	2-0	2-5	1-1	1-0	0-0		1-0	0-2	2-0	0-2	2-2
FC Metz	38	10	14	14	33	45	44	1-1	1-1	1-1	1-1	0-1	2-2	1-1	3-0	3-2	0-0	1-0	1-1	0-1	0-0	0-0		1-0	1-2	2-0	2-1
FC Nantes	38	10	13	15	33	38	43	2-2	1-3	0-0	2-0	2-2	0-0	1-0	1-1	1-0	2-2	2-1	0-1	2-2	0-0	0-1	1-0		2-0	1-1	1-0
SM Caen	38	10	12	16	36	60	42	1-0	0-0	1-0	2-2	2-3	0-0	2-0	2-0	0-0	2-0	0-0	0-0	0-2	2-2	1-1	0-1	2-1		0-1	1-1
SC Bastia	38	11	8	19	32	48	41	1-1	3-1	0-2	1-1	0-1	0-3	3-1	1-0	1-1	2-1	2-0	2-1	1-0	1-4	1-0	0-0	2-0			2-0
FC Istres	38	6	14	18	25	51	32	0-0	0-2	0-1	0-2	0-2	0-2	0-2	1-0	1-1	2-0	1-1	1-1	1-0	0-1	0-1	0-0	0-1	3-2	1-0	

6/08/2004 - 28/05/2005 • † Qualified for the UEFA Champions League • ‡ Qualified for the UEFA Cup

TOP SCORERS

FREI Alexander	Stade Rennais	20
PAGIS Mickaël	RC Strasbourg	15
PAULETA Pedro	Paris Saint-Germain	14

FRANCE 2004-05

LIGUE 2

	Pl	W	D	L	F	A	Pts	Nancy	Le Mans	Troyes	Dijon	Chat'roux	Sedan	Guingamp	Montpellier	Brest	Lorient	Grenoble	Gueugnon	Amiens	Laval	Créteil	Reims	Le Havre	Clermont	Angers	Niort
AS Nancy-Lorraine	38	21	8	9	54	33	71		1-3	1-0	2-0	1-1	1-2	2-1	1-0	2-0	1-0	2-0	1-0	1-2	2-0	1-0	2-1	3-1	1-0	2-1	3-1 3-1
Le Mans	38	20	8	10	51	30	68	1-2		2-3	2-1	0-2	3-0	0-0	2-0	1-1	3-1	1-0	1-2	1-1	3-0	1-0	0-0	1-0	2-2	3-0	1-0
Troyes	38	20	8	10	61	48	68	2-1	2-0		2-2	5-5	2-1	1-1	2-1	2-0	1-2	2-2	1-0	0-0	0-2	2-1	2-0	2-1	1-0	4-1	1-1
Dijon FCO	38	14	15	9	44	34	57	0-1	0-2	1-1		3-0	1-0	1-1	1-0	2-2	0-0	2-1	0-0	2-1	0-0	1-0	0-0	0-0	2-2	1-0	2-1
Châteauroux	38	14	15	9	51	43	57	0-0	1-3	3-1	2-1		0-0	2-0	2-0	1-2	1-1	0-1	0-1	1-0	1-0	1-0	1-0	1-0	4-1	1-1	1-1 2-0
CS Sedan Ardennes	38	16	9	13	38	38	57	2-0	1-2	2-1	0-1	2-1		3-0	2-0	0-0	3-2	1-2	3-0	0-1	0-3	1-0	2-0	1-0	2-0	1-0	0-0-0
En Avant Guingamp	38	15	11	12	53	43	56	0-0	2-1	0-1	0-1	2-0	4-0		3-1	1-2	1-1	3-1	2-0	2-1	2-1	2-0	2-0	1-0	3-1	1-0	3-1
Montpellier HSC	38	15	10	13	44	39	55	1-1	2-0	3-4	4-2	0-0	0-1	1-1		1-0	0-1	3-1	1-1	0-2	3-1	0-0	0-3	0-0	1-0	2-1	2-0
Stade Brestois	38	13	16	9	38	34	55	3-2	1-0	1-1	1-1	0-0	2-0	2-2	1-1		0-0	1-0	0-1	1-2	1-1	0-4	2-2	1-0	2-1	1-2	3-1
FC Lorient	38	14	8	16	47	51	50	1-1	1-2	1-2	0-2	2-1	2-1	1-1	1-2	3-0		2-0	3-2	1-2	1-1	3-1	3-1	2-0	1-0	1-2	3-1
Grenoble Foot	38	12	12	14	45	50	48	1-1	2-1	1-2	1-3	2-0	0-0	4-2	0-0	0-2	1-2		2-1	1-1	2-1	1-1	2-0	2-1	1-0	0-0	5-1
FC Gueugnon	38	12	12	14	30	40	48	0-2	0-0	1-2	0-1	1-3	3-2	0-0	2-1	1-2	1-0	1-1		1-1	0-1	1-1	0-2	1-0	2-1	0-2	4-1
Amiens SC	38	11	14	13	41	41	47	0-3	0-0	3-2	2-1	2-2	1-2	1-1	2-0	1-0	0-0	0-2	4-0		2-1	0-0	1-1	1-2	1-1	0-2	4-1
Stade Lavallois	38	13	8	17	43	51	47	1-2	1-2	2-1	2-1	2-3	2-2	1-0	1-3	2-1	0-0	3-1	1-0	1-0		0-0	1-2	0-1	4-3	1-1	1-0
US Créteil-Lusitanos	38	11	13	14	42	38	46	2-1	1-0	0-1	1-1	3-1	2-0	1-1	3-3	2-3	2-0	0-0	3-0	1-0	3-1		4-0	0-2	1-2	0-0	0-1
Stade de Reims	38	10	13	15	34	55	43	0-4	0-1	2-0	0-5	1-1	0-3	2-0	0-0	1-4	1-1	2-1	0-0	2-0	2-1			3-0	3-0	1-0	1-2
Le Havre AC	38	11	9	18	28	42	42	0-0	0-1	1-0	0-1	0-0	0-2	2-0	1-0	0-3	1-2	1-1	1-0	1-1	1-3	1-1			0-0	0-0	1-2
Clermont Foot	38	8	15	15	34	39	39	0-0	0-1	3-0	2-0	0-1	2-1	0-0	0-0	2-0	0-5	0-0	2-1	1-0	0-3	1-0	0-0-1			0-0	2-0
Angers SCO	38	8	14	16	32	44	38	1-1	0-2	2-1	2-2	1-2	2-2	1-0	0-1	2-0	0-0	1-3	2-0	1-1	3-2	0-1	1-3	3-0	2-1		1-2
Chamois Niortais	38	9	8	21	38	55	35	1-2	0-3	0-1	0-0	0-3	1-0	0-1	1-1	4-0	1-3	1-1	3-1	2-2	0-2	2-0	1-6	1-0	2-0	0-0	

6/08/2004 - 27/05/2005

COUPE DE FRANCE 2004-05

Seventh Round

Team	Score
AJ Auxerre	1
Calais *	0
Tarbes *	0
Vannes	3
Girondins Bordeaux *	2
FC Istres	0
Langueux *	1
Paris Saint-Germain	6
FC Nantes	3
Cournon *	0
Paris FC	2 3p
Saumur *	2 4p
Blois Foot 41	1
Epinal *	0
Avranches	0
Boulogne *	1
Sochaux-Montbéliard *	1
SC Bastia	0
Rodez *	1
FC Metz	2
Angers SCO	3
Olympique Marseille *	2
Troyes *	1
Albi	3
OGC Nice	4
Beauvais *	0
Schiltigheim *	0
Stade de Reims	2
AC Ajaccio	1 5p
AS Nancy Lorraine *	1 4p
AS Saint-Etienne	2
Nîmes Olympique	3
AS Monaco	7
Seyssinet-Pariset	0
Niort *	0
Libourne-Saint-Seurin	1
SM Caen	2
Mulhouse *	0
Brest	0
Stade Rennais *	1
Olympique Lyonnais	2
Viry-Châtillon *	0
Gambsheim	0
Toulouse	3
Toulon *	3
Montceau	0
Vesoul *	1 5p
Clermont Foot	1 6p
Grenoble Foot	3
Châteauroux *	2
Menton	0 1p
Rhône Vallée *	0 3p
RC Lens	4
Saint-Dizier *	0
Le Mans	1
Lille OSC *	2
Quevilly US *	1
En Avant Guingamp	0
Haguenau *	1
Romorantin	2
Inzinzac Montagnarde *	2
Pontivy	0
RC Strasbourg	1
CS Sedan Ardennes *	3

Eighth Round

Team	Score
AJ Auxerre	2
Vannes OC *	0
Girondins Bordeaux	1
Paris Saint-Germain *	3
FC Nantes	2
Saumur*	0
Blois Foot 41	0
Boulogne *	4
Sochaux-Montbéliard	1
FC Metz *	0
Angers SCO	0
Albi *	2
OGC Nice *	3
Stade de Reims	1
AC Ajaccio	1 3p
Nîmes Olympique *	1 4p
AS Monaco	4
Libourne-Saint-Seurin *	2
SM Caen	0
Stade Rennais *	2
Olympique Lyonnais	2
Toulouse *	1
Toulon	0
Clermont Foot *	1
Grenoble Foot	2
Rhône Vallée *	1
RC Lens	2
Lille OSC *	3
Quevilly US	1
Romorantin *	0
Inzinzac Mont	0
CS Sedan Ardennes *	4

Round of 16

Team	Score
AJ Auxerre *	3
Paris Saint-Germain	2
FC Nantes	2
Boulogne *	3
Sochaux-Montbéliard	3
Albi *	0
OGC Nice	0
Nîmes Olympique *	4
AS Monaco	1
Stade Rennais *	0
Olympique Lyonnais	1 3p
Clermont Foot *	1 4p
Grenoble Foot	3
Lille OSC *	1
Quevilly US	0
CS Sedan Ardennes *	2

* Home team

COUPE DE FRANCE 2004-05

Quarter-finals   **Semi-finals**   **Final**

AJ Auxerre	2
Boulogne *	1

AJ Auxerre	2
Nîmes Olympique	1

Sochaux-Montbéliard	3
Nîmes Olympique *	4

AJ Auxerre ‡	2
CS Sedan Ardennes	1

AS Monaco *	1
Clermont Foot	0

AS Monaco	0
CS Sedan Ardennes	1

Grenoble Foot	1
CS Sedan Ardennes *	2

COUPE DE FRANCE FINAL 2005

Stade de France, Saint-Denis, Paris, 4-06-2005, Att: 77,617, Referee: Derrien

AJ Auxerre	2	Mwaruwari 37, Kalou 93+
CS Sedan Ardennes	1	Noro 64

Auxerre: Fabien Cool; Jean-Sebastien Jaures, Johan Radet (Bacary Sagna 61), Jean-Pascal Mignot, Younes Kaboul; Yann Lachuer (Bonaventure Kalou 71), Philippe Violeau, Benoît Cheyrou, Lionel Mathis; Kanga Akale, Benjamin Mwaruwari. Tr: Guy Roux
Sedan: Patrick Regnault; Jeremy Henin, Johann Charpenet, Pierre Njanka (A Budak 90), David Ducourtioux; Nadir Belhadj, Didier Neumann, Stéphane Noro, Mickael Citony, Laurent Gagnier, Marcus Mokake. Tr: Serge Romano

‡ Qualified for the UEFA Cup

COUPE DE LA LIGUE 2004-05

Round of 16		Quarter-finals		Semi-finals		Final	
RC Strasbourg *	1 4p						
Lille OSC	1 2p	RC Strasbourg *	3				
Dijon FCO	0	Clermont Foot	2				
Clermont Foot *	4			RC Strasbourg *	1		
RC Lens	1			AS Saint-Etienne	0		
SC Bastia *	0	RC Lens *	0				
Le Havre AC *	0	AS Saint-Etienne	3				
AS Saint-Etienne	1					RC Strasbourg ‡	2
AS Monaco *	1					SM Caen	1
En Avant Guingamp	0	AS Monaco	2				
Paris Saint-Germain	0	Montpellier HSC *	1				
Montpellier HSC *	1			AS Monaco	1		
AJ Auxerre *	2			SM Caen *	3		
FC Nantes	1	AJ Auxerre *	1 5p				
Sochaux-Montbéliard *	0 3p	SM Caen	1 6p				
SM Caen	0 4p						

* Home team • ‡ Qualified for the UEFA Cup

LEAGUE CUP FINAL
30-04-2005, Att: 78 721, Ref: Veissiere
Stade de France, Saint-Denis, Paris
Scorers - Niang 38, Devaux 79 for
Strasbourg; Mazure 42 for Caen

CLUB DIRECTORY

Club	Town/City	Stadium	Phone	www.	Lge	Cup	CL
AC Ajaccio	Ajaccio	François Coty 8 927	+33 4 95503252	ac-ajaccio.com	0	0	0
AJ Auxerre	Auxerre	Abbe Deschamps 23 493	+33 3 86723232	aja.fr	1	4	0
SC Bastia	Bastia	Furiani 11 460	+33 4 95300088	sc-bastia.com	0	1	0
Girondins Bordeaux	Bordeaux	Chaban Delmas 34 462	+33 892 683433	girondins.com	5	3	0
SM Caen	Caen	Michel d'Ornano 22 816	+33 2 31291600	smcaen.fr	0	0	0
FC Istres	Istres	Stade Parsemain 17 170	+33 4 42491366	fcistres.com	0	0	0
Racing Club Lens	Lens	Felix Bollaert 41 649	+33 3 21132132	rclens.fr	1	0	0
Lille OSC	Lille	Métropole 18 185	+33 892 685672	losc.fr	2	5	0
Olympique Lyonnais	Lyon	Stade Gerland 41 044	+33 4 72767604	olweb.fr	4	3	0
Olympique Marseille	Marseille	Stade Velodrome 60 031	+33 4 91765609	om.net	9	10	1
FC Metz	Metz	Stade Symphorien 26 661	+33 3 87667215	fcmetz.com	0	2	0
AS Monaco	Monaco	Stade Louis II 18 523	+377 92057473	asm-fc.com	7	5	0
FC Nantes Atlantique	Nantes	Stade Beaujoire 38 128	+33 892 707963	fcna.fr	8	3	0
OGC Nice	Nice	Stade du Ray 18 049	+33 892 700238	ogcnice.com	4	3	0
Paris Saint-Germain	Paris	Parc des Princes 48 527	+33 1 47437171	psg.fr	2	6	0
Stade Rennais	Rennes	Parc des Sports 31 127	+33 820 000035	staderennais.com	0	2	0
AS Saint-Etienne	Saint-Etienne	Geoffroy-Guichard 35 616	+33 4 77923170	asse.fr	10	6	0
FC Sochaux	Montbeliard	Stade Bonal 20 005	+33 3 81997000	fcsochaux.fr	2	1	0
Racing Club Strasbourg	Strasbourg	Stade Meinau 27 000	+33 3 88445500	rcstrasbourg.fr	1	3	0
Toulouse FC	Toulouse	Stadium 36 580	+33 892 700831	tfc.info	0	0	0

RECENT LEAGUE AND CUP RECORD

	Championship						Cup		
Year	Champions	Pts	Runners-up	Pts	Third	Pts	Winners	Score	Runners-up
1990	Olympique Marseille	53	Girondins Bordeaux	51	AS Monaco	46	SCP Montpellier	2-1	Racing Club Paris
1991	Olympique Marseille	55	AS Monaco	51	AJ Auxerre	48	AS Monaco	1-0	Olympique Marseille
1992	Olympique Marseille	58	AS Monaco	52	Paris St-Germain	47	Unfinished due to Bastia disaster		
1993	Olympique Marseille	55	Paris St-Germain	51	AS Monaco	51	Paris St-Germain	3-0	FC Nantes
1994	Paris St-Germain	59	Olympique Marseille	51	AJ Auxerre	46	AJ Auxerre	3-0	Montpellier HSC
1995	FC Nantes	79	Olympique Lyonnais	69	Paris St-Germain	67	Paris St-Germain	1-0	RC Strasbourg
1996	AJ Auxerre	72	Paris St-Germain	68	AS Monaco	68	AJ Auxerre	2-1	Nîmes Olympique
1997	AS Monaco	79	Paris St-Germain	67	FC Nantes	64	OGC Nice	1-1 4-3p	Guingamp
1998	Racing Club Lens	68	FC Metz	68	AS Monaco	59	Paris St-Germain	2-1	Racing Club Lens
1999	Girondins Bordeaux	72	Olympique Marseille	71	Olympique Lyonnais	63	FC Nantes	1-0	CS Sedan Ardennes
2000	AS Monaco	65	Paris St-Germain	58	Olympique Lyonnais	56	FC Nantes	2-1	Calais
2001	FC Nantes	68	Olympique Lyonnais	64	Lille OSC	59	RC Strasbourg	0-0 5-4p	Amiens SC
2002	Olympique Lyonnais	66	Racing Club Lens	64	AJ Auxerre	59	FC Lorient	1-0	SC Bastia
2003	Olympique Lyonnais	68	AS Monaco	67	Olympique Marseille	65	AJ Auxerre	2-1	Paris St-Germain
2004	Olympique Lyonnais	79	Paris St-Germain	76	AS Monaco	75	Paris St-Germain	1-0	Châteauroux
2005	Olympique Lyonnais	79	Lille OSC	67	AS Monaco	63	AJ Auxerre	2-1	CS Sedan

OLYMPIQUE LYONNAIS

Date	Opponents	Score			Scorers	Att
6-08-2004	OGC Nice	W 1-0	A	Lge	De Souza [76]	14 096
14-08-2004	FC Sochaux-Montbéliard	D 1-1	H	Lge	Ribeiro Reis [70p]	38 041
22-08-2004	FC Metz	D 1-1	A	Lge	Balmont [66]	23 317
28-08-2004	Lille OSC	W 1-0	H	Lge	Frau [8]	34 107
11-09-2004	Stade Rennais	W 2-1	A	Lge	Da Silva 2 [80 87]	23 273
15-09-2004	Manchester United - ENG	D 2-2	H	CLgD	Cris [35], Frau [45]	36 000
18-09-2004	SC Bastia	D 0-0	H	Lge		33 826
21-09-2004	Toulouse FC	W 2-0	A	Lge	Essien [51], Malouda [87]	30 616
25-09-2004	AS Monaco	D 0-0	H	Lge		38 825
28-09-2004	Sparta Praha - CZE	W 2-1	A	CLgD	Essien [25], Wiltord [58]	12 050
3-10-2004	AS Saint-Etienne	W 3-2	A	Lge	Ribeiro Reis 2 [36 85], Govou [90]	34 793
15-10-2004	SM Caen	W 4-0	H	Lge	Diarra [12], Malouda [16], Essien [34], Frau [70p]	33 816
19-10-2004	Fenerbahçe - TUR	W 3-1	A	CLgD	Juninho [55], Cris [66], Frau [87]	43 000
23-10-2004	FC Istres	D 0-0	A	Lge		10 197
30-10-2004	RC Strasbourg	W 1-0	H	Lge	Frau [56]	38 220
3-11-2004	Fenerbahçe - TUR	W 4-2	H	CLgD	Essien [22], Malouda [53], Nilmar 2 [90 90]	36 000
6-11-2004	Racing Club Lens	W 1-0	A	Lge	Itandje OG [35]	39 070
10-11-2004	Lille OSC	L 2-3	A	LCr2	Abidal [89], Ben Arfa [101]	15 015
13-11-2004	FC Nantes	W 2-0	H	Lge	Frau [46], Govou [58]	35 556
19-11-2004	Paris Saint-Germain	D 0-0	A	Lge		42 478
23-11-2004	Manchester United - ENG	L 1-2	A	CLgD	Diarra [40]	66 398
27-11-2004	AJ Auxerre	W 2-1	H	Lge	Wiltord [5], Juninho [28]	37 933
4-12-2004	AC Ajaccio	D 1-1	A	Lge	Juninho [88]	2 792
8-12-2004	Sparta Praha - CZE	W 5-0	H	CLgD	Essien [7], Nilmar 2 [19 51], Idanger [53], Bergougnoux [90]	40 000
11-12-2004	Girondins Bordeaux	D 0-0	A	Lge		31 832
17-12-2004	Olympique Marseille	D 1-1	H	Lge	Govou [39]	38 728
8-01-2005	Viry-Chatillon	W 2-0	A	CDFr1	Juninho [27], Nilmar [66]	17 249
12-01-2005	FC Sochaux-Montbéliard	W 2-0	A	Lge	Bergougnoux [6], Diarra [41]	17 249
15-01-2005	FC Metz	W 2-0	H	Lge	Juninho [84], Bergougnoux [87]	38 909
23-01-2005	Lille OSC	L 1-2	A	Lge	Juninho [74p]	14 899
26-01-2005	Stade Rennais	W 2-1	H	Lge	Bergougnoux [43], Govou [44]	37 276
1-02-2005	SC Bastia	D 1-1	A	Lge	Essien [19]	4 419
5-02-2005	Toulouse FC	W 4-0	H	Lge	Juninho 2 [2 52], Malouda [45], Bergougnoux [57]	37 447
13-02-2005	Toulouse FC	W 2-1	A	CDFr2	Wiltord [65], Diarra [78p]	17 188
18-02-2005	AS Monaco	D 1-1	A	Lge	Clement [90]	
23-02-2005	Werder Bremen - GER	W 3-0	H	CLr2	Wiltord [9], Diarra [77], Juninho [80]	36 923
26-02-2005	Saint-Etienne	W 3-2	H	Lge	Wiltord [45], Malouda [47], Frau [49]	38 915
1-03-2005	Clermont Foot	D 1-1	A	CDFr3	Wiltord [94+]. L 3-4p	
4-03-2005	SM Caen	L 0-1	A	Lge		20 649
8-03-2005	Werder Bremen - GER	W 7-2	H	CLr2	Wiltord 3 [8 55 64], Essien 2 [17 30], Malouda [60], Berthod [80]	37 000
12-03-2005	FC Istres	W 2-1	H	Lge	Juninho [20], Govou [78]	37 299
19-03-2005	RC Strasbourg	W 1-0	A	Lge	Wiltord [59]	22 442
2-04-2005	RC Lens	W 1-0	H	Lge	Juninho [64]	37 669
5-04-2005	PSV Eindhoven - NED	D 1-1	A	CLqf	Malouda [12]	35 000
9-04-2005	FC Nantes	D 2-2	A	Lge	Frau 2 [36 83]	33 726
13-04-2005	PSV Eindhoven - NED	D 1-1	A	CLqf	Wiltord [10]. L 2-4p	35 000
17-04-2005	Paris Saint-Germain	L 0-1	H	Lge		37 864
24-04-2005	AJ Auxerre	W 3-0	A	Lge	Juninho [26], Essien [45], Cris [55]	14 532
8-05-2005	AC Ajaccio	W 2-1	H	Lge	Govou [36], Cacapa [64]	38 946
15-05-2005	Girondins Bordeaux	W 5-1	H	Lge	Malouda [24], Cris 2 [34 45], Govou 2 [67 84]	38 954
21-05-2005	Olympique Marseille	W 1-0	A	Lge	Juninho [55]	57 041
28-05-2005	OGC Nice	D 0-0	H	Lge		40 352

Lge = Ligue 1 • CDF = Coupe de France • LC = Coupe de la Ligue • CL = UEFA Champions League
gD = Group D • r1 = first round • r2 = second round • r3 = third round • qf = quarter-final

LEAGUE CUP FINALS

Year	Winners	Score	Runners-up
1995	Paris St-Germain	2-0	SC Bastia
1996	FC Metz	0-0 5-4p	Olympique Lyonnais
1997	RC Strasbourg	0-0 6-5p	Girondins Bordeaux
1998	Paris St-Germain	2-2 4-2p	Girondins Bordeaux
1999	RC Lens	1-0	FC Metz
2000	Gueugnon	2-0	Paris St-Germain
2001	Olympique Lyonnais	2-1	AS Monaco
2002	Girondins Bordeaux	3-0	FC Lorient
2003	AS Monaco	4-1	FC Sochaux
2004	FC Sochaux	1-1 5-4p	FC Nantes
2005	RC Strasbourg	2-1	SM Caen

FRO – FAROE ISLANDS

NATIONAL TEAM RECORD
JULY 1ST 2002 TO JUNE 30TH 2005

PL	W	D	L	F	A	%
20	4	2	14	21	50	25

FIFA/COCA-COLA WORLD RANKING

1993	1994	1995	1996	1997	1998	1999	2000	2001	2002	2003	2004	High		Low	
115	133	120	135	117	125	112	117	117	114	126	131	104	07/99	139	04/97

2004-2005											
08/04	09/04	10/04	11/04	12/04	01/05	02/05	03/05	04/05	05/05	06/05	07/05
137	137	135	130	131	132	132	133	133	133	128	126

The opening of the US$2m national association headquarters as part of a renovated National Stadium in Tórshavn has seen the return of international football to the Faroe Islands' capital with fixtures now shared with the Svangaskard in Toftir. Unfortunately results haven't improved with the national team involved in a dog fight with Cyprus to avoid finishing bottom of their 2006 FIFA World Cup™ qualifying group. It was never going to be easy in a tough group containing France, the Republic of Ireland, Israel and Switzerland but coach Henrik Larsen will be disappointed not to have had more of an influence as to how this extremely tight group has progressed. The fact

INTERNATIONAL HONOURS
None

remains, however, that since that historic win against Austria in the qualifiers for Euro 92, the Faroe Islands have only ever won competitive internationals against fellow minnows such as Malta, San Marino and Luxembourg. The 2004 League was won in style by HB Tórshavn who, after losing the first match in the campaign, went the rest of the season undefeated to finish well clear of neighbours B'36 and win a hat-trick of titles. The 2005 Cup was won by GI Gotu at the end of July when they beat IF Fuglafjørdur in the final but by then it was too late to be entered for the UEFA Cup but they do have the first confirmed place for the 2006-07 tournament!

THE FIFA BIG COUNT OF 2000

	Male	Female		Male	Female
Registered players	1 406	208	Referees	97	0
Non registered players	1 800	200	Officials	865	125
Youth players	3 317	954	Total involved	8 972	
Total players	7 885		Number of clubs	40	
Professional players	0	0	Number of teams	309	

The Faroe Islands' Football Association (FSF)
Gundadalur, PO Box 3028, Tórshavn 110, Faroe Islands
Tel +298 351979   Fax +298 319079
fsf@football.fo   www.football.fo
President: HOLM Oli   General Secretary: MIKLADAL Isak
Vice-President: A LIDARENDA Niklas   Treasurer: TBD   Media Officer: MIKLADAL Isak
Men's Coach: LARSEN Henrik   Women's Coach: HANSEN Alvur
FSF formed: 1979   UEFA: 1988   FIFA: 1988
Colours: White, Blue, White

GAMES PLAYED BY FAROE ISLANDS IN THE 2006 FIFA WORLD CUP™ CYCLE

2002 Opponents	Score		Venue	Comp	Scorers	Att	Referee
21-08 Liechtenstein	W	3-1	Tórshavn	Fr	Jacobsen.JR [70], Benjaminsen [75], Johnsson.J [84]	3 200	Orrason ISL
7-09 Scotland	D	2-2	Toftir	ECq	Petersen.J 2 [7] [13]	4 000	Granat POL
12-10 Lithuania	L	0-2	Kaunas	ECq		2 500	Delevic YUG
16-10 Germany	L	1-2	Hannover	ECq	Friedrich OG [45]	36 628	Koren ISR
2003							
27-04 Kazakhstan	W	3-2	Toftir	Fr	Borg [17]p, Petersen.J [45], Lakjuni [49]	420	Jakobsson ISL
29-04 Kazakhstan	W	2-1	Tórshavn	Fr	Flotum [65], Johnsson.J [75]	800	Bergmann ISL
7-06 Iceland	L	1-2	Reykjavik	ECq	Jacobsen.R [62]	6 038	Liba CZE
11-06 Germany	L	0-2	Tórshavn	ECq		6 130	Wegereef NED
20-08 Iceland	L	1-2	Toftir	ECq	Jacobsen.R [65]	3 416	Iturralde Gonzalez ESP
6-09 Scotland	L	1-3	Glasgow	ECq	Johnsson.J [35]	40 901	Ceferin SVN
10-09 Lithuania	L	1-3	Toftir	ECq	Olsen [43]	2 175	Trivkovic CRO
2004							
21-02 Poland	L	0-6	San Fernando	Fr		100	Cascales ESP
1-06 Netherlands	L	0-3	Lausanne	Fr		3 200	Leuba SUI
18-08 Malta	W	3-2	Toftir	Fr	Borg [20], Petersen.J [35], Benjaminsen [77]	1 932	Laursen DEN
4-09 Switzerland	L	0-6	Basel	WCq		11 880	Tudor ROU
8-09 France	L	0-2	Tórshavn	WCq		5 917	Thomson SCO
9-10 Cyprus	D	2-2	Nicosia	WCq	Jorgensen.CB [21], Jacobsen.R [43]	1 400	Gadiyev AZE
13-10 Ireland Republic	L	0-2	Dublin	WCq		36 000	Lajuks LVA
2005							
4-06 Switzerland	L	1-3	Toftir	WCq	Jacobsen.R [70]	2 047	Gumienny BEL
8-06 Ireland Republic	L	0-2	Tórshavn	WCq		5 180	Guenov BUL

Fr = Friendly match • EC = UEFA EURO 2004™ • WC = FIFA World Cup™ • q = qualifier

NATIONAL CAPS

	Caps
JOHANNESEN Oli	72
KNUDSEN Jens-Martin	63
JOHNSSON Julian	61
PETERSEN John	57
MORKORE Allan	54
HANSEN Ossur	51
HANSEN Jens Kristian	44
JÓNSSON Todi	43

NATIONAL GOALS

	Goals
JÓNSSON Todi	9
ARGE Uni	8
PETERSEN John	6
JACOBSEN Rógvi	6
JOHNSSON Julian	4
MULLER Jan Allan	4
MORKORE Kurt	3
HANSEN Jens Kristian	3

NATIONAL COACH

	Years
GUDLAUGSSON Páll	1993
NORDBUD Jogvan	1993
SIMONSEN Allan	1994-'02
LARSEN Henrik	2002-

FIFA REFEREE LIST 2005

	Int'l	DoB
ISAKSEN Lassin	1996	22-01-1961

FIFA ASSISTANT REFEREE LIST 2005

	Int'l	DoB
FREDERIKSEN Jon	1994	26-06-1964
OLSEN Tummas	1997	30-03-1960
SIMONSEN Jens Albert	2000	20-02-1974

FAROE ISLANDS COUNTRY INFORMATION

Capital	Tórshavn	Independence	Self governing division of	GDP per Capita	$22 000
Population	46 662	Status	the Kingdom of Denmark	GNP Ranking	n/a
Area km²	1 399	Language	Faroese, Danish	Dialling code	+298
Population density	33 per km²	Literacy rate	99%	Internet code	.fo
% in urban areas	n/a	Main religion	Christian	GMT + / –	0
Towns/Cities ('000)	Tórshavn 13; Klaksvik 4; Hoyvik 2; Argir 1; Fuglafjørdur 1; Vágur 1; Tvøroyri 1				
Neighbours (km)	North Atlantic Ocean 1 117				
Main stadia	Svangaskard – Toftir 7 000; Gundadalur – Tórshavn 8 020; Tórsvøllur – Tórshavn 7 000				

FAROE ISLANDS NATIONAL TEAM RECORDS AND RECORD SEQUENCES

Records			Sequence records				
Victory	3-0	SMR 1995	Wins	2	1997, 2002, 2003	Clean sheets	1
Defeat	0-9	ISL 1985	Defeats	13	1992-1995	Goals scored	5	1986
Player Caps	72	JOHANNESEN Oli	Undefeated	3	2002	Without goal	7	1991-1992
Player Goals	9	JONSSON Todi	Without win	26	1990-1995	Goals against	26	1990-1995

FAROE ISLANDS 2004

1. DEILD

	Pl	W	D	L	F	A	Pts	HB	B'36	Skála	KI	EB	NSI	VB	GI	IF	B'68
HB Tórshavn †	18	12	5	1	47	18	41		1-0	4-1	1-1	3-0	1-0	2-1	3-3	4-2	7-1
B'36 Tórshavn ‡	18	10	4	4	37	21	34	2-5		2-0	2-2	4-0	1-1	3-1	0-2	4-1	6-2
Skála	18	9	3	6	32	23	30	3-1	2-0		1-2	2-3	1-2	1-0	4-0	4-3	2-1
KI Klaksvík	18	6	8	4	25	24	26	1-1	0-1	1-1		2-2	1-0	0-0	1-1	3-2	1-0
EB/Streymur Eidi	18	7	4	7	30	25	25	0-0	0-2	0-1	4-0		2-0	1-1	1-1	7-0	2-1
NSI Runavík	18	7	4	7	28	25	25	2-2	1-2	2-0	3-1	1-0		1-1	2-1	1-2	3-2
VB Vágur	18	7	4	7	27	24	25	0-2	1-1	0-0	2-0	2-1	3-1		2-4	3-1	2-3
GI Gøtu	18	6	5	7	31	35	23	1-3	0-3	1-1	1-2	1-3	1-1	2-4		3-2	5-2
IF Fuglafjørdur	18	3	3	12	25	51	12	0-2	2-2	1-4	1-6	1-1	4-2	1-0	1-2		1-1
B'68 Toftir	18	2	2	14	19	55	8	0-5	0-2	0-4	1-1	2-4	0-5	1-3	0-2	2-0	

21/04/2004 - 2/10/2004 • † Qualified for the UEFA Champions League • ‡ Qualified for the UEFA Cup

FAROE ISLANDS 2004 — 2. DEILD

	Pl	W	D	L	F	A	Pts
TB Tvøroyri	18	12	2	4	47	24	38
B'71 Sandur	18	12	2	4	51	31	38
AB Argir	18	11	2	5	33	25	35
LIF Leirvík	18	8	5	5	30	28	29
Royn Hvalba	18	9	1	8	40	40	28
FS Vágar	18	8	3	7	56	39	27
Sumba	18	6	4	8	25	32	22
B'36 Tórshavn	18	5	3	10	28	49	18
KI Klaksvík	18	3	4	11	26	39	13
VB Vágur	18	1	4	13	19	48	7

Relegation play-off: B'71 Sandur 1-0 1-5 IF Fuglafjørdur

FFA CUP 2005

Quarter-finals		Semi-finals		Final	
GI Gøtu	3				
Skála	1	GI Gøtu	5 2		
TB Tvøroyri	2	B'71 Sandur	1 1		
B'71 Sandur	4			GI Gøtu	4
B'68 Toftir	2			IF Fuglafjørdur	1
Fram	1	B'68 Toftir	1 0		
HB Tórshavn	0	IF Fuglafjørdur	2 1	29-07-2005, Tórshavn
IF Fuglafjørdur	1				

CLUB DIRECTORY

Club	Town/City	Stadium	Phone	www.	Lge	Cup	CL
B'36 (Fótbóltsfelagid B'36)	Tórshavn	Gundadalur 8 020	+298 311936	b36.fo	7	3	0
EB/Streymur	Oyrabakki	Molini 1 000	+298 508090	eb-streymur.fo	0	0	0
GI (Gøtu Itróttarfelag)	Gøtu	Serpugerdi 3 000	+298 220818	gigotu.fo	6	5	0
HB (Havnar Bóltfelag)	Tórshavn	Gundadalur 8 020	+298 314046	hb.fo	18	14	0
IF (Itróttarfelag Fuglarfjørdur)	Fuglafjørdur	Fuglafjørdur 3 000	+298 444636	if.fo	1	0	0
KI (Klaksvikar Itróttarfelag)	Klaksvik	Klaksvik 4 000	+298 456184	ki-klaksvik.fo	16	4	0
NSI (Nes Soknar Itróttarfelag)	Runavik	Runavik 2 000	+298 449909	nsi.fo	0	2	0
Skála	Skali	Skali 1 000	+298 441574		0	0	0
TB (Tvøroyrar Bóltfelag)	Tvøroyri	Sevmyri 3 000	+298 371570	tb.fo	8	4	0
VB (Vágs Bóltfelag)	Vágur	Vestri a Eidinum 3 000	+298 373679	vb1905.fo	1	1	0

RECENT LEAGUE AND CUP RECORD

	Championship						Cup		
Year	Champions	Pts	Runners-up	Pts	Third	Pts	Winners	Score	Runners-up
1996	GI Gøta	39	KI Klaksvík	39	HB Tórshavn	32	GI Gøta	2-2 5-3	HB Tórshavn
1997	B'36 Tórshavn	48	HB Tórshavn	41	GI Gøta	35	GI Gøta	6-0	VB Vágur
1998	HB Tórshavn	45	KI Klaksvík	38	B'36 Tórshavn	37	HB Tórshavn	2-0	KI Klaksvík
1999	KI Klaksvík	41	GI Gøta	39	B'36 Tórshavn	38	KI Klaksvík	3-1	B'36 Tórshavn
2000	VB Vágur	40	HB Tórshavn	38	B'68 Tórshavn	31	GI Gøta	1-0	HB Tórshavn
2001	B'36 Tórshavn	46	GI Gøta	42	B'68 Tórshavn	31	B'36 Tórshavn	1-0	KI Klaksvík
2002	HB Tórshavn	41	NSI Runavik	36	KI Klaksvík	33	NSI Runavik	2-1	HB Tórshavn
2003	HB Tórshavn	41	B'36 Tórshavn	37	B'68 Tórshavn	35	B'36 Tórshavn	3-1	GI Gøta
2004	HB Tórshavn	41	B'36 Tórshavn	34	Skála	30	HB Tórshavn	3-1	NSI Runavik

GAB – GABON

NATIONAL TEAM RECORD
JULY 1ST 2002 TO JUNE 30TH 2005

PL	W	D	L	F	A	%
33	11	9	13	44	34	47

FIFA/COCA-COLA WORLD RANKING FOR GABON

1993	1994	1995	1996	1997	1998	1999	2000	2001	2002	2003	2004	High		Low	
60	64	67	46	63	82	74	89	102	121	111	109	45	01/96	125	05/03

2004-2005											
08/04	09/04	10/04	11/04	12/04	01/05	02/05	03/05	04/05	05/05	06/05	07/05
123	124	119	113	109	112	107	106	106	106	103	98

The ambitious recruitment of Brazilian international striker Jairzinho as national coach in October 2003 gave a clear signal that Gabon were intent on reversing the decline in their fortunes. His effect was soon felt in a 2006 FIFA World Cup™ preliminary qualifier with Burundi in Libreville that Gabon won 4-1 to send them through to a difficult group containing Nigeria and Angola. Results there have been mixed although going into the final stages a place in the 2006 Nations Cup was still a possibility. Gabon hosted the 2005 CEMAC Cup with high hopes of winning the tournament for the first time but finished third after a disappointing defeat at the hands of Chad in the

INTERNATIONAL HONOURS
None

semi-finals. Despite the disappointments Gabon have moved back into the top 100 in the FIFA/Coca-Cola World Ranking. Mangasport won the 2004 Championship losing just once to take the title although they faced a strong challenge from Télestar. The Championship was stopped early in order to create a new expanded league that began in January 2005. Mangasport couldn't manage the double however, losing 3-2 to FC 105 in the final of the Coupe du Gabon. FC 105 have built on this triumph by going on a fine run in the 2005 CAF Confederation Cup and reaching the group stages, the best performance by a Gabonese club for over a decade.

THE FIFA BIG COUNT OF 2000

	Male	Female		Male	Female
Registered players	5 000	0	Referees	100	0
Non registered players	5 000	0	Officials	800	0
Youth players	2 500	0	Total involved	13 400	
Total players	12 500		Number of clubs	50	
Professional players	0	0	Number of teams	200	

Fédération Gabonaise de Football (FGF)
Case postale 181, Libreville, Gabon
Tel +241 730460   Fax +241 564199
fegafoot@internetgabon.com   www.none
President: ABABE Leon   General Secretary: BOUASSA MOUSSADJI Barthelemy
Vice-President: ASSOUMOU Joel   Treasurer: NZE NGUEMA Jean   Media Officer: NAEMBER Jean Joseph
Men's Coach: JAIRZINHO   Women's Coach: None
FGF formed: 1962   CAF: 1967   FIFA: 1963
Colours: Green, Blue, White or Yellow, Yellow, White

GAMES PLAYED BY GABON IN THE 2006 FIFA WORLD CUP™ CYCLE

2002	Opponents	Score		Venue	Comp	Scorers	Att	Referee
25-08	Angola	L	0-1	Luanda	Fr		10 000	
1-09	Congo	D	0-0	Brazzaville	Fr			
7-09	Morocco	L	0-1	Libreville	CNq		30 000	Evehe Devine CMR
12-10	Sierra Leone	L	0-2	Freetown	CNq			Ekoue-Toulan TOG
2003								
29-03	Equatorial Guinea	W	4-0	Libreville	CNq	Moulengui [9], Yannick 2 [39 48], Bito'o [67p]		Tavares Neto STP
8-06	Equatorial Guinea	L	1-2	Malabo	CNq	Dissikadie [43]		Buenkadila COD
13-06	Andorra	W	2-0	Andorra la Vella	Fr			Ledentu FRA
20-06	Morocco	L	0-2	Rabat	CNq		15 000	Shelmani LBY
6-07	Sierra Leone	W	2-0	Libreville	CNq	Mbanangoye [33], Mintsa		
24-09	Algeria	D	2-2	Algiers	Fr	Nguéma [21], Moubamba [83], L 3-4p	2 000	Zekkini ALG
26-09	Benin	W	4-0	Algiers	Fr	Mockom [17], Mintsa [44], Nguéma 2 [65 74]		
12-10	Burundi	D	0-0	Bujumbura	WCq		10 000	Itur KEN
8-11	Burkina Faso	D	0-0	Moanda	Fr			
15-11	Burundi	W	4-1	Libreville	WCq	Nzigou [2], Mwinyi OG [16], Nguéma 2 [38 80]	15 000	Ndoye SEN
5-12	Congo	L	2-3	Brazzaville	CMr1	Nguéma [40], Edou [63]		Tchoumba CMR
9-12	Congo	D	1-1	Brazzaville	CMr1			
11-12	Central African Rep	L	0-2	Brazzaville	CMsf			
13-12	Congo	L	0-1	Brazzaville	CM3p			
2004								
29-05	Egypt	L	0-2	Cairo	Fr		15 000	Auda EGY
5-06	Zimbabwe	D	1-1	Libreville	WCq	Zue [52]	25 000	Quartey GHA
19-06	Rwanda	L	1-3	Kigali	WCq	Zue [20]	16 325	Abdulkadir TAN
3-07	Angola	D	2-2	Libreville	WCq	Issiemou [44], Zue [49]	20 000	Louzaya CGO
5-09	Algeria	W	3-0	Annaba	WCq	Aubame [56], Akieremy [73], Bito'o [84]	51 000	Ndoye SEN
3-10	Benin	W	2-0	Libreville	Fr	Djissikadie, Nguéma		
9-10	Nigeria	D	1-1	Libreville	WCq	Issiemou [29]	26 000	Yameogo BFA
2005								
3-02	Central African Rep	W	4-0	Libreville	CMr1	Akoué [32p], Nguéma [42], Yinda 2 [52 82]		
8-02	Congo	W	1-0	Libreville	CMr1	Poaty [38]		
10-02	Chad	L	2-3	Libreville	CMsf	Akoué [58p], Mabiala [69]		
12-02	Congo	W	2-1	Libreville	CM3p	Yembi, Akoué		
19-03	Congo	D	0-0	Libreville	Fr			
26-03	Nigeria	L	0-2	Port Harcourt	WCq		16 489	Hicuburundi BDI
5-06	Zimbabwe	L	0-1	Harare	WCq		55 000	Ssegonga UGA
18-06	Rwanda	W	3-0	Libreville	WCq	Djissikadie [10], Londo [55], Zue [60]	10 000	El Arjoun MAR

Fr = Friendly match • CN = CAF African Cup of Nations • CM = CEMAC Cup • WC = FIFA World Cup™
q = qualifier • r1 = first round group • sf = semi-final • 3p = third place play-off

<table>
<tr><td colspan="3">FIFA REFEREE LIST 2005</td></tr>
<tr><td></td><td>Int'l</td><td>DoB</td></tr>
<tr><td>MBERA Jean-Olivier</td><td>1998</td><td>27-01-1961</td></tr>
<tr><td>MICKOUNGUI Mathurin</td><td>2000</td><td>15-03-1973</td></tr>
<tr><td>MVE NDONG Pierre</td><td>1998</td><td>16-08-1964</td></tr>
<tr><td>NDUME Gil</td><td>2004</td><td>1-09-1965</td></tr>
<tr><td>REMBANGOUET Louis</td><td>2000</td><td>20-03-1963</td></tr>
</table>

<table>
<tr><td colspan="3">FIFA ASSISTANT REFEREE LIST 2005</td></tr>
<tr><td></td><td>Int'l</td><td>DoB</td></tr>
<tr><td>BE-MISSANG Jean-Rne</td><td>1998</td><td>27-01-1961</td></tr>
<tr><td>BIMBYO Patrick</td><td>1998</td><td>16-07-1966</td></tr>
<tr><td>LEKIBI Jean Paulin</td><td>2003</td><td>1-06-1968</td></tr>
<tr><td>LIBAMA Anselme</td><td>1998</td><td>21-04-1965</td></tr>
<tr><td>MAMBANA Jean-Bernard</td><td>2002</td><td>2-07-1966</td></tr>
<tr><td>ROTIMBO Francois</td><td>2001</td><td>19-06-1963</td></tr>
</table>

GABON COUNTRY INFORMATION

Capital	Libreville	Independence	1960 from France	GDP per Capita	5 500
Population	1 355 246	Status	Republic	GNP Ranking	121
Area km²	267 667	Language	French	Dialling code	+241
Population density	5 per km²	Literacy rate	63%	Internet code	.ga
% in urban areas	%	Main religion	Christian 75%	GMT +/−	+1
Towns/Cities ('000)	Libreville 578; Port-Gentil 109; Masuku 42; Oyem 30; Moanda 30; Mouila 22; Lambaréné 20				
Neighbours (km)	Equatorial Guinea 350; Cameroon 298; Congo 1 903				
Main stadia	Stade Omar Bongo – Libreville 40 000				

GABON NATIONAL TEAM RECORDS AND RECORD SEQUENCES

Records			Sequence records					
Victory	7-0	BEN 1995	Wins	4	1985, 1992	Clean sheets	5	1986-87, 1988
Defeat	1-6	GUI 1967	Defeats	5	1967-1971	Goals scored	14	1998-1999
Player Caps	n/a		Undefeated	11	1996	Without goal	4	2002
Player Goals	n/a		Without win	20	1977-1984	Goals against	11	1996-1997

GABON 2004

LE CHAMPIONNAT

Team	Pl	W	D	L	F	A	Pts	Mangasport	Téléstar	US Bitam	Stade d'Akébé	FC 105	USM	Wongosport	Sogéa	CMS	Munadji 76	TP Akwembé	Jeunesse
Mangasport †	15	9	5	1	27	7	32			2-1	2-1	2-0	5-0	1-0	1-2	0-0	1-0	4-1	
Téléstar	15	9	4	2	22	10	31	1-1				2-0		1-0	1-0	2-0		1-0	3-0
US Bitam	15	7	5	3	19	13	26		**3-0**			0-0	**0-3**	1-0	0-0	2-0	2-1	2-1	4-0
Stade d'Akébé	15	7	4	4	25	20	25		1-1	1-1		4-1	1-0		2-2	3-1		3-1	
FC 105 Libreville ‡	15	7	3	5	20	14	24		1-1	4-1	0-1		0-0			0-1		1-0	3-0
USM Libreville	15	7	2	6	21	20	23		0-2	0-1	1-3			1-3	3-0	4-3		2-0	2-0
Wongosport	15	6	1	8	20	18	19		1-0		2-3	1-2			2-3	1-0	1-0	3-0	
Sogéa FC	15	4	7	4	17	15	19	0-0	1-2		4-1	0-2		3-0		0-0	0-0		0-0
Centre Mbéri Sportif	15	4	4	7	11	16	16	0-0				0-2			2-2			2-0	1-0
Munadji 76	15	3	5	7	7	18	14	1-1		0-3		1-0	0-2	1-1	1-0	**3-0**			1-1
TP Akwembé	15	2	4	9	10	22	10	0-1		0-0		1-1	0-2		2-2	0-0	**3-0**		1-0
JS Libreville	15	1	4	10	8	34	7	0-6	2-2	1-1	3-2		0-2	0-4				0-1	

14/03/2004 - 7/11/2004 • † Qualified for the CAF Champions League • ‡ Teams qualifying for the CAF Confederation Cup • Matches in bold awarded 3-0 • The Championship was truncated to allow for an expanded Championship to kick-off in January 2005

COUPE DU GABON 2004

Round of 16		Quarter-finals		Semi-finals		Final	
FC 105	2						
JS Libreville	0	**FC 105**	1				
US Bitam	2 3p	Sogéa FC	0				
Sogéa FC	2 5p			**FC 105**	3 4p		
SUCAF	†			Stade d'Akébé	3 3p		
		SUCAF	0				
Aigle de Lounga	1	**Stade d'Akébé**	4				
Stade d'Akébé	12					**FC 105 ‡**	3
TP Akwembé	5					Mangasport	2
Porté Disparu	0	**TP Akwembé**	2				
Wongosport	0	Téléstar	1				
Téléstar	1			TP Akwembé	0		
Munadji 76	1			**Mangasport**	1		
USM Libreville	0	Munadji 76	0				
Cercle Mbéri Sportif	0	**Mangasport**	5				
Mangasport	1						

‡ Qualified for the CAF Confederation Cup • † Bye

CUP FINAL

24-10-2004
Omnisport, Libreville
Scorers - Ngouani 45, Boubébé 2 72 90 for FC 105; Nzinga 2 53 56 for Mangasport

RECENT LEAGUE AND CUP RECORD

	Championship						Cup		
Year	Champions	Pts	Runners-up	Pts	Third	Pts	Winners	Score	Runners-up
1995	Mangasport	40	Mbilinga	37	FC 105	32	Mbilinga		
1996	Mbilinga								
1997	FC 105						Mbilinga		
1998	FC 105						Mbilinga	3-0	Wongosport
1999	Petrosport †	63	FC 105	52	USM Libreville	46	US Bitam	2-1	Aigles Verts
2000	Mangasport	30	AO Evizo	30	FC 105	22	AO Evizo		
2001	FC 105	62	Mangasport	59	TP Akwembé	59	Mangasport	1-0	TP Akwembé
2002	USM Libreville	54	FC 105	49	Mangasport	39	USM Libreville	1-1 4-2p	Jeunesse
2003	US Bitam	45	FC 105	45	Wongosport	37	US Bitam	1-1 4-3p	USM Libreville
2004	Mangasport	32	Téléstar	31	US Bitam	26	FC 105	3-2	Mangasport

† Championship abandoned in 1999 - FC 105 were later awarded the title

5 December 2004. National Taiwan University, Taipei City, Chinese Taipei. Spain successfully defend their futsal world crown. In the final they beat Italy 2–1 having knocked out favourites Brazil in the semi-final.

12 December 2004. Estadio Doble Visera, Buenos Aires, Argentina. Newell's Old Boys coach Americo Gallego acknowledges the cheers after leading Newell's to the Apertura Championship.

12 December 2004. Abuja Stadium, Abuja, Nigeria. Obinna Nwaneri celebrates his winning penalty in the CAF African Champions League final as Enyimba become the first team since 1968 to retain the trophy.

12 December 2004. International Stadium, Yokohama, Japan. FC Porto win the last Toyota Cup beating Colombia's Once Caldas 8–7 on penalties. The event will be replaced from 2005 with the FIFA Club World Championship.

17 December 2004. La Bombonera, Buenos Aires, Argentina. South American footballer of the year Carlos Tevez holds up the Copa Sudamericana after Boca Juniors' 2–0 win over Bolivar in the final.

Right **19 December 2004. Benedito Teixeira, Sao Jose do Rio Preto, Brazil.** Robinho celebrates winning the Brazilian Championship with Santos following a 2–1 victory over Vasco da Gama.

Below **8 January 2005. Stadium Utama Senayan, Jakarta, Indonesia.** Khairul Amri scores the second goal for Singapore in a 3–1 victory over Indonesia in the first leg of the ASEAN Tiger Cup final. They claimed the trophy with a 2–1 win in the second leg in Singapore.

GAM – GAMBIA

NATIONAL TEAM RECORD
JULY 1ST 2002 TO JUNE 30TH 2005

PL	W	D	L	F	A	%
11	5	1	5	15	10	50

FIFA/COCA-COLA WORLD RANKING

1993	1994	1995	1996	1997	1998	1999	2000	2001	2002	2003	2004	High		Low	
125	117	112	128	132	135	151	155	148	143	138	154	**101**	09/94	**160**	06/01

2004-2005											
08/04	09/04	10/04	11/04	12/04	01/05	02/05	03/05	04/05	05/05	06/05	07/05
146	147	149	150	154	154	154	156	157	156	158	160

A small fish in a large pool of West African talent, Gambia have always struggled to make an impact and after an encouraging 2-0 home win against Liberia in a 2006 FIFA World Cup™ preliminary round qualifier, the Scorpions then lost 0-3 in Monrovia and were knocked out. With their involvement in the 2006 CAF Cup of Nations also over as a result of that aggregate defeat, it was more than a year and a half before another game was played. The silence at senior level focused attention on the juniors though and with great success. The country hosted the 2005 African U-17 Championship, so work with the youngsters took priority and a new crop of talent

INTERNATIONAL HONOURS
CAF African U-17 Championship 2005

was discovered that may serve them well in the future. Eight nations competed, but it was Gambia who unexpectedly triumphed by beating Ghana 1-0 in the final and booking their ticket to the FIFA U-17 World Championship in Peru in September 2005, the first time Gambia have qualified for any world event. The league programme was a close run affair with the top three finishing level on points, though it was Wallidan who collected a fourth Championship in five years on goal difference. The most successful club in the country's history couldn't complete the double though, losing 1-4 in the Cup Final against Bakau United.

THE FIFA BIG COUNT OF 2000

	Male	Female		Male	Female
Registered players	2 500	0	Referees	100	0
Non registered players	2 500	0	Officials	600	0
Youth players	1 000	0	Total involved	6 700	
Total players	6 000		Number of clubs	50	
Professional players	0	0	Number of teams	200	

Gambia Football Association (GFA)
Independence Stadium, Bakau, PO Box 523, Banjul, The Gambia
Tel +220 449980   Fax +220 449509
info@gambiafa.org   www.gambiafa.org
President: SEY Alhagi Omar   General Secretary: BOJANG Jammeh
Vice-President: KINTEH Seedy   Treasurer: JANNEH Buba   Media Officer: SAIWE Pap
Men's Coach: NDONG Sang   Women's Coach: PASUWAREH Faye
GFA formed: 1952   CAF: 1962   FIFA: 1966
Colours: Red, Red, Red or Blue, Blue, Blue

GAMES PLAYED BY GAMBIA IN THE 2006 FIFA WORLD CUP™ CYCLE

2002	Opponents	Score		Venue	Comp	Scorers	Att	Referee
25-08	Sierra Leone	W	1-0	Banjul	Fr	Samba 58		
1-09	Guinea	W	1-0	Banjul	Fr	Jatta 70		
12-10	Lesotho	W	6-0	Banjul	CNq	Nyang 2 7 40, Sarr 45, Ceesay 2 55 88, Soli	25 000	Ba MTN
2003								
16-02	Nigeria	L	0-1	Banjul	Fr		30 000	
30-03	Senegal	D	0-0	Banjul	CNq		30 000	Djingarey NIG
31-05	Mauritania	W	4-1	Banjul	Fr			
7-06	Senegal	L	1-3	Dakar	CNq	Sillah 63		Guirat TUN
6-07	Lesotho	L	0-1	Maseru	CNq		10 000	
12-10	Liberia	W	2-0	Bakau	WCq	Njie 64, Sonko 79	20 000	Codjia BEN
16-11	Liberia	L	0-3	Monrovia	WCq		10 000	Coulibaly MLI
2004								
No international matches played in 2004								
2005								
12-06	Sierra Leone	L	0-1	Freetown	Fr			

Fr = Friendly match • CN = CAF African Cup of Nations • WC = FIFA World Cup™ • q = qualifier

GAMBIA NATIONAL TEAM RECORDS AND RECORD SEQUENCES

Records			Sequence records					
Victory	6-0	LES 2002	Wins	3	2002	Clean sheets	3	1991, 2002
Defeat	0-8	GUI 1972	Defeats	9	1968-1977	Goals scored	7	1962-1971
Player Caps	n/a		Undefeated	4	Four times	Without goal	7	1998-2000
Player Goals	n/a		Without win	17	1997-2001	Goals against	16	1962-1979

FIFA REFEREE LIST 2005

	Int'l	DoB
MENDY John		21-05-1974
SARR Pa Abdou	1996	27-10-1967
SILLAH Malick	1991	8-10-1960
SOWE Modou	1998	25-11-1963

FIFA ASSISTANT REFEREE LIST 2005

	Int'l	DoB
CAMARA Lamin	1994	13-12-1963
JABANG Christian	2005	2-07-1970
MANNEH Seedy		24-12-1968

RECENT LEAGUE AND CUP RECORD

	Championship							Cup		
Year	Champions	Pts	Runners-up	Pts	Third	Pts		Winners	Score	Runners-up
1997	Real Banjul							Real Banjul	1-0	Banjul Hawks
1998	Real Banjul							Wallidan	1-1 4-3p	Ports Authority
1999	Ports Authority							Wallidan	1-1 4-3p	Mass Sosseh
2000	Real Banjul	35	Banjul Hawks	34	Wallidan	30		Steve Biko	1-1 4-2p	Wallidan
2001	Wallidan	38	Steve Biko	32	Real Banjul	27		Wallidan	3-0	Blackpool
2002	Wallidan	37	Real Banjul	34	Banjul Hawks	33		Wallidan	1-0	Real Banjul
2003	Armed Forces							Wallidan	1-0	Banjul Hawks
2004	Wallidan	38	Banjul Hawks	35	Ports Authority	28		Wallidan	1-1 9-8p	Armed Forces
2005	Wallidan	29	GAMTEL	29	Banjul Hawks	29		Bakau United	4-1	Wallidan

GAMBIA COUNTRY INFORMATION

Capital	Banjul	Independence	1965 from the UK	GDP per Capita	$1 700
Population	1 546 848	Status	Republic	GNP Ranking	172
Area km²	11 300	Language	English	Dialling code	+220
Population density	136 per km²	Literacy rate	33%	Internet code	.gm
% in urban areas	26%	Main religion	Muslim 90%	GMT +/−	0
Towns/Cities ('000)	Serekunda 218; Brikama 101; Bakau 47; Farafenni 36; Banjul 34; Lamin 16; Sukuta 15				
Neighbours (km)	Senegal 740; Atlantic Ocean 80				
Main stadia	Independence Stadium – Bakau 20 000; Brikama – Banjul 15 000				

GEO – GEORGIA

NATIONAL TEAM RECORD
JULY 1ST 2002 TO JUNE 30TH 2005

PL	W	D	L	F	A	%
23	4	4	15	22	45	26.1

FIFA/COCA-COLA WORLD RANKING

1993	1994	1995	1996	1997	1998	1999	2000	2001	2002	2003	2004	High		Low	
-	92	79	95	69	52	66	66	58	90	93	104	42	09/98	156	04/94

2004-2005											
08/04	09/04	10/04	11/04	12/04	01/05	02/05	03/05	04/05	05/05	06/05	07/05
109	112	105	107	104	106	102	100	102	100	102	103

From being one of the strongest national teams to emerge from the Soviet Bloc, Georgia have recently experienced a decline in fortunes that has seen them slip out of the top 100 in the FIFA/Coca-Cola World Ranking. In the 2006 FIFA World Cup™ qualifiers there were a series of disappointing results and in the three years following the 2002 finals Georgia have won just four times in all matches played, although one of those was a hugely satisfying win against Russia in the UEFA EURO 2004™ qualifiers. Coach Alain Giresse has not had the easiest start since taking over as coach in March 2004 but he has had to contend with a difficult group containing the

INTERNATIONAL HONOURS
None

Ukraine, Greece and Denmark and was brought in with the task of developing football for the long-term. There is certainly the history in the country to do that with twice Soviet champions and former Cup Winners Cup winners Dinamo Tbilisi still the most powerful club in the country. Coached by former national team captain Kakhaber Tskhadadze they won the 2005 Championship ahead of Torpedo and FC Tbilisi, whose game against each other on the last day of the season was abandoned after 85 minutes following a mass brawl. Lokomotivi who completed the League with fewest defeats had the consolation of winning the Cup Final against newly formed Zestafoni.

THE FIFA BIG COUNT OF 2000

	Male	Female		Male	Female
Registered players	2 700	100	Referees	87	0
Non registered players	110 000	150	Officials	1 000	0
Youth players	21 100	100	Total involved	135 237	
Total players	134 150		Number of clubs	127	
Professional players	900	0	Number of teams	728	

Georgian Football Federation (GFF)

76a Chavchavadze Avenue, Tbilisi 0162, Georgia
Tel +995 32 912680   Fax +995 32 001128
gff@gff.ge   www.gff.ge
President: AKHALKATSI Nodar   General Secretary: CHOLARIA Valeri
Vice-President: CHOLARIA Valeri   Treasurer: CHKHIKVADZE Nargiza   Media Officer: JORDANIA Bakar
Men's Coach: GIRESSE Alain   Women's Coach: KHINCHAGASHVILI Shota
GFF formed: 1990   UEFA: 1992   FIFA: 1992
Colours: White, White, White or Black, Black, Black

GAMES PLAYED BY GEORGIA IN THE 2006 FIFA WORLD CUP™ CYCLE

2002	Opponents	Score		Venue	Comp	Scorers	Att	Referee
21-08	Turkey	L	0-3	Trabzon	Fr		15 000	Agelakis GRE
8-09	Switzerland	L	1-4	Basle	ECq	Arveladze.S 62	20 500	Hrinak SVK
2003								
12-02	Moldova	D	2-2	Tbilisi	Fr	Chaladze 61, Ashvetia 83	7 000	Hovanisyan ARM
29-03	Republic of Ireland	L	1-2	Tbilisi	ECq	Kobiashvili 62	15 000	Vassaras GRE
2-04	Switzerland	D	0-0	Tbilisi	ECq		10 000	Trivkovic CRO
30-04	Russia	W	1-0	Tbilisi	ECq	Asatiani 11	11 000	Wack GER
11-06	Republic of Ireland	L	0-2	Dublin	ECq		36 000	Iturralde Gonzalez ESP
6-09	Albania	W	3-0	Tbilisi	ECq	Arveladze.S 2 9 44, Ashvetia 18	18 000	Vollquartz DEN
10-09	Albania	L	1-3	Tirana	ECq	Arveladze.S 63	10 500	Salomir ROU
11-10	Russia	L	1-3	Moscow	ECq	Iashvili 5	30 000	Plautz AUT
2004								
18-02	Romania	L	0-3	Larnaca	Fr		200	Lajuks LVA
19-02	Cyprus	L	1-3	Nicosia	Fr	Gabidauri 56		Kapitanis CYP
21-02	Armenia	L	0-2	Nicosia	Fr		200	Loizou CYP
27-05	Israel	L	0-1	Tbilisi	Fr		24 000	Oriekhov UKR
18-08	Moldova	L	0-1	Tiraspol	Fr		8 000	Godulyan UKR
4-09	Turkey	D	1-1	Trabzon	WCq	Asatiani 85	10 169	Medina Cantalejpo ESP
8-09	Albania	W	2-0	Tbilisi	WCq	Iashvili 15, Demetradze 90+1	20 000	Courtney NIR
13-10	Ukraine	L	0-2	Lviv	WCq		28 000	Stark GER
17-11	Denmark	D	2-2	Tbilisi	WCq	Demetradze 33, Asatiani 76	20 000	Ceferin SVN
2005								
9-02	Lithuania	W	1-0	Tbilisi	Fr	Ashvetia 57	1 000	Gadiyev AZE
26-03	Greece	L	1-3	Tbilisi	WCq	Asatiani 22	23 000	Rosetti ITA
30-03	Turkey	L	2-5	Tbilisi	WCq	Amisulashvili 13, Iashvili 40	10 000	Hauge NOR
4-06	Albania	L	2-3	Tirana	WCq	Burduli 85, Kobiashvili 94+	BCD	Tudor ROU

Fr = Friendly match • EC = UEFA EURO 2004™ • WC = FIFA World Cup™ • q = qualifier • BCD = Behind closed doors

NATIONAL CAPS

	Caps
NEMSADZE'Giorgi	69
JAMARAULI Gocha	62
KINKLADZE Giorgi	54
ARVELADZE Shota	53
KOBIASHVILI Levan	53
KETSBAIA Temur	52
KAVELASHVILI Mikheil	46
KALADZE Kakha	43

NATIONAL GOALS

	Goals
ARVELADZE Shota	19
KETSBAIA Temur	17
IASHVILI Aleksander	9
KAVELASHVILI Mikheil	9
KINKLADZE Giorgi	8
ARVELADZE Archil	6
JAMARAULI Gocha	6
DEMETRADZE Giorgi	6

NATIONAL COACH

	Years
CHIVADZE Aleksandre	1993-'96
KIPIANI David	1997
GUTSAEV Vladimir	1998-'99
BOSKAMP Johan	1999
KIPIANI, DZODZUASHVILI	1999-'01
CHIVADZE Aleksandre	2001-'03
SUSAK Ivo	2003
GIRESSE Alain	2004-

FIFA REFEREE LIST 2005

	Int'l	DoB
MALAGURADZE Merab	1995	31-07-1965
PANIASHVILI Levan	2000	28-10-1966
SILAGAVA Lasha		27-07-1976

FIFA ASSISTANT REFEREE LIST 2005

	Int'l	DoB
CHIGOGIDZE Guram	1999	26-09-1967
ELIKASHVILI Mamuka	1993	4-02-1966
JVARIDZE Zurab	2003	5-04-1964
MENTESHASHVILI Zaza	2000	1-09-1974
MIKRLADZE Levan	1995	4-01-1971
SAMKARADZE Avtandil	2001	5-01-1964

GEORGIA COUNTRY INFORMATION

Capital	Tbilisi	Independence	1991 from the Soviet Union	GDP per Capita	$2 500
Population	4 693 892	Status	Republic	GNP Ranking	130
Area km²	69 700	Language	Georgian	Dialling code	+995
Population density	67 per km²	Literacy rate	99%	Internet code	.ge
% in urban areas	58%	Main religion	Christian 83%	GMT + / –	+4
Towns/Cities ('000)	Tbilisi 1 049; Kutaisi 178; Batumi 118; Rustavi 109; Sukhumi 81; Zugdidi 73; Gori 46				
Neighbours (km)	Russia 723; Azerbaijan 322; Armenia 164; Turkey 252; Black Sea 310				
Main stadia	Boris Paichadze – Tbilisi 74 380; Mikheil Meshki – Tbilisi 27 223; Tsentral – Batumi 18 600				

GEORGIA NATIONAL TEAM RECORDS AND RECORD SEQUENCES

Records			Sequence records					
Victory	7-0	ARM 1997	Wins	5	1997-1998	Clean sheets	3	1997
Defeat	0-5	ROM 1996	Defeats	7	2003-2004	Goals scored	10	2001-2002
Player Caps	69	NEMSADZE Giorgi	Undefeated	8	1997-1998	Without goal	3	Four times
Player Goals	19	ARVELADZE Shota	Without win	8	1999, 2003-2004	Goals against	11	1998-1999

GEORGIA 2004-05

PREMIER LEAGUE

	Pl	W	D	L	F	A	Pts	Dinamo	Torpedo	FC Tbilisi	Lokomotivi	Zestafoni	WIT	Sioni	Batumi	Kolkheti	Dila
Dinamo Tbilisi †	36	23	6	7	73	27	75		1-2	1-2	4-1	0-1	0-0	0-0	2-0	0-1	3-2 1-0 6-0 1-0 1-0 3-0 4-0 3-0 3-0 9-0
Torpedo Kutaisi ‡	36	20	10	6	56	31	70	1-1 1-4		2-2 §	2-0 0-0	4-0 0-1	1-1 2-1	5-0 2-0	2-0 1-1	1-1 3-0	2-1 2-1
FC Tbilisi	36	21	6	9	60	40	69	5-0 1-3	1-1 2-2		3-1 4-1	2-0 0-3	0-2 2-1	3-1 1-0	3-2 1-0	3-0 3-2	4-1 2-1
Lokomotivi Tbilisi ‡	36	16	15	5	42	24	63	2-5 0-0	1-0 0-0	3-1 1-0		1-2 1-0	0-0 1-0	4-0 2-0	0-0 1-1	2-0 3-0	3-1 0-0
FC Zestafoni	36	16	5	15	38	48	53	0-2 0-0	1-1 2-1	1-3 1-0	1-4 1-1		3-1 1-3	1-0 0-0	2-1 2-0	1-2 2-1	2-0 3-0
WIT Georgia Tbilisi	36	13	9	14	54	41	48	2-3 1-0	1-3 1-2	0-2 0-0	0-0 0-1	4-0 1-2		2-1 0-2	3-2 1-1	2-1 6-0	2-0 4-0
Sioni Bolnisi	36	12	4	20	35	56	40	0-1 0-1	0-2 0-1	0-2 0-2	1-1 0-1	2-1 2-1	3-2 1-1		1-0 2-1	2-2 3-0	3-2 3-0
Dinamo Batumi	36	9	12	15	35	33	39	3-0 1-2	0-1 0-1	1-1 0-1	1-1 0-0	5-0 0-0	1-1 0-0	2-0 1-2		0-0 3-0	2-0 3-0
Kolkheti 1913 Poti	36	9	5	22	32	63	32	0-0 0-2	0-1 2-1	1-0 0-1	0-3 1-2	2-0 0-1	1-2 0-0	3-0 0-3	0-1 0-1		4-0 6-2
Dila Gori	36	2	4	30	20	88	10	1-4 0-3	0-1 1-3	2-2 0-1	0-0 0-1	0-1 1-2	1-3 0-4	2-1 0-2	0-1 0-0	2-0 1-2	

31/07/2004 - 30/05/2005 • † Qualified for the UEFA Champions League • ‡ Qualified for the UEFA Cup • § Awarded 0-3 against both teams

GEORGIA 2004-05 FIRST LEAGUE (2)

	Pl	W	D	L	F	A	Pts
Ameri Tbilisi	30	23	3	4	93	18	72
FK Borjomi	30	22	3	5	74	36	69
Spartaki Tbilisi	30	16	9	5	52	36	57
Kakheti Telavi	30	17	4	9	57	41	55
WIT Georgia-2	30	16	7	7	49	28	55
Dinamo-2 Tbilisi	30	16	1	13	64	50	49
FK Tskhinvali	30	14	4	12	39	36	46
Chikhura Sachkhere	30	12	7	11	38	35	43
Lokomotivi-2 Tbilisi	30	10	8	12	33	40	38
Guria Lanchkhuti	30	8	12	30	45	38
FK Rustavi	30	10	7	13	39	43	37
Olimpi Tbilisi	30	10	5	15	35	44	35
Iveria Khashuri	30	10	5	15	31	45	35
Milani-Merani Tsnori	30	8	4	18	35	53	28
FK Sagarejo	30	4	5	21	26	70	17
Magharoeli Chiatura	30	0	4	26	17	92	4

15/08/2004 - 6/06/2005

TOP SCORERS

MELKADZE Levani	Dinamo Tbilisi	27
MEGRELADZE Giorgi	Torpedo Tbilisi	23
FIFIA Giorgi	FC Tbilisi	13
BOBOKHIDZE Mikeili	Lokomotivi	12
MARTSVALADZE Otari	WIT Georgia	12
ODIKADZE Daviti	Dinamo Tbilisi	12

GEORGIAN CUP 2004-05

Quarter-finals		Semi-finals		Final	
Lokomotivi	0 2			‡ Qualified for the UEFA Cup	
Kolkheti 1913 *	0 0	**Lokomotivi**	2 2		
Ameri Tbilisi	2 0	WIT Georgia *	0 1		
WIT Georgia *	5 2			**Lokomotivi** ‡	2
FC Tbilisi *	2 1			FC Zestafoni	0
Torpedo Kutaisi	0 2	FC Tbilisi *	0 1	26-05-2005, Att: 20 000	
Dinamo Batumi*	0 0	**FC Zestafoni**	0 2	Boris Paichadze, Tbilisi	
FC Zestafoni	0 1	* Home team in first leg		Scorers - Bobokhidze 55, Manchkhava 60 for Lokomotivi	

RECENT LEAGUE AND CUP RECORD

	Championship						Cup		
Year	Champions	Pts	Runners-up	Pts	Third	Pts	Winners	Score	Runners-up
1990	Iberia Tbilisi	78	Guria Lanchkhuti	72	Gorda Rustavi	69	Guria Lanchkhuti	1-0	Tskhumi Sukhumi
1991	Iberia Tbilisi	47	Guria Lanchkhuti	46	FC Kutaisi	35	No tournament played		
1992	Dinamo Tbilisi	87	Tskhumi Sukhumi	76	Gorda Rustavi	75	Dinamo Tbilisi	3-1	Tskhumi Sukhumi
1993	Dinamo Tbilisi	77	Shevardeni 1906	64	Alazani Gurdzhaani	63	Dinamo Tbilisi	4-2	FC Batumi
1994	Dinamo Tbilisi	48	Kolkheti 1913 Poti	44	Torpedo Kutaisi	31	Dinamo Tbilisi	1-0	Metalurgi Rustavi
1995	Dinamo Tbilisi	78	Samtredia	74	Kolkheti 1913 Poti	63	Dinamo Tbilisi	1-0	Dinamo Batumi
1996	Dinamo Tbilisi	79	Margveti Zestafoni	68	Kolkheti 1913 Poti	68	Dinamo Tbilisi	1-0	Dinamo Batumi
1997	Dinamo Tbilisi	81	Kolkheti 1913 Poti	64	Dinamo Batumi	62	Dinamo Tbilisi	1-0	Dinamo Batumi
1998	Dinamo Tbilisi	71	Dinamo Batumi	61	Kolkheti 1913 Poti	57	Dinamo Batumi	2-1	Dinamo Tbilisi
1999	Dinamo Tbilisi	77	Torpedo Kutaisi	67	Lokomotivi Tbilisi	64	Torpedo Kutaisi	0-0 4-2p	Samgurali
2000	Torpedo Kutaisi	46	WIT Georgia Tbilisi	41	Dinamo Tbilisi	41	Lokomotivi Tbilisi	0-0 4-2p	Torpedo Kutaisi
2001	Torpedo Kutaisi	44	Lokomotivi Tbilisi	41	Dinamo Tbilisi	38	Torpedo Kutaisi	0-0 4-3p	Lokomotivi Tbilisi
2002	Torpedo Kutaisi	48	Lokomotivi Tbilisi	47	Dinamo Tbilisi	44	Lokomotivi Tbilisi	2-0	Dinamo Tbilisi
2003	Dinamo Tbilisi	48	Torpedo Kutaisi	46	WIT Georgia Tbilisi	41	Dinamo Tbilisi	3-1	Sioni Bolnisi
2004	WIT Georgia Tbilisi	41	Sioni Bolnisi	41	Dinamo Tbilisi	40	Dinamo Tbilisi	2-1	Torpedo Kutaisi
2005	Dinamo Tbilisi	75	Torpedo Kutaisi	70	FC Tbilisi	69	Lokomotivi Tbilisi	2-0	FC Zestafoni

GER – GERMANY

NATIONAL TEAM RECORD

JULY 1ST 2002 TO JUNE 30TH 2005

PL	W	D	L	F	A	%
41	21	11	9	82	51	64.6

When Germany was awarded the hosting of the 2006 FIFA World Cup™ the opportunity to revolutionise the game in the country was embraced with open arms. Most dramatic of all has been the physical transformation of the football landscape. The vast open arenas, with the ever present athletics track, have largely disappeared, replaced by ultra-modern stadia that have brought a whole new positive atmosphere to the game. When Otto Rehhagel criticised the new Zentralstadion in Leipzig as being just like any other featureless new stadium he perhaps missed the point that, for the first time, the needs of the fans were being considered and this has been reflected by a rise in attendences at Bundesliga matches, which now attract the highest average gates in the world. The appointment of Jürgen Klinsmann as national team coach in July 2004 has also contributed to the positive atmosphere and there is now a belief amongst fans that Germany have a genuine chance of winning the FIFA World Cup™ when they host it in the summer of 2006, something that did not look remotely on the cards after the shambles of UEFA EURO 2004™. The FIFA Confederations Cup, held in Germany in June 2005, has contributed to the upsurge in optimism with the national

INTERNATIONAL HONOURS

FIFA World Cup™ 1954 1974 1990   FIFA Women's World Cup 2003

Olympic Gold 1976 (GDR)   FIFA World Youth Championship 1981   FIFA Women's U-19 Championship 2004

UEFA European Championship 1972 1980 1996   UEFA Women's European Championship 1989 1991 1995 1997 2001 2005

UEFA U-19 Championship 1981 1986 (GDR)   UEFA U-17 Championship 1984 1992   UEFA Women's U-19 Championship 2000 2001 2002

UEFA Champions League Bayern München 1974 1975 1976 2001, Hamburger SV 1983, Borussia Dortmund 1997

team showing an attacking flair not evident for a long time. Germany scored 15 goals in five games but they have yet to prove that they can beat the major nations, a fact demonstrated by their semi-final defeat at the hands of Brazil. Bayern München played their last season at the Olympiastadion and celebrated their move to their futuristic new stadium by winning the double. In the Bundesliga they lost to Schalke home and away but still managed to pull away towards the end of the season to finish comfortably ahead of their rivals from the Ruhr. It was an emphatic triumph for new coach Felix Magath who had the difficult task of following in the footsteps of the hugely successful Ottmar Hitzfeld. Bayern then finished off a great first season for Magath when they beat Schalke 2-1 in a bad tempered Cup Final to win the double for the third time in six years. The lack of any consistent opposition to Bayern is a problem for German football, made worse by the near bankruptcy of Borussia Dortmund, the only club to have mounted a concerted challenge over the past 10 years, this despite having an average home attendance of 77,295 in the 2004-05 season, the highest figure anywhere in the world.

Deutscher Fussball-Bund (DFB)

Otto-Fleck-Schneise 6, Post Fach 71 02 65, Frankfurt am Main 60492, Germany

Tel +49 69 67880   Fax +49 69 6788266

info@dfb.de   www.dfb.de

President: MAYER-VORFELDER Gerhard, ZWANZIGER Theo Dr   General Secretary: SCHMIDT Horst R.

Vice-President: NELLE Engelbert   Treasurer: SCHMIDHUBER Heinrich   Media Officer: STENGER Harald

Men's Coach: KLINSMANN Jürgen   Women's Coach: NEID Silvia

DFB formed: 1900   UEFA: 1954   FIFA: 1904

Colours: White, Black, White

GAMES PLAYED BY GERMANY IN THE 2006 FIFA WORLD CUP™ CYCLE

2002	Opponents	Score		Venue	Comp	Scorers	Att	Referee
21-08	Bulgaria	D	2-2	Sofia	Fr	Ballack [23p], Jancker [57]	10 000	Bre FRA
7-09	Lithuania	W	2-0	Kaunas	ECq	Ballack [25], Stankevicius OG [58]	8 500	Poll ENG
11-10	Bosnia	D	1-1	Sarajevo	Fr	Jancker [56]	5 000	De Santis ITA
16-10	Faroe Islands	W	2-1	Hannover	ECq	Ballack [1p], Klose [59]	36 628	Koren ISR
20-11	Holland	L	1-3	Gelsenkirchen	Fr	Bobic [34]	60 601	Dallas SCO
2003								
12-02	Spain	L	1-3	Palma	Fr	Bobic [38]	20 000	Riley ENG
29-03	Lithuania	D	1-1	Nuremberg	ECq	Ramelow [8]	40 754	Esquinas Torres ESP
30-04	Serbia & Montenegro	W	1-0	Bremen	Fr	Kehl 60	22 000	De Bleeckere BEL
1-06	Canada	W	4-1	Wolfsburg	Fr	Ramelow [41], Freier [53], Bobic [61], Rau [90]	24 000	Poulat FRA
7-06	Scotland	D	1-1	Glasgow	ECq	Bobic [23]	48 037	Messina ITA
11-06	Faroe Islands	W	2-0	Tórshavn	ECq	Klose [89], Bobic [90]	6 130	Wegereef NED
20-08	Italy	L	0-1	Stuttgart	Fr		50 128	Nielsen DEN
6-09	Iceland	D	0-0	Reykjavik	ECq		7 035	Barber ENG
10-09	Scotland	W	2-1	Dortmund	ECq	Bobic [25], Ballack [50p]	67 000	Frisk SWE
11-10	Iceland	W	3-0	Hamburg	ECq	Ballack [9], Bobic [59], Kuranyi [79]	50 780	Ivanov RUS
15-11	France	L	0-3	Gelsenkirchen	Fr		53 574	Farina ITA
2004								
18-02	Croatia	W	2-1	Split	Fr	Klose [34], Ramelow [90]	15 000	Frojdfeldt SWE
31-03	Belgium	W	3-0	Cologne	Fr	Kuranyi [45], Hamann [55], Ballack [81]	46 500	Wegereef NED
28-04	Romania	L	1-5	Bucharest	Fr	Lahm [88]	12 000	Rosetti ITA
27-05	Malta	W	7-0	Freiburg	Fr	Ballack 4 [15 17 59 86], Nowotny [33], Frings [42], Bobic [90]	22 000	Stredlak SVK
2-06	Switzerland	W	2-0	Basel	Fr	Kuranyi 2 [62 84]	30 000	Messina ITA
6-06	Hungary	L	0-2	Kaiserslautern	Fr		36 590	Bennett ENG
15-06	Netherlands	D	1-1	Porto	ECr1	Frings [30]	52 000	Frisk SWE
19-06	Latvia	D	0-0	Porto	ECr1		22 344	Riley ENG
23-06	Czech Republic	L	1-2	Lisbon	ECr1	Ballack [21]	46 849	Hauge NOR
18-08	Austria	W	3-1	Vienna	Fr	Kuranyi 3 [2 61 73]	37 900	Collina ITA
8-09	Brazil	D	1-1	Berlin	Fr	Kuranyi [17]	74 315	Meier SUI
9-10	Iran	W	2-0	Tehran	Fr	Ernst [5], Bdaric [53]	110 000	Mane KUW
17-11	Cameroon	W	3-0	Leipzig	Fr	Kuranyi [71], Klose 2 [78 88]	44 200	De Santis ITA
16-12	Japan	W	3-0	Yokohama	Fr	Klose 2 [54 90], Ballack [69]	61 805	Shield AUS
19-12	Korea Republic	L	1-3	Busan	Fr	Ballack [24]	45 775	Mohd Salleh MAS
21-12	Thailand	W	5-1	Bangkok	Fr	Kuranyi 2 [34 38], Podolski 2 [73 89], Asamoah [84]	15 000	Maidin SIN
2005								
9-02	Argentina	D	2-2	Dusseldorf	Fr	Frings [28p], Kuranyi [45]	52 000	Farina ITA
26-03	Slovenia	W	1-0	Celje	Fr	Podolski [27]	8 500	Poll ENG
4-06	Northern Ireland	W	4-1	Belfast	Fr	Asamoah [17], Ballack 2 [62 66p], Podolski [81]	14 000	Richmond SCO
8-06	Russia	D	2-2	Mönchengladbach	Fr	Schweinsteiger 2 [30 69]	46 228	Plautz AUT
15-06	Australia	W	4-3	Frankfurt/Main	CCr1	Kuranyi [17], Mertesacker [23], Ballack [60p], Podolski [88]	46 466	Amarilla PAR
18-06	Tunisia	W	3-0	Cologne	CCr1	Ballack [74p], Schweinsteiger [80], Hanke [88]	44 377	Prendergast JAM
21-06	Argentina	D	2-2	Nuremberg	CCr1	Kuranyi [29], Asamoah [51]	42 088	Michel SVK
25-06	Brazil	L	2-3	Nuremberg	CCsf	Podolski [23], Ballack [48+p]	42 187	Chandia CHI
29-06	Mexico	W	4-3	Leipzig	CC3p	Podolski [37], Schweinsteiger [41], Huth [79], Ballack [97]	43 335	Breeze AUS

Fr = Friendly match • EC = UEFA EURO 2004™ • CC = FIFA Confederations Cup • q = qualifier
r1 = first round group • sf = semi-final • 3p = third place play-off • f = final

FIFA/COCA-COLA WORLD RANKING

1993	1994	1995	1996	1997	1998	1999	2000	2001	2002	2003	2004	High		Low	
1	5	2	2	2	3	5	11	12	4	12	19	1	08/93	19	12/04

2004-2005											
08/04	09/04	10/04	11/04	12/04	01/05	02/05	03/05	04/05	05/05	06/05	07/05
13	11	16	19	16	16	17	18	20	19	21	11

THE FIFA BIG COUNT OF 2000

	Male	Female		Male	Female
Registered players	1 318 250	84 050	Referees	78 67	1 567
Non registered players	2 281 614	533 832	Officials	52 752	1 000
Youth players	1 829 518	208 905	Total involved	6 390 155	
Total players	6 256 169		Number of clubs	26 697	
Professional players	870	0	Number of teams	172 716	

NATIONAL CAPS

	Caps
MATTHAUS Lothar	150
KLINSMANN Jürgen	108
KOHLER Jürgen	105
BECKENBAUER Franz	103
HABLER Thomas	101
STREICH Joachim - GDR	98
DORNER Hans-Jürgen - GDR	96
VOGTS Bertie	96
MAIER Sepp	95
RUMMENIGGE Karl-Heinz	95

NATIONAL GOALS

	Goals
MULLER Gerd	68
STREICH Joachim - GDR	53
VOLLER Rudi	47
KLINSMANN Jürgen	47
RUMMENIGGE Karl-Heinz	45
SEELER Uwe	43
BIERHOFF Oliver	37
WALTER Fritz	33
FISCHER Klaus	32
LEHNER Ernst	30

NATIONAL COACH

	Years
NERZ Otto	1926-'36
HERBERGER Sepp	1936-'63
SCHON Helmut	1963-'78
DERWALL Jupp	1978-'84
BECKENBAUER Franz	1984-'90
VOGTS Bertie	1990-'98
RIBBECK Erich	1998-'00
VOLLER Rudi	2000-'04
KLINSMANN Jürgen	2004-

GERMANY NATIONAL TEAM RECORDS AND RECORD SEQUENCES

Records			Sequence records					
Victory	16-0	RUS 1912	Wins	12	1979-1980	Clean sheets	6	1966
Defeat	0-9	ENG 1909	Defeats	7	1912-1913	Goals scored	33	1940-1952
Player Caps	150	MATTHAUS Lothar	Undefeated	23	1978-1980	Without goal	3	1985
Player Goals	68	MULLER Gerd	Without win	10	1912-1920	Goals against	15	1910-1912

FIFA REFEREE LIST 2005

	Int'l	DoB
FANDEL Herbert	1998	9-03-1964
FLEISCHER Helmut	2000	22-03-1964
KESSLER Joerg	2003	24-02-1964
KIRCHER Knut	2004	2-02-1969
MERK Markus	1992	15-03-1962
MEYER Florian	2002	21-11-1968
SIPPEL Peter	2003	6-10-1969
STARK Wolfgang	1999	20-11-1969
WACK Franz-Xaver	2000	5-03-1965
WEINER Michael	2002	21-03-1969

FIFA ASSISTANT REFEREE LIST 2005

	Int'l	DoB
EHING Harry	1999	24-06-1964
GLINDEMANN Soenke	2001	17-06-1965
HENES Peter	2002	1-05-1962
KADACH Carsten	2003	22-01-1964
MULLER Heiner	1999	30-05-1961
SALVER Jan-Hendrik	2000	1-03-1969
SATHER Harald	1995	13-07-1960
SCHEIBEL Markus	1998	30-10-1964
SCHRAER Christian	1998	15-03-1962
WEZEL Volker	2003	15-09-1965

GERMANY COUNTRY INFORMATION

Capital	Berlin	Independence	Unified in 1871, 1991	GNP per Capita	$27 600
Population	82 424 609	Status	Federal Republic	GNP Ranking	3
Area km²	357 021	Language	German	Dialling code	+49
Population density	230 per km²	Literacy rate	99%	Internet code	.de
% in urban areas	85%	Main religion	Christian 68%	GMT + / -	+1
Towns/Cities ('000)	Berlin 3 398; Hamburg 1 733; München 1 246; Köln 968; Frankfurt 648; Dortmund 594; Stuttgart 591; Düsseldorf 577; Essen 576; Bremen 546; Hannover 519; Duisburg 505; Nürnberg 497; Leipzig 492; Dresden 480; Bochum 387; Wuppertal 363; Bielefeld 327				
Neighbours (km)	Denmark 68; Poland 456; Czech Republic 646; Austria 784; Switzerland 334; France 451; Luxembourg 138; Belgium 167; Netherlands 577; North Sea & Baltic Sea 2 389				
Main stadia	Westfalenstadion – Dortmund 82 678; Olympiastadion – Berlin 76 065; Allianz Arena – München 66 000; Arena AufSchalke – Gelsenkirchen 61 027				

GERMANY 2004-05

1. BUNDESLIGA

Team	Pl	W	D	L	F	A	Pts	Bayern	Schalke	Bremen	Hertha	Stuttgart	Leverkusen	Dortmund	HSV	Wolfsburg	Hannover	Mainz	Kaiserslautern	Bielefeld	Nürnberg	Gladbach	Bochum	Rostock	Freiburg
Bayern München †	34	24	5	5	75	33	77		0-1	1-0	1-1	2-2	2-0	5-0	3-0	2-0	3-0	4-2	3-1	1-0	6-3	2-1	3-1	3-1	3-1
Schalke 04 †	34	20	3	11	56	46	63	1-0		2-1	1-3	3-2	3-3	1-2	1-2	3-0	1-0	2-1	2-1	2-1	4-1	3-2	3-2	0-2	1-1
Werder Bremen †	34	18	5	11	68	37	59	1-2	1-0		0-1	1-2	2-2	2-0	1-1	1-2	3-0	0-0	1-1	3-0	4-1	2-0	4-0	3-2	4-1
Hertha BSC Berlin ‡	34	15	13	6	59	31	58	0-0	4-1	1-1		0-0	3-1	0-1	4-1	3-1	0-0	1-1	1-1	3-0	2-1	6-2	2-1	1-1	3-1
VfB Stuttgart ‡	34	17	7	10	54	40	58	1-3	3-0	1-2	1-0		3-0	2-0	2-0	0-0	1-0	4-2	1-1	2-1	2-4	1-0	5-2	4-0	1-0
Bayer 04 Leverkusen ‡	34	16	9	9	65	44	57	4-1	0-3	2-1	3-3	1-1		0-1	3-0	2-1	2-1	2-0	2-0	3-2	2-1	5-1	4-0	3-0	4-1
Borussia Dortmund	34	15	10	9	47	44	55	2-2	0-1	1-0	2-1	0-2	1-0		0-2	1-2	1-1	3-0	4-2	1-1	2-2	1-1	1-0	2-1	2-0
Hamburger SV	34	16	3	15	55	50	51	0-2	1-2	1-2	2-1	2-1	1-1	0-2		3-1	0-2	2-1	2-1	0-2	4-3	0-0	0-1	3-0	4-0
VfL Wolfsburg	34	15	3	16	49	51	48	0-3	3-0	2-3	2-3	3-0	2-2	1-2	1-0		1-0	4-3	2-1	5-0	0-1	2-1	3-0	4-0	0-1
Hannover 96	34	13	6	15	34	36	45	0-1	1-0	1-4	0-1	0-0	0-3	1-3	2-1	3-0		2-0	3-1	0-1	1-0	2-1	3-0	0-1	2-2
1.FSV Mainz	34	12	7	15	50	55	43	2-4	2-1	2-1	0-3	2-3	2-0	1-1	2-1	0-2	2-0		3-2	0-0	1-1	1-1	1-0	3-1	5-0
1.FC Kaiserslautern	34	12	6	16	43	52	42	0-4	2-0	1-2	2-3	0-0	1-0	2-1	0-0	0-2	2-0	2-1		2-1	1-3	1-0	1-2	2-1	3-0
Arminia Bielefeld	34	11	7	16	37	49	40	3-1	0-2	2-1	1-0	0-2	1-0	0-3	4-1	2-0	1-1	1-0	0-2		3-1	1-0	1-2	1-1	3-1
1.FC Nürnberg	34	10	8	16	55	63	38	2-2	0-2	1-2	0-0	1-1	2-4	2-2	1-3	4-0	1-1	1-2	1-3	1-2		0-0	2-1	3-0	3-0
Bor. Mönchengladbach	34	8	12	14	35	51	36	2-0	1-3	1-3	2-0	0-2	2-0	1-1	2-3	1-3	0-0	1-2	1-0	2-1	1-0		2-2	2-2	3-2
VfL Bochum	34	9	8	17	47	68	35	1-3	0-2	1-4	2-2	2-0	2-2	2-2	1-2	5-1	1-0	2-6	1-1	1-1	3-1	3-0		0-1	3-1
Hansa Rostock	34	7	9	18	31	65	30	0-2	2-2	0-4	2-1	2-1	0-2	1-1	0-6	1-2	1-3	2-0	2-3	1-1	0-2	0-0	3-1		0-0
SC Freiburg	34	3	9	22	30	75	18	0-1	2-3	0-6	1-3	2-0	1-3	2-2	1-1	1-0	0-0	1-2	1-2	2-3	2-3	1-1	1-1	0-0	

6/08/2004 - 21/05/2005 • † Qualified for the UEFA Champions League • ‡ Qualified for the UEFA Cup

TOP SCORERS

MINTAL Marek	1.FC Nürnberg	24
MAKAAY Roy	Bayern München	22
BERBATOV Dimitar	Bayer Leverkusen	20
MARCELINHO	Hertha BSC Berlin	18

GERMANY 2004-05

2. BUNDESLIGA

Team	Pl	W	D	L	F	A	Pts	Köln	Duisburg	Frankfurt	TSV 1860	Fürth	Aachen	Aue	Dynamo	Burghausen	Unterhaching	Karlsruher	Saarbrücken	Ahlen	Cottbus	Trier	Oberhausen	Essen	Erfurt
1.FC Köln	34	20	7	7	62	33	67		4-0	2-0	2-0	3-2	1-0	1-0	3-2	8-1	1-0	2-2	3-1	3-0	0-0	1-2	3-2	0-0	1-1
MSV Duisburg	34	19	5	10	50	37	62	1-0		1-1	0-1	1-0	1-0	1-1	4-2	4-3	3-1	1-4	2-1	1-0	2-0	4-3	4-1	1-0	4-0
Eintracht Frankfurt	34	19	4	11	65	39	61	1-0	0-1		1-2	1-0	1-0	2-0	3-0	1-2	0-3	0-2	2-1	3-3	3-1	2-0	6-2	1-0	2-1
TSV 1860 München	34	15	12	7	52	39	57	0-0	1-0	2-1		2-1	3-0	1-0	2-0	2-4	2-2	1-1	1-1	3-4	1-0	2-0	5-1	0-0	3-1
SpVgg Greuther Fürth	34	17	5	12	51	42	56	0-1	1-3	2-1	2-3		3-2	1-0	0-1	1-1	3-1	1-0	2-0	1-0	2-0	3-3	3-2	3-2	2-0
Alemannia Aachen	34	16	6	12	60	40	54	2-3	0-0	1-1	5-1	0-1		1-5	5-1	3-1	2-3	4-0	3-1	0-2	4-0	2-0	2-1	1-1	5-1
Erzgebirge Aue	34	15	6	13	49	40	51	1-2	1-3	0-5	3-1	2-1	1-1		4-1	2-0	1-0	0-0	1-2	0-0	2-0	1-2	0-2	1-1	3-2
1.FC Dynamo Dresden	34	15	4	15	48	53	49	2-1	3-1	2-1	0-4	2-2	2-0	1-0		1-1	1-0	1-2	2-1	3-1	0-1	4-1	3-1	1-0	3-2
Wacker Burghausen	34	13	9	12	48	55	48	4-2	0-0	0-3	0-3	0-1	2-3	2-2	2-1		2-0	1-1	1-2	1-0	0-0	0-0	2-2	3-2	0-2
SpVgg Unterhaching	34	14	3	17	40	43	45	1-3	0-1	2-0	1-1	1-2	0-2	4-1	1-0	0-1		2-0	1-3	2-1	2-1	1-0	0-2	4-0	4-0
Karlsruher SC	34	11	10	13	46	47	43	0-1	0-3	3-0	1-1	2-2	0-1	0-1	4-1	1-0	1-1		1-0	0-3	0-1	3-0	4-1	2-0	
1.FC Saarbrücken	34	11	7	16	44	50	40	2-0	4-1	3-0	4-1	2-1	1-2	2-1	0-1	2-4	0-1	3-4		0-0	0-0	1-1	3-0	0-0	0-2
LR Ahlen	34	10	9	15	43	49	39	2-0	1-0	3-2	1-0	2-4	1-1	2-0	1-3	1-2	2-2	2-3			3-1	2-2	0-1	3-1	2-3
Energie Cottbus	34	10	9	15	35	48	39	3-5	1-0	0-3	1-1	2-0	1-1	2-0	4-1	1-0	0-1					2-1	1-0	0-0	3-0
Eintracht Trier	34	9	12	13	39	53	39	0-0	1-0	2-2	2-2	0-0	0-4	1-0	2-4	0-2	0-2	0-0	2-1	2-0	2-1		2-2	1-1	2-0
Rot-Weiß Oberhausen	34	8	10	16	40	62	34	0-3	0-2	0-3	0-0	1-0	0-2	0-2	1-5	2-1	1-2	0-1	2-1	2-0	0-0	1-1		1-1	4-3
Rot-Weiß Essen	34	6	15	13	35	51	33	2-2	1-0	4-4	0-0	0-2	0-2	1-5	2-1	1-2	0-1	2-1	2-0	1-0	4-2	2-2	2-2		0-0
Rot-Weiß Erfurt	34	7	9	18	34	60	30	0-1	0-0	0-3	1-2	1-0	0-3	1-1	1-0	2-0	4-2	0-1	1-3	3-3	3-0	1-1	1-1		

7/08/2004 - 22/05/2005

GERMANY 2004-05 REGIONALLIGA NORD

	Pl	W	D	L	F	A	Pts
Eintracht Braunschweig	36	20	10	6	59	35	70
SC Paderborn 07	36	20	10	6	63	40	70
VfB Lübeck	36	20	9	7	62	40	69
VfL Osnabrück	36	18	13	5	67	44	67
Wuppertaler SV	36	15	9	12	46	48	54
Hamburger SV (AM)	36	16	5	15	49	48	53
Sankt Pauli	36	13	13	10	43	39	52
Fortuna Düsseldorf	36	12	13	11	46	42	49
Holstein Kiel	36	14	6	16	54	44	48
Preußen Munster	36	12	10	14	52	58	46
1.FC Köln (AM)	36	12	10	14	58	65	46
Hertha BSC Berlin (AM)	36	12	11	13	55	57	44
Werder Bremen (AM)	36	11	9	16	48	57	42
Chemnitzer FC	36	10	10	16	33	38	40
Borussia Dortmund (AM)	36	10	10	16	57	64	40
VfL Wolfsburg (AM) §	36	7	13	16	37	58	33
Arminia Bielefeld (AM)	36	7	8	21	50	83	29
1.FC Union Berlin	36	6	9	21	32	50	27
Krefeld Uerdingen ‡	36	13	10	13	43	50	49

30/07/2004 -4/06/2005 • §One point deducted • ‡Licence withdrawn

GERMANY 2004-05 REGIONALLIGA SUD

	Pl	W	D	L	F	A	Pts
Kickers Offenbach	34	21	4	9	62	36	67
Sportfreunde Siegen	34	18	10	6	52	29	64
Wehen Taunusstein	34	19	6	9	55	38	63
FC Augsburg	34	17	10	7	62	36	61
SV Darmstadt	34	16	6	12	50	33	54
Bayern München (AM)	34	14	10	10	51	38	52
TSG Hoffenheim	34	14	8	12	57	49	50
Jahn Regensburg	34	13	9	12	47	46	48
Stuttgarter Kickers	34	12	11	11	48	43	47
SV Elversberg	34	11	11	12	45	55	44
TuS Koblenz	34	10	13	11	43	38	43
VfR Aalen	34	12	7	15	41	59	43
VfB Stuttgart (AM)	34	11	9	14	55	57	42
1.SC Feucht	34	12	6	16	42	49	42
TSV 1860 München (AM)	34	11	7	16	39	44	40
SC Pfullendorf	34	11	3	20	36	64	36
1.FSV Mainz (AM)	34	8	9	17	29	46	33
FC Nöttingen	34	3	7	24	29	83	16

6/08/2004 - 4/06/2005 • Feucht withdrew at the end of the season

CLUB DIRECTORY

Club	Stadium	Phone	www.	Lge	Cup	CL
Hertha BSC Berlin	Olympiastadion 76 065	+49 30 3009280	herthabsc.de	2	0	0
Arminia Bielefeld	Schüco Arena 26 601	+49 521 966110	arminia-bielefeld.de	0	0	0
VfL Bochum	Ruhrstadion 32 645	+49 234 951848	vfl-bochum.de	0	0	0
Werder Bremen	Weserstadion 35 800	+49 1805 937337	werder-online.de	4	5	0
Borussia Dortmund	Westfalenstadion 83 000	+49 231 90200	borussia-dortmund.de	6	2	1
SC Freiburg	Badenova-Stadion 25 000	+49 761 385510	scfreiburg.com	0	0	0
Hamburger SV	AOL Arena 55 000	+49 40 415501	hsv.de	6	3	1
Hannover 96	AWD Arena 49 000	+49 5139 8085550	hannover96.de	2	1	0
1.FC Kaiserslautern	Fritz-Walter-Stadion 46 615	+49 631 31880	fck.de	4	2	0
Bayer Leverkusen	BayArena 22 500	+49 214 86600	bayer04.de	0	1	0
1.FSV Mainz 05	Stadion am Bruchweg 18 600	+49 6131 375500	mainz05.de	0	0	0
Borussia Mönchengladbach	Borussia-Park 53 056	+49 2161 92930	borussia.de	5	3	0
Bayern München	Allianz-Arena 66 000	+49 89 699310	fcbayern.de	19	12	4
1.FC Nürnberg	Frankenstadion 44 833	+49 911 940790	fcn.de	9	3	0
FC Hansa Rostock	Ostseestadion 30 000	+49 381 499990	fc-hansa.de	1 - GDR	1 - GDR	0
Schalke 04	Arena AufSchalke 61 010	+49 209 36180	schalke04.de	7	4	0
VfB Stuttgart	Gottlieb-Daimler 54 088	+49 1805 8325463	vfb-stuttgart.de	4	3	0
VfL Wolfsburg	Volkswagen-Arena 30 000	+49 5361 89030	vfl-wolfsburg.de	0	0	0

RECENT LEAGUE AND CUP RECORD

	Championship						Cup		
Year	Champions	Pts	Runners-up	Pts	Third	Pts	Winners	Score	Runners-up
1990	Bayern München	49	1.FC Köln	43	Eintracht Frankfurt	43	1.FC Kaiserslautern	3-2	Werder Bremen
1991	1.FC Kaiserslautern	48	Bayern München	45	Werder Bremen	42	Werder Bremen	1-1 4-3p	1.FC Köln
1992	VfB Stuttgart	52	Borussia Dortmund	52	Eintracht Frankfurt	50	Hannover 96	0-0 4-3p	B. Mönchengladbach
1993	Werder Bremen	48	Bayern München	47	Eintracht Frankfurt	42	Bayer Leverkusen	1-0	Hertha Berlin (Am)
1994	Bayern München	44	1.FC Kaiserslautern	43	Bayer Leverkusen	39	Werder Bremen	3-1	Rot-Weiss Essen
1995	Borussia Dortmund	49	Werder Bremen	48	SC Freiburg	46	B. Mönchengladbach	3-0	VfL Wolfsburg
1996	Borussia Dortmund	68	Bayern München	62	Schalke 04	56	1.FC Kaiserslautern	1-0	Karlsruher SC
1997	Bayern München	71	Bayer Leverkusen	69	Borussia Dortmund	63	VfB Stuttgart	2-0	Energie Cottbus
1998	1.FC Kaiserslautern	68	Bayern München	66	Bayer Leverkusen	55	Bayern München	2-1	MSV Duisberg
1999	Bayern München	78	Bayer Leverkusen	63	Hertha BSC Berlin	62	Werder Bremen	1-1 5-4p	Bayern München
2000	Bayern München	73	Bayer Leverkusen	73	Hamburger SV	59	Bayern München	3-0	Werder Bremen
2001	Bayern München	63	Schalke 04	62	Borussia Dortmund	58	Schalke 04	2-0	1.FC Union Berlin
2002	Borussia Dortmund	70	Bayer Leverkusen	69	Bayern München	68	Schalke 04	4-2	Bayer Leverkusen
2003	Bayern München	75	VfB Stuttgart	59	Borussia Dortmund	58	Bayern München	3-1	1.FC Kaiserslautern
2004	Werder Bremen	74	Bayern München	68	Bayer Leverkusen	65	Werder Bremen	3-2	Alemannia Aachen
2005	Bayern München	77	Schalke 04	63	Werder Bremen	59	Bayern München	2-1	Schalke 04

DFB POKAL 2004-05

First Round		Second Round		Third Round	
Bayern München	6				
TSV Völpke *	0	Bayern München	3		
Erzgebirge Aue	2	VfL Osnabrück *	2		
VfL Osnabrück *	3			Bayern München	3
Rot-Weiß Oberhausen	3			VfB Stuttgart	0
Hannover 96 (Am) *	0	Rot-Weiß Oberhausen *	0		
TuS Mayen *	0	VfB Stuttgart	2		
VfB Stuttgart	6				
SC Paderborn *	4				
Hamburger SV	2	SC Paderborn *	2		
Werder Bremen (Am) *	1	MSV Duisburg	1		
MSV Duiburg	2			SC Paderborn *	2 1p
VfL Bochum	3			SC Freiburg	2 4p
Fortuna Düsseldorf *	1	VfL Bochum	2		
1.FC Union Berlin *	0	SC Freiburg *	3		
SC Freiburg	4				
Hansa Rostock	2				
TSG Hoffenheim *	1	Hansa Rostock	3 4p		
1.FC Saarbrücken *	1	1.FC Köln *	3 2p		
1.FC Köln	4			Hansa Rostock	3
1.FC Nürnberg	2			LR Ahlen *	2
FC Teningen *	1	1.FC Nürnberg *	2		
Kickers Offenbach *	1	LR Ahlen	3		
LR Ahlen	2				
Karlsruher SC	2				
1.FC Dynamo Dresden *	1	Karlsruher SC *	1 3p		
VfR Aalen *	2	1.FSV Mainz	1 0p		
1.FSV Mainz	5			Karlsruher SC	0
1.FC Köln (Am) ‡	2 (0)			Arminia Bielefeld *	4
VfL Wolfsburg	0 (3)	1.FC Köln (Am) *	2		
VfC Plauen *	1	Arminia Bielefeld	4		
Arminia Bielefeld	2				
Werder Bremen	2				
Jahn Regensburg *	0	Werder Bremen *	3		
1.FSV Mainz (Am) *	1	Bayer Leverkusen	2		
Bayer Leverkusen	3			Werder Bremen *	3
TSV 1860 München	2			Eintracht Trier	1
Germania Schöneiche *	1	TSV 1860 München *	0 3p		
SG Wattenscheid *	1	Eintracht Trier	0 4p		
Eintracht Trier	3				
Eintracht Braunschweig *	1				
Wacker Burghausen	0	Eintracht Braunschweig *	3		
TSV Aindling *	0	Hertha BSC Berlin	2		
Hertha BSC Berlin	1			Eintracht Braunschweig	2
Alemannia Aachen	2			Bayern München (Am) *	3
Rot-Weiß Essen *	0	Alemannia Aachen	1		
Borussia Mönchengladbach	1 5p	Bayern München (Am) *	2		
Bayern München (Am) *	1 6p				
Hannover 96	3				
VfR Neumünster *	0	Hannover 96	2 5p		
Sankt Pauli *	1	Energie Cottbus *	2 4p		
Energie Cottbus	3			Hannover 96 *	1
SpVgg Unterhäching	3			Borussia Dortmund	0
Jahn Regensburg II *	1	SpVgg Unterhäching	0		
VfB Lübeck *	0	Borussia Dortmund *	3		
Borussia Dortmund	1				
Eintracht Frankfurt	1				
Rot-Weiß Erfurt *	0	Eintracht Frankfurt *	4		
Carl-Zeiss Jena *	1	SpVgg Greuther Fürth	2		
SpVgg Greuther Fürth	2			Eintracht Frankfurt *	0
1.FC Kaiserslautern	15			Schalke 04	2
FC Schönberg *	0	1.FC Kaiserslautern *	4 3p		
Hertha BSC Berlin (Am) *	0	Schalke 04	4 4p		
Schalke 04	2				

‡ Tie awarded to Köln 2-0 after Wolfsburg fielded an ineligible player. Originally 3-0

DFB POKAL 2004-05

Quarter-finals	Semi-finals	Final

Bayern München 7
SC Freiburg * 0

Bayern München 2
Arminia Bielefeld * 0

Hansa Rostock 0
Arminia Bielefeld * 1

Bayern München 2
Schalke 04 1

Werder Bremen 3
Bayern München (Am) * 0

Werder Bremen 2 4p
Schalke 04 * 2 5p

DFB POKAL FINAL 2005

Olympiastadion, Berlin, 4-06-2005, Att: 74 349, Referee: Meyer

| Bayern München | 2 | Makaay 42, Salihamidzic 76 |
| Schalke 04 | 1 | Lincoln 45p |

Bayern: Oliver Kahn; Willy Sagnol (Sebastian Deisler 90), Lucio, Robert Kovac, Bixente Lizarazu; Martin Demichelis, Bastian Schweinsteiger (Hasan Salihamidzic 75), Michael Ballack, Ze Roberto (Torsten Frings 82); Roy Makaay, Claudio Pizarro.
Tr: Felix Magath
Schalke: Timo Rost; Niels Oude Kamphuis (Hamit Altintop 46), Marcelo Jose Bordon, Mladen Krstajic, Levan Kobiashvili; Christian Poulsen (Dario Rodriguez 82), Sven Vermant, Lincoln, Gerald Asamoah, Ebbe Sand, Ailton (Mike Hanke 71).
Tr: Ralf Rangnick

Hannover 96 1
Schalke 04 * 3

* Home team

FC BAYERN MUNCHEN 2004-05

Date	Opponents	Score		Comp	Scorers	Att
28-07-2004	Bayer Leverkusen	W 3-0	N	LPsf	Ze Roberto [5], Ballack [65], Frings [67]	10 100
2-08-2004	Werder Bremen	W 3-2	N	LPf	Deisler 2 [27 44], Ballack [65]	13 200
7-08-2004	Hamburger SV	W 2-0	A	BL	Ballack [22], Deisler [71]	55 500
14-08-2004	Hertha BSC Berlin	D 1-1	H	BL	Makaay [47]	58 000
21-08-2004	TSV Völpke	W 6-0	A	DPr1	Scholl [23], Santa Cruz 4 [31 57 70 89], Hargreaves [36]	21 000
28-08-2004	Bayer Leverkusen	L 1-4	A	BL	Ballack [84]	22 500
11-09-2004	Arminia Bielefeld	W 1-0	H	BL	Makaay [26]	48 000
15-09-2004	Maccabi Tel Aviv - ISR	W 1-0	A	CLgC	Makaay [64p]	25 000
18-09-2004	Borussia Dortmund	D 2-2	A	BL	Lucio [88], Makaay [90]	83 000
21-09-2004	VfL Osnabrück	W 3-2	A	DPr2	Pizarro 2 [5 74], Makaay [90]	18 415
25-09-2004	SC Freiburg	W 3-1	H	BL	Makaay [19], Frings [45], Ballack [72]	47 000
28-09-2004	Ajax - NED	W 4-0	H	CLgC	Makaay 2 [28 44 51p], Ze Roberto [55]	50 000
2-10-2004	Werder Bremen	W 2-1	A	BL	Ballack [20], Schweinsteiger [75]	42 100
16-10-2004	Schalke 04	L 0-1	H	BL		63 000
19-10-2004	Juventus - ITA	L 0-1	A	CLgC		18 089
23-10-2004	Hansa Rostock	W 2-0	A	BL	Sagnol [82], Scholl [85]	29 500
26-10-2004	VfL Wolsburg	W 2-0	H	BL	Pizarro 6 [24 45]	37 000
30-10-2004	Borussia Mönchengladbach	L 0-2	A	BL		53 466
3-11-2004	Juventus - ITA	L 0-1	H	CLgC		59 000
6-11-2004	Hannover 96	W 3-0	H	BL	Pizarro [3], Makaay [80], Guerrero [90]	62 000
10-11-2004	VfB Stuttgart	W 3-0	H	DPr3	Hargreaves [35], Ballack [69], Makaay [79]	24 000
14-11-2004	VfL Bochum	W 3-1	H	BL	Guerrero 2 [76 81], Preuss OG [82]	32 645
20-11-2004	1.FC Kaiserslautern	W 3-1	H	BL	Pizarro [12], Frings [26], Guerrero [64]	40 000
23-11-2004	Maccabi Tel Aviv - ISR	W 5-1	H	CLgC	Pizarro [12], Salihamidzic [37], Frings [44], Makaay 2 [71 80]	45 000
27-11-2004	1.FSV Mainz 05	W 4-2	H	BL	Pizarro [14], Scholl [35], Makaay [45], Ballack [88]	49 000
4-12-2004	1.FC Nürnberg	D 2-2	A	BL	Makaay [26p], Ze Roberto [60]	44 359
8-12-2004	Ajax - NED	D 2-2	A	CLgC	Makaay [9], Ballack [78]	51 000
11-12-2004	VfB Stuttgart	D 2-2	H	BL	Pizarro [66], Guerrero [89]	63 000
21-01-2005	Hamburger SV	W 3-0	H	BL	Pizarro [22], Schweinsteiger [48], Makaay [55]	39 000
30-01-2005	Hertha BSC Berlin	D 0-0	H	BL		74 500
5-02-2005	Bayer Leverkusen	W 2-0	H	BL	Makaay [45p], Guerrero [68]	45 000
13-02-2005	Arminia Bielefeld	L 1-3	A	BL	Lucio [80]	26 601
19-02-2005	Borussia Dortmund	W 5-0	H	BL	Salihamidzic [5], Makaay 3 [6 34 54], Pizarro [28]	53 000
22-02-2005	Arsenal - ENG	W 3-1	H	CLr2	Pizarro 2 [4 58], Salihamidzic [65]	59 000
26-02-2005	SC Freiburg	W 1-0	A	BL	Deisler [52]	25 000
2-03-2005	SC Freiburg	W 7-0	A	DPqf	Pizarro 4 [7 10 39 60], Ballack [27], Makaay [34], Hashemian [76]	25 000
5-03-2005	Werder Bremen	W 1-0	H	BL	Ballack [7]	53 000
9-03-2005	Arsenal - ENG	L 0-1	A	CLr2		35 463
13-03-2005	Schalke 04	L 0-1	A	BL		61 524
19-03-2005	Hansa Rostock	W 3-1	H	BL	Lucio [41], Pizarro [65], Ballack [89p]	52 000
2-04-2005	VfL Wolsburg	W 3-0	A	BL	Schweinsteiger [29], OG [45], Frings [55]	30 000
6-04-2005	Chelsea - ENG	L 2-4	A	CLqf	Schweinsteiger [52], Ballack [93p]	40 253
9-04-2005	Borussia Mönchengladbach	W 2-1	H	BL	Scholl [66], Ballack [84]	63 000
12-04-2005	Chelsea - ENG	W 3-2	H	CLqf	Pizarro [65], Guerrero [90], Scholl [95+]	59 000
16-04-2005	Hannover 96	W 1-0	A	BL	Hargreaves [90]	49 845
20-04-2005	Arminia Bielefeld	W 2-0	A	DPsf	Ballack [3], Makaay [90p]	26 601
23-04-2005	VfL Bochum	W 3-1	H	BL	Pizarro [9], Ballack [26], Makaay [63]	63 000
30-04-2005	1.FC Kaiserslautern	W 4-0	A	BL	Ballack [19], Makaay 3 [35 48 67]	40 721
7-05-2005	1.FSV Mainz 05	W 4-2	A	BL	Makaay 3 [17 82 89], Ballack [42]	20 300
14-05-2005	1.FC Nürnberg	W 6-3	H	BL	Pizarro [8], Ballack [24], Makaay 2 [31 41p], Deisler 2 [44 78]	63 000
21-05-2005	VfB Stuttgart	W 3-1	A	BL	Ballack [27], Salihamidzic [30], Makaay [71]	48 600
28-05-2005	Schalke 04	W 2-1	N	DPf	Makaay [42], Salihamidzic [76]	74 349

LP = Liga-Pokal (Super Cup) • BL = Bundesliga • CL = UEFA Champions League • DP = DFB Pokal
r1 = first round • gC = Group C • r2 = second round • r3 = third round • qf = quarter-final • sf = semi-final • f = final

FC SCHALKE 04 GELSENKIRCHEN 2004-05

Date	Opponents	Score		Comp	Scorers	Att
17-07-2004	Vardar Skopje - MKD	W 5-0	H	ITCqf	Krstajic [19], Altintop [40], Ailton [50], Kläsener [81], Tanevski OG [90+4]	56 054
24-07-2004	Vardar Skopje - MKD	W 2-1	A	ITCqf	Pander [5], Sand [15]	
28-07-2004	Esbjerg FB - DEN	W 3-1	A	ITCsf	Ailton [40], Hanke [71], Altintop [87]	8 000
3-08-2004	Esbjerg FB - DEN	W 3-0	H	ITCsf	Hanke [11], Altintop [54], Asamoah [63]	56 320
6-08-2004	Werder Bremen	L 0-1	A	BL		42 109
10-08-2004	Slovan Liberec - CZE	W 2-1	H	ITCf	Ailton [26], Asamoah [42]	54 136
14-08-2004	1.FC Kaiserslautern	W 2-1	H	BL	Asamoah 2 [25 65]	60 956
21-08-2004	Hertha BSC Berlin (Am)	W 2-0	A	DPr1	Hanke [24], Altintop [78]	4 198
24-08-2004	Slovan Liberec - CZE	W 1-0	H	ITCf	Ailton [87]	7 880
28-08-2004	Hansa Rostock	L 0-2	H	BL		60 790
11-09-2004	VfL Wolfsburg	L 0-3	A	BL		25 000
16-09-2004	Metalurgs Liepaja - LVA	W 5-1	H	UCr1	Sand 3 [20 52 60], Kobiashvili [67], Asamoah [89]	50 304
18-09-2004	Borussia Mönchengladbach	W 3-2	H	BL	Pander [35], Varela [59], Sand [66]	61 000
22-09-2004	1.FC Kaiserslautern	D 4-4	A	DPr2	Sand 2 [32 90], Lincoln [78], Krstajic [116]	22 365
25-09-2004	Hannover 96	L 0-1	A	BL		35 000
30-09-2004	Metalurgs Liepaja - LVA	W 4-0	H	UCr1	Sand [44], Hanke 3 [63 74 90]	
3-10-2004	VfL Bochum	W 3-2	H	BL	Asamoah [10], Kobiashvili [13], Lincoln [44]	61 524
16-10-2004	Bayern München	W 1-0	A	BL	Asamoah [76]	63 000
21-10-2004	FC Basle - SUI	D 1-1	H	UCgA	Kobiashvili [8]	52 870
24-10-2004	1.FSV Mainz 05	W 2-1	H	BL	Lincoln [25], Ailton [69]	61 524
27-10-2004	1.FC Nürnberg	W 2-0	A	BL	Ailton [10], Sand [45]	32 115
30-10-2004	VfB Stuttgart	W 3-2	H	BL	Ailton [1], Kobiashvili [2], Lincoln [25]	61 524
4-11-2004	Heart of Midlothian - SCO	W 1-0	A	UCgA	Lincoln [73]	27 272
7-11-2004	Hamburger SV	W 2-1	A	BL	Hanke [79], Lincoln [81]	53 487
10-11-2004	Eintracht Frankfurt	W 2-0	A	DPr3	Husterer OG [32], Hanke [77]	37 000
13-11-2004	Hertha BSC Berlin	L 1-3	H	BL	Asamoah [50]	61 524
20-11-2004	Bayer Leverkusen	W 3-0	A	BL	Sand [27], Ailton [37], Lincoln [71]	22 500
25-11-2004	Ferencváros - HUN	W 2-0	H	UCgA	Gyepes OG [16], Kobiashvili [40]	51 179
28-11-2004	Arminia Bielefeld	W 2-1	H	BL	Kobiashvili [28], Ailton [38]	61 524
1-12-2004	Feyenoord - NED	L 1-2	A	UCgA	Hanke [6]	
4-12-2004	Borussia Dortmund	W 1-0	A	BL	Ailton [17]	83 000
11-12-2004	SC Freiburg	D 1-1	H	BL	Krstajic [24]	60 433
22-01-2005	Werder Bremen	W 2-1	H	BL	Asamoah [48], Ailton [67]	61 524
29-01-2005	1.FC Kaiserslautern	L 0-2	A	BL		37 850
5-02-2005	Hansa Rostock	D 2-2	A	BL	Sand [25], Ailton [90]	24 000
12-02-2005	VfL Wolfsburg	W 3-0	H	BL	Asamoah [13], Sand [35], Hanke [85]	61 524
16-02-2005	Shakhtar Donetsk - UKR	D 1-1	A	UCr2	Ailton [9]	28 000
20-02-2005	Borussia Mönchengladbach	W 3-1	H	BL	Ailton 3 [44 66 79]	53 148
24-02-2005	Shakhtar Donetsk - UKR	L 0-1	H	UCr2		51 179
27-02-2005	Hannover 96	W 1-0	H	BL	Hanke [65]	61 524
1-03-2005	Hannover 96	W 3-1	H	DPqf	Asamoah [39], Hanke 2 [42 53]	56 932
5-03-2005	VfL Bochum	W 2-0	A	BL	Ailton [30], Lincoln [77]	32 645
13-03-2005	Bayern München	W 1-0	H	BL	Lincoln [69]	61 524
20-03-2005	1.FSV Mainz 05	L 1-2	A	BL	Lincoln [70p]	20 300
2-04-2005	1.FC Nürnberg	W 4-1	H	BL	Hanke 2 [24 36], Ailton [40], Lincoln [74]	61 524
9-04-2005	VfB Stuttgart	L 0-3	A	BL		48 600
16-04-2005	Hamburger SV	L 1-2	H	BL	Asamoah [3]	61 524
19-04-2005	Werder Bremen	D 2-2	H	DPsf	Sand [64], Ailton [96]. W 5-4p	61 524
23-04-2005	Hertha BSC Berlin	L 1-4	A	BL	Sand [17]	74 500
30-04-2005	Bayer Leverkusen	D 3-3	H	BL	Lincoln 2 [30 38], Sand [41]	61 524
7-05-2005	Arminia Bielefeld	W 2-0	A	BL	Lincoln [9p], Ailton [90]	26 601
14-05-2005	Borussia Dortmund	L 1-2	H	BL	Waldoch [19]	61 524
21-05-2005	SC Freiburg	W 3-2	A	BL	Sand [6], Bordon 2 [55 89]	24 500
28-05-2005	Bayern München	L 1-2	N	DPf	Lincoln [45p]	74 349

ITC = UEFA Intertoto Cup • BL = Bundesliga • UC = UEFA Cup • DP = DFB Pokal
gA = Group A • r1 = first round • r2 = second round • r3 = third round • qf = quarter-final • sf = semi-final • f = final

GHA – GHANA

NATIONAL TEAM RECORD
JULY 1ST 2002 TO JUNE 30TH 2005

PL	W	D	L	F	A	%
28	10	10	8	40	28	53.6

FIFA/COCA-COLA WORLD RANKING

1993	1994	1995	1996	1997	1998	1999	2000	2001	2002	2003	2004	High		Low	
37	26	29	25	57	48	48	57	59	61	78	77	15	04/96	89	06/04

2004-2005											
08/04	09/04	10/04	11/04	12/04	01/05	02/05	03/05	04/05	05/05	06/05	07/05
70	74	72	75	77	77	79	79	76	75	76	70

Having plummeted to their lowest position in the FIFA/Coca-Cola World Ranking in June 2004, the prospects for Ghana in a FIFA World Cup™ qualifying group that contained overwhelming favourites South Africa did not look good. Twelve months on there was quite a different atmosphere in the camp with the team in pole position to qualify for their first FIFA World Cup™ finals. Coach Ratomir Dujkovic has taken strong control of a side that has beaten South Africa twice and can rely on players of the calibre of Stephen Appiah and Michael Essien. It was a good

INTERNATIONAL HONOURS
FIFA World U-17 Championship 1991 1995 **Qualified for the FIFA Women's World Cup finals** 1999 2003
CAF African Cup of Nations 1963 1965 1978 1982 **CAF African Youth Championship** 1993 1999 **CAF African U-17 Championship** 1995 1999
CAF Champions League Asante Kotoko 1970 1983 Hearts of Oak 2000

year for Hearts of Oak who won their seventh Championship in eight years reclaiming the title lost in 2003 to Asante Kotoko. The single League format was abandoned for two groups of eight and Hearts and Kotoko met in the final play-off, when in front of 40,000 spectators Prince Tagoe struck the only goal of the game for a Hearts victory. The pair also met in the final of the 2004 CAF Confederation Cup with Hearts again triumphant, this time 8-7 on penalties after the two legs both ended 1-1. Real Tamale won the Cup Final with Kotoko once again the losing finalist.

THE FIFA BIG COUNT OF 2000

	Male	Female		Male	Female
Registered players	15 000	0	Referees	700	0
Non registered players	100 000	0	Officials	4 000	0
Youth players	10 000	0	Total involved	129 700	
Total players	125 000		Number of clubs	250	
Professional players	0	0	Number of teams	1 500	

Ghana Football Association (GFA)
General Secretariat, National Sports Council, PO Box 1272, Accra, Ghana
Tel +233 21 671501   Fax +233 21 668590
ghanafootball@yahoo.com   www.none
President: NYAHO-TAMAKLOE Nyaho Dr   General Secretary: NSIAH Kofi
Vice-President: NYANTAKYI Kwesi   Treasurer: TBD   Media Officer: None
Men's Coach: DUJKOVIC Ratomir   Women's Coach: ESHUN John
GFA formed: 1957   CAF: 1958   FIFA: 1958
Colours: Yellow, Yellow, Yellow

GAMES PLAYED BY GHANA IN THE 2006 FIFA WORLD CUP™ CYCLE

2002	Opponents	Score		Venue	Comp	Scorers	Att	Referee
7-09	Uganda	L	0-1	Kampala	CNq		25 000	Mohamed SOM
8-10	Lesotho	W	2-1	Accra	Fr	Taylor [40], Ofori Quaye [56]		
13-10	Rwanda	W	4-2	Accra	CNq	Kakule [25], Hamza [40], Ansampong [58], Boateng [72p]	40 000	Pare BFA
19-10	Sierra Leone	L	1-2	Freetown	Fr	Taylor [25]		Sanusie SLE
15-12	Nigeria	L	0-1	Accra	Fr			Wellington GHA
22-12	Egypt	D	0-0	Cairo	Fr			
2003								
26-01	Benin	W	3-0	Kumasi	Fr	Abbey [37], Tiero [45], Asante [87]		Amedior GHA
15-02	Benin	L	0-1	Cotonou	Fr			Lamidi BEN
27-03	Tunisia	D	2-2	Tunis	Fr	Amoah.C 2 [45 48]. L 7-8p	30 000	
30-03	Madagascar	D	3-3	Tunis	Fr	Appiah [5], Amoah.C [32], Gyan [60]. W 10-9p		
30-05	Nigeria	L	1-3	Abuja	Fr	Agyema [2]	60 000	
13-06	Kenya	L	1-3	Accra	Fr	Appiah [60]		
22-06	Uganda	D	1-1	Kumasi	CNq	Amoah.C [84]		
6-07	Rwanda	L	0-1	Kigali	CNq		40 000	
16-11	Somalia	W	5-0	Accra	WCq	Arhin Duah 2 [25 56], Boakye 2 [69 89], Gyan [82]	19 447	Bebou TOG
19-11	Somalia	W	2-0	Kumasi	WCq	Appiah [27], Adjei [90]	12 000	Chaibou NIG
2004								
28-04	Angola	D	1-1	Accra	Fr	Morgan [90]		Kotey GHA
5-06	Burkina Faso	L	0-1	Ouagadougou	WCq		25 000	Chukwujekwu NGA
14-06	Togo	D	0-0	Kumasi	Fr			
20-06	South Africa	W	3-0	Kumasi	WCq	Muntari [13], Appiah 2 [55 78]	32 000	Diatta SEN
25-06	Mozambique	W	1-0	Maputo	Fr	Gyan [72]	20 000	
3-07	Uganda	D	1-1	Kampala	WCq	Gyan [88]	20 000	El Beltagy EGY
5-09	Cape Verde Islands	W	2-0	Kumasi	WCq	Essien [24p], Veiga OG [62]	35 000	Tamuni LBY
10-10	Congo DR	D	0-0	Kumasi	WCq		30 000	Coulibaly MLI
2005								
23-03	Kenya	D	2-2	Nairobi	Fr	Gyan [23], Amoah [89]		
27-03	Congo DR	D	1-1	Kinshasa	WCq	Gyan [30]	80 000	Sowe GAM
5-06	Burkina Faso	W	2-1	Kumasi	WCq	Appiah [66], Amoah [83]	11 920	Abd el Fatah EGY
18-06	South Africa	W	2-0	Johannesburg	WCq	Amoah [59], Essien [91+]	50 000	Guezzaz MAR

Fr = Friendly match • CN = CAF African Cup of Nations • WC = FIFA World Cup™ • q = qualifier

FIFA REFEREE LIST 2005

	Int'l	DoB
AGBENYEGA Justus	2003	16-09-1964
AGBOVI William	2004	19-11-1972
ATSATSA Christian	2003	18-12-1965
DOWUONA Charles	2005	26-04-1967
KOTEY Alex	2002	31-01-1963
MCCARTHY Joseph	2005	16-06-1968
ODARTEI Joseph	2005	10-09-1974

FIFA ASSISTANT REFEREE LIST 2005

	Int'l	DoB
ANNAN Archibold	1996	23-10-1961
BOADU-AYEBOAFO Ahmed	2002	10-03-1964
DJOMOAH Nicholas	1996	27-04-1966
HARUNA Ayuba	2002	12-09-1966
QUAYE Samuel	1999	8-10-1962
SAIJAH George	2004	24-12-1969
YEBOAH Justice	1994	23-04-1961

GHANA COUNTRY INFORMATION

Capital	Accra	Independence	1957 from the UK	GDP per Capita	$2 200
Population	20 757 032	Status	Republic	GNP Ranking	108
Area km²	239 460	Language	English	Dialling code	+233
Population density	86 per km²	Literacy rate	66%	Internet code	.gh
% in urban areas	36%	Main religion	Christian 63%	GMT +/ −	0
Towns/Cities ('000)	Accra 1 963; Kumasi 1 468; Tamale 360; Tema 351; Obuasi 144; Cape Coast 143; Obuasi 119				
Neighbours (km)	Burkina Faso 549; Togo 877; Côte d'Ivoire 668; Atlantic Ocean 539				
Main stadia	Kumasi Stadium – Kumasi 51 500; Accra Stadium – Accra 35 000; Len Clay – Obuasi 25 000				

GHANA NATIONAL TEAM RECORDS AND RECORD SEQUENCES

Records			Sequence records					
Victory	9-1	NIG 1969	Wins	8	1965-1967	Clean sheets	6	1990-1991
Defeat	2-8	BRA 1996	Defeats	6	1996	Goals scored	29	1963-1967
Player Caps	n/a		Undefeated	21	1981-1983	Without goal	5	1985
Player Goals	n/a		Without win	9	1996-1997	Goals against	15	1967-1968

GHANA 2004

PREMIER FOOTBALL LEAGUE

Zone A	Pl	W	D	L	F	A	Pts	Kotoko	Faisal	Tamale	Arsenal	AshantiGold	Bafoakwa	Okwahu	BA United
Asante Kotoko †	14	9	2	3	24	10	29		1-0	1-0	4-0	4-0	2-0	3-1	4-1
King Faisal Babies ‡	14	8	3	3	19	8	27	0-1		2-0	2-1	2-0	3-0	2-0	1-0
Real Tamale United	14	7	2	5	13	13	23	1-0	0-2		2-0	2-1	1-0	1-0	2-0
Arsenal Berekum	14	6	3	5	13	16	21	0-0	1-2	2-0		0-0	2-1	1-0	1-0
AshantiGold Obuasi	14	5	5	4	18	15	20	4-1	1-1	2-0	0-0		5-2	2-0	3-2
Tano Bafoakwa	14	4	2	8	9	18	14	0-1	1-0	0-0	3-1	0-0		1-0	0-2
Okwahu United	14	2	5	7	8	16	11	1-1	2-2	1-1	1-2	0-0	1-0		1-0
Brong Ahofu United	14	3	2	9	11	19	11	2-1	0-0	2-3	1-2	1-0	0-1	0-0	

Zone B	Pl	W	D	L	F	A	Pts	Hearts	Lions	Liberty Pros	Power	Tema	Feyenoord	Hasaacas	Olympics
Hearts of Oak †	14	9	2	3	29	17	29		4-2	3-0	3-2	1-2	3-0	1-1	2-3
Heart of Lions ‡	14	6	5	3	15	13	23	1-1		2-2	2-1	0-0	0-0	1-0	1-0
Liberty Professionals	14	6	2	6	23	17	20	3-0	3-2		2-1	4-0	4-0	1-2	3-0
Power FC Koforidua	14	5	3	6	19	19	18	2-3	2-0	1-1		2-1	3-2	1-0	3-1
Real Sportive Tema	14	4	5	5	12	15	17	1-2	0-2	1-0	0-0		1-0	4-0	1-1
Feyenoord Academy	14	5	2	7	11	16	17	0-1	0-1	2-0	2-1	0-0		3-0	1-0
Hasaacas Sekondi	14	4	4	6	11	17	16	0-2	0-0	2-0	0-0	2-0	2-0		1-1
Great Olympics	14	4	3	7	13	19	15	0-3	0-1	1-0	2-0	1-1	0-1	3-1	

23/05/2004 - 21/11/2004. † Qualified for the CAF Champions League. ‡ Qualified for the CAF Confederation Cup
Championship play-off: **Hearts of Oak** 1-0 Asante Kotoko
Relegation play-off: Okwahu United 1-0 Hasaacas Sekondi

GHALCA CUP 2004

Quarter-finals

Real Tamale Utd*	2	1
Liberty Pros	0	3
Okwawu Utd	1	0
AshantiGold *	2	0
King Faisal *	1	2
Great Olympics	0	0
Real Sportive *	1	2
Asante Kotoko	2	0

Semi-finals

Real Tamale Utd	0 2	3p
AshantiGold *	2 0	0p
King Faisal	1	0
Asante Kotoko *	2	1

Final

First leg. 15-09-2004
Kumasi Sports Stadium
Scorers - Yamoah [43], Ansah [47p] for Kotoko; Weah [6] for RTU

Real Tamale Utd	1 1
Asante Kotoko *	2 0

Second leg. 6-10-2004
Accra Sports Stadium
Scorer - Abdullah [87] for RTU

* Home team in the first leg • Real Tamale won the final on away goals • Tournament organised by the Ghana League Clubs Association

RECENT LEAGUE AND CUP RECORD

	Championship							Cup		
Year	Champions	Pts	Runners-up	Pts	Third	Pts		Winners	Score	Runners-up
1996	Goldfields Obuasi	51	Asante Kotoko	50	Okwahu United	46		Hearts of Oak	1-0	Ghapoha Tema
1997	Hearts of Oak	54	Real Tamale United	51	Goldfields Obuasi	48		Ghapoha Tema	1-0	Okwahu United
1998	Hearts of Oak	52	Asante Kotoko	48	Great Olympics	39		Asante Kotoko	1-0	Real Tamale United
1999	Hearts of Oak	62	Cape Coast Dwarfs	53	Real Tamale United	52		Hearts of Oak	3-1	Great Olympics
2000	Hearts of Oak	57	Goldfields Obuasi	52	King Faisal Babies	46		Hearts of Oak	2-0	Okwahu United
2001	Hearts of Oak	64	Asante Kotoko	55	Goldfields Obuasi	45		Asante Kotoko	1-0	King Faisal Babies
2002	Hearts of Oak	78	Asante Kotoko	73	Liberty Professionals	48		Not played		
2003	Asante Kotoko	75	Hearts of Oak	66	King Faisal Babies	54		Not played		
2004	Hearts of Oak	1-0	Asante Kotoko					Real Tamale United	1-2 1-0	Asante Kotoko

GNB – GUINEA-BISSAU

NATIONAL TEAM RECORD

JULY 1ST 2002 TO JUNE 30TH 2005

PL	W	D	L	F	A	%
2	0	0	2	1	4	0

FIFA/COCA-COLA WORLD RANKING

1993	1994	1995	1996	1997	1998	1999	2000	2001	2002	2003	2004	High		Low	
131	122	118	133	148	165	173	177	174	183	186	190	**115**	07/94	**191**	02/05

2004-2005											
08/04	09/04	10/04	11/04	12/04	01/05	02/05	03/05	04/05	05/05	06/05	07/05
187	187	187	187	190	191	191	191	191	191	191	191

Relative newcomers to the international scene, Guinea-Bissau have made three attempts at FIFA World Cup™ qualification, but have so far failed to make any great impression. Knocked out at the preliminary stages of the 1998 and 2002 qualifying campaigns, the team's poor record continued for Germany 2006 when they were knocked out by Mali 4-1 on aggregate in November 2003. The team have yet to play since and there were also no entries into the recent CAF U-20 and U-17 events. As one of the poorest countries in the world the difficulties facing Guinea-Bissau run deep and the resources to develop football in the country are limited. FIFA suspended financial

INTERNATIONAL HONOURS

None

assistance in 2004 after concerns over the disappearance of funds provided for the construction of a national training centre as part of the FIFA Goal programme. However, there was some good news provided by the domestic League and for fans of Sporting Club de Bissau it's been another good year. A branch of Sporting Club de Portugal, Sporting won the League and Cup double, their third League title in four years and the 12th overall. The Taca Nacional was lifted following a 4-2 victory over Atlético Bissorã, which made up for the final defeat in 2004 and handed Sporting their first cup title in 13 years.

THE FIFA BIG COUNT OF 2000

	Male	Female		Male	Female
Registered players	1 000	0	Referees	50	0
Non registered players	3 000	0	Officials	300	0
Youth players	500	0	Total involved	4 850	
Total players	4 500		Number of clubs	40	
Professional players	0	0	Number of teams	100	

Federação de Futebol da Guiné-Bissau (FFGB)

Alto Bandim (Nova Sede), Case Postale 375, Bissau 1035, Guinea-Bissau

Tel +245 201918   Fax +245 211414

federacaofutebol@hotmail.com   www.none

President: LOBATO Jose   General Secretary: CASSAMA Infali

Vice-President: GOMES VAZ Alberto   Treasurer: DAVYES Lolita Francisca Maria   Media Officer: TCHAGO Jorge

Men's Coach: CANDE Baciro   Women's Coach: KEITA Sidico

FFGB formed: 1974   CAF: 1986   FIFA: 1986

Colours: Red, Green, Red

GAMES PLAYED BY GUINEA-BISSAU IN THE 2006 FIFA WORLD CUP™ CYCLE

2002 Opponents	Score	Venue	Comp	Scorers	Att	Referee
No international matches played after June 2002						
2003						
10-10 Mali	L 1-2	Bissau	WCq	Fernandes 50	22 000	Sowe GAM
14-11 Mali	L 0-2	Bamako	WCq		13 251	Seydou MTN
2004						
No International matches played in 2004						
2005						
No international matches played in 2005 before August						

WC = FIFA World Cup™ • q = qualifier

GUINEA-BISSAU NATIONAL TEAM RECORDS AND RECORD SEQUENCES

Records			Sequence records					
Victory	7-2	BEN 2001	Wins	3	1990-1991	Clean sheets	5	1987-1988
Defeat	1-6	MLI 1997	Defeats	5	1980-1981	Goals scored	6	1989-1991
Player Caps	n/a		Undefeated	11	1987-1989	Without goal	3	1985, 1997-2000
Player Goals	n/a		Without win	8	1979-1981	Goals against	13	1994-1997

FIFA REFEREE LIST 2005

	Int'l	DoB
CABI Antonio		11-04-1968
CANTUSSAN Silvestre	2005	13-06-1968
FAFE Joaozinho	2001	9-10-1962
GOMES Fidelis	2005	1-06-1975
SOARES DA GAMA Jono	2005	25-05-1975

FIFA ASSISTANT REFEREE LIST 2005

	Int'l	DoB
DELGADO JR. Mercelino	2005	18-05-1973
GARCES Biai	2004	3-06-1972
GRABE Rui		17-05-1966
JO Fernando	2004	4-07-1968
MENDES Antonio		20-12-1967
SEIDI Serifo	2005	28-02-1965

RECENT LEAGUE AND CUP RECORD

	Championship						Cup		
Year	Champions	Pts	Runners-up	Pts	Third	Pts	Winners	Score	Runners-up
1997	Sporting Bissau						No tournament		
1998	Sporting Bissau						No tournament		
1999	No competition held						No tournament		
2000	Sporting Bissau	38	Benfica	36	União Bissau	36	Portos Bissau	2-1	Mavegro FC
2001	No competition held						No tournament		
2002	Sporting Bissau	39	Portos Bissau	37	União Bissau	32	Mavegro FC	3-1	Sporting Bafatá
2003	União Bissau	47	Sporting Bissau	44	Sporting Bafatá	43	Tournament not finished		
2004	Sporting Bissau	39	Benfica	28	Mavegro FC	28	Mavegro FC	1-0	Sporting Bissau
2005	Sporting Bissau	45	Atlético Bissorã	38	Mavegro FC	37	Sporting Bissau	4-2	Atlético Bissorã

GUINEA-BISSAU COUNTRY INFORMATION

Capital	Bissau	Independence	1973 from Portugal	GDP per Capita	$800
Population	1 388 363	Status	Republic	GNP Ranking	184
Area km²	36 120	Language	Portuguese	Dialling code	+245
Population density	38 per km²	Literacy rate	34%	Internet code	.gw
% in urban areas	22%	Main religion	Indigenous 50%, Muslim 45%	GMT +/−	0
Towns/Cities ('000)	Bissau 388; Bafatá 22; Gabú 14; Bissorã 12; Bolama 10; Cacheu 10; Bubaque 9				
Neighbours (km)	Senegal 338; Guinea 386; Atlantic Ocean 350				
Main stadia	24 de Setembro – Bissau 20 000; Lino Correia – Bissau 12 000				

GRE – GREECE

NATIONAL TEAM RECORD
JULY 1ST 2002 TO JUNE 30TH 2005

PL	W	D	L	F	A	%
40	21	10	9	43	31	65

FIFA/COCA-COLA WORLD RANKING

1993	1994	1995	1996	1997	1998	1999	2000	2001	2002	2003	2004	High		Low	
34	28	34	35	42	53	34	42	57	48	30	18	13	02/05	66	09/98

2004-2005											
08/04	09/04	10/04	11/04	12/04	01/05	02/05	03/05	04/05	05/05	06/05	07/05
14	14	16	17	18	18	13	14	12	12	13	19

The Greeks were always likely to suffer from a hangover in the wake of their stunning European Championship success in Portugal and sure enough the return to action saw an embarrassing 2-1 defeat against Albania in Tirana. It proved to be a defeat Otto Rehhagel's men could ill afford in a FIFA World Cup™ qualifying group that was tougher than most. With Ukraine running away at the top that left the Greeks, the Turks and the Danes all chasing a single play-off spot. Should the Greeks fail to qualify for the finals they can take comfort from the fact that they won't be the first reigning European Champions missing from the FIFA World Cup™ finals. The season ended with

INTERNATIONAL HONOURS
UEFA European Championship 2004

an appearance at the FIFA Confederations Cup that Greece would rather forget. Two draws and a defeat saw them finish bottom of their group and when they failed to score against Mexico in the final game it was the team's fifth game without a goal - a new and most unwelcome record. In the domestic championship Olympiacos gained revenge over fierce rivals Panathinaikos who in 2004 had ended their run of seven consecutive Championships. Only three points separated the big three clubs from the capital at the end of the season but it was Olympiacos who stole it at the finish to win their 33rd title and to complete the double having just beaten Aris in the Cup Final.

THE FIFA BIG COUNT OF 2000

	Male	Female		Male	Female
Registered players	421 743	961	Referees	2 500	0
Non registered players	150 000	0	Officials	9 000	200
Youth players	55 311	0	Total involved	639 715	
Total players	628 015		Number of clubs	1 400	
Professional players	1 874	0	Number of teams	3 804	

Hellenic Football Federation (HFF)
137 Singrou Avenue, Nea Smirni, Athens 17121, Greece
Tel +30 210 9306000   Fax +30 210 9359666
epo@epo.gr   www.epo.gr
President: GAGATSIS Vassilis   General Secretary: ECONOMIDES Ioannis Dr
Vice-President: LYKOUREZOS Alexandros   Treasurer: GIRTZIKIS George   Media Officer: TSAPIDIS Michael
Men's Coach: REHHAGEL Otto   Women's Coach: BATSILAS Dimitrios
HFF formed: 1926   UEFA: 1954   FIFA: 1927
Colours: Blue, Blue, Blue or White, White, White

GAMES PLAYED BY GREECE IN THE 2006 FIFA WORLD CUP™ CYCLE

2002	Opponents	Score		Venue	Comp	Scorers	Att	Referee
21-08	Romania	W	1-0	Constanta	Fr	Giannakopoulos [16]	15 000	Tokat TUR
7-09	Spain	L	0-2	Athens	ECq		16 500	Merk GER
12-10	Ukraine	L	0-2	Kyiv	ECq		50 000	Temmink NED
16-10	Armenia	W	2-0	Athens	ECq	Nikolaidis 2 [2 60]	6 000	Ceferin SVN
20-11	Republic of Ireland	D	0-0	Athens	Fr		5 000	Trentalange ITA
2003								
29-01	Cyprus	W	2-1	Larnaca	Fr	Fyssas [53], Karagounis [79]	2 000	Loizou CYP
12-02	Norway	W	1-0	Irákleio	Fr	Kyrgiakos [25]	8 000	Gomes Costa POR
26-03	Austria	D	2-2	Graz	Fr	Tsartas [48p], Kafes [51]	8 500	Ovrebo NOR
2-04	Northern Ireland	W	2-0	Belfast	ECq	Charisteas 2 [3 56]	7 196	Gilewski POL
30-04	Slovakia	D	2-2	Puchov	Fr	Tsartas [13p], Choutos [77]	2 863	Messner AUT
7-06	Spain	W	1-0	Zaragoza	ECq	Giannakopoulos [42]	32 000	Sars FRA
11-06	Ukraine	W	1-0	Athens	ECq	Charisteas [87]	15 000	De Bleeckere BEL
20-08	Sweden	W	2-1	Norrköping	Fr	Giannakopoulos [63], Kafes [65]	15 018	Hyytia FIN
6-09	Armenia	W	1-0	Yerevan	ECq	Vryzas [34]	6 500	Temmink NED
11-10	Northern Ireland	W	1-0	Athens	ECq	Tsartas [69p]	15 500	Cortez Batista POR
15-11	Portugal	D	1-1	Aveiro	Fr	Lakis [47]	30 000	Esquinas Torres ESP
2004								
18-02	Bulgaria	W	2-0	Athens	Fr	Papadopoulos [25], Vryzas [60]	6 000	Poll ENG
31-03	Switzerland	W	1-0	Irákleio	Fr	Tsartas [55]	33 000	Temmink NED
28-04	Netherlands	L	0-4	Eindhoven	Fr		25 000	Bolognino ITA
29-05	Poland	L	0-1	Szczecin	Fr		17 000	Kari FIN
3-06	Liechtenstein	W	2-0	Vaduz	Fr	Vryzas [24], Charisteas [88]	2 000	Petignat SUI
12-06	Portugal	W	2-1	Porto	ECr1	Katagounis [7], Basinas [51p]	48 761	Collina ITA
16-06	Spain	D	1-1	Porto	ECr1	Charisteas [66]	25 444	Michel SVK
20-06	Russia	L	1-2	Faro-Loule	ECr1	Vryzas [43]	24 000	Veissiere FRA
25-06	France	W	1-0	Lisbon	ECqf	Charisteas [65]	45 390	Frisk SWE
1-07	Czech Republic	W	1-0	Porto	ECsf	Dellas [105 SG]	42 449	Collina ITA
4-07	Portugal	W	1-0	Lisbon	ECf	Charisteas [57]	62 865	Merk GER
18-08	Czech Republic	D	0-0	Prague	Fr		15 050	Dougal SCO
4-09	Albania	L	1-2	Tirana	WCq	Giannakopoulos [38]	15 800	Iturralde Gonzalez ESP
8-09	Turkey	D	0-0	Piraeus	WCq		32 182	Frisk SWE
9-10	Ukraine	D	1-1	Kyiv	WCq	Tsartas [83]	56 000	Mejuto Gonzalez ESP
17-11	Kazakhstan	W	3-1	Piraeus	WCq	Charisteas 2 [24 46+], Katsouranis [85]	31 838	Kostadinov BUL
2005								
9-02	Denmark	W	2-1	Piraeus	WCq	Zagorakis [25], Basinas [32p]	32 430	Collina ITA
26-03	Georgia	W	3-1	Tbilisi	WCq	Kapsis [43], Vryzas [44], Giannakopoulos [53]	23 000	Rosetti ITA
30-03	Albania	W	2-0	Piraeus	WCq	Charisteas [33], Karagounis [84]	31 700	Layec FRA
4-06	Turkey	D	0-0	Istanbul	WCq		26 700	Merk GER
8-06	Ukraine	L	0-1	Piraeus	WCq		33 500	Temmink NED
16-06	Brazil	L	0-3	Leipzig	CCr1		42 507	Michel SVK
19-06	Japan	L	0-1	Frankfurt	CCr1		34 314	Fandel GER
22-06	Mexico	D	0-0	Frankfurt	CCr1		31 285	Amarilla PAR

Fr = Friendly match • EC = UEFA EURO 2004™ • WC = FIFA World Cup™ • CC = FIFA Confederations Cup
q = qualifier • r1 = First round group • qf = quarter-final • sf = semi-final • f = final • SG = Silver goal

GREECE COUNTRY INFORMATION

Capital	Athens	Independence	1829 from Ottoman Empire	GDP per Capita	$20 000
Population	10 647 529	Status	Republic	GNP Ranking	31
Area km²	131 940	Language	Greek	Dialling code	+30
Population density	80 per km²	Literacy rate	97%	Internet code	.gr
% in urban areas	65%	Main religion	Christian 98%	GMT +/−	+2
Towns/Cities ('000)	Athens 729; Thessaloníki 354; Piraeus 172; Pátra 163; Irákleio 137; Lárisa 128; Kallithea 107; Nikaia 94; Kalamaria 91; Glifada 88; Volos 84; Akharnai 82; Nea Smirni 75				
Neighbours (km)	Albania 282; FYR Macedonia 246; Bulgaria 494; Turkey 206; Mediterranean Sea 13 676				
Main stadia	Olympic – Athens 74 767; Karaiskaki – Piraeus 33 500; Toumba – Thessaloníki 28 701				

GREECE NATIONAL TEAM RECORDS AND RECORD SEQUENCES

Records			Sequence records				
Victory	8-0	SYR 1949	Wins	6	1994-1994	Clean sheets	4	Five times
Defeat	1-11	HUN 1938	Defeats	10	1931-1933	Goals scored	17	1934-1949
Player Caps	100	ZAGORAKIS Theodorus	Undefeated	15	2002-2004	Without goal	5	2005
Player Goals	29	ANASTOPOULOS Nikolaos	Without win	12	1954-1960	Goals against	21	1957-1964

NATIONAL CAPS

	Caps
ZAGORAKIS Theodorus	106
APOSTOLAKIS Efstratos	95
SARAVAKOS Dimitris	78
MITROPOULOS Anastassios	76
TSALOHUIDIS Panayotis	75
ANASTOPOULOS Nikolaos	73
MANOLAS Steilos	70
TSARTAS Vassilis	70
DABIZAS Nikos	69
KALITZAKIS Yannis	69

NATIONAL GOALS

	Goals
ANASTOPOULOS Nikolaos	29
SARAVAKOS Dimitris	22
PAPAIOANNOU Dimitris	21
MACHLAS Nikos	18
NIKOLAIDES Themistoklis	17
TSALOHUIDIS Panayotis	16
SIDERIS Yeorgios	14
CHARISTEAS Angelos	14
TSARTAS Vassilis	12

NATIONAL COACH

	Years
SOFIANIDIS Alekos	1988-'89
GEORGIADIS Antonis	1989-'91
PETRITSIS Stefanos	1992
GEORGIADIS Antonis	1992
PANAGOULIAS Alketas	1992-'94
POLYCHRONIOU Kostas	1994-'98
IORDANESCU Anghel	1998-'99
DANIIL Vassilis	1999-'00
CHRISTIDIS Nikos	2001
REHHAGEL Otto	2001-

CLUB DIRECTORY

Club	Town/City	Stadium	Phone	www.	Lge	Cup	CL
AEK	Athens	Nikos Goumas 32 000	+30 210 6121371	aekfc.gr	11	13	0
Aris	Thessaloníki	Harilaou 18 308	+30 2310 309035	arisfc.gr	3	1	0
Chalkidona	Piraeus	Neapolis Public 7 026	+30 210 4925536	xalkhdonafc.gr	0	0	0
Egaleo	Athens	Egaleo 4 000	+30 210 5316883		0	0	0
Ergotelis	Irákleio	Pankritio 33 240	+30 2810 222246	ergotelis.gr	0	0	0
Ionikos	Piraeus	Neapolis Public 7 026	+30 210 4934106	ionikos-fc.gr	0	0	0
Iraklis	Thessaloníki	Kaftanzoglio 28 028	+30 2310 478800	iraklis-fc.gr	0	1	0
Kalamarias	Thessaloníki	Kalamaria 7 000			0	0	0
Kallithea	Athens	Kallithea 4 250	+30 210 9584990	kallitheafc.gr	0	0	0
Kérkira	Kérkira (Corfu)	Kérkira 4 000	+30 26610 46430		0	0	0
OFI Crete	Irákleio	Pankritio 33 240	+30 2810 823651	ofi.gr	0	1	0
Olympiacos	Piraeus	Karaiskaki 33 500	+30 210 4143000	olympiacos.org	33	21	0
Panathinaikos	Athens	Apostolos Nikolaidis 16 620	+30 210 8093630	pao.gr	19	16	0
Panionios	Athens	Nea Smyrni 11 700	+30 210 9311189	panionios.gr	0	2	0
PAOK	Thessaloníki	Toumba 28 701	+30 2310 950950	paokfc.gr	2	4	0
Xánthi	Xánthi	Xánthi 9 500	+30 25410 24466	skodaxanthifc.gr	0	0	0

RECENT LEAGUE AND CUP RECORD

	Championship						Cup		
Year	Champions	Pts	Runners-up	Pts	Third	Pts	Winners	Score	Runners-up
1990	Panathinaikos	53	AEK	50	PAOK	46	Olympiacos	4-2	OFI Crete
1991	Panathinaikos	54	Olympiakos	46	AEK	42	Panathinaikos	3-0 2-1	Athinaikos
1992	AEK	54	Olympiacos	51	Panathinaikos	48	Olympiacos	1-1 2-0	PAOK
1993	AEK	78	Panathinaikos	77	Olympiacos	68	Panathinaikos	1-0	Olympiacos
1994	AEK	79	Panathinaikos	72	Olympiacos	68	Panathinaikos	3-3 4-2p	AEK
1995	Panathinaikos	83	Olympiacos	67	PAOK	65	Panathinaikos	1-0	AEK
1996	Panathinaikos	83	AEK	81	Olympiacos	65	AEK	7-1	Apollon
1997	Olympiacos	84	AEK	72	OFI Crete	66	AEK	0-0 5-3p	Panathinaikos
1998	Olympiacos	88	Panathinaikos	85	AEK	74	Panionios	1-0	Panathinaikos
1999	Olympiacos	85	AEK	75	Panathinaikos	74	Olympiacos	2-0	Panathinaikos
2000	Olympiacos	92	Panathinaikos	88	AEK	66	AEK	2-0	Ionikos
2001	Olympiacos	78	Panathinaikos	66	AEK	61	PAOK	4-2	Olympiacos
2002	Olympiacos	58	AEK	58	Panathinaikos	55	AEK	2-1	Olympiacos
2003	Olympiacos	70	Panathinaikos	70	AEK	68	PAOK	1-0	Aris
2004	Panathinaikos	77	Olympiacos	75	PAOK	60	Panathinaikos	3-1	Olympiacos
2005	Olympiacos	65	Panathinaikos	64	AEK	62	Olympiacos	3-0	Aris

GREECE 2004-05

HELLENIC FOOTBALL LEAGUE A DIVISION

	Pl	W	D	L	F	A	Pts	Olympiacos	Panath'kos	AEK	Xánthi	PAOK	Egaleo	Iraklis	Chalkidona	Kallithea	Ionikos	Panionios	Kalamarias	OFI	Aris	Ergotelis	Kérkira
Olympiacos †	30	19	8	3	54	18	65	-	1-0	1-1	0-0	5-1	3-1	1-0	3-0	2-1	2-1	3-0	2-0	3-0	2-1	2-0	3-0
Panathinaikos †	30	19	7	4	51	18	64	1-0	-	0-0	3-1	2-1	0-0	0-0	6-3	1-0	3-0	4-0	5-1	5-1	0-0	1-0	1-0
AEK Athens ‡	30	17	11	2	46	22	62	0-0	1-0	-	2-1	2-0	1-0	2-1	1-0	4-1	0-1	2-0	3-0	1-1	1-0	3-0	2-0
Xánthi ‡	30	14	8	8	43	29	50	2-1	3-1	1-1	-	0-2	2-0	1-0	2-0	1-0	2-0	3-0	4-1	2-1	3-1	3-0	1-1
PAOK Thessaloníki ‡	30	13	7	10	43	39	46	1-1	1-1	1-1	1-0	-	2-4	1-0	2-1	3-1	3-0	1-0	5-2	4-1	2-2	0-2	1-0
Egaleo	30	11	12	7	31	26	45	2-2	0-1	1-1	1-1	2-1	-	1-0	2-1	1-2	1-0	0-0	0-0	2-0	2-1	2-0	1-0
Iraklis Thessaloníki	30	12	5	13	36	30	41	0-1	0-4	1-2	1-1	1-0	2-2	-	1-0	5-1	2-0	0-1	2-3	1-0	0-0	2-0	5-1
Chalkidona	30	10	8	12	34	38	38	1-1	0-2	1-1	2-1	2-0	1-1	0-0	-	4-2	0-1	1-0	2-3	2-3	1-0	2-0	0-0
Kallithea	30	9	10	11	39	44	37	1-1	0-2	1-2	2-3	1-1	0-2	1-1	3-1	-	0-0	1-1	1-1	3-1	3-1	3-0	1-2
Ionikos	30	8	12	10	22	32	36	0-4	0-0	2-3	1-1	1-1	1-1	1-0	0-0	0-0	-	0-0	2-0	0-0	2-1	1-0	0-0
Panionios	30	8	11	11	25	32	35	0-2	0-1	1-1	0-0	2-0	0-0	1-2	0-0	1-1	1-0	-	0-0	2-1	1-1	2-0	3-1
Kalamarias	30	8	9	13	31	49	33	0-2	0-1	2-1	1-1	2-1	1-1	1-3	0-2	1-2	1-1	3-3	-	1-0	0-1	1-0	3-0
OFI Crete	30	8	8	14	36	44	32	1-1	1-2	2-3	1-0	2-2	0-1	2-1	0-1	1-1	2-0	0-0	1-0	-	1-1	5-0	3-1
Aris Thessaloníki § ‡	30	5	13	12	26	37	25	0-1	1-1	1-1	2-1	1-3	0-0	0-2	1-2	2-2	0-2	1-0	0-0	3-2	-	1-1	2-0
Ergotelis	30	5	5	20	19	50	20	2-1	1-3	0-1	0-2	0-1	2-1	0-1	1-1	1-1	2-3	0-3	4-1	0-1	1-1	-	1-1
Kérkira	30	3	8	19	21	49	17	1-3	2-0	2-2	3-0	0-1	0-1	1-2	1-3	0-1	2-2	1-3	0-2	1-3	0-2	0-0	-

18/09/2004 - 25/05/2005 • † Qualified for the UEFA Champions League • ‡ Qualified for the UEFA Cup • § Three points deducted

GREECE 2004-05 B DIVISION

	Pl	W	D	L	F	A	Pts
Larisa	30	17	7	6	44	17	58
Levadiakos	30	15	11	4	30	14	56
Akratitos	30	16	8	6	33	19	56
Niki Volou	30	16	6	8	33	16	54
Olympiacos Volou	30	16	5	9	40	23	53
Panserraikos	30	15	8	7	33	21	53
Kastoria	30	13	12	5	44	21	51
Paniliakos	30	13	7	10	33	27	46
Kalamata	30	13	7	10	42	33	46
Proodeftiki	30	11	7	12	32	30	40
Ethnikos Asteras	30	11	6	13	26	27	39
Panahaiki 2005	30	10	7	13	31	34	37
Ilysiakos	30	9	9	12	43	41	36
Apollon	30	9	6	15	25	49	33
Atromitos	30	2	2	26	13	70	-31

18/09/2004 - 29/05/2005 • § 39 points deducted • Poseidonas excluded and all their opponents awarded 2-0 wins

TOP SCORERS

GEKAS Fanis	Panathinaikos	18
LUCIANO	Xánthi	16
KONSTANTINOU Michalis	Panathinaikos	15
BARKOGLOU Georgios	Egaleo	14
SALPIGGIDIS Dimitris	PAOK	14
MACHLAS Nikos	OFI	13
RIVALDO	Olympiacos	12

HELLENIC CUP 2004-05

Round of 16

Olympiacos	0	2
Iraklis Thessaloníki *	1	0
Ptolemaida	0	3
Kastoria *	2	2
Panionios	1	1
Ilysiakos *	0	0
Panathinaikos	1	1
AEK Athens *	1	3
Xánthi *	1	0
Egaleo	0	0
Chalkidona	1	1
Larisa *	3	0
Kalamaria	1	0
OFI Crete *	1	0
Ethnikos	1	1
Aris Thessaloníki *	2	2

Quarter-finals

Olympiacos	1	5
Kastoria *	2	1
Panionios *	0	0
AEK Athens	0	2
Xánthi	0	4
Larisa *	1	1
Kalamaria	0	1
Aris Thessaloníki *	0	1

Semi-finals

Olympiacos	1	2
AEK Athens *	0	1
Xánthi	2	0
Aris Thessaloníki *	1	2

Final

Olympiacos	3
Aris Thessaloníki ‡	0

CUP FINAL

21-05-2005, Att: 17 000, Ref: Kasnaferis
Panpeloponnisiako, Patras

Scorers - Djordjevic 56p, Rivaldo 2 70 90 for Olympiacos

* Home team in the first leg • ‡ Qualified for the UEFA Cup

GRN – GRENADA

NATIONAL TEAM RECORD
JULY 1ST 2002 TO JUNE 30TH 2005

PL	W	D	L	F	A	%
25	8	3	14	54	55	38

FIFA/COCA-COLA WORLD RANKING

1993	1994	1995	1996	1997	1998	1999	2000	2001	2002	2003	2004	High		Low	
143	142	141	127	111	117	121	143	133	131	154	144	105	08/97	155	02/04

2004-2005											
08/04	09/04	10/04	11/04	12/04	01/05	02/05	03/05	04/05	05/05	06/05	07/05
138	139	139	145	144	148	148	148	148	148	148	149

Ranked 149 and with a small number of UK-based player such as Wigan Athletic striker Jason Roberts, the Spice Boyz of Grenada have hopes of making their mark in the region. The 2006 FIFA World Cup™ qualifying campaign began against Guyana and an 8-1 aggregate win put them into the next round to face the USA. In the first meeting in Colombus, Grenada held out until almost half-time, finally succumbing 3-0. Back in St George's hopes of an upset were boosted because of a waterlogged pitch but the USA proved too strong and won 3-2 after Grenada were reduced to 10 men. Chasing the dream of a first appearance at the CONCACAF Gold Cup, the Spice Boyz drew

INTERNATIONAL HONOURS
None

2-2 with Surinam, lost against Trinidad and Tobago and then defeated Puerto Rico to clinch a place in the next round. They were soon stopped by St Vincent and the Grenadines, who won home and away for a 4-1 aggregate score. Ironically, the 2004 season was abandoned mid-term, with Hurricane FC topping the table, because of the devastating damage inflicted by Hurricane Ivan. A hastily convened replacement tournament was staged later in the year with Police SC of the second division beating Paradise 2-1 in the final. Neither of the youth teams made any great impression in their qualifying tournaments although the U-20s were runners-up in their group to Trinidad.

THE FIFA BIG COUNT OF 2000

	Male	Female		Male	Female
Registered players	524	0	Referees	35	0
Non registered players	1 000	125	Officials	127	5
Youth players	489	0	Total involved	2 305	
Total players	2 138		Number of clubs	30	
Professional players	0	0	Number of teams	50	

Grenada Football Association (GFA)
National Stadium, Queens Park, PO Box 326, St George's, Grenada
Tel +1 473 4409903   Fax +1 473 4409973
gfa@caribsurf.com   www.none
President: FOLKES Ashley Ram   General Secretary: DANIEL Victor
Vice-President: CHENEY Joseph   Treasurer: DANIEL Victor   Media Officer: BASCOMBE Michael
Men's Coach: DEBELLOTTE Alister   Women's Coach: SMITH Lester
GFA formed: 1924   CONCACAF: 1969   FIFA: 1978
Colours: Green & yellow stripes, Red, Yellow

GAMES PLAYED BY GRENADA IN THE 2006 FIFA WORLD CUP™ CYCLE

2002	Opponents	Score	Venue	Comp	Scorers	Att	Referee
6-07	Saint Martin	W 8-3	St George's	GCq	Phillip [10], Etienne [25], Rennie 5 [56 61 75 80 90], Charles [71]		Bynoe TRI
30-07	Chinese Taipei	W 5-2	St George's	Fr	Williams 2 [2 36], Wharwood 2 [13 31], Charles [47p]	4 500	Phillip GRN
2-08	Jamaica	L 0-1	St George's	Fr			
4-08	Saint Martin	W 7-1	Saint Martin	GCq	Bain.K [13], Phillip [23], Baptiste [54p], Bishop [64], Charles 3 [67 72 85]	200	Rouse AIA
9-11	Guadeloupe	L 4-5	St George's	GCq	Bain.C [14], Bain.K [45], Modeste [47], Williams [77]	3 000	Brizan TRI
11-11	Barbados	L 0-2	St George's	GCq		2 500	Murray TRI
13-11	Jamaica	L 1-4	St George's	GCq	Etienne [75]	3 250	Murray TRI
2003							
No international matches played in 2003							
2004							
11-01	Barbados	L 0-2	Bridgetown	Fr		2 000	Small BRB
31-01	Barbados	L 0-1	St George's	Fr			
28-02	Guyana	W 5-0	St George's	WCq	Bishop [34], Phillip [39], Augustine [72], Modeste.A [81], Rennie [91]	7 000	Archundia MEX
14-03	Guyana	W 3-1	Blairmont	WCq	Charles [15], Roberts [69], Bubb [87]	1 200	Quesada Cordero CRC
8-05	St Vincent/Grenadines	D 1-1	Kingstown	Fr			
20-05	Cuba	D 2-2	Havana	Fr	Roberts [47], Bishop [75]		
2-06	St Lucia	W 2-0	St George's	Fr	Roberts [7], Bain.K [65]	2 500	
13-06	USA	L 0-3	Columbus	WCq		10 000	Navarro CAN
20-06	USA	L 2-3	St George's	WCq	Roberts [12], Charles [77]	10 000	Brizan TRI
17-10	St Lucia	L 1-3	Castries	Fr			
13-11	St Vincent/Grenadines	L 2-6	Kingstown	Fr	Rennie [42], Bishop [81]		
20-11	St Vincent/Grenadines	W 3-2	Gouyave	Fr	Modeste.A [6], Charles 2 [13 88]	3 000	Bedeau GRN
24-11	Surinam	D 2-2	Tunapuna	GCq	Charles [46], Bishop [50]	2 000	Forde BRB
26-11	Trinidad and Tobago	L 0-2	Tunapuna	GCq			Callender BRB
28-11	Puerto Rico	W 5-2	Tunapuna	GCq	OG [1], Charles [3], Rennie [58], Williams [68], Langiagne [75]		Callender BRB
12-12	St Vincent/Grenadines	L 1-3	Kingstown	GCq	Rennie [59]		Fanus LCA
19-12	St Vincent/Grenadines	L 0-1	St George's	GCq			Small BRB
2005							
23-01	Barbados	L 0-3	Bridgetown	Fr			

Fr = Friendly match • GC = CONCACAF Gold Cup • WC = FIFA World Cup™ • q = qualifier

GRENADA NATIONAL TEAM RECORDS AND RECORD SEQUENCES

Records			Sequence records					
Victory	14-1	AIA 1998	Wins	3	1996	Clean sheets	2	1989, 1994
Defeat	0-7	TRI 1999	Defeats	5	2002-2004	Goals scored	15	2001-2002
Player Caps	n/a		Undefeated	5	1997, 2004	Without goal	3	1990
Player Goals	n/a		Without win	10	1990-1994	Goals against	17	1996-1999

RECENT LEAGUE AND CUP RECORD

Year	Champions	Pts	Runners-up	Pts	Third	Pts
1998	Fontenoy United	3-2	Saint Andrews FL			
1999	Cable Vision SAFL	30	Fontenoy United	28	GBSS	27
2000	GBSS	29	Saint John's Sports	27	Fontenoy United	20
2001	GBSS	34	Hurricane FC	22	Saint Andrews FL	22
2002	Queens Park Rangers					
2003	Hurricane FC	45	Paradise	39	Fontenoy United	31
2004	Abandoned due to Hurricane Ivan					

Cup		
Winners	Score	Runners-up
Queens Park Rangers		
Hurricane FC	3-1	GBSS
Hurricane FC		GBSS
Hurricane FC	1-0	GBSS
Police SC	2-1	Paradise

GRENADA COUNTRY INFORMATION

Capital	Saint George's	Independence	1974 from the UK	GDP per Capita	$5 500
Population	89 357	Status	Commonwealth	GNP Ranking	174
Area km²	344	Language	English	Dialling code	+1 473
Population density	259 per km²	Literacy rate	98%	Internet code	.gd
% in urban areas	37%	Main religion	Christian	GMT + / −	-4
Towns/Cities ('000)	Saint George's 4; Gouyave 3; Grenville 2; Victoria 2				
Neighbours (km)	Atlantic Ocean and the Caribbean Sea 121				
Main stadia	National Stadium – Saint George's 9 000				

GUA – GUATEMALA

NATIONAL TEAM RECORD
JULY 1ST 2002 TO JUNE 30TH 2005

PL	W	D	L	F	A	%
49	20	13	16	65	55	54.1

FIFA/COCA-COLA WORLD RANKING

1993	1994	1995	1996	1997	1998	1999	2000	2001	2002	2003	2004	High		Low	
120	149	145	105	83	73	73	56	67	78	77	71	**54**	03/03	**163**	11/95

2004-2005											
08/04	09/04	10/04	11/04	12/04	01/05	02/05	03/05	04/05	05/05	06/05	07/05
79	64	61	62	71	68	70	62	60	60	59	61

With 36 years of civil war only coming to an end in 1996, football in Guatemala has had a good deal of catching up to do and in the intervening decade the Bicolor, as the national team is known, has done its bit to raise spirits. Star striker Carlos Ruiz has been just as prolific with the team as he has been with his club side FC Dallas, scoring eight goals as Guatemala advanced to the final round of the FIFA World Cup™ qualifiers in the CONCACAF Region. With only the bottom two of the six team group missing out on a chance of making it to the finals in Germany, the tantalising prospect of a first appearance in the finals has been keeping Guatemalan fans on the edge of

INTERNATIONAL HONOURS
CONCACAF Championship 1967   UNCAF Championship 2001   CONCACAF Club Championship Municipal 1974, Comunicaciones 1978

their seats. Expectations were dampened, however, at the CONCACAF Gold Cup in July 2005. Having failed to win the UNCAF Cup, which acted as a qualifier for the finals despite hosting the event, the Guatemalans made a swift first round exit in the Gold Cup, managing only a draw against guests South Africa. Municipal continued to be the strongest team in the Championship winning their seventh title since the format of two championships a season was introduced in 1999. They finished top in the regular season of both the Apertura and Clausura and beat Comunicaciones and then Suchitepéquez in the respective finals of both.

THE FIFA BIG COUNT OF 2000

	Male	Female		Male	Female
Registered players	48 900	760	Referees	320	8
Non registered players	150 000	62 500	Officials	4 500	75
Youth players	67 500	0	Total involved	334 563	
Total players	329 660		Number of clubs	100	
Professional players	500	0	Number of teams	197	

Federación Nacional de Fútbol de Guatemala (FNFG)
2a. Calle 15-57, Zona 15, Boulevard Vista Hermosa, Guatemala City 01009, Guatemala
Tel +502 24227777   Fax +502 24227780
fedefutbol@guate.net.gt   www.fedefut.org
President: TINOCO Rafael   General Secretary: ARROYO Oscar
Vice-President: TBD   Treasurer: DE TORREBIARTE Adela   Media Officer: None
Men's Coach: MARADIAGA Ramon   Women's Coach: GARCIA Antonio
FNFG formed: 1919   CONCACAF: 1961   FIFA: 1946
Colours: Blue, White, Blue

GAMES PLAYED BY GUATEMALA IN THE 2006 FIFA WORLD CUP™ CYCLE

2002	Opponents	Score		Venue	Comp	Scorers	Att	Referee
30-10	Jamaica	D	1-1	Guatemala City	Fr	Ruiz [53]	8 000	Alfaro SLV
2003								
17-01	El Salvador	D	0-0	Santa Ana (USA)	Fr		6 000	Gack USA
19-01	El Salvador	D	0-0	Los Angeles	Fr		6 000	Jackson USA
13-02	Costa Rica	D	1-1	Panama City	GCq	Garcia [48]		Ramos Rizo MEX
16-02	Panama	L	0-2	Panama City	GCq			Pineda HON
18-02	Nicaragua	W	5-0	Panama City	GCq	Ruiz 3 [33 45 66], Garcia [77], Figueroa [81]	5 000	Moreno PAN
20-02	El Salvador	W	2-0	Panama City	GCq	Alegria.C [18], Garcia [83p]		Ramos Rizo MEX
23-02	Honduras	W	2-1	Panama City	GCq	Ramirez [7], Figueroa [56]		Ramos Rizo MEX
22-06	Honduras	L	1-2	Carson	Fr	Acevedo [16]	15 023	Saheli USA
2-07	Peru	L	1-2	San Francisco	Fr	Romero [82p]		Hall USA
8-07	El Salvador	W	2-1	Guatemala City	Fr	Plata [58], Aguirre [65]	21 047	Hall USA
15-07	Jamaica	L	0-2	Miami	GCr1		10 323	Pineda HON
17-07	Colombia	D	1-1	Miami	GCr1	Ruiz [21p]	13 000	Porras CRC
20-08	Ecuador	L	0-2	Ambato	Fr		25 000	Diaz ECU
27-08	Peru	D	0-0	Lima	Fr		2 000	Lecca PER
2004								
31-03	El Salvador	W	3-0	San Salvador	Fr	Garcia [21], Figueroa [28], Romero [90]	5 047	Aguilar SLV
1-05	Panama	L	1-2	Guatemala City	Fr	Pezzarossi [90]	11 615	Argueta Arias SLV
5-05	Haiti	W	1-0	Guatemala City	Fr	Ruiz [49]	15 000	Recinos SLV
12-06	Surinam	D	1-1	Paramaribo	WCq	Ramirez [36]	5 500	Jimenez CRC
20-06	Surinam	W	3-1	Guatemala City	WCq	Ruiz 2 [21 85], Pezzarossi [80]	19 610	Rodriguez MEX
18-07	El Salvador	W	1-0	Los Angeles	Fr	Medina [41]		Valenzuela USA
23-07	Panama	D	1-1	Panama City	Fr	Ramirez [67]	3 000	Mejia CRC
6-08	El Salvador	W	2-0	Washington DC	Fr	Ramirez [49], Mendoza [72]	20 000	Valenzuela USA
11-08	Trinidad and Tobago	W	4-1	Guatemala City	Fr	Melgar [48], Ramirez [71], Romero [78], Estrada.W [86]	9 000	
18-08	Canada	W	2-0	Vancouver	WCq	Ruiz 2 [7 59]	6 500	Sibrian SLV
5-09	Costa Rica	W	2-1	Guatemala City	WCq	Plata 2 [58 73]	27 460	Stott USA
8-09	Honduras	D	2-2	San Pedro Sula	WCq	Ruiz [20], Pezzarossi [49]	40 000	Prendergast JAM
2-10	Jamaica	D	2-2	Fort Lauderdale	Fr	Plata [56], Davilla [59]	8 500	Vaughn USA
9-10	Costa Rica	L	0-5	San Jose	WCq		18 000	Archundia MEX
13-10	Honduras	W	1-0	Guatemala City	WCq	Ruiz [44]	26 000	Brizan TRI
10-11	Mexico	L	0-2	San Antonio (USA)	Fr			Terry USA
13-11	Bolivia	W	1-0	Washington DC	Fr	Ruiz [21]	22 000	Prus USA
17-11	Canada	L	0-1	Guatemala City	WCq		18 000	Rodriguez MEX
21-12	Venezuela	W	1-0	Caracas	Fr	Ruiz [89]	5 000	Solorzano VEN
2005								
17-01	Colombia	D	1-1	Los Angeles	Fr	Ruiz [3]	15 000	Vaughn USA
23-01	Paraguay	L	1-2	Los Angeles	Fr	Rivera [36]		
9-02	Panama	D	0-0	Panama City	WCq		20 000	Prendergast JAM
13-02	Haiti	W	2-1	Fort Lauderdale	Fr	Villatoro [18], Castillo [70]	10 000	Salazar USA
19-02	Belize	W	2-0	Guatemala City	GCq	Villatoro [35], Plata [72p]	10 000	Quesada CRC
21-02	Nicaragua	W	4-0	Guatemala City	GCq	Plata [11], Sandoval 2 [30 77], Villatoro [66]	8 000	Sibrian SLV
23-02	Honduras	D	1-1	Guatemala City	GCq	Romero [22]	3 000	Moreno PAN
25-02	Costa Rica	L	0-4	Guatemala City	GCq		11 159	Archundia MEX
27-02	Panama	W	3-0	Panama City	GCq	Villatoro [7], Plata 2 [41 49]	1 491	Quesada CRC
26-03	Trinidad and Tobago	W	5-1	Guatemala City	WCq	Ramirez [17], Ruiz 2 [30 38], Pezzarossi 2 [78 87]	22 506	Stott USA
30-03	USA	L	0-2	Birmingham	WCq		31 624	Ramdhan TRI
20-04	Jamaica	L	0-1	Atlanta	Fr		7 000	Prus USA
27-04	Brazil	L	0-3	Sao Paulo	Fr		38 000	Vazquez URU
4-06	Mexico	L	0-2	Guatemala City	WCq		26 723	Hall USA
8-06	Costa Rica	L	2-3	San Jose	WCq	Villatoro [74], Rodriguez [77]	BCD	Archundia MEX
8-07	Jamaica	L	3-4	Carson	GCr1	Ruiz 3 [11p 48+ 87]	27 000	Hall USA
10-07	Mexico	L	0-4	Los Angeles	GCr1		30 710	Ruiz COL
13-07	South Africa	D	1-1	Houston	GCr1	Romero [37]	45 311	Stott USA

Fr = Friendly match • GC = CONCACAF Gold Cup • WC = FIFA World Cup™ • q = qualifier • BCD = Behind closed doors

GUATEMALA NATIONAL TEAM RECORDS AND RECORD SEQUENCES

Records			Sequence records					
Victory	9-0	HON 1921	Wins	6	1967	Clean sheets	4	1984-1985
Defeat	1-9	CRC 1955	Defeats	7	2005	Goals scored	16	1957-1965
Player Caps	n/a		Undefeated	13	1996-1997	Without goal	8	1989-1991
Player Goals	n/a		Without win	14	1989-1991	Goals against	13	1953-1961

FIFA REFEREE LIST 2005

	Int'l	DoB
BATRES Carlos	1996	2-04-1968
CASTELLANOS Ruben	2004	18-10-1971
CASTILLO Hugo	1998	26-12-1964
MEJIA Otto	1998	26-05-1963
PALMA Juan Manuel	2000	26-04-1964
RODAS Elmar	2005	15-02-1969

FIFA ASSISTANT REFEREE LIST 2005

	Int'l	DoB
ALVAREZ Marco	1999	22-03-1962
DIAZ Filadelfo	2004	13-02-1969
GONZALEZ Edwin	2004	6-04-1973
HERNANDEZ Elmer	2005	29-04-1972
MENDEZ Ariel	2005	16-07-1973
ORTIZ Francisco	1997	18-10-1961
YAT Ludwin	2004	5-01-1974

TORNEO DE COPA 2005

Round of 16			Quarter-finals			Semi-finals			Final		
Deportivo Jalapa *	4	1									
Aurora	1	3	Deportivo Jalapa *	1	1						
Sanarate *	0	0	Municipal	0	2						
Municipal	2	5				Deportivo Jalapa	1	1			
Zacapa *	2	2				Petapa *	1	0			
Cobán Imperial	1	3	Zacapa	0	1						
Deportivo Heredia	0	2	Petapa *	4	1						
Petapa *	3	0							Deportivo Jalapa *	3	0
Comunicaciones	2	4							Xelajú MC	0	2
La Gomera	0	0	Comunicaciones	2	1						
Juventud Retalteca *	1	0	Suchitepéquez *	1	1						
Suchitepéquez	1	2				Comunicaciones *	3	1			
Antigua GFC	0	3				Xelajú MC	1	4			
Xinabajul *	1	0	Antigua GFC *	0	3						
San Pedro		2	Xelajú MC	3	5						
Xelajú MC		3									

CUP FINALS
First leg. 1-06-2005
Scorers - Rosa 2 [51 85], Alegria [89] for Jalapa

Second leg. 5-06-2005
Scorers - Alvarez [13], Sumich OG [46] for Xelajú

* Home team in the first leg

RECENT LEAGUE AND CUP RECORD

Championship/Clausura from 2000				Apertura				Cup			
Year	Winners	Score	Runners-up	Winners	Score	Runners-up		Winners	Score	Runners-up	
1997	Comunicaciones	2-0 3-1	Aurora					Amatitlan	1-1 4-3	Municipal	
1998	Comunicaciones							Suchitepéquez	3-1	Cobán Imperial	
1999	Comunicaciones			Comunicaciones	1-1 2-1	Municipal		Municipal		Aurora	
2000	Municipal	0-1 2-0	Comunicaciones	Municipal	0-0 1-1	Comunicaciones		No tournament			
2001	Comunicaciones	4-0 2-3	Antigua GFC	Municipal	3-0 0-3	Cobán Imperial		No tournament			
2002	Municipal	1-2 2-0	Comunicaciones	Comunicaciones	2-1 1-1	Municipal		Deportivo Jalapa	5-2	Cobán Imperial	
2003	Comunicaciones	0-0 3-2	Cobán Imperial	Municipal	3-2 0-0	Comunicaciones		Municipal	2-1 1-0	Cobán Imperial	
2004	Cobán Imperial	3-2 2-2	Municipal	Municipal	5-1 4-1	Comunicaciones		Municipal	1-0 4-2	Deportivo Jalapa	
2005	Municipal	1-0 4-2	Suchitepéquez					Deportivo Jalapa	3-0 0-2	Xelajú MC	

GUATEMALA COUNTRY INFORMATION

Capital	Guatemala City	Independence	1821 from Spain	GDP per Capita	$4 100
Population	14 280 596	Status	Republic	GNP Ranking	64
Area km²	108 890	Language	Spanish	Dialling code	+502
Population density	131 per km²	Literacy rate	67%	Internet code	.gt
% in urban areas	41%	Main religion	Christian	GMT +/-	-6
Towns/Cities ('000)	Guatemala City 973; Mixco 460; Villa Nueva 397; Petapa 137; Quetzaltenango 127				
Neighbours (km)	Mexico 962; Belize 266; Honduras 256; El Salvador 203; Pacific Ocean & Caribbean Sea 400				
Main stadia	Mateo Flores – Guatemala City 29 950; La Pedrera – Guatemala City 17 000				

GUATEMALA 2004-05

TORNEO APERTURA

	Pl	W	D	L	F	A	Pts	Municipal	Com'ciones	Marquense	Suchit'quez	Xelajú	Herdia	Cobán	Jalapa	Antigua	Aurora
Municipal †	18	9	4	5	38	22	31		1-1	2-1	1-0	1-1	1-1	5-2	3-1	1-2	4-0
Comunicaciones †	18	9	4	5	34	20	31	2-1		0-0	0-0	1-0	3-0	3-1	5-1	3-0	3-0
Deportivo Marquense †	18	9	3	6	33	25	30	2-3	2-1		5-3	0-1	3-0	1-0	2-1	1-0	3-1
Suchitepéquez †	18	8	5	5	32	30	29	0-4	2-2	3-2		1-1	4-2	3-2	3-0	3-1	2-1
Xelajú MC †	18	6	8	4	21	22	26	0-1	3-2	1-1	1-1		1-1	2-1	3-2	2-0	1-1
Deportivo Heredia †	18	5	8	5	26	29	23	1-1	2-3	2-1	1-1	1-1		4-1	2-2	2-1	1-1
Cobán Imperial	18	7	2	9	25	29	23	3-2	0-1	0-4	3-0	3-0	0-1		1-0	1-0	3-0
Deportivo Jalapa	18	7	2	9	34	40	23	0-5	2-1	5-2	2-4	4-1	2-1	2-2		3-1	2-0
Antigua GFC	18	6	1	11	20	29	19	3-1	2-1	1-2	1-0	1-1	1-2	0-1	3-2		2-0
Aurora FC	18	3	5	10	18	35	14	2-1	3-2	1-1	1-2	0-1	2-2	1-1	1-3	3-1	

31/07/2004 - 28/11/2004 • † Qualified for the play-offs • Top two receive a bye to the semi-finals

APERTURA PLAY-OFFS

Quarter-finals

Suchitepéquez	1	1
Xelajú MC *	2	2

Deportivo Marquense	2	2
Deportivo Heredia *	3	0

Semi-finals

Municipal	0	2
Xelajú MC *	2	0

Deportivo Marquense*	3	1
Comunicaciones	1	5

* Home team in first leg

Final

First leg. 15-12-2004
Scorers - Ramírez [14], Plata 2 [17] [42], Acevedo [24p], Zorilla [39] for Municipal; Cubero [8] for Comunicaciones

Municipal	5	4
Comunicaciones *	1	1

Second leg. 19-12-2004
Scorers - Plata 2 [10] [87], Acevedo [29], Garcia [77] for Municipal; Pezarossi [12] for Comunicaciones

GUATEMALA 2004-05

TORNEO CLAUSURA

	Pl	W	D	L	F	A	Pts	Municipal	Suchit'quez	Xelajú	Com'ciones	Antigua	Cobán	Heredia	Jalapa	Aurora	Marquense
Municipal †	18	11	6	1	35	16	39		1-1	1-1	2-1	5-2	4-0	3-0	1-1	2-0	2-1
Suchitepéquez †	18	10	2	6	27	19	32	1-2		2-0	3-1	2-0	1-0	3-2	1-3	6-4	1-0
Xelajú MC †	18	8	6	4	27	17	30	1-0	0-0		1-1	3-1	3-2	5-1	3-2	4-0	2-0
Comunicaciones †	18	8	6	4	29	20	30	1-2	0-2	0-0		2-0	1-1	2-0	2-2	3-1	4-1
Antigua GFC †	18	7	4	7	20	23	25	0-0	0-1	1-1	1-2		1-0	2-1	1-0	2-0	2-0
Cobán Imperial †	18	6	3	9	17	22	21	1-3	1-0	1-0	0-0	2-0		1-0	1-1	0-0	1-1
Deportivo Heredia	18	5	5	8	27	32	20	1-1	2-1	3-1	2-2	1-1	2-1		3-0	5-1	2-2
Deportivo Jalapa	18	5	3	10	18	26	18	2-3	1-0	1-0	1-2	0-2	0-1	3-0		1-0	0-2
Aurora FC	18	5	3	10	20	33	18	0-1	1-0	1-0	1-3	2-2	4-0	2-1	1-0		1-1
Deportivo Marquense	18	3	5	10	18	30	14	2-2	1-2	0-1	0-2	1-2	0-4	1-1	3-0	2-1	

23/01/2005 - 22/05/2005 • † Qualified for the play-offs • Top two receive a bye to the semi-finals

CLAUSURA PLAY-OFFS

Quarter-finals

Antigua GFC *	1	0
Comunicaciones	1	1

Xelajú MC	0	2
Cobán Imperial *	0	1

Semi-finals

Municipal	2	3
Comunicaciones *	1	0

Xelajú MC *	1	2
Suchitepéquez	0	3

* Home team in first leg

Final

First leg. 22-06-2005
Scorers Garcia [65] for Municipal

Municipal	1	4
Suchitepéquez	0	2

Second leg. 25-06-2005
Scorers - Plata 4 [15] [38] [57] [60] for Municipal; Brown [48], OG [66] for Suchitepéquez

GUI – GUINEA

NATIONAL TEAM RECORD
JULY 1ST 2002 TO JUNE 30TH 2005

PL	W	D	L	F	A	%
27	11	7	9	36	28	53.7

FIFA/COCA-COLA WORLD RANKING FOR GUINEA

1993	1994	1995	1996	1997	1998	1999	2000	2001	2002	2003	2004	High		Low	
63	66	63	73	65	79	91	80	108	120	101	86	**51**	04/95	**123**	05/03

2004-2005											
08/04	09/04	10/04	11/04	12/04	01/05	02/05	03/05	04/05	05/05	06/05	07/05
87	89	86	84	86	88	87	88	89	93	83	89

Financial difficulties meant that no championship was organized in 2004 and it was left to the clubs of the interior to compete in the 46th National Cup tournament to determine Guinea's entrant into the 2005 Champions League. The two most financially stable clubs in the country made it to the final – Fello Stars de Labé and Club Industriel de Kamsar. Fello Stars, backed by a fishing company, came back from 2-0 down to win on penalties. Once in the Champions League they almost made it to the group stage but were denied a place after losing a penalty shoot-out to South Africa's Ajax Cape Town although that did mean a place in the Confederation Cup group stage. It was also a case

INTERNATIONAL HONOURS
Copa Amilcar Cabral 1981 1982 1987 1988   **CAF Champions League** Hafia Conakry 1972 1975 1977

of so near yet so far for the national team in the FIFA World Cup™ qualifiers. A FIFA suspension following government interference in the running of the Guinean Football Association had seen the Syli Nationale withdrawn from the 2002 FIFA World Cup™ qualifiers after a good start and once again the team got off to a flier including a 2-1 victory over African champions Tunisia. A place in the finals in Germany, however, proved a step too far for coach Patrice Neveu's team in a strong group that also contained Morocco with Guinea left to battle it out with Kenya and Botswana for the consolation of a place in the 2006 CAF African Cup of Nations finals in Egypt.

THE FIFA BIG COUNT OF 2000

	Male	Female		Male	Female
Registered players	8 000	0	Referees	300	0
Non registered players	30 000	0	Officials	2 400	0
Youth players	4 000	0	Total involved	44 700	
Total players	42 000		Number of clubs	150	
Professional players	0	0	Number of teams	700	

Fédération Guinéenne de Football (FGF)
PO Box 3645, Conakry, Guinea
Tel +224 455878   Fax +224 455879
guineefoot59@yahoo.fr   www.none
President: BANGOURA Aboubacar Bruno   General Secretary: CAMARA Fode Capi
Vice-President: CONTE Sory   Treasurer: DIALLO Mamadou   Media Officer: None
Men's Coach: NEVEU Patrice & PAPA Camara   Women's Coach: CAMARA Fabert
FGF formed: 1960   CAF: 1962   FIFA: 1962
Colours: Red, Yellow, Green

GAMES PLAYED BY GUINEA IN THE 2006 FIFA WORLD CUP™ CYCLE

2002	Opponents	Score		Venue	Comp	Scorers	Att	Referee
1-09	Gambia	L	0-1	Banjul	Fr			
8-09	Liberia	W	3-0	Conakry	CNq	Camara.T 17, Fode 56, Conte 57		Diouf SEN
12-10	Ethiopia	L	0-1	Addis Abeba	CNq			Itur KEN
2003								
12-02	Mali	L	0-1	Toulon	Fr			
30-03	Niger	W	2-0	Conakry	CNq	Mansare 40p, Sylla.A 90		Monteiro Duatre CPV
7-06	Niger	L	0-1	Niamey	CNq			Wellington GHA
21-06	Liberia	W	2-1	Accra	CNq	Soulemane 2 11 50		
6-07	Ethiopia	W	3-0	Conakry	CNq	Youla 2 32 72, Feindouno 55		
20-08	Tunisia	D	0-0	Radès/Tunis	Fr		20 000	
12-10	Mozambique	W	1-0	Conakry	WCq	Bangoura 70	13 400	Ndoye SEN
16-11	Mozambique	W	4-3	Maputo	WCq	Youla 14, Bangoura 3 21 35 54	50 000	Mochubela RSA
2004								
20-01	Burkina Faso	W	1-0	Saint-Maxime	Fr	Camara.T 72		
25-01	Congo DR	W	2-1	Tunis	CNr1	Camara.T 68, Feindouno 81	3 000	Aboubacar CIV
28-01	Rwanda	D	1-1	Bizerte	CNr1	Camara.T 48	4 000	Sowe GAM
1-02	Tunisia	D	1-1	Radès/Tunis	CNr1	Camara.T 84	18 000	Tessema ETH
7-02	Mali	L	1-2	Bizerte	CNqf	Feindouno 15	1 450	El Fatah EGY
28-04	Côte d'Ivoire	L	2-4	Aix-les-Bains	Fr	Feidouno 12, Oulare 39	2 000	
29-05	Senegal	D	1-1	Paris	Fr	Diawara 24p	2 000	Garibian FRA
20-06	Tunisia	W	2-1	Conakry	WCq	Kaba 2 12 46	15 300	Codjia BEN
3-07	Malawi	D	1-1	Lilongwe	WCq	Kaba 80	11 383	Abdulkadir TAN
5-09	Botswana	W	4-0	Conakry	WCq	Feindouno 44, Youla 54, Kaba 60, Mansare 82	25 000	Agbenyega GHA
10-10	Morocco	D	1-1	Conakry	WCq	Mansare 50	25 000	Monteiro Duatre CPV
17-11	Kenya	L	1-2	Nairobi	WCq	Feindouno 10p	16 000	Abd El Fatah EGY
2005								
9-02	Mali	D	2-2	Paris	Fr	Thiam 6, Feindouno 55		
26-03	Morocco	L	0-1	Rabat	WCq		70 000	Coulibaly MLI
5-06	Kenya	W	1-0	Conakry	WCq	Bangoura 68	21 000	Mbera GAB
11-06	Tunisia	L	0-2	Tunis	WCq		30 000	Lim Kee Chong MRI

Fr = Friendly match • CN = CAF African Cup of Nations • WC = FIFA World Cup™ • q = qualifier

FIFA REFEREE LIST 2005

	Int'l	DoB
BALDE Abdoulaye	2000	10-11-1965
BANGOURA Aboubacar	2004	21-12-1977
KABA Mamadou		13-11-1976
KEITA Yakhouba		4-06-1975
SANKHON Aboubacar	2001	12-12-1965
SOUMAH Mohamed		4-01-1976
TOURE Ahmed	2005	20-03-1978

FIFA ASSISTANT REFEREE LIST 2005

	Int'l	DoB
CAMARA Babou	2005	17-03-1975
DIALLO Mamadou	2004	1-01-1976
DIANE Alhassane	2004	3-01-1976
DOUMBOUYA Aboubacar	2004	7-01-1975
MARA Aboubacar	1999	25-07-1960
SYLLA Jean	1993	18-10-1960
SYLLA Sekou		11-12-1968

GUINEA COUNTRY INFORMATION

Capital	Conakry	Independence	1958 from France	GDP per Capita	$2 100
Population	9 246 462	Status	Republic	GNP Ranking	129
Area km²	245 857	Language	French	Dialling code	+224
Population density	37 per km²	Literacy rate	38%	Internet code	.gn
% in urban areas	30%	Main religion	Muslim 85%	GMT + / -	0
Towns/Cities ('000)	Conakry 1 871; Nzérékoré 132; Kindia 117; Kankan 114; Labé 46; Mamou 41; Siguiri 43				
Neighbours (km)	Guinea-Bissau 386; Mali 858; Côte d'Ivoire 610; Liberia 563; Sierra Leone 652; Atlantic Ocean 320				
Main stadia	Stade 28 Septembre – Conakry 40 000				

GUINEA NATIONAL TEAM RECORDS AND RECORD SEQUENCES

Records			Sequence records					
Victory	14-0	MTN 1972	Wins	7	1972-1973	Clean sheets	7	1986-1987
Defeat	2-6	GHA 1975	Defeats	4	1984, 1998-1999	Goals scored	29	1973-1977
Player Caps	n/a		Undefeated	13	1980-1981	Without goal	6	1991
Player Goals	n/a		Without win	14	1983-1984	Goals against	14	1967-1969

RECENT LEAGUE AND CUP RECORD

Championship				Cup			
Year	Champions	Score	Runners-up	Winners	Score	Runners-up
	Kaloum Stars	†		ASFAG Conakry		
1997	No championship played			Kaloum Stars		
1998	Kaloum Stars	†		Kaloum Stars	1-1 6-5p	Mineurs Sangaredi
1999	No championship played			Horoya Conakry		Kaloum Stars
2000	Hafia Conakry	†		Fello Stars Labé	2-1	Horoya Conakry
2001	Horoya Conakry	3-1	Satellite Conakry	Kaloum Stars		
2002	Satellite Conakry	3-2	Kaloum Star	Hafia Conakry	5-3	Satellite Conakry
2003	ASFAG Conakry	†		Etoile de Guinée		Etoile de Coléah
2004	No championship played			Fello Stars Labé	2-2 5-4p	CIK Kamsar

† Championship played on a league system

GUM – GUAM

NATIONAL TEAM RECORD
JULY 1ST 2002 TO JUNE 30TH 2005

PL	W	D	L	F	A	%
10	0	0	10	1	82	0

FIFA/COCA-COLA WORLD RANKING

1993	1994	1995	1996	1997	1998	1999	2000	2001	2002	2003	2004	High		Low	
-	-	-	188	191	198	200	199	199	200	201	2005	182	08/96	205	12/04

2004-2005											
08/04	09/04	10/04	11/04	12/04	01/05	02/05	03/05	04/05	05/05	06/05	07/05
204	204	204	205	205	205	205	204	204	204	204	204

Following on from the success of the Bhutan v Montserrat 'alternative' World Cup final that was played between the two bottom ranked teams in the world on the same day as the 2002 FIFA World Cup™ Final, the football authorities in Guam should perhaps start preparing for a similar match against American Samoa to coincide with the 2006 final. Throughout the past year the two have traded places at the bottom of the FIFA/Coca-Cola World Ranking. After losing heavily to Bhutan and Mongolia in an AFC Asian Cup preliminary group in April 2003 the national team went into hibernation for the best part of two years before re-emerging to take part in the East Asian

INTERNATIONAL HONOURS
None

Championship qualifiers. In a display of true Olympian spirit they lived up to the maxim that it is the taking part that counts although they were shown little mercy by Hong Kong and Korea DPR who scored 36 goals between them. A goal by Zachary James Pangelinan was a cause for celebration, however, as it was Guam's first in an official international since 1996. In an island dominated by the huge strategic US military base it is a wonder football is played at all but Guam does boast a domestic league which is split into a Spring and Fall league. In 2004 Under-18 won both to automatically win the overall championship.

THE FIFA BIG COUNT OF 2000

	Male	Female		Male	Female
Registered players	135	137	Referees	19	2
Non registered players	400	275	Officials	75	25
Youth players	1 012	153	Total involved	2 233	
Total players	2 112		Number of clubs	9	
Professional players	0	0	Number of teams	77	

Guam Football Association (GFA)
PO Box 5093, Hagatna, Guam 96932
Tel +1 671 9225423   Fax +1 671 9225424
info@guamfootball.com   www.guamfootball.com
President: LAI Richard   General Secretary: BORDALLO Michael
Vice-President: ARTERO Pascual   Treasurer: LAI George   Media Officer: CEPEDA Joseph
Men's Coach: TSUKITATE Norio   Women's Coach: CORTEZ Thomas
GFA formed: 1975   AFC: 1996   FIFA: 1996
Colours: Blue, White, Blue

GAMES PLAYED BY GUAM IN THE 2006 FIFA WORLD CUP™ CYCLE

2002	Opponents	Score	Venue	Comp	Scorers	Att	Referee
No international matches played in 2002							
2003							
24-02	Mongolia	L 0-2	Hong Kong	EACq		1 602	Huang Junjie CHN
26-02	Macao	L 0-2	Hong Kong	EACq		672	Cheung Yim Yau HKG
28-02	Chinese Taipei	L 0-7	Hong Kong	EACq		1 814	
2-03	Hong Kong	L 0-11	Hong Kong	EACq		6 862	Huang Junjie CHN
23-04	Bhutan	L 0-6	Thimphu	ACq			
25-04	Mongolia	L 0-5	Thimphu	ACq			
2004							
No international matches played in 2004							
2005							
5-03	Chinese Taipei	L 0-9	Taipei	EACq			
7-03	Hong Kong	L 0-15	Taipei	EACq			
9-03	Mongolia	L 1-4	Taipei	EACq	Pangelinan [69]		
11-03	Korea DPR	L 0-21	Taipei	EACq			

EAC = East Asian Championship • AC = AFC Asian Cup • q = qualifier

GUAM NATIONAL TEAM RECORDS AND RECORD SEQUENCES

Records			Sequence records					
Victory	-	Yet to win a match	Wins	0		Clean sheets	0	
Defeat	0-21	PRK 2005	Defeats	29	1975-	Goals scored	1	five times
Player Caps	n/a		Undefeated	0		Without goal	15	1996-2005
Player Goals	n/a		Without win	29	1975-	Goals against	29	1975-

RECENT LEAGUE AND CUP RECORD

	Overall Champions				Spring League				Fall League		
Year	Winners	Score	Runners-up		Winners	Score	Runners-up		Winners	Score	Runners-up
1998	Anderson				Anderson				Island Cargo		
1999	Silver Bullets				Carpet One				Silver Bullets		
2000	Silver Bullets	4-2	Navy		Silver Bullets				Navy	4-3	Anderson
2001					Silver Bullets	4-1	Lai National		Staywell Zoom	2-1	Guam Insurance
2002	Guam Shipyard	‡			Guam Shipyard	2-0	Guam Insurance		Guam Shipyard	4-2	IT&E Pumas
2003	Guam Shipyard	‡			Guam Shipyard	2-1	Quality Distrib's		Guam Shipyard	†	
2004	Under-18	‡			Under-18	5-0	IT&E Pumas		Under-18	4-0	Guam Shipyard
2005					Guam Shipyard	6-0	Quality Distrib's				

‡ Won both stages so automatic champions • † Played on a league system • Guam Shipyard previously known as Silver Bullets

GUAM COUNTRY INFORMATION

Capital	Hagatna	Independence	Unincorporated territory of the USA		GDP per Capita	$21 000	
Population	166 090	Status			GNP Ranking	n/a	
Area km²	549	Language	English		Dialling code	+1 671	
Population density	302 per km²	Literacy rate	99%		Internet code	.GU	
% in urban areas	n/a	Main religion	Christian 99%		GMT +/−	+10	
Towns/Cities ('000)	Tamuning 11; Mangilao 8; Yigo 8; Astumbo 5; Barrigada 4; Agat 4; Ordot 4						
Neighbours (km)	North Pacific Ocean 125						
Main stadia	Wettengel Rugby Field – Hagatna						

GUY – GUYANA

NATIONAL TEAM RECORD
JULY 1ST 2002 TO JUNE 30TH 2005

PL	W	D	L	F	A	%
7	2	1	4	8	14	35.7

FIFA/COCA-COLA WORLD RANKING

1993	1994	1995	1996	1997	1998	1999	2000	2001	2002	2003	2004	High		Low	
136	154	162	153	168	161	171	183	178	169	182	182	**133**	11/93	**185**	02/04

2004-2005											
08/04	09/04	10/04	11/04	12/04	01/05	02/05	03/05	04/05	05/05	06/05	07/05
181	181	181	181	182	182	182	182	182	182	182	180

For a country that shares a 1,000 kilometre border with Brazil, surprisingly little of the magic of football has rubbed off on Guyana. With the Georgetown cricket Test matches a major feature of the sporting calendar, football has yet to make the same inroads into the popularity of cricket as has happened in a number of the Caribbean islands. With just seven matches played by the national team in the three years since the 2002 FIFA World Cup™ Brazilian coach Nieder dos Santos has had little to work with since defeat in the 2006 FIFA World Cup™ qualifiers to Grenada in March 2004. Having initially entered the Digicel Caribbean Cup, which also doubled up as a qualifying

INTERNATIONAL HONOURS
None

tournament for the 2005 CONCACAF Gold Cup, Guyana then withdrew leaving a friendly against Barbados as the only match in the 2004-05 season. There was involvement in the CONCACAF Junior and Youth tournaments but both the U-20s and U-17s finished bottom of their preliminary groups. There has also been limited domestic competition with the National Championship not played since 2001, leaving the Georgetown League as the main source of competition. In November 2004 Western Tigers beat Fruta Conquerors 2-1 in the final while the Cup was won by Conquerors who beat invited guests Dennery from St Lucia 4-1 in the final.

THE FIFA BIG COUNT OF 2000

	Male	Female		Male	Female
Registered players	1 500	90	Referees	4	2
Non registered players	7 000	40	Officials	480	30
Youth players	1 000	0	Total involved	10 146	
Total players	9 630		Number of clubs	30	
Professional players	0	0	Number of teams	100	

Guyana Football Federation (GFF)
Lot 17 Dadanawa Street, Section K Campbellville, PO Box 10727, Georgetown, Guyana
Tel +592 2 278758   Fax +592 2 262641
gff@networksgy.com   www.gff.org.gy
President: KLASS Colin   General Secretary: RUTHERFORD George
Vice-President: CALLENDER Winston   Treasurer: HENRY Aubrey   Media Officer: WILSON Frankin
Men's Coach: DOS SANTOS Neider   Women's Coach: DOS SANTOS Neider
GFF formed: 1902   CONCACAF: 1969   FIFA: 1968
Colours: Green, Green, Yellow

GAMES PLAYED BY GUYANA IN THE 2006 FIFA WORLD CUP™ CYCLE

2002	Opponents	Score		Venue	Comp	Scorers	Att	Referee
28-07	Netherlands Antilles	W	2-1	Georgetown	GCq	Cole [6], Forbes [56]		
11-08	Netherlands Antilles	L	0-1	Willemstad	GCq	L 2-3p		Villar-Polo ARU
2003								
No international matches played in 2003								
2004								
15-02	Barbados	W	2-0	Bridgetown	Fr	Hernandez [59], Richardson [86]	1 200	Small BRB
28-02	Grenada	L	0-5	St George's	WCq		7 000	Archundia MEX
2-03	Trinidad and Tobago	L	0-1	Tunapuna	Fr			Randham TRI
14-03	Grenada	L	1-3	Blairmont	WCq		1 200	Quesada Cordero CRC
2005								
13-02	Barbados	D	3-3	Bridgetown	Fr	Richardson [21], Cadogan [36], Abrams [71]	6 000	Callender BRB

Fr = Friendly match • GC = CONCACAF Gold Cup • WC = FIFA World Cup™ • q = qualifier

GUYANA NATIONAL TEAM RECORDS AND RECORD SEQUENCES

Records			Sequence records					
Victory	14-0	AIA 1998	Wins	2	Six times	Clean sheets	2	1990-1991
Defeat	0-9	MEX 1987	Defeats	8	1987-1990	Goals scored	11	1984-1987
Player Caps	n/a		Undefeated	10	1984-1987	Without goal	7	1987-1990
Player Goals	n/a		Without win	10	1987-1990	Goals against	13	1992-1996

KASHIF & SHANGHAI CUP 2004-05

Quarter-finals		Semi-finals		Final	
Conquerors	3				
Camptown	0	**Conquerors**	0 2p		
Western Tigers	1	Topp XX	0 1p		
Topp XX	4			**Conquerors**	4
Eagles United	2			Dennery	1
Pele	0	Eagles United	0	1-01-2005	
East Coast	0	**Dennery**	2	Scorers – Abrahams 2, Parks, Hernandez for Conquerors; Edwards for Dennery	
Dennery	1				

RECENT LEAGUE AND CUP RECORD

	National Championship				Georgetown League				Cup		
Year	Winners	Score	Runners-up		Winners	Score	Runners-up		Winners	Score	Runners-up
1998					Santos				Milerock		
1999	Santos	0-0 4-2p	Conquerors		Conquerors				Khelwalaas	2-1	Real Victoria
2000						-			Top XX Linden	3-1	Conquerors
2001	Conquerors				Conquerors				Top XX Linden	1-1 4-2p	Camptown
2002						-			Real Victoria	2-2 5-4p	Netrockers
2003					Conquerors	1-0	Beacon		Conquerors	1-0	Western Tigers
2004					Western Tigers	2-1	Conquerors		Camptown	1-0	Top XX Linden
2005									Conquerors	4-1	Dennery

There are two main cup competitions - the Kashif & Shanghai Knockout tournament, which is listed above, and the Mayors Cup

GUYANA COUNTRY INFORMATION

Capital	Georgetown	Independence	1966 from the UK	GDP per Capita	$4 000
Population	705 803	Status	Republic within Commonwealth	GNP Ranking	163
Area km²	214 970	Language	English	Dialling code	+592
Population density	3 per km²	Literacy rate	98%	Internet code	.gy
% in urban areas	36%	Main religion	Christian 50%, Hindu 35%	GMT +/ –	-4
Towns/Cities ('000)	Georgetown 235; Linden 44; New Amsterdam 35; Corriverton 12; Bartica 11				
Neighbours (km)	Surinam 600; Brazil 1 119; Venezuela 743; Caribbean Sea 459				
Main stadia	Georgetown Football Stadium – Georgetown 2 000				

HAI - HAITI

NATIONAL TEAM RECORD
JULY 1ST 2002 TO JUNE 30TH 2005

PL	W	D	L	F	A	%
33	13	7	13	60	48	50

FIFA/COCA-COLA WORLD RANKING

1993	1994	1995	1996	1997	1998	1999	2000	2001	2002	2003	2004	High		Low	
145	132	153	114	125	109	99	84	82	72	96	95	72	12/02	155	04/96

2004-2005											
08/04	09/04	10/04	11/04	12/04	01/05	02/05	03/05	04/05	05/05	06/05	07/05
95	96	98	98	95	92	91	93	92	87	88	87

The past two years have seen Haiti descend into chaos with United Nations peacekeeping troops struggling to keep control of a volatile situation. In an attempt to highlight the plight of the Haitian people the Brazilian Federation organised a "Football for Peace" match that saw the likes of Roberto Carlos, Ronaldinho and Ronaldo vist the war-torn country to play the Haiti national team. It was the first of only two international matches that it has been possible to play in Haiti since the 2002 FIFA World Cup™ finals. The two home matches in the 2006 qualifying campaign were played in Miami and after knocking out the Turks and Caicos Islands 7-0 on aggregate, Haiti then

INTERNATIONAL HONOURS
Qualified for the FIFA World Cup™ finals 1974   CCCF Championship 1957   CONCACAF Champions Cup Racing Club 1963 Violette 1984

faced Jamaica who went through to the group stages after a convincing 3-0 win in Kingston. The Digicel Caribbean Cup brought slightly better results, including an 11-0 thrashing of the US Virgin Islands. After losing 1-0 at home to Cuba in the final knock-out round Haiti then led the return in Havana 1-0 at full-time, but the Cubans scored an extra-time winner to send them through to the finals. Remarkably, club football has been able to resume despite the political problems with AS Mirebalais winning the Championnat de Ouverture in the 2004-05 season after the 2004 Championship earlier in the year had been abandoned.

THE FIFA BIG COUNT OF 2000

	Male	Female		Male	Female
Registered players	8 000	0	Referees	200	0
Non registered players	75 000	0	Officials	2 000	0
Youth players	15 000	0	Total involved	100 200	
Total players	98 000		Number of clubs	300	
Professional players	0	0	Number of teams	2 000	

Fédération Haïtienne de Football (FHF)
128 Avenue Christiophe, Case postale 2258, Port-au-Prince, Haiti
Tel +509 2440115   Fax +509 2440117

jbyves@yahoo.com

President: JEAN-BART Yves Dr   General Secretary: DESIR Lionel
Vice-President: JEAN MARIE Georges   Treasurer: BERTIN Eddy   Media Officer: CHARLES M. Louis
Men's Coach: CLAVIJO Fernando   Women's Coach: ANGLADE Jean Hubert
FHF formed: 1904   CONCACAF: 1961   FIFA: 1933
Colours: Blue, Red, Blue

GAMES PLAYED BY HAITI IN THE 2006 FIFA WORLD CUP™ CYCLE

2002	Opponents	Score		Venue	Comp	Scorers	Att	Referee
18-11	Antigua and Barbuda	W	1-0	Port-au-Prince	GCq	Lormera [48]		Bowen CAY
22-11	Antigua and Barbuda	W	3-0	Port-au-Prince	GCq	Lormera [5], Gilles [45], Menelas [75]		Bowen CAY
2003								
23-02	Peru	L	1-5	Lima	Fr	Menelas [50]		Rivera PER
26-03	Martinique	W	2-1	Kingston	GCq	Menelas 2 [22 64]		Lee ANT
28-03	St Lucia	L	1-2	Kingston	GCq	Romulus [73]		Lee ANT
30-03	Jamaica	L	0-3	Kingston	GCq			Brizan TRI
29-07	St Kitts and Nevis	L	0-1	Basseterre	Fr			Matthew SKN
31-07	Trinidad and Tobago	W	2-0	Basseterre	Fr	Peguero [47], Chery [63]		Rawlins SKN
20-08	Venezuela	L	2-3	Maracaibo	Fr	Peguero [55], Maxo [69]	15 000	
31-08	China PR	W	4-3	Fort Lauderdale	Fr			
27-12	Bahamas	W	6-0	Miami	Fr			
2004								
31-01	Nicaragua	D	1-1	West Palm Beach	Fr			
18-02	Turks and Caicos Isl.	W	5-0	Miami	WCq	Peguero [6], Descouines 3 [43 45 50], Wadson [71]	3 000	Stott USA
21-02	Turks and Caicos Isl.	W	2-0	Hialeah	WCq	Roody [10p], Harvey OG [41]	3 000	Valenzuela USA
29-02	Nicaragua	D	1-1	Esteli	Fr			
13-03	USA	D	1-1	Miami	Fr	Boucicaut [69]	8 714	Prendergast JAM
5-05	Guatemala	L	0-1	Guatemala City	Fr		15 000	Recinos SLV
12-05	El Salvador	D	3-3	Houston	Fr	Peguero [10], Descouines [15], Lormera [82]	4 000	Terry USA
12-06	Jamaica	D	1-1	Miami	WCq	Peguero [50]	30 000	Stott USA
20-06	Jamaica	L	0-3	Kingston	WCq			Sibrian SLV
18-08	Brazil	L	0-6	Port-au-Prince	Fr		15 000	Oliveira BRA
24-11	US Virgin Islands	W	11-0	Kingston	GCq	Mesidor 3 [13 30 48], Ulcena 2 [15 78], Saint-Preux [33], Chery 2 [40 90], Lormera [57], Germain [64], Thelamour [87]	250	Piper TRI
26-11	Saint-Martin †	W	2-0	Montego Bay	GCq	Bruny [25], Thelamour [67]	500	Brizan TRI
28-11	Jamaica	L	1-3	Kingston	GCq	Ulcena [41]	4 000	Piper TRI
12-12	St Kitts and Nevis	W	1-0	Fort Lauderdale	GCq	Cadet [62]		McNab BAH
15-12	St Kitts and Nevis	W	2-0	Basseterre	GCq	Cadet [16], Dorcelus [70]		Bhimull TRI
2005								
9-01	Cuba	L	0-1	Port-au-Prince	GCq		15 000	Minyetti DOM
12-01	Costa Rica	D	3-3	San Jose	Fr	Cadet 2 [18 39], Germain [90]		Porras CRC
16-01	Cuba	D	1-1	Havana	GCq	Cadet [59]		Brizan TRI
1-02	Trinidad and Tobago	L	0-1	Port of Spain	Fr			
3-02	Trinidad and Tobago	L	1-2	Port of Spain	Fr	Romulus [47]		
6-02	Trinidad and Tobago	W	1-0	Scarborough	Fr	Germain [19p]		
13-02	Guatemala	L	1-2	Fort Lauderdale	Fr	Cadet [61]	10 000	Salazar USA

Fr = Friendly match • GC = CONCACAF Gold Cup • WC = FIFA World Cup™ • q = qualifier • † Not a full international

HAITI COUNTRY INFORMATION

Capital	Port-au-Prince	Independence	1804 from France	GDP per Capita	$1 600
Population	7 656 166	Status	Republic	GNP Ranking	122
Area km²	27 750	Language	French	Dialling code	+509
Population density	275 per km²	Literacy rate	52%	Internet code	.ht
% in urban areas	32%	Main religion	Christian 96%	GMT +/−	-5
Towns/Cities ('000)	Port-au-Prince 1 234; Carrefour 439; Delmas 377; Cap-Haitien 134; Pétionville 108				
Neighbours (km)	Dominican Republic 360; Atlantic Ocean & Caribbean Sea 1 771				
Main stadia	Stade Sylvio Cator – Port-au-Prince 10 500; Park St Victor – Cap-Haitien 7 500				

HAITI NATIONAL TEAM RECORDS AND RECORD SEQUENCES

Records			Sequence records					
Victory	12-1	VIR 2001	Wins	8	1979	Clean sheets	5	1997-1998
Defeat	1-9	BRA 1959	Defeats	6	1974-75, 1984-89	Goals scored	12	1997-1999
Player Caps	n/a		Undefeated	18	1977-1980	Without goal	6	1973-1974
Player Goals	n/a		Without win	12	1973-1975	Goals against	9	1974-1975

FIFA REFEREE LIST 2005

	Int'l	DoB
GRANT Rosnick	1993	26-10-1964
JEAN Wisler	1999	22-10-1963
THOMAS Deland	1999	29-02-1960

FIFA ASSISTANT REFEREE LIST 2005

	Int'l	DoB
THOMAS Jean	1998	3-07-1961
VITAL Robinson	1998	21-11-1961

HAITI 2004-05 DIVISION 1 OUVERTURE

	Pl	W	D	L	F	A	Pts
AS Mirebalais	15	9	5	1	14	6	32
Racing Club Haïtien	15	9	4	2	24	13	31
Violette AC	15	7	5	3	17	14	26
Victory FC	15	7	4	4	18	13	25
Racing FC Gônaïves	15	7	3	5	13	10	24
Zénith Cap Haïtien	15	6	4	5	15	13	22
Roulado Gônaïves	15	4	6	5	14	12	18
AS Capoise	15	5	3	7	16	15	18
Cavaly Léogâne	15	3	8	4	12	12	17
Tempête St Marc	15	3	8	4	13	19	17
Don Bosco Pétion-Ville	15	3	7	5	15	17	16
AS Carrefour	15	2	9	4	8	9	15
Aigle Noir	15	4	3	8	13	18	15
Baltimore St Marc	15	2	8	5	5	10	14
FICA Cap Haïtien	15	2	8	5	6	13	14
AS Grand-Goâve	15	2	5	8	7	16	11

26/11/2004 - 26/03/2005

HAITI 2004-05 DIVISION 1 CLOTURE

	Pl	W	D	L	F	A	Pts
Baltimore St Marc	15	8	7	0	25	9	31
Zénith Cap Haïtien	15	8	2	5	22	14	26
Tempête St Marc	15	6	4	5	17	14	22
Cavaly Léogâne	15	6	4	5	15	13	22
Violette AC	15	6	4	5	17	18	22
Racing FC Gônaïves	15	5	5	5	20	19	20
Racing Club Haitien	15	4	8	3	14	14	20
Roulado Gônaïves	15	6	2	7	14	14	20
Aigle Noir	15	6	2	7	17	18	20
FICA Cap Haïtien †	15	4	6	5	13	16	18
AS Carrefour	15	5	3	7	15	21	18
AS Grand-Goâve †	15	5	3	7	12	18	18
Don Bosco Pétion-Ville	15	4	5	6	15	16	17
Victory FC	15	4	5	6	16	19	17
AS Capoise	15	4	5	6	10	14	17
AS Mirebalais	15	4	5	6	11	16	17

9/05/2005 - 30/07/2005 • † Relegated on aggregate record

RECENT LEAGUE RECORD

	Championship					
Year	Champions	Pts	Runners-up	Pts	Third	Pts
1990	FICA Cap Haïtien					
1991	FICA Cap Haïtien					
1992	Championship unfinished					
1993	Tempête St Marc					
1994	FICA Cap Haïtien					
1995	Violette AC					
1996	Racing Gônaïves					
1997	AS Capoise					
1998	FICA Cap Haïtien					
1999	Violette AC	58	Carioca	54	Cavaly Léogâne	53
2000	Racing Club	60	Roulado Gônaïves	55	Violette AC	52
2001	FICA Cap Haïtien	60	Violette AC	54	Baltimore	51
2002A	Roulado Gônaïves	33	Aigle Noir	26	Don Bosco	25
2002C	Racing Club	31	Aigle Noir	29	Roulado Gônaïves	26
2003A	Don Bosco †	30	Cavaly Léogâne	30	AS Capoise	24
2003C	Roulado Gônaïves	27	Victory FC	27	Violette AC	26
2004	Championship cancelled ‡					
2005A	AS Mirebalais	32	Racing Club	31	Violette AC	26
2005C	Baltimore St Marc	31	Zénith Cap Haïtien	26	Tempête St Marc	22

A = Ouverture • C = Clôture • † Play-off: Don Bosco 2-0 1-0 Cavaly Léogâne •
‡ Don Bosco and Roulado played in a match of champions in October 2004 with
Roulado winning 5-4 on penalties after a 0-0 draw

HKG – HONG KONG

NATIONAL TEAM RECORD
JULY 1ST 2002 TO JUNE 30TH 2005

PL	W	D	L	F	A	%
32	12	4	16	82	57	43.7

FIFA/COCA-COLA WORLD RANKING

1993	1994	1995	1996	1997	1998	1999	2000	2001	2002	2003	2004	High		Low	
112	98	111	124	129	136	122	123	137	150	142	133	90	02/96	154	02/03

2004-2005											
08/04	09/04	10/04	11/04	12/04	01/05	02/05	03/05	04/05	05/05	06/05	07/05
145	144	144	139	133	134	134	124	126	125	123	120

Happy Valley must be sick of the sight of rivals Sun Hei. In February 2005 they lost 1-0 to them in the League Cup Final; two months later Sun Hei won 4-2 in the Challenge Shield Final and then in May the two met again in the FA Cup Final with Sun Hei winning 2-1. As if that wasn't bad enough in the week leading up to the Cup Final Sun Hei beat Happy Valley 2-1 in a vital Championship decider that left the teams level on points on the last day of the season. Happy Valley could only draw with Kitchee whilst Sun Hei beat Fukien to steal the title at the last. It was a remarkable season for Sun Hei who won the first quadruple in Hong Kong football since South China in 1991.

INTERNATIONAL HONOURS
None

One of their discoveries was striker Chan Siu Ki who scored seven times for Hong Kong in the 15-0 victory over Guam in the East Asian Championship qualifiers. Remarkably Hong Kong didn't qualify for the final tournament after they lost the top of the table clash to Korea DPR, this despite having scored 27 goals and conceded just two. With 82 goals scored in the three years after the 2002 FIFA World Cup finals, the national team have been involved in some high scoring games but in two high profile matches during the 2004-05 season Hong Kong were on the wrong end of a big score line: 0-7 against China PR in the 2006 qualifiers and 1-7 in a friendly against Brazil.

THE FIFA BIG COUNT OF 2000

	Male	Female		Male	Female
Registered players	3 652	119	Referees	143	1
Non registered players	20 000	220	Officials	500	60
Youth players	340	26	Total involved	25 061	
Total players	24 357		Number of clubs	116	
Professional players	220	0	Number of teams	574	

The Hong Kong Football Association Ltd (HKFA)

55 Fat Kwong Street, Homantin, Kowloon, Hong Kong
Tel +852 27129122   Fax +852 27604303
hkfa@hkfa.com   www.hkfa.com
President: FOK Timothy Tsun Ting   General Secretary: LAM Martin
Vice-President: HONG Martin   Treasurer: LI Sonny   Media Officer: YEUNG Andy Chun Bong
Men's Coach: LAI Sun Cheung   Women's Coach: LEUNG Chun Kun
HKFA formed: 1914   AFC: 1954   FIFA: 1954
Colours: Red, Red, Red

GAMES PLAYED BY HONG KONG IN THE 2006 FIFA WORLD CUP™ CYCLE

2002	Opponents	Score		Venue	Comp	Scorers	Att	Referee
No international matches played in 2002								
2003								
1-02	Uruguay †	L	0-3	Hong Kong	Fr		20 785	Maidin SIN
4-02	Denmark †	L	1-2	Hong Kong	Fr	Antonic 90p		
22-02	Chinese Taipei	W	2-0	Hong Kong	EACq	Kwok Tue Hung 76, Lee Wai Man 79	6 055	Matsumura JPN
24-02	Macao	W	3-0	Hong Kong	EACq	Lee Kin Wo 46p, Au Wai Lun 2 59 62	1 602	Park Sang Gu KOR
28-02	Mongolia	W	10-0	Hong Kong	EACq	Au Wai Lun 2 6 60, Yau Kin Wai 10, Chan Ho Man 3 12 40 42 Cheung Sai Ho 3 13p 26 90, Kwok Yue Hung 79	1 814	
2-03	Guam	W	11-0	Hong Kong	EACq	Lau Chi Keung 3 7 36 57, Au Wai Lun 3 9 62 86p Chan Chi Hong 40, Poon Yiu Cheuk 44 Chan Ho Man 2 47 59, Lee Wai Man 90	6 862	Huang Junjie CHN
25-03	Laos	W	5-1	Hong Kong	ACq	Chan Chi Hong 2 17 35, Kwok Yue Hung 47 Au Wai Lun 2 59p 82		
30-03	Bangladesh	D	2-2	Hong Kong	ACq	Au Wai Lun 44p, Szeto Man Chun 45		
4-08	Singapore	L	1-4	Singapore	Fr	Au Wai Lun 46		
6-11	Uzbekistan	L	1-4	Tashkent	ACq	Law Chun Bong 45		
8-11	Tajikistan	D	0-0	Tashkent	ACq			
10-11	Thailand	W	2-1	Tashkent	ACq	Siang Sai Ho 28, Wong Sun Liu 69		
17-11	Thailand	L	0-4	Bangkok	ACq			
19-11	Uzbekistan	L	0-1	Bangkok	ACq			
21-11	Tajikistan	L	0-1	Bangkok	ACq			
4-12	Korea Republic	L	1-3	Tokyo	EAC	Akandu 34	14 895	Napitupulu IDN
7-12	Japan	L	0-1	Saitama	EAC		45 145	Piromya THA
10-12	China PR	L	1-3	Yokohama	EAC	Lo Chi Kwan 75	17 400	Piromya THA
2004								
18-02	Malaysia	W	3-1	Kuantan	WCq	Ng Wai Chiu 17, Chu Siu Kei 84, Kwok Yue Hung 93+	12 000	Nagalingham SIN
31-03	China PR	L	0-1	Hong Kong	WCq		9 000	Rungklay THA
9-06	Kuwait	L	0-4	Kuwait City	WCq		9 000	Najm LIB
8-09	Kuwait	L	0-2	Hong Kong	WCq		1 500	Busurmankulov KGZ
13-10	Malaysia	W	2-0	Hong Kong	WCq	Chu Siu Kei 5, Wong Chun Yue 51	2 425	Ahamd Rakhil MAS
17-11	China PR	L	0-7	Guangzhou	WCq		20 300	Lee Jong Kuk KOR
30-11	Singapore	D	0-0	Singapore	Fr	W 6-5p	3 359	
2-12	Myanmar	D	2-2	Singapore	Fr	Feng Ji Zhi, Law Chun Bong	2 000	
2005								
9-02	Brazil	L	1-7	Hong Kong	Fr	Lee Sze Ming 85	23 425	Zhou Weixin CHN
5-03	Mongolia	W	6-0	Taipei	EACq	Chu Siu Kei 30p, Law Chun Bong 48, Wong Chun Yue 50 Lam Ka Wai 73, Chan Yiu Lun 2 92 93		
7-03	Guam	W	15-0	Taipei	EACq	Chan Wai Ho 1, Chan Siu Ki 7 8 18 28 30 36 42 87 Chan Yiu Lun 2 16 31, Wong Chun Yue 3 24 43 45 Chu Siu Kei 67, Poon Man Tik 89		
11-03	Chinese Taipei	W	5-0	Taipei	EACq	Chan Yiu Lun 2 7 45, Lam Ka Wai 20 Poon Yiu Cheuk 58p, Cheung Sai Ho 60		
13-03	Korea DPR	L	0-2	Taipei	EACq			
29-05	Macao	W	8-1	Hong Kong	Fr	Chan Siu Ki 3, Lee Chi Ho, Lam Ka Wei, Leung Sze Chung, Cheng Lai Hin		

Fr = Friendly match • EAC = East Asian Championship • AC = AFC Asian Cup • WC = FIFA World Cup™ • q = qualifier • † Hong Kong League XI

HONG KONG COUNTRY INFORMATION

Capital	Victoria	Independence		Special Administrative	GDP per Capita	$28 800
Population	6 855 125	Status		Region (SAR) of China	GNP Ranking	n/a
Area km²	1 092	Language		Cantonese, English	Dialling code	+852
Population density	6 277 per km²	Literacy rate		93%	Internet code	.hk
% in urban areas	100%	Main religion		Local religions	GMT +/−	+8
Towns/Cities ('000)	Hong Kong Island 1 320; Kowloon 1 990; New Territories 2 730					
Neighbours (km)	China 30; South China Sea 733					
Main stadia	Hong Kong Stadium – Hong Kong Island 40 000; Mongkok – Kowloon 8 500					

HONG KONG 2004-05

FIRST DIVISION

	Pl	W	D	L	F	A	Pts	Sun Hei	Happy Valley	Kitchee	Buler	Citizen	South China	Sunray CAve	Fukien	Xiangxue
Sun Hei	16	10	4	2	28	12	34		2-1	1-0	5-0	2-1	4-1	0-0	0-0	2-0
Happy Valley	16	9	5	2	45	24	32	3-2		3-3	1-1	2-2	4-1	2-1	2-2	4-1
Kitchee	16	7	6	3	29	21	27	2-2	1-1		2-4	2-1	2-1	3-2	1-0	1-1
Buler Rangers	16	7	5	4	29	22	26	1-1	2-3	0-1		1-1	3-1	1-0	1-1	3-0
Citizen	16	6	4	6	29	28	22	0-2	0-3	2-1	4-3		3-3	2-0	4-1	2-0
South China	16	4	4	8	21	33	16	0-1	1-5	1-1	1-2	4-2		3-2	1-1	2-1
Sunray Cave	16	4	3	9	18	35	15	3-0	4-1	0-1	0-1	1-1	2-0		1-1	2-0
Fukien	16	2	7	7	13	24	13	0-1	1-5	1-1	1-1	0-3	0-1	2-0		1-0
Xiangxue	16	3	2	11	12	39	11	0-3	0-5	**1-7**	0-5	3-1	0-0	**3-0**	2-1	

18/09/2004 - 15/05/2005 • Match in bold awarded 3-0

HONG KONG 2004-05 SECOND DIVISION

	Pl	W	D	L	F	A	Pts
Hong Kong FC	22	18	1	3	66	19	55
Mutual	22	12	4	6	56	35	40
Lucky Mile	22	9	9	4	33	23	36
Kwok Keung	22	9	5	8	44	38	32
Fire Services	22	9	5	8	41	36	32
Kwai Tsing	22	9	3	10	35	43	30
Tung Po	22	8	5	9	46	45	29
New Fair Kui Tan	22	8	5	9	36	42	29
Tai Po	22	9	1	12	49	45	28
Double Flower	22	6	10	6	34	37	28
Ornaments	22	5	4	13	31	59	19
Tai Po St Joseph's	22	3	2	17	29	78	11

CHALLENGE SHIELD 2004-05

Quarter-finals		Semi-finals		Final	
Sun Hei	2				
South China	1	Sun Hei	1		
Citizen	3 1p	Sunray Cave	0		
Sunray Cave	3 4p			Sun Hei	4
Kitchee	7			Happy Valley	2
Xiangxue	1	Kitchee	0 1p	23-04-2005	
Buler Rangers	1	Happy Valley	0 3p		
Happy Valley	4				

FA CUP 2004-05

Quarter-finals		Semi-finals		Final	
Sun Hei	1				
Fukien	0	Sun Hei	1		
Citizen	1	Kitchee	0		
Kitchee	5			Sun Hei	2
Sunray Cave	1			Happy Valley	1
South China	0	Sunray Cave	0	22-05-2005, Att: 1 931	
Buler Rangers	2	Happy Valley	2	Hong Kong Stadium	
Happy Valley	3			Scorers - Akosah 61, Andre 119 for Sun Hei, OG 40 for H. Valley	

LEAGUE CUP 2004-05

Semi-finals		Finals	
Sun Hei	1 4p		
Buler Rangers	1 3p	Sun Hei	1
		Happy Valley	0
Citizen	0	27-02-2005	
Happy Valley	5		

RECENT LEAGUE AND CUP RECORD

	League				FA Cup				Challenge Shield		
Year	Champions	Score	Runners-up		Winners	Score	Runners-up		Winners	Score	Runners-up
1990	South China	†	Lai Sun		South China	1-0	Lai Sun		Happy Valley	2-1	South China
1991	South China	†	Happy Valley		South China	2-1	Lai Sun		South China		Lai Sun
1992	South China	†	Eastern		Ernest Borel	1-0	Instant-Dict		Sing Tao	1-1 2-1	Instant-Dict
1993	Eastern	†	South China		Eastern	1-0	Ernest Borel		Eastern	4-0	South China
1994	Eastern	†	Instant-Dict		Eastern	4-1	Happy Valley		Eastern		Instant-Dict
1995	Eastern	†	South China		Rangers	3-0	Eastern		Rangers	2-2 3-2p	Happy Valley
1996	Instant-Dict	1-0	South China		South China	4-1	Golden		South China	2-1	Golden
1997	South China	3-2	Instant-Dict		Instant-Dict	2-1	Sing Tao		South China	3-1 1-0	Instant-Dict
1998	Instant-Dict	‡			Instant-Dict	3-1	South China		Happy Valley	1-0	Sing Tao
1999	Happy Valley	1-1 8-7p	South China		South China	1-0	Instant-Dict		South China	2-0	Sing Tao
2000	South China	2-2 4-3p	Happy Valley		Happy Valley	7-2	O & YH Union		South China	4-3	Happy Valley
2001	Happy Valley	1-0	Instant-Dict		Instant-Dict	2-1	South China		O & YH Union	1-0	Instant-Dict
2002	Sun Hei	†	Happy Valley		South China	1-0	Sun Hei		South China	3-2	Sun Hei
2003	Happy Valley	†	Sun Hei		Sun Hei	2-1	Buler Rangers		South China	2-1	Happy Valley
2004	Sun Hei	†	Kitchee		Happy Valley	3-1	Kitchee		Happy Valley	3-0	Sun Hei
2005	Sun Hei	†	Happy Valley		Sun Hei	2-1	Happy Valley		Sun Hei	4-2	Happy Valley

† Played on a league basis - in 2002 the Championship reverted to a single stage round robin format • ‡ Won both stages so automatic champions

HON – HONDURAS

NATIONAL TEAM RECORD
JULY 1ST 2002 TO JUNE 30TH 2005

PL	W	D	L	F	A	%
43	12	17	14	57	47	47.7

FIFA/COCA-COLA WORLD RANKING

1993	1994	1995	1996	1997	1998	1999	2000	2001	2002	2003	2004	High		Low	
40	53	49	45	73	91	69	46	27	40	49	59	20	09/01	98	11/98

2004-2005											
08/04	09/04	10/04	11/04	12/04	01/05	02/05	03/05	04/05	05/05	06/05	07/05
59	47	53	58	59	59	58	50	51	50	50	39

Despite losing fewer matches than rivals Costa Rica and Guatemala in their 2006 FIFA World Cup™ qualifying group, Honduras failed to progress to the second group stage. Their campaign had got off to a great start with a 5-2 away win over Costa Rica, followed by a draw away to Canada, but too many draws proved to be Honduras' downfall. The disappointment was made even more acute by the excellent performances at the CONCACAF Gold Cup finals in July 2005 where, having beaten Colombia, eventual finalists Panama and Costa Rica, they were unlucky to lose to the USA who scored twice in the last four minutes to win the semi-final 2-1. Earlier in the year

INTERNATIONAL HONOURS
Qualified for the FIFA World Cup™ finals 1982 **UNCAF Cup** 1993 1995 **CONCACAF Club Championship** Olimpia 1972 1988

Honduras had been denied a third UNCAF Cup triumph when they lost in the final to Costa Rica on penalties, a competition which also served as a qualifier for the Gold Cup. Veteran striker Wilmer Velásquez had a good season upfront for the national team and he also led Olimpia to domestic success. Once again the Championship was a fight between Olimpia from the capital Tegucigalpa and Marathón from the second city San Pedro Sula but despite winning the group stage of the Apertura Olimpia lost to Marathón in the play-off final although they did gain revenge when the two met again in the Clausura final, winning 3-2 on aggregate.

THE FIFA BIG COUNT OF 2000

	Male	Female		Male	Female
Registered players	6 000	0	Referees	250	0
Non registered players	65 000	0	Officials	1 500	100
Youth players	14 000	0	Total involved	86 850	
Total players	85 000		Number of clubs	200	
Professional players	0	0	Number of teams	1 000	

Federación Nacional Autónoma de Fútbol de Honduras (FENAFUTH)
Colonia Florencia Norte, Ave. Roble, Edificio Plaza América, Ave. Roble, 1 y 2 Nivel, Tegucigalpa, Honduras
Tel +504 2320572   Fax +504 2398826
fenafuth@fenafuth.com   www.fenafuth.com
President: CALLEJAS Rafael   General Secretary: HAWIT BANEGAS Alfredo
Vice-President: ABUDOJ Jorge   Treasurer: WILLIAMS Vicente   Media Officer: BANEGAS Martin
Men's Coach: DE LA PAZ Jose   Women's Coach: ESCALANTE Miguel
FENAFUTH formed: 1951   CONCACAF: 1961   FIFA: 1951
Colours: Blue, Blue, Blue

GAMES PLAYED BY HONDURAS IN THE 2006 FIFA WORLD CUP™ CYCLE

	Opponents	Score		Venue	Comp	Scorers	Att	Referee
2002								
20-11	Colombia	W	1-0	San Pedro Sula	Fr	Núñez[74]	25 000	Batres GUA
2003								
31-01	Argentina	L	1-3	San Pedro Sula	Fr	Martinez.S[7]		Recinos SLV
11-02	Nicaragua	W	2-0	Panama City	GCq	Martinez.J[4], De Leon[20]	500	Aguilar SLV
15-02	El Salvador	L	0-1	Colon	GCq		600	Batres GUA
18-02	Panama	D	1-1	Panama City	GCq	Martinez.J[28]	5 000	Ramos Rizo MEX
20-02	Costa Rica	L	0-1	Panama City	GCq		200	Batres GUA
23-02	Guatemala	L	1-2	Panama City	GCq	Guevara[75]	400	Ramos Rizo MEX
2-04	Paraguay	D	1-1	Tegucigalpa	Fr	Guevara[14p]	25 000	Batres GUA
25-04	Trinidad and Tobago	W	2-0	Fort-de-France	GCq	Neal[50], Ramirez[89]		Rodriguez Moreno MEX
27-04	Martinique	W	4-2	Fort-de-France	GCq	Velasquez[31], Ramirez[63], Turcios[73], Hernandez[89]		Rodriguez Moreno MEX
30-04	Colombia	D	0-0	Miami	Fr		10 441	Kennedy USA
7-06	Venezuela	L	1-2	Miami	Fr	Velasquez[44]	15 000	Terry USA
11-06	Chile	L	1-2	San Pedro Sula	Fr	Pineda[13]	25 000	Burgos GUA
22-06	Guatemala	W	2-1	Carson	Fr	Martinez.J[50], Alvarez[54]	15 023	Saheli USA
29-06	El Salvador	D	1-1	San Pedro Sula	Fr	Velasquez[64]	5 000	Porras CRC
15-07	Brazil	L	1-2	Mexico City	GCr1	Leon[90p]		Navarro CAN
17-07	Mexico	D	0-0	Mexico City	GCr1		20 000	Nery SLV
11-10	Bolivia	L	0-1	Washington DC	Fr		20 000	Kennedy USA
16-11	Finland	L	1-2	Houston	Fr	Alvarez[87]	26 000	Hall USA
2004								
25-01	Norway	L	1-3	Hong Kong	Fr	Martinez.S[30]	14 603	Chan HKG
18-02	Colombia	D	1-1	Tegucigalpa	Fr	De Leon[24]	8 000	Alfaro SLV
10-03	Venezuela	L	1-2	Maracaibo	Fr	Lopez[39]	24 000	Manzur VEN
31-03	Jamaica	D	2-2	Kingston	Fr	Martinez.E[57], Núñez[78]	28 000	Brizan TRI
7-04	Panama	D	0-0	La Ceiba	Fr		10 000	Rodriguez HON
28-04	Ecuador	D	1-1	Fort Lauderdale	Fr	Pavon[31]	15 000	Saheli USA
2-06	USA	L	0-4	Foxboro	Fr		11 533	Sibrian SLV
12-06	Netherlands Antilles	W	2-1	Willemstad	WCq	Suazo 2[9 68]	12 000	McArthur GUY
19-06	Netherlands Antilles	W	4-0	San Pedro Sula	WCq	Guevara[7], Suazo[22], Alvarez[50], Pavon[70]	30 000	Alcala MEX
28-07	Panama	D	0-0	Tegucigalpa	Fr		5 000	Zelaya HON
3-08	El Salvador	W	4-0	San Salvador	Fr	Izaguirre[4], Palacios.J 3[5 71 75]		Aguilar SLV
18-08	Costa Rica	W	5-2	Alajuela	WCq	Suazo[22], Leon[35], Guevara 2[77 87], Martinez.S[89]	14 000	Rodriguez MEX
4-09	Canada	D	1-1	Edmonton	WCq	Guevara[88p]	8 000	Archundia MEX
8-09	Guatemala	D	2-2	San Pedro Sula	WCq	Guevara[51], Suazo[65]	40 000	Prendergast JAM
9-10	Canada	D	1-1	San Pedro Sula	WCq	Turcios[92+]	42 000	Stott USA
13-10	Guatemala	L	0-1	Guatemala City	WCq		26 000	Brizan TRI
17-11	Costa Rica	D	0-0	San Pedro Sula	WCq		18 000	Sibrian SLV
2005								
19-02	Nicaragua	W	5-1	Guatemala City	GCq	Núñez 2[19 84], Velásquez 3[42 51 73]	5 306	Moreno PAN
21-02	Belize	W	4-0	Guatemala City	GCq	Velásquez[7], Núñez 2[33 80], Palacios.W[88]	3 000	Campos NCA
23-02	Guatemala	D	1-1	Guatemala City	GCq	Velásquez[72]	3 000	Moreno PAN
25-02	Panama	W	1-0	Guatemala City	GCq	Velásquez[72]	11 159	Sibrian SLV
27-02	Costa Rica	D	1-1	Guatemala City	GCq	Núñez[58], L 6-7p	1 491	Batres GUA
19-03	USA	L	0-1	Albuquerque	Fr		9 222	Navarro CAN
4-06	Jamaica	D	0-0	Atlanta	Fr		6 500	Valenzuela USA
2-07	Canada	W	2-1	Vancouver	Fr	Ramirez.F[52], Velásquez[56]	4 105	Valenzuela USA
6-07	Trinidad and Tobago	D	1-1	Miami	GCr1	Figueroa[43]	10 311	Navarro CAN
10-07	Colombia	W	2-1	Miami	GCr1	Velásquez 2[79 82]	17 292	Rodriguez MEX
12-07	Panama	W	1-0	Miami	GCr1	Caballero[81]	11 000	Wyngaarde SUR
16-07	Costa Rica	W	3-2	Foxboro	GCqf	Velásquez[6], Turcios[27], Núñez[29]	22 108	Archundia MEX
21-07	USA	L	1-2	New Jersey	GCsf	Guerrero[30]	41 721	Prendergast JAM

Fr = Friendly match • GC = CONCACAF Gold Cup • WC = FIFA World Cup™
q = qualifier • r1 = first round group • qf = quarter-final • sf = semi-final

HONDURAS NATIONAL TEAM RECORDS AND RECORD SEQUENCES

Records			Sequence records					
Victory	10-0	NCA 1946	Wins	6	1980-81, 1985-86	Clean sheets	6	1992
Defeat	1-10	GUA 1921	Defeats	6	1963-1965	Goals scored	13	Three times
Player Caps	n/a		Undefeated	14	1991-1992	Without goal	5	1988
Player Goals	n/a		Without win	14	1987-1991	Goals against	13	1993-1995

FIFA REFEREE LIST 2005

	Int'l	DoB
BARDALEZ Oscar	1996	28-08-1962
CARRANZA Marcio	1999	29-06-1966
PINEDA Jose	1999	25-03-1971
RODRIGUEZ Lucinio		12-11-1969
SORIANO Santos	2000	27-10-1967
ZELAYA Ricardo		23-03-1965

FIFA ASSISTANT REFEREE LIST 2005

	Int'l	DoB
GARCIA Rafael	2002	24-11-1966
GIRON Roberto		12-06-1968
OSORIO Florencio		19-10-1970
PASTRANA Carlos	1999	27-11-1968
RENEAU John		14-09-1965
RIVERA Walter	1993	2-01-1966
SALINAS Reynaldo	1996	17-03-1963

CLUB DIRECTORY

Club	Town/City	Stadium	Phone	www.	Lge	CL
Atlético	Olancho	Estadio Ruben Guifarro 5,000			0	0
Marathón	San Pedro Sula	Olimpico Metropolitano 40,000	+504 5541802	cdmarathon.com	4	0
Motagua	Tegucigalpa	Tiburcio Carias Andino 35,000	+504 233698	motagua.com	10	0
Olimpia	Tegucigalpa	Tiburcio Carias Andino 35,000	+504 2358337	clubolimpia.com	17	2
CD Platense	Puerto Cortés	Estadio Excelsior 7,000	+504 6656242	platensehn.com	2	0
Real España	San Pedro Sula	Estadio Francisco Morazan 18,000	+504 5591223	realcdespana.com	8	0
Universidad	Choluteca	Estadio Fausto Flores Lagos 5,000	+504 2275516		0	0
Municiapal Valencia	Choluteca	Estadio Fausto Flores Lagos 5,000			0	0
CD Victoria	La Ceiba	Estadio Nilmo Edwards 6,000	+504 4410276		1	0
CD Vida	La Ceiba	Estadio Nilmo Edwards 6,000	+504 4431454	psinet.hn/cdvida	2	0

RECENT LEAGUE RECORD

Championship/Torneo Clausura from 1998				Torneo Apertura			
Year	Champions	Score	Runners-up		Champions	Score	Runners-up
1991	Real España	0-0 2-1	Motagua				
1992	Motagua	1-0	Real España				
1993	Olimpia	‡					
1994	Real España		Motagua				
1995	Victoria	0-0 1-1	Olimpia				
1996	Olimpia	3-0 0-0	Real España				
1997	Olimpia	1-1 3-0	Platense		Motagua	3-0 2-1	Real España
1998	Motagua	0-0 1-0	Olimpia		Olimpia	0-0 1-0	Real España
1999	Season readjustment				Motagua	0-0 0-0 6-5p	Olimpia
2000	Motagua	1-1 1-1 3-2p	Olimpia		Olimpia	1-0 1-1	Platense
2001	Platense	1-0 1-1	Olimpia		Motagua	0-1 3-2	Marathón
2002	Marathón	4-1 0-1	Olimpia		Olimpia	1-1 2-1	Platense
2003	Marathón	1-0 3-1	Motagua		Real España	2-2 2-0	Olimpia
2004	Olimpia	1-1 1-0	Marathón		Marathón	3-2 2-1	Olimpia
2005	Olimpia	1-1 2-1	Marathón				

‡ Won both stages so automatic champions

HONDURAS COUNTRY INFORMATION

Capital	Tegucigalpa	Independence	1821 from Spain	GDP per Capita	$2 600
Population	6 823 568	Status	Republic	GNP Ranking	105
Area km²	112 090	Language	Spanish	Dialling code	+504
Population density	60 per km²	Literacy rate	76%	Internet code	.hn
% in urban areas	44%	Main religion	Christian	GMT +/–	-6
Towns/Cities ('000)	Tegucigalpa 850; San Pedro Sula 489; Choloma 139; La Ceiba 130; El Progreso 100; Choluteca 75				
Neighbours (km)	Guatemala 256; El Salvador 342; Nicaragua 922; Pacific Ocean & Caribbean Sea 820				
Main stadia	Olimpico Metropolitano – San Pedro Sula 40 000; Tiburcio Carias Andino – Tegucigalpa 35 000				

HONDURAS 2004-05

TORNEO APERTURA

	Pl	W	D	L	F	A	Pts	Olimpia	Marathón	R. España	Victoria	Vida	Platense	Olanchano	Valencia	Motagua	Universidad
Olimpia †	18	12	3	3	39	17	39		3-0	0-1	5-2	3-1	2-1	3-0	1-1	3-1	1-1
Marathón †	18	10	4	4	23	17	34	1-0		0-2	2-1	1-0	2-1	3-1	2-0	0-0	0-2
Real España †	18	9	4	5	23	12	31	0-0	0-2		2-2	0-1	5-0	2-1	2-1	2-0	3-0
Victoria †	18	8	7	3	32	26	31	1-1	2-3	1-0		1-0	4-4	1-1	3-1	2-0	2-1
Vida	18	6	4	8	20	23	22	4-1	0-2	0-0	1-1		1-0	1-1	2-1	1-1	3-2
Platense	18	6	3	9	21	28	21	0-3	1-2	2-1	0-1	2-1		1-1	3-0	2-0	2-0
Atlético Olanchano	18	4	8	6	23	27	20	2-3	2-2	1-0	2-2	2-1	0-1		4-2	2-2	1-0
Municipal Valencia	18	4	7	7	17	25	19	2-4	1-0	1-1	0-0	1-0	2-0	0-0		1-1	0-0
Motagua	18	4	6	8	20	25	18	0-1	1-1	0-1	3-4	1-2	2-0	2-1	1-1		2-0
Universidad Choluteca	18	2	4	12	12	30	10	0-5	0-0	0-1	0-2	3-1	1-1	1-1	1-2	1-3	

6/08/2004 - 14/11/2004 • † Qualified for the play-offs

APERTURA PLAY-OFFS

Semi-finals			Final		
Marathón	2	1	First leg 12-12-2004		
Real España *	1	1	Marathón *	3	2
Victoria *	3	0	Olimpia	2	1
Olimpia	6	5	Second leg 19-12-2004		

* Home team in the first leg

HONDURAS 2004-05

TORNEO CLAUSURA

	Pl	W	D	L	F	A	Pts	Olimpia	Marathón	Universidad	Platense	Motagua	R. España	Vida	Victoria	Valencia	Olanchano
Olimpia †	18	11	5	2	29	14	38		1-2	0-0	1-0	2-0	2-2	1-0	5-0	2-1	3-2
Marathón †	18	7	6	5	24	22	27	0-0		1-0	1-4	3-1	4-3	0-0	0-1	2-1	0-0
Universidad Choluteca †	18	6	8	4	7	8	26	0-3	2-1		1-0	0-0	0-0	1-0	0-0	0-0	1-0
Platense †	18	6	6	6	24	19	24	4-2	1-3	0-1		0-0	2-1	0-0	1-1	1-0	6-2
Motagua	18	4	11	3	18	18	23	0-0	1-1	0-0	1-1		2-1	1-1	2-1	0-0	2-2
Real España	18	5	7	6	22	22	22	1-1	1-1	1-0	3-1	1-0		3-4	0-0	0-0	1-0
Vida	18	5	7	6	16	19	22	0-1	0-0	0-1	0-0	1-3	1-0		1-3	1-1	3-2
Victoria	18	5	6	7	19	24	21	1-2	3-2	0-0	0-2	2-2	1-2	1-2		0-0	2-0
Municipal Valencia	18	3	9	6	10	13	18	0-1	2-1	0-0	1-0	0-1	0-0	1-1	1-2		1-0
Atlético Olanchano	18	3	5	10	21	31	14	1-2	1-2	2-0	1-1	2-2	3-2	0-1	2-1	1-1	

21/01/2005 - 15/05/2004 • † Qualified for the play-offs

CLAUSURA PLAY-OFFS

Semi-finals			Final		
Olimpia	1	3	First leg 22-05-2005		
Platense *	1	0	Olimpia	1	2
Universidad *	1	0	Marathón *	1	1
Marathón	1	0	Second leg 29-05-2005		

* Home team in the first leg

AGGREGATE RELEGATION TABLE

	Pl	W	D	L	F	A	Pts
Olimpia	36	23	8	5	68	31	77
Marathón	36	17	10	9	47	39	61
Real España	36	14	11	11	45	34	53
Victoria	36	13	13	10	51	50	52
Platense	36	12	9	15	45	47	45
Vida	36	11	11	14	36	42	44
Motagua	36	8	17	11	38	43	41
Municipal Valencia	36	7	16	13	27	38	37
Universidad Choluteca	36	8	12	16	19	38	36
Atlético Olanchano	36	7	13	16	44	58	34

HUN – HUNGARY

NATIONAL TEAM RECORD
JULY 1ST 2002 TO JUNE 30TH 2005

PL	W	D	L	F	A	%
34	14	6	14	55	43	50

FIFA/COCA-COLA WORLD RANKING

1993	1994	1995	1996	1997	1998	1999	2000	2001	2002	2003	2004	High		Low	
50	61	62	75	77	46	45	47	66	56	72	64	42	08/93	87	07/96

2004-2005											
08/04	09/04	10/04	11/04	12/04	01/05	02/05	03/05	04/05	05/05	06/05	07/05
77	76	68	74	64	63	65	69	69	69	65	66

It is approaching 20 years since Hungary last qualified for the finals of a major tournament and the national team is showing little sign of breaking this most unwelcome streak. In the 2006 FIFA World Cup™ qualifiers the Hungarians began by losing away to Croatia and Sweden who have both pulled away at the top of the group. Without a realistic shot at the play-offs it has been a disappointing time in charge for coach Lothar Matthäus, a former FIFA World Cup™ winner with Germany. It is a difficult time for fans in Hungary especially with the Czech Republic achieving so much in recent years when in the past the two dominated football in central and eastern Europe.

INTERNATIONAL HONOURS
Olympic Gold 1952 1964 1968

It is not just the national team that has fallen behind its neighbour. With the Czech Republic often represented in the UEFA Champions League group stage, Ferencváros are the only Hungarian club to have progressed beyond the preliminary rounds to the group stage - once back in 1995. In the 2005-06 tournament Hungary will be represented by Debrecen who won the Hungarian Championship, a first title for the club and for Hungary's second city. There was also a new name on the Cup with Matáv Sopron thrashing Ferencváros 5-1 in a controversial final in which three players were sent off, a terrible end to a nightmare season for Fradi.

THE FIFA BIG COUNT OF 2000

	Male	Female		Male	Female
Registered players	46 782	515	Referees	3 500	5
Non registered players	100 000	320	Officials	7 000	150
Youth players	73 397	288	Total involved	231 957	
Total players	221 302		Number of clubs	2 577	
Professional players	852	0	Number of teams	5 966	

Hungarian Football Federation (MLSZ)
Magyar Labdarúgó Szövetség, Róbert Kàroly krt. 61-65, Róbert Ház, Budapest 1134, Hungary
Tel +36 1 4123340   Fax +36 1 4520360
mlsz@mlsz.hu   www.mlsz.hu
President: BOZOKY Imre Dr   General Secretary: BERZI Sandor
Vice-President: PUHL Sandor   Treasurer: KRIZSO Ibolya   Media Officer: GANCZER Gabor
Men's Coach: MATTHAUS Lothar   Women's Coach: BACSO Istvan
MLSZ formed: 1901   UEFA: 1954   FIFA: 1906
Colours: Red, White, Green

GAMES PLAYED BY HUNGARY IN THE 2006 FIFA WORLD CUP™ CYCLE

2002	Opponents	Score	Venue	Comp	Scorers	Att	Referee
21-08	Spain	D 1-1	Budapest	Fr	Miriuta [72]	20 000	Fleischer GER
7-09	Iceland	W 2-0	Reykjavik	Fr	Löw [81], Dárdai [90]	3 190	Maisonlahti FIN
12-10	Sweden	D 1-1	Stockholm	ECq	Kenesei [5]	35 084	Stark GER
16-10	San Marino	W 3-0	Budapest	ECq	Gera 3 [49 60 87]	6 500	Orrason ISL
20-11	Moldova	D 1-1	Budapest	Fr	Dárdai [55]	6 000	Sowa AUT
2003							
12-02	Bulgaria †	L 0-1	Larnaca	Fr	Abandoned after 45' due to the weather	200	Theodotou CYP
29-03	Poland	D 0-0	Chorzow	ECq		48 000	De Santis ITA
2-04	Sweden	L 1-2	Budapest	ECq	Lisztes [65]	28 000	Cortez Batista POR
30-04	Luxembourg	W 5-1	Budapest	Fr	Gera [18], Szabics 2 [52 90], Lisztes [61], Kenesei [69]	1 205	Skomina SVN
7-06	Latvia	W 3-1	Budapest	ECq	Szabics 2 [50 58], Gera [86]	4 000	Merk GER
11-06	San Marino	W 5-0	Serravalle	ECq	Böör [5], Lisztes 2 [21 81], Kenesei [61], Szabics [77]	1 410	Clark SCO
20-08	Slovenia	L 1-2	Murska Sobota	Fr	Fehér.M [90]	5 000	Sowa AUT
10-09	Latvia	L 1-3	Riga	ECq	Lisztes [53]	7 500	Larsen DEN
11-10	Poland	L 1-2	Budapest	ECq	Szabics [49]	15 500	Mejuto Gonzalez ESP
19-11	Estonia	L 0-1	Budapest	Fr		1 000	Sedivy CZE
2004							
18-02	Armenia	W 2-0	Paphos	Fr	Szabics [63], Lisztes [75]	400	Gerasimou CYP
19-02	Latvia	W 2-1	Limassol	Fr	Tököli [82], Kenesei [85]	500	Kailis CYP
31-03	Wales	L 1-2	Budapest	Fr	Kenesei [17p]	10 000	Meyer GER
25-04	Japan	W 3-2	Zalaegerszeg	Fr	Kuttor [53], Juhasz [67], Huszti [90p]	7 000	Trivkovic CRO
28-04	Brazil	L 1-4	Budapest	Fr	Torghelle [56]	45 000	De Santis ITA
1-06	China PR	L 1-2	Beijing	Fr	Kenesei [4p]	18 000	Chiu HKG
6-06	Germany	W 2-0	Kaiserslautern	Fr	Torghelle 2 [7 31]	36 590	Bennett ENG
18-08	Scotland	W 3-0	Glasgow	Fr	Huszti 2 [45p 53], Marshall OG [73]	15 933	Duhamel FRA
4-09	Croatia	L 0-3	Zagreb	WCq		20 853	Riley ENG
8-09	Iceland	W 3-2	Budapest	WCq	Gera [62], Torghelle [75], Szabics [79]	5 461	Ovrebo NOR
9-10	Sweden	L 0-3	Stockholm	WCq		32 288	Dougal SCO
17-11	Malta	W 2-0	Ta'Qali	WCq	Gera [39], Kovacs.P [93+]	14 500	Asumaa FIN
30-11	Slovakia	L 0-1	Bangkok	Fr		750	Veerapool THA
2-12	Estonia	W 5-0	Bangkok	Fr	Rosa [12], Waltner [14], Kerekes [19], Rajczi [24], Pollak [63]	800	Tongkhan THA
2005							
2-02	Saudi Arabia	D 0-0	Istanbul	Fr		100	Dereli TUR
9-02	Wales	L 0-2	Cardiff	Fr		16 672	Richmond SCO
30-03	Bulgaria	D 1-1	Budapest	WCq	Rajczi [90]	11 586	Wegereef NED
31-05	France	L 1-2	Metz	Fr	Kerekes [78]	26 000	Allaerts BEL
4-06	Iceland	W 3-2	Reykjavik	WCq	Gera 2 [45p 56p], Huszti [73]	4 613	Cardoso Batista POR

Fr = Friendly match • EC = UEFA EURO 2004™ • WC = FIFA World Cup™ • q = qualifier • † Not a full international

HUNGARY NATIONAL TEAM RECORDS AND RECORD SEQUENCES

Records			Sequence records				
Victory	13-1	FRA 1927	Wins	11	1951 1952	Clean sheets	4	Five times
Defeat	0-7	ENG 1908, GER 1941	Defeats	6	1978	Goals scored	70	1949-1957
Player Caps	101	BOZSIK József	Undefeated	30	1950-1954	Without goal	4	1993
Player Goals	84	PUSKAS Ferenc	Without win	12	1994	Goals against	19	Three times

HUNGARY COUNTRY INFORMATION

Capital	Budapest	Independence	Unified in 1001	GDP per Capita	$13 900
Population	10 032 375	Status	Republic	GNP Ranking	50
Area km²	93 030	Language	Hungarian	Dialling code	+36
Population density	107 per km²	Literacy rate	99%	Internet code	.hu
% in urban areas	65%	Main religion	Christian 92%	GMT +/-	+1
Towns/Cities ('000)	Budapest 1 708; Debrecen 204; Miskolc 179; Szeged 160; Pécs 156; Győr 129; Nyiregyháza 116; Kecskemét 106; Székesfehérvár 103; Szombathely 80; Szolnok 75; Tatabánya 71; Békéscsaba 65				
Neighbours (km)	Slovakia 677; Ukraine 103; Romania 443; Serbia & Montenegro 151; Croatia 329; Slovenia 102; Austria 366				
Main stadia	Puskas Ferenc (Nep) – Budapest 68 976				

NATIONAL CAPS

	Caps
BOZSIK Jósef	101
FAZEKAS László	92
GROSICS Gyula	86
PUSKAS Ferenc	85
GARABA Imre	82
MATRAI Sándor	81
SIPOS Ferenc	77
BALINT László	76
BENE Ferenc	76
FENYVESI Máté Dr.	76

NATIONAL GOALS

	Goals
PUSKAS Ferenc	84
KOCSIS Sándor	75
SCHLOSSER Imre	59
TICHY Lajos	51
SAROSI György Dr.	42
HIDEGKUTI Nándor	39
BENE Ferenc	36
ZSENGELLER Gyula	32
NYILASI Tibor	32
ALBERT Flórián	31

NATIONAL COACH

	Years
MESZOLY Kálmán	1990-'91
GLAZER Robert	1991
JENEI Imre	1992-'93
PUSKAS Ferenc	1993
VEREBES József	1993-'94
MESZOLY Kálmán	1994-'95
CSANK János	1996-'97
BICSKEI Bertalan	1998-'01
GELLEI Imre	2001-'03
MATTHAUS Lothar	2003-

FIFA REFEREE LIST 2005

	Int'l	DoB
BEDE Ferenc	1998	16-10-1965
DUBRAVICZKY Attila	2004	26-10-1971
HANACSEK Attila	1997	11-12-1967
KASSAI Viktor	2003	10-09-1975
MEGYEBIRO Janos	2002	21-06-1969
SAPI Csaba	2005	16-09-1971
SASKOY Szabolcs	2005	10-09-1970
SZABO Zsolt	1999	1-01-1972

FIFA ASSISTANT REFEREE LIST 2005

	Int'l	DoB
EROS Gabor	2003	5-09-1971
HEGYI Peter	2002	8-04-1972
KELEMEN Attila	2004	30-01-1972
KISPAL Robert	2000	28-07-1969
KOVACS Peter	2000	12-07-1975
SZABO Peter	2003	26-01-1973
SZEKELY Ferenc	1998	2-06-1966
SZPISJAK Zsolt	2005	30-12-1973
TOMPOS Zoltan	1996	14-09-1962
VAMOS Tibor	1999	16-01-1967

CLUB DIRECTORY

Club	Town/City	Stadium	Phone	www.	Lge	Cup	CL
Békéscsabai EFC	Békéscsaba	Kórház Utcai 11 500	+36 66 444623	elorefc.hu	0	1	0
Debreceni VSC	Debrecen	Oláh Gábor Ut 7 600	+36 52 535408	dvsc.hu	1	2	0
Diósgyöri-Balaton FC	Miskolc	DVTK 22 000	+36 46 530508	balatonfc.hu	0	2	0
Fehérvár FC	Székesfehérvár	Sóstói Ut 19 000	+36 22 379493	videotonfcf.hu	0	0	0
Ferencvárosi TC	Budapest	Ullói Ut 18 100	+36 1 2190300	ftc.hu	28	20	0
Györi ETO FC	Györ	Stadion ETO 27 000	+36 96 529005	eto.hu	3	4	0
Honvéd FC	Budapest	Bozsik József 13 500	+36 1 2807240	kispesthonved.hu	13	5	0
Kaposvári Rákóczi FC	Kaposvár	Vöröshadsereg Ut 14 000			0	0	0
Matáv FC Sopron	Sopron	Városi 10 000	+36 99 317302	matavsopronfutball.hu	0	1	0
MTK-Hungária FC	Budapest	Hidegkuti Nandor 12 700	+36 1 3338386	mtkhungaria.hu	22	12	0
Nyíregyházi FC	Nyíregyháza	Sóstói Ut 16 500	+36 42 500171		0	0	0
Pápa TFC	Pápa	Várkerti 4 000			0	0	0
Pécsi MFC	Pécs	PMFC 10 000	+36 72 552880	pmfc.hu	0	1	0
Ujpest FC	Budapest	Szusza Ferenc 13 501	+36 1 2310088	ujpestfc.hu	20	8	0
Vasas SC	Budapest	Illovsky Rudolf 18 000	+36 1 3209457	vasassc.hu	6	4	0
Zalaegerszegi TE	Zalaegerszeg	ZTE 12 500	+36 92 596302	ztefc.hu	1	0	0

RECENT LEAGUE AND CUP RECORD

Year	Championship Champions	Pts	Runners-up	Pts	Third	Pts	Cup Winners	Score	Runners-up
1990	Ujpesti Dózsa	58	MTK-VM Budapest	58	Ferencvárosi TC	48	Pécsi MSC	2-0	Honvéd
1991	Honvéd	45	Ferencvárosi TC	40	Pécsi MSC	37	Ferencvárosi TC	1-0	Vac FC
1992	Ferencvárosi TC	46	Vac FC	45	Kispest-Honvéd	40	Ujpesti TE	1-0	Vac FC
1993	Kispest-Honvéd	43	Vac FC	42	Ferencvárosi TC	41	Ferencvárosi TC	1-1 1-1 5-3p	Haladás
1994	Vac FC	46	Kispest-Honvéd	43	Békéscsabai ESC	41	Ferencvárosi TC	3-0 2-1	Kispest-Honvéd
1995	Ferencvárosi TC	59	Ujpesti TE	52	Debreceni VSC	49	Ferencvárosi TC	2-0 3-4	Vac FC
1996	Ferencvárosi TC	66	BVSC	61	Ujpesti TE	48	Kispest-Honvéd	0-1 2-0	BVSC
1997	MTK-Hungária	85	Ujpesti TE	76	Ferencvárosi TC	74	MTK-Hungária	6-0 2-0	BVSC
1998	Ujpesti TE	73	Ferencvárosi TC	67	Vasas SC	64	MTK-Hungária	1-0	Ujpesti TE
1999	MTK-Hungária	83	Ferencvárosi TC	64	Ujpesti TE	63	Debreceni VSC	2-0	LFC Tatabánya
2000	Dunaferr FC	79	MTK-Hungária	63	Vasas SC	61	MTK-Hungária	3-1	Vasas SC
2001	Ferencvárosi TC	48	Dunaferr FC	46	Vasas SC	40	Debreceni VSC	5-2	Videoton Fehérvar
2002	Zalaegerszegi TE	71	Ferencvárosi TC	69	MTK-Hungária	59	Ujpesti TE	2-1	Haladás
2003	MTK-Hungária	66	Ferencvárosi TC	64	Debreceni VSC	53	Ferencvárosi TC	2-1	Debreceni VSC
2004	Ferencvárosi TC	57	Ujpesti TE	56	Debreceni VSC	56	Ferencvárosi TC	3-1	Honvéd FC
2005	Debreceni VSC	62	Ferencvárosi TC	56	MTK-Hungária	56	Mátav FC Sopron	5-1	Ferencvárosi TC

HUNGARY 2004-05

ARANY ASZOK LIGA 1.DIVISION

	Pl	W	D	L	F	A	Pts	DVSC	FTC	MTK	Ujpest	Győr	ZTE	Sopron	Fehérvár	Diósgyőr	Pécs	Honvéd	Kaposvár	Vasas	Pápa	Nyíregyháza	Békéscsaba
Debreceni VSC †	30	19	5	6	57	25	62		2-0	3-0	1-2	1-3	2-0	3-0	3-0	1-0	3-1	2-0	2-1	3-1	3-1	2-1	5-1
Ferencvárosi TC ‡	30	17	5	8	56	31	56	0-0		2-1	1-1	0-1	4-2	4-1	0-1	2-1	1-1	4-0	1-1	2-0	5-0	5-0	2-0
MTK-Hungária §1	30	16	9	5	47	26	56	2-0	3-1		3-1	1-0	2-0	3-0	2-2	0-0	1-1	3-0	0-0	2-1	1-0	3-0	1-1
Ujpest FC	30	15	10	5	60	34	55	2-0	1-1	2-0		4-1	3-2	1-4	3-0	4-1	1-1	1-2	1-1	4-0	3-1	3-3	3-0
Győri ETO	30	16	6	8	44	32	54	1-0	2-4	1-1	1-1		4-1	1-0	0-0	2-1	2-0	1-0	0-1	2-1	3-0	3-1	2-0
Zalaegerszegi TE	30	13	5	12	48	45	44	2-1	1-5	0-1	1-0	2-0		0-1	0-0	3-2	1-0	1-3	5-0	2-0	5-2	2-0	1-1
Matáv FC Sopron ‡	30	11	9	10	44	44	42	0-3	3-0	1-1	2-2	1-0	1-2		2-1	0-1	2-2	2-0	0-0	1-1	1-0	5-2	3-2
FC Fehérvár §2	30	11	10	9	44	36	40	2-2	0-1	2-3	1-2	2-1	1-1	1-1		3-0	1-0	4-1	1-1	1-0	2-1	5-3	5-0
Diósgyőri-Balaton FC	30	11	4	15	39	45	37	0-2	2-3	2-2	1-3	2-3	2-1	1-0	3-1		1-0	5-1	2-0	0-0	1-3	0-1	1-0
Pécsi MFC	30	9	9	12	33	35	36	1-1	2-0	1-0	1-0	1-1	1-0	2-3	0-2	2-1		3-1	0-0	1-0	2-1	1-1	5-0
Honvéd FC	30	10	5	15	37	58	35	1-2	0-1	1-1	1-1	2-3	3-3	2-1	1-0	2-1	2-1		1-1	1-0	3-2	3-2	2-0
Kaposvári Rákóczi FC	30	8	10	12	34	47	34	0-0	2-1	1-2	0-0	1-2	0-2	4-3	2-1	0-1	2-1	4-2		3-2	1-2	1-1	1-2
Vasas SC	30	10	3	17	34	48	33	2-5	0-1	3-1	1-2	1-0	1-0	0-1	1-1	3-1	3-0	4-1	2-1		0-6	2-0	3-0
Pápa TFC	30	8	6	16	40	47	30	1-1	1-2	0-1	1-2	1-2	1-2	0-0	2-2	1-2	1-1	1-0	4-1	2-0		0-0	2-0
Nyíregyházi FC	30	5	11	14	38	63	26	0-2	2-0	0-5	2-2	1-1	3-3	2-2	0-2	2-2	1-0	1-1	4-1	1-2	0-2		1-1
Békéscsabai EFC §3	30	4	7	19	26	65	4	0-2	0-3	0-1	0-5	1-1	1-3	3-3	0-0	0-2	2-1	3-0	2-3	3-0	1-1	2-3	

7/08/2004 - 26/05/2005 • † Qualified for the UEFA Champions League • ‡ Qualified for the UEFA Cup • §1 = one point deducted • §2 = three points deducted • §3 = 15 points deducted

HUNGARY 2004-05 2.DIVISION

	Pl	W	D	L	F	A	Pts
Tatabánya FC	26	19	5	2	74	19	62
Rákospalotai EAC	26	15	8	3	42	18	53
Vác-Duankanyar	26	13	3	10	39	38	42
Kecskeméti TE	26	11	7	8	45	36	40
Dunaújvárosi FC	26	11	3	12	43	46	36
Szolnoki MAV	26	9	9	8	30	36	36
Szeged FC §	26	11	3	12	37	36	34
BKV Előre	26	9	6	11	34	37	33
Bodajk FC	26	9	5	12	36	36	32
Mosonmagyaróvári TE	26	8	7	11	31	43	31
Orosháza FC	26	8	6	12	26	50	30
Makó FC	26	8	5	13	39	47	29
Szombathelyi Haladás	26	8	4	14	28	38	28
Hévíz FC	26	7	1	18	33	57	22

21/08/2004 - 12/06/2005 • § = two points deducted

TOP SCORERS

MEDVED Tomas	Pápa	18
BOGDANOVIC Igor	DVSC	15
OLAH Lorant	Kaposvár	15
BARANYOS Zsolt	Sopron	14
RAJCZI Peter	Ujpest	13

MAGYAR KUPA 2004-05

Round of 16		Quarter-finals		Semi-finals		Final	
Matáv FC Sopron	1						
Debreceni VSC	0	Matáv FC Sopron	2				
Dunaújvárosi FC	1	Kazincbarcika	1				
Kazincbarcika	2			Matáv FC Sopron	4		
FC Fehérvár	3			Honvéd FC	2		
Békéscsabai EFC	0	FC Fehérvár	1 1p				
Vasas SC	0	Honvéd FC	1 3p				
Honvéd FC	1					Matáv FC Sopron ‡	5
BKV Előre	1					Ferencvárosi TC	1
MTK-Hungária	0	BKV Előre	3				
Ujpest FC	0	Bodajk FC	2				
Bodajk FC	2			BKV Előre	1		
Kaposvári Rákóczi FC	2 7p			Ferencvárosi TC	3		
Pápa TFC	2 6p	Kaposvári Rákóczi FC	1				
Pécsi MFC		Ferencvárosi TC	3				
Ferencvárosi TC							

* Home team • ‡ Qualified for the UEFA Cup

CUP FINAL

11-05-2005, Att: 4 000, Ref: Trivkovic
Sóstói Ut, Székesfehérvár
Scorers - Mihály [13], Zsolt [38], Iván 2 [45 57],
András [73] for Soporon, Lpcsei [49] for FTC

IDN – INDONESIA

INDONESIA NATIONAL TEAM RECORD
JULY 1ST 2002 TO JUNE 30TH 2005

PL	W	D	L	F	A	%
36	13	10	13	70	58	50

FIFA/COCA-COLA WORLD RANKING FOR INDONESIA

1993	1994	1995	1996	1997	1998	1999	2000	2001	2002	2003	2004	High		Low	
106	134	130	119	91	87	90	97	87	110	91	91	76	09/98	152	11/95

					2004-2005						
08/04	09/04	10/04	11/04	12/04	01/05	02/05	03/05	04/05	05/05	06/05	07/05
91	92	94	99	91	91	92	92	92	90	91	92

The events of 26 December which saw more than 200 000 Indonesians lose their lives in the Tsunami disaster will remain long in the memory but in a small way football has played its part in helping the recovery process. FIFA decided the best way forward would be to provide funds for football-related projects such as the reconstruction of the stadium in Banda Aceh with US$2.5m given to Indonesia from the Solidarity fund in the first round of payments. At the time of the disaster the Indonesian national team was taking part in the ASEAN Tiger Cup with a semi-final against Malaysia scheduled to take place two days after. The decision to carry on playing was

INTERNATIONAL HONOURS
AFC Youth Championship 1961

welcomed and in the semi-final in Jakarta against Malaysia 100 000 fans turned up to pay their respects to the victims. Peter Withe's team lost the game but won the return in Kuala Lumpur to reach the final but there was no first title for Indonesians to savour after losing 5-2 on aggregate in the final to Singapore. After a long League campaign which took nearly 12 months to complete, Persebaya, from the east of Java, beat their west Javanese rivals Persija 2-1 on the final day of the season to leapfrog above them and bring the title back to Indonesia's second city, Surabaya, for the second time in the Pro League's 10 year history.

THE FIFA BIG COUNT OF 2000

	Male	Female		Male	Female
Registered players	2 525	0	Referees	669	0
Non registered players	10 000 000	0	Officials	365	0
Youth players	2 500	0	Total involved	10 006 059	
Total players	10 005 025		Number of clubs	73	
Professional players	700	0	Number of teams	73	

Football Association of Indonesia (PSSI)
Gelora Bung Karno, Pintu X-XI, Senayan, PO Box 2305, Jakarta 10023, Indonesia
Tel +62 21 5704762   Fax +62 21 5734386
pssi@pssi-online.com   www.none
President: HALID Nurdin   General Secretary: BESOES Nugraha
Vice-President: MUNZIR Ibnu   Treasurer: YANDHU Hamka   Media Officer: IRAWAN Tris
Men's Coach: WITHE Peter   Women's Coach: none
PSSI formed: 1930   AFC: 1954   FIFA: 1952
Colours: Red, White, Red

GAMES PLAYED BY INDONESIA IN THE 2006 FIFA WORLD CUP™ CYCLE

2002	Opponents	Score		Venue	Comp	Scorers	Att	Referee
10-11	Singapore	D	1-1	Singapore	Fr	Juraimi 38. L 3-4p		
15-12	Myanmar	D	0-0	Jakarta	TCr1		100 000	Ebrahim BHR
17-12	Cambodia	W	4-2	Jakarta	TCr1	Arif 36, Bambang 3 59 75 82p	20 000	Khanthachai THA
21-12	Vietnam	D	2-2	Jakarta	TCr1	Budi 11, Arif 84	35 000	Mohd Salleh MAS
23-12	Philippines	W	13-0	Jakarta	TCr1	Bambang 4 2 29 34 82, Arif 4 7 37 41 57, Budi 17, Sugiyantoro 2 53 75, Imran 80, Licuanan OG 88	30 000	Khanthachai THA
27-12	Malaysia	W	1-0	Jakarta	TCsf	Bambang 75	65 000	Ebrahim BHR
29-12	Thailand	D	2-2	Jakarta	TCf	Jaris 48, Gendut 79. L 2-4p	100 000	Mohd Salleh MAS
2003								
26-09	Malaysia	D	1-1	Kuala Lumpur	Fr	Aiboi 62		
6-10	Bhutan	W	2-0	Jeddah	ACq	Arif 2 19 50		
8-10	Yemen	W	3-0	Jeddah	ACq	Uston 2 51 90, Arif 62		
10-10	Saudi Arabia	L	0-5	Jeddah	ACq			
13-10	Bhutan	W	2-0	Jeddah	ACq	Edwarar 19, Arif 33		
15-10	Yemen	D	2-2	Jeddah	ACq	Edwarar 12p, Donald 38		
17-10	Saudi Arabia	L	0-6	Jeddah	ACq			
2004								
12-02	Jordan	L	1-2	Amman	Fr	Bambang 15		
18-02	Saudi Arabia	L	0-3	Riyadh	WCq		1 000	Al Ghafary JOR
17-03	Malaysia	D	0-0	Johor Bahru	Fr		8 000	Kim Heng MAS
31-03	Turkmenistan	L	1-3	Ashgabat	WCq	Budi 30	5 000	Sahib Shakir IRQ
3-06	India	D	1-1	Jakarta	Fr	Ponyaro 33		
9-06	Sri Lanka	W	1-0	Jakarta	WCq	Aiboi 30	30 000	Nesar BAN
18-07	Qatar	W	2-1	Beijing	ACr1	Budi 26, Ponaryo 48	5 000	Moradi IRN
21-07	China PR	L	0-5	Beijing	ACr1			Najm LIB
25-07	Bahrain	L	1-3	Jinan	ACr1	Aiboy 75	20 000	Codjia BEN
4-09	Singapore	L	0-2	Singapore	Fr			
8-09	Sri Lanka	D	2-2	Colombo	WCq	Jaya 8, Sofyan 51	4 000	Marshoud JOR
12-10	Saudi Arabia	L	1-3	Jakarta	WCq	Jaya 50	30 000	Mohd Salleh MAS
17-11	Turkmenistan	W	3-1	Jakarta	WCq	Jaya 3 20 47 59	15 000	Shaban KUW
7-12	Laos	W	6-0	Ho Chi Minh City	TCr1	Boas 26, Jaya 2 29 34. OG 53, Aiboy 60, Kurniawan 87		Rungklay THA
9-12	Singapore	D	0-0	Ho Chi Minh City	TCr1		4 000	Kwong Jong Chul KOR
11-12	Vietnam	W	3-0	Hanoi	TCr1	Lessy 18, Boas 21, Jaya 45	40 000	Ebrahim BHR
13-12	Cambodia	W	8-0	Hanoi	TCr1	Jaya 3 9 48 57, Aiboy 2 30 55, Kurniawan 2 72 74, Ortisan 82	17 000	Sun Baojie CHN
28-12	Malaysia	L	1-2	Jakarta	TCsf	Kurniawan 7	100 000	Irmatov UZB
2005								
3-01	Malaysia	W	4-1	Kuala Lumpur	TCsf	Kurniawan 59, Yulianto 74, Jaya 77, Boas 84	70 000	Kunsuta THA
8-01	Singapore	L	1-3	Jakarta	TCf	Mahyadi 90+3	120 000	Kwong Jong Chul KOR
16-01	Singapore	L	1-2	Singapore	TCf	Aiboy 76	55 000	Al Ghamdi KSA
29-03	Australia	L	0-3	Perth	Fr		14 000	Yamanishi JPN

Fr = Friendly match • TC = ASEAN Tiger Cup • AC = AFC Asian Cup • WC = FIFA World Cup™
q = qualifier • r1 = first round group • sf = semi-final • f = final

INDONESIA COUNTRY INFORMATION

Capital	Jakarta	Independence	1945 from the Netherlands	GDP per Capita	$3 200
Population	238 452 952	Status	Republic	GNP Ranking	28
Area km²	1 919 440	Language	Bahasa Indonesia	Dialling code	+62
Population density	124 per km²	Literacy rate	87%	Internet code	.id
% in urban areas	35%	Main religion	Muslim 88%	GMT +/–	+7
Cities/Towns ('000)	Jakarta 8 987; Surabaya 3 092; Bandung 2 781; Medan 2 243; Palembang 1 507; Tangerang 1 344; Semarang 1 289; Makasar 1 268				
Neighbours (km)	Malaysia 1 782; East Timor 228; Papua New Guinea 820; Pacific Ocean & Indian Ocean 54 716				
Main stadia	Utama Senayan – Jakarta 100 000; Gelora 10 November – Surabaya 40 000				

INDONESIA NATIONAL TEAM RECORDS AND RECORD SEQUENCES

Records			Sequence records					
Victory	12-0	PHI 1972	Wins	10	1968-1969	Clean sheets	4	1987
Defeat	0-9	DEN 1974	Defeats	7	1996	Goals scored	24	1967-1969
Player Caps	n/a		Undefeated	10	Three times	Without goal	5	Three times
Player Goals	n/a		Without win	18	1985-1986	Goals against	19	1985-1986

FIFA REFEREE LIST 2005

	Int'l	DoB
HIDAYAT Jajat	1998	10-12-1966
MIDI NITROREJO Setiyono	2002	24-06-1967
NAPITUPULU Jimmy	2002	13-10-1966

FIFA ASSISTANT REFEREE LIST 2005

	Int'l	DoB
ARPAN Erwin	2005	9-05-1972
EDI Budi	2005	27-02-1968
MUHAMMAD Suaidi	2005	14-07-1971
PARWO Jaka	2001	26-03-1965

INDONESIA 2004

LIGA INDONESIA DIVISI UTAMA

	Pl	W	D	L	F	A	Pts	Persebaya	PSM	Persija	PSS	Persikota	Persib	PSMS	Persita	Persik	PSIS	PKT	Persela	Persipura	Persijatim	Semen	PSPS	Pelita	Deltras
Persebaya Surabaya †	34	17	10	7	55	26	61		1-1	2-1	0-1	5-0	1-0	1-1	3-0	2-0	3-0	2-0	0-1	4-1	5-1	5-0	3-2	2-1	1-0
PSM Makassar †	34	17	10	7	46	28	61	3-1		1-1	6-2	3-1	3-0	2-1	1-0	2-0	1-0	1-0	3-0	0-0	2-1	3-1	2-0	1-0	1-0
Persija Jakarta	34	18	6	10	49	30	60	3-1	1-0		2-0	2-3	1-0	3-0	2-2	1-0	1-0	3-1	3-1	1-0	6-1	1-0	1-0	1-0	5-0
PSS Sleman	34	14	11	9	39	37	53	1-1	1-1	1-1		1-0	3-2	2-0	2-1	3-0	1-0	2-0	4-1	0-0	3-1	1-0	0-2	1-0	1-1
Persikota Tangerang	34	14	8	12	48	41	50	1-1	1-1	1-0	2-0		3-0	1-0	1-1	2-3	2-1	3-0	2-0	3-0	0-1	1-1	6-1	1-1	3-0
Persib Maung Bandung	34	12	13	9	38	37	49	1-0	3-0	0-0	2-1	1-1		1-0	1-0	2-0	1-1	3-1	2-2	1-0	2-0	2-0	1-1	2-1	2-0
PSMS Medan	34	14	5	15	34	37	47	3-0	0-1	0-1	1-0	1-0	0-0		2-1	3-0	2-0	3-0	2-0	1-0	1-3	1-0	3-1	2-1	1-0
Persita Tangerang	34	13	7	14	45	40	46	0-0	3-1	2-0	1-2	1-2	2-2	3-0		4-1	1-1	4-0	3-1	3-0	1-0	0-2	1-2	1-0	1-0
Persik Kediri	34	14	4	16	41	39	46	1-0	1-0	5-1	3-0	0-1	0-0	3-0	2-1		1-0	1-2	1-1	2-0	2-0	2-0	0-2	2-0	5-0
PSIS Semarang	34	12	10	12	35	34	46	0-0	0-2	1-0	2-0	2-0	0-0	3-1	2-2	2-1		0-0	3-0	1-0	3-1	2-0	1-0	1-0	2-2
PKT Bontang	34	12	9	13	40	42	45	1-1	0-0	1-0	0-0	2-1	3-3	3-0	0-1	1-2	0-0		3-1	2-2	1-1	1-2	1-0	4-1	3-0
Persela Lamongan	34	13	5	16	39	53	44	0-4	1-1	0-1	2-2	4-0	2-1	1-0	1-2	1-0	1-0	1-1		2-1	3-1	2-0	1-0	1-0	4-0
Persipura Jayapura	34	11	10	13	39	43	43	0-2	1-1	1-1	1-1	0-0	3-1	1-0	1-0	2-0	0-0	3-4	3-0		1-1	3-1	1-0	0-0	6-1
Persijatim Solo	34	11	9	14	35	43	42	0-1	1-1	2-1	1-1	2-3	1-1	1-0	2-0	1-0	0-0	1-0	3-1	1-0		3-1	2-0	1-1	1-0
Semen Padang	34	11	8	15	32	48	41	1-1	1-0	1-0	0-1	1-0	1-1	1-3	1-1	2-2	2-0	0-0	1-0	4-1	1-1		0-0	1-0	2-0
PSPS Pekanbaru	34	10	10	14	35	41	40	0-0	1-1	2-1	1-1	1-0	2-0	2-2	0-1	1-0	2-2	1-0	4-1	2-3	0-0	2-0		0-0	1-2
Pelita Krakatau	34	10	9	15	32	36	39	1-1	2-0	1-3	2-0	0-0	0-0	0-0	3-0	1-2	2-1	1-0	2-1	0-1	3-2	1-1	2-1		3-2
Deltra Putra Sidoarjo	34	9	4	21	31	58	31	0-1	0-2	1-0	0-1	4-3	4-0	0-0	2-0	1-0	3-4	0-1	0-1	1-2	1-0	2-0	3-1	0-2	

4/01/2004 - 23/12/2004 • † Teams qualifying for the AFC Champions League • No relegation due to the expansion of the division to 28 teams

RECENT LEAGUE RECORD

			Championship			
Year	Champions	Pts	Runners-up	Pts	Third	Pts
1990	Pelita Jaya		Tiga Berlian			
1991	No championship due to season adjustment					
1992	Arseto		Pupuk Kaltim			
1993	Arema					
1994	Pelita Jaya	1-0	Gelora Dewata			
1995	Persib	1-0	Petrokimia Putra			
1996	Bandung Raya	2-0	PSM			
1997	Persebaya	3-1	Bandung Raya			
1998	Season not finished					
1999	PSIS	1-0	Persebaya			
2000	PSM	3-2	Pupuk Kaltim			
2001	Persija	3-2	PSM			
2002	Petrokimia Putra	2-1	Persita			
2003	Persik	67	PSM	62	Persita	62
2004	Persebaya	61	PSM	61	Persija	60

End of season play-offs dropped for the 2003 season

IND – INDIA

NATIONAL TEAM RECORD
JULY 1ST 2002 TO JUNE 30TH 2005

PL	W	D	L	F	A	%
27	9	6	12	30	46	44.4

FIFA/COCA-COLA WORLD RANKING

1993	1994	1995	1996	1997	1998	1999	2000	2001	2002	2003	2004	High		Low	
100	109	121	120	112	110	106	122	121	127	127	132	**94**	02/96	**143**	07/04

					2004-2005						
08/04	09/04	10/04	11/04	12/04	01/05	02/05	03/05	04/05	05/05	06/05	07/05
142	138	138	140	132	133	133	134	135	135	135	131

Two goals conceded in the last 10 minutes of the final game of the season decided the fate of the Indian Championship in a very close fought race between Goan teams Dempo and Sporting and East Bengal from Calcutta. With just two points separating the three going into the final day, a win would have seen leaders Sporting home and dry and with 10 minutes to go they were leading Mahindra 3-1. Two late goals meant a 3-3 draw and with a home defeat for East Bengal against Vasco that left the coast clear for Dempo, who beat Tollygunge 2-0. Not only was it their first Championship but Dempo became only the second team to win the double having beaten Mohan

INTERNATIONAL HONOURS
Asian Games 1951 1962 South Asian Federation Games 1985 1987 1995 South Asian Football Federation Cup 1995

Bagan in the Federation Cup final earlier in the season. Their title triumph was dedicated to Brazilian striker Cristiano who had died on the field soon after having scored the two winning goals in the Federation Cup Final. With nine of the 12 clubs in the League coming from either Goa or Calcutta it is obvious where football is strongest in India and it would take a major cultural shift for it to challenge cricket in the rest of the country. Quite what effect this has on the performances of the national team is open to debate but once again the second most populous nation in the world barely made an impact in the 2006 FIFA World Cup™ qualifiers before bowing out.

THE FIFA BIG COUNT OF 2000

	Male	Female		Male	Female
Registered players	96 250	8 000	Referees	2 550	120
Non registered players	2 000 000	12 000	Officials	220 000	40 000
Youth players	45 000	4 000	Total involved	2 427 920	
Total players	2 165 250		Number of clubs	10 750	
Professional players	750	0	Number of teams	20 500	

All India Football Federation (AIFF)
Nehru Stadium (West Stand), Fatorda, Margoa, Goa 403 602, India
Tel +91 832 2742603   Fax +91 832 2741172
alb@sancharnet.in   www.none
President: DAS MUNSI Priya Ranjan   General Secretary: COLACO Alberto
Vice-President: PATEL Praful   Treasurer: SALGAOCAR Shivanand V.   Media Officer: None
Men's Coach: SINGH Sukwinder   Women's Coach: SINGH Moirangthem
AIFF formed: 1937   AFC: 1954   FIFA: 1948
Colours: Sky blue, Navy blue, sky blue and navy blue

GAMES PLAYED BY INDIA IN THE 2006 FIFA WORLD CUP™ CYCLE

2002	Opponents	Score		Venue	Comp	Scorers	Att	Referee
29-08	Jamaica	L	0-3	Watford	Fr			Bennett ENG
1-09	Jamaica	D	0-0	Wolverhampton	Fr		4 030	Riley ENG
2003								
10-01	Pakistan	L	0-1	Dhaka	SAr1			Shamsuzzaman BAN
12-01	Afghanistan	W	4-0	Dhaka	SAr1	Biswas 2 [30 62], D'Cunha 2 [50 85]		Gurung NEP
14-01	Sri Lanka	D	1-1	Dhaka	SAr1	Biswas [90]		Shamsuzzaman BAN
18-01	Bangladesh	L	1-2	Dhaka	SAsf	D'Cunha [80]		Kunsuta THA
20-01	Pakistan	W	2-1	Dhaka	SA3p	Vijayan [56], Yadav [100GG]		Shamsuzzaman BAN
24-03	Korea DPR	L	0-2	Pyongyang	ACq			
30-03	Korea DPR	D	1-1	Margao	ACq	Vijayan [29]		
16-10	Thailand	L	0-2	Bangkok	Fr			
22-10	Rwanda	W	3-1	Hyderabad	AAr1	Vijayan [13], Suresh [54], Biswas [79]		
24-10	Malaysia	W	2-0	Hyderabad	AAr1	Bisht [50], Vijayan [64]		
29-10	Zimbabwe	W	5-3	Hyderabad	AAsf	Vijayan 2 [25 33], Bhutia 2 [41 83p], Singh.R [58]		
31-10	Uzbekistan	L	0-1	Hyderabad	AAf			Lu Jun CHN
2004								
18-02	Singapore	W	1-0	Margao	WCq	Singh.R [50]	28 000	Yasrebi IRN
31-03	Oman	L	1-5	Kochin	WCq	Singh.R [18]	48 000	Kim Heng MAS
3-06	Indonesia	D	1-1	Jakarta	Fr	Ancheri [89p]		
9-06	Japan	L	0-7	Saitama	WCq		63 000	Huang Junjie CHN
22-08	Myanmar	W	2-1	Ho Chi Minh City	Fr	Prakash 2 [42 83]		
24-08	Vietnam	L	1-2	Ho Chi Minh City	Fr	Lawrence [87]		
8-09	Japan	L	0-4	Calcutta	WCq		90 000	Hajjar SYR
13-10	Singapore	L	0-2	Singapore	WCq		3 609	Husain BHR
5-11	Kuwait	W	3-2	Kuwait City	Fr	Singh.T [48], Zirsanga [64], Yadav [75]		
17-11	Oman	D	0-0	Muscat	WCq		2 000	Nurilddin Salman IRQ
2005								
12-06	Pakistan	D	1-1	Quetta	Fr	Chetri [65]	20 000	Khan PAK
16-06	Pakistan	W	1-0	Peshawar	Fr	Abdul Hakim [67]	15 000	Imtiaz PAK
18-06	Pakistan	L	0-3	Lahore	Fr			Asif PAK

Fr = Friendly match • SA = South Asian Football Federation Cup • AC = AFC Asian Cup • AA = Afro-Asian Games • WC = FIFA World Cup™
q = qualifier • r1 = first round group • sf = semi-final • f = final

FIFA REFEREE LIST 2005

	Int'l	DoB
BALU Sundarraj	1999	23-07-1961
BASKAR Purushothaman	2002	20-03-1964
BOSE Praveer	1999	27-05-1965
HAQ Rizwan	2000	30-04-1966
PEREIRA Manuel		8-01-1962
SARKAR Subrata	2002	6-12-1962
SINGH Binod	2000	1-12-1963
SRINIVASAN Suresh	1999	3-05-1965

FIFA ASSISTANT REFEREE LIST 2005

	Int'l	DoB
DINESH NAIR Dinesh	2004	8-07-1972
HALDER Udayan	1999	7-01-1963
KURIAN Shaji	1999	25-05-1970
PEREIRA Walter	1999	24-03-1963
ROY Mrinal	2000	30-12-1962
SANKAR Komaleeswaran	1995	10-06-1963
SILVA Benjamin	2004	31-01-1966
THALLOORI Pradeep	2003	9-11-1964

INDIA COUNTRY INFORMATION

Capital	New Delhi	Independence	1947 from the UK	GDP per Capita	2 900
Population	1 065 070 607	Status	Republic	GNP Ranking	12
Area km²	3 287 590	Language	Hindi, English	Dialling code	+91
Population density	324 per km²	Literacy rate	59%	Internet code	.in
% in urban areas	27%	Main religion	Hindu 71%, Muslim 12%	GMT +/–	+5.5
Towns/Cities ('000)	Mumbai 12 692; Delhi 10 928; Bangalore 4 931; Calcutta 4 631; Madras 4 328; Ahmadbad 3 719; Hyderabad 3 598; Pune 2 935; Surat 2 894; Kanpur 2 823; Jaipur 2 711				
Neighbours (km)	Bangladesh 4 053; Bhutan 605; Burma 1 463; China 3 380; Nepal 1 690; Pakistan 2 912; Indian Ocean 7 000				
Main stadia	Saltlake – Calcutta 120 000; Jawaharlal Nehru – Kochin 60 000; Jawaharlal Nehru – Margao 35 000				

INDIA NATIONAL TEAM RECORDS AND RECORD SEQUENCES

Records			Sequence records					
Victory	7-1	SRI 1963	Wins	7	1962-1964	Clean sheets	4	1966
Defeat	1-11	URS 1955	Defeats	8	1978-1980	Goals scored	21	1958-1961
Player Caps	n/a		Undefeated	7	1962-64, 1999	Without goal	6	1984-1985
Player Goals	n/a		Without win	11	1986-92, 1993	Goals against	15	1952-58, 1973-76

INDIA 2004-05

9TH NATIONAL FOOTBALL LEAGUE

	Pl	W	D	L	F	A	Pts	Dempo	Sporting	East Bengal	Mahindra	Fransa	Salgaocar	JCT Mills	Mohun B	Churchill	Vasco	SBT	Tollygunge
Dempo Sports Club †	22	14	5	3	28	17	47		0-4	3-2	0-0	0-1	0-0	1-0	2-0	0-0	2-0	1-0	2-0
Sporting Clube Goa †	22	14	3	5	46	23	45	1-2		1-2	1-3	2-0	1-0	2-0	1-0	1-3	5-2	3-1	3-3
East Bengal	22	13	4	5	34	16	43	2-1	2-3		1-1	0-1	1-0	2-0	0-0	2-0	1-3	2-0	5-0
Mahindra United	22	8	11	3	29	21	35	1-2	1-0	1-0		0-1	1-0	1-1	2-0	0-0	1-1	3-1	1-1
Fransa	22	8	6	8	24	26	30	1-2	1-4	0-0	2-2		2-2	0-1	2-1	2-1	2-3	2-0	0-0
Salgaocar Sports Club	22	7	7	8	26	24	28	2-3	0-1	0-0	2-2	2-1		2-0	1-0	0-1	1-0	3-4	5-1
JCT Mills	22	7	7	8	19	19	28	0-1	0-1	0-1	1-1	0-0	3-1		0-0	3-0	0-0	1-0	1-1
Mohun Bagan	22	5	8	9	16	19	23	0-0	1-0	0-1	0-1	1-2	0-0	1-0		1-1	0-1	1-1	2-1
Churchill Brothers	22	5	8	9	23	33	23	1-2	0-4	0-2	2-1	1-1	1-1	1-1	1-2		2-1	1-1	1-2
Vasco Sports Club	22	5	5	12	25	37	20	1-2	0-3	0-3	2-3	0-2	0-1	1-2	1-1	1-1		0-0	5-0
State Bank Travancore	22	4	6	12	24	34	18	1-2	0-2	2-4	1-2	2-0	1-1	1-2	1-1	3-1	4-1		0-0
Tollygunge Agragami	22	3	8	11	20	45	17	0-0	2-2	0-1	1-1	2-1	1-2	1-3	0-4	2-4	1-2	1-0	

12/01/2005 - 22/05/2005 • † Qualified for the AFC Cup

LEAGUE CLUB DIRECTORY

Club	Town/City	Stadium	Phone	www.	Lge	FC
Churchill Brothers SC	Salcete, Goa	Nehru, Margao 35 000			0	0
Dempo Sports Club	Panjim, Goa	Nehru, Margao 35 000			0	1
East Bengal Football Club	Calcutta	Saltlake 120 000	+91 33 22484642	eastbengalfootballclub.com	3	4
Fransa Football Club	Nagoa, Goa	Nehru, Margao 35 000			0	0
JCT Mills	Phagwara, Punjab	Guru Govind Singh 12 000			1	0
Mahindra United	Mumbai	The Cooperage 12 000			0	1
Mohum Bagan Club	Calcutta	Saltlake 120 000		mohunbaganclub.com	3	11
Salgaocar Sports Club	Vasco, Goa	Nehru, Margao 35 000			1	3
Sporting Clube de Goa	Goa	Nehru, Margao 35 000			0	0
State Bank of Travancore	Trivandrum, Kerala	Chandrashekar Nair			0	0
Tollygunge Agragami	Calcutta	Saltlake 120 000			0	0
Vasco Sports Club	Vasco, Goa	Nehru, Margao 35 000		vascoclub.com	0	0

RECENT LEAGUE AND CUP RECORD

National Football League

Year	Champions	Pts	Runners-up	Pts	Third	Pts
1990						
1991						
1992						
1993						
1994						
1995						
1996						
1996						
1997	JCT Mills	30	Churchill Brothers	29	East Bengal	25
1998	Mohun Bagan	34	East Bengal	31	Salgaocar	30
1999	Salgaocar	23	East Bengal	19	Churchill Brothers	15
2000	Mohun Bagan	47	Churchill Brothers	41	Salgaocar	39
2001	East Bengal	46	Mohun Bagan	45	Churchill Brothers	36
2002	Mohun Bagan	44	Churchill Brothers	42	Vasco	40
2003	East Bengal	49	Salgaocar	44	Vasco	43
2004	East Bengal	49	Dempo	45	Mahindra United	41
2005	Dempo	47	Sporting Goa	45	East Bengal	43

Federation Cup

Winners	Score	Runners-up
Kerala Police	2-1	Salgaocar
Kerala Police	2-0	Mahindra & Mahindra
Mohun Bagan	2-0	East Bengal
Mohun Bagan	1-0	Mahindra & Mahindra
Mohun Bagan	0-0 3-0p	Salgaocar
JCT Mills	1-1 7-6p	East Bengal
JCT Mills	1-1 5-3p	East Bengal
East Bengal	2-1	Dempo
Salgaocar	2-1	East Bengal
Mohun Bagan	2-1	East Bengal
	Not played	
	Not played	
Mohun Bagan	2-0	Dempo
	Not played	
Mahindra United	1-0	Mohammedan Sporting
Dempo	2-0	Mohun Bagan

INDIA 2004
SECOND DIVISION

Preliminary Round

Group I	Pl	W	D	L	F	A	Pt
Lajong SSC	4	2	2	0	4	2	**8**
Assam SEB	4	2	1	1	7	3	**7**
Rail Coach	4	1	1	2	6	8	**4**
Manipur Police	3	0	3	0	4	4	**3**
Nine Bullets	3	0	1	2	1	5	**1**

Group II	Pl	W	D	L	F	A	Pt
EverReady SA	3	3	0	0	18	3	**9**
Jammu&Kashmir	3	2	0	1	9	2	**6**
Azad SC	3	0	1	2	3	11	**1**
Uttar Pr. Police	3	0	1	2	3	17	**1**

Group III	Pl	W	D	L	F	A	Pt
Bengal Mumbai	3	2	1	0	6	2	**7**
SAI Centre	3	1	1	1	4	5	**4**
Sports College	3	1	0	2	2	4	**3**
Air Force	3	0	2	1	4	5	**2**

Group IV	Pl	W	D	L	F	A	Pt
Karnataka Police	3	2	1	0	11	3	**7**
Titanium XI	3	2	0	1	12	5	**6**
Madras SU	3	1	1	1	12	6	**4**
Young Challengers	3	0	0	3	2	23	**0**

First Round

Group A	Pl	W	D	L	F	A	Pt
Hindustan AL	5	4	1	0	10	1	**13**
Air India	5	4	1	0	9	4	**13**
Indian Bank	5	2	0	3	7	7	**6**
Border Security	5	2	0	3	6	6	**6**
Bengal Mumbai	5	1	1	3	3	7	**4**
Karnataka Police	5	0	1	4	2	12	**1**

Group B	Pl	W	D	L	F	A	Pt
Mohammedan SC	5	3	2	0	10	4	**11**
Punjab Police	5	3	1	1	13	6	**10**
Tata Academy	5	2	2	1	7	5	**8**
Hindustan Club	5	2	1	2	4	4	**7**
EverReady SA	5	1	1	3	2	5	**4**
Lajong SSC	5	0	1	4	0	12	**1**

Final Round

	Pl	W	D	L	F	A	Pt
Mohammedan SC	3	2	1	0	6	3	**7**
Air India	3	2	0	1	6	5	**6**
Punjab Police	3	1	0	2	5	5	**3**
Hindustan AL	3	0	1	2	1	5	**1**

Mohammedan SC and Air India promoted to the National Football League

FEDERATION CUP 2004

Round of 16

Dempo Sports Club	3
EverReady	1
Vasco	0 7p
Churchill Brothers	0 8p
Fransa	3
Mahindra United	2
Salgaocar	1 1p
Tollygunge Agragami	1 4p
Sporting Clube Goa	2
Mohammedan Sporting	0
Hindustan Aeronautics	0
East Bengal	1
JCT Mills	2
State Bank Travancore	1
Indian Bank	0
Mohun Bagan	1

Quarter-finals

Dempo Sports Club	1
Churchill Brothers	0
Fransa	0
Tollygunge Agragami	3
Sporting Clube Goa	1
East Bengal	0
JCT Mills	1
Mohun Bagan	4

Semi-finals

Dempo Sports Club	4
Tollygunge Agragami	3
Sporting Clube Goa	0
Mohun Bagan	1

Final

Dempo Sports Club	2
Mohun Bagan	0

CUP FINAL

5-12-2004, Bangalore
Scorer - Cristiano Junior 2 [42] [78]

(Shortly after scoring his second goal
Cristiano Junior collapsed and died on the
field of play)

All matches were played in Bangalore

INDIA 2004
CALCUTTA LEAGUE
CHAMPIONSHIP GROUP

	Pl	W	D	L	F	A	Pts
East Bengal	18	11	6	1	35	8	**39**
Mohun Bagan	18	11	5	2	27	9	**38**
EverReady SA	18	12	2	4	24	12	**38**
Tollygunge Agragami	18	6	8	4	26	24	**26**
Mohammedan Sporting	18	7	4	7	25	21	**25**
George Telegraph	18	6	4	8	13	18	**22**

28/06/2004 - 14/12/2004

INDIA 2004
7TH GOAN PRO LEAGUE

	Pl	W	D	L	F	A	Pts
Salgaocar Sports Club	14	8	5	1	28	11	**29**
Vasco Sports Club	14	6	5	3	23	17	**25**
Sporting Clube Goa	14	7	4	3	26	19	**25**
Dempo Sports Club	14	6	5	3	24	12	**23**
Churchill Brothers	14	3	6	5	13	15	**15**
Fransa FC	14	4	2	8	11	18	**14**
Cabral Sports Club	14	2	4	8	19	26	**10**
MPT Sports Council	14	2	3	9	11	38	**9**

17/08/2004 - 6/10/2004

IRL – REPUBLIC OF IRELAND

NATIONAL TEAM RECORD
JULY 1ST 2002 TO JUNE 30TH 2005

PL	W	D	L	F	A	%
33	18	11	4	43	23	71.2

FIFA/COCA-COLA WORLD RANKING

1993	1994	1995	1996	1997	1998	1999	2000	2001	2002	2003	2004	High		Low	
10	9	28	36	47	56	35	31	17	14	14	12	6	08/93	57	11/98

2004-2005											
08/04	09/04	10/04	11/04	12/04	01/05	02/05	03/05	04/05	05/05	06/05	07/05
16	16	14	14	12	12	12	12	15	15	15	15

Since taking over as national team coach in February 2003 Irishman Brian Kerr has made the Republic of Ireland a very difficult team to beat as his record of just two defeats in his first 29 games in charge shows. He arrived too late to salvage European championship qualification but has been helped since by the return of Roy Keane from his self imposed exile for the 2006 FIFA World Cup™ qualifiers. The problem for the Irish in that campaign has been the number of drawn games which has left nothing between the top four of Ireland, Israel, France and Switzerland going into the final stages of the group. The decision to go ahead with the redevelopment of Lansdowne

INTERNATIONAL HONOURS
Qualified for the FIFA World Cup™ finals 1990 1994 2002 UEFA U-17 Championship 1998

Road will be a big boost for Irish football in years to come and proof of the growing acceptance of the game in Ireland came with the decision of the GAA in April 2005 to let "foreign games" take place at Croke Park, home of the Gaelic Athletic Association, during the redevelopment. Shelbourne won the Premier Division in a close race with Cork City whilst it proved to be a good year for Longford Town in cup competitions. Having never won a trophy they won both the League Cup and the FA of Ireland Cup. Galway United made headlines in April 2005 when they appointed former Barings trader Nick Leeson as commercial manager.

THE FIFA BIG COUNT OF 2000

	Male	Female		Male	Female
Registered players	1 517	3 637	Referees	1 150	50
Non registered players	50 000	0	Officials	4 000	150
Youth players	132 527	1 615	Total involved	194 646	
Total players	189 296		Number of clubs	3 059	
Professional players	520	0	Number of teams	7 456	

The Football Association of Ireland (FAI)
80 Merrion Square South, Dublin 2
Tel +353 1 7037500   Fax +353 1 6610931
info@fai.ie   www.fai.ie
President: CORCORAN Milo   General Secretary: DELANEY John
Vice-President: BLOOD David   Treasurer: TBD   Media Officer: COSTELLO Pat
Men's Coach: KERR Brian   Women's Coach: KING Noel
FAI formed: 1921   UEFA: 1954   FIFA: 1923
Colours: Green, White, Green or White, Green, White

GAMES PLAYED BY REPUBLIC OF IRELAND IN THE 2006 FIFA WORLD CUP™ CYCLE

2002	Opponents	Score		Venue	Comp	Scorers	Att	Referee
21-08	Finland	W	3-0	Helsinki	Fr	Keane.Rb [12], Healy [74], Barrett [82]	12 225	Pedersen NOR
7-09	Russia	L	2-4	Moscow	ECq	Doherty [69], Morrison [76]	23 000	Colombo FRA
16-10	Switzerland	L	1-2	Dublin	ECq	Magnin OG [78]	40 000	Pedersen NOR
20-11	Greece	D	0-0	Athens	Fr		5 000	Trentalange ITA
2003								
12-02	Scotland	W	2-0	Glasgow	Fr	Kilbane [8], Morrison [16]	33 337	Braamhaar NED
29-03	Georgia	W	2-1	Tbilisi	ECq	Duff [18], Doherty [84]	15 000	Vassaras GRE
2-04	Albania	D	0-0	Tirana	ECq		20 000	Farina ITA
30-04	Norway	W	1-0	Dublin	Fr	Duff [17]	32 643	McCurry SCO
7-06	Albania	W	2-1	Dublin	ECq	Keane.Rb [6], Aliaj OG [90]	33 000	Mikulski POL
11-06	Georgia	W	2-0	Dublin	ECq	Doherty [43], Keane [58]	36 000	Iturralde Gonzalez ESP
19-08	Australia	W	2-1	Dublin	Fr	O'Shea [74], Morrison [81]	37 200	Vidlak CZE
6-09	Russia	D	1-1	Dublin	ECq	Duff [35]	36 000	Michel SVK
9-09	Turkey	D	2-2	Dublin	Fr	Connolly [35], Dunne [90]	27 000	Wegereef NED
11-10	Switzerland	L	0-2	Basel	ECq		31 006	Frisk SWE
18-11	Canada	W	3-0	Dublin	Fr	Duff [24], Keane.Rb 2 [60 84]	23 000	Whitby WAL
2004								
18-02	Brazil	D	0-0	Dublin	Fr		44 000	Frisk SWE
31-03	Czech Republic	W	2-1	Dublin	Fr	Harte [52], Keane.Rb [90]	42 000	Fisker DEN
28-04	Poland	D	0-0	Bydgoszcz	Fr		15 500	Shebek UKR
27-05	Romania	W	1-0	Dublin	Fr	Holland [85]	42 356	Jara CZE
29-05	Nigeria	L	0-3	London	Fr		7 438	D'Urso ENG
2-06	Jamaica	W	1-0	London	Fr	Barrett [26]	6 155	Styles ENG
5-06	Netherlands	W	1-0	Amsterdam	Fr	Keane.Rb [45]	42 000	Dean ENG
18-08	Bulgaria	D	1-1	Dublin	Fr	Reid [15]	31 887	Brines SCO
4-09	Cyprus	W	3-0	Dublin	WCq	Morrison [33], Reid [38], Keane.Rb [54]	36 000	Paniashvili GEO
8-09	Switzerland	D	1-1	Basel	WCq	Morrison [8]	28 000	Vassaras GRE
9-10	France	D	0-0	Paris	WCq		78 863	Dauden Ibanez ESP
13-10	Faroe Islands	W	2-0	Dublin	WCq	Keane.Rb 2 [14p 32]	36 000	Lajuks LVA
16-11	Croatia	W	1-0	Dublin	Fr	Keane.Rb [24]	33 200	Orrason ISL
2005								
9-02	Portugal	W	1-0	Dublin	Fr	O'Brien [21]	44 100	Messias ENG
26-03	Israel	D	1-1	Tel Aviv	WCq	Morrison [43]	32 150	Ivanov.V RUS
29-03	China PR	W	1-0	Dublin	Fr	Morrison [82]	35 222	Casha MLT
4-06	Israel	D	2-2	Dublin	WCq	Harte [5], Keane.Rb [11]	36 000	Vassaras GRE
8-06	Faroe Islands	W	2-0	Torshavn	WCq	Harte [51p], Kilbane [59]	5 180	Guenov BUL

Fr = Friendly match • EC = UEFA EURO 2004™ • WC = FIFA World Cup™ • q = qualifier

REPUBLIC OF IRELAND NATIONAL TEAM RECORDS AND RECORD SEQUENCES

Records			Sequence records					
Victory	8-0	MLT 1983	Wins	8	1987-1988	Clean sheets	5	1989, 1996-1997
Defeat	0-7	BRA 1982	Defeats	5	Six times	Goals scored	17	1954-59, 2000-01
Player Caps	102	STAUNTON Stephen	Undefeated	17	1989-1990	Without goal	5	1995-1996
Player Goals	24	KEANE Robbie	Without win	20	1968-1971	Goals against	35	1966-1973

REPUBLIC OF IRELAND COUNTRY INFORMATION

Capital	Dublin	Independence	1921 from the UK	GDP per Capita	$29 600
Population	3 969 558	Status	Republic	GNP Ranking	39
Area km²	70 280	Language	English, Irish	Dialling code	+353
Population density	56 per km²	Literacy rate	98%	Internet code	.ie
% in urban areas	58%	Main religion	Roman Catholic 91%	GMT + / −	0
Towns/Cities ('000)	Dublin 1 024; Cork 189; Limerick 90; Galway 70; Waterford 48; Drogheda 33; Dundalk 33				
Neighbours (km)	UK 360; North Atlantic & Irish Sea 1 448				
Main stadia	Lansdowne Road – Dublin 47 000; Dalymount Park – Dublin 12 200				

NATIONAL CAPS

	Caps
STAUNTON Stephen	102
QUINN Niall	91
CASCARINO Tony	88
MCGRATH Paul	83
BONNER Pat	80
HOUGHTON Ray	73
BRADY Liam	72
MORAN Kevin	71
STAPLETON Frank	71
GIVEN Shay	70

NATIONAL GOALS

	Goals
KEANE Robbie	25
QUINN Niall	21
STAPLETON Frank	20
ALDRIDGE John	19
CASCARINO Tony	19
GIVENS Don	19
CANTWELL Noel	14
DALY Gerry	13
DUNNE James	12
HARTE Ian	11

NATIONAL COACH

	Years
MEAGAN Mick	1969-'71
TUOHY Liam	1971-'73
THOMAS Sean	1973
GILES Johnny	1973-'80
KELLY Alan	1980
HAND Eoin	1980-'85
CHARLTON Jackie	1986-'95
MCCARTHY Mick	1996-'02
KERR Brian	2002-

FIFA REFEREE LIST 2005

	Int'l	DoB
BUTTIMER Anthony	2005	13-07-1965
KELLY Alan	2002	9-04-1975
MCKEON DAVID	2004	3-02-1972
STOKES Ian	2004	25-02-1972

FIFA ASSISTANT REFEREE LIST 2005

	Int'l	DoB
CASSIDY Joe	2003	25-09-1963
DELANEY Ciaran		15-02-1970
FOLEY Eddie	1995	20-03-1961
MCDONNELL Barry	2002	19-06-1965
MOLONEY Martin	2002	4-01-1968
MURRAY Kevin	2002	11-04-1962
RYAN Anthony	1998	8-06-1961
WOGAN David	2001	15-05-1964

CLUB DIRECTORY

Club	Town/City	Stadium	Phone	www.	Lge	Cup	CL
Bohemians	Dublin	Dalymount Park 12 200	+353 1 8680923	bohemians.ie	9	6	0
Bray Wanderers	Bray	Carlisle Grounds 6 500	+353 1 2828214	braywanderers.ie	0	2	0
Cork City	Cork	Turner's Cross 11 500	+353 21 4321958		1	1	0
Derry City	Londonderry	Brandywell 10 000	+44 4871 281333	derrycityfc.com	2	3	0
Drogheda United	Drogheda	United Park 5 400	+353 41 9830190	droghedaunited.ie	0	0	0
Finn Harps	Ballybofey	Finn Park 7 900	+353 74 30070	finnharps.com	0	1	0
Longford Town	Longford	Strokestown Road 10 000	+353 4 348983	longfordtownfc.com	0	2	0
St Patrick's Athletic	Dublin	Richmond Park 7 500	+353 1 4546332	stpatsfc.com	7	2	0
Shamrock Rovers	Dublin	Tallaght Stadium 6 000	+353 1 4622077	shamrockrovers.ie	15	24	0
Shelbourne	Dublin	Tolka Park 9 681	+353 1 8375754	shelbournefc.ie	11	7	0
UCD - University College Dublin	Dublin	Belfield Park 5 250	+353 1 7162183	ucd.ie/soccer	0	1	0
Waterford United	Waterford	RSC 8 200	+353 51 853222	waterford-united.ie	6	2	0

RECENT LEAGUE AND CUP RECORD

	Championship						Cup		
Year	Champions	Pts	Runners-up	Pts	Third	Pts		Winners	Score	Runners-up
1990	St Patrick's Ath	52	Derry City	49	Dundalk	42		Bray Wanderers	3-0	St Francis
1991	Dundalk	52	Cork City	50	St Patrick's Ath	44		Galway United	1-0	Shamrock Rovers
1992	Shelbourne	49	Derry City	44	Cork City	43		Bohemians	1-0	Cork City
1993	Cork City †	40	Bohemians	40	Shelbourne	40		Shelbourne	1-0	Dundalk
1994	Shamrock Rovers	66	Cork City	59	Galway United	50		Sligo Rovers	1-0	Derry City
1995	Dundalk	59	Derry City	58	Shelbourne	57		Derry City	2-1	Shelbourne
1996	St Patrick's Ath	67	Bohemians	62	Sligo Rovers	55		Shelbourne	1-1 2-1	St Patrick's Ath
1997	Derry City	67	Bohemians	57	Shelbourne	54		Shelbourne	2-0	Derry City
1998	St Patrick's Ath	68	Shelbourne	67	Cork City	53		Cork City	0-0 1-0	Shelbourne
1999	St Patrick's Ath	73	Cork City	70	Shelbourne	47		Bray Wanderers	0-0 2-2 2-1	Finn Harps
2000	Shelbourne	69	Cork City	58	Bohemians	57		Shelbourne	0-0 1-0	Bohemians
2001	Bohemians	62	Shelbourne	60	Cork City	56		Bohemians	1-0	Longford Town
2002	Shelbourne	63	Shamrock Rovers	57	St Patrick's Ath	53		Dundalk	2-1	Bohemians
2003	Bohemians	54	Shelbourne	49	Shamrock Rovers	43		Derry City	1-0	Shamrock Rovers
2003	Shelbourne	69	Bohemians	64	Cork City	53		Longford Town	2-0	St Patrick's Ath
2004	Shelbourne	68	Cork City	65	Bohemians	60		Longford Town	2-1	Waterford United

The Irish football calender was changed in 2003 to a spring - autumn season • † Cork City won a series of play-offs between the top three

REPUBLIC OF IRELAND 2004

PREMIER DIVISION

	Pl	W	D	L	F	A	Pts	Shelbourne	Cork	Bohemians	Drogheda	Waterford	Longford	Derry	St Patrick's	Shamrock	Dublin
Shelbourne †	36	19	11	6	57	37	68		2-2 0-0	0-0 1-1	3-0 0-2	1-0 2-1	1-1 3-1	1-0 0-2	2-0 3-1	1-0 1-1	2-1 4-1
Cork City ‡	36	18	11	7	52	32	65	0-2 0-1		0-1 1-1	0-0 3-2	2-3 2-0	1-0 2-0	2-1 1-1	2-1 3-0	1-1 1-0	3-1 1-1
Bohemians	36	15	15	6	51	30	60	1-1 2-0	2-3 1-0		0-1 0-0	2-2 2-2	0-0 1-1	3-0 0-1	3-1 2-2	2-2 3-2	2-4 4-0
Drogheda United	36	15	7	14	45	43	52	2-2 2-5	2-0 1-3	0-3 0-3		0-0 1-2	0-1 0-1	2-0 4-0	0-1 0-2	1-0 3-0	2-0 2-1
Waterford United	36	14	8	14	44	49	50	1-1 3-1	1-1 1-4	0-1 1-1	2-1 1-3		1-1 0-1	0-2 1-0	0-1 0-2	3-1 2-0	2-1 3-2
Longford Town ‡	36	11	13	12	32	34	46	0-2 4-1	1-1 1-2	0-2 0-1	0-0 3-1	0-2 1-1		1-0 3-0	1-3 2-1	1-0 1-1	0-0 2-0
Derry City	36	11	11	14	23	32	44	0-2 0-0	1-1 0-1	0-0 0-0	0-2 1-0	0-1 1-0	0-0 0-0		0-0 1-1	1-0 1-0	2-1 2-3
St Patrick's Athletic	36	11	9	16	38	49	42	1-2 0-0	0-2 0-3	0-2 1-2	0-2 1-1	0-1 2-1	1-1 1-0	1-1 0-1		1-2 2-0	3-1 2-2
Shamrock Rovers	36	10	8	18	41	47	38	3-0 1-4	2-1 1-1	2-1 0-1	1-2 1-2	4-0 1-2	1-1 2-0	1-0 0-0	1-2 3-1		0-0 1-3
Dublin City	36	6	7	23	39	69	25	1-3 2-3	0-1 0-1	2-1 0-0	1-1 2-3	3-1 1-3	0-1 2-1	0-2 0-2	1-1 1-2	0-4 1-2	

19/03/2004 - 22/11/2004 • † Qualified for the UEFA Champions League • ‡ Qualified for the UEFA Cup

REPUBLIC OF IRELAND 2004
FIRST DIVISION

	Pl	W	D	L	F	A	Pts
Finn Harps	33	23	7	3	60	19	76
UCD	33	22	9	2	63	19	75
Bray Wanderers	33	19	8	6	62	29	65
Kildare County	33	18	8	7	54	32	62
Galway United	33	14	10	9	55	49	52
Dundalk	33	14	4	15	46	57	46
Sligo Rovers	33	11	5	17	46	50	38
Cobh Ramblers	33	7	11	15	47	53	32
Kilkenny City	33	6	9	18	28	53	27
Athlone Town §	33	9	2	22	42	68	26
Monaghan United §	33	8	5	20	28	63	26
Limerick	33	4	8	21	18	55	20

19/03/2004 - 22/11/2005 • § Three points deducted

IRELAND LEAGUE CUP 2004

Quarter-finals

Longford Town*	2
Dublin City	0
Sligo Rovers*	1
Finn Harps	5
Limerick*	2
Cork City	0
UCD	1
Bohemians*	2

Semi-finals

Longford Town	2
Finn Harps	1
Limerick	1
Bohemians	4

* Home team

Final

Longford Town	2
Bohemians	1

30-08-2004, Flancare Park
Scorers - Dillon 4, Prunty 81, Ryan 85

FA OF IRELAND CUP 2004

Round of 16

Longford Town*	1 1
Shamrock Rovers	1 0
Cobh Ramblers	0
Athlone Town*	1
UCD*	5
Drumcondra	0
St Patrick's Athletic	0
Drogheda United*	2
Derry City	1 0 5p
Shelbourne*	1 0 3p
Bohemians*	0
Kildare County	1
Rockmount*	2
Monaghan United	0
Kilkenny City	2
Waterford United*	7

Quarter-finals

Longford Town*	2 3
Athlone Town	2 0
UCD*	0 2
Drogheda United	0 3
Derry City*	1
Kildare County	0
Rockmount	2 1
Waterford United*	2 2

Semi-finals

Longford Town	0 2
Drogheda United	0 1
Derry City	1
Waterford United	2

Final

Longford Town ‡	2
Waterford United	1

CUP FINAL
24-10-2004, Lansdowne Road, Dublin
Scorers - Kirby 85, Keegan 88 for Longford; Bruton 62 for Waterford

* Home team • ‡ Qualified for the UEFA Cup

IRN – IRAN

NATIONAL TEAM RECORD
JULY 1ST 2002 TO JUNE 30TH 2005

PL	W	D	L	F	A	%
44	28	9	7	94	37	73.9

FIFA/COCA-COLA WORLD RANKING

1993	1994	1995	1996	1997	1998	1999	2000	2001	2002	2003	2004	High		Low	
59	75	108	83	46	27	49	37	29	33	28	20	15	07/05	122	05/96

2004-2005											
08/04	09/04	10/04	11/04	12/04	01/05	02/05	03/05	04/05	05/05	06/05	07/05
24	21	20	20	20	20	20	20	19	18	17	15

After missing out on the FIFA World Cup™ finals in 2002 Iran made no mistake this time around thanks to a series of convincing displays that also saw the team climb to their highest position of 15 in the FIFA/Coca-Cola World Ranking. Iran should feel at home in the finals with the German-based quartet of Vahid Hashemian, Mehdi Mahdavikia, Fereydoon Zandi and Asian player of the year Ali Karimi, key members of a side that lost just once during the 2004-05 season – against Germany in Tehran. Iran's Croatian coach Branko Ivankovic now has the task of turning one of the

INTERNATIONAL HONOURS
Qualified for the FIFA World Cup™ finals 1978 1998 2006 **AFC Asian Cup** 1968 1972 1976 **Asian Games** 1974 1990 1998 2002
AFC Asian U-19 Championship 1973 1974 1975 1976 **AFC Champions League** Esteghlal 1970 1991

highest ranked team in Asia into a force capable of challenging the top European and South American nations. Veteran striker Ali Daei passed a significant mark in the qualifiers against Laos in November 2004 when he became the first player in history to score 100 international goals but he couldn't lead his club side Pirouzi to the League Championship in what turned out to be a bad year for the top Tehran clubs. In a season of firsts, Foolad, from the provincial town of Ahvaz near the Iraq border, won the title for the first time whilst Saba batry, a small club from Tehran, won their first trophy when they beat AbooMoslem on penalties in the Cup Final.

THE FIFA BIG COUNT OF 2000

	Male	Female		Male	Female
Registered players	251 620	1 470	Referees	4 965	56
Non registered players	400 000	0	Officials	48 600	1 050
Youth players	143 625	1 050	Total involved	852 436	
Total players	797 765		Number of clubs	2 535	
Professional players	20	0	Number of teams	16 829	

IR Iran Football Federation (IRIFF)
No. 2/2 Third St., Seoul Ave., 19958-73591 Tehran, Iran
Tel +98 21 88213306   Fax +98 21 8213302
iriff@iransports.net   www.none
President: DADGAN Mohammad Dr   General Secretary: PAHLEVAN Reza
Vice-President: NOAMOOZ Naser   Treasurer: SABRIOUN Abbas   Media Officer: None
Men's Coach: IVANKOVIC Branko   Women's Coach: None
IRIFF formed: 1920   AFC: 1958   FIFA: 1945
Colours: White, White, White

GAMES PLAYED BY IRAN IN THE 2006 FIFA WORLD CUP™ CYCLE

2002	Opponents	Score		Venue	Comp	Scorers	Att	Referee
8-08	Azerbaijan	D	1-1	Tabriz	Fr	Karimi 33	25 000	Rahimi Moghadam IRN
21-08	Ukraine	W	1-0	Kyiv	Fr	Daei 56	18 000	Khudiev AZE
30-08	Jordan	L	0-1	Damascus	WFr1		1 000	Al Zaid KSA
3-09	Lebanon	W	2-0	Damascus	WFr1	Vahedinikbakht 24, Karimi 88	2 000	Haj Khader SYR
5-09	Iraq	D	0-0	Damascus	WFsf	L 5-6p	2 000	Al Zaid KSA
7-09	Syria	D	2-2	Damascus	WF3p	Kameli 58, Vahedinikbakht 88. W 4-2p	10 000	Abu Elaish PAL
19-09	Paraguay	D	1-1	Tabriz	Fr	Daei 40. W 4-3p	25 000	Al Fadhli KUW
2003								
1-02	Denmark	W	1-0	Hong Kong	Fr	Nekoonam 48p	15 100	Chiu Sin Cheun HKG
4-02	Uruguay	D	1-1	Hong Kong	Fr	Samereh 30. L 2-4p	17 877	Fong Yau Fat HKG
13-08	Iraq	L	0-1	Tehran	Fr		20 000	Al Fadhli KUW
20-08	Belarus	L	1-2	Minsk	Fr	Nouri 84	10 000	Ivanov.N RUS
5-09	Jordan	W	4-1	Tehran	ACq	Daei 2 45 90, Vahedinikbakht 75, Mobali 82	57 000	Ebrahim BHR
26-09	Jordan	L	2-3	Amman	ACq	Golmohammadi 6, Majidi 60	27 000	Shaban KUW
12-10	New Zealand	W	3-0	Tehran	AO	Karimi 2 8 20, Kaebi 65	40 000	Kousa SYR
27-10	Korea DPR	W	3-1	Pyongyang	ACq	Karimi 2 47 79, Navidkia 87	30 000	
12-11	Korea DPR	W	3-0	Tehran	ACq	Daei 54p. Abandoned 60'. Awarded 3-0 to Iran	40 000	Haj Khader SYR
19-11	Lebanon	W	3-0	Beirut	ACq	Daei 37p, Golmohammadi 51, Vahedinikbakht 80		Al Marzouqi UAE
28-11	Lebanon	W	1-0	Tehran	ACq	Daei 22		Rungklay THA
2-12	Kuwait	L	1-3	Kuwait City	Fr	Daei 77	5 000	Al Qahtani QAT
2004								
18-02	Qatar	W	3-1	Tehran	WCq	Vahedi 8, Mahdavikia 44, Daei 62	BCD	Haj Khader SYR
31-03	Laos	W	7-0	Vientiane	WCq	Daei 2 9 17p, Enayati 2 32 36, OG 54, Taghipour 2 68 83	7 000	Yang TPE
9-06	Jordan	L	0-1	Tehran	WCq		35 000	Kamikawa JPN
17-06	Lebanon	W	4-0	Tehran	WFr1	Daei 3 15p 62 88, Nekounam 80	20 000	Issa Hazim IRQ
21-06	Syria	W	7-1	Tehran	WFr1	Daei 29, Vahedinikbakht 30, Nosrati 45, Borhani 2 55 85 Karimi 86, Majidi 89p	20 000	
23-06	Iraq	W	2-1	Tehran	WFsf	Nekounam 4, Borhani 54	15 000	Shaban KUW
25-06	Syria	W	4-1	Tehran	WFf	Karimi 34, Daei 59, Borhani 69, Nekounam 75	20 000	Shaban KUW
20-07	Thailand	W	3-0	Chongqing	ACr1	Enayati 70, Nekounam 80, Daei 86p	37 000	Kousa SYR
24-07	Oman	D	2-2	Chongqing	ACr1	Karimi 62, Nosrati 90	35 000	Al Delawar BHR
28-07	Japan	D	0-0	Chongqing	ACr1		52 000	Shield AUS
31-07	Korea Republic	W	4-3	Jinan	ACqf	Karimi 3 10 20 77, Park OG 51	32 159	Al Fadhli KUW
3-08	China PR	D	1-1	Beijing	ACsf	Alavi 38. L 3-4p	51 000	Najm LIB
6-08	Bahrain	W	4-2	Beijing	AC3p	Nekounam 9, Karimi 52, Daei 2 80p 90	23 000	Al Marzouqi UAE
8-09	Jordan	W	2-0	Amman	WCq	Vahedi 80, Daei 91+	20 000	Lu Jun CHN
9-10	Germany	L	0-2	Tehran	Fr		110 000	Mane KUW
13-10	Qatar	W	3-2	Doha	WCq	Hashemian 2 9 89, Borhani 78	8 000	Kwon Jong Chul KOR
17-11	Laos	W	7-0	Tehran	WCq	Daei 4 8 20 28 58, Nekounam 2 63 72, Borhani 69	30 000	Mamedov TKM
18-12	Panama	W	1-0	Tehran	Fr	Daei 38p	8 000	Esfahanian IRN
2005								
2-02	Bosnia-Herzegovina	W	2-1	Tehran	Fr	Daei 41, Borhani 73	15 000	
9-02	Bahrain	D	0-0	Manama	WCq		25 000	Mohd Salleh MAS
25-03	Japan	W	2-1	Tehran	WCq	Hashemian 2 13 66	110 000	Maidin SIN
30-03	Korea DPR	W	2-0	Pyongyang	WCq	Mahdavikia 32, Nekounam 79	55 000	Kousa SYR
29-05	Azerbaijan	W	2-1	Tehran	Fr	Zandi 9, Nekounam 29	30 000	Al Fadhli KUW
3-06	Korea DPR	W	1-0	Tehran	WCq	Rezaei 45	35 000	Al Ghamdi KSA
8-06	Bahrain	W	1-0	Tehran	WCq	Nosrati 47	80 000	Kwon Jong Chul KOR

Fr = Friendly match • WF = West Asian Federation Championship • AC = AFC Asian Cup • AO = AFC/OFC Challenge • WC = FIFA World Cup™
q = qualifier • r1 = first round group • qf = quarter-final • sf = semi-final • 3p = third place play-off • f = final • BCD = Behind closed doors

IRAN NATIONAL TEAM RECORDS AND RECORD SEQUENCES

Records			Sequence records					
Victory	19-0	GUM 2000	Wins	8	1974, 1996	Clean sheets	7	1977
Defeat	1-6	TUR 1950	Defeats	3	1989-1990	Goals scored	20	2000-2001
Player Caps	n/a		Undefeated	15	1996-1997	Without goal	4	1951-1958, 1988
Player Goals	n/a		Without win	10	1997	Goals against	9	1959-1963

FIFA REFEREE LIST 2005

	Int'l	DoB
ASHFARIAN Khodadad	2003	15-09-1965
BAKHSHI Siamak	1998	11-05-1964
ESFAHAN Navid		14-01-1970
GHAHREMANI Mohsen		30-06-1974
MOMBINI Hedayat	2003	21-03-1970
MORADI Masoud	1998	22-08-1965
NOOSHEHVAR Hassan	2005	1-01-1973
RAFEIE Mahmoud	2005	19-02-1967
RAHIMI Rahim	2000	1-08-1964
TORKY Mohsen	2003	11-04-1973

FIFA ASSISTANT REFEREE LIST 2005

	Int'l	DoB
JAFARI Nader	1998	21-03-1963
KARIMI Morteza	2004	22-06-1972
KHANBAN Hossein	2005	14-04-1971
KHOSRAVI Ali	1994	26-10-1961
NEJATI Hossein	1996	17-09-1962
RAFATISA.EDI Davoud	2005	2-03-1971
SAFIRI Esmaeil	1997	8-12-1962
SHAKOUR Heydar	2004	21-03-1964
SOKHANDAN Reza	2003	24-01-1973
TAGHIPOUR Javad	1999	4-04-1963

NATIONAL CAPS

	Caps
DAEI Ali	140
MAHDAVIKIA Mehdi	88
KARIMI Mohammed Ali	86
ESTILI Hamid Reza	82
BAGHERI Karim	80
ZARINCHEH Javad	80
ABEDZADEH Ahmad Reza	79
PARVIN Ali	76
CHAL Mehrdad Minavand	67
PEYROVANI Afshin	66

NATIONAL GOALS

	Goals
DAEI Ali	104
BAGHERI Karim	47
KARIMI Mohammed Ali	31
MAZLOOMI Gholamhussain	19
PEYOUS Farshad	19
ROSTA Ali Asghar Moudir	18
ROWSHAN Hassan	13
PARVIN Ali	13

NATIONAL COACH

	Years
VIERRA Valdir	1997-'98
IVIC Tomislav	1998
TALEBI Jalal	1998
POURHAYDARI Mansour	1998
TALEBI Jalal	2000
BRAGA Ademar Da Silva	2000
BLAZEVIC Miroslav	2001-'02
IVANKOVIC Branko	2002
SHAHROKHI Homayoun	2002
IVANKOVIC Branko	2002-

CLUB DIRECTORY

Club	Town/City	Stadium	Lge	Cup	CL
AbooMoslem	Mashhad	Samen 35 000	0	0	0
Bargh	Shiraz	Hafezieh 20 000	0	1	0
Esteghlal	Tehran	Azadi 110 000	5	4	2
Esteghlal	Ahvaz	Takhti 30 000	0	0	0
Fajr Sepasi	Shiraz	Hafezieh 20 000	0	1	0
Foolad	Ahvaz	Takhti 30 000	1	0	0
Malavan	Bandar Anzali	Takhti 20 000	0	3	0
Paas	Tehran	Dastgerdi 15 000	5	0	0
Pegah Gilan	Rasht	Dr Azody 20 000	0	0	0
Peykan	Tehran	Iran Khodro 10 000	0	0	0
Pirouzi (Perspolis)	Tehran	Azadi 110 000	8	3	0
Saba batry	Tehran		0	1	0
Saipa	Tehran		2	1	0
Sepahan	Esfehan	Naghsh e Jahan 75 000	1	1	0
Shamoushak	Noshahr	Sohada 10 000	0	0	0
Zob Ahan	Esfehan	Naghsh e Jahan 75 000	0	1	0

IRAN COUNTRY INFORMATION

Capital	Tehran	Formation	1502	GDP per Capita	$7 000
Population	69 018 924	Status	Republic	GNP Ranking	35
Area km²	1 648 000	Language	Persian, Turkic	Dialling code	+98
Population density	42 per km²	Literacy rate	79%	Internet code	.ir
% in urban areas	59%	Main religion	Muslim	GMT + / –	+3.5
Towns/Cities ('000)	Tehran 7 158; Mashhad 2 307; Esfahan 1 547; Karaj 1 448; Tabriz 1 424; Shiraz 1 249; Qom 1 011; Ahvaz 854; Kermanshah 766; Orumiyeh 602; Rasht 594; Kerman 577; Zahedan 551; Hamadan 514; Arak 503; Yazd 477; Ardabil 410; Abadan 370; Zanjan 357				
Neighbours (km)	Afghanistan 936; Armenia 35; Azerbaijan 611; Iraq 1458; Pakistan 909; Turkey 499; Turkmenistan 992; Caspian Sea & Arabian Gulf 2 440				
Main stadia	Azadi – Tehran 100 000; Naghsh e Jahan – Esfahan 75 000; Yadegar e Emam – Tabriz 71 000				

IRAN 2004-05

IRAN PRO LEAGUE

Team	Pl	W	D	L	F	A	Pts	Foolad	Zob Ahan	Esteghlal	Pirouzi	Esteghlal A	Paas	Malavan	AbooMoslem	Saba	Sepahan	Fajr Sepasi	Bargh	Saipa	Shamoushak	Peykan	Pegah Gilan
Foolad Ahvaz †	30	19	7	4	41	20	64		0-1	1-0	3-1	2-0	2-1	1-1	1-0	1-0	0-0	1-0	4-0	2-1	3-1	1-0	2-1
Zob Ahan Esfahan †	30	17	7	6	38	19	58	2-0		3-1	3-2	3-1	2-0	2-0	0-1	2-3	1-1	0-0	1-0	1-0	2-0	1-0	1-0
Esteghlal	30	16	10	4	51	35	58	1-2	0-3		3-2	1-1	2-1	3-1	2-2	3-1	2-2	2-1	3-2	4-3	3-0	2-1	2-0
Pirouzi	30	16	7	7	43	27	55	0-2	1-0	0-0		2-0	2-1	1-2	3-2	1-0	1-2	5-1	1-1	1-0	2-1	2-1	6-0
Esteghlal Ahvaz	30	12	8	10	41	34	44	3-1	1-2	2-2	1-1		2-1	0-1	3-2	1-0	1-1	3-0	1-1	1-0	6-0	2-1	1-0
Paas Tehran	30	11	9	10	49	40	42	1-1	2-2	1-2	1-1	1-1		3-2	1-1	2-3	2-3	1-0	5-1	3-0	4-2	0-0	3-1
Malavan Anzali	30	10	11	9	34	27	41	1-2	0-0	0-0	1-2	1-0	0-0		1-1	2-0	0-1	3-0	1-1	5-0	1-1	1-0	3-0
AbooMoslem Mashhad	30	9	11	10	33	33	38	0-0	3-2	2-3	1-0	2-2	0-1	0-0		2-3	2-1	0-1	3-2	0-1	1-0	1-0	3-0
Saba batry Tehran	30	8	11	11	38	40	35	0-0	1-2	1-1	0-0	0-0	4-3	2-0	0-0		2-1	0-1	4-4	1-2	3-0	2-2	0-0
Sepahan Esfahan	30	7	14	9	30	33	35	1-1	0-1	2-2	0-0	0-1	0-1	1-1	1-1	1-0		0-0	2-0	1-4	1-1	1-2	1-1
Fajr Sepasi Shiraz	30	9	8	13	24	32	35	0-1	0-0	0-0	0-0	1-2	0-1	0-1	4-1	3-2	0-0		1-1	1-1	2-1	2-1	0-1
Bargh Shiraz	30	7	12	11	34	43	33	1-1	0-0	0-3	1-2	2-0	2-1	1-0	0-0	1-0	1-0	1-2		0-0	3-1	1-1	4-1
Saipa	30	7	10	13	24	34	31	1-2	1-0	0-0	0-1	3-1	1-3	0-0	0-1	1-2	1-0	1-0	1-1		1-1	1-0	0-0
Shamoushak Noshahr	30	8	7	15	26	49	31	2-1	1-0	0-1	0-1	0-1	0-3	1-1	1-2	0-2	2-2	2-1	1-0	2-1		1-0	0-0
Peykan Tehran	30	5	9	16	22	34	24	0-1	0-1	0-1	0-1	0-1	2-1	0-2	2-1	1-0	1-1	1-2	1-2	0-0	0-0		2-2
Pegah Gilan Rasht	30	3	11	16	17	45	20	0-2	0-0	1-2	0-1	1-0	2-2	2-2	0-0	1-1	1-1	0-2	2-1	0-1	0-1	2-3	

13/09/2004 - 15/05/2005 • † Qualified for the AFC Champions League

JAAM HAZFI 2004-05

Eighth-finals

Saba batry Tehran *	1
Malavan Anzali	0
Sepahan Isfahan	1
Pas Tehran *	4
Sanaye Arak	2
Ansar Shahroud *	1
Pegah Rasht *	0
Esteghlal Ahvaz	1
Fajr Sepasi Shiraz	5
Iranjavan Boushehr *	2
Zob Ahan Isfahan	1
Saipa Tehran *	2
Peykhan Tehran *	3
Shahin Boushehr	1
Pirouzi *	0
AbooMoslem	1

Quarter-finals

Saba batry Tehran *	4
Pas Tehran	2
Sanaye Arak	†
Esteghlal Ahvaz *	
Fajr Sepasi Shiraz *	0 6p
Saipa Tehran	0 5p
Peykhan Tehran	0
AbooMoslem Mashhad *	1

Semi-finals

Saba batry Tehran	4 6p
Esteghlal Ahvaz	4 5p
Fajr Sepasi Shiraz	0 6p
AbooMoslem Mashhad	0 7p

Final

Saba batry Tehran	1 1 4p
AbooMoslem Mashhad	1 1 2p

CUP FINAL
First leg, 12-07-2005, Att. 12 000
Derakhshan, Saba City
Daghigi [38] for Saba; Khalatbari [82] for AbooMoslem
Second leg, 15-07-2005, Att. 35 000
Thamen, Mashhad
Fazli [47] for AbooMoslem; Markosi [86] for Saba

* Home team • † Sanaye Arak withdrew

RECENT LEAGUE AND CUP RECORD

Year	Champions	Pts	Runners-up	Pts	Third	Pts
1990	Esteghlal					
1991	Paas					
1992	Paas					
1993	Saipa					
1994	Saipa					
1995	No championship due to season readjustment					
1996	Pirouzi	57	Bahman	51	Esteghlal	51
1997	Pirouzi	59	Bahman	53	Sepahan	50
1998	Esteghlal	58	Paas	52	Zob Ahan	45
1999	Pirouzi	65	Esteghlal	53	Sepahan	53
2000	Pirouzi	54	Esteghlal	47	Fajr Sepasi	44
2001	Esteghlal	50	Pirouzi	46	Saipa	33
2002	Pirouzi	49	Esteghlal	48	Foolad	45
2003	Sepahan	52	Paas	45	Pirouzi	44
2004	Paas	53	Esteghlal	51	Foolad	47
2005	Foolad	64	Zob Ahan	58	Esteghlal	58

Year	Winners	Score	Runners-up
1990	Malavan	2-0	Khibar
1991	Pirouzi	2-1	Malavan
1992	No tournament held		
1993	No tournament held		
1994	Saipa	0-0 1-1	Jonoob
1995	Bahman	0-1 2-0	TraktorSazi
1996	Esteghlal	3-1 2-0	Bargh
1997	Bargh	1-1 3-0p	Bahman
1998	No tournament held		
1999	Pirouzi	2-1	Esteghlal
2000	Esteghlal	3-1	Bahman
2001	Fajr Sepasi	1-0 2-1	Zob Ahan
2002	Esteghlal	2-1 2-2	Fajr Sepasi
2003	Zob Ahan	2-2 2-2 6-5p	Fajr Sepasi
2004	Sepahan	3-2 2-0	Esteghlal
2005	Saba batry	1-1 2-2 4-2p	AbooMoslem

IRQ – IRAQ

NATIONAL TEAM RECORD
JULY 1ST 2002 TO JUNE 30TH 2005

PL	W	D	L	F	A	%
43	19	9	15	72	55	54.6

FIFA/COCA-COLA WORLD RANKING

1993	1994	1995	1996	1997	1998	1999	2000	2001	2002	2003	2004	High		Low	
65	88	110	98	68	94	78	79	72	53	43	44	**39**	10/04	**139**	07/96

2004-2005											
08/04	09/04	10/04	11/04	12/04	01/05	02/05	03/05	04/05	05/05	06/05	07/05
40	40	39	45	44	44	44	45	53	53	52	52

Hardly a day goes by without some reference to Iraq in the news as the country struggles to find a new identity in the post-Saddam Hussein era. With security a huge issue in the country since the second Gulf war it has not been possible to play any international matches in Iraq but still the national team provided one of the great stories of 2004. At the Athens Olympics they beat Portugal in their opening game, proceeded to win their first round group and then beat Australia in the quarter-finals. The prospect of a medal, however, was dashed first by Paraguay in the semi-final and then by Italy in the bronze medal play-off, but there was no more popular team at the Games. The lack

INTERNATIONAL HONOURS
Qualified for the FIFA World Cup™ finals 1986
Asian Games 1982 AFC Youth Championship 1975 1977 1978 1988 2000 Gulf Cup 1979 1984 1988

of home matches in the FIFA World Cup™ qualifiers probably cost Iraq a place in the final round of Asian qualifiers after they could only finish second behind Uzbekistan in the first group stage. Despite the difficult conditions at home a League competition was resumed after a break of two years. Split into four regional sections before a series of play-offs, the title was won by Al Quwa Al Jawia, the team of the Air Force, who beat Al Mina'a from Basra 2-0 in the final at the Al Sha'ab Stadium in Baghdad in July 2005.

THE FIFA BIG COUNT OF 2000

	Male	Female		Male	Female
Registered players	5 815	400	Referees	504	0
Non registered players	90 000	1 000	Officials	685	415
Youth players	1 705	250	Total involved	100 774	
Total players	99 170		Number of clubs	100	
Professional players	20	0	Number of teams	152	

Iraqi Football Association (IFA)
Al Shaab Stadium, Baghdad, Iraq
Tel +964 1 537 2010   Fax +964 1 5372021
iraqfed@yahoo.com   www.none
President: HUSSAIN Saeed   General Secretary: AHMED A. Ibrahim
Vice-President: HARIB Hamouel   Treasurer: ABDUL KHALIQ Masounel Ahmed   Media Officer: WALID Tabra
Men's Coach: MAGEED Adnan Hamad   Women's Coach: None
IFA formed: 1948   AFC: 1971   FIFA: 1950
Colours: White, White, White

GAMES PLAYED BY IRAQ IN THE 2006 FIFA WORLD CUP™ CYCLE

2002	Opponents	Score	Venue	Comp	Scorers	Att	Referee
19-07	Syria	W 2-0	Baghdad	Fr	Razzaq Farhan [69], Qusai Salah [90]		
22-07	Syria	W 2-1	Baghdad	Fr	Emad Mohammed [57], Razzaq Farhan [64]		
1-09	Palestine	W 2-0	Damascus	WFr1	Wahaib Shinayen [47], Razzaq Farhan [69]		
3-09	Syria	W 1-0	Damascus	WFr1	Ahmed Khadim [43]		
5-09	Iran	D 0-0	Damascus	WFsf	W 6-5p	2 000	Al Harbi KSA
7-09	Jordan	W 3-2	Damascus	WFf	Razzaq Farhan [32], Younes Khalef [89] Haidar Mahmoud [103GG]	10 000	
20-11	Qatar	L 1-2	Doha	Fr	Manajid Abbas [39]		Muflah OMA
23-11	Bahrain	D 2-2	Doha	Fr	Ahmed Salah [62p], Loay Salah [87]		Al Hail QAT
2003							
13-08	Iran	W 1-0	Tehran	Fr	Jassim Fayadh [53]	20 000	Al Fadhli KUW
26-08	Jordan	L 1-2	Amman	Fr	Qusai Salah [60]		Al Doseri BHR
8-10	Bahrain	W 5-1	Kuala Lumpur	ACq	Younes Khalef 4 [5 47 69 82], Jassim Swadi [24]	350	Matsumura JPN
10-10	Malaysia	D 0-0	Kuala Lumpur	ACq		5 000	Khanthama THA
12-10	Myanmar	W 3-0	Kuala Lumpur	ACq	Haydar Obaid [38], Manajid Abbas [50], Hisham Mohamed [85]	500	Yang CHN
20-10	Malaysia	W 5-1	Manama	ACq	Qusai Salah [20], Younes Khalef 3 [35 45 62] Naji Fawazi [71]	500	Al Saeedi UAE
22-10	Iraq	W 3-1	Manama	ACq	Abbas Hassan [37], Abbas Zayer [66], Jassim Fayadh [88p]	300	Yasrebi IRN
24-10	Bahrain	L 0-1	Manama	ACq		18 000	Al Saeedi UAE
12-12	Bahrain	D 2-2	Manama	Fr	Manajid Abbas [40], Hawar Tahir [76]	15 000	
15-12	Kenya	W 2-0	Manama	Fr	Hawar Taher [9], Abbas Hassan [43]		
18-12	Egypt	L 0-2	Manama	Fr			
21-12	Qatar	D 0-0	Doha	Fr			Al Qatani QAT
2004							
12-02	Japan	L 0-2	Tokyo	Fr		38 622	Kwon Jong Chul KOR
18-02	Uzbekistan	D 1-1	Tashkent	WCq	Ahmed Saleh [57]	24 000	Srinivasan IND
31-03	Palestine	D 1-1	Doha	WCq	Razak Mossa [20]	500	Al Shoufi SYR
23-05	Trinidad and Tobago	L 0-2	West Bromwich	Fr		2 000	Halsey ENG
9-06	Chinese Taipei	W 6-1	Amman	WCq	Razak Mossa 2 [2 14], Naji Fawazi [18] Manajid Abbas 2 [50 85], Jassim Fayadh [68]	2 000	Al Hail QAT
19-06	Palestine	W 2-1	Tehran	WFr1	Emad Mohammed 2 [41 83]		
21-06	Jordan	L 0-2	Tehran	WFr1			
23-06	Iran	L 1-2	Tehran	WFsf	Ahmad Abbas [30]		
25-06	Jordan	L 1-3	Tehran	WF3p	Emad Mohammed [81]		
18-07	Uzbekistan	L 0-1	Chengdu	ACr1		12 400	Kwon Jong Chul KOR
22-07	Turkmenistan	W 3-2	Chengdu	ACr1	Hawar Mohammed [12], Razzaq Farhan [81], Qusai Munir [88]		Al Fadhli KUW
26-07	Saudi Arabia	W 2-1	Chengdu	ACr1	Nashat Akram [50], Younes Khalef [86]	15 000	Kwon Jong Chul KOR
30-07	China PR	L 0-3	Beijing	ACqf			Maidin SIN
8-09	Chinese Taipei	W 4-1	Taipei	WCq	Salih Sadir 2 [4 43], Saad Attiya [75], Younes Khalef [86]	5 000	Baskar IND
7-10	Oman	L 0-1	Muscat	Fr			
13-10	Uzbekistan	L 1-2	Amman	WCq	Qusai Munir [29]	10 000	Maidin SIN
16-11	Palestine	W 4-1	Doha	WCq	Qusai Munir 2 [54 58], Emad Mohammed [65], Nashat Akram [70]	500	Al Mutlaq KSA
3-12	Yemen	W 3-1	Dubai	Fr			
10-12	Oman	L 1-3	Doha	GCr1	Razzaq Farhan [56]		
13-12	Qatar	D 3-3	Doha	GCr1	Razzaq Farhan [16], Nashat Akram [53], Haidar Hassan [90]		
16-12	UAE	D 1-1	Doha	GCr1	Qusai Munir [90p]		
2005							
26-03	Australia	L 1-2	Sydney	Fr	Mohammad Nassir [12]	30 258	O'Leary NZL
8-06	Jordan	W 1-0	Amman	Fr	Mahdi Kareem [15]		

Fr = Friendly match • WF = West Asian Federation Championship • AC = AFC Asian Cup • GC = Gulf Cup • WC = FIFA World Cup™
q = qualifier • r1 = first round group • qf = quarter-final • sf = semi-final • 3p = third place play-off • f = final • GG = golden goal

IRAQ COUNTRY INFORMATION

Capital	Baghdad	Independence	1932 from the UK	GDP per Capita	$1 500
Population	25 374 691	Status	Republic	GNP Ranking	76
Area km²	437 072	Language	Arabic, Kurdish	Dialling code	+964
Population density	58 per km²	Literacy rate	40%	Internet code	.iq
% in urban areas	75%	Main religion	Muslim	GMT +/−	+3
Towns/Cities ('000)	Baghdad 5 672; Mosul 2 066; Basra 2 016; Irbil 933; Sulimaniya 723; Kirkuk 601; Najaf 482; Karbala 434; Nasiriyah 400; Al Amarah 323; Diwaniyah 318; Al Kut 315; Al Hillah 289				
Neighbours (km)	Turkey 352; Iran 1 458; Kuwait 240; Saudi Arabia 814; Jordan 181; Syria 605; Persian Gulf 58				
Main stadia	Al Shaab - Baghdad 45 000				

IRAQ 2004-05
FIRST ROUND GROUP 1

	Pl	W	D	L	F	A	Pts
Al Quwa Al Jawia †	16	8	7	1	18	7	31
Duhok †	16	8	5	3	20	9	29
Arbil †	16	6	6	4	24	18	24
Zakho Duhok	16	6	6	4	14	15	24
Kirkuk	16	5	5	6	19	19	20
Sirwan Sulimaniya	16	4	7	5	13	16	19
Dasina Duhok	16	4	6	6	15	16	18
Sulimaniya	16	3	6	7	12	24	15
Mosul	16	2	4	10	13	24	10

21/10/2004 - 2/05/2005 • † Qualified for the next round

IRAQ 2004-05
FIRST ROUND GROUP 2

	Pl	W	D	L	F	A	Pts
Al Zawra Baghdad †	16	12	4	0	46	9	40
Al Najaf †	16	11	4	1	33	7	37
Karbala †	16	8	4	4	24	19	28
Al Sina'a Baghdad	16	7	3	6	23	19	24
Al Jaish Baghdad	16	5	3	8	20	24	18
Al Khadimiya Baghdad	16	3	7	6	15	24	16
Al Estiqlal Baghdad	16	4	4	8	13	25	16
Al Shula Baghdad	16	3	1	12	14	37	10
Babil	16	2	4	10	13	37	10

21/10/2004 - 2/05/2005 • † Qualified for the next round

IRAQ 2004-05
FIRST ROUND GROUP 3

	Pl	W	D	L	F	A	Pts
Al Talaba Baghdad †	16	8	4	4	26	13	28
Al Nafit Baghdad †	16	7	6	3	23	14	27
Al Karkh Baghdad †	16	8	3	5	20	11	27
Kahrabaa Baghdad	16	8	2	6	35	17	26
Diyala	16	6	7	3	18	16	25
Samara'a	16	6	5	5	9	13	23
Balad	16	6	3	7	15	19	21
Ramadi	16	4	4	8	15	23	16
Salah Al Deen Tikrit	16	0	4	12	6	41	4

22/10/2004 - 2/05/2005 • † Qualified for the next round

IRAQ 2004-05
FIRST ROUND GROUP 4

	Pl	W	D	L	F	A	Pts
Al Mina'a Basra †	14	9	2	3	22	5	29
Al Kut †	14	8	2	4	18	17	26
Al Shurta Baghdad †	14	7	3	4	25	11	24
Samawa	14	6	3	5	19	12	21
Maysan Umara	14	4	8	2	14	12	20
Nafit Al Janob Basra	14	4	4	6	14	24	16
Al Nasriya	14	2	3	9	15	27	9
Basra	14	1	5	8	11	30	8
Diwaniya	Excluded after 11 rounds						

20/10/2004 - 2/05/2005 • † Qualified for the next round

IRAQ 2004-05
CHAMPIONSHIP PLAY-OFFS

Second round

Group 1	Pl	W	D	L	F	A	Pt		
Al Mina'a	4	3	0	1	8	4	9	4-1	1-0
Karbala	4	1	1	2	6	8	4	0-2	1-1
Duhok	4	1	1	2	5	7	4	3-1	1-4

Group 2	Pl	W	D	L	F	A	Pt		
Al Talaba	4	2	2	0	3	0	8	0-0	2-0
Al Nafit	4	2	1	1	4	3	7	0-1	3-2
Al Karkh	4	0	1	3	2	6	1	0-0	0-1

Group 3	Pl	W	D	L	F	A	Pt		
Al Zawra	4	2	2	0	6	2	8	1-1	2-0
Al Najaf	4	2	2	0	4	1	8	0-0	2-0
Al Shurta	4	0	0	4	1	8	0	1-3	0-1

Group 4	Pl	W	D	L	F	A	Pt		
Al Quwa Al Jawia	4	3	0	1	8	2	9	4-0	3-1
Arbil	4	3	0	1	8	5	9	1-0	4-0
Al Kut	4	0	0	4	2	11	0	0-1	1-3

Al Kuwa Al Jawia champions of Iraq for the 2004-05 season

Semi-finals

Al Kuwa Al Jawia	1 2
Al Talaba	0 2

Al Zawra	0 0
Al Mina'a	1 0

Final

Al Kuwa Al Jawia	2
Al Mina'a	0

Third place play-off

Al Talaba	1 4p
Al Zawra	1 2p

RECENT LEAGUE AND CUP RECORD

Year	Champions	Pts	Runners-up	Pts	Third	Pts
1996	Al Zawra	55	Al Najaf	38	Al Shurta	37
1997	Al Quwa Al Jawia	69	Al Zawra	67	Al Talaba	60
1998	Al Shurta	73	Al Quwa Al Jawia	71	Al Zawra	70
1999	Al Zawra	57	Al Talaba	53	Al Quwa Al Jawia	47
2000	Al Zawra	114	Al Quwa Al Jawia	110	Al Shurta	110
2001	Al Zawra	70	Al Quwa Al Jawia	62	Al Shurta	60
2002	Al Talaba	91	Al Quwa Al Jawia	85	Al Shurta	80
2003	Championship abandoned					
2004	Championship abandoned					
2005	Al Quwa Al Jawia	2-0	Al Mina'a			

Cup		
Winners	Score	Runners-up
Al Zawra	2-1	Al Shurta
Al Quwa Al Jawia	1-1 8-7p	Al Shurta
Al Zawra	1-1 4-3p	Al Quwa Al Jawia
Al Zawra	1-0	Al Talaba
Al Zawra	0-0 4-3p	Al Quwa Al Jawia
No tournament held		
Al Talaba	1-0	Al Shurta
Al Talaba	1-0	Al Shurta
No tournament held		
No tournament held		

ISL – ICELAND

NATIONAL TEAM RECORD
JULY 1ST 2002 TO JUNE 30TH 2005

PL	W	D	L	F	A	%
26	7	5	14	30	45	36.5

FIFA/COCA-COLA WORLD RANKING

1993	1994	1995	1996	1997	1998	1999	2000	2001	2002	2003	2004	High		Low	
47	39	50	60	72	64	43	50	52	58	58	93	37	09/94	97	05/05

2004-2005											
08/04	09/04	10/04	11/04	12/04	01/05	02/05	03/05	04/05	05/05	06/05	07/05
79	80	88	90	93	94	94	95	95	97	90	92

Iceland's 2004-05 season got off to a sensational start with a 2-0 victory over Italy before a record crowd in Reykjavík and with players of the calibre of Chelsea's Eidur Gudjohnsen in the national team hopes ran high for the qualifiers in the 2006 FIFA World Cup™. Twelve months on and the feelings in the camp were not quite so buoyant with just one point picked up in the first six games of the campaign, a run that saw the team slump to a lowest ever position of 97 in the FIFA/Coca-Cola World Ranking. Many of the team continue to be based abroad and there are strong links with England where Gudjohnsen became the first Icelander to win an English League Championship

INTERNATIONAL HONOURS
None

medal and the hope is that Iceland can regain the form of the late 1990s and challenge for a place in the finals of the FIFA World Cup™ or the UEFA European Championship. At home there was a first trophy for FH Hafnarfjördur who comfortably won the Icelandic Championship ahead of IBV. At one stage in the season they went 22 games in all competitions without defeat before losing to Alemannia Aachen in the first round of the UEFA Cup. For the sixth year in a row Fram avoided relegation on the last day of the season whilst Keflavik won the Cup without conceding a single goal, beating KA 3-0 in the final.

THE FIFA BIG COUNT OF 2000

	Male	Female		Male	Female
Registered players	4 800	700	Referees	934	98
Non registered players	4 000	1 000	Officials	666	101
Youth players	9 000	3 500	Total involved	24 799	
Total players	23 000		Number of clubs	127	
Professional players	300	0	Number of teams	560	

Knattspyrnusamband Islands (KSI)
The Football Association of Iceland, Laugardal, Reykjavík 104, Iceland
Tel +354 5102900   Fax +354 5689793
ksi@ksi.is   www.ksi.is
President: MAGNUSSON Eggert   General Secretary: THORSTEINSSON Geir
Vice-President: JONSSON Halldor   Treasurer: STEINGRIMSSON Eggert   Media Officer: SAMARASON Omar
Men's Coach: SIGURVINSSON Asgeir & OLAFSSON Logi   Women's Coach: SVEINSSON Jorundur Aki
KSI formed: 1947   UEFA: 1954   FIFA: 1947
Colours: Blue, Blue, Blue or White, Blue, White

GAMES PLAYED BY ICELAND IN THE 2006 FIFA WORLD CUP™ CYCLE

2002	Opponents	Score	Venue	Comp	Scorers	Att	Referee
21-08	Andorra	W 3-0	Reykjavík	Fr	Gudjohnsen.E [19], Dadason 2 [26 43]	2 900	Isaksen FRO
7-09	Hungary	L 0-2	Reykjavík	Fr		3 190	Maisonlahti FIN
12-10	Scotland	L 0-2	Reykjavík	ECq		7 065	Sars FRA
16-10	Lithuania	W 3-0	Reykjavík	ECq	Helguson [49], Gudjohnsen.E 2 [61 73]	3 513	Gilewski POL
20-11	Estonia	L 0-2	Tallinn	Fr		478	Haverkort NED
2003							
29-03	Scotland	L 1-2	Glasgow	ECq	Gudjohnsen.E [48]	37 548	Temmink NED
30-04	Finland	L 0-3	Vantaa	Fr		4 005	Frojdfeldt SWE
7-06	Faroe Islands	W 2-1	Reykjavík	ECq	Sigurdsson.H [49], Gudmundsson T [88]	6 038	Liba CZE
11-06	Lithuania	W 3-0	Kaunas	ECq	Gudjónsson.Th [59], Gudjohnsen.E [72], Hreidarsson [90]	7 500	Corpodean ROU
20-08	Faroe Islands	W 2-1	Toftir	ECq	Gudjohnsen.E [55], Marteinsson [70]	3 416	Iturralde Gonzalez ESP
6-09	Germany	D 0-0	Reykjavík	ECq		7 035	Barber ENG
11-10	Germany	L 0-3	Hamburg	ECq		50 780	Ivanov RUS
19-11	Mexico	D 0-0	San Francisco	Fr		17 000	Saheli USA
2004							
31-03	Albania	L 1-2	Tirana	Fr	Gudjónsson.Th [66]	12 000	Bertini ITA
28-04	Latvia	D 0-0	Riga	Fr		6 500	Shmolik BLR
30-05	Japan	L 2-3	Manchester	Fr	Helguson 2 [5 50]	1 500	Riley ENG
5-06	England	L 1-6	Manchester	Fr	Helguson [42]	43 500	Wegereef NED
18-08	Italy	W 2-0	Reykjavík	Fr	Gudjohnsen.E [17], Einarsson [19]	20 204	Frojdfeldt SWE
4-09	Bulgaria	L 1-3	Reykjavík	WCq	Gudjohnsen.E [51p]	5 014	Hamer LUX
8-09	Hungary	L 2-3	Budapest	WCq	Gudjohnsen.E [39], Sigurdsson.I [78]	5 461	Ovrebo NOR
9-10	Malta	D 0-0	Ta'Qali	WCq		1 130	Corpodean ROU
13-10	Sweden	L 1-4	Reykjavík	WCq	Gudjohnsen.E [66]	7 037	Busacca SUI
2005							
26-03	Croatia	L 0-4	Zagreb	WCq		17 912	Damon RSA
30-03	Italy	D 0-0	Padova	Fr		16 697	Hamer LUX
4-06	Hungary	L 2-3	Reykjavík	WCq	Gudjohnsen.E [17], Sigurdsson.K [68]	4 613	Cardoso Batista POR
8-06	Malta	W 4-1	Reykjavík	WCq	Thorvaldsson.G [27], Gudjohnsen.E [33] Gudmundsson.T [74], Gunnarsson.V [84]	4 887	Skomina SVN

Fr = Friendly match • EC = UEFA EURO 2004™ • WC = FIFA World Cup™ • q = qualifier

NATIONAL CAPS

	Caps
KRISTINSSON Rúnar	104
BERGSSON Gudni	80
KRISTINSSON Birkir	74
GUDJOHNSEN Arnór	73
THORDARSON Olafur	72
GRETARSSON Arnar	71
EDVALDSSON Atli	70
JONSSON Sævar	68
GEIRSSON Marteinn	67
SVERRISSON Eyjólfur	66

NATIONAL GOALS

	Goals
JONSSON Ríkhardur	17
GUDJOHNSEN Eidur	15
DADASON Ríkhardur	14
GUDJOHNSEN Arnór	14
GUDJONSSON Thórdur	13
HALLGRIMSSON Matthías	11
PETURSSON Pétur	11
SIGURDSSON Helgi	10
SVERRISSON Eyjólfur	10
GUDMUNDSSON Tryggvi	10

NATIONAL COACH

	Years
KJARTANSSON Gudni	1980-'81
ATLASON Johannes	1982-'83
HELD Siegfried	1986-'89
KJARTANSSON Gudni	1989
JOHANNSSON Bo	1990-'91
ELIASSON Asgeir	1991-'95
OLAFSSON Logi	1996-'97
THORDARSON Gudjon	1997-'99
EDVALDSSON Atli	1999-'03
SIGURVINSSON Asgeir	2003-

ICELAND COUNTRY INFORMATION

Capital	Reykjavík	Independence	1918 from Denmark	GDP per Capita	$30 900
Population	293 966	Status	Constitutional Republic	GNP Ranking	94
Area km²	103 000	Language	Icelandic	Dialling code	+354
Population density	3 per km²	Literacy rate	99%	Internet code	.is
% in urban areas	92%	Main religion	Christian	GMT + / –	0
Towns/Cities ('000)	Reykjavík 113; Kópavogur 26; Hafnarfjördur 22; Akureyri 16; Gardabær 9; Keflavík 7				
Neighbours (km)	North Atlantic 4 988				
Main stadia	Laugardalsvöllur – Reykjavík 7 176; Akranesvöllur – Akranes 4 850				

ICELAND 2004

URVALSDEILD (1)

	Pl	W	D	L	F	A	Pts	FH	IBV	IA	Fylkir	Keflavík	KR	Grindavík	Fram	Víkingur	KA
FH Hafnarfjördur †	18	10	7	1	33	16	37		2-1	2-2	1-0	1-1	1-1	4-1	4-1	0-0	2-2
IBV Vestmannæyjar ‡	18	9	4	5	35	20	31	1-3		0-1	3-1	4-0	2-2	2-0	1-1	3-0	4-0
IA Akranes	18	8	7	3	28	19	31	2-2	2-1		1-1	2-1	0-0	0-0	0-4	0-2	2-1
Fylkir Reykjavík	18	8	5	5	26	20	29	1-0	1-2	2-2		2-0	3-1	1-1	1-0	2-1	0-1
Keflavík	18	7	3	8	31	33	24	0-1	2-5	0-2	4-2		3-1	3-4	1-1	1-0	1-0
KR Reykjavík ‡	18	6	4	8	21	22	22	0-1	0-0	1-0	1-1	1-1		2-3	3-0	2-1	2-1
Grindavík	18	5	7	6	24	31	22	0-4	1-1	1-1	0-2	3-2	0-0		3-2	3-1	2-0
Fram Reykjavík	18	4	5	9	19	28	17	1-2	1-2	0-2	1-1	1-6	1-0	2-1		3-0	0-1
Víkingur Reykjavík	18	4	4	10	19	30	16	1-1	3-2	1-4	1-3	2-3	1-2	1-0	0-0		0-1
KA Akureyri	18	4	3	11	13	30	15	1-2	0-1	0-5	0-2	1-2	3-2	1-1	0-0	0-2	

15/05/2004 - 19/09/2004 • † Qualified for the UEFA Champions League • ‡ Qualified for the UEFA Cup
Top scorers - THORVALDSON Gunnar, IBV 12; HJARTARSON Gretar, Grindavík 11; KRISTJANSSON Thorarinn, Keflavík 10

ICELAND 2004 1.DEILD (2)

	Pl	W	D	L	F	A	Pts
Valur Reykjavík	18	11	4	3	35	14	37
Thróttur Reykjavík	18	8	6	4	31	23	30
HK Kópavogur	18	9	1	8	28	28	28
Breidablik Kópavogur	18	7	5	6	31	31	26
Thór Akureyri	18	5	10	3	19	16	25
Völsungur Húsavík	18	6	4	8	27	29	22
Fjölnir Reykjavík	18	7	1	10	27	32	22
Haukar Hafnarfjördur	18	4	7	7	27	27	19
Njardvík	18	4	7	7	21	29	19
Stjarnan Gardabær	18	5	3	10	28	45	18

16/05/2004 - 17/09/2004

ICELANDIC CUP 2004

Quarter-finals		Semi-finals		Final
Keflavík	1			2-10-2004, Att: 2 049
Fylkir *	0	Keflavík	1	Laugardalsvøllur, Reykjavík
Valur	0			Scorers - Kristjánsson 2 [11 26],
HK Kópavogur *	1	HK Kópavogur	0	Sveinsson [89]
FH Hafnarfyördur	3			Keflavík ‡	3
KR *	1	FH Hafnarfyördur	0	KA Akureyri	0
IBV	0 0p	KA Akureyri	1	‡ Qualified for the UEFA Cup
KA Akureyri *	0 3p			

* Home team • Semis played at Laugardalsvøllur

CLUB DIRECTORY

Club	Town/City	Stadium	Phone	www.	Lge	Cup	CL
IA Akranes	Akranes	Akranesvöllur 4 850	+354 4313311	ia.is	18	9	0
Fram	Reykjavík	Laugardalsvöllur 7 176	+354 5335600	fram.is	18	7	0
Fylkir	Reykjavík	Fylkisvöllur 4 000	+354 5676467	fylkir.com	0	2	0
Grindavík	Grindavík	Grindavíkurvöllur 2 500	+354 4268605	umfg.is	0	0	0
FH Hafnarfjördur	Hafnarfjördur	Kaplakrikavöllur 4 800	+354 5650711	fhingar.is	1	0	0
IBV Vestmannæyjar	Vestmannæyjar	Hásteinsvöllur 3 540	+354 4812060	ibv.is	3	4	0
Keflavík	Keflavík	Keflavíkurvöllur 4 000	+354 4215388	keflavik.is	0	3	0
KR Reykjavík	Reykjavík	KR-Völlur 3 000	+354 5105310	kr.is	24	10	0
Thróttur	Reykjavík	Valbjarnarvöllur 2 500	+354 5805900	throttur.is	0	0	0
Valur	Reykjavík	Hlidarendi 3 000	+354 5623730	valur.is	19	8	0

ICELAND NATIONAL TEAM RECORDS AND RECORD SEQUENCES

Records			Sequence records				
Victory	9-0	FRO 1985	Wins	4	2000	Clean sheets	3	1984
Defeat	2-14	DEN 1967	Defeats	10	1978-1980	Goals scored	7	Three times
Player Caps	104	KRISTINSSON Rúnar	Undefeated	11	1998-1999	Without goal	6	1977-1978
Player Goals	17	JONSSON Ríkhardur	Without win	17	1977-1980	Goals against	19	1978-1981

RECENT LEAGUE AND CUP RECORD

	Championship						Cup		
Year	Champions	Pts	Runners-up	Pts	Third	Pts	Winners	Score	Runners-up
1997	IBV Vestmannæyjar	40	IA Akranes	35	Leiftur	30	Keflavík	1-1 0-0 5-4p	IBV Vestmannæyjar
1998	IBV Vestmannæyjar	38	KR Reykjavík	33	IA Akranes	30	IBV Vestmannæyjar	2-0	Leiftur
1999	KR Reykjavík	45	IBV Vestmannæyjar	38	Leiftur	26	KR Reykjavík	3-1	IA Akranes
2000	KR Reykjavík	37	Fylkir Reykjavík	35	Grindavík	30	IA Akranes	2-1	IBV Vestmannæyjar
2001	IA Akranes	36	IBV Vestmannæyjar	36	FH Hafnarfjördur	32	Fylkir Reykjavík	2-2 5-4p	KA Akureyri
2002	KR Reykjavík	36	Fylkir Reykjavík	34	Grindavík	29	Fylkir Reykjavík	3-1	Fram Reykjavík
2003	KR Reykjavík	33	FH Hafnarfjördur	30	IA Akranes	30	IA Akranes	1-0	FH Hafnarfjördur
2004	FH Hafnarfjördur	37	IBV Vestmannæyjar	31	IA Akranes	31	Keflavík	3-0	KA Akureyri

ISR – ISRAEL

NATIONAL TEAM RECORD
JULY 1ST 2002 TO JUNE 30TH 2005

PL	W	D	L	F	A	%
27	12	11	4	48	30	64.8

FIFA/COCA-COLA WORLD RANKING

1993	1994	1995	1996	1997	1998	1999	2000	2001	2002	2003	2004	High		Low	
57	42	42	52	61	43	26	41	49	46	51	48	22	06/99	71	09/93

2004-2005											
08/04	09/04	10/04	11/04	12/04	01/05	02/05	03/05	04/05	05/05	06/05	07/05
62	69	56	55	48	49	51	52	51	50	47	48

When Israel joined UEFA in 1992 it was thought that their chances of qualifying for the finals of a major tournament would be severely limited but in the 13 years since there has been a steady improvement in standards and in the 2006 FIFA World Cup™ qualifiers the national team has pushed the Republic of Ireland, France and Switzerland all the way for a place in the finals in Germany in the tightest European group of all. Having played all their home games in the UEFA EURO 2004™ qualifiers away in Italy and Turkey, there was a welcome return to Israel for home ties where they have remained unbeaten on the road to Germany, even if it did take late equalizers

INTERNATIONAL HONOURS
Qualified for the FIFA World Cup™ finals 1970 **AFC Asian Cup** 1964 **AFC Champions League** Hapoel Tel Aviv 1967 Maccabi Tel Aviv 1969 1971

against France and Ireland to secure draws. The prospect of a first appearance in the finals since 1970, when they qualified from the Oceania group, no longer seems a fanciful dream. There has also been a steady improvement in club football and in the 2004-05 season Maccabi Tel Aviv made it to the UEFA Champions League group stage where they beat Ajax and drew with Juventus. Their European campaign proved to be a distraction in the League where they finished just above the relegation zone with fierce rivals Maccabi Haifa running away with the title, their fourth in the past five seasons. There was some consolation for Maccabi Tel Aviv when they won the FA Cup.

THE FIFA BIG COUNT OF 2000

	Male	Female		Male	Female
Registered players	11 212	250	Referees	1 145	0
Non registered players	70 000	0	Officials	800	150
Youth players	25 949	150	Total involved	109 656	
Total players	107 561		Number of clubs	317	
Professional players	1 620	0	Number of teams	2 127	

The Israel Football Association (IFA)
Ramat-Gan Stadium, 299 Aba Hilell Street, Ramat-Gan 52134, Israel
Tel +972 3 6171503   Fax +972 3 5702044
r.dori@israel-football.org.il   www.israel-football.org.il
President: MENAHEM Itzhak   General Secretary: ZIMMER Haim
Vice-President: BRIKMAN Gideon   Treasurer: MENAHEM Itzhak   Media Officer: AIZENBERG Saul
Men's Coach: GRANT Avraham   Women's Coach: SCHRAIER Alon
IFA formed: 1928 & 1948   UEFA: 1992 (AFC 1956-1976)   FIFA: 1929
Colours: Blue, White, Blue or White, Blue, White

GAMES PLAYED BY ISRAEL IN THE 2006 FIFA WORLD CUP™ CYCLE

2002	Opponents	Score		Venue	Comp	Scorers	Att	Referee
21-08	Lithuania	W	4-2	Kaunas	Fr	Afek 2 [20][64], Zandberg [47], Tal [74]	3 000	Chykun BLR
5-09	Luxembourg	W	5-0	Luxembourg	Fr	Udi 2 [1][68], Badeer [24], Keisi [79], Benayoun [85]	1 400	Allaerts BEL
12-10	Malta	W	2-0	Ta'Qali	ECq	Balili [56], Revivo [77]	5 200	Shebek UKR
20-11	FYR Macedonia	W	3-2	Skopje	Fr	Zandberg [19], Nimni [28], Biton [90]	5 000	Delevic YUG
2003								
12-02	Armenia	W	2-0	Tel Aviv	Fr	Nimni [19], Zandberg [62]	8 000	Trentlange ITA
5-03	Moldova	D	0-0	Tel Aviv	Fr		8 000	Bertini ITA
29-03	Cyprus	D	1-1	Limassol	ECq	Afek [1]	8 500	McCurry SCO
2-04	France	L	1-2	Palermo	ECq	Afek [2]	4 000	Barber ENG
30-04	Cyprus	W	2-0	Palermo	ECq	Badeer [88], Holtzman [90]	1 000	Benes CZE
7-06	Slovenia	D	0-0	Antalya	ECq		2 500	Busacca SUI
20-08	Russia	W	2-1	Moscow	Fr	Nimni [52], Balili [82]	5 000	Ishchenko UKR
6-09	Slovenia	L	1-3	Ljubljana	ECq	Revivo [69]	8 000	Fandel GER
10-09	Malta	D	2-2	Antalya	ECq	Revivo [16], Abuksis [78]	300	Blareau BEL
11-10	France	L	0-3	Paris	ECq		57 900	Bolognino ITA
2004								
18-02	Azerbaijan	W	6-0	Tel Aviv	Fr	Arbeitman 3 [9][65][69], Tal [24p], Katan 2 [45][61]	13 250	Gomes Paraty POR
30-03	Lithuania	W	2-1	Tel Aviv	Fr	Balili [34], Badeer [64]	9 872	Dougal SCO
28-04	Moldova	D	1-1	Tel Aviv	Fr	Covalenco OG [31]	4 500	Corpodean ROU
27-05	Georgia	W	1-0	Tbilisi	Fr	Badeer [33]	22 000	Oriekhov UKR
18-08	Croatia	L	0-1	Zagreb	Fr		10 000	Granat POL
4-09	France	D	0-0	Paris	WCq		43 527	Temmink NED
8-09	Cyprus	W	2-1	Tel Aviv	WCq	Benayoun [64], Badeer [75]	21 872	Shmolik BLR
9-10	Switzerland	D	2-2	Tel Aviv	WCq	Benayoun 2 [9][48]	37 976	Shield AUS
17-11	Cyprus	W	2-1	Nicosia	WCq	Keisi [17], Nimni [86]	1 624	Kaldma EST
2005								
9-02	Croatia	D	3-3	Jerusalem	Fr	Balili [38], Benayoun [74], Golan [84]	4 000	Kailis CYP
26-03	Republic of Ireland	D	1-1	Tel Aviv	WCq	Souan [90]	32 150	Ivanov.V RUS
30-03	France	D	1-1	Tel Aviv	WCq	Badeer [83]	32 150	Merk GER
4-06	Republic of Ireland	D	2-2	Dublin	WCq	Yemiel [39], Nimni [46+]	36 000	Vassaras GRE

Fr = Friendly match • EC = UEFA EURO 2004™ • WC = FIFA World Cup™ • q = qualifier

ISRAEL NATIONAL TEAM RECORDS AND RECORD SEQUENCES

Records			Sequence records				
Victory	9-0	TPE 1988	Wins	7	1973-1974	Clean sheets	4	Four times
Defeat	1-7	EGY 1934, GER 2002	Defeats	8	1950-1956	Goals scored	9	1968-69, 2000-01
Player Caps	85	SHELAH Amir	Undefeated	12	1971-1973	Without goal	5	1964-1965
Player Goals	25	SPIEGLER Mordechai	Without win	22	1985-1988	Goals against	22	1934-1958

ISRAEL COUNTRY INFORMATION

Capital	Jerusalem	Formation	1948	GDP per Capita	$19 800
Population	6 199 008	Status	Republic	GNP Ranking	36
Area km²	20 770	Language	Hebrew, Arabic	Dialling code	+972
Population density	298 per km²	Literacy rate	95%	Internet code	.il
% in urban areas	91%	Main religion	Jewish 80%, Muslim 14%	GMT + / –	+2
Towns/Cities ('000)	Jerusalem 714; Tel Aviv 370; Haifa 270; Rishon LeZiyyon 222; Ashdod 202; Be'er Sheva 187				
Neighbours (km)	Lebanon 79; Syria 76; Jordan 238; West Bank 307; Egypt 266; Gaza Strip 51; Mediterranean Sea & Red Sea 273				
Main stadia	Ramat-Gan – Ramat-Gan 42 000; Teddy Maiha – Jerusalem 20 000; Bloomfield – Tel Aviv 16 500				

NATIONAL CAPS

	Caps
SHELAH Amir	85
BENADO Arik	82
HARAZI Alon	82
BANIN Tal	78
BERKOVIC Eyal	78
KLINGER Nir	77
NIMNI Avi	76
HAZAN Alon	72
REVIVO Haim	67
GINZBURG Boni	62

NATIONAL GOALS

	Goals
SPIEGLER Mordechai	25
HARAZI Ronen	23
STELMACH Nahum	22
MIZRAHI Alon	17
OHANA Eli	17
GLAZER Yehoshua	16
FEIGENBAUM Yehoshua	15
REVIVO Haim	15
NIMNI Avi	15

NATIONAL COACH

	Years
SCHMILOVICH Edmond	1970-'73
SCHWEITZER David	1973-'77
SHEFER Imanuel	1978-'79
MANSELL Jack	1980-'81
MIRMOVICH Yosef	1983-'86
MIHIC Miljenko	1986-'88
SHNEOR & GRUNDMAN	1988-'92
SCHARF Shlomo	1992-'99
MOLLER NIELSEN Richard	2000-'02
GRANT Avraham	2002-

FIFA REFEREE LIST 2005

	Int'l	DoB
JAKOV Haim	1998	3-05-1968
KENAN Asaf	2003	29-03-1968
LEVI Meir	2000	27-10-1968
YEFET Alon	2001	1-09-1972

FIFA ASSISTANT REFEREE LIST 2005

	Int'l	DoB
AL RAMILI Abed	2000	22-12-1969
BENISTY Yossef	1994	13-10-1960
BENITA Shlomo	2001	14-02-1972
KRASOKOW Danny	2001	5-02-1973
NAHMIAS Shabtai	1997	16-02-1969
OSADON Shai	1998	9-12-1960
SHTEIF Shmuel	1998	6-09-1965
ZATELMAN Erez	1994	1-09-1963

CLUB DIRECTORY

Club	Town/City	Stadium	Phone	www.	Lge	Cup	CL
FC Ashdod	Ashdod	Ashdod Stadium 8 000	+972 8 8531240		0	0	0
Beitar Jerusalem	Jerusalem	Teddy Maiha 20 000	+972 2 6528994		4	5	0
Bnei Yehuda	Tel Aviv	Bloomfield 16 500	+972 3 6876445	bnei-yehuda.co.il	1	2	0
Hapoel Beer Sheva	Beer Sheva	Vasermil 13 000	+972 8 6422986		2	1	0
Hapoel Bnei Sakhnin	Sakhnin	Ironi Sakhnin 6 000	+972 4 6746017		0	1	0
Hapoel Haifa	Haifa	Kiryat Eli'ezer 18 500	+972 4 8665000		1	3	0
Hapoel Nazareth	Nazareth Illit	Ilut 9 000	+972 4 6020188		0	0	0
Hapoel Petah Tikva	Petah Tikva	Hapoel 8 400	+972 3 9218352	hapoel-pt.co.il	6	2	0
Hapoel Tel Aviv	Tel Aviv	Bloomfield 16 500	+972 3 6821275		11	10	0
Maccabi Haifa	Haifa	Kiryat Eli'ezer 18 500	+972 4 8346626	maccabi-haifa.nana.co.il	8	5	0
Maccabi Petah Tikva	Petah Tikva	Hapoel 8 400	+972 3 9347561		0	2	0
Maccabi Tel Aviv	Tel Aviv	Bloomfield 16 500	+972 3 6817233	maccabi-tlv.nana.co.il	18	21	0

RECENT LEAGUE AND CUP RECORD

	Championship						Cup		
Year	Champions	Pts	Runners-up	Pts	Third	Pts	Winners	Score	Runners-up
1990	Bnei Yehuda	62	Hapoel Petah Tikva	58	Maccabi Haifa	50	Hapoel Kfar Saba	1-0	Shimshon Tel Aviv
1991	Maccabi Haifa	71	Hapoel Petah Tikva	70	Beitar Tel Aviv	50	Maccabi Haifa	3-1	Hapoel Petah Tikva
1992	Maccabi Tel Aviv	75	Bnei Yehuda	62	Maccabi Haifa	48	Hapoel Petah Tikva	3-1	Maccabi Tel Aviv
1993	Beitar Jerusalem	71	Maccabi Tel Aviv	62	Bnei Yehuda	56	Maccabi Haifa	1-0	Maccabi Tel Aviv
1994	Maccabi Haifa	95	Maccabi Tel Aviv	88	Hapoel Beer Sheva	65	Maccabi Tel Aviv	2-0	Hapoel Tel Aviv
1995	Maccabi Tel Aviv	63	Maccabi Haifa	58	Hapoel Beer Sheva	50	Maccabi Haifa	2-0	Hapoel Haifa
1996	Maccabi Tel Aviv	74	Maccabi Haifa	66	Beitar Jerusalem	64	Maccabi Tel Aviv	4-1	Hapoel Ironi RL
1997	Beitar Jerusalem	69	Hapoel Petah Tikva	60	Hapoel Beer Sheva	60	Hapoel Beer Sheva	1-0	Maccabi Tel Aviv
1998	Beitar Jerusalem	69	Hapoel Tel Aviv	68	Hapoel Haifa	60	Maccabi Haifa	2-0	Hapoel Jerusalem
1999	Hapoel Haifa	71	Maccabi Tel Aviv	63	Maccabi Haifa	60	Hapoel Tel Aviv	1-1 3-1p	Beitar Jerusalem
2000	Hapoel Tel Aviv	85	Maccabi Haifa	76	Hapoel Petah Tikva	74	Hapoel Tel Aviv	2-2 4-2p	Beitar Jerusalem
2001	Maccabi Haifa	82	Hapoel Tel Aviv	75	Hapoel Haifa	71	Maccabi Tel Aviv	3-0	Maccabi Petah Tikva
2002	Maccabi Haifa	75	Hapoel Tel Aviv	67	Maccabi Tel Aviv	57	Maccabi Tel Aviv	0-0 5-4p	Maccabi Haifa
2003	Maccabi Tel Aviv	69	Maccabi Haifa	69	Hapoel Tel Aviv	67	Hapoel Ramat Gan	1-1 5-4p	Hapoel Beer Sheva
2004	Maccabi Haifa	63	Maccabi Tel Aviv	57	Maccabi Petah Tikva	56	Hapoel Bnei Sakhnin	4-1	Hapoel Haifa
2005	Maccabi Haifa	71	Maccabi Petah Tikva	60	Ashdod	50	Maccabi Tel Aviv	2-2 5-3p	Maccabi Herzliya

ISRAEL 2004-05

PREMIER LEAGUE

	Pl	W	D	L	F	A	Pts	Maccabi H	Maccabi PT	Ashdod	Beitar	Hapoel NI	BY TA	Hapoel PT	Maccabi TA	Hapoel TA	Hapoel BS	Hapoel H	Hapoel BS
Maccabi Haifa †	33	21	8	4	66	27	71		0-0 2-2	6-0	1-1 1-2	3-1 3-0	5-0	1-0	3-0 3-1	1-0 3-2	1-0	3-0 2-1	4-1
Maccabi Petah Tikva ‡	33	16	12	5	47	24	60	0-2		5-1 1-0	2-0	1-1	3-0 2-1	1-0 1-1	2-1	2-0	2-0 4-2	0-0 1-0	0-0 3-1
Ashdod	33	15	5	13	48	44	50	0-1 4-0	0-0		2-3 1-2	3-1 4-2	4-3	2-0	2-0 0-0	2-1 1-1	2-2	2-0 1-1	0-2
Beitar Jerusalem	33	13	8	12	46	44	47	0-0	0-0 4-2	1-0		0-2 3-3	3-2	0-1	2-0 3-2	1-2	0-2 0-0	2-0	4-1 0-1
Hapoel Nazrat-Ilit	33	12	10	11	46	46	46	0-1	0-0 1-3	2-0	4-3		2-1 3-0	1-1	1-0 2-1	2-2	0-0 4-0	3-0	0-0
Bnei-Yehuda Tel Aviv	33	12	8	13	40	46	44	0-2 2-2	1-0	0-4 0-1	1-0 1-1	3-1		1-0 2-1	2-2	0-0 4-0	3-0	2-1	0-0
Hapoel Petah Tikva	33	11	9	13	41	46	42	2-2 1-1	0-0	2-1 1-1	1-3 0-2	1-2	3-1		1-0 4-4	1-0 1-1	1-1	2-2 1-0	4-1
Maccabi Tel Aviv ‡	33	10	10	13	32	42	40	1-0	1-0 1-3	0-1	1-1 1-2	3-1 0-0	0-0	0-1		3-0 1-0	3-2	1-2	1-0 3-2
Hapoel Tel Aviv	33	10	9	14	30	34	39	0-1	2-2 1-0	0-1	1-1 1-3	1-0 0-0	0-0	0-1	3-0 1-0		3-2	1-2	1-0 3-1
Hapoel Bnei Sakhnin	33	10	6	17	40	51	36	1-4 3-2	0-0	2-1 2-0	4-1	0-1	0-1 2-4	1-2 2-0	0-1	1-2 0-1		0-0	4-3
Hapoel Haifa	33	9	8	16	36	44	35	1-4	0-3	1-3	3-1 2-0	0-0	0-1 0-2	2-3	1-2	0-0 1-0	1-0 4-0		0-2 6-1
Hapoel Be'er Sheva	33	7	11	15	33	57	32	0-1 1-1	1-2	0-2 2-0	0-2	2-2	0-0 2-1	1-1 1-4	1-1	1-0	0-4 1-1	2-1	

21/08/2004 - 28/05/2005 • † Qualified for the UEFA Champions League • ‡ Qualified for the UEFA Cup • Match in bold awarded 2-0

ISRAEL 2004-05
LIGA LEUMIT (2)

	Pl	W	D	L	F	A	Pts
Hapoel Kfar Saba	33	15	11	7	40	27	56
Maccabi Netanya	33	14	11	8	44	31	53
Hapoel Acre	33	14	7	12	52	45	49
Hapoel Jerusalem §1	33	14	6	13	39	41	47
Hakoah Ramat Gan	33	12	10	11	31	33	46
Ironi Rishon Letzion	33	11	12	10	36	36	45
Maccabi Hertzelia	33	11	12	10	31	31	45
Hapoel Kiriat Shmona	33	11	11	11	39	41	44
Hapoel Ranana	33	11	8	14	37	40	41
Ironi Ramat HaSharon §1	33	10	11	12	33	39	40
Maccabi Akhi Nazareth §2	33	8	16	9	38	38	38
Tzafririm Holon	33	6	7	20	30	48	25

20/08/2004 - 27/05/2005 • §1 = one point deducted
§2 = two points deducted

FA CUP 2004-05

Round of 16

Maccabi Tel Aviv	3
Ashdod *	2
Maccabi Haifa	3 2p
Hapoel Haifa *	3 3p
Hakoah M. Ramat-Gan *	1
Hapoel Bnei Sakhnin	0
Hapoel Tel Aviv	0
Maccabi Petah Tikva *	1
Hapoel Ashkelon *	6
Nahlat Yehuda	0
Hapoel Raanana *	0
Beni Yehuda Tel Aviv	3
Hapoel Petah Tikva	1
Maccabi Netanya *	0
Hapoel Zafririm Holon	0
Maccabi Herzliya *	3

Quarter-finals

Maccabi Tel Aviv	2
Hapoel Haifa	1
Hakoah M. Ramat-Gan *	0
Maccabi Petah Tikva	1
Hapoel Ashkelon *	3
Beni Yehuda Tel Aviv	0
Hapoel Petah Tikva *	2
Maccabi Herzliya	3

Semi-finals

Maccabi Tel Aviv	2
Maccabi Petah Tikva	1
Hapoel Ashkelon	1 2p
Maccabi Herzliya	1 4p

Final

Maccabi Tel Aviv ‡	2 5p
Maccabi Herzliya	2 3p

CUP FINAL

18-05-2005, Ramat-Gan Stadium
Scorers - Reis [25], Meika [96] for Tel Aviv; Halwani [15], Davis [111] for Herzliya

* Home team • ‡ Qualified for the UEFA Cup

ITA – ITALY

NATIONAL TEAM RECORD
JULY 1ST 2002 TO JUNE 30TH 2005

PL	W	D	L	F	A	%
35	19	11	5	52	25	70

"Six minutes of madness" was how Milan coach Carlo Ancelotti described the incredible second half collapse in the UEFA Champions League final against Liverpool, but what a difference six minutes can have on the impression left by a whole season of football. Milan looked set for a Championship and European Cup double - something they have only ever done once before in 1994 - but they ended up with nothing. In truth their form had often been patchy with the first half of the final in Istanbul the best they had played all season but they did match Juventus all the way in Serie A before losing a crucial game between the two in early May to effectively concede the title to their Turin rivals. Fabio Capello proved his credentials as one of the all time great coaches with Juventus the third Serie A team he has led to the Scudetto, after Milan and Roma, not forgetting a Spanish Championship won with Real Madrid. It was Juventus' 28th Championship and it was achieved on the back of disciplined team work. Roberto Mancini is often regarded as a potential great coach for the future and in 2005 he took another step on that path by winning the Coppa Italia with Inter, the first Italian trophy Inter have won since 1989. The Milan club had an extraordinary

INTERNATIONAL HONOURS
FIFA World Cup™ 1934 1938 1982
Olympic Gold 1936
International Cup 1930 1935   UEFA European Championship 1968   UEFA Junior Tournament 1958 1966
UEFA U-21 Championship 1992 1994 1996 2000 2004   UEFA U-19 Championship 2003   UEFA U-17 Championship 1982 1987
UEFA Champions League Milan 1963 1969 1989 1990 1994 2003, Internazionale 1964 1965, Juventus 1985 1996

season remaining unbeaten in all competitions until February when they lost in the Milanese derby in Serie A. Indeed three of the four defeats they suffered came at the hands of Milan, two of them in the infamous Champions League quarter-final, the second leg of which had to be abandoned after Milan keeper Dida was hit by a flare thrown by an Inter fan. Too many drawn games cost Inter a challenge for the Scudetto but they were entertaining to watch and have one of the rising stars of world football in their ranks, the Brazilian striker Adriano. The Italian National team had a solid season under coach Marcelo Lippi and despite a surprising defeat away to Slovenia the Azzurri look set to keep up their record of having qualified for every FIFA World Cup™ since 1962. With all of the top sides in Italy based around a core of Italian players the Italians should be amongst the favourites in the finals in Germany but Lippi has decided the best approach is to cast his net beyond just the big clubs in an attempt to instil a club mentality into the national team. Italians fans will be hoping that pays dividends and that the team can avoid the disasters of the 2002 FIFA World Cup™ finals and the UEFA EURO 2004™ finals.

Federazione Italiana Giuoco Calcio (FIGC)
Via Gregorio Allegri 14, Roma 00198, Italy
Tel +39 06 84911   Fax +39 06 84912526
press@figc.it   www.figc.it
President: CARRARO Franco Dr   General Secretary: GHIRELLI Francesco Dr
Vice-President: ABETE Giancarlo Dr   Treasurer: GHIRELLI Francesco Dr   Media Officer: VALENTINI Antonello Dr
Men's Coach: LIPPI Marcello   Women's Coach: MORACE Carolina
FIGC formed: 1898   UEFA: 1954   FIFA: 1905
Colours: Blue, White, Blue or White, Blue, White

GAMES PLAYED BY ITALY IN THE 2006 FIFA WORLD CUP™ CYCLE

2002	Opponents	Score		Venue	Comp	Scorers	Att	Referee
21-08	Slovenia	L	0-1	Trieste	Fr		11 080	Brugger AUT
7-09	Azerbaijan	W	2-0	Baku	ECq	Akhmedov OG [33], Del Piero [65]	37 000	Vassaras GRE
12-10	Serbia & Montenegro	D	1-1	Naples	ECq	Del Piero [39]	50 000	Mejuto Gonzalez ESP
16-10	Wales	L	1-2	Cardiff	ECq	Del Piero [32]	70 000	Veissiere FRA
20-11	Turkey	D	1-1	Pescara	Fr	Vieri [38]	17 556	Garibian FRA
2003								
12-02	Portugal	W	1-0	Genoa	Fr	Corradi [62]	31 265	Fandel GER
29-03	Finland	W	2-0	Palermo	ECq	Vieri 2 [6 22]	34 074	Ivanov RUS
30-04	Switzerland	W	2-1	Geneva	ECq	Legrottaglie [10], Zanetti [75]	30 000	Ledentu FRA
3-06	Northern Ireland	W	2-0	Campobasso	Fr	Corradi [31], Delvecchio [67]	18 270	Cortez Batista POR
11-06	Finland	W	2-0	Helsinki	ECq	Totti [32], Del Piero [73]	36 850	Siric CRO
20-08	Germany	W	1-0	Stuttgart	Fr	Vieri [17]	50 128	Nielsen DEN
6-09	Wales	W	4-0	Milan	ECq	Inzaghi.F 3 [59 63 70], Del Piero [76p]	68 000	Merk GER
10-09	Serbia & Montenegro	D	1-1	Belgrade	ECq	Inzaghi.F [22]	35 000	Hamer LUX
11-10	Azerbaijan	W	4-0	Reggio Calabria	ECq	Vieri [16], Inzaghi.F 2 [24 88], Di Vaio [65]	30 000	Dougal SCO
12-11	Poland	L	1-3	Warsaw	Fr	Cassano [19]	9 000	Ovrebo NOR
16-11	Romania	W	1-0	Ancona	Fr	Di Vaio [58]	11 700	Stark GER
2004								
18-02	Czech Republic	D	2-2	Palermo	Fr	Vieri [14], Di Natale [86]	20 935	Braamhaar NED
31-03	Portugal	W	2-1	Braga	Fr	Vieri [40], Miccoli [75]	25 000	Aydin TUR
28-04	Spain	D	1-1	Genoa	Fr	Vieri [56]	30 300	Poll ENG
30-05	Tunisia	W	4-0	Tunis	Fr	Bouazizi OG [15], Cannavaro [27], Pirlo [86], Zambrotta [90]	20 000	Duhamel FRA
14-06	Denmark	D	0-0	Guimaraes	ECr1		19 595	Mejuto Gonzalez ESP
18-06	Sweden	D	1-1	Porto	ECr1	Cassano [37]	44 927	Meier SUI
22-06	Bulgaria	W	2-1	Guimaraes	ECr1	Perrotta [48], Cassano [90]	16 002	Ivanov RUS
18-08	Iceland	L	0-2	Reykjavík	Fr		20 204	Frojdfeldt SWE
4-09	Norway	W	2-1	Palermo	WCq	De Rossi [4], Toni [80]	21 463	Sars FRA
8-09	Moldova	W	1-0	Chisinau	WCq	Del Piero [32]	5 200	Benes CZE
9-10	Slovenia	L	0-1	Celje	WCq		9 262	De Bleeckere BEL
13-10	Belarus	W	4-3	Parma	WCq	Totti 2 [26p 74], De Rossi [32], Gilardino [86]	19 833	Megia Davila ESP
17-11	Finland	W	1-0	Messina	Fr	Miccoli [33]	7 043	Tudor ROU
2005								
9-02	Russia	W	2-0	Cagliari	Fr	Gilardino [56], Barone [62]	15 700	Michel SVK
26-03	Scotland	W	2-0	Milan	WCq	Pirlo 2 [35 85]	45 000	Vassaras GRE
30-03	Iceland	D	0-0	Padova	Fr		16 697	Hamer LUX
4-06	Norway	D	0-0	Oslo	WCq		24 829	Mejuto Gonzalez ESP
8-06	Serbia & Montenegro	D	1-1	Toronto	Fr	Lucarelli [83]	35 000	Depiero CAN
11-06	Ecuador	D	1-1	East Rutherford	Fr	Toni [6]	27 583	Vaughn USA

Fr = Friendly match • EC = UEFA EURO 2004™ • WC = FIFA World Cup™ • q = qualifier • r1 = first round group

FIFA/COCA-COLA WORLD RANKING

1993	1994	1995	1996	1997	1998	1999	2000	2001	2002	2003	2004	High	Low
2	4	3	10	9	7	14	4	6	13	10	10	**1** 11/93	**16** 04/98

	2004-2005										
08/04	09/04	10/04	11/04	12/04	01/05	02/05	03/05	04/05	05/05	06/05	07/05
9	9	8	10	10	10	10	10	10	10	11	14

THE FIFA BIG COUNT OF 2000

	Male	Female		Male	Female
Registered players	361 239	9 221	Referees	31 170	1 240
Non registered players	2 900 000	35 000	Officials	48 184	456
Youth players	732 864	4 563	Total involved	4 123 937	
Total players	4 042 887		Number of clubs	16 123	
Professional players	3 152	0	Number of teams	63 476	

NATIONAL CAPS

	Caps
MALDINI Paolo	126
ZOFF Dino	112
FACCHETTI Giacinto	94
CANNAVARO Fabio	85
BARESI Franco	81
BERGOMI Giuseppe	81
TARDELLI Marco	81
ALBERTINI Demetrio	79
SCIREA Gaetano	78

NATIONAL GOALS

	Goals
RIVA Luigi	35
MEAZZA Giuseppe	33
PIOLA Silvio	30
BAGGIO Roberto	27
ALTOBELLI Alessandro	25
BALONCIERI Adolfo	25
DEL PIERO Alessandro	24
GRAZIANI Francesco	23
MAZZOLA Sandro	22
VIERI Christian	22

NATIONAL COACH

	Years
VALCAREGGI Ferruccio	1967-'74
BERNARDINI Fulvio	1974-'75
BERNARDINI/BEARZOT	1975-'77
BEARZOT Enzo	1977-'86
VICINI Azeglio	1986-'91
SACCHI Arrigo	1991-'96
MALDINI Cesare	1996-'98
ZOFF Dino	1998-'00
TRAPATTONI Giovanni	2000-'04
LIPPI Marcello	2004-

ITALY NATIONAL TEAM RECORDS AND RECORD SEQUENCES

Records			Sequence records					
Victory	11-3	EGY 1928	Wins	9	1938-1939	Clean sheets	12	1972-1974
Defeat	1-7	HUN 1924	Defeats	3	Three times	Goals scored	43	1931-1937
Player Caps	126	MALDINI Paolo	Undefeated	30	1935-1939	Without goal	3	Three times
Player Goals	35	RIVA Luigi	Without win	8	1958-1959	Goals against	19	1927-1930

FIFA REFEREE LIST 2005

	Int'l	DoB
BERTINI Paolo	2003	7-07-1964
COLLINA Pierluigi	1995	13-02-1960
DE SANTIS Massimo	2000	8-04-1962
DONDARINI Paolo	2005	1-10-1968
FARINA Stefano	2001	19-09-1962
MESSINA Domenico	1998	12-08-1962
PAPARESTA Gianluca	2003	25-05-1969
RODOMONTI Pasquale	1998	1-06-1961
ROSETTI Roberto	2002	18-09-1967
TREFOLONI Matteo	2004	31-03-1971

FIFA ASSISTANT REFEREE LIST 2005

	Int'l	DoB
CALCAGNO Paolo	2005	29-01-1966
CONSOLO Andrea	2002	8-06-1963
CONTINI Gabriele	2002	23-11-1964
COPELLI Cristiano	2004	14-06-1967
GRISELLI Alessandro	2004	31-05-1974
IVALDI Marco	1999	4-07-1961
MAGGIANI Luca	2005	9-04-1968
MITRO Vincenzo	2001	30-12-1961
PISACRETA Narciso	1999	16-08-1960
STAGNOLI Alessandro	2003	2-02-1965

ITALY COUNTRY INFORMATION

Capital	Rome	Formation	1870	GDP per Capita	$26,700
Population	58 057 477	Status	Republic	GNP Ranking	7
Area km²	301 230	Language	Italian	Dialling code	+39
Population density	193 per km²	Literacy rate	98.6%	Internet code	.it
% in urban areas	67%	Main religion	Christian	GMT + / −	+1
Towns/Cities ('000)	Rome 2 643; Milan 1 156; Naples 981; Turin 846; Palermo 669; Genoa 585; Bologna 367; Florence 347; Catania 307; Bari 303; Venice 259; Verona 247; Messina 237; Padova 205; Trieste 204; Brescia 193; Taranto 191; Reggio de Calabria 181; Modena 180; Prato 178; Cagliari 157; Perugia 157; Parma 173				
Neighbours (km)	Austria 430; Slovenia 232; San Marino 39; Vatican 3; France 488; Switzerland 740; Mediterranean 7 600				
Main stadia	San Siro – Milan 85 700; Olimpico – Rome 82 307; San Paolo – Naples 82 126				

ITALY 2004-05

SERIE A

Team	Pl	W	D	L	F	A	Pts	Juventus	Milan	Inter	Udinese	Sampdoria	Palermo	Messina	Roma	Livorno	Reggina	Lecce	Cagliari	Lazio	Siena	Chievo	Fiorentina	Bologna	Parma	Brescia	Atalanta
Juventus †	38	26	8	4	67	27	86		0-0	0-1	2-1	0-1	1-1	2-1	2-0	4-2	1-0	5-2	4-2	2-1	3-0	3-0	1-0	2-1	2-0	2-0	2-0
Milan †	38	23	10	5	63	28	79	0-1		0-0	3-1	1-0	3-1	1-2	1-2	2-2	3-1	5-2	1-0	2-1	2-1	1-0	6-0	0-1	3-0	1-1	3-0
Internazionale †	38	18	18	2	65	37	72	2-2	0-1		3-1	3-2	1-1	5-0	2-0	1-0	0-0	2-1	0-1	2-0	1-1	2-0	1-1	3-2	2-2	2-2	1-0
Udinese †	38	17	11	10	56	40	62	0-1	1-1	1-1		1-1	1-0	1-1	3-3	1-1	0-2	2-1	2-0	3-0	1-0	3-0	2-2	0-1	4-0	1-2	2-1
Sampdoria ‡	38	17	10	11	42	29	61	0-3	0-1	0-1	2-0		1-0	1-0	2-1	2-0	1-2	3-2	3-3	3-3	1-0	2-0	0-0	1-1	0-1	0-1	1-2
Palermo ‡	38	12	17	9	48	44	53	1-0	0-0	0-2	1-5	2-0		2-1	2-0	1-2	1-2	3-3	3-3	1-0	2-2	0-0	1-1	1-0	1-1	3-3	
Messina	38	12	12	14	44	52	48	0-0	1-4	2-1	1-0	2-2	0-0		4-3	1-1	2-1	4-2	1-1	1-0	4-1	0-0	1-1	0-0	1-0	2-0	1-0
Roma ‡	38	11	12	15	55	58	45	1-2	0-2	3-3	3-0	3-1	1-1	1-3		3-0	1-2	2-2	5-1	0-0	0-2	0-0	1-0	1-1	5-1	2-2	2-1
Livorno	38	11	12	15	49	60	45	2-2	1-0	0-2	1-2	1-0	2-2	3-1	0-2		1-1	1-0	3-3	0-3	6-1	2-2	1-0	0-2	1-1	1-1	0-0
Reggina	38	11	11	16	48	53	44	2-1	0-1	0-0	0-0	0-1	1-0	0-2	1-0	2-1		2-2	3-2	2-1	3-3	1-0	1-2	1-1	1-3	1-3	0-0
Lecce	38	10	14	14	66	73	44	0-1	2-2	2-2	3-4	1-4	2-0	1-0	1-1	3-2	1-1		3-1	5-3	2-2	3-0	2-2	1-1	3-3	4-1	1-0
Cagliari	38	10	14	14	51	60	44	1-0	1-3	3-1	1-0	0-0	0-2	1-3	0-0	0-1	1-3	1-1		1-1	2-0	4-2	1-0	1-0	2-1	2-1	3-3
Lazio	38	10	14	14	36	45	44	0-1	1-2	1-2	1-1	1-3	2-0	3-1	3-1	1-1	3-2	2-3	1-1		0-1	1-1	1-1	1-2	1-2	0-0	2-1
Siena	38	9	16	13	44	55	43	0-3	2-1	2-2	3-2	2-1	0-0	2-2	0-4	1-1	0-0	1-1	2-1	1-0		0-1	1-0	1-1	0-1	2-3	2-1
Chievo	38	11	10	17	32	49	43	0-1	0-1	2-2	0-0	0-2	2-1	1-0	2-2	1-0	0-0	2-1	1-1	0-1	1-3		1-2	1-0	2-0	3-1	1-0
Fiorentina	38	9	15	14	42	50	42	3-3	1-2	1-1	2-2	0-2	1-2	1-1	1-2	1-1	2-1	4-0	2-1	2-3	0-0	2-0		1-0	2-1	3-0	0-0
Bologna	38	9	15	14	33	36	42	0-1	0-2	0-1	0-1	0-0	1-0	1-1	2-2	3-1	0-0	2-0	0-0	2-1	1-1	3-1	0-0		3-1	1-2	2-1
Parma	38	10	12	16	48	65	42	1-1	1-2	2-2	1-0	1-1	3-3	0-0	2-1	6-4	1-0	2-1	3-2	3-1	0-0	2-2	0-1	2-0		2-1	2-2
Brescia	38	11	8	19	37	54	41	0-3	0-0	0-3	0-1	0-1	0-2	0-1	1-0	2-3	2-0	0-2	0-0	1-1	1-1	1-1	3-1				1-0
Atalanta	38	8	11	19	34	45	35	1-2	1-2	2-3	0-1	0-0	1-0	2-1	0-1	1-0	0-1	2-2	2-1	1-1	1-1	3-0	1-2	0-1	0-0		

11/09/2004 - 29/05/2005 • † Qualified for the UEFA Champions League • ‡ Qualified for the UEFA Cup • Relegation play-off: Parma 0-1 2-0 Bologna

SERIE B PLAY-OFFS

Semi-finals

Ascoli	0	1
Torino	1	2

Treviso	0	0
Perugia	1	2

Final

Torino	2	0
Perugia	1	1

TOP SCORERS

LUCARELLI Cristiano	Livorno	24
GILARDINO	Parma	23
MONTELLA Vincenzo	Roma	21
TONI Luca	Palermo	20
VUCINIC Mirko	Lecce	19

ITALY 2004-05

SERIE B

Team	Pl	W	D	L	F	A	Pts	Genoa	Empoli	Torino	Perugia	Treviso	Ascoli	Verona	Modena	Ternana	Piacenza	AlbinoLeffe	Bari	Catania	Arezzo	Salernitana	Crotone	Cesena	Vicenza	Triestina	Pescara	Venezia	Catanzaro
Genoa	42	19	19	4	72	44	76		3-2	0-1	0-0	2-1	3-0	1-1	1-0	3-2	2-1	0-0	3-1	5-0	1-0	3-3	5-2	2-2	2-0	3-2	3-1		
Empoli	42	19	17	6	58	36	74	0-0		1-0	3-0	1-2	1-0	2-1	1-1	0-0	0-0	0-1	1-3	0-0	3-0	0-0	2-1	2-0	2-1	5-2	2-0		
Perugia	42	21	11	10	56	34	74	2-2	0-2		1-1	2-0	2-0	0-2	0-0	4-0	1-0	1-1	1-1	1-0	2-1	1-1	1-0	4-1	0-0	3-1			
Torino	42	21	11	10	49	31	74	2-1	0-0	2-0		1-2	2-1	3-1	0-3	2-1	0-1	3-1	2-0	1-0	0-0	1-0	1-0	0-1	3-1	1-1	3-0		
Treviso	42	18	10	14	58	48	64	3-0	0-1	1-0	0-1		1-1	1-1	3-1	1-1	3-1	1-2	1-1	2-0	2-1	2-0	1-1	3-0	2-0		
Ascoli	42	17	11	14	51	52	62	0-3	1-1	0-1	0-3	2-1		2-1	1-0	0-0	2-3	3-1	1-2	2-2	3-2	0-2	4-0	2-0	1-1	1-0	1-1	0-1	
Hellas Verona	42	15	16	11	60	47	61	1-1	0-1	1-2	2-0	2-1	2-2		3-0	2-2	1-0	3-2	0-0	4-0	5-3	3-1	1-0	0-2	1-5	3-0	0-1	1-0	4-1
Modena §1	42	16	14	12	47	37	61	1-1	0-1	1-0	1-0	1-0	1-1	4-0		1-0	2-2	0-0	0-1	1-0	1-0	2-0	2-1	0-0	1-0	0-1	0-0		
Ternana	42	14	15	13	51	54	57	0-1	1-1	0-1	1-3	2-2	0-1	1-1	0-1		0-1	1-3	1-1	3-1	1-0	1-1	3-0	0-2	3-2		
Piacenza	42	16	8	18	44	46	56	2-2	1-3	2-4	1-0	3-2	3-1	1-0	1-0	0-2		1-1	1-0	0-1	0-0	1-1	1-3	1-0	1-1	3-0	0-0	2-1	2-3
AlbinoLeffe	42	14	13	15	55	51	55	0-3	0-0	0-1	2-1	2-2	1-2	1-1	2-0	3-1	3-0		0-1	1-0	1-2	1-1	1-2	3-3	4-0	1-0	1-1		
Bari	42	13	17	12	41	37	55	0-1	4-1	1-1	0-1	1-1	0-1	1-0	2-2	1-2	1-0	1-1		1-0	3-0	1-1	3-2	0-1	1-2	0-1	1-1	
Catania	42	13	16	13	42	44	55	1-3	1-3	0-0	1-0	3-0	2-2	1-1	0-1	0-0	1-1	1-2	1-0		1-2	1-1	1-0	2-0	1-0	2-1	1-1	2-0	
Arezzo	42	12	15	15	51	52	51	2-2	1-1	1-2	0-0	0-1	0-0	2-1	1-2	2-0	1-1	2-1	3-1		1-0	3-0	1-1	0-3	0-1	2-1	1-2	0-2	1
Salernitana	42	12	15	15	50	57	51	4-0	1-1	0-2	0-0	0-0	2-1	1-2	2-2	1-1	3-2	1-1	2-2	1-0	2-0		1-1	6-1	3-1	3-3	0-2	0-0	0-0
Crotone §3	42	13	14	15	48	45	50	0-0	1-1	1-1	2-1	1-2	0-1	1-0	1-0	0-2	1-2	0-1	1-0	0-2	4-1	0-1		0-4	4-2	3-0	2-0	0-9	
Cesena	42	12	14	16	47	61	50	1-1	3-3	0-1	1-0	3-4	1-2	0-1	3-0	0-1	1-1	1-1	0-1	1-1	1-1	1-3	1-0		1-1	1-1	1-2	1	
Vicenza	42	12	13	17	59	67	49	2-2	2-1	2-2	1-2	0-1	1-1	0-0	2-2	1-0	4-0	4-1	0-0	2-2	1-4	1-3	2-4	2-1		0-0	2-1	5-0	
Triestina	42	12	12	18	43	54	48	0-0	3-4	0-0	1-0	1-1	1-0	1-2	0-2	3-1	0-2	3-1	0-2	3-1	2-1	1-0	1-0	0-2	1-1		3-0	1-1	1-2
Pescara	42	10	16	16	43	61	46	2-1	0-2	1-0	0-1	0-2	1-1	2-0	1-1	1-2	1-3	2-2	2-0	2-2	0-2	1-4	2-1	4-0	2-1	0-0		3-2	
Venezia	42	7	14	21	33	58	35	0-3	1-0	2-4	0-3	1-2	1-1	3-2	0-0	3-0	0-2	1-0	1-1	0-2	0-0	0-2	1-0	1-0	1-0	0-2	0-0		
Catanzaro	42	5	11	26	40	82	26	1-1	2-3	1-3	1-1	1-4	2-3	1-1	2-1	1-4	1-3	0-1	2-1	2-3	1-1	3-0	2-2	2-2	2-1	1-1	1-0	1-0	0-0

10/09/2004 - 29/05/2005 • §3 Three points deducted • §1 One point deducted • Relegation play-off: Triestina 2-0 2-0 Vicenza • Genoa later relegated to Serie C1 after they were found guilty of fixing the result of their final match, a 3-2 win over Venezia

ITALY 2004-05 SERIE C1 GROUP A

	Pl	W	D	L	F	A	Pts
Cremonese	36	22	6	8	58	36	72
Mantova ‡	36	18	10	8	45	25	64
Grosseto ‡	36	17	13	6	35	17	64
Pavia ‡	36	18	10	8	47	31	64
Frosinone ‡	36	17	8	11	42	39	59
Pistoiese	36	15	11	10	42	31	56
Spezia	36	13	13	10	46	38	52
Sangiovannese	36	13	11	12	40	32	50
Pisa	36	11	14	11	35	31	47
Pro Patria	36	10	15	11	39	37	45
Lucchese	36	10	14	12	36	44	44
Lumezzane	36	11	11	14	29	39	44
Acireale	36	9	15	12	34	41	42
Sassari Torres	36	10	12	14	36	43	42
Novara	36	9	13	14	33	43	40
Fidelis Andria	36	6	16	14	24	39	34
Vittoria	36	6	12	18	24	40	30
Como §	36	7	14	15	33	46	29
Prato	36	7	8	21	29	55	29

12/09/2004 - 15/05/2005 • ‡ Qualified for the play-offs • § Six points deducted

PLAY-OFFS

SERIE C1 GROUP A
Semi-finals

Frosinone	2	0
Mantova	4	1
Grosseto	1	0
Pavia	1	2

Final

Pavia	1	0
Mantova	3	3

SERIE C1 GROUP B
Semi-finals

Reggiana	1	2
Avellino	2	2
Sambenedettese	1	0
Napoli	1	2

Final

Napoli	0	1
Avellino	0	2

ITALY 2004-05 SERIE C1 GROUP B

	Pl	W	D	L	F	A	Pts
Rimini	34	19	13	2	50	23	70
Avellino ‡	34	18	10	6	48	29	64
Napoli ‡	34	17	10	7	45	31	61
Sambenedettese ‡	34	14	12	8	38	25	54
Reggiana ‡ §3	34	13	15	6	41	24	51
Padova	34	13	9	12	46	39	48
Lanciano	34	12	10	12	36	38	46
Benevento	34	11	12	11	31	38	45
SPAL	34	10	13	11	36	33	43
Foggia	34	9	15	10	36	35	42
Martina	34	10	12	12	31	41	42
Cittadella	34	9	14	11	36	37	41
Teramo	34	9	13	12	32	37	40
Fermana	34	10	9	15	30	45	39
Sora §2	34	8	12	14	35	42	34
Giulianova	34	7	10	17	20	43	31
Chieti	34	5	15	14	19	32	30
Vis Pesaro	34	5	10	19	21	39	25

12/09/2004 - 15/05/2005 • ‡ Qualified for the play-offs • §3 Three points deducted • §2 Two points deducted

CLUB DIRECTORY

Club	Town/City	Stadium	Phone	www.	Lge	Cup	CL
Atalanta	Bergamo	Atleti Azzurri d'Italia 26 638	+39 035 4186211	atalanta.it	0	1	0
Bologna	Bologna	Renato dall'Ara 39 561	+39 051 6111111	bolognafc.it	7	2	0
Brescia	Brescia	Mario Rigamonti 27 547	+39 030 2410751	bresciacalcio.it	0	0	0
Cagliari	Cagliari	Sant'Elia 39 905	+39 070 604201	cagliaricalcio.it	1	0	0
Chievo	Verona	Marc'Antonio Bentegodi 42 160	+39 045 575579	chievoverona.it	0	0	0
Fiorentina	Florence	Artemio Franchi 47 232	+39 055 5030191	acffiorentina.it	2	6	0
Internazionale	Milan	Giuseppe Meazza (San Siro) 85 700	+39 02 77151	inter.it	13	4	2
Juventus	Turin	Delle Alpi 71 012	+39 011 65631	juventus.com	28	9	2
Lazio	Rome	Olimpico 82 307	+39 06 976071	sslazio.it	2	4	0
Lecce	Lecce	Via del Mare 40 800	+39 0832 240211	uslecce.it	0	0	0
Livorno	Livorno	Armando Picchi 18 200	+39 0586 219295	livornocalcio.it	0	0	0
Messina	Messina	San Filippo 43 000	+39 090 2282300	mondomessina.it	0	0	0
Milan	Milan	Giuseppe Meazza (San Siro) 85 700	+39 02 62281	acmilan.com	17	5	6
Palermo	Palermo	Renzo Barbera 36 980	+39 091 6901211	ilpalermocalcio.it	0	0	0
Parma	Parma	Ennio Tardini 28 783	+39 0521 505111	fcparma.com	0	3	0
Reggina	Reggio Calabria	Oreste Granillo 27 763	+39 0965 354760	regginacalcio.it	0	0	0
Roma	Rome	Olimpico 82 307	+39 06 5061736	asromacalcio.it	3	7	0
Sampdoria	Genoa	Luigi Ferraris 41 917	+39 010 5316711	sampdoria.it	1	4	0
Siena	Siena	Artemio Franchi 13 500	+39 0577 281084	acsiena.it	0	0	0
Udinese	Udine	Friuli 41 652	+39 0432 544911	udinese.it	0	0	0

RECENT LEAGUE AND CUP RECORD

	Championship						Cup		
Year	Champions	Pts	Runners-up	Pts	Third	Pts	Winners	Score	Runners-up
1990	Napoli	51	Milan	49	Internazionale	44	Juventus	0-0 1-0	Milan
1991	Sampdoria	51	Milan	46	Internazionale	46	Roma	3-1 1-1	Sampdoria
1992	Milan	56	Juventus	48	Torino	43	Parma	0-1 2-0	Juventus
1993	Milan	50	Internazionale	46	Parma	41	Torino	3-0 2-5	Roma
1994	Milan	50	Juventus	47	Sampdoria	44	Sampdoria	0-0 6-1	Ancona
1995	Juventus	73	Lazio	63	Parma	63	Juventus	1-0 2-0	Parma
1996	Milan	73	Juventus	65	Lazio	59	Fiorentina	1-0 2-0	Atalanta
1997	Juventus	65	Parma	64	Internazionale	59	Vicenza	0-1 3-0	Napoli
1998	Juventus	74	Internazionale	69	Udinese	64	Lazio	0-1 3-1	Milan
1999	Milan	70	Lazio	69	Fiorentina	56	Parma	1-1 2-2	Fiorentina
2000	Lazio	72	Juventus	71	Milan	61	Lazio	2-1 0-0	Internazionale
2001	Roma	75	Juventus	73	Lazio	69	Fiorentina	1-0 1-1	Parma
2002	Juventus	71	Roma	70	Internazionale	69	Parma	1-2 1-0	Juventus
2003	Juventus	72	Internazionale	65	Milan	61	Milan	4-1 2-2	Roma
2004	Milan	82	Roma	71	Juventus	69	Lazio	2-0 2-2	Juventus
2005	Juventus	86	Milan	79	Internazionale	72	Internazionale	2-0 1-0	Roma

COPPA ITALIA 2004-05

First Round Group Stage **Second Round** **Third Round**

Group A	Pts
Torino	7
Genoa	4
Lumezzane	4
Empoli	1

Ternana *	1 4
Bologna	3 3

Internazionale *	3 3
Bologna	1 1

Group B	Pts
Atalanta	7
AlbinoLeffe	6
Vicenza	3
Pro Patria	1

Reggina	1 2
Atalanta *	4 3

Juventus	0 3
Atalanta *	2 3

Group C	Pts
Triestina	9
Modena	6
Treviso	1
Venezia	1

Chievo	0 1
Torino *	1 1

Sampdoria	2 1
Torino *	0 2

Group D	Pts
Livorno	7
Cesena	5
Ascoli	4
Arezzo	0

Triestina *	1 1
Cagliari	3 3

Lazio	1 3
Cagliari *	2 2

Group E	Pts
Fiorentina	7
Piacenza	7
Hellas Verona	3
Como	0

Livorno *	2 1
Lecce	1 3

Udinese	5 3
Lecce *	4 4

Group F	Pts
Ternana	6
Perugia	4
Rimini	4
Pescara	2

Palermo	1 2
Salernitana *	2 0

Palermo *	1 0
Milan	2 2

Group G	Pts
Salernitana	9
Catania	6
Catanzaro	1
Avellino	1

Fiorentina *	1 2
Brescia	1 2

Fiorentina *	2 3
Parma	0 0

Group H	Pts
Messina	9
Crotone	4
Bari	3
Acireale	1

Siena	1 1
Messina *	0 1

Siena	2 1
Roma *	1 5

Serie A clubs join in second rounds except those playing in Europe who join in the third round • * Home team in the first leg

COPPA ITALIA 2004-05

Quarter-finals	Semi-finals	Final

Internazionale	1 3
Atalanta *	0 0

Internazionale	1 3
Cagliari *	1 1

Sampdoria	0 3
Cagliari *	2 2

Internazionale	2 1
Roma * ‡	0 0

Udinese	2 4
Milan *	3 1

Udinese	1 1
Roma *	1 2

COPPA ITALIA FINAL

First leg. Stadio Olimpico, Rome, 12-06-2005, Att: 73 437, Referee: Collina

Roma	0	
Internazionale	2	Adriano 2 [30] [35]

Roma - Curci; Panucci, Ferrari, Chivu, Cufre (Scurto 82); Virga (Montella 58), Dacourt, Perrotta; Totti, Mancini (Greco 72), Cassano. Tr: Conui

Inter - Toldo; Zanetti.J, Materazzi, Mihajlovic, Favalli; Stankovic, Cambiasso, Ze Maria, Kily Gonzalez (Van der Meyde 86); Adriano, Martins (Cruz 76). Tr: Mancini

Second leg. Giuseppe Meazza, Milan, 15-06-2005, Att: 72 034, Referee: Trefoloni

Internazionale	1	Mihajlovic [52]
Roma	0	

Fiorentina	0 1 6p
Roma *	1 0 7p

Inter - Toldo; Cordoba, Materazzi, Mihajlovic, Favalli (Gamarra 87); Ze Maria (Veron 85), Zanetti.C, Stankovic (Biava 90), Kily Gonzalez; Martins, Cruz. Tr: Mancini

Roma - Curci; Panucci, Mexes, Chivu (Ferrari 79), Cufre; Perrotta, Dacourt (Montella 46) (Corvia 73), De Rossi, Mancini; Totti, Cassano. Tr: Conti

‡ Qualified for the UEFA Cup

JUVENTUS 2004-05

Date	Opponents	Score		Comp	Scorers	Att
10-08-2004	Djurgårdens IF	D 2-2	H	CLpr3	Trezeguet [50], Emerson [59]	26 146
25-08-2004	Djurgårdens IF	W 4-1	A	CLpr3	Del Piero [10], Trezeguet 2 [35 87], Nedved [54]	32 058
12-09-2004	Brescia	W 3-0	A	SA	Nedved [35], Trezeguet [38], Ibrahimovic [69]	16 504
15-09-2004	Ajax - NED	W 1-0	A	CLgC	Nedved [42]	50 000
19-09-2004	Atalanta	W 2-0	H	SA	Trezeguet 2 [14 58]	22 221
22-09-2004	Sampdoria	W 3-0	A	SA	Del Piero [18p], Ibrahimovic [69], Trezeguet [86]	32 102
25-09-2004	Palermo	D 1-1	H	SA	Ibrahimovic [53]	26 740
28-09-2004	Maccabi Tel Aviv - ISR	W 1-0	H	CLgC	Camoranesi [37]	6 494
3-10-2004	Udinese	W 1-0	A	SA	Zalayeta [61]	21 000
16-10-2004	Messina	W 2-1	H	SA	Zalayeta [26], Nedved [54]	29 622
19-10-2004	Bayern München - GER	W 1-0	H	CLgC	Nedved [75]	18 089
24-10-2004	Siena	W 3-0	A	SA	Del Piero 2 [53 60], Camoranesi [63]	14 604
28-10-2004	Roma	W 2-0	H	SA	Del Piero [31], Zalayeta [74]	27 764
31-10-2004	Chievo	W 3-0	H	SA	Zalayeta [25], Nedved [65], Ibrahimovic [79]	21 362
3-11-2004	Bayern München - GER	W 1-0	A	CLgC	Del Piero [90]	59 000
7-11-2004	Reggina	L 1-2	A	SA	Ibrahimovic [14]	20 803
10-11-2004	Fiorentina	W 1-0	H	SA	Olivera [72]	22 983
14-11-2004	Lecce	W 1-0	A	SA	Del Piero [15]	30 482
19-11-2004	Atalanta	L 0-2	A	CUPr3		
23-11-2004	Ajax - NED	W 1-0	H	CLgC	Zalayeta [15]	6 875
28-11-2004	Internazionale	D 2-2	A	SA	Zalayeta [53], Ibrahimovic [66p]	78 471
5-12-2004	Lazio	W 2-1	H	SA	Olivera [40], Ibrahimovic [75]	20 787
8-12-2004	Maccabi Tel Aviv - ISR	D 1-1	A	CLgC	Del Piero [71]	18 500
12-12-2004	Bologna	W 1-0	A	SA	Nedved [86]	28 458
18-12-2004	Milan	D 0-0	H	SA		54 181
6-01-2005	Parma	D 1-1	A	SA	Ibrahimovic [64]	23 009
9-01-2005	Livorno	W 4-2	H	SA	Del Piero [17], Camoranesi 2 [25 90p], Ibrahimovic [75]	21 445
13-01-2005	Atalanta	D 3-3	H	CUPr3	Natali OG [4], Zalayeta [33], Trezeguet [79]	4 822
16-01-2005	Cagliari	D 1-1	A	SA	Emerson [54]	13 570
23-01-2005	Brescia	W 2-0	H	SA	Trezeguet [12], Domizzi OG [43]	37 650
30-01-2005	Atalanta	W 2-1	A	SA	Olivera [23], Del Piero [78p]	18 054
2-02-2005	Sampdoria	L 0-1	H	SA		20 016
5-02-2005	Palermo	L 0-1	A	SA		34 047
13-02-2005	Udinese	W 2-1	H	SA	Ibrahimovic [1], Camoranesi [49]	20 632
19-02-2005	Messina	D 0-0	A	SA		40 000
22-02-2005	Real Madrid - ESP	L 0-1	A	CLr2		78 000
27-02-2005	Siena	W 3-0	H	SA	Del Piero 2 [34 62p], Emerson [49]	19 385
5-03-2005	Roma	W 2-1	A	SA	Cannavaro [11], Del Piero [44p]	69 488
9-03-2005	Real Madrid - ESP	W 2-0	H	CLr2	Trezeguet [57], Zalayeta [116]	59 000
13-03-2005	Chievo	W 1-0	A	SA	Olivera [87]	24 514
19-03-2005	Reggina	W 1-0	H	SA	Del Piero [65]	21 189
5-04-2005	Liverpool - ENG	L 1-2	A	CLqf	Cannavaro [63]	41 216
9-04-2005	Fiorentina	D 3-3	A	SA	Del Piero [22], Ibrahimovic 2 [59 82]	45 614
13-04-2005	Liverpool - ENG	D 0-0	H	CLqf		50 000
17-04-2005	Lecce	W 5-2	H	SA	Appiah [15], Ibrahimovic 3 [33 42 82], Nedved [55]	21 048
20-04-2005	Internazionale	L 0-1	H	SA		23 157
24-04-2005	Lazio	W 1-0	A	SA	Nedved [85]	45 462
1-05-2005	Bologna	W 2-1	H	SA	Cannavaro [18], Zalayeta [24]	35 690
8-05-2005	Milan	W 1-0	A	SA	Trezeguet [28]	79 232
15-05-2005	Parma	W 2-0	H	SA	Del Piero [6], Ibrahimovic [23]	40 000
22-05-2005	Livorno	D 2-2	A	SA	Nedved [10], Trezeguet [66]	19 756
29-05-2005	Cagliari	W 4-2	H	SA	Del Piero [44], Trezeguet 2 [51 73], Appiah [60]	52 762

SA = Serie A • CL = UEFA Champions League • CUP = Coppa Italia
pr3 = third preliminary round • gC = group C • r2 = second round • r3 = third round • qf = quarter-final • sf = semi-final • f = final

MILAN 2004-05

Date	Opponents		Score		Comp	Scorers	Att
21-08-2004	Lazio	W	3-0	H	SC	Shevchenko 3 [36 43 76]	33 274
11-09-2004	Livorno	D	2-2	H	SA	Seedorf 2 [3 47]	69 453
14-09-2004	Shakhtar Donetsk - UKR	W	1-0	A	CLgF	Seedorf [84]	30 000
19-09-2004	Bologna	W	2-0	A	SA	Shevchenko [82p], Kaká [90]	27 345
22-09-2004	Messina	L	1-2	H	SA	Pancaro [54]	59 640
26-09-2004	Lazio	W	2-1	A	SA	Shevchenko 2 [70 74]	41 738
29-09-2004	Celtic - SCO	W	3-1	H	CLqf	Shevchenko [8], Inzaghi [89], Pirlo [90]	50 000
3-10-2004	Reggina	W	3-1	H	SA	Shevchenko 2 [11 88], Kaká [66]	59 473
17-10-2004	Cagliari	W	1-0	A	SA	Pirlo [20]	23 134
20-10-2004	Barcelona - ESP	W	1-0	H	CLgF	Shevchenko [31]	76 502
24-10-2004	Internazionale	D	0-0	H	SA		79 775
27-10-2004	Atalanta	W	3-0	H	SA	Tomasson [53], Kaladze [71], Serginho [90]	57 531
30-10-2004	Sampdoria	W	1-0	A	SA	Shevchenko [76]	28 226
2-11-2004	Barcelona - ESP	L	1-2	A	CLgF	Shevchenko [17]	94 682
8-11-2004	Roma	D	1-1	H	SA	Shevchenko [6]	75 229
11-11-2004	Brescia	D	0-0	A	SA		8 093
14-11-2004	Siena	W	2-1	H	SA	Shevchenko 2 [26 37]	63 507
20-11-2004	Palermo	W	2-1	A	CUPr3	Crespo [53], Seedorf [69]	
24-11-2004	Shakhtar Donetsk - UKR	W	4-0	H	CLgF	Kaká 2 [52 90], Crespo 2 [53 85]	38 841
28-11-2004	Chievo	W	1-0	A	SA	Crespo [50]	23 406
4-12-2004	Parma	W	2-1	A	SA	Kaká [82], Pirlo [90]	19 967
7-12-2004	Celtic - SCO	D	0-0	A	CLgF		59 228
12-12-2004	Fiorentina	W	6-0	H	SA	Seedorf 2 [16 82], Crespo 2 [22 61], Shevchenko 2 [52 73]	69 226
18-12-2004	Juventus	D	0-0	A	SA		54 181
6-01-2005	Lecce	W	5-2	H	SA	Crespo 3 [23 36 57], Shevchenko [50], Tomasson [89]	76 716
9-01-2005	Palermo	D	0-0	A	SA		34 047
12-01-2005	Palermo	W	2-0	H	CUPr3	Brocchi [19], Tomasson [77p]	
16-01-2005	Udinese	W	3-1	H	SA	Shevchenko [31], Jankulovski OG [53], Kaká [90]	62 417
23-01-2005	Livorno	L	0-1	A	SA		25 000
26-01-2005	Udinese	W	3-2	H	CUPqf	Ambrosini 2 [17 67], Serginho [84]	
30-01-2005	Bologna	L	0-1	H	SA		56 756
2-02-2005	Messina	W	4-1	A	SA	Crespo 2 [9 64], Tomasson 2 [18 90]	37 582
6-02-2005	Lazio	W	2-1	H	SA	Shevchenko [72], Crespo [90]	56 845
13-02-2005	Reggina	W	1-0	A	SA	Zamboni OG [39]	19 944
19-02-2005	Cagliari	W	1-0	H	SA	Serginho [92+]	59 185
23-02-2005	Manchester United - ENG	W	1-0	A	CLr2	Crespo [78]	67 162
27-02-2005	Internazionale	W	1-0	A	SA	Kaká [74]	78 347
5-03-2005	Atalanta	W	2-1	A	SA	Ambrosini [72], Pirlo [90]	21 095
8-03-2005	Manchester United - ENG	W	1-0	H	CLr2	Crespo [6]	78 957
13-03-2005	Sampdoria	W	1-0	H	SA	Kaká [65]	69 441
16-03-2005	Udinese	L	1-4	A	CUPqf	Tomasson [77]	
20-03-2005	Roma	W	2-0	A	SA	Crespo [63], Pirlo [71p]	59 496
6-04-2005	Internazionale - ITA	W	2-0	H	CLqf	Stam [45], Shevchenko [74]	80 000
9-04-2005	Brescia	D	1-1	H	SA	Rui Costa [14]	59 726
12-04-2005	Internazionale - ITA	W	3-0	A	CLqf	Shevchenko [30]. Abandoned 75'. Match awarded 3-0 to Milan	79 000
17-04-2005	Siena	L	1-2	A	SA	Crespo [63]	13 730
20-04-2005	Chievo	W	1-0	H	SA	Seedorf [64]	54 894
23-04-2005	Parma	W	3-0	H	SA	Kaká [33], Tomasson [62], Cafu [71]	60 818
26-04-2005	PSV Eindhoven - NED	W	2-0	H	CLsf	Shevchenko [42], Tomasson [90]	71 000
30-04-2005	Fiorentina	W	2-1	A	SA	Shevchenko 2 [46 55]	45 909
4-05-2005	PSV Eindhoven - NED	L	1-3	A	CLsf	Ambrosini [90]	35 000
8-05-2005	Juventus	L	0-1	H	SA		79 232
15-05-2005	Lecce	D	2-2	A	SA	Kaladze [12], Shevchenko [53]	21 628
20-05-2005	Palermo	D	3-3	H	SA	Serginho 2 [8 16], Tomasson [32]	60 872
25-05-2005	Liverpool - ENG	D	3-3	N	CLf	Maldini [1], Crespo 2 [38 43]. L 2-3p	69 000
29-05-2005	Udinese	D	1-1	A	SA	Serginho [86]	21 397

SC = Supercoppa Italia • SA = Serie A • CL = UEFA Champions League • CUP = Coppa Italia
gF = group F • r2 = second round • r3 = third round • qf = quarter-final • sf = semi-final • f = final • N = Attaturk Olimpiyat, Istanbul

INTERNAZIONALE 2004-05

Date	Opponents	Score		Comp	Scorers	Att
11-08-2004	FC Basel - SUI	D 1-1	A	CLpr3	Adriano [19]	29 500
24-08-2004	FC Basel - SUI	W 4-1	H	CLpr3	Adriano 2 [1 52], Stankovic [12], Recoba [59]	62 000
11-09-2004	Chievo	D 2-2	A	SA	Stankovic [16], Adriano [48]	29 450
14-09-2004	Werder Bremen - GER	W 2-0	H	CLgG	Adriano 2 [34p 89]	45 000
18-09-2004	Palermo	D 1-1	H	SA	Adriano [46]	68 190
22-09-2004	Atalanta	W 3-2	A	SA	Stankovic [54], Recoba [79], Adriano [87]	21 962
26-09-2004	Parma	D 2-2	H	SA	Martins 2 [71 82]	55 303
29-09-2004	RSC Anderlecht - BEL	W 3-1	A	CLgG	Martins [9], Adriano [51], Stankovic [55]	25 000
3-10-2004	Roma	D 3-3	A	SA	Cambiasso [45], Veron [51], Recoba [54]	58 000
17-10-2004	Udinese	W 3-1	H	SA	Adriano 2 [8 12], Vieri [57]	43 500
20-10-2004	Valencia - ESP	W 5-1	A	CLgG	Stankovic [47], Vieri [49], Van der Meyde [76], Adriano [81], Cruz [91+]	40 000
24-10-2004	Milan	D 0-0	A	SA		79 775
27-10-2004	Lecce	D 2-2	A	SA	Adriano [4], Martins [33]	26 136
30-10-2004	Lazio	D 1-1	H	SA	Adriano [46]	56 016
2-11-2004	Valencia - ESP	D 0-0	H	CLgG		40 000
7-11-2004	Fiorentina	D 1-1	A	SA	Adriano [80]	43 708
10-11-2004	Bologna	D 2-2	H	SA	Mihajlovic [39], Adriano [71]	48 692
14-11-2004	Cagliari	D 3-3	A	SA	Stankovic [35], Martins 2 [76 88]	20 104
21-11-2004	Bologna	W 3-1	H	CUPr3	Vieri [45], Recoba [79], Cruz [87]	2 640
24-11-2004	Werder Bremen - GER	D 1-1	A	CLgG	Martins [55]	37 000
28-11-2004	Juventus	D 2-2	H	SA	Vieri [79], Adriano [85]	78 471
4-12-2004	Messina	W 5-0	H	SA	Adriano 3 [3 14 36], Eleftheropoulos OG [55], Vieri [84]	55 509
7-12-2004	RSC Anderlecht - BEL	W 3-0	H	CLgG	Cruzz [33], Martins 2 [60 63]	30 000
12-12-2004	Siena	D 2-2	A	SA	Adriano [36p], Vieri [90]	18 581
19-12-2004	Brescia	W 1-0	H	SA	Mihajlovic [24]	50 457
6-01-2005	Livorno	W 2-0	A	SA	Vieri 2 [42 74p]	17 835
9-01-2005	Sampdoria	W 3-2	H	SA	Martins [88], Vieri [91+], Recoba [94+]	58 989
12-01-2005	Bologna	W 3-1	A	CUPr3	Martins 3 [56 82 86]	2 990
15-01-2005	Reggina	D 0-0	A	SA		21 445
22-01-2005	Chievo	D 1-1	H	SA	Martins [83]	51 395
27-01-2005	Atalanta	W 1-0	A	CUPqf	Martins [72]	5 358
30-01-2005	Palermo	W 2-0	A	SA	Vieri 2 [5 58]	34 047
2-02-2005	Atalanta	W 1-0	H	SA	Martins [33]	48 479
6-02-2005	Parma	D 2-2	A	SA	Cordoba [76], Vieri [82p]	18 225
12-02-2005	Roma	W 2-0	H	SA	Mihajlovic 2 [23 92+]	61 116
16-02-2005	Atalanta	W 3-0	H	CUPqf	Recoba [31], Emre [36], Cruz [55]	2 400
19-02-2005	Udinese	D 1-1	A	SA	Veron [58]	23 714
23-02-2005	FC Porto - POR	D 1-1	A	CLr2	Martins [24]	38 177
27-02-2005	Milan	L 0-1	H	SA		78 347
6-03-2005	Lecce	W 2-1	H	SA	Cordoba [26], Adriano [89p]	54 305
12-03-2005	Lazio	D 1-1	A	SA	Cruz [70]	49 787
15-03-2005	FC Porto - POR	W 3-1	H	CLr2	Adriano 3 [6 63 87]	51 000
20-03-2005	Fiorentina	W 3-2	H	SA	Cambiasso [27], Veron [52], Cordoba [65]	57 157
6-04-2005	Milan - ITA	L 0-2	A	CLqf		80 000
9-04-2005	Bologna	W 1-0	A	SA	Cruz [3]	23 000
12-04-2005	Milan - ITA	L 0-3	H	CLqf	Match abandoned 75' at 0-1. Awarded 3-0 to Milan	79 000
17-04-2005	Cagliari	W 2-0	H	SA	Ze Maria [40], Martins [65]	50 367
20-04-2005	Juventus	W 1-0	A	SA	Cruz [24]	23 157
24-04-2005	Messina	L 1-2	A	SA	Cruz [46]	34 602
1-05-2005	Siena	W 2-0	H	SA	Cruz [2p], Vieri [30]	40 266
8-05-2005	Brescia	W 3-0	A	SA	Martins 2 [55 66], Vieri [90]	6 895
12-05-2005	Cagliari	D 1-1	A	CUPsf	Martins [51]	
15-05-2005	Livorno	W 1-0	H	SA	Vieri [12]	52 646
18-05-2005	Cagliari	W 3-1	H	CUPsf	Vieri 2 [26 58], Martins [90]	
22-05-2005	Sampdoria	W 1-0	A	SA	Adriano [35]	31 765
29-05-2005	Reggina	D 0-0	H	SA		50 883
12-06-2005	Roma	W 2-0	A	CUPf	Adriano 2 [30 35]	73 437
15-06-2005	Roma	W 1-0	H	CUPf	Mihajlovic [52]	72 034

SA = Serie A • CL = UEFA Champions League • CUP = Coppa Italia
pr3 = third preliminary round • gG = group G • r2 = second round • r3 = third round • qf = quarter-final • sf = semi-final • f = final

JAM – JAMAICA

NATIONAL TEAM RECORD
JULY 1ST 2002 TO JUNE 30TH 2005

PL	W	D	L	F	A	%
52	23	17	12	82	46	60.6

FIFA/COCA-COLA WORLD RANKING

1993	1994	1995	1996	1997	1998	1999	2000	2001	2002	2003	2004	High		Low	
80	96	56	32	39	33	41	48	53	51	46	49	27	08/98	96	12/94

2004-2005											
08/04	09/04	10/04	11/04	12/04	01/05	02/05	03/05	04/05	05/05	06/05	07/05
54	53	51	53	49	47	46	41	42	41	41	41

Jamaica are a shadow of the side that reached the 1998 FIFA World Cup™ finals and flattered to deceive during their 2006 campaign. After beating Haiti in round one, expectations were high but some below-par performances including defeat in Kingston to Panama, who were ranked 76 places below them, put paid to any thoughts of a trip to Europe. A week after the final FIFA World Cup™ match with the USA the Reggae Boyz got over their disappointment with a 12-0 thumping of Saint-Martin in the Copa Caribe followed two days later with an equally emphatic 11-1 win over the British Virgin Islands. Qualifying for the CONCACAF Gold Cup as the Digicel Caribbean Cup

INTERNATIONAL HONOURS
Qualified for the FIFA World Cup™ finals 1998   Caribbean Cup 1991 1998 2005

champions, Jamaica reached the quarter-finals after finishing third in their group, but lost to eventual winners, USA. In the Wray & Nephew Premier League, Portmore United beat defending champions Tivoli Gardens in the two-legged final by a single goal after a 1-1 draw in the first match. Tivoli Gardens reached the third round of the Champions Cup, but were knocked out of the competition by another Jamaican side, Harbour View, who made it to the quarter-finals before losing to DC United. Both junior sides won their groups in the CONCACAF tournaments, but the U-17s lost their play-off with Haiti, while the U-21s reached the final round only to finish bottom.

THE FIFA BIG COUNT OF 2000

	Male	Female		Male	Female
Registered players	10 110	600	Referees	150	19
Non registered players	40 000	2 000	Officials	4 000	200
Youth players	10 000	800	Total involved	67 879	
Total players	63 510		Number of clubs	570	
Professional players	110	0	Number of teams	882	

Jamaica Football Federation (JFF)
20 St Lucia Crescent, Kingston 5, Jamaica
Tel +1 876 9298036   Fax +1 876 9290438
jamff@hotmail.com   www.jamaicafootballfederation.com
President: BOXHILL Crenston   General Secretary: GIBSON Burchell
Vice-President: EVANS George   Treasurer: SPEID Rudolph   Media Officer: None
Men's Coach: DOWNSWELL Wendell   Women's Coach: BLAINE Vin
JFF formed: 1910   CONCACAF: 1961   FIFA: 1962
Colours: Gold, Black, Gold

GAMES PLAYED BY JAMAICA IN THE 2006 FIFA WORLD CUP™ CYCLE

2002	Opponents		Score	Venue	Comp	Scorers	Att	Referee
2-08	Grenada	W	1-0	St George's	Fr	Taylor [31]		
11-08	St Lucia	W	3-1	Vieux Fort	Fr	Dean 2 [73 83], Taylor [78]	8 000	
29-08	India	W	3-0	Watford	Fr	Anderson [34], Lawrence.A [73p], Goodison [88]		Bennett ENG
1-09	India	D	0-0	Wolverhampton	Fr		4 030	Riley ENG
16-10	Japan	D	1-1	Tokyo	Fr	Fuller [80]	55 427	Kim Young Joo LOR
30-10	Guatemala	D	1-1	Guatemala City	Fr	Taylor [61]	8 000	Alfaro SLV
9-11	Barbados	D	1-1	St George's	GCq	Hall [90]	3 000	Murray TRI
11-11	Guadeloupe	W	2-0	St George's	GCq	Johnson.J [56], Hall [58]	2 500	Brizan TRI
13-11	Grenada	W	4-1	St George's	GCq	Johnson.J 2 [8 40], Hall 2 [58 90]	3 250	Murray TRI
20-11	Nigeria	D	0-0	Lagos	Fr		35 000	Quartey GHA
2003								
12-01	Barbados	L	0-1	Bridgetown	Fr		7 500	
12-02	USA	L	1-2	Kingston	Fr	Lowe [52]	27 000	Bowen CAY
11-03	Cuba	D	0-0	Havana	Fr		10 000	
13-03	Cuba	L	0-1	Havana	Fr		15 000	Hernandez CUB
23-03	Barbados	W	2-1	Kingston	Fr	Taylor [20], Daley [78]		Bowen CAY
26-03	St Lucia	W	5-0	Kingston	GCq	Williams.A [9], Taylor [11], Chin-Sue [37], Davis.C [56], Daley [62]	22 000	Brizan TRI
28-03	Martinique	D	2-2	Kingston	GCq	Daley [83], Davis.C [90]	14 500	Brizan TRI
30-03	Haiti	W	3-0	Kingston	GCq	Johnson.J [15], Daley [58], Pierre OG [66]	7 200	Brizan TRI
2-04	Venezuela	L	0-2	Caracas	Fr		25 000	Diaz ECU
30-04	South Africa	D	0-0	Cape Town	Fr		18 000	Mususa ZIM
25-05	Nigeria	W	3-2	Kingston	Fr	Lowe [25], Johnson.J [40], Williams.A [90]	25 000	Brizan TRI
6-07	Cuba	L	1-2	Kingston	Fr	Langley [86]	8 500	Bowen CAY
9-07	Paraguay	W	2-0	Kingston	Fr	Byfield [11], Langley [28]	10 000	Bowen CAY
13-07	Colombia	L	0-1	Miami	GCr1		15 423	Stott USA
15-07	Guatemala	W	2-0	Miami	GCr1	Lowe [30], Williams.A [72p]	10 323	Pineda HON
20-07	Mexico	L	0-5	Mexico City	GCqf		10 000	Navarro CAN
7-09	Australia	L	1-2	Reading	Fr	Lisbie [22]	8 050	D'Urso ENG
12-10	Brazil	L	0-1	Leicester	Fr		32 000	Styles ENG
16-11	El Salvador	W	3-0	Kingston	Fr	Fuller [6], Lisbie [72], Burton [85]	15 000	Ramdhan TRI
2004								
18-02	Uruguay	W	2-0	Kingston	Fr	Lowe [9], Johnson.J [82]	27 000	Gordon TRI
31-03	Honduras	D	2-2	Kingston	Fr	Lowe [8], Davis.F [53]	28 000	Brizan TRI
28-04	Venezuela	W	2-1	Kingston	Fr	King [10], Williams.A [45]	10 000	Ford BRB
31-05	Nigeria	L	0-2	London	Fr			Bennett ENG
2-06	Republic of Ireland	L	0-1	London	Fr		6 155	Styles ENG
12-06	Haiti	D	1-1	Miami	WCq	King [39]	30 000	Stott USA
20-06	Haiti	W	3-0	Kingston	WCq	King 3 [4 14 31]	30 000	Sibrian SLV
18-08	USA	D	1-1	Kingston	WCq	Goodison [49]	30 000	Mattus CRC
4-09	Panama	L	1-2	Kingston	WCq	Ralph [77]	24 000	Batres GUA
8-09	El Salvador	W	3-0	San Salvador	WCq	King 2 [3 38], Hyde [40]	25 000	Alcala MEX
2-10	Guatemala	D	2-2	Fort Lauderdale	Fr	Hue [89], Jackson [90]	8 500	Vaughn USA
9-10	Panama	D	1-1	Panama City	WCq	Whitmore [75]	16 000	Pineda HON
13-10	El Salvador	D	0-0	Kingston	WCq		12 000	Quesada Cordero CRC
17-11	USA	D	1-1	Columbus	WCq	Williams.A [26]	9 088	Navarro CAN
24-11	Saint-Martin †	W	12-0	Kingston	GCq	Dean 3 [2 11 30], Hue [10], Shelton 4 [17 39 45 52], Stephenson [18], Scarlett 2 [20 85], West [54]	2 600	Brizan TRI
26-11	US Virgin Islands	W	11-1	Kingston	GCq	Shelton [8], Dean 2 [23 32], Hue 3 [35 53 56], Stephenson [40] Williams.A [50], Davis.F [64], Bennett [67], Priestly [68]	4 200	Piper TRI
28-11	Haiti	W	3-1	Kingston	GCq	Stephenson 20, Dean 22, Shelton 30	4 000	Piper TRI
12-12	St Lucia	D	1-1	Vieux Fort	GCq	Priestly [42]		Jeanvillier MTQ
19-12	St Lucia	W	2-1	Kingston	GCq	Dean [1], Hue [67]	2 500	Gutierrez CUB
2005								
20-02	Trinidad and Tobago	W	2-1	Bridgetown	GCq	Shelton [13], Williams.A [35]	5 000	Callender BRB
22-02	Barbados	W	1-0	Bridgetown	GCq	Williams.A [8]	2 100	Brizan TRI
24-02	Cuba	W	1-0	Bridgetown	GCq	Shelton [48]	3 000	Brizan TRI
20-04	Guatemala	W	1-0	Atlanta	Fr	Shelton [14]	7 000	Prus USA

GAMES PLAYED BY JAMAICA IN THE 2006 FIFA WORLD CUP™ CYCLE (CONTD)

2005	Opponents	Score		Venue	Comp	Scorers	Att	Referee
4-06	Honduras	D	0-0	Atlanta	Fr		6 500	Valenzuela USA
8-07	Guatemala	W	4-3	Carson	GCr1	Shelton 3, Fuller 5, Williams.A 46+p, Hue 57	27 000	Hall USA
10-07	South Africa	D	3-3	Los Angeles	GCr1	Hue 35, Stewart 43, Bennett 80	30 710	Stott USA
13-07	Mexico	L	0-1	Houston	GCr1		45 311	Quesada CRC
16-07	USA	L	1-3	Foxboro	GCqf	Fuller 88	22 108	Batres GUA

Fr = Friendly match • GC = CONCACAF Gold Cup • WC = FIFA World Cup™ • q = qualifier • r1 = first round group • qf = quarter-final
† Not a full international

JAMAICA NATIONAL TEAM RECORDS AND RECORD SEQUENCES

Records			Sequence records				
Victory	12-0	BVI 1994	Wins	7	2000	Clean sheets	5	Three times
Defeat	0-9	CRC 1999	Defeats	7	1967-68, 2001-02	Goals scored	19	1997
Player Caps	n/a		Undefeated	23	1997-1998	Without goal	7	2000
Player Goals	n/a		Without win	12	1975-79, 1988-90	Goals against	23	1966-1969

JAMAICA 2004-05 NATIONAL PREMIER LEAGUE

	Pl	W	D	L	F	A	Pts
Harbour View † (3)	33	22	5	6	60	33	74
Waterhouse † (2)	33	20	9	4	59	25	71
Portmore United † (3)	33	19	9	5	59	19	69
Tivoli Gardens †	33	19	11	3	67	26	68
Arnett Gardens	33	18	5	10	51	33	59
Village United	33	10	9	14	43	46	39
Rivoli United	33	10	6	17	52	40	36
Reno	33	7	11	15	27	42	32
Wadadah	33	8	8	17	39	72	32
Constant Spring	33	6	13	14	34	50	31
Arlington United	33	5	7	21	23	65	22
Invaders United	33	2	11	20	22	85	17

3/10/2004 - 12/06/2005 • Championship played over three stages • Bonus points for each stage indicated in brackets
† Qualified for the Championship play-offs

JNBS FEDERATION CUP 2004-05

Quarter-finals		Semi-finals		Final	
Portmore United	3				
Arnett Gardens	0	Portmore United	2		
Sandy Bay	2 1p	Reno	1		
Reno	2 3p			Portmore United	3
Waterhouse	3			Harbour View	1
Rivoli United	2	Waterhouse	2		
Tivoli Gardens	2	Harbour View	4	Final, 22-05-2005, Kingston	
Harbour View	3				

CHAMPIONSHIP PLAY-OFFS

Semi-finals		Final	
Portmore United	0 3	22-06-2005/27-06-2005	
Waterhouse	1 1	Portmore United	1 1
Harbour View	1 1	Tivoli Gardens	1 0
Tivoli Gardens	3 2		

RECENT LEAGUE AND CUP RECORD

	Championship				Cup		
Year	Champions	Score	Runners-up		Winners	Score	Runners-up
1997	Seba United	2-1 2-2	Arnett Gardens		Naggo's Head	1-0	Hazard United
1998	Waterhouse	0-0 2-1	Seba United		Harbour View	1-0	Waterhouse
1999	Tivoli Gardens	3-1 0-0	Harbour View		Tivoli Gardens	2-0	Violet Kickers
2000	Harbour View	0-0 2-1	Waterhouse		Hazard United	1-0	Wadadah
2001	Arnett Gardens	2-1 2-1	Waterhouse		Harbour View	3-0	Wadadah
2002	Arnett Gardens	1-1 2-1	Hazard United		Harbour View	2-1	Rivoli United
2003	Hazard United	1-1 3-2	Arnett Gardens		Hazard United	1-0	Harbour View
2004	Tivoli Gardens	4-1 1-2	Harbour View		Waterhouse	2-1	Village United
2005	Portmore United	1-1 1-0	Tivoli Gardens		Portmore United	3-1	Harbour View

Hazard United now known as Portmore United

JAMAICA COUNTRY INFORMATION

Capital	Kingston	Independence	1962 from the UK	GDP per Capita	$3 900
Population	2 713 130	Status	Commonweath	GNP Ranking	100
Area km²	10 991	Language	English	Dialling code	+1 876
Population density	247 per km²	Literacy rate	87%	Internet code	.jm
% in urban areas	54%	Main religion	Christian 61%	GMT +/−	-4
Towns/Cities ('000)	Kingston 584; Spanish Town 145; Portmore 102; Montego Bay 83; Mandeville 47				
Neighbours (km)	Caribbean Sea 1 022				
Main stadia	Independence Park – Kingston 35 000; Harbour View – Kingston 7 000				

JOR – JORDAN

NATIONAL TEAM RECORD
JULY 1ST 2002 TO JUNE 30TH 2005

PL	W	D	L	F	A	%
54	24	18	12	71	45	57.4

FIFA/COCA-COLA WORLD RANKING

1993	1994	1995	1996	1997	1998	1999	2000	2001	2002	2003	2004	High		Low	
87	113	143	146	124	126	115	105	99	77	47	40	37	08/04	152	07/96

2004-2005											
08/04	09/04	10/04	11/04	12/04	01/05	02/05	03/05	04/05	05/05	06/05	07/05
37	37	38	39	40	40	41	42	48	50	54	57

Since the arrival of the veteran Egyptian Mahmoud El Gohary as national team coach in April 2002 Jordan have taken huge strides forward in Asian football with the side no longer one of the whipping boys of the continent. The most notable achievement was a 1-0 away victory over Iran in the 2006 FIFA World Cup™ qualifiers. That success was no fluke as they also beat them at home on the way to qualifying for the AFC Asian Cup for the first time. In the finals in China the Jordanians made it to the quarter-finals and were only denied a place in the semis when they lost to Japan on penalties after a 1-1 draw. There was also a disappointing end to the FIFA World Cup™

INTERNATIONAL HONOURS
None

qualifying campaign when after having won the first three matches in their first round group they lost at home to Iran and then away to Qatar to finish in second place three points behind the Iranians. In the Jordanian League Al Wihdat from Amman went unbeaten through the 18-match campaign to win their eighth title comfortably ahead of Al Hussein but they were denied a double when they lost a JFA Cup semi-final clash with the most successful club in the country Al Faisaly. Faisaly then went on to beat Shabab Al Hussein 3-0 in the final to win the Cup for the 10th time in 13 years.

THE FIFA BIG COUNT OF 2000

	Male	Female		Male	Female
Registered players	3 675	0	Referees	88	0
Non registered players	20 000	100	Officials	5 000	50
Youth players	782	0	Total involved	29 695	
Total players	24 557		Number of clubs	84	
Professional players	13	0	Number of teams	120	

Jordan Football Associatiom (JFA)
Al-Hussein Youth City, PO Box 962024, Amman 11196, Jordan
Tel +962 6 5657662   Fax +962 6 565 7660
jfa@nets.com.jo   www.jfa.com.jo
President: HRH Prince Ali AL-HUSSEIN   General Secretary: ZURIEKAT Fadi
Vice-President: AL-HADID Nidal   Treasurer: MARAR Suheil   Media Officer: FAKHOURY Munem
Men's Coach: AL GOHARY Mahmoud   Women's Coach: None
JFA formed: 1949   AFC: 1970   FIFA: 191958
Colours: White, White, White or Red, Red, Red

GAMES PLAYED BY JORDAN IN THE 2006 FIFA WORLD CUP™ CYCLE

2002	Opponents	Score		Venue	Comp	Scorers	Att	Referee
17-08	Kenya	D	1-1	Amman	Fr	Shelbaieh [14]		
19-08	Sudan	D	0-0	Amman	Fr			
30-08	Iran	W	1-0	Damascus	WFr1	Shelbaieh [10]	1 000	Al Zaid KSA
1-09	Lebanon	W	1-0	Damascus	WFr1	Shelbaieh [4]		
5-09	Syria	W	2-1	Damascus	WFsf	Mansour [39], Al Zboun [118GG]		
7-09	Iraq	L	2-3	Damascus	WFf	Shehada [2], Deeb [30]	10 000	
7-12	Bahrain	W	3-0	Manama	Fr	Mansour [4], Qassem [60], Al Zboun [86]		Al Dosari KSA
9-12	China PR	D	0-0	Manama	Fr			Husain BHR
12-12	Syria	W	3-0	Manama	Fr	Al Zboun [12], Halasa [51], Mansour [56]		Al Dosari KSA
16-12	Palestine	D	1-1	Kuwait City	ARr1	Aqel [11]		
18-12	Morocco	D	1-1	Kuwait City	ARr1	Abu Zema [64p]	1 500	Al Zaid KSA
20-12	Sudan	W	2-1	Kuwait City	ARr1	Mansour [17], Abu Zema [82p]	2 000	Abbas SYR
23-12	Kuwait	W	2-1	Kuwait City	ARr1	Al Zboun 2 [69 83]	6 000	Guirat TUN
28-12	Bahrain	L	1-2	Kuwait City	ARsf	Al Zboun [43]	2 000	Hamza KUW
2003								
26-08	Iraq	W	2-1	Amman	Fr	Abu Zema [21p], Mansour [83]		Al Dosari KSA
5-09	Iran	L	1-4	Tehran	ACq	Mansour [3]	57 000	Ebrahim BHR
19-09	Syria	D	0-0	Amman	Fr			
26-09	Iran	W	3-2	Amman	ACq	Mansour [40], Shelbaieh [45], Al Shagran [80]		Shaban KUW
8-10	Oman	L	1-2	Muscat	Fr	Mansour [40]		
17-10	Lebanon	W	1-0	Amman	ACq	Aqel [85p]		
12-11	Lebanon	W	2-0	Beirut	ACq	Al Sheikh [37], Al Shagran [65]		
18-11	Korea DPR	W	3-0	Amman	ACq	Shelbaieh [7], Al Shboul [89], Al Zboun [90]		
28-11	Korea DPR	W	3-0	Pyongyang	ACq	Awarded 3-0. Jordan refused entry into Korea DPR		
2004								
12-02	Indonesia	W	2-1	Amman	Fr	Al Sheikh [39], Mansour [45]		
18-02	Laos	W	5-0	Amman	WCq	Aqel [40], Shelbaieh [45], Al Shagran [63], Ragheb [90], Shehdeh [90]	5 000	Al Mozahmi OMA
21-03	Bahrain	D	0-0	Al Muharraq	Fr			
23-03	Bahrain	W	2-0	Al Muharraq	Fr	Al Zboun, Al Shboul		
31-03	Qatar	W	1-0	Amman	WCq	Mansour [70]	15 000	Shaban KUW
28-04	Nigeria	L	0-2	Lagos	Fr			
30-04	Libya	L	0-1	Lagos	Fr			
19-05	Cyprus	D	0-0	Nicosia	Fr		2 500	Loizou CYP
30-05	Algeria	D	1-1	Annaba	Fr	Shelbaieh [18]	20 000	Zahmoul TUN
9-06	Iran	W	1-0	Tehran	WCq	Al Shboul [83]	35 000	Kamikawa JPN
17-06	Palestine	D	1-1	Tehran	WFr1	Al Shboul [3]		
21-06	Iraq	W	2-0	Tehran	WFr1	Mansour [48], Shelbaieh [79]		
23-06	Syria	D	1-1	Tehran	WFsf	Deeb [21]. L 2-3p		
25-06	Iraq	W	3-1	Tehran	WF3p	Al Shagran 2 [27 47], Abu Alieh [76]		
8-07	Thailand	D	0-0	Bangkok	Fr			
19-07	Korea Rep	D	0-0	Jinan	ACr1		26 000	Maidin SIN
23-07	Kuwait	W	2-0	Jinan	ACr1	Sa'ed [90], Al Zboun [90]	28 000	Lu Jun CHN
27-07	United Arab Emirates	D	0-0	Beijing	ACr1		25 000	Talaat LIB
31-07	Japan	D	1-1	Chongqing	ACqf	Shelbaieh [11]. L 3-4p	52 000	Salleh MAS
18-08	Azerbaijan	D	1-1	Amman	Fr	Aqel [21]	4 000	
31-08	Lebanon	D	2-2	Amman	Fr	Shelbaieh, Al Zboun		
8-09	Iran	L	0-2	Amman	WCq		20 000	Lu Jun CHN
8-10	Thailand	W	3-2	Bangkok	Fr	Al Maharmeh 2, Shehdeh		
13-10	Laos	W	3-2	Vientiane	WCq	Al Maharmeh [28], Al Shagran 2 [73 76]	3 000	Gosh BAN
20-10	Ecuador	W	3-0	Tripoli	Fr	Al Maltah [45], Shelbaieh [53], Suleiman [69]		
22-10	Libya	L	0-1	Tripoli	Fr			Bennaceur TUN
11-11	United Arab Emirates	L	0-1	Abu Dhabi	Fr			
17-11	Qatar	L	0-2	Doha	WCq		800	Yoshida JPN
2005								
28-01	Norway	D	0-0	Amman	Fr		8 000	Al Shoufi SYR
26-03	Cyprus	L	1-2	Larnaca	Fr	Ahmet [85]		
8-06	Iraq	L	0-1	Amman	Fr			

Fr = Friendly match • WF = West Asian Federation Championship • AR = Arab Cup • AC = AFC Asian Cup • WC = FIFA World Cup™
q = qualifier • r1 = first round group • qf = quarter-final • sf = semi-final • 3p = third place play-off • f = final

JORDAN COUNTRY INFORMATION

Capital	Amman	Independence	1946 from the UK	GDP per Capita	$4 300
Population	5 611 202	Status	Kingdom	GNP Ranking	90
Area km²	92 300	Language	Arabic	Dialling code	+962
Population density	61	Literacy rate	91.3%	Internet code	.jo
% in urban areas	71%	Main religion	Muslim 92%, Christian 6%	GMT + / –	+2
Towns/Cities ('000)	Amman 2 201; Irbid 1 027; Al Zarqa 915; Al Balqa 378; Al Mafraq 273; Al Karak 231				
Neighbours (km)	Syria 375; Iraq 181; Saudi Arabia 744; Israel 238; West Bank 97				
Main stadia	Al-Qwaismeh (King Abdullah International) – Amman 18 000				

FIFA REFEREE LIST 2005

	Int'l	DoB
ABU KHADIJEH Ahmad	1996	1-02-1963
ABU LOUM Mohammad	2005	28-10-1973
AL-GHAFARY Naser		1-01-1968
AL-HAFI Ismail		25-05-1965
ATARI Adham	2005	1-07-1965
HAMD Mutasem	2005	24-06-1967
MARSHOUD Hassan	1997	9-05-1963
MUJGHEF Salem	1999	1-10-1963
SHAHIN Yousef	1997	17-03-1964

FIFA ASSISTANT REFEREE LIST 2005

	Int'l	DoB
ABDEL QADER Arafat	2005	12-08-1971
ABU GHANAM Sameer	2005	7-07-1971
ARABATI Fathi	1994	5-02-1964
DIWAN Osama		20-11-1962
EYADAT Abdel-Karim	1999	25-01-1961
HASSOUNEH Awni	1994	9-01-1964
HAWWARI Deeb		18-01-1968
NAIMAT Fawwaz		25-07-1971
SALEH Mohammed		20-04-1966
SHWAIR Faisal	2005	13-12-1971

JORDAN NATIONAL TEAM RECORDS AND RECORD SEQUENCES

Records			Sequence records					
Victory	6-0	TPE 2001	Wins	5	1992	Clean sheets	4	1988, 2004
Defeat	0-6	SYR, ALG, CHN	Defeats	6	Three times	Goals scored	9	1992
Player Caps	n/a		Undefeated	14	2004	Without goal	7	1996-1997
Player Goals	n/a		Without win	13	1957-1966	Goals against	13	1992-1993

JORDAN 2004-05 FIRST DIVISION

	Pl	W	D	L	F	A	Pts
Al Wihdat	18	16	2	0	41	8	50
Al Hussein	18	11	3	4	48	27	36
Al Faisaly	18	10	1	7	31	19	31
Shabab Al Ordon	18	8	5	5	40	27	29
Al Buq'aa	18	8	4	6	25	18	28
Shabab Al Hussein	18	6	1	11	25	33	19
Kfarsoum	18	5	4	9	21	34	19
Al Ramtha	18	5	3	10	26	38	18
Al Ahli	18	4	5	9	12	28	17
That Ras	18	1	4	13	19	56	7

26/11/2004 - 26/05/2005

JFA CUP 2004-05

Quarter-finals		Semi-finals		Final	
Al Faisaly	2				
Al Ramtha	1	Al Faisaly	1		
Al Buq'aa	0 4p	Al Wihdat	0		
Al Wihdat	0 3p			Al Faisaly	3
Al Hussein	4 3p			Shabab Al Hussein	0
Al Arabi	4 0p	Al Hussein	0		
Shabab Al Ordon	0	Shabab Al Hussein	2	3-06-2005, Amman	
Shabab Al Hussein	2				

RECENT LEAGUE AND CUP RECORD

	Championship						Cup		
Year	Champions	Pts	Runners-up	Pts	Third	Pts	Winners	Score	Runners-up
1996	Al Wihdat	48	Al Ramtha	43	Al Faisaly	42	Al Wihdat	0-0 3-1p	Al Ramtha
1997	Al Wihdat	41	Al Faisaly	41	Al Ramtha	29	Al Wihdat	2-1	Al Ramtha
1997	Al Wihdat	47	Al Faisaly	46	Al Hussein	30	No tournament due to season readjustment		
1998	Al Wihdat	34	Al Faisaly	33	Al Ramtha	19	Al Faisaly	2-1	Al Wihdat
1999	Al Faisaly	57	Al Wihdat	49	Al Ramtha	48	Al Faisaly	0-0 5-4p	Al Wihdat
2000	Al Faisaly	52	Al Wihdat	44	Al Ahly	34	Al Wihdat	2-0	Al Faisaly
2001	Al Faisaly	48	Al Wihdat	44	Al Hussein	31	Al Faisaly	2-0	Al Hussein
2002	No championship due to season readjustment						No tournament due to season readjustment		
2003	Al Faisaly	48	Al Wihdat	45	Al Hussein	35	Al Faisaly	2-0	Al Hussein
2004	Al Faisaly	9	Al Hussein	4	Al Wihdat	4	Al Faisaly	3-1	Al Hussein
2005	Al Wihdat	50	Al Hussein	36	Al Faisaly	31	Al Faisaly	3-0	Shabab Al Hussein

In the 1997 play-off Al Wahdat beat Al Faisaly 4-2 on penalties following a 1-1 draw after the two clubs finished level on points

JPN – JAPAN

NATIONAL TEAM RECORD
JULY 1ST 2002 TO JUNE 30TH 2005

PL	W	D	L	F	A	%
52	29	10	13	82	43	65.4

FIFA/COCA-COLA WORLD RANKING

1993	1994	1995	1996	1997	1998	1999	2000	2001	2002	2003	2004	High		Low	
43	36	31	21	14	20	57	38	34	22	29	17	9	02/98	62	02/00

2004-2005											
08/04	09/04	10/04	11/04	12/04	01/05	02/05	03/05	04/05	05/05	06/05	07/05
20	18	19	17	17	19	18	18	17	17	18	13

Japan's recent record is impressive. In August 2004 the national team beat China PR 3-1 in Beijing to become Asian Champions for the third time; in June 2005 they were one of the first nations to qualify for the FIFA World Cup™ finals in Germany; and then at the end of the month the team did well in the FIFA Confederations Cup, only losing out on a place in the semi-finals to eventual winners Brazil on goal difference. And yet sections of the press in Japan remain critical of coach Zico and the prospects for success in Germany. With a FIFA/Coca-Cola World Ranking of 13 in July 2005 the Japanese can start regarding themselves as major players in world football but will

INTERNATIONAL HONOURS
Qualified for the FIFA World Cup™ 1998 2002 Qualified for the FIFA Women's World Cup 1991 1995 1999 20035
Asian Cup 1992 2000 2004 AFC U-16 Championship 1994 AFC Champions League Furukawa 1987, Jubilo Iwata 1999

need to prove it on a regular basis in tournaments like the FIFA World Cup™. The J.League has provided solid foundations for the improvement over the past decade and after being regarded with scepticism by some it is now firmly established and thriving with attendances continuing to rise. The 2004 Championship saw stage winners Yokohama F. Marinos and Urawa Reds meet in a play-off which was won by Marinos on penalties after both won their home legs 1-0. In a major change for 2005 the J.League will be played on a single league format instead of over two stages.

THE FIFA BIG COUNT OF 2000

	Male	Female		Male	Female
Registered players	190 206	10 357	Referees	100 545	0
Non registered players	2 500 000	0	Officials	90 346	4 970
Youth players	612 152	9 673	Total involved	3 518 249	
Total players	3 322 388		Number of clubs	700	
Professional players	1 120	0	Number of teams	28 455	

Japan Football Association (JFA)
JFA House, Football Ave., Bunkyo-ku, Tokyo 113-8311, Japan
Tel +81 3 38302004   Fax +81 3 38302005
www.jfa.or.jp/e/index.html
President: KAWABUCHI Saburo   General Secretary: HIRATA Takeo
Vice-President: OGURA Jinji   Treasurer: SAITO Koji   Media Officer: TESHIMA Hideto
Men's Coach: ZICO   Women's Coach: OHASHI Hiroshi
JFA formed: 1921   AFC: 1954   FIFA: 1929-46 & 1950
Colours: Blue, White, Blue

GAMES PLAYED BY JAPAN IN THE 2006 FIFA WORLD CUP™ CYCLE

2002 Opponents	Score	Venue	Comp	Scorers	Att	Referee
16-10 Jamaica	D 1-1	Tokyo	Fr	Ono [7]	55 427	Kim Young Joo KOR
20-11 Argentina	L 0-2	Saitama	Fr		61 816	Mane KUW
2003						
28-03 Uruguay	D 2-2	Tokyo	Fr	Nakamura [23p], Inamoto [57]	54 039	Kim Tae Young KOR
16-04 Korea Republic	W 1-0	Seoul	Fr	Nagai [90]	64 000	Kumbalingham SIN
31-05 Korea Republic	L 0-1	Tokyo	Fr		53 405	Mohd Salleh MAS
8-06 Argentina	L 1-4	Osaka	KC	Akita [55]	42 508	Fandel GER
11-06 Paraguay	D 0-0	Saitama	KC		59 891	Riley ENG
18-06 New Zealand	W 3-0	Paris	CCr1	Nakamura 2 [12 75], Nakata.H [65]	36 038	Codjia BEN
20-06 France	L 1-2	Saint-Etienne	CCr1	Nakamura [59]	33 070	Shield AUS
22-06 Colombia	L 0-1	Saint-Etienne	CCr1		24 541	Larrionda URU
20-08 Nigeria	W 3-0	Tokyo	Fr	Takahara 2 [1 39], Endo [72]	54 860	Kim Tae Young KOR
10-09 Senegal	L 0-1	Niigata	Fr		40 000	Moradi IRN
8-10 Tunisia	W 1-0	Tunis	Fr	Yanagisawa [39]		Berber ALG
11-10 Romania	D 1-1	Bucharest	Fr	Yanagisawa [58]	10 000	Carmona Mendez ESP
19-11 Cameroon	D 0-0	Oita	Fr		38 627	Lu Jun CHN
4-12 China PR	W 2-0	Tokyo	EAF	Kubo 2 [4 80]	41 742	Nagalingam SIN
7-12 Hong Kong	W 1-0	Saitama	EAF	Alex [37p]	45 145	Piromya THA
10-12 Korea Republic	D 0-0	Yokohama	EAF		62 633	Nagalingam SIN
2004						
7-02 Malaysia	W 4-0	Ibaraki	Fr	Ogasawara [10], Miyamoto [37], Yamada.N [45], Endo [46]	29 530	Moradi IRN
12-02 Iraq	W 2-0	Tokyo	Fr	Yanagisawa [47], Alex [84]	38 622	Kwon Jong Chul KOR
18-02 Oman	W 1-0	Saitama	WCq	Kubo [92+]	60 270	Abdul Hamid MAS
31-03 Singapore	W 2-1	Singapore	WCq	Takahara [33], Fujita [81]	6 000	Bae Jae Yong KOR
25-04 Hungary	L 2-3	Zalaegerszeg	Fr	Tamada [75], Kubo [78]	7 000	Trivkovic CRO
28-04 Czech Republic	W 1-0	Prague	Fr	Kubo [33]	11 802	McKeon IRL
30-05 Iceland	W 3-2	Manchester	Fr	Kubo 2 [21 36], Alex [57p]	1 500	Riley ENG
1-06 England	D 1-1	Manchester	Fr	Ono [52]	38 581	Rosetti ITA
9-06 India	W 7-0	Saitama	WCq	Kubo [12], Fukunishi [25], Nakamura [29], Suzuki.T [54], Nakazawa 2 [65 76], Ogasawara [68]	63 000	Huang CHN
9-07 Slovakia	W 3-1	Hiroshima	KC	Fukunishi [44], Suzuki.T [66], Yanagisawa [81]	34 458	Breeze AUS
13-07 Serbia & Montenegro	W 1-0	Yokohama	KC	Endo [49]	57 616	Lennie AUS
20-07 Oman	W 1-0	Chongqing	ACr1	Nakamura [34]	35 000	Shield AUS
24-07 Thailand	W 4-1	Chongqing	ACr1	Nakamura [21], Nakazawa 2 [56 87], Fukunishi [68]	45 000	Al Marzouqi UAE
28-07 Iran	D 0-0	Chongqing	ACr1		52 000	Shield AUS
31-07 Jordan	D 1-1	Chongqing	ACqf	Suzuki.T [14], W 4-3p	52 000	Mohd Salleh MAS
3-08 Bahrain	W 4-3	Jinan	ACsf	Nakata.K [48], Tamada 2 [55 93], Nakazawa [90]	32 050	Maidin SIN
7-08 China PR	W 3-1	Beijing	ACf	Fukunishi [22], Nakata.K [65], Tamada [90]	62 000	Al Fadhli KUW
18-08 Argentina	L 1-2	Shizuoka	Fr	Suzuki.T [72]	45 000	Lu Jun CHN
8-09 India	W 4-0	Calcutta	WCq	Suzuki.T [45], Ono [60], Fukunishi [71], Miyamoto [87]	90 000	Hajjar SYR
13-10 Oman	W 1-0	Muscat	WCq	Suzuki.T [52]	35 000	Lu Jun CHN
17-11 Singapore	W 1-0	Saitama	WCq	Tamada [13]	58 881	Torky IRN
16-12 Germany	L 0-3	Yokohama	Fr		61 805	Shield AUS
2005						
29-01 Kazakhstan	W 4-0	Yokohama	Fr	Tamada 2 [5 60], Matsuda [11], Alex [24]	46 941	
2-02 Syria	W 3-0	Saitama	Fr	Suzuki.T [44], Miyamoto [70], Ogasawara [90]	30 000	
9-02 Korea DPR	W 2-1	Saitama	WCq	Ogasawara [4], Oguro [92+]	60 000	Al Ghamdi KSA
25-03 Iran	L 1-2	Tehran	WCq	Fukunishi [33]	110 000	Maidin SIN
30-03 Bahrain	W 1-0	Saitama	WCq	Salmeen OG [71]	67 549	Irmatov UZB
22-05 Peru	L 0-1	Niigata	KC		39 856	Michel SVK
27-05 United Arab Emirates	L 0-1	Tokyo	KC		53 123	Michel SVK
3-06 Bahrain	W 1-0	Manama	WCq	Ogasawara [34]	32 000	Mohd Salleh MAS
8-06 Korea DPR	W 2-0	Manama	WCq	Yanagisawa [67], Oguro [89]	BCD	De Bleeckere BEL
16-06 Mexico	L 1-2	Hanover	CCr1	Yanagisawa [12]	24 036	Breeze AUS
19-06 Greece	W 1-0	Frankfurt	CCr1	Oguro [76]	34 314	Fandel GER
22-06 Brazil	D 2-2	Cologne	CCr1	Nakamura [27], Oguro [88]	44 922	Daami TUN

Fr = Friendly match • KC = Kirin Cup • CC = FIFA Confederations Cup • EAF - East Asian Federation Cup • AC = AFC Asian Cup • WC = FIFA World Cup™
q = qualifier • r1 = first round group • qf = quarter-final • sf = semi-final • f = final • BCD = behind closed doors

JAPAN NATIONAL TEAM RECORDS AND RECORD SEQUENCES

Records			Sequence records				
Victory	15-0	PHI 1966	Wins	8	Four times	Clean sheets	7	2003-2004
Defeat	2-15	PHI 1917	Defeats	9	1917-1927	Goals scored	14	1966-1968
Player Caps	123	IHARA Masami	Undefeated	12	2000, 2004	Without goal	6	1988, 1989-1990
Player Goals	56	MIURA Kazuyoshi	Without win	11	1976-1977	Goals against	31	1960-1966

NATIONAL CAPS

	Caps
IHARA Masami	123
MIURA Kazuyoshi	91
KAWAGUCHI Yoshikatsu	76
HASHIRATANI Tetsuji	71
NANAMI Hiroshi	68
NAKATA Hidetoshi	67
MORISHIMA Hiroaki	65
TSUNAMI Satoshi	64
KAMAMOTO Kunishige	61

NATIONAL GOALS

	Goals
MIURA Kazuyoshi	56
KAMAMOTO Kunishige	55
TAKAGI Takuya	28
HARA Hiromi	24
NAKAYAMA Masashi	21
YANAGISAWA Atsushi	15
KIMURA Kazushi	15
MIYAMOTO Teruki	14
NAKAMURA Shunsuke	14

NATIONAL COACH

	Years
KAWABUCHI Saburo	1980
MORI Takaji	1981-'86
ISHII Yoshinobu	1986-'87
YOKOYAMA Kenzo	1988-'92
OOFT Hans	1992-'93
FALCAO Roberto	1993-'94
KAMO Shu	1995-'97
OKADA Takeshi	1997-'98
TROUSSIER Philippe	1998-'02
ZICO	2002-

FIFA REFEREE LIST 2005

	Int'l	DoB
IEMOTO Masaaki	2005	2-06-1973
KAMIKAWA Toru	1998	8-06-1963
KASHIHARA Joji	2002	19-04-1963
MATSUMURA Kazuhiko	1999	17-07-1963
MATSUO Hajime	2005	26-09-1972
NISHIMURA Yuichi	2004	17-04-1972
SHIOKAWA Takuji	2004	24-05-1965
TAKAYAMA Hiroyoshi	2004	18-03-1974
YAMANISHI Hirofumi	2002	22-06-1963
YOSHIDA Toshimitsu	2000	29-08-1963

FIFA ASSISTANT REFEREE LIST 2005

	Int'l	DoB
AJIKI Hiroyuki	2004	17-04-1964
HIROSHIMA Yoshikazu	1994	22-05-1962
MIYAJIMA Kazushiro	2005	17-12-1967
NAGI Toshiyuki	2003	29-11-1971
NAKAI Hisashi	2005	3-12-1968
SHIBATA Masatoshi	2000	9-07-1961
TAKAHASHI Yoshihisa	2004	11-04-1964
TEZUKA Hiroshi	2002	8-06-1965
YAMAGUCHI Hiroshi	2003	5-01-1966
YAMAZAKI Yasuhiko	2004	24-06-1964

JAPAN COUNTRY INFORMATION

Capital	Tokyo	Formation	1600	GDP per Capita	$28 200
Population	127 333 002	Status	Constitutional Monarchy	GNP Ranking	2
Area km²	377 835	Language	Japanese	Dialling code	+81
Population density	337 per km²	Literacy rate	99%	Internet code	.jp
% in urban areas	78%	Main religion	Shinto & Buddhist 84%	GMT + / –	+9
Towns/Cities ('000)	Tokyo 8 336; Yokohama 3 574; Osaka 2 592; Nagoya 2 191; Sapporo 1 883; Kobe 1 528; Kyoto 1 459; Fukuoka 1 392; Kawasaki 1 306; Hiroshima 1 143; Saitama 1 077; Sendai 1 037; Kitakyushu 997; Chiba 919; Sakai 782; Kunamoto 680; Sagamihara 648; Okayama 639				
Neighbours (km)	Pacific Ocean and the Sea of Japan 29 751				
Main stadia	Yokohama International – Yokohama 72 370; Olympic Stadium – Tokyo 57 363				

JAPAN 2004

J.LEAGUE DIVISION 1 - FIRST STAGE

	Pl	W	D	L	F	A	Pts	Marinos	Jubilo	Urawa	Gamba	Antlers	FC Tokyo	JEF Uited	Nagoya	Verdy	Trinita	S-Pulse	Vissel	Sanfrecce	Albirex	Kashiwa	Cerezo
Yokohama F.Marinos ‡	15	11	3	1	26	13	36		1-1	2-1	1-0			2-1	3-1		1-1		2-0				2-1
Jubilo Iwata	15	11	1	3	31	16	34	1-2		3-1			2-0	3-2	2-0	2-1				2-2	4-2		
Urawa Reds	15	7	4	4	30	24	25					1-0	2-1	3-3				4-1		2-1		1-1	4-2
Gamba Osaka	15	7	3	5	31	23	24			0-2		3-2			2-2	0-2		4-0	6-3	1-0			
Kashima Antlers	15	7	3	5	18	14	24	1-0			1-1			0-0	3-2	3-0					2-2		
FC Tokyo	15	6	5	4	19	19	23	0-2			2-1				3-2	3-2				1-1	1-0	2-1	1-1
JEF United Ichihara	15	5	7	3	28	23	22	3-0			2-1	2-2			1-1			1-1			2-1	1-1	1-1
Nagoya Grampus Eight	15	5	5	5	24	22	20			1-3	3-0						1-2	2-1	2-2	2-2		1-1	1-0
Tokyo Verdy 1969	15	5	4	6	21	23	19			1-3	2-2	3-0	2-1					3-1				0-0	0-1
Oita Trinita	15	5	2	8	21	27	17	1-1				4-3		2-1	2-3					2-1	0-1		3-0
Shimizu S-Pulse	15	3	7	5	20	27	16			1-0	4-3					1-2	0-0		3-1	1-2			1-2
Vissel Kobe	15	3	6	6	21	25	15	0-2								1-2	1-1	0-0		5-1		2-0	2-2
Sanfrecce Hiroshima	15	3	6	6	15	19	15					0-0		0-2	1-3	1-1		1-1	2-0			1-1	3-0
Albirex Niigata	15	3	5	7	16	25	14	1-3	1-2	0-3	1-4							0-1	3-3	0-0			
Kashiwa Reysol	15	3	3	9	14	22	12	1-2	1-3							0-2	0-1	2-1		0-0			1-2
Cerezo Osaka	15	2	4	9	17	30	10	1-2			0-1	1-1					1-2	2-2		1-2	1-2	1-5	

13/03/2004 - 26/06/2004 • ‡ Qualified for the Championship play-off

JAPAN 2004

J.LEAGUE DIVISION 1 - SECOND STAGE

	Pl	W	D	L	F	A	Pts	Urawa	JEF United	Gamba	Antlers	Nagoya	Marinos	Albirex	Vissel	Verdy	FC Tokyo	Sanfrecce	Cerezo	Jubilo	S-Pulse	Kashiwa	Trinita
Urawa Reds ‡	15	12	1	2	40	15	37				2-1	1-2	0-0	4-1		7-2		1-0			3-2	2-1	
JEF United Ichihara	15	8	4	3	27	22	28	0-4			2-2				5-1	2-1			2-1	2-1			2-0
Gamba Osaka	15	8	3	4	38	25	27				2-1		0-2	6-3			1-3	1-2		7-1		5-1	3-1
Kashima Antlers	15	7	3	5	23	17	24	2-3	0-1					3-1			1-0	0-0	4-3		0-0	1-0	
Nagoya Grampus Eight	15	7	3	5	25	21	24		0-2	1-2	0-2				2-1				1-1	2-1	5-2		
Yokohama F.Marinos †	15	6	5	4	21	17	23	2-1						1-2	2-2		2-1			3-0		0-1	2-1
Albirex Niigata	15	7	2	6	31	33	23	3-3				1-0	0-0				4-2	3-2	1-2			1-3	3-0
Vissel Kobe	15	6	3	6	29	30	21	2-3			3-3	2-1	2-1			3-4			2-2			1-2	
Tokyo Verdy 1969	15	6	2	7	22	23	20				3-1	0-0	2-0		0-1				1-1		1-2	4-0	
FC Tokyo	15	4	6	5	21	22	18	1-0	3-3			0-1						3-1		0-0	1-2		1-1
Sanfrecce Hiroshima	15	3	7	5	23	28	16	2-2			2-2								3-0	1-1	3-2		0-0
Cerezo Osaka	15	4	4	7	25	34	16	0-2	3-0			1-1	1-2					4-3		2-1			1-2
Jubilo Iwata †	15	3	5	7	23	28	14				1-2	4-4	1-2		3-1			2-2			1-2	1-1	
Shimizu S-Pulse	15	4	1	10	17	26	13	1-2	0-1			1-2	1-2	2-4	1-3				3-0			2-1	
Kashiwa Reysol	15	2	7	6	15	27	13	0-4	0-0				2-2	0-3				0-2		1-1	2-1		
Oita Trinita	15	3	4	8	14	29	13	1-4		0-3	0-4			2-0	2-3			1-1	1-0	2-2			

14/08/2004 - 28/11/2004 • ‡ Qualified for the Championship play-off • † Qualified for the AFC Champions League • Due to the expansion of the J.League to 18 teams for 2005 there was no automatic relegation • The team with the worst overall record, Kashiwa Reysol, beat Avispa Fukuoka in a play-off (2-0, 2-0)

J.LEAGUE PLAY-OFF

First leg, Yokohama International, 5-12-2004, 64 899

Yokohama F.Marinos 1 Kawai 66
Urawa Reds 0

Marinos - Enomoto; Nakazawa, Matsuda, Kawai, Tanaka.H, Ueno, Nakanishi, Dutra, Oku; Shimizu (Yamazaki 89), Sakata. Tr: Okada
Urawa - Yamagishi; Alpay, Tanaka.M, Uchidate (Hirakawa 45); Yamada, Hasebe, Santos, Suzuki; Tanaka.T (Okano 75), Nagai, Emerson. Tr: Buchwald

J.LEAGUE PLAY-OFF

Second leg, Saitama Stadium 2002, 11-12-2004, 59 715

Urawa Reds 1 2p Santos 76
Yokohama F.Marinos 0 4p

Urawa - Yamagishi; Alpay, Tanaka.M, Nene; Yamada, Hasebe, Suzuki, Hirakawa (Tanaka.T 63); Nagai, Santos, Emerson. Tr: Buchwald
Marinos - Enomoto; Nakazawa, Matsuda, Kawai, Tanaka.H, Ueno, Nakanishi, Dutra, Oku; Shimizu (Yamazaki 82), Sakata. Tr: Okada

TOP SCORERS

EMERSON	Urawa Reds	27
OGURO Masashi	Gamba Osaka	20
BANDO Ryuji	Vissel Kobe	17
MARQUES	Nagoya	17
GRAL	Jubilo Iwata	16

JAPAN 2004

J.LEAGUE DIVISION 2

	Pl	W	D	L	F	A	Pts	Kawasaki	Ardija	Avispa	Montedio	Kyoto	Vegalta	Ventforet	Yokohama	Mito	Shonan	Sagan	Consadole
Kawasaki Frontale	44	34	3	7	104	38	105		1-0 0-3	1-0 3-1	2-0 1-2	1-0 3-1	4-1 2-1	2-0 4-2	2-0 4-0	5-2 5-1	5-0 2-1	3-2 5-0	6-0 2-0
Omiya Ardija	44	26	9	9	63	38	87	1-2 2-1		2-2 2-0	1-1 1-1	0-1 0-2	3-1 2-2	1-1 0-1	1-1 1-2	1-3 1-2	0-1 0-1	0-1 0-0	0-1 1-1
Avispa Fukuoka	44	23	7	14	56	41	76	0-1 2-1	2-1 0-3		1-1 0-1	0-0 1-3	2-3 1-0	1-1 1-0	0-0 1-2	1-0 2-0	3-1 2-0	3-2 2-1	0-1 1-0
Montedio Yamagata	44	19	14	11	58	51	71	2-1 1-1	1-3 1-3	0-0 1-3		1-3 1-2	0-0 2-2	1-0 3-0	1-2 0-2	2-3 2-0	2-1 1-1	1-2 2-1	1-1 1-0
Kyoto Purple Sanga	44	19	12	13	65	53	69	1-3 2-6	3-2 1-1	4-2 1-3	0-0 1-0		1-2 2-1	0-2 1-0	2-2 1-1	0-0 0-0	1-1 1-2	0-0 3-1	2-0 4-2
Vegalta Sendai	44	15	14	15	62	66	59	2-1 2-2	2-1 0-1	0-0 1-2	1-2 0-0	5-4 3-0		1-2 3-1	1-0 1-1	4-1 1-1	2-0 4-1	3-1 2-1	1-1 1-1
Ventforet Kofu	44	15	13	16	51	46	58	1-2 0-0	1-2 3-0	1-0 2-0	2-3 2-1	1-2 2-2	1-2 2-1		6-1 0-1	4-0 1-1	0-1 1-0	1-1 1-0	2-1 0-0
Yokohama FC	44	10	22	12	42	50	52	0-2 2-5	0-1 0-1	1-0 0-1	1-1 0-0	0-0 1-1	4-0 0-0	0-0 0-1		1-1 0-1	1-0 3-2	3-0 3-2	2-1 1-1
Mito Hollyhock	44	6	19	19	33	60	37	0-1 1-2	2-0 1-1	0-0 0-0	1-2 2-2	0-1 1-2	0-0 1-2	0-0 1-0	2-2 1-1		0-0 0-0	1-1 1-2	1-1 1-1
Shonan Bellmare	44	7	15	22	39	64	36	0-1 0-1	1-0 2-3	1-3 0-1	1-4 2-1	2-2 0-2	3-2 2-2	1-2 1-1	1-1 1-0	0-0 1-2		2-2 3-0	1-1 1-1
Sagan Tosu	44	8	11	25	32	66	35	1-0 0-3	0-0 0-1	0-3 1-0	0-2 0-2	0-2 3-0	1-2 2-1	0-0 1-1	0-1 1-0	2-0 0-0	0-0 2-0		2-1 0-1
Consadole Sapporo	44	5	15	24	30	62	30	0-2 1-3	1-2 0-1	1-2 0-1	2-0 1-1	2-0 0-1	0-1 0-2	2-0 2-1	1-0 0-1	2-2 1-1	1-0 0-1	2-1 1-1	

13/03/2004 - 27/11/2004 • No relegation due to the expansion of J.League Division 1

JAPAN 2004 — JAPAN FOOTBALL LEAGUE (3)

	Pl	W	D	L	F	A	Pts
Otsuka FC	30	25	3	2	74	20	78
Honda FC	30	19	5	6	64	36	62
Thespa Kusatsu	30	19	5	6	63	35	62
YKK AP	30	15	5	10	56	33	50
Ehime FC	30	14	7	9	53	42	49
Sony Sendai	30	13	8	9	50	42	47
Sagawa Tokyo	30	13	5	12	43	39	44
Gunma FC Horikoshi	30	11	8	11	48	47	41
Tochigi SC	30	11	7	12	41	47	40
Alo's Hokuriku	30	10	7	13	46	52	37
Sagawa Osaka	30	9	8	13	38	40	35
Sagawa Printing	30	10	4	16	30	45	34
Yokogawa Musashino	30	8	8	14	41	51	32
SC Tottori	30	5	7	18	36	62	22
Kokushikan University	30	5	5	20	37	73	20
Denso	30	4	6	20	29	85	18

28/03/2004 - 5/12/2004

J.LEAGUE CUP 2004

Quarter-finals		Semi-finals		Final	
FC Tokyo	4				
Gamba Osaka	1	**FC Tokyo**	4		
Shimizu S-Pulse	1	Tokyo Verdy 1969	3		
Tokyo Verdy 1969	2			**FC Tokyo**	0 4p
Nagoya Grampus	2			Urawa Reds	0 2p
Kashima Antlers	1	Nagoya Grampus	1		
Yokohama F.M	2	**Urawa Reds**	4	3-11-2005	
Urawa Reds	3			National Stadium, Tokyo	

RECENT LEAGUE AND CUP RECORD

	Championship				Emperor's Cup		
Year	**Champions**	**Score**	**Runners-up**		**Winners**	**Score**	**Runners-up**
1990	Nissan	‡	Yomiuri Nippon		Matsushita	0-0 4-3p	Nissan
1991	Yomiuri Nippon	‡	Nissan		Nissan	4-1	Yomiuri Nippon
1992	Yomiuri Nippon	‡	Nissan		Yokohama Marinos	2-1	Verdy Kawasaki
1993	Verdy Kawasaki	2-0 0-0	Kashima Antlers		Yokohama Flugels	6-2	Kashima Antlers
1994	Verdy Kawasaki	1-0 1-0	Sanfrecce Hiroshima		Bellmare Hiratsuka	2-0	Cerezo Osaka
1995	Yokohama Marinos	1-0 1-0	Verdy Kawasaki		Nagoya Grampus Eight	3-0	Sanfrecce Hiroshima
1996	Kashima Antlers	‡	Nagoya Grampus Eight		Verdy Kawasaki	3-0	Sanfrecce Hiroshima
1997	Jubilo Iwata	3-2 1-0	Kashima Antlers		Kashima Antlers	3-0	Yokohama Flugels
1998	Kashima Antlers	2-1 2-1	Jubilo Iwata		Yokohama Flugels	2-1	Shimizu S-Pulse
1999	Jubilo Iwata	2-1 1-2 4-2p	Shimizu S-Pulse		Nagoya Grampus Eight	2-0	Sanfrecce Hiroshima
2000	Kashima Antlers	0-0 3-0	Yokohama F.Marinos		Kashima Antlers	3-2	Shimizu S-Pulse
2001	Kashima Antlers	2-2 1-0	Jubilo Iwata		Shimizu S-Pulse	3-2	Cerezo Osaka
2002	Jubilo Iwata	†			Kyoto Purple Sanga	2-1	Kashima Antlers
2003	Yokohama F.Marinos	†			Jubilo Iwata	1-0	Cerezo Osaka
2004	Yokohama F.Marinos	1-0 0-1 4-2p	Urawa Reds		Tokyo Verdy 1969	2-1	Jubilo Iwata

† Both stages won by the same team so no play-off was required • ‡ Played on a single stage league system with no play-off • See club directory for pre J.League names

EMPEROR'S CUP 2004

Third Round | **Fourth Round** | **Fifth Round**

Fourth Round:
Tokyo Verdy 1969 — 2
Kyoto Purple Sanga * — 1

Third Round:
Japan Soccer College — 2
Kyoto Purple Sanga * — 11
Honda FC * — 8
Central de Chugoku — 0

Fifth Round:
Tokyo Verdy 1969 * — 2
Nagoya Grampus Eight — 1

Fourth Round:
Honda FC — 0
Nagoya Grampus Eight * — 3

Fourth Round:
Yokohama F.Marinos — 2
Montedio Yamagata * — 1

Third Round:
FC Ryukyu — 2
Montedio Yamagata * — 3

Fifth Round:
Yokohama F.Marinos * — 1
Thespa Kusatsu — 2

Fourth Round:
Cerezo Osaka * — 1
Thespa Kusatsu — 2

Third Round:
Momoyama Gauin University — 0
Thespa Kusatsu * — 1

Fourth Round:
Kashima Antlers — 1
Mito Hollyhock * — 0

Third Round:
Alouette Kumamoto — 0
Mito Hollyhock * — 4

Fifth Round:
Kashima Antlers * — 3
Kawasaki Frontale — 2

Fourth Round:
Vissel Kobe — 2
Kawasaki Frontale * — 3

Third Round:
Ehime FC — 0
Kawasaki Frontale * — 4
Yokohama FC * — 4
Oita Trinita U-18 — 0

Fourth Round:
Yokohama FC * — 1
Sanfrecce Hiroshima — 0

Fifth Round:
Yokohama FC * — 0
Gamba Osaka — 5

Third Round:
Sagan Tosu * — 2
Tochigi SC — 0

Fourth Round:
Sagan Tosu * — 1
Gamba Osaka — 3

Fourth Round:
Urawa Reds — 3
Avispa Fukuoka * — 1

Third Round:
Tenri University — 1
Avispa Fukuoka * — 9

Fifth Round:
Urawa Reds * — 3
Shonan Bellmare — 0

Fourth Round:
Albirex Niigata * — 2
Shonan Bellmare — 3

Third Round:
Hachinohe University — 0
Shonan Bellmare * — 1
Omiya Ardija * — 2
Alo's Hokuriku — 1

Fourth Round:
Omiya Ardija — 1
Shimizu S-Pulse * — 0

Fifth Round:
Omiya Ardija * — 3
FC Tokyo — 6

Third Round:
Vegalta Sendai * — 2
Sagawa Printing — 0

Fourth Round:
Vegalta Sendai * — 0
FC Tokyo — 1

Third Round:
Consadole Sapporo * — 2
Honda Lock — 1

Fourth Round:
Consadole Sapporo * — 2
JEF United Ichihara — 1

Fifth Round:
Consadole Sapporo * — 1
Oita Trinita — 0

Third Round:
Ventforet Kofu * — 1
Sony Sendai — 0

Fourth Round:
Ventforet Kofu * — 1
Oita Trinita — 2

Third Round:
Gunma FC Horikoshi — 2
Tokai University * — 1

Fourth Round:
Gunma FC Horikoshi — 1
Kashiwa Reysol * — 0

Fifth Round:
Gunma FC Horikoshi * — 1
Jubilo Iwata — 2

Third Round:
Sagawa Express Tokyo — 3
Chukyo University * — 2

Fourth Round:
Sagawa Express Tokyo * — 2
Jubilo Iwata — 3

* Home team

EMPEROR'S CUP 2004

Quarter-finals	Semi-finals	Final

Tokyo Verdy 1969	3
Thespa Kusatsu *	0

Tokyo Verdy 1969 †	3
Gamba Osaka	1

Kashima Antlers *	0
Gamba Osaka	1

Tokyo Verdy 1969	2
Jubilo Iwata	1

Urawa Reds *	2
FC Tokyo	1

Urawa Reds	1
Jubilo Iwata ‡	2

Consadole Sapporo *	0
Jubilo Iwata	1

† Played at the National Stadium, Tokyo
‡ Played at Nagai Stadium, Osaka

EMPEROR'S CUP FINAL 2004

National Stadium, Tokyo, 1-01-2005, Att: 50 233, Referee: Kashihar

Tokyo Verdy 1969	2	Iio 35, Hiramoto 53
Jubilo Iwata	1	Nishi 77

Verdy - Takagi; Lee, Yoney Ama, Tomisawa; Hayashi, Yamada, Soma, Kobayashi.D, Kobayashi.Y; Hiramoto, Iio (Yanagisawa 45). Tr: Ardiles
Jubilo - Sato; Suzuki.H, Tanaka, Kikuchi (Kawaguchi 65); Kawamura, Fukunishi, Hattori, Nishi, Nanami; Gral (Fujita 72), Maeda.
Tr: Yamamoto

YOKOHAMA F.MARINOS 2004

Date	Opponents	Score		Comp	Scorers	Att
10-02-2004	Binh Dinh - VIE	W 3-0	A	CLgG	Kurihara 2 [15 20], Shimizu [74]	n/a
24-02-2004	Persik Kediri - IDN	W 4-0	H	CLgG	Kitano 2 [12 20], Yamazaki [65], Abe [71]	3 589
26-02-2004	Tokyo Verdy 1969	D 2-2	H	SC	Ohashi [72], Tanaka [87]	21 104
13-03-2004	Urawa Reds	D 1-1	H	JL1	Ahn Jung Hwan [28]	51 052
20-03-2004	JEF United	L 0-3	A	JL1		6 813
27-03-2004	Sanfrecce Hiroshima	D 0-0	A	JLCgA		6 404
3-04-2004	Cerezo Osaka	W 2-1	H	JL1	Kubo [40], Nakazawa [79]	22 102
7-04-2004	Seongnam Chunma - KOR	L 1-2	H	CLgG	Ahn Jung Hwan [8]	9 605
10-04-2004	Albirex Niigata	W 3-1	A	JL1	Kubo [34], Oku 2 [41 44]	41 192
14-04-2004	Oita Trinita	D 1-1	A	JL1	Sakata [82]	18 463
17-04-2004	Gamba Osaka	W 2-1	H	JL1	Sakata [16], Kubo [23]	20 360
21-04-2004	Seongnam Chunma - KOR	W 1-0	A	CLgG	Kawai [75]	n/a
29-04-2004	Sanfrecce Hiroshima	W 2-1	H	JLCgA	Abe [33], Yamazaki [66]	15 655
2-05-2004	FC Tokyo	W 2-0	A	JL1	Ahn Jung Hwan [2], Oku [61]	35 680
5-05-2004	Binh Dinh - VIE	W 6-0	H	CLgG	Dutra [5], Ahn Jung-Hwan 2 [39 85], Kubo [67], Sakata [79], Oku [89]	6 374
9-05-2004	Tokyo Verdy 1969	W 3-1	H	JL1	Endo [43], Sato [89], Ahn Jung Hwan [90]	17 859
12-05-2004	Shimizu S-Pulse	D 1-1	H	JL1	Sakata [88]	13 554
15-05-2004	Jubilo Iwata	W 2-1	A	JL1	Oku [14], Nasu [64]	29 842
19-05-2004	Persik Kediri - IDN	W 4-1	A	CLgG	Dutra [1], Ahn Jung Hwan [9], Kubo [24], Yoo Sang Chul [44]	n/a
23-05-2004	Nagoya Grampus Eight	W 2-1	H	JL1	Oku [73], Sato [82]	22 011
29-05-2004	Cerezo Osaka	W 1-0	A	JLCgA	Sato [60]	7 657
5-06-2004	Tokyo Verdy 1969	L 1-2	**H**	JLCgA	Dutra [72]	9 332
12-06-2004	Vissel Kobe	W 2-0	A	JL1	Ahn Jung Hwan [20], Ueno [35]	17 880
16-06-2004	Sanfrecce Hiroshima	W 2-0	H	JL1	Ueno [9], Ahn Jung Hwan [31]	14 738
19-06-2004	Kashiwa Reysol	W 2-1	A	JL1	Tanaka [17], Ahn Jung Hwan [65]	10 399
26-06-2004	Kashima Antlers	W 1-0	H	JL1	Ahn Jung Hwan [61]	52 961
17-07-2004	Tokyo Verdy 1969	L 0-3	A	JLCgA		12 430
24-07-2004	Cerezo Osaka	W 1-0	**H**	JLCgA	Shimizu [68]	7 273
15-08-2004	Shimizu S-Pulse	W 2-1	A	JL2	Ahn Jung Hwan 2 [63 80]	19 043
21-08-2004	Oita Trinita	W 2-1	H	JL2	Ueno [12], Matsuda [89]	17 821
29-08-2004	Nagoya Grampus Eight	L 1-2	A	JL2	Kubo [13]	15 602
4-09-2004	Urawa Reds	L 2-3	A	JLCqf	Oku [12], Sakata [73]	28 977
11-09-2004	Jubilo Iwata	W 3-0	*H*	JL2	Oku [15], Sakata [31], Ahn Jung Hwan [61]	28 713
18-09-2004	Sanfrecce Hiroshima	D 2-2	H	JL2	Sakata 2 [17 66]	18 056
23-09-2004	Vissel Kobe	D 2-2	*H*	JL2	Sakata [15], Ahn Jung Hwan [30]	16 635
26-09-2004	Cerezo Osaka	D 1-1	A	JL2	Ahn Jung Hwan [45]	14 587
3-10-2004	Kashiwa Reysol	L 0-1	H	JL2		21 579
17-10-2004	Urawa Reds	D 0-0	A	JL2		58 334
23-10-2004	FC Tokyo	W 2-1	H	JL2	Oku 2 [25 88]	24 494
30-10-2004	Kashima Antlers	L 1-3	H	JL2	Sakata [48]	15 469
6-11-2004	JEF United	W 2-1	H	JL2	Shimizu [9], Sakata [80]	20 516
13-11-2004	Montedio Yamagata	W 2-1	A	ECr4		6 536
20-11-2004	Gamba Osaka	W 2-0	A	JL2	Oku 2 [67 83]	13 188
23-11-2004	Albirex Niigata	L 1-2	H	JL2	Sakata [68]	27 878
28-11-2004	Tokyo Verdy 1969	D 0-0	H	JL2		21 241
5-12-2004	Urawa Reds	W 1-0	H	JLpo	Kawai [66]	64 899
11-12-2004	Urawa Reds	L 0-1	A	JLpo	W 4-2p	59 715
15-12-2004	Thespa Kusatsu	L 1-2	H	ECr5	Oku [83]	3 392

CL = AFC Champions League • SC = Super Cup • JL1 = J.League first stage • JL2 = J.League second stage • JLC = J.League Cup • EC = Emperor's Cup
gA = Group A • gG = Group G • r4 = fourth round • r5 = fifth round • qf = quarter-final • po = play-off
H = International Stadium, Yokohama • **H** = Mitsuzawa, Yokohama • *H* = National Stadium, Tokyo

J.LEAGUE CLUB DIRECTORY (1)

Club	Town/City	Stadium	Phone	www.	Lge	Cup	CL
Albirex Niigata	Niigata	Big Swan 42 300	+81 25 2820011	albirex.co.jp	0	0	0
Cerezo Osaka	Osaka	Nagai 50 000	+81 6 66929011	cerezo.co.jp	4	3	0
Gamba Osaka	Osaka	Expo'70 23 000	+81 6 68758111	gamba-osaka.net	0	1	0
JEF United	Ichihara	Ichihara 16 933	+81 436 631201	so-net.ne.jp/jefunited	2	4	1
Jubilo Iwata	Iwata	Yamaha 16 893	+81 538 362000	jubilo-iwata.co.jp	4	2	1
Kashima Antlers	Ibaraki	Kashima 39 026	+81 299 846808	so-net.ne.jp/antlers/	4	2	0
Kashiwa Reysol	Kashiwa	Kashiwa Hitachi 15 900	+81 4 71622201	reysol.co.jp	1	2	0
Kawasaki Frontale	Kawasaki	Todoroki 25 000	+81 44 8138618	frontale.co.jp	0	0	0
Nagoya Grampus Eight	Nagoya	Nagoya Mizuho 27 000	+81 52 2429180	so-net.ne.jp/grampus	0	2	0
Oita Trinita	Oita	Oita 43 000	+81 97 5335657	oita-trinita.co.jp	0	0	0
Omiya Ardija	Saitama	Omiya 12 500	+81 48 6585511	ardija.co.jp	0	0	0

URAWA REDS 2004

Date	Opponents	Score		Comp	Scorers	Att
13-03-2004	Yokohama F.Marinos	D	1-1 A	JL1	Emerson [58]	51 052
21-03-2004	Cerezo Osaka	W	4-2 H	JL1	OG [34], Hasebe [50], Emerson 2 [73 85]	43 067
27-03-2004	Oita Trinita	L	2-3 H	JLCgC	Emerson [42]	18 543
3-04-2004	Jubilo Iwata	L	1-3 A	JL1	OG [17]	16 209
10-04-2004	Vissel Kobe	W	2-1 H	JL1	Santos [2], Hasebe [68]	20 558
14-04-2004	Shimizu S-Pulse	L	3-4 A	JL1	Tanaka.T 2 [10 32], Emerson [89]	8 354
18-04-2004	Oita Trinita	W	4-1 H	JL1	Tanaka.T [24], Emerson 3 [30p 41 82]	19 232
29-04-2004	Shimizu S-Pulse	L	0-2 A	JLCgC		13 235
2-05-2004	Sanfrecce Hiroshima	D	0-0 A	JL1		29 332
5-05-2004	Kashima Antlers	W	1-0 H	JL1	Emerson [66]	56 070
9-05-2004	Albirex Niigata	W	3-0 A	JL1	Emerson 3 [4 11 80]	41 796
15-05-2004	JEF United	D	3-3 H	JL1	Nagai [56], Tulio [72p], Okano [80]	19 618
22-05-2004	Tokyo Verdy 1969	W	3-1 A	JL1	Tanaka.T 2 [16 33], Yamase [79]	35 556
29-05-2004	Oita Trinita	W	3-0 A	JLCgC	Yamase [21], Nagai [31], Sakai [50]	18 406
5-06-2004	Shimizu S-Pulse	W	3-0 H	JLCgC	Tanaka.T [39], Tulio [43], Okano [66]	19 098
12-06-2004	Nagoya Grampus Eight	L	0-3 A	JL1		27 375
16-06-2004	Kashiwa Reysol	D	1-1 H	JL1	Tanaka.T [48]	18 029
20-06-2004	Gama Osaka	L	2-3 A	JL1	Emerson 2 [13 26]	17 282
26-06-2004	FC Tokyo	W	2-1 H	JL1	OG [44], Santos [60]	52 646
17-07-2004	JEF United	W	2-1 H	JLCgC	Hasebe [80], Okano [89]	18 475
24-07-2004	JEF United	W	2-1 A	JLCgC	Yamada 2 [8 66]	15 616
14-08-2004	Vissel Kobe	W	3-2 A	JL2	Hasebe 2 [27 39], Emerson [79]	17 261
21-08-2004	Tokyo Verdy 1969	W	7-2 H	JL2	Emerson [11], Nagai 3 [14 21 64], Yamase 3 [69 73 83]	32 296
29-08-2004	Jubilo Iwata	W	3-2 H	JL2	Emerson [15], Yamada [30], Hasebe [89]	43 746
4-09-2004	Yokohama F.Marinos	W	3-2 H	JLCqf	Yamase [16], Emerson 2 [37 66]	28 977
12-09-2004	Oita Trinita	W	4-1 A	JL2	Emerson 2 [17 40], Yamase [42], Tanaka.T [43]	27 760
18-09-2004	Albirex Niigata	W	4-1 H	JL2	Nene [17], OG 2 [25 39], Emerson [46]	49 435
23-09-2004	FC Tokyo	L	0-1 A	JL2		41 469
26-09-2004	Gamba Osaka	W	2-1 H	JL2	Yamada [16], Nagai [52]	19 497
2-10-2004	JEF United	W	4-0 H	JL2	Emerson 2 [16 71], Nagai [49], Hirakawa [89]	34 793
11-10-2004	Nagoya Grampus Eight	W	4-1 A	JLCsf	Emerson [26], Tanaka.T 3 [33 57 81]	17 473
17-10-2004	Yokohama F.Marinos	D	0-0 H	JL2		58 334
23-10-2004	Kashima Antlers	W	3-2 A	JL2	Tanaka.T 2 [10 28], Emerson [84]	31 965
30-10-2004	Cerezo Osaka	W	2-0 A	JL2	Tanaka.T [13], Emerson [67]	22 778
3-11-2004	FC Tokyo	D	0-0 N	JLCf	L 2-4p	53 236
6-11-2004	Shimizu S-Pulse	W	2-1 H	JL2	Sakai [68], Tulio [84]	43 853
14-11-2004	Avispa Fukuoka	W	3-1 A	ECr4		10 507
20-11-2004	Nagoya Grampus Eight	L	1-2 H	JL2	Emerson [88]	21 192
23-11-2004	Kashiwa Reysol	W	4-0 A	JL2	Muroi [4], Emerson 3 [50 62 83]	13 272
28-11-2004	Sanfrecce Hiroshima	W	1-0 H	JL2	Tulio [51]	52 330
15-12-2004	Shonan Bellmare	W	3-0 H	ECr5		6 027
19-12-2004	FC Tokyo	W	2-1 H	ECqf		33 480
25-12-2004	Jubilo Iwata	L	1-2 N	ECsf	Tanaka.T [72]	35 523

JL1 = J.League first stage • JL2 = J.League second stage • JLC = J.League Cup • EC = Emperor's Cup
gC = Group C • r4 = fourth round • r5 = fifth round • qf = quarter-final • sf = semi-final • f = final
H = Saitama Stadium 2002, Saitama • H = Urawa Komaba, Saitama

J.LEAGUE CLUB DIRECTORY (2)

Club	Town/City	Stadium	Phone	www.	Lge	Cup	CL
Sanfrecce Hiroshima	Hiroshima	Big Arch 50 000	+81 82 2333233	sanfrecce,co.jp	5	3	0
Shimizu S-Pulse	Shizuoka	Nihondaira 20 339	+81 543 366301	s-pulse.co.jp	0	1	0
FC Tokyo	Tokyo	Ajinomoto 50 000	+81 3 36358985	fctokyo.co.jp	0	0	0
Tokyo Verdy 1969	Tokyo	Ajinomoto 50 000	+81 3 35121969	verdy.co.jp	7	5	0
Urawa Reds	Saitama	Saitama 2002 63 700	+81 48 8323240	urawa-reds.co.jp	4	4	0
Vissel Kobe	Kobe	Kobe Wing 34 000	+81 78 6855510	vissel-kobe.co.jp	0	0	0
Yokohama F.Marinos	Yokohama	International 72 370	+81 45 4342331	so-net.ne.jp/f-marinos	5	6	0

In 1992 with the creation of the J.League the clubs changed their names as follows • Yanmar Diesel → Cerezo Osaka • Matsushita → Gamba Osaka •
Furukawa Electric and JR East Furukawa merged to form JEF United • Yamaha Motors → Jubilo Iwata • Sumitomo Honda → Kashima Antlers •
Hitachi → Kashiwa Reysol • Fujitsu → Kawasaki Frontale • Toyota FC → Nagoya Grampus Eight • NIT Kanto → Oita Trinita • Mazda FC →
Sanfrecce Hiroshima (previously Toyo Kogyo) • Yomiuri Nippon → Verdy Kawasaki and then Tokyo Verdy 1969 • Mitsubishi Motors → Urawa Reds •
Nissan → Yokohama Marinos • In 1998 Yokohama Marinos merged with Yokohama Flugels (previously All Nippon Airways) to form Yokohama F.Marinos

KAZ – KAZAKHSTAN

NATIONAL TEAM RECORD
JULY 1ST 2002 TO JUNE 30TH 2005

PL	W	D	L	F	A	%
18	0	3	15	15	48	8.3

FIFA/COCA-COLA WORLD RANKING

1993	1994	1995	1996	1997	1998	1999	2000	2001	2002	2003	2004	High		Low	
-	153	163	156	107	102	123	120	98	117	136	147	**98**	12/01	**166**	05/96

2004-2005											
08/04	09/04	10/04	11/04	12/04	01/05	02/05	03/05	04/05	05/05	06/05	07/05
144	145	145	147	147	149	149	149	149	149	148	148

When deciding to quit the AFC and join UEFA the football authorities in Kazakhstan had their eye very firmly on the long-term development of the game in the country because following the move over in 2002 it is likely that the national team will set a good number of unwanted records as they find their feet within European football. The first three years have seen 18 games played with just three draws to show for their efforts. Unsurprisingly Kazakhstan find themselves rooted to the bottom of their 2006 FIFA World Cup™ qualifying group although in fairness it was always going to be tough in a very strong group containing Ukraine, Turkey, Greece and Denmark. With the full

INTERNATIONAL HONOURS
None

support of UEFA, however, it is hoped that progress will happen sooner rather than later and with a population of 15 million Kazakhstan has the raw materials to haul the national team up from a current position of 148 in the FIFA/Coca-Cola World Ranking. Having to adhere to the strict club licensing system that UEFA applies should also benefit the Kazakhstan Championship in the long-term. After a poor start Kairat Almaty won a closely fought Championship in 2004 to qualify for the 2005-06 UEFA Champions League, but spare a thought for Yelimay Semey who finished bottom of the League. Their fans had to endure a run of 33 consecutive defeats.

THE FIFA BIG COUNT OF 2000

	Male	Female		Male	Female
Registered players	6 240	120	Referees	75	0
Non registered players	75 000	0	Officials	2 900	0
Youth players	15 040	120	Total involved	99 495	
Total players	96 520		Number of clubs	119	
Professional players	890	60	Number of teams	318	

The Football Union of Kazakhstan (FSK)
Satpayev Street 29/3, Almaty 480 072, Kazakhstan
Fax +7 3272 921885
kfo@mail.online.kz   www.fsk.kz
President: ALIYEV Rakhat   General Secretary: AKHMETOV Askar
Vice-President: AKPAYEV Tlekbek   Treasurer: KUBANOV Yuriy   Media Officer: None
Men's Coach: TIMOFEYEV Sergei   Women's Coach: JAMANTAYEV Aitpay
FSK formed: 1914   AFC: 1994-2002, UEFA: 2002   FIFA: 1994
Colours: Blue, Blue, Yellow or Yellow, Yellow, Blue

GAMES PLAYED BY KAZAKHSTAN IN THE 2006 FIFA WORLD CUP™ CYCLE

2002	Opponents	Score		Venue	Comp	Scorers	Att	Referee
7-07	Estonia	D	1-1	Almaty	Fr	Litvinenko [38]	15 000	Kapanin KAZ
2003								
12-02	Malta	D	2-2	Ta'Qali	Fr	Zhumaskaliyev [72], Tarasov [83]	200	Rogalla SUI
27-04	Faroe Islands	L	2-3	Toftir	Fr	Lunev [56], Mumanov [76]	420	Jakobsson ISL
29-04	Faroe Islands	L	1-2	Tórshavn	Fr	Lovchev [6p]	800	Bergmann ISL
6-06	Poland	L	0-3	Poznan	Fr		6 000	Fisker DEN
20-08	Portugal	L	0-1	Chaves	Fr		8 000	Rodriguez Santiago ESP
2004								
18-02	Latvia	L	1-3	Larnaca	Fr	Aksenov [23]	500	Constantinou CYP
19-02	Armenia	D	3-3	Paphos	Fr	Zhumaskaliyev 2 [53 75], Finonchenko [76]. W 3-2p	100	Loizou CYP
21-02	Cyprus	L	1-2	Larnaca	Fr	Uzdenov [68]	300	Lajaks LVA
28-04	Azerbaijan	L	2-3	Almaty	Fr	Karpovich [55], Lunev [77]	20 000	Chynybekov KGZ
8-09	Ukraine	L	1-2	Almaty	WCq	Karpovich [34]	23 000	Alves Garcia POR
9-10	Turkey	L	0-4	Istanbul	WCq		39 900	Hrinak SVK
13-10	Albania	L	0-1	Almaty	WCq		12 300	Stuchlik AUT
17-11	Greece	L	1-3	Piraeus	WCq	Baltiyev [88]	31 838	Kostadinov BUL
2005								
29-01	Japan	L	0-4	Yokohama	Fr		46 941	
26-03	Denmark	L	0-3	Copenhagen	WCq		20 980	Gilewski POL
4-06	Ukraine	L	0-2	Kyiv	WCq		45 000	Lehner AUT
8-06	Turkey	L	0-6	Almaty	WCq		20 000	Kassai HUN

Fr = Friendly match • EC = UEFA EURO 2004™ • WC = FIFA World Cup™ • q = qualifier

NATIONAL CAPS

	Caps
BALTIYEV Ruslan	34
QADIRKULOV Askhat	24
VOSKOBOYNIKOV Oleg	24
LOGINOV Vladimir	23
FAMILTSEV Aleksandr	23

NATIONAL GOALS

	Goals
ZUBAREV Viktor	12
BALTIYEV Ruslan	7
AVDEYEV Igor	6
LITVINENKO Oleg	6

NATIONAL COACH

	Years
TALGAYEV Vait	2000
FOMICHOV Vladimir	2000
MASUDOV Vahid	2001-'02
PAKHOMOV Leonid	2003-'04
TIMOFEYEV Sergei	2004-

KAZAKHSTAN NATIONAL TEAM RECORDS AND RECORD SEQUENCES

Records			Sequence records					
Victory	7-0	PAK 1997	Wins	4	1997	Clean sheets	3	1994-1995
Defeat	1-5	JPN 1997	Defeats	7	2004-	Goals scored	7	2000-2001
Player Caps	34	BALTIYEV Ruslan	Undefeated	7	2001-2003	Without goal	5	1994-1995
Player Goals	12	ZUBAREV Viktor	Without win	18	2001-	Goals against	16	2002-

KAZAKHSTAN COUNTRY INFORMATION

Capital	Astana	Independence	1991 from USSR	GDP per Capita	$6 300
Population	15 143 704	Status	Republic	GNP Ranking	61
Area km²	2 717 300	Language	Kazakh, Russian	Dialling code	+7
Population density	5 per km²	Literacy rate	98%	Internet code	.kz
% in urban areas	60%	Main religion	Muslim 47%, Orthodox 44%	GMT +/-	+4
Towns/Cities ('000)	Almaty 1 204; Shymkent 414; Karagandy 431; Taraz 358; Astana 345; Pavlodar 329; Oskamen (Ost-Kamenogorsk) 319; Semey (Semipalatinsk) 292; Aktobe 262; Kostanay 230; Uralsk 230; Petropavl (Petropavlovsk) 200; Atyrau 146; Ekibastuz 144; Kokshetau 124;				
Neighbours (km)	Russia 6 846; China 1 533; Kyrgyzstan 1 051; Uzbekistan 2 203; Turkmenistan 379				
Main stadia	Ortalyk Tsentralnyi – Almaty 26 250; Kazhimukana Munaytpasova – Astana 12 343				

KAZAKHSTAN 2004

SUPERLEAGUE

Team	Pl	W	D	L	F	A	Pts	Kairat	Irtysh	Tobol	Aktobe	Atyrau	Yesil	Taraz	Ekibast's	Shakhtyor	Zhenis	Okzheypes	Ordabasy	Vostock	Zhetysu	Yassy	Kaisar	Akzhaiyk	Almaty	Yelimay
Kairat Almaty †	36	25	8	3	70	21	83		2-1	2-2	1-1	1-1	2-0	2-0	2-0	0-0	3-2	6-1	3-0	2-1	1-0	3-0	1-0	7-1	2-1	6-0
Irtysh Pavlodar ‡	36	24	7	5	56	16	79	1-0		1-2	2-1	0-0	3-0	0-0	1-0	3-0	1-0	1-0	1-0	4-0	2-1	3-0	1-0	6-0	0-0	3-0
Tobol Kostanay	36	22	11	3	87	27	77	3-3	0-0		1-0	1-1	1-0	2-0	2-0	4-0	6-1	3-0	1-0	5-0	6-1	2-1	4-0	9-0	5-0	4-0
Aktobe Lento	36	22	8	6	52	19	74	1-3	0-1	1-1		1-0	3-1	2-0	0-1	0-0	0-0	1-0	2-1	3-2	4-0	1-0	1-0	4-1	3-0	3-1
FK Atyrau	36	20	11	5	49	31	71	2-0	1-0	4-1	0-0		2-1	4-2	0-0	1-1	2-0	3-2	1-0	4-0	3-1	1-0	3-1	2-1	3-0	2-0
Yesil Petropavl	36	18	5	13	53	40	59	1-3	1-1	1-4	0-2	0-0		4-1	1-0	2-0	2-1	4-1	2-0	5-0	4-3	3-0	**3-0**	2-0	1-0	1-0
FC Taraz	36	16	11	9	35	23	59	0-0	0-0	2-0	0-2	1-0	1-0		0-0	1-0	3-0	0-0	3-0	0-0	2-0	3-0	**3-0**	3-0	1-0	2-1
FC Ekibastuzets	36	17	7	12	42	27	58	1-0	1-2	0-0	0-1	4-0	2-1	1-0		2-0	2-0	0-0	3-0	0-1	1-2	2-0	2-1	1-1	1-0	2-1
Shakhtyor Karagandy	36	16	9	11	44	28	57	0-1	1-0	1-1	0-2	1-1	1-0	2-0	1-1		2-0	0-2	1-3	0-3	1-1	1-0	1-2	2-0	0-0	2-0
Zhenis Astana	36	15	6	15	45	44	51	0-3	1-2	3-1	0-2	1-2	1-2	0-0	2-2	3-0		2-0	0-2	2-1	3-0	3-1	**1-0**	1-2	2-0	2-0
Okzheypes Kokshetau	36	10	13	13	26	39	43	0-0	0-0	1-1	0-0	0-0	0-0	0-1	*0-3*	0-0	1-2		1-0	1-0	3-0	2-0	2-0	0-0	0-2	2-1
Ordabasy Shymkent	36	11	7	18	37	43	40	0-0	1-0	1-1	1-0	1-0	1-1	1-2	1-1	0-1	1-4	1-3		2-1	2-1	1-3	**3-0**	**5-0**	3-1	2-0
FC Vostock	36	11	7	18	42	54	40	1-2	1-3	0-4	1-2	2-2	0-2	1-1	1-2	1-0	0-0	1-1	1-1		5-0	0-2	**2-0**	1-0	0-0	4-1
Zhetysu Taldykorgan	36	11	7	18	34	55	40	0-1	0-1	0-0	1-0	2-3	1-0	1-4	1-0	2-1	0-0	1-1	3-1	1-2		2-0	**1-0**	3-1	1-1	4-2
Yassy Sayram	36	9	8	19	30	49	35	0-2	0-3	0-3	0-2	4-1	0-0	0-1	1-1	1-1	0-0	0-1	0-0	0-0			**1-0**	5-2	2-0	2-0
Kaisar Kyzylorda §	36	9	4	23	24	61	31	0-1	1-2	1-3	1-1	0-0	1-0	0-0	2-1	**0-3**	**0-3**	3-1	2-0	**0-3**	1-0	**0-3**		3-1	1-0	**0-3**
Akzhaiyk Uralsk §	36	7	4	25	24	83	25	0-2	0-2	0-3	0-1	0-3	0-1	2-2	1-0	2-1	0-2	1-2	2-0	**0-3**	1-0	0-1	**3-0**		1-1	**0-3**
FK Almaty	36	4	8	24	22	53	20	0-1	2-3	0-0	0-1	0-1	1-3	1-0	0-3	0-3	1-2	1-2	0-0	0-1	1-1	2-3	**3-0**	1-0		4-0
Yelimay Semey	36	4	1	31	25	84	13	0-1	0-0	0-2	2-3	0-2	0-1	1-2	0-1	0-2	1-2	0-1	2-1	2-0	3-0	0-4	0-1	2-2	2-3	

3/04/2004 - 2/11/2004 • † Qualified for the UEFA Champions League • ‡ Qualified for the UEFA Cup • § Kaisar expelled after round 30, Akzhaiyk expelled after round 36. Future opponents awarded games **3-0** • Relegation play-off: CSKA Temirtau 2-1 FK Almaty • Almaty retained their place after a merger between Ordabasy Shymkent and Yassy Sayram • Match in italics awarded 3-0

TOP SCORERS

BAKAYEV Ulug'bek	Tobol	22
TLEHUGOV Arsen	Kairat	22
ZHUMASKALIYEV Nurbol	Tobol	19
NIZOVTSEV Maksim	Tobol	17
BULESHEV Alibek	Kairat	14
YEREMEYEV Vyacheslav	Atyrau	14

FOOTBALL CUP OF KAZAKHSTAN 2004

Quarter-finals

FC Taraz	1 2
Aktobe Lento *	2 0
Temirzholshy *	0 0
FK Atyrau	3 2
Zhenis Astana	1 4
Zhetysu *	2 0
Vostock-2 *	0 0
Kairat Almaty	5 4

Semi-finals

FC Taraz	0 3
FK Atyrau *	1 0
Zhenis Astana *	1 2
Kairat Almaty	1 3

* Home team in first leg

Final

FC Taraz	1
Kairat Almaty	0

11-11-2004, Att:12 500
Tsentralny, Taraz
Scorer - Mazabayev 44

RECENT LEAGUE AND CUP RECORD

Championship

Year	Champions	Pts	Runners-up	Pts	Third	Pts
1992	Kairat Almaty	37	Arsenal-SKIF	36	Traktor Pavlodar	36
1993	Ansat Pavlodar	34	Batyr Ekibastuz	30	Gornyak Khromtau	30
1994	Yelimay Semey	47	Ansat Pavlodar	41	Zhiger Shymkent	40
1995	Yelimay Semey	67	Taraz Zhambul	64	Shakhtyor Karagandy	60
1996	Taraz Zhambul	76	Irtysh Pavlodar	74	Yelimay Semey	74
1997	Irtysh Pavlodar	56	FC Taraz	56	Kairat Almaty	53
1998	Yelimay Semey	63	Batyr Ekibastuz	59	Irtysh Pavlodar	57
1999	Irtysh Pavlodar	76	Yesil Petropavlovsk	72	Kairat Almaty	64
2000	Zhenis Astana	74	Yesil Petropavlovsk	72	Irtysh Pavlodar	60
2001						
2001	Zhenis Astana	81	FK Atyrau	70	Yesil Petropavlovsk	69
2002	Irtysh Pavlodar	71	FK Atyrau	63	Tobol Kostanay	52
2003	Irtysh Pavlodar	78	Tobol Kostanay	76	Zhenis Astana	64
2004	Kairat Almaty	83	Irtysh Pavlodar	79	Tobol Kostanay	77

Cup

Winners	Score	Runners-up
Kairat Almaty	5-1	Fosfor Zhambul
Dostyk Almaty	4-2	Taraz Zhambul
Vostock Oskemen	1-0	Aktyubinsk
Yelimay Semipal'sk	1-0	Ordabasy Shymkent
Kairat Almaty	2-0	Vostock Oskemen
Not played due to season readjustment		
Irtysh Pavlodar	2-1	Kaysar Kzyl-Orda
Kaysar Kzyl-Orda	1-1 2-0p	Vostock Oskemen
Kairat Almaty	5-0	Yesil Petropavlovsk
Zhenis Astana	1-1 5-4p	Irtysh Pavlodar
Kairat Almaty	3-1	Zhenis Astana
Zhenis Astana	1-0	Irtysh Pavlodar
Kairat Almaty	3-1	Tobol Kostanai
FC Taraz	1-0	Kairat Almaty

Irtysh beat Taraz 1-0 in a play-off in 1997 • Zhenis beat Petropavlovsk 2-0 in a play-off in 2000 • Two cup competitions were held in 2001

KEN – KENYA

NATIONAL TEAM RECORD
JULY 1ST 2002 TO JUNE 30TH 2005

PL	W	D	L	F	A	%
54	20	21	13	76	61	56.5

FIFA/COCA-COLA WORLD RANKING

1993	1994	1995	1996	1997	1998	1999	2000	2001	2002	2003	2004	High		Low	
74	83	107	112	89	93	103	108	104	81	72	74	70	02/04	112	12/96

2004-2005											
08/04	09/04	10/04	11/04	12/04	01/05	02/05	03/05	04/05	05/05	06/05	07/05
87	84	83	85	74	75	77	77	79	79	80	79

It has been a very mixed past couple of years for football in Kenya. The national team has showed signs of promise losing just two matches in three editions of the CECAFA CUP between 2002 and 2004, qualifying for the 2004 CAF African Cup of Nations and making a strong push to qualify for the 2006 finals in Egypt. But amongst all this there was the almost total collapse of any proper organisation of football with disputes between the national association and the government leading to the intervention of FIFA and the temporary banning of the national team just as the 2006 FIFA World Cup™ qualifiers were getting underway. With East Africa the only region on the continent

INTERNATIONAL HONOURS

Gossage Cup 1926 1931 1941 1942 1944 1946 1953 1958 1959 1960 1961 1966 **Challenge Cup** 1967 1971 **CECAFA Cup** 1975 1981 1982 1983 2002

CECAFA Club Championship Luo Union 1976 1977, AFC Leopards 1979 1982 1983 1984 1997, Gor Mahia 1985, Tusker 1988 1989 2000 2001

never to have been represented at the finals there was never any danger of that run being broken in a group dominated by Morocco and Tunisia. The administrative chaos has hit club football hardest and in the 2003-04 season there were two rival leagues. In September 2004 a unified league kicked off which was played in two groups with the top two entering the Championship play-offs. They became a tale of penalty shoot-outs with Ulinzi beating Mathare United in the semi-final and then Tusker in the final.

THE FIFA BIG COUNT OF 2000

	Male	Female		Male	Female
Registered players	12 331	1 229	Referees	2 160	110
Non registered players	750 000	5 000	Officials	30 430	2 780
Youth players	36 864	3 686	Total involved	844 590	
Total players	909 110		Number of clubs	2 956	
Professional players	43	0	Number of teams	9 002	

Kenya Football Federation (KFF)
Nyayo Stadium, PO Box 40234, Nairobi, Kenya
Tel +254 2 602310   Fax +254 2 602294
www.none
President: SAMBU Alfred Wekesa   General Secretary: KASUVE Titus Mutuku
Vice-President: HATIMY Mohammed   Treasurer: TBD   Media Officer: None
Men's Coach: KHERI Mohammed   Women's Coach: None
KFF formed: 1960   CAF: 1968   FIFA: 1960
Colours: Red, Red, Red

GAMES PLAYED BY KENYA IN THE 2006 FIFA WORLD CUP™ CYCLE

2002	Opponents		Score	Venue	Comp	Scorers	Att	Referee
3-08	Uganda	D	0-0	Kisumu	Fr			
17-08	Jordan	D	1-1	Amman	Fr	Eschesa 60		
24-08	Rwanda	D	0-0	Kigali	Fr			
7-09	Togo	W	3-0	Nairobi	CNq	Baraza 62, Otieno 68, Oliech 90	20 000	Abdulkadir TAN
13-10	Cape Verde Islands	W	1-0	Praia	CNq	Baraza 56		Aboubacar CIV
23-10	South Africa	D	1-1	Arusha	Fr	Muyoti 59p, W 5-3p		
26-10	Uganda	D	1-1	Dar es Saalam	Fr	Baraza 80, W 3-2p	6 000	Chiganga TAN
30-11	Tanzania	L	0-1	Arusha	CCr1			
3-12	Burundi	D	1-1	Arusha	CCr1	Oliech 45		
6-12	Eritrea	W	4-1	Arusha	CCr1	Baraza 2 59 90, Oliech 2 69 82		
9-12	Sudan	W	1-0	Arusha	CCr1	Oliech 75		
12-12	Uganda	W	3-1	Arusha	CCsf	Mathenge 17, Oyuga 52, Mambo 56		
14-12	Tanzania	W	3-2	Arusha	CCf	Oyuga 30, Baraza 70, Oliech 72		
2003								
15-03	Uganda	D	2-2	Nairobi	Fr	Mwalala 11, Oliech 46		
23-03	Tanzania	W	4-0	Nairobi	Fr	Mulama 2 1 4, Oliech 36, Baraza 79		
29-03	Mauritania	W	4-0	Nairobi	CNq	Mambo 2 18 70, Oyuga 45, Oliech 47	30 000	Berhane ERI
24-05	Sudan	D	1-1	Khartoum	Fr			
31-05	Trinidad and Tobago	D	1-1	Nairobi	Fr	Oliech 21	28 000	
6-06	Mauritania	D	0-0	Nouakchott	CNq		6 000	Keita GUI
13-06	Ghana	W	3-1	Accra	Fr	Mambo 2 18 44, Oliech 38		
22-06	Togo	L	0-2	Lome	CNq			Rembangouet GAB
5-07	Cape Verde Islands	W	1-0	Nairobi	CNq	Oliech 84	35 000	
14-09	Rwanda	W	1-0	Kigali	Fr	Omondi 80	10 000	
11-10	Tanzania	D	0-0	Dar es Saalam	WCq		8 864	Tessema ETH
15-11	Tanzania	W	3-0	Nairobi	WCq	Oliech 2 9 32, Okoth Origi 30	14 000	El Beltagy EGY
2-12	Eritrea	W	3-2	Kassala	CCr1	Omondi 27, Mathenge 91+, Mulama 93+		
4-12	Uganda	D	1-1	Kassala	CCr1	Sunguti 93+		
8-12	Rwanda	D	1-1	Khartoum	CCsf	Omondi 44, L 3-4p		
10-12	Sudan	W	2-1	Khartoum	CC3p	Sunguti 24, Omondi 35		
12-12	Egypt	L	0-1	Manama	Fr			
15-12	Iraq	L	0-2	Manama	Fr			
18-12	Bahrain	L	1-2	Manama	Fr	Omondi 65		
21-12	United Arab Emirates	D	2-2	Abu Dhabi	Fr	Omolisi 86, Juma 90		
2004								
16-01	Libya	L	0-2	Zawyan	Fr			
19-01	Libya	L	0-2	Tripoli	Fr			
26-01	Mali	L	1-3	Bizerte	CNr1	Mulama 58	6 000	Tessema ETH
30-01	Senegal	L	0-3	Bizerte	CNr1		13 500	Abd El Fatah EGY
2-02	Burkina Faso	W	3-0	Bizerte	CNr1	Ake 50, Oliech 63, Baraza 83	4 550	Sowe GAM
7-08	Uganda	D	1-1	Kampala	Fr	Obua 27p	25 000	
18-08	Uganda	W	4-1	Nairobi	Fr	Baraza 2 11 33, Sirengo 65, Omondi 85	5 000	
4-09	Malawi	W	3-2	Nairobi	WCq	Barasa 2 21 29, Oliech 25	13 000	Mwanza ZAM
9-10	Botswana	L	1-2	Gaborone	WCq	Oliech 5	16 500	Colembi ANG
17-11	Guinea	W	2-1	Nairobi	WCq	Oliech 10, Mukenya 61	16 000	Abd El Fatah EGY
12-12	Sudan	D	2-2	Addis Abeba	CCr1	Simiyu 37, Baraza 73		
14-12	Somalia	W	1-0	Addis Abeba	CCr1	Baraza 7		
18-12	Uganda	D	1-1	Addis Abeba	CCr1	Obua 77p		
22-12	Ethiopia	D	2-2	Addis Abeba	CCsf	Mururi 66, Baraza 85, L 4-5p	50 000	Ssegonga UGA
25-12	Sudan	L	1-2	Addis Abeba	CC3p	Baraza 82		
2005								
9-02	Morocco	L	1-5	Rabat	WCq	Otieno 93+	40 000	Tamuni LBY
12-03	Rwanda	D	1-1	Nairobi	Fr	Mkenya 25		
23-03	Ghana	D	2-2	Nairobi	Fr	Baraza 44, Sunguti 87		
26-03	Botswana	W	1-0	Nairobi	WCq	Oliech 44	15 000	Buenkadila COD
5-06	Guinea	L	0-1	Conakry	WCq		21 000	Mbera GAB
18-06	Morocco	D	0-0	Nairobi	WCq		50 000	Diatta SEN

Fr = Friendly match • CN = CAF African Cup of Nations • CC = CECAFA Cup • WC = FIFA World Cup™
q = qualifier • r1 = first round group • sf = semi-final • 3p = third place play-off • f = final

KENYA COUNTRY INFORMATION

Capital	Nairobi	Independence	1963 from the UK	GDP per Capita	$1 000
Population	32 021 586	Status	Republic	GNP Ranking	84
Area km²	582 650	Language	Kiswahili, English	Dialling code	+254
Population density	55 per km²	Literacy rate	90%	Internet code	.ke
% in urban areas	28%	Main religion	Christian 78%, Muslim 10%	GMT + / –	+3
Towns/Cities ('000)	Nairobi 2 750; Mombasa 799; Nakuru 260; Eldoret 218; Kisumu 216; Ruiru 114; Thika 99				
Neighbours (km)	Ethiopia 861; Somalia 682; Tanzania 769; Uganda 933; Sudan 232; Indian Ocean 536				
Main stadia	Kasarani – Nairobi 60 000; Nyayo – Nairobi 20 000				

KENYA NATIONAL TEAM RECORDS AND RECORD SEQUENCES

Records			Sequence records					
Victory	9-0	TAN 1956	Wins	5	1993	Clean sheets	7	1983
Defeat	0-13	GHA 1965	Defeats	7	1932-1940	Goals scored	16	1931-1948
Player Caps	n/a		Undefeated	10	1997-1998	Without goal	5	1996
Player Goals	n/a		Without win	10	1984-1985	Goals against	16	1931-1948

KENYA 2004-05 GROUP A

	Pl	W	D	L	F	A	Pts
Mumias Sugar †	22	17	5	0	43	8	56
Ulinzi Stars †	22	14	7	1	26	10	49
Dubai Bank	22	12	2	8	35	21	38
Nzoia Sugar	21	10	5	6	23	15	35
Kisumu Telkom	22	6	8	8	18	23	26
Gor Mahia	22	6	7	9	20	16	25
Kenya Commercial Bank	21	6	7	8	11	18	25
Shabana	19	6	5	8	13	19	23
AFC Leopards	18	5	7	6	14	19	22
Kangemi United	21	4	8	9	17	26	20
National Bank	20	1	8	11	14	33	11
Re-Union	18	1	3	14	5	31	6

25/09/2004 - 7/05/2005 • † Qualified for the play-offs

KENYA 2004-05 GROUP B

	Pl	W	D	L	F	A	Pts
Mathare United †	22	12	6	4	29	16	42
Tusker †	22	12	6	4	28	16	42
Chemelil Sugar	22	11	7	4	24	14	40
Red Berets	21	10	7	4	21	19	37
Thika United	22	9	5	8	16	15	32
SoNy Sugar	22	6	12	4	18	15	30
Kenya Pipeline	22	7	8	7	22	18	29
World Hope	22	7	7	8	20	23	28
Securicor	22	7	4	11	17	23	25
Sher Agencies	21	5	8	8	12	15	23
Pan Paper	21	2	6	13	14	30	12
Administration Police	21	0	8	13	12	29	8

25/09/2004 - 7/05/2005 • † Qualified for the play-offs

CHAMPIONSHIP PLAY-OFFS

Semi-finals		Finals	
Ulinzi Stars	1 3p	16-07-2005, Kasarani, Nairobi	
Mathare United	1 0p	**Ulinzi Stars**	0 4p
Mumias Sugar	0 4p	Tusker	0 2p
Tusker	0 5p		

RECENT LEAGUE AND CUP RECORD

	Championship						Cup		
Year	Champions	Pts	Runners-up	Pts	Third	Pts	Winners	Score	Runners-up
1996	Kenya Breweries	71	AFC Leopards	65	Eldoret KCC	63	Mumias Sugar	1-0	Reli
1997	Utalii	66	Gor Mahia	64	Mumias Sugar	62	Eldoret KCC	4-1	AFC Leopards
1998	AFC Leopards	69	Mumias Sugar	66	Gor Mahia	60	Mathare United	2-1	Eldoret KCC
1999	Tusker						Mumias Sugar	3-2	Coast Stars
2000	Tusker	6	Oserian Fastac	4	Mumias Sugar	4	Mathare United	2-1	AFC Leopards
2001	Oserian Fastac	88	Mathare United	81	Mumias Sugar	68	AFC Leopards	2-0	Mathare United
2002	Oserian Fastac	†	Nzoia Sugar				Pipeline	1-0	Mumias Sugar
2003	Ulinzi Stars	†	Coast Stars				Chemelil	1-0	AFC Leopards
2004	Ulinzi Stars	†	Tusker				KCB	1-0	Thika United
2005	Ulinzi Stars	†	Tusker						

† Championship play-offs • 2002: Oserian Fastac 2-2 1-0 Nzoia Sugar • 2003: Ulinzi Stars 3-3 4-2p Coast Stars • 2004: Ulinzi Stars 2-2 4-3p Tusker •
2005: Ulinzi Stars 0-0 4-2p Tusker • The original final in 2003 was won by Nzoia Sugar, who beat Tusker 2-1. It was declared void by the KFF after
a number of clubs broke away. The 2003 Moi Golden Cup was also disrupted with Utalii beating Gor Mahia 2-1 in an alternative final. The dispute
between the KFF, the breakaway clubs and the Kenyan Sports Ministry saw the 2004 season badly affected which lead to the intervention of FIFA
and the creation of Stake-holders Transition Committee (STC). Two separate championships had been played but a play-off for all the leading clubs
was organised to qualify for CAF competitions

KGZ – KYRGYZSTAN

NATIONAL TEAM RECORD
JULY 1ST 2002 TO JUNE 30TH 2005

PL	W	D	L	F	A	%
12	4	2	6	14	17	41.7

FIFA/COCA-COLA WORLD RANKING

1993	1994	1995	1996	1997	1998	1999	2000	2001	2002	2003	2004	High		Low	
-	166	172	168	140	151	159	174	164	171	157	150	**139**	09/97	**175**	11/03

2004-2005											
08/04	09/04	10/04	11/04	12/04	01/05	02/05	03/05	04/05	05/05	06/05	07/05
156	155	151	151	150	152	152	152	152	152	152	152

Members of FIFA for little more than a decade, Kyrgyzstan have yet to make much of an impact, even in Asian competition. However, in spite of losing all their group qualifying games for the 2002 FIFA World Cup™, observers did take notice of a promising team. Progress has been limited though and an early exit in preliminary qualifying for the 2004 AFC Asian Cup was another heavy blow particularly as they beat eventual group winners Nepal but missed out on goal difference through defeat to lowly Afghanistan. Hope returned with a 6-0 defeat of Pakistan in the preliminary qualifying tie for Germany 2006, but four defeats and a draw in their group matches left the side

INTERNATIONAL HONOURS
None

with only pride to play for in the final match with Syria. The subsequent victory was too late but gave the team their first win in eight matches. The country's infrastructure has been helped by FIFA's Goal project; an artificial turf pitch was inaugurated in Bishkek in 2004 and finance to upgrade the technical centre has also been granted. In the 10-team Kyrgyzstan League, a goal tally of 126 underlined the dominance of champions Dordoy Naryn who finished five points clear of SKA Shoro. Surprise winners of the League, the team had already shaken up the natural order by winning the Cup to claim their first major trophy.

THE FIFA BIG COUNT OF 2000

	Male	Female		Male	Female
Registered players	1 392	22	Referees	101	2
Non registered players	27 060	220	Officials	1 279	19
Youth players	260	0	Total involved	30 355	
Total players	28 954		Number of clubs	20	
Professional players	0	0	Number of teams	1 109	

Football Federation of Kyrgyz Republic (FFKR)
Kurenkeeva Street 195, PO Box 1484, Bishkek 720 040, Kyrgyzstan
Tel +996 312 670573　　　Fax +996 312 670573
media@ffkr.kg　　　www.ffkr.kg
President: MURALIEV Amangeldi　　General Secretary: BERDYBEKOV Klichbek
Vice-President: KUTUEV Omurbek　　Treasurer: TBD　　Media Officer: None
Men's Coach: ZAKIROV Nematjan　　Women's Coach: None
FFKR formed: 1992　　AFC: 1994　　FIFA: 1994
Colours: Red, Red, Red

GAMES PLAYED BY KYRGYZSTAN IN THE 2006 FIFA WORLD CUP™ CYCLE

2002	Opponents	Score		Venue	Comp	Scorers	Att	Referee
No international matches played in 2002								
2003								
16-03	Afghanistan	L	1-2	Kathmandu	ACq	Gulov 60		
20-03	Nepal	W	2-0	Kathmandu	ACq	Nikov 2 27 47		
29-11	Pakistan	W	2-0	Karachi	WCq	Boldygin 36, Chikishev 59	10 000	Nesar BAN
3-12	Pakistan	W	4-0	Bishkek	WCq	Chikishev 18, Chertkov 28, Boldygin 67, Krasnov 9	12 000	Mamedov TKM
2004								
18-02	Tajikistan	L	1-2	Bishkek	WCq	Berezovsky 12	14 000	Lutfullin UZB
31-03	Syria	D	1-1	Bishkek	WCq	Ishenbaev 55	17 000	Bose IND
5-06	Qatar	D	0-0	Doha	Fr			
9-06	Bahrain	L	0-5	Al Muharraq	WCq		2 800	Al Saeedi UAE
8-09	Bahrain	L	1-2	Bishkek	WCq	Kenjisariev 86	10 000	Rungklay THA
13-10	Tajikistan	L	1-2	Dushanbe	WCq	Chikishev 84	11 000	El Enezi KUW
10-11	Kuwait	L	0-3	Kuwait City	Fr			
17-11	Syria	W	1-0	Damascus	WCq	Amin 47	1 000	Tongkhan THA
2005								
No international matches played in 2005 before August								

Fr = Friendly match • AC = AFC Asian Cup • WC = FIFA World Cup™ • q = qualifier

KYRGYZSTAN NATIONAL TEAM RECORDS AND RECORD SEQUENCES

Records			Sequence records				
Victory	6-0	MDV 1997	Wins	3	2003	Clean sheets	3	2003
Defeat	0-7	IRN 1997	Defeats	8	1999-2001	Goals scored	7	2001-2004
Player Caps	30	SALO Vladimir	Undefeated	3	2003	Without goal	6	1994-1996
Player Goals	3	Four players	Without win	8	1999-2001	Goals against	8	1991-2001

NATIONAL CAPS

	Caps
SALO Vladimir	30
JALILOV Zakir	29
JUMAKEYEV Marat	25
SYDYKOV Ruslan	22
RYBAKOV Aleksey	21

NATIONAL GOALS

	Goals
CHIKISHEV Sergey	3
HAYTBAYEV Farhad	3
JUMAGULOV Zamirbek	3
KUTSOV Sergey	3

NATIONAL COACH

	Years
KOSHALIYEV Meklis	1992-'96
NOVIKOV Yevgeniy	1997-'01
ZAKIROV Nematjan	2003-

FIFA REFEREE LIST 2005

	Int'l	DoB
BUSURMANKULOV Emil		1-04-1969
CHYNYBEKOV Kadyrbek	1995	11-10-1962

FIFA ASSISTANT REFEREE LIST 2005

	Int'l	DoB
ABDULLAEV Muzaffar	2005	2-05-1971
DJANYBEKOV Damir	2004	1-01-1965
EROSHENKO Yuri	1995	4-10-1962
KOCHKOROV Bahadyr	1997	13-05-1970

KRYGYZSTAN COUNTRY INFORMATION

Capital	Bishkek	Independence	1991 from Soviet Union	GDP per Capita	$1 600
Population	5 081 429	Status	Republic	GNP Ranking	148
Area km²	198 500	Language	Kyrgyz, Russian	Dialling code	+996
Population density	25 per km²	Literacy rate	97%	Internet code	.kg
% in urban areas	39%	Main religion	Muslim 75%, Orthodox 20%	GMT +/−	+6
Towns/Cities ('000)	Bishkek 896; Os 230; Celabad 77; Karakol 70; Tokmak 63; Karabalta 63; Balikici 45				
Neighbours (km)	Kazakhstan 1 051; China 858; Tajikistan 870; Uzbekistan 1 099				
Main stadia	Spartak – Bishkek 23 000; Dynamo – Bishkek 10 000				

KYRGYZSTAN 2004

FIRST DIVISION

	Pl	W	D	L	F	A	Pts	Dordoy	SKA	Zhashtyk	Guardia	Abdysh	Alay	Zhayil	Neftchi	Shoro	U-21
Dordoy Naryn	36	32	2	2	126	17	98		0-0 1-3	5-1 4-0	1-0 7-0	3-1 6-1	3-0 4-3	5-0 4-0	7-1 3-0	4-0 3-0	4-0 4-0
SKA-Shoro Bishkek	36	30	3	3	107	20	93	1-1 0-2		1-0 2-3	3-1 4-0	4-0 0-1	5-1 1-1	10-1 6-1	3-2 3-0	3-0 3-0	4-0 3-0
Zhashtyk Kara-Su	36	25	2	9	84	38	77	0-2 0-1	0-2 0-2		4-3 2-0	5-1 1-1	1-0 3-1	7-0 3-1	5-1 3-0	4-0 3-0	5-0 3-0
Guardia Bishkek	36	20	3	13	66	55	63	0-2 4-3	0-3 0-2	2-1 0-3		5-0 2-2	2-1 3-2	5-2 3-0	0-1 1-2	3-0 2-0	3-0
Abdysh-Ata Kant	36	14	4	18	63	75	46	1-7 1-4	0-3 1-2	2-3 1-2	2-4 0-0		1-0 6-2	2-1 3-1	0-1 3-0	3-4 3-0	4-1 1-2
Alay Osh	36	13	3	20	48	60	42	0-1 0-3	0-2 0-3	1-3 0-1	2-0 1-2	2-1 0-2		1-0 2-0	2-2 3-0	0-2 3-0	3-1 4-0
Zhayil Baatyr Karabalta	36	10	3	23	44	85	33	0-2 0-6	1-4 2-3	2-0 1-1	0-1 0-1	2-5 3-2	1-0 2-2		0-0 3-0	0-2 3-0	3-1 4-0
Neftchi Kochkor-Ata	36	9	2	25	30	87	29	0-6 0-1	0-1 1-3	1-3 0-3	0-3 0-3	2-1 2-3	4-2 1-2	1-0 0-3		0-3 3-0	2-1 0-3
Shoro Bishkek	36	7	2	27	26	88	23	0-4 0-3	0-4 0-3	1-2 0-3	0-1 0-3	1-1 0-3	1-3 0-3	1-0 0-3	3-1 0-3		2-2 0-3
Kyrgyzstan U-21	36	6	2	28	25	100	20	0-5 0-5	0-5 0-6	0-4 0-2	1-4 2-2	0-2 0-2	0-3 2-0	0-1 2-1	2-3 0-1	0-6 3-0	

17/04/2004 - 10/11/2004 • Shoro Bishkek withdrew after 17 games • Neftchi withdrew after 27 games • Future oppenents awarded matches **3-0**

KYRGYZSTAN 2004 SECOND DIVISION ZONE A

	Pl	W	D	L	F	A	Pts
Nashe Pivo Kant	28	26	1	1	96	12	79
Dinamo Chuy Bishkek	28	20	1	7	87	36	61
RIK Kainda	28	18	3	7	84	43	57
FK Burana	28	16	2	10	77	51	50
Maksat Belovodsk	28	15	3	10	60	51	48
FK Shopokov	27	15	1	11	53	49	46
Egrisi Bishkek	28	14	2	12	46	44	44
FK Bishkek-90	28	13	1	14	53	61	40
FK Bishkek-88	28	11	5	12	59	42	38
FK Ysyk-Ata	28	10	4	14	50	71	34
Rassvet Sokuluk	28	11	1	16	33	63	34
Jash-Abdysh-Ata Kant	28	8	4	16	38	56	28
FK Alamudun	28	9	1	18	46	66	28
FK Bishkek-89	27	7	3	17	34	92	24
Bayzak Baatyr Bishkek	28	0	2	26	9	67	2

KYRGYZSTAN 2004 SECOND DIVISION ZONE B1

	Pl	W	D	L	F	A	Pts
Dinamo-ROVD Batken	3	3	0	0	10	2	9
FK Isfana	3	1	1	1	6	6	4
Berkut Kadamjay	3	1	1	1	4	5	4
Shumkar Suluktu	3	0	0	3	3	10	0

KYRGYZSTAN 2004 SECOND DIVISION ZONE B2

	Pl	W	D	L	F	A	Pts
Shumkar-M Kara-Su	6	6	0	0	18	8	18
Sharab-K Aravan	6	3	1	2	12	8	10
FK Kyzyl-Kiya	6	1	1	4	3	11	4
Kara-Shoro Ozgon	6	0	2	4	7	13	2

No promotion in 2004 from the any zone in the Second Division

KYRGYZSTAN CUP 2004

Quarter-finals		Semi-finals		Final	
Dordoy Naryn	8 3				
Zhayil Baatyr	0 0	**Dordoy Naryn**	1 2		
Guardia Bishkek	0 3				
SKA-Shoro Bishkek	2 2	SKA-Shoro Bishkek	2 0	**Dordoy Naryn**	1
Alay Osh	6 3			Zhashtyk Kara-Su	0
Neftchi Kochkor-Ata	4 0	Alay Osh	1 2		
FK Kyzyl-Kiya	†	**Zhashtyk Kara-Su**	3 4	Ahmatbek Suyumbayev, Osh	
Zhashtyk Kara-Su		† Kyzyl-Kiya withdrew		31-08-2004, Att: 4 000	
				Scorer - Kasymov 36	

RECENT LEAGUE AND CUP RECORD

	Championship						Cup		
Year	Champions	Pts	Runners-up	Pts	Third	Pts	Winners	Score	Runners-up
1992	Alga Bishkek	38	SKA Sokuluk	32	Alay Osh	27	Alga Bishkek	2-1	Alay Osh
1993	Alga-RIFF Bishkek	61	Spartak Tokmak	55	Alay Osh	53	Alga-RIFF Bishkek	4-0	Alga Bishkek
1994	Kant-Oil Kant	47	Semetey Kyzyl-Kiya	44	Ak-Maral Tokmak	43	Ak-Maral Tokmak	2-1	Alay Osh
1995	Kant-Oil Kant	31	AiK Bishkek	30	Semetey Kyzyl-Kiya	28	Semetey Kyzyl-Kiya	2-0	Dinamo Bishkek
1996	Metallurg Kadamjay	56	AiK Bishkek	56	Alay Osh	45	AiK Bishkek		Metallurg Kadamjay
1997	Dinamo Bishkek	46	Alga-PVO Bishkek	41	AiK Bishkek	40	Alga-PVO Bishkek	1-0	Alay Osh
1998	Dinamo Bishkek	36	SKA-PVO Bishkek	31	AiK Bishkek	28	SKA-PVO Bishkek	3-0	Alay Osh
1999	Dinamo Bishkek	54	SKA-PVO Bishkek	48	Polyot & Zhashtyk	47	SKA-PVO Bishkek	3-0	Semetey Kyzyl-Kiya
2000	SKA-PVO Bishkek	64	Dinamo Bishkek	52	Polyot Bishkek	48	SKA-PVO Bishkek	2-0	Alay Osh
2001	SKA-PVO Bishkek	66	Zhashtyk Kara-Su	57	Dordoy Naryn	53	SKA-PVO Bishkek	1-0	Zhashtyk Kara-Su
2002	SKA-PVO Bishkek	48	Zhashtyk Kara-Su	43	Dordoy Naryn	39	SKA-PVO Bishkek	1-0	Zhashtyk Kara-Su
2003	Zhashtyk Kara-Su	36	SKA-PVO Bishkek	31	Dordoy Naryn	29	SKA-PVO Bishkek	1-0	Zhashtyk Kara-Su
2004	Dordoy Naryn	98	SKA-Shoro Bishkek	93	Zhashtyk Kara-Su	77	Dordoy Naryn	1-0	Zhashtyk Kara-Su

Play-off in 1996: Metallurg 1-0 AiK (now Guardia) • SKA-Shoro Bishkek previously named Alga Bishkek, Alga-PVO Bishkek then SKA-PVO Bishkek

KOR – KOREA REPUBLIC

NATIONAL TEAM RECORD
JULY 1ST 2002 TO JUNE 30TH 2005

PL	W	D	L	F	A	%
44	21	11	12	81	32	60.2

FIFA/COCA-COLA WORLD RANKING

1993	1994	1995	1996	1997	1998	1999	2000	2001	2002	2003	2004	High		Low	
41	35	46	44	27	17	51	40	42	20	22	22	**17**	12/98	**62**	02/96

2004-2005											
08/04	09/04	10/04	11/04	12/04	01/05	02/05	03/05	04/05	05/05	06/05	07/05
22	23	25	24	22	21	21	22	22	21	20	21

The heroics of the 2002 FIFA World Cup™ will be a tough act to follow in future years for the Koreans but under new coach Jo Bonfrere the Taeguk Warriors made sure of qualification for Germany, their sixth consecutive appearance in the finals of the FIFA World Cup™. Such a consistent record has not been reflected in senior Asian football with the Koreans having to go back to 1960 since they last won the AFC Asian Cup. In the 2004 finals they lost a titanic struggle against Iran in the quarter-finals although the U-20s did win the Asian Youth Championship after

INTERNATIONAL HONOURS

Qualified for the FIFA World Cup™ finals 1954 1986 1990 1994 1998 2002 Qualified for the FIFA Women's World Cup finals 2003

AFC Asian Cup 1956 1960 Asian Games Football Tournament 1970 (shared) 1978 (shared) 1986 East Asian Championship 2003

AFC Youth Championship 1959 1960 1963 1978 1980 1982 1990 1996 1998 2002 2004 AFC U-17 Championship 1986 2002

AFC Champions League Daewoo Royals 1986, Ilhwa Chunma 1996, Pohang Steelers 1997 1998, Suwon Samsung Bluewings 2001 2002

beating China PR 2-0 in the final in Malaysia. At home there was a return to winning ways for Suwon Samsung Bluewings. The two-time Asian Champions won their first K-League title since 1999 beating Pohang Steelers on penalties after both legs of the play-off final finished 0-0. Busan won the FA Cup, also on penalties whilst Ilhwa Chunma looked set to be crowned Asian champions before losing 5-1 at home to Saudi's Al Ittihad having won the first leg in Jeddah 3-1.

THE FIFA BIG COUNT OF 2000

	Male	Female		Male	Female
Registered players	2 157	180	Referees	559	6
Non registered players	500 000	4 000	Officials	968	106
Youth players	13 182	879	Total involved	522 037	
Total players	520 398		Number of clubs	54	
Professional players	417	0	Number of teams	615	

Korea Football Association (KFA)

1-131 Sinmunno, 2-ga, Jongno-Gu, Seoul 110-062, Korea Republic

Tel +82 2 7336764   Fax +82 2 7352755

fantasista@kfa.or.kr   www.kfa.or.kr

President: CHUNG Mong Joon Dr   General Secretary: ROH Heung Sub

Vice-President: CHO Chung Yun   Treasurer: TBD   Media Officer: None

Men's Coach: BONFRERE Jo   Women's Coach: None

KFA formed: 1928   AFC: 1954   FIFA: 1948

Colours: Red, Blue, Red

GAMES PLAYED BY KOREA REPUBLIC IN THE 2006 FIFA WORLD CUP™ CYCLE

2002	Opponents		Score	Venue	Comp	Scorers	Att	Referee
7-09	Korea DPR †	D	0-0	Seoul	Fr		60 000	Kwon Jong Chul KOR
20-11	Brazil	L	2-3	Seoul	Fr	Seol Ki Hyeon [8], Ahn Jung Hwan [58]	63 000	Lu Jun CHN
2003								
27-03	Colombia	D	0-0	Busan	Fr		56 248	Katayama JPN
16-04	Japan	L	0-1	Seoul	Fr		64 703	Kumbalingam SIN
31-05	Japan	W	1-0	Tokyo	Fr	Ahn Jung Hwan [86]	53 405	Mohd Salleh MAS
8-06	Uruguay	L	0-2	Seoul	Fr		63 691	-Yoshida JPN
11-06	Argentina	L	0-1	Seoul	Fr		62 000	Rungklay THA
25-09	Vietnam	W	5-0	Incheon	ACq	Lee Ki Hyung [35], Cho Jae Jin [49], Kim Do Hoon [68], Kim Dae Eui [72], Woo Sung Yong [86]	14 327	Lazar SIN
27-09	Oman	W	1-0	Incheon	ACq	Choi Sung Gook [46]	18 750	Okada JPN
29-09	Nepal	W	16-0	Incheon	ACq	Kim Dae Eui 2 [18 37], Woo Sung Yong 3 [21 45 48], Park Jin Sub 5 [22 28 64 67 89], Lee Eul Yong [54], Lee Gwan Woo [58], Kim Do Hoon 3 [75 84 86], Chung Kyung Ho [80]	6 521	Okada JPN
19-10	Vietnam	L	0-1	Muscat	ACq		25 000	Hanlumyaung THA
21-10	Oman	L	1-3	Muscat	ACq	Chung Kyung Ho [49]	22 000	
24-10	Nepal	W	7-0	Muscat	ACq	Cho Jae Jin [1], Lee Ki Hyung 2 [6 51], Kim Do Hoon 3 [16 32 34], Chung Kyung Ho [37]	100	
18-11	Bulgaria	L	0-1	Seoul	Fr		38 257	Mohd Salleh MAS
4-12	Hong Kong	W	3-1	Tokyo	EAC	Kim Do Heon [23], Kim Do Hoon [50], Ahn Jung Hwan [57]	14 895	Napitupulu IDN
7-12	China PR	W	1-0	Saitama	EAC	Yoo Sang Chul [45]	27 715	Abdul Hamid MAS
10-12	Japan	D	0-0	Yokohama	EAC		62 633	Nagalingam SIN
2004								
14-02	Oman	W	5-0	Ulsan	Fr	OG 2 [9 86], Seol Ki Hyeon [25], Ahn Jung Hwan 2 [41p 60]	26 514	Yoshida JPN
18-02	Lebanon	W	2-0	Suwon	WCq	Cha Du Ri [32], Cho Byung Kuk [51]	22 000	Al Dosari KSA
31-03	Maldives	D	0-0	Male	WCq		12 000	Vidanagamage SRI
28-04	Paraguay	D	0-0	Incheon	Fr		26 237	Kamikawa JPN
2-06	Turkey	L	0-1	Seoul	Fr		51 185	Maidin SIN
5-06	Turkey	W	2-1	Daegu	Fr	Yoo Sang Chul [66p], Kim Eun Jong [77]	45 284	Yoshida JPN
9-06	Vietnam	W	2-0	Daejeon	WCq	Ahn Jung Hwan 2 [11], Kim Do Heon [61]	40 019	Al Mehannah KSA
10-07	Bahrain	W	2-0	Gwangju	Fr	Lee Dong Gook [2], Choi Jin Cheul [40]	35 241	Fong HKG
14-07	Trinidad and Tobago	D	1-1	Seoul	Fr	Cha Du Ri [52]	18 025	Matsumura JPN
19-07	Jordan	D	0-0	Jinan	ACr1		26 000	Maidin SIN
23-07	United Arab Emirates	W	2-0	Jinan	ACr1	Lee Dong Gook [41], Ahn Jung Hwan [91+]	30 000	Irmatov UZB
27-07	Kuwait	W	4-0	Jinan	ACr1	Lee Dong Gook 2 [24 40], Cha Du Ri [45], Ahn Jung Hwan [75]	20 000	Maidin SIN
31-07	Iran	L	3-4	Jinan	ACqf	Seol Ki Hyun [16], Lee Dong Gook [25], Kim Nam Il [68]	20 000	Al Fadhli KUW
8-09	Vietnam	W	2-1	Ho Chi Minh City	WCq	Lee Dong Gook [63], Lee Chun Soo [76]	25 000	Yoshida JPN
13-10	Lebanon	D	1-1	Beirut	WCq	Choi Jin Cheul [8]	38 000	Irmatov UZB
17-11	Maldives	W	2-0	Seoul	WCq	Kim Do Heon [66], Lee Dong Gook [80]	64 000	Lazar SIN
19-12	Germany	W	3-1	Busan	Fr	Kim Dong Jin [16], Lee Dong Gook [71], Cho Jae Jin [87]	45 775	Mohd Salleh MAS
2005								
15-01	Colombia	L	1-2	Los Angeles	Fr	Chung Kyung Ho [2]	20 000	
19-01	Paraguay	D	1-1	Los Angeles	Fr	Kim Jin Kyu [46]	9 000	Hall USA
22-01	Sweden	D	1-1	Carson	Fr	Chung Kyung Ho [70]	9 941	Stott USA
4-02	Egypt	L	0-1	Seoul	Fr		16 054	Huang Junjie CHN
9-02	Kuwait	W	2-0	Seoul	WCq	Lee Dong Gook [24], Lee Young Pyo [81]	53 287	Maidin SIN
20-03	Burkina Faso	W	1-0	Dubai	Fr	Kim Sang Sik		
25-03	Saudi Arabia	L	0-2	Dammam	WCq		25 000	Mohd Salleh MAS
30-03	Uzbekistan	W	2-1	Seoul	WCq	Lee Young Pyo [54], Lee Dong Gook [61]	62 857	Najm LIB
3-06	Uzbekistan	D	1-1	Tashkent	WCq	Park Chu Young [90]	40 000	Moradi IRN
8-06	Kuwait	W	4-0	Kuwait City	WCq	Park Chu Young [19], Lee Dong Gook [29], Chung Kyung Ho [55], Park Ji Sung [61]	15 000	Khanthama THA

Fr = Friendly match • AC = AFC Asian Cup • EAC = East Asian Championship • WC = FIFA World Cup™
q = qualifier • r1 = first round group • qf = quarter-final • † Not a full international

KOREA REPUBLIC NATIONAL TEAM RECORDS AND RECORD SEQUENCES

Records			Sequence records				
Victory	16-0	NEP 2003	Wins	11	1975, 1978	Clean sheets	9	1970, 1988-1989
Defeat	0-12	SWE 1948	Defeats	3	Seven times	Goals scored	23	1975-76, 1977-78
Player Caps	135	HONG Myung Bo	Undefeated	32	1977-1978	Without goal	3	Four times
Player Goals	55	CHA Bum Kun	Without win	8	1981-1982	Goals against	11	1948-1953

KOREA REPUBLIC 2004 — K-LEAGUE FIRST STAGE

	Pl	W	D	L	F	A	Pts
Pohang Steelers	12	6	5	1	16	12	23
Chonbuk Hyundai Motors	12	5	5	2	16	9	20
Ulsan HyundaiHorang-i	12	5	5	2	11	8	20
Suwon Samsung Bluewings	12	5	3	4	19	16	18
FC Seoul	12	3	7	2	12	10	16
Chunnam Dragons	12	3	6	3	17	13	15
Gwangju Sangmu Phoenix	12	3	6	3	11	12	15
Seongnam Ilhwa Chunma	12	4	3	5	13	16	15
Busan Icons	12	2	8	2	7	8	14
Daegu FC	12	3	3	6	19	19	12
Daejeon Citizen	12	2	6	4	9	11	12
Bucheon SK	12	1	8	3	7	12	11
Incheon United	12	2	3	7	9	20	9

3/04/2004 - 27/06/2004

KOREA REPUBLIC 2004 — K-LEAGUE SECOND STAGE

	Pl	W	D	L	F	A	Pts
Suwon Samsung Bluewings	12	7	2	3	12	8	23
Chunnam Dragons	12	6	4	2	12	7	22
Ulsan Hyundai Horang-i	12	6	3	3	11	6	21
Incheon United	12	4	5	3	11	9	17
FC Seoul	12	4	5	3	8	7	17
Busan Icons	12	4	4	4	14	11	16
Daegu FC	12	4	4	4	11	12	16
Gwangju Sangmu Phoenix	12	3	5	4	7	8	14
Seongnam Ilhwa Chunma	12	3	5	4	10	12	14
Bucheon SK	12	3	4	5	12	15	14
Daejeon Citizen	12	4	2	6	9	15	14
Chonbuk Hyundai Motors	12	3	3	6	7	9	12
Pohang Steelers	12	2	3	7	7	12	9

29/08/2004 - 20/11/2004

KOREA REPUBLIC 2004 — K-LEAGUE OVERALL

	Pl	W	D	L	F	A	Pts	Ulsan	Suwon	Chunnam	Seoul	Chonbuk	Pohang	Busan	Gwangju	Seongnam	Daegu	Daejon	Incheon	Bucheon
Ulsan Hyundai Horang-i ‡	24	11	8	5	22	14	41		0-2	1-1	2-1	1-0	0-1	0-0	0-0	2-1	0-0	0-0	2-1	2-0
Suwon Samsung Bluewings †	24	12	5	7	31	24	41	1-0		2-1	1-0	2-1	1-2	1-2	3-2	1-2	1-0	1-2	3-2	3-1
Chunnam Dragons ‡	24	9	10	5	29	20	37	1-0	2-2		0-0	0-0	2-2	0-1	1-0	1-0	4-1	3-1	2-1	0-0
FC Seoul	24	7	12	5	20	17	33	0-0	1-0	0-0		0-0	1-1	1-1	1-0	2-0	1-1	0-1	1-0	1-1
Chonbuk Hyundai Motors	24	7	8	8	23	18	32	1-2	1-1	2-1	1-1		1-0	2-0	0-0	2-0	0-2	1-1	0-1	3-1
Pohang Steelers †	24	8	8	8	23	24	32	0-1	0-1	1-0	0-1	0-2		1-1	1-1	1-1	2-1	1-2	2-1	1-1
Busan Icons	24	6	12	6	21	19	30	0-0	0-1	1-2	2-0	0-0	1-0		0-0	1-1	2-1	2-0	1-1	0-0
Gwangju Sangmu Phoenix	24	6	11	7	18	20	29	0-0	1-0	2-2	0-1	1-0	2-3	1-0		1-0	0-0	1-1	1-0	0-1
Seongnam Ilhwa Chunma	24	7	8	9	23	28	29	0-2	2-2	1-0	1-2	1-0	1-2	1-1	1-2		1-0	2-1	0-0	1-1
Daegu FC	24	7	7	10	30	31	28	1-0	0-1	1-1	2-2	2-3	1-0	1-0	4-2	2-3		2-0	5-0	1-2
Daejon Citizen	24	6	8	10	18	26	26	1-3	1-0	0-2	0-0	1-0	0-1	2-0	1-1	1-1	1-1		0-1	1-1
Incheon United	24	6	8	10	20	29	26	2-3	0-0	0-2	1-3	0-0	1-0	2-2	0-0	1-1	1-0			3-1
Bucheon SK	24	4	13	7	19	27	25	0-1	1-1	1-1	1-1	0-3	0-0	0-3	0-0	1-1	4-0	1-0	0-0	

† Qualified for the play-offs as stage winners • ‡ Qualified for play-offs thanks to overall record • Matches in bold played in the first stage

K-LEAGUE PLAY-OFFS 2004

Semi-finals

Suwon Samsung Bluewings *	1
Chunnam Dragons	0

Ulsan Hyundai Horang-i	0
Pohang Steelers *	1

Finals

Suwon Samsung Bluewings	0 0 4p
Pohang Steelers	0 0 3p

* At home as stage winners

TOP SCORERS

JOAO SOARES	Chunnam	14
RAIMUNDO	Daegu	13
NADSON	Suwon	12
WOO Seong Jung	Pohang	10
KIM Eun Jung	Seoul	8
MARCEL	Suwon	8

KOREA REPUBLIC COUNTRY INFORMATION

Capital	Seoul	Independence	1945 from Japan	GDP per Capita	$17 800
Population	48 598 175	Status	Republic	GNP Ranking	13
Area km²	98 480	Language	Korean	Dialling code	+82
Population density	493 per km²	Literacy rate	98%	Internet code	.kr
% in urban areas	81%	Main religion	Christian 26%, Buddhist 26%	GMT + / –	+9

Towns/Cities ('000)	Seoul 10 349; Pusan 3 678; Inchon 2 580; Taegu 2 566; Taejon 1 475; Kwangju 1 416; Suwon 1 242; Koyang 1 195, Songnam 1 032; Ulsan 962; Puchon 829; Chonju 711; Ansan 650; Chongju 634; Anyang 634; Shihung 621; Changwon 526; Uijongbu 479; Chonan 365
Neighbours (km)	North Korea 238; Sea of Japan & Yellow Sea 2 413
Main stadia	Olympic Stadium – Seoul 69 841; Seoul Sang-am World Cup Stadium – Seoul 64 677

KOREA REPUBLIC 2004
K2-LEAGUE FIRST STAGE

	Pl	W	D	L	F	A	Pts
Goyang Kookmin Bank	9	7	2	0	17	5	23
Ulsan Hyundai Dockyard	9	6	3	0	19	7	21
Icheon Sangmu 2	9	6	1	2	12	9	19
Daejon Hydro & Nuclear	9	3	3	3	9	9	12
Suwon City Office	9	2	4	3	7	10	10
Gangneung City Office	9	2	3	4	9	10	9
Incheon National Railway	9	2	3	4	6	9	9
Gimpo Halleluja	9	2	3	4	11	15	9
Seosan Citizen	9	1	2	6	8	14	5
Uijeongbu Hummel	9	1	2	6	12	22	5

10/04/2004 - 7/06/2004
Goyang qualified to meet second stage winners for the title

KOREA REPUBLIC 2004
K2-LEAGUE SECOND STAGE

	Pl	W	D	L	F	A	Pts
Gangneung City Office	9	6	2	1	11	8	20
Ulsan Hyundai Dockyard	9	5	4	0	19	7	19
Suwon City Office	9	3	4	2	12	10	13
Goyang Kookmin Bank	9	3	3	3	9	8	12
Incheon National Railway	9	1	7	1	10	10	10
Icheon Sangmu 2	9	2	4	3	11	12	10
Uijeongbu Hummel	9	2	4	3	8	9	10
Daejon Hydro & Nuclear	9	2	3	4	10	15	9
Seosan Citizen	9	2	2	5	9	14	8
Gimpo Halleluja	9	0	5	4	7	13	5

28/08/2004 - 14/11/200
K2-League championship play-off: Goyang 2-1 2-0 Gangneung

KOREA REPUBLIC 2004
SAMSUNG HAUZEN CUP

	Pl	W	D	L	F	A	Pts
Seongnam Ilhwa Chunma	12	6	4	2	20	14	22
Daejeon Citizen	12	5	5	2	16	13	20
Chonbuk Hyundai Motors	12	5	4	3	16	12	19
Suwon Samsung Bluewings	12	4	7	1	14	9	19
Ulsan Hyundai Horang-i	12	4	5	3	17	13	17
Chunnam Dragons	12	5	1	6	13	17	16
Pohang Steelers	12	4	3	5	18	15	15
Incheon United	12	3	6	3	13	14	15
Daegu FC	12	2	9	1	21	20	15
Gwangju Sangmu Phoenix	12	4	2	6	12	14	14
Bucheon SK	12	2	6	4	7	9	12
FC Seoul	12	2	4	6	11	18	10
Busan Icons	12	2	4	6	17	27	10

11/07/2004 - 21/08/2004

RECENT LEAGUE CUP RECORD

Year	Winners
1992	Ilhwa Chunma
1993	POSCO Atoms
1994	Yukong Elephants
1995	Ulsan Horang-i
1996	Puchon Yukong
1997	Pusan Daewoo Royals
1998	Pusan Daewoo Royals
	Not organised from 1999-2003
2004	Seongnam Ilhwa Chunma

Adidas Cup 1992-97 • Hauzen Cup 2003-

RECENT LEAGUE AND CUP RECORD

	Championship						Cup		
Year	Champions	Pts	Runners-up	Pts	Third	Pts	Winners	Score	Runners-up
1990	Lucky Goldstar	39	Daewoo Royals	35	POSCO Atoms	28			
1991	Daewoo Royals	52	Ulsan Horang-i	42	POSCO Atoms	39			
1992	POSCO Atoms	35	Ilhwa Chunma	34	Ulsan Horang-i	32			
1993	Ilhwa Chunma	68	Anyang Cheetahs	59	Ulsan Horang-i	56			
1994	Ilhwa Chunma	54	Yukong Elephants	51	POSCO Atoms	50			
1995	Ilhwa Chunma	†	Pohang Atoms						
1996	Ulsan Horang-i	†	Suwon Bluewings						
1997	Pusan Royals	37	Chunnam Dragons	36	Ulsan Horang-i	30	Pohang Steelers	0-0 7-6p	Suwon Bluewings
1998	Suwon Bluewings	†					Chunnam Dragons	1-0	Ilhwa Chunma
1999	Suwon Bluewings	59	Bucheon SK	47	Chunnam Dragons	38	Anyang Cheetahs	2-1	Ulsan Horang-i
2000	Anyang Cheetahs	†	Bucheon SK				Chonbuk Hyundai	2-0	Ilhwa Chunma
2001	Ilhwa Chunma	45	Anyang Cheetahs	43	Suwon Bluewings	41	Daejeon Citizen	1-0	Pohang Steelers
2002	Ilhwa Chunma	49	Ulsan Horang-i	47	Suwon Bluewings	45	Suwon Bluewings	1-0	Pohang Steelers
2003	Ilhwa Chunma	91	Ulsan Horang-i	73	Suwon Bluewings	72	Chonbuk Hyundai	2-2 4-2p	Chunnam Dragons
2004	Suwon Bluewings	†	Pohang Steelers				Busan Icons	1-1 4-3p	Bucheon SK

† End of season play-offs: 1995 Seongnam Ilhwa Chunma 1-1 3-3 1-0 Pohang Atoms • 1996 Ulsan Hyundai Horang-i 0-1 3-1 Suwon Samsung Bluewings • 1998 Suwon Samsung Bluewings 1-0 0-0 Ulsan Hyundai Horang-i • 2000 Anyang LG Cheetahs 4-1 1-1 (4-2p) Bucheon SK 2004 Suwon Samsung Bluewings 0-0 0-0 4-3p Pohang Steelers

HANA BANK FA CUP 2004

First Round		Second Round		Quarter-finals		Semi-finals		Final	
Busan Icons ††	4								
Hongik University	0	Busan Icons ††	2						
Jeonju University	1	Suwon Samsung Bluewings	1	Busan Icons ††	2 6p				
Suwon Samsung Bluewings †‡	2			Chonbuk Hyundai Motors	2 5p				
Ajou University †‡	5	Ajou University	0			Busan Icons †	5		
Bundang Joma	0	Chonbuk Hyundai Motors ††	3			Ulsan Hyundai Horang-i	1		
								Busan Icons	1 4p
Gimpo Halleluja ‡‡	3	Gimpo Halleluja ‡‡	3					Bucheon SK	1 3p
Daegu FC	1	JEI	1	Gimpo Halleluja	0				
Konkuk University	0			Ulsan Hyundai Horang-i ††	5				
JEI ‡‡	1	Incheon National Railway	2						
Incheon National Railway	1 5p	Ulsan Hyundai Horang-i ‡‡	5						
Incheon United	1 4p								
Gangneung City Office	1								
Ulsan Hyundai Horang-i §§	3								
Daejeon Citizen †	4	Daejeon Citizen †	2						
Kyunghee University	0	Suwon City Office	0	Daejeon Citizen †	1				
Seongnam Ilhwa Chunma	1			Chunnam Dragons	0				
Suwon City Office †	3	Goyang Kookmin Bank	0			Daejeon Citizen	0 2p		
Goyang Kookmin Bank ††	3	Chunnam Dragons †	2			Bucheon SK †	0 4p		
Hanmin University	1								
Ulsan Mipo Dockyard	0								
Chunnam Dragons ††	2								
Gwangju Sangmu Phoenix §	9	Gwangju Sangmu Phoenix ‡	3						
Yongin City Office	0	FC Seoul	2	Gwangju Sangmu Phoenix	0				
Paju Beomu FC	1			Bucheon SK †	2				
FC Seoul §	10	Dongeui University	1						
Dongeui University ‡	1	Bucheon SK ‡	2						
Pohang Steelers	0								
Myongji University	0								
Bucheon SK ‡	3								

CUP FINAL

Civil Stadium, Changwong
25-12-2004
Scorers – Meb 5 for Busan;
Byeon Jae Seop 6 for Bucheon

† Played in Changwon • †† Played in Masan • ‡ Played in Gimhae • ‡‡ Played in Tongyeong • § Played in Yangsan • §§ Played in Haman • †† Played in Namhae (All in Kyongsangnam-do Province)

SUWON SAMSUNG BLUEWINGS 2004

Date	Opponents	Score		Comp	Scorers	Att
10-04-2004	Chonbuk Hyundai Motors	D 1-1	A	KL1	Nadson [69]	11 135
17-04-2004	Pohang Steelers	L 1-2	H	KL1	Jo Jae Jin [19]	23 179
24-04-2004	Seongnam Ilhwa Chunma	D 2-2	A	KL1	Marcel [15], OG [34]	7 953
5-05-2004	Daegu FC	W 1-0	H	KL1	Nadson [12]	38 163
8-05-2004	Ulsan Hundai Horang-i	W 2-0	A	KL1	Nadson [3], Marcel [65]	7 452
15-05-2004	Busan Icons	L 1-2	H	KL1	Marcel [27]	20 376
23-05-2004	FC Seoul	L 0-1	A	KL1		30 751
26-05-2004	Bucheon SK	W 3-1	H	KL1	Marcel [3], Choi Seong Yong [55], Kim Dong Hyeon [85]	23 160
30-05-2004	Chunnam Dragons	D 2-2	H	KL1	Marcel [32], Kim Dae Ui [68]	13 650
13-06-2004	Gwangju Sangmu Phoenix	W 3-2	H	KL1	Nadson 3 [11 30 45]	26 487
20-06-2004	Daejeon Citizen	L 0-1	A	KL1		15 121
27-06-2004	Incheon United	W 3-2	H	KL1	Kim Dae Ui [64p], Seo Jeong Won [80], Kim Dong Hyeon [89]	27 326
11-07-2004	Gwangju Sangmu Phoenix	W 1-0	H	HC	Marcel [5]	13 467
15-07-2004	Pohang Steelers	W 3-2	H	HC	Nadson [24], Kim Dae-Ui [67], Marcel [90]	8 367
18-07-2004	Seongnam Ilhwa Chunma	D 2-2	A	HC	Kim Dae Ui [7], Nadson [21]	6 253
22-07-2004	Ulsan Hyundai Horang-i	D 1-1	A	HC	Park Geon Ha [3]	22 315
25-07-2004	Bucheon SK	W 3-1	H	HC	Kim Dae Ui [20], Marcel [86], Kim Dong Hyeon [97+]	25 311
1-08-2004	Daegu FC	D 1-1	A	HC	Marcel [34]	12 365
4-08-2004	Daejeon Citizen	D 0-0	H	HC		22 136
8-08-2004	FC Seoul	D 0-0	A	HC		14 823
11-08-2004	Incheon United	D 0-0	A	HC		5 632
14-08-2004	Chunnam Dragons	L 0-1	H	HC		20 317
18-08-2004	Busan Icons	W 2-0	A	HC	Kim Dae Ui [30], Urumov [62]	1 823
21-08-2004	Chonbuk Hyundai Motors	D 1-1	H	HC	Jo Seong Hwan [78]	21 362
29-08-2004	Daejeon Citizen	L 1-2	H	KL2	Nadson [81p]	18 639
1-09-2004	Gwangju Sangmu Phoenix	L 0-1	A	KL2		27 863
7-09-2004	Chunnam Dragons	W 2-1	H	KL2	Nadson [63], Marcel [81]	6 637
19-09-2004	Bucheon SK	D 1-1	A	KL2	Jo Byeong Guk [13]	2 523
3-10-2004	FC Seoul	W 1-0	H	KL2	Kim Du Hyeon [82]	19 836
6-10-2004	Busan Icons	W 1-0	A	KL2	Nadson [15]	942
16-10-2004	Ulsan Hyundai Horang-i	W 1-0	H	KL2	Nadson [34]	17 362
31-10-2004	Daegu FC	W 1-0	A	KL2	Kim Dong Hyeon [69]	25 462
3-11-2004	Seongnam Ilhwa Chunma	L 1-2	H	KL2	Marcel [36]	18 365
7-11-2004	Pohang Steelers	W 1-0	A	KL2	Nadson [66]	11 702
10-11-2004	Chonbuk Hyundai Motors	W 2-1	H	KL2	Nadson [7], Marcel [44]	12 351
20-11-2004	Incheon United	D 0-0	A	KL2		23 595
5-12-2004	Chunnam Dragons	W 1-0	H	KLsf	Musa 4	26 445
8-12-2004	Pohang Steelers	D 0-0	A	KLf		15 206
12-12-2004	Pohang Steelers	D 0-0	H	KLf		36 490
14-12-2004	Jeonju University	W 2-1	N	FACr1	Kim Gi Beom [50], Yun Hwa Pyeong [100]	
16-12-2004	Busan Icons	L 1-2	N	FACr2	Yun Hwa Pyeong [43]	

KL1 = K-League Stage 1 • HC = Samsung Hauzen Cup • KL2 = K-League Stage 2 • FAC = Hana Bank FA Cup
r1 = first round • r2 = second round • f = final • **A** = Civil Stadium, Changwon • N = Sports Park Namhae • **N** = Masan Stadium, Masan

CLUB DIRECTORY

Club	Town/City	Stadium	Phone	www.	Lge	Cup	CL
Bucheon SK (1)	Bucheon	Bucheon Lesports Park 35 000	+82 2 21215271	skfc.com	1	0	0
Busan I-Park (2)	Busan	Busan Asiad Main Stadium 55 982	+82 51 5557101	busanipark.co.kr	4	1	0
Chonbuk Hyundai Motors	Jeonju	Jeonju World Cup Stadium 42 477	+82 63 2731763	hyundai-motorsfc.co.kr	0	2	0
Chunnam Dragons	Gwangyang	Gwangyang Football Stadium 14 284	+82 61 7925600	dragons.co.kr	0	1	0
Daegu FC	Daegu	Daegu World Cup Stadium 68 014	+82 53 2562003	daegufc.co.kr	0	0	0
Daejeon Citizen	Daejeon	Daejeon World Cup Stadium 42 176	+82 42 8242002	fcdaejeon.com	0	1	0
Gwangju Sangmu Phoenix	Gwangju	Guus Hidink Stadium 42 880	+82 2 34006151	gwangjusmfc.co.kr	0	0	0
Incheon United	Incheon	Incheon Munhak 51 179	+82 32 4231500	incheonutd.com	0	0	0
Pohang Steelers (3)	Pohang	Steel Yard 25 000	+82 54 2217700	steelers.co.kr	3	1	2
Seongnam Ilhwa Chunma (4)	Seongnam	Seongnam Stadium 27 000	+82 31 7533956	seongnamilhwafc.co.kr	6	1	1
FC Seoul	Seoul	Seoul World Cup Stadium 64 677	+82 2 3065050	fcseoul.com	0	0	0
Suwon Samsung Bluewings	Suwon	Suwon World Cup Stadium 44 047	+82 31 2472002	fcbluewings.com	3	1	2
Ulsan Hyundai Horang-i	Ulsan	Ulsan Big Crown 43 550	+82 52 2306141	horangifc.co.kr	1	0	0

Name changes (1) Yukong Elephants → Puchong Yukong → Puchong SK → Bucheon SK
(2) Daewoo Royals → Pusan Daewoo Royals → Pusan Icons → Busan Icons → Busan I-Park
(3) POSCO Dolphins → POSCO Atoms → Pohang Atoms → Pohang Steelers
(4) Ilhwa Chunma → Seongnam Ilhwa Chunma
(Others) Lucky Goldstar → Anyang LG Cheetahs

KSA – SAUDI ARABIA

NATIONAL TEAM RECORD
JULY 1ST 2002 TO JUNE 30TH 2005

PL	W	D	L	F	A	%
47	28	12	7	91	30	72.3

FIFA/COCA-COLA WORLD RANKING

1993	1994	1995	1996	1997	1998	1999	2000	2001	2002	2003	2004	High		Low	
38	27	54	37	33	30	39	36	31	38	26	28	21	07/04	63	09/00

2004-2005											
08/04	09/04	10/04	11/04	12/04	01/05	02/05	03/05	04/05	05/05	06/05	07/05
26	27	27	30	28	30	30	30	31	31	31	28

Jeddah's Al Ittihad were responsible for one of the most remarkable comebacks ever in international club football when they won the AFC Champions League in December 2004. In the final against Ilhwa Chuma they lost the first leg 1-3 at home in Jeddah but then won the return 5-1 in Korea Republic to win the title for the first time. It was Al Hilal, the only other Saudi club to have been Asian champions, who dominated domestic club football and they completed the League and Cup double for the first time in their history. Despite finishing second to 2004 champions Al Shabab in the regular season Hilal won the play-off final between the two thanks to a great free-kick from

INTERNATIONAL HONOURS
Qualified for the FIFA World Cup™ finals 1994 1998 2002 **FIFA U-17 World Championship** 1989 **AFC Asian Cup** 1984 1988 1996 **AFC Asian Youth Cup** 1986 1992 **AFC Asian U-17** 1985 1988 **AFC Champions League** Al Hilal 1992 2000, Al Ittihad 2004

their Brazilian midfielder Camacho. Two months previously they had beaten Al Qadisiya to win the Crown Prince Cup. The Saudis made relatively easy work of qualifying for the 2006 FIFA World Cup™ finals in Germany with the Argentine Gabriel Calderon at the helm for the final stages of the campaign having taken over in December 2004. His task will be to make sure that first and foremost there is no repeat of the 2002 finals debacle and build a belief in the squad that they can repeat the performances of the 1994 finals in the USA.

THE FIFA BIG COUNT OF 2000

	Male	Female		Male	Female
Registered players	6 402	0	Referees	602	0
Non registered players	100 000	0	Officials	612	0
Youth players	10 316	0	Total involved	117 932	
Total players	116 718		Number of clubs	153	
Professional players	458	0	Number of teams	700	

Saudi Arabian Football Federation (SAFF)
Al Mather Quarter, Prince Faisal Bin Fahad Street, PO Box 5844, Riyadh 11432, Saudi Arabia
Tel +966 1 4822240   Fax +966 1 4821215
www.saff.com.sa
President: TBD   General Secretary: AL-ABDULHADI Faisal
Vice-President: HRH Prince Nawaf Bin Faisal B.F. BIN ABDULAZIZ   Treasurer: AL-ATHEL Abdullah
Men's Coach: CALDERON Gabriel   Women's Coach: None
SAFF formed: 1959   AFC: 1972   FIFA: 1959
Colours: White, Green, White

GAMES PLAYED BY SAUDI ARABIA IN THE 2006 FIFA WORLD CUP™ CYCLE

2002	Opponents	Score		Venue	Comp	Scorers	Att	Referee
17-12	Bahrain	W	2-1	Kuwait City	ARr1	Al Abili 33, Al Meshal 71	7 000	Guezzaz MAR
19-12	Lebanon	W	1-0	Kuwait City	ARr1	Tamim 90	700	El Beltagy EGY
24-12	Syria	W	3-0	Kuwait City	ARr1	Takar 1, Khariri 71 Al Meshal 90	2 000	Zekrini ALG
26-12	Yemen	D	2-2	Kuwait City	ARr1	Al Qahtani 2		
28-12	Morocco	W	2-0	Kuwait City	ARsf	Al Waked 20, Al Meshal 57	2 000	Abbas SYR
30-12	Bahrain	W	1-0	Kuwait City	ARf	Noor 94GG	7 500	Zekrini ALG
2003								
30-04	Liechtenstein	L	0-1	Vaduz	Fr		1 200	Rogalla SUI
30-09	Syria	D	1-1	Jeddah	Fr	Al Basha 22		
6-10	Yemen	W	7-0	Jeddah	ACq	Al Basha 4 15 20 25 35, Noor 64, Al Shlhoub 72p Al Meshal 78		
8-10	Bhutan	W	6-0	Jeddah	ACq	Al Basha 7, Jumaan 2 9 25, Al Qahtani 28 Al Janoubi 43, Al Wadani 90		
10-10	Indonesia	W	5-0	Jeddah	ACq	Al Meshal 3 34 55 56, Al Basha 2 47 76		
13-10	Yemen	W	3-1	Jeddah	ACq	Al Montasheri 18, Al Wakad 20, Al Shlhoub 82p		
15-10	Bhutan	W	4-0	Jeddah	ACq	Al Wakad 4 3 24 70 80		
17-10	Indonesia	W	6-0	Jeddah	ACq	Al Meshal 2 21 85, Al Shlhoub 45p, Noor 52 Al Dosari 78, Al Janoubi 89		
17-12	Estonia	D	1-1	Dammam	Fr	Tukar 28	1 500	Al Mehannah KSA
20-12	Azerbaijan	W	1-0	Riyadh	Fr	Al Meshal 86		
26-12	United Arab Emirates	W	2-0	Kuwait City	GC	Al Shlhoub 15p, Tukar 83		Ebrahim BHR
29-12	Qatar	D	0-0	Kuwait City	GC			Meier SUI
2004								
1-01	Bahrain	W	1-0	Kuwait City	GC	Suwaid 74		
4-01	Kuwait	D	1-1	Kuwait City	GC	Al Shlhoub 76		
6-01	Oman	W	2-1	Kuwait City	GC	Noor 69, Al Qahtani 90		
8-01	Yemen	W	2-0	Kuwait City	GC	Al Qahtani 2 9 31		
18-02	Indonesia	W	3-0	Riyadh	WCq	Al Shahrani 2 4 39, Al Qahtani 45	1 000	Al Ghafary JOR
31-03	Sri Lanka	W	1-0	Colombo	WCq	Al Shahrani 51	6 000	Chynybekov KGZ
9-06	Turkmenistan	W	3-0	Riyadh	WCq	Al Meshal 2 27 45, Noor 32	1 000	Khanthama THA
18-07	Turkmenistan	D	2-2	Chengdu	ACr1	Al Qahtani 2 9p 59	12 400	Al Fadhli KUW
22-07	Uzbekistan	L	0-1	Chengdu	ACr1		22 000	Kwon Jong Chul KOR
26-07	Iraq	L	1-2	Chengdu	ACr1	Al Montasheri 56	15 000	Kwon Jong Chul KOR
1-09	Kuwait	D	1-1	Riyadh	Fr			
8-09	Turkmenistan	W	1-0	Ashgabat	WCq	Al Qahtani 47	5 000	Kwon Jong Chul KOR
6-10	Syria	D	2-2	Riyadh	Fr	Muwaled 26, Suwaid 69p		
12-10	Indonesia	W	3-1	Jakarta	WCq	Al Meshal 9, Sulaimani 13, Al Qahtani 80	30 000	Mohd Salleh MAS
17-11	Sri Lanka	W	3-0	Dammam	WCq	Al Harthi 6, Al Shlhoub 45p, Fallata 65	2 000	Muflah OMA
11-12	Kuwait	L	1-2	Doha	GCr1	Al Qahtani 13		
14-12	Yemen	W	2-0	Doha	GCr1	Al Otaibi 34, Al Saweyed 47		
17-12	Bahrain	L	0-3	Doha	GCr1			
2005								
25-01	Tajikistan	W	3-0	Riyadh	Fr	Edris 42, Al Jamaan 60, Al Saqri 66		
29-01	Turkmenistan	W	1-0	Riyadh	Fr	Al Shamrani 90		
2-02	Hungary	D	0-0	Istanbul	Fr		100	Dereli TUR
29-02	Uzbekistan	D	1-1	Tashkent	WCq	Al Jaber 76	45 000	Kamikawa JPN
14-03	Egypt	L	0-1	Dammam	Fr			
18-03	Finland	L	1-4	Dammam	Fr	Al Basha 48		
25-03	Korea Republic	W	2-0	Dammam	WCq	Khariri 29, Al Qahtani 74	25 000	Mohd Salleh MAS
30-03	Kuwait	D	0-0	Kuwait City	WCq		25 000	Moradi IRN
27-05	Bahrain	D	1-1	Riyadh	Fr	Khariri 35		
3-06	Kuwait	W	3-0	Riyadh	WCq	Al Shlhoub 2 19 50, Al Harthi 82	72 000	Kamikawa JPN
8-06	Uzbekistan	W	3-0	Riyadh	WCq	Al Jaber 2 8 61, Al Harthi 88	72 000	Huang Junjie CHN

Fr = Friendly match • AR = Arab Cup • AC = AFC Asian Cup • GC = Gulf Cup • WC = FIFA World Cup™
q = qualifier • r1 = first round group • sf = semi-final • f = final • GG = Golden Goal

FIFA REFEREE LIST 2005

	Int'l	DoB
AL AMRI Abdulrahman		24-09-1968
AL DOSARI Muageb		8-12-1961
AL GHAMDI Khalil	2002	2-09-1970
AL HAMDAN Naser	1996	6-11-1964
AL HARBI Abdulrahman	2005	16-10-1966
AL MIRDASI Mamdouh		17-09-1969
AL MUTLAQ Ali	2004	25-10-1965
AL NAFISAH Ibrahim	1999	1-01-1962
AL SHEHRI Daffer	2004	24-09-1968

FIFA ASSISTANT REFEREE LIST 2005

	Int'l	DoB
AL ABAD Abdullah		23-09-1968
AL BEGAMI Mohammed	1999	8-12-1961
AL GHAMDI Mohammed	2004	26-10-1966
AL KATHIRI Abdul Aziz	2005	5-10-1969
AL MULHIM Fahad		8-12-1961
AL NAMI Ibrahim	2005	4-10-1977
AL SHOPAKY Mohina	1997	28-11-1962
AL TRAIFI Ali	1998	19-12-1960
DEBASI Ibrahim	2004	16-10-1966
RUSTOM Yosef	2004	26-10-1965

NATIONAL COACH

	Years
PARREIRA Carlos Alberto	1998
AL KHARASHI Mohammad	1999
PFISTER Otto	1999
MACALA Milan	2000
AL JOHOR Nasser	2000
SANTRAC Slobodan	2001
AL JOHOR Nasser	2002
VAN DER LEM Gerard	2002-'04
AL ABODULAZIZ Nasser	2004
CALDERON Gabriel	2004-

SAUDI ARABIA NATIONAL TEAM RECORDS AND RECORD SEQUENCES

Records			Sequence records					
Victory	8-0	MAC 1993	Wins	11	2001	Clean sheets	9	2001
Defeat	0-13	EGY 1961	Defeats	6	1995	Goals scored	15	2001
Player Caps	170	AL DAEYEA Mohamed	Undefeated	19	2003-2004	Without goal	5	1998
Player Goals	67	ABDULLAH Majed	Without win	10	1988	Goals against	10	1981-1982

CLUB DIRECTORY

Club	Town/City	Stadium	Lge	Cup	CL
Al Ahly	Jeddah	Prince Sultan bin Fahd 15 000	2	12	0
Al Ansar	Medina	Prince Mohammed bin Abdul Aziz 10 000	0	0	0
Al Hilal	Riyadh	Prince Faisal bin Fahd 27 000	10	10	2
Al Ittifaq	Dammam	Prince Mohamed bin Fahd 35 000	2	2	0
Al Ittihad	Jeddah	Prince Abdullah Al Faisal 24 000	6	10	1
Al Nasr	Riyadh	Prince Faisal bin Fahd 27 000	6	7	0
Ohod	Medina	Prince Mohammed bin Abdul Aziz 10 000	0	0	0
Al Qadisiya	Khobar	Prince Saud bin Jalawi 10 000	0	1	0
Al Riyadh	Riyadh	Prince Faisal bin Fahd 27 000	0	1	0
Al Shabab	Riyadh	Prince Faisal bin Fahd 27 000	4	3	0
Al Ta'ee	Ha'il	Prince bin Masaad bin Jalawi 10 000	0	0	0
Al Wahda	Mecca	King Abdul Aziz 33 500	0	2	0

SAUDI ARABIA COUNTRY INFORMATION

Capital	Riyadh	Formation	1932	GDP per Capita	$11 800
Population	25 795 938	Status	Monarchy	GNP Ranking	23
Area km²	1 960 582	Language	Arabic	Dialling code	+966
Population density	13 per km²	Literacy rate	78%	Internet code	.sa
% in urban areas	80%	Main religion	Muslim	GMT + / –	+3
Towns/Cities ('000)	Riyadh 3 469; Jeddah 2 545; Mecca 1 199; Medina 824; Ad Damman 568; At Taif 514; Tabuk 355; Buraydah 341; Khamis Mushayt 276; Al Hufuf 266; Al Mubarraz 258; Ha'il 236				
Neighbours (km)	Jordan 744; Iraq 814; Kuwait 222; Qatar 60; UAE 457; Oman 676; Yemen 1 458; Persian Gulf & Red Sea 2 640				
Main stadia	King Fahd International – Riyadh 70 000; Prince Abdullah Al Faisal – Jeddah 24 000				

SAUDI ARABIA 2004-05

THE CUSTODIAN OF THE TWO HOLY MOSQUES LEAGUE CUP

	Pl	W	D	L	F	A	Pts	Shabab	Hilal	Ittihad	Nasr	Ahly	Wahda	Qadisiya	Ta'ee	Ittifaq	Ansar	Riyadh	Ohod
Al Shabab †	22	14	6	2	42	16	48		1-2	1-1	1-1	1-1	2-1	2-0	2-1	0-0	4-0	3-1	3-1
Al Hilal †‡	22	13	6	3	41	21	45	1-1		4-2	2-0	2-1	1-1	1-0	4-0	1-0	0-1	1-1	2-0
Al Ittihad ‡	22	11	5	6	53	37	38	0-2	2-1		1-1	3-2	3-3	2-0	3-0	4-3	4-0	4-1	4-1
Al Nasr ‡	22	11	5	6	37	31	38	0-2	1-1	3-2		3-1	6-2	2-1	0-1	1-0	3-2	3-1	2-0
Al Ahly	22	10	4	8	41	29	34	1-0	3-0	2-4	2-3		1-0	2-0	3-0	0-3	6-1	2-0	3-0
Al Wahda	22	7	7	8	35	36	28	1-1	0-3	2-2	2-2	3-0		3-2	3-2	1-0	1-1	3-2	5-0
Al Qadisiya	22	7	7	8	32	33	28	1-2	3-3	3-2	1-2	2-1	1-1		3-1	1-1	6-3	1-1	2-1
Al Ta'ee	22	8	2	12	24	36	26	0-2	1-2	2-0	2-0	1-1	1-0	1-2		1-0	1-1	3-1	2-0
Al Ittifaq	22	6	7	9	26	23	25	0-3	0-3	1-1	0-0	0-1	2-0	0-0	4-0		4-0	3-1	1-1
Al Ansar	22	6	6	10	31	52	24	3-6	1-3	3-2	1-2	1-1	1-0	0-1	3-2	1-1		2-1	3-1
Al Riyadh	22	4	7	11	27	42	19	0-1	1-1	1-4	3-1	2-2	1-2	1-1	2-1	2-1	1-1		1-0
Ohod	22	2	4	16	18	51	10	0-2	1-3	1-3	3-1	0-5	2-1	1-1	0-1	1-2	2-2	2-2	

27/08/2004 - 16/06/2005 • † Qualified for the play-off final • †‡ Qualified for the play-off semi-final • ‡ Qualified for the play-off first round

SAUDI ARABIA 2004-05 FIRST DIVISION (2)

	Pl	W	D	L	F	A	Pts
Al Hazm Raas	26	16	7	3	46	20	55
Abha	26	13	8	5	54	31	47
Al Ra'ed Beraida	26	11	8	7	38	30	41
Hajr Ihsa'a	26	11	8	7	30	30	41
Al Taawun Beraida	26	11	7	8	45	33	40
Al Sho'ala Karj	26	12	3	11	38	30	39
Al Faysali	26	10	8	8	28	16	38
Al Khaleej Saihat	26	9	9	8	27	33	36
Al Jabalain	26	8	9	9	29	27	33
Al Fat'h	26	7	10	9	32	30	31
Faiha'a	26	6	9	11	21	31	27
Najran	26	5	12	9	25	37	27
Hamada	26	6	6	14	31	54	24
Al Najma Onayzah	26	3	4	19	20	62	13

18/11/2004 - 19/05/2005

CHAMPIONSHIP PLAY-OFFS 2004-05

First round		Semi-final		Final	
		Al Hilal	1		
Al Nasr	0	Al Ittihad	0	Al Hilal	1
Al Ittihad	6			Al Shabab ‡	0

15-07-2005
Scorer - Marcelo Camacho 57 for Hilal

‡ Qualified for AFC Champions League as Al Hilal had already qualified via the Crown Prince Cup

RECENT LEAGUE AND CUP RECORD

	Championship				Cup		
Year	Champions	Score	Runners-up		Winners	Score	Runners-up
1990	Al Hilal	†	Al Ahly				
1991	Al Shabab				Al Ittihad	0-0 5-4p	Al Nasr
1992	Al Shabab	1-1 4-3p	Al Ittifaq		Al Qadisiya	0-0 4-2p	Al Shabab
1993	Al Shabab	1-0	Al Hilal		Al Shabab	1-1 5-3p	Al Ittihad
1994	Al Nasr	1-0	Al Riyadh		Al Riyadh	1-0	Al Shabab
1995	Al Nasr	3-1	Al Hilal		Al Hilal	1-0	Al Riyadh
1996	Al Hilal	2-1	Al Ahly		Al Shabab	3-0	Al Nasr
1997	Al Ittihad	2-0	Al Hilal		Al Ittihad	2-0	Al Ta'ee
1998	Al Hilal	3-2	Al Shabab		Al Ahly	3-2	Al Riyadh
1999	Al Ittihad	1-0	Al Ahly		Al Shabab	1-0	Al Hilal
2000	Al Ittihad	2-1	Al Ahly		Al Hilal	3-0	Al Shabab
2001	Al Ittihad	1-0	Al Nasr		Al Ittihad	3-0	Al Ittifaq
2002	Al Hilal	2-1	Al Ittihad		Al Ahly	2-1	Al Ittihad
2003	Al Ittihad	3-2	Al Ahly		Al Hilal	1-0	Al Ahly
2004	Al Shabab	1-0	Al Ittihad		Al Ittihad	1-0	Al Ahly
2005	Al Hilal	1-0	Al Shabab		Al Hilal	2-1	Al Qadisiya

† Played on a league basis • The Crown Prince Cup took over as the main Cup competition in 1991

CROWN PRINCE CUP 2004-05

Round of 16		Quarter-finals		Semi-finals		Final	
Al Hilal *	1						
Al Ra'ed	0	Al Hilal	1				
Ohod	2	Al Wahda *	0				
Al Wahda *	4			Al Hilal *	1 1		
Al Ta'ee *	4			Al Ittihad	0 1		
Al Ittifaq	3	Al Ta'ee	1				
Najran	0	Al Ittihad *	5				
Al Ittihad *	5					Al Hilal ‡	2
Al Nasr *	4					Al Qadisiya	1
Al Ansar	1	Al Nasr *	1				
Al Ahly	2 3p	Al Watani	0				
Al Watani *	2 5p			Al Nasr	1 1		
Al Shabab *	4			Al Qadisiya *	2 1		
Al Khaleej	0	Al Shabab *	2 3p				
Al Riyadh *	1	Al Qadisiya	2 4p				
Al Qadisiya	3						

* Home team in the first leg • ‡ Qualified for AFC Champions League

CUP FINAL

13-05-2005
Scorers - Al Shlhoub 35, Al Anbar 83 for Hilal; Souza 18 for Qadisiya

AL ITTIHAD 2004-05

Date	Opponents	Score			Scorers
27-08-2004	Ohod	W 4-0	H	LGE	Qahwaji 2 23 39, Al Waked 56, Idris 81
2-09-2004	Al Ta'ee	L 0-2	A	LGE	
6-09-2004	Al Ittifaq	D 1-1	A	LGE	Qahwaji 27
14-09-2004	Dalian Shide - CHN	D 1-1	A	ACLqf	Carevic 23
21-09-2004	Dalian Shide - CHN	W 1-0	H	ACLqf	Tukar 68
26-09-2004	Al Ahly	W 4-2	H	LGE	Noor 11p, Idris 40, OG 60, Suwaid 64
1-10-2004	Al Ansar	W 4-0	H	LGE	Idris 2 3 64, Suwaid 16, Al Yami 80
8-10-2004	Al Qadisiya	W 2-0	H	LGE	Al Otaibi 15, Idris 90
15-10-2004	Al Wahda	D 2-2	A	LGE	Idris 17, Chico 62
19-10-2004	Chonbuk Motors - KOR	W 2-1	H	ACLsf	Noor 22, Al Montashari 89
26-10-2004	Chonbuk Motors - KOR	D 2-2	A	ACLsf	Chico 70p, Al Harbi 88
8-11-2004	Al Riyadh	W 4-1	H	LGE	Chico 2 21 29, Idris 58p, Sergio 74p
19-11-2004	Al Shabab	D 1-1	A	LGE	Chico 33
24-11-2004	Seognam Ihlwa Chunma - KOR	L 1-3	H	ACLf	Tukar 28
1-12-2004	Seognam Ihlwa Chunma - KOR	W 5-1	A	ACLf	Tukar 27, Idris 45, Noor 2 56 78, Abushgeer 95+
28-12-2004	Al Nasr	D 1-1	H	LGE	Sergio 24
5-01-2005	Ohod	W 3-1	A	LGE	Al Saqri 35, Sergio 52p, Al Otaibi 83
14-01-2005	Al Ta'ee	W 3-0	H	LGE	Sergio 2 56p 58, Al Saqri 84
30-01-2005	Al Hilal	L 2-4	A	LGE	Al Otaibi 2 50 64
5-02-2005	Al Ittifaq	W 4-3	H	LGE	Al Otaibi 15, Sergio 2 25 42, Petkovic 32
18-02-2005	Najran	W 5-0	H	CPCr2	
26-02-2005	Al Ahly	W 3-2	H	LGE	Herrera 9, Sergio 2 46 87
7-03-2005	Al Ta'ee	W 5-1	H	CPCqf	
10-03-2005	Al Ansar	L 2-3	A	LGE	Al Muwallid 31, Al Saqri 43
15-03-2005	Al Qadisiya	L 2-3	A	LGE	Al Wada'ani 26, Sergio 76
20-03-2004	Al Riyadh	W 4-1	A	LGE	Sergio 3 27 44 73, Herrera 52
26-04-2005	Al Hilal	L 0-1	H	CPCsf	
30-04-2005	Al Hilal	D 1-1	H	CPCsf	
4-05-2005	Al Wahda	D 3-3	H	LGE	Sergio 2 33p 68, Al Shamrani 40
28-05-2005	Al Hilal	W 2-1	H	LGE	Al Otaibi 76, Sergio 90p
12-06-2005	Al Nasr	L 2-3	A	LGE	Al Otaibi 13, Suwaid 58
16-06-2005	Al Shabab	L 0-2	H	LGE	
20-06-2005	Al Nasr	W 6-0	H	LGEpo	Al Wuwallid 3, OG 36, Al Otaibi 2 37 61, Sergio 49, Al Saqri 85
7-07-2005	Al Hilal	L 0-1	A	LGEpo	

LGE = Custodian of the Two Holy Mosques League Cup • CPC = Crown Prince Cup • ACL = AFC Asian Champions League
r2 = second round • qf = quarter-final • sf = semi-final • f = final • po = play-off

KUW – KUWAIT

NATIONAL TEAM RECORD
JULY 1ST 2002 TO JUNE 30TH 2005

PL	W	D	L	F	A	%
59	25	15	19	87	74	55.1

FIFA/COCA-COLA WORLD RANKING

1993	1994	1995	1996	1997	1998	1999	2000	2001	2002	2003	2004	High		Low	
64	54	84	62	44	24	82	74	74	83	48	54	24	12/98	96	08/03

2004-2005											
08/04	09/04	10/04	11/04	12/04	01/05	02/05	03/05	04/05	05/05	06/05	07/05
54	55	60	60	54	55	56	54	55	55	56	55

With over 20 years having passed since their first appearance in the FIFA World Cup™ finals the Kuwaiti national team put themselves in position to qualify for a second time when they dramatically knocked out China PR on the last day of the first group stage having scored one more goal but with identical points and goal difference. Despite not getting a guaranteed spot in the finals from the next group stage there was still a play-off position to aim for. In other competitions the story was not quite so upbeat with an embarrassing first round exit in the AFC Asian Cup finals in China PR, thanks largely due to a 0-2 defeat at the hands of Jordan. In the Gulf Cup, a tournament they

INTERNATIONAL HONOURS
Qualified for the FIFA World Cup™ finals 1982   Asian Cup 1980   Gulf Cup 1970 1972 1974 1976 1982 1986 1990 1996 1998

dominated for many years, they were beaten in the semi-finals by hosts Qatar and have now gone three editions without winning it, their worst run to date. Al Qadisiya from Kuwait City won a third successive Championship when after having won the regular season they also won the Golden Four play-offs but they were denied a third consecutive double when they lost in the semi-final of the Emir Cup. That was won by Al Arabi who beat Kazma 6-5 on penalties after a 1-1 draw. Al Qadisiya did win the Crown Prince Cup, a relative newcomer to the calendar that is played on a group basis in the first phase, when they won a penalty shoot-out in the final against Al Kuwait.

THE FIFA BIG COUNT OF 2000

	Male	Female		Male	Female
Registered players	1 000	0	Referees	70	0
Non registered players	6 000	0	Officials	300	0
Youth players	1 000	0	Total involved	8 370	
Total players		8 000	Number of clubs	40	
Professional players	0	0	Number of teams	100	

Kuwait Football Association (KFA)
Udailiya, Block 4, Al-Ittihad Street, PO Box 2029, Safat 13021, Kuwait
Tel +965 2555851   Fax +965 2549955
info@kfa.org.kw   www.kfa.org.kw
President: AL-SABAH Shk. Ahmad   General Secretary: TAHER Naser Abdul-Latif
Vice-President: AL-SABAH Shk. Khaled Fahad A.   Treasurer: AL-MUTAIRY Haiyef Hussain   Media Officer: None
Men's Coach: STOICHITA Mihai   Women's Coach: None
KFA formed: 1952   AFC: 1962   FIFA: 1962
Colours: Blue, Blue, Blue

GAMES PLAYED BY KUWAIT IN THE 2006 FIFA WORLD CUP™ CYCLE

2002 Opponents	Score		Venue	Comp	Scorers	Att	Referee
16-12 Morocco	D	1-1	Kuwait City	ARr1	Laheeb [46]	7 000	Abbas SYR
18-12 Sudan	W	1-0	Kuwait City	ARr1	Nada [90]	2 000	Zekrini ALG
23-12 Jordan	L	1-2	Kuwait City	ARr1	Bashar [86]	6 000	Guirat TUN
25-12 Palestine	D	3-3	Kuwait City	ARr1	Shaker [15], Allam [38], Al Jaish [46]		
2003							
4-09 Singapore	W	3-1	Singapore	ACq	Al Enezi [10], Al Mutwa [68], Al Fadli [90]		
14-09 Qatar	W	2-1	Kuwait City	ACq	Bashar [56], Wabran [86]		
20-09 Qatar	D	2-2	Doha	ACq	Asel [25], Al Atiqi [70]		
27-09 Singapore	W	4-0	Kuwait City	ACq	Bashar 2 [25 78], Al Mutwa [47], Asel [53]		
5-10 Palestine	W	2-1	Kuwait City	ACq	Wabran [24], Al Mutwa [59]		
8-10 Palestine	W	4-0	Kuwait City	ACq	Bashar 2 [36 57p], Al Mutwa 2 [42 47]		
19-11 Portugal	L	0-8	Leiria	Fr		22 000	Ingvarsson SWE
2-12 Iran	W	3-1	Kuwait City	Fr	Bashar 2 [23p 33], Jumah [63]	5 000	Al Qahtani QAT
10-12 Slovakia	L	0-2	Larnaca	Fr			
16-12 Lebanon	W	2-0	Larnaca	Fr	Al Shemali [24], Abdulkudous [26]		
18-12 Lebanon	D	0-0	Larnaca	Fr			
20-12 Latvia	W	2-0	Larnaca	Fr	Jumah [6], Bashar [69]		Kapitanis CYP
26-12 Oman	D	0-0	Kuwait City	GC			Al Saeedi UAE
29-12 United Arab Emirates	L	0-2	Kuwait City	GC			Kassai HUN
2004							
1-01 Yemen	W	4-0	Kuwait City	GC	Abdulkudous [33], Bashar [40p], Al Mutwa [63], Salama [87]		
4-01 Saudi Arabia	D	1-1	Kuwait City	GC	Abdulkudous [89]		
8-01 Qatar	L	1-2	Kuwait City	GC	Bashar [5]		
10-01 Bahrain	L	0-4	Kuwait City	GC			
18-02 China PR	L	0-1	Guangzhou	WCq		50 000	Roman UZB
31-03 Malaysia	W	2-0	Kuantan	WCq	Al Mutwa [75], Al Harbi [87]	9 327	Matsumura JPN
1-06 Syria	L	0-1	Kuwait City	Fr			
3-06 Syria	L	1-2	Kuwait City	Fr	Mousa [50]		
9-06 Hong Kong	W	4-0	Kuwait City	WCq	Seraj [12], Al Mutwa [38], Al Enezi [45], Al Dawood [75]	9 000	Najm LIB
19-07 United Arab Emirates	W	3-1	Jinan	ACr1	Bashar [25], Al Mutwa 2 [40 45]	31 250	Al Hamdan KSA
23-07 Jordan	L	0-2	Jinan	ACr1		28 000	Lu Jun CHN
27-07 Korea Republic	L	0-4	Jinan	ACr1			Maidin SIN
26-08 Bahrain	D	0-0	Al Muharraq	Fr			
1-09 Saudi Arabia	D	1-1	Riyadh	Fr			
8-09 Hong Kong	W	2-0	Hong Kong	WCq	Al Enezi [38], Humaidan [70]	1 500	Busurmankulov KGZ
29-09 Syria	D	1-1	Tripoli	Fr			
3-10 Lebanon	W	3-1	Tripoli	Fr	Bashar [42p], Al Harbi [80], Sobeih [87]		
6-10 Lebanon	D	1-1	Beirut	Fr	Seraj [60]		
13-10 China PR	W	1-0	Kuwait City	WCq	Jumah [47]	10 000	Kunsuta THA
5-11 India	L	2-3	Kuwait City	Fr	Al Fahed [35], Bashar [54]		
10-11 Kyrgyzstan	W	3-0	Kuwait City	Fr			
17-11 Malaysia	W	6-1	Kuwait City	WCq	Al Mutwa [17], Bashar 2 [60 70], Saeed 2 [75 85], Al Hamad [82]	15 000	Lutfullin UZB
27-11 United Arab Emirates	W	1-0	Abu Dhabi	Fr	Al Harbi [50]		
3-12 United Arab Emirates	D	1-1	Dubai	Fr	Al Fahad [80]		
6-12 Tajikistan	W	3-0	Kuwait City	Fr	Bashar [19], Laheeb [90], Al Humaidan [90]		
11-12 Saudi Arabia	W	2-1	Doha	GCr1	Al Enezi [75], Al Mutwa [86]		
14-12 Bahrain	D	1-1	Doha	GCr1	Jarragh [16]		
17-12 Yemen	W	3-0	Doha	GCr1	Bashar 2 [18 90], Al Mutwa [82]		
20-12 Qatar	L	0-2	Doha	GCsf			
23-12 Bahrain	L	1-3	Doha	GC3p	Khodeir [35]		
2005							
22-01 Norway	D	1-1	Kuwait City	Fr	Bashar [27]	200	Shaban KUW
26-01 Syria	W	3-2	Kuwait City	Fr	OG [8], Mussa [70], Al Humaidan [83]		
2-02 Korea DPR	D	0-0	Beijing	Fr			
9-02 Korea Republic	L	0-2	Seoul	WCq		53 287	Maidin SIN
12-03 Finland	L	0-1	Kuwait City	Fr		10 000	
18-03 Armenia	W	3-1	Al Ain	Fr	Abdulreda [70], Al Mutwa [79], Al Subaih [90]		
25-03 Uzbekistan	W	2-1	Kuwait City	WCq	Bashar 2 [7 62]	12 000	Sun Baojie CHN
30-03 Saudi Arabia	D	0-0	Kuwait City	WCq		25 000	Moradi IRN
27-05 Egypt	L	0-1	Kuwait City	Fr			
3-06 Saudi Arabia	L	0-3	Riyadh	WCq		72 000	Kamikawa JPN
8-06 Korea Republic	L	0-4	Kuwait City	WCq		15 000	Khanthama THA

Fr = Friendly match • AR = Arab Cup • AC = AFC Asian Cup 2004 • GC = Gulf Cup • WC = FIFA World Cup™
q = qualifier • r1 = first round group • sf = semi-final • 3p = third place play-off

KUWAIT COUNTRY INFORMATION

Capital	Kuwait City	Independence	1961 from the UK	GDP per Capita	$19 000
Population	2 257 549	Status	Constitutional Monarchy	GNP Ranking	54
Area km²	17 820	Language	Arabic	Dialling code	+965
Population density	126 per km²	Literacy rate	83%	Internet code	.kw
% in urban areas	97%	Main religion	Muslim 85%	GMT +/-	+3
Towns/Cities ('000)	Hitan-al-Janubiyah 203; as-Sabahiyah 187; Jalib as-Suyuh 166; as-Salimiyah 158				
Neighbours (km)	Iraq 240; Saudi Arabia 222; Persian Gulf 499				
Main stadia	Kazma Stadium – Kuwait City 20 000; National Stadium – Kuwait City 16 000				

KUWAIT NATIONAL TEAM RECORDS AND RECORD SEQUENCES

Records			Sequence records				
Victory	20-0	BHU 2000	Wins	7	1974	Clean sheets	7	1988
Defeat	0-8	EGY 1961, POR 2003	Defeats	5	1964-1965	Goals scored	17	1986-1987
Player Caps	n/a		Undefeated	21	1985-1987	Without goal	5	1988
Player Goals	n/a		Without win	12	1988	Goals against	18	1964-1971

KUWAIT 2004-05 PREMIER LEAGUE

	Pl	W	D	L	F	A	Pts
Al Qadisiya †	13	10	1	2	33	10	31
Al Kuwait †	13	8	3	2	27	12	27
Al Yarmouk †	13	8	1	4	28	16	25
Al Arabi †	13	7	3	3	23	13	24
Al Sahel ‡	13	7	3	3	22	17	24
Kazma ‡	13	7	2	4	19	9	23
Al Nasr ‡	13	7	0	6	14	16	21
Salmiya ‡	13	4	4	5	17	13	16
Fehayheel	13	4	3	6	20	29	15
Al Tadamon	13	4	2	7	21	34	14
Solaybeekhat	13	4	1	8	14	22	13
Jahra	13	3	4	6	11	21	13
Khitan	13	3	2	8	16	28	11
Al Shabab	13	0	1	12	9	34	1

28/01/2005 - 12/04/2005 • † Qualified for Golden Four play-offs • ‡ Qualified for Silver Four play-offs

KUWAIT 2004-05 GOLDEN FOUR PLAY-OFFS

	Pl	W	D	L	F	A	Pts	Ku	Ar	Ya
Al Qadisiya (3)	3	2	0	1	6	4	9	3-2	0-2	3-0
Al Kuwait (2)	3	2	0	1	10	4	8		2-0	6-1
Al Arabi	3	2	0	1	6	3	6			4-1
Al Yarmouk (1)	3	0	0	3	2	13	1			

23/04/2005 - 28/04/2005 • Bonus points in brackets

KUWAIT 2004-05 SILVER FOUR PLAY-OFFS

	Pl	W	D	L	F	A	Pts	Ka	Na	Sa
Salmiya	3	3	0	0	9	1	9	4-0	3-1	2-0
Kazma (2)	3	1	1	1	4	4	6		0-0	1-0
Al Nasr (1)	3	1	1	1	3	4	5			2-1
Al Sahel (3)	3	0	0	3	1	5	3			

23/04/2005 - 28/04/2005 • Bonus points in brackets

EMIR CUP 2004-05

Quarter-finals		Semi-finals		Final	
Al Arabi	1 3p				
Salmiya	1 2p	Al Arabi	2		
Al Shabab	0	Al Tadamon	0		8-05-2005
Al Tadamon	1			Al Arabi	1 6p
Al Qadisiya	1 5p			Kazma	1 5p
Al Sahel	1 3p	Al Qadisiya	2 2p	Third Place Play-off	
Khitan	0 0p	Kazma	2 3p	Al Tadamun	1 3p
Kazma	0 3p			Al Qadisiya	1 1p

CROWN PRINCE CUP 2004-05

Semi-finals		Final	
Al Qadisiya	2		
Al Nasr	1	1-05-2005	
		Al Qadisiya	1 3p
		Al Kuwait	1 1p
Salmiya	0		
Al Kuwait	2		

RECENT LEAGUE AND CUP RECORD

	Championship						Cup		
Year	Champions	Pts	Runners-up	Pts	Third	Pts	Winners	Score	Runners-up
1996	Kazma	24	Salmiya	22	Al Qadisiya	15	Al Arabi	2-1	Jahra
1997	Al Arabi						Kazma	2-0	Al Qadisiya
1998	Salmiya	64	Kazma	55	Al Qadisiya	50	Kazma	3-1	Al Arabi
1999	Al Qadisiya	1-0	Al Tadamon				Al Arabi	2-1	Al Sahel
2000	Salmiya	23	Al Qadisiya	20	Al Kuwait	15	Al Arabi	2-1	Al Tadamon
2001	Al Kuwait	28	Salmiya	24	Al Arabi	24	Salmiya	3-1	Kazma
2002	Al Arabi	26	Al Qadisiya	25	Salmiya	23	Al Kuwait	1-0	Jahra
2003	Al Qadisiya	28	Al Arabi	26	Kazma	24	Al Qadisiya	2-2 4-1p	Al Salimiya
2004	Al Qadisiya	2-1	Salmiya				Al Qadisiya	2-0	Al Kuwait
2005	Al Qadisiya	9	Al Kuwait	8	Al Arabi	6	Al Arabi	1-1 6-5p	Kazma

LAO – LAOS

NATIONAL TEAM RECORD
JULY 1ST 2002 TO JUNE 30TH 2005

PL	W	D	L	F	A	%
17	2	2	13	13	66	17.6

FIFA/COCA-COLA WORLD RANKING

1993	1994	1995	1996	1997	1998	1999	2000	2001	2002	2003	2004	High	Low
146	160	152	147	143	144	156	165	162	170	167	162	**134** 09/98	**175** 06/04

2004-2005											
08/04	09/04	10/04	11/04	12/04	01/05	02/05	03/05	04/05	05/05	06/05	07/05
173	171	170	166	162	162	164	164	164	162	163	163

As with much of southeast Asia, football is booming in Laos and it is the youth that is helping to drive the sport forward as demonstrated by the U-20s and the U-17s. Both teams reached the finals of their respective Asian Championships and although they didn't progress further, qualification was some achievement. Meanwhile, the seniors found themselves in the second round of the 2006 FIFA World Cup™ as lucky losers after Guam and Nepal withdrew. Competition proved stiffer in a group with Iran, Qatar and Jordan, all teams that had reached the 2004 AFC Asian Cup finals. Six matches, no points and a goals against column reading 33 gave Laos a clearer picture of how

INTERNATIONAL HONOURS
None

much progress was required to compete at the next level. Matters improved slightly at the Tiger Cup in Vietnam and Malaysia where Laos registered their only win of the year by beating Cambodia 2-1. However, defeats to Indonesia, Singapore and Vietnam meant an early departure and Laos have not played since. The 2005 L-League was won by Ventiane FC who prevented MCPTC (Ministry of Communications, Transportation and Construction) from winning the title for a fourth straight year. The Championship followed their success the previous year when the club won the Prime Minister's Cup 2-1 in extra-time against Savannakhet.

THE FIFA BIG COUNT OF 2000

	Male	Female		Male	Female
Registered players	1 100	0	Referees	50	0
Non registered players	20 000	0	Officials	300	0
Youth players	1 000	0	Total involved	22 450	
Total players		22 100	Number of clubs	50	
Professional players	0	0	Number of teams	150	

Lao Football Federation (LFF)

National Stadium, Konboulo Street, PO Box 3777, Vientiane 856-21, Laos
Tel +856 21 251593   Fax +856 21 213460
laosff@laotel.com   www.none
President: PHISSAMAY Bountiem   General Secretary: VONGSOUTHI Phouvanh
Vice-President: VONGSOUTHI Phouvanh   Treasurer: KEOMANY Khammoui   Media Officer: VILAYSAK Sisay
Men's Coach: KHENKITISACK Bounlab   Women's Coach: BOUTSAVATH Kingmano
LFF formed: 1951   AFC: 1980   FIFA: 1952
Colours: Red, Red, Red

GAMES PLAYED BY LAOS IN THE 2006 FIFA WORLD CUP™ CYCLE

2002	Opponents	Score	Venue	Comp	Scorers	Att	Referee
18-12	Thailand	L 1-5	Singapore	TCr1	Phaphouvanin 66	7 000	Rahmanvijay SIN
20-12	Singapore	L 1-2	Singapore	TCr1	Phaphouvanin 19	10 000	Setiyono IDN
22-12	Malaysia	D 1-1	Singapore	TCr1	Phaphouvanin 29	350	Lee Young Chun KOR
2003							
25-03	Hong Kong	L 1-5	Hong Kong	ACq	Phaphouvanin 66		
27-03	Bangladesh	W 2-1	Hong Kong	ACq	Phonephachan 30, Phaphouvanin 38		
29-11	Sri Lanka	D 0-0	Vientiane	WCq		4 500	Luong VIE
3-12	Sri Lanka	L 0-3	Colombo	WCq		6 000	Saleem MDV
2004							
18-02	Jordan	L 0-5	Amman	WCq		5 000	Al Mozahmi OMA
31-03	Iran	L 0-7	Vientiane	WCq		7 000	Yang Mu Sheng TPE
9-06	Qatar	L 0-5	Doha	WCq		500	Abu Armana PAL
8-09	Qatar	L 1-6	Vientiane	WCq	Chanthalome 88	2 900	Napitupulu IDN
13-10	Jordan	L 2-3	Vientiane	WCq	Phaphouvanin 13, Thongphachan 53	3 000	Gosh BAN
17-11	Iran	L 0-7	Tehran	WCq		30 000	Mamedov TKM
7-12	Indonesia	L 0-6	Ho Chi Minh City	TCr1			Mongkol THA
11-12	Cambodia	W 2-1	Hanoi	TCr1	Chalana 2 63 73	20 000	Kwong Jong Chul KOR
13-12	Singapore	L 2-6	Hanoi	TCr1	Phaphouvanin 22, Chalana 72p	17 000	Supian MAS
15-12	Vietnam	L 0-3	Hanoi	TCr1		20 000	Mongkul THA
2005							

No international matches played before August 2005

TC = Tiger Cup • AC = AFC Asian Cup 2004 • WC = FIFA World Cup™ • q = qualifier • r1 = first round group

LAOS NATIONAL TEAM RECORDS AND RECORD SEQUENCES

Records			Sequence records					
Victory	4-1	PHI	Wins	3	1993-1995	Clean sheets	3	1995
Defeat	0-12	OMA 2001	Defeats	11	1970-1974	Goals scored	9	1996-1998
Player Caps	n/a		Undefeated	4	1993-1995	Without goal	8	2000-2001
Player Goals	n/a		Without win	19	1970-1993	Goals against	14	1961-1969

FIFA REFEREE LIST 2005

	Int'l	DoB
PHOMMAKOUN Somphone	2004	11-06-1976
SINBANDITH Sipaseuth	2005	23-01-1974

FIFA ASSISTANT REFEREE LIST 2005

	Int'l	DoB
PHONESIRIGNAVONG Thongp'th	1999	2-03-1963
SINTHALAVONG Keung	2005	8-01-1965

RECENT LEAGUE AND CUP RECORD

	Championship	Cup
Year	Champions	Winners
2000	Vientiane Municipality	
2001		
2002	MCPTC	
2003	MCPTC	
2004	MCPTC	MCPTC
2005	Vientiane FC	Vientiane FC

LAOS COUNTRY INFORMATION

Capital	Vientiane	Independence	1953 from France	GDP per Capita	$1 700
Population	6 068 117	Status	Republic	GNP Ranking	143
Area km²	236 800	Language	Lao	Dialling code	+856
Population density	25.5 per km²	Literacy rate	66%	Internet code	.la
% in urban areas	22%	Main religion	Buddhist 60%	GMT +/–	+7
Towns/Cities ('000)	Vientiane 196; Pakxe 88; Savannakhet 66; Luang Prabang 47; Xam Nua 39; Xaignabury 31				
Neighbours (km)	China 423; Vietnam 2 130; Cambodia 541; Thailand 1 754; Burma 235				
Main stadia	National Stadium – Vientiane 18 000				

LBR – LIBERIA

NATIONAL TEAM RECORD
JULY 1ST 2002 TO JUNE 30TH 2005

PL	W	D	L	F	A	%
17	4	1	12	9	30	26.5

FIFA/COCA-COLA WORLD RANKING

1993	1994	1995	1996	1997	1998	1999	2000	2001	2002	2003	2004	High		Low	
123	127	87	94	94	108	105	95	73	88	110	123	**66**	07/01	**136**	07/94

2004-2005											
08/04	09/04	10/04	11/04	12/04	01/05	02/05	03/05	04/05	05/05	06/05	07/05
114	114	115	117	123	124	124	124	125	126	127	128

Long gone are the days when George Weah weaved his magic spell over football in Liberia and the ranking of the national team is now back down to the levels of the early 1990s. The 2006 FIFA World Cup™ qualifiers turned out to be a disaster, especially in light of how close the Liberians came to qualifying for 2002 when they finished only a point behind group winners and finalists Nigeria. The campaign started off well with wins against Gambia and Mali but the following seven games saw just a single point won as the team slumped to the bottom of the table, which meant a place in the 2006 CAF African Cup of Nations finals was also out of reach. Weah has turned his

INTERNATIONAL HONOURS
None

attention from football to politics and is hoping to be elected president of Liberia in October 2005 and if successful he would certainly raise the profile of the country on a number of levels, not least in football. It is hoped that the elections will bring a new era of stability and peace to a country in which more than 200,000 were left dead in the fighting of the last decade. As one of the initial recipients in 1999 of aid from FIFA's Goal programme very little has been done since the laying of the artificial pitch at the Antoinette Tubman Stadium and questions have been asked about how the money was spent.

THE FIFA BIG COUNT OF 2000

	Male	Female		Male	Female
Registered players	1 360	0	Referees	42	0
Non registered players	10 000	0	Officials	400	0
Youth players	1 000	264	Total involved	13 066	
Total players	12 624		Number of clubs	80	
Professional players	25	0	Number of teams	157	

Liberia Football Association (FLFA)
Antoinette Tubman Stadium (ATS), PO Box 10-1066, Monrovia 1000, Liberia
Fax +231 227223
yansbor@yahoo.com   www.liberiansoccer.com
President: WESLEY Sombo   General Secretary: BORSAY Yanqueh
Vice-President: SHERIF Siaka A.   Treasurer: KOON Joseph S.   Media Officer: None
Men's Coach: SAYON Joseph   Women's Coach: None
FLFA formed: 1936   CAF: 1962   FIFA: 1962
Colours: Blue, White, Red

GAMES PLAYED BY LIBERIA IN THE 2006 WORLD CUP CYCLE

2002	Opponents	Score		Venue	Comp	Scorers	Att	Referee
8-09	Guinea	L	0-3	Conakry	CNq		35 000	Diouf.AS SEN
13-10	Niger	W	1-0	Monrovia	CNq	Daye [80]	40 000	
2003								
30-03	Ethiopia	L	0-1	Addis Ababa	CNq		40 000	Ali Mohamed DJI
8-06	Ethiopia	W	1-0	Monrovia	CNq	Mennoh [57]	14 000	Aguidissou BEN
21-06	Guinea	L	1-2	Accra	CNq	Daye [20]		Sowe GAM
5-07	Niger	L	0-1	Niamey	CNq			
12-10	Gambia	L	0-2	Bakau	WCq		20 000	Codjia BEN
16-11	Gambia	W	3-0	Monrovia	WCq	Roberts [10], Tondo 2 [76 83]	10 000	Coulibaly MLI
2004								
6-06	Mali	W	1-0	Monrovia	WCq	Kieh [85]	30 000	Codjia BEN
20-06	Congo	L	0-3	Brazzaville	WCq		25 000	Lemghambodj MTN
4-07	Togo	D	0-0	Monrovia	WCq		30 000	Soumah GUI
4-09	Zambia	L	0-1	Lusaka	WCq		30 000	Nchengwa BOT
10-10	Senegal	L	0-3	Monrovia	WCq		26 000	Aboubacar CIV
2005								
26-03	Senegal	L	1-6	Dakar	WCq	Tondo [86]	50 000	Shelmani LBY
5-06	Mali	L	1-4	Segou	WCq	Toe [54]	11 000	Pare BFA
10-06	Sierra Leone	L	0-2	Freetown	Fr			
19-06	Congo	L	0-2	Paynesville	WCq		5 000	Sillah GAM

CN = CAF African Cup of Nations • WC = FIFA World Cup™ • q = qualifier

LIBERIA NATIONAL TEAM RECORDS AND RECORD SEQUENCES

Records			Sequence records				
Victory	4-0	GAM 1996, MRI 2000	Wins	4	2001	Clean sheets	4	1987-1995
Defeat	2-7	TUN 2001	Defeats	7	1971-1975	Goals scored	8	2001, 2001-02
Player Caps	n/a		Undefeated	11	1994-1995	Without goal	4	1971-75, 1981-82
Player Goals	n/a		Without win	17	1971-1980	Goals against	13	1984-1986

FIFA REFEREE LIST 2005

	Int'l	DoB
KONAH Ebenezer		31-12-1970
KORTI Sam		5-05-1968
PAYE Patrick		20-08-1969
YARSIAH Benedict		5-10-1964

FIFA ASSISTANT REFEREE LIST 2005

	Int'l	DoB
FLANJAY Jay		4-06-1968
GOODING Augustine		25-04-1967
JOHNSON Sylvester		4-04-1967
KORMAH Jallah		17-06-1970
SNYDER Buster		7-02-1965

RECENT LEAGUE AND CUP RECORD

	Championship		Cup
Year	Champions		Winners
1996	Junior Professional		Junior Professional
1997	Invincible Eleven		Invincible Eleven
1998	Invincible Eleven		Invincible Eleven
1999	LPRC Oilers		LPRC Oilers
2000	Mighty Barolle		LPRC Oilers
2001	Mighty Barolle		
2002	LPRC Oilers		Mighty Blue Angels
2003	Not finished		
2004	Mighty Barolle		LISCR FC

LIBERIA COUNTRY INFORMATION

Capital	Monrovia	Independence	1847	GDP per Capita	$1 000
Population	3 390 635	Status	Republic	GNP Ranking	171
Area km²	111 370	Language	English	Dialling code	+231
Population density	30 per km²	Literacy rate	57%	Internet code	.lr
% in urban areas	45%	Main religion	Christian & Indigenous 40%	GMT +/–	0
Cities/Towns ('000)	Monrovia 935; Gbarnga 45; Bensonville 33; Harper 33; Buchanan 26; Zwedru 26				
Neighbours (km)	Guinea 563; Côte d'Ivoire 716; Sierra Leone 306; Atlantic Ocean 579				
Main stadia	Samuel Doe Sports Complex – Monrovia 35 000; Antoinette Tubman – Monrovia 10 000				

LBY – LIBYA

NATIONAL TEAM RECORD
JULY 1ST 2002 TO JUNE 30TH 2005

PL	W	D	L	F	A	%
30	17	5	8	54	30	65

FIFA/COCA-COLA WORLD RANKING

1993	1994	1995	1996	1997	1998	1999	2000	2001	2002	2003	2004	High		Low	
152	167	175	184	147	147	131	116	116	104	83	61	61	12/04	187	07/97

2004-2005											
08/04	09/04	10/04	11/04	12/04	01/05	02/05	03/05	04/05	05/05	06/05	07/05
71	73	68	61	61	62	63	64	67	70	66	73

In mid-1997 there were only five teams below the Libyan national team in the FIFA/Coca-Cola World Ranking but since then progress has been steady to a point where Libya felt confident enough to put in a bid to host the FIFA World Cup™ in 2010. The main figure behind the failed bid was Saadi Al Gadhafi, a professional footballer in Italy with Perugia who also happens to be son of the Libyan president Muammar Gadhafi. Having such a well known figure involved has given football in Libya a profile that for many years it lacked. Hopes were high for the 2006 FIFA World Cup™ qualifiers and although those ambitions floundered in a very tough group there was

INTERNATIONAL HONOURS
None

the consolation of a place in the 2006 CAF African Cup of Nations in Egypt, the first time Libya have qualified for the finals since hosting the event in 1982. There was drama in the 2005 Libyan Championship when Al Ittihad of Tripoli won the title as they were helped in no small part by the expulsion of city rivals Al Ahly in the final stages of the campaign. Ittihad then went on to do the double. Progress in the CAF club competitions has been slow in recent years but with a mixture of finance and ambition Libya is intent on building a better future, both at national and club level, having spent far too long amongst the minnows of the continent.

THE FIFA BIG COUNT OF 2000

	Male	Female		Male	Female
Registered players	5 000	0	Referees	300	0
Non registered players	20 000	0	Officials	1 900	0
Youth players	2 500	0	Total involved	29 700	
Total players	27 500		Number of clubs	100	
Professional players	0	0	Number of teams	500	

Libyan Football Federation (LFF)
General Sports Federations Building, Sports City, Gorji, PO Box 5137, Tripoli, Libya
Tel +218 21 4782001   Fax +218 21 4782006
libyaff@hotmail.com@   www.none
President: AL GATHAFI Mohamad Maamar   General Secretary: ABOUSHWESHA Abdulmagid
Vice-President: KHALED Tuhami   Treasurer: EL YAZIDI Ahmed   Media Officer: BEN TAHIA Mohamad
Men's Coach: EL SELINE Mohamed   Women's Coach: None
LFF formed: 1962   CAF: 1965   FIFA: 1963
Colours: Green/black, Black, Black

GAMES PLAYED BY LIBYA IN THE 2006 FIFA WORLD CUP™ CYCLE

2002	Opponents	Score		Venue	Comp	Scorers	Att	Referee
27-08	Egypt	W	1-0	Alexandria	Fr	Al Mossily 72		
1-09	Togo	W	4-0	Lomé	Fr			
2-09	Togo	W	4-0	Misurata	Fr			
8-09	Congo DR	W	3-2	Tripoli	CNq	Al Mallian 15, Montasser 37, Ragab 41p		El Arjoun MAR
13-10	Swaziland	L	1-2	Mbabane	CNq	Nader 20		Colembi ANG
2003								
12-02	Canada	L	2-4	Tripoli	Fr	Al Taied 2 27p 59p	45 000	
30-03	Botswana	D	0-0	Tripoli	CNq			Pare BFA
30-04	Argentina	L	1-3	Tripoli	Fr	El Taib 65	25 000	Zahmoul TUN
7-06	Botswana	W	1-0	Gaborone	CNq	Masli 89		Nunkoo MRI
22-06	Congo DR	L	1-2	Kinshasa	CNq	Hamed 49		
5-07	Swaziland	W	6-2	Tripoli	CNq	El Taib 2, Al Mirghani, Tarhouni, Al Milyan		
11-10	São Tomé e Príncipe	W	1-0	São Tomé	WCq	Masli 85	4 000	Yameogo BFA
16-11	São Tomé e Príncipe	W	8-0	Benghazi	WCq	Masli 3 14 17 20, El Taib 2 45 63, Suliman 54 Osman.A 74, El Rabty 88	20 000	Guirat TUN
2004								
16-01	Kenya	W	2-0	Zawyan	Fr	Kara, El Kikli		
19-01	Kenya	W	2-0	Tripoli	Fr	Saad 27, Hussain 56		
18-02	Ukraine	D	1-1	Tripoli	Fr	Kara 55		
26-03	Qatar	W	1-0	Rome	Fr	Kara 48		
30-04	Jordan	W	1-0	Lagos	Fr	Rewani 37		
30-05	Burkina Faso	L	2-3	Ouagadougou	Fr	El Hamail 21, Rewani 54		Pare BFA
6-06	Côte d'Ivoire	L	0-2	Abidjan	WCq		40 827	Colembi ANG
18-06	Cameroon	D	0-0	Misurata	WCq		7 000	Lim Kee Chong MRI
3-07	Sudan	W	1-0	Khartoum	WCq	Kara 93+	10 000	Bennett RSA
3-09	Benin	W	4-1	Tripoli	WCq	Al Shibani 9, Kara 47, Osman.A 51, Suliman 70	30 000	Kidane Tesfu ERI
8-10	Egypt	W	2-1	Tripoli	WCq	Kara 31, Osman.A 85	40 000	Haïmoudi ALG
20-10	Nigeria	W	2-1	Tripoli	Fr	Kara 2 23 44		
22-10	Jordan	W	1-0	Tripoli	Fr	Kara 59p		
2005								
27-03	Egypt	L	1-4	Cairo	WCq	Ferjani 50	30 000	Poulat FRA
27-05	Malawi	D	1-1	Tripoli	Fr			
3-06	Côte d'Ivoire	D	0-0	Tripoli	WCq		45 000	Lim Kee Chong MRI
19-06	Cameroon	L	0-1	Yaoundé	WCq		36 000	Coulibaly MLI

Fr = Friendly match • CN = CAF African Cup of Nations • WC = FIFA World Cup™ • q = qualifier

FIFA REFEREE LIST 2005

	Int'l	DoB
ABDALLA Mohamed	1994	1-06-1963
AMBAYA Jamel	2001	11-03-1964
EL MUSRATI Naser	1999	27-08-1966
IMHAMED Mohamed		3-04-1965
MOHAMED Abdalla	2000	10-11-1961
SHELMANI Abdullhakim	1994	12-06-1961
TAMUNI Wahid	1999	29-05-1974

FIFA ASSISTANT REFEREE LIST 2005

	Int'l	DoB
ABULKHIR Khalid	2005	3-04-1977
EL MAGHRABI Foaad	2005	17-07-1977
ELARIBI Mohamed	2005	5-11-1975
FARKASH Ibrahim	2000	11-01-1972
MEHMED Naseraldin		1-07-1968
OTMAN Bashir	1998	11-11-1962
ZAIED Mohammed	1999	1-09-1971

LIBYA COUNTRY INFORMATION

Capital	Tripoli	Independence	1951 from Italy	GDP per Capita	$6 400
Population	5 631 585	Status	Republic	GNP Ranking	59
Area km²	1 759 540	Language	Arabic	Dialling code	+218
Population density	3 per km²	Literacy rate	82%	Internet code	.ly
% in urban areas	86%	Main religion	Muslim	GMT +/−	+1
Towns/Cities ('000)	Tripoli 1 150; Benghazi 650; Misurata 386; Al Aziziyah 287; Tarhunah 210; Al-Hums 201; Az-Zawiyah 186; Zuwarah 180; Ajdabiya 134; Surt 128; Sabha 126; Tubruq 121				
Neighbours (km)	Egypt 1 115 km; Sudan 383; Chad 1 055; Niger 354; Algeria 982; Tunisia 459; Mediterranean 1 770				
Main stadia	11 June Stadium – Tripoli 80 000; 28 March Stadium – Benghazi 60 000				

LIBYA NATIONAL TEAM RECORDS AND RECORD SEQUENCES

Records			Sequence records					
Victory	21-0	OMA 1966	Wins	5	2003-04, 2004	Clean sheets	4	1996, 2003-04
Defeat	2-10	EGY 1953	Defeats	5	1953-1960	Goals scored	15	1998-1999
Player Caps	n/a		Undefeated	7	1982-1983	Without goal	4	1966
Player Goals	n/a		Without win	7	1967	Goals against	16	1953-65, 1992-99

LIBYA 2004-05

PREMIER LEAGUE

	Pl	W	D	L	F	A	Pts	Ittihad	Uruba	Olympique	Akhdar	Hilal	Madina	Wifak	Shat	Mustaqbal	Rafik	Swihli	Tahaddi	Ahly	Nasr
Al Ittihad Tripoli †	22	16	3	3	41	13	51		1-0	1-0	1-0	4-0	1-1	2-1	2-0	5-0	1-2	2-0	3-0	1-1	2-0
Al Uruba ‡	22	12	7	3	39	21	43	2-1		0-0	1-1	5-2	4-2	5-2	0-0	1-0	2-2	3-1	1-0	1-2	1-1
Olympique Az Zwiyah	22	12	6	4	25	15	42	0-0	1-1		3-2	3-1	0-1	1-1	2-0	2-1	2-1	1-0	1-0	1-0	
Al Akhdar Darnah	22	9	7	6	23	16	34	1-1	2-2	2-1		0-1	2-1	0-1	1-1	2-0	1-1	1-0	2-0	0-1	
Al Hilal Benghazi	22	9	4	9	29	32	31	0-2	0-0	1-2	1-0		2-2	1-0	0-2	2-1	2-0	2-0	1-1	2-1	0-3
Al Madina Tripoli	22	6	8	8	27	27	26	3-3	1-2	0-1	1-0	0-1		0-0	4-0	1-2	0-0	1-1	2-0		0-1
Al Wifak Sabrata	22	5	11	6	18	24	26	1-2	0-2	1-1	0-0	0-4	0-0		2-1	1-1	0-0	3-1	0-0	1-2	0-0
Al Shat Tripoli	22	7	5	10	19	32	26	0-1	2-5	1-0	0-1	2-1	0-2	0-0		1-1	0-2	3-0	3-2		1-1
Al Mustaqbal Tripoli	22	6	5	11	30	32	23	0-3	0-1	0-1	0-1	3-2	1-1	2-2	5-0		0-1	4-0	1-2		3-2
Rafik Sorman	22	5	8	9	20	25	23	0-2	0-1	0-1	0-0	2-2	2-1	0-1	1-1	2-2		0-1	3-1	2-2	1-2
Al Swihli Misurata	22	7	1	14	21	34	22	2-3	1-0	0-1	0-3	3-1	4-0	0-1	0-1	1-3	2-0		2-0	1-3	1-2
Al Tahaddi Benghazi	22	3	5	14	15	36	14	2-2	0-1	1-1	1-1	0-2	1-3	1-1	0-1	0-3	2-1	1-2		1-4	1-0
Al Ahly Tripoli		Record annulled						0-2	2-0			1-0	2-0	3-2	2-1	2-1	3-1		3-0		
Al Nasr Tripoli		Record annulled						0-1	5-0	2-1	0-1			2-1					4-0	1-2	

10/09/2004 - 12/07/2005 • † Qualified for the CAF Champions League • ‡ Qualified for the CAF Confederation Cup

AL FATIH CUP 2004-05

Round of 16		Quarter-finals		Semi-finals		Final	
Al Ittihad Tripoli	1 2						
Rafik *	0 0	Al Ittihad Tripoli *	0 1				
Olympique Az Zwiyah	0 2	Al Uruba	0 0				
Al Uruba *	1 1						
				Al Ittihad Tripoli *	5 3		
				Al Wifak Sabrata	0 2		
Al Nasr Tripoli *	2 1						
Al Shat Tripoli	0 2	Al Nasr Tripoli §	3				
Al Mustaqbal Tripoli *	0 0	Al Wifak Sabrata	1				
Al Wifak Sabrata	1 0					Al Ittihad Tripoli	3
Al Ahly Tripoli *	4 4					Al Akhdar Darnah	0
Al Dhahra	2 0	Al Ahly Tripoli	2 3				
Al Madina Tripoli *	1 0 2p	Al Swihli Misurata *	2 1	Al Ahly Tripoli §	0 -		
Al Swihli Misurata	0 1 3p			Al Akhdar Darnah *	3 -		
Al Ahly Benghazi *	2 1						
Al Hilal Benghazi	1 1	Al Ahly Benghazi §	1 -				
Al Sawaed	0 1 2p	Al Akhdar Darnah	0 -				
Al Akhdar Darnah *	1 0 4p						

CUP FINAL

16-07-2005; Att. 45 000
11th June Stadium, Tripoli

Scorers - Tarhouni 75p, Merghani 80, Raouani 90 for Ittihad

* Home team in the first leg • § Expelled from the tournament

RECENT LEAGUE AND CUP RECORD

	Championship						Cup		
Year	Champions	Pts	Runners-up	Pts	Third	Pts	Winners	Score	Runners-up
1996	Al Shaat Tripoli						Al Ahly Benghazi	2-0	Al Ittihad Al Asskary
1997	Al Tahaddi Benghazi						Al Nasr Benghazi	1-1 4-3p	Al Yarmouk
1998	Al Mahalah Tripoli						Al Shaat Tripoli	1-1 4-2p	Al Hilal Benghazi
1999	Al Mahalah Tripoli	30	Al Shat Tripoli	23	Al Hilal Benghazi	21	Al Ittihad Ytipoli	2-0	Al Tahaddi Benghazi
2000	Al Ahly Tripoli	1-0	Al Hilal Benghazi				Al Ahly Tripoli	2-0	Al Shawehly Misurata
2001	Al Medina Tripoli	1-1	Al Tahaddi Benghazi						
2002	Al Ittihad Tripoli	67	Al Nasr Benghazi	67	Al Hilal Benghazi	52			
2003	Al Ittihad Tripoli	65	Al Nasr Benghazi	52	Al Hilal Benghazi	43			
2004	Olympique Az-Zwiyah	57	Al Ittihad Tripoli	52	Al Ahly Tripoli	51	Al Ittihad Tripoli	0-0 8-7p	Al Hilal
2005	Al Ittihad Tripoli	51	Al Uruba	43	Olympique Az-Zwiyah	42	Al Ittihad Tripoli	3-0	Al Akhdar

Al Medina won the 2001 Championship on penalties after a 1-1 draw

LCA – ST LUCIA

NATIONAL TEAM RECORD
JULY 1ST 2002 TO JUNE 30TH 2005

PL	W	D	L	F	A	%
22	9	3	10	45	39	47.7

FIFA/COCA-COLA WORLD RANKING

1993	1994	1995	1996	1997	1998	1999	2000	2001	2002	2003	2004	High		Low	
139	157	114	134	142	139	152	135	130	112	130	114	108	04/03	157	12/94

2004-2005											
08/04	09/04	10/04	11/04	12/04	01/05	02/05	03/05	04/05	05/05	06/05	07/05
128	128	128	122	114	117	118	117	118	118	118	118

In 17 years as FIFA members, St Lucia have managed to climb to 118th in the FIFA/Coca-Cola World Ranking, but without making the breakthrough they so desire. With players in other Caribbean countries and in the USA, experience is developing although results have not really reflected that. Thirteen international games in 2004 netted just four wins and their 2006 FIFA World Cup™ campaign ended quickly. Kicking off with an undemanding tie against British Virgin Islands, St Lucia won 1-0 away in Tortola before a 9-0 drubbing at Vieux Fort set the side up for a meeting with Panama. However, the away match did not go as planned and a 4-0 defeat left St

INTERNATIONAL HONOURS
None

Lucia needing a miracle and that didn't materialise as Panama won 3-0. In the Digicel Caribbean Cup the side finished as runners-up to St Kitts and Nevis in their group before being edged out over two legs by Jamaica 3-2 on aggregate in the first knockout round. In 2003 FIFA's Goal Bureau approved the construction of a technical centre on the island, but progress has been minimal if at all, so St Lucia's football association has been given until November 2005 to either begin or resume work on the project. Roots Alley Ballers won their third League title in five years while the FA Cup went to Northern United.

THE FIFA BIG COUNT OF 2000

	Male	Female		Male	Female
Registered players	2 025	100	Referees	37	4
Non registered players	1 500	0	Officials	300	15
Youth players	500	0	Total involved	4 481	
Total players	4 125		Number of clubs	39	
Professional players	25	0	Number of teams	119	

St Lucia Football Association (SLFA)
La Clery, PO Box 255, Castries, St Lucia
Tel +1 758 4530687   Fax +1 758 4560510
gs_slfa@hotmail.com   www.none
President: LARCHER Oswald W.   General Secretary: JOSEPH Germaine
Vice-President: SEALEY John   Treasurer: JOSEPH Germaine   Media Officer: HALL Gilroy
Men's Coach: MILLAR Carson   Women's Coach: ANDERSON Trevor
SLFA formed: 1979   CONCACAF: 1988   FIFA: 1988
Colours: White with yellow/blue/black stripe, White with yellow/blue/black stripe, White/blue/yellow

GAMES PLAYED BY ST LUCIA IN THE 2006 FIFA WORLD CUP™ CYCLE

2002	Opponents	Score		Venue	Comp	Scorers	Att	Referee
14-07	British Virgin Islands	W	3-1	Tortola	GCq	Joseph.V [15], McVane [40], Jean-Marie [60]		
28-07	British Virgin Islands	W	8-1	Castries	GCq	Walter [2], Joseph.V [7], McVane [43], Jean-Marie 2 [52 75] Mark [54], Joseph.E [58], Elva [82]		Forde BRB
11-08	Jamaica	L	1-3	Vieux Fort	Fr	Joseph.V [18]	8 000	
6-10	Barbados	L	2-3	Bridgetown	Fr	Burrows 2		
9-10	Martinique †	L	0-4	Riviere-Pilote	Fr			
6-11	Martinique †	L	0-2	Vieux Fort	Fr			
13-11	St Kitts and Nevis	L	1-2	Port of Spain	GCq	Lastic [78]		Forde BRB
17-11	Trinidad and Tobago	W	1-0	Port of Spain	GCq	McVane [54]		Forde BRB
2003								
26-03	Jamaica	L	0-5	Kingston	GCq		22 000	Brizan TRI
28-03	Haiti	W	2-1	Kingston	GCq	Emmanuel [45], Flavius [90]	14 500	Lee ATG
30-03	Martinique	L	4-5	Kingston	GCq	Elva [21], Mark [38], Jean [52], Joseph.V [56]	7 200	Lee ATG
2004								
1-02	Guadeloupe †	L	0-2		Fr			
8-02	St Vincent/Grenadines	L	1-2	Castries	Fr			
22-02	British Virgin Islands	W	1-0	Tortola	WCq	Elva [55]	800	Stewart JAM
21-03	St Vincent/Grenadines	D	1-1	Kingstown	Fr	Elva [15]		
28-03	British Virgin Islands	W	9-0	Vieux Fort	WCq	Emmanuel 2 [13p 66], Joseph.E [26], Jean 2 [28 52] Skeete 2 [49 55], Elva [69], Baptiste [90]	665	Corrivault CAN
2-06	Grenada	L	0-2	St George's	Fr		2 500	
13-06	Panama	L	0-4	Panama City	WCq		15 000	Phillip GRN
20-06	Panama	L	0-3	Vieux Fort	WCq		400	Gurley VIN
17-10	Grenada	W	3-1	Castries	Fr	Gilbert 3		
2-11	St Kitts and Nevis	D	1-1	Basseterre	GCq	Gilbert [67]		Bedeau GRN
4-11	Montserrat	W	3-0	Basseterre	GCq	St Lucia awarded match 3-0		
6-11	Antigua and Barbuda	W	2-1	Basseterre	GCq	Elva [22], Gilbert [27]		Bedeau GRN
12-12	Jamaica	D	1-1	Vieux Fort	GCq	Joseph.E [23]		Jeanvillier MTQ
19-12	Jamaica	L	1-2	Kingston	GCq	Elva [23]	2 500	Gutierrez CUB
2005								

No international matches played before August 2005

Fr = Friendly match • GC = CONCACAF Gold Cup • WC = FIFA World Cup™ • q = qualifier • † Not a full international

NATIONAL TEAM RECORDS AND RECORD SEQUENCES

Records			Sequence records					
Victory	14-1	VIR 2001	Wins	5	2000	Clean sheets	5	1990-1991
Defeat	0-5	TRI 1995, JAM 2003	Defeats	5	1996	Goals scored	14	1999-2000
Player Caps	n/a		Undefeated	7	1982-1983	Without goal	3	2004
Player Goals	n/a		Without win	6	1996-1997	Goals against	12	2001-02

RECENT LEAGUE AND CUP RECORD

	Championship	Cup
Year	Champions	Winners
2000	Roots Alley Ballers	Rovers United
2001	VSADC	VSADC
2002	VSADC	VSADC
2003	season readjustment	18 Plus
2004	Roots Alley Ballers	Northern United

ST LUCIA COUNTRY INFORMATION

Capital	Castries	Independence	1979 from the UK	GDP per Capita	$5 400
Population	164 213	Status	Parliamentary democracy	GNP Ranking	165
Area km²	616	Language	English	Dialling code	+1758
Population density	266 per km²	Literacy rate	67%	Internet code	.lc
% in urban areas	48%	Main religion	Christian	GMT +/−	-4
Towns/Cities ('000)	Castries 13; Vieux Fort 4; Micoud 3; Dennery 3; Soufrière 3; Gros Islet 2				
Neighbours (km)	Atlantic Ocean & Carribbean Sea 158				
Main stadia	Bones Park – Castries 20 000; National Stadium – Vieux Fort				

LES – LESOTHO

NATIONAL TEAM RECORD
JULY 1ST 2002 TO JUNE 30TH 2005

PL	W	D	L	F	A	%
25	5	7	13	21	39	34

FIFA/COCA-COLA WORLD RANKING

1993	1994	1995	1996	1997	1998	1999	2000	2001	2002	2003	2004	High		Low	
138	135	149	162	149	140	154	136	126	132	120	144	120	12/03	165	04/97

2004-2005											
08/04	09/04	10/04	11/04	12/04	01/05	02/05	03/05	04/05	05/05	06/05	07/05
129	130	133	138	144	141	142	142	144	144	144	146

With elimination in the 2006 FIFA World Cup™ qualifiers by local rivals Botswana at the very first hurdle, the calendar for the national team since November 2003 has looked relatively barren and it has been left to the U-20 Crocodiles to write most of the headlines. In the qualifiers they remarkably knocked out both South Africa and Zimbabwe to become the first team from Lesotho to qualify for the finals of a CAF competition. In the final tournament in Benin they even added Angola to their list of scalps before finishing third in the group behind Egypt and Morocco. The senior side under German coach Antoine Hey, who was appointed in 2004, have had to be content with entry into the

INTERNATIONAL HONOURS
None

COSAFA Castle Cup but the 2005 edition didn't bring a repeat of the heroics of 2000 when they reached the final. Instead they were knocked out after one game in the first round tournament held in Lusaka. With Lesotho totally surrounded by South Africa there should be plenty of opportunities for the national team to gain experience against top class sides wishing to sample the region ahead of the 2010 finals. The battle for supremacy between Maseru giants Matlama and Lesotho Defence Force continued in the 2004 League Championship with LDF equalling Matlama's record of eight titles.

THE FIFA BIG COUNT OF 2000

	Male	Female		Male	Female
Registered players	27 400	0	Referees	70	0
Non registered players	5 000	0	Officials	2 000	0
Youth players	2 000	10 000	Total involved	43 770	
Total players	41 700		Number of clubs	100	
Professional players	0	0	Number of teams	910	

Lesotho Football Association (LEFA)
Old Polo Ground, PO Box 1879, Maseru-100, Lesotho
Tel +266 22311879   Fax +266 22310586
lefa@leo.co.ls
www.lesothofa.com
President: PHAFANE Salemane   General Secretary: MOKALANYANE Boniface
Vice-President: MOSOTHOANE Pitso   Treasurer: TBD   Media Officer: MONNE
Men's Coach: HEY Antoine   Women's Coach: MASIMONA Lethoia
LEFA formed: 1932   CAF: 1964   FIFA: 1964
Colours: Blue, Green, White

GAMES PLAYED BY LESOTHO IN THE 2006 FIFA WORLD CUP™ CYCLE

2002	Opponents	Score		Venue	Comp	Scorers	Att	Referee
26-08	Botswana	W	1-0	Gaborone	Fr	Shale [30]		
30-08	Zimbabwe	L	0-2	Harare	Fr			
8-09	Senegal	L	0-1	Maseru	CNq			Langwenya SWZ
6-10	Swaziland	D	0-0	Big Bend	Fr		4 000	
8-10	Ghana	L	1-2	Accra	Fr	Makhele [55]		
12-10	Gambia	L	0-6	Banjul	CNq		25 000	Ba MTN
2003								
9-03	Botswana	W	1-0	Gaborone	Fr	Mpakanyane [13]		
16-03	Congo DR	D	2-2	Maseru	Fr			
19-03	Swaziland	L	0-1	Mbabane	Fr		400	
22-03	Mozambique	D	0-0	Maputo	CCr1	L 4-5p		Lwanja MWI
16-05	Botswana	L	1-2	Maseru	Fr			
21-05	Malawi	D	0-0	Maseru	Fr			
25-05	Swaziland	W	2-1	Maseru	Fr	Potse 2 [87 89]		
14-06	Senegal	L	0-3	Dakar	CNq			
6-07	Gambia	W	1-0	Maseru	CNq	Makhele [87]		
4-10	Swaziland	W	5-2	Maseru	Fr			
8-10	South Africa	L	0-3	Maseru	Fr			
11-10	Botswana	L	1-4	Gaborone	WCq	Ramafole [64]	10 000	Manuel Joao ANG
16-11	Botswana	D	0-0	Maseru	WCq		9 000	Shikapande ZIM
2004								
29-02	Botswana	D	0-0	Maseru	CCr1	L 10-11p	10 000	Mufeti NAM
15-12	Botswana	D	1-1	Maseru	Fr			
2005								
19-03	Namibia	L	1-2	Maseru	Fr			
1-06	Swaziland	L	3-4	Maseru	Fr			
11-06	Malawi	L	1-2	Lusaka	CCr1	Potse [46]		Mpanisi ZAM
26-06	Mozambique	L	0-1	Maputo	Fr			

Fr = Friendly match • CN = CAF African Cup of Nations • CC = COSAFA Castle Cup • WC = FIFA World Cup™ • q = qualifier • r1 = first round group

LESOTHO NATIONAL TEAM RECORDS AND RECORD SEQUENCES

Records			Sequence records				
Victory	4-0	BOT 1992	Wins	3	1979	Clean sheets	3	1992
Defeat	0-7	COD 1993	Defeats	6	1995-1997	Goals scored	6	1992
Player Caps	n/a		Undefeated	7	1992	Without goal	3	Three times
Player Goals	n/a		Without win	11	1981-1992	Goals against	12	2000-2001

FIFA REFEREE LIST 2005

	Int'l	DoB
KELEPA Albert	2004	13-07-1968
LETSIE Daniel	2004	7-03-1974
MOEKETSI Samuel	1993	16-11-1962
MPOPO Moeti	1993	15-09-1966
PHOMANE Paul	1999	18-06-1966
SENTSO Mohau	2000	10-03-1973
TSENOLI Thabiso	2001	4-02-1965

FIFA ASSISTANT REFEREE LIST 2005

	Int'l	DoB
KHIBA Paul	2001	28-12-1962
MOEPI Nephtali	2002	20-11-1969
MOHLAKALA Tseliso	2002	1-01-1963
MOKHEMISA John	2004	4-06-1972
SEEISO Sekhonyana	2001	21-01-1969
SEKOATI Letuka	2000	12-03-1965
SHALE Fusi	2002	6-12-1963

LESOTHO COUNTRY INFORMATION

Capital	Maseru	Independence	1966 from the UK	GDP per Capita	3 000
Population	1 865 040	Status	Constutional Monarchy	GNP Ranking	153
Area km²	30 355	Language	Sesotho, English	Dialling code	+266
Population density	61 per km²	Literacy rate	84%	Internet code	.ls
% in urban areas	23%	Main religion	Christian 80%	GMT +/-	+2
Towns/Cities ('000)	Maseru 194; Hlotse 46; Mafeteng 40; Maputsoa 31; Teyateyaneng 25; Mohale's Hoek 22				
Neighbours (km)	South Africa 909				
Main stadia	National Stadium – Maseru 20 000				

LIB – LEBANON

NATIONAL TEAM RECORD
JULY 1ST 2002 TO JUNE 30TH 2005

PL	W	D	L	F	A	%
33	7	8	18	33	58	33.3

FIFA/COCA-COLA WORLD RANKING

1993	1994	1995	1996	1997	1998	1999	2000	2001	2002	2003	2004	High		Low	
108	129	134	97	90	85	111	110	93	119	115	105	85	12/98	145	11/95

2004-2005											
08/04	09/04	10/04	11/04	12/04	01/05	02/05	03/05	04/05	05/05	06/05	07/05
108	110	109	109	105	107	108	109	112	112	113	114

After years of civil war, football received a welcome boost when Lebanon hosted the 2000 Asian Cup. Since then, the national side have continued to make some progress but are still waiting for a real breakthrough. Failure to qualify for the 2004 Asian Cup finals in China cost French coach Richard Tardi his position leaving Mohamad Kwid to guide the team through the qualifiers for the 2006 FIFA World Cup™. A missed penalty in the first match with Korea Republic was to cost Lebanon dear. The Koreans went on to win 2-0 and then won the group after the 'decider' between the two sides resulted in a 1-1 draw. The Lebanese were left to rue the missed opportunities as they

INTERNATIONAL HONOURS
None

finished second in the group three points behind Korea. More disappointment came at the West Asian Football Federation Cup in Iran sandwiched between FIFA World Cup™ fixtures where a primarily home-based squad soon returned home after defeats to Syria and the hosts. The battle for the League title went to the wire with the reigning champions Al Nijmeh travelling to Al Ansar on the final day with both team level on points. A 2-2 draw meant Al Nijmeh retained the title on goal difference. They also won their 2005 AFC Cup group with maximum points to reach the quarter-finals along with Al Ahed.

THE FIFA BIG COUNT OF 2000

	Male	Female		Male	Female
Registered players	21 912	0	Referees	155	0
Non registered players	300 000	0	Officials	2 680	0
Youth players	5 000	0	Total involved	329 747	
Total players	326 912		Number of clubs	174	
Professional players	62	0	Number of teams	2 070	

Lebanese Football Association (FLFA)
Verdun Street - Bristol, Radwan Center, PO Box 4732, Beirut, Lebanon
Tel +961 1 745745   Fax +961 1 349529
libanfa@cyberia.net.lb   www.lebanesefa.com
President: HAYDAR Hachem   General Secretary: AZOU HAMZEH Bahij
Vice-President: YAMMINE Kabalan   Treasurer: MAKKI Moussa   Media Officer: None
Men's Coach: KWID Mohamad   Women's Coach: None
FLFA formed: 1933   AFC: 1964   FIFA: 1935
Colours: Red, White, Red

GAMES PLAYED BY LEBANON IN THE 2006 FIFA WORLD CUP™ CYCLE

2002	Opponents	Score		Venue	Comp	Scorers	Att	Referee
1-09	Jordan	L	0-1	Damascus	WAr1			
3-09	Iran	L	0-2	Damascus	WAr1		2 000	Haj Khader SYR
19-12	Saudi Arabia	L	0-1	Kuwait City	ARr1		700	El Beltagy EGY
21-12	Syria	L	1-4	Kuwait City	ARr1	Kassas 54	1 000	Guezzaz MAR
24-12	Yemen	W	4-2	Kuwait City	ARr1	Antar.R 3 11 51 60, Hojeij 62	1 000	Hamza KUW
26-12	Bahrain	D	0-0	Kuwait City	ARr1		1 000	Guirat TUN
2003								
15-08	Syria	D	0-0	Damascus	Fr	Abandoned at half-time		
22-08	Syria	W	1-0	Beirut	Fr	Ali Atwi 57		
4-09	Korea DPR	W	1-0	Pyongyang	ACq	Farah 56		
19-09	Bahrain	L	3-4	Manama	Fr	Kassas 53, Mohammed 69, Al Jamal 86		
17-10	Jordan	L	0-1	Amman	ACq			
3-11	Korea DPR	D	1-1	Beirut	ACq	Hamieh 58	25 000	
12-11	Jordan	L	0-2	Beirut	ACq		15 000	
19-11	Iran	L	0-3	Beirut	ACq			Al Marzouqi UAE
28-11	Iran	L	0-1	Tehran	ACq			Rungklay THA
16-12	Kuwait	L	0-2	Larnaca	Fr			
18-12	Kuwait	D	0-0	Larnaca	Fr			
2004								
8-02	Bahrain	W	2-1	Beirut	Fr	Chahoud 90, Al Jamal 90		
18-02	Korea Republic	L	0-2	Suwon	WCq		22 000	Al Dosari KSA
23-03	Syria	L	0-1	Jounieh	Fr			
31-03	Vietnam	W	2-0	Nam Dinh	WCq	Antar.R 83, Hamieh 88	25 000	Irmatov UZB
26-05	Bahrain	D	2-2	Beirut	Fr	Ali Atwi 70, Balout 81		
9-06	Maldives	W	3-0	Beirut	WCq	Zein 21, Antar.R 87, Nasseredine 93+	18 000	Nurilddin Salman IRQ
17-06	Iran	L	0-4	Tehran	WAr1			
19-06	Syria	L	1-3	Tehran	WAr1	Zein 65		
3-07	China PR	L	0-6	Chongqing	Fr			
31-08	Jordan	D	2-2	Amman	Fr			
8-09	Maldives	W	5-2	Male	WCq	Nasseredine 2 4 58, Antar.F 44, Chahoud 63, Antar.R 75	12 000	Al Ajmi OMA
3-10	Kuwait	L	1-3	Tripoli	Fr	Chahoud 64		
6-10	Kuwait	D	1-1	Beirut	Fr	Chahoud 45		
13-10	Korea Republic	D	1-1	Beirut	WCq	Nasseredine 27	38 000	Irmatov UZB
17-11	Vietnam	D	0-0	Beirut	WCq		1 000	Ebrahim BHR
1-12	Qatar	L	1-4	Doha	Fr	Nasseredine		
2005								
2-02	Bahrain	L	1-2	Doha	Fr	Ali Atwi		

Fr = Friendly match • WA = West Asian Federation Cup • AR = Arab Cup • AC = AFC Asian Cup • WC = FIFA World Cup™
q = qualifier • r1 = first round group

LEBANON NATIONAL TEAM RECORDS AND RECORD SEQUENCES

Records			Sequence records					
Victory	11-1	PHI 1967	Wins	6	1995-1996	Clean sheets	4	1997
Defeat	0-8	IRQ 1959	Defeats	5	1979-1985	Goals scored	10	1993-1996
Player Caps	n/a		Undefeated	9	1993-96, 1996-97	Without goal	11	1974-1988
Player Goals	n/a		Without win	11	1998	Goals against	11	1997-1998

LEBANON COUNTRY INFORMATION

Capital	Beirut	Independence	1944 from France	GDP per Capita	$4 800
Population	3 777 218	Status	Republic	GNP Ranking	70
Area km²	10 400	Language	Arabic	Dialling code	+961
Population density	363 per km²	Literacy rate	87%	Internet code	.lb
% in urban areas	87%	Main religion	Muslim 60%, Christian 39%	GMT +/−	+2
Towns/Cities ('000)	Beirut 1 252; Tripoli 229; Sidon 163; Sour 135; Nabatiye 98; Jounieh 96; Zahlah 78				
Neighbours (km)	Syria 375; Israel 79; Mediterranean Sea 225				
Main stadia	Camille Chamoun – Beirut 57 000; International Olympic – Tripoli 22 400				

LEBANON 2004-05

PREMIER LEAGUE

	Pl	W	D	L	F	A	Pts	Nijmeh	Ansar	Ahed	Olympic	Safa	Tadamon	Mabarra	Rayyan	Sagesse	Shabab	Akha Ahly
Al Nijmeh †	20	13	5	2	56	18	44		2-2	2-0	4-1	2-1	3-0	2-2	0-1	0-2	1-1	5-1
Al Ansar	20	13	5	2	35	17	44	2-2		1-0	1-0	0-1	4-2	1-1	2-2	5-0	2-1	1-0
Al Ahed	20	11	3	6	37	22	36	2-4	1-2		1-5	1-1	2-0	2-0	2-1	4-0	1-0	4-0
Olympic Beirut	20	9	6	5	33	22	33	1-0	3-0	1-1		2-1	3-2	0-1	3-1	0-0	1-1	3-1
Safa	20	7	7	6	26	23	28	1-2	1-1	1-3	2-1		2-0	2-3	0-0	1-0	4-2	3-4
Al Tadamon Tyre	20	6	6	8	17	26	24	2-2	0-1	0-3	1-1	1-1		2-0	1-0	0-1	1-1	0-0
Al Mabarra	20	6	6	8	18	28	24	0-7	0-2	2-1	1-2	0-0	0-1		0-1	1-2	1-0	2-0
Al Rayyan	20	5	6	9	19	28	21	0-6	1-2	0-1	2-2	0-2	2-2	1-1		3-0	0-0	1-0
La Sagesse	20	6	3	11	12	32	21	0-4	0-2	0-2	1-0	0-0	0-1	1-2	1-0		1-2	1-1
Shabab Al Sahel	20	3	7	10	23	31	16	0-2	0-3	2-2	2-3	0-1	0-2	1-1	1-0	1-2		6-1
Akha Ahly §	20	1	6	13	16	45	3	1-4	0-1	0-4	1-1	1-1	0-1	0-0	2-3	1-2	2-2	

21/11/2004 - 16/06/2005 • † Qualified for AFC Cup • § Six points deducted

FA CUP 2004-05

Round of 16

Al Ahed	1
Al Nijmah Sahra	0

Al Rayyan *	1 3p
Shabab Al Sahel	1 4p

Riyada wal Adab *	5
Shabab Al Ghazieh	2

Mahba Tripoli	1
Akha Ahly	4

Al Mabarra *	1 10p
Al Ansar	1 9p

Racing Beirut *	2
Al Nijmeh	3

Bourj	1
Tadamon Nabatiye	0

Safa *	1 3p
Olympic Beirut	1 5p

Quarter-finals

Al Ahed	2 1
Shabab Al Sahel *	0 0

Riyada wal Adab *	1 1
Akha Ahly	2 3

Al Mabarra *	4 1
Al Nijmeh	0 2

Bourj *	3 0
Olympic Beirut	3 2

Semi-finals

Al Ahed *	5 2
Akha Ahly	1 0

Al Mabarra *	0 1
Olympic Beirut	2 1

Final

25-06-2005

Al Ahed †	2
Olympic Beirut	1

* Home team/Home team in the first leg • † Qualified for AFC Cup

RECENT LEAGUE AND CUP RECORD

	Championship						Cup		
Year	Champions	Pts	Runners-up	Pts	Third	Pts	Winners	Score	Runners-up
1995	Al Ansar	61	Al Nijmeh	54	Homenetmen	51	Al Ansar	1-0	Safa
1996	Al Ansar	60	Safa	49	Al Nijmeh	42	Al Ansar	4-2	Al Nijmeh
1997	Al Ansar	65	Al Nijmeh	58	Homenetmen	49	Al Nijmeh	2-0	Al Ansar
1998	Al Ansar	63	Al Nijmeh	53	Al Tadamon	43	Al Nijmeh	2-1	Homenmen
1999	Al Ansar	48	Safa	38	Al Tadamon	36	Al Ansar	2-1	Homenmen
2000	Al Njmeh	47	Al Ansar	44	Al Akha 'a-Ahly	33	Shabab Al Sahel	1-1 5-4p	Safa
2001	Championship cancelled due to match fixing scandal						Al Tadamon	2-1	Al Ansar
2002	Al Nijmeh	61	La Sagesse	60	Al Tadamon	59	Al Ansar	2-0	Al Ahed
2003	Olympic Beirut	54	Al Nijmeh	53	Al Ahed	50	Olympic Beirut	3-2	Al Nijmeh
2004	Al Nijmeh	54	Al Ahed	47	Olympic Beirut	35	Al Ahed	2-1	Al Nijmeh
2005	Al Nijmeh	44	Al Ansar	44	Al Ahed	36	Al Ahed	2-1	Olympic Beirut

LIE – LIECHTENSTEIN

NATIONAL TEAM RECORD
JULY 1ST 2002 TO JUNE 30TH 2005

PL	W	D	L	F	A	%
23	2	3	18	15	53	15.2

FIFA/COCA-COLA WORLD RANKING

1993	1994	1995	1996	1997	1998	1999	2000	2001	2002	2003	2004	High		Low	
160	156	157	154	158	159	125	147	150	147	148	142	125	12/99	165	09/98

2004-2005											
08/04	09/04	10/04	11/04	12/04	01/05	02/05	03/05	04/05	05/05	06/05	07/05
154	152	151	140	142	144	144	144	142	141	140	138

There has huge disappointment once again in Liechtenstein when for the third year running FC Vaduz just missed out on promotion to the Swiss Super League. What made the failure even more disappointing was the fact that Vaduz had led the Second Division table before slipping back in the final weeks to finish a point behind Yverdon-Sport who won automatic promotion. For the second successive year that left a play-off with Super League opposition, this time against Schaffhausen, and once again Vaduz lost. With clubs from Liechtenstein competing in the Swiss Leagues the only national competition is the Cup, which Vaduz once again easily claimed beating USV

INTERNATIONAL HONOURS
None

Eschen/Mauren 4-1 in the final for their eighth straight success. The 2004-05 UEFA Cup saw a notable first when Vaduz beat Ireland's Longford Town to progress through a round of European competition for the first time and there were also some notable firsts for the national team. A sensational 2-2 draw at home to Portugal was the first point the team had ever won in the FIFA World Cup™ and it was followed four days later with a 4-0 away win over Luxembourg – the first time Liechtenstein had ever won away from home with what was their biggest ever win. The two results earned the national team the title of 'Team of the Year' in Liechtenstein.

THE FIFA BIG COUNT OF 2000

	Male	Female		Male	Female
Registered players	708	22	Referees	30	0
Non registered players	300	40	Officials	200	0
Youth players	745	50	Total involved	2 095	
Total players	1 865		Number of clubs	7	
Professional players	8	0	Number of teams	100	

Liechtensteiner Fussballverband (LFV)
Altenbach 11, Postfach 165, 9490 Vaduz, Liechtenstein
Tel +423 2374747   Fax +423 2374748
info@lfv.li   www.lfv.li
President: WALSER Reinhard   General Secretary: GERSTGRASSER Oliver
Vice-President: HILTI Fredi   Treasurer: EGGENBERBER Rolf   Media Officer: FROMMELT Judith
Men's Coach: ANDERMATT Martin   Women's Coach: None
LFV formed: 1934   UEFA: 1992   FIFA: 1974
Colours: Blue, Red, Blue

GAMES PLAYED BY LIECHTENSTEIN IN THE 2006 FIFA WORLD CUP™ CYCLE

2002	Opponents	Score		Venue	Comp	Scorers	Att	Referee
21-08	Faroe Islands	L	1-3	Tórshavn	Fr	Hetta [40p]	3 200	Orrason ISL
8-09	Macedonia FYR	D	1-1	Vaduz	ECq	Stocklasa.Mk [90]	2 300	Godulyan UKR
16-10	Turkey	L	0-5	Istanbul	ECq		8 000	Baskakov RUS
2003								
29-03	England	L	0-2	Vaduz	ECq		3 548	Kasnaferis GRE
2-04	Slovakia	L	0-4	Trnava	ECq			Ceferin SVN
30-04	Saudi Arabia	W	1-0	Vaduz	Fr	Burgmeier.F [22]	1 200	Rogalla SUI
7-06	Macedonia FYR	L	1-3	Skopje	ECq	Beck.R [18]	6 000	Jara CZE
20-08	San Marino	D	2-2	Vaduz	Fr	Frick.M [16], Burgmeier.F [23]	850	Wildhaber SUI
6-09	Turkey	L	0-3	Vaduz	ECq		3 548	Van Egmond NED
10-09	England	L	0-2	Manchester	ECq		64 931	Fisker DEN
11-10	Slovakia	L	0-2	Vaduz	ECq		800	Hyytia FIN
2004								
28-04	San Marino	L	0-1	Serravalle	Fr		700	Sammut MLT
3-06	Greece	L	0-2	Vaduz	Fr		2 000	Petignat SUI
6-06	Switzerland	L	0-1	Zürich	Fr		10 200	Drabek AUT
18-08	Estonia	L	1-2	Vaduz	WCq	D'Elia [49]	912	Bozinovski MKD
3-09	Netherlands	L	0-3	Utrecht	Fr		15 000	Brines SCO
8-09	Slovakia	L	0-7	Bratislava	WCq		5 620	Delevic SCG
9-10	Portugal	D	2-2	Vaduz	WCq	Burgmeier.F [48], Beck.T [76]	3 548	Panic BIH
13-10	Luxembourg	W	4-0	Luxembourg	WCq	Stocklasa.Mt [41], Burgmeier.F 2 [44 85], Frick.M [57p]	3 748	Jara CZE
17-11	Latvia	L	1-3	Vaduz	WCq	Frick.M [32]	1 460	Szabo HUN
2005								
26-03	Russia	L	1-2	Vaduz	WCq	Beck.T [40]	2 400	Bernsten NOR
4-06	Estonia	L	0-2	Tallinn	WCq		3 000	Whitby WAL
8-06	Latvia	L	0-1	Riga	WCq		8 000	Eriksson SWE

Fr = Friendly match • EC = UEFA EURO 2004™ • WC = FIFA World Cup™ • q = qualifier

NATIONAL CAPS

	Caps
HASLER Daniel	62
FRICK Mario	58
TELSER Martin	54
STOCKLASA Martin	51
STOCKLASA Michael	42

NATIONAL GOALS

	Goals
FRICK Mario	7
BURGMEIER Franz	5
STOCKLASA Martin	5
BECK Thomas	2

NATIONAL COACH

	Years
WEISE Dietrich	1994-'96
RIEDL Alfred	1997
BURZLE Erich	1998
LOOSE Ralf	1998-03'
HORMANN Walter	2003-'04
ANDERMATT Martin	2004-

Liechtenstein has no referees or assistant referees on the FIFA list. There is also no league competition as teams compete in the Swiss regional leagues

LIECHTENSTEIN NATIONAL TEAM RECORDS AND RECORD SEQUENCES

Records			Sequence records					
Victory	4-1	LUX 2004	Wins	3	1981-1982	Clean sheets	2	1981-82, 1999
Defeat	1-11	MKD 1996	Defeats	17	1995-1998	Goals scored	4	2004-2005
Player Caps	62	HASLER Daniel	Undefeated	3	1981-1982	Without goal	11	1994-96, 2000-02
Player Goals	7	FRICK Mario	Without win	29	1984-1998	Goals against	22	1995-1999

LIECHTENSTEIN COUNTRY INFORMATION

Capital	Vaduz	Formation	1719	GDP per Capita	$25 000
Population	33 436	Status	Constitutional Monarchy	GNP Ranking	144
Area km²	160	Language	German	Dialling code	+423
Population density	208 per km²	Literacy rate	100%	Internet code	.li
% in urban areas	21%	Main religion	Christian 83%	GMT + / –	+1
Towns/Cities ('000)	Schaan 6; Vaduz 5; Triesen 5; Balzers 4; Eschen 4; Mauren 3; Triesenberg 2				
Neighbours (km)	Austria 34; Switzerland 41				
Main stadia	Rheinpark Stadion – Vaduz 8 000				

LTU – LITHUANIA

NATIONAL TEAM RECORD
JULY 1ST 2002 TO JUNE 30TH 2005

PL	W	D	L	F	A	%
27	7	4	16	31	42	33.3

FIFA/COCA-COLA WORLD RANKING

1993	1994	1995	1996	1997	1998	1999	2000	2001	2002	2003	2004	High		Low	
85	59	43	48	45	54	50	85	97	100	101	100	42	08/97	118	09/04

2004-2005											
08/04	09/04	10/04	11/04	12/04	01/05	02/05	03/05	04/05	05/05	06/05	07/05
116	118	111	103	100	100	100	102	98	98	94	94

Despite slipping to their lowest position in the FIFA/Coca-Cola World Ranking in September 2004, the Lithuanian national team has had a surprisingly successful time in the 2006 FIFA World Cup™ qualifiers. Five games into the campaign Lithuania remained unbeaten although a defeat at the hands of Spain in June 2005 has damaged any realistic hopes of a place in the finals in Germany. A number of players are gaining experience abroad, notably Tomas Danilevicius with Livorno in Italy, while there has been a Lithuanian revolution at Heart of Midlothian in Scotland's capital city Edinburgh. Since being bought by wealthy tycoon Vladimir Romanov the list of Lithuanian

INTERNATIONAL HONOURS
None

players at the club is growing with Edgaras Jankauskas the latest addition. There was an exciting finale to the 2004 Championship in Lithuania when Ekranas met Kaunas on the last day of the season with both level on 62 points. Despite enjoying home advantage and having won all three previous matches between the two (the only games Kaunas lost all season) Ekranas collapsed in the second half, handing their rivals a sixth successive title and losing out on the chance of a first Championship since 1993. The win also saw Kaunas clinch the double having beaten Atlantas on penalties in the Cup Final two weeks before.

THE FIFA BIG COUNT OF 2000

	Male	Female		Male	Female
Registered players	17 069	100	Referees	125	5
Non registered players	35 000	500	Officials	1 200	100
Youth players	12 179	450	Total involved	66 728	
Total players	65 298		Number of clubs	60	
Professional players	224	0	Number of teams	1 135	

Lithuanian Football Federation (LFF)
Seimyniskiu 15, 2005 Vilnius, Lithuania
Tel +370 52638741   Fax +370 52638740
info@futbolas.lt   www.futbolas.lt
President: VARANAVICIUS Liutauras   General Secretary: KVEDARAS Julius
Vice-President: BABRAVICIUS Gintautas   Treasurer: TBD   Media Officer: ZIZAITE Vaiva
Men's Coach: LIUBINSKAS Algimantas   Women's Coach: TUTLYS Vytautas
LFF formed: 1922   UEFA: 1992   FIFA: 1923-1943 & 1992
Colours: Yellow, Green, Yellow

GAMES PLAYED BY LITHUANIA IN THE 2006 FIFA WORLD CUP™ CYCLE

2002	Opponents	Score	Venue	Comp	Scorers	Att	Referee
21-08	Israel	L 2-4	Kaunas	Fr	Fomenka [10], Poskus [32]	3 000	Chykun BLR
7-09	Germany	L 0-2	Kaunas	ECq		8 500	Poll ENG
12-10	Faroe Islands	W 2-0	Kaunas	ECq	Razanauskas [23p], Poskus [37]	2 500	Delevic YUG
16-10	Iceland	L 0-3	Reykjavík	ECq		3 513	Gilewski POL
2003							
12-02	Latvia	L 1-2	Antalya	Fr	OG [34]	700	
29-03	Germany	D 1-1	Nuremberg	ECq	Razanauskas [73]	40 754	Esquinas Torres ESP
2-04	Scotland	W 1-0	Kaunas	ECq	Razanauskas [75p]	8 000	Stuchlik AUT
30-04	Romania	L 0-1	Kaunas	Fr		5 000	Sipailo LVA
11-06	Iceland	L 0-3	Kaunas	ECq		7 500	Corpodean ROU
3-07	Estonia	W 5-1	Valga	BC	Morinas [39], Cesnauskis.D [45], Velicka [72] Bezykornovas [84], Cesnauskas.E [90]	800	Ingvarsson SWE
4-07	Latvia	L 1-2	Valga	BC	Tamosauskas [73]	500	Frojdfeldt SWE
20-08	Bulgaria	L 0-3	Sofia	Fr		2 000	Bolognino ITA
10-09	Faroe Islands	W 3-1	Toftir	ECq	Morinas 2 [23 57], Vencevicius [88]	2 175	Trivcovic CRO
11-10	Scotland	L 0-1	Glasgow	ECq		50 343	Colombo FRA
14-12	Poland	L 1-3	Ta'Qali	Fr	Butrimavicius [5]	100	Attard MLT
2004							
30-03	Israel	L 1-2	Tel Aviv	Fr	OG [43]	9 782	Dougal SCO
28-04	Belarus	L 0-1	Minsk	Fr		8 000	Ivanov RUS
5-06	Portugal	L 1-4	Alcochete	Fr	Vencevicius [74p]	25 000	Wilmes LUX
18-08	Russia	L 3-4	Moscow	Fr	Danilevicius [40], Poskus [83], Barasa [89]	3 500	Mikulski POL
4-09	Belgium	D 1-1	Charleroi	WCq	Jankauskas [73]	19 218	Loizou CYP
8-09	San Marino	W 4-0	Kaunas	WCq	Jankauskas 2 [18 50], Danilevicius [65], Gedgaudas [92+]	4 000	Jareci ALB
13-10	Spain	D 0-0	Vilnius	WCq		9 114	Poulat FRA
17-11	San Marino	W 1-0	Serravalle	WCq	Cesnauskis.D [41]	1 457	Nalbandyan ARM
2005							
9-02	Georgia	L 0-1	Tbilisi	Fr		1 000	Gadiyev AZE
30-03	Bosnia-Herzegovina	D 1-1	Sarajevo	WCq	Stankevicius [60]	6 000	Baskakov RUS
21-05	Latvia	W 2-0	Kaunas	BC	Morinas 2 [25 81]		
4-06	Spain	L 0-1	Valencia	WCq		25 000	Farina ITA

Fr = Friendly match • EC = UEFA EURO 2004™ • BC = Baltic Cup • WC = FIFA World Cup™ • q = qualifier

NATIONAL CAPS

	Caps
SKARBALIUS Aurelijus	62
STAUCE Gintaras	61
TERESKINAS Andrius	56
MIKALAJUNAS Saulius	50
ZIUKAS Tomas	45

NATIONAL GOALS

	Goals
LINGIS Antanas	12
BALTUSNIKAS Virginijus	9
CITAVICIUS Jaroslavas	8
IVANAUSKAS Valdas	8
JANKAUSKAS Edgaras	8

NATIONAL COACH

	Years
TAUTKUS Robertas	1999-'00
STANKUS Stasys	2000
KVEDARAS Julius	2000
ZELKEVICIUS Benjaminas	2000-'03
LIUBINSKAS Algimantas	2003-

LITHUANIA NATIONAL TEAM RECORDS AND RECORD SEQUENCES

Records			Sequence records					
Victory	7-0	EST 1995	Wins	3	1992	Clean sheets	3	2004
Defeat	0-10	EGY 1924	Defeats	10	1936-1938	Goals scored	15	1934-1937
Player Caps	62	SKARBALIUS Aurelijus	Undefeated	5	1935, 1992	Without goal	4	1993, 1997
Player Goals	12	LINGIS Antanas	Without win	13	1936-1939	Goals against	18	1923-1936

LITHUANIA COUNTRY INFORMATION

Capital	Vilnius	Independence	1991 from the USSR	GDP per Capita	$11 400
Population	3 607 899	Status	Republic	GNP Ranking	82
Area km²	65 200	Language	Lithuanian, Russian	Dialling code	+370
Population density	55 per km²	Literacy rate	99%	Internet code	lt
% in urban areas	72%	Main religion	Christian	GMT +/-	+2
Towns/Cities ('000)	Vilnius 542; Kaunas 374; Klaipeda 192; Siauliai 130; Panevezys 117; Alytus 70				
Neighbours (km)	Latvia 453; Belarus 502; Poland 91; Russia 227; Baltic Sea 99				
Main stadia	Zalgirio – Vilnius 15 030; Aukstaitijos – Panevezys 10 000; Darius Girenas – Kaunas 8 476				

LITHUANIA 2004

A LYGA

	Pl	W	D	L	F	A	Pts	FBK	Ekranas	Atlantas	Zalgiris	Vetra	FK Silute	Süduva	FK Vilnius
FBK Kaunas †	28	20	5	3	49	19	65		0-2 0-3	0-0 5-1	1-0 3-0	1-1 1-0	2-1 2-1	3-0 1-1	1-0 2-0
Ekranas Panevezys ‡	28	20	2	6	59	22	62	1-0 0-2		1-0 3-0	4-0 3-1	2-2 2-0	0-1 1-0	5-0 4-3	3-0 4-1
Atlantas Klaipeda ‡	28	15	5	8	36	29	50	0-1 1-2	2-1 1-0		1-0 1-0	2-0 2-1	2-0 5-3	2-1 0-1	0-1 3-2
Zalgiris Vilnius	28	10	7	11	32	38	37	0-0 1-5	3-1 1-3	0-0 0-3		0-0 1-2	1-0 2-1	3-1 1-1	0-0 1-1
Vetra Vilnius	28	9	8	11	29	33	35	1-2 0-2	1-3 0-3	1-1 4-0	0-0 0-3		1-1 0-1	1-1 1-1	2-0 2-1
FK Silute	28	6	7	15	34	44	25	2-2 0-4	0-1 2-1	0-1 1-1	1-4 4-0	0-1 0-1		1-1 1-1	0-3 1-1
Süduva Marijampole	28	5	7	16	31	55	22	1-2 2-3	1-2 1-2	1-1 0-1	1-3 0-3	0-1 2-1	2-6 3-1		2-0 0-2
FK Vilnius	28	4	5	19	19	49	17	0-1 0-1	0-4 0-0	0-1 0-4	0-2 1-2	0-2 1-3	0-4 1-1	4-1 0-2	

18/04/2004 - 7/11/2004 • † Qualified for the UEFA Champions League • ‡ Qualified for the UEFA Cup • No relegation in 2004

LITHUANIA 2004 LFF 1 LYGA (2)

	Pl	W	D	L	F	A	Pts
KFK Siauliai	32	22	5	5	81	21	71
Kauno Jegeriai †	32	21	7	4	73	26	70
Nevezis Kedainiai	32	19	7	6	62	31	64
Gelezinis Vilkas	32	17	7	8	61	37	58
Polonija Vilnius	32	17	3	12	53	34	54
FK Mazeikiai	32	15	4	13	54	51	49
Lietava Jonava	32	13	7	12	45	54	46
Babrungas Plunge	32	13	6	13	55	47	45
Rodovitas Klaipeda	32	12	8	12	55	60	44
Vetra-2 Vilnius	32	12	6	14	59	62	42
Ekranas-2 Panevezys	32	10	7	15	45	48	37
LKKA Kaunas	32	9	8	15	44	68	35
Utenis Utena	32	10	4	18	29	66	34
Alytis Alytus	32	8	10	14	23	41	34
Atletas Kaunas	32	8	9	15	25	44	33
Tauras Taurage	32	9	2	21	29	73	29
KF Vilnius-2	32	4	6	22	26	56	18

17/04/2004 - 30/10/2004 • † Kauno Jegeriai ineligible for promotion due to their links with FBK Kaunas

FA CUP 2004-05

Quarter-finals		Semi-finals		Final	
FBK Kaunas	1 2				
Ekranas	1 1	FBK Kaunas	1 0 4p		
FK Silute	1 0	Vetra	0 1 3p		
Vetra	1 1			FBK Kaunas	0 2p
Zalgiris	2 4			Atlantas ‡	0 1p
FK Vilnius	0 2	Zalgiris	1 0	27-10-2004, Att.500	
Süduva	2 2	Atlantas	0 2	Ref: Malzinskas	
Atlantas	3 3	‡ Qualified for the UEFA Cup		Savlvaldybes, Siauliai	

FIFA REFEREE LIST 2005

	Int'l	DoB
MALZINSKAS Paulius	2001	21-06-1970
ZUTA Audrius		5-01-1969

CLUB DIRECTORY

Club	Town/City	Stadium	Phone	www.	Lge	Cup	CL
Atlantas	Klaipeda	Centrinis 5 000	+370 46 312606	atlantas.lt	0	2	0
Ekranas	Panevezys	Aukstaitijos 10 000	+370 45 435515	fk-ekranas.lt	1	2	0
FBK Kaunas	Kaunas	Darius Girenas 8 476	+370 37 361613	fbk.rodiklis.lt	6	2	0
Nevezis	Kedainiai	Kedainlu 3 000	+370 3 4750669		0	0	0
KFK Siauliai	Siauliai	Savlvaldybes 2 430	+370 41 422829		0	0	0
FK Silute	Silute	Centrinis 5 000	+370 44 151133		0	0	0
Suduva	Marijampole	Suduvos 4 000	+370 34 391065	fksuduva.lt	0	0	0
Vetra	Vilnius		+370 52 639270	fkvetra.lt	0	0	0
FK Vilnius	Vilnius	Zalgirio 15 030	+370 52 730629	zalgiris-vilnius.lnx.lt	0	0	0
Zalgiris	Vilnius	Zalgirio 15 030	+370 52 342360		3	5	0

RECENT LEAGUE AND CUP RECORD

	Championship						Cup		
Year	Champions	Pts	Runners-up	Pts	Third	Pts	Winners	Score	Runners-up
1995	Inkaras Kaunas	36	Zalgiris Vilnius	36	ROMAR	34	Inkaras Kaunas	2-1	Zalgiris Vilnius
1996	Inkaras Kaunas	56	Kareda Siauliai	52	Zalgiris Vilnius	50	Kareda Siauliai	1-0	Inkaras Kaunas
1997	Kareda Siauliai	64	Zalgiris Vilnius	56	Inkaras Kaunas	53	Zalgiris Vilnius	1-0	Inkaras Kaunas
1998	Kareda Siauliai	79	Zalgiris Vilnius	77	Ekranas Panevezys	68	Ekranas Panevezys	1-0	FBK Kaunas
1999	Zalgiris Vilnius	59	Kareda Siauliai	58	FBK Kaunas	57	Kareda Siauliai	3-0	FBK Kaunas
1999	FBK Kaunas	41	Zalgiris Vilnius	36	Atlantas Klaipeda	33			
2000	FBK Kaunas	86	Zalgiris Vilnius	83	Atlantas Klaipeda	67	Ekranas Panevezys	1-0	Zalgiris Vilnius
2001	FBK Kaunas	85	Atlantas Klaipeda	69	Zalgiris Vilnius	69	Atlantas Klaipeda	1-0	Zalgiris Vilnius
2002	FBK Kaunas	78	Atlantas Klaipeda	67	Ekranas Panevezys	55	FBK Kaunas	3-1	Süduva Marijampole
2003							Atlantas Klaipeda	1-1 3-1p	Vetra
2003	FBK Kaunas	68	Ekranas Panevezys	62	Vetra	47	Zalgiris Vilnius	3-1	Ekranas Panevezys
2004	FBK Kaunas	65	Ekranas Panevezys	62	Atlantas Klaipeda	50	FBK Kaunas	0-0 2-1p	Atlantas Klaipeda

Two leagues were played in 1999 and an extra cup competition held in 2003 due to a change in the season calendar

LUX – LUXEMBOURG

NATIONAL TEAM RECORD
JULY 1ST 2002 TO JUNE 30TH 2005

PL	W	D	L	F	A	%
25	0	2	23	9	77	4

FIFA/COCA-COLA WORLD RANKING

1993	1994	1995	1996	1997	1998	1999	2000	2001	2002	2003	2004	High		Low	
111	128	100	123	138	143	124	139	142	148	153	155	**93**	04/96	**157**	08/04

2004-2005											
08/04	09/04	10/04	11/04	12/04	01/05	02/05	03/05	04/05	05/05	06/05	07/05
157	157	155	155	155	155	154	155	156	155	155	155

The Luxembourg national team continues to confound observers with a winless run now stretching back to 1995. It was hoped that with the expansion of UEFA and the increase in members who could be termed as 'minnows' that runs like this, which were all too common in the past, would be consigned to history. Of particular embarrassment was the 0-4 home defeat in the 2006 FIFA World Cup™ qualifiers at the hands of Liechtenstein, a country with a tenth of the population of Luxembourg. It's a far cry from the EURO 96™ qualifiers when Luxembourg picked up 10 points and beat the Czech Republic, who then went on to reach the final. The 2004-05 season saw Guy

INTERNATIONAL HONOURS
None

Heller's side concede at least three goals in every match with the 4-0 defeat at home to Slovakia the 15th consecutive loss. The only comforting fact is that in the battle to avoid being the worst team in Europe, San Marino are some seven places below Luxembourg in the FIFA/Coca-Cola World Ranking. The extraordinary thing is that the Championship in Luxembourg continues to be relatively competitive and in 2005 it was won for the fourth time in six seasons by F'91 Dudelange. In the Cup, however, there was a new name on the trophy with CS Petange winning their first major title after convincingly beating surprise finalists Cebra from the Third Division, 5-0.

THE FIFA BIG COUNT OF 2000

	Male	Female		Male	Female
Registered players	17 148	403	Referees	225	6
Non registered players	4 000	0	Officials	1 000	50
Youth players	9 434	0	Total involved	32 266	
Total players	30 985		Number of clubs	120	
Professional players	150	0	Number of teams	490	

Fédération Luxembourgeoise de Football (FLF)
68 rue de Gasperich, 1617 Luxembourg
Tel +352 4886651   Fax +352 488 66582
flf@football.lu   www.football.lu
President: PHILIPP Paul   General Secretary: WOLFF Joel
Vice-President: SCHAACK Charles   Treasurer: DECKER Erny   Media Officer: DIEDERICH Marc
Men's Coach: HELLERS Guy   Women's Coach: JEAN Romain
FLF formed: 1908   UEFA: 1954   FIFA: 1910
Colours: Red, Red, Red

GAMES PLAYED BY LUXEMBOURG IN THE 2006 FIFA WORLD CUP™ CYCLE

2002	Opponents	Score		Venue	Comp	Scorers	Att	Referee
21-08	Morocco	L	0-2	Luxembourg	Fr		1 650	
5-09	Israel	L	0-5	Luxembourg	Fr		1 400	Allaerts BEL
12-10	Denmark	L	0-2	Copenhagen	ECq		40 259	Bede HUN
16-10	Romania	L	0-7	Luxembourg	ECq		2 000	Lajuks LVA
20-11	Cape Verde Islands	D	0-0	Hesperange	Fr			
2003								
29-03	Bosnia-Herzegovina	L	0-2	Zenica	ECq		10 000	Hyytia FIN
2-04	Norway	L	0-2	Luxembourg	ECq		3 000	Dobrinov BUL
30-04	Hungary	L	1-5	Budapest	Fr	Strasser 25	1 205	Skomina SVN
11-06	Denmark	L	0-2	Luxembourg	ECq		6 869	Baskakov RUS
19-08	Malta	D	1-1	Luxembourg	Fr	Strasser 53p		Lehner AUT
6-09	Romania	L	0-4	Ploesti	ECq		4 500	Yefet ISR
10-09	Bosnia-Herzegovina	L	0-1	Luxembourg	ECq		3 500	Kapitanis CYP
11-10	Norway	L	0-1	Oslo	ECq		22 255	Szabo HUN
20-11	Moldova	L	1-2	Hesperange	Fr	Schauls 77	623	
2004								
31-03	Bosnia-Herzegovina	L	1-2	Luxembourg	Fr	Huss 87	2 000	Rogalla SUI
28-04	Austria	L	1-4	Innsbruck	Fr	Huss 63	9 400	Skomina SVN
29-05	Portugal	L	0-3	Agueda	Fr		9 000	Styles ENG
18-08	Slovakia	L	1-3	Bratislava	WCq	Strasser 2	5 016	Kassai HUN
4-09	Estonia	L	0-4	Tallinn	WCq		3 000	Kelly IRL
8-09	Latvia	L	3-4	Luxembourg	WCq	Braun 11, Leweck 55, Cardoni 62	2 125	Kasnaferis GRE
9-10	Russia	L	0-4	Luxembourg	WCq		3 670	Braamhaar NED
13-10	Liechtenstein	L	0-4	Luxembourg	WCq		3 478	Jara CZE
17-11	Portugal	L	0-5	Luxembourg	WCq		8 045	Godulyan UKR
2005								
30-03	Latvia	L	0-4	Riga	WCq		8 203	Kovacic CRO
8-06	Slovakia	L	0-4	Luxembourg	WCq		2 108	Styles ENG

Fr = Friendly match • EC = UEFA EURO 2004™ • WC = FIFA World Cup™ • q = qualifier

LUXEMBOURG NATIONAL TEAM RECORDS AND RECORD SEQUENCES

Records			Sequence records					
Victory	6-0	AFG 1948	Wins	3	1939-1943	Clean sheets	3	1995
Defeat	0-9	GER 1936, ENG 1960 1982	Defeats	32	1980-1985	Goals scored	7	1948-1951
Player Caps	87	WEIS Carlo	Undefeated	4	1963	Without goal	9	1980-81, 1984-85
Player Goals	16	MART Léon	Without win	78	1980-1995	Goals against	31	1987-1995

NATIONAL CAPS

	Caps
WEIS Carlo	87
KONTER François	77
LANGERS Roby	73
CARDONI Manuel	69
BRENNER Ernest	67

NATIONAL GOALS

	Goals
MART Léon	16
KEMP Gustave	15
LIBAR Camille	14
KETTEL Nicolas	13
MULLER François	12

NATIONAL COACH

	Years
PHILIPP Paul	1985-'01
SIMONSEN Allan	2001-'04
HELLERS Guy	2004-

LUXEMBOURG COUNTRY INFORMATION

Capital	Luxembourg	Independence	1839 from the Netherlands	GDP per Capita	$55 100
Population	462 690	Status	Constitutional Monarchy	GDP Ranking	
Area km²	2 586	Language	Luxembourgish, German, French	Dialling code	+352
Population density	179 per km²	Literacy rate	100%	Internet code	.lu
% in urban areas	89%	Main religion	Christian	GMT + / –	+1
Towns/Cities ('000)	Luxembourg 76; Esch-sur-Alzette 28; Dudelange 18; Schifflange 8; Battembourg 7				
Neighbours (km)	Germany 138; France 73; Belgium 148;				
Main stadia	Stade Josy Barthel – Luxembourg 8 250; Stade de la Frontière – Esch-sur-Alzette 5 400				

LUXEMBOURG 2004-05

DIVISION NATIONALE

	Pl	W	D	L	F	A	Pts	Dudelange	Etzella	Jeunesse	Victoria	Grev'cher	Swift	Alliance	Petange	Wiltz	Spora	Union	Avenir
F'91 Dudelange †	22	18	2	2	56	13	56		0-1	5-1	4-2	2-1	2-1	3-0	2-0	3-1	7-0	1-1	3-0
Etzella Ettelbruck †	22	17	1	4	57	23	52	0-1		3-1	3-1	2-1	3-0	2-4	3-1	2-0	3-0	5-0	5-0
Jeunesse d'Esch †	22	12	5	5	50	28	41	0-3	2-2		3-0	0-2	0-0	2-2	0-3	1-0	4-2	3-1	1-1
Victoria Rosport †	22	12	5	5	43	33	41	2-2	4-1	1-6		2-1	1-2	3-0	1-0	2-1	1-1	5-1	1-1
CS Grevenmacher ‡	22	9	5	8	40	27	32	1-5	0-1	1-1	0-2		3-0	5-0	0-0	3-0	1-1	1-2	2-1
Swift Hesperange ‡‡	22	8	5	9	28	34	29	2-1	0-1	0-1	1-1	1-5		1-1	3-3	1-2	2-0	2-2	1-3
Alliance Luxembourg ‡	22	8	4	10	31	47	28	0-2	1-4	0-7	1-3	1-1	0-1		3-2	1-0	2-5	3-1	2-2
CS Petange ‡‡	22	8	3	11	38	34	27	0-2	1-4	1-3	2-3	3-1	2-0	0-3		4-0	1-2	1-1	1-0
FC Wiltz 71 ‡	22	8	1	13	25	37	25	0-2	3-4	1-3	1-2	2-2	0-2	1-0	2-1		2-0	1-0	3-2
Spora Luxembourg ‡‡	22	5	3	14	24	54	18	0-4	2-0	0-4	2-5	0-3	0-2	2-4	0-4	2-1		1-2	3-0
Union Luxembourg ‡	22	3	5	14	14	44	14	0-1	0-3	0-3	0-0	0-3	0-2	0-4	0-1	1-0			2-2
Avenir Beggen ‡‡	22	2	5	15	20	52	11	0-1	1-5	0-4	0-1	1-3	3-4	0-2	1-4	0-3	1-1	1-0	

7/08/2004 - 24/04/2005 • † Qualified for championship play-off • ‡ To relegation Group A • ‡‡ To relegation Group B

LUXEMBOURG 2004-05

CHAMPIONSHIP PLAY-OFF

	Pl	W	D	L	F	A	Pts	FD	EE	JE	VR
F'91 Dudelange †	28	22	4	2	74	15	70		1-1	7-1	5-0
Etzella Ettelbruck ‡	28	20	4	4	68	29	64	0-0		1-1	2-0
Jeunesse d'Esch	28	13	6	9	58	45	45	0-4	3-4		1-0
Victoria Rosport	28	13	5	10	45	47	44	0-1	1-3	1-0	

30/04/2005 - 5/06/2005 • † Qualified for the UEFA Champions League • ‡ Qualified for the UEFA Cup

LUXEMBOURG 2004-05

RELEGATION PLAY-OFF

Group A	Pl	W	D	L	F	A	Pts	AL	CG	FW	UL
Alliance Luxembourg	28	12	5	11	45	54	41		2-2	4-0	3-1
CS Grevenmacher	28	11	7	10	57	40	40	2-3		4-3	2-3
FC Wiltz 71	28	8	2	18	30	56	26	0-2	0-5		0-0
Union Luxembourg	28	6	7	15	26	53	25	2-0	2-2	4-2	

Group B	Pl	W	D	L	F	A	Pts	SH	CP	AB	SL
Swift Hesperange	28	11	6	11	39	46	39		1-0	0-3	1-1
CS Petange	28	10	5	13	50	45	35	4-3		1-3	1-1
Avenir Beggen	28	6	6	16	37	60	24	2-3	3-3		1-0
Spora Luxembourg	28	5	5	18	29	68	20	2-3	0-3	1-5	

30/04/2005 - 5/06/2005

LUXEMBOURG 2004-05

PROMOTION HONNEUR (2)

	Pl	W	D	L	F	A	Pts
UN Kaerjeng	26	17	8	1	71	19	59
US Rumelange	26	17	5	4	77	33	56
FC Mondercange	26	17	4	5	70	24	55
FC Differdange 03	26	12	8	6	58	45	44
Sporting Mertzig	26	13	4	9	44	39	43
FC 72 Erpeldange	26	12	6	8	43	38	42
Union Mertert	26	10	6	10	49	41	36
FC Hamm 37	26	9	6	11	38	31	33
Progres Niedercorn	26	9	5	12	33	53	32
FC Wormeldange	26	8	7	11	41	45	31
CS Obercorn	26	8	5	13	39	46	29
Echternach	26	6	2	18	29	55	20
CS Fola Esch	26	4	7	15	28	55	19
Young Boys Diekirch	26	3	1	22	20	86	10

22/08/2004 - 28/05/2005

COUPE DE LUXEMBOURG 2004-05

Quarter-finals		Semi-finals		Final	
Petange	5				
Union Luxembourg	0	Petange	1		
Rumelange	0				
Grevenmacher	4	Grevenmacher	0		
Hamm	1			Petange ‡	5
F'91 Dudelange	0			Cebra	0
Ell	4	Hamm	0	15-05-2005	
Cebra	5	Cebra	2	Stade Josy Barthel	

‡ Qualified for the UEFA Cup

RECENT LEAGUE AND CUP RECORD

	Championship						Cup		
Year	Champions	Pts	Runners-up	Pts	Third	Pts	Winners	Score	Runners-up
1996	Jeunesse d'Esch	48	CS Grevenmacher	47	Union Luxembourg	42	Union Luxembourg	3-1	Jeunesse d'Esch
1997	Jeunesse d'Esch	56	CS Grevenmacher	50	Union Luxembourg	38	Jeunesse d'Esch	2-0	Union Luxembourg
1998	Jeunesse d'Esch	54	Union Luxembourg	53	CS Grevenmacher	43	CS Grevenmacher	2-0	Avenir Beggen
1999	Jeunesse d'Esch	51	F'91 Dudelange	47	Avenir Beggen	45	Jeunesse d'Esch	3-0	FC Mondercange
2000	F'91 Dudelange	57	CS Grevenmacher	46	Jeunesse d'Esch	46	Jeunesse d'Esch	4-1	FC Mondercange
2001	F'91 Dudelange	63	CS Grevenmacher	59	CS Hobscheid	46	Etzella Ettelbruck	5-3	FC Wiltz
2002	F'91 Dudelange	62	CS Grevenmacher	58	Union Luxembourg	47	Avenir Beggen	1-0	F'91 Dudelange
2003	CS Grevenmacher	59	F'91 Dudelange	58	Jeunesse d'Esch	52	CS Grevenmacher	1-0	Etzella Ettelbruck
2004	Jeunesse d'Esch	68	F'91 Dudelange	59	Etzella Ettelbruck	48	F'91 Dudelange	3-1	Etzella Ettelbruck
2005	F'91 Dudelange	70	Etzella Ettelbruck	64	Jeunesse d'Esch	45	CS Petange	5-0	Cebra

LVA – LATVIA

NATIONAL TEAM RECORD
JULY 1ST 2002 TO JUNE 30TH 2005

PL	W	D	L	F	A	%
41	14	10	17	49	61	46.3

FIFA/COCA-COLA WORLD RANKING

1993	1994	1995	1996	1997	1998	1999	2000	2001	2002	2003	2004	High		Low	
86	69	60	82	75	77	62	92	106	79	51	65	51	12/03	107	03/02

2004-2005											
08/04	09/04	10/04	11/04	12/04	01/05	02/05	03/05	04/05	05/05	06/05	07/05
56	60	63	67	65	66	67	67	65	65	64	65

Matching the exploits of the UEFA EURO 2004™ campaign was never going to be an easy task for the Latvian national team, especially when coach Aleksandrs Starkovs quit after one game of the 2006 FIFA World Cup™ qualifiers to take up the Spartak Moskva job. His replacement Jurjis Andrejevs kept up the momentum although key defeats away to Slovakia and Russia damaged the prospects of a play-off place. Andrejevs also took over from Starkovs as coach of Skonto Riga just in time to be part of a world record breaking performance. Going into the penultimate round of fixtures in the Championship both Skonto and Metalurgs were equal on points before they met in

INTERNATIONAL HONOURS
Baltic Cup 1928 1932 1933 1936 1937 1993 1995 2001 2003

a top of the table clash. With Skonto winning 3-2 Metalurgs were awarded a last minute penalty which if scored would have kept them at the top of the table. Genadijs Solonicins missed and it cost his team the title. It also handed Skonto a world record 14th consecutive Championship. No other team has won the League since independence and given that Norway's Rosenborg look unlikely to add to their tally of 13 in 2005, Skonto's record looks as though it will stand for many years to come. They missed out on an eighth double, however, when for the second year running they lost to Ventspils in the Cup Final.

THE FIFA BIG COUNT OF 2000

	Male	Female		Male	Female
Registered players	1 420	10	Referees	215	0
Non registered players	14 000	0	Officials	400	30
Youth players	5 640	235	Total involved	21 950	
Total players	21 305		Number of clubs	51	
Professional players	210	0	Number of teams	256	

Latvian Football Federation (LFF)
Latvijas Futbola Federacija, Augsiela 1, Riga LV1009, Latvia
Tel +371 7292988   Fax +371 7315604
futbols@lff.lv   www.lff.lv
President: INDRIKSONS Guntis   General Secretary: MEZECKIS Janis
Vice-President: GORKSS Juris   Treasurer: TBD   Media Officer: KALNS Nils
Men's Coach: ANDREJEVS Jurjis   Women's Coach: BANDOLIS Agris
LFF formed: 1921   UEFA: 1992   FIFA: 1923-43, 1992
Colours: Carmine red, Carmine red, Carmine red

GAMES PLAYED BY LATVIA IN THE 2006 FIFA WORLD CUP™ CYCLE

2002	Opponents	Score		Venue	Comp	Scorers	Att	Referee
6-07	Azerbaijan	D	0-0	Riga	Fr		2 000	Miezelis LTU
21-08	Belarus	L	2-4	Riga	Fr	Verpakovskis [17], Laizans [26]	4 200	Kaasik EST
7-09	Sweden	D	0-0	Riga	ECq		8 500	De Bleeckere BEL
12-10	Poland	W	1-0	Warsaw	ECq	Laizans [29]	12 000	Busaca SUI
20-11	San Marino	W	1-0	Serravalle	ECq	OG [89]	600	Khudiev AZE
2003								
12-02	Lithuania	W	2-1	Antalya	Fr	Rubins [31], Miholaps [58]	700	
2-04	Ukraine	L	0-1	Kyiv	Fr		3 700	Michel SVK
30-04	San Marino	W	3-0	Riga	ECq	Prohorenkovs [10], Bleidelis 2 [21 75]	7 500	Byrne IRL
7-06	Hungary	L	1-3	Budapest	ECq	Verpakovskis [38]	4 000	Merk GER
4-07	Lithuania	W	2-1	Valga	BC	Laizans [28], Rubins [32]	500	Frojdfeldt SWE
5-07	Estonia	D	0-0	Tallinn	BC			Ingvarsson SWE
20-08	Uzbekistan	L	0-3	Riga	Fr		4 000	Shandor UKR
6-09	Poland	L	0-2	Riga	ECq		9 000	Vassaras GRE
10-09	Hungary	W	3-1	Riga	ECq	Verpakovskis 2 [38 51], Bleidelis [42]	7 500	Larsen DEN
11-10	Sweden	W	1-0	Stockholm	ECq	Verpakovskis [23]	32 095	De Santis ITA
15-11	Turkey	W	1-0	Riga	ECpo	Verpakovskis [29]	8 000	Veissiere FRA
19-11	Turkey	D	2-2	Istanbul	ECpo	Laizans [66], Verpakovskis [77]	25 000	Frisk SWE
20-12	Kuwait	L	0-2	Larnaca	Fr			Kapitanis CYP
2004								
18-02	Kazakhstan	W	3-1	Larnaca	Fr	Pahars [40], Laizans 2 [45 56]	500	Constantinou CYP
19-02	Hungary	L	1-2	Limassol	Fr	Stepanovs [64]	100	Kailis CYP
21-02	Belarus	L	1-4	Limassol	Fr	Zemlinskis [37p]	100	Theodotou CYP
31-03	Slovenia	W	1-0	Celje	Fr	Verpakovskis [36]	1 500	Stredak SVK
28-04	Iceland	D	0-0	Riga	Fr		6 500	Shmolik BLR
6-06	Azerbaijan	D	2-2	Riga	Fr	Verpakovskis [53], Zemlinskis [82p]	8 000	Maisonlahti FIN
15-06	Czech Republic	L	1-2	Aveiro	ECr1	Verpakovskis [45]	21 744	Veissiere FRA
19-06	Germany	D	0-0	Porto	ECr1		22 344	Riley ENG
23-06	Netherlands	L	0-3	Braga	ECr1		27 904	Milton Nielsen DEN
18-08	Wales	L	0-2	Riga	Fr		6 500	Ivanov RUS
4-09	Portugal	L	0-2	Riga	WCq		9 500	Poll ENG
8-09	Luxembourg	W	4-3	Luxembourg	WCq	Verpakovskis [4], Zemlinskis [40p], OG [65], Prohorenkovs [67]	2 125	Kasnaferis GRE
9-10	Slovakia	L	1-4	Bratislava	WCq	Verpakovskis [3]	13 025	Farina ITA
13-10	Estonia	D	2-2	Riga	WCq	Astafjevs [65], Laizans [82]	8 500	Meyer GER
17-11	Liechtenstein	W	3-1	Vaduz	WCq	Verpakovskis [7], Zemlinskis [57], Prohorenkovs [89]	1 460	Szabo HUN
1-12	Oman	L	2-3	Manama	Fr	Rimkus [66], Rubins [68]		
3-12	Bahrain	D	2-2	Manama	Fr	Kolesnicenko [22p], Zakresevskis [35]. L 2-4p	2 000	Al Hilali OMA
2005								
8-02	Finland	L	1-2	Nicosia	Fr	Zemlinskis [62p]	102	Kailis CYP
9-02	Austria	D	1-1	Limassol	Fr	Visnakovs [70]. W 5-3p	50	Theodotou CYP
30-03	Luxembourg	W	4-0	Riga	WCq	Bleidelis [32], Laizans [38p], Verpakovskis 2 [73 90]	8 203	Kovacic CRO
21-05	Lithuania	L	0-2	Kaunas	BC			
4-06	Russia	L	0-3	St Petersburg	WCq		21 575	Poulat FRA
8-06	Liechtenstein	W	1-0	Riga	WCq	Bleidelis [17]	8 000	Eriksson SWE

Fr = Friendly match • EC = UEFA EURO 2004™ • BC = Baltic Cup • WC = FIFA World Cup™
q = qualifier • po = play-off • r1 = first round group

LATVIA COUNTRY INFORMATION

Capital	Riga	Independence	1991 from the Soviet Union	GDP per Capita	$10 200
Population	2 306 306	Status	Republic	GNP Ranking	98
Area km²	64 589	Language	Latvian, Russian	Dialling code	+371
Population density	35 per km²	Literacy rate	99%	Internet code	.lv
% in urban areas	73%	Main religion	Christian	GMT +/−	+2
Towns/Cities ('000)	Riga 742; Daugavpils 111; Liepāja 82; Jelgava 62; Jurmala 54; Ventspils 42				
Neighbours (km)	Estonia 339; Russia 217; Belarus 141; Lithuania 453; Baltic Sea 531				
Main stadia	Stadions Skonto – Riga 9 300				

LATVIA NATIONAL TEAM RECORDS AND RECORD SEQUENCES

Records			Sequence records			
Victory	8-1	EST 1942	Wins	4	1936	Clean sheets	2	
Defeat	0-12	SWE 1927	Defeats	5	1999-2000	Goals scored	10	Three times
Player Caps	114	ASTAFJEVS Vitalijs	Undefeated	6	1937, 1938	Without goal	5	1998-1999
Player Goals	24	PETERSONS Eriks	Without win	10	1995-1997	Goals against	21	1933-1937

NATIONAL CAPS

	Caps
ASTAFJEVS Vitalijs	114
ZEMLINSKIS Mihails	103
BLEIDELIS Imants	91
STEPANOVS Igors	81
STOLCERS Andrejs	78
BLAGONADEZDINS Olegs	70
IVANOVS Valerijs	69
RUBINS Andrejs	69
LAIZANS Juris	68
PAHARS Marians	63

NATIONAL GOALS

	Goals
PETERSONS Eriks	24
VERPAKOVSKIS Maris	18
PAHARS Marians	15
SEIBELIS Albert	14
VESTERMANS Ilja	13
ZEMLINSKIS Mihails	12
ASTAFJEVS Vitalijs	11
TAURINS Arnold	10
BLEIDELIS Imants	10

NATIONAL COACH

	Years
GILIS Janis	1992-'97
DZODZUASHVILI Revaz	1997-'99
JOHNSON Gary	1999-'01
STARKOVS Alexandrs	2001-'04
ANDREJEVS Jurijs	2004-

FIFA REFEREE LIST 2005

	Int'l	DoB
LAJUKS Romans	1993	19-06-1964
SIPAILO Andrejs	2000	7-01-1971

FIFA ASSISTANT REFEREE LIST 2005

	Int'l	DoB
BRAGA Sergejs	1996	22-03-1962
GRABEJS Deniss	2001	14-09-1971
POPOVICENKO Jurijs	2004	26-03-1963
PUKIJANS Janis	1999	16-06-1965

CLUB DIRECTORY

Club	Town/City	Stadium	Phone	www.	Lge	Cup	CL
FC Dinaburg	Daugavpils	Celtnieka Stadions 4 070	+371 5 439235	dinaburg.com	0	0	0
FK Jurmala	Jurmala		+371 78 11156	fcjurmala.lv	0	0	0
FHK Leipajas Metalurgs	Liepaja	Daugavas Stadions 5 000	+371 3 455912	sport.metalurgs.lv	0	0	0
Olimps	Riga	Stadions Skonto 9 300			0	0	0
FK Riga	Riga	Latvijas Universitates 5 000	+371 7 242889		0	1	0
Skonto FC	Riga	Stadions Skonto 9 300	+371 7 282669	skontofc.lv	14	7	0
Venta	Kuldiga				0	0	0
FK Ventspils	Ventspils	Olimpiska Centra 3 200	+371 36 81254	fkventspils.lv	0	2	0

LATVIAN CUP 2004

Fourth Round		Quarter-finals		Semi-finals		Final	
FK Ventspils	14						
Aloja Starkelsen *	0	FK Ventspils *	2				
JFC Skonto Riga *	0	Dinaburg Daugavpils	1				
Dinaberg Daugavpils	3			FK Ventspils	2		
Auda Riga	1			Ditton Daugavpils	0		
Zibens Ilukste *	0	Auda Riga *	0				
FK Saldus/Broceni *	0	Ditton Daugavpils	1				
Ditton Daugavpils	9					FK Ventspils ‡	2
Liepajas Metalurgs	4					Skonto Riga	1
Dizvanagi Rezekne *	1	Liepajas Metalurgs	1 5p				
FK Valmiera *	0	FK Riga *	1 4p				
FK Riga	8			Liepajas Metalurgs	1	CUP FINAL	
FK Jurmala	9			Skonto Riga	2	26-09-2004, Att: 4 700, Ref: Sipailo	
RFS Flaminko Riga *	0	FK Jurmala *	1			Skonto, Riga	
Fortuna/OSC Ogre *	0	Skonto Riga	2			Scorers - Rimkus 40, Bicka 71 for Ventspils;	
Skonto Riga	13	* Home teams • ‡ Qualified for the UEFA Cup				Buitkus 86 for Skonto	

LATVIA 2004

VIRSLIGA

	Pl	W	D	L	F	A	Pts	Skonto	Metalurgs	Ventspils	Dinaburg	Jurmala	Riga	Ditton	Auda
Skonto Riga †	28	22	3	3	65	18	69		1-0 1-2	1-0 0-0	1-1 3-0	3-2 0-2	1-0 4-1	2-0 6-0	3-0 2-0
Liepajas Metalurgs ‡	28	21	3	4	85	27	66	3-1 2-3		3-4 4-0	2-1 4-0	1-1 1-0	2-2 2-1	5-1 3-0	4-1 10-1
FK Ventspils ‡	28	16	7	5	64	28	55	1-1 0-3	0-2 1-1		1-2 3-1	3-2 4-0	1-1 1-0	3-0 0-0	5-1 2-1
Dinaburg Daugavpils	28	10	6	12	35	36	36	0-1 1-2	1-4 3-0	0-2 0-2		0-0 0-1	2-1 3-3	1-0 4-0	2-0 3-1
FK Jurmala	28	8	10	10	30	33	34	0-1 0-1	0-2 1-4	1-1 2-2	2-0 0-0		1-1 2-0	0-2 4-1	1-1 2-0
FK Riga	28	6	9	13	32	43	27	0-2 2-4	0-2 1-2	1-4 1-3	1-1 0-0	1-0 1-1		1-2 1-1	2-1 3-1
Ditton Daugavpils	28	7	5	16	20	62	26	0-4 0-4	0-3 0-4	0-8 0-4	0-1 2-0	1-1 1-1	0-0 0-1		1-0 4-0
Auda Riga	28	0	1	27	13	97	1	0-4 1-6	1-7 1-6	0-3 0-6	0-5 0-3	1-2 0-1	0-2 0-4	0-2 1-2	

4/04/2004 - 11/11/2004 • † Qualified for the UEFA Champions League • ‡ Qualified for the UEFA Cup
Relegation/promotion play-off: Venta Ventspils 1-0 1-0 Ditton Daugavpils

LATVIA 2004
PIRMALIGA (2)

	Pl	W	D	L	F	A	Pts
FK Ventspils-2	26	20	4	2	74	11	64
Skonto-2 Riga	26	18	6	2	79	17	60
Liepajas Metalurgs-2	26	19	3	4	105	23	60
Zibens Ilukste	26	16	6	4	71	33	54
Venta	26	13	6	7	65	33	45
Dizvanagi Rezekne	26	13	3	10	60	57	42
FK Valmiera	26	12	3	11	53	42	39
JFC Skonto Riga	26	11	5	10	68	34	38
FK Riga-2	26	10	4	12	50	45	34
RFS Flaminko Riga	26	8	2	16	45	64	26
FK Jelgava	26	7	5	14	43	68	26
Balvu Vilki	26	5	0	21	38	112	15
Alberts Riga	26	4	1	21	37	117	13
Fortuna Ogre	26	2	0	24	15	147	6

1/05/2004 - 6/11/2004 • The top three teams were ineligible for promotion due to their links with teams in the Virsliga • Zibens declined to take up their place in the Virsliga which went instead to a new team Olimps Riga

RECENT LEAGUE AND CUP RECORD

	Championship						Cup		
Year	Champions	Pts	Runners-up	Pts	Third	Pts	Winners	Score	Runners-up
1991	Skonto Riga	32	Pardaugava Riga	26	Olimpija Liepaja	25	Celtnieks	0-0 3-1p	Skonto Riga
1992	Skonto Riga	38	RAF Jelgava	38	VEF Riga	33	Skonto Riga	1-0	Daugava Kompar
1993	Skonto Riga	34	Olimpija Riga	26	RAF Jelgava	26	RAF Jelgava	1-0	Pardaugava Riga
1994	Skonto Riga	42	RAF Jelgava	33	DAG Riga	29	Olimpija Riga	2-0	DAG Riga
1995	Skonto Riga	78	Vilan-D Daugavpils	51	RAF Jelgava	48	Skonto Riga	3-0	DAG Liepaja
1996	Skonto Riga	73	Daugava Riga	61	Dinaburg Daugavpils	47	RAF Jelgava	2-1	Skonto Riga
1997	Skonto Riga	64	Daugava Riga	43	Dinaburg Daugavpils	42	Skonto Riga	2-1	Dinaburg Daugavpils
1998	Skonto Riga	67	Liepajas Metalurgs	57	FK Ventspils	54	Skonto Riga	1-0	Liepajas Metalurgs
1999	Skonto Riga	69	Liepajas Metalurgs	60	FK Ventspils	56	FK Riga	1-1 6-5p	Skonto Riga
2000	Skonto Riga	75	FK Ventspils	65	Liepajas Metalurgs	55	Skonto Riga	4-1	Liepajas Metalurgs
2001	Skonto Riga	68	FK Ventspils	67	Liepajas Metalurgs	64	Skonto Riga	2-0	Dinaburg Daugavpils
2002	Skonto Riga	73	FK Ventspils	71	Liepajas Metalurgs	51	Skonto Riga	3-0	Liepajas Metalurgs
2003	Skonto Riga	73	Liepajas Metalurgs	68	FK Ventspils	61	FK Ventspils	4-0	Skonto Riga
2004	Skonto Riga	69	Liepajas Metalurgs	66	FK Ventspils	55	FK Ventspils	2-1	Skonto Riga

Play-off in 1992: Skonto 3-2 RAF • Skonto are the only club to have won the title since independence • Their 14 triumphs represent a world record

MAC – MACAO

NATIONAL TEAM RECORD
JULY 1ST 2002 TO JUNE 30TH 2005

PL	W	D	L	F	A	%
9	2	0	7	7	24	22.2

FIFA/COCA-COLA WORLD RANKING

1993	1994	1995	1996	1997	1998	1999	2000	2001	2002	2003	2004	High		Low	
166	175	180	172	157	174	176	180	180	188	184	188	156	09/97	190	03/05

					2004-2005						
08/04	09/04	10/04	11/04	12/04	01/05	02/05	03/05	04/05	05/05	06/05	07/05
188	188	189	189	188	190	190	190	190	190	190	190

Minnows in most competitions in Asia, Macao has a sound football infrastructure but no real power at international level. Reflecting the FIFA/Coca-Cola World Ranking of 190, victories have been few and far between in the 60 matches played since joining FIFA in 1978, while heavy defeats have been all too frequent as two 10-0 drubbings by Japan in qualifying for the 1998 World Cup™ testify. In the 2003 East Asian Football Federation Cup, Macao took part in a qualifying group with Hong Kong, Mongolia, Guam and Chinese Taipei but while recording their only two wins in recent years they didn't make it to the finals. Since then Macao have lost every match played – in the AFC

INTERNATIONAL HONOURS
None

Asian Cup against Pakistan and Singapore and most disappointingly to Chinese Taipei in the preliminary round of the 2006 FIFA World Cup™ Asian qualifiers. It was 18 months before the national side took to the field again, an enforced layoff that included a period when the national association was suspended by FIFA because of government interference. They may have wished they hadn't resumed as Hong Kong knocked eight past them in a friendly. The 2004-05 Campenonato da 1 Divisao do Futebol was contested by eight teams with Policia de Seguranca Publica emerging as champions for the third time, losing just two of their 14 fixtures.

THE FIFA BIG COUNT OF 2000

	Male	Female		Male	Female
Registered players	3 710	0	Referees	60	0
Non registered players	2 000	10	Officials	600	4
Youth players	622	0	Total involved	7 006	
Total players		6 342	Number of clubs	174	
Professional players	0	0	Number of teams	276	

Macao Football Association (AFM)
Avenida Dr. Sun Yat Sen, Edificio Wa Fung Kok, 15 Andar, Bloco A, Taipa, Macao
Tel +853 830287   Fax +853 830409
futebol@macau.ctm.net   www.none
President: CHEUNG Vitor Lup Kwan   General Secretary: REGO Alexander
Vice-President: CHONG Coc Veng   Treasurer: CHIO Kam Vai   Media Officer: None
Men's Coach: DOS SANTOS LOPES João   Women's Coach: None
AFM formed: 1939   AFC: 1976   FIFA: 1976
Colours: Green, Green, Green

GAMES PLAYED BY MACAO IN THE 2006 FIFA WORLD CUP™ CYCLE

2002	Opponents	Score	Venue	Comp	Scorers	Att	Referee
No international matches played in 2002							
2003							
22-02	Mongolia	W 2-0	Hong Kong	EAq	Che Chi Man 34p, Chan Man Hei 82	6 055	Matsumura JPN
24-02	Hong Kong	L 0-3	Hong Kong	EAq		1 602	Park Sang Gu KOR
26-02	Guam	W 2-0	Hong Kong	EAq	De Sousa 2 37 77	672	Cheung Yim Yau HKG
2-03	Chinese Taipei	L 1-2	Hong Kong	EAq	Hoi Man Io 35	6 862	
21-03	Pakistan	L 0-3	Singapore	ACq			
23-03	Singapore	L 0-2	Singapore	ACq			
23-11	Chinese Taipei	L 0-3	Taipei	WCq		2 000	Napitupulu IDN
29-11	Chinese Taipei	L 1-3	Macau	WCq	Lei Fu Weng 87	250	Zhou Weixin CHN
2004							
No international matches played in 2004							
2005							
21-05	Hong Kong	L 1-8	Hong Kong	Fr	Chung Koon Kan 86		

Fr = Friendly match • EA = East Asian Championship • AC = AFC Asian Cup • WC = FIFA World Cup™ • q = qualifier

MACAO NATIONAL TEAM RECORDS AND RECORD SEQUENCES

Records			Sequence records					
Victory	5-1	PHI	Wins	2	1997-1990	Clean sheets	1	Six times
Defeat	0-10	JPN 1997 (Twice)	Defeats	9	2000-2001	Goals scored	5	1975-1978
Player Caps	n/a		Undefeated	2	Three times	Without goal	5	1985-1987
Player Goals	n/a		Without win	9	2000-2001	Goals against	15	1992-1997

FIFA REFEREE LIST 2005

	Int'l	DoB
None		

FIFA ASSISTANT REFEREE LIST 2005

	Int'l	DoB
None		

MACAO 2005 CAMPEONATO 1° DIVISAO

	Pl	W	D	L	F	A	Pts
Polícia	14	10	2	2	41	12	32
Lam Pak	14	9	2	3	37	13	29
Monte Carlo	14	6	5	3	32	24	23
Va Luen	14	6	4	4	23	21	22
Alfândega	14	6	3	5	24	23	21
Heng Tai	14	4	2	8	29	40	14
Kuan Tai	14	1	5	8	17	43	8
Kei Lun	14	2	1	11	13	40	7

4/01/2005 - 22/04/2005

RECENT LEAGUE RECORD

Year	Champions
1996	GD Artilheiros
1997	GD Lam Park
1998	GD Lam Park
1999	GD Lam Park
2000	Polícia de Segurança Pública
2001	GD Lam Park
2002	Monte Carlo
2003	Monte Carlo
2004	Monte Carlo
2005	Polícia de Segurança Pública

MACAO COUNTRY INFORMATION

Capital	Macao	Status	Special administrative region of China	GDP per Capita	$19 400
Population	445 286			GNP Ranking	n/a
Area km²	25.4 per km²	Language	Portuguese, Cantonese	Dialling code	+853
Population density	17 530	Literacy rate	94%	Internet code	.mo
% in urban areas	100%	Main religion	Buddhist 50%, Christian 15%	GMT +/–	+8
Towns/Cities ('000)	Macao 445				
Neighbours (km)	China 0.34; South China Sea 41				
Main stadia	Campo Desportivo – Macao 15 000				

MAD – MADAGASCAR

NATIONAL TEAM RECORD
JULY 1ST 2002 TO JUNE 30TH 2005

PL	W	D	L	F	A	%
18	3	4	11	13	35	27.8

FIFA/COCA-COLA WORLD RANKING

1993	1994	1995	1996	1997	1998	1999	2000	2001	2002	2003	2004	High		Low	
89	111	132	140	163	150	134	114	122	101	118	147	**81**	08/93	**169**	05/98

2004-2005											
08/04	09/04	10/04	11/04	12/04	01/05	02/05	03/05	04/05	05/05	06/05	07/05
131	132	136	142	147	150	150	149	150	150	150	150

When drawn with Benin there was hope that Madagascar could qualify for the main group stage of the 2006 FIFA World Cup™ and thus ensure a structured fixture list throughout 2004 and 2005. Even with Benin below them in the FIFA/Coca-Cola World Ranking it was the West Africans, boosted by having qualified for the CAF African Cup of Nations for the first time, who went through 4-3 on aggregate. Since then, Madagascar have played just two COSAFA Castle Cup games, losing both at the hands of Mozambique and Mauritius. Coach Jean Francois Dhebon faces a big challenge to improve the island's fortunes, which was not helped by the failure to take part

INTERNATIONAL HONOURS
Indian Ocean Games 1990 1993

in either of the CAF youth competitions. With the focus firmly on domestic football, 2004 saw new champions in both the League and in the Cup. USJF/Ravinala won the local Antananarivo League to qualify for the last six in the National Championship in which they reached the final. There they came from behind to beat Fortior Toamasina 2-1 and then completed an historic double by winning the Coupe de Madagascar two weeks later. Their 2005 Champions League campaign ended in the first round when they lost 5-1 on aggregate to South Africa's Kaizer Chiefs, the defeat made worse when two fans died in a crush at the home leg in Antananarivo.

THE FIFA BIG COUNT OF 2000

	Male	Female		Male	Female
Registered players	15 000	800	Referees	316	18
Non registered players	40 000	300	Officials	525	20
Youth players	400	0	Total involved	57 106	
Total players	56 500		Number of clubs	200	
Professional players	0	0	Number of teams	800	

Fédération Malagasy de Football (FMF)
26 rue de Russie Isoraka, PO Box 4409, Tananarive 101, Madagascar
Tel +261 20 2268374   Fax +261 20 2268373
www.none
President: AHMAD   General Secretary: RABIBISOA Anselme
Vice-President: RAZAFINDKIAKA Sylvain   Treasurer: ZAFINANDRO René   Media Officer: RANJALAHY Sylvain
Men's Coach: DHEBON Jean Francois   Women's Coach: ANDRIANTANASASOA Herihaja
FMF formed: 1961   CAF: 19   FIFA: 1962
Colours: Red/green, White/green, Green/White

GAMES PLAYED BY MADAGASCAR IN THE 2006 FIFA WORLD CUP™ CYCLE

2002	Opponents		Score	Venue	Comp	Scorers	Att	Referee
21-07	South Africa	D	0-0	Port Elizabeth	CCqf	L 1-4p	8 000	Colembi ANG
8-09	Egypt	W	1-0	Antananarivo	CNq	Menakely 73		Nkole ZAM
12-10	Mauritius	W	1-0	Port Louis	CNq	Menakely 18	1 819	Maillet SEY
2003								
22-02	Mauritius	W	2-1	Antananarivo	CCr1	Menakely 16p, Radonamahafalison 33	25 000	Motau RSA
27-03	Cameroon	L	0-2	Tunis	Fr		14 000	Zahmoul TUN
29-03	South Africa	L	0-2	Johannesburg	Fr		5 000	Shikapande ZAM
30-03	Ghana	D	3-3	Tunis	Fr	OG 47, Rasonaivo 82, Randriandelison 88. L 9-10p		
24-04	Algeria	L	1-3	Amiens	Fr	Menakely 78p	1 295	Garibian FRA
27-04	Mali	L	0-2	Paris	Fr			
20-06	Egypt	L	0-6	Port Said	CNq			
6-07	Mauritius	L	0-2	Antananarivo	CNq			
13-07	Swaziland	L	0-2	Mbabane	CCqf		8 000	Mpofu BOT
28-08	Seychelles	D	1-1	Curepipe	IOG	Menakely 32	1 000	Lim Kee Chong MRI
30-08	Mauritius	L	1-3	Curepipe	IOG	Ralaitafika 54	4 500	Ramsamy REU
11-10	Benin	D	1-1	Antananarivo	WCq	Edmond 28	5 131	Maillet SEY
16-11	Benin	L	2-3	Cotonou	WCq	Radonamahafalison 15, Rakotondramanana 23	20 000	Imiere NGA
2004								
18-04	Mozambique	L	0-2	Maputo	CCr1		28 000	Damon RSA
2005								
26-02	Mauritius	L	0-2	Curepipe	CCq			Fakude SWZ

Fr = Friendly match • CN = CAF African Cup of Nations • CC = COSAFA Cup • IOG = Indian Ocean Games • WC = FIFA World Cup™
q = qualifier • r1 = first round group • qf = quarter-final

MADAGASCAR NATIONAL TEAM RECORDS AND RECORD SEQUENCES

Records			Sequence records					
Victory	8-1	CGO 1960	Wins	8	1957-1963	Clean sheets	4	1990, 1992-93
Defeat	0-7	MRI 1952	Defeats	8	2001	Goals scored	14	1957-1965
Player Caps	n/a		Undefeated	10	1979-1980	Without goal	6	2001
Player Goals	n/a		Without win	14	2003-	Goals against	17	1971-1980

FIFA REFEREE LIST 2005

	Int'l	DoB
RAKOTOARIMANANA Lova	2004	14-03-1974
RAMANAMPAMONJY Lanto	2000	21-09-1969
RAOLIMANANA Floriant	2000	29-04-1965
TSISAROTINA Mena	1993	21-08-1964
VAHINY Doudou	1998	5-10-1960

FIFA ASSISTANT REFEREE LIST 2005

	Int'l	DoB
DIMASY Paul	2005	2-12-1964
RAKOTOARISOA Paul	1999	23-02-1962
RAKOTOSON Eli	1999	5-10-1966
RAKOTOTIANA Andriamaholisoa	2000	18-08-1968
RAZAFITSITAMY Alberto	2004	20-01-1973
ZAFITSARA Jackot	2004	30-10-1970

MADAGASCAR COUNTRY INFORMATION

Capital	Antananarivo	Independence	1960 from France	GDP per Capita	$800
Population	17 501 871	Status	Republic	GNP Ranking	119
Area km²	587 040	Language	French, Malagasy	Dialling code	+261
Population density	29 per km²	Literacy rate	68%	Internet code	.mg
% in urban areas	27%	Main religion	Indigenous 52%, Christian 41%	GMT +/–	+3
Towns/Cities ('000)	Antananarivo 1 391; Toamasina 206; Antsirabé 183; Fianarantsoa 167; Mahajanga 155; Toliary 115; Antsiranana 82; Antanifotsy 70; Ambovombe 66; Amparafaravola 51				
Neighbours (km)	Indian Ocean 4 828				
Main stadia	Mahamasina – Antananarivo 22 000				

MADAGASCAR 2004 NATIONAL CHAMPIONSHIP FIRST STAGE

Group A in Mahajanga	Pl	W	D	L	F	A	Pts
Léopards Transfoot †	5	4	1	0	11	1	13
Adema Antananarivo †	5	3	1	1	16	2	10
Jirama Mahajanga	5	2	1	2	5	5	7
Espoir Afoma Ambositra	5	1	3	1	6	10	6
JOS Nosy Be	5	1	1	3	3	7	4
FC TAM Morondava	5	0	1	4	3	19	1

Group B in Toamasina	Pl	W	D	L	F	A	Pts
USJF/Ravinala †	5	4	1	0	14	5	13
Fortior Toamasina †	5	2	3	0	8	4	9
SAF/FJKM Mahajanga	5	2	2	1	6	5	8
Herin' i Sambava	5	2	1	2	12	8	7
Fornela Ambalavao	5	1	1	3	9	12	4
Scorpions Morondava	5	0	0	5	7	22	0

Group C in Fianarantsoa	Pl	W	D	L	F	A	Pts
Jirama Fianarantsoa †	5	4	1	0	11	3	13
USCA Foot †	5	3	2	0	10	3	11
Eco Redipharm	5	3	1	1	21	3	10
Kohinoor SC	5	1	1	3	5	11	4
ASUT Toliara	5	1	1	3	2	11	4
AJSM	5	0	0	5	0	18	0

11/09/2004 - 19/09/2004 • † Qualified for the second stage
• The top three teams from the regional leagues of
Antananarivo, Fianarantsoa, Toamasina, Antsiranana,
Mahajanga and Toliary qualified for this first stage.

MADAGASCAR 2004 NATIONAL CHAMPIONSHIP SECOND STAGE

Played in Toamasina	Pl	W	D	L	F	A	Pts
Adema Antananarivo †	5	3	0	2	11	5	9
USJF/Ravinala †	5	2	2	1	6	3	8
Jirama Fianarantsoa †	5	2	2	1	8	7	8
Fortior Toamasina †	5	2	1	2	6	3	7
Léopards Transfoot	5	2	0	3	7	17	6
USCA Foot	5	1	1	3	5	8	4

16/10/2004 - 24/10/2004 • † Qualified for the play-offs

MADAGASCAR 2004 CHAMPIONSHIP PLAY-OFFS

Semi-finals

USJA/Ravinala	2
Jirama Fianarantsao	1

Adema Antananarivo	1
Fortior Toamasina	2

Finals

31-10-2004
Mahamasina, Antananarivo

USJA/Ravinala	2
Fortior Toamasina	1

Scorers - Rata 45, Coco 55 for USJA;
Lova 23 for Fortior

COUPE DE MADAGASCAR 2004

Round of 16		Quarter-finals		Semi-finals		Final	
USJF/Ravinala †							
Adema		USJF/Ravinala	1				
COSPN	0 4p	Fortior Club Mahajanga	0				
Fortior Club Mahajanga	0 5p			USJF/Ravinala	2		
DSA Antananarivo	2			Tanambao	0		
AS Port	0	DSA Antananarivo	0				
FC Casino	1 3p	Tanambao	1				
Tanambao	1 4p					USJF/Ravinala	2
Eco Redipharm	2					USCA Foot	1
Jirama Fianar	1	Eco Redipharm	0 4p				
USERJ Fénérive	0	ASUT Toliara	0 3p				
ASUT Toliara	1			Eco Redipharm	1 3p	CUP FINAL	
Ny Antsika	2			USCA Foot	1 4p		
CNaPS	1	Ny Antsika	1			14-11-2004	
FC SAP	0	USCA Foot	2			Mahamasina, Antananarivo	
USCA Foot	7	† Walkover after Adema withdrew with the score at 1-1					

RECENT LEAGUE AND CUP RECORD

	Championship		Cup		
Year	Champions	Winners	Score	Runners-up
1998	DSA Antananarivo	FC Djivan Farafangana	2-0	Fortior Club Mahajanga
1999	Fortior Toamasina	FC Djivan Farafangana	3-0	Akon'Ambatomena
2000	Fortior Toamasina	FC Djivan Farafangana	1-0	FC Jirama Antsirabe
2001	SOE Antananarivo	US Transfoot Toamasina	1-0	Fortior Toamasina
2002	Adema Antananarivo	Fortior Toamasina	3-0	US Transfoot Toamasina
2003	Eco Redipharm Tamatave	Léopards Transfoot	1-0	SOE Antananarivo
2004	USJF/Ravinala	USJF/Ravinala	2-1	USCA Foot

ACTION IMAGES

Above **15 February 2005. Camp Nou, Barcelona, Spain.** The world's top footballers turn out in the 'Football for Hope' match to help raise funds for the victims of the Asian tsunami which struck on 26 December 2004. By July 2005 over US$10m had been donated to football-related projects.

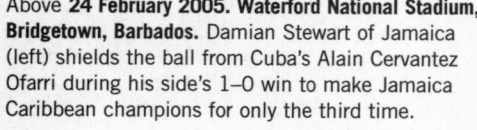

Above **24 February 2005. Waterford National Stadium, Bridgetown, Barbados.** Damian Stewart of Jamaica (left) shields the ball from Cuba's Alain Cervantez Ofarri during his side's 1–0 win to make Jamaica Caribbean champions for only the third time.

Right **27 February 2005. La Bombonera, Buenos Aires, Argentina.** Diego Maradona waves to the Boca Juniors crowd from his private box in the stadium.

27 February 2005. Mateo Flores, Guatemala City, Guatemala. Costa Rica are Central American champions for the 12th time after beating Honduras on penalties in the final of the UNCAF Cup.

11 March 2005. Soccer Field, Gothenburg, Sweden. Anders Frisk walks across the pitch where he first refereed a match in 1978. He decided to retire after receiving death threats following the Barcelona v Chelsea UEFA Champions League match.

MAR – MOROCCO

NATIONAL TEAM RECORD
JULY 1ST 2002 TO JUNE 30TH 2005

PL	W	D	L	F	A	%
40	22	10	8	65	25	67.5

FIFA/COCA-COLA WORLD RANKING

1993	1994	1995	1996	1997	1998	1999	2000	2001	2002	2003	2004	High		Low	
30	33	38	27	15	13	24	28	36	35	38	33	10	04/98	41	08/02

2004-2005											
08/04	09/04	10/04	11/04	12/04	01/05	02/05	03/05	04/05	05/05	06/05	07/05
33	33	34	34	33	34	34	34	35	35	33	35

In the seven matches played in the 2004-05 season the Moroccan national team remained unbeaten but they still could not guarantee themselves a place at the 2006 FIFA World Cup™ finals as their titanic struggle with African champions Tunisia saw the two stay neck and neck throughout the campaign. After failing to qualify for the 2002 finals on goal difference and with South Africa winning the race to host the 2010 finals, failure to make it to Germany would be a huge setback for a nation with such big aspirations in football. Although many Moroccan players are based with clubs in Europe, the Championship remains one of the strongest in Africa and the 2005 title race

INTERNATIONAL HONOURS
Qualified for the FIFA World Cup™ finals 1970 1986 1994 1998   CAF African Cup of Nations 1976
African Youth Championship 1997   CAF Champions League FAR Rabat 1985, Raja Casablanca 1989 1997 1999, Wydad Casablanca 1992

was between the three giants of the club game – Raja and Wydad from Casablanca and FAR from the capital Rabat. It was FAR who lasted the pace to win a record 11th title, their first since 1989. Of concern was the paucity of goals in the League with only the top three scoring more goals than games played. Over one weekend of the season there were just three scored in eight games while one in five games in the campaign as a whole finished 0-0. The lack of fire-power may help explain the relatively poor record of Moroccan clubs in the CAF Champions League in recent seasons.

THE FIFA BIG COUNT OF 2000

	Male	Female		Male	Female
Registered players	30 639	913	Referees	1 556	0
Non registered players	120 000	0	Officials	6 000	0
Youth players	100 119	1 737	Total involved	260 964	
Total players	253 408		Number of clubs	400	
Professional players	100	0	Number of teams	3 374	

Fédération Royale Marocaine de Football (FRMF)
51 Bis Avenue Ibn Sina, Agdal, Case Postale 51, Rabat 10 000, Morocco
Tel +212 37 672706   Fax +212 37 671070
contact@fedefoot.ma   www.frmf.ma
President: BENSLIMANE Housni   General Secretary: AMMOR Ahmed
Vice-President: AOUZAL Mohamed   Treasurer: EL AOUFIR Larbi   Media Officer: MOUFID Mohamed
Men's Coach: BADOU Zaki   Women's Coach: ALAOUI Slimani
FRMF formed: 1955   CAF: 1966   FIFA: 1960
Colours: Green, Green, Green

GAMES PLAYED BY MOROCCO IN THE 2006 FIFA WORLD CUP™ CYCLE

2002	Opponents	Score		Venue	Comp	Scorers	Att	Referee
21-08	Luxembourg	W	2-0	Luxembourg	Fr	Jabrane 72, Kacemi 84	1 654	Steinborn GER
7-09	Gabon	W	1-0	Libreville	CNq	Chippo 16	30 000	Evehe Devine CMR
3-10	Niger	W	6-1	Rabat	Fr	Bidodane 9, Bouden 29p, El Assas 50, Jabrane 70, Hassi 78, Zerouali 83	4 300	Rouaissi MAR
13-10	Equatorial Guinea	W	5-0	Rabat	CNq	Ramzi 9, Bidoudane 25, Safri 28, Rokki 45, Kacemi 55	25 000	Boukthir TUN
20-11	Mali	L	1-3	Rabat	Fr	Rokki 5	15 000	Tahri MAR
16-12	Kuwait	D	1-1	Kuwait City	ARr1	Lembarki 26	7 000	Abbas SYR
18-12	Jordan	D	1-1	Kuwait City	ARr1	Qaissi 4	1 500	Al Zeid KSA
20-12	Palestine	W	3-1	Kuwait City	ARr1	Armomen 2 30 40, Al Kharazi 88	700	Omar UAE
25-12	Sudan	L	0-1	Kuwait City	ARsf			
28-12	Saudi Arabia	L	0-2	Kuwait City	AR3p		2 000	Abbas SYR
2003								
12-02	Senegal	W	1-0	Paris	Fr	Saber 64	8 000	Piccirillo FRA
29-03	Sierra Leone	D	0-0	Freetown	CNq			Kabu LBR
30-04	Côte d'Ivoire	L	0-1	Rabat	Fr		20 000	Arjoune LBY
8-06	Sierra Leone	W	1-0	Casablanca	CNq	Chippo 25		Abd El Fatah EGY
20-06	Gabon	W	2-0	Rabat	CNq	El Yaagoubi 22, Jaziri 75	15 000	Shelmani LBY
6-07	Equatorial Guinea	W	1-0	Malabo	CNq	Akadar 61		
10-09	Trinidad and Tobago	W	2-0	Marrakech	Fr	Chamarh 2 38 49		Yaacoubi TUN
11-10	Tunisia	D	0-0	Tunis	Fr		13 000	Layec FRA
15-11	Burkina Faso	W	1-0	Meknès	Fr	Ouaddou 24	25 000	Boukthir TUN
18-11	Mali	L	0-1	Casablanca	Fr		6 000	Shelmani LBY
19-11	Mali	L	0-1	Meknès	Fr			
2004								
27-01	Nigeria	W	1-0	Monastir	CNr1	Youssef Hadji 77	15 000	Ndoye SEN
31-01	Benin	W	4-0	Sfax	CNr1	Chamarh 15, Mokhtari 73, Ouaddou 75, El Karkouri 80	20 000	Maillet SEY
4-02	South Africa	D	1-1	Sousse	CNr1	Safri 38p	6 000	Guirat TUN
8-02	Algeria	W	3-1	Sfax	CNqf	Chamarh 90, Youssef Hadji 113, Zairi 120	22 000	Shelmani LBY
11-02	Mali	W	4-0	Sousse	CNsf	Mokhtari 2 14 58, Youssef Hadji 80, Baha 90	15 000	Sharaf CIV
14-02	Tunisia	L	1-2	Tunis	CNf	Mokhtari 38	60 000	Ndoye SEN
18-02	Switzerland	W	2-1	Rabat	Fr	Adjou 78, Iajour 82	1 700	Berber ALG
31-03	Angola	W	3-1	Casablanca	Fr	Baha 2 67 74, Zairi 77	7 000	Risha EGY
28-04	Argentina	L	0-1	Casablanca	Fr		65 000	Ndoye SEN
28-05	Mali	D	0-0	Bamako	Fr		35 000	Sidibe MLI
5-06	Malawi	D	1-1	Blantyre	WCq	Safri 25	30 040	Mususa ZIM
3-07	Botswana	W	1-0	Gaborone	WCq	Mokhtari 30	22 000	Dlamini SWZ
4-09	Tunisia	D	1-1	Rabat	WCq	El Karkouri 74	45 000	Auda EGY
10-10	Guinea	D	1-1	Conakry	WCq	Chamarh 5	25 000	Monteiro Duarte CPV
17-11	Burkina Faso	W	4-0	Rabat	Fr	Oulmers 52, Boukhari 68, Sarssar 78, Abdessadki 82	5 000	Keita MLI
2005								
9-02	Kenya	W	5-1	Rabat	WCq	Zairi 3 12 39 90, Diane 46, Youssef Hadji 81	40 000	Tamuni LBY
26-03	Guinea	W	1-0	Rabat	WCq	Youssef Hadji 62	70 000	Coulibaly MLI
4-06	Malawi	W	4-1	Rabat	WCq	Chamarh 16, Youssef Hadji 2 21 75, Kharja 72	48 000	Buenkadila COD
18-06	Kenya	D	0-0	Nairobi	WCq		50 000	Diatta SEN

Fr = Friendly match • AR = Arab Cup • CN = CAF African Cup of Nations • WC = FIFA World Cup™
q = qualifier, r1 = first round group • qf = quarter-final • sf = semi-final • 3p = third place play-off • f = final

MOROCCO NATIONAL TEAM RECORDS AND RECORD SEQUENCES

Records			Sequence records					
Victory	7-0	TOG 1979	Wins	8	1997	Clean sheets	9	1997
Defeat	0-6	HUN 1964	Defeats	4	1994	Goals scored	12	1975-1976
Player Caps	n/a		Undefeated	15	1983-84, 1996-97	Without goal	6	1983
Player Goals	n/a		Without win	7	1988	Goals against	9	1959-1961

MOROCCO COUNTRY INFORMATION

Capital	Rabat	Independence	1956 from France	GDP per Capita	$4 000
Population	32 209 101	Status	Constitutional Monarchy	GNP Ranking	57
Area km²	446 550	Language	Arabic, French, Berber	Dialling code	+212
Population density	72 per km²	Literacy rate	51%	Internet code	.ma
% in urban areas	48%	Main religion	Muslim 99%	GMT +/–	0
Towns/Cities ('000)	Casablanca 3 609; Rabat 1 894; Fès 1 160; Marrakech 942; Tanger 825; Agadir 656; Meknès 583; Salé 521; Oujda 433; Kénitra 420; Tetouan 365; Safi 278; Mohammedia 156;				
Neighbours (km)	Spain (Ceuta & Melilla) 15; Algeria 1 559; Western Sahara 443; North Atlantic & Mediterranean Sea 1 835				
Main stadia	Stade Mohammed V – Casablanca 67 000; Stade Moulay Abdallah – Rabat 52 000				

FIFA REFEREE LIST 2005

	Int'l	DoB
BARHMI Slimane	1999	12-07-1962
EL ACHIRI Abdellah	2005	25-03-1967
EL ARJOUN Abderrahim	1994	18-07-1963
GUEZZAZ Mohamed	1997	1-10-1962
ROUAISSI Khalil	2002	21-04-1965
TAHRI Said	2001	25-01-1964

FIFA ASSISTANT REFEREE LIST 2005

	Int'l	DoB
AYOUB Mohammed	2002	10-09-1964
BEL KHATIR Ahmed	2000	13-09-1961
FANNANE Abdelwahab	1999	1-01-1962
GUOUR Yahya	1999	4-09-1960
HARAKI Driss	2005	5-05-1966
JEDDIOUI Abdelmajid	1997	27-09-1961
QUARQORI Abdelhak	2005	25-01-1967

CLUB DIRECTORY

Club	Town/City	Stadium	Phone	www.	Lge	Cup	CL
AS Salé (ASS)	Salé	Narche Verte 4 000			0	0	0
SC Chabab (SCCM)	Mohammedia	El Bachir 5 000		chabab.org	1	1	0
COD Meknès (CODM)	Meknès	Stade d'Honneur 20 000	+212 55 402073	codm-meknes.com	1	1	0
Forces Armées Royales (FAR)	Rabat	Moulay Abdallah 52 000	+212 37 833394	supporters-asfar.com	11	8	1
Hassania US (HUSA)	Agadir	Al Inbiaâte 15 000	+212 48 827828		2	0	0
Ittihad Zemmouri (IZK)	Khemisset	Stade du 20 Août 6 000	+212 37 671695		0	0	0
Ittihad Riadi (IRT)	Tanger	Stade de Marchan 14 000	+212 39 935141		0	0	0
Jeunesse Al Massira (JSM)	Laâyoune	Cheikh Laaghdef 40 000	+212 48 893910		0	0	0
Kawkab AC (KACM)	Marrakech	El Harti 25 000	+212 44 480666		2	6	0
Maghreb AS (MAS)	Fès	Complexe Sportif 45 000	+212 55 944464	massawi.com	4	2	0
Mouloudia Club (MCO)	Oujda	Stade d'Honneur 35 000			1	4	0
Olympique Club (OCK)	Khouribga	Stade Municipal 5 000	+212 23 491506	ock.ma	0	0	0
Olympique Club (OCS)	Safi			ocs.ma	0	0	0
Raja CA (RCA)	Casablanca	Stade Mohammed V 67 000	+212 22 259954	rajacasablanca.com	8	5	3
Union Touarga (UST)	Rabat				0	0	0
Wydad AC (WAC)	Casablanca	Stade Mohammed V 67 000	+212 22 988787	wydad.com	10	9	1

RECENT LEAGUE AND CUP RECORD

		Championship						Cup		
Year	Champions	Pts	Runners-up	Pts	Third	Pts		Winners	Score	Runners-up
1990	Wydad Casablanca	72	Ittihad Riadi Tanger	66	Kawkab Marrakech	65		Olympic Casablanca	0-0 4-2p	FAR Rabat
1991	Wydad Casablanca	72	FAR Rabat	68	Ittihad Riadi Tanger	63		Kawkab Marrakech	1-0	KAC Kénitra
1992	Kawkab Marrakech	74	Raja Casablanca	66	Wydad Casablanca	64		Olympic Casablanca	1-0	Raja Casablanca
1993	Wydad Casablanca	72	Raja Casablanca	64	Renaissance Settat	64		Kawkab Marrakech	1-0	Maghreb Fès
1994	Olympic Casablanca	76	Wydad Casablanca	66	FAR Rabat	64		Wydad Casablanca	1-0	Olympic Khouribga
1995	COD Meknès	66	Olympic Casablanca	65	Kawkab Marrakech	65		FUS Rabat	2-0	Olympic Khouribga
1996	Raja Casablanca	57	Olympic Khouribga	48	Wydad Casablanca	47		Raja Casablanca	1-0	FAR Rabat
1997	Raja Casablanca	55	Wydad Casablanca	53	Renaissance Settat	53		Wydad Casablanca	1-0	Kawkab Marrakech
1998	Raja Casablanca	67	Kawkab Marrakech	53	Wydad Casablanca	51		Wydad Casablanca	2-1	FAR Rabat
1999	Raja Casablanca	62	Kawkab Marrakech	58	Olympic Khouribga	54		FAR Rabat	1-0	Chabab Mohammedia
2000	Raja Casablanca	59	Wydad Casablanca	54	Maghreb Fès	53		Majd Casablanca	1-1 8-7p	Renaissance Settat
2001	Raja Casablanca	64	FUS Rabat	55	Maghreb Fès	48		Wydad Casablanca	1-0	Maghreb Fès
2002	Hassania Agadir	65	Wydad Casablanca	62	Raja Casablanca	55		Raja Casablanca	2-0	Maghreb Fès
2003	Hassania Agadir	54	Raja Casablanca	52	Wydad Casablanca	52		FAR Rabat	1-0	Wydad Casablanca
2004	Raja Casablanca	56	FAR Rabat	56	AS Salé	51		FAR Rabat	0-0 3-0p	Wydad Casablanca
2005	FAR Rabat	62	Raja Casablanca	60	Wydad Casablanca	50		Raja Casablanca	0-0 5-4p	Olympic Khouribga

MOROCCO 2004-05

CHAMPIONNAT DU GNFE1

	Pl	W	D	L	F	A	Pts	FAR	RCA	WAC	OCS	JSM	IZK	HUSA	OCK	UST	SCCM	ASS	MCO	CODM	IRT	MAS	KACM
FAR Rabat †	30	17	11	2	35	9	62		2-0	0-0	2-1	3-0	1-1	0-0	0-0	1-0	1-0	3-1	3-0	2-0	1-1	2-1	2-1
Raja Casablanca †	30	18	6	6	42	17	60	0-2		1-1	2-1	3-0	1-1	2-0	1-1	2-1	1-0	2-0	3-0	2-0	5-1	2-0	5-0
Wydad Casablanca	30	12	14	4	32	14	50	1-0	0-1		0-0	1-1	1-1	2-0	3-1	2-0	0-0	1-1	1-0	1-0	4-1	0-0	2-0
Olympique Safi	30	10	11	9	25	22	41	0-0	0-1	0-0		1-0	1-1	0-0	3-1	1-2	2-0	0-0	1-0	1-0	1-0	1-1	1-0
JS Massira	30	9	12	9	26	24	39	0-1	0-1	2-0	1-2		1-0	1-1	3-0	3-0	1-0	3-1	0-2	0-0	1-0	0-0	0-0
IZ Khemisset	30	7	16	7	18	21	37	0-0	2-1	0-0	1-0	2-4		1-0	0-1	1-1	0-0	0-0	2-1	0-1	0-0	0-0	0-0
Hassania Agadir	30	6	18	6	19	21	36	0-0	0-0	0-0	0-0	1-0	0-0		1-0	1-1	1-0	2-2	2-0	1-0	1-0	2-2	0-0
Olympique Khouribga	30	7	15	8	24	29	36	0-1	1-0	1-1	0-0	0-0	0-1	3-3		2-0	3-1	0-0	1-0	2-0	1-1	0-0	1-1
US Touarga	30	9	9	12	27	33	36	1-1	0-2	1-1	0-0	2-2	1-0	3-1	1-2		0-2	1-0	1-0	2-0	1-0	1-1	1-0
Chabab Mohammedia	30	8	10	12	18	24	34	0-2	0-0	0-3	1-0	0-0	1-2	0-0	1-1	2-1		1-0	1-0	1-0	1-1	0-0	3-0
AS Salé §	30	9	8	13	24	33	34	0-3	0-1	0-2	1-1	2-1	0-0	1-0	4-1	2-1	1-0		0-1	2-1	1-1	1-0	2-0
Mouloudia Oujda	30	7	12	11	21	27	33	0-1	3-1	1-1	1-0	0-0	2-0	0-0	0-0	2-1	0-1	1-0		1-1	1-1	2-2	0-0
COD Meknès	30	8	9	13	16	22	33	0-0	0-1	1-0	1-2	2-0	0-0	0-0	2-0	0-0	0-0	1-0	1-1		0-1	2-1	2-0
IR Tanger	30	6	15	9	19	28	33	0-0	1-0	0-3	2-2	0-0	0-1	0-0	0-0	2-1	1-0	2-0	1-1	0-0		0-0	1-0
Maghreb Fès	30	6	14	10	22	26	32	0-1	0-0	0-1	2-0	1-1	2-0	1-0	0-0	0-2	1-0	1-2	1-1	0-1	2-1		1-2
Kawkab Marrakech	30	5	12	13	17	35	27	1-0	0-1	1-0	1-3	0-1	1-1	2-2	1-1	0-0	2-2	2-1	0-0	1-0	0-0	0-1	

16/08/2003 – 15/05/2004 • † Qualified for the CAF Champions League • § One point deducted

MOROCCO 2004-05
CHAMPIONNAT DU GNFE2

	Pl	W	D	L	F	A	Pts
MA Tetouan	30	17	8	5	29	16	59
DH Jadida	30	16	9	5	45	23	57
FUS Rabat	30	15	11	4	36	19	56
Kénitra AC	30	12	15	3	31	17	51
CAY Berrechid	30	13	11	6	32	23	50
Hilal Nador	30	11	9	10	29	26	42
Stade Marocain	30	11	7	12	26	30	40
NR Marrakech	30	9	12	9	28	23	39
Rachad Bernoussi	30	9	10	11	27	31	37
US Mohamedia	30	9	8	13	18	24	35
Racing Casablanca	30	9	8	13	25	29	35
RS Settat	30	7	13	10	15	22	34
Fath Riadi Nador	30	8	11	11	24	28	33
RS Berkane	30	9	6	15	28	39	33
USY El Mansour	30	4	8	18	17	39	20
Wydad Fès	30	2	12	16	15	36	18

26/09/2004 – 4/06/2005

COUPE DU TRONE 2004-05

Round of 16

Raja Casablanca	3
Kawkab Marrakech *	1
Union IF Ben Saleh	0
CODM Meknès *	2
Wydad Fès *	3
Difaa Hassani Jadidi	2
Mouloudia Oujda *	1 3p
FUS Rabat	1 4p
JS Massira *	1
FAR Rabat	0
Fath Riadi Nador	0
JC Houara *	1
Maghreb Fès *	3
Union Touarga	1
Hassania Agadir *	1
Olympique Khouribga	2

Quarter-finals

Raja Casablanca	2
CODM Meknès *	0
Wydad Fès *	1 3p
FUS Rabat	1 4p
JS Massira *	2
JC Houara	0
Maghreb Fès *	0
Olympique Khouribga	1

* Home team

Semi-finals

Raja Casablanca	1
FUS Rabat *	0
JS Massira	0
Olympique Khouribga*	1

Final

Raja Casablanca	0 5p
Olympique Khouribga	0 4p

CUP FINAL

16-07-2005
Stade Prince Moulay Abdallah, Rabat

MAS – MALAYSIA

NATIONAL TEAM RECORD
JULY 1ST 2002 TO JUNE 30TH 2005

PL	W	D	L	F	A	%
36	12	5	19	51	61	40.3

FIFA/COCA-COLA WORLD RANKING

1993	1994	1995	1996	1997	1998	1999	2000	2001	2002	2003	2004	High		Low	
79	89	106	96	87	113	117	107	111	128	116	120	**75**	08/93	**128**	12/02

2004-2005											
08/04	09/04	10/04	11/04	12/04	01/05	02/05	03/05	04/05	05/05	06/05	07/05
118	114	117	120	120	114	114	114	114	113	111	111

Chosen as co-hosts for the 2007 Asian Cup, Malaysia will be hoping for a dramatic improvement in the interim if any success can be gleaned. A long history in the game is not matched by any great rewards except for four South East Asian Games titles, the last of which came in 1989, and the national team has stagnated while football has surged forward in other parts of Asia. The draw for the 2006 FIFA World Cup™ qualifiers was none too kind, pitting Malaysia against Hong Kong, Kuwait and China PR and hopes were virtually extinguished from the beginning with two straight home defeats against Hong Kong and Kuwait. After losing 4-0 in China PR, former Hungary coach

INTERNATIONAL HONOURS
Southeast Asian Games 1961 1977 1979 1989

Bertalan Bicskei became Malaysia's third trainer of the campaign but he could not salvage anything. Spirits were lifted at the 2004 Tiger Cup where the team took bronze after winning the third play play-off against Myanmar. Hosting the Asian Youth Finals exempted the U-20 side from qualifying and two wins at the first stage set up a quarter-final with China PR which they lost 3-0. The U-17s qualified for their finals in Japan but soon left after failing to win any of their three games. The eight-team Malaysian Super League (MSL), which features many players from Africa and South America, was won by Perlis who finished 10 points clear of defending champs Pahang.

THE FIFA BIG COUNT OF 2000

	Male	Female		Male	Female
Registered players	2 400	250	Referees	3 500	0
Non registered players	300 000	800	Officials	16 000	100
Youth players	800	100	Total involved	323 950	
Total players	304 350		Number of clubs	600	
Professional players	800	0	Number of teams	2 800	

Football Association of Malaysia (FAM)
3rd Floor Wisma FAM, Jalan SS5A/9, Kelana Jaya, Selangor Darul Ehsan 47301, Malaysia
Tel +60 3 78733100   Fax +60 3 78757984
gensec@fam.org.my   www.fam.org.my
President: HRH Sultan AHMAD SHAH   General Secretary: AKBAR KHAN Dato' Dell
Vice-President: RITHAUDDEEN Tengka   Treasurer: KEAP TAI Cheong   Media Officer: KHAWARI Ahmad
Men's Coach: BICSKEI Bertalan   Women's Coach: ZHANG Hong
FAM formed: 1933   AFC: 1954   FIFA: 1956
Colours: Yellow/black, Yellow/black, Yellow/black

GAMES PLAYED BY MALAYSIA IN THE 2006 FIFA WORLD CUP™ CYCLE

2002	Opponents	Score		Venue	Comp	Scorers	Att	Referee
16-07	Singapore	L	1-2	Kuantan	Fr	Bin Jamlus [35]	25 000	
11-12	Cambodia	W	5-0	Kuala Lumpur	Fr	Marjan 2, Omar, Mahayuddin, Rakhli		
18-12	Singapore	W	4-0	Singapore	TCr1	Rakhli [30], Mahayuddin 2 [49 65], Yusoff [69]	40 000	Lee Young Chun KOR
20-12	Thailand	W	3-1	Singapore	TCr1	Rakhli [43], Tengku [66], Mahayudin [86]	7 000	Luong The Tai VIE
22-12	Laos	D	1-1	Singapore	TCr1	Jamil [28]	350	Lee Young Chun KOR
27-12	Indonesia	L	0-1	Jakarta	TCsf		65 000	Ebrahim BHR
29-12	Vietnam	L	1-2	Jakarta	TC3p	Mahayuddin [56]	25 000	Midi Nitrorejo IDN
2003								
26-09	Indonesia	D	1-1	Kuala Lumpur	Fr	Saari [90]		
8-10	Myanmar	W	4-0	Kuala Lumpur	ACq	Tengku 2 [34 79], Gilbert [67p], OG [85]	4 500	Yang CHN
10-10	Iraq	D	0-0	Kuala Lumpur	ACq		5 000	Kunthama THA
12-10	Bahrain	D	2-2	Kuala Lumpur	ACq	Shukor [80], Yosri [90]	15 000	Matsumura JPN
20-10	Iraq	L	1-5	Manama	ACq	Omar [53]	500	Al Saeedi UAE
22-10	Bahrain	L	1-3	Manama	ACq	Mahayuddin [32]	18 000	Najm LIB
24-10	Myanmar	L	1-2	Isa Town	ACq	Omar [86]	200	Al Harrassi OMA
24-10	India	L	0-2	Hyderabad	AAG			
26-10	Rwanda	L	1-2	Hyderabad	AAG	Amri [28]		
2004								
7-02	Japan	L	0-4	Ibaraki	Fr		29 530	Moradi IRN
18-02	Hong Kong	L	1-3	Kuantan	WCq	Talib [39p]	12 000	Nagalimgam SIN
17-03	Indonesia	D	0-0	Johor Bahru	Fr		8 000	Kim Heng MAS
31-03	Kuwait	L	0-2	Kuantan	WCq		9 327	Matsumura JPN
9-06	China PR	L	0-4	Tianjin	WCq		35 000	Park Sang Gu KOR
12-07	Singapore	W	2-0	Kuala Lumpur	Fr			
19-08	Thailand	W	2-1	Bangkok	Fr	Kit Hong [8], Vellu [57]		
8-09	China PR	L	0-1	Penang	WCq		14 000	Karim BHR
13-10	Hong Kong	L	0-2	Hong Kong	WCq		2 425	Ghandour LIB
1-11	Singapore	W	2-1	Singapore	Fr	Bin Jamlus [68], Amri [90]	3 293	Luong The Tai VIE
17-11	Kuwait	L	1-6	Kuwait City	WCq	Mohd [19]	15 000	Lutfullin UZB
8-12	East Timor †	W	5-0	Kuala Lumpur	TCr1	Kit Kong [27], Amri 2 [47 83], Saari [67], Adan [85]	6 000	Lazar SIN
10-12	Philippines	W	4-1	Kuala Lumpur	TCr1	Kit Kong [17], Bin Jamlus 2 [67 77p], Hussein [74]		Napitupulu IDN
12-12	Myanmar	L	0-1	Kuala Lumpur	TCr1		10 000	Hsu Chao Lo TPE
14-12	Thailand	W	2-1	Kuala Lumpur	TCr1	Bin Jamlus 2 [63 65]	10 000	Moradi IRN
28-12	Indonesia	W	2-1	Jakarta	TCsf	Kit Kong 2 [28 47]	100 000	Irmatov UZB
2005								
3-01	Indonesia	L	1-4	Kuala Lumpur	TCsf	Bin Jamlus [26]	70 000	Kunsuta THA
15-01	Myanmar	W	2-1	Kuala Lumpur	TC3p	Bin Jamlus [15], Nor [56]	2 000	Vo Minh Tri VIE
4-06	Singapore	L	0-2	Singapore	Fr		18 000	Kunsuta THA
8-06	Singapore	L	1-2	Penang	Fr	Ayob [25]	10 000	Napitupulu IDN

Fr = Friendly match • TC = ASEAN Tiger Cup • AC = AFC Asian Cup • AAG = Afro-Asian Games • WC = FIFA World Cup™
q = qualifier • r1 = first round group • sf = semi-final • 3p = third place play-off • † not a full international

MALAYSIA COUNTRY INFORMATION

Capital	Kuala Lumpur	Independence	1963 from the UK	GDP per Capita	$9 000
Population	23 522 482	Status	Constitutional Monarchy	GNP Ranking	42
Area km²	329 750	Language	Malay, English, Chinese	Dialling code	+60
Population density	71 per km²	Literacy rate	88%	Internet code	.my
% in urban areas	54%	Main religion	Muslim 45%, Buddhist 15%	GMT +/–	+8
Towns/Cities ('000)	Kuala Lumpur 1 453; Klang 879; Subang Jaya 833; Johor Bahru 802; Ipoh 673; Ampang Jaya 644; Kuching 570; Petaling Jaya 520; Shah Alam 481; Kota Kinabalu 457; Sandakan 392; Kuantan 366				
Neighbours (km)	Brunei 381; Indonesia 1 782; Thailand 506; South China Sea 4 675				
Main stadia	Bukit Jalil – Kuala Lumpur 100 200; Shah Alam – Shah Alam 69 372; Darul Makmur – Kuantan 40 000				

MALAYSIA NATIONAL TEAM RECORDS AND RECORD SEQUENCES

Records			Sequence records					
Victory	15-1	PHI 1962	Wins	6	1975, 1989	Clean sheets	5	1979
Defeat	2-8	NZL 1967	Defeats	7	1980-81, 2003-04	Goals scored	14	1999-2000
Player Caps	n/a		Undefeated	10	1961-1962, 1971	Without goal	5	1997-1998
Player Goals	n/a		Without win	12	2003-2004	Goals against	15	1970-1971

FIFA REFEREE LIST 2005

	Int'l	DoB
ABDUL HAMID Halim	1999	13-06-1962
CHAPPANIMUTU Ravichandran	2002	27-09-1965
KIM HENG Danny	2003	11-07-1967
MAT AMIN Mohamad	1999	1-01-1965
MOHD SALLEH Subkhiddin	2000	17-11-1966
RAMACHANDRAN Krishnan	2001	11-11-1965
SHAHARUL Rosdi	2004	1-01-1971
SUPIAN Ahmad	2001	27-01-1961

FIFA ASSISTANT REFEREE LIST 2005

	Int'l	DoB
ISHAK Nasaruddin	2002	20-05-1966
MOHAMAD Saadon	2000	25-01-1965
SALIM Idzha	2005	4-04-1966
SULONG Azman	2004	6-03-1968
TUMIN Mohd	2004	9-05-1971
VAITHILINGHAM Thiruch	2005	5-03-1965
YACOB Mohamad	2000	27-05-1967

MALAYSIA 2004

SUPER LEAGUE

	Pl	W	D	L	F	A	Pts	Pahang	Selangor	Perlis	Perak	Penang	Sabah	Sarawak	Kedah
Pahang †	21	14	5	2	48	29	47		2-1 3-3	3-3	1-0	3-1	4-2 2-0	1-1 3-2	4-3 2-1
Selangor Public Bank	21	11	5	5	38	29	38	2-4		2-0 4-2	1-1 4-1	3-1 0-3	1-0 2-0	2-2	2-1
Perlis	21	10	6	5	41	30	36	2-2 2-1	1-1		2-3	2-1 1-1	2-1	4-0	4-0 6-3
Perak	21	10	6	5	35	27	36	0-0 3-2	2-0	0-0 1-3		4-0 4-1	2-0 2-2	2-1	1-0
Penang	21	8	3	10	29	38	27	1-4 0-2	0-1	1-3	4-2		3-0 1-0	0-0 2-1	3-2 2-1
Sabah	21	4	5	12	22	35	17	0-1	0-0	4-1 1-0	0-2	2-2		2-1 2-2	2-1 1-2
Sarawak	21	3	7	11	28	38	16	1-2	1-2 1-0	1-1 0-1	4-2 1-1	1-2	3-1		1-2
Kedah	21	4	3	14	30	45	15	1-2	3-4 1-3	0-1	1-2 0-0	2-0	1-1	2-2 3-2	

14/02/2004 - 3/08/2004 • † Qualified for the AFC Cup

MALAYSIA 2004 PREMIER LEAGUE (2) GROUP A

	Pl	W	D	L	F	A	Pts
Melaka Telecom	24	17	1	6	41	24	52
Selangor	24	16	2	6	52	35	50
Johor FC	24	14	5	5	43	25	47
Selangor PKNS	24	13	4	7	47	35	43
Kelantan TNB	24	11	3	10	32	27	36
Police	24	7	7	10	34	44	28
Brunei	24	8	2	14	48	49	26
Armed Forces	24	7	2	15	37	49	23
Kelantan JPS	24	2	0	22	27	73	6

14/02/2004 - 8/08/2004

PLAY-OFF PREMIER LEAGUE

Selangor MPPJ	3
Melaka Telekom	2

MALAYSIA 2004 PREMIER LEAGUE (2) GROUP B

	Pl	W	D	L	F	A	Pts
Selangor MMPJ	24	13	6	5	49	28	45
Selangor MK Land	24	13	3	8	42	31	42
Kuala Lumpur	24	10	8	6	44	33	38
Negeri Sembilan	24	10	8	6	45	35	38
Terengganu	24	8	11	5	33	27	35
Johor	24	8	8	8	30	31	32
Melaka	24	6	9	9	32	38	27
Kelantan SKMK	24	8	2	14	24	47	26
Kelantan	24	1	7	16	13	42	10

14/02/2004 - 8/08/2004

RECENT LEAGUE AND CUP RECORD

	Championship					
Year	Champions	Pts	Runners-up	Pts	Third	Pts
1995	Pahang	65	Selangor	54	Sarawak	54
1996	Sabah	58	Kedah	57	Negri Sembilan	57
1997	Sarawak	54	Kedah	50	Sabah	49
1998	Penang	41	Pahang	40	Brunei	35
1999	Pahang	34	Penang	31	Negeri Sembilan	29
2000	Selangor	45	Penang	43	Perak	41
2001	Penang	50	Terengganu	41	Kelantan	38
2002	Perak	60	Selangor	56	Sabah	47
2003	Perak	47	Kedah	45	Perlis	45
2004	Pahang	47	Selangor Public Bank	38	Perlis	36

	FA Cup	
Winners	Score	Runners-up
Sabah	3-1	Pahang
Kedah	1-0	Sarawak
Selangor	1-0	Penang
Johor	1-0	Sabah
Kuala Lumpur	0-0 5-3p	Terengganu
Terengganu	1-1 4-3p	Penang
Selangor	1-0	Sarawak
Penang	1-0	Perak
Negeri Sembilan	2-1	Perlis
Perak	3-0	Terengganu

FA CUP 2004

Third Round		Quarter-finals		Semi-finals		Final	
Perak	2 0						
Melaka Telecom *	1 0	Perak	2 6				
Melaka *	2 1	Negeri Sembilan *	3 0				
Negeri Sembilan	2 3			Perak *	1 2		
Armed Forces *	3 0			Selangor PKNS	0 0		
Police	1 1	Armed Forces	1 0				
Selangor MK Land *	1 3	Selangor PKNS *	1 4				
Selangor PKNS	3 2					Perak †	3
Pahang	6 6					Terengganu	0
Kelantan JPS *	0 1	Pahang	2 5				
Selangor MPPJ *	3 1 2p	Johor FC *	1 3				
Johor FC	2 2 4p			Pahang	0 2		
Sabah	1 1			Terengganu *	2 1		
Perlis *	1 0	Sabah *	2 2				
Selangor	1 1	Terengganu	4 1				
Terengganu *	2 2						

* Home team in the first leg • † Qualified for the AFC Cup

CUP FINAL

10-10-2004, Att: 60 000
Bukit Jalil, Kuala Lumpur
Scorers - Goux [103], Jamlus 2 [107] [110]

MALAYSIA CUP 2004

Quarter-finals		Semi-finals		Final	
Perlis	2 1 5p				
Negeri Sembilan	3 0 4p	Perlis	2 1		
Selangor	1 0	Pahang	0 2		
Pahang	1 2			Perlis	1
Sabah	1 2			Kedah	0
Penang	0 1	Sabah	1 0		
Selangor PB	2 0	Kedah	1 1		
Kedah	0 3				

4-12-2004, Kula Lumpur
Scorer - Faisal OG [7]

MALAYSIA CUP

Year	Winners	Score	Runners-up
1995	Selangor	1-0	Pahang
1996	Selangor	1-1 5-3p	Sabah
1997	Selangor	1-0	Pahang
1998	Perak	1-1 5-3p	Terengganu
1999	Brunei	2-1	Sarawak
2000	Perak	2-0	Negeri Sembilan
2001	Terengganu	2-1	Perak
2002	Selangor	1-0	Sabah
2003	Selangor MPPJ	3-0	Sabah
2004	Perlis	1-0	Kedah

CLUB DIRECTORY

Club	Town/City	Stadium	Phone	Lge	Cup	MC	CL
Brunei	Bandar Seri Begawan	Sultan Hassan Bolkiah 30 000	+673 2 382761	0	0	1	0
Jenderata	Perak		+60 5 6411411	0	0	0	0
Johor	Johor Bharu	Tan Sri Hassan Yunus 30 000	+60 7 2247034	1	1	2	0
Johor FC	Pasir Gudang	Pasir Gudang Corporation 15 000	+60 7 2552603	0	0	0	0
Kedah	Alor Setar		+60 4 7339190	1	1	2	0
Kelantan TNB	Kota Bharu	Sultan Mohammad IV 30 000	+60 9 7482020	0	0	0	0
Kuala Lumpur	Kuala Lumpur	KLFA Stadium 18 000	+60 3 91315757	0	3	3	0
Melaka	Melaka	Hang Jebat 20 000	+60 6 2834008	1	0	0	0
Melaka Telecom	Kuala Lumpur		+60 3 22401563	0	0	0	0
Negeri Sembilan	Seremban	Tuanku Abdul Rahman 30 000	+60 6 7628494	0	1	1	0
NTFA	Penang		+60 4 5073904	0	0	0	0
Pahang	Kuantan	Darul Makmur 40 000	+60 9 5121280	5	0	2	0
PDRM	Kuala Lumpur		+60 3 26938373	0	0	0	0
Penang	Pulau Pinang	Bandaraya 40 000	+60 4 2289454	3	1	4	0
Perak	Ipoh	Stadium Perak 40 000	+60 5 5478812	2	2	7	0
Perlis	Kangar	Utama Negeri 30 000	+60 4 9761867	0	0	1	0
Sabah	Kota Kinabalu	Likas Stadium 35 000	+60 88 261623	1	1	0	0
Sarawak	Kuching	Sarawak State 26 000	+60 82 442343	1	1	0	0
Selangor	Kelana Jaya	Shah Alam 69 372	+60 3 78037054	4	3	31	0
Selangor MK Land	Petaling Jaya		+60 3 77266591	0	0	0	0
Selangor MPPJ	Petaling Jaya	MPPJ Stadium 25 000	+60 3 78740284	0	0	1	0
Selangor PKNS	Petaling Jaya		+60 3 79574144	0	0	0	0
Selangor Public Bank	Kuala Lumpur	Shah Alam 69 372	+60 3 21766249	0	0	0	0
Terengganu	Kuala Terenggabu	Sultan Nasiruddin Shah 25 000	+60 9 6234004	0	1	1	0

MC = Malaysia Cup

MDA – MOLDOVA

NATIONAL TEAM RECORD
JULY 1ST 2002 TO JUNE 30TH 2005

PL	W	D	L	F	A	%
27	5	8	14	15	41	33.3

FIFA/COCA-COLA WORLD RANKING

1993	1994	1995	1996	1997	1998	1999	2000	2001	2002	2003	2004	High		Low	
-	118	109	117	131	116	93	94	103	111	106	114	89	02/00	149	07/94

2004-2005											
08/04	09/04	10/04	11/04	12/04	01/05	02/05	03/05	04/05	05/05	06/05	07/05
110	104	113	112	114	116	115	114	115	115	117	115

A 1-0 victory over Georgia at the start of the 2004-05 season gave the national team hope that they could have a say in the outcome of their 2006 FIFA World Cup™ qualifying group and although there were no wins to celebrate both Scotland and Norway left Moldova with draws instead of the expected wins while Italy only managed a 1-0 victory. It was not enough, however, to keep coach Viktor Pasulko in his job in the long-term with his contract due to be terminated once the qualifiers have finished. For the 2-0 defeat against Scotland in June 2005 there wasn't a single home-based player in the squad with the majority playing in Russia and Ukraine. Two players – goalkeeper

INTERNATIONAL HONOURS
None

Evgheni Hmaruc and defender Vladislav Lungu – won Championship medals abroad, the former with CSKA in Bulgaria and the latter with Gorica in Slovenia. At home Sherif Tiraspol have well and truly turned the tables on Zimbru Chisinau, who for the first time since independence failed to finish in the top three in the Championship. Sheriff were never in danger of missing out on a fifth consecutive title after winning 14 of their first 15 games. Their only challengers were Nistru from Otaci but they ended up 16 points behind. There was huge satisfaction for Nistru, however, when they beat Dacia in the Cup Final to win their first trophy.

THE FIFA BIG COUNT OF 2000

	Male	Female		Male	Female
Registered players	793	85	Referees	316	18
Non registered players	63 000	2 500	Officials	252	20
Youth players	2 300	165	Total involved	57 106	
Total players	68 843		Number of clubs	200	
Professional players	0	0	Number of teams	800	

Football Association of Moldova (FMF)
Federatia Moldoveneasca de Fotbal, Str. Tricolorului nr. 39, Chisinau MD-2012, Moldova
Tel +373 22 210413   Fax +373 22 210432
fmf@mfotbal.mldnet.com   www.fmf.md
President: CEBANU Pavel   General Secretary: CEBOTARI Nicolai
Vice-President: COJUHARI Valentin   Treasurer: ROMAN Constantin   Media Officer: VATAMANU Vasile
Men's Coach: PASULKO Viktor   Women's Coach: PUSICOV Evgheni
FMF formed: 1990   UEFA: 1992   FIFA: 1994
Colours: Red, Blue, Red

GAMES PLAYED BY MOLDOVA IN THE 2006 FIFA WORLD CUP™ CYCLE

2002	Opponents	Score		Venue	Comp	Scorers	Att	Referee
21-08	Estonia	L	0-1	Tallinn	Fr		1 500	Kaldma EST
7-09	Austria	L	0-2	Vienna	ECq		18 300	Dougal SCO
12-10	Czech Republic	L	0-2	Chisinau	ECq		4 000	Irvine NIR
20-11	Hungary	D	1-1	Budapest	Fr	Patula 16	6 000	Sowa AUT
2003								
12-02	Georgia	D	2-2	Tbilisi	Fr	Golban 75, Dadu 84p	7 000	Hovanisyan ARM
5-03	Israel	D	0-0	Tel Aviv	Fr		8 000	Bertini ITA
29-03	Belarus	L	1-2	Minsk	ECq	Cebotari 14	7 500	Verbist BEL
2-04	Netherlands	L	1-2	Tiraspol	ECq	Boret 16	12 000	Sars FRA
7-06	Austria	W	1-0	Tiraspol	ECq	Frunza 60	10 000	Paraty Silva POR
11-06	Czech Republic	L	0-5	Olomouc	ECq		12 907	Jakobsson ISL
20-08	Turkey	L	0-2	Ankara	Fr		15 300	Plautz AUT
10-09	Belarus	W	2-1	Tiraspol	ECq	Dadu 23, Covaliciuc 88	7 000	Delevic SCG
11-10	Netherlands	L	0-5	Eindhoven	ECq		30 995	Siric CRO
20-11	Luxembourg	W	2-1	Hesperange	Fr	Golban 19, Dadu 90	623	Duhamel FRA
2004								
14-02	Malta	D	0-0	Ta'Qali	Fr		600	Vialichka BLR
16-02	Belarus	L	0-1	Ta'Qali	Fr		40	Attard MLT
18-02	Estonia	L	0-1	Ta'Qali	Fr		100	Sammut MLT
31-03	Azerbaijan	W	2-1	Chisinau	Fr	Dadu 2 42p 84	5 500	Godulyan UKR
28-04	Israel	D	1-1	Tel Aviv	Fr	Rogaciov 71	4 500	Corpodean ROU
18-08	Georgia	W	1-0	Tiraspol	Fr	Miterev 68	8 000	Godulyan UKR
4-09	Slovenia	L	0-3	Celje	WCq		3 620	Hyytia FIN
8-09	Italy	L	0-1	Chisinau	WCq		5 200	Benes CZE
9-10	Belarus	L	0-4	Minsk	WCq		21 000	Dereli TUR
13-10	Scotland	D	1-1	Chisinau	WCq	Dadu 28	7 000	Jakobsson ISL
2005								
9-02	Azerbaijan	D	0-0	Baku	Fr		1 500	
30-03	Norway	D	0-0	Chisinau	WCq		5 000	Meyer GER
4-06	Scotland	L	0-2	Glasgow	WCq		45 317	Braamhaar NED

Fr = Friendly match • EC = UEFA EURO 2004™ • WC = FIFA World Cup™ • q = qualifier

MOLDOVA NATIONAL TEAM RECORDS AND RECORD SEQUENCES

Records			Sequence records					
Victory	2-0	Four times	Wins	3	1994	Clean sheets	2	2000, 2005
Defeat	0-6	SWE 2001	Defeats	9	1996-1998	Goals scored	7	1998-1999
Player Caps	63	CLESCENKO Serghei	Undefeated	3	Five times	Without goal	7	1997-98, 2000-01
Player Goals	10	CLESCENKO Serghei	Without win	10	1996-98, 2002-03	Goals against	25	1994-1998

NATIONAL CAPS

	Caps
CLESCENKO Serghei	63
REBEJA Radu	54
TESTIMITANU Ion	49
GAIDAMASCIUC Vladimir	45
STROENCO Serghei	45

NATIONAL GOALS

	Goals
CLESCENKO Serghei	10
MITEREV Iurie	8
DADU Serghei	6
TESTIMITANU Ion	6

NATIONAL COACH

	Years
CARAS Ion	1993-'97
DANILIANT Ivan	1998-'99
MATIURA Alexandr	1999-'01
SPIRIDON Alexandr	2001-'02
PASULKO Victor	2002-

MOLDOVA COUNTRY INFORMATION

Capital	Chisinau	Independence	1991 from the USSR	GDP per Capita	$1 800
Population	4 446 455	Status	Republic	GNP Ranking	146
Area km²	33 843	Language	Moldovan, Russian	Dialling code	+373
Population density	131 per km²	Literacy rate	99%	Internet code	.md
% in urban areas	52%	Main religion	Christian	GMT +/-	+2
Towns/Cities ('000)	Chisinau 713; Tiraspol 196; Balti 150; Tighina 128; Rabnita 61; Orhei 49; Cahul 44				
Neighbours (km)	Ukraine 939; Romania 450				
Main stadia	Complex Sheriff – Tiraspol 14 000; Stadionul Republica – Chisinau 8 084				

MOLDOVA 2004-05

DIVIZIA NATIONALA

	Pl	W	D	L	F	A	Pts	Sheriff	Nistru	Dacia	Tiraspol	Zimbru	Tiligul	Unisport	Steaua
Sheriff Tiraspol †	28	22	4	2	54	12	70		2-0 4-1	2-0 2-0	1-0 2-3	2-1 1-3	2-0 0-0	6-1 1-0	3-0 5-0
Nistru Otaci ‡	28	17	3	8	51	27	54	0-1 0-0		4-2 2-0	1-0 1-0	0-1 1-1	2-1 0-0	2-0 4-1	4-0 7-2
Dacia Chisinau ‡	28	14	3	11	38	31	45	1-1 0-1	1-3 2-1		0-0 4-1	0-1 1-0	1-1 1-0	2-0 3-0	3-0 3-0
FC Tiraspol	28	12	8	8	41	23	44	1-3 0-1	0-1 2-0	2-1 1-0		1-1 0-0	1-1 1-1	0-0 2-1	7-0 5-1
Zimbru Chisinau	28	12	7	9	29	15	43	0-1 0-0	2-0 0-0	0-1 0-1	0-1 0-2		3-0 0-0	5-1 3-0	1-0 3-0
Tiligul-Tiras Tiraspol	28	11	8	9	32	27	41	0-1 1-2	1-3 4-2	3-1 3-2	1-0 0-1	0-1 1-0		1-0 2-0	4-0 3-1
Unisport-Auto Chisinau	28	3	5	20	16	51	14	0-2 0-2	0-2 0-1	1-2 1-2	1-1 0-4	0-0 0-1	0-0 1-2		4-1 2-0
Steaua Chisinau	28	0	4	24	8	83	4	0-4 0-2	0-3 0-5	0-2 1-2	1-1 0-4	0-0 0-2	1-1 0-1	0-0 0-2	

14/08/2004 - 12/06/2005 • † Qualified for the UEFA Champions League • ‡ Qualified for the UEFA Cup • Relegation play-off: Politehnica 4-0 Unisport-Auto

MOLDOVA 2004-05 DIVIZIA A (2)

	Pl	W	D	L	F	A	Pts
Dinamo Bender	30	24	3	3	68	16	75
Politehnica Chisinau	30	23	2	4	90	18	71
Olimpia Balti	30	21	6	3	63	22	69
Sheriff Tiraspol 2	30	19	8	3	76	22	65
Roso Floreni	30	16	6	8	51	36	54
Victoria Chisnau	30	11	11	8	39	31	44
Zimbru Chisnau 2	30	11	10	9	48	36	43
Tiligul-Tiras Tiraspol 2	30	15	5	10	45	35	40
Iskra-Stali Ribnita	30	9	9	12	27	40	36
Intersport Aroma	30	10	5	15	27	41	35
USC Gagauziya	30	6	10	14	16	39	28
FC Orhei	30	7	6	17	24	70	27
FC Otaci	30	5	6	19	20	58	21
Steaua Chisinau 2	30	4	8	18	18	56	20
Agro-Goliador	30	5	2	23	17	56	17
Energetic Dubasari	30	4	3	23	17	70	15

7/08/2004 - 12/06/2005

CUPA MOLDOVEI 2004-05

Quarter-finals		Semi-finals		Final	
Nistru Otaci	-				
Petrocub §	-	Nistru Otaci	1 0		
Zimbru Chisnau	1 1	Tiligul-Tiras *	1 0		
Tiligul-Tiras *	2 1			Nistru Otaci ‡	1
Politehnica	2 0			Dacia Chisinau	0
FC Tiraspol *	2 0	Politehnica	0 0	21-05-2005, Att: 5 500
Sheriff Tiraspol	0 0	Dacia Chisinau *	1 0	Ref: Orlic
Dacia Chisinau *	1 0			Republica, Chisinau
				Scorer - Zharov [89] for Nistru

* Home team in the first leg • ‡ Qualified for the UEFA Cup • § Petrocub withdrew

CLUB DIRECTORY

Club	Town/City	Stadium	Phone	www.	Lge	Cup	CL
FC Dacia	Chisinau	Baza CSF Zimbru	+373 22 245597	fcdacia.com	0	0	0
FC Nistru	Otaci	Calarasauca	+373 71 24965		0	1	0
FC Sheriff	Tiraspol	Complex Sheriff 14 000	+373 33 63500	fc.sheriff.md	5	3	0
CS Steaua	Chisinau	Speia	+373 22 733522		0	0	0
CS Tiligul-Tiras	Tiraspol	Orasenesc	+373 33 71195		0	3	0
FC Tiraspol	Tiraspol	Complex Sheriff 14 000	+373 33 26314		0	0	0
FC Unisport-Auto	Chisinau	Dinamo	+373 22 272289		0	0	0
CSF Zimbru	Chisinau	Baza CSF Zimbru	+373 22 772400	zimbru.md	8	4	0

RECENT LEAGUE AND CUP RECORD

	Championship						Cup		
Year	Champions	Pts	Runners-up	Pts	Third	Pts	Winners	Score	Runners-up
1992	Zimbru Chisinau	35	Tiligul Tiraspol	35	Bugeac Comrat	33	Bugeac Comrat	5-0	Tiligul Tiraspol
1993	Zimbru Chisinau	50	Tiligul Tiraspol	47	Moldova Boroseni	41	Tiligul Tiraspol	1-0	Dinamo Chisinau
1994	Zimbru Chisinau	52	Tiligul Tiraspol	49	Codru Calarasi	40	Tiligul Tiraspol	1-0	Nistru Otaci
1995	Zimbru Chisinau	67	Tiligul Tiraspol	66	Olimpia Balti	57	Tiligul Tiraspol	1-0	Zimbru Chisinau
1996	Zimbru Chisinau	81	Tiligul Tiraspol	74	Constructorul	74	Constructorul	2-1	Tiligul Tiraspol
1997	Constructorul	81	Zimbru Chisinau	70	Tiligul Tiraspol	68	Zimbru Chisinau	0-0 7-6p	Nistru Otaci
1998	Zimbru Chisinau	69	Tiligul Tiraspol	59	Constructorul	54	Zimbru Chisinau	1-0	Constructorul
1999	Zimbru Chisinau	61	Constructorul	51	Tiligul Tiraspol	39	Sheriff Tiraspol	2-1	Constructorul
2000	Zimbru Chisinau	82	Sheriff Tiraspol	81	Constructorul	65	Constructorul	1-0	Zimbru Chisinau
2001	Sheriff Tiraspol	67	Zimbru Chisinau	66	Tiligul Tiraspol	41	Sheriff Tiraspol	0-0 5-4p	Nistru Otaci
2002	Sheriff Tiraspol	67	Nistru Otaci	52	Zimbru Chisinau	46	Sheriff Tiraspol	3-2	Nistru Otaci
2003	Sheriff Tiraspol	60	Zimbru Chisinau	50	Nistru Otaci	42	Zimbru Chisinau	0-0 4-2p	Nistru Otaci
2004	Sheriff Tiraspol	65	Nistru Otaci	57	Zimbru Chisinau	49	Zimbru Chisinau	2-1	Sheriff Tiraspol
2005	Sheriff Tiraspol	70	Nistru Otaci	54	Dacia Chisinau	45	Nistru Otaci	1-0	Dacia Chisinau

MDV – MALDIVES

NATIONAL TEAM RECORD
JULY 1ST 2002 TO JUNE 30TH 2005

PL	W	D	L	F	A	%
21	6	4	11	33	35	38.1

FIFA/COCA-COLA WORLD RANKING

1993	1994	1995	1996	1997	1998	1999	2000	2001	2002	2003	2004	High		Low	
148	162	169	176	160	166	143	154	147	152	141	139	136	11/04	183	09/97

	2004-2005										
08/04	09/04	10/04	11/04	12/04	01/05	02/05	03/05	04/05	05/05	06/05	07/05
141	142	142	136	139	140	141	141	141	142	142	142

One of the countries hit by the tsunami disaster of December 2004, FIFA came to the aid of the Maldives through the Tsunami Task Force that was set up to raise funds and offer assistance to football organisations affected. Initially granted US$1 million in April 2005, a further US$441,509 was awarded in July to assist in repairing damage at the association's headquarters and training centre, as well as the reconstruction of an artificial pitch and two other football facilities. Unsurprisingly the national side have not featured in 2005 and the islanders will hope they can return to the international scene where they are regarded as a skilful side in South Asia. This was

INTERNATIONAL HONOURS
None

proved in the 2003 SAFF Cup where they finished runners-up to Bangladesh only on penalties after a 1-1 draw in the final. Although finishing bottom of their second round group in the 2006 FIFA World Cup™ qualifiers, the Maldives team provided some memorable moments including a goalless draw with the 2002 FIFA World Cup™ semi-finalists Korea Republic and a 3-0 victory over Vietnam. Domestic football has continued with Valencia winning the Cup Winners Cup in May 2005 and then losing to New Radiant the following week in the Cup Final. The two had met in the 2004 National Championship final in December with New Radiant again the victors.

THE FIFA BIG COUNT OF 2000

	Male	Female		Male	Female
Registered players	3 305	0	Referees	130	0
Non registered players	13 600	1 200	Officials	20	0
Youth players	1 556	55	Total involved	19 866	
Total players	19 716		Number of clubs	127	
Professional players	105	0	Number of teams	367	

Football Association of Maldives (FAM)
Ujaalaa Hin'gun, Maafannu, Male 20388, Maldives
Tel +960 317006   Fax +960 317005
famaldvs@dhivehinet.net.mv   www.famaldives.gov.mv
President: SHAKOOR Abdul   General Secretary: ISMAIL Ibrahim
Vice-President: TBD   Treasurer: RASHEED Hussain   Media Officer: JAMEEL Ahmedullah
Men's Coach: GONCALVES Manuel   Women's Coach: GONCALVES Manuel
FAM formed: 1982   AFC: 1986   FIFA: 1986
Colours: Red, Green, White

GAMES PLAYED BY MALDIVES IN THE 2006 FIFA WORLD CUP™ CYCLE

2002	Opponents		Score	Venue	Comp	Scorers	Att	Referee
No international matches played in 2002 after June								
2003								
11-01	Bhutan	W	6-0	Dhaka	SAFr1	Nizam [2], Luthfy [11], Shiham 3 [24 25 67], Umar [80]		Vidanagamage SRI
13-01	Bangladesh	L	0-1	Dhaka	SAFr1		20 000	Vidanagamage SRI
15-01	Nepal	W	3-2	Dhaka	SAFr1	Nizam [63], Luthfy [75], Umar [85]	15 000	Kunsuta THA
18-01	Pakistan	W	1-0	Dhaka	SAFsf	Fazeel [12]		Gurung NEP
20-01	Bangladesh	D	1-1	Dhaka	SAFf	Umar [58], L 3-5p	46 000	Vidanagamage SRI
4-03	Singapore	L	1-4	Singapore	Fr	Umar [44]		Abdul Bashir SIN
21-03	Brunei Darussalam	D	1-1	Malé	ACq	Umar [42]		
25-03	Myanmar	L	0-2	Malé	ACq			
29-11	Mongolia	W	1-0	Ulaan-Baatar	WCq	Nizam [24]	2 000	Yang Zhiqiang CHN
3-12	Mongolia	W	12-0	Malé	WCq	Ashfaq 4 [4 61 63 68], Nizam [42], Fazeel 2 [46+ 49+], Ghani [65], Thariq [74], OG [75], Nazeeh [80]	9 000	Arambekade SRI
2004								
18-02	Vietnam	L	0-4	Hanoi	WCq		25 000	Fong KKG
31-03	Korea Republic	D	0-0	Malé	WCq		12 000	Vidanagamage SRI
31-05	Oman	L	0-3	Muscat	Fr			
3-06	Oman	L	1-4	Muscat	Fr			
9-06	Lebanon	L	0-3	Beirut	WCq		18 000	Nurilddin Salman IRQ
31-08	Oman	L	0-1	Malé	Fr			
3-09	Oman	L	1-2	Malé	Fr			
8-09	Lebanon	L	2-5	Malé	WCq	Fazeel [79], Umar [88]	12 000	Al Ajmi OMA
13-10	Vietnam	W	3-0	Malé	WCq	Thariq [29], Ashfaq 2 [68 85]	10 000	Haq IND
17-11	Korea Republic	L	0-2	Seoul	WCq		64 000	Lazar SIN
18-12	Sri Lanka	D	0-0	Malé	Fr			
2005								
No internationals played in 2005 before August								

Fr = Friendly match • SAF = South Asian Football Federation Cup • AC = AFC Asian Cup • WC = FIFA World Cup™
q = qualifier • r1 = first round group • sf = semi-final • f = final

MALDIVES NATIONAL TEAM RECORDS AND RECORD SEQUENCES

Records			Sequence records				
Victory	6-0	CAM 2001	Wins	3	1999	Clean sheets	2	1993, 1999, 2003
Defeat	0-17	IRN 1997	Defeats	12	1996-1997	Goals scored	7	1999
Player Caps	n/a		Undefeated	4	2000	Without goal	6	1997
Player Goals	n/a		Without win	23	1985-1997	Goals against	14	1996-1997

FIFA ASSISTANT REFEREE LIST 2005

	Int'l	DoB
ABEER Ahmed	1995	11-07-1969
AMEEZ Ahmed	2001	3-06-1972
HAKEEM Abdul	1994	20-11-1961
SAEED Mohamed	1993	14-01-1962
THAUFEEQ Ibrahim	2005	21-08-1970
UMMEED Ahmed	2005	28-03-1968

FIFA REFEREE LIST 2005

	Int'l	DoB
RASHEED Riyaz	2001	18-06-1969
SALEEM Ali	195	10-04-1969

MALDIVES COUNTRY INFORMATION

Capital	Malé	Independence	1965 from the UK	GDP per Capita	$3 900
Population	339 330	Status	Republic	GNP Ranking	168
Area km²	300	Language	Maldivian Dhiveti	Dialling code	+960
Population density	1 131 per km²	Literacy rate	97%	Internet code	.mv
% in urban areas	27%	Main religion	Muslim	GMT +/−	+5
Towns/Cities ('000)	Malé 85; Hithadoo 9; Fuvammulah 8; Kulhudhuffushi 8; Thinadhoo 5; Naifaru 4				
Neighbours (km)	Indian Ocean 644				
Main stadia	Galolhu National Stadium – Male				

MALDIVES 2004

MALE LEAGUE

	Pl	W	D	L	F	A	Pts	Radiant	Victory	Valencia	IFC	Hurriyya	Guraid.	Mecano	United
New Radiant	7	7	0	0	34	7	21		3-2	3-2	4-1	3-1	3-1	2-0	16-0
Victory	7	6	0	1	41	9	18			2-1	2-1	3-2	2-1	13-0	17-1
Valencia	7	4	1	2	33	11	13				1-1	3-0	5-2	7-2	14-1
IFC	7	4	1	2	22	11	13					3-2	1-0	12-1	3-1
Hurriyya	7	3	0	4	13	12	9						1-0	3-0	4-0
Guraidhoo ZJ	7	2	0	5	12	14	6							3-2	5-2
Mecano	7	1	0	6	6	42	3								3-2
United Victory	7	0	0	7	7	62	0								

11/05/2004 - 16/07/2004 • Top six qualify for the Dhivehi League

MALDIVES 2004

DHIVEHI LEAGUE

	Pl	W	D	L	F	A	Pts	Valencia	Radiant	Hurriyya	Victory	IFC	Guraid.	DX	Mahib.
Valencia	12	9	1	2	35	17	28		2-1	2-0	0-2	1-1	4-0	4-0	8-0
New Radiant	12	6	4	2	40	13	22	2-4		1-0	1-1	0-0	2-2	9-1	6-1
Hurriyya	12	6	2	4	27	11	20	1-2	2-2		0-2	4-1	1-1	4-0	5-0
Victory	12	6	1	5	24	13	19	8-1	0-3	0-2		1-2	1-2	3-0	5-0
IFC	12	3	4	5	19	23	13	0-4	0-5	0-1	2-0		1-3	2-2	8-0
Guraidhoo ZJ	12	3	4	5	18	33	13	2-3	0-8	0-7	0-1	2-2		2-2	4-1
DX Sports Club	7	0	3	4	6	25	3								1-1
Mahibadhoo ZG	7	0	1	6	3	37	1								

19/07/2004 - 26/09/2004 • Top four qualify for the National Championship play-offs

NATIONAL CHAMPIONSHIP 2004

Quarter-finals	Semi-finals	Final
	New Radiant 2	
	Valencia 1	
		New Radiant 1 6p
Hurriyya 1		Valencia 1 5p
Victory 0	Hurriyya	8-12-2005
	Valencia	Scorers - Simeonov 25 for New Radiant; Ashfaq 43 for Valencia

CUP WINNERS CUP 2005

	Pl	W	D	L	F	A	Pts
Victory	4	4	0	0	8	1	12
Valencia	4	2	1	1	20	7	7
New Radiant	4	1	2	1	10	5	5
IFC	4	0	2	2	3	7	2
United Victory	4	0	1	3	2	23	1

Final: Valencia 2-1 Victory • Played 13/05/2004 • Scorers - Ashfaq 2 45 90 for Valencia; Batchou 73 for Victory

FA CUP 2005

Quarter-finals	Semi-finals	Final
New Radiant 2		
Hurriyya 1	New Radiant 0 3p	
Vyansa 1	Victory 0 0p	
Victory 2		New Radiant 2
IFC 3		Valencia 0
Guraidhoo ZJ 0	IFC 2	20-05-2005
Mazia SRC 0	Valencia 5	National Stadium, Male
Valencia 9		Goals - Mohamed 12, Nimal 75 for New Radiant

RECENT LEAGUE AND CUP RECORD

	National Championship				FA Cup			Cup Winners Cup		
Year	Winners	Score	Runners-up		Winners	Score	Runners-up	Winners	Score	Runners-up
1997	New Radiant	2-1	Hurriyya		New Radiant	2-0	Valencia	Valencia		
1998	Valencia	1-1 2-0	Victory		New Radiant	1-0	Hurriyya	Valencia	2-0	New Radiant
1999	Valencia	2-1	Hurriyya		Valencia	2-2 2-1	New Radiant	New Radiant	3-1	Victory
2000	Victory				Victory	3-0	Hurriyya	New Radiant		
2001	Victory	2-1	Valencia		New Radiant	1-1 2-0	Valencia	Victory	1-1 5-4p	Valencia
2002	Victory	4-2	Valencia		IFC	2-0	New Radiant	Victory	4-3	Valencia
2003	Victory	2-1	Valencia		IFC	1-0	Valencia	New Radiant	1-1 3-1p	Valencia
2004	New Radiant	1-1 6-5p	Valencia		Valencia	2-0	Victory	Valencia	1-0	IFC
2005					New Radiant	2-0	Valencia	Valencia	2-1	Victory

MEX – MEXICO

NATIONAL TEAM RECORD
JULY 1ST 2002 TO JUNE 30TH 2005

PL	W	D	L	F	A	%
51	27	15	9	99	37	67.6

A longstanding powerhouse of CONCACAF, Mexico usually have one foot in the FIFA World Cup™ finals before qualifying has even begun. The 2006 campaign has been no different with 12 of their first 13 games won, including a victory over arch rivals USA. Only Panama managed to take a point off the Mexicans during that run in which they scored 36 goals and let in just four. In the past Mexico have struggled when they have played outside of their region but that is beginning to change and at the 2005 FIFA Confederations Cup in Germany they were very impressive, winning their group courtesy of a victory over eventual winners Brazil before losing to Argentina on penalties in the semis. Defeat against Germany in a dramatic third place play-off was their first in 22 games. Shortly afterwards the squad decamped to the USA to defend their CONCACAF Gold Cup title, but after winning their first round group, during which Jared Borgetti equalled the all-time Mexican goalscoring record, they surprisingly lost in the quarter-finals to Colombia. At youth level there was also a major surprise when the U-20 team failed to qualify for the FIFA World Youth Championship in the Netherlands, finishing behind both Canada and Honduras in their

INTERNATIONAL HONOURS

Qualified for the FIFA World Cup™ finals 1930 1950 1954 1958 1962 1966 1970 (hosts) 1978 1986 (hosts) 1994 1998 2002
FIFA Confederations Cup 1999   **Qualified for the FIFA Women's World Cup finals** 1999
North American Championship 1947 1949   **CONCACAF Championship** 1965 1971   **CONCACAF Gold Cup** 1993 1996 1998 2003
CONCACAF U-20 1962 1970 1973 1976 1978 1980 1984 1990 1992   **CONCACAF U-17** 1985 1987 1991 1996
CONCACAF Club Championship Guadalajara 1962 Toluca 1968 2003 Cruz Azul 1969 1970 1971 1996 1997 America 1977 1990 1992
UAG Tecos 1978 UNAM Pumas 1980 1982 1989 Atlante 1983 Puebla 1991 Necaxa 1999 Pachuca 2002

qualifying group although the U-17 team did make it through to the FIFA finals in Peru. The 18-team Mexican League, in which most of the national squad are involved, is regarded as perhaps the strongest on the American continent and, as elsewhere, there are two Championships a year. Hugo Sanchez's UNAM Pumas won the 2004-05 Apertura after beating Monterrey over two legs in the final while glamour club América recovered from a very poor campaign in the Apertura to lose just one match on the way to capturing the Clausura title. The second leg of the final against UAG Tecos saw a nine goal thriller, the highest number of goals scored in a final, with America winning 6-3 to take the title 7-4 on aggregate. Straddling the two Americas, Mexican clubs enter both the Copa Libertadores and CONCACAF Champions Cup and in the former Tigres UANL, Pachuca and Chivas Guadalajara all reached the knockout stages with Guadalajara making the last four. UNAM Pumas made the final of the CONCACAF Champions Cup, but lost to Saprissa of Costa Rica who had prevented an all-Mexican final by beating Monterrey in the semis.

Federación Mexicana de Fútbol Asociación, A.C. (FMF)
Colima No. 373, Colonia Roma, Mexico D.F. 06700, Mexico
Tel +52 55 52410166   Fax +52 55 52410191
ddemaria@femexfut.org.mx   www.femexfut.org.mx
President: DE LA TORRE BOUVET Jose   General Secretary: DE MARIA SERRANO Decio
Vice-President: TBD   Treasurer: TBD   Media Officer: KOCHEN Juan Jose
Men's Coach: LA VOLPE Ricardo   Women's Coach: CUELLAR Leonardo
FMF formed: 1927   CONCACAF: 19   FIFA: 1929
Colours: Green, White, Red

GAMES PLAYED BY MEXICO IN THE 2006 FIFA WORLD CUP™ CYCLE

2002	Opponents	Score	Venue	Comp	Scorers	Att	Referee
No international matches played in 2002 after June							
2003							
4-02	Argentina	L 0-1	Los Angeles	Fr			Stott USA
12-02	Colombia	D 0-0	Mexico City	Fr		28 764	Valenzuela USA
19-03	Bolivia	W 2-0	Dallas	Fr	Pardo 27, Olalde 72	40 000	Terry USA
26-03	Paraguay	D 1-1	San Diego	Fr	Patino 72	35 000	Kennedy USA
30-04	Brazil	D 0-0	Guadalajara	Fr		60 000	Ruiz COL
8-05	USA	D 0-0	Houston	Fr		69 582	Prendergast JAM
6-07	El Salvador	L 1-2	Carson	Fr	Osorno 77	19 271	Hall USA
13-07	Brazil	W 1-0	Mexico City	GCr1	Borgetti 70	60 000	Sibrian SLV
17-07	Honduras	D 0-0	Mexico City	GCr1			Nery SLV
20-07	Jamaica	W 5-0	Mexico City	GCqf	Bravo 38, Garcia.R 42, Osorno 55, Borgetti 61, Rodriguez.J 63	10 000	Navarro CAN
24-07	Costa Rica	W 2-0	Mexico City	GCsf	Marquez 19, Borgetti 28	35 000	Alfaro SLV
27-07	Brazil	W 1-0	Mexico City	GCf	Osorno 97GG	80 000	Navarro CAN
20-08	Peru	L 1-3	New Jersey	Fr	Trujillo 54	30 143	Hall USA
15-10	Uruguay	L 0-2	Chicago	Fr		41 587	Kennedy USA
19-11	Iceland	D 0-0	San Francisco	Fr		17 000	Saheli USA
2004							
18-02	Chile	D 1-1	Carson	Fr	Bravo 49	26 000	Cruz USA
10-03	Ecuador	W 2-1	Tuxtla Gutierrez	Fr	Martinez.D 18p, Bravo 30	20 000	Batres GUA
31-03	Costa Rica	W 2-0	Carson	Fr	Garcia.R 13, Martinez.D 41 .	27 000	Stott USA
28-04	USA	L 0-1	Dallas	Fr		45 048	Navarro CAN
19-06	Dominica	W 10-0	San Antonio, USA	WCq	Bautista 2 9 38, Borgetti 2 11 36, Marquez 16, Osorno 49, Lozano 74 87, Davino 77, Palencia 92+	36 451	Callender BRB
27-06	Dominica	W 8-0	Aguascalientes	WCq	Bautista 2 2 36, Lozano 2 17 61, Borgetti 2 33 38, Oteo 59, Altamirano 76	17 000	Stott USA
7-07	Uruguay	D 2-2	Chiclayo	CAr1	Osorio 47+, Pardo 68	25 000	Hidalgo PER
10-07	Argentina	W 1-0	Chiclayo	CAr1	Morales 9	25 000	Rezende BRA
13-07	Ecuador	W 2-1	Piura	CAr1	Altamirano 26p, Bautista 42	21 000	Lecca PER
18-07	Brazil	L 0-4	Piura	CAqf		22 000	Ruiz COL
8-09	Trinidad and Tobago	W 3-1	Port of Spain	WCq	Arellano 2 1 80, Borgetti 19	20 000	Navarro CAN
6-10	St Vincent/Grenadines	W 7-0	Pachuca	WCq	Borgetti 4 31 68 77 89, Lozano 2 54 63, Santana 81	21 000	Liu CAN
10-10	St Vincent/Grenadines	W 1-0	Kingstown	WCq	Borgetti 25	2 500	Alfaro SLV
13-10	Trinidad and Tobago	W 3-0	Puebla	WCq	Naelson 19, Lozano 2 55 84	37 000	Sibrian SLV
27-10	Ecuador	W 2-1	New Jersey	Fr	Fonseca 2 42 47		Prus USA
10-11	Guatemala	W 2-0	San Antonio, USA	Fr	Osorno 67, Medina.A 69	21 921	Terry USA
13-11	St Kitts and Nevis	W 5-0	Miami	WCq	Altamirano 31, Fonseca 2 40 57, Santana 2 49 91	18 312	Moreno PAN
17-11	St Kitts and Nevis	W 8-0	Monterrey	WCq	Altamirano 10p, Perez.L 3 21 49 78, Fonseca 2 44 56, Osorno 52, Santana 67	12 000	Stott USA
2005							
26-01	Sweden	D 0-0	San Diego	Fr		35 521	Hall USA
9-02	Costa Rica	W 2-1	San Jose	WCq	Lozano 2 8 10	22 000	Batres GUA
23-02	Colombia	D 1-1	Culiacan	Fr	Fonseca 5	10 000	Gasso MEX
9-03	Argentina	D 1-1	Los Angeles	Fr	OG 23	51 345	Hall USA
27-03	USA	W 2-1	Mexico City	WCq	Borgetti 30, Naelson 32	84 000	Sibrian SLV
30-03	Panama	D 1-1	Panama City	WCq	Morales 26	13 000	Pineda HON
27-04	Poland	D 1-1	Chicago	Fr	Morales 52	54 427	Kennedy USA
4-06	Guatemala	W 2-0	Guatemala City	WCq	Zinha 41, Cabrera OG 45	26 723	Hall USA
8-06	Trinidad and Tobago	W 2-0	Monterrey	WCq	Borgetti 63, Perez.L 88	32 833	Stott USA
16-06	Japan	W 2-1	Hanover	CCr1	Zinha 39, Fonseca 64	24 036	Breeze AUS
19-06	Brazil	W 1-0	Hanover	CCr1	Borgetti 59	43 677	Rosetti ITA
22-06	Greece	D 0-0	Frankfurt	CCr1		31 285	Amarilla PAR
26-06	Argentina	D 1-1	Hanover	CCsf	Salcido 104	40 718	Rosetti ITA
29-06	Germany	L 3-4	Leipzig	CCsf	Fonseca 40, Borgetti 2 58 85	43 335	Breeze AUS
8-07	South Africa	L 1-2	Carson	GCr1	Rodriguez.F 83	27 000	Quesada CRC
10-07	Guatemala	W 4-0	Los Angeles	GCr1	Borgetti 2 5 14, Galindo 54, Bravo 65	30 710	Ruiz COL
13-07	Jamaica	W 1-0	Houston	GCr1	Medina 19	45 311	Quesada CRC
17-07	Colombia	L 1-2	Houston	GCqf	Pineda 65	60 050	Sibrian SLV

Fr = Friendly match • GC = CONCACAF Gold Cup • CA = Copa America • CC = FIFA Confederations Cup • WC = FIFA World Cup™
q = qualifier • r1 = first round group • qf = quarter-final • sf = semi-final • f = final

THE FIFA BIG COUNT OF 2000

	Male	Female		Male	Female
Registered players	208 481	1 518	Referees	3 832	95
Non registered players	5 000 000	2 000 000	Officials	20 000	600
Youth players	215 696	6 030	Total involved	7 456 252	
Total players	7 431 725		Number of clubs	1 493	
Professional players	15 000	0	Number of teams	20 009	

MEXICO NATIONAL TEAM RECORDS AND RECORD SEQUENCES

Records			Sequence records					
Victory	11-0	VIN 1992	Wins	8	1947-49, 2004	Clean sheets	6	1965-1966
Defeat	0-8	ENG 1961	Defeats	7	1950-1952	Goals scored	22	1930-1950
Player Caps	172	SUAREZ Claudio	Undefeated	21	2004-2005	Without goal	5	1975-1976
Player Goals	35	Three players	Without win	11	1971	Goals against	12	1957-1960

NATIONAL CAPS

	Caps
SUAREZ Claudio	172
CAMPOS Jorge	130
RAMIREZ Ramón	121
PARDO Pavel	115
GARCIA ASPE Alberto	109
HERMOSILLO Carlos	90
HERNANDEZ Luis	85
ALVES Zague Luis Roberto	84
CARMONA Salvador	84
BLANCO Cuauhtmémoc	83

NATIONAL GOALS

	Goals
HERMOSILLO Carlos	35
HERNANDEZ Luis	35
BORGETTI Jared	35
BORJA Enrique	31
ALVES Zague Luis Roberto	30
BLANCO Cuauhtémoc	30
FLORES Luis	29
GARCIA Postigo Luis	29
SANCHEZ Hugo	29
GALINDO Benjamin	28

NATIONAL COACH

	Years
VELARDE Mario	1987-'89
GUERRA Alberto	1990
LAPUENTE Manuel	1991
MENOTTI Luis Cesar	1992
BARON Miguel	1993-'95
MILUTINOVIC Bora	1995-'97
LAPUENTE Manuel	1997-'00
MEZA Enrique	2000-'01
AGUIRRE Javier	2001-'02
LA VOLPE Ricardo	2002-

FIFA REFEREE LIST 2005

	Int'l	DoB
ALCALA Gilbert	1994	25-07-1963
ARCHUNDIA Benito	1993	21-03-1966
ARREDONDO German	2001	27-05-1968
GASSO Jorge	1999	9-06-1969
GLOWER Manuel	2004	17-04-1972
LEON Hugo	2004	29-08-1970
MORALES Mauricio	2004	27-11-1967
RODRIGUEZ Marco	1999	10-11-1973

FIFA ASSISTANT REFEREE LIST 2005

	Int'l	DoB
CAMARGO Jose Luis	2005	25-09-1972
CRUZ Alejandro	1997	17-07-1964
DELGADILLO Hector	1997	30-08-1970
DELGADO Alfonso	2004	19-11-1967
MUNOZ Ramon	2001	24-02-1964
PEREZ Francisco	2005	27-11-1972
RAMIREZ JOSE	1999	27-11-1962
REBOLLAR Pedro	2004	11-09-1966
TREJO Oscar	1995	7-04-1960
VELAQUEZ Arturo	2003	15-12-1965

FIFA/COCA-COLA WORLD RANKING

1993	1994	1995	1996	1997	1998	1999	2000	2001	2002	2003	2004	High		Low	
16	15	12	11	5	10	10	12	9	8	7	7	4	02/98	19	11/94

2004-2005												
08/04	09/04	10/04	11/04	12/04	01/05	02/05	03/05	04/05	05/05	06/05	07/05	
8	8	10	8	7	7	6	6	8	7	6	5	

MEXICO COUNTRY INFORMATION

Capital	Mexico City	Independence	1836 from Spain	GDP per Capita	$9 000
Population	104 959 594	Status	Federal Republic	GNP Ranking	10
Area km²	1 972 550	Language	Spanish	Dialling code	+52
Population density	53 per km²	Literacy rate	92%	Internet code	.mx
% in urban areas	75%	Main religion	Christian	GMT + / -	-6
Towns/Cities ('000)	Mexico City 8 657; Guadalajara 1 640; Juárez 1 403; Puebla 1 392; Tijuana 1 376; Nezahualcóyotl 1 232; Monterrey 1 122; Léon 1 114; Zapopan 987; Naucalpan 846; Guadalupe 724; Mérida 717; Tlalnepantla 715; Chihuahua 708; Aguascalientes 658; Acapulco 652; Querétaro 611				
Neighbours (km)	Belize 250; Guatemala 962; USA 3 141; Pacific & Gulf of Mexico 9 330				
Main stadia	Azteca – Mexico City 101 000; Jalisco – Guadalajara 63 163; Universitario – Monterrey 45 000				

MEXICO 2004-05

PRIMERA DIVISION NACIONAL (APERTURA)

Group 1	Pl	W	D	L	F	A	Pts	Atlante	Pumas	Morelia	América	Dorados	UAG Tecos	Toluca	Atlas	Guadalajara	Tigres	Puebla	Cruz Azul	Veracruz	Pachuca	Monterrey	Necaxa	Santos	Jaguares
Atlante †	17	7	3	7	27	33	24		0-1	1-6	1-0			4-0	2-1	3-2		1-2	2-1				7-1		
UNAM Pumas †	17	7	2	8	25	31	23					3-2	0-1		1-5			1-3	2-3	2-3			1-3	2-1	2-1
Monarcas Morelia	17	6	4	7	29	30	22				0-0		3-2	2-0				1-1	1-2	0-2			1-5	1-1	2-1
América	17	5	5	7	17	23	20					0-3	2-3	3-2					0-1	2-1	1-1	1-1	1-0		
Dorados	17	4	4	9	25	32	16	0-1								0-1	0-1	2-0	3-3				3-2	2-1	0-0
UAG Tecos	17	4	4	9	17	29	16				1-0	1-2				2-3			1-1			3-2	0-1	1-0	0-1

Group 2	Pl	W	D	L	F	A	Pts	Atlante	Pumas	Morelia	América	Dorados	UAG Tecos	Toluca	Atlas	Guadalajara	Tigres	Puebla	Cruz Azul	Veracruz	Pachuca	Monterrey	Necaxa	Santos	Jaguares
Toluca †	17	10	2	5	27	15	32		0-1	3-1	0-1		1-1		0-2		4-1	1-0				3-2	4-0		
Atlas †	17	9	4	4	34	24	31			3-1	3-3		1-1				0-1	3-3	2-0	1-2	3-3				
Guadalajara †	17	8	5	4	34	22	29	7-0					2-1	1-1			2-2	1-1	1-3	3-1	3-1	1-0			
Tigres UANL	17	6	5	6	37	27	23			3-1	3-0	0-1		2-2	1-3				4-0		7-1	0-0	6-2		
Puebla	17	5	6	6	17	23	21			2-3	0-3				1-1					3-1	0-0	1-1	1-1	1-0	
Cruz Azul	17	4	4	9	30	37	16	2-0						3-3	5-2	1-3	2-4	1-1					0-1	1-0	3-4

Group 3	Pl	W	D	L	F	A	Pts	Atlante	Pumas	Morelia	América	Dorados	UAG Tecos	Toluca	Atlas	Guadalajara	Tigres	Puebla	Cruz Azul	Veracruz	Pachuca	Monterrey	Necaxa	Santos	Jaguares
Veracruz †	17	11	2	4	27	25	35	6-2				2-1	1-0	1-0		1-0			3-2				1-0	3-2	*0-2*
Pachuca †	17	9	5	3	30	19	32	1-1				1-0	2-0			1-1			3-1	1-2			4-1	2-1	3-0
Monterrey †	17	8	3	6	36	34	27		1-1	2-1			6-2						3-0	2-0	4-1			1-0	5-1
Necaxa	17	6	3	8	27	26	21		1-1				4-1			0-1	2-0	4-1	2-1		2-3				
Santos Laguna	17	5	3	9	22	22	18	2-1			1-1					0-1	2-0	4-1	2-1			1-1			4-2
Jaguares	17	4	6	7	20	29	18	0-0			2-1					1-3	1-2	0-0	1-1	1-1		2-2			

14/08/2004 - 20/11/2004 • † Qualified for the play-offs • Match in italics awarded 2-0 to Jaguares after Veracruz failed to turn up

MEXICO 2004-05

PRIMERA DIVISION NACIONAL (CLAUSURA)

Group 1	Pl	W	D	L	F	A	Pts	Morelia	América	UAG Tecos	Dorados	Atlante	Pumas	Cruz Azul	Tigres	Guadalajara	Toluca	Puebla	Atlas	Necaxa	Santos	Monterrey	Jaguares	Pachuca	Veracruz
Monarcas Morelia †	17	11	2	4	27	16	35		1-1			2-1		2-1	4-2	1-0	3-1	4-1					1-2		
América †	17	7	9	1	38	27	30			3-3		1-1		1-1	3-3	0-0				5-2	2-0	4-2		4-1	
UAG Tecos †	17	8	5	4	31	21	29	2-0					3-0	1-0	3-3	2-0	3-2	4-2						1-0	1-1
Dorados	17	7	5	5	23	19	26	0-1	0-1	1-0				2-1	1-1		0-0					1-0	3-1	2-0	
Atlante	17	5	5	7	24	21	20						1-1	2-0			1-1				2-3	3-0	2-0	1-1	5-1
UNAM Pumas	17	4	2	11	19	28	14	0-2	2-3			0-1		2-1			1-2	1-0	3-2			1-2			

Group 2	Pl	W	D	L	F	A	Pts	Morelia	América	UAG Tecos	Dorados	Atlante	Pumas	Cruz Azul	Tigres	Guadalajara	Toluca	Puebla	Atlas	Necaxa	Santos	Monterrey	Jaguares	Pachuca	Veracruz
Cruz Azul †	17	9	4	4	36	19	31	1-0	2-3						2-2		3-1	1-2				6-1		4-0	3-0
Tigres †	17	6	6	5	25	19	24					1-0	2-1	0-3			2-2	6-0		2-0	3-1		0-0		
Guadalajara	17	6	5	6	29	31	23							1-1	2-1		1-1			2-0	5-1		0-2	0-4	2-0
Toluca	17	6	5	6	17	22	23					1-2	1-0	0-2		2-1				1-0	2-0		1-2		1-1
Puebla	17	4	4	9	19	29	16		2-2	0-3		2-1		0-3	4-1	0-0				5-2	0-1		1-0		
Atlas	17	2	5	10	21	35	11					1-1	2-3	2-2		1-1	2-3	0-0		2-0	1-2		0-1		

Group 3	Pl	W	D	L	F	A	Pts	Morelia	América	UAG Tecos	Dorados	Atlante	Pumas	Cruz Azul	Tigres	Guadalajara	Toluca	Puebla	Atlas	Necaxa	Santos	Monterrey	Jaguares	Pachuca	Veracruz
Necaxa †	17	9	1	7	28	20	28	0-1		1-0	4-3	3-1	0-1									4-2	2-0	5-0	4-0
Santos Laguna †	17	9	1	7	31	31	28	3-1		4-2	2-1	1-1	2-0				2-0					3-1		2-0	4-1
Monterrey †	17	8	3	6	24	25	27		4-2	2-1		1-0		1-1	0-1	1-3	4-1	1-0	1-1						
Jaguares	17	6	4	7	19	23	22	0-2		1-1	2-2	2-0	1-3				2-0	1-1			0-1				4-3
Pachuca	17	5	5	7	20	27	20	0-1	2-2					1-3			1-1	1-1	1-1	3-1		2-0			
Veracruz	17	3	5	9	15	33	14	1-1	1-1			1-0		2-0			2-1	0-0		0-2			1-2		

15/01/2005 - 8/05/2005 • † Qualified for the play-offs.

APERTURA PLAY-OFFS

Quarter-finals		Semi-finals		Final
UNAM *	3 1			
Veracruz	0 1	UNAM *	4 2	
Guadalajara*	0 3	Atlas	3 1	8-12-2004/11-12-2004
Atlas	1 3			UNAM * 2 1
Atlante *	4 4			Monterrey 1 0
Toluca	2 3	Atlante *	2 1	
Pachuca	1 1	Monterrey	4 3	
Monterrey *	2 1	* Home team in the first leg		

APERTURA FINAL

First Leg. Olimpico, Mexico City, 8-12-2004. Ref: Morales

UNAM Pumas	2	Beltran [50], Toledo [81]
Monterrey	1	Franco [21]

Second Leg. Tecnologico, Monterrey, 11-12-2004. Ref: Archundia

Monterrey	0	
UNAM Pumas	1	Fonseca [46]

MEXICO 2004-05
PRIMERA A (2) APERTURA

Group 1	Pl	W	D	L	F	A	Pts
San Luis †	19	10	4	5	46	25	34
Atlético Mexiquense †	19	9	5	5	28	19	32
Broncos †	19	8	6	5	25	20	30
Colima	19	6	6	7	21	25	24
Chivas	19	4	5	10	28	41	17
Group 2							
Pioneros †	19	7	5	7	24	24	26
Mérida †	19	5	10	4	31	30	25
Durango	19	5	9	5	27	25	24
Lagartos	19	5	7	7	25	39	22
Coatzacoalcos	19	5	4	10	24	32	19
Group 3							
León †	19	9	5	5	26	18	32
Cruz Azul Oaxaca †	19	7	5	5	29	28	26
Atlético Celaya	19	6	6	8	23	24	26
Pachuca Jr	19	5	5	6	26	25	21
Potros Neza	19	5	5	4	21	30	19
Group 4							
Querétaro †	19	9	5	5	37	32	32
Cobras †	19	9	3	7	24	17	30
Correcaminos †	19	8	6	5	24	24	30
BUAP	19	8	5	6	25	23	29
Estudiantes	19	3	6	10	19	32	14

7/08/2004 - 19/12/2004 • † Qualified for the play-offs •
Repechaje: Pioneros 2-1 0-2 Broncos; Cruz Azul 3-0 0-4
Correcaminos

APERTURA PLAY-OFFS

Quarter-finals		Semi-finals		Final
San Luis	0 4			
Merida *	1 3	San Luis	1 5	
León	1 1	Cobras *	1 1	
Cobras *	2 2			San Luis 0 3
Querétaro	3 2			Mexiquense* 1 1
Broncos *	2 2	Querétaro	0 3	
Correcaminos*	0 1	Mexiquense	1 4	
Mexiquense	0 2	* Home team in the first leg		

CLAUSURA PLAY-OFFS

Quarter-finals		Semi-finals		Final
América	2 1			
Santos *	2 1	América *	3 3	
Monterrey *	0 3	Cruz Azul	1 1	26-05-2005/29-05-2005
Cruz Azul	0 3			América 1 6
Morelia	2 2			UAG Tecos* 1 3
Tigres *	3 1	Morelia	0 1	
Necaxa	0 1	UAG Tecos*	1 1	
UAG Tecos	2 2	* Home team in the first leg		

CLAUSURA FINAL

First Leg. 3 de Marzo, Guadalajara, 26-05-2005. Ref: Rodriguez

UAG Tecos	1	Colotto [59]
América	1	Blanco [87]

Second Leg. Azteca, Mexico City, 11-06-2005. Ref: Alcala

América	6	Padilla 2 [2 37], Lopez 3 [4 67 90], Blanco [62]
UAG Tecos	3	Lillingston [21], Morales [60], Davino [85]

MEXICO 2004-05
PRIMERA A (2) CLAUSURA

Group 1	Pl	W	D	L	F	A	Pts
San Luis †	19	9	6	4	33	21	33
Colima †	19	9	4	6	31	21	31
Broncos	19	9	2	8	36	40	29
Atlético Mexiquense	19	5	4	10	24	33	19
Chivas	19	3	8	8	14	32	17
Group 2							
Coatzacoalcos †	19	8	5	6	29	23	29
Durango †	19	8	4	7	22	22	28
Pioneros	19	6	6	7	25	28	24
Mérida	19	6	5	8	32	32	23
Lagartos	19	3	8	8	27	34	17
Group 3							
Cruz Azul Oaxaca †	19	10	5	4	42	29	35
Pachuca Jr †	19	10	3	6	25	23	33
León †	19	10	2	7	34	25	32
Atlético Celaya	19	9	5	5	26	23	32
Potros Neza	19	8	4	7	29	27	28
Group 4							
Querétaro †	19	7	5	7	28	25	26
Cobras	19	5	9	5	26	25	24
BUAP	19	5	6	8	24	27	21
Estudiantes	19	4	8	7	20	23	20
Correcaminos	19	5	3	11	29	43	18

15/01/2005 - 5/05/2005 • † Qualified for the play-offs •
Repechaje: Cobras 0-0 1-5 León; Durango 2-1 2-1 Celaya

CLAUSURA PLAY-OFFS

Quarter-finals		Semi-finals		Final
Querétaro *	1 2			
Cruz Azul	0 2	Querétaro *	3 3	
Durango *	2 1	Colima	0 0	
Colima	2 2			Querétaro * 2 1
Coat'coalcos*	2 1			León 1 1
San Luis	1 1	Coat'coalcos*	2 1	
Pachuca Jr	0 1	León	2 4	
León *	2 4	* Home team in the first leg		

CHAMPIONSHIP PLAY-OFF

Querétaro 2-1 0-2 San Luis

San Luis promoted to replace Puebla

UNAM PUMAS 2004

Date	Opponents	Score		Comp	Scorers
15-08-2004	UAG Tecos	L 0-1	H	AP	
21-08-2004	Atlante	W 1-0	A	AP	Del Olmo [64]
8-09-2004	Pachuca	L 2-3	H	AP	Del Olmo [28], Delgado [37]
11-09-2004	Toluca	W 1-0	A	AP	Oteo OG [68]
15-09-2004	Veracruz	L 2-3	H	AP	Verón [10], Lozano [11]
18-09-2004	Tigres UNAL	L 1-3	A	AP	Alonso [42]
26-09-2004	Cruz Azul	L 1-3	H	AP	Botero [39]
30-09-2004	Atlas	L 1-3	A	AP	Botero [54]
3-10-2004	Dorados	W 3-2	H	AP	Botero [11], Lozano [40], Iñiguez [51]
17-10-2004	América	W 3-0	A	AP	Botero [23], Davino OG [29], Iñiguez [32]
21-10-2004	Santos Laguna	W 2-1	H	AP	Botero [11], Iñiguez [30]
24-10-2004	Puebla	W 3-2	A	AP	Toledo [42], Botero [62], Alonso [90]
31-10-2004	Jaguares	W 2-1	H	AP	Alonso 2 [46 48]
4-11-2004	Monterrey	D 1-1	A	AP	Botero [1]
7-11-2004	Necaxa	L 1-3	H	AP	Alonso [7]
12-11-2004	Monarcas Morelia	D 0-0	A	AP	
21-11-2004	Guadalajara	L 1-5	H	AP	Toledo [87]
24-11-2004	Veracruz	W 3-0	H	APqf	Botero 2 [5 81], Lozano [73]
27-11-2004	Veracruz	D 1-1	A	APqf	Alonso [43]
2-12-2004	Atlas	W 4-3	H	APsf	Fonseca [10], Botero 2 [12 47], Alonso [83]
5-12-2004	Atlas	W 2-1	A	APsf	Fonseca [44], Lopez [48]
8-12-2004	Monterrey	W 2-1	H	APf	Beltrán [50], Toledo [81]
11-12-2004	Monterrey	W 1-0	A	APf	Fonseca [46]
16-01-2005	UAG Tecos	L 0-1	A	TC	
23-01-2005	Atlante	L 0-1	H	TC	
30-01-2005	Pachuca	W 3-2	A	TC	Lozano [73], Alonso 2 [74 81]
6-02-2005	Toluca	L 1-2	H	TC	Augusto [74]
12-02-2005	Veracruz	L 0-1	A	TC	
20-02-2005	Tigres UNAL	W 2-1	H	TC	Alonso [26], Lozano [31]
26-02-2005	Cruz Azul	D 2-2	A	TC	Lopez [28], Marioni [74]
6-03-2005	Atlas	W 3-2	H	TC	Galindo [42], Alonso [46], Beltrán [48]
9-03-2005	Olimpia - HON	D 1-1	A	CLqf	Alonso [83p]
12-03-2005	Dorados	L 1-2	A	TC	Marioni [46]
16-03-2005	Olimpia - HON	W 2-1	H	CLqf	Botero [17], Marioni [118]
20-03-2005	América	L 2-3	H	TC	Alonso [53], Lozano [74]
6-04-2005	DC United - USA	D 1-1	A	CLsf	Da Silva [51p]
10-04-2005	Puebla	W 1-0	H	TC	Marioni [42]
13-04-2005	DC United - USA	W 5-0	A	CLsf	Marioni [11], Beltrán 2 [48 73], Toledo [85], Lozano [88]
16-04-2005	Jaguares	L 0-2	A	TC	
20-04-2005	Monterrey	L 1-2	H	TC	Lozano [50]
23-04-2005	Necaxa	L 1-3	A	TC	Alonso [69]
27-04-2005	Santos Laguna	D 1-1	A	TC	Alonso [87]
1-05-2005	Monarcas Morelia	L 0-2	H	TC	
4-05-2005	Deportivo Saprissa - CRC	L 0-2	A	CLf	
8-05-2005	Guadalajara	L 1-2	A	TC	Da Silva [61]
11-05-2005	Deportivo Saprissa - CRC	W 2-1	H	CLf	Del Olmo [66], Augusto [89]

AP = Apertura • TC = Clausura • CL = CONCACAF Champions Cup • qf = quarter-final • sf = semi-final • f = final

RECENT LEAGUE RECORD

	Championship Play-off/Clausura				Apertura		
Year	Champions	Score	Runners-up		Winners	Score	Runners-up
1990	Puebla	2-1 4-3	Universidad Guadalajara				
1991	UNAM Pumas	1-0 2-3	América				
1992	León	2-0 0-0	Puebla				
1993	Atlante	1-0 3-0	Monterrey				
1994	UAG Tecos	2-0 0-1	Santos Laguna				
1995	Necaxa	2-0 1-1	Cruz Azul				
1996	Necaxa	1-1 0-0	Atlético Celaya				
1997	Guadalajara	1-1 6-1	Neza				
1998	Toluca	1-2 5-2	Necaxa				
1999	Toluca	3-3 2-2 5-4p	Atlas		Santos Laguna	0-1 4-2	Necaxa
2000	Toluca	2-0 5-1	Santos Laguna		Cruz Azul	1-0 1-1	Leon
2001	Santos Laguna	1-2 3-1	Pachuca		Necaxa	0-0 2-0	Guadalajara
2002	América	0-2 3-0	Necaxa		Pachuca	2-2 1-0	Cruz Azul
2003	Monterrey	3-1 0-0	Monarcas Morelia		Monarcas Morelia	3-1 0-2 5-4p	Toluca
2004	UNAM Pumas	1-1 0-0 5-4p	Guadalajara		Pachuca	2-0 1-1	Tigres UANL
2005	América	1-1 6-3	UAG Tecos		Toluca	0-1 4-1	Monarcas Morelia
					Pachuca	3-1 0-1	Tigres UANL
					UNAM Pumas	2-1 1-0	Monterrey

AMERICA 2004

Date	Opponents	Score			Comp	Scorers
15-08-2004	Dorados	W	3-2	H	AP	Lopez ^{14}, Navia ^{38}, Torres ^{79}
22-08-2004	UAG Tecos	L	0-1	A	AP	
29-08-2004	Santos Laguna	D	1-1	A	AP	Djalminha ^{88}
12-09-2004	Puebla	L	0-1	H	AP	
16-09-2004	Jaguares	L	1-2	A	AP	Padilla ^{77}
19-09-2004	Monterrey	W	1-0	H	AP	Perez ^{62}
25-09-2004	Necaxa	L	1-4	A	AP	Lopez ^{66}
29-09-2004	Monarcas Morelia	L	2-3	H	AP	Davino ^{73}, Navia ^{87}
2-10-2004	Guadalajara	D	1-1	A	AP	Mendoza ^{88}
17-10-2004	UNAM Pumas	L	0-3	H	AP	
21-10-2004	Atlante	L	0-1	A	AP	
24-10-2004	Pachuca	D	1-1	H	AP	Lopez ^{50}
30-10-2004	Toluca	W	1-0	A	AP	Padilla ^{77}
3-11-2004	Veracruz	D	1-1	H	AP	Pardo ^{61}
6-11-2004	Tigres UNAL	W	1-0	A	AP	Lopez ^{77}
13-11-2004	Cruz Azul	W	2-1	H	AP	Padilla ^{84}, Ortiz ^{90}
21-11-2004	Atlas	D	1-1	A	AP	Mendoza ^{71}
15-01-2005	Dorados	W	1-0	A	TC	Sanchez OG ^{49}
23-01-2005	UAG Tecos	D	3-3	H	TC	Rojas ^{1}, Padilla ^{26}, Torres ^{78}
30-01-2005	Santos Laguna	W	4-2	H	TC	Kleber 3 $^{6\ 61\ 90}$, Padilla ^{87}
6-02-2005	Puebla	D	2-2	A	TC	Kleber 2 $^{43\ 73}$
13-02-2005	Jaguares	W	4-1	H	TC	Rojas ^{11}, Kleber ^{24}, Lopez 2 $^{63\ 84}$
19-02-2005	Monterrey	L	2-4	A	TC	Lopez 2 $^{21\ 50}$
27-02-2005	Necaxa	W	2-0	H	TC	Kleber 2 $^{8\ 36}$
5-03-2005	Monarcas Morelia	D	1-1	A	TC	Lopez ^{53}
13-03-2005	Guadalajara	D	3-3	H	TC	Pardo ^{15}, Rojas ^{38}, Lopez ^{78}
20-03-2005	UNAM Pumas	W	3-2	A	TC	Rojas ^{13}, Kleber ^{51}, Lopez ^{70}
6-04-2005	Atlante	D	1-1	H	TC	Blanco ^{38}
10-04-2005	Pachuca	D	2-2	A	TC	Hurtado OG ^{13}, Blanco ^{18}
17-04-2005	Toluca	D	0-0	H	TC	
20-04-2005	Veracruz	D	1-1	A	TC	Kleber ^{1}
24-04-2005	Tigres UNAL	D	1-1	H	TC	Lopez ^{75}
30-04-2005	Cruz Azul	W	3-2	A	TC	Kleber ^{24}, Blanco ^{72}, Ortiz ^{72}
8-05-2005	Atlas	W	5-2	H	TC	Padilla 2 $^{17\ 57}$, Kleber ^{56}, Blanco ^{56}, Lopez ^{76}
12-05-2005	Santos Laguna	D	2-2	A	TCqf	Kleber ^{15}, Lopez ^{67}
15-05-2005	Santos Laguna	D	1-1	H	TCqf	Kleber ^{33}. América qualified due to a better record in the season
19-05-2005	Cruz Azul	W	3-1	A	TCsf	Blanco 2 $^{3\ 57}$, Lopez ^{82}
22-05-2005	Cruz Azul	W	3-1	H	TCsf	Padilla ^{14}, Torres ^{38}, Lopez ^{43}
26-05-2005	UAG Tecos	D	1-1	A	TCf	Blanco ^{87}
29-05-2005	UAG Tecos	W	6-3	H	TCf	Padilla 2 $^{2\ 37}$, Lopez 3 $^{4\ 67\ 90}$, Blanco ^{62}

AP = Apertura • TC = Clausura • CL = CONCACAF Champions Cup • qf = quarter-final • sf = semi-final • f = final

CLUB DIRECTORY

Club	Town/City	Stadium	Phone	www.	Lge	Cup	CL
América	Mexico City	Azteca 101 000	+52 5 6771781	esmas.com/clubamerica	14	6	3
Atlante	Mexico City	Azteca 101 000	+52 5 6110871	club-atlante.com	4	3	1
Atlas	Guadalajara	Jalisco 65 000	+52 3 6423232	atlas.com.mx	1	4	0
Cruz Azul	Mexico City	Azul 35 161	+52 5 6416416	cruz-azul.com.mx	8	2	5
Dorados	Culiacan	Carlos Gonzalez 13 717			0	0	0
Guadalajara	Guadalajara	Jalisco 65 000	+52 3 8175130	chivasdecorazon.com.mx	10	2	1
Jaguares	Tuxtla Gutierrez	Victor Manuel Reyna 25 000			0	0	0
Monarcas Morelia	Morelia	Jose Morelos y Pavon 41 552	+52 431 41188		1	0	0
Monterrey	Monterrey	Tecnologico 32 662	+52 8 3465401		2	1	0
Necaxa	Aguascalientes	Victoria 20 000	+52 5 8804742		7	7	1
Pachuca	Pachuca	Hidalgo 25 000	+52 771 87290	tuzos.com.mx	6	2	1
Puebla	Puebla	Cuauhtemoc 42 600	+52 22 222166	pueblafc.com.mx	2	4	1
Santos Laguna	Torreón	Corona 20 010	+52 17 174818		2	0	0
Tigres UANL	Monterrey	Universitario 43 000	+52 8 3760528	tigres.com.mx	2	2	0
Toluca	Toluca	Nemesio Diez 27 000	+52 72 155149	deportivotolucafc.com	7	2	2
UAG Tecos	Guadalajara	3 de Marzo 22 988	+52 3 6410237		1	1	1
UNAM Pumas	Mexico City	Olimpico 72 449	+52 5 6655775	pumasunam.com.mx	5	1	3
Veracruz	Veracruz	Luis Pirata Fuente 35 000	+52 55 248058		2	1	0

MGL – MONGOLIA

NATIONAL TEAM RECORD
JULY 1ST 2002 TO JUNE 30TH 2005

PL	W	D	L	F	A	%
12	3	2	7	11	42	33.3

FIFA/COCA-COLA WORLD RANKING

1993	1994	1995	1996	1997	1998	1999	2000	2001	2002	2003	2004	High		Low	
-	-	-	-	-	196	198	196	187	193	179	185	**179**	12/03	**200**	02/00

2004-2005											
08/04	09/04	10/04	11/04	12/04	01/05	02/05	03/05	04/05	05/05	06/05	07/05
185	184	184	184	185	185	185	182	182	183	183	183

Since joining FIFA in 1998, Mongolia have played just 24 internationals and those have been with limited success. In only their second game, they were beaten into submission by Uzbekistan who scored 15 without reply. Similarly hefty defeats have been inflicted by Hong Kong and most recently the Maldives in the preliminary qualifying round for the 2006 FIFA World Cup™. Having lost by just the one goal in the home leg to keep the tie finely balanced, Mongolia then collapsed in Malé to a 12-0 score line after being reduced to 10 men. After a 15-month hiatus the 2005 East Asian Federation Cup qualifiers provided the national team's next challenge where they started

INTERNATIONAL HONOURS
None

badly against Hong Kong and Korea DPR, but then beat Guam 4-0 (the only nation they have ever beaten) and drew with the hosts Chinese Taipei. FIFA's Goal programme had provided Mongolia in 2002 with an artificial pitch that offered a surface on which international matches could be played. The second phase of the project, which won approval in 2004, was for a mini-stadium to be built around the pitch that also incorporates a technical centre, spectator stands, dressing rooms and meeting rooms. The plan is that both domestic and international matches will be played here. Contested by six teams the MFF League was won in July 2005 by Khoromkhon for the first time.

THE FIFA BIG COUNT OF 2000

	Male	Female		Male	Female
Registered players	650	0	Referees	10	0
Non registered players	10 000	0	Officials	70	0
Youth players	700	30	Total involved	11 460	
Total players	11 380		Number of clubs	27	
Professional players	150	0	Number of teams	74	

Mongolia Football Federation (MFF)
PO Box 259, Ulaan-Baatar 210646, Mongolia
Tel +976 11 312145   Fax +976 11 312145
ubmaya@yahoo.com   www.none
President: AMARJARGAL Renchinnyam   General Secretary: GANBOLD Buyannemekh
Vice-President: TBD   Treasurer: OYUNTSETSEG Davaa   Media Officer: BAYARTSOGT Ganjuur
Men's Coach: OTGONBAYAR Ishdorj   Women's Coach: OTGONBAYAR Ishdorj
MFF formed: 1959   AFC: 1998   FIFA: 1998
Colours: White, Red, White

GAMES PLAYED BY MONGOLIA IN THE 2006 FIFA WORLD CUP™ CYCLE

2002	Opponents		Score	Venue	Comp	Scorers	Att	Referee
	No international matches played in 2002							
2003								
22-02	Macao	L	0-2	Hong Kong	EAq		6 055	Chan Siu Kee HKG
24-02	Guam	W	2-0	Hong Kong	EAq	Tugsbayar 52, Lumbengarav 59	1 602	Huang Junjie CHN
26-02	Chinese Taipei	L	0-4	Hong Kong	EAq		672	Chan Siu Kee HKG
28-02	Hong Kong	L	0-10	Hong Kong	EAq		1 814	
25-04	Guam	W	5-0	Thimphu	ACq	Batyalat 20, Tugsbayar 3 26 56 90, Lunmbengaran 61		
27-04	Bhutan	D	0-0	Thimphu	ACq			
29-11	Maldives	L	0-1	Ulaan-Baatar	WCq		2 000	Yang Zhiqiang CHN
3-12	Maldives	L	0-12	Malé	WCq		9 000	Arambekade SRI
2004								
	No international matches played in 2004							
2005								
5-03	Hong Kong	L	0-6	Taipei	EAq			
7-03	Korea DPR	L	0-6	Taipei	EAq			
9-03	Guam	W	4-1	Taipei	EAq	Tugsbayar 2 31 34, Bayarzorig 46, Buman-Uchral 81		
13-03	Chinese Taipei	D	0-0	Taipei	EAq			

EA = EAFF East Asian Championship • AC = AFC Asian Cup • WC = FIFA World Cup™ • q = qualifier

MONGOLIA NATIONAL TEAM RECORDS AND RECORD SEQUENCES

Records			Sequence records					
Victory	5-0	GUM 2003	Wins	1		Clean sheets	2	2003
Defeat	0-15	UZB 1998	Defeats	11	1998-2001	Goals scored	1	
Player Caps	n/a		Undefeated	2	2003, 2005	Without goal	5	2001, 2003-2005
Player Goals	n/a		Without win	13	1998-2003	Goals against	13	1998-2003

RECENT LEAGUE RECORD

	Championship		
Year	Champions	Score	Runners-up
1997	Delger	2-1	Erchim
1998	Erchim		Delger
1999	ITI Bank Bars		Erchim
2000	Erchim		Sonor
2001	Khangarid		Mon Uran
2002	Erchim		Khangarid
2003	Khangarid	2-1	Mon Uran
2004	Khangarid	1-0	Khoromkon
2005	Khoromkhon	1-0	Khangarid

MONGOLIA COUNTRY INFORMATION

Capital	Ulaan-Baatar	Independence	1921 from China	GDP per Capita	$1 800
Population	2 751 314	Status	Republic	GNP Ranking	156
Area km²	1 564 116	Language	Khalkha Mongol	Dialling code	+976
Population density	2 per km²	Literacy rate	97%	Internet code	.mn
% in urban areas	61%	Main religion	Buddhist 50%, None 40%	GMT + / –	+8
Towns/Cities ('000)	Ulaan-Baatar 844; Èrdènèt 76; Darhan 72; Cojbalsan 44; Ölgij 30; Sahnsand 28; Ulaangom 28				
Neighbours (km)	China 4 677; Russia 3 543				
Main stadia	National Sports Stadium – Ulaan-Baatar 20 000				

MKD – FYR MACEDONIA

NATIONAL TEAM RECORD
JULY 1ST 2002 TO JUNE 30TH 2005

PL	W	D	L	F	A	%
30	8	8	14	39	44	40

FIFA/COCA-COLA WORLD RANKING

1993	1994	1995	1996	1997	1998	1999	2000	2001	2002	2003	2004	High		Low	
-	90	94	86	92	59	68	76	89	85	92	92	58	01/99	147	05/94

2004-2005											
08/04	09/04	10/04	11/04	12/04	01/05	02/05	03/05	04/05	05/05	06/05	07/05
92	88	92	91	92	93	93	94	96	96	94	94

On the one hand the Macedonian national team holds a powerful Netherlands to a 2-2 draw in Skopje in the 2006 FIFA World Cup™ qualifiers and then four days later they lose to Andorra – the first nation ever to be beaten by the Andorrans in a competitive international. Inconsistency seems to be a fairly consistent trait with Macedonia. Qualification for the finals in Germany was never going to be on the cards in a very tough group but the defeat to Andorra was embarrassing as was a record defeat at the hands of the Czech Republic, the latter coming after the appointment of the Serb Slobodan Santrac as coach. Previous coach Dragan Kanatlarovski had resigned following

INTERNATIONAL HONOURS
None

the 0-0 draw in the return match against Andorra which saw another landmark for the Andorrans, their first ever away point. It was all change in Macedonian domestic football with new names on both the Championship trophy and the Cup. Club football remains relatively competitive with no team able to dominate, a fact that has seen six different teams win trophies over the past three years, with four of them first-time winners. Rabotnicki got the better of their Skopje rivals Vardar in the title race, with the two a long way ahead of 2004 Champions Pobeda, whilst Baskimi beat relegated Madzar with an injury-time winner in the Cup Final.

THE FIFA BIG COUNT OF 2000

	Male	Female		Male	Female
Registered players	11 223	0	Referees	820	0
Non registered players	17 000	0	Officials	1 000	0
Youth players	11 500	0	Total involved	41 543	
Total players	39 723		Number of clubs	594	
Professional players	223	0	Number of teams	919	

Football Federation of Macedonia (FFM)

8-ma Udarna brigada 31-a, Skopje 1000, FYR Macedonia
Tel +389 2 3229042   Fax +389 2 3165448
fsm@fsm.org.mk   www.ffm.com.mk
President: HADZIRISTESKI Haralampie   General Secretary: MITROVSKI Lazar
Vice-President: BEDZETI Redzep   Treasurer: TBD   Media Officer: None
Men's Coach: SANTRAC Slobodan   Women's Coach: DIMOVSKI Dobre
FFM formed: 1908   UEFA: 1994   FIFA: 1994
Colours: Red, Red, Red

GAMES PLAYED BY FYR MACEDONIA IN THE 2006 FIFA WORLD CUP™ CYCLE

2002	Opponents		Score	Venue	Comp	Scorers	Att	Referee
21-08	Malta	W	5-0	Skopje	Fr	Stojkov [37], Sakiri 2 [40 60], Hristov [54], Pandev [86]	4 000	Supraha CRO
8-09	Liechtenstein	D	1-1	Vaduz	ECq	Hristov [7]	2 300	Godulyan UKR
12-10	Turkey	L	1-2	Skopje	ECq	Grozdanovski [2]	15 000	Fisker DEN
16-10	England	D	2-2	Southampton	ECq	Sakiri [10], Trajanov [24]	32 095	Dauden Ibanez ESP
20-11	Israel	L	2-3	Skopje	Fr	Vasoski [63], Sedloski [89]	5 000	Delevic SCG
2003								
9-02	Croatia	D	2-2	Sibenik	Fr	Sedloski [10p], Toleski [60]	4 000	Zrnic BIH
14-02	Poland	L	0-3	Split	Fr		500	Trivkovic POL
29-03	Slovakia	L	0-2	Skopje	ECq		11 000	Duhamel FRA
2-04	Portugal	L	0-1	Lausanne	Fr		14 258	Nobs SUI
7-06	Liechtenstein	W	3-1	Skopje	ECq	Sedloski [39p], Krstev [51], Stojkov [82]	6 000	Jara CZE
11-06	Turkey	L	2-3	Istanbul	ECq	Grozdanovski [24], Sakiri [28]	23 000	Rosetti ITA
20-08	Albania	W	3-1	Prilep	Fr	Naumoski [9], Pandev [36], Dimitrovski [77]	3 000	Mihajlevic SCG
6-09	England	L	1-2	Skopje	ECq	Hristov [28]	20 500	De Bleeckere BEL
10-09	Slovakia	D	1-1	Zilina	ECq	Dimitrovski [62]	2 286	Sundell SWE
11-10	Ukraine	D	0-0	Kyiv	Fr		13 000	Orlic MDA
2004								
27-01	China PR	D	0-0	Shanghai	Fr		25 000	Lee Yu CHN
29-01	China PR	L	0-1	Shanghai	Fr		17 500	Zhig Yang CHN
18-02	Bosnia-Herzegovina	W	1-0	Skopje	Fr	Pandev [20]	8 000	Vrajkov BUL
31-03	Ukraine	W	1-0	Skopje	Fr	Stavrevski [26]	16 000	Karagic SCG
28-04	Croatia	L	0-1	Skopje	Fr		15 000	Arzuman TUR
11-06	Estonia	W	4-2	Tallinn	Fr	Sedloski [11], Popov [15], Pandev [31], Grozdanovski [65]	1 500	Fröjfeldt SWE
18-08	Armenia	W	3-0	Skopje	WCq	Pandev [5], Sakiri [37], Sumolikoski [90]	4 375	Guenov BUL
4-09	Romania	L	1-2	Craiova	WCq	Vasoski [70]	14 500	Plautz AUT
9-10	Netherlands	D	2-2	Skopje	WCq	Pandev [45], Stojkov [71]	15 000	Frojdfeldt SWE
13-10	Andorra	L	0-1	Andorra La Vella	WCq		350	Podeschi SMR
17-11	Czech Republic	L	0-2	Skopje	WCq		7 000	Meier SUI
2005								
9-02	Andorra	D	0-0	Skopje	WCq		5 000	Verbist BEL
30-03	Romania	L	1-2	Skopje	WCq	Maznov [31]	15 000	Ovrebo NOR
4-06	Armenia	W	2-1	Yerevan	WCq	Pandev 2 [29p 47]	2 870	Mikulski POL
8-06	Czech Republic	L	1-6	Teplice	WCq	Pandev [13]	14 150	Dauden Ibanez ESP

Fr = Friendly match • EC = UEFA EURO 2004™ • WC = FIFA World Cup™ • q = qualifier

FYR MACEDONIA NATIONAL TEAM RECORDS AND RECORD SEQUENCES

Records			Sequence records					
Victory	11-1	LIE 1996	Wins	4	1993-1994	Clean sheets	2	
Defeat	1-6	CZE 2005	Defeats	3	Four times	Goals scored	8	2002-2003
Player Caps	67	SHAKIRI Artim	Undefeated	8	1998	Without goal	4	2001-2002
Player Goals	16	HRISTOV Giorgji	Without win	19	2000-2002	Goals against	13	2001-2002

NATIONAL CAPS

	Caps
SHAKIRI Artim	67
SEDLOSKI Goce	62
HRISTOV Giorgji	47

NATIONAL GOALS

	Goals
HRISTOV Giorgji	16
SHAKIRI Artim	15
PANDEV Goran	9
CIRIC Sasa	8

NATIONAL COACH

	Years
KANATLAROVSKI Dragan	1999-'01
JOVANOVSKI Gjore	2001-'02
ILIEVSKI Nikola	2002-'04
KANATLAROVSKI Dragan	2004-'05
SANTRAC Slobodan	2005-

FYR MACEDONIA COUNTRY INFORMATION

Capital	Skopje	Independence	1991 from Yugoslavia	GDP per Capita	$6 700
Population	2 071 210	Status	Republic	GNP Ranking	126
Area km²	25 333	Language	Macedonian, Albanian	Dialling code	+389
Population density	82 per km²	Literacy rate	n/a	Internet code	.mk
% in urban areas	60%	Main religion	Christian 70%, Muslim 29%	GMT +/-	+1
Towns/Cities ('000)	Skopje 475; Kumanovo 108; Bittola 86; Prilep 74; Tetovo 73; Veles 58; Ohrid 55; Gostivar 51				
Neighbours (km)	Serbia and Montenegro 221; Bulgaria 148; Greece 246; Albania 151				
Main stadia	City Stadium - Skopje 22 000; City Stadium - Tetovo 20 500				

FYR MACEDONIA 2004-05

PRVA LIGA

Team	Pl	W	D	L	F	A	Pts	Rabotnicki	Vardar	Pobeda	Sileks	Shkendija	Baskimi	Belasica	Bregalnica	Cement'ca	Madzari	Sloga	Napredok
Rabotnicki Skopje †	33	25	3	5	66	23	78	—	0-0 1-3	3-2	3-0 3-0	3-0	0-2 1-0	1-1 2-0	2-1	3-0	4-0 3-0	1-0 1-0	3-1
Vardar Skopje ‡	33	22	6	5	68	34	72	0-1	—	2-0 4-2	1-1	1-0 3-0	4-1	2-1	2-1 4-1	3-2 3-3	3-1 1-0	3-1	1-3 3-0
Pobeda Prilep	33	16	7	10	59	49	55	0-4 0-0	1-0	—	1-0 2-1	1-1	3-1 2-1	4-0 2-1	5-2	2-0	3-1 3-3	4-1 1-0	4-1
Sileks Kratovo	33	15	6	12	56	37	51	0-1	1-2 0-2	2-2	—	2-0 3-1	1-0	2-0	1-0 0-1 3-0 1-3	1-3	5-1	5-1	4-0 8-0
Shkendija Tetovo	33	15	5	13	59	40	50	0-1 2-1	0-0	4-1 3-2	4-0	—	3-0 1-1	4-2 2-1	3-4	1-0	1-0 2-1	3-0 7-0	2-0
Baskimi Kumanovo ‡	33	14	7	12	53	47	49	1-2	0-1 4-2	0-2	2-2 2-1	2-1	—	2-1	4-0 2-2 1-0 4-3	1-2 1-1	0-2	3-1	6-1
Belasica Strumica	33	14	6	13	53	47	48	3-1	3-1 2-1	3-0	1-1 3-2	1-1	1-3 0-0	—	2-0	0-0 2-1	1-1	3-1 5-3	3-2
Bregalnica Stip	33	14	6	13	55	60	48	1-4 4-2	2-3	0-0 1-1	0-0	2-1 2-1	2-2 1-1	1-0	—	1-0	2-1	4-1	4-1 6-1
Cementarnica Skopje	33	13	7	13	54	50	43	1-3 0-1	1-1	0-2 5-3	2-0	1-0 2-1	2-1	2-2 6-1 1-1	2-1	—	2-1	2-1	5-2 5-1
Madzari Skopje	33	12	5	16	35	46	41	0-2	1-2	2-1	0-2	0-0	0-1	1-0 0-3	1-0 2-0	0-0 0-1 2	—	3-2 1-0	1-0 3-0
Sloga Jugomagnat	33	5	2	26	37	80	17	1-3	1-2 1-4	3-2	0-1 0-1	1-7	0-1 2-2	1-2	4-1 2-3	0-2 2-3	1-2	—	3-0
Napredok Kicevo	33	1	4	28	17	99	7	0-3 0-3	0-4	0-0 0-1	0-5	0-3 2-0	1-2	0-1 1-5	0-3	0-0	0-3 0-1	1-1	—

8/08/2004 - 15/05/2005 • † Qualified for the UEFA Champions League • ‡ Qualified for the UEFA Cup • Matches in bold awarded 3-0 • § Three points deducted
Relegation play-offs: Makedonija 2-1 Madzari; Cementarnica 2-1 Turnovo

FYR MACEDONIA 2004-05 VTORA LIGA (2)

	Pl	W	D	L	F	A	Pts
Vlazrimi Kicevo	33	24	3	6	70	34	75
Renova Cepchiste	33	22	5	6	63	27	71
Makedonija Skopje	33	22	5	6	76	34	71
Turnovo	33	18	4	11	59	40	58
Teteks Tetovo	33	17	5	11	46	31	56
Pelister Bitola	33	12	7	14	40	43	43
Skopje	33	11	8	14	46	49	41
Bratstvo Resen	33	9	10	14	32	45	37
Mladost Susica	33	10	7	16	32	46	37
Tikves Kavadarci	33	9	4	20	36	55	13
Bregalnitsa Delcevo	33	6	5	22	29	76	23
Shkendija Skopje	33	5	3	25	30	79	18

7/08/2004 - 28/05/2005

FA CUP 2004-05

Quarter-finals		Semi-finals		Final	
Baskimi	0 1				
Bregalnica *	0 0	Baskimi	0 2		
Rabotnicki *	0 0	Sileks *	1 0		
Sileks	2 0			Baskimi ‡	2
Turnovo *	2 2			Madzari	1
Vlazrimi	1 1	Turnovo	0 0		
Sloga	0 1	Madzari *	1 0		
Madzari *	2 0				

* Home team • ‡ Qualified for the UEFA Cup

24-05-2005, Att:10 000
Gradski, Skopje
Scorers - Presilski 2 78 92 + for Baskimi; Aleksovski 11 for Madzari

CLUB DIRECTORY

Club	Town/City	Stadium	Phone	www.	Lge	Cup	CL
Baskimi	Kumanovo	Gradski Arena 7 000	+389 31 322200		0	1	0
Belasica Geras Cunev	Strumica	Mladost 6 370	+389 34 329211	belasica.com.mk	0	0	0
Bregalnica	Stip	City Stadium 10 000	+389 32 389500		0	0	0
Cementarnica	Skopje	Cementarnica 2 000	+389 22 782528		0	1	0
Madzari	Skopje	Madzari 5 000	+389 22 530819		0	0	0
Napredok	Kicevo	City Stadium 5 000	+389 45 226000		0	0	0
Pobeda	Prilep	Goce Delcev 15 000	+389 48 423380		1	1	0
Rabotnicki	Skopje	City Stadium 22 000	+389 23 164044		1	0	0
Shkendija	Tetovo	City Stadium 20 500	+389 44 341812		0	0	0
Sileks	Kratovo	Sileks 3 000	+389 31 481830		3	2	0
Sloga Jugomagnat	Skopje	Cair 4 500	+389 22 616694	sloga-jugomagnat.com.mk	3	3	0
Vardar	Skopje	City Stadium 22 000	+389 23 222271	fkvardar.com.mk	5	4	0

RECENT LEAGUE AND CUP RECORD

Year	Champions	Pts	Runners-up	Pts	Third	Pts	Winners	Score	Runners-up
1993	Vardar Skopje	61	Sileks Kratovo	40	Balkan Skopje	40	Vardar Skopje	1-0	Pelister Bitola
1994	Vardar Skopje	51	Sileks Kratovo	44	Balkan Stokokomerc	37	Sileks Kratovo	1-1 4-2p	Pelister Bitola
1995	Vardar Skopje	76	Sileks Kratovo	60	Sloga Jugomagnat	58	Vardar Skopje	2-1	Sileks Kratovo
1996	Sileks Kratovo	70	Sloga Jugomagnat	58	Vardar Skopje	57	Sloga Jugomagnat	0-0 5-3p	Vardar Skopje
1997	Sileks Kratovo	62	Pobeda Prilep	54	Sloga Jugomagnat	42	Sileks Kratovo	4-2	Sloga Jugomagnat
1998	Sileks Kratovo	48	Sloga Jugomagnat	43	Makedonija Skopje	42	Vardar Skopje	2-0	Sloga Jugomagnat
1999	Sloga Jugomagnat	60	Sileks Kratovo	57	Pobeda Prilep	53	Vardar Skopje	2-0	Sloga Jugomagnat
2000	Sloga Jugomagnat	61	Pobeda Prilep	52	Rabotnicki Skopje	50	Sloga Jugomagnat	6-0	Pobeda Prilep
2001	Sloga Jugomagnat	63	Vardar Skopje	63	Pobeda Prilep	56	Pelister Bitola	2-1	Sloga Jugomagnat
2002	Vardar Skopje	37	Belasica Strumica	36	Cementarnica	27	Pobeda Prilep	3-1	Cementarnica
2003	Vardar Skopje	72	Belasica Strumica	69	Pobeda Prilep	65	Cementarnica	4-4 3-2p	Sloga Jugomagnat
2004	Pobeda Prilep	71	Sileks Kratovo	66	Vardar Skopje	60	Sloga Jugomagnat	1-0	Napredok Kicevo
2005	Rabotnicki Skopje	78	Vardar Skopje	72	Pobeda Prilep	55	Baskimi Kumanovo	2-1	Madzari Skopje

MLI – MALI

NATIONAL TEAM RECORD
JULY 1ST 2002 TO JUNE 30TH 2005

PL	W	D	L	F	A	%
34	19	6	9	52	28	64.7

FIFA/COCA-COLA WORLD RANKING

1993	1994	1995	1996	1997	1998	1999	2000	2001	2002	2003	2004	High		Low	
70	52	52	67	80	70	72	98	112	73	54	51	**43**	09/04	**117**	10/01

2004-2005											
08/04	09/04	10/04	11/04	12/04	01/05	02/05	03/05	04/05	05/05	06/05	07/05
46	43	44	47	51	51	53	54	57	61	59	59

Mali looked to be on the cusp of something great when, after earning semi-final places at the 2002 and 2004 African Cup of Nations tournaments and the quarter-finals of the 2004 Olympics, they qualified for the group stage of the 2006 FIFA World Cup™. With a growing number of professional players, many considered the Eagles a good outside bet to reach Germany, but having gone on an unbeaten run between October 2002 and February 2004, a run that included 15 wins in 16 games, Mali's good form deserted them in disastrous fashion. It left the team struggling at the bottom of their qualifying group and without even a place at the 2006 CAF African Cup of Nations

INTERNATIONAL HONOURS
None

finals in Egypt. Despondent fans decided enough was enough causing a riot after a 2-1 home defeat to Togo in March 2005. Locally it was a great season for Djoliba FC of Bamako, who after four years as bridesmaids to Stade Malien, finally pipped their arch-rivals to the League title. Opening the season with a defeat, Djoliba put together an unbeaten run of 25 games scoring 73 goals. They completed the double by retaining the Coupe du Mali after beating Nianan de Koulikoro 2-0 in the final. The Champions League proved more difficult though and the double winners were eliminated by AS Douanes of Senegal.

THE FIFA BIG COUNT OF 2000

	Male	Female		Male	Female
Registered players	3 900	0	Referees	462	8
Non registered players	1 000 000	1 500	Officials	4 336	462
Youth players	6 980	510	Total involved	1 018 158	
Total players	1 012 890		Number of clubs	407	
Professional players	0	0	Number of teams	103 400	

Fédération Malienne de Football (FMF)
Avenue du Mali, Hamdallaye ACI 2000, PO Box 1020, Bamako 12582, Mali
Tel +223 2238844   Fax +223 2224254
malifoot@afribone.net.ml   www.none
President: KEITA Salif   General Secretary: TRAORE Jacouba
Vice-President: KEITA Karounga   Treasurer: TRAORE Brehima   Media Officer: KOUYATE Mamadou
Men's Coach: LECHANTRE Pierre   Women's Coach: LAICO Moustapha
FMF formed: 1960   CAF: 1963   FIFA: 1962
Colours: Green, Yellow, Red

GAMES PLAYED BY MALI IN THE 2006 FIFA WORLD CUP™ CYCLE

2002	Opponents	Score		Venue	Comp	Scorers	Att	Referee
8-09	Zimbabwe	L	0-1	Harare	CNq		50 000	Mochubela RSA
2-10	Mauritania	W	2-1	Bamako	Fr			
5-10	Mauritania	W	2-0	Bamoko	Fr			
13-10	Seychelles	W	3-0	Bamako	CNq	Keita.S [31], Sidibe.M [77], Coulibaly.Dr [85]	50 000	Sorie SLE
20-11	Morocco	W	3-1	Rabat	Fr	Sidibe.D [56], Coulibaly.Dr 2 [80][90]	15 000	Tahiri MAR
2003								
12-02	Guinea	W	1-0	Toulon	Fr	Doukantie [20]		
30-03	Eritrea	W	2-0	Asmara	CNq	Thiam [54], Coulibaly.Dr [90]		Abdulkadir TAN
27-04	Madagascar	W	2-0	Paris	Fr	Toure.B [25], Bagayoko [73]		
7-06	Eritrea	W	1-0	Bamako	CNq	Coulibaly.S [20]		Aboubacar CIV
22-06	Zimbabwe	D	0-0	Bamako	CNq			
5-07	Seychelles	W	2-0	Victoria	CNq	Traore.S [60], Bagayoko [90]	5 000	Lim Kee Chong MRI
10-10	Guinea-Bissau	W	2-1	Bissau	WCq	Keita.S [8], Coulibaly.S [69]	22 000	Sowe GAM
14-11	Guinea-Bissau	W	2-0	Bamako	WCq	Coulibaly.S [15], Sidibe.D [84p]	13 251	Seydou MTN
19-11	Morocco	W	1-0	Meknes	Fr	Coulibaly.Dv [35]	6 000	Shelmani LBY
2004								
15-01	Algeria	W	2-0	Algiers	Fr	Traore.D [4], Toure.B [57]	7 000	Zehmoun TUN
26-01	Kenya	W	3-1	Bizerte	CNr1	Sissoko [27], Kanoute 2 [63][82]	6 000	Tessema ETH
30-01	Burkina Faso	W	3-1	Tunis	CNr1	Kanoute [33], Diarra.M [37], Coulibaly.S [78]	1 500	Shelmani LBY
2-02	Senegal	D	1-1	Tunis	CNr1	Traore.D [33]	7 550	Evehe CAM
7-02	Guinea	W	2-1	Bizerte	CNqf	Kanoute [45], Diarra.M [90]	1 450	Abd El Fatah EGY
11-02	Morocco	L	0-4	Sousse	CNsf		15 000	Aboubacar CIV
13-02	Nigeria	L	1-2	Monastir	CN3p	Abouta [70]	2 500	Sowe GAM
28-04	Tunisia	L	0-1	Sfax	Fr		8 000	Shelmani LBY
28-05	Morocco	D	0-0	Bamako	Fr		35 000	
6-06	Liberia	L	0-1	Monrovia	WCq		30 000	Codjia BEN
19-06	Zambia	D	1-1	Bamako	WCq	Kanoute [80]	19 000	Sowe GAM
4-07	Congo	L	0-1	Brazzaville	WCq		20 000	Evehe CMR
18-08	Congo DR	W	3-0	Paris	Fr	Keita.S 2 [2][21], Kanoute [81]		Bruno FRA
5-09	Senegal	D	2-2	Bamako	WCq	Diallo.M [4], Kanoute [54]	45 000	Guezzaz MAR
10-10	Togo	L	0-1	Lome	WCq		45 000	Njike CMR
2005								
9-02	Guinea	D	2-2	Paris	Fr	Traore.D [8], Diao [51]	2 000	
27-03	Togo	L	1-2	Bamako	WCq	Coulibaly.S [12]	45 000	Agbenyega GHA
5-06	Liberia	W	4-1	Liberia	WCq	Coulibaly.D 2 [7p][34], Diamoutene [48p], Diarra.M [75]	11 000	Pare BFA
12-06	Algeria	W	3-0	Arles	Fr	Coulibaly.D [33], Dissa 2 [58][79]	2 000	Derrien FRA
17-06	Zambia	L	1-2	Chililabombwe	WCq	Coulibaly.S [73]	29 000	Colembi ANG

Fr = Friendly match • CN = CAF African Cup of Nations • WC = FIFA World Cup™
q = qualifier • r1 = first round group • qf = quarter-final • sf = semi-final • 3p = third place play-off

MALI NATIONAL TEAM RECORDS AND RECORD SEQUENCES

Records			Sequence records				
Victory	6-0	MTN 1975	Wins	8	2002-2003	Clean sheets	6	2003
Defeat	1-8	KUW 1997	Defeats	5	1997	Goals scored	11	1971-1972
Player Caps	n/a		Undefeated	18	2002-2004	Without goal	4	Three times
Player Goals	n/a		Without win	8	1989-90, 1995-96	Goals against	12	1987-1988

MALI COUNTRY INFORMATION

Capital	Bamako	Independence	1960 from France	GDP per Capita	$900
Population	11 956 788	Status	Republic	GNP Ranking	134
Area km²	1 240 000	Language	French, Bambara	Dialling code	+223
Population density	10 per km²	Literacy rate	46%	Internet code	.ml
% in urban areas	27%	Main religion	Muslim 90%	GMT +/−	0
Towns/Cities ('000)	Bamako 1 297; Sikasso 144; Mopti 109; Koutiala 100; Kayes 97; Ségou 95; Nioro 72				
Neighbours (km)	Algeria 1 376; Niger 821; Burkina Faso 1 000; Cote d'Ivoire 532; Guinea 858; Senegal 419; Mauritania 2 237				
Main stadia	Stade 26 Mars – Bamako 50 000; Stade Omnisports – Sikasso 20 000				

MALI 2004

PREMIERE DIVISION

	Pl	W	D	L	F	A	Pts	Djoliba	Stade	CSK	CO	AS	Real	USFAS	Comune II	Biton	Nianan	Mande	Sigui	Tata	Moribab.
Djoliba Bamako †	26	19	6	1	73	18	63		1-0	1-0	0-0	2-1	2-2	0-1	3-0	2-1	5-0	3-1	9-0	4-1	6-1
Stade Malien Bamako	26	18	4	4	51	17	58	0-3		1-1	1-1	2-0	2-2	2-0	4-0	3-0	1-0	1-0	3-0	2-0	3-2
Centre Salif Keita	26	18	4	4	52	20	58	0-2	**1-0**		0-2	0-2	2-0	3-0	4-1	4-0	2-0	2-2	3-1	3-0	2-0
Cercle Olympique	26	14	8	4	40	18	50	1-1	1-0	1-1		3-1	**0-1**	0-0	1-1	**0-1**	4-0	0-0	4-0	2-0	3-0
AS Bamako	26	13	5	8	33	26	44	2-2	0-0	1-2	0-2		0-0	1-0	1-0	2-1	2-0	2-0	3-0	2-1	1-0
Real Bamako	26	12	7	7	36	26	43	0-2	1-4	0-1	1-3	2-4		**1-0**	0-0	3-1	0-0	1-0	5-0	5-0	1-1
USFAS Bamako	26	9	6	11	25	32	33	1-7	1-3	1-2	0-2	1-1	0-1		0-1	2-0	0-2	0-0	4-1	1-1	0-0
Comune II	26	8	5	13	26	41	29	1-1	1-3	1-6	2-2	0-1	0-3	0-1		0-1	0-1	1-0	0-0	0-2	1-0
Biton Ségou	26	9	1	16	22	40	28	0-3	1-4	1-2	1-0	1-0	1-2	0-1	0-1		**0-1**	2-1	1-0	1-1	2-0
Nianan Koulikoro ‡	26	8	3	15	22	36	27	1-1	0-2	0-2	0-1	1-2	0-1	1-2	2-3	3-1		2-0	3-1	1-0	0-1
Mande Bamako	26	6	5	15	20	34	23	2-4	0-1	2-2	0-1	1-0	0-1	0-2	2-1	0-2	1-0		2-0	1-1	3-1
Sigui Kayes	26	7	2	17	24	66	23	1-4	1-5	0-3	2-3	3-1	1-0	0-2	2-3	1-3	3-2	1-0		2-1	1-0
Tata National Sikasso	26	4	8	14	25	46	20	1-2	0-3	0-2	5-2	1-1	2-2	1-3	1-3	2-0	0-0	1-2	1-1		1-1
Moribabougou Koulikoro	26	3	4	19	17	46	13	0-3	0-1	1-2	0-1	1-2	0-1	2-2	0-5	2-0	1-2	2-0	1-2	0-1	

28/02/2004 - 27/09/2004 • † Qualified for the CAF Champions League • ‡ Qualified for the CAF Confederation Cup • Matches in bold were awarded by the Federation • Relegation play-off: Tata National 1-0 Bakaridjan Baroueli

COUPE DU MALI 2004

Round of 16

Djoliba Bamako	2
Bakaridjan Baroueli	1
Sigui Kayes	0
Moribabougou	2
Biton Ségou	2
Union Sportive Kita	1
Al Farouk Tombouctou	1
Stade Malien	3
Real Bamoko	4
Stade Malien Sikasso	0
Sonni Gao	0
Tata National	1
Centre Salif Keita	3
Maliano-Belge Mopti	0
Debo Club Mopti	1
Nianan Koulikoro	2

Quarter-finals

Djoliba Bamako	2
Moribabougou	0
Biton Ségou	0
Stade Malien	1
Real Bamoko	1
Tata National	0
Centre Salif Keita	1
Nianan Koulikoro	2

Semi-finals

Djoliba Bamako	1
Stade Malien	0
Real Bamoko	0
Nianan Koulikoro	1

Final

Djoliba Bamako	2
Nianan Koulikoro	0

CUP FINAL

19-09-2004, Att: 20 000
Stade 26 Mars, Bamako.
Scorers - Tamboura 34, Abouta 70

RECENT LEAGUE AND CUP RECORD

	Championship							Cup		
Year	Champions	Pts	Runners-up	Pts	Third	Pts		Winners	Score	Runners-up
1996	Djoliba		Real Bamako		Stade Malien			Djoliba	2-1	Real Bamako
1997	Djoliba							Stade Malien	2-0	Real Bamako
1998	Djoliba		Centre Salif Keita		USFAS			Djoliba	1-0	Stade Malien
1999	Djoliba	54	USFAS	53	Centre Salif Keita	50		Stade Malien	1-0	Nianan
2000	Stade Malien	52	Djoliba	47	Centre Salif Keita	40		Cercle Olympique	1-0	Stade Malien
2001	Stade Malien	66	Djoliba	54	Cercle Olympique	45		Stade Malien	5-0	Mamahira Kati
2002	Stade Malien	68	Djoliba	61	Centre Salif Keita	54		Cercle Olympique	2-1	Stade Malien
2003	Stade Malien	62	Djoliba	60	Cercle Olympique	53		Djoliba	2-1	Tata National
2004	Djoliba	63	Stade Malien	58	Centre Salif Keita	58		Djoliba	2-0	Nianan

MLT – MALTA

NATIONAL TEAM RECORD
JULY 1ST 2002 TO JUNE 30TH 2005

PL	W	D	L	F	A	%
26	1	5	20	18	83	13.5

FIFA/COCA-COLA WORLD RANKING

1993	1994	1995	1996	1997	1998	1999	2000	2001	2002	2003	2004	High		Low	
83	78	90	122	133	130	116	119	131	122	129	134	**66**	09/94	**137**	03/05

2004-2005											
08/04	09/04	10/04	11/04	12/04	01/05	02/05	03/05	04/05	05/05	06/05	07/05
131	130	133	132	134	135	136	137	137	136	137	137

It was more of the same for Malta in the 2004-05 season with the top three in the League unchanged from the previous season whilst the national team continued to struggle even against smaller nations like themselves. There have been a couple of opportunities to add to the single game won in the three years since the 2002 FIFA World Cup™ finals but the 5-2 victory over Estonia in February 2004 is still all that the team have managed. Given the run of four wins and two draws in late 2001 and early 2002 the drop in form is especially disappointing. In the 2006 FIFA World Cup™ qualifiers a single point from a draw against Iceland left Malta rooted to the

INTERNATIONAL HONOURS
None

bottom of the table going into the final stages with little hope of improving on that position. That is something the team have managed just once before, in the 1994 qualifiers, coinciding with their only win in a FIFA World Cup™ match against the unfortunate Estonians. In the Maltese Championship Sliema Wanderers completed a hat-trick of titles with Birkirkara also finishing as runners-up for the third year in a row. It was a record 26th title for Sliema who move one ahead of rivals Floriana. The consolation for Birkirkara was a third Cup triumph in the past four years after they beat first time finalists Msida St Joseph 2-1 in the National Stadium in Ta'Qali.

THE FIFA BIG COUNT OF 2000

	Male	Female		Male	Female
Registered players	6 350	200	Referees	101	5
Non registered players	3 000	0	Officials	2 000	50
Youth players	4 000	75	Total involved	15 781	
Total players	13 625		Number of clubs	56	
Professional players	350	0	Number of teams	198	

Malta Football Association (MFA)
280 St Paul Street, Valletta VLT 07, Malta
Tel +356 21 232581   Fax +356 21 245136
info@mfa.com.mt   www.mfa.com.mt
President: MIFSUD Joseph Dr   General Secretary: GAUCHI Joseph
Vice-President: BARTOLO Carmelo   Treasurer: MANFRE Alex   Media Officer: VELLA Alex
Men's Coach: HEESE Horst & BUSUTTIL Carmel   Women's Coach: BRINCAT Pierre
MFA formed: 1900   UEFA: 1960   FIFA: 1959
Colours: Red, White, Red

GAMES PLAYED BY MALTA IN THE 2006 FIFA WORLD CUP™ CYCLE

2002	Opponents	Score	Venue	Comp	Scorers	Att	Referee
21-08	FYR Macedonia	L 0-5	Skopje	Fr		4 000	Supraha CRO
7-09	Slovenia	L 0-3	Ljubljana	ECq		7 000	Borovilos GRE
12-10	Israel	L 0-2	Ta'Qali	ECq		5 200	Shebek UKR
16-10	France	L 0-4	Ta'Qali	ECq		10 000	Tudor ROU
20-11	Cyprus	L 1-2	Nicosia	ECq	Mifsud.Mc [90]	5 000	Guenov BUL
2003							
12-02	Kazakhstan	D 2-2	Ta'Qali	Fr	Bogdanovic [15], Nwoko [61]	200	Rogalla SUI
29-03	France	L 0-6	Lens	ECq		40 775	Bozinovski MKD
30-04	Slovenia	L 1-3	Ta'Qali	ECq	Mifsud.Mc [90]	5 000	Hanacsek HUN
7-06	Cyprus	L 1-2	Ta'Qali	ECq	Dimech [72]	3 000	Brugger AUT
19-08	Luxembourg	D 1-1	Luxembourg	Fr	Giglio [55]	2 000	Lehner AUT
10-09	Israel	D 2-2	Antalya	ECq	Mifsud.Mc [51p], Carabott [52]	300	Blareau BEL
11-12	Poland	L 0-4	Larnaca	Fr		300	Kasnaferis GRE
2004							
14-02	Moldova	D 0-0	Ta'Qali	Fr		600	Vialichka BLR
16-02	Estonia	W 5-2	Ta'Qali	Fr	Barbara 2 [12 60], Said [28], Turner [57], Zahra [87]		Orlic MDA
18-02	Belarus	L 0-4	Ta'Qali	Fr			Kaldma EST
31-03	Finland	L 1-2	Ta'Qali	Fr	Mifsud.Mc [90]		Trefoloni ITA
27-05	Germany	L 0-7	Freiburg	Fr		22 000	Stredak SVK
18-08	Faroe Islands	L 2-3	Toftir	Fr	Giglio [50], Mifsud.Mc [65]	1 932	Laursen DEN
4-09	Sweden	L 0-7	Ta'Qali	WCq		4 200	Jakov ISR
9-10	Iceland	D 0-0	Ta'Qali	WCq		1 130	Corpodean ROU
13-10	Bulgaria	L 1-4	Sofia	WCq	Mifsud.Mc [11]	16 800	Richards WAL
17-11	Hungary	L 0-2	Ta'Qali	WCq		14 500	Asumaa FIN
2005							
9-02	Norway	L 0-3	Ta'Qali	Fr		1 000	Malcolm NIR
30-03	Croatia	L 0-3	Zagreb	WCq		15 510	Kapitanis CYP
4-06	Sweden	L 0-6	Gothenburg	WCq		35 593	Ivanov.N RUS
8-06	Iceland	L 1-4	Reykjavík	WCq	Said [58]	4 887	Skomina SVN

Fr = Friendly match • EC = UEFA EURO 2004™ • WC = FIFA World Cup™ • q = qualifier

NATIONAL CAPS

	Caps
CARABOTT David	121
BUSUTTIL Carmel	111
BRINCAT Joe	102
BUTTIGIEG John	95
VELLA Silvio	90

NATIONAL GOALS

	Goals
BUSUTTIL Carmel	23
CARABOTT David	12
MIFSUD Michael	11
SUDA Hubert	8

NATIONAL COACH

	Years
GATT Robert	1996
KOSANOVIC Milorad	1996-'97
ILIC Josef	1997-'01
HELD Siggi	2001-'03
HEESE/BUSUTTIL	2003-

MALTA NATIONAL TEAM RECORDS AND RECORD SEQUENCES

Records			Sequence records					
Victory	5-0	AZE 1994	Wins	3	1981, 1999-2000	Clean sheets	4	1999-2000
Defeat	1-12	ESP 1983	Defeats	16	1982-1985	Goals scored	7	1991-1992
Player Caps	121	CARABOTT David	Undefeated	6	2001-2002	Without goal	8	2000-2001
Player Goals	23	BUSUTTIL Carmel	Without win	34	1994-1998	Goals against	29	1996-19999

MALTA COUNTRY INFORMATION

Capital	Valletta	Independence	1964 from the UK	GDP per Capita	$17 700
Population	396 851	Status	Republic	GNP Ranking	124
Area km²	316	Language	Maltese, English	Dialling code	+356
Population density	1 255 per km²	Literacy rate	92%	Internet code	.mt
% in urban areas	89%	Main religion	Christian	GMT + / −	+1
Towns/Cities ('000)	Birkirkara 22; Qormi 18; Mosta 18; Sliema 11; Hamrun 11; Naxxar 10; Gzira 7; Valletta 7				
Neighbours (km)	Mediterranean Sea 196				
Main stadia	Ta'Qali Stadium – Ta'Qali 17 797				

MALTA 2004-05

PREMIER LEAGUE

	Pl	W	D	L	F	A	Pts	Sliema	Birkirkara	Hibernians	Valletta	Marsaxlokk	Floriana	Pietà H	Msida SJ	St Patrick	Lija
Sliema Wanderers †(21)	28	18	7	3	47	23	40		0-0 1-1	1-1 1-1	3-1 0-0	2-1 2-0	1-0 2-1	1-0	1-1	2-1	0-1
Birkirkara ‡(16)	28	15	9	4	69	36	38	0-2 3-1		2-1 1-1	1-2 6-3	1-1 2-2	3-0 3-0	2-3	5-3	7-2	4-0
Hibernians ‡(18)	28	14	11	3	49	32	35	2-3 1-1	4-2 2-2		2-1 0-3	3-3 3-0	2-0 1-1	2-1	1-1	2-2	2-1
Valletta (18)	28	16	4	8	57	41	34	3-2 0-3	0-1 1-2	2-2 0-2		3-1 4-1	3-2 2-1	4-1	5-1	5-0	4-1
Marsaxlokk (13)	28	8	6	14	41	47	17	1-3 1-2	1-1 0-3	1-2 1-3	1-1 0-1		0-1	4-1	2-1	3-1	5-1
Floriana (12)	28	7	7	14	28	39	16	0-2 0-1	1-3 0-2	1-1 0-1	0-0 0-1	1-0 4-3		1-1	1-1	2-1	4-0
Pietà Hotspurs (10)	24	8	5	11	44	38	20	2-3	1-1	1-3	2-3	0-3	2-3		2-2 1-1	4-0 4-0	3-0 1-0
Msida St Joseph (8)	24	7	8	9	38	41	19	1-2	0-2	0-2	4-1	1-2	1-1	1-1 2-1		3-1 3-0	2-1 2-0
St Patrick (5)	24	5	3	16	27	56	14	0-1	3-3	0-1	1-2	0-0	0-2	0-5 2-0	3-2 4-2		2-0 4-1
Lija (4)	24	3	2	19	13	60	8	0-4	1-6	0-1	1-2	0-3	1-1	0-4 0-3	1-2 1-1	1-0 1-0	

16/08/2004 - 15/05/2005 • † Qualified for the UEFA Champions League • ‡ Qualified for the UEFA Cup • Points taken forward for the final round in brackets

MALTA 2004-05 FIRST DIVISION

	Pl	W	D	L	F	A	Pts
Hamrun Spartans	18	10	5	3	30	19	35
Mosta	18	9	5	4	37	24	32
Mqabba	18	9	4	5	33	19	31
Senglea Athletic	18	7	7	4	31	27	28
Marsa	18	7	5	6	38	33	26
Naxxar Lions	18	7	2	9	29	35	23
San Gwann	18	6	5	7	21	27	23
St George's §	18	6	6	6	23	25	22
Balzan Youths	18	5	3	10	23	31	18
Gozo	18	1	4	13	14	39	7

5/09/2004 - 15/05/2005 • § Deducted two points

FA TROPHY 2004-05

Quarter-finals		Semi-finals		Final	
Birkirkara	3				
Floriana	2	Birkirkara	0 5p		
Mqabba	2	Sliema W	0 4p		
Sliema W	3			Birkirkara ‡	2
Marsaxlokk	4			Msida SJ	1
Valletta	2	Marsaxlokk	2 4p	20-05-2005, Ta'Qali, Ref: Borg	
Hibernians	0	Msida SJ	2 5p	Scorers - Galea.L 52, Galea.M 84	
Msida SJ	1			for Birkirkara; Boni 83 for Msida	

‡ Qualified for the UEFA Cup

CLUB DIRECTORY

Club	Town/City	Stadium	Phone	www.	Lge	Cup	CL
Birkirkara	Birkirkara	Ta'Qali 17 797	+356 21 447005	birkirkarafc.com	1	3	0
Floriana	Floriana	Ta'Qali 17 797	+356 79 474141	florianafc.com	25	18	0
Hibernians	Paola	Hibernians Ground 8 000	+356 21 677627	hibernians.com	9	6	0
Lija	Lija	Ta'Qali 17 797	+356 21 435868		0	0	0
Marsaxlokk	Marsaxlokk	Ta'Qali 17 797	+356 21 652966	marsaxlokkfc.com	0	0	0
Msida St Joseph	Msida	Ta'Qali 17 797	+356 21 340401	msidastjoseph.com	0	0	0
Pietà Hotspurs	Pietà	Ta'Qali 17 797	+356 21 231336	pietahotspurs.com	0	0	0
Sliema Wanderers	Sliema	Ta'Qali 17 797	+356 21 340073	eswfc.com	26	19	0
Saint Patrick	Zabbar	Ta'Qali 17 797	+356 21 664889		0	0	0
Valletta	Valletta	Ta'Qali 17 797	+356 25 967136	vallettafcofficial.net	18	11	0

RECENT LEAGUE AND CUP RECORD

	Championship						Cup		
Year	Champions	Pts	Runners-up	Pts	Third	Pts	Winners	Score	Runners-up
1990	Valletta	28	Sliema Wanderers	24	Hamrun Spartans	23	Sliema Wanderers	1-0	Birkirkara
1991	Hamrun Spartans	24	Valletta	19	Floriana	18	Valletta	2-1	Sliema Wanderers
1992	Valletta	33	Floriana	24	Hamrun Spartans	23	Hamrun Spartans	3-3 2-1	Valletta
1993	Floriana	29	Hamrun Spartans	24	Valletta	24	Floriana	5-0	Sliema Wanderers
1994	Hibernians	31	Floriana	28	Valletta	27	Floriana	2-1	Valletta
1995	Hibernians	43	Sliema Wanderers	39	Valletta	37	Valletta	1-0	Hamrun Spartans
1996	Sliema Wanderers	46	Valletta	42	Floriana	37	Valletta	0-0 1-0	Sliema Wanderers
1997	Valletta	67	Birkirkara	60	Floriana	53	Valletta	2-0	Hibernians
1998	Valletta	65	Birkirkara	63	Sliema Wanderers	56	Hibernians	2-1	Valletta
1999	Valletta	70	Birkirkara	68	Sliema Wanderers	47	Valletta	1-0	Birkirkara
2000	Birkirkara	46	Sliema Wanderers	39	Valletta	36	Sliema Wanderers	4-1	Birkirkara
2001	Valletta	46	Sliema Wanderers	40	Birkirkara	36	Valletta	3-0	Birkirkara
2002	Hibernians	43	Sliema Wanderers	36	Birkirkara	31	Birkirkara	1-0	Sliema Wanderers
2003	Sliema Wanderers	42	Birkirkara	37	Valletta	35	Birkirkara	1-0	Sliema Wanderers
2004	Sliema Wanderers	43	Birkirkara	39	Hibernians	35	Sliema Wanderers	2-0	Marsaxlokk
2005	Sliema Wanderers	40	Birkirkara	38	Hibernians	35	Birkirkara	2-1	Msida St Joseph

MOZ – MOZAMBIQUE

NATIONAL TEAM RECORD
JULY 1ST 2002 TO JUNE 30TH 2005

PL	W	D	L	F	A	%
21	7	5	9	18	26	45.2

FIFA/COCA-COLA WORLD RANKING

1993	1994	1995	1996	1997	1998	1999	2000	2001	2002	2003	2004	High		Low	
104	94	76	85	67	80	101	112	128	125	127	126	66	11/97	134	07/05

					2004-2005						
08/04	09/04	10/04	11/04	12/04	01/05	02/05	03/05	04/05	05/05	06/05	07/05
125	125	125	128	126	126	126	127	129	129	132	134

The Black Mambas, as the Mozambique national team are commonly referred to, have rather lost their venom in recent years. After the long civil war ground to a halt in 1992, football began to flourish resulting in qualification for the 1996 and 1998 CAF African Cup of Nations finals. The catastrophic floods in 2000 and 2001 followed by drought in 2002 have since had a devastating effect on the country and football hasn't been exempt. From a high of 66 in the FIFA/Coca-Cola World Ranking in 1997, Mozambique slipped to an all-time low of 134 in July 2005. A close aggregate defeat to Guinea in the preliminary round of the 2006 FIFA World Cup™ qualifiers in

INTERNATIONAL HONOURS
None

November 2003 hasn't helped with the COSAFA Castle Cup providing the only competitive internationals since then. There were four Ferroviario clubs in the top division of the 2004 Championship and it was the branch based in Nampula that surprised pundits by winning a first Championship to follow up their Cup success of 2003. The more famous and historically successful Ferroviario Maputo convincingly beat Textáfrica Chimoio 5-1 in the Cup Final to complete a great year for the Ferroviaro organisation. Neither fared well, however, in the 2005 CAF African club competitions with both knocked-out in the first ties they played.

THE FIFA BIG COUNT OF 2000

	Male	Female		Male	Female
Registered players	5 259	100	Referees	415	0
Non registered players	50 000	0	Officials	4 597	25
Youth players	5 725	0	Total involved	66 121	
Total players	61 084		Number of clubs	150	
Professional players	168	0	Number of teams	208	

Federação Moçambicana de Futebol (FMF)
Av. Samora Machel, Número 11-2 Andar, Maputo 1467, Mozambique
Tel +258 1 300366   Fax +258 1 300367
fmf@tvcabo.co.mz   www.none
President: COLUNA Mario   General Secretary: MONTEIRO Manuel
Vice-President: GAFUR Amir Abdul   Treasurer: NHANCOLO Luis   Media Officer: None
Men's Coach: SEMEDO Artur   Women's Coach: ABDULA Abdil
FMF formed: 1976   CAF: 1978   FIFA: 1980
Colours: Red, Black, Red

GAMES PLAYED BY MOZAMBIQUE IN THE 2006 FIFA WORLD CUP™ CYCLE

2002	Opponents	Score		Venue	Comp	Scorers	Att	Referee
6-07	Zambia	L	0-3	Lusaka	CCqf			Ndoro ZIM
9-09	Central African Rep.	D	1-1	Bangui	CNq	Fumo 60		Ndong EQG
13-10	Congo	L	0-3	Maputo	CNq			Lwanja MWI
2003								
22-03	Lesotho	D	0-0	Maputo	CCrl	W 5-4p		Lwanja MWI
30-03	Burkina Faso	W	1-0	Maputo	CNq	Monteiro Dario 89		Nunkoo MRI
7-06	Burkina Faso	L	0-4	Ouagadougou	CNq		25 000	Ould Mohamed MTN
22-06	Central African Rep.	W	1-0	Maputo	CNq	Jossias 73p	15 000	
6-07	Congo	D	0-0	Brazzaville	CNq			
27-07	Zambia	L	2-4	Lusaka	CCqf	To 44, Tico-Tico 60	10 000	Katjimune NAM
12-10	Guinea	L	0-1	Conakry	WCq		13 400	Ndoye SEN
9-11	Swaziland	W	2-0	Maputo	Fr			
16-11	Guinea	L	3-4	Maputo	WCq	Monteiro Dario 3 75 80 89	50 000	Mochubela RSA
2004								
11-04	Swaziland	W	2-0	Maputo	Fr	Nando 42, Amilcar 72		
18-04	Madagascar	W	2-0	Maputo	CCrl	Tico-Tico 64, Fala-Fala 89	28 000	Damon RSA
26-05	Botswana	D	0-0	Maputo	Fr		2 000	
31-05	Swaziland	D	1-1	Maputo	Fr	Nelinho 43	5 000	
13-06	Malawi	W	2-0	Maputo	CCqf	Mabedi OG 42, To 62	30 000	Kaoma ZAM
25-06	Ghana	L	0-1	Maputo	Fr			
19-09	Angola	L	0-1	Maputo	CCsf		50 000	Jovinala MWI
2005								
16-04	Zimbabwe	L	0-3	Windhoek	CCrl			Mufeti NAM
26-06	Lesotho	W	1-0	Maputo	Fr			

Fr = Friendly match • CN = CAF African Cup of Nations • CC = COSAFA Cup • WC = FIFA World Cup™ • q = qualifier

MOZAMBIQUE NATIONAL TEAM RECORDS AND RECORD SEQUENCES

Records			Sequence records					
Victory	6-1	LES 1980	Wins	5	1989-1990	Clean sheets	4	1983, 1984, 1985
Defeat	0-6	ZIM 1979, ZIM 1980	Defeats	7	1998	Goals scored	15	1980-1982
Player Caps	n/a		Undefeated	7	1995	Without goal	3	1986, 1989, 1991
Player Goals	n/a		Without win	18	1985-1989	Goals against	17	1985-1989

FIFA REFEREE LIST 2005

	Int'l	BoB
CHIRINDZA Alfredo		6-02-1963
FADUCO Justino	1999	7-10-1964
INFANTE Mateus	1996	14-05-1967
JANNA Andre		24-09-1965
LOFORTE Pascoal Da Fonseca	1996	30-06-1963
MASSANGO Antonio	1996	9-08-1969
MUSSANE Venildo	1996	23-10-1960

FIFA ASSISTANT REFEREE LIST 2005

	Int'l	DoB
LANGA Henriques	2000	16-06-1966
MACHEL Francisco		15-02-1968
MASSAVANHANE Fernando	1993	13-01-1963
MUNGOI Julio	1996	30-01-1963
PELEMBE Agostinho	2000	23-02-1964
PIQUENINO Domingos	1996	1-01-1960
VICTOR Acacio	1996	20-06-1961

MOZAMBIQUE COUNTRY INFORMATION

Capital	Maputo	Independence	1975 from Portugal	GDP per Capita	$1 200
Population	18 811 731	Status	Republic	GNP Ranking	123
Area km²	801 590	Language	Portuguese, Makhuwa, Tsonga	Dialling code	+258
Population density	23 per km²	Literacy rate	47%	Internet code	.mz
% in urban areas	34%	Main religion	Indigenous 50%, Christian 30%	GMT +/−	+2
Towns/Cities ('000)	Maputo 1 191; Matola 544; Beira 531; Nampula 388; Chomoio 257; Nacala 225; Quelimane 188				
Neighbours (km)	South Africa 491; Swaziland 105; Zimbabwe 1 231; Zambia 419; Malawi 1 569; Tanzania 756; Indian Ocean 2 470				
Main stadia	Estádio da Machava – Maputo 6 000; Estádio do Ferroviário – Beira 7 000				

MOZAMBIQUE 2004

CAMPEONATO NACIONAL DA 1ª DIVISAO

	Pl	W	D	L	F	A	Pts	F. Nampula	Desportivo	F. Maputo	F. Beira	Maxaquene	Lichinga	Matchedje	Costa do Sol	Têxtil	F. Pemba	Textáfrica	Des. Matola
Ferroviário Nampula †	22	12	8	2	24	8	44		0-1	0-0	1-1	1-0	1-1	2-0	1-1	4-0	3-0	2-0	1-0
Desportivo Maputo	22	11	9	2	25	8	42	0-0		1-0	0-0	1-2	0-0	1-0	0-0	4-0	1-0	3-0	1-0
Ferroviário Maputo ‡	22	9	8	5	22	11	35	2-0	0-0		3-0	0-0	2-1	0-0	2-0	2-1	2-0	2-0	0-1
Ferroviário Beira	22	9	7	6	25	22	34	1-1	3-1	2-1		4-2	2-1	2-1	0-0	1-0	1-0	2-0	2-0
Maxaquene	22	7	8	7	16	15	29	0-1	1-1	1-0	2-0		1-0	0-0	0-2	2-0	0-1	3-1	0-0
Lichinga	22	7	7	8	18	16	28	0-1	0-0	0-1	2-0	1-0		1-0	1-0	2-0	1-0	1-1	2-0
Matchedje	22	6	7	9	17	19	25	1-2	0-3	0-2	1-0	0-0	0-0		1-0	1-0	5-0	3-1	0-0
Costa do Sol	22	5	10	7	15	16	25	0-0	0-0	0-0	1-0	0-0	1-0	1-1		4-1	1-1	1-1	0-1
Têxtil Púnguè	22	6	5	11	21	31	23	0-1	0-0	2-2	0-0	1-1	2-1	1-2	2-1		2-0	3-0	0-0
Ferroviário Pemba	22	6	5	11	16	25	23	0-1	1-2	0-0	1-0	0-1	2-1	1-1	3-1	1-0		0-0	4-0
Textáfrica Chimoio	22	5	7	10	15	30	22	0-1	0-1	0-0	2-2	1-0	1-1	1-0	1-0	1-4	1-0		2-0
Desportivo Matola	22	4	9	9	12	25	21	0-0	0-1	2-1	2-2	0-0	1-1	1-0	0-1	1-2	1-2	1-1	

24/04/2004 - 21/11/2004 • † Qualified for the CAF Champions League • ‡ Qualified for the CAF Confederation Cup

TAÇA NACIONAL 2004

Round of 16

- Ferroviário Maputo
- Munhuanense Azar
- Clube Gaza
- Ferroviário Mahotas
- Ferroviário Quelimane
- Têxtil Púnguè
- Matchedje Chimoio 0
- Ferroviário Beira 2
- Matchedje Maputo
- Desportivo Matola
- ECMEP Nampula 0
- Lichinga 1
- Costa do Sol
- Ferroviário Inhambane
- Chingale Tete 0
- Textáfrica Chimoio 2

Quarter-finals

- Ferroviário Maputo 4
- Ferroviário Mahotas 0
- Ferroviário Quelimane
- Ferroviário Beira
- Matchedje Maputo 1 7p
- Lichinga 1 5p
- Costa do Sol
- Textáfrica Chimoio

‡ Qualified for the CAF Confederation Cup

Semi-finals

- Ferroviário Maputo 2
- Ferroviário Beira 1
- Matchedje Maputo 0
- Textáfrica Chimoio 1

Final

- Ferroviário Maputo ‡ 5
- Textáfrica Chimoio 1

CUP FINAL

Estádio da Machava, Maputo, 5-12-2004
Scorers - Macamo 47+, Chana 2 47 65, Chinwa, Mauricio 69 for Ferroviário; Arlindo for Textáfrica

CLUB DIRECTORY

Club	City/Town	Stadium	Lge	Cup	CL
Costa do Sol	Maputo	Costa do Sol 10 000	8	9	0
Desportivo	Maputo	Desportivo 4 000	5	1	0
Ferroviário	Beira	Ferroviário 7 000	0	1	0
Ferroviário	Maputo	Machava 60 000	6	4	0
Ferroviário	Nampula	Nampula 4 000	1	1	0
Lichinga	Lichinga	Lichinga 3 000	0	0	0
Matchedje	Maputo	Costa do Sol 10 000	2	1	0
Maxaquene	Maputo	Maxaquene 15 000	4	6	0
Têxtil Púnguè	Beira	Chiveve 5 000	1	0	0

RECENT LEAGUE AND CUP RECORD

Championship

Year	Champions	Pts	Runners-up	Pts	Third	Pts
1999	Ferroviário Maputo	23	Costa do Sol	23	Chingale Tete	14
2000	Costa do Sol	51	Ferroviário Maputo	47	Matchadje	38
2001	Costa do Sol	45	Ferroviário Maputo	38	Maxaquene	33
2002	Ferroviário Maputo	50	Maxaquene	46	Costa do Sol	43
2003	Maxaquene	47	Costa do Sol	43	Desportivo Maputo	40
2004	Ferroviário Nampula	44	Desportivo Maputo	42	Ferroviário Maputo	35

Cup

Winners	Score	Runners-up
Costa do Sol	5-0	Sporting Nampula
Costa do Sol	1-0	Matchadje
Maxaquene	3-1	Textáfrica Chimoio
Costa do Sol	2-0	Académica Maputo
Ferroviário Nampula	1-1 5-4p	Ferroviário Maputo
Ferroviário Maputo	5-1	Textáfrica Chimoio

MRI – MAURITIUS

NATIONAL TEAM RECORD
JULY 1ST 2002 TO JUNE 30TH 2005

PL	W	D	L	F	A	%
17	8	2	7	18	21	52.9

FIFA/COCA-COLA WORLD RANKING

1993	1994	1995	1996	1997	1998	1999	2000	2001	2002	2003	2004	High		Low	
133	146	154	150	151	148	118	118	124	126	123	140	**116**	08/00	**158**	05/96

	2004-2005											
08/04	09/04	10/04	11/04	12/04	01/05	02/05	03/05	04/05	05/05	06/05	07/05	
127	127	130	134	140	143	143	143	143	143	143	143	

In June 2003 Mauriitius suffered their worst ever defeat when they lost 7-0 in Cairo but since then they have slowly improved and in the three years since the 2002 FIFA World Cup™ finals have actually posted a positive record in international matches. A 2-0 victory over South Africa in January 2004 in the COSAFA Castle Cup gave an indication of the potential of the island while it is hoped that the opening of the new Goal-financed Football Home will help give the island the infrastucture it needs to move up a level. With a close defeat at the hands of Uganda in the 2006 FIFA World Cup™ qualifiers, the COSAFA Castle Cup has been the main feature of a truncated

INTERNATIONAL HONOURS
None

fixture list but new coach Rajesh Gunesh has his sights set on qualification for the 2008 CAF African Cup of Nations. Once again in domestic football AS Port Louis 2000 proved that they are the team to beat by securing a treble of League, Cup and Republic Cup. In the League they finished comfortably ahead of Savanne SC in second place to win a fourth consecutive title. The club is also proving to be no walk-over in CAF club competitions and although they lost 3-2 on aggregate to South Africa's Kaizer Chiefs in the preliminary round of the 2005 Champions League, they did win the home leg 2-1.

THE FIFA BIG COUNT OF 2000

	Male	Female		Male	Female
Registered players	11 250	522	Referees	88	2
Non registered players	6 000	200	Officials	4 000	0
Youth players	4 170	0	Total involved	26 232	
Total players	22 142		Number of clubs	62	
Professional players	0	0	Number of teams	637	

Mauritius Football Association (MFA)
Football House, Trianon, Mauritius
Tel +230 4652200   Fax +230 4547909
mfaho@intnet.mu   www.none
President: PERSUNNOO Dinnanathlall   General Secretary: VUDDAMALAY Ananda
Vice-President: CHITBAHAL Bhai Mustapha   Treasurer: BOWUD A.H. Nazir   Media Officer: NG PING MAN Laval
Men's Coach: GUNESH Rajesh   Women's Coach: ROSE Eddy
MFA formed: 1952   CAF: 1962   FIFA: 1962
Colours: Red, Red, Red

GAMES PLAYED BY MAURITIUS IN THE 2006 FIFA WORLD CUP™ CYCLE

2002	Opponents		Score	Venue	Comp	Scorers	Att	Referee
1-08	Swaziland	W	1-0	Mbabane	Fr	Zuel [2]		
3-08	Swaziland	D	0-0	Big Bend	Fr			Sitriongomyane SWZ
26-09	Seychelles	W	1-0	Port Louis	Fr	Laboiteuse [70]	166	Roopnah MRI
12-10	Madagascar	L	0-1	Port Louis	CNq		1 819	Maillet SEY
2003								
22-02	Madagascar	L	1-2	Antananarivo	CCr1	Appou [50]	25 000	Motau RSA
29-03	Egypt	L	0-1	Port Louis	CNq		800	
8-06	Egypt	L	0-7	Cairo	CNq		40 000	Abdalla LBY
6-07	Madagascar	W	2-0	Antananarivo	CNq	Perle [13], Appou [30p]		
30-08	Madagascar	W	3-1	Curepipe	IOr1	Appou 2 [11p 56], Perle [15]	4 500	Ramsamy REU
2-09	Seychelles	D	0-0	Curepipe	IOr1			
4-09	Comoros †	W	5-0	Curepipe	IOsf	Perle 2 [8 87], Appou 2 [42p 70], Cundasamy [49]	4 500	Labrosse SEY
6-09	Reunion	W	2-1	Curepipe	IOf	Cundasamy [41], Ithier [83]	10 000	Labrosse SEY
11-10	Uganda	L	0-3	Kampala	WCq		6 800	Tangawarima ZIM
16-11	Uganda	W	3-1	Curepipe	WCq	Naboth [37], Mourgine [70], Louis [82]	2 465	Maillet SEY
2004								
10-01	South Africa	W	2-0	Curepipe	CCr1	Lekgetho OG [53], Perle [81]	5 230	Raolimanana MAD
31-07	Zambia	L	1-3	Lusaka	CCqf	Appou [70]		Manuel ZIM
2005								
26-02	Madagascar	W	2-0	Curepipe	CCr1	Appou [44], Louis [48]		Fakude SWZ
27-02	South Africa	L	0-1	Curepipe	CCr1			Mnkantjo ZIM

Fr = Friendly match • CN = CAF African Cup of Nations • CC = COSAFA Cup • IO = Indian Ocean Games • WC = FIFA World Cup™
q = qualifier • r1 = first round group • qf = quarter-final • sf = semi-final • f = final • † not a full international

MAURITIUS NATIONAL TEAM RECORDS AND RECORD SEQUENCES

Records			Sequence records					
Victory	15-0	REU 1950	Wins	17	1947-1955	Clean sheets	4	1957-1958
Defeat	0-7	EGY 2003	Defeats	6	1974-1975	Goals scored	25	1947-1958
Player Caps	n/a		Undefeated	17	1947-1955	Without goal	6	1994-1995
Player Goals	n/a		Without win	9	Three times	Goals against	10	1999-2000

FIFA REFEREE LIST 2005

	Int'l	DoB
LIM KEE CHONG An-Yan	1988	15-05-1960
MADARBOCUS Abdool	1998	17-11-1960
RAMLUCHUMUN Auruduth	2004	24-01-1966
ROHEEMUN Ahmad	1999	28-09-1964
ROOPNAH Dharmanand		15-10-1966
SEECHURN Rajindraparsad	2004	3-06-1970
SIMISSE Louis	2002	8-12-1963

FIFA ASSISTANT REFEREE LIST 2005

	Int'l	DoB
BOOTUN Balkrishna	2005	24-07-1973
CHANGEA Sanjaye	2002	28-10-1964
CHOYTAH Toolsy	2001	17-02-1961
JUGGURNATH Iswarduth		19-02-1962
KRISTNAMA Appanah	2004	30-12-1964
RAMPHUL Raj		11-07-1964
RUNGIEN Damalingum	2001	11-03-1961

MAURITIUS COUNTRY INFORMATION

Capital	Port Louis	Independence	1968 from the UK	GDP per Capita	$11 400
Population	1 220 481	Status	Republic	GNP Ranking	116
Area km²	2 040	Language	French, English	Dialling code	+230
Population density	598 per km²	Literacy rate	85%	Internet code	.mu
% in urban areas	41%	Main religion	Hindu 52%, Christian 28%	GMT +/−	+4
Towns/Cities ('000)	Port Louis 155; Beau Bassin-Rose Hill 110; Vascoas-Pheinix 107; Curepipe 84; Quatre Bras 80				
Neighbours (km)	Indian Ocean 2 740				
Main stadia	George V Stadium – Curepipe 10 000; Auguste Vollaire – Port Louis				

MAURITIUS 2004-05

PREMIER LEAGUE FIRST STAGE

	Pl	W	D	L	F	A	Pts	ASPL 2000	Savanne	Pampl'ses	Olympique	ASVP	Starlight	USBB/RH	Faucon	Grand Port	Sodnac	Rivière	Arsenal
AS Port Louis 2000 †	11	7	2	2	23	8	23		2-0			1-1	0-3		0-1	3-1		4-0	
Savanne SC †	11	7	2	2	20	11	23			3-1	3-0	2-1			0-0	1-1			5-2
Pamplemousses SC †	11	7	0	4	19	13	21	1-2				4-1		4-1			1-0		2-0
Olympique Moka †	11	5	3	3	19	20	18	0-0					1-0		1-1	2-2	6-4	4-0	
AS Vacoas-Phoenix †	11	5	2	4	20	13	17			3-1	4-0			0-1	1-1		4-2		1-2
Curepipe Starlight †	11	5	2	4	17	15	17		2-3			3-1		1-0		3-2		1-2	
US Beau-Basin/Rose Hill†	11	4	3	4	15	10	15	1-2		1-3	1-2				1-1		2-0		4-0
Faucon Flacq SC †	11	3	6	2	10	9	15			0-1			0-0			1-2		1-1	2-1
Grand Port United ‡	11	3	3	5	13	17	12		2-0	0-1		0-3	1-1						0-0
Sodnac Quatre-Bornes ‡	11	3	1	7	16	23	10	0-4	0-2					1-1	0-1	2-1		4-0	
AS Rivière Rempart ‡	11	2	1	8	6	22	7		0-1		**2-0**	0-1		0-3		1-2			
Arsenal Wanderers ‡	11	2	1	8	9	26	7	0-5			1-2			1-2			1-3	1-0	

9/10/2004 - 19/12/2004 • † Qualified for the Super League play-offs • ‡ Entered the promotion/relegation group • Match in bold awarded 2-0

MAURITIUS 2004-05

PREMIER LEAGUE SUPER LEAGUE PLAY-OFFS

	Pl	W	D	L	F	A	Pts	ASPL 2000	Savanne	USBB/RH	Pampl'ses	Starlight	ASVP	Faucon	Olympique
AS Port Louis 2000	14	9	4	1	33	9	31		2-2	4-3	1-1	4-0	3-0	4-1	3-0
Savanne SC	14	7	5	2	29	12	26	1-1		2-0	1-1	1-2	0-0	1-1	4-1
US Beau-Basin/Rose Hill	14	7	2	5	27	21	23	0-0	0-3		3-1	2-1	2-0	2-1	1-0
Pamplemousses SC	14	5	4	5	20	21	19	0-4	1-2	2-1		2-0	2-0	2-3	2-1
Curepipe Starlight	14	6	1	7	21	27	19	0-1	2-1	3-0	2-1		0-3	1-1	6-2
AS Vacoas-Phoenix	14	5	3	6	16	19	18	0-2	1-2	2-2	1-1	1-0		3-1	3-0
Faucon Flacq SC	14	5	2	7	28	31	17	1-0	0-5	1-3	1-3	7-2	4-1		1-3
Olympique Moka	14	1	1	12	11	45	4	0-4	0-4	1-8	1-1	1-2	0-1	1-5	

9/03/2005 - 28/05/2005 • † Qualified for the CAF Champions League • ‡ Qualified for the CAF Confederation Cup

MAURITIUS 2004-05 PROMOTION/RELEGATION

	Pl	W	D	L	F	A	Pts
Arsenal Wanderers	7	5	1	1	21	10	16
Petite Rivière Noire	7	5	1	1	19	8	16
Grand Port United	7	4	1	2	17	9	13
Sodnac Quatre-Bornes	7	4	0	3	14	11	12
Henrietta YC	7	3	1	3	14	9	10
AS Rivière Rempart	7	2	1	4	10	13	7
Jeunesse Olivia	7	2	1	4	11	19	7
AS Quatre-Bornes	7	0	0	7	4	31	0

19/03/2005 - 28/05/2005

MFA CUP 2004-05

Quarter-finals

ASPL 2000	2
Arsenal Wan	1
Grand Port Utd	0
Blue Birds	1
USBB/RH	1 4p
ASVP	1 3p
Petite R-Noire	0
PAS Mates	1

Semi-finals

ASPL 2000	7
Blue Birds	1
USBB/RH	0
PAS Mates	1

Final

ASPL 2000	2
PAS Mates	0

12-06-2005

RECENT LEAGUE AND CUP RECORD

Year	Champions	Pts	Runners-up	Pts	Third	Pts	Winners	Score	Runners-up
1996	Sunrise Flacq						Sunrise Flacq	2-1	Scouts Club
1997	Sunrise Flacq						Fire Brigade BB/RH	3-1	Sunrise Flacq
1998	Scouts Club	28	Fire Brigade BB/RH	21	Sunrise Flacq	20	Fire Brigade BB/RH	3-0	Scouts Club
1999	Fire Brigade BB/RH	39	Scouts Club	38	Sunrise Flacq	35			
2000									
2001	Olympique Moka	57	AS Port Louis 2000	44	US Beau-Basin/RH		US Beau-Basin/RH	2-1	Olympique Moka
2002	AS Port Louis 2000	58	US Beau-Basin/RH	52	Faucon Flacq	40	AS Port Louis 2000	3-0	Olympique Moka
2003	AS Port Louis 2000	26	Faucon Flacq SC	21	US Beau-Basin/RH	21	Savanne SC	1-1 4-2p	AS Port Louis 2000
2004	AS Port Louis 2000	56	Pamplemousses SC	43	Savanne SC	37	Savanne SC	3-2	Faucon Flacq SC
2005	AS Port Louis 2000	31	Savanne SC	26	US Beau-Basin/RH	23	AS Port Louis 2000	2-0	PAS Mates

In 2000 there was a major re-organisation of football in Mauritius after major incidents on the pitch that year • Sunrise Flacq became Olympique de Moka; Fire Brigade merged with Real Pamplemousses to form Pamplemousses SC; Mahebourg United became Grand Port United

MSR - MONTSERRAT

NATIONAL TEAM RECORD
JULY 1ST 2002 TO JUNE 30TH 2005

PL	W	D	L	F	A	%
5	0	0	5	5	34	0

FIFA/COCA-COLA WORLD RANKING

1993	1994	1995	1996	1997	1998	1999	2000	2001	2002	2003	2004	High		Low	
-	-	-	-	-	-	201	202	203	203	204	202	**201**	12/99	**205**	10/04

2004-2005											
08/04	09/04	10/04	11/04	12/04	01/05	02/05	03/05	04/05	05/05	06/05	07/05
205	205	205	201	202	202	202	202	202	202	202	202

On the day of the 2002 FIFA World Cup™ final in Yokohama, Bhutan hosted Montserrat in an alternative Cup Final featuring the bottom two nations in the FIFA/Coca-Cola World Ranking. Bhutan won 4-0, but for the smallest national association affiliated to FIFA, Montserrat were grateful to make the headlines on the pitch for a change. In the face of volcanic eruptions that devastated the country and forced an estimated half of the islanders to flee abroad, it's a wonder the residents find the time or the inclination to play football, but the national team still took part in the 2006 FIFA World Cup™ qualifiers. A preliminary round match with Bermuda saw the team six goals

INTERNATIONAL HONOURS
None

down at half-time in the first leg before slumping to a record 13-0 defeat. The return leg in Montserrat was only marginally better as Bermuda triumphed 7-0 to win 20-0 on aggregate. With such a small pool of talent available, the chances of Montserrat making any success internationally are severely limited; winning their first match since 1995 would be a good start though. The four-team Premier League was played on the island's one pitch with Ideal FC emerging as champions. The club entered the 2005 CONCACAF Champions Cup, but were clearly out of their depth as Jamaica's Harbour View dispatched Ideal with an aggregate 30-1 scoreline.

THE FIFA BIG COUNT OF 2000

	Male	Female		Male	Female
Registered players	100	0	Referees	5	0
Non registered players	100	0	Officials	20	0
Youth players	100	0	Total involved	325	
Total players	300		Number of clubs	4	
Professional players	0	0	Number of teams	7	

Montserrat Football Association Inc. (MFA)
PO Box 505, Woodlands, Montserrat
Tel +1 664 4918744   Fax +1 664 4918801
monfa@candw.ms   www.montserrat-football.com
President: CASSELL Vincent   General Secretary: TBD
Vice-President: POLLIDORE Clement   Treasurer: TBD   Media Officer: None
Men's Coach: COOPER Scott   Women's Coach: READ Darren & LABORDE Ottley
MFA formed: 1994   CONCACAF: 1996   FIFA: 1996
Colours: Green with black and white stripes, Green with white stripes, Green with black and white stripes

GAMES PLAYED BY MONTSERRAT IN THE 2006 FIFA WORLD CUP™ CYCLE

2002	Opponents		Score	Venue	Comp	Scorers	Att	Referee
No international matches played in 2002 after June								
2003								
No international matches played in 2003								
2004								
29-02	Bermuda	L	0-13	Hamilton	WCq		3 000	Kennedy USA
21-03	Bermuda	L	0-7	Plymouth	WCq		250	Charles DMA
31-10	St Kitts and Nevis	L	1-6	Basseterre	GCq	Adams 81		Bedeau GRN
2-11	Antigua and Barbuda	L	4-5	Basseterre	GCq	Bramble 36, Fox 41, Mendes 50, Farrel 61		Phillip GRN
4-11	St Lucia	L	0-3	Basseterre	GCq	St Lucia awarded the match 3-0		
2005								
No international matches played in 2005 before August								

Fr = Friendly match • GC = CONCACAF Gold Cup • WC = FIFA World Cup™ • q = qualifier

MONTSERRAT NATIONAL TEAM RECORDS AND RECORD SEQUENCES

Records			Sequence records				
Victory	3-2	AIA 1995	Wins	2	1995	Clean sheets	1	1995
Defeat	0-13	BER 2004	Defeats	16	1995-2004	Goals scored	3	1996-99, 2000-01
Player Caps	n/a		Undefeated	2	1995	Without goal	4	2004-2004
Player Goals	n/a		Without win	16	1995-2004	Goals against		

FIFA REFEREE LIST 2005

	Int'l	DoB
None		

FIFA ASSISTANT REFEREE LIST 2005

	Int'l	DoB
None		

RECENT LEAGUE RECORD

Championship	
Year	Champions
1996	Royal Montserrat Police Force
1997	Abandoned
1998	Not held
1999	Not Held
2000	Royal Montserrat Police Force
2001	Royal Montserrat Police Force
2002	Not held due to season readjustment
2003	Royal Montserrat Police Force
2004	Ideal SC

MONTSERRAT COUNTRY INFORMATION

Capital	Plymouth	Status	UK Dependent Territory	GDP per Capita	$3 400
Population	9 245			GNP Ranking	n/a
Area km²	102	Language	English	Dialling code	+1 664
Population density	91 per km²	Literacy rate	97%	Internet code	.ms
% in urban areas	n/a	Main religion	Christian	GMT +/–	-4
Towns/Cities	Cork Hill 732; Salem 680; Saints Johns 627; Bransby Point 550; Davy Hill 366; Geralds 314				
Neighbours (km)	Caribbean Sea 40				
Main stadia	Blakes Estate Football Ground – Plymouth				

MTN – MAURITANIA

MAURITANIA NATIONAL TEAM RECORD
JULY 1ST 2002 TO JUNE 30TH 2005

PL	W	D	L	F	A	%
11	1	2	8	4	22	18.2

FIFA/COCA-COLA WORLD RANKING FOR MAURITANIA

1993	1994	1995	1996	1997	1998	1999	2000	2001	2002	2003	2004	High		Low	
144	137	85	113	135	142	160	161	177	180	165	175	85	12/95	182	05/03

2004-2005											
08/04	09/04	10/04	11/04	12/04	01/05	02/05	03/05	04/05	05/05	06/05	07/05
174	174	174	174	175	175	175	175	175	175	176	176

Although Mauritania were knocked out of the 2006 FIFA World Cup™ qualifiers 4-2 on aggregate by Zimbabwe, their second leg win in Nouakchott in November 2003 was notable for two reasons. Not only was it Mauritania's first win in a FIFA World Cup™ match but it also ended a run of 34 games without a win stretching back to 1995. The win wasn't enough to overturn a 3-0 deficit from the first leg in Harare and because the qualifiers for Germany also doubled up as qualifiers for the 2006 CAF African Cup of Nations, the national team has not played since. With a population of just under three million Mauritania will always struggle as underdogs even in their own region of

INTERNATIONAL HONOURS
None

West Africa. Their best achievement to date came when they hosted the Amilcar Cabral Cup in 1995. They reached the final but were denied a first trophy when they lost to Sierra Leone on penalties. It is hoped that Mauritanian football will benefit in the long-term from the opening in 2003 of a new House of Football built with the assistance of the FIFA Goal Programme that combines a headquarters for the national association as well as a technical centre. The 2004 League saw ASC Ksar finish as champions, nine points clear of second placed NASR of Sebkha but they were denied a double when they lost to Nouadhibou in the Cup Final.

THE FIFA BIG COUNT OF 2000

	Male	Female		Male	Female
Registered players	2 933	0	Referees	90	5
Non registered players	6 000	0	Officials	200	0
Youth players	1 288	0	Total involved	10 516	
Total players	10 221		Number of clubs	52	
Professional players	10	0	Number of teams	160	

Fédération de Foot-Ball de la République Islamique de Mauritanie (FFM)
Case postale 566, Nouakchott, Mauritania
Tel +222 5 241860　　Fax +222 5 241861
ffrim@mauritel.mr　　www.none
President: ABBAS Moulay Mohamed　　General Secretary: BOUGHOURBAL Moulaye Abdel Aziz
Vice-President: OULD KLEIB Abdallahi　　Treasurer: OULD LIMAM AHMED Sidi Mohamed　　Media Officer: None
Men's Coach: TOSI Noel　　Women's Coach: None
FFM formed: 1961　　CAF: 1968　　FIFA: 1964
Colours: Green and yellow, Yellow, Green

GAMES PLAYED BY MAURITANIA IN THE 2006 FIFA WORLD CUP™ CYCLE

2002	Opponents	Score		Venue	Comp	Scorers	Att	Referee
6-09	Cape Verde Islands	L	0-2	Nouakchott	CNq			Sillah GAM
2-10	Mali	L	1-2	Bamako	Fr			
5-10	Mali	L	0-2	Bamako	Fr			
13-10	Togo	L	0-1	Lome	CNq			Kaba LBR
2003								
29-03	Kenya	L	0-4	Nairobi	CNq		30 000	Berhane ERI
31-05	Gambia	L	1-4	Banjul	Fr			
6-06	Kenya	D	0-0	Nouakchott	CNq		6 000	Keita GUI
21-06	Cape Verde Islands	L	0-3	Praia	CNq			
5-07	Togo	D	0-0	Nouakchott	CNq		2 000	Djingarey NIG
12-10	Zimbabwe	L	0-3	Harare	WCq		55 000	Damon RSA
14-11	Zimbabwe	W	2-1	Nouakchott	WCq	Langlet [3], Sidibe.A [10]	3 000	Keita GUI
2004								

No international matches played in 2004

2005

No international matches played in 2005 before August

Fr = Friendly match • CN = CAF African Cup of Nations • WC = FIFA World Cup™ • q = qualifier

MAURITANIA NATIONAL TEAM RECORDS AND RECORD SEQUENCES

Records			Sequence records				
Victory	3-0	LBR 1984	Wins	2	1983, 1995	Clean sheets	4	1994-95, 1995-96
Defeat	0-14	GUI 1972	Defeats	11	1976-1979	Goals scored	9	1979-1980
Player Caps	n/a		Undefeated	7	1994-95, 1995-96	Without goal	5	1983-1984
Player Goals	n/a		Without win	34	1995-2003	Goals against	25	1963-1979

FIFA REFEREE LIST 2005

	Int'l	DoB
BOURGE Mohamed		1-01-1966
HAIDARA Houssein	1999	13-07-1965
OULD ALI Lemghaifry	2005	
OULD LEMGHAMBODJ Mohamed	1998	9-11-1966
OULD MOHAMED Samba	1995	17-09-1962
SECK Moussa		22-04-1962
SOUMARE Yacouba	2005	31-10-1966

FIFA ASSISTANT REFEREE LIST 2005

	Int'l	DoB
DIA El Haassane	2005	28-10-1974
DIARRA Mamadou		1-01-1963
GUEYE Moussa	1993	16-12-1961
MOUNTAGA Sada	1998	1-12-1967
NIANG Oumar	2004	1-01-1969
OULD IDY Abdallahi	2001	25-12-1970
SALL Abdoul		31-07-1969

RECENT LEAGUE AND CUP RECORD

Championship		Cup			
Year	Champions	Winners	Score	Runners-up	
1995	ASC Sonalec	Air Mauritanie			
1996	No Tournament held	ASC Imarguens			
1997	No tournament held	ASC Sonalec	2-0	AS Garde Nationale	
1998	AS Garde Nationale	ASC Sonalec	3-2	SDPA Trarza	
1999	SDPA Rosso	ASC Police	2-1	AS Garde Nationale	
2000	ASC Mauritel	Air Mauritanie	4-0	ASC Gendrim	
2001	FC Nouadhibou	AS Garde Nationale			
2002	FC Nouadhibou	No tournament held			
2003	NASR Sebkha	ASC Entente Sebkha	1-0	ACS Ksar	
2004	ACS Ksar	FC Nouadhibou	1-0	ACS Ksar	

MAURITANIA COUNTRY INFORMATION

Capital	Nouakchott	Independence	1960 from France	GDP per Capita	$1 800
Population	2 998 563	Status	Republic	GNP Ranking	154
Area km²	1 030 700	Language	Arabic, French, Pulaar	Dialling code	+222
Population density	3 per km²	Literacy rate	47%	Internet code	.mr
% in urban areas	54%	Main religion	Muslim	GMT +/–	0
Towns/Cities ('000)	Nouakchott 709; Nouadhibou 80; Kifah 68; Kayhaydi 51; Zuwarat 44; an-Na'mah 36				
Neighbours (km)	Western Sahara 1 561; Algeria 463; Mali 2 237; Senegal 813; North Atlantic 754				
Main stadia	Stade National – Nouakchott 40 000				

MWI – MALAWI

NATIONAL TEAM RECORD
JULY 1ST 2002 TO JUNE 30TH 2005

PL	W	D	L	F	A	%
36	7	12	17	37	63	36.1

FIFA/COCA-COLA WORLD RANKING

1993	1994	1995	1996	1997	1998	1999	2000	2001	2002	2003	2004	High		Low	
67	82	89	88	97	89	114	113	120	95	105	109	67	12/93	124	06/01

2004-2005											
08/04	09/04	10/04	11/04	12/04	01/05	02/05	03/05	04/05	05/05	06/05	07/05
102	104	108	109	109	112	113	108	108	108	108	108

By beating Ethiopia in the preliminary round of the 2006 FIFA World Cup™ qualifiers in November 2003, Malawi avoided the fate of a drastically reduced fixture list although results in the group stage since then have been disappointing to say the least with questions even asked in Parliament about the embarrassing state of the team. Going into the final stages of the campaign Malawi were left rooted to the bottom of their group way behind local rivals Botswana with a 7-0 thrashing at the hands of African Champions Tunisia in early 2005 the low point. The national association were also handed an $11,000 fine from FIFA because of crowd trouble at the home leg

INTERNATIONAL HONOURS
None

with Tunisia. Although new coach Yassin Osman has few resources to hand he believes his young side can develop and hopefully improve on their Castle Cup campaigns of 2002 and 2003 when they managed to reach consecutive finals. The former President of Malawi, Bakili Muluzi, is an avid fan; the owner of Bakili Bullets he sponsored the 2004 Super League which the Bullets won handsomely for the sixth successive season (under three different guises). The Bullets unexpectedly reached the group stage of the 2004 Champions League, but did not enter for 2005 while League runners-up MTL Wanderers won the only domestic cup tournament of the year, the Charity Shield.

THE FIFA BIG COUNT OF 2000

	Male	Female		Male	Female
Registered players	2 704	63	Referees	10	0
Non registered players	27 000	0	Officials	1 680	0
Youth players	2 000	63	Total involved	33 520	
Total players	31 830		Number of clubs	66	
Professional players	4	0	Number of teams	105	

Football Association of Malawi (FAM)
Mpira House, Old Chileka Road, PO Box 865, Blantyre, Malawi
Tel +265 1 623197   Fax +265 1 623204
gensec@fam.mw   www.none
President: NYAMILANDU MANDA Walter   General Secretary: ROOSEVELT Mpinganjira
Vice-President: ANDERSON Zimba   Treasurer: TBD   Media Officer: TAKOMANA Harold
Men's Coach: YASSIN Osman   Women's Coach: MBOLEMBOLE Stuart
FAM formed: 1966   CAF: 1968   FIFA: 1967
Colours: Red, White, Red

GAMES PLAYED BY MALAWI IN THE 2006 FIFA WORLD CUP™ CYCLE

2002	Opponents	Score		Venue	Comp	Scorers	Att	Referee
7-07	Zimbabwe	W	3-2	Blantyre	Fr	Kanyenda [13p], Maduka [37], Nundwe [51]	35 000	Kafatiya MWI
8-07	Zimbabwe	D	2-2	Lilongwe	Fr	Kondowe [28], Nkhwazi [87]	20 000	
10-08	Zambia	W	1-0	Blantyre	CCsf	Kanyenda [66p]	60 000	Phomane LES
21-09	South Africa	L	1-3	Blantyre	CCf	Mabedi [44p]	60 000	Shikapande ZAM
28-09	South Africa	L	0-1	Durban	CCf		20 000	Mususa ZIM
12-10	Angola	W	1-0	Lilongwe	CNq	Mwafulirwa [87]	40 000	Tangawarima ZIM
2003								
22-02	Congo DR	D	1-1	Blantyre	Fr			
23-02	Congo DR	L	2-3	Lilongwe	Fr			
16-03	Zimbabwe	D	0-0	Harare	Fr		10 000	Bwanya ZIM
29-03	Nigeria	L	0-1	Blantyre	CNq		60 000	Nkole ZAM
17-05	Zambia	L	0-1	Blantyre	Fr			Lwanja MWI
21-05	Lesotho	D	0-0	Maseru	Fr			
25-05	Botswana	D	1-1	Gaborone	CCqf	Chavula [86]. W 3-1p	25 000	Infante MOZ
7-06	Nigeria	L	1-4	Lagos	CNq	Kanyenda [7]		Ndoye SEN
6-07	Angola	L	1-5	Luanda	CNq	Mgangira [78]	10 000	
16-08	Zambia	D	1-1	Blantyre	CCsf	Mwafulirwa [35]		Mnkantjo ZIM
27-09	Zimbabwe	L	1-2	Blantyre	CCf	Mwafulirwa [83]	60 000	Bennett RSA
5-10	Zimbabwe	L	0-2	Harare	CCf		25 000	Nkole ZAM
12-10	Ethiopia	W	3-1	Addis Abeba	WCq	Kanyenda 2 [39 55], Mgangira [88]	20 000	Abd El Fatah EGY
15-11	Ethiopia	D	0-0	Lilongwe	WCq		20 000	Abdel Rahman SUD
2004								
22-05	Zambia	W	2-0	Kitwe	Fr	Mwakasungula [15], Munthali [70]	20 000	Nkole ZAM
5-06	Morocco	D	1-1	Blantyre	WCq	Munthali [35]	30 040	Mususa ZIM
13-06	Mozambique	L	0-2	Maputo	CCqf		30 000	Kaoma ZAM
19-06	Botswana	L	0-2	Gaborone	WCq		15 000	Awuye UGA
3-07	Guinea	D	1-1	Lilongwe	WCq	Mpinganjira [71]	11 383	Abdulkadir TAN
6-07	Swaziland	L	1-2	Blantyre	Fr			
8-07	Swaziland	D	1-1	Lilongwe	Fr			
4-09	Kenya	L	2-3	Nairobi	WCq	Munthali [41], Mabedi [90p]	13 000	Mwanza ZAM
9-10	Tunisia	D	2-2	Blantyre	WCq	Mwafulirwa [19], Chipatala [37]	20 000	Awuye UGA
2005								
27-02	Zimbabwe	W	2-1	Blantyre	Fr	Tambala [45], Phiri.V [51]		
26-03	Tunisia	L	0-7	Tunis	WCq		30 000	Abdel Rahman SUD
27-05	Libya	D	1-1	Tripoli	Fr			
4-06	Morocco	L	1-4	Rabat	WCq	Chipatala [10]	48 000	Buenkadila COD
11-06	Lesotho	W	2-1	Lusaka	CCr1	Chitsulo [54], Zakazaka [73]		Mpanisi ZAM
12-06	Zambia	L	1-2	Lusaka	CCr1	Maduka [55]		Nhlapo RSA
18-06	Botswana	L	1-3	Blantyre	WCq	Mwafulirwa [48]	20 000	Gabonamong BOT

Fr = Friendly match • CN = CAF African Cup of Nations • CC = COSAFA Cup • WC = FIFA World Cup™
q = qualifier • r1 = first round group • qf = quarter-final • sf = semi-final • f = final

MALAWI COUNTRY INFORMATION

Capital	Lilongwe	Independence	1964 from the UK	GDP per Capita	$600
Population	11 906 855	Status	Republic	GNP Ranking	
Area km²	118 480	Language	English, Chichewa	Dialling code	+265
Population density	100 per km²	Literacy rate	62%	Internet code	.mw
% in urban areas	14%	Main religion	Christian 75%, Muslim 20%	GMT +/–	+2
Towns/Cities ('000)	Lilongwe 647; Blantyre 585; Mzuzu 128; Zomba 81; Kasungu 42; Mangochi 40; Karonga 34				
Neighbours (km)	Mozambique 1 569; Zambia 837; Tanzania 475				
Main stadia	Chichiri – Blantyre 60 000; Chivo – Lilongwe 40 000				

MALAWI NATIONAL TEAM RECORDS AND RECORD SEQUENCES

Records			Sequence records				
Victory	8-1	BOT 1968	Wins	8	1984	Clean sheets	5	1989
Defeat	0-7	ZAM 1969, TUN 2005	Defeats	9	1962-1968	Goals scored	13	1986-1987
Player Caps	n/a		Undefeated	15	1989-1990	Without goal	5	Three times
Player Goals	n/a		Without win	14	1998-2000	Goals against	18	1971-1975

FIFA REFEREE LIST 2005

	Int'l	DoB
BANDA Bester	2005	19-07-1975
CHILINDA Youngson	1998	20-02-1962
JOVINALA Simon	2003	20-02-1975
KAPANGA Patrick	2003	14-05-1970
LWANJA Verson	2001	21-04-1968
NGOSI Kalyoto	2003	14-09-1968
NTUTHA Hastings	2002	13-03-1967

FIFA ASSISTANT REFEREE LIST 2005

	Int'l	DoB
BANDA Damson	2002	12-06-1963
CHAMPITI Moffat	2002	18-08-1967
MHANGO Paul	2004	12-12-1970
MPENI McGovern	1998	8-08-1961
NGOLANGA John	2005	4-11-1974
NYONDO Zuza	2002	7-08-1966
SINAGO Wistard	1995	23-08-1962

RECENT LEAGUE AND CUP RECORD

Year	Championship						Cup		
	Champions	Pts	Runners-up	Pts	Third	Pts	Winners	Score	Runners-up
1996	Telecom Wanderers								
1997	Telecom Wanderers								
1998	Telecom Wanderers								
1999	Bata Bullets	62	Telecom Wanderers	60	Red Lions	44	Bata Bullets	3-0	MDC United
2000	Bata Bullets	44	MDC United	41	Silver Strikers	40	Telecom Wanderers	2-1	Bata Bullets
2001	Total Big Bullets	69	MTL Wanderers	66	MDC United	44	Moyale Barracks	1-0	Super ESCOM
2002	Total Big Bullets	62	Silver Strikers	50	MDC United	45	Total Big Bullets	1-0	MTL Wanderers
2003	Bakili Bullets	70	MTL Wanderers	69	MDC United	60	Final between Wanderers and Bullets abandoned		
2004	Bakili Bullets		MTL Wanderers		Silver Strikers				

Bakili Bullets previously known as Bata Bullets and Total Big Bullets • MTL Wanderers previously known as Limbe Leaf Wanderers and Telecom Wanderers

MYA - MYANMAR

NATIONAL TEAM RECORD
JULY 1ST 2002 TO JUNE 30TH 2005

PL	W	D	L	F	A	%
24	8	3	13	39	47	39.6

FIFA/COCA-COLA WORLD RANKING

1993	1994	1995	1996	1997	1998	1999	2000	2001	2002	2003	2004	High		Low	
110	124	115	104	114	115	126	124	151	162	140	144	97	04/96	162	12/02

2004-2005											
08/04	09/04	10/04	11/04	12/04	01/05	02/05	03/05	04/05	05/05	06/05	07/05
148	149	150	153	144	147	147	147	147	146	146	145

Withdrawing from the qualifiers for the 2002 FIFA World Cup™ cost Myanmar dear when FIFA banned them from competing in the 2006 edition and the national team have yet to play a competitive fixture in the competition. This is a far cry from the 1960s and 1970s when Myanmar (then Burma) were twice Asian Games winners and Asian Youth Champions seven times. However, the appointment of Bulgarian Ivan Kolev as coach appears to be paying dividends; at the 2004 Tiger Cup, Myanmar advanced to the semi-finals before losing to Singapore over two legs. Further success was found by an U-21 side at the 2005 ASEAN finals in Brunei where they finished runners-up to Thailand

INTERNATIONAL HONOURS
Asian Games 1966 1970 **SEA Games** 1965 1967 1969 1971 **AFC Youth Championship** 1961 1963 1964 1966 1968 1969 1970

after losing the final 3-0. The country has benefited from FIFA's Goal programme with the construction of a multi-purpose centre and the development of a football academy in Rangoon. The 2005 Premier League was won by Finance & Revenue who won all 15 of their League matches to finish as runaway champions and they then took the double by beating Cons 3-1 in the Premier Knock-out Cup Final. Finance & Revenue had earlier travelled to India to contest the IFA Shield for the first time and won the title after beating Mohun Bagan on penalties in the final. With no team entered for the AFC Cup, it provided the only international competition.

THE FIFA BIG COUNT OF 2000

	Male	Female		Male	Female
Registered players	79 500	2 000	Referees	188	18
Non registered players	180 000	3 500	Officials	2 500	100
Youth players	10 000	1 200	Total involved	279 006	
Total players	276 200		Number of clubs	573	
Professional players	0	0	Number of teams	3 620	

Myanmar Football Federation (MFF)
National Football Training Centre, Thuwunna Thingankyun, Township, Yangon, Myanmar
Tel +951 577366   Fax +951 570000
mff@myanmar.com.mm   www.myanmarfootball.org
President: ZAW Zaw   General Secretary: AUNG Tin
Vice-President: NAING Zaw Win   Treasurer: ZAW Than   Media Officer: OO Tin Tun
Men's Coach: KOLEV Ivan   Women's Coach: AYE Maung
MFF formed: 1947   AFC: 1954   FIFA: 1957
Colours: Red, White, Red

GAMES PLAYED BY MYANMAR IN THE 2006 FIFA WORLD CUP™ CYCLE

2002 Opponents		Score	Venue	Comp	Scorers	Att	Referee
15-12 Indonesia	D	0-0	Jakarta	TCr1		100 000	Ebrahim BHR
17-12 Philippines	W	6-1	Jakarta	TCr1	Aung Kyaw Moe 2 [7 52], Zaw Htike [35], Soe Lynn Tun [44] Zaw Zaw [56], Tint Naing Tun Thein [63]	2 500	Subkhiddin MAS
19-12 Cambodia	W	5-0	Jakarta	TCr1	Zaw Zaw [47], Lwin Oo 2 [57 77], Zaw Htike [69] Tint Naing Tun Thein [83]	2 000	Ebrahim BHR
23-12 Vietnam	L	2-4	Jakarta	TCr1	Lwin Oo [29], Htay Aung [80]	2 000	Nagalingham SIN
2003							
23-03 Brunei Darussalam	W	5-0	Malé	ACq	Win Htike [10], Aung Kyaw Moe [14], Yan Paing 2 [45 66] Lwin Oo [75]		
25-03 Maldives	W	2-0	Malé	ACq	Win Htike [52], Zaw Zaw [65]		
8-10 Malaysia	L	0-4	Kuala Lumpur	ACq		4 500	Yang Zhiqiang CHN
10-10 Bahrain	L	1-3	Kuala Lumpur	ACq	Soe Myat Min [77]	500	Naglingham SIN
12-10 Iraq	L	0-3	Kuala Lumpur	ACq		500	Yang Zhiqiang CHN
20-10 Bahrain	L	0-4	Manama	ACq		15 000	Al Harrassi OMA
22-10 Iraq	L	1-3	Manama	ACq	Zaw Zaw [45]	300	Yasrebi IRN
24-10 Malaysia	W	2-1	Isa Town	ACq	Soe Myat Min [25], Fadzli OG [43]	200	Al Harrassi OMA
2004							
17-03 China PR	L	0-2	Guangzhou	Fr			
20-08 Vietnam	L	0-5	Ho Chi Minh	Fr			
22-08 India	L	1-2	Ho Chi Minh	Fr	Win Nawng [81]		
27-11 Singapore	L	0-1	Singapore	Fr			
2-12 Hong Kong	D	2-2	Singapore	Fr	Yan Paing 2 [28 84]		
8-12 Philippines	W	1-0	Kuala Lumpur	TCr1	San Day Thien [92+]	1 000	Vo Minh Tri VIE
10-12 Thailand	D	1-1	Kuala Lumpur	TCr1	Zaw Lynn Tun [89]		Moradi IRN
12-12 Malaysia	W	1-0	Kuala Lumpur	TCr1	Soe Myat Min [20]	10 000	Hsu Chao Lo TPE
16-12 East Timor †	W	3-1	Kuala Lumpur	TCr1	Soe Myat Min [4], San Day Thien [43], Myo Hlaing Win [51]	1 000	Hsu Chao Lo TPE
29-12 Singapore	L	3-4	Kuala Lumpur	TCsf	Soe Myat Min 2 [34 90], Min Thu [36]	12 000	Rungklay THA
2005							
2-01 Singapore	L	2-4	Singapore	TCsf	Soe Myat Min [15], Aung Kyaw Moe [50]	30 000	Kamikawa JPN
15-01 Malaysia	L	1-2	Singapore	TC3p	Soe Myat Min [52]	2 000	Vo Minh Tri VIE

Fr = Friendly match • TC = Tiger Cup • AC = AFC Asian Cup
q = qualifier • r1 = 1st round • sf = semi-final • 3p = 3rd place play-off • † Not a full international

MYANMAR NATIONAL TEAM RECORDS AND RECORD SEQUENCES

Records			Sequence records					
Victory	9-0	SIN 1969	Wins	8	1971-1972	Clean sheets	7	1966-1967
Defeat	1-9	MAS 1977	Defeats	7	1957-1961	Goals scored	14	1964-1966
Player Caps	n/a		Undefeated	14	1970-1971	Without goal	4	1987-1991
Player Goals	n/a		Without win	9	1987-1993	Goals against	11	2003-2004

RECENT LEAGUE RECORD

Championship		Interstate Championship		
Year	Champions	Winners	Score	Runners-up
2002	Finance & Revenue Yangon	Mandalay		Sagaing
2003	Finance & Revenue Yangon	Shan State	2-0	Kayin State
2004	Custom			
2005	Finance & Revenue Yangon			

MYANMAR COUNTRY INFORMATION

Capital	Yangon (Rangoon)	Independence	1948 from the UK	GDP per Capita	$1 800
Population	42 720 196	Status	Republic	GNP Ranking	52
Area km²	678 500	Language	Burmese	Dialling code	+95
Population density	63 per km²	Literacy rate	85%	Internet code	.mm
% in urban areas	29%	Main religion	Buddhist 90%	GMT +/−	+6.5
Towns/Cities ('000)	Yangon 4 477; Mandalay 1 208; Mawlamyine 439; Bago 244; Pathein 237; Monywa 182				
Neighbours (km)	China 2 185; Laos 235; Thailand 1 800; Bangladesh 193; India 1 463; Indian Ocean 1 930				
Main stadia	Bogyoke Aung San – Yangon 40 000; Thuwanna YTC – Yangon 30 000				

NAM – NAMIBIA

NATIONAL TEAM RECORD
JULY 1ST 2002 TO JUNE 30TH 2005

PL	W	D	L	F	A	%
13	2	3	8	8	19	26.9

FIFA/COCA-COLA WORLD RANKING

1993	1994	1995	1996	1997	1998	1999	2000	2001	2002	2003	2004	High	Low
156	123	116	103	86	69	80	87	101	123	144	158	68 11/98	161 07/94

2004-2005											
08/04	09/04	10/04	11/04	12/04	01/05	02/05	03/05	04/05	05/05	06/05	07/05
150	150	154	154	158	158	158	159	159	158	159	160

After joining FIFA in 1992 Namibia made quick progress culiminating in an appearance at the CAF African Cup of Nations finals in Burkina Faso in 1998, but rather than acting as a stepping stone for further success, the national team has since struggled to maintain that standard. Namibia may be a sizeable country but with a population of just under two million it is always going to be a difficult task to keep up with even their regional rivals let alone the rest of Africa. The qualification system for the 2006 FIFA World Cup™ which doubled up as a qualifying tournament for the 2006 CAF African Cup of Nations hasn't helped either. After two matches against Rwanda at the end of

INTERNATIONAL HONOURS
None

2003, the Brave Warriors found themselves out of both competitions and with only the COSAFA Castle Cup to fill the fixture list for the following two and a half years. From a high of 68 in the November 1998 FIFA/Coca-Cola World Ranking, Namibia now find themselves nearly 100 places lower down the order. The lack of national team action has seen domestic football take on added significence and in 2005 both the League and the Cup saw teams victorious for the first time. In the League Civics finished two points ahead of defending champions Blue Water after losing just one game all season while Ramblers beat Black Africans on penalties in the Cup Final.

THE FIFA BIG COUNT OF 2000

	Male	Female		Male	Female
Registered players	4 000	0	Referees	100	0
Non registered players	8 000	0	Officials	600	0
Youth players	2 000	0	Total involved	14 700	
Total players	14 000		Number of clubs	50	
Professional players	0	0	Number of teams	200	

Namibia Football Association (NFA)
Council of Churches, Abraham Mashego Street, CCN Building, Katutura, PO Box 1345, Windhoek 9000, Namibia
Tel +264 61 265691   Fax +264 61 265693
nfass@iafrica.com.na   www.none
President: DAMASEB Petrus   General Secretary: GAWESEB Alpheus
Vice-President: MUINJO John   Treasurer: RIJATUA Tjeripo   Media Officer: none
Men's Coach: JOHNSON Max   Women's Coach: none
NFA formed: 1990   CAF: 1990   FIFA: 1992
Colours: Red, Red, Red

GAMES PLAYED BY NAMIBIA IN THE 2006 FIFA WORLD CUP™ CYCLE

2002	Opponents		Score	Venue	Comp	Scorers	Att	Referee
7-09	Algeria	L	0-1	Windhoek	CNq		13 000	Tangawarima ZIM
2003								
16-03	Botswana	L	0-1	Windhoek	CCr1			Kakudze SWA
30-03	Chad	L	0-2	N'Djamena	CNq			Dimanche CTA
7-06	Chad	W	2-1	Windhoek	CNq	Diergaardt 24, Hummel 76p	5 000	Bernardo Colembi ANG
20-06	Algeria	L	0-1	Blida	CNq		30 000	Auda EGY
7-09	Angola	L	0-2	Luanda	Fr		5 000	Antonio De Sousa ANG
20-09	Angola	L	1-3	Windhoek	Fr	Hindjou 4		
12-10	Rwanda	L	0-3	Kigali	WCq		22 000	Abdulkadir TAN
15-11	Rwanda	D	1-1	Windhoek	WCq	Shipanga 39	9 000	Mbera GAB
2004								
28-04	Botswana	D	0-0	Windhoek	Fr		1 500	
9-05	Angola	L	1-2	Luanda	CCr1	Petrus 70	4 000	Ngcamphalala SWA
2005								
19-03	Lesotho	W	2-1	Maseru	Fr	Guriras, Malgas		
16-04	Botswana	D	1-1	Windhoek	CCr1	Botes 35, L 4-5p		Sentso LES

Fr = Friendly match • CN = CAF African Cup of Nations • CC = COSAFA Cup • WC = FIFA World Cup™ • q = qualifier • r1 = first round group

NAMIBIA NATIONAL TEAM RECORDS AND RECORD SEQUENCES

Records			Sequence records					
Victory	8-2	BEN 2000	Wins	3	1997	Clean sheets	3	1995-1996, 1996
Defeat	2-8	EGY 2001	Defeats	7	2001-03	Goals scored	15	1997-1998
Player Caps	n/a		Undefeated	8	1995-1996	Without goal	5	1992-1993, 2001
Player Goals	n/a		Without win	8	1998	Goals against	25	1997-1998

FIFA REFEREE LIST 2005

	Int'l	DoB
KATJIMUNE Mathews		17-09-1974
MUFETI Arvo	2003	25-01-1969
SHIGWEDHA Lazarus	2004	8-12-1969

FIFA ASSISTANT REFEREE LIST 2005

	Int'l	DoB
EKSTEEN Piet	1997	22-01-1962
KAMUKWANYAMA Daniel	2005	14-06-1970
KWEYO Sakeus	2003	2-05-1967
NASHENDA Benedictus	2005	22-09-1975
SHILUNGA Erastus	2000	6-07-1968
SHIPANGA Alfeus	2005	25-05-1972
SWARTBOOI Hendrik	2005	9-02-1971

NAMIBIA COUNTRY INFORMATION

Capital	Windhoek	Independence	1990 from South Africa	GDP per Capita	$7 200
Population	1 954 033	Status	Republic	GNP Ranking	125
Area km²	825 415	Language	English, Afrikaans, Oshivambo	Dialling code	+264
Population density	2 per km²	Literacy rate	84%	Internet code	.na
% in urban areas	37%	Main religion	Christian 80%	GMT + / –	+2
Towns/Cities ('000)	Windhoek 268; Rundu 58; Walvis Bay 52; Oshakati 34; Swakopmund 25; Katima Mulilo 25				
Neighbours (km)	Angola 1 376; Zambia 233; Botswana 1 360; South Africa 967; South Atlantic 1 572				
Main stadia	Independence Stadium – Windhoek 25 000				

NAMIBIA 2004-05 PREMIER LEAGUE

	Pl	W	D	L	F	A	Pts
Civics	30	21	8	1	71	28	71
Blue Waters	30	21	6	3	80	28	69
Ramblers	30	19	4	7	64	39	61
United Africa Tigers	30	17	7	6	57	30	58
Orlando Pirates	30	14	8	8	58	36	50
Black Africa	30	11	10	9	48	41	43
African Stars	30	11	9	10	33	33	42
Eleven Arrows	30	12	5	13	54	45	41
Oshakati City	30	10	7	13	45	49	37
Chief Santos	30	8	10	12	44	44	34
Golden Bees	30	8	6	16	36	53	30
Benfica	30	6	10	14	37	51	28
King Kauluma Palace	30	7	7	16	34	56	28
Friends	30	8	4	18	42	75	28
Life Fighters	30	7	5	18	35	55	26
Deportivo Alaves	30	4	6	20	32	107	18

9/10/2004 - 25/05/2005

NFA CUP 2004-05

Round of 16 †		Quarter-finals ‡		Semi-finals †‡		Final	
Ramblers	3						
African Stars	2	Ramblers	4				
Orlando Pirates	1	Friends	0				
Friends	4			Ramblers	2		
UA Tigers	2			Blue Waters	1		
Life Fighters	0	UA Tigers	1				
Julinho	2	Blue Waters	2				
Blue Waters	3					Ramblers	2 5p
Golden Bees	3					Black Africa	2 4p
Benfica	0	Golden Bees	1				
Chief Santos	0	Eleven Arrows	0				
Eleven Arrows	2			Golden Bees	0		
Rundu Chiefs	0 5p			Black Africa	2		
Oshakati City	0 3p	Rundu Chiefs	0				
KK Palace	0	Black Africa	3				
Black Africa	3						

† Played in Otjiwarongo • ‡ Played in Walvis Bay • †‡ Played in Gobais

CUP FINAL
18-06-2005
Independence Stadium, Windhoek
Scorers - Jacobs 20, Helu 120 for Ramblers; Aoseb 32, John 115 for Black Africa

CLUB DIRECTORY

Club	Town/City	Lge	Cup	CL
Benfica	Tsumeb	1	0	0
Black Africans	Windhoek	5	3	0
Blue Waters	Walvis Bay	4	1	0
Chief Santos	Tsumeb	2	4	0
Civics	Windhoek	1	1	0
Eleven Arrows	Walvis Bay	1	0	0
Orlando Pirates	Walvis Bay	1	1	0
Ramblers	Windhoek	1	1	0
Tigers	Windhoek	0	2	0

RECENT LEAGUE AND CUP RECORD

Year	Champions	Pts	Runners-up	Pts	Third	Pts	Winners	Score	Runners-up
1998	Black Africans	46	Civics	39	Chief Santos	37	Chief Santos	1-0	Tigers
1999	Black Africans	56	Life Fighters	43	Blue Waters	40	Chief Santos	1-0	Tigers
2000	Blue Waters	54	Black Africans	45	Nashua Young Ones	40	Chief Santos	4-2	Life Fighters
2001	No Championship due to season readjustment						Not held due to season readjustment		
2002	Liverpool	57	Blue Waters	56	Chief Santos	56	Orlando Pirates	2-1	Tigers
2003	Chief Santos						Civics	4-2	Tigers
2004	Blue Waters	72	Civics	69	Orlando Pirates	62	Black Africans	2-0	Life Fighters
2005	Civics	71	Blue Waters	69	Ramblers	61	Ramblers	2-2 5-4p	Black Africa

NCA – NICARAGUA

NATIONAL TEAM RECORD
JULY 1ST 2002 TO JUNE 30TH 2005

PL	W	D	L	F	A	%
18	5	3	10	15	38	36.1

FIFA/COCA-COLA WORLD RANKING

1993	1994	1995	1996	1997	1998	1999	2000	2001	2002	2003	2004	High		Low	
155	168	174	179	182	188	193	191	188	186	173	158	150	08/93	193	05/01

2004-2005												
08/04	09/04	10/04	11/04	12/04	01/05	02/05	03/05	04/05	05/05	06/05	07/05
160	159	158	160	158	158	158	156	154	156	156	157

Although Nicaragua has a relatively long tradition in football, the country's international players are more spectators than participants at international events. Unlike other parts of Central America, the game has not really caught on in a country dominated by baseball and at 157 in the FIFA/Coca-Cola World Ranking, Nicaragua are regarded as one of the minnows of the region. In 2004, the national side, known as the Pinoleros, won just two of their nine matches and their participation in the 2006 FIFA World Cup™ was short-lived; in Diriamba, Nicaragua managed a 2-2 draw with St Vincent and the Grenadines, but the return in Kingstown was more straightforward with the

INTERNATIONAL HONOURS
None

home side winning 4-1. Competing in the 2005 UNCAF Cup didn't offer much more encouragement when in spite of a rare victory – against Belize – defeats to Honduras and Guatemala meant no qualification for the CONCACAF Gold Cup. The Campeonato Nacional proved successful for Diriangen who won both the Apertura and Clausura tournaments while Parmalat secured the second spot for the 2006 CONCACAF Champions Cup. Neither of the two entrants in the 2005 competition progressed too far; while Diriangen lost to FAS of El Salvador 9-0 on aggregate in the first round, Real Esteli lost 5-0 on aggregate to Saprissa of Costa Rica at the next stage.

THE FIFA BIG COUNT OF 2000

	Male	Female		Male	Female
Registered players	10 000	600	Referees	1 197	15
Non registered players	50 000	1 000	Officials	1 500	100
Youth players	25 480	1 400	Total involved	91 292	
Total players	88 480		Number of clubs	200	
Professional players	0	0	Number of teams	1 879	

Federación Nicaragüense de Fútbol (FENIFUT)
Hospital Bautista 1, Cuadra abajo, 1 cuadra al Sur y 1/2 cuadra abajo, Managua 976, Nicaragua
Tel +505 2227035   Fax +505 2227885
fenifut@tmx.com.ni   www.fenifut.org.ni
President: ROCHA LOPEZ Julio   General Secretary: LOPEZ SANDERS Rolando
Vice-President: QUINTANILLA Manuel   Treasurer: TBD   Media Officer: ROSALES Marlon
Men's Coach: CRUZ Mauricio   Women's Coach: URROZ Edward
FENIFUT formed: 1931   CONCACAF: 1968   FIFA: 1950
Colours: Blue, White, Blue

GAMES PLAYED BY NICARAGUA IN THE 2006 FIFA WORLD CUP™ CYCLE

2002	Opponents	Score		Venue	Comp	Scorers	Att	Referee
17-11	Cayman Islands	W	1-0	Grand Cayman	Fr			
2003								
11-02	Honduras	L	0-2	Panama City	GCq			Aguilar SLV
13-02	El Salvador	L	0-3	Panama City	GCq			Moreno PAN
15-02	Costa Rica	L	0-1	Colon	GCq			Aguilar SLV
18-02	Guatemala	L	0-5	Panama City	GCq		5 000	Moreno PAN
21-02	Panama	W	1-0	Panama City	GCq	Palacios [83]		Aguilar SLV
2004								
31-01	Haiti	D	1-1	West Palm Beach	Fr	Palacios [41]	53	
29-02	Haiti	D	1-1	Esteli	Fr	Calero [58]		
31-03	Bermuda	L	0-3	Hamilton	Fr			Crockwell BER
2-04	Bermuda	L	1-2	Hamilton	Fr	Palacios [72p]		Raynor BER
30-04	Bermuda	W	2-0	Diriamba	Fr	Solorzano [4], Palacios [30]	800	
2-05	Bermuda	W	2-0	Esteli	Fr	Rocha [8], Palacios [46]	4 000	Reyes NCA
4-06	Costa Rica	L	1-5	San Carlos	Fr	Lopez.F [1]	BCD	
13-06	St Vincent/Grenadines	D	2-2	Diriamba	WCq	Palacios [37], Calero [79]	7 500	Delgado CUB
20-06	St Vincent/Grenadines	L	1-4	Kingstown	WCq	Palacios [60]	5 000	Brohim DMA
2005								
19-02	Honduras	L	1-5	Guatemala City	GCq	Bustos [54]	5 306	Moreno PAN
21-02	Guatemala	L	0-4	Guatemala City	GCq		8 000	Sibrian SLV
23-02	Belize	W	1-0	Guatemala City	GCq	Vilchez [85]	3 000	Quesada CRC

Fr = Friendly match • GC = CONCACAF Gold Cup • WC = FIFA World Cup™ • q = qualifier • BCD = behind closed doors

NICARAGUA NATIONAL TEAM RECORDS AND RECORD SEQUENCES

Records			Sequence records					
Victory	3-1	PAN 1967	Wins	2	2004	Clean sheets	2	2004
Defeat	1-11	ANT 1950	Defeats	25	1986-2001	Goals scored	7	2004-2005
Player Caps	n/a		Undefeated	3	2003-2004	Without goal	8	1999-2001
Player Goals	n/a		Without win	33	1975-2001	Goals against	55	1966-2002

FIFA ASSISTANT REFEREE LIST 2005

	Int'l	DoB
ABURTO Luis	1995	30-05-1964
AGUIRRE Gustavo	1996	18-10-1960
ARIAS Silvio	1997	25-03-1971
CALERO Hugo	1992	4-05-1967
GUZMAN Angel	1999	2-10-1972
QUINTERO Mariano	1996	17-04-1971

FIFA REFEREE LIST 2005

	Int'l	DoB
GARCIA Paulo	2002	24-04-1975
GUERRERO Jose	2003	14-11-1973
MENDOZA Williams	1997	1-03-1968

NICARAGUA COUNTRY INFORMATION

Capital	Managua	Independence	1838 from Spain	GDP per Capita	$2 300
Population	5 359 759	Status	Republic	GNP Ranking	140
Area km²	129 494	Language	Spanish	Dialling code	+505
Population density	41 per km²	Literacy rate	67%	Internet code	.ni
% in urban areas	63%	Main religion	Christian 85%	GMT +/−	-6
Towns/Cities ('000)	Managua 1 140; Léon 150; Chinandega 128; Masaya 123; Granada 92; Estelí 92; Tipitapa 89				
Neighbours (km)	Costa Rica 309; Honduras 922; Caribbean Sea & Pacific Ocean 910				
Main stadia	Estadio Dennis Martinez – Managua 30 000; Cacique Diriangen – Diriamba				

NICARAGUA 2004-05

PRIMERA DIVISION TORNEO APERTURA

	Pl	W	D	L	F	A	Pts	Diriangén	Real Estelí	Parmalat	Masatepe	Jalapa	Madriz	W. Ferreti	Bluefields	At. Estelí	Masachapa
Diriangén †	18	14	2	2	54	14	44		3-2	0-2	6-1	2-3	3-0	1-1	5-0	6-1	6-0
Real Estelí †	18	12	3	3	41	9	39	0-1		0-0	1-2	3-0	4-0	6-0	3-0	2-1	7-0
Parmalat †	18	11	4	3	45	15	37	1-3	1-2		0-0	1-0	8-2	3-0	3-1	2-0	4-0
Masatepe †	18	11	4	3	38	23	37	0-4	0-0	1-0		1-1	3-1	2-1	5-0	4-2	4-1
Deportivo Jalapa	18	11	3	4	51	27	36	1-2	0-0	3-3	3-2		6-0	5-0	4-0	2-1	8-1
Real Madriz	18	5	5	8	28	37	20	0-3	0-1	2-2	0-0	7-2		2-2	5-0	4-1	1-0
Dep. Walter Ferreti	18	4	4	10	13	38	16	0-4	0-1	0-1	0-3	1-3	0-0		2-1	3-2	1-0
Deportivo Bluefields	17	3	1	13	10	52	10	1-3	0-4	0-7	0-4	1-2	2-1	0-0		2-1	2-1
Atlético Estelí	18	2	2	14	21	44	8	1-2	0-3	0-5	2-3	0-2	0-0	4-0	2-0		1-1
Deportivo Masachapa	17	1	2	14	12	54	5	0-0	1-2	1-2	1-3	2-6	0-3	0-2	-	3-2	

3/07/2004 - 31/10/2004 • † Qualified for the Apertura play-offs • Matches in bold were awarded 3-0

NICARAGUA 2004-05

PRIMERA DIVISION TORNEO CLAUSURA

	Pl	W	D	L	F	A	Pts	Real Estelí	Masatepe	Diriangén	Madriz	Parmalat	Jalapa	Bluefields	W. Ferreti	At. Estelí	Masachapa
Real Estelí †	9	6	2	1	32	5	20		5-0				1-1	4-0	4-0		7-0
Masatepe †	9	5	2	2	21	10	17			2-0	2-0	2-1		5-0		1-1	
Diriangén †	9	4	4	1	19	5	16	1-1			1-0	4-1		1-1		0-0	
Real Madriz †	9	4	2	3	10	7	14	1-0				2-2			0-0		3-0
Parmalat †	9	4	1	4	29	16	13	2-5					1-2		3-1		3-0
Deportivo Jalapa †	9	3	4	2	13	11	13		1-1	0-0	1-3					2-0	
Deportivo Bluefields	9	4	1	4	9	24	13			1-0	0-12	3-1			1-0		
Dep. Walter Ferreti	9	2	3	4	8	15	9		1-0	0-4			2-2			1-1	
Atlético Estelí	9	2	3	4	6	14	9	0-5			0-1	0-4		1-0			3-0
Deportivo Masachapa	9	0	0	9	1	41	0		1-8	0-8			0-3	0-3	0-3		

26/12/2004 - 27/02/2005 • † Qualified for the Clausura Hexagonal • Masachapa withdrew after three rounds - Future opponents were awarded games 3-0

APERTURA PLAY-OFFS

Semi-finals

Diriangén	3 3
Masatepe	3 1
Parmalat	0 1
Real Estelí	4 2

Finals

28-11-2004/5-12-2004

Diriangén	0 1
Real Estelí	0 0

CLAUSURA PLAY-OFFS

Semi-finals

Diriangén	1 1
Real Estelí	0 1
Real Madriz	1 2
Parmalat	1 3

Finals

8-05-2005/15-05-2005

Diriangén	1 0 3p
Parmalat	0 1 2p

CLAUSURA HEXAGONAL

	Pl	W	D	L	F	A	Pts	Pa	Di	RE	RM	Ma	DJ
Parmalat †	5	3	1	1	9	3	10						6-1
Diriangén †	5	2	3	0	6	3	9	0-0		0-0	1-0	2-0	
Real Estelí †	5	2	2	1	4	3	8	0-1			1-1	2-1	
Real Madriz †	5	2	1	2	6	6	7	2-1				0-1	3-2
Masatepe	5	2	0	3	5	5	6	0-1					
Deportivo Jalapa	5	0	1	4	6	16	1		3-3	0-1		0-3	

12/03/2005 - 17/04/2005 • † Qualified for the Clausura play-offs

RECENT LEAGUE RECORD

Championship/Clausura from 2004				Apertura		
Year	Champions	Score	Runners-up	Winners	Score	Runners-up
1998	Deportivo Walter Ferreti	1-0	Deportivo Masachapa			
1999	Real Estelí	0-0 3-1p	Diriangén			
2000	Diriangén	1-0	Deportivo Walter Ferreti			
2001	Deportivo Walter Ferreti	0-0 0-0 5-3p	Diriangén			
2002	Deportivo Jalapa	1-1 4-0	Deportivo Walter Ferreti			
2003	Real Estelí	0-1 3-0	Diriangén			
2004	Real Estelí	1-0 0-0	Diriangén	Real Estelí	0-0 1-0	Diriangén
2005	Diriangén	1-0 0-1 3-2p	Parmalat	Diriangén	0-0 1-0	Real Estelí

NCL – NEW CALEDONIA

NEW CALEDONIA NATIONAL TEAM RECORD
JULY 1ST 2002 TO JUNE 30TH 2005

PL	W	D	L	F	A	%
12	5	2	5	28	19	50

FIFA/COCA-COLA WORLD RANKING

1993	1994	1995	1996	1997	1998	1999	2000	2001	2002	2003	2004	High		Low	
-	-	-	-	-	-	-	-	-	-	-	186	185	07/05	185	06/05

	2004-2005										
08/04	09/04	10/04	11/04	12/04	01/05	02/05	03/05	04/05	05/05	06/05	07/05
186	186	186	186	186	186	186	186	186	186	186	185

One of FIFA's newest recruits, New Caledonia have not played any games as actual members. The tiny island of just over 200,000 people were granted membership at the FIFA Congress on 20 May, the day after New Caledonia's last match, an 8-0 thrashing of Tonga. That game marked the end of their World Cup™ qualifying campaign having seen off the Cook Islands by the same score two days previously. The two other results were a defeat to Tahiti and a draw with the Solomon Islands that left the country third in the group, and a point away from qualifying for the second stage. A campaign like that would have been regarded as success enough for a country debuting on the

INTERNATIONAL HONOURS
None

international arena but for New Caledonia it was perhaps a missed opportunity; the team had already competed regularly on the Oceanic scene for many years and were South Pacific Games runners-up in 2003. AS Magenta took the Division d'Honneur title for the third straight year, 12 points clear of runners-up JS Baco and won the National Championship contested by the top four teams. The club rounded off the season by claiming the Caledonia Cup for the sixth successive year beating JS Baco in the final again. Qualifying for the Oceania Champions Cup, Magenta surpassed all expectations by reaching the final where they lost 2-0 to Sydney FC.

THE FIFA BIG COUNT OF 2000

	Male	Female		Male	Female
Registered players	n/a	n/a	Referees	n/a	n/a
Non registered players	n/a	n/a	Officials	n/a	n/a
Youth players	n/a	n/a	Total involved	n/a	
Total players		n/a	Number of clubs	n/a	
Professional players	n/a	n/a	Number of teams	n/a	

Fédération Calédonienne de Football (FCF)
7 bis, rue Suffren Quartien latin, BP 560, 99845 Nouméa CEDEX 99845, New Caledonia
Tel +687 272383   Fax +687 263249
fedcalfoot@canl.nc   www.none
President: FOURNIER Claude   General Secretary: VIRCONDELET Laurent
Vice-President: TOGNA Daniel   Treasurer: PALAOU Chanel   Media Officer: none
Men's Coach: MARTINENGO Serge   Women's Coach: none
FCF formed: 1928   OFC: 19   FIFA: 2004
Colours: Grey, Red, Grey

GAMES PLAYED BY NEW CALEDONIA IN THE 2006 FIFA WORLD CUP™ CYCLE

2002	Opponents		Score	Venue	Comp	Scorers	Att	Referee
6-07	Fiji	L	1-2	Auckland	OCr1	Sinedo [79]	1 000	Rugg NZL
8-07	Australia	L	0-11	Auckland	OCr1		200	Rugg NZL
10-07	Vanuatu	L	0-1	Auckland	OCr1		500	Ariiotima TAH
2003								
30-06	Papua New Guinea	W	2-0	Suva	SPr1	Djamali [69], Hmae [81]		Shah FIJ
1-07	Micronesia †	W	18-0	Suva	SPr1	Hmae 4 [3 41 49 53], Poatinda 6 [8 9 29 33 66 76] Wajoka 3 [15 62 85], Elmour [16], Joseph [71], Jacques [78] Theodore [80], Jacky [84]	3 000	Moli SOL
3-07	Tonga	W	4-0	Suva	SPr1	Djamali [10], Dokunengo [30], Cawa [54], Kabeu [74]	700	Shah FIJ
5-07	Tahiti	W	4-0	Nadi	SPr1	Lameu 2 [10 41], Djamali [31], Poatinda [88]	3 000	Shah FIJ
9-07	Vanuatu	D	1-1	Lautoka	SPsf	Kabeu [44]. W 4-3p	7 000	Shah FIJ
11-07	Fiji	L	0-2	Suva	SPf		10 000	Attison VAN
2004								
12-05	Tahiti	D	0-0	Honiara	WCq		14 000	Rakaroi FIJ
15-05	Solomon Islands	L	0-2	Honiara	WCq		20 000	Attison VAN
17-05	Cook Islands	W	8-0	Honiara	WCq	Wajoka [3], Hmae 6 [20 35 40 42 52 85], Djamali [25]	400	Singh FIJ
19-05	Tonga	W	8-0	Honiara	WCq	Hmae 2 [4 45], Poatinda 3 [26 42 79], Wajoka 2 [54 58] Kaume [72]	14 000	Fred VAN
2005								
No international matches played in 2005 before August								

Fr = Friendly match • OC = OFC Oceania Nations Cup • SP = South Pacific Games • WC = FIFA World Cup™
q = qualifier • r1 = first round group • sf = semi-final • f = final • † Not a full international

NEW CALEDONIA NATIONAL TEAM RECORDS AND RECORD SEQUENCES

Records			Sequence records					
Victory	18-0	GUM 1991	Wins	6	1964-1966	Clean sheets	4	1987
Defeat	0-8	AUS 1980	Defeats	6	1995-1998	Goals scored	31	1951-1966
Player Caps	n/a		Undefeated	9	1969	Without goal	3	1988
Player Goals	n/a		Without win	6	1995-1998	Goals against	15	1969-1973

RECENT LEAGUE AND CUP RECORD

	Championship				Cup		
Year	Champions	Score	Runners-up		Winners	Score	Runners-up
1997	JS Baco	2-1	CA Saint-Louis		CA Saint-Louis	1-1 4-3p	FC Gaïcha
1998	AS Poum	4-2	JS Traput Lifou		JS Traput Lifou	1-1 4-3p	CS Nékoué
1999	FC Gaïcha	2-2 4-3p	AS Auteuil		JS Traput Lifou	1-0	AS Auteuil
2000	JS Baco	1-0	JS Traput Lifou		AS Magenta Nouméa	1-1 4-1p	JS Traput Lifou
2001	JS Baco	1-0	AS Mont-Doré		AS Magenta Nouméa	4-3	AS Mont-Doré
2002	AS Mont-Doré	2-2 4-3p	JS Baco		AS Magenta Nouméa	5-2	JS Ouvéa
2003	AS Magenta Nouméa	5-3	JS Baco		AS Magenta Nouméa	1-0	JS Baco
2004	AS Magenta Nouméa	3-1	AS Mont-Doré		AS Magenta Nouméa	2-1	AS Mont-Doré
2005	AS Magenta Nouméa	3-2	AS Mont-Doré		AS Magenta Nouméa	2-1	JS Baco

NEW CALEDONIA COUNTRY INFORMATION

Capital	Nouméa	Status	French overseas territory	GDP per Capita	$15 000
Population	213 679			GNP Ranking	n/a
Area km²	19 060	Language	French	Dialling code	+687
Population density	11 per km²	Literacy rate	91%	Internet code	.nc
% in urban areas	n/a	Main religion	Christian 60%	GMT +/–	+11
Towns/Cities ('000)	Nouméa 93; Mont-Doré 26; Dumbéa 21; Wé 11; Paita 10; Tadine 8; Poindimié 5; Houailu 5				
Neighbours (km)	South Pacific Ocean 2 254				
Main stadia	Nouméa-Daly Magenta – Nouméa				

NED – NETHERLANDS

NATIONAL TEAM RECORD
JULY 1ST 2002 TO JUNE 30TH 2005

PL	W	D	L	F	A	%
37	22	9	6	73	23	71.6

FIFA/COCA-COLA WORLD RANKING

1993	1994	1995	1996	1997	1998	1999	2000	2001	2002	2003	2004	High		Low	
7	6	6	9	22	11	19	8	8	6	4	6	2	11/93	25	05/98

2004-2005											
08/04	09/04	10/04	11/04	12/04	01/05	02/05	03/05	04/05	05/05	06/05	07/05
6	6	5	6	6	6	6	7	5	5	4	3

Rarely has there been a more successful or convincing baptism for an international coach as that experienced by Marco van Basten since taking the Dutch job in the aftermath of UEFA EURO 2004™. If the Dutch can overcome their propensity to fall apart at final tournaments they should be amongst the favourites to win the 2006 FIFA World Cup™. Providing they qualify that is, given that they are grouped with the equally successful Czech team with whom they are neck and neck in the race for the one automatic qualifying place. In his first year in charge Van Basten was unbeaten in 11 games which included a victory over the Czech Republic in Amsterdam. With a good crop of

INTERNATIONAL HONOURS
Qualified for the FIFA World Cup™ finals 1934 1938 1974 1978 1990 1994 1998 UEFA European Championship 1988
UEFA Champions League Feyenoord 1970 Ajax 1971 1972 1973 1995 PSV Eindhoven 1988

young talent like Arjen Robben and Robin van Persie much is expected of this Dutch team. The 2004-05 season also proved to a good one for Guus Hiddink as his PSV side won the double and were desperately unlucky to miss out on the UEFA Champions League final, having outclassed Milan in both legs of the semi-final. In the League PSV's main challenge came from AZ Alkmaar, who also reached the UEFA Cup semi-final, and they registered a rare Cup win – only the second in the past 15 years – after comfortably beating Willem II in the final.

THE FIFA BIG COUNT OF 2000

	Male	Female		Male	Female
Registered players	527 900	35 000	Referees	76 000	10 000
Non registered players	250 000	0	Officials	5 400	400
Youth players	418 000	30 000	Total involved	1 352 700	
Total players	1 260 900		Number of clubs	4 050	
Professional players	900	0	Number of teams	58 868	

Koninklijke Nederlandse Voetbalbond (KNVB)
Woudenbergseweg 56-58, PO Box 515, Am Zeist 3700, Netherlands
Tel +31 343 499201   Fax +31 343 499189
concern@knvb.nl   www.knvb.nl
President: SPRENGERS Mathieu Dr   General Secretary: BEEN Harry
Vice-President: LESTERHUIS Hans   Treasurer: HOOGENDOORN Jan Willem   Media Officer: DE LEEDE Rob
Men's Coach: VAN BASTEN Marco   Women's Coach: PAUW Vera
KNVB formed: 1889   UEFA: 1954   FIFA: 1904
Colours: Orange, White, Orange

GAMES PLAYED BY NETHERLANDS IN THE 2006 FIFA WORLD CUP™ CYCLE

2002	Opponents	Score		Venue	Comp	Scorers	Att	Referee
21-08	Norway	W	1-0	Oslo	Fr	Davids [71]	15 356	Stuchlik AUT
7-09	Belarus	W	3-0	Eindhoven	ECq	Davids [34], Kluivert [36], Hasselbaink [72]	34 000	Barber ENG
16-10	Austria	W	3-0	Vienna	ECq	Seedorf [16], Cocu [20], Makaay [30]	46 300	Collina ITA
20-11	Germany	W	3-1	Gelsenkirchen	Fr	Kluivert [22], Hasselbaink [69], Van Nistelrooij [79]	60 601	Dallas SCO
2003								
12-02	Argentina	W	1-0	Amsterdam	Fr	Van Bronckhorst [86]	40 090	Milton Nielsen DEN
29-03	Czech Republic	D	1-1	Rotterdam	ECq	Van Nistelrooij [45]	51 180	Milton Nielsen DEN
2-04	Moldova	W	2-1	Tiraspol	ECq	Van Nistelrooij [37], Van Bommel [85]	12 000	Sars FRA
30-04	Portugal	D	1-1	Eindhoven	Fr	Kluivert [27]	31 500	Meier SUI
7-06	Belarus	W	2-0	Minsk	ECq	Overmars [62], Kluivert [68]	28 000	Ovrebo NOR
20-08	Belgium	D	1-1	Brussels	Fr	Makaay [55]	38 000	Fandel GER
6-09	Austria	W	3-1	Rotterdam	ECq	Van der Vaart [30], Lkuivert [60], Cocu [64]	47 000	Poulat FRA
10-09	Czech Republic	L	1-3	Prague	ECq	Van der Vaart [62]	18 356	Cortez Batista POR
11-10	Moldova	W	5-0	Eindhoven	ECq	Kluivert [43], Sneijder [51], Van Hooijdonk [74p] Van der Vaart [80], Robben [89]	30 995	Siric CRO
15-11	Scotland	L	0-1	Glasgow	ECpo		50 670	Hauge NOR
19-11	Scotland	W	6-0	Amsterdam	ECpo	Sneijder [14], Ooijer [32], Van Nistelrooij 3 [37 51 67] De Boer.F [65]	51 000	Michel SVK
2004								
18-02	United States	W	1-0	Amsterdam	Fr	Robben [56]	29 700	Ovrebo NOR
31-03	France	D	0-0	Rotterdam	Fr		50 000	Stark GER
28-04	Greece	W	4-0	Eindhoven	Fr	Makaay [50], Zenden [58], Heitinga [61], Van Hooijdonk [89]	25 000	Bolognino ITA
29-05	Belgium	L	0-1	Eindhoven	Fr		32 500	Colombo FRA
1-06	Faroe Islands	W	3-0	Lausanne	Fr	Van der Vaart [29], Makaay [51], Overmars [58]	3 200	Leuba SUI
5-06	Republic of Ireland	L	0-1	Amsterdam	Fr		42 000	Dean ENG
15-06	Germany	D	1-1	Porto	ECr1	Van Nistelrooij [81]	52 000	Frisk SWE
19-06	Czech Republic	L	2-3	Aveiro	ECr1	Bouma [4], Van Nistelrooij [19]	29 935	Mejuto Gonzalez ESP
23-06	Latvia	W	3-0	Braga	ECr1	Van Nistelrooij 2 [27p 35], Makaay [84]	27 904	Milton Nielsen DEN
26-06	Sweden	D	0-0	Faro-Loule	ECqf	W 5-4p	27 286	Michel SVK
30-06	Portugal	L	1-2	Lisbon	ECsf	Jorge Andrade OG [63]	46 679	Frisk SWE
18-08	Sweden	D	2-2	Stockholm	Fr	Sneijder [17], Van Bommel [43]	20 377	Styles ENG
3-09	Liechtenstein	W	3-0	Utrecht	Fr	Van Bommel [23], Ooijer [56], Landzaat [78]	15 000	Brines SCO
8-09	Czech Republic	W	2-0	Amsterdam	WCq	Van Hooijdonk 2 [34 84]	48 488	Merk GER
9-10	FYR Macedonia	D	2-2	Skopje	WCq	Bouma [42], Kuyt [65]	15 000	Frojdfeldt SWE
13-10	Finland	W	3-1	Amsterdam	WCq	Sneijder [39], Van Nistelrooij 2 [41 63]	50 000	Bennett ENG
17-11	Andorra	W	3-0	Barcelona	WCq	Cocu [21], Robben [31], Sneijder [78]	2 000	Yefet ISR
2005								
9-02	England	D	0-0	Birmingham	Fr		40 705	Frojdfeldt SWE
26-03	Romania	W	2-0	Bucharest	WCq	Cocu [1], Babel [84]	19 000	Medina Cantalejo ESP
30-03	Armenia	W	2-0	Eindhoven	WCq	Castelen [3], Van Nistelrooij [33]	35 000	Trefoloni ITA
4-06	Romania	W	2-0	Rotterdam	WCq	Robben [26], Kuyt [47]	47 000	De Santis ITA
8-06	Finland	W	4-0	Helsinki	WCq	Van Nistelrooij [36], Kuyt [76], Coco [85], Van Persie [87]	37 786	Hamer LUX

Fr = Friendly match • EC = UEFA EURO 2004™ • WC = FIFA World Cup™ • q = qualifier • r1 = first round group • qf = quarter-final

NETHERLANDS COUNTRY INFORMATION

Capital	The Hague	Formation	1579	GDP per Capita	$28 600
Population	16 318 199	Status	Constitutional Monarchy	GNP Ranking	14
Area km2	41 526	Language	Dutch	Dialling code	+31
Population density	393 per km2	Literacy rate	99%	Internet code	.nl
% in urban areas	89%	Main religion	Christinan 52%	GMT + / –	+1
Towns/Cities ('000)	Amsterdam 745; Rotterdam 603; The Hague 476; Utrecht 267; Eindhoven 210; Tilburg 206; Almere 186; Groningen 179; Breda 168; Nijmegen 158; Apeldoorn 157; Enschede 154; Haarlem 147; Arnhem 144; Zaanstad 141; Amersfoort 139; 's-Hertogenbosch 135				
Neighbours (km)	Germany 577; Belgium 450; North Sea 451				
Main stadia	Amsterdam ArenA – Amsterdam 51 859; Stadion Feijenoord (De Kuip) – Rotterdam 51 180; Philips Stadion – Eindhoven 36 500; Gelredome – Arnhem 29 000				

NATIONAL CAPS

	Caps
DE BOER Frank	112
VAN DER SAR Edwin	100
COCU Philip	90
OVERMARS Marc	86
WINTER Aron	84
KROL Ruud	83
BERGKAMP Dennis	79
KLUIVERT Patrick	79
KOEMAN Ronald	78
SEEDORF Clarence	77

NATIONAL GOALS

	Goals
KLUIVERT Patrick	40
BERGKAMP Dennis	37
WILKES Faas	35
LENSTRA Abe	33
CRUIJFF Johan	33
BAKHUYS Bep	28
SMIT Kick	26
VAN BASTEN Marco	24
VAN NISTELROOIJ Ruud	22
VENTE Leen	19

NATIONAL COACH

	Years
LIBREGTS Thijs	1988-'89
DE RUITER Nol	1990
BEENHAKKER Leo	1990
MICHELS Rinus	1990-'92
ADVOCAAT Dick	1992-'94
HIDDINK Guus	1994-'98
RIJKAARD Frank	1998-'00
VAN GAAL Louis	2000-'01
ADVOCAAT Dick	2002-'04
VAN BASTEN Marco	2004-

NETHERLANDS NATIONAL TEAM RECORDS AND RECORD SEQUENCES

Records			Sequence records					
Victory	9-0	FIN 1912, NOR 1972	Wins	7	1971-72, 2002-03	Clean sheets	6	1987, 2004-05
Defeat	2-12	ENG 1907	Defeats	8	1949-1950	Goals scored	23	1912-1920
Player Caps	112	DE BOER Frank	Undefeated	17	2001-2003	Without goal	3	1949-50, 1968
Player Goals	40	KLUIVERT Patrick	Without win	12	1951-1953	Goals against	24	1938-1948

CLUB DIRECTORY

Club	Town/City	Stadium	Phone	www.	Lge	Cup	CL
ADO Den Haag	The Hague	Zuiderpark 11 000	+31 70 3054500	adodenhaag.nl	2	1	0
Ajax	Amsterdam	Amsterdam ArenA 51,859	+31 20 3111444	ajax.nl	29	15	4
AZ Alkmaar	Alkmaar	Alkmaarderhout 8,372	+31 72 5154744	az.nl	1	3	0
Den Bosch	's-Hertogenbosch	Ecco Stadion 9 000	+31 73 6464700	fcdenbosch.nl	0	0	0
Feyenoord	Rotterdam	De Kuip 51 180	+31 10 2926870	feyenoord.nl	14	10	1
De Graafschap	Doetinchem	De Vijverberg 10 900	+31 314 368450	degraafschap.nl	0	0	0
FC Groningen	Groningen	Oosterpark 13 000	+31 50 5878787	fcgroningen.nl	0	0	0
SC Heerenveen	Heerenveen	Abe Lenstra 17 653	+31 513 612100	sc-heerenveen.nl	0	0	0
NAC Breda	Breda	MyCom Stadion 17 064	+31 76 5214500	nac.nl	1	1	0
NEC Nijmegan	Nijmegen	De Goffert 12 500	+31 24 3590360	nec-nijmegan.nl	0	0	0
PSV Eindhoven	Eindhoven	Philips Stadion 36 500	+31 40 2505514	psv.nl	18	8	1
RBC Roosendaal	Roosendaal	Vast & Goed 4 995	+31 165 540133	rbconline.nl	0	0	0
RKC Waalwijk	Waalwijk	Mandemakers 7 500	+31 416 334356	rkcwaalwijk.nl	0	0	0
Roda JC	Kerkrade	Parkstad Limburg 19 200	+31 45 6317000	rodajc.nl	0	2	0
FC Twente	Enschede	Arke Stadion 13 500	+31 53 8525572	fctwente.nl	0	2	0
FC Utrecht	Utrecht	Nieuw Galgenwaard 18 500	+31 30 8885503	fc-utrecht.nl	0	3	0
Vitesse	Arnhem	Gelredome 29 000	+31 26 8807888	vitesse.com	0	0	0
Willem II	Tilburg	Willem II 14 700	+31 13 5490590	willem-ii.nl	3	2	0

RECENT LEAGUE AND CUP RECORD

		Championship					Cup		
Year	Champions	Pts	Runners-up	Pts	Third	Pts	Winners	Score	Runners-up
1990	Ajax	49	PSV Eindhoven	48	Twente Enschede	42	PSV Eindhoven	1-0	Vitesse Arnhem
1991	PSV Eindhoven	53	Ajax	53	FC Groningen	46	Feyenoord	1-0	BVV Den Bosch
1992	PSV Eindhoven	58	Ajax	55	Feyenoord	49	Feyenoord	3-0	Roda JC Kerkrade
1993	Feyenoord	53	PSV Eindhoven	51	Ajax	49	Ajax	6-2	SC Heerenveen
1994	Ajax	54	Feyenoord	51	PSV Eindhoven	44	Feyenoord	2-1	NEC Nijmegan
1995	Ajax	61	Roda JC Kerkrade	54	PSV Eindhoven	47	Feyenoord	2-1	FC Volendam
1996	Ajax	83	PSV Eindhoven	77	Feyenoord	63	PSV Eindhoven	5-2	Sparta Rotterdam
1997	PSV Eindhoven	77	Feyenoord	73	Twente Enschede	65	Roda JC Kerkrade	4-2	SC Heerenveen
1998	Ajax	89	PSV Eindhoven	72	Vitesse Arnhem	70	SC Heerenveen	3-1	Twente Enschede
1999	Feyenoord	80	Willem II Tilburg	65	PSV Eindhoven	61	Ajax	2-0	Fortuna Sittard
2000	PSV Eindhoven	84	SC Heerenveen	68	Feyenoord	64	Roda JC Kerkrade	2-0	NEC Nijmegan
2001	PSV Eindhoven	83	Feyenoord	66	Ajax	61	Twente Enschede	0-0 4-3p	PSV Eindhoven
2002	Ajax	73	PSV Eindhoven	68	Feyenoord	64	Ajax	3-2	FC Utrecht
2003	PSV Eindhoven	84	Ajax	83	Feyenoord	80	FC Utrecht	4-1	Feyenoord
2004	Ajax	80	PSV Eindhoven	74	Feyenoord	68	FC Utrecht	1-0	Twente Enschede
2005	PSV Eindhoven	87	Ajax	77	AZ Alkmaar	64	PSV Eindhoven	4-0	Willem II Tilburg

AMSTEL CUP 2004-05

Second Round | **Third Round** | **Fourth Round**

			PSV Eindhoven *	4
			FC Volendam	0
Heracles Almelo	3			
Fortuna Sittard *	1	Heracles Almelo	1	
Lisse *	1	**FC Volendam ***	3	
FC Volendam	2			
RKC Waalwijk *	1			
FC Eindhoven	0	**RKC Waalwijk**	1 4p	
VVV Venlo *	0	Feyenoord 2 *	1 3p	
Feyenoord 2	2			
Helmond Sport *	3			RKC Waalwijk	1 5p
De Treffers/Kegro	1	Helmond Sport *	2	**TOP Oss ***	1 6p
Haarlem	2	**TOP Oss**	4	
TOP Oss *	4			
NAC Breda	2			
FC Groningen *	1	**NAC Breda**	3	
ROHDA Raalte	0	ADO '20 *	0	
ADO '20 *	3			NAC Breda *	2
				FC Utrecht	1

			AZ Alkmaar *	1
			Feyenoord	3

			Ajax *	2
			SC Heerenveen	0

FC Twente Enschede *	3			
Baronie	0	**FC Twente Enschede**	2	
RBC Roosendaal	0	NEC Nijmegan *	0	
NEC Nijmegan *	4			
Emmen *	5			FC Twente Enschede	1 3p
WHC	1	Emmen	1	**ADO Den Haag ***	1 4p
FC Zwolle	0	**ADO Den Haag ***	3	
ADO Den Haag *	3			
FC Ben Bosch *	8			
Quick '20	0	**FC Ben Bosch ***	1	
AGOVV Apeldorn *	0	Vitesse Arnhem	0	
Vitesse Arnhem	2			FC Ben Bosch	3
Stormvogels/Telstar	2			FC Dordrecht *	1
Cambuur Leeuwarden *	0	Stormvogels/Telstar *	0	
Quick Boys	1	**FC Dordrecht**	2	
FC Dordrecht *	6			
Go Ahead Eagles	4			
De Graafschap *	0	**Go Ahead Eagles ***	2	
Excelsior	0	Roda JC Kerkrade	0	
Roda JC Kerkrade *	3			Go Ahead Eagles *	0
BV Veendam	4			**Willem II Tilburg**	1
IJsselmeervogels *	3	BV Veendam *	4	
Sparta Rotterdam	0	**Willem II Tilburg**	5	
Willem II Tilburg *	2			

* Home team • Clubs playing in Europe join in at the fourth round

AMSTEL CUP 2004-05

Quarter-finals   **Semi-finals**   **Final**

PSV Eindhoven *	6
TOP Oss	1

PSV Eindhoven	1	4p
Feyenoord *	1	2p

NAC Breda	0
Feyenoord *	4

PSV Eindhoven	4
Willem II Tilburg ‡	0

Ajax	2
ADO Den Haag *	0

Ajax	0
Willem II Tilburg *	1

FC Den Bosch	0
Willem II Tilburg *	3

AMSTEL CUP FINAL 2005

De Kuip, Rotterdam, 29-05-2005, Att: 35 000, Referee: Braamhaar

PSV Eindhoven   4   Bouma [45], Cocu [51], Park [74], Hesselink [90]

Willem II Tilburg   0

PSV – Gomes; Lee, Alex, Bouma (Ooijer 70), Lucius; Van Bommel, Vogel, Cocu (Afellay 70); Vennegoor of Hesselink, Farfán, Park. Tr: Guus Hiddink
Willem II – Moens; van der Haar, Wau, Van Mosselveld (Redan 70), Van der Struijk; Augustien (Delanoy 85), Victoria (Kreek 46), Caluwé; Ceesay, Bobson, Reuser. Tr: Maaskant

‡ Qualified for the UEFA Cup

NETHERLANDS 2004-05

EREDIVISIE

Team	Pl	W	D	L	F	A	Pts	PSV	Ajax	AZ	Feyenoord	Heerenveen	Twente	Vitesse	Roda	Waalwijk	Willem II	Utrecht	Groningen	NEC	ADO	NAC	RBC	Graafschap	Den Bosch
PSV Eindhoven †	34	27	6	1	89	18	87	—	2-0	5-1	4-2	4-0	2-0	3-0	0-2	1-0	1-0	2-0	3-0	4-1	4-0	4-0	4-1	4-1	3-0
Ajax †	34	24	5	5	74	33	77	0-4	—	4-2	1-1	1-3	1-2	1-0	1-0	4-0	2-0	1-1	2-1	1-0	0-0	6-2	4-1	1-0	2-0
AZ Alkmaar ‡	34	19	7	8	71	41	64	0-0	0-0	—	4-1	1-1	5-0	3-0	1-1	3-0	3-1	4-0	2-1	1-1	2-0	1-1	1-3	3-2	5-0
Feyenoord ‡	34	19	5	10	90	51	62	3-3	2-3	4-2	—	1-3	3-1	1-2	4-1	4-0	7-0	0-3	1-2	2-1	6-3	4-0	3-0	6-1	4-2
SC Heerenveen ‡	34	18	6	10	64	52	60	0-3	2-1	1-3	2-2	—	1-2	0-3	3-4	1-2	2-2	2-1	1-0	2-1	1-0	3-0	7-1	2-0	2-1
FC Twente Enschede	34	15	9	10	48	38	54	2-2	2-3	3-0	0-0	4-1	—	1-4	2-3	3-1	0-0	0-1	1-2	2-1	2-1	0-0	3-0	0-0	4-0
Vitesse Arnhem	34	16	6	12	53	49	54	0-2	0-2	0-3	1-1	1-3	1-1	—	3-0	3-1	2-0	2-1	1-0	1-0	3-4	1-2	1-3	3-1	0-0
Roda JC Kerkrade	34	13	8	13	60	55	47	0-0	1-2	1-1	0-2	2-3	1-2	2-3	—	1-1	4-0	3-2	5-1	1-0	1-1	2-1	3-1	2-1	5-0
RKC Waalwijk	34	13	8	13	44	51	47	1-4	1-2	2-1	4-0	1-0	2-2	1-0	1-0	—	1-0	2-2	3-0	2-2	1-3	1-0	2-0	2-2	2-2
Willem II Tilburg ‡	34	13	6	15	44	56	45	0-1	1-3	1-3	0-4	2-2	0-3	3-2	3-1	3-0	—	0-0	4-2	3-1	1-0	0-1	3-0	4-1	2-1
FC Utrecht	34	12	8	14	40	43	44	0-0	0-2	3-2	0-2	0-1	2-2	1-2	1-1	3-2	0-3	—	1-2	1-0	2-0	2-0	5-1	1-0	1-0
FC Groningen	34	11	7	16	50	58	40	0-1	0-4	1-2	0-2	1-2	1-0	0-0	4-4	0-0	1-1	3-0	—	0-0	4-3	2-3	3-0	1-0	3-1
NEC Nijmegen	34	9	10	15	41	47	37	0-3	0-1	1-2	2-0	3-2	0-2	1-1	1-1	2-0	0-0	4-3		—	1-1	3-3	3-0	3-0	2-2
ADO Den Haag	34	10	6	18	44	59	36	0-2	3-3	2-1	2-0	0-2	0-1	0-4	1-4	0-0	0-1	1-0	0-3	1-2	—	6-2	5-1	2-0	2-0
NAC Breda	34	9	8	17	43	67	35	2-2	1-2	0-3	0-2	1-1	1-1	1-2	4-0	0-4	1-2	3-2	1-4	1-2	1-1	—	1-2	3-2	3-0
RBC Roosendaal	34	10	2	22	38	77	32	2-5	1-4	0-2	0-4	1-3	0-1	4-1	3-1	0-1	2-0	0-0	1-2	1-0	2-0	0-0	—	3-0	1-1
De Graafschap	34	4	7	23	32	78	19	0-4	0-5	1-3	2-7	2-1	0-0	1-2	2-0	2-4	2-2	0-0	2-3	2-1	1-2	0-2	0-1	—	1-1
FC Den Bosch	34	5	4	25	23	75	19	0-3	0-5	0-1	4-1	2-4	1-0	1-2	0-3	0-2	1-2	0-3	1-2	0-0	1-0	0-2	2-1	0-2	—

13/08/2004 - 29/05/2005 • † Qualified for the UEFA Champions League • ‡ Qualified for the UEFA Cup

TOP SCORERS

KUIJT Dirk	Feyenoord	29
KALOU Salomon	Feyenoord	20
VENNEGOOR OF HESSELINK Jan	PSV Einhoven	19
HUNTELAAR Klaas-Jan	Heerenveen	16
NEVLAND Erik	Groningen	16
N'KUFO Blaise	Twente	16
KONE Arouna	Roda	15
VAN BOMMEL Mark	PSV	14

NETHERLANDS 2004-05 EERSTE DIVISIE

Team	Pl	W	D	L	F	A	Pts
Heracles Almelo	36	23	6	7	67	34	75
Sparta Rotterdam †	36	21	11	4	93	39	74
VVV Venlo †	36	18	8	10	56	36	62
FC Zwolle †	36	17	10	9	66	50	61
FC Volendam †	36	18	7	11	52	38	61
Helmond Sport †	36	16	9	11	61	44	57
Stormvogels/Telstar †	36	15	11	10	58	46	56
FC Dordrecht	36	15	8	13	46	51	53
Cambuur Leeuwarden	36	13	8	15	44	54	47
AGOVV Apeldoorn	36	15	1	20	55	60	46
BV Veendam	36	11	12	13	47	56	45
Excelsior Rotterdam	36	12	8	16	56	59	44
Haarlem	36	11	9	16	47	56	42
MVV Maastricht	36	9	12	15	40	46	39
FC Eindhoven	36	10	9	17	60	80	39
TOP Oss	36	10	9	17	41	66	39
Go Ahead Eagles §3	36	9	11	16	40	60	35
Emmen	36	7	9	20	38	71	30
Fortuna Sittard §6	36	8	10	18	46	67	28

13/08/2004 - 22/05/2005 • † Qualified for the play-offs •
§3 Three points deducted • §6 Six points deducted

PROMOTION/RELEGATION NACOMPETITIE GROUP A

Team	Pl	W	D	L	F	A	Pts	Ro	Vo	ST	Ve
RBC Roosendaal	6	3	2	1	9	3	11	—	4-0	2-1	2-0
FC Volendam	6	2	3	1	11	9	9	0-0	—	3-1	4-1
Stormvogels/Telstar	6	2	2	2	9	10	8	0-0	0-3	—	2-1
VVV Venlo	6	1	1	4	6	13	4	2-1	1-1	1-3	—

25/05/2005 - 9/06/2005 • RBC retain their place in the Eredivisie

PROMOTION/RELEGATION NACOMPETITIE GROUP B

Team	Pl	W	D	L	F	A	Pts	Sp	HS	Gr	Zw
Sparta Rotterdam	6	5	0	1	13	5	15	—	0-1	1-0	3-1
Helmond Sport	6	2	3	1	11	6	9	1-2	—	1-1	5-0
De Graafschap	6	2	2	2	11	10	8	1-3	2-2	—	3-2
FC Zwolle	6	0	1	5	6	20	1	1-4	1-1	1-4	—

25/05/2005 - 9/06/2005

PSV EINDHOVEN 2004-05

Date	Opponents	Score		Comp	Scorers	Att
11-08-2004	Crvena Zvezda Beograd - SCG	L 2-3	A	CLpr3	Park [8], De Jong [65]	
14-08-2004	RBC Roosendaal	W 5-2	A	ED	Hesselink 3 [31 62 74], Sibon [59], Beasley [76]	4 850
21-08-2004	AZ Alkmaar	W 5-1	H	ED	Van Bommel [21], Ooijer [60], De Jong 2 [70 88], Park [76]	32 500
25-08-2004	Crvena Zvezda Beograd - SCG	W 5-0	H	CLpr3	Van Bommel 2 [9p 56], Beasley [32], De Jong [57], Hesselink [80]	
28-08-2004	NAC Breda	D 2-2	A	ED	Van Bommel [1], Sibon [61]	13 072
11-09-2004	RKC Waalwijk	W 1-0	H	ED	Hesselink [46]	34 500
14-09-2004	Arsenal - ENG	L 0-1	A	CLgE		34 068
18-09-2004	NEC Nijmegan	W 3-0	A	ED	Van Bommel [29p], Lamey [72], Vonlanthen [89]	12 000
25-09-2004	SC Heerenveen	W 4-0	H	ED	Lucius [49], Farfán [57], Hesselink 2 [63 74]	31 000
29-09-2004	Panathinaikos - GRE	W 1-0	H	CLgE	Hesselink [80]	26 500
2-10-2004	FC Groningen	W 3-0	H	ED	Elshot OG [5], Beasley [32], De Jong [65]	30 500
16-10-2004	ADO Den Haag	W 2-0	A	ED	Vonlanthen 2 [1 53]. Abandoned 80'. Result stood	7 500
20-10-2004	Rosenborg BK - NOR	W 2-1	A	CLgE	Farfán [26], De Jong [86]	20 950
24-10-2004	Ajax	W 2-0	H	ED	Lee [39], De Jong [49]	35 000
29-10-2004	FC Utrecht	D 0-0	A	ED		22 286
2-11-2004	Rosenborg BK - NOR	W 1-0	H	CLgE	Beasley [10]	26 250
7-11-2004	Den Bosch	W 3-0	A	ED	Farfán [41], Alex [68], Cocu [74]	6 477
13-11-2004	Willem II Tilburg	W 1-0	H	ED	Hesselink [16]	31 000
21-11-2004	Vitesse Arnhem	W 2-0	A	ED	Sibon [56], Beasley [90]	17 349
24-11-2004	Arsenal - ENG	D 1-1	H	CLgE	Ooijer [8]	26 100
27-11-2004	FC Twente Enscede	W 2-0	H	ED	Sibon [15], Cocu [66]	30 500
4-12-2004	De Graafschap	W 4-0	A	ED	Alex [20], Van Bommel [66p], Farfán 2 [77 82]	11 500
7-12-2004	Panathinaikos - GRE	L 1-4	A	CLgE	Beasley [37]	10 196
12-12-2004	Feyenoord	D 3-3	A	ED	Cocu [6], Farfán [24], Beasley [70]	45 000
18-12-2004	Roda JC Kerkrade	L 0-2	H	ED		31 300
22-01-2005	NAC Breda	W 4-0	H	ED	Hesselink 2 [28 38], Penders OG [71], Van Bommel [76]	31 000
25-01-2005	FC Volendam	W 4-0	H	ACr4	Hesselink [37], Park [44], Van Bommel 2 [49 52]	
30-01-2005	RKC Waalwijk	W 4-1	A	ED	Beasley [35], Hesselink 3 [38 69 82]	7 000
2-02-2005	RBC Roosendaal	W 4-1	H	ED	Van Bommel 2 [51p 58], Hesselink [75p], De Jong [83]	30 200
12-02-2005	AZ Alkmaar	D 0-0	A	ED		8 683
19-02-2005	NEC Nijmegan	W 4-1	H	ED	Park [21], Beasley [45], Hesselink [71], Ooijer [77]	30 800
22-02-2005	Monaco - FRA	W 1-0	H	CLr2	Alex [8]	31 225
27-02-2005	SC Heerenveen	W 3-0	A	ED	Park [39], Farfán 2 [82 90]	19 500
3-03-2005	TOP Oss	W 6-1	H	ACqf	Lamey [2], Robert 3 [11 26 58], Beasley [36], Van Bommel [83]	
9-03-2005	Monaco - FRA	W 2-0	A	CLr2	Hesselink [27], Beasley [69]	15 523
13-03-2005	ADO Den Haag	W 4-0	H	ED	Park 2 [6 42], Van Bommel [28], Alex [88]	31 000
17-03-2005	FC Groningen	W 1-0	A	ED	Farfán [45]	12 500
20-03-2005	Ajax	W 4-0	H	ED	Cocu [24], Van Bommel 3 [45 54 59]	50 765
2-04-2005	FC Utrecht	W 2-0	H	ED	Hesselink [37], Park [42]	31 600
5-04-2005	Olympique Lyonnais - FRA	D 1-1	A	CLqf	Cocu [79]	35 000
9-04-2005	Den Bosch	W 3-0	H	ED	Cocu [30], Bouma [61], Van Bommel [89]	31 200
13-04-2005	Olympique Lyonnais - FRA	D 1-1	H	CLqf	Alex [50]. W 4-2p	35 000
17-04-2005	Willem II Tilburg	W 1-0	A	ED	Robert [62]	12 700
20-04-2005	Feyenoord	D 1-1	A	ACsf	Beasley [89]. W 4-2p	
23-04-2005	Vitesse Arnhem	W 3-0	H	ED	Park [23], Van Bommel [44], Sibon [87]	33 600
26-04-2005	Milan - ITA	L 0-4	A	CLsf		71 000
29-04-2005	FC Twente Enschede	D 2-2	A	ED	Sibon [67], Hesselink [76]	13 100
4-05-2005	Milan - ITA	W 3-1	H	CLsf	Park [9], Cocu 2 [65 90]	35 000
7-05-2005	De Graafschap	W 4-1	H	ED	Hesselink 2 [2 10], Cocu [12], Vogel [55]	32 000
15-05-2005	Feyenoord	W 4-2	H	ED	Afellay 2 [13 71], Hesselink [40], Van Bommel [52]	33 000
22-05-2005	Roda JC Kerkrade	D 0-0	A	ED		15 500
29-05-2005	Willem II Tilburg	W 4-0	N	ACf	Bouma [45], Cocu [51], Park [74], Hesselink [90]	35 000

ED = Eredivisie • AC = Amstel Cup • CL = UEFA Champions League
pr3 = third preliminary round • gE = Group E • r2 = second round • r4 = fourth round • qf = quarter-final • sf = semi-final • f = final

NEP – NEPAL

NATIONAL TEAM RECORD
JULY 1ST 2002 TO JUNE 30TH 2005

PL	W	D	L	F	A	%
11	2	0	9	8	49	18.2

FIFA/COCA-COLA WORLD RANKING

1993	1994	1995	1996	1997	1998	1999	2000	2001	2002	2003	2004	High		Low	
124	138	147	151	155	176	157	166	156	165	165	177	**124**	12/93	**178**	07/05

2004-2005											
08/04	09/04	10/04	11/04	12/04	01/05	02/05	03/05	04/05	05/05	06/05	07/05
175	175	175	176	177	176	177	177	178	177	178	178

The decision not to enter the qualifying rounds for the 2006 FIFA World Cup™ gives an indication of the state of football in Nepal today. The 1984 and 1993 South Asian Federation Games champions experienced a dreadful 2004 Asian Cup qualifying campaign in which a 4-0 victory over Afghanistan was followed by seven straight defeats including a particularly gruelling 16-0 reverse at the hands of Korea Republic. The decision not to enter the FIFA World Cup™ was taken in order to concentrate resources on re-organisation in order to improve results over time. However, with no senior international match played in nearly two years, the road to progress may be a long one.

INTERNATIONAL HONOURS
South Asian Games 1984 1993

With no national League football is mostly centred on the capital and the 13-team Kathmandu League is the nearest thing to a high level competition with the top six progressing to the Super League stage. Three Star Club won the title undefeated three points clear of runners-up Mahendra Police Club. The two teams met in the final fixture where, watched by 20,000 spectators, Star secured the draw they needed for the Championship. Police got some revenge in the inaugural Himalayan Bank Cup when they beat Three Star 3-2 in the final. At youth level the U-20s reached the Asian finals in Malaysia where they beat Vietnam, but lost to Japan and the hosts.

THE FIFA BIG COUNT OF 2000

	Male	Female		Male	Female
Registered players	2 500	0	Referees	200	0
Non registered players	100 000	0	Officials	800	0
Youth players	2 500	0	Total involved	106 000	
Total players	105 000		Number of clubs	100	
Professional players	0	0	Number of teams	400	

All-Nepal Football Association (ANFA)
ANFA House, Ward No.4, Bishalnagar, PO Box 12582, Kathmandu, Nepal
Tel +977 1 5539059　　　　Fax +977 1 4424314
ganesht@ntc.net.np　　　　www.none
President: THAPA Ganesh　　　General Secretary: THAPA Kumar
Vice-President: BISTA Mahesh　　　Treasurer: SHAH Birat Jun　　　Media Officer: None
Men's Coach: THAPA Krishna　　　Women's Coach: KISHOR K.C.
ANFA formed: 1951　　　AFC: 1971　　　FIFA: 1970
Colours: Red, Red, Red

GAMES PLAYED BY NEPAL IN THE 2006 FIFA WORLD CUP™ CYCLE

2002	Opponents	Score		Venue	Comp	Scorers	Att	Referee
No international matches played in 2002								
2003								
11-01	Bangladesh	L	0-1	Dhaka	SAFr1		55 000	Kunsuta THA
13-01	Bhutan	W	2-0	Dhaka	SAFr1	Rayamajhi [14], Thapa [87]	25 000	Raj IND
15-01	Maldives	L	2-3	Dhaka	SAFr1	Rayamajhi [56], Chaudhary [90p]	15 000	Kunsata THA
18-03	Afghanistan	W	4-0	Kathmandu	ACq	Rayamajhi 2 [35 88], Khadka [39], Lama [90]		Haq IND
20-03	Kyrgyzstan	L	0-2	Kathmandu	ACq			
25-09	Oman	L	0-7	Incheon	ACq			
27-09	Vietnam	L	0-5	Incheon	ACq			
29-09	Korea Republic	L	0-16	Incheon	ACq			
19-10	Oman	L	0-6	Muscat	ACq			Al Ghafary JOR
21-10	Vietnam	L	0-2	Muscat	ACq			
24-10	Korea Republic	L	0-7	Muscat	ACq			
2004								
No international matches played in 2004								
2005								
No international matches played in 2005 before August								

Fr = Friendly match • SAF = South Asian Football Federation Cup • AC = AFC Asian Cup • q = qualifier • r1 = first round group

NEPAL NATIONAL TEAM RECORDS AND RECORD SEQUENCES

Records			Sequence records					
Victory	7-0	BHU 1999	Wins	3	1982	Clean sheets	2	Four times
Defeat	0-16	KOR 2003	Defeats	10	1997-1998	Goals scored	4	1995
Player Caps	n/a		Undefeated	3	1982, 1993	Without goal	13	1987-1989
Player Goals	n/a		Without win	20	1987-93, 1995-98	Goals against	21	1996-1999

RECENT LEAGUE AND CUP RECORD

	Championship	Cup
Year	Champions	Winners
1995	New Road Team	
1996	No Tournament	
1997	Three Star Club	Tribhuvan Army Club
1998	Three Star Club	Mahendra Police
1999	No tournament	Mahendra Police
2000	Manang Marsyangdi	
2001	No tournament	
2002	No tournament	Mahendra Police
2003	Manang Marsyangdi	Manang Marsyangdi
2004	Three Star Club	Mahendra Police

The Cup from 1997 to 1999 refers to the National League Cup, in 2002 to the Tribhuvan Challenge Shield and for 2003 and 2004 to the Khukuri Gold Cup

NEPAL 2004 KATHMANDU LEAGUE

	Pl	W	D	L	F	A	Pts
Three Star Club	17	12	5	0	37	8	**41**
Mahendra Police Club	17	11	5	1	35	7	38
Tribhuvan Army Club	17	9	6	2	36	13	33
Manang Marsyangdi	17	9	4	4	32	13	31
Friends Club	17	5	5	7	20	38	20
Jawalakhel Youth Club	17	3	7	7	18	27	16
New Road Team	12	4	3	5	14	14	15
Sankata Boys Sports Club	12	3	5	4	13	15	14
Brigade Boys Club	12	2	5	5	11	33	11
Ranipokhari Corner Team	12	2	4	6	7	12	10
Boys Union Club	12	2	3	7	14	30	9
Mahavir Club	12	1	5	6	10	21	8
Kathmandu Club	12	1	1	10	9	25	4

17/04/2004 - 18/07/2004 • Top six played an extra five rounds

NEPAL COUNTRY INFORMATION

Capital	Kathmandu	Formation	1769	GDP per Capita	$1 400
Population	27 070 666	Status	Constitutional Monarchy	GNP Ranking	107
Area km²	140 800	Language	Nepali	Dialling code	+977
Population density	19 per km²	Literacy rate	45%	Internet code	.np
% in urban areas	14%	Main religion	Hindu 86%, Buddhism 8%	GMT +/−	5.75
Towns/Cities ('000)	Kathmandu 790; Pokhara 186; Laltipur 183; Biratnagar 183; Birganj 133; Bharatpur 107				
Neighbours (km)	China 1 236; India 1 690				
Main stadia	Dasarath Rangasala – Kathmandu 25 000				

NGA – NIGERIA

NATIONAL TEAM RECORD
JULY 1ST 2002 TO JUNE 30TH 2005

PL	W	D	L	F	A	%
34	17	10	7	51	31	64.7

Enyimba once again proved to be the story of the year in Nigeria by defending their CAF Champions League title – the first club to do so since TP Englebert in 1968 – proving that the triumph in 2003 was no fluke. Once again they beat North African opposition in the final although it did take a penalty shoot-out to beat Tunisia's Etoile du Sahel after both teams won their home legs 2-1. The team from the provincial town of Aba proved that good organisation can take you a long way in Nigerian football and that Europe does not have to be the chosen destination of every good player - at least not intially. Enyimba couldn't defend their League title, however, losing out to neighbours Dolphins from Port Harcourt. With just 20 away wins beyween all 18 clubs all season, the Championship proved to be relatively evenly matched, harking back to the days when an away trip posed genuine obstacles. Away from the glare of saturation television coverage, there were stories of teams being held up and robbed whilst driving to games and intimidation by fans and officials of the home teams, none more so than the players of Lobi Stars who claimed they were forced back on to the pitch by armed officials until Bendel Insurance scored a fourth goal which

INTERNATIONAL HONOURS
Qualified for the FIFA World Cup™ finals 1994 1998 2002   Qualified for the FIFA Women's World Cup finals 1991 1995 1999 2003
Olympic Games Gold 1996   FIFA U-17 World Championship 1985 1993
CAF African Cup of Nations 1980 1994   African Women's Championship 1991 1995 1998 2000 2002 2004
African Youth Championship 1983 1985 1987 1989 2005   African U-17 Championship 2001   African Women's U-19 Championship 2002 2004
CAF Champions League Enyimba 2003 2004

meant that Insurance and not Pillars qualified for the CAF Confederation Cup. After winning the Championship Dolphin finished the season in style by winning the NFA Cup. In Benin City they beat Enugu Rangers by a single goal to win the trophy for the second time. Once again the national team was a topic of much debate, especially the position of experienced coach Christian Chukwu. Despite a fine overall record too many draws in the 2006 FIFA World Cup™ qualifiers cost Chukwu his job when with just two games to go Nigeria found themselves in too close a fight with Angola and Zimbabwe for the one place in the finals. Once more it opened up the debate as to the benefits or not of a local coach managing highly paid European based stars vis-à-vis a European coach unfamiliar with the customs of local football. It is a debate that may be resolved soon as the success of the youth team at the FIFA World Youth Championship in the Netherlands showed. Coached by Samson Siasia, a Nigerian with many years experience in Europe, the Flying Eagles went all the way to the final before losing to Argentina. With Stephen Keshi doing well with Togo this new generation of coaches offers perhaps the best way forward for African football.

Nigeria Football Association (NFA)
Plot 2033, Olusegun Obasanjo Way, Zone 7, Wuse Abuja, PO Box 5101 Garki, Abuja, Nigeria
Tel +234 9 5237326   Fax +234 9 5237327
info@nigeriafa.com   www.nigeriafa.com
President: GALADIMA Ibrahim   General Secretary: OGUNJOBI Taiwo Chief
Vice-President: CHUKWUMA Gabriel   Treasurer: OKE Olubode   Media Officer: SAMUEL Kaalu
Men's Coach: TBD   Women's Coach: IZILEIN Godwin
NFA formed: 1945   CAF: 1959   FIFA: 1959
Colours: Green, Green, Green

GAMES PLAYED BY NIGERIA IN THE 2006 FIFA WORLD CUP™ CYCLE

2002	Opponents	Score		Venue	Comp	Scorers	Att	Referee
8-09	Angola	D	0-0	Luanda	CNq		10 000	Mathabela RSA
12-10	Senegal	D	2-2	Dakar	Fr	Okechukwu [46], Idahor [48]	50 000	Diatta SEN
20-11	Jamaica	D	0-0	Lagos	Fr		35 000	Quartey GHA
25-11	Egypt	D	1-1	Lagos	Fr	Moneke [73]	8 000	
15-12	Ghana	W	1-0	Accra	Fr	Yeboah.D OG [12]	15 000	Wellington GHA
2003								
16-02	Gambia	W	1-0	Banjul	Fr	Ugochukwu [10]	30 000	
29-03	Malawi	W	1-0	Blantyre	CNq	Utaka [10]	60 000	Nkole ZAM
25-05	Jamaica	L	2-3	Kingston	Fr	Ugochukwu [65], Kanu [80]	25 000	Brizan TRI
30-05	Ghana	W	3-1	Abuja	Fr	Aiyegbeni 2 [49p 71], Enakhire [82]	8 000	
7-06	Malawi	W	4-1	Lagos	CNq	Aiyegbeni 2 [10 17], Kanu 2 [22 35]	40 000	Ndoye SEN
11-06	Brazil	L	0-3	Abuja	Fr		30 000	Quartey GHA
21-06	Angola	D	2-2	Benin City	CNq	Uche [56], Odemwigie [62p]	15 000	
26-07	Venezuela	W	1-0	Watford	Fr	Okocha [8]	1 000	
20-08	Japan	L	0-3	Tokyo	Fr		54 860	Kim Tae Young KOR
2004								
27-01	Morocco	L	0-1	Monastir	CNr1		15 000	Ndoye SEN
31-01	South Africa	W	4-0	Monastir	CNr1	Yobo [4], Okocha [64p], Odemwingie 2 [81 83]	15 000	Bujsaim UAE
4-02	Benin	W	2-1	Sfax	CNr1	Lawal [35], Utaka [76]	15 000	Abd el Fatah EGY
8-02	Cameroon	W	2-1	Monastir	CNqf	Okocha [45], Utaka [73]	14 750	Guezzaz MAR
11-02	Tunisia	D	1-1	Tunis	CNsf	Okocha [57p], L 3-5p	56 000	Coffi BEN
13-02	Mali	W	2-1	Monastir	CN3p	Okocha [16], Odemwingie [47]	2 500	Sowe GAM
28-04	Jordan	W	2-0	Lagos	Fr	Akueme [16], Nworgu [82]	40 000	
29-05	Republic of Ireland	W	3-0	London	Fr	Ogbeche 2 [36 69], Martins [49]	7 438	D'Urso ENG
31-05	Jamaica	W	2-0	London	Fr	Utaka [17], Ogbeche [55]	15 000	Bennett ENG
5-06	Rwanda	W	2-0	Abuja	WCq	Martins 2 [55 88]	35 000	Pare BFA
20-06	Angola	L	0-1	Luanda	WCq		40 000	Nkole ZAM
3-07	Algeria	W	1-0	Abuja	WCq	Yobo [84]	35 000	Hisseine CHA
5-09	Zimbabwe	W	3-0	Harare	WCq	Aghahowa [3], Enakahire [28], Aiyegbeni [48p]	60 000	Mandzioukouta CGO
9-10	Gabon	D	1-1	Libreville	WCq	Aiyegbeni [50]	26 000	Yameogo BFA
20-10	Libya	L	1-2	Tripoli	Fr	Ezeji [17]	50 000	Guirat TUN
22-10	Ecuador	D	2-2	Tripoli	Fr	Ademola, Ezeji [78], L 3-4p	50 000	
17-11	South Africa	L	1-2	Johannesburg	Fr	Makinwa [62]	39 817	Marange ZIM
2005								
26-03	Gabon	W	2-0	Port Harcourt	WCq	Aghahowa [79], Kanu [81]	16 489	Hicuburundi BDI
5-06	Rwanda	D	1-1	Kigali	WCq	Martins [78]	30 000	Kidane ERI
18-06	Angola	D	1-1	Kano	WCq	Okocha [5]	17 000	Abd el Fatah EGY

Fr = Friendly match • CN = CAF African Cup of Nations • WC = FIFA World Cup™
q = qualifier • r1 = first round group • qf = quarter-final • sf = semi-final • 3p = third place play-off

FIFA/COCA-COLA WORLD RANKING

1993	1994	1995	1996	1997	1998	1999	2000	2001	2002	2003	2004	High		Low	
18	12	27	63	71	65	76	52	40	29	35	21	5	04/94	82	11/99

2004-2005											
08/04	09/04	10/04	11/04	12/04	01/05	02/05	03/05	04/05	05/05	06/05	07/05
18	20	18	21	21	21	21	23	24	25	29	29

THE FIFA BIG COUNT OF 2000

	Male	Female		Male	Female
Registered players	35 000	660	Referees	737	151
Non registered players	500 000	17 000	Officials	10 353	714
Youth players	25 000	0	Total involved	589 615	
Total players	577 660		Number of clubs	365	
Professional players	1 400	0	Number of teams	1 320	

NATIONAL CAPS

	Caps
LAWAL Muda	86
RUFAI Peter	61
ATUEGBU Aloy	60
NWOSU Henry	59
YEKINI Rashidi	58
KESHI Stephen	57
CHUKWU Christian	54
ADESINA Ademola	52
OKALA Emma	51
GEORGE Finidi, SIASIA Samson	50

NATIONAL GOALS

	Goals
YEKINI Rashidi	37
ODEGBAMI Segun	23
OYAREKHUA Sunday	16
SIASIA Samson	16
USIYEN Thompson	15
AGHAHOWA Julius	13
AMOKACHI Daniel	12
EKPE Asuquo	12
OLAYOMBO Kenneth	12
LAWAL Muda	11

NATIONAL COACH

	Years
BONFRERE Jo	1995-'96
AMODU Shuaibu	1996-'97
SINCLAIR Monday	1997
TROUSSIER Philippe	1997-'98
MILUTINOVIC Bora	1988
LIBREGTS Thijs	1988-'89
BONFRERE Jo	1999-'01
AMODU Shuaibu	2001-'02
ONIGBINDE Adegboye	2002
CHUKWU Christian	2002-'05

NIGERIA NATIONAL TEAM RECORDS AND RECORD SEQUENCES

Records			Sequence records					
Victory	8-1	UGA 1991	Wins	5	Four times	Clean sheets	6	1992-1993
Defeat	0-7	GHA 1955	Defeats	5	1963-1964	Goals scored	26	1972-1976
Player Caps	86	LAWAL Muda	Undefeated	12	1993-94, 1999-00	Without goal	4	Three times
Player Goals	37	YEKINI Rashidi	Without win	9	1985-1987	Goals against	11	1965-1967

FIFA REFEREE LIST 2005

	Int'l	DoB
AIGBE Osareniye	1999	30-09-1961
CHUKWUJEKWU Chukwudi	1995	7-09-1961
IMIERE Emmanuel	2001	27-04-1965
MANA Sule	1995	1-10-1964
ODENIRAN James		1-11-1965
ONAH Emmanuel	1995	7-07-1970
SAULAWA Aliu	1996	5-06-1964

FIFA ASSISTANT REFEREE LIST 2005

	Int'l	DoB
AUNDUGH Robert	2005	23-11-1972
BAKO Abdullahi	1999	17-03-1962
EDIBE Peter	2004	5-01-1970
ERO Samuel	1993	7-06-1961
MADAKI Sani	1998	13-01-1961
OGINNI Toyin	1998	22-01-1962
SANI Zubairu	2004	2-06-1970

NIGERIA COUNTRY INFORMATION

Capital	Abuja	Independence	1960 from the UK	GDP per Capita	$900
Population	137 253 133	Status	Republic	GNP Ranking	
Area km²	923 768	Language	English, Hausa, Yoruba, Igbo	Dialling code	+234
Population density	148 per km²	Literacy rate	68%	Internet code	.ng
% in urban areas	39%	Main religion	Muslim 50%, Christian 40%	GMT + / –	+1

Cities/Towns ('000)	Lagos 8 789; Kano 3 626; Ibadan 3 565; Kaduna 1 582; Port Harcourt 1 148; Benin 1 125; Maiduguri 1 112; Zaria 975; Aba 897; Ogbomosho 861; Jos 816; Ilorin 814; Oyo 736; Enugu 653; Abeokuta 593; Sokoto 563; Onitsha 561; Warri 536; Oshogbo 499; Okene 479
Neighbours (km)	Chad 87; Cameroon 1 690; Benin 773; Niger 1 497; Atlantic Ocean (Gulf of Guinea) 853
Main stadia	Abuja Stadium – Abuja 60 000; Surulere – Lagos 45 000; Liberty Stadium – Ibadan 35 000

NIGERIA 2004

PREMIER LEAGUE

Premier League	Pl	W	D	L	F	A	Pts	Dolphin	Enyimba	Insurance	Pillars	Nationale	Rangers	Lobi	Gombe	Gabros	Shooting	NPA	Berger	Tornados	El Kanemi	Wikki	Kwara	Plateau	Jets
Dolphin †	34	19	5	10	44	30	62		1-1	1-0	2-0	4-0	1-1	3-1	2-1	1-1	3-1	1-0	2-1	3-0	1-0	2-0	1-0	1-0	2-0
Enyimba †	34	18	6	10	44	24	60	0-1		5-0	1-0	2-1	1-0	3-0	1-0	3-0	3-1	2-0	2-0	1-0	3-0	1-1	1-0	1-0	2-0
Bendel Insurance ‡	34	17	5	12	45	29	56	2-1	1-0		1-0	2-0	2-0	4-0	1-0	2-2	4-1	3-0	0-0	1-0	**3-0**	1-0	**3-0**	1-1	2-1
Kano Pillars	34	17	5	12	43	27	56	3-0	1-1	2-1		2-1	1-1	1-0	7-1	2-0	1-0	1-0	2-0	3-0	1-1	2-2	1-0	4-0	1-0
Iwuanyanwu Nationale	34	17	5	12	31	23	56	2-0	0-0	2-0	1-0		1-0	1-0	1-0	1-0	0-1	1-0	1-0	1-0	1-0	4-0	4-0	1-0	2-0
Enugu Rangers ‡	34	14	10	10	28	21	52	1-1	2-0	1-0	2-0	0-0		1-0	2-0	1-0	2-0	2-0	0-0	2-0	1-0	2-0	1-0	1-0	1-0
Lobi Stars	34	15	5	14	44	34	50	1-0	1-0	2-1	0-1	1-1	2-0		4-0	0-2	4-0	3-1	3-0	2-0	4-0	2-0	4-1	2-0	3-0
Gombe United	34	15	3	16	30	40	48	2-1	1-1	1-0	1-0	1-0	2-0	0-0		1-0	2-0	1-0	1-1	2-1	2-0	1-0	2-1	**3-0**	1-0
Gabros International	34	14	5	15	23	27	47	1-0	1-0	0-0	2-0	1-0	1-0	1-0	0-2		2-0	1-0	2-1	0-0	0-0	2-0	1-0	2-0	2-0
Shooting Stars	34	14	5	15	39	47	47	2-0	2-0	0-0	2-1	2-0	2-1	1-1	1-0	1-0		3-0	1-0	0-0	2-0	2-1	3-1	1-1	4-0
Ports Authority	34	14	4	16	35	35	46	0-1	1-2	1-0	1-0	0-0	0-0	2-1	2-0	2-0	4-1		2-1	2-0	2-1	4-1	2-0	1-1	2-1
Julius Berger	34	13	7	14	36	37	46	1-0	1-2	2-1	**0-3**	1-0	1-1	3-2	3-0	1-0	2-1	1-0		2-1	3-0	2-0	3-2	0-0	3-1
Niger Tornados	34	14	4	16	32	46	46	1-0	1-0	2-0	2-1	0-1	1-1	1-1	2-1	1-0	1-0	1-0	1-0		2-0	2-0	1-0	1-0	**3-0**
El Kanemi Warriors	34	14	4	16	25	37	46	3-1	1-0	1-0	0-0	1-0	1-1	2-0	1-0	2-0	1-0	1-0	0-0	2-0		**0-3**	2-0	1-0	2-0
Wikki Tourists	34	14	3	17	36	42	45	1-2	2-0	**0-3**	1-0	2-0	1-0	2-0	1-0	3-0	2-3	2-1	0-0	2-1	1-1		2-1	2-1	0-1
Kwara United	34	12	6	16	37	43	42	2-2	1-0	1-0	3-0	0-1	2-2	1-0	2-0	3-0	1-0	3-1	1-1	1-0	1-0	3-1		0-0	2-0
Plateau United	34	8	11	15	26	36	35	0-1	0-2	0-3	3-0	0-0	2-0	0-0	1-0	2-0	4-0	1-1	2-2	2-1	1-0	2-1	1-1		0-1
Mighty Jets	34	7	7	20	20	49	28	1-2	2-2	**0-3**	0-1	1-1	0-0	0-0	3-1	1-0	1-1	0-2	1-0	1-0	1-0	1-0	1-2	1-1	

28/02/2004 - 22/09/2004 • † Qualified for the CAF Champions League • ‡ Qualified for the CAF Confederation Cup • Matches in bold awarded 3-0

CLUB DIRECTORY

Club	Town/City	Stadium	Lge	Cup	CL
Bendel Insurance	Benin City	Samuel Ogbemudia 20 000	2	3	0
Dolphin	Port Harcourt	Liberation Stadium 25 000	2	2	0
El Kanemi Warriors	Maiduguri	El Kanemi Stadium 10 000	0	2	0
Enugu Rangers	Enugu	Nnamdi Azikiwe 25 000	6	5	0
Enyimba	Aba	Enyimba Sports Stadium 10 000	3	0	2
Gabros International	Nnewi	Nnewi Township Stadium 5 000	0	0	0
Gombe United	Gombe	Abubakar Umar Memorial 10 000	0	0	0
Iwuanyanwu Nationale	Owerri	Dan Anyiam 10 000	5	1	0
Julius Berger	Lagos	Kashimawo Abiola 15 000	2	2	0
Kano Pillars	Kano	Sani Abacha 25 000	0	1	0
Kwara United	Ilorin	Kwara State Stadium 10 000	0	0	0
Lobi Stars	Makurdi	Aper Aku 15 000	1	1	0
Mighty Jets	Jos	Rwang Pam 15 000	1	0	0
Niger Tornados	Minna	Minna Township Stadium 5 000	0	1	0
Nigerian Ports Authority	Warri	Warri Township Stadium 20 000	0	2	0
Plateau United	Jos	Rwang Pam 15 000	0	1	0
Shooting Stars	Ibadan	Lekan Salami 18 000	5	8	0
Wikki Tourists	Bauchi	Abubakar Balewa 25 000	0	1	0

RECENT LEAGUE AND CUP RECORD

Year	Champions	Pts	Runners-up	Pts	Third	Pts	Cup Winners	Score	Cup Runners-up
1990	Iwuanyanwu Nat.						Stationery Stores	0-0 5-4p	Enugu Rangers
1991	Julius Berger	58	Shooting Stars	57	Plateau United	54	El Kanemi Warriors	3-2	Kano Pillars
1992	Stationery Stores	63	Shooting Stars	62	Iwuanyanwu Nat.	57	El Kanemi Warriors	1-0	Stationery Stores
1993	Iwuanyanwu Nat.	57	Bendel Insurance	56	Concord	54	BCC Lions	1-0	Plateau United
1994	BCC Lions	63	Shooting Stars	59	Enyimba	59	BCC Lions	1-0	Julius Berger
1995	Shooting Stars						Shooting Stars	2-0	Katsina United
1996	Udoji United	58	Jasper United	58	Sharks	58	Julius Berger	1-0	Katsina United
1997	Eagle Cement	59	Jasper United	58	Shooting Stars	51	BCC Lions	1-0	Katsina United
1998	Shooting Stars	57	Kwara United	53	Enugu Rangers	53	Wikki Tourists	0-0 3-2	Plateau United
1999	Lobi Stars	5	Iwuanyanwu Nat.	5	Plateau United	4	Plateau United	1-0	Iwuanyanwu Nat.
2000	Julius Berger	7	Katsina United	6	Lobi Stars	3	Niger Tornados	1-0	Enugu Rangers
2001	Enyimba	9	Ports Authority	4	Gombe United	3	Dolphin	2-0	El Kanemi Warriors
2002	Enyimba	61	Enugu Rangers	57	Kano Pillars	56	Julius Berger	3-0	Yobe Stars
2003	Enyimba	63	Julius Berger	58	Enugu Rangers	58	Lobi Stars	2-0	Sharks
2004	Dolphin	62	Enyimba	60	Bendel Insurance	56	Dolphin	1-0	Enugu Rangers

Dolphin were known previously as Eagle Cement

NFA CUP 2004

Third Round

Team	Score
Dolphin	2
Lobi Stars	1
Zamfara United	1
Bisalo Babes	3
JC Raiders	1
Bayelsa United	0
Shooting Stars	1 5p
Jigawa Stars	1 6p
Sunshine Stars ††	1 4
Gabros International	0 1
Yerima Strikers	0
Nasarawa United	1
Makwada	1 7p
Buffalo	1 6p
Gombe Lions	0
Julius Berger	3
Bendel Insurance	1
Kwara United	0
Diskaborg	1
Talba	3
Dynamos	3
Commaise	1
Enyimba Feeders	0
Sharks	1
El Kanemi Warriors	1 5p
Owina United	1 3p
Ebonyi Angels	0
Yobe Desert Stars	2
Adamawa United	5
Gassol Taraba	0
Niger Tornados	0
Enugu Rangers	1

Fourth Round

Team	Score
Dolphin *	4 0
Bisalo Babes	2 0
JC Raiders	0 0 6p
Jigawa Stars *	0 0 7p
Sunshine Stars *	2 3
Nasarawa United	1 1
Makwada	0 1
Julius Berger *	3 0
Bendel Insurance	0 2
Talba *	0 0
Dynamos *	2 0
Sharks	2 3
El Kanemi Warriors	0 2
Yobe Desert Stars *	1 0
Adamawa United *	1
Enugu Rangers §	0

Quarter-finals

Team	Score
Dolphin *	4 1
Jigawa Stars	0 1
Sunshine Stars	0 3
Julius Berger *	2 1
Bendel Insurance §§	0
Sharks *	3
El Kanemi Warriors	0 1
Enugu Rangers *	3 0

Semi-finals

Team	Score
Dolphin ‡	3
Julius Berger	0
Bendel Insurance	0
Enugu Rangers †	1

Final

Team	Score
Dolphin	1
Enugu Rangers ††	0

CUP FINAL

2-10-2004
Samuel Ogbemudia Stadium, Benin City

Scorer - Bola Bello 44 for Dolphin

* Home team in the first leg • Third round ties played in neutral venues • †† Replay ordered after Gabros protest • § Rangers through by forfeit
§§ Awarded to Insurance after Sharks walked off in the second leg • † Played in Warri • ‡ Played in Kaduna • †† Qualified for the CAF Confederation Cup

NIG – NIGER

NATIONAL TEAM RECORD
JULY 1ST 2002 TO JUNE 30TH 2005

PL	W	D	L	F	A	%
10	3	1	6	7	20	35

FIFA/COCA-COLA WORLD RANKING

1993	1994	1995	1996	1997	1998	1999	2000	2001	2002	2003	2004	High		Low	
81	70	93	129	150	154	164	182	191	184	164	173	**68**	11/94	**196**	08/02

2004-2005											
08/04	09/04	10/04	11/04	12/04	01/05	02/05	03/05	04/05	05/05	06/05	07/05
172	173	173	172	173	173	174	174	174	174	174	175

These are troubled times for Niger. Ranked as the second poorest country in the world the harvest in 2004 was badly affected by drought and an invasion of locusts that have left many in the south of the country facing famine. With the cities less affected football has continued although it too has been beset by problems but not of a life-threatening kind. After the 2006 FIFA World Cup™ exit at the hands of Algeria in the preliminary round coach Martial Yeo was fired and the team has been inactive since. The Nigerian Olympic Committee chief Doula Talata blamed the national association for lack of ambition and when the government got involved it resulted in a full blown crisis with

INTERNATIONAL HONOURS
None

FIFA suspending the association because of "repeated interference from political authorities." The suspension was lifted after assurances from the Prime Minister and the implementation of a roadmap to reorganise the association. Sahel Sporting Club from the capital Niamey won both the League and Cup in mid-2004 and although the 2004-05 season kicked off in December there have been delays and disruptions caused by the problems in the country and within the association. The roadmap should ensure the long-term development of the game which should be helped by the opening of the new Goal programme funded-headquaters for the association.

THE FIFA BIG COUNT OF 2000

	Male	Female		Male	Female
Registered players	6 377	0	Referees	50	1
Non registered players	30 000	0	Officials	609	25
Youth players	1 054	0	Total involved	38 116	
Total players	37 431		Number of clubs	127	
Professional players	20	0	Number of teams	922	

Fédération Nigerienne de Football (FENIFOOT)
FENIFOOT, 93 Avenue de la Grande Chancellerie, Case postale 12 628, Niamey - Plateau, Niger
Tel +227 725663   Fax +227 725664
www.none
President: HIMA SOULEY Amadou   General Secretary: TBD
Vice-President: TBD   Treasurer: TBD   Media Officer: None
Men's Coach: TBD   Women's Coach: ACOSTA Frederic
FENIFOOT formed: 1967   CAF: 1967   FIFA: 1967
Colours: Orange, White, Green

GAMES PLAYED BY NIGER IN THE 2006 FIFA WORLD CUP™ CYCLE

2002	Opponents	Score		Venue	Comp	Scorers	Att	Referee
7-09	Ethiopia	W	3-1	Niamey	CNq	Tankary 2 55 61, Abdoulaye 80	35 000	Pare BFA
3-10	Morocco	L	1-6	Rabat	Fr	Hamidou	4 300	Rouaissi MAR
13-10	Liberia	L	0-1	Monrovia	CNq		40 000	
2003								
7-03	Benin	D	1-1	Cotonou	Fr	L 1-3p		
30-03	Guinea	L	0-2	Conakry	CNq		25 000	Monteiro Duarte CPV
7-06	Guinea	W	1-0	Niamey	CNq	Tankary 69	50 000	Wellington GHA
22-06	Ethiopia	L	0-2	Addis Abeba	CNq		25 000	
5-07	Liberia	W	1-0	Niamey	CNq	Alhassan 90p		
11-10	Algeria	L	0-1	Niamey	WCq		20 126	Coulibaly MLI
14-11	Algeria	L	0-6	Algiers	WCq		50 000	El Arjoun MAR
2004								
No international matches played in 2004								
2005								
No international matches played in 2005 before August								

Fr = Friendly match • CN = CAF African Cup of Nations • WC = FIFA World Cup™ • q = qualifier

NIGER NATIONAL TEAM RECORDS AND RECORD SEQUENCES

Records			Sequence records					
Victory	7-1	MTN 1990	Wins	2	1981	Clean sheets	2	1983
Defeat	1-9	GHA 1969	Defeats	9	1969-1972	Goals scored	5	1994-1995
Player Caps	n/a		Undefeated	4	Three times	Without goal	5	1987-1988
Player Goals	n/a		Without win	23	1963-1976	Goals against	25	1963-1980

CHAMPIONSHIP PLAY-OFFS 2004

Semi-finals		Finals	
Sahel SC Niamey	2		
Urana	0		
		Sahel SC Niamey	4
		ASFNIS	0
Akokana Agadez	0		
ASFNIS	3	6-06-2004, Seyni Kountche, Niamey	

COUPE NATIONALE 2004

Semi-finals		Finals	
Sahel SC Niamey	1 4	3-08-2004	
Dan Gourmou Tahoua	0 0	Seyni Kountche, Niamey	
		Sahel SC Niamey	2
		Akokana	1
Espoir Zinder	0 2	Scorers - Harakoye, Konaté for	
Akokana Agadez	2 2	Sahel; Abdullahi for Akokana	

RECENT LEAGUE AND CUP RECORD

	Championship	Cup			
Year	Champions	Winners	Score	Runners-up	
1995	No competition held	ASFAN Niamey	3-1	Liberté FC Niamey	
1996	Sahel SC Niamey	Sahel SC Niamey	3-2	JS Ténéré Niamey	
1997	No competition held	JS Ténéré Niamey	6-2	Jangorzo Maradi	
1998	Olympic FC Niamey	JS Ténéré Niamey	4-0	Liberté FC Niamey	
1999	Olympic FC Niamey	JS Ténéré Niamey	2-0	Sahel SC Niamey	
2000	JS Ténéré Niamey	JS Ténéré Niamey	3-1	Olympic FC Niamey	
2001	JS Ténéré Niamey	Akokana Agadez	1-1 5-4p	Jangorzo Maradi	
2002	No competition held	Tournament not held			
2003	Sahel SC Niamey	Olympic FC Niamey	4-1	Alkali Nassara Zinder	
2004	Sahel SC Niamey	Sahel SC Niamey	2-1	Akokana Agadez	

NIGER COUNTRY INFORMATION

Capital	Niamey	Independence	1960 from France	GDP per Capita	$800
Population	11 360 538	Status	Republic	GNP Ranking	138
Area km²	1 267 000	Language	French, Hausa, Djerma	Dialling code	+227
Population density	9 per km²	Literacy rate	17%	Internet code	.ne
% in urban areas	17%	Main religion	Muslim 80%	GMT +/–	+1
Towns/Cities ('000)	Niamey 774; Zinder 191; Maradi 163; Agadez 88; Arlit 83; Tahoua 80; Dosso 49				
Neighbours (km)	Chad 1 175; Nigeria 1 497; Benin 266; Burkina Faso 628; Mali 821; Algeria 956; Libya 354				
Main stadia	General Seyni Kountche – Niamey 30 000; Municipal – Zinder 10 000; Municipal – Maradi 10 000				

NIR – NORTHERN IRELAND

NATIONAL TEAM RECORD
JULY 1ST 2002 TO JUNE 30TH 2005

PL	W	D	L	F	A	%
26	3	10	13	15	35	30.8

FIFA/COCA-COLA WORLD RANKING

1993	1994	1995	1996	1997	1998	1999	2000	2001	2002	2003	2004	High		Low	
39	45	45	64	93	86	84	93	88	103	122	107	33	05/94	124	03/04

2004-2005											
08/04	09/04	10/04	11/04	12/04	01/05	02/05	03/05	04/05	05/05	06/05	07/05
110	109	110	107	107	109	111	111	113	114	114	112

In a sign of the changing times in Northern Ireland, the finals of the UEFA European Under-19 Championship were held in the country in July 2005 coinciding with the announcement that the IRA were renouncing the armed struggle. In the 10 years since the ceasefire Belfast has become a much changed city but the fact remains that football has not kept up with the new mood in the country. The national team recently suffered their worst run without scoring a goal, whilst club football continues to be plagued by the fact that every weekend most fans get on a ferry to watch either Celtic or Rangers play in the Scottish Premier League. There have been many ideas mooted

INTERNATIONAL HONOURS
Qualified for the FIFA World Cup™ finals 1958 1982 1986   **British International Championship** 1903 1914 1956 1958 1959 1964 1980 1984

to improve the game in the country not least the creation of an All-Ireland national team, as is the case with rugby, and an All-Ireland League, though neither would be universally popular. The return of Belfast Celtic, who last played in 1949 but who still exist as a club, could revitalise club football but whether it is still too premature for that to happen so soon after the Troubles is open to debate. In the 2006 FIFA World Cup™ qualifiers there was a distinctly British feel to the group Northern Ireland found themselves in but going in to the final stages they found themselves marooned at the bottom with Wales and Azerbaijan.

THE FIFA BIG COUNT OF 2000

	Male	Female		Male	Female
Registered players	20 370	1 000	Referees	425	2
Non registered players	17 000	0	Officials	3 000	50
Youth players	15 000	2 000	Total involved	58 847	
Total players	55 370		Number of clubs	1 278	
Professional players	370	0	Number of teams	2 128	

Irish Football Association (IFA)
20 Windsor Avenue, Belfast, BT9 6EE, United Kingdom
Tel +44 28 90669458   Fax +44 28 90667620
enquiries@irishfa.com   www.irishfa.com
President: BOYCE Jim   General Secretary: WELLS Howard J C
Vice-President: KENNEDY Raymond   Treasurer: MARTIN David   Media Officer: BRUNT Heather Jan
Men's Coach: SANCHEZ Lawrie   Women's Coach: WYLIE Alfie
IFA formed: 1880   UEFA: 1954   FIFA: 1911-20, 1924-28, 1946
Colours: Green, White, Green

GAMES PLAYED BY NORTHERN IRELAND IN THE 2006 FIFA WORLD CUP™ CYCLE

2002	Opponents		Score	Venue	Comp	Scorers	Att	Referee
21-08	Cyprus	D	0-0	Belfast	Fr		6 922	Jones WAL
12-10	Spain	L	0-3	Albacete	ECq		16 000	Michel SVK
16-10	Ukraine	D	0-0	Belfast	ECq		9 288	Bolognino ITA
2003								
12-02	Finland	L	0-1	Belfast	Fr		6 137	McDonald SCO
29-03	Armenia	L	0-1	Yerevan	ECq		10 321	Beck LIE
2-04	Greece	L	0-2	Belfast	ECq		7 196	Gilewski POL
3-06	Italy	L	0-2	Campobasso	Fr		18 270	Cortez Batista POR
11-06	Spain	D	0-0	Belfast	ECq		11 365	Larsen DEN
6-09	Ukraine	D	0-0	Donetsk	ECq		24 000	Stark GER
10-09	Armenia	L	0-1	Belfast	ECq		8 616	Stredak SVK
11-10	Greece	L	0-1	Athens	ECq		15 500	Cortez Batista POR
2004								
18-02	Norway	L	1-4	Belfast	Fr	Healy 56	11 288	Thomson SCO
31-03	Estonia	W	1-0	Tallinn	Fr	Healy 45	2 900	Petteri FIN
28-04	Serbia & Montenegro	D	1-1	Belfast	Fr	Quinn 18	9 690	Richards WAL
30-05	Barbados	D	1-1	Bridgetown	Fr	Healy 71	8 000	Brizan TRI
2-06	St Kitts and Nevis	W	2-0	Basseterre	Fr	Healy 78, Jones 82	5 000	Matthew SKN
6-06	Trinidad and Tobago	W	3-0	Port of Spain	Fr	Healy 2 4 65, Elliott 41	5 500	Callender BRB
18-08	Switzerland	D	0-0	Zurich	Fr		4 000	Vollquartz DEN
4-09	Poland	L	0-3	Belfast	WCq		12 487	Wegereef NED
8-09	Wales	D	2-2	Cardiff	WCq	Whitley 10, Healy 21	63 500	Messina ITA
9-10	Azerbaijan	D	0-0	Baku	WCq		6 460	Hanacsek HUN
13-10	Austria	D	3-3	Belfast	WCq	Healy 36, Murdock 58, Elliott 93+	11 810	Shield AUS
2005								
9-02	Canada	L	0-1	Belfast	Fr		11 156	Attard MLT
26-03	England	L	0-4	Manchester	WCq		62 239	Stark GER
30-03	Poland	L	0-1	Warsaw	WCq		13 515	Frojdfeldt SWE
4-06	Germany	L	1-4	Belfast	Fr	Healy 15p	14 000	Richmond SCO

Fr = Friendly match • EC = UEFA EURO 2004™ • WC = FIFA World Cup™ • q = qualifier

NORTHERN IRELAND NATIONAL TEAM RECORDS AND RECORD SEQUENCES

Records			Sequence records					
Victory	7-0	WAL 1930	Wins	3	1968, 1984	Clean sheets	6	1985-1986
Defeat	0-13	ENG 1882	Defeats	11	1884-87, 1959-61	Goals scored	13	1933-1938
Player Caps	119	JENNING Pat	Undefeated	9	1979-80, 1985-86	Without goal	13	2002-2003
Player Goals	17	HEALEY David	Without win	21	1947-1953	Goals against	46	1882-1897

NORTHERN IRELAND COUNTRY INFORMATION

Capital	Belfast			GDP per Capita	$27 700
Population	1 716 942	Status	Part of the UK	GNP Ranking	4
Area km²	14 120	Language	English	Dialling code	+44
Population density	121 per km²	Literacy rate	99%	Internet code	.uk
% in urban areas	89%	Main religion	Christian	GMT +/-	0
Towns/Cities ('000)	Belfast 585; Londonderry 86; Bangor 62; Newtonabbey 59; Craigavon 57; Lisburn 45				
Neighbours (km)	Ireland Republic 360; Irish Sea & North Atlantic				
Main stadia	Windsor Park – Belfast 20 332; The Oval – Belfast 15 000				

NATIONAL CAPS

	Caps
JENNINGS Pat	119
DONHAGY Mal	91
MCILROY Sammy	88
NICHOLL Jimmy	73
HUGHES Michael	71
MCCREERY David	67
WORTHINGTON Nigel	66
O'NEILL Martin	64
ARMSTRONG Gerry	63
GILLESPIE Keith	62

NATIONAL GOALS

	Goals
HEALY David	17
CLARKE Colin	13
ARMSTRONG Gerry	12
BAMBRICK Joe	12
DOWIE Iain	12
GILLESPIE William	12
QUINN Jimmy	12
STANFIELD Olphert	11
Four players with 10 goals	

NATIONAL COACH

	Years
PEACOCK Bertie	1962-'67
BINGHAM Billy	1967-'71
NEILL Terry	1971-'75
CLEMENTS Dave	1975-'76
BLANCHFLOWER Danny	1976-'79
BINGHAM Billy	1980-'93
HAMILTON Bryan	1994-'98
MCMENEMY Lawrie	1998-'99
MCILROY Sammy	2000-'03
SANCHEZ Lawrie	2004-

FIFA REFEREE LIST 2005

	Int'l	DoB
COURTNEY Mark	2002	26-04-1972
MALCOLM David	1999	8-05-1969
MCCOURT ADRIAN	2003	13-07-1972
ROSS Michael	1996	5-03-1961

FIFA ASSISTANT REFEREE LIST 2005

	Int'l	DoB
FLYNN Gerard	2002	20-08-1963
GLASGOW Keith	2002	26-03-1964
MCCLENAGHAN	1997	19-09-1960
MCDOWELL John	1997	20-03-1965
MUNN Paul	2003	27-04-1967
REDFERN David	1995	7-12-1962
SHANKS Eamon	2003	28-03-1968
TODD David	1997	9-02-1972

IRISH CUP 2004-05

Round of 16

Portadown *	2
Bangor	1
Institute *	1
Ards	2
Coleraine	1
Crusaders *	0
Linfield	1 0
Glentoran *	1 3
Ballymena United *	4
Kilmore	1
Lisburn Distillery *	1 1
HW Welders	1 2
Loughgall *	0 2
Banbridge Town	0 0
Dungannon Swifts *	1
Larne	2

Quarter-finals

Portadown	1
Ards *	0
Coleraine *	1
Glentoran	2
Ballymena United *	0 4
HW Welders	0 0
Loughgall *	1 0
Larne	1 3

Semi-finals

Portadown ††	0 1
Glentoran	0 0
Ballymena United	0
Larne †	1

Final

Portadown ‡	5
Larne	1

CUP FINAL

7-05-2005
Windsor Park, Belfast
Scorers - Arkins 2 [15] [59], Convery [34],
McCann [36], Kelly [48] for Portadown;
Kelly [48] for Larne

* Home team • ‡ Qualified for the UEFA Cup • † At the Oval • †† At Windsor Park

CLUB DIRECTORY

Club	Town/City	Stadium	Phone	www.	Lge	Cup	CL
Ards	Newtownards	Taylor's Avenue 6 000	+44 2891 814970		1	4	0
Ballymena United	Ballymena	The Showgrounds 8 000	+44 2825 652049	ballymenaunited.com	0	6	0
Cliftonville	Belfast	Solitude 6 000	+44 2890 754628	cliftonvillefc.net	3	8	0
Coleraine	Coleraine	The Showgrounds 6 500	+44 2870 353655	colerainefc.com	1	5	0
Crusaders	Belfast	Seaview 6 500	+44 2890 370777		4	2	0
Dungannon Swifts	Dungannon	Stangmore Park 3 000	+44 2887 724114	dungannonswifts.co.uk	0	0	0
Glentoran	Belfast	The Oval 15 000	+44 2890 456137	glentoran.net	22	20	0
Institute	Drumahoe	YMCA Grounds 2 000	+44 2871 302129		0	0	0
Larne	Larne	Inver Park 6 000	+44 2828 274292	wwwlarnefc.net	0	0	0
Limavady United	Limavady	The Showgrounds 1 500	+44 2877 764351		0	0	0
Linfield	Belfast	Windsor Park 20 332	+44 2890 244198	linfieldfc.com	45	36	0
Lisburn Distillery	Lisburn	New Grosvenor 8 000	+44 2890 301148	lisburn-distillery.net	6	12	0
Loughgall	Loughgall	Lakeview Park 3 000	+44 2838 891400	loughgallfc.org	0	0	0
Newry City	Newry	The Showgrounds 6 500	+44 2830 257168		0	0	0
Omagh	Omagh	St Julians Road 4 500	+44 2862 242223		0	0	0
Portadown	Portadown	Shamrock Park 8 000	+44 2838 332726	portadownfc.co.uk	4	3	0

NORTHERN IRELAND 2004-05

PREMIER LEAGUE

	Pl	W	D	L	F	A	Pts	Glentoran	Linfield	Portadown	Swifts	Limavady	Coleraine	Distillery	Ballymena	Institute	Newry	Cliftonville	Loughgall	Larne	Ards	Crusaders	Omagh
Glentoran †	30	24	2	4	73	22	74		3-2	1-2	5-0	2-0	1-0	1-0	4-2	2-0	3-1	4-0	2-0	3-0	2-0	4-1	3-0
Linfield ‡	30	22	6	2	78	23	72	1-1		0-0	2-1	4-1	4-1	5-2	0-1	3-1	2-0	3-1	3-0	1-1	3-0	2-1	6-1
Portadown ‡	30	18	4	8	64	29	58	4-3	0-1		1-2	0-1	2-0	2-1	3-0	4-0	2-3	3-0	2-2	3-0	2-3	0-0	9-0
Dungannon Swifts	30	15	5	10	57	39	50	2-0	1-1	1-3		1-1	0-1	1-1	1-2	3-0	1-0	3-1	1-0	3-1	7-0	0-0	2-1
Limavady United	30	13	9	8	52	36	48	2-2	0-1	0-2	3-2		0-3	2-2	2-1	5-1	3-2	0-0	1-1	6-0	0-1	1-1	2-0
Coleraine	30	14	5	11	62	47	47	0-1	0-4	2-2	4-2	1-2		1-3	0-2	2-4	6-1	3-1	2-0	3-0	3-0	1-1	3-4
Lisburn Distillery	30	13	8	9	49	42	47	2-1	0-4	2-0	2-0	1-1	2-2		0-2	3-2	1-3	3-1	3-1	2-1	1-1	3-2	6-1
Ballymena United	30	11	12	7	40	37	45	0-3	3-4	2-0	1-2	2-1	2-2	2-1		1-1	2-1	1-1	2-1	0-0	2-2	1-1	1-1
Institute	30	11	3	16	36	50	36	0-1	0-1	2-1	3-2	0-3	3-1	1-3	1-1		2-1	1-2	3-0	3-0	1-1	2-0	0-1
Newry City	30	10	5	15	38	63	35	0-4	0-3	0-6	0-4	2-2	0-1	0-0	1-1	4-1		4-2	2-5	1-3	1-0	2-0	2-1
Cliftonville	30	9	7	14	29	44	34	0-1	0-0	0-2	1-1	0-2	1-4	1-0	0-0	1-0	0-1		1-3	2-0	3-1	1-0	2-1
Loughgall	30	8	6	16	34	53	30	1-3	0-4	0-2	1-2	1-1	1-5	2-1	1-0	0-1	1-1	0-0		0-2	3-1	2-0	1-3
Larne	30	7	7	16	31	60	28	0-5	0-2	2-3	3-2	0-4	1-5	0-0	0-0	2-0	0-1	0-2	2-3		2-2	5-2	2-0
Ards	30	6	8	16	33	54	26	0-3	2-2	0-1	1-3	0-1	1-2	0-1	1-1	1-2	5-1	3-0	0-0	0-3		2-2	2-0
Crusaders	30	5	9	16	27	48	24	0-2	1-2	0-1	0-3	1-0	1-1	0-0	2-3	1-0	0-1	0-2	3-2	1-1	0-2		3-1
Omagh Town	30	5	2	23	32	88	17	2-3	1-8	1-2	1-4	2-5	1-3	2-3	0-2	0-1	2-2	0-5	0-2	3-0	2-1	1-3	

25/09/2004 - 30/04/2005 • † Qualified for the UEFA Champions League • ‡ Qualified for the UEFA Cup • Play-off: **Glenavon** 1-1 2-1 Crusaders

NORTHERN IRELAND 2004-05
FIRST DIVISION (2)

	Pl	W	D	L	F	A	Pts
Armagh City	22	15	7	0	35	11	52
Glenavon	22	14	4	4	43	17	46
Donegal Celtic	22	10	6	6	34	19	36
HW Welders	22	10	6	6	35	29	36
Bangor	22	9	6	7	33	29	33
Coagh United	22	8	5	9	39	42	29
Ballyclare Comrades	22	7	7	8	22	24	28
Dundela	22	7	6	9	28	33	27
Moyola Park	22	6	5	11	18	29	23
Carrick Rangers	22	6	4	12	25	37	22
Ballymoney United	22	6	2	14	29	45	20
Ballinamallard United	22	3	4	15	14	40	13

25/09/2004 - 30/04/2005

LEAGUE CUP 2004-05

Quarter-finals		Semi-finals		Final	
Glentoran*	1			9-11-2004	
Ballymena Utd	0	**Glentoran ‡**	2	Windsor Park, Belfast	
Coleraine	0	Lisburn Distillery	0		
Lisburn Distillery*	1			**Glentoran**	2
Cliftonville*	2			Linfield	1
Ards	1	Cliftonville	1	Scorers - Lockhart 5,	
Dungannon Swifts	1	**Linfield †**	2	Morgan 114, Picking 85	
Linfield*	3	* Home team • † At the Oval • ‡ At Windsor Park			

RECENT LEAGUE AND CUP RECORD

	Championship							Cup		
Year	Champions	Pts	Runners-up	Pts	Third	Pts		Winners	Score	Runners-up
1990	Portadown	55	Glenavon	54	Glentoran	44		Glentoran	3-0	Portadown
1991	Portadown	71	Bangor City	61	Glentoran	60		Portadown	2-1	Glenavon
1992	Glentoran	77	Portadown	65	Linfield	60		Glenavon	2-1	Linfield
1993	Linfield	66	Crusaders	66	Bangor	64		Bangor	1-0	Ards
1994	Linfield	70	Portadown	68	Glenavon	68		Linfield	2-0	Bangor
1995	Crusaders	67	Glenavon	60	Portadown	50		Linfield	3-1	Carrick Rangers
1996	Portadown	56	Crusaders	52	Glentoran	46		Glentoran	1-0	Glenavon
1997	Crusaders	46	Coleraine	43	Glentoran	41		Glenavon	1-0	Cliftonville
1998	Cliftonville	68	Linfield	64	Portadown	60		Glentoran	1-0	Glenavon
1999	Glentoran	78	Linfield	70	Crusaders	62		Portadown	w/o	Cliftonville
2000	Linfield	79	Coleraine	61	Glenavon	61		Glentoran	1-0	Portadown
2001	Linfield	75	Glenavon	62	Glentoran	57		Glentoran	1-0	Linfield
2002	Portadown	75	Glentoran	74	Linfield	62		Linfield	2-1	Portadown
2003	Glentoran	90	Portadown	80	Coleraine	73		Coleraine	1-0	Glentoran
2004	Linfield	73	Portadown	70	Lisburn Distillery	55		Glentoran	1-0	Coleraine
2005	Glentoran	74	Linfield	72	Portadown	58		Portadown	5-1	Larne

NOR – NORWAY

NATIONAL TEAM RECORD

JULY 1ST 2002 TO JUNE 30TH 2005

PL	W	D	L	F	A	%
41	20	12	9	56	33	63.4

FIFA/COCA-COLA WORLD RANKING

1993	1994	1995	1996	1997	1998	1999	2000	2001	2002	2003	2004	High		Low	
4	8	10	14	13	14	7	14	26	26	42	35	2	10/93	42	01/04

2004-2005											
08/04	09/04	10/04	11/04	12/04	01/05	02/05	03/05	04/05	05/05	06/05	07/05
38	38	37	35	35	36	35	35	36	36	35	36

In an extraordinary finish to the Norwegian Championship, a last minute goal in the last game of the season by Frode Johnsen gave Rosenborg a world record-equalling 13th consecutive title, ahead of Vålerenga, who finished with the same points and goal difference as Rosenborg but who had scored fewer goals. It was the closest Rosenborg have come to seeing their domination of Norwegian football come to an end and they live to fight another day in their duel with Estonia's Skonto Riga to establish the all-time record, although within days Skonto took the record back by winning a 14th title. Once again the Cup provided the other teams with the best opportunity for a

INTERNATIONAL HONOURS

Qualified for the FIFA World Cup™ finals 1938 1994 1998

FIFA Women's World Cup 1995   Women's Olympic Gold 2000   European Women's Championship 1987 1993

trophy and before a capacity crowd in the Ullevaal, Brann convincingly beat Lyn in the Cup Final to win their first trophy for nearly a quarter of a century. After missing out on the finals of UEFA Euro 2004™ after a play-off defeat at the hands of Spain, the national team made a nervous start to the 2006 FIFA World Cup™ qualifiers with an away defeat to Italy and then a home draw with Belarus and although unbeaten for the rest of the 2004-05 season the group remained very tight going into the final stages.

THE FIFA BIG COUNT OF 2000

	Male	Female		Male	Female
Registered players	90 292	21 319	Referees	4 000	1 000
Non registered players	60 000	25 000	Officials	4 000	1 000
Youth players	162 846	53 367	Total involved	422 824	
Total players	412 824		Number of clubs	1 820	
Professional players	800	30	Number of teams	15 431	

Norges Fotballforbund (NFF)

Ullevaal Stadion, Sognsveien 75J, Serviceboks 1 Ullevaal Stadion, Oslo 0840, Norway

Tel +47 21029300   Fax +47 21029301

nff@fotball.no   www.fotball.no

President: KAAFJORD Sondre   General Secretary: ESPELUND Karen

Vice-President: HELGELAND Per Olav   Treasurer: RIBERG Rune   Media Officer: SOLHEIM Roger

Men's Coach: HAREIDE Age   Women's Coach: BERNTSEN Bjarne

NFF formed: 1902   UEFA: 1954   FIFA: 1908

Colours: Red, White, Blue

GAMES PLAYED BY NORWAY IN THE 2006 FIFA WORLD CUP™ CYCLE

2002 Opponents	Score	Venue	Comp	Scorers	Att	Referee
21-08 Netherlands	L 0-1	Oslo	Fr		15 356	Stuchlik AUT
7-09 Denmark	D 2-2	Oslo	ECq	Riise 54, Carew 90	24 141	Dallas SCO
12-10 Romania	W 1-0	Bucharest	ECq	Iversen 83	25 000	Ivanov RUS
16-10 Bosnia-Herzegovina	W 2-0	Oslo	ECq	Lundekvam 7, Riise 27	24 169	Benes CZE
20-11 Austria	W 1-0	Vienna	Fr	Kah 81	15 800	Abraham HUN
2003						
26-01 United Arab Emirates	D 1-1	Dubai	Fr	Helstad 72	800	Al Saeedi UAE
28-01 Oman	W 2-1	Muscat	Fr	Karadas 62, Rushfeldt 82	500	Al Ajmi OMA
12-02 Greece	L 0-1	Irakleio	Fr		8 000	Gomes Costa POR
2-04 Luxembourg	W 2-0	Luxembourg	ECq	Rushfeldt 58, Solskjaer 73	3 000	Dobrinov BUL
30-04 Republic of Ireland	L 0-1	Dublin	Fr		32 643	McCurry SCO
22-05 Finland	W 2-0	Oslo	Fr	Leonhardsen 22, Flo.TA 80	13 436	Clark SCO
7-06 Denmark	L 0-1	Copenhagen	ECq		41 824	Poll ENG
11-06 Romania	D 1-1	Oslo	ECq	Solskjaer 78p	24 890	Michel SVK
20-08 Scotland	D 0-0	Oslo	Fr		12 858	Vuorela FIN
6-09 Bosnia-Herzegovina	L 0-1	Zenica	ECq		18 000	Bre FRA
10-09 Portugal	L 0-1	Oslo	Fr		11 014	Bennett ENG
11-10 Luxembourg	W 1-0	Oslo	ECq	Flo.TA 18	22 255	Szabo HUN
15-11 Spain	L 1-2	Valencia	ECpo	Iversen 14	53 000	Poll ENG
19-11 Spain	L 0-3	Oslo	ECpo		25 106	Collina ITA
2004						
22-01 Sweden	W 3-0	Hong Kong	Fr	Johnsen.F 44, Flo.H 2 54 63	10 000	Fong HKG
25-01 Honduras	W 3-1	Hong Kong	Fr	Brattbakk 27, Johnsen.F 39, Hoseth 86	14 603	Chan HKG
28-01 Singapore	W 5-2	Singapore	Fr	Stadheim 18, Aas 42, Flo.H 2 59 70, Brattbakk 67	5 000	Supian MAS
18-02 Northern Ireland	W 4-1	Belfast	Fr	Gamst Pedersen 3 17 35, Iversen 43, OG 57	11 288	Thomson SCO
31-03 Serbia & Montenegro	W 1-0	Belgrade	Fr	Andresen 76p	8 000	Panic BIH
28-04 Russia	W 3-2	Oslo	Fr	Andresen 25, Rushfeldt 43, Solli 62	11 435	Wegereef NED
27-05 Wales	D 0-0	Oslo	Fr		14 137	Hansson SWE
18-08 Belgium	D 2-2	Oslo	Fr	Johnsen.F 32, Riseth 59	16 669	Slupik POL
4-09 Italy	L 1-2	Palermo	WCq	Carew 1	21 463	Sars FRA
8-09 Belarus	D 1-1	Oslo	WCq	Riseth 39	25 272	Costa POR
9-10 Scotland	W 1-0	Glasgow	WCq	Iversen 54p	51 000	Allaerts BEL
13-10 Slovenia	W 3-0	Oslo	WCq	Carew 7, Pedersen.M 60, Odegaard 89	24 907	Ivanov RUS
16-11 Australia	D 2-2	London	Fr	Iversen 42, Gamst Pedersen 72	7 364	Styles ENG
2005						
22-01 Kuwait	D 1-1	Kuwait City	Fr	Kvisvik 49	200	Shaban KUW
25-01 Bahrain	W 1-0	Manama	Fr	Kvisvik 49	4 000	Al Bannai UAE
28-01 Jordan	D 0-0	Amman	Fr		8 000	Al Shoufi SYR
9-02 Malta	W 3-0	Ta'Qali	Fr	Rushfeldt 2 71 80, Riise 82	1 000	Malcolm NIR
30-03 Moldova	D 0-0	Chisinau	WCq		5 000	Meyer GER
20-04 Estonia	W 2-1	Tallinn	Fr	Johnsen.F 24, Braaten 54	2 500	Vink NED
24-05 Costa Rica	W 1-0	Oslo	Fr	Johnsen.F 77	21 251	Van Egmond NED
4-06 Italy	D 0-0	Oslo	WCq		24 829	Mejuto Gonzalez ESP
8-06 Sweden	W 3-2	Stockholm	Fr	Riise 60, Helstad 64, Iversen 65	15 345	Jara CZE

Fr = Friendly match • EC = UEFA EURO 2004™ • WC = FIFA World Cup™ • q = qualifier • po = qualifying play-off

NORWAY COUNTRY INFORMATION

Capital	Oslo	Independence	1905 from Sweden	GDP per Capita	$37 800
Population	4 574 560	Status	Constitutional Monarchy	GNP Ranking	27
Area km²	324 220	Language	Norwegian	Dialling code	+47
Population density	14 per km²	Literacy rate	100%	Internet code	.no
% in urban areas	73%	Main religion	Christian	GMT +/–	+1
Towns/Cities ('000)	Oslo 808; Bergen 214; Stavanger 173; Trondheim 145; Fredrikstad-Sarpsborg 97; Kristiansand 67; Tromsø 53; Bodø 34; Larvik 23; Halden 22; Harstad 19; Lillehammer 19				
Neighbours (km)	Russia 196; Finland 736; Sweden 1 619; North Sea & North Atlantic 21 925				
Main stadia	Ullevaal Stadion – Oslo 25 572; Lerkendal – Trondheim 21 166				

NORWAY NATIONAL TEAM RECORDS AND RECORD SEQUENCES

Records			Sequence records					
Victory	12-0	FIN 1946	Wins	9	1999	Clean sheets	6	Three times
Defeat	0-12	DEN 1917	Defeats	9	1908-1913	Goals scored	21	1929-1933
Player Caps	104	SVENSSEN Thorbjørn	Undefeated	17	1997-98	Without goal	7	1975-1976
Player Goals	33	JUVE Jørgen	Without win	27	1908-18	Goals against	20	1908-1916

NATIONAL CAPS

	Caps
SVENSSEN Thorbjørn	104
BERG Henning	100
THORSTVEDT Erik	97
LEONHARDSEN Oyvind	86
REKDAL Kjetil	83
MYKLAND Erik	78
GRONDALEN Svein	77
FLO Tore André	76
BJORNEBYE Stig Inge	75
FJORTOFT Jan Age	71

NATIONAL GOALS

	Goals
JUVE Jørgen	33
GUNDERSEN Einar	26
HENNUM Harald	25
FLO Tore André	23
THORESEN Gunnar	22
SOLSKJAER Ole Gunnar	21
FJORTOFT Jan Age	20
IVERSEN Odd	19
LEONHARDSEN Oyvind	19
NILSEN Olav	18

NATIONAL COACH

	Years
JOHANNESSEN Oivind	1970-'71
CURTIS George	1972-'74
ANDREASSEN Kjell / EGGEN Nils Arne	1974-'77
FOSSEN Tor Røste	1978-'87
GRIP Tord	1987-'88
STADHEIM Ingvar	1988-'90
OLSEN Egil	1990-'98
SEMB Nils Johan	1998-'03
HAREIDE Age	2003-

FIFA REFEREE LIST 2005

	Int'l	DoB
BERNTSEN Espen	2002	12-05-1967
HAUGE Terje	1993	5-10-1965
MOEN Svein Oddvar	2005	22-01-1979
OVREBO Tom	1994	26-06-1966
SANDMOEN Btage	2003	22-03-1967
SKJERVEN Tommy	2001	25-07-1967
STABERG Per Ivar	2003	16-10-1969

FIFA ASSISTANT REFEREE LIST 2005

	Int'l	DoB
BORGAN Ole Hermann	1996	10-10-1964
HOLEN Geir Age	2001	25-08-1967
HOLVIK Steinar	2000	21-07-1968
KARLSEN Ole Hermann	2003	17-06-1967
LIEN Roe Vidar	2000	27-01-1960
RAESTAD Erik	1996	14-07-1964
RANDEN Jan Petter	2004	20-07-1965
SUNDET Arild	1995	6-03-1962
TOSSE Magne	2001	8-09-1961
VANGEN Odd Arne	2001	27-09-1964

NM-CUP 2004

Round of 16		Quarter-finals		Semi-finals		Final	
SL Brann	3 6p						
FK Bodø/Glimt *	3 5p	SK * Brann	3				
Bærum	1	Bryne FK	2				
Bryne FK *	2			SK Brann	3		
Sandefjord	3			Stabæk *	1		
Kongsvinger *	0	Sandefjord *	3				
Moss FK	1	Stabæk	4				
Stabæk *	3					SK Brann ‡	4
Lillestrøm	1 5p					SFK Lyn	1
Tromsø IL *	1 3p	Lillestrøm *	3				
Haugesund *	1	Rosenborg BK	2				
Rosenborg BK	2			Lillestrøm	0	CUP FINAL	
Hamarkameratene	2			SFK Lyn *	1	7-11-2004, Ullevaal, Oslo	
Mandalskameratene *	0	Hamarkameratene	1			Att: 25 458, Ref: Bernsten	
Vard Haugesund *	0	SFK Lyn *	3			Scorers - Sæternes 3 4 13 34, Winters 8 for	
SFK Lyn	5	* Home team • ‡ Qualified for the UEFA Cup				Brann; Markstedt 11 for Lyn	

NORWAY 2004

TIPPELIGAEN

	Pl	W	D	L	F	A	Pts	Rosenborg	Vålerenga	Brann	Tromsø	Ham-Kam	Lyn	Lillestrøm	Odd	Viking	Fredrikstad	Molde	Bodø/Glimt	Stabæk	Sogndal
Rosenborg BK †	26	14	6	6	52	34	48		1-4	1-0	3-0	5-0	4-1	4-1	2-0	0-0	3-1	0-2	3-0	1-2	3-1
Vålerenga IF †	26	13	9	4	40	22	48	2-2		1-0	1-1	2-0	1-2	2-0	1-0	0-0	3-0	4-1	1-0	3-0	0-0
SK Brann ‡	26	12	4	10	46	40	40	3-4	1-1		1-0	2-0	5-1	1-5	1-1	1-0	4-2	3-0	3-1	1-2	2-1
Tromsø IL ‡	26	12	4	10	38	32	40	4-1	2-0	0-1		0-3	0-1	1-0	2-0	4-0	3-2	2-1	2-0	2-1	3-1
Hamarkameratene	26	10	8	8	34	33	38	2-0	0-1	2-1	1-1		1-0	1-1	2-4	1-2	3-2	5-1	0-2	0-0	3-2
SFK Lyn Oslo	26	9	10	7	30	31	37	0-2	1-1	1-2	2-1	1-1		1-1	2-2	2-0	2-2	1-2	1-0	2-0	2-0
Lillestrøm SK	26	8	11	7	45	33	35	2-2	0-1	2-2	2-2	0-1	1-1		0-4	5-1	2-0	1-1	0-0	3-0	1-0
Odd Grenland	26	9	8	9	47	44	35	3-0	2-4	0-2	3-1	2-2	0-0	3-2		1-0	5-2	1-1	3-5	2-0	4-4
Viking SK	26	7	12	7	31	33	33	1-1	1-1	4-2	1-2	0-1	0-0	1-1	2-2		5-2	1-1	1-1	1-0	4-2
Fredrikstad FK	26	9	5	12	42	54	32	0-2	2-2	3-2	1-0	2-1	2-4	1-4	3-0	0-0		2-1	1-0	0-2	3-3
Molde FK	26	7	10	9	34	37	31	1-1	1-1	2-3	1-1	0-0	2-0	2-2	2-1	1-1	0-1		3-0	3-0	1-1
FK Bodø/Glimt	26	7	6	13	28	41	27	0-1	1-2	1-1	2-1	0-2	0-0	0-4	0-2	2-2	0-3	0-0		3-1	3-1
Stabæk	26	7	6	13	25	40	27	1-1	2-0	2-1	1-2	1-1	0-1	0-1	0-0	0-1	1-1	1-3	2-5		3-1
Sogndal	26	5	7	14	39	57	22	3-3	2-1	3-1	2-1	1-1	1-1	0-4	4-2	0-2	2-4	2-1	1-2	1-2	

12/04/2004 - 30/10/2004 • † Qualified for the UEFA Champions League • ‡ Qualified for the UEFA Cup

NORWAY 2004 ADECCOLIGAEN (2)

	Pl	W	D	L	F	A	Pts
IK Start Kristiansand	30	24	2	4	71	28	74
Aalesunds FK	30	21	1	8	67	36	64
Kongsvinger	30	16	5	9	53	42	53
Sandefjord	30	15	6	9	60	32	51
Mandalskameratene	30	13	6	11	51	55	45
IL Hødd	30	14	2	14	63	59	44
Bryne FK	30	11	9	10	54	45	42
Skeid	30	12	6	12	57	56	42
Strømsgodset IF	30	11	7	12	42	45	40
Moss FK	30	11	5	14	48	47	38
Pors Grenland §	30	11	7	12	56	60	38
Hønefoss BK	30	11	4	15	52	54	37
Raufoss	30	10	7	13	42	47	37
FK Haugesund	30	11	4	15	44	59	37
Vard Haugesund	30	7	3	20	43	83	24
Tromsdalen	30	3	4	23	29	84	13

12/04/2004 - 31/10/2004 • § Two points deducted

TOP SCORERS

JOHNSEN Frode	Rosenborg	19
ODEGAARD Alexander	Sogndal	15
SUNDGOT Arild	Lillestrøm	14
OCCEAN Olivier	Odd Grenland	14
KVISVIK Raymond	Brann	13
WINTERS Robbie	Brann	13

RECENT LEAGUE AND CUP RECORD

	Championship						Cup		
Year	Champions	Pts	Runners-up	Pts	Third	Pts	Winners	Score	Runners-up
1990	Rosenborg BK	44	Tromsø IL	42	Molde FK	40	Rosenborg BK	5-1	Fyllingen
1991	Viking SK	41	Rosenborg BK	36	IK Start	34	Strømsgodset	3-2	Rosenborg BK
1992	Rosenborg BK	46	Kongsvinger	40	IK Start	39	Rosenborg BK	3-2	Lillestrøm
1993	Rosenborg BK	47	FK Bodø/Glimt	45	Lillestrøm	42	FK Bodø/Glimt	2-0	Strømsgodset
1994	Rosenborg BK	49	Lillestrøm	41	Viking SK	39	Molde FK	3-2	SFK Lyn
1995	Rosenborg BK	62	Molde FK	47	FK Bodø/Glimt	43	Rosenborg BK	1-1 3-1	SK Brann
1996	Rosenborg BK	59	Lillestrøm	46	Viking SK	43	Tromsø IL	2-1	FK Bodø/Glimt
1997	Rosenborg BK	61	SK Brann	50	Strømsgodset	46	Vålerenga	4-2	Strømsgodset
1998	Rosenborg BK	63	Molde FK	54	Stabæk	53	Stabæk	3-1	Rosenborg BK
1999	Rosenborg BK	56	Molde FK	50	SK Brann	49	Rosenborg BK	2-0	SK Brann
2000	Rosenborg BK	54	SK Brann	47	Viking SK	45	Odd Grenland	2-1	Viking SK
2001	Rosenborg BK	57	Lillestrøm	56	Viking SK	49	Viking SK	3-0	Bryne FK
2002	Rosenborg BK	56	Molde FK	50	SFK Lyn	47	Vålerenga	1-0	Odd Grenland
2003	Rosenborg BK	61	FK Bodø/Glimt	47	Stabæk	42	Rosenborg BK	3-1	FK Bodø/Glimt
2004	Rosenborg BK	48	Vålerenga	48	SK Brann	40	SK Brann	4-1	SFK Lyn

ROSENBORG BK 2004

Date	Opponents	Score		Comp	Scorers	Att
26-02-2004	Benfica - POR	L 0-1	A	UCr3		40 000
3-03-2004	Benfica - POR	W 2-1	H	UCr3	Berg [9], Karadas [16]	18 238
12-04-2004	SK Brann	W 1-0	H	TL	Strand [83]	14 667
18-02-2004	Fredrikstad FK	W 2-0	A	TL	Johnsen.F [43], Stensaas [90]	10 106
25-04-2004	Viking FK	D 0-0	H	TL		12 915
2-05-2004	Lillestrøm SK	D 2-2	A	TL	Powell OG [6], Karadas [78]	9 655
5-05-2004	Rissa	W 15-0	A	CUPr1	Hoftun [4], Brattbakk 6 [11 19 39 65 83 87], Karadas 2 [17 44], Stensaas [59], Storflor 2 [70 86], Olsen 2 [71 85], Winsnes [74]	1 964
10-05-2004	Tromsø IL	L 1-4	A	TL	Johnsen.F [71]	9 435
16-05-2004	Molde FK	L 0-2	H	TL		21 366
19-05-2004	Vålerenga	D 2-2	A	TL	Johnsen.F [57], Brattbakk [87]	18 434
23-05-2004	Odd Grenland	W 2-0	H	TL	Johnsen [32], Berg [47]	15 402
26-05-2004	Levanger	W 7-2	A	CUPr2	Brattbakk 3 [6 33 83], Johnsen.F 2 [29 41], Karadas [45], Hoftun [63]	3 500
31-05-2004	Sogndal	D 3-3	A	TL	Riseth 2 [13 83], Johnsen.F [18]	2 738
3-06-2004	Strindheim	W 6-1	H	CUPr3	Winsnes [17], Brattbakk [22], Johnsen.F 3 [48 65 71], Stensaas [81]	1 328
6-06-2004	Hamarkameratane	W 5-0	H	TL	Karadas 2 [24 53], Riseth [32], Strand [64], Johnsen.F [69]	15 721
9-06-2004	FK Bodø/Glimt	W 3-0	H	TL	Stensaas [11], Johnsen.F [22], Strand [29]	18 691
14-06-2004	Stabæk	D 1-1	A	TL	Brattbakk [21]	5 012
23-06-2004	Haugesund	W 2-1	A	CUPr4	Brattbakk [4], Strand [8]	3 033
28-06-2004	SFK Lyn	W 2-0	A	TL	Brattbakk [26], Strand [43]	6 637
5-07-2004	SK Brann	W 4-3	A	TL	Winsnes [25], Olsen [27], Brattbakk [59], Johnsen.F [77]	15 539
25-07-2004	Fredrikstad FK	W 3-1	H	TL	Johnsen.F 2 [8 51], Berg [32]	17 040
28-07-2004	Sheriff Tiraspol - MDA	W 2-1	H	CLpr2	Johnsen.F [24], George [85]	10 909
1-08-2004	Viking FK	D 1-1	A	TL	Winsnes [74]	12 688
4-08-2004	Sheriff Tiraspol - MDA	W 2-0	A	CLpr2	Berg [36], Brattbakk [39]	8 000
8-08-2004	Lillestrøm SK	W 4-1	H	TL	Johnsen.F [11], Dorsin [80], Storflor [88], Braaten [90]	19 170
11-08-2004	Maccabi Haifa - ISR	W 2-1	H	CLpr3	Brattbakk [1], Solli [9]	18 432
14-08-2004	Lillestrøm SK	L 2-3	A	CUPqf	Johnsen.F [49], George [86]	9 035
21-08-2004	Tromsø IL	W 3-0	H	TL	Johnsen.F 2 [9 55], Braaten [81]	20 024
25-08-2004	Maccabi Haifa - ISR	W 3-2	A	CLpr3	Brattbakk [90], Braaten [95], Berg [116]	20 000
29-08-2004	Molde FK	W 3-1	A	TL	Braaten 2 [14 89], Riseth [84]	9 142
11-09-2004	Vålerenga	L 1-4	H	TL	Johnsen.F [28]	16 444
14-09-2004	Panathinaikos - GRE	L 1-2	A	CLgE	Johnsen.F [90]	13 204
19-09-2004	Odd Grenland	L 0-3	A	TL		7 816
25-09-2004	Sogndal	W 3-1	H	TL	Storflor [10], Johnsen.F 2 [23 26]	12 739
29-09-2004	Arsenal - ENG	D 1-1	A	CLgE	Strand [52]	21 195
3-10-2004	Hamarkameratane	L 0-2	A	TL		7 418
16-10-2004	Stabæk	L 1-2	H	TL	Helstad [67]	20 276
20-10-2004	PSV Eindhoven - NED	L 1-2	H	CLgE	Storflor [42]	20 950
24-10-2004	FK Bodø/Glimt	W 1-0	A	TL	Winsnes [69]	6 507
30-10-2004	SFK Lyn	W 4-1	H	TL	Braaten [58], Johnsen.F 3 [62 70 89]	21 228
2-11-2004	PSV Eindhoven - NED	L 0-1	A	CLgE		26 000
11-11-2004	Djurgårdens IF - SWE	D 4-4	H	RL	Brattbakk 2 [13 17], Helstad 2 [61 90]	7 925
20-11-2004	Vålerenga - NOR	L 2-3	A	RL	Braaten 57, Johnsen 74	11 535
24-11-2004	Panathinaikos - GRE	D 2-2	H	CLgE	Helstad 2 [68 76]	20 591
2-12-2004	Esbjerg FB - DEN	W 2-1	A	RL	Stensaas 69, Johnsen.F 90	
7-12-2004	Arsenal - ENG	L 1-5	A	CLgE	Hoftun [38]	35 421

TL = Tippeligaen • UC = UEFA Cup • CUP = NM-Cup • CL = UEFA Champions League • RL = Royal League
pr2 = second preliminary round • pr3 = third preliminary round • r1 = first round • r2 = second round • r3 = third round • r4 = fourth round •
gE = group E • qf = quarter-final

CLUB DIRECTORY

Club	Town/City	Stadium	Phone	www.	Lge	Cup	CL
Aalesunds FK	Aalesund	Kråmyra 9 600	+47 70 107780	aafk.no	0	0	0
FK Bodø/Glimt	Bodø	Aspmyra 6 100	+47 75 545500	glimt.no	0	2	0
SK Brann	Bergen	Brann Stadion 17 600	+47 55 598500	brann.no	2	6	0
Fredrikstad FK	Fredrikstad	Fredrikstad Stadion 10 000	+47 69 313171	fredrikstadfk.no	9	10	0
Hamarkameratane	Hamar	Briskeby 8 000	+47 62 553080	hamkam.no	0	0	0
Lillestrøm SK	Lillestrøm	Aråsen 12 250	+47 63 805660	lsk.no	5	4	0
SFK Lyn	Oslo	Ullevaal 25 572	+47 23 005190	lyn.no	2	8	0
Molde FK	Molde	Molde Stadion 11 167	+47 71 202500	moldefk.no	0	1	0
Odd Grenland	Skien	Odd Stadion 9 008	+47 35 900140	oddgrenland.no	0	12	0
Rosenborg BK	Trondheim	Lerkendal 21 166	+47 73 822100	rosenborg.no	19	9	0
IK Start	Kristiansand	Kristiansand Stadion 12 000	+47 38 106666	ikstart.no	2	0	0
Tromsø IL	Tromsø	Alfheim 9 362	+47 77 602600	til.no	0	2	0
Vålerenga IF	Oslo	Ullevaal 25 572	+47 23 247800	vif.no	4	3	0
Viking FK	Stavanger	Viking Stadion 15 300	+47 51 329700	viking-fk.no	8	5	0

NZL – NEW ZEALAND

NATIONAL TEAM RECORD
JULY 1ST 2002 TO JUNE 30TH 2005

PL	W	D	L	F	A	%
19	8	1	10	45	30	44.7

FIFA/COCA-COLA WORLD RANKING

1993	1994	1995	1996	1997	1998	1999	2000	2001	2002	2003	2004	High		Low	
77	99	102	132	120	103	100	91	84	49	88	95	47	08/02	136	11/96

2004-2005											
08/04	09/04	10/04	11/04	12/04	01/05	02/05	03/05	04/05	05/05	06/05	07/05
86	86	90	92	95	96	98	98	99	99	106	107

The friendly with Australia in London in June 2005 was New Zealand's first match in a year but it was also the last between the two as fellow members of Oceania. The Socceroos' defection to the Asian Football Confederation will leave New Zealand as the dominant force in Oceania, a fact welcomed by the new All Whites coach Ricki Herbert. Not only will the junior sides be more likely to qualify for World Championships and gain valuable experience but with the prospect of a place in the FIFA Club World Championship each year it could also provide the boost club football needs. In March 2005 Auckland City won the inaugural New Zealand Football Championship,

INTERNATIONAL HONOURS
Oceania Nations Cup 1973 1998 2002   Oceania Women's Championship 1983 1991
Oceania Youth Championship 1980 1992   Oceania U-17 Championship 1997

beating runners-up Waitakere United in the end of season Grand Final and winning a place in the Oceania Club Championship in Tahiti. Rather disappointingly, however, they didn't get past the group stage, showing there is still much work to be done. Waitakere lost out again, in the Chatham Cup, when they lost 1-0 to Miramar Rangers in the final, but there will be much focus on how the renamed NZ Knights fare in the inaugural Hyundai A-League. Should they do well it is possible that the FIFA Club World Championship in Tokyo could feature two clubs from New Zealand.

THE FIFA BIG COUNT OF 2000

	Male	Female		Male	Female
Registered players	17 525	6 700	Referees	400	7
Non registered players	35 000	2 000	Officials	9 240	6 160
Youth players	60 725	14 098	Total involved	151 855	
Total players	136 048		Number of clubs	311	
Professional players	25	0	Number of teams	7 088	

New Zealand Soccer Inc (NZS)
Albany, PO Box 301 043, Auckland, New Zealand
Tel +64 9 4140175   Fax +64 9 4140176
billmac@soccernz.co.nz   www.nzsoccer.com
President: MORRIS John   General Secretary: SEATTER Graham
Vice-President: TBD   Treasurer: HAYTON Alex   Media Officer: DEWHURST Andrew
Men's Coach: HERBERT Ricki   Women's Coach: DAVIE Sandie
NZS formed: 1891   OFC: 1966   FIFA: 1948
Colours: White, White, White

GAMES PLAYED BY NEW ZEALAND IN THE 2006 FIFA WORLD CUP™ CYCLE

2002	Opponents		Score	Venue	Comp	Scorers	Att	Referee
5-07	Tahiti	W	4-0	Auckland	OCr1	Nelsen [30], Vicelich [49], Urlovic [80], Campbell [88]	1 000	Atisson VAN
7-07	Papua New Guinea	W	9-1	Auckland	OCr1	Killen 4 [9 10 28 51], Campbell 2 [27 85], Nelsen [54], Burton [87], De Gregorio [90]	2 200	Rakaroi FIJ
9-07	Solomon Islands	W	6-1	Auckland	OCr1	Vicelich 2 [28 45], Urlovic [42], Campbell 2 [50 75], Burton [88]	300	Atisson VAN
12-07	Vanuatu	W	3-0	Auckland	OCsf	Burton 2 [13 65], Killen [23]	1 000	Breeze AUS
14-07	Australia	W	1-0	Auckland	OCf	Nelsen [78]	4 000	Ariiotima TAH
12-10	Estonia	L	2-3	Tallinn	Fr	Hickey [41], Lines [45]	800	Pedersen NOR
16-10	Poland	L	0-2	Ostrowiec	Fr		8 000	Layec FRA
2003								
27-05	Scotland	D	1-1	Edinburgh	Fr	Nelsen [47]	10 016	Ingvarsson SWE
8-06	USA	L	1-2	Richmond	Fr	Coveny [23]	9 116	Liu CAN
18-06	Japan	L	0-3	Paris	CCr1		36 038	Codjia BEN
20-06	Colombia	L	1-3	Lyon	CCr1	De Gregorio [27]	22 811	Batres GUA
22-06	France	L	0-5	Paris	CCr1		36 842	Moradi IRN
12-10	Iran	L	0-3	Tehran	AO		40 000	Kousa SYR
2004								
29-05	Australia	L	0-1	Adelaide	WCq		12 100	Larsen DEN
31-05	Solomon Islands	W	3-0	Adelaide	WCq	Fisher [36], Oughton [81], Lines [90]	217	Iturralde Gonzalez ESP
2-06	Vanuatu	L	2-4	Adelaide	WCq	Coveny 2 [61 75]	356	Farina ITA
4-06	Tahiti	W	10-0	Adelaide	WCq	Coveny 3 [6 38 46+], Fisher 3 [16 22 63], Jones [72], Oughton [74], Nelsen 2 [82 87]	200	Shield AUS
6-06	Fiji	W	2-0	Adelaide	WCq	Bunce [8], Coveny [56]	300	Larsen DEN
2005								
9-06	Australia	L	0-1	London	Fr		9 023	Dean ENG

Fr = Friendly match • OC = OFC Oceania Nations Cup • CC = FIFA Confederations Cup • AO = Asia/Oceania Challenge • WC = FIFA World Cup™ • q = qualifier • r1 = first round group

FIFA REFEREE LIST 2005

	Int'l	Birth date
FOX Neil	1996	16-02-1963
O'LEARY Peter	2003	3-03-1972

FIFA ASSISTANT REFEREE LIST 2005

	Int'l	Birth date
BEST Brent	2004	12-02-1968
DUNHAM Paul	2003	31-07-1962
MITCHELL Darrin	2004	9-04-1965

NATIONAL CAPS

	Caps
SUMNER Steve	105
TURNER Brian	102
COLE Duncan	92
ELRICK Adrian	91
MCGARRY Michael	87
EVANS Ceri	85
SIBLEY Tony	85
ZORICICH Chris	77
JACKSON Chris	72

Caps/Goals include unofficial games

NATIONAL GOALS

	Goals
COVENY Vaughan	28
NEWALL Jock	28
SUMNER Steve	27
NELSON Keith	26
TURNER Brian	25
MCGARRY Michael	22
COXON ROY	20
TURNER Grant	19
THOMAS Earle	18
WALKER Colin	18

NATIONAL COACH

	Years
JONES Allan	1983-'84
FALLON Kevin	1985-'88
ADSHEAD John	1989
MARSHALL Ian	1989-'94
CLARK Bobby	1994-'95
PRITCHETT Keith	1996-'97
MCGRATH Joe	1997-'98
DUGDALE Ken	1998-'02
WAITT Mick	2002-'04
HERBERT Ricki	2004-

NEW ZEALAND COUNTRY INFORMATION

Capital	Wellington	Independence	1907 from the UK	GDP per Capita	$21 600
Population	3 993 817	Status	Commonwealth	GNP Ranking	48
Area km²	268 680	Language	English, Maori	Dialling code	+64
Population density	15 per km²	Literacy rate	99%	Internet code	.nz
% in urban areas	86%	Main religion	Christian	GMT +/-	+12
Towns/Cities ('000)	Aukland 417; Manukau 383; Christchurch 364; North Shore 207; Wellington 179; Waitakere 166; Hamilton 152; Dunedin 114; Tauranga 110; Lower Hutt 101; Palmerston North 75; Hastings 61				
Neighbours (km)	South Pacific Ocean 15 134				
Main stadia	Ericsson Stadium – Auckland 50 000; North Harbour Stadium – Albany, Auckland 25 000				

NEW ZEALAND NATIONAL TEAM RECORDS AND RECORD SEQUENCES

Records			Sequence records					
Victory	13-0	FIJ 1981	Wins	9	1951-1954	Clean sheets	10	1981
Defeat	0-10	AUS 1936	Defeats	16	1927-1951	Goals scored	22	1951-1967
Player Caps	105	SUMNER Steve	Undefeated	11	1981	Without goal	5	1997-1998
Player Goals	28	COVENY/NEWALL	Without win	16	1927-1951	Goals against	19	1927-1951

NEW ZEALAND 2004-05

NEW ZEALAND FOOTBALL CHAMPIONSHIP

	Pl	W	D	L	F	A	Pts	Auckland	Waitakere	Waikato	Canterbury	Napier	Wellington	Otago	Manawatu
Auckland City †	21	14	4	3	53	24	46		1-0 4-2	0-0	5-0	3-3	5-1 2-1	0-1	4-1
Waitakere United ‡	21	12	4	5	39	19	40	1-3		1-2	5-2	3-0 4-0	1-1 1-1	2-0 4-0	1-0 3-0
Waikato FC ‡	21	9	4	8	27	25	31	1-2 0-2	0-3 3-0		1-2 1-2	0-2 3-1	3-2	0-2	0-0
Canterbury United	21	7	6	8	31	38	27	1-1 0-3	0-0 0-1	1-2		3-0 3-1	2-1	1-5 2-2	0-0 1-1
Napier City	21	7	5	9	39	48	26	1-3 4-2	0-0	0-3	3-2		2-2 3-3	3-0	2-3 4-3
Team Wellington	21	5	8	8	35	40	23	1-4	1-4	0-0 3-0	2-2 2-1	1-4		2-2 2-0	1-2
Otago United	21	5	5	11	26	46	20	0-3 2-3	0-1	2-1 1-1	2-5	3-3 0-2	0-5		2-1 1-1
YoungHeart Manawatu	21	4	6	11	26	36	18	2-2 1-2	1-2	0-4 0-1	0-1	4-1	1-2 1-1	4-1	

15/10/2004 - 12/03/2005 • † Qualified for the Grand Final • ‡ Qualified for the Elimination Final
Elimination Final: Waitakere United 4-1 Waikato FC • Grand Final: **Auckland City** 3-2 Waitakere United • Auckland qualify for the OFC Champions Cup • Cities and Stadia: Auckland City - Kiwitea St, Auckland • Canterbury United - English Park, Christchurch • Napier City - Park Island, Napier • Otago United - Caledonian Ground, Dunedin • Team Wellington - Newtown Park, Wellington • Waikato FC - Waikato Stadium, Hamilton • Waitakere United - The Trust Stadium, Henderson • YoungHeart Manawatu - Memorial Park, Palmerston North

CHATHAM CUP 2004

Eighth-finals		Quarter-finals		Semi-finals		Final	
Miramar Rangers *	3						
Wellington Olympic	2	**Miramar Rangers**	2				
Caversham	0	Western *	1				
Western *	2			**Miramar Rangers**	1		
Lower Hutt City *	5			Eastern Suburbs *	0		
Upper Hutt City	0	Lower Hutt City *	2				
Kerikeri *	0	**Eastern Suburbs**	3				
Eastern Suburbs	10					**Miramar Rangers**	1
Palmerston North Marist	3					Waitakere City	0
Nelson Suburbs *	2	**Palmerston N. Marist ***	1				
Takapuna *	0	Central United	0				
Central United	7			Palmerston North Marist	1	CUP FINAL	
East Coast Bays	2			**Waitakere City ***	2		
Lynn Avon United *	1	East Coast Bays *	2			6-09-2004, Att: 3 000, Ref: O'Leary	
Mangere United *	1	**Waitakere City**	3			North Harbour Stadium, Auckland	
Waitakere City	2	* Home team				Scorer - Zannoto [106] for Rangers	

RECENT LEAGUE AND CUP RECORD

	Championship				Chatham Cup		
Year	Champions	Score	Runners-up		Winners	Score	Runners-up
1993	Napier City Rovers	4-3	Waitakere City		Napier City Rovers	6-0	Rangers
1994	North Shore United	3-1	Napier City Rovers		Waitakere City	1-0	Wellington Olympic
1995	Waitakere City	4-0	Waikato United		Waitakere City	4-0	North Shore United
1996	Waitakere City	5-2	Miramar Rangers		Waitakere City	3-1	Mt Wellington
1997	Waitakere City	3-1	Napier City Rovers		Central United	3-2	Napier City Rovers
1998	Napier City Rovers	5-2	Central United		Central United	5-0	Dunedin Technical
1999	Central United	3-1	Dunedin Technical		Dunedin Technical	4-0	Waitakere City
2000	Napier City Rovers	0-0 4-2p	University Mt Wellington		Napier City Rovers	4-1	Central United
2001	Central United	3-2	Miramar Rangers		University Mt Wellington	3-3 5-4p	Central United
2002	Miramar Rangers	3-1	Napier City Rovers		Napier City Rovers	2-0	Tauranga City United
2003	Miramar Rangers	3-2	East Auckland		University Mt Wellington	3-1	Melville United
2004	No tournament held				Miramar Rangers	1-0	Waitakere City
2005	Auckland City	3-2	Waitakere United				

OMA – OMAN

NATIONAL TEAM RECORD
JULY 1ST 2002 TO JUNE 30TH 2005

PL	W	D	L	F	A	%
41	26	6	9	86	35	70.7

FIFA/COCA-COLA WORLD RANKING

1993	1994	1995	1996	1997	1998	1999	2000	2001	2002	2003	2004	High		Low	
97	71	98	91	81	58	92	106	91	96	62	56	**50**	08/04	**117**	07/03

2004-2005											
08/04	09/04	10/04	11/04	12/04	01/05	02/05	03/05	04/05	05/05	06/05	07/05
50	50	50	55	56	56	57	57	59	59	63	64

Oman enjoyed possibly their finest year in international football in 2004 when they reached the Asian Cup finals for the first time and finished as runners-up to Qatar in the Gulf Cup, their best ever finish. Under Czech coach Milan Macala, the team shook off its modest history and looked a more professional outfit emphasised by their rise up the FIFA/Coca-Cola World Rankings to the fringes of the top 50. The 2006 FIFA World Cup™ qualifying draw, however, was not kind to Oman. With a population of just under three million it was always going to be a tall order to match their main group rivals Japan, although they did finish second ahead of both India and Singapore.

INTERNATIONAL HONOURS
AFC U-17 Championship 1996 2000

Oman runs a 13-team semi-professional League won in 2005 by Dhofar for the ninth time after edging ahead of runners-up Al Arooba in the closing weeks. Dhofar were one of only four clubs anywhere in the world to go through the past season unbeaten although with more games drawn than won they were never runaway leaders. By winning the Championship they also completed the double having won the Sultan Qaboos Cup the previous October. There wasn't a clean sweep of trophies though; in the end of season Champions Cup between the top four in the League Dhofar lost 2-1 to Muscat, a defeat in their final match of the season.

THE FIFA BIG COUNT OF 2000

	Male	Female		Male	Female
Registered players	1 765	0	Referees	120	0
Non registered players	10 000	0	Officials	600	0
Youth players	5 110	0	Total involved	17 595	
Total players	16 875		Number of clubs	51	
Professional players	0	0	Number of teams	153	

Oman Football Association (OFA)
Al Farahidy Street, PO Box 3462, Ruwi 112, Oman
Tel +968 24 787636   Fax +968 24 787632
omanfa@omantel.net.om   www.none
President: AL KHALILI Shk. Khalil   General Secretary: AL RAISI Fahad
Vice-President: AL FARSI Abdullah Shaaban   Treasurer: AL LAWATI Jamil Ali Sultan   Media Officer: AL RAWAHI Aiman
Men's Coach: MACALA Milan   Women's Coach: None
OFA formed: 1978   AFC: 1979   FIFA: 1980
Colours: White, White, White

GAMES PLAYED BY OMAN IN THE 2006 FIFA WORLD CUP™ CYCLE

2002	Opponents	Score		Venue	Comp	Scorers	Att	Referee
25-09	United Arab Emirates	W	2-1	Muscat	Fr			
2003								
28-01	Norway	L	1-2	Muscat	Fr	Yousef Shaaban [50]	500	Al Ajmi OMA
10-09	Bahrain	W	1-0	Muscat	Fr	Bashir [31]		
16-09	Singapore	W	3-1	Singapore	Fr	Bashir 2 [32 68], OG 50		Abdul Hamid MAS
25-09	Nepal	W	7-0	Incheon	ACq	Bashir [1], Badar Mubarak 2 [3 51], Mustahil 2 [5 11], Hassan Yousuf [25], Al Dhabat [90]		
27-09	Korea Republic	L	0-1	Incheon	ACq			
29-09	Vietnam	W	6-0	Incheon	ACq	Bashir 2 [14 42], Al Dhabat 2 [15 26], Thuwaini [19], Mohamed Mubarak [86]		
8-10	Jordan	W	2-1	Muscat	Fr	Saleh [11], Al Dhabat [14]		
19-10	Nepal	W	6-0	Muscat	ACq	Bashir 3 [18 62 82], Yousuf Mubarak [20], Thuwaini [44], Saleh [78]		Al Ghafary JOR
21-10	Korea Republic	W	3-1	Muscat	ACq	Al Dhabat [60], Saleh [64], Bashir [88]		
24-10	Vietnam	W	2-0	Muscat	ACq	Al Dhabat [47], Thuwaini [68]		
18-12	Azerbaijan	W	1-0	Muscat	Fr	Saleh [84]		
20-12	Estonia	W	3-1	Muscat	Fr	Saleh 2 [6 71], Al Dhabat [80]	1 000	Al Harrassi OMA
26-12	Kuwait	D	0-0	Kuwait City	GC			Al Saeedi UAE
28-12	Yemen	D	1-1	Kuwait City	GC	Bashir [65]		Sadeq KUW
31-12	United Arab Emirates	W	2-0	Kuwait City	GC	Ahmed Mubarak [32], Saleh [51]		Al Qahtani QAT
2004								
3-01	Bahrain	L	0-1	Kuwait City	GC			
6-01	Saudi Arabia	L	1-2	Kuwait City	GC	Amad Ali [62]		
11-01	Qatar	W	2-0	Kuwait City	GC	Bashir [45p], Al Maimani [77]		
14-02	Korea Republic	L	0-5	Ulsan	Fr		26 514	Yoshida JPN
18-02	Japan	L	0-1	Saitama	WCq		60 270	Abdul Hamid MAS
31-03	India	W	5-1	Kochin	WCq	Amad Ali [12], Ahmed Mubarak 2 [26 49], Al Hinai 2 [60 88]	48 000	Kim Heng MAS
31-05	Maldives	W	3-0	Muscat	Fr			
3-06	Maldives	W	4-1	Muscat	Fr			
9-06	Singapore	W	7-0	Muscat	WCq	Al Maimani 4 [9 44 64 86], Khalifa Ayil 2 [25 53], Hahdid [39]	2 000	Ebrahim BHR
20-07	Japan	L	0-1	Chongqing	ACr1		35 000	Shield AUS
24-07	Iran	D	2-2	Chongqing	ACr1	Amad Ali 2 [32 41]	35 000	Al Delawar BHR
28-07	Thailand	W	2-0	Chengdu	ACr1	OG [11], Amad Ali [49]	13 000	Lu Jun CHN
31-08	Maldives	W	1-0	Malé	Fr			
3-09	Maldives	W	2-1	Malé	Fr			
8-09	Singapore	W	2-0	Singapore	WCq	Yousef Shaaban [3], Amad Ali [82]	4 000	Arambekade SRI
7-10	Iraq	W	1-0	Muscat	Fr			
13-10	Japan	L	0-1	Muscat	WCq		35 000	Lu Jun CHN
17-11	India	D	0-0	Muscat	WCq		2 000	Nurilddin Salman IRQ
1-12	Latvia	W	3-2	Manama	Fr	Ahmed Mubarak [39], Khalifa Ayil [62], Kamouna [90]		
3-12	Finland	D	0-0	Manama	Fr	W 4-3p		
10-12	Iraq	W	3-1	Doha	GCr1	Amad Ali 2 [29 46], Khalifa Ayil [53]		
13-12	United Arab Emirates	W	2-1	Doha	GCr1	Mudhafir [74], Al Maimani [85]		
16-12	Qatar	L	1-2	Doha	GCr1	Kamouna [26]		
20-12	Bahrain	W	3-2	Doha	GCsf	Amad Ali 2 [44 83], Al Maimani [50]		
24-12	Qatar	D	2-2	Doha	GCf	Al Maimani [26], L 4-5p		
2005								

No international matches played in 2005 before August

Fr = Friendly match • GC = Gulf Cup • AC = AFC Asian Cup • WC = FIFA World Cup™
q = qualifier • r1 = first round group • sf = semi-final • f = final

OMAN COUNTRY INFORMATION

Capital	Muscat	Independence	1650 Portuguese Expulsion	GDP per Capita	$13 100
Population	2 903 165	Status	Monarchy	GNP Ranking	75
Area km²	212 460	Language	Arabic	Dialling code	+968
Population density	13 per km²	Literacy rate	75%	Internet code	.om
% in urban areas	13%	Main religion	Muslim	GMT +/−	+4
Towns/Cities ('000)	Muscat 871; Salalah 178; Suhar 138; 'Ibri 88; Nizwa 86; as-Suwayq 86; Sur 77; Saham 76				
Neighbours (km)	Saudi Arabia 676; UAE 410; Yemen 288; Arabian Sea & Persian Gulf 2 092				
Main stadia	Sultan Qaboos – Muscat 39 000, Nizwa Complex – Nizwa 11 000				

OMAN NATIONAL TEAM RECORDS AND RECORD SEQUENCES

Records			Sequence records		
Victory	12-0	LAO 2001	Wins	7	2003
Defeat	0-21	LBY 1966	Defeats	17	1976-1984
Player Caps	n/a		Undefeated	10	2003
Player Goals	n/a		Without win	29	1965-1984
			Clean sheets	5	2001
			Goals scored	11	1994, 2001
			Without goal	8	1965-1976
			Goals against	28	1965-1984

OMAN 2004-05

PREMIER LEAGUE

	Pl	W	D	L	F	A	Pts	Dhofar	Al Urooba	Muscat	Al Nahda	Sur	Oman	Al Nasr	Seeb	Bahla	Al Tali'aa	Ahly	Al Ittihad	Khaboora
Dhofar Salalah †	24	11	13	0	37	19	46		0-0	2-0	3-2	1-1	1-1	0-0	0-0	0-0	1-1	3-1	2-0	3-1
Al Urooba Sur †	24	12	8	4	42	27	44	2-3		1-3	1-2	2-0	1-1	2-1	1-1	2-3	3-0	3-1	3-0	
Muscat	24	10	10	4	36	24	40	1-1	1-1		2-1	2-1	0-0	4-2	0-0	2-3	2-0	2-3	2-0	2-2
Al Nahda	24	11	3	10	42	37	36	0-1	1-2	1-1		2-3	2-1	2-0	2-4	6-2	3-0	2-1	1-0	2-0
Sur	24	9	8	7	42	35	35	3-5	1-2	0-0	1-1		0-0	4-1	0-0	2-2	3-1	2-0	6-3	3-1
Oman	24	8	11	5	24	20	35	0-1	0-0	0-1	0-0	1-0		1-1	3-2	0-0	1-1	1-0	4-0	1-0
Al Nasr Salalah	24	9	7	8	38	38	34	1-1	1-1	1-1	2-1	2-1	2-2		2-1	5-3	0-1	4-2	1-0	2-1
Seeb	24	8	8	8	44	36	32	0-2	3-4	3-3	4-1	2-2	0-1	2-2		1-2	1-0	0-2	3-2	2-1
Bahla	24	7	10	7	38	41	31	1-1	1-1	1-0	4-2	1-1	2-3	1-2	1-1		3-2	1-1	2-0	4-2
Al Tali'aa	24	6	7	11	31	38	25	1-1	1-2	0-2	0-2	1-2	3-2	2-0	1-1	3-0		2-0	2-2	1-2
Ahly/Sedab	24	5	9	10	27	37	24	2-2	2-2	1-1	1-2	4-1	0-0	1-0	1-3	1-1	1-1		0-2	0-0
Al Ittihad	24	6	3	15	29	48	21	1-3	1-2	0-2	2-1	0-1	0-1	2-1	1-4	2-1	3-3	1-1		3-2
Khaboora	24	4	3	17	26	56	15	0-0	0-2	0-2	2-3	1-4	3-0	2-6	1-6	2-1	2-1	1-2	0-3	

23/09/2004 - 19/05/2005 • † Qualified for the AFC Cup

SULTAN QABOOS CUP 2004-05

Round of 16

Dhofar	3
Al Ittihad	1
Saham	1
Al Urooba	4
Al Tali'aa	2
Masna'aa	1
Nazwa	0
Al Nasr	4
Sur	1
Al Nahda	0
Oman Club	2
Suwaiq	3
Khaboora	2 5p
Seeb	2 4p
Sohar	1
Muscat	2

Quarter-finals

Dhofar	2 2
Al Urooba	2 1
Al Tali'aa	0 1
Al Nasr	1 3
Sur	1 3
Suwaiq	0 1
Khaboora	2 1
Muscat	2 3

Semi-finals

Dhofar	2 1
Al Nasr	2 0
Sur	0 1
Muscat	2 1

Final

Dhofar	1
Muscat	0

CUP FINAL

23-11-2004
Scorer - Hani Al Dhabet 45 for Dhofar

RECENT LEAGUE AND CUP RECORD

Championship

Year	Champions	Pts	Runners-up	Pts	Third	Pts
1996	Sur	56	Oman Club	50	Dhofar	48
1997	Oman Club	49	Sur	36	Al Ittihad	36
1998	Al Nasr	38	Sur	28	Al Urooba	27
1999	Dhofar	34	Al Nasr	27	Suwaiq	27
2000	Al Urooba	42	Al Nasr	36	Seeb	31
2001	Dhofar	41	Al Urooba	36	Seeb	36
2002	Al Urooba	38	Sur	37	Seeb	30
2003	Rowi	65	Dhofar	63	Al Nasr	55
2004	Al Nasr	46	Muscat	45	Al Urooba	41
2005	Dhofar	46	Al Urooba	44	Muscat	40

Cup

Year	Winners	Score	Runners-up
1996	Seeb		
1997	Seeb	1-0	Al Urooba
1998	Seeb	1-0	Sedab
1999	Dhofar	2-1	Al Nasr
2000	Al Nasr	2-1	Al Urooba
2001	Al Urooba	1-0	Al Nasr
2002	Al Nasr	2-1	Dhofar
2003	Rowi	2-0	Seeb
2004	Dhofar	1-0	Muscat

Muscat were formed by the merger of Rowi and Bustan

PAK – PAKISTAN

NATIONAL TEAM RECORD
JULY 1ST 2002 TO JUNE 30TH 2005

PL	W	D	L	F	A	%
12	5	1	6	12	15	45.8

FIFA/COCA-COLA WORLD RANKING

1993	1994	1995	1996	1997	1998	1999	2000	2001	2002	2003	2004	High		Low	
142	158	160	173	153	168	179	190	181	178	168	177	141	02/94	192	05/01

2004-2005											
08/04	09/04	10/04	11/04	12/04	01/05	02/05	03/05	04/05	05/05	06/05	07/05
176	176	176	177	177	176	177	177	178	177	175	170

Although introduced to the Indian subcontinent by British soldiers in the 19th Century football has never drawn the enthusiasm in Pakistan that is reserved for cricket and hockey. Even with a population of some 150 million the game has failed to develop, thus providing an answer as to why Pakistan languish 170th in the FIFA/Coca-Cola World Ranking. Their 2006 FIFA World Cup™ preliminary qualifying campaign ended as quickly as it began losing 6-0 on aggregate to Kyrgyzstan and the team didn't play again for 18 months until a three-match friendly series with India. Befitting the intense rivalry between the two nations the matches revived some competitive

INTERNATIONAL HONOURS
South Asian Federation Games 1989 1991 2004

spirit in Pakistan and the record of won one, drew one and lost one was a solid return against a team ranked 40 places above them. Although winners of the South Asian Federation Games in 1989, 1991 and 2004, Pakistan have had to endure India, Bangladesh and Sri Lanka all claiming the top prize in the region, the South Asian Football Federation Gold Cup. In December 2005 they have the chance to change that when they host the tournament and try to make home advantage count. The National League A Division ended with WAPDA claiming the title on goal difference after finishing level on points with Army after the pair drew 2-2 on the final day of the season.

THE FIFA BIG COUNT OF 2000

	Male	Female		Male	Female
Registered players	37 000	0	Referees	340	0
Non registered players	800 000	0	Officials	6 750	0
Youth players	20 000	0	Total involved	864 090	
Total players	857 000		Number of clubs	2 500	
Professional players	0	0	Number of teams	2 570	

Pakistan Football Federation (PFF)
6-National Hockey Stadium, Feroze Pure Road, Lahore, Pakistan
Tel +92 42 9230821   Fax +92 42 9230823
pff@nexlinx.net.pk   www.pff.com.pk
President: SALEH HAYAT Makhdoom Syed   General Secretary: ARSHAD KHAN LODHI Muhammad
Vice-President: LIAQAT ALI Agha Syed   Treasurer: SAEED MIR Pervaiz   Media Officer: None
Men's Coach: LUFTI Tariq   Women's Coach: None
PFF formed: 1948   AFC: 1954   FIFA: 1948
Colours: Green, Green, Green

GAMES PLAYED BY PAKISTAN IN THE 2006 FIFA WORLD CUP™ CYCLE

2002	Opponents	Score		Venue	Comp	Scorers	Att	Referee
No international matches played in 2002 after June								
2003								
10-01	India	W	1-0	Dhaka	SAr1	Sarfraz Rasool [50]		Hossain BAN
12-01	Sri Lanka	W	2-1	Dhaka	SAr1	Zahid Niaz [50], Sarfraz Rasool [86]		Ghosh BAN
14-01	Afghanistan	W	1-0	Dhaka	SAr1	Sarfraz Rasool [9]		Ghosh BAN
18-01	Maldives	L	0-1	Dhaka	SAsf			Gurung NEP
20-01	India	L	1-2	Dhaka	SA3p	Sarfraz Rasool [66]		Hassan BAN
21-03	Macao	W	3-0	Singapore	ACq	Qadeer Ahmed 2 [27 65], Sarfraz Rasool [51]		
25-03	Singapore	L	0-3	Singapore	ACq			
29-11	Kyrgyzstan	L	0-2	Karachi	WCq		10 000	Nesar BAN
3-12	Kyrgyzstan	L	0-4	Bishkek	WCq		12 000	Mamedov TKM
2004								
No international matches played in 2004								
2005								
12-06	India	D	1-1	Quetta	Fr	Essa [81]	20 000	Khan PAK
16-06	India	L	0-1	Peshawar	Fr		15 000	Imtiaz PAK
18-06	India	W	3-0	Lahore	Fr	Essa [2], Tanveer Ahmed [45+], Arif Mehmood [46]		Asif PAK

Fr = Friendly match • SA = South Asian Federation Cup • AC = AFC Asian Cup • WC = FIFA World Cup™
q = qualifier • r1 = first round group • sf = semi-final • f = final

PAKISTAN NATIONAL TEAM RECORDS AND RECORD SEQUENCES

Records			Sequence records					
Victory	7-0	THA 1960	Wins	3	2003	Clean sheets	5	1952-1953
Defeat	1-9	IRN 1969	Defeats	14	1992-1993	Goals scored	13	1953-1959
Player Caps	n/a		Undefeated	5	1952-1953	Without goal	6	Three times
Player Goals	n/a		Without win	19	1992-1993	Goals against	21	1965-1981

FIFA REFEREE LIST 2005

	Int'l	DoB
ASIF Muhammad	2005	2-03-1979
IMTIAZ Ali		2-06-1971
KHAN Jehangir		15-10-1968

FIFA ASSISTANT REFEREE LIST 2005

	Int'l	DoB
IQBAL Muhammad	1999	14-10-1965
KHAN Muhammad	2005	13-11-1968
KHAN Saleem		10-01-1965
RANA Ahmad		1-06-1974
ULLAH Hidayat		8-07-1968

CLUB DIRECTORY

Club	Abbreviation	Town/City	Lge	Cup	CL
Afghan Club		Chaman	0	0	0
Allied Bank Ltd		Lahore	3	4	0
Baloch FC		Quetta	0	0	0
Habib Bank Ltd	HBL	Karachi	1	1	0
Karachi Port Trust	KPT	Karachi	0	1	0
Khan Research Laboratories	KRL	Rawalpindi	0	0	0
Mauripur Baloch		Karachi	0	0	0
Pakistan Army		Rawalpindi	2	2	0
Pakistan Navy		Islamabad	0	0	0
Pakistan Telecommunication Company Ltd	PTCL	Islamabad	0	1	0
Panther Club		Faisalabad	0	0	0
Water and Power Development Authority	WAPDA	Lahore	5	0	0
Wohaib Club		Lahore	0	0	0
Young XI Dera Ismail Khan			0	0	0

PAKISTAN COUNTRY INFORMATION

Capital	Islamabad	Independence	1947 from the UK	GDP per Capita	$2 100
Population	159 196 336	Status	Republic	GNP Ranking	44
Area km²	803 940	Language	Punjabi 48%, English	Dialling code	+92
Population density	198 per km²	Literacy rate	45%	Internet code	.pk
% in urban areas	35%	Main religion	Muslim	GMT + / –	+5
Towns/Cities ('000)	Karachi 11 627; Lahore 6 312; Faisalabad 2 507; Rawalpindi 1 743; Multan 1 437; Hyderabad 1 386; Gujranwala 1 384; Peshawar 1 219; Islamabad 756; Quetta 733; Bahawalpur 552				
Neighbours (km)	China 523; India 2 912; Iran 909; Afghanistan 2 430; Arabian Sea 1 046				
Main stadia	Jinnah Sport Stadium – Islamabad 48 200; National Stadium – Karachi 34 228				

PAKISTAN 2004

NATIONAL FOOTBALL LEAGUE A DIVISION

Team	Pl	W	D	L	F	A	Pts	WAPDA	Army	KRL	KPT	PTCL	Navy	Habib Bank	Allied Bank	Afghan	Wohaib	Panther	Young XI	Mauripur	Baloch	Naka	Mardan
WAPDA †	30	23	5	2	98	12	74		2-2	4-0	2-0	1-0	1-1	5-1	2-0	6-0	3-0	1-1	4-1	6-0	3-1	8-0	10-0
Pakistan Army	30	23	5	2	98	16	74	0-0		0-0	1-1	2-1	3-1	2-0	1-0	6-0	2-0	2-0	4-2	4-1	5-0	12-0	8-0
Khan Research Labs	30	23	4	3	98	24	73	0-1	1-0		3-1	2-2	1-0	1-1	1-1	3-1	4-1	10-0	7-1	4-0	10-0	7-1	
Karachi Port Trust	30	18	7	5	68	34	60	1-3	2-1	1-0		3-2	1-1	2-2	4-0	4-1	4-0	6-0	3-0	3-0	1-3	7-3	4-1
Pakistan Telecoms	30	18	6	6	63	29	60	2-1	2-3	1-4	0-0		1-1	2-0	1-0	2-0	1-0	1-1	4-2	2-1	3-0	2-0	4-1
Pakistan Navy	30	14	11	5	62	28	53	0-0	2-2	0-0	1-1	2-1		1-1	0-1	1-0	2-1	1-1	8-1	4-0	2-1	10-0	4-0
Habib Bank	30	14	7	9	67	35	49	0-1	0-2	1-2	2-2	2-0	2-2		3-1	5-1	0-2	0-0	1-1	5-0	2-0	6-2	3-1
Allied Bank	30	15	3	12	52	40	48	1-3	0-3	1-5	0-1	0-5	0-0	3-1		0-1	4-1	4-0	2-0	2-0	5-1	5-1	5-0
Afghan Club	30	10	7	13	43	46	37	1-0	0-2	1-2	0-1	0-0	3-4	1-1	1-2		1-0	3-1	1-1	0-0	2-0	5-0	4-0
Wohaib Club	30	9	3	18	37	53	30	0-4	0-3	0-1	2-2	1-4	0-2	2-1	1-0	1-1		1-0	2-3	0-1	4-2	4-1	5-0
Panther Club	30	8	6	16	43	67	30	0-4	0-2	2-7	2-3	0-2	1-4	1-3	1-4	2-0	1-0		4-1	1-2	1-1	8-2	3-0
Young XI DIK	30	7	4	19	38	90	25	0-4	0-5	2-4	2-2	1-4	1-4	0-2	0-4	2-0	0-3	2-2		2-1	2-3	2-0	3-1
Mauripur Baloch	30	6	4	20	25	64	22	0-4	1-5	1-2	0-2	0-2	1-1	1-1	0-0	2-3	1-0	0-1	0-4		2-1	4-0	1-2
Baloch FC	30	5	5	20	26	62	20	0-3	0-2	0-2	1-2	0-4	0-1	0-1	0-1	2-2	0-0	1-2	1-1	2-1		2-0	2-0
Naka Muhammadan	30	5	0	25	32	154	15	0-5	0-5	1-8	1-3	1-3	2-1	0-15	1-5	1-8	1-6	2-3	1-3	1-0	3-1		3-1
Mardan FC	30	3	1	26	20	116	10	0-7	0-9	0-6	0-3	0-3	0-2	1-4	0-1	2-4	3-0	1-2	2-0	0-3	1-1	2-5	

16/08/2003 - 15/05/2004 • † Qualified for the AFC Presidents Cup

16TH PRESIDENT PFF FOOTBALL TOURNAMENT 2003

First Round Groups (Pts)

	Pts
Karachi Port Trust	7
Allied Bank	6
Pakistan Police	4
Pakistan Int. Airlines	0
Pakistan Telecoms	7
Habib Bank	5
Pakistan Railways	4
Pakistan Air Force	0
Pakistan Navy	3
Pakistan Army	2
Karachi Electric	1
Khan Research Labs	9
WAPDA	6
National Bank	3
Sui Southern Gas	0

Quarter-finals

Pakistan Telecoms	1
Allied Bank	0
Pakistan Army	0
Khan Research Labs	1
Pakistan Navy	0 4p
WAPDA	0 3p
Habib Bank	1
Karachi Port Trust	2

Semi-finals

Pakistan Telecoms	1
Khan Research Labs	0
Pakistan Navy	0
Karachi Port Trust	3

Final

Pakistan Telecoms	1
Karachi Port Trust	1

CUP FINAL

Quetta, 5-10-2003
Scorers - Zahid Hameed 58 for Telecoms; Akhtar 78p for Karachi Port Trust
Telecoms won on the toss of a coin

Tournament held in Quetta from September 17th to October 5th

RECENT LEAGUE AND CUP RECORD

	Championship				Cup		
Year	Champions	Score	Runners-up		Winners	Score	Runners-up
1990	Punjub Red		Pakistan Int. Airlines		Karachi Port Trust		HBFC
1991	WAPDA		Habib Bank		Marker Club		Karachi Port Trust
1992	Pakistan Int. Airlines	†	Pakistan Army		Crescent Textile Mills		Marker Club
1993	Pakistan Army	†	WAPDA		National Bank		Pakistan Steel
1994	Crescent Textile Mills	1-0	WAPDA		Frontier Constabulary		Pakistan Air Force
1995	Pakistan Army		Allied Bank		No tournament held		
1996	No tournament held				Allied Bank	3-1	Pakistan Army
1997	Allied Bank	0-0 3-0p	Pakistan Int. Airlines		No tournament held		
1998	Pakistan Int. Airlines	1-1 3-1p	Allied Bank		Allied Bank	1-0	Karachi Port Trust
1999	Allied Bank	0-0 4-3p	Pakistan Navy		Allied Bank	1-1 5-4p	Khan Research Labs
2000	Allied Bank	1-0	Habib Bank		Pakistan Army	1-0	Allied Bank
2001	WAPDA	1-1 4-3p	Khan Research Labs		Pakistan Army		Khan Research Labs
2002	No tournament held				Allied Bank	1-1 4-2p	WAPDA
2003	WAPDA	0-0 4-2p	Pakistan Army		Pakistan Telecoms	1-1 ‡	Karachi Port Trust
2004	WAPDA	†	Pakistan Army		No tournament held		

† Played on a league basis • ‡ Won on the toss of a coin • The PFF does not recognise the National Championships in 1992, 1993 and 1994 as official tournaments

PAL – PALESTINE

NATIONAL TEAM RECORD
JULY 1ST 2002 TO JUNE 30TH 2005

PL	W	D	L	F	A	%
23	2	8	13	26	43	26.1

FIFA/COCA-COLA WORLD RANKING

1993	1994	1995	1996	1997	1998	1999	2000	2001	2002	2003	2004	High		Low	
-	-	-	-	-	184	170	171	145	151	139	126	125	11/04	191	08/99

2004-2005											
08/04	09/04	10/04	11/04	12/04	01/05	02/05	03/05	04/05	05/05	06/05	07/05
129	129	129	125	126	126	126	128	128	127	130	131

A new political order in the Palestinian territories brings with it the chance for football to develop along something resembling normal lines for the first time ever. Since admission to FIFA in 1998 the intifada has seriously impinged on football and for years the best Palestinian players have opted to play for Israeli clubs and the Israeli national team. For its part the Palestinian national team has been left to scour South America for players of Palestinian descent of which, fortunately, there are a good number. It is a process which is likely to unearth even more though it may be a while before they play matches staged in either the West Bank or Gaza. For the FIFA World Cup 2006™

INTERNATIONAL HONOURS
None

qualifiers, the Palestinians opted to play their home matches in Qatar, but apart from two wins over Chinese Taipei – including a record 8-0 triumph – the World Cup qualifiers yielded very little. At the heart of the future development of the game will be the provision of safe and secure facilities, especially for the kids. There is no lack of goodwill, with a number of high profile visitors to the region, notably Chelsea manager Jose Mourinho who was keen to use football to help the peace process. There is undoubted potential amongst the Palestine people as far as football is concerned but there is a tough job ahead to build up the foundations for future prosperity.

THE FIFA BIG COUNT OF 2000

	Male	Female		Male	Female
Registered players	5 000	0	Referees	285	0
Non registered players	20 000	130	Officials	980	8
Youth players	12 000	60	Total involved	38 463	
Total players	37 190		Number of clubs	377	
Professional players	0	0	Number of teams	1 215	

Palestine Football Association (PFA)
Al Yarmuk, Gaza
Tel +970 8 2834339   Fax +970 8 2825208
info@palfa.com   www.palfa.com
President: AFIFI Ahmed   General Secretary: MEKKY Bader Yassin
Vice-President: ALBEDD Georg   Treasurer: ZAQOUI Jamal   Media Officer: HASAN Khwalda
Men's Coach: NASSER Asmi   Women's Coach: SHAHWAN Necola & HANIA Bish
PFA formed: 1928, 1962   AFC: 1998   FIFA: 1998
Colours: White, Black, White

GAMES PLAYED BY PALESTINE IN THE 2006 FIFA WORLD CUP™ CYCLE

2002 Opponents		Score	Venue	Comp	Scorers	Att	Referee
30-08 Syria	L	1-2	Damascus	WAr1			
1-09 Iraq	L	0-2	Damascus	WAr1			
10-12 Chile	L	1-3	Santiago	Fr			
16-12 Jordan	D	1-1	Kuwait City	ARr1	Alkord 5		
20-12 Morocco	L	1-3	Kuwait City	ARr1	Alkord 52	700	Al Saeedi UAE
23-12 Sudan	D	2-2	Kuwait City	ARr1	Salem 31, Alkord 53	2 000	Al Zeid KSA
25-12 Kuwait	D	3-3	Kuwait City	ARr1	Shaker 15, Allam 38, Al Jaish 46		
2003							
24-09 Qatar	D	1-1	Doha	ACq	Aziz 90		
27-09 Qatar	L	1-2	Doha	ACq	Florentio 77		
5-10 Kuwait	L	1-2	Kuwait City	ACq	Abdullah 62		
8-10 Kuwait	L	0-4	Kuwait City	ACq			
19-10 Singapore	L	0-2	Singapore	ACq		2 787	Sarkar IND
22-10 Singapore	D	0-0	Singapore	ACq		3 076	Vidanagamage SRI
2004							
18-02 Chinese Taipei	W	8-0	Doha	WCq	Alkord 10, Habaib 2 20 32, Atura 43, Beshe 2 52 86, Amar 76, Keshkesh 82	1 000	Al Yarimi YEM
26-03 Syria	D	1-1	Damascus	Fr			
31-03 Iraq	D	1-1	Doha	WCq	Beshe 72	500	Al Shoufi SYR
9-06 Uzbekistan	L	0-3	Tashkent	WCq		35 000	Moradi IRN
17-06 Jordan	D	1-1	Tehran	WAr1	Alkord 12		
19-06 Iraq	L	1-2	Tehran	WAr1	Alkord 40		
2-09 Bahrain	L	0-1	Al Muharraq	Fr			
8-09 Uzbekistan	L	0-3	Rayyan	WCq		400	Maidin SIN
14-10 Chinese Taipei	W	1-0	Taipei	WCq	Amar 94+	500	Rasheed MDV
16-11 Iraq	L	1-4	Doha	WCq	Zaatara 71	500	Al Mutlaq KSA
2005							

No international matches played in 2005 before August

Fr = Friendly match • AC = AFC Asian Cup • AR = Arab Cup • WA = West Asian Championship • WC = FIFA World Cup™
q = qualifier • r1 = 1st round

PALESTINE NATIONAL TEAM RECORDS AND RECORD SEQUENCES

Records			Sequence records					
Victory	8-0	TPE 2004	Wins	2	1999	Clean sheets	3	1976-1992
Defeat	1-8	EGY 1953	Defeats	4	2001-02, 2003	Goals scored	8	1953-1965
Player Caps	n/a		Undefeated	4	1999	Without goal	3	2003
Player Goals	n/a		Without win	14	2001-2003	Goals against	13	2001-2003

The organisation of a Palestinian championship and cup tournament is sporadic and often haphazrad due to the political and geographical difficulties. Champions in the past have included Rafah Services club in 1996, Shabab Al Amari in 1997, Khadamat Rafah in 1998 and Al Aqsa in 2002

PALESTINE COUNTRY INFORMATION

Capital	Ramallah	Independence	1993	GDP per Capita	$600
Population	3 636 195	Status	Republic	GNP Ranking	n/a
Area km²	6 220	Language	Arabic	Dialling code	+972
Population density	584 per km²	Literacy rate	n/a	Internet code	.il
% in urban areas	n/a	Main religion	Muslim	GMT +/−	+2
Towns/Cities	Ramallah; Nablus; Jericho; Hebron; Gaza; Bethlehem				
Neighbours (km)	For the West Bank and Gaza: Israel 358; Jordan 97; Egypt 11; Mediterranean Sea 40				
Main stadia	None				

PAN – PANAMA

NATIONAL TEAM RECORD
JULY 1ST 2002 TO JUNE 30TH 2005

PL	W	D	L	F	A	%
44	12	14	18	43	54	43.2

FIFA/COCA-COLA WORLD RANKING

1993	1994	1995	1996	1997	1998	1999	2000	2001	2002	2003	2004	High		Low	
132	140	126	101	119	131	138	121	109	129	125	100	97	03/05	150	10/95

2004-2005											
08/04	09/04	10/04	11/04	12/04	01/05	02/05	03/05	04/05	05/05	06/05	07/05
106	106	103	101	100	101	101	97	97	95	98	83

Panama is enjoying its most successful year with the U-20s reaching the FIFA World Youth Championship while the national team featured in the final round of the 2006 FIFA World Cup™ qualifiers and most impressively finished runners-up at the 2005 CONCACAF Gold Cup. Having broken into the top 100 in the FIFA/Coca-Cola World Ranking for the first time, Panama came tantalisingly close to their first senior trophy when they lost to hosts USA 3-1 on penalties after a goalless final. Although struggling in their World Cup™ group and unlikely to qualify for Germany 2006, Panama's fans can be pleased at the huge progress made by the national team during the

INTERNATIONAL HONOURS
None

course of the past two years. The U-20s efforts in the final stages of the CONCACAF U-20 Championship were enough to send them to the Netherlands, but they received a stern lesson, losing all three of their group games against China PR, Ukraine and Turkey. There were some familiar faces in the Torneo ANAPROF in 2004 where the Dely Valdes twins led Deportivo Arabe Unido to both the Apertura and Clausura titles. That meant there was no need for an end of season play-off while in the 2005 CONCACAF Champions Cup, Plaza Amador beat Cabron International before bowing out to FAS of El Salvador 2-6 on aggregate.

THE FIFA BIG COUNT OF 2000

	Male	Female		Male	Female
Registered players	25 300	3 250	Referees	263	20
Non registered players	25 000	6 000	Officials	1 500	0
Youth players	20 080	1 075	Total involved	82 488	
Total players	80 705		Number of clubs	100	
Professional players	300	250	Number of teams	860	

Federación Panameña de Fútbol (FEPAFUT)

Estadio Rommel Fernández, Puerta 24, Ave. Jose Aeustin Araneo, Apartado postal 8-391 Zona 8, Panama
Tel +507 2333896   Fax +507 2330582
fepafut@sinfo.net   www.marearoja.com
President: ALVARADO Ariel   General Secretary: ALVAREZ Ruben
Vice-President: ARCE Fernando   Treasurer: DURAN Ricardo   Media Officer: PITTY Ricardo
Men's Coach: HERNANDEZ Jose   Women's Coach: Fernandez Ezequiel
FEPAFUT formed: 1937   CONCACAF: 1961   FIFA: 1938
Colours: Red, Red, Red

GAMES PLAYED BY PANAMA IN THE 2006 FIFA WORLD CUP™ CYCLE

2002 Opponents	Score	Venue	Comp	Scorers	Att	Referee
No international matches played in 2002						
2003						
9-02 El Salvador	L 1-2	Panama City	GCq	Díaz 34	8 000	Pineda HON
16-02 Guatemala	W 2-0	Panama City	GCq	Mendez 29, Brown 36		Pineda HON
18-02 Honduras	D 1-1	Panama City	GCq	Mendieta 61	5 000	Rizo MEX
21-02 Nicaragua	L 0-1	Panama City	GCq		7 000	Aguilar SLV
23-02 Costa Rica	L 0-1	Panama City	GCq		550	Batres GUA
27-06 Cuba	W 2-0	Panama City	Fr	Tejada 23, Garces 81		Moreno PAN
29-06 Cuba	W 1-0	Panama City	Fr	Tejada 55		Vidal PAN
20-08 Paraguay	L 1-2	Panama City	Fr	Solis 77		Porras CRC
31-08 Bolivia	L 0-3	La Paz	Fr			Ortube BOL
2004						
28-01 El Salvador	D 1-1	San Salvador	Fr	Garces 10		
16-03 Cuba	D 1-1	Havana	Fr	Phillips 7		Rojas Corbeas CUB
18-03 Cuba	L 0-3	Havana	Fr			Yero Rodriguez CUB
7-04 Honduras	D 0-0	La Ceiba	Fr		10 000	Rodriguez HON
28-04 Bermuda	W 4-1	Panama City	Fr	Phillips 2 25 90, Dely Valdes.JC 66, Tejada 68		
1-05 Guatemala	W 2-1	Guatemala City	Fr	Dely Valdes.JC 2 35 64p	11 615	Argueta SLV
13-06 St Lucia	W 4-0	Panama City	WCq	Dely Valdes.JC 5, Tejada 18, Phillips 39, Brown 75		Phillip GRN
20-06 St Lucia	W 3-0	Vieux Fort	WCq	Tejada 14, Dely Valdes.JC 88, Blanco 89	400	Gurley VIN
23-07 Guatemala	D 1-1	Panama City	Fr	Dely Valdes.J 72	3 000	Mejia CRC
28-07 Honduras	D 0-0	Tegucigalpa	Fr		6 000	Zelaya HON
18-08 El Salvador	L 1-2	San Salvador	WCq	Dely Valdes.JC 36	11 400	Navarro CAN
4-09 Jamaica	W 2-1	Kingston	WCq	Brown 2, Dely Valdes.JC 90	24 000	Batres GUA
8-09 USA	D 1-1	Panama City	WCq	Brown 69	15 000	Rodriguez MEX
9-10 Jamaica	D 1-1	Panama City	WCq	Brown 24	16 000	Pineda HON
13-10 USA	L 0-6	Washington DC	WCq		22 000	Ramdhan TRI
17-11 El Salvador	W 3-0	Panama City	WCq	Brown 4, Baloy 7, Garces 21	9 502	Archundia MEX
18-12 Iran	L 0-1	Tehran	Fr			Esfahanian IRN
2005						
26-01 Ecuador	L 0-2	Ambato	Fr		5 000	Vasco ECU
29-01 Ecuador	L 0-2	Babahoyo	Fr			
9-02 Guatemala	D 0-0	Panama City	WCq		20 000	Prendergast JAM
19-02 El Salvador	W 1-0	Guatemala City	GCq	Solis 77	10 000	Archundia MEX
23-02 Costa Rica	L 0-1	Guatemala City	GCq		3 000	Archundia MEX
25-02 Honduras	L 0-1	Guatemala City	GCq		11 159	Sibrian SLV
27-02 Guatemala	L 0-3	Guatemala City	GCq		1 491	Quesada CRC
26-03 Costa Rica	L 1-2	San Jose	WCq	Brown 58p	8 000	Rodriguez MEX
30-03 Mexico	D 1-1	Panama City	WCq	Tejada 75	13 000	Pineda HON
25-05 Venezuela	D 1-1	Caracas	Fr	Brown 34	15 000	Brand VEN
4-06 Trinidad and Tobago	L 0-2	Port of Spain	WCq		18 000	Prendergast JAM
8-06 USA	L 0-3	Panama City	WCq		15 000	Navarro CAN
6-07 Colombia	W 1-0	Miami	GCr1	Tejada 70	10 311	Batres GUA
10-07 Trinidad and Tobago	D 2-2	Miami	GCr1	Tejada 2 24 90	17 292	Wyngaarde SUR
12-07 Honduras	L 0-1	Miami	GCr1		11 000	Wyngaarde SUR
17-07 South Africa	D 1-1	Houston	GCqf	Dely Valdes.JL 48 W 5-3p	60 050	Prendergast JAM
21-07 Colombia	W 3-2	New Jersey	GCsf	Phillips 2 11 72, Dely Valdes.JL 26	41 721	Sibrian SLV
24-07 USA	D 0-0	New Jersey	GCf	L 1-3p	31 018	Batres GUA

Fr = Friendly match • GC = CONCACAF Gold Cup • WC = FIFA World Cup™
q = qualifier • r1 = first round group • qf = quarter-final • sf = semi-final • f = final

PANAMA COUNTRY INFORMATION

Capital	Panamá	Independence	1903	GDP per Capita	$6 300
Population	3 000 463	Status	Republic	GNP Ranking	87
Area km²	78 200	Language	Spanish	Dialling code	+507
Population density	38 per km²	Literacy rate	92%	Internet code	.pa
% in urban areas	53%	Main religion	Christian	GMT +/–	-5
Towns/Cities ('000)	Panamá 408; San Miguelito 321; Tocumen 88; David 82; Arraiján 77; Colón 76; Las Cumbres 69				
Neighbours (km)	Colombia 225; Costa Rica 330; Caribbean and North Pacific 2 490				
Main stadia	Rommel Fernandez – Panamá 25 000; Armando Dely Valdez – Colón 3 000				

PANAMA 2004

ANAPROF PRIMERA PROFESIONAL APERTURA

	Pl	W	D	L	F	A	Pts	Arabe Unido	Tauro	Plaza	Chorrillo	San Fran	Veraguense	Coclé	Alianza	River	Azúcar
Deportivo Arabe Unido	18	14	1	3	31	16	43		3-2	1-0	0-3	2-1	1-0	1-1	1-0	3-1	6-0
Tauro	18	10	3	5	25	11	33	0-1		0-2	0-0	0-1	2-0	3-0	2-1	2-0	6-0
Plaza Amador	18	10	3	5	25	15	33	2-0	0-0		1-1	1-0	1-0	2-1	3-2	4-1	2-0
El Chorrillo	18	8	8	2	26	12	32	1-2	1-1	1-0		3-3	1-2	1-0	1-1	4-0	1-0
San Francisco	18	9	5	4	22	14	32	2-0	0-1	0-1	1-1		2-1	2-2	2-0	2-0	1-0
Atlético Veraguense	18	7	4	7	23	16	25	1-3	0-1	1-0	0-0	0-0		1-0	3-0	3-1	3-0
Sporting Coclé	18	5	6	7	21	25	21	0-1	1-2	3-2	0-2	2-2	1-0		1-0	3-3	3-1
Alianza	18	3	5	10	10	24	14	0-1	1-0	0-0	0-0	0-1	0-5	1-1		1-2	1-0
River Plate Colón	18	2	4	12	20	39	10	1-3	0-1	2-3	1-2	0-1	2-2	1-1	0-1		2-0
Pan de Azúcar	18	1	3	14	10	41	6	1-2	1-3	2-1	0-3	0-1	1-1	0-1	1-1	3-1	

13/02/2004 - 12/05/2004 • † Qualified for the Apertura play-offs

APERTURA PLAY-OFFS 2004

Semi-finals

Arabe Unido	1 2
El Chorrillo	0 0

Tauro	1 1
Plaza Amador	3 0

Finals

Arabe Unido	1
Plaza Amador	0

23-05-2004
Rommel Fernandez, Panama City

CLAUSURA PLAY-OFFS 2004

Semi-finals

Arabe Unido	1 3
El Chorrillo	0 3

Tauro	1 0
San Francisco	1 1

Finals

First leg, 31-10-2004
Muquita Sanchez, La Chorrera

Arabe Unido	1 5
San Francisco	1 3

Second leg, 7-11-2004
Armando Dely Valdez, Colón

PANAMA 2004

ANAPROF PRIMERA PROFESIONAL CLAUSURA

	Pl	W	D	L	F	A	Pts	Arabe Unido	Tauro	San Fran	Chorrillo	Plaza	Alianza	River	Coclé	Veraguense	Azúcar
Deportivo Arabe Unido	18	12	4	2	32	14	40		4-1	1-0	1-5	2-1	2-0	2-1	3-0	3-0	2-0
Tauro	18	11	3	4	36	11	36	1-0		2-0	2-0	2-0	2-0	3-0	0-0	3-2	7-0
San Francisco	18	11	2	5	38	17	35	1-1	0-2		1-3	3-0	3-2	3-0	3-0	4-1	3-0
El Chorrillo	18	11	2	5	32	19	35	0-0	1-0	2-2		1-0	0-2	2-0	2-1	2-0	1-0
Plaza Amador	17	8	5	4	34	18	29	1-1	0-0	1-0	4-1		3-1	2-1	1-1		4-1
Alianza	18	9	1	8	28	29	28	0-1	2-1	0-3	1-0	0-4		3-0	4-1	2-2	2-1
Colón River	18	5	3	10	21	39	18	1-1	0-5	0-5	2-1	3-6	1-0		2-1	1-1	5-1
Sporting Coclé	18	4	3	11	21	35	15	1-3	1-5	0-3	2-3	0-0	1-2	2-1		2-0	2-0
Atlético Veraguense	17	3	3	11	15	36	12	0-2	1-0	1-2	1-2	0-6	1-3	0-2	2-1		2-0
Pan de Azúcar	18	0	4	14	12	51	4	1-3	0-0	1-2	0-6	1-1	3-4	1-1	1-5	1-1	

16/07/2004 - 21/10/2004 • † Qualified for the Clausura play-offs • Pan de Azúcar relegated

CLUB DIRECTORY

Club	Town/City	Lge	CL
Alianza		0	0
Deportivo Arabe Unido	Colón	3	0
Atlético Chiriquí	San Cristobal	0	0
Atlético Veraguense	Veraguas	0	0
Colón River	Colón	0	0
El Chorrillo	Balboa	0	0
Plaza Amador	Panama City	4	0
Sporting 89	San Miguelito	0	0
San Francisco	La Chorrera	2	0
Tauro	Panama City	6	0

RECENT LEAGUE RECORD

	Championship		
Year	Winners	Score	Runners-up
1997	Tauro	1-0	Euro Kickers
1998	Tauro	1-0	Deportivo Arabe Unido
1999	Deportivo Arabe Unido	3-0	Tauro
2000	Tauro	2-0	Plaza Amador
2001	Panama Viejo	4-3	Tauro
2001	Deportivo Arabe Unido	†	
2002	Plaza Amador	2-0	Deportivo Arabe Unido
2003	Tauro	†	
2004	Deportivo Arabe Unido	†	

† Won both Apertura and Clausura so automatic champions

PANAMA NATIONAL TEAM RECORDS AND RECORD SEQUENCES

Records			Sequence records					
Victory	12-0	PUR 1946	Wins	4	2001, 2003	Clean sheets	3	2000
Defeat	0-11	CRC 1938	Defeats	9	1976-1977	Goals scored	11	1946-50, 1974-75
Player Caps	n/a		Undefeated	7	2001, 2003	Without goal	6	1984-1985
Player Goals	n/a		Without win	13	1950-1963	Goals against	17	1975-1979

PAR – PARAGUAY

NATIONAL TEAM RECORD
JULY 1ST 2002 TO JUNE 30TH 2005

PL	W	D	L	F	A	%
35	13	13	9	38	39	55.7

FIFA/COCA-COLA WORLD RANKING

1993	1994	1995	1996	1997	1998	1999	2000	2001	2002	2003	2004	High		Low	
61	87	64	38	29	25	17	10	13	18	22	30	8	03/01	103	05/95

2004-2005											
08/04	09/04	10/04	11/04	12/04	01/05	02/05	03/05	04/05	05/05	06/05	07/05
22	23	23	24	30	29	29	28	28	29	30	34

The highlight of the past season for Paraguayan fans has been the silver medal performance of the U-23 team at the Athens Olympics. Victories over Japan, Italy, Korea Republic and Iraq earned the players their medals although there was obvious disappointment at missing out on gold after the 1-0 defeat to Argentina in the final. As the senior team came to the end of the marathon 2006 FIFA World Cup™ qualifying campaign they were no nearer knowing whether they would be in the finals in Germany than when they started out in September 2003, with five or six nations grouped

INTERNATIONAL HONOURS
Qualified for the FIFA World Cup™ finals 1930 1950 1958 1986 1998 2002   Copa America 1953 1979
South America U-23 1992   Juventud de America 1971   South America U-16 2004   Copa Libertadores Olimpia 1979 1990 2002

in mid-table aiming for two automatic qualifying spots and a single play-off place. Domestic football in 2004 was dominated by Cerro Porteno and their Argentine coach Gerardo Martino. Cerro won both the Apertura and Clausura Championships to automatically win the overall title but for Martino it secured his hat-trick, having won the Championship in 2002 and 2003 with Libertad. The decline in fortunes of Olimpia has been dramatic with the 2002 Copa Libertadores winners finishing bottom of the Clausura and forced to watch the Copa Libertadores in 2005 from the sidelines, the first time they had not qualified in eight years.

THE FIFA BIG COUNT OF 2000

	Male	Female		Male	Female
Registered players	200 000	0	Referees	400	0
Non registered players	500 000	0	Officials	2 000	150
Youth players	20 000	251	Total involved	722 801	
Total players	720 251		Number of clubs	1 100	
Professional players	180	0	Number of teams	2 000	

Asociación Paraguaya de Fútbol (APF)
Estadio de los Defensores del Chaco, Calle Mayor Martinez 1393, Asuncion, Paraguay
Tel +595 21 480120   Fax +595 21 480124
apf@telesurf.com.py   www.apf.org.py
President: HARRISON Oscar   General Secretary: FILARTIGA Arturo
Vice-President: NAPOUT BARRETO Angel   Treasurer: ZACARIAZ PEREIRA Emilio   Media Officer: BATTILANA Guillermo Eloy
Men's Coach: RUIZ Anibal   Women's Coach: VON LUCKEN Esteban
APF formed: 1906   CONMEBOL: 1921   FIFA: 1925
Colours: Red and white stripes, Blue, Blue

GAMES PLAYED BY PARAGUAY IN THE 2006 FIFA WORLD CUP™ CYCLE

2002	Opponents	Score		Venue	Comp	Scorers	Att	Referee
21-08	Brazil	W	1-0	Fortaleza	Fr	Cuevas 28	30 000	Ruiz COL
19-09	Iran	D	1-1	Tabriz	Fr	Bareiro 35. L 3-4p	25 000	Kameel KUW
16-10	Spain	D	0-0	Logrono	Fr		15 000	Benquerenca POR
2003								
26-03	Mexico	D	1-1	San Diego	Fr	Cardozo 74		Kennedy USA
29-03	Costa Rica	L	1-2	Alajuela	Fr	Cáceres 53		Quesada CRC
2-04	Honduras	D	1-1	Tegucigalpa	Fr	Quintana 55		Batres GUA
30-04	Peru	W	1-0	Lima	Fr	Alvarenga 73		Lopez Buitrago COL
6-06	Portugal	D	0-0	Braga	Fr			Kasnaferis GRE
11-06	Japan	D	0-0	Saitama	Fr			Riley ENG
2-07	El Salvador	W	1-0	San Francisco	Fr	Samudio 3		Valenzuela USA
6-07	USA	L	0-2	Columbus	Fr			Navarro CAN
9-07	Jamaica	L	0-2	Kingston	Fr			Bowen CAY
20-08	Panama	W	2-1	Panama City	Fr	Campos 6, Gamarra 17		Porras CRC
6-09	Peru	L	1-4	Lima	WCq	Gamarra 24	42 557	Baldassi ARG
10-09	Uruguay	W	4-1	Asuncion	WCq	Cardozo 3 26 58 72, Paredes 53	15 000	Ruiz COL
15-11	Ecuador	W	2-1	Asuncion	WCq	Santa Cruz 29, Cardozo 75	12 000	Arandia BOL
18-11	Chile	W	1-0	Santiago	WCq	Paredes 30	61 923	Mendez URU
2004								
31-03	Brazil	D	0-0	Asuncion	WCq		40 000	Ruiz COL
28-04	Korea Republic	D	0-0	Incheon	Fr		26 237	Kamikawa JPN
1-06	Bolivia	L	1-2	La Paz	WCq	Cardozo 33	23 013	Rezende BRA
6-06	Argentina	D	0-0	Buenos Aires	WCq		37 000	Simon BRA
8-07	Costa Rica	W	1-0	Arequipa	CAr1	Dos Santos 85p	30 000	Ruiz COL
11-07	Chile	D	1-1	Arequipa	CAr1	Cristaldo 79	15 000	Mendez URU
14-07	Brazil	W	2-1	Arequipa	CAr1	González.J 29, Bareiro 71	8 000	Hidalgo PER
18-07	Uruguay	L	1-3	Tacna	CAqf	Gamarra 16	20 000	Baldassi ARG
5-09	Venezuela	W	1-0	Asuncion	WCq	Gamarra 52	30 000	Mendez URU
9-10	Colombia	D	1-1	Barranquilla	WCq	Gavilan 77	25 000	Elizondo ARG
13-10	Peru	D	1-1	Asuncion	WCq	Paredes 13	30 000	Ruiz COL
17-11	Uruguay	L	0-1	Montevideo	WCq		35 000	Simon BRA
2005								
19-01	Korea Republic	D	1-1	Los Angeles	Fr	Cardozo 45p	10 000	Hall USA
23-01	Guatemala	W	2-1	Los Angeles	Fr	Cuevas 14, Dos Santos 74		
27-03	Ecuador	L	2-5	Quito	WCq	Cardozo 10p, Cabanas 14	32 449	Mendez URU
30-03	Chile	W	2-1	Asuncion	WCq	Morinigo 37, Cardozo 59	10 000	Elizondo ARG
5-06	Brazil	L	1-4	Porto Alegre	WCq	Santa Cruz 72	45 000	Vazquez URU
7-06	Bolivia	W	4-1	Asuncion	WCq	Gamarra 17, Santa Cruz 46+, Caceres 54, Nunez 68	5 534	Brand VEN

Fr = Friendly match • CA = Copa America • WC = FIFA World Cup™ • q = qualifier • r1 = 1st round • qf = quarter-final

PARAGUAY COUNTRY INFORMATION

Capital	Asunción	Independence	1811	GDP per Capita	$4 700
Population	6 191 368	Status	Republic	GNP Ranking	99
Area km²	406 750	Language	Spanish, Guarani	Dialling code	+595
Population density	15 per km²	Literacy rate	94%	Internet code	.py
% in urban areas	53%	Main religion	Christian	GMT +/−	-4
Towns/Cities ('000)	Asunción 508; Ciudad del Este 260; San Lorenzo 228; Luque 210; Capiatá 199; Lambaré 126				
Neighbours (km)	Brazil 1 290; Argentina 1 880; Bolivia 750				
Main stadia	Defensores del Chaco – Asuncion 40 000; Feliciano Cáceres – Luque 24 000				

PARAGUAY NATIONAL TEAM RECORDS AND RECORD SEQUENCES

Records			Sequence records					
Victory	7-0	BOL 1949	Wins	8	1947-1949	Clean sheets	5	1947-49, 1988
Defeat	0-8	ARG 1926	Defeats	8	1959-1961	Goals scored	15	1958-1960
Player Caps	99	GAMARRA Carlos	Undefeated	14	1985-1986	Without goal	4	1981-83, 1993
Player Goals	24	CARDOZA Jose	Without win	20	1959-1962	Goals against	20	1931-1942

NATIONAL CAPS

	Caps
GAMARRA Carlos Alberto	99
AYALA Celso	85
ACUNA Roberto	84
FERNANDEZ Roberto	78
CARDOZO Jose	77
TORALES Juan	77
CHILAVERT Jose-Luis	74
STRUWAY Estanislao	74
ENCISO Julio Cesar	70
CANIZA Denis	65

NATIONAL GOALS

	Goals
CARDOZO Jose	24
ARRUA Saturnino	13
ROMERO Julio Cesar	13
RIVAS Gerardo	12
BENITEZ Miguel Angel	11
GAMARRA Carlos Alberto	10
GONZALEZ AURELIO	10
PAREDES Carlos Alberto	10
SANTA CRUZ Roque	10
VILLALBA Juan	10

FIFA REFEREE LIST 2005

	Int'l	DoB
AMARILLA Carlos	1997	26-10-1970
CHAMORRO Ramon	2005	28-08-1965
GRANCE Ricardo	1997	12-12-1963
INVERNIZZI Atilio	2001	17-10-1965
LUGO Benito	2002	25-04-1964
TORRES Carlos	1998	27-04-1970
VALENZUELA Nelson	1995	5-03-1966

FIFA ASSISTANT REFEREE LIST 2005

	Int'l	DoB
ANDINO Amelio		24-12-1962
BERNAL Manuel	1999	17-06-1963
CANO Nelson	1999	10-10-1961
GALVAN Celestino	1994	6-04-1963
RUIZ Emigdio		20-04-1966
SERVIAN Nelson		4-04-1964
YEGROS Nicolas		10-10-1967

CLUB DIRECTORY

Club	Town/City	Stadium	Phone	www.	Lge	CL
3 de Febrero	Ciudad del Este	Ciudad del Este 25 000			0	0
12 de Octubre	Itaugua	Juan Pettengil 8 000			0	0
Cerro Porteño	Asuncion	General Pablo Rojas 25 000	+595 21 371022	clubcerro.com	26	0
General Caballero	Zeballos Cue				0	0
Guarani	Asuncion	Rogelio Livieres 10 000	+595 21 227080		9	0
Libertad	Asuncion	Alfredo Stroessner 16 000	+595 21 224342		10	0
Nacional	Asuncion	Arsenio Erico 4 500	+595 21 371590		6	0
Olimpia	Asuncion	Manuel Ferreira 20 000	+595 21 200680	clubolimpia.com.py	38	3
Sportivo Luqueño	Luque	Feliciano Cáceres 24 000	+595 64 3299		2	0
Tacuary	Tacuary	Toribio Vargas 4 000	+595 21 206033		0	0

RECENT LEAGUE RECORD

	Championship		
Year	Winners	Score	Runners-up
1990	Cerro Porteño	2-0 2-1	Libertad
1991	Sol de América	1-1 2-1	Cerro Porteño
1992	Cerro Porteño	2-2 0-0 5-0	Libertad
1993	Olimpia	†	Cerro Porteño
1994	Cerro Porteño	1-1 0-0 4-3p	Olimpia
1995	Olimpia	2-1 0-1 8-7p	Cerro Porteño
1996	Cerro Porteño	1-2 5-1	Guaraní
1997	Olimpia	1-0 1-1	Cerro Porteño
1998	Olimpia	2-2 3-1	Cerro Porteño
1999	Olimpia	1-0 3-2	Cerro Porteño
2000	Olimpia	†	
2001	Cerro Porteño	†	Sportivo Luqueño
2002	Libertad	2-1 4-1	12 de Octubre
2003	Libertad	†	Guarani
2004	Cerro Porteño	†	

† Won both Apertura and Clausura so automatic champions

PARAGUAY 2004

DIVISION PROFESIONAL APERTURA

	Pl	W	D	L	F	A	Pts	Cerro	Libertad	Tacuary	Guaraní	Olimpia	Nacional	Sol	12 Octobre	Luqueño	Colombia
Cerro Porteño ‡	18	12	5	1	31	13	41		2-2	1-0	3-1	1-1	2-1	3-0	1-2	1-1	1-0
Libertad ‡	18	11	5	2	44	13	38	0-0		2-1	3-0	4-1	0-1	1-0	1-1	6-1	3-0
Tacuary	18	8	4	6	25	13	28	0-1	1-1		0-1	3-0	2-1	0-1	4-1	5-1	3-0
Guaraní	18	8	4	6	20	25	28	1-3	0-6	1-1		0-0	2-0	1-1	2-1	1-0	2-1
Olimpia	18	6	5	7	21	28	23	1-1	0-3	0-1	1-3		1-1	2-0	1-0	2-1	5-3
Nacional	18	5	5	8	19	24	20	2-3	2-1	0-2	1-0	2-3		1-2	1-0	1-1	1-1
Sol de América	18	5	4	9	14	24	19	0-2	1-2	0-1	0-1	0-0	1-0		1-0	2-2	1-0
12 de Octobre	18	5	3	10	18	28	18	1-4	1-4	0-0	2-1	1-0	1-2	3-1		0-1	2-1
Sportivo Luqueño	18	3	8	7	19	30	17	0-1	1-1	0-0	0-0	2-3	1-1	4-2	0-0		2-1
Sport Colombia	18	4	3	11	21	34	15	0-1	0-4	2-1	2-3	2-0	1-1	1-1	3-2	3-1	

7/02/2004 - 27/06/2004 • Cerro are Apertura Champions and qualify to meet the Clausura champions for the 2004 title
‡ Qualified for the Copa Sudamericana 2004

PARAGUAY 2004

DIVISION PROFESIONAL CLAUSURA

	Pl	W	D	L	F	A	Pts	Cerro	Libertad	Nacional	Guaraní	Tacuary	Colombia	Luqueño	Sol	12 Octobre	Olimpia
Cerro Porteño †	18	12	2	4	30	13	38		0-1	3-0	5-0	2-0	2-1	2-0	1-0	2-0	3-1
Libertad †	18	9	4	5	26	21	31	4-3		3-0	1-0	0-0	0-0	3-2	4-1	0-0	1-0
Nacional	18	7	6	5	29	24	27	1-3	2-1		7-0	1-1	4-1	0-0	1-3	1-1	1-2
Guaraní	18	5	8	5	21	29	23	3-0	1-3	1-2		0-0	1-0	0-0	0-0	4-4	3-1
Tacuary †	18	3	13	2	14	14	22	0-0	1-1	0-0	0-0		0-0	0-0	1-1	1-0	3-2
Sport Colombia	18	5	6	7	21	23	21	0-1	3-1	1-2	2-2	0-1		1-1	3-2	0-0	3-2
Sportivo Luqueño	18	4	9	5	23	28	21	1-0	3-1	3-3	2-2	2-2	3-2		1-2	1-1	1-1
Sol de América	18	5	5	8	25	27	20	1-2	1-2	0-1	0-1	1-1	1-2	4-1		2-2	1-0
12 de Octubre	18	3	9	6	19	22	18	0-0	2-0	0-2	1-2	1-1	0-0	3-0	2-3		0-2
Olimpia	18	4	4	10	22	29	16	0-1	2-0	1-1	1-1	3-2	0-2	1-2	2-2	1-2	

7/08/2004 - 5/12/2004 • Cerro are Clausura Champions and having won the Apertura are automatically the overall champions for 2004
† Qualified for the Copa Libertadores 2005 • Sport Colombia and Sol de América relegated based on a three year average

PARAGUAY 2004
DIVISION INTERMEDIA (2)

	Pl	W	D	L	F	A	Pts
3 de Febrero	18	9	7	2	32	17	34
General Caballero	18	9	5	4	30	23	32
Cerro Porteño PF	18	8	6	4	29	23	30
Fernando de la Mora	18	7	8	3	20	17	29
Sportivo Iteño	18	7	4	7	24	23	25
River Plate	18	7	4	7	20	21	25
2 de Mayo	18	6	4	8	27	34	22
Universal	18	4	8	6	16	26	20
Sportivo San Lorenzo	18	4	2	12	21	22	14
Cerro Corá	18	3	4	11	19	32	13

26/03/2004 - 31/07/2004

PER – PERU

NATIONAL TEAM RECORD
JULY 1ST 2002 TO JUNE 30TH 2005

PL	W	D	L	F	A	%
35	10	12	13	45	45	45.7

FIFA/COCA-COLA WORLD RANKING

1993	1994	1995	1996	1997	1998	1999	2000	2001	2002	2003	2004	High		Low	
73	72	69	54	38	72	42	45	43	82	74	66	34	09/97	86	02/03

2004-2005											
08/04	09/04	10/04	11/04	12/04	01/05	02/05	03/05	04/05	05/05	06/05	07/05
61	63	68	70	66	67	69	70	65	66	69	73

There wasn't a dull moment in the 2004 Championship in Peru. Coming hot on the heels of a two month players' strike which severely disrupted the 2003 season, there was drama and controversy right to the end when Alianza beat fierce rivals Sporting Cristal on penalties to win the title. Having won the Apertura Alianza qualified for the end of season title play-off against the Clausura winners – as long as they finished in the top six of the Clausura. That very nearly didn't happen and only a controversial 2-2 draw against Cienciano on the final day saw them achieve sixth spot on goal difference. The season also saw Estudiantes withdraw from the Championship due to a

INTERNATIONAL HONOURS
Qualified for the FIFA World Cup™ finals 1930 1970 1978 1982   Copa America 1939 1975

financial crisis while a bounced cheque to the league cost Deportivo Wanka their place in the top flight. As a punishment the League overturned a 1-0 win over San Martin and awarded a 2-0 defeat against them. In a fit of pique Wanka decided they would play the rest of their matches in Cerro de Pasco, at 4,338 metres one of the highest cities in the world, but the tactic failed and they were still relegated. Having hosted the 2004 Copa America it was back to business in the 2006 FIFA World Cup™ qualifiers for the national team although a first appearance in the finals since 1982 never looked on with too many draws costing the team dear and coach Paulo Autuori his job.

THE FIFA BIG COUNT OF 2000

	Male	Female		Male	Female
Registered players	262 500	800	Referees	1 940	40
Non registered players	750 000	30 000	Officials	1 300	300
Youth players	150 800	1 000	Total involved	1 198 680	
Total players	1 195 100		Number of clubs	2 500	
Professional players	2 500	0	Number of teams	11 000	

Federación Peruana de Fútbol (FPF)
Av. Aviación 2085, San Luis, Lima 30, Peru
Tel +51 1 2258236   Fax +51 1 2258240
fepefutbol@fpf.org.pe   www.fpf.com.pe
President: BURGA Manuel Dr   General Secretary: QUINTANA Javier
Vice-President: LOMBARDI Francisco   Treasurer: ALEMAN Lander   Media Officer: None
Men's Coach: TERNERO Freddy   Women's Coach: None
FPF formed: 1922   CONMEBOL: 1926   FIFA: 1926
Colours: White with a red sash, White, White

GAMES PLAYED BY PERU IN THE 2006 FIFA WORLD CUP™ CYCLE

2002	Opponents	Score		Venue	Comp	Scorers	Att	Referee
No international matches played in 2002								
2003								
23-02	Haiti	W	5-1	Lima	Fr	SotoJs 2 [13p 83], Serrano [19], SotoJg [26], Farfan [84]		Rivera PER
30-03	Chile	L	0-2	Santiago	Fr		39 662	Amarilla PAR
2-04	Chile	W	3-0	Lima	Fr	Quinteros [17], Pizarro 2 [48 49]	25 000	Ruiz COL
30-04	Paraguay	L	0-1	Lima	Fr			Lopez COL
11-06	Ecuador	D	2-2	New Jersey	Fr	Silva [42], Mendoza [52]		Terry USA
26-06	Venezuela	W	1-0	Miami	Fr	Carmona [74]		Kennedy USA
2-07	Guatemala	W	2-1	San Francisco	Fr	Silva [15], Orejuela [35]		Hall USA
24-07	Uruguay	L	3-4	Lima	Fr	Farfan 2 [27 56], Marengo [46]		Garay PER
30-07	Uruguay	L	0-1	Montevideo	Fr			Mendez URU
20-08	Mexico	W	3-1	New Jersey	Fr	Pizarro [1], Zegarra [31], Solano [33]		Hall USA
27-08	Guatemala	D	0-0	Lima	Fr			Lecca PER
6-09	Paraguay	W	4-1	Lima	WCq	Solano [34], Mendoza [42], SotoJg [83], Farfan [90]	42 557	Baldassi ARG
9-09	Chile	L	1-2	Santiago	WCq	Mendoza [57]	54 303	Gimenez ARG
16-11	Brazil	D	1-1	Lima	WCq	Solano [50]	70 000	Ruiz COL
19-11	Ecuador	D	0-0	Quito	WCq		34 361	Gonzalez Chaves PAR
2004								
18-02	Spain	L	1-2	Barcelona	Fr	Solano [21]	23 580	Layec FRA
31-03	Colombia	L	0-2	Lima	WCq		29 325	Rezende BRA
28-04	Chile	D	1-1	Antofagasta	Fr	Zúñiga [91+]	23 000	Amarilla PAR
1-06	Uruguay	W	3-1	Montevideo	WCq	Solano [13], Pizarro [18], Farfan [61]	30 000	Selman CHI
6-06	Venezuela	D	0-0	Lima	WCq		40 000	Larrionda URU
30-06	Argentina	L	1-2	East Rutherford	Fr	Solano [36p]	41 013	Stott USA
6-07	Bolivia	D	2-2	Lima	CAr1	Pizarro [68p], Palacios [86]	45 000	Baldassi ARG
9-07	Venezuela	W	3-1	Lima	CAr1	Farfan [34], Solano [62], Acasiete [72]	43 000	Selman CHI
12-07	Colombia	D	2-2	Trujillo	CAr1	Solano [58], Maestri [60]	25 000	Rodriguez Moreno MEX
17-07	Argentina	L	0-1	Chiclayo	CAqf		25 000	Amarilla PAR
4-09	Argentina	L	1-3	Lima	WCq	SotoJg [62]	28 000	Simon BRA
9-10	Bolivia	L	0-1	La Paz	WCq		23 729	Reinoso ECU
13-10	Paraguay	D	1-1	Asuncion	WCq	Solano [74]	30 000	Ruiz COL
17-11	Chile	W	2-1	Lima	WCq	Farfan [56], Guerrero [85]	39 752	Baldassi ARG
2005								
27-03	Brazil	L	0-1	Goiania	WCq		49 163	Amarilla PAR
30-03	Ecuador	D	2-2	Lima	WCq	Guerrero [1], Farfan [58]	40 000	Chandia CHI
22-05	Japan	W	1-0	Niigata	Fr	Vassallo [94+]	39 856	Michel SVK
24-05	United Arab Emirates	D	0-0	Toyota	Fr		6 536	Nishimura JPN
4-06	Colombia	L	0-5	Barranquilla	WCq		15 000	Torres PAR
7-06	Uruguay	D	0-0	Lima	WCq		31 515	Baldassi ARG

Fr = Friendly match • CA = Copa América • WC = FIFA World Cup™ • q = qualifier • r1 = first round group • qf = quarter-final

PERU COUNTRY INFORMATION

Capital	Lima	Independence	1821 from Spain	GDP per Capita	$5 100
Population	27 544 305	Status	Constitutional Republic	GNP Ranking	46
Area km²	1 285 220	Language	Spanish, Quechua	Dialling code	+51
Population density	21 per km²	Literacy rate	90%	Internet code	.pe
% in urban areas	72%	Main religion	Christian	GMT +/−	-5
Towns/Cities ('000)	Lima 7 646; Arequipa 844; Trujillo 750; Chiclayo 582; Iquitos 439; Huancayo 380; Piura 326; Chimbote 320; Cusco 313; Pucallpa 311; Tacna 280; Juliaca 247; Ica 247; Sullana 162				
Neighbours (km)	Ecuador 1 420; Colombia 1 496; Brazil 1 560; Bolivia 900; Chile 160; South Pacific 2 414				
Main stadia	Estadio Nacional – Santiago 45 574; Monumental 'U' – Santiago 80 093				

PERU NATIONAL TEAM RECORDS AND RECORD SEQUENCES

Records			Sequence records					
Victory	9-1	ECU 1938	Wins	9	1937-1939	Clean sheets	4	1996
Defeat	0-7	BRA 1997	Defeats	9	1965-1968	Goals scored	12	1937-1941
Player Caps	113	PALACIOS Roberto	Undefeated	12	1937-1941	Without goal	3	Seven times
Player Goals	26	CUBILLAS Teófilo	Without win	15	1965-1969	Goals against	16	1959-1965

NATIONAL CAPS

	Caps
PALACIOS Roberto	113
CHUMPITAZ Héctor	105
SOTO Jorge	97
DIAZ Rubén Toribio	89
JAYO Juan José	86
REYNOSO Juan	84
OLIVARES Percy	83
VELASQUEZ José	82
CUBILLAS Teófilo	81
SOTO José	75

NATIONAL GOALS

	Goals
CUBILLAS Teófilo	26
FERNANDEZ Teodoro	24
SOLANO Nolberto	20
PALACIOS Roberto	19
SOTIL Hugo	18
RAMIREZ Oswaldo	17
NAVARRO Franco	16
LEON Pedro Pablo	15
GOMEZ SANCHEZ Oscar	14
ALCALDE Jorge	13

FIFA REFEREE LIST 2005

	Int'l	DoB
CABALLERO Albert	2005	15-01-1966
CARRILLO Victor	2004	30-10-1975
GARAY Manuel	2002	28-04-1970
HIDALGO Gilberto	1999	25-06-1961
LECCA Eduardo	1999	14-02-1962
MORALES David	2004	23-06-1977
RIVERA Victor	2001	11-01-1967

FIFA ASSISTANT REFEREE LIST 2005

	Int'l	DoB
ABADIE Luis	2005	9-05-1966
AVILA Luis	2000	13-10-1966
ESCANO Cesar	2002	8-02-1970
GUILLEN Cesar	2004	10-10-1967
ORLANDINI Alfonso	2002	14-06-1969
REATEGUI Winston	2001	1-04-1969
SULCA Juan	1994	12-01-1964

CLUB DIRECTORY

Club	Town/City	Stadium	Phone	www.	Lge	CL
Alianza Atlético	Sullana	Campeones del '36 10 000	+51 74 503695		0	0
Alianza Lima	Lima	Alejandro Villanueva 35 000	+51 1 4235352	alianzalima.net	19	0
Coronel Bolognesi	Tacna	Modelo 19 850	+51 54 659183		0	0
Cienciano	Cusco	Inca Garcilaso de la Vega 42 056	+51 84 245323	cienciano.com	0	0
FBC Melgar	Arequipa	Mariano Melgar 20 000	+51 54 233091	fbcmelgar.com	1	0
Sport Boys	Callao	Miguel Grau 15 000	+51 1 4296827	clubsportboys.com.pe	6	0
Sporting Cristal	Lima	San Martin de Porres 18 000	+51 1 4812183		14	0
Unión Huaral	Huaral	Julio Lores Colan 10 000			2	0
Atlético Universidad	Arequipa	Monumental UNSA 40 217			0	0
Universidad César Vallejo	Trujillo	Mansiche 25 036			0	0
Universitario	Lima	Teodoro Fernández 80 093	+51 1 3482278	universitario.com.pe	24	0

RECENT LEAGUE RECORD

Year	Champions	Pts	Runners-up	Pts	Third	Pts
1990						
1991						
1992	Universitario	43	Sporting Cristal	40	FBC Melgar	37
1993	Universitario	45	Alianza Lima	41	Sport Boys	41
1994	Sporting Cristal	53	Universitario	42	Alianza Lima	40
1995	Sporting Cristal	96	Alianza Lima	84	Universitario	84
1996	Sporting Cristal	69	Alianza Lima	60	Universitario	58
1997						
1998						
1999						
2000						
2001						
2002						
2003						
2004						

Championship Play-off		
Winners	Score	Runners-up
Universitario	4-2	Sport Boys
Sporting Cristal	†	
Alianza Lima	†	
Universitario	2-1 1-2 4-2p	Sporting Cristal
Universitario	3-0 0-1	Alianza Lima
Universitario	†	
Alianza Lima	3-2 0-1 4-2p	Cienciano
Sporting Cristal	‡	
Alianza Lima	2-1	Sporting Cristal
Alianza Lima	0-0 5-4p	Sporting Cristal

† Won both Apertura and Clausura so automatic champions. ‡ Apertura champions Universitario forfeited their place in the play-off by failing to finish in the top 4 of the Clausura

PERU 2004

PRIMERA DIVISION APERTURA

	Pl	W	D	L	F	A	Pts	Alianza	Cienciano	Alianza At.	Cristal	Universitario	Unión	Univ. CV	Bolognesi	Melgar	Estudiantes	Wanka	Sport Boys	At. Univ.	San Martín
Alianza Lima	26	19	4	3	48	16	61		0-1	2-1	1-0	1-0	2-1	1-0	3-1	4-0	2-0	3-0	1-0	2-0	2-0
Cienciano	26	18	3	5	53	28	57	1-0		1-2	1-0	1-1	3-1	2-2	3-2	4-0	4-0	2-1	4-1	4-0	1-0
Alianza Atlético	26	15	5	6	46	29	50	1-1	2-4		1-1	2-0	1-1	1-0	1-2	2-2	0-1	6-1	2-0	3-2	2-1
Sporting Cristal	26	13	6	7	50	24	45	0-5	3-0	0-1		2-2	4-2	5-0	1-1	3-0	4-0	1-2	4-0	3-0	3-0
Universitario	26	11	8	7	31	25	41	0-1	3-0	1-3	2-1		0-0	0-0	1-0	4-2	1-0	3-1	1-0	2-0	1-0
Unión Huaral	26	10	7	9	32	29	37	1-1	0-2	0-2	0-0	3-1		0-1	1-0	3-1	1-1	0-0	2-0	4-0	1-0
Univ. César Vallejo	26	9	8	9	24	33	35	1-1	2-1	2-1	0-3	1-1	1-0		1-2	1-1	1-2	1-0	0-2	0-0	1-0
Coronel Bolognesi	26	9	3	14	40	44	30	2-6	2-4	0-2	1-3	1-0	0-2	4-1		2-3	3-0	4-0	3-0	3-2	4-1
FBC Melgar	26	8	6	12	31	41	30	4-0	2-0	0-1	2-1	1-1	2-3	0-1	1-1		2-2	1-0	2-0	0-1	3-1
Estudiantes	26	7	9	10	21	37	30	0-2	0-1	0-1	1-1	1-0	2-1	2-1	0-0	1-0		2-0	1-1	0-0	2-2
Deportivo Wanka	26	7	7	12	28	43	28	0-1	0-3	3-1	1-1	1-1	1-1	1-2	2-1	0-0	4-1		2-2	3-1	2-1
Sport Boys	26	6	7	13	28	40	25	0-1	1-2	2-2	0-2	1-2	3-0	2-2	3-1	3-1	0-0	2-0		1-1	2-0
Atlético Universidad	26	5	9	12	28	42	24	*1-1	2-3	1-2	0-1	1-1	0-2	1-1	2-0	2-0	3-0	2-2	1-1		1-1
Univ. San Martín	26	2	4	20	21	50	10	1-4	1-1	1-3	1-3	1-2	1-2	0-1	1-0	0-1	2-2	0-1	3-1	2-4	

28/02/2004 - 22/08/2004 • Alianza qualified to meet the winners of the Clausura in the 2004 Championship decider

PERU 2004

PRIMERA DIVISION CLAUSURA

	Pl	W	D	L	F	A	Pts	Cristal	San Martín	Cienciano	Universitario	Alianza At.	Alianza	Unión	Sport Boys	At. Univ.	Melgar	Bolognesi	Univ. CV	Wanka	Estudiantes
Sporting Cristal	26	16	2	8	55	37	50		1-0	1-2	4-2	2-0	4-3	1-0	1-3	1-2	2-1	3-0	2-0	6-1	4-2
Univ. San Martín	26	14	5	7	40	26	47	2-1		1-1	2-0	2-1	1-3	0-2	0-0	1-0	2-1	5-2	3-0	2-1	1-0
Cienciano	26	11	11	4	41	26	44	2-2	0-0		2-0	1-0	2-2	3-0	6-2	2-2	1-0	2-1	4-0	0-0	2-0
Universitario	26	11	10	5	34	28	43	3-4	1-0	1-0		1-1	0-0	2-2	1-0	0-0	2-1	3-2	1-1	5-2	1-0
Alianza Atlético	26	12	6	8	41	34	42	4-3	1-4	3-3	0-0		1-0	2-1	5-0	3-2	3-1	1-2	2-1	2-0	1-0
Alianza Lima	26	10	8	8	31	23	38	2-1	2-1	0-0	0-2	3-0		1-1	0-1	1-0	0-0	0-0	2-1	4-0	2-0
Unión Huaral	26	10	8	8	35	30	38	1-2	0-1	1-1	0-1	2-1	0-0		1-0	4-2	2-0	1-2	1-1	3-1	**2-0**
Sport Boys	26	10	7	9	38	40	37	2-2	2-0	1-1	0-1	1-1	1-0	3-2		2-2	3-2	5-2	0-1	3-0	1-0
Atlético Universidad	26	8	9	9	37	38	33	1-3	2-1	4-1	1-0	0-0	0-0	1-1	2-2		2-2	3-0	2-1	3-0	3-3
FBC Melgar	26	9	5	12	47	41	32	1-2	4-4	2-3	2-2	2-4	2-0	0-1	2-1	2-0		3-3	4-1	5-0	3-0
Coronel Bolognesi	26	8	6	12	45	42	30	0-1	0-0	1-1	0-0	0-1	1-2	1-2	4-1	4-0	2-3		4-1	7-1	1-0
Univ. César Vallejo	26	7	7	12	24	39	28	1-0	1-2	0-1	0-0	1-1	1-0	0-1	1-1	1-0	1-0	0-4		3-0	1-1
Deportivo Wanka	26	7	4	15	27	62	25	2-1	**0-2**	1-0	2-2	1-0	3-2	1-1	3-1	2-1	0-2	1-1	2-4		**2-0**
Estudiantes	26	3	4	19	19	48	13	0-1	0-3	1-0	2-3	1-3	0-2	3-3	0-2	1-2	0-2	2-1	1-1	2-1	

11/09/2004 - 26/12/2004 • Sporting Cristal qualified to meet the winners of the Apertura in the 2004 championship decider
2004 Championship Play-off: 29-12-2004 **Alianza Lima** 0-0 5-4p Sporting Cristal • Alianza are the 2004 champions
Estudiantes and Deportivo Wanka are relegated • Matches in bold awarded 2-0. Estudiantes withdrew from the league in December

COPA PERU (2ND DIVISION) 2004

Round of 16		Quarter-finals		Semi-finals		Final	
Sport Ancash	1 3						
Flamengo	0 0	**Sport Ancash**	4 2 1				
Universidad Chiclayo	1 1	José Gálvez	1 3 0				
José Gálvez	2 1			**Sport Ancash**	2 1		
San José	4 2 2			Alfonso Ugarte	1 1		
Santa Rita	1 3 1	San José	1 0				
Echa Muni	1 1	**Alfonso Ugarte**	3 0				
Alfonso Ugarte	1 5					**Sport Ancash**	1 3
Senati	1 1 2					Deportivo Municipal	0 1
Franciscano San Román	0 3 1	**Senati**	2 0 1				
Juventus Corazón	1 1 1	Unión Grauína	1 1 0				
Unión Grauína	0 3 2			Senati	2 1 1		
Olímpico Somos Peru	5 0			**Deportivo Municipal**	8 0 3		
At. Independiente	1 1	Olímpico Somos Peru	2 0 2				
Un. Nacional Amazonia	0 1 1	**Deportivo Municipal**	1 2 3				
Deportivo Municipal	1 0 5						

Sport Ancash promoted to the Primera Division

PHI – PHILIPPINES

NATIONAL TEAM RECORD
JULY 1ST 2002 TO JUNE 30TH 2005

PL	W	D	L	F	A	%
8	0	0	8	5	34	0

FIFA/COCA-COLA WORLD RANKING

1993	1994	1995	1996	1997	1998	1999	2000	2001	2002	2003	2004	High		Low	
163	171	166	166	175	175	181	179	175	181	189	188	162	08/93	193	11/04

2004-2005											
08/04	09/04	10/04	11/04	12/04	01/05	02/05	03/05	04/05	05/05	06/05	07/05
191	192	193	193	188	187	187	187	187	187	187	187

Although one of the founding members of the Asian Football Confederation, football has stagnated on the vast island archipelago of the Philippines while American influence has encouraged the rise of basketball since the end of the Second World War. There was a revival in the 1970s, but the national team did not enter the the the FIFA World Cup™ until 1998 and then with little success. Four years later they managed one point from their six matches but the Federation decided not to enter for 2006, instead focusing on youth development and competing in regional tournaments. The 2004 Tiger Cup saw the Philippines gain their first victory in the competition when they beat East

INTERNATIONAL HONOURS
Far-Eastern Games 1913

Timor, 2-1 but three defeats against Myanmar, Malaysia and Thailand meant they progressed no further. However, their performances were a huge improvement on their last excursion in the competition two years previously when they lost to Indonesia, 13-1. The eight-team adidas National Men's Open Championship ended with NCR defeating Negros Occidental 4-3 on penalties after a goalless draw to retain the title. However, for the size and population of the country, the League is small and exists at a low level. In their respective regional competitions, neither the U-20s nor the U-17s got past the first stage, inspiring little confidence for the future.

THE FIFA BIG COUNT OF 2000

	Male	Female		Male	Female
Registered players	4 000	2 500	Referees	178	0
Non registered players	400 000	1 000	Officials	150	80
Youth players	12 000	4 000	Total involved	423 908	
Total players	423 500		Number of clubs	500	
Professional players	0	0	Number of teams	1 320	

Philippine Football Federation (PFF)
Room 405, Building B, Philsports Complex, Meralco Avenue, Pasig City, Metro Manila 1604, Philippines
Tel +63 2 6871594   Fax +63 2 6871598
philfutbol@hotmail.com   www.philfootball.net
President: ROMUALDEZ Juan Miguel   General Secretary: GARAMENDI Domeka Gaizka B.
Vice-President: TBD   Treasurer: MORAN Daniel   Media Officer: None
Men's Coach: CASLIB Jose Ariston   Women's Coach: MARO Marlon
PFF formed: 1907   AFC: 1954   FIFA: 1930
Colours: Blue, Blue, Blue

GAMES PLAYED BY PHILIPPINES IN THE 2006 FIFA WORLD CUP™ CYCLE

2002	Opponents		Score	Venue	Comp	Scorers	Att	Referee
11-12	Singapore	L	0-2	Singapore	Fr			Nagalingham SIN
17-12	Myanmar	L	1-6	Jakarta	TCr1	Gonzales 81		Mohd Salleh MAS
19-12	Vietnam	L	1-4	Jakarta	TCr1	Canedo 71		Nagalingham SIN
21-12	Cambodia	L	0-1	Jakarta	TCr1			Napitupulu IDN
23-12	Indonesia	L	1-13	Jakarta	TCr1	Go 78		Khanthachai THA
2003								
No international matches played in 2003								
2004								
8-12	Myanmar	L	0-1	Kuala Lumpur	TCr1		1 000	Napitupulu IDN
10-12	Malaysia	L	1-4	Kuala Lumpur	TCr1	Gould 93+		Napitupulu IDN
14-12	East Timor †	W	2-1	Kuala Lumpur	TCr1	Caligdong 2 89 92+	100	Napitupulu IDN
16-12	Thailand	L	1-3	Kuala Lumpur	TCr1	Caligdong 27	300	Lazar SIN
2005								
No international matches played in 2005 before August								

Fr = Friendly match • TC = ASEAN Tiger Cup • r1 = 1st round • † Not a full international

PHILIPPINES NATIONAL TEAM RECORDS AND RECORD SEQUENCES

Records			Sequence records					
Victory	15-2	JPN 1917	Wins	2	1972	Clean sheets	2	1972
Defeat	0-15	JPN 1967	Defeats	23	1958-1971	Goals scored	6	1923-1930
Player Caps	n/a		Undefeated	3	1972, 1991	Without goal	14	1980-1983
Player Goals	n/a		Without win	38	1977-1990	Goals against	33	1972-1982

FIFA REFEREE LIST 2005

	Int'l	DoB
ANDRES Jerry	1993	18-11-1961
MARTINEZ Allan	2002	25-11-1974
NICOLAU Jaime	2002	17-01-1966

FIFA ASSISTANT REFEREE LIST 2005

	Int'l	DoB
ESTREMOS Randolph	2002	20-09-1966
MONTANA Ariel	2002	17-03-1967
PINERO Chrislie	1999	3-01-1968
SAGANSAY Arnel	2002	9-11-1965
SOLDEVILLA Celso	1999	15-09-1961

RECENT LEAGUE RECORD

Year	Winners	Score	Runners-up
1998	National Capital Region South	3-1	Negros Occidental
1999	National Capital Region-B		Davao
2000			
2001			
2002			
2003			
2004	National Capital Region	4-1	Laguna
2005	National Capital Region	0-0 4-3p	Negros Occidental

PHILIPPINES COUNTRY INFORMATION

Capital	Manila	Independence	1946 from the USA	GDP per Capita	$4 600
Population	86 241 697	Status	Republic	GNP Ranking	41
Area km²	300 000	Language	Filipino, English	Dialling code	+63
Population density	274 per km²	Literacy rate	92%	Internet code	.ph
% in urban areas	54%	Main religion	Christian	GMT + / –	+8
Towns/Cities ('000)	Manila 10 443; Davao 1 212; Cebu 758; Antipolo 549; Zamboanga 460; Bacolod 454; Cagayan 445; Dasmariñas 441; Dadiangas 432; Iloilo 387; San Jose del Monte 357				
Neighbours (km)	Philippine Sea & South China Sea 36 289				
Main stadia	José Rizal Memorial Stadium – Manilla 30 000; Pana-ad Stadium – Bacolod 15 000				

PNG – PAPUA NEW GUINEA

NATIONAL TEAM RECORD
JULY 1ST 2002 TO JUNE 30TH 2005

PL	W	D	L	F	A	%
11	2	3	6	24	30	31.8

FIFA/COCA-COLA WORLD RANKING

1993	1994	1995	1996	1997	1998	1999	2000	2001	2002	2003	2004	High		Low	
-	-	-	169	167	172	183	192	196	167	172	161	**160**	06/04	197	02/02

					2004-2005						
08/04	09/04	10/04	11/04	12/04	01/05	02/05	03/05	04/05	05/05	06/05	07/05
164	163	162	161	161	161	163	162	162	161	162	164

After joining FIFA in 1963 it took Papua New Guinea 17 years to play their first international at the 1980 Oceania Nations Cup. With a population of more than five million, the potential resources exist but the sport has always struggled to compete with rugby union and league. The national team's crowning moment came in the qualifiers for the 1998 FIFA World Cup™ when they sensationally beat New Zealand. Although they didn't come close to qualifying it proved they could compete. 2006 marked Papua New Guinea's second stab at the tournament and nearly began with another superb result when they were within a minute of beating a much-fancied Vanuatu

INTERNATIONAL HONOURS
South Pacific Mini Games 1989

team; a last-minute equaliser spoilt the celebrations though. The team eventually finished third in the group thanks to two resounding victories over American Samoa and Samoa, 10-0 and 4-1 respectively. Papua New Guinea has benefited from FIFA's Goal project and in 2003 a new national headquarters and training centre was inaugurated. The 2004 National Club Championship involved 28 teams in four pools with the winners progressing to the knockout stages. Sobou, who were turning out for their 12th successive finals, beat HC West in the Grand Final to progress to the Champions Club Cup in Tahiti. There they struggled, losing 1-5 to AS Pirae and 2-9 against Sydney City.

THE FIFA BIG COUNT OF 2000

	Male	Female		Male	Female
Registered players	7 000	0	Referees	500	0
Non registered players	23 000	0	Officials	1 800	0
Youth players	8 000	0	Total involved	40 300	
Total players	38 000		Number of clubs	400	
Professional players	0	0	Number of teams	2 500	

Papua New Guinea Football Association (PNGFA)
Fenridge Estate, 11 Mile, Lae, PO Box 957, Lae, Papua New Guinea
Tel +675 4751357   Fax +675 4751399
pngsoka@datec.net.pg   www.none
President: CHUNG Davy   General Secretary: TBD
Vice-President: DANIELS Seth   Treasurer: TBD   Media Officer: None
Men's Coach: PEKA Ludwig   Women's Coach: MOIYAP Francis
PNGFA formed: 1962   OFC: 1966   FIFA: 1963
Colours: Red/yellow, Black, Yellow

GAMES PLAYED BY PAPUA NEW GUINEA IN THE 2006 FIFA WORLD CUP™ CYCLE

2002	Opponents	Score		Venue	Comp	Scorers	Att	Referee
5-07	Solomon Islands	D	0-0	Auckland	OCr1		1 000	Breeze AUS
7-07	New Zealand	L	1-9	Auckland	OCr1	Aisa 35p	1 000	Rakaroi FIJ
9-07	Tahiti	L	1-3	Auckland	OCr1	Davani 43	800	Rakaroi FIJ
2003								
14-06	Solomon Islands	L	3-5	Port Moresby	Fr			
30-06	New Caledonia	L	0-2	Suva	SPr1			Shah FIJ
1-07	Tonga	D	2-2	Suva	SPr1	Sow 41, Habuka 76	3 000	Singh FIJ
3-07	Tahiti	L	0-3	Suva	SPr1		1 000	Attison VAN
2004								
10-05	Vanuatu	D	1-1	Apia	WCq	Wasi 73	500	Breeze AUS
12-05	Fiji	L	2-4	Apia	WCq	Davani 12, Komboi 44	400	Diomis AUS
17-05	American Samoa	W	10-0	Apia	WCq	Davani 4 23 24 40 79, Lepani 3 26 28 64, Wasi 34 Komboi 37, Lohai 71	150	Afu SOL
19-05	Samoa	W	4-1	Apia	WCq	Davani 16, Lepani 2 37 55, Komeng 68	300	Diomis AUS
2005								

No international matches played in 2005 before August

Fr = Friendly match • OC = OFC Nations Cup • SP = South Pacific Games • WC = FIFA World Cup™ • q = qualifier • r1 = first round group

PAPUA NEW GUINEA NATIONAL TEAM RECORDS AND RECORD SEQUENCES

Records			Sequence records					
Victory	10-0	ASA 2004	Wins	4	2002	Clean sheets	2	2002
Defeat	2-11	AUS 1980	Defeats	6	1998-2000	Goals scored	7	2000-2002
Player Caps	n/a		Undefeated	5	1993-97, 2002	Without goal	4	1990-1993
Player Goals	n/a		Without win	10	1985-1986	Goals against	12	1980-1993

RECENT LEAGUE AND CUP RECORD

	National Championship			Port Moresby			Lae			Lahi		
Year	Winners	Score	Finalist	Winners	Score	Finalist	Winners	Score	Finalist	Winners	Score	Finalist
1997	ICF Univ'sity	2-0	Babaka							Guria		Sobou
1998	ICF Univ'sity	1-0	Blue Kumuls	ICF Univ'sity	2-1	Rapatona	Mopi	3-2	Bulolo Utd	Sobou	4-2	Guria
1999	Guria	2-1	Rapatona	Defence	1-1 4-2p	PS United	Bara	1-0	Buresong	Sobou	1-1 5-4p	Guria
2000	Unitech	3-2	Guria	PS United	1-0	Rapatona	Poro SC	1-1 4-3p	Blue Kumuls	Sobou	1-0	Unitech
2001	Sobou	3-1	ICF Univ'sity	ICF Univ'sity	1-0	PS United	Blue Kumuls	2-1	Goro	Unitech	2-0	Sobou
2002	Sobou	1-0	PS United	ICF Univ'sity	3-1	Rapatona	Tarangau	2-0	Poro SC	Sobou	w/o	Unitech
2003	Sobou	1-0	Unitech	Cosmos	2-1	ICF Univ'sity	Blue Kumuls		HC West	Unitech	2-0	Sobou
2004	Sobou	2-0	HC Water	Rapatona	1-0	PS Rutz	HC West	2-1	Tarangau	Sobou	3-0	Bismarck

The National Championship is held over the course of a week with representatives from the regional leagues. The most successful of the regional leagues in the National Championship are Port Moresby, Lae and Lahi. Others include Alotau, East Sepik, Enga, Goroka, Kerema, Kompian, Kokopo, Madang, Manus, Mount Hagen, New Ireland, Popondetta, Sogeri, Tari, Wabag, Wau and Wewak.

PAPUA NEW GUINEA COUNTRY INFORMATION

Capital	Port Moresby	Independence	1975 from Australia	GDP per Capita	$2 200
Population	5 420 280	Status	Constitutional Monarchy	GNP Ranking	131
Area km²	462 840	Language	Melanesian Pidgin, English	Dialling code	+675
Population density	12 per km²	Literacy rate	64%	Internet code	.pg
% in urban areas	16%	Main religion	Christian	GMT + / −	+10
Towns/Cities ('000)	Port Moresby 283; Lae 76; Arawa 40; Mount Hagen 33; Popondetta 28; Madang 27; Kokopo 26				
Neighbours (km)	Indonesia 820; South Pacific Ocean & Coral Sea 5 152				
Main stadia	Hubert Murray – Port Moresby 10 000				

POL – POLAND

NATIONAL TEAM RECORD
JULY 1ST 2002 TO JUNE 30TH 2005

PL	W	D	L	F	A	%
39	22	7	10	74	38	

FIFA/COCA-COLA WORLD RANKING

1993	1994	1995	1996	1997	1998	1999	2000	2001	2002	2003	2004	High		Low	
28	29	33	53	48	31	32	43	33	34	25	25	**20**	08/93	**61**	03/98

2004-2005											
08/04	09/04	10/04	11/04	12/04	01/05	02/05	03/05	04/05	05/05	06/05	07/05
28	29	29	26	25	25	25	27	25	24	23	24

There was a sense of déjà-vu when Poland and England were drawn togther for the 2006 FIFA World Cup™ qualifiers. Since EURO 88 the two nations have been kept apart in just two qualifying campaigns with the English having the upper hand but memories were rekindled of the last time the FIFA World Cup™ finals were played in neighbouring Germany, in 1974. Then, on the way to finishing third, the Poles knocked England out in the qualifiers. A repeat of that did not look on the cards after losing the home fixture to England in the second game of the campaign but the team responded in fine style winning their next five. That put them ahead of their rivals going into the

INTERNATIONAL HONOURS
Qualified for the FIFA World Cup Finals 1938 1974 1978 1982 1986 2002

2005 summer break in the battle for the one automatic qualifying place. Poland may not be a match yet for the team of the 1970s but should they qualify for Germany they would be able to count on a huge following at the finals. Domestically Wisla Krakow continue to dominate, winning a hat-trick of titles and making it five Championships in the past seven seasons, while Dyskobolia won their first trophy by beating Zaglebie Lubin in the Cup Final. It is nearly 10 years, however, since a Polish club was last represented in the group stage of the UEFA Champions League, a fact that Wilsa in particular are keen to address.

THE FIFA BIG COUNT OF 2000

	Male	Female		Male	Female
Registered players	382 703	540	Referees	8 570	22
Non registered players	380 000	6 300	Officials	15 000	400
Youth players	217 068	950	Total involved	1 011 553	
Total players	987 561		Number of clubs	7 763	
Professional players	1 150	65	Number of teams	27 107	

Polish Football Association (PZPN)
Polski Zwiazek Pilki Noznej, Miodowa 1, Warsaw 00-080, Poland
Tel +48 22 5512200   Fax +48 22 5512240
pzpn@pzpn.pl   www.pzpn.pl
President: LISTKIEWICZ Michal   General Secretary: KRECINA Zdzislaw
Vice-President: KOLATOR Eugeniusz   Treasurer: SPECZIK Stanislaw   Media Officer: KOCIEBA Michal
Men's Coach: JANAS Pawel   Women's Coach: STEPCZAK Jan
PZPN formed: 1919   UEFA: 1954   FIFA: 1923
Colours: White, Red, White

GAMES PLAYED BY POLAND IN THE 2006 FIFA WORLD CUP™ CYCLE

2002	Opponents		Score	Venue	Comp	Scorers	Att	Referee
21-08	Belgium	D	1-1	Szczecin	Fr	Zurawski 6	19 000	Ingvarsson SWE
7-09	San Marino	W	2-0	Serravalle	ECq	Kaczorowski 75, Kukielka 88	2 000	McKeon IRL
12-10	Latvia	L	0-1	Warsaw	ECq		12 000	Busacca SUI
16-10	New Zealand	W	2-0	Ostrowiec	Fr	Ratajczyk 52, Kukielka 88	8 000	Layec FRA
20-11	Denmark	L	0-2	Copenhagen	Fr		15 364	Bossen NED
2003								
12-02	Croatia	D	0-0	Split	Fr		1 000	Wack GER
14-02	FYR Macedonia	W	3-0	Split	Fr	Niedzielan 27, Rasiak 38, Lasocki 44	500	Trivkovic CRO
29-03	Hungary	D	0-0	Chorzow	ECq		48 000	De Santis ITA
2-04	San Marino	W	5-0	Ostrowiec	ECq	Szymkowiak 4, Kosowski 27, Kuzba 2 55 90, Karwan 82	8 500	Loizou CYP
30-04	Belgium	L	1-3	Brussels	Fr	Krzynowek 81	27 000	McDonald SCO
6-06	Kazakhstan	W	3-0	Posnan	Fr	Wichniarek 2, Dawidowski 50, Kzzynowek 82p	6 000	Fisker DEN
11-06	Sweden	L	0-3	Stockholm	ECq		35 220	Veissiere FRA
20-08	Estonia	W	2-1	Tallinn	Fr	Sobolewski 52, Wichniarek 90	4 500	Johannesson SWE
6-09	Latvia	W	2-0	Riga	ECq	Szymkowiak 36, Klos 38	9 000	Vassaras GRE
10-09	Sweden	L	0-2	Chorzow	ECq		20 000	Riley ENG
11-10	Hungary	W	2-1	Budapest	ECq	Niedzielan 2 10 62	15 500	Mejuto Gonzalez ESP
12-11	Italy	W	3-1	Warsaw	Fr	Bak 6, Klos 18, Krzynowek 85	9 000	Ovrebo NOR
16-11	Serbia & Montenegro	W	4-3	Plock	Fr	Niedzielan 27, Rasiak 30, Kosowski 73, Zurawski 82	9 000	Weiner GER
11-12	Malta	W	4-0	Ta'Qali	Fr	Bieniuk 54, Mila 57, Sikora 83, Burkhardt 88	300	Kasnaferis GRE
14-12	Lithuania	W	3-1	Ta'Qali	Fr	Rasiak 8, Mila 11, Jelen 50	100	Attard MLT
2004								
18-02	Slovenia	W	2-0	Cadiz	Fr	Mila 24, Niedzielan 65	100	Barea Lopez ESP
21-02	Faroe Islands	W	6-0	San Fernando	Fr	Kryszalowicz 4 9 39 41 42, Klos 60, Kukielka 86	100	Cascales ESP
31-03	USA	L	0-1	Plock	Fr		10 500	Skjerven NOR
28-04	Republic of Ireland	D	0-0	Bydgoszcz	Fr		15 500	Shebek UKR
29-05	Greece	W	1-0	Szczecin	Fr	Kapsis OG 17	17 000	Kari FIN
5-06	Sweden	L	1-3	Stockholm	Fr	Gorawski 89	28 281	Kelly IRL
11-07	USA	D	1-1	Chicago	Fr	Wlodarczyk 76	39 529	Petrescu CAN
18-08	Denmark	L	1-5	Poznan	Fr	Zurawski 76	4 500	Bebek CRO
4-09	Northern Ireland	W	3-0	Belfast	WCq	Zurawski 4, Wlodarczyk 36, Krzynowek 56	12 487	Wegereef NED
8-09	England	L	1-2	Chorzow	WCq	Zurawski 47	30 000	Farina ITA
9-10	Austria	W	3-1	Vienna	WCq	Kaluzny 10, Krzynowek 78, Frankowski 90	46 100	Cardoso Batista POR
13-10	Wales	W	3-2	Cardiff	WCq	Frankowski 72, Zurawski 81, Krzynowek 85	56 685	Sars FRA
17-11	France	D	0-0	Paris	Fr		50 480	Benquerenca POR
2005								
9-02	Belarus	L	1-3	Warsaw	Fr	Zurawski 51	6 000	Zuta LTU
26-03	Azerbaijan	W	8-0	Warsaw	WCq	Frankowski 3 12 63 66, Hajiyev OG 16, Kosowski 40, Krzynowek 72, Saganowski 2 84 90	9 000	Vollquartz DEN
30-03	Northern Ireland	W	1-0	Warsaw	WCq	Zurawski 87	13 515	Frojdfeldt SWE
27-04	Mexico	D	1-1	Chicago	Fr	Brozek 71	54 427	Kennedy USA
29-05	Albania	W	1-0	Szczecin	Fr	Zurawski 1	14 000	Weiner GER
4-06	Azerbaijan	W	3-0	Baku	WCq	Frankowski 28, Klos 57, Zurawski 81	10 458	Undiano Mallenco ESP

Fr = Friendly match • EC = UEFA EURO 2004™ • WC = FIFA World Cup™ • q = qualifier

POLAND COUNTRY INFORMATION

Capital	Warsaw	Independence	1918	GDP per Capita	$11 100
Population	38 626 349	Status	Republic	GNP Ranking	26
Area km2	312 685	Language	Polish	Dialling code	+48
Population density	123 per km2	Literacy rate	99%	Internet code	.pl
% in urban areas	65%	Main religion	Christian	GMT +/−	+1
Towns/Cities ('000)	Warsaw 1 651; Lódz 768; Kraków 755; Wroclaw 634; Poznan 570; Gdánsk 461; Szczecin 413; Bydgoszcz 366; Lublin 360; Katowice 317; Bialystok 291; Gdynia 253; Czestochowa 248				
Neighbours (km)	Russia 206; Lithuania 91; Belarus 407; Ukraine 526; Slovakia 444; Czech Republic 658; Germany 456; Baltic Sea 491				
Main stadia	Slaski – Chorzow 43 000; Florian Kryger – Szczecin 17 783; Wojska Polskiego – Warsaw 15 278				

POLAND NATIONAL TEAM RECORDS AND RECORD SEQUENCES

Records			Sequence records					
Victory	9-0	NOR 1963	Wins	7	Three times	Clean sheets	4	1978, 1979, 2003
Defeat	0-8	DEN 1948	Defeats	6	1933-1934	Goals scored	28	1978-1980
Player Caps	100	LATO Grzegorz	Undefeated	13	2000-2001	Without goal	6	1999-2000
Player Goals	48	LUBANSKI Wlodzimeirz	Without win	13	1995-1996	Goals against	17	1957-1960

NATIONAL CAPS

	Caps
LATO Grzegorz	100
DEYNA Kazimierz	97
ZMUDA Wladyslaw	91
SZYMANOWSKI Antoni	82
BONIEK Zbigniew	80
LUBANSKI Wlodzimierz	75
WALDOCH Tomasz	74
SWIERCZEWSKI Piotr	70
KOSECKI Roman	69

NATIONAL GOALS

	Goals
LUBANSKI Wlodzimierz	48
LATO Grzegorz	45
DEYNA Kazimierz	41
POL Ernest	39
CIESLIK Gerard	27
SZARMACH Andrzej	25
BONIEK Zbigniew	24
WILIMOWSKI Ernest	21
DZIEKANOWSKI Dariusz	20
KOSECKI Roman	19

NATIONAL COACH

	Years
LAZAREK Wojciech	1986-'89
STREJLAU Andrzej	1989-'93
CMIKIEWICZ Leslaw	1993
APOSTEL Henryk	1994-'95
STACHURSKI Wladyslaw	1996
PIECHNICZEK Antoni	1996-'97
WOJCIK Janusz	1997-'99
ENGEL Jerzy	2000-'02
BONIEK Zbigniew	2002
JANAS Pawel	2002-

FIFA REFEREE LIST 2005

	Int'l	DoB
GILEWSKI Grzegorz	2001	24-02-1973
GRANAT Jacek	1994	22-02-1966
MALEK Robert	2001	15-03-1971
MIKOLAJEWSKI Marek	2004	21-03-1972
MIKULSKI Tomasz	1995	21-06-1968
RYSZKA Miroslaw	1999	26-01-1960
SLUPIK Krzysztof	1998	21-08-1964

FIFA ASSISTANT REFEREE LIST 2005

	Int'l	DoB
JAREMKO Andrzej	2002	31-08-1972
KOWALSKI Mariusz	1999	10-12-1961
MYRMUS Krysztof	2002	4-06-1974
ROSTKOWSKI Rafal	2000	6-08-1972
SADCZUK Piotr	2002	13-06-1973
SAPELA Konrad	1998	10-07-1971
SIEJKA Radoslav	2004	17-09-1974
STEMPNIEWSKI Slawomir	1997	26-09-1961
SZYMANIK Maciej	2004	15-01-1970
WIERZBOWSKI Maciej	1998	15-02-1971

CLUB DIRECTORY

Club	Town/City	Stadium	Phone	www.	Lge	Cup	CL
Amica Sport	Wronki	Amiki 5 296	+48 67 2545550	amica.com.pl	0	3	0
Cracovia	Kraków	Jana Pawla II 10 000	+48 12 2929100	cracovia.pl	5	0	0
Górnik Zabrze	Zabrze	Górnika 18 000	+48 32 2714926	gornikzabrze.pl	14	6	0
Groclin Grodzisk	Grodzisk	Groclin 7 000	+48 61 4436250	dyskobolia.com.pl	0	1	0
GKS Katowice	Katowice	GKS 12 000	+48 32 6085592	gkskatowice.pl	0	3	0
GKS Górnik Leczna	Leczna	Górnik 7 000	+48 81 7521740	gornik.leczna.com	0	0	0
Legia Warszawa	Warsaw	Wojska Polskiego 15 278	+48 22 6284303	legia.pl	7	12	0
MKS Odra Wodzislaw	Wodzislaw	Odry 6 607	+48 32 4551394	odra.wodzislaw.pl	0	0	0
Wisla Plock	Plock	Gorskiego 12 500	+48 24 3663010	wisla.plock.pl	0	0	0
Pogon Szczecin	Szczecin	Florian Kryger 17 783	+48 91 4860099	pogonszczecin.pl	0	0	0
KSP Polonia Warszawa	Warsaw	Polonia 6 200	+48 22 6351637	ksppolonia.pl	2	2	0
Lech Poznan	Poznan	Lecha 27 500	+48 61 8673061	lech.poznan.pl	5	4	0
Wisla Kraków	Kraków	Wisly 10 410	+48 12 6307600	wislaw.krakow.pl	10	4	0
Zaglebie Lubin	Lubin	Zaglebia 32 420	+48 76 8478644	zaglebie-lubin.pl	1	0	0

POLAND 2004-05

LIGA POLSKA I LIGA

	Pl	W	D	L	F	A	Pts	Wisla	Dyskobolia	Legia	Wisla Pl	Cracovia	Amica	Górnik L	Lech	Pogon	Polonia	Górnik Z	Zaglebie	Odra	Katowice
Wisla Kraków †	26	19	5	2	70	23	62		3-0	2-0	4-0	0-0	1-1	5-1	4-1	1-1	4-0	2-1	6-0	3-1	1-0
Groclin Grodzisk ‡	26	16	3	7	46	28	51	2-4		3-2	1-2	3-1	4-0	0-0	1-0	2-0	5-0	3-1	3-1	1-0	3-2
Legia Warszawa ‡	26	13	8	5	42	19	47	5-1	0-1		2-1	2-1	1-1	1-1	3-0	3-0	4-1	2-1	0-0	0-1	2-0
Wisla Plock ‡	26	12	5	9	35	30	41	1-1	0-1	0-0		3-0	2-0	3-0	2-1	3-2	4-1	0-0	2-0	1-0	0-0
Cracovia	26	12	4	10	37	29	40	0-1	2-0	1-0	4-0		0-1	0-0	2-0	4-2	2-1	0-0	1-0	2-3	2-0
Amica Wronki	26	10	8	8	29	28	38	0-1	1-3	1-1	2-1	3-2		1-0	1-0	0-0	1-0	1-1	0-2	2-2	1-0
Górnik Leczna	26	10	6	10	36	36	36	2-2	2-1	1-2	3-2	3-1	1-0		2-0	1-1	1-1	2-0	2-1	1-2	4-2
Lech Poznan	26	10	4	12	34	40	34	3-1	2-2	1-1	4-2	0-2	0-4	3-0		1-1	1-1	2-1	2-0	1-0	3-1
Pogon Szczecin	26	7	10	9	34	43	31	0-5	1-0	1-2	2-0	1-1	1-0	2-1	3-1		1-1	0-2	1-1	4-1	4-2
Polonia Warszawa	26	8	5	13	27	52	29	1-3	1-0	0-5	1-4	2-3	1-1	1-0	0-2	3-3		2-1	1-1	1-0	2-0
Górnik Zabrze	26	7	7	12	27	30	28	1-3	0-1	0-0	1-0	1-0	1-1	0-3	1-2	4-0	0-1		1-1	2-0	4-1
Zaglebie Lubin	26	6	10	10	31	41	28	1-7	1-1	0-0	0-1	2-5	1-1	1-0	2-0	2-2	3-0	1-1		1-1	7-0
Odra Wodzislaw Slaski	26	7	3	16	27	41	24	1-2	1-2	0-1	0-1	0-1	1-2	0-5	3-1	1-0	2-1	1-2	1-2		2-2
GKS Katowice	26	4	4	18	23	58	16	0-3	1-3	0-3	0-0	1-0	1-4	4-0	0-3	1-1	2-3	1-0	2-0	0-3	

30/07/2004 - 12/06/2005 • † Qualified for the UEFA Champions League • ‡ Qualified for the UEFA Cup • Relegation play-off: Widzew Lódz 1-3 1-0 Odra
Match in bold awarded 3-0

POLAND 2004-05 II LIGA

	Pl	W	D	L	F	A	Pts
Korona Kielce	34	18	13	3	51	33	67
GKS Belchatow	34	19	9	6	58	35	66
Arka Gdynia	34	18	10	6	44	23	64
Widzew Lodz	34	16	10	8	44	26	58
Podbeskidzie	34	17	7	10	39	33	58
Jagiellonia Bialystok	34	14	12	8	45	29	54
Zaglebie Sosnowiec	34	17	3	14	48	44	54
Kujawiak Wloclawek	34	15	9	10	48	36	54
Lódzki KS	34	13	12	9	48	42	51
KSZO Ostrowiec	34	14	8	12	43	41	50
Swit Nowy Dwór	34	13	10	11	34	30	49
Górnik Polkowice	34	10	11	13	29	42	41
Piast Gliwice	34	10	6	18	29	37	36
Ruch Chorzów	34	8	11	15	36	50	35
Szczakowianka	34	8	9	17	37	38	33
Radomiak Radom	34	8	7	19	34	48	31
MKS Mlawa	34	7	7	20	25	47	28
RKS Radomsko	34	3	2	29	28	86	11

30/07/2004 - 11/06/2005

PUCHAR POLSKI 2004-05

Quarter-finals

Groclin	4	2
Korona Kielce *	2	2
Lech Poznan *	0	1
Legia Warszawa	0	2
Wisla Kraków	0	1
Pogón Szczecin*	0	0
Wisla Plock *	1	0
Zaglebie Lubin	1	3

Semi-finals

Groclin	1 1	4p
Legia Warszawa*	1 1	1p
Wisla Kraków *	1	1
Zaglebie Lubin	0	3

* Home team in the first leg

Final

First leg, 18-06-2005 Grodzisk, Att: 4 000 Scorers - Piechniak 28, Slusarski 31

Groclin	2	0
Zaglebie Lubin	0	1

Second leg, 21-06-2005 Lubin, Att: 8 000 Scorer - Iwanski 22

RECENT LEAGUE AND CUP RECORD

	Championship						Cup		
Year	Champions	Pts	Runners-up	Pts	Third	Pts	Winners	Score	Runners-up
1990	Lech Poznan	42	Zaglebie Lubin	40	GKS Katowice	40	Legia Warszawa	2-0	GKS Katowice
1991	Zaglebie Lubin	44	Górnik Zabrze	40	Wisla Kraków	40	GKS Katowice	1-0	Legia Warszawa
1992	Lech Poznan	49	GKS Katowice	44	Widzew Lódz	43	Miedz Legnica	1-1 4-3p	Górnik Zabrze
1993	Legia Warszawa †	47	LKS Lódz †	47	Lech Poznan †	47	GKS Katowice	1-1 5-4p	Ruch II Chorzów
1994	Legia Warszawa	48	GKS Katowice	47	Górnik Zabrze	46	Legia Warszawa	2-0	LKS Lódz
1995	Legia Warszawa	51	Widzew Lódz	45	GKS Katowice	42	Legia Warszawa	2-0	GKS Katowice
1996	Widzew Lódz	88	Legia Warszawa	85	Hutnik Kraków	52	Ruch Chorzów	1-0	GKS Belchatów
1997	Widzew Lódz	81	Legia Warszawa	77	Odra Wodzislaw	55	Legia Warszawa	2-0	GKS Katowice
1998	LKS Lódz	66	Polonia Warszawa	63	Wisla Kraków	61	Amica Wronki	5-3	Aluminium Konin
1999	Wisla Kraków	73	Widzew Lódz	56	Legia Warszawa	56	Amica Wronki	1-0	GKS Belchatów
2000	Polonia Warszawa	65	Wisla Kraków	56	Ruch Chorzów	55	Amica Wronki	2-2 3-0	Wisla Kraków
2001	Wisla Kraków	62	Pogon Szczecin	53	Legia Warszawa	50	Polonia Warszawa	2-1 2-2	Górnik Zabrze
2002	Legia Warszawa	42	Wisla Kraków	41	Amica Wronki	36	Wisla Kraków	4-2 4-0	Amica Wronki
2003	Wisla Kraków	68	Groclin Grodzisk	62	GKS Katowice	61	Wisla Kraków	0-1 3-0	Wisla Plock
2004	Wisla Kraków	65	Legia Warszawa	60	Amica Wronki	48	Lech Poznan	2-0 0-1	Legia Warszawa
2005	Wisla Kraków	62	Groclin Grodzisk	51	Legia Warszawa	47	Groclin Grodzisk	2-0 0-1	Zaglebie Lubin

† Lech Poznan proclaimed champions following match fixing involving Legia and LKS

POR – PORTUGAL

NATIONAL TEAM RECORD
JULY 1ST 2002 TO JUNE 30TH 2005

PL	W	D	L	F	A	%
37	21	10	6	78	32	70.3

FIFA/COCA-COLA WORLD RANKING

1993	1994	1995	1996	1997	1998	1999	2000	2001	2002	2003	2004	High		Low	
20	20	16	13	30	36	15	6	4	11	17	9	4	03/01	43	08/98

2004-2005											
08/04	09/04	10/04	11/04	12/04	01/05	02/05	03/05	04/05	05/05	06/05	07/05
12	11	8	8	9	9	9	9	9	9	8	10

Given the events of UEFA EURO 2004™ when as hosts they were surprisingly beaten in the final by Greece, the Portuguese should be used to the unexpected but there was no hiding the blushes when the national team could only draw away to tiny Liechtenstein in the 2006 FIFA World Cup™ qualifying campaign. In the event it proved to be only a small hiccup with other results putting the team in pole position to qualify for successive finals for the first time. Brazilian coach Luiz Felipe Scolari is building a strong attacking side with Cristiano Ronaldo emerging as the star attraction

INTERNATIONAL HONOURS
Qualified for FIFA World Cup™ finals 1966 1986 2002 FIFA World Youth Championship 1989 1991
UEFA Youth Tournament 1961   UEFA U-18 Championship 1994 1999 UEFA U-17 Championship 1989 1995 1996 2000 2003
Intercontinental Cup FC Porto 1987 2004   UEFA Champions League Benfica 1961 1962, FC Porto 1987 2004

and should they qualify Portugal would go to Germany as one of the teams to watch. In the League Benfica, coached for the season by Giovanni Trappatoni, ended their 10-year wait for a title in one of the more absorbing title races in Europe although they did miss out on the double after losing the Cup Final to Vitória Setúbal. There was disappointment for Sporting when they lost the UEFA Cup Final, played in their own stadium, to CSKA Moskva while Porto brightened up an otherwise unremarkable season by winning the last Toyota Cup against Colombia's Once Caldas.

THE FIFA BIG COUNT OF 2000

	Male	Female		Male	Female
Registered players	40 169	2 593	Referees	3 967	27
Non registered players	170 000	3 600	Officials	8 000	200
Youth players	47 198	722	Total involved	303 476	
Total players	291 282		Number of clubs	2 530	
Professional players	2 244	0	Number of teams	10 382	

Federaçao Portuguesa de Futebol (FPF)
Rua Alexandre Herculano, no.58, Apartado 24013, Lisbon 1250-012, Portugal
Tel +351 21 3252700   Fax +351 21 3252780
secretario_geral@fpf.pt   www.fpf.pt
President: MADAIL Gilberto, Dr   General Secretary: TBD
Vice-President: BROU Angelo   Treasurer: PACHECO LAMAS Carlos   Media Officers: FELIX Filipe & HENRIQUE Bruno
Men's Coach: SCOLARI Luiz Felipe   Women's Coach: AUGUSTO Jose
FPF formed: 1914   UEFA: 1954   FIFA: 1923
Colours: Red, Green, Red

GAMES PLAYED BY PORTUGAL IN THE 2006 FIFA WORLD CUP™ CYCLE

2002	Opponents	Score		Venue	Comp	Scorers	Att	Referee
7-09	England	D	1-1	Birmingham	Fr	Costinha [79]	40 058	Ovrebo NOR
12-10	Tunisia	D	1-1	Lisbon	Fr	Pauleta [3]	10 000	Allaerts BEL
16-10	Sweden	W	3-2	Gothenburg	Fr	Sergio Conceiçao [34p], Romeu [53], Rui Costa [88]	30 047	Vassaras GRE
20-11	Scotland	W	2-0	Braga	Fr	Pauleta 2 [8 17]	8 000	Anghelinei ROU
2003								
12-02	Italy	L	0-1	Genoa	Fr		31 265	Fandel GER
29-03	Brazil	W	2-1	Porto	Fr	Pauleta [6], Deco [81]		Yefet ISR
2-04	FYR Macedonia	W	1-0	Lausanne	Fr	Figo [23]	14 258	Nobs SUI
30-04	Netherlands	D	1-1	Eindhoven	Fr	Simão [78]	31 500	Meier SUI
6-06	Paraguay	D	0-0	Braga	Fr		17 000	Kasnaferis GRE
10-06	Bolivia	W	4-0	Lisbon	Fr	Jorge Andrade [7], Couto [13], Postiga 2 [40 47]	10 000	Kenan ISR
20-08	Kazakhstan	W	1-0	Chaves	Fr	Simão [63]	8 000	Rodriguez Santiago ESP
6-09	Spain	L	0-3	Lisbon	Fr		21 176	Salomir ROU
10-09	Norway	W	1-0	Oslo	Fr	Pauleta [9]	11 014	Bennett ENG
11-10	Albania	W	5-3	Lisbon	Fr	Figo [6], Simão [48], Rui Costa [55], Pauleta [57], Miguel [64]	5 000	Garibian FRA
15-11	Greece	D	1-1	Aveiro	Fr	Pauleta [60]	30 000	Esquinas Torres ESP
19-11	Kuwait	W	8-0	Leiria	Fr	Pauleta 4 [10 20 45 52], Figo [33], Nuno Gomes 3 [69 75 87]	22 000	Ingvarsson SWE
2004								
18-02	England	D	1-1	Faro/Loule	Fr	Pauleta [68]	27 000	Kassai HUN
31-03	Italy	L	1-2	Braga	Fr	Nuno Valente [5]	25 000	Aydin TUR
28-04	Sweden	D	2-2	Coimbra	Fr	Pauleta [33], Nuno Gomes [90]	15 000	Ceferin SVN
29-05	Luxembourg	W	3-0	Agueda	Fr	Figo [13], Nuno Gomes [28], Rui Costa [36]	9 000	Styles ENG
5-06	Lithuania	W	4-1	Alcochete	Fr	Couto [3], Pauleta [13], Nuno Gomes [81], Postiga [90]	25 000	Wilmes LUX
12-06	Greece	L	1-2	Porto	ECr1	Ronaldo [90]	48 761	Collina ITA
16-06	Russia	W	2-0	Lisbon	ECr1	Maniche [7], Rui Costa [89]	55 000	Hauge NOR
20-06	Spain	W	1-0	Lisbon	ECr1	Nuno Gomes [57]	52 000	Frisk SWE
24-06	England	D	2-2	Lisbon	ECqf	Postiga [83], Rui Costa [110], W 6-5p	65 000	Meier SUI
30-06	Netherlands	W	2-1	Lisbon	ECsf	Ronaldo [26], Maniche [58]	46 679	Frisk SWE
4-07	Greece	L	0-1	Lisbon	ECf		62 865	Merk GER
4-09	Latvia	W	2-0	Riga	WCq	Ronaldo [57], Pauleta [58]	9 500	Poll ENG
8-09	Estonia	W	4-0	Leiria	WCq	Ronaldo [75], Postiga 2 [83 91+], Pauleta [86]	27 214	Demirlek TUR
9-10	Liechtenstein	D	2-2	Vaduz	WCq	Pauleta [23], Hasler OG [39]	3 548	Panic BIH
13-10	Russia	W	7-1	Lisbon	WCq	Pauleta [26], Ronaldo 2 [39 69], Deco [45], Simão [82] Petit 2 [89 92+]	27 258	Vassaras GRE
17-11	Luxembourg	W	5-0	Luxembourg	WCq	Federspiel OG [11], Ronaldo [28], Maniche [52] Pauleta 2 [67 82]	8 045	Godulyan UKR
2005								
9-02	Republic of Ireland	L	0-1	Dublin	Fr		44 100	Messias ENG
26-03	Canada	W	4-1	Barcelos	Fr	Manuel Fernandes [2], Pauleta [11], Postiga [81] Nuno Gomes [90]	13 000	Ishchenko UKR
30-03	Slovakia	D	1-1	Bratislava	WCq	Postiga [62]	21 000	Sars FRA
4-06	Slovakia	W	2-0	Lisbon	WCq	Fernando Meira [21], Ronaldo [42]	64 000	Collina ITA
8-06	Estonia	W	1-0	Tallinn	WCq	Ronaldo [32]	10 280	Riley ENG

Fr = Friendly match • EC = UEFA EURO 2004™ • WC = FIFA World Cup™
q = qualifier • r1 = first round group • qf = quarter-final • sf = semi-final • f = final

PORTUGAL NATIONAL TEAM RECORDS AND RECORD SEQUENCES

Records			Sequence records					
Victory	8-0	LIE, LIE, KUW	Wins	9	1966	Clean sheets	8	1998-1999
Defeat	0-10	ENG 1947	Defeats	7	1957-59, 1961-62	Goals scored	16	1966-1967
Player Caps	112	FIGO Luis	Undefeated	13	1998-2000	Without goal	4	1996-1997
Player Goals	41	EUSEBIO	Without win	13	1949-1953	Goals against	17	1949-1953

NATIONAL CAPS

	Caps
FIGO Luis	112
FERNANDO COUTO Manuel	110
RUI COSTA Manuel	94
JOAO PINTO Manuel	81
VITOR BAIA Manuel	80
PAULETA	72
JOAO PINTO Domingos	70
NENE	66
EUSEBIO	64
HUMBERTO COELHO	64

NATIONAL GOALS

	Goals
EUSEBIO	41
PAULETA	37
FIGO Luis	31
RUI COSTA Manuel	26
JOAO PINTO Manuel	23
NENE	22
NUNO GOMES	22
JORDAO	15
PEYROTEO Fernando	14
TORRES José	14

NATIONAL COACH

	Years
RUI SEABRA	1986-'87
JUCA	1987-'89
JORGE Artur	1989
QUEIROZ Carlos	1990-'93
VINGADA Eduardo	1994
OLIVEIRA Antonio	1994-'96
JORGE Artur	1996-'97
HUMBERTO COELHO	1998-'00
OLIVEIRA Antonio	2000-'02
SCOLARI Luiz Felipe	2002-

FIFA REFEREE LIST 2005

	Int'l	DoB
BENQUERENCA Olegario	2001	18-10-1969
CARDOSO BATISTA Lucilio	1996	26-04-1965
COSTA Antonio	1999	6-12-1960
COSTA Paulo	1999	2-12-1964
FERREIRA Joao	2003	25-09-1967
GOMES Joaquim	1997	17-12-1962
GOMES Duarte	2002	16-01-1973
PAIXAO Bruno	2004	18-05-1974
PROENCA Pedro	2003	3-11-1970

FIFA ASSISTANT REFEREE LIST 2005

	Int'l	DoB
CARDINAL Jose	1997	19-01-1967
JANIARIO Paulo	1997	8-06-1972
LACROIX Sergio	2003	6-07-1969
MIRANDA Bertino	1999	18-05-1972
NOGUEIRA Serafim	2001	23-02-1967
PERDIGAO Antonio	2001	13-09-1961
PINHEIRO Jose	1997	30-04-1967
RAMALHO Jose	2001	28-08-1966
SANTOS Joao	2003	5-11-1968

CLUB DIRECTORY

Club	Town/City	Stadium	Phone	www.	Lge	Cup	CL
SC Beira-Mar	Aveiro	Municipal de Aveiro 31 498	+351 234 377420	beiramar.pt	0	1	0
CF Os Belenenses	Belem - Lisbon	Estádio do Restelo 32 500	+351 21 3010461	osbelenenses.com	1	3	0
SL Benfica	Lisbon	Estádio da Luz 65 647	+351 21 7219555	slbenfica.pt	31	24	2
Boavista FC	Porto	Estádio do Bessa 28 263	+351 22 6071020	boavistafc.pt	1	5	0
SC Braga	Braga	Municipal de Braga 30 359	+351 253 205150	scbraga.pt	0	1	0
Académica de Coimbra	Coimbra	Cidade de Coimbra 30 154	+351 239 793890		0	1	0
FC Penafiel	Penafiel	Municipal 15 000	+351 255 212369	fcpenafiel.pt	0	0	0
FC Porto	Porto	Estádio do Dragão 50 948	+351 22 5070500	fcporto.fc	20	12	2
Rio Ave FC	Villa do Conde	Estádio dos Arcos 12 815	+351 252 640590		0	0	0
Sporting CP	Lisbon	José Alvalade 46 955	+351 21 7516000	sporting.pt	18	13	0
Vitória SC	Guimarães	Alfonso Henriques 29 865	+351 253 432570	vitoriasc.pt	0	0	0
Vitória FC	Setúbal	Estádio do Bonfim 25 000	+351 265 521460		0	3	0
GD Estoril-Praia	Estoril	Da Mota 15 000	+351 21 4680019		0	0	0
Gil Vicente FC	Barcelos	Municipal de Barcelos 12 540	+351 253 811573	gilvicente.bcl.pt	0	0	0
União Leiria	Leiria	Magalhães Pessoa 29 869	+351 244 831774		0	0	0
CS Marítimo	Funchal	Estádio dos Barreiros 14 000	+351 291 708300	csmaritimo-madeira.pt	0	0	0
Moreirense FC	Moreira de Cónegos	Almeida Freitas 8 000	+351 253 561836	moreirensefc.com	0	0	0
CD Nacional	Funchal	Estádio dos Barreiros 14 000	+351 291 227324	nacional-da-madeira.com	0	0	0

PORTUGAL COUNTRY INFORMATION

Capital	Lisbon	Independence	1640	GDP per Capita	$18 000
Population	10 524 145	Status	Republic	GNP Ranking	34
Area km²	92 391	Language	Portuguese	Dialling code	+351
Population density	114 per km²	Literacy rate	93%	Internet code	.pt
% in urban areas	36%	Main religion	Christian	GMT + / −	0

Towns/Cities ('000)	Lisbon 2 561; Porto 1 218; Braga 121; Coimbra 106; Funchal 98; Aveiro 54; Evora 45; Leiria 45; Faro 41; Sesimbra 41; Guimarães 40; Portimão 38; Castelo Branco 33
Neighbours (km)	Spain 1 214; North Atlantic 1 793
Main stadia	Estadio da Luz – Lisbon 65 647; Estadio do Dragão – Porto 50 948; Estadio José Alvalade – Lisbon 46 955; Estadio Algarve – Faro-Loulé 30 305; Dr. Magalhães Pessoa – Leiria 29 869

PORTUGAL 2004-05

SUPERLIGA

	Pl	W	D	L	F	A	Pts	Benfica	Porto	Sporting	Braga	Guimarães	Boavista	Marítimo	Rio Ave	Belenenses	Setúbal	Penafiel	Nacional	Gil Vicente	Académica	Leiria	Moreirense	Estoril	Beira-Mar
SL Benfica †	34	19	8	7	51	31	65		0-1	1-0	0-0	2-1	4-0	4-3	3-3	1-0	4-0	1-0	2-1	2-0	3-0	1-1	2-0	2-1	0-2
FC Porto †	34	17	11	6	39	26	62	1-1		3-0	1-3	0-0	0-1	1-0	1-1	3-0	2-1	2-0	0-4	1-0	1-1	1-1	1-0	2-2	0-1
Sporting CP †	34	18	7	9	66	36	61	2-1	2-0		0-0	1-0	6-1	0-1	5-0	2-0	1-1	0-2	2-4	3-2	0-0	2-2	4-1	4-0	1-0
Sporting Braga ‡	34	16	10	8	45	28	58	0-0	1-1	0-3		1-0	3-0	1-1	3-0	2-0	2-3	0-1	3-2	2-1	2-0	1-0	0-0	2-0	1-1
Vitória SC Guimarães ‡	34	15	9	10	38	29	54	1-2	0-1	2-4	1-0		2-0	1-1	0-0	1-0	3-1	2-1	1-1	2-1	1-1	1-1	0-1	1-0	1-0
Boavista	34	13	11	10	39	43	50	1-1	1-0	0-4	1-2	2-1		3-2	0-1	2-0	1-1	2-1	1-2	2-2	1-0	0-0	1-1	0-0	3-0
CS Marítimo Funchal	34	12	13	9	39	32	49	1-1	1-1	3-0	2-0	1-2	2-1		1-1	0-0	3-1	3-0	2-1	1-1	1-1	2-0	1-0	2-1	0-0
Rio Ave	34	10	17	7	35	35	47	1-0	0-2	0-0	1-1	1-1	2-2	0-0		3-3	1-0	1-0	4-1	0-1	3-1	2-0	1-0	2-1	1-1
Os Belenenses	34	13	7	14	38	34	46	4-1	0-1	1-0	1-2	1-0	1-2	3-0	2-1		0-0	4-1	1-0	0-1	0-0	2-1	3-0	3-0	2-0
Vitória FC Setúbal ‡	34	11	11	12	46	45	44	0-2	0-1	2-0	1-4	1-0	0-0	2-0	2-0	1-2		4-0	1-0	0-0	1-0	0-0	2-1	2-2	2-1
Penafiel	34	13	4	17	39	53	43	1-0	1-2	0-3	1-0	1-3	1-1	0-1	1-1	0-0	1-4		0-1	1-3	3-1	3-0	1-0	2-1	2-1
CD Nacional Funchal	34	12	5	17	46	48	41	0-1	2-2	3-2	1-0	1-0	0-2	1-1	0-0	2-0	1-3	1-3		0-0	2-1	0-3	4-1	4-1	2-1
Gil Vicente	34	11	7	16	34	40	40	1-1	0-2	0-3	0-1	1-3	0-1	1-0	3-1	1-0	2-1	0-1	3-2		0-1	1-3	1-1	2-0	2-0
Académica Coimbra	34	9	11	14	29	41	38	0-1	0-0	2-3	2-2	0-2	1-0	1-0	0-0	1-1	3-3	4-1	1-0	2-1		0-1	0-4	1-0	1-1
União Leiria	34	8	14	12	29	36	38	1-0	0-1	0-0	0-0	0-1	0-3	0-0	0-3	1-0	0-2	1-2	1-0	1-1	1-2		0-0	4-2	5-1
Moreirense	34	7	13	14	30	43	34	1-2	1-1	3-1	2-1	0-0	1-1	0-0	0-1	2-2	2-2	3-2	3-2	1-0	0-0	1-0		1-2	0-0
GD Estoril-Praia	34	8	6	20	38	55	30	1-2	1-2	1-4	0-1	0-1	3-3	0-1	0-0	1-0	2-1	3-2	2-0	2-0	0-1	1-1	2-0		5-0
SC Beira-Mar	34	6	12	16	30	56	30	2-3	0-1	2-2	1-4	2-2	1-0	2-2	0-0	3-3	1-1	1-3	0-3	1-0	0-0	0-1	1-3	2-1	

28/08/2004 - 22/05/2005 • † Qualified for the UEFA Champions League • ‡ Qualified for the UEFA Cup

PORTUGAL 2004-05
LIGA DE HONRA

	Pl	W	D	L	F	A	Pts
Paços Ferreira	34	20	9	5	60	34	69
Naval 1. de Maio	34	17	11	6	52	30	62
Estrela Amadora	34	17	9	8	47	30	60
FC Marco	34	13	12	9	51	43	51
Desportivo Aves	34	15	6	13	45	35	51
Leixões	34	14	8	12	40	33	50
Feirense	34	14	7	13	45	48	49
FC Maia	34	13	10	11	46	36	49
Olhanense	34	11	11	12	32	31	44
Varzim SC	34	11	10	13	37	42	43
Felgueiras	34	11	9	14	37	44	42
AD Ovarense	34	11	8	15	40	51	41
FC Alverca	34	11	6	17	26	38	39
Portimonense SC	34	10	9	15	40	49	39
CD Santa Clara	34	11	6	17	39	49	39
Gondomar	34	10	6	18	36	43	39
GD Chaves	34	9	10	15	24	38	37
Sporting Espinho	34	9	9	16	37	51	36

29/08/2004 - 22/05/2005

TOP SCORERS

LIEDSON	Sporting	25
JOAO TOMAS	Braga	15
SIMAO	Benfica	15
WESLEY	Penafiel	14
ANTCHOUET Henri	Belenenses	12
MEYONG Albert	Setúbal	11
McCARTHY Benni	Porto	11
ZE MANUEL	Boavista	10

RECENT LEAGUE AND CUP RECORD

Year	Champions	Pts	Runners-up	Pts	Third	Pts
1992	FC Porto	56	Benfica	46	Sporting CP	44
1993	FC Porto	54	Benfica	52	Sporting CP	45
1994	Benfica	54	FC Porto	52	Sporting CP	51
1995	FC Porto	62	Sporting CP	53	Benfica	49
1996	FC Porto	84	Benfica	73	Sporting CP	67
1997	FC Porto	85	Sporting CP	72	Benfica	58
1998	FC Porto	77	Benfica	68	Vitória Guimarães	59
1999	FC Porto	79	Boavista	71	Benfica	65
2000	Sporting CP	77	FC Porto	73	Benfica	69
2001	Boavista	77	FC Porto	76	Sporting CP	62
2002	Sporting CP	75	Boavista	70	FC Porto	68
2003	FC Porto	86	Benfica	75	Sporting CP	59
2004	FC Porto	82	Benfica	74	Sporting CP	73
2005	Benfica	65	FC Porto	62	Sporting CP	61

Cup Winners	Score	Runners-up
Boavista	2-1	FC Porto
Benfica	5-2	Boavista FC
FC Porto	0-0 2-1	Sporting CP
Sporting CP	2-0	Marítimo
Benfica	3-1	Sporting CP
Boavista	3-2	Benfica
FC Porto	3-1	SC Braga
Beira-Mar	1-0	Campomaiorense
FC Porto	1-1 2-0	Sporting CP
FC Porto	2-0	Marítimo
Sporting CP	1-0	Leixões
FC Porto	1-0	União Leiria
Benfica	2-1	FC Porto
Vitória Setúbal	2-1	Benfica

TAÇA DE PORTUGAL 2004-05

First Round

Team	Score
Vitória Setúbal	3
Académico Viseu *	1
Aliados Lordelo *	0
Vitória Guimarães	2
Oliveira Hospital *	2
Moreirense	1
Odivelas *	1
Sporting Braga	2
Marítimo Funchal	0 4p
Flães *	0 1p
Rio Ave *	2
Académica Coimbra	2
Nacional Funchal	1
União Leiria *	2
Vianense *	1
Boavista	3
Estrela Amadora *	1
Louletano	0
Maia	2
Penafiel *	3
Pinhalnovense *	3
Leça	0
Pombal	0
Os Belenenses *	3
Beira-Mar *	2 4p
Espinho	2 3p
Sporting CP *	4
Pampilhosa	1
AD Oliveirense	1
Benfica *	4

Second Round

Team	Score
Vitória Setúbal *	3
Vitória Guimarães	1
Oliveira Hospital *	0
Sporting Braga	1
Marítimo Funchal	2
Académica Coimbra *	1
Nacional Funchal *	3
Boavista	4
Estrela Amadora *	1
Panafiel	0
Pinhalnovense *	1
Os Belenenses	2
Beira-Mar	
Sporting CP	3 6p
Benfica *	3 7p

Quarter-finals

Team	Score
Vitória Setúbal *	3
Sporting Braga	2
Marítimo Funchal *	0
Boavista	2
Estrela Amadora *	0 8p
Os Belenenses	0 7p
Beira-Mar	0
Benfica *	1

Semi-finals

Team	Score
Vitória Setúbal *	2
Boavista	1
Estrela Amadora *	0
Benfica	3

Final

Team	Score
Vitória Setúbal ‡	2
Benfica	1

CUP FINAL

29-05-2005, Estádio Nacional, Lisbon

Scorers – Ricardo Rocha OG 26, Meyong 72 for Setúbal; Simão 59 for Benfica

Setúbal: Moretto; Eder, Auri, Hugo Alcântara, Nandinho; Manuel José (Binho 79), Sandro, Ricardo Chaves, Bruno Ribeiro; Jorginho, Meyong (Igor 89). Tr: José Rachão

Benfica: Moreira; Miguel, Alcides, Ricardo Rocha, Fyssas (Dos Santos 55); Manuel Fernandes, Petit, Nuno Assis (Mantorras 74); Geovanni, Simão, Nuno Gomes (Delibasic 85). Tr: Trapattoni

* Home team ‡ Qualified for the UEFA Cup

SPORT LISBOA E BENFICA 2004-2005

Date	Opponents	Score		Comp	Scorers
10-08-2004	RSC Anderlecht - BEL	W 1-0	H	CLpr3	Zahovic [13]
20-08-2004	FC Porto	L 0-1	N	SC	
24-08-2004	RSC Anderlecht - BEL	L 0-3	A	CLpr3	
29-08-2004	Beira-Mar	W 3-2	A	SL	Karadas 2 [42 53], Petit [48]
11-09-2004	Moreirense	W 2-0	H	SL	Petit [23], Simão [82]
16-09-2004	Banská Bystrica - SVK	W 3-0	A	UCr1	Simão 2 [38 65], João Pereira [72]
19-09-2004	Académica Coimbra	W 1-0	A	SL	Simão [74]
26-09-2004	SC Braga	D 0-0	H	SL	
30-09-2004	Banská Bystrica - SVK	W 2-0	H	UCr1	Zahovic [13], Nuno Gomes [17]
3-10-2004	Vitória Guimarães	W 2-1	A	SL	Simão [70], Geovanni [92+]
17-10-2004	FC Porto	L 0-1	H	SL	
21-10-2004	SC Heerenveen - NED	W 4-2	H	UCgG	Dos Santos [14], Nuno Gomes 2 [32 78], Karadas [73]
24-10-2004	Nacional	W 2-1	H	SL	Karadas [64], Sokota [83]
27-10-2004	Oriental	W 3-1	H	TPr4	Sokota 2 [27 71], Geovanni [61]
31-10-2004	Gil Vicente	D 1-1	A	SL	Simão [97+]
4-11-2004	VfB Stuttgart - GER	L 0-3	A	UCgG	
7-11-2004	Vitória Setubal	W 4-0	H	SL	Karadas [31], Sokota [52], Geovanni [73], Simão [91+]
13-11-2044	Marítimo	D 1-1	A	SL	Simão [15]
20-11-2004	Rio Ave	D 3-3	H	SL	Simão 2 [3 22], Sokota [30]
25-11-2004	Dinamo Zagreb - CRO	W 2-0	H	UCgG	Sokota [11], Simão [29p]
28-11-2004	União Leiria	L 0-1	A	SL	
2-12-2004	KSK Beveren - BEL	W 3-0	A	UCgG	Simão [5p], Zahovic 2 [21 59]
6-12-2004	Estoril-Praia	W 2-1	H	SL	Simão 2 [33 44p]
12-12-2004	Belenenses	L 1-4	A	SL	Sokota [76]
18-12-2004	Penafiel	W 1-0	H	SL	Argel [22]
21-12-2004	Oliveirense	W 4-1	H	TPr5	Simão [49p], Cristiano OG [96], Sokota [112], Geovanni [114]
8-01-2005	Sporting CP	L 1-2	A	SL	Nuno Gomes [26]
16-01-2005	Boavista	W 4-0	H	SL	Simão [40p], Nuno Gomes 2 [62 71], Mantorras [99+]
22-01-2005	Beira-Mar	L 0-2	H	SL	
26-01-2005	Sporting CP	D 3-3	H	TPr6	Geovanni 2 [3 22], Simão [116]. W 7-6p
29-01-2005	Moreirense	W 2-1	A	SL	Nuno Gomes [9], Nuno Assis [36]
6-02-2005	Académica Coimbra	W 3-0	H	SL	Geovanni [32], Simão 2 [60 83]
12-02-2005	SC Braga	D 0-0	A	SL	
17-02-2005	CSKA Moskva - RUS	L 0-2	A	UCr3	
21-02-2005	Vitória Guimarães	W 2-1	H	SL	Geovanni [12], Nuno Assis [44]
24-02-2005	CSKA Moskva - RUS	D 1-1	H	UCr3	Karadas [63]
28-02-2005	FC Porto	D 1-1	A	SL	Geovanni [77]
3-03-2005	Beira-Mar	W 1-0	H	TPqf	João Pereira [27]
6-03-2005	Nacional	W 1-0	A	SL	Nuno Gomes [50]
12-03-2005	Gil Vicente	W 2-0	H	SL	Mantorras [53], Miguel [91+]
19-03-2005	Vitória Setubal	W 2-0	H	SL	Manuel Fernandes [42], Geovanni [67]
3-04-2005	Marítimo	W 4-3	H	SL	Nuno Gomes 2 [6 22], Miguel [12], Mantorras [89]
10-04-2005	Rio Ave	L 0-1	A	SL	
16-04-2005	União Leiria	D 1-1	H	SL	Mantorras [93+]
20-04-2005	Estrela Amadorra	W 3-0	A	TPsf	Nuno Gomes 2 [37 74], Nuno Assis [66]
24'-04-2005	Estoril-Praia	W 2-1	A	SL	Luisão [75], Mantoras [82]
30-04-2005	Belenenses	W 1-0	H	SL	Simão [68]
7-05-2005	Panafiel	L 0-1	A	SL	
14-05-2005	Sporting CP	W 1-0	H	SL	Luisão [83]
22-05-2005	Boavista	D 1-1	A	SL	Simão [38p]
29-05-2005	Vitória Setubal	L 1-2	N	TPf	Simão [5p]

SL = SuperLiga • TP = Taça de Portugal • CL = UEFA Champions League • UC = UEFA Cup • SC = Portuguese Super Cup
pr3 = third preliminary round • r1 = first round • gG = group G • r3 = third round • r4 = fourth round • r5 = fifth round • r6 = sixth round
qf = quarter-final • sf = semi-final • f = final

PRK – KOREA DPR

NATIONAL TEAM RECORD
JULY 1ST 2002 TO JUNE 30TH 2005

PL	W	D	L	F	A	%
28	8	8	12	54	38	42.9

FIFA/COCA-COLA WORLD RANKING

1993	1994	1995	1996	1997	1998	1999	2000	2001	2002	2003	2004	High		Low	
62	84	117	144	166	158	172	142	136	124	117	95	57	11/93	181	11/98

2004-2005											
08/04	09/04	10/04	11/04	12/04	01/05	02/05	03/05	04/05	05/05	06/05	07/05
113	112	102	96	95	97	95	91	91	88	94	91

Mention Korea DPR and the feats of the team at the 1966 FIFA World Cup™ usually spring to mind, or the name Pak Do Ik, scorer of the winner against Italy in those finals. The minimal contact that this secretive country has with the rest of the world does little to dispel the stereotype but the Koreans have produced a number of good teams in recent years especially in women's football where the national team has successfully challenged China PR for supremacy in the region, twice winning the Asian Women's Championship and twice qualifying for the FIFA Women's World Cup finals. The men have yet to match that but in the 2006 FIFA World Cup™ qualifiers they did win

INTERNATIONAL HONOURS
Qualified for the FIFA World Cup™ finals 1966   Qualified for the FIFA Women's World Cup finals 1999 2003
Asian Games 1978   Asian Women's Championship 2001 2003   Women's Asian Games 2002

a potentially difficult first round group containing Thailand, the United Arab Emirates and Yemen. That meant a place in the final group stage which included a politically sensitive trip to Japan. Defeats in their first five games put an end to any hopes of qualifying for the finals, even via the play-offs and after incidents in the home defeats against Bahrain and Iraq the Koreans were ordered to play their last home match, against Japan, in Bangkok. Little news filters out from the country about league football but the 2004 Championship was won by Pyongyang City Sports Group.

THE FIFA BIG COUNT OF 2000

	Male	Female		Male	Female
Registered players	5 000	0	Referees	300	0
Non registered players	100 000	0	Officials	1 000	0
Youth players	5 000	0	Total involved	111 300	
Total players	110 000		Number of clubs	150	
Professional players	0	0	Number of teams	800	

DPR Korea Football Association (PRK)
Kumsongdong, Kwangbok Street, Mangyongdae Dist., PO Box 56, Pyongyang, Korea DPR
Tel +850 2 18222   Fax +850 2 3814403
noc-kp@co.chesin.com   www.none
President: RI Kwang Gun   General Secretary: RI Hi Yen
Vice-President: RI Tong Ho   Treasurer: TBD   Media Officer: None
Men's Coach: PAEK Kil Son   Women's Coach: WON Kyong Hak
PRK formed: 1945   AFC: 1974   FIFA: 1958
Colours: White, White, White

GAMES PLAYED BY KOREA DPR IN THE 2006 FIFA WORLD CUP™ CYCLE

2002	Opponents	Score		Venue	Comp	Scorers	Att	Referee
No international matches played in 2002 after June								
2003								
16-02	Thailand	D	2-2	Bangkok	Fr	Kim Yong Jun [54], Kim Myong Won [87]		
18-02	Sweden	D	1-1	Bangkok	Fr	Pak Yong Chol [84]		Rungklay THA
20-02	Qatar	D	2-2	Bangkok	Fr	Nam Song Chol [12], Jon Yong Chol [20]		
22-02	Sweden	L	0-4	Bangkok	Fr			Kunsuta THA
24-03	India	W	2-0	Pyongyang	ACq	So Hyok Chol 2 [22 80]		
30-03	India	D	1-1	Margao	ACq	Choe Hyun U [85]		
4-09	Lebanon	L	0-1	Pyongyang	ACq			
27-10	Iran	L	1-3	Pyongyang	ACq	Myong Song Chol [65]	30 000	
3-11	Lebanon	D	1-1	Beirut	ACq	Kim Yong Chol [61]		
12-11	Iran	L	0-3	Tehran	ACq			
18-11	Jordan	L	0-3	Amman	ACq			
28-11	Jordan	L	0-3	Pyongyang	ACq	Match awarded 3-0 to Jordan		
2004								
18-02	Yemen	D	1-1	Sana'a	WCq	Hong Yong Jo [85]	15 000	Husain BHR
31-03	United Arab Emirates	D	0-0	Pyongyang	WCq		20 000	Zhou Weixin CHN
9-06	Thailand	W	4-1	Bangkok	WCq	Kim Yong Su 2 [42 71], Sin Yong Nam [52], Hong Yong Jo [67]	30 000	Tseytlin UZB
8-09	Thailand	W	4-1	Pyongyang	WCq	An Yonh Hak 2 [49 73], Hong Yong Jo [55], Ri Hyok Chol [60]	20 000	Moradi IRN
13-10	Yemen	W	2-1	Pyongyang	WCq	Ri Han Ja [1], Hong Yong Jo [64]	15 000	Vo Minh Tri VIE
17-11	United Arab Emirates	L	0-1	Dubai	WCq		2 000	Abdul Hamid MAS
2005								
2-02	Kuwait	D	0-0	Beijing	Fr			
9-02	Japan	L	1-2	Saitama	WCq	Nam Song Chol [61]	60 000	Al Ghamdi KSA
7-03	Mongolia	W	6-0	Taipei	EAq	Kim Kwang Hyok 3 [18 39 66], Ri Hyok Chol 2 [22 30] Hong Yong Jo [64]		
9-03	Chinese Taipei	W	2-0	Taipei	EAq	Choe Chol Man 2 [13 14]		
11-03	Guam	W	21-0	Taipei	EAq	Hong Yong Jo 2 [6 17], Choe Chol Man 3 [10 37 54] Kim Kwang Hyok 7 [21 43 61 63 71 76 77], Park Nam Chol [83] Kim Yong Jun 3 [29 39 49], Kang Jin Hyok 5 [31 44 65 84 91+]		
13-03	Hong Kong	W	2-0	Taipei	EAq	Kang Jin Hyok [43], Ri Myong Sam [64]		
25-03	Bahrain	L	1-2	Pyongyang	WCq	Pak Song Gwan [63]	50 000	Rungklay THA
30-03	Iran	L	0-2	Pyongyang	WCq		55 000	Kousa SYR
3-06	Iran	L	0-1	Tehran	WCq		35 000	Al Ghamdi KSA
8-06	Japan	L	0-2	Bangkok	WCq		BCD	De Bleeckere BEL

Fr = Friendly match • AC = AFC Asian Cup 2004 • EA = East Asian Championship • WC = FIFA World Cup™ • q = qualifier

KOREA DPR NATIONAL TEAM RECORDS AND RECORD SEQUENCES

Records			Sequence records				
Victory	21-0	GUM 2005	Wins	8	1993	Clean sheets	4	Four times
Defeat	1-6	BUL 1974	Defeats	5	1993	Goals scored	18	1992-1993
Player Caps	n/a		Undefeated	13	1978-1980	Without goal	4	1989-1990
Player Goals	n/a		Without win	15	1993-2000	Goals against	12	1993-2000

KOREA DPR COUNTRY INFORMATION

Capital	Pyongyang	Independence	1945 from Japan	GDP per Capita	$1 400
Population	22 912 177	Status	Communist Republic	GNP Ranking	68
Area km²	120 540	Language	Korean	Dialling code	+850
Population density	190 per km²	Literacy rate	99%	Internet code	.kp
% in urban areas	61%	Main religion	None	GMT +/−	+9
Towns/Cities ('000)	Pyongyang 2 787; Hamhung 840; Chongjin 689, Nampo 670; Sinuiju 385; Wonsan 355; Phyongsong 323; Sariwon 300; Haeju 271; Kanggye 264; Kimchaek 237; Hyesan 210				
Neighbours (km)	Korea Republic 238; China 1 416; Russia 19; Sea of Japan & Yellow Sea 2 495				
Main stadia	Kim Il-Sung Stadium – Pyongyang 70 000; Yanggakdo – Pyongyang 30 000				

PUR – PUERTO RICO

NATIONAL TEAM RECORD
JULY 1ST 2002 TO JUNE 30TH 2005

PL	W	D	L	F	A	%
5	0	1	4	3	17	10

FIFA/COCA-COLA WORLD RANKING

1993	1994	1995	1996	1997	1998	1999	2000	2001	2002	2003	2004	High		Low	
105	112	128	149	169	182	186	195	195	198	200	194	97	03/94	202	11/04

2004-2005											
08/04	09/04	10/04	11/04	12/04	01/05	02/05	03/05	04/05	05/05	06/05	07/05
201	201	201	202	194	194	194	194	194	194	194	194

A commonwealth territory of the USA, American influence pervades Puerto Rico and it is unsurprising that football does not play a major part of the island's life. However, it is by far the most populous non-independent country and with four million people could be regarded as a potential candidate for development of the game. Currently ranked 194th in the world, there is a long way to go if Puerto Rico are to make any impression on the Caribbean region, let alone the world. Their last international success was victory over Barbados in 1994 so it is not surprising that the side did not enter the 2006 FIFA World Cup™ qualifiers, instead deciding to concentrate on reorganising

INTERNATIONAL HONOURS
None

their football structures with the help of FIFA and CONCACAF. However, the team did enter the Digicel Caribbean Cup, forcing a draw with Surinam, but defeats to Grenada and Trinidad and Tobago meant they went no further and a place at the CONCACAF Gold Cup must wait. Regarded as one of the weaker leagues in the region, the 2004 Liga Major was contested by eight clubs with Sporting de San Lorenzo claiming their first title. Sporting and Huracanes Caguas finished the regular season in the top two places to meet again in the final that Sporting won with a golden goal from Montero after a goalless 90 minutes.

THE FIFA BIG COUNT OF 2000

	Male	Female		Male	Female
Registered players	8 000	0	Referees	300	0
Non registered players	36 000	0	Officials	2 000	1 000
Youth players	10 000	0	Total involved	56 400	
Total players	54 000		Number of clubs	200	
Professional players	0	0	Number of teams	800	

Federación Puertorriquena de Fútbol (FPF)
392 Juan B. Rodriguez, Parque Central Hato Rey, PR 00918, San Juan 00918, Puerto Rico

Tel +1 787 7652895   Fax +1 787 7672288

jserralta@yahoo.com   www.fedefutbolpr.com

President: SERRALTA Joe   General Secretary: RODRIGUEZ ESTRELLA Esteban

Vice-President: COLLAZO Dariel   Treasurer: VILLEGAS Miguel   Media Officer: ARIAS Ana Rosa

Men's Coach: VILLAREJO Luis   Women's Coach: ROSA Oscar

FPF formed: 1940   CONCACAF: 1962   FIFA: 1960

Colours: White with red stripes and Blue sleeves, White, White

GAMES PLAYED BY PUERTO RICO IN THE 2006 FIFA WORLD CUP™ CYCLE

2002	Opponents	Score		Venue	Comp	Scorers	Att	Referee
7-07	Guadeloupe	L	0-4	Baie-Mahault	GCq			Ibrahim DMA
21-07	Guadeloupe	L	0-2	San Juan	GCq			Richard DMA
2003								
No international matches played in 2003								
2004								
24-11	Trinidad and Tobago	L	0-5	Tunapuna	GCq		2 000	Callender BRB
26-11	Surinam	D	1-1	Marabella	GCq	Ortiz [80]		Forde BRB
28-11	Grenada	L	2-5	Malabar	GCq	Garcia [85], Nieves [86]		Callender BRB
2005								
No international matches played in 2005 before August								

GC = CONCACAF Gold Cup • q = qualifier

PUERTO RICO NATIONAL TEAM RECORDS AND RECORD SEQUENCES

Records			Sequence records					
Victory	4-0	CAY 1993	Wins	4	1993	Clean sheets	4	1993
Defeat	0-9	CUB 1995	Defeats	15	1949-1965	Goals scored	6	1988-1992
Player Caps	n/a		Undefeated	4	1993	Without goal	6	1982-1988
Player Goals	n/a		Without win	37	1940-1970	Goals against	26	1949-1970

Puerto Rico has no referees or assistant referees on the FIFA lists

PUERTO RICO 2004 LIGA MAYOR

	Pl	W	D	L	F	A	Pts
Sporting San Lorenzo†	14	11	1	2	28	13	34
Huracanes Caguas †	13	9	0	4	39	15	27
San Juan Reales ‡	14	8	3	3	44	20	27
Añasco Atlético ‡	13	8	3	2	32	18	27
Vaqueros Bayamón ‡	13	6	3	4	28	22	21
Borikén Yabucoa ‡	13	5	0	8	21	39	15
Humacao Tornados	14	2	0	12	15	51	3
Brujos Guayama	14	0	0	14	5	34	0

7/08/2004 - 24/10/2005 • † Qualified for the semi-finals
‡ Qualified for the quarter-finals

LIGA MAYOR PLAY-OFFS

Quarter-finals	Semi-finals	Final
	Sp. San Lorenzo 2 2	
Vaq'os Bayamón 0 0	Añasco Atlético 2 1	
Añasco Atlético 2 5		Sp. San Lorenzo 1
San Juan Reales 1 0		Hurac's Caguas 0
Borikén Yabucoa 0 1	San Juan Reales	12-12-2004
	Hurac's Caguas	Country Club, San Juan Scorer - Montero [100] for San Lorenzo

RECENT LEAGUE RECORD

Championship		Liga Mayor		
Year	Champions	Winners	Score	Runners-up
1997	Académicos Quintana	Leones Maunabo		Islanders San Juan
1998	Académicos Quintana	Islanders San Juan	3-0	Brujos Guayama
1999	CF Nacional Carolina	Islanders San Juan		Cardenales
2000	Académicos Quintana	Vaqueros Bayamón	1-0	Gigantes Carolina
2001	Académicos Quintana	Islanders San Juan	4-3	Brujos Guayama
2002	Académicos Quintana	Vaqueros Bayamón	3-0	Islanders San Juan
2003	Not held	Sporting Carolina	2-1	Vaqueros Bayamón
2004	Not held	Sporting San Lorenzo	1-0	Huracanes Caguas

PUERTO RICO COUNTRY INFORMATION

Capital	San Juan	Status	Commonwealth associated with the US	GDP per Capita	$16 800
Population	3 897 960			GNP Ranking	n/a
Area km²	9 104	Language	Spanish, English	Dialling code	+1 787
Population density	428 per km²	Literacy rate	94%	Internet code	.pr
% in urban areas	71%	Main religion	Christian	GMT +/-	-5
Towns/Cities ('000)	San Juan 418; Bayamón 203; Carolina 170; Ponce 152; Caguas 86; Guaynabo 81; Mayagüez 76				
Neighbours (km)	Caribbean Sea & North Atlantic 501				
Main stadia	Estadio Sixto Escobar – San Juan 18 000; Country Club – San Juan 2 500				

QAT – QATAR

NATIONAL TEAM RECORD
JULY 1ST 2002 TO JUNE 30TH 2005

PL	W	D	L	F	A	%
41	15	13	13	66	49	52.4

FIFA/COCA-COLA WORLD RANKING

1993	1994	1995	1996	1997	1998	1999	2000	2001	2002	2003	2004	High		Low	
54	60	83	69	70	60	107	102	80	62	65	66	51	08/93	107	12/99

					2004-2005						
08/04	09/04	10/04	11/04	12/04	01/05	02/05	03/05	04/05	05/05	06/05	07/05
59	61	62	65	66	65	67	68	67	67	74	75

Considering the size and population of Qatar, the national team have been punching well above their weight for some time. 2004, however, was a mixed year for the Qataris beginning with two straight defeats in their 2006 FIFA World Cup™ qualifiers. A 5-0 victory over Laos put the team back on course only to be derailed a month later with a disastrous Asian Cup. Coach Philippe Troussier was dismissed after the first game, a 2-1 defeat to Indonesia, and the team left China earlier than many observers had expected. Although they partially recovered for the remaining World Cup™ qualifiers the damage had been done and Qatar failed to progress. With home advantage

INTERNATIONAL HONOURS
Gulf Cup 1992 2004

for the 2004 Gulf Cup, Qatar repaid their fans by winning the tournament for only the second time beating Oman in the final 5-4 on penalties and the country will be hoping for similar rewards when it hosts the 2006 Asian Games. Both junior sides reached their respective regional finals with the U-17s the most successful as they finished third to book their place at the FIFA U-17 World Championship in Peru. The Q-League was once again brimming with stars from around the world and was won by Al Gharafa, captained by Marcel Desailly, who finished 14 points clear of an Al Rayyan team boasting the talents of the De Boer twins and Sonny Anderson.

THE FIFA BIG COUNT OF 2000

	Male	Female		Male	Female
Registered players	1 943	0	Referees	85	0
Non registered players	2 370	0	Officials	1 040	0
Youth players	1 598	0	Total involved	7 036	
Total players		5 911	Number of clubs	16	
Professional players	4	0	Number of teams	45	

Qatar Football Association (QFA)
7th Floor, QNOC Building, Cornich, PO Box 5333, Doha, Qatar
Tel +974 4944411   Fax +974 4944414
football@qatarolympics.org   www.qatar-football.com
President: AL-THANI Shk. Hamad Bin Khalifa   General Secretary: AL-MOHANNADI Saud
Vice-President: TBD   Treasurer: AL-OBAIDLY Abdulaziz Hassan   Media Officer: AL-KAWARI Khalid
Men's Coach: MUSOVIC Dzemaludin   Women's Coach: None
QFA formed: 1960   AFC: 1972   FIFA: 1970
Colours: White, White, White

GAMES PLAYED BY QATAR IN THE 2006 FIFA WORLD CUP™ CYCLE

2002	Opponents	Score	Venue	Comp	Scorers	Att	Referee
20-11	Iraq	W 2-1	Doha	Fr	Mujib Hamid [79], Rahmi OG [83]		Muflah OMA
2003							
16-02	Sweden	L 2-3	Bangkok	Fr	Yaser Abdulrahman [54], Salem Al Enazi [90p]	5 000	Hanlunyaung THA
18-02	Thailand	D 1-1	Bangkok	Fr	Salem Al Enazi [86]		Lee Gi Young KOR
20-02	Korea DPR	D 2-2	Bangkok	Fr	Salem Al Enazi 2 [25 52]		
22-02	Thailand	L 1-3	Bangkok	Fr	Ali Bechir [57]		
19-03	Egypt	L 0-6	Port Said	Fr			El Beltagy EGY
4-09	Algeria	L 0-1	Paris	Fr		400	
14-09	Kuwait	L 1-2	Kuwait City	ACq	Ghanim Al Shemmari [27]	20 000	
20-09	Kuwait	D 2-2	Doha	ACq	Sayed Al Bashir 2 [20 82]		Al Hamdan KSA
24-09	Palestine	D 1-1	Doha	ACq	Meshal Abdullah [47]		Abdul Kadir Nema IRQ
27-09	Palestine	W 2-1	Doha	ACq	Muhyeddin [68], Hamza [90]		Mujghef JOR
19-11	Singapore	W 2-0	Doha	ACq	Ali Bechir [11], Mubarak Mustafa [29]		
29-11	Singapore	W 2-0	Singapore	ACq	Abdullah Kouni [42], Ali Bechir [55]		Hanlumyaung THA
21-12	Iraq	D 0-0	Doha	Fr			Al Qatani QAT
27-12	Bahrain	D 0-0	Kuwait City	GC			Kassai HUN
29-12	Saudi Arabia	D 0-0	Kuwait City	GC			Meier SUI
2004							
3-01	United Arab Emirates	D 0-0	Kuwait City	GC			
5-01	Yemen	W 3-0	Kuwait City	GC	Mubarak Mustafa [22], Meshal Abdulla [39], Salmeen [58]		
8-01	Kuwait	W 2-1	Kuwait City	GC	Salmeen [41], Mubarak Mustafa [58]		
11-01	Oman	L 0-2	Kuwait City	GC			
13-02	Bahrain	W 2-0	Doha	Fr			
18-02	Iran	L 1-3	Tehran	WCq	Waleed Rasoul [70]		Haj Khader SYR
26-03	Libya	L 0-1	Rome	Fr			
31-03	Jordan	L 0-1	Amman	WCq		15 000	Shaban KUW
31-05	Turkmenistan	W 5-0	Doha	Fr	Mijbel [2], Ali Bechir 3 [15 60 88], Moussa [44]		
5-06	Kyrgyzstan	D 0-0	Doha	Fr			
9-06	Laos	W 5-0	Doha	WCq	Fazli 2 [17 37], Waleed Jassim 2 [69 86], Ali Bechir [89]	500	Abu Armana PAL
18-07	Indonesia	L 1-2	Beijing	ACrl	Magid [83]	5 000	Moradi IRN
21-07	Bahrain	D 1-1	Beijing	ACrl	Wesam Rizak [58p]		Toru JPN
25-07	China PR	L 0-1	Beijing	ACrl		60 000	Moradi IRN
8-09	Laos	W 6-1	Vientiane	WCq	Abdulmajid [36], Nasser Mubarak [42], Ali Bechir [50], Waleed Rasoul [70], Meshal Abdulla [86], Saad Al Shammari [89]	2 900	Napitupulu IDN
8-10	Syria	L 1-2	Doha	Fr			
13-10	Iran	L 2-3	Doha	WCq	Bilal Rajab [18], Golmohammadi OG [75]	8 000	Kwon Jong Chul KOR
17-11	Jordan	W 2-0	Doha	WCq	Salem Al Hamad [60], Nayef Al Khater [75]	800	Yoshida JPN
1-12	Lebanon	W 4-1	Doha	Fr			
5-12	Yemen	W 3-0	Doha	Fr			
10-12	United Arab Emirates	D 2-2	Doha	GCrl	Waleed Jassim [90], Wisam Rizq [93+]		
13-12	Iraq	D 3-3	Doha	GCrl	Bilal Mohammed [38], Waleed Jassim 2 [43p 57]		
16-12	Oman	W 2-1	Doha	GCrl	Sattam Al Shamari [10], Ali Bechir [27]		
20-12	Kuwait	W 2-0	Doha	GCsf	Ali Bechir [39], Nasir Kamil [90p]		
24-12	Oman	D 1-1	Doha	GCf	Wissam Rizq [4]. W 5-4p		
2005							

No international matches played in 2005 before July

Fr = Friendly match • AC = AFC Asian Cup • GC = Gulf Cup • WC = FIFA World Cup™ • q = qualifier • r1 = first round group • sf = semi-final • f = final

QATAR COUNTRY INFORMATION

Capital	Doha	Independence	1971 from the UK	GDP per Capita	$21 500
Population	840 290	Status	Monarchy	GNP Ranking	92
Area km²	11 437	Language	Arabic	Dialling code	+974
Population density	73 per km²	Literacy rate	82%	Internet code	.qa
% in urban areas	91%	Main religion	Muslim	GMT +/−	+3
Towns/Cities ('000)	Doha 344; Al Rayyan 272; Umm Salal 29; Al Wakra 26; Khor 19				
Neighbours (km)	Saudi Arabia 60; Persain Gulf 563				
Main stadia	Khalifa International – Doha 45 000				

QATAR NATIONAL TEAM RECORDS AND RECORD SEQUENCES

Records			Sequence records					
Victory	8-0	AFG 1984, LIB 1985	Wins	5	1988, 1996, 2001	Clean sheets	7	2003-2004
Defeat	0-9	KUW 1973	Defeats	8	1972-1974	Goals scored	12	1996
Player Caps	n/a		Undefeated	11	2001, 2003-04	Without goal	4	1998, 2003-04
Player Goals	n/a		Without win	11	1970-1974	Goals against	15	1994-1996

FIFA REFEREE LIST 2005

	Int'l	DoB
ABDOU Abdulrahman		1-10-1972
AL ALI Juma	1998	2-05-1964
AL BALOSHI Abdulla		4-02-1970
AL HAIL Jassim	1998	15-09-1963
AL KHORI Jassem	1996	26-09-1956
AL MANSOURI Haroun	1998	2-10-1968

FIFA ASSISTANT REFEREE LIST 2005

	Int'l	DoB
AL BOENAIN Ali	2003	1-07-1964
AL KHALIFI Ali	1998	10-08-1965
AL REMAIHI Khaled	2005	19-09-1965
MANSOOR Salah	2004	28-02-1964
MOHD Ibrahim Ali	2001	2-08-1967
NE AMA Mohamed	1999	17-12-1961

QATAR 2004-05

Q-LEAGUE	Pl	W	D	L	F	A	Pts	Gharrafa	Rayyan	Khor	Qatar	Arabi	Wakra	Sadd	Ahli	Shamal	Khritiyat
Al Gharrafa †	27	20	6	1	71	23	66		2-0	3-0 1-1	4-0 3-2	2-2 2-1	2-1 1-0	3-1 2-4	2-2	6-1 6-0	0-0
Al Rayyan †	27	15	7	5	66	34	52	2-2 1-3		1-0	1-0 0-1	4-0 1-1	3-3 2-0	4-2 3-1	1-0	4-2 2-0	8-2 5-1
Khor	27	14	6	7	46	30	48	1-3	1-0 1-1		2-1 2-1	2-1 1-2	1-0 0-1	1-1 2-1	1-1 3-0	3-0	3-0
Qatar SC	27	14	3	10	40	34	45	0-1	1-2	1-1		1-0 1-4	0-1	2-1	2-3	4-2 2-0	3-1 3-1
Al Arabi	27	12	8	7	53	35	44	1-2	2-5 1-1	5-2	0-1		1-1	0-1	3-1	1-0	3-2
Al Wakra	27	9	7	11	37	35	34	1-3	1-4	3-1	1-2 1-1	1-1 2-2		0-1	1-1	2-1	0-3 2-0
Al Sadd	27	9	7	11	35	35	34	0-3	2-2	1-1	0-0 0-1	1-2 0-0	0-4 0-0		0-1	3-0 3-1	2-0 2-1
Al Ahly	27	7	7	13	35	55	28	0-0 2-3	2-2	0-2	1-3 1-3	0-3 2-4	0-2 2-1	2-1 0-3		1-0	3-3 3-3
Shamal	27	4	3	20	22	67	15	0-1	3-1	0-1 0-8	1-2	1-1 0-4	3-2 0-3	0-0	3-1 2-3		1-1 0-2
Al Khritiyat	27	2	4	21	24	81	10	0-6 0-5	0-6	1-3 1-2	0-2	1-2 1-6	0-3	0-4	0-3	0-1	

23/09/2004 - 25/04/2005 • † Qualified for AFC Champions League

AMIR CUP 2004-05

Quarter-finals		Semi-finals		Final	
Al Sadd	2 5p				
Khor	2 4p	Al Sadd	1 1		
Al Gharrafa	0	Al Ahly	0 0		
Al Ahly	1			Al Sadd	0 5p
Al Arabi	5			Al Wakra	0 4p
Qatar SC	1	Al Arabi	1 1		
Al Rayyan	2	Al Wakra	0 4	4-06-2005	
Al Wakra	4				

RECENT LEAGUE AND CUP RECORD

	Championship						Amir Cup		
Year	Champions	Pts	Runners-up	Pts	Third	Pts	Winners	Score	Runners-up
1996	Al Arabi	36	Al Rayyan	35	Al Wakra	35	Al Ittihad	5-2	Al Rayyan
1997	Al Arabi	34	Al Rayyan	32	Al Ittihad	29	Al Ittihad	1-1 3-2p	Al Rayyan
1998	Al Ittihad	32	Al Rayyan	29	Al Sadd	26	Al Ittihad	4-3	Al Ahli
1999	Al Wakra	39	Al Ittihad	34	Al Sadd	33	Al Rayyan	2-1	Al Ittihad
2000	Al Sadd	38	Al Rayyan	34	Al Arabi	26	Al Sadd	2-0	Al Rayyan
2001	Al Wakra	32	Al Arabi	29	Al Taawun	28	Qatar SC	3-2	Al Sadd
2002	Al Ittihad	41	Qatar SC	29	Al Rayyan	25	Al Ittihad	3-1	Al Sadd
2003	Qatar SC	34	Al Sadd	31	Khor	31	Al Sadd	2-1	Al Ahli
2004	Al Sadd	42	Qatar SC	34	Al Arabi	31	Al Rayyan	3-2	Qatar SC
2005	Al Gharrafa	66	Al Rayyan	52	Khor	48	Al Sadd	0-0 5-4p	Al Wakra

Name changes: Al Ittihad → Al Gharrafa; Al Taawun → Khor

ROU – ROMANIA

NATIONAL TEAM RECORD
JULY 1ST 2002 TO JUNE 30TH 2005

PL	W	D	L	F	A	%
30	16	5	9	56	29	61.7

FIFA/COCA-COLA WORLD RANKING

1993	1994	1995	1996	1997	1998	1999	2000	2001	2002	2003	2004	High		Low	
13	11	11	16	7	12	8	13	15	24	27	29	3	09/97	35	08/04

					2004-2005						
08/04	09/04	10/04	11/04	12/04	01/05	02/05	03/05	04/05	05/05	06/05	07/05
35	32	26	28	29	28	28	29	30	32	32	31

It was Romania's great misfortune to be placed in a 2006 FIFA World Cup™ qualifying group with perhaps two of the best and most in-form teams in Europe – the Czech Republic and the Netherlands. Despite winning their first three matches the Romanians found themselves trailing in the wake of their rivals and after a 1-1 draw in Yerevan against Armenia in November 2004 experienced coach Anghel Iordanescu decided to quit. Having been the architect of the successful team of the 1990s he took the job in 2002 to try and revive the fortunes of the team but was unable to weave the same magic and decided to concentrate his efforts on a political career instead. His

INTERNATIONAL HONOURS
Balkan Cup 1931 1933 1936 1980   **UEFA Junior Tournament** 1962   **UEFA Champions League** Steaua Bucuresti 1986

replacement Victor Piturca had led Romania to qualification for UEFA Euro 2000™ and although going into the final stages there was a chance of making it to the finals in Germany it was slim at best. The domestic scene was enlived by the arrival of Walter Zenga as coach of Steaua Bucuresti and the Italian led the former European champions to their first title for four years. Remarkably he wasn't there to see the team clinch the title having been sacked with just three games to go due to poor results! Dinamo continued their domination of the Cup with a 1-0 victory over Farul in the final, their fifth victory in the past six years.

THE FIFA BIG COUNT OF 2000

	Male	Female		Male	Female
Registered players	52 650	176	Referees	6 085	17
Non registered players	500 000	4 000	Officials	13 252	35
Youth players	54 890	1 500	Total involved	632 605	
Total players	613 216		Number of clubs	2 276	
Professional players	3 920	0	Number of teams	3 852	

Romanian Football Federation (FRF)
Federatia Romana de Fotbal, House of Football, Str. Serg. Serbanica Vasile 12, Bucharest 022186, Romania
Tel +40 21 3250678   Fax +40 21 3250679
frf@frf.ro   www.frf.ro
President: SANDU Mircea   General Secretary: KASSAI Adalbert
Vice-President: COSTINESCU Corneliu   Treasurer: FILIMON Vasile   Media Officer: ZAHARIA Paul Daniel
Men's Coach: PITURCA Victor   Women's Coach: STAICU Gheorghe
FRF formed: 1909   UEFA: 1954   FIFA: 1923
Colours: Yellow, Yellow, Yellow

GAMES PLAYED BY ROMANIA IN THE 2006 FIFA WORLD CUP™ CYCLE

2002	Opponents	Score		Venue	Comp	Scorers	Att	Referee
21-08	Greece	L	0-1	Constanta	Fr		15 000	Toat TUR
7-09	Bosnia-Herzegovina	W	3-0	Sarajevo	ECq	Chivu [8], Munteanu.D [8], Ganea [27]	4 000	Cortez Batista POR
12-10	Norway	L	0-1	Bucharest	ECq		25 000	Ivanov RUS
16-10	Luxembourg	W	7-0	Luxembourg	ECq	Moldovan 2 [2 5], Radoi [24], Contra 3 [45 47 86], Ghioane [80]	2 000	Lajuks LVA
20-11	Croatia	L	0-1	Timisoara	Fr		40 000	Megyebiro HUN
2003								
12-02	Slovakia	W	2-1	Larnaca	Fr	Munteanu.D [39], Ganea [41]	150	Papaioannou GRE
29-03	Denmark	L	2-5	Bucharest	ECq	Mutu [5], Munteanu.D [47]	55 000	Mejuto Gonzalez ESP
30-04	Lithuania	W	1-0	Kaunas	Fr	Bratu [63]	5 000	Sipailo LVA
7-06	Bosnia-Herzegovina	W	2-0	Craiova	ECq	Mutu [46], Ganea [88]	36 000	Bossen NED
11-06	Norway	D	1-1	Oslo	ECq	Ganea [64]	24 890	Michel SVK
20-08	Ukraine	W	2-0	Donetsk	Fr	Mutu 2 [25p 57]	28 000	Yegorov RUS
6-09	Luxembourg	W	4-0	Ploiesti	ECq	Mutu [39], Pancu [42], Ganea [44], Bratu [77]	4 500	Yefet ISR
10-09	Denmark	D	2-2	Copenhagen	ECq	Mutu [61], Pancu [72]	42 049	Meier SUI
11-10	Japan	D	1-1	Bucharest	Fr	Mutu [17]	10 000	Carmona Mendez ESP
16-11	Italy	L	0-1	Ancona	Fr		11 700	Stark GER
2004								
18-02	Georgia	W	3-0	Larnaca	Fr	Mutu 2 [30 70], Cernat [87]	300	Lajuks LVA
31-03	Scotland	W	2-1	Glasgow	Fr	Chivu [37], Pancu [51]	20 433	Hyytia FIN
28-04	Germany	W	5-1	Bucharest	Fr	Plesan [21], Rat [23], Danciulescu 2 [35 43], Caramarin [85]	12 000	Rosetti ITA
27-05	Republic of Ireland	L	0-1	Dublin	Fr		42 356	Jara CZE
18-08	Finland	W	2-1	Bucharest	WCq	Mutu [50], Petre [90]	17 500	Gilewski POL
4-09	FYR Macedonia	W	2-1	Craiova	WCq	Pancu [15], Mutu [88]	14 500	Plautz AUT
8-09	Andorra	W	5-1	Andorra la Vella	WCq	Cernat 2 [1 17], Pancu 2 [5 83], Niculae [70]	1 100	Kircher GER
9-10	Czech Republic	L	0-1	Prague	WCq		16 028	Rosetti ITA
17-11	Armenia	D	1-1	Yerevan	WCq	Ciprian [29]	1 403	De Bleeckere BEL
2005								
9-02	Slovakia	D	2-2	Larnaca	Fr	Nicolae [35], Ilie [87]	500	Kapitanis CYP
26-03	Netherlands	L	0-2	Bucharest	WCq		19 000	Medina Cantalejo ESP
30-03	FYR Macedonia	W	2-1	Skopje	WCq	Mitea 2 [18 58]	15 000	Ovrebo NOR
24-05	Moldova	W	2-0	Bacau	Fr	Niculescu [8], Dica [55]		
4-06	Netherlands	L	0-2	Rotterdam	WCq		47 000	De Santis ITA
8-06	Armenia	W	3-0	Constanta	WCq	Petre [29], Bucur 2 [40 78]	5 146	Briakos GRE

Fr = Friendly match • EC = UEFA EURO 2004™ • WC = FIFA World Cup™ • q = qualifier

ROMANIA NATIONAL TEAM RECORDS AND RECORD SEQUENCES

Records			Sequence records					
Victory	9-0	FIN 1973	Wins	8	1996-1997	Clean sheets	5	1996-97, 1999
Defeat	0-9	HUN 1948	Defeats	4	1924-25, 1979	Goals scored	16	1971-1972
Player Caps	125	HAGI Gheorghe	Undefeated	17	1989-1990	Without goal	4	1947-1948
Player Goals	35	HAGI Gheorghe	Without win	20	1968-1971	Goals against	21	1933-1937

ROMANIA COUNTRY INFORMATION

Capital	Bucharest	Independence	1878 from Ottoman Empire	GDP per Capita	$7 000	
Population	22 355 551	Status	Republic	GNP Ranking	53	
Area km²	237 500	Language	Romanian, Hungarian	Dialling code	+40	
Population density	94 per km²	Literacy rate	98%	Internet code	.ro	
% in urban areas	55%	Main religion	Christian	GMT +/−	+2	
Towns/Cities ('000)	Bucharest 1 877; Iasi 318; Cluj-Napoca 316; Timisoara 315; Craiova 304; Constanta 303; Galati 294; Brasov 276; Ploiesti 228; Braila 213; Oradea 203; Bacau 171; Arad 169; Pitesti 167					
Neighbours (km)	Ukraine 531; Moldova 450; Bulgaria 608; Serbia 476; Hungary 443; Black Sea 225					
Main stadia	Stadionul Lia Manoliu – Bucharest 60 120; Stadionul Giulesti – Bucharest 19 100					

NATIONAL CAPS

	Caps
HAGI Gheorghe	125
MUNTEANU Dorinel	122
POPESCU Gheorghe	115
BOLONI Ladislau	104
PETRESCU Dan	95
STELEA Bogdan	91
KLEIN Michael	90
LACATUS Marius	84
REDNIC Mircea	83
LUNG Silviu	77

NATIONAL GOALS

	Goals
HAGI Gheorghe	35
BODOLA Iuliu	30
MOLDOVAN Dinu	25
BOLONI Ladislau	24
CAMATARU Rodion	22
IORDANESCU Anghel	22
GEORGESCU Dudu	21
RADUCIOIU Florin	21
DOBAY Stefan	20
DUMITRESCU Ilie	20

NATIONAL COACH

	Years
CONSTANTIN Gheorghe	1990-'91
RADULESCU Mircea	1991-'92
DINU Cornel	1992-'93
IORDANESCU Anghel	1993-'98
PITURCA Victor	1998-'99
IENEI Emeric	2000
BOLONI Ladislau	2000-'01
HAGI Gheorghe	2001
IORDANESCU Anghel	2002-'04
PITURCA Victor	2004-

FIFA REFEREE LIST 2005

	Int'l	DoB
BALAJ Pavel	2003	17-08-1971
CONSTANTIN Augustus	2002	7-07-1974
CORPODEAN Sorin	1997	29-03-1965
DEACONU Alexandru	2005	3-03-1972
SALOMIR Marian	1999	3-07-1968
SEREA Ionica	2004	6-09-1969
TUDOR Alexandru	2001	13-09-1971

FIFA ASSISTANT REFEREE LIST 2005

	Int'l	DoB
COJOCARU Ispas	2002	2-08-1965
ILIESCU Mihai	2005	4-01-1975
MARODIN Nicolae	2000	22-02-1963
NICA Cristian	2004	13-08-1968
ONITA Aurel	2004	19-10-1969
POPA Ionel	2005	19-07-1966
SAVINU Marcel	2001	16-11-1964
SOVRE Octavian	2005	19-07-1973
SZEKELY Zoltan	2004	30-08-1967
VIDAN George	2000	27-05-1968

CLUB DIRECTORY

Club	Town/City	Stadium	Phone	www.	Lge	Cup	CL
Apulum Alba Iulia	Iulia	Cetate 18 000	+40 258 835834		0	0	0
Arges Pitesti	Pitesti	Nicolae Dobrin 15 170	+40 248 217214		2	0	0
FCM Bacau	Bacau	Dumitru Sechelariu 17 500	+40 234 570617	fcmbacau.ro	0	0	0
FC Brasov	Brasov	Tineretului 12 670	+40 268 325454	fcbrasov.ro	0	0	0
CFR Cluj	Cluj	Gruia 6 000	+40 264 406325		0	0	0
Universitatea Craiova	Craiova	Ion Oblemenco 27 915	+40 251 414726	fcuniversitatea.ro	4	6	0
Dinamo Bucuresti	Bucuresti	Dinamo 15 138	+40 21 2106974	fcdinamo.ro	17	12	0
Farul Constanta	Constanta	Gheorghe Hagi 15 520	+40 241 616142	fcfarul.ro	0	0	0
Gloria Bistrita	Bistrita	Gloria 15 000	+40 263 212998	cfgloria.ro	0	1	0
Politehnica Iasi	Iasi	Emil Alexandrescu 12 500	+40 232 213018	politehnicaiasi.ro	0	0	0
National Bucuresti	Bucuresti	Cotroceni 14 542	+40 21 4106606	nationalfc.ro	0	1	0
Otelul Galati	Galati	Otelul 13 932	+40 236 464677		0	0	0
Politehnica AEK Timisoara	Timisoara	Dan Paltinisanu 40 000	+40 256 198808		0	2	0
Rapid Bucuresti	Bucuresti	Giulesti 19 100	+40 21 2234390	fcrapid.ro	3	11	0
Sportul Studentesc	Bucuresti	Aurica Radulescu 15 000	+40 21 2125059	fcsportulstudentesc.ro	0	0	0
Steaua Bucuresti	Bucuresti	Ghencea 27 063	+40 21 4034250	steaua.ro	22	21	1

RECENT LEAGUE AND CUP RECORD

	Championship						Cup		
Year	Champions	Pts	Runners-up	Pts	Third	Pts	Winners	Score	Runners-up
1990	Dinamo Bucuresti	57	Steaua Bucuresti	56	Universit. Craiova	44	Dinamo Bucuresti	6-4	Steaua Bucuresti
1991	Universit. Craiova	50	Steaua Bucuresti	50	Dinamo Bucuresti	43	Universit. Craiova	2-1	FC Bacau
1992	Dinamo Bucuresti	55	Steaua Bucuresti	48	Electroput. Craiova	39	Steaua Bucuresti	1-1 4-3p	Politehn. Timisoara
1993	Steaua Bucuresti	48	Dinamo Bucuresti	47	Universit. Craiova	37	Universit. Craiova	2-0	Dacia Unirea Braila
1994	Steaua Bucuresti	53	Universit. Craiova	40	Dinamo Bucuresti	39	Gloria Bistrita	1-0	Universit. Craiova
1995	Steaua Bucuresti	77	Universit. Craiova	68	Dinamo Bucuresti	65	Petrolul Ploiesti	1-1 5-3p	Rapid Bucuresti
1996	Steaua Bucuresti	71	National Bucuresti	60	Rapid Bucuresti	59	Steaua Bucuresti	3-1	Gloria Bistrita
1997	Steaua Bucuresti	73	National Bucuresti	68	Dinamo Bucuresti	59	Steaua Bucuresti	4-2	National Bucuresti
1998	Steaua Bucuresti	80	Rapid Bucuresti	78	Arges Pitesti	65	Rapid Bucuresti	1-0	Universit. Craiova
1999	Rapid Bucuresti	89	Dinamo Bucuresti	82	Steaua Bucuresti	66	Steaua Bucuresti	2-2 4-2p	Rapid Bucuresti
2000	Dinamo Bucuresti	84	Rapid Bucuresti	72	Ceahlaul P. Neamt	57	Dinamo Bucuresti	2-0	Universit. Craiova
2001	Steaua Bucuresti	60	Dinamo Bucuresti	51	FC Brasov	50	Dinamo Bucuresti	4-2	Rocar Bucuresti
2002	Dinamo Bucuresti	60	National Bucuresti	58	Rapid Bucuresti	50	Rapid Bucuresti	2-1	Dinamo Bucuresti
2003	Rapid Bucuresti	63	Steaua Bucuresti	56	Gloria Bistrita	45	Dinamo Bucuresti	1-0	National Bucuresti
2004	Dinamo Bucuresti	70	Steaua Bucuresti	64	Rapid Bucuresti	55	Dinamo Bucuresti	2-0	Otelul Galati
2005	Steaua Bucuresti	63	Dinamo Bucuresti	62	Rapid Bucuresti	57	Dinamo Bucuresti	1-0	Farul Constanta

ROMANIA 2004-05

DIVIZIA A

	Pl	W	D	L	F	A	Pts	Steaua	Dinamo	Rapid	National	Farul	Poli'nica	Sportul	Otelul	Poli	Arges	Cluj	Bacau	Gloria	Apulum	Brasov	Craiova
Steaua Bucuresti †	30	19	6	5	47	18	63		1-0	0-0	5-1	3-1	2-1	1-0	1-0	0-1	2-0	1-0	2-0	2-0	3-0	3-2	5-0
Dinamo Bucuresti ‡	30	20	2	8	60	30	62	0-1		2-2	0-1	2-0	1-0	2-1	4-0	2-0	4-0	4-0	3-0	4-1	4-2	3-1	5-0
Rapid Bucuresti ‡	30	16	9	5	51	27	57	2-1	2-1		3-0	3-1	0-3	3-0	2-0	3-2	3-0	2-0	3-1	2-2	2-0	4-0	
National Bucuresti	30	17	6	7	50	33	57	1-0	5-1	3-3		2-2	1-2	2-1	0-0	6-0	2-1	2-2	2-1	1-0	3-0	2-1	3-1
Farul Constanta	30	15	7	8	42	28	52	1-0	1-0	2-0	2-1		4-0	1-1	2-0	2-1	3-0	0-1	1-0	1-0	4-0	3-2	2-1
Politehnica Timisoara	30	13	6	11	37	34	45	1-1	2-3	1-1	1-4	1-0		2-0	2-1	2-0	0-2	3-0	2-1	2-1	1-1	2-1	2-0
Sportul Studentesc	30	12	9	9	37	27	45	1-2	0-1	0-0	1-0	1-1	0-0		3-2	1-1	0-0	2-1	1-0	1-0	1-2	2-0	
Otelul Galati	30	12	4	14	31	32	40	1-0	2-0	1-0	0-2	1-0	1-0	1-0		1-0	1-2	1-2	1-0	2-1	2-0	1-1	0-0
Poli Unirea Iasi	30	10	8	12	28	41	38	0-0	2-3	1-2	1-2	2-2	3-1	1-3	1-0		1-1	0-0	1-0	1-0	1-0	2-1	1-0
Arges Pitesti	30	8	12	10	32	37	36	2-2	0-1	0-0	0-1	1-1	0-0	2-2	1-1	3-0		2-0	0-0	4-3	1-1	0-1	1-1
Ecomax Cluj	30	9	9	12	33	44	36	0-2	4-2	1-1	0-1	0-0	2-1	1-1	1-0	1-1	1-1		2-0	1-2	2-1	2-1	1-1
FCM Bacau	30	8	9	13	20	28	33	2-2	0-2	2-1	1-0	1-0	2-1	1-1	1-0	0-1	1-0	2-0		3-0	0-0	0-0	1-1
Gloria Bistrita	30	9	5	16	38	46	32	0-2	0-1	0-2	0-0	1-2	0-0	0-5	3-0	2-2	3-0	2-0	1-0		6-1	2-0	4-3
Apulum Alba-Iulia	30	6	8	16	28	62	26	1-1	1-3	1-1	0-1	2-3	2-1	0-4	0-4	2-1	1-3	2-4	0-0	1-1		1-0	1-0
FC Brasov	30	5	6	19	28	45	21	0-1	1-1	0-1	1-1	1-0	0-1	1-0	0-1	0-1	2-1	1-2	0-1	2-2	0-0		1-3
Universitatea Craiova	30	4	8	18	24	54	20	0-1	0-1	2-0	3-0	0-0	0-1	0-1	0-6	0-0	1-2	3-2	1-1	1-1	1-2	1-3	

30/07/2004 - 15/05/2005 • † Qualified for the UEFA Champions League • ‡ Qualified for the UEFA Cup

ROMANIA 2004-05
DIVIZIA B SERIA 1

	Pl	W	D	L	F	A	Pts
FC Vaslui	30	19	7	4	50	20	64
Midia Navodari	30	15	9	6	41	26	54
Dunarea Galati	30	15	7	8	39	33	52
Dacia Unirea Braila	30	14	8	8	43	20	50
Ceahlaul Piatra Neamt	30	13	7	10	34	20	46
Gloria Buzau	30	12	10	8	38	25	46
Petrolul Moinesti	30	13	7	10	35	26	46
Callatis Mangalia	30	11	13	6	34	24	46
FC Botosani	30	13	6	11	31	22	45
Precizia Sacele	30	11	9	10	28	25	42
Altay Constanta	30	10	9	11	37	42	39
FCM Targoviste	30	8	10	12	28	42	34
Laminorul Roman	30	9	6	15	29	35	33
FC Ghimbav	30	5	9	16	26	47	24
Unirea Focsani	30	6	6	18	17	44	24
Politehnica Timisoara	30	4	1	25	18	77	13

21/08/2004 - 11/06/2005

ROMANIA 2004-05
DIVIZIA B SERIA 2

	Pl	W	D	L	F	A	Pts
Pandurii Lignitul	30	19	8	3	51	16	65
FC Sibiu	30	19	7	4	48	25	64
CS Otopeni	30	18	5	7	51	27	59
Petrolul Ploiesti	30	17	7	6	59	21	58
Unirea Valahorum	30	14	5	11	55	46	47
Electromagnetica	30	11	8	11	48	49	41
Dacia Mioveni	30	12	5	13	49	52	41
Dinamo II Bucuresti	30	11	7	12	39	35	40
FC Caracal	30	11	6	13	31	32	39
Minerul Motru	30	10	6	14	31	49	36
Inter-Gaz Bucuresti	30	9	9	12	38	42	36
Juventus Colentina	30	10	5	15	28	46	35
International Pitesti	30	9	5	16	29	50	32
Oltul Slatina	30	7	9	14	19	36	30
Turnu Severin	30	7	9	14	28	35	30
Rulmentul Alexandria	30	2	7	21	13	56	13

21/08/2004 - 11/06/2005

ROMANIA 2004-05
DIVIZIA B SERIA 3

	Pl	W	D	L	F	A	Pts
Jiul Petrosani	28	20	5	3	64	19	65
Gaz Metan Medias	28	20	5	3	48	19	65
FC Oradea	28	16	6	6	45	21	54
Olimpia Satu Mare	28	15	4	9	37	23	49
Liberty Salonta	28	11	9	8	37	34	42
Armatura Zalau	28	10	11	7	44	32	41
Universitatea Cluj	28	12	4	12	41	33	40
Campia Turzii	28	11	7	10	28	36	40
Unirea Sannicolau	28	10	7	11	36	38	37
UT Arad	28	9	6	13	31	40	33
Tricotaje Ineu	28	9	5	14	39	57	32
CS Deva	28	8	6	14	30	39	30
Unirea Dej	28	6	4	18	21	47	22
Oasul Negresti	28	7	1	20	24	56	22
ACU Arad	28	1	10	17	16	47	13
Corvinul Hunedoara	Excluded after 12 rounds						

21/08/2004 - 11/06/2005

CUPA ROMANIEI 2004-05

Quarter-finals			Semi-finals			Final		
Dinamo Bucuresti	1	2						
Dacia Braila	0	0	Dinamo Bucuresti	1	4			
Sportul Bucuresti	2	0	National Bucuresti	2	0			
National Bucuresti	0	3				Dinamo Bucuresti	1	
Univ. Craiova	1	1				Farul Constanta	0	
Arges Pitesti	0	1	Univ. Craiova	0	2			
Otelul Galati	1	0	Farul Constanta	1	1	11-05-2005 National, Bucharest		
Farul Constanta	2	2						

RSA – SOUTH AFRICA

NATIONAL TEAM RECORD
JULY 1ST 2002 TO JUNE 30TH 2005

PL	W	D	L	F	A	%
43	21	11	11	57	42	61.6

FIFA/COCA-COLA WORLD RANKING

1993	1994	1995	1996	1997	1998	1999	2000	2001	2002	2003	2004	High		Low	
95	56	40	19	31	26	30	20	35	30	36	38	16	08/96	109	08/93

2004-2005											
08/04	09/04	10/04	11/04	12/04	01/05	02/05	03/05	04/05	05/05	06/05	07/05
41	39	40	41	38	38	40	40	37	38	39	38

Founder members of CAF, South Africa found themselves banned by the organisation and FIFA during much of the apartheid era before rejoining the fold in 1992. Football has since made great progress and the national team have a record of which many established nations would be envious. The rehabilitation will be complete in 2010 when South Africa hosts the FIFA World Cup™. However, qualification for 2006 has proved a stern task as Bafana Bafana found their status as group favourites undermined by Ghana. A place at the CAF African Cup of Nations was on offer too, a competition that South Africa won just four years after being readmitted by FIFA, were

INTERNATIONAL HONOURS
CAF African Cup of Nations 1996 CAF Champions League Orlando Pirates 1995

runners-up in 1998 and third in 2000. With such a successful record, failure to qualify is not seen as an option. Invited to the 2005 CONCACAF Gold Cup in the USA and amid lowered expectations, South Africa performed well including a victory over Mexico to reach the quarter-finals. Kaizer Chiefs won the League title for the 10th time along with the Coca-Cola League Cup, while SuperSport United took the main Cup competition, the ABSA Cup after beating Wits University 1-0 in the final. However, Chiefs also earned themselves a three-year ban from CAF after withdrawing from a Confederation Cup tie with Ismaili of Egypt.

THE FIFA BIG COUNT OF 2000

	Male	Female		Male	Female
Registered players	40 000	4 000	Referees	700	0
Non registered players	400 000	8 000	Officials	10 000	0
Youth players	60 000	2 000	Total involved	524 700	
Total players	514 000		Number of clubs	300	
Professional players	250	0	Number of teams	2 000	

South African Football Association (SAFA)
First National Bank Stadium, PO Box 910, Johannesburg 2000, South Africa
Tel +27 11 4943522   Fax +27 11 4943013
safa@safa.net   www.safa.net
President: OLIPHANT Molefi   General Secretary: HACK Raymond
Vice-President: KHOZA Irvin   Treasurer: HULYO Gronie   Media Officer: MARAWA Gugu
Men's Coach: BAXTER Stuart   Women's Coach: TBD
SAFA formed: 1991   CAF: 1992   FIFA: 1992
Colours: White with yellow stripes, White, White

GAMES PLAYED BY SOUTH AFRICA IN THE 2006 FIFA WORLD CUP™ CYCLE

2002	Opponents	Score		Venue	Comp	Scorers	Att	Referee
21-07	Madagascar	D	0-0	Port Elizabeth	CCqf	W 4-1p	8 000	Colembi ANG
24-08	Swaziland	W	4-1	Polokwane	CCsf	Mokoena 2 [28 64], Pule [77p], Fredricks [90]	30 000	Katjimune NAM
8-09	Côte d'Ivoire	D	0-0	Abidjan	CNq		30 000	Coulibaly MLI
21-09	Malawi	W	3-1	Blantyre	CCf	Mayo 2 [42 58], Kauleza [88]	60 000	Shikapande ZAM
28-09	Malawi	W	1-0	Durban	CCf	Vilakazi [90]		Musasa ZIM
12-10	Burundi	W	2-0	Bloemfontein	CNq	Mayo [12], Buckly [39]	30 000	Madarbocus MRI
23-10	Kenya	D	1-1	Arusha	Fr	Kukame [51]. L 4-5p		
26-10	Tanzania	D	1-1	Dar es Saalam	Fr	Ntsoane [73]. W 4-3p		
19-11	Senegal	D	1-1	Johannesburg	Fr	Bartlett [66]. L 1-4p	40 000	Tangawarima ZIM
2003								
29-03	Madagascar	W	2-0	Johannesburg	Fr	Manyathela [42], Ramarojaona OG [82]	5 000	Shikapande
30-04	Jamaica	D	0-0	Cape Town	Fr			Musasa ZIM
22-05	England	L	1-2	Durban	Fr	McCarthy [18p]	48 000	Lim Kee Chong MRI
14-06	Trinidad and Tobago	W	2-1	Port Elizabeth	Fr	Manyathela 2 [20 71p]		Mpofu BOT
22-06	Côte d'Ivoire	W	2-1	Johannesburg	CNq	Bartlett [21], Nomvete [65]	35 000	Maillet SEY
6-07	Burundi	W	2-0	Bujumbura	CNq	Mokoena [1], Fredricks [30]	8 000	Teshome ETH
19-07	Zimbabwe	L	0-1	East London	CC		7 000	Raolimanana MAD
8-10	Lesotho	W	3-0	Maseru	Fr	Moshoeu [23], Seema OG [66], Raselemane [72]	20 000	
11-10	Costa Rica	W	2-1	Johannesburg	Fr	Nomvete [75], Mayo [87]		Bwanya ZIM
15-11	Egypt	L	1-2	Cairo	Fr	McCarthy [50]	10 000	Mohammed LBY
19-11	Tunisia	L	0-2	Tunis	Fr		12 000	Chaibu NGA
2004								
10-01	Mauritius	L	0-2	Curepipe	CC		5 230	Raolimanana MAD
18-01	Senegal	L	1-2	Dakar	Fr	Nomvete [15]	50 000	El Achiri MAR
27-01	Benin	W	2-0	Sfax	CNr1	Nomvete 2 [58 76]	12 000	Coulibaly MLI
31-01	Nigeria	L	0-4	Monastir	CNr1		15 000	Bujsaim UAE
4-02	Morocco	D	1-1	Sousse	CNr1	Mayo [29]	6 000	Guirat TUN
30-03	Australia	L	0-1	London	Fr		16 108	Halsey ENG
5-06	Cape Verde Islands	W	2-1	Bloemfontein	WCq	Mabizela 2 [40 68]	30 000	Tessema ETH
20-06	Ghana	L	0-3	Kumasi	WCq		32 000	Diatta SEN
3-07	Burkina Faso	W	2-0	Johannesburg	WCq	Pienaar [14], Bartlett [42]	25 000	Ramanampamony MAD
18-08	Tunisia	W	2-0	Tunis	Fr	McCarthy [2], Arsendse [82]	4 000	Zekrini ALG
5-09	Congo DR	L	0-1	Kinshasa	WCq		85 000	Hicuburundi BDI
10-10	Uganda	W	1-0	Kampala	WCq	McCarthy [68p]	50 000	Gasingwa RWA
17-11	Nigeria	W	2-1	Johannesburg	Fr	Bartlett [2], Vilakazi [60]	39 817	Marang ZIM
2005								
9-02	Australia	D	1-1	Durban	Fr	McCarthy [12]		Lim Kee Chong MRI
26-02	Seychelles	W	3-0	Curepipe	CCr1	Mphela 2 [12 16], Chabangu [44]	3 000	Roheemun MRI
27-02	Mauritius	W	1-0	Curepipe	CCr1	Mphela [36]	3 500	Mnkantjo ZIM
26-03	Uganda	W	2-1	Johannesburg	WCq	Fortune [21p], Pienaar [71]	20 000	Chukwujekwu NGA
4-06	Cape Verde Islands	W	2-1	Praia	WCq	McCarthy [10], Buckley [12]	6 000	Benouza ALG
18-06	Ghana	L	0-2	Johannesburg	WCq		50 000	Guezzaz MAR
8-07	Mexico	W	2-1	Carson	GCr1	Evans [28], Van Heerden [41]	27 000	Sibrian SLV
10-07	Jamaica	D	3-3	Los Angeles	GCr1	Raselemane [35], Ndela [41], Nomvete [56]	30 710	Stott USA
13-07	Guatemala	D	1-1	Houston	GCr1	Nkosi [45]	45 311	Sott USA
17-07	Panama	D	1-1	Houston	GCqf	Ndlela [68]	60 050	Prendergast JAM

Fr = Friendly match • CN = CAF African Cup of Nations • CC = COSAFA Cup • GC = CONCACAF Gold Cup • WC = FIFA World Cup™
q = qualifier • r1 = first round group • qf = quarter-final • sf = semi-final • f = final

SOUTH AFRICA COUNTRY INFORMATION

Capital	Pretoria	Independence	1934	GDP per Capita	$10 700
Population	42 718 530	Status	Republic	GNP Ranking	30
Area km²	1 219 912	Language	Afrikaans, English, Zulu	Dialling code	+27
Population density	35 per km²	Literacy rate	86%	Internet code	.za
% in urban areas	51%	Main religion	Christian	GMT +/–	+2

Towns/Cities ('000)	Johannesburg 5 226; Cape Town 4 302; Durban 3 120; Pretoria 1 884; Port Elizabeth 1 224; Pietermaritzburg 750; Vereeniging 730; Bloemfontein 463; Welkom 432; East London 421
Neighbours (km)	Mozambique 491; Swaziland 430; Lesotho 909; Botswana 1 840; Namibia 967; Zimbabwe 225; South Atlantic & Indian Ocean 2 798
Main stadia	FNB – Johannesburg 90 000; ABSA – Durban 55 000; Newlands – Cape Town 50 900

SOUTH AFRICA NATIONAL TEAM RECORDS AND RECORD SEQUENCES

Records			Sequence records					
Victory	8-0	AUS 1955	Wins	7	1947-50, 1954-92	Clean sheets	7	1997-1997, 2002
Defeat	1-5	AUS 1947	Defeats	3	Five times	Goals scored	12	1947-1950
Player Caps	73	MOSHOEU John	Undefeated	15	1994-1996	Without goal	2	Six times
Player Goals	27	McCARTHY Benedict	Without win	9	1997-1998	Goals against	11	1998

NATIONAL CAPS

	Caps
MOSHOEU John	73
BARTLETT Shaun	72
RADEBE Lucas	70
ARENDSE Andre	67
MKHALELE Helman	66
FISH Mark	62
MCCARTHY Benedict	59

NATIONAL GOALS

	Goals
MCCARTHY Benedict	27
BARTLETT Shaun	26
MASINGA Philemon	19
NOMVETE Siyabonga	13
WILLIAMS Mark	9
KHUMALO Theophilus	9
MOSHOEU John	8

NATIONAL COACH

	Years
MOLOTO Trott	2002
SONO Jomo	2002
MASHABA Ephraim	2002-'03
KUBHEKA Kenneth	2003
MASHABA Ephraim	2003
PHUMO April	2004
BAXTER Stuart	2004-

FIFA REFEREE LIST 2005

	Int'l	DoB
BENNETT Daniel	2003	22-08-1976
DAMON Jerome	2000	4-04-1972
NCOBO Aldrin	2004	10-10-1967
NHLAPO Jonas	2004	4-12-1969

FIFA ASSISTANT REFEREE LIST 2005

	Int'l	DoB
JIBILIZA Siphiwo	2001	31-03-1971
MALEBO Toko	2004	11-09-1975
MATELA Lazarus	1995	18-08-1965
MDLULI Andrew	1998	15-08-1960
MOLEFE Tshotleno	2000	4-06-1968
MOTLOUNG Reginald	1994	27-07-1967
RADEBE Happy	2001	1-01-1968

CLUB DIRECTORY

Club	Town/City	Stadium	Phone	www.	Lge	Cup	CL
Ajax	Capetown	Newlands 50 900	+27 21 9306001	ajaxct.com	0	0	0
Black Leopards	Johannesburg	Thohoyandou	+27 11 8349571	blackleopardsfc.com	0	0	0
Bloemfontein Celtic	Bloemfontein	Seisa Ramabodu 20 000	+27 51 4471183	bloemfonteincelticfc.co.za	0	1	0
Bush Bucks	East London	Absa	+27 43 7312890	bushbucks.co.za	1	0	0
Dynamos	Pietersburg	Giyani 35 000	+27 15 2911391		0	0	0
Golden Arrows	Durban	King Zwelithini 25 000	+27 31 3039848		0	0	0
Jomo Cosmos	Johannesburg	Makhulong	+27 11 6836120	jomocosmos.co.za	1	1	0
Kaizer Chiefs	Johannesburg	FNB 90 000	+27 11 9411465	kaizerchiefs.co.za	5	3	0
Manning Rangers	Durban	Chatsworth 35 000	+27 31 3685844		2	0	0
Moroka Swallows	Johannesburg	Rand 30 000	+27 11 4846138	morokaswallows.co.za	0	3	0
Orlando Pirates	Johannesburg	JHB	+27 11 4842084	orlandopiratesfc.com	3	2	1
Santos	Cape Town	Athlone 25 000			1	2	0
Silver Stars	Johannesburg	Peter Mokaba	+27 11 6159028		0	0	0
SuperSport United	Pretoria	Securicor Loftus 52 000	+27 11 6867675	sufc.co.za	0	2	0
Sundowns	Pretoria	Securicor Loftus 52 000	+27 11 3935007	sundownsfc.com	6	2	0
Wits University	Johannesburg	BidVest	+27 11 7177677	witsfc.co.za	0	0	0

RECENT LEAGUE AND CUP RECORD

	Championship						Cup		
Year	Champions	Pts	Runners-up	Pts	Third	Pts	Winners	Score	Runners-up
1990	Mamelodi Sundowns	55	Kaizer Chiefs	55	Orlando Pirates	48	Jomo Cosmos	1-0	Amazulu
1991	Kaizer Chiefs	57	Mamelodi Sundowns	53	Fairway Stars	46	Moroka Swallows	3-1 2-0	Jomo Cosmos
1992	Kaizer Chiefs	60	Hellenic	57	Wits University	51	Kaizer Chiefs	1-1 1-0	Jomo Cosmos
1993	Mamelodi Sundowns	55	Moroka Swallows	52	Amazulu	48	Witbank Aces	1-0	Kaizer Chiefs
1994	Orlando Pirates	50	Cape Town Spurs	49	Umtata Bucks	41	Vaal Professionals	1-0	Qwa Qwa Stars
1995	Cape Town Spurs	71	Mamelodi Sundowns	66	Orlando Pirates	60	Cape Town Spurs	3-2	Pretoria City
1996	Not played due to season adjustment						Orlando Pirates	1-0	Jomo Cosmos
1997	Manning Rangers	74	Kaizer Chiefs	66	Orlando Pirates	64	No tournament played		
1998	Mamelodi Sundowns	68	Kaizer Chiefs	63	Orlando Pirates	57	Mamelodi Sundowns	1-1 1-1 6-5p	Orlando Pirates
1999	Mamelodi Sundowns	75	Kaizer Chiefs	75	Orlando Pirates	60	SuperSport United	2-1	Kaizer Chiefs
2000	Mamelodi Sundowns	75	Orlando Pirates	64	Kaizer Chiefs	60	Kaiser Chiefs	1-0	Mamelodi Sundowns
2001	Orlando Pirates	61	Kaizer Chiefs	60	Mamelodi Sundowns	59	Santos Cape Town	1-0	Mamelodi Sundowns
2002	Santos Cape Town	64	SuperSport United	59	Orlando Pirates	57	No tournament played		
2003	Orlando Pirates	61	SuperSport United	55	Wits University	54	Santos Cape Town	2-0	Ajax Cape Town
2004	Kaizer Chiefs	63	Ajax Cape Town	57	SuperSport United	53	Moroka Swallows	3-1	Manning Rangers
2005	Kaizer Chiefs	62	Orlando Pirates	60	Mamelodi Sundowns	56	SuperSport United	1-0	Wits University

SOUTH AFRICA 2004-05

PREMIER SOCCER LEAGUE

	Pl	W	D	L	F	A	Pts	Chiefs	Pirates	Sundowns	S'Sport	Swallows	Ajax	Silver Stars	Celtic	Arrows	Dynamos	Bucks	Santos	Cosmos	Leopards	Rangers	Wits
Kaizer Chiefs	30	17	11	2	55	26	62		1-1	1-1	0-0	2-0	2-2	2-1	4-1	2-2	1-1	2-2	1-0	0-0	3-0	3-0	1-0
Orlando Pirates †	30	17	9	4	52	29	60	2-1		0-4	2-1	1-1	6-0	2-1	1-1	3-2	3-1	1-1	1-2	1-0	1-0	3-1	1-1
Sundowns †	30	16	8	6	54	28	56	3-4	1-2		1-2	1-1	4-0	1-0	3-1	0-0	0-0	2-0	2-1	2-0	3-0	5-1	3-2
SuperSport United ‡	30	13	12	5	37	27	51	0-1	4-3	0-1		2-2	1-1	0-0	1-1	2-1	1-1	3-1	1-0	1-1	2-2	1-2	0-0
Moroka Swallows ‡	30	13	10	7	38	29	49	1-0	2-2	0-0	0-0		3-0	1-0	2-1	2-0	1-0	2-3	1-1	2-1	1-1	2-1	1-0
Ajax Cape Town	30	11	8	11	31	37	41	1-2	0-1	1-1	1-3	1-2		1-0	3-0	1-0	0-3	1-1	1-0	2-0	1-1	3-1	2-1
Silver Stars	30	9	11	10	33	30	38	0-0	0-2	2-2	0-1	0-1	1-0		1-1	2-1	0-2	2-1	2-0	1-1	1-1	4-1	3-3
Bloemfontein Celtic	30	9	9	12	32	40	36	0-2	1-0	1-2	0-1	2-1	1-1	0-2		2-0	2-1	0-1	3-1	0-1	1-1	1-0	4-3
Golden Arrows	30	8	9	13	29	34	33	1-1	0-0	5-2	1-1	1-0	0-2	1-1	0-2		0-1	3-1	1-0	1-0	1-0	1-1	0-1
Dynamos	30	7	12	11	38	45	33	1-4	0-3	1-2	1-2	3-2	1-2	2-4	1-1	1-1		2-3	0-0	1-1	4-3	0-0	1-1
Bush Bucks	30	8	9	13	39	48	33	3-4	1-2	0-3	0-1	1-0	2-0	1-1	0-1	1-1	2-2		1-1	1-0	0-0	4-1	2-0
Santos	30	8	7	15	27	36	31	0-1	0-0	0-2	2-0	1-0	1-2	1-1	2-0	2-1	1-3	3-0		0-2	0-3	0-0	0-2
Jomo Cosmos	30	7	10	13	27	38	31	0-3	0-3	0-2	1-4	1-1	2-1	0-0	1-2	0-2	4-1	1-1	4-1		3-1	1-0	0-0
Black Leopards	30	6	13	11	30	42	31	0-2	2-3	2-1	1-1	2-2	0-0	0-2	2-2	1-1	0-0	2-1	0-2	0-0		1-0	1-2
Manning Rangers	30	7	8	15	28	49	29	2-2	1-1	1-0	0-1	1-2	0-2	2-1	1-0	1-1	3-2	1-4	4-2	0-1			0-0
Wits University	30	5	12	13	24	34	27	1-2	0-1	0-0	1-2	0-2	0-0	0-0	0-0	2-1	0-2	4-2	0-0	0-0	0-2	1-1	

6/08/2004 - 24/05/2005 • † Qualified for the CAF Champions League • ‡ Qualified for the CAF Confederation Cup

SOUTH AFRICA 2004-05
MVELA GOLDEN LEAGUE (2)

	Pl	W	D	L	F	A	Pts
Free State Stars	34	19	10	5	46	23	67
Durban Stars	34	17	9	8	48	35	60
Hellenic	34	18	5	11	60	43	59
Classic	34	18	5	11	54	41	59
Maritzburg United	34	16	9	9	54	36	57
Zulu Royals	34	15	8	11	44	31	53
Vasco da Gama	34	14	11	9	43	39	53
FC Fortune	34	11	13	10	36	33	46
Pietersburg Pillars	34	11	10	13	43	44	43
B'fontein Young Tigers	34	11	9	14	51	51	42
Winners Park	34	10	12	12	37	43	42
Pretoria University	34	10	11	13	48	44	41
Mabopane Young Masters	34	9	11	14	45	51	38
Uthukela	34	9	11	14	33	45	38
Dangerous Darkies	34	7	15	12	34	45	36
North-West Tigers	34	7	14	13	27	40	35
Avendale Athletico	34	8	8	18	47	65	32
Louisvale Pirates	34	6	9	19	22	63	27

28/08/2004 - 22/05/2005

ABSA CUP 2004-05

Second Round

SuperSport United *	8
Tornado	0
Jomo Cosmos *	1
Sundowns	2
Bush Bucks	2 4p
People's Bank Spurs *	2 3p
Cemforce	0
Santos *	6
Dynamos *	2
Dangerous Darkies	1
Black Leopards	0
Orlando Pirates *	4
Moroka Swallows	1 4p
Manning Rangers *	1 2p
Kaizer Chiefs *	0 3p
Wits University	0 4p

Quarter-finals

SuperSport United	3
Sundowns *	2
Bush Bucks	0
Santos *	3
Dynamos *	2
Orlando Pirates	0
Moroka Swallows	1
Wits University *	2

Semi-finals

SuperSport United	5
Santos	0
Dynamos	0
Wits University	2

Final

SuperSport United	1
Wits University	0

CUP FINAL

28-05-2005, Rustenburg

Scorer - Ndlela 44 for SuperSport

* Home team

ORLANDO PIRATES 2004-2005

Date	Opponents	Score		Comp	Scorers
9-07-2004	Sable Batié - CMR	W 4-2	H	CCir	Kauleza [13], Vilakazi [21], Makhanya [44], Mokoena [75]
25-07-2004	Sable Batié - CMR	D 0-0	A	CCir	Abandoned 50' due to rain
31-07-2004	Sundowns	L 0-1	N	TCsf	
6-08-2004	Jomo Cosmos	W 1-0	H	PSL	Leremi [51]
15-08-2004	Sable Batié - CMR	-	A	CCir	Pirates did not turn up and were disqualified
22-08-2004	Wits University	L 1-2	A	SEqf	Kauleza [18]
29-08-2004	Golden Arrows	D 0-0	A	PSL	
8-09-2004	Manning Rangers	D 1-1	A	PSL	
11-09-2004	Black Leopards	W 3-2	A	PSL	Arendse 2 [65 70], Leremi [85p]
22-09-2004	Ajax Cape Town	W 6-0	H	PSL	Vilakazi [25], Arense [42], Manenzhe 2 [50 54], Leremi [68], Netshodwe [88]
26-09-2004	Moroka Swallows	D 2-2	A	PSL	Lekoelea [63], Arendse [69]
13-10-2004	Bloemfontein Celtic	D 1-1	H	PSL	Mothibi [30]
17-10-2004	Dynamos	W 3-0	A	PSL	Vilakazi [9], Lekoelea [69], Mokoena [86]
30-10-2004	Kaizer Chiefs	W 2-1	H	PSL	Leremi [1], Vilakazi [87]
7-11-2004	Sundowns	L 1-3	A	LCr1	
14-11-2004	Sundowns	W 2-1	A	PSL	Manenzhe [20], Dinha [32]
28-11-2004	Silver Stars	W 2-0	A	PSL	Manenzhe [40], Dinha [77p]
11-12-2004	SuperSport United	W 2-0	H	PSL	Lekoelea [33], Mokoena [91+]
19-12-2004	Santos	D 0-0	A	PSL	
8-01-2005	Wits University	D 1-1	H	PSL	Manenzhe [28]
15-01-2005	Bush Bucks	W 2-1	A	PSL	Arendse [48], Mutapa [71]
19-01-2005	Jomo Cosmos	W 3-0	A	PSL	Lekoelea 2 [33 65], Manenzhe [81]
22-01-2005	Golden Arrows	W 3-2	H	PSL	Arendse 2 [37 65], Leremi [45]
29-01-2005	SuperSport United	L 3-4	A	PSL	Lekgwathi [24], Leremi [26], OG [53]
5-02-2005	Black Leopards	W 1-0	H	PSL	Vilakazi [50]
12-02-2005	Moroka Swallows	D 1-1	H	PSL	Manenzhe [92+]
16-02-2005	Manning Rangers	W 3-1	H	PSL	Vilakazi [12], Lekgwathi [27], Dinha [55]
27-02-2005	Silver Stars	W 1-0	H	CUPr1	Kauleza [54]
2-03-2005	Bloemfontein Celtic	L 0-1	A	PSL	
6-03-2005	Dynamos	W 3-1	H	PSL	Manenzhe 2 [33 51], Lekgwathi [81]
12-03-2005	Black Leopards	W 4-0	H	CUPr2	Manenzhe [26], Tau [47], Lekoelea 2 [83 88]
2-04-2005	Sundowns	L 0-4	H	PSL	
9-04-2005	Silver Stars	W 2-1	H	PSL	Lekoelea [53], Mutapa [85]
17-04-2005	Dynamos	L 0-2	A	CUPqf	
23-04-2005	Santos	L 1-2	H	PSL	Mutapa [57]
30-04-2005	Kaizer Chiefs	D 1-1	A	PSL	Vilakazi [64]
3-05-2005	Ajax Cape Town	W 1-0	A	PSL	Vilakazi [5]
8-05-2005	Wits University	W 1-0	A	PSL	Leremi [31]
22-05-2005	Bush Bucks	D 1-1	H	PSL	OG [12]

CC = CAF Confederation Cup • TC = Telekom Charity Cup • PSL = Premier Soccer League • SE = SAA Supa8 Cup • LC = Coca-Cola League Cup
CUP = ABSA Cup • ir = Intermediate round • r1 = first round • r2 = second round • qf = quarter-final • sf = semi-final
H = JHB Stadium • **H** = Ellis Park • *H* = FNB Stadium

COCA-COLA LEAGUE CUP 2004

First Round		Quarter-finals		Semi-finals		Final
Kaizer Chiefs	2					
Golden Arrows *	1	**Kaizer Chiefs ***	4			
Ajax Cape Town	0	Dynamos	0			
Dynamos *	2			**Kaizer Chiefs**	2 2p	
Black Leopards	2			Moroka Swallows	2 0p	
Silver Stars *	1	Black Leopards *	0			
Bloemfontein Celtic *	2	**Moroka Swallows**	2			**Kaizer Chiefs** 1
Moroka Swallows	3					SuperSport United 0
Wits University *	3					
Manning Rangers	0	**Wits University ***	2			
Orlando Pirates	1	Sundowns	1			
Sundowns *	3			Wits University	0 3p	**CUP FINAL**
Jomo Cosmos *	3			**SuperSport United**	0 4p	
Santos	1	Jomo Cosmos	0			18-12-2004
Bush Bucks	1	**SuperSport United ***	1			Vodacom Park, Bloemfontein
SuperSport United *	4			* Home team		Scorer - Mbesuma [79] for Chiefs

KAIZER CHIEFS 2004-2005

Date	Opponents		Score	Comp	Scorers
31-07-2004	Black Leopards	W	2-0	N	TCsf	Moshoeu [35], Nengomasha [81]
31-07-2004	Sundowns	D	0-0	N	TCf	L 4-5p
7-08-2004	Dynamos	W	4-1	A	PSL	Mbesuma 3 [11 64 75], Mabedi [82]
14-08-2004	Black Leopards	W	2-1	H	SEr1	Mbesuma 2 [45 95]
28-08-2004	Manning Rangers	W	3-0	H	PSL	McCarthy 2 [32 45], Moshoeu [55]
11-09-2004	Silver Stars	W	2-1	H	PSL	Moshoeu [35], Mbesuma [66]
19-09-2004	Moroka Swallows	W	1-0	H	SEsf	Mbesuma [27]
2-10-2004	SuperSport United	L	0-1	N	SEf	
16-10-2004	Bush Bucks	D	2-2	H	PSL	Moshoeu [44], Mooki [63]
24-10-2004	Golden Arrows	W	2-1	A	LCr1	Zwane [14], Mbesuma [48]
30-10-2004	Orlando Pirates	L	1-2	A	PSL	Zwane [51]
6-11-2004	Wits University	W	2-1	A	PSL	Nengomasha [70], Radebe [76]
13-11-2004	Golden Arrows	D	2-2	H	PSL	Mbesuma 2 [2 75]
20-11-2004	Dynamos	W	4-0	H	LCqf	Zwane [28], Moshoeu [37], Radebe 2 [55 86]
27-11-2004	Sundowns	D	1-1	H	PSL	Mbesuma [40]
4-12-2004	Moroka Swallows	D	2-2	A	LCsf	Mayo [12], Mbesuma [86], W 2-0p
11-12-2004	Black Leopards	W	3-0	A	PSL	Mathebula [75], Mbesuma 2 [77 92+]
18-12-2004	SuperSport United	W	1-0	N	LCf	Mbesuma [79]
5-01-2005	Santos	W	1-0	H	PSL	Ngobese [57]
9-01-2005	Moroka Swallows	L	0-1	A	PSL	
15-01-2005	Bloemfontein Celtic	W	4-1	H	PSL	Radebe 2 [19 91+], Ngobese [34], Mooki [38]
19-01-2005	Dynamos	D	1-1	H	PSL	Zwane [87]
23-01-2005	Manning Rangers	D	2-2	A	PSL	Zwane [26], Mbesuma [55]
26-01-2005	Jomo Cosmos	W	3-0	A	PSL	Mbesuma [7], Chalwe [25], Sibeko [40]
29-01-2005	Port Louis 2000 - MRI	W	2-0	H	CLpr	Chalwe [7], Mbesuma [59p]
2-02-2005	Black Leopards	W	3-0	H	PSL	Mbesuma 2 [16 50], Sibeko [65]
6-02-2005	Silver Stars	D	0-0	A	PSL	
13-02-2005	Port Louis 2000 - MRI	L	1-2	A	CLpr	Zwane [32]
19-02-2005	Sundowns	W	4-3	A	PSL	Radebe [43], Mbesuma 3 [45 59 61]
23-02-2005	SuperSport United	D	0-0	H	PSL	
26-02-2005	Bilika All Stars	W	4-0	A	CUPr1	Radebe 2 [36 75], Mbambo [50], Mzizi [91+]
1-03-2005	Jomo Cosmos	D	0-0	H	PSL	
6-03-2005	USJF/Ravinala - MAD	W	1-0	A	CLr1	Mbesuma [75]
13-03-2005	Wits University	D	0-0	H	CUPr2	L 3-4p
16-03-2005	Santos	W	1-0	A	PSL	Mbesuma [68]
19-03-2005	USJF/Ravinala - MAD	W	4-1	H	CLr1	Mbesuma 2 [6 22], Mbambo [26], Zwane [69]
31-03-2005	Ajax Cape Town	D	2-2	H	PSL	Zwane 2 [28 84]
3-04-2005	Golden Arrows	D	1-1	A	PSL	Radebe [74]
9-04-2005	Espérance - TUN	L	0-4	A	CLr2	
17-04-2005	Ajax Cape Town	W	2-1	H	PSL	Mbesuma [9], Radebe [75]
23-04-2005	Espérance - TUN	W	2-1	H	CLr2	Moshoeu [63], Mbambo [90]
26-04-2005	Wits University	W	1-0	H	PSL	Mbesuma [88p]
30-04-2005	Orlando Pirates	D	1-1	H	PSL	Ngobese [7]
7-05-2005	Moroka Swallows	W	2-0	H	PSL	Mbesuma 2 [47 52]
14-05-2005	Bush Bucks	W	4-3	A	PSL	Ngobese [35], Mbesuma 2 [40 87p], Radebe [91+]
18-05-2005	SuperSport United	W	1-0	A	PSL	Ngobese [88]
22-05-2005	Bloemfontein Celtic	W	2-0	A	PSL	Mbesuma 2 [54 63]

TC = Telekom Charity Cup • PSL = Premier Soccer League • SE = SAA Supa 8 Cup • LC = Coca-Cola League Cup • CL = CAF Champions League
CUP = ABSA Cup • pr = preliminary round • r1 = first round • r2 = second round • qf = quarter-final • sf = semi-final • f = final
H = FNB Stadium • **H** = Olympia Stadium,

SAA SUPA 8 CUP 2004

First Round		Semi-finals		Final	
SuperSport United *	2 5p				
Santos	2 3p	**SuperSport United ***	1 6p		
Orlando Pirates	1	Wits University	1 5p		
Wits University *	2			**SuperSport United**	1
Moroka Swallows *	3			Kaizer Chiefs	0
Ajax Cape Town	1	Moroka Swallows	0	2-10-2004	
Black Leopards	1	**Kaizer Chiefs ***	1	ABSA Park, Durban	
Kaizer Chiefs *	2	* Home team		Scorer - Evans [47p]	

RUS – RUSSIA

NATIONAL TEAM RECORD
JULY 1ST 2002 TO JUNE 30TH 2005

PL	W	D	L	F	A	%
29	11	9	9	49	42	53.4

FIFA/COCA-COLA WORLD RANKING

1993	1994	1995	1996	1997	1998	1999	2000	2001	2002	2003	2004	High		Low	
14	13	5	7	12	40	18	21	21	23	24	32	3	04/96	40	12/98

2004-2005											
08/04	09/04	10/04	11/04	12/04	01/05	02/05	03/05	04/05	05/05	06/05	07/05
27	26	33	33	32	32	32	33	31	30	27	30

2005 may well prove to be a seminal year for Russian football with the historic win by CSKA Moskva in the UEFA Cup helping to change the perception the outside world has of football in this huge country. But it wasn't just CSKA's UEFA Cup triumph which marked a new era in Russian football. Just as Roman Abramovich's millions have helped change the face of English football, the money of Russia's new wealthy elite is also changing the game at home. From being a city where the best route to fame and fortune was to leave, Moscow is now a destination of choice for many footballers. Spearheading the new elite are not only CSKA but also Lokomotiv and the pair

INTERNATIONAL HONOURS
Qualified for the FIFA World Cup™ finals 1994 2002

of them dominated the championship in 2004. Lokomotiv's title was only their second ever but with the best stadium in Russia they now look to be a force to be reckoned with. Ironically, the boom in club football has come at a time when the national team is struggling as never before, with the 1-7 thrashing at the hands of Portugal in the World Cup qualifiers a particularly sobering moment. It was unsurprising therefore that Lokomotiv's long serving coach Yuri Syomin was asked to take over the national team following the dismissal of Georgi Yartsev in the wake of the away draw against Estonia in March 2005.

THE FIFA BIG COUNT OF 2000

	Male	Female		Male	Female
Registered players	603 920	2 290	Referees	44 000	36
Non registered players	2 955 000	8 000	Officials	17 000	1 000
Youth players	192 000	1 300	Total involved	3 824 546	
Total players	3 762 510		Number of clubs	17 816	
Professional players	3 920	190	Number of teams	155 980	

Football Union of Russia (RFU)
8 Luzhnetskaya Naberezhnaja, Moscow 119 992, Russia
Tel +7 095 2011637   Fax +7 501 4981010
rfs@roc.ru   www.rfs.ru
President: MUTKO Vitaliy   General Secretary: RADIONOV Vladimir
Vice-President: SIMONIAN Nikita   Treasurer: GROUZDEV Victor   Media Officer: CHERNOV Alexander
Men's Coach: SYOMIN Yuri   Women's Coach: BYSTRITSKIY Yury
RFU formed: 1912   UEFA: 1992   FIFA: 1992
Colours: White, White, White

GAMES PLAYED BY RUSSIA IN THE 2006 FIFA WORLD CUP™ CYCLE

2002	Opponents		Score	Venue	Comp	Scorers	Att	Referee
21-08	Sweden	D	1-1	Moscow	Fr	Kerzhakov 55	23 000	Poulat FRA
7-09	Republic of Ireland	W	4-2	Moscow	ECq	Karyaka 20, Beschastnykh 24, Kerzhakov 71, OG 88	23 000	Colombo FRA
16-10	Albania	W	4-1	Volgograd	ECq	Kerzhakov 3, Semak 2 42 55, Onopko 52	18 000	Sundell SWE
2003								
12-02	Cyprus	W	1-0	Limassol	Fr	Khokhlov 43	300	Efthimiadis GRE
29-03	Albania	L	1-3	Shkoder	ECq	Karyaka 77	16 000	Allaerts BEL
30-04	Georgia	L	0-1	Tbilisi	ECq		11 000	Wack GER
7-06	Switzerland	D	2-2	Basel	ECq	Ignashevich 2 24 67p	30 500	Dauden Ibanez ESP
20-08	Israel	L	1-2	Moscow	Fr	Semak 86	5 000	Ishchenko UKR
6-09	Republic of Ireland	D	1-1	Dublin	ECq	Ignashevich 42	36 000	Michel SVK
10-09	Switzerland	W	4-1	Moscow	ECq	Bulykin 3 20 33 59, Mostovoi 72	29 000	Collina ITA
11-10	Georgia	W	3-1	Moscow	ECq	Bulykin 29, Titov 45, Sychev 73	30 000	Plautz AUT
15-11	Wales	D	0-0	Moscow	ECpo		29 000	Cortez Batista POR
19-11	Wales	L	0-1	Cardiff	ECpo		73 062	Mejuto Gonzalez ESP
2004								
31-03	Bulgaria	D	2-2	Sofia	Fr	Sychev 2 9 31	14 938	Alves Garcia POR
28-04	Norway	L	2-3	Oslo	Fr	Radimov 85, Kirichenko 90	11 435	Wegereef NED
25-05	Austria	D	0-0	Graz	Fr		9 600	Vuorela FIN
12-06	Spain	L	0-1	Faro-Loule	ECr1		28 182	Meier SUI
16-06	Portugal	L	0-2	Lisbon	ECr1		59 273	Hauge NOR
20-06	Greece	W	2-1	Faro-Loule	ECr1	Kirichenko 2, Bulykin 17	24 347	Veissiere FRA
18-08	Lithuania	W	4-3	Moscow	Fr	Khokhlov 22, Karyaka 53, Bulykin 66, Sychev 88	3 500	Mikulski POL
4-09	Slovakia	D	1-1	Moscow	WCq	Bulykin 14	11 500	Mejuto Gonzalez ESP
9-10	Luxembourg	W	4-0	Luxembourg	WCq	Sychev 3 56 69 86, Arshavin 62	3 670	Braamhaar NED
13-10	Portugal	L	1-7	Lisbon	WCq	Arshavin 79	27 258	Vassaras GRE
17-11	Estonia	W	4-0	Krasnodar	WCq	Karyaka 23, Izmailov 25, Sychev 32, Loskov 67p	29 000	Busacca SUI
2005								
9-02	Italy	L	0-2	Cagliari	Fr		15 700	Michel SVK
26-03	Liechtenstein	W	2-1	Vaduz	WCq	Kerzhakov 23, Karyaka 37	2 400	Berntsen NOR
30-03	Estonia	D	1-1	Tallinn	WCq	Arshavin 18	8 850	Paparesta ITA
4-06	Latvia	W	2-0	Sankt Peterburg	WCq	Arshavin 56, Loskov 78p	21 575	Poulat FRA
8-06	Germany	D	2-2	Mönchengladbach	Fr	Anyukov 26, Arshavin 91+	46 228	Plautz AUT

Fr = Friendly match • EC = UEFA EURO 2004™ • WC = FIFA World Cup™ • q = qualifier • po = play-off • r1 = first round group

RUSSIA NATIONAL TEAM RECORDS AND RECORD SEQUENCES

Records			Sequence records				
Victory	7-0	SMR 1995	Wins	12	1995-1996	Clean sheets	4	1992-93, 2000
Defeat	0-16	GER 1912	Defeats	6	1998	Goals scored	23	1998-2001
Player Caps	109	ONOPKO Victor	Undefeated	17	1995-1996	Without goal	3	1912
Player Goals	26	BESCHASTNYKH Vladimir	Without win	8	1912-1914, 1998	Goals against	8	Three times

RUSSIA COUNTRY INFORMATION

Capital	Moscow	Independence	1991 from Soviet Union	GDP per Capita	$8 900
Population	143 782 238	Status	Republic	GNP Ranking	19
Area km²	17 075 200	Language	Russian	Dialling code	+7
Population density	8 per km²	Literacy rate	99%	Internet code	.ru
% in urban areas	76%	Main religion	Christian	GMT +/–	+2-12

Towns/Cities ('000)	Moscow 10 381; Sankt Peterburg 4 039; Novosibirsk 1 419; Yekaterinburg 1 287; Nizhny Novgorod 1 284; Samara 1 134; Omsk 1 129; Kazan 1 104; Rostov-na-Donu 1 074; Chelyabinsk 1 062; Ufa 1 033; Volgograd 1 010; Perm 982; Krasnoyarsk 907; Saratov 863
Neighbours (km)	Korea DPR 19; China 3 645; Mongolia 3 485; Kazakhstan 6 846; Azerbaijan 284; Georgia 723; Ukraine 1 576; Belarus 959; Poland 206; Lithuania 227; Latvia 217; Estonia 294; Finland 1 340; Norway 196; Arctic Ocean & Pacific Ocean 37 653
Main stadia	Luzhniki – Moscow 84 745; Kirov – Sankt Peterburg; Metallurg – Samara 35 330; Tsentralnyi – Volgograd 32 120; Lokomotiv – Moscow 30 979; Kuban – Krasnodar 28 800

RUSSIA 2004

PREMIER LEAGUE

	Pl	W	D	L	F	A	Pts	Lokomotiv	CSKA	Krylya	Zenit	Torpedo	Shinnik	Saturn	Spartak	Moskva	Rubin	Amkar	Rostov	Dinamo	Alania	Kuban	Rotor
Lokomotiv Moskva †	30	18	7	5	44	19	61		1-0	1-0	0-1	3-1	3-0	2-0	0-0	0-1	0-0	0-0	1-1	2-1	3-0	3-0	0-1
CSKA Moskva ‡	30	17	9	4	53	22	60	0-1		1-1	3-3	3-3	1-1	2-0	2-1	0-0	1-0	3-0	2-0	0-0	1-0	3-1	3-0
Krylya Sovetov Samara ‡	30	17	5	8	50	41	56	1-0	1-1		0-1	2-5	1-2	1-1	4-2	2-1	2-1	1-0	2-1	4-1	4-2	2-1	1-0
Zenit Sankt-Peterburg ‡	30	17	5	8	55	37	56	0-2	0-3	1-2		3-1	1-0	2-2	2-0	2-3	4-3	0-0	0-1	2-0	3-2	1-0	3-2
Torpedo Moskva	30	16	6	8	53	37	54	1-1	0-1	0-1	3-1		2-0	1-2	2-1	1-0	1-0	3-2	4-1	3-1	3-2	3-1	1-0
Shinnik Yaroslavl	30	12	8	10	29	29	44	0-2	2-1	0-1	2-1	3-1		1-0	1-1	1-1	1-1	2-1	1-0	1-0	1-1	1-0	2-1
Saturn Moskovskaya	30	10	11	9	37	30	41	1-2	0-1	1-2	1-3	1-1	0-0		2-2	1-1	1-1	1-1	2-0	0-0	5-1	2-1	2-0
Spartak Moskva	30	11	7	12	43	44	40	1-3	0-2	3-1	0-3	1-2	1-0	0-2		3-2	2-0	6-0	1-0	2-2	0-1	1-1	1-0
FK Moskva	30	10	10	10	38	39	40	1-2	1-4	5-1	1-1	0-2	3-2	2-1	2-3		1-0	3-1	2-2	1-0	0-	2-2	1-0
Rubin Kazan	30	7	12	11	32	31	33	0-0	2-1	1-3	1-1	2-0	0-1	0-1	2-0	3-0		2-2	1-1	2-2	4-1	2-0	1-1
Amkar Perm	30	6	12	12	27	42	30	0-1	0-0	3-1	0-2	2-1	1-1	1-1	0-2	1-0	2-2		2-0	0-1	1-0	1-2	1-1
FK Rostov	30	7	8	15	28	42	29	1-2	1-3	0-1	2-1	0-4	0-0	1-2	3-1	1-2	1-0	0-0		2-0	0-0	1-1	4-1
Dinamo Moskva	30	6	11	13	27	38	29	2-4	1-1	1-1	0-2	1-1	1-0	0-2	1-1	1-0	0-0	3-1	0-1		1-0	0-1	5-0
Alania Vladikavkaz	30	7	7	16	28	52	28	1-2	1-4	1-4	0-3	0-0	2-1	0-3	0-2	1-0	0-0	1-2	0-0	4-2		2-0	1-1
Kuban Krasnodar	30	6	10	14	26	42	28	2-1	0-3	1-1	1-3	1-2	1-0	0-0	1-2	0-0	1-0	0-0	3-1	0-0	2-3		1-1
Rotor Volgograd	30	4	10	16	28	53	22	2-2	1-3	3-2	2-5	0-1	0-2	1-0	2-3	1-1	0-1	2-2	3-2	0-0	0-1	1-1	

12/03/2004 - 12/11/2004 • † Qualified for the UEFA Champions League • ‡ Qualified for the UEFA Cup • Torpedo-Metall renamed FK Moskva

RUSSIA 2004 FIRST DIVISION (2)

	Pl	W	D	L	F	A	Pts
Terek Groznyi	42	32	4	6	70	22	100
Tom Tomsk	42	27	5	10	70	38	86
Sokol Saratov	42	25	8	9	69	38	83
KamAZ Chelny	42	19	12	11	52	49	69
FK Khimki	42	17	10	15	39	33	61
FK Oryol	42	16	13	13	37	34	61
SHA-Energiya Khabarovsk	42	16	13	13	42	37	61
Anzhi Makhachkala	42	16	12	14	50	53	60
Metalurg Lipetsk	42	15	15	12	48	43	60
Lokomotiv Chita	42	17	8	17	47	48	59
Dinamo Makhachkala	42	16	11	15	44	48	59
Spartak Nalchik	42	16	10	16	53	46	58
Arsenal Tula	42	15	13	14	39	32	58
Luch-En. Vladivostock	42	15	11	16	50	50	56
Dinamo Bryansk	42	14	13	15	49	51	55
Metallurg Novokuznetsk	42	14	10	18	53	53	52
Chernomorets Novorossiysk	42	13	12	17	47	44	51
Uralan Elista	42	13	11	18	48	57	50
Nef'himik Nizhnekamsk	42	11	12	19	38	57	45
Baltika Kaliningrad	42	10	9	23	37	60	39
Lisma Saransk	42	5	11	26	24	62	26
Gazovik Izhevsk	42	5	7	30	40	91	22

28/03/2004 - 6/11/2004

TOP SCORERS

KERZHAKOV Aleksandr	Zenit	18
KARYAKA Andrei	Krylya Sovetov	17
PANOV Aleksandr	Torpedo	15
SYCHEV Dmitriy	Lokomotiv	15
BRACAMONTE Hector	FK Moskva	11
PAVLYUCHENKO Roman	Spartak	10
SPIVAK Oleksandr	Zenit	10
YESIPOV Valeriy	Rotor	10

RECENT LEAGUE AND CUP RECORD

	Championship						Cup		
Year	Champions	Pts	Runners-up	Pts	Third	Pts	Winners	Score	Runners-up
1992	Spartak Moskva	24	Spartak Vladikavkaz	17	Dinamo Moskva	16	Torpedo Moskva	1-1 5-3p	CSKA Moskva
1993	Spartak Moskva	53	Rotor Volgograd	42	Dinamo Moskva	42	Spartak Moskva	2-2 4-2p	CSKA Moskva
1994	Spartak Moskva	39	Dinamo Moskva	39	Lokomotiv Moskva	36	Dinamo Moskva	0-0 8-7p	Rotor Volograd
1995	Spartak Vladikavkaz	71	Lokomotiv Moskva	65	Spartak Moskva	63	Lokomotiv Moskva	3-2	Spartak Moskva
1996	Spartak Moskva	72	Alania Vladikavkaz	72	Rotor Volgograd	70	Lokomotiv Moskva	2-0	Dinamo Moskva
1997	Spartak Moskva	73	Rotor Volgograd	68	Dinamo Moskva	68	Spartak Moskva	1-0	Lokomotiv Moskva
1998	Spartak Moskva	59	CSKA Moskva	56	Lokomotiv Moskva	55	Zenit St-Peterburg	3-1	Dynamo Moskva
1999	Spartak Moskva	72	Lokomotiv Moskva	65	CSKA Moskva	55	Lokomotiv Moskva	3-2	CSKA Moskva
2000	Spartak Moskva	70	Lokomotiv Moskva	62	Torpedo Moskva	55	Lokomotiv Moskva	2-1	Anzhi Makhachkala
2001	Spartak Moskva	60	Lokomotiv Moskva	56	Zenit St-Peterburg	56	CSKA Moskva	2-0	Zenit St-Peterburg
2002	Lokomotiv Moskva	66	CSKA Moskva	66	Spartak Moskva	55	Spartak Moskva	1-0	FK Rostov
2003	CSKA Moskva	59	Zenit St-Peterburg	56	Rubin Kazan	53	Terek Groznyi	1-0	Krylya S. Samara
2004	Lokomotiv Moskva	61	CSKA Moskva	60	Krylya S. Samara	56	CSKA Moskva	1-0	FK Khimki
2005									

RUSSIAN CUP 2004-05

Fifth Round			Sixth Round			Quarter-finals			Semi-finals			Final	
CSKA Moskva *	0	3	CSKA Moskva	3	3	CSKA Moskva *	2	0	CSKA Moskva	0	2	CSKA Moskva	1
Sokol Saratov *	2	0	FK Moskva *	1	1	Saturn Moskovskaya	1	0	Zenit Sankt Peterburg *	1	0	FK Khimki	0
FK Yelets *	1	0											
FK Moskva	3	5											
FK Rostov	2	2	FK Rostov *	1	0								
Sodovik Sterlitamak *	1	1	Saturn Moskovskaya	2	0								
KamAZ Chelny	0	1											
Saturn Moskovskaya *	3	3											
Shinnik Yaroslavl	0	4	Shinnik Yaroslavl	†		Shinnik Yaroslavl	0	1					
SKA-Energiya Khabarovsk *	3	0	Rotor Volgograd			Zenit Sankt Peterburg *	4	4					
Lokomotiv Chita *	1	0											
Rotor Volgograd	0	5											
Kuban Krasnodar	1	3	Kuban Krasnodar	0	0								
Tom Tomsk *	1	1	Zenit Sankt Peterburg *	0	1								
Irtysh Omsk *	0	1											
Zenit Sankt Peterburg	2	7											
Amkar Perm	1	0	Amkar Perm	†		Amkar Perm *	1	1	Amkar Perm	0	0		
Terek Groznyi *	0	0	Ch'morets Novorossiysk			Krylya Sovetov Samara	0	1	FK Khimki *	2	0		
Lokomotiv Moskva	0	1											
Ch'morets Novorossiysk *	1	0											
Dinamo Moskva *	2	3	Dinamo Moskva *	1	0								
Dinamo Makhachkala	0	0	Krylya Sovetov Samara	1	1								
Olimpia Volgograd	1	1											
Krylya Sovetov Samara *	3	4											
Torpedo Moskva	2	2	Torpedo Moskva *	3	1	Torpedo Moskva	1	0					
Dinamo Bryansk *	0	0	Metalurg Lipetsk	0	1	FK Khimki *	1	3					
Spartak Moskva *	0	1											
Metalurg Lipetsk	2	1											
Alania Vladikavkav	0	5	Alania Vladikavkav *	0	1								
Arsenal Tula *	0	2	FK Khimki	2	1								
Rubin Kazan *	0	1											
FK Khimki	1	3											

RUSSIAN CUP FINAL

29-05-2005, Att: 25 000, Referee: Kayumov Lokomotiv, Moscow

Scorer - Zhirkov 58 for CSKA

CSKA - Akinfeyev, Berezutskiy V (Krasic 46), Ignashevich, Berezutskiy A, Gusev (Odiah 55), Aldonin, Semberas, Carvalho, Zhirkov, Olic (Laizans 71), Vagner Love
Khimki - Lomaia, Yeshchenko, Prigantuc, Jovanovic, Grishin, Kalachou, Perov, Prodsyn, Nakhushev (Ivanov 82), Tikhonov, Danishbevsky (Antipenko 82)

* Home team in the first leg • † Rotor Volgograd and Chernomorets Novorossiysk expelled

LOKOMOTIV MOSKVA 2004

Date	Opponents	Score				Scorers	Crowd
24-02-2004	AS Monaco - FRA	W	2-1	H	CLr2	Izmailov [32], Maminov [59]	26 000
29-02-2004	FK Khimki	W	1-0	A	CUPr5	Cesnauskis [38]	5 000
4-03-2004	Rubin Kazan	D	1-1	A	CUPr6	Sychov [45]	15 000
10-03-2004	AS Monaco - FRA	L	0-1	A	CLr2		18 000
15-03-2004	Shinnik Yaroslavl	W	3-0	H	PL	Izmailov [4], Sychov 2 [33 39]	4 000
21-03-2004	Amkar Perm	D	0-0	H	PL		7 000
24-03-2004	Rubin Kazan	W	1-0	H	CUPr6	Izmailov [20]	6 409
28-03-2004	Torpedo Moskva	D	1-1	A	PL	Bilyaletdinov [17]	5 500
3-04-2004	Rubin Kazan	D	0-0	A	PL		10 000
7-04-2004	Torpedo-Metall	L	0-1	H	PL		7 000
10-04-2004	Saturn Moskovskaya Oblast	W	2-1	A	PL	Sychov [73], Pimenov [90]	13 500
14-04-2004	Shinnik Yaroslavl	L	0-3	A	CUPqf		10 000
17-04-2004	CSKA Moskva	W	1-0	H	PL	Khokhlov [56]	21 834
21-04-2004	Shinnik Yaroslavl	W	4-1	H	CUPqf	Loskov [42p], Khokhlov [53], Hurenka [56], Sychov [72]	7 500
24-04-2004	Rotor Volgograd	D	2-2	A	PL	Sychov 2 [2 96+]	9 500
1-05-2004	FC Rostov	W	2-1	A	PL	Sychov 2 [9 61]	11 000
8-05-2004	Kuban Krasnodar	W	3-0	H	PL	Khokhlov [15], Sychov [42], Loskov [45]	8 170
15-05-2004	Alania Vladikavkaz	W	2-1	A	PL	Loskov [76], Obiorah [84]	20 000
19-05-2004	Zenit Sankt Peterburg	L	0-1	H	PL		18 623
22-05-2004	Krylya Sovetov Samara	L	0-1	A	PL		32 500
7-07-2004	Dinamo Moskva	W	4-2	A	PL	Yevseyev [49], Sychov 2 [59 82], Parks [75]	6 500
10-07-2004	Krylya Sovetov Samara	W	1-0	H	PL	Khokhlov [79]	9 723
17-07-2004	Zenit Sank Peterburg	W	2-0	A	PL	Sychov [17], Pimenov [93+]	21 650
24-07-2004	Dinamo Moskva	W	2-1	H	PL	Khokhlov [56], Yevseyev [76]	11 722
31-07-2004	Chernomorets Novorossiysk	L	0-1	A	CUPr5		6 000
7-08-2004	Spartak Moskva	D	0-0	H	PL		20 200
14-08-2004	Spartak Moskva	W	3-1	A	PL	Bilyaletdinov 2 [58 75], Pimenov [78]	12 000
22-08-2004	FC Rostov	D	1-1	H	PL	Sychov [79]	9 321
29-08-2004	Kuban Krasnodar	L	1-2	A	PL	Khokhlov [69]	18 000
8-09-2004	Chernomorets Novorossiysk	D	1-1	H	CUPr5	Izmailov 65	2 805
12-09-2004	Alania Vladikavkaz	W	3-0	H	PL	Asatiani [40], Pimenov [60], Yevseyev [78]	7 200
19-09-2004	Rotor Volgograd	L	0-1	H	PL		7 983
25-09-2004	CSKA Moskva	W	1-0	A	PL	Loskov [73]	15 500
3-10-2004	Saturn Moskovskaya Oblast	W	2-0	H	PL	Bilyaletdinov [58], Izmailov [60]	7 839
16-10-2004	FC Moskva	W	2-1	A	PL	Sychov [3], Maminov [36]	6 500
24-10-2004	Rubin Kazan	D	0-0	H	PL		8 200
30-10-2004	Amkar Perm	W	1-0	A	PL	Yevseyev [29]	15 800
8-11-2004	Torpedo Moskva	W	3-1	H	PL	Sychov [9], Loskov [64], Khokhlov [87]	12 500
12-11-2004	Shinnik Yaroslavl	W	2-0	A	PL	Bilyaletdinov [4], Sychov [21]	10 000

CL = UEFA Champions League • CUP = Russian Cup • PL = Premier League
r2 = second round • r5 = fifth round • r6 = sixth round • qf = quarter-final

CLUB DIRECTORY

Club	Town/City	Stadium	Phone	www.	Lge	Cup	CL
Alania Vladikavkaz	Vladikavkaz	Republikan 32 574	+7 8672 530340	fc-alania.ru	1 - 0	0 - 0	0
Amkar Perm	Perm	Zvezda 20 000	+7 3422 440281	amkar.ru	0 - 0	0 - 0	0
CSKA Moskva	Moskva	Eduard Streltsov 14 274	+7 095 2134372	cska-football.ru	1 - 7	1 - 5	0
Dinamo Moskva	Moskva	Dinamo 36 540	+7 095 2128432	fcdynamo.ru	0 - 11	1 - 6	0
Lokomotiv Moskva	Moskva	Lokomotiv 30 979	+7 095 1619704	fclm.ru	2 - 0	4 - 2	0
FC Moskva	Moskva	Eduard Streltsov 14 274	+7 095 5444366	fcmoscow.ru	0 - 0	0 - 0	0
FC Rostov	Rostov-na-Donu	Olimp 21-Vek 15 600	+7 8632 519539	fc-rostov.ru	0 - 0	0 - 0	0
Rubin Kazan	Kazan	Tsentralnyi 25 000	+7 8432 711404	rubin-kazan.ru	0 - 0	0 - 0	0
Krylya Sovetov Samara	Samara	Metallurg 35 330	+7 8462 351635	kc-kampara.ru	0 - 0	0 - 0	0
Saturn Moskovskaya Oblast	Ramenskoe	Saturn 16 726	+7 096 4679372	Saturn-fc.ru	0 - 0	0 - 0	0
Shinnik Yaroslavl	Yaroslavl	Shinnik 22 984	+7 0852 720626	shinnik.yar.ru	0 - 0	0 - 0	0
Spartak Moskva	Moskva	Luzhniki 84 745	+7 095 9808674	rus.spartak.com	9 - 12	3 - 10	0
Terek Grozny	Grozny	Uvays Akhtayev 15 000			0 - 0	1 - 0	0
Tom Tomsk	Tomsk	Trud 15 500	+7 3822 527967	football.tomsk.ru	0 - 0	0 - 0	0
Torpedo Moskva	Moskva	Luzhniki 84 745	+7 095 2011301	torpedo.ru	0 - 3	1 - 6	0
Zenit Sankt Peterburg	Sankt Peterburg	Petrovski 21 838	+7 812 2750330	fc-zenit.ru	0 - 1	1 - 1	0

In the championships and cups column, the first of the two figures indicates titles won in Russia, the second titles won in the Soviet era

CSKA MOSKVA 2004

Date	Opponents	Score			Scorers	Crowd
7-03-2004	Spartak Moskva	W	3-1	N SC	Semak [40], Carvalho [111], Kirichenko [113]	18 000
23-03-2004	Uralan Elista	W	1-0	A CUPr6	Kirichenko [20]	6 000
12-03-2004	Torpedo-Metall	D	0-0	H PL		10 000
20-03-2004	Dinamo Moskva	D	1-1	A PL	Kirichenko [57]	14 000
27-03-2004	Krylya Sovetov Samara	D	1-1	A PL	Gusev [23]	30 000
3-04-2004	Zenit Sankt Peterburg	D	3-3	H PL	Kirichenko [6], Zhirkov [39], Rahimic [56]	11 000
7-04-2004	FC Rostov	W	3-1	A PL	Zhirkov [38], Kirichenko [68], Ignashevich [90]	12 000
10-04-2004	Kuban Krasnodar	W	3-1	H PL	Kirichenko [8], Gusev [17], Semak [73]	8 000
14-04-2004	Krylya Sovetov Samara	L	1-2	A CUPqf	Olic [93+]	25 000
17-04-2004	Lokomotiv Moskva	L	0-1	A PL		21 834
21-04-2004	Krylya Sovetov Samara	L	0-1	H CUPqf		7 000
24-05-2004	Alania Vladikavkaz	W	1-0	H PL	Kirichenko [59]	7 000
1-05-2004	Rotor Volgograd	W	3-1	A PL	Olic 3 [45 59p 76]	10 000
9-05-2004	Saturn Moskovskaya Oblast	W	2-0	H PL	Zhirkov [26], Semak [71]	8 000
15-05-2004	Spartak Moskva	W	2-0	A PL	OG [9], Olic [78]	18 500
19-05-2004	Shinnik Yaroslavl	D	1-1	H PL	Semak [70]	3 500
22-05-2004	Amkar Perm	D	0-0	A PL		19 000
3-07-2004	Torpedo Moskva	D	3-3	H PL	Jarosik [33], Olic [54], Kirichenko [86]	8 000
7-07-2004	Rubin Kazan	L	1-2	A PL	Jarosik [52]	14 000
11-07-2004	Amkar Perm	W	3-0	H PL	Zhirkov 2 [36 61], Jarosik [65]	7 000
17-07-2004	Torpedo Moskva	W	1-0	A PL	Olic [39]	9 000
23-07-2004	Rubin Kazan	W	1-0	H PL	Olic [43]	7 000
27-07-2004	Neftchi Baku - AZE	D	0-0	A CLpr2		
31-07-2004	Sokol Saratov	L	0-2	A CUPr5		13 200
4-08-2004	Neftchi Baku - AZE	W	2-0	H CLpr2	Gusev [68], Vágner Love [72]	
10-08-2004	Rangers - SCO	W	2-1	H CLpr3	Vágner Love [4], Jarosik [46]	
14-08-2004	Shinnik Yaroslavl	L	1-2	A PL	Kirichenko [42p]	12 000
20-08-2004	Rotor Volgograd	W	3-0	H PL	Olic [28], Vágner Love 2 [42 70]	6 000
25-08-2004	Rangers - SCO	D	1-1	A CLpr3	Vágner Love [60]	
29-08-2004	Saturn Moskovskaya Oblast	W	1-0	A PL	Kirichenko [89]	15 500
10-09-2004	Spartak Moskva	W	2-1	H PL	Jarosik [18], Olic [89]	23 000
14-09-2004	FC Porto - POR	D	0-0	A CLgH		39 309
19-09-2004	Alania Vladikavkaz	W	4-1	A PL	Vágner Love 2 [15 51], Gusev [32], Ferreyra [65]	7 000
25-09-2004	Lokomotiv Moskva	L	0-1	H PL		15 500
29-09-2004	Paris Saint-Germain - FRA	W	2-0	H CLgH	Sernak [64], Vágner Love [77p]	29 000
3-10-2004	Kuban Krasnodar	W	3-0	A PL	Ferreyra [33], Semak [50], Kirichenko [92+]	25 000
16-10-2004	FC Rostov	W	2-0	H PL	Jarosik [37], Vágner Love [81p]	9 000
20-10-2004	Chelsea - ENG	L	0-2	A CLgH		33 945
25-10-2004	Zenit Sankt Peterburg	W	3-0	A PL	Gusev [12], Zhirkov [68], Vágner Love [94+]	22 000
30-10-2005	Krylya Sovetov Samara	D	1-1	H PL	Vágner Love [3]	8 500
2-11-2004	Chelsea - ENG	L	0-1	H CLgH		28 000
8-11-2004	Dinamo Moskva	D	0-0	H PL		12 000
12-11-2004	FC Moskva	W	4-1	A PL	Vágner Love 2 [49 67], Carvalho [60]	9 000
20-11-2004	Sokol Saratov	W	3-0	H CUPr5	Awarded 3-0 to CSKA	
24-11-2004	FC Porto - POR	L	0-1	H CLgH		21 500
7-12-2004	Paris Saint-Germain - FRA	W	3-1	A CLgH	Semak 3 [28 64 70]	40 000

SC = Super Cup • CUP = Russian Cup • PL = Premier League • CL = UEFA Champions League
pr2 = second preliminary round • pr3 = third preliminary round • r6 = sixth round • qf = quarter-final • gH = group H

NATIONAL CAPS		NATIONAL GOALS		NATIONAL COACH	
	Caps		Goals		Years
ONOPKO Viktor	109	BESCHASTNYKH Vladimir	26	SADYRIN Pavel	1992-'94
KARPIN Valeri	72	KARPIN Valeri	17	ROMANTSEV Oleg	1994-'96
BESCHASTNYKH Vladimir	71	KOLYVANOV Igor	12	IGNATIEV Boris	1996-'98
ALENICHEV Dmitri	55	KIRYAKOV Sergei	10	BYSHOVETS Anatoliy	1998
NIKIFOROV Yuri	55	MOSTOVOI Alexsandr	10	ROMANTSEV Oleg	1998-'02
KHOKHLOV Dmitri	52	SYCHEV Dmitri	10	GAZZAEV Valeriy	2002-'03
KHLESTOV Dmitri	50	RADCHENKO Dimitri	9	YARTSEV Georgy	2003-'05
KOVTUN Yuri	50	SIMUTENKOV Igor	9	SYOMIN Yuri	2005-
MOSTOVOI Alexsandr	50				
SMERTIN Aleksei	49				

RWA – RWANDA

NATIONAL TEAM RECORD
JULY 1ST 2002 TO JUNE 30TH 2005

PL	W	D	L	F	A	%
42	12	12	18	45	61	42.9

FIFA/COCA-COLA WORLD RANKING

1993	1994	1995	1996	1997	1998	1999	2000	2001	2002	2003	2004	High		Low	
-	-	168	159	172	107	146	128	144	130	109	99	97	10/04	178	07/99

2004-2005											
08/04	09/04	10/04	11/04	12/04	01/05	02/05	03/05	04/05	05/05	06/05	07/05
99	98	97	97	99	98	99	100	101	100	99	104

Less than 10 years after genocide swept the country, Rwanda took their place at the top table of African football when they made their debut at the CAF African Cup of Nations. Their presence in Tunisia marked the end of a decade of recovery for the national team that climbed back up the FIFA/Coca-Cola World Ranking and also picked up the 1999 CECAFA Cup title along the way. Progress began with regular fixtures and as the players gained experience, results improved and then coach Ratomir Dujkovic led them to an historic win against Ghana and a place in Tunisia. There they performed respectably even picking up a victory over Congo DR. The 2006 FIFA World

INTERNATIONAL HONOURS
CECAFA Cup 1999

Cup™ qualifiers were not such a happy hunting ground and in spite of early success over Gabon the Wasps soon crumbled to leave them rooted to the bottom of the table without even a place at the 2006 Cup of Nations. The national team has played an important part in national re-integration, and as well as winning and hosting the CECAFA Cup in 1999, Rwanda staged the event again two years later. Rayon Sport won the 2004 Championnat National to claim their fourth title claiming the double when they beat Makura Victory in the Cup final. However, their Champions League campaign was short after defeat in the preliminary round.

THE FIFA BIG COUNT OF 2000

	Male	Female		Male	Female
Registered players	4 000	0	Referees	200	0
Non registered players	25 000	0	Officials	1 400	0
Youth players	2 000	0	Total involved	32 600	
Total players	31 000		Number of clubs	100	
Professional players	0	0	Number of teams	500	

Fédération Rwandaise de Football Amateur (FERWAFA)
Case Postale 2000, Kigali, Rwanda
Tel +250 518525   Fax +250 518523
ferwafa@yahoo.fr   www.none
President: KAYIZARI Cesar   General Secretary: RWAGATARE Janvier
Vice-President: MUSABYIMANA Celestin   Treasurer: MUREGO Jean Bosco   Media Officer: None
Men's Coach: PALMGREN Roger   Women's Coach: None
FERWAFA formed: 1972   CAF: 1976   FIFA: 1978
Colours: Green with red and yellow, Green, Red

GAMES PLAYED BY RWANDA IN THE 2006 FIFA WORLD CUP™ CYCLE

2002	Opponents	Score		Venue	Comp	Scorers	Att	Referee
24-08	Kenya	D	0-0	Kigali	Fr			
13-10	Ghana	L	2-4	Accra	CNq	Karekezi [16], Ndikumana [43p]	40 000	Lassina BFA
30-11	Zanzibar †	W	1-0	Arusha	CCr1	Gatete [12]		
3-12	Somalia	W	1-0	Arusha	CCr1	Karekezi [53]		
6-12	Uganda	L	1-2	Arusha	CCr1	OG [30]		
9-12	Ethiopia	W	1-0	Arusha	CCr1	Nsengiyumve [85]		
11-12	Tanzania	L	0-3	Mwanza	CCsf			
14-12	Uganda	W	2-1	Arusha	CC3p	Sibomana, Baliwuza		
2003								
15-03	Burundi	W	4-2	Kigali	Fr			
22-03	Zambia	D	1-1	Kigali	Fr			
24-03	Zambia	L	0-3	Kigali	Fr			
29-03	Uganda	D	0-0	Kigali	CNq			Bakhit SUD
7-06	Uganda	W	1-0	Kampala	CNq	Gatete [39]	50 000	Gizate ETH
6-07	Ghana	W	1-0	Kigali	CNq	Gatete [49]	40 000	
14-09	Kenya	L	0-1	Kigali	Fr		10 000	
12-10	Namibia	W	3-0	Kigali	WCq	Elias [43], Karekezi [52], Lomani [58]	22 000	Abdulkadir TAN
22-10	India	L	1-3	Hyderabad	AA	Balinda [61]		
26-10	Malaysia	W	2-1	Hyderabad	AA	Iraguha 2 [81 87]		
29-10	Uzbekistan	L	1-2	Hyderabad	AA	Mulisa [73]		
31-10	Zimbabwe	D	2-2	Hyderabad	AA	Milly [37], Iraguha [75]. L 3-5p		
15-11	Namibia	D	1-1	Windhoek	WCq	Lomani [37]	9 000	Mbera GAB
2-12	Zanzibar †	D	2-2	Khartoum	CCr1	Kerekezi 2 [40p 56]		Segonga UGA
4-12	Sudan	L	0-3	Khartoum	CCr1			
8-12	Kenya	D	1-1	Khartoum	CCsf	Lomani [30]. W 4-3p		
10-02	Uganda	L	0-2	Khartoum	CCf			Itur KEN
2004								
8-01	Egypt	L	1-5	Port Said	Fr	Said [87]	10 000	
24-01	Tunisia	L	1-2	Tunis	CNr1	Elias [31]	60 000	Evehe CMR
28-01	Guinea	D	1-1	Bizerte	CNr1	Kamanazi [90]	4 000	Sowe GAM
1-02	Congo DR	W	1-0	Bizerte	CNr1	Said [74]	700	N'Doye SEN
28-05	Uganda	D	1-1	Kigali	Fr	Kamanazi [5]		
5-06	Nigeria	L	0-2	Abuja	WCq		35 000	Pare BFA
19-06	Gabon	W	3-1	Kigali	WCq	Said 2 [4 64], Mulisa [27]	16 325	Abdulkadir TAN
3-07	Zimbabwe	L	0-2	Kigali	WCq			Chilinda MWI
14-08	Uganda	W	2-1	Kampala	Fr	Mulisa, Karekezi		
28-08	Zambia	L	1-2	Kitwe	Fr	Gaseruka [71]	15 000	Mwanza ZAM
5-09	Angola	L	0-1	Luanda	WCq		30 000	Damon RSA
9-10	Algeria	D	1-1	Kigali	WCq	Said [9]	20 000	Abdel Rahman SUD
11-12	Zanzibar †	W	4-2	Addis Abeba	CCr1	Lomani 3 [8 28 48], Karekezi [24]	20 000	
13-12	Burundi	L	1-3	Addis Abeba	CCr1	Gatete [59]		
15-12	Ethiopia	D	0-0	Addis Abeba	CCr1		20 000	
19-12	Tanzania	W	5-1	Addis Abeba	CCr1	Lomani 3, Karekezi, Sibomana		
2005								
12-03	Kenya	D	1-1	Niarobi	Fr	Bolla [10]		
27-03	Algeria	L	0-1	Oran	WCq		20 000	Abd El Fatah EGY
5-06	Nigeria	D	1-1	Kigali	WCq	Gatete [53]	30 000	Kidane ERI
18-06	Gabon	L	0-3	Libreville	WCq		10 000	El Arjoun MAR

Fr = Friendly match • CN = CAF African Cup of Nations • CC = CECAFA Cup • AA = Afro-Asian Games • WC = FIFA World Cup™
q = qualifier • r1 = first round group • sf = semi-final • f = final • † Not a full international

RWANDA NATIONAL TEAM RECORDS AND RECORD SEQUENCES

Records			Sequence records				
Victory	4-1	DJI 1999	Wins	3	2000	Clean sheets	4	1999
Defeat	1-6	COD 1976	Defeats	5	1976-77, 1983-86	Goals scored	14	2000-2001
Player Caps	n/a		Undefeated	10	1998-2000	Without goal	3	1983-1986
Player Goals	n/a		Without win	16	1983-1996	Goals against	8	2003-04, 2004

FIFA REFEREE LIST 2005

	Int'l	DoB
BENIJAMBO Landouard	2001	28-07-1971
BUREGEYA Janvier		6-01-1969
GASINGWA Michel	1997	25-09-1964
KAGABO Issa		23-03-1970
MUNYEMANA Hudu	2001	10-10-1974
MUTANGUHA Idi Saidi		2-04-1972

FIFA ASSISTANT REFEREE LIST 2005

	Int'l	DoB
BAMPORIKI Desire	2001	19-05-1974
KABANDA Felicien		19-07-1971
KAMBANDA Innocent	2001	24-12-1964
NKUBITO Athanase		29-03-1964
NTAGUNGIRA Celestin	1997	11-05-1966
NZEYIMANA Jean-Baptiste	1999	29-06-1965
UGIRASHEBUJA Zuberi		3-03-1964

COUPE AMAHORO 2005

Quarter-finals			Semi-finals			Final	
Rayon Sport	1	0					
La Jeunesse	0	0	Rayon Sport	2	1		
Zebres FC		0	Kigali FC	1	1		
Kigali FC		2				Rayon Sport	3
Police FC	1	2				Mukura Victory	0
APR FC	1	1	Police FC		0		
Kiyovu Sport	1	0	Mukura Victory		1		
Mukura Victory	1	1					

4-07-2005
Amahoro, Kigali
Scorers - Sibomana 2 [12] [89p], OG [87]

RECENT LEAGUE AND CUP RECORD

	Championship	Cup		
Year	Champions	Winners	Score	Runners-up
1995	APR FC Kigali			
1996	APR FC Kigali			
1997	Rayon Sports Butare			
1998	Rayon Sports Butare			
1999	APR FC Kigali			
2000	APR FC Kigali			
2001	APR FC Kigali	Citadins	0-0 6-5p	APR FC
2002	Rayon Sports Butare	APR FC Kigali	2-1	Rayon Sports Butare
2003	APR FC Kigali			
2004	Rayon Sports Butare			
2005		Rayon Sport	3-0	Mukura Victory

RWANDA COUNTRY INFORMATION

Capital	Kigali	Independence	1962 from Belgium	GDP per Capita	$1 300
Population	7 954 013	Status	Repulblic	GNP Ranking	139
Area km²	26 338	Language	Kinyarwanda, English, French	Dialling code	+250
Population density	301 per km²	Literacy rate	70%	Internet code	.rw
% in urban areas	6%	Main religion	Christian	GMT + / –	+2
Towns/Cities ('000)	Kigali 745; Butare 89; Gitarama 87; Ruhengeri 86; Gisenyi 83; Byumba 70; Cyangugu 63				
Neighbours (km)	Tanzania 217; Burundi 290; Congo DR 217; Uganda 169				
Main stadia	Stade Amahoro – Kigali 15 000				

Left **12 April 2005. San Siro, Milan, Italy.** Milan's goalkeeper Dida is hit by a flare thrown by an Inter fan during the UEFA Champions League quarter-final tie between the Milanese rivals. The match was abandoned and later awarded to Milan.

Middle left **4 May 2005. Estadio Ricardo Saprissa, San Jose, Costa Rica.** Deportivo Saprissa players celebrate their second goal against Mexico's UNAM Pumas in the final of the CONCACAF Champions Cup. Saprissa won 3–2 on aggregate.

Below left **22 May 2005. Stamford Bridge, London, England.** The fifty year itch. In their centenary Chelsea celebrate a second Championship, fifty years after the first. The fans are unlikely to have to wait as long again for a third.

Below **8 May 2005. San Siro, Milan, Italy.** Milan lose at home to Juventus and see the Scudetto slip from their hands. Not for the last time in May 2005, the players of Milan can't quite believe what has happened.

15 May 2005. Copacabana, Rio de Janeiro, Brazil. Inspired by coach Eric Cantona, France win the first FIFA Beach Soccer World Cup beating Portugal on penalties in the final.

28 May 2005. Olympiastadion, Berlin, Germany. For the third time this century Bayern München do the double after beating Schalke 2–1 in the Cup final.

25 May 2005. Ataturk Olimpiyat, Istanbul, Turkey. A dramatic finale to the UEFA Champions League final as Jerzy Dudek saves Andriy Shevchenko's penalty to win the European Cup for Liverpool.

Below **31 May 2005. Allianz Arena, Munich, Germany.** Football enters the space age as the new home of Bayern München and TSV 1860 is opened.

SAM – SAMOA

NATIONAL TEAM RECORD
JULY 1ST 2002 TO JUNE 30TH 2005

PL	W	D	L	F	A	%
5	1	1	3	5	11	30

FIFA/COCA-COLA WORLD RANKING

1993	1994	1995	1996	1997	1998	1999	2000	2001	2002	2003	2004	High		Low	
-	-	-	177	183	164	180	173	172	163	176	179	**166**	03/02	**186**	06/00

					2004-2005						
08/04	09/04	10/04	11/04	12/04	01/05	02/05	03/05	04/05	05/05	06/05	07/05
177	177	178	178	179	179	177	177	176	179	178	178

With one of the best rugby union teams in the Polynesian and Melanesian islands the main focus of Samoan sporting attention is most definitely the oval ball. With rugby league also strong, the difficulty in attracting support for football among a population of less than 200,000 spread over nine islands cannot be underestimated. However, the sport has moved forward with the help of FIFA's Goal projects that funded the creation of the Toleafoa J.S. Blatter football pitches and a football complex that will house the association and teaching facilities. On the international stage, Samoa's FIFA World Cup™ qualifying campaign began on familiar territory as the country hosted

INTERNATIONAL HONOURS
None

Group 2 of the Oceania Zone. However, home advantage didn't work as only victory over neighbours American Samoa kept them off the foot of the table. The J.S. Blatter Fields hosted all the matches of the 10-team Samoa League that was won by the undefeated Strickland Brothers. A quick name change meant the Brothers were now Tunaimato Breeze, but that detail didn't hinder the team as they went on to win the Champion of Champions series (Premier League Cup), beating Central United 3-2 in the final. Breeze couldn't maintain the success though as they lost 7-0 on aggregate to Sobou of Papua new Guinea in the preliminary round of the Oceania Champions Club Cup.

THE FIFA BIG COUNT OF 2000

	Male	Female		Male	Female
Registered players	1 000	0	Referees	50	0
Non registered players	1 000	0	Officials	250	0
Youth players	1 000		Total involved	3 300	
Total players	3 000		Number of clubs	50	
Professional players	0	0	Number of teams	200	

Samoa Football Soccer Federation (SFSF)
Tuanaimato, PO Box 6172, Apia, Samoa
Tel +685 7783210   Fax +685 22855
www.soccersamoa.ws
President: ROEBECK Tautulu   General Secretary: SOLIA Tilomai
Vice-President: PAPALII Seiuli Poasa   Treasurer: LINO Maiava Visesio   Media Officer: SOLIA Tilomai
Men's Coach: BRAND David   Women's Coach: Brand David
SFSF formed: 1968   OFC: 1984   FIFA: 1986
Colours: Blue, Blue, Red

GAMES PLAYED BY SAMOA IN THE 2006 FIFA WORLD CUP™ CYCLE

2002	Opponents	Score	Venue	Comp	Scorers	Att	Referee
No international matches played in 2002 after June							
2003							
No international matches played in 2003							
2004							
5-05	Cook Islands	D 0-0	Auckland	Fr			
10-05	American Samoa	W 4-0	Apia	WCq	Bryce 12, Fasavalu 2 30 53, Michael 66	500	Afu SOL
15-05	Vanuatu	L 0-3	Apia	WCq		650	Breeze AUS
17-05	Fiji	L 0-4	Apia	WCq		450	Diomis AUS
19-05	Papua New Guinea	L 1-4	Apia	WCq	Michael 69	300	Diomis AUS
2005							
No international matches played in 2005 before August							

Fr = Friendly match • WC = FIFA World Cup™ • q = qualifier

SAMOA NATIONAL TEAM RECORDS AND RECORD SEQUENCES

Records			Sequence records				
Victory	5-0	ASA 2002	Wins	3	1998-2000	Clean sheets	2	2002, 2004
Defeat	0-13	TAH 1981	Defeats	8	1979-1981	Goals scored	8	1998-2000
Player Caps	n/a		Undefeated	3	1998-2000	Without goal	4	1983-1988
Player Goals	n/a		Without win	8	1979-1981	Goals against	22	1979-1998

FIFA ASSISTANT REFEREE LIST 2005

	Int'l	DoB
AIMAASU Fiti	2001	24-04-1978
AUVELE Collins	2001	10-07-1977

SAMOA 2004 PREMIER LEAGUE

	Pl	W	D	L	F	A	Pts
Strickland Brothers	9	7	2	0	24	5	23
Lupe Ole Soaga	9	7	1	1	15	7	22
Gold Star Sogi	9	5	2	2	22	8	17
Kiwi	9	5	2	2	20	10	17
Central United	9	5	0	4	16	14	15
Moa Moa	9	3	1	5	6	17	10
Hosanna	9	2	1	6	6	19	7
OSM Sinamoga	9	1	3	5	12	22	6
Moata'a	9	2	0	7	7	22	6
Vaivase-tai	9	1	2	6	6	10	5

17/07/2004 - 18/09/2004

PREMIER LEAGUE CUP 2004-05

Quarter-finals		Semi-finals		Final	
Tunaimato Breeze	2				
Sinamoga	1	Tunaimato Breeze	2	4-12-2004	
Manumea U-20	0	Gold Star Sogi	0		
Gold Star Sogi	1			Tunaimato Breeze	3
Moata'a	3			Central United	2
Vaivase-tai	1	Moata'a	0		
Kiwi	1	Central United	2		
Central United	5				

RECENT LEAGUE AND CUP RECORD

Championship		Cup		
Year	Champions	Winners	Score	Runners-up
1997	Kiwi	Kiwi		Vaivase-tai
1998	Vaivase-tai	Togafuafua		
1999	Moata'a	Moaula		Moata'a
2000	Titavi	Gold Star	4-1	Faatoia
2001	Gold Star	Strickland Brothers	3-3 5-4p	Moata'a
2002	Strickland Brothers	Vaivase-tai		Hosanna
2003	Strickland Brothers	Strickland Brothers	5-2	Moata'a
2004	Strickland Brothers	Tunaimato Breeze	3-2	Central United

SAMOA COUNTRY INFORMATION

Capital	Apia	Independence	1962 from New Zealand	GDP per Capita	$5 600
Population	177 714	Status	Constitutional Monarchy	GNP Ranking	178
Area km²	2 944	Language	Samoan, English	Dialling code	+685
Population density	60 per km²	Literacy rate	99%	Internet code	.ws
% in urban areas	21%	Main religion	Christian	GMT +/−	-11
Towns/Cities ('000)	Apia 40; Vaitele 5; Faleasiu3; Vailele 3; Leauvaa 3; Faleula 2; Siusega 2; Malie 2; Fasitoouta 2				
Neighbours (km)	South Pacific Ocean 403				
Main stadia	Toleafoa J.S. Blatter Complex – Apia				

SCG – SERBIA AND MONTENEGRO

NATIONAL TEAM RECORD
JULY 1ST 2002 TO JUNE 30TH 2005

PL	W	D	L	F	A	%
28	8	10	10	33	33	46.4

FIFA/COCA-COLA WORLD RANKING

1993	1994	1995	1996	1997	1998	1999	2000	2001	2002	2003	2004	High		Low	
-	-	-	-	-	-	-	-	-	19	41	46	19	12/02	55	10/04

2004-2005											
08/04	09/04	10/04	11/04	12/04	01/05	02/05	03/05	04/05	05/05	06/05	07/05
44	51	55	54	46	46	46	46	47	46	49	49

Where once there was a single nation of 23 million Yugoslavs, there are now five different countries and it is a testament to the huge talent produced in the Balkans that football is still played to such a high standard throughout the region. With a population of 10 million Serbia and Montenegro is the most populous of the former Yugoslav republics but unlike Croatia and Slovenia they have yet to qualify for FIFA World Cup™ finals. In the past Yugoslav teams were noted for their attacking flare, but at the heart of Serbia and Montenegro's attempt to qualify for the finals in Germany has been a formidable defence that after the qualifiers in June 2005 had still to concede a goal, a

INTERNATIONAL HONOURS
UEFA Champions League Crvena Zvezda 1991

feat no other nation could match. Concerns remain, however, about the level of competition within club football in the country as once again Partizan and Red Star completely dominated the League. Partizan remained undefeated throughout the 30 game campaign while Red Star lost just twice and although neither defeat was at the hands of Partizan it proved to be the difference between the two clubs. In an example of just how precarious a situation many of the clubs find themselves in, not longer after causing a big upset by beating Red Star in the Cup Final, Zeleznik folded.

THE FIFA BIG COUNT OF 2000

	Male	Female		Male	Female
Registered players	250 800	450	Referees	8 000	30
Non registered players	120 000	2 000	Officials	375 000	150
Youth players	100 100	120	Total involved	856 650	
Total players	473 470		Number of clubs	2 821	
Professional players	800	0	Number of teams	7 527	

Football Association of Serbia and Montenegro (FSSCG)

Fudbalski savez Srbije i Crne Gore, Terazije 35, PO Box 263, Belgrade 11000, Serbia and Montenegro

Tel +381 11 3234253   Fax +381 11 3233433

fsj@beotel.yu   www.fsj.co.yu

President: KARADZIC Tomislav   General Secretary: DAMJANOVIC Zoran

Vice-President: SAVICEVIC Dejan   Treasurer: TBD   Media Officer: None

Men's Coach: PETKOVIC Ilija   Women's Coach: KRSTIC Perica

FSSCG formed: 1919   UEFA: 1954   FIFA: 1919

Colours: Blue, White, Red

GAMES PLAYED BY SERBIA AND MONTENEGRO IN THE 2006 FIFA WORLD CUP™ CYCLE

2002	Opponents	Score		Venue	Comp	Scorers	Att	Referee
21-08	Bosnia-Herzegovina	W	2-0	Sarajevo	Fr	Krstajic [34], Kovacevic.D [41]	9 000	Siric CRO
6-09	Czech Republic	L	0-5	Prague	Fr		5 435	Baskakov RUS
12-10	Italy	D	1-1	Naples	ECq	Mijatovic [27]	50 000	Mejuto Gonzalez ESP
16-10	Finland	W	2-0	Belgrade	ECq	Kovacevic.D [56], Mihajlovic [84p]	30 000	Wegereef NED
20-11	France	L	0-3	Paris	Fr		60 000	Iturralde Gonzalez ESP
2003								
12-02	Azerbaijan	D	2-2	Podgorica	ECq	Mijatovic [34p], Lazetic [52]	8 000	Granat POL
27-03	Bulgaria	L	1-2	Krusevac	Fr	Kovacevic.D [29]	10 000	Lazarevski MKD
30-04	Germany	L	0-1	Bremen	Fr		22 000	De Bleeckere BEL
3-06	England	L	1-2	Leicester	Fr	Jestrovic [45]	30 900	Allaerts BEL
7-06	Finland	L	0-3	Helsinki	ECq		17 343	Colombo FRA
11-06	Azerbaijan	L	1-2	Baku	ECq	Boskovic [27]	5 000	Fisker DEN
20-08	Wales	W	1-0	Belgrade	ECq	Mladenovic [73]	25 000	Frisk SWE
10-09	Italy	D	1-1	Belgrade	ECq	Ilic [82]	35 000	Hamer LUX
11-10	Wales	W	3-2	Cardiff	ECq	Vukic [4], Milosevic [82], Ljuboja [87]	72 514	Stuchlik AUT
16-11	Poland	L	3-4	Plock	Fr	Boskovic [70], Vukic [79], Iliev [89]	9 000	Weiner GER
2004								
31-03	Norway	L	0-1	Belgrade	Fr		3 000	Panic BIH
28-04	Northern Ireland	D	1-1	Belfast	Fr	Paunovic [7]	9 690	Richards WAL
11-07	Slovakia	W	2-0	Fukuoka	Fr	Milosevic [6], Jestrovic [90]	6 100	Yoshida JPN
13-07	Japan	L	0-1	Yokohama	Fr		57 616	Lennie AUS
18-08	Slovenia	D	1-1	Ljubljana	Fr	Jestrovic [49]	7 000	Ovrebo NOR
4-09	San Marino	W	3-0	Serravalle	WCq	Vukic [4], Jestrovic 2 [15 83]	1 137	Kholmatov KAZ
9-10	Bosnia-Herzegovina	D	0-0	Sarajevo	WCq		22 440	Veissiere FRA
13-10	San Marino	W	5-0	Belgrade	WCq	Milosevic [35], Stankovic 2 [45 50], Koroman [53], Vukic [69]	4 000	Isaksen FRO
17-11	Belgium	W	2-0	Brussels	WCq	Vukic [7], Kezman [60]	28 350	Frojdfeldt SWE
2005								
9-02	Bulgaria	D	0-0	Sofia	Fr		3 000	Guenov BUL
30-03	Spain	D	0-0	Belgrade	WCq		48 910	Busacca SUI
4-06	Belgium	D	0-0	Belgrade	WCq		16 662	Ivanov.V RUS
8-06	Italy	D	1-1	Toronto	Fr	Zigic [25]	35 000	Depiero CAN

Fr = Friendly match • EC = UEFA EURO 2004™ • WC = FIFA World Cup™ • q = qualifier

FIFA REFEREE LIST 2005

	Int'l	DoB
DELEVIC Dejan	1998	24-01-1961
KARADZIC Milan	2004	16-01-1967
MIHALJEVIC Goran	2003	5-05-1969
RABRENOVIC Nebojsa	2003	12-12-1971
STANISIC Dejan	2001	3-04-1967
TANOVIC Dragomir	2002	28-04-1965

FIFA ASSISTANT REFEREE LIST 2005

	Int'l	DoB
BOROVIC Jovan	2005	18-08-1965
CUPIC Zoran	2002	22-12-1966
NEDIC Dejan	2004	24-06-1965
RADOJCIC Igor	2005	12-10-1968
RADULOVIC Milos	2004	11-04-1967
SAVIJA Jovica	2004	27-01-1969
SIMOVIC Vitomir	2000	24-06-1963
SIPCIC Zoran	1999	20-12-1960
STEPANOVIC Radovan	2005	18-03-1969
TOMICIC Nikola	2003	14-03-1966

SERBIA AND MONTENEGRO COUNTRY INFORMATION

Capital	Belgrade	Independence	1992 (break up of Yugoslavia)	GDP per Capita	$2 200
Population	10 825 900	Status	Republic	GNP Ranking	86
Area km²	102 350	Language	Serbian, Albanian	Dialling code	+381
Population density	105 per km²	Literacy rate	93%	Internet code	.yu
% in urban areas	57%	Main religion	Christian 70%, Muslim 19%	GMT + / −	+1
Towns/Cities ('000)	Belgrade 1 115; Pristina 254; Novi Sad 194; Nis 173; Prizren 159; Podgorica 157				
Neighbours (km)	Romania 476; Bulgaria 318; FYR Macedonia 221; Albania 287; Bosnia and Herzegovina 527; Croatia 266; Hungary 151				
Main stadia	Maracana – Belgrade 51 328; Partizana – Belgrade 30 887				

SERBIA AND MONTENEGRO NATIONAL TEAM RECORDS AND RECORD SEQUENCES

Records			Sequence records					
Victory	10-0	VEN 1972	Wins	10	1978-1980	Clean sheets	7	2004-2005
Defeat	0-7	CZE, URU, CZE	Defeats	6	1931-1932	Goals scored	36	1959-1962
Player Caps	90	MILOSEVIC Savo	Undefeated	16	1996-1998	Without goal	4	1971-72, 1977-78
Player Goals	38	BOBEK Stjepan	Without win	7	2002-2003	Goals against	19	1920-1927

NATIONAL CAPS

	Caps
MILOSEVIC Savo	90
DZAJIC Dragan	85
STOJKOVIC Dragan	84
MIJATOVIC Predrag	73
VUJOVIC Zlatko	70
ZEBEC Branko	65
JOKANOVIC Slavisa	64
BOBEK Stjepan	63
MIHAJLOVIC Sinisa	63

NATIONAL GOALS

	Goals
BOBEK Stjepan	38
GALIC Milan	37
MARJANOVIC Blagoje	36
MILOSEVIC Savo	35
MITIC Rajko	32
BAJEVIC Dusan	29
VESELINOVIC Todor	28
MIJATOVIC Predrag	27
KOSTIC Borivoje	26
VUJOVIC Zlatko	25

NATIONAL COACH

	Years
SANTRAC Slobodan	1994-'98
ZIVADINOVIC Milan	1998-'99
BOSKOV Vujadin	1999-'00
PETKOVIC Ilija	2000-'01
DJORIC Milovan	2001
3 man commision	2001
SAVICEVIC Dejan	2001-'03
PETKOVIC Ilija	2003-

CLUB DIRECTORY

Club	Town/City	Stadium	Phone	www.	Lge	Cup	CL
FK Borac	Cacak	Gradski 6 000	+381 32 225458		0	0	0
Crvena Zvezda (Red Star)	Beograd	Crvena Zvezda 51 328	+381 11 3672060	fc-redstar.net	23	20	1
FK Cukaricki	Beograd	Cukaricki 5 000	+381 11 558627		0	0	0
FK Hajduk Beograd	Beograd	Hajduk 4 000	+381 11 2417338		0	0	0
FK Hajduk Kula	Kula	Hajduk 11 000	+381 25 723569	fchajduk.com	0	0	0
FK Obilic	Beograd	Milos Obilic 4 508	+381 11 3807426	fcobilic.co.yu	1	0	0
OFK Beograd	Beograd	Omladinski 13 912	+381 11 2765425	ofkbeograd.com	0	4	0
FK Partizan	Beograd	Partizana 30 887	+381 11 3229691	partizan.co.yu	19	9	0
FK Buducnost Podgorica	Podgorica	Pod Goricom 17 000	+381 81 244955	fkbuducnost.co.yu	0	0	0
FK Radnicki Novi Beograd	Beograd	Cika Daca 22 058	+381 11 2699119		0	0	0
FK Smederevo	Smederevo	Kraj Stare Zelezare 16 565	+381 26 223030	fcsartid.co.yu	0	1	0
FK Sutjeska	Niksic	Gradski 10 800	+381 83 246874	sutjeska.cg.yu	0	0	0
FK Vojvodina	Novi Sad	Gradski 15 745	+381 21 421688	fcvojvodina.co.yu	2	0	0
FK Zeleznik	Zeleznik	Zeleznik 8 350	+381 11 577164	fczeleznik.co.yu	0	0	0
FK Zemun	Zemun	Gradski 10 000	+381 11 2196057	fkzemun.co.yu	0	0	0
FK Zeta	Golubovci	Tresnjica 5 000	+381 81 873141		0	0	0

RECENT LEAGUE AND CUP RECORD

	Championship						Cup		
Year	Champions	Pts	Runners-up	Pts	Third	Pts	Winners	Score	Runners-up
1990	Crvena Zvezda	51	Dinamo Zagreb	42	Hajduk Split	38	Crvena Zvezda	1-0	Hajduk Split
1991	Crvena Zvezda	54	Dinamo Zagreb	46	Partizan Beograd	41	Hajduk Split	1-0	Crvena Zvezda
1992	Crvena Zvezda	50	Partizan Beograd	46	Vojvodina Novi Sad	42	Partizan Beograd	1-0 2-2	Crvena Zvezda
1993	Partizan Beograd	65	Crvena Zvezda	51	Vojvodina Novi Sad	46	Crvena Zvezda	0-1 1-0 5-4p	Partizan Beograd
1994	Partizan Beograd	42	Crvena Zvezda	37	Vojvodina Novi Sad	31	Partizan Beograd	3-2 6-1	Spartak Subotica
1995	Crvena Zvezda	42	Partizan Beograd	38	Vojvodina Novi Sad	37	Crvena Zvezda	4-0 0-0	FK Obilic
1996	Partizan Beograd	60	Crvena Zvezda	48	Vojvodina Novi Sad	43	Crvena Zvezda	3-0 3-1	Partizan Beograd
1997	Partizan Beograd	84	Crvena Zvezda	78	Vojvodina Novi Sad	53	Crvena Zvezda	0-0 1-0	Vojvodina Novi Sad
1998	FK Obilic	86	Crvena Zvezda	84	Partizan Beograd	70	Partizan Beograd	0-0 2-0	FK Obilic
1999	Partizan Beograd	66	FK Obilic	64	Crvena Zvezda	51	Crvena Zvezda	4-2	Partizan Beograd
2000	Crvena Zvezda	105	Partizan Beograd	101	FK Obilic	89	Crvena Zvezda	4-0	Napredak Krusevac
2001	Crvena Zvezda	88	Partizan Beograd	86	FK Obilic	63	Partizan Beograd	1-0	Crvena Zvezda
2002	Partizan Beograd	81	Crvena Zvezda	66	Sartid Smederevo	58	Crvena Zvezda	1-0	Sartid Smederevo
2003	Partizan Beograd	89	Crvena Zvezda	70	OFK Beograd	63	Sartid Smederevo	1-0	Crvena Zvezda
2004	Crvena Zvezda	74	Partizan Beograd	63	FK Zeleznik	58	Crvena Zvezda	1-0	Buducnost Dvor
2005	Partizan Beograd	80	Crvena Zvezda	74	Zeta Golubovci	59	Zeleznik Beograd	1-0	Crvena Zvezda

Croatian and Slovenian clubs withdrew from the league after the 1991 season • Bosnian and Macedonian clubs followed after the 1992 season

SERBIA AND MONTENEGRO 2004-05

PRVA SAVEZNA LIGA

	Pl	W	D	L	F	A	Pts	Partizan	Red Star	Zeta	OFK	Zemun	Buducnost	Kula	Vojvodina	Zeleznik	Smederevo	Obilic	Radnicki	Borac	Cukaricki	Sutjeska	Hajduk
Partizan Beograd †	30	25	5	0	81	20	80		0-0	3-2	3-2	3-1	1-0	5-0	1-0	4-1	4-1	4-1	1-0	1-1	3-1	3-0	7-0
Crvena Zvezda ‡	30	23	5	2	66	18	74	1-1		2-1	4-2	1-0	1-2	2-1	3-0	3-1	1-1	4-1	4-0	0-1	5-0	3-0	5-0
Zeta Golubovci ‡	30	18	5	7	52	30	59	1-1	1-1		2-0	2-1	0-0	3-0	1-0	1-0	2-2	2-1	2-0	4-0	2-0	2-1	5-2
OFK Beograd ‡	30	16	2	12	51	36	50	0-2	0-1	0-1			4-0	1-0	4-1	2-0	1-0	3-0	2-1	3-2	2-0	2-0	6-0
FK Zemun	30	12	7	11	31	34	43	0-5	0-0	2-1	3-2		5-3	1-0	0-0	1-1	2-0	2-0	3-1	2-2	0-0	1-0	2-1
Buducnost Podgorica	30	12	5	13	37	37	41	0-2	1-3	1-0	1-0	0-1		1-1	3-1	0-0	0-1	3-1	1-0	1-2	0-0	1-0	4-0
Hajduk Kula	30	10	9	11	34	37	39	0-1	0-1	3-2	0-0	0-1	0-1		2-0	3-0	0-0	0-0	2-1	1-1	1-0	0-0	1-1
Vojvodina Novi Sad	30	10	8	12	31	37	38	1-3	1-3	2-2	0-1	1-0	2-1	1-1		2-0	2-0	4-2	2-1	1-0	1-0	3-0	1-1
FK Zeleznik	30	11	5	14	38	45	38	1-2	3-5	1-3	3-2	1-0	2-2	2-1	2-2		0-1	4-3	3-2	3-1	2-1	1-0	3-0
FK Smederevo	30	9	10	11	28	36	37	1-3	0-2	0-2	3-0	1-0	2-1	3-1	1-0	0-2		1-1	3-0	1-4	0-0	1-1	1-1
Obilic Beograd	30	10	6	14	35	47	36	0-4	0-1	3-1	2-0	0-2	4-2	1-3	1-0	2-0	1-0		1-1	3-2	1-0	1-1	1-0
Radnicki Novi Beograd	30	10	5	15	33	38	35	1-2	0-1	3-0	1-2	0-0	2-1	2-2	1-1	1-0	0-2	1-0		1-0	3-0	0-1	2-0
Borac Cacak	30	9	7	14	34	44	34	1-3	0-2	0-2	0-2	0-0	0-2	0-2	3-0	1-0	1-0	0-0	1-1		1-1	5-2	2-0
Cukaricki Beograd	30	8	8	14	32	41	32	2-2	0-1	0-1	1-1	2-1	3-1	1-3	1-0	2-1	0-2	1-1	2-1	0-2		3-0	5-0
Sutjeska Niksic	30	5	7	18	21	48	22	1-4	1-2	0-2	3-2	1-0	0-1	0-2	1-1	1-0	1-1	0-0	0-1	3-1	1-2		0-0
Hajduk Beograd	30	2	6	22	20	76	12	0-3	0-4	1-2	2-3	2-0	2-3	2-3	0-1	0-0	0-0	1-2	0-3	1-2	0-3	3-2	

7/08/2004 - 28/05/2005 • † Qualified for the UEFA Champions League • ‡ Qualified for the UEFA Cup

II LIGA GRUPA SRBIJA (2)

	Pl	W	D	L	F	A	Pts
Buducnost Banatski Dvor	38	22	10	6	69	34	76
Javor Ivanjica	38	22	8	8	44	30	74
Rad Beograd	38	21	8	9	64	30	71
Mladost Apatin	38	17	12	9	50	31	63
Bezanija Novi Beograd	38	17	7	14	59	53	58
Napredak Krusevac	38	14	13	11	46	37	55
Jedinstvo Ub	38	13	14	11	44	35	53
Spartak Subotica	38	13	13	12	53	44	52
Srem	38	15	7	16	50	48	52
Novi Pazar	38	14	10	14	37	39	52
Macva Sabac	38	14	10	14	44	51	52
Vozdovac Beograd	38	12	15	11	46	37	51
OFK Nis	38	15	6	17	43	40	51
Novi Sad	38	13	11	14	39	47	50
Radnicki Nis	38	13	10	15	44	44	49
Vlasina Vlasotince	38	15	3	20	45	53	48
Radnicki Obrenovac	38	11	10	17	26	50	43
Proleter Zrenjanin	38	11	7	20	38	59	40
Kosanica Kursumlija	38	6	11	21	22	64	29
Mladost Lucani	38	7	5	26	27	60	26

14/08/2004 - 18/06/2005

II LIGA GRUPA CRNA GORA (2)

	Pl	W	D	L	F	A	Pts
Jedinstvo Bijelo Polje	36	19	11	6	57	26	68
Kom Podgorica	36	16	10	10	54	30	58
Decic Tuzi	36	12	19	5	40	27	55
Rudar Pljevlja	36	13	12	11	38	39	51
Petrovac	36	12	9	15	34	38	45
Mogren Budva	36	11	12	13	40	46	45
Grbalj Radanovici	36	11	10	15	36	50	43
Bokelj Kotor	36	11	15	10	30	40	41
Mornar Bar	36	10	9	17	31	46	39
Mladost Podgorica	36	9	11	16	31	49	38

13/08/2004 - 3/06/2005

KUP SCG 2004-05

Eighth-finals

FK Zeleznik	1
Zeta Golubovci *	0
Buducnost B. Dvor	1
Cukaricki Beograd *	3
Radnicki Pirot	1 3p
Crvena Stijena *	1 1p
OFK Beograd	0 4p
Rad Beograd *	0 5p
Partizan Beograd	3
Vojvodina Novi Sad *	1
Kom Podgorica	0
Obilic Beograd *	2
FK Smederevo	0 3p
Buducnost Podgorica*	0 1p
Javor Ivanjica	0
Crvena Zvezda *	2

Quarter-finals

FK Zeleznik *	1 3p
Cukaricki Beograd	1 2p
Radnicki Pirot *	0
Rad Beograd	1
Partizan Beograd *	1
Obilic Beograd	0
FK Smederevo	1
Crvena Zvezda *	2

Semi-finals

FK Zeleznik	3
Rad Beograd	0
Partizan Beograd	0
Crvena Zvezda	2

Final

FK Zeleznik	1
Crvena Zvezda	0

SERBIAN CUP FINAL
24-05-2005, Att:7 000, Ref: Stojanovic
Belgrade
Scorer - Radjenovic 91+ for Zeleznik

* Home team

SCO – SCOTLAND

NATIONAL TEAM RECORD
JULY 1ST 2002 TO JUNE 30TH 2005

PL	W	D	L	F	A	%
31	9	8	14	28	43	41.9

FIFA/COCA-COLA WORLD RANKING

1993	1994	1995	1996	1997	1998	1999	2000	2001	2002	2003	2004	High		Low	
24	32	26	29	37	38	20	25	50	59	54	86	**20**	10/99	**88**	03/05

2004-2005											
08/04	09/04	10/04	11/04	12/04	01/05	02/05	03/05	04/05	05/05	06/05	07/05
62	67	68	77	86	86	87	88	86	85	83	85

An extraordinary finale to the Scottish Premier League saw Rangers snatch the title from Celtic in the final minutes of the final match of the season. With just three minutes remaining Celtic were beating Motherwell 1-0 and were champions bar the shouting, but then in an extraordinary twist they conceded twice in the final minutes to hand the title to their fierce cross-town rivals. Never before had the Championship gone so close to the wire. There was some consolation for Celtic the following weekend when they beat Dundee United in the Cup Final in what was Martin O'Neill's final match in charge after five hugely successful years during which he transformed the fortunes

INTERNATIONAL HONOURS
British International Championship 41 times from 1884 to 1977   UEFA Champions League Celtic 1967

of the club. Fans in Scotland will be hoping Walter Smith will have the same effect on the national team following his replacement of Bertie Vogts after a disappointing start to the FIFA World Cup™ qualifying campaign. The Scots never really warmed to their first foreign coach but the roots of the Scottish decline probably lie closer to home. In 1967 Celtic won the European Cup with 11 players born within 10 miles of Celtic Park but now the production line that produced such talent no longer seems to work. Remarkably, however, having won just one of the first six games, Scotland were still in with a chance of making it to the finals in Germany.

THE FIFA BIG COUNT OF 2000

	Male	Female		Male	Female
Registered players	30 000	0	Referees	2 097	33
Non registered players	50 000	7 500	Officials	8 000	150
Youth players	95 000	2 000	Total involved	194 780	
Total players	184 500		Number of clubs	5 879	
Professional players	2 785	0	Number of teams	8 969	

The Scottish Football Association (SFA)
Hampden Park, Glasgow G42 9AY, United Kingdom
Tel +44 141 6166000   Fax +44 141 6166001
info@scottishfa.co.uk   www.scottishfa.co.uk
President: McBETH John   General Secretary: TAYLOR David
Vice-President: PEAT George   Treasurer: TBD   Media Officer: MITCHELL Andrew
Men's Coach: SMITH Walter   Women's Coach: SIGNEUL Anna
SFA formed: 1873   UEFA: 1954   FIFA: 1910-20, 1924-28, 1946
Colours: Dark blue, White, Dark blue

GAMES PLAYED BY SCOTLAND IN THE 2006 FIFA WORLD CUP™ CYCLE

2002	Opponents	Score		Venue	Comp	Scorers	Att	Referee
21-08	Denmark	L	0-1	Glasgow	Fr		28 766	Irvine NIR
7-09	Faroe Islands	D	2-2	Toftir	ECq	Lambert 62, Ferguson 83	4 000	Granat POL
12-10	Iceland	W	2-0	Reykjavik	ECq	Dailly 6, Naysmith 63	7 065	Sars FRA
15-10	Canada	W	3-1	Edinburgh	Fr	Crawford 2 11 73, Thompson 50	16 207	Huyghe BEL
20-11	Portugal	L	0-2	Braga	Fr		8 000	Anghelinei ROM
2003								
12-02	Republic of Ireland	L	0-2	Glasgow	Fr		33 337	Braamhaar NED
29-03	Iceland	W	2-1	Glasgow	ECq	Miller.K 12, Wilkie 70	37 548	Temmink NED
2-04	Lithuania	L	0-1	Kaunas	ECq		8 000	Stuchlik AUT
30-04	Austria	L	0-2	Glasgow	Fr		12 189	Vollquartz DEN
27-05	New Zealand	D	1-1	Edinburgh	Fr	Crawford 10	10 016	Ingvarsson SWE
7-06	Germany	D	1-1	Glasgow	ECq	Miller.K 69	48 037	Messina ITA
20-08	Norway	D	0-0	Oslo	Fr		12 858	Vuorela FIN
6-09	Faroe Islands	W	3-1	Glasgow	ECq	McCann 7, Dickov 45, McFadden 74	40 901	Ceferin SVN
10-09	Germany	L	1-2	Dortmund	ECq	McCann 60	67 000	Frisk SWE
11-10	Lithuania	W	1-0	Glasgow	ECq	Fletcher 70	50 343	Colombo FRA
15-11	Netherlands	W	1-0	Glasgow	ECpo	McFadden 22	50 670	Hauge NOR
19-11	Netherlands	L	0-6	Amsterdam	ECpo	-	51 000	Michel SVK
2004								
18-02	Wales	L	0-4	Cardiff	Fr		47 124	Ross NIR
31-03	Romania	L	1-2	Glasgow	Fr	McFadden 57	20 433	Hyytia FIN
28-04	Denmark	L	0-1	Copenhagen	Fr		22 485	Ingvarsson SWE
27-05	Estonia	W	1-0	Tallinn	Fr	McFadden 76	4 000	Poulsen DEN
30-05	Trinidad and Tobago	W	4-1	Edinburgh	Fr	Fletcher 6, Holt 14, Caldwell.G 23, Quashie 34	16 187	Vink NED
18-08	Hungary	L	0-3	Glasgow	Fr		15 933	Duhamel FRA
3-09	Spain	D	1-1	Valencia	Fr	McFadden 17. Abandoned 59'	11 000	Bre FRA
8-09	Slovenia	D	0-0	Glasgow	WCq		38 279	Larsen DEN
9-10	Norway	D	0-1	Glasgow	WCq		51 000	Allaerts BEL
13-10	Moldova	D	1-1	Chisinau	WCq	Thompson 31	7 000	Jakobsson ISL
17-11	Sweden	L	1-4	Edinburgh	Fr	McFadden 78p	15 071	Jara CZE
2005								
26-03	Italy	L	0-2	Milan	WCq		45 000	Vassaras GRE
4-06	Moldova	W	2-0	Glasgow	WCq	Dailly 52, McFadden 88	45 317	Braamhaar NED
8-06	Belarus	D	0-0	Minsk	WCq		28 287	Benquerenca POR

Fr = Friendly match • EC = UEFA EURO 2004™ • WC = FIFA World Cup™ • q = qualifier

SCOTLAND NATIONAL TEAM RECORDS AND RECORD SEQUENCES

Records			Sequence records				
Victory	11-0	NIR 1901	Wins	13	1879-1985	Clean sheets	7	1925-27,1996-97
Defeat	0-7	URU 1954	Defeats	5	2002	Goals scored	32	1873-1988
Player Caps	102	DALGLISH Kenny	Undefeated	22	1879-1887	Without goal	4	1971
Player Goals	30	LAW Denis/DALGLISH	Without win	9	1997-1998	Goals against	14	1957-1958

SCOTLAND COUNTRY INFORMATION

Capital	Edinburgh	Status	Part of the UK	GDP per Capita	$27 300
Population	5 057 400			GNP Ranking	4
Area km²	77 000	Language	English	Dialling code	+44
Population density	66 per km²	Literacy rate	99%	Internet code	.uk
% in urban areas	89%	Main religion	Christian	GMT +/–	0
Towns/Cities ('000)	Glasgow 610; Edinburgh 435; Aberdeen 183; Dundee 151; Paisley 73; East Kilbride 74				
Neighbours (km)	England 164				
Main stadia	Hampden Park – Glasgow 50 670; Parkhead – Glasgow 60 506; Ibrox – Glasgow 50 420				

NATIONAL CAPS

	Caps
DALGLISH Kenny	102
LEIGHTON Jim	91
MCLEISH Alex	77
MCSTAY Paul	76
BOYD Tom	72
MILLER Willie	65
MCGRAIN Danny	62
GOUGH Richard	61
MCCOIST Ally	61
COLLINS John	58

NATIONAL GOALS

	Goals
DALGLISH Kenny	30
LAW Denis	30
GALLACHER Hugh	23
REILLY Lawrie	22
MCCOIST Ally	19
HAMILTON Robert	14
JOHNSTON Mo	14
MCCOLL Robert	13
SMITH John	13
WILSON Andrew Nesbit	13

NATIONAL COACH

	Years
BROWN Bobby	1967-'71
DOCHERTY Tommy	1971-'72
ORMOND Wille	1972-'77
MCLEOD Ally	1977-'78
STEIN Jock	1978-'85
FERGUSON Alex	1985-'86
ROXBURGH Andy	1986-'93
BROWN Craig	1993-'02
VOGTS Bertie	2002-'04
SMITH Walter	2004-

FIFA REFEREE LIST 2005

	Int'l	DoB
BRINES Iain	2003	22-07-1967
CLARK Kenny	1993	1-11-1961
DOUGAL Stuart	1996	6-11-1962
MC DONALD Douglas	2000	8-10-1965
MURRAY Calum	2005	7-07-1967
RICHMOND Charlie	2003	13-05-1968
THOMSON Craig	2003	20-06-1972

FIFA ASSISTANT REFEREE LIST 2005

	Int'l	DoB
ANDREWS Francis	2004	24-08-1966
BEE James	2004	12-09-1967
CRYANS Martin	2002	4-02-1969
CUNNINGHAM Alan	2001	22-02-1966
DAVIS Andrew	2000	11-07-1961
LYON Jim	2003	6-07-1969
MACAULAY Stuart	2004	31-12-1966
MIDDLETON Gordon	2004	23-06-1967
MURPHY Tom	2003	8-09-1965
SORBIE Keith	2005	25-05-1965

CLUB DIRECTORY

Club	Town/City	Stadium	Phone	www.	Lge	Cup	CL
Aberdeen	Aberdeen	Pittodrie 21 487	+44 8779 837903	afc.co.uk	4	7	0
Celtic	Glasgow	Celtic Park 60 355	+44 141 5562611	celticfc.net	39	33	1
Dundee	Dundee	Dens Park 11 760	+44 1382 889966	thedees.co.uk	1	1	0
Dundee United	Dundee	Tannadice Park 14 223	+44 1382 833166	dundeeunitedfc.co.uk	1	1	0
Dunfermline Athletic	Dunfermline	East End Park 12 500	+44 1383 724295	dafc.co.uk	0	2	0
Heart of Midlothian	Edinburgh	Tynecastle 18 000	+44 131 2007222	heartsfc.co.uk	4	6	0
Hibernian	Edinburgh	Easter Road 17 500	+44 131 6612159	hibernianfc.co.uk	4	2	0
Inverness Caledion Thistle	Inverness	Caledonian Stadium 6 500	+44 1463 222880	sportnetwork.net	0	0	0
Kilmarnock	Kilmarnock	Rugby Park 18 128	+44 1563 545300	kilmarnockfc.co.uk	1	3	0
Livingston	Livingston	City Stadium 10 024	+44 1506 417000	livingstonfc.co.uk	0	0	0
Motherwell	Motherwell	Fir Park 13 742	+44 1698 333333	motherwellfc.co.uk	1	2	0
Rangers	Glasgow	Ibrox 50 444	+44 870 6001972	rangers.co.uk	51	31	0

RECENT LEAGUE AND CUP RECORD

	Championship						Cup		
Year	Champions	Pts	Runners-up	Pts	Third	Pts	Winners	Score	Runners-up
1990	Rangers	51	Aberdeen	44	Heart of Midlothian	44	Aberdeen	0-0 9-8p	Celtic
1991	Rangers	55	Aberdeen	53	Celtic	41	Motherwell	4-3	Dundee United
1992	Rangers	72	Heart of Midlothian	63	Celtic	62	Rangers	2-1	Airdrieonians
1993	Rangers	73	Aberdeen	64	Celtic	60	Rangers	2-1	Aberdeen
1994	Rangers	58	Aberdeen	55	Motherwell	54	Dundee United	1-0	Rangers
1995	Rangers	69	Motherwell	54	Hibernian	53	Celtic	1-0	Airdrieonians
1996	Rangers	87	Celtic	83	Aberdeen	55	Rangers	5-1	Heart of Midlothian
1997	Rangers	80	Celtic	75	Dundee United	60	Kilmarnock	1-0	Falkirk
1998	Celtic	74	Rangers	72	Heart of Midlothian	67	Heart of Midlothian	2-1	Rangers
1999	Rangers	77	Celtic	71	St. Johnstone	57	Rangers	1-0	Celtic
2000	Rangers	90	Celtic	69	Heart of Midlothian	54	Rangers	4-0	Aberdeen
2001	Celtic	97	Rangers	82	Hibernian	66	Celtic	3-0	Hibernian
2002	Celtic	103	Rangers	85	Livingston	58	Rangers	3-2	Celtic
2003	Rangers	97	Celtic	97	Heart of Midlothian	63	Rangers	1-0	Dundee
2004	Celtic	98	Rangers	81	Heart of Midlothian	68	Celtic	3-1	Dunfermline Ath.
2005	Rangers	93	Celtic	92	Hibernian	61	Celtic	1-0	Dundee United

SCOTLAND 2004-05

PREMIER LEAGUE

	Pl	W	D	L	F	A	Pts	Rangers	Celtic	Hibs	Aberdeen	Hearts	Motherwell	Kilmarn'k	Inverness	Dundee U	Livingston	D'fermline	Dundee
Rangers †	38	29	6	3	78	22	93		2-0 1-2	4-1 3-0	5-0 3-1	3-2 2-1	4-1 4-1	2-0 2-1	1-0 1-1	1-1 0-1	4-0 3-0	3-0	3-0
Celtic †	38	30	2	6	85	35	92	1-0 0-2		2-1 1-3	2-3 3-2	3-0 0-2	2-0 2-0	2-1	3-0	1-0	2-1	3-0 6-0	3-0 3-0
Hibernian ‡	38	18	7	13	64	57	61	0-1 0-1	2-2 1-3		2-1 1-2	1-2 2-1	1-0 2-2	0-1 3-0	2-1	2-0 3-2	2-1 0-3	2-1	4-4 4-0
Aberdeen	38	18	7	13	44	39	61	0-0 1-2	0-1 0-2	0-1 3-0		0-1 2-0	2-1 1-3	3-2	0-0	1-0	2-0 2-0	2-1	1-1 1-1
Heart of Midlothian	38	13	11	14	43	41	50	0-0 1-2	0-2 1-2	2-1 1-2	0-0 1-0		0-1 0-0	3-0 3-0	1-0 0-2	3-2	0-0 3-1	3-0	3-0
Motherwell	38	13	9	16	46	49	48	0-2 2-3	2-3 2-1	1-2 1-1	0-0 1-2	0-2 0-0		0-1 1-1	1-2	4-2 2-0	2-0	2-1	3-0
Kilmarnock	38	15	4	19	49	55	49	0-1	2-4 0-1	3-1	0-1 0-1	1-1	2-0		2-2 0-1	5-2 3-0	1-3 2-0	1-0 2-1	3-1 1-0
Inverness CT	38	11	11	16	41	47	44	1-1	1-3 0-2	1-2 3-0	1-3 0-1	1-1	1-1 1-0	0-2 1-2		1-1 0-1	2-0 0-1	2-0 2-0	2-1 3-2
Dundee United	38	8	12	18	41	59	36	1-1	0-3 2-3	1-4	1-1 1-2	1-1 2-1	0-1	3-0 1-1	2-1 1-1		1-0 1-1	1-2 0-1	1-2 2-2
Livingston	38	9	8	21	34	61	35	1-4	2-4 0-4	0-2	0-2	1-2	2-3 1-1	0-2 3-1	3-0 1-4	1-1 0-2		2-0 1-1	1-0 1-1
Dunfermline Athletic	38	8	10	20	34	60	34	1-2 0-1	0-2	1-1 4-0	1-2 1-1	0-1 1-1	1-0 4-1	0-4 1-0	0-0 1-1	1-1 1-0	0-0 0-2		3-1 5-0
Dundee	38	8	9	21	37	71	33	0-2 0-2	2-2	1-4	1-0	0-1 1-1	1-2 2-1	3-1 1-0	3-1 1-1	1-0 1-2	0-0 0-1	1-2 2-1	

16/08/2004 - 22/05/2005 • † Qualified for the UEFA Champions League • ‡ Qualified for the UEFA Cup • Matches in bold are away not home matches

FIRST DIVISION (2)

	Pl	W	D	L	F	A	Pts
Falkirk	36	22	9	5	66	30	74
St Mirren	36	15	15	6	41	23	60
Clyde	36	16	12	8	35	29	60
Queen of the South	36	14	9	13	36	38	51
Airdrie United	36	14	8	14	44	48	50
Ross County	36	13	8	15	40	37	47
Hamilton Academical	36	12	11	13	35	36	47
St Johnstone	36	12	10	14	38	39	46
Partick Thistle	36	10	9	17	38	52	39
Raith Rovers	36	3	7	26	26	67	16

7/08/2004 - 7/05/2005

SECOND DIVISION (3)

	Pl	W	D	L	F	A	Pts
Brechin City	36	22	6	8	81	43	72
Stranraer	36	18	9	9	48	41	63
Greenock Morton	36	18	8	10	60	37	62
Stirling Albion	36	14	9	13	56	55	51
Forfar Athletic	36	13	8	15	51	45	47
Alloa Athletic	36	12	10	14	66	68	46
Dumbarton	36	11	9	16	43	53	42
Ayr United	36	11	9	16	39	54	42
Arbroath	36	10	8	18	49	73	38
Berwick Rangers	36	8	10	18	40	64	34

7/08/2004 - 7/05/2005

THIRD DIVISION (4)

	Pl	W	D	L	F	A	Pts
Gretna	36	32	2	2	130	29	98
Peterhead	36	23	9	4	81	38	78
Cowdenbeath	36	14	9	13	54	61	51
Queen's Park	36	13	9	14	51	50	48
Montrose	36	13	7	16	47	53	46
Elgin City	36	12	7	17	39	61	43
Stenhousemuir	36	10	12	14	58	58	42
East Fife	36	10	8	18	40	56	38
Albion Rovers	36	8	10	18	40	78	34
East Stirlingshire	36	5	7	24	32	88	22

7/08/2004 - 7/05/2005

RECENT LEAGUE CUP RECORD

Year	Winners	Score	Runners-up
1996	Aberdeen	2-0	Dundee
1997	Rangers	4-3	Heart of Midlothian
1998	Celtic	3-0	Dundee United
1999	Rangers	2-1	St Johnstone
2000	Celtic	2-0	Aberdeen
2001	Celtic	3-0	Kilmarnock
2002	Rangers	4-0	Ayr United
2003	Rangers	2-1	Celtic
2004	Livingston	2-0	Hibernian
2005	Rangers	5-1	Motherwell

SCOTTISH LEAGUE CUP 2004-05

Third Round

Rangers	2
Aberdeen *	0
Falkirk	1
Celtic *	8
Hibernian	3
Albion Rovers *	1
Clyde	0
Dundee United *	4
Heart of Midlothian *	2
Kilmarnock	1
Partick Thistle	1
Dunfermline Athletic *	3
Livingston *	2
Dundee	1
Inverness CT *	1
Motherwell	3

Quarter-finals

Rangers *	2
Celtic	1
Hibernian	1
Dundee United *	2
Heart of Midlothian	3
Dunfermline Athletic *	1
Livingston *	0
Motherwell	5

Semi-finals

Rangers ‡	7
Dundee United	1
Heart of Midlothian	2
Motherwell †	3

Final

Rangers	5
Motherwell	1

LEAGUE CUP FINAL

20-03-2005, Att: 50 182, Ref. McCurry
Hampden Park, Glasgow
Scorers - Ross [5], Kyrgiakos 2 [9 86]
Ricksen [33], Novo [48], for Rangers;
Partridge [13] for Motherwell

* Home team • † Easter Road, Edinburgh • ‡ Hampden Park, Glasgow

SCOTTISH FA CUP 2004-05

Third Round

Team	Score
Celtic*	2
Rangers	1
East Fife*	0 1
Dunfermline Athletic	0 3
Ross County*	4
Airdrie United	1
Falkirk	0
Clyde*	3
Livingston*	2
Greenock Morton	1
Raith Rovers*	0
Alloa Athletic	2
Kilmarnock*	2
Motherwell	0
Partick Thistle*	0 1
Heart of Midlothian	0 2
Hibernian*	2
Dundee	0
Berwick Rangers*	0
Brechin City	3
Ayr United*	3 2
Stranraer	3 0
Hamilton Academical	0
St Mirren*	3
Aberdeen	2
Arbroath*	0
St Johnstone	1
Inverness CT*	2
Queen of the South	2
Montrose*	1
Gretna*	3
Dundee United	4

Second Round

Team	Score
Celtic	3
Dunfermline Athletic*	0
Ross County*	0 1
Clyde	0 2
Livingston*	1
Alloa Athletic*	0
Kilmarnock	2 1
Heart of Midlothian*	2 3
Hibernian*	4
Brechin City	0
Ayr United*	0
St Mirren	2
Aberdeen*	2
Inverness CT	1
Queen of the South*	0
Dundee United	3

Quarter-finals

Team	Score
Celtic	5
Clyde*	0
Livingston	1
Heart of Midlothian*	2
Hibernian*	2
St Mirren	0
Aberdeen	1
Dundee United*	4

Semi-finals

Team	Score
Celtic	2
Heart of Midlothian	1
Hibernian	1
Dundee United	2

Final

Team	Score
Celtic	1
Dundee United	0

SCOTTISH CUP FINAL

28-05-2005. Att: 50,635. Referee: Rowbotham
Hampden Park, Glasgow

Scorer: Thompson 11 for Celtic

Celtic – Douglas, Agathe, Balde, Varga, McNamara, Petrov, Lennon, Sutton, Thompson (McGeady 86), Hartson (Valgaeren 73), Bellamy. Tr: O'Neill
Dundee Utd – Bullock, Wilson, Ritchie, Kenneth, Archibald, Kerr, McInnes (Samuel 76), Brebner (Duff 83), Robson, Crawford (Grady 83), Scotland. Tr: Chisholm

* Home team • Both semi-finals played at Hampden Park

RANGERS 2004-2005

Date	Opponents	Score		Comp	Scorers	Att
7-08-2004	Aberdeen	D 0-0	A	SPL		19 028
10-08-2004	CSKA Moskva - RUS	L 1-2	A	CLpr3	Novo [37]	11 000
14-08-2004	Livingston	W 4-0	H	SPL	Prso [5], Hughes 2 [31 78], Arveladze [87]	48 102
21-08-2004	Hibernian	W 4-1	H	SPL	Arveladze [11], Prso [15], Boumsong [58], Lovenkrands [84]	48 702
25-08-2004	CSKA Moskva - RUS	D 1-1	H	CLpr3	Thompson [87]	49 010
29-08-2004	Celtic	L 0-1	A	SPL		58 935
12-09-2004	Heart of Midlothian	D 0-0	A	SPL		14 601
16-09-2004	Maritimo - POR	L 0-1	A	UCr1		5 000
19-09-2004	Inverness Caledonian Thistle	W 1-0	H	SPL	Prso [17]	47 063
22-09-2004	Aberdeen	W 2-0	A	LCr1	Ricksen [45], Thompson [89]	14 876
26-09-2004	Dundee	W 2-0	A	SPL	Novo 2 [78 80]	9 404
30-09-2004	Maritimo - POR	W 1-0	H	UCr1	Prso [70]. W 4-2p	47 360
3-10-2004	Kilmarnock	W 2-0	H	SPL	Andrews [10], Novo [82]	46 278
17-10-2004	Motherwell	W 2-0	A	SPL	Prso 2 [7 83]	10 946
21-10-2004	Amica Wronki - POL	W 5-0	H	UCgF	Lovenkrands [18], Novo [58], Ricksen [70], Arveladze [73p], Thompson [88]	3 100
24-10-2004	Dundee United	D 1-1	H	SPL	Novo [69]	46 796
27-10-2004	Dunfermline Athletic	W 2-1	H	SPL	Boumsong [47], Novo [58p]	8 678
31-10-2004	Aberdeen	W 5-0	H	SPL	Thompson [39], Lovenkrands [68], Novo 2 [75 90p], Ricksen [88]	48 918
7-11-2004	Livingston	W 4-1	A	SPL	Lovenkrands [37], Novo [55], Thompson [67], Namouchi [84]	8 780
10-11-2004	Celtic	W 2-1	H	LCqf	Prso [85], Arveladze [100]	47 298
14-11-2004	Hibernian	W 1-0	H	SPL	Prso [65p]	13 829
20-11-2004	Celtic	W 2-0	H	SPL	Novo [15p], Prso [36]	50 043
25-11-2004	Grazer AK - AUT	W 3-0	H	UCgF	Novo [58], Arveladze [86], Namouchi [90]	46 453
28-11-2004	Heart of Midlothian	W 3-2	H	SPL	McAllister OG [45], Novo 2 [56 81]	48 494
2-12-2004	AZ Alkmaar - NED	L 0-1	A	UCgF		8 000
5-12-2004	Inverness Caledonian Thistle	D 1-1	A	SPL	Prso [51]	6 543
11-12-2004	Dundee	W 3-0	H	SPL	Novo [3p], Prso [4], Malcolm [50]	48 114
15-12-2004	AJ Auxerre - FRA	L 0-2	H	UCgF		48 847
19-12-2004	Kilmarnock	W 1-0	A	SPL	Arveladze [16]	11 156
27-12-2004	Motherwell	W 4-1	H	SPL	Novo 2 [3 15], Aveladze [53], Thompson [86]	49 909
1-01-2005	Dundee United	D 1-1	A	SPL	Namouchi [90]	10 461
9-01-2005	Celtic	L 1-2	A	SCr3	Ricksen [47]	58 622
15-01-2005	Dunfermline Athletic	W 3-0	H	SPL	Thompson [6], Andrews [38], Rae [64]	48 055
23-01-2005	Aberdeen	W 2-1	A	SPL	Prso [9], McNaughton OG [16]	17 495
29-01-2005	Livingston	W 3-0	H	SPL	Prso [14], Ricksen [63], Novo [68]	48 579
2-02-2005	Dundee United	W 7-1	N	LCsf	Novo 2 [7 85], Prso [18], Buffel [67], Ricksen [77], Thompson 2 [80 88]	25 622
12-02-2005	Hibernian	W 3-0	H	SPL	Prso 2 [35 50], Buffel [61]	50 143
20-02-2005	Celtic	W 2-0	H	SPL	Vignal [71], Novo [82]	59 041
26-02-2005	Kilmarnock	W 2-1	H	SPL	Prso [29], Novo [41]	48 575
2-03-2005	Heart of Midlothian	W 2-1	A	SPL	Novo [49], Ricksen [90p]	13 842
5-03-2005	Inverness Caledonian Thistle	D 1-1	H	SPL	Ferguson [57]	49 345
13-03-2005	Dundee	W 2-0	A	SPL	Andrews [82], Ricksen [84]	9 876
20-03-2005	Motherwell	W 5-1	N	LCf	Ross [5], Krygiakos 2 [9 86], Ricksen [33], Novo [48]	50 182
3-04-2005	Motherwell	W 3-2	A	SPL	Vignal 2 [4 32], Prso [51]	10 210
12-04-2005	Dundee United	L 0-1	H	SPL		49 302
17-04-2005	Dunfermline Athletic	W 1-0	A	SPL	Prso [7]	8 266
24-04-2005	Celtic	L 1-2	H	SPL	Thompson [87]	49 593
1-05-2005	Aberdeen	W 3-1	A	SPL	Ferguson 10, Prso 2 [43 59]	17 198
7-05-2005	Heart of Midlothian	W 2-1	H	SPL	Buffel [9], Andrews [42]	49 342
14-05-2005	Motherwell	W 4-1	A	SPL	Buffel 2 [12 57], Arveladze 2 [17 54]	49 495
22-05-2005	Hibernian	W 1-0	A	SPL	Novo [59]	17 450

SPL = Scottish Premier League • CL = UEFA Champions League • UC = UEFA Cup • LC = League Cup • SC = Scottish FA Cup
pr3 = third preliminary round • r1 = first round • gF = Group F • r3 = third round • qf = quarter-final • sf = semi-final • f = final

CELTIC 2004-2005

Date	Opponents	Score			Comp	Scorers	Att
8-08-2004	Motherwell	W	2-0	H	SPL	McNamara [7], Sutton [55]	57 245
14-08-2004	Kilmarnock	W	4-2	A	SPL	Hartson 2 [15 70], Thompson 2 [36 44]	10 500
22-08-2004	Inverness Caledonian Thistle	W	3-1	A	SPL	Hartson 2 [25 76], Petrov [68]	8 736
29-08-2004	Rangers	W	1-0	H	SPL	Thompson [85]	58 935
11-09-2004	Dundee	W	3-0	H	SPL	Camara 2 [23 87], Hartson [36]	56 936
14-09-2004	Barcelona - ESP	L	1-3	H	CLgF	Sutton [59]	58 589
19-09-2004	Hibernian	D	2-2	A	SPL	Camara [34], Hartson [45]	13 500
21-09-2004	Falkirk	W	8-1	H	LCr3	Sylla [2], Wallace 3 [5 57 74], Balde [39], Lambert [45], McManus [48] McGeady [90]	
25-09-2004	Dunfermline Athletic	W	3-0	H	SPL	Varga [19], Camara 2 [39 55]	58 213
29-09-2004	Milan - ITA	L	1-3	A	CLgF	Varga [73]	50 000
3-10-2004	Dundee United	W	3-0	A	SPL	Sutton 2 [8 36], Petrov [17]	10 329
16-10-2004	Heart of Midlothian	W	3-0	H	SPL	Camara [42], Juninho [55], Hartson [80]	58 869
20-10-2004	Shakhtar Donetsk - UKR	L	0-3	H	ECgF		30 000
24-10-2004	Livingston	W	4-2	A	SPL	Petrov [2], Camara [13], Hartson [19], Sutton [32]	7 695
27-10-2004	Aberdeen	L	2-3	H	SPL	Hartson 2 [45 68]	57 151
30-10-2004	Motherwell	W	3-2	A	SPL	McGeady [41], Thompson [65p], Beattie [77]	10 592
2-11-2004	Shakhtar Donetsk - UKR	W	1-0	H	CLgF	Thompson [24]	58 347
6-11-2004	Kilmarnock	W	2-1	H	SPL	McGeady [43], Thompson [63p]	57 348
10-11-2004	Rangers	L	1-2	A	LCqf	Hartson [66]	
13-11-2004	Inverness Caledonian Thistle	W	3-0	H	SPL	Sutton [3], Hartson 2 [53 75]	
20-11-2004	Rangers	L	0-2	A	SPL		50 043
24-11-2004	Barcelona - ESP	D	1-1	A	CLgF	Hartson [44]	74 119
28-11-2004	Dundee	D	2-2	A	SPL	Camara [53], Hartson [61]	9 539
4-12-2004	Hibernian	W	2-1	H	SPL	Hartson 2 [17 83]	58 384
7-12-2004	Milan - ITA	D	0-0	H	CLgF		59 228
12-12-2004	Dunfermline Athletic	W	2-0	H	SPL	Sutton [15], Petrov [31]	7 650
18-12-2004	Dundee United	W	1-0	H	SPL	Sutton [19]	56 318
26-12-2004	Heart of Midlothian	W	2-0	A	SPL	McGeady [9], Petrov [68]	16 163
2-01-2005	Livingston	W	2-1	H	SPL	Hartson [18], Sutton [54p]	57 593
9-01-2005	Rangers	W	2-1	H	SCr3	Sutton [38], Hartson [77]	58 622
16-01-2005	Aberdeen	W	1-0	A	SPL	Sutton [24]	17 051
22-01-2005	Motherwell	W	2-0	H	SPL	Petrov [30], Sutton [60]	58 438
30-01-2005	Kilmarnock	W	1-0	A	SPL	Sutton [38p]	9 723
6-02-2005	Dunfermline Athletic	W	3-0	A	SCr4	Hartson 2 [8 43], Sutton [10]	8 014
20-02-2005	Rangers	L	0-2	H	SPL		59 041
27-02-2005	Clyde	W	5-0	A	SCqf	Varga 2 [40 68], Thompson [48p], Petrov [60], Bellamy [72]	8 200
2-03-2005	Dundee	W	3-0	H	SPL	Petrov [49], Balde 2 [60 87]	52 500
6-03-2005	Hibernian	W	3-1	A	SPL	Petrov [5], Hartson [30], Bellamy [70]	15 787
12-03-2005	Dunfermline Athletic	W	6-0	H	SPL	Hartson 2 [8 67], McGeady [62], Petrov 2 [71 73], Beattie [88]	58 908
16-03-2005	Inverness Caledonian Thistle	W	2-0	H	SPL	Bellamy [62], Thompson [83p]	7 045
19-03-2005	Dundee United	W	3-2	A	SPL	Bellamy 3 [5 34 80]	10 828
2-04-2005	Heart of Midlothian	L	0-2	H	SPL		59 562
10-04-2005	Heart of Midlothian	W	2-1	N	SCsf	Sutton [2], Bellamy [49]	38 505
13-04-2005	Livingston	W	4-0	A	SPL	Hartson 3 [43 75 86p], Varga [90]	8 750
16-04-2005	Aberdeen	W	3-2	A	SPL	Varga [26], Hartson [50], Bellamy [57]	59 998
24-04-2005	Rangers	W	2-1	A	SPL	Petrov [21], Bellamy [35]	49 593
30-04-2005	Hibernian	L	1-3	H	SPL	Beattie [55]	58 322
8-05-2005	Aberdeen	W	2-0	H	SPL	Hartson 2 [47 70]	59 498
15-05-2005	Heart of Midlothian	W	2-1	A	SPL	Thompson [24], Beattie [75]	15 927
22-05-2005	Motherwell	L	1-2	A	SPL	Sutton [29]	12 944
28-05-2005	Dundee United	W	1-0	N	SCf	Thompson [11]	50 635

SPL = Scottish Premier League • CL = UEFA Champions League • LC = League Cup • SC = Scottish FA Cup
gF = Group F • r3 = third round • r4 = fourth round • qf = quarter-final • sf = semi-final • f = final • N = Hampden Park, Glasgow

SEN – SENEGAL

NATIONAL TEAM RECORD
JULY 1ST 2002 TO JUNE 30TH 2005

PL	W	D	L	F	A	%
30	14	9	7	44	25	61.7

FIFA/COCA-COLA WORLD RANKING

1993	1994	1995	1996	1997	1998	1999	2000	2001	2002	2003	2004	High		Low	
56	50	47	58	85	95	79	88	65	27	33	31	26	06/04	95	12/98

2004-2005											
08/04	09/04	10/04	11/04	12/04	01/05	02/05	03/05	04/05	05/05	06/05	07/05
31	31	31	31	31	30	31	32	33	33	37	39

Since stunning the world with their 2002 FIFA World Cup™ exploits, Senegal's star has waned. After coach Bruno Metsu left, the national team disappointed at the 2004 CAF African Cup of Nations and now find themselves under siege as Togo and Zambia vie for a place at the 2006 FIFA World Cup™. Even with a large crop of quality European-based players, the Lions of Terranga have not coped with the pressure and have slid to their lowest FIFA/Coca-Cola World Ranking position since before the 2002 finals. Their two remaining fixtures with Mali and Zambia are must-win matches if Senegal are to make a quick return to the finals. With qualification for the

INTERNATIONAL HONOURS
Copa Amilcar Cabral 1979 1980 1983 1984 1985 1986 1991 2001

Nations Cup virtually assured, Senegal will be anxious to achieve success similar to their 2002 runners-up spot and reinvigorate a nervous team. ASC Diaref Dakar won their first Championnat National title in four years doggedly keeping a four-point margin between them and runners-up AS Douanes Dakar over the final five fixtures. Douanes were compensated with winning the Coupe Nationale for the third year in a row, beating the new League champions 2-1 in the final. The juniors missed the chance of a short trip to Gambia for the Africa U-17 Championship finals when they failed to get past Cote d'Ivoire, losing 6-5 on aggregate over two entertaining ties.

THE FIFA BIG COUNT OF 2000

	Male	Female		Male	Female
Registered players	6 593	0	Referees	3 230	0
Non registered players	40 000	0	Officials	2 700	0
Youth players	146 689	0	Total involved	199 212	
Total players	193 282		Number of clubs	82	
Professional players	50	0	Number of teams	12 200	

Fédération Sénégalaise de Football (FSF)
VDN-Ouest-Foire en face du CICES, Case Postale 13021, Dakar, Senegal
Tel +221 8692828   Fax +221 8205600
fsf@senegalfoot.sn   www.senegalfoot.sn
President: NDOYE Mbaye   General Secretary: CISSE Victor
Vice-President: NDOYE Mbaye   Treasurer: DIAGNE Blaise   Media Officer: SECK Mbacke
Men's Coach: STEPHAN Guy   Women's Coach: DIABY Bassouare
FSF formed: 1960   CAF: 1963   FIFA: 1962
Colours: White, White, White

GAMES PLAYED BY SENEGAL IN THE 2006 FIFA WORLD CUP™ CYCLE

2002	Opponents	Score		Venue	Comp	Scorers	Att	Referee
8-09	Lesotho	W	1-0	Maseru	CNq	Camara.H [44]	60 000	Mangaliso SWZ
12-10	Nigeria	D	2-2	Dakar	Fr	Camara.S [84], Sarr [90]	50 000	Diatta SEN
19-11	South Africa	D	1-1	Johannesburg	Fr	Niang [58], W 4-1p	40 000	Tangawarima ZIM
2003								
12-02	Morocco	L	0-1	Paris	Fr		8 000	Piccirillo FRA
30-03	Gambia	D	0-0	Banjul	CNq		30 000	Djingarey NIG
30-04	Tunisia	L	0-1	Tunis	Fr			
31-05	Cape Verde Islands	W	2-1	Dakar	Fr	Camara.S [50], Diao [62]	20 000	Santos GNB
7-06	Gambia	W	3-1	Dakar	CNq	Diatta [5], Camara.H [36], Diouf [73]		Guirat TUN
14-06	Lesotho	W	3-0	Dakar	CNq	Diouf [26p], Camara 2 [66 71]		
10-09	Japan	W	1-0	Niigata	Fr	Diop.PB [6]	40 000	Moradi IRN
10-10	Egypt	L	0-1	Cairo	Fr		20 000	
15-11	Côte d'Ivoire	W	1-0	Dakar	Fr	Diouf [89]	50 000	Daami TUN
2004								
18-01	South Africa	W	2-1	Dakar	Fr	Diop.PM [29], Mabizela OG [83]	50 000	El Achiri MAR
26-01	Burkina Faso	D	0-0	Tunis	CNr1		2 000	Guezzaz MAR
30-01	Kenya	W	3-0	Bizerte	CNr1	Niang 2 [4 31], Diop.PB [19]	13 500	Abd El Fatah EGY
2-02	Mali	D	1-1	Tunis	CNr1	Beye [45]	7 550	Evehe CMR
7-02	Tunisia	L	0-1	Tunis	CNqf		57 000	Bujsaim UAE
29-05	Guinea	D	1-1	Paris	Fr	Guaye [82]	2 000	Garibian FRA
5-06	Congo	W	2-0	Dakar	WCq	Diatta [55], Ndiaya [77]	18 000	Benouza ALG
13-06	Cape Verde Islands	W	3-1	Praia	Fr	Gueye [65], Kamara.D 2 [71 74]	10 000	
20-06	Togo	L	1-3	Lome	WCq	Diop.PB [81]	25 000	El Arjoun MAR
3-07	Zambia	W	1-0	Dakar	WCq	Gueye [21]	50 000	Monteiro Duarte CPV
18-08	Côte d'Ivoire	L	1-2	Avignon	Fr	Camara [12]	5 000	
5-09	Mali	D	2-2	Bamako	WCq	Camara.H [45], Dia [84]	45 000	Guezzaz MAR
10-10	Liberia	W	3-0	Monrovia	WCq	Diop.PB [41], Camara.H 2 [50 73]	26 000	Aboubacar CIV
17-11	Algeria	W	2-1	Toulon	Fr	Niang [35], Gueye [41]	4 000	Bata FRA
2005								
9-02	Cameroon	L	0-1	Creteil	Fr			
26-03	Liberia	W	6-1	Dakar	WCq	Fadiga [19], Diouf 2 [45p 84], Faye [56], Camara.H [72], Ndiaye [75]	50 000	Shelmani LBY
5-06	Congo	D	0-0	Brazzaville	WCq		40 000	Damon RSA
18-06	Togo	D	2-2	Dakar	WCq	Niang [15], Camara.H [30]	50 000	Guirat TUN

Fr = Friendly match • CN = CAF African Cup of Nations • WC = FIFA World Cup™ • q = qualifier • r1 = first round group • qf = quarter-final

SENEGAL NATIONAL TEAM RECORDS AND RECORD SEQUENCES

Records			Sequence records					
Victory	6-0	MTN 1984	Wins	11	1985-1986	Clean sheets	6	1999-2000
Defeat	0-4	Seven times	Defeats	4	1969-1970	Goals scored	14	1999
Player Caps	n/a		Undefeated	12	1987-1989	Without goal	7	1987
Player Goals	n/a		Without win	12	2000-2001	Goals against	22	1965-1970

SENEGAL COUNTRY INFORMATION

Capital	Dakar	Independence	1960 from France	GDP per Capita	$1 600	
Population	10 852 147	Status	Republic	GNP Ranking	115	
Area km²	196 190	Language	French, Wolof, Pulaar	Dialling code	+221	
Population density	55 per km²	Literacy rate	40%	Internet code	.sn	
% in urban areas	42%	Main religion	Muslim	GMT +/–	+0	
Towns/Cities ('000)	Dakar 2 702; Thiès 320; Kaolack 289; Ziguinchor 255; Mbour 194; Saint Louis 176; Diourbel 126					
Neighbours (km)	Mauritania 813; Mali 419; Guinea 330; Guinea-Bissau 338; Gambia 740; Atlantic Ocean 531					
Main stadia	Stade Léopold Senghor (Stade de l'Amitié) – Dakar 60 000					

SENEGAL 2004

CHAMPIONNAT NATIONAL 1ERE DIVISION

Team	Pl	W	D	L	F	A	Pts	Diaraf	Douanes	Ndiambour	DUC	Sonacos	CSS	US Rail	Gorée	Jeanne d'Arc	Port Auto.	Casa	Guédiawaye	HLM	Ouakam	Mbour	Saloum	Linguère	Khombole	Police	ASFA
ASC Diaraf Dakar †	38	20	12	6	54	22	72	—	0-0	1-0	1-0	0-0	1-1	1-1	1-0	1-1	2-0	2-0	6-1	1-2	3-0	2-0	4-0	1-0	5-1	3-2	2-0
AS Douanes Dakar †	38	19	12	7	37	16	69	2-0	—	0-0	1-0	0-0	2-0	2-1	3-0	0-1	1-1	1-0	2-0	1-0	1-0	2-0	1-2	0-0	0-0	2-1	2-0
ASC Ndiambour Louga‡	38	19	8	11	29	20	65	0-0	0-0	—	1-1	1-0	1-0	1-2	0-1	1-0	1-0	1-0	0-0	3-2	1-0	1-0	1-0	2-1	1-0		
DUC Dakar ‡	38	18	9	11	41	27	63	0-1	0-2	2-1	—	1-2	0-0	1-2	1-1	1-0	2-1	2-0	2-1	1-0	2-1	1-2	1-0	1-0	3-0	2-0	1-2
Sonacos Djourbel	38	14	17	7	32	19	59	0-0	0-0	1-0	0-1	—	0-0	1-1	0-0	0-1	0-0	0-1	0-0	2-0	0-0	0-0	2-2	2-1	2-1	0-1	2-0
CSS Richard-Toll	38	13	16	9	29	25	55	1-1	1-1	0-0	0-0	0-0	—	0-3	0-0	0-0	1-0	2-2	0-1	0-0	2-0	2-1	1-1	2-0	0-0	1-0	
US Rail Thiès	38	14	13	11	36	36	55	0-1	3-0	1-2	0-2	0-0	3-1	—	1-1	0-0	2-0	1-0	1-1	1-2	2-1	0-0	0-0	0-1	0-1	1-0	1-0
US Gorée	38	13	15	10	32	21	54	0-1	0-1	0-1	0-0	0-0	1-3	8-2	—	0-1	0-1	0-0	1-2	0-0	0-0	2-0	0-0	2-0	0-0	0-0	2-0
Jeanne d'Arc Dakar	38	13	14	11	41	26	53	1-0	0-0	1-1	1-1	0-1	0-1	2-0	2-0	—	0-2	3-0	0-0	1-1	3-2	1-1	1-0	2-0	5-0	6-0	0-0
Port Autoname Dakar	38	13	13	12	29	26	52	1-1	0-2	0-0	1-0	0-1	0-3	2-2	0-0	1-1	—	0-1	0-2	0-0	2-0	0-1	3-0	0-0	1-0	1-1	1-0
Casa Sport Ziguinchor	38	15	7	16	23	22	52	2-1	0-1	0-1	0-2	0-1	2-0	0-1	1-0	3-0	0-1	—	0-1	2-0	0-0	0-1	0-0	1-0	1-0	1-0	1-0
Guédiawaye Dakar	38	12	16	10	35	38	52	2-2	2-0	0-3	1-2	1-1	1-0	0-0	0-0	2-0	1-1	0-0	—	2-1	0-3	3-1	0-0	0-0	3-1	3-1	0-0
ASC HLM Dakar	38	11	18	9	26	22	51	0-2	0-0	0-0	1-0	1-1	1-2	1-0	0-1	0-0	1-0	0-0		—	0-1	0-0	0-0	2-1	3-1	0-0	2-1
US Ouakam	38	11	15	12	27	27	48	0-0	1-0	1-0	1-1	0-2	0-1	0-0	0-1	3-1	0-0	1-0	0-0	0-0	—	0-0	1-1	0-2	0-1	3-1	2-0
Stade de Mbour	38	10	16	12	24	29	46	0-0	1-1	0-1	1-0	0-0	0-2	1-1	0-0	0-0	0-0	0-0				—	1-0	1-1	2-1	0-0	0-0
ASC Saloum Kaolack	38	12	10	16	29	36	46	0-1	0-2	2-0	1-1	3-1	1-2	1-3	0-0	1-0	1-0	0-0	3-1	0-2	0-1	2-1	—	2-0	2-0	1-0	1-1
Linguère St Louis	38	11	12	15	19	26	45	0-1	1-0	0-2	0-2	1-0	0-1	1-1	1-2	1-0	1-0	0-1	1-0	0-0	1-1	0-0	1-0	—	2-0	0-0	0-0
ASC Khombole	38	8	6	24	17	50	30	2-1	0-1	1-0	0-1	1-1	1-0	0-1	0-1	1-2	0-3	0-2	0-0	1-1	0-2	1-0	0-1	0-1	—	1-0	1-0
ASC Police Dakar	38	4	16	18	19	46	28	2-1	1-1	0-1	0-1	0-0	0-1	1-0	0-0	0-3	0-2	1-0	0-3	2-0	0-2	1-0	0-1	0-0		—	1-1
ASFA Dakar	38	3	9	26	11	56	18	0-3	0-3	0-1	0-2	0-5	0-2	0-1	0-3	0-4	0-1	0-2	1-2	0-0	0-1	0-1	2-0	2-1	1-1		—

13/12/2003 - 9/10/2004 • † Qualified for the CAF Champions League • ‡ Qualified for the CAF Confederation Cup

COUPE NATIONALE 2004

Eighth-finals

AS Douanes Dakar	2
USCTT	1
ASC Khombole	0
Jeanne d'Arc Dakar	1
ASEC Ndiambour	1
US Gorée	0
ASC HLM	1 1p
CSS Richard-Toll	1 4p
Linguère St Louis	1
AS Saloum	0
AS Police	1
Stade de Mbour	2
ASFA Dakar	0 4p
US Ouakam	0 2p
US Rail	1
Diaraf Dakar	2

Quarter-finals

AS Douanes Dakar	4
Jeanne d'Arc Dakar	1
ASC Ndiambour	2
CSS Richard-Toll	3
Linguère St Louis	1
Stade de Mbour	0
ASFA Dakar	1
Diaraf Dakar	3

Semi-finals

AS Douanes Dakar	2
CSS Richard-Toll	1
Linguère St Louis	0
Diaraf Dakar	2

Final

AS Douanes Dakar	2
Diaraf Dakar	1

CUP FINAL

24-10-2004
Stade Leopold Sedar Senghor, Dakar
Scorers - Samb [9], Cisse [57] for Douane; Ndoye [72] for Diaraf

RECENT LEAGUE AND CUP RECORD

Year	Champions	Pts	Runners-up	Pts	Third	Pts	Winners	Score	Runners-up
1991	Port Autoname	40	ASC Ndiambour	38	SIDEC Dakar	37	ASC Diaraf	2-1	Jeanne d'Arc
1992	ASC Ndiambour	41	Jeanne d'Arc	39	Port Autoname	37	US Gorée	2-1	ASC Diaraf
1993	AS Douanes	54	ASC Diaraf	52	Jeanne d'Arc	46	ASC Diaraf	2-0	Linguère
1994	ASC Ndiambour	†	US Rail Thiès				ASC Diaraf	1-0	CSS
1995	ASC Diaraf	2-1	ESO				ASC Diaraf	2-0	AS Douanes
1996	Sonacas	‡	Linguère				US Gorée	1-0	ASC Ndiambour
1997	ASC Douanes	46	Jeanne d'Arc	45	Linguère	43	AS Douanes	3-1	Linguère
1998	ASC Ndiambour	47	ASC Diaraf	46	AS Douanes	39	ASC Yeggo	1-0	US Gorée
1999	Jeanne d'Arc	53	ASC Ndiambour	46	CSS Richard-Toll	43	ASC Ndiambour	1-1 3-0p	Sonacos
2000	ASC Diaraf	37	Port Autonome	36	ASC Ndiambour	35	Port Autonome	4-0	AS Saloum
2001	Jeanne d'Arc	47	ASC Ndiambour	45	US Gorée	44	Sonacos	1-0	US Gorée
2002	Jeanne d'Arc	52	Sonacos	42	ASC Ndiambour	39	AS Douanes	1-1 4-1p	Sonacos
2003	Jeanne d'Arc	51	ASC Diaraf	47	AS Douanes	43	AS Douanes	1-0	ASC Thiès
2004	ASC Diaraf	72	AS Douanes	69	ASC Ndiambour	65	AS Douanes	2-1	ASC Diaraf

† Ndiambour won 4-3 on penalties after a 0-0 draw • ‡ Sonacos 3-0 0-1 Linguère

SEY – SEYCHELLES

NATIONAL TEAM RECORD
JULY 1ST 2002 TO JUNE 30TH 2005

PL	W	D	L	F	A	%
13	2	3	8	6	21	26.9

FIFA/COCA-COLA WORLD RANKING

1993	1994	1995	1996	1997	1998	1999	2000	2001	2002	2003	2004	High		Low	
157	175	176	175	181	181	192	188	192	185	163	173	**152**	08/93	**195**	07/02

2004-2005											
08/04	09/04	10/04	11/04	12/04	01/05	02/05	03/05	04/05	05/05	06/05	07/05
171	172	172	172	173	173	173	173	173	173	173	174

Since joining FIFA nearly 20 years ago, Seychelles have made little impact on the international arena. With 59 matches played, they have won just nine and their Cup campaigns have failed to progress beyond the first stages. The 2006 FIFA World Cup™ marked Seychelles' second attempt to qualify, but a tie with Zambia, ranked 30 places above them, was always going to prove difficult. Losing 4-0 at home, the islanders didn't give up hope though and forced a creditable 1-1 draw in front of 30,000 fans in Lusaka. It was more than a year later before the team played again, this time in a COSAFA Castle Cup first round match with South Africa, which they lost 3-0. The country's

INTERNATIONAL HONOURS
None

Football Federation aims to make a concerted effort to develop youth football and the latest FIFA Goal project funds are being used with that in mind as new facilities are added to the artificial turf pitches already built to create a training centre. However, with neither the U-20s nor the U-17s entering their respective African Championships there is still a long way to go. La Passe FC, who won the Sunkiss'd Division One, rounded off a miserable season for bottom-of-the-table Plaisance by beating them 16-0 in the final match of the campaign that was abandoned on 77 minutes when Plaisance were reduced to seven men.

THE FIFA BIG COUNT OF 2000

	Male	Female		Male	Female
Registered players	1 328	140	Referees	39	5
Non registered players	400	0	Officials	295	0
Youth players	1 028	0	Total involved	3 235	
Total players	2 896		Number of clubs	55	
Professional players	0	0	Number of teams	55	

Seychelles Football Federation (SFF)
People's Stadium, PO Box 843, Victoria, Mahe, Seychelles
Tel +248 324632   Fax +248 225468
sff@seychelles.net   www.none
President: PATEL Suketu   General Secretary: BONIFACE Wilhem
Vice-President: ADAM Hugh   Treasurer: MATHIOT Justin   Media Officer: none
Men's Coach: TBD   Women's Coach: none
SFF formed: 1979   CAF: 1986   FIFA: 1986
Colours: Red, Red, Red

GAMES PLAYED BY SEYCHELLES IN THE 2006 FIFA WORLD CUP™ CYCLE

2002	Opponents		Score	Venue	Comp	Scorers	Att	Referee
8-09	Eritrea	W	1-0	Victoria	CNq	Victor 50	3 000	Ravelontsalama MAD
26-09	Mauritius	L	0-1	Port Louis	Fr		166	Roopnah MRI
13-10	Mali	L	0-3	Bamako	CNq		50 000	Sorie SLE
2003								
30-03	Zimbabwe	L	1-3	Harare	CNq	Zialor 90	60 000	Bernardo Colembi ANG
7-06	Zimbabwe	W	2-1	Victoria	CNq	Balde 73p, Zialor 87	12 000	Mangaliso SWZ
21-06	Eritrea	L	0-1	Asmara	CNq			
5-07	Mali	L	0-2	Victoria	CNq		5 000	Lim Kee Chong MRI
28-08	Madagascar	D	1-1	Curepipe	IOr1	Balde 87	1 000	Lim Kee Chong MRI
2-09	Mauritius	D	0-0	Curepipe	IOr1			
4-09	Reunion	L	0-1	Curepipe	IOr1		1 000	
11-10	Zambia	L	0-4	Victoria	WCq		2 700	Lim Kee Chong MRI
15-11	Zambia	D	1-1	Lusaka	WCq	Suzette 69	30 000	Abdulkadir TAN
2004								
No international matches played in 2004								
2005								
26-02	South Africa	L	0-3	Curepipe	CCr1			Roheemun MRI

Fr = Friendly match • CN = CAN African Cup of Nations • IO = Indian Ocean Games • CC = COSAFA Castle Cup • WC = FIFA World Cup™
q = qualifier • r1 = first round group

SEYCHELLES NATIONAL TEAM RECORDS AND RECORD SEQUENCES

Records			Sequence records				
Victory	9-0	MDV 1979	Wins	1		Clean sheets	1	
Defeat	0-6	MAD 1990	Defeats	11	1992-1996	Goals scored	4	1979-1983
Player Caps	n/a		Undefeated	2	Four times	Without goal	3	Three times
Player Goals	n/a		Without win	14	1992-1998	Goals against	17	1990-1998

SEYCHELLES 2004 FIRST DIVISION

	Pl	W	D	L	F	A	Pts
La Passe	18	13	4	1	55	9	43
St Louis Victoria	18	11	4	3	47	24	36
Red Star Anse-aux-Pins	18	11	1	6	42	18	34
Anse Reunion	17	7	7	3	33	17	28
Light Stars Grande Anse	18	8	2	8	28	29	26
St Michel United	18	5	6	7	24	19	21
Sunshine SC Victoria	17	6	3	8	23	25	21
Seychelles MB Victoria	18	4	7	7	20	20	19
Northern Dynamo Glacis	18	4	5	9	24	30	17
Plaisance	18	1	0	17	9	114	3

27/05/2004 - 30/10/2004

RECENT LEAGUE AND CUP RECORD

	Championship		Cup		
Year	Champions	Winners	Score	Runners-up
1995	Sunshine	Red Star		
1996	St Michel United	St Louis		
1997	St Michel United	St Michel		
1998	Red Star	St Michel United	4-0	Ascot
1999	St Michel United	Red Star	2-1	Sunshine
2000	St Michel United	Sunshine	1-1 4-2p	Red Star
2001	Red Star	St Michel United	2-1	Sunshine
2002	La Passe	Anse Reunion	2-1	Red Star
2003	St Michel United	St Louis	2-1	Light Stars
2004	La Passe	Red Star	1-0	Anse Reunion

SEYCHELLES COUNTRY INFORMATION

Capital	Victoria	Independence	1976 from the UK	GDP per Capita	$7 800
Population	80 832	Status	Republic	GNP Ranking	169
Area km²	455	Language	English, French, Creole	Dialling code	+248
Population density	177 per km²	Literacy rate	58%	Internet code	.sc
% in urban areas	54%	Main religion	Christian	GMT +/−	+4
Towns/Cities	Victoria 26 361				
Neighbours (km)	Indian Ocean 491				
Main stadia	Stade Linité – Victoria 12 000				

SIN – SINGAPORE

NATIONAL TEAM RECORD
JULY 1ST 2002 TO JUNE 30TH 2005

PL	W	D	L	F	A	%
40	19	6	15	62	59	55

FIFA/COCA-COLA WORLD RANKING

1993	1994	1995	1996	1997	1998	1999	2000	2001	2002	2003	2004	High		Low	
75	95	104	92	103	81	104	101	115	118	106	112	**73**	08/93	**121**	09/04

2004-2005											
08/04	09/04	10/04	11/04	12/04	01/05	02/05	03/05	04/05	05/05	06/05	07/05
118	121	120	118	112	104	104	104	104	104	99	99

After winning the ASEAN Tiger Cup at the beginning of the year by beating Indonesia 5-2 on aggregate Singapore's stock is riding high. Watched by a total of 175,000 fans in Jakarta and Singapore over the two legs, it was the second occasion Singapore had lifted the trophy. Clearly with much support in the country as well as money and decent facilities, conditions are ripe for football to develop and with the national team creeping into the top 100 of the FIFA/Coca-Cola World Ranking progress is being made. An early exit from the 2006 World Cup™ qualifying campaign cannot be regarded as too disastrous because expectations were muted once Singapore

INTERNATIONAL HONOURS
Tiger Cup 1998 2002

found themselves in a group with Oman, India and regional heavyweights Japan. It took Singapore until their penultimate match to register a win and, as expected, they finished bottom of the group. The 2004 S-League closed with Tampine Rovers as champions and also double winners. Losing just four games, they were 10 points clear of 2003 double winners Home United at the season's end and it was United who Rovers beat in the Cup Final 4-1 although it took them three goals in extra-time to claim the trophy. Home United and Geylang United made a big impact in the inaugural AFC Cup with both reaching the semi-finals before losing to Syrian opposition.

THE FIFA BIG COUNT OF 2000

	Male	Female		Male	Female
Registered players	1 280	0	Referees	125	0
Non registered players	50 000	300	Officials	120	20
Youth players	5 700	0	Total involved	57 545	
Total players	57 280		Number of clubs	136	
Professional players	200	0	Number of teams	563	

Football Association of Singapore (FAS)
100 Tyrwhitt Road, Singapore 207542
Tel +65 63483477   Fax +65 62933728
johnkoh@fas.org.sg   www.fas.org.sg
President: HO Peng Kee   General Secretary: KOH John
Vice-President: NORDIN Zainudin   Treasurer: CHAN Ket Teck   Media Officer: LEE Winston
Men's Coach: AVRAMOVIC Radojko   Women's Coach: ISMAIL Hassan
FAS formed: 1892   AFC: 1954   FIFA: 1952
Colours: Red, Red, Red

GAMES PLAYED BY SINGAPORE IN THE 2006 FIFA WORLD CUP™ CYCLE

2002	Opponents	Score	Venue	Comp	Scorers	Att	Referee
16-07	Malaysia	W 2-1	Kuantan	Fr	Zainal [89], Nazri Nasri Mohd [95]	25 000	
10-11	Indonesia	D 1-1	Singapore	Fr	Juraimi [37], W 4-3p		
12-12	Philippines	W 2-0	Singapore	Fr	Goncalves [72], Indra Sahdan Daud [90]		Nagalingam SIN
18-12	Malaysia	L 0-4		TCr1		40 000	Lee Young Chun KOR
20-12	Laos	W 2-1	Singapore	TCr1	Noh Alam Shah [6], Noor Ali [52]	10 000	Midi Nitrorejo IDN
22-12	Thailand	D 1-1	Singapore	TCr1	Noor Ali [45]	20 000	Anders PHI
2003							
4-03	Maldives	W 4-1	Singapore	Fr	Baksin [8], Indra Sahdan Daud [17], Fadhil [22], Juraimi [67]		Bashir MAS
23-03	Macao	W 2-0	Singapore	ACq	Baksin [18], Indra Sahdan Daud [59]		
25-03	Pakistan	W 3-0	Singapore	ACq	Indra Sahdan Daud 2 [4 33p], Noh Alam Shah [66]		
4-08	Hong Kong	W 4-1	Singapore	Fr	Bennett [7], Juaimi [16], Indra Sahdan Daud 2 [67 77]		
4-09	Kuwait	L 1-3	Singapore	ACq	Goncalves [50]		Sun Baojie CHN
16-09	Oman	L 1-3	Singapore	Fr	Indra Sahdan Daud [66]		Abdul Hamid MAS
27-09	Kuwait	L 0-4	Kuwait City	ACq			
19-10	Palestine	W 2-0	Singapore	ACq	Juraimi [18], Noh Alam Shah [89]		Sarkar IND
22-10	Palestine	D 0-0	Singapore	ACq			Vidanagamage SRI
19-11	Qatar	L 0-2	Doha	ACq			
29-11	Qatar	L 0-2	Singapore	ACq			Hamlumyaung THA
2004							
28-01	Norway	L 2-5	Singapore	Fr	Bennett [45], Ishak [51]	5 000	Supian MAS
18-02	India	L 0-1	Margoa	WCq		28 000	Yasrebi IRN
31-03	Japan	L 1-2	Singapore	WCq	Indra Sahdan Daud [62]	6 000	Bae Jae Yong KOR
9-06	Oman	L 0-7	Muscat	WCq		2 000	Ebrahim BHR
12-07	Malaysia	L 0-2	Kuala Lumpur	Fr		2 000	
4-09	Indonesia	W 2-0	Singapore	Fr		3 030	Vo Minh Tri VIE
8-09	Oman	L 0-2	Singapore	WCq		4 000	Arambekade SRI
8-10	United Arab Emirates	L 1-2	Singapore	Fr	Masturi [60]	2 809	Ong MAS
13-10	India	W 2-0	Singapore	WCq	Indra Sahdan Daud [73], Kairul Amri Mohd [76]	3 609	Husain BHR
1-11	Malaysia	L 1-2	Singapore	Fr	Dickson [21]	3 293	Luong VIE
17-11	Japan	L 0-1	Saitama	WCq		58 881	Torky IRN
27-11	Myanmar	W 1-0	Singapore	Fr	Noh Alam Shah [78]	4 881	Hadi IDN
30-11	Hong Kong	D 0-0	Singapore	Fr	L 5-6p	3 359	Phaengsupha THA
7-12	Vietnam	D 1-1	Ho Chi Minh City	TCr1	Indra Sahdan Daud [70]	20 000	Sun Baojie CHN
9-12	Indonesia	D 0-0	Ho Chi Minh City	TCr1		4 000	Kwon Jong Chul KOR
13-12	Laos	W 6-2	Hanoi	TCr1	Jailani [7], Indra Sahdan Daud 2 [19 74], OG [41], Casmir 2 [45 90p]	17 000	Supian MAS
15-12	Cambodia	W 3-0	Hanoi	TCr1	Dickson [21], Khaizan [27], Khairul Amri [54]	2 000	Ebrahim BHR
29-12	Myanmar	W 4-3	Kuala Lumpur	TCsf	Bennet [21], Casmir [39], Noh Alam Shah [64], Ishak [82]	12 000	Rungklay THA
2005							
2-01	Myanmar	W 4-2	Singapore	TCsf	Noh Alam Shah 3 [74 94 95], Casmir [110]	30 000	Kamikawa JPN
8-01	Indonesia	W 3-1	Jakarta	TCf	Bennett [5], Khairul Amri [39], Casmir [69]	120000	Kwon Jong Chul KOR
16-01	Indonesia	W 2-1	Singapore	TCf	Indra Sahdan Daud [5], Casmir [40p]	55 000	Al Ghamdi KSA
4-06	Malaysia	W 2-0	Singapore	Fr	Noh Alam Shah 2 [32 93+]	18 000	Kunsuta THA
8-06	Malaysia	W 2-1	Pinang	Fr	Noh Alam Shah [19], Bennett [66]	10 000	Napitupulu IDN

Fr = Friendly match • AC = AFC Asian Cup • TC = ASEAN Tiger Cup • WC = FIFA World Cup™
q = qualifier • r1 = first round group • sf = semi-final • f = final

SINGAPORE COUNTRY INFORMATION

Capital	Singapore City	Independence	1965 from Malaysia	GDP per Capita	$23 700
Population	4 353 893	Status	Republic	GNP Ranking	38
Area km²	693	Language	Chinese, English, Malay	Dialling code	+65
Population density	6 282 per km²	Literacy rate	92%	Internet code	.sg
% in urban areas	100%	Main religion	Buddhist 54%, Muslim 15%	GMT +/−	+8
Towns/Cities ('000)	Singapore City 3 547				
Neighbours (km)	Strait of Singapore & Johore Strait 193				
Main stadia	Jalan Besar – Singapore 6 000; National Stadium – Singapore 55 000				

SINGAPORE NATIONAL TEAM RECORDS AND RECORD SEQUENCES

Records			Sequence records					
Victory	8-1	IDN 1986	Wins	8	2004-2005	Clean sheets	4	1985
Defeat	0-9	MYA 1969	Defeats	9	1977	Goals scored	14	1993-1995
Player Caps	n/a		Undefeated	12	2004-2005	Without goal	5	1976-1977
Player Goals	n/a		Without win	19	1966-1968	Goals against	36	1966-1970

SINGAPORE 2004

S.LEAGUE

	Pl	W	D	L	F	A	Pts	Tampines	Home Utd	Young Lions	SAF	Albirex	Woodlands	Geylang	Balestier	Sinchi	Tanjong
Tampines Rovers †	27	20	3	4	76	29	63		2-2 2-1	6-3 6-2	2-1	5-1	1-1 5-1	1-0	3-1 4-0	2-1	9-0 1-0
Home United †	27	17	2	8	76	43	53	2-1		1-2	1-2 8-1	2-2 4-2	6-1 1-0	4-2	3-2	5-1	4-1 6-2
Young Lions	27	14	5	8	74	52	47	4-0	2-0 4-1		2-2	1-0 2-3	2-1	2-2 1-3	2-2 6-0	4-1 7-1	4-2
Sing. Armed Forces	27	14	3	10	45	48	45	2-1 0-2	1-6	6-6 0-5		3-2	0-2 0-1	2-0	2-1	2-0 3-0	4-0 2-0
Albirex Niigata	27	12	8	7	50	42	44	1-0 0-3	2-4	1-1	1-0 3-1		2-0	4-1 1-1	3-2	2-2 2-1	1-1
Woodlands Wellington	27	12	4	11	48	49	40	1-4	0-2	4-3 4-0	1-2	3-2 1-2		2-1	3-2 2-3	3-2 0-0	1-1
Geylang United	27	10	7	10	43	43	37	3-3 0-2	2-4 2-0	2-1	2-1 1-3	1-1	1-2 1-0		1-0 1-2	2-2	2-2
Balestier Khalsa	27	6	2	19	36	73	20	1-4	3-2 2-0	1-2	0-1 0-2	2-2 0-3	1-2	1-4		1-4	2-1 0-6
Sinchi TV	27	4	5	18	36	62	17	1-2 0-2	1-2 1-3	1-2	0-1	1-1	1-5	0-1 1-1	6-3		3-2 3-1 2-0
Tanjong Pagar United	27	4	5	18	29	72	17	0-3	0-2	0-3 2-1	1-1	0-3 0-3	1-4 3-3	1-2 0-4	2-1	2-1	

2/03/2004 - 26-09-2004/2004 • † Qualified for the AFC Cup

SINGAPORE CUP 2004

Eighth-finals

Tampines Rovers	6
Cosmoleague	0
Albirex Niigata	3
Balestier Khalsa	4
Woodlands Wellington	2
DPMM Brunei	1
Geylang United	Bye
Sinchi TV	4
Tampines Rovers SC	1
Sembawang	0
Young Lions	7
Singapore Armed Forces	4
Tanjong Pagar United	0
Home United	Bye

Quarter-finals

Tampines Rovers	2	2
Balestier Khalsa *	4	0
Woodlands Wellington	2	1
Geylang United *	3	2
Sinchi TV	2	1
Young Lions *	3	0
Singapore Armed Forces	1	1
Home United *	0	3

Semi-finals

Tampines Rovers	1	3
Geylang United *	2	0
Sinchi TV *	1	4
Home United	5	5

Final

Tampines Rovers	4
Home United	1

CUP FINAL

3-10-2004, Att: 17 000
National Stadium, Singapore
Scorers - Tan Kim Leng 36, Noh Alam Shah 93, Grabovac 111, Azlan Alipah 119 for Tampines; Indra Sahdan Daud 45 for Home United

* Home Team in the first leg

RECENT LEAGUE AND CUP RECORD

	Championship							Cup		
Year	Champions	Pts	Runners-up	Pts	Third	Pts		Winners	Score	Runners-up
1997	Sing. Armed Forces	37	Tanjong Pagar Utd	34	Woodlands Well'ton	33		Sing. Armed Forces	4-2	Woodlands Well'ton
1998	Sing. Armed Forces	46	Tanjong Pagar Utd	46	Geylang United	38		Tanjong Pagar Utd	2-0	Sing. Armed Forces
1999	Home United	51	Sing. Armed Forces	49	Tanjong Pagar Utd	41		Sing. Armed Forces	3-1	Jurong
2000	Sing. Armed Forces	52	Tanjong Pagar Utd	43	Geylang United	41		Home United	1-0	Sing. Armed Forces
2001	Geylang United	76	Sing. Armed Forces	74	Home United	72		Home United	8-0	Geylang United
2002	Sing. Armed Forces	84	Home United	64	Geylang United	59		Tampines Rovers	1-0	Jurong
2003	Home United	85	Geylang United	71	Sing. Armed Forces	69		Home United	2-1	Geylang United
2004	Tampines Rovers	63	Home United	53	Young Lions	47		Tampines Rovers	4-1	Home United

SKN – ST KITTS AND NEVIS

NATIONAL TEAM RECORD
JULY 1ST 2002 TO JUNE 30TH 2005

PL	W	D	L	F	A	%
28	13	2	13	49	49	50

FIFA/COCA-COLA WORLD RANKING

1993	1994	1995	1996	1997	1998	1999	2000	2001	2002	2003	2004	High		Low	
166	175	150	121	127	132	137	146	129	109	134	118	**108**	07/04	**176**	11/94

					2004-2005						
08/04	09/04	10/04	11/04	12/04	01/05	02/05	03/05	04/05	05/05	06/05	07/05
112	110	115	115	118	119	119	119	119	120	120	122

For a country with a population of 46,000 to be holding 122nd place in the FIFA/Coca-Cola World Ranking after little more than a decade as FIFA members is a pretty remarkable achievement and one that St Kitts and Nevis fully deserve. Although never in danger of qualifying for the 2006 FIFA World Cup™, the national team played 20 games throughout 2004, gaining valuable experience against bigger and better sides and their qualifiers were not without success. First up were the US Virgin Islands who were comfortably dispatched 11-0 on aggregate to set up a meeting with Barbados. St Kitts won away in Bridgetown before claiming a thrilling 3-2 home win and a place

INTERNATIONAL HONOURS
None

at the second preliminary group stage. Sadly, that's where the journey ended as the strength of the other teams in the group – Mexico, Trinidad and Tobago and St Vincent and the Grenadines – showed and St Kitts finished bottom and without a point. However, the experience looked to have helped the team as they came close to qualifying for the CONCACAF Gold Cup for the first time thanks to three matches unbeaten before two defeats to Haiti shattered the dream. For the first time, a play-off was held between the winners of the islands' two Leagues with Village Superstars from St Kitts beating Bath FC from Nevis.

THE FIFA BIG COUNT OF 2000

	Male	Female		Male	Female
Registered players	825	0	Referees	0	0
Non registered players	500	0	Officials	100	
Youth players	500	75	Total involved	2 000	
Total players	1 900		Number of clubs	31	
Professional players	0	0	Number of teams	32	

St Kitts and Nevis Football Association (SKNFA)
Warner Park, PO Box 465, Basseterre, St Kitts and Nevis
Tel +1 869 4668502   Fax +1 869 4659033
info@sknfa.com   www.sknfa.com
President: JENKINS Peter   General Secretary: AMORY Spencer Leonard
Vice-President: GILLARD II Frederick   Treasurer: AMORY Spencer Leonard   Media Officer: None
Men's Coach: LAKE Lennie & BROWNE Elvis   Women's Coach: none
SKNFA formed: 1932   CONCACAF: 1992   FIFA: 1992
Colours: Green, Red, Yellow

GAMES PLAYED BY ST KITTS AND NEVIS IN THE 2006 FIFA WORLD CUP™ CYCLE

2002	Opponents	Score		Venue	Comp	Scorers	Att	Referee
25-07	Chinese Taipei	W	3-0	Basseterre	Fr			
27-07	Barbados	W	3-0	Basseterre	Fr	Issac, Francis, Gumbs		
28-07	Trinidad and Tobago	W	2-1	Basseterre	Fr	Sargeant [49], Issac [75]	800	
29-10	Antigua and Barbuda	D	1-1	Basseterre	Fr			
13-11	St Lucia	W	2-1	Port of Spain	GCq	Isaac 2 [38 56]		Forde BRB
15-11	Trinidad and Tobago	L	0-2	Port of Spain	GCq		3 500	Faneijte ANT
2003								
29-07	Haiti	W	1-0	Basseterre	Fr	Isaac [3]		Matthew SKN
2-08	Trinidad and Tobago	L	1-2	Basseterre	Fr	Francis [50]		
2004								
1-02	Antigua and Barbuda	L	0-1	St John's	Fr			
18-02	US Virgin Islands	W	4-0	St Thomas	WCq	Huggins [26], Lake 2 [50 64], Isaac [62]	225	Brizan TRI
20-03	British Virgin Islands	W	4-0	Basseterre	Fr			
21-03	Antigua and Barbuda	L	2-3	Basseterre	Fr			
31-03	US Virgin Islands	W	7-0	Basseterre	WCq	Lake 5 [8 38 46 56 77], Isaac 2 [80 90]	800	Recinos SLV
23-05	St Vincent/Grenadines	W	3-2	Basseterre	Fr	Lake [9], Hodge [25], Willock [63]		Matthew SKN
2-06	Northern Ireland	L	0-2	Basseterre	Fr		5 000	Matthew SKN
13-06	Barbados	W	2-0	Bridgetown	WCq	Gumbs [78], Newton [88]	3 700	Alfaro SLV
19-06	Barbados	W	3-2	Basseterre	WCq	Gomez [16], Willock 2 [22 29]	3 500	Pineda HON
4-09	Trinidad and Tobago	L	1-2	Basseterre	WCq	Isaac [40]	2 800	Castillo GUA
10-09	St Vincent/Grenadines	L	0-1	Kingstown	WCq		4 000	Delgado CUB
10-10	Trinidad and Tobago	L	1-5	Marabella	WCq	Gumbs [43p]	7 000	Valenzuela USA
13-10	St Vincent/Grenadines	L	0-3	Basseterre	WCq		500	Whittaker CAY
31-10	Montserrat	W	6-1	Basseterre	GCq	Francis 3 [9 45 86], Connonier [36], Isaac [57], Hodge [83]		Bedeau GRN
2-11	St Lucia	D	1-1	Basseterre	GCq	Francis [14]		Bedeau GRN
4-11	Antigua and Barbuda	W	2-0	Basseterre	GCq	Sargeant [34], Isaac [45]		Phillip GRN
13-11	Mexico	L	0-5	Miami	WCq		18 312	Moreno PAN
17-11	Mexico	L	0-8	Monterrey	WCq		12 000	Stott USA
12-12	Haiti	L	0-1	Fort Lauderdale	GCq		2 500	McNab BAH
15-12	Haiti	L	0-2	Basseterre	GCq		1 000	Bhimull TRI
2005								

No international matches played in 2005 before August

Fr = Friendly match • GC = CONCACAF Gold Cup • WC = FIFA World Cup™ • q = qualifier

ST KITTS AND NEVIS COUNTRY INFORMATION

Capital	Basseterre	Independence	1983 from the UK	GDP per Capita	$8 800
Population	38 836	Status	Constitutional Monarchy	GNP Ranking	177
Area km²	261	Language	English	Dialling code	+1869
Population density	148 per km²	Literacy rate	97%	Internet code	.kn
% in urban areas	42%	Main religion	Christian	GMT +/–	-4
Towns/Cities	Basseterre 12 920; Charlestown 1 538; Saint Paul's 1 483; Sadlers 986; Middle Island 887				
Neighbours (km)	Caribbean Sea 135				
Main stadia	Warner Park – Basseterre 6 000				

ST KITTS AND NEVIS NATIONAL TEAM RECORDS AND RECORD SEQUENCES

Records			Sequence records					
Victory	9-1	MSR 1994	Wins	4	1996, 2002	Clean sheets	3	1991-1992
Defeat	0-8	MEX 2004	Defeats	4	2004	Goals scored	10	1998-99, 2001
Player Caps	n/a		Undefeated	10	2001-2002	Without goal	4	2004
Player Goals	n/a		Without win	5	1996	Goals against	14	1998-2000

FIFA REFEREE LIST 2005

	Int'l	DoB
MATTHEW James	2003	30-01-1969

FIFA ASSISTANT REFEREE LIST 2005

	Int'l	DoB
JOSEPH Alexis	2002	6-08-1971
TECHEIRA Steadroy	1994	2-04-1961

ST KITTS 2004-05
PREMIER DIVISION

	Pl	W	D	L	F	A	Pts
Village Superstars †	12	7	2	3	21	12	23
Newtown United †	12	6	4	2	27	10	22
Garden Hotspurs †	12	5	3	4	15	11	18
St Peter's †	12	5	3	4	20	17	18
St Paul's United	12	3	6	3	13	11	13
St Thomas Strikers	12	3	3	6	14	28	12
Old Road	12	1	3	8	8	29	6

21/11/2004 - 5/03/2005 • † Qualified for play-offs
Relegation play-off: Conaree 1-0 Strikers • Conaree promoted
Strikers had won a first game 2-1 but that was awarded to
Conaree after Strikers fielded an ineligible player

ST KITTS 2004-05
PREMIER DIVISION SUPER FOUR

	Pl	W	D	L	F	A	Pts
Village Superstars †	3	2	0	1	4	3	6
St Peter's †	3	2	0	1	4	4	6
Garden Hotspurs	3	1	0	2	6	5	3
Newtown United	3	1	0	2	3	5	3

12/03/2005 - 23/03/2005 • † Qualified for the final

ST KITTS AND NEVIS 2004-05
PREMIER DIVISION FINAL

Champions	Score	Runners-up
Village Superstars	1-0 2-1	St Peter's

ST KITTS AND NEVIS 2004-05
CHAMPION OF CHAMPIONS

Champions	Score	Runners-up
Village Superstars	1-0	Bath United

Played between the champions of St Kitts and the champions of Nevis

RECENT LEAGUE AND CUP RECORD

	Championship				Cup		
Year	Champions	Score	Runners-up		Winners	Score	Runners-up
1996	Newtown United						
1997	Newtown United						
1998	Newtown United						
1999	St Paul's United	3-0 0-1 4-2	Garden Hotspurs				
2000	No tournament due to season adjustment						
2001	Garden Hotspurs	3-0 0-0 3-4p 1-0	Village Superstars				
2002	Cayon Rockets	0-0 3-2p 3-0	Garden Hotspurs		Cayon Rockets		
2003	Village Superstars	0-1 2-1 0-0 5-4p	Newtown United		Village Superstars	1-0	Newtown United
2004	Newtown United	0-1 1-0 2-0	Village Superstars		Village Superstars	3-1	Cayon Rockets
2005	Village Superstars	1-0 2-1	St Peter's				

SLE – SIERRA LEONE

NATIONAL TEAM RECORD
JULY 1ST 2002 TO JUNE 30TH 2005

PL	W	D	L	F	A	%
11	5	2	4	11	8	54.5

FIFA/COCA-COLA WORLD RANKING

1993	1994	1995	1996	1997	1998	1999	2000	2001	2002	2003	2004	High		Low	
76	76	58	84	84	111	120	129	138	133	146	160	51	01/96	163	04/05

2004-2005											
08/04	09/04	10/04	11/04	12/04	01/05	02/05	03/05	04/05	05/05	06/05	07/05
153	153	156	157	160	160	162	162	163	162	164	156

Football finally returned to Sierra Leone after a period of disputes and controversy that had led to clubs boycotting the national League. With the long-term effects of the civil war in the mid-1990s still being felt, it's hoped some stability will enable football to fulfil its potential in the country. To set the national team back on the international road, Sierra Leone hosted the Peace Cup with Gambia, Guinea and Liberia invited to take part. Victorious in all three matches, the tournament marked a successful return for the Leone Stars after more than 18 months without a fixture. The team had come close to qualifying for the 2004 CAF African Cup of Nations, but defeat to Gabon

INTERNATIONAL HONOURS
Copa Amilcar Cabral 1993 1995

in their last match allowed Zimbabwe to snatch the place for best group runner-up. In spite of the side's failure in the 2006 FIFA World Cup™ qualifiers where they lost 2-1 on aggregate to Congo, there is some hope for the future after the U-17s reached the 2003 World Youth Championships although this year neither the U-20s nor the U-17s made much impression in their respective events. After a two-year break from league football when only friendlies were played, competitive football has made a welcome return and it is hoped that next year's continental competitions will feature clubs from Sierra Leone for the first time in more than a decade.

THE FIFA BIG COUNT OF 2000

	Male	Female		Male	Female
Registered players	600	240	Referees	246	17
Non registered players	15 000	150	Officials	2 120	80
Youth players	5 640	0	Total involved	24 093	
Total players	21 630		Number of clubs	24	
Professional players	0	0	Number of teams	196	

Sierra Leone Football Association (SLFA)
21 Battery Street, Kingtom, PO Box 672, Freetown, Sierra Leone
Tel +232 22 240071   Fax +232 22 241339
Starssierra@yahoo.com   www.slfa.net
President: KHADI Nahim   General Secretary: KABBA Abu Bakahr
Vice-President: BANGURA Bassie   Treasurer: TBD   Media Officer: none
Men's Coach: SHERINGTON J.J.   Women's Coach: MOSES
SLFA formed: 1967   CAF: 1967   FIFA: 1967
Colours: Green, Green, Green

GAMES PLAYED BY SIERRA LEONE IN THE 2006 FIFA WORLD CUP™ CYCLE

2002	Opponents	Score		Venue	Comp	Scorers	Att	Referee
25-08	Gambia	L	0-1	Banjul	Fr			
8-09	Equatorial Guinea	W	3-1	Malabo	CNq	Bah [38], Sesay [46], Mansaray [68]		Neto STP
12-10	Gabon	W	2-0	Freetown	CNq	Kpaka [45], Bah [52]		Ekoue TOG
19-10	Ghana	W	2-1	Freetown	Fr	Massaquoi [24], Kemokai Kallon [36]		Sanusie SLE
2003								
29-03	Morocco	D	0-0	Freetown	CNq			Kabu LBR
8-06	Morocco	L	0-1	Casablanca	CNq			Abd El Fatah EGY
22-06	Equatorial Guinea	W	2-0	Freetown	CNq	Mohanned Kallon [71], Kabbah [90]		
6-07	Gabon	L	0-2	Libreville	CNq			
12-10	Congo	L	0-1	Brazzaville	WCq		4 800	Mana NGA
16-11	Congo	D	1-1	Freetown	WCq	Koroma [58]	20 000	Monteiro Lopes CPV
2004								
No international matches played in 2004								
2005								
12-06	Gambia	W	1-0	Freetown	Fr	Kpaka [56]		

Fr = Friendly match • CN = CAF African Cup of Nations • WC = FIFA World Cup™ • q = qualifier

SIERRA LEONE NATIONAL TEAM RECORDS AND RECORD SEQUENCES

Records			Sequence records					
Victory	5-1	NIG 1976, NIG 1995	Wins	4	1986	Clean sheets	5	1984, 1991-92
Defeat	0-5	MWI 1978, GHA 2000	Defeats	6	1982-83, 1996	Goals scored	11	1985-1987
Player Caps	n/a		Undefeated	14	1991-1993	Without goal	6	1982-83, 1996
Player Goals	n/a		Without win	9	1971-1973	Goals against	19	1976-1983

FIFA REFEREE LIST 2005

	Int'l	DoB
FREEMAN Mohamed	2002	16-08-1967
PARKINSON Edward	1996	11-07-1966
SANUSI Abdul	2003	24-12-1968
SANUSIE Rashid	1999	24-07-1964
SORIE Denis	1995	12-01-1962

FIFA ASSISTANT REFEREE LIST 2005

	Int'l	DoB
BANGALI Charles	1996	18-04-1962
BANGURA Sorie	1996	20-01-1961
JONES Frederick	2003	1-09-1968
KARGBO Daniel	2003	3-02-1977
MASSAQUOI Bockarie	1999	17-04-1966
NEWLAND Sheriff	2002	7-11-1972
SENESIE Emmanuel	1995	14-11-1960

RECENT LEAGUE AND CUP RECORD

	Championship		Cup
Year	Champions		Winners
1995	Mighty Blackpool		
1996	Mighty Blackpool		
1997	East End Lions		
1998	Mighty Blackpool		
1999	East End Lions		
2000	Mighty Blackpool		Mighty Blackpool
2001	Mighty Blackpool		Old Edwardians
2002	No tournament		No tournament
2003	No tournament		
2004	No tournament		

SIERRA LEONE COUNTRY INFORMATION

Capital	Freetown	Independence	1961 from UK	GDP per Capita	$500
Population	5 883 889	Status	Republic	GNP Ranking	160
Area km²	71 740	Language	English, Mende, Krio	Dialling code	+232
Population density	82 per km²	Literacy rate	31%	Internet code	.sl
% in urban areas	36%	Main religion	Muslim 60%	GMT +/–	0
Towns/Cities ('000)	Freetown 1 190; Koidu 111; Bo 80; Kenema 70; Makeni 54; Lunsar 21; Waterloo 21				
Neighbours (km)	Guinea 652; Liberia 306; North Atlantic Ocean 402				
Main stadia	National Stadium – Freetown 36 000				

SLV – EL SALVADOR

NATIONAL TEAM RECORD
JULY 1ST 2002 TO JUNE 30TH 2005

PL	W	D	L	F	A	%
33	7	7	19	24	54	31.8

FIFA/COCA-COLA WORLD RANKING

1993	1994	1995	1996	1997	1998	1999	2000	2001	2002	2003	2004	High		Low	
66	80	82	65	64	92	96	83	86	94	95	106	60	10/93	116	07/05

2004-2005											
08/04	09/04	10/04	11/04	12/04	01/05	02/05	03/05	04/05	05/05	06/05	07/05
103	103	106	102	106	108	110	110	110	111	110	116

After competing at two FIFA World Cups™ in 1970 and 1982, hopes are that El Salvador will once again grace the finals. However, their third appearance won't be in Germany 2006 after they disappointed fans by crashing out in the second stage. To cap a less than vintage year for the country, the team then failed to qualify for the 2005 CONCACAF Gold Cup. Poor results in the 2006 FIFA World Cup™ qualifiers led to the dismissal of coach Juan Roman Paredes, but his replacement Armando Contreras could not revive their fortunes before the end of the group stage with Panama and not the Salvadorians accompanying the USA into the next qualifying round. Domestically El

INTERNATIONAL HONOURS
Central American Championship 1943   Central American and Caribbean Games 1954 2002
CONCACAF Champions Cup Alianza 1967 Aguila 1976 Deportivo FAS 1979

Salvador follows the system of two Championships a year. Deportivo FAS won the group stage of both the Apertura and Clausura and confirmed their domination by winning the play-offs of both. In the Apertura final they beat Balboa 4-3 on penalties and in the Clausura final they beat Luis Angel Firpo 3-1. While Alianza exited the Champions Cup in the second round, FAS fared better reaching the third round group stage but there they found Municipal, Saprissa and Olimpia too strong and were the only one of the four not to reach the final knock-out stage.

THE FIFA BIG COUNT OF 2000

	Male	Female		Male	Female
Registered players	24 497	310	Referees	258	0
Non registered players	250 000	0	Officials	610	0
Youth players	5 546	0	Total involved	281 221	
Total players	280 353		Number of clubs	200	
Professional players	216	0	Number of teams	15 630	

Federacion Salvadorena de Futbol (FESFUT)
Avenida José Matias Delgado, Frente al Centro Español, Colonia Escalón, Zona 10, San Salvador CA 1029, El Salvador
Tel +503 2096200   Fax +503 2637583
presidfsf@hotmail.com   www.fesfut.org.sv
President: TORRES Jose Humberto   General Secretary: VILLALTA Hugo
Vice-President: CABRERA RAJO Jorge   Treasurer: SORTO Aristides   Media Officer: MARTINEZ Julio Ruiz
Men's Coach: CONTRERAS Armando   Women's Coach: HERRERA Jose
FESFUT formed: 1935   CONCACAF: 1961   FIFA: 1938
Colours: Blue, Blue, Blue

GAMES PLAYED BY EL SALVADOR IN THE 2006 FIFA WORLD CUP™ CYCLE

2002	Opponents	Score	Venue	Comp	Scorers	Att	Referee
17-11	USA	L 0-2	Washington DC	Fr		13 590	Prendergast JAM
2003							
17-01	Guatemala	D 0-0	Santa Ana, USA	Fr		6 000	Gack USA
19-01	Guatemala	D 0-0	Los Angeles	Fr		6 000	Jackson USA
9-02	Panama	W 2-1	Panama City	GCq	Galdamez 70, Corrales 77	7 000	Pineda HON
11-02	Costa Rica	L 0-1	Panama City	GCq		500	Batres GUA
13-02	Nicaragua	W 3-0	Panama City	GCq	Corrales 5, Velasquez 27, Mejia 89		Moreno PAN
15-02	Honduras	W 1-0	Colon	GCq	Murgas 81	600	Batres GUA
20-02	Guatemala	L 0-2	Panama City	GCq		500	Ramos MEX
29-06	Honduras	D 1-1	San Pedro Sula	Fr	Mejia 80	5 000	Porras CRC
2-07	Paraguay	L 0-1	San Francisco	Fr			Valenzuela USA
6-07	Mexico	W 2-1	Carson	Fr	Mejia 30, Corrales 60	19 271	Hall USA
8-07	Guatemala	L 1-2	Houston	Fr	Murgas 68	21 047	Hall USA
12-07	USA	L 0-2	Boston	GCr1		33 652	Ramos MEX
16-07	Martinique	W 1-0	Boston	GCr1	Gonzalez.M 76	10 361	Batres GUA
19-07	Costa Rica	L 2-5	Boston	GCqf	Murgas 34p, Pacheco 53	15 627	Ramos MEX
16-11	Jamaica	L 0-3	Kingston	Fr		12 000	Ramdhan TRI
2004							
28-01	Panama	D 1-1	San Salvador	Fr	Velasquez 36		
31-03	Guatemala	L 0-3	San Salvador	Fr		5 047	Aguilar Chicas SLV
28-04	Colombia	L 0-2	Washington DC	Fr		23 000	Vaughn USA
12-05	Haiti	D 3-3	Houston	Fr	Gochez 29, Murgas 43p, Martinez.J 72	4 000	Terry USA
13-06	Bermuda	W 2-1	San Salvador	WCq	Martinez.J 14, Velasquez 54	12 000	Campos NCA
20-06	Bermuda	D 2-2	Hamilton	WCq	Pacheco 2 20 41p	4 000	Whittaker CAY
18-07	Guatemala	L 0-1	Los Angeles	Fr			Valenzuela USA
3-08	Honduras	L 0-4	San Salvador	Fr			Aguilar Chicas SLV
6-08	Guatemala	L 0-2	Washington DC	Fr		20 000	Valenzuela USA
18-08	Panama	W 2-1	San Salvador	WCq	Velasquez 7, Rodriguez.J 45	11 400	Navarro CAN
4-09	USA	L 0-2	Boston	WCq		25 266	Brizan TRI
8-09	Jamaica	L 0-3	San Salvador	WCq		25 000	Alcala MEX
9-10	USA	L 0-2	San Salvador	WCq		20 000	Batres GUA
13-10	Jamaica	D 0-0	Kingston	WCq		12 000	Quesada Cordero CRC
17-11	Panama	L 0-3	Panama City	WCq		9 502	Archundia MEX
2005							
19-02	Panama	L 0-1	Guatemala City	GCq		10 000	Archundia MEX
21-02	Costa Rica	L 1-2	Guatemala City	GCq	Alas 40	3 000	Batres GUA

Fr = Friendly match • GC = CONCACAF Gold Cup • WC = FIFA World Cup™ • q = qualifier

EL SALVADOR NATIONAL TEAM RECORDS AND RECORD SEQUENCES

Records			Sequence records					
Victory	9-0	NCA 1929	Wins	5	1967-1968	Clean sheets	5	1981-1982
Defeat	0-8	MEX 1988	Defeats	7	1989	Goals scored	11	1999-2000
Player Caps	n/a		Undefeated	10	1981-1982	Without goal	6	1971-72, 2004-05
Player Goals	n/a		Without win	10	1989	Goals against	18	1930-1941

EL SALVADOR COUNTRY INFORMATION

Capital	San Salvador	Independence	1841 from Spain	GDP per Capita	$4 800
Population	6 587 541	Status	Republic	GNP Ranking	80
Area km²	21 040	Language	Spanish	Dialling code	+503
Population density	313 per km²	Literacy rate	80%	Internet code	.sv
% in urban areas	45%	Main religion	Christian	GMT +/−	-6
Towns/Cities ('000)	San Salvador 526; Soyapango 329; Santa Ana 176; San Miguel 161; Mejicanos 160				
Neighbours (km)	Guatemala 203; Honduras 342; North Pacific Ocean 307				
Main stadia	Estadio Cuscatlán – San Salvador 39 000				

EL SALVADOR 2004-05

PRIMERA DIVISION PROFESIONAL TORNEO APERTURA

	Pl	W	D	L	F	A	Pts	FAS	San Sal'dor	Balboa	LA Firpo	Metapán	Aguila	Alianza	Lobos	Municipal	Limeño
Deportivo FAS †	18	9	5	4	26	19	32		1-1	2-1	1-0	2-1	3-1	3-0	2-1	1-0	2-1
San Salvador †	18	9	5	4	30	33	32	1-1		1-1	0-6	1-4	2-0	2-1	1-0	3-1	2-0
Atlético Balboa †	18	7	9	2	26	13	30	1-0	6-1		0-0	1-1	0-0	2-2	1-1	2-0	0-0
Luis Angel Firpo	18	7	8	3	26	13	29	3-1	1-1	1-1		1-1	1-1	1-0	1-1	3-0	3-1
Isidro-Metapán †	18	8	5	5	25	24	29	2-1	1-3	0-2	0-0		2-1	1-0	3-3	3-2	2-1
Aguila	18	5	8	5	24	20	23	1-1	3-3	1-1	0-0	3-0		1-1	2-1	5-0	1-0
Alianza	18	6	3	9	19	25	21	1-2	2-3	0-2	1-0	2-1	2-0		1-0	0-1	3-1
Once Lobos	18	4	7	7	22	21	19	2-1	1-2	3-1	1-2	0-0	2-2	3-0		0-1	2-0
Once Municipal	18	5	4	9	15	26	19	1-1	2-0	0-2	3-1	0-1	1-1	1-2	0-0		0-0
Municipal Limeño	18	0	6	12	12	31	6	1-1	2-3	0-2	0-2	1-2	0-2	1-1	1-1	2-2	

7/08/2004 - 28/11/2004 • † Qualified for the play-offs • Play-off for 4th place: Isidro-Metapán 2-0 Luis Angel Firpo

APERTURA PLAY-OFFS

Semi-finals		Finals	
Deportivo FAS		19-12-2004, Cuscatlán, San Salvador	
Isidro-Metapán		Deportivo FAS	0 4p
San Salvador		Atlético Balboa	0 3p
Atlético Balboa			

CLAUSURA PLAY-OFFS

Semi-finals		Finals	
Deportivo FAS	0 4	26-06-2005, Cuscatlán, San Salvador	
Alianza	1 1	Deportivo FAS	3
Municipal Limeño	1 1	Luis Angel Firpo	1
Luis Angel Firpo	6 1		

EL SALVADOR 2004-05

PRIMERA DIVISION PROFESIONAL TORNEO CLAUSURA

	Pl	W	D	L	F	A	Pts	FAS	Limeño	LA Firpo	Alianza	Municipal	Metapán	Balboa	Aguila	San Sal'dor	Lobos
Deportivo FAS †	18	10	5	3	30	19	35		1-2	2-1	2-1	1-0	1-2	1-1	2-1	3-2	2-1
Municipal Limeño †	18	8	6	4	25	19	30	1-1		4-2	2-3	4-2	1-0	1-1	1-1	0-0	3-1
Luis Angel Firpo †	18	8	5	5	29	21	29	3-2	3-0		1-1	3-0	2-0	1-1	2-1	0-1	3-1
Alianza †	18	7	7	4	25	17	28	1-1	0-0	0-1		0-1	1-1	2-1	0-0	1-1	2-0
Once Municipal	18	8	3	7	19	24	27	1-1	1-0	0-0	0-3		3-2	1-2	2-1	1-0	1-1
Isidro-Metapán	18	6	4	8	20	25	22	1-2	1-0	1-0	1-1	2-0		0-1	1-0	1-2	2-1
Atlético Balboa	18	5	6	7	22	21	21	1-2	1-2	1-1	1-2	1-2	3-0		3-1	0-0	1-1
Aguila	18	5	5	8	24	27	20	0-3	0-2	0-0	4-1	2-0	4-2	2-1		3-3	1-1
San Salvador	18	5	5	8	24	32	20	0-3	0-1	1-5	0-2	1-3	2-2	1-2	1-0		6-3
Once Lobos	18	2	6	10	22	35	12	0-0	1-1	5-1	0-4	0-1	1-1	1-0	2-3	2-3	

29/01/2005 - 5/06/2005 • † Qualified for the play-offs • Once Lobos and Municpal Limeño relegated

CLUB DIRECTORY

Club	Town/City	Stadium	www.	Lge	CL
CD Aguila	San Miguel	Juan Francisco Barraza 10 000	cdaguila.com.sv	13	1
Alianza FC	San Salvador	Jorge Mágico González 25 000	alianzafc.com.sv	9	1
Atlético Balboa	La Unión	Marcelino Imbers		0	0
Club Deportivo FAS	Santa Ana	Oscar Alberto Quiteño 15 000	clubdeportivofas.com	16	1
Luis Angel Firpo	Cuscatlán	Sergio Torres 5 000	firpo.com.sv	7	0
AD Isidro Metapán	Metapán	Jorge Calero Suárez	isidrometapan.com	0	0
CD Municipal Limeño	Santa Rosa de Lima	Ramón Flores Berrios 5 000	cdmunicipallimeno.com.sc	0	0
Once Lobos	Chalchuapa	Cesar Hernández		0	0
Once Municipal	Ahuachapan	Simeón Magaña		1	0
San Salvador FC (Prev El Transito)	San Salvador	Cuscatlán 39 000	sansalvadorfc.com	0	0

RECENT LEAGUE AND CUP RECORD

	Championship/Clausura from 2000			Apertura		
Year	Champions	Score	Runners-up	Winners	Score	Runners-up
1999	Luis Angel Firpo	1-1 5-4p	Deportivo FAS	Aguila	1-0	Municipal Limeño
2000	Luis Angel Firpo	1-1 10-9p	AD El Tránsito	Aguila	3-2	Municipal Limeño
2001	Aguila	1-1 2-1	Deportivo FAS	Alianza	2-1	Luis Angel Firpo
2002	Deportivo FAS	4-0	Alianza	Deportivo FAS	3-1	San Salvador
2003	San Salvador	3-1	Luis Angel Firpo	Deportivo FAS	2-2 5-3p	Aguila
2004	Alianza	1-1 3-2p	Deportivo FAS	Deportivo FAS	0-0 4-3p	Atlético Balboa
2005	Deportivo FAS	3-1	Luis Angel Firpo			

SMR – SAN MARINO

NATIONAL TEAM RECORD
JULY 1ST 2002 TO JUNE 30TH 2005

PL	W	D	L	F	A	%
17	1	1	15	5	55	8.8

FIFA/COCA-COLA WORLD RANKING

1993	1994	1995	1996	1997	1998	1999	2000	2001	2002	2003	2004	High		Low	
121	131	951	165	173	179	150	168	158	160	162	164	**118**	09/03	**180**	11/98

2004-2005											
08/04	09/04	10/04	11/04	12/04	01/05	02/05	03/05	04/05	05/05	06/05	07/05
167	169	167	166	164	165	161	161	160	162	161	162

If there is any consolation for San Marino in being ranked as the worst team in Europe it's in the fact that there are a number of much bigger nations elsewhere in the world who are below them in the FIFA/Coca-Cola World Ranking. The 2004-05 season didn't see a repeat of the historic first win which the national team gained against Liechtenstein in April 2004 but if achievement is measured in goals scored then it wasn't a bad season and for one player it was an exceptional year. In the 2006 FIFA World Cup™ qualifiers Andy Selva scored against both Belgium and Bosnia-Herzegovina to take his personal tally to six for the national team, a total which also includes the

INTERNATIONAL HONOURS
None

goal that beat Liechtenstein. The fact remains, however, that in 65 competitive games San Marino have drawn just two matches – away to Latvia and at home to Turkey. One area in which this tiny republic is the undisputed master is in the organisation of complicated play-offs to determine the champions for the year. With the top three of two first round groups qualifying both Domagnano and Murata emerged from the play-off maze to contest the final which was won by Domagnano. The Cup is not a straightforward knock-out either and it was won by Pennarosa who beat Tre Fiore in the final.

THE FIFA BIG COUNT OF 2000

	Male	Female		Male	Female
Registered players	800	0	Referees	30	0
Non registered players	300	0	Officials	200	10
Youth players	600	0	Total involved	1 940	
Total players	1 700		Number of clubs	32	
Professional players	0	0	Number of teams	60	

Federazione Sammarinese Giuoco Calcio (FSGC)
Viale Campo dei Giudei 14, Rep. San Marino 47890
Tel +378 054 9990515   Fax +378 054 9992348
fsgc@omniway.sm   www.fsgc.sm
President: CRESCENTINI Giorgio   General Secretary: CASADEI Luciano
Vice-President: CECCOLI Pier Luigi   Treasurer: GUIDI Joseph   Media Officer: ELISA Felici
Men's Coach: MAZZA Gianpaolo   Women's Coach: none
FSGC formed: 1931   UEFA: 1988   FIFA: 1988
Colours: Light blue, Light blue, Light blue

GAMES PLAYED BY SAN MARINO IN THE 2006 FIFA WORLD CUP™ CYCLE

2002	Opponents	Score		Venue	Comp	Scorers	Att	Referee
7-09	Poland	L	0-2	Serravalle	ECq		2 000	McKeon IRE
16-10	Hungary	L	0-3	Budapest	ECq		6 500	Orrason ISL
20-11	Latvia	L	0-1	Serravalle	ECq		600	Khudiev AZE
2003								
2-04	Poland	L	0-5	Ostrowiec	ECq		8 500	Loizou CYP
30-04	Latvia	L	0-3	Riga	ECq		7 500	Byrne IRE
7-06	Sweden	L	0-6	Serravalle	ECq		2 184	Delevic SCG
11-06	Hungary	L	0-5	Serravalle	ECq		1 410	Clark SCO
20-08	Liechtenstein	D	2-2	Vaduz	Fr	Gasperoni 39, Ciacci 45	850	Wildhaber SUI
6-09	Sweden	L	0-5	Gothenburg	ECq		31 098	Messner AUT
2004								
28-04	Liechtenstein	W	1-0	Serravalle	Fr	Selva 5	700	Sammut MLT
4-09	Serbia & Montenegro	L	0-3	Serravalle	WCq		1 137	Kholmatov KAZ
8-09	Lithuania	L	0-4	Kaunas	WCq		4 000	Jareci ALB
13-10	Serbia & Montenegro	L	0-5	Belgrade	WCq		4 000	Isaksen FRO
17-11	Lithuania	L	0-1	Serravalle	WCq		1 457	Nalbandyan ARM
2005								
9-02	Spain	L	0-5	Almeria	WCq		12 580	Clark SCO
30-03	Belgium	L	1-2	Serravalle	WCq	Selva 41	871	Kasnaferis GRE
4-06	Bosnia-Herzegovina	L	1-3	Serravalle	WCq	Selva 39	750	Demirlek TUR

Fr = Friendly match • EC = UEFA EURO 2004™ • WC = FIFA World Cup™ • q = qualifier

SAN MARINO NATIONAL TEAM RECORDS AND RECORD SEQUENCES

Records			Sequence records					
Victory	1-0	LIE 2004	Wins	1	2004	Clean sheets	1	1993, 2004
Defeat	0-10	NOR	Defeats	36	1993-2001	Goals scored	2	2005
Player Caps	48	GENNARI Mirco	Undefeated	1	Four times	Without goal	10	1995-1998
Player Goals	6	SELVA Andy	Without win	64	1990-2004	Goals against	50	1993-2004

NATIONAL CAPS

	Caps
GENNARI Mirco	48
MATTEONI Ivan	44
GOBBI Luca	41
GASPERONI Federico	40
GUERRA William	40

NATIONAL GOALS

	Goals
SELVA Andy	6

NATIONAL COACH

	Years
LEONI Giorgio	1990-'95
BONINI Massimo	1996-'98
MAZZA Gianpaolo	1998-

FIFA REFEREE LIST 2005

	Int'l	DoB
PODESCHI Stefano	2002	30-08-1967
ROSSI Gabriele	2004	26-03-1966

FIFA ASSISTANT REFEREE LIST 2005

	Int'l	DoB
BUSIGNANI Marcello	1995	11-11-1960
GIUSTI Manuel	2001	11-04-1967

SAN MARINO COUNTRY INFORMATION

Capital	San Marino	Formation	301	GDP per Capita	$34 600
Population	28 503	Status	Republic	GNP Ranking	185
Area km2	61	Language	Italian	Dialling code	+378
Population density	467 per km2	Literacy rate	96%	Internet code	.sm
% in urban areas	94%	Main religion	Christian	GMT +/-	+1
Towns/Cities	Serravalle 9 258; Borgo Maggiore 6 627; San Marino 4 598; Domagnano 2 724; Fiorentino 2 082				
Neighbours (km)	Italy 39				
Main stadia	Stadio Olimpico – Serravalle 2 210				

SAN MARINO 2004-05
CAMPIONATO DILETTANTI
GIRONE A

	Pl	W	D	L	F	A	Pts
Tre Penne †	20	14	2	4	43	23	44
Murata †	20	11	6	3	39	23	39
Tre Fiori †	20	10	4	6	38	24	34
Pennarossa	20	9	7	4	40	26	34
La Fiorita	20	6	7	7	27	28	25
Cailungo	20	4	5	11	27	42	17
Cosmos	20	1	2	17	16	71	5

16/08/2004 - 15/05/2005 • † Qualified for the play-offs

SAN MARINO 2004-05
CAMPIONATO DILETTANTI
GIRONE B

	Pl	W	D	L	F	A	Pts
Libertas †	21	15	3	3	46	22	48
Domagnano †	21	11	7	3	50	25	40
Virtus †	21	11	4	6	37	22	37
Faetano	21	9	6	6	42	27	33
Juvenes Dogana	21	9	6	6	35	22	33
Folgore Falciano	21	4	6	11	26	40	18
Montevito	21	3	6	12	22	40	15
San Giovanni	21	1	1	19	16	69	4

16/08/2004 - 15/05/2005 • † Qualified for the play-offs

CAMPIONATO DILETTANTI
PLAY-OFFS

First round: Virtus 2-1 Murata; Domagnano 3-2 Tre Fiori
Second round: Domagnano 1-1 5-4p Tre Penne; Libertas 1-0 Virtas
Third round: Murata 7-1 Tre Penne; Virtus 2-0 Tre Fioro
Fourth round: Domagnano 3-0 Libertas; Murata 1-0 Virtus
Semi-final: Murata 1-1 3-2p Libertas

FINAL

Champions	Score	Runners-up
Domagnano	2-1	Murata

CLUB DIRECTORY

Club	Phone	Lge	Cup
Cailungo	+378 0549 903322	0	1
Cosmos	+378 0549 900236	1	3
Dogana	+378 0549 905156	0	0
Domagnano	+378 0549 906864	4	3
Faetano		3	1
Folgore	+378 0549 908088	3	2
La Fiorita	+378 0549 996728	2	2
Libertas	+378 0549 906475	1	3
Montevito	+378 0549 878208	1	0
Murata	+378 0549 992311	0	0
Pennarossa	+378 0549 924130	1	2
San Giovanni		0	0
Tre Fiori	+378 0549 878026	4	2
Tre Penne	+378 0549 906699	0	0
Virtus	+378 0549 999168	0	1

COPPA TITANO 2004-05

Quarter-finals		Semi-finals		Final	
Pennarossa	1				
Tre Penne	0	Pennarossa	3		
Libertas	2	Tre Fiori	0		
Tre Fiore	3			Pennarossa	4
				Tre Penne	1
		Tre Fiore	1		
Libertas	2	Tre Penne	5	4-07-2005	
Tre Penne	3			Olimpico, Serravalle	

RECENT LEAGUE AND CUP RECORD

	Championship				Cup		
Year	Champions	Score	Runners-up		Winners	Score	Runners-up
1990	La Fiorita	1-0	Cosmos		Domagnano	2-0	Juvenes
1991	Faetano	1-0	Tre Fiori		Libertas	2-0	Faetano
1992	Montevito	4-2	Libertas		Domagnano	1-1 4-2p	Tre Fiori
1993	Tre Fiori	2-0	Domagnano		Faetano	1-0	Libertas
1994	Tre Fiori	2-0	La Fiorita		Faetano	3-1	Folgore
1995	Tre Fiori	1-0	La Fiorita		Cosmos	0-0 3-1p	Faetano
1996	Libertas	4-1	Cosmos		Domagnano	2-0	Cosmos
1997	Folgore Falciano	2-1	La Fiorita		Murata	2-0	Virtus
1998	Folgore Falciano	2-1	Tre Fiori		Faetano	4-1	Cosmos
1999	Faetano	1-0	Folgore Falciano		Cosmos	5-1	Domagnano
2000	Folgore Falciano	3-1	Domagnano		Tre Penne	3-1	Folgore
2001	Cosmos	3-1	Folgore Falciano		Domagnano	1-0	Tre Fiori
2002	Domagnano	1-0	Cailungo		Domagnano	6-1	Cailungo
2003	Domagnano	2-1	Pennarossa		Domagnano	1-0	Pennarossa
2004	Pennarossa	2-2 4-2p	Domanano		Pennarossa	3-0	Domagnano
2005	Domagnano	2-1	Murata		Pennarossa	4-1	Tre Penne

SOL – SOLOMON ISLANDS

NATIONAL TEAM RECORD
JULY 1ST 2002 TO JUNE 30TH 2005

PL	W	D	L	F	A	%
19	9	4	6	39	36	57.9

FIFA/COCA-COLA WORLD RANKING

1993	1994	1995	1996	1997	1998	1999	2000	2001	2002	2003	2004	High		Low	
149	163	170	171	130	128	144	130	134	142	156	130	124	10/98	177	08/96

2004-2005											
08/04	09/04	10/04	11/04	12/04	01/05	02/05	03/05	04/05	05/05	06/05	07/05
126	126	125	129	130	130	130	131	130	132	134	135

On current form, the Solomon Islands are prime candidates to fill the void left by Australia's defection to the Asian Football Confederation. Following their historic run through the 2006 FIFA World Cup™ qualifiers that resulted in a play-off with the Socceroos, the Solomon Islands broke the New Zealand/Australia stranglehold on the region. With one part of that duopoly gone, the Solomons are in a superb position to take advantage because of the infrastructure that has been established on the Islands. The country was among the first recipients of funds from FIFA's Goal programme and the refurbished Lawson Tama stadium in Honiara now provides one of the best playing

INTERNATIONAL HONOURS
Melanesian Cup 1994

surfaces in the region while a new football academy with administrative offices is being built. With such facilities available development at senior and even more crucially at junior level can continue apace. However, it won't be an easy ride for the national team as the 11-1 aggregate defeat to Australia in the 2004 Oceania Nations Cup final demonstrated and if the team aims to play a bigger part in football beyond the region, much work is still required, not least the ability to beat New Zealand. JP Su'uria, often known as Makuru FC, won the 2005 S-League group stage and then won the knock-out stage beating East Harbour Strikers 4-2 in the final.

THE FIFA BIG COUNT OF 2000

	Male	Female		Male	Female
Registered players	1 000	0	Referees	100	0
Non registered players	2 000	0	Officials	300	0
Youth players	1 000	0	Total involved	4 400	
Total players	4 000		Number of clubs	100	
Professional players	0	0	Number of teams	200	

Solomon Islands Football Federation (SIFF)
Lawson Tama, PO Box 854, Honiara, Solomon Islands
Tel +677 26496   Fax +677 26497
administration@siff.com.sb   www.siff.com.sb
President: WICKHAM Adrian   General Secretary: OHOTOONA Philip
Vice-President: SHANEL Peter   Treasurer: TBD   Media Officer: PITUVAKA Francis
Men's Coach: GILLET Alan   Women's Coach: MASUAKU Rex
SIFF formed: 1978   OFC: 1988   FIFA: 1988
Colours: Green, Blue, White

GAMES PLAYED BY SOLOMON ISLANDS IN THE 2006 FIFA WORLD CUP™ CYCLE

2002	Opponents	Score		Venue	Comp	Scorers	Att	Referee
5-07	Papua New Guinea	D	0-0	Auckland	OCq		1 000	Breeze AUS
7-07	Tahiti	L	2-3	Auckland	OCq	Daudau 8, Menapi 25	1 000	Breeze AUS
9-07	New Zealand	L	1-6	Auckland	OCq	Faarodo 73	300	Atisson VAN
2003								
14-06	Papua New Guinea	W	5-3	Port Moresby	Fr	Samani 12, Menapi 2 ?? ??p, Mehau ??, Suri ??p		
1-07	Vanuatu	D	2-2	Suva	SPr1	Menapi 2 49 57		Shah FIJ
3-07	Kiribati †	W	7-0	Suva	SPr1	Waita 8, Menapi 5 43 48 52 55 74, Mehau 78	700	Ariiotima TAH
5-07	Tuvalu †	W	4-0	Nausori	SPr1	Maniadalo 16, Menapi 2 27 87, Suri 80	2 500	Bayung PNG
7-07	Fiji	L	1-2	Lautoka	SPr1	Menapi 68	6 000	Ariiotima TAH
2004								
3-04	Vanuatu	W	2-1	Port Vila	Fr	Menapi 2 52 71	4 000	Lencie VAN
6-04	Vanuatu	W	2-1	Port Vila	Fr	Suri 34, Menapi ??		
10-05	Tonga	W	6-0	Honiara	WCq	Faarodo 3 12 30 77, Maemae 2 62 76, Samani 79	12 385	Attison VAN
12-05	Cook Islands	W	5-0	Honiara	WCq	Waita 21, Omokirio 27, Samani 45, Maemae 70, Leo 81	14 000	Fred VAN
15-05	New Caledonia	W	2-0	Honiara	WCq	Omokirio 10, Suri 42	20 000	Attison VAN
19-05	Tahiti	D	1-1	Honiara	WCq	Suri 80	18 000	Rakaroi FIJ
29-05	Vanuatu	W	1-0	Adelaide	WCq	Suri 51p	200	Shield AUS
31-05	New Zealand	L	0-3	Adelaide	WCq		217	Iturralde Gonzalez ESP
2-06	Tahiti	W	4-0	Adelaide	WCq	Faarodo 9, Menapi 2 14 80, Suri 42	50	Rakaroi FIJ
4-06	Fiji	W	2-1	Adelaide	WCq	Kakai 16, Houkarawa 82	1 500	Attison VAN
6-06	Australia	D	2-2	Adelaide	WCq	Menapi 2 43 75	1 500	Iturralde Gonzalez ESP
9-10	Australia	L	1-5	Honiara	OCf	Suri 60	21 000	O'Leary NZL
12-10	Australia	L	0-6	Sydney	OCf		19 208	Rakaroi FIJ
2005								

No international matches played in 2005 before August

Fr = Friendly match • OC = OFC Oceania Nations Cup • SP = South Pacific Games • WC = FIFA World Cup™
q = qualifier • r1 = first round group • f = final • † Not a full international

SOLOMON ISLANDS NATIONAL TEAM RECORDS AND RECORD SEQUENCES

Records			Sequence records					
Victory	16-0	COK 1995	Wins	5	1994, 2004	Clean sheets	3	Three times
Defeat	0-8	NCL 1966	Defeats	5	1992-1993	Goals scored	14	2002-2004
Player Caps	n/a		Undefeated	7	2004	Without goal	4	1989-1990
Player Goals	n/a		Without win	9	1963-1975	Goals against	21	1997-2001

FIFA REFEREE LIST 2005

	Int'l	DoB
AFU Michael	2004	14-11-1969
MOLI Andrew	2003	17-08-1969
SOGO Nelson	2002	14-02-1971

FIFA ASSISTANT REFEREE LIST 2005

	Int'l	DoB
ERE ANIMAE Silas	2005	14-09-1974
INDU Joash	2003	24-06-1965
POLOSO Neil	2002	9-02-1969
SIAU Hamilton	2005	6-02-1980
TARO Matthew	2002	16-05-1967

SOLOMON ISLANDS COUNTRY INFORMATION

Capital	Honiara	Independence	1978 from the UK	GDP per Capita	$1 700
Population	523 617	Status	Constitutional Monarchy	GNP Ranking	180
Area km²	28 450	Language	Melanesian, English	Dialling code	+677
Population density	18 per km²	Literacy rate	n/a	Internet code	.sb
% in urban areas	17%	Main religion	Christian	GMT +/−	+11
Towns/Cities ('000)	Honiara 56; Gizo 6; Auki 4; Buala 2; Tulagi 1; Kirakira 1				
Neighbours (km)	South Pacific Ocean 5 313				
Main stadia	Lawson Tama Stadium – Honiara 10 000				

CUP 2004

Quarter-finals		Semi-finals		Final	
Wan Toks	3				
Eastern Knights	0	Wan Toks	5		
Real Reds	0	Agfa Hana	1		
Agfa Hana	3			Wan Toks	3
Systek Kingz	1			JP Su'uria	2
East Harbour Strikers	0	Systek Kingz	3		
Fair West	1	JP Su'uria	5		
JP Su'uria	5				

28-08-2004, Lawson Tama, Honiara
Billy 3 for Wan Toks; Menapi, Lui for
JP Su'uria

S-LEAGUE KNOCKOUT STAGE 2005

Quarter-finals		Semi-finals		Final	
JP Su'uria	6				
Agfa Hana	2	JP Su'uria	4		
Systek Kingz	1	Wan Toks	1		
Wan Toks	2			JP Su'uria	4
Fair West	4			East Harbour Strikers	2
Real Red	0	Fair West	0		
Eastern Knights	0	East Harbour Strikers	1		
East Harbour Strikers	2				

2-08-2005, Lawson Tama, Honiara
Scorers - Menapi 2, Meovle, Tavake for
JP Su'uria; Houkarawa, Ratu for Strikers

SOM – SOMALIA

NATIONAL TEAM RECORD
JULY 1ST 2002 TO JUNE 30TH 2005

PL	W	D	L	F	A	%
8	1	0	7	1	17	12.5

FIFA/COCA-COLA WORLD RANKING

1993	1994	1995	1996	1997	1998	1999	2000	2001	2002	2003	2004	High		Low	
-	159	165	178	187	190	197	194	197	190	191	193	158	04/95	199	04/00

2004-2005											
08/04	09/04	10/04	11/04	12/04	01/05	02/05	03/05	04/05	05/05	06/05	07/05
193	193	192	192	193	189	189	189	189	189	189	188

Somalia is a country of eight million people that has had no effective central government for well over a decade. Unsurprisingly football has been hard hit but in spite of the difficult security situation the national team have remarkably managed to play the odd game albeit with little success with just one win in nine fixtures over nearly four years. Somalia is a country ripe for financial assistance from FIFA's Goal project, but aid was cut to the federation because of a lack of accountability. There are no easy solutions to the problems that football faces in the country, but with a new football association recently installed, organisation and development may return along

INTERNATIONAL HONOURS
None

with badly-needed facilities and resources. League football is also at a low ebb and just eight teams contested the Somali Football League which was won by Elman FC, a team founded in 1992 as a sports club to rehabilitate child soldiers and street children. They went on to compete in the CECAFA Club Championship in Tanzania, but lost all four games. No clubs entered continental competition, but there was some international activity in the junior ranks with the U-20s losing 3-1 on aggregate to Sudan in an African Youth Championship preliminary match. However, the U-17s were withdrawn from their qualifier with Eritrea.

THE FIFA BIG COUNT OF 2000

	Male	Female		Male	Female
Registered players	1 560	120	Referees	1 000	0
Non registered players	25 000	590	Officials	3 120	30
Youth players	2 080	160	Total involved	33 660	
Total players	29 510		Number of clubs	32	
Professional players	0	0	Number of teams	112	

Somali Football Federation (SFF)
DHL Mogadishu, Mogadishu BN 03040, Somalia
Tel +252 1 216199   Fax +252 1 251777
sofofed@yahoo.com   www.none
President: SALAD Mohamed   General Secretary: ARAB Abdiqani Said
Vice-President: ABDULLE Abdulkadir   Treasurer: ARAB Abdiqani Said   Media Officer: MOHAMMED Abdulkadir Ali
Men's Coach: ABDI FARAH Ali   Women's Coach: HUSSEIN ALI Abdule
SFF formed: 1951   CAF: 1968   FIFA: 1960
Colours: Sky blue, Sky blue, White

GAMES PLAYED BY SOMALIA IN THE 2006 FIFA WORLD CUP™ CYCLE

2002	Opponents	Score	Venue	Comp	Scorers	Att	Referee
1-12	Uganda	L 0-2	Arusha	CCr1			Juma Ali TAN
3-12	Rwanda	L 0-1	Arusha	CCr1			
5-12	Zanzibar †	L 0-1	Arusha	CCr1			
7-12	Ethiopia	W 1-0	Arusha	CCr1			
2003							
16-11	Ghana	L 0-5	Accra	WCq		19 447	Bebou TOG
19-11	Ghana	L 0-2	Kumasi	WCq		12 000	Chaibou NIG
2004							
12-12	Uganda	L 0-2	Addis Abeba	CCr1			
14-12	Kenya	L 0-1	Addis Abeba	CCr1			
18-12	Sudan	L 0-4	Addis Abeba	CCr1			
2005							

No international matches played in 2005 before August

Fr = Friendly match • CC = CECAFA Cup • WC = FIFA World Cup™ • q = qualifier • r1 = first round group • † Not a full international

SOMALIA NATIONAL TEAM RECORDS AND RECORD SEQUENCES

Records			Sequence records					
Victory	5-2	MTN 1985	Wins	1		Clean sheets	1	
Defeat	2-9	CMR 1960	Defeats	7	1995-2000	Goals scored	4	Six times
Player Caps	n/a		Undefeated	4	1978-1980	Without goal	8	2000-2002
Player Goals	n/a		Without win	17	1995-2002	Goals against	10	1994-2000

FIFA REFEREE LIST 2005

	Int'l	DoB
ABDULLE AHMED Abdi	1998	11-08-1968
HASSAN HAILE Abdulkadir		10-07-1975
HUSSEIN OMAR Ahmed		20-03-1976
JAMA DIRA Osman	1998	19-07-1962
OLAD ARAB Bashir		20-05-1974
OSMAN MOHAMED Salad		12-04-1960

FIFA ASSISTANT REFEREE LIST 2005

	Int'l	DoB
ABDI OSMAN Osman		20-12-1967
ABDULAHI ALASOW Abdi	2001	12-09-1973
HASSAN FIDO Mohamed	2004	12-09-1978
MOHAMED AHMED Ali	2001	20-03-1975
OMAR ABUKAR Salah	2001	7-02-1975
SHIRE HAYDAR Bashir	1998	28-10-1969

RECENT LEAGUE RECORD

	Championship
Year	Champions
1995	Alba
1996	No tournament
1997	No tournament
1998	Ports Authority
1999	No tournament
2000	Elman
2001	Elman
2002	Elman
2003	Elman
2004	Elman

SOMALIA COUNTRY INFORMATION

Capital	Mogadishu	Independence	1960	GDP per Capita	$500
Population	8 304 601	Status	Republic	GNP Ranking	151
Area km²	637 657	Language	Somali	Dialling code	+252
Population density	13 per km²	Literacy rate	37%	Internet code	.so
% in urban areas	26%	Main religion	Muslim	GMT +/−	+3
Towns/Cities ('000)	Mogadishu 2 590; Hargeysa 478; Marka 320; Berbera 242; Kismayo 234; Jamame 185				
Neighbours (km)	Kenya 682; Ethiopia 1 600; Djibouti 58; Gulf of Aden & Indian Ocean 3 025				
Main stadia	Mogadishu Stadium - Mogadishu 35 000				

SRI – SRI LANKA

NATIONAL TEAM RECORD
JULY 1ST 2002 TO JUNE 30TH 2005

PL	W	D	L	F	A	%
23	4	7	12	20	45	32.6

FIFA/COCA-COLA WORLD RANKING

1993	1994	1995	1996	1997	1998	1999	2000	2001	2002	2003	2004	High		Low	
126	139	135	126	136	134	153	149	143	139	135	140	122	08/98	164	06/00

2004-2005											
08/04	09/04	10/04	11/04	12/04	01/05	02/05	03/05	04/05	05/05	06/05	07/05
143	143	141	137	140	139	140	140	140	140	141	140

Sri Lanka was one of the worst hit countries when the tsunami of 26 December 2004 struck southeast Asia, leaving thousands dead and many more homeless. It was no surprise then that the country was forced to forgo hosting the South East Asia Games in August 2005. Without a win in 2004, the national side have not played since their last friendly against another tsunami-affected country, the Maldives, eight days before the disaster. As part of the country's rebuilding, FIFA's Tsunami Task Force quickly agreed to donate US$2.5 million to Sri Lanka that was designated for reconstruction of 12 regional centres for the association, 12 football pitches and 30 club buildings. A few months later

INTERNATIONAL HONOURS
None

a further US$1.95 million was awarded for 13 projects among the regional associations in the country. Before the Maldives match, all of Sri Lanka's games that year had been World Cup™ qualifiers. Having beaten Laos 3-0 on aggregate in the preliminary round, the Sri Lankans were grouped with Turkmenistan, Saudi Arabia and Indonesia in a difficult group. Drawing twice, they failed to win a match and finished bottom. Saunders FC won the Kit Premier League which resumed just weeks after the tsunami while runners-up Rattnam earned some consolation by beating Saunders 2-1 in the Cup Final in front of 10,000 in Colombo.

THE FIFA BIG COUNT OF 2000

	Male	Female		Male	Female
Registered players	20 560	200	Referees	258	0
Non registered players	70 000	0	Officials	5 000	150
Youth players	22 000	0	Total involved	118 168	
Total players	112 760		Number of clubs	1 110	
Professional players	0	0	Number of teams	1 366	

Football Federation of Sri Lanka (FFSL)
100/9 Independence Avenue, Colombo 07, Sri Lanka
Tel +94 11 2686120   Fax +94 11 2682471
ffsl@srilankafootball.com   www.srilankafootball.com
President: PANDITHARATHNE Thilina   General Secretary: SALLY B.H.H.
Vice-President: GAMINI Randeni   Treasurer: RANJITH Rodrigo   Media Officer: PERERA Rukmal
Men's Coach: SAMPATH PERERA Kolomage   Women's Coach: DE SILVA Clement
FFSL formed: 1939   AFC: 1958   FIFA: 1950
Colours: White, White, White

GAMES PLAYED BY SRI LANKA IN THE 2006 FIFA WORLD CUP™ CYCLE

2002	Opponents	Score		Venue	Comp	Scorers	Att	Referee
27-11	Vietnam	L	1-2	Colombo	Fr	Channa [78]		Deshapriya SRI
29-11	Vietnam	D	1-1	Colombo	Fr	Nazar [90]		Pingamage SRI
1-12	Vietnam	D	2-2	Colombo	Fr	Steinwall [??], Maduranga [??]		
2003								
10-01	Afghanistan	W	1-0	Dhaka	SAFr1	Steinwall [43]		Gurung NEP
12-01	Pakistan	L	1-2	Dhaka	SAFr1	Siyaguna [90]		Gosh BAN
14-01	India	D	1-1	Dhaka	SAFr1	Abeysekera [90]		Shamsuzzaman BAN
21-03	East Timor	W	3-2	Colombo	ACq	Weerarathne 2 [36 89], Channa [44]		
25-03	Chinese Taipei	W	2-1	Colombo	ACq	Kumara [13], Channa [79]		
15-10	Syria	L	0-5	Damascus	ACq			
18-10	Syria	L	0-8	Damascus	ACq			
9-11	Turkmenistan	L	0-1	Balkanabat	ACq			
12-11	Turkmenistan	L	0-3	Ashgabat	ACq			
18-11	United Arab Emirates	L	1-3	Dubai	ACq	Channa [31]		
22-11	United Arab Emirates	L	0-3	Dubai	ACq			
29-11	Laos	D	0-0	Vientiane	WCq		4 500	Luong The Tai VIE
3-12	Laos	W	3-0	Colombo	WCq	Edribandanage [35], Weerarathna [59], Hameed [93+]	6 000	Saleem MDV
2004								
18-02	Turkmenistan	L	0-2	Ashgabat	WCq		11 000	Al Bannai UAE
31-03	Saudi Arabia	L	0-1	Colombo	WCq		6 000	Chynybekov KGZ
9-06	Indonesia	L	0-1	Jakarta	WCq		30 000	Nesar BAN
8-09	Indonesia	D	2-2	Colombo	WCq	Steinwall [81], Karunaratne [82]	4 000	Marshoud JOR
9-10	Turkmenistan	D	2-2	Colombo	WCq	Perera [47], Mudiyanselage [57]	4 000	Al Bannai UAE
17-11	Saudi Arabia	L	0-3	Dammam	WCq		2 000	Muflah OMA
18-12	Maldives	D	0-0	Male	Fr			
2005								

No international matches played in 2005 before August

Fr = Friendly match • SAF = South Asian Federation Cup • AC = AFC Asian Cup • WC = FIFA World Cup™ • q = qualifier • r1 = first round group

FIFA REFEREE LIST 2005

	Int'l	DoB
ARAMBEKADE Deshapryia	1998	1-08-1961
MUHANDIRAM Ranutt		6-09-1965
NAKANDALAGE DON Indika	2005	19-09-1976
PEIRIS Bemminahennedige	2005	2-01-1969
PERERA Hettikamkanamge	2004	19-09-1978
PINGAMAGE Nishaniha	2002	9-09-1975

FIFA ASSISTANT REFEREE LIST 2005

	Int'l	DoB
ALPONSU Rohan	2002	5-06-1964
BURAH Tuan Horirah	2002	18-11-1964
DISSANAYAKE Keerthi	2001	20-01-1962
MIRANDA Johanne	2005	21-05-1970
MOHAMED Cader	2004	23-08-1969
MURUGIAH Vadivel	2005	17-11-1967
PALLIYAGURUGE Priyanga	2005	3-06-1976
PANDIGE Mahendra Jayantha	2002	20-04-1968
RATNAYAKE Daya	2004	12-02-1967
SERASINGHE Premadasa		14-10-1967

SRI LANKA COUNTRY INFORMATION

Capital	Colombo	Independence	1948 from UK	GDP per Capita	$3 700
Population	19 905 165	Status	Republic	GNP Ranking	73
Area km²	65 610	Language	Sinhala, Tamil, English	Dialling code	+94
Population density	303 per km²	Literacy rate	92.3%	Internet code	.lk
% in urban areas	22%	Main religion	Buddhist, Hindu	GMT +/−	+5.5
Towns/Cities ('000)	Colombo 648; Dehiwala-Mount Lavinia 215; Jaffna 169; Negombo 137; Chavakachcheri 121; Kotte 118; Kandy 111; Trincomalee 108; Kalmunai 100; Galle 93; Point Pedro 89				
Neighbours (km)	Indian Ocean 1 340				
Main stadia	Sugathadasa Stadium – Colombo 25 000				

SRI LANKA NATIONAL TEAM RECORDS AND RECORD SEQUENCES

Records			Sequence records				
Victory	4-0	SIN, NEP, PAK	Wins	3	1996-97, 2002	Clean sheets	2	Five times
Defeat	0-8	IDN 1972, SYR 2003	Defeats	12	1972-79, 1979-84	Goals scored	12	2002-2003
Player Caps	n/a		Undefeated	7	2001-2002	Without goal	10	1991-1993
Player Goals	n/a		Without win	15	1954-72, 1984-93	Goals against	35	1952-1979

SRI LANKA 2004-05

PREMIER LEAGUE

	Pl	W	D	L	F	A	Pts	Saunders	Ratnams	Blue Star	Negombo	Army	Air Force	Renown	Java Lane	Police	Jupiters	Navy	York	Matara	Old Bens	Victory	New Young
Saunders	30	21	6	3	63	28	69		2-1	4-1	0-0	1-4	1-0	1-0	2-1	0-0	4-1	3-2	3-0	3-1	5-0	1-0	2-2
Ratnams	30	20	4	6	61	31	64	1-2		2-1	0-0	4-1	0-1	1-1	4-1	2-1	3-2	1-0	4-0	2-0	3-2	1-0	5-1
Blue Star	30	19	5	6	62	37	62	0-1	1-1		2-3	2-1	3-1	1-1	4-1	1-1	1-0	3-2	2-0	4-0	2-3	2-0	7-3
Negombo Youth	30	17	11	2	61	25	62	3-3	3-1	4-1		4-3	2-0	3-1	1-1	3-0	2-0	2-1	2-1	0-1	0-0	4-0	7-0
Army	30	15	4	11	63	41	49	0-3	1-1	1-2	0-0		0-1	2-3	1-3	4-1	1-3	3-1	2-0	3-2	3-0	7-0	5-0
Air Force	30	13	8	9	44	33	47	2-1	0-1	1-1	1-1	0-3		2-3	1-1	2-2	2-2	0-1	2-0	3-0	3-1	2-0	7-1
Renown	30	12	8	10	37	36	44	0-1	1-3	0-3	0-2	1-3	1-1		0-0	0-0	3-0	2-1	3-1	3-2	0-0	0-2	3-1
Java Lane	30	11	10	9	54	48	43	3-2	2-3	1-2	2-2	3-1	1-1	1-1		1-2	2-2	2-1	0-2	2-0	2-1	2-1	2-2
Police	30	11	10	9	42	34	43	1-1	1-2	0-2	3-1	2-1	1-2	0-1	3-1		1-1	0-1	2-1	3-1	2-0	1-0	5-0
Jupiters	30	9	7	14	40	44	34	0-1	0-4	0-1	0-2	0-1	2-0	1-3	2-2	2-0		3-3	5-0	4-0	1-0	0-1	2-1
Navy	30	7	8	15	33	38	29	1-1	1-2	1-2	0-4	1-2	0-1	0-0	0-1	0-0	0-0		0-0	5-0	0-1	2-2	
Kandy York	30	8	5	17	25	56	29	0-6	1-0	1-2	0-1	1-1	1-3	1-3	2-6	1-1	2-1	1-0		0-2	1-1	1-0	2-1
Matara	30	8	4	18	29	56	28	2-3	3-0	1-1	1-1	1-1	0-2	1-0	2-1	1-5	2-1	0-2	0-2		0-2	2-0	2-2
Old Bens	30	6	6	18	33	54	24	1-2	1-2	1-2	1-1	1-5	0-1	0-1	1-6	1-1	0-1	0-1	0-0	1-0		2-1	9-0
Victory	30	6	6	18	21	51	24	1-2	0-5	1-2	2-2	0-2	1-1	2-1	1-2	1-1	1-1	2-2	2-1	0-2	1-0		0-0
New Young	30	3	6	21	29	85	15	0-2	1-2	1-4	0-1	0-1	2-1	0-1	1-1	0-2	1-3	0-1	1-2	2-0	2-4	2-0	

4/06/2004 - 23/02/2005

HOLCIM FA CUP 2004-05

Quarter-finals		Semi-finals		Final	
Ratnams	3				
Java Lane	0	Ratnams	1		
Super Beach	0	Navy	0		
Navy	2				
New Young	3			Ratnams	3
Air Force	2	New Young	0	Saunders	1
Army	1	Saunders	2		
Saunders	2				

Final: 24-07-2005
Scorers - Mohideen 2 [10][83], Kumara [27] for Ratnams; Amanulla [8] for Saunders

CLUB DIRECTORY

Club	Town/City	Lge	Cup
Blue Stars	Kalutara	1	0
Jupiters	Colombo	0	0
Negombo Youth	Negombo	1	0
Old Bens	Colombo	1	1
Pettah United	Colombo	1	0
Ratnams	Colombo	2	3
Renown	Colombo	3	5
Saunders	Colombo	12	6
York	Kandy	0	1

RECENT LEAGUE AND CUP RECORD

Championship		Cup		
Year	Champions	Winners	Score	Runners-up
1996	Saunders	Old Benedictans		Renown
1997	Saunders	Saunders	1-0	Police
1998	Ratnams			
1999	Saunders	Saunders	3-2	Renown
2000	Saunders	Ratnams	2-1	Saunders
2001	Saunders	Saunders	4-0	Negombo Youth
2002	Saunders			
2003	Negombo Youth	Renown	1-0	Air Force
2004	Blue Stars	Ratnams	6-5	Renown
2005	Saunders	Ratnams	3-1	Saunders

STP – SAO TOME E PRINCIPE

NATIONAL TEAM RECORD
JULY 1ST 2002 TO JUNE 30TH 2005

PL	W	D	L	F	A	%
3	0	0	3	1	12	0

FIFA/COCA-COLA WORLD RANKING

1993	1994	1995	1996	1997	1998	1999	2000	2001	2002	2003	2004	High		Low	
-	-	-	-	-	194	187	181	186	191	192	195	**179**	08/00	**196**	11/99

2004-2005											
08/04	09/04	10/04	11/04	12/04	01/05	02/05	03/05	04/05	05/05	06/05	07/05
194	194	194	194	195	195	195	195	195	195	195	195

Firmly in the bottom 10 of the FIFA/Coca-Cola World Ranking, São Tomé e Príncipe are one of the weakest African national teams. Made up of two islands in the Atlantic Ocean, isolation has resulted in just 19 international matches played since the association was established in 1975. Just two of them have been won, the last in 2000 – a 2-0 defeat of Sierra Leone. Without a match between July of that year and October 2003, there was little hope of success when the national team was drawn with Libya in the first preliminary qualifier for the 2006 FIFA World Cup™. The first leg in São Tomé drew a 5,000-strong crowd where the visitors edged it, 1-0. The return in Benghazi

INTERNATIONAL HONOURS
None

was more straightforward as Libya thrashed the islanders 8-0 and the São Tomé e Príncipe side has not reconvened since. With close ties to Portugal, there is a pool of players from which the country could draw, but unlike Cape Verde, Angola and Mozambique, the players aren't willing to commit to the country. Separate leagues run on each island with the champions playing off for the title. Operarios from Príncipe picked up their fourth title after drawing 2-2 with UDESCAI from São Tomé and winning the penalty shoot-out 5-4. In doing so they became the first Príncipe club to claim the Championship since 1998.

THE FIFA BIG COUNT OF 2000

	Male	Female		Male	Female
Registered players	500	0	Referees	20	0
Non registered players	500	0	Officials	100	0
Youth players	150	0	Total involved	1 270	
Total players	1 150		Number of clubs	10	
Professional players	0	0	Number of teams	20	

Federação Santomense de Futebol (FSF)
Rua Ex-João de Deus No QXXIII - 426/26, Casa postale 440, São Tomé, São Tomé e Príncipe
Tel +239 2 224231   Fax +239 2 21333
futebol@cstome.net   www.fsf.st
President: DENDE Manuel   General Secretary: BARROS Ricardino
Vice-President: LIMA Emilio   Treasurer: DA GRACA ANDRADE Celestino   Media Officer: none
Men's Coach: FERRAZ Jose   Women's Coach: N'VUBA Eustave
FSF formed: 1975   CAF: 1986   FIFA: 1986
Colours: Green, Yellow, Green

GAMES PLAYED BY SAO TOME E PRINCIPE IN THE 2006 FIFA WORLD CUP™ CYCLE

2002 Opponents		Score	Venue	Comp	Scorers	Att	Referee
No international matches played in 2002 after June							
2003							
11-10 Libya	L	0-1	São Tomé	WCq		4 000	Yameogo JPN
12-11 Equatorial Guinea	L	1-3	Malabo	Fr			
16-11 Libya	L	0-8	Benghazi	WCq		20 000	Guirat TUN
2004							
No international matches played in 2004							
2005							
No international matches played in 2005 before August							

Fr = Friendly match • WC = FIFA World Cup™ • q = qualifier

SAO TOME E PRINCIPE NATIONAL TEAM RECORDS AND RECORD SEQUENCES

Records			Sequence records					
Victory	2-0	EQG 1999, SLE 2000	Wins	2	1999-2000	Clean sheets	2	1999-2000
Defeat	0-11	CGO 1976	Defeats	6	1998-1999	Goals scored	2	1999-2000, 2000
Player Caps	n/a		Undefeated	2	1999-2000	Without goal	3	1999
Player Goals	n/a		Without win	11	1976-1999	Goals against	11	1976-1999

FIFA REFEREE LIST 2005

	Int'l	DoB
CASSANDRA COSTA Valdemar	2002	19-09-1972
DA GRACA FERREIRA Gastao	1999	09-01-1963
ESPIRITO SANTO Helio	1999	11-05-1970
TAVARES NETO Lourenco	1999	10-08-1962

FIFA ASSISTANT REFEREE LIST 2005

	Int'l	DoB
DA COSTA CHEQUE Wilson	2000	17-09-1976
DE BARROS SEMEDO Edgar	2005	01-01-1978
DO ESPIRITO SANTO Eusebio	1998	25-06-1965
DO ESPIRITO SANTO Gilberto	2000	05-07-1972
DOS RAMOS ARAGAO Ilirio	1999	11-07-1977
LEAL DUARTE Jose	1998	27-07-1962

RECENT LEAGUE AND CUP RECORD

	League	Cup			São Tomé	Príncipe
Year	Champions	Winners	Score	Finalist	Champions	Champions
1995	Inter Bom-Bom	Caixão Grande			Inter Bom-Bom	
1996	Caixão Grande	Aliança Nacional				
1997	No Tournament	No Tournament				
1998	Os Operários	Sporting Praia Cruz				
1999	Sporting Praia Cruz	Vitória Riboque	3-2	Os Operários	Sporting Praia Cruz	Os Operários
2000	Inter Bom-Bom	Sporting Praia Cruz	3-1	Caixão Grande	Inter Bom-Bom	GD Sundy
2001	Bairros Unidos	GD Sundy	4-3	Vitória Riboque	Bairros Unidos	GD Sundy
2002	No tournament	No Tournament				
2003	Inter Bom Bom	Os Operários	1-0	UDESCAI	Inter Bom-Bom	1º de Maio
2004	Os Operários				UDESCAI	Os Operários

SAO TOME E PRINCIPE COUNTRY INFORMATION

Capital	Sao Tomé	Independence	1975 from Portugal	GDP per Capita	$1 200
Population	181 565	Status	Republic	GNP Ranking	190
Area km²	1 001	Language	Portuguese	Dialling code	+239
Population density	185 per km²	Literacy rate	79%	Internet code	.st
% in urban areas	46%	Main religion	Christian	GMT +/–	0
Towns/Cities ('000)	Sao Tomé 62; Santo Amaro 8; Neves 7; Santana 7; Trinidade 7; Sao José dos Agnolares 2				
Neighbours (km)	Atlantic Ocean/Gulf of Guinea 209				
Main stadia	Estadio Nacional 12 de Julho – São Tomé 6 500				

SUD – SUDAN

NATIONAL TEAM RECORD
JULY 1ST 2002 TO JUNE 30TH 2005

PL	W	D	L	F	A	%
47	16	13	18	60	62	47.9

FIFA/COCA-COLA WORLD RANKING

1993	1994	1995	1996	1997	1998	1999	2000	2001	2002	2003	2004	High		Low	
119	116	86	74	108	114	132	132	118	106	103	114	74	12/96	137	04/00

2004-2005											
08/04	09/04	10/04	11/04	12/04	01/05	02/05	03/05	04/05	05/05	06/05	07/05
106	108	112	113	114	104	106	107	103	102	101	102

As one of CAF's founders and one of Africa's first FIFA members, Sudan have a long history in the game. Sadly, in spite of such a distinguished background, football has suffered and Sudan find themselves at 102 in the FIFA/Coca-Cola World Ranking after years of decline. Although they were only the third country from Africa to enter the FIFA World Cup™, in 1958, they have never qualified and their 2006 campaign was no different. In a strong group that contained Cote d'Ivoire, Cameroon and Egypt as well as Libya and Benin, Sudan were never in the running. They finished massively adrift of the group leaders and even a place at the CAF African Cup of Nations was

INTERNATIONAL HONOURS
CAF African Cup of Nations 1970 CECAFA Cup 1980

nowhere within their reach. Some pride was restored at the 2004 CECAFA Cup in Ethiopia where Sudan got their act together and reached the last four but they had to settle for third place overall beating Kenya in the third place play-off after losing to Burundi in the semi-final. The Sudanese League was a straight fight between the two most powerful clubs in the country – Al Hilal and Al Merreikh – that went to the wire. The two met each other on the final day of the season with both level on points and it was Al Hilal who snatched the title with a 2-1 win. Hilal then beat Merreikh 3-2 on penalties in the Cup Final to secure the double.

THE FIFA BIG COUNT OF 2000

	Male	Female		Male	Female
Registered players	18 000	0	Referees	1 000	0
Non registered players	80 000	0	Officials	7 000	0
Youth players	10 000	0	Total involved	116 000	
Total players	108 000		Number of clubs	400	
Professional players	0	0	Number of teams	2 500	

Sudan Football Association (SFA)
Bladia Street, Khartoum, Sudan
Tel +249 183 773495   Fax +249 183 776633
www.none
President: SHADDAD Kamal, Dr   General Secretary: EL DIN Magdi Shams
Vice-President: EL MAZZAL Ahmed Elhag   Treasurer: EL KHATEM Mustasim Gaffar Dr   Media Officer: none
Men's Coach: AHMED Mohamed   Women's Coach: None
SFA formed: 1936   CAF: 1957   FIFA: 1948
Colours: Red, White, Black

GAMES PLAYED BY SUDAN IN THE 2006 FIFA WORLD CUP™ CYCLE

2002	Opponents	Score		Venue	Comp	Scorers	Att	Referee
26-07	Chad	W	2-0	Khartoum	Fr			Abdel Rahman SUD
28-07	Uganda	W	2-0	Khartoum	Fr			Mour SUD
30-07	Ethiopia	W	3-0	Khartoum	Fr			Abdel Rahman SUD
19-08	Jordan	D	0-0	Amman	Fr			
23-08	Egypt	L	0-3	Cairo	Fr			
8-09	Zambia	L	0-1	Khartoum	CNq			Berhane ETH
12-10	Tanzania	W	2-1	Mwanza	CNq	Samson [49p]	20 000	Tessema ETH
2-12	Tanzania	D	1-1	Arusha	CCrl	Kabir [82]		
4-12	Eritrea	L	1-2	Arusha	CCrl	Agabishido [85]		
7-12	Burundi	W	2-1	Arusha	CCrl	Gomal [38], Khalid Mohammed [75]		
9-12	Kenya	L	0-1	Arusha	CCrl			
18-12	Kuwait	L	0-1	Kuwait City	ARrl		2 000	Zakrini ALG
20-12	Jordan	L	1-2	Kuwait City	ARrl	Mohamed Ali [84]	2 000	Abbas SYR
23-12	Palestine	D	2-2	Kuwait City	ARrl	Farjallah [51], Al Tijani [88]	2 000	Al Zeid KSA
25-12	Morocco	W	1-0	Kuwait City	ARrl	Farouq [45]		
2003								
5-03	Congo DR	L	1-3	Khartoum	Fr			
29-03	Benin	W	3-0	Khartoum	CNq	Tambal 2 [34 71], Motaz [68]	20 000	Buenkadila COD
21-05	Uganda	D	0-0	Kampala	Fr			
24-05	Kenya	D	1-1	Khartoum	Fr			
8-06	Benin	L	0-3	Cotonou	CNq			Coulibaly MLI
21-06	Zambia	D	1-1	Lusaka	CNq	Galag [23]		Maxim KEN
17-09	Yemen	L	2-3	Sana'a	Fr	Ammar Ibrahim [64], Amir Damir [83]		
19-09	Yemen	W	2-1	Sana'a	Fr			
12-10	Eritrea	W	3-0	Khartoum	WCq	Tambal [68], El Rasheed [72], Ahmed Mugahid [89p]	18 000	Tamuni LBY
16-11	Eritrea	D	0-0	Asmara	WCq		12 000	Abdulle Ahmed SOM
30-11	Zanzibar †	W	4-0	Khartoum	CCrl	El Rasheed 2 [10 45], Aldoud [50], Saleh Mohammed [90p]		
4-12	Rwanda	W	3-0	Khartoum	CCrl	El Rasheed [11], Gibril [60], Onsa [87]		
8-12	Uganda	D	0-0	Khartoum	CCsf	L 3-4p		
10-12	Kenya	L	1-2	Khartoum	CC3p	Almazir Muhamoud [30p]		
2004								
19-04	Syria	L	1-2	Khartoum	Fr	Kabir [65]		
21-04	Syria	D	0-0	Khartoum	Fr			
22-05	Uganda	W	2-1	Khartoum	Fr	Muhaned Mohamed, Ali Musa		
25-05	Zambia	L	0-2	Khartoum	Fr			
6-06	Egypt	L	0-3	Khartoum	WCq		10 000	Kidane Tesfu ERI
20-06	Benin	D	1-1	Cotonou	WCq	Abd Iaziz [47+]	20 000	Guezzaz MAR
3-07	Libya	L	0-1	Khartoum	WCq		10 000	Bennett RSA
5-09	Côte d'Ivoire	L	0-5	Abidjan	WCq		20 000	Mana NGA
9-10	Cameroon	D	1-1	Omdurman	WCq	Agab Sido [17]	30 000	Buenkadila COD
12-12	Kenya	D	2-2	Addis Abeba	CCrl	Mustafa Ali [45p], Kamal [79]		
14-12	Uganda	W	2-1	Addis Abeba	CCrl	Kamal [3], El Rasheed [75]		
18-12	Somalia	W	4-0	Addis Abeba	CCrl	Mustafa Haitham [46], Hameedama [63], Tambal [69], Omar Mohamed [90]		
22-12	Burundi	L	1-2	Addis Abeba	CCsf	Mustafa Haitham [54p]		
25-12	Kenya	W	2-1	Addis Abeba	CC3p	Kamal 2 [30 60]	30 000	
2005								
12-03	Ethiopia	W	3-1	Khartoum	Fr			
27-03	Cameroon	L	1-2	Yaoundé	WCq	Tambal [41]	30 000	Diatta SEN
22-05	Chad	W	4-1	Khartoum	Fr			
27-05	Chad	D	1-1	Khartoum	Fr			
5-06	Egypt	L	1-6	Cairo	WCq	Tambal [83]	20 000	Mususa ZIM

Fr = Friendly match • CN = CAF African Cup of Nations • CC = CECAFA Cup • AR = Arab Cup • WC = FIFA World Cup™
q = qualifier • r1 = first round group • sf = semi-final • 3p = third place play-off • † Not an official international

SUDAN NATIONAL TEAM RECORDS AND RECORD SEQUENCES

Records			Sequence records					
Victory	15-0	OMA 1965	Wins	5	1965	Clean sheets	5	2003
Defeat	0-8	KOR 1979	Defeats	5	2000-2001	Goals scored	12	1996-1998
Player Caps	n/a		Undefeated	9	1968-1969	Without goal	4	2000-2001
Player Goals	n/a		Without win	9	1980-1982	Goals against	15	1996-1998

FIFA REFEREE LIST 2005

	Int'l	DoB
ABDEL GADIR Badr	2004	1-01-1974
ABDEL RAHMAN Khalid	2001	16-01-1968
BABIKER Sharaf	2003	1-01-1967
EL NIGOMI Ahmed	2004	1-01-1968
HAKIM Mubarak	2005	25-05-1967
RASSAS Sabit	2002	1-01-1970

FIFA ASSISTANT REFEREE LIST 2005

	Int'l	DoB
BAKHEIT Awad	2004	3-01-1968
EL FAKI Ahmed	2001	1-01-1964
ELTOM Aarif	2005	15-12-1970
HAMAD EL NEEL Aymen	2002	1-01-1970
KHALAFALLA Abdel	2004	1-01-1976
MOHAMED Abdalla	2001	1-01-1964
MOHAMED Tarig	2001	22-09-1965

SUDAN 2004

PREMIER LEAGUE

	Pl	W	D	L	F	A	Pts	Hilal	Merreikh	Khartoum	Merghani	Mawrada	Amal	Hilal PS	Taka	Shambat	Hay Al Arab	Ahli	Merreikh PS
Al Hilal Omdurman †	22	17	3	2	59	11	54		2-0	2-0	0-0	2-1	8-0	7-3	2-0	3-0	5-0	2-0	2-0
Al Merreikh Omdurman‡	22	16	3	3	43	15	51	1-2		0-2	1-0	4-0	1-0	3-1	1-0	3-1	4-0	3-1	2-0
Khartoum-3	22	10	5	7	35	23	35	0-1	0-1		4-1	1-0	3-0	0-1	0-0	3-2	3-0	1-1	4-1
Al Merghani Kassala	22	8	7	7	25	27	31	0-8	1-2	2-2		2-0	2-0	1-1	1-1	0-1	1-1	2-0	2-2
Al Mawrada Omdurman	22	9	3	10	30	34	30	2-4	0-5	1-2	3-2		3-1	2-0	1-2	0-0	4-1	2-1	3-0
Al Amal Atbara	22	9	3	10	16	29	30	2-1	0-1	1-1	1-0	2-1		0-0	3-2	0-1	1-0	1-0	1-0
Al Hilal Port Sudan	22	7	7	8	21	29	28	1-0	1-1	2-0	0-0	0-1	0-1		1-0	2-0	1-4	1-1	0-1
Al Taka Kassala	22	5	10	7	20	22	25	0-0	1-1	1-1	0-2	2-2	2-1	1-1		0-1	0-0	0-2	3-0
Al Shambat Khartoum	22	6	6	10	18	31	24	0-4	2-4	0-2	0-1	1-1	0-0	3-4	0-2		2-0	0-0	0-0
Hay Al Arab Pt. Sudan	22	5	7	10	17	31	22	1-1	0-1	3-2	0-1	0-1	2-0	0-0	1-1	1-1		0-0	0-1
Al Ahli Wad Medani	22	4	6	12	21	31	18	0-1	1-1	1-3	0-2	1-2	1-0	3-0	1-1	1-2	1-2		3-2
Al Merreikh Pt. Sudan	22	5	2	15	13	35	17	0-2	0-3	2-1	0-2	1-0	0-1	0-1	0-1	0-1	0-1	3-2	

16/08/2004 - 15/05/2005 • † Qualified for the CAF Champions League • ‡ Qualified for the CAF Confederations Cup

RECENT LEAGUE AND CUP RECORD

Championship		Cup		
Year	Champions	Winners	Score	Runners-up
1998	Al Hilal	Al Morada		
1999	Al Hilal	Al Morada		
2000	Al Merreikh	Al Hilal	3-0	Al Ahly
2001	Al Merreikh	Al Merreikh	1-0	Al Mourada
2002	Al Merreikh			
2003	Al Hilal			
2004	Al Hilal	Al Hilal	0-0 3-2p	Al Merreikh

SUDAN COUNTRY INFORMATION

Capital	Khartoum	Independence	1956 from Egypt and UK	GDP per Capita	$1 900
Population	39 148 162	Status	Republic	GNP Ranking	83
Area km²	2 505 810	Language	Arabic, English, Nubian	Dialling code	+249
Population density	15 per km²	Literacy rate	61%	Internet code	.sd
% in urban areas	25%	Main religion	Muslim	GMT + / –	+2
Towns/Cities ('000)	Omdurman 2 810; Khartoum 1 974; Khartoum North 1 530; Niyala 499; Port Sudan 459; Kassala 401; El Obeid 393; Kusti 345; Wad Madani 332; Gadaref 322, El Fasher 252				
Neighbours (km)	Eritrea 605; Ethiopia 1 606; Kenya 232; Uganda 435; Congo DR 628; Central African Republic 1 165; Chad 1 360; Libya 383; Egypt 1 273; Red Sea 853				
Main stadia	National Stadium – Khartoum 20 000; El Merriekh – Omdurman 30 000				

SUI – SWITZERLAND

NATIONAL TEAM RECORD
JULY 1ST 2002 TO JUNE 30TH 2005

PL	W	D	L	F	A	%
28	11	8	8	44	35	53.6

FIFA/COCA-COLA WORLD RANKING

1993	1994	1995	1996	1997	1998	1999	2000	2001	2002	2003	2004	High		Low	
12	7	18	47	62	83	47	58	63	44	44	51	3	08/93	83	12/98

2004-2005											
08/04	09/04	10/04	11/04	12/04	01/05	02/05	03/05	04/05	05/05	06/05	07/05
47	49	42	45	51	51	49	49	45	45	42	42

The staging of UEFA EURO 2008™ in Switzerland has prompted something of a revolution in Swiss football. Where there once stood quaint but antiquated stadia in Basel, Berne and Geneva there are now sleek modern arenas with Zurich, the fourth of the cities to host matches in the finals, to follow suit in 2007. FC Basel in particular have benefited and are enjoying a golden spell that in 2005 saw them win their third Super League title in four years. Thanks in part to the stadium the club is now able to compete in the market for players and the Argentine duo of Christian Giménez and Julio Rossi have been instrumental in the recent success. Servette on the other hand proved

INTERNATIONAL HONOURS
Qualified for the FIFA World Cup™ finals 1934 1938 1950 1954 1962 1966 1994

that football can still be a risky business and after Canal+ sold their 43.2 per cent stake in the club in 2002 debts mounted and they were forced to pull out from the League after going bankrupt midway through the season. The national team has been bolstered by a generation of fine young players - notably Arsenal's Philippe Senderos and PSV's Johan Vonlanthen - inspired by the prospect of playing at a major tournament at home. Drawn in a very tough 2006 FIFA World Cup™ group the Swiss have had a battle with France, Israel and the Republic of Ireland to make it to their first finals since 1994 and went through the 2004-05 season unbeaten in eight games

THE FIFA BIG COUNT OF 2000

	Male	Female		Male	Female
Registered players	89 980	4 000	Referees	4 540	60
Non registered players	200 000	25 000	Officials	250 000	200
Youth players	115 800	3 000	Total involved	692 580	
Total players	437 780		Number of clubs	1 453	
Professional players	300	0	Number of teams	11 800	

Schweizerischer Fussball-Verband (SFV/ASF)
Worbstrasse 48, Postfach, Bern 15 3000, Switzerland
Tel +41 31 9508111   Fax +41 31 9508181
sfv.asf@football.ch   www.football.ch
President: ZLOCZOWER Ralph   General Secretary: GILLIERON Peter
Vice-President: CORNELLA Guido   Treasurer: POMA Giuseppe   Media Officer: BENOIT Pierre
Men's Coach: KUHN Koebi   Women's Coach: VON SIEBENTHAL Beatrice
SFV/ASF formed: 1895   UEFA: 1954   FIFA: 1904
Colours: Red, White, Red

GAMES PLAYED BY SWITZERLAND IN THE 2006 FIFA WORLD CUP™ CYCLE

2002	Opponents	Score		Venue	Comp	Scorers	Att	Referee
21-08	Austria	W	3-2	Basel	Fr	Yakin.H [19], Frei [41], Yakin.M [76]	23 500	Rosetti ITA
8-09	Georgia	W	4-1	Basel	ECq	Frei [37], Yakin.H [62], Muller.P [74], Chapuisat [81]	20 500	Hrinak SVK
12-10	Albania	D	1-1	Tirana	ECq	Yakin.M [37]	15 000	Erdemir TUR
16-10	Republic of Ireland	W	2-1	Dublin	ECq	Yakin.H [45], Celestini [87]	40 000	Pedersen NOR
2003								
12-02	Slovenia	W	5-1	Nova Gorica	Fr	Yakin.H [3], Haas [29], Frei 2 [36 78], Cabanas [49]	3 500	Abraham HUN
2-04	Georgia	D	0-0	Tbilisi	ECq		10 000	Trivkovic CRO
30-04	Italy	L	1-2	Geneva	Fr	Frei 6	30 000	Ledentu FRA
7-06	Russia	D	2-2	Basel	ECq	Frei 2 [14 16]	30 500	Dauden Ibanez ESP
11-06	Albania	W	3-2	Geneva	ECq	Haas [11], Frei [32], Cabanas [72]	26 000	Bennett ENG
20-08	France	L	0-2	Geneva	Fr		30 000	Allaerts BEL
10-09	Russia	L	1-4	Moscow	ECq	Karyaka OG [12]	29 000	Collina ITA
11-10	Republic of Ireland	W	2-0	Basel	ECq	Yakin.H [6], Frei [60]	31 006	Frisk SWE
2004								
18-02	Morocco	L	1-2	Rabat	Fr	Frei [90]	3 000	Berber ALG
31-03	Greece	L	0-1	Heraklion	Fr		33 000	Temmink NED
28-04	Slovenia	W	2-1	Geneva	Fr	Celestini [66], Yakin.H [85]	7 500	Bossen NED
2-06	Germany	L	0-2	Basel	Fr		30 000	Messina ITA
6-06	Liechtenstein	W	1-0	Zurich	Fr	Gygax [90]	10 200	Drabek AUT
13-06	Croatia	D	0-0	Leiria	ECr1		24 090	Cortez Batista POR
17-06	England	L	0-3	Coimbra	ECr1		28 214	Ivanov.V RUS
21-06	France	L	1-3	Coimbra	ECr1	Vonlanthen [26]	28 111	Michel SVK
18-08	Northern Ireland	D	0-0	Zurich	Fr		4 000	Vollquartz DEN
4-09	Faroe Islands	W	6-0	Basel	WCq	Vonlanthen 3 [10 14 57], Rey 3 [29 44 55]	11 880	Tudor ROM
8-09	Republic of Ireland	D	1-1	Basel	WCq	Yakin.H [17]	28 000	Vassaras GRE
9-10	Israel	D	2-2	Tel Aviv	WCq	Frei [26], Vonlanthen [34]	37 976	Shield AUS
2005								
9-02	United Arab Emirates	W	2-1	Dubai	Fr	Gygax [9], Muller.P [79]	1 000	El Hilali OMA
26-03	France	D	0-0	Paris	WCq		79 373	De Santis ITA
30-03	Cyprus	W	1-0	Zurich	WCq	Frei [87]	16 066	Dougal SCO
4-06	Faroe Islands	W	3-1	Toftir	WCq	Wicky [25], Frei 2 [72 84]	2 047	Gumienny BEL

Fr = Friendly match • EC = UEFA EURO 2004™ • WC = FIFA World Cup™ • q = qualifier

SWITZERLAND NATIONAL TEAM RECORDS AND RECORD SEQUENCES

Records			Sequence records		
Victory	9-0	LTU 1924	Wins	5	1960-1961	Clean sheets	4	1973
Defeat	0-9	ENG 1909, HUN 1911	Defeats	11	1928-1930	Goals scored	22	1921-1924
Player Caps	117	HERMANN Heinz	Undefeated	13	1992-1993	Without goal	5	1985
Player Goals	34	ABEGGLEN/TURKYILMAZ	Without win	16	1928-1930	Goals against	45	1926-1932

SWITZERLAND COUNTRY INFORMATION

Capital	Bern	Formation	1291	GDP per Capita	$32 700
Population	7 450 867	Status	Federal Republic	GNP Ranking	17
Area km²	41 290	Language	German 64%, French 19%, Italian 7%	Dialling code	.ch
Population density	180 per km²	Literacy rate	99%	Internet code	+41
% in urban areas	61%	Main religion	Christian	GMT + / –	+1
Towns/Cities ('000)	Zürich 346; Geneva 181; Basel 164; Bern 123; Lausanne 118; Winterthur 91; St Gallen 72; Luzern 57; Biel 49; Thun 41; La Chaux-de-Fonds 36; Köniz 35; Schaffhausen 34, Neuchâtel 31				
Neighbours (km)	Austria 164; Liechtenstein 41; Italy 740; France 573; Germany 334				
Main stadia	St Jakob Park – Basel 42 500; Stade de Genève – Geneva 30 000; Letzigrund – Zürich 30 000				

NATIONAL CAPS

	Caps
HERMANN Heinz	117
GEIGER Alain	112
CHAPUISAT Stéphane	103
MINELLI Severino	80
SFORZA Ciriaco	79
EGLI André	79
VOGEL Johan	74
HENCHOZ Stéphane	72
BICKEL Alfred	71
ABEGGLEN Max	68

NATIONAL GOALS

	Goals
TURKYILMAZ Kubilay	34
ABEGGLEN Max	34
ABEGGLEN André	29
FATTON Jacques	29
KNUP Adrian	26
HUGI Josef	23
ANTENEN Charles	22
AMADO Lauro	21
CHAPUISAT Stéphane	21
BALLAMAN Robert	19

NATIONAL COACH

	Years
JEANDUPEUX Daniel	1986-'89
WOLFISBERG Paul	1989
STIELIKE Ueli	1989-'91
HODGSON Roy	1992-95
JORGE Artur	1996
FRINGER Rolf	1996-'97
GRESS Gilbert	1998-'99
ZAUGG Hanspeter	2000
TROSSERO Enzo	2000-'01
KUHN Koebi	2001-

FIFA REFEREE LIST 2005

	Int'l	DoB
BERTOLINI Carlo	1997	16-09-1965
BUSACCA Massimo	1998	6-02-1969
CIRCHETTA Claudio	2005	18-11-1970
LEUBA Philippe	1997	9-12-1965
NOBS Markus	2001	17-06-1966
ROGALLA Rene	2000	19-12-1963
WILDHABER Guido		24-05-1962

FIFA ASSISTANT REFEREE LIST 2005

	Int'l	DoB
ARNET Matthias	2000	2-06-1968
BARRAUD Armand	2002	14-10-1962
BURAGINA Francesco	2001	7-01-1966
CUHAT Stephane	1999	8-10-1963
FERNANDEZ Antonio	2003	2-02-1967
HIDBER Beat	2003	18-03-1971
ISELI Martin	1999	14-01-1964
KAEPPELI Rudolf	1998	24-04-1960
REMY Jean-Paul	2004	13-04-1966
SALERNO Carmelo	2002	20-09-1969

CLUB DIRECTORY

Club	Town/City	Stadium	Phone	www.	Lge	Cup	CL
FC Aarau	Aarau	Brügglifeld Stadion 13 500	+41 62 8321414	fcaarau.ch	3	1	0
FC Basel	Basel	St Jakob Park 31 539	+41 61 3751010	fcb.ch	11	7	0
Grasshopper-Club	Zürich	Hardturm Stadion 17 666	+41 1 4474646	gcz.ch	26	18	0
FC Schaffhausen	Schaffhausen	Breite Stadion 6 000	+41 52 6300180	fcschaffhausen.ch	0	0	0
Servette FC	Geneva	Stade de Genève 31 124	+41 22 3088989	servettefc.ch	17	7	0
FC St. Gallen	St. Gallen	Espenmoos Stadion 11 300	+41 71 2430909	fcsg.ch	2	1	0
FC Thun	Thun	Lachen Stadion 7 250	+41 33 3361698	fcthun.ch	0	0	0
Neuchâtel Xamax FC	Neuchâtel	Stade La Maladière 13 300	+41 32 7254428	xamax.ch	2	0	0
BSC Young Boys	Berne	Neufeld Stadion 12 000	+41 31 3304488	bscyb.ch	11	6	0
FC Zürich	Zürich	Letzigrund Stadion 19 400	+41 1 4927474	fcz.ch	9	7	0

RECENT LEAGUE AND CUP RECORD

	Championship						Cup		
Year	Champions	Pts	Runners-up	Pts	Third	Pts	Winners	Score	Runners-up
1990	Grasshopper-Club	31	Lausanne-Sports	31	Neuchâtel Xamax	30	Grasshopper-Club	2-1	Neuchâtel Xamax
1991	Grasshopper-Club	33	FC Sion	29	Neuchâtel Xamax	29	FC Sion	3-2	BSC Young Boys
1992	FC Sion	33	Neuchâtel Xamax	31	Grasshopper-Club	30	FC Luzern	3-1	FC Lugano
1993	FC Aarau	34	BSC Young Boys	28	FC Lugano	27	FC Lugano	4-1	Grasshopper-Club
1994	Servette FC	34	Grasshopper-Club	33	FC Sion	31	Grasshopper-Club	4-0	FC Schaffhausen
1995	Grasshopper-Club	37	FC Lugano	30	Neuchâtel Xamax	28	FC Sion	4-2	Grasshopper-Club
1996	Grasshopper-Club	52	FC Sion	47	Neuchâtel Xamax	43	FC Sion	3-2	Servette FC
1997	FC Sion	49	Neuchâtel Xamax	46	Grasshopper-Club	45	FC Sion	3-3 5-4p	FC Luzern
1998	Grasshopper-Club	57	Servette FC	41	Lausanne-Sports	40	Lausanne-Sports	2-2 4-3p	FC St. Gallen
1999	Servette FC	46	Grasshopper-Club	46	Lausanne-Sports	45	Lausanne-Sports	2-0	Grasshopper-Club
2000	FC St. Gallen	54	Lausanne-Sports	44	FC Basel	40	FC Zürich	2-2 3-0p	Lausanne-Sports
2001	Grasshopper-Club	46	FC Lugano	41	FC St. Gallen	40	Servette FC	3-0	Yverdon-Sports
2002	FC Basel	55	Grasshopper-Club	45	FC Lugano	42	FC Basel	2-1	Grasshopper-Club
2003	Grasshopper-Club	57	FC Basel	56	Neuchâtel Xamax	35	FC Basel	6-0	Neuchâtel Xamax
2004	FC Basel	85	BSC Young Boys	72	Servette FC	52	FC Wil	3-2	Grasshopper-Club
2005	FC Basel	70	FC Thun	60	Grasshopper-Club	50	FC Zürich	3-1	FC Luzern

SWITZERLAND 2004-05

AXPO SUPER LEAGUE

	Pl	W	D	L	F	A	Pts	Basel	Thun	Grasshoppers	Young Boys	Zürich	Neuchâtel	St. Gallen	Aarau	Schaf'sen	Servette
FC Basel †	34	21	7	6	81	45	70		3-3 4-1	8-1 4-1	2-1 1-1	2-1 3-2	1-1 2-0	1-0 3-1	6-0 4-2	1-1 4-3	2-1
FC Thun †	34	18	6	10	69	42	60	4-1 3-0		0-1 2-5	3-1 1-1	0-1 5-1	3-0 2-1	1-1 3-1	0-0 5-0	2-1 4-0	3-0
Grasshopper-Club ‡	34	12	14	8	51	50	50	2-3 4-1	0-0 1-0		0-1 1-1	1-1 1-1	2-1 1-1	0-0 4-0	1-1 1-1	1-0 3-1	0-2
BSC Young Boys	34	12	13	9	60	52	49	1-1 2-5	2-1 2-4	1-1 3-2		2-4 1-1	2-1 1-0	0-1 2-3	1-1 1-1	6-1 4-1	1-1
FC Zürich ‡	34	13	9	12	55	57	48	0-0 2-2	1-0 6-3	2-0 1-1	2-3 0-5		1-2 0-0	3-1 0-2	1-3 2-0	1-1 2-0	2-1
Neuchâtel Xamax	34	10	8	16	36	48	38	1-2 0-4	0-2 0-0	2-0 1-2	3-1 0-1	1-1 1-2		3-0 2-1	2-1 1-1	1-0 0-1	3-0
FC St. Gallen	34	8	12	14	51	60	36	0-1 3-1	3-1 1-2	0-0 3-3	3-3 2-2	1-2 4-5	4-2 5-0		2-1 0-0	2-2 1-1	1-1
FC Aarau	34	7	11	16	42	64	32	1-0 0-5	0-1 1-7	1-2 2-3	1-3 1-1	3-1 2-3	0-0 1-2	4-1 3-1		2-1 0-1	4-0
FC Schaffhausen	34	7	11	16	36	59	32	1-0 0-2	0-1 0-1	1-2 2-2	1-1 0-1	2-1 2-1	1-1 2-1	3-2 0-0	3-3 1-1		1-4
Servette FC	18	6	5	7	24	28	20	1-2	3-1	2-2	2-1	2-1	1-2	1-1	1-0	1-1	

17/07/2004 - 29/05/2005 • † Qualified for the UEFA Champions League • ‡ Qualified for the UEFA Cup • Servette went bankrupt durining the winter break and withdrew from the league. They had 3 points deducted already • Relegation play-off: FC Schaffhausen 1-1 1-0 FC Vaduz

SWITZERLAND 2004-05
CHALLENGE LEAGUE (2)

	Pl	W	D	L	F	A	Pts
Yverdon-Sports	34	20	10	4	59	26	70
FC Vaduz	34	21	6	7	58	28	69
FC Sion	34	19	11	4	63	33	68
FC Chiasso	34	20	5	9	60	37	65
FC Luzern	34	19	2	13	73	53	59
AC Bellinzona	34	17	6	11	58	46	57
FC Concordia	34	13	12	9	52	40	51
AC Lugano	34	14	8	12	49	46	50
SC Kriens	34	11	15	8	46	37	48
FC La Chaux-de-Fonds	34	12	7	15	57	56	43
FC Winterthur	34	11	8	15	46	53	41
FC Baulmes	34	12	5	17	31	54	41
FC Wil 1900	34	10	10	14	45	54	40
FC Meyrin	34	9	8	17	39	61	35
FC Wohlen	34	8	7	19	38	63	31
SCYF Juventus Zürich	34	8	5	21	43	71	29
FC Baden	34	7	7	20	39	62	28
FC Bulle	34	6	6	22	43	79	24

30/07/2004 - 28/05/2005

SWISSCOM CUP 2004-05

Eighth-finals

FC Zürich	2
Neuchâtel Xamax *	0
Juventus Zürich *	0
AC Bellinzona	2
FC Thun *	1 4p
FC Basel	1 3p
FC Sion *	1
BSC Young Boys	2
FC Aarau	2
FC Baulmes *	0
FC Schaffhausen *	2 3p
FC Sankt Gallen	2 5p
FC Chiasso *	1
Yverdon-Sports	0
Concordia Basel	1
FC Luzern *	4

Quarter-finals

FC Zürich	2
AC Bellinzona *	0
FC Thun	0
BSC Young Boys *	2
FC Aarau	3 4p
FC Sankt Gallen *	3 3p
FC Chiasso *	0
FC Luzern	4

Semi-finals

FC Zürich	3
BSC Young Boys	1
FC Aarau	1
FC Luzern	2

Final

FC Zürich ‡	3
FC Luzern	1

SWISS CUP FINAL
16-05-2005, Att:32 000
St Jakob Park, Basel

Scorers - Schneider 39, Keita 62, Tararache 74 for FC Zürich; Andreoli 87 for FC Luzern

* Home team • ‡ Qualified for the UEFA Cup

SUR – SURINAM

NATIONAL TEAM RECORD
JULY 1ST 2002 TO JUNE 30TH 2005

PL	W	D	L	F	A	%
11	4	4	3	24	13	54.5

FIFA/COCA-COLA WORLD RANKING

1993	1994	1995	1996	1997	1998	1999	2000	2001	2002	2003	2004	High		Low	
117	104	124	131	145	160	162	164	141	141	158	149	**92**	07/94	**168**	04/01

2004-2005											
08/04	09/04	10/04	11/04	12/04	01/05	02/05	03/05	04/05	05/05	06/05	07/05
147	146	148	149	149	151	151	151	151	151	151	151

Surinam may border Brazil, but the two countries share little else in terms of footballing heritage. A member of FIFA since 1929 and with close links to the Dutch KNVB, more may have been expected from the national team, but they have been consistent underperformers. The qualifiers for the 2006 FIFA World Cup™ began with a tie against Aruba. A 10-2 aggregate victory gave Surinam a fixture with Guatemala and after a 1-1 draw in Paramaribo, Surinam looked to be onto a surprise win when they led 1-0 in the away leg. Guatemala fought back for a comfortable 3-1 win though and Surinam's attention turned towards the Gold Cup, but qualifying for that also ended

INTERNATIONAL HONOURS
CONCACAF Champions Cup Transvaal 1973 1981

quickly. For a country that could follow the Jamaican model and draw on Netherlands-based players, the potential for improvement exists but has not yet been grasped with most players preferring to try and follow in the footsteps of numerous Surinamese descended players who have played for the Dutch national team. The Hoofdklasse League was won by Robinhood, who finished the season nine points ahead of nearest rivals Royal 95. Inter Moengotapoe and Walking Bout Co entered the 2005 Champion Clubs Cup, the latter exiting at the first round while Inter made it to the next stage only to lose 6-9 on aggregate to Harbour View of Jamaica.

THE FIFA BIG COUNT OF 2000

	Male	Female		Male	Female
Registered players	4 659	750	Referees	125	20
Non registered players	12 500	200	Officials	250	50
Youth players	1 463	0	Total involved	20 017	
Total players	19 572		Number of clubs	30	
Professional players	0	0	Number of teams	257	

Surinaamse Voetbal Bond (SVB)
Letitia Vriesdelaan 7, PO Box 1223, Paramaribo, Surinam
Tel +597 473112   Fax +597 479718
svb@sr.net   www.none
President: GISKUS Louis   General Secretary: FELTER Harold
Vice-President: KOORNDIJK Ronald   Treasurer: GOBARDHAN Waldo   Media Officer: POCORNI Dennis
Men's Coach: KOSWAL Leo   Women's Coach: JALIENS Kenneth
SVB formed: 1920   CONCACAF: 1964   FIFA: 1929
Colours: White, Green, Green

GAMES PLAYED BY SURINAM IN THE 2006 FIFA WORLD CUP™ CYCLE

2002	Opponents		Score	Venue	Comp	Scorers	Att	Referee
28-07	Aruba	W	2-0	Oranjestad	GCq	Kejansi 55, Sandvliet 62		Faneijte ATG
11-08	Aruba	W	6-0	Paramaribo	GCq	Zinhagel 2 28 47, Kejansi 3 35 57 84, Kinsaini 63	2 500	Mercera ATG
2003								
No international matches played in 2003								
2004								
10-01	Netherlands Antilles	D	1-1	Paramaribo	Fr	Sandvliet 53		Jol NED
17-01	Netherlands Antilles	L	0-2	Willemstad	Fr			
28-02	Aruba	W	2-1	Oranjestad	WCq	Felter 54p, Zinhagel 63	2 108	Moreno PAN
27-03	Aruba	W	8-1	Paramaribo	WCq	Kinsaini 2 6 49, Loswijk 14, Felter 3 18 65 66, Sandvliet 42, Zinhagel 90	4 000	Prendergast JAM
12-06	Guatemala	D	1-1	Paramaribo	WCq	Purperhart 14	5 500	Jimenez CRC
20-06	Guatemala	L	1-3	Guatemala City	WCq	Brandon 82	19 610	Rodriguez MEX
24-11	Grenada	D	2-2	Tunapuna	GCq	Modeste OG 27, Sandvliet 59	2 000	Forde BRB
26-11	Puerto Rico	D	1-1	Marabella	GCq	Sandvliet 45		Forde BRB
28-11	Trinidad and Tobago	L	0-1	Malabar	GCq			Forde BRB
2005								
No international matches played in 2005 before August								

Fr = Friendly match • GC = CONCACAF Gold Cup • WC = FIFA World Cup™ • q = qualifier

SURINAM NATIONAL TEAM RECORDS AND RECORD SEQUENCES

Records			Sequence records					
Victory	8-1	ARU 2004	Wins	4	1992	Clean sheets	4	1980
Defeat	1-8	MEX 1977	Defeats	5	1997	Goals scored	9	1990-1992
Player Caps	n/a		Undefeated	9	1990-1992	Without goal	2	Six times
Player Goals	n/a		Without win	6	Four times	Goals against	22	1994-1999

SVB CUP 2003-04

Quarter-finals		Semi-finals		Final	
Super Red Eagles	2				
Vorwaarts †	1	**Super Red Eagles**	1		
Transvaal	1	Amardeep	0	15-08-2004	
Amardeep	2			**Super Red Eagles**	2
				Walking Bout Co	1
		Voorwaarts	1		
FCS National	0	**Walking Bout Co**	2		
Walking Bout Co	1	† Vorwaarts given passage to semis as best loser			

RECENT LEAGUE RECORD

	Championship					
Year	Champions	Pts	Runners-up	Pts	Third	Pts
1999	SNL	64	Robin Hood	53	Transvaal	46
2000	Transvaal	57	SNL	54	Royal '95	49
2001	No Competition					
2002	Voorwaarts	67	SNL	63	Royal '95	52
2003	FCS National	52	Robin Hood	50	House of Billiards	43
2004	Walking Bout Co	55	Inter Moengotapoe	47	Transvaal	46
2005						

SURINAM COUNTRY INFORMATION

Capital	Paramaribo	Independence	1975 from the Netherlands	GDP per Capita	$4 000
Population	436 935	Status	Republic	GNP Ranking	158
Area km²	163 270	Language	Dutch, English, Surinamese	Dialling code	+597
Population density	2.6 per km²	Literacy rate	93%	Internet code	.sr
% in urban areas	50%	Main religion	Christian, Hindu, Muslim,	GMT +/-	-3
Cities/Towns ('000)	Paramaribo 220; Lelydorp 17; Nieuw Nickerie 13; Moengo 7; Meerzorg 6; Nieuw Amsterdam 5				
Neighbours (km)	French Guiana 510; Brazil 597; Guyana 600; North Atlantic Ocean 386				
Main stadia	André Kamperveen Stadion – Paramaribo 18 000				

SVK – SLOVAKIA

NATIONAL TEAM RECORD
JULY 1ST 2002 TO JUNE 30TH 2005

PL	W	D	L	F	A	%
32	11	11	10	50	37	51.6

FIFA/COCA-COLA WORLD RANKING

1993	1994	1995	1996	1997	1998	1999	2000	2001	2002	2003	2004	High		Low	
150	43	35	30	34	32	21	24	47	55	50	53	17	05/97	150	12/93

2004-2005											
08/04	09/04	10/04	11/04	12/04	01/05	02/05	03/05	04/05	05/05	06/05	07/05
71	71	57	55	53	53	54	54	48	48	43	45

The Slovakian national team has been one of the revelations of the 2006 FIFA World Cup™ qualifiers. After finding thelmselves in a group with UEFA EURO 2004™ finalists, Portugal, Russia and Latvia, little was expected of them but they surprised many observers by winning four of their first six matches and drawing the other two before a defeat in Lisbon brought a reality check. With Slovakia producing more than its fair share of players for the old Czechoslovakia team, especially the side that won the European Championship in 1976, perhaps the success should not be surprising. With a number of players based with clubs in Germany and Britain, coach Dusan

INTERNATIONAL HONOURS
None

Galis has experienced players to help the younger generation through and there is no reason why Slovakia should not match rivals Czech Republic and be a force in years to come. Where Slovakia lags behind the Czechs is in club football. Since independence in 1993 clubs like Slovan Bratislava have experienced a decline allowing a new order to be established, epitomised by Artmedia Bratislava. In 2005 they won the title for the first time and then made headlines by beating former European champions Celtic in the UEFA Champions League preliminaries. Artmedia also made it to the Cup Final but missed out on the double after losing 2-1 against Dukla Banská Bystrica.

THE FIFA BIG COUNT OF 2000

	Male	Female		Male	Female
Registered players	115 680	578	Referees	92	15
Non registered players	75 000	1 500	Officials	696	100
Youth players	127 175	397	Total involved	321 233	
Total players	320 330		Number of clubs	2 427	
Professional players	1 918	0	Number of teams	7 298	

Slovak Football Association (SFZ)
Slovensky futbalovy zväz, Junácka 6, 832 80, Bratislava, Slovakia
Tel +421 2 49249151   Fax +421 2 49249595
international@futbalsfz.sk   www.futbalsfz.sk
President: LAURINEC Frantisek   General Secretary: TITTEL Dusan
Vice-President: OBLOZINSKY Juraj   Treasurer: VENCEL Stanislav   Media Officer: LAMACOVA Karolina
Men's Coach: GALIS Dusan   Women's Coach: URVAY Frantisek
SFZ formed: 1993   UEFA: 1994   FIFA: 1907/1994
Colours: Blue, Blue, Blue

GAMES PLAYED BY SLOVAKIA IN THE 2006 FIFA WORLD CUP™ CYCLE

2002	Opponents		Score	Venue	Comp	Scorers	Att	Referee
21-08	Czech Republic	L	1-4	Olomouc	Fr	Nemeth.S [16]	11 986	Douros GRE
7-09	Turkey	L	0-3	Istanbul	ECq		19 750	Lopez Nieto ESP
12-10	England	L	1-2	Bratislava	ECq	Nemeth.S [24]	30 000	Messina ITA
20-11	Ukraine	D	1-1	Bratislava	Fr	Karhan [61p]	2 859	Marczyk POL
2003								
12-02	Romania	L	1-2	Larnaca	Fr	Vittek [6]	150	Papaioannou GRE
13-02	Cyprus	W	3-1	Larnaca	Fr	Reiter [1], Vittek 2 [62 82]	250	Kapitanis CYP
29-03	FYR Macedonia	W	2-0	Skopje	ECq	Petras [28], Reiter [90]	11 000	Duhamel FRA
2-04	Liechtenstein	W	4-0	Trnava	ECq	Reiter [19], Nemeth.S 2 [51 64], Janocko [90]	BCD	Ceferin SVN
30-04	Greece	D	2-2	Puchov	Fr	Nemeth.S 2 [13 87]	2 863	Messner AUT
7-06	Turkey	L	0-1	Bratislava	ECq		15 000	Hauge NOR
11-06	England	L	1-2	Middlesbrough	ECq	Janocko [31]	35 000	Stark GER
20-08	Colombia	D	0-0	New Jersey	Fr		16 000	Stott USA
10-09	FYR Macedonia	D	1-1	Zilina	ECq	Nemeth.S [25]	2 286	Sundell SWE
11-10	Liechtenstein	W	2-0	Vaduz	ECq	Vittek 2 [40 56]	800	Hyytia FIN
10-12	Kuwait	W	2-0	Larnaca	Fr	Breska [53], Dovicovic [71]		
2004								
31-03	Austria	D	1-1	Bratislava	Fr	Mintal [72]	4 500	Vidlak CZE
28-04	Ukraine	D	1-1	Kyiv	Fr	Varga [65]	18 000	Ryszka POL
29-05	Croatia	L	0-1	Rijeka	Fr		10 000	Kassai HUN
9-07	Japan	L	1-3	Hiroshima	Fr	Babnic [65]	34 458	Breeze AUS
11-07	Serbia & Montenegro	L	0-2	Fukuoka	Fr		6 100	Yoshida JPN
18-08	Luxembourg	W	3-1	Bratislava	WCq	Vittek [26], Gresko [48], Demo [89]	5 016	Kassai HUN
4-09	Russia	D	1-1	Moscow	WCq	Vittek [87]	11 500	Mejuto Gonzalez ESP
8-09	Liechtenstein	W	7-0	Bratislava	WCq	Vittek 3 [15 59 81], Karhan [42], Nemeth.S [84], Mintal [85], Zabavnik [92+]	5 620	Delevic SCG
9-10	Latvia	W	4-1	Bratislava	WCq	Nemeth.S [36], Reiter [50], Karhan 2 [55 87]	13 025	Farina ITA
17-11	Slovenia	D	0-0	Trnava	Fr		5 482	Skjerven NOR
30-11	Hungary	W	1-0	Bangkok	Fr	Porazik [47]	750	Veerapool THA
2-12	Thailand	D	1-1	Bangkok	Fr	Durica [65p], W 5-4p	5 000	Chappanimutu MAS
2005								
9-02	Romania	D	2-2	Larnaca	Fr	Vittek [12], Karhan [44]	500	Kapitanis CYP
26-03	Estonia	W	2-1	Tallinn	WCq	Mintal [58], Reiter [65]	3 051	Frojdfeldt SWE
30-03	Portugal	D	1-1	Bratislava	WCq	Karhan [8]	21 000	Sars FRA
4-06	Portugal	L	0-2	Lisbon	WCq		64 000	Collina ITA
8-06	Luxembourg	W	4-0	Luxembourg	WCq	Nemeth [5], Mintal [15], Kisel [54], Reiter [60]	2 108	Styles ENG

Fr = Friendly match • EC = UEFA EURO 2004™ • WC = FIFA World Cup™ • q = qualifier • BCD = Behind closed doors

SLOVAKIA COUNTRY INFORMATION

Capital	Bratislava	Independence	1993 from Czechoslovakia	GDP per Capita	$13 300
Population	5 423 567	Status	Republic	GNP Ranking	60
Area km²	48 845	Language	Slovak, Hungarian	Dialling code	+421
Population density	111 per km²	Literacy rate	n/a	Internet code	.sk
% in urban areas	59%	Main religion	Christian	GMT +/−	+1
Cities/Towns ('000)	Bratislava 423; Kosice 236; Presov 94; Nitra 86; Zilna 86; Banska Bystrica 82; Trnava 69				
Neighbours (km)	Ukraine 97; Hungary 677; Austria 91; Czech Republic 215; Poland 444				
Main stadia	Tehelné Pole – Bratislava 30 087; Anton Malatinsky – Trnava 18 448				

SLOVAKIA NATIONAL TEAM RECORDS AND RECORD SEQUENCES

Records			Sequence records				
Victory	7-0	LIE 2004	Wins	3	Five times	Clean sheets	4	2000
Defeat	1-6	CRO 1942	Defeats	5	2001	Goals scored	8	1996-1997
Player Caps	73	KARHAN Miroslav	Undefeated	12	2000-2001	Without goal	4	2001
Player Goals	20	NEMETH Slizard	Without win	6	Four times	Goals against	11	2002-2003

NATIONAL CAPS

	Caps
KARHAN Miroslav	73
TOMASCHEK Robert	53
NEMETH Szilard	52
VARGA Stanislav	52
DZURIK Peter	45
KONIG Miroslav	45
TITTEL Dusan	45
BALIS Igor	41

NATIONAL GOALS

	Goals
NEMETH Szilard	20
DUBOVSKY Peter	12
VITTEK Robert	12
JANCULA Tibor	9
REITER Lubomir	9
KARHAN Miroslav	7
TIMKO Jaroslav	7
TITTEL Dusan	7
MORAVCIK Lubomir	6
MINTAL Marek	6

NATIONAL COACH

	Years
VENGLOS Jozef Dr	1993-'95
JANKECH Jozef	1995-'98
GALIS Dusan	1998
RADOLSKY Dusan	1998-'99
ADEMEC Jozef	1999-'01
JURKEMIK Ladislav	2001-'03
GALIS Dusan	2003-

FIFA ASSISTANT REFEREE LIST 2005

	Int'l	DoB
BALKO Martin	1998	8-03-1972
BARTOS Ivan	1997	13-08-1962
CSABAY Roman	1995	15-01-1965
LASKOVSKY Vlastislav	1999	9-10-1965
MEDVED Vladimir	1999	3-05-1961
MUSAK Vladimir	1999	22-08-1967
RUZBARSKY Marian	1999	30-08-1968
SLYSKO Roman	2003	4-08-1973
SOMOLANI Tomas	2005	23-12-1977
SUNIAR Jan	1998	10-08-1968

FIFA REFEREE LIST 2005

	Int'l	DoB
HAVRILLA Richard	2003	31-03-1966
HRINAK Vladimir	1993	25-02-1964
MICHEL Lubos	1993	16-05-1968
OLSIAK Pavel	2005	28-10-1972
STREDAK Anton	1995	24-07-1963

CLUB DIRECTORY

Club	Town/City	Stadium	Phone	www.	Lge	Cup	CL
Artmedia Petrzalka	Bratislava	Petrzalka Stadion 8 000	+421 2 62525717	fcartmedia.sk	1	1	0
Dukla Banská Bystrica	Banská Bystrica	DAC Stadion 16 490	+421 48 4230444	fkdukla.sk	0	1	0
Inter Bratislava	Bratislava	Pasienky Stadion 13 295	+421 2 44371007	askinter.sk	2	3	0
Matador Púchov	Púchov	Matador 5 964	+421 42 4631761	fkmatadorpuchov.sk	0	1	0
FC Rimavská Sobota	Rimavská Sobota	Rimavská Sobota 8 000	+421 47 5631208		0	0	0
MFK Ruzomberok	Ruzomberok	MFK Stadion 5 030	+421 44 4322506	futbalruza.sk	0	0	0
FK AS Trencin	Trencin	Mestsky Stadion 15 712	+421 32 7432346	astn.sk	0	0	0
Spartak Trnava	Trnava	Anton Malatinsky 18 448	+421 33 5503804	spartak.sk	0	1	0
MSK Zilina	Zilina	Pod Dubnon 6 233	+421 41 5626955	mskzilina.sk	3	0	0
ZTS Dubnica	Dubnica Nad	Mestsky Stadion 8 000	+421 42 4420025	fkdubnica.sk	0	0	0

RECENT LEAGUE AND CUP RECORD

	Championship						Cup		
Year	Champions	Pts	Runners-up	Pts	Third	Pts	Winners	Score	Runners-up
1994	Slovan Bratislava	50	Inter Bratislava	40	Dunajska Streda	36	Slovan Bratislava	2-1	Tatran Presov
1995	Slovan Bratislava	72	1.FC Kosice	52	Inter Bratislava	50	Inter Bratislava	1-1 3-1p	Dunajska Streda
1996	Slovan Bratislava	75	1.FC Kosice	65	Spartak Trnava	63	Chemlon Humenné	2-1	Spartak Trnava
1997	1.FC Kosice	70	Spartak Trnava	69	Slovan Bratislava	50	Slovan Bratislava	1-0	Tatran Presov
1998	1.FC Kosice	68	Spartak Trnava	66	Inter Bratislava	60	Spartak Trnava	2-0	1.FC Kosice
1999	Slovan Bratislava	70	Inter Bratislava	68	Spartak Trnava	64	Slovan Bratislava	3-0	Dukla B. Bystrica
2000	Inter Bratislava	70	1.FC Kosice	61	Slovan Bratislava	57	Inter Bratislava	1-1 4-2p	1.FC Kosice
2001	Inter Bratislava	80	Slovan Bratislava	71	SCP Ruzomberok	55	Inter Bratislava	1-0	SCP Ruzomberok
2002	MSK Zilina	69	Matador Púchov	62	Inter Bratislava	56	Koba Senec	1-1 4-2p	Matador Púchov
2003	MSK Zilina	70	Artmedia Bratislava	67	Slovan Bratislava	63	Matador Púchov	2-1	Slovan Bratislava
2004	MSK Zilina	64	Dukla B. Bystrica	64	SCP Ruzomberok	55	Artmedia Bratislava	2-0	Trans Licartovce
2005	Artmedia Bratislava	72	MSK Zilina	65	Dukla B. Bystrica	52	Dukla B. Bystrica	2-1	Artmedia Bratislava

Slovak clubs took part in the Czechoslovak League until the end of the 1992-1993 season

SLOVAKIA 2004-05

CORGON LIGA

	Pl	W	D	L	F	A	Pts	Artmedia	Zilina	Dukla	Dubnica	Trnava	Puchov	Ruzomberok	Trencin	Inter	Rimavská
Artmedia Bratislava	36	20	12	4	64	28	72		1-1 0-0	2-1 3-1	1-1 1-0	3-1 0-0	4-0 6-1	1-2 3-1	1-0 6-1	2-1 3-1	7-1 2-0
MSK Zilina	36	19	8	9	73	34	65	5-1 0-1		4-0 2-1	2-2 5-0	2-1 1-0	3-0 0-1	6-0 3-0	2-2 1-0	1-1 7-3	3-0 5-0
Dukla Banská Bystrica	36	13	13	10	45	38	52	0-0 0-0	1-1 1-0		3-0 3-1	4-2 0-0	1-1 2-0	0-0 2-1	2-1 1-1	1-2 2-0	3-0 3-2
ZTS Dubnica nad Vahom	36	13	12	11	42	43	51	1-1 0-2	3-1 0-0	2-2 1-0		2-0 0-1	2-0 1-1	0-3 3-2	1-1 0-0	2-2 0-0	2-0 3-0
Spartak Trnava	36	12	10	14	39	37	46	1-0 0-1	0-1 3-1	2-0 3-0	1-0		3-1 1-0	1-2 1-2	1-1 1-2	0-0 1-1	1-1 1-0
Matador Púchov	36	12	10	14	31	43	46	0-1 1-1	1-0 0-1	0-0 0-0	1-2 0-1	3-2 1-0		0-1 1-0	2-1 3-0	2-1 1-0	2-0 1-1
MFK Ruzomberok	36	11	10	15	50	57	43	1-1 2-2	2-1 2-3	2-2 0-0	0-2 1-2	2-2 0-3	1-2 0-0		1-1 2-0	2-2 6-0	4-1 0-0
AS Trencin	36	12	7	17	36	50	43	1-0 0-1	4-2 2-1	3-2 0-1	0-4 1-1	0-1 2-1	0-1 2-0	3-0 0-2		2-0 0-1	1-0 1-0
Inter Bratislava	36	9	11	16	37	60	38	1-3 1-1	1-4 2-0	0-1 3-1	1-1 1-1	1-1 0-0	1-0 1-5	2-1 1-2	2-0		2-2 1-0
Rimavská Sobota	36	7	11	18	30	57	32	0-1 1-1	0-0 0-3	1-1 0-1	1-1 1-0	0-0 2-1	1-1 3-3	2-0 3-0	2-1 3-0	1-0 0-1	

24/07/2004 - 15/06/2005 • † Qualified for the UEFA Champions League • ‡ Qualified for the UEFA Cup

SLOVAKIA 2004-05
II LIGA (2)

	Pl	W	D	L	F	A	Pts
FC Nitra	30	21	6	3	59	16	69
Trans Licartovce	30	18	6	6	66	26	60
Slovan Bratislava	30	14	8	8	37	24	50
Zemplin Michalovce	30	14	5	11	44	35	47
Tatran Presov	30	12	8	10	38	33	44
Slovan Duslo Sala	30	12	7	11	34	32	43
OFK Velky Lapas	30	10	12	8	41	34	42
DAC Dunajská Streda	30	12	6	12	33	45	42
Sport Podbrezová	30	11	8	11	28	22	41
KOBA Senec	30	11	8	12	40	37	41
Druzstevnik Bác	30	11	8	11	38	43	41
Zlaté Moravce	30	9	10	11	32	37	37
Rapid Bratislava	30	7	9	14	37	50	30
Slavoj Trebisov	30	8	7	17	28	50	29
HFK Prievidza	30	7	8	15	26	57	29
SK Kremnicka	30	5	2	23	25	65	17

24/07/2004 - 15/06/2005

SLOVENSKY POHAR 2004-05

Second Round

Dukla Banská Bystrica*	4
HFK Prievidza	1
SK Kremnicka *	1
Inter Bratislava	2
Vion Zlaté Moravce	1
Spartak Trnava *	0
Slovan Duslo Sala	0
MSK Zilina *	3
Trans Licartovce *	2
MFK Ruzomberok	1
Matador Púchov	1 2p
Rimavská Sobota *	1 4p
Slovan Bratislava	0 5p
AS Trencin *	0 3p
FC Nitra	0
Artmedia Petrzalka *	2

Quarter-finals

Dukla Banská Bystrica	2 0
Inter Bratislava *	0 1
Vion Zlaté Moravce	1 0
MSK Zilina *	3 2
Trans Licartovce	1 3
Rimavská Sobota *	0 0
Slovan Bratislava *	0 0
Artmedia Petrzalka	0 4

Semi-finals

Dukla Banská Bystrica	0 2
MSK Zilina *	0 1
Trans Licartovce	1 1
Artmedia Petrzalka *	2 2

Final

Dukla Banská Bystrica ‡	2
Artmedia Petrzalka	1

CUP FINAL

8-05-2005, Att: 2 474, Ref: Michel
Nitra Stadion, Nitra

Scorers - Pecovsky [5], Jakubko [24] for Dukla; Soltis [65] for Artmedia

* Home team/home team in the first leg • ‡ Qualified for the UEFA Cup

SVN – SLOVENIA

NATIONAL TEAM RECORD
JULY 1ST 2002 TO JUNE 30TH 2005

PL	W	D	L	F	A	%
26	8	8	10	28	35	46.2

FIFA/COCA-COLA WORLD RANKING

1993	1994	1995	1996	1997	1998	1999	2000	2001	2002	2003	2004	High		Low	
134	81	71	77	95	88	40	35	25	36	31	42	25	12/01	134	02/94

2004-2005											
08/04	09/04	10/04	11/04	12/04	01/05	02/05	03/05	04/05	05/05	06/05	07/05
43	46	43	40	42	42	43	44	46	46	44	47

For the last five or six years the Slovenian national team has punched well above its weight with qualification for the finals of UEFA EURO 2000™ and the finals of the 2002 FIFA World Cup™ an incredible achievement for this small Alpine nation of just two million people in which winter sports are the abiding passion. The question is can Slovenia maintain these high standards? The qualifiers for the 2006 FIFA World Cup™ did nothing to dispel the feeling that they can especially in light of the 1-0 victory over Italy in Celje, the second time since the 2002 finals that Slovenia have managed to beat the Italians. Indeed, the Slovenians have become a bit of a bogey team for

INTERNATIONAL HONOURS
Qualified for the FIFA World Cup™ finals 2002

their neighbours and are one of the very few sides who historically do not have a negative record against the Azzurri. For the second season in a row NK Gorica won the Championship firmly ending Maribor's undisputed reign as the top team in the country. After winning seven consecutive titles between 1997 and 2003, Maribor had a terrible season, ending up in the relegation group when the Championship split after 22 rounds and for only the third time since independence finished the season trophyless. Publikum Celje denied Gorica the double when the two met in the Cup Final with an own goal giving Publikum their first trophy.

THE FIFA BIG COUNT OF 2000

	Male	Female		Male	Female
Registered players	15 072	90	Referees	912	2
Non registered players	50 000	200	Officials	4 500	40
Youth players	10 063	55	Total involved	80 934	
Total players	75 480		Number of clubs	243	
Professional players	354	0	Number of teams	1 510	

Football Association of Slovenia (NZS)
Nogometna Zveza Slovenije, Cerinova 4, PO Box 3986, Ljubljana 1001, Slovenia
Tel +386 1 5300400   Fax +386 1 5300410
nzs@nzs.si   www.nzs.si
President: ZAVRL Rudi   General Secretary: JOST Danijel
Vice-President: ILESIC Marko   Treasurer: SPACAPAN Ertomir   Media Officer: SINKOVC Rok
Men's Coach: OBLAK Branko   Women's Coach: SKRINJAR Anton
NZS formed: 1920   UEFA: 1992   FIFA: 1992
Colours: White with green sleeves, White, White

GAMES PLAYED BY SLOVENIA IN THE 2006 FIFA WORLD CUP™ CYCLE

2002	Opponents	Score		Venue	Comp	Scorers	Att	Referee
21-08	Italy	W	1-0	Trieste	Fr	Cimirotic [32]	11 080	Brugger AUT
7-09	Malta	W	3-0	Ljubljana	ECq	OG [37], Siljak [59], Cimirotic [90]	7 000	Borovilos GRE
12-10	France	L	0-5	Paris	ECq		77 619	Milton Nielsen DEN
2003								
12-02	Switzerland	L	1-5	Nova Gorica	Fr	Rakovic [79]	3 500	Abraham HUN
2-04	Cyprus	W	4-1	Ljubljana	ECq	Siljak 2 [5 14], Zahovic [39p], Ceh.N [43]	5 000	Gomes Costa POR
30-04	Malta	W	3-1	Ta'Qali	ECq	Zahovic [15], Siljak 2 [37 57]	5 000	Hanacsek HUN
7-06	Israel	D	0-0	Antalya	ECq		2 500	Busacca SUI
20-08	Hungary	W	2-1	Murska Sobota	Fr	Sukalo [3], Cimirotic [75]	5 000	Sowa AUT
6-09	Israel	W	3-1	Ljubljana	ECq	Siljak [35], Knavs [37], Ceh.N [78]	8 000	Fandel GER
10-09	France	L	0-2	Ljubljana	ECq		8 000	Messina ITA
11-10	Cyprus	D	2-2	Limassol	ECq	Siljak 2 [12 42]	2 346	Ovrebo NOR
15-11	Croatia	D	1-1	Zagreb	ECpo	Siljak [22]	35 000	Merk GER
19-11	Croatia	L	0-1	Ljubljana	ECpo		9 000	Meier SUI
2004								
18-02	Poland	L	0-2	Cadiz	Fr		100	Barea Lopez ESP
31-03	Latvia	L	0-1	Celje	Fr		1 500	Stredak SVK
28-04	Switzerland	L	1-2	Geneva	Fr	Zahovic [45]	7 500	Bossen NED
18-08	Serbia & Montenegro	D	1-1	Ljubljana	Fr	Ceh.N [83]	8 000	Ovrebo NOR
4-09	Moldova	W	3-0	Celje	WCq	Acimovic 3 [5 27 48]	3 620	Hyytia FIN
8-09	Scotland	D	0-0	Glasgow	WCq		38 279	Larsen DEN
9-10	Italy	W	1-0	Celje	WCq	Cesar [82]	9 262	De Bleeckere BEL
13-10	Norway	L	0-3	Oslo	WCq		24 907	Ivanov.V RUS
17-11	Slovakia	D	0-0	Trnava	Fr		5 482	Skjerven NOR
2005								
9-02	Czech Republic	L	0-3	Celje	Fr		4 000	Strahonja CRO
26-03	Germany	L	0-1	Celje	Fr		9 000	Poll ENG
30-03	Belarus	D	1-1	Celje	WCq	Rodic [44]	6 450	Al Ghamdi KSA
4-06	Belarus	D	1-1	Minsk	WCq	Ceh.N [17]	29 042	Hansson SWE

Fr = Friendly match • EC = UEFA EURO 2004™ • WC = FIFA World Cup™ • q = qualifier • po = play-off

SLOVENIA COUNTRY INFORMATION

Capital	Ljubljana	Independence	1991 from Yugoslavia	GDP per Capita	$19 000
Population	2 011 473	Status	Republic	GNP Ranking	65
Area km²	20 273	Language	Slovenian, Serbo-Croat	Dialling code	+386
Population density	99 per km²	Literacy rate	99%	Internet code	.si
% in urban areas	64%	Main religion	Christian	GMT + / −	+1
Towns/Cities ('000)	Ljubljana 255; Maribor 89; Celje 37; Kranj 35; Velenje 26; Koper 23; Ptuj 18; Trbovlje 16				
Neighbours (km)	Hungary 102; Croatia 670; Italy 232; Austria 330; Adriatic Sea 46				
Main stadia	Ljudski Vrt – Maribor 10 210; Sportni Park – Celje 8 600; Bezigrad – Ljubljana 8 211				

SLOVENIA NATIONAL TEAM RECORDS AND RECORD SEQUENCES

Records			Sequence records					
Victory	7-0	OMA 1999	Wins	4	1998	Clean sheets	4	2002
Defeat	0-5	FRA 1999, FRA 2002	Defeats	4	1997, 1998	Goals scored	9	2001-2002
Player Caps	80	ZAHOVIC Zlatko	Undefeated	8	2001	Without goal	4	2004-2005
Player Goals	35	ZAHOVIC Zlatko	Without win	8	2003-2004	Goals against	13	1997-1998

NATIONAL CAPS

	Caps
ZAHOVIC Zlatko	80
CEH Ales	74
NOVAK Dzoni	71
GALIC Marinko	66
RUDONJA Mladen	65
KARIC Amir	64
ACIMOVIC Milenko	63
PAVLIN Miran	63
KNAVS Aleksander	58
SIMEUNOVIC Marko	57

NATIONAL GOALS

	Goals
ZAHOVIC Zlatko	35
UDOVIC Saso	16
SILJAK Ermin	14
ACIMOVIC Milenko	13
GLIHA Primoz	10
OSTERC Milan	8
CEH Nastja	6
PAVLIN Miran	5
CIMIROTIC Sebastjan	4

NATIONAL COACH

	Years
PRASNIKAR Bojan	1992-'93
VERDENIK Zdenko	1993-'97
PRASNIKAR Bojan	1997-'98
KATANEC Srecko	1998-'02
PRASNIKAR Bojan	2002-'04
OBLAK Branco	2004-

FIFA REFEREE LIST 2005

	Int'l	DoB
CEFERIN Darko	2000	11-07-1968
KOS Drago	1998	13-01-1961
KRANJC Robert	2002	18-01-1969
SKOMINA Damir	2003	5-08-1976

FIFA ASSISTANT REFEREE LIST 2005

	Int'l	DoB
AHAR Primoz	2003	19-05-1968
KOGEJ Milan	2005	30-07-1967
KOKOLJ Andrej	1999	29-01-1969
STANCIN Marko	2005	5-04-1968
ZIRNSTEIN Robert	2003	30-06-1965
ZUPANCIC Igor	2001	9-04-1968

CLUB DIRECTORY

Club	Town/City	Stadium	Phone	www.	Lge	Cup	CL
NK Bela Krajina	Crnomelj	Bela Krajina Stadion 1 500	+386 73 052500		0	0	0
NK Domzale	Domzale	Sportni Park 3 212	+386 17 226550	nogometniklub-domzale.si	0	0	0
NK Drava	Ptuj	Mestni Stadion 1 950	+386 27 797431	nkptuj-klub.si	0	0	0
NK Gorica	Nova Gorica	Sportni Park 4 200	+386 5 3334086	nd-gorica.com	3	2	0
FC Koper	Koper	SRC Bonifika Stadion 3 557	+386 56 395050	nkkoper.net	0	0	0
NK Ljubljana	Ljubljana	ZSD Ljubljana Stadion 5 000	+386 1 4386470		0	0	0
NK Maribor	Maribor	Ljudski vrt Stadion 10 210	+386 22 284700	nkmaribor.com	7	5	0
NK Mura	Murska Sobota	Fazanerija Stadion 5 400	+386 25 349290	snkmura.com	0	1	0
NK Olimpija Ljubljana	Ljubljana	Bezigrad Stadion 8 211	+386 1 5300300	nkolimpija.com	4	4	0
NK Primorje	Ajdovscina	Primorje Stadion 3 000	+386 53 661042	nkprimorje.com	0	0	0
NK Publikum	Celje	Sportni Park 8 600	+386 35 482250	publikum.com	0	1	0
NK Zagorje	Zagorje Obsavi	Zagorje Stadion 2 000	+386 35 668915		0	0	0

RECENT LEAGUE AND CUP RECORD

	Championship						Cup		
Year	Champions	Pts	Runners-up	Pts	Third	Pts	Winners	Score	Runners-up
1992	Olimpija Ljubljana	66	NK Maribor	59	Izola Belvedur	56	NK Maribor	0-0 4-3p	Olimpija Ljubljana
1993	Olimpija Ljubljana	52	NK Maribor	48	Mura Murska Sobota	46	Olimpija Ljubljana	2-1	Publikum Celje
1994	Olimpija Ljubljana	51	Mura Murska Sobota	45	NK Maribor	42	NK Maribor	0-1 3-1	Mura Murska Sobota
1995	Olimpija Ljubljana	44	NK Maribor	42	ND Gorica	41	Mura Murska Sobota	1-1 1-0	Publikum Celje
1996	ND Gorica	67	Olimpija Ljubljana	64	Mura Murska Sobota	58	Olimpija Ljubljana	1-0 1-1	Primorje Ajdovscina
1997	NK Maribor	71	Primorje Ajdovscina	66	ND Gorica	65	NK Maribor	0-0 3-0	Primorje Ajdovscina
1998	NK Maribor	67	Mura Murska Sobota	57	ND Gorica	65	Rudar Velenje	1-2 3-0	Primorje Ajdovscina
1999	NK Maribor	66	ND Gorica	62	Rudar Velenje	56	NK Maribor	3-2 2-0	Olimpija Ljubljana
2000	NK Maribor	81	ND Gorica	62	Rudar Velenje	58	Olimpija Ljubljana	1-2 2-0	Korotan Prevalje
2001	NK Maribor	62	Olimpija Ljubljana	60	Primorje Ajdovscina	56	ND Gorica	0-1 4-2	Olimpija Ljubljana
2002	NK Maribor	66	Primorje Ajdovscina	60	FC Koper	56	ND Gorica	4-0 2-1	Aluminij Kidricevo
2003	NK Maribor	62	Publikum Celje	55	Olimpija Ljubljana	54	Olimpija Ljubljana	1-1 2-2	Publikum Celje
2004	ND Gorica	56	Olimpija Ljubljana	55	NK Maribor	54	NK Maribor	4-0 3-4	Koroska Dravograd
2005	ND Gorica	65	Domzale	52	Publikum Celje	52	Publikum Celje	1-0	ND Gorica

Slovenian clubs played in the Yugoslav League until the end of the 1990-1991 season

SLOVENIA 2004-05

SIMOBIL LIGA

	Pl	W	D	L	F	A	Pts	Gorica	Domzale	Celje	Ajdovscina	Ptuj	Olimpija	Maribor	Mura	Ljubljana	Bela	Koper	Zagorje
ND Gorica †	32	18	11	3	49	23	65		2-0 0-0	0-1 2-0	0-0 1-1	1-2 0-0	2-0 2-0	2-1	2-0	0-0	1-1	2-0	6-0
Domzale ‡	32	14	10	8	48	36	52	1-2 1-1		2-0 1-0	1-2 1-1	3-2 3-3	0-1 3-0	2-1	0-0	6-1	3-1	1-1	0-0
Publikum Celje ‡	32	16	4	12	47	28	52	1-1 0-1	2-3 3-1		2-0 1-0	0-1 1-2	4-1 2-1	2-2	2-0	3-0	2-0	3-0	2-0
Primorje Ajdovscina	32	12	10	10	37	30	46	2-3 0-2	3-1 0-1	1-0 2-0		0-0 1-1	2-0 0-0	3-1	3-1	0-0	4-0	2-1	0-0
Drava Ptuj	32	12	10	10	40	36	46	2-2 0-0	0-1 0-1	1-0 0-1	0-2 1-1		0-0 4-1	2-0	2-0	2-4	0-1	3-2	2-1
Olimpija Ljubljana §	32	10	7	15	34	52	37	2-3 1-1	1-1 1-3	1-4 0-6	2-1 2-3	2-0 2-1		1-0	0-2	4-1	2-0	2-0	1-0
NK Maribor	32	15	6	11	47	36	51	1-2	1-1	2-0	1-0	2-1	0-3		1-1 2-0	0-2 3-0	5-0 2-0	0-0 1-1	2-0 3-0
Mura Murska Sobota	32	11	11	10	43	38	44	1-2	2-0	0-0	2-2	3-1	1-1	2-3 1-3		1-2 1-1	3-1 0-0	1-3 3-2	2-0 2-1
Ljubljana	32	10	12	10	38	43	42	4-0	1-1	0-2	3-0	1-1	0-1	1-2 1-0	1-4 0-0		1-0 0-2	2-0 0-1	1-3 1-1
Bela Krajina Crnomelj	32	9	10	13	31	44	37	0-1	1-2	2-1	1-0	2-3	1-0	1-2 3-0	2-2 1-1	1-1 3-0		1-4 1-0	1-0 0-0
FC Koper	32	9	9	14	38	41	36	0-2	0-2	0-1	1-0	0-0	1-1	1-3 3-1	0-0 2-2	2-1 1-1	1-1 1-0		3-0 5-0
Zagorje	32	2	8	22	17	62	14	1-3	3-2	1-1	0-1	0-1	2-2	0-0 0-2	0-3 0-2	1-1 1-3	1-1 1-3	1-0 2-4	

30/07/2004 - 28/05/2005 • † Qualified for the UEFA Champions League • ‡ Qualified for the UEFA Cup • § Olimpija relegated on financial grounds

SLOVENIA 2004-05 2.SNL (2)

	Pl	W	D	L	F	A	Pts
Rudar Velenje	33	23	3	7	76	40	72
Nafta Lendava	33	20	10	3	67	28	70
Svoboda Ljubljana	33	18	7	8	52	33	61
Dravinja	33	18	4	11	43	36	58
Koroska Dravograd	33	15	9	9	55	43	54
Livar Ivancna Gorica	33	15	4	14	48	38	49
Aluminij Kidricevo	33	14	5	14	68	51	47
Supernova Kranj	33	12	10	11	50	39	46
Factor Ljubljana	33	12	2	19	49	58	38
Krsko	33	11	5	17	46	59	38
Izola-Argeta	33	4	7	22	25	71	19
Smartno ob Paki §	33	2	2	29	25	108	5

8/08/2004 - 5/06/2005 • § Three points deducted

POKAL HERVIS 2004-05

Eighth-finals

Publikum Celje *	2
Izola Argeta	0
Factor Ljubljana	0
Olimpija Ljubljana *	2
Mura Murska Sobota *	4
Smartno ob Paki	0
FC Koper *	1
NK Maribor	2
Nafta Lendava	2
Aluminij Kidricevo *	1
Primorje Ajdovscina	2
Koroska Dravograd *	5
Domzale *	2
Ljubljana	1
Zavrc	0
ND Gorica *	6

Quarter-finals

Publikum Celje *	1 4p
Olimpija Ljubljana	1 2p
Mura Murska Sobota	0
NK Maribor *	2
Nafta Lendava *	9
Koroska Dravograd	2
Domzale *	2
ND Gorica	4

Semi-finals

Publikum Celje	1 3
NK Maribor *	2 1
Nafta Lendava	0 0
ND Gorica *	2 1

Final

Publikum Celje ‡	1
ND Gorica	0

* Home team/home team in the first leg • ‡ Qualified for the UEFA Cup

CUP FINAL

17-05-2005, Att: 4 000, Ref: Kos
Arena Petrol, Celje

Scorer - Lungu OG [17] for Publicum

SWE – SWEDEN

NATIONAL TEAM RECORD
JULY 1ST 2002 TO JUNE 30TH 2005

PL	W	D	L	F	A	%
41	18	13	10	90	42	59.8

FIFA/COCA-COLA WORLD RANKING

1993	1994	1995	1996	1997	1998	1999	2000	2001	2002	2003	2004	High		Low	
9	3	13	17	18	18	16	23	16	25	19	13	2	11/94	31	08/98

2004-2005											
08/04	09/04	10/04	11/04	12/04	01/05	02/05	03/05	04/05	05/05	06/05	07/05
20	22	22	15	13	13	13	13	13	13	12	17

The 2004 Championship in Sweden went right to the wire. With Halmstad leading Malmö on goal difference going into the final game they could only manage a 1-1 draw against IFK Göteborg. The match between Malmö and Elfsborg was decided by a penalty and although Niklas Skoog missed the initial kick Norwegian defender Jon-Inge Höiland scored from the rebound to give Malmö a 1-0 victory and their first title for 15 years. Defending champions Djurgården IF missed out on a hat-trick of titles but they had the consolation of beating IFK Göteborg in the Cup Final to continue their revival of recent years. For IFK there was also the heartbreak of defeat in the final

INTERNATIONAL HONOURS

Olympic Games Gold 1948 Qualified for the FIFA World Cup™ finals 1934 1938 1950 1959 (Hosts) 1970 1974 1978 1990 1994 2002
Women's European Championship 1984 Qualified for the FIFA Women's World Cup 1991 1995 1999 2003

of the inaugural Scandinavian Royal League. In the final played in Gothenburg they drew 1-1 with FC København but then lost a dramatic penalty shoot-out 11-10 when George Mourad missed with his second spot-kick. In the 2006 FIFA World Cup™ qualifying campaign the Swedes got off to the worst possible start when they lost at home to an in-form Croatia in what turned out to be a very tight battle between the two for the one automatic qualifying spot while the women's team lost to Norway in the semi-finals of the UEFA European Women's Championship.

THE FIFA BIG COUNT OF 2000

	Male	Female		Male	Female
Registered players	123 612	25 535	Referees	15 300	1 200
Non registered players	300 000	75 000	Officials	10 000	200
Youth players	37 397	14 864	Total involved	603 108	
Total players	576 408		Number of clubs	3 228	
Professional players	1 500	0	Number of teams	25 000	

Svenska Fotbollförbundet (SVFF)
PO Box 1216, Solna 17 123, Sweden
Tel +46 8 7350900   Fax +46 8 7350901
svff@svenskfotboll.se   www.svenskfotboll.se
President: LAGRELL Lars-Ake   General Secretary: HELLSTROMER Sune
Vice-President: MADSEN Bengt   Treasurer: SAHLSTROEM Kjell   Media Officer: NYSTEDT Jonas
Men's Coach: LAGERBACK Lars   Women's Coach: DOMANSKI LYFORS Marika
SVFF formed: 1904   UEFA: 1954   FIFA: 1954
Colours: Yellow, Blue, Yellow

GAMES PLAYED BY SWEDEN IN THE 2006 FIFA WORLD CUP™ CYCLE

2002 Opponents	Score	Venue	Comp	Scorers	Att	Referee
21-08 Russia	D 1-1	Moscow	Fr	Ibrahimovic [90]	23 000	Poulat FRA
7-09 Latvia	D 0-0	Riga	ECq		8 500	De Bleeckere BEL
12-10 Hungary	D 1-1	Stockholm	ECq	Ibrahimovic [76]	35 084	Stark GER
16-10 Portugal	L 2-3	Gothenburg	Fr	Pettersson [6], Allback [24]	30 047	Vassaras GRE
20-11 Czech Republic	D 3-3	Teplice	Fr	Nilsson.M 2 [29 43], Allback [65]	10 238	Bosat TUR
2003						
12-02 Tunisia	L 0-1	Tunis	Fr		20 000	Haimoudi ALG
16-02 Qatar	W 3-2	Bangkok	Fr	Elmander 2 [16 24], Skoog [82]	5 000	Hanlumyaung THA
18-02 Korea DPR	D 1-1	Bangkok	Fr	Skoog [21]	4 000	Rungklay THA
20-02 Thailand	W 4-1	Bangkok	Fr	OG [47], Elmander [63], Farnerud.A [66], Majstorovic [69]	4 000	Lee Gui Young PRK
22-02 Korea DPR	W 4-0	Bangkok	Fr	Skoog 2 [3 77], Grahn [26], Johannesson [56]	10 000	Kunsuta THA
2-04 Hungary	W 2-1	Budapest	ECq	Allback 2 [34 66]	28 000	Cortez Batista POR
30-04 Croatia	L 1-2	Stockholm	Fr	Ibrahimovic [33]	15 109	Van Egmond NED
7-06 San Marino	W 6-0	Serravalle	ECq	Jonson.M 3 [16 60 71], Allback 2 [52 86], Ljungberg [55]	2 184	Delevic SCG
11-06 Poland	W 3-0	Stockholm	ECq	Svensson.A 2 [15 71], Allback [43]	35 220	Veissiere FRA
20-08 Greece	L 1-2	Norrköping	Fr	Svensson.A [16]	15 018	Hyytia FIN
6-09 San Marino	W 5-0	Gothenburg	ECq	Jonson.M [33], Jakobsson [49], Ibrahimovic 2 [56 83p], Kallstrom [68p]	31 098	Messner AUT
10-09 Poland	W 2-0	Chorzow	ECq	Nilsson [2], Mellberg [36]	20 000	Riley ENG
11-10 Latvia	L 0-1	Stockholm	ECq		32 095	De Santis ITA
18-11 Egypt	L 0-1	Cairo	Fr		15 000	Abdallah LBY
2004						
22-01 Norway	L 0-3	Hong Kong	Fr		10 000	Fong HKG
18-02 Albania	L 1-2	Tirana	Fr	Selakovic [50]	15 000	Paparesta ITA
31-03 England	W 1-0	Gothenburg	Fr	Ibrahimovic [54]	40 464	Ovrebo NOR
28-04 Portugal	D 2-2	Coimbra	Fr	Kallstrom [17], OG [86]	15 000	Ceferin SVN
28-05 Finland	W 3-1	Tammerfors	Fr	Anders Andersson [30], Allback 2 [45 82]	16 500	Undiano Mallenco ESP
5-06 Poland	W 3-1	Stockholm	Fr	Larsson [42], Jakobsson [54], Allback [72]	28 281	Kelly IRL
14-06 Bulgaria	W 5-0	Lisbon	ECr1	Ljungberg [32], Larsson 2 [57 58], Ibrahimovic [78p], Allback [90]	31 652	Riley ENG
18-06 Italy	D 1-1	Porto	ECr1	Ibrahimovic [85]	44 927	Meier SUI
22-06 Denmark	D 2-2	Porto	ECr1	Larsson [47p], Jonson.M [89]	26 115	Merk GER
26-06 Netherlands	D 0-0	Faro-Loule	ECqf		27 286	Michel SVK
18-08 Netherlands	D 2-2	Stockholm	Fr	Jonson.M [4], Ibrahimovic [69]	20 377	Styles ENG
4-09 Malta	W 7-0	Ta'Qali	WCq	Ibrahimovic 4 [4 11 14 71], Ljungberg 2 [46 74], Larsson [76]	4 200	Jakov ISR
8-09 Croatia	L 0-1	Gothenburg	WCq		40 023	Dauden Ibanez ESP
9-10 Hungary	W 3-0	Stockholm	WCq	Ljungberg [26], Larsson [50], Svensson.A [67]	32 288	Dougal SCO
13-10 Iceland	W 4-1	Reykjavik	WCq	Larsson 2 [24 39], Allback [27], Wilhelmsson [45]	7 037	Busacca SUI
17-11 Scotland	W 4-1	Edinburgh	Fr	Allback 2 [27 49], Elmander [72], Berglund [73]	15 071	Jara CZE
2005						
22-01 Korea Republic	D 1-1	Carson	Fr	Rosenberg [86]	9 941	Stott USA
26-01 Mexico	D 0-0	San Diego	Fr		35 521	Hall USA
9-02 France	D 1-1	Paris	Fr	Ljungberg [11]	59 923	Rodriguez Santiago ESP
26-03 Bulgaria	W 3-0	Sofia	WCq	Ljungberg 2 [17 92+p], Edman [74]	42 530	Fandel GER
4-06 Malta	W 6-0	Gothenburg	WCq	Jonson [6], Svensson.A [18], Wilhelmsson [29], Ibrahimovic [40], Ljungberg [57], Elmander [81]	35 593	Ivanov.N RUS
8-06 Norway	L 2-3	Stockholm	Fr	Kallstrom [16], Elmander [68]	15 345	Jara CZE

Fr = Friendly match • EC = UEFA EURO 2004™ • WC = FIFA World Cup™ • q = qualifier • r1 = first round group • qf = quarter-final

SWEDEN COUNTRY INFORMATION

Capital	Stockholm	Independence	1523	GDP per Capita	$26 800
Population	8 986 400	Status	Constitutional monarchy	GNP Ranking	21
Area km²	449 964	Language	Swedish	Dialling code	+46
Population density	20 per km²	Literacy rate	99%	Internet code	.se
% in urban areas	83%	Main religion	Lutheran	GMT +/-	+1
Towns/Cities ('000)	Stockolm 1 253; Göteborg 515; Malmö 261; Uppsala 127; Västeras 107; Örebro 98; Linköping 96; Helsingborg 91; Jönköping 83; Norrköping 82; Lund 76; Umeå 74; Gävle 63; Borås 63;				
Neighbours (km)	Finland 614; Norway 1 619; Baltic Sea & Gulf of Bothnia 3 218				
Main stadia	Råsunda – Solna, Stockholm 37 000; Nya Ullevi – Göteborg 43 200				

NATIONAL CAPS

	Caps
RAVELLI Thomas	143
NILSSON Roland	116
NORDQVIST Björn	115
ANDERSSON Patrick	96
BERGMARK Orvar	94
ANDERSSON Kennet	83
LARSSON Henrik	82
HELLSTROM Ronnie	77
ALEXANDERSSON Niclas	77

NATIONAL GOALS

	Goals
RYDELL Sven	49
NORDAHL Gunnar	43
GREN Gunnar	32
LARSSON Henrik	32
ANDERSSON Kennet	31
DAHLIN Martin	29
SIMONSSON Agne	27
BROLIN Tomas	26
KAUFELDT Per	23

NATIONAL COACH

	Years
NYMAN Lennart	1962-'65
BERGMARK Orvar	1966-'70
ERICSON Georg	1971-'79
ARNESSON Lars	1980-'85
NORDIN Olle	1986-'90
ANDERSSON Nils	1990
SVENSSON Tommy	1991-'97
SVENSSON/SODERBERG	1997
SODERBERG/LAGERBACK	1998-'04
LAGERBACK Lars	2004-

SWEDEN NATIONAL TEAM RECORDS AND RECORD SEQUENCES

Records			Sequence records				
Victory	12-0	LVA 1927, KOR 1948	Wins	11	2001	Clean sheets	9	2001
Defeat	1-12	ENG 1908	Defeats	6	1908-1909	Goals scored	28	1958-1962
Player Caps	143	RAVELLI Thomas	Undefeated	23	2000-2002	Without goal	4	1998
Player Goals	49	RYDELL Sven	Without win	15	1920-1921	Goals against	17	1925-1927

CLUB DIRECTORY

Club	Town/City	Stadium	Phone	www.	Lge	Cup	CL
Assyriska Föreningen	Södertälje	Bara IP 7 600	+46 8 55067018	assyria.se	0	0	0
Djurgårdens IF	Stockholm	Stockholms Stadion 14 500	+46 8 54515800	dif.se	10	3	0
IF Elfsborg	Borås	Borås Arena 14 500	+46 33 139191	elfsborg.se	4	2	0
Gefle IF	Gävle	Strömvallen 6 200	+46 26 652233	geflefotboll.com	0	0	0
BK Häcken	Gothenburg	Rambergsvallen 8 480	+46 31 506790	hacken.o.se	0	0	0
Halmstads BK	Halmstad	Orjans Vall 15 500	+46 35 171880	halmstadsbk.se	4	1	0
Hammarby	Stockholm	Söderstadion 16 000	+46 8 4628810	hammarbyfotboll.se	1	0	0
Helsingborgs IF	Helsingborg	Olympia Stadion 16 673	+46 42 377000	hif.se	6	2	0
IFK Göteborg	Gothenburg	Gamla Ullevi 15 845	+46 31 7037300	ifkgoteborg.se	17	4	0
Kalmar FF	Kalmar	Fredriksskans 8 500	+46 480 444430	kalmarff.se	0	2	0
Landskrona BoIS	Landskrona	Landskrona IP 11 500	+46 41 856190	landskronobois.com	0	1	0
Malmö FF	Malmö	Malmö Stadion 26 500	+46 40 326600	mff.se	15	14	0
Orgryte IS	Gothenburg	Gamla Ullevi 15 845	+46 31 866770	ois.o.se	14	1	0
GIF Sundsvall	Sundsvall	Idrottsparken 8 800	+46 60 663770	sundsvall.nu/gifsundsvall	0	0	0

RECENT LEAGUE AND CUP RECORD

Championship						Cup		
Year	Champions	Pts	Runners-up	Pts	Third	Pts	Winners	Score	Runners-up
1991	IFK Göteborg	36	IFK Norrköping	31	Orebro SK	28	IFK Göteborg	3-2	AIK Stockholm
1992	AIK Stockholm	34	IFK Norrköping	32	Osters IF	30	No tournament due to a season readjustment		
1993	IFK Göteborg	59	IFK Norrköping	54	AIK Stockholm	46	Degerfors IF	3-0	Landskrona BoIS
1994	IFK Göteborg	54	Orebro SK	52	Malmö FF	49	IFK Norrköping	4-3	Helsingborgs IF
1995	IFK Göteborg	46	Helsingborgs IF	42	Halmstads BK	41	Halmstads BK	3-1	AIK Stockholm
1996	IFK Göteborg	56	Malmö FF	46	Helsingborgs IF	44	AIK Stockholm	1-0	Malmö FF
1997	Halmstads BK	52	IFK Göteborg	49	Malmö FF	46	AIK Stockholm	2-1	IF Elfsborg
1998	AIK Stockholm	46	Helsingborgs IF	44	Hammarby IF	42	Helsingborgs IF	1-1 1-1 3-0p	Orgryte IS
1999	Helsingborgs IF	54	AIK Stockholm	53	Halmstads BK	48	AIK Stockholm	1-0 0-0	IFK Göteborg
2000	Halmstads BK	52	Helsingborgs IF	46	AIK Stockholm	45	Orgryte IS	2-0 0-1	IFK Göteborg
2001	Hammarby IF	48	Djurgårdens IF	47	AIK Stockholm	45	IF Elfsborg	1-1 9-8p	AIK Stockholm
2002	Djurgårdens IF	52	Malmö FF	46	Orgryte IS	44	Djurgårdens IF	1-0	AIK Stockholm
2003	Djurgårdens IF	58	Hammarby IF	51	Malmö FF	48	IF Elfsborg	2-0	Assyriska
2004	Malmö FF	52	Halmstads BK	50	IFK Göteborg	47	Djurgårdens IF	3-1	IFK Göteborg

SWEDEN 2004

ALLSVENSKAN

	Pl	W	D	L	F	A	Pts	Malmö	Halmstad	Göteborg	Djurgården	Kalmar	Hammarby	Orebro	Sundsvall	Elfsborg	Helsingborg	Landskrona	Orgryte	AIK	Trelleborg
Malmö FF †	26	15	7	4	44	21	52		2-1	1-0	2-0	0-0	4-3	5-1	0-0	1-0	1-1	0-1	1-0	0-0	4-2
Halmstads BK ‡	26	14	8	4	53	27	50	2-2		1-1	2-2	1-0	2-1	5-0	1-0	3-0	3-2	5-3	2-2	1-2	1-0
IFK Göteborg	26	14	5	7	33	20	47	1-2	0-0		2-0	1-0	0-1	1-0	0-1	3-0	2-2	1-1	4-0	1-0	2-0
Djurgårdens IF ‡	26	11	8	7	38	32	41	0-2	1-1	1-2		0-3	1-0	5-1	3-1	3-2	2-1	1-1	2-1	3-1	5-0
Kalmar FF	26	10	10	6	27	18	40	1-0	1-3	0-0	1-1		1-2	0-1	2-1	0-1	0-0	1-1	1-1	1-1	2-0
Hammarby IF	26	10	7	9	28	28	37	0-0	1-1	1-2	3-0	0-3		1-1	1-0	1-0	2-1	3-1	0-1	1-1	0-1
Orebro SK	26	9	6	11	32	45	33	1-2	2-5	0-0	0-2	1-2	1-2		3-3	2-2	3-1	2-0	1-0	2-1	3-0
GIF Sundsvall	26	8	8	10	28	30	32	3-2	1-0	2-1	0-1	0-1	2-0	1-0		0-0	3-3	0-0	1-1	1-1	1-0
Elfsborg IF	26	8	8	10	25	32	32	1-5	1-1	1-0	0-0	0-1	0-1	3-0	3-1		1-1	1-1	1-2	1-0	3-1
Helsingborgs IF	26	7	9	10	41	33	30	0-2	1-2	1-2	1-1	1-2	3-1	0-0	1-0	4-0		0-1	3-0	3-0	2-0
Landskrona BoIS	26	7	9	10	27	33	30	2-1	0-4	0-1	2-0	0-2	0-0	0-1	3-2	0-0	1-1		0-2	0-1	4-0
Orgryte IS	26	6	10	10	25	33	28	0-2	1-2	0-1	0-1	1-1	0-0	2-2	1-3	0-2	1-1	1-1		1-1	1-0
AIK Stockholm	26	5	10	11	23	35	25	0-2	0-2	3-1	1-1	1-1	0-1	1-2	1-0	1-1	2-2	1-3	0-3		0-0
Trelleborgs FF	26	2	7	17	18	55	13	1-1	0-4	2-3	2-2	0-0	2-2	1-2	1-1	0-1	1-6	2-1	1-1	1-3	

3/04/2004 - 30/10/2004 • † Qualified for the UEFA Champions League • ‡ Qualified for the UEFA Cup • § Orebro SK were relegated after being refused a license for 2005 • Relegation play-off: Assyriska 2-1 0-1 Orgryte IS. Despite losing on away goals Assyriska were promoted thanks to the relegation of Orebro

SWEDEN 2004
SUPERETTAN (2)

	Pl	W	D	L	F	A	Pts
BK Häcken	30	19	8	3	60	31	65
Gefle IF	30	17	7	6	50	28	58
Assyriska	30	17	3	10	48	39	54
IFK Norrköping	30	14	8	8	58	37	50
Osters IF	30	14	8	8	51	36	50
GAIS	30	13	10	7	45	40	49
Atvidabergs FF	30	14	6	10	55	47	48
Västerås SK	30	12	8	10	47	47	44
Café Opera	30	10	10	10	45	39	40
IF Brommapojkarna	30	9	9	12	43	42	36
Västra Frölunda IF	30	10	6	14	40	48	36
Falkenbergs FF	30	8	5	17	30	52	29
Bodens BK	30	5	13	12	32	40	28
Enköpings SK	30	5	11	14	31	44	26
IK Brage	30	5	10	15	41	62	25
Friska Viljor	30	6	2	22	30	74	20

17/04/2004 - 23/10/2004

SVENSKA CUPEN 2004

4th Round

Djurgårdens IF *	3
GIF Sundsvall	2
Café Opera	1
IFK Norrköping *	3
Assyriska *	2 4p
IF Brommapojkarna	2 3p
Orgryte IS	2
Osters IF *	3
Hammarby IF	2 4p
IFK Värnamo *	2 2p
Lärje/Angereds *	0
GAIS	4
Orebro SK	4
Halmstads BK *	2
Friska Viljor *	0
IFK Göteborg	4

Quarter-finals

Djurgårdens IF	1
IFK Norrköping *	0
Assyriska	0
Osters IF *	2
Hammarby IF	1
GAIS *	0
Orebro SK	2
IFK Göteborg *	3

* Home team • ‡ Qualified for the UEFA Cup

Semi-finals

Djurgårdens IF	2
Osters IF	0
Hammarby IF	0
IFK Göteborg	2

Final

Djurgårdens IF ‡	3
IFK Göteborg	1

CUP FINAL

6-11-2004, Att. 9 417, Ref: Sundell
Råsunda, Stockholm

Scorers - Sjölund 2 [11] [66], Johansson.A [56] for
Djurgården; Alexandersson [52] for IFK

SWZ – SWAZILAND

NATIONAL TEAM RECORD
JULY 1ST 2002 TO JUNE 30TH 2005

PL	W	D	L	F	A	%
26	6	7	13	24	51	36.5

FIFA/COCA-COLA WORLD RANKING

1993	1994	1995	1996	1997	1998	1999	2000	2001	2002	2003	2004	High		Low	
99	125	148	160	165	149	127	137	132	116	114	126	92	10/93	174	10/97

2004-2005											
08/04	09/04	10/04	11/04	12/04	01/05	02/05	03/05	04/05	05/05	06/05	07/05
121	122	122	124	126	128	128	129	130	131	126	128

In the 114 internationals Swaziland have played since foundation in 1968 they have won only 24, explaining their rather modest status. However, Swaziland's prospects looked brighter in 2003. A new headquarters for the football association was opened that year and the country hosted the African U-17 Championship while the national team managed to reach the semi-finals of the COSAFA Castle Cup. However, if there was ever any hope of breaking their record of failing to get past the preliminary round in a World Cup™ campaign, it soon disappeared at Dakar Airport. Following a 1-1 home leg with Cape Verde, six of Swaziland's players were held en route because

INTERNATIONAL HONOURS
None

of passport problems. With a weakened squad, coach Werner Bicklehaupt watched Swaziland's World Cup™ dreams disappear quickly followed by his job. In the tightest Championship race in 10 years, Mbabane Swallows pipped Green Mamba to the MTN Premier League title on goal difference but in hugely controversial circumstances. Having beaten Mhlume in their last game of the season Green Mamba thought they had won the Championship but the victory was overturned due to a player ineligibility, a decision that also saved Mhlume from relegation. In the Swazi Bank Cup Final, relegated Hub Sundowns beat Malanti Chiefs to win their first trophy.

THE FIFA BIG COUNT OF 2000

	Male	Female		Male	Female
Registered players	3 000	0	Referees	100	0
Non registered players	3 500	0	Officials	700	0
Youth players	1 500	0	Total involved	8 800	
Total players	8 000		Number of clubs	50	
Professional players	0	0	Number of teams	200	

National Football Association of Swaziland (NFAS)
Sigwaca House, Plot 582, Sheffield Road, PO Box 641, Mbabane H100, Swaziland
Tel +268 4046852   Fax +268 4046206
kenmakh@realnet.co.sz   www.nfas.org.sz
President: MKHALIPHI Philemon   General Secretary: MNGOMEZULU Frederick
Vice-President: SHONGWE Timothy   Treasurer: LES Jacobs   Media Officer: None
Men's Coach: MAHLALELA Dumisa   Women's Coach: DU-PONT Naomi
NFAS formed: 1968   CAF: 1976   FIFA: 1978
Colours: Blue, Gold, Red

GAMES PLAYED BY SWAZILAND IN THE 2006 FIFA WORLD CUP™ CYCLE

2002	Opponents	Score		Venue	Comp	Scorers	Att	Referee
1-08	Mauritius	L	0-1	Mbabane	Fr			
3-08	Mauritius	D	0-0	Big Bend	Fr			Sitriongomyane SWZ
24-08	South Africa	L	1-4	Polokwane	CCsf	Sibusiso Dlamini 58	30 000	Katjimune NAM
7-09	Botswana	D	0-0	Gaborone	CNq			Moeketsi LES
6-10	Lesotho	D	0-0	Big Bend	Fr		4 000	
13-10	Libya	W	2-1	Mbabane	CNq	Gamedze 81, Nhleko 83		Bernardo Colembi ANG
2003								
19-03	Lesotho	W	1-0	Mbabane	Fr	Mfanizle Dlamini 51	400	
30-03	Congo DR	D	1-1	Mbabane	CNq	Mfanizle Dlamini 9		Katjimune NAM
25-05	Lesotho	L	1-2	Maseru	Fr	Mkhwanazi 35	5 000	
8-06	Congo DR	L	0-2	Kinshasa	CNq		60 000	Benjamin MRI
22-06	Botswana	W	3-2	Mbabane	CNq	Siza Dlamini 2 7 25, Sibusiso Dlamini 18	35 000	
5-07	Libya	L	2-6	Tripoli	CNq	Bongali Dlamini 2		
13-07	Madagascar	W	2-0	Mbabane	CCqf	Siza Dlamini 30, Mfanizle Dlamini 51	8 000	Mpofu BOT
31-08	Zimbabwe	L	0-2	Harare	CCsf		25 000	Antonio De Souza ANG
6-09	Botswana	L	0-3	Mbabane	Fr			
4-10	Lesotho	L	2-5	Maseru	Fr			
12-10	Cape Verde Islands	D	1-1	Mbabane	WCq	Siza Dlamini 64	5 000	Teshome ERI
9-11	Mozambique	L	0-2	Maputo	Fr			
16-11	Cape Verde Islands	L	0-3	Praia	WCq		6 000	Aboubacar CIV
2004								
11-04	Mozambique	L	0-2	Maputo	Fr			
31-05	Mozambique	D	1-1	Maputo	Fr	Maziya 83p	5 000	
27-06	Zimbabwe	L	0-5	Mbabane	CCqf			Infante MOZ
6-07	Malawi	W	2-1	Blantyre	Fr			
8-07	Malawi	D	1-1	Lilongwe	Fr			
2005								
1-06	Lesotho	W	4-3	Maseru	Fr			
11-06	Zambia	L	0-3	Lusaka	CCr1			Chidoda BOT

Fr = Friendly match • CN = CAF African Cup of Nations • CC = COSAFA Castle Cup • WC = FIFA World Cup™
q = qualifier • r1 = first round group • qf = quarter-final • sf = semi-final

SWAZILAND NATIONAL TEAM RECORDS AND RECORD SEQUENCES

Records			Sequence records				
Victory	4-1	LES 1999	Wins	3	1999, 2001-2002	Clean sheets	2	1968, 2001, 2002
Defeat	1-9	ZAM 1978	Defeats	8	1969-1989	Goals scored	8	1998-1999
Player Caps	n/a		Undefeated	9	2001-2002	Without goal	6	1993-1997
Player Goals	n/a		Without win	18	1969-1990	Goals against	15	1981-1990

SWAZILAND COUNTRY INFORMATION

Capital	Mbabane	Independence	1968 from the UK	GDP per Capita	$4 900
Population	1 169 241	Status	Monarchy	GNP Ranking	147
Area km²	17 363	Language	English, siSwati	Dialling code	+46
Population density	67 per km²	Literacy rate	81%	Internet code	.sz
% in urban areas	31%	Main religion	Christian 60%	GMT +/−	+1
Towns/Cities ('000)	Manzini 110; Mbabane 76; Big Bend 10; Malkerns 9; Nhlangano 9; Mhlume 8; Hluti 6				
Neighbours (km)	Mozambique 105; South Africa 430				
Main stadia	Somholo National Stadium – Mbabane 30 000				

SWAZILAND 2004-05

MTN PREMIER LEAGUE

	Pl	W	D	L	F	A	Pts	Swallows	Mamba	Leopards	Sundowns	Highlanders	Wanderers	Rovers	Pirates	Mhlume Utd	Buffaloes	Illovo	Hub
Mbabane Swallows †	22	13	4	5	42	19	43		2-0	2-0	1-0	1-0	1-1	2-4	1-0	7-1	1-0	4-0	4-1
Green Mamba ‡	22	13	4	5	40	21	43	1-3		3-4	2-1	2-1	4-2	1-0	5-1	3-0	1-0	3-0	0-0
Royal Leopards	22	12	3	7	34	23	39	1-1	2-1		1-2	1-0	1-0	2-1	0-1	1-0	2-1	0-1	1-1
Denver Sundowns	22	9	8	5	29	25	35	1-4	1-1	1-0		3-1	1-3	1-1	0-0	3-1	1-1	1-0	1-0
Mbabane Highlanders	22	9	4	9	24	23	31	2-1	0-1	0-1	1-1		1-1	0-2	2-0	1-0	0-0	3-1	2-1
Manzini Wanderers	22	7	9	6	21	20	30	1-0	0-0	2-1	1-1	2-1		1-1	0-2	0-0	0-0	0-1	0-0
Mhlambanyatsi Rovers	22	7	7	8	32	26	28	2-0	2-2	2-2	0-1	3-0	1-1		0-1	1-0	1-1	0-1	1-1
Moneni Pirates	22	7	5	10	20	29	26	2-1	0-3	0-3	1-1	0-3	1-2	0-1		1-1	1-1	2-1	5-1
Mhlume United	22	7	5	10	18	28	26	0-0	2-0	1-3	3-1	0-1	1-0	2-1	0-0		2-0	2-2	1-0
Young Buffaloes	22	5	10	7	21	27	25	2-3	0-2	1-4	2-2	2-2	0-0	3-2	1-1	2-1		0-0	1-0
Illovo Ubombo	22	7	3	12	15	31	24	0-0	0-2	0-3	1-2	0-1	2-1	0-3	0-2	2-0	0-1		1-0
Hub Sundowns	22	2	6	14	13	37	12	0-3	0-3	2-1	0-3	0-2	1-2	2-2	1-0	0-0	1-2	1-2	

16/08/2004 - 23/04/2005 • † Qualified for the CAF Champions League • ‡ Qualified for the CAF Confederation Cup • Match in bold awarded 2-0
Green Mamba had won the game, played on the last day of the season, to win the Championship. The match was then awarded to Mbabane Swallows.
Green Mamba launched an appeal but it was rejected

SWAZI BANK CUP 2004-05

Eighth-finals

Hub Sundowns	5
Young Buffaloes	4
Highway Never Die	0
Green Mamba	3
Moneni Pirates	2
Vento Umoya	1
Simunye	0
Manzini Wanderers	3
Royal Leopards	1
Mbabane Swallows	0
Lusushwane Rhinos	1
Mhlanbanyatsi Rovers	3
Mbabane Highlanders	1 †
Eleven Men in Flight	2 †
Denver Sundowns	2
Malanti Chiefs	4

Quarter-finals

Hub Sundowns	2
Green Mamba	1
Moneni Pirates	1 1p
Manzini Wanderers	1 2p
Royal Leopards	2
Mhlámbanyatsi Rovers	1
Mbabane Highlanders	1
Malanti Chiefs	2

† Awarded to Highlanders

Semi-finals

Hub Sundowns	1 5p
Manzini Wanderers	1 4p
Royal Leopards	0
Malanti Chiefs	1

Final

Hub Sundowns	2
Malanti Chiefs	0

CUP FINAL

10-04-2005, Att:12 000
Somhlolo, Mbabane

Scorers - Nkambue 30, Mathunjwa 39 for Sundowns

RECENT LEAGUE AND CUP RECORD

	Championship						Cup		
Year	Champions	Pts	Runners-up	Pts	Third	Pts	Winners	Score	Runners-up
1996	XI Men in Flight	69	Denver Sundowns	66	C&M Eagles	56			
1997	Mbabane Highlanders	54	XI Men in Flight	52	Mbabane Swallows	52	Mbabane Highlanders		
1998	No championship due to season readjustment								
1999	Manzini Wanderers	48	Mbabane Highlanders	45	Mbabane Swallows	44	Mbabane Highlanders		
2000	Mbabane Highlanders	52	Green Mamba	45	Mbabane Swallows	37	Mhlume United		
2001	Mbabane Highlanders	48	Manzini Wanderers	42	Mbabane Swallows	40	XI Men in Flight	1- 4-3p	Mbabane Swallows
2002	Manzini Wanderers	46	Mhlam'yatsi Rovers	43	Mbabane Swallows	43			
2003	Manzini Wanderers	45	Mhlam'yatsi Rovers	42	Mbabane Swallows	38			
2004	Mhlam'yatsi Rovers	50	Mbabane Highlanders	45	Green Mamba	37	Green Mamba	5-1	Denver Sundowns
2005	Mbabane Swallows	43	Green Mamba	43	Royal Leopards	39	Hub Sundowns	2-0	Malanti Chiefs

SYR – SYRIA

NATIONAL TEAM RECORD
JULY 1ST 2002 TO JUNE 30TH 2005

PL	W	D	L	F	A	%
46	16	11	19	73	74	46.7

FIFA/COCA-COLA WORLD RANKING

1993	1994	1995	1996	1997	1998	1999	2000	2001	2002	2003	2004	High		Low	
82	105	136	115	98	84	109	100	90	91	85	85	78	08/03	145	05/96

2004-2005											
08/04	09/04	10/04	11/04	12/04	01/05	02/05	03/05	04/05	05/05	06/05	07/05
82	84	87	89	85	85	86	86	86	85	93	97

Although active on the Asian football scene for more than half a century, Syria have remained lesser lights in an increasingly competitive region. Renowned for being difficult to beat at home, Syria can't match that with results on the road. Winning just one of their three away matches in their FIFA World Cup™ group put paid to any hopes of progress and after a dismal 1-0 defeat at home to basement side Kyrgyzstan, Syria finished runners-up behind Bahrain but six points adrift. Better luck came in the West Asian Football Federation Cup in Iran where Syria reached the final against the hosts after beating Jordan 3-2 on penalties in the semis. Having already lost to Iran 7-1 at the

INTERNATIONAL HONOURS
Asian Youth Championship 1994

group stage, the team were ready for a stern test but enjoyed a dream start when Raja Rafe scored after just three minutes. However, Iran proved too strong again and ran out 4-1 winners. The U-20s surpassed themselves by qualifying for the World Youth Championship in the Netherlands. After finishing as group runners-up they narrowly missed out on a semi-final place when they lost to Brazil by a single penalty. Al Ittihad won the First Division title and the Syria Cup while in an all-Syrian final in the inaugural 2004 AFC Cup, Al Jaish beat Al Wahda, a result that promoted the country's teams to the 2005 AFC Champions League.

THE FIFA BIG COUNT OF 2000

	Male	Female		Male	Female
Registered players	4 263	0	Referees	600	0
Non registered players	194 750	0	Officials	3 240	0
Youth players	27 007		Total involved	229 860	
Total players	226 020		Number of clubs	157	
Professional players	20	0	Number of teams	694	

Syrian Arab Federation for Football (FASF)
Maysaloon Street, PO Box 22296, Damascus, Syria
Tel +963 11 3335866   Fax +963 11 3331511
toafiksarhan@hotmail.com   www.none
President: AHMAD Jappan Dr   General Secretary: SARHAN Toufik
Vice-President: SWAIDAN Hassan   Treasurer: SELOU Aref   Media Officer: none
Men's Coach: REFAAT Ahmad   Women's Coach: None
FASF formed: 1936   AFC: 1970   FIFA: 1937
Colours: Red, Red, Red

GAMES PLAYED BY SYRIA IN THE 2006 FIFA WORLD CUP™ CYCLE

2002	Opponents	Score		Venue	Comp	Scorers	Att	Referee
19-07	Iraq	L	0-2	Baghdad	Fr			
22-07	Iraq	L	1-2	Baghdad	Fr	Ahmed Azzam 77		
30-08	Palestine	W	2-1	Damascus	WAr1			
3-09	Iraq	L	0-1	Damascus	WAr1			
5-09	Jordan	L	1-2	Damascus	WAsf	Raghdan Shehada 54		
7-09	Iran	D	2-2	Damascus	WA3p	Anas Sari 2 16 89, L 2-4p	10 000	Abu Elaish PAL
7-12	China PR	L	1-3	Manama	Fr	Jehad Al Houssain 35		Al Khabbaz BHR
9-12	Bahrain	W	3-2	Manama	Fr	Feras Al Khateeb 2 15 70, Jomard Mousa 77p		Al Hail QAT
12-12	Jordan	L	0-3	Manama	Fr			Al Dosari KSA
17-12	Yemen	W	4-0	Kuwait City	ARr1	Raja Rafe 26, Maher Al Sayyed 52, Feras Al Khatib 2 57p 70	300	Al Saeedi UAE
19-12	Bahrain	L	0-2	Kuwait City	ARr1			Shaban KUW
21-12	Lebanon	W	4-1	Kuwait City	ARr1	Feras Al Khatib 44, Raja Rafe 3 46 52 59	1 000	Guezzaz MAR
24-12	Saudi Arabia	L	0-3	Kuwait City	ARr1		2 000	Zekrini ALG
2003								
22-08	Lebanon	L	0-1	Beirut	Fr	Abandoned after 45'		
19-09	Jordan	D	0-0	Amman	Fr			
27-09	Yemen	W	8-2	Jeddah	Fr			
30-09	Saudi Arabia	D	1-1	Jeddah	Fr	Maher Al Sayed 49		
15-10	Sri Lanka	W	5-0	Damascus	ACq	Iyad Mandou 2 34 82, Maher Al Sayed 2 54 84, Feras Al Khatib 73p		
18-10	Sri Lanka	W	8-0	Damascus	ACq	Feras Al Khatib 3 40 49 55, Maher Al Sayed 2 45 65, Iyad Mandou 60, Nabil Shuhmeh 2 80 83		
7-11	United Arab Emirates	L	1-3	Damascus	ACq	Feras Al Khatib 50		Moradi IRN
14-11	United Arab Emirates	L	1-3	Sharjah	ACq	Raja Rafe 36		
28-11	Turkmenistan	D	1-1	Damascus	ACq	Anas Sari 10		Sadeq KUW
3-12	Turkmenistan	L	0-3	Ashgabat	ACq	Match not played but awarded 3-0 to Turkemistan		
2004								
18-02	Bahrain	L	1-2	Al Muharraq	WCq	Shekh Eleshra 80	5 000	Khanthama THA
23-03	Lebanon	W	1-0	Jounieh	Fr			
26-03	Palestine	D	1-1	Damascus	Fr			
31-03	Kyrgyzstan	D	1-1	Bishkek	WCq	Meaataz Kailouni 86	17 000	Bose IND
19-04	Sudan	W	2-1	Khartoum	Fr			
21-04	Sudan	D	0-0	Khartoum	Fr			
1-06	Kuwait	W	1-0	Kuwait City	Fr			
3-06	Kuwait	W	2-1	Kuwait City	Fr	Raja Rafe 22, Maher Al Sayed 55p		
10-06	Tajikistan	W	2-1	Homs	WCq	Yahia Al Mhd. 76, Raja Rafe 80	18 000	Al Fadhli KUW
19-06	Lebanon	W	3-1	Tehran	WAr1	Maen Al Rashed 7, Shekh Eleshra 27, Raja Rafe 45		
21-06	Iran	L	1-7	Tehran	WAr1	Maher Al Sayed 82		
23-06	Jordan	D	1-1	Tehran	WAsf	Raja Rafe 55, W 3-2p		
25-06	Iran	L	1-4	Tehran	WAf	Raja Rafe 3		
26-08	Yemen	W	2-1	Sana'a	Fr			
28-08	Yemen	L	1-2	Sana'a	Fr			
8-09	Tajikistan	W	1-0	Dushanbe	WCq	Raja Rafe 35	18 000	Mohd Salleh MAS
29-09	Kuwait	D	1-1	Tripoli (LIB)	Fr			
6-10	Saudi Arabia	D	2-2	Riyadh	Fr	Raja Rafe 7, Raafat 90p		
8-10	Qatar	W	2-1	Doha	Fr			
13-10	Bahrain	D	2-2	Damascus	WCq	Shekh Eleshra 12, Jehad Al Houssain 18	35 000	Moradi IRN
17-11	Kyrgyzstan	L	0-1	Damascus	WCq		1 000	Tongkhan THA
2005								
26-01	Kuwait	L	2-3	Kuwait City	Fr	Amneh 39, Raja Rafe 74		
2-02	Japan	L	0-3	Saitama	Fr			

Fr = Friendly match • WA = West Asian Championship • AR = Arab Championship • AC = AFC Asian Cup • WC = FIFA World Cup™
q = qualifier • r1 = first round group • sf = semi-final • 3p = third place play-off • f = final

SYRIA NATIONAL TEAM RECORDS AND RECORD SEQUENCES

Records			Sequence records				
Victory	13-0	OMA 1965	Wins	4	1998, 2001, 2004	Clean sheets	5	1985
Defeat	0-8	GRE 1949, EGY 1951	Defeats	9	1977-1978	Goals scored	14	2004
Player Caps	n/a		Undefeated	10	1987-1988	Without goal	4	Three times
Player Goals	n/a		Without win	13	1981-1983	Goals against	15	1981-1983

SYRIA 2004-05

FIRST DIVISION

	Pl	W	D	L	F	A	Pts	Ittihad	Karama	Wahda	Jaish	Qardaha	Taliya	Majd	Teshrin	Horriya	Foutoua	Jabala	Hottin	Umayya	Shorta
Al Ittihad Aleppo	26	15	8	3	50	20	53		1-1	2-2	1-1	3-1	3-1	1-1	1-2	5-0	3-0	1-1	2-0	2-0	3-1
Al Karama Homs	26	14	8	4	38	24	50	1-2		1-1	1-0	1-0	0-4	1-1	2-0	2-1	2-1	1-1	2-0	1-0	0-0
Al Wahda Damascus	26	12	8	6	35	25	44	0-0	3-1		2-1	0-1	1-0	3-2	2-1	2-1	1-1	3-1	0-0	3-0	1-0
Al Jaish Damascus	26	12	7	7	34	20	43	1-0	0-1	2-0		3-1	3-1	1-2	2-1	1-0	2-1	4-0	2-0	0-0	2-1
Qardaha	26	13	4	9	32	30	43	1-3	1-0	0-3	2-2		2-0	1-0	2-1	1-2	1-0	0-1	2-1	1-0	5-2
Al Taliya Hama	26	12	6	8	38	29	42	2-2	2-3	0-1	1-0	1-0		1-1	3-2	0-0	1-1	2-0	2-1	2-1	3-0
Al Majd Damascus	26	9	11	6	35	24	38	1-3	0-2	2-0	1-0	1-2	2-2		1-1	0-0	1-1	1-0	2-0	5-0	2-1
Teshrin Latakia	26	7	10	9	29	31	31	0-2	0-0	1-1	2-2	2-0	0-1	1-1		4-3	1-1	2-0	0-2	0-1	2-0
Al Horriya Aleppo	26	8	7	11	26	32	31	0-0	0-3	1-2	0-1	0-0	0-3	1-0	0-1		3-0	2-0	2-1	3-1	0-0
Al Foutoua Deir ez-Zor	26	5	12	9	20	31	27	0-3	0-0	1-0	1-0	0-0	0-0	1-1	1-1	1-2		0-2	1-2	2-2	1-0
Jabala	26	6	7	13	18	36	25	0-3	1-2	1-0	0-3	0-0	2-0	0-5	0-0	1-1	1-2		2-0	1-2	2-0
Hottin Latakia	26	6	6	14	21	34	24	1-0	2-3	3-2	0-0	1-2	1-0	1-0	0-1	0-2	0-0	1-1		1-1	1-0
Umayya Idlib	26	4	11	11	24	39	23	0-1	2-2	1-1	1-1	2-3	1-3	0-1	1-1	2-2	2-2	0-0	2-1		2-0
Al Shorta Damascus	26	3	7	16	18	43	16	2-3	1-5	1-1	0-0	1-3	2-3	0-0	2-2	1-0	0-1	1-2	2-1	0-0	

16/08/2004 - 15/05/2005 • † Qualified for the AFC Cup

FASF CUP 2004-05

Round of 16		Quarter-finals		Semi-finals		Final	
Al Ittihad *	2 3						
Umayya	1 1	Al Ittihad *	2 0				
Al Wathba	2 1	Al Taliya	1 0				
Al Taliya *	2 2			Al Ittihad *	2 1		
Al Foutoua *	2 0			Hottin	0 1		
Al Jaish	0 1	Al Foutoua *	3 0				
Al Wahda	1 1 3p	Hottin	1 5				
Hottin *	1 1 4p					Al Ittihad	3
Al Karama	3 2					Al Majd	1
Teshrin *	2 0	Al Karama *	5 2				
Jabla *	2 2 2p	Al Arabi	0 0				
Al Arabi	2 2 3p			Al Karama	1 1		
Horriya *	2 2			Al Majd *	0 2	CUP FINAL	
Al Shorta	1 2	Horriya *	1 3				
Al Qardaha *	1 1	Al Majd	2 3				
Al Majd	2 2	* Home team in the first leg					

CUP FINAL
15-07-2005, Abbasiyyin, Damascus
Scorers - Anas Sari 2 [26] [52], Mahmoud
Amneh [77] for Ittihad;
Samer Awadh [90p] for Majd

SYRIA COUNTRY INFORMATION

Capital	Damascus	Independence	1946 from France	GDP per Capita	$3 300
Population	18 016 874	Status	Republic	GNP Ranking	72
Area km²	185 180	Language	Arabic, Kurdish, Armenian	Dialling code	+963
Population density	97 per km²	Literacy rate	76%	Internet code	.sy
% in urban areas	52%	Main religion	Muslim	GMT + / −	+2
Towns/Cities ('000)	Aleppo 2 139; Damascus 1 576; Homs 736; Latakia 431; Hama 348; ar-Raqqah 261				
Neighbours (km)	Iraq 605; Jordan 375; Israel 76; Lebanon 375; Turkey 822; Mediterranean Sea 193				
Main stadia	Abbasiyyin – Damascus 45 000				

AL JAISH 2004-2005

Date	Opponents		Score	Comp	Scorers
10-02-2004	Olympic Beirut - LIB	D	0-0	A	ACgC
25-02-2004	Nebitchi Balkanabat - TKM	W	6-0	H	ACgC Ziad Sha'abo [36], Raghdan Shehade [50], Rabih Hassan 2 [55][64] Ahmed Omair 2 [69][87]
5-05-2004	Olympic Beirut - LIB	W	2-0	H	ACgC Alaomer [8], Ziad Sha'abo [86]
18-05-2004	Nebitchi Balkanabat - TKM	D	0-0	A	ACgC
15-09-2004	East Bengal - IND	D	0-0	A	ACqf
22-09-2004	East Bengal - IND	W	3-0	H	ACqf Adel Abdullah [16], Mohamed Zeino [50], Firas Ismail [87]
16-10-2004	Al Wahda	W	2-0	H	LGE Ziad Sha'abo [33], Amer Al Abtah [73]
20-10-2004	Home United - SIN	W	4-0	H	ACsf Mohamed Zeino [34], Firas Ismail 2 [53][62], Iyad Hilou [76]
27-10-2004	Home United - SIN	W	2-1	A	ACsf Mohamed Zeino [76], Ziad Sha'abo [90]
1-11-2004	Teshrin	D	2-2	A	LGE Adib Barakat [60], Ziad Sha'abo [87]
6-11-2004	Al Shorta	W	2-1	H	LGE Raghdan Shehade [23], Mohamed Zeino [90]
9-11-2004	Al Ittihad	D	1-1	A	LGE Mohamed Zeino [65]
19-11-2004	Al Wahda - SYR	W	3-2	A	ACf Ziad Sha'abo [3], Firas Ismail [32], Amer al Abtah [55p]
26-11-2004	Al Wahda - SYR	L	0-1	H	ACf
30-11-2004	Qardaha	D	2-2	A	LGE Ziad Sha'abo [49p], Tareq Jabban [74]
4-12-2004	Al Karama	L	0-1	H	LGE
10-12-2004	Hottin	D	0-0	A	LGE
14-12-2004	Jabala	W	3-0	H	LGE Ahmed Hariri [2], Ziad Sha'abo [63], Mohamed Zeino [72]
17-12-2004	Al Majd	L	1-2	H	LGE Mohamed Zeino [77]
21-12-2004	Al Taliya	W	3-1	H	LGE
24-12-2004	Horriya	W	1-0	A	LGE Ahmed Al Hariri [41]
2-01-2005	Umayya	D	0-0	H	LGE
7-01-2005	Foutoua	L	0-1	A	LGE
18-02-2005	Al Wahda	L	1-2	A	LGE Firas Ismail [83]
26-02-2005	Jabala	W	4-0	H	LGE Raghdan Shehade [22], Mohamed Zeino [55], Ziad Sha'abo [61] Majed Al Haji [68]
4-03-2005	Teshrin	W	2-1	H	LGE Firas Ismail [33], Ziad Sha'abo [82]
9-03-2005	Pakhtakor Tashkent - UZB	L	0-2	H	CLgD
12-03-2005	Al Shorta	D	0-0	A	LGE
16-03-2005	Al Ahly - JOR	L	1-3	A	CLgD Mohamed Zeino [69]
20-03-2005	Al Ittihad	W	1-0	H	LGE Mohamed Zeino [55]
22-03-2005	Al Forat	W	2-1	A	CUPr1
25-03-2005	Al Taliya	L	0-1	A	LGE
29-03-2005	Al Forat	W	2-0	H	CUPr1
1-04-2005	Qardaha	W	3-1	H	LGE Mohamed Khalaf [30], Tareq Jabban [71], Mohamed Zeino [78]
5-04-2005	Al Zawra - IRQ	W	5-1	A	CLgD Mohamed Zeino 3 [19][30][48], Ziad Sha'abo [66], Ahmed Al Hariri [90]
9-04-2005	Al Karama	L	0-1	A	LGE
20-04-2005	Al Zawra - IRQ	D	0-0	H	CLgD
24-04-2005	Hottin	W	2-0	H	LGE Nouhad Hajj-Mustapha [4], Mohamed Zeino [77]
30-04-2005	Al Majd	L	0-1	A	LGE
6-05-2005	Horriya	W	1-0	H	LGE Ahmed Al Hariri [61]
11-05-2005	Pakhtakor Tashkent - UZB	L	1-4	A	CLgD Ahmed Al Hariri [69]
21-05-2005	Umayya	D	1-1	A	LGE Tareq Jabban [66]
25-05-2005	Al Ahly - JOR	L	0-4	H	CLgD
30-05-2005	Al Foutoua	L	0-2	H	CUPr2
3-06-2005	Foutoua	W	2-1	H	LGE Firas Ismail 2 [35][66]
11-06-2005	Al Foutoua	W	1-0	H	CUPr2

AC = AFC Cup • LGE = Syrian First Division • CUP = Syrian Cup • CL = AFC Champions League
gC = group C • gD = group D • r1 = first round • r2 = second round • qf = quarter-final • sf = semi-final • final

RECENT LEAGUE AND CUP RECORD

Year	Champions	Pts	Runners-up	Pts	Third	Pts	Winners	Score	Runners-up
1990	Al Foutoua	43	Al Karama	43	Al Wathba	34	Al Foutoua	1-0	Al Karama
1991	Al Foutoua	44	Jabala	37	Al Shourta	34	Al Foutoua	1-0	Yaqaza
1992	Al Horriya	42	Jabala	41	Al Ittihad	38	Al Horriya	1-0	Al Ittihad
1993	Al Ittihad						Al Wahda	4-0	Hottin
1994	Al Horriya						Al Ittihad		
1995	Al Ittihad						Al Karama	3-0	Hottin
1996	Al Karama	62	Hottin	51	Teshrin	45	Al Karama	3-0	Jabala
1997	Teshrine	60	Al Jaish	57	Al Karama	49	Al Jaish	2-0	Jabala
1998	Al Jaish	62	Al Karama	48	Hottine	46	Al Jaish	5-2	Al Karama
1999	Al Jaish	58	Al Karama	55	Al Wahda	44	Jabala	2-2 3-0p	Hottin
2000	Jabala	51	Hottin	50	Teshrine	50	Al Jaish	4-1	Jabala
2001	Al Jaish	60	Al Karama	51	Al Ittihad	49	Hottin	1-0	Al Jaish
2002	Al Jaish	37	Al Ittihad	35	Al Wahda	29	Al Jaish	3-0	Jabala
2003	Al Jaish	57	Al Ittihad	54	Qardah	47	Al Wahda	5-2	Al Ittihad
2004	Al Wahda	60	Al Karama	58	Teshrine	54	Al Jaish	0-0 4-2p	Teshrine
2005	Al Ittihad	53	Al Karama	50	Al Wahda	44	Al Ittihad	3-1	Al Majd

TAH – TAHITI

NATIONAL TEAM RECORD
JULY 1ST 2002 TO JUNE 30TH 2005

PL	W	D	L	F	A	%
19	8	3	8	23	41	50

FIFA/COCA-COLA WORLD RANKING

1993	1994	1995	1996	1997	1998	1999	2000	2001	2002	2003	2004	High		Low	
141	148	156	158	161	123	139	131	127	115	33	124	111	08/02	172	09/98

2004-2005											
08/04	09/04	10/04	11/04	12/04	01/05	02/05	03/05	04/05	05/05	06/05	07/05
123	123	124	125	124	125	125	126	127	127	130	133

According to the FIFA/Coca-Cola World Ranking Tahiti are Oceania's third best side although with the Solomon Islands' recent World Cup™ exploits that could be disputed. However, the French overseas territory of just over half a million people have always played a full part on the region's football scene. Occasional club entries into the early rounds of the French Cup have added extra colour as well as giving some players the chance to play professionally in France. After a relatively successful 2003 South Pacific Games in which they finished fourth, Tahiti began their 2006 FIFA World Cup™ qualification by finishing runners-up to the Solomon Islands in their first stage

INTERNATIONAL HONOURS
South Pacific Games & Mini Games 1966 1975 1979 1981 1983 1985 1993 1995

group. Their unbeaten run stretched to five games with a goalless draw against Fiji before it all came to an abrupt halt when Australia scored nine without reply to inflict on Tahiti their heaviest international defeat. Worse came four days later when New Zealand made it 10-0 and Tahiti's campaign ended. In the 2005 Championnat Federal, Tefana won their first title two points ahead of AS Pirae and 2004 champions Manu Ura Paea. The latter won the Coupe de Tahiti beating Pirae 10-9 on penalties in the final. With Tahiti hosting the 2005 Oceania Champion Cup, both clubs were allowed to compete with Pirae faring better as they reached the semi-finals.

THE FIFA BIG COUNT OF 2000

	Male	Female		Male	Female
Registered players	5 582	152	Referees	55	3
Non registered players	4 050	135	Officials	55	4
Youth players	3 660	86	Total involved	13 782	
Total players	13 665		Number of clubs	184	
Professional players	0	0	Number of teams	589	

Fédération Tahitienne de Football (FTF)
Rue Coppenrath, Stade de Fautaua, Case postale 50858, Pirae 98716, Tahiti, French Polynesia
Tel +689 540954   Fax +689 419629
ftf@mail.pf   www.none
President: HAERERAAROA Eugene   General Secretary: DAVIO Vairani
Vice-President: ARIIOTIMA Henri Thierry   Treasurer: MARTIN Jean-François   Media Officer: None
Men's Coach: KAUTAI Gerard   Women's Coach: KAUTAI Gerard
FTF formed: 1989   OFC: 1990   FIFA: 1990
Colours: Red, White, Red

GAMES PLAYED BY TAHITI IN THE 2006 FIFA WORLD CUP™ CYCLE

2002	Opponents	Score		Venue	Comp	Scorers	Att	Referee
5-07	New Zealand	L	0-4	Auckland	OCr1		1 000	Attison VAN
7-07	Solomon Islands	W	3-2	Auckland	OCr1	Booene [42], Tagawa [57], Fatupua-Lecaill [90]	1 000	Breeze AUS
9-07	Papua New Guinea	W	3-1	Auckland	OCr1	Garcia [29], Tagawa 2 [49 64]	800	Rakaroi FIJ
12-07	Australia	L	1-2	Auckland	OCsf	Zaveroni [38]	400	Rugg NZL
14-07	Vanuatu	W	1-0	Auckland	OC3p	Auraa [65]	1 000	Rakaroi FIJ
2003								
30-06	Micronesia †	W	17-0	Suva	SPr1	Tagawa 4 [8 10 19 33], OG [17], Guyon 3 [32 41 56], Bennett 4 [48 70 76 86], Tchen [69], Papaaura [71], Senechal [72], Lecaill [78], Terevaura [81]		Rakaroi FIJ
3-07	Papua New Guinea	W	3-0	Suva	SPr1	Bennett 2 [13 69], Tagawa [62]	1 000	Attison VAN
5-07	New Caledonia	L	0-4	Nadi	SPr1		3 000	Shah FIJ
7-07	Tonga	W	4-0	Lautoka	SPr1	Tagawa 2 [2 27], Bennett 2 [81 83]	3 000	Shah FIJ
9-07	Fiji	L	1-2	Lautoka	SPsf	Papura [4]	8 000	Attison VAN
11-07	Vanuatu	L	0-1	Suva	SP3p		6 000	Rakaroi FIJ
2004								
10-05	Cook Islands	W	2-0	Honiara	WCq	Temataua [2], Moretta [80]	12 000	Singh FIJ
12-05	New Caledonia	D	0-0	Honiara	WCq		14 000	Rakaroi FIJ
17-05	Tonga	W	2-0	Honiara	WCq	Wajoka [1], Temataua [78]	400	Sosongan PNG
19-05	Solomon Islands	D	1-1	Honiara	WCq	Simon [30]	18 000	Rakaroi FIJ
29-05	Fiji	D	0-0	Adelaide	WCq		3 000	Farina ITA
31-05	Australia	L	0-9	Adelaide	WCq		1 200	Attison VAN
2-06	Solomon Islands	L	0-4	Adelaide	WCq		50	Rakaroi FIJ
4-06	New Zealand	L	0-10	Adelaide	WCq		200	Shield AUS
6-06	Vanuatu	W	2-1	Adelaide	WCq	Temataua [40], Wajoka [89]	300	Rakaroi FIJ
2005								

No international matches played in 2005 before August

Fr = Friendly match • OC = OFC Oceania Cup • SP = South Pacific Games • WC = FIFA World Cup™
q = qualifier • r1 = first round group • sf = semi-final • 3p = third place play-off • † Not a full international

TAHITI NATIONAL TEAM RECORDS AND RECORD SEQUENCES

Records			Sequence records				
Victory	30-0 COK 1971	Wins	10	1978-1980	Clean sheets	5	1995
Defeat	0-10 NZL 2004	Defeats	5	1996-1997	Goals scored	17	1981-1983
Player Caps	n/a	Undefeated	17	1981-1983	Without goal	4	2004
Player Goals	n/a	Without win	17	1959-1963	Goals against	20	1953-1963

RECENT LEAGUE AND CUP RECORD

	Championship	Cup		
Year	Champions	Winners	Score	Runners-up
2000	AS Vénus Mahina	AS Vénus Mahina	6-0	Central Sport
2001	AS Pirae	AS Dragon Papeete	2-1	AS Vénus Mahina
2002	AS Vénus Mahina	AS Pirae	1-0	AS Vénus Mahina
2003	AS Pirae	AS Manu-Ura Paea	0-0 4-3p	AS Pirae
2004	AS Manu-Ura Paea	AS Tefana	1-1 5-4p	AS Pirae
2005	AS Tefana	AS Manu-Ura Paea	0-0 10-9p	AS Pirae

TAHITI COUNTRY INFORMATION

Capital	Papeete	Status	French Overseas Possession, part of French Polynesia	GDP per Capita	$17 920
Population	266 339			GNP Ranking	n/a
Area km²	4 167	Language	French, Tahitian	Dialling code	+689
Population density	62 per km²	Literacy rate	98%	Internet code	.pf
% in urban areas	n/a	Main religion	Christian	GMT +/–	-10
Towns/Cities ('000)	Faaa 29; Papeete 26; Punaauia 25; Pirae 14; Mahina 14; Paea 13; Papara 10; Arue 9				
Neighbours (km)	South Pacific Ocean 2 525				
Main stadia	Stade de Fautaua – Pirae; Stade Pater – Papeete 15 000				

TAN – TANZANIA

NATIONAL TEAM RECORD
JULY 1ST 2002 TO JUNE 30TH 2005

PL	W	D	L	F	A	%
23	3	5	15	15	40	23.9

FIFA/COCA-COLA WORLD RANKING

1993	1994	1995	1996	1997	1998	1999	2000	2001	2002	2003	2004	High		Low	
98	74	70	89	96	118	128	140	149	153	159	172	65	02/95	172	05/05

2004-2005											
08/04	09/04	10/04	11/04	12/04	01/05	02/05	03/05	04/05	05/05	06/05	07/05
168	168	169	171	172	172	172	172	172	172	172	173

"This team is like an orphan; nobody cares", were the words of one of Tanzania's national team after an 1800km trip to Zambia in a bus had resulted in yet another defeat. Without a win in nearly three years and just two draws from 14 matches, there is much to be said about that opinion. Tanzania's last victory came in the 2002 CECAFA Cup semi-finals when they beat Rwanda to set up a final with neighbours and long-time rivals Kenya. Tanzania twice squandered a lead to lose 3-2 and missed the chance to win the trophy for the first time since 1994. Thus, when the draw for the 2006 FIFA World Cup™ paired the two sides again in the preliminary round there was little

INTERNATIONAL HONOURS
CECAFA Cup 1974 1994

hope of progress. After a goalless draw at home in the first leg Tanzania were 3-0 down after half an hour in Nairobi and soon out of the FIFA World Cup™ altogether. Worse followed at the 2004 CECAFA Cup when the team lost to Zanzibar, an island officially part of Tanzania but which enters the competition in its own right. Tanzania's Mainland League, which is split into two groups of 10 with the top four in each progressing to the Super Eight League, was won by Simba FC for the third time in four years. For the 2005 continental cups CAF gave Zanzibar the right to enter its own team thus ending the traditional end of season play-off with the Mainland League champions.

THE FIFA BIG COUNT OF 2000

	Male	Female		Male	Female
Registered players	12 000	0	Referees	400	0
Non registered players	100 000	0	Officials	3 500	0
Youth players	12 000	0	Total involved	127 900	
Total players	124 000		Number of clubs	400	
Professional players	0	0	Number of teams	2 000	

The Football Association of Tanzania (FAT)
Uhuru/Shaurimoyo Street, PO Box 1574, Dar-es-Salaam, Tanzania
Tel +255 74 4264181   Fax +255 22 2861815
www.none
President: TENGA Leodgar   General Secretary: TBD
Vice-President: MAGORI Crescentius John   Treasurer: TBD   Media Officer: None
Men's Coach: HAFIDH Badru   Women's Coach: BAKARI Mohamed
FAT formed: 1930   CAF: 1960   FIFA: 1964
Colours: Green, Black, Green

GAMES PLAYED BY TANZANIA IN THE 2006 FIFA WORLD CUP™ CYCLE

2002	Opponents	Score	Venue	Comp	Scorers	Att	Referee
8-09	Benin	L 0-4	Cotonou	CNq		10 000	Chukwujekwu NGA
12-10	Sudan	L 1-2	Mwanza	CNq	Rajab [17]	20 000	Tessema ETH
23-10	Uganda	L 0-2	Arusha	Fr			Masondo RSA
26-10	South Africa	D 1-1	Dar-es-Salaam	Fr	Fred Morris [88]		Kaunda KEN
30-11	Kenya	W 1-0	Arusha	CCr1	Henry Morris [9]		
2-12	Sudan	D 1-1	Arusha	CCr1	Edward [81]		
5-12	Burundi	W 2-0	Arusha	CCr1	Machupa 2 [4 41]		
8-12	Eritrea	D 1-1	Arusha	CCr1	Mwakingwe [24]		
11-12	Rwanda	W 3-0	Arusha	CCsf	Mtiro [44], Edward [69], Machupa [83]		
14-12	Kenya	L 2-3	Arusha	CCf	Gabriel [28], Maxime [59p]		
2003							
12-03	Uganda	D 0-0	Arusha	Fr		30 000	
23-03	Kenya	L 0-4	Nairobi	Fr			
29-03	Zambia	L 0-1	Dar-es-Salaam	CNq		23 000	Haislemelk ETH
29-05	Uganda	L 1-3	Kampala	Fr	Kapirima [84p]		
31-05	Uganda	L 0-1	Kampala	Fr			
7-06	Zambia	L 0-2	Lusaka	CNq		30 000	Chilinda MWI
22-06	Benin	L 0-1	Dar-es-Salaam	CNq		20 000	
11-10	Kenya	D 0-0	Dar-es-Salaam	WCq		8 864	Tessema ETH
11-11	Uganda	L 1-2	Kampala	Fr	Abu Masula		
15-11	Kenya	L 0-3	Nairobi	WCq		14 000	El Beltagy EGY
2004							
13-12	Zanzibar †	L 2-4	Addis Abeba	CCr1	Maxime [23], Machupa [32]		
15-12	Burundi	L 0-2	Addis Abeba	CCr1			
17-12	Ethiopia	L 0-2	Addis Abeba	CCr1			
19-12	Rwanda	L 1-5	Addis Abeba	CCr1			
2005							

No international matches played in 2005 before August

Fr = Friendly match • CN = CAF African Cup of Nations • CC = CECAFA Cup • WC = FIFA World Cup™
q = qualifier • r1 = first round group • sf = semi-final • f = final • † Not a full international

TANZANIA NATIONAL TEAM RECORDS AND RECORD SEQUENCES

Records			Sequence records				
Victory	7-0	SOM 1995	Wins	5	1994	Clean sheets	5	1994
Defeat	0-9	KEN 1956	Defeats	6	Four times	Goals scored	11	1993-1994
Player Caps	n/a		Undefeated	9	1973-1975	Without goal	4	Four times
Player Goals	n/a		Without win	28	1984-1990	Goals against	12	2001-2002

TANZANIA COUNTRY INFORMATION

Capital	Dodoma	Independence	1964 from the UK	GDP per Capita	$600
Population	36 588 225	Status	Republic	GDP Ranking	88
Area km²	945 087	Language	Swahili, English	Dialling code	+255
Population density	38 per km²	Literacy rate	78%	Internet code	.tz
% in urban areas	24%	Main religion	Muslim 35%, Christian 30%	GMT +/−	+3
Towns/Cities ('000)	Dar es Salaam 2 698; Mwanza 436; Zanzibar 403; Arusha 341; Mbeya 291; Morogoro 250; Tanga 224; Dodoma 180; Kigoma 164; Moshi 156; Tabora 145; Songea 126, Musoma 121				
Neighbours (km)	Mozambique 756; Malawi 475; Zambia 338; Congo DR 459; Burundi 451; Rwanda 217; Uganda 396; Kenya 769; Indian Ocean 1 424				
Main stadia	National Stadium – Dar-es-Salaam 15 000; CCM Kirumba – Mwanza 30 000				

FIFA REFEREE LIST 2005

	Int'l	DoB
BAIJUKA Frederick	2002	10-07-1964
CHAULA Emmanuel	1997	14-02-1962
CHIGANGA Pascal	2000	10-04-1964
IBADA Ramadhan	2004	9-02-1969
KAZI Osman	2005	2-10-1973
MWANDIKE Victor	2002	15-01-1967
WAZIRI Sheha		27-03-1971

FIFA ASSISTANT REFEREE LIST 2005

	Int'l	Birth date
ABDI Soud	2000	1-04-1962
BWIRE Manyama	2000	1-01-1961
CHANGWALU Hamis	2005	24-06-1977
CHARLES Mchau	2000	26-03-1960
MOHAMED Ramadhani	2002	4-04-1963
NDAGALA Charles	2004	24-08-1968
NYANDWI David	1996	19-04-1961

TANZANIA 2004 FIRST STAGE GROUP A

	Pl	W	D	L	F	A	Pts
Prisons Mbeya †	16	10	3	3	16	7	33
Young Africans †	16	8	5	3	28	14	29
Police Dodoma †	15	8	3	4	20	14	27
Arusha FC †	16	7	1	8	21	20	22
Maji Maji Songea	16	4	8	4	13	14	20
Trans Camp	15	5	2	8	9	12	17
Karume Rangers	16	4	3	9	8	20	15
Vijana	15	2	8	5	7	11	14
Bandari Mtwara	15	3	5	7	9	19	14
Reli Kigoma	Disqualified after 12 rounds						

17/04/2004 - 26/07/2004 • † Qualified for Super 8 League

TANZANIA 2004 FIRST STAGE GROUP B

	Pl	W	D	L	F	A	Pts
Simba SC †	14	9	2	3	19	9	29
Moro Utd Morogoro †	14	7	3	4	17	9	24
Ruvu Stars Dodoma †	14	4	7	3	12	8	19
Mtibwa Sugar Turiani †	13	5	4	4	12	9	19
Kahama Utd Shinyanga	13	4	6	3	11	10	18
Twiga Sports	13	4	3	6	8	13	15
Mji Mpwapwa	13	3	4	6	8	12	13
Tukuyu Stars Mbeya	14	1	5	8	6	23	8
Kariakoo Lindi	Disqualified after 8 rounds						
Pallsons Arusha	Disqualified after 8 rounds						

17/04/2004 - 25/07/2004 • † Qualified for Super 8 League

TANZANIA 2004

SUPER EIGHT LEAGUE

	Pl	W	D	L	F	A	Pts	Simba	Sugar	Yanga	Prisons	Moro Utd	Police	Kahama	Arusha
Simba SC †	14	10	4	0	18	6	34		1-1	2-1	1-0	1-0	1-0	3-1	1-1
Mtibwa Sugar	14	7	4	3	25	16	25	0-1		3-3	2-1	5-0	2-1	4-2	
Young Africans	14	7	2	5	20	12	23	0-1	0-1		1-1	1-0	1-0	3-0	3-0
Prisons ‡	14	6	4	4	14	11	22	0-0	2-1	1-0		1-1	0-1	1-2	2-0
Moro United	14	4	8	2	18	11	20	1-1	4-2	1-0	1-1		1-1	3-0	4-1
Police	14	4	3	7	11	17	15	0-1	0-1	2-3	1-2	1-1		2-0	1-0
Kahama United	14	1	3	10	4	21	6	0-1	**0-2**	**0-2**	0-1	0-0	0-1		0-0
Arusha FC	14	0	6	8	8	24	6	1-3	1-1	0-2	0-1	1-1	1-1	0-0	

31/07/2004 - 23/10/2004 • † Qualified for the CAF Champions League • ‡ Qualified for the CAF Confederation Cup • Matches in bold were awarded 2-0 after both had originally finished 0-0

RECENT LEAGUE AND CUP RECORD

Year	Union League Champions	Tanzanian Mainland Champions	Islands League Champions	FAT Cup Winners
1990	Pamba Shinyanga	Simba SC Dar es Salaam	Malindi	Small Simba
1991	Young Africans Dar es Salaam	Young Africans Dar es Salaam	Small Simba	Railways Morogoro
1992	Malindi	Young Africans Dar es Salaam	Malindi	Pamba FC Mwamba
1993	Simba SC Dar es Salaam	Young Africans Dar es Salaam	Shengini	Malindi
1994	Simba SC Dar es Salaam	Simba SC Dar es Salaam	Shengini	Young Africans Dar es Salaam
1995	Simba SC Dar es Salaam	Simba SC Dar es Salaam	Small Simba	Simba SC Dar es Salaam
1996	Young Africans Dar es Salaam	Young Africans Dar es Salaam	Mlandege	Sigara
1997	Young Africans Dar es Salaam	Young Africans Dar es Salaam	-	Tanzania Stars
1998	Maji Maji Songea	Young Africans Dar es Salaam	Mlandege	Tanzania Stars
1999	Prisons Mbeya	Mtibwa Sugar	Mlandege	Young Africans Dar es Salaam
2000	Young Africans Dar es Salaam	Mtibwa Sugar	Kipanga	Simba SC Dar es Salaam
2001	Simba SC Dar es Salaam	Simba SC Dar es Salaam	Mlandege	Polisi Zanzibar
2002	Simba SC Dar es Salaam	Young Africans Dar es Salaam	Mlandege	Ruvu Stars
2003	Discontinued	Simba SC Dar es Salaam	Jamhuri Pemba	
2004		Simba SC Dar es Salaam		

The Union League was a play-off between the top teams from the Mainland League and the Islands League • The Island of Zanzibar is now eligible to enter a team by right into CAF competitions

TCA – TURKS AND CAICOS ISLANDS

NATIONAL TEAM RECORD
JULY 1ST 2002 TO JUNE 30TH 2005

PL	W	D	L	F	A	%
2	0	0	2	0	7	0

FIFA/COCA-COLA WORLD RANKING

1993	1994	1995	1996	1997	1998	1999	2000	2001	2002	2003	2004	High		Low	
-	-	-	-	-	-	196	200	200	202	203	203	192	05/99	203	05/05

2004-2005											
08/04	09/04	10/04	11/04	12/04	01/05	02/05	03/05	04/05	05/05	06/05	07/05
202	202	202	203	203	203	203	203	203	203	203	203

Propping up the CONCACAF nations, the Turks and Caicos Islands are also just two places off the bottom of the FIFA/Coca-Cola World Ranking and struggling to make any impact internationally. After being inactive for more than three years, the national side re-emerged in 2004 to play twice against Haiti in the 2006 FIFA World Cup™ preliminary round qualifiers. Although they lost both legs 7-0 on aggregate against one of the region's stronger teams, the Turks could be pleased with their first competitive games in four years against a nation ranked more than 100 places above them. A new national training centre was opened in Providenciales with help from the Goal

INTERNATIONAL HONOURS
None

programme and FIFA's Financial Assistance Programme that has been used primarily by the islands' youngsters. However, a youth programme has not developed and neither an U-20 nor an U-17 side featured in regional tournaments. The 2004-05 MFL League was won by KPMG United FC for the second year running, finishing five points ahead of second place Caribbean All Stars in the five-team championship. KPMG failed to take the double though when they lost to Police FC in the final of the Fidelity Cup. It took a Police goal two minutes from the end of extra-time to seal the match after a 3-3 draw in normal time.

THE FIFA BIG COUNT OF 2000

	Male	Female		Male	Female
Registered players	120	30	Referees	15	0
Non registered players	200	200	Officials	30	20
Youth players	400	0	Total involved	1 015	
Total players	950		Number of clubs	6	
Professional players	0	0	Number of teams	6	

Turks and Caicos Islands Football Association (TCIFA)
Tropicana Plaza, Leeward Highway, PO Box 626, Providenciales, Turks and Caicos Islands
Tel +1 649 9415532   Fax +1 649 9415554
tcifa@tciway.tc   www.football.tc
President: SMITH Thomas   General Secretary: BRYAN Christopher
Vice-President: SLATTERY James   Treasurer: BRUTON Dax   Media Officer: None
Men's Coach: CROSBIE Paul   Women's Coach: CROSBIE Paul
TCIFA formed: 1996   CONCACAF: 1998   FIFA: 1998
Colours: White, White, White

GAMES PLAYED BY TURKS AND CAICOS ISLANDS IN THE 2006 FIFA WORLD CUP™ CYCLE

2002	Opponents	Score	Venue	Comp	Scorers	Att	Referee
	No international matches played in 2002						
2003							
	No international matches played in 2003						
2004							
18-02	Haiti	L 0-5	Miami †	WCq		3 000	Stott USA
21-02	Haiti	L 0-2	Hialeah †	WCq		3 000	Valenzuela USA
2005							
	No international matches played in 2005 before August						

WC = FIFA World Cup™ • q = qualifier • † Both matches played in the USA

TURKS AND CAICOS ISLANDS NATIONAL TEAM RECORDS AND RECORD SEQUENCES

Records			Sequence records					
Victory	-		Wins	0		Clean sheets	0	
Defeat	0-8	SKN 2000	Defeats	6	2000-2004	Goals scored	1	1999, 2000
Player Caps			Undefeated	1	1999	Without goal	3	2000
Player Goals			Without win	8	1999-2004	Goals against	8	1999-2004

Turks and Caicos have no referees or assistant referees on the FIFA list

TURKS AND CAICOS ISLANDS 2004-05 MFL LEAGUE

	Pl	W	D	L	F	A	Pts
KPMG United	11	10	0	1	46	15	**30**
Caribbean All Stars	11	8	1	2	39	15	**25**
Cost Right	11	4	2	5	18	25	**14**
SWA Sharks	12	2	1	9	15	40	**7**
ProvoPool Celtic	11	1	2	8	19	42	**5**

16/10/2004 - 18/05/2005

RECENT LEAGUE AND CUP RECORD

	Championship							Cup		
Year	Champions	Pts	Runners-up	Pts	Third	Pts		Winners	Score	Runners-up
1999	Tropic All Stars	15	Fleches Rapides	13	Provo	7		No tournament		
2000	Masters	16	Beaches	10	Sans Complex	4		Masters	2-0	Beaches
2001	Sharks	1-0	Projetech					No tournament		
2002	Beaches †	2-2	Barefoot					No tournament		
2003	Caribbean All Stars	28	Master Hammer	25	KPMG United	13		Caribbean All Stars	2-1	Master Hammer
2004	KPMG United	27	Caribbean All Stars	22	Police	14		Police	4-3	KPMG United
2005	KPMG United	30	Caribbean All Stars	25	Cost Right	14				

† Final abandoned at 2-2. Beaches declared champions

TURKS AND CAICOS ISLANDS COUNTRY INFORMATION

Capital	Cockburn Town	Status	Overseas territory of the UK	GDP per Capita	$9 600
Population	19 956			GNP Ranking	n/a
Area km²	430	Language	English	Dialling code	+1649
Population density	46 per km²	Literacy rate	98%	Internet code	.tc
% in urban areas	n/a	Main religion	Christian	GMT +/−	-4
Towns/Cities	Cockburn Town 5 525; Cockburn Harbour 1 744				
Neighbours (km)	North Atlantic Ocean 389				
Main stadia	National Development Facility – Providenciales 1 500				

TGA – TONGA

NATIONAL TEAM RECORD
JULY 1ST 2002 TO JUNE 30TH 2005

PL	W	D	L	F	A	%
7	1	1	5	4	27	21.4

FIFA/COCA-COLA WORLD RANKING

1993	1994	1995	1996	1997	1998	1999	2000	2001	2002	2003	2004	High		Low	
-	-	-	164	174	163	178	185	173	175	180	183	**163**	10/98	**185**	05/04

2004-2005											
08/04	09/04	10/04	11/04	12/04	01/05	02/05	03/05	04/05	05/05	06/05	07/05
182	182	182	182	183	183	183	184	184	184	184	184

For a country whose sporting profile is dominated by rugby, Tonga are making solid progress in establishing football on its many islands. Admitted to FIFA in 1994, the country has since proved to be one of Oceania's most ambitious nations with a careful programme of continuous development. This has partly manifested itself through the FIFA Goal project, the first instalment of which involved construction of a football academy, while the second and most recent development has been to improve the academy and incorporate the national association's headquarters. On the field, results have not been as successful. Participation in the South Pacific Games brought just one win

INTERNATIONAL HONOURS
None

in four matches, a 7-0 victory over Micronesia, while the subsequent FIFA World Cup™ campaign was equally disappointing. Opening with a 6-0 defeat against the Solomon Islands, Tonga registered their only victory in the group against the Cook Islands before succumbing to Tahiti and New Caledonia. Results may take time to improve but with a football-mad monarch who provided the land for the academy, football can rely on high-level support. SC Lotoha'apa Nuku'alofa won the Major League title for the seventh year in a row qualifying for the Oceania Champion Clubs Cup. There they made little impact, losing 1-7 to Tafea of Vanuatu in the preliminary round.

THE FIFA BIG COUNT OF 2000

	Male	Female		Male	Female
Registered players	1 824	272	Referees	78	24
Non registered players	500	100	Officials	87	36
Youth players	864	288	Total involved	4 073	
Total players	3 848		Number of clubs	91	
Professional players	0	0	Number of teams	203	

Tonga Football Association (FTF)
Loto Tonga Soko Center, Off Taufa'Ahau Road - 'Atele, PO Box 852, Nuku'alofa, Tonga
Tel +676 30233   Fax +676 30240
tfa@kalianet.to   www.tongafootball.com
President: VEEHALA Hon   General Secretary: FUSIMALOHI Ahongalu
Vice-President: FUSITUA Hon   Treasurer: AHO Lui   Media Officer: None
Men's Coach: JANKOVIC Milan   Women's Coach: None
FTF formed: 1965   OFC: 1994   FIFA: 1994
Colours: Red, White, Red

GAMES PLAYED BY TONGA IN THE 2006 FIFA WORLD CUP™ CYCLE

2002	Opponents	Score		Venue	Comp	Scorers	Att	Referee
No international matches played in 2002 after June								
2003								
1-07	Papua New Guinea	D	2-2	Suva	SPr1		3 000	Singh FIJ
3-07	New Caledonia	L	0-4	Suva	SPr1		700	Shah FIJ
5-07	Micronesia †	W	7-0	Nausori	SPr1	Fonua 5, Tevi 15, Uhatahi 2 22 36, Feao 2 34 55, Uele 72	1 000	Moli SOL
7-07	Tahiti	L	0-4	Lautoka	SPr1		3 000	Shah FIJ
2004								
10-05	Solomon Islands	L	0-6	Honiara	WCq		12 385	Attison VAN
15-05	Cook Islands	W	2-1	Honiara	WCq	Uhatahi 46, Vaitaki 61	15 000	Sosongan PNG
17-05	Tahiti	L	0-2	Honiara	WCq		400	Sosongan PNG
19-05	New Caledonia	L	0-8	Honiara	WCq		14 000	Fred VAN
2005								
No international matches played in 2005 before August								

Fr = Friendly match • SP = South Pacific Games • WC = FIFA World Cup™ • q = qualifier • r1 = first round group • † Not a full international

TONGA NATIONAL TEAM RECORDS AND RECORD SEQUENCES

Records			Sequence records					
Victory	5-0	ASA 2001	Wins	3	1994-1996	Clean sheets	2	1996
Defeat	0-22	AUS 2001	Defeats	4	1998-2000	Goals scored	4	1994-96, 2000-01
Player Caps	n/a		Undefeated	4	1994-1996	Without goal	4	1993-1994
Player Goals	n/a		Without win	6	1983-1994	Goals against	12	2001-2004

FIFA ASSISTANT REFEREE LIST 2005

	Int'l	DoB
MAILE Ngase	2004	9-06-1972
VAKATAPU Koliniasi	2005	1-07-1975

TONGA CHAMPIONS

Year	Champions
1998	SC Lotoha'apai Nuku'alofa
1999	SC Lotoha'apai Nuku'alofa
2000	SC Lotoha'apai Nuku'alofa
2001	SC Lotoha'apai Nuku'alofa
2002	SC Lotoha'apai Nuku'alofa
2003	SC Lotoha'apai Nuku'alofa
2004	SC Lotoha'apai Nuku'alofa

TONGA COUNTRY INFORMATION

Capital	Nuku'alofa	Independence	1970 from the UK	GDP per Capita	$2 200
Population	110 237	Status	Constitutional Monarchy	GNP Ranking	186
Area km²	748	Language	Tongan, English	Dialling code	+676
Population density	147 per km²	Literacy rate	98%	Internet code	.to
% in urban areas	41%	Main religion	Christian	GMT +/–	+13
Towns/Cities ('000)	Nuku'alofa 23; Mu'a 5; Neiafu 4; Haveloloto 3; Vaini 3; Tofoa-Koloua 2; Pangai 2				
Neighbours (km)	South Pacific Ocean 419				
Main stadia	Mangweni Stadium – Nuku'alofa 3 000				

THA – THAILAND

NATIONAL TEAM RECORD
JULY 1ST 2002 TO JUNE 30TH 2005

PL	W	D	L	F	A	%
37	12	9	16	57	61	44.6

FIFA/COCA-COLA WORLD RANKING

1993	1994	1995	1996	1997	1998	1999	2000	2001	2002	2003	2004	High		Low	
69	85	77	57	54	45	60	61	61	66	60	79	43	09/98	103	11/95

					2004-2005						
08/04	09/04	10/04	11/04	12/04	01/05	02/05	03/05	04/05	05/05	06/05	07/05
64	67	74	72	79	80	80	80	83	84	88	96

Chosen as co-hosts for the 2007 Asian Cup, Thailand will be seeking to improve on a modest record in the tournament. Coach Peter Withe did much to improve the team including winning the 2002 Tiger Cup before leaving in September 2003, since when the side has slid back down the FIFA/Coca-Cola World Ranking. At the 2004 Asian Cup finals, Thailand lost all three of their matches to make an early departure from China while the defence of their Tiger Cup crown also ended prematurely at the group stage. Interspersed between these tournaments were the 2006 FIFA World Cup™ qualifiers which were equally as unimpressive as the Thais took just seven points

INTERNATIONAL HONOURS
SEA Games 1965 1975 1981 1983 1985 1993 1995 1997 1999 2001 2003 **Tiger Cup** 1996 2000 2002
AFC Champions League Thai Farmers Bank 1994 1995

from six games to finish third in the group behind Korea DPR and the United Arab Emirates. The tsunami of December 2004 caused widespread destruction and loss of life in the southern parts of the country and FIFA's Tsunami Task Force provided nearly US$1 million in aid, money that has been used to construct the Tsunami Memorial Football Centre and other projects. In the Premier Division, Thailand Tobacco won the title for the first time while newly-promoted Electrical Authority surprised everyone by claiming the runners-up spot.

THE FIFA BIG COUNT OF 2000

	Male	Female		Male	Female
Registered players	9 680	100	Referees	1 000	3
Non registered players	300 000	10 000	Officials	5 000	3
Youth players	15 000	0	Total involved	340 786	
Total players	334 780		Number of clubs	132	
Professional players	480	0	Number of teams	1 624	

The Football Association of Thailand (FAT)
National Stadium, Gate 3, Rama 1 Road, Patumwan, Bangkok 10330, Thailand
Tel +66 2 2164691   Fax +66 2 2154494
www.none

President: GETKAEW Vijit Dr   General Secretary: MAKUDI Worawi
Vice-President: WATTANAWONGKEEREE Pisarn   Treasurer: MULULIM Samart   Media Officer: None
Men's Coach: HELD Siegfried   Women's Coach: PONGPANICH Prapol
FAT formed: 1916   AFC: 1957   FIFA: 1925
Colours: Red, Red, Red

GAMES PLAYED BY THAILAND IN THE 2006 FIFA WORLD CUP™ CYCLE

2002	Opponents	Score	Venue	Comp	Scorers	Att	Referee
8-12	Vietnam	W 2-1	Bangkok	Fr	Chaiman 2 [24 56]		
18-12	Laos	W 5-1	Singapore	TCr1	Srimaka 2 [1 24], Senamuang 3 [8 83 90]	7 000	Rahman SIN
20-12	Malaysia	L 1-3	Singapore	TCr1	Chaiman [23]	7 000	Luong MYA
22-12	Singapore	D 1-1	Singapore	TCr1	Srimaka [15]	20 000	Anders PHI
27-12	Vietnam	W 4-0	Jakarta	TCsf	Srimaka [24], Vachiraban [42], Noyvach [75], Joemdee [90]	10 000	Nagalingham SIN
29-12	Indonesia	D 2-2	Jakarta	TCf	Noosalung [26], Chaiman [38], W 4-2p	100 000	Mohd Salleh MAS
2003							
16-02	Korea DPR	D 2-2	Thailand	Fr	Chaikamdee [27], Thonglao [55]		
18-02	Qatar	D 1-1	Bangkok	Fr	Chaiman [55p]		Lee Gi Young KOR
20-02	Sweden	L 1-4	Bangkok	Fr	Vachiraban [80]		Lee Gi Young KOR
22-02	Qatar	W 3-1	Bangkok	Fr	Noyvach 2 [24 33], Cheoychiew [76]		
16-10	India	W 2-0	Bangkok	Fr	Phorueundee [64], Chaikamdee [78]		
6-11	Takijistan	L 0-1	Tashkent	ACq			
8-11	Uzbekistan	L 0-3	Tashkent	ACq			
10-11	Hong Kong	L 1-2	Tashkent	ACq	Thonglao [64]		
17-11	Hong Kong	W 4-0	Bangkok	ACq	Noyvech [24], Thonglao [35], Chaikamdee 2 [79 88p]		
19-11	Tajikistan	W 1-0	Bangkok	ACq	Chaiman [83p]		
21-11	Uzbekistan	W 4-1	Bangkok	ACq	Noyvech [38], Surasiang [56], Tongmaen [78], Chaikamdee [81]		
2004							
18-02	United Arab Emirates	L 0-1	Al Ain	WCq		4 000	Sun Baojie CHN
31-03	Yemen	W 3-0	Sana'a	WCq	Chaikamdee [69], Surasiang [71], Senamuang [88]	25 000	Mansour LIB
9-06	Korea DPR	L 1-4	Bangkok	WCq	Senamuang [51]	30 000	Tseytlin UZB
5-07	Bahrain	L 0-2	Bangkok	Fr			
8-07	Jordan	D 0-0	Bangkok	Fr			
10-07	Trinidad and Tobago	W 3-2	Bangkok	Fr	Vachiraban [47], Suksomkit [53], Pichitpong [87]		
20-07	Iran	L 0-3	Chongqing	ACr1		37 000	Kousa SYR
24-07	Japan	L 1-4	Chongqing	ACr1	Suksomkit [11]	45 000	Al Marzouqi UAE
28-07	Oman	L 0-2	Chengdu	ACr1		13 000	Lu Jun CHN
19-08	Malaysia	L 1-2	Bangkok	Fr	Chaiman [90]		
8-09	Korea DPR	L 1-4	Pyongyang	WCq	Suksomkit [72]	20 000	Moradi IRN
8-10	Jordan	L 2-3	Bangkok	Fr			
13-10	United Arab Emirates	W 3-0	Bangkok	WCq	Jakapong [10], Nanok [30], Chaiman [67]	15 000	Nishimura JPN
17-11	Yemen	D 1-1	Bangkok	WCq	Siriwong [95+]	15 000	Baskar IND
30-11	Estonia	D 0-0	Bangkok	Fr	W 4-3p	35 000	Mat Amin MAS
2-12	Slovakia	D 1-1	Bangkok	Fr	Joemdee [15p], L 4-5p	5 000	Chappanimutu MAS
10-12	Myanmar	D 1-1	Kuala Lumpur	TCr1	Chaiman [14]		Moradi IRN
12-12	East Timor †	W 8-0	Kuala Lumpur	TCr1	Yodyingyong [17], Domthaisong [41], Jitkuntod [53], Chaiman [59], Chaikamdee 3 [63 65 67], Konjan [84]		Vo Minh Try VIE
14-12	Malaysia	L 1-2	Kuala Lumpur	TCr1	Chaikamdee [45]	10 000	Moradi IRN
16-12	Philippines	W 3-1	Kuala Lumpur	TCr1	Poolsap [42], Sainui [56], Domthaisong [89]	300	Vo Minh Try VIE
21-12	Germany	L 1-5	Bangkok	Fr	Chaikamdee [57]	15 000	Maidin SIN
2005							

No international matches played in 2005 before August

Fr = Friendly match • TC = ASEAN Tiger Cup • AC = AFC Asian Cup • WC = FIFA World Cup™
q = qualifier • r1 = 1st round • sf = semi-final • f = final • † Not a full international

THAILAND COUNTRY INFORMATION

Capital	Bangkok	Foundation	1238	GDP per Capita	$7 400
Population	64 865 523	Status	Constitutional Monarchy	GNP Ranking	32
Area km²	514 000	Language	Thai	Dialling code	+66
Population density	126 per km²	Literacy rate	92%	Internet code	.th
% in urban areas	20%	Main religion	Buddhist	GMT +/–	+7
Towns/Cities ('000)	Bangkok 5 104; Samut Prakan 388; Nonthaburi 375; Udon Thani 247; Chon Buri 219; Nakhon Ratchasima 208; Chiang Mai 201; Hat Yai 191; Pak Kret 183; Si Racha 179				
Neighbours (km)	Laos 1 754; Cambodia 803; Malaysia 506; Myanmar 1 800; Gulf of Thailand 3 219				
Main stadia	Rajamangala – Bangkok 65 000; Suphachalasai – Bangkok 30 000				

THAILAND NATIONAL TEAM RECORDS AND RECORD SEQUENCES

Records			Sequence records					
Victory	10-0	BRU 1970	Wins	8	1993	Clean sheets	4	Five times
Defeat	0-8	CZE 1968	Defeats	11	1959-1961	Goals scored	19	1960-1963
Player Caps	n/a		Undefeated	11	1995-1996	Without goal	9	1990-1991
Player Goals	n/a		Without win	23	1959-1963	Goals against	31	1959-1965

FIFA REFEREE LIST 2005

	Int'l	DoB
KHANTHAMA Adunyachart	1999	14-08-1969
KUNSUTA Chaiwat	1999	25-07-1965
PHAENGSUPHA Natthanai		19-11-1962
ROONGSANG Tossaporn	2005	13-03-1972
RUNGKLAY Mongkol		2-04-1960
SANANWAI Chawalit	2005	9-10-1969
TONGKHAN Satop		22-06-1963
VEERAPOOL Prayoon		3-04-1972
WAIYABOT Anucha	1998	29-07-1963

FIFA ASSISTANT REFEREE LIST 2005

	Int'l	DoB
BORIKUT Thanom	2005	17-06-1969
KAETKUANG Apichart		1-09-1962
KLIENKLARD Sitthikhun	1998	24-08-1962
KONGTONGKAI Sunchai	2005	23-04-1969
PERMPANICH Prachya	1995	13-08-1962
PREMSUK Somchai	1999	1-12-1963
PUTSORN Pornchai	2005	5-04-1965
SAIWAEW Sumate		2-01-1970
SRIDEE Uthen		13-04-1963
TONGSUWIMON Surasak	1999	18-01-1960

THAILAND 2004-05

PREMIER LEAGUE

	Pl	W	D	L	F	A	Pts	Tobacco	PEA	Osotpa	Port	KTB	BEC Tero	University	BBL	TOT	Navy
Thailand Tobacco	18	9	7	2	26	11	34		0-0	1-2	0-2	0-0	0-0	0-0	3-0	0-0	4-0
Electrical Authority	18	9	5	4	23	19	32	0-2		2-1	4-1	3-2	1-1	3-2	1-2	1-0	2-1
Osotspa	18	9	5	4	34	20	32	1-1	1-2		2-4	1-1	1-0	2-1	5-1	3-2	4-0
Port Authority	18	7	5	6	26	27	26	1-4	11-	1-1		1-2	1-3	2-0	1-0	0-3	1-2
Krung Thai Bank	18	6	7	5	24	22	25	1-3	0-0	0-1	0-0		3-1	2-3	2-1	2-2	2-1
BEC Tero Sasana	18	6	7	5	19	18	25	0-1	3-0	1-1	0-3	3-2		0-0	1-2	2-2	1-0
Bangkok University	18	5	7	6	16	21	22	0-0	1-0	2-1	0-0	0-0	0-1		2-2	1-1	1-0
Bangkok Bank	18	5	5	8	25	28	20	2-3	1-1	1-1	1-2	0-1	1-1	4-0		1-1	1-2
Telephone Organisation	18	3	7	8	20	25	16	1-2	0-1	0-3	3-4	1-1	0-0	1-2	1-2		1-0
Royal Thai Navy	18	3	1	14	11	33	10	1-2	0-1	0-3	1-1	1-3	0-1	2-1	0-3	0-1	

28/11/2004 - 7/05/2005 • † Qualified for the AFC Champions League

RECENT LEAGUE RECORD

	Championship						
Year	Champions	Pts	Runners-up	Pts	Third	Pts	
1996	Bangkok Bank						
1997	Bangkok Bank	2-0	Stock Exchange				
1997	Royal Thai Air Force	42	Sinthana	42	Bangkok Bank	38	
1998	Sinthana	42	Royal Thai Air Force	40	BEC Tero Sasana	38	
1999	Royal Thai Air Force	39	Port Authority	39	BEC Tero Sasana	39	
2000	BEC Tero Sasana	49	Royal Thai Air Force	41	Thai Farmers Bank	37	
2002	BEC Tero Sasana	50	Osotapa	44	Bangkok Bank	35	
2003	Krung Thai Bank	36	BEC Tero Sasana	35	Port Authority	33	
2004	Krung Thai Bank	38	BEC Tero Sasana	34	Osotapa	33	
2005	Thailand Tobacco	34	Electical Authority	32	Osotapa	32	

TJK – TAJIKISTAN

NATIONAL TEAM RECORD

JULY 1ST 2002 TO JUNE 30TH 2005

PL	W	D	L	F	A	%
16	6	3	7	12	20	

FIFA/COCA-COLA WORLD RANKING

1993	1994	1995	1996	1997	1998	1999	2000	2001	2002	2003	2004	High		Low	
-	155	164	163	118	120	119	134	154	168	137	136	114	07/97	180	10/03

					2004-2005							
08/04	09/04	10/04	11/04	12/04	01/05	02/05	03/05	04/05	05/05	06/05	07/05	
136	136	137	133	136	135	136	137	138	137	138	139	

Tajikistan joined FIFA in 1994 following the break-up of the Soviet Union and are beginning to show small signs of progress. Entered for the 1998 and 2002 FIFA World Cup™, the national team exited early at the preliminary round stage but not without registering some notable scalps including a 5-0 victory over Turkmenistan and a 16-0 pounding of Guam. In the 2006 qualifying tournament opponents didn't quite know what to expect because of the few international games that Tajikistan have played. Bangladesh were dismissed with little fuss and the Tajiks were grouped with Bahrain, Kyrgyzstan and Syria. A goalless draw with Bahrain in which two penalties were saved put

INTERNATIONAL HONOURS

None

Tajikistan at the top of the group, but that was as good as it got and Tajikistan were soon eliminated. Having only played twice since, more fixtures are needed if Tajikistan are to develop. With Uzbekistan, Turkmenistan and Kyrgysztan there is good opposition available in the region. In 2002 the Federation received approval from FIFA's Goal project to build a new headquarters, but problems delayed its construction and it was expected to be completed in 2005. The Tajiki Premier Division was won by Regar-Tursunzoda who edged out Vaksh Qurghonteppa for their fifth title in as many years.

THE FIFA BIG COUNT OF 2000

	Male	Female		Male	Female
Registered players	750	0	Referees	45	0
Non registered players	30 000	0	Officials	240	0
Youth players	1 600	0	Total involved	32 635	
Total players	32 350		Number of clubs	125	
Professional players	0	0	Number of teams	200	

Tajikistan Football Federation (TFF)

14/ Ainy Street, Dushanbe 734 025, Tajikistan

Tel +992 372 212447   Fax +992 372 510157

tff@tajikfootball.org   www.none

President: KOSIMOV Sukhrob   General Secretary: DAVLATOV Sherali

Vice-President: TURSUNOV Valery   Treasurer: KHOLOV Sherali   Media Officer: BURIEV Aloviddin

Men's Coach: BABAEV Zoir   Women's Coach: GASANOVA Zebo

TFF formed: 1936   AFC: 1994   FIFA: 1994

Colours: White, White, White

GAMES PLAYED BY TAJIKISTAN IN THE 2006 FIFA WORLD CUP™ CYCLE

2002 Opponents	Score	Venue	Comp	Scorers	Att	Referee
No international matches played in 2002						
2003						
6-11 Thailand	W 1-0	Tashkent	ACq	Fuzailov [79]		
8-11 Hong Kong	D 0-0	Tashkent	ACq			
10-11 Uzbekistan	D 0-0	Tashkent	ACq			
17-11 Uzbekistan	L 1-4	Bangkok	ACq	Burkhanov [65]		
19-11 Thailand	L 0-1	Bangkok	ACq			
21-11 Hong Kong	W 1-0	Bangkok	ACq	Muhidinov [68]		
26-11 Bangladesh	W 2-0	Dhaka	WCq	Hamidov [11], Hakimov [51]	6 000	Khanthachai THA
30-11 Bangladesh	W 2-0	Dushanbe	WCq	Kholomatov [15], Rabiev [83]	12 000	Pereira IND
2004						
18-02 Kyrgyzstan	W 2-1	Bishkek	WCq	Burkhanon 2 [31 53]	14 000	Lutfullin UZB
31-03 Bahrain	D 0-0	Dushanbe	WCq		17 000	Maidin SIN
10-06 Syria	L 1-2	Homs	WCq	Kholomatov [35]	18 000	Al Fadhli KUW
8-09 Syria	L 0-1	Dushanbe	WCq		18 000	Mohd Salleh MAS
13-10 Kyrgyzstan	W 2-1	Dushanbe	WCq	Rabiev [19], Hakimov [37]	11 000	Naser Al Enezi KUW
17-11 Bahrain	L 0-4	Manama	WCq		15 000	Sun Baojie CHN
6-12 Kuwait	L 0-3	Kuwait City	Fr			
2005						
25-01 Saudi Arabia	L 0-3	Riyadh	Fr			

Fr = Friendly match • AC = AFC Asian Cup • WC = FIFA World Cup™ • q = qualifier

TAJIKISTAN NATIONAL TEAM RECORDS AND RECORD SEQUENCES

Records			Sequence records				
Victory	16-0	GUM 2000	Wins	4	2003-2004	Clean sheets	3	1997, 2003, 2003
Defeat	0-5	UZB 1996, IRN 1998	Defeats	3	Three times	Goals scored	5	1997-98, 1998-99
Player Caps	n/a		Undefeated	5	2003-2004	Without goal	3	1993-94, 2004-05
Player Goals	n/a		Without win	5	1998-1999	Goals against	7	1998-1999

TAJIKISTAN 2004 PREMIER DIVISION

	Pl	W	D	L	F	A	Pts
Regar Tursunzoda	36	26	8	2	111	32	86
Vakhsh Qurghonteppa	36	26	7	3	89	24	85
Aviator B. Gafurov	36	22	5	9	87	33	71
FK Khujand	36	17	9	10	56	36	60
BDA Dushanbe	36	15	7	14	65	56	52
FK Uroteppa	36	11	8	17	52	65	41
CSKA Dushanbe	36	11	4	21	55	76	37
FK Danghara	36	10	7	19	47	67	37
Olimp-Ansol Kulob	36	10	6	20	55	70	36
Safarbek Gazimalik	36	0	1	35	15	179	1

Safarbek withdrew after round 22 • Uroteppa withdrew after round 31 • All their remaining matches were awarded 3-0
Tajikistan Cup Final 2004: Aviator 5-0 Uroteppa

RECENT LEAGUE RECORD

	Championship					
Year	Champions	Pts	Runners-up	Pts	Third	Pts
1992	Pamir Dushanbe	33	Regar Tursunzoda	26	Vakhsh Qur'teppa	24
1993	Sitora Dushanbe	55	Pamir Dushanbe	52	P'takor Proletarsk	42
1994	Sitora Dushanbe	47	Pamir Dushanbe	45	P'takor Proletarsk	43
1995	Pamir Dushanbe	67	Istravshan	57	Sitora Dushanbe	52
1996	Dinamo Dushanbe	73	Sitora Dushanbe	71	Khojent	64
1997	Vakhsh Qur'teppa	59	Ranjbar Vosse	55	Khujand	52
1998	Varzob Dushanbe	56	Khujand	44	Saddam Sarband	42
1999	Varzob Dushanbe	57	Khuja Gazimalik	49	Ravshan Kulyab	46
2000	Varzob Dushanbe	87	Regar Tursunzoda	77	Khujand	68
2001	Regar Tursunzoda	50	Panjsher Kolk'bad	38	Pamir Dushanbe	32
2002	Regar Tursunzoda	58	Khujand	53	Farrukh Ghissar	44
2003	Regar Tursunzoda	81	Khujand	72	Aviator	71
2004	Regar Tursunzoda	86	Vakhsh Qur'teppa	85	Aviator	71

Tajik clubs took part in the Soviet league until the end of the 1991 season

TAJIKISTAN COUNTRY INFORMATION

Capital	Dushanbe	Independence	1991 from the USSR	GDP per Capita	$1 000
Population	7 011 556	Status	Republic	GNP Ranking	152
Area km²	143 100	Language	Tajik, Russian	Dialling code	+992
Population density	49 per km²	Literacy rate	99%	Internet code	.tj
% in urban areas	32%	Main religion	Muslim	GMT +/–	+5
Towns/Cities ('000)	Dushanbe 543; Khujand 144; Kulob 78; Qurgonteppa 60; Uroteppa 52; Konibodom 50				
Neighbours (km)	China 414; Afghanistan 1 206; Uzbekistan 1 161 Kyrgyzstan 870;				
Main stadia	National Stadium – Dushanbe 20 000				

TKM – TURKMENISTAN

NATIONAL TEAM RECORD
JULY 1ST 2002 TO JUNE 30TH 2005

PL	W	D	L	F	A	%
21	9	4	8	37	26	52.4

FIFA/COCA-COLA WORLD RANKING

1993	1994	1995	1996	1997	1998	1999	2000	2001	2002	2003	2004	High		Low	
-	108	133	141	134	122	129	125	114	134	99	98	86	04/04	150	04/97

2004-2005											
08/04	09/04	10/04	11/04	12/04	01/05	02/05	03/05	04/05	05/05	06/05	07/05
90	91	93	93	98	99	96	99	100	103	105	105

Turkmenistan suffered an extraordinary reversal of fortunes in the 2004-05 season. Having qualified for the Asian Cup finals on the back of an unbeaten sequence of nine victories and two draws that included an 11-0 thrashing of Afghanistan, they conspired to lose eight and draw two of their next 10 games. The end result was that Turkmenistan failed to get past the group stage in China and finished a distant second behind Saudi Arabia in their 2006 FIFA World Cup™ qualifying group. In spite of the recent decline in fortunes on the pitch, Turkmenistan has prospered reasonably well since joining FIFA in 1994 after the dismantling of the Soviet Union and rose to a high of 86th in

INTERNATIONAL HONOURS
None

the FIFA/Coca-Cola World Ranking last year. Nebitchi Balkanabad were the surprise champions of the 2004 Turkmen League although they had a comfortable six-point cushion over runners-up Nisa Ashgabat by the end of the season. The club completed the double by winning the Turkmenbashi Cup for the second successive year beating Asudalyk Ashgabat 1-0 in the final. The U-20s qualified for the Asian Youth Championship in Malaysia after victories over Kyrgyzstan and India but then withdrew, while the U-17s were involved in two entertaining matches with Iran and Tajikistan, losing 2-4 and 3-4 respectively.

THE FIFA BIG COUNT OF 2000

	Male	Female		Male	Female
Registered players	868	0	Referees	50	0
Non registered players	15 000	0	Officials	112	0
Youth players	300	0	Total involved	16 330	
Total players	16 168		Number of clubs	12	
Professional players	264	0	Number of teams	95	

Football Association of Turkmenistan (FFT)

15 A. Niyazova Street, Stadium Kopetdag, Ashgabat 744 001, Turkmenistan
Tel +993 12 362392   Fax +993 12 3632355
footballtkm@mail.ru   www.none
President: YUSUPOV Aman   General Secretary: SATYLOV Meret
Vice-President: TBD   Treasurer: LEONOVA Natalya   Media Officer: IVANNIKOV Evgeniy
Men's Coach: KURBANMAMEDOV Rakhim   Women's Coach: None
FFT formed: 1992   AFC: 1994   FIFA: 1994
Colours: Green, White, Green

GAMES PLAYED BY TURKMENISTAN IN THE 2006 FIFA WORLD CUP™ CYCLE

2002	Opponents	Score		Venue	Comp	Scorers	Att	Referee
No international matches played in 2002								
2003								
19-10	United Arab Emirates	W	1-0	Ashgabat	ACq	Bayramov.V [43]		
30-10	United Arab Emirates	D	1-1	Sharjah	ACq	Bayramov.V [40]		
9-11	Sri Lanka	W	1-0	Balkanabat	ACq	Agabaev [9]		
12-11	Sri Lanka	W	3-0	Ashgabat	ACq	Agayev 2 [25 70], Bayramov.V [45]		
19-11	Afghanistan	W	11-0	Ashgabat	WCq	Ovekov 2 [6 35], Kuliev 3 [8 22 81], Bayramov.N [27] Berdyev [42], Agabaev 3 [49 65 67], Urazov [90]	12 000	Busurmankulov KGZ
23-11	Afghanistan	W	2-0	Kabul	WCq	Kuliev 2 [85 91+]	6 000	Khan PAK
28-11	Syria	D	1-1	Damascus	ACq	Urazov [16]		Sadeq KUW
3-12	Syria	W	3-0	Ashgabat	ACq	Not played. Turkmenistan awarded match 3-0		
2004								
18-02	Sri Lanka	W	2-0	Ashgabat	WCq	Ovekov [40], Bayramov.N [56]	11 000	Al Bannai UAE
17-03	Yemen	W	2-1	Sana'a	Fr			
31-03	Indonesia	W	3-1	Ashgabat	WCq	Bayramov.V 2 [10 74], Kuliev [35]	5 000	Sahib Shakir IRQ
28-04	Armenia	L	0-1	Yerevan	Fr		7 500	
31-05	Qatar	L	0-5	Doha	Fr			
9-06	Saudi Arabia	L	0-3	Riyadh	WCq		1 000	Khanthama THA
18-07	Saudi Arabia	D	2-2	Chengdu	ACr1	Bayramov.N [7], Kuliev [90]	12 400	Al Qahtani KSA
22-07	Iraq	L	2-3	Chengdu	ACr1	Bayramov.V [15], Kuliev [85]	22 000	Al Fadhli KUW
26-07	Uzbekistan	L	0-1	Chongqing	ACr1		34 000	Kousa SYR
8-09	Saudi Arabia	L	0-1	Ashgabat	WCq		5 000	Kwon Jong Chul KOR
9-10	Sri Lanka	D	2-2	Colombo	WCq	Bayramov.D [20], Nazarov [70]	4 000	Al Bannai UAE
17-11	Indonesia	L	1-3	Jakarta	WCq	Durdiyev [25]	15 000	Shaban KUW
2005								
29-01	Saudi Arabia	L	0-1	Riyadh	Fr			

Fr = Friendly match • AC = AFC Asian Cup • WC = FIFA World Cup™ • q = qualifier

TURKMENISTAN NATIONAL TEAM RECORDS AND RECORD SEQUENCES

Records			Sequence records					
Victory	11-0	AFG 2003	Wins	4	2003, 2003-2004	Clean sheets	4	2003
Defeat	1-6	KUW 2000	Defeats	3	Four times	Goals scored	14	2001-2004
Player Caps	n/a		Undefeated	13	2001-2004	Without goal	3	2004
Player Goals	n/a		Without win	10	2004-2005	Goals against	12	2004-2005

FIFA REFEREE LIST 2005

	Int'l	DoB
MAMEDOV Mamed	1996	12-11-1967
SAPAEV Allabergen	1996	10-10-1962

FIFA ASSISTANT REFEREE LIST 2005

	Int'l	DoB
ALLABERDYEV Bengech	2000	15-02-1966
ATAJANOV Bahtiyar	2005	7-07-1966
KURBANOV Charymurat	2003	5-12-1977
NIYAZDURDYEV Berdimyrat	2003	28-01-1978
PALVANOV Rashid	2004	24-04-1966
SEIDOV Kakabai	2001	20-03-1973

TURKMENISTAN COUNTRY INFORMATION

Capital	Ashgabat	Independence	1991 from the USSR	GDP per Capita	$5 800
Population	4 863 169	Status	Republic	GNP Ranking	113
Area km²	488 100	Language	Turkmen, Russian, Uzbek	Dialling code	+993
Population density	10 per km²	Literacy rate	98%	Internet code	.tm
% in urban areas	45%	Main religion	Muslim	GMT +/-	+5
Cities/Towns ('000)	Ashgabat 979; Turkmenabat 234; Dasoguz 199; Mari 114; Balkanabat 87; Bayramali 75				
Neighbours (km)	Uzbekistan 1 621; Afghanistan 744; Iran 992; Kazakhstan 379; Caspian Sea 1 768				
Main stadia	Olympic Stadium – Ashgabat 30 000; Köpetdag – Ashgabat 26 000				

TURKMENISTAN 2004
FIRST DIVISION

	Pl	W	D	L	F	A	Pts
Nebitchi Balkanabat	36	27	3	6	78	23	84
Nisa Ashgabat	36	24	6	6	84	29	78
Merv Mary	36	20	7	9	55	38	67
Sagadam Turkmenbasy	36	19	10	7	70	34	67
ITTU Ashgabat	36	16	4	16	67	64	52
Asudalyk Ashgabat	36	15	5	16	38	40	50
Ahal Annau	36	11	5	20	24	64	38
Kopetdag Ashgabat	36	9	4	23	41	68	31
Turan Dasoguz	36	5	10	21	22	61	25
Gazcy Gaz-Acak	36	4	6	26	34	92	18

TURKMENISTAN CUP 2004

Quarter-finals		Semi-finals		Final	
Nebitchi *	6 4				
FK Merw	2 1	Nebitchi *	8 0	28-10-2004	
ITTU	2 2	Gazcy	0 1		
Gazcy *	1 3			Nebitchi	1
Nisa *	1 4			Asudalyk	0
Kopetdag	0 2	Nisa *	1 0		
Sagadam	0 2	Asudalyk	1 0		
Asudalyk *	3 0	* Home team in the first leg			

RECENT LEAGUE AND CUP RECORD

	Championship						Cup		
Year	Champions	Pts	Runners-up	Pts	Third	Pts	Winners	Score	Runners-up
1992	Kopetdag Ashgabat	54	Nebitchi Balkanabat	47	Akhal Akdashayak	46			
1993	Kopetdag Ashgabat	14	Byuzmeyin	11	Nebitchi Balkanabat	9	Kopetdag Ashgabat	4-0	Merv Mary
1994	Kopetdag Ashgabat	31	Nisa Ashgabat	24	Merv Mary	20	Kopetdag Ashgabat	2-0	Turan Dasoguz
1995	Kopetdag Ashgabat	84	Nisa Ashgabat	79	Nebitchi Balkanabat	61	Turan Dasoguz	4-3	Kopetdag Ashgabat
1996	Nisa Ashgabat	83	Kopetdag Ashgabat	74	Exkavatorshchik	60	No tournament due to season re-adjustment		
1997	No tournament due to season re-adjustment						Kopetdag Ashgabat	2-0	Nisa Ashgabat
1998	Kopetdag Ashgabat		Nisa Ashgabat				Nisa Ashgabat	3-0	Nebitchi Balkanabat
1999	Nisa Ashgabat	78	Kopetdag Ashgabat	67	Dagdan Ashgabat	60	Kopetdag Ashgabat	3-1	Nebitchi Balkanabat
2000	Kopetdag Ashgabat	56	Nebitchi Balkanabat	41	Nisa Ashgabat	37	Kopetdag Ashgabat	5-0	Nisa Ashgabat
2001	Nisa Ashgabat	77	Kopetdag Ashgabat	68	Nebitchi Balkanabat	60	Kopetdag Ashgabat	2-0	Nebitchi Balkanabat
2002	Sagadam Turk'basy	67	Nisa Ashgabat	63	Garagam Turk'abat	59	Garagam Turk'abat	0-0 4-2p	Sagadam Turk'basy
2003	Nisa Ashgabat	92	Nebitchi Balkanabat	79	Sagadam Turk'basy	76	Nebitchi Balkanabat	2-1	Nisa Ashgabat
2004	Nebitchi Balkanabat	84	Nisa Ashgabat	78	Merv Mary	67	Nebitchi Balkanabat	1-0	Asudalyk Ashgabat

Turkmen clubs took part in the Soviet league until the end of the 1991 season

TOG – TOGO

NATIONAL TEAM RECORD
JULY 1ST 2002 TO JUNE 30TH 2005

PL	W	D	L	F	A	%
22	11	5	6	28	23	61.4

FIFA/COCA-COLA WORLD RANKING

1993	1994	1995	1996	1997	1998	1999	2000	2001	2002	2003	2004	High		Low	
113	86	92	87	78	68	87	81	71	86	94	89	65	07/01	123	06/94

2004-2005											
08/04	09/04	10/04	11/04	12/04	01/05	02/05	03/05	04/05	05/05	06/05	07/05
96	97	91	85	89	89	90	87	79	79	67	67

Togo may have been beset by political difficulties since the death of the long standing President General Eyadema in February 2005, but the stadium that bears his name has been at the centre of a revival in Togolese football that has seen the national team top their 2006 FIFA World Cup™ qualifying group well into the campaign to qualify for Germany. Just once since the turn of the century – against Cameroon in January 2001 – have Togo lost in Lomé in a competitive international, and it is this home form that has been the foundation for their surge in fortunes. Senegal, Mali and Zambia all left Lomé empty-handed and should they qualify for the finals there would be no more

INTERNATIONAL HONOURS
None

popular team in Germany than Togo. Coached by the Nigerian Stephen Keshi, who was one of the first Africans to make a successful career in Europe, the Togolese have also benefitted from a number of their players gaining experience in Europe, notably Sheyi Adebayor at Monaco who has been prolific during the campaign, scoring nine goals in the first eight games to top the scoring charts in Africa. At home AS Douanes won the Championship ahead of Dynamic Togolais with both clubs having dominated the local scene in recent years. Another club from Lomé, Agaza, did make it to the Cup Final but were beaten 1-0 by Dynamic.

THE FIFA BIG COUNT OF 2000

	Male	Female		Male	Female
Registered players	1 535	162	Referees	585	40
Non registered players	14 000	235	Officials	2 410	190
Youth players	4 015	85	Total involved	23 257	
Total players	20 032		Number of clubs	565	
Professional players	35	0	Number of teams	565	

Fédération Togolaise de Football (FTF)
Case postale 5, Lome, Togo
Tel +228 2212698   Fax +228 2221413
eperviers@ftf.tg   www.ftf-enligne.tg
President: GNASSINGBE Balakiyem Rock   General Secretary: ASSOGBAVI Komlan
Vice-President: DOGBATSE Winny   Treasurer: ADJETE Tino   Media Officer: ATTOLOU Messan
Men's Coach: KESHI Stephan   Women's Coach: ZOUGBEDE Messan
FTF formed: 1960   CAF: 1963   FIFA: 1962
Colours: White, Green, Red

GAMES PLAYED BY TOGO IN THE 2006 FIFA WORLD CUP™ CYCLE

2002	Opponents	Score		Venue	Comp	Scorers	Att	Referee
1-09	Libya	L	0-4	Lomé	Fr			
2-09	Libya	L	0-4	Misurata	Fr			
7-09	Kenya	L	0-3	Nairobi	CNq		20 000	Abdulkadir TAN
13-10	Mauritania	W	1-0	Lomé	CNq	Adebayor 23		Kaba LBR
2003								
29-03	Cape Verde Islands	L	1-2	Praia	CNq	Wondu 37		Nandigna GNB
8-06	Cape Verde Islands	W	5-2	Lomé	CNq	Sania 2, Touré.S 2 23 32, De Souza 72, Adebayor 78		Pare BFA
22-06	Kenya	W	2-0	Lomé	CNq	Faria 2 21 56p		Rembangouet GAB
5-07	Mauritania	D	0-0	Nouakchott	CNq		2 000	Djingarey NIG
11-10	Equatorial Guinea	L	0-1	Bata	WCq		25 000	Evehe CMR
16-11	Equatorial Guinea	W	2-0	Lomé	WCq	Adebayor 43, Salifou 53	12 000	Mandzioukouta CGO
2004								
20-05	Benin	W	1-0	Cotonou	Fr	Kadafi 53		
23-05	Benin	D	1-1	Lomé	Fr	Salou 50p		
5-06	Zambia	L	0-1	Lusaka	WCq		40 000	Damon RSA
14-06	Ghana	D	0-0	Kumasi	Fr			
20-06	Senegal	W	3-1	Lomé	WCq	Adebayor 30, Senaya 2 76 85	25 000	El Arjoun MAR
4-07	Liberia	D	0-0	Monrovia	WCq		30 000	Soumah GUI
5-09	Congo	W	2-0	Lomé	WCq	Adebayor 2 37 80	20 000	Mbera GAB
10-10	Mali	W	1-0	Lomé	WCq	Adebayor 23	45 000	Njike CMR
2005								
27-03	Mali	W	2-1	Bamako	WCq	Salifou 78, Mamam 91+	45 000	Agbenyega GHA
29-05	Burkina Faso	W	1-0	Lomé	Fr			
5-06	Zambia	W	4-1	Lomé	WCq	Adebayor 2 12 88, Toure.S 44, Coubadja 65	15 000	Guezzaz MAR
18-06	Senegal	D	2-2	Dakar	WCq	Olufade 11, Adebayor 71	50 000	Guirat TUN

Fr = Friendly match • CN = CAF African Cup of Nations • WC = FIFA World Cup™ • q = qualifier

TOGO NATIONAL TEAM RECORDS AND RECORD SEQUENCES

Records			Sequence records					
Victory	4-0	Six times	Wins	5	2004-2005	Clean sheets	3	Six times
Defeat	0-7	MAR 1979, TUN 2000	Defeats	5	1977-79, 1999-00	Goals scored	12	1956-1957
Player Caps	n/a		Undefeated	9	1994-95, 2004-05	Without goal	5	2002
Player Goals	n/a		Without win	14	1992-94, 1999-00	Goals against	9	1983-1984

RECENT LEAGUE AND CUP RECORD

	Championship						Cup		
Year	Champions	Pts	Runners-up	Pts	Third	Pts	Winners	Score	Runners-up
1997	Dynamic Togolais	43	Etoile Filante Lomé	40	Agaza Lomé	37	No tournament		
1998	No tournament						No tournament		
1999	Semassi Sokodé						Agaza Lomé	1-0	Entente 2 Lomé
2000	Season unfinished						No tournament		
2001	Dynamic Togolais	17	Maranatha Fiokpo	16	ASKO Kara	14	Dynamic Togolais	3-0	Sara Sport Bafilo
2002	AS Douanes	63	Maranatha Fiokpo	63	Dynamic Togolais	51	Dynamic Togolais	2-0	Doumbé
2003	No tournament due to season readjustment						Maranatha Fiokpo		
2004	Dynamic Togolais	59	Maranatha Fiokpo	54	Kakadle Defale	51	AS Douanes	2-1	Foadam Dapaong
2005	AS Douanes	31	Dynamic Togolais	26	Togo Télécom	20	Dynamic Togolais	1-0	Agaza Lomé

TOGO COUNTRY INFORMATION

Capital	Lomé	Independence	1960 from France	GDP per Capita	$1 500
Population	5 556 812	Status	Republic	GNP Ranking	149
Area km²	56 785	Language	French	Dialling code	+228
Population density	97 per km²	Literacy rate	60%	Internet code	.tg
% in urban areas	31%	Main religion	Indigenous 51% Christian 29%	GMT +/-	0
Towns/Cities ('000)	Lomé 726; Kpalimé 110; Sokodé 108; Kara 94; Atakpamé 92; Bassar 55; Tsévié 55; Aného 47				
Neighbours (km)	Benin 644; Ghana 877; Burkina Faso 126; Atlantic Ocean/Bight of Benin 56				
Main stadia	Stade General Eyadema (Kegue) – Lomé 20 000				

TPE – CHINESE TAIPEI

NATIONAL TEAM RECORD
JULY 1ST 2002 TO JUNE 30TH 2005

PL	W	D	L	F	A	%
21	8	1	12	38	47	40.5

FIFA/COCA-COLA WORLD RANKING

1993	1994	1995	1996	1997	1998	1999	2000	2001	2002	2003	2004	High		Low	
161	170	178	174	154	169	174	162	170	166	150	155	**149**	04/97	**180**	07/96

2004-2005											
08/04	09/04	10/04	11/04	12/04	01/05	02/05	03/05	04/05	05/05	06/05	07/05
155	155	153	152	155	155	156	153	153	153	153	153

It was in the immediate aftermath of the creation of Chinese Taipei in 1949 that the country experienced its only really successful spell in football when the national team twice won the football tournament of the Asian Games, in 1954 and 1958. The strong American influence in the country, however, soon encouraged baseball and basketball to become the most popular sports while football has always remained relatively low key. After beating Macao in the preliminary round of qualifiers in Asia Chinese Taipei then had a miserable campaign in the first group stage losing all six matches against Uzbekistan, Iraq and Palestine with a total of just three goals scored and a hefty 26 against.

INTERNATIONAL HONOURS
Asian Games 1954 1958

At the end of 2004 the country hosted its first FIFA tournament – the finals of the FIFA Futsal World Championship, but once again the national team was on the end of some heavy defeats, losing all three matches to Spain, the eventual champions, Ukraine and Egypt. Then in early 2005 Taipei hosted the qualifying round for the East Asian Championship with a place in the four-team finals alongside Japan, Korea Republic and China PR up for grabs. Despite a 9-0 victory over Guam there was never a chance of making it to the finals with Korea DPR finishing top of the group. In domestic football Taipower won the championship for the 10th season in a row.

THE FIFA BIG COUNT OF 2000

	Male	Female		Male	Female
Registered players	500	250	Referees	110	10
Non registered players	80 000	600	Officials	480	155
Youth players	1 520	420	Total involved	84 045	
Total players	83 290		Number of clubs	50	
Professional players	0	0	Number of teams	127	

Chinese Taipei Football Association (CTFA)
2F No. Yu Men St., 104 Taipei, Taiwan 104
Tel +886 2 25961184   Fax +886 2 25951594
ctfa7155@ms59.hinet.net   www.chinesetaipeifa.com
President: LU Kun Shan   General Secretary: TBD
Vice-President: TBD   Treasurer: TBD   Media Officer: None
Men's Coach: LEE Po Houng   Women's Coach: LU Kuei Hua
CTFA formed: 1924   AFC: 1954-75, 1990   FIFA: 1954
Colours: Blue, Blue, White

GAMES PLAYED BY CHINESE TAIPEI IN THE 2006 FIFA WORLD CUP™ CYCLE

2002	Opponents	Score		Venue	Comp	Scorers	Att	Referee
25-07	St Kitts and Nevis	L	0-3	Basseterre	Fr			
27-07	Trinidad and Tobago	W	1-0	Basseterre	Fr			
30-07	Grenada	L	2-5	St George's	Fr	Hsiao Hsien Chang, Chen Kun Shan	4 500	
2003								
22-02	Hong Kong	L	0-2	Hong Kong	EAq		6 055	Matsumura JPN
26-02	Mongolia	W	4-0	Hong Kong	EAq	Huang Che Ming 2 26 54, Chiang Shih Lu 71, Yang Cheng Hsing 90p	672	Chan Siu Kee HKG
28-02	Guam	W	7-0	Hong Kong	EAq	Tu Chu Hsein 2 24 34, Sheu Sheau Bao 3 48 54 90, Hsu Jui Chen 55, Tu Ming Feng 64	1 814	
2-03	Macao	W	2-1	Hong Kong	EAq	Wu Chun I 43, Huang Che Ming 53	6 862	Huang Junjie CHN
23-03	East Timor	W	3-0	Colombo	ACq	Huang Che Ming 6, Chen Jiunn Ming 38, Chang Wu Yeh 55		
25-03	Sri Lanka	L	1-2	Colombo	ACq	Chang Wu Yeh 47		
23-11	Macao	W	3-0	Taipei	WCq	Chuang Yao Tsung 23, Chen Jui Te 52, Chang Wu Yeh 57	2 000	Napitupulu IDN
29-11	Macao	W	3-1	Macao	WCq	Chen Jui Te 2 14 69, Chiang Shih Lu 66	250	Zhou Weixin CHN
2004								
18-02	Palestine	L	0-8	Doha	WCq		1 000	Al Yarimi YEM
31-03	Uzbekistan	L	0-1	Taipei	WCq		2 500	Midi Nitrorejo IDN
9-06	Iraq	L	1-6	Amman	WCq	Huang Wei Yi 57	2 000	Al Hail QAT
8-09	Iraq	L	1-4	Taipei	WCq	Huang Wei Yi 82	5 000	Baskar IND
14-10	Palestine	L	0-1	Taipei	WCq		500	Rasheed MDV
17-11	Uzbekistan	L	1-6	Tashkent	WCq	Huang Wei Yi 64	20 000	Basma SYR
2005								
5-03	Guam	W	9-0	Taipei	EAq	Tu Ming Feng 8, Kuo Yin Hung 3 10 20 69, Chiang Shih Lu 2 56 70, He Ming Chan 3 66 83 93+		
9-03	Korea DPR	L	0-2	Taipei	EAq			
11-03	Hong Kong	L	0-5	Taipei	EAq			
13-03	Mongolia	D	0-0	Taipei	EAq			

Fr = Friendly match • EA = East Easian Championship • AC = AFC Asian Cup • WC = FIFA World Cup™ • q = qualifier

CHINESE TAIPEI NATIONAL TEAM RECORDS AND RECORD SEQUENCES

Records			Sequence records					
Victory	9-0	PHI 1967, GUM 2005	Wins	8	1958-1960	Clean sheets	3	1981
Defeat	1-10	IDN 1968	Defeats	9	1988-92, 1992-96	Goals scored	15	1966-1967
Player Caps	n/a		Undefeated	11	1957-1960	Without goal	12	2000-2002
Player Goals	n/a		Without win	19	1988-1996	Goals against	15	1867-1968

RECENT LEAGUE RECORD

Year	Champions
1997	Taipower Taipei
1998	Taipower Taipei
1999	Taipower Taipei
2000	No tournament
2001	Taipower Taipei
2002	Taipower Taipei
2003	Taipower Taipei
2004	Taipower Taipei

CHINESE TAIPEI COUNTRY INFORMATION

Capital	Taipei	Independence	1949	GDP per Capita	$23 400
Population	22 749 838	Status	Republic	GNP Ranking	16
Area km²	35 980	Language	Mandarin, Min	Dialling code	+886
Population density	632 per km²	Literacy rate	96%	Internet code	.tw
% in urban areas	69%	Main religion	Buddhist, Confucian, Taoist	GMT + / −	+8
Towns/Cities ('000)	Taipei 2 514; Kaoshiung 1 512; Taichung 1 083; Tainan 734; Panchiao 491; Hsinchu 413				
Neighbours (km)	Taiwan Strait, East China Sea, Philippine Sea & South China Sea 1 566				
Main stadia	Chung Shan Soccer Stadium – Taipei 25 000				

TRI – TRINIDAD AND TOBAGO

NATIONAL TEAM RECORD
JULY 1ST 2002 TO JUNE 30TH 2005

PL	W	D	L	F	A	%
64	28	9	27	89	82	50.8

FIFA/COCA-COLA WORLD RANKING

1993	1994	1995	1996	1997	1998	1999	2000	2001	2002	2003	2004	High		Low	
88	91	57	41	56	51	44	29	32	47	70	63	25	06/01	95	04/94

					2004-2005						
08/04	09/04	10/04	11/04	12/04	01/05	02/05	03/05	04/05	05/05	06/05	07/05
67	65	64	64	63	61	62	60	61	62	58	58

Over the past 15 years Trinidad and Tobago have been one of the leading Caribbean nations but without quite making the breakthrough that they have threatened. Since missing out on the World Cup™ in 1990 when the USA pipped them thanks to a last-minute goal, the national side did not come close again until 2002. The current campaign presents Trinidad with another fantastic opportunity and although Mexico and the USA have dominated the final qualifying group, third place and the fourth play-off spot are both still realistic targets particularly with the likes of Dwight Yorke and Shaka Hislop playing. Futsal on the island was given a boost when the Goal project gave

INTERNATIONAL HONOURS
Caribbean Cup 1981 1989 1992 1994 1995 1996 1997 1999 2001 **CONCACAF Champions Cup** Defence Force 1978 1985

approval to the construction of a national centre in Macoya and the Federation hopes it will help to lift the sport throughout the Caribbean. Like the seniors, the two junior sides underperformed; the U-20s won their first round group which they hosted but then lost all three matches against USA, Costa Rica and Panama in the regional finals. The U-17s won their group convincingly scoring 27 goals in three matches against St Lucia, Bahamas and Barbados only to lose to Cuba at the next stage. The 2004 Professional League was won by North Star who lost just three of their 26 matches to finish six points ahead of Vibe CT105 W Connection.

THE FIFA BIG COUNT OF 2000

	Male	Female		Male	Female
Registered players	2 362	230	Referees	380	16
Non registered players	13 000	1 500	Officials	570	75
Youth players	10 100	500	Total involved	28 733	
Total players	27 692		Number of clubs	135	
Professional players	200	0	Number of teams	963	

Trinidad and Tobago Football Federation (TTFF)

24-26 Dundonald Street, PO Box 400, Port of Spain, Trinidad and Tobago
Tel +1 868 6237312   Fax +1 868 6238109
RGrodenTT@aol.com   www.tnt.fifa.com
President: CAMPS Oliver   General Secretary: GRODEN Richard
Vice-President: TIM KEE Raymond   Treasurer: RUDOLPH Thomas   Media Officer: FUENTES Shaun
Men's Coach: BEENHAKER Leo   Women's Coach: SHABAZZ Jamaal
TTFF formed: 1908   CONCACAF: 1964   FIFA: 1963
Colours: Red, Red, Red

GAMES PLAYED BY TRINIDAD AND TOBAGO IN THE 2006 FIFA WORLD CUP™ CYCLE

2002	Opponents		Score	Venue	Comp	Scorers	Att	Referee
25-07	Barbados	D	0-0	Basseterre	Fr		700	
27-07	Chinese Taipei	L	0-1	Basseterre	Fr			
28-07	St Kitts and Nevis	L	1-2	Basseterre	Fr	Toussaint 40	800	
15-11	St Kitts and Nevis	W	2-0	Port of Spain	GCq	Glasgow 39, Noray 60	3 500	Faneijte ANT
17-11	St Lucia	L	0-1	Macoya	GCq			Forde BRB
2003								
29-01	Finland	L	1-2	Port of Spain	Fr	Scotland 31		Forde BRB
26-03	Antigua and Barbuda	W	2-0	Port of Spain	GCq	Wise 3, John 55	6 000	James GUY
28-03	Guadeloupe	W	1-0	Macoya	GCq	John 88p	4 000	Callender BRB
30-03	Cuba	L	1-3	Marabella	GCq	John 18	5 000	James GUY
23-04	Martinique	L	2-3	Fort de France	GCq	Dwarika 13, Scotland 41		Archundia MEX
25-04	Honduras	L	0-2	Fort de France	GCq			Rodriguez Moreno MEX
30-04	Venezuela	L	0-3	San Cristobal	Fr			Rivero VEN
31-05	Kenya	D	1-1	Nairobi	Fr	Sam 7p		
10-06	Botswana	D	0-0	Gaborone	Fr			
14-06	South Africa	L	1-2	Port Elizabeth	Fr	Coyle OG 24		Mpofu BOT
3-07	Venezuela	D	2-2	Port of Spain	Fr	John 2 48p 73	7 500	Piper TRI
31-07	Haiti	L	0-2	Basseterre	Fr			Rawlins SKN
2-08	St Kitts and Nevis	W	2-1	Basseterre	Fr	Toussaint 5, Prosper 35		
10-09	Morocco	L	0-2	Marrakech	Fr			Yacoubi TUN
19-11	Cuba	W	2-1	Port of Spain	Fr	Whitley 12, Márquez OG 23	8 000	
2004								
10-02	Bermuda	W	1-0	Hamilton	Fr	Glenn 64		Raynor BER
12-02	Bermuda	D	2-2	Hamilton	Fr	Smith.C 37, Glenn 75		Crockwell BER
2-03	Guyana	W	1-0	Tunapuna	Fr	Celestine 32		Ramdhan TRI
31-03	Egypt	L	1-2	Cairo	Fr	John 79	13 000	El Beltagy EGY
23-05	Iraq	W	2-0	West Bromwich	Fr	John 2 30 66	1 464	Halsey ENG
30-05	Scotland	L	1-4	Edinburgh	Fr	John 56	16 187	Vink NED
6-06	Northern Ireland	L	0-3	Tobago	Fr		7 500	Callender BRB
13-06	Dominican Republic	W	2-0	Santo Domingo	WCq	Andrews 62, John 90	2 500	Moreno PAN
20-06	Dominican Republic	W	4-0	Marabella	WCq	Scotland 49, John 71, Theobald 73, Sealt 85	5 500	Pinas SUR
10-07	Thailand	L	2-3	Bangkok	Fr	Rougier 17, Glasgow 30	3 000	
14-07	Korea Republic	D	1-1	Seoul	Fr	Scotland 77	18 025	Matsumura JPN
11-08	Guatemala	L	1-4	Guatemala City	Fr	Smith.C 89	9 000	
18-08	St Vincent/Grenadines	W	2-0	Kingstown	WCq	McFarlane 2 80 85	5 000	Vaughn USA
4-09	St Kitts and Nevis	W	2-1	Basseterre	WCq	McFarlane 45, John 89	2 800	Castillo GUA
8-09	Mexico	L	1-3	Port of Spain	WCq	John 39	20 000	Navarro CAN
10-10	St Kitts and Nevis	W	5-1	Marabella	WCq	Riley OG 8, John 2 24 80, Glenn 71, Nixon 88	7 000	Valenzuela USA
13-10	Mexico	L	0-3	Puebla	WCq		37 000	Sibrian SLV
17-11	St Vincent/Grenadines	W	2-1	Port of Spain	WCq	Sam 84, Eve 91+	10 000	Batres GUA
24-11	Puerto Rico	W	5-0	Tunapuna	GCq	Glenn 3 13 43 48, King 81p, Smith.C 89	2 000	Callender BRB
26-11	Grenada	W	2-0	Marabella	GCq	Pierre.N 22p, Gray 50		Callender BRB
28-11	Surinam	W	1-0	Malabar	GCq	Glenn 65		Forde BRB
12-12	British Virgin Islands	W	4-0	Tortola	GCq	Pierre.N 2 7 65, Jemmott 75, Spann 90	1 600	Arthur LCA
19-12	British Virgin Islands	W	2-0	Tunapuna	GCq	Pierre.N 21, Eve 61		Lancaster GUY
2005								
9-01	St Vincent/Grenadines	W	3-1	Marabella	GCq	Glasgow 51, Fitzpatrick 2 54 62	1 688	Chance ANT
12-01	Antigua and Barbuda	L	1-2	St John's	Fr	Pierre.N 55	2 000	
16-01	St Vincent/Grenadines	L	0-1	Kingstown	GCq		1 450	Pine JAM
21-01	Azerbaijan	W	1-0	Port of Spain	Fr	Sealy 41	500	
23-01	Azerbaijan	W	2-0	Marabella	Fr	Pierre.N 21, Smith.C 67	1 000	Gordon TRI
1-02	Haiti	W	1-0	Port of Spain	Fr	Pierre.A 59	1 500	
3-02	Haiti	W	2-1	Port of Spain	Fr	John 21, Glenn 43		
6-02	Haiti	L	0-1	Scarborough	Fr			
9-02	USA	L	1-2	Port of Spain	WCq	Eve 87	11 000	Archundia MEX
20-02	Jamaica	L	1-2	Bridgetown	GCq	Pierre.N 37	5 000	Callender BRB

GAMES PLAYED BY TRINIDAD AND TOBAGO IN THE 2006 FIFA WORLD CUP™ CYCLE (CONTINUED)

2005	Opponents		Score	Venue	Comp	Scorers	Att	Referee
22-02	Cuba	L	1-2	Bridgetown	GCq	Glen [13]	2 100	Lancaster GUY
24-02	Barbados	W	3-2	Bridgetown	GCq	Smith.C [11], Glenn [30], Eve [84]	3 000	Prendergast JAM
26-03	Guatemala	L	1-5	Guatemala City	WCq	Edwards [32]	22 506	Stott USA
30-03	Costa Rica	D	0-0	Port of Spain	WCq		8 000	Navarro CAN
25-05	Bermuda	W	4-0	Port of Spain	Fr	OG [34], Jones.K [46], Lawrence [51], John [65]	400	
27-05	Bermuda	W	1-0	Marabella	Fr	John [17]		
4-06	Panama	W	2-0	Port of Spain	WCq	John [34], Lawrence [71]		Prendergast JAM
8-06	Mexico	L	0-2	Monterrey	WCq			
6-07	Honduras	D	1-1	Miami	GCr1	Birchall [28]	10 311	Navarro CAN
10-07	Panama	D	2-2	Miami	GCr1	Andrews [17], Glen [91+]	17 292	Wyngaarde SUR
12-07	Colombia	L	0-2	Miami	GCr1		11 000	Rodriguez MEX

Fr = Friendly match • GC = CONCACAF Gold Cup • WC = FIFA World Cup™ • q = qualifier • r1 = first round group

TRINIDAD AND TOBAGO NATIONAL TEAM RECORDS AND RECORD SEQUENCES

Records			Sequence records					
Victory	11-0	ARU 1989	Wins	8	1996, 1999	Clean sheets	5	2000, 2004
Defeat	0-7	MEX 2000	Defeats	6	1955-1957	Goals scored	19	1998-1999
Player Caps	n/a		Undefeated	9	1996, 1999	Without goal	4	1990
Player Goals	n/a		Without win	13	1983-1985	Goals against	15	1976-1979

FIFA REFEREE LIST 2005

	Int'l	DoB
BRIZAN Neal	2002	01-11-1969
BYNOE Noel	1997	15-01-1962
GORDON Ted	2003	14-09-1965
PIPER Richard	2001	12-11-1966
RAMDHAN Ramesh	1991	25-07-1960

FIFA ASSISTANT REFEREE LIST 2005

	Int'l	DoB
BAPTISTE Simon	2003	25-02-1967
BREWSTER Solomon	2000	13-10-1961
BURTON Lyndon	2000	22-03-1964
RAGOONATH Michael	1998	23-04-1967
TAYLOR Joseph	2000	6-10-1964

CLUB DIRECTORY

Club	Town/City	Stadium	Lge	CL
Caledonia AIA Fire	Tunapuna	Marvin Lee 8 000	0	0
Defence Force	Chaguaramas	Hasely Crawford 27 000	20	2
Joe Public	Arouca	Marvin Lee 8 000	1	0
National Quarries North East Stars	Sangre Grande	Marvin Lee 7 000	0	0
CL Financial San Juan Jabloteh	Port of Spain	Hasely Crawford 27 000	2	0
Tobago United	Bacolet	Dwight Yorke 7 500	0	0
United Petrotrin			0	0
Vibe CT 105 Williams Connection	Point Lisas	Manny Ramjohn 10 000	2	0

TRINIDAD AND TOBAGO COUNTRY INFORMATION

Capital	Port of Spain	Independence	1962 from the UK	GDP per Capita	$9 500
Population	1 096 585	Status	Republic	GNP Ranking	96
Area km²	5 128	Language	English, Hindi	Dialling code	+1 868
Population density	213 per km²	Literacy rate	98%	Internet code	.tt
% in urban areas	72%	Main religion	Christian 43%, Hindu 23%	GMT +/−	+4
Towns/Cities ('000)	Chaguanas 72; San Juan 56; San Fernando 56; Port of Spain 49; Arima 35; Marabella 26				
Neighbours (km)	Caribbean Sea & Atlantic Ocean 362				
Main stadia	Hasely Crawford Stadium – Port of Spain 27 000; Manny Ramjohn Stadium – Marabella 10 000; Marvin Lee Stadium – Tunapuna 8 000; Dr João Havelange Centre of Excellence – Macoya				

TRINIDAD AND TOBAGO 2004

PROFESSIONAL LEAGUE

	Pl	W	D	L	F	A	Pts	NE Stars	Connection	Jabloteh	Strikers	Defence	Arima Fire	Drillers	Tobago Utd
North East Stars †	26	17	6	3	80	33	57		2-0 1-1	0-1 1-1	3-3 3-2	5-2 3-1	2-2 0-0	2-0 8-0	5-1 4-1
Williams Connection †	26	15	6	5	67	26	51	0-0 3-1		0-3 1-1	4-2 0-0	2-0 3-1	4-2 3-0	5-0 2-0	3-1 18-1
San Juan Jabloteh	26	15	6	5	65	24	51	1-2 1-3	0-2 2-1		0-0 4-2	2-2 1-1	0-1 2-0	8-0 4-2	3-0 8-1
South Starworld Strikers	26	10	9	7	64	41	39	5-2 3-4	1-0 1-1	0-3 0-4		1-0 0-2	0-0 2-1	2-0 2-2	9-0 13-1
Defence Force	26	11	6	9	45	43	39	1-3 0-3	1-5 2-3	1-1 2-0	1-1 1-1		3-0 2-1	0-0 2-0	4-2 6-4
Morvant-Arima Fire	26	8	5	13	42	42	29	0-3 2-5	1-1 2-0	0-3 1-3	1-2 2-2	1-2 1-2		1-0 5-0	3-0 6-0
South West Drillers	21	3	2	16	17	61	11	1-2	0-2	1-2	0-7	0-3	1-2		3-0 3-1
Tobago United	21	0	0	21	18	128	0	1-13	1-3	0-7	2-3	0-3	0-7	1-4	

18/04/2004 - 7/11/2004 • † Qualified for the CONCACAF Champions Cup

TRINIDAD AND TOBAGO 2004 NATIONAL SUPER LEAGUE (2)

	Pl	W	D	L	F	A	Pts
Joe Public	26	22	2	2	102	20	68
Crab Connection	26	17	3	6	105	52	54
Superstar Rangers	26	16	4	6	62	36	52
Police	26	15	4	7	58	34	49
Stokely Vale	26	13	7	6	62	40	46
Phoenix	26	12	4	10	60	50	40
WASA Clean & White	26	11	3	12	69	82	36
Caroni	26	10	5	11	54	40	35
The Harvard Club	26	10	3	13	61	56	33
East San Juan United	26	8	4	14	50	65	28
Maraval Youth Academy	26	7	5	14	34	53	26
Club Sando	26	7	2	17	37	86	23
Carib	26	4	4	18	49	96	16
Morgua United	26	4	2	20	23	116	14

4/06/2004 - 19/09/2005

FIRST CITIZENS BANK CUP 2004

Quarter-finals		Semi-finals		Final	
W Connection	2				
SW Drillers	0	W Connection	2		
Arima Fire	1	Strikers	1		
Strikers	5				
North East Stars	8			W Connection	2 3p
Tobago United	2	North East Stars	0	Defence Force	2 2p
SJ Jabloteh	2 1p	Defence Force	2	1-10-2004	
Defence Force	2 3p			Manny Ramjohn, Marabella	

PRO BOWL 2004

Quarter-finals		Semi-finals		Final	
W Connection	8				
Tobago United	0	W Connection	1		
NE Stars	0	Arima Fire	0		
Arima Fire	1				
Strikers	4			W Connection	2 3p
SW Drillers	0	Strikers	0	SJ Jabloteh	2 0p
Defence Force	0	SJ Jabloteh	3		
SJ Jabloteh	3				

RECENT LEAGUE AND CUP RECORD

	Championship						Cup		
Year	Champions	Pts	Runners-up	Pts	Third	Pts	Winners	Score	Runners-up
1996	Defence Force						Defence Force		Police
1997	Defence Force	53	Joe Public	52	Caledonia AIA	44	United Petrotrin		Superstar Rangers
1998	Joe Public	51	Caledonia AIA	45	Queen's Park	44	San Juan Jabloteh	3-2	Defence Force
1999	Defence Force	64	Joe Public	55	Williams Connection	55	Williams Connection		Joe Public
2000	Williams Connection	52	Defence Force	51	San Juan Jabloteh	47	Williams Connection	1-1 5-4p	Joe Public
2001	Williams Connection	37	Joe Public	35	Defence Force	24	Joe Public	1-0	Carib
2002	San Juan Jabloteh	65	Williams Connection	62	Joe Public	48	Williams Connection	5-1	Arima Fire
2003	San Juan Jabloteh	92	Williams Connection	80	North East Stars	64	North East Stars	2-2 4-1p	Williams Connection
2004	North East Strikers	57	Williams Connection	51	San Juan Jabloteh	51			

The semi-pro league was introduced in 1996, followed by a professional league in 1999

TUN – TUNISIA

NATIONAL TEAM RECORD
JULY 1ST 2002 TO JUNE 30TH 2005

PL	W	D	L	F	A	%
38	18	10	7	54	33	60.5

FIFA/COCA-COLA WORLD RANKING

1993	1994	1995	1996	1997	1998	1999	2000	2001	2002	2003	2004	High		Low	
32	30	22	23	23	21	31	26	28	41	45	35	19	02/98	46	11/03

2004-2005											
08/04	09/04	10/04	11/04	12/04	01/05	02/05	03/05	04/05	05/05	06/05	07/05
36	36	36	36	35	35	36	38	39	40	38	32

Despite having a population of just 10 million Tunisia has arguably the most professional football set-up in Africa and over the past decade that has paid handsome dividends with a first African Cup of Nations title in 2004 for the national team and appearances in 12 continental finals by their clubs since Espérance won the Champions Cup in 1994. Coach Roger Lemerre achieved a unique double when he led Tunisia to the African title having coached France to their UEFA EURO 2000™ triumph but it has not been plain sailing in the 2006 FIFA World Cup qualifiers where the Tunisians dropped points to both Guinea and Malawi in the close race with Morocco for a place in the finals.

INTERNATIONAL HONOURS
Qualified for the FIFA World Cup™ finals 1978 1998 2002 CAF African Cup of Nations 2004
CAF Champions League Club Africain 1991, Esperance 1994

At the FIFA Confederations Cup in Germany there was an admirable win against Australia although defeats against Argentina and Germany saw the team knocked out in the first round. In an exciting Championship race just three points seperated the top four teams going into the final day. With all of them winning, the title went to CS Sfaxien on goal difference over Etoile, who earlier in the year had lost the CAF Champions League final to Enyimba of Nigeria. There was also an unexpected winner in the Cup with Espérance losing to Zarzis in the final.

THE FIFA BIG COUNT OF 2000

	Male	Female		Male	Female
Registered players	26 271	0	Referees	910	10
Non registered players	45 000	0	Officials	5 920	0
Youth players	6 262	0	Total involved	84 373	
Total players	77 533		Number of clubs	552	
Professional players	311	0	Number of teams	1 309	

Fédération Tunisienne de Football (FTF)
Maison des Fédérations Sportives, Cité Olympique, Tunis 1003, Tunisia
Tel +216 71 233303   Fax +216 71 767929
directeur@ftf.org.tn   www.ftf.org.tn
President: BEN AMMAR Hamouda   General Secretary: DARRAGI Amor
Vice-President: BACCAR Mohieddine   Treasurer: HAMMAMI Mahmoud   Media Officer: None
Men's Coach: LEMERRE Roger   Women's Coach: None
FTF formed: 1956   CAF: 1960   FIFA: 1960
Colours: Red, White, Red

GAMES PLAYED BY TUNISIA IN THE 2006 FIFA WORLD CUP™ CYCLE

2002	Opponents	Score		Venue	Comp	Scorers	Att	Referee
21-08	France	D	1-1	Radès/Tunis	Fr	Zitouni [38]	59 223	Bolognino ITA
12-10	Portugal	D	1-1	Lisbon	Fr	Zitouni [41]	10 000	Allaerts BEL
20-11	Egypt	D	0-0	Tunis	Fr			Ambaya LBY
2003								
12-02	Sweden	W	1-0	Radès/Tunis	Fr	Braham [49]	20 000	Haimoudi ALG
27-03	Ghana	D	2-2	Radès/Tunis	Fr	Mhadhebi [46], Missaoui [55], W 8-7p	30 000	
30-03	Cameroon	W	1-0	Radès/Tunis	Fr	Bouazizi [80]	40 000	Guezzaz MAR
30-04	Senegal	W	1-0	Radès/Tunis	Fr	Braham [45]	50 000	Benouza ALG
20-08	Guinea	D	0-0	Radès/Tunis	Fr		20 000	Abdalla LBY
10-09	Côte d'Ivoire	W	3-2	Tunis	Fr	Chedli [18p], Melki [69], Seghaier [83]	17 000	Djaballah ALG
8-10	Japan	L	0-1	Tunis	Fr			Berber ALG
11-10	Morocco	D	0-0	Tunis	Fr		13 000	Layec FRA
19-11	South Africa	W	2-0	Tunis	Fr	Braham [43], Ayari [88]	12 000	Diabate SEN
2004								
14-01	Benin	W	2-0	Djerba	Fr	Jaziri [31], Hagui [43]	6 000	
17-01	Benin	W	2-1	Tunis	Fr	Santos [9], Saidi [90]	25 000	
24-01	Rwanda	W	2-1	Radès/Tunis	CNr1	Jaziri [26], Santos [56]	60 000	Evehe CMR
28-01	Congo DR	W	3-0	Radès/Tunis	CNr1	Santos 2 [55 87], Braham [65]	20 000	Damon RSA
1-02	Guinea	D	1-1	Radès/Tunis	CNr1	Ben Achour [58]	18 000	Tessema ETH
7-02	Senegal	W	1-0	Radès/Tunis	CNqf	Mnari [65]	57 000	Ali Bujsaim UAE
11-02	Nigeria	D	1-1	Radès/Tunis	CNsf	Badra [82p]. W 5-3p	56 000	Codjia BEN
14-02	Morocco	W	2-1	Radès/Tunis	CNf	Santos [5], Jaziri [52]	60 000	Ndoye SEN
31-03	Côte d'Ivoire	L	0-2	Tunis	Fr		10 000	Haimoudi ALG
28-04	Mali	W	1-0	Sfax	Fr	Jedidi [56]	8 000	Shelmani LBY
30-05	Italy	L	0-4	Radès/Tunis	Fr		30 000	Duhamel FRA
5-06	Botswana	W	4-1	Radès/Tunis	WCq	Ribabro [9], Hagui 2 [35 79], Zitouni [74]	2 844	Abdel Rahman SUD
20-06	Guinea	L	1-2	Conakry	WCq	Braham [67]	15 300	Codjia BEN
18-08	South Africa	L	0-2	Tunis	Fr		4 000	Zekrini ALG
4-09	Morocco	D	1-1	Rabat	WCq	Santos [11]	45 000	Auda EGY
9-10	Malawi	D	2-2	Blantyre	WCq	Jaziri [82], Ghodhbane [89]	20 000	Awuye UGA
2005								
26-03	Malawi	W	7-0	Radès/Tunis	WCq	Guemamdia [3], Santos 4 [12 52 75 77], Clayton [60p], Ghodbane [80]	30 000	Abdel Rahman SUD
27-05	Angola	W	4-1	Tunis	Fr	Zitouni 2 [20 70], Mehedhebi 2 [51 89]	4 000	
4-06	Botswana	W	3-1	Gaborone	WCq	Nafti [20], Santos [44], Wissem [76]	20 000	Mana NGA
11-06	Guinea	W	2-0	Tunis	WCq	Clayton [36p], Chadli [78]	30 000	Lim Kee Chong MRI
15-06	Argentina	L	1-2	Cologne	CCr1	Guemamdia [72p]	28 033	Rosetti ITA
18-06	Germany	L	0-3	Cologne	CCr1		44 377	Prendergast JAM
21-06	Australia	W	2-0	Leipzig	CCr1	Santos 2 [26 70]	23 952	Chandia CHI

Fr = Friendly match • CN = CAF African Cup of Nations • CC = FIFA Confederations Cup • WC = FIFA World Cup™
q = qualifier • r1 = first round group • qf = quarter-final • sf = semi-final • f = final

TUNISIA COUNTRY INFORMATION

Capital	Tunis	Independence	1956 from France	GDP per Capita	$6 900
Population	9 974 722	Status	Republic	GNP Ranking	62
Area km²	163 610	Language	Arabic, French	Dialling code	+216
Population density	61 per km²	Literacy rate	74%	Internet code	.tn
% in urban areas	57%	Main religion	Muslim	GMT +/−	+1
Towns/Cities ('000)	Tunis 1 160; Sfax 276; Sousse 163; Kairouan 119; Bizerte 115; Gabès 111; Kasserine 82; Gafsa 81; Jarjis 79; Ben Arous 78; Masakin 64; Medenine 64; Monastir 64; Djerba 62				
Neighbours (km)	Algeria 965; Libya 459; Mediterranean Sea 1 148				
Main stadia	Stade 7 Novembre – Rades (Tunis) 60 000; El Menzah – Tunis 45 000; Stade Olympique – Sousse 28 000; Stade Taïeb-Mhiri – Sfax 22 000; Moustapha Ben Jenat – Monastir 20 000				

TUNISIA NATIONAL TEAM RECORDS AND RECORD SEQUENCES

Records			Sequence records				
Victory	7-0	TOG 2000, MWI 2005	Wins	7	1963	Clean sheets	6	1965
Defeat	1-10	HUN	Defeats	5	1988	Goals scored	14	1961-1963
Player Caps	n/a		Undefeated	11	1975-1977	Without goal	7	2002
Player Goals	n/a		Without win	14	2002	Goals against	13	1960-1962

FIFA REFEREE LIST 2005

	Int'l	DoB
BENNACEUR Kacem	2004	12-07-1977
DAAMI Mourad	1996	15-08-1962
GUIRAT Hichem	1998	11-10-1960
HERZI Riadh	2005	11-03-1965
MAROUANI SLIM	2005	16-03-1965
YACOUBI Atef	1998	19-07-1962
ZAHMOUL Adel	2000	19-08-1964

FIFA ASSISTANT REFEREE LIST 2005

	Int'l	DoB
ADJENGUI Taoufik	1997	27-05-1960
AZOUZ Jaloul	1997	30-11-1963
FEHMI Ridha	2003	27-10-1964
HAMOUDA Lotfi	2004	17-03-1971
HASSANI Bechir	2003	22-09-1969
OUESLATI Taoufik	1999	4-11-1960
SAADALLAH Chokri	2004	25-07-1965

NATIONAL COACH

	Years
MAHJOUB Mrad	1990-'93
AKACHA Salah	1993
ZOUAOUI Youssef	1993-'94
BENZARTI Faouzi	1994
KASPERCZAK Henri	1994-'98
SCOGLIO Francesco	1998-'00
KRAUTZUN Eckhard	2000-'01
MICHEL Henri	2001-'02
SOUAYAH/LAABIDI	2002
LEMERRE Roger	2002-

CLUB DIRECTORY

Club	Town/City	Stadium	www.	Lge	Cup	CL
ASM - Avenir Sportif de la Marsa	Marsa, Tunis	Stade Chtioui 6 000		0	5	0
CA - Club Africain	Tunis	El Menzah 45 000	club-africain.com	9	11	1
CAB - Club Athletic Bizertin	Bizerte	Stade Municipal 20 000	cabizertin.com	1	2	0
CSHL - Club Sportif de Hammam Lif	Hammam Lif	Stade Boui Kournine 8 000		1	2	0
CSS - Club Sportif Sfaxien	Sfax	Stade Taïeb-Mhiri 22 000	css.org.tn	7	3	0
EGSG - El Gawafel Sportives de Gafsa	Gafsa			0	0	0
EOGK - EO Goulette et Kram	Kram			0	0	0
ESBK - Etoile Sportive Beni Khalled	Beni Khalled	Stade Habib Tajouri 5 000		0	0	0
ESS - Etoile Sportive du Sahel	Sousse	Stade Olympique 28 000	etoile-du-sahel.com	7	7	0
EST - Espérance Sportive de Tunis	Tunis	El Menzah 45 000	est.org.tn	19	10	1
ESZ - Espérance Sportive de Zarzis	Zarzis	Stade Jlidi 7 000		0	1	0
OB - Olympique de Béjà	Béjà	Stade Municipal 8 000		0	1	0
ST - Stade Tunisien	Tunis	Stade Zouiten 18 000	stadetunisien.com	4	6	0
USMO - Union Sportive Monastir	Monastir	Moustapha Benn Jenat 20 000	usmonastir.com	0	0	0

RECENT LEAGUE AND CUP RECORD

	Championship						Cup		
Year	Champions	Pts	Runners-up	Pts	Third	Pts	Winners	Score	Runners-up
1990	Club Africain	83	Espérance Tunis	83	Stade Tunisien	82	AS Marsa	3-2	Stade Tunisien
1991	Espérance Tunis	82	Club Africain	75	Etoile du Sahel	65	Espérance Tunis	2-1	Etoile du Sahel
1992	Club Africain	84	CA Bizertin	83	Espérance Tunis	67	Club Africain	2-1	Stade Tunisien
1993	Espérance Tunis	43	JS Kairouan	32	CA Bizertin	27	Olympique Béja	0-0 3-1p	AS Marsa
1994	Espérance Tunis	43	Club Africain	33	Etoile du Sahel	32	AS Marsa	1-0	Etoile du Sahel
1995	CS Sfaxien	38	Espérance Tunis	37	Etoile du Sahel	37	CS Sfaxien	2-1	Olympique Béja
1996	Club Africain	63	Etoile du Sahel	58	Espérance Tunis	52	Etoile du Sahel	2-1	JS Kairouan
1997	Etoile du Sahel	64	Espérance Tunis	61	CS Sfaxien	45	Espérance Tunis	2-1	Club Africain
1998	Espérance Tunis	69	Cub Africain	59	Etoile du Sahel	48	Club Africain	1-1 4-2p	Olympique Béja
1999	Espérance Tunis	38	CA Bizertin	25	CS Sfaxien	24	Espérance Tunis	2-1	Club Africain
2000	Espérance Tunis	60	Etoile du Sahel	53	CS Sfaxien	35	Club Africain	0-0 4-2p	CS Sfaxien
2001	Espérance Tunis	57	Etoile du Sahel	38	Club Africain	36	CS Hammam-Lif	1-0	Etoile du Sahel
2002	Espérance Tunis	46	Etoile du Sahel	39	Club Africain	35	Tournament not finished		
2003	Espérance Tunis	57	Etoile du Sahel	38	Club Africain	35	Stade Tunisien	1-0	Club Africain
2004	Espérance Tunis	53	Etoile du Sahel	44	Club Africain	42	CS Sfaxien	2-0	Espérance Tunis
2005	CS Sfaxien	58	Etoile du Sahel	58	Club Africain	56	ES Zarzis	2-0	Espérance Tunis

TUNISIA 2004-05
LIGUE NATIONALE A

	Pl	W	D	L	F	A	Pts	Sfaxien	Etoile	Club Africain	Espérance	Marsa	Kram	Bizertin	Monastir	Gafsa	Stade	Hammam-L	Zarzis	B. Khalled	Béjà
CS Sfaxien †	26	17	7	2	44	12	58		2-0	0-0	0-0	1-0	3-1	1-0	2-0	2-0	0-0	0-0	2-1	2-0	2-0
Etoile du Sahel †	26	17	7	2	38	11	58	1-1		3-1	0-0	1-0	2-0	4-0	1-0	2-0	1-0	1-0	1-0	4-0	3-2
Club Africain ‡	26	16	8	2	46	16	56	1-1	1-0		2-2	3-0	1-0	3-2	2-1	5-1	4-0	2-1	1-0	5-0	2-0
Espérance ‡	26	15	10	1	43	15	55	1-2	0-0	1-1		1-0	3-1	3-0	2-1	1-1	3-2	0-0	3-1	4-0	5-2
AS Marsa	26	10	3	13	21	22	33	0-2	0-1	1-2	0-1		0-1	0-0	1-1	0-1	3-1	0-1	2-0		
EOG Kram	26	7	9	10	22	28	30	0-1	1-1	0-0	0-1	0-1		2-1	2-1	**0-2**	1-1	2-1	1-0	2-0	0-0
CA Bizerin	26	7	9	10	26	34	30	2-1	0-0	0-2	1-2	1-0	3-3		1-1	5-0	1-0	2-2	**0-2**	0-0	1-0
US Monastir	26	6	11	9	27	30	29	2-1	1-1	1-1	0-0	0-2	3-1	1-1		1-0	2-2	2-0	0-0	4-1	0-0
EGS Gafsa	26	6	9	11	22	33	27	1-2	0-1	0-0	0-0	0-1	1-1	1-2	3-1		1-1	2-1	2-2	0-0	2-0
Stade Tunisien	26	6	8	12	28	40	26	1-4	0-3	1-1	0-1	3-2	1-1	1-1	1-2	2-1		0-3	2-0	4-1	0-0
CS Hammam Lif	26	6	7	13	19	31	25	0-2	1-2	0-3	0-3	0-2	0-0	0-1	2-0	1-1	0-2		2-1	0-0	3-1
ES Zarzis	26	5	9	12	17	26	24	1-1	0-2	1-0	0-2	0-1	0-0	0-1	0-0	3-1	0-0	1-1		1-0	0-0
ES Béni Khalled	26	4	8	14	14	45	20	0-5	1-1	0-1	0-3	0-0	1-0	0-0	2-1	0-1	2-1	2-0	0-0		2-2
Olympique Béjà	26	3	9	14	15	39	18	0-4	0-2	**0-2**	1-1	0-2	**0-2**	2-0	1-1	1-0	0-2	0-0	1-1	2-1	

27/08/2004 - 15/05/2005 • † Qualified for the CAF Champions League • ‡ Qualified for the CAF Confederation Cup • Matches in bold awarded 0-2

TUNISIA 2004-05
LIGUE NATIONAL B (2)

	Pl	W	D	L	F	A	Pts
Jendouba Sport	26	13	7	6	27	18	46
JS Kairouan	26	13	5	8	34	28	44
AS Gabès	26	11	6	9	30	25	39
Stade Gabésian	26	10	9	7	27	20	39
AS Djerba	26	11	6	9	29	29	39
EM Mafdia	26	10	7	9	32	32	37
AS Kasserine	26	8	13	5	25	25	37
ES Hammam-Sousse	26	9	8	9	28	26	35
Stir Zarzouna Bizerte	26	9	6	11	30	32	33
CS Korba	26	9	6	11	28	40	33
CO Médenine	26	10	2	14	20	28	32
AS Ariana	26	8	8	10	26	20	32
CO Transports Tunis	26	7	8	11	26	31	29
Olympique Kef	26	5	7	14	26	34	22

12/09/2004 - 15/05/2005

COUPE NATIONALE 2004-05

Fourth Round

ES Zarzis	2
ES Radès	1
Stir Zarzouna	5 4p
CA Bizerte	5 5p
CS Sfaxien	2
Ghazel Oum Larayess	1
Mechaal Souassi	0
Olympique Béja	5
Club Africain	3
Jendouba Sport	2
Stade Tunisien	2
JS Kairouan	3
US Ben Guerdane	2
AS Gabès	1
Etoile du Sahel	0 3p
Espérance	0 4p

Quarter-finals

ES Zarzis	0 10p
CA Bizerte	0 9p
CS Sfaxien	0
Olympique Béja	1
Club Africain	2
JS Kairouan	1
US Ben Guerdane	0
Espérance	1

Semi-finals

ES Zarzis	1
Olympique Béja	0
Club Africain	0
Espérance	4

Final

ES Zarzis	2
Espérance	0

CUP FINAL
22-05-2005, Att: 30 000, Ref: Guirat
Stade 7 Novembre, Rades, Tunis

Scorers - Ali Ghariani 65, Bouzommita 90 for Zarzis

TUR – TURKEY

NATIONAL TEAM RECORD
JULY 1ST 2002 TO JUNE 30TH 2005

PL	W	D	L	F	A	%
38	19	11	8	67	39	64.5

FIFA/COCA-COLA WORLD RANKING

1993	1994	1995	1996	1997	1998	1999	2000	2001	2002	2003	2004	High		Low	
52	48	30	31	43	57	29	30	23	9	8	14	5	06/04	67	10/93

2004-2005											
08/04	09/04	10/04	11/04	12/04	01/05	02/05	03/05	04/05	05/05	06/05	07/05
10	13	12	12	14	14	15	15	14	14	14	12

Since finishing third in the 2002 FIFA World Cup™ the Turkish national team has experienced mixed fortunes. Beaten in a play-off by Latvia for a place in the finals of UEFA EURO 2004™ they were then drawn in one of the toughest European qualifying groups for the 2006 FIFA World Cup™ with the Ukraine, Greece and Denmark providing formidable opposition. The two matches with European Champions Greece marked the first occasion the two neighbours and fierce rivals had met in official competition. In the event both games were an anti-climax with neither side managing a single goal nor gaining a decisive advantage over the other in a group dominated by

INTERNATIONAL HONOURS
Qualified for the FIFA World Cup™ finals 2002   UEFA European U-17 Championship 1994 2005

the Ukraine. In domestic football there was a close title race between Fenerbahçe, Trabzonspor and Galatatasaray in the 2005 Super Lig. Coached by Christophe Daum Fenerbahçe won a second successive title - a record 16th overall - prompting club president Aziz Yildirim to state that he wanted to see the club crowned European champions within two years. High hopes indeed but with the opening of their renovated stadium in 2003 Fenerbahçe are certainly in a much better position to achieve that than in the past. They fell short of completing the double, however, when they lost heavily in the Cup Final to a Galatasaray team celebrating its centenary.

THE FIFA BIG COUNT OF 2000

	Male	Female		Male	Female
Registered players	575 327	327	Referees	4 567	141
Non registered players	750 000	50	Officials	200 000	200
Youth players	350 076	85	Total involved	1 880 773	
Total players	1 675 865		Number of clubs	5 240	
Professional players	5 577	0	Number of teams	14 405	

Türkiye Futbol Federasyonu (TFF)
Konaklar Mah. Ihlamurlu Sok. 9, 4. Levent, Istanbul, Turkey
Tel +90 212 2827020   Fax +90 212 2827016
tff@tff.org.tr   www.tff.org
President: BICAKCI Levent   General Secretary: ARIBOGAN Lütfi
Vice-President: DOGAN Hasan   Treasurer: CAGALIKOC Osman   Media Officer: None
Men's Coach: TERIM Fatih   Women's Coach: TBD
TFF formed: 1923   UEFA: 1962   FIFA: 1923
Colours: White, White, White

GAMES PLAYED BY TURKEY IN THE 2006 FIFA WORLD CUP™ CYCLE

2002	Opponents	Score		Venue	Comp	Scorers	Att	Referee
21-08	Georgia	W	3-0	Trabzon	Fr	Arif Erdem [9], Cihan Haspolatli [51], Nihat Kahveci [71]	15 000	Agelakis GRE
7-09	Slovakia	W	3-0	Istanbul	ECq	Serhat Akin [14], Arif Erdem 2 [45 65]	19 750	Lopez Nieto ESP
12-10	FYR Macedonia	W	2-1	Skopje	ECq	Okan Buruk [29], Nihat Kahveci [53]	15 000	Fisker DEN
16-10	Liechtenstein	W	5-0	Istanbul	ECq	Okan Buruk [7], Umit Davala [14], Ilhan Mansiz [23], Serhat Akin 2 [81 90]	8 000	Baskakov RUS
20-11	Italy	D	1-1	Pescara	Fr	Emre Belozoglu [29]	17 556	Garibian FRA
2003								
12-02	Ukraine	D	0-0	Izmir	Fr		40 000	Attard MLT
2-04	England	L	0-2	Sunderland	ECq		47 667	Meier SUI
30-04	Czech Republic	L	0-4	Teplice	Fr		14 156	Szabo HUN
7-06	Slovakia	W	1-0	Bratislava	ECq	Nihat Kahveci [12]	15 000	Hauge NOR
11-06	FYR Macedonia	W	3-2	Istanbul	ECq	Nihat Kahveci [27], Karadeniz [48], Hakan Sukur [60]	23 000	Rosetti ITA
19-06	USA	W	2-1	St Etienne	CCr1	Okan Yilmaz 39p, Tuncay Sanli 70	16 944	Larrionda URU
21-06	Cameroon	L	0-1	Paris	CCr1		43 743	Amarilla PAR
23-06	Brazil	D	2-2	St Etienne	CCr1	Karadeniz [53], Okan Yilmaz [81]	29 170	Merk GER
26-06	France	L	2-3	Paris	CCsf	Karadeniz [42], Tuncay Sanli [48]	41 195	Larrionda URU
28-06	Colombia	W	2-1	St Etienne	CC3p	Tuncay Sanli [2], Okan Yilmaz [86]	18 237	Shield AUS
20-08	Moldova	W	2-0	Ankara	Fr	Nihat Kahveci [30], Okan Yilmaz [55]	15 300	Plautz AUT
6-09	Liechtenstein	W	3-0	Vaduz	ECq	Tumer Metin [14], Okan Buruk [41], Hakan Sukur [50]	3 548	Van Egmond NED
9-09	Republic of Ireland	D	2-2	Dublin	Fr	Hakan Sukur [52], Okan Yilmaz [86]	27 000	Wegereef NED
11-10	England	D	0-0	Istanbul	ECq		42 000	Collina ITA
15-11	Latvia	L	0-1	Riga	ECpo		8 000	Veissiere FRA
19-11	Latvia	D	2-2	Istanbul	ECpo	Ilhan Mansiz [21], Hakan Sukur [64]	25 000	Frisk SWE
2004								
18-02	Denmark	L	0-1	Adana	Fr		15 000	Wack GER
31-03	Croatia	D	2-2	Zagreb	Fr	Zafer Biryol [73], Cagdas Atan [78]	12 000	Lopes Ferreira POR
28-04	Belgium	W	3-2	Brussels	Fr	Basturk [43], Tolga Seyhan [68], Karadeniz [89]	25 000	Van Egmond NED
21-05	Australia	W	3-1	Sydney	Fr	Umit Ozat [42], Hakan Sukur 2 [69 76]	28 326	Kamikawa JPN
24-05	Australia	W	1-0	Melbourne	Fr	Nihat Kahveci [45]	28 953	Rugg NZL
2-06	Korea Republic	W	1-0	Seoul	Fr	Hakan Sukur [22]	51 185	Maidin SIN
5-06	Korea Republic	L	1-2	Daegu	Fr	Hakan Sukur [44]	45 284	Yoshida JPN
18-08	Belarus	W	2-1	Denizli	Fr	Hakan Sukur [14]	18 000	Mrkovic BIH
4-09	Georgia	D	1-1	Trabzon	WCq	Fatih Tekke [49], Malkhaz Asatiani [85]	10 169	Medina Cantalejpo ESP
8-09	Greece	D	0-0	Piraeus	WCq		32 182	Frisk SWE
9-10	Kazakhstan	W	4-0	Istanbul	WCq	Karadeniz [17], Nihat Kahveci [50], Fatih Tekke 2 [90 93+]	39 900	Hrinak SVK
13-10	Denmark	D	1-1	Copenhagen	WCq	Nihat Kahveci [70]	41 331	De Santis ITA
17-11	Ukraine	L	0-3	Istanbul	WCq		40 468	Cardoso Batista POR
2005								
26-03	Albania	W	2-0	Istanbul	WCq	Necati Ates 3p, Basturk [5]	32 000	Plautz AUT
30-03	Georgia	W	5-2	Tbilisi	WCq	Tolga Seyhan [12], Fatih Tekke 2 [20 35], Koray Avci [72], Tuncay Sanli [89]	10 000	Hauge NOR
4-06	Greece	D	0-0	Istanbul	WCq		26 700	Merk GER
8-06	Kazakhstan	W	6-0	Almaty	WCq	Fatih Tekke 2 [13 85], Ibrahim Toraman [15], Tuncay Sanli 2 [41 90], Halil Altintop [88]	20 000	Kassai HUN

Fr = Friendly match • EC = UEFA EURO 2004™ • CC = FIFA Confederation Cup • WC = FIFA World Cup™
q = qualifier • po = play-off • r1 = first round group • sf = semi-final • 3p = third place play-off

TURKEY COUNTRY INFORMATION

Capital	Ankara	Independence	1923 out of Ottoman Empire	GDP per Capita	$6 700
Population	68 893 918	Status	Republic	GNP Ranking	24
Area km²	780 580	Language	Turkish, Kurdish	Dialling code	+90
Population density	88 per km²	Literacy rate	86%	Internet code	.tr
% in urban areas	69%	Main religion	Muslim 99%	GMT +/–	+2
Towns/Cities ('000)	Istanbul 9 797; Ankara 3 519; Izmir 2 501; Bursa 1 413; Adana 1 249; Gaziantep 1 066; Konya 876; Antalya 758; Diyarbakir 645; Mersin 612; Kayseri 593; Eskisehir 515; Urfa 449				
Neighbours (km)	Georgia 252; Armenia 268; Azerbaijan 9; Iran 499; Iraq 352; Syria 822; Greece 206; Bulgaria 240; Mediterranean Sea & Black Sea 7 200				
Main stadia	Olimpiyat – Istanbul 81 653; Atatürk – Izmir 63 000; Sükrü Saracoglu – Istanbul 46 231				

TURKEY NATIONAL TEAM RECORDS AND RECORD SEQUENCES

Records			Sequence records					
Victory	7-0	SYR, KOR, SMR	Wins	5	1995, 2002	Clean sheets	4	1958-1959
Defeat	0-8	POL, ENG, ENG	Defeats	8	1980-1982	Goals scored	15	1925-1931
Player Caps	102	RUSTU Reçber	Undefeated	15	1998-1999	Without goal	8	1980-1982
Player Goals	46	HAKAN Sükür	Without win	17	1989-1992	Goals against	19	1923-1931

NATIONAL CAPS

	Caps
RUSTU Reçber	102
BULENT Korkmaz	101
HAKAN Sükür	97
TUGAY Kerimoglu	92
ALPAY Ozalan	84
OGUN Temizkanoglu	76
ABDULLAH Ercan	71
OGUZ Cetin	70
FATIH Akyel	64
ARIF Erdem	60

NATIONAL GOALS

	Goals
HAKAN Sükür	46
LEFTER Kücükandonyadis	20
OKTAY Metin	19
TURAN Cemil	19
ZEKI-RIZA Sporel	15
ARIF Erdem	11
ERTUGRUL Saglam	11
TANJU Colak	10
NIHAT Kahveci	8
HAMI Mandirali	8

NATIONAL COACH

	Years
OZARI Coskun	1986
DENIZLI Mustafa	1987-'88
TERPAN Tinaz	1988-'89
TERIM Fatih	1990
PIONTEK Sepp	1990-'93
TERIM Fatih	1993-'96
DENIZLI Mustafa	1996-'00
GUNES Senol	2000-'04
YANAL Ersun	2004-'05
TERIM Fatih	2005-

CLUB DIRECTORY

Club	Town/City	Stadium	Phone	www.	Lge	Cup	CL
Akçaabat Sebatspor	Trabzon	Fatih Stadi 6 200	+90 462 2481418	akcaabatsebatspor.org.tr	0	0	0
MKE Ankaragücü	Ankara	19 Mayis Stadi 21 250	+90 312 2153263	ankaragucu.org.tr	0	2	0
BB Ankaraspor	Ankara	19 Mayis Stadi 21 250	+90 312 3574770	ankaraspor.net	0	0	0
Besiktas JK	Istanbul	Inönü Stadi 32 750	+90 212 3101000	bjk.com.tr	10	5	0
Denizlispor	Denizli	Atatürk Stadi 15 000	+90 258 2659014	denizlispor.cc	0	0	0
Diyarbakirspor	Diyarbakir	Atatürk Stadi 16 000	+90 412 2247580	diyarbakirspor.com	0	0	0
Fenerbahçe SK	Istanbul	Sükrü Saracoglu 46 231	+90 216 4146464	fenerbahce.org	16	4	0
Galatasaray SK	Istanbul	Ali Sami Yen 18 000	+90 212 2515707	galatasaray.org	15	14	0
Gaziantepspor	Gaziantep	Kamil Ocak Stadi 19 000	+90 342 3222000	gaziantepspor.org.tr	0	0	0
Gençlerbirligi SK	Ankara	19 Mayis Stadi 21 250	+90 312 2153000	genclerbirligi.org.tr	0	2	0
Istanbulspor AS	Istanbul	Zeytinburnu 17 500	+90 212 6612273	istanbulspor.com.tr	0	0	0
Kayserispor	Kayseri	Atatürk Stadi 21 300	+90 352 3512727	kayserispor.org.tr	0	0	0
Konyaspor	Konya	Atatürk Stadi 19 440	+90 332 3531522	konyaspor.org.tr	0	0	0
Malatyaspor	Malatya	Inönü Stadi 15 000	+90 422 3240505	malatyaspor.org.tr	0	0	0
Caykur Rizespor	Rize	Atatürk Stadi 10 800	+90 464 2121012		0	0	0
Sakaryaspor	Sakarya	Atatürk Stadi 14 500	+90 264 2818155	sakaryasporluyuz.com	0	1	0
Samsunspor	Samsun	19 Mayis Stadi 13 500	+90 362 2383696	samsunspor.org.tr	0	0	0
Trabzonspor	Trabzon	Hüseyin Avni Aker 21 700	+90 462 3250967	trabzonspor.org.tr	6	7	0

TÜRKIYE KUPASI 2004-05

Third Round		Quarter-finals		Semi-finals		Final		
Galatasaray *	1							
Bursaspor	0	Galatasaray	1					
Caykur Rizespor	0	Diyarbakirspor *	0					
Diyarbakirspor *	1			Galatasaray	1 4p			
Gaziantepspor	3			Trabzonspor	1 2p			
Samsunspor *	2	Gaziantepspor	0					
Malatyaspor	0	Trabzonspor *	3					
Trabzonspor *	2					Galatasaray ‡		5
Denizlispor	4					Fenerbahçe		1
Kayseri Erciyesspor *	1	Denizlispor *	1 5p					
Besiktas *	1	Konyaspor	1 4p					
Konyaspor	3			Denizlispor	1 3p			
Kayserispor	2 6p			Fenerbahçe	1 4p			
Mardinspor *	2 5p	Kayserispor	0					
Ankaragücü	2	Fenerbahçe *	4					
Fenerbahçe *	3							

* Home team • ‡ Qualified for the UEFA Cup

CUP FINAL

11-05-2005, Ref: Tatil
Atatürk Olimpiyat Stadi, Istanbul
Scorers - Ribery [16], Necati Ates [25], OG [38],
Hakan Sükür 2 [72 89] for Galatasaray;
Luciano [41] for Fenerbahçe

TURKEY 2004-05

SUPER LIG

	Pl	W	D	L	F	A	Pts	F'bahçe	Trabzon	Gala	Besiktas	G'birligi	Denizli	Ankarasp.	Konya	Gaz'tep	Rizespor	Malatya	Samsun	Ank'gücü	Kayseri	D'bakir	Sakarya	Istanbul	Akçaabat
Fenerbahçe †	34	26	2	6	77	24	80		2-1	1-0	3-4	3-2	2-0	1-0	3-0	2-0	2-0	3-1	2-1	5-0	7-0	3-0	6-0	4-0	2-0
Trabzonspor †	34	24	5	5	73	29	77	0-2		0-1	1-0	3-1	3-0	2-2	4-2	0-0	1-0	3-0	3-0	3-1	3-1	4-1	4-3	1-1	3-1
Galatasaray ‡	34	24	4	6	64	25	76	1-0	0-2		1-0	1-2	4-0	4-2	3-1	5-1	2-1	1-1	3-1	2-1	5-1	1-0	1-0	4-1	2-0
Besiktas ‡	34	20	9	5	70	39	69	2-1	1-0	0-0		0-0	2-0	2-3	2-1	3-4	2-2	1-0	2-0	4-1	3-2	4-0	2-1	2-1	6-1
Gençlerbirligi	34	14	9	11	52	41	51	1-2	0-1	1-3	1-1		1-3	1-1	2-1	2-1	2-1	5-3	0-0	4-0	0-0	2-0	1-0	1-0	1-1
Denizlispor	34	13	10	11	46	45	49	2-0	0-2	0-0	3-1	1-1		1-1	2-1	2-1	3-0	0-0	2-0	2-0	2-1	0-0	6-1	2-2	4-2
Ankaraspor	34	13	9	12	52	48	48	0-1	1-1	0-2	2-4	2-1	3-2		1-3	1-0	1-0	1-3	0-1	2-0	4-1	3-0	1-1	3-2	2-1
Konyaspor	34	11	12	11	62	62	45	4-2	1-1	0-2	2-2	3-2	0-0	2-3		2-2	0-0	2-0	3-0	3-4	3-1	2-1	2-0	2-1	3-1
Gaziantepspor	34	13	5	16	49	55	44	0-1	3-2	1-0	0-1	1-0	3-1	2-1	2-0		0-1	4-3	1-3	2-0	1-2	1-1	1-0	0-1	6-4
Caykur Rizespor	34	11	10	13	36	37	43	2-2	1-2	0-3	0-1	1-1	2-0	1-1	1-1	1-1		0-1	2-0	1-2	2-1	3-0	2-0	1-1	2-1
Malatyaspor	34	12	7	15	47	53	43	0-2	3-4	0-1	1-1	0-2	2-2	2-1	5-0	2-1	0-1		1-2	1-0	0-1	2-1	4-2	3-0	2-2
Samsunspor	34	10	8	16	40	55	38	1-1	0-4	2-1	2-4	2-0	4-0	0-0	1-1	1-3	0-1	0-1		1-1	3-3	0-1	1-1	2-1	3-0
Ankaragücü	34	10	8	16	37	61	38	1-0	0-2	0-1	1-4	1-0	1-1	2-5	1-1	2-1	0-0	3-0	1-2		2-2	4-1	2-7	0-0	2-1
Kayserispor	34	8	10	16	42	65	34	0-2	0-3	2-2	1-2	1-2	1-0	0-0	2-2	3-1	2-1	1-1	1-4	1-1		3-0	1-0	0-0	4-1
Diyarbakirspor	34	9	7	18	31	53	34	0-2	0-1	2-0	0-0	1-3	0-1	1-0	3-3	0-1	1-1	1-2	3-0	0-1	2-1		1-0	1-0	1-0
Sakaryaspor	34	9	5	20	51	72	32	0-1	1-2	1-4	2-2	1-2	1-1	1-4	2-2	3-1	4-1	4-2	1-0	4-2	3-2			1-3	4-2
Istanbulspor	34	5	12	17	32	59	27	0-3	0-5	0-3	1-1	1-3	1-1	1-1	2-2	1-3	0-3	0-2	1-1	1-2	2-0	1-1	3-0		1-0
Akçaabat Sebatspor	34	3	10	21	40	78	19	1-4	0-1	1-3	2-2	0-5	2-1	1-3	3-5	2-0	0-0	1-1	3-0	0-0	0-0	2-2	0-1	2-2	

16/08/2004 - 15/05/2005 • † Qualified for the UEFA Champions League • ‡ Qualified for the UEFA Cup

TURKEY 2004-05 — 2. LIG A

	Pl	W	D	L	F	A	Pts
Sivasspor	34	23	5	6	58	24	74
Vestel Manisaspor	34	20	9	5	55	26	69
Kayseri Erciyesspor	34	21	5	8	64	46	68
Bursaspor	34	18	9	7	61	26	63
Kocaelispor	34	17	11	6	49	28	62
Elazigspor	34	17	6	11	53	45	57
Mersin Idman Yurdu	34	15	8	11	49	53	53
Türk Telecom Ankara	34	13	10	11	44	42	49
Istanbul BB	34	12	10	12	34	35	46
Mardinspor	34	12	9	13	33	34	45
Altay Izmir	34	11	7	16	41	49	40
Dardanel Canakkale	34	11	6	17	54	57	39
Karpiyaka Izmir	34	11	5	18	41	50	38
Antalyaspor	34	9	10	15	42	45	37
Yimpas Yozgatspor	34	8	9	17	48	64	33
Sariyer Istanbul	34	7	6	21	32	56	27
Adanaspor	34	7	6	21	38	70	27
Karagümrük Istanbul	34	6	5	23	31	77	23

28/08/2004 - 22/05/2005

TOP SCORERS

FATIH Tekke	Trabzonspor	31
ALEX	Fenerbahçe	24
ZAFER Biryol	Konyaspor	18
HAKAN Sükür	Galatasaray	18
JABA	Ankaraspor	17
MARCIO NOBRE	Fenerbahçe	17

RECENT LEAGUE AND CUP RECORD

Championship

Year	Champions	Pts	Runners-up	Pts	Third	Pts
1990	Besiktas	75	Fenerbahçe	70	Trabzonspor	68
1991	Besiktas	69	Galatasaray	64	Trabzonspor	51
1992	Besiktas	76	Fenerbahçe	71	Galatasaray	60
1993	Galatasaray	66	Besiktas	66	Trabzonspor	60
1994	Galatasaray	70	Fenerbahçe	69	Trabzonspor	59
1995	Besiktas	79	Trabzonspor	76	Galatasaray	69
1996	Fenerbahçe	84	Trabzonspor	82	Besiktas	69
1997	Galatasaray	82	Besiktas	74	Fenerbahçe	73
1998	Galatasaray	75	Fenerbahçe	71	Trabzonspor	66
1999	Galatasaray	78	Besiktas	77	Fenerbahçe	72
2000	Galatasaray	79	Besiktas	75	Gaziantepspor	62
2001	Fenerbahçe	76	Galatasaray	73	Gaziantepspor	68
2002	Galatasaray	78	Fenerbahçe	75	Besiktas	62
2003	Besiktas	85	Galatasaray	77	Gençlerbirligi	66
2004	Fenerbahçe	76	Trabzonspor	72	Besiktas	62
2005	Fenerbahçe	80	Trabzonspor	77	Galatasaray	76

Cup

Winners	Score	Runners-up
Besiktas	2-0	Trabzonspor
Galatasaray	3-1	Ankaragücü
Trabzonspor	0-3 5-1	Bursaspor
Galatasaray	1-0 2-2	Besiktas
Besiktas	3-2 0-0	Galatasaray
Trabzonspor	3-2 1-0	Galatasaray
Galatasaray	1-0 1-1	Fenerbahçe
Kocaelispor	1-0 1-1	Trabzonspor
Besiktas	1-1 1-1 4-2p	Galatasaray
Galatasaray	0-0 2-0	Besiktas
Galatasaray	5-3	Antalyaspor
Gençlerbirligi	2-2 4-1p	Fenerbahçe
Kocaelispor	4-0	Besiktas
Trabzonspor	3-1	Gençlerbirligi
Trabzonspor	4-0	Gençlerbirligi
Galatasaray	5-1	Fenerbahçe

FENERBAHCE 2004-2005

Date	Opponents	Score		Comp	Scorers
6-08-2004	Caykur Rizespor	D 2-2	A	SL	Van Hooijdonk 2 [13 45]
14-08-2004	Samsunspor	W 2-1	H	SL	Luciano [52], Tuncay Sanli [65]
21-08-2004	Istanbulspor	W 3-0	A	SL	Tuncay Sanli [50], Van Hooijdonk [53], Alex [89]
28-08-2004	Kayserispor	W 2-0	A	SL	Van Hooijdonk 2 [44 73]
11-09-2004	Akçaabat Sebatspor	W 4-1	A	SL	Ogün OG [7], Alex [84], Márcio Nobre 2 [86 88]
15-09-2004	Sparta Praha - CZE	W 1-0	H	CLgD	Van Hooijdonk [16]
18-09-2004	Malatyaspor	W 3-1	H	SL	Márcio Nobre 2 [43 58], Deniz Baris [72]
24-09-2004	Gençlerbirligi	W 2-1	A	SL	Alex 2 [85 89]
28-09-2004	Manchester United - ENG	L 2-6	A	CLgD	Márcio Nobre [46], Tuncay Sanli [59]
2-10-2004	Denizlispor	W 2-0	H	SL	Márcio Nobre [68], Alex [87]
16-10-2004	Gaziantepspor	W 1-0	A	SL	Van Hooijdonk [61]
19-10-2004	Olympique Lyonnais - FRA	L 1-3	H	CLgD	Márcio Nobre [68]
24-10-2004	Sakaryaspor	W 6-0	H	SL	Mehmet Yozgatli [22], Márcio Nobre 2 [26 32], Serhat Akin [73], Servet Cetin [77], Van Hooijdonk [81]
30-10-2004	Besiktas	L 1-2	A	SL	Van Hooijdonk [68]
3-11-2004	Olympique Lyonnais - FRA	L 2-3	A	CLgD	Selçuk Sahin [14], Tuncay Sanli [73]
6-11-2004	Ankaraspor	W 1-0	H	SL	Márcio Nobre [34]
20-11-2004	Trabzonspor	W 2-0	A	SL	Alex [19], Tuncay Sanli [76]
23-11-2004	Sparta Praha - CZE	W 1-0	A	CLgD	Kovác OG [20]
27-11-2004	Diyarbakirspor	W 3-0	H	SL	Marco Aurélio [6], Alex 2 [43 87]
3-12-2004	Ankaragücü	W 5-0	H	SL	Alex 3 [42 74 82], Servet Cetin [66], Tuncay Sanli [75]
8-12-2004	Manchester United - ENG	W 3-0	A	CLgD	Tuncay Sanli 3 [47 62 90]
12-12-2004	Galatasaray	L 0-1	A	SL	
18-12-2004	Konyaspor	W 3-0	H	SL	Alex [37], Tuncay Sanli [47], Márcio Nobre [90p]
22-12-2004	Usakspor	W 6-2	A	CUPr2	Selçuk Sahin [14], Alex 2 [15 45], Márcio Nobre 2 [55 70], Mahmut Hanefi [80]
23-01-2005	Ankaragücü	W 3-2	H	CUPr3	Marco Aurélio [20], Fabio Luciano [58], Tuncay Sanli [60]
30-01-2005	Caykur Rizespor	W 2-0	H	SL	Alex [19p], Servet Cetin [54]
5-02-2005	Samsunspor	D 1-1	A	SL	Alex [78]
13-02-2005	Istanbulspor	W 4-0	H	SL	Márcio Nobre 2 [27 58], Anelka [63], Fabio Luciano [80]
17-02-2005	Real Zaragoza - ESP	L 0-1	H	UCr2	
20-02-2005	Kayserispor	W 7-0	H	SL	Umit Ozat [22], Alex [56], Tuncay Sanli [58], Márcio Nobre 2 [68 70], Marco Aurélio [81], Serhat Akin [90]
24-02-2005	Real Zaragoza - ESP	L 1-2	A	UCr2	Alex [88]
27-02-2005	Akçaabat Sebatspor	W 2-0	H	SL	Anelka [48], Alex [54]
2-03-2005	Kayserispor	W 4-0	H	CUPqf	Alex [5], Márcio Nobre [10], Servet Cetin [16], Van Hooijdonk [62]
6-03-2005	Malatyaspor	W 2-0	A	SL	Anelka [81], Márcio Nobre [90]
13-03-2005	Gençlerbirligi	W 3-2	H	SL	Alex 3 [26p 45p 90]
18-03-2005	Denizlispor	L 0-2	A	SL	
2-04-2005	Gaziantepspor	W 2-0	H	SL	Umit Ozat [45], Alex [90]
9-04-2005	Sakaryaspor	W 1-0	A	SL	Fabio Luciano [93+]
17-04-2005	Besiktas	L 3-4	H	SL	Fabio Luciano [34], Alex 2 [69 83p]
21-04-2005	Denizlispor	D 1-1	H	CUPsf	Fabio Luciano [111]. W 4-3p
24-04-2005	Ankaraspor	W 1-0	A	SL	Alex [44]
30-04-2005	Trabzonspor	W 2-1	H	SL	Márcio Nobre [16], Alex [65p]
7-05-2005	Diyarbakirspor	W 2-0	A	SL	Tuncay Sanli [42], Márcio Nobre [70]
11-05-2005	Galatasaray	L 1-5	N	CUPf	Fabio Luciano [41]
15-05-2005	Ankaragücü	L 0-1	A	SL	
22-05-2005	Galatasaray	W 1-0	H	SL	Márcio Nobre [65]
27-05-2005	Konyaspor	L 2-4	A	SL	Onder Turaci [7], Anelka [83]

SL = Super Lig • CUP = Turkisg Cup • CL = UEFA Champions League • UC = UEFA Cup
gD = group D • r2 = second round • r3 = third round • qf = quarter-final • sf = semi-final • f = final

UAE – UNITED ARAB EMIRATES

NATIONAL TEAM RECORD
JULY 1ST 2002 TO JUNE 30TH 2005

PL	W	D	L	F	A	%
41	12	13	16	56	57	45.1

FIFA/COCA-COLA WORLD RANKING

1993	1994	1995	1996	1997	1998	1999	2000	2001	2002	2003	2004	High		Low	
51	46	75	60	50	42	54	64	60	89	75	82	42	11/98	111	10/03

2004-2005											
08/04	09/04	10/04	11/04	12/04	01/05	02/05	03/05	04/05	05/05	06/05	07/05
75	77	84	88	82	83	83	83	85	88	86	87

Affiliated to FIFA in 1970, the United Arab Emirates didn't play their first competitive match in the FIFA World Cup™ until the 1986 qualifiers, but just four years later they found themselves among the 24 finalists at Italia '90. Although they haven't reached such heights since, the UAE only just missed out in 2002 when they lost a play-off with Iran and for Germany 2006 the side were pipped to a place in the final group stage. Drawn with Korea DPR, Thailand and Yemen, UAE led the group after three matches. However, a shock 3-0 defeat to Yemen let in Korea DPR who held on to take the group by a solitary point. The was also huge disappointment at the AFC Asian

INTERNATIONAL HONOURS
None

Cup finals with just a draw against Jordan to show for their efforts while the Gulf Cup at the end of the year offered no comfort after two draws and a defeat sent the team packing at the group stage. After hosting and reaching the quarter-finals of the 2003 World Youth Championships, more of the same was expected from the U-20s in the Asian Championship. Unfortunately, the UAE were eliminated at the group stage without losing a match. Al Wahda ended three years of League domination by Al Ain, winning the Premier League by five points although Al Ain turned the tables in the Presidents Cup, winning the final 3-1 in extra-time.

THE FIFA BIG COUNT OF 2000

	Male	Female		Male	Female
Registered players	727	0	Referees	150	0
Non registered players	10 000	0	Officials	300	0
Youth players	2 047	0	Total involved	13 224	
Total players	12 774		Number of clubs	10	
Professional players	0	0	Number of teams	29	

United Arab Emirates Football Association (UAEFA)
PO Box 916, Abu Dhabi, United Arab Emirates
Tel +971 2 4445600   Fax +971 2 4448558
uaefa@uae-football.org.ae   www.none
President: AL SERKAL Yousuf   General Secretary: BIN DAKHAN Mohammed Abdul Wahab
Vice-President: AL ROAMITHI Mohamed Khalfan Matar   Treasurer: AL KHOURI Younes Haji   Media Officer: None
Men's Coach: DE MOS Aad   Women's Coach: None
UAEFA formed: 1971   AFC: 1974   FIFA: 1972
Colours: White, White, White

GAMES PLAYED BY UNITED ARAB EMIRATES IN THE 2006 FIFA WORLD CUP™ CYCLE

2002	Opponents	Score	Venue	Comp	Scorers	Att	Referee
25-09	Oman	L 1-2	Muscat	Fr			
16-12	Egypt	L 1-2	Abu Dhabi	Fr	Abdullah Ali [50]		
2003							
26-01	Norway	D 1-1	Dubai	Fr	Mohamed Sirour [63]	800	Al Saeedi UAE
27-09	Bahrain	L 1-4	Sharjah	Fr	Faisal Khalil [61]		
11-10	Uzbekistan	D 2-2	Dubai	Fr	Faisal Khalil [23], Nawaf Mubarak [49]		
19-10	Turkmenistan	L 0-1	Ashgabat	ACq			
30-10	Turkmenistan	D 1-1	Sharjah	ACq	Ismail Matar [60]		
7-11	Syria	W 3-1	Damascus	ACq	Rami Yaslem [74], Moh'd Sirour [80], Abdulrahim Juma [89]		Moradi IRN
14-11	Syria	W 3-1	Sharjah	ACq	Rami Yaslem [45], Moh'd Omar [63], Rashed Al Kalbani [78]		
18-11	Sri Lanka	W 3-1	Dubai	ACq	Moh'd Omar [11p], Subait Khatir [40], Ismail Mattar [61]		
22-11	Sri Lanka	W 3-0	Dubai	ACq	Abdulrahim Juma 2 [45 79], Mohamed Omar [87]		
14-12	Azerbaijan	D 3-3	Dubai	Fr	Nawaf Mubarak [5], Moh'd Sirour [54], Moh'd Omar [72p]		Mohamed UAE
21-12	Kenya	D 2-2	Abu Dhabi	Fr	Mohamed Omar 2 [41p 45]		
26-12	Saudi Arabia	L 0-2	Kuwait City	GC			Ebrahim BHR
29-12	Kuwait	W 2-0	Kuwait City	GC	Rashed Al Kalbani [70], Mohamed Sirour [77]		Kassai HUN
31-12	Oman	L 0-2	Kuwait City	GC			Al Qahtani QAT
2004							
3-01	Qatar	D 0-0	Kuwait City	GC			
7-01	Bahrain	L 1-3	Kuwait City	GC	Faysal Khalil 7		
11-01	Yemen	W 3-0	Kuwait City	GC	Moh'd Omar [6], Moussa Hatab [21], Moh'd Sirour [89]		
18-02	Thailand	W 1-0	Al Ain	WCq	Mohamed Rashid [22]	4 000	Sun Baojie CHN
31-03	Korea DPR	D 0-0	Pyongyang	WCq		20 000	Zhou Weixin CHN
31-05	Bahrain	L 2-3	Dubai	Fr			
9-06	Yemen	W 3-0	Al Ain	WCq	Rashid Abdulrahman [24], Mohamed Omar 2 [28 73]	5 000	Sapaev TKM
10-07	China PR	D 2-2	Hohhot	Fr	Khamis [48], Ismail Matar [60]		
19-07	Kuwait	L 1-3	Jinan	ACr1	Mohamed Rashid [47]	31 250	Al Hamdan KSA
23-07	Korea Republic	L 0-2	Jinan	ACr1		30 000	Irmatov UZB
27-07	Jordan	D 0-0	Beijing	ACr1		25 000	Najm LIB
8-09	Yemen	L 1-3	Sana'a	WCq	Mohamed Omar [26]	17 000	Al Ghamdi KSA
8-10	Singapore	W 2-1	Singapore	Fr	Fahed Masoud [25], Khamis [26]		
13-10	Thailand	L 0-3	Bangkok	WCq		15 000	Nishimura JPN
11-11	Jordan	W 4-0	Abu Dhabi	Fr			
17-11	Korea DPR	W 1-0	Dubai	WCq	Saleh Obeid [58]	2 000	Abdul Hamid MAS
22-11	Belarus	L 2-3	Dubai	Fr	Saleh Obeid [21], Fahed Masoud [75]	600	Kaliq BHR
27-11	Kuwait	L 0-1	Abu Dhabi	Fr			
3-12	Kuwait	D 1-1	Dubai	Fr	Basheer Saeed [26]		
10-12	Qatar	D 2-2	Doha	GCr1	Subait Khatir [41p], Ismail Matar [83]		
13-12	Oman	L 1-2	Doha	GCr1	Fahed Masoud [46+]		
16-12	Iraq	D 1-1	Doha	GCr1	Faisal Khalil [68]		
2005							
9-02	Switzerland	L 1-2	Dubai	Fr	Ismail Matar [21]		
24-05	Peru	D 0-0	Tokyo	Fr			
27-05	Japan	W 1-0	Tokyo	Fr	Haidar Ali [68]		

Fr = Friendly match • AC = AFC Asian Cup • GC = Gulf Cup • WC = FIFA World Cup™ • q = qualifier • r1 = first round group

UNITED ARAB EMIRATES COUNTRY INFORMATION

Capital	Abu Dhabi	Independence	1971 from the UK	GDP per Capita	$23 200
Population	2 523 915	Status	Federation	GNP Ranking	49
Area km²	82 880	Language	Arabic	Dialling code	+971
Population density	30 per km²	Literacy rate	77%	Internet code	.ae
% in urban areas	84%	Main religion	Muslim	GMT +/−	+4
Towns/Cities ('000)	Dubai 1 137; Abu Dhabi 603; Sharjah 543; al-Ayn 408; Ras al-Haymah 115; al-Fujayrah 62				
Neighbours (km)	Oman 410; Saudi Arabia 457; Persian Gulf & Gulf of Oman 1 318				
Main stadia	Zayed – Abu Dhabi 49 500; Al Ahli Club – Dubai 12 000; Al Ain Club – Al Ain 12 000				

UNITED ARAB EMIRATES NATIONAL TEAM RECORDS AND RECORD SEQUENCES

Records			Sequence records						
Victory	12-0	BRU 2001	Wins	5	1993, 1998	Clean sheets	4	1985, 1993, 1996
Defeat	0-7	KUW 1972, KUW 1979	Defeats	9	1990-1992	Goals scored	18	1999-2000
Player Caps	n/a		Undefeated	16	1996-1997	Without goal	4	1974-1976, 1980
Player Goals	n/a		Without win	14	1974-1979	Goals against	14	2002-2003

FIFA REFEREE LIST 2005

	Int'l	DoB
AL BANNAI Abdulla	2004	1-07-1964
AL BLOUSHI Musallam	2000	14-12-1969
AL MARZOUQI Fareed	2000	1-01-1965
AL SAEEDI Mohamed	2001	15-07-1966
AL SENAN Khalid	2005	4-06-1972
ALBADWAWI Ali Hamad	2005	2-02-1972
ALJUNAIBI Mohamed Ali	2005	1-08-1966
ALMULLA Ali Mohamed	2005	1-07-1967
MOHAMED Salah	2003	30-12-1966
ZAROUNI Mohamed	2002	6-02-1972

FIFA ASSISTANT REFEREE LIST 2005

	Int'l	DoB
AHMAD Nasser	2000	1-04-1966
AL HAMMADI Nasser	1998	10-02-1967
AL MARZOUQI Saleh Mohamed	2005	2-12-1970
AL MEHAIRI Mohamed Jasem	2005	9-01-1974
AL NEAIMI Bader	2003	9-09-1964
GHULOUM Eisa	2002	1-03-1966
KHALFAN Ali Abdulla	1998	1-02-1962
MAKHLOUF Ali Abdulla	1997	3-06-1963
MOHAMED Ahmed Yaqqob	1992	1-12-1960
MOHAMED Hamza Qambar	2000	1-07-1964

CLUB DIRECTORY

Club	Towns/City	Stadium	Lge	Cup	CL
Al Ahly	Dubai	Al Maktoum 12 000	3	6	0
Al Ain	Al Ain	Tahnoon Bin Mohammed 10 000	9	2	1
Dhafra	Dhafra		0	0	0
Dubai	Dubai		0	0	0
Emirates	Ras Al Khaima		0	0	0
Al Ittihad	Kalba		0	0	0
Al Jazeera	Abu Dhabi	Mohammed Bin Zayed 15 000	0	0	0
Al Khaleej	Khor Fakkan		0	0	0
Al Nasr	Dubai	Al Maktoum 12 000	3	3	0
Al Sha'ab	Sharjah	Sharjah Stadium 12 000	0	1	0
Al Shabab	Dubai	Al Maktoum 12 000	2	4	0
Sharjah	Sharjah	Sharjah Stadium 12 000	4	8	0
Al Wahda	Dubai	Al Nuhayyan 12 000	3	1	0
Al Wasl	Dubai	Al Maktoum 12 000	6	1	0

RECENT LEAGUE AND CUP RECORD

	Championship						Cup		
Year	Champions	Pts	Runners-up	Pts	Third	Pts	Winners	Score	Runners-up
1990	Al Wasl	40	Al Shabab	40	Sharjah	39	Al Shabab		
1991	Tournament not finished						Sharjah		
1992	Al Wasl	46	Sharjah	45	Bani Yas	44	Bani Yas	2-1	Al Nasr
1993	Al Ain	35	Al Wasl	27	Sharjah	26	Al Sha'ab		
1994	Sharjah	29	Al Ain	29	Al Nasr	23	Al Shabab	1-0	Al Ain
1995	Al Shabab	29	Al Ain	23	Al Wasl	18	Sharjah	0-0 5-4p	Al Ain
1996	Sharjah	39	Al Wasl	35	Al Ain	25	Al Ahli	4-1	Al Wahda
1997	Al Wasl	19	Al Nasr	16	Al Wahda	16	Al Shabab	1-1 5-4p	Al Nasr
1998	Al Ain	32	Sharjah	30	Al Wasl	23	Sharjah	3-2	Al Wasl
1999	Al Wahda	65	Al Ain	57	Al Nasr	56	Al Ain	1-0	Al Shabab
2000	Al Ain	47	Al Nasr	46	Al Wahda	45	Al Wahda	1-1 8-7p	Al Wasl
2001	Al Wahda	50	Al Ahly	42	Al Jazeera	38	Al Ain	3-2	Al Sha'ab
2002	Al Ain	47	Al Jazeera	38	Al Sha'ab	37	Al Ahli	3-1	Al Jazeera
2003	Al Ain	48	Al Wahda	43	Al Ahli	34	Sharjah	1-1 6-5p	Al Wahda
2004	Al Ain	15	Al Ahli	13	Al Shabab	7	Al Ain	2-1	Al Sha'ab
2005	Al Wahda	62	Al Ain	57	Al Jazeera	53			

1990 title play-off: Al Shabab 2-1 1994 title play-off: Sharjah 1-0 Al Ain

UNITED ARAB EMIRATES 2004-05

PREMIER LEAGUE

	Pl	W	D	L	F	A	Pts	Wahda	Ain	Jazeera	Nasr	Sharjah	Shabab	Ahli	Wasl	Sha'ab	Emirates	Dubai	Khaleej	Ittihad	Dhafra
Al Wahda	26	20	2	4	75	35	62		2-1	4-3	3-2	4-2	3-0	2-1	2-0	4-0	4-2	4-1	3-0	0-2	5-2
Al Ain	26	18	3	5	54	26	57	2-1		2-1	2-1	3-1	2-1	2-0	5-2	1-3	1-0	3-0	2-0	7-0	2-1
Al Jazeera	26	16	5	5	62	41	53	1-0	2-0		3-0	4-4	4-1	3-2	3-0	2-1	2-1	4-0	2-1	3-1	4-3
Al Nasr	26	13	7	6	48	33	46	3-1	3-0	5-2		2-0	2-2	1-1	2-1	4-1	5-1	2-1	2-2	0-0	2-0
Sharjah	26	12	6	8	59	44	42	1-3	2-1	4-4	4-3		0-2	4-2	2-1	3-0	0-1	2-1	5-3	4-0	1-2
Al Shabab	26	11	7	8	43	44	40	1-3	0-1	1-1	2-2	2-2		0-5	0-2	2-1	4-1	1-1	0-3	5-2	5-1
Al Ahli	26	11	6	9	58	40	39	2-5	0-2	4-2	2-0	1-1	1-2		1-0	1-2	5-0	2-1	5-1	5-0	3-1
Al Wasl	26	9	7	10	36	36	34	2-2	1-1	0-1	1-1	1-1	1-2			1-0	1-0	1-1	2-0	1-0	4-0
Al Sha'ab	26	10	4	12	37	44	34	0-2	1-1	1-2	0-0	1-5	1-2	2-2	1-0		3-0	3-5	3-1	2-0	3-1
Emirates	26	7	5	14	26	47	26	1-4	0-2	0-2	0-1	0-0	0-0	3-3	0-1	0-1		3-1	2-1	1-0	1-0
Dubai ‡	26	6	6	14	30	53	24	2-4	0-3	1-3	2-0	1-0	1-2	0-4	1-1	3-2	1-1		0-1	1-1	1-0
Al Khaleej	26	5	4	17	36	62	19	1-1	0-3	3-1	1-2	1-4	0-1	4-3	1-2	1-3	1-2	1-1		1-0	2-2
Al Ittihad	26	4	7	15	27	55	19	1-1	1-2	0-0	0-1	0-4	3-4	0-0	2-2	1-2	2-4	3-0	5-3		2-1
Dhafra	26	2	7	17	36	67	13	1-5	2-2	1-3	2-2	1-3	1-2	1-1	2-5	0-1	2-2	2-3	6-3	1-1	

16/08/2004 - 15/05/2005 • † Qualified for the AFC Champions League • ‡ Relegation play-off: Dibba Al Hisn 1-1 Dubai

UNITED ARAB EMIRATES 2004-05
SECOND DIVISION

	Pl	W	D	L	F	A	Pts
Bani Yas †	26	19	5	2	64	26	62
Ahli Fujeira †	26	16	6	4	68	32	54
Ras Al Khaima †	26	16	6	4	48	31	54
Dibba Al Hisn †	26	16	3	7	76	42	51
Hatta	26	12	3	11	56	50	39
Al Arabi	26	12	2	12	64	51	38
Al Urooba	26	10	8	8	48	41	38
Himriya	26	11	5	10	44	46	38
Ajman	26	11	1	14	42	49	34
Ramms	26	8	9	9	49	56	31
Thaid	26	9	2	15	38	52	29
Masafi	26	4	6	16	21	52	21
Hamra Island	26	4	2	20	33	77	14
Dibba	26	3	4	19	28	74	13

16/09/2004 - 30/03/2005 • † Qualified for play-offs

SECOND DIVISION PLAY-OFFS

	Pl	W	D	L	F	A	Pts
Bani Yas	6	2	4	0	11	6	10
Dibba Al Hisn ‡	6	2	3	1	9	3	9
Ras Al Khaima	6	2	2	2	5	11	8
Ahli Fujeira	6	1	1	4	8	13	4

7/04/2005- 12/05/2005 • ‡ Qualified for play-off

UAE CUP 2004-05

Round of 16

Al Ain *	7
Al Urooba	1
Al Nasr	0
Al Jazeera *	1
Al Shabab *	2
Al Kaleej	0
Dhafra	0 2p
Al Wasl *	0 3p
Al Ahli *	2
Ras Al Khaima	1
Emirates *	0
Al Ittihad	1
Sharjah	0 5p
Al Sha'ab *	0 4p
Dubai	1
Al Wahda *	4

Quarter-finals

Al Ain *	1
Al Jazeera	0
Al Shabab	1 2p
Al Wasl *	1 4p
Al Ahli	1
Al Ittihad	0
Sharjah *	4
Al Wahda	5

Semi-finals

Al Ain *	2
Al Wasl	0
Al Ahli *	2
Al Wahda	3

Final

Al Ain	3
Al Wahda	1

CUP FINAL
15-06-2005

* Home team

UGA – UGANDA

NATIONAL TEAM RECORD
JULY 1ST 2002 TO JUNE 30TH 2005

PL	W	D	L	F	A	%
49	15	16	18	49	55	46.9

FIFA/COCA-COLA WORLD RANKING

1993	1994	1995	1996	1997	1998	1999	2000	2001	2002	2003	2004	High		Low	
94	93	74	81	109	105	108	103	119	102	103	109	66	04/95	121	07/02

2004-2005											
08/04	09/04	10/04	11/04	12/04	01/05	02/05	03/05	04/05	05/05	06/05	07/05
100	102	104	106	109	109	111	112	110	110	115	110

Uganda remain a major power in East African football but it's a sobering fact that their last appearance in the finals of the African Cup of Nations was way back in 1978. After winning the CECAFA Cup for a record ninth time in 2003 the Cranes failed to get past the group stage of the 2004 tournament held in Addis Abeba to compound the disappointment of a poor 2006 FIFA World Cup™ which also saw them miss out on a place in the 2006 Cup of Nations finals in Egypt. Uganda almost didn't make it to the group stage in the first place having squandered a 3-0 first leg lead against Mauritius in the return and only an extra-time goal by David Obua spared their blushes. The 2004 TOP Radio

INTERNATIONAL HONOURS
CECAFA Cup 1973 1976 1977 1989 1990 1992 1996 2000 2003

Super League was won for the seventh year in a row by SC Villa who finished well clear of runners-up Express Red Eagles. Going for a fourth consecutive Cup triumph, Express also finished as runners-up in that competition losing the final 3-2 on penalties to Kampala City Council after a 1-1 draw. At the 2005 CECAFA Club Championship held in Tanzania in April and May, Villa confirmed their status as the top team in East Africa winning the title for the second time in three years. They topped their first group unbeaten in four matches, beat Tanzania's Mtibwa Suger in the semi-final and then Rwanda's APR 3-0 in the final.

THE FIFA BIG COUNT OF 2000

	Male	Female		Male	Female
Registered players	17 000	0	Referees	600	0
Non registered players	60 000	0	Officials	5 000	0
Youth players	10 000	0	Total involved	92 600	
Total players	87 000		Number of clubs	400	
Professional players	0	0	Number of teams	2 000	

Federation of Uganda Football Associations (FUFA)
FUFA House, Plot No. 879, Kyadondo Block 8, Mengo Wakaliga Road, PO Box 22518, Kampala, Uganda
Tel +256 41 272702   Fax +256 41 272702
fufaf@yahoo.com   www.none
President: SEKAJUGO James Dr   General Secretary: ISIAGI Patrick
Vice-President: KWIZERN Godfrey   Treasurer: ISIAGI Patrick   Media Officer: None
Men's Coach: ABBAS Mohammed   Women's Coach: None
FUFA formed: 1924   CAF: 1959   FIFA: 1959
Colours: Yellow, Yellow, Yellow

GAMES PLAYED BY UGANDA IN THE 2006 FIFA WORLD CUP™ CYCLE

2002	Opponents		Score	Venue	Comp	Scorers	Att	Referee
26-07	Ethiopia	D	0-0	Khartoum	Fr			Salih SUD
28-07	Sudan	L	0-2	Khartoum	Fr			Mour SUD
30-07	Chad	W	2-0	Khartoum	Fr	Mubiru, Kinene		Salih SUD
3-08	Kenya	D	0-0	Kisumu	Fr			
2G-08	Egypt	L	0-2	Alexandria	Fr			
31-08	Zambia	D	2-2	Kampala	Fr			
7-09	Ghana	W	1-0	Kampala	CNq	Obwiny 52	25 000	Hassan Mohamed SOM
24-09	Algeria	D	1-1	Annaba	Fr	Mubiru 36		Benaissa ALG
23-10	Tanzania	W	2-0	Arusha	Fr	Isabirye 32, Kinene 87		Masondo RSA
26-10	Kenya	D	1-1	Dar es Salaam	Fr	Okello 14		Chiganga TAN
1-12	Somalia	W	2-0	Arusha	CCr1	Ssozi, Mulyanga		
4-12	Ethiopia	W	3-0	Arusha	CCr1	Almirew OG 17, Kawesa 49, Sserunkuma 52		Abdulkadir TAN
6-12	Rwanda	W	2-1	Arusha	CCr1	Kinene 3, Sserunkuma 43		
8-12	Zanzibar †	W	2-0	Arusha	CCr1	Masaba 29, Tabula 88		Nimubona BDI
12-12	Kenya	L	1-3	Arusha	CCsf	Obwin 33		
14-12	Rwanda	L	1-2	Arusha	CC3p	Mulyanga		
2003								
25-01	Algeria	L	0-1	Kampala	Fr		5 000	Awuye UGA
12-03	Tanzania	D	0-0	Arusha	Fr		30 000	
15-03	Kenya	D	2-2	Nairobi	Fr	Tabula 75, Okello 84		
29-03	Rwanda	D	0-0	Kigali	CNq			Bakhit SUD
21-05	Sudan	D	0-0	Kigali	Fr			
29-05	Tanzania	W	3-1	Kampala	Fr	Kasongo 2 39 88, Ssozi 44p		
31-05	Tanzania	W	1-0	Kampala	Fr			
7-06	Rwanda	L	0-1	Kampala	CNq		50 000	Gizate ETH
22-06	Ghana	D	1-1	Kumasi	CNq	Bajaba 16		
11-10	Mauritius	W	3-0	Kampala	WCq	Bajope 52, Mubiru 68, Obua 92+	6 800	Tangwarima ZIM
11-11	Tanzania	W	2-1	Kampala	Fr	Ssali, Lubega		Kalyango UGA
16-11	Mauritius	L	1-3	Curepipe	WCq	Obua 113	2 465	Maillet SEY
30-11	Eritrea	W	2-1	Kassala	CCr1	Kabagambe 43, Kabeta 60		
4-12	Kenya	D	1-1	Kassala	CCr1	Obua 47		
8-12	Sudan	D	0-0	Khartoum	CCsf	W 4-3p		
10-12	Rwanda	W	2-0	Khartoum	CCf	Lubega 48, Obua 54		Itur KEN
2004								
22-05	Sudan	L	1-2	Khartoum	Fr	Ojara		
28-05	Rwanda	D	1-1	Kigali	Fr	Tabala 71		
6-06	Congo DR	W	1-0	Kampala	WCq	Sekajja 75	45 000	Maillet SEY
19-06	Cape Verde Islands	L	0-1	Praia	WCq		5 000	Coulibaly MLI
3-07	Ghana	D	1-1	Kampala	WCq	Obua 46+	20 000	El Beltagy EGY
7-08	Kenya	D	1-1	Kampala	Fr	Obua 27p	25 000	
14-08	Rwanda	L	1-2	Kampala	Fr	Sebalata		
18-08	Kenya	L	1-4	Nairobi	Fr	Tabula 55	5 000	
22-08	Zimbabwe	L	0-2	Harare	Fr		3 000	
4-09	Burkina Faso	L	0-2	Ouagadougou	WCq		30 000	Ould Lemghambodj MTN
10-10	South Africa	L	0-1	Kampala	WCq		50 000	Gasingwa RWA
12-12	Somalia	W	2-0	Addis Abeba	CCr1	Kalungi 2 30 42		
14-12	Sudan	L	1-2	Addis Abeba	CCr1	Mwesigwa 83		
18-12	Kenya	D	1-1	Addis Abeba	CCr1	Obua 77p		
2005								
8-01	Egypt	L	0-3	Cairo	Fr			
26-03	South Africa	L	1-2	Johennesburg	WCq	Obua 63p	20 000	Chukwujekwu NGA
5-06	Congo DR	L	0-4	Kinshasa	WCq		80 000	Daami TUN
17-06	Cape Verde Islands	W	1-0	Kampala	WCq	Serunkuma 36	5 000	Kidane ERI

Fr = Friendly match • CN = CAF African Cup of Nations • CC = CECAFA Cup • WC = FIFA World Cup™
q = qualifier • r1 = first round group • sf = semifinal • 3p = third place play-off • f = final • † Not a full international

UGANDA NATIONAL TEAM RECORDS AND RECORD SEQUENCES

Records			Sequence records					
Victory	13-1	KEN 1932	Wins	7	1932-1940	Clean sheets	5	1996-1998
Defeat	0-6	TUN 1999	Defeats	5	1978-1979, 2004	Goals scored	19	1931-1952
Player Caps	n/a		Undefeated	15	1996-1998	Without goal	4	1995, 1999
Player Goals	n/a		Without win	11	1995-1996	Goals against	15	1999-2000

FIFA REFEREE LIST 2005

	Int'l	DoB
AWUYE Yusuf	1994	22-12-1967
BUKENYA Arthur	1998	27-07-1971
KAKOOZA Fred	2000	9-10-1963
KALYANGO Ali	2004	22-02-1973
KAYINDI-NGOBI Fredrick	2003	23-12-1973
KIRUMIRA Festus	2002	27-03-1964
SSEGONGA Muhmed	2002	12-12-1970

FIFA ASSISTANT REFEREE LIST 2005

	Int'l	DoB
BUGEMBE Hussein	2003	4-01-1974
BUKENYA Robert	2004	11-11-1970
KAYONDO Samuel	2004	18-11-1970
KITTI Yahaya	2003	18-10-1968
MUBANDA Nelson	1993	25-06-1967
OJWEE Dennis	2004	10-01-1969
TOMUSANGE Ali	1993	12-12-1964

UGANDA 2004 SUPER LEAGUE

	Pl	W	D	L	F	A	Pts
SC Villa	28	21	4	3	47	10	67
Express Red Eagles	29	16	9	4	47	20	57
URA Kampala	29	16	9	4	41	17	57
Kampala City Council	28	16	7	5	48	25	55
Police Jinja	29	11	8	10	38	23	41
SC Simba	29	11	7	11	34	31	40
Kinyara Sugar	29	11	7	11	35	33	40
Masaka Local Council	29	11	7	11	28	27	40
Ggaba United	29	11	6	12	32	35	39
Mityana UTODA	28	10	8	10	39	35	38
Tower of Praise	29	10	7	12	30	35	37
Iganga Town Council	29	8	7	14	21	40	31
Mbale Heroes	28	5	11	12	18	34	26
Ruhinda	29	6	6	17	21	57	24
Old Timers Bugiri	27	3	9	15	24	49	18
Moyo Town Council	15	0	0	15	9	41	0

31/01/2004 - 20/10/2004 • Moyo expelled

KAKUNGULU CUP 2004

Quarter-finals		Semi-finals			Final	
Kampala CC*	6 1					
Butukirwa	0 0	Kampala CC	1 1 4p			
SC Villa*	2 0	URA	1 1 2p			
URA	2 0				Kampala CC	1 3p
Top TV	1				Express	1 2p
Maji FC *	0	Top TV ‡	0 -		12-11-2004	
Makerere Univ.*	1	Express	0 -		National Stadium, Kampala	
Express	2					

* Home team in the first leg • ‡ Top TV withdrew

RECENT LEAGUE AND CUP RECORD

	Championship							Cup		
Year	Champions	Pts	Runners-up	Pts	Third	Pts		Winners	Score	Runners-up
1995	Express	74	Umeme Jinja	61	SC Villa	52		Express	2-0	Posta
1996	Express	75	Kampala CC	65	SC Villa	65		Umeme Jinja	1-0	Nile FC
1997	Kampala CC	76	Umeme Jinja	73	Express	72		Express	4-1	Umeme Jinja
1998	SC Villa	45	Express	44	SC Simba	39		SC Villa	2-0	SC Simba
1999	SC Villa	94	Express	92	SC Simba	76		Mbale Heroes	0-0 3-0p	Lyantonde
2000	SC Villa	75	Kampala CC	70	Express	65		SC Villa	1-0	Military Police
2001	SC Villa	70	Kampala CC	65	Mbale Heroes	48		Express	3-1	SC Villa
2002	SC Villa	79	Express	63	Kampala CC	61		SC Villa	2-1	Express
2003	SC Villa	72	Express	72	Kampala CC	53		Express	3-1	Police
2004	SC Villa	67	Express	57	URA Kampala	57		Kampala CC	1-1 3-2	Express

UGANDA COUNTRY INFORMATION

Capital	Kampala	Independence	1962 from the UK	GDP per Capita	$1 400
Population	26 404 543	Status	Republic	GNP Ranking	106
Area km²	236 040	Language	English, Ganda	Dialling code	+3
Population density	111 per km²	Literacy rate	69%	Internet code	.ug
% in urban areas	13%	Main religion	Christian 66%, Muslim 16%	GMT + / −	+3
Towns/Cities ('000)	Kampala 1 353; Gulu 146; Lira 119; Jinja 93; Mbarara 79; Mbale 76; Mukono 67; Kasese 67				
Neighbours (km)	Kenya 933; Tanzania 396; Rwanda 169; Congo DR 765; Sudan 435;				
Main stadia	National Stadium – Kampala 40 000				

UKR – UKRAINE

NATIONAL TEAM RECORD
JULY 1ST 2002 TO JUNE 30TH 2005

PL	W	D	L	F	A	%
29	10	11	8	30	25	53.4

FIFA/COCA-COLA WORLD RANKING

1993	1994	1995	1996	1997	1998	1999	2000	2001	2002	2003	2004	High		Low	
90	77	71	59	49	47	27	34	45	45	60	57	**22**	04/99	**132**	09/93

2004-2005											
08/04	09/04	10/04	11/04	12/04	01/05	02/05	03/05	04/05	05/05	06/05	07/05
85	87	80	67	57	57	49	46	42	39	35	36

Ukraine put their poor form of the 2003-04 season behind them in devastating fashion by completely dominating their difficult 2006 FIFA World Cup™ qualifying group. Excellent away victories in Istanbul against Turkey and in Athens against Greece saw the team surge ahead at the top of the table. An appearance in the finals in Germany would crown the excellent progress the country has made on all fronts. In the aftermath of the breakdown of the Soviet Union much was expected of Ukraine which had dominated football in the Soviet era, but with many Ukrainians ending up playing for Russia progress was slow at first. A number of players have since made their

INTERNATIONAL HONOURS
None

name abroad, notably Andrij Shevchenko at Milan but a huge rise in standards of the League at home has also done much to change the perception of Ukrainian football. When Rinat Akhmetov, the richest man in the country, became president of Shakhtar Donetsk in 1996 he set in motion a revolution that saw a number of high profile internationals from abroad sign for the club in the attempt to end the domination of Dynamo Kyiv who won nine consecutive championships between 1993 and 2001. Shakhtar won their first Championship in 2002 and won it for the second time in 2005 but were denied the double by Kyiv who beat them 1-0 in the Cup Final.

THE FIFA BIG COUNT OF 2000

	Male	Female		Male	Female
Registered players	27 059	1 100	Referees	12 000	7
Non registered players	600 000	5 000	Officials	15 200	33
Youth players	120 000	100	Total involved	780 499	
Total players	753 259		Number of clubs	1 088	
Professional players	2 010	300	Number of teams	8 487	

Football Federation of Ukraine (FFU)
Laboratorna Str. 1, PO Box 293, Kyiv 03150, Ukraine
Tel +380 44 2528498   Fax +380 44 2528513
ffu@ffu.org.ua   www.ffu.org.ua
President: SURKIS Grigoriy   General Secretary: BANDURKO Oleksandr
Vice-President: BANDURKO Oleksandr   Treasurer: MISCHENKO Lyudmyla   Media Officer: None
Men's Coach: BLOKHIN Oleg   Women's Coach: LYTVYN Mykola
FFU formed: 1991   UEFA: 1992   FIFA: 1992
Colours: Yellow, Yellow, Yellow

GAMES PLAYED BY UKRAINE IN THE 2006 FIFA WORLD CUP™ CYCLE

2002	Opponents	Score		Venue	Comp	Scorers	Att	Referee
21-08	Iran	L	0-1	Kyiv	Fr		15 000	Khudiyev AZE
7-09	Armenia	D	2-2	Yerevan	ECq	Serebrennikov 2, Zubov 33	9 000	Vuorela FIN
12-10	Greece	W	2-0	Kyiv	ECq	Vorobei 51, Voronin 90	50 000	Temmink NED
16-10	Northern Ireland	D	0-0	Belfast	ECq		9 288	Bolognino ITA
20-11	Slovakia	D	1-1	Bratislava	Fr	Melaschenko 84	2 859	Marczyk POL
2003								
12-02	Turkey	D	0-0	Izmir	Fr		40 000	Attard MLT
29-03	Spain	D	2-2	Kyiv	ECq	Voronin 11, Horshkov 90	82 000	Riley ENG
2-04	Latvia	W	1-0	Kyiv	Fr	Kalinichenko 83p	3 700	Michel SVK
30-04	Denmark	L	0-1	Copenhagen	Fr		15 599	Mikulski POL
7-06	Armenia	W	4-3	Lviv	ECq	Horshkov 28, Shevchenko 2 66p 73, Fedorov 90	35 000	Albrecht GER
11-06	Greece	L	0-1	Athens	ECq		15 000	De Bleckere BEL
20-08	Romania	L	0-2	Donetsk	Fr		28 000	Egorov RUS
6-09	Northern Ireland	D	0-0	Donetsk	ECq		24 000	Stark GER
19-09	Spain	L	1-2	Elche	ECq	Shevchenko 84	38 000	Hauge NOR
11-10	FYR Macedonia	D	0-0	Kyiv	Fr		13 000	Orlic MDA
2004								
18-02	Libya	D	1-1	Tripoli	Fr	Pukanych 14	40 000	El Arjoun MAR
31-03	FYR Macedonia	L	0-1	Skopje	Fr		16 000	Karagic SCG
28-04	Slovakia	D	1-1	Kyiv	Fr	Venhlynskyi 13	18 000	Ryszka POL
6-06	France	L	0-1	Paris	Fr		66 646	Ceferin SVN
18-08	England	L	0-3	Newcastle	Fr		35 387	McCurry SCO
4-09	Denmark	D	1-1	Copenhagen	WCq	Husin 56	36 335	Meier SUI
8-09	Kazakhstan	W	2-1	Almaty	WCq	Byelik 14, Rotan 90	23 000	Oliveira POR
9-10	Greece	D	1-1	Kyiv	WCq	Shevchenko 48	56 000	Mejuto Gonzalez ESP
13-10	Georgia	W	2-0	Lviv	WCq	Byelik 12, Shevchenko 79	28 000	Stark GER
17-11	Turkey	W	3-0	Istanbul	WCq	Husyev 8, Shevchenko 2 17 88	40 468	Cardoso Batista POR
2005								
9-02	Albania	W	2-0	Tirana	WCq	Rusol 40, Gusin 59	12 000	Bennett ENG
30-03	Denmark	W	1-0	Kyiv	WCq	Voronin 68	60 000	Michel SVK
4-06	Kazakhstan	W	2-0	Kyiv	WCq	Shevchenko 18, Avdeyev OG 83	45 000	Lehner AUT
8-06	Greece	W	1-0	Piraeus	WCq	Gusin 82	33 500	Temmink NED

Fr = Friendly match • EC = UEFA EURO 2004™ • WC = FIFA World Cup™ • q = qualifier

UKRAINE NATIONAL TEAM RECORDS AND RECORD SEQUENCES

Records			Sequence records					
Victory	4-0	GEO 1998, AND 1999	Wins	6	2004-2005	Clean sheets	6	2004-2005
Defeat	0-4	CRO 1995	Defeats	2	Six times	Goals scored	10	1995-1996
Player Caps	65	REBROV Serhiy	Undefeated	13	1998-1999	Without goal	3	2003
Player Goals	27	SHEVCHENKO Andriy	Without win	11	2003-2004	Goals against	8	2004

UKRAINE COUNTRY INFORMATION

Capital	Kiev	Independence	1991 from the USSR	GDP per Capita	$5 400
Population	47 732 079	Status	Republic	GNP Ranking	56
Area km2	603 700	Language	Ukrainian, Russian	Dialling code	+380
Population density	79 per km2	Literacy rate	99%	Internet code	.ua
% in urban areas	70%	Main religion	Christian	GMT + / −	+2
Towns/Cities ('000)	Kyiv 2 514; Kharkiv 1 430; Dnipropetrovsk 1 032; Odessa 1 001; Donetsk 987; Zaporizhzhya 796; Lviv 725; Kryvyi Rih 652; Mykolayiv 510; Mariupol 481; Luhansk 451; Makiyivka 376; Vinnytsya 352; Simferopol 342; Sevastopol 332; Kherson 320; Poltava 317; Chernihiv 307; Cherkasy 297				
Neighbours (km)	Russia 1 576; Romania 531; Moldova 939; Hungary 103; Slovakia 97; Poland 526; Belarus 891; Black Sea & Caspian Sea 2 782				
Main stadia	NSK Olimpiyskiy − Kyiv 83 160; Shakhtor − Donetsk 31 547; Ukrajina − Lviv 28 058				

NATIONAL CAPS

	Caps
REBROV Serhiy	65
SHEVCHENKO Andriy	60
SHOVKOVSKYI Olexandr	60
HOLOVKO Olexandr	58
POPOV Serhiy	54
HUSIN Andriy	54
LUZHNY Oleg	52
VASHCHUK Vladyslav	49
TYMOSCHUK Anatoliy	46

NATIONAL GOALS

	Goals
SHEVCHENKO Andriy	27
REBROV Serhiy	13
GUSEINOV Timerlan	8
HUSIN Andriy	7
LEONENKO Viktor	6
POPOV Serhiy	5
VOROBEI Andriy	5
MAXIMOV Yuriy	5

NATIONAL COACH

	Years
PROKOPENKO Viktor	1992
PAVLOV Nikolay	1992
BAZYLEVYCH Oleg	1993-'94
SZABO Jozsef	1994
KONKOV Anatoliy	1995
SZABO Jozsef	1996-'99
LOBANOVSKYI Valeriy	2000-'01
BURYAK Leonid	2001-'03
BLOKHIN Oleg	2003-

FIFA REFEREE LIST 2005

	Int'l	DoB
BEREZKA Sergiy	2003	19-01-1972
GODULYAN Vitaliy	2001	18-09-1968
ISHCHENKO Igor	2001	21-02-1967
ORIEKHOV Oleh	2003	20-08-1967
SHANDOR Andriy	2002	5-01-1966
SHEBEK Sergiy	2000	14-06-1960

FIFA ASSISTANT REFEREE LIST 2005

	Int'l	DoB
BILORUS Oleksandr	2004	8-12-1965
KRAVCHENKO Olexsandr	2000	13-03-1960
OLSHANETSKYY Vasyl	2003	8-12-1963
PRYYMAK Andriy	2004	22-03-1963
SOBOTYUK Sergiy	2003	12-11-1963
SUSLO Viktor	2003	15-01-1961
TSYMBAL Sergiy	2004	20-01-1963
ZHURBA Olexsandr	1999	8-03-1961

CLUB DIRECTORY

Club	Town/City	Stadium	Phone	www.	Lge	Cup	CL
FC Arsenal	Kyiv	CSK ZSU 12 000	+380 44 2468504		0	0	0
FC Borysfen Boryspil	Kyiv	Stadion Kolos 7 500	+380 44 2055237	fcborisfen.kiev.ua	0	0	0
FC Chernomorets	Odesa	Tsentralnyi 30 767	+380 482 684894	chernomorets.odessa.ua	0	2	0
FC Dnipro	Dnipropetrovsk	Stadion Meteor 26 345	+380 562 342989	fcdnipro.dp.ua	0 - 2	0 - 1	0
FC Dynamo Kyiv	Kyiv	Valeriy Lobanovskyi 16 888	+380 44 2797624	fcdynamo.kiev.ua	11 - 13	7 - 9	0
FC Illychivets	Mariupil	Stadion Illchivets 13 000	+380 629 534486	fcilyich.com.au	0	0	0
FC Kryvbas	Kryvyi Rih	Stadion Metalurh 29 782	+380 564 236045	fckrivbass.dp.ua	0	0	0
FC Metallist	Kharkiv	Stadion Metallist 28 000	+380 572 277936	metallist.kharkov.ua	0	0 - 1	0
FC Metalurh	Donetsk	RSK Olimpiyskiy 24 510	+380 62 3850488	metalurg.donetsk.ua	0	0	0
FC Metalurh	Zaporizhya	Stadion Metalurh 24 000	+380 61 2240656	fcmetalurg.com.ua	0	0	0
FC Obolon	Kyiv	Stadion Obolon 6 000	+380 44 4113910	fc.obolon.ua	0	0	0
FC Shakhtar Donetsk	Donetsk	Stadion Shakhtor 31 547	+380 62 3349898	shakhtar.com	1	5 - 4	0
FC Tavriya	Simferopol	Stadion Tavriya 20 013	+380 652 548501	fctavriya.crimea.ua	1	0	0
FC Volyn	Lutsk	Stadion Avanhard 11 574	+380 332 240557	fcvolyn.com	0	0	0
FC Vorskla	Poltava	Stadion Vorskla 24 810	+380 532 221670	vorskla.com.au	0	0	0
FC Zakarpattya	Uzhgorod	Stadion Avanhard 12 000	+380 312 243398		0	0	0

Where clubs have won trophies in both the Soviet era and post independence, the figure for the Soviet era is given second

FFU CUP 2004-05

Third Round		Quarter-finals		Semi-finals		Final	
Dynamo Kyiv	1						
Karpaty Lviv *	0	**Dynamo Kyiv**	2 4				
Illychivets Mariupil *	1	Volyn Lutsk	1 0				
Volyn Lutsk	2			**Dynamo Kyiv**	1 2		
Nyva Vinnytsja *	1			Kryvbas Kryvyi Rih	1 0		
Metalurh Zaporizhya	0	Nyva Vinnytsja	2 0				
Desna Chernihiv *	1	**Kryvbas Kryvyi Rih**	1 2				
Kryvbas Kryvyi Rih	4					**Dynamo Kyiv**	1
Dnipro Dnipropetrovsk	2					Shakhtar Donetsk	0
Stal Alchevsk *	1	**Dnipro Dnipropetrovsk**	2 2				
Metalurh Donetsk	1	Naftovyk-Ukrnafta	0 2				
Naftovyk-Ukrnafta *	2			Dnipro Dnipropetrovsk	1 0		
Tavrija Simferopol	1 5p			**Shakhtar Donetsk**	2 0		
Cherkasy	1 4p	Tavrija Simferopol	0 0				
CSCA Kyiv *	1	**Shakhtar Donetsk**	3 4				
Shakhtar Donetsk	2						

* Home team in the 1st leg

CUP FINAL

29-05-2004, Att: 68 000
Olimpiyskiy, Kyiv

Scorer - Rincon 11p for Dynamo

UKRAINE 2004-05

PREMIER LEAGUE

	Pl	W	D	L	F	A	Pts	Shakhtar	Dynamo	Metalurg	Dnipro	Illychivets	Ch'morets	Tavriya	Volyn	Arsenal	Metalurg	Metalist	Kryvbas	Uzhgorod	Vorskla	Borysten	Obolon
Shakhtar Donetsk †	30	26	2	2	63	19	80		3-2	3-0	2-0	4-1	1-0	1-0	3-1	3-0	2-1	0-1	4-2	1-0	1-0	2-0	5-2
Dynamo Kyiv †	30	23	4	3	58	14	73	0-2		1-0	2-0	2-0	3-1	1-0	3-0	1-1	1-2	3-0	2-0	3-0	1-0	2-0	3-1
Metalurh Donetsk ‡	30	14	7	9	38	35	49	1-3	1-2		2-1	2-1	1-0	2-1	1-0	1-0	1-0	3-1	1-1	2-0	2-0	1-3	2-1
Dnipro Dnipropetrovsk‡	30	13	9	8	38	34	48	1-3	1-2	3-3		2-0	1-0	3-1	1-0	1-0	1-1	4-2	2-1	0-3	3-1	0-0	3-0
Illychivets Mariupil	30	12	8	10	38	34	44	0-1	1-1	3-0	3-0		2-1	2-2	1-0	0-0	2-2	1-1	2-0	3-0	2-0	1-0	1-1
Chernomorets Odesa	30	12	6	12	29	29	42	1-3	0-3	1-0	2-0	0-1		1-0	2-1	1-0	1-0	2-1	3-1	1-0	0-0	1-1	0-1
Tavriya Simferopol	30	11	9	10	34	28	42	2-1	0-1	0-0	1-1	2-0	2-2		4-1	1-1	1-1	1-0	1-2	0-0	4-0	2-1	0-1
Volyn Lutsk	30	11	7	12	35	37	40	1-3	0-1	1-2	1-1	3-2	1-0	1-0		1-0	2-2	4-2	3-1	3-0	1-0	0-0	1-0
Arsenal Kyiv	30	9	10	11	30	33	37	1-1	0-0	2-1	1-2	5-2	2-1	2-2	1-2		1-0	0-0	0-2	2-2	1-0	2-1	1-0
Metalurh Zaporizhya	30	8	11	11	25	32	35	0-2	0-0	1-1	0-2	0-2	1-2	1-1	0-0			1-4	2-0	1-0	1-0	2-1	1-0
Metalist Kharkiv	30	9	7	14	25	37	34	0-1	0-2	1-4	0-2	1-0	0-1	1-1	1-0	1-1	0-0			0-1	1-0	3-1	0-1
Kryvbas Kryvyi Rih	30	7	10	13	24	38	31	1-2	0-2	1-1	1-2	0-0	0-0	0-2	0-0	0-3	0-0	3-1		1-0	1-0	1-1	1-1
Zakarpattya Uzhgorod	30	7	10	13	21	30	31	0-0	1-2	1-1	0-0	1-0	2-1	0-0	2-2	2-0	0-1	0-0	1-1		1-0	1-0	1-2
Vorskla Poltava	30	8	6	16	18	35	30	0-2	0-2	0-3	1-1	0-2	1-0	2-0	0-0	0-2	3-0	1-0	0-1	2-1		1-1	2-1
Borysfen Boryspil	30	4	9	17	18	43	21	0-2	0-0	0-1	1-1	1-1	0-1	1-0	0-1	1-0	0-1	0-0	1-0	0-0	1-3		0-0
Obolon Kyiv	30	3	11	16	15	31	20	0-1	0-7	0-1	0-1	1-2	1-1	0-1	1-2	2-1	0-0	0-0	0-1	0-0	0-1	0-0	

16/08/2004 - 15/05/2005 • † Qualified for the UEFA Champions League • ‡ Qualified for the UEFA Cup

UKRAINE 2004-05 FIRST DIVISION (2)

	Pl	W	D	L	F	A	Pts
Stal Alchevsk	34	22	11	1	60	24	77
Arsenal Kharkiv	34	23	4	7	47	24	73
Zorja Luhansk	34	19	9	6	54	21	66
Dynamo 2 Kyiv	34	16	6	12	48	33	54
Nyva Vinnytsya	34	15	8	11	49	38	53
Karpaty Lviv	34	15	7	12	39	35	52
CSCA Kyiv	34	15	6	13	28	38	51
Spartak Ivano-Frank'sk	34	15	5	14	34	33	50
Stal Dniprodzerzhinsk	34	14	7	13	42	47	49
Naftovyk-Ukrnafta	34	13	10	11	37	26	49
Shakhtar 2 Donetsk	34	13	5	16	45	53	44
Hazovyk-Skala Stryj	34	12	7	15	34	39	43
Podillja Khmelnytskyj	34	12	7	15	45	54	43
Dynamo Simferopol	34	12	5	17	38	57	41
Spartak-Horobyna Sumy	34	9	12	13	34	41	39
Nafkom Brovary	34	9	10	15	26	38	37
FK Mykolajiv	34	8	7	19	15	40	31
Polissja Zhytomyr §	34	1	2	31	5	39	5

15/07/2004 - 19/06/2005 • § Withdrew after 17 games

TOP SCORERS

KOSYRIN Olexandr	Chernomorets	14
BRANDAO	Shakhtar	12
MENDOZA	Metalurh Donetsk	12
SACHKO Vasil	Volyn	12
ZAKARLIUKA Serhiy	Illychivets	12
SHATSKIKH Maksim	Dynamo Kyiv	11
RINCON	Dynamo Kyiv	10

RECENT LEAGUE AND CUP RECORD

Championship

Year	Champions	Pts	Runners-up	Pts	Third	Pts
1992	Tavriya Simferopol	1-0	Dynamo Kyiv			
1993	Dynamo Kyiv	44	Dn. Dnipropetrovsk	44	Ch'morets Odesa	38
1994	Dynamo Kyiv	56	Shakhtar Donetsk	49	Ch'morets Odesa	48
1995	Dynamo Kyiv	83	Ch'morets Odesa	73	Dn. Dnipropetrovsk	65
1996	Dynamo Kyiv	79	Ch'morets Odesa	73	Dn. Dnipropetrovsk	63
1997	Dynamo Kyiv	73	Shakhtar Donetsk	62	Vorskla Poltava	58
1998	Dynamo Kyiv	72	Shakhtar Donetsk	67	Karpaty L'viv	57
1999	Dynamo Kyiv	74	Shakhtar Donetsk	65	Kryvbas Kryvyi Rih	59
2000	Dynamo Kyiv	84	Shakhtar Donetsk	66	Kryvbas Kryvyi Rih	60
2001	Dynamo Kyiv	64	Shakhtar Donetsk	63	Dn. Dnipropetrovsk	55
2002	Shakhtar Donetsk	66	Dynamo Kyiv	65	Metalurh Donetsk	42
2003	Dynamo Kyiv	73	Shakhtar Donetsk	70	Metalurh Donetsk	60
2004	Dynamo Kyiv	73	Shakhtar Donetsk	70	Dn. Dnipropetrovsk	57
2005	Shakhtar Donetsk	80	Dynamo Kyiv	73	Metalurh Donetsk	

Cup

Winners	Score	Runners-up
Ch'morets Odesa	1-0	Metalist Kharkiv
Dynamo Kyiv	2-1	Karpaty L'viv
Ch'morets Odesa	0-0 5-3p	Tavriya Simferopol
Shakhtar Donetsk	1-1 7-6p	Dn. Dnipropetrovsk
Dynamo Kyiv	2-0	Nyva Vinnitsa
Shakhtar Donetsk	1-0	Dn. Dnipropetrovsk
Dynamo Kyiv	2-1	CSCA Kyiv
Dynamo Kyiv	3-0	Karpaty L'viv
Dynamo Kyiv	1-0	Kryvbas Kryvyi Rih
Shakhtar Donetsk	2-1	CSCA Kyiv
Shakhtar Donetsk	3-2	Dynamo Kyiv
Dynamo Kyiv	2-1	Shakhtar Donetsk
Shakhtar Donetsk	2-0	Dn. Dnipropetrovsk
Dynamo Kyiv	1-0	Shakhtar Donetsk

Ukrainian clubs played in the Soviet league until the end of the 1991 season

URU – URUGUAY

NATIONAL TEAM RECORD
JULY 1ST 2002 TO JUNE 30TH 2005

PL	W	D	L	F	A	%
32	12	11	9	50	50	54.7

Since winning the first Copa America in 1916 not a single decade has passed without either the Uruguay national team or a Uruguayan club winning a major international honour; but time is running out in the current decade if that record is to be kept alive. Uruguayan clubs show little sign of recovering the position that once saw Peñarol and Nacional the most feared clubs on the continent and beyond. In the 45-year history of the Intercontinental Cup between the winners of the European Cup and the Copa Libertadores both Peñarol and Nacional sit at the top of the all-time winners list alongside Milan, Real Madrid and Boca Juniors but it may be some time before either make a first appearance in the new FIFA Club World Championship. Indeed, the 2004 season in Uruguay showed that Peñarol and Nacional can no longer even take supremacy within their own country for granted with Danubio winning the League after beating Nacional in the end of season play-off, the first time since 1991 that the title has been prised away from the big two. Both Nacional and Danubio qualified for the Championship play-off semi-finals after Nacional won the Apertura and Danubio won the Clausura. The winner of that match would play the team

INTERNATIONAL HONOURS
FIFA World Cup™ 1930 1950   Olympic Gold 1924 1928
Qualified for the FIFA World Cup™ finals 1930 (hosts) 1950 1954 1962 1966 1970 1986 1990 2002
Copa América 1916 1917 1920 1923 1924 1926 1935 1942 1956 1959 1967 1983 1987 1995
Panamerican Games 1983 Juventud de América 1954 1958 1964 1975 1977 1979 1981
Copa Toyota Libertadores Peñarol 1960 1961 1966 1982 1987   Nacional 1971 1980 1988

with the best overall record in the season – Danubio. So despite losing against Nacional in the semi-final, Danubio had a second chance in the final which they took, winning 1-0 with a late injury-time winner from Brazilian Jadson Viera. The first half of 2005 saw the staging of a short League season, won by Nacional, in order that the Championship could be changed to a September to June cycle instead of being based on the calender year. It was yet another unsuccessful year for Uruguayan clubs in both the Copa Sudamericana and the Copa Libertadores with Peñarol knocked out by Paraguay's Cerro Porteño in the early rounds of the former while neither Danubio or Nacional made it past the group stage of the latter. The national team made a solid start to the 2006 FIFA World Cup™ qualifiers but a dreadful run in the first half of 2004, including home defeats to Venezuela and Peru and a 5-0 mauling at the hands of Colombia undermined the team's chances of qualifying for the finals in Germany. Under coach Jorge Fossati, who was appointed after the Venezuela debacle, the team clawed its way back into contention although too many draws have left Uruguay just off the pace going into the final stages.

Asociación Uruguaya de Fútbol (AUF)
Guayabo 1531, Montevideo 11200, Uruguay
Tel +59 82 4004814   Fax +59 82 4090550
auf@auf.org.uy   www.auf.org.uy
President: FIGUEREDO Eugenio   General Secretary: ALMADA Jorge Dr
Vice-President: DAMIANI Juan Pedro   Treasurer: PASTORINI Daniel Dr   Media Officer: GONZALEZ Heber
Men's Coach: FOSSATI Jorge   Women's Coach: DUARTE Juan
AUF formed: 1900   CONMEBOL: 1916   FIFA: 1923
Colours: Sky blue, Black, Black

GAMES PLAYED BY URUGUAY IN THE 2006 FIFA WORLD CUP™ CYCLE

2002	Opponents		Score	Venue	Comp	Scorers	Att	Referee
20-11	Venezuela	L	0-1	Caracas	Fr		27 000	Solorzano VEN
2003								
1-02	Hong Kong	W	3-0	Hong Kong	Fr	Rodriguez.J [84], Peralta [86], Munhoz [89]	20 785	Maidin SIN
4-02	Iran	D	1-1	Hong Kong	Fr	Estoyanoff [83], W 4-2p	17 877	Fong HKG
28-03	Japan	D	2-2	Tokyo	Fr	Forlan [21], Lembo [25]	54 039	Kim Tae Young KOR
8-06	Korea Republic	W	2-0	Seoul	Fr	Hiornos [12], Abreu [53]		Yoshida JPN
16-07	Argentina	D	2-2	La Plata	Fr	Chevanton [7], Milito OG [37]	35 000	Gonzalez PAR
24-07	Peru	W	4-3	Lima	Fr	Liguera 2 [10 72], Sosa [49], Vigneri [79]		Garay Evia PER
30-07	Peru	W	1-0	Montevideo	Fr	Liguera [54]	9 000	Mendez URU
20-08	Argentina	L	2-3	Florence	Fr	Forlan [2], Abreu [57]	3 000	De Santis ITA
7-09	Bolivia	W	5-0	Montevideo	WCq	Forlan [17], Chevanton 2 [40 61], Abeijon [83], Bueno [88]	39 253	Ricaldi
10-09	Paraguay	L	1-4	Asuncion	WCq	Chevanton [24]	15 000	Ruiz COL
15-10	Mexico	W	2-0	Chicago	Fr	Perrone 2 [27 63]		Kennedy USA
15-11	Chile	W	2-1	Montevideo	WCq	Chevanton [31], Romero [49]	60 000	Martin ARG
19-11	Brazil	D	3-3	Curitiba	WCq	Forlan 2 [57 76], Gilberto Silva OG [78]	28 000	Elizondo ARG
2004								
18-02	Jamaica	L	0-2	Kingston	Fr		27 000	Gordon TRI
31-03	Venezuela	L	0-3	Montevideo	WCq		40 094	Ortube BOL
1-06	Peru	L	1-3	Montevideo	WCq	Forlan [72]	30 000	Selman CHI
6-06	Colombia	L	0-5	Barranquilla	WCq		7 000	Amarilla PAR
7-07	Mexico	D	2-2	Chiclayo	CAr1	Bueno [42], Montero [87]	25 000	Hidalgo PER
10-07	Ecuador	W	2-1	Chiclayo	CAr1	Forlan [61], Bueno [79]	25 000	Brand VEN
13-07	Argentina	L	2-4	Piura	CAr1	Estoyanoff [7], Sanchez.V [39]	24 000	Selman CHI
18-07	Paraguay	W	3-1	Tacna	CAqf	Bueno [40p], Silva 2 [65 88]	20 000	Baldassi ARG
21-07	Brazil	D	1-1	Lima	CAsf	Sosa [22], L 3-5p	10 000	Rodriguez Moreno MEX
24-07	Colombia	W	2-1	Cusco	CA3p	Estoyanoff [4], Sanchez.V [88]	35 000	Ortube BOL
5-09	Ecuador	W	1-0	Montevideo	WCq	Bueno [57]	28 000	Hidalgo PER
9-10	Argentina	L	2-4	Buenos Aires	WCq	Rodriguez.C [63], Chevanton [86]	50 000	Souza BRA
12-10	Bolivia	D	0-0	La Paz	WCq		24 349	Rezende BRA
17-11	Paraguay	W	1-0	Montevideo	WCq	Montero [78]	35 000	Simon BRA
2005								
26-03	Chile	D	1-1	Santiago	WCq	Regueiro [4]	55 000	Ruiz COL
30-03	Brazil	D	1-1	Montevideo	WCq	Forlan [48]	60 000	Baldassi ARG
4-06	Venezuela	D	1-1	Maracaibo	WCq	Forlan [2]	12 504	Brazenas ARG
7-06	Peru	D	0-0	Lima	WCq		31 515	Baldassi ARG

Fr = Friendly match • CA = Copa América • WC = FIFA World Cup™
q = qualifier • r1 = first round group • qf = quarter-final • sf = semi-final • 3p = third place play-off

FIFA/COCA-COLA WORLD RANKING

1993	1994	1995	1996	1997	1998	1999	2000	2001	2002	2003	2004	High		Low	
17	37	32	43	40	76	46	32	22	28	21	16	**14**	05/94	**76**	12/98

2004-2005											
08/04	09/04	10/04	11/04	12/04	01/05	02/05	03/05	04/05	05/05	06/05	07/05
19	19	17	19	16	17	18	15	16	16	18	18

THE FIFA BIG COUNT OF 2000

	Male	Female		Male	Female
Registered players	107 873	600	Referees	400	0
Non registered players	85 000	1 000	Officials	2 000	100
Youth players	7 212	100	Total involved	204 285	
Total players	201 785		Number of clubs	1 100	
Professional players	1 000	0	Number of teams	2 000	

NATIONAL CAPS

	Caps
RODRIGUEZ Rodolfo	78
FRANCESCOLI Enzo	72
ROMANO Angel	68
AGUILERA Carlos	65
BARRIOS Jorge	61
RECOBA Alvaro	58
MONTERO Paolo	57
GUTIERREZ Nelson	56
HERRERA José	56

NATIONAL GOALS

	Goals
SCARONE Héctor	31
ROMANO Angel	28
MIGUEZ Omar	27
PETRONE Pedro	24
AGUILERA Carlos	23
MORENA Fernando	22
PIENDIBENE Jos	21
CASTRO Héctor	20
VARELA Severino	19
SCARONE Carlos	18

NATIONAL COACH

	Years
MANEIRO Ildo	1993-'94
FLEITAS Roberto	1994
NUNEZ Hector	1994-'96
AHUNTCHAIN Juan	1996-'97
MASPOLI Roque	1997
PUA Victor	1997-'99
PASSARELLA Daniel	1999-'00
PUA Victor	2001-'03
CARRASCO Juan	2003-'04
FOSSATI Jorge	2004-

URUGUAY NATIONAL TEAM RECORDS AND RECORD SEQUENCES

Records			Sequence records			
Victory	9-0	BOL 1927	Wins	7	1941-42, 1980-81	Clean sheets	6	1969-1970
Defeat	0-6	ARG 1902	Defeats	5	1916	Goals scored	20	1953-1956
Player Caps	78	RODRIGUEZ Rodolfo	Undefeated	14	1967-1968	Without goal	4	1925, 1968. 1976
Player Goals	31	SCARONE Héctor	Without win	9	1986	Goals against	18	1961-1963

FIFA REFEREE LIST 2005

	Int'l	DoB
CABRERA Fernando	2005	13-03-1968
KOMJETAN Sergio	2005	11-12-1966
LARRIONDA Jorge	1998	9-03-1968
MENDEZ Gustavo	1997	24-11-1967
SIEGLER Gustavo		17-09-1969
SILVERA Roberto	2005	30-01-1971
VAZQUEZ Martin	2005	14-01-1969
VIERA Olivier	1998	5-08-1962

FIFA ASSISTANT REFEREE LIST 2005

	Int'l	DoB
ACOSTA Edgardo	2005	21-06-1963
COSTA Marcelo	1999	5-02-1968
CRESCI Fernando	1998	27-05-1969
ESPINOSA Mauricio		6-05-1972
FANDINO Pablo	2001	11-10-1966
GADEA Marcelo	2001	29-08-1971
RIAL Walter	1999	9-01-1964
SACARELO Alvaro	2005	19-11-1964

URUGUAY COUNTRY INFORMATION

Capital	Montevideo	Independence	1828 from Spain	GDP per Capita	$12 800
Population	3 339 237	Status	Republic	GNP Ranking	66
Area km²	176 220	Language	Spanish	Dialling code	+598
Population density	19 per km²	Literacy rate	98%	Internet code	uy
% in urban areas	90%	Main religion	Christian	GMT +/-	-3
Towns/Cities ('000)	Montevideo 1 305; Ciudad de la Costa 112; Salto 104; Paysandú 78; Las Piedras 73; Rivera 68				
Neighbours (km)	Argentina 579; Brazil 985; South Atlantic Ocean 660				
Main stadia	Estadio Centenario – Montevideo 73 609				

URUGUAY 2004

TABLA ANUAL

	Pl	W	D	L	F	A	Pts	Danubio	Defensor	Nacional	Peñarol	Liverpool	Rentistas	Wanderers	Cerrito	Fénix	Plaza
Danubio †	27	18	7	2	40	11	61		0-0	2-1	2-0	2-0	2-1	2-1	1-0	3-1	1-0
Defensor Sporting	27	13	10	4	43	29	49	0-1		2-1	2-1	1-1	0-0	2-1	4-0	5-1	1-0
Nacional	27	12	9	6	43	25	45	1-1	0-0		3-2	2-1	6-1	0-0	1-0	2-1	2-2
Peñarol	27	12	8	7	51	41	44	1-5	1-1	1-2		3-3	3-1	0-0	2-1	5-3	3-1
Liverpool	27	12	5	10	44	42	41	1-0	1-2	1-4	4-0		2-0	2-2	2-3	1-1	3-1
Rentistas	27	6	10	11	29	43	28	2-1	1-2	0-1	2-2	3-0		2-1	1-1	1-1	2-1
Wanderers	27	6	9	12	18	34	27	1-1	1-2	1-3	1-2	0-2	0-0		0-3	1-1	1-0
Cerrito	27	7	5	15	30	45	26	0-2	0-2	2-2	1-1	0-1	2-3	0-1		2-4	2-0
Fénix	27	5	9	13	35	47	24	1-2	0-0	0-3	0-3	2-3	4-0	0-0	0-1		0-0
Plaza Colonia	27	2	12	13	28	44	18	0-0	1-2	1-1	2-0	1-2	1-1	0-1	3-1	3-3	

† Danubio qualified for the 2004 championship final against the winner of Apertura/Clausura play-off • Only the Apertura and Clausura results are listed in the table with the Apertura results in the shaded boxes

URUGUAY 2004 CLASIFICATORIO

	Pl	W	D	L	F	A	Pts
Danubio †	17	12	5	0	32	11	41
Cerrito †	17	10	3	4	25	17	33
Peñarol †	17	9	5	3	34	17	32
Nacional †	17	8	5	4	26	15	29
Liverpool †	17	8	5	4	24	19	29
Rentistas †	17	6	7	4	23	18	25
Wanderers †	17	7	4	6	15	18	25
Fénix †	17	6	6	5	27	21	24
Defensor Sporting † ‡	17	5	7	5	22	24	22
Cerro ‡	17	7	1	9	21	26	22
Miramar Misiones	17	5	6	6	24	25	21
Plaza Colonia † ‡	17	3	9	5	29	32	18
Colonia ‡	17	3	9	5	19	24	18
Rocha	17	3	8	6	22	33	17
Bella Vista	17	4	4	9	15	26	16
Tacuarembó	17	3	4	10	18	28	13
Central Español	17	2	6	9	14	25	12
Maldonado	17	1	8	8	12	23	11

19/03/2004 - 29/08/2004 • † Qualified for Apertura/Clausura
‡ Teams involved in the Montevideo/interior play-off

CHAMPIONSHIP PLAY-OFFS

Semi-finals		Finals	
		Danubio	1
Danubio	1	Nacional	0
Nacional	4		

CHAMPIONSHIP FINAL 2004

Estadio Jardines del Hipódromo, 15-12-2004, Ref: Silvera

| Danubio | 1 | Viera [93+] |
| Nacional | 0 | |

As winners of the Tabla Anual and the Clausura, Danubio needed to win just one game in the final series to become champions.

Danubio - Barbat; Barbosa, Viera, Rodriguez.G; Rariz (Artigas 60), Pouso, Gargano, Lima (Báez 56); Gonzalez.I (Perrone 76); Salgueiro, Risso. Tr: Pelusso
Nacional - Viera; Rariz (Machado 69), Valdez, Cichero, La Luz; Mendez.G, Morales, Eguren; Liguera; Medina (Abreu 69), Castro.G (Albin 80). Tr: De León

URUGUAY 2004 TORNEO APERTURA

	Pl	W	D	L	F	A	Pts
Nacional †	9	6	3	0	17	6	21
Defensor Sporting	9	6	2	1	18	7	20
Danubio	9	5	3	1	11	5	18
Liverpool	9	3	4	2	13	15	13
Peñarol	9	3	3	3	16	14	12
Rentistas	9	3	2	4	13	13	11
Plaza Colonia	9	1	4	4	8	12	7
Cerrito	9	2	1	6	8	14	7
Wanderers	9	1	4	4	7	13	7
Fénix	9	0	4	5	7	19	4

11/09/2004 - 31/10/2004 • † Qualified for play-off semi-final

URUGUAY 2004 TORNEO CLAUSURA

	Pl	W	D	L	F	A	Pts
Danubio †	9	7	1	1	17	6	22
Defensor Sporting	9	5	4	0	10	4	19
Nacional	9	4	3	2	18	12	15
Liverpool	9	5	0	4	17	12	15
Peñarol	9	4	2	3	16	18	14
Rentistas	9	2	4	3	8	17	10
Fénix	9	2	3	4	16	16	9
Wanderers	9	2	3	4	6	9	9
Cerrito	9	2	2	5	11	16	8
Plaza Colonia	9	0	2	7	7	16	2

2/11/2004 - 8/12/2004 • † Qualified for play-off semi-final

URUGUAY LEAGUE RECORD

Year	Winners	Score	Runners-up
1994	Peñarol	1-1 1-1 2-1	Defensor Sporting
1995	Peñarol	1-0 1-2 3-1	Nacional
1996	Peñarol	1-0 1-1	Nacional
1997	Peñarol	1-0 3-0	Defensor Sporting
1998	Nacional	†	
1999	Peñarol	1-1 1-1 2-1	Nacional
2000	Nacional	1-0 1-1	Peñarol
2001	Nacional	2-2 2-1	Danubio
2002	Nacional	2-1 2-1	Danubio
2003	Peñarol	1-0	Nacional
2004	Danubio	1-0	Nacional

† Automatic champions as winners of both the Apertura and Clausura

DANUBIO 2004

Date	Opponents	Score		Comp	Scorers
21-03-2004	Rocha	D 3-3	A	LGE	Curbelo [14], González.I [41], Oliveira [57]
4-04-2004	Defensor	W 2-0	H	LGE	Grosnile [25], Oliveira [80]
11-04-2004	Nacional	W 1-0	H	LGE	Oliveira [70]
18-04-2004	Colonia	D 1-1	H	LGE	Grosnile [70]
21-04-2004	Peñarol	W 2-0	A	LGE	Viera [17], Pouso [41]
25-04-2004	Bella Vista	W 3-1	H	LGE	Gutiérrez.E [9], González.I [52], Rariz [82]
28-04-2004	Central Español	W 3-2	A	LGE	Gutiérrez.E [8], Guglielmone 2 [22 83]
2-05-2004	Fénix	W 4-0	A	LGE	Oliveira [4], Viera [67], González.I [73], Grosnile [78p]
9-05-2004	Miramar Misiones	W 4-3	H	LGE	Oliveira 4 [16p 39p 45 52]
15-05-2004	Tacuarembó	W 2-0	A	LGE	Pouso [25], Guglielmone [60]
22-05-2004	Cerrito	W 2-0	H	LGE	Lima [16], Guglielmone [80]
29-05-2004	Liverpool	W 1-0	H	LGE	Guglielmone [78]
12-06-2004	Maldonado	W 2-0	A	LGE	Rodríguez.G [77], Guglielmone [83]
16-06-2004	Cerro	W 2-1	H	LGE	Guglielmone [5], González.I [66]. Last 66 minutes from 19-05-2004
20-06-2004	Plaza	D 0-0	A	LGE	
23-06-2004	Rentistas	D 0-0	H	LGE	
29-08-2004	Wanderers	D 0-0	A	LGE	
9-09-2004	Peñarol	L 1-2	H	CSpr	Risso [71]
12-09-2004	Wanderers	D 1-1	A	AP	Risso [34]
15-09-2004	Nacional	D 1-1	A	AP	Risso [55]
18-09-2004	Fénix	W 3-1	H	AP	Ortiz [6], Rariz [24], Báez [87]
21-09-2004	Peñarol	D 1-1	A	CSpr	Viera [9]
26-09-2004	Cerrito	W 1-0	H	AP	Risso [26]
28-09-2004	Plaza	D 0-0	A	AP	
3-10-2004	Rentistas	W 2-1	H	AP	Risso [68p], González.I [80]
16-10-2004	Defensor	W 1-0	A	AP	Risso [68]
23-10-2004	Liverpool	L 0-1	A	AP	
31-10-2004	Peñarol	W 2-0	H	AP	Risso [22], Salgueiro [77]
3-11-2004	Wanderers	W 2-1	H	CL	Salgueiro 2 [10 29]
6-11-2004	Nacional	W 2-1	H	CL	Ortiz 2 [49 68]
9-11-2004	Fénix	W 2-1	A	CL	Silva [67], Perrone [69]
20-11-2004	Cerrito	W 2-0	A	CL	Salgueiro [2], Artigas [53]
24-11-2004	Plaza	W 1-0	H	CL	Salgueiro [47]
27-11-2004	Rentistas	L 1-2	A	CL	Risso [63]
1-12-2004	Defensor	D 0-0	H	CL	
5-12-2004	Liverpool	W 2-0	H	CL	Risso [34], González.I [65]
8-12-2004	Peñarol	W 5-1	A	CL	Risso [5], Rodríguez.G [12], Báez [31], Salgueiro 2 [45 50]
12-12-2004	Nacional	L 1-4	A	PO	Risso [26]
15-12-2004	Nacional	W 1-0	H	PO	Viera [93+]

LGE = Clasificatorio • AP = Apertura • CL = Clausura • PO = Championship final • CS = Copa Sudamericana • pr = preliminary round

CLUB DIRECTORY

Club	Town/City	Stadium	www.	Lge	CL
Club Bella Vista	Montevideo	Jose Nasazzi 15 000		1	0
CS Cerrito	Montevideo	Estadio Charrua 12 000		0	0
CA Cerro	Montevideo	Luis Troccoli 25 000		0	0
Danubio FC	Montevideo	Jardines del Hipodromo 16 000	danubio.org.uy	2	0
Defensor Sporting Club	Montevideo	Luis Franzini 18 000		3	0
CA Fénix	Montevideo	Parque Capurro 10 000		0	0
Liverpool FC	Montevideo	Estadio Belvedere 9 500		0	0
Club Nacional de Fútbol	Montevideo	Parque Central 16 000	nacional.com.uy	39	3
CA Peñarol	Montevideo	Estadio Charrua 12 000	penarol.org	47	5
Rampla Juniors FC	Montevideo	Estadio Olimpico 9 500	rampla.com	1	0
River Plate	Montevideo	Federico Saroldi 12 000		4	0
Montevideo Wanderers	Montevideo	Alfredo Victor Viera 12 500	mwfc.com.uy	0	0

USA – UNITED STATES OF AMERICA

NATIONAL TEAM RECORD
JULY 1ST 2002 TO JUNE 30TH 2005

PL	W	D	L	F	A	%
46	29	10	7	85	27	73.9

The USA continues to make steady progress on all fronts and although soccer is still regarded as un-American by many, such is the number of people involved with the game that this hardly seems a relevant point anymore. The hard facts show that 18m Americans are actively engaged in soccer, compared to six million in Germany or four million in Italy and with a growing Hispanic population these figures will only get bigger in the future. Success of course doesn't depend on numbers alone but in July 2005 the national team rose to a highest ever position of sixth in the FIFA/Coca-Cola World Ranking and then finished off a great month by winning the 2005 CONCACAF Gold Cup in the Giants Stadium in New Jersey. The team also has its sights firmly set on qualification for the 2006 FIFA World Cup™ for what would be a fifth successive appearance in the finals, something that 20 years ago no-one would have thought possible. Central to the rise in standards has been Major League Soccer and such is the optimism for the future that two expansion teams were given franchises for the 2005 season. It is ironic that while European football is run unregulated on almost pure capitalist lines, in the home of capitalism all sports are regulated to a degree that would

INTERNATIONAL HONOURS

FIFA Women's World Cup 1991 1999   **Women's Olympic Gold** 1996 2004   **FIFA U-19 Women's World Championship** 2002
Qualified for the FIFA World Cup™ 1930 1934 1950 1990 1994 1998 2002
CONCACAF Gold Cup 1991 2002   **CONCACAF Women's Gold Cup** 1991 1993 1994 2000 2002
Panamerican Games 1991   **CONCACAF U-17** 1983 1992
CONCACAF Champions Cup DC United 1998, Los Angeles Galaxy 2000

not have looked out of place in the old Soviet Bloc. With strict salary guidelines and control over players MLS has ensured that no team can dominate to the extent that has happened in many European leagues and although many players have left to earn more in Europe, the pitfalls that sent the NASL crashing down in the mid-1980s have been avoided. In the first 11 seasons of the League no fewer than five teams were crowned champions although 2004 did see DC United win the trophy for the fourth time when they beat Kansas City Wizards in the MLS Cup. There was some consolation for the Wizards when they won the Lamar Hunt US Open Cup, a tournament which celebrated its 90th anniversary, making it the longest running competition in the country. Having set the pace for many years the women's game in America finds itself challenged on a number of fronts, notably by Germany and Brazil, but at the 2004 Olympic Games some of the older generation, including Mia Hamm, added another gold medal to the collection when they beat Brazil 2-1 in a hard-fought final. The U-19 team, however, couldn't defend their world title at the FIFA U-19 Women's World Championship in Thailand after losing to Germany in the semi-finals.

US Soccer Federation (USSF)
US Soccer House, 1801 S. Prairie Avenue, Chicago IL 60616, USA
Tel +1 312 8081300   Fax +1 312 8081301
communications@ussoccer.org   www.ussoccer.com
President: CONTIGUGLIA Robert Dr   General Secretary: FLYNN Dan
Vice-President: GULATI Sunil   Treasurer: GOAZIOU Bill   Media Officer: MOORHOUSE Jim
Men's Coach: ARENA Bruce   Women's Coach: RYAN Greg
USSF formed: 1913   CONCACAF: 1961   FIFA: 1914
Colours: White, Blue, White

GAMES PLAYED BY USA IN THE 2006 FIFA WORLD CUP™ CYCLE

2002	Opponents	Score	Venue	Comp	Scorers	Att	Referee
17-11	El Salvador	W 2-0	Washington	Fr	Olsen [31], Victorine [60]	13 590	Prendergast JAM
2003							
18-01	Canada	W 4-0	Fort Lauderdale	Fr	Bocanegra [7], Mathis [31], Klein [32], Ralston [61]	6 549	Sibrian SLV
8-02	Argentina	L 0-1	Miami	Fr		27 196	Batres GUA
12-02	Jamaica	W 2-1	Kingston	Fr	Bocanegra [11], Klein [12]	27 000	Bowen CAY
29-03	Venezuela	W 2-0	Seattle	Fr	Kirovski [52], Donovan [76]	17 819	Seifert CAN
8-05	Mexico	D 0-0	Houston	Fr		69 582	Prendergast JAM
26-05	Wales	W 2-0	San Jose	Fr	Donovan [41p], Lewis [59]	12 282	Archundia MEX
8-06	New Zealand	W 2-1	Richmond	Fr	Klein [20], Kirovski [65]	9 116	Liu CAN
19-06	Turkey	L 1-2	St Etienne	CCr1	Beasley [36]	16 944	Larrionda URU
21-06	Brazil	L 0-1	Lyon	CCr1		20 306	Cardoso Batista POR
23-06	Cameroon	D 0-0	Lyon	CCr1		19 206	Shield AUS
6-07	Paraguay	W 2-0	Columbus	Fr	Donovan [12], Stewart [90]	14 103	Navarro CAN
12-07	El Salvador	W 2-0	Boston	GCr1	Lewis [28], McBride [76]	33 652	Ramos MEX
14-07	Martinique	W 2-0	Boston	GCr1	McBride 2 [39 43]	8 780	Moreno PAN
19-07	Cuba	W 5-0	Boston	GCqf	Donovan 4 [22 25 55 76], Ralston [42]	15 627	Prendergast JAM
23-07	Brazil	L 1-2	Miami	GCsf	Bocanegra [62]	35 211	Batres GUA
26-07	Costa Rica	W 3-2	Miami	GC3p	Bocanegra [29], Stewart [56], Convey [67]	5 093	Piper TRI
2004							
18-01	Denmark	D 1-1	Carson	Fr	Donovan [76p]	10 461	Mendoza MEX
18-02	Netherlands	L 0-1	Amsterdam	Fr		29 700	Ovrebo NOR
13-03	Haiti	D 1-1	Miami	Fr	Califf [94+]	8 714	Prendergast JAM
31-03	Poland	W 1-0	Plock	Fr	Beasley [26]	10 500	Skjerven NOR
28-04	Mexico	W 1-0	Dallas	Fr	Pope [93+]	45 048	Navarro CAN
2-06	Honduras	W 4-0	Boston	Fr	McBride 2 [22 37], Lewis [77], Sanneh [81]	11 533	Sibrian SLV
13-06	Grenada	W 3-0	Columbus	WCq	Beasley 2 [45 71], Vanney [90]	9 137	Navarro CAN
20-06	Grenada	W 3-2	St George's	WCq	Donovan [6], Wolff [19], Beasley [76]	15 267	Brizan TRI
11-07	Poland	D 1-1	Chicago	Fr	Bocanegra	39 529	
18-08	Jamaica	D 1-1	Kingston	WCq	Ching [88]	27 000	Mattus CRC
4-09	El Salvador	W 2-0	Boston	WCq	Ching [5], Donovan [68]	25 266	Brizan TRI
8-09	Panama	D 1-1	Panama City	WCq	Jones.C [91+]	14 500	Rodriguez MEX
9-10	El Salvador	W 2-0	San Salvador	WCq	McBride [29], Johnson [75]	20 000	Batres GUA
13-10	Panama	W 6-0	Washington	WCq	Donovan 2 [21 56], Johnson 3 [69 84 86], Torres OG [89]	19 793	Ramdhan TRI
17-11	Jamaica	D 1-1	Columbus	WCq	Johnson [15]	9 088	Navarro CAN
2005							
9-02	Trinidad and Tobago	W 2-1	Port of Spain	WCq	Johnson [23], Lewis [53]	11 000	Archundia MEX
9-03	Colombia	W 3-0	Fullerton	Fr	Noonan [25], Marshall [33], Mathis [66]	7 086	Rodriguez MEX
19-03	Honduras	W 1-0	Albuquerque	Fr	Johnson [45]	9 222	Navorro CAN
27-03	Mexico	L 1-2	Mexico City	WCq	Lewis [58]	84 000	Sibrian SLV
30-03	Guatemala	W 2-0	Birmingham	WCq	Johnson [11], Ralston [69]	31 624	Ramdhan TRI
28-05	England	L 1-2	Chicago	Fr	Dempsey [79]	47 637	Archundia MEX
4-06	Costa Rica	W 3-0	Salt Lake City	WCq	Donovan 2 [10 62], McBride [87]	40 576	Batres GUA
8-06	Panama	W 3-0	Panama City	WCq	Bocanegra [6], Donovan [19], McBride [39]	15 000	Navarro CAN
7-07	Cuba	W 4-1	Seattle	GCr1	Dempsey [44], Donovan 2 [87 92+], Beasley [89]	15 831	Pineda HON
9-07	Canada	W 2-0	Seattle	GCr1	Hutchinson OG [48], Donovan [90]	15 109	Brizan TRI
12-07	Costa Rica	D 0-0	Boston	GCr1		15 211	Archundia MEX
16-07	Jamaica	W 3-1	Boston	GCqf	Wolff [6], Beasley 2 [42 83]	22 108	Batres GUA
21-07	Honduras	W 2-1	New Jersey	GCsf	O'Brien [86], Onyewu [92+]	41 721	Prendergast JAM
24-07	Panama	D 0-0	New Jersey	GCf		31 018	Batres GUA

Fr = Friendly match • CC = FIFA Confederations Cup • GC = CONCACAF Gold Cup • WC = FIFA World Cup™
q = qualifier • r1 = first round group • qf = quarter-final • sf = semi-final • 3p = third place play-off • f = final

FIFA/COCA-COLA WORLD RANKING

1993	1994	1995	1996	1997	1998	1999	2000	2001	2002	2003	2004	High		Low	
22	23	19	18	26	23	22	16	24	10	11	11	7	07/04	35	10/97

2004-2005											
08/04	09/04	10/04	11/04	12/04	01/05	02/05	03/05	04/05	05/05	06/05	07/05
10	10	11	11	11	11	11	10	10	10	10	6

NATIONAL CAPS

	Caps
JONES Cobi	164
AGOOS Jeff	134
BALBOA Marcelo	128
CALIGIURI Paul	110
REYNA Claudio	106
WYNALDA Eric	106
STEWART Earnie	101
MOORE Joe-Max	100
MEOLA Tony	99
LALAS Alexi	96

NATIONAL GOALS

	Goals
WYNALDA Eric	34
MCBRIDE Brian	28
DONOVAN Landon	25
MOORE Joe-Max	24
MURRAY Bruce	21
STEWART Earnie	17
JONES Cobi	15
BALBOA Marcelo	13
PEREZ Hugo	13
MATHIS Clint	12

NATIONAL COACH

	Years
SCHELLSCHEIDT Manny	1975
CHYZOWYCH Walter	1976-'80
GANSLER Bob	1982
PANAGOULIAS Alkis	1983-'85
OSIANDER Lothar	1986-'88
GANSLER Bob	1989-'91
KOWALSKI John	1991
MILUTINOVIC Bora	1991-'95
SAMPSON Steve	1996-'98
ARENA Bruce	1998-'04

USA NATIONAL TEAM RECORDS AND RECORD SEQUENCES

Records			Sequence records					
Victory	8-1	CAY 1993	Wins	6	1997-1998	Clean sheets	5	2003
Defeat	0-11	NOR 1948	Defeats	13	1973-1975	Goals scored	23	2004-2005
Player Caps	164	JONES Cobi	Undefeated	16	2004-2005	Without goal	5	1990-1991
Player Goals	34	WYNALDA Eric	Without win	16	1973-1976	Goals against	14	1973-1976

USA THE FIFA BIG COUNT OF 2000

	Male	Female		Male	Female
Registered players	159 928	102 049	Referees	87 150	17 850
Non registered players	8 400 000	5 600 000	Officials	487 500	262 500
Youth players	2 178 000	1 452 000	Total involved	18 746 977	
Total players	17 891 977		Number of clubs	1 690	
Professional players	6 928	49	Number of teams	10 945	

USA COUNTRY INFORMATION

Capital	Washington DC	Independence	1776 from Great Britain	GDP per Capita	$37 800
Population	293 027 571	Status	Republic	GNP Ranking	1
Area km²	9 631 418	Language	English, Spanish	Dialling code	+1
Population density	30 per km²	Literacy rate	97%	Internet code	.us
% in urban areas	76%	Main religion	Christian	GMT +/–	-6 to -11

Towns/Cities ('000)	New York 22 313; Los Angeles 17 542; Chicago 9 418; Washington-Baltimore 8 036; San Francisco 7 533; Philadelphia 6 254; Boston 5 908; Dallas 5 896; Detroit 5 885; Houston 5 194; Atlanta 4 716; San Diego 4 688; Miami 4 286; Phoenix 3 792; Seattle 3 769; Minneapolis 3 162; Cleveland 2 956; Denver 2 685; Saint Louis 2 629; Tampa 2 584; Portland 2 467; Pittsburgh 2 332; Cincinnati 2 038; Sacramento 1 980; Las Vegas 1 952
Neighbours (km)	Canada 8 893; Mexico 3 141; North Atlantic, North Pacific & Gulf of Mexico 19 924
Main stadia	Rose Bowl – Pasadena 92 542; Gillette Stadium – Foxboro/Boston 68 756; RFK Memorial – Washington 56 454; Home Depot Centre – Carson 27 000; Crew Stadium – Columbus 22 555

USA 2004

MAJOR LEAGUE SOCCER REGULAR SEASON

Eastern Conference	Pl	W	D	L	F	A	Pts	Columbus	DC United	MetroStars	N. England	Chicago	Kansas	Los Angeles	Colorado	San Jose	Dallas
Columbus Crew †	30	12	13	5	40	32	49		2-2 1-0	1-3 4-2	1-0 1-1	2-0 3-3	2-2 2-1	3-1	1-2	1-0	0-0 2-1
DC United †	30	11	9	10	43	42	42	1-1 3-1		6-2 3-2	2-2 1-0	0-1 3-1	1-0	2-4 1-1	0-0 3-1	2-1	3-0
MetroStars †	30	11	7	12	47	49	40	1-1 1-1	3-2 0-1		1-1 3-2	1-1 2-1	1-0	2-1 3-0	2-3	2-0	0-2 0-1
New England Revolution †	30	8	9	13	42	43	33	1-2 2-2	0-1 0-0	1-1 2-1		3-1 2-1	1-3 1-2	2-1	6-1	1-3 0-1	2-0
Chicago Fire	30	8	9	13	36	44	33	1-3 0-1	3-0 3-1	3-0 1-1	1-1 2-0		3-1	0-1	1-0 0-3	1-1 2-1	0-2

Western Conference	Pl	W	D	L	F	A	Pts	Columbus	DC United	MetroStars	N. England	Chicago	Kansas	Los Angeles	Colorado	San Jose	Dallas
Kansas City Wizards †	30	14	7	9	38	30	49	1-0	1-0	1-2 1-0	2-3	0-0 2-2		2-2 1-0	2-0 1-0	0-2 1-0	2-0 5-1
Los Angeles Galaxy †	30	11	10	9	42	40	43	2-0 0-0	1-1	0-3	3-2	3-2 1-1	1-2 1-1		1-1 2-0	2-1 2-1	4-1 2-0
Colorado Rapids †	30	10	11	9	29	32	41	0-0 1-1	2-1	1-0	0-0 1-0	2-0	0-1 3-1	1-1 0-0		1-0 1-1	1-1 2-1
San Jose Earthquakes †	30	9	11	10	41	35	38	0-1	1-1 2-0	5-5 3-1	2-2		1-0 0-0	4-2 0-0	3-1 0-0		1-2 3-0
Dallas Burn	30	10	6	14	34	45	36	0-0	1-1 5-1	0-2	3-1 0-3	4-1	1-0 0-1	1-3 2-0	1-1 1-0	1-2 2-2	

16/08/2004 - 15/05/2005 • † Qualified for the play-offs

MLS PLAY-OFFS 2004

Quarter-finals

DC United	2	2
MetroStars	0	0
Columbus Crew	0	1
New England Revolution	1	1
Los Angeles Galaxy	0	2
Colorado Rapids	1	0
San Jose Earthquakes	2	0
Kansas City Wizards	0	3

Semi-finals

DC United	3 4p
New England Revolution	3 3p
Los Angeles Galaxy	0
Kansas City Wizards	2

Final

DC United	3
Kansas City Wizards	2

USA 2004 A-LEAGUE (2)

Eastern Conference	Pl	W	D	L	F	A	Pts
Montreal Impact †	28	17	5	6	36	15	56
Richmond Kickers †	28	17	3	8	44	29	54
Syracuse Salty Dogs †	28	15	5	8	40	29	50
Rochester Rhinos †	28	15	3	10	36	32	48
Atlanta Silverbacks	28	14	3	11	41	48	45
Virginia Mariners	28	11	3	14	43	41	36
Toronto Lynx	28	10	2	16	38	50	32
Charleston Battery	28	7	6	15	30	39	27
Puerto Rico Islanders	28	5	6	17	22	48	21

Western Conference	Pl	W	D	L	F	A	Pts
Portland Timbers †	28	18	3	7	58	30	57
Vancouver Whitecaps †	28	14	5	9	38	29	47
Minnesota Thunder †	28	13	6	9	33	23	45
Seattle Sounders †	28	13	4	11	40	34	43
Milwaukee Wave Utd	28	12	4	12	44	48	40
Edmonton Aviators	28	4	6	18	19	56	18
Calgary Mustangs	28	4	6	18	30	51	18

A-LEAGUE PLAY-OFFS

Western Conference: Semi-finals: Seattle 1-2 2-0 Portland; Minnesota 0-2 0-1 Vancouver; Final: Vancouver 0-1 1-1 Seattle;
Eastern Conference: Semi-finals: Syracuse 1-0 1-2 5-4p Richmond; Montreal 1-0 1-0 Rochester; Final: Montreal 2-0 1-1 Syracuse
A-League Final: Montreal 2-0 Seattle

ATTENDANCES MLS 2004

	Total	Average
Los Angeles Galaxy	357 137	23 809
DC United	258 484	17 232
MetroStars	257 923	17 195
Chicago Fire	257 295	17 153
Columbus Crew	253 079	16 872
Kansas City Wizards	222 235	14 816
Colorado Rapids	212 925	14 195
San Jose Earthquakes	195 015	13 001
New England Revolution	183 385	12 226
Dallas Burn	136 319	9 088
Total	2 333 797	15 559

RECENT LEAGUE AND CUP RECORD

	Championship				Cup		
Year	Champions	Score	Runners-up		Winners	Score	Runners-up
1996	DC United	3-2	Los Angeles Galaxy		DC United	3-0	Rochester Rhinos
1997	DC United	2-1	Colorado Rapids		Dallas Burn	0-0 5-3p	DC United
1998	Chicago Fire	2-0	DC United		Chicago Fire	2-1	Columbus Crew
1999	DC United	2-0	Los Angeles Galaxy		Rochester Rhinos	2-0	Colorado Rapids
2000	Kansas City Wizards	1-0	Chicago Fire		Chicago Fire	2-1	Miami Fusion
2001	San Jose Earthquakes	2-1	Los Angeles Galaxy		Los Angeles Galaxy	2-1	New England Revolution
2002	Los Angeles Galaxy	1-0	New England Revolution		Columbus Crew	1-0	Los Angeles Galaxy
2003	San Jose Earthquakes	4-2	Chicago Fire		Chicago Fire	1-0	MetroStars
2004	DC United	3-2	Kansas City Wizards		Kansas City Wizards	1-0	Chicago Fire

LAMAR HUNT US OPEN CUP 2004

Third Round	Fourth Round	Quarter-finals	Semi-finals	Final

Third Round

| Carolina Dynamo * | 2 |
| Atlanta Silverbacks | 3 |

| Virginia Beach Mariners | 2 |
| Dallas Burn * | 0 |

| Minnesota Thunder * | 2 |
| Boulder Rapids Reserve | 1 |

| Portland Timbers | 2 |
| Utah Blitzz * | 1 |

| Charleston Battery * | 2 |
| Wilmington Hammerheads | 0 |

| Chicago Fire Reserves | 0 |
| Rochester Rhinos * | 1 |

| Richmond Kickers * | 1 |
| Cape Cod Crusaders | 0 |

| Columbus Crew * | 2 |
| Syracuse Salty Dogs | 1 |

Fourth Round

| Kansas City Wizards | 4 |
| Atlanta Silverbacks * | 1 |

| Colorado Rapids | 0 |
| Dallas Burn * | 3 |

| Minnesota Thunder * | 1 |
| Los Angeles Galaxy | 0 |

| Portland Timbers * | 0 |
| San Jose Earthquakes | 3 |

| Charleston Battery * | 1 |
| MetroStars | 0 |

| New England Revolution* | 1 | 1p |
| Rochester Rhinos | 1 | 3p |

| Richmond Kickers * | 2 |
| DC United | 1 |

| Columbus Crew * | 1 |
| Chicago Fire | 2 |

Quarter-finals

| Kansas City Wizards * | 4 |
| Dallas Burn | 0 |

| Minnesota Thunder * | 2 | 4p |
| San Jose Earthquakes | 2 | 5p |

| Charleston Battery | 1 |
| Rochester Rhinos * | 0 |

| Richmond Kickers * | 0 |
| Chicago Fire | 1 |

Semi-finals

| Kansas City Wizards * | 1 |
| San Jose Earthquakes | 0 |

| Charleston Battery | 0 |
| Chicago Fire * | 1 |

Final

| Kansas City Wizards | 1 |
| Chicago Fire | 0 |

CUP FINAL

22-09-2004. Att: 8 819. Ref. Vaughn
Arrowhead Stadium, Kansas City
Scorer - Simutenkov 95 for Kansas

Kansas: Tony Meola, Alex Zotinca, Nick Garcia, Jimmy Conrad, Jose Burciaga, Francisco Gomez (Igor Simutenkov 46), Kerry Zavagnin, Diego Gutierrez, Jack Jewsbury (Taylor Graham 68), Josh Wolff, Davy Arnaud. Tr. Bob Gansler
Chicago: Henry Ring, Kelly Gray, CJ Brown, Jim Curtin, Evan Whitfield, Logan Pause (Chris Armas 80), Jesse Marsch, Andy Williams, Dipsy Selowine, Nate Jaqua, Damani Ralph. Tr. Dave Sarachan

* Home team

DC UNITED 2004

Date	Opponents	Score		Comp	Scorers	Att
3-04-2004	San Jose Earthquakes	W 2-1	H	MLS	Moreno [12], Eskandarian [39]	24 603
10-04-2004	Los Angeles Galaxy	D 1-1	A	MLS	Cerritos [68]	27 000
17-04-2004	MetroStars	L 2-3	A	MLS	Olsen [26], Adu [75]	31 419
24-04-2004	Chicago Fire	L 0-1	H	MLS		21 235
1-05-2004	San Jose Earthquakes	D 1-1	A	MLS	Kovalenko [66]	17 667
8-05-2004	Columbus Crew	D 1-1	H	MLS	Kovalenko [66]	18 376
15-05-2004	Kansas City Wizards	W 1-0	H	MLS	Moreno [75]	16 147
19-05-2004	Los Angeles Galaxy	L 2-4	H	MLS	Cerritos [45], Adu [67]	13 043
22-05-2004	Colorado Rapids	L 1-2	A	MLS	Gros [48]	31 443
29-05-2004	New England Revolution	W 1-0	A	MLS	Kamler OG [5]	19 314
5-06-2004	Chicago Fire	L 0-3	A	MLS		25 810
12-06-2004	Colorado Rapids	D 0-0	H	MLS		21 742
19-06-2004	Columbus Crew	W 3-1	H	MLS	Moreno [6], Eskandarian 2 [33 45]	17 176
26-06-2004	Dallas Burn	D 1-1	H	MLS	Eskandarian [58]	13 833
3-07-2004	MetroStars	W 6-2	H	MLS	Nelsen [30], Moreno [37], Eskandarian 2 [41 69], Stewart [57], Olsen [90]	16 177
10-07-2004	Kansas City Wizards	L 0-1	A	MLS		26 223
17-07-2004	Los Angeles Galaxy	D 1-1	H	MLS	Nelsen [45]	17 671
21-07-2004	Richmond Kickers	L 1-2	A	OCr4	Kuffour [82]	8 776
24-07-2004	Dallas Burn	L 1-5	A	MLS	Gibbs OG [34]	11 088
7-08-2004	San Jose Earthquakes	L 0-2	A	MLS		19 324
11-08-2004	Colorado Rapids	W 3-1	H	MLS	Adu [35], Stewart [40], Kotschau OG [64]	10 848
14-08-2004	New England Revolution	D 2-2	H	MLS	Moreno 2 [39 56]	13 298
21-08-2004	Columbus Crew	D 2-2	A	MLS	Eskandarian [35], Moreno [76]	23 849
28-08-2004	New England Revolution	D 0-0	A	MLS		17 236
4-09-2004	Chicago Fire	L 1-3	A	MLS	Stewart [58]	
11-09-2004	Dallas Burn	W 3-0	H	MLS	Eskandarian 2 [45 82], Adu [84]	13 024
18-09-2004	Chicago Fire	W 3-1	H	MLS	Gomez [8], Eskandarian [20], Olsen [40]	15 851
25-09-2004	Columbus Crew	L 0-1	A	MLS		23 375
2-10-2004	MetroStars	W 1-0	H	MLS	Adu [16]	32 864
9-10-2004	New England Revolution	W 1-0	H	MLS	Gomez [32]	19 461
17-10-2004	MetroStars	W 3-2	H	MLS	Gomez 2 [23 29], Petke [64]	19 832
23-10-2004	MetroStars	W 2-0	A	MLSqf	Stewart [67], Eskandarian [88]	11 161
30-10-2004	MetroStars	W 2-0	H	MLSqf	Moreno [85], Namoff [89]	15 763
6-11-2004	New England Revolution	D 3-3	H	MLSsf	Eskandarian [11], Moreno [21], Gomez [67]	21 201
14-11-2004	Kansas City Wizards	W 3-2	N	MLSf	Eskandarian 2 [19 23], Zotinca OG [26]	25 797

MLS = Major League Soccer • OC = Lamar Hunt US Open Cup • qf = Conference semi-final • sf = Conference final • f = MLS Cup 2004

MLS CUP 2004

Home Depot Centre, Carson, 14-11-2004, Att: 25 797 Referee: Vaughn

DC United 3 Eskandarian 2 [19 23], Zotinca OG [26]
Kansas City Wizards 2

DC United - Nick Rimando; Bryan Namoff, Ryan Nelsen, Mike Petke, Earnie Stewart (Brandon Prideaux 82); Brian Carroll, Christian Gomez (Joshua Gros 59), Ben Olsen, Dema Kovalenko; Jamie Moreno, Alecko Eskandarian (Freddy Adu 65). Tr: Peter Nowak
Kansas - Bo Oshoniyi; Alex Zotinca (Diego Walsh 82), Jimmy Conrad, Nick Garcia, Jose Burciaga; Khari Stephenson (Igor Simutenkov 46), Diego Gutierrez, Kerry Zavagnin, Jack Jewsbury (Matt Taylor 66); Josh Wolff, Davy Arnaud. Tr: Bob Gansler

MLS AWARDS 2004

MVP	GUEVARA Amado	MetroStars
Defender	FRASER Robin	Columbus
Goalkeeper	CANNON Joe	Colorado
Coach	ANDRULIS Greg	Columbus
Comback	CHING Brian	San Jose
Rookie	DEMPSEY Clint	New England
Referee	OKULAJA Abiodun	
Goal	DE ROSARIO Dwayne	San Jose
Play	ADU Freddy	DC United
Fair Play	POPE Eddie	MetroStars
Humanitarian	HENDERSON Chris	Colorado

CLUB DIRECTORY

Club	Town/City	Stadium	Phone	www.	Lge	Cup	CL
Chicago Fire	Chicago	Soldier Field 20 000		chicagofire.mlsnet.com	1	3	0
Chivas USA	Carson/Los Angeles	Home Depot Centre 27 000		chivas.usa.mlsnet.com	0	0	0
Colorado Rapids	Denver	Invesco Field 76 125		coloradorapids.com	0	0	0
Columbus Crew	Columbus	Crew Stadium 22 555		thecrew.com	0	1	0
FC Dallas	Dallas	Frisco (FSEC) 21 193	+1 214 9790303	fcdallas.mlsnet.com	0	1	0
DC United	Washington	RFK Memorial 56 454		dcunited.mlsnet.com	4	1	1
Kansas City Wizards	Kansas City	Arrowhead 79 451		kc.wizards.mlsnet.com	1	1	0
Los Angeles Galaxy	Carson/Los Angeles	Home Depot Centre 27 000	+1 310 6302200	la.galaxy.mlsnet.com	1	1	1
MetroStars	New York/New Jersey	Giants Stadium 80 242		metrostars.mlsnet.com	0	0	0
New England Revolution	Foxboro/Boston	Gillette Stadium 68 756		revolutionsoccer.net	0	0	0
Real Salt Lake	Salt Lake	Rice-Eccles 46 500		real.saltlake.mlsnet.com	0	0	0
San Jose Earthquakes	San Jose	Spartan Stadium 26 525		sjearthquakes.com	2	0	0

KANSAS CITY WIZARDS 2004

Date	Opponents		Score		Comp	Scorers	Att
3-04-2004	Chicago Fire	D	0-0	H	MLS		20 229
17-04-2004	Columbus Crew	W	1-0	H	MLS	Arnaud [42]	9 682
24-04-2004	Dallas Burn	L	0-1	A	MLS		10 269
1-05-2004	Colorado Rapids	W	2-0	H	MLS	Klein [64], Wolff [84]	27 969
8-05-2004	Chicago Fire	D	2-2	H	MLS	Klein [9], Arnaud [64]	11 094
15-05-2004	DC United	L	0-1	A	MLS		16 147
22-05-2004	Dallas Burn	W	2-0	H	MLS	Jewsbury [57], Wolff [60]	10 013
30-05-2004	MetroStars	L	0-1	A	MLS		9 101
2-06-2004	New England Revolution	L	2-3	H	MLS	Wolff [33], Arnaud [37]	8 014
5-06-2004	Los Angeles Galaxy	W	2-1	H	MLS	Gomez [65], Gutierrez [86]	22 774
9-06-2004	Colorado Rapids	W	1-0	A	MLS	Wolff [90p]	12 546
12-06-2004	Columbus Crew	D	2-2	A	MLS	Conrad [21], Thomas [24]	13 680
19-06-2004	New England Revolution	W	3-1	A	MLS	Arnaud [41], Taylor 2 [70 90]	10 038
26-06-2004	San Jose Earthquakes	D	1-1	A	MLS	Burciaga [45]	10 188
3-07-2004	Dallas Burn	W	5-1	H	MLS	Arnaud 3 [22 79 90], Klein [72], Wolff [75]	20 011
10-07-2004	DC United	W	1-0	H	MLS	Taylor [17]	26 223
17-07-2004	Dallas Burn	W	1-0	H	MLS	Gutierrez [42]	6 942
20-07-2004	Atlanta Silverbacks	W	4-1	A	OCr4	Arnaud 2 [10 52], Gomez [54], Gutierrez [81]	2 212
24-07-2004	Los Angeles Galaxy	D	2-2	H	MLS	Arnaud [59], Jewsbury [61]	9 505
28-07-2004	MetroStars	L	1-2	H	MLS	Klein [37p]	
4-08-2004	Dallas Burn	W	4-0	H	OCqf	Klein [52], Arnaud [57], Detter [72], Zotinca [88]	2 143
14-08-2004	San Jose Earthquakes	L	0-2	H	MLS		11 545
18-08-2004	Columbus Crew	L	1-2	H	MLS	Graham [79]	14 580
21-08-2004	New England Revolution	W	2-1	A	MLS	Wolff [39], Arnaud [66]	7 410
24-08-2004	San Jose Eathquakes	W	1-0	H	OCsf	Simutenkov [45p]	2 162
1-09-2004	Chicago Fire	L	1-3	A	MLS	Wolff [36]	7 723
4-09-2004	MetroStars	W	1-0	H	MLS	Wolff [43]	10 430
10-09-2004	Colorado Rapids	L	1-3	A	MLS	Wolff [11p]	11 986
18-09-2004	San Jose Earthquakes	W	1-0	H	MLS	Gutierrez [83]	10 873
22-09-2004	Chicago Fire	W	1-0	H	OCf	Simutenkov 95	8 819
25-09-2004	Colorado Rapids	W	1-0	H	MLS	Simutenkov [55]	18 074
2-10-2004	Los Angeles Galaxy	D	1-1	A	MLS	Victorine OG [89]	27 000
9-10-2004	San Jose Earthquakes	D	0-0	A	MLS		25 311
16-10-2004	Los Angeles Galaxy	W	1-0	H	MLS	Wolff [23]	20 435
24-10-2004	San Jose Earthquakes	L	0-2	A	MLSqf		8 659
30-10-2004	San Jose Earthquakes	W	3-0	H	MLSqf	Stephenson [26], Ching OG [48], Jewsbury [90]	10 022
5-11-2004	Los Angeles Galaxy	W	2-0	H	MLSsf	Arnaud 2 [24 69]	11 931
14-11-2004	DC United	L	2-3	N	MLSf	Burciaga [6], Wolff [58]	25 797

MLS = Major League Soccer • OC = Lamar Hunt US Open Cup • qf = Conference semi-final • sf = Conference final • f = MLS Cup 2004

FIFA REFEREE LIST 2005

	Int'l	DoB
HALL Brian	1992	5-06-1961
KENNEDY Michael	1999	16-04-1961
PRUS Arkadiusz	2004	6-02-1964
SALAZAR Ricardo	2005	6-09-1972
STOTT Kevin	1995	9-07-1967
VALENZUELA Ricardo	1999	7-02-1964
VAUGHN Terry	2004	1-04-1973

FIFA ASSISTANT REFEREE LIST 2005

	Int'l	DoB
BARKEY Gregory	1995	20-08-1963
CLEMENT Nathan	1999	2-04-1961
DAVIDSON Steven	2003	2-05-1967
FEREDAY Robert	2000	18-05-1962
GANSNER George	2002	13-10-1971
LOWRY Craig	1998	21-04-1961
QUISENBERRY Kermit	2004	27-09-1968
STRICKLAND Chris	2002	29-11-1966
SUPPLE Thomas	2004	17-12-1965
VERGARA George	1999	4-08-1960

UZB – UZBEKISTAN

NATIONAL TEAM RECORD
JULY 1ST 2002 TO JUNE 30TH 2005

PL	W	D	L	F	A	%
31	16	8	7	52	33	64.5

FIFA/COCA-COLA WORLD RANKING

1993	1994	1995	1996	1997	1998	1999	2000	2001	2002	2003	2004	High		Low	
-	78	97	109	79	66	55	71	62	98	81	47	**46**	03/05	**119**	11/96

2004-2005											
08/04	09/04	10/04	11/04	12/04	01/05	02/05	03/05	04/05	05/05	06/05	07/05
51	51	54	51	47	47	48	46	54	54	54	53

Uzbekistan have enjoyed a Jekyll and Hyde existence in the years since the demise of the Soviet Union. Success came quickly and surprisingly with the 1994 Asian Games triumph and with players from clubs that had featured at the top level of Soviet football, Uzbekistan were in a strong position from the start. The potential of the country is evident, but the breakthrough that could see them ranked alongside Japan, Iran and the like just hasn't happened yet. In spite of political tension in the region generated by the strict control of President Karimov, football still thrives and in 2004 Uzbekistan reached the quarter-finals of the Asian Cup. That momentum has carried into the 2006

INTERNATIONAL HONOURS
Asian Games 1994

FIFA World Cup™ qualifiers in which Uzbekistan impressively won their second stage group dropping just two points from six matches. Through to the last eight they encountered a tough group in which Saudi Arabia and Korea Republic firmly controlled the top two places leaving Uzbekistan and Kuwait fighting for the reward of the third place play-off. The leading club in the country, Pakhtakor Tashkent, won the 2004 Oloy Liga for the third year in a row, losing just once in 26 games. Success continued with their fifth Uzbekistan Cup title in as many years and also in the 2005 AFC Champions League where they reached the semi-finals for the second straight year.

THE FIFA BIG COUNT OF 2000

	Male	Female		Male	Female
Registered players	4 000	0	Referees	200	0
Non registered players	130 000	0	Officials	1 300	0
Youth players	4 000	0	Total involved	139 500	
Total players	138 000		Number of clubs	150	
Professional players	0	0	Number of teams	600	

Uzbekistan Football Federation (UFF)
O'zbekiston Futbol Federatsiyasi, Massiv Almazar, Furkat Street 15/1, Tashkent 700 003, Uzbekistan
Tel +998 71 1441684   Fax +998 71 1441683
info@uzfootball.com   www.uzfootball.com
President: ALMATOV Zakirjon Almatovich   General Secretary: RAKHMATULLAEV Sardor
Vice-President: RAKHIMOV Botyr   Treasurer: ISKHAKOVA Zemfira   Media Officer: RIZAEV Sanjar
Men's Coach: HOUGHTON Bob   Women's Coach: SARKISYAN Pavel
UFF formed: 1946   AFC: 1994   FIFA: 1994
Colours: White, White, White

GAMES PLAYED BY UZBEKISTAN IN THE 2006 FIFA WORLD CUP™ CYCLE

2002	Opponents	Score		Venue	Comp	Scorers	Att	Referee
21-08	Azerbaijan	L	0-2	Baku	Fr		7 000	Abdullayev AZE
2003								
2-04	Belarus	D	2-2	Minsk	Fr	Khvostunov 66p, Geynrikh 69	4 000	Lajuks LVA
30-04	Belarus	L	1-2	Tashkent	Fr	Shishelov 43	4 000	Kolpakov KGZ
20-08	Latvia	W	3-0	Riga	Fr	Akopyants 41, Soliev 80, Geynrikh 86	4 000	Shandor UKR
11-10	United Arab Emirates	D	2-2	Dubai	Fr	Karpenko 40, Djeparov 86		
25-10	Burkina Faso	W	1-0	Hyderabad	AArl	Krusheinitskiy 66		
27-10	Zimbabwe	D	1-1	Hyderabad	AArl	Suyunov 50		
29-10	Rwanda	W	2-1	Hyderabad	AAsf	Saidov 63, Boyev 102		
31-10	India	W	1-0	Hyderabad	AAf	Inomov 90		Lu Jun CHN
6-11	Hong Kong	W	4-1	Tashkent	ACq	Akopyants 1, Shishelov 2 17 65, Soliev 28		
8-11	Thailand	W	3-0	Tashkent	ACq	Shatskikh 23, Shishelov 2 27 70		
10-11	Tajikistan	D	0-0	Tashkent	ACq			
17-11	Tajikistan	W	4-1	Bangkok	ACq	Shishelov 2 8 36, Kapadze 50, Koshekev 61		
19-11	Hong Kong	W	1-0	Bangkok	ACq	Shirshov 32		
21-11	Thailand	L	1-4	Bangkok	ACq	Koshekev 88		
2004								
18-02	Iraq	D	1-1	Tashkent	WCq	Soliev 78	24 000	Srinivasan IND
31-03	Chinese Taipei	W	1-0	Taipei	WCq	Koshekev 59	2 500	Midi Nitrorejo IDN
28-05	Azerbaijan	L	1-3	Baku	Fr	Tadjiyev 45	12 000	
9-06	Palestine	W	3-0	Tashkent	WCq	Soliev 93+	45 000	Kamikawa JPN
18-07	Iraq	W	1-0	Chengdu	ACrl	Kasimov 22	12 400	Kwon Jong Chul KOR
22-07	Saudi Arabia	W	1-0	Chengdu	ACrl	Geynrikh 11	22 000	Codjia BEN
26-07	Turkmenistan	W	1-0	Chongqing	ACrl	Kasimov 57	34 000	Kousa SYR
30-07	Bahrain	D	2-2	Chengdu	ACqf	Geynrikh 60, Shishelov 86, L 3-4p	18 000	Salmeen BHR
8-09	Palestine	W	3-0	Rayyan	WCq	Kasimov 9, Djeparov 32, Bikmoev 78	400	Maidin SIN
13-10	Iraq	W	2-1	Amman	WCq	Shatskikh 10, Geynrikh 22	10 000	Maidin SIN
17-11	Chinese Taipei	W	6-1	Tashkent	WCq	Geynrikh 5, Kasimov 3 12 45 85, Shatskikh 18, Koshekev 34	20 000	Basma SYR
2005								
9-02	Saudi Arabia	D	1-1	Tashkent	WCq	Soliev 93+	45 000	Kamikawa JPN
25-03	Kuwait	L	1-2	Kuwait City	WCq	Geynrikh 77	12 000	Sun Baojie CHN
30-03	Korea Republic	L	1-2	Seoul	WCq	Geynrikh 78	62 857	Najm LIB
3-06	Korea Republic	D	1-1	Tashkent	WCq	Shatskikh 63	40 000	Moradi IRN
8-06	Saudi Arabia	L	0-3	Riyadh	WCq		72 000	Huang Junjie CHN

Fr = Friendly match • AA - Afo-Asian Games • AC = AFC Asian Cup • WC = FIFA World Cup™
q = qualifier • r1 = first round group • qf = quarter-final • sf = semi-final • f = final

UZBEKISTAN NATIONAL TEAM RECORDS AND RECORD SEQUENCES

Records			Sequence records				
Victory	15-0	MGL 1998	Wins	8	1994	Clean sheets	4	2004
Defeat	1-8	JPN 2000	Defeats	4	2000-2001	Goals scored	18	2003-2005
Player Caps	n/a		Undefeated	11	1994, 2001	Without goal	3	2000-2001
Player Goals	n/a		Without win	6	1997	Goals against	8	1997

UZBEKISTAN COUNTRY INFORMATION

Capital	Tashkent	Independence	1991 from the USSR	GDP per Capita	$1 700
Population	26 410 416	Status	Republic	GNP Ranking	78
Area km²	447 400	Language	Uzbek, Russian	Dialling code	+7
Population density	59 per km²	Literacy rate	99%	Internet code	.uz
% in urban areas	41%	Main religion	Muslim	GMT +/-	+5
Cities/Towns ('000)	Tashkent 1 978; Namangan 432; Samarkand 319; Andijon 318; Bukhara 247; Nukus 230; Karshi 222; Kukon 187; Chirchik 167; Fergana 164; Cizak 152; Urganch 150; Termiz 140				
Neighbours (km)	Kyrgyzstan 1 099; Tajikistan 1 161; Afghanistan 137; Turkmenistan 1 621; Kazakhstan 2 203				
Main stadia	Pakhtakor – Tashkent 54 000; Markaziy – Bukhara 40 000				

UZBEKISTAN 2004

PREMIER DIVISION

	Pl	W	D	L	F	A	Pts	Pakhtakor	Neftchi	Navbahor	Nasaf	Traktor	Lok'motiv	Bukhara	Sogdiana	Metallurg	Mashal	Kizilgum	Sam'kand	Surhon	Andijon
Pakhtakor Tashkent †	26	22	3	1	81	15	69		6-1	3-0	2-1	4-4	2-0	4-0	3-1	3-1	4-1	4-1	4-0	8-0	2-0
Neftchi Fergana †	26	21	2	3	61	26	65	1-1		0-3	1-0	5-2	4-0	3-1	3-0	3-2	3-0	4-0	4-1	3-0	2-0
Navbahor Namangan	26	18	3	5	66	2	57	1-0	1-1		6-0	1-0	0-0	3-1	4-0	3-0	1-0	5-2	2-0	6-0	5-0
Nasaf Karshi	26	17	3	6	66	31	54	0-0	3-1	3-1		5-2	5-1	1-0	2-3	7-0	2-1	3-2	2-1	4-0	8-1
Traktor Tashkent	26	13	2	11	46	50	41	0-5	1-3	2-1	0-1		3-1	2-1	3-1	1-0	1-0	1-0	2-0	2-1	4-0
Lokomotiv Tashkent	26	10	6	10	37	35	36	0-4	0-1	3-2	2-0	1-3		0-1	3-0	4-0	1-0	5-0	4-0	0-0	3-2
FK Bukhara §	26	10	3	13	31	45	30	0-3	0-4	0-4	0-0	3-1	1-1		1-2	2-0	2-2	1-0	3-2	3-1	3-0
Sogdiana Jizak	26	9	2	15	27	47	29	0-2	0-2	1-2	1-4	1-2	2-0	3-2		1-0	1-3	2-0	2-1	3-0	1-1
Metallurg Bekobod	26	8	3	15	26	48	27	0-2	0-2	2-3	4-3	0-2	2-1	1-1	3-0		1-0	3-2	1-1	1-0	3-2
Mashal Muborak	26	8	3	15	34	43	27	1-3	0-1	1-2	4-3	3-2	0-1	2-1	0-1	1-1		2-2	3-0	1-0	3-1
Kizilgum Zarafshon	26	6	7	13	28	48	25	0-3	0-2	2-2	0-2	1-1	0-0	1-2	1-1	1-0	1-0		2-0	2-1	4-1
Samarkand Dinamo	26	6	2	18	25	48	20	1-2	0-1	0-3	1-1	3-4	3-1	0-1	4-0	1-0	1-0	1-1		1-0	3-0
Surhon Termiz §	26	7	2	17	24	55	20	1-2	1-2	0-4	0-5	6-2	0-0	0-1	1-0	1-0	3-1	2-1	3-0		2-1
FK Andijon	26	6	1	19	30	68	19	0-5	2-3	0-1	1-2	1-0	1-5	3-1	2-0	3-0	2-3	2-1	2-1	2-1	

16/08/2004 - 15/05/200 • † Qualified for the AFC Champions League • § Three points deducted

UZBEKISTAN 2004 FIRST DIVISION WEST (2)

	Pl	W	D	L	F	A	Pts
Topolon Sariasia †	40	28	3	9	119	61	87
Shurton Guzor †	40	26	1	13	117	46	79
FK Vobkent	40	23	5	12	82	66	74
Zarafshon Navai	40	22	3	15	90	61	69
FK Hazorasp	40	20	3	17	75	65	63
Xorazm-2003 Urganch	40	16	5	19	61	76	53
FK Yangier	40	15	7	18	66	82	52
Gallakor Gallaorol	40	16	4	20	59	74	52
FK Shorchi	40	16	2	22	70	90	50
Chagoniyon Denov	40	8	6	26	52	107	30
Hisor Shahrisabz	40	8	5	27	59	122	29

4/04/2004 - 14/11/2004 • † Qualified for play-offs

UZBEKISTAN 2004 FIRST DIVISION EAST (2)

	Pl	W	D	L	F	A	Pts
Sementchi Kuvasoy †	40	27	4	9	95	57	85
NBU Osiyo Taskent †	40	25	7	8	102	38	82
Kimyogar Chirchik	40	23	7	10	91	42	76
FK Guliston	40	22	9	9	82	46	75
Shakhontohur Taskent	40	19	7	14	83	88	64
OTMK Olmalik	40	18	5	17	73	75	59
FK Shahrixon	40	16	5	19	58	75	53
Lokomotiv-2 Tashkent	40	10	12	18	65	75	42
Pop-Fen Namangan	40	10	7	23	64	94	37
FK Kosonsoy	40	6	8	26	51	116	26
Pakhtakor-2 Tashkent	40	6	5	29	43	101	23

4/04/2004 - 14/11/2004 • † Qualified for play-offs

FIRST DIVISION PLAY-OFFS

	Pl	W	D	L	F	A	Pts
Shurton Guzor	3	2	1	0	6	3	7
Topolon Sariosia	3	2	0	1	8	4	6
NBU Osiyo Taskent	3	0	2	1	4	7	2
Sementchi Kuvasoy	3	0	1	2	2	6	1

23/11/2004 - 27/11/2004

UZBEKISTAN CUP 2004-05

Second Round

Pakhtakor Tashkent	3
FK Vobkent *	0
Sementchi Kuvasoy *	2
Sogdiana Jizak	3
Lokomotiv Tashkent *	3
FK Andijon	0
Hisor Shahrisabz *	1
Neftchi Fergana	5
Mashal Muborak	4
Shakhontohur Taskent*	0
Pakhtakor-2 Tashkent *	2 3p
Kizilgum Zarafshon	2 5p
FK Bukhara	2
FK Guliston *	1
Nasaf Karshi	0
Traktor Tashkent *	4

Quarter-finals

Pakhtakor Tashkent	2 4
Sogdiana Jizak *	2 2
Lokomotiv Tashkent *	1 2
Neftchi Fergana	3 3
Mashal Muborak	0 2
Kizilgum Zarafshon *	1 0
FK Bukhara	1 0
Traktor Tashkent *	1 1

Semi-finals

Pakhtakor Tashkent *	1 2
Neftchi Fergana	0 1
Mashal Muborak *	3 0
Traktor Tashkent	2 2

Final

Pakhtakor Tashkent	3
Traktor Tashkent	2

* Home team/home team in the first leg

CUP FINAL

1-10-2004, Att: 10 000, Ref: Roman Pakhtakor, Tashkent

Scorers - Shishelov 15, Djeparov 23 Soliev 44 for Pakhtakor; Hasanov 48, Ayzatullov 58 for Traktor

PAKHTAKOR TASHKENT 2004

Date	Opponents	Score		Comp	Scorers	Att
11-02-2004	Zob Ahan - IRN	L 0-1	A	CLgA		
25-02-2005	Qatar SC - QAT	W 1-0	H	CLgA	Nikolaev [43]	
4-03-2004	Traktor Tashkent	W 5-0	A	LGE	Tojiev 2 [47 67], Koshekev [49], Djeparov [85], Vahobov [90]	6 000
10-03-2004	Samarkand Dinamo	W 4-0	H	LGE	Koshekev [71], Ashurmatov [78], Bikmoev 2 [92+ 94+]	6 000
15-03-2004	FK Bukhara	W 3-0	A	LGE	Djeparov [20], Gocguliev [36], Magdeev [55]	10 000
20-03-2004	Kizilgum Zarafshon	W 4-1	H	LGE	Gocguliev 2 [34 70p], OG [53], Soliev [78]	2 500
8-04-2004	Sogdiana Jizak	W 2-0	A	LGE	Tojiev [55], Bikmoev [70]	5 000
15-04-2004	Navbahor Namangan	W 3-0	H	LGE	Koshekev [11], Tojiev 2 [45 70]	7 000
26-04-2004	Nasaf Karshi	D 0-0	A	LGE		12 000
5-05-2004	Zob Ahan - IRN	W 2-0	H	CLgA	Koshekev [27], Bikmoev [90]	
8-05-2004	FK Vobkent	W 3-0	A	CUPr2	Vahobov 2 [20 47], Koshekev [53]	7 000
14-05-2004	FK Andijon	W 5-0	A	LGE	Kapadze [4], Ashurmatov [19], Koshekev [55], Gocguliev [84p] Vlasichev [90]	6 000
19-05-2004	Qatar SC - QAT	D 0-0	A	CLgA		
24-05-2004	Lokomotiv Tashkent	W 2-0	H	LGE	Soliev [16], Djeparov [47]	5 000
3-06-2004	Surhom Termiz	W 2-1	A	LGE	Tojiev [5], Bikmoev [76]	10 000
14-06-2004	Neftchi Fergana	W 6-1	H	LGE	Magdeev 2 [2 82], Gocguliev [13p], Ponomarov [44], Kapadze [79], Vahobov [92+]	6 000
19-06-2004	Metallurg Bekobod	W 3-1	H	LGE	Soliev 2 [50 63], Djeparov [72]	2 500
22-06-2004	Sogdiana Jizak	D 2-2	A	CUPqf	Abdullaev [20], Vlasichev [48]	2 500
25-06-2004	Mashal Muborak	W 3-1	A	LGE	Inomov 2 [28 90], Djeparov [45]	2 500
28-06-2004	Sogdiana Jizak	W 4-2	H	CUPqf	Djeparov [5], Tojiev 2 [16 71], Soliev [19]	100
10-08-2004	Neftchi Fergana	W 1-0	H	CUPsf	Nikolaev [32]	6 000
14-08-2004	Mashal Muborak	W 4-1	H	LGE	Koshekev 3 [1 37 68], Tojiev [59]	6 000
17-08-2004	Lokomotiv Tashkent	W 4-0	A	LGE	Ponomarov [53], Vahobov [62], Soliev [71], Gocguliev [87]	3 000
21-08-2004	Metallurg Bekobod	W 2-0	A	LGE	Koshekev [24], Gocguliev [26]	4 000
28-08-2004	Surhom Termiz	W 8-0	H	LGE	Djeparov 2 [20 64], Soliev [34], Shishelov 3 [45 45 48], Ponomarov 2 [80 86]	200
2-09-2004	Neftchi Fergana	W 2-1	A	CUPsf	Gocguliev [44], Shishelov [62]	15 000
15-09-2004	Al Wahda - UAE	D 1-1	A	CLqf	Magdeev [85]	
19-09-2004	FK Andijon	W 2-0	H	LGE	Soliev [26], Koshekev [91+]	1 000
22-09-2004	Al Wahda - UAE	W 4-0	H	CLqf	Soliev [21], Shishelov 2 [44 90], OG [86]	
26-09-2004	Neftchi Fergana	D 1-1	A	LGE	Shishelov [53]	15 500
1-10-2004	Traktor Tashkent	W 3-2	H	CUPf	Shishelov [15], Djeparov [23], Soliev [44]	10 000
6-10-2004	Nasaf Karshi	W 2-1	H	LGE	OG [10], Soliev [50]	2 000
22-10-2004	Seognam Ilhwa Chunma - KOR	D 0-0	A	CLsf		
24-10-2004	Sogdiana Jizak	W 3-1	H	LGE	Koshekev [21], Vahobov [63], Soliev [69]	500
27-10-2004	Seognam Ilhwa Chunma - KOR	L 0-2	H	CLsf		
1-11-2004	Kizilgum Zarafshon	W 3-0	A	LGE	Tojiev [15], Djeparov 2 [26 64p]	4 500
5-11-2004	FK Bukhara	W 4-0	H	LGE	Kiryan [4], Tojiev [25], Koshekev [64], Djeparov [70]	1 000
9-11-2004	Navbahor Namangan	L 0-1	A	LGE		11 500
13-11-2004	Samarkand Dinamo	W 2-1	A	LGE	Alikulov [20], Ponomarov [38]	2 000
20-11-2004	Traktor Tashkent	D 4-4	A	LGE	Tojiev 2 [39 70], Djeparov [67], Koshekev [78]	1 000

LGE = Premier Division • CUP = Uzbekistan Cup • CL = AFC Champions League
gA = group A • r2 = second round • qf = quarter-final • sf = semi-final • f = final

RECENT LEAGUE AND CUP RECORD

	Championship						Cup		
Year	Champions	Pts	Runners-up	Pts	Third	Pts	Winners	Score	Runners-up
1992	Pakhtakor Tashkent	51	Neftchi Fergana	51	Sogdiana Jizak	48	Navbahor Nam'gan	0-0 6-5p	Temirulchi Kukon
1993	Neftchi Fergana	52	Pakhtakor Tashkent	47	Navbahor Nam'gan	43	Pakhtakor Tashkent	3-0	Navbahor Nam'gan
1994	Neftchi Fergana	51	Nurafshon Bukhara	44	Navbahor Nam'gan	40	Neftchi Fergana	2-0	FK Yangier
1995	Neftchi Fergana	76	MHSK Tashkent	74	Navbahor Nam'gan	72	Navbahor Nam'gan	1-0	MHSK Tashkent
1996	Navbahor Nam'gan	74	Neftchi Fergana	72	MHSK Tashkent	62	Neftchi Fergana	0-0 5-4p	Pakhtakor Tashkent
1997	MHSK Tashkent	90	Neftchi Fergana	81	Navbahor Nam'gan	68	Pakhtakor Tashkent	3-2	Neftchi Fergana
1998	Pakhtakor Tashkent	76	Neftchi Fergana	70	Navbahor Nam'gan	59	Navbahor Nam'gan	2-0	Neftchi Fergana
1999	Dustlik Tashkent	64	Neftchi Fergana	63	Navbahor Nam'gan	61	No tournament		
2000	Dustlik Tashkent	94	Navbahor Nam'gan	90	Nasaf Karshi	85	Dustlik Tashkent	4-1	Samarkand Dinamo
2001	Neftchi Fergana	84	Pakhtakor Tashkent	72	Nasaf Karshi	71	Pakhtakor Tashkent	2-1	Neftchi Fergana
2002	Pakhtakor Tashkent	74	Neftchi Fergana	69	Kizilgum Zarafshon	59	Pakhtakor Tashkent	6-3	Neftchi Fergana
2003	Pakhtakor Tashkent	77	Neftchi Fergana	71	Navbahor Nam'gan	63	Pakhtakor Tashkent	3-1	Nasaf Karshi
2004	Pakhtakor Tashkent	69	Neftchi Fergana	65	Navbahor Nam'gan	57	Pakhtakor Tashkent	3-2	Traktor Tashkent

Uzbek clubs played in the Soviet league until the end of the 1991 season • Pakhtakor and Neftch shared the title in 1992

VAN – VANUATU

NATIONAL TEAM RECORD
JULY 1ST 2002 TO JUNE 30TH 2005

PL	W	D	L	F	A	%
20	7	4	9	29	24	45

FIFA/COCA-COLA WORLD RANKING

1993	1994	1995	1996	1997	1998	1999	2000	2001	2002	2003	2004	High		Low	
164	172	179	180	186	177	184	167	168	156	160	143	139	08/04	188	04/00

2004-2005											
08/04	09/04	10/04	11/04	12/04	01/05	02/05	03/05	04/05	05/05	06/05	07/05
139	140	139	144	143	145	145	145	145	147	147	147

Vanuatu pulled off one of the biggest shocks in Oceanian football when they beat New Zealand in a 2006 FIFA World Cup™ qualifier – witnessed by just 356 spectators. The victory enabled the Solomon Islands to claim the group runners-up spot and a play-off with Australia while hastening the departure of New Zealand coach Mick Waitt. Although Vanuatu lost all their other games to finish bottom of the group, they had enjoyed a successful run. The team finished top of their first round group unbeaten in four matches including a 9-1 demolition of American Samoa and a 3-0 victory against group runners-up Fiji. Prior to the World Cup™ campaign, Vanuatu had also

INTERNATIONAL HONOURS
Melanesian Cup 1990

enjoyed success at the 2002 OFC Oceania Cup and the 2003 South Pacific Games taking third and fourth place respectively. The juniors have provided more success with the U-17s reaching the final of the OFC tournament before an agonising 1-0 defeat to Australia thanks to an 82nd-minute goal while the U-20s won their third place play-off with Fiji. The absence of a national league is an area of weakness with the Port Vila League the strongest in the country but that has been virtually monopolised by Tafea FC for many years and 2004 was no exception. They won the title for the 11th successive time before reaching the semi-finals of the 2005 Oceania Champion Clubs Cup.

THE FIFA BIG COUNT OF 2000

	Male	Female		Male	Female
Registered players	1 000	0	Referees	100	0
Non registered players	1 000	0	Officials	200	0
Youth players	1 000	0	Total involved	3 300	
Total players	3 000		Number of clubs	100	
Professional players	0	0	Number of teams	200	

Vanuatu Football Federation (VFF)
PO Box 266, Port Vila, Vanuatu
Tel +678 25236   Fax +678 25236
jimmy_nipo@yahoo.com   www.none
President: LULU Johnny   General Secretary: MALTOCK Lambert
Vice-President: TRONQUET Jacques   Treasurer: IAPSON Georges   Media Officer: STEVENS Moses
Men's Coach: BUZZETTI Juan   Women's Coach: BUZZETTI Juan
VFF formed: 1934   OFC: 1988   FIFA: 1988
Colours: Gold, Black, Gold

GAMES PLAYED BY VANUATU IN THE 2006 FIFA WORLD CUP™ CYCLE

2002	Opponents	Score		Venue	Comp	Scorers	Att	Referee
6-07	Australia	L	0-2	Auckland	OCr1		1 000	Ariiotima TAH
8-07	Fiji	W	1-0	Auckland	OCr1	Marango [6]	800	Sosongan PNG
10-07	New Caledonia	W	1-0	Auckland	OCr1	Iwai [76]	500	Ariiotima TAH
12-07	New Zealand	L	0-3	Auckland	OCsf		1 000	Breeze AUS
14-07	Tahiti	L	0-1	Auckland	OC3p		1 000	Rakaroi FIJ
2003								
30-06	Fiji	D	0-0	Suva	SPr1			Ariiotima TAH
1-07	Solomon Islands	D	2-2	Suva	SPr1	Mermer [22], Qorig [47]		Shah FIJ
3-07	Tuvalu †	W	1-0	Suva	SPr1	Tabe [86]	700	Bayung PNG
7-07	Kiribati †	W	18-0	Lautoka	SPr1	Mermer 4 [4 15 51 53], Chillia 4 [10 22 29 30], Iwai 5 [27 40 41 63 64], Tabe [35], Vava [47], Thomsen [54], Demas [62], Pita [83]	2 000	Bayung PNG
9-07	New Caledonia	D	1-1	Lautoka	SPsf	Laki [54], L 3-4p	7 000	Shah FIJ
11-07	Tahiti	W	1-0	Suva	SP3p	Mermer [57]	6 000	Rakaroi FIJ
2004								
3-04	Solomon Islands	L	1-2	Port-Vila	Fr	Chillia [41]	4 000	Fred VAN
6-04	Solomon Islands	L	1-2	Port-Vila	Fr			
10-05	Papua New Guinea	D	1-1	Apia	WCq	Lauru [92+]	500	Breeze AUS
12-05	American Samoa	W	9-1	Apia	WCq	Qorig 2 [30 47+], Mermer 3 [37 56 91+], Poida [55], Chilea [65], Maleb 2 [80 92+]	400	Fox NZL
15-05	Samoa	W	3-0	Apia	WCq	Mermer [13], Chillia 55, Maleb 57	650	Breeze AUS
19-05	Fiji	W	3-0	Apia	WCq	Thomsen [46+], Lauru 2 [63 65]	200	Breeze AUS
29-05	Solomon Islands	L	0-1	Adelaide	WCq		200	Shield AUS
31-05	Fiji	L	0-1	Adelaide	WCq		500	Ariiotima TAH
2-06	New Zealand	W	4-2	Adelaide	WCq	Chillia [37], Bibi [64], Maleb [72], Qoriz [88]	356	Farina ITA
4-06	Australia	L	0-3	Adelaide	WCq		4 000	Ariiotima TAH
6-06	Tahiti	L	1-2	Adelaide	WCq	Iwai [23]	300	Rakaroi FIJ
2005								

No international matches played in 2005 before August

Fr = Friendly match • OC = OFC Oceania Cup • SP = South Pacific Games • WC = FIFA World Cup™
q = qualifier • r1 = first round group • sf = semi-final • 3p = third place play-off • † Not a full international

VANUATU NATIONAL TEAM RECORDS AND RECORD SEQUENCES

Records			Sequence records					
Victory	13-1	SAM 1981	Wins	3	2004	Clean sheets	2	Five times
Defeat	0-9	NZL 1951	Defeats	6	Three times	Goals scored	13	1996-2000
Player Caps	n/a		Undefeated	6	2003	Without goal	3	1992, 2003-2004
Player Goals	n/a		Without win	9	1979-1981	Goals against	23	1951-1979

RECENT LEAGUE RECORD

Year	Port Vila Football League
1999	Tafea FC
2000	Tafea FC
2001	Tafea FC
2002	Tafea FC
2003	Tafea FC
2004	Tafea FC

VANUATU COUNTRY INFORMATION

Capital	Port-Vila	Independence	1980 from UK and France	GDP per Capita	$2 900
Population	202 609	Status	Republic	GNP Ranking	183
Area km²	12 200	Language	English, French, Bislama	Dialling code	+678
Population density	16 per km²	Literacy rate	53%	Internet code	.vu
% in urban areas	19%	Main religion	Christian	GMT +/–	+11
Towns/Cities ('000)	Port-Vila 35; Luganville 13; Norsup 3; Port Olry 2; Isangel ; Sola 1				
Neighbours (km)	South Pacific Ocean 2 528				
Main stadia	Korman Stadium – Port-Vila				

VEN – VENEZUELA

NATIONAL TEAM RECORD
JULY 1ST 2002 TO JUNE 30TH 2005

PL	W	D	L	F	A	%
36	13	7	16	45	46	45.8

FIFA/COCA-COLA WORLD RANKING

1993	1994	1995	1996	1997	1998	1999	2000	2001	2002	2003	2004	High		Low	
93	110	127	111	115	129	110	111	81	69	57	62	48	04/04	129	12/98

2004-2005											
08/04	09/04	10/04	11/04	12/04	01/05	02/05	03/05	04/05	05/05	06/05	07/05
53	55	59	52	62	63	61	65	70	70	70	68

Venezuela has taken huge strides forward in football over the past few years and there has been no more symbolic a result than the 3-0 victory over Uruguay in Montevideo in the 2006 FIFA World Cup™ qualifiers. In early 2004 after a run of three victories there was even the possibility that Richard Paez's side could, for the first time, make a serious challenge to qualify for a place in the finals. The campaign faltered later on in the year but no longer can the other nations bank on three easy points when they play Venezuela. The challenge is to prove that this is not a temporary rise in fortunes and that football can challenge the popularity of baseball and basketball on a more

INTERNATIONAL HONOURS
None

permenant basis. The hosting of the 2007 Copa America should keep the impetus going and there is even the hope that their winless streak in the competition dating back to 1967 could come to an end. Club football is also showing signs of improvement with the Championship more competitive than ever before. In 2005 there was a first title for Unión Atlético Maracaibo. On the last day of the Apertura they leapfrogged Caracas who surprisingly lost to bottom club ItalChacao. It was a slip up Caracas were to regret as Unión went on to win the Clausura and were declared champions without the need for an end of season play-off.

THE FIFA BIG COUNT OF 2000

	Male	Female		Male	Female
Registered players	7 592	1 289	Referees	512	68
Non registered players	500 000	10 000	Officials	8 000	300
Youth players	22 563	2 115	Total involved	552 439	
Total players	543 559		Number of clubs	400	
Professional players	372	0	Number of teams	1 557	

Federación Venezolana de Fútbol (FVF)
Avda. Santos Erminy Ira, Calle las Delicias Torre Mega II, P.H. Sabana Grande, Caracas 1050, Venezuela
Tel +58 212 7624472   Fax +58 212 7620596
fvfcnav@hotmail.com   www.fvf.org.ve
President: ESQUIVEL Rafael   General Secretary: GARCIA-REGALADO Jesus
Vice-President: ALMARZA Rafael   Treasurer: BOUTUREIRA Serafin   Media Officer: None
Men's Coach: HERNANDEZ Ramon & PAEZ Richard   Women's Coach: ALONSO Lino
FVF formed: 1926   CONMEBOL: 1965   FIFA: 1952
Colours: Burgundy, White, White

GAMES PLAYED BY VENEZUELA IN THE 2006 FIFA WORLD CUP™ CYCLE

2002	Opponents	Score		Venue	Comp	Scorers	Att	Referee
21-08	Bolivia	W	2-0	Caracas	Fr	Noriega [17], González.H [20]	25 000	Ibarra VEN
20-10	Ecuador	W	2-0	Caracas	Fr	Rey [30], Moreno [79]	24 000	Brand VEN
20-11	Uruguay	W	1-0	Caracas	Fr	Páez [49]	26 000	Solorzano VEN
2003								
29-03	USA	L	0-2	Seattle	Fr		17 819	Seifert CAN
2-04	Jamaica	W	2-0	Caracas	Fr	Urdaneta [11p], Páez [38]	25 000	Díaz ECU
30-04	Trinidad and Tobago	W	3-0	San Cristobal	Fr	Arango 2 [30 38], Noriega [75]	25 000	Rivero VEN
7-06	Honduras	W	2-1	Miami	Fr	Urdaneta [14], Arango [36]	15 000	Terry USA
26-06	Peru	L	0-1	Miami	Fr			Kennedy USA
3-07	Trinidad and Tobago	D	2-2	Port of Spain	Fr	Casseres 2 [1 49]	7 500	Piper TRI
26-07	Nigeria	L	0-1	Watford	Fr		1 000	
20-08	Haiti	W	3-2	Maracaibo	Fr	Vielma [78], González.H [83], Rivero [87]	15 000	Manzur VEN
6-09	Ecuador	L	0-2	Quito	WCq		14 997	Selman CHI
9-09	Argentina	L	0-3	Caracas	WCq		24 783	Vazquez URU
15-11	Colombia	W	1-0	Barranquilla	WCq	Arango [9]	20 000	Chandia CHI
18-11	Bolivia	W	2-1	Maracaibo	WCq	Rey [90], Arango [92+]	30 000	Reinoso ECU
2004								
18-02	Australia	D	1-1	Caracas	Fr	Arango [91+]	16 000	Ruiz COL
10-03	Honduras	W	2-1	Maracaibo	Fr	Vera [35p], Noriega [53]	24 000	Manzur VEN
31-03	Uruguay	W	3-0	Montevideo	WCq	Urdaneta [19], González.H [67], Arango [77]	40 094	Ortube BOL
28-04	Jamaica	L	1-2	Kingston	Fr	Arango [27]	10 000	Ford BRB
1-06	Chile	L	0-1	San Cristobal	WCq		23 040	Torres PAR
6-06	Peru	D	0-0	Lima	WCq		40 000	Larrionda URU
6-07	Colombia	L	0-1	Lima	CAr1		45 000	Rezende BRA
9-07	Peru	L	1-3	Lima	CAr1	Margiotta [74]	43 000	Selman CHI
12-07	Bolivia	D	1-1	Trujillo	CAr1	Moran [27]	25 000	Mattus CRC
18-08	Spain	L	2-3	Las Palmas	Fr	Rojas.J [46+], Castellin [92+]	32 000	Rodomonti ITA
5-09	Paraguay	L	0-1	Asuncion	WCq		30 000	Mendez URU
9-10	Brazil	L	2-5	Maracaibo	WCq	Moran 2 [79 90]	26 133	Chandia CHI
14-10	Ecuador	W	3-1	San Cristobal	WCq	Urdaneta [20p], Moran 2 [72 80]	13 800	Lecca PER
17-11	Argentina	L	2-3	Buenos Aires	WCq	Moran [31], Vielma [72]	30 000	Hidalgo PER
21-12	Guatemala	L	0-1	Caracas	Fr		6 000	Solorzano VEN
2005								
9-02	Estonia	W	3-0	Maracaibo	Fr	Paez [20], Margiotta [33], Maldonado [83]	12 000	Vazquez ECU
26-03	Colombia	D	0-0	Maracaibo	WCq		18 000	Simon BRA
29-03	Bolivia	L	1-3	La Paz	WCq	Maldonado [71]	7 908	Lecca PER
25-05	Panama	D	1-1	Caracas	Fr	Maldonado [4]	15 000	Brand VEN
4-06	Uruguay	D	1-1	Maracaibo	WCq	Maldonado [74]	12 504	Brazenas ARG
8-06	Chile	L	1-2	Santiago	WCq	Moran [82]	35 506	Torres PAR

Fr = Friendly match • CA = Copa América • WC = FIFA World Cup™ • q = qualifier • r1 = first round group

VENEZUELA COUNTRY INFORMATION

Capital	Caracas	Independence	1821 from Spain	GDP per Capita	$4 800
Population	25 017 387	Status	Republic	GNP Ranking	33
Area km²	912 050	Language	Spanish	Dialling code	+58
Population density	27 per km²	Literacy rate	93%	Internet code	.ve
% in urban areas	93%	Main religion	Christian	GMT + / −	-4
Towns/Cities ('000)	Maracaibo 1 948; Caracas 1 815; Valencia 1 385; Barquisimeto 809; Ciudad Guayana 746; Barcelona 424; Maturin 410; Maracay 395; Petare 365; Turmero 344; Ciudad Bolivar 291				
Neighbours (km)	Guyana 743; Brazil 2 200; Colombia 2 050; Atlantic Ocean & Caribbean Sea 2 800				
Main stadia	Pachenricho Romero – Maracaibo 35 000; Pueblo Nuevo – San Cristobal 27 500; Olimpico – Caracas 25 000				

VENEZUELA NATIONAL TEAM RECORDS AND RECORD SEQUENCES

Records			Sequence records					
Victory	6-0	PUR 1946	Wins	4	2001	Clean sheets	4	2002
Defeat	0-11	ARG 1975	Defeats	9	1989-1991	Goals scored	8	1946-1956
Player Caps	74	URDANETA Gabriel	Undefeated	6	1946-1956	Without goal	5	1990-1991
Player Goals	14	MORAN Ruberth	Without win	26	1989-1993	Goals against	21	1993-96, 1999-01

NATIONAL CAPS

	Caps
URDANETA Gabriel	74
REY José Manuel	69
JIMENEZ Leopoldo	62
VALLENILLA Luis	60
MORAN Ruberth	59
DUDAMEL Rafael	52
ROJAS Jorge	51
ARANGO Juan	49
GARCIA Juan	47
MEA VITALI Miguel	47

NATIONAL GOALS

	Goals
MORAN Ruberth	14
ARANGO Juan	10
URDANETA Gabriel	9
GARCIA Juan	7
DOLGETTA José Luis	6
REY José Manuel	6
CASTELLIN Rafael	5
FEBLES Pedro	5
NORIEGA Daniel	5
PAEZ Ricardo	5

FIFA REFEREE LIST 2005

	Int'l	DoB
ANDARCIA Candelario	2005	18-09-1971
BRAND Gustavo	1999	3-08-1961
IBARRA Edixon	1999	28-10-1966
MANZUR Jorge	2000	23-04-1961
RIVERA Jorge	2002	11-06-1960
SOTO Juan	2005	14-10-1977
TORREALBA Rafael	1996	5-10-1966

FIFA ASSISTANT REFEREE LIST 2005

	Int'l	DoB
ALDANA Robinson	1999	1-01-1971
CHUELLO Placido	2000	5-10-1974
QUINTERO Gerardo	1999	11-11-1965
RINCON Jose	2002	29-10-1961
SÁNCHEZ Luis	2005	18-07-1972
YANEZ Rafael	1998	11-04-1967

CLUB DIRECTORY

Club	Town/City	Stadium	Lge	CL
Carabobo FC	Valencia	Missael Delgado 15 000	0	0
Caracas FC	Caracas	Estadio Olimpico 25 000	7	0
Deportivo Táchira	San Cristobal	Pueblo Nuevo 30 000	4	0
Estudiantes FC	Merida	Guillermo Soto Rosas 15 000	2	0
Deportivo ItalChacao	Caracas	Brigido Iriarte 15 000	5	0
Deportivo ItalMaracaibo	Maracaibo	Pachenricho Romero 35 000	0	0
AC Mineros de Guayana	Puerto Ordaz	Polideportivo Cachamay 15 000	1	0
Monagas SC	Maturin	Polideportivo Maturin 4 000	0	0
Trujillanos FC	Valera	Luis Loreto Lira 15 000	0	0
Unión Atlético Maracaibo	Maracaibo	Pachenricho Romero 35 000	1	0

RECENT LEAGUE RECORD

	Championship						Championship Play-off		
Year	Champions	Pts	Runners-up	Pts	Third	Pts	Winners	Score	Runners-up
1990	CS Maritimo	43	Unión At. Táchira	43	Minervén	42			
1991	Univ. de Los Andes	39	CS Maritimo	37	Atlético Zamora	36			
1992	Caracas FC	43	Minervén	42	CS Maritimo	39			
1993	CS Maritimo	41	Minervén	41	Caracas FC	40	CS Maritimo	0-1 1-0 7-6p	Minervén
1994	Caracas FC	43	Trujillanos	40	Minervén	39			
1995	Caracas FC	17	Minervén	16	Trullianos	14			
1996	Minervén	22	Mineros de Guayana	20	Caracas FC	19			
1997	Caracas FC						Caracas	3-1 5-0	Atlético Zulia
1998	Atlético Zulia						Atlético Zulia	1-0 4-0	Estudiantes
1999	ItalChalcao						ItalChalcao	5-1 2-1	Unión At. Táchira
2000	Deportivo Táchira	15	ItalChacao	7	Estudiantes	6			
2001	Caracas FC	35	Trujillanos	33	ItalChacao	32			
2002	Nacional Táchira						Nacional Táchira	3-3 0-0 5-3p	Estudiantes
2003	Caracas FC						Caracas FC	1-1 3-0	Unión At. Maracaibo
2004	Caracas FC	†							
2005	Unión At. Maracaibo	†							

† Automatic champions as winners of both the Apertura and Clausura

VENEZUELA 2004-05

PRIMERA DIVISION
TORNEO APERTURA 2004

	Pl	W	D	L	F	A	Pts	Unión	Caracas	Mineros	Táchira	Trujillanos	Carabobo	Monagas	Estudiantes	ItalMara'bo	ItalChacao
Unión At. Maracaibo	18	9	7	2	27	12	34		3-1	2-0	0-0	1-1	0-0	2-0	2-2	2-0	5-1
Caracas FC	18	9	5	4	23	19	32	2-1		0-0	1-1	1-0	3-2	2-1	0-0	3-0	2-1
Mineros de Guayana	18	8	6	4	28	18	30	1-1	2-0		4-1	2-2	0-0	1-4	1-0	3-1	3-0
Deportivo Táchira	18	9	3	6	23	19	30	1-0	2-2	1-0		1-0	2-1	1-0	3-2	3-0	3-0
Trujillanos FC	18	8	5	5	21	16	29	0-0	1-0	1-1	1-0		1-0	2-0	2-1	1-1	1-0
Carabobo FC	18	4	9	5	23	25	21	1-1	0-1	2-1	3-1	0-4		3-1	2-1	1-1	1-1
Monagas SC	18	5	4	9	21	27	19	1-2	2-1	0-2	2-0	2-1	1-1		2-0	0-0	1-1
Estudiantes FC	18	4	5	9	24	31	17	1-2	0-1	2-2	2-1	2-0	2-2	3-0		2-1	2-2
Dep. ItalMaracaibo	18	4	5	9	18	30	17	0-2	1-2	1-3	1-0	3-1	2-2	1-3	2-0		1-0
Dep. ItalChacao	18	3	5	10	22	33	14	0-1	2-0	0-2	0-2	1-2	2-2	3-1	6-2	2-2	

7/08/2004 - 12/12/2004 • Unión Atlético Maracaibo are Apertura Champions and qualify for the championship final

VENEZUELA 2004-05

PRIMERA DIVISION
TORNEO CLAUSURA 2005

	Pl	W	D	L	F	A	Pts	Unión	Caracas	Táchira	Estudiantes	Monagas	Mineros	Carabobo	ItalMara'bo	Trujillanos	ItalChacao
Unión At. Maracaibo	18	12	3	3	30	12	39		0-0	3-0	3-1	6-0	1-0	3-2	2-1	0-1	2-1
Caracas FC	18	9	6	3	28	14	33	0-1		2-0	0-1	4-0	1-0	2-2	2-1	3-1	2-2
Deportivo Táchira	18	9	5	4	25	20	32	0-2	2-1		1-1	1-1	3-0	3-2	4-0	0-3	2-1
Estudiantes FC	18	6	7	5	18	19	25	1-0	0-0	1-1		0-2	2-0	0-1	2-2	2-1	0-0
Monagas FC	18	6	5	7	26	36	23	2-1	0-1	0-2	0-1		3-2	1-1	2-1	2-2	2-1
Mineros de Guayana	18	5	6	7	22	23	21	0-0	2-2	0-1	3-2	2-0		1-1	0-0	3-2	5-1
Carabobo FC	18	4	9	5	21	22	21	1-1	0-0	2-2	2-0	2-2	0-1		1-2	2-0	1-0
Dep. ItalMaracaibo	18	4	5	9	19	26	17	1-2	0-3	0-1	0-1	2-4	1-1	3-0		0-0	1-0
Trujillanos FC	18	4	5	9	21	29	17	0-1	2-4	0-1	2-2	2-2	1-0	1-1	0-3		2-0
Dep. ItalChacao	18	2	7	9	20	29	13	1-2	0-1	1-1	1-1	5-3	2-2	0-0	1-1	3-1	

9/01/2005 - 15/05/2005 •

PRIMERA DIVISION AGGREGATE

	Pl	W	D	L	F	A	Pts
Unión At. Marcaibo †	36	12	3	3	30	12	73
Caracas FC †	36	9	6	3	28	14	65
Deportivo Táchira ‡	36	9	5	4	25	20	62
Mineros de Guayana ‡	36	6	7	5	18	19	51
Trujillanos FC	36	6	7	5	26	36	46
Carabobo FC	36	5	6	7	22	23	42
Estudiantes FC	36	4	9	5	21	22	42
Monagas SC	36	4	5	9	19	26	42
Dep. ItalMaracaibo ††	36	4	5	9	21	29	34
Dep. ItalChacao	36	2	7	9	20	29	27

† Qualified for Copa Libertadores 2006 • ‡ Qualified for Copa Sudamericana 2005 • †† Relegation play-off

VENEZUELA 2004-05 ASCENSO APERTURA (2)

	Pl	W	D	L	F	A	Pts
Dep. Maracaibo †	20	12	3	5	33	19	39
UPEL Nacional	20	10	5	5	41	29	35
Dep. Anzoátegui	20	10	5	5	37	30	35
Unión Lara	20	10	4	6	41	27	34
Llaneros de Guanare	20	10	2	8	42	31	32
Aragua Maracay	20	9	5	6	29	23	32
Zamora Barinas	20	7	5	8	29	26	26
Hermandad Gallega	20	5	5	10	19	29	20
UA El Vigía	20	6	1	13	26	44	19
Portuguesa	20	5	3	12	22	41	18
Nueva Cádiz	20	4	6	10	19	39	18

21/08/2004 - 19/12/2004 • † Qualified for play-off

PROMOTION PLAY-OFFS

ACSENSO CHAMPIONSHIP AND AUTOMATIC PROMOTION

Aragua *	2	3
Dep. Maracaibo	0	2

LOSERS VERSUS PRIMERA DIVISION 9TH PLACED TEAM

D. ItalMaracaibo*	0	1
Dep. Maracaibo	0	1

* Home team in first leg

VENEZUELA 2004-05 ASCENSO CLAUSURA (2)

	Pl	W	D	L	F	A	Pts
Aragua Maracay †	20	14	5	1	39	11	47
Unión Lara	20	12	6	2	44	17	42
Dep. Maracaibo	20	11	6	3	38	18	39
UA El Vigía	20	7	6	7	26	30	27
Portuguesa	20	7	5	8	22	29	26
Dep. Anzoátegui	20	5	8	7	20	18	23
Zamora Barinas	20	6	4	10	22	29	22
Llaneros de Guanare	20	6	4	10	19	41	22
Hermandad Gallega	20	4	9	7	14	16	21
UPEL Nacional	20	3	7	10	24	38	16
Nueva Cádiz	20	4	2	14	23	44	14

15/01/2005 - 1/05/2005 • † Qualified for play-off

VGB – BRITISH VIRGIN ISLANDS

NATIONAL TEAM RECORD
JULY 1ST 2002 TO JUNE 30TH 2005

PL	W	D	L	F	A	%
15	4	1	10	15	38	30

FIFA/COCA-COLA WORLD RANKING

1993	1994	1995	1996	1997	1998	1999	2000	2001	2002	2003	2004	High		Low	
-	-	-	-	180	187	161	172	163	161	175	165	**160**	03/00	**187**	02/99

2004-2005											
08/04	09/04	10/04	11/04	12/04	01/05	02/05	03/05	04/05	05/05	06/05	07/05
179	179	177	175	165	163	165	165	165	165	165	165

With a population of just 22,000 to draw on, the national team of the British Virgin Islands has done reasonably well in the decade since joining FIFA, rising to 165 in the FIFA/Coca-Cola World Ranking. With most action confined to years when there are either FIFA World Cup™ qualifiers or Caribbean Cup matches taking part in the competitions is an achievement in itself but to then put in some good performanaces and win matches deserves credit. For the second FIFA World Cup™ in a row the British Virgin Islands drew St Lucia in the preliminary round, a much bigger Caribbean island some fifty places higher in the rankings. Once again a narrow defeat in the home

INTERNATIONAL HONOURS
None

leg in Tortola was followed by a heavy defeat in Castries with St Lucia winning 10-0 on aggregate. Next up later in the year was the Digicel Caribbean Cup. Grouped with St Vincent and the Grenadines, Cayman Islands and Bermuda, BVI remarkably qualified for the knock-out stage thanks to a 2-0 win over Bermuda. Many expected heavy defeats against Trinidad and Tobago in the next round but the scores were kept respectable with Trinidad winning 6-0 on aggregate. Both Tortola and Virgin Gorda, the two biggest of the 60 islands that make up the country, run their own Leagues with Valencia victorious in 2004 in Tortola and Spice United champions of Virgin Gorda.

THE FIFA BIG COUNT OF 2000

	Male	Female		Male	Female
Registered players	208	28	Referees	11	1
Non registered players	100	15	Officials	4	0
Youth players	214	93	Total involved	674	
Total players	658		Number of clubs	10	
Professional players	0	0	Number of teams	21	

British Virgin Islands Football Association (BVIFA)
Botanic Station Road, Road Town, PO Box 4269, Tortola, British Virgin Islands
Tel +1 284 4945655   Fax +1 284 4948968
bvifa@surfbvi.com   www.bvifa.com
President: GRANT Kenrick   General Secretary: DASENT Llewellyn
Vice-President: LIBURD Aubrey   Treasurer: DASENT Llewellyn   Media Officer: FAYE Anatole
Men's Coach: DAVIES Ben   Women's Coach: PETERSON Azille
BVIFA formed: 1974   CONCACAF: 1996   FIFA: 1996
Colours: Gold, Green, Green

GAMES PLAYED BY BRITISH VIRGIN ISLANDS IN THE 2006 FIFA WORLD CUP™ CYCLE

2002	Opponents	Score		Venue	Comp	Scorers	Att	Referee
6-07	Anguilla	W	2-1	Tortola	Fr	Baptiste [42], Huggins [44]		
14-07	St Lucia	L	1-3	Tortola	GCq	Huggins [53]		
28-07	St Lucia	L	1-8	Castries	GCq	Azile [36]		
2003								
No international matches played in 2003								
2004								
28-01	Dominica	L	0-1	Tortola	Fr			Matthew SKN
30-01	US Virgin Islands	W	5-0	Tortola	Fr	OG [18], Williams [24], Morris 2 [26 56], Ferron [88]		
1-02	Dominica	L	1-2	Tortola	Fr	Morris [28]		Charles DMA
22-02	St Lucia	L	0-1	Tortola	WCq		800	Stewart JAM
20-03	St Kitts and Nevis	L	0-4	Basseterre	Fr			
28-03	St Lucia	L	0-9	Vieux Fort	WCq		665	Corrivault CAN
25-09	US Urgin Islands	W	2-1	Tortola	Fr	Heileger [48], Ettienne [55]		
24-11	St Vincent/Grenadines	D	1-1	Kingstown	GCq	Haynes [53]	300	Prendergast JAM
26-11	Cayman Islands	L	0-1	Kingstown	GCq			
28-11	Bermuda	W	2-0	Kingstown	GCq	James 2 [12 24]	400	Matthews SKN
12-12	Trinidad and Tobago	L	0-4	Tortola	GCq		16 000	Arthur LCA
19-12	Trinidad and Tobago	L	0-2	Tunapuna	GCq			Lancaster GUY
2005								
No international matches played in 2005 before August								

Fr = Friendly match • GC = CONCACAF Gold Cup • WC = FIFA World Cup™ • q = qualifier

BRITISH VIRGIN ISLANDS NATIONAL TEAM RECORDS AND RECORD SEQUENCES

	Records			Sequence records				
Victory	5-0	PUR, AIA, VIR	Wins	2	1999	Clean sheets	2	1999, 2001
Defeat	0-12	JAM 1994	Defeats	8	1997-1998	Goals scored	6	1999-2000
Player Caps	n/a		Undefeated	6	2000-2001	Without goal	3	Five times
Player Goals	n/a		Without win	10	1991-1997	Goals against	18	1992-1999

British Virgin Islands has no referees or assistant referees on the FIFA lists

RECENT LEAGUE RECORD

	Tortola	Virgin Gorda
Year	Champions	Champions
1996	Black Lions	Spice United
1997	No tournament	Beverly Hills
1998	BDO Binder Stingers	United Kickers
1999	Veterans	
2000	HBA Panthers	Rangers
2001	HBA Panthers	
2001	Future Stars United	Rangers
2002	HBA Panthers	No tournament
2003		Rangers
2004	Valencia	Rangers

BRITISH VIRGIN ISLANDS COUNTRY INFORMATION

Capital	Road Town	Status	Overseas territory of the UK	GDP per Capita	$16 000
Population	22 187			GNP Ranking	n/a
Area km²	153	Language	English	Dialling code	+1284
Population density	145 per km²	Literacy rate	97%	Internet code	.vg
% in urban areas	NA	Main religion	Christian	GMT + / –	-4
Towns/Cities	Road Town 8 449; Spanish Town 355				
Neighbours (km)	Caribbean Sea & Atlantic Ocean 80				
Main stadia	Shirley Recreational Field – Road Town, Tortola 2 000				

VIE – VIETNAM

NATIONAL TEAM RECORD
JULY 1ST 2002 TO JUNE 30TH 2005

PL	W	D	L	F	A	%
29	13	5	11	60	51	53.4

FIFA/COCA-COLA WORLD RANKING

1993	1994	1995	1996	1997	1998	1999	2000	2001	2002	2003	2004	High		Low	
135	151	122	99	104	98	102	99	105	108	98	103	84	09/98	156	11/95

2004-2005											
08/04	09/04	10/04	11/04	12/04	01/05	02/05	03/05	04/05	05/05	06/05	07/05
101	94	96	109	103	102	102	105	107	107	107	106

Co-hosting the 2007 Asian Cup may mark an important milestone in the development of football in Vietnam. Since the end of the civil war in the 1970s, the sport has grown; the V-League was expanded to 12 clubs a few years ago with the teams attracting the best players in the country and also from the surrounding area and the national side complemented the League's progress. 2002 proved a high point in FIFA World Cup™ competition as the side finished runners-up in their qualifying group behind Saudi Arabia. The latest campaign proved more disappointing as Vietnam exited at the second stage after poor performances left them third behind Korea Republic and

INTERNATIONAL HONOURS
South East Asian Games 1959

Lebanon and level with the Maldives at the second group stage. In the Tiger Cup, big wins over Cambodia and Laos were nullified by defeat to Indonesia and a draw with Singapore that once again put Vietnam out at a group stage. Perhaps 2007's Asian Cup will offer a clearer indication of any short-term progress when Vietnam line up against the region's top nations. Gach Dong Tam won their first V-League title denying Hoang Anh Gia Lia their third successive Championship and preventing Binh Dinh from adding the League title to their 2004 Vietnam Cup victory. Both national junior sides reached their respective Asian finals but made early exits at the group stages.

THE FIFA BIG COUNT OF 2000

	Male	Female		Male	Female
Registered players	1 652	176	Referees	180	20
Non registered players	985 000	50 000	Officials	18 000	2 000
Youth players	1 948	0	Total involved	1 058 976	
Total players	1 038 776		Number of clubs	200	
Professional players	0	0	Number of teams	18 300	

Vietnam Football Federation (VFF)
Liên Doàn Bong Dá Viêt Nam, 18 Ly van Phuc, Dong Da District, Hanoi 844, Vietnam
Tel +84 4 8452480   Fax +84 4 8233119
ldbd@hn.vnn.vn   www.vff.org.vn
President: NGUYEN Trong Hy   General Secretary: TRAN Quoc Tuan
Vice-President: LE The Tho   Treasurer: LE Hung Dung   Media Officer: NGUYEN Trung Lan
Men's Coach: RIEDL Alfred   Women's Coach: MAI Chung Duc
VFF formed: 1962   AFC: 1954   FIFA: 1964
Colours: Red, Red, Red

GAMES PLAYED BY VIETNAM IN THE 2006 FIFA WORLD CUP™ CYCLE

2002	Opponents		Score	Venue	Comp	Scorers	Att	Referee
27-11	Sri Lanka	W	2-1	Colombo	Fr	Nguyen Minh Phuong [32], Nhuyen Duc Thang [62]		Arambakade SRI
29-11	Sri Lanka	D	1-1	Colombo	Fr	Trinh Xuan Thanh [49]		Pingamage SRI
1-12	Sri Lanka	D	2-2	Colombo	Fr	Le Huynh Duc		
8-12	Thailand	L	1-2	Bangkok	Fr	Huynh Hong Son [13]		
15-12	Cambodia	W	9-2	Jakarta	TCr1	Huynh Hong Son [10], Tran Truong Giang 2 [14 41], Nguyen Quoc Trung [24], Le Huynh Duc 2 [58 73], Nguyen Minh Phuong [70], Trinh Xuan Thanh [83], Pham Van Quyen [89]	5 000	Nagalingam SIN
19-12	Philippines	W	4-1	Jakarta	TCr1	Huynh Hong Son 2 [55 69], Le Huynh Duc 2 [68p 72]	2 000	Nagalingam SIN
21-12	Indonesia	D	2-2	Jakarta	TCr1	Phan Van Tai Em [53], Le Huynh Duc [57]	35 000	Mohd Salleh MAS
23-12	Myanmar	W	4-2	Jakarta	TCr1	Trinh Xuan Thanh [37], Dang Phuong Nam 2 [49 67], Le Huynh Duc [72]	2 000	Nagalingam SIN
27-12	Thailand	L	0-4	Jakarta	TCsf		10 000	Nagalingam SIN
29-12	Malaysia	W	2-1	Jakarta	TC3p	Tran Truong Giang [45], Nguyen Minh Phuong [59]	25 000	Midi Nitrorejo IDN
2003								
12-02	Albania	L	0-5	Bastia Umbra	Fr			Nicoletti ITA
25-09	Korea Republic	L	0-5	Incheon	ACq			
27-09	Nepal	W	5-0	Incheon	ACq	Pham Van Quyen 3 [14 22 36], Nguyen Huu Thang [23], Pham Thanh Binh [90]		
29-09	Oman	L	0-6	Incheon	ACq			
19-10	Korea Republic	W	1-0	Muscat	ACq	Pham Van Quyen [73]		
21-10	Nepal	W	2-0	Muscat	ACq	Nguyen Minh Phuong [49], Phan Thanh Binh [51]		
24-10	Oman	L	0-2	Muscat	ACq			
2004								
18-02	Maldives	W	4-0	Hanoi	WCq	Phan Van Tai Em 2 [9 60], Nguyen Van Hai [13], Pham Van Quyen [80p]	25 000	Fong HKG
31-03	Lebanon	L	0-2	Nam Dinh	WCq		25 000	Irmatov UZB
9-06	Korea Republic	L	0-2	Daejeon	WCq		40 019	Al Mehannah KSA
20-08	Myanmar	W	5-0	Ho Chi Minh City	Fr	Le Cong Vinh 2, Thach Boa Khanh, Nguyen Minh Phuong, Pham Van Quyen		
24-08	India	W	2-1	Ho Chi Minh City	Fr	Le Cong Vinh [21], Thach Boa Khanh [57]		
8-09	Korea Republic	L	1-2	Ho Chi Minh City	WCq	Phan Van Tai Em [49]	25 000	Yoshida JPN
13-10	Maldives	L	0-3	Male	WCq		10 000	Haq IND
17-11	Lebanon	D	0-0	Beirut	WCq		1 000	Ebrahim BHR
7-12	Singapore	D	1-1	Ho Chi Minh City	TCr1	Thach Boa Khanh [51]	20 000	Sun Baojie CHN
9-12	Cambodia	W	9-1	Ho Chi Minh City	TCr1	Thach Boa Khanh 2 [8 23], Le Cong Vinh 3 [58 87 89], OG [63], Dang Van Thanh 2 [71 83], Nguyen Huu Thang [83]	8 000	Supian MAS
11-12	Indonesia	L	0-3	Hanoi	TCr1		40 000	Sun Baojie CHN
15-12	Laos	W	3-0	Hanoi	TCr1	Le Cong Vinh [9], Nguyen Minh Phuong [41], Thach Bao Khanh [74]	20 000	Rungklay THA
2005								

No international matches played in 2005 before August

Fr = Friendly match • TC = ASEAN Tiger Cup • AC = AFC Asian Cup • WC = FIFA World Cup™
q = qualifier • r1 = first round group • sf = semi-final • 3p = third place play-off

VIETNAM COUNTRY INFORMATION

Capital	Hanoi	Independence	1954 from France	GDP per Capita	$2 500
Population	82 689 518	Status	Republic	GNP Ranking	58
Area km²	329 560	Language	Vietnamese	Dialling code	+84
Population density	251 per km²	Literacy rate	90%	Internet code	.vn
% in urban areas	21%	Main religion	Buddhist, Hoa Hao, Cao Dai	GMT +/−	+7
Towns/Cities ('000)	Ho Chi Minh City 3 467; Hanoi 1 431; Hai Phong 602; Da Nang 472; Bien Hoa 407; Hue 287				
Neighbours (km)	Cambodia 1 228; China 1 281; Laos 2 130; South China Sea & Gulf of Tonkin 3 444				
Main stadia	My Dinh – Hanoi 40 000; San Chi Lang – Da Nang 28 000; Thong Nhat – Ho Chi Minh City 25 000				

VIETNAM 2005

V-LEAGUE

	Pl	W	D	L	F	A	Pts	GDT	Da Nang	Binh Duong	HAGL	SLNA	SD Nam D.	Hai Pong	CSG	Hoa Phat	HL Binh D.	LG Hanoi	Dong Thap
Gach Dong Tam †	22	12	6	4	43	25	42		1-0	1-1	4-3	1-2	2-1	3-1	4-1	2-0	1-1	5-0	2-0
Da Nang †	22	10	8	4	33	19	38	2-2		5-0	3-0	0-0	2-0	2-0	1-2	2-1	1-1	0-0	1-0
Binh Duong	22	11	5	6	40	32	38	1-2	3-0		3-1	3-1	4-2	4-3	0-1	0-1	1-0	1-0	4-1
Hoang Anh Gia Lai	22	9	5	8	30	24	32	1-1	1-1	3-2		3-1	0-1	1-0	0-0	2-0	0-0	0-1	3-0
Song Lam Nghe An	22	8	7	7	33	28	31	2-0	1-0	2-2	0-0		1-0	4-4	2-0	2-3	2-2	0-0	6-2
Song Da Nam Dinh	22	7	7	8	27	31	28	1-0	0-3	3-3	2-0	1-1		2-1	2-1	1-1	2-2	0-0	3-1
Hai Phong	22	6	9	7	31	34	27	3-2	2-2	2-1	1-0	1-0	1-1		3-2	0-0	0-1	0-0	2-2
Cang Saigon	22	6	9	7	26	30	27	2-2	0-1	1-1	3-2	0-3	3-1	3-2		0-0	0-0	0-1	2-2
Hoa Phat	22	6	7	9	24	29	25	0-0	2-3	1-2	1-3	1-2	3-2	1-1	1-3		2-0	2-0	2-1
Hoa Lam Binh Dinh	22	5	10	7	17	21	25	1-2	1-1	0-1	0-2	1-0	1-0	1-2	0-0	0-0		2-1	2-1
LG Hanoi	22	5	9	8	18	27	24	2-3	2-2	1-2	0-4	3-1	1-1	1-1	1-1	1-1	1-0		2-0
Delta Dong Thap	22	3	6	13	18	40	15	0-3	0-1	1-1	0-1	1-0	0-1	1-1	1-1	1-1	2-1	1-1	

30/01/2005 - 11/08/2005 • † Qualified for the AFC Champions League

VIETNAM 2005 FIRST DIVISION (2)

	Pl	W	D	L	F	A	Pts
Khatoco Khanh Hoa	22	12	5	5	35	17	41
Tien Giang	22	13	2	7	24	17	41
NHDA Thep Pomina	22	10	9	3	28	18	39
Can Tho	22	11	5	6	23	20	38
Huda Hue	22	8	8	6	28	27	32
The Công	22	8	4	10	22	31	28
Thanh Hoa	22	7	6	9	19	18	27
Da My Nghe	22	7	5	10	21	30	26
An Giang	22	5	10	7	24	24	25
Dong Nai	22	6	5	11	25	27	23
Quang Nam	22	5	7	10	16	21	22
Buu Dien	22	4	6	12	16	30	18

29/01/2005 - 6/08/2005

VIETNAM CUP 2004

Semi-finals

Binh Dinh	3
Binh Duong	1

Sông Lam Nghe An	1
The Công	2

Finals

Binh Dinh	2
The Công	0

10-07-2004, Vinh Stadium, Vinh
Scorers - Phuong, Issawa

VIETNAM NATIONAL TEAM RECORDS AND RECORD SEQUENCES

Records			Sequence records					
Victory	11-0	GUM 2000	Wins	6	1966	Clean sheets	6	1999
Defeat	1-9	IDN 1971	Defeats	10	1997	Goals scored	23	1949-1958
Player Caps	n/a		Undefeated	8	1954-1956	Without goal	4	1997
Player Goals	n/a		Without win	12	1974-1993	Goals against	22	1956-1959

RECENT LEAGUE AND CUP RECORD

	Championship						Cup		
Year	Champions	Pts	Runners-up	Pts	Third	Pts	Winners	Score	Runners-up
1996	Dong Thap	6-1	Cong An HCMC				Hai Quan	0-0 6-5p	Cang Saigon
1997	Cang Saigon						Hai Quan	3-0	Cang Saigon
1998	The Cong		Song Lam Nghe An		Cong An HCMC		Cong An HCMC	2-0	Hai Quan
1999	Championship not played						No tournament		
2000	Song Lam Nghe An	43	Cong An HCMC	42	Cong An Hanoi	37	Cang Saigon	2-1	Cong An HCMC
2001	Song Lam Nghe An	36	Nam Dinh	34	The Cong	29	Cong An HCMC	2-1	Cong An Hanoi
2002	Cang Saigon	32	Song Lam Nghe An	28	Ngan Hang Dong	26	Song Lam Nghe An	1-0	Thua Thien
2003	Hoang Anh Gia Lai	43	Gach Dong Tam	40	Nam Dinh	36	Binh Dinh	2-1	Ngan Hang Dong
2004	Hoang Anh Gia Lai	46	Nam Dinh	44	Gach Dong Tam	38	Binh Dinh	2-0	The Cong
2005									

Cong An = Police • The Cong = Army • Cang Saigon = Saigon Port • HCMC = Ho Chi Minh City

VIN – ST VINCENT AND THE GRENADINES

NATIONAL TEAM RECORD
JULY 1ST 2002 TO JUNE 30TH 2005

PL	W	D	L	F	A	%
22	9	5	8	40	37	52.3

FIFA/COCA-COLA WORLD RANKING

1993	1994	1995	1996	1997	1998	1999	2000	2001	2002	2003	2004	High		Low	
129	144	95	93	122	138	141	127	125	144	169	137	**80**	08/96	**170**	02/04

2004-2005											
08/04	09/04	10/04	11/04	12/04	01/05	02/05	03/05	04/05	05/05	06/05	07/05
151	150	146	146	137	138	135	135	134	133	132	128

A small multi-island nation, St Vincent and the Grenadines have caused more than the odd upset in the past with a place at the CONCACAF Gold Cup finals in 1996 a notable achievement. Currently ranked 128th in the world, the national team had a busy year in 2004 playing 19 matches after two years of inactivity. The 2006 FIFA World Cup™ qualifiers began with a visit to Nicaragua where they had to settle for a 2-2 draw after leading twice, but they made sure of progress in Kingstown with a 4-1 victory. Being drawn in a group with Mexico, Trinidad and Tobago and St Kitts and Nevis did not inspire confidence and sure enough third place in the group was the end

INTERNATIONAL HONOURS
None

of the road. However, the islanders could take some comfort in that they only lost to Mexico by the one goal in Kingstown, a far better result than the 11-0 thrashing they received in 1992. Serbian coach Zoran Vranes joined the side midway through the campaign and he guided the team through a good run in the Digicel Caribbean Cup in which St Vincent eliminated Grenada before narrowly losing to Trinidad and Tobago. Because of the many islands that make up the country there is no single league structure, rather 14 different championships that give little coherence and focus for sponsors and fans.

THE FIFA BIG COUNT OF 2000

	Male	Female		Male	Female
Registered players	1 000	106	Referees	4	0
Non registered players	1 100	170	Officials	410	15
Youth players	3 000	40	Total involved	5 845	
Total players	5 416		Number of clubs	272	
Professional players	5	0	Number of teams	272	

Saint Vincent and the Grenadines Football Federation (SVGFF)
Murray's Road, PO Box 1278, Saint George, St Vincent and the Grenadines
Tel +1 784 4561092   Fax +1 784 4572193
svgfootball@vincysurf.com   www.svgnetworks.com
President: LEACOCK St Clair   General Secretary: BENNETT Earl
Vice-President: TBD   Treasurer: HUGGINS Trevor   Media Officer: WILLIAMS Asberth
Men's Coach: VRANES Zoran   Women's Coach: ALEXANDER Rodwell
SVGFF formed: 1979   CONCACAF: 1988   FIFA: 1988
Colours: Green, Blue, Green

GAMES PLAYED BY ST VINCENT AND THE GRENADINES IN THE 2006 FIFA WORLD CUP™ CYCLE

2002	Opponents	Score	Venue	Comp	Scorers	Att	Referee
No international matches played in 2002							
2003							
No international matches played in 2003							
2004							
8-02	St Lucia	W 2-1	Castries	Fr			
21-03	St Lucia	D 1-1	Kingstown	Fr	Charles [39]		
8-05	Grenada	D 1-1	Kingstown	Fr	Guy [6]		
23-05	St Kitts and Nevis	L 2-3	Basseterre	Fr	Haynes [10], Samuel [32]		Matthew SKN
13-06	Nicaragua	D 2-2	Diriamba	WCq	Haynes [9], Samuel [43]	7 500	Delgado CUB
20-06	Nicaragua	W 4-1	Kingstown	WCq	Samuel 2 [14 79], James [15], Alonso OG [86]	5 000	Brohim DMA
18-08	Trinidad and Tobago	L 0-2	Kingstown	WCq		5 000	Vaughn USA
10-09	St Kitts and Nevis	W 1-0	Kingstown	WCq	Jack [23]	4 000	Delgado CUB
6-10	Mexico	L 0-7	Pachuca	WCq		21 000	Liu CAN
10-10	Mexico	L 0-1	Kingstown	WCq		2 500	Alfaro SLV
13-10	St Kitts and Nevis	W 3-0	Basseterre	WCq	Velox 2 [19 85], Samuel [65]	500	Whittaker CAY
13-11	Grenada	W 6-2	Kingstown	Fr	James 2 [12 27], John [19], Joseph [71], Gonsalves [74], Velox [88]		Moss VIN
17-11	Trinidad and Tobago	L 1-2	Port of Spain	WCq	Haynes [49]	10 000	Batres GUA
20-11	Grenada	L 2-3	Gouyave	Fr	Gonsalves [18], Haynes [58]	3 000	Bedeau CAN
24-11	British Virgin Islands	D 1-1	Kingstown	GCq	Forde [69]	300	Prendergast JAM
26-11	Bermuda	D 3-3	Kingstown	GCq	Pierre [7], Haynes [52], Samuel [54]		
28-11	Cayman Islands	W 4-0	Kingstown	GCq	Samuel [20], Forde [43p], Haynes [51], Gonsalves [80]	850	Prendergast JAM
12-12	Grenada	W 3-1	Kingstown	GCq	Samuel [10], Guy [23], Velox [64]		Fanus LCA
19-12	Grenada	W 1-0	St George's	GCq	Francis [6]	1 000	Small BRB
2005							
9-01	Trinidad and Tobago	L 1-3	Port of Spain	GCq	Haynes [25]	1 688	Chance ATG
16-01	Trinidad and Tobago	W 1-0	Kingstown	GCq	Forde [66p]	1 450	Pine JAM
30-01	Barbados	L 1-3	Bridgetown	Fr	Guy [14]		

Fr = Friendly match • GC = CONCACAF Gold Cup • WC = FIFA World Cup™ • q = qualifier

ST VINCENT AND THE GRENADINES NATIONAL TEAM RECORDS AND RECORD SEQUENCES

Records			Sequence records					
Victory	9-0	MSR 1995, VIR 2000	Wins	5	1999-2000	Clean sheets	4	1995
Defeat	0-11	MEX 1992	Defeats	7	1992-1993, 2000	Goals scored	21	1996-2000
Player Caps	n/a		Undefeated	8	1995	Without goal	7	1992-1993
Player Goals	n/a		Without win	10	1996	Goals against	12	1996-1998

FIFA ASSISTANT REFEREE LIST 2005

	Int'l	DoB
ALEXANDER Rodwell	2004	26-10-1964
BRAMBLE Andrew	1997	19-03-1964
FRANCOIS Clemroy	1996	3-01-1964
HAYNES Earl	1997	9-06-1973

FIFA REFEREE LIST 2005

	Int'l	DoB
HAZELWOOD Timothy	1995	16-08-1962
MOSS Lyndon	1995	25-03-1965

ST VINCENT AND THE GRENADINES COUNTRY INFORMATION

Capital	Kingstown	Independence	1979 from the UK	GDP per Capita	$2 900
Population	117 193	Status	Parliamentary Democracy	GNP Ranking	176
Area km²	389	Language	English	Dialling code	+1809
Population density	301 per km²	Literacy rate	96%	Internet code	.vc
% in urban areas	46%	Main religion	Christian	GMT +/−	-4
Towns/Cities ('000)	Kingstown 17; Barroualie 2; Georgetown 2; Layou 2; Byera 1; Biabou 1				
Neighbours (km)	Caribbean Sea & Atlantic Ocean 84				
Main stadia	Arnos Vale Playing Ground – Kingstown 18 000				

VIR – US VIRGIN ISLANDS

NATIONAL TEAM RECORD
JULY 1ST 2002 TO JUNE 30TH 2005

PL	W	D	L	F	A	%
9	0	0	9	4	56	0

FIFA/COCA-COLA WORLD RANKING

1993	1994	1995	1996	1997	1998	1999	2000	2001	2002	2003	2004	High		Low	
-	-	-	-	-	-	194	198	198	197	199	196	**190**	04/99	**200**	09/04

2004-2005											
08/04	09/04	10/04	11/04	12/04	01/05	02/05	03/05	04/05	05/05	06/05	07/05
200	200	199	199	196	196	196	196	196	196	196	196

Joining the FIFA family in 1998 the US Virgin Islands were not regarded as natural football territory and their subsequent results have done little to refute the theory. Having beaten the British Virgin Islands in an unofficial match in 1998 before joining FIFA, the national side are still looking for their second victory although they did manage a 2-2 draw with the Turks and Caicos Islands the following year. Since that victory there have been some heavy defeats including a 14-1 setback against St Lucia in 2002 and most recently 11-0 and 11-1 thrashings at the hands of Haiti and Jamaica respectively in the Digicel Caribbean Cup which also doubled up as a qualifying compe-

INTERNATIONAL HONOURS
None

tition for the 2005 CONCACAF Gold Cup. With those setbacks and no games so far in 2005, it is little surprise the Islands are ranked 196th in the world. The USVI Championship returned in 2005 after a two-year absence featuring the top two from the St Croix and St Thomas Leagues. The final pitted Positive Vibes from St Thomas against St Croix's Helenites with Vibes clinching the title thanks to a 2-0 victory. The U-20s met an ignominious fate in the region's junior event; drawn against Saint Martin, the side lost 2-1 away and then could only draw 3-3 in the return leg against a side from a country not yet a FIFA member.

THE FIFA BIG COUNT OF 2000

	Male	Female		Male	Female
Registered players	200	85	Referees	1	0
Non registered players	800	50	Officials	13	4
Youth players	600	275	Total involved	2 028	
Total players	2 010		Number of clubs	9	
Professional players	0	60	Number of teams	22	

U.S.V.I. Soccer Federation Inc. (USVISA)
AQ Building Contant, Suite 205, PO Box 306627, St Thomas VI 0080-6627, US Virgin Islands
Tel +1 340 7142828　　　Fax +1 340 7142830
usvisoccer@vipowernet.net　　　www.none
President: MARTIN Derrick　　General Secretary: MONTICEUX Glen
Vice-President: FAHIE Collister　　Treasurer: TBD　　Media Officer: none
Men's Coach: ST ROSE Felix　　Women's Coach: WOREDE Yohannes
USVISA formed: 1992　　CONCACAF: 1998　　FIFA: 1998
Colours: Royal blue, Royal blue, Royal blue

GAMES PLAYED BY US VIRGIN ISLANDS IN THE 2006 FIFA WORLD CUP™ CYCLE

2002	Opponents	Score		Venue	Comp	Scorers	Att	Referee
16-08	Dominican Republic	L	1-6	Santo Domingo	GCq	Sheppard 44		Forde BRB
18-08	Dominican Republic	L	1-5	Santo Domingo	GCq	Sheppard 69		Jean Lesly HAI
2003								
No international matches played in 2003								
2004								
30-01	British Virgin Islands	L	0-5	Road Town	Fr			
31-01	Dominica	L	0-5	St Thomas	Fr			Matthew SKN
18-02	St Kitts and Nevis	L	0-4	St Thomas	WCq		225	Brizan TRI
31-03	St Kitts and Nevis	L	0-7	Basseterre	WCq		800	Recinos SLV
25-09	British Virgin Islands	L	1-2	Road Town	Fr	Challenger 65		
24-11	Haiti	L	0-11	Kingston	GCq		250	Piper TRI
26-11	Jamaica	L	1-11	Kingston	GCq	Lauro 72	4 200	Piper TRI
28-11	St Martin †	D	0-0	Kingston	GCq		200	Brizan TRI
2005								
No international matches played in 2005 before August								

Fr = Friendly match • GC = CONCACAF Gold Cup • WC = FIFA World Cup™ • q = qualifier • † Not a full international

US VIRGIN ISLANDS NATIONAL TEAM RECORDS AND RECORD SEQUENCES

Records			Sequence records					
Victory	1-0	BVI 1998	Wins	1	1998	Clean sheets	1	1998, 1999
Defeat	1-14	LCA 2001	Defeats	17	2000-2004	Goals scored	3	2001-2002
Player Caps	n/a		Undefeated	3	1998-1999	Without goal	4	1999-2000, 2004
Player Goals	n/a		Without win	19	1999-2004	Goals against	17	2000-2004

FIFA REFEREE LIST 2005

	Int'l	DoB
None		

FIFA ASSISTANT REFEREE LIST 2005

	Int'l	DoB
None		

RECENT LEAGUE RECORD

	Overall Championship			St Thomas/St John	St Croix
Year	Champions	Score	Runners-up	Champions	Champions
1998				MI Roc Masters	Helenites
1999				MI Roc Masters	Unique FC
2000	United We Stand Upsetters	5-1	Helenites	United We Stand Upsetters	Helenites
2001	United We Stand Upsetters				Helenites
2002	Hatian Stars	1-0	United We Stand Upsetters	Waitikubuli United	Helenites
2003		Not played		Waitikubuli United	Helenites
2004		Not played			Helenites
2005	Positive Vibes	2-0	Helenites	Positive Vibes	Helenites

US VIRGIN ISLANDS COUNTRY INFORMATION

Capital	Charlottte Amalie	Status	US Unincorpoated Territory	GDP per Capita	$17 500
Population	108 775			GNP Ranking	n/a
Area km²	352	Language	English, Spanish, Creole	Dialling code	+1340
Population density	309 per km²	Literacy rate	n/a	Internet code	.vi
% in urban areas	n/a	Main religion	Christian	GMT +/−	-4
Towns/Cities ('000)	Charlotte Amalie 10; Anna's Retreat 8; Charlotte Amalie West 5; Frederiksted Southeast 3				
Neighbours (km)	Caribbean Sea & Atlantic Ocean 188				
Main stadia	Lionel Roberts – Charlotte Amalie, St Thomas 9 000				

11 June 2005. Vicente Calderon, Madrid, Spain.
Assunção holds the Copa del Rey after Betis won
the trophy for only the second time in their history.

19 June 2005. Ewood Park, Blackburn, England. FIFA women's
world player of the year Birgit Prinz scores Germany's third
goal as they win the UEFA European Women's Championship
for the sixth time in succession.

29 June 2005. Waldstadion, Frankfurt, Germany. Four of the best. Brazil beat Argentina 4–1
to win the FIFA Confederations Cup.

2 July 2005. Galgenwaard, Utrecht, Netherlands. Argentina raise the FIFA World Youth Championship trophy for a record fifth time after beating Nigeria 2–1 in the final.

14 July 2005. Morumbi, São Paulo, Brazil. São Paulo win the Copa Libertadores for a third time. In an all Brazilian final they beat Atlético Paranaense 5–1 on aggregate.

24 July 2005. Giants Stadium, New Jersey, USA. Penalty despair for brave Panama as the USA win the CONCACAF Gold Cup after a 0–0 draw in the final.

WAL – WALES

NATIONAL TEAM RECORD
JULY 1ST 2002 TO JUNE 30TH 2005

PL	W	D	L	F	A	%
25	9	7	9	32	28	50

FIFA/COCA-COLA WORLD RANKING

1993	1994	1995	1996	1997	1998	1999	2000	2001	2002	2003	2004	High		Low	
29	41	61	80	102	97	98	109	100	52	66	68	27	08/93	113	09/00

2004-2005											
08/04	09/04	10/04	11/04	12/04	01/05	02/05	03/05	04/05	05/05	06/05	07/05
64	57	57	63	68	68	65	71	73	74	79	80

Having come so close to qualifying for the finals of UEFA EURO 2004™ there was genuine belief amongst Welsh fans that Mark Hughes could take the national team to their first FIFA World Cup™ finals since 1958 but after two draws and two defeats in the opening four games that dream was firmly extinguished. The defeat at home to Poland was also the last game in charge for Hughes who took the Blackburn Rovers job believing that he had achieved all that he could with Wales. His replacement was the hugely experienced John Toshack but there was little he could do to salvage the campaign. Until 1993 Wales had no league of its own with clubs integrated into the English

INTERNATIONAL HONOURS
British International Championship 1907 1920 1924 1928 1933 1934 1937 1939 1952 1956 1960 1970

football pyramid and although the top clubs like Cardiff City, Swansea City and Wrexham remain there, since 1993 the League of Wales has provided an excellent focus for the rest of the clubs. Dominated for much of its first decade by Barry Town the 2004-05 season saw ambitious TNS Llansantffraid complete the double finishing four points ahead of defending champions Rhyl and beating Carmarthen Town in the Cup Final. The League of Wales clubs do still have some contact with the English-based clubs in the FAW Premier Cup; TNS lost on penalties to Swansea in the semi-final who then went on to beat Wrexham in the final.

THE FIFA BIG COUNT OF 2000

	Male	Female		Male	Female
Registered players	38 946	400	Referees	1 062	12
Non registered players	30 000	0	Officials	10 500	125
Youth players	28 700	600	Total involved	110 345	
Total players	98 646		Number of clubs	1 830	
Professional players	320	0	Number of teams	4 615	

The Football Association of Wales, Ltd (FAW)
Plymouth Chambers, 3 Westgate Street, Cardiff, CF10 1DP, United Kingdom
Tel +44 29 20372325   Fax +44 29 20343961
info@faw.co.uk   www.faw.org.uk
President: EVANS Tegwyn MBE   General Secretary: COLLINS David
Vice-President: REES Peter   Treasurer: WILLIAMS Idwal   Media Officer: COLLINS David
Men's Coach: TOSHACK John MBE   Women's Coach: BEATTIE Andy
FAW formed: 1876   UEFA: 1954   FIFA: 1910-20, 1924-28, 1946
Colours: Red, Red, Red

GAMES PLAYED BY WALES IN THE 2006 FIFA WORLD CUP™ CYCLE

2002	Opponents	Score		Venue	Comp	Scorers	Att	Referee
21-08	Croatia	D	1-1	Varazdin	Fr	Davies.S [11]	6 000	Frohlich GER
7-09	Finland	W	2-0	Helsinki	ECq	Hartson [30], Davies.S [72]	35 833	Plautz AUT
6-10	Italy	W	2-1	Cardiff	ECq	Davies.S [11], Bellamy [70]	70 000	Vessiere FRA
20-11	Azerbaijan	W	2-0	Baku	ECq	Speed [10], Hartson [70]	8 000	Huyghe BEL
2003								
12-02	Bosnia-Herzegovina	D	2-2	Cardiff	Fr	Earnshaw [8], Hartson [74]	25 000	Malcolm NIR
29-03	Azerbaijan	W	4-0	Cardiff	ECq	Bellamy [1], Speed [40], Hartson [44], Giggs [52]	72 500	Leuba SUI
26-05	USA	L	0-2	San Jose	Fr		12 282	Archundia MEX
20-08	Serbia & Montenegro	L	0-1	Belgrade	ECq		25 000	Frisk SWE
6-09	Italy	L	0-4	Milan	ECq		68 000	Merk GER
10-09	Finland	D	1-1	Cardiff	ECq	Davies.S [3]	72 500	Dauden Ibanez ESP
11-10	Serbia & Montenegro	L	2-3	Cardiff	ECq	Hartson [24p], Earnshaw [90]	72 514	Stuchlik AUT
15-11	Russia	D	0-0	Moscow	ECpo		29 000	Cortez Batista POR
19-11	Russia	L	0-1	Cardiff	ECpo		73 062	Mejuto Gonzalez ESP
2004								
18-02	Scotland	W	4-0	Cardiff	Fr	Earnshaw 3 [1 35 58], Taylor [78]	47 124	Ross NIR
31-03	Hungary	W	2-1	Budapest	Fr	Koumas [20], Earnshaw [81]	10 000	Meyer GER
27-05	Norway	D	0-0	Oslo	Fr		14 137	Hansson SWE
30-05	Canada	W	1-0	Wrexham	Fr	Parry [21]	10 805	McKeon IRL
18-08	Latvia	W	2-0	Riga	Fr	Hartson [80], Bellamy [89]	10 000	Ivanov RUS
4-09	Azerbaijan	D	1-1	Baku	WCq	Speed [47]	8 000	Trivkovic CRO
8-09	Northern Ireland	D	2-2	Cardiff	WCq	Hartson [32], Earnshaw [74]	63 500	Messina ITA
9-10	England	L	0-2	Manchester	WCq		65 224	Hauge NOR
13-10	Poland	L	2-3	Cardiff	WCq	Earnshaw [56], Hartson [90]	56 685	Sars FRA
2005								
9-02	Hungary	W	2-0	Cardiff	Fr	Bellamy 2 [63 80]	16 672	Richmond SCO
26-03	Austria	L	0-2	Cardiff	WCq		47 760	Allaerts BEL
30-03	Austria	L	0-1	Vienna	WCq		29 500	Mejuto Gonzalez ESP

Fr = Friendly match • EC = UEFA EURO 2004™ • WC = FIFA World Cup™ • q = qualifier

WALES NATIONAL TEAM RECORDS AND RECORD SEQUENCES

Records			Sequence records					
Victory	11-0	NIR 1888	Wins	6	1980-1981	Clean sheets	4	1981, 1991
Defeat	0-9	SCO 1878	Defeats	8	1897-1900	Goals scored	16	1950-1954
Player Caps	92	SOUTHALL Neville	Undefeated	8	1980-1981	Without goal	6	1971-72, 1973-74
Player Goals	28	RUSH Ian	Without win	12	1896-00, 1999-01	Goals against	28	1891-1900

WALES COUNTRY INFORMATION

Capital	Cardiff	Status	Part of the UK	GDP per Capita	$22 160
Population	2 935 283			GNP Ranking	4
Area km²	20 798	Language	English, Welsh	Dialling code	+44
Population density	141 per km²	Literacy rate	99%	Internet code	.uk
% in urban areas	89%	Main religion	Christian	GMT +/–	0
Towns/Cities ('000)	Cardiff 305; Swansea 223; Newport 137; Wrexham 128; Rhondda 59; Merthyr Tydfil 55; Barry 51; Cwmbran 48; Llanelli 47; Neath 46; Bridgend 41; Pontypool 35; Port Talbot 35				
Neighbours (km)	England 468				
Main stadia	Millennium Stadium – Cardiff 74 500; Racecourse Ground – Wrexham 15 891				

NATIONAL CAPS

	Caps
SOUTHALL Neville	92
SPEED Gary	85
SAUNDERS Dean	75
NICHOLAS Peter	73
RUSH Ian	73
HUGHES Mark	72
JONES Joey	72
ALLCHURCH Ivor	68
FLYNN Bryan	66
MELVILLE Andrew	65

NATIONAL GOALS

	Goals
RUSH Ian	28
ALLCHURCH Ivor	23
FORD Trevor	23
SAUNDERS Dean	22
HUGHES Mark	16
JONES Cliff	16
CHARLES John	15
HARTSON John	14
TOSHACK John	13
LEWIS Billy	12

NATIONAL COACH

	Years
SMITH Mike	1974-'79
ENGLAND Mike	1980-'88
WILLIAMS David	1988
YORATH Terry	1988-'93
TOSHACK John	1994
SMITH Mike	1994-'95
GOULD Bobby	1995-'99
HUGHES Mark	1999-'04
TOSHACK John	2004-

FIFA REFEREE LIST 2005

	Int'l	DoB
LAWLOR Brian	1995	31-01-1963
RICHARDS Ceri	1994	28-06-1965
WHITBY Mark	2003	12-08-1973

FIFA ASSISTANT REFEREE LIST 2005

	Int'l	DoB
ADIE Darren	2003	8-07-1966
BATES Phil	2000	8-11-1964
EVANS Lee	2003	13-10-1975
JONES Mike	1997	16-11-1974
KING Eddie	1999	5-11-1972
WILLIAMS Maldwyn	2001	3-09-1963

CLUB DIRECTORY

Club	Town/City	Stadium	Phone	www.	Lge	Cup	CL
Aberystwyth Town	Aberystwyth	Park Avenue 2 300	+44 1970 612122	atfcnews.co.uk	0	1	0
Afan Lido	Port Talbot	Sports Ground 4 200	+44 1639 892960	afanlidofc.co.uk	0	0	0
Airbus UK	Broughton		+44 1244 522356		0	0	0
Bangor City	Bangor	Farrar Road 2 000	+44 1248 355852	bangorcityfc.com	2	5	0
Caernarfon Town	Caernarfon	The Oval 2 000	+44 1286 675002	caernarfontownfc.net	0	0	0
Caersws	Caersws	Recreation Ground 2 500	+44 1686 688753	caerswsfc.com	0	0	0
Carmarthen Town	Carmarthen	Richmond Park 2 300	+44 1267 232101	carmarthentownafc.net	0	0	0
Cefn Druids	Wrexham	Plaskynaston Lane 2 500	+44 1978 824332	cefndruids.co.uk	0	0	0
Connah's Quay Nomads	Connah's Quay	Deeside Stadium 4 000	+44 1244 816418	nomadsfc.co.uk	0	0	0
Cwmbran Town	Cwmbran	Cwmbran Stadium 7 877	+44 1633 627100	cwmbrantownafc.org.uk	1	0	0
Haverfordwest County	Haverfordwest	Bridge Meadow 2 500	+44 1437 769048	haverfordwestcounty.com	0	0	0
Llanelli	Llanelli	Stebonheath Park 3 700	+44 1554 772973	llanelli-afc.co.uk	0	0	0
TNS Llansantffraid	Llansantffraid	Treflan 2 000	+44 1691 664053	tnsfc.co.uk	2	2	0
Newtown	Newtown	Latham Park 5 000	+44 1686 623120	newtonafc.co.uk	0	1	0
Porthmadog	Porthmadog	Y Traeth 4 000	+44 1766 514687	geocities.com/port_fc	0	0	0
Port Talbot Town	Port Talbot	Victoria Road 2 000	+44 1639 882465	porttalbotafc.co.uk	0	0	0
Rhyl	Rhyl	Belle View 3 000	+44 1745 338327	rhylfc.com	1	3	0
Welshpool Town	Welshpool	Maes-y-Dre 3 000	+44 1938 555140		0	0	0

RECENT LEAGUE AND CUP RECORD

Year	Champions	Pts	Runners-up	Pts	Third	Pts	Winners	Score	Runners-up
1993	Cwmbran Town	87	Inter Cardiff	83	Aberystwyth Town	78	Cardiff City	5-0	Rhyl
1994	Bangor City	83	Inter Cardiff	81	Ton Petre	71	Barry Town	2-1	Cardiff City
1995	Bangor City	88	Afan Lido	79	Ton Petre	77	Wrexham	2-1	Cardiff City
1996	Barry Town	97	Newtown	80	Conwy United	76	TNS Llansantffraid	3-3 3-2p	Barry Town
1997	Barry Town	105	Inter Cardiff	84	Ebbw Vale	78	Barry Town	2-1	Cwmbran Town
1998	Barry Town	104	Newtown	78	Ebbw Vale	77	Bangor City	1-1 4-2p	Nomads
1999	Barry Town	76	Inter Cardiff	63	Cwmbran Town	57	Inter Cardiff	1-1 4-2p	Carmarthen Town
2000	TNS Llansantffraid	76	Barry Town	74	Cwmbran Town	69	Bangor City	1-0	Cwmbran Town
2001	Barry Town	77	Cwmbran Town	74	Carmarthen Town	58	Barry Town	2-0	TNS Llansantffraid
2002	Barry Town	77	TNS Llansantffraid	70	Bangor City	69	Barry Town	4-1	Bangor City
2003	Barry Town	83	TNS Llansantffraid	80	Bangor City	71	Barry Town	2-2 4-3	Cwmbran Town
2004	Rhyl	77	TNS Llansantffraid	76	Haverfordwest Cty	62	Rhyl	1-0	TNS Llansantffraid
2005	TNS Llansantffraid	78	Rhyl	74	Bangor City	67	TNS Llansantffraid	1-0	Carmarthen Town

Welsh clubs playing in the English league system have been ineligible to take part in the Welsh Cup since 1995

WALES 2004-05

LEAGUE OF WALES

	Pl	W	D	L	F	A	Pts	Llans'fraid	Rhyl	Bangor	Hav'west	Caersws	Carmarthen	Cwmbran	Aberystwyth	Welshpool	Newtown	Porthmadog	Nomads	Port Talbot	Llanelli	Caernarfon	Airbus UK	Druids	Afan Lido
TNS Llansantffraid †	34	23	9	2	83	25	78		2-2	1-1	2-0	5-0	2-0	2-0	3-1	1-0	3-0	2-1	2-1	1-1	4-2	5-0	1-1	1-0	2-1
Rhyl ‡	34	23	5	6	70	31	74	1-2		2-3	0-0	3-0	3-1	0-0	1-0	2-2	3-0	3-1	4-2	1-0	2-0	5-1	2-0	3-2	3-1
Bangor City	34	20	7	7	73	44	67	1-0	2-1		1-1	1-0	0-1	0-3	4-2	4-2	2-3	0-2	2-0	3-2	6-0	2-0	5-0	2-0	1-0
Haverfordwest County	34	17	12	5	50	28	63	0-0	2-1	1-1		0-0	0-0	1-0	4-1	3-0	2-1	0-0	0-0	3-1	3-0	1-1	6-1	1-1	2-1
Caersws	34	19	5	10	67	39	62	0-0	1-4	2-2	1-0		1-2	5-2	4-1	2-1	2-0	0-1	1-2	2-2	2-0	3-1	3-0	7-0	4-1
Carmarthen Town ‡	34	17	10	7	60	34	61	0-1	0-3	3-3	4-2	1-1		1-1	4-1	1-1	3-2	2-1	2-2	2-0	5-1	1-3	0-1	1-1	1-1
Cwmbran Town	34	15	8	11	52	47	53	2-2	0-1	0-3	0-2	1-4	0-2		2-3	2-3	1-2	2-1	1-0	3-1	2-0	2-1	4-4	3-3	1-0
Aberystwyth Town	34	15	8	11	45	40	53	1-1	1-2	1-2	4-0	1-0	0-0	0-1		0-0	1-1	0-0	1-0	0-0	2-0	5-0	1-0	2-1	1-1
Welshpool Town	34	14	9	11	55	46	51	5-2	1-2	1-5	1-1	2-3	3-0	0-2	2-0		2-1	1-1	0-1	0-0	4-0	1-1	2-1	2-0	2-1
Newtown	34	13	7	14	49	55	46	0-3	0-1	3-0	0-2	0-1	3-2	1-1	2-0	1-1		1-1	2-1	3-2	4-0	3-3	0-0	2-0	
Porthmadog	34	11	12	11	38	39	45	1-2	0-3	3-0	0-2	0-1	3-2	1-1	2-0	1-1	0-2		0-0	1-0	1-1	2-0	3-3	0-0	2-0
Connah's Quay Nomads	34	9	9	16	48	58	36	0-7	1-1	3-4	2-2	2-1	1-2	1-2	0-2	1-1	0-3	3-1		0-2	1-3	1-2	1-2	4-0	4-2
Port Talbot Town	34	6	11	17	36	49	29	2-2	1-3	1-4	0-1	0-0	3-0	0-4	2-3	1-2	2-2	1-1	0-1		4-0	0-0	3-2	1-1	1-2
Llanelli	34	8	5	21	42	85	29	0-4	2-1	5-1	0-3	2-4	0-3	0-4	2-3	1-2	2-2	1-1	0-2	1-2		2-1	2-2	1-4	3-1
Caernarfon Town	34	7	7	20	29	72	28	0-7	1-4	2-1	0-2	0-1	0-5	1-1	0-2	1-3	1-2	3-1	1-1	3-1	1-4		0-3	2-0	0-0
Airbus UK	34	5	9	20	36	76	24	0-6	1-0	0-0	1-2	0-3	0-1	0-1	1-2	0-2	2-2	0-1	3-3	3-1	0-3	1-1		1-2	1-4
Newi Cefn Druids §	34	5	7	22	30	72	22	1-3	0-3	0-4	0-2	0-5	0-1	1-3	0-1	2-1	0-2	1-2	0-5	1-2	2-3	0-1	2-2		3-0
Afan Lido §	34	6	6	22	29	52	21	0-2	1-2	2-3	0-1	1-0	0-2	0-2	0-0	0-1	1-3	1-1	0-1	0-1	1-1	1-0	4-0	1-0	

14/08/2004 - 29/04/2005 • † Qualified for the UEFA Champions League • ‡ Qualified for the UEFA Cup • § Three points deducted

FAW PREMIER CUP 2004-05

Quarter-finals		Semi-finals		Final	
Swansea City	5				
Caernarfon Town *	0	Swansea City	1 4p		
Rhyl	1	TNS Llansantffraid *	1 2p		
TNS Llansantffraid *	2			Swansea City	2
Brangor City *	1			Wrexham	1
Cardiff City	0	Bangor City *	1		
Haverfordwest County *	1	Wrexham	2		
Wrexham	2	* Home team			

11-05-2005, Ref: Lawlor
Vetch Field, Swansea
Scorers - Pejic 68, Robinson 76 for Swansea; Ugarte 60 for Wrexham

WELSH CUP 2004-05

Eighth-finals		Quarter-finals		Semi-finals		Final	
TNS Llansantffraid *	2						
Bangor City	1	TNS Llansantffraid *	4				
Barry Town *	2	Afan Lido	1				
Afan Lido	5			TNS Llansantffraid †	3		
Bala Town	2			Rhyl	1		
Welshpool Town *	1	Bala Town	4				
Llangefni	0	Rhyl *	1				
Rhyl *	4					TNS Llansantffraid	1
Haverfordwest County	4					Carmarthen Town ‡	0
UWIC Inter Cardiff *	1	Haverfordwest County	2				
Caernarfon Town	2	Aberystwyth Town *	0				
Aberystwyth Town *	3			Haverfordwest County	0		
Caersws	4			Carmarthen Town §	1		
Halkyn *	0	Caersws *	0				
Cwmbran Town	0	Carmarthen Town	1	‡ Qualified for the UEFA Cup			
Carmarthen Town *	1	* Home team • † Played in Wrexham • § Played in Llanelli					

CUP FINAL

8-05-2005, Ref: Jones
Stebonheath Park, Llanelli

Scorer - Lawless 76 for TNS

YEM – YEMEN

NATIONAL TEAM RECORD
JULY 1ST 2002 TO JUNE 30TH 2005

PL	W	D	L	F	A	%
34	5	7	22	42	88	25

FIFA/COCA-COLA WORLD RANKING

1993	1994	1995	1996	1997	1998	1999	2000	2001	2002	2003	2004	High		Low	
91	103	123	139	128	146	158	160	135	145	132	124	**90**	08/93	**163**	07/00

2004-2005											
08/04	09/04	10/04	11/04	12/04	01/05	02/05	03/05	04/05	05/05	06/05	07/05
135	135	127	131	124	123	123	123	124	124	124	124

Very much minnows in the Middle East, Yemen still sprang a few surprises in 2004 in spite of losing 13 of 19 matches played. Victory over United Arab Emirates and draws with Korea DPR and Thailand didn't prevent Yemen from finishing bottom of their FIFA World Cup™ qualifying group, but did mark them out as a team with some potential and their FIFA/Coca-Cola World Ranking of 124 reflects their progress. Unfortunately, the national side was unable to make any great impact at their first Gulf Cup; a 1-1 draw with Bahrain was followed by defeats to Saudi Arabia and Kuwait sending the team home early. After such a busy year, any momentum has been

INTERNATIONAL HONOURS
None

lost as Yemen have not played a match in 2005. The Yemeni League was expanded to 14 teams in 2005 with Al Tilal Aden winning the title after losing their first three matches denying defending champions Al Sha'ab Ibb their third crown in as many years. They had previously been denied the double in 2004 when they lost the final of the Presidents Cup to Al Ahly San'a. There were high hopes for those U-20s players who had graduated from the U-17 side that reached the 2003 FIFA World Youth Championship finals. As expected the U-20s made the finals in Malaysia, but three defeats to Thailand, Korea Republic and Iraq meant it was a short visit.

THE FIFA BIG COUNT OF 2000

	Male	Female		Male	Female
Registered players	2 000	0	Referees	100	0
Non registered players	60 000	0	Officials	400	0
Youth players	2 000	0	Total involved	64 500	
Total players	64 000		Number of clubs	100	
Professional players	0	0	Number of teams	200	

Yemen Football Association (YFF)
Ouarter fo Sport - Al Jeraf, Behind the Stadium of Ali Mushen, PO Box 908, Sanaa-Yemen, Al Thawra City, Yemen
Tel +967 1 310923   Fax +967 1 310921
www.none
President: ABD AL AHMAR Sh. Hussein   General Secretary: SALEM Ahmed Mahdi
Vice-President: AL EASEE Ahmed Salah   Treasurer: AL SHAREEF Hussein   Media Officer: None
Men's Coach: AL RAEA Ahmad S.   Women's Coach: None
YFF formed: 1962   AFC: 1972   FIFA: 1980
Colours: Green, Green, Green

GAMES PLAYED BY YEMEN IN THE 2006 FIFA WORLD CUP™ CYCLE

2002	Opponents		Score	Venue	Comp	Scorers	Att	Referee
17-12	Syria	L	0-4	Kuwait City	ARr1		300	Al Saeedi UAE
21-12	Bahrain	L	1-3	Kuwait City	ARr1	Al Slimi [89]	1 000	Al Baltaji EGY
24-12	Lebanon	L	2-4	Kuwait City	ARr1	Al Qadimi [24], Ali Abboud [70]	1 000	Hamza KUW
26-12	Saudi Arabia	D	2-2	Kuwait City	ARr1			
2003								
17-09	Sudan	W	3-2	Sana'a	Fr	Al Minj [17], Ali Mubarak [54], Al Shihri [76]		
19-09	Sudan	L	1-2	Sana'a	Fr			
27-09	Syria	L	2-8	Jeddah	Fr			
6-10	Saudi Arabia	L	0-7	Jeddah	ACq			
8-10	Indonesia	L	0-3	Jeddah	ACq			
10-10	Bhutan	W	8-0	Jeddah	ACq	Al Qassayi 3 [20 25 82], Al Habishi [36], Al Shiri [60], Al Salmi 2 [67 88], Al Hijam [74]		
13-10	Saudi Arabia	L	1-3	Jeddah	ACq	Al Qassayi [12]		
15-10	Indonesia	D	2-2	Jeddah	ACq	Al Salmi [31p], Al Omqi [59]		
17-10	Bhutan	W	4-0	Jeddah	ACq	Al Hijam 2 [3 20], Al Omqi [33], Al Salmi [81]		
28-12	Oman	D	1-1	Kuwait City	GC	Fawzi Bashir [65]		Abdul Sadeq KUW
30-12	Bahrain	L	1-5	Kuwait City	GC	Al Salmi [14p]		Al Hamdan KSA
2004								
1-01	Kuwait	L	0-4	Kuwait City	GC			
5-01	Qatar	L	0-3	Kuwait City	GC			
8-01	Saudi Arabia	L	0-2	Kuwait City	GC			
11-01	United Arab Emirates	L	0-3	Kuwait City	GC			
18-02	Korea DPR	D	1-1	Sana'a	WCq	Al Selwi [73]	15 000	Husain BHR
17-03	Turkmenistan	L	1-2	Sana'a	Fr			
31-03	Thailand	L	0-3	Sana'a	WCq		25 000	Mansour LIB
9-06	United Arab Emirates	L	0-3	Al Ain	WCq		5 000	Sapaev TKM
26-08	Syria	L	1-2	Sana'a	Fr			
28-08	Syria	W	2-1	Sana'a	Fr			
8-09	United Arab Emirates	W	3-1	Sana'a	WCq	Al Nono 2 [22 77], Abduljabar [49]	17 000	Al Ghamdi KSA
13-10	Korea DPR	L	1-2	Pyongyang	WCq	Jaber [76]	15 000	Vo Minh Tri VIE
1-11	Zambia	D	2-2	Dubai	Fr	Al Nono [83], Al Qaar [90]		
17-11	Thailand	D	1-1	Bangkok	WCq	Al Shehri [69]	15 000	Baskar IND
3-12	Iraq	L	1-3	Dubai	Fr			
5-12	Qatar	L	0-3	Doha	Fr			
11-12	Bahrain	D	1-1	Doha	GCr1	Nasser Ghazi [47]		
14-12	Saudi Arabia	L	0-2	Doha	GCr1			
17-12	Kuwait	L	0-3	Doha	GCr1			
2005								

No international matches played in 2005 before August

Fr = Friendly match • GC = Gulf Cup • AC = AFC Asian Cup • AR = Arab Cup • WC = FIFA World Cup™ • q = qualifier • r1 = first round group

YEMEN COUNTRY INFORMATION

Capital	Sana'a	Unification	1990	GDP per Capita	$800
Population	20 024 867	Status	Republic	GNP Ranking	93
Area km²	527 970	Language	Arabic	Dialling code	+967
Population density	38 per km²	Literacy rate	50%	Internet code	.ye
% in urban areas	34%	Main religion	Muslim	GMT +/−	+3
Towns/Cities ('000)	Sana'a 1 937; Hudayda 617; Taizz 615; Aden 550; Mukalla 258; Ibb 234; Damar 158;				
Neighbours (km)	Oman 288; Saudi Arabia 1 458; Red Sea & Arabian Sea 1 906				
Main stadia	Ali Moshen – Sana'a 25 000				

YEMEN NATIONAL TEAM RECORDS AND RECORD SEQUENCES

Records			Sequence records					
Victory	11-2	BHU 2000	Wins	2	1989-1990	Clean sheets	4	1989-1990
Defeat	1-15	ALG 1973	Defeats	10	1965-1975	Goals scored	7	2001
Player Caps	n/a		Undefeated	5	2001	Without goal	5	1994-1996
Player Goals	n/a		Without win	12	1981-1989	Goals against	17	1976-1990

FIFA REFEREE LIST 2005

	Int'l	DoB
AL GUNAID Fouad	2001	25-12-1975
AL LABANY Khalaf	2001	13-07-1970
AL YARIMI Mukhtar	2001	2-12-1972

FIFA ASSISTANT REFEREE LIST 2005

	Int'l	DoB
ANAAM Ahmed Qiad	1998	25-06-1967
KURMA Hasson	2001	3-03-1973
SHUKRAN Hussain	2001	1-09-1969

YEMEN 2003-04

PREMIER LEAGUE

	Pl	W	D	L	F	A	Pts	Sha'ab Ibb	Ahly Sana'a	Tilal	Wahda	Hilal	May 22	Shabab	Saqr	Sha'ab Muk	Yarmuk	Hassan	Ahly Hu'da
Al Sha'ab Ibb	22	13	7	2	29	13	46		2-0	1-3	1-1	1-0	2-0	2-1	2-1	2-0	1-0	3-0	0-0
Al Ahly Sana'a	22	14	2	6	47	25	44	2-2		3-2	2-3	1-0	3-1	1-1	1-0	0-1	3-2	5-0	3-0
Al Tilal Aden	22	12	3	7	32	24	39	0-2	2-1		1-0	1-4	4-1	2-1	0-0	2-1	0-1	1-0	5-0
Al Wahda Sana'a	22	11	4	7	32	25	37	2-1	3-2	2-1		0-0	2-1	4-1	2-4	1-1	1-2	1-0	3-0
Al Hilal Hudayda	22	10	6	6	29	23	36	1-1	1-3	0-2	0-1		1-0	1-1	1-0	2-1	0-0	2-0	2-0
May 22 Sana'a	22	9	3	10	36	32	30	1-0	2-5	1-1	0-1	5-0		2-0	3-2	3-0	1-0	1-0	6-1
Shabab Al Baydaa	22	7	7	8	29	31	28	0-1	1-4	2-0	2-1	2-4	2-1		1-1	2-1	3-1	1-1	4-0
Al Saqr Taizz	22	5	9	8	28	26	24	0-1	1-0	1-2	1-1	1-1	2-2	1-1		1-1	1-2	0-0	4-1
Al Sha'ab Mukalla	22	6	6	10	18	26	24	1-1	0-2	0-1	1-0	3-3	0-1	1-0	1-0		2-1	1-0	1-1
Yarmuk Al Radwa Sana'a	22	6	4	12	23	32	22	1-1	0-1	2-0	1-2	0-2	1-2	1-1	2-2	1-0		3-4	1-0
Hassan Abyan	22	5	4	13	22	32	19	0-1	1-2	1-2	1-0	0-2	1-1	1-2	1-2	1-1	4-1		3-0
Al Ahly Hudayda	22	4	5	13	10	46	17	0-0	0-3	0-0	2-1	0-2	3-2	0-0	0-3	1-0	1-0	0-3	

5/12/2003 - 14/05/2004 • Yemen is reverting to the calender year season and the 2005 tournament started on 3/2/2005

PRESIDENTS CUP 2003-04

Quarter-finals		Semi-finals		Final	
Al Ahly Sana'a	6				
Shamsan	1	Al Ahly Sana'a	5		
Nassir Al Dalaa	1	Al Sha'ab Sana'a	0		
Al Sha'ab Sana'a	3			Al Ahly Sana'a	2
Al Ittihad Ibb	1 4p			Al Sha'ab Ibb	0
Al Sha'ab Mukalla	1 2p	Al Ittihad Ibb	0		
Yarmuk Al Radwa	0 2p	Al Sha'ab Ibb	2	23-07-2004, Al Murisi, Sana'a	
Al Sha'ab Ibb	0 4p			Scorers - Al Dabhani 68, Aziz 70 for Ahly	

RECENT LEAGUE AND CUP RECORD

	Championship						Cup		
Year	Champions	Pts	Runners-up	Pts	Third	Pts	Winners	Score	Runners-up
1997	Al Wahda Sana'a	42	Al Tilal Aden	39	Al Ahly Hudayda	37	Al Ahly Hudayda	1-0	Al Sha'ab Mukalla
1998	Al Wahda Sana'a	48	Al Ahly Sana'a	47	Al Shoala Aden	44	Al Ittihad Ibb	1-0	Al Shoala Aden
1999	Al Ahly Sana'a						No tournament		
2000	Al Ahly Sana'a	†	Al Tali'aa Taizz				Al Sha'ab Mukalla	0-0 5-4p	Al Shoala Aden
2001	Al Ahly Sana'a						Al Ahly Sana'a	2-1	Al Tilal Aden
2002	Al Wahda Sana'a	63	Al Ahly Sana'a	50	Al Hilal Hudayda	39	Al Sha'ab Ibb	4-0	Al Tadamun
2003	Al Sha'ab Ibb	46	Al Tilal Aden	43	Al Hilal Hudayda	36	Al Sha'ab Ibb	2-1	Al Sha'ab Mukalla
2004	Al Sha'ab Ibb	46	Al Ahly Sana'a	44	Al Tilal Aden	39	Al Ahly Sana'a	2-0	Al Sha'ab Ibb

† 1999 championship final: Al Ahly 1-2 5-1 Al Tali'aa

ZAM – ZAMBIA

NATIONAL TEAM RECORD
JULY 1ST 2002 TO JUNE 30TH 2005

PL	W	D	L	F	A	%
39	18	14	7	52	32	64.1

FIFA/COCA-COLA WORLD RANKING

1993	1994	1995	1996	1997	1998	1999	2000	2001	2002	2003	2004	High		Low	
27	21	25	20	21	29	36	49	64	67	68	70	15	02/96	80	05/04

					2004-2005						
08/04	09/04	10/04	11/04	12/04	01/05	02/05	03/05	04/05	05/05	06/05	07/05
69	72	67	65	70	71	71	72	70	68	73	62

Zambia's reputation as one of the top ranked footballing nations in Africa has come under threat in recent years but with the appointment of Kalusha Bwalya as national team coach in the wake of the failure to qualify for the 2004 African Cup of Nations there is once again a sense of optimism amongst the fans. Not since the qualifiers for the 1994 FIFA World Cup™ has the national team had such a good campaign with Kalusha even coming off the bench to score the odd vital goal at the ripe old age of 40. Along with Stephen Keshi in Togo and Zaki Badou in Morocco, Bwalya represents the new face of coaches in Africa - players who have competed at the highest level in

INTERNATIONAL HONOURS
CECAFA Cup 1984   COSAFA Castle Cup 1997 1998

Europe but who have returned to use that experience to the benefit of the national team and local football as a whole. The team still relies on the production line of talent that emerges from the Copperbelt but this once stronghold of club football is experiencing a decline in the wake of the privatisations that have swept through the industry and in the 2004 domestic season clubs from the capital Lusaka dominated the Championship with Red Arrows winning the title for the first time. Arrows lost in the final of the four-year-old Coca-Cola Cup against Lusaka based Zanaco while Lusaka Celtic completed a clean sweep for the capital by beating Kabwe in the Mosi Cup final.

THE FIFA BIG COUNT OF 2000

	Male	Female		Male	Female
Registered players	7 409	720	Referees	497	9
Non registered players	728 100	3 450	Officials	3 800	79
Youth players	3 173	450	Total involved	747 687	
Total players	743 302		Number of clubs	428	
Professional players	49	0	Number of teams	24 350	

Football Association of Zambia (FAZ)
Football House, Alick Nkhata Road, Long Acres, PO Box 34751, 34751 Lusaka, Zambia
Tel +260 1 250940   Fax +260 1 250946
faz@zamnet.zm   www.faz.co.zm
President: MULONGA Teddy   General Secretary: MUSONDA Brig Gen
Vice-President: BWALYA Kalusha   Treasurer: MWEEMBA Rix   Media Officer: MWANSA Mbulakulima
Men's Coach: BWALYA Kalusha   Women's Coach: KASHIMOTO Fredrick
FAZ formed: 1929   CAF: 1964   FIFA: 1964
Colours: Copper, Black, Copper

GAMES PLAYED BY ZAMBIA IN THE 2006 FIFA WORLD CUP™ CYCLE

2002	Opponents		Score	Venue	Comp	Scorers	Att	Referee
6-07	Mozambique	W	3-0	Lusaka	CCqf	Kilambe 2 10 57, Nsofwa 38		Ndoro ZIM
10-08	Malawi	L	0-1	Blantyre	CCsf		60 000	Phomane LES
31-08	Uganda	D	2-2	Kampala	Fr			
8-09	Sudan	W	1-0	Khartoum	CNq	Nsofwa 89		Dagnew ERI
28-09	Zimbabwe	D	0-0	Harare	Fr			
12-10	Benin	D	1-1	Lusaka	CNq	Kilambe 76	30 000	Mochubela ZIM
14-12	Botswana	L	0-1	Gaborone	Fr			
2003								
22-03	Rwanda	D	1-1	Kigali	Fr	Chilembe 42		
24-03	Rwanda	W	3-0	Kigali	Fr	Kombe, Phiri.M, Lungu		
29-03	Tanzania	W	1-0	Dar es Salaam	CNq	Lungu 25	23 000	Haislemelk ETH
17-05	Malawi	W	1-0	Blantyre	Fr	Mumbi 88		Lwanja MWI
7-06	Tanzania	W	2-0	Lusaka	CNq	Milanzi 2 44 71	30 000	Chilinda MWI
21-06	Sudan	D	1-1	Lusaka	CNq	Chalwe 72		Maxim KEN
6-07	Benin	L	0-3	Cotonou	CNq		40 000	Monteiro Duarte CPV
27-07	Mozambique	W	4-2	Lusaka	CCqf	Mwandila 2 51 80, Milanzi 84, Msesuma 89	10 000	Katjimune ZIM
16-08	Malawi	D	1-1	Blantyre	CCsf	Chalwe 89. L 2-4p	55 000	Mnkantjo ZIM
11-10	Seychelles	W	4-0	Victoria	WCq	Kampamba 8, Fichite 44, Milanzi 52, Numba 75	2 700	Lim Kee Chong MRI
15-11	Seychelles	D	1-1	Lusaka	WCq	Milanzi 7	30 000	Abdulkadir TAN
2004								
1-05	Zimbabwe	D	1-1	Lusaka	Fr	Chansa 79		
16-05	Zimbabwe	D	0-0	Harare	Fr			
22-05	Malawi	L	0-2	Kitwe	Fr		20 000	Nkole ZAM
25-05	Sudan	W	2-0	Khartoum	Fr	Numba 9, Chalwe 39		
5-06	Togo	W	1-0	Lusaka	WCq	Mulenga 11	40 000	Damon RSA
19-06	Mali	D	1-1	Bamako	WCq	Milanzi 25	19 000	Sowe GAM
3-07	Senegal	L	0-1	Dakar	WCq		50 000	Monteiro Duarte CPV
31-07	Mauritius	W	3-1	Lusaka	CCqf	Mulenga 11, Numba 55, Bwalya.K 68		Manuel ZIM
28-08	Rwanda	W	2-1	Kitwe	Fr	Kaposa 8, Mwamdila 38	15 000	Mwanza ZAM
4-09	Liberia	W	1-0	Lusaka	WCq	Bwalya.K 91+	30 000	Nchengwa BOT
30-09	Botswana	L	0-1	Gaborone	Fr			Chidoda BOT
10-10	Congo	W	3-2	Brazzaville	WCq	Mbesuma 3 2 37 65	20 000	Yacoubi TUN
24-10	Zimbabwe	D	0-0	Harare	CCsf	W 5-4p	25 000	Simisse MRI
1-11	Yemen	D	2-2	Dubai	Fr	Mwale 32, Nsofwa 58		
20-11	Angola	D	0-0	Lusaka	CCf	L 4-5p		Lwanja MWI
2005								
26-02	Botswana	D	0-0	Gaborone	Fr			
26-03	Congo	W	2-0	Chililabombwe	WCq	Tana 1, Mbesuma 44	20 000	Maillet SEY
5-06	Togo	L	1-4	Lome	WCq	Kampamba 15	15 000	Guezzaz MAR
11-06	Swaziland	W	3-0	Lusaka	CCr1	Mbesuma 2 44 46, Kalaba 56		Chidoda BOT
12-06	Malawi	W	2-1	Lusaka	CCr1	Mbesuma 2 79 85		Nhlapo RSA
18-06	Mali	W	2-1	Chililabombwe	WCq	Chalwe 26, Mbesuma 85	29 000	Colembi ANG

Fr = Friendly match • CC = COSAFA Castle Cup • CN = CAF African Cup of Nations • WC = FIFA World Cup™ • q = qualifier

ZAMBIA COUNTRY INFORMATION

Capital	Lusaka	Independence	1964 from the UK	GDP per Capita	$800
Population	10 462 436	Status	Republic	GNP Ranking	128
Area km²	752 614	Language	English, Bemba, Kaonda	Dialling code	+260
Population density	14 per km²	Literacy rate	80%	Internet code	.zm
% in urban areas	43%	Main religion	Christian 63%	GMT +/-	+2
Towns/Cities ('000)	Lusaka 1 267; Kitwe 400; Ndola 394; Kabwe 189; Chingola 148; Mufulira 120; Luanshya 113				
Neighbours (km)	Tanzania 338; Malawi 837; Mozambique 419; Zimbabwe 797; Namibia 233; Angola 1 110; Congo DR 1 930				
Main stadia	Independence Stadium – Lusaka 30 000; Dola Hill – Ndola 23 000; Nchanga – Chingola 20 000				

ZAMBIA NATIONAL TEAM RECORDS AND RECORD SEQUENCES

Records			Sequence records					
Victory	9-0	KEN 1978	Wins	8	1964-1966	Clean sheets	7	1997-1998, 2000
Defeat	1-10	COD 1969	Defeats	4	Four times	Goals scored	19	1966-1971
Player Caps	n/a		Undefeated	11	Three times	Without goal	4	2001
Player Goals	n/a		Without win	11	1999-2000	Goals against	10	1966-1968

ZAMBIA 2004

PREMIER LEAGUE

Team	Pl	W	D	L	F	A	Pts	Red Arrows	Buffaloes	Zanaco	N. Assembly	Warriors	ZESCO	Dynamos	Kitwe	Y. Arrows	Nchanga	Nkwazi	Chambishi	Blades	Nkana	Forest Ran.	Celtic
Red Arrows †	30	19	5	6	43	18	62		2-1	2-0	2-0	0-2	2-0	0-1	2-2	2-1	1-0	2-1	0-0	2-0	0-0	2-0	0-1
Green Buffaloes ‡	30	16	7	7	48	31	55	1-2		2-2	1-2	1-2	0-0	2-1	0-0	2-0	3-2	2-1	3-0	1-1	0-0	1-0	4-3
Zanaco	30	15	8	7	41	24	53	3-1	0-1		1-0	1-2	1-0	1-2	1-0	0-0	0-0	3-2	3-1	2-0	1-0	**3-0**	6-1
National Assembly	30	16	5	9	33	23	53	0-3	3-1	0-0		2-2	2-0	1-0	0-1	1-0	1-2	0-1	1-0	1-1	2-1	0-0	2-0
Kabwe Warriors	30	13	10	7	31	26	49	0-3	3-1	0-0	2-2		2-1	0-0	0-0	0-3	1-0	3-0	0-0	2-0	0-1	1-0	2-0
ZESCO United	30	13	8	9	34	24	47	1-0	2-3	1-1	2-0	5-2		1-0	0-0	0-1	3-0	3-1	2-2	2-1	1-0	1-0	1-0
Power Dynamos	30	11	12	7	32	27	45	1-2	1-1	1-2	2-1	1-1	0-0		1-1	1-0	1-1	4-3	0-2	0-0	0-1	1-0	1-0
Kitwe United	30	10	13	7	26	16	43	0-2	0-1	1-0	1-1	0-0	0-2	2-0		0-1	0-0	0-0	**3-0**	2-0	1-0	1-1	1-0
Young Arrows	30	10	10	10	25	23	40	0-0	1-2	1-1	1-0	1-1	1-2	0-0	0-3		1-1	0-0	2-0	1-1	0-1	**3-0**	0-0
Nchanga Rangers	30	9	11	10	25	25	38	0-2	1-1	2-0	0-1	2-1	0-1	0-0	1-1	0-1		0-2	1-1	0-0	1-0	2-0	2-0
Nkwazi	30	10	8	12	27	32	38	0-0	1-3	0-1	0-1	0-0	1-0	3-1	1-1	1-0	0-0		1-1	0-2	0-0	3-1	2-0
Chambishi §	30	8	9	13	24	36	30	0-2	0-4	0-1	1-1	0-1	2-1	1-2	0-1	2-0	1-1	3-0		1-0	1-0	1-0	1-0
Konkola Blades	30	6	7	17	20	38	25	1-4	2-1	0-0	0-2	0-1	1-1	0-1	1-0	0-2	1-3	0-1	2-0		3-1	0-0	2-1
Nkana	30	5	9	16	9	25	24	0-1	0-2	0-1	0-1	1-0	0-0	1-3	0-2	0-1	0-2	2-2	0-0	0-1		0-0	1-0
Forest Rangers §	30	6	9	15	16	33	24	1-0	0-1	1-1	1-2	0-0	1-1	0-0	2-1	1-2	0-1	1-0	2-1	0-1	1-0		0-1
Lusaka Celtic	30	5	5	20	15	48	20	1-4	0-2	1-4	0-3	1-2	1-1	0-3	0-3	0-0	1-0	0-1	1-0	1-0	1-0	1-1	

25/04/2004 - 1/12/2004 • † Qualified for the CAF Champions League • ‡ Qualified for the CAF Confederation Cup • Matches in bold awarded 3-0
§ Three points deducted

MOSI CUP 2004

Eighth-finals		Quarter-finals		Semi-finals		Final	
Lusaka Celtic	2						
National Assembly *	1	Lusaka Celtic *	0 4p				
Prison Leopards	0	Green Bullets	0 2p				
Green Bullets *	1			Lusaka Celtic †	2 4p		
INDENI	0 5p			Power Dynamos	2 3p		
Kitwe United *	0 4p	INDENI	1				
Green Buffaloes *	1	Power Dynamos *	6				
Power Dynamos	3					Lusaka Celtic	2
Red Arrows *	2					Kabwe Warriors	1
Chilanga Heroes	0	Red Arrows	2				
Lusaka City Council	0	Mufulira Wanderers *	1				
Mufulira Wanderers *	2			Red Arrows	0		
Roan United *	0 4p			Kabwe Warriors ‡	1		
Nchanga Rangers	0 2p	Roan United *	0 8p				
Riflemen	0	Kabwe Warriors	0 9p				
Kabwe Warriors *	4						

* Home team • † played at Nkoloma, Lusaka • ‡ Played at Sunset, Lusaka

CUP FINAL
4-12-2004
Independence Stadium, Lusaka
Scorers - Chikomo [22], Lungu [53] for Celtic; Mangumu [6p] for Kabwe

RECENT LEAGUE AND CUP RECORD

Championship						Cup		
Year	Champions	Pts	Runners-up	Pts	Third	Pts	Winners	Score	Runners-up
1997	Power Dynamos	66	Nkana	64	Nchanga Rangers	56	Power Dynamos	1-0	City of Lusaka
1998	Nchanga Rangers	56	Kabwe Warriors	49	Nkana	48	Konkola Blades	2-1	Zanaco
1999	Nkana	57	Zamsure	55	Nchanga Rangers	54	Zamsure		Power Dynamos
2000	Power Dynamos	56	Nkana	52	Zanaco	50	Nkana	0-0 7-6p	Green Buffaloes
2001	Nkana	60	Zanaco	57	Kabwe Warriors	55	Power Dynamos	1-0	Kabwe Warriors
2002	Zanaco	61	Power Dynamos	60	Green Buffaloes	60	Zanaco	2-2 3-2p	Power Dynamos
2003	Zanaco	69	Green Buffaloes	59	Kabwe Warriors	57	Power Dynamos	1-0	Kabwe Warriors
2004	Red Arrows	62	Green Buffaloes	55	Zanaco	53	Lusaka Celtic	2-1	Kabwe Warriors

ZIM – ZIMBABWE

NATIONAL TEAM RECORD
JULY 1ST 2002 TO JUNE 30TH 2005

PL	W	D	L	F	A	%
45	22	13	10	70	42	63.3

FIFA/COCA-COLA WORLD RANKING

1993	1994	1995	1996	1997	1998	1999	2000	2001	2002	2003	2004	High	Low
46	51	59	71	74	74	67	68	68	57	53	60	**40** 04/95	**92** 03/98

2004-2005											
08/04	09/04	10/04	11/04	12/04	01/05	02/05	03/05	04/05	05/05	06/05	07/05
47	44	51	59	60	60	60	63	62	57	53	53

There was only one team in Zimbabwe in 2004 as CAPS United from Harare swept all before them, winning both League and Cup in some style. CAPS won their first 10 games in the league and extended their unbeaten run to 16 before losing 4-3 to Highlanders in Harare. It was the only game they lost all season although two weeks previously the two had played each other in another entertaining match that had to be abandoned due to crowd trouble when CAPS scrambled a last-minute penalty equaliser in a 3-3 draw. In the final table CAPS finished 15 points ahead of Highlanders and they then wrapped up the double with a 1-0 victory over Wankie in the ZIFA Unity

INTERNATIONAL HONOURS
CECAFA Cup 1985 COSAFA Castle Cup 2000 2003

Cup final. Earlier in the season they had won the inaugural and lucrative Buddie Challenge Cup to win all three major tournaments in the season. The national team continues to flourish and on the back of their 2003 triumph in the COSAFA Castle Cup and their first appearance at the finals of the African Cup of Nations in Tunisia in 2004, the Warriors had a very good campaign in the 2006 FIFA World Cup™ qualifiers. In a difficult group containing strong favourites Nigeria, Charles Mhlauri's team retained the hope of qualification going into the final stages although a place in the finals of the 2006 Cup of Nations in Egypt would be an achievement in its own right.

THE FIFA BIG COUNT OF 2000

	Male	Female		Male	Female
Registered players	25 548	490	Referees	703	11
Non registered players	42 000	600	Officials	2 015	51
Youth players	5 374	0	Total involved	76 792	
Total players	74 012		Number of clubs	27	
Professional players	68	0	Number of teams	1 134	

Zimbabwe Football Association (ZIFA)
Causeway, PO Box CY 114, Harare, Zimbabwe
Tel +263 4 721026   Fax +263 4 721045
zifa@africaonline.co.zw   www.zimbabwesoccer.com
President: KHAN Rafiq   General Secretary: MASHINGAIDZE Jonathan
Vice-President: MPOFU Wyatt   Treasurer: DUBE Cuthbert   Media Officer: None
Men's Coach: MHLAURI Charles   Women's Coach: KAGOGODA Bendick
ZIFA formed: 1965   CAF: 1965   FIFA: 1965
Colours: Green, Yellow, Green

GAMES PLAYED BY ZIMBABWE IN THE 2006 FIFA WORLD CUP™ CYCLE

2002	Opponents	Score		Venue	Comp	Scorers	Att	Referee
7-07	Malawi	L	2-3	Blantyre	Fr	Chandida [57], Matola [63]	35 000	Kafatiya MWI
8-07	Malawi	D	2-2	Lilongwe	Fr	Mguni 2 [25 63]	20 000	
30-08	Lesotho	W	2-0	Harare	Fr	Johnson 2 [22 87]		
8-09	Mali	W	1-0	Harare	CNq	Muhoni [32]	50 000	Mochubela RSA
28-09	Zambia	D	0-0	Harare	Fr			
12-10	Eritrea	W	1-0	Asmara	CNq	Ndlovu [10]	10 000	Rirache DJI
2003								
16-03	Malawi	D	0-0	Harare	Fr		10 000	Bwanya ZIM
30-03	Seychelles	W	3-1	Harare	CNq	Ndlovu.P 2 [20p 90p], Ndlovu.A [89]	60 000	Bernardo Colembi ANG
20-04	Angola	W	1-0	Harare	CCr1	Ndlovu.A [20]	20 000	Nkuna ZAM
7-06	Seychelles	L	1-2	Victoria	CNq	Charles [80]	12 000	Mangaliso SWZ
22-06	Mali	D	0-0	Bamako	CNq			
5-07	Eritrea	W	2-0	Harare	CNq	Ndlovu.P 2 [11 17p]		
19-07	South Africa	W	1-0	East London	CCqf	Muhoni [15]	7 000	Raolimanana MAD
31-08	Swaziland	W	2-0	Harare	CCsf	Ndlovu.P 2 [3 53]	25 000	De Sousa ANG
27-09	Malawi	W	2-1	Blantyre	CCf	Mbano 2 [7 57]	60 000	Bennett RSA
5-10	Malawi	W	2-0	Harare	CCf	Yohane [36], Ndlovu [66]	15 000	Nkole ZAM
12-10	Mauritania	W	3-0	Harare	WCq	Ndlovu.A [23], Tembo [47], Ndlovu.P [57]	55 000	Damon RSA
23-10	Burkina Faso	W	4-1	Hyderabad	AAr1	Nyoni 2 [3 74], Mbano 2 [26 82]		
27-10	Uzbekistan	D	1-1	Hyderabad	AAr1	Tsipa [12]		
29-10	India	L	3-5	Hyderabad	AAsf	Mbano [4], Mashiri [81], Chipunza [87]		Mohd Salleh MAS
31-10	Rwanda	D	2-2	Hyderabad	AA3p	Nyoni [65], Mbano [90]. W 5-3p		
14-11	Mauritania	L	1-2	Nouakchott	WCq	Mbwando [81]	3 000	Keita GUI
13-12	Botswana	W	2-0	Selibe-Phikwe	Fr	Chandida [30], Sandaka [80]	7 000	
2004								
25-01	Egypt	L	1-2	Sfax	CNr1	Ndlovu.P [46]	22 000	Pare BFA
29-01	Cameroon	L	3-5	Sfax	CNr1	Ndlovu.P 2 [8 47p], Nyandoro [89]	15 000	Aboubacar CIV
3-02	Algeria	W	2-1	Sousse	CNr1	Luphahala 2 [65 71]	10 000	Maillet SEY
1-05	Zambia	D	1-1	Lusaka	Fr	Ndlovu.B [89]		
16-05	Zambia	D	0-0	Harare	Fr			
24-05	Egypt	L	0-2	Cairo	Fr		10 000	
5-06	Gabon	D	1-1	Libreville	WCq	Kaondera [82]	25 000	Quartey GHA
20-06	Algeria	D	1-1	Harare	WCq	Raho OG [60]	65 000	Ntambidila COD
27-06	Swaziland	W	5-0	Mbabane	CCqf	Kasinuayo [7], Ndlovu.P 3 [41 58 81], OG [54]. Abandoned 83'		Infante MOZ
3-07	Rwanda	W	2-0	Kigali	WCq	Ndlovu.P [41], Nengomasha [79]		Chilinda MWI
18-08	Botswana	W	2-0	Bulawayo	Fr	Ncube [67], Sibanda [87]	5 000	
22-08	Uganda	W	2-0	Harare	Fr	Moyo [28], Ncube [81]	3 000	
5-09	Nigeria	L	0-3	Harare	WCq		60 000	Mandzioukouta COD
10-10	Angola	L	0-1	Luanda	WCq		17 000	Lwanja MWI
24-10	Zambia	D	0-0	Harare	CCsf	L 4-5p	25 000	Simisse MRI
2005								
27-02	Malawi	L	1-2	Blantyre	Fr	Tsipa [54]		
16-03	Botswana	D	1-1	Harare	Fr	Chimedza [53]	3 000	
27-03	Angola	W	2-0	Harare	WCq	Kaondera [60], Mwaruwari [69]		Codjia BEN
16-04	Mozambique	W	3-0	Windhoek	CCr1	Chimedza 2 [66p 78], Sandaka [82]		Mufeti NAM
17-04	Botswana	W	2-0	Windhoek	CCr1	Badza [21], Sandaka [58]		Braga Mavunza ANG
5-06	Gabon	W	1-0	Harare	WCq	Ndlovu.P [52]	55 000	Ssegonga UGA
19-06	Algeria	D	2-2	Oran	WCq	Kaondera [33], Ndlovu.P [87]	15 000	Pare BFA

Fr = Friendly match • CN = CAF African Cup of Nations • CC = COSAFA Castle Cup • AA = Afro-Asian Games • WC = FIFA World Cup™
q = qualifier • r1 = first round group • qf = quarter-final • sf = semi-final • 3p = third place play-off • f = final

ZIMBABWE COUNTRY INFORMATION

Capital	Harare	Independence	1980	GDP per Capita	$1 900
Population	12 671 860	Status	Republic	GNP Ranking	104
Area km²	390 580	Language	English, Shona, Sindebele	Dialling code	+263
Population density	32 per km²	Literacy rate	90%	Internet code	.zw
% in urban areas	32%	Main religion	Christian	GMT +/−	+2
Towns/Cities ('000)	Harare 2 213; Bulawayo 897; Chitungwiza 456; Mutare 253; Gweru 201; Kwekwe 116; Kadoma 100				
Neighbours (km)	Mozambique 1 231; South Africa 225; Botswana 813; Zambia 797				
Main stadia	National Sports Stadium – Harare 60 000; Barbourfields – Bulawayo 25 000				

ZIMBABWE NATIONAL TEAM RECORDS AND RECORD SEQUENCES

Records			Sequence records					
Victory	7-0	BOT 1990	Wins	6	2003	Clean sheets	5	2002-2003
Defeat	0-5	CIV 1989, COD 1995	Defeats	5	1997-1998	Goals scored	12	2003-2004
Player Caps	n/a		Undefeated	13	1981-1982	Without goal	4	1988
Player Goals	n/a		Without win	9	1995-96, 1997-98	Goals against	11	1995-1996

ZIMBABWE 2004

NATIONAL PREMIER SOCCER LEAGUE

	Pl	W	D	L	F	A	Pts	CAPS Utd	Highlanders	Shabanie	AmaZulu	Motor Action	Dynamos	Rhinos	Masvingo	Wankie	Railstars	L'shire Steel	Eiffel Flats	Sundowns	Kwekwe	Lions	Saints
CAPS United †	30	25	4	1	71	19	79		3-4	3-0	4-1	2-1	1-0	3-1	5-0	5-1	2-1	3-0	1-0	1-0	0-0	2-0	1-0
Highlanders	30	19	7	4	46	21	64	3-3		2-0	0-1	3-2	2-1	0-0	0-0	1-0	2-1	1-1	3-0	2-1	5-1	3-1	2-0
Shabanie Mine	30	15	6	9	53	38	51	0-1	0-2		4-1	1-2	1-1	4-4	0-0	2-1	4-3	1-0	4-2	1-5	1-2	2-0	3-1
AmaZulu	30	14	5	11	52	47	47	1-4	0-2	1-1		1-1	1-1	1-0	0-2	3-2	3-1	0-1	3-0	2-1	1-0	6-1	2-1	4-1
Motor Action	30	12	9	9	41	28	45	1-1	0-0	1-0	2-0		0-1	1-2	1-1	3-0	1-0	2-0	1-0	1-0	0-1	2-2	3-0
Dynamos	30	10	13	7	40	29	43	1-2	0-1	1-1	3-1	1-1		0-0	2-0	0-0	2-2	0-0	1-1	2-0	1-1	3-0	2-4
Black Rhinos	30	11	9	10	43	41	42	0-2	1-0	0-1	2-0	2-5	1-0		1-1	3-1	1-2	1-1	2-0	1-0	4-0	2-0	1-1
Masvingo United	30	10	9	11	40	37	39	1-2	1-2	1-3	1-2	2-0	3-3	2-2		2-0	2-1	2-1	3-0	1-0	6-1	2-0	0-0
Wankie	30	10	9	11	34	42	39	0-4	1-0	1-0	2-2	2-1	0-0	0-0	2-0		1-1	1-1	1-1	2-0	1-0	2-1	3-1
Railstars	30	10	8	12	44	44	38	0-1	0-1	0-4	4-1	1-1	2-0	4-2	0-0	1-2		4-2	0-0	1-1	3-2	0-0	2-1
Lancashire Steel	30	9	11	10	37	38	38	0-0	0-0	1-1	3-3	0-1	1-1	2-1	1-0	2-2	2-0		4-0	4-2	1-2	4-1	1-1
Eiffel Flats	30	10	6	14	29	39	36	0-1	1-0	0-2	1-2	0-0	1-2	0-0	0-0	1-0	2-1	2-0		3-0	1-3	1-1	2-1
Njube Sundowns	30	11	2	17	40	42	35	1-2	0-1	0-3	2-1	2-2	2-3	3-1	1-0	3-2	4-0	2-0	2-0		1-2	2-1	0-2
Kwekwe Cables	30	10	5	15	31	60	35	1-5	1-1	0-2	0-3	0-2	0-3	3-2	1-3	1-0	0-0	2-1	0-3	1-0		0-2	1-1
Sporting Lions	30	5	4	21	26	56	19	0-2	0-1	0-2	0-1	0-2	0-3	1-2	3-2	2-4	2-4	0-1	3-1	1-3	1-0		2-0
Zimbabwe Saints	30	2	7	21	24	70	13	1-5	1-2	2-5	0-5	0-3	0-2	2-2	0-2	1-1	1-5	0-1	0-2	0-3	1-4	1-1	

6/03/2004 - 15/12/2004 • † Qualified for the CAF Champions League • Matches in bold awarded 2-0 • Sporting Lions withdrew from the League with four games to play

ZIFA UNITY CUP 2004

Eighth-finals		Quarter-finals		Semi-finals		Final	
CAPS United	6						
Buffaloes	0	CAPS United	3				
Lancashire Steel		Eiffel Flats	1				
Eiffel Flats				CAPS United	1 4p		
CTC Stars				Motor Action	1 3p		
Sporting Lions		CTC Stars	1				
Dynamos	1	Motor Action	3				
Motor Action	5					CAPS United	1
AmaZulu	2					Wankie ‡	0
Zimbabwe Saints	0	AmaZulu	4				
Railstars	1	Shabanie Mine	0				
Shabanie Mine	4			AmaZulu	2		
Njube Sundowns	2			Wankie	4		
Highlanders	1	Njube Sundowns	1 1p				
Masvingo United	1	Wankie	1 3p				
Wankie	2	‡ Qualified for the Confederation Cup					

CUP FINAL

22-12-2004, Att: 10 000
National Sports Stadium, Harare

Scorer - Undi [70] for CAPS United

RECENT LEAGUE AND CUP RECORD

	Championship						Cup		
Year	Champions	Pts	Runners-up	Pts	Third	Pts	Winners	Score	Runners-up
1997	Dynamos	68	CAPS United	57	Black Aces	50	CAPS United	3-2	Dynamos
1998	No championship due to calender reorganisation						CAPS United		
1999	Highlanders	72	Dynamos	71	Zimbabwe Saints	54			
2000	Highlanders	78	AmaZulu	76	Dynamos	66	No tournament		
2001	Highlanders	62	AmaZulu	59	Shabanie Mine	51	Highlanders	4-1	Shabanie Mine
2002	Highlanders	72	Black Rhinos	52	AmaZulu	50	Masvingo United	2-2 4-3p	Railstars
2003	AmaZulu	51	Highlanders	50	Dynamos	48	Dynamos	2-0	Highlanders
2004	CAPS United	79	Highlanders	64	Shabanie Mine	51	CAPS United	1-0	Wankie

PART THREE

THE
CONFEDERATIONS

AFC

ASIAN FOOTBALL CONFEDERATION

Celebrating its 50th anniversary, the third biggest Confederation may be about to get bigger if East Timor and Australia are given the go-ahead from FIFA to join. The Socceroos' case has been controversial given that they will leave behind a weaker Oceania Football Confederation with its long-term future in question. AFC President Mohamed Bin Hammam has courted the Australians and believes that their presence will not only benefit the image of the confederation but also improve standards. Away from the politics, following on from the AFC Asian Cup triumph by Japan in China PR in early August 2004, the Chinese made some amends by winning the AFC U-17 Championship in Japan the next month. China PR then made a hat-trick of final appearances in AFC events but missed out on a youth 'double' to South Korea in the AFC Youth Cup in Malaysia. The focus for the senior national teams in 2004-05 was the 2006 FIFA World Cup™ qualifying campaign which saw the expected quartet of Iran, Japan, Korea Republic and Saudi Arabia all

THE FIFA BIG COUNT OF 2000 FOR THE AFC

	Male	Female		Male	Female
Registered players	963 054	26 771	Referees	127 289	294
Non registered players	31 932 830	125 355	Officials	506 876	81 735
Youth players	1 278 492	25 867	Total involved	99 836 726	6 180 338
Children & Occasional	65 020 000	5 920 000	in football	106 008 563	
Professionals	8 185	316	Number of clubs	29 095	
Total players	105 300 870		Number of teams	134 876	

make it to Germany. At club level the AFC Champions League final witnessed a spectacular come-back by Saudi Arabia's Al Ittihad against Seongnam Ilhwa Chunma of South Korea. After being 3-1 down from the first leg at home in Jeddah, they travelled to Korea with little hope but won 5-0 to become Asian Champions for the first time. 2004 also saw the first edition of the AFC Cup for nations ranked in the second tier of club football, which was won by Syria's Al Jaish. On the domestic front, China PR were once again in the news. Their failure to qualify for the 2006 FIFA World Cup™ was compounded by a number of problems in the inaugural Super League, including unpaid wages to players of champions Shenzhen Jianlibao. In Japan on the other hand, the momentum since the 2002 FIFA World Cup™ has been maintained. The J.League moved into its 13th year with a new single league format, rising attendances, an expanded line-up of 18 clubs and looking at its most competitive.

Asian Football Confederation (AFC)

AFC House, Jalan 1/155B, Bukit Jalil, 57000 Kuala Lumpur, Malaysia
Tel +60 3 89943388   Fax +60 3 89946168
media@the-afc.com   www.the-afc.com
President: BIN HAMMAM Mohamed QAT   General Secretary: VELAPPAN Peter Dato' MAS
AFC Formed: 1954

AFC EXECUTIVE COMMITTEE

President: BIN HAMMAM Mohamed QAT	Vice-President: TAQI Asad KUW	Vice-President: ZHANG Jilong CHN
Vice-President: FERNANDO V. Manilal SRI	Vice-President: TENGKU Abdullah Ibni Ahmad Shah	Hon Treasurer: BOUZO Farouk, Gen SYR
FIFA Vice-President: CHUNG Mong Joon, Dr KOR	FIFA Executive Member: MAKUDI Worawi	FIFA Executive Member: OGURA Junji

MEMBERS OF THE EXECUTIVE COMMITTEE

DAS MUNSHI Priya Ranjan IND	NOOMOOZ Naser Gen IRN	HUSSAIN Mohammed Saeed IRQ
TAHIR Dali IDN	THAPA Ganesh NEP	AL DAHAB Mohamed, Dr OMA
ADAD Rene PHI	RAHIMOV Bahtier UZB	AL DABAL Abdullah Khaled KSA
General Secretary: VELAPPAN Peter Dato' MAS		Legal Advisor: GANESAN N. SIN

ASIAN TOURNAMENTS

AFC ASIAN CUP

Year	Host Country	Winners	Score	Runners-up	Venue
1956	Hong Kong	Korea Republic	2-1	Israel	Government Stadium, Hong Kong
1960	Korea Republic	Korea Republic	3-0	Israel	Hyochang Park, Seoul
1964	Israel	Israel	2-0	India	Bloomfield, Jaffa
1968	Iran	Iran	3-1	Burma	Amjadieh, Tehran
1972	Thailand	Iran	2-1	Korea Republic	Suphachalasai, Bangkok
1976	Iran	Iran	1-0	Kuwait	Azadi, Tehran
1980	Kuwait	Kuwait	3-0	Korea Republic	Kuwait City
1984	Singapore	Saudi Arabia	2-0	China PR	National Stadium, Singapore
1988	Qatar	Saudi Arabia	0-0 4-3p	Korea Republic	Khalifa, Doha
1992	Japan	Japan	1-0	Saudi Arabia	Main Stadium, Hiroshima
1996	UAE	Saudi Arabia	0-0 4-2p	United Arab Emirates	Zayed, Abu Dhabi
2000	Lebanon	Japan	1-0	Saudi Arabia	Camille Chamoun, Beirut
2004	China PR	Japan	3-1	China PR	Workers' Stadium, Beijing

From 1956 to 1968 the tournament was played as a league. The result listed is that between the winners and runners-up

The four major powers in Asia – Iran, Japan, Korea Republic and Saudia Arabia – have shared all bar two of the titles in Asia's premier competition for national teams, although of the six editions played since 1984, Japan and Saudi have been crowned Asian champions three times each. The most surprising aspect has been the failure of Korea Republic, despite qualifying for every FIFA World Cup™ since 1986, to add another title to the two won in 1956 and 1960. From the late 1960s to the late 1970s Iran were the undisputed kings of the continent winning every game they played and a hat-trick of titles. Kuwait became the first Arab nation to win the tournament, in 1980, but since then it has been all Japan and Saudi Arabia. The lack of any real success on the part of China PR is another surprising feature and in 2004 they became only the second nation to lose a final on home soil, eight years after the United Arab Emirates had done so. Traditionally held every four years, the next tournament, to be co-hosted by Indonesia, Malaysia, Thailand and Vietnam, will be held after a break of three years to avoid clashing with other continental championships.

AFC WOMEN'S CHAMPIONSHIP

Year	Host Country	Winners	Score	Runners-up	Venue
1975	Hong Kong	New Zealand	3-1	Thailand	Hong Kong
1977	Chinese Tapei	Chinese Taipei	3-1	Thailand	Taipei
1979	India	Chinese Taipei	2-0	India	Calicut
1981	Hong Kong	Chinese Taipei	5-0	Thailand	Hong Kong
1983	Thailand	Thailand	3-0	India	Bangkok
1986	Hong Kong	China PR	2-0	Japan	Hong Kong
1989	Hong Kong	China PR	1-0	Chinese Taipei	Hong Kong
1991	Japan	China PR	5-0	Japan	Fukuoka
1993	Malaysia	China PR	3-0	Korea DPR	Sarawak
1995	Malaysia	China PR	2-0	Japan	Sabah
1997	China PR	China PR	2-0	Korea DPR	Guangdong
1999	Philippines	China PR	3-0	Chinese Taipei	Bacalod
2001	Chinese Taipei	Korea DPR	2-0	Japan	Taipei
2003	Thailand	Korea DPR	2-1	China PR	Bangkok

The AFC Women's Championship is the longest running of all the continental championships for women though not surprisingly it has been dominated by East Asia with the countries of the Middle East having failed to enter a single tournament. Played every other year, China PR has emerged as the most successful nation with seven consecutive titles though they were recently knocked off their perch by the North Koreans, winners of the past two events. Japan have made it to four finals but have yet to win the trophy.

FOOTBALL TOURNAMENT OF THE ASIAN GAMES

Year	Host Country	Winners	Score	Runners-up	Venue
1951	India	India	1-0	Iran	New Delhi
1954	Philippines	Chinese Taipei	5-2	Korea Republic	Manilla
1958	Japan	Chinese Taipei	3-2	Korea Republic	Tokyo
1962	Indonesia	India	2-1	Korea Republic	Djakarta
1966	Thailand	Burma	1-0	Iran	Bangkok
1970	Thailand	Burma	0-0 †	Korea Republic	Bangkok
1974	Iran	Iran	1-0	Israel	Tehran
1978	Thailand	Korea Republic	0-0 †	Korea DPR	Bangkok
1982	India	Iraq	1-0	Kuwait	New Delhi
1986	Korea Republic	Korea Republic	2-0	Saudi Arabia	Seoul
1990	China PR	Iran	0-0 4-1p	Korea DPR	Beijing
1994	Japan	Uzbekistan	4-2	China PR	Hiroshima
1998	Thailand	Iran	2-0	Kuwait	Bangkok
2002	Korea Republic	Iran	2-1	Japan	Busan

† Gold medal shared in 1970 and 1978

For many years the Football Tournament of the Asian Games rivalled the Asian Cup in importance meaning the continent had a major championship every other year. The range of winners has been more diverse than in the Asian Cup with Japan and Saudi Arabia yet to win gold. The first six tournaments saw India, Chinese Taipei and Burma (now Myanmar) dominate winning two titles apiece and in the eight Games since, Iran have won half. As a result they are the most successful nation followed by Korea Republic with three titles. The Asian Games operate as a regional version of the Olympics so in the amateur days this was not an issue given the lack of professional players on the continent. In 2002, as with the Olympics, the football tournament was turned into a U-23 tournament with three older players allowed, although in practice many nations had fielded under strength or youth teams in 1998. One of the most notable matches came in the 1978 final when North and South Korea played each other for the first time. Honours were even after a 0-0 draw and they shared the title. Doha in Qatar is the next venue in 2006.

WOMEN'S FOOTBALL TOURNAMENT OF THE ASIAN GAMES

Year	Host Country	Winners	Score	Runners-up	Venue
1990	China PR	China PR	5-0	Japan	Beijing
1994	Japan	China PR	2-0	Japan	Hiroshima
1998	Thailand	China PR	1-0	Korea DPR	Bangkok
2002	Korea Republic	Korea DPR	0-0	China PR	Busan

In 1990 and 1994 the tournament was played as a league. The result listed is that between the winners and runners-up

Given the strength of women's football in East Asia and in particular in China PR, it was a natural progression to introduce the sport to the Games when Beijing was host in 1990. The Chinese won that year and have remained dominant although they have faced a strong challenge at the past two Games from the North Koreans, which has also been the case at the AFC Women's Championship. The 2006 Asian Games will represent a major breakthrough for the women's game when Qatar are the hosts. It will only be the second time that a West Asian country has hosted the Games and the first since Iran in 1974, and it means that for the first time a major women's football tournament will be held in an Arab country.

AFC UNDER 17 CHAMPIONSHIP WINNERS

Year	Host Country	Winners	Runners-up
1984	Qatar	Saudi Arabia	Qatar
1986	Qatar	Korea Republic	Qatar
1988	Thailand	Saudi Arabia	Bahrain
1990	UAE	Qatar	UAE
1992	Saudi Arabia	China PR	Qatar
1994	Qatar	Japan	Qatar

AFC UNDER 17 CHAMPIONSHIP WINNERS

Year	Host Country	Winners	Runners-up
1996	Thailand	Oman	Thailand
1998	Qatar	Thailand	Qatar
2000	Vietnam SR	Oman	Iran
2002	UAE	Korea Republic	Yemen
2004	Japan	China PR	Korea DPR

AFC YOUTH CHAMPIONSHIP WINNERS

Year	Host Country	Winners	Runners-up
1959	Malaysia	Korea Republic	Malaysia
1960	Malaysia	Korea Republic	Malaysia
1961	Thailand	Burma & Indonesia	
1962	Thailand	Thailand	Korea Republic
1963	Malaysia	Burma & Korea Republic	
1964	Vietnam	Burma & Israel	
1965	Japan	Israel	Burma
1966	Philippines	Burma & Israel	
1967	Thailand	Israel	Indonesia
1968	Korea Republic	Burma	Malaysia
1969	Thailand	Burma & Thailand	
1970	Philippines	Burma	Indonesia
1971	Japan	Israel	Korea Republic
1972	Thailand	Israel	Korea Republic
1973	Iran	Iran	Japan
1974	Thailand	India & Iran	
1975	Kuwait	Iran & Iraq	

AFC YOUTH CHAMPIONSHIP WINNERS

Year	Host Country	Winners	Runners-up
1976	Thailand	Iran & Korea DPR	
1977	Iran	Iraq	Iran
1978	Bangladesh	Iraq & Korea Republic	
1980	Thailand	Korea Republic	Qatar
1982	Thailand	Korea Republic	China PR
1984	UAE	China PR	Saudi Arabia
1986	Saudi Arabia	Saudi Arabia	Bahrain
1988	Qatar	Iraq	Syria
1990	Indonesia	Korea Republic	Korea DPR
1992	UAE	Saudi Arabia	Korea Republic
1994	Indonesia	Syria	Japan
1996	Korea Republic	Korea Republic	China PR
1998	Thailand	Korea Republic	Japan
2000	Iran	Iraq	Japan
2002	Qatar	Korea Republic	Japan
2004	Malaysia	Korea Republic	China PR

Asia has a long history of youth tournaments dating back to the 1950s when the Youth Championship was held annually although it was largely confined to the countries of East and South-East Asia. Burma (now Myanmar) had the best record before the 1970s with seven titles but since then they have won none as the countries of the Middle East joined the AFC and began flexing their muscles. Iran won their first title in 1973 while two years later Iraq claimed the first of their five titles. Since the 1980s the Championship has been held every two years to tie in with the FIFA World Youth Championship for which it serves as a qualifying tournament. The South Koreans remain the most successful nation in the history of the AFC Youth Championship with 11 titles. The AFC U-17 Championship was introduced in 1984 to coincide with the launch of the FIFA U-17 World Championship. No country has won that title more than twice although Saudi Arabia did follow up their 1988 Championship victory by winning the world title a year later.

ASIAN CHAMPIONS CUP AND AFC CHAMPIONS LEAGUE FINALS

Year	Winners	Country	Score	Country	Runners-up
1967	Hapoel Tel Aviv	ISR	2-1	MAS	Selangor
1968	Maccabi Tel Aviv	ISR	1-0	KOR	Yangzee
1970	Taj Club	IRN	2-1	ISR	Hapoel Tel Aviv
1971	Maccabi Tel Aviv	ISR	W-O	IRQ	Police Club
1986	Daewoo Royals	KOR	3-1	KSA	Al Ahly
1987	Furukawa	JPN	4-3	KSA	Al Hilal
1988	Yomiuri	JPN	W-O	KSA	Al Hilal
1989	Al Saad	QAT	2-3 1-0	IRQ	Al Rasheed
1990	Liaoning	CHN	2-1 1-1	JPN	Nissan
1991	Esteghlal SC	IRN	2-1	CHN	Liaoning
1992	Al Hilal	KSA	1-1 4-3p	IRN	Esteghlal SC
1993	Pas	IRN	1-0	KSA	Al Shabab
1994	Thai Farmers Bank	THA	2-1	OMA	Omani Club
1995	Thai Farmers Bank	THA	1-0	QAT	Al Arabi
1996	Ilhwa Chunma	KOR	1-0	KSA	Al Nasr
1997	Pohang Steelers	KOR	2-1	KOR	Ilhwa Chunma
1998	Pohang Steelers	KOR	0-0 6-5p	CHN	Dalian
1999	Jubilo Iwata	JPN	2-1	IRN	Esteghlal SC
2000	Al Hilal	KSA	3-2	JPN	Jubilo Iwata
2001	Suwon Samsung Bluewings	KOR	1-0	JPN	Jubilo Iwata
2002	Suwon Samsung Bluewings	KOR	0-0 4-2p	KOR	Anyang LG Cheetahs
2003	Al Ain	UAE	2-0 0-1	THA	BEC Tero Sasana
2004	Al Ittihad	KSA	1-3 5-0	KOR	Seongnam Ilhwa Chunma

It is in club football where Asia has seriously lagged behind the rest of the world and nowhere was this been more evident than in the Asian Champion Teams' Cup, or the AFC Champions League as the competition is now known. After an initial burst of enthusiasm in the 1960s, mainly thanks to Israeli and Iranian clubs, it went into a prolonged hibernation to finally re-emerge in 1986. Support for the new tournament was still patchy and the logistics remained cumbersome thanks to the large distances clubs were forced to travel to play games given the geographical spread of the AFC. As part of his Vision Asia development strategy, AFC President Mohamed bin Hammam placed the development of club football at the heart of this strategy, hence the launch of the AFC Champions League in 2002. A key element was the streaming of the nations in the Confederation so that the AFC Champions League is now open to only the top 14 ranked 'mature' countries. A second tier of 14 'developing' countries entered the new AFC Cup while the President's Cup for the lowest ranked nations was launched in the 2005 season. Historically Saudi and Korean clubs have been the most successful in the Champions Cup and AFC Champions League with nine titles between them whilst Iran, Japan and China PR have underachieved given the strength of their domestic leagues. Six clubs have been Asian Champions twice - Maccabi Tel Aviv, Esteghlal (once as Taj), Al Hilal, Thai Farmers Bank, Pohang Steelers and Suwon Bluewings - although no club has managed to win it more.

ASIAN CUP WINNERS' CUP FINALS

Year	Winners	Country	Score	Country	Runners-up
1991	Pirouzi	IRN	0-0 1-0	BHR	Al Muharraq
1992	Nissan	JPN	1-1 5-0	KSA	Al Nasr
1993	Nissan	JPN	1-1 1-0	IRN	Pirouzi
1994	Al-Qadisiyah	KSA	4-2 2-0	HKG	South China
1995	Yokohama Flugels	JPN	2-1	UAE	Al Shaab
1996	Bellmare Hiratsuka	JPN	2-1	IRQ	Al Talaba
1997	Al Hilal	KSA	3-1	JPN	Nagoya Grampus Eight
1998	Al Nasr	KSA	1-0	KOR	Suwon Samsung Bluewings
1999	Al Ittihad	KSA	3-2	KOR	Chunnam Dragons
2000	Shimizu S-Pulse	JPN	1-0	IRQ	Al Zawra
2001	Al Shabab	KSA	4-2	CHN	Dalian Shide
2002	Al Hilal	KSA	2-1	KOR	Chonbuk Hyundai Motors

Discontinued after 2002 following the creation of the AFC Champions League

ASIAN SUPER CUP

Year	Winners	Country	Score	Country	Runners-up
1995	Yokohama Flugels	JPN	1-1 3-2	THA	Thai Farmers Bank
1996	Ilhwa Chunma	KOR	5-3 1-0	JPN	Bellmare Hiratsuka
1997	Al Hilal	KSA	1-0 1-1	KOR	Pohang Steelers
1998	Al Nasr	KSA	1-1 0-0	KOR	Pohang Steelers
1999	Jubilo Iwata	JPN	1-0 1-2	KSA	Al Ittihad
2000	Al Hilal	KSA	2-1 1-1	JPN	Shimizu S-Pulse
2001	Suwon Samsung Bluewings	KOR	2-2 2-1	KSA	Al Shabab
2002	Suwon Samsung Bluewings	KOR	1-0 0-1 4-2p	KSA	Al Hilal

Discontinued after 2002 following the creation of the AFC Champions League

AFC CUP

Year	Winners	Country	Score	Country	Runners-up
2004	Al Jaish	SYR	3-2 0-1	SYR	Al Wahda

The AFC Cup is reserved for nations ranked in the second tier of Asian club football with the aim of increasing the competitive nature of the club game in these countries by holding out the real prospect of honours for nations unlikely to win the Champions League. The first edition in 2004 proved to be a huge success and was won by Al Jaish in an all-Damascus final against Al Wahda. The success of the Syrians earned their country a move up into the AFC Champions League for the 2005 tournament.

WEST ASIAN FOOTBALL FEDERATION CHAMPIONSHIP

Year	Host Country	Winners	Score	Runners-up	Venue
2000	Jordan	Iran	1-0	Syria	Malek Abdullah, Amman
2002	Syria	Iraq	3-2	Jordan	Al Abbassiyyine, Damascus
2004	Iran	Iran	4-1	Syria	Tehran

GULF CUP

Year	Host Country	Winners	Runners-up
1970	Bahrain	Kuwait	Bahrain
1972	Saudi Arabia	Kuwait	Saudi Arabia
1974	Kuwait	Kuwait	Saudi Arabia
1976	Qatar	Kuwait	Iraq
1979	Iraq	Iraq	Kuwait
1982	UAE	Kuwait	Bahrain
1984	Oman	Iraq	Qatar
1986	Bahrain	Kuwait	UAE
1988	Saudi Arabia	Iraq	UAE

GULF CUP

Year	Host Country	Winners	Runners-up
1990	Kuwait	Kuwait	Qatar
1992	Qatar	Qatar	Bahrain
1994	UAE	Saudi Arabia	UAE
1996	Oman	Kuwait	Qatar
1998	Bahrain	Kuwait	Saudi Arabia
2002	Saudi Arabia	Saudi Arabia	Qatar
2004	Kuwait	Saudi Arabia	Bahrain
2005	Qatar	Qatar	Oman

FOOTBALL TOURNAMENT OF THE SOUTH ASIAN GAMES

Year	Host Country	Winners	Score	Runners-up	Venue
1984	Nepal	Nepal	4-2	Bangladesh	Dasharath Rangashala, Kathmandu
1985	Bangladesh	India	1-1 4-1p	Bangladesh	Dhaka
1987	India	India	1-0	Nepal	Salt Lake, Calcutta
1989	Pakistan	Pakistan	1-0	Bangladesh	Islamabad
1991	Sri Lanka	Pakistan	2-0	Maldives	Colombo
1993	Bangladesh	Nepal	2-2 4-3p	India	Dhaka
1995	India	India	1-0	Bangladesh	Madras
1999	Nepal	Bangladesh	1-0	Nepal	Dasharath Rangashala, Kathmandu
2004	Pakistan	Pakistan	1-0	India	Jinnah Stadium, Islamabad

SOUTH ASIAN FOOTBALL FEDERATION CUP

Year	Host Country	Winners	Score	Runners-up	Venue
1993	Pakistan	India	2-0	Sri Lanka	Lahore
1995	Sri Lanka	Sri Lanka	1-0	India	Colombo
1997	Nepal	India	5-1	Maldives	Dasharath Rangashala, Kathmandu
1999	Goa	India	2-0	Bangladesh	Margao
2003	Bangladesh	Bangladesh	1-1 5-3p	Maldives	Bangabandu, Dhaka

In 2003 the tournament was played as a league. The result listed is that between the winners and runners-up

ASEAN TIGER CUP

Year	Host Country	Winners	Score	Runners-up	Venue
1996		Thailand	1-0	Malaysia	
1998	Vietnam	Singapore	1-0	Vietnam	Hanoi Stadium, Hanoi
2000	Thailand	Thailand	4-1	Indonesia	Bangkok
2002	Indonesia/Sin'pore	Thailand	2-2 4-2p	Indonesia	Gelora Senayan, Jakarta
2004	Malaysia/Vietnam	Singapore	3-1 2-1	Indonesia	Jakarta, Singapore

EAST ASIAN CHAMPIONSHIP

Year	Host Country	Winners	Score	Runners-up	Venue
2003	Japan	Korea Republic	0-0	Japan	International, Yokohama

The 2003 tournament was played as a league. The result listed is that between the winners and runners-up

Regional tournaments in Asia are particularly strong dating back to 1911, when the Far East Olympics were first held, and they play a hugely important role given the vast size of the continent. The Middle East has the West Asian Football Federation Championship and the Gulf Cup; Central Asia has the South Asian Games and the South Asian Football Federation Cup; an the nations of Eastern Asia take part in either the ASEAN Tiger Cup or the East Asian Championship.

AFC CHAMPIONS LEAGUE 2004

AFC CHAMPIONS LEAGUE 2004

Group Stage			Quarter-finals			Semi-finals			Final		

Group A — Pts

Pakhtakor Tashkent	UZB	7
Zob-Ahan Isfahan	IRN	5
Qatar SC	QAT	3
Riffa ‡	BHR	0

Group B — Pts

Al Wahda	UAE	6
Al Sadd	QAT	5
Al Quwa Al Jawiya	IRQ	4
Al Qadisiya ‡	KUW	0

Quarter-finals:
Al Ittihad	1	1
Dalian Shide	1	0

Semi-finals:
Al Ittihad	2	2
Chonbuk Hyundai	1	2

Group C — Pts

Sharjah	UAE	10
Al Hilal	KSA	7
Al Shurta	IRQ	0
Al Ahly ‡	BHR	0

Quarter-finals:
Al Ain †	0	1
Chonbuk Hyundai	1	4

Group D — Pts

Al Ittihad	KSA	13
Sepahan	IRN	13
Al Arabi	KUW	8
Neftchi Fergana	UZB	0

Final:
Al Ittihad	1	5
Seongnam Ilhwa	3	0

Group E — Pts

Chonbuk Hyundai	KOR	12
Jubilo Iwata	JPN	12
Shanghai Shenhua	CHN	9
BEC Tero Sasana	THA	3

Quarter-finals:
Pakhtakor Tashkent	1	4
Al Wahda	1	0

Semi-finals:
Pakhtakor Tashkent	0	0
Seongnam Ilhwa	2	0

Group F — Pts

Dalian Shide	CHN	15
Krung Thai Bank	THA	7
Hoang Anh Gia Lai	VIE	7
PSM Makassar	IDN	6

Quarter-finals:
Sharjah	0	2
Seongnam Ilhwa	6	5

Group G — Pts

Seongnam Ilhwa	KOR	15
Yokohama F.Marinos	JPN	15
Persik Kediri	IDN	4
Binh Dinh	VIE	1

† Al Ain (UAE) given a bye to the quater-finals as holders
‡ Riffa and Al Ahly withdrew while Al Qadisiya were expelled from the tournament

GROUP A

		Pl	W	D	L	F	A	Pts	UZB	IRN	QAT	BHR
Pakhtakor Tashkent †	UZB	4	2	1	1	3	1	7		2-0	1-0	
Zob Ahan	IRN	4	1	2	1	4	5	5	1-0		3-3	
Qatar SC	QAT	4	0	3	1	3	4	3	0-0	0-0		2-0
‡Riffa	BHR	0	0	0	0	0	0	0		0-0		

† Qualified for the knock-out stage • ‡ Riffa withdrew from the group after two games

GROUP A MATCHDAY 1	
Foolad Shahr, Esfahan	
11-02-2004	
Zob Ahan	**1**
Ezukam 77	
Pakhtakor	**0**

GROUP A MATCHDAY 1	
Rayyan Stadium, Doha	
11-02-2004	
Qatar SC	**2**
Mostafa 28, Akwa 73	
Riffa	**0**

GROUP A MATCHDAY 2	
Pakhtakor Stadium, Tashkent	
25-02-2004	
Pakhtakor	**1**
Nikoleaev 43	
Qatar SC	**0**

GROUP A MATCHDAY 2	
Isa Town Stadium, Isa Town	
25-02-2004	
Riffa	**0**
Zob Ahan	**0**

GROUP A MATCHDAY 3	
Pakhtakor Stadium, Tashkent	
6-04-2004	
Pakhtakor	**-**
Riffa	**-**
Match postponed for security reasons	

GROUP A MATCHDAY 3	
Foolad Shahr, Esfahan	
6-04-2004	
Zob Ahan	**3**
Tahmasebi 15, Azizi 65, Azizzadeh 84	
Qatar SC	**3**
Mubarak 2 47 50, Caniggia 58	

GROUP A MATCHDAY 4	
21-04-2004	
Riffa	**-**
Pakhtakor	**-**
Riffa withdrew from the AFC Champions League	

GROUP A MATCHDAY 4	
Rayyan Stadium, Doha	
21-04-2004	
Qatar SC	**0**
Zob Ahan	**0**

GROUP A MATCHDAY 5	
Sheikh Ali bin Mohammed, Muharraq	
5-05-2004	
Riffa	**-**
Qatar SC	**-**
Riffa withdrew from the AFC Champions League	

GROUP A MATCHDAY 5	
Pakhtakor Stadium, Tasknet	
5-05-2004	
Pakhtakor	**2**
Koshelev 27, Bikmoev 90	
Zob Ahan	**0**

GROUP A MATCHDAY 6	
Foolad Shahr, Esfahan	
19-05-2004	
Zob Ahan	**-**
Riffa	**-**
Riffa withdrew from the AFC Champions League	

GROUP A MATCHDAY 6	
Rayyan Stadium, Doha	
19-05-2004	
Qatar SC	**0**
Pakhtakor	**0**

GROUP B

		Pl	W	D	L	F	A	Pts	UAE	QAT	IRQ	KUW
Al Wahda †	UAE	4	1	3	0	3	0	6		0-0	3-0	
Al Sadd	QAT	4	1	2	1	1	1	5	0-0		1-0	0-1
Al Quwa Al Jawiya	IRQ	4	1	1	2	1	4	4	0-0	1-0		0-1
Al Qadisiya ‡	KUW	0	0	0	0	0	0	0	1-3	0-0	1-0	

† Qualified for the knock-out stage • ‡ Al Qadisiya expelled from the tournament on 28 May after a mass brawl at the Al Qadisiya v Al Sadd match on 20 April

GROUP B MATCHDAY 1	
Teshrine, Damascus	
10-02-2004	
Al Quwa Al Jawiya	**0**
Al Qadisiya	**1**
Glaucio de Jesus 65	

GROUP B MATCHDAY 1	
Al Nahyan, Abu Dhabi	
11-02-2005	
Al Wahda	**0**
Al Sadd	**0**

GROUP B MATCHDAY 2	
Mohammed Al Hamad, Kuwait City	
25-02-2005	
Al Qadisiya	**1**
Al Mutari.K 44	
Al Wahda	**3**
Abiodun 2, Abdulrazzaq 18, Matar 22	

GROUP B MATCHDAY 2
Al Etehad, Doha
25-02-2004

Al Sadd	1
	Tenorio [47]
Al Quwa Al Jawiya	0

GROUP B MATCHDAY 3
Al Nahyan, Abu Dhabi
6-04-2004

Al Wahda	3
Abiodun [1], Omar Ali [41], Younes Mahmoud [65]	
Al Quwa Al Jawiya	0

GROUP B MATCHDAY 3
Al Sadd, Doha
7-04-2204

Al Sadd	0
Al Qadisiya	1
	Al Mutari.N [4]

GROUP B MATCHDAY 4
Teshrine, Damascus
20-04-2004

| Al Quwa Al Jawiya | 0 |
| Al Wahda | 0 |

GROUP B MATCHDAY 4
Mohammed Al Hamad, Kuwait City
20-04-2005

| Al Qadisiya | 0 |
| Al Sadd | 0 |

GROUP B MATCHDAY 5
Al Etehad, Doha
5-05-2004

| Al Sadd | 0 |
| Al Wahda | 0 |

GROUP B MATCHDAY 5
Mohammed Al Hamad, Kuwait City
6-05-2004

Al Qadisiya	1
	Rashed [49]
Al Quwa Al Jawiya	0

GROUP B MATCHDAY 6
Teshrine, Damascus
18-05-2004

Al Quwa Al Jawiya	1
	Loay Salah [88]
Al Sadd	0

GROUP B MATCHDAY 6
Al Nahyan, Abu Dhabi

| Al Wahda | - |
| Al Qadisiyah | - |

GROUP C

		Pl	W	D	L	F	A	Pts	UAE	KSA	IRQ	BHR
Sharjah †	UAE	4	3	1	0	10	4	10		5-2	2-0	
Al Hilal	KSA	4	2	1	1	6	6	7	0-0		2-0	
Al Shorta	IRQ	4	0	0	0	3	9	0	2-3	1-2		
Al Ahly ‡	BHR	0	0	0	0	0	0	0				

† Qualified for the knock-out stage • ‡ Al Ahli withdrew before the start of the tournament

GROUP C MATCHDAY 1
Al Sharjah Club, Sharjah
10-02-2004

Sharjah	2
	El Assas [80], Al Kaas [86]
Al Shorta	0

GROUP C MATCHDAY 1
King Fahad, Riyadh
25-02-2004

| Al Hilal | 0 |
| Sharjah | 0 |

GROUP C MATCHDAY 2
Teshrine, Damascus
6-04-2004

Al Shorta	1
	Amar Abbas [54]
Al Hilal	2
	Al Suwailh [45], Ceesay [72]

GROUP C MATCHDAY 2
King Fahad, Riyadh
21-04-2004

Al Hilal	2
	Traore 2 [30 90]
Al Shorta	0

GROUP C MATCHDAY 3
Teshrine, Damascus
4-05-2004

Al Shorta	2
Taysir Abdulhassan [23], Amar Abbas [45p]	
Sharjah	3
	Barbosa 2 [30 44], El Assas [68p]

GROUP C MATCHDAY 3
Al Sharjah Club, Sharjah
18-05-2004

Sharjah	5
Al Kass [13], Barbosa 2 [48 90],	
Nawaf Mubarak [53], Al Anbari [70]	
Al Hilal	2
	Al Jaber [19], Shariedah [40]

GROUP D

		Pl	W	D	L	F	A	Pts	KSA	IRN	KUW	UZB
Al Ittihad †	KSA	6	4	1	1	14	4	13		4-0	2-0	3-0
Sepahan	IRN	6	4	1	1	15	10	13	3-2		3-1	4-0
Al Arabi	KUW	6	2	2	2	8	10	8	0-0	2-2		3-2
Neftchi Fergana	UZB	6	0	0	6	5	18	0	1-3	1-3	1-2	

† Qualified for the knock-out stage

GROUP D MATCHDAY 1
Naghsh-E-Jahan, Esfahan
10-02-2004

Sepahan	4
Karimi 2 44 57, Salehi 2 62 68	
Neftchi Fergana	0

GROUP D MATCHDAY 1
Prince Abdullah Al Faisal, Jeddah
11-02-2004

Al Ittihad	2
Demba 41, Abu Shgeer 71	
Al Arabi	0

GROUP D MATCHDAY 2
Neftchi, Fergana
24-02-2004

Neftchi Fergana	1
Lebedev 20	
Al Ittihad	3
Demba 7, Falatah.H 43, Falatah.R 63	

GROUP D MATCHDAY 2
Sabah Al Salem, Kuwait City
24-02-2004

Al Arabi	2
Al Qallaf 67, Al Khatib 84	
Sepahan	2
Khatibi 17, Karimi 79	

GROUP D MATCHDAY 3
Naghsh-E-Jahan, Esfahan
7-04-2004

Sepahan	3
Karimi 2 48 62, Khatibi 53	
Al Ittihad	2
Haidar 51, Demba 83	

GROUP D MATCHDAY 4
Prince Abdullah Al Faisal, Jeddah
20-04-2004

Al Ittihad	4
Al Oteibi 3 11 14 37, Demba 58	
Sepahan	0

GROUP D MATCHDAY 4
Sabah Al Salem, Kuwait City
21-04-2004

Al Arabi	3
Al Khatib 2 38 59, Dago 51	
Neftchi Fergana	2
Isakov 53, Holmatov 88	

GROUP D MATCHDAY 5
Neftchi, Fergana
4-05-2004

Neftchi Fergana	1
Isakov 11	
Sepahan	3
Farshbaf 31, Salehi 45, Talebnasab 57	

GROUP D MATCHDAY 5
Sabah Al Salem, Kuwait City
4-05-2004

Al Arabi	0
Al Ittihad	0

GROUP D MATCHDAY 6
Naghsh-E-Jahan, Esfahan
18-05-2004

Sepahan	3
Farshbaf 55, Karimi 57, Talebnasab 74	
Al Arabi	1
Al Khatib 3	

GROUP D MATCHDAY 6
Prince Abdullah Al Faisal, Jeddah
18-05-2004

Al Ittihad	3
Noor 30, Al Oteibi 2 64 76	
Neftchi Fergana	0

GROUP D MATCHDAY 7
Neftchi, Fergana
26-05-2004

Neftchi Fergana	1
Kovalenko 65	
Al Arabi	2
Muham 47, Qallaf 68	

GROUP E

		Pl	W	D	L	F	A	Pts	KOR	JPN	CHN	THA
Chonbuk Hyundai Motors †	KOR	6	4	0	2	14	5	12		1-2	0-1	4-0
Jubilo Iwata	JPN	6	4	0	2	14	11	12	2-4		2-1	3-0
Shanghai Shenhua	CHN	6	3	0	3	7	9	9	0-1	3-2		1-0
BEC Tero Sasana	THA	6	1	0	5	6	16	3	0-4	2-3	4-1	

† Qualified for the knock-out stage

GROUP E MATCHDAY 1
Gang Chang Hak, Seogwipo
11-02-2004

Chonbuk Hyundai Motors	1
Edmilson 40	
Jubilo Iwata	2
Nanami 52, Nishino 67	

GROUP E MATCHDAY 1
Thai Japanese Stadium, Bangkok
11-02-2004

BEC Tero Sasana	4
Worrawoot 40, Narongchai 46, Datsakorn 82, Panai 90	
Shanghai Shenhua	1
Martinez 71	

GROUP E MATCHDAY 2
Hong Kou, Shanghai
25-02-2004

Shanghai Shenhua	0
Chonbuk Hyundai Motors	1
Sena 87	

GROUP E MATCHDAY 2
Yamaha Stadium, Shizuoka
25-02-2004

Jubilo Iwata	3
Gral 2 44 48, Hattori 81p	
BEC Tero Sasana	0

GROUP E MATCHDAY 3
Yamaha Stadium, Shizuoka
6-04-2004

Jubilo Iwata	2
Naruoka 44, Gral 80	
Shanghai Shenhua	1
Zhang Yuning 7	

GROUP E MATCHDAY 3
World Cup Stadium, Jeonju
7-04-2004

Chonbuk Hyundai Motors	4
Kim Yeon Gun 3 34 57 65, Botti 47	
BEC Tero Sasana	0

GROUP E MATCHDAY 4
Supachalasai, Bangkok
20-04-2004

BEC Tero Sasana	0

Chonbuk Hyundai Motors	4
Nam Kung Do [19], Edu 3 [60 62 90]

GROUP E MATCHDAY 4
Hong Kou, Shanghai
22-04-2004

Shanghai Shenhua	3
Li Chengming [5], Wang Ke [7], Martinez [83]

Jubilo Iwata	2
Nakayama [11], Nishi [45]

GROUP E MATCHDAY 5
Hong Kou, Shanghai
5-05-2004

Shanghai Shenhua	1
Li Dawei [89]

BEC Tero Sasana	0

GROUP E MATCHDAY 5
Yamaha Stadium, Shizuoka
12-05-2004

Jubilo Iwata	2
Fukunishi [50], Maeda [71]

Chonbuk Hyundai Motors	4
Suzuki OG [27], Edu [65], Park Dong Hyuk [86], Nam Kung Do [90]

GROUP E MATCHDAY 6
Thai Japanese Stadium, Bangkok
19-05-2004

BEC Tero Sasana	2
Pituratana [16], Sukngam [79]

Jubilo Iwata	3
Cullen [20], Naruoka [33], Gaviao [70]

GROUP E MATCHDAY 6
World Cup Stadium, Jeonju
19-05-2004

Chonbuk Hyundai Motors	0

Shanghai Shenhua	1
Luo Xiao [67]

GROUP F

		Pl	W	D	L	F	A	Pts	CHN	VIE	THA	IDN
Dalian Shide †	CHN	6	5	0	1	11	5	15		2-0	3-1	2-1
Hoang Anh Gia Lai	VIE	6	2	1	3	10	10	7	3-1		0-1	5-1
Krung Thai	THA	6	2	1	3	8	11	7	0-2	2-2		1-2
PSM Makassar	IDN	6	2	0	4	9	12	6	0-1	3-0	2-3	

† Qualified for the knock-out stage

GROUP F MATCHDAY 1
Thai Japanese Stadium, Bangkok
10-02-2004

Krung Thai	0

Dalian Shide	2
Siljak 2 [44 69]

GROUP F MATCHDAY 1
Gia Lai Stadium, Pleiku City
11-02-2004

Hoang Anh Gia Lai	5
Dusit [15], Kiatisuk 3 [29 46 90], Quang Truong [37]

PSM Makassar	1
Cristian [72]

GROUP F MATCHDAY 2
Chengdu Sports Center
24-02-2004

Dalian Shide	2
Siljak 2 [20 27]

Hoang Anh Gia Lai	0

GROUP F MATCHDAY 2
Mattoangin Stadium, Makassar
25-02-2004

PSM Makassar	2
Salossa [37], Rasyid [75]

Krung Thai	3
Piyawat [13], Chirawat [17], Phichitpong [28]

GROUP F MATCHDAY 3
Gia Lai Stadium, Pleiku City
6-04-2004

Hoang Anh Gia Lai	0

Krung Thai	1
Phichitpong [90]

GROUP F MATCHDAY 3
Mattoangin Stadium, Makassar
7-04-2004

PSM Makassar	0

Dalian Shide	1
Siljak [6]

GROUP F MATCHDAY 4
Supachalasai, Bangkok
21-04-2004

Krung Thai	2
Anon [17], Phichitpong [44]

Hoang Anh Gia Lai	2
Nguyen Van Dan [26], Kiatisuk [57]

GROUP F MATCHDAY 4
People's Stadium, Dalian
21-04-2004

Dalian Shide	2
Siljak [31], Li Yao [78]

PSM Makassar	1
Ronaldo [10]

GROUP F MATCHDAY 5
People's Stadium, Dalian
4-05-2004

Dalian Shide	3
Siljak 2 [45 80], Hao Haidong [81]

Krung Thai	1
Sawangsri [20]

GROUP F MATCHDAY 5
Mattoangin Stadium, Makassar
5-05-2004

PSM Makassar	3
Astaman [16], Moestamu [86], Bachri [89]

Hoang Anh Gia Lai	0

GROUP F MATCHDAY 6
Gia Lai Stadium, Pleiku City
18-05-2004

Hoang Anh Gia Lai	3
Kiatisuk [19], Nguyen Minh Hai [62], Ro Chom Tien [86]

Dalian Shide	1
Wang Peng [82]

GROUP F MATCHDAY 6
Thai Japanese Stadium, Bangkok
18-05-2004

Krung Thai	1
Tootone [13]

PSM Makassar	2
Fagundez [53], Moestamu [82]

GROUP G

		Pl	W	D	L	F	A	Pts	KOR	JPN	IDN	VIE
Seongnam Ilhwa Chunma †	KOR	6	5	0	1	24	4	15		0-1	15-0	2-0
Yokohama F¥Marinos	JPN	6	5	0	1	19	3	15	1-2		4-0	6-0
Persik Kediri	IDN	6	1	1	4	5	27	4	1-2	1-4		1-0
Binh Dinh	VIE	6	0	1	5	3	17	1	1-3	0-3	2-2	

† Qualified for the knock-out stage

GROUP G MATCHDAY 1
Quy Nhon, Binh Dinh
10-02-2004

Binh Dinh	0

Yokohama F¥Marinos	3
Kurihara 2 [15] [20], Shimuzu [74]

GROUP G MATCHDAY 1
Brawijaya Kediri, Kediri
11-02-2004

Persik Kediri	1
Tapia [90]

Seongnam Ilhwa Chunma	2
Kim Do Hoon 2 [29] [30]

GROUP G MATCHDAY 2
Mitsuzawa, Yokohama
24-02-2004

Yokohama F¥Marinos	4
Kitano 2 [12] [20], Yamazaki [65], Abe [71]

Persik Kediri	0

GROUP G MATCHDAY 2
Sports Complex, Seongnam
25-02-2004

Seongnam Ilhwa Chunma	2
Do Jae Joon [8] ,Chun Dae Hwan [38]

Binh Dinh	0

GROUP G MATCHDAY 3
Quy Nhon, Binh Dinh
7-04-2004

Binh Dinh	2
Pipat 2 [21] [25]

Persik Kediri	2
Ikenwa [21], Harianto [84]

GROUP G MATCHDAY 3
Mitsuzawa, Yokohama
7-04-2004

Yokohama F¥Marinos	1
Ahn Jung Hwan [8]

Seongnam Ilhwa Chunma	2
Laktionov [44], Adhemar [69]

GROUP G MATCHDAY 4
Brawijaya Kediri, Kediri
21-04-2004

Persik Kediri	1
Wibowo [30]

Binh Dinh	0

GROUP G MATCHDAY 4
Sports Complex, Seongnam
21-04-2004

Seongnam Ilhwa Chunma	0

Yokohama F¥Marinos	1
Kawai [75]

GROUP G MATCHDAY 5
International Stadium, Yokohama
5-05-2004

Yokohama F¥Marinos	6
Dutra [5], Ahn Jung Hwan 2 [39] [85], Kubo [67], Sakata [79], Oku [89]

Binh Dinh	0

GROUP G MATCHDAY 5
Sports Complex, Seongnam
11-05-2004

Seongnam Ilhwa Chunma	15
Sabitovic 4 [3] [73] [74] [86], Adhemar 2 [5] [25], Shin Tae Yong [12], Laktionov 4 [39] [42] [45p] [65], Kim Do Hoon 3 [60] [71] [88], Cho Sung Rae [82]

Persik Kediri	0

GROUP G MATCHDAY 6
Quy Nhon, Binh Dinh
19-05-2004

Binh Dinh	1
Pipat [40]

Seongnam Ilhwa Chunma	3
Adhemar 2 [9] [29], Shin Tae Yong [80]

GROUP G MATCHDAY 6
Brawijaya Kediri, Kediri
19-05-2004

Persik Kediri	1
Yuana Putra [85]

Yokohama F¥Marinos	4
Dutra [1], Ahn Jung Hwa [9], Kubo [24], Yoo Sang Chul [44]

QUARTER-FINAL FIRST LEG
People's Stadium, Dalian
14-09-2004

Dalian Shide	1
Zou Jie [66]

Al Ittihad	1
Carevic [23]

QUARTER-FINAL SECOND LEG
Prince Abdullah Al Faisal, Jeddah
21-09-2004

Al Ittihad	1
Redha Tukar [68]

Dalian Shide	0

QUARTER-FINAL FIRST LEG
Tahnon Bin Mohammed, Al Ain
14-09-2004

Al Ain	0

Chonbuk Hyundai Motors	1
Gomez [93+]

QUARTER-FINAL SECOND LEG
World Cup Stadium, Jeonju
21-09-2004

Chonbuk Hyundai Motors	4
Nam Kung Do [53], Rink [69], Gomes [91+], Park Dong Hyuk [93+]

Al Ain	1
Rami Yaslam [88]

QUARTER-FINAL FIRST LEG
Al Nahyan, Abu Dhabi
15-09-2004

Al Wahda	1
Nantcho [10]

Pakhtakor Tashkent	1
Magdeev [85]

QUARTER-FINAL SECOND LEG
Pakhtakor, Tashkent
22-09-2004

Pakhtakor Tashkent	4
Soliev [21], Shishelov [44], Salem OG [86], Koshelev [94+]

Al Wahda	0

QUARTER-FINAL FIRST LEG
Sports Complex, Seognam
15-09-2004

Seognam Ilhwa Chunma	6
Kim Do Hoon 20, Lee Ki Hyung 49, Dudu 2 52p 65, Laktionov 89	
Sharjah	0

QUARTER-FINAL SECOND LEG
Al Sharjah Club, Sharjah
22-09-2004

Sharjah	2
N'Diaye 44, Barbosa 66p	
Seognam Ilhwa Chunma	5
Dudu 2 11p 25, Marcedo 20, Kim Do Hoon 32, Laktionov 74	

SEMI-FINAL FIRST LEG
Prince Abdullah Al Faisal, Jeddah
19-10-2004

Al Ittihad	2
Noor 22, Al Montashari 89	
Chonbuk Hyundai Motors	1
Botti 85	

SEMI-FINAL SECOND LEG
World Cup Stadium, Jeonju
26-10-2004

Chonbuk Hyundai Motors	2
Rink 31, Botti 43	
Al Ittihad	2
Chico 70p, Al Harbi 88	

SEMI-FINAL FIRST LEG
Sports Complex, Seognam
20-10-2004

Seognam Ilhwa Chunma	0
Pakhtakor Tashkent	0

SEMI-FINAL SECOND LEG
Pakhtakor, Tashkent
27-10-2004

Pakhtakor Tashkent	0
Seognam Ilhwa Chunma	2
Kim Do Hoon 37, Dudu 56	

AFC CHAMPIONS LEAGUE FINAL FIRST LEG
Prince Abdullah Al Faisal, Jeddah
24-11-2004; 19:35; 21 000; Moradi IRN

AL ITTIHAD	1	3	SEOGNAM

Redha Tukar 28

Laktionov 27, Kim Do Hoon 81, Jang Hak Young 90

	Al Ittihad				Seognam Ilhwa Chunma	
22	AL SADIG Hussain				YANG Young Min	21
4	FALLATAH Redha Tukar				LEE Ki Hyung	5
9	FALATA Hamzah				KIM Do Hoon	9
11	LUCIANO Anderson Chico	67		88	DA SILVA NETO Eduardo	10
16	AL ZAHRANI Khamees	70		63	LAKTIONOV Denis	11
18	HAWSAWI Mohammed Noor				KIM Cheol Ho	15
21	AL MONTASHARI Hamad				CHEON Kwang Jin	25
27	KHARIRI Saud				DO Jae Joon	28
33	AL HARBI Osama				PARK Woo Hyun	29
41	CAREUIC Mario	46			JANG Hack Young	33
55	AL SAEED Mishal			24	TESTEMITANU Ivan	40
	Tr: IVIC Tomislav				Tr: CHA Kyoung Bok	
	Substitutes				Substitutes	
6	AL DOSREI Khamees	70		88	KIM Sang Hoon	2
8	ABUSHGEER Manaf	67		24	KIM Sung Il	3
20	AL YAMI Al Hasan	70		63	SEO Hyuk Su	6

AFC CHAMPIONS LEAGUE FINAL SECOND LEG
Seongnam Sports Complex, Seongnam
1-12-2004; 19:00; 26 000; Lu Jun CHN

SEONGNAM	0	5	AL ITTIHAD

Redha Tukar 27, Hamzah 46+, Noor 2 56 78, Abushgeer 95+

	Seognam Ilhwa Chunma				Al Ittihad	
21	YANG Young Min				AL SADIG Hussain	22
3	KIM Sung Il				FALLATAH Redha Tukar	4
5	LEE Ki Hyung				AL DOSREI Khamees	6
9	KIM Do Hoon				ABUSHGEER Manaf	8
10	DA SILVA NETO Eduardo			85	FALATA Hamzah	9
11	LAKTIONOV Denis			63	LUCIANO Anderson Chico	11
15	KIM Cheol Ho				AL OTAIBI Marzouk	17
25	CHEON Kwang Jin	60			HAWSAWI Mohammed Noor	18
28	DO Jae Joon	46			AL MONTASHARI Hamad	21
29	PARK Woo Hyun				AL HARBI Osama	33
33	JANG Hack Young			71	AL SAEED Mishal	55
	Tr: CHA Kyoung Bok				Tr: TALAGIC Dragan	
	Substitutes				Substitutes	
6	SEO Hyuk Su	46		63	KHARIRI Saud	27
18	VACEDO Marcelo	60		71	AL GARNI Ali	31
				85	AL SHAHRANI Ibrahim	70

AFC CUP 2004

The AFC Cup is an innovative idea that may well serve as a template for other Confederations in the future. It acts as a 'second division' for Asian club football with the 2004 edition restricted to clubs from Jordan, Lebanon, Oman, Syria, Turkmenistan and Yemen from West and Central Asia and to clubs from Bangladesh, Hong Kong, India, Malaysia, Maldives, Myanmar, Korea DPR and Singapore from East Asia. The theory is that rather than compete in the AFC Champions League where historically the prospect of success is remote, the development of clubs from these countries would be better served by a competition in which the standards are more even and with the possibility of winning the trophy. This certainly proved to be the case for clubs from Syria and Singapore who between them claimed the four semi-final berths with the two Syrian teams meeting in the final. The Damascus derby between army club Al Jaish and Al Wahda was settled by the away goal even though both matches were played in the Al Abbasiyyin Stadium. A 3-2 'away' victory in the first leg was enough for Al Jaish to become the inaugural winners. Syria moved up into the AFC Champions League so when the 2005 AFC Cup got underway, Al Jaish were not present to defend their title.

AFC CUP 2004

Group Stage	Quarter-finals	Semi-finals	Final

Group A		Pts
Al Nijmeh	LIB	16
Nisa Ashgabat	TKM	7
Al Sha'ab	YEM	7
Muktijoddha	BAN	1

Al Jaish	0 3
East Bengal	0 0

Group B		Pts
Al Wahda	SYR	8
Dhofar	OMA	4
Mahindra United	IND	4
Al Wahda †	YEM	0

Al Jaish	4 2
Home United	0 1

Olympic Beirut	3 1
Home United	3 2

Group C		Pts
Al Jaish	SYR	8
Olympic Beirut	LIB	7
Nebitchi	TKM	1
Mohammedan SC †	BAN	0

Al Jaish	3 0
Al Wahda	2 1

Group D		Pts
Home United	SIN	14
Perak	MAS	14
Happy Valley	HKG	3
Valencia	MDV	3

Geylang United	2 3
Perak	1 2

Geylang United	1 0
Al Wahda	1 1

Group E		Pts
East Bengal	IND	13
Geylang United	IND	13
Negri Sembilan	MAS	6
Island FC	MDV	3

Al Nejmeh	1 3
Al Wahda	2 2

† Yemen's Al Wahda and Mohammedan Sporting from Bangladesh withdrew before the tournament kicked-off
Group winners and the three second placed teams with the best records qualify for the quarter-finals

GROUP A

		Pl	W	D	L	F	A	Pts	LIB	TKM	YEM	BAN
Al Nijmeh †	LIB	6	5	1	0	11	2	**16**		3-1	3-0	2-0
Nisa Ashgabat	TKM	5	2	1	2	3	4	7	0-1		–	1-0
Al Sha'ab Ibb	YEM	5	2	1	2	7	7	7	1-1	0-1		**3-0**
Muktijoddha Sangsad	BAN	6	0	1	5	2	10	1	0-1	0-0	2-3	

† Qualified for the knock-out stage • Match in bold awarded 3-0 to Al Sha'ab

GROUP A MATCHDAY 1	
11-02-2004	
Al Nijmeh	**3**
Ivankovic 62, Nasereddine 2 82 89	
Al Sha'ab Ibb	0

GROUP A MATCHDAY 1	
11-02-2004	
Nisa Ashgabat	**1**
Nazarov 69p	
Muktijoddha Sangsad	0

GROUP A MATCHDAY 2	
Sana'a	
25-02-2004	
Al Sha'ab Ibb	0
Nisa Ashgabat	**1**
Konchaev 50	

GROUP A MATCHDAY 2	
25-02-2004	
Muktijoddha Sangsad	0
Al Nijmeh	**1**
Qassas 72	

GROUP A MATCHDAY 3	
6-04-2004	
Al Nijmeh	**3**
Qassas 2 12p 47, Nasserreddine 37	
Nisa Ashgabat	1
Hajiev 34	

GROUP A MATCHDAY 3	
Sana'a	
7-04-2004	
Al Sha'ab Ibb	**3**
Match awarded 3-0 to Al Sha'ab	
Muktijoddha Sangsad	0

GROUP A MATCHDAY 4

20-04-2004

Muktijoddha Sangsad	2
Ghansa 1, Moni 38	
Al Sha'ab Ibb	3
Al Gharbani 2 34 60, Ahmed 78	

GROUP A MATCHDAY 4

20-04-2004

Nisa Ashgabat	0
Al Nijmeh	1
Qassas 71	

GROUP A MATCHDAY 5

4-05-2004

Al Sha'ab Ibb	1
Al Nuno 51	
Al Nijmeh	1
Qassas 8	

GROUP A MATCHDAY 5

5-05-2004

Muktijoddha Sangsad	0
Nisa Ashgabat	0

GROUP A MATCHDAY 6

19-05-2004

Nisa Ashgabat	-
Al Sha'ab Ibb	-

GROUP A MATCHDAY 6

19-05-2004

Al Nijmeh	2
McFarlane 8, Hojeij 90	
Muktijoddha Sangsad	0

GROUP B

		Pl	W	D	L	F	A	Pts	SYR	OMA	IND	YEM
Al Wahda Damascus †	SYR	4	2	2	0	8	2	8		2-0	5-1	
Dhofar	OMA	4	1	1	2	6	7	4	1-1		4-2	
Mahindra United	IND	4	1	1	2	5	10	4	0-0	2-1		
Al Wahda Sana'a ‡	YEM	0	0	0	0	0	0	0				

† Qualified for the knock-out stage. ‡ Al Wahda Sana'a withdrew before the start of the tournament

GROUP B MATCHDAY 1

11-02-2004

Mahindra United	2
Venkatesh 21, Yadav 66	
Dhofar	1
Al Seem 55	

GROUP B MATCHDAY 2

25-02-2004

Dhofar	1
Al Ghafri 83	
Al Wahda Damascus	1
Al Shohmoh 22	

GROUP B MATCHDAY 3

7-04-2004

Mahindra United	0
Al Wahda Damascus	0

GROUP B MATCHDAY 4

21-04-2004

Al Wahda Damascus	5
Al Shihmih 36, Mando 2 39 53, Traore.M 2 69 73	
Mahindra United	1
Abaoagye 84	

GROUP B MATCHDAY 5

5-05-2004

Dhofar	4
Sultan 2 27 47, Al Shidad 35, Gabriel 61	
Mahindra United	2
Abaoagye 55, Akakpo 80	

GROUP B MATCHDAY 6

19-05-2004

Al Wahda Damascus	2
Maher Al Sayed 20, Traore.M 54	
Dhofar	0

GROUP C

		Pl	W	D	L	F	A	Pts	SYR	LIB	TKM	BAN
Al Jaish †	SYR	4	2	2	0	8	0	8		2-0	6-0	
Olympic Beirut †	LIB	4	2	1	1	4	3	7	0-0		2-0	
Nebitchi Balkanabat	TKM	4	0	1	3	1	10	1	0-0	1-2		
Mohammedan Sporting	BAN	0	0	0	0	0	0	0				

† Qualified for the knock-out stage. ‡ Mohammedan Sporting withdrew before the start of the tournament

GROUP C MATCHDAY 1

10-02-2004

Olympic Beirut	0
Al Jaish	0

GROUP C MATCHDAY 2

25-02-2004

Al Jaish	6
Sha'abo 36, Shehade 50, Rabih Hassan 2 55 64, Ahmed Omair 2 69 87	
Nebitchi Balkanabat	0

GROUP C MATCHDAY 3

7-04-2004

Olympic Beirut	2
Issa 65, Wassef Mohamed 75	
Nebitchi Balkanabat	0

GROUP C MATCHDAY 4	
21-04-2004	
Nebitchi Balkanabat	1
Olympic Beirut	2

GROUP C MATCHDAY 5	
5-05-2004	
Al Jaish	2
Alaomer 8, Sha'abo 86	
Olympic Beirut	0

GROUP C MATCHDAY 6	
18-05-2004	
Nebitchi Balkanabat	0
Al Jaish	0

GROUP D

		Pl	W	D	L	F	A	Pts	SIN	MAS	HKG	MDV
Home United †	SIN	6	4	2	0	18	5	14		2-2	5-1	5-0
Perak †	MAS	6	4	2	0	12	6	14	2-2		2-1	2-0
Happy Valley	HKG	6	1	0	5	7	14	3	0-2	1-2		3-1
Valencia	MDV	6	1	0	5	3	15	3	0-3	0-1	2-1	

† Qualified for the knock-out stage

GROUP D MATCHDAY 1	
11-02-2004	
Home United	5
Goncalves 3 30 66 72, De Oliveira 53, Indra Sahdan Daud 61	
Happy Valley	1
Jancula 69	

GROUP D MATCHDAY 1	
11-02-2004	
Perak	2
Seator 2 45 60	
Valencia	0

GROUP D MATCHDAY 2	
25-02-2004	
Valencia	0
Home United	3
Goncalves 2 37 43, De Oliveira 60	

GROUP D MATCHDAY 2	
25-02-2004	
Happy Valley	1
Ambassa 6	
Perak	2
Seator 72, Khalid Jamlus 80	

GROUP D MATCHDAY 3	
6-04-2004	
Valencia	2
Ali Ashfag 2 43 60	
Happy Valley	1
Akandu 50	

GROUP D MATCHDAY 3	
6-04-2004	
Perak	2
Khalid Jamlus 56, Seator 77	
Home United	2
Goncalves 2, Sutee 18	

GROUP D MATCHDAY 4	
20-04-2004	
Home United	2
Sutee 7p, Liew Kit Kong OG 35	
Perak	2
Khalid Jamlus 14, Saravanan 90	

GROUP D MATCHDAY 4	
21-04-2004	
Happy Valley	3
Akandu 2 2 42, Ambassa 82	
Valencia	1
Ali Ashfag 72	

GROUP D MATCHDAY 5	
5-05-2004	
Valencia	0
Perak	1
Goux 41	

GROUP D MATCHDAY 5	
5-05-2004	
Happy Valley	0
Home United	2
Indra Sahdan Daud 15, De Oliveira 90	

GROUP D MATCHDAY 6	
19-05-2004	
Home United	5
Indra Sahdan Daud 3 32 45 71, Nazim OG 78, De Oliveira 90	
Valencia	0

GROUP D MATCHDAY 6	
19-05-2004	
Perak	2
Seator 71, Khalid Jamlus 80	
Happy Valley	1
Ambassa 6	

GROUP E

		Pl	W	D	L	F	A	Pts	IND	SIN	MAS	MDV
East Bengal †	IND	6	4	1	1	14	8	13		1-1	4-2	3-0
Geylang United †	SIN	6	4	1	1	12	5	13	2-3		2-1	1-0
Negeri Sembilan	MAS	6	2	0	4	11	9	6	2-1	0-1		6-0
Island FC	MDV	6	1	0	5	2	17	3	1-2	0-5	1-0	

† Qualified for the knock-out stage

GROUP E MATCHDAY 1

10-02-2004

Geylang United	2
Hafiz Rahim [40], Jeyapal [90]	
East Bengal	3
Cristiano Junior 2 [45 76], Bijen Singh [83]	

GROUP E MATCHDAY 1

10-02-2004

Negeri Sembilan	6
Effiong 3 [19 64 71], Ekpoki 2 [30 90], Rajan.K [28]	
Island FC	0

GROUP E MATCHDAY 2

24-02-2004

Island FC	0
Geylang United	5
Hafiz Rahim [5], Johari [44], Nahar Daud [49], Noor Ali 2 [67 84]	

GROUP E MATCHDAY 2

25-02-2004

East Bengal	4
Okoro [9], Cristiano Junior 2 [34p 70], Bhutia [77]	
Negeri Sembilan	2
Rajan Koran [45], Shahrin Majid [64]	

GROUP E MATCHDAY 3

7-04-2004

Island FC	1
Ahmed Sunain [72p]	
East Bengal	2
Bhutia [36], Okoro [90]	

GROUP E MATCHDAY 3

7-04-2004

Negeri Sembilan	0
Geylang United	1
Duric [10]	

GROUP E MATCHDAY 4

21-04-2004

East Bengal	3
Da Silva [9], Cristiano Junior [36], Okoro [85]	
Island FC	0

GROUP E MATCHDAY 4

21-04-2004

Geylang United	2
Chang Hui [49], Duric [71]	
Negeri Sembilan	1
Efendi Malek [27]	

GROUP E MATCHDAY 5

4-05-2004

Island FC	1
Ismail Mohamed [14]	
Negeri Sembilan	0

GROUP E MATCHDAY 5

5-05-2004

East Bengal	1
Okoro [76]	
Geylang United	1
Hill [33]	

GROUP E MATCHDAY 6

18-05-2004

Geylang United	1
Khairon [29]	
Island FC	0

GROUP E MATCHDAY 6

18-05-2004

Negeri Sembilan	2
Suharmin Yusof 2 [23 49]	
East Bengal	1
Cristiano Junior [24]	

QUARTER-FINAL FIRST LEG

15-09-2004

East Bengal	0
Al Jaish	0

QUARTER-FINAL SECOND LEG

22-09-2004

Al Jaish	3
Adel Abdullah [16], Zeino [50], Firas Ismail [87]	
East Bengal	0

QUARTER-FINAL FIRST LEG

15-09-2004

Olympic Beirut	3
Atwi [18], Alozian [40], Antar [60]	
Home United	1
Indra Sahdan Daud 2 [28 79], Goncalves [83]	

QUARTER-FINAL SECOND LEG

22-09-2004

Home United	2
Fahmie Abdullah 2 [69 74]	
Olympic Beirut	1
Abbas Ali [63]	

QUARTER-FINAL FIRST LEG

14-09-2004

Perak	1
Seator [92+]	
Geylang United	2
Duric [49], Nawaz [60]	

QUARTER-FINAL SECOND LEG

21-09-2004

Geylang United	3
Jailani [12], Duric [27], Fazrul Nawaz [60]	
Perak	2
Mohamed Saad [55], Surendran.R [90]	

QUARTER-FINAL FIRST LEG

14-09-2004

Al Wahda	2
Iyad Mandou [86], Maher Al Sayed [89]	
Al Nijmeh	1
Qassas [50]	

QUARTER-FINAL SECOND LEG

21-09-2004

Al Nijmeh	3
Hjeij [21], Savane [33], Nasserredine [65]	
Al Wahda	2
Traore.M [19], Iyad Mandou [34]	

SEMI-FINAL FIRST LEG

20-10-2004	
Al Jaish	**4**
Zeino 34, Firas Ismail 2 53 62, Iyad Al Hilou 76	
Home United	**0**

SEMI-FINAL SECOND LEG

27-10-2004	
Home United	**1**
Siva Kumar 17	
Al Jaish	**2**
Zeino 76, Ziad Shaabou 90	

SEMI-FINAL FIRST LEG

19-10-2004	
Al Wahda	**1**
Jaafar 85	
Geylang United	**1**
Duric 63	

SEMI-FINAL SECOND LEG

26-10-2004	
Geylang United	**0**
Al Wahda	**1**
Traore.M 12	

AFC CUP FINAL FIRST LEG

Al Abbasiyyin, Damascus
19-11-2004; 17:00; 30 000; Najm LIB

AL WAHDA	2	3	AL JAISH

Darar Radawi 49, Omar Akik 92+

Ziad Sha'abo 3, Firas Ismail 32, Amer Al Abtah 55p

	Al Wahda				Al Jaish	
1	AZZOUR Badreddir				AL AZHAR Redwan	25
4	KICHANI Houssain		70		ISMAIL Firas	3
5	REDAWI Dirar				JABBAN Tareq	5
6	ABAZA Yanal				AL ZEINO Mohammed	10
9	AL SAYED Maher		51		AL SHEHADE Raghdan	12
10	MANDO Iyad	44			KHALAF Mohamad	15
15	SAYED Houssam				AL ABTAH Amer	18
17	MOHAMMAD Rafa				ABDULLAH Adel	19
18	ALMAOU Jamal	34	80		SHA'ABO Ziad	20
21	ALAYA Mootassam	75			AL SHAAR Basel	21
23	TRAORE Moussa				AL HILOU Iyad	24
	Tr: STAVRIC Nenad				Tr: COSTICA Stefanescu	
	Substitutes				Substitutes	
8	MUSTAFA Maher	44	70		ALI Kazzafi	8
11	SHAHMEH Nabil	75	51		AL HAJ Majed	14
25	A'AQEL Omar	34	80		AZZAM Ahmad	17

AFC CUP FINAL SECOND LEG

Al Abbasiyyin, Damascus
26-11-2004; 17:00; 17 000; Shaban KUW

AL JAISH	0	1	AL WAHDA

Al Jaish won on away goals

Kichani 72

	Al Jaish				Al Wahda	
25	AL AZHAR Redwan				AZZOUR Badreddir	1
3	ISMAIL Firas	67	59		MAATOUQ Ghassan	3
5	JABBAN Tareq				KICHANI Houssain	4
10	AL ZEINO Mohammed	90			REDAWI Dirar	5
12	AL SHEHADE Raghdan				ABAZA Yanal	6
15	KHALAF Mohamad				AL SAYED Maher	9
18	AL ABTAH Amer				SHAHMEH Nabil	11
19	ABDULLAH Adel				SAYED Houssam	15
20	SHA'ABO Ziad	84			MOHAMMAD Rafa	17
21	AL SHAAR Basel		84		ALAYA Mootassam	21
24	AL HILOU Iyad				TRAORE Moussa	23
	Tr: COSTICA Stefanescu				Tr: STAVRIC Nenad	
	Substitutes				Substitutes	
9	AL HARIRI Ahmad		59		SHAREEF Walid	2
14	AL HAJ Majed		84		AJL Kamial	7
17	AZZAM Ahmad					

AFC U-17 CHAMPIONSHIP JAPAN 2004

Qualifying Group 1
	Pl	W	D	L	F	A	Pts	KUW	JOR
Kuwait	2	1	1	0	4	3	4		2-1
Jordan	2	0	1	1	3	4	1	2-2	

Qualifying Group 2
	Pl	W	D	L	F	A	Pts	OMA	PAL
Oman	2	2	0	0	10	0	6		5-0
Palestine	2	0	0	2	0	10	0	0-5	

Qualifying Group 3
	Pl	W	D	L	F	A	Pts	UAE	KSA
Iraq	2	2	0	0	5	2	6	4-2	1-0
UAE	2	1	0	1	3	4	3		1-0
Saudi Arabia	2	0	0	2	0	2	0		

Qualifying Group 4
	Pl	W	D	L	F	A	Pts	BHR	LIB
Qatar	2	2	0	0	13	1	6	4-1	9-0
Bahrain	2	1	0	1	2	4	3		1-0
Lebanon	2	0	0	2	0	10	0		

Qualifying Group 5
	Pl	W	D	L	F	A	Pts	TJK	TKM
Iran	2	1	1	0	5	3	4	1-1	4-2
Tajikistan	2	1	1	0	5	4	4		4-3
Turkmenistan	2	0	0	2	5	8	0		

Qualifying Group 6
	Pl	W	D	L	F	A	Pts	NEP	AFG
India	2	1	1	0	5	1	4	1-1	4-1
Nepal	2	1	1	0	3	1	4		2-0
Afghanistan	2	0	0	2	0	6	0		

Qualifying Group 7
	Pl	W	D	L	F	A	Pts	SRI	BHU
Uzbekistan	2	2	0	0	10	1	6	4-1	6-0
Sri Lanka	2	1	0	1	4	4	3		3-0
Bhutan	2	0	0	2	0	9	0		

Qualifying Group 8
	Pl	W	D	L	F	A	Pts	BAN	KGZ
Bangladesh	2	2	0	0	3	0	6		2-0
Kyrgyzstan	2	0	0	2	0	3	0	0-1	

Qualifying Group 9
	Pl	W	D	L	F	A	Pts	THA	SIN
Thailand	2	2	0	0	7	1	6		4-0
Singapore	2	0	0	2	1	7	0	1-3	

Qualifying Group 10
	Pl	W	D	L	F	A	Pts	MYA	MDV
Laos	2	2	0	0	8	0	6	2-0	6-0
Myanmar	2	1	0	1	3	2	3		3-0
Maldives	2	0	0	2	0	9	0		

Qualifying Group 11
	Pl	W	D	L	F	A	Pts	CAM	PHI
Vietnam	2	2	0	0	10	0	6	4-0	6-0
Cambodia	2	1	0	1	4	6	3		4-2
Philippines	2	0	0	2	2	10	0		

Qualifying Group 12
	Pl	W	D	L	F	A	Pts	MAS	IDN
Malaysia	2	1	1	0	4	2	4		3-1
Indonesia	2	0	1	1	2	4	1	1-1	

Qualifying Group 13
	Pl	W	D	L	F	A	Pts	HKG	GUM
Korea Republic	2	2	0	0	28	0	6	10-0	18-0
Hong Kong	2	1	0	1	7	12	3		7-2
Guam	2	0	0	2	2	25	0		

Qualifying Group 14
	Pl	W	D	L	F	A	Pts	PRK	MGL
Korea DPR	2	2	0	0	20	0	6		0-0
Mongolia	2	0	0	2	0	20	0	0-11	

Japan qualified as host nation

Qualifying Group 15
	Pl	W	D	L	F	A	Pt	TPE	MAC
China PR	2	2	0	0	30	0	6	7-0	23-0
Chinese Taipei	2	1	0	1	8	7	3		8-0
Macau	2	0	0	2	0	31	0		

AFC U-17 CHAMPIONSHIP JAPAN 2004

First round groups

Group A	Pl	W	D	L	F	A	Pts	PRK	JPN	THA
China PR	3	2	0	1	5	5	6	2-1	1-3	2-1
Korea DPR	3	1	1	1	5	3	4		0-0	4-1
Japan	3	1	1	1	4	3	4			1-2
Thailand	3	1	0	2	4	7	3			

Group B	Pl	W	D	L	F	A	Pts	OMA	LAO	VIE
Korea Republic	3	3	0	0	9	3	9	3-0	8-0	1-0
Oman	3	2	0	1	4	4	6		2-0	2-1
Laos	3	1	0	2	2	11	3			2-1
Vietnam	3	0	0	3	2	5	0			

Group C	Pl	W	D	L	F	A	Pts	KUW	IND	MAS
Iran	3	3	0	0	9	1	9	3-1	1-0	5-0
Kuwait	3	1	1	1	3	4	4		2-1	0-0
India	3	1	0	2	3	4	3			2-1
Malaysia	3	0	1	2	1	7	1			

Group D	Pl	W	D	L	F	A	Pts	IRQ	UZB	BAN
Qatar	3	2	1	0	9	3	7	1-0	2-2	6-1
Iraq	3	2	0	1	7	3	6		4-1	3-1
Uzbekistan	3	0	2	1	4	7	2			1-1
Bangladesh	3	0	1	2	3	10	1			

China PR, Korea DPR and Qatar qualify for the FIFA U-17 World Championship in Peru

Quarter-finals
China PR	1
Oman	0

Iraq	0
Iran	3

Qatar	4
Kuwait	3

Korea Republic	0
Korea DPR	1

Semi-finals
China PR	3
Iran	0

Qatar	0 6p
Korea DPR	0 7p

Final
China PR	1
Korea DPR	0

Third Place Play-off
Qatar	2
Iran	1

AFC YOUTH CHAMPIONSHIP MALAYSIA 2004

Qualifying Group 1

	Pl	W	D	L	F	A	Pts	UAE	LIB
Qatar	2	1	1	0	2	1	4	1-1	1-0
UAE	2	0	2	0	2	2	2		1-1
Lebanon	2	0	1	1	1	2	1		

Qualifying Group 2

	Pl	W	D	L	F	A	Pts	BHR	JOR
Iraq	2	2	0	0	3	0	6	1-0	2-0
Bahrain	2	1	0	1	1	1	3		1-0
Jordan	2	0	0	2	0	3	0		

Qualifying Group 3

	Pl	W	D	L	F	A	Pts	KUW	PAL
Syria	2	2	0	0	10	2	6	4-1	6-1
Kuwait	2	1	0	1	8	5	3		7-1
Palestine	2	0	0	2	2	13	0		

Qualifying Group 4

	Pl	W	D	L	F	A	Pts	OMA	KSA
Yemen	2	2	0	0	3	0	6	1-0	2-0
Oman	2	1	0	1	1	1	3		1-0
Saudi Arabia	2	0	0	2	0	3	0		

Qualifying Group 5

	Pl	W	D	L	F	A	Pts	BAN	PAK
Nepal	2	1	1	0	4	1	4	1-1	3-0
Bangladesh	2	1	1	0	2	1	4		1-0
Pakistan	2	0	0	2	0	4	0		

Qualifying Group 6

	Pl	W	D	L	F	A	Pts	SRI	BHU
Uzbekistan	2	2	0	0	8	0	6	3-0	5-0
Sri Lanka	2	0	1	1	0	3	1		0-0
Bhutan	2	0	1	1	0	5	1		

Qualifying Group 7

	Pl	W	D	L	F	A	Pts	TJK	AFG
Iran	2	2	0	0	8	1	6	2-1	6-0
Tajikistan	2	1	0	1	4	3	3		3-1
Afghanistan	2	0	0	2	1	9	0		

Qualifying Group 8

	Pl	W	D	L	F	A	Pts	IND	KGZ
Turkmenistan	2	2	0	0	4	0	6	2-0	2-0
India	2	0	1	1	0	2	1		0-0
Kyrgyzstan	2	0	1	1	0	2	1		

Qualifying Group 9

	Pl	W	D	L	F	A	Pts	MYA	BRU
Vietnam	2	2	0	0	9	2	6	1-0	8-2
Myanmar	2	1	0	1	5	2	3		5-1
Brunei	2	0	0	2	3	13	0		

Qualifying Group 10

	Pl	W	D	L	F	A	Pts	LAO	CAM
Laos	2	2	0	0	6	0	6		1-0
Cambodia	2	0	0	2	0	6	0	0-5	

Qualifying Group 11

	Pl	W	D	L	F	A	Pts	MDV	PHI
Indonesia	2	2	0	0	7	0	6	3-0	4-0
Maldives	2	1	0	1	2	3	3		2-0
Philippines	2	0	0	2	0	6	0		

Qualifying Group 12

	Pl	W	D	L	F	A	Pts	THA	SIN
Thailand	2	2	0	0	4	0	6		2-0
Singapore	2	0	0	2	0	4	0	0-2	

Qualifying Group 13

	Pl	W	D	L	F	A	Pts	TPE	MAC
Japan	2	2	0	0	14	0	6	7-0	7-0
Chinese Taipei	2	1	0	1	3	7	3		3-0
Macau	2	0	0	2	0	10	0		

Qualifying Group 14

	Pl	W	D	L	F	A	Pts	KOR	MGL
Korea Republic	2	2	0	0	22	0	6		12-0
Mongolia	2	0	0	2	0	22	0	0-10	

Malaysia qualified as host nation

Qualifying Group 15

	Pl	W	D	L	F	A	Pts	HKG	GUM
China PR	2	2	0	0	17	0	6	8-0	9-0
Hong Kong	2	1	0	1	6	11	3		6-3
Guam	2	0	0	2	3	15	0		

AFC YOUTH CHAMPIONSHIP MALAYSIA 2004

First round groups

Group A

	Pl	W	D	L	F	A	Pts	MAS	NEP	VIE
Japan	3	3	0	0	7	0	9	3-0	3-0	1-0
Malaysia	3	2	0	1	4	3	6		3-0	1-0
Nepal	3	1	0	2	1	6	3			1-0
Vietnam	3	0	0	3	0	3	0			

Group B

	Pl	W	D	L	F	A	Pts	QAT	IRN	IDN
China PR	3	2	1	0	6	1	7	1-0	0-0	5-1
Qatar	3	2	0	1	3	2	6		2-1	1-0
Iran	3	1	1	1	7	4	4			6-2
Indonesia	3	0	0	3	3	12	0			

Group C

	Pl	W	D	L	F	A	Pts	SYR	LAO	IND
Uzbekistan	3	2	1	0	8	4	7	1-1	5-2	2-1
Syria	3	2	1	0	7	3	7		4-1	2-1
Laos	3	1	0	2	4	9	3			1-0
India	3	0	0	3	2	5	0			

Group D

	Pl	W	D	L	F	A	Pts	KOR	THA	YEM
Iraq	3	3	0	0	9	3	9	3-0	2-0	2-0
Korea Republic	3	1	1	1	5	4	4		1-1	4-0
Thailand	3	1	1	1	3	4	4			2-1
Yemen	3	0	0	3	1	8	0			

Quarter-finals

Korea Republic	2
Uzbekistan	1

Qatar	0 3p
Japan	0 5p

Syria	1
Iraq	0

Malaysia	0
China PR	3

Semi-finals

Korea Republic	2 3p
Japan	2 1p

Syria	0
China PR	1

Final

Korea Republic	2
China PR	0

Third Place Play-off

Japan	1 4p
Syria	1 3p

Korea Republic, China PR, Japan and Syria qualified for the FIFA World Youth Championship in the Netherlands

REGIONAL TOURNAMENTS IN ASIA

GULF CUP QATAR 2004

First Round Group Stage

	Pl	W	D	L	F	A	Pts	QAT	UAE	IRQ
Oman	3	2	0	1	6	4	6	1-2	2-1	3-1
Qatar	3	1	2	0	7	6	5		2-2	3-3
United Arab Emirates	3	0	2	1	4	5	2			1-1
Iraq	3	0	2	1	5	7	2			

	Pl	W	D	L	F	A	Pts	BHR	KSA	YEM
Kuwait	3	2	1	0	6	2	7	1-1	2-1	3-0
Bahrain	3	1	2	0	5	2	5		3-0	1-1
Saudi Arabia	3	1	0	2	3	5	3			2-0
Yemen	3	0	1	2	1	6	1			

Semi-finals

Qatar	2
Kuwait	0

Bahrain	2
Oman	3

Final

Qatar	1	5p
Oman	1	4p

ASEAN TIGER CUP 2004-05

First Round Group Stage

Group A - Vietnam	Pl	W	D	L	F	A	Pts	SIN	VIE	LAO	CAM
Indonesia	4	3	1	0	17	0	10	0-0	3-0	6-0	8-0
Singapore	4	2	2	0	10	3	8		1-1	6-2	3-0
Vietnam	4	2	1	1	13	5	7			3-0	9-1
Laos	4	1	0	3	4	16	3				2-1
Cambodia	4	0	0	4	2	22	0				

Group B - Malaysia	Pl	W	D	L	F	A	Pts	MAS	THA	PHI	TIM
Myanmar	4	3	1	0	6	2	10	1-0	1-1	1-0	3-1
Malaysia	4	3	0	1	11	3	9		2-1	4-1	5-0
Thailand	4	2	1	1	12	4	7			3-1	8-0
Philippines	4	1	0	3	4	9	3				2-1
East Timor	4	0	0	4	2	17	0				

Semi-finals

Singapore	4 4
Myanmar *	3 2

Malaysia	2 1
Indonesia *	1 4

* At home in the first leg
Third place play-off held
in Singapore.

Final

Singapore	3 2
Indonesia *	1 1

Third Place Play-off

Malaysia	2
Myanmar	1

Tiger Cup Final first Leg, Utama Senayan, Jakarta
8-01-2005, 19:45, 120 000, Kwong Jong Chul KOR

IDN	1	3	SIN

Mahyadi Panggabean 90

Bennett 5, Khairul Amri 39
Agu Casmir 69

INDONESIA			SINGAPORE	
1 KARTIKO Hendro			LIONEL Lewis	18
2 YULIANTO Charis			ISKANDAR Aide	5
18 AGUS Firmansyah			KHAIZAN Baihakki	6
3 SALOSSA Ortisan			SUBRAMANI Shunmugham	14
6 MAULY Mohammad			BENNETT Daniel	16
8 AIBOI Elie	74		JAILANI Hasrin	4
11 ASTAMAN Ponario (c)		46	CHUAN Goh	7
16 BACHRI Syamsul			ISHAK Shahril	17
7 SALOSSA Boas	30	41	MOHD Khairul Amri	19
9 JAYA Ilham	84	87	SHAH Noh Alam	8
10 KURNIAWAN Dwi			CASMIR Agu	20
Tr: WITHE Peter			Tr: AVRAMOVIC Raddy	
14 UTINA Firman	30	87	ZAINOL Ishak	3
20 SINAGA Saktiawan	84	46	RAHMAN Noh	13
21 PANGGABEAN Mahyadi	74	41	DICKSON Itimi	22

Tiger Cup Final second Leg, National Stadium, Singapore
16-01-2005, 19:30, 55 000, Al Ghamdi KSA

SIN	2	1	IDN

Daud 5, Casmir 40p

Aiboi 76

SINGAPORE			INDONESIA	
18 LIONEL Lewis			KARTIKO Hendro	1
5 ISKANDAR Aide	87		HAMZAH Hamka	17
6 KHAIZAN Baihakki			AGUS Firmansyah	18
14 SUBRAMANI Shunmugham			INDARTO Aris	19
16 BENNETT Daniel		56	SALOSSA Ortisan	3
4 JAILANI Hasrin			AIBOI Elie	8
7 CHUAN Goh			(c) ASTAMAN Ponario	11
17 ISHAK Shahril			SALIMIN Supriyono	15
10 DAUD Indra Sahdan	63		BACHRI Syamsul	16
20 CASMIR Agu			JAYA Ilham	9
22 DICKSON Itimi	90		KURNIAWAN Dwi	10
Tr: AVRAMOVIC Raddy			Tr: WITHE Peter	
13 RAHMAN Noh	90	83	UTINA Firman	14
19 MOHD Khairul Amri	63	56 83	PANGGABEAN Mahyadi	21

CAF

CONFEDERATION AFRICAINE DE FOOTBALL

To ease fixture congestion after persistent grumbles from European clubs about releasing players, CAF decided to use the qualifying groups for the 2006 FIFA World Cup™ as the qualifiers for the 2006 CAF African Cup of Nations in Egypt as well. The decision has restored some order to the fixture list but for the 20 countries eliminated after the knock-out preliminary round, matches have been few and far between as a consequence. With only the winner of each group qualifying for Germany the decision has helped keep the interest alive with the top three clubs qualifying for the finals in Egypt. There was controversy even before the qualifiers began when FIFA docked Cameroon six points for wearing an illegal all-in-one kit during the 2004 African Cup of Nations. No strangers to sartorial controversy, Cameroon were reprimanded for sporting a sleeveless number at the 2002 tournament, but this time their punishment was seen as harsh and the Centennial Congress rescinded the penalty. At club level, Enyimba of Nigeria were the first team

THE FIFA BIG COUNT OF 2000 FOR CAF

	Male	Female		Male	Female
Registered players	610 997	13 724	Referees	26 798	499
Non registered players	5 607 300	111 329	Officials	189 443	5 392
Youth players	621 238	19 932	Total involved	21 332 631	1 451 476
Children & Occasional	14 300 000	1 300 000	in football	22 806 652	
Professionals	3 653	600	Number of clubs	13 302	
Total players	22 584 520		Number of teams	195 886	

in 36 years to retain the Champions League title beating Tunisia's Etoile Sahel 5-3 on penalties after a 3-3 aggregate draw in the final. In the Super Cup, the Nigerians lost to Hearts of Oak who had beaten Ghanaian rivals Asanta Kotoko 8-7 on penalties to become the first winners of the Confederation Cup, the trophy that replaced two previous CAF competitions, the African Winner's Cup and the CAF Cup. Meanwhile, South Africa's league champions Kaizer Chiefs won't play in the Champions League after being banned by CAF from African club competitions for three years after withdrawing from the Confederation Cup. At junior level, Nigeria won the African Youth Championships while in Gambia there was a huge shock when the host nation beat Nigeria 1-0 in the African U-17 Championship final. In October the Super Falcons of Nigeria won the CAF African Women's Championship for the fourth time in a row. CAF faces a number of challenges, not least amongst them continued disorder in stadia and ensuring that the stadia themselves are up to the standard required to host international matches.

Confédération Africaine de Football (CAF)

PO Box 23, 3 Abdel Khalek Sarwat Street, El Hay El Motamayez, 6th October City, Egypt

Tel +20 2 8371000   Fax +20 2 8370006

info@cafonline.com   www.cafonline.com

President: HAYATOU Issa CMR   General Secretary: FAHMY Mustapha EGY

CAF Formed: 1957

CAF EXECUTIVE COMMITTEE

President: HAYATOU Issa CMR   Vice-President: MEMENE Seyi TOG   Vice-President: OLIPHANT Molefi RSA

ORDINARY MEMBERS OF THE EXECUTIVE COMMITTEE

PATEL Suketu SEY	ADAMU Amos Dr. NGA	RAOURAOUA Mohamed ALG
SYLVESTRE Mbongo CGO	DIAKITE Amadou MLI	WADE Mawade SEN
REDA Hani Abu EGY	SHADDAD Kamal SUD	DJIBRINE Adoum CHA
BARANSANANIYE Moses BDI	General Secretary: FAHMY Mustapha EGY	Co-opted: ALOULOU Slim

AFRICAN TOURNAMENTS

CAF AFRICAN CUP OF NATIONS

Year	Host Country	Winners	Score	Runners-up	Venue
1957	Sudan	Egypt	4-0	Ethiopia	Khartoum Stadium, Khartoum
1959	Egypt	Egypt	2-1	Sudan	Al Ahli Stadium, Cairo
1962	Ethiopia	Ethiopia	2-0	Egypt	Haile Selassie, Addis Abeba
1963	Ghana	Ghana	3-0	Sudan	Accra Stadium, Accra
1965	Tunisia	Ghana	3-2	Tunisia	Zouiten, Tunis
1968	Ethiopia	Congo Kinshasa	1-0	Ghana	Haile Selassie, Addis Abeba
1970	Sudan	Sudan	1-0	Ghana	Municipal, Khartoum
1972	Cameroon	Congo	3-2	Mali	Omnisports, Yaoundé
1974	Egypt	Zaire	2-2 2-0	Zambia	International, Cairo
1976	Ethiopia	Morocco	1-1	Guinea	Addis Abeba Stadium
1978	Ghana	Ghana	2-0	Uganda	Accra Stadium, Accra
1980	Nigeria	Nigeria	3-0	Algeria	Surulere, Lagos
1982	Libya	Ghana	1-1 7-6p	Libya	11th June Stadium, Tripoli
1984	Côte d'Ivoire	Cameroon	3-1	Nigeria	Houphouët Boigny, Abidjan
1986	Egypt	Egypt	0-0 5-4p	Cameroon	International, Cairo
1988	Morocco	Cameroon	1-0	Nigeria	Mohamed V, Casablanca
1990	Algeria	Algeria	1-0	Nigeria	Stade Olympique, Algiers
1992	Senegal	Côte d'Ivoire	0-0 11-10p	Ghana	Stade de l'Amite, Dakar
1994	Tunisia	Nigeria	2-1	Zambia	El Menzah, Tunis
1996	South Africa	South Africa	2-0	Tunisia	Soccer City, Johannesburg
1998	Burkina Faso	Egypt	2-0	South Africa	Stade du 4 Août, Ouagadougou
2000	Ghana/Nigeria	Cameroon	2-2 4-3p	Nigeria	Surulere, Lagos
2002	Mali	Cameroon	0-0 3-2p	Senegal	Stade du 26 Mars, Bamako
2004	Tunisia	Tunisia	2-1	Morocco	Rades, Tunis

That 13 different countries have triumphed at the 24 CAF African Cup of Nations tournaments bears witness to the high quality of football across the continent. This lack of domination by one country and the fact that it is played every two years means the competition gives a very good indication of the footballing prowess on the continent. The great teams from the past have all managed to inscribe their name on the trophy - the Egyptian team of the late 1950s; Ghana at the time of independence in the 1960s; Zaire in the early 1970s; Cameroon in the 1980s; and the Nigerians of the mid-1990s. Fifteen different nations have hosted the tournament which has grown from a three team round robin in the early years into a 16 team spectacular nowadays. For the 2006 edition the FIFA World Cup™ qualifiers doubled up as Nations Cup qualifiers to ease the fixture load and this remains the plan for those editions played in future FIFA World Cup™ years. In 2006 Egypt will host the tournament for the fourth time and hope to win an outright record fifth title, as will current joint record holders Ghana when they are hosts in 2008. Remarkably the other joint record holders, Cameroon, have won all their four titles away from home.

CAF AFRICAN WOMEN'S CHAMPIONSHIP

Year	Host Country	Winners	Score	Runners-up	Venue
1991		Nigeria	2-0 4-0	Cameroon	
1995		Nigeria	4-1 7-1	South Africa	
1998	Nigeria	Nigeria	2-0	Ghana	Abeokuta
2000	South Africa	Nigeria	2-0	South Africa	Johannesburg
2002	Nigeria	Nigeria	2-0	Ghana	Lagos
2004	South Africa	Nigeria	5-0	Cameroon	Johannesburg

With relatively little empowerment of women on the continent the game is not particulary widespread but the chance of a place in the FIFA Women's World Cup provided the spur for CAF to introduce a women's Championship. To date Nigeria has won all six tournaments with Cameroon, South Africa and Ghana each losing in the final twice.

AFRICAN YOUTH CHAMPIONSHIP

Year	Host Country	Winners	Score	Runners-up	Venue
1979		Algeria	2-1 2-3	Guinea	Algiers, Conakry
1981		Egypt	1-1 2-0	Cameroon	Douala, Cairo
1983		Nigeria	2-2 2-1	Côte d'Ivoire	Abidjan, Lagos
1985		Nigeria	1-1 2-1	Tunisia	Tunis, Lagos
1987		Nigeria	2-1 3-0	Togo	Lomé, Lagos
1989		Nigeria	2-1 2-0	Mali	Bamako, Lagos
1991	Egypt	Egypt	2-1	Côte d'Ivoire	Cairo
1993	Mauritius	Ghana	2-0	Cameroon	Bellevue
1995	Nigeria	Cameroon	4-0	Burundi	Lagos
1997	Morocco	Morocco	1-0	South Africa	Meknès
1999	Ghana	Ghana	1-0	Nigeria	Accra
2001	Ethiopia	Angola	2-0	Ghana	Addis Abeba
2003	Burkina Faso	Egypt	4-3	Côte d'Ivoire	Ouagadougou
2005	Benin	Nigeria	2-0	Egypt	Cotonou

AFRICAN U–17 CHAMPIONSHIP

Year	Host Country	Winners	Score	Runners-up	Venue
1995	Mali	Ghana	3-1	Nigeria	Bamako
1997	Botswana	Egypt	1-0	Mali	Gaborone
1999	Guinea	Ghana	3-1	Burkina Faso	Conakry
2001	Seychelles	Nigeria	3-0	Burkina Faso	Victoria
2003	Swaziland	Cameroon	1-0	Sierra Leone	Mbabane
2005	Gambia	Gambia	1-0	Ghana	Bakau

AFRICAN WOMEN'S U–19 CHAMPIONSHIP

Year	Host Country	Winners	Score	Runners-up	Venue
2002		Nigeria	6-0 3-2	South Africa	
2004		Nigeria	1-0 0-0	South Africa	

Africa's youth tournaments came from the need to play qualifiers for the FIFA age-restricted competitions. Until the 1990s they were played on a home and away basis but since 1991 in the Youth Championship and 1995 in the U-17s, there has been a final tournament in a designated country. This has given those countries unlikely to host the CAF African Cup of Nations a chance to organise a major football tournament.

FOOTBALL TOURNAMENT OF THE AFRICAN GAMES

Year	Host Country	Winners	Score	Runners-up	Venue
1965	Congo	Congo	0-0 †	Mali	Brazzaville
1973	Nigeria	Nigeria	2-0	Guinea	Lagos
1978	Algeria	Algeria	1-0	Nigeria	Algiers
1987	Kenya	Egypt	1-0	Kenya	Nairobi
1991	Egypt	Cameroon	1-0	Tunisia	Cairo
1995	Zimbabwe	Egypt	3-1	Zimbabwe	Harare
1999	South Africa	Cameroon	0-0 4-3p	Zambia	Johannesburg
2003	Nigeria	Cameroon	2-0	Nigeria	Abuja

† Decided on number of corner-kicks awarded. Congo won 7-2

WOMEN'S FOOTBALL TOURNAMENT OF THE AFRICAN GAMES

Year	Host Country	Winners	Score	Runners-up	Venue
2003	Nigeria	Nigeria	1-0	South Africa	Abuja

At one time the football tournament of the African Games carried enormous prestige but it is only since 1987 that it has been played on a regular basis. Cameroon and Egypt have dominated since then although it is now staged as an age-restricted tournament as at the Olympics. The 1965 final at the Brazzaville Games threw up an interesting historical curiosity. After the hosts Congo and Mali could only draw 0-0, the game was decided not on penalties but by the number of corner kicks won which many believe is a much fairer system.

CAF CHAMPIONS LEAGUE

Year	Winners	Country	Score	Country	Runners-up
1965	Oryx Douala	CMR	2-1	MLI	Stade Malien
1966	Stade Abidjan	CIV	1-3 4-1	MLI	AS Real Bamako
1967	Tout Puissant Englebert	ZAI	1-1 2-2	GHA	Asante Kotoko
1968	Tout Puissant Englebert	ZAI	5-0 1-4	TOG	Etoile Filante
1969	Al Ismaili	EGY	2-2 3-1	ZAI	Tout Puissant Englebert
1970	Asante Kotoko	GHA	1-1 2-1	ZAI	Tout Puissant Englebert
1971	Canon Yaoundé	CMR	0-3 2-0 1-0	GHA	Asante Kotoko
1972	Hafia FC Conakry	GUI	4-2 3-2	UGA	Simba FC
1973	AS Vita Kinshasa	ZAI	2-4 3-0	GHA	Asante Kotoko
1974	CARA Brazzaville	CGO	4-2 2-1	EGY	Mehalla Al Kubra
1975	Hafia FC Conakry	GUI	1-0 2-1	NGA	Enugu Rangers
1976	Mouloudia d'Algiers	ALG	3-0 0-3 4-1p	GUI	Hafia FC Conakry
1977	Hafia FC Conakry	GUI	1-0 3-2	GHA	Hearts of Oak
1978	Canon Yaoundé	CMR	0-0 2-0	GUI	Hafia FC Conakry
1979	Union Douala	CMR	0-1 1-0 5-3p	GHA	Hearts of Oak
1980	Canon Yaoundé	CMR	2-2 3-0	ZAI	AS Bilima
1981	JE Tizi-Ouzou	ALG	4-0 1-0	ZAI	AS Vita Kinshasa
1982	Al Ahly Cairo	EGY	3-0 1-1	GHA	Asante Kotoko
1983	Asante Kotoko	GHA	0-0 1-0	EGY	Al Ahly Cairo
1984	Zamalek	EGY	2-0 1-0	NGA	Shooting Stars
1985	FAR Rabat	MAR	5-2 1-1	ZAI	AS Bilima
1986	Zamalek	EGY	2-0 0-2 4-2p	CIV	Africa Sports
1987	Al Ahly Cairo	EGY	0-0 2-0	SUD	Al Hilal
1988	Entente Setif	ALG	0-1 4-0	NGA	Iwuanyanwu Owerri
1989	Raja Casablanca	MAR	1-0 0-1 4-2p	ALG	Mouloudia d'Oran
1990	JS Kabylie	ALG	1-0 0-1 5-3p	ZAM	Nkana Red Devils
1991	Club Africain	TUN	5-1 1-1	UGA	Nakivubo Villa
1992	Wydad Casablanca	MAR	2-0 0-0	SUD	Al Hilal
1993	Zamalek	EGY	0-0 0-0 7-6p	GHA	Asante Kotoko
1994	Espérance Tunis	TUN	0-0 3-1	EGY	Zamalek
1995	Orlando Pirates	RSA	2-2 1-0	CIV	ASEC Mimosas
1996	Zamalek	EGY	1-2 2-1 4-2p	NGA	Shooting Stars
1997	Raja Casablanca	MAR	0-1 1-0 5-4p	GHA	Obuasi Goldfields
1998	ASEC Mimosas	CIV	0-0 4-1	ZIM	Dynamos
1999	Raja Casablanca	MAR	0-0 0-0 4-3p	TUN	Espérance Tunis
2000	Hearts of Oak	GHA	2-1 3-1	TUN	Espérance Tunis
2001	Al Ahly Cairo	EGY	1-1 3-0	RSA	Pretoria Sundowns
2002	Zamalek	EGY	0-0 1-0	MAR	Raja Casablanca
2003	Enyimba	NGA	2-0 0-1	EGY	Al Ismaili
2004	Enyimba	NGA	1-2 2-1 5-3p	TUN	Etoile du Sahel

Previously known the African Cup of Champion Clubs, the CAF Champions League is unpredictable and never short of controversy, but it remains hugely entertaining despite the growing number of African players who will never compete in it thanks to moves to Europe at increasingly young ages. The heart of the rivalry in the tournament lies between the Arab North African countries and the sub-Saharan countries. Until the 1980s the latter held the upper hand but for 17 years between 1981 and 1997 only Ghana's Asante Kotoko and Orlando Pirates from South Africa managed to prise the cup from the north. Since Pirates' win in 1995 the honours have been split evenly with five apiece, although it is fair to say that club football in North Africa is run along more professional lines and suffers less from an exodus of leading players. It has proved difficult for any club, however, to maintain a consistant presence in the tournament with the possible exception of the two Egyptian giants Al Ahly and record title holders Zamalek. In 2003 Enyimba became the first Nigerian African champions, retaining their title in 2004 but they were only the second club to do so and the first since 1968. They were also the 19th different club from 13 different countries to have won the title. No other continent has such a range of winners.

CAF CUP WINNERS' CUP

Year	Winners	Country	Score	Country	Runners-up
1975	Tonnerre Yaoundé	CMR	1-0 4-1	CIV	Stella Abidjan
1976	Shooting Stars	NGA	4-1 0-1	CMR	Tonnerre Yaoundé
1977	Enugu Rangers	NGA	4-1 1-1	CMR	Canon Yaoundé
1978	Horoya AC Conakry	GUI	3-1 2-1	ALG	MA Hussein-Dey
1979	Canon Yaoundé	CMR	2-0 6-0	KEN	Gor Mahia
1980	TP Mazembe	ZAI	3-1 1-0	CIV	Africa Sports
1981	Union Douala	CMR	2-1 0-0	NGA	Stationery Stores
1982	Al Mokaoulum	EGY	2-0 2-0	ZAM	Power Dynamos
1983	Al Mokaoulum	EGY	1-0 0-0	TOG	Agaza Lomé
1984	Al Ahly Cairo	EGY	1-0 0-1 4-2p	CMR	Canon Yaoundé
1985	Al Ahly Cairo	EGY	2-0 0-1	NGA	Leventis United
1986	Al Ahly Cairo	EGY	3-0 0-2	GAB	AS Sogara
1987	Gor Mahia	KEN	2-2 1-1	TUN	Espérance Tunis
1988	CA Bizerte	TUN	0-0 1-0	NGA	Ranchers Bees
1989	Al Merreikh	SUD	1-0 0-0	NGA	Bendel United
1990	BCC Lions	NGA	3-0 1-1	TUN	Club Africain
1991	Power Dynamos	ZAM	2-3 3-1	NGA	BCC Lions
1992	Africa Sports	CIV	1-1 4-0	BDI	Vital'O
1993	Al Ahly Cairo	EGY	1-1 1-0	CIV	Africa Sports
1994	DC Motema Pembe	ZAI	2-2 3-0	KEN	Kenya Breweries
1995	JS Kabylie	ALG	1-1 2-1	NGA	Julius Berger
1996	Al Mokaoulum	EGY	0-0 4-0	ZAI	Sodigraf
1997	Etoile du Sahel	TUN	2-0 0-1	MAR	FAR Rabat
1998	Espérance Tunis	TUN	3-1 1-1	ANG	Primeiro Agosto
1999	Africa Sports	CIV	1-0 1-1	TUN	Club Africain
2000	Zamalek	EGY	4-1 0-2	CMR	Canon Yaoundé
2001	Kaiser Chiefs	RSA	1-1 1-0	ANG	Inter Luanda
2002	Wydad Casablanca	MAR	1-0 1-2	GHA	Asante Kotoko
2003	Etoile du Sahel	TUN	0-2 3-0	NGA	Julius Berger

Discontinued after the 2003 tournament and replaced by the CAF Confederation Cup

CAF CUP

Year	Winners	Country	Score	Country	Runners-up
1992	Shooting Stars	NGA	0-0 3-0	UGA	Nakivubo Villa
1993	Stella Abidjan	CIV	0-0 2-0	TAN	SC Simba
1994	Bendel Insurance	NGA	0-1 3-0	ANG	Primeiro de Maio
1995	Etoile du Sahel	TUN	0-0 2-0	GUI	Kaloum Star
1996	Kawkab Marrakech	MAR	1-3 2-0	TUN	Etoile du Sahel
1997	Esperance Tunis	TUN	0-1 2-0	ANG	Petro Atlético
1998	CS Sfaxien	TUN	1-0 3-0	SEN	ASC Jeanne d'Arc
1999	Etoile du Sahel	TUN	1-0 1-2	MAR	Wydad Casablanca
2000	JS Kabylie	ALG	1-1 0-0	EGY	Al Ismaili
2001	JS Kabylie	ALG	1-2 1-0	TUN	Etoile du Sahel
2002	JS Kabylie	ALG	4-0 0-1	CMR	Tonnerre Youndé
2003	Raja Casablanca	MAR	2-0 0-0	CMR	Cotonsport Garoua

Discontinued after the 2003 tournament and replaced by the CAF Confederation Cup

CAF CONFEDERATION CUP

Year	Winners	Country	Score	Country	Runners-up
2004	Hearts of Oak	GHA	1-1 1-1 8-7p	GHA	Asante Kotoko

With the decision to allow more than one team from each country into the CAF Champions League, CAF decided in 2003 to discarded the Cup Winners' Cup and the CAF Cup in favour of a 'best of the rest' tournament - the CAF Confederation Cup. As with the UEFA Cup in Europe the Confederation Cup also takes teams knocked out in early rounds of the Champions League and both finalists in the first edition in 2004 came via that route. As with the CAF Champions League there is a group stage with the winners of both groups going through to the final.

COSAFA CUP

Year	Host Country	Winners	Score	Runners-up	Venue
1997	Home and away	Zambia	1-1	Namibia	Windhoek
1998	Home and away	Zambia	1-0	Zimbabwe	Harare
1999	Home and away	Angola	1-0 1-1	Namibia	Luanda & Windhoek
2000	Home and away	Zimbabwe	3-0 3-0	Lesotho	Maseru & Bulawayo
2001	Home and away	Angola	0-0 1-0	Zimbabwe	Luanda & Harare
2002	Home and away	South Africa	3-1 1-0	Malawi	Blantyre & Durban
2003	Home and away	Zimbabwe	2-1 2-0	Malawi	Blantyre & Harare
2004	Home and away	Angola	0-0 5-4p	Zambia	Lusaka

The 1997 and 1998 tournaments were played as a league. The result listed is that between the winners and runners-up

COPA AMILCAR CABRAL

Year	Host Country	Winners	Score	Runners-up	Venue
1979	Guinea-Bissau	Senegal	1-0	Mali	Bissau
1980	Gambia	Senegal	1-0	Gambia	Banjul
1981	Mali	Guinea	0-0 6-5p	Mali	Bamako
1982	Cape Verde	Guinea	3-0	Senegal	Praia
1983	Mauritania	Senegal	3-0	Guinea-Bissau	Nouakchott
1984	Sierra Leone	Senegal	0-0 5-3p	Sierra Leone	Freetown
1985	Gambia	Senegal	1-0	Gambia	Banjul
1986	Senegal	Senegal	3-1	Sierra Leone	Dakar
1987	Guinea	Guinea	1-0	Mali	Conakry
1988	Guinea-Bissau	Guinea	3-2	Mali	Bissau
1989	Mali	Mali	3-0	Guinea	Bamako
1991	Senegal	Senegal	1-0	Cape Verde Islands	Dakar
1993	Sierra Leone	Sierra Leone	2-0	Senegal	Freetown
1995	Mauritania	Sierra Leone	0-0 4-2p	Mauritania	Nouakchott
1997	Gambia	Mali	1-0	Senegal	Banjul
2000	Cape Verde	Cape Verde Islands	1-0	Senegal	Praia
2001	Mali	Senegal	3-1	Gambia	Bamako
2005	Guinea Bissau				

COUPE CEMAC

Year	Host Country	Winners	Score	Runners-up	Venue
2003	Congo	Cameroon	3-2	Central African Rep.	Brazzaville
2005	Gabon	Cameroon	1-0	Chad	Libreville

There is a long and rich history of regional tournaments in Africa dating back to 1926 when William Gossage sponsored an annual competition between Kenya and Uganda. From 1945 it was extended to include Tanganyika and then Zanzibar from 1949 and was a popular feature of the football calendar. With independence the name of the competition was changed to the Challenge Cup in 1967. With the creation in 1973 of CECAFA – the Confederation of East and Central African Football Associations – the tournament was renamed as the CECAFA Cup and expanded to include Zambia and Somalia; Malawi joined in 1975, Sudan in 1980, Zimbabwe in 1982, Ethiopia in 1983, Seychelles in 1992, Eritrea and Djibouti in 1994, Rwanda in 1995 and finally Burundi in 1998. The Southern African contingent left to join COSAFA in the aftermath of South Africa's return to international football with the first COSAFA Castle Cup held in 1997 and contested since by Angola, Botswana, Lesotho, Madagascar, Malawi, Mauritius, Mozambique, Namibia, Seychelles, South Africa, Swaziland, Zambia and Zimbabwe. The situation in West Africa has been much more fragmented although the Copa Amilcar Cabral has stood the test of time unlike many other tournaments in the region. The Coupe CEMAC is the latest addition to the list of tournaments. Introduced in 2003 entries come from the member states of the Communauté Economique et Monétaire de l'Afrique Central.

CECAFA CUP

Year	Host Country	Winners	Score	Runners-up
1973	Uganda	Uganda	2-1	Tanzania
1974	Tanzania	Tanzania	1-1 5-3p	Uganda
1975	Zambia	Kenya	0-0 5-4p	Malawi
1976	Zanzibar	Uganda	2-0	Zambia
1977	Somalia	Uganda	0-0 5-3p	Zambia
1978	Malawi	Malawi	3-2	Zambia
1979	Kenya	Malawi	3-2	Kenya
1980	Sudan	Sudan	1-0	Tanzania
1981	Tanzania	Kenya	1-0	Tanzania
1982	Uganda	Kenya	1-1 5-3p	Uganda
1983	Kenya	Kenya	1-0	Zimbabwe
1984	Uganda	Zambia	0-0 3-0p	Malawi
1985	Zimbabwe	Zimbabwe	2-0	Kenya
1986	Sudan	Not held		
1987	Ethiopia	Ethiopia	1-1 5-4p	Zimbabwe
1988	Malawi	Malawi	3-1	Zambia
1989	Kenya	Uganda	3-3 2-1	Malawi
1990	Zanzibar	Uganda	2-0	Sudan
1991	Uganda	Zambia	2-0	Kenya
1992	Tanzania	Uganda	1-0	Tanzania
1993	Uganda	Not held		
1994	Kenya	Tanzania	2-2 4-3p	Uganda
1995	Uganda	Zanzibar	1-0	Uganda
1996	Sudan	Uganda	1-0	Sudan
1997		Not held		
1998	Rwanda	Not held		
1999	Rwanda	Rwanda B	3-1	Kenya
2000	Uganda	Uganda	2-0	Uganda B
2001	Rwanda	Ethiopia	2-1	Kenya
2002	Tanzania	Kenya	3-2	Tanzania
2003	Sudan	Uganda	2-0	Rwanda
2004	Ethiopia	Ethiopia	3-0	Burundi

CECAFA CLUB CHAMPIONSHIP

Year	Winners	Country	Score	Country	Runners-up
1974	Simba SC	TAN	1-0 †	KEN	Abaluhya FC
1975	Young Africans	TAN	2-0	TAN	Simba SC
1976	Luo Union	KEN	2-1	TAN	Young Africans
1977	Luo Union	KEN	2-1	SOM	Horsed
1978	Kamapala City Council	UGA	0-0 3-2p	TAN	Simba SC
1979	Abaluhya FC	KEN	1-0	UGA	Kampala City Council
1980	Gor Mahia	KEN	3-2	KEN	Abaluhya FC
1981	Gor Mahia	KEN	1-0	TAN	Simba SC
1982	AFC Leopards	KEN	1-0	ZIM	Rio Tinto
1983	AFC Leopards	KEN	2-1	MWI	Admarc Tigers
1984	AFC Leopards	KEN	2-1	KEN	Gor Mahia
1985	Gor Mahia	KEN	2-0	KEN	AFC Leopards
1986	El Merreikh	SUD	2-2 4-2p	TAN	Young Africans
1987	Nakivubo Villa	UGA	1-0	SUD	El Merreikh
1988	Kenya Breweries	KEN	2-0	SUD	El Merreikh
1989	Kenya Breweries	KEN	3-0	TAN	Coastal Union
1990	Not held				
1991	Simba SC	TAN	3-0	UGA	Nikivubo Villa
1992	Simba SC	TAN	1-1 5-4p	TAN	Young Africans
1993	Young Africans	TAN	2-1	UGA	Nakivubo Villa
1994	El Merreikh	SUD	2-1	UGA	Express FC

CECAFA CLUB CHAMPIONSHIP (CONT'D)

Year	Winners	Country	Score	Country	Runners-up
1995	Simba SC	TAN	1-1 5-3p	UGA	Express FC
1996	Simba SC	TAN	1-0	RWA	APR FC
1997	AFC Leopards	KEN	1-0	KEN	Kenya Breweries
1998	Rayyon Sport	RWA	2-1	ZAN	Mlandege
1999	Young Africans	TAN	1-1 4-1p	UGA	SC Villa
2000	Tusker FC	KEN	3-1	RWA	APR FC
2001	Tusker FC	KEN	0-0 3-0p	KEN	Oserian
2002	Simba SC	TAN	1-0	BDI	Prince Louis
2003	SC Villa	UGA	1-0	TAN	Simba SC
2004	APR FC	RWA	3-1	KEN	Ulinzi Stars
2005	SC Villa	UGA	3-0	RWA	APR FC

PAST AFRICAN PLAYER OF THE YEAR AWARDS

PLAYER OF THE YEAR 1970

KEITA Salif	Saint-Étienne	MLI	54
POKOU Laurent	ASEC Abidjan	CIV	28
ABOUGREISHA Ali	Ismaili	EGY	28
KALALA Pierre	TP Englebert	ZAI	19
LALMAS Hacène	CR Belcourt	ALG	15
SORY Petit	Hafia	GUI	9
ALLAL Ben Kassou	FAR Rabat	MAR	5
MENSAH Robert	Asante Kotoko	GHA	5
KOFI Osei	Asante Kotoko	GHA	5
Four players with four votes			

PLAYER OF THE YEAR 1971

SUNDAY Ibrahim	Asante Kotoko	GHA	29
MENSAH Robert	Asante Kotoko	GHA	15
OBENGUE Lea	Canon	CMR	13
POKOU Laurent	ASEC Abidjan	CIV	8
ATTOUGA Sadok	Club Africain	TUN	8
KIBONGE Mafu	Victoria Club	ZAI	6
M'PELE Francois	Ajaccio	CGO	6
KOUM Emmanuel	Monaco	CMR	6
LALMAS Hacène	CR Belcourt	ALG	6
KALLET BIALY Ernest	Africa Sports	CIV	6

PLAYER OF THE YEAR 1972

SOULEYMANE Cherif	Hafia	GUI	21
BWANGA Tshimen	TP Mazembe	ZAI	16
SORY Petit	Hafia	GUI	14
HANY Moustafa	Al Ahly	EGY	12
FARRAS Ahmed	Mohammedia	MAR	11
HADEFI Miloud	MO Oran	ALG	11
MALIK Jabir	Asante Kotoko	GHA	10
ABOUGREISHA Ali	Ismaili	EGY	8
MINGA Jean-Noel	CARA	CGO	8
N'TUMBA Kalala	Vita	ZAI	8

PLAYER OF THE YEAR 1973

BWANGA Tshimen	TP Mazembe	ZAI	49
KAZADI Mwamba	TP Mazembe	ZAI	44
POKOU Laurent	ASEC Abidjan	CIV	41
KAKOKO Etepe	Imana	ZAI	29
FARRAS Ahmed	Mohammedia	MAR	18
SAM Yaw	Asante Kotoko	GHA	16
KEMBO Kembo Uba	Vita	ZAI	15
SOULEYMANE Cherif	Hafia	GUI	9
Three players with eight votes			

PLAYER OF THE YEAR 1974

MOUKILA Paul	CARA	CGO	57
LOBILO Boba	Vita	ZAI	32
SHEHATA Hassan	Zamalek	EGY	28
CHAMA Dickson	Gr'n Buffaloes	ZAM	16
FARRAS Ahmed	Mohammedia	MAR	14
N'DAYE Mulamba	Vita	ZAI	10
KAKOKO Etepe	Imana	ZAI	8
Five players with six votes			

PLAYER OF THE YEAR 1975

FARRAS Ahmed	Mohammedia	MAR	28
N'JO LEA Mamadou	Hafia	GUI	24
MILLA Roger	Canon	CMR	24
DHIAB Tarak	Esperance	TUN	16
SAGNA Christophe	Jeanne d'Arc	SEN	15
SORY Petit	Hafia	GUI	10
LARBI Ahardane	Wydad	MAR	9
GAAFAR Farouk	Zamalek	EGY	7
ATTOUGA Sadok	Club Africain	TUN	7
Three players with five votes			

PLAYER OF THE YEAR 1976

MILLA Roger	Tonnerre	CMR	33
CAMARA Papa	Hafia	GUI	32
BENCHEIKH Ali	MC Alger	ALG	27
SYLLA Bengally	Hafia	GUI	26
FARRAS Ahmed	Mohammedia	MAR	12
BETROUNI Rachid	MC Alger	ALG	12
LARBI Ahardane	Wydad	MAR	11
ATTOUGA Sadok	Club Africain	TUN	11
DHIAB Tarak	Esperance	TUN	10
SORY Petit	Hafia	GUI	10

PLAYER OF THE YEAR 1977

DHIAB Tarak	Espérance	TUN	45
CAMARA Papa	Hafia	GUI	33
ODEGBAMI Segun	Shooting Stars	NGA	29
POLO Mohamed	Olympics	GHA	15
BWALYA Thomas	Mufulira	ZAM	6
BENCHEIKH Ali	MC Alger	ALG	5
ATTOUGA Sadok	Club Africain	TUN	4
GAAFAR Farouk	Zamalek	EGY	3
BAHAMBOULA Jonas	Diable Noir	CGO	3
SOULEYMANE Cherif	Hafia	GUI	3

PLAYER OF THE YEAR 1978

ABDUL RAZAK Karim	Asante Kotoko	GHA	58
BENCHEIKH Ali	MP Algiers	ALG	33
N'KONO Thomas	Canon	CMR	29
CHUKWU Christian	Enugu Rangers	NGA	25
SYLLA Bengally	Hafia	GUI	20
DHIAB Tarak	Al Ahly Jeddah	TUN	18
LAHZANI Temime	Espérance	TUN	12
MANGA-ONGUENE J	Canon	CMR	10
OMONDI Philip	Kampala CC	UGA	9
Four players with four votes			

PLAYER OF THE YEAR 1979

N'KONO Thomas	Canon	CMR	55
ARMAH Adolf	Hearts of Oak	GHA	23
BANGOURA Kerfalla	Horoya	GUI	15
CAMPAORE Abdoulaye	Bobo Dioulasso	BFA	13
OLUOCH Nahashion	Gor Mahia	KEN	9
KIYIKA Tokodia	Imana	ZAI	8
AGBONIFO Felix	Shooting Stars	NGA	7
MIEZAN Pascal	ASEC Abidjan	CIV	6
LAWAL Muda	Shooting Stars	NGA	5
Four players with four votes			

PLAYER OF THE YEAR 1980

MANGA-ONGUENE J	Canon	CMR	64
ODEGBAMI Segun	Shooting Stars	NGA	41
ABEGA Théophile	Canon	CMR	18
BELLOUMI Lakhdar	GCR Mascara	ALG	13
MAYELE Ayel	AS Bilima	ZAI	12
N'KONO Thomas	Canon	CMR	12
KOUICI Mustapha	CR Belcourt	MAR	11
MASSENGO Elunga	TP Mazembe	ZAI	7
BENSAOULA Tadj	MC Oran	ALG	6
KAZADI Mwamba	TP Mazembe	ZAI	6

PLAYER OF THE YEAR 1981

BELLOUMI Lakhdar	GCR Mascara	ALG	78
N'KONO Thomas	Canon	CMR	54
FERGANI Ali	JE Tizi-Ouzou	ALG	26
EKOULE Eugène	Union Douala	CMR	18
ABEGA Théophile	Canon	CMR	16
BOUDERBALA Aziz	Wydad	MAR	16
ODEGBAMI Segun	Shooting Stars	NGA	8
KEITA Cheik	Kaloum Stars	GUI	6
KOUADIO Koffi	ASEC Abidjan	CIV	4
ZAKI Badou	Wydad	MAR	4

PLAYER OF THE YEAR 1982

N'KONO Thomas	Español	CMR	83
ASSAD Salah	Mulhouse	ALG	54
BELLOUMI Lakhdar	GCR Mascara	ALG	36
EL KHATIB Mahmoud	Al Ahly Cairo	EGY	28
ABEGA Théophile	Canon	CMR	23
KAUMBA Peter	Power Dynamos	ZAM	23
ASASE Albert	Asante Kotoko	GHA	22
AFRIYIE Opoku	Asante Kotoko	GHA	13
MADJER Rabah	Hussein Dey	ALG	9
MERZEKANE Chaabane	Hussein Dey	ALG	8

PLAYER OF THE YEAR 1983

EL KHATIB Mahmoud	Al Ahly Cairo	EGY	98
N'TI Opoku	Asante Kotoko	GHA	89
MOUTAIROU Rafiou	Agaza Lomé	TOG	19
ABEGA Théophile	Canon	CMR	18
BELL Joseph Antoine	Al Mokaouloum	CMR	18
ABDUL RAZAK Karim	Al Mokaouloum	GHA	18
SECK Cheikh	Diaraf Dakar	SEN	11
NASSER Mohamed Ali	Al Ahly Cairo	EGY	7
HADDAOUI Mustapha	Rajan	MAR	7
MADJER Rabah	Racing Paris	ALG	7

PLAYER OF THE YEAR 1984

ABEGA Théophile	Toulouse	CMR	124
YOUSSEF Ibrahim	Zamalek	EGY	65
BELL Joseph Antoine	Al Mokaouloum	CMR	65
NWOSU Henry	Nigerian Bank	NGA	47
ABOU ZEID Taher	Al Ahly Cairo	EGY	28
FOFANA Youssouf	Cannes	CIV	28
EL KHATIB Mahmoud	Al Ahly Cairo	EGY	28
KESHI Stephen	Nigerian Bank	NGA	16
BELLOUMI Lakhdar	GCR Mascara	ALG	12
MSIYA Clifton	Berrick Power	MWI	12

PLAYER OF THE YEAR 1985

TIMOUMI Mohamed	FAR Rabat	MAR	113
MADJER Rabah	Porto	ALG	45
MENAD Djamel	JE Tizi-Ouzou	ALG	39
YOUSSEF Ibrahim	Zamalek	EGY	39
ZAKI Badou	Wydad	MAR	33
FOFANA Youssouf	Monaco	CIV	31
BELLOUMI Lakhdar	GCR Mascara	ALG	20
PELE Abedi	Dragons	GHA	19
BOCANDE Jules	Metz	SEN	17
Two players with 16 votes			

PLAYER OF THE YEAR 1986

ZAKI Badou	Real Mallorca	MAR	125
BOUDERBALA Aziz	Sion	MAR	88
MILLA Roger	Montpellier	CMR	80
ABOU ZEID Taher	Al Ahly	EGY	47
TIMOUMI Mohamed	Real Murcia	MAR	35
BOCANDE Jules	PSG	SEN	13
DOLMY Abdelmajid	Raja	MAR	13
PELE Abedi	Niort	GHA	13
CHABALA Efford	Nkana	ZAM	11
DRID Nacer	MP Oran	ALG	11

PLAYER OF THE YEAR 1987

MADJER Rabah	Porto	ALG	130
FOFANA Youssouf	Monaco	CIV	63
OMAM BIYIK François	Laval	CMR	52
ABDELGHANI Magdi	Al Ahly Cairo	EGY	37
ABOU ZEID Taher	Al Ahly Cairo	EGY	25
MALUNGA Kennedy	Club Brugge	MWI	24
DAWO Peter	Gor Mahia	KEN	21
PELE Abedi	Marseille	GHA	17
AYOYI Ambrose	AFC Leopards	KEN	15
MILLA Roger	Montpellier	CMR	14

PLAYER OF THE YEAR 1988

BWALYA Kalusha	Cercle Brugge	ZAM	111
MILLA Roger	Montpellier	CMR	68
FOFANA Youssouf	Monaco	CIV	40
WEAH George	Monaco	LBR	32
BOUDERBALA Aziz	Racing Paris	MAR	27
RUFAI Peter	Lokeren	NGA	27
KESHI Stephen	Anderlecht	NGA	14
KUNDE Emmanuel	Reims	CMR	14
KINGAMBO Jacques	St Truidense	ZAI	13
BELL Joseph Antoine	Toulon	CMR	12

PLAYER OF THE YEAR 1989

WEAH George	Monaco	LBR	133
BELL Joseph Antoine	Bordeaux	CMR	105
BWALYA Kalusha	PSV	ZAM	49
PELE Abedi	Lille OSC	GHA	40
OMAM BIYIK François	Laval	CMR	31
ABDELGHANI Magdi	Beira Mar	EGY	30
SHOUBEIR Ahmed	Al Ahly Cairo	EGY	28
TATAW Stephen	Tonnerre	CMR	19
KESHI Stephen	Anderlecht	NGA	18
HASSAN Hossam	Al Ahly Cairo	EGY	17

PLAYER OF THE YEAR 1990

MILLA Roger	No Club	CMR	209
EL OUAZANI Cherif	Aydinspor	ALG	64
MADJER Rabah	Porto	ALG	60
OMAM BIYIK François	Stade Rennais	CMR	60
SHOUBEIR Ahmed	Al Ahly Cairo	EGY	49
RAMZY Hany	Neuchâtel	EGY	41
MAKANAKY Cyrille	Málaga	CMR	34
WEAH George	Monaco	LBR	26
PELE Abedi	Marseille	GHA	23
HASSAN Hossam	PAOK	EGY	22

PLAYER OF THE YEAR 1991

PELE Abedi	Marseile	GHA	159
WEAH George	Monaco	LBR	106
OMAM BIYIK François	Cannes	CMR	52
BWALYA Kalusha	PSV	ZAM	30
LAMPETY Nii	Anderlecht	GHA	29
YEBOAH Anthony	Ein. Frankfurt	GHA	20
MENDY Roger	Monaco	SEN	18
TRAORE Abdoulaye	ASEC Abidjan	CIV	16
FOFANA Youssouf	Monaco	CIV	14
BOUDERBALA Aziz	Lyon	EGY	13

PLAYER OF THE YEAR 1992

PELE Abedi	Marseille	GHA	198
WEAH George	PSG	LBR	161
YEBOAH Anthony	Ein. Frankfurt	GHA	64
TRAORE Abdoulaye	ASEC Abidjan	CIV	36
GOUAMENE Alain	Raja	CIV	33
N'DORAM Japhet	Nantes	CHA	30
NDLOVU Peter	Coventry City	ZIM	24
YEKINI Rashidi	Vitoria Setubal	NGA	20
BWALYA Kalusha	PSV	ZAM	15
DAOUDI Rachid	Wydad	MAR	14

PLAYER OF THE YEAR 1993

PELE Abedi	Lyonnais	GHA	119
YEBOAH Anthony	Ein. Frankfurt	GHA	117
YEKINI Rashidi	Vitoria Setubal	NGA	104
IKPEBA Victor	Monaco	NGA	57
WEAH George	PSG	LBR	56
BWALYA Kalusha	PSV	ZAM	48
OMAM BIYIK François	RC Lens	CMR	28
DAOUDI Rachid	Wydad	MAR	20
NDLOVU Peter	Coventry City	ZAM	19
TRAORE Abdoulaye	ASEC Abidjan	CIV	16

PLAYER OF THE YEAR 1994

WEAH George	PSG	LBR	148
AMUNIKE Emmanuel	Sporting CP	NGA	133
AMOKACHI Daniel	Everton	NGA	99
YEKINI Rashidi	Olympiakos	NGA	87
BWALYA Kalusha	América	ZAM	37
YEBOAH Anthony	Ein. Frankfurt	GHA	32
GEORGE Finidi	Ajax	NGA	31
TIEHI Joël	Le Havre	CIV	22
N'DORAM Japhet	Nantes	CHA	18
OKOCHA Jay-Jay	Ein. Frankfurt	NGA	18

CAF PLAYER OF THE YEAR 1992

PELE Abedi	Marseille	GHA
GOUAMENE Alain	Raja	CIV
YEKINI Rashidi	Vitoria Setubal	NGA
WEAH George	PSG	LBR
DAOUDI Rachid	Wydad	MAR
MAGUY Serge Alain	Africa Sports	CIV
YEBOAH Anthony	Ein. Frankfurt	GHA
RAMZY Hany	Neuchatel	EGY
NDAW Moussa	Wydad	SEN
AMOKACHI Daniel	Club Brugge	NGA

CAF PLAYER OF THE YEAR 1993

YEKINI Rashidi	Vitoria Setubal	NGA
PELE Abedi	Marseille	GHA
WEAH George	PSG	LBR
YEBOAH Anthony	Ein. Frankfurt	GHA
OMAM BIYIK François	RC Lens	CMR
NAYBET Nouredine	Nantes	MAR
IKPEBA Victor	Monaco	NGA
BELL Joseph Antoine	Saint-Etienne	CMR
Three players in 9th place		

CAF PLAYER OF THE YEAR 1994

AMUNIKE Emmanuel	Sporting CP	NGA
WEAH George	PSG	LBR
YEKINI Rashidi	Olympiakos	NGA
GEORGE Finidi	Ajax	NGA
AMOKACHI Daniel	Everton	NGA
N'DORAM Japhet	Nantes	CHA
TIEHI Joel	Le Havre	CIV
OKOCHA Jay-Jay	Ein. Frankfurt	NGA
MAGUY Serge Alain	Africa Sports	CIV
OLISEH Sunday	FC Liège	NGA

CAF PLAYER OF THE YEAR 1995

WEAH George	Milan	LBR
N'DORAM Japhet	Nantes	CHA
GEORGE Finidi	Ajax	NGA
YEBOAH Anthony	Leeds	GHA
KANU Nwankwo	Ajax	NGA
AMUNIKE Emmanuel	Sporting CP	NGA
AMOKACHI Daniel	Everton	NGA
TIEHI Joel	Martigues	CIV
ONDO Valery	Mbilinga	GAB
Two players in 10th place		

CAF PLAYER OF THE YEAR 1996

KANU Nwankwo	Internazionale	NGA
WEAH George	Milan	LBR
AMOKACHI Daniel	Besiktas	NGA
FISH Mark	Lazio	RSA
GEORGE Finidi	Betis	NGA
N'DORAM Japhet	Nantes	CHA
BWALYA Kalusha	América	ZAM
AMUNIKE Emmanuel	Sporting CP	NGA
OLISEH Sunday	1.FC Köln	NGA
YEBOAH Anthony	Leeds United	GHA

CAF PLAYER OF THE YEAR 1997

IKPEBA Victor	Monaco	NGA	56
N'DORAM Japhet	Monaco	CHA	40
WEST Taribo	Internazionale	NGA	35
OLISEH Sunday	Ajax	NGA	24
SONGO'O Jacques	Deportivo LC	CMR	17
WEAH George	Milan	LBR	15
SELLIMI Adel	Nantes	TUN	12
GEORGE Finidi	Betis	NGA	9
PAULAO	Coimbra	ANG	7
M'BOMA Patrick	Gamba Osaka	CMR	6

CAF PLAYER OF THE YEAR 1998

HADJI Mustapha	Deportivo LC	MAR	76
OKOCHA Jay-Jay	PSG	NGA	74
OLISEH Sunday	Ajax	NGA	58
HASSAN Hossam	Al Ahly Cairo	EGY	34
MCCARTHY Benni	Ajax	RSA	24
GUEL Tchiressoua	ASEC Abidjan	CIV	16
AKONNOR Charles	Fortuna Köln	GHA	12
FOE Marc-Vivien	RC Lens	CMR	10
GEORGE Finidi	Betis	NGA	8
SONG Rigobert	Salernitana	CMR	6

CAF PLAYER OF THE YEAR 1999

KANU Nwankwo	Arsenal	NGA	46
KUFFOUR Samuel	Bayern	GHA	44
BAKAYOKO Ibrahima	Marseille	CIV	42
WEAH George	Milan	LBR	40
OKOCHA Jay-Jay	PSG	NGA	30
DINDANE Aruna	ASEC Abidjan	CIV	28
IKPEBA Victor	Dortmund	NGA	26
BENARBIA Ali	PSG	ALG	24
HADJI Mustapha	Coventry City	MAR	24
BADRA Khaled	Espérance	TUN	22

CAF PLAYER OF THE YEAR 2000

M'BOMA Patrick	Parma	CMR	123
LAUREN Etame-Mayer	Arsenal	CMR	36
ETO'O Samuel	Real Mallorca	CMR	29
GEREMI Njitap	Real Madrid	CMR	27
KANU Nwankwo	Arsenal	NGA	21
NAYBET Nouredine	Deportivo LC	MAR	20
HASSAN Hossam	Zamalek	EGY	17
NONDA Shabani	Monaco	COD	11
BARTLETT Shaun	Charlton	RSA	10
RAMY Hani	Werder	EGY	10

CAF PLAYER OF THE YEAR 2001

DIOUF El-Hadji	RC Lens	SEN	93
KUFFOUR Samuel	Bayern	GHA	66
ETO'O Samuel	Real Mallorca	CMR	34
KALLON Mohamed	Internazionale	SLE	28
NAYBET Nouredine	Deportivo LC	MAR	26
FADIGA Khalilou	Auxerre	SEN	22
BAGAYOKO Mamadou	Strasbourg	MLI	16
M'BOMA Patrick	Sunderland	CMR	15
RAMY Hani	Werder	EGY	12
Two players with 10 votes			

CAF PLAYER OF THE YEAR 2002

DIOUF El-Hadji	Liverpool	SEN	93
DIOP Papa Bouba	RC Lens	SEN	46
HOSSAM Ahmed	Celta Vigo	EGY	42
FADIGA Khalilou	Auxerre	SEN	41
LAUREN Etame-Mayer	Arsenal	CMR	35
CAMARA Henri	Sedan	SEN	20
AGHAHOWA Julius	Shakhtar	NGA	19
TRABELSI Hatem	Ajax	TUN	19
DIAO Salif	Liverpool	SEN	17
KEITA Seydou	RC Lens	MLI	16

CAF PLAYER OF THE YEAR 2003

ETO'O Samuel	Mallorca	CMR

CAF PLAYER OF THE YEAR 2004

ETO'O Samuel	Barcelona	CMR	116
DROGBA Didier	Chelsea	CIV	90
OKOCHA Jay-Jay	Bolton	NGA	68
MCCARTHY Benni	Porto	RSA	31
ADEBAYOR Emmanuel	Monaco	TOG	21

CAF CHAMPIONS LEAGUE 2004

2004 saw a restructuring of African club football with the scrapping of the Cup Winners' Cup and CAF Cup, the expansion of the CAF Champions League with the top 12 ranked nations – Algeria, Angola, Cameroon, Congo DR, Côte d'Ivoire, Egypt, Ghana, Morocco, Nigeria, Senegal, South Africa and Tunisia – allowed to enter two teams and the creation of a new tournament, the CAF Confederation Cup. The elite nations now have four clubs in continental club competition with two places also in the Confederation Cup. As with the UEFA Cup, CAF have adopted the system whereby teams knocked out in the second round of the Champions League enter the Confederation Cup at the intermediate round. The 2004 CAF Champions League was won by Nigeria's Enyimba, the first club to retain the title since TP Englebert did so in 1968 and the Nigerians will be hoping that they make it a hat-trick of titles as the 2005 winners will qualify for theFIFA Club World Championship in Japan in December 2005. The 2004 campaign began with Egypt's Ismailia still campaigning to get the result of the 2003 final overturned in their favour but Enyimba proved that when properly run, clubs from sub-Saharan Africa can be a match for their counterparts in North Africa. Hearts of Oak and Asante Kotoko made it an all-Ghanaian final in the Confederation Cup, having both been knocked out of the Champions League before the group stage. Hoping for a first continental title since 1983 Kotoko came close but it was their fierce rivals from Accra who took the Cup after a penalty shoot-out following two 1-1 draws.

PRELIMINARY ROUND 1ST LEG	
Conakry	
7-03-2004	
ASFAG Conakry	**0**
ASC Diaraf	**1**

PRELIMINARY ROUND 2ND LEG	
Dakar	
20-03-2004	
ASC Diaraf	**2**
Ndoye [20], Ayanda [34]	
ASFAG Conakry	**1**
Sylla [53]	

PRELIMINARY ROUND 1ST LEG	
Bulawayo	
7-03-2004	
Amazulu	**3**
Nyoni [20], Sandaka [49], Komani [75]	
Maxaquene	**1**
Mabui [44]	

PRELIMINARY ROUND 2ND LEG	
Maputo	
21-03-2004	
Maxaquene	**3**
Helder [3], Miro [57], Mabui [90]	
Amazulu	**4**
Nyandoro [15], Zvavanhu [30], Komani [39], Nyoni [51]	

PRELIMINARY ROUND 1ST LEG	
Luanda	
6-03-2004	
Petro Atlético	**3**
Flávio [43], Lopes [70], Faial [93+]	
Atlético Malabo	**1**
Edouthá [17]	

PRELIMINARY ROUND 2ND LEG	
Malabo	
21-03-2004	
Atlético Malabo	**1**
Ndongui [7]	
Petro Atlético	**3**
Tana [25], Flávio [58], Lopes [81]	

PRELIMINARY ROUND 1ST LEG	
Kigali	
6-03-2004	
APR FC	**7**
Zoweldi [13], Hassan [42], Koy [44], Karekezi [45+], Nsengiyumva 2 [57][71], Silenge [83]	
Anseba	**1**

PRELIMINARY ROUND 2ND LEG	
Asmara	
21-03-2004	
Anseba	**2**
APR FC	**4**

PRELIMINARY ROUND 1ST LEG	
Cotonou	
7-03-2004	
Dragons de l'Ouémé	**1**
Monde [78]	
AS Douanes	**1**
Seibou [74]	

PRELIMINARY ROUND 2ND LEG	
Lomé	
21-03-2004	
AS Douanes	**0**
Dragons de l'Ouémé	**0**

PRELIMINARY ROUND 1ST LEG	
Blantyre	
6-03-2004	
Bakili Bullets	**2**
Khondowe	
SC Villa	**1**
Isabirye	

PRELIMINARY ROUND 2ND LEG	
Kampala	
21-03	
SC Villa	**0**
Bakili Bullets	**0**

CAF CHAMPIONS LEAGUE 2004

Preliminary Round

Team	Country	Score
ASC Diaraf	SEN	1 2
ASFAG Conakry *	GUI	0 1
Maxaquene	MOZ	1 3
Amazulu *	ZIM	3 4
Petro Atlético *	ANG	3 3
Atlético Malabo	EQG	1 1
Anseba SC	ERI	1 2
APR FC *	RWA	7 4
Dragons de l'Ouémé *	BEN	1 0
AS Douanes	TOG	1 0
SC Villa	UGA	1 0
Bakili Bullets *	MWI	2 0
Zanaco	ZAM	0 3
Simba SC *	TAN	1 1
Eco Redipharm *	MAD	0 0
Saint Michael United	SEY	0 2
Orlando Pirates	RSA	3 4
Matlama *	LES	0 0
Saint Michel d'Ouenzé *	CGO	2 0 4p
US Bitam	GAB	0 2 3p
Al Ittihad Tripoli *	LBY	1 0
Sahel SC	NIG	0 2
Armed Forces *	GAM	0 0
Jeanne d'Arc	SEN	3 3
Ulinzi Stars ‡	KEN	-
AS Vita Club *	COD	-
AS Tempête Mocaf ‡	CTA	-
Asante Kotoko	GHA	-
Julius Berger	NGA	2 0
ASFA Yennega *	BFA	3 0
Civics CC	NAM	0 0
SuperSport United *	RSA	5 1
AS Port Louis 2000	MRI	-
US Stade Tamponnaise ‡	REU	-
Al Hilal Omdurman	SUD	2 1
Saint George SC *	ETH	1 1
Stade Malien *	MLI	0 0
Hearts of Oak	GHA	0 2
Atlético Aviação *	ANG	1 1
SC Cimenterie	COD	1 0
ASC Nasr de Sebkha	MTN	0
Hassania US Agadir *	MAR	7

First Round

Team	Country	Score
Enyimba *	NGA	3 0
ASC Diaraf	SEN	0 2
Amazulu *	ZIM	0 1
Petro Atlético	ANG	0 2
APR FC	RWA	2 4
Zamalek *	EGY	3 1
AS Douanes	TOG	1 0
Africa Sports *	CIV	4 1
Bakili Bullets	MWI	1 0 6p
Zanaco *	ZAM	0 1 5p
Saint Michael United *	SEY	2 1
Orlando Pirates	RSA	3 5
Cotonsport Garoua *	CMR	4 0
Saint Michel d'Ouenzé	CGO	1 1
Sahel SC	NIG	0 0
Espérance *	TUN	4 1
Jeanne d'Arc	SEN	0 2 5p
Raja Casablanca *	MAR	2 0 4p
AS Vita Club	COD	0 1
Canon Yaoundé *	CMR	3 1
Asante Kotoko	GHA	1 0
ASEC Mimosas *	CIV	1 0
ASFA Yennega	BFA	1 2
USM Alger *	ALG	8 2
SuperSport United	RSA	1 2
AS Port Louis 2000 *	MRI	1 0
Al Ahly *	EGY	0 0
Al Hilal Omdurman	SUD	1 0
Hearts of Oak *	GHA	4 1
Atlético Aviação	ANG	1 1
Hassania US Agadir	MAR	0 0
Etoile du Sahel *	TUN	2 0

Second Round

Team	Score
Enyimba *	1 2
Petro Atlético	1 1
APR FC *	1 0 1p
Africa Sports	0 1 3p
Bakili Bullets	1 1
Orlando Pirates *	2 0
Cotonsport Garoua	0 1
Espérance *	3 0
Jeanne d'Arc *	2 1
Canon Yaoundé	0 2
Asante Kotoko	0 2 1p
USM Alger *	2 0 3p
SuperSport United *	2 0
Al Hilal Omdurman	0 0
Hearts of Oak *	1 0 4p
Etoile du Sahel	0 1 5p

* Home club in the 1st leg • Losing teams in the second round enter the CAF Confederation Cup • ‡ Team withdrew

CAF CHAMPIONS LEAGUE 2004

Champions League Stage **Semi-finals** **Final**

Group A		Pts	TUN	NGA	CIV	MWI
Etoile du Sahel	TUN	11		1-0	2-0	1-1
Enyimba	NGA	8	1-1		0-1	6-0
Africa Sports	CIV	7	3-2	0-3		1-1
Bakili Bullets	MWI	6	0-1	1-1	2-1	

Enyimba *	1 1 6p
Espérance	1 1 5p

Enyimba	1 2 5p
Etoile du Sahel *	2 1 3p

Jeanne d'Arc *	2 0
Etoile du Sahel	1 3

Group B		Pts	TUN	SEN	ALG	RSA
Espérance	TUN	12		5-0	2-1	2-0
Jeanne d'Arc	SEN	11	2-1		2-1	2-0
USM Alger	ALG	7	3-0	1-1		2-1
SuperSport United	RSA	4	1-2	1-1	2-0	

PRELIMINARY ROUND 1ST LEG
Dar es Salaam
7-03-2004

Simba SC	1
John [62]	
Zanaco	0

PRELIMINARY ROUND 2ND LEG
Lusaka
21-03-2004

Zanaco	3
Banda [14], Mwewa [55], Kalengo [93+]	
Simba SC	1
Gabriel [77]	

PRELIMINARY ROUND 1ST LEG
Tamatave
8-03-2004

Eco Redipharm	0
Saint Michael United	0

PRELIMINARY ROUND 2ND LEG
Mahé
20-03-2004

Saint Michael United	2
Onyango [61], Rath [82]	
Eco Redipharm	0

PRELIMINARY ROUND 1ST LEG
Maseru
6-03-2004

Matlama	0
Orlando Pirates	3
Vilakazi 2 [33 56], Lekoelea	

PRELIMINARY ROUND 2ND LEG
Johannesburg
20-03-2004

Orlando Pirates	4
Phakathi [10], Kauleza [37], Mokoena 2 [50 72]	
Matlama	0

PRELIMINARY ROUND 1ST LEG
Brazzaville
7-03-2004

Saint Michel d'Ouenzé	2
Bouithys [75], Nzembe [90]	
US Bitam	0

PRELIMINARY ROUND 2ND LEG
Libreville
21-03-2004

US Bitam	2 3p
Nieme [33], Mabiala [64]	
Saint Michel d'Ouenzé	0 4p

PRELIMINARY ROUND 1ST LEG
Tripoli
7-03-2004

Al Ittihad Tripoli	1
Sahel SC	0

PRELIMINARY ROUND 2ND LEG
Niamey
20-03-2004

Sahel SC	2
Al Ittihad Tripoli	0

PRELIMINARY ROUND 1ST LEG
Bakau
7-03-2004

Armed Forces	0
Jeanne d'Arc	3
Ndoye [24], Ndiaye [30], Fall [44]	

PRELIMINARY ROUND 2ND LEG
Dakar
21-03-2004

Jeanne d'Arc	3
Ndoye 2 [40 62], Diarra [90]	
Armed Forces	0

PRELIMINARY ROUND 1ST LEG
Kinshasa
7-03-2004

AS Vita Club	-
Ulinzi Stars	-
Ulinzi withdrew. Vita Club qualify	

PRELIMINARY ROUND 1ST LEG
Kumasi
7-03-2004

Asante Kotoko	-
AS Tempête Mocaf	-
Tempête Mocaf withdrew. Kotoko qualify	

PRELIMINARY ROUND 1ST LEG
Ouagadougou
6-03-2004

ASFA Yennega	3
Gorogo [75], Konvelbo [88], Dagano [90]	
Julius Berger	2
Ishola [37], Idahor [51]	

PRELIMINARY ROUND 2ND LEG
Abeokuta
20-03-2004

Julius Berger	0
ASFA Yennega	0

PRELIMINARY ROUND 1ST LEG
Pretoria
6-03-2004

SuperSport United	5
Takutchie [8], Raselmane 2 [49 89], Sibeko [64], Tsweu [85]	
Civics CC	0

PRELIMINARY ROUND 2ND LEG
Windhoek
19-03-2004

Civics CC	0
SuperSport United	1
Tsweu [13]	

PRELIMINARY ROUND 1ST LEG
St Denis
6-03-2004

US Stade Tamponnaise	-
AS Port Louis 2000	-
Stade withdrew. Port Louis qualify	

PRELIMINARY ROUND 1ST LEG
Addis Abeba
7-03-2004

Saint George SC	1
Francis [21]	
Al Hilal Omdurman	2
Mutaz Kabair 2 [53 72]	

PRELIMINARY ROUND 2ND LEG
Omdurman
21-03-2004

Al Hilal Omdurman	1
Saint George SC	1

PRELIMINARY ROUND 1ST LEG	
Bamako	
7-03-2004	
Stade Malien	0
Hearts of Oak	0

PRELIMINARY ROUND 2ND LEG	
Accra	
21-03-2004	
Hearts of Oak	2
Kuffour [18], Quaye [83p]	
Stade Malien	0

PRELIMINARY ROUND 1ST LEG	
Luanda	
7-03-2004	
Atlético Aviação	1
Malamba [24]	
SC Cimenterie	1
Matondo [83]	

PRELIMINARY ROUND 2ND LEG	
Kinshasa	
21-03-2004	
SC Cimenterie	0
Atlético Aviação	1
Kabungula	

PRELIMINARY ROUND 1ST LEG	
Agadir	
7-03-2004	
Hassania US Agadir	7
Ouchrif 3 [26 76 90], Allouli [50], Ouaaliti [80], Boukmouch [82], OG [87]	
ASC Nasr de Sebkha	0
Nasr withdrew before the 2nd leg	

FIRST ROUND 1ST LEG	
Aba	
11-04-2004	
Enyimba	3
Osim [33p], Anumunu [36], Tyakase [42]	
ASC Diaraf	0

FIRST ROUND 2ND LEG	
Dakar	
24-04-2004	
ASC Diaraf	2
Mbengue [23], Coulibaly [69]	
Enyimba	0

FIRST ROUND 1ST LEG	
Bulawayo	
11-04-2004	
Amazulu	0
Petro Atlético	0

FIRST ROUND 2ND LEG	
Luanda	
27-04-2004	
Petro Atlético	2
Litana 2 [68 83]	
Amazulu	1
Nyoni [61]	

FIRST ROUND 1ST LEG	
Cairo	
9-04-2004	
Zamalek	3
Hamza [19], Abdulhamid [53], Emam [77]	
APR FC	2
Gatete [39], Karekezi [42]	

FIRST ROUND 2ND LEG	
Kigali	
24-04-2004	
APR FC	4
Silengo [26], Gatete [32], Makombe [43], Mulisa [81]	
Zamalek	1
Abdulhamid [11]	

FIRST ROUND 1ST LEG	
Abidjan	
10-04-2004	
Africa Sports	4
Nantcho [4], Dagbei [45], Kassiaty [72], Kouassi [73]	
AS Douanes	1
Houessou [89]	

FIRST ROUND 2ND LEG	
Lome	
25-04-2004	
AS Douanes	0
Africa Sports	1
Nazé	

FIRST ROUND 1ST LEG	
Lusaka	
10-04-2004	
Zanaco	0
Bakili Bullets	1
Zakazaka [19]	

FIRST ROUND 2ND LEG	
Blantyre	
24-04-2004	
Bakili Bullets	0 6p
Zanaco	1 5p
Banda [27]	

FIRST ROUND 1ST LEG	
Mahé	
10-04-2004	
Saint Michael United	2
Amanaka [2], Bonne [92+]	
Orlando Pirates	3
Vilakazi [23], Dinha [39p], Phakatih [49]	

FIRST ROUND 2ND LEG	
Johannesburg	
25-04-2004	
Orlando Pirates	5
Dinha [12p], Thakathi 2 [35 63], Mokoena [38], Vilakazi [58]	
Saint Michael United	1
Onyango [17]	

FIRST ROUND 1ST LEG	
Garoua	
11-04-2004	
Cotonsport Garoua	4
Amungwa 2 [43 83], Minusu [65], Dikoume [73]	
Saint Michel d'Ouenzé	1
Gautier [69]	

FIRST ROUND 2ND LEG	
Brazzaville	
25-04-2004	
Saint Michel d'Ouenzé	1
Cotonsport Garoua	0

FIRST ROUND 1ST LEG	
Monastir	
10-04-2004	
Espérance	4
Narbaoui [33], Jaidi [60], Souayah [70p], Diaky [88]	
Sahel SC	0

FIRST ROUND 2ND LEG	
Niamey	
25-04-2004	
Sahel SC	0
Espérance	1
Harbaoui 80	

FIRST ROUND 1ST LEG	
Rabat	
10-04-2004	
Raja Casablanca	2
Misbah 69, Bidoudane 90	
Jeanne d'Arc	0

FIRST ROUND 2ND LEG	
Dakar	
25-04-2004	
Jeanne d'Arc	2 5p
Diarra 11, Gaye 23	
Raja Casablanca	0 4p

FIRST ROUND 1ST LEG	
Yaoundé	
11-04-2004	
Canon Yaoundé	3
Mebega 34, Maemble 83, Ndjoum 89	
AS Vita Club	0

FIRST ROUND 2ND LEG	
Kinshasa	
25-04-2004	
AS Vita Club	1
Mungunu 85	
Canon Yaoundé	1
Ndenga 32	

FIRST ROUND 1ST LEG	
Abídjan	
11-04-2004	
ASEC Mimosas	1
Foneye 55	
Asante Kotoko	1
Al Hassan 77	

FIRST ROUND 2ND LEG	
Kumasi	
25-04-2004	
Asante Kotoko	0
ASEC Mimosas	0

FIRST ROUND 1ST LEG	
Algiers	
10-04-2004	
USM Alger	8
Dziri 2 20 47, Ammour 21, Diallo 3 31 62 88, Metref 79, Balbone 87	
ASFA Yennega	1
Konte 64	

FIRST ROUND 2ND LEG	
Ouagadougou	
24-04-2004	
ASFA Yennega	2
Konte 2 36 85p	
USM Alger	2
Diallo 2 44 75	

FIRST ROUND 1ST LEG	
Port Louis	
10-04-2004	
AS Port Louis 2000	1
Appou 62p	
SuperSport United	1
Raselemane 14	

FIRST ROUND 2ND LEG	
Pretoria	
24-04-2004	
SuperSport United	2
Raselemane 21, OG 82	
AS Port Louis 2000	0

FIRST ROUND 1ST LEG	
Cairo	
10-04-2004	
Al Ahly	0
Al Hilal Omdurman	1
Gustin 8	

FIRST ROUND 2ND LEG	
Omdurman	
25-04-2004	
Al Hilal Omdurman	0
Al Ahly	0

FIRST ROUND 1ST LEG	
Accra	
11-04-2004	
Hearts of Oak	4
Agyeman 15, Kuffour 37, Tetteh 68, Morgan 88	
Atlético Aviação	1
Cabungula 19	

FIRST ROUND 2ND LEG	
Luanda	
25-04-2004	
Atlético Aviação	1
Love 14	
Hearts of Oak	1
Agyeman 62	

FIRST ROUND 1ST LEG	
Sousse	
10-04-2004	
Etoile du Sahel	2
Mhadhebi 14p, Hagui 61	
Hassania US Agadir	0

FIRST ROUND 2ND LEG	
Agadir	
24-04-2004	
Hassania US Agadir	0
Etoile du Sahel	0

SECOND ROUND 1ST LEG	
Aba	
16-05-2004	
Enyimba	1
Nwanna 67	
Petro Atlético	1
Flávio 27	

SECOND ROUND 2ND LEG	
Luanda	
30-05-2004	
Petro Atlético	1
Lopes 70	
Enyimba	2
Nwanna 11, Tyankale 86	

SECOND ROUND 1ST LEG	
Kigali	
15-05-2004	
APR FC	1
Karekezi 60	
Africa Sports	0

SECOND ROUND 2ND LEG

Abidjan
30-05-2004

Africa Sports	1 3p
Nantcho [83]	
APR FC	0 1p

SECOND ROUND 1ST LEG

Port Elizabeth
15-05-2004

Orlando Pirates	2
Dinha [19p], Vilakazi [38]	
Bakili Bullets	1
Malunga [74]	

SECOND ROUND 2ND LEG

Blantyre
29-05-2004

Bakili Bullets	1
Malidadi [78]	
Orlando Pirates	0

SECOND ROUND 1ST LEG

Monastir
16-05-2004

Espérance	3
Diaky 2 [11 70], Zitouni [20]	
Cotonsport Garoua	0

SECOND ROUND 2ND LEG

Garoua
30-05-2004

Cotonsport Garoua	1
Kameni [41p]	
Espérance	0

SECOND ROUND 1ST LEG

Dakar
16-05-2004

Jeanne d'Arc	2
Ndiaye 2 [45p 61]	
Canon Yaoundé	0

SECOND ROUND 2ND LEG

Yaoundé
30-05-2004

Canon Yaoundé	2
Moukake [34], Inobe [75]	
Jeanne d'Arc	1
Ndiaye [28]	

SECOND ROUND 1ST LEG

Algiers
15-05-2004

USM Alger	2
Meftah [16], Ouichaoui [77]	
Asante Kotoko	0

SECOND ROUND 2ND LEG

Kumasi
30-05-2004

Asante Kotoko	2 1p
Duah [5], Chibsah [81]	
USM Alger	0 3p

SECOND ROUND 1ST LEG

Pretoria
16-05-2004

SuperSport United	2
Takuchie, Raselemane	
Al Hilal Omdurman	0

SECOND ROUND 2ND LEG

Omdurman
30-05-2004

Al Hilal Omdurman	0
SuperSport United	0

SECOND ROUND 1ST LEG

Accra
16-05-2004

Hearts of Oak	1
Boffman [43]	
Etoile du Sahel	0

SECOND ROUND 2ND LEG

Sousse
28-05-2004

Etoile du Sahel	1 5p
Hearts of Oak	1 4p

GROUP A

		Pl	W	D	L	F	A	Pts	TUN	NGA	CIV	MWI
Etoile du Sahel †	TUN	6	3	2	1	8	5	11		1-0	2-0	1-1
Enyimba †	NGA	6	2	2	2	11	4	8	1-1		0-1	6-0
Africa Sports	CIV	6	2	1	3	6	10	7	3-2	0-3		1-1
Bakili Bullets	MWI	6	1	3	2	5	11	6	0-1	1-1	2-1	

† Qualified for the semi-finals

GROUP A MATCHDAY 1

10-07-2004

Bakili Bullets	0
Etoile du Sahel	1
Okpara [89]	

GROUP A MATCHDAY 1

10-07-2004

Africa Sports	0
Enyimba	3
Okonkwo [27], Nwaneri [47], Anumnu [76]	

GROUP A MATCHDAY 2

25-07-2004

Etoile du Sahel	2
Ben Fraj [10p], Obiakor [81]	
Africa Sports	0

GROUP A MATCHDAY 2	
25-07-2004	
Enyimba	6
Frimpong 26, Anumunu 32, Okonkwo 47p, Ogunbiyi 2 80 89, Ozurumba 85	
Bakili Bullets	0

GROUP A MATCHDAY 3	
7-08-2004	
Etoile du Sahel	1
	Beya 89
Enyimba	0

GROUP A MATCHDAY 3	
8-08-2004	
Bakili Bullets	2
	Lungu 34, Malidili 38
Africa Sports	1
	Olosipe 31

GROUP A MATCHDAY 4	
12-09-2004	
Enyimba	1
	Nwaneri 48p
Etoile du Sahel	1
	Opara 2

GROUP A MATCHDAY 4	
12-09-2004	
Africa Sports	1
	Nikiewa 48p
Bakili Bullets	1
	Ngambi 18

GROUP A MATCHDAY 5	
26-09-2004	
Etoile du Sahel	1
	Traoré 25
Bakili Bullets	1
	Kondowe 44

GROUP A MATCHDAY 5	
26-09-2004	
Enyimba	0
Africa Sports	1
	Oyasipe 37

GROUP A MATCHDAY 6	
16-10-2004	
Africa Sports	3
	Kouassi 3 25p 30 45p
Etoile du Sahel	2
	Bouchhioua 8, Ben Frej 13p

GROUP A MATCHDAY 6	
16-10-2004	
Bakili Bullets	1
	Ngami 62
Enyimba	1
	Nwanna 35

GROUP B

		Pl	W	D	L	F	A	Pts	TUN	SEN	ALG	RSA
Espérance †	TUN	6	4	0	2	12	7	12		5-0	2-1	2-0
Jeanne d'Arc †	SEN	6	3	2	1	8	9	11	2-1		2-1	2-0
USM Alger	ALG	6	2	1	3	8	8	7	3-0	1-1		2-1
SuperSport United	RSA	6	1	1	4	5	9	4	1-2	1-1	2-0	

† Qualified for the semi-finals

GROUP B MATCHDAY 1	
10-07-2004	
SuperSport United	1
	Randjies 60
Espérance	2
	Zitouni 2 26 47

GROUP B MATCHDAY 1	
11-07-2004	
Jeanne d'Arc	2
	Ndiaye 30, Diarra 80
USM Alger	1
	Diallo 73

GROUP B MATCHDAY 2	
23-07-2004	
USM Alger	2
	Diallo 2 34 94+
SuperSport United	1
	Raselemane 84

GROUP B MATCHDAY 2	
Sfax	
24-07-2004	
Espérance	5
Zitouni 2 29 63, Souayah 31, Daoud 79, Mnari 87	
Jeanne d'Arc	0

GROUP B MATCHDAY 3	
6-08-2004	
Espérance	2
	Zitouni 2 23 67
USM Alger	1
	Dziri 57

GROUP B MATCHDAY 3	
7-08-2004	
SuperSport United	1
	Katza 53
Jeanne d'Arc	1
	Ndiaye 89

GROUP B MATCHDAY 4	
10-09-2004	
USM Alger	3
	Bourahli 2 15 55, Diallo 50
Espérance	0

GROUP B MATCHDAY 4	
11-09-2004	
Jeanne d'Arc	2
	Gaye 60, Ndiaye 70
SuperSport United	0

GROUP B MATCHDAY 5	
25-09-2005	
USM Alger	1
	Diallo 72
Jeanne d'Arc	1
	Ndoye 14

GROUP B MATCHDAY 5	
26-09-2004	
Espérance	2
Zitouni 36, Mnari 58	
SuperSport United	0

GROUP B MATCHDAY 6	
17-10-2004	
Jeanne d'Arc	2
Mendy 77, Diarra 80	
Espérance	1
Triki 40p	

GROUP B MATCHDAY 6	
17-10-2004	
SuperSport United	2
Mokoro 77, Mahlangu 86	
USM Alger	0

SEMI-FINAL 1ST LEG	
Aba	
31-10-2004	
Enyimba	1
Fasindo 90	
Espérance	1
Mnari 77	

SEMI-FINAL 2ND LEG	
Tunis	
14-11-2004	
Espérance	1 5p
Zitouni 43	
Enyimba	1 6p
Tyavkase 60	

SEMI-FINAL 1ST LEG	
Dakar	
30-10-2004	
Jeanne d'Arc	2
Diarra 2 61 70	
Etoile du Sahel	1
Opara 51	

SEMI-FINAL 2ND LEG	
Stade Olympique, Sousse	
14-11-2004	
Etoile du Sahel	3
Traoré 2 5 76, Opara	
Jeanne d'Arc	0

CAF CHAMPIONS LEAGUE FINAL 1ST LEG

Stade Olympique, Sousse
4-12-2004; 35 000; Benouza ALG

ETOILE DU SAHEL 2   1   ENYIMBA

Mhadhebi 44p, Traoré 53   Nwanna 15

Etoile du Sahel			Enyimba	
16	EJIDE Austin		ENYEAMA Vincent	1
27	KALABANE Omar		NWANERI Obinna	3
14	ZOUAGHI Kais		ALIYU Musa	4
5	MILADI Mohamed	88	EZOBA Jerome	6
6	HAMMI Ahmed		OMOLADE Ajibade	13
26	BARGUI Hakim		YUSUF Mohamed	7
7	BEYA Zoubeir (c)	31	OKONKWO Onyekachi	26
25	MHADHEBI Imed	64	TYAVKASE David	29
15	SELLEMI Lotfi	72 89	OGUNBIYI Mouri	28
12	OPARA Emeka		NWANNA Emeka	23
30	TRAORE Kandia	81	EZENWA Ekene	8
	Tr: CHETALI Abdelmajid		Tr: EMORDI Okey	
	Substitutes		Substitutes	
29	EL BOKRI Marouane	88 89	FRIMPONG Joetex	21
8	JEDIDI Mohhamed	64 47	UDEH Damian	14
		81	FASINDO Eric	10

CAF CHAMPIONS LEAGUE FINAL 2ND LEG

Abuja Stadium, Abuja
12-12-2004; Codja Coffi BEN

ENYIMBA   2   1   ETOILE DU SAHEL

Enyeama 44p, Ogunbiyi 53   Zouaghi 63

Enyimba			Etoile du Sahel	
1	ENYEAMA Vincent	90	EJIDE Austin	16
3	NWANERI Obinna		KALABANE Omar	27
4	ALIYU Musa		ZOUAGHI Kais	14
6	EZOBA Jerome		MILADI Mohamed	5
13	OMOLADE Ajibade		HAMMI Ahmed	6
7	YUSUF Mohamed		EL BOKRI Marouane	29
29	TYAVKASE David		(c) BEYA Zoubeir	7
28	OGUNBIYI Mouri		MHADHEBI Imed	25
14	UDEH Damian		BEN FREJ Saber	13
23	NWANNA Emeka	80 60	ETTRAOUI Mejdi	18
9	ANUMNU Ndidi		TRAORE Kandia	30
	Tr: EMORDI Okey		Tr: CHETALI Abdelmajid	
	Substitutes		Substitutes	
21	FRIMPONG Joetex	64 46 54	OPARA Emeka	12
8	EZENWA Ekene	80 54	OBIAKOR Ogochukwu	9
16	AIYENUGBA Dele	90 60	BARGUI Hakim	26

PENALTY SHOOT-OUT

Enyimba First		Etoile Second	
EZOBA Jerome	✔	MILADI Mohamed	✔
ALIYU Musa	✔	BEN FREJ Saber	✘
FRIMPONG Joetex	✔	TRAORE Kandia	✔
UDEH Damian	✔	BEYA Zoubeir	✔
NWANERI Obinna	✔		

Enyimba win CAF Champions League 5-3 on penalties

CAF CONFEDERATION CUP 2004

Preliminary Round

ASC Thiès	SEN	0	3
Stade Tunisien *	TUN	6	0
Olympic Real * ‡	CTA	-	
Petro Huambo	ANG	-	
Olympique Niamey	NIG	2	1
Bouaflé *	CIV	3	0
Djoliba *	MLI	1	1
Wallidan	GAM	0	3
ASC Entente *	MTN	0	0
Etoile de Guinea	GUI	2	2
Mogas 90 *	BEN	1	0
Al Nasr Benghazi	LBY	0	5
El Merreikh Omdurman *	SUD	1	0
Green Buffaloes	ZAM	0	2
Ethiopian Coffee	ETH	1	0
Express *	UGA	2	0
Dynamos *	ZIM	0	3
Savanne *	MRI	0	0
Chemelil Sugar *	TAN	0	1
Mtibwa Sugar	KEN	2	2
USM Libreville	GAB	1	2
Kiyovu Sports *	RWA	0	1
Ferroviário *	MOZ	1	0
Wits University	RSA	2	4
Léopards Transfoot	MAD	2	4
Saint Louis *	SEY	2	0
Deportivo Mongomo	EQG	2	0
Diables Noirs *	CGO	2	0
Dynamic Togolais	TOG	0	0
Etoile Filante *	BFA	2	0

First Round

AS Douanes	SEN	2	2
Inter Luanda *	ANG	1	1
TP Mazembe	COD	0	2
PWD Bamenda *	CMR	1	1
Stade Tunisien	TUN	1	2
Ismaili *	EGY	2	0
Petro Huambo *	ANG	1	1
Liberty Professionals	GHA	0	5
FAR Rabat *	MAR	3	3
Olympique Niamey	NIG	0	2
Wallidan *	GAM	2	0
Club Africain	TUN	1	3
Etoile de Guinea *	GUI	1	1
CR Belouizdad	ALG	0	2
Al Nasr Benghazi *	LBY	1	0
Enugu Rangers	NGA	0	4
Green Buffaloes *	ZAM	6	1
DC Motema Pembe	COD	1	2
Express *	UGA	1	0
Lobi Stars	NGA	1	3
King Faisal Babies	GHA	1	4
Dynamos *	ZIM	0	0
Mtibwa Sugar *	TAN	0	
Santos Cape Town	RSA	3	
Sable Batié	CMR	2	1
USM Libreville *	GAB	2	1
Wits University	RSA	1	2
Léopards Transfoot *	MAD	1	2
Stella Abidjan	CIV	1	2
Deportivo Mongomo *	EQG	1	0
Etoile Filante *	BFA	0	0
Wydad Casablanca	MAR	1	0

Second Round

AS Douanes	2	3
PWD Bamenda *	2	0
Stade Tunisien	2	1
Liberty Professionals *	3	1
FAR Rabat *	0	1
Club Africain	0	1
Etoile de Guinea *	0	1
Enugu Rangers	0	2
Green Buffaloes	1	4
Lobi Stars *	2	2
King Faisal Babies *	1	1
Santos Cape Town	1	2
Sable Batié *	4	2
Léopards Transfoot	1	1
Stella Abidjan *	0	1
Wydad Casablanca	0	2

* Home team in the first leg • Losing teams in the second round of the CAF Champions League enter at the Intermediate round • ‡ Team withdrew

CAF CONFEDERATION CUP 2004

Intermediate Round

Hearts of Oak *	GHA	1	0
AS Douanes	SEN	0	0

Liberty Professionals	GHA	0 1 0p	
Al Hilal Omdurman *	SUD	1 0 3p	

Petro Atlético *	ANG	0	1
FAR Rabat	MAR	0	0

APR FC *	RWA	1	0
Enugu Rangers	NGA	0	3

Cotonsport Garoua *	CMR	3	1
Green Buffaloes	ZAM	0	1

Canon Yaoundé *	CMR	1	0
Santos Cape Town	RSA	1	2

Sable Batié	CMR	2	
Orlando Pirates * †	RSA	4	

Wydad Casablanca	MAR	0	1
Asante Kotoko *	GHA	2	1

† Second leg was abandoned due to rain and Pirates did not turn up for the replay

Group Stage

Group A

	Pts				
Asante Kotoko	10		3-1	3-0	2-1
Enugu Rangers	10	2-1		4-0	4-0
Al Hilal Omdurman	9	2-0	2-1		1-0
Petro Atlético	5	1-1	0-0	3-1	

Group B

	Pts				
Hearts of Oak	13		3-2	5-1	1-0
Cotonsport Garoua	11	0-0		1-0	4-0
Sable Batié	7	2-0	0-0		3-2
Santos Cape Town	3	0-1	0-2	1-0	

Final

Hearts of Oak *	1 1	8p
Asante Kotoko	1 1	7p

CAF AFRICAN WOMEN'S CHAMPIONSHIP 2005

CAF AFRICAN WOMEN'S CHAMPIONSHIP SOUTH AFRICA 2005
PRELIMINARY ROUNDS

First Round: Equatorial Guinea 2-2 0-2 **Congo**; **Uganda** w-o Malawi; **Tanzania** 4-0 1-1 Eritrea. **Second Round:** Congo 0-2 0-0 **Cameroon**; Congo DR v Gabon (both withdrew); Guinea 0-13 0-9 **Ghana**; Malawi 0-4 0-5 **Ethiopia**; Mali 2-2 0-1 **Algeria**; Senegal 2-8 1-4 **Nigeria**; Tanzania 0-3 0-4 **Zimbabwe**. South Africa qualified as hosts. Mali qualified as best losers due to the withdrawal of Congo DR and Gabon

FINAL TOURNAMENT

First Round Group Stage

	Pl	W	D	L	F	A	Pts	ETH	ZIM	RSA
Ghana †	3	3	0	0	7	1	9	2-1	2-0	3-0
Ethiopia †	3	1	1	1	4	4	4		1-1	2-1
Zimbabwe	3	1	1	1	3	4	4			2-1
South Africa	3	0	0	3	2	7	0			

	Pl	W	D	L	F	A	Pts	CMR	ALG	MLI
Nigeria †	3	2	1	0	9	2	7	2-2	4-0	3-0
Cameroon †	3	1	2	0	7	5	5		3-1	2-2
Algeria	3	1	0	2	4	7	3			3-0
Mali	3	0	1	2	2	8	1			

Semi-finals

Nigeria	4
Ethiopia	0

Ghana	0
Cameroon	1

Final

Nigeria	5
Cameroon	0

3rd place play-off

Ghana	0 6p
Ethiopia	0 5p

† Qualified for the semi-finals • Tournament played in South Africa from 18-09-2004 to 3-10-2004

AFRICAN YOUTH AND JUNIOR CHAMPIONSHIPS

AFRICAN YOUTH CHAMPIONSHIP 2005 QUALIFIERS

Prelim Round			First Round			Second Round		
Namibia	0	0	Angola	3	2			
Botswana	0	5	Botswana	0	2	Angola †	1	0
			Mozambique	1	0	Rwanda	0	0
Eritrea	0	0	Rwanda	0	4			
Rwanda	1	0	Ghana	w-o				
			Gabon			Ghana	0	1
			Côte d'Ivoire	2 0 5p		Côte d'Ivoire†	1	1
			Guinea	0 2 4p				
			Mali	3	0			
Burundi			Senegal	1	0	Mali †	1	1
Congo	w-o		Cameroon	w-o		Cameroon	0	2
			Congo					
Sierra Leone	0	1	Morocco	3	0			
Gambia	0	1	Sierra Leone	0	1	Morocco †		4
			Algeria	1	0	Niger		0
Libya	2	0	Niger	2	1			
Niger	2	0	Congo DR					
			Nigeria	w-o		Nigeria †	2	3
			Tunisia	1 0 3p		Burkina Faso	0	2
			Burkina Faso	0 1 5p				
			Ethiopia					
			Zambia	w-o		Zambia	2	0
			Egypt	4	0	Egypt †	0	3
Sudan	1	2	Sudan	0	0			
Somalia	0	1	Zimbabwe	w-o				
			Tanzania			Zimbabwe	0	0
Lesotho	w-o		South Africa	2	0	Lesotho †	0	3
Mauritius			Lesotho	1	1			

† Qualified for the finals in Benin • Benin qualified as hosts
Home team in the first leg listed above in each match
w-o = walk over after opponents withdraw

AFRICAN JUNIOR CHAMPIONSHIP 2005 QUALIFIERS

Prelim Round			First Round			Second Round		
			Angola	w-o				
Botswana	1	1	Lesotho			Angola	1	0
Lesotho	2	2	Sierra Leone	1	0	Nigeria †	3	3
			Nigeria	1	0			
			Congo DR					
Burundi	1	1	Burundi	w-o		Burundi	2	1
Namibia	1	0	Cameroon	2	0	Burkina Faso†	0	5
			Burkina Faso	1	1			
			Ethiopia	w-o				
			Egypt			Ethiopia	2	0
			Ghana	3	2	Ghana †	1	3
			Tunisia	1	1			
			Mali	3	1			
			Guinea	1	2	Mali †	3	1
			Gabon			C. African Rep	0	1
C. African Rep	3	0	C. African Rep	w-o				
Congo	0	1	Libya					
			Morocco	w-o		Morocco	0	0
			Senegal	1	4	Côte d'Ivoire†	2	1
			Côte d'Ivoire	4	2			
			Mozambique	0	1			
			South Africa	3	5	South Africa †	5	3
Somalia			Sudan	1	0	Sudan	0	0
Eritrea	w-o		Eritrea	0	0			
			Zambia	1	0			
Rwanda	1	0	Tanzania	2	2	Tanzania ‡	3	1
Tanzania	1	1	Zimbabwe	w-o		Zimbabwe †	1	0
			Madagascar					

† Qualified for the finals in Gambia • Gambia qualified as hosts
‡ Tanzania disqualified • w-o = walk over after opponents withdrew
Home team in the first leg listed above in each match

CAF AFRICAN U-17 CHAMPIONSHIP GAMBIA 2005

First Round Group Stage

Group A	Pl	W	D	L	F	A	Pts	GAM	MLI	BFA
Ghana †	3	2	0	1	5	4	6	1-0	3-2	1-2
Gambia †	3	2	0	1	4	3	6		3-2	1-0
Mali	3	1	0	2	7	7	3			3-1
Burkina Faso	3	1	0	2	3	5	3			

Group B	Pl	W	D	L	F	A	Pts	CIV	NGA	ZIM
South Africa †	3	2	1	0	7	3	7	1-0	2-2	4-1
Côte d'Ivoire †	3	2	0	1	5	3	6		3-2	2-0
Nigeria	3	1	1	1	8	6	4			4-1
Zimbabwe	3	0	0	3	2	10	0			

Semi-finals

Gambia	2
South Africa	1

Côte d'Ivore	0
Ghana	2

Final

Gambia	1
Ghana	0

Third place play-off

Côte d'Ivoire	1
South Africa	0

† Qualified for the semi-finals • Tournament played in Gambia from 7-05-2005 to 22-05-2005 • Gambia, Ghana and Côte d'Ivoire qualify for the FIFA World U-17 Championship in Peru

CAF AFRICAN YOUTH CHAMPIONSHIP BENIN 2005

First Round Group Stage

Group A	Pl	W	D	L	F	A	Pts	BEN	CIV	MLI
Nigeria †	3	3	0	0	7	1	9	3-0	1-0	3-1
Benin †	3	1	1	1	7	7	4		4-1	3-3
Côte d'Ivoire	3	1	0	2	2	5	3			1-0
Mali	3	0	1	2	4	7	1			

Group B	Pl	W	D	L	F	A	Pts	MAR	LES	ANG
Egypt †	3	2	1	0	7	3	7	2-2	4-1	1-0
Morocco †	3	2	1	0	5	2	7		2-0	1-0
Lesotho	3	1	0	2	3	7	3			2-1
Angola	3	0	0	3	1	4	0			

Semi-finals

Nigeria	2	5p
Morocco	2	3p

Benin	1	1p
Egypt	1	3p

Final

Nigeria	2
Egypt	0

Third place play-off

Benin	1	5p
Morocco	1	3p

† Qualified for the semi-finals • Tournament played in Benin from 15-01-2005 to 29-01-2005 • Nigeria, Egypt, Benin and Morocco qualify for the FIFA World Youth Championship in the Netherlands

REGIONAL TOURNAMENTS IN AFRICA

CECAFA KAGAME INTER-CLUB CUP TANZANIA 2005

First round groups

Group A		Pl	W	D	L	F	A	Pts	RWA	TAN	BDI	SOM
SC Villa †	UGA	4	3	1	0	8	0	10	0-0	1-0	2-0	5-0
Rayon Sport †	RWA	4	2	1	1	7	2	7	1-2	5-0	1-0	
Simba SC	TAN	4	2	1	1	4	2	7		0-0	2-0	
Atletico Olympique	BDI	4	1	1	2	3	9	4			3-2	
Elman	SOM	4	0	0	4	2	11	0				

Group B		Pl	W	D	L	F	A	Pts	TAN	ETH	KEN	ZAN
APR FC †	RWA	4	4	0	0	10	1	12	2-0	2-1	2-0	4-0
Mtibwa Sugar †	TAN	4	2	1	1	6	5	7	1-1	3-2	2-0	
Awassa Kenema	ETH	4	1	2	1	4	4	5		1-1	1-0	
Ulinzi Stars	KEN	4	1	1	2	4	6	4			1-0	
KMKM	ZAN	4	0	0	4	0	8	0				

Semi-finals

SC Villa	1
Mtibwa Sugar	0

Rayon Sport	1	3p
APR FC	1	4p

Final

SC Villa	3
APR FC	0

Third place play-off

Rayon Sport	0	4p
Mtibwa Sugar	0	2p

† Qualified for the semi-finals • The tournament took place in Tanzania from 23-04-2005 to 8-05-2005 and was played in Mwanza and Arusha

CECAFA CUP ETHIOPIA 2004

First Round Group Stage

Group A	Pl	W	D	L	F	A	Pts	BDI	RWA	ZAN	TAN
Ethiopia †	4	3	1	0	7	1	10	2-1	0-0	3-0	2-0
Burundi †	4	3	0	1	8	4	9		3-1	2-1	2-0
Rwanda	4	2	1	1	10	6	7			2-1	5-1
Zanzibar	4	1	0	3	7	11	3				4-2
Tanzania	4	0	0	4	3	13	0				

Group B	Pl	W	D	L	F	A	Pts	KEN	UGA	SOM
Sudan †	3	2	1	0	8	3	7	2-2	2-1	4-0
Kenya †	3	1	2	0	4	3	5		1-1	1-0
Uganda	3	1	1	1	4	3	4			2-0
Somalia	3	0	0	3	0	7	0			

† Qualified for the semi-finals • Played in Ethiopia from 11-12-2004 to 25-12-2004

Semi-finals

Ethiopia	2 5p
Kenya	2 4p

Sudan	1
Burundi	2

Final

Ethiopia	3
Burundi	0

Third place play-off

Sudan	2
Kenya	1

COSAFA CASTLE CUP 2004

First Round

Angola *	2
Namibia	1

Lesotho *	0 10p
Botswana	0 11p

Madagascar	0
Mozambique *	2

Mauritius *	2
South Africa	0

Quarter-finals

Angola *	1 5p
Botswana	1 3p

Malawi	0
Mozambique *	2

Zimbabwe	5
Swaziland *	0

Mauritius	1
Zambia *	3

Semi-finals

Angola	1
Mozambique *	0

Zimbabwe *	0 4p
Zambia	0 5p

Final

Angola	0 5p
Zambia *	0 4p

* Home team

COSAFA Cup Final, Independence Stadium, Lusaka
20-11-2004, Lwanja MWI

ZAM	4p 0	0 5p	ANG

Angola won the COSAFA Cup 5-4 on penalties

ZAMBIA			ANGOLA
MWEENE Kennedy			LAMA
HACHILENSA Clive			JACINTO
MUSONDA Joseph			JAMBA
TANA Elijah			LEBO-LEBO
LUNGU Misheck			YAMBA ASHA
KATONGO Christopher		89	ITO
CHANSA Isaac	81	78	FOFANA
BAKALA Ian			SIMAO
KATONGO Felix	65	66	STOPIRRA
MULENGA Jacob	101		MAURITO
MILANZI Harry			FLAVIO
Tr: BWALYA Kalusha			Tr: DE OLIVEIRA GONCALVES Luis
NSOFWA Chaswe	65	66	RATS
BWALYA Kalusha	81	78	LOVE
MWAPE Davies	101	89	KADIMA

PENALTY SHOOT-OUT			
Zambia first		Angola second	
BAKALA Ian	✔	FLAVIO	✔
HACHILENSA Clive	✔	YAMBA ASHA	✔
LUNGU Misheck	✔	SIMAO	✔
BWALYA Kalusha	✗	RATS	✔
TANA Elijah	✔	LOVE	✔
Angola win the COSAFA Cup 5-4 on penalties			

CONCACAF

CONFEDERATION OF NORTH, CENTRAL AMERICAN AND

CARIBBEAN ASSOCIATION FOOTBALL

With the focus on the 2006 FIFA World Cup™ and the 2005 CONCACAF Gold Cup qualifiers, it has been a busy year for the teams of North America, Central America and the Caribbean. There were few surprises in the FIFA World Cup™ qualifiers with Mexico and the USA making steady progress towards the finals in Germany. Mexico were rightly regarded as the revelation of the FIFA Confederations Cup 2005 in Germany and only a penalty shoot-out defeat against Argentina saw them miss out on a place in the final. They then went on to take part in the CONCACAF Gold Cup which was won by the USA at the end of July, although only just after Panama played the tournament of their lives and losing the final to the Americans on penalties. It was a busy year for the Caribbean nations with the launch of the Digicel Caribbean Cup. Twenty-one of the islands took part with Jamaica winning only their second Caribbean crown since 1991 and qualifying along with Trinidad and Cuba for the CONCACAF Gold Cup finals. Costa Rica cemented a good year

THE FIFA BIG COUNT OF 2000 FOR CONCACAF

	Male	Female		Male	Female
Registered players	625 537	147 782	Referees	102 257	24 083
Not registered players	15 656 500	7 877 050	Officials	635 916	314 045
Youth players	3 064 691	1 698 518	Total involved in football	28 809 582	10 851 837
Children & Occasional	8 700 000	790 000		39 636 379	
Professionals	24 681	359	Number of clubs	12 852	
Total players	38 560 078		Number of teams	115 830	

with a fifth Central American title. Earlier Deportivo Saprissa had beaten Mexico's UNAM Pumas to win the Champions' Cup, the second Costa Rican team in succession to beat off competition from Mexico and the USA to take the title. The spoils are growing for the CONCACAF Champions Cup with Saprissa taking a berth at the FIFA Club World Championship in Tokyo at the end of 2005. Mexican clubs also missed out on a spot via the Copa Libertadores when Chivas Guadalajara were knocked out by Brazil's Atletico Paranaense. Mexican influence beyond their own borders remains strong in the Americas with Chivas setting up a satelitte club, Chivas USA in Los Angeles, one of two expansion clubs in Major League Soccer. As MLS Commissioner Don Garber said: "This nation is now undergoing a big demographic change, with a new wave of immigration coming mostly from the south – fortunately for us, it's from soccer-playing countries. We have a great opportunity with the 70 million Hispanics in this country."

Confederation of North, Central American and Caribbean Association Football (CONCACAF)
725, Fifth Avenue, Trump Tower, 17th Floor, New York, NY 1022, USA
Tel +1 212 3080 044   Fax +1 212 3081 851
mail@concacaf.net   www.concacaf.com
President: WARNER Jack A. TRI   General Secretary: BLAZER Chuck USA
CONCACAF Formed: 1961

CONCACAF EXECUTIVE COMMITTEE
President: WARNER Jack A. TRI
Vice-President: AUSTIN Lisle BRB   Vice-President: SALGUERO Rafael GUA   Vice-President: ROTHENBURG Alan USA
ORDINARY MEMBERS OF THE EXECUTIVE COMMITTEE
JAMES Anthony JAM   BANEGAS Alfredo HON   KIESE Hugo MEX

CENTRAL AMERICAN, NORTH AMERICAN AND CARIBBEAN TOURNAMENTS

CCCF CHAMPIONSHIP WINNERS

Year	Host Country	Winners	Runners-up
1941	Costa Rica	Costa Rica	El Salvador
1943	El Salvador	El Salvador	Guatemala
1946	Costa Rica	Costa Rica	Guatemala
1948	Costa Rica	Costa Rica	Guatemala
1951	Panama	Panama	Costa Rica
1953	Costa Rica	Costa Rica	Honduras
1955	Costa Rica	Costa Rica	Neth. Antilles
1957	Haiti	Haiti	Curacao
1960	Costa Rica	Costa Rica	Neth. Antilles
1961	Costa Rica	Costa Rica	El Salvador

CONCACAF CHAMPIONSHIP WINNERS

Year	Host Country	Winners	Runners-up
1963	El Salvador	Costa Rica	El Salvador
1965	Guatemala	Mexico	Guatemala
1967	Honduras	Guatemala	Mexico
1969	Costa Rica	Costa Rica	Guatemala
1971	Trinidad	Mexico	Haiti
1973	Haiti	Haiti	Trinidad
1977	Mexico	Mexico	Haiti
1981	Honduras	Honduras	El Salvador
1985	Home & Away	Canada	Honduras
1989	Home & Away	Costa Rica	USA

CONCACAF GOLD CUP

Year	Host Country	Winners	Score	Runners-up	Venue
1991	USA	USA	0-0 4-3p	Honduras	Coliseum, Los Angeles
1993	Mexico/USA	Mexico	4-0	USA	Azteca, Mexico City
1995	USA	Mexico	2-0	Brazil	Coliseum, Los Angeles
1998	USA	Mexico	1-0	USA	Coliseum, Los Angeles
2000	USA	Canada	2-0	Colombia	Coliseum, Los Angeles
2002	USA	USA	2-0	Costa Rica	Rose Bowl, Pasadena
2003	Mexico/USA	Mexico	1-0	Brazil	Azteca, Mexico City
2005	USA	USA	0-0 3-1	Panama	Giants Stadium, New Jersey

Not until the introduction of the CONCACAF Gold Cup in 1991 did the region have a proper continental championship. Prior to the creation of CONCACAF in 1961 there had been a tournament based largely around Central America with occasional Caribbean entrants, which had been dominated by Costa Rica. In 1963 CONCACAF introduced a championship staged every other year until 1971 but they singularly failed in their attempts to make the Americans and especially the Mexicans take it seriously. From 1991 either Mexico or the USA have hosted every tournament and provided the winners with the exception of Canada in 2000.

CONCACAF WOMEN'S GOLD CUP

Year	Host Country	Winners	Score	Runners-up	Venue
1991	Haiti	United States	5-0	Canada	Port au Prince
1993	USA	United States	1-0	Canada	Long Island
1994	Canada	United States	6-0	Canada	Montreal
1998	Canada	Canada	1-0	Mexico	Toronto
2000	USA	United States	1-0	Brazil	Foxboro, Boston
2002	USA/Canada	United States	2-1	Canada	Rose Bowl, Pasadena

CONCACAF WOMEN'S U–19 GOLD CUP

Year	Host Country	Winners	Score	Runners-up	Venue
2004	Canada	Canada	2-1	USA	Frank Clair, Ottawa

If there is one area in which CONCACAF can claim to be world beaters it is in women's football with both the USA and Canada ranked amongst the highest levels of the game. The Women's Gold Cup coincided with the launch of the men's competition and since then the USA have won five of the six tournaments played, beating Canada in the final of four of them. Canada won on home soil in 1998, beating the USA in an historic semi-final before defeating Mexico in the final, the only other team from the CONCACAF area to reach the final. It is hard to imagine any nation seriously threatening the North American dominance in either this or the U-19 event.

CONCACAF YOUTH CHAMPIONS

Year	Host Country	Winners	Runners-up
1954	Costa Rica	Costa Rica	Panama
1956	El Salvador	El Salvador	Neth. Antilles
1958	Guatemala	Guatemala	Honduras
1960	Honduras	Costa Rica	Honduras
1962	Panama	Mexico	Guatemala
1964	Guatemala	El Salvador	
1970	Cuba	Mexico	Cuba
1973	Mexico	Mexico	Guatemala
1974	Canada	Mexico	Cuba
1976	Puerto Rico	Mexico	Honduras

CONCACAF YOUTH CHAMPIONS

Year	Host Country	Winners	Runners-up
1978	Honduras	Mexico	Canada
1980	USA	Mexico	USA
1982	Guatemala	Honduras	USA
1984	Trinidad	Mexico	Canada
1986	Trinidad	Canada	USA
1988	Guatemala	Costa Rica	Mexico
1990	Guatemala	Mexico	Trinidad
1992	Canada	Mexico	USA
1994	Honduras	Honduras	Costa Rica
1996	Mexico	Canada	Mexico

CONCACAF UNDER 17 CHAMPIONS

Year	Host Country	Winners	Runners-up
1983	Trinidad	USA	Trinidad
1985	Mexico	Mexico	Costa Rica
1987	Honduras	Mexico	USA
1988	Trinidad	Cuba	USA

CONCACAF UNDER 17 CHAMPIONS

Year	Host Country	Winners	Runners-up
1991	Trinidad	Mexico	USA
1992	Cuba	USA	Mexico
1994	El Salvador	Costa Rica	USA
1996	Trinidad	Mexico	USA

Youth tournaments have a long, if patchy, history in the CONCACAF region. At both U-19 and U-17 levels they have served as qualifiers for the FIFA events but since 1996 once the qualifying nations have been identified the principle of determining the champions at each level has been abandoned.

CARIBBEAN CUP

Year	Host Country	Winners	Score	Runners-up	Venue
1989	Barbados	Trinidad & Tobago	2-1	Grenada	Bridgetown
1990	Trinidad	Not completed			
1991	Jamaica	Jamaica	2-0	Trinidad & Tobago	Kingston
1992	Trinidad	Trinidad & Tobago	3-1	Jamaica	Port of Spain
1993	Jamaica	Martinique	0-0 6-5p	Jamaica	Kingston
1994	Trinidad	Trinidad & Tobago	7-2	Martinique	Port of Spain
1995	Cayman/Jamaica	Trinidad & Tobago	5-0	St Vincent	George Town
1996	Trinidad	Trinidad & Tobago	2-0	Cuba	Port of Spain
1997	Antigua/St Kitts	Trinidad & Tobago	4-0	St Kitts	St John's
1998	Jamaica/Trinidad	Jamaica	2-1	Trinidad & Tobago	Port of Spain
1999	Trinidad	Trinidad & Tobago	2-1	Cuba	Port of Spain
2001	Trinidad	Trinidad & Tobago	3-0	Haiti	Port of Spain
2005	Barbados	Jamaica	1-0 †	Cuba	Waterford

† Final tournament played as a league. The match listed is that between the top two.

UNCAF CUP

Year	Host Country	Winners	Score	Runners-up	Venue
1991	Costa Rica	Costa Rica	2-0	Honduras	San José
1993	Honduras	Honduras	2-0	Costa Rica	Tegucigalpa
1995	El Salvador	Honduras	3-0	Guatemala	San Salvador
1997	Guatemala	Costa Rica	1-1	Guatemala	Mateo Flores, Guatemala City
1999	Costa Rica	Costa Rica	1-0	Guatemala	San José
2001	Honduras	Guatemala	2-0	Costa Rica	Tegucigalpa
2003	Panama	Costa Rica	1-1	Guatemala	Rommel Fernández, Panama City
2005	Guatemala	Costa Rica	1-1 7-6p	Honduras	Mateo Flores, Guatemala City

All Final tournaments played as a league except for 1995 and 2005. The matches listed are those between the top two

The UNCAF Cup, played between the nations of Central America, is a prestigious event that doubles up as a qualifying competition for the Gold Cup, as does the Caribbean Cup. Trinidad and Tobago along with Jamaica have dominated the latter tournament with Martinique in 1993 the only country to break the duopoly whilst Costa Rica have won five of the eight UNCAF championships.

CONCACAF CHAMPIONS' CUP

Year	Winners	Country	Score	Country	Runners-up
1962	Guadalajara CD	MEX	1-0 5-0	GUA	Comunicaciones
1963	Racing Club Haïtienne	HAI	W-O	MEX	Guadalajara CD
1964	Not completed				
1965	Not completed				
1966	-				
1967	Alianza	SLV	1-2 3-0 5-3	ANT	Jong Colombia
1968	Toluca	MEX	W-O †		
1969	Cruz Azul	MEX	0-0 1-0	GUA	Comunicaciones
1970	Cruz Azul	MEX	W-O †		
1971	Cruz Azul	MEX	5-1	CRC	LD Alajuelense
1972	Olimpia	HON	0-0 2-0	SUR	Robin Hood
1973	Transvaal	SUR	W-O †		
1974	Municipal	GUA	2-1 2-1	SUR	Transvaal
1975	Atletico Español	MEX	3-0 2-1	SUR	Transvaal
1976	Aguila	SLV	6-1 2-1	SUR	Robin Hood
1977	América	MEX	1-0 0-0	SUR	Robin Hood
1978	Universidad Guadalajara	MEX	W-O †		
1979	Deportivo FAS	SLV	1-0 8-0	ANT	Jong Colombia
1980	UNAM Pumas	MEX	2-0	HON	Universidad de Honduras
1981	Transvaal	SUR	1-0 1-1	SLV	Atlético Marte
1982	UNAM Pumas	MEX	2-2 3-0	SUR	Robin Hood
1983	Atlante	MEX	1-1 5-0	SUR	Robin Hood
1984	Violette	HAI	W-O †		
1985	Defence Force	TRI	2-0 0-1	HON	Olimpia
1986	LD Alajuelense	CRC	4-1 1-1	SUR	Transvaal
1987	América	MEX	2-0 1-1	TRI	Defence Force
1988	Olimpia	HON	2-0 2-0	TRI	Defence Force
1989	UNAM Pumas	MEX	1-1 3-1	CUB	Piñar del Rio
1990	América	MEX	2-2 6-0	CUB	Piñar del Rio
1991	Puebla	MEX	3-1 1-1	TRI	Police FC
1992	América	MEX	1-0	CRC	LD Alajuelense
1993	Deportivo Saprissa	CRC	2-2 ‡	MEX	Leon
1994	CS Cartagines	CRC	3-2	MEX	Atlante
1995	Deportivo Saprissa	CRC	1-0 ‡	GUA	Municipal
1996	Cruz Azul	MEX	1-1 ‡	MEX	Necaxa
1997	Cruz Azul	MEX	5-3	USA	Los Angeles Galaxy
1998	DC United	USA	1-0	MEX	Toluca
1999	Necaxa	MEX	2-1	CRC	LD Alajuelense
2000	LA Galaxy	USA	3-2	HON	Olimpia
2001	Not completed				
2002	Pachuca	MEX	1-0	MEX	Morelia
2003	Toluca	MEX	3-3 2-1	MEX	Morelia
2004	LD Alajuelense	CRC	1-1 4-0	CRC	Deportivo Saprissa
2005	Deportivo Saprissa	CRC	2-0 1-2	MEX	UNAM Pumas

† 1968 Toluca were champions after Aurora GUA and Transvaal SUR were disqualified • 1970 Cruz Azul were champions after Deportivo Saprissa CRC and Transvaal SUR withdrew • 1978 Universidad Guadalajara are listed as the winners by default though Comunicaciones GUA and Defence Force TRI are also considered joint winners by CONCACAF • 1984 Violette were champions after Guadalajara and New York Freedoms withdrew
‡ 1993, 1995 & 1996 finals played as a league • The match listed is that between the top two

The CONCACAF Champions Cup is the weakest of all of the continental club championships with the exception of Oceania. Mexican clubs remain the mainstay of the tournament winning the title on 21 occasions although their focus remains largely on the Copa Libertadores. The presence of MLS clubs since the late 1990s has significantly helped the profile of the tournament although they have not experienced the success they might have hoped for. Costa Rican clubs have provided an unexpected challenge in recent years and along with Mexico and the USA are the only countries to have provided the winners since 1989. Cruz Azul remain the most successful team with five titles.

CONCACAF GOLD CUP 2005™

The USA walked off with the CONCACAF Gold Cup 2005™ title on home soil but it was a close run thing, especially in the final where brave Panama held the Americans to a scoreless draw over 120 minutes before losing in the penalty shoot-out. In a closely fought game both sides squandered chances with the veteran Panamanian striker Jorge Luis Dely Valdes hitting the crossbar with a second half shot. It was the USA's third title and moves them to within one of Mexico's record of four. For the first time the final was held on the east coast with the Giants Stadium in New York/New Jersey host to both semi-finals and the final. It capped a great season for the USA who climbed to sixth in the FIFA/Coca-Cola World Ranking even if their tiumph had in parts been less than convincing. For the first time there was an African flavour to the tournament with an invitation to the 2010 FIFA World Cup™ hosts South Africa to take part along with regular guests Colombia. Both made it through from the first phase which was played in three groups with Miami, Seattle, Boston, Carson, Los Angeles and Houston all staging matches. In all 18 first round games were played to eliminate just four teams – Trinidad and Tobago, Canada, Cuba and Guatemala. In Group A Panama set out their intentions from the start with a 1-0 victory over the Colombians thanks to a goal from Luis Tejada, one of three players in the squad based with clubs in Colombia and they made it out of the group as runners-up to Honduras. Group B was dominated by the USA and Costa Rica although the Americans left it very late to beat Cuba in their first game, scoring three times in the last five minutes to win 4-1, while Group C was won by a Mexican team that had just impressed a world audience with their displays at the FIFA Confederations Cup in Germany. The possibility of a team from outside of the CONCACAF region winning the tournament was reduced when Panama beat South Africa on penalties in the quarter-finals and although Colombia ensured a guest presence in the last four when they beat Mexico thanks to a freak goal, they then lost to Panama for the second time, in the semi-finals. The most unexpected result of the quater-finals was Honduras' 3-2 victory over Costa Rica which set up a semi-final with the States. Once again the Americans left it late with two goals in the last six minutes snatching victory from the jaws of defeat, after Honduras had led 1-0, to set up the finale with Panama.

CONCACAF GOLD CUP 2005™

First round groups		Quarter-finals		Semi-finals		Final		
Group A	**Pts**							
Honduras	7							
Panama	4	**USA**	3					
Colombia	3	Jamaica	1					
Trinidad and Tobago	2							
				USA	2			
				Honduras	1			
		Costa Rica	2					
GroupB	**Pts**	**Honduras**	3					
USA	7							
Costa Rica	7					**USA**	0	3p
Canada	3					Panama	0	1p
Cuba	0							
		Colombia	2					
		Mexico	1					
				Colombia	2			
Group C	**Pts**			**Panama**	3			
Mexico	6							
South Africa	5	South Africa	1 3p					
Jamaica	4	**Panama**	1 5p					
Guatemala	1							

GROUP A		PL	W	D	L	F	A	PTS
1	Honduras	3	2	1	0	4	2	7
2	Panama	3	1	1	1	3	3	4
3	Colombia	3	1	0	2	3	3	3
4	Trinidad and Tobago	3	0	2	1	3	5	2

	PAN	COL	TRI
	1-0	2-1	1-1
		1-0	2-2
			2-0

Orange Bowl, Miami
6-07-2005, 19:00, 10 311, Carlos GUA

COL 0 1 PAN

Tejada 70

COLOMBIA		
1	MONDRAGON Farid (c)	
3	DE LA CUESTA Jose	
4	MENDOZA Humberto	
6	RAMIREZ Juan Carlos	
9	RENTERIA Wason	
10	MORENO Tressor	46
13	ANCHICO Yulian	87
16	HURTADO Hector	69
17	PATINO Jairo	
18	ARZUAGA Martin	18
23	PASSO Oscar Enrique	46
Tr: RUEDA Reinaldo		
8	RAMIREZ Aldo	46
21	AGUILAR Abel	69
23	BRICENO Oscar	80

PANAMA		
46	PENEDO Jaime	1
	RIVERA Carlos	2
	MORENO Luis	3
	TORRES Jose Anthony	4
	BALOY Felipe	5
	GOMEZ Gabriel	6
87	(c) DELY VALDES Julio Cesar	9
85	MEDINA Julio	11
	PHILLIPS Ricardo	15
	TEJADA Luis	18
46	MITRE Engin	20
Tr: HERNANDEZ Jose		
46	DELY VALDES Jorge Luis	7
85	BLANCO Alberto	8
87	AVILA Gustavo	19

Orange Bowl, Miami
6-07-2005, 21:00, 10 311, Navarro CAN

HON 1 1 TRI

Figueroa 43 — Birchall 28

HONDURAS		
1	COELLO Victor	86
2	HENRIQUEZ Astor	
3	FIGUEROA Maynor	
6	IZAGUIRRE Junior	
9	RAMIREZ Jose Francisco	46
10	VELASQUEZ Wilmer (c)	71
13	BERRIOS Mario	
14	GARCIA Oscar	
19	TURCIOS Elvis	65
21	VALLECILLO Erick	
23	GUERRERO Mario	
Tr: DE LA PAZ HERRERA Jose		
8	PALACIOS Wilson	65 71
11	NUNEZ Milton	46 65
22	MORALES Junior	86

TRINIDAD/TOBAGO		
	JOHN Avery	3
	ANDREWS Marvin	4
	LAWRENCE Dennis	6
	BIRCHALL Christopher	7
	WHITLEY Aurtis	9
71	SCOTLAND Jason	10
	RAHIM Brent	12
	(c) JOHN Stern	14
	THEOBALD Densil	18
	JACK Kelvin	21
	GRAY Cyd	24
Tr: BEENHAKKER Leo		
71	JONES Kenwyne	15
65	SAMUEL Colin	20

Orange Bowl, Miami
9-07-2005, 19:00, 17 292, Wyngaarde SUR

PAN 2 2 TRI

Tejada 2 24 90 — Andrews 17, Glen 91+

PANAMA		
1	PENEDO Jaime	
2	RIVERA Carlos	
3	MORENO Luis	
4	TORRES Jose Anthony	
5	BALOY Felipe	69
6	GOMEZ Gabriel	46
9	DELY VALDES Julio Cesar (c)	74
10	MEDINA Julio	
15	PHILLIPS Ricardo	88
18	TEJADA Luis	
20	MITRE Engin	
Tr: HERNANDEZ Jose		
8	BLANCO Alberto	46 69
11	BROWN Roberto	74 83
19	AVILA Gustavo	88

TRINIDAD/TOBAGO		
	JOHN Avery	3
	ANDREWS Marvin	4
	LAWRENCE Dennis	6
	BIRCHALL Christopher	7
69	SCOTLAND Jason	10
69	(c) JOHN Stern	14
	THEOBALD Densil	18
	SPANN Silvio	19
83	SAMUEL Colin	20
	JACK Kelvin	21
	GRAY Cyd	24
Tr: BEENHAKKER Leo		
69	EVE Angus	8
83	GLEN Cornell	13
69	JONES Kenwyne	15

Orange Bowl, Miami
9-07-2005, 21:00, 17 292, Rodriguez MEX

HON 2 1 COL

Velasquez 2 79 82 — Moreno 30p

HONDURAS		
1	COELLO Victor	
2	HENRIQUEZ Astor	72
3	FIGUEROA Maynor	
6	IZAGUIRRE Junior	
10	VELASQUEZ Wilmer (c)	
11	NUNEZ Milton	76
13	BERRIOS Mario	62
14	GARCIA Oscar	
19	TURCIOS Elvis	
21	VALLECILLO Erick	46
23	GUERRERO Mario	67
Tr: DE LA PAZ HERRERA Jose		
8	PALACIOS Wilson	72 67
24	GUIFARRO Luis	62 76
		46

COLOMBIA		
	(c) MONDRAGON Farid	1
	DE LA CUESTA Jose	3
	MENDOZA Humberto	4
	BENITEZ Jair	5
	RAMIREZ Juan Carlos	6
76	RENTERIA Wason	9
	MORENO Tressor	10
	PALACIO Hayder	14
	CASTRILLON Jaime	15
46	PATINO Jairo	17
67	ARZUAGA Martin	18
Tr: RUEDA Reinaldo		
67	VALOYES Cesar	11
76	TORRES Macnelly	20
46	AGUILAR Abel	21

Orange Bowl, Miami
11-07-2005, 19:00, 11 000, Rodriguez MEX

COL 2 0 TRI

Aguilar 77, Hurtado 79

COLOMBIA		
1	MONDRAGON Farid (c)	
3	DE LA CUESTA Jose	75
4	MENDOZA Humberto	
8	RAMIREZ Aldo	
13	ANCHICO Yulian	
15	CASTRILLON Jaime	
17	PATINO Jairo	67
18	ARZUAGA Martin	81
19	LEAL Juan Fernando	52
21	AGUILAR Abel	
23	PASSO Oscar Enrique	
Tr: RUEDA Reinaldo		
6	RAMIREZ Juan Carlos	81 75
9	RENTERIA Wason	52 46
16	HURTADO Hector	67 46

TRINIDAD/TOBAGO		
	JOHN Avery	3
75	ANDREWS Marvin	4
	LAWRENCE Dennis	6
	BIRCHALL Christopher	7
46	SCOTLAND Jason	10
46	GLEN Cornell	13
	(c) JOHN Stern	14
	SPANN Silvio	19
	SAMUEL Colin	20
	JACK Kelvin	21
	GRAY Cyd	24
Tr: BEENHAKKER Leo		
75	CHARLES David	2
46	EVE Angus	8
46	RAHIM Brent	12

Orange Bowl, Miami
11-07-2005, 21:00, 11 000, Wyngaarde SUR

HON 1 0 PAN

Caballero 81

HONDURAS		
1	COELLO Victor	
3	FIGUEROA Maynor	
4	CABALLERO Jorge	
6	IZAGUIRRE Junior	
8	PALACIOS Wilson	
9	RAMIREZ Jose Francisco	61
11	NUNEZ Milton	
14	GARCIA Oscar	
20	THOMAS Hendry	
23	GUERRERO Mario	75
24	GUIFARRO Luis	62
Tr: DE LA PAZ HERRERA Jose		
10	VELASQUEZ Wilmer (c)	61
18	MORAN Carlos	75
19	TURCIOS Elvis	62

PANAMA		
	PENEDO Jaime	1
	RIVERA Carlos	2
	MORENO Luis	3
	TORRES Jose Anthony	
	DELY VALDES Jorge Luis	7
	BLANCO Alberto	8
85	MEDINA Julio	10
	PHILLIPS Ricardo	15
	HENRIQUEZ Luis	17
46	TEJADA Luis	18
56	MITRE Engin	20
Tr: HERNANDEZ Jose		
85	(c) DELY VALDES Julio Cesar	9
56	AVILA Gustavo	19
46	RODRIGUEZ Angel	21

GROUP B	PL	W	D	L	F	A	PTS
1 USA	3	2	1	0	6	1	7
2 Costa Rica	3	2	1	0	4	1	7
3 Canada	3	1	0	2	2	4	3
4 Cuba	3	0	0	3	3	9	0

	CRC	CAN	CUB
	0-0	2-0	4-1
		1-0	3-1
			2-1

Quest Field, Seattle
7-07-2005, 17:30, 15 831, Prendergast JAM

CAN 0   1 CRC

Soto 30p

CANADA			COSTA RICA	
1 SUTTON Greg			(c) PORRAS Jose Francisco	18
2 BRAZ Adam			MILLER Roy	3
4 MCKENNA Kevin (c)	81		UMANA Michael	4
6 BERNIER Patrice			FONSECA Danny	6
9 GERBA Ali	70		LOPEZ Jose Luis	8
11 BRENNAN Jim		76	RUIZ Bryan	9
12 GRANDE Sandro	90		SOTO Jafet	10
13 BRENNAN Jim			BOLANOS Cristian	11
14 DEROSARIO Dwayne		56	CORDERO Victor	13
15 SIMPSON Josh		85	WALLACE Harold	15
16 LEDUC Patrick	83		BRYCE Steven	17
Tr: YALLOP Frank			Tr: GUIMARAES Alexander	
7 HUME Iain	70	76	ROJAS Oscar	7
8 SERIOUX Adrian	83	56	SEGURA Geiner	14
17 PETERS Jaime	90	85	SEQUEIRA Douglas	20

Quest Field, Seattle
7-07-2005, 19:30, 15 831, Pineda HON

CUB 1   4 USA

More 18

Dempsey 44, Landon 2 87 92+
Beasley 89

CUBA		USA	
1 MOLINA Odelin (c)		HAHNEMANN Marcus	1
2 MINOZO Silvio Pedro	90	HEDJUK Frankie	2
3 MARQUEZ Yenier		BEASLEY DaMarcus	7
5 CRUZATA Alexander		DEMPSEY Clint	8
6 VILLAURRUTIA Enrique		QUARANTA Santino	9
8 AQUINO Disney		CASEY Conor	11
9 CERVANTES Alain		CASEY Conor	12
10 MORE Lester	57	(c) ARMAS Chris	14
13 GALINDO Maikel	77	OLSEN Ben	15
14 COLOME Jaime	50	DAVIS Brad	21
16 CERVANTES Reysander		SANNEH Tony	22
Tr: GARCIA Luis		Tr: ARENA Bruce	
11 GIL Mario	77	O'BRIEN John	5
18 DUARTE Leonel	57	DONOVAN Landon	10
19 MUNOZ Jensis	90	WOLFF Josh	16

Quest Field, Seattle
9-07-2005, 11:30, 15 109, Archundia MEX

CUB 1   3 CRC

Galindo 72

Randall 2 61 85, Soto 81p

CUBA			COSTA RICA	
1 MOLINA Odelin (c)			(c) MESEN Alvaro	1
2 MINOZO Silvio Pedro	68		UMANA Michael	4
3 MARQUEZ Yenier			BADILLA Gabriel	5
5 CRUZATA Alexander			ROJAS Oscar	7
6 VILLAURRUTIA Enrique		46	RUIZ Bryan	9
9 CERVANTES Alain			SOTO Jafet	10
10 MORE Lester		75	BOLANOS Cristian	11
13 GALINDO Maikel		46	DIAZ Junior	12
15 MORALES Gisbel	85		SEGURA Geiner	14
16 CERVANTES Reysander			WRIGHT Mauricio	19
17 FAIFE Pedro	60		SEQUEIRA Douglas	20
Tr: GARCIA Luis			Tr: GUIMARAES Alexander	
7 RAMIREZ Jorge	60	46	MILLER Roy	3
18 DUARTE Leonel	85	75	BRYCE Steven	17
19 MUNOZ Jensis	68		BRENES Randall	21

Quest Field, Seattle
9-07-2005, 13:30, 15 109, Brizan TRI

USA 2   0 CAN

Hutchinson 48, Donovan 90

USA			CANADA	
1 KELLER Kasey (c)			SUTTON Greg	1
3 VANNEY Greg			BRAZ Adam	2
4 ONYEWU Oguchi			GERVAIS Gabriel	5
5 O'BRIEN John	67		BERNIER Patrice	6
6 CHERUNDOLO Steve		82	SERIOUX Adrian	8
10 DONOVAN Landon		70	OCCEAN Oliver	10
13 NOONAN Patrick	81	79	BRENNAN Jim	11
16 WOLFF Josh			BRENNAN Jim	13
19 RALSTON Steve			DEROSARIO Dwayne	14
23 POPE Eddie	46		SIMPSON Josh	15
25 MASTROENI Pablo	67		LEDUC Patrick	16
Tr: ARENA Bruce			Tr: YALLOP Frank	
7 BEASLEY DaMarcus	67	70	GERBA Ali	9
12 CONRAD Jimmy	46	79	GRANDE Sandro	12
14 ARMAS Chris	81	67	PETERS Jaime	17

Foxboro, Boston
12-07-2005, 19:00, 15 211, Archundia MEX

USA 0   0 CRC

USA			COSTA RICA	
18 KELLER Kasey (c)			(c) PORRAS Jose Francisco	18
2 HEJDUK Frankie			MILLER Roy	3
5 O'BRIEN John	58		UMANA Michael	4
6 CHERUNDOLO Steve			FONSECA Danny	6
8 DEMPSEY Clint	78		ROJAS Oscar	7
12 CONRAD Jimmy		67	LOPEZ Jose Luis	8
13 NOONAN Patrick	66	76	SOTO Jafet	10
14 ARMAS Chris			CORDERO Victor	13
15 OLSEN Ben			WALLACE Harold	15
19 RALSTON Steve			BRYCE Steven	17
22 SANNEH Tony		62	BRENES Randall	21
Tr: ARENA Bruce			Tr: GUIMARAES Alexander	
7 BEASLEY DaMarcus	58	76	RUIZ Bryan	9
10 DONOVAN Landon	66	62	BOLANOS Cristian	11
16 WOLFF Josh	78	67	SEQUEIRA Douglas	20

Foxboro, Boston
12-07-2005, 21:00, 15 211, Moreno PAN

CAN 2   1 CUB

Gerba 69, Hutchinson 87

Cervantes 90

CANADA			CUBA	
1 SUTTON Greg			AVILES Alexis	12
2 BRAZ Adam		76	MINOZO Silvio Pedro	2
3 POZNIAK Chris	63		MARQUEZ Yenier	3
4 MCKENNA Kevin			CRUZATA Alexander	5
5 GERVAIS Gabriel		59	VILLAURRUTIA Enrique	6
6 BERNIER Patrice			CERVANTES Alain	9
9 GERBA Ali			MORE Lester	10
10 OCCEAN Oliver		25	GIL Mario	11
12 GRANDE Sandro	56		COLOME Jaime	14
13 HUTCHINSON Atiba			MORALES Gisbel	15
14 DEROSARIO Dwayne			CERVANTES Reysander	16
Tr: YALLOP Frank			Tr: GARCIA Luis	
15 SIMPSON Josh	63	59	FAIFE Pedro	17
17 PETERS Jaime	56	25	DUARTE Leonel	18
		76	MUNOZ Jensis	19

GROUP C

		PL	W	D	L	F	A	PTS
1	Mexico	3	2	0	1	6	2	6
2	South Africa	3	1	2	0	6	5	5
3	Jamaica	3	1	1	1	7	7	4
4	Guatemala	3	0	1	2	4	9	1

	RSA	JAM	GUA
	1-2	1-0	4-0
		3-3	1-1
			4-3

Home Depot Centre, Carson, Los Angeles
8-07-2005, 19:00, 27 000, Sibrian SLV

RSA 2　1 MEX

Evans 28, Van Heerden 41 — Rodriguez 83

SOUTH AFRICA				MEXICO
1 MARLIN Calvin				CORONA Jose de Jesus 12
2 LEKGWATHI Lucky			2	RODRIGUEZ Francisco
3 THWALA Lucas			3	SALCIDO Carlos Arnaldo
4 EVANS Phillip			4	OSARIO Ricardo
5 KATZA Ricardo		71	5	LOPEZ Israel
6 GAXA Sibiniso		53	7	NAELSON Antonio
7 SIPHIKA Siyabinga		46	8	GARCIA Rafael
9 MOKOENA Lebohang	65		9	BORGETTI Jared
11 VAN HEERDEN Elrio	91		14	PINEDA Gonzalo
14 NOMVETE Siyabango	71		17	LUGO Rafael Marquez
19 NDLELA Lungisani			22	ALTAMIRANO Hector
Tr: BAXTER Stuart				Tr: LA VOLPE Ricardo
10 BIANCHI Craig	91	53	10	BRAVO Omar
17 c	65	46	19	MEDINA Alberto
21 LEREMI Gift	71	71	23	PEREZ Luis Ernesto

Home Depot Centre, Carson, Los Angeles
8-07-2005, 21:00, 27 000, Hall USA

GUA 3　4 JAM

Ruiz 3 11p 48+ 87 — Shelton 3, Fuler 5, Williams 46+p, Hue 57

GUATEMALA				JAMAICA
22 MOLINA Luis Pedro				RICKETTS Donovan 30
2 MORALES Nelson	29		3	STEWART Damion
3 MELGAR Pablo			5	SAWYERS Tyrone
6 CABRERA Gustavo			6	SCARLETT Robert
7 THOMPSON Fredy		75	9	WILLIAMS Andrew
8 ROMERO Gonzalo			10	FULLER Ricardo
10 VILLATORO Edwin	75		14	MARSHALL Tyrone
11 RAMIREZ Guillermo		65	17	HUE Jermaine
14 PONCIANO Elmer	62		18	STEPHENSON Khari
20 RUIZ Carlos		56	21	SHELTON Luton
26 SANABRIA Angel			25	DAVIS Claude
Tr: MARADIAGA Ramon				Tr: DOWNSWELL Wendell
12 FIGUEROA Carlos	29	75	12	JOHNSON Jermaine
23 SANDOVAL Hernan	62	65	16	DALEY Omar
24 DAVILA Maynor	75	56	20	RALPH Damani

Memorial Coliseum, Los Angeles
10-07-2005, 12:00, 30 710, Ruiz COL

MEX 4　0 GUA

Borgetti 2 5 14, Galindo 54, Bravo 65

MEXICO				GUATEMALA
1 MUNOZ Moises				KLEE Miguel Angel 1
2 RODRIGUEZ Francisco		69	4	CHEN Dennis
3 SALCIDO Carlos Arnaldo			5	HERNANDEZ Victor
4 OSARIO Ricardo			6	CABRERA Gustavo
7 NAELSON Antonio	73		7	THOMPSON Fredy
9 BORGETTI Jared	46	64	10	VILLATORO Edwin
15 MORALES Carlos	88		11	RAMIREZ Guillermo
16 MENDEZ Mario			12	FIGUEROA Carlos
19 MEDINA Alberto	67		13	MARTINEZ Nestor
21 GALINDO Gerardo			20	RUIZ Carlos
23 PEREZ Luis Ernesto	77		24	DAVILA Maynor
Tr: LA VOLPE Ricardo				Tr: MARADIAGA Ramon
10 BRAVO Omar	46	77	8	ROMERO Gonzalo
18 PADILLA Aaron	73	64	23	SANDOVAL Hernan
20 GARCIA Juan Pablo	67	69	26	SANABRIA Angel

Memorial Coliseum, Los Angeles
10-07-2005, 14:00, 30 710, Stott USA

RSA 3　3 JAM

Raselemane 35, Ndela 41, Nomvete 56 — Hue 35, Stewart 43, Bennett 80

SOUTH AFRICA				JAMAICA
16 RADEBE Thabang				RICKETTS Donovan 30
2 LEKGWATHI Lucky			3	STEWART Damion
3 THWALA Lucas			4	TAYLOR Jermaine
4 EVANS Phillip	74		5	SAWYERS Tyrone
5 KATZA Ricardo			6	SCARLETT Robert
6 GAXA Sibiniso	48		9	WILLIAMS Andrew
8 SIPHIKA Siyabinga	46		10	FULLER Ricardo
11 VAN HEERDEN Elrio		64	12	JOHNSON Jermaine
14 NOMVETE Siyabango	87	83	14	MARSHALL Tyrone
18 RASELEMANE Abram	56		17	HUE Jermaine
19 NDLELA Lungisani			18	STEPHENSON Khari
Tr: BAXTER Stuart				Tr: DOWNSWELL Wendell
10 BIANCHI Craig	56	83	16	DALEY Omar
13 NKOSI Bongani	46	74	20	RALPH Damani
17 BIANCHI Craig	87	64	23	BENNETT Teofore

Reliant Stadium, Houston
13-07-2005, 19:00, 45 311, Stott USA

RSA 1　1 GUA

Nkosi 45 — Romero 37

SOUTH AFRICA				GUATEMALA
1 MARLIN Calvin				MOTTA Paulo Cesar 25
2 LEKGWATHI Lucky			3	MELGAR Pablo
4 EVANS Phillip		73	6	CABRERA Gustavo
5 KATZA Ricardo		65	8	ROMERO Gonzalo
10 BIANCHI Craig			12	FIGUEROA Carlos
11 VAN HEERDEN Elrio	81		14	PONCIANO Elmer
13 NKOSI Bongani			16	GIRON Julio
14 NOMVETE Siyabango	81		20	RUIZ Carlos
18 RASELEMANE Abram	66		21	GOMEZ Rigoberto
19 NDLELA Lungisani			24	DAVILA Maynor
20 PETERSON Peter			26	SANABRIA Angel
Tr: BAXTER Stuart				Tr: MARADIAGA Ramon
7 KLATE Diane	66	73	2	MORALES Nelson
17 NOBLE Reagan	81	65	9	ZACARIAS Jose
21 LEREMI Gift	81			

Reliant Stadium, Houston
13-07-2005, 21:00, 45 311, Quesada CRC

MEX 1　0 JAM

Medina 19

MEXICO				JAMAICA
1 MUNOZ Moises				SAWYERS Shawn 1
2 RODRIGUEZ Francisco			3	STEWART Damion
3 SALCIDO Carlos Arnaldo			4	TAYLOR Jermaine
4 OSARIO Ricardo			9	WILLIAMS Andrew
7 NAELSON Antonio	69		18	STEPHENSON Khari
9 BORGETTI Jared	71	71	16	DALEY Omar
14 PINEDA Gonzalo			17	HUE Jermaine
19 MEDINA Alberto	58		19	REID Garfield
21 GALINDO Gerardo	61		20	RALPH Damani
22 ALTAMIRANO Hector	60		23	BENNETT Teofore
23 PEREZ Luis Ernesto	82		25	DAVIS Claude
Tr: LA VOLPE Ricardo				Tr: DOWNSWELL Wendel
5 LOPEZ Israel	58	61	10	FULLER Ricardo
10 BRAVO Omar	82	60	12	JOHNSON Jermaine
17 LUGO Rafael Marquez	69			

QUARTER-FINALS

Foxboro, Boston
16-07-2005, 13:00, 22 108, Archundia MEX

HON 3 2 CRC

Velasquez [6], Turcios [27], Nunez [29] | Bolanos [39], Ruiz [81]

HONDURAS			COSTA RICA	
1 COELLO Victor			MESEN Alvaro	1
2 HENRIQUEZ Astor			MILLER Roy	3
3 FIGUEROA Maynor			UMANA Michael	4
4 CABALLEROS Jorge		73	FONSECA Danny	6
6 IZAGUIRRE Junior			ROJAS Oscar	7
10 VELASQUEZ Wilmer			SOTO Jafet	10
11 NUNEZ Milton			CORDERO Victor	13
13 BERRIOS Mario	83		WALLACE Harold	15
14 GARCIA Oscar	82	62	BRYCE Steven	17
19 TURCIOS Elvis	69		SEQUEIRA Douglas	20
23 GUERRERO Mario		35	BRENES Randall	21
Tr: DE LA PAZ HERRERA Jose			Tr: GUIMARAES Alexander	
8 PALACIOS Wilson	82	73	LOPEZ Jose Luis	8
21 VALLECILLO Erick	83	62	RUIZ Bryan	9
24 GUIFARRO Luis	69	35	BOLANOS Cristan	11

Foxboro, Boston
16-07-2005, 16:00, 22 108, Batres GUA

USA 3 1 JAM

Wolff [6], Beasley 2 [42][83] | Fuller [88]

USA			JAMAICA	
18 KELLER Kasey			RICKETTS Donovan	30
3 VANNEY Greg			STEWART Damion	3
4 ONYEWU Oguchi		66	TAYLOR Jermaine	4
5 O'BRIEN John		60	SAWYERS Tyrone	5
6 CHERUNDOLO Steve	25		SCARLETT Robert	6
7 BEASLEY DaMarcus			WILLIAMS Andrew	9
10 DONOVAN Landon			FULLER Ricardo	10
12 CONRAD Jimmy			MARSHALL Tyrone	14
16 WOLFF Josh	80	78	HUE Jermaine	17
19 RALSTON Steve	84		STEPHENSON Khari	18
25 MASTROENI Pablo		69	SHELTON Luton	21
Tr: ARENA Bruce			Tr: DOWNSWELL Wendell	
9 QUARANTA Santino	84	69	JOHNSON Jermaine	12
14 ARMAS Chris	80	78	REID Garfield	19
15 OLSEN Ben	25 56	60	RALPH Damani	20

Reliant Stadium, Houston
17-07-2005, 60 050, Sibrian SLV

MEX 1 2 COL

Pineda [64] | Castrillon [58], Aguilar [74]

MEXICO			COLOMBIA	
1 MUNOZ Moises			MONDRAGON Farid	1
2 RODRIGUEZ Francisco			DE LA CUESTA Jose Julian	3
3 SALCIDO Carlos			MENDOZA Humberto	4
4 OSORIO Ricardo		71	RENTERIA Wason	9
7 NAELSON Antonio	63		MORENO Tressor	10
14 PINEDA Gonzalo			ANCHICO Yulian	13
16 MENDEZ Mario	61		CASTRILLON Jaime	15
17 MARQUEZ LUGO Rafael	32	93	PATINO Jairo	17
19 MEDINA Alberto	91	71	LEAL Juan Fernando	19
21 GALINDO Gerardo			AGUILAR Abel	21
23 PEREZ Luis Ernesto			PASSO Oscar	23
Tr: LAVOLPE Ricardo			Tr: RUEDA Reinaldo	
10 BRAVO Omar	61	93	RAMIREZ Juan Carlos	6
18 PADILLA Aaron	63	71	HURTADO Hector	16
22 ALTAMIRANO Hector	32	71	ARZUAGA Martin	18

Reliant Stadium, Houston
17-07-2005, 60 050, Prendergast JAM

RSA 1 1 PAN

Ndlela [68] | Dely Valdes [48]

SOUTH AFRICA			PANAMA	
1 MARLIN Calvin			PENEDO Jaime	1
2 LEKGWATHI Lucky			RIVERA Carlos	2
3 THWALA Lucas			TORRES Jose Anthony	4
4 EVANS Phillip			BALOY Felipe	5
5 KATZA Ricardo			GOMEZ Gabriel	6
6 GAXA Siboniso		104	DELY VALDES Jorge Luis	7
7 KLATE Daine	82		BLANCO Alberto	8
11 VAN HEERDEN Elrio	65		PHILLIPS Ricardo	15
13 NKOSI Bongani		100	GUARDIA Ubaldo	16
14 NOMVETE Slyabango	117	99	HENRIQUEZ Luis	17
18 NDLELA Lungisani			TEJADA Luis	18
Tr: BAXTER Stuart			Tr: HERNANDEZ Jose	
12 KGATLE Stanley	117	100	TORRES Roman	14
17 NOBLE Reagan	82	104	AVILA Gustavo	19
18 RASELEMANE Abram	65	99	RODRIGUEZ Angel Luis	21

SEMI-FINALS

Giants Stadium, New York/New Jersey
21-07-2005, 18:00, 41 721, Prendergast JAM

USA 2 1 HON

O'Brien [86], Onyewu [92] | Guerrero [30]

USA			HONDURAS	
18 KELLER Kasey		46	COELLO Victor	1
4 ONYEWU Oguchi		89	HENRIQUEZ Astor	2
3 O'BRIEN John			FIGUEROA Maynor	3
7 BEASLEY DaMarcus			CABALLEROS Jorge	4
10 DONOVAN Landon			VELASQUEZ Wilmer	10
12 CONRAD Jimmy			NUNEZ Milton	11
14 ARMAS Chris			BERRIOS Mario	13
16 WOLFF Josh	63		GARCIA Oscar	14
19 RALSTON Steve		75	TURCIOS Elvis	19
23 POPE Eddie	15		VALLECILLO Erick	21
25 MASTROENI Pablo	58		GUERRERO Mario	23
Tr: ARENA Bruce			Tr: DE LA PAZ HERRERA Jose	
2 HEJDUK Frankie	15	75	PALACIOS Wilson	8
8 DEMPSEY Clint	58	46	MORALES Junior	22
13 NOONAN Patrick	63	89	GUIFARRO Luis	24

Giants Stadium, New York/New Jersey
21-07-2005, 21:00, 41 721, Sibrian SLV

COL 2 3 PAN

Patino 2 [62][88] | Phillips 2 [11][72], Dely Valdes [26]

COLOMBIA			PANAMA	
1 MONDRAGON Farid			PENEDO Jaime	1
3 DE LA CUESTA Jose			RIVERA Carlos	2
4 MENDOZA Humberto	39	52	MORENO Luis	3
9 RENTERIA Wason	63		TORRES Jose Anthony	4
10 MORENO Tressor			BALOY Felipe	5
13 ANCHICO Yulian		63	GOMEZ Gabriel	6
15 CASTRILLON Jaime	46	55	DELY VALDES Jorge Luis	7
17 PATINO Jairo			BLANCO Alberto	8
19 LEAL Juan Fernando	39	69	MEDINA Julio	10
21 AGUILAR Abel			PHILLIPS Ricardo	15
23 PASSO Oscar			TEJADA Luis	18
Tr: RUEDA Reinaldo			Tr: HERNANDEZ Jose	
5 BENITEZ Jair	46	55	GUARDIA Ubaldo	16
6 RAMIREZ Aldo Leo	39	69	HENRIQUEZ Luis	17
18 ARZUAGA Martin	63	63	MITRE Engin	20

CONCACAF Gold Cup Final   **Giants Stadium, New York/New Jersey**   **24-07-2005**

Kick-off: 15:00   Attendance: 31 018

USA   0   0   PAN

		USA			MATCH STATS			PANAMA		
18	GK	KELLER Kasey			Shots		PENEDO Jaime	GK	1
2	DF	HEJDUK Frankie			Shots on Goal		RIVERA Carlos	DF	2
3	MF	VANNEY Greg			Fouls Committed		MORENO Luis	DF	3
4	DF	ONYEWU Oguchi			Corner Kicks		TORRES Jose Anthony	DF	4
5	MF	O'BRIEN John			Offside		BALOY Felipe	DF	5
7	MF	BEASLEY Da Marcus	116		Possession %		GOMEZ Gabriel	MF	6
8	MF	DEMPSEY Clint	85				DELY VALDES Jorge Luis	FW	7
10	FW	DONOVAN Landon					BLANCO Alberto	MF	8
12	DF	CONRAD Jimmy			MATCH OFFICIALS	87	MEDINA Julio	MF	10
14	MF	ARMAS Chris			Referee		TEJADA Luis	FW	18
16	FW	WOLFF Josh	62		BATRES Carlos	43	MITRE Engin	MF	20
		Tr: ARENA Bruce			Assistant Referees		Tr: HERNANDEZ Jose		
		Substitutes			VEGARA Hector		Substitutes		
9	FW	QUARANTA Santino	62		VELASQUEZ Arturo	87	HENRIQUEZ Luis	DF	17
15	MF	OLSEN Ben	116		4th Official	43	RODRIGUEZ Angel Luis	MF	21
21	MF	DAVIS Brad	85		PRENDERGAST Peter				

PENALTY SHOOT-OUT Q-FINAL

Panama First		South Africa Second	
TEJADA Luis	✔	EVANS Phillip	✔
RODRIGUEZ Angel	✔	GAXA Siboniso	✔
BALOY Felipe	✔	KATZA Ricardo	✘
BLANCO Alberto	✔	LEKGWATHI Lucky	✔
GOMEZ Gabriel	✔		
Panama win 5-3 to qualify for the semi-finals			

PENALTY SHOOT-OUT FINAL

Panama First		USA Second	
TEJADA Luis	✘	QUARANTA Santino	✔
DELY VALDES Jorge	✘	ARMAS Chris	✘
BALOY Felipe	✔	DONOVAN Landon	✔
BLANCO Alberto	✘	DAVIS Brad	✔
USA win 3-1			

TOP SCORERS

BEASLEY DaMarcus	USA	3
DONOVAN Landon	USA	3
RUIZ Carlos	Guatemala	3
VELAZQUEZ Wilmer	Honduras	3
TEJADA Luis	Panama	3

CONCACAF CHAMPIONS' CUP 2004–05

Costa Rican clubs continued their excellent recent form in the tournament with Deportivo Saprissa claiming the title for the third time in their history, this despite having to go through two more rounds than the American and Mexican clubs, who joined in at the quarter-final stage. The preliminary rounds of the Champions' Cup involve the UNCAF Club Championship of Central America from which the top three qualify for the quarter-finals, and the Caribbean Championship, the winners of which join the seven others in the quarter-finals. Jamaica's Harbour View beat compatriots Tivoli Gardens to claim the Caribbean crown, but it was Guatemala's Municipal who won the Central American title and not Saprissa. Once again the form of the MLS teams was disappointing with DC United losing heavily to UNAM Pumas in the semi-finals.

CONCACAF CHAMPIONS' CUP 2004-05

First Round

Real Esteli *	NCA	1	3
Real España	HON	1	3
Plaza Amador *	PAN	2	2
Cobán Imperial	GUA	1	3
Driangén	NCA	0	0
Deportivo FAS	SLV	2	7
Boca FC *	BLZ	0	0
Olimpia	HON	1	5
Tauro *	PAN	0	0
Herediano	CRC	3	3
Kulture Yabra *	BLZ	0	2
Alianza	SLV	0	5
Harour View	JAM	15	15
Ideal FC ‡	MSR	1	1
Juventus St Martin	SXM	0	1
Inter Meongo Tapu*	SUR	2	1
San Juan Jabloteh *	TRI	3	0
Walking Boys	SUR	1	0
Bassa SC †	ATG	2	0
Tivoli Gardens	JAM	1	3

Second Round

Deportivo Saprissa	CRC	1	4
Real Esteli *	NCA	0	0
Plaza Amador	PAN	2	0
Deportivo FAS *	SLV	5	1
Olimpia	HON	3	0
Herediano *	CRC	2	1
Alianza *	SLV	0	1
Municipal	GUA	1	3
Harbour View	JAM	6	3
Inter Meongo Tapu*	SUR	4	2
San Juan Jabloteh *	TRI	1	0
Tivoli Gardens	JAM	1	1

Third Round

		Pts
Municipal	GUA	6
Deportivo Saprissa	CRC	4
Olimpia	HON	4
Deportivo FAS	SLV	3

Harbour View *	JAM	1	2
Tivoli Gardens	JAM	1	1

Quarter-finals

Deportivo Saprissa	CRC	0	2
Kansas City Wiz. *	USA	0	1
Municipal	GUA	1	0
Monterrey *	MEX	2	0
DC United *	USA	2	2
Harbour View	JAM	1	1
Olimpia *	HON	1	1
UNAM Pumas	MEX	1	2

Semi-finals

Deportivo Saprissa*	CRC	2	15p
Monterrey	MEX	2	13p
DC United *	USA	1	0
UNAM Pumas	MEX	1	5

Final

Deportivo Saprissa*	CRC	2	1
UNAM Pumas	MEX	0	2

* Home club in the first leg • † Both legs played in Antigua • ‡ Both legs played in Montserrat • Two clubs from each of Mexico and USA qualify directly to the quarter-finals

FIRST ROUND UNCAF 1ST LEG
MCC Grounds Belize City
21-09-2004, 3 000, Mendoza NCA

Kulture Yabra	0
Alianza	0

FIRST ROUND UNCAF 2ND LEG
Magico Gonzalez, San Salvador
30-09-2004, 1 143, Melendez PAN

Alianza	5
Cerritos [1], Espindola [19], Curbelo [55], Martin Garcia 2 [66] [85]	
Kulture Yabra	2
Nunez [16], Symms [23]	

FIRST ROUND UNCAF 1ST LEG
Cacique Diriangén
21-09-2004, 1 444, Palma GUA

Diriangén	0
Deportivo FAS	2
Bentos [65], Mafla [75]	

FIRST ROUND UNCAF 2ND LEG
Oscar Quiteño, Santa Ana
30-09-2004, 1 004, Zelaya HON

Deportivo FAS	7
Munoz 2 [18] [33], Mafla [51], De la Cruz [55], Panameno 2 [73] [84], Reyes [80]	
Diriangén	0

FIRST ROUND UNCAF 1ST LEG
Rommel Fernandez, Panama City
22-09-2004, Quesada CRC

Plaza Amador	2
Justavino [61], Mitre [63]	
Cobán Imperial	1
Cifuentes [31]	

FIRST ROUND UNCAF 2ND LEG
José Angel Rossi, Cobán
28-09-2004, 2 000, Aguilar SLV

Cobán Imperial	3
Dos Santos [12], Montepeque 2 [56] [59]	
Plaza Amador	2
Osudo [48], Hernandez [50]	

FIRST ROUND UNCAF 1ST LEG
Michael Ashcroft, Mango Creek
22-09-2004, Castellanos GUA

Boca FC	0
Olimpia	1
Ferreira [57]	

FIRST ROUND UNCAF 2ND LEG
Tiburcio Andino, Tegucigalpa
28-09-2004, 3 125, Guerrero NCA

Olimpia	5
Emilio 3 [13] [50] [54], Ferreira [48], Morales [59]	
Boca FC	0

FIRST ROUND UNCAF 1ST LEG
Rommel Fernandez, Panama City
23-09-2004, Rodriguez HON

Tauro	0
Herediano	3
Bernard [44], Diaz [53], Soto [83p]	

FIRST ROUND UNCAF 2ND LEG
Eladio Cordero, Heredia
29-09-2004, 3 000, Alfaro SLV

Herediano	3
Aparicio OG [75], Cortez [78], Berry [83]	
Tauro	0

FIRST ROUND UNCAF 1ST LEG
Independencia, Estelí
23-09-2004, 1 000, Jimenez CRC

Real Estelí	1
Mejio [38]	
Real España	1
Altamirano [90]	

FIRST ROUND UNCAF 2ND LEG
Metropolitano, San Pedro Sula
29-09-2004, 997, Vidal PAN

Real España	3
Hernandez [15], Nunez [38], Ciccia [63]	
Real Estelí	3
Calero 2 [50] [76], Rodriguez [53]	

FIRST ROUND CFU 1ST LEG
Hasely Crawford, Port of Spain
22-09-2004, Forde BRB

San Juan Jabloteh	3
Baptiste [32], Daniel [57], Mitchell [90]	
Walking Boys Company	1
Donavan [13]	

FIRST ROUND CFU 2ND LEG
Andre Kamperveen, Paramaribo
26-09-2004, 100, McArthur GUY

Walking Boys Company	0
San Juan Jabloteh	0

FIRST ROUND CFU 1ST LEG
Andre Kamperveen, Paramaribo
24-09-2004, 500, McArthur GUY

Inter Meongo Tapu	2
Pinas [7], Vlijter [90]	
Juventus Saint Martin	0

FIRST ROUND CFU 2ND LEG
Alberic Richard, Saint Martin
29-09-2004, Charles DMA

Juventus Saint Martin	1
Cherubin [40]	
Inter Meongo Tapu	1
Bron [78]	

FIRST ROUND CFU 1ST LEG
Recreation Ground, St John's
15-10-2004, 2 700, Matthew SKN

Bassa Sports Club	2
O'Garro-Williams, Thomas	
Tivoli Gardens	1
Morgan	

FIRST ROUND CFU 2ND LEG
Recreation Ground, St John's
17-10-2004, 3 200, Matthew SKN

Tivoli Gardens	3
Dean 2 [4] [54], Hyde 59	
Bassa Sports Club	0

FIRST ROUND CFU 1ST LEG
Blakes Stadium, Blakes
22-10-2004, 150, Charin GPE

Harbour View	15
Grant 2 [27] [61], Shelton 4 [35] [36] [44] [50], Hue 3 [39] [45] [56], Waugh [42], Gordon 3 [65] [86] [88], Fraser [85], Priestly [89]	
Ideal FC	1
Munroe [38]	

FIRST ROUND CFU 2ND LEG
Blakes Stadium, Blakes
24-10-2004, 250, Charin GPE

Ideal FC	0
Harbour View	15
McCreath 4 [5] [14] [19] [45], Stewart [8p], Shelton [10], Priestly [12], Stewart 2 [44] [49], Gordon 4 [56] [65] [66] [75], Richards [84], Palmer [90]	

SECOND ROUND UNCAF 1ST LEG
Magico Gonzalez, San Salvador
19-10-2004, Pineda HON

Alianza	0
Municipal	1
Acevedo [49]	

SECOND ROUND UNCAF 2ND LEG
Mateo Flores, Guatemala City
27-10-2004, Campos NCA

Municipal	3
Acevedo [9], Ponciano [28], Rodriguez [86]	
Alianza	1
Sanchez [67]	

SECOND ROUND UNCAF 1ST LEG
Oscar Quiteño, Santa Ana
20-10-2004, Castillo GUA

Deportivo FAS	5
Pacheco 2 [18 24], Reyes 2 [44 71]p, De la Cruz [84]	
Plaza Amador	2
Lombardo [19], Cox [61]	

SECOND ROUND UNCAF 2ND LEG
Rommel Fernandez, Panama City
26-10-2004, Porras CRC

Plaza Amador	0
Deportivo FAS	1
Pacheco [76p]	

SECOND ROUND UNCAF 1ST LEG
Independencia, Estelí
20-10-2004, Carranza HON

Real Estelí	0
Deportivo Saprissa	1
Gonzalez [53p]	

SECOND ROUND UNCAF 2ND LEG
Ricardo Saprissa, San José
28-10-2004

Deportivo Saprissa	4
Benwell 20, Phillips 2 [44p 69], Bolanos [49]	
Real Estelí	0

SECOND ROUND UNCAF 1ST LEG
Eladio Cordero, Heredia
21-10-2004, Moreno PAN

Herediano	2
Umana [37], Oviedo [77]	
Olimpia	3
Velazquez [22], Lopez [55], Emilio [90]	

SECOND ROUND UNCAF 2ND LEG
Tiburcio Carias, Tegucigalpa
27-10-2004, Recinos SLV

Olimpia	0
Herediano	1
Vargas [89]	

SECOND ROUND CFU 1ST LEG
Andre Kamerveen, Paramaribo
3-11-2004, Chance ANT

Inter Meongo Tapu	4
Bron 2 [9 76], OG [39], Pinas [60]	
Harbour View	6
Stewart [4], Shelton 3 [16 57 90], Gordon [4], McCreath [80]	

SECOND ROUND CFU 2ND LEG
Andre Kamerveen, Paramaribo
5-11-2004, 2 500, Valentino ANT

Harbour View	3
Shelton [31], Hue [80], Gordon [84]	
Inter Meongo Tapu	2
Pinas [43], Vlyter [52]	

SECOND ROUND CFU 1ST LEG
Hasley Crawford; Port of Spain
3-11-2004, Callender BRB

San Juan Jobloteh	1
Daniel [83]	
Tivoli Gardens	1
Davis [58]	

SECOND ROUND CFU 2ND LEG
Edward Seaga, Kingston
10-11-2004, Whittaker CAY

Tivoli Gardens	1
Gillings [57]	
San Juan Jabloteh	0

THIRD ROUND CFU 1ST LEG
Harbour View Mini-Stadium, Kingston
8-12-2004, 4 000, Campbell JAM

Harbour View	1
Priestley [81]	
Tivoli Gardens	1
Nicholas [14]	

THIRD ROUND CFU 2ND LEG
Edward Seaga, Kingston
15-12-2004, 3 000, Prendergast JAM

Tivoli Gardens	1
Davis [58]	
Harbour View	2
Stewart [25], Gordon [90]	

THIRD ROUND UNCAF CLUB CHAMPIONSHIP FINALS

		Pl	W	D	L	F	A	Pts	CRC	HON	SLV
Municipal	GUA	3	2	0	1	3	1	6	1-0	0-1	2-0
Deportivo Saprissa	CRC	3	1	1	1	3	2	4		0-0	3-1
Olimpia	HON	3	1	1	1	2	3	4			1-3
Deportivo FAS	SLV	3	1	0	2	4	6	3			

Top three qualify for the quarter-finals

THIRD ROUND UNCAF
Cementos Progreso, Guatemala City
1-12-2004, Mejias CRC

Municipal	2
Acevedo [2], Plata [64]	
Deportivo FAS	0

THIRD ROUND UNCAF
Cementos Progreso, Guatemala City
1-12-2004, Batres GUA

Deportivo Saprissa	0
Olimpia	0

THIRD ROUND UNCAF
Cementos Progreso, Guatemala City
3-12-2004, Sibrian SLV

Municipal	0
Olimpia	1
Morales [44]	

THIRD ROUND UNCAF
Cementos Progreso, Guatemala City
3-12-2004, Pineda HON

Deportivo Saprissa	3
Sequeira 2 [24 41], Solís [31]	
Deportivo FAS	1
Flores [45]	

THIRD ROUND UNCAF
Cementos Progreso, Guatemala City
5-12-2004, Batres GUA

Municipal	1
Rodriguez [77]	
Deportivo Saprissa	0

THIRD ROUND UNCAF
Cementos Progreso, Guatemala City
5-12-2004, Sibrian SLV

Olimpia	1
Garcia [37]	
Deportivo FAS	3
Muñoz [22], Góchez [43], Ventos [87]	

QUARTER-FINAL 1ST LEG
Arrowhead, Kansas City
9-03-2005, 1 207, Alcala MEX

Kansas City Wizards	0
Deportivo Saprissa	0

QUARTER-FINAL 2ND LEG
Estadio Ricardo Saprissa, San José
17-03-2005, Moreno PAN

Deportivo Saprissa	2
Drummond.G 2 [90 95]	
Kansas City Wizards	1
Burciaga [78]	

QUARTER-FINAL 1ST LEG
Estadio Tecnologico, Monterrey
9-03-2005, 20 000, Stott USA

Monterrey	2
Martinez [3], Rotchen [43]	
Municipal	1
Muller [70]	

QUARTER-FINAL 2ND LEG
Mateo Flores, Guatemala City
16-03-2005, 15 000, Pineda HON

Municipal	0
Monterrey	0

QUARTER-FINAL 1ST LEG
Maryland SoccerPlex, Germantown
9-03-2005, 3 825, Quesada CRC

DC United	2
Eskandarian [5], Gros [64]	
Harbour View	1
Shelton [23]	

QUARTER-FINAL 2ND LEG
Harbour View, Kingston
16-03-2005, Brizan TRI

Harbour View	1
Stewart [45]	
DC United	2
Walker [74], Moreno [77]	

QUARTER-FINAL 1ST LEG
Tiburcio Carias, Tegucigalpa
9-03-2005, Batres GUA

Olimpia	1
Palacios [48]	
UNAM Pumas	1
Alonso [83p]	

QUARTER-FINAL 2ND LEG
Estadio Olímpico, Mexico City
16-03-2005, 25 200, Hall USA

UNAM Pumas	2
Botero [17], Marioni [118]	
Olimpia	1
Palacios [30]	

SEMI-FINAL 1ST LEG
Estadio Ricardo Saprissa, San José
7-04-2005, Sibrian SLV

Deportivo Saprissa	2
Gomez [45p], Alemán [85]	
Monterrey	2
Martinez [43], Veiga [67]	

SEMI-FINAL 2ND LEG
Estadio Tecnologico, Monterrey
13-04-2005, 30 000, Castillo GUA

Monterrey	1 3p
Casartelli [40]	
Deportivo Saprissa	1 5p
Gomez [71p]	

SEMI-FINAL 1ST LEG
RFK Stadium, Washington
6-04-2005, 21 185, Navarro CAN

DC United	1
Gomez [10]	
UNAM Pumas	1
Da Silva [51p]	

SEMI-FINAL 2ND LEG
Estadio Olímpico, Mexico City
13-04-2005, 22 000, Pineda HON

UNAM Pumas	5
Marioni [11], Beltran 2 [48 73], Toledo [85], Lozano [88]	
DC United	0

CONCACAF CHAMPIONS CUP FINAL 1ST LEG
Estadio Ricardo Saprissa, San José
4-05-2005, 20 000, Hall USA

SAPRISSA 2 0 UNAM PUMAS

Bolaños [21], Badilla [43]

	Deportivo Saprissa			UNAM Pumas	
GK	PORRAS José Francisco			BERNAL Sergio	GK
DF	BADILLA Gabriel			CASTRO Israel	DF
DF	BENNETH Try			BELTRAN Joaquín	DF
MF	BOLANOS Cristian			VERON Darío	DF
MF	BRENES Pablo	67	62	PINEDA Gonzalo	DF
DF	CORDERO Victor			TOLEDO David	MF
DF	DRUMMOND Jervis			GALINDO Gerardo	MF
DF	ESQUIVEL Juan Bautista			AUGUSTO Leandro	MF
MF	LOPEZ José Luis			LOZANO Jaime	MF
MF	SOLIS Alonso	83		BOTERO Joaquín	FW
MF	ALEMAN Allan	77		MARIONI Bruno	FW
	Tr: MEDFORD Hernán			Tr: SANCHEZ Hugo	
	Substitutes			Substitutes	
MF	MUNOZ Wilson	67	62	INIGUEZ Ismael	FW
FW	DRUMMOND Gerrold	77			
DF	GONZALEZ Ronald	83			

CONCACAF CHAMPIONS CUP FINAL 2ND LEG
Estadio Olímpico, Mexico City
11-05-2005, 40 000, Stott USA

UNAM PUMAS 2 1 SAPRISSA

Del Olmo [66], Augusto [89]

Gomez [33]

	UNAM Pumas			Deportivo Saprissa	
GK	BERNAL Sergio			PORRAS José Francisco	GK
DF	CASTRO Israel			BADILLA Gabriel	DF
DF	VERON Darío			BENNETH Try	DF
DF	PINEDA Gonzalo		73	BOLANOS Cristian	MF
MF	LOZANO Jaime		90	CENTENO Walter	MF
MF	TOLEDO David	46		CORDERO Victor	DF
MF	AUGUSTO Leandro			DRUMMOND Jervis	DF
FW	DA SILVA Jose Ailton			ESQUIVEL Juan Bautista	DF
FW	BOTERO Joaquín	79		GOMEZ Ronald	FW
FW	ALONSO Diego			LOPEZ José Luis	MF
MF	ESPINOSA Fernando	46	69	SOLIS Alonso	MF
	Tr: SANCHEZ Hugo			Tr: MEDFORD Hernán	
	Substitutes			Substitutes	
DF	DEL OLMO Joaquin	46	73 69	ALEMAN Allan	MF
MF	PALACIOS Marco	46	73	PHILLIPS Saul	DF
FW	BONELLS Pablo	79	90	NUNEZ Andres	DF

CONCACAF YOUTH TOURNAMENTS

CONCACAF JUNIOR TOURNAMENT 2005

Qualifying Rounds

Group A	Pl	W	D	L	F	A	Pts		BRB	BAH	LCA
Trinidad & T	3	3	0	0	27	2	9		5-0	14-1	8-1
Barbados	3	2	0	1	4	5	6			1-0	3-0
Bahamas	3	1	0	2	6	17	3				5-2
St Lucia	3	0	0	3	3	16	0				

British V.I. * 0 1
Antigua & B 6 8

Group B	Pl	W	D	L	F	A	Pts		DOM	GRN	ATG
Jamaica	3	3	0	0	14	1	9		4-1	2-0	8-0
Dominican R	3	2	0	1	7	4	6			2-0	4-0
Grenada	3	0	1	2	2	6	1				2-2
Antigua & B	3	0	1	2	2	14	1				

Group C	Pl	W	D	L	F	A	Pts		SUR	ANT	ARU
Haiti	3	3	0	0	14	1	9		4-0	5-0	2-0
Surinam	3	2	0	1	7	6	6			3-1	4-1
Neth. Antilles	3	1	0	2	3	9	3				2-1
Aruba	3	0	0	3	2	8					

Trinidad & T* 1 1
Cuba 3 3

Jamaica * 0 1
Haiti 4 0

* Home team in first leg

Group Hosts
A: Trinidad
B: Jamaica
C: Neth Antilles
D: Cuba
UNCAF A: El Salvador
UNCAF B: Honduras

Group D	Pl	W	D	L	F	A	Pts		BER	VIN	GUY
Cuba	3	3	0	0	9	0	9		3-0	3-0	3-0
Bermuda	3	1	1	1	3	5	4			1-1	2-1
St Vincent & G	3	1	1	1	3	5	4				2-1
Guyana	3	0	0	3	2	7	0				

UNCAF A	Pl	W	D	L	F	A	Pts		GUA	NCA
El Salvador	2	2	0	0	10	0	6		1-0	9-0
Guatemala	2	1	0	1	3	1	3			3-0
Nicaragua	2	0	0	2	0	12	0			

UNCAF B	Pl	W	D	L	F	A	Pts		PAN	BLZ
Honduras	2	2	0	0	7	1	6		2-1	5-0
Panama	2	1	0	1	7	3	3			6-1
Belize	2	0	0	2	1	11	0			

Final Tournament

Group A	Pl	W	D	L	F	A	Pts		CRC	CUB	SLV
USA †	3	2	1	0	6	2	7		2-1	1-1	3-0
Costa Rica	3	2	0	1	6	3	6			3-0	2-1
Cuba	3	0	2	1	5	4	3				2-2
El Salvador	3	0	1	2	3	7	1				

Play-off for third place in the finals
Costa Rica * 2
Honduras 1

Group B	Pl	W	D	L	F	A	Pts		HON	CAN	HAI
Mexico †	3	3	0	0	7	0	9		3-0	2-0	2-0
Honduras	3	1	1	1	3	4	4			2-0	1-1
Canada	3	1	0	2	5	4	3				5-0
Haiti	3	0	1	2	1	8	1				

† qualified for the FIFA U-17 World Championship in Peru
Group A played in Heredia, Costa Rica from 12-01-2005 to 16-01-2005 • Group B played in Culiacan, Mexico from 17-05-2005 to 21-05-2005 • Mexico, Costa Rica, Canada and USA qualified automatically for the finals

CONCACAF YOUTH TOURNAMENT 2005

Qualifying Rounds

Group A	Pl	W	D	L	F	A	Pts		GRN	BRB	GUY
Trinidad & T	3	2	1	0	7	3	7		1-1	4-2	2-0
Grenada	3	1	1	1	2	2	4			0-1	1-0
Barbados	3	1	0	2	5	7	3				2-3
Guyana	3	1	0	2	3	5	3				

Dominica * 0 1
St Kitts/Nevis 1 2

Group B	Pl	W	D	L	F	A	Pts		LCA	BER	ATG
Jamaica	3	3	0	0	17	0	9		2-0	3-0	12-0
St Lucia	3	2	0	1	6	3	6			2-0	4-1
Bermuda	3	1	0	2	2	6	3				2-1
Antigua & B	3	0	0	3	2	18	0				

St Martin * 2 3
US Virgin Isl 1 3

Group C	Pl	W	D	L	F	A	Pts		ANT	VIN	ARU
Haiti	3	3	0	0	11	0	9		5-0	3-0	3-0
Neth. Antilles	3	1	1	1	2	5	4			2-0	0-0
St Vincent & G	3	1	0	2	2	6	3				2-1
Aruba	3	0	1	2	1	5	1				

Surinam * 3 0
Aruba 2 2

Trinidad & T* 3 3
Cuba 2 3

Jamaica * 4
Haiti 0

* Home team in first leg

Group Hosts
A: Trinidad
B: Jamaica
C: Neth Antilles
D: Cuba
UNCAF: Costa Rica

Group D	Pl	W	D	L	F	A	Pts		DOM	SKN
Cuba	2	2	0	0	10	2	6		6-2	4-0
Dominican R.	2	0	1	1	5	9	1			3-3
St Kitts/Nevis	2	0	1	1	3	7	1			

St Martin withdrew

UNCAF Group	Pl	W	D	L	F	A	Pts		PAN	SLV	GUA	NCA
Costa Rica	4	3	1	0	9	2	10		1-1	1-0	5-1	2-0
Panama	4	3	1	0	6	1	10			2-0	1-0	2-0
El Salvador	4	2	0	2	9	6	6				5-2	4-1
Guatemala	4	1	0	3	6	13	3					3-2
Nicaragua	4	0	0	4	3	11	0					

Belize withdrew

Final Tournament

Group A	Pl	W	D	L	F	A	Pts		PAN	CRC	TRI
USA †	3	3	0	0	10	1	9		2-0	2-0	6-1
Panama †	3	1	1	1	4	4	4			1-1	3-1
Costa Rica	3	1	1	1	3	4	4				2-1
Trinidad & T	3	0	0	3	3	11	0				

Group B	Pl	W	D	L	F	A	Pts		HON	MEX	JAM
Canada †	3	3	0	0	4	1	9		1-0	2-1	1-0
Honduras †	3	2	0	1	6	3	6			2-0	4-2
Mexico	3	1	0	2	2	4	3				1-0
Jamaica	3	0	0	3	2	6	0				

† qualified for the FIFA World Youth Championship in the Netherlands
Group A played in Carson, Los Angeles from 12-01-2005 to 16-01-2005 • Group B played in San Pedro Sula in Honduras from 26-01-2005 to 30-01-2005 • Mexico, Honduras, Canada and USA qualified automatically for the finals

REGIONAL TOURNAMENTS IN CONCACAF

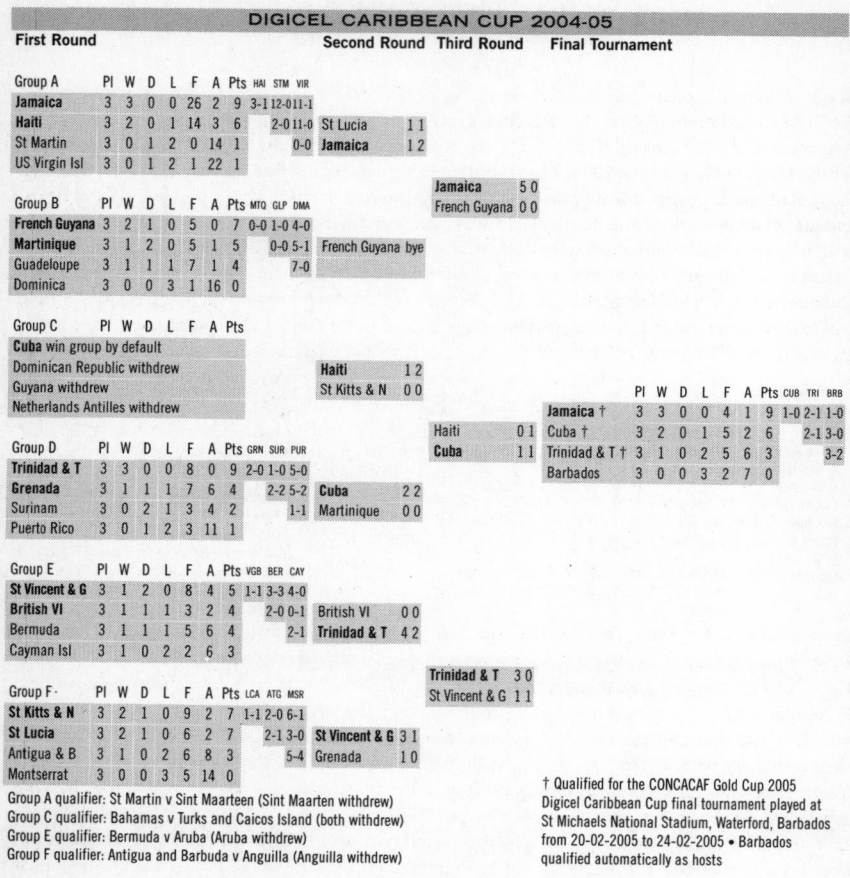

DIGICEL CARIBBEAN CUP 2004-05

First Round / **Second Round** / **Third Round** / **Final Tournament**

Group A
	Pl	W	D	L	F	A	Pts	HAI	STM	VIR
Jamaica	3	3	0	0	26	2	9	3-1	12-0	11-1
Haiti	3	2	0	1	14	3	6		2-0	11-0
St Martin	3	0	1	2	0	14	1			0-0
US Virgin Isl	3	0	1	2	1	22	1			

Second Round: St Lucia 1 1 / Jamaica 1 2

Third Round: Jamaica 5 0 / French Guyana 0 0

Group B
	Pl	W	D	L	F	A	Pts	MTQ	GLP	DMA
French Guyana	3	2	1	0	5	0	7	0-0	1-0	4-0
Martinique	3	1	2	0	5	1	5		0-0	5-1
Guadeloupe	3	1	1	1	7	1	4			7-0
Dominica	3	0	0	3	1	16	0			

Second Round: French Guyana bye

Group C
	Pl	W	D	L	F	A	Pts
Cuba win group by default							
Dominican Republic withdrew							
Guyana withdrew							
Netherlands Antilles withdrew							

Second Round: Haiti 1 2 / St Kitts & N 0 0

Third Round: Haiti 0 1 / Cuba 1 1

Final Tournament
	Pl	W	D	L	F	A	Pts	CUB	TRI	BRB
Jamaica †	3	3	0	0	4	1	9	1-0	2-1	1-0
Cuba †	3	2	0	1	5	2	6		2-1	3-0
Trinidad & T †	3	1	0	2	5	6	3			3-2
Barbados	3	0	0	3	2	7	0			

Group D
	Pl	W	D	L	F	A	Pts	GRN	SUR	PUR
Trinidad & T	3	3	0	0	8	0	9	2-0	1-0	5-0
Grenada	3	1	1	1	7	6	4		2-2	5-2
Surinam	3	0	2	1	3	4	2			1-1
Puerto Rico	3	0	1	2	3	11	1			

Second Round: Cuba 2 2 / Martinique 0 0

Group E
	Pl	W	D	L	F	A	Pts	VGB	BER	CAY
St Vincent & G	3	1	2	0	8	4	5	1-1	3-3	4-0
British VI	3	1	1	1	3	2	4		2-0	0-1
Bermuda	3	1	1	1	5	6	4			2-1
Cayman Isl	3	1	0	2	2	6	3			

Second Round: British VI 0 0 / Trinidad & T 4 2

Third Round: Trinidad & T 3 0 / St Vincent & G 1 1

Group F
	Pl	W	D	L	F	A	Pts	LCA	ATG	MSR
St Kitts & N	3	2	1	0	9	2	7	1-1	2-0	6-1
St Lucia	3	2	1	0	6	2	7		2-1	3-0
Antigua & B	3	1	0	2	6	8	3			5-4
Montserrat	3	0	0	3	5	14	0			

Second Round: St Vincent & G 3 1 / Grenada 1 0

Group A qualifier: St Martin v Sint Maarteen (Sint Maarten withdrew)
Group C qualifier: Bahamas v Turks and Caicos Island (both withdrew)
Group E qualifier: Bermuda v Aruba (Aruba withdrew)
Group F qualifier: Antigua and Barbuda v Anguilla (Anguilla withdrew)

† Qualified for the CONCACAF Gold Cup 2005
Digicel Caribbean Cup final tournament played at St Michaels National Stadium, Waterford, Barbados from 20-02-2005 to 24-02-2005 • Barbados qualified automatically as hosts

UNCAF CUP GUATEMALA 2005

First Round Group Stage / **Semi-finals** / **Final**

	Pl	W	D	L	F	A	Pts	GUA	NCA	BLZ
Honduras	3	2	1	0	10	2	7	1-1	5-1	4-0
Guatemala	3	2	1	0	7	1	7		4-0	2-0
Nicaragua	3	1	0	2	2	9	3			1-0
Belize	3	0	0	3	0	7	0			

Semi-finals: Costa Rica 4 / Guatemala 0

	Pl	W	D	L	F	A	Pts	PAN	SLV
Costa Rica	2	2	0	0	3	1	6	1-0	2-1
Panama	2	1	0	1	1	1	3		1-0
El Salvador	2	0	0	2	1	3	0		

Semi-finals: Panama 0 / Honduras 1

Final: Costa Rica 1 7p / Honduras 1 6p

Third place play-off: Guatemala 3 / Panama 0

Tournament held in the Mateo Flores Stadium, Guatemala City from 19-02-2005 to 27-02-2005
All four semi-finalists qualified for the CONCACAF Gold Cup 2005

CONMEBOL

CONFEDERACION SUDAMERICANA DE FUTBOL

South American football finished the season on a high when Brazil met Argentina in the final of the FIFA Confederations Cup. The Brazilians made up for their defeat earlier in the month against Argentina in the FIFA World Cup™ qualifiers, winning 4-1 with a powerful display that bodes well for the finals in Germany in 2006. The marathon campaign for the finals continued with Argentina the first nation to qualify. Most of the interest centred around the pack chasing Argentina and Brazil and the scrabble for third and fourth places was intense throughout amongst the eight other nations, with fifth spot also bringing the possibility of qualification via a play-off against the winners from Oceania. Brazil and Argentina's duel continued in the semi-finals of the FIFA World Youth Championship in the Netherlands, a goal deep into injury time sending Argentina into the final where they won a record fifth title beating Nigeria 2-1. In the Copa Libertadores, however, it was all Brazil when São Paulo FC and Atlético Paranaense met in the final, the first time in the history of

THE FIFA BIG COUNT OF 2000 FOR CONMEBOL

	Male	Female		Male	Female
Registered players	1 619 285	13 019	Referees	17 265	203
Not registered players	11 345 000	97 300	Officials	114 835	3 070
Youth players	2 122 337	9 666	Total involved	21 533 624	693 436
Children & Occasional	6 280 000	570 000	in football	22 191 980	
Professionals	34 902	178	Number of clubs	23 334	
Total players	22 056 607		Number of teams	95 241	

the competition that two clubs from the same country made up the final two. São Paulo FC ensured River's poor record in the Copa Libertadores continued with a 5-2 aggregate victory in the semi-finals before winning the title for the third time with a 5-1 aggregate victory over Atlético Paranaense. After using only reserve teams, Argentina's Boca Juniors fielded a full-strength side to win the Copa Sudamericana when it became clear it was their only chance of winning a trophy in their centenary year. In the final they beat Bolivar, the first Bolivian team to make it through to a South American club competition final. One of the biggest stories of the year concerned the mysterious investment into Brazilian club Corinthians by London-based Media Sports Investments. Results didn't go as smoothly as hoped with poor results and disunity from players to boardroom following a US$30 million spending spree including the extraordinary signing of Argentine sensation Carlos Tevez, whom many thought would be bound for a top European club.

Confederación Sudamericana de Fútbol (CONMEBOL)
Autopista Aeropuerto Internacional y Leonismo Luqueño, Luque (Gran Asuncion), Paraguay
Tel +595 21 645781   Fax +595 21 645791
conmebol@conmebol.com.py   www.conmebol.com
President: LEOZ Nicolás, Dr PAR   General Secretary: DELUCA Eduardo ARG
CONMEBOL Formed: 1916

CONMEBOL EXECUTIVE COMMITTEE

President: LEOZ Nicolás, Dr PAR

Vice-President: FIGUEREDO Eugenio URU   General Secretary: DELUCA Eduardo ARG   Treasurer: OSUNA Romer BOL

ORDINARY MEMBERS OF THE EXECUTIVE COMMITTEE

ESQUIVEL Rafael VEN	DELFINO Nicolás PER	HARRISON Oscar PAR
CHEDID Nabí Abí BRA	CHIRIBOGA Luis ECU	FINA Alvaro COL
	ABDALAH José CHI	

SOUTH AMERICAN TOURNAMENTS

COPA AMERICA

Year	Host Country	Winners	Score	Runners-up	Venue
1910	Argentina ††	Argentina	4-1	Uruguay	‡ Racing Club, Buenos Aires
1916	Argentina †	Uruguay	0-0	Argentina	‡ Racing Club, Buenos Aires
1917	Uruguay	Uruguay	1-0	Argentina	‡ Parque Pereira, Montevideo
1919	Brazil	Brazil	1-0	Uruguay	§ Laranjeiras, Rio de Janeiro
1920	Chile	Uruguay	1-1	Argentina	* Sporting Club, Vina del Mar
1921	Argentina	Argentina	1-0	Brazil	* Sportivo Barracas, Buenos Aires
1922	Brazil	Brazil	3-0	Paraguay	§ Laranjeiras, Rio de Janeiro
1923	Uruguay	Uruguay	2-0	Argentina	‡ Parque Central, Montevideo
1924	Uruguay	Uruguay	0-0	Argentina	‡ Parque Central, Montevideo
1925	Argentina	Argentina	2-2	Brazil	‡ Bombonera, Buenos Aires
1926	Chile	Uruguay	2-0	Argentina	* Sport de Nunoa, Santiago
1927	Peru	Argentina	3-2	Uruguay	* Estadio Nacional, Lima
1929	Argentina	Argentina	4-1	Paraguay	* San Lorenzo, Buenos Aires
1935	Peru †	Uruguay	3-0	Argentina	‡ Estadio Nacional, Lima
1937	Argentina	Argentina	2-0	Brazil	‡ San Lorenzo, Buenos Aires
1939	Peru	Peru	2-1	Uruguay	‡ Estadio Nacional, Lima
1941	Chile †	Argentina	1-0	Uruguay	* Estadio Nacional, Santiago
1942	Uruguay	Uruguay	1-0	Argentina	‡ Centenario, Montevideo
1945	Chile †	Argentina	3-1	Brazil	* Estadio Nacional, Santiago
1946	Argentina †	Argentina	2-0	Brazil	‡ Monumental, Buenos Aires
1947	Ecuador	Argentina	6-0	Paraguay	* Estadio Capwell, Guayaquil
1949	Brazil	Brazil	7-0	Paraguay	§ Sao Januario, Rio de Janeiro
1953	Lima	Paraguay	3-2	Brazil	§ Estadio Nacional, Lima
1955	Chile	Argentina	1-0	Chile	‡ Estadio Nacional, Santiago
1956	Uruguay †	Uruguay	1-0	Argentina	‡ Centenario, Montevideo
1957	Peru	Argentina	3-0	Brazil	‡ Estadio Nacional, Lima
1959	Argentina	Argentina	1-1	Brazil	‡ Monumental, Buenos Aires
1959	Ecuador †	Uruguay	5-0	Argentina	* Modelo, Guayaquil
1963	Bolivia	Bolivia	5-4	Brazil	‡ Felix Capriles, Cochabamba
1967	Uruguay	Uruguay	1-0	Argentina	‡ Centenario, Montevideo
1975		Peru	0-1 2-0 1-0	Colombia	Bogota, Lima, Caracas
1979		Paraguay	3-0 0-1 0-0	Chile	Asuncion, Santiago, Buenos Aires
1983		Uruguay	2-0 1-1	Brazil	Montevideo & Salvador
1987	Argentina	Uruguay	1-0	Chile	Monumental, Buenos Aires
1989	Brazil	Brazil	1-0	Uruguay	‡ Maracana, Rio de Janeiro
1991	Chile	Argentina	3-2	Brazil	* Estadio Nacional, Santiago
1993	Ecuador	Argentina	2-1	Mexico	Monumental, Guayaquil
1995	Uruguay	Uruguay	1-1 5-3p	Brazil	Centenario, Montevideo
1997	Bolivia	Brazil	3-1	Bolivia	Hernando Siles, La Paz
1999	Paraguay	Brazil	3-0	Uruguay	Defensores del Chaco, Asuncion
2001	Colombia	Colombia	1-0	Mexico	El Campin, Bogota
2004	Peru	Brazil	2-2 4-2p	Argentina	Estadio Nacional, Lima
2006	Venezuela				

† Extraordinario tournaments are recognised as official tournaments though the teams did not compete for the Copa America • †† Unofficial tournament that is not part of the official records • ‡ Tournament played on a league system. The final game was between the top two teams
** Tournament played on a league system. The game listed between the top two teams was not the final match in the tournament • § Tournament played on a league system. The game listed was a play-off after the top two teams finished level on points.

Following the demise of the British International Championship, the Copa América is now the longest-running international competition in the world, dating back to 1916 though some historians like to point to a tournament played in 1910 that was referred to at the time as the "South American Championship". Argentina and Uruguay have always been the most enthusiastic proponents of the Copa América and each has been champions 14 times lending credence to the belief among many

South Americans that the real home of football on the continent lies around the River Plate estuary and the cities of Montevideo and Buenos Aires and not further north in Brazil. In the first 33 editions spanning 73 years the Brazilians won the title just three times and never outside of Rio de Janeiro. Aside from these three, Peru in 1939 and 1975, and Paraguay in 1953 and 1979, have been champions twice while Bolivia in 1963 and Colombia in 2001 have both won the title once. Only Venezuela, Ecuador and Chile have failed to win it with Venezuela yet to win a single match since beating Bolivia the first time they took part in 1967. Historically the tournament has usually been played on a league system although since the 1970s a group stage followed by knock-out rounds has been the preferred format. Another innovation has been the invitation extended to Mexico to take part since 1993, along with another guest, most commonly Costa Rica or the USA. Now held every two years the Copa América has finally caught the imagination of the Brazilians and in recent years they have been the most successful nation winning three of the past four editions and their 1997 triumph in Bolivia was their first away from home. The past three FIFA World Cup™ qualifying campaigns in South America, in which each of the ten nations plays each other home and away, has to a certain extent cast a shadow over the Copa América. It is difficult to argue against the fact that the top team, at the end of what amounts to a three-year campaign, should be regarded as the best team on the continent rather than the Copa America champions. However, the Copa América remains an important landmark in the fixture list and it rarely fails to entertain.

SOUTH AMERICAN WOMEN'S CHAMPIONSHIP

Year	Host Country	Winners	Score	Runners-up	Venue
1991	Brazil	Brazil	6-1	Chile	‡ Maringá
1995	Brazil	Brazil	2-0	Argentina	Uberlândia
1998	Argentina	Brazil	7-1	Argentina	Mar del Plata
2003	Peru	Brazil	3-2	Argentina	** Lima

‡ Tournament played on a league system. The final game was between the top two teams • ** Tournament played on a league system. The game listed between the top two teams was not the final match in the tournament.

SOUTH AMERICAN WOMEN'S U-19 CHAMPIONSHIP

Year	Host Country	Winners	Score	Runners-up	Venue
2004		Brazil	5-2	Paraguay	

‡ Tournament played on a league system. The final game was between the top two teams

The South American Women's Championship was introduced in 1991 as a qualifying tournament for the FIFA Women's World Cup and has been played as such ever since. Brazil have dominated since the start, a position reinforced when the U-19 competition was introduced in 2004. Ranked fourth in the world at the end of 2004, Brazil's nearest challenger Colombia was ranked 31 places below them, so it could be some time before the name of another nation is engraved on either trophy.

SOUTH AMERICA PRE-OLIMPICO

Year	Host Country	Winners	Runners-up
1960	Peru	Argentina	Peru
1964	Peru	Argentina	Brazil
1968	Colombia	Brazil	Colombia
1971	Colombia	Brazil	Colombia
1976	Brazil	Brazil	Uruguay
1980	Colombia	Argentina	Colombia
1984	Ecuador	Brazil	Chile
1987	Bolivia	Brazil	Argentina
1992	Paraguay	Paraguay	Colombia
1996	Argentina	Brazil	Argentina
2000	Brazil	Brazil	Chile
2004	Chile	Argentina	Paraguay

Open to non-professionals only prior to 1984 • The 1987 tournament was open to any player who had not played in a FIFA World Cup™ match • Since 1992 it has been an U-23 tournament

SUDAMERICANA SUB-17

Year	Host Country	Winners	Runners-up
1985	Argentina	Argentina	Brazil
1986	Peru	Bolivia	Brazil
1988	Ecuador	Brazil	Argentina
1991	Paraguay	Brazil	Uruguay
1993	Colombia	Colombia	Chile
1995	Peru	Brazil	Argentina
1997	Paraguay	Brazil	Argentina
1999	Uruguay	Brazil	Paraguay
2002	Peru	Brazil	Argentina
2003	Bolivia	Argentina	Brazil
2005	Venezuela	Brazil	Uruguay

From 1985-1988 the championship was a U-16 tournament but since 1991 it has operated as an U-17 championship

SUDAMERICANA SUB-20

Year	Host Country	Winners	Runners-up
1954	Venezuela	Uruguay	Brazil
1958	Chile	Uruguay	Argentina
1964	Colombia	Uruguay	Paraguay
1967	Paraguay	Argentina	Paraguay
1971	Paraguay	Paraguay	Uruguay
1974	Chile	Brazil	Uruguay
1975	Peru	Uruguay	Chile
1977	Venezuela	Uruguay	Brazil
1979	Uruguay	Uruguay	Argentina
1981	Ecuador	Uruguay	Brazil
1983	Bolivia	Brazil	Uruguay

SUDAMERICANA SUB-20

Year	Host Country	Winners	Runners-up
1985	Paraguay	Brazil	Paraguay
1987	Colombia	Colombia	Brazil
1988	Argentina	Brazil	Colombia
1991	Venezuela	Brazil	Argentina
1992	Colombia	Brazil	Uruguay
1995	Bolivia	Brazil	Argentina
1997	Chile	Argentina	Brazil
1999	Argentina	Argentina	Uruguay
2001	Ecuador	Brazil	Argentina
2003	Uruguay	Argentina	Brazil
2005	Colombia	Colombia	Brazil

SUPERCOPA JOAO HAVELANGE

Year	Winners	Country	Score	Country	Runners-up
1988	Racing Club	ARG	2-1 1-1	BRA	Cruzeiro
1989	Boca Juniors	ARG	0-0 0-0 5-3p	ARG	Independiente
1990	Olimpia	PAR	3-0 3-3	URU	Nacional Montevideo
1991	Cruzeiro	BRA	0-2 3-0	ARG	River Plate
1992	Cruzeiro	BRA	4-0 0-1	ARG	Racing Club
1993	São Paulo FC	BRA	2-2 2-2 5-3p	BRA	Flamengo
1994	Independiente	ARG	1-1 1-0	ARG	Boca Juniors
1995	Independiente	ARG	2-0 0-1	BRA	Flamengo
1996	Velez Sarsfield	ARG	1-0 2-0	BRA	Cruzeiro
1997	River Plate	ARG	0-0 2-1	BRA	São Paulo FC

Discontinued in 1997 and replaced by the Copa Mercosur and Copa Merconorte

COPA MERCOSUR

Year	Winners	Country	Score	Country	Runners-up
1998	Palmeiras	BRA	1-2 3-1 1-0	BRA	Cruzeiro
1999	Flamengo	BRA	4-3	BRA	Palmeiras
2000	Vasco da Gama	BRA	2-0 0-1 4-3	BRA	Palmeiras
2001	San Lorenzo	ARG	0-0 1-1 4-3p	BRA	Flamengo

COPA MERCONORTE

Year	Winners	Country	Score	Country	Runners-up
1998	Atlético Nacional Medellin	COL	3-1 1-0	COL	Deportivo Cali
1999	América Cali	COL	1-2 1-0	COL	Independiente Santa Fé
2000	Atlético Nacional Medellin	COL	0-0 2-1	COL	Millonarios
2001	Millonarios	COL	1-1 1-1 3-1p	ECU	Emelec

Both the Copa Mercosur and Copa Merconorte were discontinued in 2001 and were replaced by the Copa Sudamericana

COPA CONMEBOL

Year	Winners	Country	Score	Country	Runners-up
1992	Atlético Mineiro	BRA	2-0 0-1	PAR	Olimpia
1993	Botafogo	BRA	1-1 2-2 3-1p	URU	Peñarol
1994	São Paulo FC	BRA	6-1 0-3	URU	Peñarol
1995	Rosario Central	ARG	0-4 4-0 4-3p	BRA	Atlético Mineiro
1996	Lanús	ARG	2-0 0-1	COL	Independiente Santa Fé
1997	Atlético Mineiro	BRA	4-1 1-1	ARG	Lanús
1998	Santos	BRA	1-0 0-0	ARG	Rosario Central
1999	Talleres Cordoba	ARG	2-4 3-0	BRA	CSA

Discontinued in 1999

COPA SUDAMERICANA

Year	Winners	Country	Score	Country	Runners-up
2002	San Lorenzo	ARG	4-0 0-0	COL	Atlético Nacional Medellin
2003	Cienciano	PER	3-3 1-0	ARG	River Plate
2004	Boca Juniors	ARG	0-1 2-0	BOL	Bolivar

COPA LIBERTADORES DE AMERICA

Year	Winners	Country	Score	Country	Runners-up
1960	Peñarol	URU	1-0 1-1	PAR	Olimpia
1961	Peñarol	URU	1-0 1-1	BRA	Palmeiras
1962	Santos	BRA	2-1 2-3 3-0	URU	Peñarol
1963	Santos	BRA	3-2 2-1	ARG	Boca Juniors
1964	Independiente	ARG	0-0 1-0	URU	Nacional Montevideo
1965	Independiente	ARG	1-0 1-3 4-1	URU	Peñarol
1966	Peñarol	URU	2-0 2-3 4-2	ARG	River Plate
1967	Racing Club	ARG	0-0 0-0 2-1	URU	Nacional Montevideo
1968	Estudiantes LP	ARG	2-1 1-3 2-0	BRA	Palmeiras
1969	Estudiantes LP	ARG	1-0 2-0	URU	Nacional Montevideo
1970	Estudiantes LP	ARG	1-0 0-0	URU	Peñarol
1971	Nacional Montevideo	URU	0-1 1-0 2-0	ARG	Estudiantes LP
1972	Independiente	ARG	0-0 2-1	PER	Universitario
1973	Independiente	ARG	1-1 0-0 2-1	CHI	Colo Colo
1974	Independiente	ARG	1-2 2-0 1-0	BRA	São Paulo FC
1975	Independiente	ARG	0-1 3-1 2-0	CHI	Union Española
1976	Cruzeiro	BRA	4-1 1-2 3-2	ARG	River Plate
1977	Boca Juniors	ARG	1-0 0-1 0-0 5-4p	BRA	Cruzeiro
1978	Boca Juniors	ARG	0-0 4-0	COL	Deportivo Cali
1979	Olimpia	PAR	2-0 0-0	ARG	Boca Juniors
1980	Nacional Montevideo	URU	0-0 1-0	BRA	Internacional PA
1981	Flamengo	BRA	2-1 0-1 2-0	CHI	Cobreloa
1982	Peñarol	URU	0-0 1-0	CHI	Cobreloa
1983	Grêmio	BRA	1-1 2-1	URU	Peñarol
1984	Independiente	ARG	1-0 0-0	BRA	Grêmio
1985	Argentinos Juniors	ARG	1-0 0-1 1-1 5-4p	COL	América Cali
1986	River Plate	ARG	2-1 1-0	COL	América Cali
1987	Peñarol	URU	0-2 2-1 1-0	COL	América Cali
1988	Nacional Montevideo	URU	0-1 3-0	ARG	Newell's Old Boys
1989	Atlético Nacional Medellín	COL	0-2 2-0 5-4p	PAR	Olimpia
1990	Olimpia	PAR	2-0 1-1	ECU	Barcelona
1991	Colo Colo	CHI	0-0 3-0	PAR	Olimpia
1992	São Paulo FC	BRA	1-0 0-1 3-2p	ARG	Newell's Old Boys
1993	São Paulo FC	BRA	5-1 0-2	CHI	Universidad Catolica
1994	Velez Sarsfield	ARG	1-0 0-1 5-3p	BRA	São Paulo FC
1995	Grêmio	BRA	3-1 1-1	COL	Atlético Nacional Medellin
1996	River Plate	ARG	0-1 2-0	COL	América Cali
1997	Cruzeiro	BRA	0-0 1-0	PER	Sporting Cristal
1998	Vasco da Gama	BRA	2-0 2-1	ECU	Barcelona
1999	Palmeiras	BRA	0-1 2-1 4-3p	COL	Deportivo Cali
2000	Boca Juniors	ARG	2-2 0-0 4-2p	BRA	Palmeiras
2001	Boca Juniors	ARG	1-0 0-1 3-1p	MEX	Cruz Azul
2002	Olimpia	PAR	0-1 2-1 4-2p	BRA	São Caetano
2003	Boca Juniors	ARG	2-0 3-1	BRA	Santos
2004	Once Caldas	COL	0-0 1-1 2-0p	ARG	Boca Juniors
2005	São Paulo FC	BRA	1-1 4-0	BRA	Atlético Paranaense

The Copa Libertadores de América is the premier South American club event. Prior to its inception in 1960, there had been no continent-wide tournament organised by CONMEBOL. A still-born Campeonato Sudamericano de Campeones, organised by Colo Colo in Chile in 1948, and won by Vasco da Gama, attracted the champion teams from all but Colombia, Venezuela and Paraguay but it was a financial disaster and was not organised the following year. The success of the European Champions Cup persuaded CONMEBOL to give the idea another try and at a meeting in Brazil in 1958 the idea was approved in principle. That same year Henri Delaunay, the General Secretary of UEFA, suggested to CONMEBOL an annual meeting between the winners of the European Cup and the winners of a South American tournament. The prospect of a World Club Championship was very appealing to the top clubs and it was this more than anything else that got the idea off the ground. The first series was organised in 1960 with seven of the continent's champions taking part. Missing were Ecuador, Peru and Venezuela but for the second tournament the following year, all bar Venezuela entered, however, by 1964 they too found the lure of the competition too hard to resist. The Copa Libertadores has enjoyed a rich and varied history with moments of high drama. It has always been dominated by clubs from around the River Plate and, as in the South American Championship, Brazil's record is lamentable. The first two tournaments were played on a knock-out basis with home and away legs in each tie, including the final. Although the format of the rounds prior to the final has varied over the years, the final itself has always been played over two legs and is decided on a points basis, with goal difference only counting if the play-off has not produced a winner. Penalties were introduced in the late 1980s as the logistics of organising a third match became more difficult in a crowded calender. A group stage was introduced in 1962 – some 30 years before the idea caught on in Europe and elsewhere around the world and the Copa Libertadores was also the first continental championship to see more than just the champions of each country take part, with the runners-up in each League qualifying as far back as 1966. Now Brazil and Argentina have as many as five teams taking part each year. Since 1998, Mexico, although not a member of CONMEBOL, has been invited to enter teams into the Copa Libertadores, but so far without the success that was first anticipated. 1988 brought the introduction of the Supercopa Joao Havelange for former winners of the Copa Libertadores whilst a 'best of the rest' Copa Conmebol briefly ran between 1992 and 1999, but both tournaments didn't stand the test of time. They were replaced by the Copa Mercosur and the Copa Merconorte, which were in turn superseded by the Copa Sudamericana in 2002.

PAST SOUTH AMERICAN PLAYER OF THE YEAR AWARDS

Historically there have been two different awards for South American Footballer of the Year. From 1971 until 1992 *El Mundo* newspaper in Caracas awarded the accolade which was open to South Americans playing anywhere in the world. Since 1986 *El Pais* of Montevideo has given the award to the best South American playing within the Americas.

PLAYER OF THE YEAR 1971

TOSTAO	Cruzeiro	BRA	24
PASTORIZA Omar	Independiente	ARG	21
ARTIME Luis	Nacional	ARG	19
CUBILLAS Teófilo	Alianza	PER	17
GERSON	São Paulo FC	BRA	16
PELE	Santos	BRA	15
MAZURKIEWICZ Lad.	Atlético MG	URU	13
JAIRZINHO	Botafogo	BRA	11
RIVELINO Roberto	Corinthians	BRA	10
CHUMPITAZ Hector	Universitario	PAR	9

PLAYER OF THE YEAR 1972

CUBILLAS Teófilo	Alianza	PER	41
PELE	Santos	BRA	32
JAIRZINHO	Botafogo	BRA	28
TOSTAO	Vasco	BRA	16
ADEMIR da Guia	Palmeiras	BRA	15
M. CASTILLO Julio	Peñarol	URU	15
ALONSO Norberto	River Plate	ARG	11
FIGUEROA Elias	Internacional	CHI	11
FISCHER Rodolfo	Botafogo	ARG	9
REINOSO Carlos	América, Mex	CHI	6

PLAYER OF THE YEAR 1973

PELE	Santos	BRA	54
BRINDISI Miguel	Huracán	ARG	43
RIVELINO Roberto	Corinthians	BRA	33
MORENA Fernando	Peñarol	URU	19
CASZELY Carlos	Colo Colo	CHI	17
FIGUEROA Elias	Internacional	CHI	10
JAIRZINHO	Botafogo	BRA	6
SOTIL Hugo	CF Barcelona	PER	6
AYALA Ruben	Atlético Madrid	ARG	6
Two players with five votes			

PLAYER OF THE YEAR 1974

FIGUEROA Elias	Internacional	CHI	39
MARINHO Francisco	Botafogo	BRA	24
BABINGTON Carlos	Wattenschied	ARG	22
PEREIRA Luis	Palmeiras	BRA	20
PELE		BRA	15
MORENA Fernando	Peñarol	URU	14
BOCHINI Ricardo	Independiente	ARG	14
HOUSEMAN Rene	Huracán	ARG	11
CASZELY Carlos	Levante	CHI	8
RIVELINO	Fluminense	BRA	7

PLAYER OF THE YEAR 1975

FIGUEROA Elias	Internacional	CHI	50
ALONSO Norberto	River Plate	ARG	24
MORENA Fernando	Peñarol	URU	23
NELINHO	Cruzeiro	BRA	20
PEREIRA Luis	Atlético Madrid	BRA	16
SOTIL Hugo	CF Barcelona	ARG	12
SCOTTA Horacio	San Lorenzo	ARG	11
CUBILLAS Teófilo	FC Porto	PER	10
BOCHINI Ricardo	Independiente	ARG	10
LEIVINHA	Atlético Madrid	BRA	7

PLAYER OF THE YEAR 1976

FIGUEROA Elias	Palestino	CHI	51
ZICO	Flamengo	BRA	34
RIVELINO Roberto	Fluminense	BRA	31
GATTI Hugo	Boca Juniors	ARG	29
PEREIRA Luis	Atlético Madrid	BRA	19
MORENA Fernando	Peñarol	URU	12
PASSARELLA Daniel	River Plate	ARG	10
PAULO CESAR	Fluminense	BRA	10
ALONSO Norberto	River Plate	ARG	10
LEIVINHA	Atlético Madrid	BRA	9

PLAYER OF THE YEAR 1977

ZICO	Flamengo	BRA
RIVELINO Roberto	Fluminense	BRA
FIGUEROA Elias	Palestino	CHI
PELE	NY Cosmos	BRA
FILLOL Ubaldo	River Plate	ARG
BOCHINI Ricardo	Independiente	ARG
CUBILLAS Teófilo	Alianza	PER
GATTI Hugo	Boca Juniors	ARG
BERTONI Daniel	Independiente	ARG
HOUSEMAN Rene	Huracán	ARG

PLAYER OF THE YEAR 1978

KEMPES Mario	Valencia	ARG	78
FILLOL Ubaldo	River Plate	ARG	59
DIRCEU Guimaraes	América, Mex	BRA	48
PASSARELLA Daniel	River Plate	ARG	29
CUBILLAS Teófilo	Alianza	PER	19
FIGUEROA Elias	Palestino	CHI	7
BOCHINI Ricardo	Independiente	ARG	6
CUETO César	Alianza	PER	5
RIVELINO Roberto	Fluminense	BRA	4
ARDILES Osvaldo	Tottenham	ARG	3

PLAYER OF THE YEAR 1979

MARADONA Diego	Argentinos J	ARG	80
ROMERO Julio Cesar	Sp. Luqueño	PAR	40
FALCAO Roberto	Internacional	BRA	29
FILLOL Ubaldo	River Plate	ARG	26
ZICO	Flamengo	BRA	15
MORENA Fernando	Rayo Vallecano	URU	13
CASZELY Carlos	Colo Colo	CHI	11
PASSARELLA Daniel	River Plate	ARG	9
KEMPES Mario	Valencia	ARG	9
DIAZ Ramón	River Plate	ARG	7

PLAYER OF THE YEAR 1980

MARADONA Diego	Argentinos J	ARG
ZICO	Flamengo	BRA
VICTORINO Waldemar	Nacional	URU
FILLOL Ubaldo	River Plate	ARG
PAZ Ruben	Peñarol	URU
PASSARELLA Daniel	River Plate	ARG
TONINHO CEREZO	Atlético MG	BRA
SOCRATES	Corinthians	BRA
RODRIGUES Rodolfo	Nacional	URU
ROMERO Julio Cesar	NY Cosmos	PAR

PLAYER OF THE YEAR 1981

ZICO	Flamengo	BRA
MARADONA Diego	Boca Juniors	ARG
JUNIOR	Flamengo	BRA
URIBE Julio	Sporting Cristal	PER
YANEZ Patricio	San Luis	CHI
PASSARELLA Daniel	River Plate	ARG
FALCAO Roberto	Roma	BRA
SOCRATES	Corinthians	BRA
FIGUEROA Elias	Ft Lauderdale	CHI
PAZ Ruben	Peñarol	URU

PLAYER OF THE YEAR 1982

ZICO	Flamengo	BRA
FALCAO Roberto	Roma	BRA
MARADONA Diego	Barcelona	ARG
MORENA Fernando	Peñarol	URU
JUNIOR	Flamengo	BRA
SOCRATES	Corinthians	BRA
PASSARELLA Daniel	Fiorentina	ARG
SANCHEZ Hugo	Atlético Madrid	MEX

PLAYER OF THE YEAR 1983

SOCRATES	Corinthians	BRA	59
FILLOL Ubaldo	Argentinos J	ARG	30
EDER	Atlético MG	BRA	29
MORENA Fernando	Peñarol	URU	25
DIOGO Victor	Peñarol	URU	17
GARECA Ricardo	Boca Juniors	ARG	15
RODRIGUEZ Rodolfo	Santos	URU	13
AGUILERA Ramon	Nacional	URU	10
JUNIOR	Flamengo	BRA	9
PAZ Ruben	Peñarol	URU	8

PLAYER OF THE YEAR 1984

FRANCESCOLI Enzo	River Plate	URU	43
FILLOL Ubaldo	Flamengo	ARG	36
BOCHINI Ricardo	Independiente	ARG	25
RODRIGUEZ Rodolfo	Santos	URU	20
GARECA Ricardo	Boca Juniors	ARG	17
DE LEON Hugo	Grêmio	URU	17
BURRUCHAGA Jorge	Independiente	ARG	13
MARCICO Alberto	FC Oeste	ARG	11
DIOGO Victor	Palmeiras	URU	8
MORENA Fernando	Peñarol	URU	7

PLAYER OF THE YEAR 1985

ROMERO Julio Cesar	Fluminense	PAR
FRANCESCOLI Enzo	River Plate	URU
BORGHI Claudio	Argentinos J	ARG
CABANAS Roberto	América Cali	PAR
CASAGRANDE Walter	Corinthians	BRA
FERNANDEZ Roberto	América Cali	PAR
ZICO	Flamengo	BRA
BATISTA Daniel	Argentinos J	ARG
RENATO GAUCHO	Grêmio	BRA
RODRIGUEZ Rodolfo	Santos	URU

PLAYER OF THE YEAR 1986

MARADONA Diego	Napoli	ARG
CARECA	São Paulo FC	BRA
SANCHEZ Hugo	Real Madrid	MEX
BURRUCHAGA Jorge	FC Nantes	ARG
ROMERO Julio Cesar	Fluminense	PAR
VALDANO Jorge	Real Madrid	ARG
FRANCESCOLI Enzo	Racing Paris	URU
JOSIMAR	Botafogo	BRA
RUGGERI Oscar	River Plate	ARG
NEGRETE Manuel	Sporting CL	MEX

PLAYER OF THE YEAR 1987

VALDERRAMA Carlos	Deportivo Cali	COL
CABANAS Roberto	América Cali	PAR
ALZAMENDI Antonio	River Plate	URU
AGUIRRE Diego	Peñarol	URU
ROJAS Roberto	Colo Colo	CHI
MARANGONI Claudio	Independiente	ARG
PERDOMO Jose	Peñarol	URU
LETELIER Juan Carlos	Cobreloa	CHI
REDIN Bernardo	Deportivo Cali	COL
RODRIGUEZ Rodolfo	Santos	URU

PLAYER OF THE YEAR 1988

PAZ Ruben	Racing Club	URU
DE LEON Hugo	Nacional	URU
GEOVANI SILVA	Vasco	BRA
TAFFAREL Claudio	Internacional	BRA
FABBRI Nestor	Racing Club	ARG
REDIN Bernardo	Deportivo Cali	COL
BATISTA Daniel	River Plate	ARG
URIBE Julio	Sporting Cristal	PER
POLILLA	River Plate	BRA

PLAYER OF THE YEAR 1989

MARADONA Diego	Napoli	ARG
SOSA Ruben	Lazio	URU
BEBETO	Vasco	BRA
ROMARIO	PSV	BRA
CARECA	Napoli	BRA
HIGUITA Rene	At. Nacional	COL
BATISTA Daniel	River Plate	ARG
ALEMAO	Napoli	BRA
DUNGA Carlos	Fiorentina	BRA
REDIN Bernardo	Deportivo Cali	COL

PLAYER OF THE YEAR 1990

MARADONA Diego	Napoli	ARG
CANIGGIA Claudio	Atalanta	ARG
HIGUITA Rene	At. Nacional	COL
CARECA	Napoli	BRA
ALEMAO	Napoli	BRA
GOYCOECHEA Sergio	Racing Club	ARG
SANCHEZ Hugo	Real Madrid	MEX
CONEJO Luis	Albacete	CRC
VALDERRAMA Carlos	Montpellier	COL

PLAYER OF THE YEAR 1991

BATISTUTA Gabriel	Fiorentina	ARG
CANIGGIA Claudio	Atalanta	ARG
ZAMORANO Ivan	Sevilla	CHI
ROCHA Ricardo	Real Madrid	BRA
RUGGERI Oscar	Vélez	ARG
RODRIGUEZ Leonardo	Toulon	ARG
LATORRE Diego	Boca Juniors	ARG
VALDERRAMA Carlos	Real Valladolid	COL

PLAYER OF THE YEAR 1992

MARADONA Diego	Sevilla	ARG	32
BEBETO	Deportivo LC	BRA	31
RAI	São Paulo FC	BRA	25
BATISTUTA Gabriel	Fiorentina	ARG	24
CANIGGIA Claudio	Roma	ARG	21
FONSECA Daniel	Napoli	URU	18
ROMARIO	PSV	BRA	17
CABANAS Roberto	Boca Juniors	PAR	14
ZAMORANO Ivan	Real Madrid	CHI	13
MULLER	São Paolo FC	BRA	10

PLAYER OF THE YEAR 1986

ALZAMENDI Antonio	River Plate	URU
CARECA	São Paulo FC	BRA
ROMERO Julio Cesar	Fluminense	PAR

PLAYER OF THE YEAR 1987

VALDERRAMA Carlos	Deportivo Cali	COL	56
TRASANTE Obdulio	Peñarol	URU	27
PERDOMO José	Peñarol	URU	25
DOMINGUEZ Alfonso	Peñarol	URU	23
ALZAMENDI Antonio	River Plate	URU	23
JOSIMAR	Flamengo	BRA	18
GUTIERREZ Nelson	River Plate	URU	17
AGUIRRE Diego	Peñarol	URU	15
PAZ Ruben	Racing Club	URU	10
2 players with 9 votes			

PLAYER OF THE YEAR 1988

PAZ Ruben	Racing Club	URU
DE LEON Hugo	Nacional	URU
SALDANHA José	Nacional	URU

PLAYER OF THE YEAR 1989

BEBETO	Vasco	BRA	74
MAZINHO	Vasco	BRA	42
HIGUITA Rene	At. Nacional	COL	34
OSTOLAZA Santiago	Nacional	URU	32
BATISTA Sergio	River Plate	ARG	30
DE LEON Hugo	Nacional	URU	29
AGUINAGA Alex	Necaxa	ECU	28
SIMON Juan	Boca Juniors	ARG	23
DOMINGUEZ Alfonso	Peñarol	URU	22
MORENO Carlos	Independiente	ARG	21

PLAYER OF THE YEAR 1990

AMARILLA Raúl	Olimpia	PAR	57
DA SILVA Ruben	River Plate	URU	32
ALVAREZ Leonel	At. Nacional	COL	25
HIGUITA René	At. Nacional	COL	25
BASUALDO Fabian	River Plate	ARG	23

PLAYER OF THE YEAR 1991

RUGGERI Oscar	ARG	44
DIAZ Ramón	ARG	28
TOLEDO Patricio	CHI	23
ASTRADA Leonardo	ARG	21
BORRELLI Juan José	ARG	18
TILICO Mario	BRA	18
MENDOZA Gabriel	CHI	15
BASUALDO Fabian	ARG	13
DEL SOLAR José	PER	13
Three players with 12 votes		

PLAYER OF THE YEAR 1992

RAI	São Paulo FC	BRA	55
GOYCOECHEA Sergio	Olimpia	ARG	24
ACOSTA Alberto	Newell's OB	ARG	20
GAMBOA Fernando	San Lorenzo	ARG	20
CAFU	São Paulo FC	BRA	18
RENATO Gaúcho	Cruzeiro	BRA	17
JUNIOR	Flamengo	BRA	14
BOIADEIRO	Boca Juniors	BRA	13
MARCICO Alberto	Cruzeiro	ARG	13
ISLAS Luis	Independiente	ARG	10

PLAYER OF THE YEAR 1993

VALDERRAMA Carlos	Atlético Junior	COL	46
ETCHEVERRY Marco	Colo Colo	BOL	30
CAFU	São Paulo FC	BRA	28
RINCON Freddy	Palmeiras	COL	28
ALVAREZ Leonel	América Cali	COL	18
MULLER	São Paulo FC	BRA	18
GOYCOECHEA Sergio	Olimpia	ARG	12
PEREA Luis Carlos	Ind. Medellín	COL	11
KANAPKIS Fernando	Mandiyu	URU	11
MARADONA Diego	Newell's OB	ARG	11

PLAYER OF THE YEAR 1994

CAFU	São Paulo FC	BRA	36
CHILAVERT Jose Luis	Vélez	PAR	35
LOPEZ Gustavo	Independiente	ARG	22
RAMBERT Sebastian	Independiente	ARG	21

PLAYER OF THE YEAR 1995

FRANCESCOLI Enzo	River Plate	URU	34
MARADONA Diego	Boca Juniors	ARG	28
EDMUNDO	Flamengo	BRA	24
ROMARIO	Flamengo	BRA	23
CHILAVERT Jose Luis	Vélez	PARA	21

PLAYER OF THE YEAR 1996

CHILAVERT Jose Luis	Vélez	PAR	80
FRANCESCOLI Enzo	River Plate	URU	69
ORTEGA Ariel	River Plate	ARG	41
VALDERRAMA Carlos	Tampa Bay	COL	41
ARCE Francisco	Grêmio	PAR	27
GAMARRA Carlos	Cerro Porteño	PAR	26
SALAS Marcelo	River Plate	CHI	23
ACUNA Roberto	Independiente	PAR	18
SORIN Juan Pablo	River Plate	ARG	18
AYALA Celso	River Plate	PAR	17

PLAYER OF THE YEAR 1997

SALAS Marcelo	River Plate	CHI	87
SOLANO Nolberto	Boca Juniors	PER	39
CHILAVERT Jose Luis	Vélez	PAR	37
AYALA Celso	River Plate	PAR	36
GALLARDO Marcelo	River Plate	ARG	35
FRANCESCOLI Enzo	River Plate	URU	28
DENILSON	São Paulo FC	BRA	27
BERMUDEZ Jorge	Boca Juniors	COL	26
ASTRADA Leonardo	River Plate	ARG	23
EDMUNDO	Vasco	BRA	23

PLAYER OF THE YEAR 1998

PALERMO Martin	Boca Juniors	ARG	73
GAMARRA Carlos	Corinthians	PAR	70
CHILAVERT Jose Luis	Vélez	PAR	63
ARCE Francisco	Palmeiras	PAR	44
SERNA Mauricio	Boca Juniors	COL	41
FELIPE	Vasco	BRA	27
GALLARDO Marcelo	River Plate	ARG	27
MARCELINO	Corinthians	BRA	24
BERMUDEZ Jorge	Boca Juniors	COL	22
CAGNA Diego	Boca Juniors	ARG	21

PLAYER OF THE YEAR 1999

SAVIOLA Javier	River Plate	ARG	55
ARCE Francisco	Palmeiras	PAR	45
RIQUELME Juan	Boca Juniors	ARG	42
CHILAVERT Jose Luis	Vélez	PAR	36
Cordoba Ivan	San Lorenzo	COL	33
ALEX	Palmeiras	BRA	28
AIMAR Pablo	River Plate	ARG	27
VAMPETA	Corinthians	BRA	23
Three players with 22 votes			

PLAYER OF THE YEAR 2000

ROMARIO	Vasco	BRA	67
RIQUELME Juan	Boca Juniors	ARG	64
CORDOBA Oscar	Boca Juniors	COL	53
PALERMO Martin	Boca Juniors	ARG	53
AIMAR Pablo	River Plate	ARG	38
SERNA Mauricio	Boca Juniors	COL	38
SORIN Juan Pablo	Cruzeiro	ARG	37
ARCE Francisco	Palmeiras	PAR	36
BERMUDEZ Jorge	Boca Juniors	COL	36
GAMARRA Carlos	Flamengo	PAR	32

PLAYER OF THE YEAR 2001

RIQUELME Juan	Boca Juniors	ARG	88
CORDOBA Oscar	Boca Juniors	COL	59
ROMARIO	Vasco	BRA	41
ARCE Francisco	Palmeiras	PAR	39
SORIN Juan Pablo	Cruzeiro	ARG	37
YEPES Mario	River Plate	COL	36
ORTEGA Ariel	River Plate	ARG	31
LEMBO Alejandro	Nacional	URU	29
SERNA Mauricio	Boca Juniors	COL	27
Two players with 20 votes			

PLAYER OF THE YEAR 2002

CARDOZO José	Toluca	PAR	39
ORTEMAN Sergio	Olimpia	URU	32
LEMBO Alejandro	Nacional	URU	30
D'ALESSANDRO Andrés	River Plate	ARG	29
KAKA	São Paulo FC	BRA	27
MILITO Gabriel	Independiente	ARG	25
ARCE Francisco	Palmeiras	PAR	24
SAJA Sebastian	San Lorenzo	ARG	23
DELGADO Marcelo	Boca Juniors	ARG	18
ROBINHO	Santos	BRA	16

PLAYER OF THE YEAR 2003

TEVEZ Carlos	Boca Juniors	ARG	73
CARDOZO José	Toluca	PAR	39
DIEGO	Santos	BRA	33
BATTAGLIA Sebastián	Boca Juniors	ARG	26
RODRIGUEZ Clemente	Boca Juniors	ARG	18
SCHIAVI Rolando	Boca Juniors	ARG	17
ALEX	Cruzeiro	BRA	16
ROBINHO	Santos	BRA	14
ABBONDANZIERI Rob.	Boca Juniors	ARG	14
SOSA Marcelo	Danubio	URU	13

PLAYER OF THE YEAR 2004

TEVEZ Carlos	Boca Juniors	ARG	76
MASCHERANO Javier	River Plate	ARG	56
GONZALEZ Luis	River Plate	ARG	37
ROBINHO	Santos	BRA	37
HENAO Juan Carlos	Once Caldas	COL	32
CARDOZO José	Toluca	PAR	26
LEO	Santos	BRA	24
ELANO	Santos	BRA	23
LUGANO Diego	São Paulo FC	URU	22
SCHIAVI Rolando	Boca Juniors	ARG	22

COPA TOYOTA LIBERTADORES 2005

COPA LIBERTADORES 2005

Preliminary Round

Mineros de Guayana	VEN	0	1
América Cali ‡	COL	2	3
LDU Quito ‡	ECU	3	1
Peñarol	URU	0	4
Quilmes ‡	ARG	0	2
Colo Colo	CHI	0	2
Tacuary Asunción	PAR	2	0
Palmeiras ‡	ARG	2	2
Atlético Junior ‡	COL	2	3
Oriente Petrolero	BOL	1	1
Guadalajara ‡	MEX	3	5
Cienciano	PER	1	1

Group Stage

Grupo 1

		Pts	COL	BRA	COL	PAR
Independiente Medellín †	COL	10		2-2	2-0	4-2
Atlético Paranaense †	BRA	10	0-4		2-1	1-0
América Cali	COL	9	1-0	3-1		0-1
Libertad	PAR	6	3-2	1-2	1-2	

Grupo 2

		Pts	BRA	ECU	URU	BOL
Santos †	BRA	12		3-1	3-2	6-0
LDU Quito †	ECU	8	2-1		1-1	1-0
Danubio	URU	7	1-2	3-0		2-0
Bolívar	BOL	7	4-3	2-2	2-0	

Grupo 3

		Pts	BRA	CHI	ARG	BOL
São Paulo FC †	BRA	12		4-2	3-1	3-0
Universidad de Chile †	CHI	9	1-1		3-2	2-1
Quilmes	ARG	5	2-2	1-1		1-0
The Strongest	BOL	5	3-3	0-0	2-1	

Grupo 4

		Pts	PAR	BRA	BRA	VEN
Cerro Porteño †	PAR	12		1-1	1-0	3-1
Palmeiras †	BRA	9	0-0		1-1	3-0
Santo André	BRA	8	2-2	2-1		6-0
Deportivo Táchira	VEN	3	0-3	1-2	1-0	

Grupo 5

		Pts	ARG	COL	ECU	URU
River Plate †	ARG	16		2-1	1-1	1-0
Atlético Junior †	COL	9	0-2		2-0	3-2
Olmedo	ECU	7	2-3	3-1		2-3
Nacional Montevideo	URU	3	1-3	0-1	1-2	

Grupo 6

		Pts	MEX	ARG	PER	VEN
Tigres UNAL †	MEX	12		2-2	0-0	3-1
Banfield †	ARG	11	0-3		3-2	3-1
Alianza Lima	PER	5	0-0	0-1		2-1
Caracas FC	VEN	4	2-5	1-1	2-0	

Grupo 7

		Pts	MEX	COL	CHI	ARG
Guadalajara †	MEX	11		0-0	3-1	2-1
Once Caldas †	COL	9	4-2		0-0	0-0
Cobreloa	CHI	8	1-3	2-1		2-0
San Lorenzo	ARG	3	0-0	0-1	0-0	

Grupo 8

		Pts	ARG	MEX	PER	ECU
Boca Juniors †	ARG	13		4-0	3-0	3-0
Pachuca †	MEX	10	3-1		2-0	2-1
Sporting Cristal	PER	7	0-3	2-0		1-0
Deportivo Cuenca	ECU	3	0-0	1-1	2-2	

‡ Qualified for the group stage • † Qualified for the knockout phase

COPA LIBERTADORES 2005

2nd Round			Quarter-finals			Semi-finals			Final		
São Paulo FC	1	2									
Palmeiras *	0	0									
			São Paulo FC *	4	1						
			Tigres UNAL	0	2						
Once Caldas *	1	1									
Tigres UNAL	1	2									
						São Paulo FC *	2	3			
						River Plate	0	2			
Banfield *	3	2									
Indep'nte Medellín	0	0									
			Banfield *	1	2						
			River Plate	1	3						
LDU Quito *	2	2									
River Plate	1	4									
									São Paulo FC	1	4
									Atlético Paranaense*	1	0
Chivas Guadalajara	1	3									
Pachuca *	1	1									
			Chivas Guadalajara *	4	0						
			Boca Juniors	0	0						
Atlético Junior *	3	0									
Boca Juniors	3	4									
						Chivas Guadalajara	0	2			
						Atlético Paranaense*	3	2			
Santos	1	3									
Universidad de Chile*	2	0									
			Santos	2	0						
			Atlético Paranaense*	3	2						
Cerro Porteño	1 2 4p										
Atlético Paranaense*	2 1 5p										

PRLEMINARY ROUND 1ST LEG
Cachamay, Puerto Ordaz
1-02-2005, Ramos ECU

Mineros de Guayana	0

América Cali	2
Ferreira [14p], Chará [20]	

PRLEMINARY ROUND 2ND LEG
Pascual Guerrero, Cali
8-02-2005, Rezende BRA

América Cali	3
Villareal [14], Bustos [43], Ferreira [88]	

Mineros de Guyana	1
Parra [10]	

PRLEMINARY ROUND 1ST LEG
Jalisco, Guadalajara
2-02-2005, Larrionda URU

Guadalajara	3
Medina [9], Bautista [68], Bravo [73]	

Cienciano	1
Silva [42]	

PRLEMINARY ROUND 2ND LEG
Inca Garcilaso de la Vega, Cusco
9-02-2005, Baldassi ARG

Cienciano	1
Lobatón [58]	

Guadalajara	5
Bravo 2 [49 76], Palencia [55], Vela [73], Medina [75]	

PRLEMINARY ROUND 1ST LEG
Centenario, Quilmes
1-02-2005, Duque COL

Quilmes	0

Colo Colo	0

PRLEMINARY ROUND 2ND LEG
Monumental, Santiago
8-02-2005, Torres PAR

Colo Colo	2
Donoso [10], Aceval [27]	

Quilmes	2
Torres [27], Riffo OG [75]	

PRLEMINARY ROUND 1ST LEG
Roberto Bettega, Asuncion
2-02-2005, Ortubé BOL

Tacuary	2
Silva [26], Leite [81]	

Palmeiras	2
Magrão [36], Warley [57]	

PRLEMINARY ROUND 2ND LEG
Palestra Italia, São Paulo
9-02-2005, Selman CHI

Palmeiras	2
Ricardinho 2 [3 90]	

Tacuary	0

PRLEMINARY ROUND 1ST LEG
Metropolitano, Barranquilla
3-02-2005, Carpio ECU

Atlético Junior	2
Leal [4], Acuña [41]	

Oriente Petrolero	1
Villagra [66]	

PRLEMINARY ROUND 2ND LEG
Ramón Aguilera, Santa Cruz
10-02-2005, Lecca PER

Oriente Petrolero	1
Espínola [32]	

Atlético Junior	3
Acuña [21], Leal [23], Pérez [66]	

PRLEMINARY ROUND 1ST LEG
Casa Blanca, Quito
3-02-2005, Hidalgo PER

Liga Deportiva Universitaria	3
Salas [55], Palacios [67], Aguinaga [81]	

Peñarol	0

PRLEMINARY ROUND 2ND LEG
Centenario, Montevideo
10-02-2005, Oliveira BRA

Peñarol	4
Obregón OG [5], Gaglianone [46], Pierre [70], Tejera [91+]	

Liga Deportiva Universitaria	1
Méndez [21]	

GROUP 1

		Pl	W	D	L	F	A	Pts	COL	BRA	COL	PAR
Independiente Medellín †	COL	6	3	1	2	14	8	10		2-2	2-0	4-2
Atlético Paranaense †	BRA	6	3	1	2	8	11	10	0-4		2-1	1-0
América Cali	COL	6	3	0	3	7	7	9	1-0	3-1		0-1
Libertad	PAR	6	2	0	4	8	11	6	3-2	1-2	1-2	

† Qualified for the knockout phase

GROUP 1 MATCHDAY 1
Atanasio Girardot, Medellín
15-02-2005, Reinoso ECU

Independiente Medellín	2
GonzálezJD [82], Morantes [90]	

Atlético Paranaense	2
Marcão [12], Denis Marques [50]	

GROUP 1 MATCHDAY 1
Defensores de Chaco, Asuncion
17-02-2005, Vázquez URU

Libertad	1
Devaca [48]	

América Cali	2
Salazar [35], Chará [57]	

GROUP 1 MATCHDAY 2
Pascual Guerrero, Cali
22-02-2005, Hoyos COL

América Cali	1
Londoño [87]	

Independiente Medellín	0

GROUP 1 MATCHDAY 2
Arena da Baixada, Curitiba
1-03-02005, Elizondo ARG

Atlético Paranaense	1
Maciel [57]	

Libertad	0

GROUP 1 MATCHDAY 3
Defensores de Chaco, Asuncion
8-03-2005, Chandía CHI

Libertad	3
Samudio 3 [38 42 44]	

Independiente Medellín	2
Castrillón [20], Valoyes [55]	

GROUP 1 MATCHDAY 3
Pascual Guerrero, Cali
10-03-2005, Baldassi ARG

América Cali	3
Mina [36], Salazar [44], Ferreira [64]	

Atlético Paranaense	1
Marín [51]	

GROUP 1 MATCHDAY 4
Atanasio Girardot, Medellín
17-03-2005, Brazenas ARG

Independiente Medellín	4
Montoya [8], Alvarez 2 [13 23], Serna [82]	
Libertad	2
Caballero [5], Blanco [19]	

GROUP 1 MATCHDAY 4
Arena da Baixada, Curitiba
14-04-2005, Larrionda URU

Atlético Paranaense	2
Fabrício [40], Lima [89]	
América Cali	1
Banguero [44]	

GROUP 1 MATCHDAY 5
Defensores de Chaco, Asuncion
20-04-2005, Ortubé BOL

Libertad	1
Blanco [90]	
Atlético Paranaense	2
Denis Marques [58], Maciel [70]	

GROUP 1 MATCHDAY 5
Atanasio Girardot, Medellín
26-04-2005, Paneso COL

Independiente Medellín	2
Alvarez [35], Montoya [60]	
América Cali	0

GROUP 1 MATCHDAY 6
Pascual Guerrero, Cali
10-05-2005, Reinoso ECU

América Cali	0
Libertad	1
Devaca [40]	

GROUP 1 MATCHDAY 6
Arena da Baixada, Curitiba
10-05-2005, Pezzotta ARG

Atlético Paranaense	0
Independiente Medellín	4
Valoyes 2 [63 74], Serna [82], Montoya [85]	

GROUP 2

		Pl	W	D	L	F	A	Pts	BRA	ECU	URU	BOL
Santos †	BRA	6	4	0	2	18	10	12		3-1	3-2	6-0
Liga Deportiva Universitaria †	ECU	6	2	2	2	7	10	8	2-1		1-1	1-0
Danubio	URU	6	2	1	3	9	8	7	1-2	3-0		2-0
Bolivar	BOL	6	2	1	3	8	14	7	4-3	2-2	2-0	

† Qualified for the knockout phase

GROUP 2 MATCHDAY 1
Hernando Siles, La Paz
16-02-2005, Torres PAR

Bolívar	4
Zermatten 3 [2 52 86], Cabrera [88]	
Santos	3
Deivid 2 [25 56], Cabrera [88]	

GROUP 2 MATCHDAY 1
Luis Frazini, Montevideo
24-02-2005, Grance PAR

Danubio	3
Risso [1], González.IM [7], Pouso [79]	
Liga Deportiva Universitaria	0

GROUP 2 MATCHDAY 2
Vila Belmiro, Santos
3-03-2005, Brazenas ARG

Santos	3
Léo [38], Robinho [70], Ricardinho [89]	
Danubio	2
González.IM [1], Viera [86]	

GROUP 2 MATCHDAY 2
Casa Blanca, Quito
8-03-2005, Ruiz COL

Liga Deportiva Universitaria	1
Méndez [25]	
Bolívar	0

GROUP 2 MATCHDAY 3
Luis Frazini, Montevideo
15-03-2005, Garay PER

Danubio	2
Pouso [40], Silva [47]	
Bolívar	0

GROUP 2 MATCHDAY 3
Casa Blanca, Quito
17-03-2005, Amarilla PAR

Liga Deportiva Universitaria	2
Graziani [8], Salas [13]	
Santos	1
Ricardinho [26]	

GROUP 2 MATCHDAY 4
Vila Belmiro, Santos
6-04-2005, Elizondo ARG

Santos	3
Robinho 2 [20 60], Ricardinho [48]	
Liga Deportiva Universitaria	1
Urrutai [2]	

GROUP 2 MATCHDAY 4
Hernando Siles, La Paz
12-04-2005, Amarilla PAR

Bolívar	2
Cabrera 2 [14 64]	
Danubio	0

GROUP 2 MATCHDAY 5
Luis Frazini, Montevideo
20-04-2005, Baldassi ARG

Danubio	1
Pouso [52]	
Santos	2
Deivid [75], Risso OG [83]	

GROUP 2 MATCHDAY 5
Hernando Siles, La Paz
27-04-2005, Duque COL

Bolívar	2
Zermatten [18], Gutiérrez [33]	
Liga Deportiva Universitaria	2
Espínola [55], Palacios [63]	

GROUP 2 MATCHDAY 6
Casa Blanca, Quito
11-05-2005, Ruiz COL

Liga Deportiva Universitaria	1
Méndez [77]	
Danubio	1
Risso [27]	

GROUP 2 MATCHDAY 6
Vila Belmiro, Santos
11-05-2005, Larrionda URU

Santos	6
Ricardo Bóvio [2], Avalos [13], Paulo César [42], Ricardinho [57], Basílio [69], Deivid [74]	
Bolívar	0

GROUP 3

		Pl	W	D	L	F	A	Pts	BRA	CHI	ARG	BOL
São Paulo FC †	BRA	6	3	3	0	16	9	12		4-2	3-1	3-0
Universidad de Chile †	CHI	6	2	3	1	9	9	9	1-1		3-2	2-1
Quilmes	ARG	6	1	2	3	8	11	5	2-2	1-1		1-0
The Strongest	BOL	6	1	2	3	6	10	5	3-3	0-0	2-1	

† Qualified for the knockout phase

GROUP 3 MATCHDAY 1
Estadio Nacional, Santiago
22-02-2005, Méndez URU

Universidad de Chile	3
Olea 35, Ponce 45, Martínez 93+	
Quilmes	2
Vivas 33, Torres 59	

GROUP 3 MATCHDAY 1
Hernando Siles, La Paz
3-03-2005, Méndez URU

The Strongest	3
Cuba 23, Sosa 39, Escobar 54	
São Paulo FC	3
Danilo 21, Luizão 57, Grafite 97+	

GROUP 3 MATCHDAY 2
Morumbí, São Paulo
9-03-2005, Larrionda URU

São Paulo FC	4
Lugano 2, Rogério 20, Cicinho 47, Grafite 64	
Universidad de Chile	2
Gioino 2 7 38	

GROUP 3 MATCHDAY 2
Centenario, Quilmes
10-03-2005, Grance PAR

Quilmes	1
Osorio 42	
The Strongest	0

GROUP 3 MATCHDAY 3
Estadio Nacional, Santiago
15-03-2005, Viera URU

Universidad de Chile	2
Rivarola 2 64 80	
The Strongest	1
Ponce OG 9	

GROUP 3 MATCHDAY 3
Centenario, Quilmes
16-03-2005, Ruiz COL

Quilmes	2
Osorio 13, Caneo 76	
São Paulo FC	2
Diego Tardelli 47, Grafite 68	

GROUP 3 MATCHDAY 4
Hernando Siles, La Paz
13-04-2005, Torres PAR

The Strongest	0
Universidad de Chile	0

GROUP 3 MATCHDAY 4
Morumbí, São Paulo
13-04-2005, Vázquez URU

São Paulo FC	3
Diego Tardelli 2 32 55, Cicinho 83	
Quilmes	1
Rueda 57	

GROUP 3 MATCHDAY 5
Estadio Nacional, Santiago
21-04-2005, Amarilla PAR

Universidad de Chile	1
Gioino 47	
São Paulo FC	1
Luizão 27	

GROUP 3 MATCHDAY 5
Hernando Siles, La Paz
28-04-2005, Ruiz COL

The Strongest	2
Tufiño 36, Desabato OG 49	
Quilmes	1
Alayes 44	

GROUP 3 MATCHDAY 6
Morumbí, São Paulo
11-05-2005, Elizondo ARG

São Paulo FC	3
Edcarlos 30, Luizão 38, Grafite 52	
The Strongest	0

GROUP 3 MATCHDAY 6
Centenario, Quilmes
11-05-2005, Morales PER

Quilmes	1
Rueda 52	
Universidad de Chile	1
Iturra 23	

GROUP 4

		Pl	W	D	L	F	A	Pts	PAR	BRA	BRA	VEN
Cerro Porteño †	PAR	6	3	3	0	10	4	12		1-1	1-0	3-1
Palmeiras †	BRA	6	2	3	1	8	5	9	0-0		1-1	3-0
Santo André	BRA	6	2	2	2	11	6	8	2-2	2-1		6-0
Deportivo Táchira	VEN	6	1	0	5	3	17	3	0-3	1-2	1-0	

† Qualified for the knockout phase

GROUP 4 MATCHDAY 1
Pueblo Nuevo, San Cristóbal
2-03-2005, Ortubé BOL

Deportivo Táchira	1
Alvarado 14	
Santo André	0

GROUP 4 MATCHDAY 1
Pablo Rojas, Asunción
2-03-2005, Baldassi ARG

Cerro Porteño	1
Salcedo 44	
Palmeiras	1
Osmar 72	

GROUP 4 MATCHDAY 2
Bruno Daniel, Santo André
10-03-2005, Selman CHI

Santo André	2
Rodrigão 2 40 53	
Cerro Porteño	2
Salcedo 17, Ramírez 44	

GROUP 4 MATCHDAY 2
Palestra Italia, São Paulo
10-03-2005, Vázquez URU

Palmeiras	3
Lúcio [10], Osmar [12], Warley [83]	
Deportivo Táchira	0

GROUP 4 MATCHDAY 3
Palestra Italia, São Paulo
16-03-2005, Oliveira BRA

Palmeiras	1
Pedrinho [76]	
Santo André	1
Rafinha [81]	

GROUP 4 MATCHDAY 3
Pablo Rojas, Asunción
7-04-2005, Tardelli BRA

Cerro Porteño	3
Salcedo 3 [42 54 64]	
Deportivo Táchira	1
Pérez [78]	

GROUP 4 MATCHDAY 4
Pueblo Nuevo, San Cristóbal
19-04-2005, Ruiz COL

Deportivo Táchira	0
Cerro Porteño	3
Salcedo 2 [17 43], Achucaroo [68]	

GROUP 4 MATCHDAY 4
Bruno Daniel, Santo André
19-04-2004, Pereira BRA

Santo André	2
Fernando [19], Rodrigão [87]	
Palmeiras	1
Osmar [37]	

GROUP 4 MATCHDAY 5
Pablo Rojas, Asunción
28-04-2005, Elizondo ARG

Cerro Porteño	1
Salcedo [58]	
Santo André	0

GROUP 4 MATCHDAY 5
Pueblo Nuevo, San Cristóbal
4-05-2005, Chandía CHI

Deportivo Táchira	1
Boada [26]	
Palmeiras	2
Osmar [21], Ricardinho [35]	

GROUP 4 MATCHDAY 6
Bruno Daniel, Santo André
12-05-2005, Silvera URU

Santo André	6
Sandro Gaúcho [36], Rodrigão 2 [53 63], Romerito [59], Leandrinho [60], Richarlyson [88]	
Deportivo Táchira	0

GROUP 4 MATCHDAY 6
Palestra Italia, São Paulo
12-05-2005, Giménez ARG

Palmeiras	0
Cerro Porteño	0

GROUP 5

		Pl	W	D	L	F	A	Pts	ARG	COL	ECU	URU
River Plate †	ARG	6	5	1	0	12	5	16		2-1	1-1	1-0
Atlético Junior †	COL	6	3	0	3	8	9	9	0-2		2-0	3-2
Olmedo	ECU	6	2	1	3	10	11	7	2-3	3-1		2-3
Nacional Montevideo	URU	6	1	0	5	7	12	3	1-3	0-1	1-2	

† Qualified for the knockout phase

GROUP 5 MATCHDAY 1
Centenario, Montevideo
15-02-2005, Pozo CHI

Nacional	0
Atlético Junior	1
Arzuaga [83]	

GROUP 5 MATCHDAY 1
Olímpico, Riobamba
23-02-2005, Simón BRA

Olmedo	2
Rodríguez.FD 2 [88 90]	
River Plate	3
Patiño [8], Mascherano [18], Farías [67]	

GROUP 5 MATCHDAY 2
Metropolitano, Barranquilla
1-03-2005, Garay PER

Atlético Junior	2
Arzuaga [31], Pérez.S [53]	
Olmedo	0

GROUP 5 MATCHDAY 2
Monumental, Buenos Aires
3-03-2005, Amarilla PAR

River Plate	1
Gallardo [6]	
Nacional	0

GROUP 5 MATCHDAY 3
Parque Central, Montevideo
16-03-2005, Lecca PER

Nacional	1
Abreu [73p]	
Olmedo	2
Rodríguez.FD [62], Brito [80]	

GROUP 5 MATCHDAY 3
Metropolitano, Barranquilla
17-03-2005, Chandía CHI

Atlético Junior	0
River Plate	2
Farías [91+], Sambueza [95+]	

GROUP 5 MATCHDAY 4
Monumental, Buenos Aires
7-04-2005, Selman CHI

River Plate	2
Farías [42], Gallardo [52]	
Atlético Junior	1
Arzuaga [45]	

GROUP 5 MATCHDAY 4
Olímpico, Riobamba
7-04-2005, Paniagua BOL

Olmedo	2
González.HM [6], Rodríguez.FD [72]	
Nacional	3
Medina [26], Vázquez [62], Castro [83]	

GROUP 5 MATCHDAY 5
Olímpico, Riobamba
19-04-2005, Pozo CHI

Olmedo	3
Caicedo [3], Hurtado [64], Gómez [70]	
Atlético Junior	1
Acuña [73]	

GROUP 5 MATCHDAY 5
Centenario, Montevideo
21-04-2005, Souza Mendonça BRA

Nacional	1
Méndez [5]	
River Plate	3
Ahumada [33], Sand [64], Méndez [78]	

GROUP 5 MATCHDAY 6
Metropolitano, Barranquilla
3-05-2005, Lopes BRA

Atlético Junior	3
Arzuaga 2 [18 89], Palacio [87p]	
Nacional	2
Castro [14], Albin [86]	

GROUP 5 MATCHDAY 6
Monumental, Buenos Aires
3-05-2005, Ortubé BOL

River Plate	1
Sand [39]	
Olmedo	1
Zandoná [76]	

GROUP 6

		Pl	W	D	L	F	A	Pts	MEX	ARG	PER	VEN
Tigres UNAL †	MEX	6	3	3	0	13	5	12		2-2	0-0	3-1
Banfield †	ARG	6	3	2	1	10	9	11	0-3		3-2	3-1
Alianza Lima	PER	6	1	2	3	4	7	5	0-0	0-1		2-1
Caracas FC	VEN	6	1	1	4	8	14	4	2-5	1-1	2-0	

† Qualified for the knockout phase

GROUP 6 MATCHDAY 1
Estadio Nacional, Lima
15-02-2005, Rezende BRA

Alianza Lima	0
Tigres UANL	0

GROUP 6 MATCHDAY 1
Brígido Iriarte, Caracas
17-02-2005, López COL

Caracas FC	1
Noriega [17]	
Banfield	1
Piriz Alvez [47]	

GROUP 6 MATCHDAY 2
Florencio Sola, Buenos Aires
23-02-2005, Carvalho BRA

Banfield	3
Bilos [29], Andrizzi [63], Ceballos [88]	
Alianza Lima	2
Olcese 2 [64 80]	

GROUP 6 MATCHDAY 2
Universitario, Monterrey
23-02-2005, Chandía CHI

Tigres UANL	3
Sánchez.H [38], Silvera [50], Núñez [57]	
Caracas FC	1
Castellín [60]	

GROUP 6 MATCHDAY 3
Estadio Nacional, Lima
1-03-2005, Duque COL

Alianza Lima	2
Olcese [46], Soto [61]	
Caracas FC	1
García.G [30]	

GROUP 6 MATCHDAY 3
Universitario, Monterrey
15-03-2005, Souza Mendonça BRA

Tigres UNAL	2
Gaitán [31], Peralta [62]	
Banfield	2
Barijho [12], Bilos [73]	

GROUP 6 MATCHDAY 4
Brígido Iriarte, Caracas
5-04-2005, Vasco ECU

Caracas FC	2
García.G [25], Carpintero [63]	
Alianza Lima	0

GROUP 6 MATCHDAY 4
Florencio Sola, Buenos Aires
6-04-2005, Vázquez URU

Banfield	0
Tigres UNAL	3
Morales [13], Silvera [62], Peralta [66]	

GROUP 6 MATCHDAY 5
Estadio Nacional, Lima
12-04-2005, Lopes BRA

Alianza Lima	0
Banfield	1
Barijho [51]	

GROUP 6 MATCHDAY 5
Brígido Iriarte, Caracas
13-04-2005, Paneso COL

Caracas FC	2
Carpintero 2 [1 18]	
Tigres UNAL	5
Núñez 2 [6 32], Soares 2 [64 86], De Nigris [81]	

GROUP 6 MATCHDAY 6
Universitario, Monterrey
3-05-2005, Manzur VEN

Tigres UANL	0
Alianza Lima	0

GROUP 6 MATCHDAY 6
Florencia Sola, Buenos Aires
3-05-2005, Silvera URU

Banfield	3
Fernández.PC [18], Ceballos [58], Bilos [61]	
Caracas FC	1
García.G [76]	

GROUP 7

		Pl	W	D	L	F	A	Pts	MEX	COL	CHI	ARG
Guadalajara †	MEX	6	3	2	1	10	7	11		0-0	3-1	2-1
Once Caldas †	COL	6	2	3	1	6	4	9	4-2		0-0	0-0
Cobreloa	CHI	6	2	2	2	6	7	8	1-3	2-1		2-0
San Lorenzo	ARG	6	0	3	3	1	5	3	0-0	0-1	0-0	

† Qualified for the knockout phase

GROUP 7 MATCHDAY 1
Municipal, Calama
16-02-2005, Rivera PER

Cobreloa	1
González.JL [89]	
Guadalajara	3
García.J [10], Palencia [48], Bravo [59]	

GROUP 7 MATCHDAY 1
Palogrande, Manizales
24-02-2005, Larrionda URU

Once Caldas	0
San Lorenzo	0

GROUP 7 MATCHDAY 2
Jalisco, Guadalajara
2-03-2005, Souza Mendonça BRA

Guadalajara	0
Once Caldas	0

GROUP 7 MATCHDAY 2
Nuevo Gasometro, Buenos Aires
9-03-2005, Torres PAR

San Lorenzo	0
Cobreloa	0

GROUP 7 MATCHDAY 3
Municipal, Calama
22-03-2005, Ortubé BOL

Cobreloa	2
Fuentes [79], Díaz [95+]	
Once Caldas	1
Alvarez [49]	

GROUP 7 MATCHDAY 3
Jalisco, Guadalajara
23-03-2005, Rezende BRA

Guadalajara	2
Morales 2 [49 60]	
San Lorenzo	1
García.W [66]	

GROUP 7 MATCHDAY 4
Nuevo Gasometro, Buenos Aires
5-04-2005, Grance PAR

San Lorenzo	0
Guadalajara	0

GROUP 7 MATCHDAY 4
Palogrande, Manizales
5-04-2005, Brand VEN

Once Caldas	0
Cobreloa	0

GROUP 7 MATCHDAY 5
Palogrande, Manizales
12-04-2005, Garay PER

Once Caldas	4
Soto [1], Moreno [4], Viáfara [20], Fabbro [35]	
Guadalajara	2
García.J [39], Bravo [78]	

GROUP 7 MATCHDAY 5
Municipal, Calama
26-04-2005, Simón BRA

Cobreloa	2
Díaz.JL 2 [2 34]	
San Lorenzo	0

GROUP 7 MATCHDAY 6
Jalisco, Guadalajara
5-05-2005, Brazenas ARG

Guadalajara	3
Morales [46], Bautista 2 [58 66]	
Cobreloa	1
Díaz.JL [67]	

GROUP 7 MATCHDAY 6
Nuevo Gasometro, Buenos Aires
5-05-2005, Gamboa BOL

San Lorenzo	0
Once Caldas	1
Viáfara [43]	

GROUP 8

		Pl	W	D	L	F	A	Pts	ARG	MEX	PER	ECU
Boca Juniors †	ARG	6	4	1	1	14	3	13		4-0	3-0	3-0
Pachuca †	MEX	6	3	1	2	8	9	10	3-1		2-0	2-1
Sporting Cristal	PER	6	2	1	3	5	10	7	0-3	2-0		1-0
Deportivo Cuenca	ECU	6	0	3	3	4	9	3	0-0	1-1	2-2	

† Qualified for the knockout phase

GROUP 8 MATCHDAY 1
Estadio Nacional, Lima
16-02-2005, Lopes BRA

Sporting Cristal	2
Zegarra [66], Bonnet [84]	
Pachuca	0

GROUP 8 MATCHDAY 1
Alejandro Serrano Aguilar, Cuenca
17-02-2005, Selman CHI

Deportivo Cuenca	0
Boca Juniors	0

GROUP 8 MATCHDAY 2
Hidalgo, Pachuca
24-02-2004, Brand VEN

Pachuca	2
Pinto [21], Vidrio [45]	
Deportivo Cuenca	1
Quiñónez [38]	

GROUP 8 MATCHDAY 2
La Bombonera, Buenos Aires
2-03-2005, Chandía CHI

Boca Juniors	3
Palermo 2 [16 65], Baiano [29]	
Sporting Cristal	0

GROUP 8 MATCHDAY 3
Estadio Nacional, Lima
8-03-2005, López COL

Sporting Cristal	1
Bonnet [65]	
Deportivo Cuenca	0

GROUP 8 MATCHDAY 3
El Huracán, Pachuca
16-03-2005, Rezende BRA

Pachuca	3
Cacho [37], De Anda [50], Rodríguez.A [90]	
Boca Juniors	1
Barros Schelotto.G [55]	

GROUP 8 MATCHDAY 4
La Bombonera, Buenos Aires
6-04-2005, Amarilla PAR

Boca Juniors	4

Cagna [28], Guglielminpietro [32], Palacio [75],
Baiano [88]

Pachuca	0

GROUP 8 MATCHDAY 4
Alejandro Serrano Aguilar, Cuenca
14-04-2005, Ortubé BOL

Deportivo Cuenca	2

Calderón 2 [12 39]

Sporting Cristal	2

Figueroa [51], Prado [78]

GROUP 8 MATCHDAY 5
Estadio Nacional, Lima
27-04-2005, Larrionda URU

Sporting Cristal	0

Boca Juniors	3

Ledesma [11], Delgado [29], Palermo [43]

GROUP 8 MATCHDAY 5
Alejandro Serrano Aguilar, Cuenca
27-04-2005, Chandía CHI

Deportivo Cuenca	1

Carnero [8]

Pachuca	1

Chitiva [63]

GROUP 8 MATCHDAY 6
El Huracán, Pachuca
4-05-2005, Brand VEN

Pachuca	2

Santana [3], Borgetti [37]

Sporting Cristal	0

GROUP 8 MATCHDAY 6
La Bombonera, Buenos Aires
4-05-2005, Vázquez URU

Boca Juniors	3

Guglielminpietro 2 [35 42], Palermo [39]

Deportivo Cuenca	0

SECOND ROUND 1ST LEG
Palestra Italia, São Paulo
18-05-2005, Fagundes BRA

Palmeiras	0

São Paulo FC	1

Cicinho [59]

SECOND ROUND 2ND LEG
Morumbi, São Paulo
25-05-2005, Fagundes BRA

São Paulo FC	2

Rogerio [81p], Cicinho [89]

Palmeiras	0

SECOND ROUND 1ST LEG
Palogrande, Manizales
19-05-2005, Pezzota ARG

Once Caldas	1

Alvarez [83]

Tigres UNAL	1

Gaitan [34]

SECOND ROUND 2ND LEG
Universitario, Monterrey
26-05-2005, Mendez URU

Tigres UNAL	2

De Nigris [52], Saavedra [64]

Once Caldas	1

Fabbro [34]

SECOND ROUND 1ST LEG
Florencio Sola, Buenos Aires
18-05-2005, Amarilla PAR

Banfield	3

Bilos 2 [59 69], Ceballos [72]

Independiente Medellin	0

SECOND ROUND 2ND LEG
Atanasio Giradot, Medellin
24-05-2005, Souza Mendonça BRA

Independiente Medellin	0

Banfield	2

Barijho [51], Paletta [70]

SECOND ROUND 1ST LEG
Casa Blanca, Quito
17-05-2005, Chandia CHI

LDU Quito	2

Urrutia 2 [35p 72]

River Plate	1

Patiño [40]

SECOND ROUND 2ND LEG
Monumental, Buenos Aires
26-05-2005, Amarilla PAR

River Plate	4

Salas 3 [6 11 48], González.L [60]

LDU Quito	2

Palacios [46], Espinola [66]

SECOND ROUND 1ST LEG
Hidalgo, Pachuca
18-05-2005, Archundia MEX

Pachuca CF	1

Borgetti [26]

Chivas Guadalajara	1

Palencia 48

SECOND ROUND 2ND LEG
Jalisco, Guadalajara
24-05-2005, Alcala MEX

Chivas Guadalajara	3

Alfaro [35], Vela [50], Medina [57]

Pachuca CF	1

Santana [15]

SECOND ROUND 1ST LEG
Metropolitano, Barranquilla
17-05-2005, Selman CHI

Atlético Junior	3

Perez.S [10], Arzuaga [13], Acuña [36]

Boca Juniors	3

Schiavi [7], Palacio [59], Delgado [92+]

SECOND ROUND 2ND LEG
La Bombonera, Buenos Aires
14-06-2005, Vázquez URU

Boca Juniors	4

Guglielminpietro 2 [1 55], Palermo 2 [39 71]

Atlético Junior	0

SECOND ROUND 1ST LEG
Estadio Nacional, Santiago
19-05-2005, Ruiz COL

Universidad de Chile	2

Rivarola [50], Galaz [72]

Santos	1

Ricardinho [57]

SECOND ROUND 2ND LEG
Vila Belmiro, Santos
25-05-2005, Elizondo ARG

Santos	3

Flavio [34], Robinho 2 [72 89]

Universidad de Chile	0

SECOND ROUND 1ST LEG
Arena da Baixada, Curitiba
19-05-2005, Brazenas ARG

Atlético Paranaense	2

Lima [30], Cleverson [50]

Cerro Porteño	1

Dos Santos [48]

SECOND ROUND 2ND LEG
Asuncion
26-05-2005, Ruiz COL

Cerro Porteño	2
Dos Santos [6], Salcedo [38]	
Atlético Paranaense	1
Lima [9]. Atlético won 5-4 on penalties	

QUARTER-FINAL 1ST LEG
Morumbi, São Paulo
1-06-2005, Giménez ARG

São Paulo FC	4
Rogerio 2 [30 58], Luizão [39], Souza [61]	
Tigres UNAL	0

QUARTER-FINAL 2ND LEG
Universitario, Monterrey
15-06-2005, Baldassi ARG

Tigres UNAL	2
Silvera 2 [61 74]	
São Paulo FC	1
Souza [87]	

QUARTER-FINAL 1ST LEG
Florencio Sola, Buenos Aires
2-06-2006, Elizondo ARG

Banfield	1
Bilos [55]	
River Plate	1
Gallardo [9]	

QUARTER-FINAL 2ND LEG
Monumental, Buenos Aires
16-06-2005, Brazenas ARG

River Plate	3
Farias 2 [28 32], Zapata [35]	
Banfield	2
Bilos [34], Barijho [48]	

QUARTER-FINAL 1ST LEG
Jalisco, Guadalajara
2-06-2005, Torres PAR

Chivas Guadalajara	4
Garcia J [47+], Bravo [55], Alfaro [60], Bautista [67]	
Boca Juniors	0

QUARTER-FINAL 2ND LEG
La Bombonera, Buenos Aires
14-06-2005, Vázquez URU

Boca Juniors	0
Chivas Guadalajara	0

QUARTER-FINAL 1ST LEG
Arena da Baixada, Curitiba
1-06-2005, Souza Mendonça BRA

Atlético Paranaense	3
Evandro [25], Marcão [40], Lima [71]	
Santos	2
Ricardinho [12], Deivid [44]	

QUARTER-FINAL 2ND LEG
Vila Belmiro, Santos
15-06-2005, Simon BRA

Santos	0
Atlético Paranaense	2
Aloisio 2 [16 52]	

SEMI-FINAL 1ST LEG
Morumbi, São Paulo
22-06-2005, Méndez URU

São Paulo FC	2
Danilo [76], Rogerio [89]	
River Plate	0

SEMI-FINAL 2ND LEG
Monumental, Buenos Aires
29-06-2005, Selman CHI

River Plate	2
Farias [35], Salas [84]	
São Paulo FC	3
Danilo [11], Marcio Amoroso [59], Fabão [80]	

SEMI-FINAL 1ST LEG
Arena da Baixada, Curitiba
23-06-2005, Selman CHI

Atlético Paranaense	3
Aloisio [22], Fernandinho [44], Fabricio [78]	
Chivas Guadalajara	0

SEMI-FINAL 2ND LEG
Jalisco, Guadalajara
30-06-2005, Torres PAR

Chivas Guadalajara	2
Palencia 2 [24 86]	
Atlético Paranaense	2
Lima 2 [68 80]	

FINAL **BEIRA RIO, PORTO ALEGRE** **6-07-2005**

Kick-off: 21:45 Attendance: 35 000

ATLETICO 1 1 SAO PAULO

Aloisio [14] Durval OG [52]

ATLETICO PARANAENSE		
1	DIEGO	
2	JANCARLOS	82
4	COCITO	
5	MARCAO	
7	ALAN BAHIA	
9	ALOISIO	
10	FERNANDINHO	66
13	DANILO	
14	DURVAL	
23	FABRICIO	
25	LIMA	
Tr: LOPES Antonio		
Substitutes		
17	ANDRE ROCHA	82
20	EVANDRO	66

MATCH OFFICIALS
Referee
LARRIONDA Jorge URU
Assistant Referees
CRESCI Fernando URU
RIAL Walter URU
4th Official
SILVERA Roberto URU

SAO PAULO FC		
	ROGERIO	1
	CICINHO	2
	FABAO	3
	LUGANO	5
	JUNIOR	6
	MINEIRO	7
	JOSUE	8
	MARCIO AMOROSO	9
	DANILO	10
	LUIZAO	11
	ALEX	25
Tr: AUTUORI Paulo		
Substitutes		

FINAL **MORUMBI, SAO PAULO** **14-07-2005**

Kick-off: 21:45 Attendance: 75 000

SAO PAULO 4 0 ATLETICO

Marcio Amoroso [16], Fabão [52], Luizão [70], Diego Tardelli [89]

SAO PAULO FC		
1	ROGERIO	
2	CICINHO	
3	FABAO	
5	LUGANO	
6	JUNIOR	85
7	MINEIRO	
8	JOSUE	
9	MARCIO AMOROSO	78
10	DANILO	
11	LUIZAO	72
25	ALEX	
Tr: AUTUORI Paulo		
Substitutes		
16	FABIO SANTOS	85
19	DIEGO TARDELLI	78
21	SOUZA	72

MATCH OFFICIALS
Referee
ELIZONDO Horacio ARG
Assistant Referees
OTERO Rodolfo ARG
REBOLLO Juan Carlos ARG
4th Official
PEZZOTTA Sergio ARG

ATLETICO PARANAENSE		
	DIEGO	1
	JANCARLOS	2
	COCITO	4
60	MARCAO	5
	ALOISIO	9
	DANILO	13
	DURVAL	14
82	ANDRE ROCHA	17
	EVANDRO	20
	FABRICIO	23
60	LIMA	25
Tr: LOPES Antonio		
Substitutes		
82	ALAN BAHIA	7
60	RODRIGO ALMEIDA	8
60	FERNANDINHO	10

COPA NISSAN SUDAMERICANA 2004

QUARTER-FINAL 1ST LEG		QUARTER-FINAL 2ND LEG		QUARTER-FINAL 1ST LEG	
Padre Martearena, Salta		Defensores del Chaco, Asunción		Beira Rio, Porto Alegre	
27-10-2004; Rezende BRA		10-11-2004; Larrionda URU		3-11-2004; Larrionda URU	
Boca Juniors	1	Cerro Porteño	0 7p	Internacional	1
Cascini [50]				Fernandão [2]	
Cerro Porteño	1	Boca Juniors	0 8p	Atlético Junior	0
Benítez [20]					

QUARTER-FINAL 2ND LEG		QUARTER-FINAL 1ST LEG		QUARTER-FINAL 2ND LEG	
Metropolitano, Barranquilla		Casa Blanca, Quito		Vila Belmiro, Santos	
10-11-2004; Giménez ARG		3-11-2004; Ortube BOL		10-11-2004; Torres PAR	
Atlético Junior	1	LDU Quito	3	Santos	1
Arzuaga [87]		Murillo [14], Ambrosi [37], Salas [84]		Elano [83]	
Internacional	1	Santos	2	LDU Quito	2
Edinho [13]		William [20], Basilio [51]		Aguinaga [7], Murillo [88]	

QUARTER-FINAL 1ST LEG		QUARTER-FINAL 2ND LEG		SEMI-FINAL 1ST LEG	
Julio Grondona, Buenos Aires		Hernando Siles, La Paz		La Bombonera, Buenos Aires	
28-10-2004; Lecca PER		4-11-2004; Torres PAR		24-11-2004; Ruiz COL	
Arsenal	1	Bolivar	3	Boca Juniors	4
Casteglione [3]		Ferreira [36], Chiorazzo [49], Tufiño [54]		Traverso [54], Cagna [60], Palermo [67], Cardozo [70]	
Bolivar	0	Arsenal	0	Internacional	2
				Sobis [46], Diego [80]	

SEMI-FINAL 2ND LEG		SEMI-FINAL 1ST LEG		SEMI-FINAL 2ND LEG	
Beira Rio, Porto Alegre		Casa Blanca, Quito		Hernando Siles, La Paz	
1-12-2004; Torres PAR		25-11-2004; Selman CHI		2-12-2004; Hidalgo PER	
Internacional	0	LDU Quito	1	Bolivar	2
		Murillo [63]		Chiorazzo [11], Garcia [48]	
Boca Juniors	0	Bolivar	1	LDU Quito	1
		Chiorazzo [69]		Espinoza [50]	

COPA SUDAMERICANA FINAL 1ST LEG
Hernando Siles, La Paz
8-12-2004; 20:15; Simon BRA

BOLIVAR   1   0   BOCA JUNIORS

Chiorazzo [75]

BOLIVAR			BOCA JUNIORS	
1	MACHADO Mauro		ABBONDANZIERI Roberto	1
16	PACHI Dani Jesus		SCHIAVI Rolando Carlos	2
6	SANCHEZ Oscar Carmelo		MATELLAN Anibal	6
14	FERREIRA Julio César		TRAVERSO Cristian	13
3	SANDY Marco Antonio		CALVO José María	15
24	GALINDO Gonzalo	66	CASCINI Alfredo Raúl	5
21	TUFINO Rubén Darío		82	GUGLIELMINPIETRO Andrés	23
22	GARCIA Ronald Lázaro	74	65	VARGAS Fabián Andrés	11
18	GUTIERREZ Limberg		89	B. SCHELOTTO Guillermo	7
17	SUAREZ Roger			TEVEZ Carlos Alberto	10
8	CHIORAZZO Horacio			Tr: BENITEZ Jorge	
	Tr: SORIA Vladimir				
	Substitutes			Substitutes	
10	GUIBERGUIS Pedro	74	82	DONNET Matias Abel	18
11	COLQUE Percy	66	65	CARDOZO Nery Raúl	19
			89	CARRENO Ariel Sebastián	16

COPA SUDAMERICANA FINAL 2ND LEG
La Bombonera, Buenos Aires
17-12-2004; 21:15; Chandia CHI

BOCA JUNIORS   2   0   BOLIVAR

Palermo [14], Tévez [28]

BOCA JUNIORS			BOLIVAR	
1	ABBONDANZIERI Roberto		MACHADO Mauro	1
15	CALVO José María		SANCHEZ Oscar Carmelo	6
2	SCHIAVI Rolando Carlos		FERREIRA Julio César	14
13	TRAVERSO Cristian		SANDY Marco Antonio	3
6	MATELLAN Anibal	46	COLQUE Percy	11
8	CAGNA Diego	67	TUFINO Rubén Darío	21
5	CASCINI Alfredo Raúl		PIZARRO Limbert Percy	2
23	GUGLIELMINPIETRO Andrés	82	GALINDO Gonzalo	24
10	TEVEZ Carlos Alberto	75	GARCIA Ronald Lázaro	22
7	B. SCHELOTTO Guillermo		GUTIERREZ Limberg	18
9	PALERMO Martín		CHIORAZZO Horacio	8
	Tr: BENITEZ Jorge		Tr: SORIA Vladimir	
	Substitutes		Substitutes	
11	VARGAS Fabián Andrés	75	46	SUAREZ Roger	17
14	LEDESMA Pablo Martín	67			
19	CARDOZO Nery Raúl	82			

COPA SUDAMERICANA 2004

Preliminary Round			First Round			Second Round	
			Boca Juniors	ARG	Bye		
						Boca Juniors	0 2 4p
						San Lorenzo *	1 1 1p
			Quilmes *	ARG	0 0		
			San Lorenzo	ARG	2 0		
			Peñarol	URU	2 1		
			Danubio *	URU	1 1		
						Peñarol *	1 2
						Cerro Porteño	3 1
			Libertad	PAR	1 0		
			Cerro Porteño *	PAR	1 2		
			Atlético Junior	COL	0 2		
			Millonarios *	COL	1 0		
						Atlético Junior	2 4
						Alianza Atlético *	0 1
			Coronel Bolognesi *	PER	1 1		
			Alianza Atlético	PER	0 4		
Goiás *	BRA	4 1	Cruzeiro	BRA	2 3		
Atlético Mineiro	BRA	2 1	Goiás *	BRA	2 2		
						Cruzeiro	1 0
						Internacional *	3 1
Figueirense *	BRA	0 1 2p	Grêmio	BRA	0 2		
Internacional	BRA	0 1 4p	Internacional *	BRA	2 1		
			LDU Quito *	ECU	1 1		
			Aucas	ECU	0 1		
						LDU Quito *	4 2
Deportivo Italchaco *	VEN	0 0				Cienciano	0 2
Carabobo	VEN	0 2	Carabobo *	VEN	1 1		
			Cienciano	PER	2 6		
			São Paulo FC	BRA	1 1 4p		
Coritiba *	BRA	1 2	São Caetano *	BRA	1 1 1p		
São Caetano	BRA	2 2					
						São Paulo FC	0 1
						Santos *	1 1
			Flamengo	BRA	0 2 4p		
Paraná *	BRA	2 0	Santos *	BRA	0 2 5p		
Santos	BRA	1 3					
			Arsenal *	ARG	1 4		
			Banfield	ARG	1 3		
						Arsenal *	2 0
						River Plate	1 0
			River Plate	ARG	Bye		
			Univ. de Concepción *	CHI	2 1		
			Santiago Wanderers	CHI	1 0		
						Univ. de Concepción *	0 2
						Bolívar	0 4
			Aurora *	BOL	1 1		
			Bolívar	BOL	2 3		

* Home team in the first leg

COPA SUDAMERICANA 2004

Quarter-finals   **Semi-finals**   **Final**

Boca Juniors *	1 0 8p	
Cerro Porteño	1 0 7p	

Boca Juniors *	4 0	
Internacional	2 0	

Atlético Junior	0 1	
Internacional *	1 1	

Boca Juniors	0 2	
Bolivar *	1 0	

LDU Quito *	3 2	
Santos	2 1	

LDU Quito *	1 1	
Bolivar	1 2	

Arsenal *	1 0	
Bolivar	0 3	

CONMEBOL YOUTH TOURNAMENTS 2005

SUDAMERICANO SUB-16 PARAGUAY 2004

First Round Group Stage

Group A	Pl	W	D	L	F	A	Pts	CHI	PER	BOL
Paraguay	3	2	0	1	5	2	6	0-2	4-0	1-0
Chile	3	1	1	1	3	3	4		0-0	1-3
Peru	3	1	1	1	1	4	4			1-0
Bolivia	3	1	0	2	3	3	3			

Group B	Pl	W	D	L	F	A	Pts	URU	USA	ECU
Argentina	3	3	0	0	7	1	9	2-0	2-1	3-0
Uruguay	3	2	0	1	3	3	6		1-0	2-1
USA	3	0	1	2	3	5	1			2-2
Ecuador	3	0	1	2	3	7	1			

Group C	Pl	W	D	L	F	A	Pts	BRA	VEN	MEX
Colombia	3	2	1	0	3	1	7	1-0	1-1	1-0
Brazil	3	2	0	1	11	4	6		6-2	5-1
Venezuela	3	0	2	1	5	9	2			2-2
Mexico	3	0	1	2	3	8	1			

Quarter-finals

Paraguay	7
Venezuela	0

Brazil	0 5p
Uruguay	0 6p

Argentina	1
Peru	0

Chile	0
Colombia	2

Semi-finals

Paraguay	3
Uruguay	2

Argentina	0
Colombia	2

Final

Paraguay	0 5p
Colombia	0 3p

Tournament held from 17-09-2004 to 26-09-2004

Host cities: Ciudad del Este, Encarnacion, Pedro Juan Caballero, Itagua and Luque

SUDAMERICANO SUB-17 VENEZUELA 2005

First Round Group Stage

Group A	Pl	W	D	L	F	A	Pts	ECU	PAR	BOL	VEN
Brazil	4	3	0	1	18	7	9	5-1	2-3	4-2	7-1
Ecuador	4	3	0	1	12	8	9		3-1	3-1	5-1
Paraguay	4	3	0	1	12	8	9			5-2	3-1
Bolivia	4	1	0	3	8	14	3				3-2
Venezuela	4	0	0	4	5	18	0				

Group B	Pl	W	D	L	F	A	Pts	COL	CHI	ARG	PER
Uruguay	4	3	0	1	8	1	9	0-1	4-0	1-0	3-0
Colombia	4	2	1	1	4	2	7		0-1	0-0	3-1
Chile	4	2	0	2	6	7	6			2-3	3-0
Argentina	4	1	1	2	6	7	4				3-4
Peru	4	1	0	3	5	12	3				

Final Round Group

	Pl	W	D	L	F	A	Pts	URU	ECU	COL
Brazil †	3	2	1	0	9	4	7	2-2	4-1	3-1
Uruguay †	3	2	1	0	7	4	7		4-2	1-0
Ecuador	3	1	0	2	5	9	3			2-1
Colombia	3	0	0	3	2	6	0			

† qualified for the FIFA U-17 World Championship in Peru
Tournament played in Maracaibo, Venezuela from 1-04-2005 to 13-04-2005

SUDAMERICANO SUB-20 COLOMBIA 2005

First Round Group Stage

Group A	Pl	W	D	L	F	A	Pts	COL	VEN	BOL	PER
Argentina	4	3	1	0	14	1	10	1-1	3-0	4-0	6-0
Colombia	4	3	1	0	9	1	10		2-0	5-0	1-0
Venezuela	4	1	1	2	6	8	4			3-3	3-0
Bolivia	4	0	2	2	4	13	2				1-1
Peru	4	0	1	3	1	11	1				

Group B	Pl	W	D	L	F	A	Pts	CHI	URU	PAR	ECU
Brazil	4	2	2	0	10	3	8	4-2	0-0	1-1	5-0
Chile	4	2	1	1	10	7	7		0-0	3-2	5-1
Uruguay	4	1	3	0	6	6	6			0-0	6-0
Paraguay	4	1	2	1	7	6	5				4-2
Ecuador	4	0	0	4	3	20	0				

Final Round Group

	Pl	W	D	L	F	A	Pts	BRA	ARG	CHI	URU	VEN
Colombia †	5	4	1	0	11	5	13	1-0	1-1	4-3	3-1	2-0
Brazil †	5	3	0	2	8	6	9		1-2	2-1	4-2	1-0
Argentina †	5	2	3	0	5	3	9			1-1	0-0	1-0
Chile †	5	1	2	2	10	11	5				2-2	3-2
Uruguay	5	1	2	2	7	10	5					2-1
Venezuela	5	0	0	5	3	9	0					

† qualified for the FIFA World Youth Championship in the Netherlands
Tournament played in Armenia, Manizales and Pereira, Colombia from 13-01-2005 to 6-02-2005

OFC

OCEANIA FOOTBALL CONFEDERATION

January 1, 2006 will mark a watershed in the history of the Oceania Football Confederation. On that day Australia will resign from the Confederation and join the Asian Football Confederation, leaving behind an already critically weak OFC even weaker. New Zealand intends to turn the situation to its advantage especially when it comes to qualifying for FIFA tournaments but how long the OFC can survive is open to question. Should New Zealand decide to follow suit the writing would surely be on the wall. As the executive committee of the OFC unanimously approved the move and the AFC welcomed the application, FIFA did not raise any objections although it remained wary of similar moves in the future. "If it's too easy to change Confederation in the end you will have a Confederation of all the big countries, and that leaves those that are not so big alone. This is not solidarity. But we can't see any hurdles that would not allow such a movement," FIFA President Joseph S. Blatter said. The reasoning behind the Socceroos' decision is that the

THE FIFA BIG COUNT OF 2000 FOR OFC

	Male	Female		Male	Female
Registered players	106 469	13 677	Referees	4 483	104
Not registered players	322 100	10 285	Officials	18 602	6 650
Youth players	153 149	20 482	Total involved	1 205 028	101 198
Children & Occasional	600 000	50 000	in football	1 306 001	
Professionals	225	0	Number of clubs	2 801	
Total players	1 276 162		Number of teams	24 968	

OFC is too uncompetitive for them, but also it is a reaction to FIFA's withdrawal of the promised automatic qualifying place for the 2006 FIFA World Cup™. Instead Australia and the Solomon Islands must play a two-legged final for the right to meet the fifth placed team from the CONMEBOL group in a final qualifier for Germany. The two sides previously met in October 2004 in the OFC Nations Cup final to decide the OFC representative in the 2005 FIFA Confederations Cup, Australia coming away with an 11-1 aggregate victory. Sydney FC made it a double for Australia after beating AS Magenta of New Caledonia in the OFC Club Championship final only a year after the island had been welcomed as a FIFA association. It also earned Sydney a place at the FIFA Club World Championship in Japan in December 2005, although qualification for Australian sides in the future will be more difficult as they will have to now win the AFC Champions League. That leaves the door open for some very interesting OFC qualifiers in the future.

Oceania Football Confederation (OFC)

Ericsson Stadium, 12 Maurice Road, Penrose, PO Box 62 586, Auckland 6, New Zealand

Tel +64 9 5258161   Fax +64 9 5258164

info@ofcfoot.org.nz   www.oceaniafootball.com

President: TEMARII Reynald TAH

General Secretary: NICHOLAS Tai COK

Vice-President: LULU Johnny VAN   Treasurer: HARMON Lee COK

OFC Formed: 1966

OFC EXECUTIVE COMMITTEE

President: TEMARII Reynald TAH

Senior Vice-President: LULU Johnny VAN	2nd Vice-President: WICKHAM Adrian SOL	Treasurer: HARMON Lee COK
HARVEY Ron AUS	FUSIMALOHI 'Ahongalu TGA	1st Vice-President: BURGESS Mark NZL
ANDREW Madiu PNG	3rd Vice-President: OTT Richard ASA	General Secretary NICHOLAS Tai COK

OCEANIA TOURNAMENTS

OCEANIA NATIONS CUP

Year	Host Country	Winners	Score	Runners-up	Venue
1973	New Zealand	New Zealand	2-0	Tahiti	Auckland
1980	New Caledonia	Australia	4-2	Tahiti	Nouméa
1996	Home & away	Australia	6-0 5-0	Tahiti	Papeete & Canberra
1998	Australia	New Zealand	1-0	Australia	Brisbane
2000	Tahiti	Australia	2-0	New Zealand	Stade de Pater, Papeete
2002	New Zealand	New Zealand	1-0	Australia	Ericsson Stadium, Auckland
2004	Home & away	Australia	5-1 6-0	Solomon Islands	Honaria & Sydney

Only since the advent of the FIFA Confederations Cup has the Oceania Nations Cup become a permanent fixture in the calender and unsurprisingly it has only ever been won by Australia or New Zealand. Following the departure of Australia from the OFC on January 1, 2006, New Zealand may think that they will have it all their way, although the Solomon Islands, finalists in the latest tournament in 2004 might think otherwise. Indeed, all of the smaller members of the OFC will be buoyed by the fact that at least one of them will be guaranteed a place in the future finals.

OCEANIA WOMEN'S CHAMPIONSHIP

Year	Host Country	Winners	Score	Runners-up	Venue
1983	New Caledonia	New Zealand	3-2	Australia	Nouméa
1986	New Zealand	Chinese Taipei	4-1	Australia	Christchurch
1989	Australia	Chinese Taipei	1-0	New Zealand	Brisbane
1991	Australia	New Zealand	1-0 0-1 †	Australia	Sydney
1995	Papua New Guinea	Australia	1-2 1-0 †	New Zealand	Port Moresby
1998	New Zealand	Australia	3-1	New Zealand	Mount Smart, Auckland
2003	Australia	Australia	2-0 †	New Zealand	Belconnen, Canberra

† The 1991, 1995 and 2003 tournaments were played as leagues • The results shown are those between the top two teams

OCEANIA WOMEN'S U-19 CHAMPIONSHIP

Year	Host Country	Winners	Score	Runners-up	Venue
2002	Tonga	Australia	6-0	New Zealand	Nuku'alofa
2004	Papua New Guinea	Australia	14-1	Papua New Guinea	Lloyd Robson Oval, Port Moresby

Australia have developed into the most consistent power in women's football in the OFC so their departure will be a loss to the confederation with only New Zealand having a team of any great strength.

OCEANIA YOUTH CHAMPIONSHIP

Year	Host Country	Winners	Score	Runners-up	Venue
1974	Tahiti	Tahiti	2-0	New Zealand	Papeete
1978	New Zealand	Australia	5-1 †	Fiji	Auckland
1980	Fiji	New Zealand	2-0	Australia	Suva
1982	Papua New Guinea	Australia	4-3	New Zealand	Port Moresby
1985	Australia	Australia	3-2 †	Israel	Sydney
1987	New Zealand	Australia	1-1 †	Israel	Auckland
1988	Fiji	Australia	1-0	New Zealand	Suva
1990	Fiji	Australia	6-0 †	New Zealand	Suva
1992	Tahiti	New Zealand	1-0 †	Tahiti	Papeete
1994	Fiji	Australia	1-0	New Zealand	Suva
1996	Tahiti	Australia	2-1	New Zealand	Papeete
1998	Samoa	Australia	2-0	Fiji	Apia
2001	New Cal/Cook Is	Australia	1-2 3-1	New Zealand	Auckland & Coffs Harbour
2003	Vanuatu/Fiji	Australia	11-0 4-0	Fiji	Melbourne & Ba
2005	Solomon Islands	Australia	3-0	Solomon Islands	Honiara

† The 1978, 1985, 1987, 1990 and 1992 tournaments were played as leagues • The results shown are those between the top two teams

OCEANIA U-17 CHAMPIONSHIP

Year	Host Country	Winners	Score	Runners-up	Venue
1983	New Zealand	Australia	2-1	New Zealand	Mount Smart, Auckland
1986	Chinese Taipei	Australia	0-1	New Zealand	CKF Stadium, Kaohsiung
1989	Australia	Australia	5-1	New Zealand	
1991	New Zealand	Australia	1-1 1-0	New Zealand	Napier
1993	New Zealand	Australia	3-0	Soloman Islands	
1995	Vanuatu	Australia	1-0	New Zealand	
1997	New Zealand	New Zealand	1-0	Australia	
1999	Fiji	Australia	5-0	Fiji	Churchill Park, Lautoka
2001	Samoa/Cook Isl	Australia	3-0 6-0	New Zealand	Canberra & Auckland
2003	Home & away	Australia	3-1 4-0	New Caledonia	Nouméa
2005	New Caledonia	Australia	1-0	Vanuatu	Nouméa

From 1983 to 1991 the tournaments were played as leagues. The results shown are those between the top two teams

With a guaranteed place for Oceania at the FIFA World Youth Championship and the FIFA U-17 World Championship, Australia has long been a regular qualifier at these events which has helped enormously at encouraging young talent in the country. The challenge will now be for the other countries to develop their youth systems to take advantage of Australia's absence.

SOUTH PACIFIC GAMES WINNERS

Year	Host Country	Winners	Runners-up
1963	Fiji	New Caledonia	Fiji
1966	New Caledonia	Tahiti	New Caledonia
1969	Papua New Guinea	New Caledonia	Tahiti
1971	Tahiti	New Caledonia	Tahiti
1975	Guam	Tahiti	New Caledonia
1979	Fiji	Tahiti	Fiji
1983	Western Samoa	Tahiti	Fiji
1987	New Caledonia	New Caledonia	Tahiti
1991	Papua New Guinea	Fiji	Solomon Isl
1995	Tahiti	Tahiti	Solomon Isl
1999	Guam	Not played	
2003	Fiji	Fiji	New Caledonia

MELANESIAN CUP WINNERS

Year	Host Country	Winners	Runners-up
1988	Solomon Islands	Fiji	Solomon Isl
1989	Fiji	Fiji	New Caledonia
1990	Vanuatu	Vanuatu	New Caledonia
1992	Vanuatu	Fiji	New Caledonia
1994	Solomon Islands	Solomon Isl	Fiji
1996	Papua New Guinea	Papua NG	Solomon Isl
1998	Vanuatu	Fiji	Vanuatu
2000	Fiji	Fiji	Solomon Isl

SOUTH PACIFIC MINI GAMES WINNERS

Year	Host Country	Winners	Runners-up
1981	Solomon Islands	Tahiti	New Caledonia
1985	Cook Islands	Tahiti	
1989	Tonga	Papua NG	
1993	Vanuatu	Tahiti	Fiji

POLYNESIAN CUP WINNERS

Year	Host Country	Winners	Runners-up
1994	Samoa	Tahiti	Tonga
1996	Tonga	Tonga	Samoa
1998	Cook Islands	Tahiti	Cook Islands
2000	Tahiti	Tahiti	Cook Islands

For the Pacific islands, these smaller tournaments have been the lifeblood of football, representing until now the only real prospect of success and as a result they are very popular with the fans. Tahiti and Fiji have been the most consistent performers.

OCEANIA CHAMPIONS CUP

Year	Winners	Country	Score	Country	Runners-up
1987	Adelaide City	AUS	1-1 4-1p	NZL	Mount Wellington
1999	South Melbourne	AUS	5-1	FIJ	Nadi
2001	Wollongong City Wolves	AUS	1-0	VAN	Tafea FC
2005	Sydney FC	AUS	2-0	NCL	AS Magenta

The Oceania Champions Cup has, with one exception, only been contested when a club from the Confederation needs to qualify for the FIFA Club World Championship. All four titles have been won by Australian clubs with South Melbourne and Sydney FC making it to the FIFA tournament. Wollongong missed out when the 2001 FIFA Club World Championship was cancelled.

OFC NATIONS CUP 2004

OFC Nations Cup Final 1st leg, Lawson Tama, Honiara
9-10-2004, 14:00, 21 000, O'Leary NZL

SOL 1 5 AUS

Suri [60]

Skoko 2 [5 28], Milicic [18]
Emerton [43], Elrich [79]

SOLOMON ISLANDS		AUSTRALIA	
1 RAY Jr Felix		SCHWARZER Mark 1	
2 LEO Leslie		MUSCAT Kevin 2	
3 HOUKARAWA Mahlon		COLOSIMO Simon 3	
5 SURI George	71	NEILL Lucas 4	
6 KILIFA Nelson		VIDMAR Tony 5	
7 MAEMAE Alick		POPOVIC Tony 6	
10 SURI Batram	60	EMERTON Brett 7	
11 MENAPI Commins		SKOKO Josip 8	
13 LUI George	60	GRELLA Vince 13	
14 SAMANI Jack		ELRICH Ahmad 21	
18 FA'ARODO Henry		MILICIC Ante 22	
Tr: GILLETT Alan		Tr: FARINA Frank	
	60	STERJOVSKI Mile 11	
	60	WILKSHIRE Luke 15	
	71	MVKAIN Jonathon 16	

OFC Nations Cup Final 2nd leg, Stadium Australia, Sydney
12-10-2004, 19:30, 19 208, Rakaroi FIJ

AUS 6 0 SOL

Milicic [5], Kewell [8], Vidmar [60],
Thompson [79], Elrich [82], Emerton [86]

AUSTRALIA		SOLOMON ISLANDS	
1 SCHWARZER Mark		RAY Jr Felix 1	
2 MUSCAT Kevin	45	HOUKARAWA Mahlon 3	
3 COLOSIMO Simon		SURI George 5	
4 NEILL Lucas		KILIFA Nelson 6	
5 VIDMAR Tony		MAEMAE Alick 7	
6 POPOVIC Tony		KONOFILIA Joel 8	
7 EMERTON Brett	45	SURI Batram 10	
8 SKOKO Josip	45	MENAPI Commins 11	
10 KEWELL Harry	45	LUI George 13	
15 WILKSHIRE Luke		OMOKIRIO Gideon 17	
22 MILICIC Ante		FA'ARODO Henry 18	
Tr: FARINA Frank		Tr: GILLETT Alan	
16 MVKAIN Jonathon	45	45 KIDSON Billy 9	
17 THOMPSON Archie	45		
21 ELRICH Ahmad	45		

The OFC Nations Cup Final was played between the winners and runners-up of stage two of the FIFA World Cup™ qualifiers in Oceania, held in Adelaide, Australia in May/June 2004

OFC YOUTH TOURNAMENTS 2005

OFC YOUTH CHAMPIONSHIP SOLOMON ISLANDS 2005

First Round Group Stage

Group A	Pl	W	D	L	F	A	Pts	VAN	NCL	TGA
Australia	3	3	0	0	40	3	9	9-2	12-1	19-0
Vanuatu	3	2	0	1	7	11	6		3-2	2-0
New Caledonia	3	1	0	2	10	16	3			7-1
Tonga	3	0	0	3	1	28	0			

Group B	Pl	W	D	L	F	A	Pts	FIJ	NZL	SAM
Solomon Islands	3	3	0	0	9	1	9	1-0	2-1	6-0
Fiji	3	2	0	1	10	2	6		1-0	9-1
New Zealand	3	1	0	2	8	3	3			7-0
Samoa	3	0	0	3	1	22	0			

Tournament held in Honiara, Solomon Islands

Semi-finals

Australia	3
Fiji	2

Vanuatu	1
Solomon Islands	3

Final

† Qualified for the FIFA World Youth Championship in the Netherlands

Australia †	3
Solomon Islands	0

Third place play-off

Vanuatu	4
Fiji	1

OFC U–17 CHAMPIONSHIP NEW CALEDONIA 2005

First Round Group Stage

Group A	Pl	W	D	L	F	A	Pts	VAN	TAH	TGA
Australia	3	3	0	0	35	0	9	4-0	5-0	26-0
Vanuatu	3	2	0	1	22	5	6		2-1	20-0
Tahiti	3	1	0	2	16	7	3			15-0
Tonga	3	0	0	3	0	61	0			

Group B	Pl	W	D	L	F	A	Pts	SOL	FIJ	PNG	COK
New Caledonia	4	3	0	1	11	6	9	0-5	2-0	3-1	6-0
Solomon Islands	4	2	2	0	17	5	8		2-2	3-3	7-0
Fiji	4	2	1	1	9	6	7			5-2	2-0
Papua New Guinea	4	1	1	2	10	11	4				4-0
Cook Islands	4	0	0	4	0	19	0				

Tournament held in Nouméa, New Caledonia

Semi-finals

Australia	2
Solomon Islands	0

New Caledonia	1
Vanuatu	4

Final

† Qualified for the FIFA U-17 World Championship in Peru

Australia †	1
Vanuatu	0

Third place play-off

Solomon Islands	3
New Caledonia	1

OFC CLUB CHAMPIONSHIP TAHITI 2005

OFC CLUB CHAMPIONSHIP TAHITI 2005

Prelim Round			First Round Group Stage											Semi-finals		Final	
Manumea	ASA																
Auckland City	NZL	w-o	Group A		Pl	W	D	L	F	A	Pts	TAH	NZL	PNG			
			Sydney FC	AUS	3	3	0	0	18	4	9	6-0	3-2	9-2			
Nikao Sokattack	COK	0 1	AS Pirae	TAH	3	2	0	1	6	7	6		1-0	5-1			
AS Magenta	NCL	4 5	Auckland City	NZL	3	1	0	2	8	5	3			6-1	Sydney FC	6	
			Sobou FC	PNG	3	0	0	3	4	20	0				Tafea FC	0	
Sobou FC	PNG	5 2															Sydney FC	2
Tuinaimato Breeze	SAM	0 0															AS Magenta	0
			Group B		Pl	W	D	L	F	A	Pts	VAN	SOL	TAH	AS Pirae	1	
Lotoha 'apai	TGA	1 0	AS Magenta	NCL	3	2	1	0	10	2	7	1-1	5-0	4-1	AS Magenta	4	
Tafea FC	VAN	2 5	Tafea FC	VAN	3	2	1	0	6	3	7		3-2	2-0			
			Makuru FC	SOL	3	1	0	2	4	9	3			2-1	Third place play-off		
Electric Ba	FIJ	1 1	AS Manu ura	TAH	3	0	0	3	2	8	0				Tafea FC	3	
Makuru FC	SOL	4 4	Tournament played in Papeete, Tahiti from 30-05-2005 to 10-06-2005												AS Pirae	1	

GROUP A

Stade Pater, Papeete, 31-05-2005, 18:30	
Sydney FC	**3**
Ceccoli 32, Talay 47, Corica 93+	
Auckland City	
Seaman 37, SmithJ 78	

Stade Pater, Papeete, 2-06-2005, 21:00	
Sobou FC	**2**
Wate 57, Daniel 90	
Sydney FC	**9**
Fyfe 5, Petrovski 3 14 43 71, Zdrilic 3 19 40 42,	
Brodie 79, Salazar 82	

Stade Pater, Papeete, 31-05-2005, 21:00	
Sobou FC	**1**
Kassam 87	
AS Pirae	**5**
Bennett 3 9 35 49, Zaveroni 2 18 28	

Stade Pater, Papeete, 4-06-2005, 15:00	
Sydney FC	**6**
Zdrilic 4, 11 25 35 39, Buonavoglia 43, Carney 85	
AS Pirae	**0**

Stade Pater, Papeete, 2-06-2005, 18:00	
AS Pirae	**1**
Bennett 50	
Auckland City	**0**

Stade Pater, Papeete, 5-06-2005, 18:30	
Auckland City	**6**
Mulrooney 2 6 30, Urlovic 13, Coombes 18	
Uhlmann 21, McIvor 87	
Sobou FC	**1**
Deno 45	

GROUP B

Stade Pater, Papeete, 1-06-2005, 18:30	
AS Magenta	**4**
Watrone 2 32 56, Wajoka 43, Poatinda 62	
AS Manu ura	**1**
Diaike 46	

Stade Pater, Papeete, 3-06-2005, 21:00	
AS Magenta	
Watrone 39	
Tafea FC	**1**
Naprapol 13	

Stade Pater, Papeete, 1-06-2005, 21:00	
Tafea FC	**3**
Poida 4, Obed 18, Naprapol 56	
Makuru FC	**2**
Suri 54, Maemae 79	

Stade Pater, Papeete, 5-06-2005, 13:00	
AS Manu ura	**0**
Tafea FC	**2**
Qorig 18, Naprapol 54	

Stade Pater, Papeete, 3-06-2005, 18:30	
AS Manu ura	**1**
Lee-Tham 4	
Makuru FC	**2**
Maemae 6, Afia 66	

Stade Pater, Papeete, 5-06-2005, 15:30	
Makuru FC	**0**
AS Magenta	**5**
Hmae 3 33 62 81, Elmour 76p, Kaudre 87	

SEMI-FINAL	
Stade Pater, Papeete, 7-06-2005, 18:00	
Sydney FC	**6**
Petrovski 26, Zdrilic 39, Bingley 44p	
Corica 2 65 90, Salazar 87	
Tafea FC	**0**

SEMI-FINAL	
Stade Pater, Papeete, 7-06-2005, 21:00	
AS Magenta	**4**
Elmour 45, Sinedo 61, Kaudre 2 90 91+	
AS Pirea	**1**
Wadriako OG 17	

THIRD PLACE PLAY-OFF	
Stade Pater, Papeete, 10-06-2005, 18:00	
Tafea FC	**3**
Poida 30, Mermer 2 48 69	
AS Pirea	
Bennett 74	

Final, Stade Pater, Papeete		
10-06-2005, 21:00, 4 000, Fox NZL, Tauaroa TAH, Doriri VAN		
SYDNEY FC	**2 0**	**AS MAGENTA**

Bingley 16, Zdrilic 59

	SYDNEY FC			AS MAGENTA	
1	BOLTON Clint			HNE Michel	1
2	FYFE Iain			OUKA Nicolas	2
3	CECCOLI Alex			SINEDO Andre	4
6	TALAY Ufuk	62		WIAKO Jacky	5
7	MIDDLEBY Robert	76		ELMOUR Gil	6
8	BINGLEY Matthew			LONGUE Stevens	7
9	ZDRILIC David	89		WEA Jules	8
11	PETROVSKI Sasho		46	POATINDA Paul	9
13	SALAZAR Alejandro			WAJOKA Pierre	10
14	PACKER Andrew		78	HMAE Michael	11
15	MCFLYNN Terence			WADRIAKO Robert	17
	Tr: LITTBARSKI Pierre			Tr: CUREAU Jean Paul	
10	CORICA Stephen	62	78	WATRONE Francis	12
12	CARNEY David	89	46	KAUDRE Noel	16
16	BRODIE Todd	76			

UEFA

UNION DES ASSOCIATIONS EUROPEENNES DE FOOTBALL

As ever, European football continued to make headlines in the 2004-05 season, not least in the remarkable UEFA Champions League final in Istanbul between Liverpool and Milan. Never had there been such an extraordinary about turn in fortunes from one half to the next with Milan seemingly in complete control and 3-0 up at half-time. But three goals in six second half minutes and then a desperate rearguard action in extra-time saw the game go to penalties with Liverpool winning the Cup for a fifth time. Controversy reigned as Liverpool were refused a place in next season's tournament because they finished outside the top four in the Premier League. However, they had UEFA President Lennart Johansson on their side who insisted that the winners "should have a chance to defend the title" and a place was found. Twenty years after Heysel, crowd problems still persist with missiles raining down at the San Siro in the all-Milan UEFA Champions League quarter-final while Anders Frisk abandoned the match after he was hit during the Dynamo Kyiv

THE FIFA BIG COUNT OF 2000 FOR UEFA

	Male	Female		Male	Female
Registered players	8 562 596	276 323	Referees	399 919	16 650
Not registered players	17 351 201	967 291	Officials	1 752 808	17 936
Youth players	8 553 560	429 883	Total involved	51 773 742	3 078 790
Children & Occasional	15 100 000	1 370 000	in football	54 798 167	
Professionals	53 658	707	Number of clubs	223 676	
Total players	52 610 854		Number of teams	981 345	

and Roma UEFA Champions League group game. He then quit refereeing altogther following death threats in the aftermath of the Barcelona v Chelsea tie. Chelsea owner Roman Ambramovich celebrated victory in a European competition, but probably not the one he was expecting. Instead of cheering Chelsea to Champions League glory, he saw CSKA Moscow, sponsored by his oil company Sibneft, win the UEFA Cup and hand Russia its first European title. Michel Platini declared an interest in Lennart Johansson's job when he retires in 2007 and is seen by many as an ideal candidate to preserve the balance between business and football interests in Europe. UEFA decided to act on the issue of home-grown players (or the lack of) with clubs competing in European competition from 2006-07 obliged to include four local players in a 25-man squad. The European season ended with Germany winning the UEFA Women's Championship for a fourth consecutive time in a tournament played before record crowds in the North-West of England.

Union des associations européennes de football (UEFA)
Route de Genève 46, 1260 Nyon, Switzerland
Tel +41 22 9944444   Fax +41 22 9944488
info@uefa.com   www.uefa.com
President: JOHANSSON Lennart SWE   Chief Executive: OLSSON Lars-Christer SWE
UEFA Formed: 1954

UEFA EXECUTIVE COMMITTEE
President: JOHANSSON Lennart SWE   1st Vice-President: ERZIK Senes TUR   2nd Vice-President: OMDAL Per Ravn NOR
3rd Vice-President: VILLAR LLONA Angel Maria ESP   4th Vice-President: THOMPSON Geoffrey ENG   Treasurer: SPRENGERS Mathieu, Dr
ORDINARY MEMBERS OF THE EXECUTIVE COMMITTEE
CARRARO Franco ITA   KOLOSKOV Viacheslav, Dr RUS   LEFKARITIS Marios CYP
MAGNUSSON Eggert ISL   MAYER-VORFELDER Gerhard GER   MIFSUD Joseph, Dr MLT
PLATINI Michel FRA   SPIESS Giangiorgio SUI   ROEMER Henri LUX
Co-opted: SURKIS Grigory UKR   Co-opted: MADAIL Gilberto, Dr POR   FIFA vice-president: WILL David SCO
FIFA Exco member: D'HOOGHE Michel, Dr BEL   Chief Executive: OLSSON Lars-Christer SWE

EUROPEAN TOURNAMENTS

UEFA EUROPEAN CHAMPIONSHIP

Year	Host Country	Winners	Score	Runners-up	Venue
1960	France	Soviet Union	2-1	Yugoslavia	Parc des Princes, Paris
1964	Spain	Spain	2-1	Soviet Union	Bernabeu, Madrid
1968	Italy	Italy	1-1 2-0	Yugoslavia	Stadio Olimpico, Roma
1972	Belgium	Germany FR	3-0	Soviet Union	Heysel, Brussels
1976	Yugoslavia	Czechoslovakia	2-2 5-4p	Germany FR	Crvena Zvezda, Belgrade
1980	Italy	Germany FR	2-1	Belgium	Stadio Olimpico, Rome
1984	France	France	2-0	Spain	Parc des Princes, Paris
1988	Germany FR	Netherlands	2-0	Soviet Union	Olympiastadion, Munich
1992	Sweden	Denmark	2-0	Germany	Nya Ullevi, Gothenburg
1996	England	Germany	2-1	Czech Republic	Wembley, London
2000	Belgium/Netherlands	France	2-1	Italy	Feijenoord Stadion, Rotterdam
2004	Portugal	Greece	1-0	Portugal	Stadio da Luz, Lisbon

The UEFA European Championship is the second youngest of the Confederation championships after the Oceania Nations Cup. At first there was a patchy response to the tournament and it was not until the third edition that the Germans, the most succesful nation to date with three titles, bothered to enter. The French are the only other team to have been European Champions more than once and the wide range of winners has been a prominent feature and one of the major reasons for the continued success of the tournament. Only England of the traditional powers has failed to win the title but it has been the triumphs of the smaller nations such as Czechoslovakia, Netherlands, Denmark and most recently Greece that have caught the imagination. Only since 1980 has the UEFA European Championship had a final tournament along the lines of the current system. From 1980 to 1992 the finals had eight teams which was expanded to 16 in 1996 in no small part because UEFA's membership had grown from 32, which it had been for much of the post-war period, to beyond 50 as the political boundaries of Europe were redrawn. Eleven nations have hosted the finals but home advantage has never been a serious factor. On seven occasions the hosts have been beaten in the semi-finals, and in only three of the 12 tournaments have they actually won the title – and not since 1984 – while in 2004 Portugal became the first host nation to lose the final itself. Belgium and the Netherlands co-hosted Euro 2000™ and this system is likely to prove popular in the future with Austria and Switzerland scheduled to do the same in 2008.

UEFA EUROPEAN WOMEN'S CHAMPIONSHIP

Year	Host Country	Winners	Score	Runners-up	Venue
1984		Sweden	1-0 0-1 4-3p	England	Gothenburg & Luton
1987	Norway	Norway	2-1	Sweden	Oslo
1989	Germany FR	Germany FR	4-1	Norway	Osnabrück
1991	Denmark	Germany	3-1	Norway	Aalborg
1993	Italy	Norway	1-0	Italy	Cesena
1995	Germany	Germany	3-2	Sweden	Kaiserslautern
1997	Norway/Sweden	Germany	2-0	Italy	Oslo
2001	Germany	Germany	1-0	Sweden	Donaustadion, Ulm
2005	England	Germany	3-1	Norway	Ewood Park, Blackburn

The UEFA Women's Championship is now a flourishing event in its own right drawing good crowds into the stadiums and earning widespread coverage in the media. An unofficial European Championship was played in Italy in 1979 but since then there have been nine official tournaments, six of which have been won by Germany. The Scandinavian countries remain strong and provided the two other winners in Norway and Sweden. The eight-team final tournament was introduced for 1997 in Norway and Sweden. Although early editions often doubled up as FIFA Women's World Cup qualifiers, these are now held separately.

UEFA EUROPEAN UNDER–21 CHAMPIONSHIP

Year	Host Country	Winners	Score	Runners-up	Venue
1978		Yugoslavia	1-0 4-1	German DR	Halle & Mostar
1980		Soviet Union	0-0 1-0	German DR	Rostock & Moscow
1982		England	3-1 2-3	Germany FR	Sheffield & Bremen
1984		England	1-0 2-0	Spain	Seville & Sheffield
1986		Spain	1-2 2-1 3-0p	Italy	Rome & Valladolid
1988		France	0-0 3-0	Greece	Athens & Besançon
1990		Soviet Union	4-2 3-1	Yugoslavia	Sarajevo & Simferopol
1992		Italy	2-0 0-1	Sweden	Ferrara & Växjö
1994	France	Italy	1-0	Portugal	Montpellier
1996	Spain	Italy	1-1 4-2p	Spain	Barcelona
1998	Romania	Spain	1-0	Greece	Bucharest
2000	Slovakia	Italy	2-1	Czech Republic	Bratislava
2002	Switzerland	Czech Republic	0-0 3-1p	France	Basel
2004	Germany	Italy	3-0	Serbia & Montenegro	Bochum

Since 1992 the tournament has doubled as a qualifying tournament for the Olympic Games in the respective years

UEFA EUROPEAN UNDER–19 CHAMPIONSHIP

Year	Host Country	Winners	Score	Runners-up	Venue
1981	West Germany	Germany FR	1-0	Poland	Düsseldorf
1982	Finland	Scotland	3-1	Czechoslovakia	Helsinki
1983	England	France	1-0	Czechoslovakia	White Hart Lane, London
1984	Soviet Union	Hungary	0-0 3-2p	Soviet Union	Zentralny, Moscow
1986	Yugoslavia	German DR	3-1	Italy	Subotica
1988	Czechoslovakia	Soviet Union	3-1	Portugal	Frydek-Mistek
1990	Hungary	Soviet Union	0-0 4-2p	Portugal	Bekescsaba
1992	Germany	Turkey	2-1	Portugal	Bayreuth
1993	England	England	1-0	Turkey	City Ground, Nottingham
1994	Spain	Portugal	1-1 4-1p	Germany	Merida
1995	Greece	Spain	4-1	Italy	Katerini
1996	France/Luxemb	France	1-0	Spain	Besançon
1997	Iceland	France	1-0	Portugal	Reykjavík
1998	Cyprus	Republic of Ireland	1-1 4-3p	Germany	Larnaca
1999	Sweden	Portugal	1-0	Italy	Norrköping
2000	Germany	France	1-0	Ukraine	Nürnberg
2001	Finland	Poland	3-1	Czech Republic	Helsinki
2002	Norway	Spain	1-0	Germany	Ullevaal, Oslo
2003	Liechtenstein	Italy	2-0	Portugal	Rheinpark Stadion, Vaduz
2004	Switzerland	Spain	1-0	Turkey	Nyon
2005	Nth. Ireland	France	3-1	England	Windsor Park, Belfast

Played as an U-18 tournament from 1981 to 2001

UEFA EUROPEAN WOMEN'S UNDER–19 CHAMPIONSHIP

Year	Host Country	Winners	Score	Runners-up	Venue
1998		Denmark	2-0 2-3	France	Aabenraa & Niederbronn-les-Bains
1999	Sweden	Sweden	1-0	Germany	Bromölla
2000	France	Germany	4-2	Spain	La Libération, Boulogne
2001	Norway	Germany	3-2	Norway	Aråsen, Lillestrom
2002	Sweden	Germany	3-1	France	Olympia, Helsingborg
2003	Germany	France	2-0	Norway	Alfred Kunze Sportpark, Leipzig
2004	Finland	Spain	2-1	Germany	Pohjola Stadion, Vantaa
2005	Hungary	Russia	2-2 6-5p	France	ZTE, Zalaegerszeg

The first three tournaments were played as U-18 championships

UEFA EUROPEAN UNDER-17 CHAMPIONSHIP

Year	Host Country	Winners	Score	Runners-up	Venue
1982	Italy	Italy	1-0	Germany FR	Falconara
1984	Germany FR	Germany FR	2-0	Soviet Union	Ulm
1985	Hungary	Soviet Union	4-0	Greece	Budapest
1986	Greece	Spain	2-1	Italy	Athens
1987	France	Italy	1-0	Soviet Union	Paris
1988	Spain	Spain	0-0 4-2p	Portugal	Teresa Rivero, Madrid
1989	Denmark	Portugal	4-1	German DR	Vejle
1990	East Germany	Czechoslovakia	3-2	Yugoslavia	Erfurt
1991	Swtzerland	Spain	2-0	Germany	Wankdorf, Berne
1992	Cyprus	Germany	2-1	Spain	Ammokostos, Larnaca
1993	Turkey	Poland	1-0	Italy	Inönü, Istanbul
1994	Rep. Ireland	Turkey	1-0	Denmark	Tolka Park, Dublin
1995	Belgium	Portugal	2-0	Spain	Brussels
1996	Austria	Portugal	1-0	France	Wien
1997	Germany	Spain	0-0 5-4p	Austria	Celle
1998	Scotland	Republic of Ireland	2-1	Italy	McDiarmid Park, Perth
1999	Czech Republic	Spain	4-1	Poland	Olomouc
2000	Israel	Portugal	2-1	Czech Republic	Ramat Gan, Tel Aviv
2001	England	Spain	1-0	France	Stadium of Light, Sunderland
2002	Denmark	Switzerland	0-0 4-2p	France	Farum
2003	Portugal	Portugal	2-1	Spain	Viseu
2004	France	France	2-1	Spain	
2005	Italy	Turkey	2-0	Netherlands	Pontedera

Played as an U-16 tournament prior to 2002

Europe has a long history of youth football dating back to the launch of the International Youth Tournament by the English FA in 1948. UEFA took over the running of that event in 1956 and it remained largely unaltered until 1980 when it was replaced by two new tournaments, for players under 16 and players under 18. These have since changed to Under-17 and Under-19 Championships to tie in with the systems used by FIFA for their World Championships at these levels. In 1998 and before any other confederation, UEFA launched their Under-19 Championship for women which has since been played annually and which, like the men's events, doubles up when required as a qualifying tournament for the FIFA World Championships. UEFA has one other age-restricted event, the UEFA European Under-21 Championship which mirrors the qualifying groups of the senior men's team, with games often played the previous day. As with the seniors' team tournaments are played over two years and since 1992 every second edition has doubled up as a qualifing tournament for the Olympic Games. Unlike South America, youth football has been viewed with varying degrees of scepticism in Europe and this has showed in results at world level although the French and particularly the Spanish are helping to change this.

UEFA WOMEN'S CUP

Year	Winners	Country	Score	Country	Runners-up
2002	1.FFC Frankfurt	GER	2-0	SWE	Umeå IK
2003	Umeå IK	SWE	4-1 3-0	DEN	Fortuna Hjørring
2004	Umeå IK	SWE	3-0 5-0	GER	1.FFC Frankfurt
2005	1.FFC Turbine Potsdam	GER	2-0 3-1	SWE	Djurgården/Alvsjö

Of all of the recent additions to the UEFA calendar the UEFA Women's Cup is potentially the most interesting. Whereas women's football in the USA has had its foundations in the college system, in Europe the link with men's clubs has been stronger and could develop further if the UEFA Women's Cup fulfils its potential and prompts clubs to become more serious about funding their female sections. For the 2005 tournament 42 of UEFA's 52 members entered teams, up from 22 in the first tournament in 2001, although it is the German and Scandinavian teams that have so far been the most successful.

UEFA CHAMPIONS LEAGUE

Year	Winners	Country	Score	Country	Runners-up
1956	Real Madrid	ESP	4-3	FRA	Stade de Reims
1957	Real Madrid	ESP	2-0	ITA	Fiorentina
1958	Real Madrid	ESP	3-2	ITA	Milan
1959	Real Madrid	ESP	2-0	FRA	Stade de Reims
1960	Real Madrid	ESP	7-3	FRG	Eintracht Frankfurt
1961	Benfica	POR	3-2	ESP	Barcelona
1962	Benfica	POR	5-3	ESP	Real Madrid
1963	Milan	ITA	2-1	POR	Benfica
1964	Internazionale	ITA	3-1	ESP	Real Madrid
1965	Internazionale	ITA	1-0	POR	Benfica
1966	Real Madrid	ESP	2-1	YUG	Partizan Beograd
1967	Celtic	SCO	2-1	ITA	Internazionale
1968	Manchester United	ENG	4-1	POR	Benfica
1969	Milan	ITA	4-1	NED	Ajax
1970	Feyenoord	NED	2-1	SCO	Celtic
1971	Ajax	NED	2-0	GRE	Panathinaikos
1972	Ajax	NED	2-0	ITA	Internazionale
1973	Ajax	NED	1-0	ITA	Juventus
1974	Bayern München	FRG	1-1 4-0	ESP	Atlético Madrid
1975	Bayern München	FRG	2-0	ENG	Leeds United
1976	Bayern München	FRG	1-0	FRA	AS Saint-Étienne
1977	Liverpool	ENG	3-1	FRG	Borussia Mönchengladbach
1978	Liverpool	ENG	1-0	BEL	Club Brugge
1979	Nottingham Forest	ENG	1-0	SWE	Malmö FF
1980	Nottingham Forest	ENG	1-0	FRG	Hamburger SV
1981	Liverpool	ENG	1-0	ESP	Real Madrid
1982	Aston Villa	ENG	1-0	FRG	Bayern München
1983	Hamburger SV	FRG	1-0	ITA	Juventus
1984	Liverpool	ENG	1-1 4-2p	ITA	Roma
1985	Juventus	ITA	1-0	ENG	Liverpool
1986	Steaua Bucuresti	ROU	0-0 2-0p	ESP	Barcelona
1987	FC Porto	POR	2-1	FRG	Bayern München
1988	PSV Eindhoven	NED	0-0 6-5p	POR	Benfica
1989	Milan	ITA	4-0	ROO	Steaua Bucuresti
1990	Milan	ITA	1-0	POR	Benfica
1991	Crvena Zvezda Beograd	YUG	0-0 5-3p	FRA	Olympique Marseille
1992	Barcelona	ESP	1-0	ITA	Sampdoria
1993	Olympique Marseille	FRA	1-0	ITA	Milan
1994	Milan	ITA	4-0	ESP	Barcelona
1995	Ajax	NED	1-0	ITA	Milan
1996	Juventus	ITA	1-1 4-2p	NED	Ajax
1997	Borussia Dortmund	GER	3-1	ITA	Juventus
1998	Real Madrid	ESP	1-0	ITA	Juventus
1999	Manchester United	ENG	2-1	GER	Bayern München
2000	Real Madrid	ESP	3-0	ESP	Valencia
2001	Bayern München	GER	1-1 5-4p	ESP	Valencia
2002	Real Madrid	ESP	2-1	GER	Bayer Leverkusen
2003	Milan	ITA	0-0 3-2p	ITA	Juventus
2004	FC Porto	POR	3-0	FRA	Monaco
2005	Liverpool	ENG	3-3 3-2p	ITA	Milan

Europe's top club competition needs little introduction although how it is referred to may need a little explanation. Launched in 1955 as the European Champion Clubs' Cup it was often known simply as the European Cup. In 1992 it was rebranded as the UEFA Champions League, although technically speaking many of the teams taking part are not the champions of their respective leagues and half of the competition is actually run on a knock-out basis and not a league system.

There are few higher honours for a footballer than lifting the European Champions Clubs' Cup, as the trophy itself is still known, and the final in May remains one of the major highlights of the year. Before 1955 clubs from different countries only met in friendly matches with two major exceptions. The annual Mitropa Cup, which started in 1927, brought together the top teams from Italy, Czechoslovakia, Hungary, Austria, Switzerland and Yugoslavia and was at its most powerful before the Second World War; and the Latin Cup, played in the post-war period between the champions of Spain, Portugal, France and Italy. Ironically the 1955 Latin Cup final was contested by Real Madrid and Stade de Reims, the two teams which a year later made it to the final of the first European Cup. The southern European nations benefited from the competitive edge that the Latin Cup had given them and it wasn't until Celtic's victory in 1967 that a club from outside of Spain, Italy or Portugal won the Cup. Most notable was Real Madrid's achievement in winning the first five tournaments and with nine triumphs they remain the most successful team. Milan are second with six although their titles have been more widespread over time than Real's showing slightly more consistency than their rivals. 1967 marked a complete shift in the balance of power with clubs from northern Europe completely dominating the competition for most of the next two decades. English clubs won six titles in a row between 1977 and 1982 while Bayern München and Ajax each won a hat-trick of titles. Heysel in 1985 marked the next watershed. That one of the worst disasters in European football should come in the European Cup final was difficult to take but it meant that UEFA could ban English clubs and the fans that had followed them abroad. It also meant the balance of power shifted south once again coinciding with the rise of the great Milan team of the late 1980s and early 1990s, a team that, in the eyes of many, rivals the Real Madrid of the 1950s as the greatest in the history of the competition. The 1991-92 season saw the first shake up in the European Cup with two groups of four replacing the quarter-finals, the winners of which qualified for the final, while the following year it was rebranded the UEFA Champions League. Since then the format has been tinkered with on a number of occasions with four first round groups introduced for the 1994-95 season, six first round groups for the 1997-98 season and finally eight first round groups and four second round groups for the 1999-2000 season. Most dramatically of all perhaps was the decision taken for the 1997-98 season which allowed more than the champions from each country to take part. For the top countries that now means entry for the top four teams, a situation which has led to some criticism, but it does satisfy the needs of the clubs whilst balancing the integrity of the national leagues. It has often been said that a European League is inevitable one day, but in many respects it is already with us in the form of the UEFA Champions League and much to UEFA's credit it has come without the clubs breaking away to form an independent body. Since the formation of the UEFA Champions League there has been a remarakble leveling of standards with no one team able to dominate the competition. Only a revived Real Madrid have come close but the past 15 tournaments have been won by 12 different clubs from eight countries. 2005 marked the 50th final with English, Italian and Spanish clubs all holding 10 titles each.

FAIRS CUP

Year	Winners	Country	Score	Country	Runners-up
1958	Barcelona	ESP	2-2 6-0	ENG	London Select XI
1960	Barcelona	ESP	0-0 4-1	ENG	Birmingham City
1961	Roma	ITA	2-2 2-0	ENG	Birmingham City
1962	Valencia	ESP	6-2 1-1	ESP	Barcelona
1963	Valencia	ESP	2-1 2-0	YUG	Dinamo Zagreb
1964	Real Zaragoza	ESP	2-1	ESP	Valencia
1965	Ferencváros	HUN	1-0	ITA	Juventus
1966	Barcelona	ESP	0-1 4-2	ESP	Real Zaragoza
1967	Dinamo Zagreb	YUG	2-0 0-0	ENG	Leeds United
1968	Leeds United	ENG	1-0 0-0	HUN	Ferencváros
1969	Newcastle United	ENG	3-0 3-2	HUN	Ujpesti Dózsa
1970	Arsenal	ENG	1-3 3-0	BEL	RSC Anderlecht
1971	Leeds United	ENG	2-2 1-1	ITA	Juventus

UEFA CUP

Year	Winners	Country	Score	Country	Runners-up
1972	Tottenham Hotspur	ENG	2-1 1-1	ENG	Wolverhampton Wanderers
1973	Liverpool	ENG	3-0 0-2	FRG	Borussia Mönchengladbach
1974	Feyenoord	NED	2-2 2-0	ENG	Tottenham Hotspur
1975	Borussia Mönchengladbach	FRG	0-0 5-1	NED	FC Twente Enschede
1976	Liverpool	ENG	3-2 1-1	BEL	Club Brugge
1977	Juventus	ITA	1-0 1-2	ESP	Athletic Bilbao
1978	PSV Eindhoven	NED	0-0 3-0	FRA	SEC Bastia
1979	Borussia Mönchengladbach	FRG	1-1 1-0	YUG	Crvena Zvezda Beograd
1980	Eintracht Frankfurt	FRG	2-3 1-0	FRG	Borussia Mönchengladbach
1981	Ipswich Town	ENG	3-0 2-4	NED	AZ 67 Alkmaar
1982	IFK Göteborg	SWE	1-0 3-0	FRG	Hamburger SV
1983	RSC Anderlecht	BEL	1-0 1-1	POR	Benfica
1984	Tottenham Hotspur	ENG	1-1 1-1 4-3p	BEL	RSC Anderlecht
1985	Real Madrid	ESP	3-0 0-1	HUN	Videoton SC
1986	Real Madrid	ESP	5-1 0-2	FRG	1.FC Köln
1987	IFK Göteborg	SWE	1-0 1-1	SCO	Dundee United
1988	Bayer Leverkusen	FRG	0-3 3-0 3-2p	ESP	Español
1989	Napoli	ITA	2-1 3-3	FRG	VfB Stuttgart
1990	Juventus	ITA	3-1 0-0	ITA	Fiorentina
1991	Internazionale	ITA	2-0 0-1	ITA	Roma
1992	Ajax	NED	2-2 0-0	ITA	Torino
1993	Juventus	ITA	3-1 3-0	GER	Borussia Dortmund
1994	Internazionale	ITA	1-0 1-0	AUT	Austria Salzburg
1995	Parma	ITA	1-0 1-1	ITA	Juventus
1996	Bayern München	GER	2-0 3-1	FRA	Bordeaux
1997	Schalke 04	GER	1-0 0-1 4-1p	ITA	Internazionale
1998	Internazionale	ITA	3-0	ITA	Lazio
1999	Parma	ITA	3-0	FRA	Olympique Marseille
2000	Galatasaray	TUR	0-0 4-1p	ENG	Arsenal
2001	Liverpool	ENG	5-4	ESP	CD Alavés
2002	Feyenoord	NED	3-2	GER	Borussia Dortmund
2003	FC Porto	POR	3-2	SCO	Glasgow Celtic
2004	Valencia	ESP	2-0	FRA	Olympique Marseille
2005	CSKA Moskva	RUS	3-1	POR	Sporting CP

There was a time when winning the UEFA Cup was seen as a more challenging task than winning the European Champions Clubs' Cup. With up to three or four clubs from the top nations taking part, compared to just one in the European Cup, the depth of opposition was stronger, not just in terms of numbers but also due to the fact that unless they successfully defended their national title, the teams in the European Cup were not necessarily the form teams of the season or the ones challenging for the title at home. More often than not these teams were playing in the UEFA Cup. Rather bizarrely the tournament was at first restricted to teams from cities that had staged a major international trade fair. Renamed in 1971 the UEFA Cup enjoyed its golden era over the next three decades. Juventus, Inter, Liverpool and Barcelona are the most successful clubs in its history with three titles, while Italy and England share 10 titles apiece with Spain on nine. Despite this fine and glorious history, the UEFA Cup now finds itself in a crisis which UEFA has tried to address by rebranding it and introducing a group stage to try and appeal to the fans. The problem, however, dates back to the decision in 1997 to allow more than one club per country into the UEFA Champions League. Qualifying for the UEFA Cup and not the UEFA Champions League is now seen by the top clubs as a major disaster, hardly good for the credibility of the tournament. Furthermore, the problem is exacerbated by the clubs finishing third in the Champions League groups then playing in the UEFA Cup and more often than not going on to win it. This decline in prestige has had one good side effect; perhaps because the pressure is not so intense or the fear of failure so great, every final in recent years has been an entertaining and classic extravaganza.

EUROPEAN CUP WINNERS' CUP

Year	Winners	Country	Score	Country	Runners-up
1961	Fiorentina	ITA	2-0 2-1	SCO	Rangers
1962	Atlético Madrid	ESP	1-1 3-0	ITA	Fiorentina
1963	Tottenham Hotspur	ENG	5-1	ESP	Atlético Madrid
1964	Sporting CP	POR	3-3 1-0	HUN	MTK Budapest
1965	West Ham United	ENG	2-0	FRG	TSV München 1860
1966	Borussia Dortmund	FRG	2-1	ENG	Liverpool
1967	Bayern München	FRG	1-0	SCO	Rangers
1968	Milan	ITA	2-0	FRG	Hamburger SV
1969	Slovan Bratislava	CZE	3-2	ESP	Barcelona
1970	Manchester City	ENG	2-1	POL	Gornik Zabrze
1971	Chelsea	ENG	1-1 2-1	ESP	Real Madrid
1972	Rangers	SCO	3-2	URS	Dynamo Moskva
1973	Milan	ITA	1-0	ENG	Leeds United
1974	1.FC Magdeburg	GDR	2-0	ITA	Milan
1975	Dynamo Kyiv	URS	3-0	HUN	Ferencváros
1976	RSC Anderlecht	BEL	4-2	ENG	West Ham United
1977	Hamburger SV	FRG	2-0	BEL	RSC Anderlecht
1978	RSC Anderlecht	BEL	4-0	AUT	FK Austria
1979	Barcelona	ESP	4-3	FRG	Fortuna Düsseldorf
1980	Valencia	ESP	0-0 5-4p	ENG	Arsenal
1981	Dynamo Tbilisi	URS	2-1	GDR	Carl Zeiss Jena
1982	Barcelona	ESP	2-1	BEL	Standard CL
1983	Aberdeen	SCO	2-1	ESP	Real Madrid
1984	Juventus	ITA	2-1	POR	FC Porto
1985	Everton	ENG	3-1	AUT	SK Rapid Wien
1986	Dynamo Kyiv	URS	3-0	ESP	Atlético Madrid
1987	Ajax	NED	1-0	GDR	Lokomotive Leipzig
1988	KV Mechelen	BEL	1-0	NED	Ajax
1989	Barcelona	ESP	2-0	ITA	Sampdoria
1990	Sampdoria	ITA	2-0	BEL	RSC Anderlecht
1991	Manchester United	ENG	2-1	ESP	Barcelona
1992	Werder Bremen	GER	2-0	FRA	Monaco
1993	Parma	ITA	3-1	BEL	Royal Antwerp FC
1994	Arsenal	ENG	1-0	ITA	Parma
1995	Real Zaragoza	ESP	2-1	ENG	Arsenal
1996	Paris Saint-Germain	FRA	1-0	AUT	SK Rapid Wien
1997	Barcelona	ESP	1-0	FRA	Paris Saint-Germain
1998	Chelsea	ENG	1-0	GER	VfB Stuttgart
1999	Lazio	ITA	2-1	ESP	Real Mallorca

Played between the winners of the various cup competitions around the continent for a period of 39 years, the Cup Winners' Cup was often seen as the weakest of the three UEFA tournaments given the varying degrees of public support for domestic Cup competitions. Another problem was the fact that it often resembled a cup runners-up cup given that the Cup winners often won the Championship as well and didn't take part. The expansion of the UEFA Champions League after 1997 to include more than just the champions meant that the writing was on the wall for the Cup Winners' Cup given the possibility of having to trawl the semi-finals to find an entrant and the last final was played in 1999. A glance at the list of winners, however, shows some classic teams and great games. English and Spanish clubs were especially strong, unsurprising perhaps given the prestige of the FA Cup and Copa del Rey and it is Barcelona who go down in history as the all time leading winners with four titles. England was the most sucessful nation overall with a total of eight triumphs compared to seven for both Spain and Italy. Perhaps UEFA should have bitten the bullet and scrapped the UEFA Cup at the same time as the Cup Winners' Cup and given Cup winners entry into an even further expanded UEFA Champions league.

PAST UEFA AWARDS

MOST VALUABLE PLAYER

1998	RONALDO	BRA	Internazionale
1999	BECKHAM David	ENG	Manchester United
2000	REDONDO Fernando	ARG	Real Madrid
2001	EFFENBERG Stefan	GER	Bayern München
2002	ZIDANE Zinedine	FRA	Real Madrid
2003	BUFFON Gianluigi	ITA	Juventus
2004	DECO	POR	FC Porto

BEST GOALKEEPER

1998	SCHMEICHEL Peter	DEN	Manchester United
1999	KAHN Oliver	GER	Bayern München
2000	KAHN Oliver	GER	Bayern München
2001	KAHN Oliver	GER	Bayern München
2002	KAHN Oliver	GER	Bayern München
2003	BUFFON Gianluigi	ITA	Juventus
2004	BAIA Vitor	POR	FC Porto

BEST DEFENDER

1998	HIERRO Fernando	ESP	Real Madrid
1999	STAM Jaap	NED	Manchester United
2000	STAM Jaap	NED	Manchester United
2001	AYALA Fabian	ARG	Valencia
2002	ROBERTO CARLOS	BRA	Real Madrid
2003	ROBERTO CARLOS	BRA	Real Madrid
2004	CARVALHO Ricardo	POR	FC Porto

BEST MIDFIELDER

1998	ZIDANE Zinedine	FRA	Juventus
1999	BECKHAM David	ENG	Manchester United
2000	MENDIETA Gaizka	ESP	Valencia
2001	MENDIETA Gaizka	ESP	Lazio
2002	BALLACK Michael	GER	Bayern München
2003	NEDVED Pavel	CZE	Juventus
2004	DECO	POR	FC Porto

BEST FORWARD

1998	RONALDO	BRA	Internazionale
1999	SHEVCHENKO Andriy	UKR	Milan
2000	RAUL	ESP	Real Madrid
2001	RAUL	ESP	Real Madrid
2002	VAN NISTELROOIJ Ruud	NED	Manchester United
2003	RAUL	ESP	Real Madrid
2004	MORIENTES Fernando	ESP	Monaco

COACH OF THE YEAR

1998	LIPPI Marcelo	ITA	Juventus
1999	FERGUSON Alex	SCO	Manchester United
2000	CUPER Hector	ARG	Valencia
2001	HITZFELD Ottmar	GER	Bayern München
2002	DEL BOSQUE Vicente	ESP	Real Madrid
2003	ANCELOTTI Carlo, ITA, Milan & MOURINHO Jose, POR, FC Porto		
2004	MOURINHO Jose, POR, FC Porto & BENITEZ Raffa, ESP, Valencia		

PAST EUROPEAN PLAYER OF THE YEAR AWARDS

The Ballon d'Or is awarded by *France Football* magazine and since 1995 has been open to non Europeans playing with European clubs

BALLON D'OR 1956

MATTHEWS Stanley	Blackpool	ENG	47
DI STEFANO Alfredo	Real Madrid	ESP	44
KOPA Raymond	Reims	FRA	33
PUSKAS Ferenc	Honved	HUN	32
YACHIN Lev	Dyn. Moskva	URS	19
BOZSIK Jozsef	Honved	HUN	15
OCWIRK Ernst	Sampdoria	AUT	9
KOCSIS Sandor	Honved	HUN	6
Three players with four votes			

BALLON D'OR 1957

DI STEFANO Alfredo	Real Madrid	ESP	72
WRIGHT Billy	Wolves	ENG	19
KOPA Raymond	Real Madrid	FRA	16
EDWARDS Duncan	Man United	ENG	16
KUBALA Lazslo	Barcelona	ESP	15
CHARLES John	Juventus	WAL	14
STRELITSOV Edward	Torp. Moskva	URS	12
TAYLOR Tommy	Man Utd	ENG	10
BOZSIK Jozsef	Honved	HUN	9
NETTO Igor	Dyn. Moskva	URS	9

BALLON D'OR 1958

KOPA Raymond	Real Madrid	FRA	71
RAHN Helmut	RW Essen	FRG	40
FONTAINE Just	Reims	FRA	23
HAMRIN Kurt	Fiorentina	SWE	15
CHARLES John	Juventus	WAL	15
WRIGHT Billy	Wolves	ENG	9
HAYNES Johnny	Fulham	ENG	7
GREGG Harry	Man United	NIR	6
SZYMANIAK Horst	Wuppertaler SV	FRG	6
LIEDHOLM Nils	Milan	SWE	6

BALLON D'OR 1959

DI STEFANO Alfredo	Real Madrid	ESP	80
KOPA Raymond	Reims	FRA	42
CHARLES John	Juventus	WAL	24
SUAREZ Luis	Barcelona	ESP	22
SIMONSSON Agne	Örgryte IS	SWE	20
TICHY Lajos	Honved	HUN	18
PUSKAS Ferenc	Real Madrid	HUN	16
GENTO Francisco	Real Madrid	ESP	12
RAHN Helmut	1.FC Köln	FRG	11
SZYMANIAK Horst	Karlsruher SC	FRG	8

BALLON D'OR 1960

SUAREZ Luis	Barcelona	ESP	54
PUSKAS Ferenc	Real Madrid	HUN	37
SEELER Uwe	Hamburger SV	FRG	33
DI STEFANO Alfredo	Real Madrid	ESP	32
YACHIN Lev	Dyn. Moskva	URS	28
KOPA Raymond	Reims	FRA	14
CHARLES John	Juventus	WAL	11
CHARLTON Bobby	Man United	ENG	11
SIVORI Omar	Juventus	ITA	9
SZYMANIAK Horst	Karlsruher SC	FRG	9

BALLON D'OR 1961

SIVORI Omar	Juventus	ITA	46
SUAREZ Luis	Internazionale	ESP	40
HAYNES Johnny	Fulham	ENG	22
YACHIN Lev	Dyn. Moskva	URS	21
PUSKAS Ferenc	Real Madrid	ESP	16
DI STEFANO Alfredo	Real Madrid	ESP	13
SEELER Uwe	Hamburger SV	FRG	13
CHARLES John	Juventus	WAL	10
GENTO Francisco	Real Madrid	ESP	8
Seven players with five votes			

BALLON D'OR 1962

MASOPUST Josef	Dukla Praha	CZE	65
EUSEBIO	Benfica	POR	53
SCHNELLINGER K-H	1.FC Köln	FRG	33
SEKULARAC Dragoslav	Crvena Zvezda	YUG	26
JURION Joseph	Anderlecht	BEL	15
RIVERA Gianni	Milan	ITA	14
GREAVES Jimmy	Tottenham	ENG	11
GALIC Milan	Partizan	YUG	10
CHARLES John	Roma	WAL	9
GOROCS Janos	Ujpesti Dózsa	HUN	6

BALLON D'OR 1963

YACHIN Lev	Dyn. Moskva	URS	73
RIVERA Gianni	Milan	ITA	56
GREAVES Jimmy	Tottenham	ENG	51
LAW Denis	Man United	SCO	45
EUSEBIO	Benfica	POR	19
SCHNELLINGER K-H	Mantova	FRG	16
SEELER Uwe	Hamburger SV	FRG	9
SUAREZ Luis	Internazionale	ESP	5
TRAPATTONI Giovanni	Milan	ITA	5
CHARLTON Bobby	Man United	ENG	5

BALLON D'OR 1964

LAW Denis	Man United	SCO	61
SUAREZ Luis	Internazionale	ESP	43
AMANCIO	Real Madrid	ESP	38
EUSEBIO	Benfica	POR	31
VAN HIMST Paul	Anderlecht	BEL	28
GREAVES Jimmy	Tottenham	ENG	19
CORSO Mario	Internazionale	ITA	17
YACHIN Lev	Dyn. Moskva	URS	15
RIVERA Gianni	Milan	ITA	14
VORONIN Valerie	Torp. Moskva	URS	13

BALLON D'OR 1965

EUSEBIO	Benfica	POR	67
FACCHETTI Giacinto	Internazionale	ITA	59
SUAREZ Luis	Internazionale	ITA	45
VAN HIMST Paul	Anderlecht	BEL	25
CHARLTON Bobby	Man United	ENG	19
ALBERT Florian	Ferencváros	HUN	14
RIVERA Gianni	Milan	ITA	10
ASPARUCHOV Georgi	Levski Sofia	BUL	9
MAZZOLA Sandro	Internazionale	ITA	9
VORONIN Valerie	Torp. Moskva	URS	9

BALLON D'OR 1966

CHARLTON Bobby	Man United	ENG	81
EUSEBIO	Benfica	POR	80
BECKENBAUER Franz	Bayern	FRG	59
MOORE Bobby	West Ham Utd	ENG	31
ALBERT Florian	Ferencváros	HUN	23
BENE Ferenc	Ujpesti Dózsa	HUN	8
YACHIN Lev	Dyn. Moskva	URS	6
BALL Alan	Everton	ENG	6
FARKAS János	Vasas	HUN	6
TORRES José	Benfica	POR	5

BALLON D'OR 1967

ALBERT Florian	Ferencváros	HUN	68
CHARLTON Bobby	Man United	ENG	40
JOHNSTONE Jimmy	Celtic	SCO	39
BECKENBAUER Franz	Bayern	FRG	37
EUSEBIO	Benfica	POR	26
GEMMEL Tommy	Celtic	SCO	21
MULLER Gerd	Bayern	FRG	19
BEST George	Man United	NIR	18
CHISLENKO Igor	Torp. Moskva	URS	9
Three players with eight votes			

BALLON D'OR 1968

BEST George	Man United	NIR	61
CHARLTON Bobby	Man United	ENG	53
DZAJIC Dragan	Crvena Zvezda	YUG	46
BECKENBAUER Franz	Bayern	FRG	36
FACCHETTI Giacinto	Internazionale	ITA	30
RIVA Gigi	Cagliari	ITA	22
AMANCIO	Real Madrid	ESP	20
EUSEBIO	Benfica	POR	15
RIVERA Gianni	Milan	ITA	13
Two players with eight votes			

BALLON D'OR 1969

RIVERA Gianni	Milan	ITA	83
RIVA Gigi	Cagliari	ITA	79
MULLER Gerd	Bayern	FRG	38
CRUYFF Johan	Ajax	NED	30
KINDVALL Ove	Feyenoord	SWE	30
BEST George	Man United	ENG	21
BECKENBAUER Franz	Bayern	FRG	18
PRATI Pierino	Milan	ITA	17
JEKOV Peter	CSKA Sofia	BUL	14
CHARLTON Jackie	Leeds United	ENG	10

BALLON D'OR 1970

MULLER Gerd	Bayern	FRG	77
MOORE Bobby	West Ham Utd	ENG	69
RIVA Gigi	Cagliari	ITA	65
BECKENBAUER Franz	Bayern	FRG	32
Wolfgang Overath	1.FC Köln	FRG	29
DZAJIC Dragan	Crvena Zvezda	YUG	24
CRUYFF Johan	Ajax	NED	13
BANKS Gordon	Stoke City	ENG	8
MAZZOLA Sandro	Internazionale	ITA	8
Four players with seven votes			

BALLON D'OR 1971

CRUYFF Johan	Ajax	NED	116
MAZZOLA Sandro	Internazionale	ITA	57
BEST George	Man United	NIR	56
NETZER Gunter	Gladbach	FRG	30
BECKENBAUER Franz	Bayern	FRG	27
MULLER Gerd	Bayern	FRG	18
SKOBLAR Josip	Marseille	YUG	18
CHIVERS Martin	Tottenham	ENG	13
KEIZER Piet	Ajax	NED	9
Two players with seven votes			

BALLON D'OR 1972

BECKENBAUER Franz	Bayern	FRG	81
MULLER Gerd	Bayern	FRG	79
NETZER Gunter	Gladbach	FRG	79
CRUYFF Johan	Ajax	NED	73
KEIZER Piet	Ajax	NED	13
DEYNA Kazimierz	Legia	POL	6
BANKS Gordon	Stoke City	ENG	4
HULSHOFF Barry	Ajax	NED	4
LUBANSKI Wlodzmierz	Gornik Zabrze	POL	4
MOORE Bobby	West Ham Utd	ENG	4

BALLON D'OR 1973

CRUYFF Johan	Barcelona	NED	96
ZOFF Dino	Juventus	ITA	47
MULLER Gerd	Bayern	FRG	44
BECKENBAUER Franz	Bayern	FRG	30
BREMNER Billy	Leeds United	SCO	22
DEYNA Kazimierz	Legia	POL	16
EUSEBIO	Benfica	POR	14
RIVERA Gianni	Milan	ITA	12
EDSTROM Ralf	Eindhoven	SWE	11
HOENESS Uli	Bayern	FRG	11

BALLON D'OR 1974

CRUYFF Johan	Barcelona	NED	116
BECKENBAUER Franz	Bayern	FRG	105
DEYNA Kazimierz	Legia	POL	35
BREITNER Paul	Real Madrid	FRG	32
NEESKENS Johan	Barcelona	NED	21
LATO Grzegorz	Stal Mielec	POL	16
MULLER Gerd	Bayern	FRG	14
GADOCHA Robert	Legia	POL	11
BREMNER Billy	Leeds United	SCO	9
Three players with four votes			

BALLON D'OR 1975

BLOKHIN Oleg	Dynamo Kiev	URS	122
BECKENBAUER Franz	Bayern	FRG	42
CRUYFF Johan	Barcelona	NED	27
VOGTS Berti	Gladbach	FRG	25
MAIER Sepp	Bayern	FRG	20
GEELS Ruud	Ajax	NED	18
HEYNCKES Jupp	Gladbach	FRG	17
BREITNER Paul	Real Madrid	FRG	14
TODD Colin	Derby County	ENG	12
GEORGESCU Dudu	Din. Bucuresti	ROM	11

BALLON D'OR 1976

BECKENBAUER Franz	Bayern	FRG	91
RENSENBRINK Rob	Anderlecht	NED	75
VIKTOR Ivo	Dukla Praha	CZE	52
KEEGAN Kevin	Liverpool	ENG	32
PLATINI Michel	AS Nancy	FRA	19
ONDRUS Anton	Slovan	CZE	16
CRUYFF Johan	Barcelona	NED	12
CURKOVIC Ivan	Saint-Etienne	YUG	12
Three players with nine votes			

BALLON D'OR 1977

SIMONSEN Allan	Gladbach	DEN	74
KEEGAN Kevin	Liverpool	ENG	71
PLATINI Michel	AS Nancy	FRA	70
BETTEGA Roberto	Juventus	ITA	39
CRUYFF Johan	Barcelona	NED	23
FISCHER Klaus	Schalke 04	FRG	21
NYILASI Tibor	Ferencváros	HUN	13
RENSENBRINK Rob	Anderlecht	NED	13
GEORGESCU Dudu	Din. Bucuresti	ROU	6
3 players with 5 votes			

BALLON D'OR 1978

KEEGAN Kevin	Hamburger SV	ENG	87
KRANKL Hans	Rapid Wien	AUT	81
RENSENBRINK Rob	Anderlecht	NED	50
BETTEGA Roberto	Juventus	ITA	28
ROSSI Paolo	Vicenza	ITA	23
HELLSTROM Ronnie	Kaiserslautern	SWE	20
KROL Ruud	Ajax	NED	20
DALGLISH Kenny	Liverpool	SCO	10
SIMONSEN Allan	Gladbach	DEN	10
SHILTON Peter	Nottm Forest	ENG	9

BALLON D'OR 1979

KEEGAN Kevin	Hamburger SV	ENG	118
RUMMENIGGE K-H	Bayern	FRG	52
KROL Ruud	Ajax	NED	41
KALTZ Manni	Hamburger SV	FRG	27
PLATINI Michel	Saint-Etienne	FRA	23
ROSSI Paolo	Perugia	ITA	16
BRADY Liam	Arsenal	IRL	13
FRANCIS Trevor	Nottm Forest	ENG	13
BONIEK Zbigniew	Wisla Krakow	POL	9
NEHODA Zdenek	Dukla Praha	CZE	9

BALLON D'OR 1980

RUMMENIGGE K-H	Bayern	FRG	122
SCHUSTER Bernd	Barcelona	FRG	34
PLATINI Michel	Saint-Etienne	FRA	33
VAN MOER Wilfred	SK Beveren	BEL	27
CEULEMANS Jan	Club Brugge	BEL	20
HRUBESCH Horst	Hamburger SV	FRG	18
PROHASKA Herbert	Internazionale	AUT	16
MULLER Hansi	VfB Stuttgart	FRG	11
BRADY Liam	Juventus	IRL	11
KALTZ Manni	Hamburger SV	FRG	10

BALLON D'OR 1981

RUMMENIGGE K-H	Bayern	FRG	106
BREITNER Paul	Bayern	FRG	64
SCHUSTER Bernd	Barcelona	FRG	39
PLATINI Michel	Saint-Etienne	FRA	36
BLOKHIN Oleg	Dynamo Kyiv	URS	14
ZOFF Dino	Juventus	ITA	13
SHENGELIA Ramas	Dynamo Tbilisi	URS	10
CHIVADZE Alexander	Dynamo Tbilisi	URS	9
BRADY Liam	Juventus	IRL	7
WARK John	Ipswich Town	SCO	7

BALLON D'OR 1982

ROSSI Paolo	Juventus	ITA	115
GIRESSE Alain	Bordeaux	FRA	64
BONIEK Zbigniew	Juventus	POL	53
RUMMENIGGE K-H	Bayern	FRG	51
CONTI Bruno	Roma	ITA	48
DASAYEV Rinat	Spartak Moskva	URS	17
LITTBARSKI Pierre	1.FC Köln	FRG	10
ZOFF Dino	Juventus	ITA	9
PLATINI Michel	Juventus	FRA	5
SCHUSTER Bernd	Barcelona	FRG	4

BALLON D'OR 1983

PLATINI Michel	Juventus	FRA	110
DALGLISH Kenny	Liverpool	SCO	26
SIMONSEN Allan	Vejle BK	DEN	25
STRACHAN Gordon	Aberdeen	SCO	24
MAGATH Felix	Hamburger SV	FRG	20
DASAYEV Rinat	Spartak Moskva	URS	15
PFAFF Jean-Marie	Bayern	BEL	15
OLSEN Jesper	Ajax	DEN	14
RUMMENIGGE K-H	Bayern	FRG	14
ROBSON Bryan	Man United	ENG	13

BALLON D'OR 1984

PLATINI Michel	Juventus	FRA	128
TIGANA Jean	Bordeaux	FRA	57
ELKJAER Preben	Hellas Verona	DEN	48
RUSH Ian	Liverpool	WAL	44
CHALANA	Bordeaux	POR	18
SOUNESS Graeme	Sampdoria	SCO	16
SCHUMACHER Harald	1.FC Köln	FRG	12
RUMMENIGGE K-H	Internazionale	FRG	10
GIRESSE Alain	Bordeaux	FRA	9
ROBSON Bryan	Man United	ENG	7

BALLON D'OR 1985

PLATINI Michel	Juventus	FRA	127
ELKJAER Preben	Hellas Verona	DEN	71
SCHUSTER Bernd	Barcelona	FRG	46
LAUDRUP Michael	Juventus	DEN	14
RUMMENIGGE K-H	Internazionale	FRG	13
BONIEK Zbigniew	Roma	POL	12
PROTASOV Oleg	Dnepr	URS	10
BRIEGEL Hans-Peter	Hellas Verona	FRG	9
DASAYEV Rinat	Spartak Moskva	URS	8
ROBSON Bryan	Man United	ENG	8

BALLON D'OR 1986

BELANOV Igor	Dynamo Kyiv	URS	84
LINEKER Gary	Barcelona	ENG	62
BUTRAGUENO Emilio	Real Madrid	ESP	59
AMOROS Manuel	Monaco	FRA	22
ELKJAER Preben	Hellas Verona	DEN	22
RUSH Ian	Liverpool	WAL	20
ZAVAROV Alexander	Dynamo Kyiv	URS	20
VAN BASTEN Marco	Ajax	NED	10
DUCADAM Helmut	Steaua	ROU	10
ALTOBELLI Alessandro	Internazionale	ITA	9

BALLON D'OR 1987

GULLIT Ruud	Milan	NED	106
FUTRE Paolo	Atlético Madrid	POR	91
BUTRAGUENO Emilio	Real Madrid	ESP	61
MICHEL Gonzales	Real Madrid	ESP	29
LINEKER Gary	Barcelona	ENG	13
BARNES John	Liverpool	ENG	10
VAN BASTEN Marco	Milan	NED	10
VIALLI Gianluca	Sampdoria	ITA	9
ROBSON Bryan	Man United	ENG	7
ALLOFS Klaus	Marseille	FRG	6

BALLON D'OR 1988

VAN BASTEN Marco	Milan	NED	129
GULLIT Ruud	Milan	NED	88
RIJKAARD Frank	Milan	NED	45
MIKHAILICHENKO Alex	Dynamo Kyiv	URS	41
KOEMAN Ronald	PSV	NED	39
MATTHAUS Lothar	Bayern	FRG	10
VIALLI Gianluca	Sampdoria	ITA	7
BARESI Franco	Milan	ITA	5
KLINSMANN Jürgen	VfB Stuttgart	FRG	5
ZAVAROV Alexander	Juventus	URS	5

BALLON D'OR 1989

VAN BASTEN Marco	Milan	NED	119
BARESI Franco	Milan	ITA	80
RIJKAARD Frank	Milan	NED	43
MATTHAUS Lothar	Internazionale	FRG	24
SHILTON Peter	Derby County	ENG	22
STOJKOVIC Dragan	Crvena Zvezda	YUG	19
GULLIT Ruud	Milan	NED	16
HAGI Georgi	Steaua	ROU	11
KLINSMANN Jürgen	Internazionale	FRG	11
Two players with 10 votes			

BALLON D'OR 1990

MATTHAUS Lothar	Internazionale	FRG	137
SCHILLACI Salvadore	Juventus	ITA	84
BREHME Andreas	Internazionale	FRG	68
GASCOIGNE Paul	Tottenham	ENG	43
BARESI Franco	Milan	ITA	37
KLINSMANN Jürgen	Internazionale	FRG	12
SCIFO Enzo	AJ Auxerre	BEL	12
BAGGIO Roberto	Juventus	ITA	8
RIJKAARD Frank	Milan	NED	7
BUCHWALD Guido	VfB Stuttgart	FRG	6

BALLON D'OR 1991

PAPIN Jean-Pierre	Marseille	FRA	141
PANCEV Darko	Crvena Zvezda	YUG	42
SAVICEVIC Dejan	Crvena Zvezda	YUG	42
MATTHAUS Lothar	Internazionale	FRG	42
PROSINECKI Robert	Real Madrid	YUG	34
LINEKER Gary	Tottenham	ENG	33
VIALLI Gianluca	Sampdoria	ITA	18
BELODEDIC Miodrag	Crvena Zvezda	YUG	15
HUGHES Mark	Man United	WAL	12
WADDLE Chris	Marseille	ENG	11

BALLON D'OR 1992

VAN BASTEN Marco	Milan	NED	98
STOICHKOV Hristo	Barcelona	BUL	80
BERGKAMP Dennis	Ajax	NED	53
HASSLER Thomas	Roma	GER	42
SCHMEICHEL Peter	Man United	DEN	41
LAUDRUP Brian	Fiorentina	DEN	32
LAUDRUP Michael	Barcelona	DEN	22
KOEMAN Ronald	Barcelona	NED	14
CHAPUISAT Stéphane	Dortmund	SUI	10
Two players with eight votes			

BALLON D'OR 1993

BAGGIO Roberto	Juventus	ITA	142
BERGKAMP Dennis	Internazionale	NED	83
CANTONA Eric	Man United	FRA	34
BOKSIC Alen	Lazio	CRO	29
LAUDRUP Michael	Barcelona	DEN	27
BARESI Franco	Milan	ITA	24
MALDINI Paolo	Milan	ITA	19
KOSTADINOV Emil	FC Porto	BUL	11
CHAPUISAT Stéphane	Dortmund	SUI	9
GIGGS Ryan	Man United	WAL	9

BALLON D'OR 1994

STOICHKOV Hristo	Barcelona	BUL	210
BAGGIO Roberto	Juventus	ITA	136
MALDINI Paolo	Milan	ITA	109
BROLIN Tomas	Parma	SWE	68
HAGI Georghe	Barcelona	ROU	68
KLINSMANN Jürgen	Tottenham	GER	43
RAVELLI Thomas	IFK Göteborg	SWE	21
LITMANEN Jari	Ajax	FIN	12
DESAILLY Marcel	Milan	FRA	8
SAVICEVIC Dejan	Milan	YUG	8

BALLON D'OR 1995

WEAH George	Milan	LBR	144
KLINSMANN Jürgen	Bayern	GER	108
LITMANEN Jari	Ajax	FIN	67
DEL PIERO Alex	Juventus	ITA	57
KLUIVERT Patrick	Ajax	NED	47
ZOLA Gianfranco	Parma	ITA	41
MALDINI Paolo	Milan	ITA	36
OVERMARS Marc	Ajax	NED	33
SAMMER Matthias	Dortmund	GER	18
LAUDRUP Michael	Real Madrid	DEN	17

BALLON D'OR 1996

SAMMER Matthias	Dortmund	GER	144
RONALDO	Barcelona	BRA	141
SHEARER Alan	Newcastle Utd	ENG	109
DEL PIERO Alex	Juventus	ITA	65
KLINSMANN Jürgen	Bayern	GER	60
SUKER Davor	Real Madrid	CRO	38
CANTONA Eric	Man United	FRA	24
DESAILLY Marcel	Milan	FRA	22
DJORKAEFF Youri	Internazionale	FRA	20
WEAH George	Milan	LBR	17

BALLON D'OR 1997

RONALDO	Internazionale	BRA	222
MIJATOVIC Predrag	Real Madrid	YUG	72
ZIDANE Zinedine	Juventus	FRA	63
BERGKAMP Dennis	Arsenal	NED	53
ROBERTO CARLOS	Real Madrid	BRA	47
MOLLER Andreas	Dortmund	GER	40
RAUL	Real Madrid	ESP	35
SCHMEICHEL Peter	Man United	DEN	19
KOHLER Jürgen	Dortmund	GER	17
Two players with 16 votes			

BALLON D'OR 1998

ZIDANE Zinedine	Juventus	FRA	244
SUKER Davor	Real Madrid	CRO	68
RONALDO	Internazionale	BRA	66
OWEN Michael	Liverpool	ENG	51
RIVALDO	Barcelona	BRA	45
BATISTUTA Gabriel	Fiorentina	ARG	43
THURAM Lilian	Parma	FRA	36
BERGKAMP Dennis	Arsenal	NED	28
DAVIDS Edgar	Juventus	NED	28
DESAILLY Marcel	Chelsea	FRA	19

BALLON D'OR 1999

RIVALDO	Barcelona	BRA	219
BECKHAM David	Man United	ENG	154
SHEVCHENKO Andriy	Milan	UKR	64
BATISTUTA Gabriel	Fiorentina	ARG	48
FIGO Luis	Barcelona	POR	38
KEANE Roy	Man United	IRL	36
VIERI Christian	Internazionale	ITA	33
VERON Juan Seb.	Lazio	ARG	30
RAUL	Real Madrid	ESP	27
MATTHAUS Lothar	Bayern	GER	16

BALLON D'OR 2000

FIGO Luis	Real Madrid	POR	197
ZIDANE Zinedine	Juventus	FRA	181
SHEVCHENKO Andriy	Milan	UKR	85
HENRY Thierry	Arsenal	FRA	57
NESTA Alessandro	Lazio	ITA	39
RIVALDO	Barcelona	BRA	39
BATISTUTA Gabriel	Roma	ARG	26
MENDIETA Gaizka	Valencia	ESP	22
RAUL	Real Madrid	ESP	18
Two players with 10 votes			

BALLON D'OR 2001

OWEN Michael	Liverpool	ENG	176
RAUL	Real Madrid	ESP	140
KAHN Oliver	Bayern	GER	114
BECKHAM David	Man United	ENG	102
TOTTI Francesco	Roma	ITA	57
FIGO Luis	Real Madrid	POR	56
RIVALDO	Barcelona	BRA	20
SHEVCHENKO Andriy	Milan	UKR	18
HENRY Thierry	Arsenal	FRA	14
ZIDANE Zinedine	Real Madrid	FRA	14

BALLON D'OR 2002

RONALDO	Real Madrid	BRA	171
ROBERTO CARLOS	Real Madrid	BRA	145
KAHN Oliver	Bayern	GER	114
ZIDANE Zinedine	Real Madrid	FRA	78
BALLACK Michael	Bayern	GER	67
HENRY Thierry	Arsenal	FRA	54
RAUL	Real Madrid	ESP	38
RIVALDO	Milan	BRA	29
BASTURK Yildiray	Leverkusen	TUR	13
DEL PIERO Alex	Juventus	ITA	12

BALLON D'OR 2003

NEDVED Pavel	Juventus	CZE	190
HENRY Thierry	Arsenal	FRA	128
MALDINI Paolo	Milan	ITA	123
SHEVCHENKO Andriy	Milan	UKR	67
ZIDANE Zinedine	Real Madrid	FRA	64
VAN NISTELROOY Ruud	Man United	NED	61
RAUL	Real Madrid	ESP	32
ROBERTO CARLOS	Real Madrid	BRA	27
BUFFON Gianluigi	Juventus	ITA	19
BECKHAM David	Real Madrid	ENG	17

BALLON D'OR 2004

SHEVCHENKO Andriy	Milan	UKR	175
DECO	Barcelona	POR	139
RONALDINHO	Barcelona	BRA	133
HENRY Thierry	Arsenal	FRA	80
ZAGORAKIS Theodoros	Bologna	GRE	44
ADRIANO	Internazionale	BRA	23
NEDVED Pavel	Juventus	CZE	23
ROONEY Wayne	Man United	ENG	22
RICARDO CARVALHO	Chelsea	POR	18
VAN NISTELROOY Ruud	Man United	NED	18

UEFA CHAMPIONS LEAGUE 2004-05

First Preliminary Round

Team			
Flora Tallinn	EST	2	1
Gorica	SVN	4	3
KR Reykjavík	ISL	2	0
Shelbourne	IRL	2	0
WIT Georgia	GEO	5	0
HB Tórshavn	FRO	0	3
Skonto Riga	LVA	4	3
Rhyl	WAL	0	1
Sliema Wanderers	MLT	0	1
FBK Kaunas	LTU	2	4
Linfield	NIR	0	0
HJK Helsinki	FIN	1	1
Gomel	BLR	0	1
SK Tiranë	ALB	2	0
Sheriff Tiraspol	MDA	2	0
Jeuness d'Esch	LUX	0	1
Pobeda	MKD	1	1
Pyunik Yerevan	ARM	3	1
Siroki Brijeg	BIH	2	0
Neftchi Baku	AZE	1	1

Second Preliminary Round

Team			
Gorica	SVN	1	5
FC København	DEN	2	0
Hajduk Split	CRO	3	0
Shelbourne	IRL	2	2
WIT Georgia	GEO	2	0
Wisla Krakow	POL	8	3
Skonto Riga	LVA	1	0
Trabzonspor	TUR	1	3
Djurgårdens IF	SWE	0	2
FBK Kaunas	LTU	0	0
HJK Helsinki	FIN	0	0
Maccabi Tel Aviv	ISR	0	1
MSK Zilina	SVK	0	0
Dinamo Bucuresti	ROM	1	1
SK Tiranë	ALB	2	1
Ferencváros	HUN	3	0
APOEL Nicosia	CYP	2	1
Sparta Praha	CZE	2	2
Young Boys Berne	SUI	2	0
Crvena Zvezda	SCG	2	3
Rosenborg BK	NOR	2	2
Sheriff Tiraspol	MDA	1	0
Pyunik Yerevan	ARM	1	0
Shakhtar Donetsk	UKR	3	1
Club Brugge	BEL	2	4
Lokomotiv Plovdiv	BUL	0	0
Neftchi Baku	AZE	0	0
CSKA Moskva	RUS	0	2

Third Preliminary Round

Team			
Gorica	SVN	0	0
Monaco	FRA	3	6
Grazer AK	AUT	0	1
Liverpool	ENG	2	0
Shelbourne	IRL	0	0
Deportivo La Coruna	ESP	0	3
Bayer Leverkusen	GER	5	1
Banik Ostrava	CZE	0	2
Wisla Krakow	POL	0	1
Real Madrid	ESP	2	3
Dynamo Kyiv	UKR	1	2
Trabzonspor	TUR	2	0
Juventus	ITA	2	4
Djurgårdens IF	SWE	2	1
PAOK Salonika	GRE	1	0
Maccabi Tel Aviv †	ISR	2	1
Dinamo Bucuresti	ROM	1	0
Manchester United	ENG	2	3
Ferencváros	HUN	1	0
Sparta Praha	CZE	0	2
Crvena Zvezda	SCG	3	0
PSV Eindhoven	NED	2	5
Rosenborg BK	NOR	2	3
Maccabi Haifa	ISR	1	2
Shakhtar Donetsk	UKR	4	2
Club Brugge	BEL	1	2
FC Basel	SUI	1	1
Internazionale	ITA	1	4
Benfica	POR	1	0
RSC Anderlecht	BEL	0	3
CSKA Moskva	RUS	2	1
Rangers	SCO	1	1

Group Stage

Group A		Pts
Monaco	FRA	12
Liverpool	ENG	10
Olympiacos	GRE	10
Deportivo La Coruna	ESP	2

Group B		Pts
Bayer Leverkusen	GER	11
Real Madrid	ESP	11
Dynamo Kyiv	UKR	10
Roma	ITA	1

Group C		Pts
Juventus	ITA	16
Bayern München	GER	10
Ajax	NED	4
Maccabi Tel Aviv	ISR	4

Group D		Pts
Olymp. Lyonnais	FRA	13
Manchester United	ENG	11
Fenerbahçe	TUR	9
Sparta Praha	CZE	1

Group E		Pts
Arsenal	ENG	10
PSV Eindhoven	NED	10
Panathinaikos	GRE	9
Rosenborg BK	NOR	2

Group F		Pts
Milan	ITA	13
Barcelona	ESP	10
Shakhtar Donetsk	UKR	6
Celtic	SCO	5

Group G		Pts
Internazionale	ITA	14
Werder Bremen	GER	13
Valencia	ESP	7
RSC Anderlecht	BEL	0

Group H		Pts
Chelsea	ENG	13
FC Porto	POR	8
CSKA Moskva	RUS	7
Paris Saint-Germain	FRA	5

† Maccabi Tel Aviv awarded first leg 3-0 after PAOK fielded an ineligible player • In each preliminary round tie the home team in the first leg is listed above their opponents • Teams placed third in the group stage qualify for the UEFA Cup

UEFA CHAMPIONS LEAGUE 2004-05

Second Round			Quarter-finals			Semi-finals			Final		
Liverpool *	3	3									
Bayer Leverkusen	1	1									
			Liverpool *	2	0						
			Juventus	1	0						
Real Madrid *	1	0									
Juventus	0	2									
						Liverpool	0	1			
						Chelsea *	0	0			
Bayern München *	3	0									
Arsenal	1	1									
			Bayern München	2	3						
			Chelsea *	4	2						
Barcelona *	2	2									
Chelsea	1	4									
									Liverpool	3	3p
									Milan	3	2p
PSV Eindhoven *	1	2									
AS Monaco	0	0									
			PSV Eindhoven	1	1 4p						
			Olympique Lyonnais*	1	1 2p						
Werder Bremen *	0	2									
Olympique Lyonnais	3	7									
						PSV Eindhoven	0	3			
						Milan *	2	1			
Internazionale	1	3									
FC Porto *	1	1									
			Internazionale	0	0						
			Milan *	2	3						
Manchester United *	0	0									
Milan	1	1									

* Home team in first leg

1ST PRELIM ROUND 1ST LEG
A Le Coq Arena, Tallinn
14-07-2004, Thomson SCO

Flora Tallinn	2
Zahovalko [81], Post [90]	
NK Gorica	4
Srebrnic [30], Krsic [73], Rodic [75], Panic [90]	

1ST PRELIM ROUND 2ND LEG
Sportni Park, Nova Gorica
21-07-2004, Zografos GRE

NK Gorica	3
Kokot [17p], Sturm 2 [50] [52]	
Flora Tallinn	1
Zahovaiko [68]	

1ST PRELIM ROUND 1ST LEG
Laugardalsvöllur, Reykjavík
14-07-2004, Vervecken BEL

KR Reykjavík	2
Sigurgeirsson [47], Olafsson [54]	
Shelbourne	2
Moore [83], Sigurdsson OG [86]	

1ST PRELIM ROUND 2ND LEG
Tolka Park, Dublin
21-07-2004, Svendsen DEN

Shelbourne	0
KR Reykjavík	0

1ST PRELIM ROUND 1ST LEG
Boris Palchadze, Tbilisi
14-07-2004, Theodotou CYP

WIT Georgia	5
Gochashvili [20], Martsvaladze [32], Digmelashvili [43], Intskirveli [47], Ebanoldze [57]	
HB Tórshavn	0

1ST PRELIM ROUND 2ND LEG
Tórsvøllur, Tórshavn
21-07-2004, Stokes IRL

HB Tórshavn	3
Thorsteinsson [66], Jespersen [69], Eliasen [88]	
WIT Georgia	0

1ST PRELIM ROUND 1ST LEG
Skonto, Riga
14-07-2004, Haverkort NED

Skonto Riga	4
Miholaps 2 [10] [56], Dedura [65], Visnakovs [78]	
Rhyl	0

1ST PRELIM ROUND 2ND LEG
Belle Vue, Rhyl
21-07-2004, Sowa AUT

Rhyl	1
Powell [50]	
Skonto Riga	3
Dedura [45], Miholaps 2 [80] [88]	

1ST PRELIM ROUND 1ST LEG
Ta'Qali Stadium, Ta'Qali
13-07-2004, McCourt NIR

Sliema Wanderers	0
FBK Kaunas	2
Zutautas [55], Sanajevas [77]	

1ST PRELIM ROUND 2ND LEG
Dariaus ir Gireno, Kaunas
21-07-2004, Matejek CZE

FBK Kaunas	4
Gedgaudas [28], Sanajevas [43], Mikoliunas [53], Zaliukas [90]	
Sliema Wanderers	1
Mifsud [71]	

1ST PRELIM ROUND 1ST LEG
Windsor Park, Belfast
14-07-2004, Johannesson SWE

Linfield	0
HJK Helsinki	1
Kottila [76]	

1ST PRELIM ROUND 2ND LEG
Pohjola, Vantaa
21-07-2004, Berezka UKR

HJK Helsinki	1
Kottila [27]	
Linfield	0

1ST PRELIM ROUND 1ST LEG
Tsentralny, Gomel
14-07-2004, Sandmoen NOR

FC Gomel	0
SK Tiranë	2
Mukaj [75], Fortuzi [89]	

1ST PRELIM ROUND 2ND LEG
Qemal Stafa, Tirana
21-07-2004, Serea ROM

SK Tiranë	0
FC Gomel	1
Blizniuk [38]	

1ST PRELIM ROUND 1ST LEG
Sheriff, Tiraspol
14-07-2004, Megyebiro HUN

Sheriff Tiraspol	2
Priganiuc [32], Kuznetsov [67]	
Jeunesse d'Esch	0

1ST PRELIM ROUND 2ND LEG
La Frontière, Esch sur Alzette
21-07-2004, Kovacic CRO

Jeunesse d'Esch	1
Cardoni [61]	
Sheriff Tiraspol	0

1ST PRELIM ROUND 1ST LEG
Gradski, Skopje
13-07-2004, Skomina SVN

FC Pobeda	1
Gesoski [80]	
Pyunik Yerevan	3
Manucharyan 2 [15] [41], Hovhannisyan [26]	

1ST PRELIM ROUND 2ND LEG
Republican, Yerevan
21-07-2004, Wildhaber SUI

Pyunik Yerevan	1
Galust Petrosyan [77]	
FC Pobeda	1
Dimitrovski [21]	

1ST PRELIM ROUND 1ST LEG
Pecara, Siroki Brijeg
13-07-2004, Ryszka POL

NK Siroki Brijeg	2
Tabi [67], Jurcic [75]	
Neftchi Baku	1
Tagizade [90]	

1ST PRELIM ROUND 2ND LEG
Tofikh Bakhramov, Baku
21-07-2004, Havrilla SVK

Neftchi Baku	1
Guliyev [80]	
NK Siroki Brijeg	0

2ND PRELIM ROUND 1ST LEG

Sportni Park, Nova Gorica

27-07-2004, Malcolm NIR

NK Gorica	1
	Rodic [57]
FC København	2
	Santos [44], Møller [77]

2ND PRELIM ROUND 2ND LEG

Parken, Copenhagen

4-08-2004, Lehner AUT

FC København	0
NK Gorica	5
	Rodic 2 [28 52], Sturm 2 [39 77], Srebrnic [45]

2ND PRELIM ROUND 1ST LEG

Poljud, Split

28-07-2004, Kassai HUN

Hajduk Split	3
	Blatnjak 2 [18 85], Suto [48]
Shelbourne	2
	Fitzpatrick [5], Moore [89]

2ND PRELIM ROUND 2ND LEG

Tolka Park, Dublin

4-08-2004, Sukhina RUS

Shelbourne	2
	Rogers [78], Moore [90]
Hajduk Split	0

2ND PRELIM ROUND 1ST LEG

Boris Paichadze, Tbilisi

27-07-2004, Staberg NOR

WIT Georgia	2
	Kobiashvili [13], Adamia [51]
Wisla Krakow	8
	Frankowski 4 [4 5 26 51], Gorawski [24], Zurawski 2 [58 67], Kuzba [76]

2ND PRELIM ROUND 2ND LEG

Wisly, Krakow

4-08-2004, Panic BIH

Wisla Krakow	3
	Kuzba [23], Omeonu [35], Gorawski [63]
WIT Georgia	0

2ND PRELIM ROUND 1ST LEG

Skonto, Riga

28-07-2004, Kircher GER

Skonto Riga	1
	Kalnins [67]
Trabzonspor	1
	Mehmet Yilmaz [86]

2ND PRELIM ROUND 2ND LEG

Hüseyin Avni Aker, Trabzon

4-04-2004, Gumienny BEL

Trabzonspor	3
	Yattara [57], Mehmet Yilmaz [65], Fatih Tekke [83]
Skonto Riga	0

2ND PRELIM ROUND 1ST LEG

Råsunda, Stockholm

28-07-2004, Balaj ROM

Djurgårdens IF	0
FBK Kaunas	0

2ND PRELIM ROUND 2ND LEG

Darius & Gireno, Kaunas

4-08-2004, Tanovic

FBK Kaunas	0
Djurgårdens IF	2
	Johansson.A [25], Barsom [68]

2ND PRELIM ROUND 1ST LEG

Pohjola, Vantaa

27-07-2004, Tiumin RUS

HJK Helsinki	0
Maccabi Tel Aviv	0

2ND PRELIM ROUND 2ND LEG

Bloomfield, Tel Aviv

4-08-2004, Bebek, CRO

Maccabi Tel Aviv	1
	Cohen.L [88]
HJK Helsinki	0

2ND PRELIM ROUND 1ST LEG

Pod Dubnon, Zilina

28-07-2004, Dereli TUR

MSK Zilina	0
Dinamo Bucuresti	1
	Danciulescu [89]

2ND PRELIM ROUND 2ND LEG

Dinamo, Bucharest

4-08-2004, Kelly IRL

Dinamo Bucuresti	1
	Danciulescu [19]
MSK Zilina	0

2ND PRELIM ROUND 1ST LEG

Qemal Stafa, Tirana

27-07-2004, Demirlek TUR

SK Tiranë	2
	Mukaj 2 [58 68]
Ferencváros	3
	Huszti 2 [41p 90], Hajdari OG [88]

2ND PRELIM ROUND 2ND LEG

Üllöi úti, Budapest

4-08-2004, Richmond SCO

Ferencváros	0
SK Tiranë	1
	Mukaj [13]

2ND PRELIM ROUND 1ST LEG

GSP, Nicosia

28-07-2004, Undiano Mallenco ESP

APOEL Nicosia	2
	Alexandrou [6], Charalambides [47]
Sparta Praha	2
	Pacanda [82], Sivok [89]

2ND PRELIM ROUND 2ND LEG

Letna, Prague

4-08-2004, Dean ENG

Sparta Praha	2
	Poborsky [31], Pacanda [55]
APOEL Nicosia	1
	Charalambides [52]

2ND PRELIM ROUND 1ST LEG

Hardturm, Zurich

28-07-2004, Vink NED

Young Boys Berne	2
	Chapuisat [6], Eugster [65]
Crvena Zvezda Beograd	2
	Zigic 2 [79 88]

2ND PRELIM ROUND 2ND LEG

Crvena Zvezda, Belgrade

4-08-2004, Ledentu FRA

Crvena Zvezda Beograd	3
	Miladinovic [39], Dudic [49], Zigic [69]
Young Boys Berne	0

2ND PRELIM ROUND 1ST LEG

Lerkendal, Trondheim

28-07-2004, Sipailo LVA

Rosenborg BK	2
	Johnsen.F [24], George [85]
Sheriff Tiraspol	1
	Cocis [34]

2ND PRELIM ROUND 2ND LEG
Sheriff, Tiraspol
4-08-2004, Rogalla SUI

Sheriff Tiraspol	0
Rosenborg BK	2
	Berg 36, Brattbakk 40

2ND PRELIM ROUND 1ST LEG
Republican, Yerevan
27-07-2004, Douros GRE

Pyunik Yerevan	1
	Nazaryan 49
Shakhtar Donetsk	3
	Marica 2 30 74, Aghahowa 86

2ND PRELIM ROUND 2ND LEG
Shakhtar, Donetsk
4-08-2004, Asumaa FIN

Shakhtar Donetsk	1
	Hübschman 31
Pyunik Yerevan	0

2ND PRELIM ROUND 1ST LEG
Jan Breydel, Brugge
28-07-2004, Pereira Gomes POR

Club Brugge	2
	Balaban 2 71 88
Lokomotiv Plovdiv	0

2ND PRELIM ROUND 2ND LEG
Naftex, Burgas
4-08-2004, Trefoloni ITA

Lokomotiv Plovdiv	0
Club Brugge	4
	Balaban 2 14 44, Sæternes 74, Ceh 84

2ND PRELIM ROUND 1ST LEG
Tofikh Bakhramov, Baku
27-07-2004, Kenan ISR

Neftchi Baku	0
CSKA Moskva	0

2ND PRELIM ROUND 2ND LEG
Dinamo, Moscow
4-08-2004, Stalhammar SWE

CSKA Moskva	2
	Gusev 68, Vágner Love 72
Neftchi Baku	0

3RD PRELIM ROUND 1ST LEG
Sportni Park, Nova Gorica
11-08-2004, 3 000, Temmink NED

NK Gorica	0
AS Monaco	3
	Kallon 2 8 89, Chevantón 77

3RD PRELIM ROUND 2ND LEG
Stade Louis II, Monaco
24-08-2004, 7 000, Riley ENG

AS Monaco	6
	Chevantón 18, Bernardi 32, El Fakiri 42
	Kallon 47, Farnerud 66, Adebayor 84p
NK Gorica	0

3RD PRELIM ROUND 1ST LEG
Arnold Schwarzenegger, Graz
10-08-2004, 15 000, Sars FRA

Grazer AK	0
Liverpool	2
	Gerrard 2 22 78

3RD PRELIM ROUND 2ND LEG
Anfield, Liverpool
24-08-2004, 42 950, Medina Cantalejo ESP

Liverpool	0
Grazer AK	1
	Tokic 54

3RD PRELIM ROUND 1ST LEG
Lansdowne Road, Dublin
11-08-2004, 24 000, Benes CZE

Shelbourne	0
Deportivo La Coruña	0

3RD PRELIM ROUND 2ND LEG
Riazor, La Coruña
24-08-2004, 26 000, Hamer LUX

Deportivo La Coruña	3
	Victor 2 59 65, Pandiani 88
Shelbourne	0

3RD PRELIM ROUND 1ST LEG
BayArena, Leverkusen
11-08-2004,20 000, Dougal SCO

Bayer Leverkusen	5
	França 3 11 67 88, Juan 74, Berbatov 82
Banik Ostrava	0

3RD PRELIM ROUND 2ND LEG
Bazaly, Ostrava
25-08-2004, 5 369, Mejuto González ESP

Banik Ostrava	2
	Papadopulos 38, Zurek 82
Bayer Leverkusen	1
	Berbatov 76

3RD PRELIM ROUND 1ST LEG
Wisly, Krakow
11-08-2004, 10 000, Busacca SUI

Wisla Krakow	0
Real Madrid	2
	Morientes 2 72 90

3RD PRELIM ROUND 2ND LEG
Bernabeu, Madrid
25-08-2004, Milton Nielsen DEN

Real Madrid	3
	Ronaldo 2 3 31, Pavón 85
Wisla Krakow	1
	Gorawski 89

3RD PRELIM ROUND 1ST LEG
Valery Lobanovskiy, Kyiv
10-08-2004, 18 000, De Bleeckere BEL

Dynamo Kyiv	1
	Verpakovskis 21
Trabzonspor	2
	Gökdeniz 34, Yattara 65

3RD PRELIM ROUND 2ND LEG
Hüseyin Avni Aker, Trabzon
25-08-2004, Messina ITA

Trabzonspor	0
Dynamo Kyiv	2
	Gavrancic 6, Diogo Rincón 28

3RD PRELIM ROUND 1ST LEG
Delle Alpi, Turin
10-08-2004, 26 146, Fandel GER

Juventus	2
Trezeguet 50, Emerson 59	
Djurgårdens IF	2
Johansson.A 45p, Hysén 49	

3RD PRELIM ROUND 2ND LEG
Råsunda, Stockholm
25-08-2004, 32 058, Poll ENG

Djurgårdens IF	1
Arneng 19	
Juventus	4
Del Piero 10, Trezeguet 2 35 87, Nedved 54	

3RD PRELIM ROUND 1ST LEG
Toumba, Thessalonika
10-08-2004, 14 000, Dauden Ibañez ESP

PAOK Salonika	1
Yasemakis 50. Maccabi awarded game 3-0	
Maccabi Tel Aviv	2
Addo 12, Mesika 42	

3RD PRELIM ROUND 2ND LEG
Bloomfield, Tel Aviv
25-08-2004, Michel SVK

Maccabi Tel Aviv	1
Cohen.L 8	
PAOK Salonika	0

3RD PRELIM ROUND 1ST LEG
Lia Manoliu, Bucharest
11-08-2004, 58 000, Gomes Costa POR

Dinamo Buçuresti	1
Danciulescu 9	
Manchester United	2
Giggs 37, Alistar OG 70	

3RD PRELIM ROUND 2ND LEG
Old Trafford, Manchester
25-08-2004, 61 041, Merk GER

Manchester United	3
Smith 2 47 50, Bellion 70	
Dinamo Buçuresti	0

3RD PRELIM ROUND 1ST LEG
Üllöi úti, Budapest
11-08-2004, 11 000, Meyer SUI

Ferencváros	1
Vagner 26	
Sparta Praha	0

3RD PRELIM ROUND 2ND LEG
Letna, Prague
25-08-2004, Meier SUI

Sparta Praha	2
Zelenka 45, Homola 114	
Ferencváros	0

3RD PRELIM ROUND 1ST LEG
Crvena Zvezda, Belgrade
11-08-2004, 58 000, Collina ITA

Crvena Zvezda Beograd	3
Dudic 20, Jankovic 39, Pantelic 59	
PSV Eindhoven	2
Park 8, De Jong 65	

3RD PRELIM ROUND 2ND LEG
Philips Stadion, Eindhoven
25-08-2004, 29 794, Ivanov.V RUS

PSV Eindhoven	5
Van Bommel 2 9p 56, Beasley 32, De Jong 57, Vennegoor 80	
Crvena Zvezda Beograd	0

3RD PRELIM ROUND 1ST LEG
Lerkendal, Trondheim
11-08-2004, 18 482, Plautz AUT

Rosenborg BK	2
Brattbakk 1, Solli 8	
Maccabi Haifa	1
Rosso 45	

3RD PRELIM ROUND 2ND LEG
Ramat Gan, Tel Aviv
24-08-2004, Veissière FRA

Maccabi Haifa	2
Badir 31, Boccoli 38	
Rosenborg BK	3
Brattbakk 90, Braaten 94, Berg 120	

3RD PRELIM ROUND 1ST LEG
Shakhtar, Donetsk
11-08-2004, 25 000, Ovrebo NOR

Shakhtar Donetsk	4
Aghahowa 15, Marica 70, Vorobey 77, Brandão 90	
Club Brugge	1
Balaban 50	

3RD PRELIM ROUND 2ND LEG
Jan Breydel, Brugge
25-08-2004, Bennett ENG

Club Brugge	2
Ceh 2 15 34p	
Shakhtar Donetsk	2
Vukic 2 6 52	

3RD PRELIM ROUND 1ST LEG
St Jakob Park, Basel
11-08-2004, 29 500, Poll ENG

FC Basel	1
Huggel 25	
Internazionale	1
Adriano 19	

3RD PRELIM ROUND 2ND LEG
San Siro, Milan
24-08-2004, 62 000, Frisk SWE

Internazionale	4
Adriano 2 1 52, Stankovic 12, Recoba 59	
FC Basel	1
Sterjovski 49	

3RD PRELIM ROUND 1ST LEG
Estádio da Luz, Lisbon
10-08-2004, 2 000, Fröjdfeldt SWE

Benfica	1
Zahovic 13	
RSC Anderlecht	0

3RD PRELIM ROUND 2ND LEG
Constant Vanden Stock, Brussels
24-08-2004, 20 107, Farina ITA

RSC Anderlecht	3
Aruna 2 34 59, Jestrovic 73p	
Benfica	0

3RD PRELIM ROUND 1ST LEG
Lokomotiv, Moscow
10-08-2004, 11 000, Wegereef NED

CSKA Moskva	2
Vágner Love 4, Jarosik 46	
Rangers	1
Novo 37	

3RD PRELIM ROUND 1ST LEG
Ibrox, Glasgow
25-08-2004, 49 010, Stark GER

Rangers	1
Thompson 87	
CSKA Moskva	1
Vágner Love 60	

GROUP A

		Pl	W	D	L	F	A	Pts	FRA	ENG	GRE	ESP
AS Monaco †	FRA	6	4	0	2	10	4	12		1-0	2-1	2-0
Liverpool †	ENG	6	3	1	2	6	3	10	2-0		3-1	0-0
Olympiacos ‡	GRE	6	3	1	2	5	5	10	1-0	1-0		1-0
Deportivo La Coruña	ESP	6	0	2	4	0	9	2	0-5	0-1	0-0	

† Qualified for the knockout phase • ‡ Entered the UEFA Cup at the knockout stage

GROUP A MATCHDAY 1
Riazor, La Coruña
15-09-2004, 23 000, De Bleeckere BEL

Deportivo La Coruña	0
Olympiacos	0

GROUP A MATCHDAY 1
Anfield, Liverpool
15-09-2004, 33 517, Hauge NOR

Liverpool	2
	Cissé 22, Baros 84
AS Monaco	0

GROUP A MATCHDAY 2
Karaiskakis, Piraeus
28-09-2004, 33 000, Collina ITA

Olympiacos	1
	Stoltidis 17
Liverpool	0

GROUP A MATCHDAY 2
Stade Louis II, Monaco
28-09-2004, 13 673, Farina ITA

AS Monaco	2
	Kallon 5, Saviola 10
Deportivo La Coruña	0

GROUP A MATCHDAY 3
Stade Louis II, Monaco
19-10-2004, 16 624, Wegereef NED

AS Monaco	2
	Saviola 3, Chevantón 10
Olympiacos	1
	Okkas 60

GROUP A MATCHDAY 3
Anfield, Liverpool
19-10-2004, 40 236, Frisk SWE

Liverpool	0
Deportivo La Coruña	0

GROUP A MATCHDAY 4
Karaiskakis, Piraeus
3-11-2004, 33 000, Merk GER

Olympiacos	1
	Schürrer 84
AS Monaco	0

GROUP A MATCHDAY 4
Riazor, La Coruña
3-11-2004, 32 000, Stark GER

Deportivo La Coruña	0
Liverpool	1
	Andrade OG 14

GROUP A MATCHDAY 5
Stade Louis II, Monaco
23-11-2004, 15 000, Larsen DEN

AS Monaco	1
	Saviola 55
Liverpool	0

GROUP A MATCHDAY 5
Karaiskakis, Piraeus
23-11-2004, 33 000, Hauge NOR

Olympiacos	1
	Djordjevic 68
Deportivo La Coruña	0

GROUP A MATCHDAY 6
Anfield, Liverpool
8-12-2004, 42 045, Mejuto Gonzalez ESP

Liverpool	3
	Pongolle 47, Mellor 80, Gerrard 86
Olympiacos	1
	Rivaldo 27

GROUP A MATCHDAY 6
Riazor, La Coruña
8-12-2004, 16 000, Baskakov RUS

Deportivo La Coruña	0
AS Monaco	5
Chevantón 22, Givet 37, Saviola 39, Maicon 55, Adebayor 76	

GROUP B

		Pl	W	D	L	F	A	Pts	GER	ESP	UKR	ITA
Bayer Leverkusen †	GER	6	3	2	1	13	7	11		3-0	3-0	3-1
Real Madrid †	ESP	6	3	2	1	11	8	11	1-1		1-0	4-2
Dynamo Kyiv ‡	UKR	6	3	1	2	11	8	10	4-2	2-2		2-0
Roma	ITA	6	0	1	5	4	16	1	1-1	0-3	0-3	

† Qualified for the knockout phase • ‡ Entered the UEFA Cup at the knockout stage

GROUP B MATCHDAY 1
BayArena, Leverkusen
15-09-2004, 22 500, Poll ENG

Bayer Leverkusen	3
	Krzynówek 39, França 50, Berbatov 55
Real Madrid	0

GROUP B MATCHDAY 1
Olimpico, Rome
15-09-2004, Frisk SWE

Roma	0
Abandoned 45'. Match awarded 3-0 to Kyiv	
Dynamo Kyiv	1
	Gavrancic 29

GROUP B MATCHDAY 2
Olimpiyskyi, Kyiv
28-09-2004, 83 000, Milton Nielsen DEN

Dynamo Kyiv	4
	Diogo Rincón 2 30 69, Cernat 2 74 90
Bayer Leverkusen	2
	Voronin 59, Nowotny 68

GROUP B MATCHDAY 2	
Bernabeu, Madrid	
28-09-2004, 60 000, Ivanov RUS	
Real Madrid	**4**
Raúl 2 [39 72], Figo [53p], Roberto Carlos [79]	
Roma	**2**

GROUP B MATCHDAY 3	
Bernabeu, Madrid	
19-10-2004, 45 000, Veissière FRA	
Real Madrid	**1**
Owen [35]	
Dynamo Kyiv	**0**

GROUP B MATCHDAY 3	
BayArena, Leverkusen	
19-10-2004, 22 500, Poulat FRA	
Bayer Leverkusen	**3**
Roque Junior [48], Krzynówek [59], França [94+]	
Roma	**1**
Berbatov OG [26]	

GROUP B MATCHDAY 4	
Olimpiyskyi, Kyiv	
3-11-2004, 83 000, Vassaras GRE	
Dynamo Kyiv	**2**
Yussuf [13], Verpaskis [23]	
Real Madrid	**2**
Raúl [37], Figo [44p]	

GROUP B MATCHDAY 4	
Olimpico, Rome	
3-11-2004, Cortez Batista POR	
Roma	**1**
Montella [93+]	
Bayer Leverkusen	**1**
Berbatov [82]	

GROUP B MATCHDAY 5	
Bernabeu, Madrid	
23-11-2004, 40 000, Hamer LUX	
Real Madrid	**1**
Raúl [70]	
Bayer Leverkusen	**1**
Berbatov [36]	

GROUP B MATCHDAY 5	
Olimpiyskyi, Kyiv	
23-11-2004, 40 000, Riley ENG	
Dynano Kyiv	**2**
Dellas OG [73], Shatskikh [82]	
Roma	**0**

GROUP B MATCHDAY 6	
BayArena, Leverkusen	
8-12-2004, 22 500, Collina ITA	
Bayer Leverkusen	**3**
Juan [51], Voronin [77], Babic [86]	
Dynamo Kyiv	**0**

GROUP B MATCHDAY 6	
Olimpico, Rome	
8-12-2004, 0, Temmink NED	
Roma	**0**
Real Madrid	**3**
Ronaldo [8], Figo 2 [60p 82]	

GROUP C											
		Pl	W	D	L	F	A	Pts	ITA	GER	NED	ISR
Juventus †	ITA	6	5	1	0	6	1	16		1-0	1-0	1-0
Bayern München †	GER	6	3	1	2	12	5	10	0-1		4-0	5-1
Ajax ‡	NED	6	1	1	4	6	10	4	0-1	2-2		3-0
Maccabi Tel Aviv	ISR	6	1	1	4	4	12	4	1-1	0-1	2-1	

† Qualified for the knockout phase • ‡ Entered the UEFA Cup at the knockout stage

GROUP C MATCHDAY 1	
Amsterdam ArenA	
15-09-2004, 50 000, Meier SUI	
Ajax	**0**
Juventus	**1**
Nedved [42]	

GROUP C MATCHDAY 1	
Ramat Gan, Tel Aviv	
15-09-2004, 25 000, Bennett ENG	
Maccabi Tel Aviv	**0**
Bayern München	**1**
Makaay [64p]	

GROUP C MATCHDAY 2	
Olympiastadion, Munich	
28-09-2004, 50 000, Sars FRA	
Bayern München	**4**
Makaay 3 [28 44 51p], Zé Roberto [55]	
Ajax	**0**

GROUP C MATCHDAY 2	
Delle Alpi, Turin	
28-09-2004, 6 494, Hamer LUX	
Juventus	**1**
Camoranesi [37]	
Maccabi Tel Aviv	**0**

GROUP C MATCHDAY 3	
Delle Alpi, Turin	
19-10-2004, 18 089, Mejuto González ESP	
Juventus	**1**
Nedved [75]	
Bayern München	**0**

GROUP C MATCHDAY 3	
Amsterdam ArenA	
19-10-2004, 49 500, Iturralde González ESP	
Ajax	**3**
Sonck [4], De Jong [21], Van der Vaart [33]	
Maccabi Tel Aviv	**0**

GROUP C MATCHDAY 4	
Olympiastadion, Munich	
3-11-2004, 59 000, Poll ENG	
Bayern München	**0**
Juventus	**1**
Del Piero [90]	

GROUP C MATCHDAY 4	
Ramat Gan, Tel Aviv	
3-11-2004, 35 000, Hrinak SVK	
Maccabi Tel Aviv	**2**
Dego 2 [49 57]	
Ajax	**1**
De Ridder [88]	

GROUP C MATCHDAY 5	
Delle Alpi, Turin	
23-11-2004, 6 875, Plautz AUT	
Juventus	**1**
Zalayeta [15]	
Ajax	**0**

GROUP C MATCHDAY 5
Olympiastadion, Munich
23-11-2004, 45 000, Medina Cantalejo ESP
Bayern München   **5**
Pizarro [12], Salihamidzic [37], Frings [44],
Makaay 2 [71 80]
Maccabi Tel Aviv   **1**
Dego [56p]

GROUP C MATCHDAY 6
Amsterdam ArenA
8-12-2004, 51 000, Cortez Batista POR
Ajax   **2**
Galásek [38], Mitea [64]
Bayern München   **2**
Makaay [9], Ballack [78]

GROUP C MATCHDAY 6
Ramat Gan, Tel Aviv
8-12-2004, 18 500, Sars FRA
Maccabi Tel Aviv   **1**
Dego [29p]
Juventus   **1**
Del Piero [71]

GROUP D

		Pl	W	D	L	F	A	Pts	FRA	ENG	TUR	CZE
Olympique Lyonnais †	FRA	6	4	1	1	17	8	13		2-2	4-2	5-0
Manchester United †	ENG	6	3	2	1	14	9	11	2-1		6-2	4-1
Fenerbahçe ‡	TUR	6	3	0	3	10	13	9	1-3	3-0		1-0
Sparta Praha	CZE	6	0	1	5	2	13	1	1-2	0-0	0-1	

† Qualified for the knockout phase • ‡ Entered the UEFA Cup at the knockout stage

GROUP D MATCHDAY 1
Sükrü Saracoglu, Istanbul
15-09-2004, 45 000, Cortez Batista POR
Fenerbahçe   **1**
Van Hooijdonk [16]
Sparta Praha   **0**

GROUP D MATCHDAY 1
Stade Gerland, Lyon
15-09-2004, 40 000, Stark GER
Olympique Lyonnais   **2**
Cris [35], Frau [45]
Manchester United   **2**
Van Nistelrooy 2 [56 61]

GROUP D MATCHDAY 2
Old Trafford, Manchester
28-09-2004, 67 128, De Bleeckere BEL
Manchester United   **6**
Giggs [7], Rooney 3 [17 28 54], Van Nistelrooy [78],
Bellion [81]
Fenerbahçe   **2**
Márcio Nobre [46], Tuncay Sanli [59]

GROUP D MATCHDAY 2
Letna, Prague
28-09-2004, 12 050, Dauden Ibañez ESP
Sparta Praha   **1**
Jun [7]
Olympique Lyonnais   **2**
Essien [25], Wiltord [58]

GROUP D MATCHDAY 3
Letna, Prague
19-10-2004, 20 654, De Santis ITA
Sparta Praha   **0**
Manchester United   **0**

GROUP D MATCHDAY 3
Sükrü Saracoglu, Istanbul
19-10-2004, 49 000, Baskakov RUS
Fenerbahçe   **1**
Márcio Nobre [68]
Olympique Lyonnais   **3**
Juninho [55], Cris [66], Frau [87]

GROUP D MATCHDAY 4
Old Trafford, Manchester
3-11-2004, 66 706, Hamer LUX
Manchester United   **4**
Van Nistelrooy 4 [14 25p 60 91+]
Sparta Praha   **1**
Zelenka [53]

GROUP D MATCHDAY 4
Stade Gerland, Lyon
3-11-2004, 36 000, Farina ITA
Olympique Lyonnais   **4**
Essien [22], Malouda [53], Nilmar 2 [94+ 96+]
Fenerbahçe   **2**
Selçuk [14], Tuncay Sanli [73]

GROUP D MATCHDAY 5
Letna, Prague
23-11-2004, 11 507, Stark GER
Sparta Praha   **0**
Fenerbahçe   **1**
Kovác OG [20]

GROUP D MATCHDAY 5
Old Trafford, Manchester
23-11-2004, 66 398, Milton Nielsen DEN
Manchester United   **2**
Neville.G [19], Van Nistelrooy [53]
Olympique Lyonnais   **1**
Diarra [40]

GROUP D MATCHDAY 6
Sükrü Saracoglu, Istanbul
8-12-2004, 35 000, Dauden Ibañez ESP
Fenerbahçe   **3**
Tuncay Sanli 3 [47 62 90]
Manchester United   **0**

GROUP D MATCHDAY 6
Stade Gerland, Lyon
8-12-2004, 40 000, Plautz AUT
Olympique Lyonnais   **5**
Essien [7], Nilmar 2 [19 51], Idanger [83],
Bergougnoux [90]
Sparta Praha   **0**

GROUP E

		Pl	W	D	L	F	A	Pts	ENG	NED	GRE	NOR
Arsenal †	ENG	6	2	4	0	11	6	10		1-0	1-1	5-1
PSV Eindhoven †	NED	6	3	1	2	6	7	10	1-1		1-0	1-0
Panathinaikos ‡	GRE	6	2	3	1	11	8	9	2-2	4-1		2-1
Rosenborg BK	NOR	6	0	2	4	6	13	2	1-1	1-2	2-2	

† Qualified for the knockout phase • ‡ Entered the UEFA Cup at the knockout stage

GROUP E MATCHDAY 1
Apostolos Nikolaidis, Athens
14-09-2004, 13 204, Allaerts BEL

Panathinaikos	2
González 2 [43] [79]	
Rosenborg BK	1
Johnsen.J [90]	

GROUP E MATCHDAY 1
Highbury, London
14-09-2004, 34 068, Messina ITA

Arsenal	1
Alex OG [41]	
PSV Eindhoven	0

GROUP E MATCHDAY 2
Philips Stadion, Eindhoven
29-09-2004, 26 500, Plautz AUT

PSV Eindhoven	1
Vennegoor [80]	
Panathinaikos	0

GROUP E MATCHDAY 2
Lerkendal, Trondheim
29-09-2004, 21 100, Meyer GER

Rosenborg BK	1
Strand [52]	
Arsenal	1
Ljungberg [6]	

GROUP E MATCHDAY 3
Lerkendal, Trondheim
20-10-2004, 20 950, Sars FRA

Rosenborg BK	1
Storflor [42]	
PSV Eindhoven	2
Farfán [26], De Jong [86]	

GROUP E MATCHDAY 3
Apostolos Nikolaidis, Athens
20-10-2004, 12 345, Ivanov RUS

Panathinaikos	2
González [65], Olisadebe [82]	
Arsenal	2
Ljungberg [18], Henry [74]	

GROUP E MATCHDAY 4
Philips Stadion, Eindhoven
2-11-2004, 26 250, Dauden Ibañez ESP

PSV Eindhoven	1
Beasley [10]	
Rosenborg BK	0

GROUP E MATCHDAY 4
Highbury, London
2-11-2004, 35 137, Medina Cantalejo ESP

Arsenal	1
Henry [16p]	
Panathinaikos	1
Cygan OG [75]	

GROUP E MATCHDAY 5
Lerkendal, Trondheim
24-11-2004, 18 000, De Santis ITA

Rosenborg BK	2
Helstad 2 [68] [76]	
Panathinaikos	2
Konstantinou [16], Stácel [71]	

GROUP E MATCHDAY 5
Philips Stadion, Eindhoven
24-11-2004, 26 100, Fandel GER

PSV Eindhoven	1
Ooijer [8]	
Arsenal	1
Henry [31]	

GROUP E MATCHDAY 6
Apostolos Nikolaidis, Athens
7-12-2004, 10 196, Fröjdfeldt SWE

Panathinaikos	4
Papadopoulos 2 [30] [45p], Münch [57], Sanmartean [81]	
PSV Eindhoven	1
Beasley [37]	

GROUP E MATCHDAY 6
Highbury, London
7-12-2004, 35 421, Farina ITA

Arsenal	5
Reyes [3], Henry [24], Fabregas [29], Pires [41p], Van Persie [84]	
Rosenborg BK	1
Hoftun [38]	

GROUP F

		Pl	W	D	L	F	A	Pts	ITA	ESP	UKR	SCO
Milan †	ITA	6	4	1	1	10	3	13		1-0	4-0	3-1
Barcelona †	ESP	6	3	1	2	9	6	10	2-1		3-0	1-1
Shakhtar Donetsk ‡	UKR	6	2	0	4	5	9	6	0-1	2-0		3-0
Celtic	SCO	6	1	2	3	4	10	5	0-0	1-3	1-0	

† Qualified for the knockout phase • ‡ Entered the UEFA Cup at the knockout stage

GROUP F MATCHDAY 1
Shakhtar, Donetsk
14-09-2004, 30 000, Fandel GER

Shakhtar Donetsk	0
Milan	1
Seedorf [84]	

GROUP F MATCHDAY 1
Celtic Park, Glasgow
14-09-2004, 58 589, Merk GER

Celtic	1
Sutton [59]	
Barcelona	3
Deco [20], Guily [78], Larsson [82]	

GROUP F MATCHDAY 2
Camp Nou, Barcelona
29-09-2004, 64 148, Hauge NOR

Barcelona	3
Deco [15], Ronaldinho [64p], Eto'o [89]	
Shakhtar Donetsk	0

GROUP F MATCHDAY 2
San Siro, Milan
29-09-2004, 50 000, Veissière FRA

Milan	3
Shevchenko [8], Inzaghi [89], Pirlo [90]	
Celtic	1
Varga [74]	

GROUP F MATCHDAY 3
San Siro, Milan
20-10-2004, 76 502, Poll ENG

Milan	1
Shevchenko [31]	
Barcelona	0

GROUP F MATCHDAY 3
Shakhtar, Donetsk
20-10-2004, 30 000, Temmink NED

Shakhtar Donetsk	3
Matuzalem 2 [57] [62], Brandão [78]	
Celtic	0

GROUP F MATCHDAY 4
Camp Nou, Barcelona
2-11-2004, 94 682, Meier SUI

Barcelona	2
Eto'o [37], Ronaldinho [89]	
Milan	1
Shevchenko [17]	

GROUP F MATCHDAY 4
Celtic Park, Glasgow
2-11-2004, 58 347, Poulat FA

Celtic	1
Thompson [25]	
Shakhtar Donetsk	0

GROUP F MATCHDAY 5
San Siro, Milan
24-11-2004, 38 841, De Bleeckere BEL

Milan	4
Kaka 2 [52 90], Crespo 2 [53 85]	
Shakhtar Donetsk	0

GROUP F MATCHDAY 5
Camp Nou, Barcelona
24-11-2004, 74 119, Michel SVK

Barcelona	1
Eto'o [24]	
Celtic	1
Hartson [45]	

GROUP F MATCHDAY 6
Shakhtar, Donetsk
7-12-2004, 25 000, Larsen DEN

Shakhtar Donetsk	2
Aghahowa 2 [14 22]	
Barcelona	0

GROUP F MATCHDAY 6
Celtic Park, Glasgow
7-12-2004, 59 228, Vassaras GRE

Celtic	0
Milan	0

GROUP G

		Pl	W	D	L	F	A	Pts	ITA	GER	ESP	BEL
Internazionale †	ITA	6	4	2	0	14	3	14	-	2-0	0-0	3-0
Werder Bremen †	GER	6	4	1	1	12	6	13	1-1		2-1	5-1
Valencia ‡	ESP	6	2	1	3	6	10	7	1-5	0-2		2-0
RSC Anderlecht	BEL	6	0	0	6	4	17	0	1-3	1-2	1-2	

† Qualified for the knockout phase • ‡ Entered the UEFA Cup at the knockout stage

GROUP G MATCHDAY 1
Mestalla, Valencia
14-09-2004, 39 000, Layec FRA

Valencia	2
Vicente [16], Baraja [45]	
RSC Anderlecht	0

GROUP G MATCHDAY 1
San Siro, Milan
14-09-2004, 45 000, Michel SVK

Internazionale	2
Adriano 2 [34p 89]	
Werder Bremen	0

GROUP G MATCHDAY 2
Weserstadion, Bremen
29-09-2004, 36 000, Riley ENG

Werder Bremen	2
Klose [60], Charisteas [84]	
Valencia	1
Vicente [2]	

GROUP G MATCHDAY 2
Constant Vanden Stock, Brussels
29-09-2004, 25 000, Vassaras GRE

RSC Anderlecht	1
Baseggio [90]	
Internazionale	3
Martins [9], Adriano [51], Stankovic [55]	

GROUP G MATCHDAY 3
Constant Vanden Stock, Brussels
20-10-2004, 22 000, Larsen DEN

RSC Anderlecht	1
Wilhelmsson [26]	
Werder Bremen	2
Klasnic 2 [36 59]	

GROUP G MATCHDAY 3
Mestalla, Valencia
20-10-2004, 40 000, Meier SUI

Valencia	1
Aimar [73]	
Internazionale	5
Stankovic [47], Vieri [49], Van der Meyde [76], Adriano [81], Cruz [91+]	

GROUP G MATCHDAY 4
Weserstadion, Bremen
2-11-2004, 37 579, Busacca SUI

Werder Bremen	5
Klasnic 3 [2 16 79], Klose [33], Jensen [90]	
RSC Anderlecht	1
Iachtchouk [30]	

GROUP G MATCHDAY 4
San Siro, Milan
2-11-2004, 40 000, Ivanov RUS

Internazionale	0
Valencia	0

GROUP G MATCHDAY 5
Constant Vanden Stock, Brussels
24-11-2004, 23 000, Ovrebo NOR

RSC Anderlecht	1
Wilhelmsson [24]	
Valencia	2
Corradi [19], Di Vaio [48]	

GROUP G MATCHDAY 5
Weserstadion, Bremen
24-11-2004, 37 000, Veissière FRA

Werder Bremen	1
Ismaël [49p]	
Internazionale	1
Martins [55]	

GROUP G MATCHDAY 6
Mestalla, Valencia
7-12-2004, 40 000, Frisk SWE

Valencia	0
Werder Bremen	2
Valdez 2 [83 90]	

GROUP G MATCHDAY 6
San Siro, Milan
7-12-2004, 30 000, Riley ENG

Internazionale	3
Cruz [33], Martins 2 [60 63]	
RSC Anderlecht	0

GROUP H

		Pl	W	D	L	F	A	Pts	ENG	POR	RUS	FRA
Chelsea †	ENG	6	4	1	1	10	3	13		3-1	2-0	0-0
FC Porto †	POR	6	2	2	2	4	6	8	2-1		0-0	0-0
CSKA Moskva ‡	RUS	6	2	1	3	5	5	7	0-1	0-1		2-0
Paris Saint-Germain	FRA	6	1	2	3	3	8	5	0-3	2-0	1-3	

† Qualified for the knockout phase • ‡ Entered the UEFA Cup at the knockout stage

---

GROUP H MATCHDAY 1
Parc des Princes, Paris
14-09-2004, 40 000, Mejuto González ESP

Paris Saint-Germain	0

Chelsea	3
Terry [29], Drogba 2 [45 76]	

GROUP H MATCHDAY 1
O Dragão, Porto
14-09-2004, 39 309, Milton Nielsen DEN

FC Porto	0

CSKA Moskva	0

GROUP H MATCHDAY 2
Lokomotiv, Moscow
29-09-2004, 29 000, Busacca SUI

CSKA Moskva	2
Semak [64], Vágner Love [77p]	

Paris Saint-Germain	0

GROUP H MATCHDAY 2
Stamford Bridge, London
29-09-2004, 39 237, Fandel GER

Chelsea	3
Smertin [7], Drogba [50], Terry [70]	
FC Porto	1
McCarthy [68]	

GROUP H MATCHDAY 3
Stamford Bridge, London
20-10-2004, 33 945, Michel SVK

Chelsea	2
Terry [9], Gudjohnsen [45]	
CSKA Moskva	0

GROUP H MATCHDAY 3
Parc des Princes, Paris
20-10-2004, 41 000, Collina ITA

Paris Saint-Germain	2
Coridon [30], Pauleta [31]	
FC Porto	0

GROUP H MATCHDAY 4
Lokomotiv, Moscow
2-11-2004, 28 000, De Santis ITA

CSKA Moskva	0

Chelsea	1
Robben [24]	

GROUP H MATCHDAY 4
O Dragão, Porto
2-11-2004, 30 210, Dougal SCO

FC Porto	0

Paris Saint-Germain	0

GROUP H MATCHDAY 5
Stamford Bridge, London
24-11-2004, 39 626, Temmink NED

Chelsea	0

Paris Saint-Germain	0

GROUP H MATCHDAY 5
Lokomotiv, Moscow
24-11-2004, 21 500, Mejuto González ESP

CSKA Moskva	0

FC Porto	1
McCarthy [28]	

GROUP H MATCHDAY 6
Parc des Princes, Paris
7-12-2004, 40 000, Merk GER

Paris Saint-Germain	1
Pancrate [37]	
CSKA Moskva	3
Semak 3 [28 64 70]	

GROUP H MATCHDAY 6
O Dragão, Porto
7-12-2004, 42 409, Busacca SUI

FC Porto	2
Diego [61], McCarthy [86]	
Chelsea	1
Duff [34]	

SECOND ROUND 1ST LEG
Anfield, Liverpool
22-02-2005, 40 942, Vassaras GRE

Liverpool	3
Luis Garcia [15], Riise [35], Hamann [92+]	
Bayer Leverkusen	1
França [93+]	

SECOND ROUND 2ND LEG
BayArena, Leverkusen
9-03-2005, 23 000, Sars FRA

Bayer Leverkusen	1
Krzynówek [88]	
Liverpool	3
Luis Garcia 2 [28 32], Baros [67]	

SECOND ROUND 1ST LEG
Benabeu, Madrid
22-02-2004, 78 000, Michel LUX

Real Madrid	1
Helguera [31]	
Juventus	0

SECOND ROUND 2ND LEG
Delle Alpi, Turin
9-03-2005, 59 000, Merk GER

Juventus	2
Trezeguet [57], Zalayeta [116]	
Real Madrid	0

SECOND ROUND 1ST LEG
Olympiastadion, Munich
22-02-2005, 59 000, Milton Nielsen DEN

Bayern München	3
Pizarro 2 [4 58], Salihamidzic [65]	
Arsenal	1
Touré [88]	

SECOND ROUND 2ND LEG
Highbury, London
9-03-2005, 35 463, De Santis ITA

Arsenal	1
Henry [66]	
Bayern München	0

SECOND ROUND 1ST LEG
Camp Nou, Barcelona
23-02-2005, 89,000, Frisk SWE

Barcelona	2
López 67, Eto'o 73	
Chelsea	1
Bellett OG 33	

SECOND ROUND 2ND LEG
Stamford Bridge, London
8-03-2005, 41 515, Collina ITA

Chelsea	4
Gudjohnsen 8, Lampard 17, Duff 19, Terry 76	
Barcelona	2
Ronaldinho 2 27p 38	

SECOND ROUND 1ST LEG
Philips Stadion, Eindhoven
22-02-2005, 32 000, Medina Cantalejo ESP

PSV Eindhoven	1
Alex 8	
AS Monaco	0

SECOND ROUND 2ND LEG
Stade Louis II, Monaco
9-03-2005, 15 523, Bennett ENG

AS Monaco	0
PSV Eindhoven	2
Vennegoor 26, Beasley 69	

SECOND ROUND 1ST LEG
Weserstadion, Bremen
23-02-2005, 36 923, De Bleeckere BEL

Werder Bremen	0
Olympique Lyonnais	3
Wiltord 9, Diarra 77, Juninho 80	

SECOND ROUND 2ND LEG
Stade Gerland, Lyon
8-03-2005, 37 000, Ivanov RUS

Olympique Lyonnais	7
Wiltord 3 8 55 64, Essien 2 17 30, Malouda 60, Berthod 80p	
Werder Bremen	2
Micoud 32, Ismaël 57p	

SECOND ROUND 1ST LEG
O Dragão, Porto
23-02-2005, 38 177, Poll ENG

FC Porto	1
Ricardo Costa 61	
Internazionale	1
Martins 24	

SECOND ROUND 2ND LEG
San Siro, Milan
15-03-2005, 51 000, Hauge NOR

Internazionale	3
Adriano 3 6 63 87	
FC Porto	1
Jorge Costa 69	

SECOND ROUND 1ST LEG
Old Trafford, Manchester
23-02-2005, 67 162, Mejuto Gonzalez ESP

Manchester United	0
Milan	1
Crespo 78	

SECOND ROUND 2ND LEG
Giuseppe Meazza, Milan
8-03-2005, 78 957, Fandel GER

Milan	1
Crespo 61	
Manchester United	0

QUARTER-FINAL 1ST LEG
Anfield, Liverpool
5-04-2005, 41 216, De Bleeckere BEL

Liverpool	2
Hyypia 10, Luis Garcia 25	
Juventus	1
Cannavaro 63	

QUARTER-FINAL 2ND LEG
Delle Alpi, Turin
13-04-2005, 50 000, Ivanov RUS

Juventus	0
Liverpool	0

QUARTER-FINAL 1ST LEG
Stamford Bridge, London
6-04-2005, 40 253, Temmink NED

Chelsea	4
Cole 4, Lampard 2 60 70, Drogba 81	
Bayern München	2
Schweinsteiger 52, Ballack 93+p	

QUARTER-FINAL 2ND LEG
Olympiastadion, Munich
12-04-2005, 59 000, Mejuto Gonzalez ESP

Bayern München	3
Pizarro 65, Guerrero 90, Scholl 95+	
Chelsea	2
Lampard 30, Drogba 80	

QUARTER-FINAL 1ST LEG
Stade Gerland, Lyon
5-04-2005, 35 000, Collina ITA

Olympique Lyonnais	1
Malouda 12	
PSV Eindhoven	1
Cocu 79	

QUARTER-FINAL 2ND LEG
Philips Stadion, Eindhoven
13-04-2005, 35 000, Milton Nielsen DEN

PSV Eindhoven	1 4p
Alex 50	
Olympique Lyonnais	1 2p
Wiltord 10	

QUARTER-FINAL 1ST LEG
San Siro, Milan
6-04-2005, 80 000, Sars FRA

Milan	2
Stam 45, Shevchenko 74	
Internazionale	0

QUARTER-FINAL 2ND LEG
San Siro, Milan
12-04-2005, 79 000, Merk GER

Internazionale	0
Abandoned 74'. Awarded 3-0 to Milan	
Milan	1
Shevchenko 30	

SEMI-FINAL 1ST LEG
Stamford Bridge, London
27-04-2005, 40 497, Sars FRA

Chelsea	0
Liverpool	0

SEMI-FINAL 2ND LEG
Anfield, Liverpool
3-05-2005, 42 529, Michel SVK

Liverpool	1
Luis Garcia 4	
Chelsea	0

SEMI-FINAL 1ST LEG	
San Siro, Milan	
26-04-2005, 71 000, Vassaras GRE	
Milan	**2**
Shevchenko [42], Tomasson [90]	
PSV Eindhoven	**0**

SEMI-FINAL 2ND LEG	
Philips Stadion, Eindhoven	
4-05-2005, 35 000, Hauge NOR	
PSV Eindhoven	**3**
Park [9], Cocu 2 [65][92+]	
Milan	**1**
Ambrosini [91+]	

FINAL   ATTATURK OLIMPIYAT, ISTANBUL   **25-05-2005**

Kick-off: 20:45   Attendance: 69 000

LIVERPOOL   3   3   MILAN

3-2p

Gerrard [54], Smicer [56], Xabi Alonso [60]   Maldini [1], Crespo 2 [39][44]

		LIVERPOOL	
1	GK	DUDEK Jerzy	
3	DF	FINNAN Steve	46
4	DF	HYYPIA Sami	
5	FW	BAROS Milan	85
6	MF	RIISE John Arne	
7	FW	KEWELL Harry	23
8	MF	GERRARD Steven	
10	MF	LUIS GARCIA	
14	MF	XABI ALONSO	
21	DF	TRAORE Djimi	
23	DF	CARRAGHER Jamie	
		Tr: BENITEZ Rafael	
		Substitutes	
9	FW	CISSE Djibril	85
11	MF	SMICER Vladimír	23
16	MF	HAMANN Dietmar	46

MATCH STATS		
14	Shots	18
7	Shots on Goal	10
23	Fouls Committed	16
4	Corner Kicks	10
5	Offside	7
45	Possession %	55

MATCH OFFICIALS

Referee
MEJUTO GONZALEZ Manuel

Assistant Referees
AYETE PLOU Clemente
MARTINEZ SAMANIEGO Oscar

4th Official
DAUDEN IBANEZ Arturo

	MILAN		
	DIDA	GK	1
	CAFU	DF	2
	MALDINI Paolo	DF	3
	SHEVCHENKO Andriy	FW	7
112	GATTUSO Gennaro	MF	8
85	CRESPO Hernán	FW	11
	NESTA Alessandro	DF	13
86	SEEDORF Clarence	MF	20
	PIRLO Andrea	MF	21
	KAKA	MF	22
	STAM Jaap	DF	31
	Tr: ANCELOTTI Carlo		
	Substitutes		
112	RUI COSTA	MF	10
85	TOMASSON Jon Dahl	FW	15
86	SERGINHO	MF	27

We tried to change things at half-time and said it would be different if we scored - and it was. But the players believed and we won. Steven Gerrard was the key player for us.

Rafael Benitez

I think Milan played a marvellous final. The defeat was not deserved but we have to accept it. The team should be proud. I told my players that I wasn't disappointed in them.

Carlo Ancelotti

MATCH REPORT

The pundits had predicted a dull 0-0 draw between two teams renowned for their defensive capabilities, but the tone for this exhilarating climax to the European season was set after just 50 seconds when Paolo Maldini scored the fastest goal in the 50 finals played so far. Milan then proceeded to play their best football in the competition, totally outplaying a shell-shocked Liverpool team, to go in 3-0 ahead at half-time. Milan fans were perhaps thinking of record scores at half-time, but instead Liverpool created history of their own. No team had ever come back from 3-0 down but after an hour they were level following an extraordinary six minutes of play. They had the best of the last 30 minutes but in extra-time clung on grimly for the draw. With memories of Grobelaar in 1984, Jerzy Dudek performed a shuffle and pulled off two heroic saves to win the shoot-out for Liverpool.

PENALTY SHOOT-OUT			
Milan first		**Liverpool second**	
Serginho	✗	Hamann	✔
Pirlo	✗	Cissé	✔
Tomasson	✔	Riise	✗
Kaka	✔	Smicer	✔
Shevchenko	✗		
Liverpool win the European Cup 3-2 on penalties			

UEFA CUP 2004-05

First Preliminary Round

FK Ekranas	LTU	1	2
F91 Dudelange	LUX	0	1
Osters IF	SWE	2	2
TNS	WAL	0	1
B36 Tórshavn	FRO	1	1
Metalurgs Liepaja	LVA	3	8
Omonia Nicosia	CYP	4	4
Sloga Jugomagnat	MKD	0	1
Sileks	MKD	0	1
NK Maribor	SVN	1	1
Levadia Tallinn	EST	0	3
Bohemians	IRL	0	1
Nistru Otaci	MDA	1	2
Shakhtyor Soligorsk	BLR	1	1
Illychivets Mariupil	UKR	2	2
Banants Yerevan	ARM	0	0
FC Tbilisi	GEO	1	4
FK Shamkir	AZE	0	1
Partizani Tiranë	ALB	4	1
Birkirkara	MLT	2	2
Haka Valkeakoski	FIN	2	3
Etzella Ettelbrück	LUX	1	1
BATE Borisov	BLR	2	0
Dinamo Tbilisi	GEO	3	1
IA Akranes	ISL	4	2
TVMK Tallinn	EST	2	1
Otelul Galati	ROU	4	4
Dinamo Tiranë	ALB	0	1
Shirak Gyumri	ARM	1	0
FC Tiraspol	MDA	2	2
Portadown	NIR	2	0
Zalgiris Vilnius	LTU	2	2
Pennarossa	SMR	1	0
Zeljeznicar	BIH	5	4
B 68 Toftir	FRO	0	0
AJ FK Ventspils	LVA	3	8
MIKA Ashtarak	ARM	0	1
Honvéd	HUN	1	1
Banská Bystrica	SVK	3	1
FK Karabakh	AZE	0	0
Marsaxlokk	MLT	0	0
NK Primorje	SVN	1	2
Glentoran	NIR	2	2
Allianssi	FIN	2	1
Santa Coloma	AND	0	0
FK Modrica	BIH	1	3
FC Vaduz	LIE	1	3
Longford Town	IRL	0	2
Haverfordwest	WAL	0	1
FH Hafnarfjördur	FRO	1	3

Second Preliminary Round

Odd Grenland	NOR	3	1
FK Ekranas	LTU	1	2
Osters IF	SWE	2	1
Metalurgs Liepaja	LVA	2	1
Terek Grozny	RUS	1	1
Lech Poznan	POL	0	0
Zeleznik Beograd	SCM	2	2
Steaua Bucuresti	ROM	4	1
Omonia Nicosia	CYP	1	1
CSKA Sofia	BUL	1	3
Banatski Dvor	SCG	1	1
NK Maribor	SVN	2	0
FK Bodø/Glimt	NOR	2	18p
Levadia Tallinn	EST	1	27p
Artmedia	SVK	0	1
Dnipro	UKR	3	1
Nistru Otaci	MDA	1	0
Sigma Olomouc	CZE	2	4
Illychivets Mariupil	UKR	0	0
FK Austria Wien	AUT	0	3
FC Tbilisi	GEO	0	0
Legia Warszawa	POL	1	6
Hapoel Bnei Sak.	ISR	3	3
Partizani Tiranë	ALB	0	1
Stabæk IF	NOR	3	3
Haka Valkeakoski	FIN	1	1
SK Rapid Wien	AUT	0	3
Rubin Kazan	RUS	2	0
Slavia Praha	CZE	3	0
Dinamo Tbilisi	GEO	1	2
Hammarby IF	SWE	2	2
IA Akranes	ISL	0	1
Otelul Galati	ROU	0	0
Partizan Beograd	SCG	0	1
Metalurg Donetsk	UKR	3	2
FC Tiraspol	MDA	0	1
Gençlerbirligi	TUR	1	1
HNK Rijeka	CRO	0	2
Zalgiris Vilnius	LTU	1	0
AaB Aalborg	DEN	3	0
Zeljeznicar	BIH	1	0
Litex Lovech	BUL	2	7
FK Ventspils	LVA	0	1
Brøndby IF	DEN	0	1
Amica Wronki	POL	1	05p
Honvéd	HUN	0	14p
Ujpest	HUN	3	2
Servette	SUI	1	0
Banská Bystrica	SVK	3	1
FC Wil	SUI	1	1
AEK Larnaca	CYP	3	0
Maccabi P-Tikva	ISR	0	4
Dinamo Zagreb	CRO	4	0
NK Primorje	SVN	0	2
Glentoran	NIR	0	1
IF Elfsborg	SWE	1	2
Levski Sofia	BUL	5	3
FK Modrica	BIH	0	0
SK Beveren	BEL	3	2
FC Vaduz	LIE	1	1
FH Hafnarfjördur	FRO	2	2
Dunfermline Ath.	SCO	1	0
SV Pasching	AUT	3	0
Zenit St Peterburg	RUS	1	2

First Round

Odd Grenland	NOR	0	1
Feyenoord	NED	1	4
FC Schalke 04	GER	5	4
Metalurgs Liepaja	LVA	1	0
Terek Grozny	RUS	1	0
FC Basel	SUI	1	2
Millwall	ENG	1	1
Ferencváros	HUN	1	3
Heart of Midlothian	SCO	3	2
SC Braga	POR	1	2
Trabzonspor	TUR	3	0
Athletic Bilbao	ESP	2	2
Steaua Bucuresti	ROM	2	2
CSKA Sofia	BUL	1	2
Parma	ITA	3	0
NK Maribor	SVN	2	0
FK Bodø/Glimt	NOR	1	0
Besiktas	TUR	1	1
Standard CL	BEL	0	1
VfL Bochum	GER	0	1
Maccabi Haifa	ISR	1	0
Dnipro	UKR	0	2
Real Zaragoza	ESP	1	3
Sigma Olomouc	CZE	0	2
FK Austria Wien	AUT	1	3
Legia Warszawa	POL	0	1
Club Brugge	BEL	4	2
Châteauroux	FRA	0	1
FC Utrecht	NED	4	0
Djurgardens IF	SWE	0	3
Newcastle United	ENG	2	5
Hapoel Bnei Sak.	ISR	0	1
Sochaux	FRA	4	5
Stabæk IF	NOR	0	0
Sporting CP	POR	2	0
SK Rapid Wien	AUT	0	0
Panionios	GRE	3	0
Udinese	ITA	1	1
Wisla Krakow	POL	4	1
Dinamo Tbilisi	GEO	3	2
Middlesbrough	ENG	3	1
Banik Ostrava	CZE	0	0
Hammarby IF	SWE	1	0
Villarreal	ESP	2	3
Partizan Beograd	SCG	3	0
Dinamo Bucuresti	ROM	1	0
Metalurg Donetsk	UKR	0	0
Lazio	ITA	3	3
Gençlerbirligi	TUR	0	1
Egaleo	GRE	1	1
PAOK Salonika	GRE	2	1
AZ Alkmaar	NED	3	2
AaB Aalborg	DEN	1	0
AJ Auxerre	FRA	1	2
Grazer AK	AUT	0	1
Litex Lovech	BUL	0	1
Maritimo	POR	1	02p
Rangers	SCO	1	04p
FK Ventspils	LVA	1	0
Amica Wronki	POL	1	1
Ujpest	HUN	1	0
VfB Stuttgart	GER	3	4
Banská Bystrica	SVK	0	0
Benfica	POR	3	2
Maccabi P-Tikva	ISR	-	0
Heerenveen	NED	-	5
Dinamo Zagreb	CRO	2	0
IF Elfsborg	SWE	0	0
Levski Sofia	BUL	1	0
SK Beveren	BEL	1	1
Shelbourne	IRL	2	0
Lille OSC	FRA	2	2
Sevilla	ESP	2	2
CD Nacional	POR	0	1
FH Hafnarfjördur	FRO	1	0
Alemannia Aachen	GER	5	0
Zenit St Peterburg	RUS	4	2
Crvena Zvezda	SCM	0	1
NK Gorica	SVN	1	0
AEK Athens	GRE	1	1

Group Stage

Group A		Pts
Feyenoord	NED	7
FC Schalke 04	GER	7
FC Basel	SUI	7
Ferencváros	HUN	4
Heart of Midlothian	SCO	3

Group B		Pts
Athletic Bilbao	ESP	9
Steaua Bucuresti	ROM	6
Parma	ITA	6
Besiktas	TUR	4
Standard CL	BEL	4

Group C		Pts
Dnipro Dnipropetrovsk	UKR	9
Real Zaragoza	ESP	7
FK Austria Wien	AUT	7
Club Brugge	BEL	5
FC Utrecht	NED	0

Group D		Pts
Newcastle United	ENG	10
Sochaux	FRA	9
Sporting CP	POR	7
Panionios	GRE	3
Dinamo Tbilisi	GEO	0

Group E		Pts
Middlesbrough	ENG	9
Villarreal	ESP	8
Partizan Beograd	SCM	5
Lazio	ITA	3
Egaleo	GRE	1

Group F		Pts
AZ Alkmaar	NED	9
AJ Auxerre	FRA	7
Grazer AK	AUT	7
Rangers	SCO	6
Amica Wronki	POL	0

Group G		Pts
VfB Stuttgart	GER	9
Benfica	POR	7
Heerenveen	NED	7
Dinamo Zagreb	CRO	4
SK Beveren	BEL	0

Group H		Pts
Lille OSC	FRA	9
Sevilla	ESP	7
Alemannia Aachen	GER	7
Zenit Sankt Peterburg	RUS	5
AEK Athens	GRE	0

In each tie the home team in the first leg is listed above their opponents

UEFA CUP 2004-05

Third Round			Fourth Round			Quarter-Final			Semi-Final			Final	
CSKA Moskva *	2	1											
Benfica	0	1											
			CSKA Moskva	1	2								
			Partizan B'grad*	1	0								
Dnipro	2	0											
Partizan B'grad *	2	1											
						CSKA Moskva *	4	0					
						AJ Auxerre	0	2					
Lille OSC	0	2											
FC Basel *	0	0											
			Lille OSC *	0	0								
			AJ Auxerre	1	0								
Ajax *	1	1											
AJ Auxerre	0	3											
									CSKA Moskva	0	3		
									Parma *	0	0		
FK Austria *	0	2											
Athletic Bilbao	0	1											
			FK Austria *	1	2								
			Real Zaragoza	1	2								
Fenerbahçe *	0	1											
Real Zaragoza	1	2											
						FK Austria *	1	0					
						Parma	1	0					
Sevilla	0	2											
Panathinaikos *	1	0											
			Sevilla *	0	0								
			Parma	0	1								
VfB Stuttgart	0	0											
Parma *	0	2											
												CSKA Moskva	3
												Sporting CP	1
AZ Alkmaar	0	2											
Alem. Aachen *	0	1											
			AZ Alkmaar	3	2								
			Shakhtar D'tsk *	1	1								
FC Schalke 04	1	0											
Shakhtar D'tsk *	1	1											
						AZ Alkmaar	2	1					
						Villarreal *	1	1					
Steaua B'resti	0 2 4p												
Valencia *	2 0 3p												
			Steaua B'resti *	0	0								
			Villarreal	0	2								
Dynamo Kyiv *	0	0											
Villarreal	0	2											
									AZ Alkmaar	1	3		
									Sporting CP *	2	2		
Newcastle Utd	2	2											
Heerenveen *	1	1											
			Newcastle Utd	3	4								
			Olympiacos *	1	0								
Sochaux	0	0											
Olympiacos *	1	1											
						Newcastle Utd *	1	1					
						Sporting CP	0	4					
Middlesbrough	2	2											
Grazer AK *	2	1											
			Middlesbrough *	2	0								
			Sporting CP	3	1								
Feyenoord	1	1											
Sporting CP *	2	2											

* Home team in the first leg

UEFA CUP 2005 FINAL ROUNDS

QUARTER-FINAL 1ST LEG
Lokomotiv, Moscow
7-04-2005, Medina Cantalejo ESP

CSKA Moskva	**4**
Odiah [21], Ignashevich [63p], Vágner Love [71], Gusev [77]	
AJ Auxerre	**0**

QUARTER-FINAL 2ND LEG
Abbé-Deschamps, Auxerre
14-04-2005, Stark GER

AJ Auxerre	**2**
Lachuer [9], Kalou [78p]	
CSKA Moskva	**0**

QUARTER-FINAL 1ST LEG
Ernst Happel, Vienna
7-04-2005, Poulat FRA

FK Austria	**1**
Mila [61]	
Parma	**1**
Pisanu [34]	

QUARTER-FINAL 2ND LEG
Ennio Tardini, Parma
14-04-2005, Bennett ENG

Parma	**0**
FK Austria	**0**

QUARTER-FINAL 1ST LEG
El Madrigal, Villarreal
7-04-2005, Plautz AUT

Villarreal	**1**
Riquelme [13]	
AZ Alkmaar	**2**
Landzaat [11], Nelisse [74]	

QUARTER-FINAL 2ND LEG
Alkmaarderhout, Alkmaar
14-04-2005, Rosetti ITA

AZ Alkmaar	**1**
Perez [8]	
Villarreal	**1**
Lucho [72]	

QUARTER-FINAL 1ST LEG
St James' Park, Newcastle
7-04-2005, Baskakov RUS

Newcastle United	**1**
Shearer [37]	
Sporting CP	**0**

QUARTER-FINAL 2ND LEG
José Alvalade, Lisbon
14-04-2005, Fröjdfeldt SWE

Sporting CP	**4**
Niculae [40], Sa Pinto [71], Beto [76], Rochemback [91+]	
Newcastle United	**1**
Dyer [20]	

SEMI-FINAL 1ST LEG
Ennio Tardini, Parma
28-04-2005, Busacca SUI

Parma	**0**
CSKA Moskva	**0**

SEMI-FINAL 2ND LEG
Lokomotiv, Moscow
5-05-2005, Hamer LUX

CSKA Moskva	**3**
Carvakho 2 [10] [53], Berezoutski [60]	
Parma	**0**

SEMI-FINAL 1ST LEG
José Alvalade, Lisbon
28-04-2005, De Santis ITA

Sporting CP	**2**
Doula [36], Pinilla [80]	
AZ Alkmaar	**1**
Landzaat [76]	

SEMI-FINAL 2ND LEG
Alkmaarderhout, Alkmaar
5-05-2005, Bo Larsen DEN

AZ Alkmaar	**3**
Perez [6], Huysegems [79], Jaliens [108]	
Sporting CP	**2**
Liedson [49+], Miguel Garcia [122+]	

FINAL, Jose Alvalade, Lisbon, 18-05-2005
19:45, 47 085, Poll ENG, Tingey ENG, Turner ENG

SPORTING CP   1   3   CSKA MOSKVA

Rogerio [29]

Berezoutski.A [56], Zhirkov [65]
Vágner Love [75]

SPORTING CLUBE				CSKA MOSKVA			
76	GK	RICARDO		AKINFEEV Igor	GK	35	
8	MF	PEDRO BARBOSA		IGNASHEVICH Sergei	DF	4	
10	FW	SA PINTO Ricardo	72	BEREZOUTSKI Aleksei	DF	6	
14	DF	ENAKARHIRE Joseph		CARVALHO Daniel	MF	7	82
15	DF	MIGUEL GARCIA		OLIC Ivica	FW	9	67
22	DF	BETO		VAGNER LOVE	FW	11	
26	MF	ROCHEMBACK Fabio		ODIAH Chidi	DF	15	
28	MF	MOUTINHO João	87	ZHIRKOV Yuri	MF	18	
31	FW	LIEDSON		ALDONIN Evgeni	MF	22	86
37	MF	ROGERIO	79	BEREZOUTSKI Vassili	DF	24	
11	MF	TELLO Rodrigo		RAHIMIC Elvir	MF	25	
		Tr: PESEIRO José					
9	FW	NICULAE Marius	72	SEMBERAS Deividas	DF	2	82
17	FW	DOUALA Roudolphe	79	GUSEV Rolan	MF	8	86
45	MF	HUGO VIANA	87	KRASIC Milos	MF	17	67

UEFA WOMEN'S EURO 2005™ ENGLAND

Germany's extraordinary record in the UEFA Women's Championship continued when they won a fouth consecutive title in a tournament that was notable for the interest generated, not only in England where it was staged, but across Europe. England's opening game, in the City of Manchester Stadium, drew a record European crowd of 29,092 while the final itself pulled in 21,105, a fantastic figure given that England had been knocked out in the first round. Once again it was the Scandinavian countries that posed the biggest threat to Germany although Finland's semi-final appearance was the surprise of the tournament. Germany then proved a step too far for the inexperienced Finns but the other semi-final, between Sweden and Norway, was a much closer affair with the fans in Warrington witnessing one of the best women's matches of recent years. Norway's victory was hard fought and it took its toll in the final when they found themselves 2-0 behind early on. They staged a gallant comeback and with more luck may have won but it was the Germans' day again, holding on for their sixth title in the past seven tournaments.

First Category Qualifying Group 1

	Pl	W	D	L	F	A	Pts	SWE	ITA	FIN	SUI	SCG
Sweden	8	6	1	1	26	5	19		5-0	2-1	6-0	5-1
Italy	8	4	3	1	15	9	15	2-1		1-1	0-0	8-0
Finland	8	3	4	1	12	6	13	1-1	1-1		1-1	4-0
Switzerland	8	1	2	5	2	13	5	0-2	0-1	0-2		1-0
Serbia/Montenegro	8	1	0	7	3	25	3	0-4	1-2	0-1	1-0	

First Category Qualifying Group 2

	Pl	W	D	L	F	A	Pts	DEN	NOR	ESP	NED	BEL
Denmark	8	7	1	0	26	4	22		2-1	2-0	3-0	6-0
Norway	8	6	1	1	22	4	19	1-1		2-0	2-0	6-0
Spain	8	2	1	5	10	10	7	0-1	0-2		0-0	9-1
Netherlands	8	2	1	5	7	13	7	1-5	0-2	0-1		3-0
Belgium	8	1	0	7	5	39	3	1-6	1-6	2-0	0-3	

First Category Qualifying Group 3

	Pl	W	D	L	F	A	Pts	FRA	RUS	ISL	HUN	POL
France	8	7	0	1	32	7	21		2-5	2-0	6-0	7-1
Russia	8	5	2	1	22	8	17	0-3		1-1	4-0	6-0
Iceland	8	4	1	3	23	11	13	0-3	0-2		4-1	10-0
Hungary	8	1	1	6	6	28	4	0-4	1-3	0-5		2-2
Poland	8	0	2	6	7	36	2	1-5	1-1	2-3	0-2	

First Category Qualifying Group 4

	Pl	W	D	L	F	A	Pts	GER	CZE	SCO	UKR	POR
Germany	8	8	0	0	50	2	24		4-0	5-0	6-0	13-0
Czech Republic	8	4	1	3	15	15	13	0-5		2-0	4-1	5-1
Scotland	8	4	0	4	19	16	12	1-3	3-2		5-1	2-1
Ukraine	8	2	1	5	7	21	7	1-3	1-1	1-0		0-1
Portugal	8	1	0	7	5	42	3	0-11	0-1	1-8	1-2	

First Category Play-offs

Home team 1st Leg	Score	Home team 2nd leg
Finland	1-0 3-1	Russia
Iceland	2-7 1-2	Norway
Italy	2-1 3-0	Czech Republic

Second Category Qualifying Group 5

	Pl	W	D	L	F	A	Pts	IRL	ROM	CRO	BIH	MLT
Republic of Ireland	8	5	3	0	35	5	18		2-2	8-1	6-0	5-0
Romania	8	5	3	0	29	5	18	1-1		10-0	2-0	3-0
Croatia	8	4	1	3	17	22	13	0-0	2-3		6-0	3-0
Bosnia-Herzegov.	8	2	1	5	4	19	7	1-4	0-0	0-1		0-0
Malta	8	0	0	8	1	35	0	0-9	0-8	1-4	0-2	

Second Category Qualifying Group 6

	Pl	W	D	L	F	A	Pts	BLR	ISR	EST	KAZ
Belarus	6	5	1	0	21	3	16		1-1	5-0	8-1
Israel	6	3	2	1	20	6	11	0-2		12-1	3-1
Estonia	6	1	1	4	6	26	4	1-3	1-4		3-2
Kazakhstan	6	0	2	4	4	16	2	0-2	0-0	0-0	

Second Category Qualifying Group 7

	Pl	W	D	L	F	A	Pts	AUT	GRE	SVK	ARM
Austria	6	5	0	1	31	4	15		1-2	3-0	11-0
Greece	6	4	1	1	23	6	13	0-2		3-1	7-0
Slovakia	6	2	1	3	20	11	7	2-3	2-2		5-0
Armenia	6	0	0	6	0	53	0	0-11	0-9	0-10	

UEFA EUROPEAN WOMEN'S CHAMPIONSHIP 2005

First Round Group Stage

Group A	Pl	W	D	L	F	A	Pts	FIN	DEN	ENG
Sweden	3	1	2	0	2	1	5	0-0	1-1	1-0
Finland	3	1	1	1	4	4	4		2-1	2-3
Denmark	3	1	1	1	4	4	4			2-1
England	3	1	0	2	4	5	3			

Semi-finals

Germany	4
Finland	1

Final

Germany	3
Norway	1

Group B	Pl	W	D	L	F	A	Pts	NOR	FRA	ITA
Germany	3	3	0	0	8	0	9	1-0	3-0	4-0
Norway	3	1	1	1	6	5	4	1-1	5-3	
France	3	1	1	1	5	4	4		3-1	
Italy	3	0	0	3	4	12	0			

Sweden	2
Norway	3

GROUP A

Bloomfield Road, Blackpool
5-06-2005, 17:00, 3 231, Seitz USA

SWE 1 1 DEN

Ljungberg 21 — Rasmussen 29

SWEDEN				DENMARK	
12	LINDAHL Hedvig			CEDERQVIST Tine	1
3	TORNQVIST Jane			FALK Bettina	2
4	MARKLUND Hanna		85	(c) PEDERSEN Katrine	3
5	BENGTSSON Kristin (c)			ANDERSEN Gitte	4
6	MOSTROM Malin			KNUDSEN Mariann G.	5
7	LARSSON Sara			HANSEN Louise	6
8	OSTBERG Frida			SORENSEN Catherine	7
10	LJUNGBERG Hanna			NIELSEN Anne	10
11	SVENSSON Victoria			PEDERSEN Merete	11
13	SCHELIN Lotta	85	79	RASMUSSEN Johanna	13
16	SEGER Caroline	55	85	JOHANSEN Nanna	17
	Tr: LYFORS Marika Domanski			Tr: BONDE Peter	
15	SJOGRAN Therese	55	85	JENSEN Lene	9
20	OQVIST Josephine	85	79	JENSEN Dorte Dalum	12
			85	OLSEN Mie	18

City of Manchester Stadium, Manchester
5-06-2005, 19:00, 29 092, Gaal HUN

ENG 3 2 - FIN

Valkonen OG 18, Barr 40, Carney 91+ — Rantanen 56, Kalmari 88

ENGLAND				FINLAND	
1	FLETCHER Josephine			KUNNAS Satu	1
2	SCOTT Alex			VAELMA Petra	2
3	UNITT Rachel			JULIN Jessica	3
4	CHAPMAN Katie			(c) VALKONEN Sanna	4
5	WHITE Faye (c)	85		SALMEN Tiina	5
6	PHILLIP Mary Rose			SARAPAA Evelina	6
8	WILLIAMS Fara			MAKINEN Anne	7
9	BARR Amanda	73		KALMARI Laura	9
11	YANKEY Rachel			RANTANEN Anna-Kaisa	10
12	SMITH Kelly	46	81	KACKUR Heidi	11
14	CARNEY Karen		74	THORN Jessica	13
	Tr: POWELL Hope			Tr: KALD Michael	
10	WESTWOOD Emily	46	74	MUSTONEN Minna	8
18	ALUKO Eniola	73	81	TALONEN Sanna	18
19	JOHNSON Lindsay	85			

Ewood Park, Blackburn
8-06-2005, 18:00, 14 695, Ihringova SVK

DEN 2 1 ENG

Pedersen.M 80, Sørensen 88 — Williams 52p

DENMARK				ENGLAND	
1	CEDERQVIST Tine			FLETCHER Josephine	1
2	FALK Bettina			SCOTT Alex	2
3	PEDERSEN Katrine (c)			UNITT Rachel	3
4	ANDERSEN Gitte			CHAPMAN Katie	4
5	KNUDSEN Mariann G.			(c) WHITE Faye	5
6	HANSEN Louise			PHILLIP Mary Rose	6
7	SORENSEN Catherine			WILLIAMS Fara	8
10	NIELSEN Anne	71	64	BARR Amanda	9
11	PEDERSEN Merete			YANKEY Rachel	11
13	RASMUSSEN Johanna		46	SMITH Kelly	12
17	JOHANSEN Nanna	57		CARNEY Karen	14
	Tr: BONDE Peter			Tr: POWELL Hope	
9	JENSEN Lene	57	46	EXLEY Vicky	16
15	CHRISTENSEN Tanja	71	64	ALUKO Eniola	18

Bloomfield Road, Blackpool
8-06-2005, 20:00, 1 491, Damkova CZE

SWE 0 0 FIN

SWEDEN				FINLAND	
12	LINDAHL Hedvig			KUNNAS Satu	1
3	TORNQVIST Jane			VAELMA Petra	2
4	MARKLUND Hanna			JULIN Jessica	3
5	BENGTSSON Kristin (c)			(c) VALKONEN Sanna	4
6	MOSTROM Malin			SALMEN Tiina	5
7	LARSSON Sara			SARAPAA Evelina	6
9	ANDERSSON Malin			MAKINEN Anne	7
10	LJUNGBERG Hanna		71	MUSTONEN Minna	8
11	SVENSSON Victoria			KALMARI Laura	9
13	SCHELIN Lotta	56	90	RANTANEN Anna-Kaisa	10
15	SJOGRAN Therese	71	46	KACKUR Heidi	11
	Tr: LYFORS Marika Domanski			Tr: KALD Michael	
17	SJOSTROM Anna	71	46	THORN Jessica	13
20	OQVIST Josephine	56	90	MALASKA Sanna	15
			71	TALONEN Sanna	18

Ewood Park, Blackburn
11-06-2005, 18:00, 25 694, Petignat SUI

ENG 0 1 SWE

Sjöström 3

ENGLAND				SWEDEN	
13	BROWN Rachel			LINDAHL Hedvig	12
2	SCOTT Alex			TORNQVIST Jane	3
3	UNITT Rachel			MARKLUND Hanna	4
4	CHAPMAN Katie		75	(c) BENGTSSON Kristin	5
5	WHITE Faye (c)			MOSTROM Malin	6
6	PHILLIP Mary Rose			LARSSON Sara	7
8	WILLIAMS Fara			LJUNGBERG Hanna	10
11	YANKEY Rachel	93		SVENSSON Victoria	11
12	SMITH Kelly			SJOGRAN Therese	15
14	CARNEY Karen	69	54	SEGER Caroline	16
18	ALUKO Eniola			SJOSTROM Anna	17
	Tr: POWELL Hope			Tr: LYFORS Marika Domanski	
9	BARR Amanda	69	75	WESTBERG Karolina	2
			54	OSTBERG Frida	8
			93	OQVIST Josephine	20

Bloomfield Road, Blackpool
11-06-2005, 18:00, 2 500, Ihringova SVK

FIN 2 1 DEN

Kalmari 6, Kackur 16 — Sørensen 45

FINLAND				DENMARK	
1	KUNNAS Satu			CEDERQVIST Tine	1
2	VAELMA Petra			(c) PEDERSEN Katrine	3
3	JULIN Jessica			ANDERSEN Gitte	4
4	VALKONEN Sanna (c)		70	HANSEN Louise	6
5	SALMEN Tiina			SORENSEN Catherine	7
6	SARAPAA Evelina			NIELSEN Anne	10
7	MAKINEN Anne	79		PEDERSEN Merete	11
9	KALMARI Laura	89		JENSEN Dorte Dalum	12
10	RANTANEN Anna-Kaisa			RASMUSSEN Johanna	13
11	KACKUR Heidi		63	JOHANSEN Nanna	17
13	THORN Jessica	59	70	OLSEN Mie	18
	Tr: KALD Michael			Tr: BONDE Peter	
8	MUSTONEN Minna	89	63	JENSEN Stine Kjær	8
15	MALASKA Sanna	59	70	CHRISTENSEN Tanja	15
19	LINDSTROM Heidi	74	70	NIELSEN Helle	19

GROUP B

Halliwell Jones, Warrington
6-06-2005, 18:00, 1 600, Petignat SUI

GER	1	0	NOR

Pohlers 61

GERMANY			NORWAY	
1 ROTTENBERG Silke			NORDBY Bente	1
2 STEGEMANN Kerstin			(c) STANGELAND Ane	2
4 JONES Stephanie			FOLSTAD Gunhild	3
6 GRINGS Inka	71		STENSLAND Ingrid	4
10 LINGOR Renate (c)			CHRISTENSEN Marit	6
11 MITTAG Anja			RONNING Trine	7
13 MINNERT Sandra			GULBRANDSEN Solveig	8
16 POHLERS Conny	80	66	LEHN Unni	10
17 HINGST Ariane			MELLGREN Dagny	14
18 GAREFREKES Kerstin			PAULSEN Marianne	17
19 OMILADE Navina	62	83	FRANTZEN Stine	19
Tr: THEUNE-MEYER Tina			Tr: BERNTSEN Bjarne	
8 SMISEK Sandra	71	83	HERLOVSEN Isabell	9
14 CARLSON Britta	62	66	KLAVENESS Lise	20
20 WIMBERSKY Petra	80			

Deepdale, Preston
6-06-2005, 20:00, 957, Toms ENG

FRA	3	1	ITA

Lattaf 16, Pichon 2 20 30   Di Filippo 83

FRANCE			ITALY	
20 BOUHADDI Sarah			BRUNOZZI Carla	1
4 GEORGES Laura			ZORRI Tatiana	3
5 DIACRE Corinne			DI FILIPPO Sara	4
6 SOUBEYRAND Sandrine			TONA Elisabetta	5
7 MUGNERET-B. Stephanie		46	GAZZOLI Chiara	7
8 BOMPASTOR Sonia (c)			(c) PANICO Patrizia	9
9 PICHON Marinette	85		CAMPORESE Elisa	10
11 DUSANG Sandrine	91		PASQUI Ilaria	11
13 CASSELEUX Anne Laure		39	MASIA Gioia	13
18 LATTAF Hoda	72		SCHIAVI Viviana	15
19 BUSSAGLIA Elise		69	CONTI Pamela	18
Tr: LOISEL Elisabeth			Tr: MORACE Carolina	
3 PROVOST Peggy	91	69	DOMENICHETTI Giulia	2
12 ABILY Camille	85	39	FICARELLI Elena	16
15 THOMIS Elodie	72	46	GANNIADINI Melania	17

Deepdale, Preston
9-06-2005, 17:15, 1 279, Seitz USA

ITA	0	4	GER

Prinz 11, Pohlers 18, Jones 55, Mittag 74

ITALY			GERMANY	
1 BRUNOZZI Carla			ROTTENBERG Silke	1
3 ZORRI Tatiana	75	19	STEGEMANN Kerstin	2
4 DI FILIPPO Sara			JONES Stephanie	4
5 TONA Elisabetta			PRINZ Birgit	9
9 PANICO Patrizia (c)			(c) LINGOR Renate	10
10 CAMPORESE Elisa		77	MITTAG Anja	11
11 PASQUI Ilaria			MINNERT Sandra	13
13 MASIA Gioia			CARLSON Britta	14
15 SCHIAVI Viviana	46		POHLERS Conny	16
16 FICARELLI Elena			HINGST Ariane	17
18 CONTI Pamela	51		GAREFREKES Kerstin	18
Tr: MORACE Carolina			Tr: THEUNE-MEYER Tina	
2 DOMENICHETTI Giulia	51	19	GRINGS Inka	6
8 DEIANA Damiana	46	77	SMISEK Sandra	8
19 BONI Valentina	75			

Halliwell Jones, Warrington
9-06-2005, 20:00, 3 263, Gaal HUN

FRA	1	1	NOR

Mugneret-Béghé 20   Herlovsen 66

FRANCE			NORWAY	
20 BOUHADDI Sarah			NORDBY Bente	1
3 PROVOST Peggy			(c) STANGELAND Ane	2
4 GEORGES Laura			FOLSTAD Gunhild	3
5 DIACRE Corinne			STENSLAND Ingrid	4
6 SOUBEYRAND Sandrine			NORDBY Siri	5
7 MUGNERET-B. Stephanie	54		CHRISTENSEN Marit	6
8 BOMPASTOR Sonia (c)			RONNING Trine	7
9 PICHON Marinette			GULBRANDSEN Solveig	8
11 DUSANG Sandrine		46	LEHN Unni	10
18 LATTAF Hoda			MELLGREN Dagny	14
19 BUSSAGLIA Elise		64	FRANTZEN Stine	19
Tr: LOISEL Elisabeth			Tr: BERNTSEN Bjarne	
17 KRAMO Marie-Ange	54	46	HERLOVSEN Isabell	9
		64	KLAVENESS Lise	20

Halliwell Jones, Warrington
12-06-2005, 15:00, 3 835, Ionescu ROU

GER	3	0	FRA

Grings 72, Lingor 77p, Minnert 83

GERMANY			FRANCE	
1 ROTTENBERG Silke			BOUHADDI Sarah	20
4 JONES Stephanie			PROVOST Peggy	3
6 GRINGS Inka			GEORGES Laura	4
9 PRINZ Birgit			DIACRE Corinne	5
10 LINGOR Renate (c)	80		SOUBEYRAND Sandrine	6
11 MITTAG Anja	46	32	MUGNERET-B. Stephanie	7
13 MINNERT Sandra			(c) BOMPASTOR Sonia	8
16 POHLERS Conny	46	80	PICHON Marinette	9
17 HINGST Ariane			DUSANG Sandrine	11
18 GAREFREKES Kerstin			ABILY Camile	12
19 OMILADE Navina			NECIB Louisa	14
Tr: THEUNE-MEYER Tina			Tr: LOISEL Elisabeth	
3 FUSS Sonja	46	80	HERBERT Candie	10
7 WUNDERLICH Pia	46	32	KRAMO Marie-Ange	17
14 CARLSON Britta	80			

Deepdale, Preston
12-06-2005, 15:00, 1 154, Damkova CZE

NOR	5	3	ITA

Klaveness 2 7 57, Christensen 30   Gabbiadini 2 8 52, Camporese 68
Gulbrandsen 35, Mellgren 45

NORWAY			ITALY	
1 NORDBY Bente			BRUNOZZI Carla	1
2 STANGELAND Ane (c)		54	DOMENICHETTI Giulia	2
3 FOLSTAD Gunhild			ZORRI Tatiana	3
4 STENSLAND Ingrid			TONA Elisabetta	5
6 CHRISTENSEN Marit			(c) PANICO Patrizia	9
7 RONNING Trine	46		CAMPORESE Elisa	10
8 GULBRANDSEN Solveig	69	91	PASQUI Ilaria	11
9 HERLOVSEN Isabell	83	63	LANZIERI Valentina	14
14 MELLGREN Dagny			FICARELLI Elena	16
17 PAULSEN Marianne			GANNIADINI Melania	17
20 KLAVENESS Lise			CONTI Pamela	18
Tr: BERNTSEN Bjarne			Tr: MORACE Carolina	
10 LEHN Unni	46	36	DEIANA Damiana	8
18 KNUTSEN Marie	69	91	SCHIAVI Viviana	15
19 FRANTZEN Stine	83	54	BONI Valentina	19

SEMI-FINALS

Deepdale, Preston		
15-06-2005, 18:30, 2 785, Damkova CZE		

GER	**4**	**1**	**FIN**

Grings 2 [3 12], Pohlers [8], Prinz [62]
Mustonen [15]

GERMANY			FINLAND	
1	ROTTENBERG Silke		KUNNAS Satu	1
4	JONES Stephanie		VAELMA Petra	2
6	GRINGS Inka	81	JULIN Jessica	3
9	PRINZ Birgit		(c) VALKONEN Sanna	4
10	LINGOR Renate (c)	75	SALMEN Tiina	5
11	MITTAG Anja	46	69	SARAPAA Evelina	6
13	MINNERT Sandra		MAKINEN Anne	7
14	CARLSON Britta		46	MUSTONEN Minna	8
16	POHLERS Conny		KALMARI Laura	9
17	HINGST Ariane		RANTANEN Anna-Kaisa	10
18	GAREFREKES Kerstin	62	KACKUR Heidi	11
	Tr: THEUNE-MEYER Tina		Tr: KALD Michael	
3	FUSS Sonja	46	46	UUSI-LUOMALAHTI Terhi	16
5	GUNTHER Sarah	75	69	THORN Jessica	13
20	WIMBERSKY Petra	62	81	MALASKA Sanna	15

Halliwell Jones, Warrington		
16-06-2005, 18:30, 5 722, Seitz USA		

NOR	**3**	**2**	**SWE**

Gulbrandsen 2 [41 109]
Herlovesen [65]
Ljungberg 2 [43 89]

NORWAY			SWEDEN	
1	NORDBY Bente		LINDAHL Hedvig	12
2	STANGELAND Ane (c)		TORNQVIST Jane	3
3	FOLSTAD Gunhild		MARKLUND Hanna	4
4	STENSLAND Ingrid		(c) BENGTSSON Kristin	5
6	CHRISTENSEN Marit	83	MOSTROM Malin	6
8	GULBRANDSEN Solveig		LARSSON Sara	7
9	HERLOVSEN Isabell	65	LJUNGBERG Hanna	10
10	LEHN Unni	60	49	SVENSSON Victoria	11
14	MELLGREN Dagny		71	SJOGRAN Therese	15
17	PAULSEN Marianne		46	SEGER Caroline	16
20	KLAVENESS Lise		SJOSTROM Anna	17
	Tr: BERNTSEN Bjarne		Tr: LYFORS Marika Domanski	
7	RONNING Trine	60	46	OSTBERG Frida	8
11	KAUFMANN Maritha	83	49	SCHELIN Lotta	13
19	FRANTZEN Stine	65	71	OQVIST Josephine	20

FINAL

Ewood Park, Blackburn		
19-06-2005, 15:15, 21 105, Ihringova SVK, Parga Rodriguez ESP, Logarusic CRO		

GER	**3**	**1**	**NOR**

Grings [21], Lingor [24], Prinz [63]
Mellgren [41]

GERMANY				NORWAY		
1	GK	ROTTENBERG Silke		NORDBY Bente	GK	1
4	DF	JONES Stephanie		(c) STANGELAND Ane	DF	2
6	FW	GRINGS Inka	68	FOLSTAD Gunhild	DF	3
9	FW	PRINZ Birgit		STENSLAND Ingrid	MF	4
10	MF	LINGOR Renate (c)		CHRISTENSEN Marit	DF	6
11	FW	MITTAG Anja	58	83	RONNING Trine	MF	7
13	DF	MINNERT Sandra		GULBRANDSEN Solveig	MF	8
14	MF	CARLSON Britta	81	MELLGREN Dagny	FW	14
16	MF	POHLERS Conny		PAULSEN Marianne	DF	17
17	DF	HINGST Ariane	59	FRANTZEN Stine	FW	19
18	MF	GAREFREKES Kerstin	87	KLAVENESS Lise	FW	20
		Tr: THEUNE-MEYER Tina		Tr: BERNTSEN Bjarne		
5	DF	GUNTHER Sarah	81	59	HERLOVSEN Isabell	FW	9
8	FW	SMISEK Sandra	68	87	BLYSTAD-BJERKE Kristin	FW	16
20	FW	WIMBERSKY Petra	58	83	KNUTSEN Marie	MF	18

UEFA WOMEN'S CUP 2004–05

The UEFA Women's Cup has now established itself as an important part of the women's game with European clubs beginning to attract players from other parts of the world, notably Brazil. Played in two group stages followed by a knock-out tournament for the surving eight clubs the UEFA Women's Cup attracted entries from 42 nations for the 2005 tournament. The winners of the nine first round groups joined seven clubs with byes in the four second round groups with the top two from each group qualifying for the quarter-finals. Defending champions Umeå IK were surprisingly eliminated by compatriots Djurgården/Alvsjö who then went on to beat Arsenal in the semi-finals to meet 1.FFC Turbine Potsdam in the final. Potsdam made it a good year for German football with their 5-1 aggregate victory over the Swedes with goals from Pohlers, Mittag and Wimbersky, who all went on to do the double with the national team a month later in England.

UEFA WOMEN'S CUP 2004–05

First round Groups

Team		Pl	W	D	L	F	A	Pts			
Alma KTZH	KAZ	3	3	0	0	11	2	9	2-1	5-1	4-0
SK Slavia Praha	CZE	3	2	0	1	8	2	6		3-0	4-0
LP Super Sport Sofia	BUL	3	1	0	2	2	10	3			2-2
MSK Žiar nad Hronom	SVK	3	0	0	1	2	10	1			
FC Energy Voronezh	RUS	3	3	0	0	27	0	9	3-0	11-0	13-0
Gömrükçü Baku	AZE	3	2	0	1	16	4	6		3-0	13-1
Gintra-Universitetas	LTU	3	1	0	2	14	3	3			1-0
KFF Sžiponjat	MKD	3	0	0	3	1	27	0			
FC Bobruichanka	BLR	3	3	0	0	7	2	9	2-0	3-1	2-1
FC Codru Anenii Noi	MDA	3	2	0	1	6	4	4		1-0	5-1
Viktoria Szombathe	HUN	3	1	0	2	6	4	4			4-0
Pärnu JK	EST	3	0	0	3	2	11	0			
ZNK KRKA Novo Mesto	SVN	3	2	0	1	4	4	6	2-1	0-2	2-1
KR Reykjavik	ISL	3	1	0	1	5	3	6		1-0	3-1
Ter Leede Sassenheim	NED	3	1	0	2	3	2	4			1-1
Malmö PS Helsinki	FIN	3	0	0	3	3	6	1			
ZFK Masinac Nis	SCG	3	3	0	0	10	2	9	4-1	4-1	2-0
Hibernian LFC	SCO	3	2	0	1	9	6	6		3-2	5-0
KFC Rapide Wezemaal	BEL	3	1	0	2	5	7	3			2-0
ZNK Maksimir Zagreb	CRO	3	0	0	3	3	9	0			
KS AZS Wroclaw	POL	3	3	0	0	9	2	9	2-0	5-1	2-1
Metalist Kharkiv	UKR	3	2	0	1	10	4	6		2-1	8-1
Ki Klaksvik	ISL	3	1	0	2	6	7	3			4-0
Cardiff LFC	WAL	3	0	0	3	2	14	0			
Athletic Club Bilbao	ESP	3	2	1	0	16	4	7	5-0	1-1	10-3
CFF Clujana	ROU	3	1	1	1	5	5	4		0-0	3-0
Maccabi Holon	ISR	3	1	0	3	3	3	3			2-2
Newtonabbey Strikers	NIR	3	0	1	2	5	15	1			
AE Aegina	GRE	3	3	0	0	10	0	9	1-0	2-0	7-0
FFC Zuchwil	SUI	3	2	0	1	17	2	6		4-0	13-1
SFK 2000 Sarajevo	BIH	3	1	0	2	5	6	3			5-0
Ledra	CYP	3	0	0	3	1	25	0			
Montpellier HSC	FRA	3	3	0	0	13	0	9	7-0	1-0	5-0
SV Neulengbach	AUT	3	2	0	1	7	10	6		3-1	4-2
União 1° Dezembro	POR	3	1	0	2	2	2	5			1-1
Univ. College Dublin	IRL	3	0	0	3	3	10	1			

Second Round Groups

Team		Pl	W	D	L	F	A	Pts			
1.FFC Turbine Potsdam	GER	3	3	0	0	17	6	9	7-5	4-1	6-0
Torres Terra Sarda	ITA	3	2	0	1	12	8	6		5-0	2-1
KS AZS Wroclaw	POL	3	1	0	2	9	9	3			2-0
Montpellier HSC	FRA	3	0	0	3	1	10	0			
Umeå IK	SWE	3	3	0	0	20	2	9	5-1	8-0	7-1
FC Bobruichanka	BLR	3	1	1	1	5	5	4		0-0	4-0
ZFK Masinac Nis	SCG	3	1	1	1	8	4	4			2-0
ZNK KRKA Novo Mesto	SVN	3	0	0	3	3	13	0			
SK Trondheims-Orn	NOR	3	2	1	0	6	1	7	1-1	2-0	3-0
FC Energy Voronezh	RUS	3	2	0	1	6	3	6		1-1	4-1
Brøndby IF	DEN	3	1	1	1	3	3	4			2-0
Alma KTZH	KAZ	3	0	0	3	1	9	0			
Arsenal	ENG	3	2	1	0	8	3	7	1-0	2-0	7-0
Djurgården / Älvsjö	SWE	3	2	1	0	10	3	6		3-2	5-1
Athletic Club Bilbao	ESP	3	1	1	1	9	6	4			5-1
AE Aegina	GRE	3	0	0	3	2	17	0			

Seven clubs received byes to the second round

Quarter-finals

1.FFC Turbine Potsdam	1	4
FC Energy Voronezh	1	1
FC Bobruichanka	0	1
SK Trondheims-Orn	4	2
Arsenal	2	1
Torres Terra Sarda	0	4
Umeå IK	1	0
Djurgården / Älvsjö	3	2

Semi-finals

1.FFC Turbine Potsdam	4	3
SK Trondheims-Orn	0	1
Arsenal	1	0
Djurgården / Älvsjö	1	1

Final

FINAL 1ST LEG

1.FFC Turbine Potsdam	2	3
Djurgården/Älvsjö	0	1

15-05-2005, Ref. De Toni ITA
Stockholms Stadion
Scorers - Pohlers 34, Mittag 53 for Potsdam
Djurgården - Aström, Fagerström, Törnqvist, Ekblom, Thunebro, Nykvist, Bengtsson, Fagerström, Hall, Norlin (Callebaut 76), James. Tr. Södermann
Potsdam - Angerer, Fuss (Thomas 68), Carlson, Omilade, Becher, Pohlers, Zietz, Hingst, Odebrecht, Wimbersky (Sousa Silva 82), Mittag. Tr. Schröder

FINAL 2ND LEG

Arsenal	1	0
Djurgården / Älvsjö	1	1

21-05-2005, Ref. Laìa Orta TUR
Karl Liebknecht, Potsdam
Scorers - Wimbersky 2, Pohlers 2 9 15 for Potsdam. Bengtsson 10 for Djurgården
Potsdam - Angerer, Fuss, Carlson, Omilade, Becher, Pohlers (Sousa Silva 74), Zietz, Hingst, Odebrecht, Wimbersky (Thomas 79), Mittag. Tr. Schröder
Djurgården - Aström, Fagerström (Curtsdotter 46), Ekblom, Thunebro (Lekander 46), Nykvist, Bengtsson, Fagerström, Svensson, Norlin (Hall 53), James, Törnqvist. Tr. Södermann

UEFA EUROPEAN WOMEN'S U–19 CHAMPIONSHIP 2005

First Qualifying Round Group 1

	Pl	W	D	L	F	A	Pts	AUT	SVN	BIH
Netherlands	3	3	0	0	11	0	9	1-0	7-0	3-0
Austria	3	2	0	1	13	2	6		8-0	5-1
Slovenia	3	1	0	2	5	15	3			5-0
Bosnia-Herzegov.	3	0	0	3	1	13	0			

First Qualifying Round Group 2

	Pl	W	D	L	F	A	Pts	UKR	MDA	BLR
Scotland	3	3	0	0	24	0	9	6-0	5-0	13-0
Ukraine	3	2	0	1	10	7	6		8-1	2-0
Moldova	3	1	0	2	3	13	3			2-0
Belarus	3	0	0	3	0	17	0			

First Qualifying Round Group 3

	Pl	W	D	L	F	A	Pts	DEN	AZE	LTU
France	3	3	0	0	22	0	9	2-0	10-0	10-0
Denmark	3	2	0	1	28	2	6		20-0	8-0
Azerbaijan	3	1	0	2	2	31	3			2-1
Lithuania	3	0	0	3	1	20	0			

First Qualifying Round Group 4

	Pl	W	D	L	F	A	Pts	WAL	ROM	BUL
England	3	3	0	0	11	0	9	2-0	3-0	6-0
Wales	3	2	0	1	9	3	6		4-1	5-0
Romania	3	1	0	2	5	7	3			4-0
Bulgaria	3	0	0	3	0	15	0			

First Qualifying Round Group 5

	Pl	W	D	L	F	A	Pts	ISR	KAZ	LVA
Russia	3	3	0	0	19	0	9	3-0	9-0	7-0
Israel	3	2	0	1	6	5	6		3-0	3-2
Kazakhstan	3	1	0	2	5	13	3			5-1
Latvia	3	0	0	3	3	15	0			

First Qualifying Round Group 6

	Pl	W	D	L	F	A	Pts	IRL	GRE	ISL
Switzerland	3	2	1	0	9	1	7	0-0	5-0	4-1
Rep. of Ireland	3	2	1	0	3	0	7		2-0	1-0
Greece	3	1	0	2	4	7	3			4-0
Iceland	3	0	0	3	1	9	0			

First Qualifying Round Group 7

	Pl	W	D	L	F	A	Pts	ITA	ARM	EST
Sweden	3	3	0	0	31	1	9	5-1	11-0	15-0
Italy	3	2	0	1	18	5	6		9-0	8-0
Armenia	3	1	0	2	2	21	3			2-1
Estonia	3	0	0	3	1	25	0			

First Qualifying Round Group 8

	Pl	W	D	L	F	A	Pts	SCG	POR	SVK
Finland	3	3	0	0	9	1	9	1-0	6-1	2-0
Serbia/Montenegro	3	1	1	1	8	6	4		5-2	3-3
Portugal	3	1	0	2	6	12	3			3-1
Slovakia	3	0	1	2	4	8	1			

First Qualifying Round Group 9

	Pl	W	D	L	F	A	Pts	POL	CRO	FRO
Belgium	3	2	1	0	6	1	7	1-1	1-0	4-0
Poland	3	1	2	0	6	3	5		2-2	3-0
Croatia	3	1	1	1	3	3	4			1-0
Faroe Islands	3	0	0	3	0	8	0			

First Qualifying Round Group 10

	Pl	W	D	L	F	A	Pts	CZE	NIR	MKD
Spain	3	3	0	0	17	1	9	5-1	3-0	9-0
Czech Republic	3	2	0	1	9	5	6		1-0	7-0
Northern Ireland	3	1	0	2	6	5	3			6-1
FYR Macedonia	3	0	0	3	1	22	0			

Second Qualifying Round Group 1

	Pl	W	D	L	F	A	Pts	SWE	CZE	DEN
Germany	3	3	0	0	6	1	9	1-0	4-1	1-0
Sweden	3	2	0	1	9	2	6		6-0	3-1
Czech Republic	3	0	1	2	2	11	1			1-1
Denmark	3	0	1	2	2	5	1			

Second Qualifying Round Group 2

	Pl	W	D	L	F	A	Pts	NOR	ITA	MDA
England	3	2	0	1	7	2	6	2-0	1-2	4-0
Norway	3	2	0	1	10	4	6		3-1	7-1
Italy	3	2	0	1	8	4	6			5-0
Moldova	3	0	0	3	1	16	0			

Second Qualifying Round Group 3

	Pl	W	D	L	F	A	Pts	NED	WAL	GRE
Finland	3	2	1	0	3	1	7	1-0	1-1	1-0
Netherlands	3	2	0	1	5	2	6		3-1	2-0
Wales	3	1	1	1	4	5	4			2-1
Greece	3	0	0	3	1	5	0			

Second Qualifying Round Group 4

	Pl	W	D	L	F	A	Pts	AUT	SCG	ROM
Russia	3	3	0	0	14	1	9	3-1	5-0	6-0
Austria	3	2	0	1	8	5	6		3-2	4-0
Serbia/Montenegro	3	1	0	2	5	8	3			3-0
Romania	3	0	0	3	0	13	0			

Second Qualifying Round Group 5

	Pl	W	D	L	F	A	Pts	POR	ISR	BEL
Scotland	3	3	0	0	9	1	9	2-0	4-1	3-0
Portugal	3	2	0	1	5	3	6		4-1	1-0
Israel	3	1	0	2	4	9	3			2-1
Belgium	3	0	0	3	1	6	0			

Second Qualifying Round Group 6

	Pl	W	D	L	F	A	Pts	POL	NIR	UKR
Switzerland	3	3	0	0	11	5	9	4-1	4-2	3-2
Poland	3	2	0	1	5	5	6		3-1	1-0
Northern Ireland	3	1	0	2	5	7	3			2-0
Ukraine	3	0	0	3	2	6	0			

Second Qualifying Round Group 7

	Pl	W	D	L	F	A	Pts	ESP	IRL	CRO
France	3	3	0	0	9	1	9	1-0	1-0	7-1
Spain	3	2	0	1	9	1	6		5-0	4-0
Rep. of Ireland	3	1	0	2	4	7	3			4-1
Croatia	3	0	0	3	2	15	0			

UEFA EUROPEAN WOMEN'S U-19 CHAMPIONSHIP 2005

First Round Group Stage

Group A	Pl	W	D	L	F	A	Pts	FIN	SUI	HUN
Germany	3	3	0	0	10	3	9	3-1	5-2	2-0
Finland	3	2	0	1	7	5	6		4-2	2-0
Switzerland	3	1	0	2	8	10	3			4-1
Hungary	3	0	0	3	1	8	0			

Semi-finals

Russia	3
Germany	1
Finland	0
France	1

Final

Russia	2 6p
France	2 5p

Group B	Pl	W	D	L	F	A	Pts	RUS	ENG	SCO
France	3	2	1	0	8	2	7	4-0	1-1	3-1
Russia	3	2	0	1	7	5	6		2-1	5-0
England	3	1	1	1	5	4	4			3-1
Scotland	3	0	0	3	2	11	0			

Tournament held in Hungary from 20-07-2005 to 31-07-2005

UEFA EUROPEAN U-17 CHAMPIONSHIP 2005

First Qualifying Round Group 1

	Pl	W	D	L	F	A	Pts	ROM	POL	EST
Bulgaria	3	2	0	1	8	3	6	2-1	1-2	5-0
Romania	3	2	0	1	5	4	6		1-0	3-2
Poland	3	2	0	1	5	2	6			3-0
Estonia	3	0	0	3	2	11	0			

First Qualifying Round Group 2

	Pl	W	D	L	F	A	Pts	LVA	BIH	BEL
France	3	3	0	0	5	0	9	1-0	2-0	2-0
Latvia	3	0	2	1	2	3	2		1-1	1-1
Bosnia-Herzegov.	3	0	2	1	2	4	2			1-1
Belgium	3	0	2	1	2	4	2			

First Qualifying Round Group 3

	Pl	W	D	L	F	A	Pts	IRL	ISL	LTU
Germany	3	2	1	0	6	1	7	1-1	1-0	4-0
Rep. of Ireland	3	1	2	0	7	2	5		1-1	5-0
Iceland	3	0	2	1	3	4	2			2-2
Lithuania	3	0	1	2	2	11	1			

First Qualifying Round Group 4

	Pl	W	D	L	F	A	Pts	RUS	CYP	KAZ
Ukraine	3	2	1	0	8	0	7	0-0	5-0	3-0
Russia	3	2	1	0	5	2	7		1-0	4-2
Cyprus	3	1	0	2	2	7	3			2-1
Kazakhstan	3	0	0	3	3	9	0			

First Qualifying Round Group 5

	Pl	W	D	L	F	A	Pts	SCO	NOR	FRO
Israel	3	2	1	0	8	5	7	1-1	3-2	4-2
Scotland	3	2	1	0	4	1	7		1-0	2-0
Norway	3	1	0	2	5	5	3			3-1
Faroe Islands	3	0	0	3	3	9	0			

First Qualifying Round Group 6

	Pl	W	D	L	F	A	Pts	DEN	SWE	SVN
Czech Republic	3	2	1	0	6	1	7	2-0	1-1	3-0
Denmark	3	1	1	1	3	4	4		0-1	2-2
Sweden	3	1	1	1	3	2	4			2-0
Slovenia	3	0	1	2	2	7	1			

First Qualifying Round Group 7

	Pl	W	D	L	F	A	Pts	CRO	ALB	AND
Serbia/Montenegro	3	3	0	0	13	2	9	3-1	4-1	6-0
Croatia	3	2	0	1	15	5	6		3-2	11-0
Albania	3	1	0	2	8	7	3			5-0
Andorra	3	0	0	3	0	22	0			

First Qualifying Round Group 8

	Pl	W	D	L	F	A	Pts	GRE	GEO	MKD
Finland	3	2	0	1	5	4	6	1-2	1-0	3-2
Greece	3	1	2	0	3	2	5		0-0	1-1
Georgia	3	1	1	1	4	2	4			4-1
FYR Macedonia	3	0	1	2	4	8	1			

First Qualifying Round Group 9

	Pl	W	D	L	F	A	Pts	NED	WAL	ARM
Turkey	3	1	2	0	4	3	5	1-1	1-1	2-1
Netherlands	3	1	2	0	7	2	5		0-0	6-1
Wales	3	1	2	0	3	2	5			2-1
Armenia	3	0	0	3	3	10	0			

First Qualifying Round Group 10

	Pl	W	D	L	F	A	Pts	NIR	SVK	LIE
Switzerland	3	2	1	0	12	1	7	1-1	2-0	9-0
Northern Ireland	3	2	1	0	9	1	7		3-0	5-0
Slovakia	3	1	0	2	4	5	3			4-0
Liechtenstein	3	0	0	3	0	18	0			

First Qualifying Round Group 11

	Pl	W	D	L	F	A	Pts	BLR	MLT	SMR
Portugal	3	3	0	0	14	1	9	4-1	2-0	8-0
Belarus	3	2	0	1	9	4	6		3-0	5-0
Malta	3	1	0	2	1	5	3			1-0
San Marino	3	0	0	3	0	14	0			

First Qualifying Round Group 12

	Pl	W	D	L	F	A	Pts	AZE	LUX	MDA
Austria	3	2	1	0	5	2	7	3-2	2-0	0-0
Azerbaijan	3	2	0	1	5	4	6		2-1	1-0
Luxembourg	3	1	0	2	3	4	3			2-0
Moldova	3	0	1	2	0	3	1			

Elite Round Group 1

	Pl	W	D	L	F	A	Pts	ESP	DEN	POL
Switzerland	3	2	1	0	6	3	7	1-1	2-1	3-1
Spain	3	2	1	0	3	1	7		1-0	1-0
Denmark	3	0	1	2	2	4	1			1-1
Poland	3	0	1	2	2	5	1			

Elite Round Group 2

	Pl	W	D	L	F	A	Pts	SCG	IRL	NIR
England	3	3	0	0	9	2	9	3-1	3-1	3-0
Serbia/Montenegro	3	2	0	1	9	5	6		2-1	6-1
Rep. of Ireland	3	1	0	2	4	6	3			2-1
Northern Ireland	3	0	0	3	2	11	0			

Elite Round Group 3

	Pl	W	D	L	F	A	Pts	UKR	POR	HUN
Croatia	3	2	1	0	5	3	7	1-1	2-1	2-1
Ukraine	3	1	2	0	4	1	5		3-0	0-0
Portugal	3	1	0	2	3	5	3			2-0
Hungary	3	0	1	2	1	4	1			

Elite Round Group 4

	Pl	W	D	L	F	A	Pts	RUS	BUL	FIN
Belarus	3	2	0	1	5	2	6	2-0	3-1	0-1
Russia	3	2	0	1	5	4	6		1-0	4-2
Bulgaria	3	1	0	2	4	3	3			2-0
Finland	3	1	0	2	3	6	3			

Elite Round Group 5

	Pl	W	D	L	F	A	Pts	GRE	ROM	AUT
Israel	3	2	1	0	3	1	7	1-0	1-1	1-0
Greece	3	2	0	1	3	2	6		1-0	2-1
Romania	3	1	1	1	2	2	4			1-0
Austria	3	0	0	3	1	4	0			

Elite Round Group 6

	Pl	W	D	L	F	A	Pts	SCO	FRA	AZE
Turkey	3	3	0	0	6	1	9	2-1	1-0	3-0
Scotland	3	1	0	2	4	3	3		0-1	3-0
France	3	1	0	2	1	3	3			0-2
Azerbaijan	3	1	0	2	2	6	3			

Elite Round Group 7

	Pl	W	D	L	F	A	Pts	GER	CZE	LVA
Netherlands	3	2	0	1	8	4	6	3-2	1-2	4-0
Germany	3	2	0	1	8	4	6		2-1	4-0
Czech Republic	3	2	0	1	5	3	6			2-0
Latvia	3	0	0	3	0	10	0			

UEFA EUROPEAN U-17 CHAMPIONSHIP 2005

First Round Group Stage

Group A	Pl	W	D	L	F	A	Pts	ITA	ENG	BLR
Turkey	3	2	0	1	8	4	6	0-1	3-2	5-1
Italy	3	2	0	1	2	1	6		1-0	0-1
England	3	1	0	2	6	4	3			4-0
Belarus	3	1	0	2	2	9	3			

Semi-finals

Turkey	3
Croatia	1

Final

Turkey	2
Netherlands	0

Group B	Pl	W	D	L	F	A	Pts	NED	SUI	ISR
Croatia	3	2	1	0	11	6	7	2-2	5-2	4-2
Netherlands	3	1	2	0	4	3	5		0-0	2-1
Switzerland	3	1	1	1	5	5	4			3-0
Israel	3	0	0	3	3	9	0			

Italy	0
Netherlands	1

3rd place play-off

Italy	2
Croatia	1

Final tournament held in Italy from 3-05-2005 to 14-05-2005

UEFA EUROPEAN U–19 CHAMPIONSHIP 2005

First Qualifying Round Group 1

	Pl	W	D	L	F	A	Pts	GRE	WAL	FRO
Hungary	3	2	0	1	5	2	6	2-1	0-1	3-0
Greece	3	1	1	1	6	2	4		0-0	5-0
Wales	3	1	1	1	2	3	4			1-3
Faroe Islands	3	1	0	2	3	9	3			

First Qualifying Round Group 2

	Pl	W	D	L	F	A	Pts	POL	MDA	SUI
Ukraine	3	2	0	1	3	2	6	2-1	0-1	1-0
Poland	3	1	1	1	4	3	4		0-0	3-1
Moldova	3	1	1	1	3	3	4			2-3
Switzerland	3	1	0	2	4	6	3			

First Qualifying Round Group 3

	Pl	W	D	L	F	A	Pts	GER	SVN	LVA
Serbia/Montenegro	3	2	1	0	7	3	7	1-1	4-2	2-0
Germany	3	1	2	0	5	2	5		3-0	1-1
Slovenia	3	1	0	2	4	8	3			2-1
Latvia	3	0	1	2	2	5	1			

First Qualifying Round Group 4

	Pl	W	D	L	F	A	Pts	ARM	MKD	AZE
France	3	3	0	0	9	2	9	2-1	4-1	3-0
Armenia	3	1	1	1	4	4	4		2-1	1-1
FYR Macedonia	3	1	0	2	3	6	3			1-0
Azerbaijan	3	0	1	2	1	5	1			

First Qualifying Round Group 5

	Pl	W	D	L	F	A	Pts	LTU	GEO	MLT
Slovakia	3	2	0	1	7	6	6	3-1	2-4	2-1
Lithuania	3	2	0	1	5	5	6		3-2	1-0
Georgia	3	1	1	1	7	6	4			1-1
Malta	3	0	1	2	2	4	1			

First Qualifying Round Group 6

	Pl	W	D	L	F	A	Pts	DEN	FIN	LUX
Albania	3	2	0	1	5	7	6	3-0	1-7	1-0
Denmark	3	2	0	1	6	6	6		3-2	3-1
Finland	3	1	1	1	10	5	4			1-1
Luxembourg	3	0	1	2	2	5	1			

First Qualifying Round Group 7

	Pl	W	D	L	F	A	Pts	ISR	BLR	EST
Netherlands	3	3	0	0	11	1	9	2-1	3-0	6-0
Israel	3	1	1	1	5	2	4		0-0	4-0
Belarus	3	1	1	1	4	5	4			4-2
Estonia	3	0	0	3	2	14	0			

First Qualifying Round Group 8

	Pl	W	D	L	F	A	Pts	SCO	TUR	SMR
Belgium	3	2	1	0	8	2	7	1-1	3-1	4-0
Scotland	3	1	2	0	7	3	5		2-2	4-0
Turkey	3	1	1	1	13	5	4			10-0
San Marino	3	0	0	3	0	18	0			

First Qualifying Round Group 9

	Pl	W	D	L	F	A	Pts	IRL	CYP	AND
Russia	3	2	0	1	11	3	6	1-2	5-1	5-0
Rep. of Ireland	3	2	0	1	6	2	6		0-1	4-0
Cyprus	3	2	0	1	7	5	6			5-0
Andorra	3	0	0	3	0	14	0			

First Qualifying Round Group 10

	Pl	W	D	L	F	A	Pts	CRO	ROM	LIE
Sweden	3	3	0	0	9	2	9	3-1	2-1	4-0
Croatia	3	1	1	1	9	5	4		2-2	6-0
Romania	3	1	1	1	5	5	4			2-1
Liechtenstein	3	0	0	3	1	12	0			

First Qualifying Round Group 11

	Pl	W	D	L	F	A	Pts	ITA	KAZ	BIH
Portugal	3	2	1	0	6	1	7	0-0	2-0	4-1
Italy	3	2	1	0	4	0	7		2-0	2-0
Kazakhstan	3	1	0	2	1	4	3			1-0
Bosnia-Herzegov.	3	0	0	3	1	7	0			

First Qualifying Round Group 12

	Pl	W	D	L	F	A	Pts	NOR	ISL	BUL
Austria	3	2	1	0	7	2	7	0-0	5-2	2-0
Norway	3	2	1	0	6	1	7		3-0	3-1
Iceland	3	1	0	2	5	10	3			3-2
Bulgaria	3	0	0	3	3	8	0			

Elite Round Group 1

	Pl	W	D	L	F	A	Pts	SWE	DEN	MDA
England	3	3	0	0	3	0	9	1-0	1-0	1-0
Sweden	3	2	0	1	8	3	6		3-2	5-0
Denmark	3	0	1	2	3	5	1			1-1
Moldova	3	0	1	2	1	7	1			

Elite Round Group 2

	Pl	W	D	L	F	A	Pts	CZE	NED	CRO
Germany	3	3	0	0	7	1	9	2-1	2-0	3-0
Czech Republic	3	1	0	2	3	4	3		0-2	2-0
Netherlands	3	1	0	2	2	4	3			0-2
Croatia	3	1	0	2	2	5	3			

Elite Round Group 3

	Pl	W	D	L	F	A	Pts	ESP	ISR	POR
France	3	3	0	0	5	2	9	1-0	1-0	3-2
Spain	3	2	0	1	5	1	6		3-0	2-0
Israel	3	1	0	2	4	4	3			2-0
Portugal	3	0	0	3	2	7	0			

Elite Round Group 4

	Pl	W	D	L	F	A	Pts	BEL	ITA	HUN
Armenia	3	2	1	0	6	1	7	1-0	0-0	5-1
Belgium	3	2	0	1	6	2	6		2-0	4-1
Italy	3	1	1	1	3	2	4			3-0
Hungary	3	0	0	3	2	12	0			

Elite Round Group 5

	Pl	W	D	L	F	A	Pts	SCO	SVK	AUT
Greece	3	3	0	0	5	1	9	1-0	2-0	2-1
Scotland	3	2	0	1	5	3	6		2-0	3-2
Slovakia	3	1	0	2	2	4	3			2-0
Austria	3	0	0	3	3	7	0			

Elite Round Group 6

	Pl	W	D	L	F	A	Pts	UKR	RUS	LTU
Norway	3	2	1	0	8	2	7	5-1	1-1	2-0
Ukraine	3	2	0	1	5	5	6		1-0	3-0
Russia	3	1	1	1	4	2	4			3-0
Lithuania	3	0	0	3	0	8	0			

Elite Round Group 7

	Pl	W	D	L	F	A	Pts	POL	IRL	ALB
Serbia/Montenegro	3	3	0	0	10	2	9	2-1	1-0	7-1
Poland	3	2	0	1	4	2	6		1-0	2-0
Rep. of Ireland	3	0	1	2	1	3	1			1-1
Albania	3	0	1	2	2	10	1			

UEFA EUROPEAN U-19 CHAMPIONSHIP 2005

First Round Group Stage

Group A	Pl	W	D	L	F	A	Pts	GER	GRE	NIR
Serbia/Montenegro	3	3	0	0	8	2	9	4-2	3-0	1-0
Germany	3	2	0	1	7	5	6		3-0	2-1
Greece	3	1	0	2	1	6	3			1-0
Northern Ireland	3	0	0	3	1	4	0			

Group B	Pl	W	D	L	F	A	Pts	ENG	NOR	ARM
France	3	2	1	0	5	2	7	1-1	3-1	1-0
England	3	1	2	0	5	4	5		3-2	1-1
Norway	3	1	0	2	5	6	3			2-0
Armenia	3	0	1	2	1	4	1			

Semi-finals

France	3
Germany	2

Serbia/Montenegro	1
England	3

Final

France	3
England	1

Final tournament held in Northern Ireland from 18-07-2005 to 29-07-2005

ADDITIONAL INFORMATION FOR PART TWO

FIFA REFEREE LIST 2005 - ALB

Continuation from page 204	Int'l	DoB
JANKU Albano	2002	13-08-1967
JARECI Sokol	2000	15-09-1967

FIFA ASSISTANT REFEREE LIST 2005 - ALB

Continuation from page 204	Int'l	DoB
AVDO Sokol	1998	10-10-1961
MALI Arjan	1999	7-08-1964
MALOKU Genc	1997	25-02-1962
PREGJA Arben	1999	31-07-1962
SALAJ Dritan	2004	23-11-1976

FIFA ASSISTANT REFEREE LIST 2005 – AZE

Continuation from page 243	Int'l	DoB
ABDULLAYEV Munis	2000	26-07-1965
ALAKABAROV Aydin	2004	2-01-1966
ALIYEV Ilkham	2001	20-06-1966
ASADOV Ramiz	1997	24-07-1964
HUSEYNOV Azad	1996	12-06-1963
NAGIBEKOV Eldar	2001	7-05-1964

FIFA ASSISTANT REFEREE LIST 2005 – AZE

Continuation from page 243	Int'l	DoB
GADIYEV Zohrab	2003	22-05-1964
MAMMEDOV Khagani	1995	15-10-1961
SULTANI Imankhan	2000	16-01-1963

FIFA REFEREE LIST 2005 – BDI

Continuation from page 251	Int'l	DoB
BIGERE Deo	2004	2-06-1966
HICUBURUNDI Jean-Marie	1992	10-05-1963
NDAYISHIMYE Faustin	2000	17-07-1967
NDUWARUGIRA Jean-Marie	1999	13-01-1963
NIYONGABO Athanase	2000	15-09-1968
NIYONGABO Jean-Claude	2004	16-06-1971

FIFA ASSISTANT REFEREE LIST 2005 – BDI

Continuation from page 251	Int'l	DoB
BAZUBWABO Felix	2004	25-12-1966
BIRUMUSHAHU Jean-Claude	2004	13-02-1972
BIZIMANA Jean Marie	2004	2-09-1966
GAHUNGU Desire	1999	1-06-1967
HAKIZIMANA Jean-Marie	2000	1-04-1969
NIZIGIYIMANA Charles	2000	1-01-1966
NZISABIRA Emmanuel	2001	25-12-1965

FIFA REFEREE LIST 2005 – BEN

Continuation from page 258	Int'l	DoB
AGUIDISSOU Crespin	1998	24-10-1967
CODIJA Coffi	1994	9-12-1967
IGUE Brice	2004	1-01-1969
LAMIDI Cocou	2000	1-01-1964
SAHI Chabi	2004	1-01-1965
TOKPEME Guy	1997	10-01-1964
ZODEOUGAN Gislain	2004	13-02-1970

FIFA ASSISTANT REFEREE LIST 2005 – BEN

Continuation from page 258	Int'l	DoB
ADERODJOU Abodou	1992	13-02-1961
ADJOVI Hugues	1992	25-11-1962
ATOYO Horus	2003	20-12-1967
FASSINOU Alexis	2004	13-08-1978
LOUIS Joel	2001	25-01-1966
ZOUNTCHEME Adrien	2005	5-05-1967

FIFA REFEREE LIST 2005 – BRU

Continuation from page 302	Int'l	DoB
ABDULLAH Mohd	1998	22-06-1965
ANAK LUNGAN Jampong	2005	19-02-1974
HAJI AHMAD Haji	2005	4-07-1968
HAJI DURAMAN Zulkifle	1997	19-04-1966
HAJI SERUDIN Mohd	2005	26-03-1966

FIFA ASSISTANT REFEREE LIST 2005 – BRU

Continuation from page 302	Int'l	DoB
ABDULLAH CHUA Mohd	2005	21-10-1969
ABDULLAH Modh	2000	12-01-1966
CHANDAU Degat	2002	31-05-1970
OMAR Roslan	2005	13-05-1966

FIFA REFEREE LIST 2005 – BUL

Continuation from page 304	Int'l	DoB
DIMITROV Dimitar	2001	17-05-1966
GEORGIEV Tsvetan	2003	30-01-1975
GUENOV Anton	1999	10-10-1966
KOSTADINOV Kostadin	2000	6-05-1963
MOSKALEV Galin	2005	25-06-1972
RISTOSKOV Hristo	2004	23-03-1971

FIFA ASSISTANT REFEREE LIST 2005 – BUL

Continuation from page 304	Int'l	DoB
ANGELOV Nikolay	2003	18.06.1969
DJUGANSKI Nikola	2001	11.10.1965
GAVRILOV Venzislav	2003	27.05.1967
GULEV Iordan	1998	31.05.1960
KEREZOV Krassimir	1998	27.04.1964
PETROV Nikolay	2004	30.01.1968
PETROV Petar	1998	16.04.1960
STOILOV Krum	2002	03.01.1970
TCHAKAROV Nedeltcho	2001	23.12.1962
VALTCHEV Ivan	2001	30.05.1971

FIFA REFEREE LIST 2005 – CGO

Continuation from page 315	Int'l	DoB
BANSIMBA Serge	1999	08.10.1965
EBATTA John-Rollin	2000	16.02.1965
KAYA Michel	1993	23.08.1962
LOUZAYA Rene	2000	14.11.1970
MANDZIOUKOUTA Joseph	1995	05.03.1961
MOUKOKO Jean-Michel	2003	29.09.1974
POUNGUI Alain	2000	17.05.1963

FIFA ASSISTANT REFEREE LIST 2005 – CGO

Continuation from page 315	Int'l	DoB
BOUENDE-MALONGA Richard	2004	25-03-1974
DAMBA Daniel	1999	19-05-1965
ENGANDZA Antoine	2004	12-08-1970
IWANGOU-AHYI Mabick	2002	06-01-1970
KIMBATSA Robert	1993	28-04-1962
MAKOUMBOU Albert	1996	06-12-1960
MAMBOTI Francois	1999	28-06-1965

FIFA REFEREE LIST 2005 – CPV

Continuation from page 349	Int'l	DoB
ALMEIDA ROCHA Francisco	2000	12-06-1963
FAIAL Jorge	2000	26-02-1963
MONTEIRO DUARTE Manuel	1997	10-01-1960
MONTEIRO LOPES Herminio	1997	24-04-1964
MORENO BARBOSA Claudio	2004	2-04-1964

FIFA ASSISTANT REFEREE LIST 2005 – CPV

Continuation from page 349	Int'l	DoB
ALEM COSTA Humberto	1997	27-08-1967
BARROS Rui Antonio	2000	3-03-1964
PIRES FERNANDES Ramiro	1997	25-11-1963
SOARES ROSA Jose	1997	15-01-1960
XAVIER MONIZ Mario	1997	15-05-1962

FIFA REFEREE LIST 2005 – CRC

Continuation from page 351	Int'l	DoB
DURAN Edgar	2000	7-07-1965
JIMENEZ Alexandro	2002	16-09-1967
MEJIAS OVARES Olger	1995	11-09-1960
PORRAS Greivin	1995	18-07-1963
QUESADA Walter	2001	9-05-1970
ZAMORA Freddy	2001	15-02-1965

FIFA ASSISTANT REFEREE LIST 2005 – CRC

Continuation from page 351	Int'l	DoB
AZOFEIFA Alejandro	2005	24-01-1969
FLORES Miguel	1998	30-11-1960
LEAL Leonel	2001	21-11-1976
LUNA Osvaldo	2005	24-12-1972
MORA Edgar	2001	30-12-1971
MORA Erick	1997	16-03-1960
PEREIRA Jose Manuel	1996	25-11-1965
ROMAN Luis	2001	25-09-1965

FIFA REFEREE LIST 2005 – CYP

Continuation from page 364	Int'l	DoB
KAILIS Panicos	2005	12-06-1965
KAPITANIS Costas	1996	21-05-1964
THEODOTOU Costas	2002	28-06-1965

FIFA ASSISTANT REFEREE LIST 2005 – CYP

Continuation from page 364	Int'l	DoB
ARGYROU Vassos	2004	21-07-1963
IOANNOU Michael	1998	11-09-1960
PAPAPANAYIOTOU Andreas	2004	31-07-1964
PETROU Frixos	1999	29-06-1963
PROCOPIOU Stavros	1999	14-09-1963
XANTHOU Andreas	1998	2-07-1964

FIFA REFEREE LIST 2005 – ECU

Continuation from page 381	Int'l	DoB
ALARCON Tomas	2005	22-12-1965
CARPIO Jose	1997	19-10-1966
HARO Samuel	2005	26-10-1978
MENDOZA Charles	2003	5-08-1966
RAMOS Pedro	2001	2-05-1968
REINOSO	1996	16-03-1967
VASCO Luis	1999	27-02-1960

FIFA ASSISTANT REFEREE LIST 2005 – ECU

Continuation from page 381	Int'l	DoB
BADARACO Felix	1996	20-06-1963
BAUTISTA Javier	2005	7-08-1972
CEDENO Juan	2001	4-07-1967
HERRERA Carlos		12-07-1970
JORDAN Ivan	2003	4-02-1967
MUZO Marco	2004	2-03-1969
TAMAYO Fernando	2001	17-10-1963

FIFA REFEREE LIST 2005 – EST

Continuation from page 414	Int'l	DoB
KALDMA Sten	1998	2-08-1968

FIFA ASSISTANT REFEREE LIST 2005 – EST

Continuation from page 414	Int'l	DoB
REINVALD Hannes	2000	29-07-1971
ROZOV Eduard	2003	17-11-1963

FIFA REFEREE LIST 2005 – GRE

Continuation from page 461	Int'l	DoB
BRIAKOS Athanassios	2001	6-04-1967
DOUROS Georgios	2000	17-02-1962
KASNAFERIS George	1995	10-02-1967
TSACHEILIDIS Ioannis	2002	11-09-1968
TSIKINIS Iraklis	2001	11-11-1968
VASSARAS Kyros	1998	1-02-1966
ZOGRAFOS Christoforos	2004	24-03-1969

FIFA ASSISTANT REFEREE LIST 2005 – GRE

Continuation from page 461	Int'l	DoB
BOZATZIDIS Dimitrios	2002	11-02-1971
DALAS Konstantinos	2003	26-09-1968
GALANOS Konstantinos	2004	25-11-1966
GENNAIOS Cristos	2004	22-11-1967
MAVROPOULOS Panagiotis	1999	24-03-1966
PAPADOPOULOS Dimitrios	2001	13-10-1968
SARAIDARIS Dimitrios	2002	13-08-1970
TAPRANTZIS George	2000	24-08-1961
TSOLAKIDIS Simeon	1996	17-03-1966
TSORTANIDIS Dimitrios	2004	26-07-1968

FIFA REFEREE LIST 2005 – GRN

Continuation from page 465	Int'l	DoB
BEDEAU Valman	1997	3-12-1969
PHILLIP George	1999	30-01-1964

FIFA ASSISTANT REFEREE LIST 2005 – GRN

Continuation from page 465	Int'l	DoB
CHARLES Finbar	1998	16-05-1963
PHILLIP Allison	2003	6-05-1969
PHILLIP Wayne	2000	26-02-1968
RICHARDSON Earnest	2005	4-03-1971

FIFA REFEREE LIST 2005 – GUY

Continuation from page 476	Int'l	DoB
CALLENDER John	2000	14-12-1961
JAMES Otis	1999	14-10-1970
LANCASTER Stanley	2004	12-10-1970
MCARTHUR Roy	2002	29-12-1965

FIFA ASSISTANT REFEREE LIST 2005 – GUY

Continuation from page 476	Int'l	DoB
BLAIR Selwyn	2005	7-03-1970
HAMID Abdulla	2002	6-08-1967
INNISS Dion	2004	26-02-1976
MARS Venton	2004	15-03-1980

FIFA REFEREE LIST 2005 – HKG

Continuation from page 481	Int'l	DoB
CHAN Siu Kee	1998	17-11-1962
CHIU Sin Chuen Albert	2000	29-08-1965
FONG Yau Fat Jame	2000	21-10-1961
NG Kai Lam	2004	26-10-1971

FIFA ASSISTANT REFEREE LIST 2005 – HKG

Continuation from page 481	Int'l	DoB
FUNG Ka Yu	2001	4-02-1962
LEE Yau Tak	2000	22-09-1963
LUI Siu Chuen	2005	23-07-1965
NG Chiu Kok	2004	25-11-1975
POON Ming Fai	2003	8-07-1963
YEUNG Chi Ming	2004	9-03-1973

FIFA REFEREE LIST 2005 – IRQ

Continuation from page 507	Int'l	DoB
ABDUL Ala	1997	19-03-1965
ABID Sabah	2003	5-09-1966
AKOOL Samir	2004	1-02-1965
AUDA Kadhum	2003	7-05-1966
BAKIR Serwan	2004	1-07-1965
ISSA Hussein	1995	12-12-1961
KASIM Sabah	1997	1-07-1965
MWENA Nagim	1999	1-01-1966
NURILDDIN Mahmoud	1994	12-12-1963
SAHIB Muhammad	1996	12-12-1961

FIFA ASSISTANT REFEREE LIST 2005 – IRQ

Continuation from page 507	Int'l	DoB
AHMED Sabban	2003	25-10-1967
GADIR Arsalan	1997	5-11-1965
IBRAHIM Khalil	1998	5-04-1963
KADOM Mohammad	1998	3-02-1963
KARIM Aziz	1996	1-01-1967
KHUDHEIR Ahmed	1994	1-07-1962
MEHANA Samir	1996	1-01-1963
MOHAMMAD Ali	2004	1-07-1967
SAEED Ahmad	2004	1-07-1967
SUBHI Luay	2003	20-09-1970

FIFA REFEREE LIST 2005 – ISL

Continuation from page 510	Int'l	DoB
HINRIKSSON Gardar	2005	10-12-1971
JAKOBSSON Kristinn	1997	11-06-1969
MARKUSSON Egill	1999	25-10-1964
VALGEIRSSON Johannes	2004	1-06-1968

FIFA ASSISTANT REFEREE LIST 2005 – ISL

Continuation from page 510	Int'l	DoB
FINNSSON Eyjolfur	1999	5-03-1966
GUDFINNSSON Olafur	2004	25-09-1965
GUNNARSSON Gunnar	2005	26-05-1974
GYLFASON Gunnar	2000	17-01-1971
SIGURDSSON Einar	2003	7-07-1963
SIGURDSSON Pjetur	1992	2-07-1964
TORLEIFSSON Sigurdur	2005	18-11-1975

FIFA REFEREE LIST 2005 – JAM

Continuation from page 527	Int'l	DoB
CAMPBELL Courtney	2004	16-11-1968
PINE Raymond	2001	26-10-1961
PRENDERGAST Peter	1994	23-09-1963
STEWART Victor	1998	11-01-1962

FIFA ASSISTANT REFEREE LIST 2005 – JAM

Continuation from page 527	Int'l	DoB
GARWOOD Anthony	1998	15-12-1972
MEIKLE Dave	1995	19-10-1962
MORGAN Ricardo	1998	30-01-1972
THOBOURNE Rohan	2000	14-07-1967
TULLOCH Triston	2004	5-04-1972

FIFA REFEREE LIST 2005 – KAZ

Continuation from page 542	Int'l	DoB
KHOLMATOV Akmalkhan	2003	1-01-1968
KISTER Igor	2003	6-10-1965
SALIY Pavel	2003	6-12-1967
TSAREGRADSKIY Sergey	1995	29-01-1962

FIFA ASSISTANT REFEREE LIST 2005 – KAZ

Continuation from page 542	Int'l	DoB
DUZMAMBETOV Ruslan	2003	21-04-1968
KARLIBAYEV Bolat	2003	15-07-1975
KENETAYEV Bolat	2003	14-09-1966
KOPZHASSAROV Bagytpek	2003	2-12-1970
KOZHABERGENOV Nurlan	2003	20-07-1967
MAMASHEV Viktor	2003	6-04-1974
SLAMBEKOV Kairat	2003	26-06-1966
SOKOLOV Oleg	2003	6-09-1969

FIFA REFEREE LIST 2005 – KEN

Continuation from page 545	Int'l	DoB
AMWAYI Caleb	2003	22-05-1968
GONA Simon	2004	16-02-1975
KALUME Jumaa	2005	27-01-1970
KAUNDA Paul	1998	10-01-1962
KIRWA Sylvester	2003	3-04-1971
NDINYA Alfred	1999	10-04-1969
UKIRU Joseph	2004	7-06-1967

FIFA ASSISTANT REFEREE LIST 2005 – KEN

Continuation from page 545	Int'l	DoB
GIKONYO David	2003	6-08-1970
KIEREINI Peter	2005	19-09-1969
LIKHOTIO Sylvester	2003	7-07-1964
MBOGO Hesborn	2005	23-07-1966
MUHINDI Samuel	2001	25-02-1968
MWACHIA Evans	1999	31-01-1965
OGOLLA George	2001	25-09-1962

FIFA REFEREE LIST 2005 – KOR

Continuation from page 551	Int'l	DoB
BAE Jae Yong	2001	26-03-1966
KIM Dong Jin	2005	9-06-1973
KWON Jong Chul	1997	11-09-1963
LEE Gi Young	2001	15-11-1965
LEE Jong Kuk	2003	8-09-1964
LEE Min Hu	2005	14-09-1979
PARK Sang Gu	2000	21-07-1962
YU Byung Seob	2002	23-08-1962

FIFA ASSISTANT REFEREE LIST 2005 – KOR

Continuation from page 551	Int'l	DoB
EUN Jong Bok	2005	22-01-1969
JEONG Hae Sang	2004	1-06-1971
KANG Chang Goo	1998	29-12-1965
KIM Bu Keun	2001	26-08-1967
KIM Dae Young	1998	15-08-1962
KIM Hee Wook	1996	25-06-1962
KIM Kye Soo	1999	18-12-1962
KIM Yong Su	2005	7-03-1965
YANG Byoung Eun	2005	1-03-1976

FIFA REFEREE LIST 2005 – KUW

Continuation from page 562	Int'l	DoB
ABUL SADEQ Mansour	1996	20-05-1962
AL DAWAS Abdullatif	1997	27-04-1963
AL ENEZI Atallah	2005	6-10-1966
AL ENEZI Naser	2001	4-10-1966
AL FADHLI Saad	1994	6-01-1963
AL SHATTI Waleed	2005	1-05-1968
AL SHEMMARI Mahammad	1998	24-01-1964
ARAB Hamid	2004	21-01-1964
SADEQ Khaled	1995	22-01-1963
SHABAN Qasem	1997	26-03-1961

FIFA ASSISTANT REFEREE LIST 2005 – KUW

Continuation from page 562	Int'l	DoB
AKBAR Abdullah	2004	12-02-1975
AL ANEZI Murshed	1996	18-10-1960
AL KHABBAZ Yosuf	1999	17-04-1961
AL RASHEED Rasheed	2001	20-11-1961
AL RHBIAN Fuad	1999	18-03-1962
AL SAHALI Ghanim	1996	28-08-1961
AL SHAMMARI Sulaiman	2004	1-09-1967
MARAD Yaser	2004	14-08-1969

FIFA REFEREE LIST 2005 – LCA

Continuation from page 572	Int'l	DoB
ARTHUR Gilles	1997	7-02-1964
FANUS Francis	1997	16-01-1967
WILLIAMS Alexander	1999	17-10-1966

FIFA ASSISTANT REFEREE LIST 2005 – LCA

Continuation from page 572	Int'l	DoB
EUGENE-MARC Maurinus	2000	3-03-1963
GEORGE John	2001	25-04-1968
POPO Fitz Gerald		3-04-1973

FIFA REFEREE LIST 2005 – LIB

Continuation from page 576	Int'l	DoB
DAHER ALi	1998	18-01-1963
GHANDOUR Radwan	2003	30-10-1975
HOUMANI Mohamad	1996	28-08-1969
MANSOUR Mohammad	1994	4-08-1964
NAJM Tallat	1994	18-09-1968

FIFA ASSISTANT REFEREE LIST 2005 – LIB

Continuation from page 576	Int'l	DoB
ADI Ali	2002	22-09-1966
EL KAWAS Ahmad	2002	30-08-1973
EL MASRI Samer	2002	8-03-1973
EL MHAJER Ziad	2002	10-01-1968
ISMAIL Azzam	1992	17-04-1961
KOLEIT Haidar	1990	10-02-1963
TALEB Mustafa	1994	20-04-1964

FIFA ASSISTANT REFEREE LIST 2005 – LTU

Continuation from page 581	Int'l	DoB
DIRDA Saulius	2005	31-10-1972
PIPIRAS Arturas	1996	6-07-1967
SESKUS Arunas		28-11-1979
SIMKUS Vytautas		13-01-1975

FIFA REFEREE LIST 2005 – LUX

Continuation from page 584	Int'l	DoB
HAMER Alain	1993	10-12-1965
JOHNSDORF Robert	2002	27-12-1974
WILMES Luc	2002	21-09-1968

FIFA ASSISTANT REFEREE LIST 2005 – LUX

Continuation from page 584	Int'l	DoB
CRELO Francis	1999	27-02-1963
DE CAROLIS Antonio	2005	9-03-1968
HOLTGEN Christian	2005	21-04-1967
MANGEN Franaois	1998	12-10-1965
NOBER Luc	2000	29-09-1966
ROLLING Guy	2001	8-05-1962

FIFA REFEREE LIST 2005 – MDA

Continuation from page 606	Int'l	DoB
BANARI Veaceslav	2003	1-02-1975
ORLIC Ghenadie	2001	14-04-1961

FIFA ASSISTANT REFEREE LIST 2005 – MDA

Continuation from page 606	Int'l	DoB
BERCO Veaceslav	2002	18-05-1971
BODEAN Anatolie	2000	2-03-1974
BODEAN Andrei		6-04-1978
MOLCEANOV Oleg	2002	13-05-1971

FIFA REFEREE LIST 2005 – MKD

Continuation from page 621	Int'l	DoB
BOZINOVSKI Emil	2000	10-01-1964
JAKIMOVSKI Delce	1999	28-02-1961
LAZAREVSKI Saso	1995	6-01-1963

1036APPENDIX 1

FIFA ASSISTANT REFEREE LIST 2005 – MKD

Continuation from page 621	Int'l	DoB
BAUTA Bekim	1995	22-07-1961
GLIGOROV Toni	2002	1-01-1970
JOSIFOV Zoran	2001	11-09-1964
KODOVSKI Petre	2005	12-10-1966
KRSTEVSKI Ljubomir	2000	24-04-1966
MIHAJLOV Mijalce	2002	26-11-1961

FIFA REFEREE LIST 2005 – MLT

Continuation from page 627	Int'l	DoB
ATTARD Joseph	1995	1-07-1965
CASHA Adrian	2002	12-10-1968
LAUTIER Christopher	2005	23-11-1972
ZAMMIT Anton	1995	17-02-1964

FIFA ASSISTANT REFEREE LIST 2005 – MLT

Continuation from page 627	Int'l	DoB
AGIUS Philip	1992	19-06-1965
BORG Konrad	2002	12-09-1976
CAMILLERI Alan	2003	21-12-1979
CAMILLERI Joseph	2003	11-09-1966
DE BATTISTA Nicholas	2004	23-12-1979
MICALLEF Charles	1997	7-08-1964
RAPA Joseph	2002	20-04-1970
SPITERI Ingmar	2000	16-01-1976

FIFA REFEREE LIST 2005 – MYA

Continuation from page 643	Int'l	DoB
U HLA THAN Maung		7-09-1967
U HLA Tint	2004	20-08-1973
U MAUNG MAUNG Kyi		21-09-1970
U SOE MOE Kyaw	2005	10-12-1968
U THEIN Myaing	1995	30-11-1962
U TUN Tun	1999	10-12-1969
U TUN Wla		18-10-1972
U WIN Cho	2004	10-08-1974
U WIN Oo	1997	15-10-1961

FIFA ASSISTANT REFEREE LIST 2005 – MYA

Continuation from page 643	Int'l	DoB
U AUNG Myint	1999	7-12-1970
U HLA Myint Latt	1999	9-12-1968
U HMWE Kyaing		4-12-1965
U KYAW Win		5-04-1973
U MYO Win	2004	30-01-1971
U THAN Htun		16-12-1969
U TIN TUN Tin	1996	28-12-1960
U TUN Yee	2004	10-08-1968

FIFA REFEREE LIST 2005 – NED

Continuation from page 653	Int'l	DoB
BLOM Kevin	2005	21-02-1974
BOSSEN Ruud		11-01-1962
BRAAMHAAR Eric	2002	13-10-1966
TEMMINK Rene	1995	24-06-1960
VAN EGMOND Dick	1997	13-05-1961
VINK Pieter	2004	13-03-1967
WEGEREEF Jan	1993	17-01-1962

FIFA ASSISTANT REFEREE LIST 2005 – NED

Continuation from page 653	Int'l	DoB
BRINK Arie	2002	18-08-1968
DROSTE Coen	2005	23-12-1967
GERRITSEN Patrick	2005	29-12-1967
INIA Adriaan	2000	27-12-1963
LOBBERT Wilco	2005	9-02-1968
MEENHUIS Rob	2005	12-01-1967
MEINTS Jantinus	2000	16-11-1961
RUTGERS Wynand	2005	9-08-1962
SLOT Richard	2005	3-02-1967
TEN HOOVE Hans	2004	20-09-1966

FIFA REFEREE LIST 2005 – NEP

Continuation from page 660	Int'l	DoB
BISTA Devendra	1997	25-11-1962
GURUNG Buddhi	1993	20-01-1962
PANDE Birendra	2001	28-08-1969
POKHEREL Ambar	2003	16-04-1969
RAJAK Dilip	1999	23-11-1966
SHRESTHA Gyanu	1993	20-01-1968
SIKHRAKAR Surendra	1997	30-01-1970

FIFA ASSISTANT REFEREE LIST 2005 – NEP

Continuation from page 660	Int'l	DoB
GIRI Kiran	1997	27-11-1970
JOSHI Sailesh	2001	11-02-1968
KC Binod	1997	22-02-1965
KHANAL Madhusudan	1999	26-02-1970
LAMA Shyam	1992	5-08-1964
SHRESTHA Ganesh	2003	15-08-1967
SINGH Gajendra	1992	24-02-1963

FIFA REFEREE LIST 2005 – NIG

Continuation from page 667	Int'l	DoB
ABANI Salissou	2002	14-04-1963
DJIBO Ahamadou	1998	23-08-1964
DJINGAREY Ibrahim	1993	31-10-1964

FIFA ASSISTANT REFEREE LIST 2005 – NIG

Continuation from page 667	Int'l	DoB
DIALLO Deydou	1998	6-07-1966
IBRAHIM Mahamadou	2005	1-01-1975
KONE Amadou	2005	1-01-1966
NASSIROU Elhadji	2005	30-08-1972

FIFA REFEREE LIST 2005 – OMA

Continuation from page 681	Int'l	DoB
AL AJMI Hassan	1996	30-12-1963
AL GHATRIFI Mahmood		26-06-1964
AL HARRASI Abdullah		5-11-1971
AL Hilali Abdullah	2002	1-09-1970
AL MOZAHMI Sultan	1996	29-08-1966
AL SHAMMAKI Khamis	2003	1-01-1970
MUFLAH Mohamed	1998	1-12-1965

FIFA ASSISTANT REFEREE LIST 2005 – OMA

Continuation from page 667	Int'l	DoB
AL AMBO Suliman	1994	1-01-1965
AL AMOURI Abdullah	2002	1-01-1970
AL BATTASHI Salim	2002	3-11-1967
AL QASIMI Ali	1996	1-01-1967
AL RASHDY Salim	1997	13-09-1965

FIFA REFEREE LIST 2005 – PAL

Continuation from page 687	Int'l	DoB
ABU ARMANA Naji		13-08-1968
ABU ELAISH		30-09-1961
ABU MARKHYA		14-09-1960
AL JAISH Mahmoud		1-01-1964
AL JAMAL Aref		14-09-1965
AL SHAKHRIT Mohammed		1-01-1968
AMAR Khaled		31-03-1964
EED Abd El Qader		16-03-1961
HANANIA Michael		24-04-1968

FIFA ASSISTANT REFEREE LIST 2005 – PAL

Continuation from page 687	Int'l	DoB
ABU FARA Khaled		9-04-1968
AL BASHA Fayez		18-10-1967
AL BHAISI Mahmoud		30-07-1961
EL RAWAGH Anan		2-07-1970
EL SALHI Waleed		30-01-1965
EL SHAKH KHALEL Mohamad		12-01-1969
HAMAD Soud		27-01-1961
SADEQ Mahyoub		9-03-1971
SHUIBAT Walid		25-04-1966
TAQATEQ Husain		25-04-1966

FIFA REFEREE LIST 2005 – PAN

Continuation from page 689	Int'l	DoB
GARCIA Basilio	2001	4-05-1964
MORENO Roberto	1996	5-04-1970
RODRIGUEZ José	2001	2-11-1965
VIDAL Rolando	2002	15-03-1974

FIFA ASSISTANT REFEREE LIST 2005 – PAN

Continuation from page 689	Int'l	DoB
BERTIAGA Vladimir	1996	19-05-1969
ESTE Alfonso	1996	26-07-1961
FUENTES Hairo	2004	4-08-1977
RODRIGUEZ Baltazar	1998	6-01-1964
SMITH Jaime	2000	2-12-1967
WILLIAMSON Daniel	2002	30-07-1977

FIFA REFEREE LIST 2005 – PRK

Continuation from page 714	Int'l	DoB
HWANG Thae Ho	2005	13-04-1967
HYON Myong Song	1998	28-02-1965
YU Yong MOK	1992	12-06-1965

FIFA ASSISTANT REFEREE LIST 2005 – PRK

Continuation from page 714	Int'l	DoB
CHOE Hae Il	1990	16-09-1962
JANG Myong Ho	1998	29-09-1968
JI Chol Song	2005	1-12-1975
KANG Song Jun	2005	7-01-1975
RI Il Myong	1989	1-03-1962
SO Myong Son	1997	4-05-1968

FIFA REFEREE LIST 2005 – RUS

Continuation from page 731	Int'l	DoB
BASKAKOV Yuri	1998	10-05-1964
EGOROV Igor	2003	4-11-1968
GVARDIS Alexander	2003	2-03-1965
IVANOV Nikolai	2000	24-01-1964
IVANOV Valentin	1997	4-07-1961
SUKHINA Stanislav	2003	16-08-1968
ZAKHAROV Igor	2005	8-06-1966

FIFA ASSISTANT REFEREE LIST 2005 – RUS

Continuation from page 731	Int'l	DoB
ANTONOV Lev	2000	10-11-1961
ENIUTIN Vladimir	1998	5-11-1960
GOLUBEV Nikolay	2003	9-11-1970
KALUGIN Tihon	2001	3-12-1974
KHODEEV Vladislav	2004	21-09-1965
KRASYUK Gennady	2000	1-02-1964
LEBEDEV Victor	1995	11-07-1960
MONAHOV Alexey	2000	8-03-1961
SEMENOV Viatcheslav	2005	20-10-1977
VOLNIN Evgueni	2001	27-06-1962

FIFA REFEREE LIST 2005 – SEN

Continuation from page 755	Int'l	DoB
AOUDY Khalil	1995	26-08-1968
DIATTA Badara	1999	2-08-1969
DIOUF Abdou	1997	30-12-1970
DIOUF Ousmane	1999	11-11-1962
DJIBA Yaya		10-03-1965
NDIAYE Samba	1999	19-09-1962
NDOYE Falla	1993	4-03-1960

FIFA ASSISTANT REFEREE LIST 2005 – SEN

Continuation from page 755	Int'l	DoB
BA Mouhamadou	1999	15-11-1963
GOUDIABY Elhadji		18-04-1974
MBENGUE Mouhamadou	1997	1-04-1961
NDOYE Mamadou	1999	27-12-1961
SARR Saliou	1999	30-01-1961
SENE El Hadji	1999	28-12-1963
SOW Magueye	1997	29-07-1962

FIFA REFEREE LIST 2005 – SEY

Continuation from page 758	Int'l	DoB
ANDRE Jacques	2005	28-11-1966
BENSTRONG Jourdan	2003	01-01-1968
LABROSSE Jean-Claude	2001	28-09-1968

FIFA ASSISTANT REFEREE LIST 2005 – SEY

Continuation from page 758	Int'l	DoB
CEDRAS Jossy	2003	13-11-1968
DAMOO Jason	2003	01-05-1975
FRANCOISE Winsley	2003	15-04-1962
OMATH David	2002	18-09-1963

FIFA REFEREE LIST 2005 – SIN

Continuation from page 760	Int'l	DoB
BASHIR Abdul	2002	11-01-1968
KUMBALINGAM Kennedy	1994	21-05-1964
LAZAR Subash	2000	16-11-1971
MAIDIN Shamsul	1996	16-04-1966
MINIAM Ganesan	1996	29-06-1964
NAGALINGAM Santhan	1996	26-11-1961
RAHMAN Vijay	1999	24-08-1960

FIFA ASSISTANT REFEREE LIST 2005 – SIN

Continuation from page 760	Int'l	DoB
EMIR Lutfi	2000	26-07-1966
ENG WAH John Chia	2002	27-12-1963
HAJA Haja	2005	22-07-1968
KEE SIANG JARROD Lim	2004	10-02-1980
NAZEER Hussain	1999	13-10-1967
SAMAD Mohd Ali	1997	2-08-1963
TAN YEW CHONG Tan	2005	28-07-1971
TANG Yew Mun	2002	27-08-1976

FIFA REFEREE LIST 2005 – SLV

Continuation from page 768	Int'l	DoB
AGUILAR Joel	2001	2-07-1975
ALFARO Nery	1996	26-04-1968
ARGUETA Ramon	1999	24-12-1962
BONILLA Elmer	2004	22-10-1978
SIBRIAN Rodolfo	1999	30-11-1963

FIFA ASSISTANT REFEREE LIST 2005 – SLV

Continuation from page 768	Int'l	DoB
BERMUDEZ Douglas	2005	5-06-1979
DELSID Mauricio	1998	9-08-1961
FERNANDEZ Vladimir	1993	19-04-1961
GONZALEZ Gilberto	1998	23-09-1965
VELASQUEZ Juan	1996	23-06-1966

FIFA REFEREE LIST 2005 – SUR

Continuation from page 791	Int'l	DoB
BUDEL Jerry		25-06-1964
KIA Henry	1999	23-11-1969
PINAS Antonius	1996	12-01-1971
WIJNGAARDE Enrico		11-01-1974

FIFA ASSISTANT REFEREE LIST 2005 - SUR

Continuation from page 791	Int'l	DoB
KRAAG Jerrel	2000	17-10-1969
LOUISVILLE Ramon		19-10-1970
RATHIPAL Rewiedath	1999	11-12-1967
SOMAI Shyamdew	1995	14-02-1964

FIFA REFEREE LIST 2005 – SWE

Continuation from page 801	Int'l	DoB
ERIKSSON Jonas	2002	28-03-1974
FRISK Anders	1991	18-02-1963
FROJDFELDT Peter	2001	14-11-1963
HANSSON Martin	2001	6-04-1971
INGVARSSON Martin	1997	9-12-1965
JOHANNESSON Stefan	2003	22-11-1971
STALHAMMAR Daniel	2004	20-10-1974

FIFA ASSISTANT REFEREE LIST 2005 – SWE

Continuation from page 801	Int'l	DoB
ANDREN Henrik	1999	21-07-1968
BERGSTEN Erik	2001	26-03-1970
EKSTROM Peter	1996	19-05-1964
FLINK JOAKIM	2004	20-03-1970
LARSSON Ingemar	1995	4-05-1961
MARTINSSON Peter	2005	20-06-1971
NILSSON Fredrik	2004	17-01-1972
PETERSSON Kenneth	1993	6-09-1964
PRUNER Edvard	2001	6-04-1971
WITTBERG Stefan	1997	2-09-1968

FIFA REFEREE LIST 2005 – SWZ

Continuation from page 805	Int'l	DoB
DLAMINI Gilbert		24-12-1968
FAKUDZE Mbongseni		7-05-1975
MLANGENI Frank	2000	20-02-1972
NGCAMPHALALA Elphas	1998	9-05-1967

FIFA ASSISTANT REFEREE LIST 2005 – SWZ

Continuation from page 805	Int'l	DoB
GAMA Mandla	2005	22-07-1974
KUNENE Sabelo		19-11-1970
KUNENE Sipho		4-05-1968
MKHABELA Bhekisizwe	2000	24-02-1973
NHLEKO Simanga	2002	12-03-1974
SIBIYA Lybnah		24-06-1970

FIFA REFEREE LIST 2005 – SYR

Continuation from page 808	Int'l	DoB
ABBAS Mahmoud	1997	19-09-1964
ABO ALLO Suleman	2004	13-12-1961
AL SHOUFI Hassan	2004	1-01-1962
ALOULO Ziad	2005	1-01-1965
BASMA Muhsen	2004	21-10-1966
DELLO Ahmad	2004	5-06-1966
HAJ KHADER Khader	1999	2-02-1965
HAJJAR Basel	1999	22-12-1966
KOUSA Mohammed	2001	10-02-1961
TURKI Mahmoud	2004	1-09-1967

FIFA ASSISTANT REFEREE LIST 2005 – SYR

Continuation from page 808	Int'l	DoB
AL ABDULLA Mohammed	1997	11-05-1964
AL HMIDI Chaker	2004	10-02-1964
AL KADRI Hamdi	1997	12-04-1965
AL NAHLAWI Mohammed	2003	21-09-1967
ATTAL Mohammad	2005	1-01-1965
DAYOB Alam-Aldin	1999	12-05-1969
HAMDAN Mashhour	2004	20-08-1965
HAMDOUN Tammam	1999	7-09-1967
KAZZAZ Ahmad	2004	1-05-1965
RABBAT Mohammed	1999	17-06-1962

FIFA REFEREE LIST 2005 – TAH

Continuation from page 812	Int'l	DoB
ARIIOTIMA Charles		18-01-1966

FIFA ASSISTANT REFEREE LIST 2005 – TAH

Continuation from page 812	Int'l	DoB
TAUAROA Daniel		7-03-1968
TAUOTAHA Raimana		16-04-1974

FIFA REFEREE LIST 2005 – TJK

Continuation from page 824	Int'l	DoB
MURTAZOEV Rakhmon	2005	9-04-1964
ORZUEV Dilovar	2005	13-02-1970
SAFAROV Kiyomiddin	1996	3-02-1964

FIFA ASSISTANT REFEREE LIST 2005 – TJK

Continuation from page 824	Int'l	DoB
AZIZOV Nasriddin	1997	15-06-1964
DJURAEV Orif	1996	15-06-1960
KARAEV Alisher	1995	10-05-1968
KARIMOV Kurbon	2005	1-03-1969
KHUDOJEROV Furkat	1999	13-02-1971
PIROV Hamza	2005	7-06-1963
SHOIMARDQNOV Safarmahrnad	2005	23-07-1966

FIFA REFEREE LIST 2005 – TOG

Continuation from page 829	Int'l	DoB
ATSOO Kokou	2003	25-10-1972
AZIAKA Kudzo	2003	1-01-1972
BEBOU Bakoubebile	1997	4-03-1960
DJAOUPE Kokou	2001	10-07-1968
FAGLA Kokou	2003	3-07-1977
SEDJRO Kossi	2003	31-12-1970
SOUSSOU Komlan	2002	4-11-1976

FIFA ASSISTANT REFEREE LIST 2005 – TOG

Continuation from page 829	Int'l	DoB
AYENA Nouwagnon	2000	24-02-1966
DJOUKERE Biagui	2000	1-01-1965
ELO Kokou	1997	1-01-1962
KAPOU Koffi	1998	26-06-1964
KONYOH Komi	2003	18-12-1972
KOUMA Komi	2003	17-01-1970
OUROTOU Agba	1996	23-11-1961

FIFA REFEREE LIST 2005 – TPE

Continuation from page 831	Int'l	DoB
KAO Tsai Hu	2005	2-10-1975
LIU Sung Ho	2000	16-03-1961
YANG Mu Sheng	1999	3-03-1964

FIFA ASSISTANT REFEREE LIST 2005 – TPE

Continuation from page 831	Int'l	DoB
HSU Min Yu	2005	14-09-1974
LEE Chi Lu	2001	2-11-1966
LIN Cheng Chiu	1999	20-03-1960
NIEN San Hua	2005	4-08-1970
TSAI Chen Hsiung	1998	2-01-1966
YU Ming Hsun	2002	1-10-1974

FIFA REFEREE LIST 2005 – TUR

Continuation from page 841	Int'l	DoB
ARZUMAN Ismet		7-07-1964
AYDOGAN Metin	2005	16-04-1970
CULCU Mustafa	1997	1-01-1960
DEMIRLEK Bulent		9-09-1975
DERELI Selcuk	2000	6-06-1969
MUFTUOGLU Kuddusi		4-03-1970
PAPILA Cem	2005	18-11-1966

FIFA ASSISTANT REFEREE LIST 2005 – TUR

Continuation from page 841	Int'l	DoB
BAKI TUNCAY Akkin	2005	26-06-1972
DURAN Bahattin		26-09-1975
EYISOY Mustafa		22-11-1980
GEMICI Cemal	2005	2-01-1970
GOKCU Bulent		28-09-1970
GURSES Muhittin	2005	14-05-1974
KAN Ekrem		6-02-1980
OK Serkan		17-10-1978
SINEM Adil		10-08-1972
SONMEZ Erhan		10-02-1979

FIFA REFEREE LIST 2005 – UZB

Continuation from page 869	Int'l	DoB
IRMATOV Ravshan	2003	9-08-1977
ISMAILOV Marat	2001	13-06-1966
LUTFULLIN Nail	1996	13-06-1961
SAIDOV Rustam	1997	21-06-1963
SMIRNOV Konstantin	2002	1-03-1962
TSEYTLIN Vladislav	2002	23-08-1971

FIFA ASSISTANT REFEREE LIST 2005 – UZB

Continuation from page 869	Int'l	DoB
ABDULLAEV Farkhad	2001	17-06-1975
ILYASOV Rafael	2001	20-12-1973
KHATAMOV Arslan	1997	22-02-1962
KOVALENKO Valentin	2002	9-08-1975
NADJAFALIEV Viloyat	2002	14-07-1972
NIZOMOV Gofurjon	1998	25-03-1963
POPOV Alexander	1998	5-08-1961
SERAZITDINOV Viktor	2002	11-08-1974
SHAKURBANOV Davron	2004	9-03-1972
TAGAYEV Bakhtiyor	2005	7-05-1966

FIFA REFEREE LIST 2005 – VAN

Continuation from page 873	Int'l	DoB
ATTISON Harry	1998	12-11-1969
FRED Lencie	2000	21-03-1968
WILBUR Ron	1999	19-12-1965

FIFA ASSISTANT REFEREE LIST 2005 – VAN

Continuation from page 873	Int'l	DoB
DORIRI Elise	1999	9-02-1972
MAEL Kiddley	2000	16-11-1973
MELTETAMAT Tony	1994	7-03-1969
RAKRAK Athanas	1997	5-07-1971

FIFA REFEREE LIST 2005 – VIE

Continuation from page 881	Int'l	DoB
DANG Thanh Ha	2002	25-04-1965
DUONG Van Hien	2002	25-12-1966
LE Van Tu	2005	1-01-1969
LUONG The Tai	1995	3-04-1966
PHAM Huu Loc	2003	26-01-1965
VO Minh Tri	2001	3-04-1972
VU Trong Chien	2004	4-09-1966

FIFA ASSISTANT REFEREE LIST 2005 – VIE

Continuation from page 881	Int'l	DoB
NGUYEN Duc Vu		23-12-1975
NGUYEN Truong Xuan	2000	6-02-1972
PHAM Manh Long	2002	24-10-1976
PHUNG Dinh Dung	2005	12-09-1972
TRUONG The Toan	1997	23-10-1963

FIFA REFEREE LIST 2005 – ZAM

Continuation from page 897	Int'l	DoB
CHIPAMPA George	2000	5-12-1967
CHISANGA Gracious	2005	10-08-1969
KAOMA Wellington	2000	15-08-1974
MPANISI Wilson	2002	3-06-1966
MWANZA Cornelius	2000	8-07-1965
SHIKAPANDE Harris	1997	4-12-1963
ZIWA Timmy	2005	11-09-1969

FIFA ASSISTANT REFEREE LIST 2005 – ZAM

Continuation from page 897	Int'l	DoB
CHICHENGA Kenneth	1997	29-11-1967
CHUNGU Andrew	1997	26-11-1964
JERE Lovemore	2004	1-01-1976
KAMUNGOMA Stephen	2005	31-05-1967
SHISHEKANU Francis		17-04-1973
SICHONE Felix		10-10-1966
SIWAKWI Enos	1998	18-07-1960

FIFA REFEREE LIST 2005 – ZIM

Continuation from page 900	Int'l	DoB
BWANYA Tendayi	2003	19-08-1965
CHAPFIKA Tichaona	2005	25-07-1970
CHIHOWA Masimba	2003	17-12-1966
MANUEL Christopher	2003	15-07-1968
MARANGE Kenias	1998	9-10-1964
MNKANTJO Tabani	2002	27-05-1965
MUSUSA Joseph	1998	5-05-1960

FIFA ASSISTANT REFEREE LIST 2005 – ZIM

Continuation from page 900	Int'l	DoB
BOUYED Ngoni	1998	6-04-1966
CHAFA Cosmas	2005	17-11-1971
KALOTA Wonder	2001	25-11-1966
KUSOSA Nelson	1998	15-04-1961
MUDZAMIRI Brighton	1991	16-03-1960
NYONI Cosmas	2003	18-05-1964
ZINDOVE Alfred	2002	29-03-1967

BENIN NATIONAL TEAM RECORDS AND RECORD SEQUENCES
Continuation from page 258

Records			Sequence records					
Victory	6-2	CHA 1963	Wins	3	2003	Clean sheets	3	2003
Defeat	1-10	NGA 1959	Defeats	9	1991-1993	Goals scored	7	1963-1965, 2004
Player Caps	n/a		Undefeated	7	1963-1965	Without goal	5	1988-1990, 1991
Player Goals	n/a		Without win	24	1984-1991	Goals against	14	1963-1969

MAJOR WORLD RECORDS

NATIONAL CAPS – MEN

		First	Last	Caps
AL DEAYEA Mohamed	KSA	1990	2004	173
SUAREZ Claudio	MEX	1992	2004	172
JONES Cobi	USA	1992	2004	164
AL TALYANI Adnan	UAE	1984	1987	164
HASSAN Hossan	EGY	1985	2004	163
AL JABER Sami	KSA	1992	2005	152
MATTHAUS Lothar	GER	1980	2000	150
AL KHILAIWI Mohamed	KSA	1990	2001	143
KRISTAL Marko	EST	1992	2005	143
RAVELLI Thomas	SWE	1981	1987	143
REIM Martin	EST	1992	2005	143
DAEI Ali	IRN	1993	2005	140
ABDULLAH Majed	KSA	1978	1994	139
HONG Myung Bo	KOR	1990	2002	135
AGOOS Jeff	USA	1988	2003	134
CAFU	BRA	1990	2005	133
CAMPOS Jorge	MEX	1991	2003	130
SCHMEICHEL Peter	DEN	1987	2001	129
BALBOA Marcelo	USA	1988	2000	128
MALDINI Paolo	ITA	1988	2002	126
SAEED Hussein	IRQ	1977	1990	126
ZUBIZARRETA Andoni	ESP	1985	1998	126
HAGI Gheorghe	ROM	1983	2000	125
HASSAN Ibrahim	EGY	1988	2002	125
HURTADO Ivan	ECU	1992	2005	125
SHILTON Peter	ENG	1970	1990	125

NATIONAL GOALS – MEN

		First	Last	Goals
DAEI Ali	IRN	1993	2005	104
PUSKAS Ferenc	HUN	1945	1956	84
PELE	BRA	1957	1971	77
KOCSIS Sandor	HUN	1948	1956	75
WOODWARD Vivian	ENG	1903	1914	73
MULLER Gerd	GER	1966	1974	68
ABDULLAH Majed	KSA	1978	1994	67
HASSAN Hossam	EGY	1985	2004	64
SENAMUANG Kiatisuk	THA	1993	2004	64
Al HOUWAIDI Jassem	KUW	1992	2002	63
SAEED Hussein	IRQ	1977	1990	61
JOHN Stern	TRI	1995	2005	59
SCHLOSSER Imre	HUN	1906	1927	59
BATISTUTA Gabriel	ARG	1991	2002	56
MIURA Kazuyoshi	JPN	1990	2000	56
RONALDO	BRA	1994	2005	56
ABDULLAH Bashar	KUW	1996	2004	55
CHA Bum Kun	KOR	1972	1986	55
KAMAMOTO Kunishige	JPN	1964	1977	55
ROMARIO	BRA	1987	2005	55
STREICH Joachim	GDR	1969	1984	53
AL TALYANI Adnan	UAE	1984	1997	53
NIELSEN Poul	DEN	1910	1925	52
ZICO	BRA	1976	1986	52
TICHY Lajos	HUN	1955	1964	51
HWANG Seong Hong	KOR	1993	2003	50

NATIONAL COACHES

	First	Last	Games
MILUTINOVIC Bora	1983	2004	276
MATURANA Francisco	1987	2003	172
HERBERGER Sepp	1936	1964	167
MEISL Hugo	1912	1937	155
SCHON Helmut	1953	1978	148
VOGTS Berti	1990	2004	144
PIONTEK Sepp	1979	1993	143
WINTERBOTTOM Walter	1946	1962	139
PETTERSSON John	1921	1936	138
TIRNANIC Alexander	1946	1966	128
STABILE Guillermo	1939	1960	127
KACHALIN Gavril	1954	1970	123
GOMEZ Hernan Dario	1995	2004	122
THYS Guy	1976	1991	114
RAMSEY Alf	1963	1974	113
BUSCHNER Georg	1970	1981	106

NATIONAL CAPS – WOMEN

		First	Last	Caps
LILLY Kristine	USA	1987	2005	296
HAMM Mia	USA	1987	2004	275
FOUDY Julie	USA	1988	2004	271
FAWCETT Joy	USA	1987	2004	239
MILBRETT Tiffeny	USA	1991	2005	200
CHASTAIN Brandi	USA	1988	2005	192
FAN Yunjie	CHN	1992	2004	192
RIISE Hege	NOR	1990	2004	188
ZHAO Lihong	CHN	1992	2003	182
AILING Liu	CHN	1987	2001	173
MACMILLAN Shannon	USA	1993	2005	173
OVERBECK Carla	USA	1988	2000	168
LIRONG Wen	CHN	1987	2001	163
WANG Liping	CHN	1992	2004	162
WEN Sun	CHN	1990	2003	162
PARLOW Cindy	USA	1996	2005	157

UNBEATEN RUN – NATIONAL TEAM

	Years	Games
England (includes Amateur Team)	1906-1910	36
Brazil	1993-1995	36
Argentina	1991-1993	31
Spain	1994-1998	31
Hungary	1950-1954	30
France	1994-1996	30
Brazil	1970-1973	29
Colombia	1992-1994	27
Brazil	1975-1978	24
Ghana	1981-1983	23
Czechoslovakia	1974-1976	23
Germany	1978-1980	23
Brazil	1981-1982	23
Brazil	1997-1998	23

UNBEATEN RUN – CLUBS

	Years	Games
ASEC Abidjan	1989-1994	108
Steaua Bucuresti	1986-1989	104
Espérance Tunis	1997-2001	85
Celtic	1915-1917	62
Union Saint-Gilloise	1933-1935	60
Boca Juniors	1924-1927	59
Pyunik Yerevan	2002-2004	59
Milan	1991-1993	58
Olympiacos	1972-1974	58
Skonto Riga	1993-1996	58
Benfica	1976-1978	56
Peñarol	1966-1969	56
Shakhtar Donetsk	2000-2002	55
Dalian Wanda	1995-1997	55

CONSECUTIVE WINS – NATIONAL TEAM

	Years	Games
England (includes Amateur Team)	1908-1909	23
Australia	1996-1997	14
Brazil	1997	14
France	2003-2004	14
Scotland	1879-1885	13
Brazil	1960-1962	13
Germany DR	1973-1974	12
Germany FR	1979-1980	12
France	1984-1985	12
Mexico	1987-1990	12

The 2002 FIFA World Cup™ qualifier between Australia and American Samoa on 11 April 2001, set two major records. The 31-0 victory recorded by the Australians is the highest ever win in an international match. 13 of the goals were scored by Archie Thompson, the largest haul by a single player in a match. Records results in international matches for all 205 associations can be found in part two of the Almanack listed under each country. Record victories and defeats are shown for each country along with record sequences. Once FIFA has published the official list of every game ever played, it is our intention to expand this section of the Almanack to reflect the findings of that research.

CALENDAR FOR THE 2005–2006 SEASON

Week starting

Month	Week	Events
September 2005	Sat 3	Fixed date for Official Competition matches 3/09-7/09
	Sat 10	CAF CL group • CAF CC group • AFC CLqf 1L (m/w) • UEFA CL group (m/w) • UEFA CUPr1 1L (m/w)
	Sat 17	AFC CLqf 2L (m/w) • AFC CUPqf 2L (m/w)
	Sat 24	CAF CLsf 1L • CAF CC group • AFC CLsf 1L (m/w) • AFC CUPsf 1L (m/w) • UEFA CL group (m/w) • UEFA CUPr1 2L (m/w)
October 2005	Sat 1	
	Sat 8	FIFA Congress Marrakech 11/09-12/09 • AFC CLsf 2L (m/w) • AFC CUP sf 2L (m/w) Fixed date for Official Competition matches 8/10-12/10
	Sat 15	FIFA U-17 World Championship Peru 16/09-2/10 • CAF CLsf 2L • CAF CC Group • AFC CUPf 1L (m/w) • CONMEBOL SAqf 1L (m/w) UEFA CL group (m/w) • UEFA CUP group (m/w)
	Sat 22	AFC CLf 1L (m/w) • AFC CUPf 2L (m/w) • CONMEBOL SAqf 1L (m/w)
	Sat 29	CAF CLf 1L • AFC CLf 2L (m/w) • CONMEBOL SAqf 2L (m/w) • UEFA CL group (m/w) • UEFA CUP group (m/w)
November 2005	Sat 5	CAF CCf 1L • CONMEBOL SAqf 2L (m/w)
	Sat 12	CAF CLf 2L • Fixed date for Official Competition matches 12/11-16/11 • OFC Congress Sydney (12th)
	Sat 19	CAF CCf 2L • CONMEBOL SAsf 1L (m/w) • UEFA CL group (m/w) • UEFA CUP group (m/w)
	Sat 26	CONMEBOL SAsf 2L (m/w) • UEFA CUP group (m/w)
December 2005	Sat 3	FIFA World Cup™ qualifying draw Leipzig (9th) • CONMEBOL SAf 1L (7) • UEFA CL group (m/w)
	Sat 10	FIFA Club World Championship Japan 11/12-18/12 • SAFF Championship Pakistan 8/12-18/12 • AFC Awards • CONMEBOL SAf 2L (14th) UEFA CUP group (m/w)
	Sat 17	FIFA World Player Gala 2005 Zurich (19th)
	Sat 24	
	Sat 31	
January 2006	Sat 7	
	Sat 14	
	Sat 21	CAF Cup of Nations Egypt 20/01-10/02
	Sat 28	
February 2006	Sat 4	Fixed date for international matches (8th) • Copa Libertadores 2006 kicks-off (TBC) • CAF Champions League kicks-off (TBC)
	Sat 11	UEFA CUPr2 1L (m/w)
	Sat 18	UEFA CLr2 1L (m/w) • UEFA CUPr2 2L (m/w)
	Sat 25	
March 2006	Sat 4	UEFA CLr2 2L (m/w) • UEFA CUPr3 1L (m/w) • AFC Champions League kicks-off (TBC)
	Sat 11	UEFA CUPr3 2L (m/w)
	Sat 18	
	Sat 25	Fixed date for international matches (29th) • UEFA CLqf 1L (m/w) • UEFA CUPqf 1L (m/w)
April 2006	Sat 1	UEFA CLqf 2L (m/w) • UEFA CUPqf 2L (m/w)
	Sat 8	
	Sat 15	UEFA CLsf 1L (m/w) • UEFA CUPsf 1L (m/w)
	Sat 22	UEFA CLsf 2L (m/w) • UEFA CUPsf 2L (m/w)
	Sat 29	UEFA U-17 Championship finals 3/05-14/05
May 2006	Sat 6	UEFA CUPf (10th)
	Sat 13	UEFA CLf Paris (17th)
	Sat 20	UEFA U-21 Championship finals 25/05-6/06 • UEFA Womens Cupf 1L
	Sat 27	UEFA Women's Cupf 2L
June 2006	Sat 3	
	Sat 10	FIFA World Cup™ Germany 9/06-9/07
	Sat 17	
	Sat 24	
July 2006	Sat 1	
	Sat 8	FIFA World Cup™ Final (9th)
	Sat 15	
	Sat 22	
	Sat 29	

CL = Champions League (according to the confederation indicated) • SA = Copa Sudamericana • CC = Confederation Cup
r1 = first round • r2 = second round • r3 = third round • qf = quarter-final • sf = semi-final • f = final
1L - first leg • 2L = second leg • m/w = mid-week after the week-end indicated • TBC = dates to be confirmed